O'Connor's Family Code Plus

Author

Sydney Aaron Beckman

Jones McClure Publishing, Inc.
Houston, Texas

O'Connor's Annotated Codes Series

Suggested cite form: ***O'Connor's Family Code Plus*** (2002-2003)

Jones McClure Publishing, Inc.
Product List

Texas Litigation Series

*O'Connor's Texas Rules * Civil Trials*

Texas civil pretrial, trial, and post-trial procedure explained in plain English. *O'Connor's Texas Rules* provides the entire Texas Rules of Civil Procedure and Texas Rules of Evidence, both with up-to-date quotations from relevant, controlling cases. Also included are the Texas Rules of Appellate Procedure and timetables for tracking important deadlines. Thoroughly researched and revised each year to bring you every important rule or case-law change in a clear and concise manner.

O'Connor's Texas Civil Forms

Covers pleadings and motions from the trial's beginning to end with easy-to-use, plain-English forms. Provides forms for every common motion, as well as original petition, answer, and discovery forms for cases involving breach of contract, personal injury (auto accident & slip and fall), DTPA, Texas Tort Claims Act, bill of review, and suit on account.

O'Connor's Texas Civil Forms on CD

Every form from *O'Connor's Texas Civil Forms* in a convenient electronic format compatible with your favorite word processing program. Save hours of typing time.

O'Connor's Texas Civil Appeals

Provides comprehensive coverage of appellate procedure. Includes the Texas Rules of Appellate Procedure annotated with case quotations, commentaries that explain every phase of the appeal, forms used for appeals, timetables for tracking all-important appellate deadlines, and helpful descriptions of local procedures for all appellate courts. The appellate forms are also available on CD.

Federal Litigation Series

*O'Connor's Federal Rules * Civil Trials*

Ten chapters of detailed commentaries explain Federal Civil Procedure in plain English. Provides entire Federal Rules of Civil Procedure and Federal Rules of Evidence, both with up-to-date quotations from relevant, controlling cases. Also included are the Federal Rules of Appellate Procedure and important Advisory Committee Notes, plus Title 28 of the U.S.C., and timetables for tracking deadlines.

*O'Connor's Federal Forms * Civil Trials*

Comprehensive collection of trial forms written in plain English and formatted for quick, efficient completion. Complete sets of forms are included for cases involving Admiralty-Jones Act, trademark infringement, Age Discrimination in Employment Act, Family and Medical Leave Act, breach of contract, the Federal Tort Claims Act, copyright infringement, employment discrimination and sexual harassment suits under Title VII and the ADA, civil rights suits under 42 U.S.C. §1983, negligence under the Federal Employer's Liability Act, and personal injury in an auto accident.

O'Connor's Federal Forms on CD

Create forms quickly and efficiently on your computer with fill-in-the-blank word processing files for every form in *O'Connor's Federal Forms * Civil Trials.*

Texas Expert Series

Texas Rules of Evidence Handbook 4th edition

Evidence explained in ten detailed chapters of expert commentary citing the most recent case law and most authoritative sources, updated by Cathy Cochran, Justice on the Texas Court of Criminal Appeals and member of the Administration of the Rules of Evidence Committee of the State Bar, to reflect the current Texas Rules of Evidence.

JONES MCCLURE PUBLISHING, INC.
PRODUCT LIST

O'Connor's Texas Causes of Action

Over 900 pages of comprehensive commentary discussing the most common causes of action pleaded by Texas attorneys. Lists and explains the elements of each cause of action, referring to the definitive authority on each point and providing cross references to both the relevant state pattern jury charges and law journal articles discussing the cause of action. Covers torts, contracts, negligence, and statutory causes of action.

O'Connor's Family Law Handbook *(coming soon)*

Complete resource for the family law practitioner. Detailed commentary covering all aspects of family practice, including cites to the most recent case law and expert practice tips. Incorporates the most up-to-date changes to the Texas Family Code.

TEXAS ANNOTATED CODES SERIES

O'Connor's CPRC Plus

Includes the Civil Practice & Remedies Code, annotated with case quotations, along with the full text of the DTPA, the Medical Practice Act, the Medical Liability & Insurance Act, and Insurance Code Arts. 21.21 & 21.28. Also provides relevant excerpts from the codes cited in *O'Connor's Texas Rules * Civil Trials.*

O'Connor's Criminal Codes Plus

Includes the Code of Criminal Procedure, Penal Code, and selected provisions from the Government Code, Transportation Code, and Water Code. Includes the Texas Rules of Evidence and Texas Rules of Appellate Procedure as well as timetables for criminal appeals based on the rules. Combines all commonly used criminal codes and statutes into one user-friendly volume with annotations carefully selected by George McCall "Mac" Secrest, Jr.

O'Connor's Family Code Plus

Includes the Family Code, Texas Rules of Civil Procedure, and Texas Rules of Evidence with case quotations carefully selected to explain how the courts interpret each section. Also includes selected sections from various codes that family lawyers need. The contents and quotations were carefully selected by Sydney Aaron Beckman.

O'Connor's Business Organizations Codes Plus

Complete reference manual for organizing and maintaining all varieties of corporations and partnerships. Contains the Business Corporation Act and Texas Securities Act, as well as all relevant partnership, limited liability, and nonprofit corporation statutes. Provides incorporation forms suitable for filing with the Secretary of State.

O'Connor's Business & Commerce Code Plus

Includes the Business & Commerce Code, annotated with case quotations. Contains both the new and old Chapter 9. Supplemented with helpful charts regarding secured transactions, the DTPA, and covenants not to compete.

O'Connor's Texas Employment Codes Plus

Comprehensive Texas employment law reference manual. Contains the entire Labor Code and selected provisions from other codes and statutes, including whistleblower; concealed handgun; employment contract; arbitration; access to criminal history; public health; and state, municipal, and educator employment. All are annotated with quotations from controlling cases. Also includes a variety of charts and timetables.

JONES McCLURE PUBLISHING INC.

Mail to:
P.O. Box 3348
Houston, TX 77253-3348

Ship to:
1113 Vine, Suite 240
Houston, TX 77002

Tel: (713) 223-2727
(800) OCONNOR
(800) 626-6667
Fax: (713) 223-9393

Internet: www.JonesMcClure.com

Print date: June 19, 2002
Printed in the United States of America.

ISBN 1-884554-58-X

This publication is intended to provide lawyers with current and accurate information about selected Texas codes, rules, and statutes. The information in this book, however, may not be sufficient in dealing with a client's particular legal problem, and Jones McClure Publishing, Inc., Michol O'Connor, and Sydney Beckman do not warrant or represent its suitability for such purpose. Lawyers using this publication do so with the understanding that the information published in this book should not be relied on as a substitute for independent research to original sources of authority.

INTRODUCTION

This book contains the Texas Family Code, Texas Rules of Civil Procedure, and Texas Rules of Evidence with case annotations, plus selections from other codes and statutes used most often in daily family law practice. The book contains the most recent legislative changes from 2001 along with code sections that were superseded in 2001 but that still may govern some pending cases.

The book is laid out in the form familiar to practitioners using *O'Connor's* code books. Family lawyers will find this book particularly useful; the entire design and contents have been selected with the practitioner in mind. This book enables you to carry only one volume to the courthouse and to have on your desktop all the necessary codes, statutes, and rules. Cross references and caution tips have been included in the Rules of Civil Procedure and Evidence to help guide you to sections of the Family Code that supplant or affect the rules. In addition, we provide annotations in the Rules of Civil Procedure and Evidence that are particular to family law practice. Finally, pains were taken to develop a comprehensive yet easy-to-use index.

2001 LEGISLATIVE CHANGES

The Legislature met in 2001 and made a number of changes that are important to the family lawyer. In this book, the 2001 legislative changes are marked with: Ⓐ, Ⓔ, or Ⓒ, depending on whether the section was amended, enacted, or codified. Former sections that are still in effect for suits commenced before the effective dates of the amendments are shaded in gray. Where the Legislature numbered different new sections with duplicate numbers, we labeled them with bracketed letters, *e.g.*, [A*], to help distinguish them. Where the Legislature passed two irreconcilable amendments to the same code provision, we marked the text with a ☠ directing the reader to consult the Code Construction Act (Govt. Code ch. 311) to resolve the conflict. To conserve space, we made liberal use of abbreviations in the annotations. A chart of these abbreviations is on the inside front cover of this book.

2002 ADDITIONS

Annotations. The Family Code, Rules of Civil Procedure, and Rules of Evidence have all been updated with new case annotations from 2001 and 2002. In an attempt to provide the family lawyer with case law that is pertinent only to family practice, we have streamlined the annotations under the Rules of Civil Procedure and Evidence.

Statutes. In a continuing effort to provide coverage of statutes that affect family practice, we have added new provisions from the Code of Criminal Procedure, Penal Code, United States Code, and Code of Federal Regulations.

- **Code of Criminal Procedure**. From the Code of Criminal Procedure, we have added chapter 5 and article 14.03, which provide for the powers and duties of peace officers and officials in preventing family violence, articles 17.29-17.293, which authorize emergency protection orders issued by magistrates, and the newly enacted article 42.23, which requires the notification of a court of continuing jurisdiction of a family violence conviction.

- **Penal Code.** From the Penal Code, we have added §46.04, which prohibits the possession of firearms by persons subject to a protective order under Family Code chapter 88.

- **United States Code.** From the U.S.C., we have added §§921 & 922, which prohibit the sale of firearms to persons subject to a protective order or convicted of a domestic violence misdemeanor, and §§2261-2262, which deal with interstate domestic violence, stalking, and violations of protective orders.

- **Code of Federal Regulations.** From the C.F.R., we have added Internal Revenue Service regulations, §1.71-1T (maintenance payments), §1.152-4T (dependency exemption—child of divorced parents), §§1.215-1, 1.215-1T (alimony payment deductions), and §1.1041-1T (transfer of property between spouses).

Charts. This year's edition includes the new 2002 Child Support Tax Table and a new Statute of Limitations Chart for family law actions. The limitations chart also provides limitations periods for some commonly filed tort actions.

CASE-LAW DEVELOPMENTS

Ad litem fees. In ***Gonzalez v. Gonzalez***, 26 S.W.3d 657 (Tex.App.—San Antonio 2000, no pet.), the San Antonio Court of Appeals held that because Family Code §107.015 expressly provides that the trial court shall set the amount of attorney ad litem fees, the trial court did not err in refusing to submit the issue to the jury.

Alter ego. In ***Lifshutz v. Lifshutz***, 61 S.W.3d 511 (Tex.App.—San Antonio 2001, pet. denied), the San Antonio Court of Appeals held that to pierce the corporate veil in a divorce context, the trial court must find (1) unity between the separate property corporation and the spouse such that the separateness of the corporation has ceased to exist and (2) that the spouse's improper use of the corporation damaged the community estate beyond that which may be remedied by a claim for reimbursement.

Arbitration. In ***In re Cartwright***, __ S.W.3d __ (Tex.App.—Houston [1st Dist.] 2002, n.p.h.) (No. 01-01-00948-CV; 4-4-02), the Houston First Court of Appeals held that the Texas Arbitration Act applies to binding arbitration under the Family Code.

Child support—administrative writ of withholding. In ***In re A.D.***, __ S.W.3d __ (Tex.2002) (No. 00-0337; 4-11-02), the Texas Supreme Court held that the Legislature's decision to remove the four-year limitations period to issue an administrative writ of withholding for past due support obligations did not violate the Texas Constitution's ban on retroactive laws.

Conservatorship—grandparent's role. In ***In re Edwards***, __ S.W.3d __ (Tex.App.—Texarkana 2002, n.p.h.) (No. 06-00-00130-CV; 4-11-02), the Texarkana Court of Appeals held that a trial court does not err in considering the role grandparents or other family members will play in a child's life when determining the best interests of that child.

Division of property—fault. In ***Phillips v. Phillips***, __ S.W.3d __ (Tex.App.—Beaumont 2002, n.p.h.) (No. 09-01-346-CV; 5-2-02), the Beaumont Court of Appeals held that a court may not consider fault in making a just and right division of the marital estate if the sole ground for divorce was insupportability.

Fraud on the community—preempted. In ***Barnett v. Barnett***, 67 S.W.3d 107 (Tex.2001), the Texas Supreme Court held that a wife's claim for fraud on the community and a request for a constructive trust after her husband died was preempted by ERISA because the husband's life insurance policy was part of an employee welfare benefit plan covered by ERISA.

Geographical restrictions—binding jury issues. In ***Lenz v. Lenz***, __ S.W.3d __ (Tex.2002) (No. 01-0232; 6-6-02), the Texas Supreme Court held that Family Code §105.001 prevents a trial court from disregarding a jury's verdict giving a parent the exclusive right to establish her children's primary residence by imposing a geographical restriction on their primary residence.

Geographical restrictions—modification. In ***Lenz v. Lenz***, __ S.W.3d __ (Tex.2002) (No. 01-0232; 6-6-02), the Texas Supreme Court held that a court should consider the public policy concerns under Family Code §153.001 when modifying a court's residency restrictions.

Grandparents—access. In ***Roby v. Adams***, 68 S.W.3d 822 (Tex.App.—El Paso 2002, n.p.h.), the El Paso Court of Appeals held that a grandparent seeking access under Family Code §153.433 had the burden to overcome the presumption established by the United States Supreme Court in ***Troxel v. Granville***, 530 U.S. 57 (2000), that a fit parent acts in the best interest of the parent's child.

Parental notification—fact findings. In ***In re Jane Doe 10***, __ S.W.3d __ (Tex.2002), the Texas Supreme Court held that a trial court must make fact findings for each ground asserted for judicial bypass and issue particularized findings when credibility or maturity issues are involved.

Protective order—continuance. In ***Martinez v. Martinez***, 52 S.W.3d 429 (Tex.App.—Fort Worth 2001, pet. denied), the Fort Worth Court of Appeals held that the need to conduct discovery is not one of the statutory bases to grant a continuance for a hearing on a protective order.

Protective order—criminal enforceability. In ***Martinez v. Martinez***, 52 S.W.3d 429 (Tex.App.—Fort Worth 2001, pet. denied), the Fort Worth Court of Appeals held that a temporary protective order is not a criminally enforceable order as is a final protective order after hearing.

Protective order—final appealable order. In ***Kelt v. Kelt***, 67 S.W.3d 364 (Tex.App.—Waco 2001, no pet.), the Waco Court of Appeals reexamined their earlier decision in ***Normand v. Fox***, 940 S.W.2d 401, and held that a protective order that disposes of all issues and parties is a final, appealable order.

Stock options—determining value. In ***Boyd v. Boyd***, 67 S.W.3d 398 (Tex.App.—Fort Worth 2002, n.p.h.), the Fort Worth Court of Appeals held that any post-divorce increases or decreases in the value of stock options that are not attributable to the spouse's post-divorce work will be community property.

UCCJEA. In ***In re Bellamy***, 67 S.W.3d 482 (Tex.App.—Texarkana 2002, n.p.h.), the Texarkana Court of Appeals held that §152.202 of the UCCJEA prevails over §155.003(b)(1) in determining which court has continuing exclusive jurisdiction to modify conservatorship.

Venue—establishing residency. In ***In re Salgado***, 53 S.W.3d 752 (Tex.App.—El Paso 2001, no pet.), the El Paso Court of Appeals looked to the Supreme Court's elements of residency under the general civil venue statute to define "residency" of a child applicant for purposes of establishing venue under §82.003.

ABOUT THE AUTHOR

Sydney Aaron Beckman is Board Certified in Family Law by the Texas Board of Legal Specialization and currently is in private practice in Fort Worth, Texas. Mr. Beckman is an officer and a Barrister in the Eldon B. Mahon Inn of Court and has been actively involved in the Inn since 1994. He serves on the Inn's Executive Committee and has served as Chair of the Membership Committee and Chair of the Program Committee. Mr. Beckman serves on the Family Law Section of the State Bar of Texas as Co-Chair of the Publications Committee and as a member of the Legislative Committee. In 2000, Mr. Beckman was elected to the Board of Directors of the Texas Academy of Family Law Specialists. Mr. Beckman serves on the Tarrant County Bar Association Fee Arbitration Committee and has previously served on the Publications Committee and the Editorial Board.

In addition to his private practice, Mr. Beckman has served as a Municipal Judge Pro Tem for the City of Fort Worth since August of 2000 and currently serves as an Adjunct Professor of Law at Texas Wesleyan University School of Law.

Mr. Beckman is a frequent lecturer and author at continuing legal education seminars and has also served on planning committees for various CLE seminars. He served on the committees that authored Checklists for Family Law and Checklists 2 for Family Law. He is also an author of the Family Lawyer's Essential Tool Kit. Mr. Beckman is currently working on the *O'Connor's Family Law Handbook* with an anticipated publication date in late 2002 and the *O'Connor's Family Law Form Book* with an anticipated publication date in 2003. He also co-authored Texas Family Law: Direct & Cross Examination (Suggested Questions, Ideas and Outlines) and is currently working on a second volume devoted entirely to children's issues.

Mr. Beckman is a member of the International Brotherhood of Magicians, the Society of American Magicians, the Texas Association of Magicians, and the Aircraft Owner's and Pilots Association.

YOUR SUGGESTIONS

We invite your comments. If you see anything that needs correction, amendment, or supplementation, please let us know. If you are in a hurry, just photocopy the page in the book, make a note in the margin, include your card so we can contact you, and send it to us at the address or the fax number on the copyright page. We appreciate constructive criticism; if you feel a significant case was omitted, please let us know. Also, if you feel an included case is inappropriate, please let us know that as well. This book is designed by a practitioner for practitioners. Your thoughts are appreciated and welcomed.

CAVEAT

This book provides you with citations to important opinions that interpret the Family Code, Texas Rules of Civil Procedure, and Texas Rules of Evidence through June 2002. You may disagree with the choice of cases for the various codes and rules in this book. You should therefore use this book only as a research guide. Read the codes, the rules, and the cases in full and make your own evaluation of them.

SPECIAL THANKS

As with the first edition, the creation of this book would not have happened but for the patience, understanding, and incredible amount of work performed by the attorneys and staff at Jones McClure Publishing, Inc. As always, my managing legal editors spent a great deal of time on this project and had much patience with me; I cannot thank them enough for their attention to detail and continuing drive to make this book excellent. Special thanks must also go to the former Allyson Torres—on April 13, 2002 she became my wife; as always, she was kind and patient when I devoted much more time to this work than to her. Last but not least, I have to thank my parents, Bill and Eleanor McKee, for their never-ending support in all my endeavors.

PERMISSION

We would like to thank the National Conference of Commissioners on Uniform State Laws for use of the official comments to uniform acts adopted by the Texas Legislature.

RESEARCH & VERIFICATION

As always, the editorial staff of Jones McClure worked especially hard in ensuring the accuracy of this publication both for substantive citation to the law and for precision of the layout and page design. The persons who worked on this second edition of ***O'Connor's Texas Family Code Plus*** are listed below.

EXECUTIVE LEGAL EDITOR
Jason E. Wilson, J.D.

MANAGING LEGAL EDITORS
Gregory S. Otterson, J.D.
Jeffrey C. Hunter, J.D.

PRODUCTION MANAGERS
Amy Krivohlavek
Donna E. Vass

LAYOUT EDITORS
Michael A. Hauenstein
Erin Mann
Amanda Schlatre

ASSISTANT LEGAL EDITORS
James Coggeshall, J.D.
Nicole H. Davis, J.D.
Carlos Goenaga, J.D.
Douglas Haldane, J.D.
Shanna Kuzdzal
David Schultz, J.D.

LEGAL INTERNS
Jonathan Ichikawa
Kristy Gabrielova
Robyn Letness
Ellic Sahualla

SYDNEY A. BECKMAN

Fort Worth, Texas

Master Table of Contents

FAMILY CODE—TITLE 1
THE MARRIAGE RELATIONSHIP
TABLE OF CONTENTS

FAMILY CODE—TITLE 1

THE MARRIAGE RELATIONSHIP

TABLE OF CONTENTS

FAMILY CODE—TITLE 1
THE MARRIAGE RELATIONSHIP
TABLE OF CONTENTS

FAMILY CODE—TITLE 1
THE MARRIAGE RELATIONSHIP
TABLE OF CONTENTS

TITLE 1. THE MARRIAGE RELATIONSHIP

SUBTITLE A. MARRIAGE

CHAPTER 1. GENERAL PROVISIONS

SUBCHAPTER A. DEFINITIONS

FAM §1.001. APPLICABILITY OF DEFINITIONS

(a) The definitions in this subchapter apply to this title.

(b) Except as provided by this subchapter, the definitions in Chapter 101 apply to terms used in this title.

(c) If, in another part of this title, a term defined by this subchapter has a meaning different from the meaning provided by this subchapter, the meaning of that other provision prevails.

History of Fam §1.001: Acts 1997, 75th Leg., ch. 7, §1, eff. April 17, 1997.

FAM §1.002. COURT

"Court" means the district court, juvenile court having the jurisdiction of a district court, or other court expressly given jurisdiction of a suit under this title.

History of Fam §1.002: Acts 1997, 75th Leg., ch. 7, §1, eff. April 17, 1997.

FAM §1.003. SUIT FOR DISSOLUTION OF MARRIAGE

"Suit for dissolution of a marriage" includes a suit for divorce or annulment or to declare a marriage void.

History of Fam §1.003: Acts 1997, 75th Leg., ch. 7, §1, eff. April 17, 1997.

Sections 1.004-1.100 reserved for expansion

SUBCHAPTER B. PUBLIC POLICY

FAM §1.101. EVERY MARRIAGE PRESUMED VALID

In order to promote the public health and welfare and to provide the necessary records, this code specifies detailed rules to be followed in establishing the marriage relationship. However, in order to provide stability for those entering into the marriage relationship in good faith and to provide for an orderly determination of parentage and security for the children of the relationship, it is the policy of this state to preserve and uphold each marriage against claims of invalidity unless a strong reason exists for holding the marriage void or voidable. Therefore, every marriage entered into in this state is presumed to be valid unless expressly made void by Chapter 6 or unless expressly made voidable by Chapter 6 and annulled as provided by that chapter.

History of Fam §1.101: Acts 1997, 75th Leg., ch. 7, §1, eff. April 17, 1997. Source: Former Fam §2.01.

Author's Comment: Texas courts no longer use terms such as "legitimate" and "bastard" when referring to children.

Texas Employers' Ins. Ass'n v. Elder, 282 S.W.2d 371, 373 (Tex.1955). "The presumption in favor of the validity of a marriage which, as in this case, has been duly shown to have been contracted is one of the strongest, if, indeed, not the strongest, known to law. The presumption is, in itself, evidence, and may even outweigh positive evidence to the contrary. The strength of the presumption increases with the lapse of time, acknowledgments by the parties to the marriage, and the birth of children; and the fact that the legitimacy of a child may be involved is a factor in sustaining the validity of the marriage. It is well that the presumption should be so regarded, for it is grounded upon a sound public policy which favors morality, innocence, marriage, and legitimacy rather than immorality, guilt, concubinage, and bastardy." (Internal quotations omitted.)

Black v. Shell Oil Co., 397 S.W.2d 877, 881 (Tex. App.—Texarkana 1965, writ ref'd n.r.e.). "The marriage license and certificate having been placed in evidence, all reasonable presumptions will be indulged in favor of the validity of the marriage."

FAM §1.102. MOST RECENT MARRIAGE PRESUMED VALID

When two or more marriages of a person to different spouses are alleged, the most recent marriage is presumed to be valid as against each marriage that precedes the most recent marriage until one who asserts the validity of a prior marriage proves the validity of the prior marriage.

History of Fam §1.102: Acts 1997, 75th Leg., ch. 7, §1, eff. April 17, 1997. Source: Former Fam §2.01.

Estate of Claveria v. Claveria, 615 S.W.2d 164, 165 (Tex.1981). "The presumption that the most recent marriage is a valid one continues until one proves the impediment of a prior marriage and its continuing validity. *At 166:* After some evidence of a prior and continuing marriage has been introduced, the weight of such evidence must be determined by the finder of fact."

Davis v. Davis, 521 S.W.2d 603, 605 (Tex.1975). "It is not necessary in order to rebut the presumption that [respondent] prove the nonexistence of divorce in every jurisdiction where proceedings could have been possible; it is only necessary to rule out those proceedings where [decedent husband] might reasonably have been expected to have pursued them." *See also **Jordan v. Jordan***, 938 S.W.2d 177, 179 (Tex.App.—Houston [1st Dist.] 1997, no writ).

Chandler v. Chandler, 842 S.W.2d 829, 834 (Tex. App.—El Paso 1992, writ denied). "While it is unclear from a cursory reading of the statute whether the above presumption only applies when the most recent marriage was performed in Texas, the portion of §2.01 [now §1.102] providing for the presumption does not limit it solely to Texas marriages. Moreover, cases prior and subsequent to enactment of §2.01 have applied the presumption to 'foreign' marriages."

Loera v. Loera, 815 S.W.2d 910, 911 (Tex.App.—Corpus Christi 1991, no writ). "Because the presumption is, in itself, considered evidence, the party attacking the validity of the marriage has a burden to 'introduce sufficient evidence, standing alone, to negate the dissolution of the prior marriage.' *At 912:* To prevail, [husband] was required to adduce evidence establishing the continued validity of the prior marriage at the time of the parties' marriage. Death terminates marriage as a matter of law, and death is presumed after seven years of absence; therefore, [husband's] failure to present any evidence establishing that [former husband] was alive within seven years before the parties' marriage, or thereafter, requires us to sustain [respondent's] point of error."

FAM §1.103. PERSONS MARRIED ELSEWHERE

The law of this state applies to persons married elsewhere who are domiciled in this state.

History of Fam §1.103: Acts 1997, 75th Leg., ch. 7, §1, eff. April 17, 1997. Source: Former Fam §4.01.

Littleton v. Prange, 9 S.W.3d 223, 226 (Tex.App.—San Antonio 1999, pet. denied). The Defense of Marriage Act "defines marriage for federal purposes as a legal union between one man and one woman, and provides that no state shall be required to give effect to any public act, record, or judicial proceeding of any other state respecting a relationship between persons of the same sex that is treated as a marriage under the laws of such other State ... or a right or claim arising from such relationship. So even if one state were to recognize same-sex marriages it would not need to be recognized in any other state, and probably would not be." (Internal quotations omitted.)

Seth v. Seth, 694 S.W.2d 459, 462 (Tex.App.—Fort Worth 1985, no writ). "Traditionally, courts have chosen and used the law of the place a divorce or marriage purportedly occurs to determine the validity of the ceremony. Two recent decisions by the Supreme Court of Texas, however, indicate that choice-of-law decisions should not be made on the basis of the mechanical test of where the act occurred (lex loci) but should instead be made on the basis of the most significant relationship approach, using the factors set forth in the Restatement (2d) of Conflict of Laws §6 (1971). Thus, based on [these decisions], we hold that §6 criteria, and not the place of celebration test, should be applied to determine choice of law in a marriage or divorce context. *At 463:* We now list the §6 choice of law principles: ... (1) A court, subject to constitutional restrictions, will follow a statutory directive of its own state on choice of law. (2) When there is no such directive, the factors relevant to the choice of the applicable rule of law include (a) the needs of the interstate and international systems, (b) the relevant policies of the forum, (c) the relevant policies of other interested states and the relative interests of those states in the determination of the particular issue, (d) the protection of justified expectations, (e) the basic policies underlying the particular field of law, (f) certainty, predictability and uniformity of result, and (g) ease in the determination and application of the law to be applied."

FAM §1.104. CAPACITY OF SPOUSE

Except as expressly provided by statute or by the constitution, a person, regardless of age, who has been married in accordance with the law of this state has the capacity and power of an adult, including the capacity to contract.

History of Fam §1.104: Acts 1997, 75th Leg., ch. 7, §1, eff. April 17, 1997. Source: Former Fam §4.03.

Husband v. Pierce, 800 S.W.2d 661, 663 (Tex. App.—Tyler 1990, orig. proceeding). "Under Texas law, a minor who 'has been married in accordance with the laws of this state ... has the power and capacity of an adult.' The parents' rights and obligations in relation to their child end upon the child's emancipation by marriage."

FAM §1.105. JOINDER IN CIVIL SUITS

(a) A spouse may sue and be sued without the joinder of the other spouse.

(b) When claims or liabilities are joint and several, the spouses may be joined under the rules relating to joinder of parties generally.

History of Fam §1.105: Acts 1997, 75th Leg., ch. 7, §1, eff. April 17, 1997. Source: Former Fam §4.04.

Cooper v. Texas Gulf Indus., 513 S.W.2d 200, 202 (Tex.1974). "While [§4.04, now §1.105] provides that a spouse may sue and be sued without the joinder of the other, *neither* spouse may virtually represent the other. The rights of the wife, like the rights of the husband and the rights of any other joint owner, may be affected only by a suit in which the wife is called to answer. If one of the spouses wishes the other to represent him or her, §5.22(c) [now §3.102(c)] permits that arrangement provided the consenting spouse authorizes that representation by a power of attorney or other agreement in writing."

FAM §1.106. CRIMINAL CONVERSATION NOT AUTHORIZED

A right of action by one spouse against a third party for criminal conversation is not authorized in this state.

History of Fam §1.106: Acts 1997, 75th Leg., ch. 7, §1, eff. April 17, 1997. Source: Former Fam §4.05.

Truitt v. Carnley, 836 S.W.2d 786, 787 (Tex.App.—Fort Worth 1992, writ denied). Section 4.05, now §1.106, "abolished actions against third parties based upon criminal conversation.... Criminal conversation is a tort based on adultery." *See also* ***McMillan v. Felsenthal***, 482 S.W.2d 9, 11 (Tex.App.—Tyler 1972), *aff'd*, 493 S.W.2d 729 (Tex.1973).

FAM §1.107. ALIENATION OF AFFECTION NOT AUTHORIZED

A right of action by one spouse against a third party for alienation of affection is not authorized in this state.

History of Fam §1.107: Acts 1997, 75th Leg., ch. 7, §1, eff. April 17, 1997. Source: Former Fam §4.06.

Helena Lab. Corp. v. Snyder, 886 S.W.2d 767, 768-69 (Tex.1994). The Texas Supreme Court "has never recognized an independent cause of action for negligent interference with the familial relationship. In some circumstances, damages may be recovered for such injuries; but, such recovery is allowed only in connection with some recognized tort. [¶] An independent cause of action for negligent interference with the familial relationship would allow an employer to be held responsible for an employee's conduct, even though the employee is shielded from responsibility for that conduct by §4.06 [now §1.107]. Exposing employers to this form of liability would be inconsistent with §4.06." *See also* ***Stites v. Gillum***, 872 S.W.2d 786, 791-92 (Tex.App.—Fort Worth 1994, no writ).

FAM §1.108. PROMISE OR AGREEMENT MUST BE IN WRITING

A promise or agreement made on consideration of marriage or nonmarital conjugal cohabitation is not enforceable unless the promise or agreement or a memorandum of the promise or agreement is in writing and signed by the person obligated by the promise or agreement.

History of Fam §1.108: Acts 1997, 75th Leg., ch. 7, §1, eff. April 17, 1997. Source: Bus. & Com. Code §26.01.

O'Farrill Avila v. Gonzalez, 974 S.W.2d 237, 243-44 (Tex.App.—San Antonio 1998, pet. denied). "A contract ... must be supported by consideration, and this agreement recites no consideration. [Female partner] testified at trial that she gave consideration for [male partner's] promise: her promise to remain in San Antonio and to stay at home with the couple's daughter. [¶] The [contract to make monthly payments to female partner] presented to the trial court is, on its face, no more than a unilateral promise to pay, which is not an enforceable contract. [Female partner] argues that extrinsic evidence is allowed to prove that mutual promises were exchanged. We agree. 'The rule is that it may in fact be shown [with extrinsic evidence] that consideration exists even if the consideration takes the form of a promise.' The rationale for this rule is that, without consideration on both sides, the agreement is at best a partial integration, and a showing of consideration would not contradict any of its terms. [¶] Even if promises were not mutual at the time of contracting, the parties' performance on the agreement renders the contracts enforceable."

Zaremba v. Cliburn, 949 S.W.2d 822, 826-27 (Tex.App.—Fort Worth 1997, writ. denied). "This is a 'palimony' suit by nature. [Male partner #1] first filed this suit in a Tarrant County Family Court. This shows that although [male partner #1] has raised his claims as arising from a purported oral or implied partnership agreement, he considered the suit a 'family' matter. [Male partner #1] claims that he and [male partner #2] became close friends and sexual partners over 30 years ago. [Male partner #1] alleges that when [male partner #2] asked him to move in with him in 1977, he agreed to provide services like shopping, doing the mail, paying the bills, drafting checks, dealing with accountants, creditors and real estate agents, and co-managing the household in exchange for a share in [male partner #2's] income. However, pleading ancillary items of consideration does not take the agreement outside the statute of frauds and render it enforceable. The performance of [male partner #1's] household services were collateral to a nonmarital, conjugal cohabitation agreement. Each claim put forth in [male partner #1's] petition as arising from a purported oral or implied partnership agreement is an attempt to disguise the palimonial nature of the suit…."

Tatum v. Tatum, 606 S.W.2d 31, 33 (Tex.App.—Corpus Christi 1980, no writ). "It is settled in Texas that an oral promise based upon a consideration of marriage is unenforceable under the statute of frauds. Furthermore, the rendition of services by the plaintiff spouse is not sufficient part performance to render the promise enforceable."

Tex. Atty. Gen. Op. No. JC-0156 (12-16-99). "You have asked this office whether the County Clerk … is required to accept for filing a document styled a 'declaration of domestic partnership,' in which two unmarried persons who reside together declare under oath 'that the two individuals share in each other's lives in a committed relationship and that they agree to be jointly responsible for each other's financial responsibilities.' [¶] Texas recognizes two forms of marriage, ceremonial and informal. [¶] Generally, such affidavits as these are apparently made in an attempt to secure some legal recognition for unions of persons of the same sex. However, the laws of Texas do not recognize marriages between persons of the same sex, whether ceremonial or informal. Neither the county clerk, by registration of such instruments as those in question here, nor private persons by the creation of them, may alter the laws of Texas. [¶] Because such an affidavit as you describe is not, therefore, one 'required or permitted by law to be recorded,' the County Clerk … is not required to accept it for recording."

CHAPTER 2. THE MARRIAGE RELATIONSHIP

Subchapter A. Application for Marriage License

Subchapter B. Underage Applicants

Subchapter C. Ceremony & Return of License

Subchapter D. Validity of Marriage

Subchapter E. Marriage Without Formalities

Subchapter F. Rights & Duties of Spouses

SUBCHAPTER A. APPLICATION FOR MARRIAGE LICENSE

FAM §2.001. MARRIAGE LICENSE

(a) A man and a woman desiring to enter into a ceremonial marriage must obtain a marriage license from the county clerk of any county of this state.

(b) A license may not be issued for the marriage of persons of the same sex.

History of Fam §2.001: Acts 1997, 75th Leg., ch. 7, §1, eff. April 17, 1997. Source: Former Fam §1.01.

Littleton v. Prange, 9 S.W.3d 223, 225 (Tex.App.—San Antonio 1999, pet. denied). "Can there be a valid marriage between a man and a person born as a man, but surgically altered to have the physical characteristics of a woman? [¶] There is no dispute that [the decedent and the plaintiff] went through a ceremonial marriage ritual. [¶] [Plaintiff] is medically termed a transsexual.... *At 226:* She has been surgically and chemically altered to be a woman. *At 231:* We hold, as a matter of law, that [plaintiff] is a male. As a male, [plaintiff] cannot be married to another male. Her marriage to [the decedent] was invalid...."

Husband v. Pierce, 800 S.W.2d 661, 664 (Tex. App.—Tyler 1990, orig. proceeding). "[W]e conclude that even in the absence of a valid marriage license authorizing a marriage ceremony, whether conducted by a person authorized by §1.83 [now §2.202] or not, is nevertheless valid 'if there was a reasonable appearance of authority by that person, and at least one party to the marriage participated in the ceremony in good faith and that party treats the marriage as valid.' Moreover, it is noteworthy that historically ... Texas law has never mandated any particular vows, oaths, or other responses in the marriage ceremony."

FAM §2.002. APPLICATION FOR LICENSE

Except as provided by Section 2.006, each person applying for a license must:

(1) appear before the county clerk;

(2) submit the person's proof of identity and age as provided by this subchapter;

(3) provide the information applicable to that person for which spaces are provided in the application for a marriage license;

(4) mark the appropriate boxes provided in the application; and

(5) take the oath printed on the application and sign the application before the county clerk.

History of Fam §2.002: Acts 1997, 75th Leg., ch. 7, §1, eff. April 17, 1997. Source: Former Fam §1.02.

FAM §2.003. APPLICATION FOR LICENSE BY MINOR

In addition to the other requirements provided by this chapter, a person under 18 years of age applying for a license must provide to the county clerk:

(1) documents establishing, as provided by Section 2.102, parental consent for the person to the marriage;

(2) documents establishing that a prior marriage of the person has been dissolved; or

(3) a court order granted under Section 2.103 authorizing the marriage of the person.

History of Fam §2.003: Acts 1997, 75th Leg., ch. 7, §1, eff. April 17, 1997. Source: Former Fam §1.02(2)(B).

FAM §2.004. APPLICATION FORM

(a) The county clerk shall furnish the application form as prescribed by the bureau of vital statistics.

(b) The application form must contain:

(1) a heading entitled "Application for Marriage License, ____________ County, Texas";

(2) spaces for each applicant's full name, including the woman's maiden surname, address, social security number, if any, date of birth, and place of birth, including city, county, and state;

(3) a space for indicating the document tendered by each applicant as proof of identity and age;

(4) spaces for indicating whether each applicant has been divorced within the last 30 days;

(5) printed boxes for each applicant to check "true" or "false" in response to the following statement: "I am not presently married.";

(6) printed boxes for each applicant to check "true" or "false" in response to the following statement: "The other applicant is not related to me as:

(A) an ancestor or descendant, by blood or adoption;

(B) a brother or sister, of the whole or half blood or by adoption;

(C) a parent's brother or sister, of the whole or half blood or by adoption; or

(D) a son or daughter of a brother or sister, of the whole or half blood or by adoption.";

(7) printed boxes for each applicant to check "true" or "false" in response to the following statement: "I am not presently delinquent in the payment of court-ordered child support.";

(8) a printed oath reading: "I SOLEMNLY SWEAR (OR AFFIRM) THAT THE INFORMATION I HAVE GIVEN IN THIS APPLICATION IS CORRECT.";

(9) spaces immediately below the printed oath for the applicants' signatures;

(10) a certificate of the county clerk that:

(A) each applicant made the oath and the date and place that it was made; or

(B) an applicant did not appear personally but the prerequisites for the license have been fulfilled as provided by this chapter;

(11) spaces for indicating the date of the marriage and the county in which the marriage is performed; and

(12) a space for the address to which the applicants desire the completed license to be mailed.

History of Fam §2.004: Acts 1997, 75th Leg., ch. 7, §1, eff. April 17, 1997. Amended by Acts 1997, 75th Leg., ch. 776, §1, eff. Sept. 1, 1997. Source: Former Fam §1.03.

FAM §2.005. PROOF OF IDENTITY & AGE

(a) The county clerk shall require proof of the identity and age of each applicant.

(b) The proof must be established by a certified copy of the applicant's birth certificate or by some certificate, license, or document issued by this state or another state, the United States, or a foreign government.

History of Fam §2.005: Acts 1997, 75th Leg., ch. 7, §1, eff. April 17, 1997. Source: Former Fam §1.04.

FAM §2.006. ABSENT APPLICANT

(a) If an applicant is unable to appear personally before the county clerk to apply for a marriage license, any adult person or the other applicant may apply on behalf of the absent applicant.

(b) The person applying on behalf of an absent applicant shall provide to the clerk:

(1) the affidavit of the absent applicant as provided by this subchapter;

(2) proof of the identity and age of the absent applicant as provided by this subchapter; and

(3) if required because the absent applicant is a person under 18 years of age, the documents establishing parental consent, documents establishing that a prior marriage has been dissolved, or a court order authorizing the marriage of the absent, underage applicant.

History of Fam §2.006: Acts 1997, 75th Leg., ch. 7, §1, eff. April 17, 1997. Source: Former Fam §1.05(a), (b).

FAM §2.007. AFFIDAVIT OF ABSENT APPLICANT

The affidavit of an absent applicant must include:

(1) the absent applicant's full name, including the maiden surname of a female applicant, address, date of birth, place of birth, including city, county, and state, citizenship, and social security number, if any;

(2) a declaration that the absent applicant has not been divorced within the last 30 days;

(3) a declaration that the absent applicant is:

(A) not presently married; or

(B) married to the other applicant and they wish to marry again;

(4) a declaration that the other applicant is not related to the absent applicant as:

(A) an ancestor or descendant, by blood or adoption;

(B) a brother or sister, of the whole or half blood or by adoption;

(C) a parent's brother or sister, of the whole or half blood or by adoption; or

(D) a son or daughter of a brother or sister, of the whole or half blood or by adoption;

(5) a declaration that the absent applicant desires to marry and the name, age, and address of the person to whom the absent applicant desires to be married;

(6) the approximate date on which the marriage is to occur;

(7) the reason the absent applicant is unable to appear personally before the county clerk for the issuance of the license; and

(8) if the absent applicant will be unable to attend the ceremony, the appointment of any adult, other than the other applicant, to act as proxy for the purpose of participating in the ceremony.

History of Fam §2.007: Acts 1997, 75th Leg., ch. 7, §1, eff. April 17, 1997. Source: Former Fam §1.05(c).

FAM §2.008. EXECUTION OF APPLICATION BY CLERK

(a) The county clerk shall:

(1) determine that all necessary information, other than the date of the marriage ceremony, the county in which the ceremony is conducted, and the name of the person who performs the ceremony, is recorded on the application and that all necessary documents are submitted;

(2) administer the oath to each applicant appearing before the clerk;

(3) have each applicant appearing before the clerk sign the application in the clerk's presence; and

(4) execute the clerk's certificate on the application.

(b) A person appearing before the clerk on behalf of an absent applicant is not required to take the oath on behalf of the absent applicant.

History of Fam §2.008: Acts 1997, 75th Leg., ch. 7, §1, eff. April 17, 1997. Source: Former Fam §1.06.

FAM §2.009. ISSUANCE OF LICENSE

(a) Except as provided by Subsections (b) and (d), the county clerk may not issue a license if either applicant:

(1) fails to provide the information required by this subchapter;

(2) fails to submit proof of age and identity;

(3) is under 14 years of age and has not been granted a court order as provided by Section 2.103;

(4) is 14 years of age or older but under 18 years of age and has not presented at least one of the following:

(A) parental consent as provided by Section 2.102;

(B) documents establishing that a prior marriage of the applicant has been dissolved; or

(C) a court order as provided by Section 2.103;

(5) checks "false" in response to a statement in the application, except as provided by Subsection (b) or (d), or fails to make a required declaration in an affidavit required of an absent applicant; or

(6) indicates that the applicant has been divorced by a decree of a court of this state within the last 30 days, unless:

(A) the applicants were divorced from each other; or

(B) the prohibition against remarriage is waived as provided by Section 6.802.

(b) If an applicant checks "false" in response to the statement "I am not presently married," the county clerk shall inquire as to whether the applicant is presently married to the other applicant. If the applicant states that the applicant is currently married to the other applicant, the county clerk shall record that statement on the license before the administration of the oath. The county clerk may not refuse to issue a license on the ground that the applicants are already married to each other.

(c) On the proper execution of the application, the clerk shall:

(1) prepare the license;

(2) enter on the license the names of the licensees, the date that the license is issued, and, if applicable, the name of the person appointed to act as proxy for an absent applicant, if any;

(3) record the time at which the license was issued;

(4) distribute to each applicant printed materials about acquired immune deficiency syndrome (AIDS) and human immunodeficiency virus (HIV) and note on the license that the distribution was made; and

(5) distribute to each applicant a premarital education handbook provided by the attorney general under Section 2.014.

(d) The county clerk may not refuse to issue a license to an applicant on the ground that the applicant checked "false" in response to the statement "I am not presently delinquent in the payment of court-ordered child support."

History of Fam §2.009: Acts 1997, 75th Leg., ch. 7, §1, eff. April 17, 1997. Amended by Acts 1997, 75th Leg., ch. 776, §2, eff. Sept. 1, 1997; Acts 1999, 76th Leg., ch. 185, §1 (eff. Sept. 1, 1999), ch. 62, §6.01(a) (eff. Sept. 1, 1999). Source: Former Fam §1.07.

FAM §2.010. AIDS INFORMATION

Materials providing information about acquired immune deficiency syndrome (AIDS) and human immunodeficiency virus (HIV) shall be prepared and provided to the clerk by the Texas Department of Health and shall be designed to inform the applicants about:

(1) the incidence and mode of transmission of AIDS and HIV;

(2) the local availability of medical procedures, including voluntary testing, designed to show or help show whether a person has AIDS or HIV infection, antibodies to HIV, or infection with any other probable causative agent of AIDS; and

(3) available and appropriate counseling services regarding AIDS and HIV infection.

History of Fam §2.010: Acts 1997, 75th Leg., ch. 7, §1, eff. April 17, 1997. Source: Former Fam §1.07(e).

FAM §2.011. RECORDING

The county clerk shall record all licenses issued by the clerk and all documents submitted with an application for a license or note a summary of the documents on the application.

History of Fam §2.011: Acts 1997, 75th Leg., ch. 7, §1, eff. April 17, 1997. Source: Former Fam §1.08.

FAM §2.012. VIOLATION BY COUNTY CLERK; PENALTY

A county clerk or deputy county clerk who violates or fails to comply with this subchapter commits an offense. An offense under this section is a misdemeanor punishable by a fine of not less than $200 and not more than $500.

History of Fam §2.012: Acts 1997, 75th Leg., ch. 7, §1, eff. April 17, 1997. Source: Former Fam §1.09.

FAM §2.013. PREMARITAL EDUCATION REQUIREMENTS; WAIVER

(a) Each person applying for a marriage license is encouraged to attend a premarital education course of at least four hours during the year preceding the date of the application for the license.

(b) The course under Subsection (a) may be completed by:

(1) personal instruction;

(2) videotape instruction;

(3) instruction through an electronic medium; or

(4) a combination of these methods.

(c) A premarital education course should include instruction in:

(1) conflict management;

(2) communication skills;

(3) children and parenting responsibilities; and

(4) financial responsibilities.

(d) A course under this section should be offered by:

(1) a mental health professional who holds at least a master's degree with a background in family therapy; or

(2) a religious practitioner who performs counseling consistent with the laws of this state or another person designated as a program counselor by a church or religious institution.

(e) Each county clerk may maintain a roster of area course providers who meet the requirements of this section, including providers who offer the course on a sliding scale or without charge. The clerk may provide a copy of the roster on request to an applicant for a marriage license.

(f) An applicant for a marriage license who takes a course under this section shall pay any fee charged for the course.

(g) A person who seeks to be listed as a course provider on a list maintained under Subsection (e) shall notify the county clerk of the county in which the person intends to offer a course. The notification must include the applicant's professional license number or evidence of the person's position or affiliation with a church or religious institution, as appropriate, and an address at which the course provider may be contacted.

History of Fam §2.013: Acts 1999, 76th Leg., ch. 185, §2, eff. Sept. 1, 1999.

FAM §2.014. FAMILY TRUST FUND

(a) The family trust fund is created as a trust fund with the state comptroller and shall be administered by the attorney general for the beneficiaries of the fund.

(b) Money in the trust fund is derived from depositing $3 of each marriage license fee as authorized under Section 118.018(c), Local Government Code, and may be used only for:

(1) the development and distribution of a premarital education handbook;

(2) grants to institutions of higher education having academic departments that are capable of research on marriage and divorce that will assist in determining programs, courses, and policies to help strengthen families and assist children whose parents are divorcing;

(3) support for counties to create or administer free or low-cost premarital education courses;

(4) programs intended to reduce the amount of delinquent child support; and

(5) other programs the attorney general determines will assist families in this state.

(c) The premarital education handbook under Subsection (b)(1) shall be distributed to each applicant for a marriage license as provided by Section 2.009(c)(5) and shall contain information on:

(1) conflict management;

(2) communication skills;

(3) children and parenting responsibilities; and

(4) financial responsibilities.

(d) The attorney general shall appoint an advisory committee to assist in the development of the premarital education handbook. The advisory committee shall consist of nine members, including at least three members who are eligible under Section 2.013(d) to provide a premarital education course. A member of the advisory committee is not entitled to reimbursement of the member's expenses.

History of Fam §2.014: Acts 1999, 76th Leg., ch. 185, §2, eff. Sept. 1, 1999.

Sections 2.015-2.100 reserved for expansion

SUBCHAPTER B. UNDERAGE APPLICANTS

FAM §2.101. GENERAL AGE REQUIREMENT

Except as otherwise provided by this subchapter or on a showing that a prior marriage has been dissolved, a county clerk may not issue a marriage license if either applicant is under 18 years of age.

History of Fam §2.101: Acts 1997, 75th Leg., ch. 7, §1, eff. April 17, 1997. Source: Former Fam §1.51.

FAM §2.102. PARENTAL CONSENT FOR UNDERAGE APPLICANT

(a) If an applicant is 14 years of age or older but under 18 years of age, the county clerk shall issue the license if parental consent is given as provided by this section.

(b) Parental consent must be evidenced by a written declaration on a form supplied by the county clerk in which the person consents to the marriage and swears that the person is a parent (if there is no judicially designated managing conservator or guardian of the applicant's person) or a judicially designated managing conservator or guardian (whether an individual, authorized agency, or court) of the applicant's person.

(c) Except as otherwise provided by this section, consent must be acknowledged before a county clerk.

(d) If the person giving parental consent resides in another state, the consent may be acknowledged before an officer authorized to issue marriage licenses in that state.

(e) If the person giving parental consent is unable because of illness or incapacity to comply with the provisions of Subsection (c) or (d), the consent may be acknowledged before any officer authorized to take acknowledgments. A consent under this subsection must be accompanied by a physician's affidavit stating that the person giving parental consent is unable to comply because of illness or incapacity.

(f) Parental consent must be given at the time the application for the marriage license is made or not earlier than the 30th day preceding the date the application is made.

History of Fam §2.102: Acts 1997, 75th Leg., ch. 7, §1, eff. April 17, 1997. Source: Former Fam §1.52.

FAM §2.103. COURT ORDER FOR UNDERAGE APPLICANT

(a) A minor may petition the court in the minor's own name for an order granting permission to marry. In a suit under this section, the trial judge may advance the suit if the best interest of the applicant would be served by an early hearing.

(b) The petition must be filed in the county where a parent resides if a managing conservator or a guardian of the person has not been appointed. If a managing conservator or a guardian of the person has been appointed, the petition must be filed in the county where the managing conservator or the guardian of the person resides. If no person authorized to consent to marriage for the minor resides in this state, the petition must be filed in the county where the minor lives.

(c) The petition must include:

(1) a statement of the reasons the minor desires to marry;

(2) a statement of whether each parent is living or is dead;

(3) the name and residence address of each living parent; and

(4) a statement of whether a managing conservator or a guardian of the person has been appointed for the minor.

(d) Process shall be served as in other civil cases on each living parent of the minor or, if a managing conservator or a guardian of the person has been appointed, on the managing conservator or guardian of the person. Citation may be given by publication as in other civil cases, except that notice shall be published one time only.

(e) The court shall appoint a guardian ad litem to represent the minor in the proceeding and to speak for or against the petition in the manner the guardian ad litem believes to be in the best interest of the minor. The court shall specify a fee to be paid by the minor for the services of the guardian ad litem. The fee shall be collected in the same manner as other costs of the proceeding.

(f) If after a hearing the court, sitting without a jury, believes marriage to be in the best interest of the minor, the court, by order, shall grant the minor permission to marry.

History of Fam §2.103: Acts 1997, 75th Leg., ch. 7, §1, eff. April 17, 1997. Source: Former Fam §1.53.

Sections 2.104-2.200 reserved for expansion

SUBCHAPTER C. CEREMONY & RETURN OF LICENSE

FAM §2.201. EXPIRATION OF LICENSE

If a marriage ceremony has not been conducted before the 31st day after the date the license is issued, the marriage license expires.

History of Fam §2.201: Acts 1997, 75th Leg., ch. 7, §1, eff. April 17, 1997. Source: Former Fam §1.81(a).

FAM §2.202. PERSONS AUTHORIZED TO CONDUCT CEREMONY

(a) The following persons are authorized to conduct a marriage ceremony:

(1) a licensed or ordained Christian minister or priest;

(2) a Jewish rabbi;

(3) a person who is an officer of a religious organization and who is authorized by the organization to conduct a marriage ceremony; and

(4) a justice of the supreme court, judge of the court of criminal appeals, justice of the courts of appeals, judge of the district, county, and probate courts, judge of the county courts at law, judge of the courts of domestic relations, judge of the juvenile courts, retired justice or judge of those courts, justice of the peace, retired justice of the peace, or judge or magistrate of a federal court of this state.

(b) For the purposes of this section, a retired judge or justice is a former judge or justice who is vested in the Judicial Retirement System of Texas Plan One or the Judicial Retirement System of Texas Plan Two or who has an aggregate of at least 12 years of service as judge or justice of any type listed in Subsection (a)(4).

History of Fam §2.202: Acts 1997, 75th Leg., ch. 7, §1, eff. April 17, 1997. Source: Former Fam §1.83(a), (b).

Husband v. Pierce, 800 S.W.2d 661, 664 (Tex. App.—Tyler 1990, orig. proceeding). "[E]ven in the absence of a valid marriage license authorizing a marriage ceremony, whether conducted by a person authorized by §1.83 [now §2.202] or not, is nevertheless valid 'if there was a reasonable appearance of authority by that person, and at least one party to the marriage participated in the ceremony in good faith and that party treats the marriage as valid.'"

FAM §2.203. CEREMONY

(a) On receiving an unexpired marriage license, an authorized person may conduct the marriage ceremony as provided by this subchapter.

(b) A person unable to appear for the ceremony may assent to marriage by the appearance of a proxy appointed in the affidavit authorized by Subchapter A.

History of Fam §2.203: Acts 1997, 75th Leg., ch. 7, §1, eff. April 17, 1997. Source: Former Fam §1.82(a), (b).

Coulter v. Melady, 489 S.W.2d 156, 158 (Tex. App.—Texarkana, 1972, writ ref'd n.r.e.). "The Code prescribes no set form for a marriage ceremony or the procedure therein. The official conducting the ceremony is not required to elicit particular or specific information or answers from a party to the marriage, nor are participants required to speak or respond in a given way. [Purported wife's] failure to audibly respond to questions during the ceremony does not raise a fact issue as to her consent to the marriage, as her prior action shows consent as a matter of law."

FAM §2.204. 72-HOUR WAITING PERIOD; EXCEPTIONS

(a) Except as provided by this section, a marriage ceremony may not take place during the 72-hour period immediately following the issuance of the marriage license.

(b) The 72-hour waiting period after issuance of a marriage license does not apply to an applicant who:

(1) is a member of the armed forces of the United States and on active duty; or

(2) obtains a written waiver under Subsection (c).

(c) An applicant may request a judge of a court with jurisdiction in family law cases, a justice of the supreme court, a judge of the court of criminal appeals, a county judge, or a judge of a court of appeals for a written waiver permitting the marriage ceremony to take place during the 72-hour period immediately following the issuance of the marriage license. If the judge finds that there is good cause for the marriage to take place during the period, the judge shall sign the waiver. Notwithstanding any other provision of law, a judge under this section has the authority to sign a waiver under this section.

History of Fam §2.204: Acts 1997, 75th Leg., ch. 7, §1, eff. April 17, 1997. Amended by Acts 1999, 76th Leg., ch. 1052, §1, eff. Sept. 1, 1999. Source: Former Fam §1.82(c), (d).

Tex. Atty. Gen. Op. No. LO-89-28 (3-21-89). "A retired district judge may be assigned to a district court pursuant to §74.054 of the ... Government Code. A retired district judge may exercise the powers and duties of the district court judge of the court to which he is assigned. If a retired district judge is assigned to a court, he would have the authority to issue an order waiving the 72-hour waiting period provided for in §1.82 [now §2.204]. The retired judge's authority to do so would stem from his assignment to a court, however, not from his authority to perform marriages. The retired judge's authority to perform marriages would not by itself authorize him to issue a court order waiving a statutory requirement any more than a federal judge's authority to perform marriages in Texas would give him authority to issue such an order."

FAM §2.205. DISCRIMINATION IN CONDUCTING MARRIAGE PROHIBITED

(a) A person authorized to conduct a marriage ceremony by this subchapter is prohibited from discriminating on the basis of race, religion, or national origin against an applicant who is otherwise competent to be married.

(b) On a finding by the State Commission on Judicial Conduct that a person has intentionally violated Subsection (a), the commission may recommend to the supreme court that the person be removed from office.

History of Fam §2.205: Acts 1997, 75th Leg., ch. 7, §1, eff. April 17, 1997. Source: Former Fam §1.83(c), (d).

Tex. Atty. Gen. Op. No. JM-1 (3-8-83). "[A] justice of the peace, when conducting a marriage ceremony, is clothed with the State power, and acts in the name and for the State. As a result, the equal protection clause is applicable to his performance of that ceremony. The United States Supreme Court has held that a state may not, consistent with that constitutional provision, restrict the freedom to marry on racial grounds. Once a justice of the peace undertakes to exercise the authority granted him by §1.83 [now §2.202], he may not refuse to exercise it on racial grounds. We conclude that a justice of the peace is barred by the equal protection clause from imposing a racial test upon the right to marry." (Internal quotations omitted.)

FAM §2.206. RETURN OF LICENSE; PENALTY

(a) The person who conducts a marriage ceremony shall record on the license the date on which and the county in which the ceremony is performed and the person's name, subscribe the license, and return the license to the county clerk who issued it not later than the 30th day after the date the ceremony is conducted.

(b) A person who fails to comply with this section commits an offense. An offense under this section is a misdemeanor punishable by a fine of not less than $200 and not more than $500.

History of Fam §2.206: Acts 1997, 75th Leg., ch. 7, §1, eff. April 17, 1997. Source: Former Fam §1.84.

FAM §2.207. MARRIAGE CONDUCTED AFTER LICENSE EXPIRED; PENALTY

(a) A person who is to conduct a marriage ceremony shall determine whether the license has expired from the county clerk's endorsement on the license.

(b) A person who conducts a marriage ceremony after the marriage license has expired commits an offense. An offense under this section is a misdemeanor punishable by a fine of not less than $200 and not more than $500.

History of Fam §2.207: Acts 1997, 75th Leg., ch. 7, §1, eff. April 17, 1997. Source: Former Fam §1.81.

FAM §2.208. RECORDING & DELIVERY OF LICENSE

(a) The county clerk shall record a returned marriage license and mail the license to the address indicated on the application.

(b) On the application form the county clerk shall record:

(1) the date of the marriage ceremony;

(2) the county in which the ceremony was conducted; and

(3) the name of the person who conducted the ceremony.

History of Fam §2.208: Acts 1997, 75th Leg., ch. 7, §1, eff. April 17, 1997. Source: Former Fam §1.85.

FAM §2.209. DUPLICATE LICENSE

(a) On the application and proof of identity of a person whose marriage is recorded in the records of the county clerk, the county clerk shall issue a duplicate marriage license completed with information as contained in the records.

(b) On the application and proof of identity of both persons to whom a marriage license was issued but not recorded as required by Section 2.208, the county clerk shall issue a duplicate license if each person applying submits to the clerk an affidavit stating:

(1) that the persons to whom the original license was issued were married to each other before the expiration date of the original license by a person authorized to conduct a marriage ceremony;

(2) the name of the person who conducted the ceremony; and

(3) the date of the ceremony.

History of Fam §2.209: Acts 1997, 75th Leg., ch. 7, §1, eff. April 17, 1997. Source: Former Fam §1.86.

Sections 2.210-2.300 reserved for expansion

SUBCHAPTER D. VALIDITY OF MARRIAGE

FAM §2.301. FRAUD, MISTAKE, OR ILLEGALITY IN OBTAINING LICENSE

Except as otherwise provided by this chapter, the validity of a marriage is not affected by any fraud, mistake, or illegality that occurred in obtaining the marriage license.

History of Fam §2.301: Acts 1997, 75th Leg., ch. 7, §1, eff. April 17, 1997. Source: Former Fam §2.02.

Foster v. State, 20 S.W. 823, 824 (Tex.Crim. App.1892). "That the officer signed the license as district clerk instead as county clerk could not and did not operate to render the marriage void. The evidence clearly manifests a sufficient marriage, duly solemnized by a Catholic priest according to the ritual of that church. This was sufficient. This court cannot agree to the proposition that a mistake of the clerk in issuing a marriage license can invalidate a marriage solemnly consummated between the parties."

Williams v. White, 263 S.W.2d 666, 668 (Tex. App.—Austin 1953, writ ref'd n.r.e.). "[O]ur courts have held that statutes regulating the mode of entering into the marriage relations including the consent of the parents and provisions requiring that a license be obtained before performance of the marriage ceremony, are merely directory, and that, although marriage is entered into otherwise than in accordance with the provisions of such statutes, it is nevertheless a valid marriage unless, of course, the statute declares that its violation shall render the marriage void."

FAM §2.302. CEREMONY CONDUCTED BY UNAUTHORIZED PERSON

The validity of a marriage is not affected by the lack of authority of the person conducting the marriage ceremony if:

(1) there was a reasonable appearance of authority by that person; and

(2) at least one party to the marriage participated in the ceremony in good faith and that party treats the marriage as valid.

History of Fam §2.302: Acts 1997, 75th Leg., ch. 7, §1, eff. April 17, 1997. Source: Former Fam §2.03.

Husband v. Pierce, 800 S.W.2d 661, 664 (Tex. App.—Tyler 1990, orig. proceeding). See Annotation in §2.202.

Sections 2.303-2.400 reserved for expansion

SUBCHAPTER E. MARRIAGE WITHOUT FORMALITIES

FAM §2.401. PROOF OF INFORMAL MARRIAGE

(a) In a judicial, administrative, or other proceeding, the marriage of a man and woman may be proved by evidence that:

(1) a declaration of their marriage has been signed as provided by this subchapter; or

(2) the man and woman agreed to be married and after the agreement they lived together in this state as husband and wife and there represented to others that they were married.

(b) If a proceeding in which a marriage is to be proved as provided by Subsection (a)(2) is not commenced before the second anniversary of the date on which the parties separated and ceased living together, it is rebuttably presumed that the parties did not enter into an agreement to be married.

(c) A person under 18 years of age may not:

(1) be a party to an informal marriage; or

(2) execute a declaration of informal marriage under Section 2.402.

History of Fam §2.401: Acts 1997, 75th Leg., ch. 7, §1, eff. April 17, 1997. Amended by Acts 1997, 75th Leg., ch. 1362, §1, eff. Sept. 1, 1997. Source: Former Fam §1.91.

Generally

Mossler v. Shields, 818 S.W.2d 752, 754 (Tex.1991). "Because [alleged wife] has never proved that she was the common-law wife of [alleged husband], estoppel pursuant to a dismissal with prejudice does not condemn the two parties to a life sentence in marriage; rather, it functions as a bar to any future claims of whether a common-law marriage existed prior to the dismissal of the original claim. [¶] Moreover, it is well established that a dismissal with prejudice functions as a final determination on the merits. ... Allowing [alleged wife] to raise the identical matters in Beaumont that were dismissed with prejudice in Houston ... would 'allow a party who had a fair opportunity to present his claims in one suit, and whose cause was dismissed with prejudice for failure to comply with discovery orders, to present those same claims ... in a subsequent suit between the same parties.'"

Tompkins v. State, 774 S.W.2d 195, 209 (Tex. Crim.App.1987). "[T]estimony of a witness that merely constitutes a conclusion that a common law marriage exists is not sufficient, standing alone, to establish a common law marriage."

Amaye v. Oravetz, 57 S.W.3d 581, 584 (Tex.App.—Houston [14th Dist.] 2001, pet. denied). Husband's "motion for summary judgment asserted he was entitled to judgment *as a matter of law* because, under §2.401(b) ..., [wife] failed to prove the existence of her common-law marriage within the required two-year period. We hold that [husband]'s motion provided [wife] with sufficient specificity to afford her the chance to avoid summary judgment, notwithstanding the fact that his legal conclusion about the effect of the §2.401 presumption was incorrect."

Ballesteros v. Jones, 985 S.W.2d 485, 489 (Tex. App.—San Antonio 1998, pet. denied). "A valid common law marriage consists of three elements: (1) an agreement presently to be husband and wife; (2) living together in Texas as husband and wife; and (3) representing to others in Texas that they are married. All three elements must exist at the same time."

Georgiades v. Di Ferrante, 871 S.W.2d 878, 881 (Tex.App.—Houston [14th Dist.] 1994, writ denied). The "marital status of parties is a proper subject for declaratory relief, but only where an actual, justiciable controversy exists. Where marital status is clear, no declaratory judgment can be had."

Texas Employers' Ins. Ass'n v. Borum, 834 S.W.2d 395, 399 (Tex.App.—San Antonio 1992, writ denied). "Proof of a common-law marriage pursuant to the Texas Family Code requires: 1) an agreement presently to be married; 2) living together *in this state* as husband and wife; and 3) holding each other out to the public *in this state* as husband and wife. The language in subsections (2) and (3) preclude proof of a common-law marriage when the acts occurred in a state other than Texas."

Tatum v. Tatum, 478 S.W.2d 629, 631 (Tex.App.—Fort Worth 1972, writ dism'd). "A common law marriage is a legal and valid marriage. It can only be terminated by death, divorce or annulment. Because of this, the validity of the common law marriage which was consummated by the parties to this suit ... could not be vitiated by subsequent acts of the parties ... after some five years of marriage to one another."

Present Agreement

Russell v. Russell, 865 S.W.2d 929, 933 (Tex.1993). "Proof of cohabitation and representations to others that the couple are married may constitute circumstantial evidence of an agreement to be married. However, the circumstances of each case must be determined based upon its own facts. We conclude that §1.91 [now §2.401] does not require direct evidence of an agreement to be married in order to establish a common law marriage, but that the agreement may be proved by circumstantial evidence."

Collora v. Navarro, 574 S.W.2d 65, 68 (Tex.1978). "The only direct evidence relating to the first element—a present agreement to be husband and wife—was [alleged wife's] testimony that she and [her alleged husband] had 'agreed to a marriage.' Her testimony was direct, positive, and uncontradicted. [Husband's attorney] chose not to cross-examine her, nor did he call her as an adverse witness. There was no other direct evidence produced at trial that proved or disproved her testimony. Under these circumstances, the court of civil appeals held that [the alleged wife's] testimony, standing alone, could do no more than raise a fact issue of credibility and could not support a directed verdict. With this conclusion we cannot agree."

Flores v. Flores, 847 S.W.2d 648, 650 (Tex.App.—Waco 1993, writ denied). "The evidence must show that the parties intended to have a present, immediate, and permanent marital relationship and that they did in fact agree to be husband and wife. *At 652:* Occasional references to 'my wife' or 'my husband' do not prove a tacit agreement to be married without corroboration. If the statement is made in a self-serving context ... it may not have great weight. On the other hand, a forthright assertion of marriage with the consequences of liability ... may be far more probative of such an agreement."

Faglie v. Williams, 569 S.W.2d 557, 565 (Tex. App.—Austin 1978, writ ref'd n.r.e.). "No distinction exists between cases in which the evidence of an agreement is express and those in which the evidence is implied, and the existence of the agreement to be married remains a fact question in either instance."

Cohabitation

Ex parte Threet, 333 S.W.2d 361, 363 (Tex.1960). "All of the acts of intercourse ... occurred at her parents' house or at the home of defendant's parents. After such meetings, the one away from home would 'go home.' [¶] The plaintiff candidly admitted that she and the defendant never established a home together. She never moved in with defendant at his house, nor he into hers. She continued to give her parents' residence as her residence. Neither moved any of his or her clothes or personal effects into any common room or apartment. *At 364:* It is our opinion that the facts above set out do not constitute evidence that the couple lived together *as man and wife*...."

Allen v. Allen, 966 S.W.2d 658, 661 (Tex.App.—San Antonio 1998, pet. denied). "[W]e do not believe 'cohabitation' would encompass, without more, situations involving a frequent overnight guest or someone who stores personal property at someone else's home."

De Shazo v. Christian, 191 S.W.2d 495, 496-97 (Tex.App.—Amarillo 1945, writ ref'd n.r.e.). "There was ... testimony ... which indicated strongly that appellant was not cohabitating with [her alleged common law husband] in the usual manner but that they occupied separate rooms.... One witness testified that ... appellant told her she did not spend her nights at their farm home but that after dark she went to her sister's home a short distance from the farm, spent the nights there, and returned to the farm before daylight the following mornings. This witness and her husband purchased some of the furniture belonging to appellant and [her alleged common law husband], and she said that she and her husband observed there were two beds in the [farm] home and that it was evident that each of them was being occupied by someone. [¶] From the foregoing resume of the testimony, we think it is conclusive that appellant wholly failed to show by legal and competent evidence that she was the common-law wife...."

Holding Out

Estate of Claveria v. Claveria, 615 S.W.2d 164, 166 (Tex.1981). "[P]roof of common-law marriage may be shown by the conduct of the parties, or by such circumstances as their addressing each other as husband and wife, acknowledging their children as legitimate, joining in conveyances as spouses, and occupying the same dwelling place. [¶] When two persons not living together occasionally refer to each other as a spouse, those isolated references have been held, in some instances as a matter of law, not to have established a common-law marriage. Further, the act of one of the parties to an alleged common-law marriage in celebrating a ceremonial marriage with another person without having first obtained a divorce tends to discredit the first relationship and to show that it was not valid. Still, the circumstances of each case must be determined based upon its own facts."

Ex parte Threet, 333 S.W.2d 361, 364-65 (Tex. 1960). "[T]he introduction of defendant as her husband to two close friends, and telling two or three others that she was married to defendant, constituted no evidence that plaintiff and [defendant] were living together as husband and wife and holding themselves out to the public as man and wife. Under the Texas decisions, there can be no secret common law marriage as such. The secrecy is inconsistent and irreconcilable with the requirement of a public holding out that the couple are living together as husband and wife." *See also* ***Eris v. Phares***, 39 S.W.3d 708, 714-715 (Tex. App.—Houston [1st Dist.] 2001, pet. denied).

Lee v. Lee, 981 S.W.2d 903, 906 (Tex.App.—Houston [1st Dist.] 1998, no pet.). "The statutory requirement of 'represented to others' is synonymous with the judicial requirement of 'holding out to the public.' It is well settled that 'holding out' may be established by conduct and actions of the parties. Spoken words are not necessary to establish representation as husband and wife."

Dalworth Trucking Co. v. Bulen, 924 S.W.2d 728, 735 (Tex.App.—Texarkana 1996, no writ). The statement by the decedent's father that appellee and decedent entered into a common law marriage "could be construed as a legal opinion, was actually a lay person's opinion based on observations and not on special knowledge. It was relevant to the question of whether [decedent and appellee] held themselves out as husband and wife, one of the elements of a common law marriage."

Capacity

Villegas v. Griffin Indus., 975 S.W.2d 745, 749 (Tex.App.—Corpus Christi 1998, pet. denied). "[I]n order to establish a valid marriage, the parties must possess the legal capacity to marry and there must not be any legal impediment prohibiting the marriage contract. *At 750:* Informal marriages, like ceremonial marriages, can only be dissolved by legal proceedings decreeing annulment or divorce, or by the death of one spouse. A marriage contracted while one party is married to another person is void *ab initio* as a matter of law, but an informal marriage will be recognized as beginning on the date the prior marriage is dissolved."

FAM §2.402. DECLARATION & REGISTRATION OF INFORMAL MARRIAGE

(a) A declaration of informal marriage must be signed on a form prescribed by the bureau of vital statistics and provided by the county clerk. Each party to the declaration shall provide the information required in the form.

(b) The declaration form must contain:

(1) a heading entitled "Declaration and Registration of Informal Marriage, ___________ County, Texas";

(2) spaces for each party's full name, including the woman's maiden surname, address, date of birth, place of birth, including city, county, and state, and social security number, if any;

(3) a space for indicating the type of document tendered by each party as proof of age and identity;

(4) printed boxes for each party to check "true" or "false" in response to the following statement: "The other party is not related to me as:

(A) an ancestor or descendant, by blood or adoption;

(B) a brother or sister, of the whole or half blood or by adoption;

(C) a parent's brother or sister, of the whole or half blood or by adoption; or

(D) a son or daughter of a brother or sister, of the whole or half blood or by adoption.";

(5) a printed declaration and oath reading: "I SOLEMNLY SWEAR (OR AFFIRM) THAT WE, THE UNDERSIGNED, ARE MARRIED TO EACH OTHER BY VIRTUE OF THE FOLLOWING FACTS: ON OR ABOUT (DATE) WE AGREED TO BE MARRIED, AND AFTER THAT DATE WE LIVED TOGETHER AS HUSBAND AND WIFE AND IN THIS STATE WE REPRESENTED TO OTHERS THAT WE WERE MARRIED. SINCE THE DATE OF MARRIAGE TO THE OTHER PARTY I HAVE NOT BEEN MARRIED TO ANY OTHER PERSON. THIS DECLARATION IS TRUE AND THE INFORMATION IN IT WHICH I HAVE GIVEN IS CORRECT.";

(6) spaces immediately below the printed declaration and oath for the parties' signatures; and

(7) a certificate of the county clerk that the parties made the declaration and oath and the place and date it was made.

(c) Repealed by Acts 1997, 75th Leg., ch. 1362, Sec. 4, eff. Sept. 1, 1997.

History of Fam §2.402: Acts 1997, 75th Leg., ch. 7, §1, eff. April 17, 1997. Amended by Acts 1997, 75th Leg., ch. 1362, §4, eff. Sept. 1, 1997. Source: Former Fam §1.92.

Amaye v. Oravetz, 57 S.W.3d 581, 584 n.3 (Tex. App.—Houston [14th Dist.] 2001, pet. denied). "A declaration and registration is simply a method of establishing a common law marriage; it is not an independent basis, as [wife] suggests, upon which a marriage may be founded. Accordingly, [wife's] failure to present evidence to rebut the presumption of no common law marriage negates this 'basis' as well."

FAM §2.403. PROOF OF IDENTITY & AGE

The county clerk shall require proof of the identity and age of each party to the declaration of informal marriage to be established by a certified copy of the party's birth certificate or by some certificate, license, or document issued by this state or another state, the United States, or a foreign government.

History of Fam §2.403: Acts 1997, 75th Leg., ch. 7, §1, eff. April 17, 1997. Source: Former Fam §1.93.

FAM §2.404. RECORDING OF DECLARATION OF INFORMAL MARRIAGE

(a) The county clerk shall:

(1) determine that all necessary information is recorded on the declaration of informal marriage form and that all necessary documents are submitted to the clerk;

(2) administer the oath to each party to the declaration;

(3) have each party sign the declaration in the clerk's presence; and

(4) execute the clerk's certificate to the declaration.

(b) The county clerk may not certify or record the declaration if:

(1) either party fails to supply any information or provide any document required by this subchapter;

(2) either party is under 18 years of age; or

(3) either party checks "false" in response to the statement of relationship to the other party.

(c) On execution of the declaration, the county clerk shall record the declaration and all documents submitted with the declaration or note a summary of them on the declaration form, deliver the original of the declaration to the parties, and send a copy to the bureau of vital statistics.

(d) A declaration recorded as provided in this section is prima facie evidence of the marriage of the parties.

(e) At the time the parties sign the declaration, the clerk shall distribute to each party printed materials about acquired immune deficiency syndrome (AIDS) and human immunodeficiency virus (HIV). The clerk shall note on the declaration that the distribution was made. The materials shall be prepared and provided to the clerk by the Texas Department of Health and shall be designed to inform the parties about:

(1) the incidence and mode of transmission of AIDS and HIV;

(2) the local availability of medical procedures, including voluntary testing, designed to show or help show whether a person has AIDS or HIV infection, antibodies to HIV, or infection with any other probable causative agent of AIDS; and

(3) available and appropriate counseling services regarding AIDS and HIV infection.

History of Fam §2.404: Acts 1997, 75th Leg., ch. 7, §1, eff. April 17, 1997. Amended by Acts 1997, 75th Leg., ch. 1362, §2, eff. Sept. 1, 1997. Source: Former Fam §1.94.

Colburn v. State, 966 S.W.2d 511, 514 (Tex. Crim.App.1998). "A properly recorded declaration of informal marriage constitutes *prima facie* proof of the informal marriage. Thus, the trial court may find the common law marriage proven based upon the declaration alone, but evidence may be offered rebutting the existence of the marriage as sworn to or stated in the declaration. In other words, the trial court is not bound to find a marriage as stated in the declaration when there is evidence to the contrary."

FAM §2.405. VIOLATION BY COUNTY CLERK; PENALTY

A county clerk or deputy county clerk who violates this subchapter commits an offense. An offense under this section is a misdemeanor punishable by a fine of not less than $200 and not more than $500.

History of Fam §2.405: Acts 1997, 75th Leg., ch. 7, §1, eff. April 17, 1997. Source: Former Fam §1.95.

Sections 2.406-2.500 reserved for expansion

SUBCHAPTER F. RIGHTS & DUTIES OF SPOUSES

FAM §2.501. DUTY TO SUPPORT

(a) Each spouse has the duty to support the other spouse.

(b) A spouse who fails to discharge the duty of support is liable to any person who provides necessaries to the spouse to whom support is owed.

History of Fam §2.501: Acts 1997, 75th Leg., ch. 7, §1, eff. April 17, 1997. Source: Former Fam §4.02.

Ex parte Hall, 854 S.W.2d 656, 658 (Tex.1993). "The obligation which the law imposes on spouses to support one another ... is not considered a 'debt' within Article I, §18 [of the Texas Constitution], but a legal duty arising out of the status of the parties. ... However, a person may also contract to support his spouse ..., and that obligation, to the extent it exceeds his legal duty, is a debt."

Smoak v. Smoak, 525 S.W.2d 888, 891 (Tex.App.—Texarkana 1975, writ dism'd). "The wife's recovery of attorney fees in a divorce action is founded upon the husband's liability to furnish necessaries." (Internal quotations omitted.)

Gabel v. Blackburn Operating Corp., 442 S.W.2d 818, 820 (Tex.App.—Amarillo 1969, no writ). "It is undisputed that at the time the various charges were made at appellee's store, the appellant was married to the codefendant in this case, and actually lived with her for several months thereafter. Although a marriage relationship does not make the wife a general agent of the husband, it does confer upon the wife agency to purchase, and contract for necessities for which the husband will be liable. [T]he husband has a duty to support his wife and children, as well as the wife a duty to support a husband that is unable to support himself. Therefore, it was not necessary that the appellant have actually purchased the merchandise himself to become liable for the payment therefor."

SUBTITLE B. PROPERTY RIGHTS & LIABILITIES

CHAPTER 3. MARITAL PROPERTY RIGHTS & LIABILITIES

SUBCHAPTER A. GENERAL RULES FOR SEPARATE & COMMUNITY PROPERTY

FAM §3.001. SEPARATE PROPERTY

A spouse's separate property consists of:

(1) the property owned or claimed by the spouse before marriage;

(2) the property acquired by the spouse during marriage by gift, devise, or descent; and

(3) the recovery for personal injuries sustained by the spouse during marriage, except any recovery for loss of earning capacity during marriage.

History of Fam §3.001: Acts 1997, 75th Leg., ch. 7, §1, eff. April 17, 1997. Source: Former Fam §5.01(a).

Generally

Welder v. Lambert, 44 S.W. 281, 286 (Tex.1898). "In this cause the title [to disputed land] originated in the contract of [father] with the state of ... Texas. That contract ... was the 'cause' of the title. [Father] was single when it was entered into, and the right to earn the lands acquired by it was his separate property. The title relates to its origin, and must take the impress of its character from it."

Rusk v. Rusk, 5 S.W.3d 299, 303 (Tex.App.—Houston [14th Dist.] 1999, pet. denied). "The characterization of property as either 'community' or 'separate' is determined by the inception of title to the property. The major consideration in determining the characterization of property as community or separate is the intention of spouses shown by the circumstances surrounding the inception of title. Inception of title occurs when a party first has right of claim to the property by virtue of which title is finally vested."

Lipsey v. Lipsey, 983 S.W.2d 345, 350 (Tex.App.—Fort Worth 1998, no pet.). "[W]hen separate property produces income and that income is acquired by a spouse, it is community property. However, an increase in the value of an item of separate property is an inherent part of the item and cannot be separated from it."

Ridgell v. Ridgell, 960 S.W.2d 144, 148 (Tex.App.—Corpus Christi 1997, no pet.). "Property acquired in exchange for separate property becomes the separate property of the spouse who exchanged the property."

Harris v. Harris, 765 S.W.2d 798, 803 (Tex.App.—Houston [14th Dist.] 1989, writ denied). "As in the case of stock splits and increases, analogous to this situation involving 'units' of a partnership, mutations and increases in separate property remain separate property."

Cook v. Cook, 679 S.W.2d 581, 583 (Tex.App.—San Antonio 1984, no writ). "Where property is purchased partly with community funds and partly with separate funds, the property is community property to the extent and in the proportion that the purchase price is paid by the community, while the spouse providing the separate funds will have a separate interest in the property to the amount of investment of separate funds."

Property Owned Before Marriage

Jensen v. Jensen, 665 S.W.2d 107, 109 (Tex.1984). "[A]ll property held by either a husband or a wife before marriage remains the separate property of such spouse and the status of the property is to be determined by the origin of the title to the property, and not by the acquisition of the final title."

Gift, Devise, or Descent

In re Marriage of Case, 28 S.W.3d 154, 158-59 (Tex.App.—Texarkana 2000, no pet.). "The general rule in divorce cases is that, when a spouse uses separate property to acquire property during marriage and takes title to that property in the names of both spouses, a presumption arises that the purchasing spouse intended to make a gift of one half of the separate funds to the other spouse. [¶] However, in 1979 the Nontestamentary Transfers Chapter of the Texas Probate Code was adopted. This chapter of the Probate Code contains specific provisions governing the ownership of joint bank accounts. The provisions govern the basic ownership and withdrawal rights both during and after the life of a depositor. [¶] The Texas Probate Code ... provides, 'A joint account belongs, during the lifetime of all parties, to the parties in proportion to the net contributions by each to the sums on deposit, unless there is clear and convincing evidence of a different intent.' This statutory provision of the Probate Code has the effect of overriding any common-law gift presumptions on bank accounts. The Probate Code specifically spells out how the ownership of the property is to be determined. [¶] Section 437 of the Texas Probate Code specifically provides, 'a multiple-party account created with community funds is subject to Article XVI, §15 of the Texas Constitution, and will not in any way alter community property rights.' However, the gift presumption is not a community property right, but rather a separate property presumption."

Dutton v. Dutton, 18 S.W.3d 849, 852 (Tex.App.—Eastland 2000, pet. denied). "A joint gift to a husband and wife is not community property; rather, each gets a one-half undivided separate interest in the gift." *See also* ***Roosth v. Roosth***, 889 S.W.2d 445, 457 (Tex. App.—Houston [14th Dist.] 1994, writ denied) (each spouse gets one-half undivided separate interest in wedding gifts).

Powell v. Powell, 822 S.W.2d 181, 183 (Tex.App.—Houston [1st Dist.] 1991, writ denied). "All property acquired during marriage by gift is the separate property of that spouse. [¶] A gift is a transfer of property made voluntarily and gratuitously. A gift requires: (1) an intent to make a gift, (2) delivery of the property, and (3) acceptance of the property. The burden of proving a gift is on the party claiming the gift."

Pemelton v. Pemelton, 809 S.W.2d 642, 646 (Tex. App.—Corpus Christi 1991), *rev'd on other grounds*, 836 S.W.2d 145 (Tex.1992). "Proof that the property was acquired by gift during the marriage may rebut the community presumption. A presumption of separate property arises when (1) one spouse is grantor and the other spouse is grantee, or (2) one spouse furnishes separate property consideration and title is taken in the name of the other spouse, or (3) the instrument of conveyance contains a significant recital that states that the consideration is paid from the separate funds of a spouse or that the property is conveyed to a spouse as his or her separate property. Furthermore, a grantor may make a gift of encumbered property and a conveyance may be a gift even if the grantee assumes an obligation to extinguish the encumbrance. *At 647:* A gift is a transfer of property made voluntarily and gratuitously, without consideration. The burden of proving a gift is on the person claiming the gift was made. Although a conveyance of title from parent to child is presumed a gift, such presumption is rebuttable by evidence showing the facts and circumstances surrounding the deed's execution in addition to the deed's recitations. [¶] Lack of consideration is an essential characteristic of a gift. An exchange of consideration precludes a gift. Gift and onerous consideration are exact antitheses. A recital of onerous consideration in a deed negatives the idea of a gift." (Internal quotations omitted.)

Personal Injury

Douglas v. Delp, 987 S.W.2d 879, 883 (Tex.1999). "Any mental anguish damages recovered are part of the injured spouse's separate property."

Lewis v. Lewis, 944 S.W.2d 630, 630 (Tex.1997). "The character of [workers'] compensation benefits paid during marriage is determined not by when the injury occurred, but by when the loss of earning capacity occurred."

Graham v. Franco, 488 S.W.2d 390, 397 (Tex. 1972). "In any event, the reason for the rule that the negligence of the husband should be imputed to the wife (that he would profit from his own wrong) falls where the recovery for her injuries is her separate property. We have held that such recovery is her separate property, and the recovery will not be to him or the community. Therefore, the contributory negligence of the husband does not bar the recovery by the wife."

Slaton v. Slaton, 987 S.W.2d 180, 184 (Tex.App.—Houston [14th Dist.] 1999, pet. denied). Money "received as the result of a settlement agreement for personal injuries sustained by a spouse during the marriage has been found to be separate property, minus loss of earnings and other consequential damages to the community estate. Thus, we reject appellant's contention that the settlement agreement was merely a contract that proceeds should be viewed as community property."

Osborn v. Osborn, 961 S.W.2d 408, 414 (Tex.App.—Houston [1st Dist.] 1997, writ denied). "There is no presumption that a potential recovery for a personal injuries to the body of a spouse is community property. ... The damages that are the separate property of the injured spouse include those for disfigurement and for physical pain and suffering in the past and in the future. [¶] To the extent the marital partnership was injured, the community estate is entitled to recover damages. The damages that belong to the community estate include lost wages of the injured spouse, damages for medical expenses, and other expenses associated with the injury to the community estate. To the extent the other spouse was injured by loss of consortium, those damages are the separate property of the other spouse." *See also* ***Licata v. Licata***, 11 S.W.3d 269, 273 (Tex. App.—Houston [14th Dist.] 1999, no pet.).

Kirkpatrick v. Hurst, 472 S.W.2d 295, 303 (Tex. App.—Texarkana 1971), *rev'd on other grounds*, 484 S.W.2d 587 (Tex.1972). "[W]hen a husband and wife are joined in marriage they each bring with them as their separate property their bodies. Thus, an injury to the body of either spouse after marriage is such that leaves it in a diminished condition. The recovery for this diminished condition is the separate property of the spouse who recovers damages for the depleted or diminished condition."

Putative Marriage

Garduno v. Garduno, 760 S.W.2d 735, 739 (Tex. App.—Corpus Christi 1988, no writ). "The effect of a putative marriage is to give the putative spouse who acted in good faith the same right in property acquired during the marital relationship as if he or she were a lawful spouse. However, there being no legally recognized marriage, property acquired during a putative marriage is not community property, but jointly owned separate property."

FAM §3.002. COMMUNITY PROPERTY

Community property consists of the property, other than separate property, acquired by either spouse during marriage.

History of Fam §3.002: Acts 1997, 75th Leg., ch. 7, §1, eff. April 17, 1997. Source: Former Fam §5.01(b).

Generally

Lee v. Lee, 247 S.W. 828, 832-33 (Tex.1923). "The word 'acquired' is not to be construed in any restricted sense, but must necessarily have that broad signification as will include all effects or gains or property of every kind coming to the husband or wife during coverture in any manner other than by 'gift, devise or descent.'"

McClary v. Thompson, 65 S.W.3d 829, 836 (Tex. App.—Fort Worth 2002, pet. denied). Although we agree with ***Dewey v. Dewey***, 745 S.W.2d 514 (Tex. App.—Corpus Christi 1988, writ denied) "that the inception-of-title rule has no application in the context of retirement benefits, the fact is that whether we characterize the Texas rule as one of apportionment or inception-of-title, the result is the same, i.e., apportionment. Therefore, we reject [wife]'s argument that the character of the entire retirement account must be determined based on the inception-of-title rule. We conclude that, under either theory, the contributions and interest earned during the marriage constituted community property."

Wilson v. Wilson, 44 S.W.3d 597, 601 (Tex.App.—Fort Worth 2001, no pet.). "Because [husband and wife] were still married even after their separation in 1990, the property they continued to acquire between the date of separation and divorce was still considered community property, unless either spouse could establish that the property was separate property under §3.001."

Camp v. Camp, 972 S.W.2d 906, 908 n.1 (Tex. App.—Corpus Christi 1998, pet. denied). "The characterization of property as either 'community' or 'separate' is determined by the inception of title to the property. Inception of title occurs when a party first has right of claim to the property by virtue of which title is finally vested."

Business Interest—Corporations

Vallone v. Vallone, 644 S.W.2d 455, 458 (Tex.1982). "Consideration of whether a corporation is an *alter ego* for purposes of determining whether assets held in the corporation's name should be treated as community property is an issue of fact from which the status of the property is determined."

Lifshutz v. Lifshutz, 61 S.W.3d 511, 516-17 (Tex. App.—San Antonio 2001, pet. denied). "In exceptional circumstances, the principles of alter ego and piercing the corporate veil have been applied to divorce cases in what could be termed 'reverse piercing.' Piercing the corporate veil in a divorce case allows the divorce court to characterize as community property corporate assets that would otherwise be the separate property of one spouse. [P]iercing in the divorce context allows the trial court to move assets out of the corporation and divide them between spouses as part of the shareholder's community estate. The concepts of alter ego and piercing are applied in divorce cases to achieve an equitable result, that is, a just and right settlement of the marital estate. [¶] Generally, the trial court pierces in a divorce case to avoid leaving the community estate with virtually no property. Other courts have considered whether the conduct of the stockholder resulted in fraud upon the other spouse or third parties. [¶] Thus to properly pierce in a divorce case, the trial court must find something more than mere dominance of the corporation by the spouse. At the least, a finding of alter ego sufficient to justify piercing in the divorce context requires the trial court to find: (1) unity between the separate property corporation and the spouse such that the separateness of the corporation has ceased to exist, and (2) the spouse's improper use of the corporation damaged the community estate beyond that which might be remedied by a claim for reimbursement."

Hunt v. Hunt, 952 S.W.2d 564, 567 (Tex.App.—Eastland 1997, no writ). "When a corporation is funded with separate property, the corporation is separate property."

Siefkas v. Siefkas, 902 S.W.2d 72, 79 (Tex.App.—El Paso 1995, no writ). "[U]nless the corporation is a spouse's alter ego, a court may only award a spouse's interest in the corporation, not specific corporate property."

Thomas v. Thomas, 738 S.W.2d 342, 343 (Tex. App.—Houston [1st Dist.] 1987, writ denied). Wife "admits that in an ordinary corporation, retained earnings are a corporate asset. They are not marital property, separate or community. [Wife] contends, however, that retained earnings of a Subchapter S corporation should be treated as community property because the community has paid federal income tax on them. This, she argues, justifies the recognition of a community interest in the retained earnings. We disagree. [¶] Subchapter S status does not determine who owns the corporation's earnings. It merely provides an alternate method to tax the corporation's income. A Subchapter S corporation may distribute its income, but, like any other corporation, it is not required to do so. Corporate distributions, regardless of form, are controlled by state law. The shareholder in a Subchapter S corporation has no greater rights over corporate property than a shareholder in any other corporation."

Business Interest—Goodwill

Salinas v. Rafati, 948 S.W.2d 286, 291 (Tex.1997). "The goodwill of the company, apart from the goodwill associated with the [professional] himself, [can] be considered in dividing the community estate upon divorce."

Nail v. Nail, 486 S.W.2d 761, 764 (Tex.1972). "[I]t cannot be said that the accrued good will in [a professional practice] was an earned or vested property right at the time of the divorce or that it qualifies as property subject to division by decree of the court. It did not possess value or constitute an asset separate and apart from his person, or from his individual ability to practice his profession. It would be extinguished in event of his death, or retirement, or disablement, as well as in event of the sale of his practice or the loss of his patients, whatever the cause. ... Accordingly, we hold that the good will of petitioner's medical practice [personal goodwill] that may have accrued at the time of the divorce was not property in the estate of the parties.... [¶] It is to be understood that in resolving the question at hand we are not concerned with good will as an asset incident to the sale of a professional practice, or that may exist in a professional partnership or corporation apart from the person of an individual member, or that may be an element of damage by reason of tortious conduct."

Finn v. Finn, 658 S.W.2d 735, 740-41 (Tex.App.—Dallas 1983, writ ref'd n.r.e.). "[A] two-pronged test [is used] to determine whether the goodwill attached to a professional practice is subject to division upon divorce. First, goodwill must be determined to exist independently of the personal ability of the professional spouse. Second, if such goodwill is found to exist, then it must be determined whether that goodwill has a commercial value in which the community estate is entitled to share. [¶] Evidence in the present case indicates that the husband's law firm has goodwill independent of his professional ability. [¶] The inquiry does not stop here ..., but must continue to determine whether his goodwill has commercial value to which the community estate is entitled. [¶] The community estate is not entitled to a greater interest than that to which the husband is entitled in the firm's goodwill. The extent of the husband's interest is governed by the partnership agreement. *At 742:* The [partnership] agreement does not provide any compensation for accrued goodwill to a partner who ceases to practice law with the firm, nor does it provide any mechanism to realize the value of the firm's goodwill. [¶] The lack of any legal right of the husband to realize the value of the firm's goodwill is a decisive factor. ... Such realization in the future is no more than an expectancy entirely dependent on the husband's continued participation in the firm, and, therefore, is not property in the community estate."

Austin v. Austin, 619 S.W.2d 290, 291 (Tex.App.—Austin 1981, no writ). "When good will is not attached to the person of the professional man or woman, it is property that may be divided as community property. *At 292:* Once a professional practice is sold, the good will is no longer attached to the person of the professional man or woman. The seller's actions will no longer have significant effect on the good will. The value of the good will is fixed and it is now property that may be divided as community property."

Business Interest—Partnership

Harris v. Harris, 765 S.W.2d 798, 802 (Tex.App.—Houston [14th Dist.] 1989, writ denied). "Under the entity theory of partnership, adopted by Texas in the Uniform Partnership Act [now Texas Revised Partnership Act], partnership property is owned by the partnership entity, not the individual partners. A partner's rights in specific partnership property are wholly subordinated to the rights of the partnership entity as owner of the property. He may possess the property only for partnership purposes. Partnership property is therefore neither separate nor community in character. The only partnership property right the partner has which is subject to a community or separate property characterization is his interest in the partnership, that is his right to receive his share of the partnership profits and surplus. Distributions of the partner's share of profits and surplus (income) received during marriage are community property even if the partner's interest in the partnership is separate property."

Business Interest—Sole Proprietorship

In re Marriage of York, 613 S.W.2d 764, 770 (Tex.App.—Amarillo 1981, no writ). "In Texas, the profits derived from a business enterprise carried on by either the husband or wife are community property, even though the capital of the business is the separate property of one of the spouses."

Debts/Loans

Cockerham v. Cockerham, 527 S.W.2d 162, 171 (Tex.1975). "It is well established that debts contracted during marriage are presumed to be on the credit of the community and thus are joint community obligations, unless it is shown the creditor agreed to look solely to the separate estate of the contracting spouse for satisfaction."

Nesmith v. Berger, 64 S.W.3d 110, 117 (Tex.App.—Austin 2001, pet. denied). Wife "contends that the mortgage signed by [husband] lacks the 'magic words' stating that the creditor agreed to look solely to [husband]'s separate property for satisfaction. [¶] A question of fact is raised as to the character of the property when the documentary evidence fails to reflect an express agreement by the lender to look only to the purchasing spouse's separate estate for payment. We must look to the totality of the circumstances in which the debt arose to determine the character of the debt. Evidence showing, for example, that the down payment was paid with separate funds, and the parties agreed that the property would remain separate property and the balance of the debt was to be paid from separate funds is sufficient to overcome the presumption of community debt. 'The effect of such proof would not be altered by the fact that the [non-purchasing spouse] joined in the promise to pay the balance of the purchase money.'"

Jones v. Jones, 890 S.W.2d 471, 475-76 (Tex. App.—Corpus Christi 1994, writ denied). "When establishing whether the debt incurred and the property purchased during marriage was the separate property of one of the spouses, the lender's knowledge of the spouses' intentions is of significant importance. The intention of one spouse alone to repay a loan out of separate funds and then hold the property purchased with the proceeds of that loan as separate property has never been controlling. Therefore, the intention of the lender to look solely to the property of one spouse is an evidentiary factor of prime importance in showing by clear and convincing evidence that the spouses intended to hold the property as one spouse's separate property, especially where there is no evidence of such an agreement."

Goodridge v. Goodridge, 591 S.W.2d 571, 574 (Tex. App.—Dallas 1979, writ dism'd). "Property acquired on the credit of the community is community property."

Uranga v. Uranga, 527 S.W.2d 761, 765 (Tex. App.—San Antonio 1975, writ dism'd). "The evidence reveals that during the time the parties were married husband borrowed $145,000.00 for the purpose of constructing an apartment complex on his separate realty. The nature of this loan transaction is completely unexplained, and since money borrowed during marriage is presumed to be community property, it must be concluded that the $145,000.00 which husband invested in improving his separate realty was community property."

Income—Child's

Insurance Co. of Tex. v. Stratton, 287 S.W.2d 320, 323 (Tex.App.—Waco 1956, writ ref'd n.r.e.). "[E]arnings of an unemancipated minor, as well as any property that might be purchased with proceeds derived from such earnings, belong to and become a part of the community property of the father and mother of such minor."

Income—Property

Walston v. Walston, 971 S.W.2d 687, 696 (Tex. App.—Waco 1998, writ denied). "In Texas, the general rule is that income from a spouse's separate property, generated during the marriage, is community property."

McElwee v. McElwee, 911 S.W.2d 182, 188-89 (Tex. App.—Houston [1st Dist.] 1995, writ denied). "Rents and revenues from separate property are community property."

Income—Spouse's

Keller v. Keller, 141 S.W.2d 308, 311 (Tex.1940). "It is urged on [husband's] behalf that under the trial court's findings the community owned no claim for salary at the time of the divorce. It is undisputed that the item was not paid by the corporation until a few days after the divorce was granted. [¶] Whether the salaries were drawn during the current year is immaterial. When paid they were paid for that year and were paid as salaries. [¶] The parties at interest, including [husband], treated the amounts received as salary, according to the undisputed testimony. [¶] Regardless of whether the corporation could have elected to treat the item in question as dividends on the stock, it did not do so; nor could [husband] lawfully waive his claim to salary already set up and by his mere ipse dixit convert it into dividends, or some form of profit incident to stock ownership, and thereby convert his salary, which was community property, into his separate property."

Chubb Lloyds Ins. Co. v. Kizer, 943 S.W.2d 946, 952 n.3 (Tex.App.—Fort Worth 1997, writ denied). "The personal earnings of either spouse during marriage are characterized as community property."

Moore v. Moore, 192 S.W.2d 929, 930 (Tex.App.—Fort Worth 1946, no writ). "Moneys received by [a spouse] after marriage for services rendered ... prior to marriage become [the spouse's] separate property."

Life Insurance

Brown v. Lee, 371 S.W.2d 694, 696 (Tex.1963). "[T]he right to receive insurance proceeds payable at a future but uncertain date is 'property.' Such property is said to be in the nature of a chose in action which matures at the death of the insured. [¶] When purchased with community funds, the ownership of the unmatured chose logically belongs to the community, unless it has been irrevocably given away under the terms of the policy, *i.e.*, where the purchaser has, without fraud, foreclosed any right to change the named beneficiary....

The proceeds at maturity are likewise community in character, except where the named beneficiary is in fact surviving, in which case a gift of the policy rights to such beneficiary is presumed to have been intended and completed by the death of the insured. [¶] Under circumstances where the uninsured spouse predeceases the insured spouse, settlement of the decedent's community interest in the unmatured chose has ordinarily been resolved by allocating one-half of the cash surrender value to the deceased's estate and the other one-half, plus ownership of the unmatured chose, to the surviving spouse. But ..., where settlement of the deceased wife's community interest in the policies was not made prior to the death of the insured and her heirs were not guilty of laches in failing to seek such compensation, the wife's community interest was never extinguished and the policies retained their community status up to the time of maturity. Consequently, the proceeds are community."

Camp v. Camp, 972 S.W.2d 906, 908-09 (Tex.App.—Corpus Christi 1998, writ denied). Decedent's mother "contended that the inception of title rule governs the disposition of this case, *i.e.*, because [decedent] acquired title to the insurance policy before his marriage to [his wife], it is his separate property and his designation of his mother as beneficiary stands. It is undisputed that [decedent] acquired title to the insurance policy through his employment compensation prior to his marriage to [his wife] and that [his mother] is the named beneficiary. Texas case law supports the conclusions that the policy was his separate property with his wife entitled to reimbursement for her share of the premiums paid with community funds ([decedent's] earnings during the marriage). [¶] [Wife] would argue that, as applied to the instant case, inception of title analysis is inapposite because term life insurance is too ephemeral to constitute property. Unlike other life insurance, she argues, term life insurance does not build up cash value; it merely pays upon the insured's death; thus it would not seem something which [decedent] could have acquired as property, especially separate property. [Wife] presents no Texas authority in support of this position. As per the government code, property contemplated by family code provisions relating to the characterization of marital property must be understood to include not only life insurance policies, but also 'the effects of life insurance policies.' The undisputed effect of the term life policy [decedent] acquired was that it would pay $35,000 to a named beneficiary upon his ... death. Thus, even if it does not build up cash value, the term life insurance policy produces a tangible effect, and [decedent's] title to it relates back to a time prior to his marriage to [his wife]."

Seaman v. Seaman, 756 S.W.2d 56, 58 (Tex.App.—Texarkana 1988, no writ). "A life insurance policy that is an incident of employment during marriage is community property. This is true even if premiums are not deducted from the employee's salary because the policy is a benefit earned by employment. Even though the policy provides only for term insurance and has no cash value, it is still a property right that can be awarded to one of the spouses on divorce."

Dent v. Dent, 689 S.W.2d 521, 522 (Tex.App.—Fort Worth 1985, no writ). "The proceeds of life insurance policies purchased during the marriage on the life of a third person with one of the spouses named as the beneficiary are community property."

Givens v. Girard Life Ins. Co., 480 S.W.2d 421, 423 (Tex.App.—Dallas 1972, writ ref'd n.r.e.). "Life insurance is defined as property ..., and earnings during marriage are community property.... Since the premiums paid by [husband's] employer were part of the compensation for his services, this insurance is deemed to be purchased out of his earnings and therefore community property."

Mineral Interest

Norris v. Vaughan, 260 S.W.2d 676, 679 (Tex.1953). "When royalty is paid for oil or gas produced from the separate property of the lessor, the courts of this state have held that such royalty is payment for the extraction or waste of the separate estate and therefore remains separate property."

Cone v. Cone, 266 S.W.2d 480, 483-84 (Tex.App.—Amarillo 1953), *writ dism'd*, 266 S.W.2d 860 (Tex.1954). "No citation of authority should be required as to the proposition that oil in place is a part of the realty and that if such oil is separate property when a part of the realty it remains separate property when produced and separated therefrom."

McGarraugh v. McGarraugh, 177 S.W.2d 296, 301 (Tex.App.—Amarillo 1943, writ dism'd). "Inasmuch as the items here involved were delay rentals and accrued merely by lapse of time like other rentals, did not depend upon the finding or production of oil or gas, and did not exhaust the substance of the land, we think they constituted personal property and belonged to the community estate."

Real Property

In re Marriage of Morris, 12 S.W.3d 877, 881-82 (Tex.App.—Texarkana 2000, no pet.). "Once separate property character attaches, that character does not change because community funds are spent to improve the property. Any improvements made on separate property, including a residence, are considered the separate property of the land owner." (Internal quotations omitted.)

Wilkerson v. Wilkerson, 992 S.W.2d 719, 722 (Tex. App.—Austin 1999, no pet.). "Real property acquired before marriage is separate property. ... When real property is acquired under a contract for deed or installment contract, the inception of title relates back to the time the contract was executed, not the time when legal title is conveyed. Thus, if one spouse entered into a contract for deed before marriage, the property is separate property even if the conveyance of legal title occurs during the marriage and the deed names both spouses as grantees."

Carter v. Carter, 736 S.W.2d 775, 779 (Tex.App.—Houston [14th Dist.] 1987, no writ). "Ownership of real property is governed by the rule that 'the character of title to property as separate or community depends upon the existence or nonexistence of the marriage at the time of the incipiency of the right in virtue of which the title is finally extended, and that the title, when extended, relates back to that time.' [Husband] acquired a right to title to the property when he entered into the earnest money contract. As the date of execution of the earnest money contract was prior to the marriage, [husband's] right to title preceded the marriage and the separate character of the property was thereby established."

Retirement Benefits

Cearley v. Cearley, 544 S.W.2d 661, 665-66 (Tex. 1976). "Although a serviceman's military pension is not payable before the date of its maturity, it is not 'earned' on that day. Rather it is a form of deferred compensation which is earned during each month of his military service. The portion that he earned during the months of coverture became contingent earnings of the community which may or may not bloom into full maturity at some future date. We hold that such rights, prior to accrual and maturity, constitute a contingent interest in property and a community asset subject to consideration...."

Boyd v. Boyd, 67 S.W.3d 398, 407 (Tex.App.—Fort Worth 2002, n.p.h.). "An employee spouse's accrued benefits in a defined benefit retirement plan that have been earned during marriage, but have not vested and matured at the time of divorce, are a contingent property interest and a community asset subject to division upon divorce. *At 408:* Post-divorce increases in the value of an individual's defined-benefit retirement plans that are attributable to the person's continued employment, such as raises, promotions, services rendered, and post-divorce contributions, are the individual's separate property and are not subject to division. But post-divorce cost-of-living increases and other increases in value that are not attributable to the employee's continued employment after divorce are community property subject to division. *At 409-410:* Our research has not revealed any cases in which a court has addressed whether a nonemployee spouse is entitled to post-divorce increases in the value of a defined contribution plan that are not attributable to the employee spouse's continued employment.... Thus, the future increases in [wife's] share will not be [husband's] separate property, and they were subject to the trial court's just and right division. To the extent that the future increases in value are attributable to [husband's] continued employment or to contributions of his separate property, however, they will be [husband's] separate property and were not subject to division at divorce."

McElwee v. McElwee, 911 S.W.2d 182, 188 (Tex. App.—Houston [1st Dist.] 1995, writ denied). "Matured private retirement, annuity and pension benefits earned by a spouse during marriage are part of the community estate. Disability plans which are part of an employee benefit package are also community property."

Morris v. Morris, 894 S.W.2d 859, 863 (Tex.App.—Fort Worth 1995, no writ). "[M]ilitary retirement benefits earned from years of service during the marriage are community property. Military retirement pay is a vested community property right, subject to division by the divorce court, and it is not alimony."

Williamson v. Williamson, 457 S.W.2d 311, 314 (Tex.App.—Austin 1970, no writ). "[R]etirement benefits and pension plan benefits of the husband are earned property rights belonging to the community estate and are distributable to the wife when the marriage is dissolved, even though payment under the plans may be contingent and are to take place, if at all, in the future."

Stocks

Boyd v. Boyd, 67 S.W.3d 398, 411-12 (Tex.App.—Fort Worth 2002, n.p.h.). Husband "contends that the trial court should have valued the stock options as of the date of divorce rather than giving [wife] the benefit of the value of the options attributable to his post-divorce employment. [¶] [Husband's] company was privately held, not publicly traded. If [husband] left his employment before he was 100% vested in his stock options, he could sell the options to the company for the price he paid for them. But [husband's] ability to exercise his stock options for a profit was contingent upon his employer becoming a publicly traded company or being wholly or partially acquired by a third party. In either of these circumstances, [husband] would have the opportunity to sell his stock options for the price the company received for its shares. [¶] The trial court determined that [husband's] 'fair value' stock options had a contingent value at divorce of $5,628,776. This value was determined by using a formula that did not take into account [husband's] post-divorce work for his company or the company's future productivity. The formula was fixed at the time of the divorce. [¶] The contingent value of the stock options could not be realized, however, until between 2002 and 2004, during which time a third-party corporation had the option to acquire all of the remaining stock in [husband's] company. If [husband] was not employed by the company at that time, he would not make any more profit on his 'fair value' stock options because he would no longer be a company stockholder. In addition, even if his employment continued after divorce, [husband] would not make any more profit on the stock options if the sale did not occur or if his company's stock did not become publicly traded after 2004. [¶] To date, no Texas court has considered how to determine the community property value of stock options at divorce. The cases have only addressed whether stock options are community property. The factors presented here cause us to conclude that the contingent value of the stock options was community property. The method for calculating this contingent value was fixed at divorce, and the minimum price for the stock options was also fixed. [Husband] would either be able to exercise the stock options in the future for their contingent value ..., or he would only be able to recover what he paid for them. Further, the contingent value of the options was not dependent on [husband's] post-divorce *work* for his company, even though he had to be employed to receive it. [¶] If [husband] is no longer employed when the stock options are sold, [wife's] contingent community property interest will be extinguished. Any post-divorce increases or decreases in the value of these stock options that are not attributable to [husband's] post-divorce work will not be his separate property. [Wife] will be entitled to 50% of the increases, and the contingent value of her interest will be reduced by any decreases. [Wife] will not be entitled to any post-divorce increases in the value of these stock options that *are* attributable to [husband's] post-divorce work for the company because these post-divorce increases will be his separate property."

Charriere v. Charriere, 7 S.W.3d 217, 221-22 (Tex. App.—Dallas 1999, no pet.). "We ... reject [wife's] 'alternative' suggestion that we analogize the stock options to retirement benefits and, as with retirement benefits, allocate them proportionally between the parties on a 'time rule' basis. In our view, this analogy is unwarranted. This case involves a stock option plan, not retirement benefits. Unlike retirement benefits, the stock options in this case are not benefits earned over the entire period of [wife's] employment; to the contrary, they have already been earned. Because their value is fixed and cannot be changed except by market forces, we conclude (1) the options are distinguishable from retirement benefits, and (2) treating them the same would therefore be improper."

Bodin v. Bodin, 955 S.W.2d 380, 381 (Tex.App.—San Antonio 1997, no pet.). "[U]nvested stock options constitute a contingent interest in property and are a community asset subject to consideration along with other property in the disposition of the parties' estate...."

Bakken v. Bakken, 503 S.W.2d 315, 317-18 (Tex. App.—Dallas 1973, no writ). "Mutual funds assets usually consist of the stocks, bonds and other securities of a number of other corporations. Their income is generally of two kinds: (1) cash dividends received from the corporations whose stock they own, and (2) the profit or gain realized from the sale of such stocks. When these cash dividends are passed on to married owners of mutual fund shares who hold them as separate property, there is no question that these dividends become community property of the spouses. The question before us is whether the distributed capital gains retain their nature as separate property or become community property when passed on to married owners of the mutual fund shares. [¶] We hold that since appellee's original shares in the two mutual funds were admittedly her separate property the profit or gain realized from the sale of capital assets of the mutual funds is also her separate property."

Wohlenberg v. Wohlenberg, 485 S.W.2d 342, 347 (Tex.App.—El Paso 1972, no writ). "A stock dividend normally is separate if the stock ownership out of which it springs is separate."

Trusts

Lipsey v. Lipsey, 983 S.W.2d 345, 351 (Tex.App.—Fort Worth 1998, no pet.). "Absent fraud, a spouse may create a trust from separate property, and so long as the income remains undistributed during marriage and there is no right to compel distribution, the income is not acquired during marriage and remains separate trust property."

Ridgell v. Ridgell, 960 S.W.2d 144, 148 (Tex.App.—Corpus Christi 1997, no pet.). "Income received by a married beneficiary on the trust corpus to which the beneficiary is entitled, or becomes entitled, is community property. [¶] If appellee does not receive income from the trusts and has no more than an expectancy interest in the corpuses, the income remains separate property."

In re Marriage of Burns, 573 S.W.2d 555, 557-58 (Tex.App.—Texarkana 1978, writ dism'd). The "determination of whether the undistributed income earned during a marriage by either a separate property trust or estate should be characterized as community property is governed by §5.01(b) [now §3.002]. ... It is unquestioned but that *the property* in question is income and thereby would normally be characterized as community property; however, the issue presented for our determination is whether *the property was acquired by either spouse* during the marriage. By definition, the undistributed trust and estate income had not been distributed to [husband] nor did he have a present or past right to require its distribution so as to compel a finding that there was a constructive acquisition. The income was actually acquired by the trusts and estates and not by either [husband or wife]. As stated, there was no constructive acquisition. Since neither spouse actually or constructively acquired the undistributed trust and estate income during the marriage, such income, though earned during the marriage, remained a part of the respective trust or estate and was not subject to division by the court. Such income was not community property."

FAM §3.003. PRESUMPTION OF COMMUNITY PROPERTY

(a) Property possessed by either spouse during or on dissolution of marriage is presumed to be community property.

(b) The degree of proof necessary to establish that property is separate property is clear and convincing evidence.

History of Fam §3.003: Acts 1997, 75th Leg., ch. 7, §1, eff. April 17, 1997. Source: Former Fam §5.02.

Generally

Tarver v. Tarver, 394 S.W.2d 780, 783 (Tex.1965). "The plain wording of the statute creates a rebuttable presumption that all property possessed by a husband and wife when their marriage is dissolved is their community property and imposes the burden upon one asserting otherwise to prove the contrary by satisfactory evidence. [¶] The general rule is that to discharge the burden imposed by the statute, a spouse, or one claiming through a spouse, must trace and clearly identify property claimed as separate property, and that when the evidence shows that separate and community property have been so commingled as to defy resegregation and identification, the burden is not discharged and the statutory presumption that the entire mass is community controls its disposition."

Smith v. Lanier, 998 S.W.2d 324, 331 (Tex.App.—Austin 1999, pet. denied). "Texas is a community property state. All property possessed by either spouse during or on dissolution of marriage is presumed to be community property. The presumption which obtains when the marriage is dissolved applies to dissolution by death as well as divorce."

Ellebracht v. Ellebracht, 735 S.W.2d 658, 659 (Tex.App.—Austin 1987, no writ). "Any doubt as to the character of property should be resolved in favor of the community estate."

Rebutting the Presumption

Evans v. Evans, 14 S.W.3d 343, 346 (Tex.App.—Houston [14th Dist.] 2000, no pet.). "To overcome the [community property] presumption, a party must present clear and convincing evidence that the property is separate. This evidence must generally trace and clearly identify the property as separate."

Bahr v. Kohr, 980 S.W.2d 723, 728 (Tex.App.—San Antonio 1998, no pet.). "The requirement of clear and convincing evidence is merely another way of stating that there must be factually sufficient evidence. To rebut the presumption, the party must generally trace and clearly identify property claimed as separate property. The issue of whether property is separate or community property is determined by the facts which, according to rules of law, give character to the property. Mere testimony that property was purchased with separate property funds, without any tracing of the funds, is generally insufficient to rebut the presumption." (Internal quotations omitted.)

Faram v. Gervitz-Faram, 895 S.W.2d 839, 842 (Tex.App.—Fort Worth 1995, no writ). "Tracing involves establishing the separate origin of the property through evidence showing the time and means by which the spouse originally obtained possession of the property. Separate property will retain its character through a series of exchanges so long as the party asserting separate ownership can overcome the presumption of community property by tracing the assets on hand during the marriage back to property that, because of its time and manner of acquisition, is separate in character." *See also* ***Celso v. Celso***, 864 S.W.2d 652, 654 (Tex.App.—Tyler 1993, no writ).

In re Marriage of Moore, 890 S.W.2d 821, 834 (Tex.App.—Amarillo 1994, no writ). "The burden of proof of rebutting this presumption rests on the party who claims separate ownership of such property. ... A necessary corollary of this burden is that [the party rebutting the presumption has] the obligation of requesting the necessary and proper jury questions as to the separate or community status of the [property]."

Latham v. Allison, 560 S.W.2d 481, 485 (Tex. App.—Fort Worth 1977, writ ref'd n.r.e.). "When tracing separate property, it is not enough to show that separate funds *could have been* the source of a subsequent deposit of funds. Such conjecture does not constitute sufficient evidence to sustain appellant's burden of tracing to overcome the community property presumption of ... §5.02 [now §3.003]."

Method of Tracing—Clearinghouse

Estate of Hanau v. Hanau, 730 S.W.2d 663, 667 (Tex.1987). "The account here has not been commingled, as it was stipulated that the decedent had always kept the property in his own name and that his wife had no power over the account. It certainly does not appear that the property has so radically changed as to 'defy resegregation and identification'.... Further, the petitioner has shown the chain of events leading from the Texaco stock to the TransWorld purchase and shown that no other transactions occurred on the days in question, which would have planted the seeds of doubt upon the possible source of the funds used to buy the stocks."

McKinley v. McKinley, 496 S.W.2d 540, 542-43 (Tex.1973). "In late 1964, [husband] had $9,500 on deposit in a First Federal Savings & Loan savings account. It is uncontroverted that this $9,500 was [husband's] separate property. By December 31, 1965, the interest earned by this account was $472.03, and on January 5, 1966, $472.03 was withdrawn. The $9,500 originally deposited remained in the account and continued to earn interest until, on December 31, 1967, the account balance was $10,453.81. From January 5, 1966, to December 31, 1967, no withdrawals were made from this account, and all deposits are shown on the account statement to have been dividends. On January 2, 1968, $10,400 was withdrawn from the savings account and, on the same date, was used to purchase First Federal Savings & Loan savings certificate No. 101046 in the amount of $10,400. The First Federal certificate remained on account and untouched until [husband's] death on October 15, 1970. [¶] [I]t seems clear that the $9,500 originally on deposit with the First Federal Savings & Loan was traced in its entirety into savings certificate No. 101046, and that $9,500 of that certificate was clearly identified as separate property. We therefore hold that $9,500 of savings certificate No. 101046 in the face amount of $10,400 is separate property."

Peterson v. Peterson, 595 S.W.2d 889, 892 (Tex. App.—Austin 1980, writ dism'd). Husband "testified that he sold inherited property and deposited funds in excess of $35,000 into his personal bank account. He subsequently paid the balance of the purchase price from that same account. [Wife] argues that no evidence was introduced to establish the beginning balance of that account on the date of marriage or to establish what deposits or withdrawals were made between the date of the marriage and the date of closing. [¶] In reviewing [wife's] 'no evidence' point, after examining only that evidence in favor of the trial court's finding, we find probative evidence to support the trial court's finding that the community property presumption was overcome by tracing the entire purchase price to [husband's] separate funds."

Method of Tracing—Community-out-first

Smith v. Smith, 22 S.W.3d 140, 146 (Tex.App.—Houston [14th Dist.] 2000, no pet.). "Generally, when separate property and community property are commingled in a single bank account, we presume that the community funds are drawn out first, before separate funds are withdrawn, and where there are sufficient funds at all times to cover the separate property balance in the account at the time of divorce, we presume that the balance remains separate property. *At 147:* We assume, without deciding, that the community-out-first presumption is a rebuttable one. *At n.5:* We also note that a blind application of the community-out-first presumption does not uphold the policy reason for the presumption's original application. [M]echanical application of the community-out-first presumption leads to the husband's preserving his separate estate at the expense of the community. Were we to view the husband as a trustee acting in the best interest of the beneficiary, we would apply not the community-out-first presumption, but a separate-out-first presumption. We would presume the husband spent his own funds before spending the community funds thus leaving community funds in the account for possible disbursement to the beneficiary—the wife—upon dissolution of the marriage. The husband would have the burden of rebutting the separate-out-first presumption. We apply the community-out-first presumption because it seems to be established law."

Welder v. Welder, 794 S.W.2d 420, 433-34 (Tex. App.—Corpus Christi 1990, no writ). "Our courts have developed rules of tracing to distinguish the character of funds which are withdrawn from an account of mixed separate and community funds. Where a joint bank account contains both community and separate funds, we presume that the community funds are drawn out first, before separate funds are withdrawn, and where there are sufficient funds at all times to cover the separate property balance in the account at the time of divorce, we presume that the balance remains separate property. [¶] Appellant argues that the community-out-first presumption should be limited to situations where one party is acting in a special position of trust with regard to the other's funds, over and above the trust relationship inherent in the very nature of a joint account. ***Sibley***, however, does not limit itself in this way. As in the present case, ***Sibley*** determined rights to a joint account held by the parties during marriage and used to pay community expenditures, in which one of the parties had deposited separate funds. The only requirement for tracing and the application of the community-out-first presumption is that the party attempting to overcome the community presumption produce clear evidence of the transactions affecting the commingled account."

Sibley v. Sibley, 286 S.W.2d 657, 659 (Tex.App.—Dallas 1955, writ dism'd). "The presumption is that where funds are commingled so as to prevent their proper identity as separate or community funds, they must be held to be community funds. However, there are exceptions to the rule or presumption. In divorce proceedings our courts have found no difficulty in following separate funds through bank accounts. Equity impresses a resulting trust on such funds in favor of the wife and where a trustee draws checks on a fund in which trust funds are mingled with those of the trustee, the trustee is presumed to have checked out his own money first, and is therefore an exception to the general rule. [¶] The community moneys in joint bank account of the parties are therefore presumed to have been drawn out first, before the separate moneys are withdrawn."

Method of Tracing—Item Tracing

Cockerham v. Cockerham, 527 S.W.2d 162, 167 (Tex.1975). "In order to overcome this presumption, the party asserting separate ownership must clearly trace the original separate property into the particular assets on hand during the marriage."

Mortenson v. Trammell, 604 S.W.2d 269, 274 (Tex. App.—Corpus Christi 1980, writ ref'd n.r.e.). "To prove by clear and convincing evidence that a certain asset is the separate property of one spouse, it is generally necessary to trace the origin of the asset. Value tracing is commonly accepted as the means by which cash assets are traced, while item tracing is required of other assets. This requirement for tracing to the origin not only necessitates a showing of how one spouse obtained the property but also requires evidence which clearly establishes the origin of the asset."

Method of Tracing—Minimum Sum Balance

Padon v. Padon, 670 S.W.2d 354, 357 (Tex.App.—San Antonio 1984, no writ). "The evidence elicited at trial shows the following: During the marriage of the parties, [husband's] father died leaving [husband] an amount in excess of $160,000.00. On February 25, 1977, $160,490.00 was deposited ... to open an account styled 'R.H. Pat Padon or Carolyn Padon.' Both parties agree [husband] inherited and deposited $160,000.00 into this account. Both parties also agree that in early 1977 a house was purchased for $89,900.00, which was paid for by check. The March bank statement of the [spouse's] account shows no additional deposits from the time of the initial $160,490.00 deposit until March 4, 1977. On March 1, 1977, the statement shows a check cleared the account in the amount of $89,900.00. [¶] Both parties testified that all monies received from all sources during the marriage were subsequently deposited into this account. The March 1977 statement is the only statement in evidence. [¶] We hold [husband] established as a matter of law that the house ... is his separate property...."

Snider v. Snider, 613 S.W.2d 8, 11 (Tex.App.—Dallas 1981, no writ). "On the date of the marriage, the balance in the account was $27,642.45. Upon dissolution of the community by the husband's death, the balance was $35,809.80. The account grew by *interest* from time to time, as well as by new deposits, and was reduced by withdrawals from time to time. The witness ... testified that an additional deposit of $10,000.00 of separate funds of the husband was made after the marriage and that the remaining deposits, as well as withdrawals, were made by the community. The passbook for this account was introduced into evidence and supports the separate character and balance of the account on the date of marriage. Between the marriage on October 3, 1972, and October 20, 1972, no interest was earned and no deposits were made, but withdrawals reduced the balance to $19,642.45. Between October 20, 1972, and April 23, 1973, there were entries of earned interest, deposits of unknown character, and withdrawals, but the balance was never below $19,642.45. On April 23, 1973, a separate property deposit of $10,000.00 was made and the identifiable separate property interest in the account became $19,642.45 plus $10,000.00 or $29,642.45. Subsequent interest earned, deposits, and withdrawals to the date of the husband's death never reduced the account balance to or below $29,642.45. We hold that this record traces and identifies the husband's separate interest in the Mercantile savings account to the extent of $29,642.45 with the remainder of the account being deemed community for want of tracing or identity."

Method of Tracing—Pro Rata

Marineau v. General Am. Life Ins. Co., 898 S.W.2d 397, 403 (Tex.App.—Fort Worth 1995, writ denied). "[O]nce [insurance company] proved that embezzled funds were commingled into the [spouse's account] used to pay the insurance policy premiums, the burden shifted to [wife] to prove that part or all of the insurance premiums were paid with funds belonging to [husband]. [Insurance company] contends that [wife] failed to meet this burden by only offering evidence of the proportion of embezzled money to personal money deposited into the Account used to pay the insurance premiums. In [insurance company's] view, [wife] would have had to prove the ownership proportion of each payment to calculate the ownership of the policy, and absent such proof, the presumption is that all of the commingled funds are held in trust. We disagree. Neither party has cited any Texas case addressing the proof necessary to rebut the presumption that the commingled funds belong to the trust, or the extent of recovery allowed the owner of the embezzled funds when those funds only paid for part of the premiums. After reviewing the case law of other jurisdictions on this point, we feel the reasoning of the court in ***G & M Motor Co. v. Thompson***, 567 P.2d 80 (Okla.1977), is appropriate in this case. The court there held that the employer of the embezzling employee was entitled to a pro rata share of the life insurance policy proceeds where the wrongfully acquired funds were partially used to pay the premiums. Recovery was limited to the total amount of embezzled monies, interest, and costs."

Method of Tracing—Value Tracing

Trawick v. Trawick, 671 S.W.2d 105, 110 (Tex. App.—El Paso 1984, no writ). "The party with the burden of tracing is aided by the rule that one dollar has the same value as another. Under the law, there can be no commingling by the mixing of dollars where the number owned by each claimant is known."

Mortenson v. Trammell, 604 S.W.2d 269, 274 (Tex. App.—Corpus Christi 1980, writ ref'd n.r.e.). "To prove by clear and convincing evidence that a certain asset is the separate property of one spouse, it is generally necessary to trace the origin of the asset. Value tracing is commonly accepted as the means by which cash assets are traced, while item tracing is required of other assets. This requirement for tracing to the origin not only necessitates a showing of how one spouse obtained the property but also requires evidence which clearly establishes the origin of the asset."

In re Marriage of Tandy, 532 S.W.2d 714, 717 (Tex. App.—Amarillo 1976, no writ). "The account from which the Federal Land Bank payment was made contained proceeds of grain sales as well as proceeds from the sale of real estate that was the separate property of [ex-husband] and his two sons. It was undisputed that the proceeds from the grain sales were community property. [Husband] claims, however, that since the exact amount of money that went into the account was known and the exact amount of money that came out of the account was known, the requirements of tracing were satisfied. We agree. There was evidence that the proceeds from the real estate sale, $25,000, were deposited in February, 1974. In February and March, 1974, $6,250 was disbursed to each of [husband's] two sons as their ownership share of the total. Of the $25,000 deposit, $12,500 remained, which amount [husband] paid to the Federal Land Bank in March, 1974 on his separate property debt. One dollar has the same value as another; there can be no commingling of dollars where the number owned by each claimant is known."

FAM §3.004. RECORDATION OF SEPARATE PROPERTY

(a) A subscribed and acknowledged schedule of a spouse's separate property may be recorded in the deed records of the county in which the parties, or one of them, reside and in the county or counties in which the real property is located.

(b) A schedule of a spouse's separate real property is not constructive notice to a good faith purchaser for value or a creditor without actual notice unless the instrument is acknowledged and recorded in the deed records of the county in which the real property is located.

History of Fam §3.004: Acts 1997, 75th Leg., ch. 7, §1, eff. April 17, 1997. Source: Former Fam §5.03.

FAM §3.005. GIFTS BETWEEN SPOUSES

If one spouse makes a gift of property to the other spouse, the gift is presumed to include all the income and property that may arise from that property.

History of Fam §3.005: Acts 1997, 75th Leg., ch. 7, §1, eff. April 17, 1997. Source: Former Fam §5.04.

In re Marriage of Morris, 12 S.W.3d 877, 881 (Tex. App.—Texarkana 2000, no pet.). "It is well established law that when a spouse uses separate property to acquire property during marriage and takes title to that property in the names of both spouses, a presumption arises that the purchasing spouse intended to make a gift of one half of the separate funds to the other spouse. In order to rebut this presumption, evidence of the absence of an intent to make a gift must be shown."

Roberts v. Roberts, 999 S.W.2d 424, 432 (Tex. App.—El Paso 1999, no pet.). "A gift is a voluntary transfer of property to another made gratuitously and without consideration. Three elements are required to establish the existence of a gift: (1) intent to make a gift; (2) delivery of the property; and (3) acceptance of the property. Generally speaking, one who is claiming the existence of a gift has the burden of proof. However, where the conveyance is from one spouse to the other spouse, there is a presumption of gift. [¶] A gift by one spouse to another may be set aside if it is induced by duress or undue influence. In such a case, the burden rests with the donee to show that the gift was fair and equitable."

Celso v. Celso, 864 S.W.2d 652, 655 (Tex.App.—Tyler 1993, no writ). "The spouse that makes a deposit to a joint bank account of his or her separate property does not make a gift to the other spouse."

Ⓐ FAM §3.006. PROPORTIONAL OWNERSHIP OF PROPERTY BY MARITAL ESTATES

If the community estate of the spouses and the separate estate of a spouse have an ownership interest in property, the respective ownership interests of the marital estates are determined by the rule of inception of title.

History of Fam §3.006: Acts 1999, 76th Leg., ch. 692, §1, eff. Sept. 1, 1999. Amended by Acts 2001, 77th Leg., ch. 838, §3, eff. Sept. 1, 2001.

Sections 3.007-3.100 reserved for expansion

SUBCHAPTER B. MANAGEMENT, CONTROL, & DISPOSITION OF MARITAL PROPERTY

FAM §3.101. MANAGING SEPARATE PROPERTY

Each spouse has the sole management, control, and disposition of that spouse's separate property.

History of Fam §3.101: Acts 1997, 75th Leg., ch. 7, §1, eff. April 17, 1997. Source: Former Fam §5.21.

Vallone v. Vallone, 644 S.W.2d 455, 458 (Tex.1982). "It is fundamental that any property or rights acquired by one of the spouses after marriage by toil, talent, industry or other productive faculty belongs to the community estate. Nevertheless, the law contemplates that a spouse may expend a reasonable amount of talent or labor in the management and preservation of his or her separate estate without impressing a community character upon that estate."

Whittlesey v. Miller, 572 S.W.2d 665, 669 (Tex. 1978). "In the absence of evidence showing authority, the mere relationship of husband and wife does not give the husband authority to contract with regard to the wife's separate property."

FAM §3.102. MANAGING COMMUNITY PROPERTY

(a) During marriage, each spouse has the sole management, control, and disposition of the community property that the spouse would have owned if single, including:

(1) personal earnings;

(2) revenue from separate property;

(3) recoveries for personal injuries; and

(4) the increase and mutations of, and the revenue from, all property subject to the spouse's sole management, control, and disposition.

(b) If community property subject to the sole management, control, and disposition of one spouse is mixed or combined with community property subject to the sole management, control, and disposition of the other spouse, then the mixed or combined community property is subject to the joint management, control, and disposition of the spouses, unless the spouses provide otherwise by power of attorney in writing or other agreement.

(c) Except as provided by Subsection (a), community property is subject to the joint management, control, and disposition of the spouses unless the spouses provide otherwise by power of attorney in writing or other agreement.

History of Fam §3.102: Acts 1997, 75th Leg., ch. 7, §1, eff. April 17, 1997. Source: Former Fam §5.22.

Sole Management

Douglas v. Delp, 987 S.W.2d 879, 883 (Tex.1999). "Sole-management community property is that property which, though acquired during the marriage, would have belonged to that spouse if single. [¶] [Husband's] loss of earning capacity during the marriage constitutes his sole-management community property. [Husband's] credit reputation is also his sole-management community property, as it was acquired, at least in part, during the marriage and would have belonged solely to him were he not married."

Medenco, Inc. v. Myklebust, 615 S.W.2d 187, 189 (Tex.1981). "During marriage, community property employment benefits acquired through employment are subject to the sole management, control and disposition of the employee spouse."

Valdez v. Ramirez, 574 S.W.2d 748, 750 (Tex.1978). "While [wife] was employed by the federal government and earning future rights to a retirement annuity, those contingent rights were community property, but such inchoate rights are characterized by the Family Code as 'special community' under the wife's sole management and control. *At 751:* Thus, while being earned, the right to a future Civil Service retirement annuity was the special community of [wife], subject to her sole management, control and disposition. As manager of this 'special community' asset, she had the contract right to select a mode of payment."

Bell v. Moores, 832 S.W.2d 749, 752 (Tex.App.—Houston [14th Dist.] 1992, writ denied). "Personal earnings are community property if earned during marriage. Though personal earnings are community property, Texas law has classified this kind of community property as 'special community.' 'Special community' is community property that is subject to one spouse's sole management, control, and disposition. Personal earnings are subject to the sole management, control, and disposition of the employee spouse. [¶] Courts have held that an employee spouse, because of his exclusive managerial power over personal earnings, has the sole authority to bring an action for recovery of the community property under his sole management. *At 753:* At the time [wife] intervened in the suit against the appellees, she was still married to [her husband]. At that time, the royalties in question were community property under his sole management. ... Thus, when the suit was commenced by [wife], she was without standing to assert such a claim. The property involved was subject to the sole management of [her husband], and as such, only he had the power to sue for recovery of the royalties because of his management power."

Joint Management

Cockerham v. Cockerham, 527 S.W.2d 162, 170 (Tex.1975). "With regard to the 320-acre tract, the record reveals [husband] and his wife in effect borrowed the cash necessary to purchase the community interest by giving a note secured by a deed of trust on the property in return. Title to the property was taken in the name of both husband and wife; both husband and wife were obligated on the note. Under virtually identical circumstances these facts were considered sufficient to establish that the community interest was subject to the joint management of the husband and wife...."

Cooper v. Texas Gulf Indus., Inc., 513 S.W.2d 200, 202 (Tex.1974). "Section 5.22 [now §3.102] takes away the husband's sole right to manage all of the couple's community property. When joint management community property is involved, the husband and wife are now *joint* managers. The wife is her husband's equal with respect to management; she stands in the same position as any other joint owner of property. While another section provides that a spouse may sue and be sued without the joinder of the other, *neither* spouse may virtually represent the other. The rights of the wife, like the rights of the husband and the rights of any other joint owner, may be affected only by a suit in which the wife is called to answer. If one of the spouses wishes the other to represent him or her, §5.22(c)... permits that arrangement provided the consenting spouse authorizes that representation by a power of attorney or other agreement in writing. No such writing is in evidence here. [¶] [Wife] was not a party to the first suit; the doctrine of virtual representation was abolished by the new Family Code; there was no writing authorizing her husband to represent her. Accordingly, her interest in [their] joint management community property is untouched by the judgment of dismissal with prejudice of the first suit."

Caulley v. Caulley, 777 S.W.2d 147, 150 (Tex.App.—Houston [14th Dist.] 1989), *rev'd in part on other grounds*, 806 S.W.2d 795 (Tex.1991). "Absent evidence that the community property farm is subject to the wife's sole management, control, and disposition, the farm is presumed to be jointly managed."

Vallone v. Miller, 663 S.W.2d 97, 99 (Tex.App.—Houston [14th Dist.] 1983, writ ref'd n.r.e.). "One spouse cannot alone convey or encumber joint management community property unless the spouses have otherwise agreed. ... Without a 'power of attorney in writing or other agreement' to the contrary, [husband] had no authority to contract to dispose of the entire joint management community property without his wife joining in the contract."

LeBlanc v. Waller, 603 S.W.2d 265, 267 (Tex. App.—Houston [14th Dist.] 1980, no writ). "This 'agreement' referred to in [§5.22(c), now §3.102(c)] is not a partition agreement of the community, but rather an agreement to transfer the power of management, control, and disposition over certain community property assets from one spouse to the other. Appellant contends that the oral agreement for division of their property falls within the 'other agreement' provision of subsection (c) above. We agree. Prior to 1974, §5.22(c) read, '... unless the spouses provide otherwise by power of attorney or other agreement in writing.' In 1973 that section was amended to read, '... unless the spouses provide otherwise by power of attorney in writing or other agreement.' This amendment became effective on January 1, 1974. Applying the standard rules of statutory construction, it is apparent that the Texas Legislature chose to remove the requirement that such an agreement be in writing."

Fraud on the Community

Schlueter v. Schlueter, 975 S.W.2d 584, 585 (Tex. 1998). "Because a wronged spouse has an adequate remedy for fraud on the community through the 'just and right' property division upon divorce, we hold that there is no independent tort cause of action between spouses for damages to the community estate."

Carnes v. Meador, 533 S.W.2d 365, 370-71 (Tex. App.—Dallas 1975, writ ref'd n.r.e.). "Although a spouse has the right to dispose of community property under his or her control under §5.22 [now §3.102], he may not dispose of his spouse's interest in community funds if actual or constructive fraud exists. Without specific proof of fraudulent intent, Texas courts nevertheless have set aside any gift of community funds as a constructive fraud on the other spouse if the gift is capricious, excessive or arbitrary. [¶] Constructive fraud is the breach of a legal or equitable duty which the law declares fraudulent because it violates a fiduciary relationship. A trust relationship exists between husband and wife as to that community property controlled by each spouse. Thus, a presumption of constructive fraud arises when a spouse unfairly disposes of the other spouse's one-half interest in community property. The burden of proof is, therefore, upon the disposing spouse or his donee to prove the fairness of the disposition of the other spouse's one-half community ownership. Implicit in these holdings is the recognition that each spouse owns a one-half interest in all community funds regardless of which spouse has management and control."

Horlock v. Horlock, 533 S.W.2d 52, 55 (Tex.App.—Houston [14th Dist.] 1975, writ dism'd). "In considering the wife's claim of a constructive fraud against her share of the community property the courts have considered three primary factors. Those factors are the size of the gift in relation to the total size of the community estate, the adequacy of the estate remaining to support the wife in spite of the gift, and the relationship of the donor to the donee."

Ⓐ FAM §3.103. MANAGING EARNINGS OF MINOR

Except as provided by Section 264.0111, during the marriage of the parents of an unemancipated minor for whom a managing conservator has not been appointed, the earnings of the minor are subject to the joint management, control, and disposition of the parents of the minor, unless otherwise provided by agreement of the parents or by judicial order.

History of Fam §3.103: Acts 1997, 75th Leg., ch. 7, §1, eff. April 17, 1997. Amended by Acts 2001, 77th Leg., ch. 964, §1, eff. Sept. 1, 2001. Source: Former Fam §5.23.

FAM §3.104. PROTECTION OF THIRD PERSONS

(a) During marriage, property is presumed to be subject to the sole management, control, and disposition of a spouse if it is held in that spouse's name, as shown by muniment, contract, deposit of funds, or other evidence of ownership, or if it is in that spouse's possession and is not subject to such evidence of ownership.

(b) A third person dealing with a spouse is entitled to rely, as against the other spouse or anyone claiming from that spouse, on that spouse's authority to deal with the property if:

(1) the property is presumed to be subject to the sole management, control, and disposition of the spouse; and

(2) the person dealing with the spouse:

(A) is not a party to a fraud on the other spouse or another person; and

(B) does not have actual or constructive notice of the spouse's lack of authority.

History of Fam §3.104: Acts 1997, 75th Leg., ch. 7, §1, eff. April 17, 1997. Source: Former Fam §5.24.

Anton v. Merrill Lynch, 36 S.W.3d 251, 258 (Tex. App.—Austin 2001, pet. denied). Husband "was the only person involved in the establishment of the IRA or the designation of death beneficiaries, and that he was the only person with contractual authority to direct the [brokers]. The [brokers] were entitled to rely on [husband's] authority to manage solely an IRA bearing his name and containing funds rolled over from his 401k plan."

Fajkus v. First Nat'l Bank, 735 S.W.2d 882, 886 (Tex.App.—Austin 1987, writ denied). "The 206 acres were held in the name of [husband] only, therefore, it is presumed that the property was subject to his sole management, control and disposition. [Wife] asserts that the presumption was rebutted by evidence that both spouses signed in all other transactions involving the property. This evidence, however, is insufficient to show joint management. [J]oint execution of documents relating to liens on property does not render that property subject to the joint management of both spouses." *See also* ***Thomas v. Rhodes***, 701 S.W.2d 943, 945 (Tex.App.—Fort Worth 1986, writ ref'd n.r.e.).

Williams v. Portland State Bank, 514 S.W.2d 124, 126 (Tex.App.—Beaumont 1974, writ dism'd). "[I]t is presumed that property held in the name of one spouse alone, is subject to the sole management, control and disposition of such spouse, and a third person dealing with that spouse is entitled to rely upon that spouse's authority to deal with the property in the absence of fraud or notice of the spouse's lack of authority. From the factual situation before us in this case, we meet the question as to whether knowledge by the president of the Bank making this loan that [wife] had refused to execute the first note and deed of trust was notice that [husband] lacked the authority to encumber [wife's] interest in this tract of land. [¶] There is ... no evidence in this record that the Bank had actual specific knowledge that [husband] had no authority from [wife] to encumber her interest in this tract of land. However, [§5.24] does not require knowledge of lack of authority, but uses the term notice. ... Whatever puts a person on inquiry ordinarily amounts in law to notice, provided inquiry has become a duty and would lead to knowledge of the facts by the exercise of ordinary diligence and understanding. In other words, one who has knowledge of such facts as would cause a prudent man to make further inquiry, is chargeable with notice of the facts which, by use of ordinary intelligence, he would have ascertained. [¶] [W]e hold the actual knowledge by the Bank that [wife] had refused to sign the first note and deed of trust was sufficient as a matter of law to put the Bank on notice to make further inquiry as to the extent to [husband's] authority to encumber [wife's] interest in this tract of land." (Internal quotations omitted.) *See also* ***Flack v. First Nat'l Bank***, 226 S.W.2d 628, 632 (Tex.1950).

Sections 3.105-3.200 reserved for expansion

SUBCHAPTER C. MARITAL PROPERTY LIABILITIES

FAM §3.201. SPOUSAL LIABILITY

(a) A person is personally liable for the acts of the person's spouse only if:

(1) the spouse acts as an agent for the person; or

(2) the spouse incurs a debt for necessaries as provided by Subchapter F, Chapter 2.

(b) Except as provided by this subchapter, community property is not subject to a liability that arises from an act of a spouse.

(c) A spouse does not act as an agent for the other spouse solely because of the marriage relationship.

History of Fam §3.201: Acts 1997, 75th Leg., ch. 7, §1, eff. April 17, 1997. Source: Former Fam §4.031.

Kimsey v. Kimsey, 965 S.W.2d 690, 695 (Tex. App.—El Paso 1998, writ denied). "Generally, both spouses are jointly and severally liable for the tax due on a joint return. Thus, a spouse may be liable for the entire tax liability although the income was totally earned by the other spouse. If a husband and wife file as married filing separately, each is liable only for the tax due on his or her own return. [¶] Generally if husband and wife are separated, they are considered married for the entire year if no final decree of divorce has been entered by the last day of the tax year. If they are considered married, they may file jointly or as married filing separately and they may file a joint return even if one had no income or deductions. The difficulty here is that for the years prior to the year of divorce, the trial court made no order as to whether the parties are to file jointly or as married filing separately. As for the year of divorce, if the final decree is obtained on or before the last day of the tax year, the parties are considered unmarried and cannot file a joint return. As a result, each spouse is still liable for taxes on half of the community income for the part of the year before dissolution."

Coker v. Weatheread, 852 S.W.2d 764, 766 (Tex. App.—Tyler 1993, no writ). "Although not a party to the suit, [husband] intentionally signed the pleading, apparently as an agent for [his wife], without the authority to do so. [¶] [T]he purpose of a signature requirement in the pleadings is to fix the responsibility for the allegations. We cannot conclude that the signature of a stranger to a law suit, although a party's spouse, effectively fixes the responsibility for what is stated in the pleading."

Carr v. Houston Business Forms, Inc. 794 S.W.2d 849, 852 (Tex.App.—Houston [14th Dist.] 1990, no writ). Section 4.031, now §3.201, "provides that a person is personally liable for his or her spouse's debts only if the debt is for necessaries or if the spouse acts as the person's agent when incurring the debt. The marital relationship alone is insufficient evidence that a spouse acted as the other spouse's agent."

Brooks v. Brooks, 515 S.W.2d 730, 732 (Tex.App.—Eastland 1974, writ ref'd n.r.e.). "Texas statutes do not define the term 'community debt.' We hold that the term does not include a potential income tax obligation."

FAM §3.202. RULES OF MARITAL PROPERTY LIABILITY

(a) A spouse's separate property is not subject to liabilities of the other spouse unless both spouses are liable by other rules of law.

(b) Unless both spouses are personally liable as provided by this subchapter, the community property subject to a spouse's sole management, control, and disposition is not subject to:

(1) any liabilities that the other spouse incurred before marriage; or

(2) any nontortious liabilities that the other spouse incurs during marriage.

(c) The community property subject to a spouse's sole or joint management, control, and disposition is subject to the liabilities incurred by the spouse before or during marriage.

(d) All community property is subject to tortious liability of either spouse incurred during marriage.

History of Fam §3.202: Acts 1997, 75th Leg., ch. 7, §1, eff. April 17, 1997. Source: Former Fam §5.61.

Carlton v. Estate of Estes, 664 S.W.2d 322, 323 (Tex.1983). "[A] spouse's interest in community property subject to joint management, control, and disposition may be reached to satisfy the liabilities of the other spouse without joinder of both spouses in the suit."

Cockerham v. Cockerham, 527 S.W.2d 162, 171-72 (Tex.1975). "To determine whether a debt is only that of the contracting party or if it is instead that of both the husband and wife, it is necessary to examine the totality of the circumstances in which the debt arose. Of particular importance ... is the consideration of implied assent to the debt by the noncontracting party.... [¶] Characterization of the debts as community liabilities is only one aspect of the circumstances to be considered in determining whether the debts are joint. [¶] In the instant case the record is replete with factors which point to the conclusion that the dress shop debts were joint liabilities of both the husband and the wife. For example, it was the husband who advanced the wife the necessary capital to pay for the initial inventory of the store. In addition, it was the wife's practice, acquiesced in by her husband, to write checks for personal and family expenses on his personal checking account by signing his name rather than hers.... After the wife opened the dress shop she continued to write checks on her husband's account and often paid for merchandise for the store in this manner. The husband never forbade her to do so nor did he stop payment on any of the checks. ... Though the husband now claims he did not authorize the dress shop liabilities, his actions were consistent with an implied assent to their establishment. [¶] In view of the record presented to this court, we hold the dress shop debts are joint liabilities of both the husband and the wife."

Butler v. Butler, 975 S.W.2d 765, 769 (Tex.App.—Corpus Christi 1998, no pet.). "Debts established during marriage which do not involve the exclusive use of one spouse's separate property or sole management community property may be satisfied from joint management community property. However, this presumption can be rebutted by showing that the creditor agreed to look solely to the separate estate of the obligor for satisfaction. [¶] A spouse's child support obligations depend on the spouse's net resources, as determined according to §154.062. ... The net resources of a spouse of the child support obligor are not considered. We conclude that, because [appellee's] net resources are excluded from consideration in setting [appellant's] child support obligation, the obligee is restricted to looking only to [appellant] for satisfaction of [appellant's] child support obligation." *See also* ***Farish v. Farish***, 982 S.W.2d 623, 627 (Tex.App.—Houston [1st Dist.] 1998, no pet.).

Blake v. Amoco Fed. Credit Un., 900 S.W.2d 108, 111 (Tex.App.—Houston [14th Dist.] 1995, no writ). "It is well-settled law in Texas that divorce courts cannot disturb the rights of a creditor to collect from either of the divorcing parties on a joint obligation. *At 112:* [T]he divorce court could not prejudice the creditor's right to take a judgment against both spouses when dividing responsibility for payment of debts."

Nelson v. Citizens Bank & Trust Co., 881 S.W.2d 128, 131 (Tex.App.—Houston [14th Dist.] 1994, no writ). "[E]ither spouse can incur contractual liability that will bind the share of the noncontracting spouse's community property subject to the sole or joint control of the contracting spouse, but the noncontracting spouse is not 'personally liable' for the obligation."

Pemelton v. Pemelton, 809 S.W.2d 642, 650-51 (Tex.App.—Corpus Christi 1991), *rev'd on other grounds*, 836 S.W.2d 145 (Tex.1992). "Because the businesses were created during the marriage and benefited the community, their income and debts were joint management community property. A joint liability, being a personal liability of each spouse individually, can be collected from both spouses' non-exempt property, be it separate or community."

Humphrey v. Taylor, 673 S.W.2d 954, 956 (Tex. App.—Tyler 1984, no writ). "The proceeds of the note were never under the sole management and control of [the wife]. [¶] [Wife] had no knowledge of the note transaction between [the husband] and [creditors] until she was advised by telephone that the note was in default. There is no evidence that she took any action to ratify [her husband's] act or to acknowledge any liability. She did not participate in the transaction; she did not realize any gain from it. There is no evidence of assent, implied or expressed, to [her husband's] incurring the debt. The facts and circumstances will not support the conclusion that there is joint liability."

FAM §3.203. ORDER IN WHICH PROPERTY IS SUBJECT TO EXECUTION

(a) A judge may determine, as deemed just and equitable, the order in which particular separate or community property is subject to execution and sale to satisfy a judgment, if the property subject to liability for a judgment includes any combination of:

(1) a spouse's separate property;

(2) community property subject to a spouse's sole management, control, and disposition;

(3) community property subject to the other spouse's sole management, control, and disposition; and

(4) community property subject to the spouses' joint management, control, and disposition.

(b) In determining the order in which particular property is subject to execution and sale, the judge shall consider the facts surrounding the transaction or occurrence on which the suit is based.

History of Fam §3.203: Acts 1997, 75th Leg., ch. 7, §1, eff. April 17, 1997. Source: Former Fam §5.62.

Sections 3.204-3.300 reserved for expansion

SUBCHAPTER D. MANAGEMENT, CONTROL, & DISPOSITION OF MARITAL PROPERTY UNDER UNUSUAL CIRCUMSTANCES

FAM §3.301. MISSING, ABANDONED, OR SEPARATED SPOUSE

A *Section 3.301 below is effective for proceedings in which original petitions are filed on or after Sept. 1, 2001.*

(a) A spouse may file a sworn petition stating the facts that make it desirable for the petitioning spouse to manage, control, and dispose of community property described or defined in the petition that would otherwise be subject to the sole or joint management, control, and disposition of the other spouse if:

(1) the other spouse has disappeared and that spouse's location remains unknown to the petitioning spouse, unless the spouse is reported to be a prisoner of war or missing on public service;

(2) the other spouse has permanently abandoned the petitioning spouse; or

(3) the spouses are permanently separated.

(b) The petition may be filed in a court in the county in which the petitioner resided at the time the separation began, or the abandonment or disappearance occurred, not earlier than the 60th day after the date of the occurrence of the event. If both spouses are nonresidents of this state at the time the petition is filed, the petition may be filed in a court in a county in which any part of the described or defined community property is located.

History of Fam §3.301: Acts 1997, 75th Leg., ch. 7, §1, eff. April 17, 1997. Amended by Acts 2001, 77th Leg., ch. 217, §23, eff. Sept. 1, 2001. Source: Former Fam §5.25(a), (b).

FAM §3.301. INCAPACITATED, MISSING, ABANDONED, OR SEPARATED SPOUSE

Section 3.301 below is effective for proceedings in which original petitions were filed before Sept. 1, 2001.

(a) A spouse may file a sworn petition stating the facts that make it desirable for the petitioning spouse to manage, control, and dispose of community property described or defined in the petition that would otherwise be subject to the sole or joint management, control, and disposition of the other spouse if:

(1) because of physical or mental incapacity, the other spouse is unable to manage, control, or dispose of the community property subject to that spouse's sole or joint management, control, and disposition;

(2) the other spouse has disappeared and that spouse's location remains unknown to the petitioning spouse, unless the spouse is reported to be a prisoner of war or missing on public service;

(3) the other spouse has permanently abandoned the petitioning spouse; or

(4) the spouses are permanently separated.

(b) The petition may be filed in a court in the county in which the petitioner resided at the time the incapacity or separation began, or the abandonment or disappearance occurred, not earlier than the 60th day after the date of the occurrence of the event. If both spouses are nonresidents of this state at the time the petition is filed, the petition may be filed in a court in a county in which any part of the described or defined community property is located.

FAM §3.302. SPOUSE MISSING ON PUBLIC SERVICE

(a) If a spouse is reported by an executive department of the United States to be a prisoner of war or missing on the public service of the United States, the spouse of the prisoner of war or missing person may file a sworn petition stating the facts that make it desirable for the petitioner to manage, control, and dispose of the community property described or defined in the petition that would otherwise be subject to the sole or joint management, control, and disposition of the imprisoned or missing spouse.

(b) The petition may be filed in a court in the county in which the petitioner resided at the time the report was made not earlier than six months after the date of the notice that a spouse is reported to be a prisoner of war or missing on public service. If both spouses were nonresidents of this state at the time the report was made, the petition shall be filed in a court in a county in which any part of the described or defined property is located.

History of Fam §3.302: Acts 1997, 75th Leg., ch. 7, §1, eff. April 17, 1997. Source: Former Fam §5.26(a), (b).

FAM §3.303. APPOINTMENT OF ATTORNEY

(a) Except as provided by Subsection (b), the court may appoint an attorney in a suit filed under this subchapter for the respondent.

(b) The court shall appoint an attorney in a suit filed under this subchapter for a respondent reported to be a prisoner of war or missing on public service.

(c) The court shall allow a reasonable fee for an appointed attorney's services as a part of the costs of the suit.

History of Fam §3.303: Acts 1997, 75th Leg., ch. 7, §1, eff. April 17, 1997. Source: Former Fam §§5.25(c), 5.26(c).

FAM §3.304. NOTICE OF HEARING; CITATION

(a) Notice of the hearing, accompanied by a copy of the petition, shall be issued and served on the attorney representing the respondent, if an attorney has been appointed.

(b) If an attorney has not been appointed for the respondent, citation shall be issued and served on the respondent as in other civil cases.

History of Fam §3.304: Acts 1997, 75th Leg., ch. 7, §1, eff. April 17, 1997. Source: Former Fam §§5.25(d), 5.26(d).

FAM §3.305. CITATION BY PUBLICATION

(a) If the residence of the respondent, other than a respondent reported to be a prisoner of war or missing on public service, is unknown, citation shall be published in a newspaper of general circulation published in the county in which the petition was filed. If that county has no newspaper of general circulation, citation shall be published in a newspaper of general circulation in an adjacent county or in the nearest county in which a newspaper of general circulation is published.

(b) The notice shall be published once a week for two consecutive weeks before the hearing, but the first notice may not be published after the 20th day before the date set for the hearing.

History of Fam §3.305: Acts 1997, 75th Leg., ch. 7, §1, eff. April 17, 1997. Source: Former Fam §5.25(e).

FAM §3.306. COURT ORDER FOR MANAGEMENT, CONTROL, & DISPOSITION OF COMMUNITY PROPERTY

(a) After hearing the evidence in a suit under this subchapter, the court, on terms the court considers just and equitable, shall render an order describing or defining the community property at issue that will be subject to the management, control, and disposition of each spouse during marriage.

(b) The court may:

(1) impose any condition and restriction the court deems necessary to protect the rights of the respondent;

(2) require a bond conditioned on the faithful administration of the property; and

(3) require payment to the registry of the court of all or a portion of the proceeds of the sale of the property, to be disbursed in accordance with the court's further directions.

History of Fam §3.306: Acts 1997, 75th Leg., ch. 7, §1, eff. April 17, 1997. Source: Former Fam §§5.25(f), 5.26(e).

FAM §3.307. CONTINUING JURISDICTION OF COURT; VACATING ORIGINAL ORDER

(a) The court has continuing jurisdiction over the court's order rendered under this subchapter.

(b) On the motion of either spouse, the court shall amend or vacate the original order after notice and hearing if:

A *Subsections (1) through (3) below are effective for proceedings in which original petitions are filed on or after Sept. 1, 2001.*

(1) the spouse who disappeared reappears;

(2) the abandonment or permanent separation ends; or

(3) the spouse who was reported to be a prisoner of war or missing on public service returns.

Subsections (1) through (4) below are effective for proceedings in which original petitions were filed before Sept. 1, 2001.

(1) the incapacitated spouse's capacity is restored;

(2) the spouse who disappeared reappears;

(3) the abandonment or permanent separation ends; or

(4) the spouse who was reported to be a prisoner of war or missing on public service returns.

History of Fam §3.307: Acts 1997, 75th Leg., ch. 7, §1, eff. April 17, 1997. Amended by Acts 2001, 77th Leg., ch. 217, §24, eff. Sept. 1, 2001. Source: Former Fam §§5.25(g), 5.26(f).

FAM §3.308. RECORDING ORDER TO AFFECT REAL PROPERTY

An order authorized by this subchapter affecting real property is not constructive notice to a good faith purchaser for value or to a creditor without actual notice unless the order is recorded in the deed records of the county in which the real property is located.

History of Fam §3.308: Acts 1997, 75th Leg., ch. 7, §1, eff. April 17, 1997. Source: Former Fam §§5.25(h), 5.26(g).

FAM §3.309. REMEDIES CUMULATIVE

The remedies provided in this subchapter are cumulative of other rights, powers, and remedies afforded spouses by law.

History of Fam §3.309: Acts 1997, 75th Leg., ch. 7, §1, eff. April 17, 1997. Source: Former Fam §5.27.

Sections 3.310-3.400 blank

A SUBCHAPTER E. CLAIMS FOR ECONOMIC CONTRIBUTION & REIMBURSEMENT

FAM §3.401. DEFINITIONS

E *Section 3.401 below is effective for suits for dissolution of marriage or annulments pending on or filed on or after Sept. 1, 2001.*

In this subchapter:

(1) "Claim for economic contribution" means a claim made under this subchapter.

(2) "Economic contribution" means the contribution to a marital estate described by Section 3.402.

(3) "Equity" means, with respect to specific property owned by one or more marital estates, the amount computed by subtracting from the fair market value of the property as of a specific date the amount of a lawful lien specific to the property on that same date.

(4) "Marital estate" means one of three estates:

(A) the community property owned by the spouses together and referred to as the community marital estate;

(B) the separate property owned individually by the husband and referred to as a separate marital estate; or

(C) the separate property owned individually by the wife, also referred to as a separate marital estate.

(5) "Spouse" means a husband, who is a man, or a wife, who is a woman. A member of a civil union or similar relationship entered into in another state between persons of the same sex is not a spouse.

History of Fam §3.401: Enacted by Acts 2001, 77th Leg., ch. 838, §2, eff. Sept. 1, 2001. Subchapter amended by Acts 2001, 77th Leg., ch. 838, §2, eff. Sept. 1, 2001.

History of Former Fam §3.401: Acts 1999, 76th Leg., ch. 692, §2, eff. Sept. 1, 1999. Deleted by Acts 2001, 77th Leg., ch. 838, §2, eff. Sept. 1, 2001.

FAM §3.402. ECONOMIC CONTRIBUTION

E *Section 3.402 below is effective for suits for dissolution of marriage or annulments pending on or filed on or after Sept. 1, 2001.*

(a) For purposes of this subchapter, "economic contribution" is the dollar amount of:

(1) the reduction of the principal amount of a debt secured by a lien on property owned before marriage, to the extent the debt existed at the time of marriage;

(2) the reduction of the principal amount of a debt secured by a lien on property received by a spouse by gift, devise, or descent during a marriage, to the extent the debt existed at the time the property was received;

(3) the reduction of the principal amount of that part of a debt, including a home equity loan:

(A) incurred during a marriage;

(B) secured by a lien on property; and

(C) incurred for the acquisition of, or for capital improvements to, property;

(4) the reduction of the principal amount of that part of a debt:

(A) incurred during a marriage;

(B) secured by a lien on property owned by a spouse;

(C) for which the creditor agreed to look for repayment solely to the separate marital estate of the spouse on whose property the lien attached; and

(D) incurred for the acquisition of, or for capital improvements to, property;

(5) the refinancing of the principal amount described by Subdivisions (1)-(4), to the extent the refinancing reduces that principal amount in a manner described by the appropriate subdivision; and

(6) capital improvements to property other than by incurring debt.

(b) "Economic contribution" does not include the dollar amount of:

(1) expenditures for ordinary maintenance and repair or for taxes, interest, or insurance; or

(2) the contribution by a spouse of time, toil, talent, or effort during the marriage.

History of Fam §3.402: Enacted by Acts 2001, 77th Leg., ch. 838, §2, eff. Sept. 1, 2001.

History of Former Fam §3.402: Acts 1999, 76th Leg., ch. 692, §2, eff. Sept. 1, 1999. Deleted by Acts 2001, 77th Leg., ch. 838, §2, eff. Sept. 1, 2001.

FAM §3.403. CLAIM BASED ON ECONOMIC CONTRIBUTION

E *Section 3.403 below is effective for suits for dissolution of marriage or annulments pending on or filed on or after Sept. 1, 2001.*

(a) A marital estate that makes an economic contribution to property owned by another marital estate has a claim for economic contribution with respect to the benefited estate.

(b) The amount of the claim under this section is equal to the product of:

(1) the equity in the benefited property on the date of dissolution of the marriage, the death of a spouse, or disposition of the property; multiplied by

(2) a fraction of which:

(A) the numerator is the economic contribution to the property by the contributing estate; and

(B) the denominator is an amount equal to the sum of:

(i) the economic contribution to the property by the contributing estate;

(ii) the equity in the property as of the date of the marriage or, if later, the date of the first economic contribution by the contributing estate; and

(iii) the economic contribution to the property by the benefited estate during the marriage.

(c) The amount of a claim under this section may be less than the total of the economic contributions made by the contributing estate, but may not cause the contributing estate to owe funds to the benefited estate.

(d) The amount of a claim under this section may not exceed the equity in the property on the date of dissolution of the marriage, the death of a spouse, or disposition of the property.

(e) The use and enjoyment of property during a marriage for which a claim for economic contribution to the property exists does not create a claim of an offsetting benefit against the claim.

History of Fam §3.403: Enacted by Acts 2001, 77th Leg., ch. 838, §2, eff. Sept. 1, 2001.

History of Former Fam §3.403: Acts 1999, 76th Leg., ch. 692, §2, eff. Sept. 1, 1999. Renumbered as §3.404 by Acts 2001, 77th Leg., ch. 838, §2, eff. Sept. 1, 2001.

A FAM §3.404. APPLICATION OF INCEPTION OF TITLE RULE; OWNERSHIP INTEREST NOT CREATED

(a) This subchapter does not affect the rule of inception of title under which the character of property is determined at the time the right to own or claim the property arises.

(b) The claim for economic contribution created under this subchapter does not create an ownership interest in property, but does create a claim against the property of the benefited estate by the contributing estate. The claim matures on dissolution of the marriage or the death of either spouse.

History of Fam §3.404: Acts 1999, 76th Leg., ch. 692, §2, eff. Sept. 1, 1999. Renumbered from §3.403 and amended by Acts 2001, 77th Leg., ch. 838, §2, eff. Sept. 1, 2001.

A FAM §3.405. MANAGEMENT RIGHTS

This subchapter does not affect the right to manage, control, or dispose of marital property as provided by this chapter.

History of Fam §3.405: Acts 1999, 76th Leg., ch. 692, §2, eff. Sept. 1, 1999. Renumbered from §3.404 and amended by Acts 2001, 77th Leg., ch. 838, §2, eff. Sept. 1, 2001.

History of Former Fam §3.405: Acts 1999, 76th Leg., ch. 692, §2, eff. Sept. 1, 1999. Deleted by Acts 2001, 77th Leg., ch. 838, §2, eff. Sept. 1, 2001.

FAM §3.406. EQUITABLE LIEN

A (a) On dissolution of a marriage, the court shall impose an equitable lien on property of a marital estate to secure a claim for economic contribution in that property by another marital estate.

E *Subsections (b) & (c) below are effective for suits for dissolution of marriage or annulments pending on or filed on or after Sept. 1, 2001.*

(b) On the death of a spouse, a court shall, on application for a claim of economic contribution brought by the surviving spouse, the personal representative of the estate of the deceased spouse, or any other person interested in the estate, as defined by Section 3, Texas Probate Code, impose an equitable lien on the property of a benefited marital estate to secure a claim for economic contribution by a contributing marital estate.

(c) Subject to homestead restrictions, an equitable lien under this section may be imposed on the entirety of a spouse's property in the marital estate and is not limited to the item of property that benefited from an economic contribution.

History of Fam §3.406: Acts 1999, 76th Leg., ch. 692, §2, eff. Sept. 1, 1999. Amended by Acts 2001, 77th Leg., ch. 838, §2, eff. Sept. 1, 2001.

FAM §3.407. OFFSETTING CLAIMS

E *Section 3.407 below is effective for suits for dissolution of marriage or annulments pending on or filed on or after Sept. 1, 2001.*

The court shall offset a claim for one marital estate's economic contribution in a specific asset of a second marital estate against the second marital estate's claim for economic contribution in a specific asset of the first marital estate.

History of Fam §3.407: Enacted by Acts 2001, 77th Leg., ch. 838, §2, eff. Sept. 1, 2001.

FAM §3.408. CLAIM FOR REIMBURSEMENT

E *Section 3.408 below is effective for suits for dissolution of marriage or annulments pending on or filed on or after Sept. 1, 2001.*

(a) A claim for economic contribution does not abrogate another claim for reimbursement in a factual circumstance not covered by this subchapter. In the case of a conflict between a claim for economic contribution under this subchapter and a claim for reimbursement, the claim for economic contribution, if proven, prevails.

(b) A claim for reimbursement includes:

(1) payment by one marital estate of the unsecured liabilities of another marital estate; and

(2) inadequate compensation for the time, toil, talent, and effort of a spouse by a business entity under the control and direction of that spouse.

(c) The court shall resolve a claim for reimbursement by using equitable principles, including the principle that claims for reimbursement may be offset against each other if the court determines it to be appropriate.

(d) Benefits for the use and enjoyment of property may be offset against a claim for reimbursement for expenditures to benefit a marital estate on property that does not involve a claim for economic contribution to the property.

History of Fam §3.408: Enacted by Acts 2001, 77th Leg., ch. 838, §2, eff. Sept. 1, 2001.

Payment of Unsecured Liabilities

Penick v. Penick, 783 S.W.2d 194, 196 (Tex.1988). "[T]he payment by one marital estate of the debt of another creates a prima facie right of reimbursement."

Time, Toil, Talent, and Effort

Jensen v. Jensen, 665 S.W.2d 107, 109 (Tex.1984). The reimbursement "theory requires adoption of the rule that the community will be reimbursed for the value of time and effort expended by either or both spouses to enhance the separate estate of either, other than that reasonably necessary to manage and preserve the separate estate, less the remuneration received for that time and effort in the form of salary, bonus, dividends and other fringe benefits, those items being community property when received." *See also* ***Vallone v. Vallone***, 644 S.W.2d 455, 459 (Tex.1982).

Pearce v. Pearce, 824 S.W.2d 195, 200 (Tex.App.—El Paso 1991, writ denied). "[W]hen time, toil, talent and effort have been expended for the betterment of a marital estate, it is clear that a spouse has the option of pursuing a claim for reimbursement. If the spouse has entered, as in this case, a post-nuptial agreement, one must determine whether such a claim has been waived. [¶] The Trust Indenture involved in this case does not mention 'reimbursement,' nor does it contain a release or waiver of such a claim. In fact, there is no provision in the agreement that specifically addresses the issue of future wages and/or time, toil, talent and effort of either spouse. Instead, the agreement only refers to community property and/or other rights to the separate property of [husband]. Reimbursement, however, is not a property right, it is an equitable claim that arises upon dissolution of the marriage through death, divorce or annulment. [¶] We find that the language of the Trust Indenture cannot be construed as a bar to Appellant's claim for reimbursement. There is no manifestation of intent to exclude such a claim."

Equity

Vallone v. Vallone, 644 S.W.2d 455, 458-59 (Tex. 1982). "The rule of reimbursement is purely an equitable one. It obtains when the community estate in some way improves the separate estate of one of the spouses (or vice versa). The right of reimbursement is not an interest in property or an enforceable debt, per se, but an equitable right which arises upon dissolution of the marriage through death, divorce, or annulment. [¶] The party claiming the right of reimbursement has the burden of pleading and proving that the expenditures and improvements were made and that they are reimbursable."

Dakan v. Dakan, 83 S.W.2d 620, 627 (Tex.1935). "[T]he general right of reimbursement ... is not a fixed right..., but is an equity ... and the final determination of the rights of the respective parties is to be determined upon equitable principles as to the amount of reimbursement, as well as the means of enforcing the same. It is not a mere question of balancing ledger accounts."

Zieba v. Martin, 928 S.W.2d 782, 787 (Tex.App.—Houston [14th Dist.] 1996, no writ). "Reimbursement is an equitable doctrine, and a court of equity is bound to look at all the facts and circumstances and determine what is fair, just and equitable. The trier of fact should consider the benefits and detriments to each estate. 'Reimbursement is not available as a matter of law but lies in the discretion of the court.' Great latitude must be given to the trial court in applying equitable principles to value a claim for reimbursement. ... The discretion to be exercised in evaluating a claim for reimbursement is equally as broad as the discretion exercised in making a just and right division of the community estate." *See also* ***Jones v. Jones***, 804 S.W.2d 623, 626 (Tex.App.—Texarkana 1991, no writ).

Offsets

Penick v. Penick, 783 S.W.2d 194, 197 (Tex.1988). "The outright rejection of offsetting benefits is inconsistent with the equitable nature of a claim for reimbursement."

Kimsey v. Kimsey, 965 S.W.2d 690, 700 (Tex.App.—El Paso 1998, pet. denied). "Off-setting benefits to the paying estate must be considered. The party claiming the right of reimbursement has the burden of proof."

Grossnickle v. Grossnickle, 935 S.W.2d 830, 841 (Tex.App.—Texarkana 1996, writ denied). "Reimbursement for expenditures made on property may be offset by benefits such as usage by the party making these expenditures."

Measure of Reimbursement

Penick v. Penick, 783 S.W.2d 194, 197 (Tex.1988). The "court of appeals held that the best rule was to reimburse the community for every dollar advanced on the principal of [husband's] prenuptial, purchase money debt. [¶] This 'dollar for dollar' reimbursement rule is inconsistent with the equitable approach we advocated in ***Anderson***. The court of appeals, however, distinguishes ***Anderson*** because it concerned reimbursement for a capital improvement to separate property rather than reimbursement for a prenuptial, purchase money debt. [¶] We view the advancement of funds by one marital estate to another under either transaction, payment of a purchase money debt or as a capital improvement, as essentially identical and therefore subject to the same kind of measurement."

Anderson v. Gilliland, 684 S.W.2d 673, 675 (Tex. 1985). "We hold that a claim for reimbursement for funds expended by an estate for improvements to another estate is to be measured by the enhancement in value to the benefited estate. This rule is more likely to insure equitable treatment of both the contributing and benefited estates in most situations."

Kimsey v. Kimsey, 965 S.W.2d 690, 700 (Tex.App.—El Paso 1998, pet. denied). "A claim for reimbursement of funds expended by an estate for improvements to another estate is to be measured by the enhancement value to the benefited estate. This measurement is to be applied whether the claim for reimbursement is based on funds expended for payment of a purchase money debt or for a capital improvement to another estate."

Magill v. Magill, 816 S.W.2d 530, 535 (Tex.App.—Houston [1st Dist.] 1991, writ denied). "Testimony regarding the value of the property before the improvements and the value after the improvements is sufficient to sustain a finding of enhanced value."

Liens

Heggen v. Pemelton, 836 S.W.2d 145, 146 (Tex. 1992). "When dividing marital property on divorce, trial courts may impose equitable liens on one spouse's *separate real property* to secure the other spouse's right of reimbursement for community improvements to that property. Although courts may impress equitable liens on separate real property to secure reimbursement rights, they may not impress such liens, absent any compensable reimbursement interest, simply to ensure a just and right division. *At 148:* The lien imposed on [wife's] separate property homestead was invalid for two reasons. First, it burdened her separate real property for reasons other than to secure [husband's] reimbursement interest; that is, the trial court impermissibly imposed it to secure a just and right division. And second, it imposed a lien on [wife's] homestead that, based on the record, did not fit into any of the categories allowed by the Texas Constitution...."

Winkle v. Winkle, 951 S.W.2d 80, 87 (Tex.App.—Corpus Christi 1997, pet. denied). "[T]rial courts generally may impose equitable liens on one spouse's separate property as a means for securing the discharge of payments owed by one spouse to the other. Such liens, however, are permissible only against the separate property to which improvement was made at community expense."

FAM §3.409. NONREIMBURSABLE CLAIMS

Ⓔ *Section 3.409 below is effective for suits for dissolution of marriage or annulments pending on or filed on or after Sept. 1, 2001.*

The court may not recognize a marital estate's claim for reimbursement for:

(1) the payment of child support, alimony, or spousal maintenance;

(2) the living expenses of a spouse or child of a spouse;

(3) contributions of property of a nominal value;

(4) the payment of a liability of a nominal amount; or

(5) a student loan owed by a spouse.

History of Fam §3.409: Enacted by Acts 2001, 77th Leg., ch. 838, §2, eff. Sept. 1, 2001.

Living Expenses

Norris v. Vaughan, 260 S.W.2d 676, 683 (Tex.1953). "It is fundamental that the husband is obligated to furnish support for the community living and if no community funds are available he should utilize his separate funds. It is his duty to provide for the community and in this instance he chose to expend a portion of his separate estate so that the community standard of living could be as it was. Separate funds spent for community living in such a manner should be deemed a gift to the community for its well-being and use. Allowing a right of reimbursement at a later date would be inconsistent with the fundamental concept that a man should provide for his home and community."

In re Marriage of Case, 28 S.W.3d 154, 161 (Tex. App.—Texarkana 2000, no pet.). "[W]hen separate funds are expended for normal community living expenses, such as rent, food, etc., there is no right to reimbursement because these merely extinguish the obligation of each spouse to support the family. ... The use of separate funds in a lump sum to retire community obligations does not constitute a living expense of the community and gives a prima facie right to reimbursement."

Pelzig v. Berkebile, 931 S.W.2d 398, 400 (Tex. App.—Corpus Christi 1996, no writ). "The cases which exempt 'living expenses' from reimbursement all deal with claims for separate property expended by one spouse for the living expenses of the married couple and their family. The child support, college expenses, and alimony payments were legal obligations [of husband] brought with him into the marriage. There is no evidence that [wife] was deceived about these obligations. There is no evidence that [wife] ever sought to require [husband] to meet these obligations out of his separate estate, either during their marriage or in the form of a prenuptial agreement. There is no evidence that these expenses benefited [husband's] separate estate. The trial court, therefore, did not abuse its discretion in equitably determining that no right of reimbursement attaches to these payments."

Graham v. Graham, 836 S.W.2d 308, 310-11 (Tex. App.—Texarkana 1992, no writ). Husband "established that the Auburn house was his separate property. The record shows that the proceeds from its sale were used to retire community obligations on a house purchased during marriage. [¶] [Wife] contends that the trial court abused its discretion in ordering reimbursement because the proceeds of the Auburn house were a gift of separate funds to the marriage partners for community living. [¶] Spouses are obligated to furnish support for community living expenses using separate property, if necessary. Separate property expended for community living is deemed to be a gift for the benefit of the well-being and use of the community estate. However, no cases have applied this rule to a situation where separate funds have been used to retire a community obligation in a lump sum payment. [¶] [Husband] proved that the proceeds from the sale of his separate property were used to retire the corpus of a community debt. There was no evidence that any of the funds were used to pay normal living expenses. The use of separate property to retire a community debt gives rise to reimbursement regardless of the purpose of the debt." *See also* ***Hilton v. Hilton***, 678 S.W.2d 645, 648 (Tex.App.—Houston [14th Dist.] 1984, no writ).

Spouse's Student Loan

Halbert v. Halbert, 794 S.W.2d 535, 536 (Tex. App.—Tyler 1990, no writ). "'Although the trial court did not specifically award the wife reimbursement for her husband's education in its division of the community property, we caution the trial court on remand that the cost of [husband's] veterinary degree is not a reimbursable community expenditure.'"

E FAM §3.410. EFFECT OF MARITAL PROPERTY AGREEMENTS

A premarital or marital property agreement, whether executed before, on, or after September 1, 1999, that satisfies the requirements of Chapter 4 is effective to waive, release, assign, or partition a claim for economic contribution under this subchapter to the same extent the agreement would have been effective to waive, release, assign, or partition a claim for reimbursement under the law as it existed immediately before September 1, 1999, unless the agreement provides otherwise.

History of Fam §3.410: Enacted by Acts 2001, 77th Leg., ch. 838, §2, eff. Sept. 1, 2001.

CHAPTER 4. PREMARITAL & MARITAL PROPERTY AGREEMENTS

Editor's note: Changes have been made to the official comments to reflect the Texas Legislature's omission of sections and changing section numbers. The full uniform act and official comments can be found at http://www.nccusl.org.

SUBCHAPTER A. UNIFORM PREMARITAL AGREEMENT ACT

Official Prefatory Comment

The number of marriages between persons previously married and the number of marriages between persons each of whom is intending to continue to pursue a career is steadily increasing. For these and other reasons, it is becoming more and more common for persons contemplating marriage to seek to resolve by agreement certain issues presented by the forthcoming marriage. However, despite a lengthy legal history for these premarital agreements, there is a substantial uncertainty as to the enforceability of all, or a portion, of the provisions of these agreements and a significant lack of uniformity of treatment of these agreements among the states. The problems caused by this uncertainty and nonuniformity are greatly exacerbated by the mobility of our population. Nevertheless, this uncertainty and nonuniformity seem reflective not so much of basic policy differences between the states but rather a result of spasmodic, reflexive response to varying factual circumstances at different times. Accordingly, uniform legislation conforming to modern social policy which provides both certainty and sufficient flexibility to accommodate different circumstances would appear to be both a significant improvement and a goal realistically capable of achievement.

This Act is intended to be relatively limited in scope. Section 4.001 defines a "premarital agreement" as "an agreement between prospective spouses made in contemplation of marriage and to be effective upon marriage." Section 4.002 requires that a premarital agreement be in writing and signed by both parties. Section 4.004 provides that a premarital agreement becomes effective upon the marriage of the parties. These sections establish significant parameters. That is, the UPAA does not deal with agreements between persons who live together but who do not contemplate marriage or who do not marry. Nor does the UPAA provide for postnuptial or separation agreements or with oral agreements.

On the other hand, agreements which are embraced by the UPAA are permitted to deal with a wide variety of matters and Section 4.003 provides an **illustrative** list of those matters, including spousal support, which may properly be dealt with in a premarital agreement.

Section 4.006 is the key operative section of the UPAA and sets forth the conditions under which a premarital agreement is not enforceable. An agreement is not enforceable if the party against whom enforcement is sought proves that (a) he or she did not execute the agreement voluntarily or that (b) the agreement was unconscionable when it was executed and, before execution of the agreement, he or she (1) was not provided a fair and reasonable disclosure of the property or financial obligations of the other party, (2) did not voluntarily and expressly waive, in writing, any right to disclosure of the property or financial obligations of the other party beyond the disclosure provided, and (3) did not have, or reasonably could not have had, an adequate knowledge of the property and financial obligations of the other party.

These sections form the heart of the UPAA; the remaining sections deal with more tangential issues. Section 4.005 prescribes the manner in which a premarital agreement may be amended or revoked; Section 4.007 provides for very limited enforcement where a marriage is subsequently determined to be void; and Section 8 tolls any statute of limitations applicable to an action asserting a claim for relief under a premarital agreement during the parties' marriage.

FAM §4.001. DEFINITIONS

In this subchapter:

(1) "Premarital agreement" means an agreement between prospective spouses made in contemplation of marriage and to be effective on marriage.

(2) "Property" means an interest, present or future, legal or equitable, vested or contingent, in real or personal property, including income and earnings.

History of Fam §4.001: Acts 1997, 75th Leg., ch. 7, §1, eff. April 17, 1997. Source: Former Fam §5.41.

Official Comment

The definition of "premarital agreement" set forth in subsection (1) is limited to an agreement between prospective spouses made in contemplation of and to be effective upon marriage. Agreements between persons living together but not contemplating marriage (see *Marvin v. Marvin*, 18 Cal. 3d 660 (1976), judgment after trial modified, 122 Cal. App. 3d 871 (1981)) and postnuptial or separation agreements are outside the scope of this Act. Formal requirements are prescribed by Section 4.002. An illustrative list of matters which may be included in an agreement is set forth in Section 4.003.

Subsection (2) is designed to embrace all forms of property and interests therein. These may include rights in a professional license or practice, employee benefit plans, pension and retirement accounts, and so on. The reference to income or earnings includes both income from property and earnings from personal services.

Beck v. Beck, 814 S.W.2d 745, 749 (Tex.1991). "We hold that the 1980 amendment to article XVI, §15, of the Texas Constitution demonstrates an intention on the part of the legislature and the people of Texas to not only authorize future premarital agreements, but to impliedly validate §5.41 [now §4.001] and all premarital agreements entered into before 1980 pursuant to that statute. The legislature and the people of Texas have made the public policy determination that premarital agreements should be enforced."

Williams v. Williams, 569 S.W.2d 867, 870 (Tex. 1978). Section 5.41, now §4.001, "should be construed as broadly as possible in order to allow the parties as much flexibility to contract with respect to property or other rights incident to the marriage, provided the constitutional and statutory definitions of separate and community property or the requirements of public policy are not violated."

FAM §4.002. FORMALITIES

A premarital agreement must be in writing and signed by both parties. The agreement is enforceable without consideration.

History of Fam §4.002: Acts 1997, 75th Leg., ch. 7, §1, eff. April 17, 1997. Source: Former Fam §5.42.

Official Comment

Section 4.002 restates the common requirement that a premarital agreement be reduced to writing and signed by both parties (see Ariz. Rev. Stats. §25-201; Ark. Stats. §55-310; Cal. Civ. C. §5134; 13 Dela. Code 1974 §301; Idaho Code §32-917; Ann. Laws Mass. ch. 209, §25; Minn. Stats. Ann. §519.11; Montana Rev. C. §36-123; New Mex Stats. Ann. 1978 40-2-4; Ore. Rev. Stats. §108.140; Vernon's Texas Codes Ann. §5.44; Vermont Stats. Ann. Title 12, §181). Many states also require other formalities, including notarization or an acknowledgement (see, *e.g.*, Arizona, Arkansas, California, Idaho, Montana, New Mexico) but may then permit the formal statutory requirement to be avoided or satisfied subsequent to execution (see *In re Marriage of Cleveland*, 76 Cal. App. 3d 357 (1977) (premarital agreement never acknowledged but "proved" by sworn testimony of parties in dissolution proceeding)). This act dispenses with all formal requirements except a writing signed by both parties. Although the section is framed in the singular, the agreement may consist of one or more documents intended to be part of the agreement and executed as required by this section.

Section 4.002 also restates what appears to be the almost universal rule regarding the marriage as consideration for a premarital agreement (see, *e.g.*, Ga. Code §20-303; *Barnhill v. Barnhill*, 386 So. 2d 749 (Ala. Civ. App. 1980); *Estate of Gillilan v. Estate of Gillilan*, 406 N.E. 2d 981 (Ind. App. 1980); *Friedlander v. Friedlander*, 494 P.2d 208 (Wash. 1972); but cf. *Wilson v. Wilson*, 170 A. 2d 679, 685 (Me. 1961)). The primary importance of this rule has been to provide a degree of mutuality of benefits to support the enforceability of a premarital agreement. A marriage is a prerequisite for the effectiveness of a premarital agreement under this act (see Section 4.004). This requires that there be a ceremonial marriage. Even if this marriage is subsequently determined to have been void, Section 4.007 may provide limits of enforceability of an agreement entered into in contemplation of that marriage. Consideration as such is not required and the standards for enforceability are established by Sections 4.006 and 4.007. Nevertheless, this provision is retained here as a desirable, if not essential, restatement of the law. On the other hand, the fact that marriage is deemed to be consideration for the purpose of this act does not change the rules applicable in other areas of law (see, *e.g.*, 26 U.S.C.A. §2043 (release of certain marital rights not treated as consideration for federal estate tax), 2512; *Merrill v. Fahs*, 324 U.S. 308, rehearing denied 324 U.S. 888 (release of marital rights in premarital agreement not adequate and full consideration for purposes of federal gift tax).

Finally, a premarital agreement is a contract. As required for any other contract, the parties must have the capacity to contract in order to enter into a binding agreement. Those persons who lack the capacity to contract but who under other provisions of law are permitted to enter into a binding agreement may enter into a premarital agreement under those other provisions of law.

FAM §4.003. CONTENT

(a) The parties to a premarital agreement may contract with respect to:

(1) the rights and obligations of each of the parties in any of the property of either or both of them whenever and wherever acquired or located;

(2) the right to buy, sell, use, transfer, exchange, abandon, lease, consume, expend, assign, create a

security interest in, mortgage, encumber, dispose of, or otherwise manage and control property;

(3) the disposition of property on separation, marital dissolution, death, or the occurrence or nonoccurrence of any other event;

(4) the modification or elimination of spousal support;

(5) the making of a will, trust, or other arrangement to carry out the provisions of the agreement;

(6) the ownership rights in and disposition of the death benefit from a life insurance policy;

(7) the choice of law governing the construction of the agreement; and

(8) any other matter, including their personal rights and obligations, not in violation of public policy or a statute imposing a criminal penalty.

(b) The right of a child to support may not be adversely affected by a premarital agreement.

History of Fam §4.003: Acts 1997, 75th Leg., ch. 7, §1, eff. April 17, 1997. Source: Former Fam §5.43.

Official Comment

Section 4.003 permits the parties to contract in a premarital agreement with respect to any matter listed and any other matter not in violation of public policy or any statute imposing a criminal penalty. The matters are intended to be illustrative, not exclusive. Paragraph (4) of subsection (a) specifically authorizes the parties to deal with spousal support obligations. There is a split in authority among the states as to whether an premarital agreement may control the issue of spousal support. Some few states do not permit a premarital agreement to control this issue (see, *e.g.*, *In re Marriage of Winegard*, 278 N.W. 2d 505 (Iowa 1979); *Fricke v. Fricke*, 42 N.W. 2d 500 (Wis. 1950)). However, the better view and growing trend is to permit a premarital agreement to govern this matter if the agreement and the circumstances of its execution satisfy certain standards (see, *e.g.*, *Newman v. Newman*, 653 P.2d 728 (Colo. Sup. Ct. 1982); *Parniawski v. Parniawski*, 359 A.2d 719 (Conn. 1976); *Volid v. Volid*, 286 N.E. 2d 42 (Ill. 1972); *Osborne v. Osborne*, 428 N.E. 2d 810 (Mass. 1981); *Hudson v. Hudson*, 350 P.2d 596 (Okla. 1960); *Unander v. Unander*, 506 P.2d 719 (Ore. 1973)) (see Sections 4.007 and 4.008).

Paragraph (8) of subsection (a) makes clear that the parties may also contract with respect to other matters, including personal rights and obligations, not in violation of public policy or a criminal statute. Hence, subject to this limitation, an agreement may provide for such matters as the choice of abode, the freedom to pursue career opportunities, the upbringing of children, and so on. However, subsection (b) of this section makes clear that an agreement may not adversely affect what would otherwise be the obligation of a party to a child.

Williams v. Williams, 569 S.W.2d 867, 870 (Tex. 1978). Spouse may waive rights to the homestead and exempt property in a premarital agreement.

Dokmanovic v. Schwarz, 880 S.W.2d 272, 275-76 (Tex.App.—Houston [14th Dist.] 1994, no writ). "The agreement in this case ... indicated the parties' intent to exchange their community interests in income from separate property and in earnings. [¶] [W]e hold that the antenuptial agreement in this case was valid as an exchange of income to be acquired by the parties during their future marriage. Because the agreement was valid, there were no commingled funds with which property was acquired during marriage. Furthermore, no partition was required where a valid exchange occurred."

Winger v. Pianka, 831 S.W.2d 853, 858 (Tex.App.—Austin 1992, writ denied). "We hold that ... persons about to marry [may] partition or exchange between themselves salaries and earnings to be acquired by the parties during their future marriage."

FAM §4.004. EFFECT OF MARRIAGE

A premarital agreement becomes effective on marriage.

History of Fam §4.004: Acts 1997, 75th Leg., ch. 7, §1, eff. April 17, 1997. Source: Former Fam §5.44.

Official Comment

This section establishes a marriage as a prerequisite for the effectiveness of a premarital agreement. As a consequence, the act does not provide for a situation where persons live together without marrying. In that situation, the parties must look to the other law of the jurisdiction (see *Marvin v. Marvin*, 18 Cal. 3d 660 (1976); judgment after trial modified, 122 Cal. App. 3d 871 (1981)).

Marshall v. Marshall, 735 S.W.2d 587, 592 (Tex. App.—Dallas 1987, writ ref'd n.r.e.). "We conclude from [the premarital agreement] provisions that the parties were contracting in relation to the [first] marriage only. It is unreasonable to assume that they anticipated a series of remarriages and divorces. The first divorce is the ascertainable contingency that determined the duration of the agreement; consequently, the agreement has no bearing on either the second marriage or the second divorce."

FAM §4.005. AMENDMENT OR REVOCATION

After marriage, a premarital agreement may be amended or revoked only by a written agreement signed by the parties. The amended agreement or the revocation is enforceable without consideration.

History of Fam §4.005: Acts 1997, 75th Leg., ch. 7, §1, eff. April 17, 1997. Source: Former Fam §5.45.

Official Comment

This section requires the same formalities of execution for an amendment or revocation of a premarital agreement as are required for its original execution (cf. *Estate of Gillilan v. Estate of Gillilan*, 406 N.E. 2d 981 (Ind. App. 1980) (agreement may be altered by subsequent agreement but not simply by inconsistent acts)).

FAM §4.006. ENFORCEMENT

(a) A premarital agreement is not enforceable if the party against whom enforcement is requested proves that:

(1) the party did not sign the agreement voluntarily; or

(2) the agreement was unconscionable when it was signed and, before signing the agreement, that party:

(A) was not provided a fair and reasonable disclosure of the property or financial obligations of the other party;

(B) did not voluntarily and expressly waive, in writing, any right to disclosure of the property or financial obligations of the other party beyond the disclosure provided; and

(C) did not have, or reasonably could not have had, adequate knowledge of the property or financial obligations of the other party.

(b) An issue of unconscionability of a premarital agreement shall be decided by the court as a matter of law.

(c) The remedies and defenses in this section are the exclusive remedies or defenses, including common law remedies or defenses.

History of Fam §4.006: Acts 1997, 75th Leg., ch. 7, §1, eff. April 17, 1997. Source: Former Fam §5.46.

Official Comment

This section sets forth the conditions which must be proven to avoid the enforcement of a premarital agreement. If prospective spouses enter into a premarital agreement and their subsequent marriage is determined to be void, the enforceability of the agreement is governed by Section 7.

The conditions stated under subsection (a) are comparable to concepts which are expressed in the statutory and decisional law of many jurisdictions. Enforcement based on disclosure and voluntary execution is perhaps most common (see, *e.g.*, Ark. Stats. §55-309; Minn. Stats. Ann. §519.11; *In re Kaufmann's Estate*, 171 A. 2d 48 (Pa. 1961) (alternate holding)). However, knowledge or reason to know, together with voluntary execution, may also be sufficient (see, *e.g.*, Tenn. Code Ann. §36-606; *Barnhill v. Barnhill*, 386 So. 2d 749 (Ala. Civ. App. 1980); *Del Vecchio v. Del Vecchio*, 143 So. 2d 17 (Fla. 1962); *Coward and Coward*, 582 P. 2d 834 (Or. App. 1978); but see *Matter of Estate of Lebsock*, 618 P.2d 683 (Colo. App. 1980)) and so may a voluntary, knowing waiver (see *Hafner v. Hafner*, 295 N.W. 2d 567 (Minn. 1980)). In each of these situations, it should be underscored that execution must have been voluntary (see *Lutgert v. Lutgert*, 338 So. 2d 1111 (Fla. 1976); see also 13 Dela. Code 1974 §301 (10 day waiting period)). Finally, a premarital agreement is enforceable if enforcement would not have been unconscionable at the time the agreement was executed (cf. *Hartz v. Hartz*, 234 A.2d 865 (Md. 1967) (premarital agreement upheld if no disclosure but agreement was fair and equitable under the circumstances)).

The test of "unconscionability" is drawn from Section 306 of the Uniform Marriage and Divorce Act (UMDA) (see *Ferry v. Ferry*, 586 S.W. 2d 782 (Mo. 1979); see also *Newman v. Newman*, 653 P.2d 728 (Colo. Sup. Ct. 1982) (maintenance provisions of premarital agreement tested for unconscionability at time of marriage termination)). The following discussion set forth in the Commissioner's Note to Section 306 of the UMDA is equally appropriate here:

"In order to determine whether the agreement is unconscionable, the court may look to the economic circumstances of the parties resulting from the agreement, and any other relevant evidence such as the conditions under which the agreement was made, including the knowledge of the other party. If the court finds the agreement not unconscionable, its terms respecting property division and maintenance may not be altered by the court at the hearing." (Commissioner's Note, Sec. 306, Uniform Marriage and Divorce Act.)

Nothing in Section 4.006 makes the absence of assistance of independent legal counsel a condition for the unenforceability of a premarital agreement. However, lack of that assistance may well be a factor in determining whether the conditions stated in Section 6 may have existed (*see, e.g., Del Vecchio v. Del Vecchio*, 143 So.2d 17 (Fla. 1962)).

No special provision is made for enforcement of provisions of a premarital agreement relating to personal rights and obligations. However, a premarital agreement is a contract and these provisions may be enforced to the extent that they are enforceable are under otherwise applicable law (see *Avitzur v. Avitzur*, 459 N.Y.S. 2d 572 (Ct. App.).

Section 4.006 is framed in a manner to require the party who alleges that a premarital agreement is not enforceable to bear the burden of proof as to that allegation. The statutory law conflicts on the issue of where the burden of proof lies (contrast Ark. Stats. §55-313; 31 Minn. Stats. Ann. §519.11 with Vernon's Texas Codes Ann. §5.45). Similarly, some courts have placed the burden on the attacking spouse to prove the invalidity of the agreement. *Linker v. Linker*, 470 P.2d 921 (Colo. 1970); *Matter of Estate of Benker*, 296 N.W. 2d 167 (Mich. App. 1980); *In re Kauffmann's Estate*, 171 A.2d 48 (Pa. 1961). Some have placed the burden upon those relying upon the agreement to prove its validity. *Hartz v. Hartz*, 234 A.2d 865 (Md. 1967). Finally, several have adopted a middle ground by stating that a premarital agreement is presumptively valid but if a disproportionate disposition is made for the wife, the husband bears the burden of proof of showing adequate disclosure. (*Del Vecchio v. Del Vecchio*, 143 So.2d 17 (Fla. 1962); *Christians v. Christians*, 44 N.W.2d 431 (Iowa 1950); *In re Neis' Estate*, 225 P.2d 110 (Kans. 1950); *Truitt v. Truitt's Adm'r*, 162 S.W. 2d 31 (Ky. 1942); *In re Estate of Strickland*, 149 N.W. 2d 344 (Neb. 1967); *Kosik v. George*, 452 P.2d 560 (Or. 1969); *Friedlander v. Friedlander*, 494 P.2d 208 (Wash. 1972).

Osorno v. Osorno, ___ S.W.3d ___ (Tex.App.—Houston [14th Dist.] 2002, n.p.h.) (No. 14-00-00070-CV; 2-21-02). "In August, [wife-to-be] discovered she was pregnant. According to her, [husband-to-be] wanted her to have an abortion, which she refused for religious reasons. In September, [husband-to-be] agreed to marry her if she signed a premarital agreement. Both [husband-to-be] and [wife-to-be] signed an Agreement in Contemplation of Marriage on October 9, 1992, and were married the following day. [¶] [A]side from his moral duties, [husband-to-be] had no legal duty to marry [wife-to-be]. His threat to do something he had the legal right to do is insufficient to invalidate the premarital agreement. [Wife-to-be] was faced with difficult choices, but we cannot find her decision to sign the agreement was involuntary."

Fazakerly v. Fazakerly, 996 S.W.2d 260, 265 (Tex. App.—Eastland 1999, pet. denied). "[T]o invalidate an antenuptial agreement, a party must first show either that he did not sign voluntarily or that the agreement is unconscionable and then that certain conditions regarding disclosure of the other party's estate were not met. The issue of unconscionability must be decided by the trial court as a matter of law before the disclosure questions are addressed."

Marsh v. Marsh, 949 S.W.2d 734, 739 (Tex.App.—Houston [14th Dist.] 1997, no writ). "[N]either the legislature nor Texas courts have defined 'unconscionable' in the context of marital or premarital property agreements. *At 741-42:* In reviewing the validity of a marital property agreement, this court has considered such factors as the maturity of the individuals, their business backgrounds, their educational levels, their experiences in prior marriages, their respective ages and their motivations to protect their respective children. [¶] The fact that the premarital agreement was signed shortly before the wedding does not make the agreement unconscionable. Likewise, the fact that [the husband] was not represented by independent counsel is not dispositive. [¶] [Additionally,] even though a premarital agreement may be disproportionate, unfairness is not material to the enforceability of the agreement. A factual finding that a premarital agreement is unfair does not satisfy the burden of proof required to establish unconscionability. [¶] [Further,] [t]he fact that [husband] denied reading the premarital agreement is not grounds for avoiding the contract. [¶] [Finally,] [f]or an agreement to be unconscionable, it must be 'so far one-sided that no reasonable person could consider it to be an arm's length transaction.'"

FAM §4.007. ENFORCEMENT: VOID MARRIAGE

If a marriage is determined to be void, an agreement that would otherwise have been a premarital agreement is enforceable only to the extent necessary to avoid an inequitable result.

History of Fam §4.007: Acts 1997, 75th Leg., ch. 7, §1, eff. April 17, 1997. Source: Former Fam §5.47.

Official Comment

Under section 4.007 a void marriage does not completely invalidate an premarital agreement but does substantially limit its enforceability. Where parties have married and lived together for a substantial period of time and one or both have relied on the existence of a premarital agreement, the failure to enforce the agreement may well be inequitable. This section, accordingly, provides the court discretion to enforce the agreement to the extent necessary to avoid the inequitable result (see Annot., 46 A.L.R. 3d 1403).

FAM §4.008. LIMITATION OF ACTIONS

A statute of limitations applicable to an action asserting a claim for relief under a premarital agreement is tolled during the marriage of the parties to the agreement. However, equitable defenses limiting the time for enforcement, including laches and estoppel, are available to either party.

History of Fam §4.008: Acts 1997, 75th Leg., ch. 7, §1, eff. April 17, 1997. Source: Former Fam §5.48.

Official Comment

In order to avoid the potentially disruptive effect of compelling litigation between the spouses in order to escape the running of an applicable statute of limitations, Section 4.008 tolls any applicable statute during the marriage of the parties (contrast *Dykema v. Dykema*, 412 N.E. 2d 13 (Ill. App. 1980) (statute of limitations not tolled where fraud not adequately pleaded, hence premarital agreement enforced at death)). However, a party is not completely free to sit on his or her rights because the section does preserve certain equitable defenses.

FAM §4.009. APPLICATION & CONSTRUCTION

This subchapter shall be applied and construed to effect its general purpose to make uniform the law with respect to the subject of this subchapter among states enacting these provisions.

History of Fam §4.009: Acts 1997, 75th Leg., ch. 7, §1, eff. April 17, 1997. Source: Former Fam §5.49.

FAM §4.010. SHORT TITLE

This subchapter may be cited as the Uniform Premarital Agreement Act.

History of Fam §4.010: Acts 1997, 75th Leg., ch. 7, §1, eff. April 17, 1997. Source: Former Fam §5.50.

Sections 4.011-4.100 reserved for expansion

SUBCHAPTER B. MARITAL PROPERTY AGREEMENT

FAM §4.101. DEFINITION

In this subchapter, "property" has the meaning assigned by Section 4.001.

History of Fam §4.101: Acts 1997, 75th Leg., ch. 7, §1, eff. April 17, 1997. Source: Former Fam §5.51.

FAM §4.102. PARTITION OR EXCHANGE OF COMMUNITY PROPERTY

At any time, the spouses may partition or exchange between themselves any part of their community property, then existing or to be acquired, as the spouses may desire. Property or a property interest transferred to a spouse by a partition or exchange agreement becomes that spouse's separate property.

History of Fam §4.102: Acts 1997, 75th Leg., ch. 7, §1, eff. April 17, 1997. Source: Former Fam §5.52.

Byrnes v. Byrnes, 19 S.W.3d 556, 559 (Tex.App.—Fort Worth 2000, no pet.). "The term 'partition' as used in this section contemplates a division of property among the parties, not a complete forfeiture or assignment. Absent a specific reference to a partition or language indicating that such a division was intended, Texas courts have refused to uphold transactions between spouses as partitions. [¶] Because the parties' agreement makes no specific reference to a partition, contains no language indicating that the parties intended a partition, and provides for a forfeiture of [husband's] interest, the document is not a valid partition under §4.102…. *At 559 n.2:* The parties' agreement also specifically provides that it is subject to judicial approval. A partition agreement does not require judicial approval, while an agreement incident to divorce does."

In re Marriage of Morrison, 913 S.W.2d 689, 693 (Tex.App.—Texarkana 1995, writ denied). "Although a partition and exchange agreement is one mechanism by which spouses may convert community property into their separate property, it is not the only method by which such a transformation can be effected."

FAM §4.103. AGREEMENT BETWEEN SPOUSES CONCERNING INCOME OR PROPERTY FROM SEPARATE PROPERTY

At any time, the spouses may agree that the income or property arising from the separate property that is then owned by one of them, or that may thereafter be acquired, shall be the separate property of the owner.

History of Fam §4.103: Acts 1997, 75th Leg., ch. 7, §1, eff. April 17, 1997. Source: Former Fam §5.53.

FAM §4.104. FORMALITIES

A partition or exchange agreement must be in writing and signed by both parties.

History of Fam §4.104: Acts 1997, 75th Leg., ch. 7, §1, eff. April 17, 1997. Source: Former Fam §5.54.

Texas Farmers Ins. Co. v. Murphy, 996 S.W.2d 873, 881 (Tex.1999). "Partition agreements require the [written] consent of both spouses."

Collins v. Collins, 752 S.W.2d 636, 637 (Tex.App.—Fort Worth 1988, writ ref'd). "[W]e find that a joint income tax return signed by both spouses, in which the income of various assets is listed as separate and community, absent specific language indicating that the document is intended by the parties to constitute an agreement to partition, as a matter of law does not constitute a partition agreement in writing and signed by the parties as required by … §5.54 [now §4.104]. [¶] We do not find the requirements of the Statute of Frauds to be applicable to the requirements for the writing required by [§5.54], because §5.54 requires an agreement in writing signed by both parties, whereas the Statute of Frauds requires only a memorandum of an agreement and not an agreement itself. *At 638:* To allow the establishment of the existence of the agreement by parol evidence would be to destroy the requirement set forth by [§5.54] that the agreement be in writing."

Dalton v. Don J. Jackson, Inc., 691 S.W.2d 765, 768 (Tex.App.—Austin 1985, no pet.). "[O]ne spouse may not convey his or her interest in joint community property to a third party [without the other spouse's consent], so as to effectuate a partition by creating a tenancy-in-common between the remaining spouse and the third party."

FAM §4.105. ENFORCEMENT

(a) A partition or exchange agreement is not enforceable if the party against whom enforcement is requested proves that:

(1) the party did not sign the agreement voluntarily; or

(2) the agreement was unconscionable when it was signed and, before execution of the agreement, that party:

(A) was not provided a fair and reasonable disclosure of the property or financial obligations of the other party;

(B) did not voluntarily and expressly waive, in writing, any right to disclosure of the property or financial obligations of the other party beyond the disclosure provided; and

(C) did not have, or reasonably could not have had, adequate knowledge of the property or financial obligations of the other party.

(b) An issue of unconscionability of a partition or exchange agreement shall be decided by the court as a matter of law.

(c) The remedies and defenses in this section are the exclusive remedies or defenses, including common law remedies or defenses.

History of Fam §4.105: Acts 1997, 75th Leg., ch. 7, §1, eff. April 17, 1997. Source: Former Fam §5.55.

Nesmith v. Berger, 64 S.W.3d 110, 115 (Tex.App.—Austin 2001, pet. denied). "In light of the bargaining that accompanied every step of the relationship between the parties before and during their marriage, we cannot say that [husband]'s proposed bargain to finalize the terms of the long-contemplated agreement before leaving on a honeymoon exerted such undue influence as to deprive [wife] of her free will in signing the agreement."

Pletcher v. Goetz, 9 S.W.3d 442, 445 (Tex.App.—Fort Worth 1999, pet. denied). "The party challenging the enforceability of a partition and exchange agreement bears the burden of proving the agreement was involuntary or unconscionable. However, neither the legislature nor the supreme court has defined the term 'unconscionable' in the context of marital property agreements. As a result, appellate courts have turned to the commercial context for guidance in evaluating 'unconscionability.' [¶] The issue of whether a partition and exchange agreement is unconscionable is a question of law for the court. In assessing the conscionability of an agreement, the court should consider all of the circumstances in which the agreement was made."

Matthews v. Matthews, 725 S.W.2d 275, 278 (Tex. App.—Houston [1st Dist.] 1986, writ ref'd n.r.e.). "[W]hether duress exists in a particular situation is a question of fact dependent on all the circumstances, including the mental effect on the party claiming duress. *At 279:* It is never duress to threaten to do that which one has a legal right to do. However, a vice arises when one employs extortive measures or, lacking good faith, makes improper demands. [¶] [Husband's] demands and threats to initiate custody litigation, if [wife] did not execute the agreement, may have been lawful. However, under the circumstances of this case, the trial court, as the trier of fact, did not have to believe [husband's] testimony and could have reasonably concluded that [husband] failed to prove, by clear and convincing evidence, that appellee's consent was not procured by duress or overreaching."

FAM §4.106. RIGHTS OF CREDITORS & RECORDATION UNDER PARTITION OR EXCHANGE AGREEMENT

(a) A provision of a partition or exchange agreement made under this subchapter is void with respect to the rights of a preexisting creditor whose rights are intended to be defrauded by it.

(b) A partition or exchange agreement made under this subchapter may be recorded in the deed records of the county in which a party resides and in the county in which the real property affected is located. An agreement made under this subchapter is constructive notice to a good faith purchaser for value or a creditor without actual notice only if the instrument is acknowledged and recorded in the county in which the real property is located.

History of Fam §4.106: Acts 1997, 75th Leg., ch. 7, §1, eff. April 17, 1997. Source: Former Fam §5.56.

Sections 4.107-4.200 blank

SUBCHAPTER C. AGREEMENT TO CONVERT SEPARATE PROPERTY TO COMMUNITY PROPERTY

FAM §4.201. DEFINITION

In this subchapter, "property" has the meaning assigned by Section 4.001.

History of Fam §4.201: Acts 1999, 76th Leg., ch. 692, §3, eff. Jan. 1, 2000.

FAM §4.202. AGREEMENT TO CONVERT TO COMMUNITY PROPERTY

At any time, spouses may agree that all or part of the separate property owned by either or both spouses is converted to community property.

History of Fam §4.202: Acts 1999, 76th Leg., ch. 692, §3, eff. Jan. 1, 2000.

FAM §4.203. FORMALITIES OF AGREEMENT

(a) An agreement to convert separate property to community property:

(1) must be in writing and:

(A) be signed by the spouses;

(B) identify the property being converted; and

(C) specify that the property is being converted to the spouses' community property; and

(2) is enforceable without consideration.

(b) The mere transfer of a spouse's separate property to the name of the other spouse or to the name of both spouses is not sufficient to convert the property to community property under this subchapter.

History of Fam §4.203: Acts 1999, 76th Leg., ch. 692, §3, eff. Jan. 1, 2000.

FAM §4.204. MANAGEMENT OF CONVERTED PROPERTY

Except as specified in the agreement to convert the property and as provided by Subchapter B, Chapter 3, and other law, property converted to community property under this subchapter is subject to:

(1) the sole management, control, and disposition of the spouse in whose name the property is held;

(2) the sole management, control, and disposition of the spouse who transferred the property if the property is not subject to evidence of ownership;

(3) the joint management, control, and disposition of the spouses if the property is held in the name of both spouses; or

(4) the joint management, control, and disposition of the spouses if the property is not subject to evidence of ownership and was owned by both spouses before the property was converted to community property.

History of Fam §4.204: Acts 1999, 76th Leg., ch. 692, §3, eff. Jan. 1, 2000.

FAM §4.205. ENFORCEMENT

(a) An agreement to convert property to community property under this subchapter is not enforceable if the spouse against whom enforcement is sought proves that the spouse did not:

(1) execute the agreement voluntarily; or

(2) receive a fair and reasonable disclosure of the legal effect of converting the property to community property.

(b) An agreement that contains the following statement, or substantially similar words, prominently displayed in bold-faced type, capital letters, or underlined, is rebuttably presumed to provide a fair and reasonable disclosure of the legal effect of converting property to community property:

"THIS INSTRUMENT CHANGES SEPARATE PROPERTY TO COMMUNITY PROPERTY. THIS MAY HAVE ADVERSE CONSEQUENCES DURING MARRIAGE AND ON TERMINATION OF THE MARRIAGE BY DEATH OR DIVORCE. FOR EXAMPLE:

"EXPOSURE TO CREDITORS. IF YOU SIGN THIS AGREEMENT, ALL OR PART OF THE SEPARATE PROPERTY BEING CONVERTED TO COMMUNITY PROPERTY MAY BECOME SUBJECT TO THE LIABILITIES OF YOUR SPOUSE. IF YOU DO NOT SIGN THIS AGREEMENT, YOUR SEPARATE PROPERTY IS GENERALLY NOT SUBJECT TO THE LIABILITIES OF YOUR SPOUSE UNLESS YOU ARE PERSONALLY LIABLE UNDER ANOTHER RULE OF LAW.

"LOSS OF MANAGEMENT RIGHTS. IF YOU SIGN THIS AGREEMENT, ALL OR PART OF THE SEPARATE PROPERTY BEING CONVERTED TO COMMUNITY PROPERTY MAY BECOME SUBJECT TO EITHER THE JOINT MANAGEMENT, CONTROL, AND DISPOSITION OF YOU AND YOUR SPOUSE OR THE SOLE MANAGEMENT, CONTROL, AND DISPOSITION OF YOUR SPOUSE ALONE. IN THAT EVENT, YOU WILL LOSE YOUR MANAGEMENT RIGHTS OVER THE PROPERTY. IF YOU DO NOT SIGN THIS AGREEMENT, YOU WILL GENERALLY RETAIN THOSE RIGHTS.

"LOSS OF PROPERTY OWNERSHIP. IF YOU SIGN THIS AGREEMENT AND YOUR MARRIAGE IS SUBSEQUENTLY TERMINATED BY THE DEATH OF EITHER SPOUSE OR BY DIVORCE, ALL OR PART OF THE SEPARATE PROPERTY BEING CONVERTED TO COMMUNITY PROPERTY MAY BECOME THE SOLE PROPERTY OF YOUR SPOUSE OR YOUR SPOUSE'S HEIRS. IF YOU DO NOT SIGN THIS AGREEMENT, YOU GENERALLY CANNOT BE DEPRIVED OF OWNERSHIP OF YOUR SEPARATE PROPERTY ON TERMINATION OF YOUR MARRIAGE, WHETHER BY DEATH OR DIVORCE."

History of Fam §4.205: Acts 1999, 76th Leg., ch. 692, §3, eff. Jan. 1, 2000.

FAM §4.206. RIGHTS OF CREDITORS; RECORDING

(a) A conversion of separate property to community property does not affect the rights of a preexisting creditor of the spouse whose separate property is being converted.

(b) A conversion of separate property to community property may be recorded in the deed records of the county in which a spouse resides and of the county in which any real property is located.

(c) A conversion of real property from separate property to community property is constructive notice to a good faith purchaser for value or a creditor without actual notice only if the agreement to convert the property is acknowledged and recorded in the deed records of the county in which the real property is located.

History of Fam §4.206: Acts 1999, 76th Leg., ch. 692, §3, eff. Jan. 1, 2000.

CHAPTER 5. HOMESTEAD RIGHTS

Subchapter A. Sale of Homestead; General Rule

Subchapter B. Sale of Homestead Under Unusual Circumstances

SUBCHAPTER A. SALE OF HOMESTEAD; GENERAL RULE

FAM §5.001. SALE, CONVEYANCE, OR ENCUMBRANCE OF HOMESTEAD

Whether the homestead is the separate property of either spouse or community property, neither spouse may sell, convey, or encumber the homestead without the joinder of the other spouse except as provided in this chapter or by other rules of law.

History of Fam §5.001: Acts 1997, 75th Leg., ch. 7, §1, eff. April 17, 1997. Source: Former Fam §5.81.

Benchmark Bank v. Crowder, 919 S.W.2d 657, 662 (Tex.1996). "When a homestead is subject to foreclosure of a federal tax lien on an indebtedness owed by a taxpayer, the taxpayer's spouse, who does not owe any of that indebtedness, has a separate homestead interest and must be compensated for the loss of the homestead estate."

Grissom v. Anderson, 79 S.W.2d 619, 621 (Tex. 1935). "A conveyance by a husband, not joined by his wife, of the homestead property, is merely inoperative while the property continues to be a homestead, or until such time as the homestead may be abandoned, or the deed ratified in accordance with law."

Skelton v. Washington Mut. Bank, 61 S.W.3d 56, 60 (Tex.App.—Amarillo 2001, no pet.) Wife "argues that the lien is unenforceable because she did not execute any documentation creating it. Although it may be good practice to require that purchase money and vendor's lien transactions be evidenced by documentation signed by the grantees, a vendor's lien is enforceable to secure payment of purchase money even without documentation. Moreover, §5.001 does not apply because the lien note was part of the purchase price and [the lien] holder of the superior title, could enforce the vendor's lien even if [wife] did not sign or acknowledge the loan instruments because the homestead interest and the lien were created simultaneously and no interest was transferred after creation in violation of §5.001."

Ⓐ FAM §5.002. SALE OF SEPARATE HOMESTEAD AFTER SPOUSE JUDICIALLY DECLARED INCAPACITATED

If the homestead is the separate property of a spouse and the other spouse has been judicially declared incapacitated by a court exercising original jurisdiction over guardianship and other matters under Chapter XIII, Texas Probate Code, the owner may sell, convey, or encumber the homestead without the joinder of the other spouse.

History of Fam §5.002: Acts 1997, 75th Leg., ch. 7, §1, eff. April 17, 1997. Amended by Acts 2001, 77th Leg., ch. 217, §25, eff. Sept. 1, 2001. Source: Former Fam §5.82.

Ⓐ FAM §5.003. SALE OF COMMUNITY HOMESTEAD AFTER SPOUSE JUDICIALLY DECLARED INCAPACITATED

If the homestead is the community property of the spouses and one spouse has been judicially declared incapacitated by a court exercising original jurisdiction over guardianship and other matters under Chapter XIII, Texas Probate Code, the competent spouse may sell, convey, or encumber the homestead without the joinder of the other spouse.

History of Fam §5.003: Acts 1997, 75th Leg., ch. 7, §1, eff. April 17, 1997. Renumbered from §5.107 and amended by Acts 2001, 77th Leg., ch. 217, §29, eff. Sept. 1, 2001. Source: Former Fam §5.84.

Sections 5.004-5.100 reserved for expansion

SUBCHAPTER B. SALE OF HOMESTEAD UNDER UNUSUAL CIRCUMSTANCES

FAM §5.101. SALE OF SEPARATE HOMESTEAD UNDER UNUSUAL CIRCUMSTANCES

If the homestead is the separate property of a spouse, that spouse may file a sworn petition that gives a description of the property, states the facts that make it desirable for the spouse to sell, convey, or encumber the homestead without the joinder of the other spouse, and alleges that the other spouse:

Ⓐ *Subsections (1) through (4) below are effective for proceedings in which original petitions are filed on or after Sept. 1, 2001.*

(1) has disappeared and that the location of the spouse remains unknown to the petitioning spouse;

(2) has permanently abandoned the homestead and the petitioning spouse;

(3) has permanently abandoned the homestead and the spouses are permanently separated; or

(4) has been reported by an executive department of the United States to be a prisoner of war or missing on public service of the United States.

Subsections (1) through (5) below are effective for proceedings in which original petitions were filed before Sept. 1, 2001.

(1) is incapacitated, whether judicially declared incapacitated or not;

(2) has disappeared and that the location of the spouse remains unknown to the petitioning spouse;

(3) has permanently abandoned the homestead and the petitioning spouse;

(4) has permanently abandoned the homestead and the spouses are permanently separated; or

(5) has been reported by an executive department of the United States to be a prisoner of war or missing on public service of the United States.

History of Fam §5.101: Acts 1997, 75th Leg., ch. 7, §1, eff. April 17, 1997. Amended by Acts 2001, 77th Leg., ch. 217, §26, eff. Sept. 1, 2001. Source: Former Fam §§5.83(a), 5.831(a).

Caulley v. Caulley, 806 S.W.2d 795, 797 (Tex.1991). "Once homestead rights are shown to exist in property, they are presumed to continue, and anyone asserting abandonment has the burden of proving it by competent evidence."

FAM §5.102. SALE OF COMMUNITY HOMESTEAD UNDER UNUSUAL CIRCUMSTANCES

If the homestead is the community property of the spouses, one spouse may file a sworn petition that gives a description of the property, states the facts that make it desirable for the petitioning spouse to sell, convey, or encumber the homestead without the joinder of the other spouse, and alleges that the other spouse:

A *Subsections (1) through (4) below are effective for proceedings in which original petitions are filed on or after Sept. 1, 2001.*

(1) has disappeared and that the location of the spouse remains unknown to the petitioning spouse;

(2) has permanently abandoned the homestead and the petitioning spouse;

(3) has permanently abandoned the homestead and the spouses are permanently separated; or

(4) has been reported by an executive department of the United States to be a prisoner of war or missing on public service of the United States.

Subsections (1) through (5) below are effective for proceedings in which original petitions were filed before Sept. 1, 2001.

(1) is incapacitated, whether judicially declared incapacitated or not;

(2) has disappeared and that the location of the spouse remains unknown to the petitioning spouse;

(3) has permanently abandoned the homestead and the petitioning spouse;

(4) has permanently abandoned the homestead and the spouses are permanently separated; or

(5) has been reported by an executive department of the United States to be a prisoner of war or missing on public service of the United States.

History of Fam §5.102: Acts 1997, 75th Leg., ch. 7, §1, eff. April 17, 1997. Amended by Acts 2001, 77th Leg., ch. 217, §27, eff. Sept. 1, 2001. Source: Former Fam §§5.85(a), 5.87(a).

FAM §5.103. TIME FOR FILING PETITION

A *Section 5.103 below is effective for proceedings in which original petitions are filed on or after Sept. 1, 2001.*

The petitioning spouse may file the petition in a court of the county in which any portion of the property is located not earlier than the 60th day after the date of the occurrence of an event described by Sections 5.101(1)-(3) and 5.102(1)-(3) or not less than six months after the date the other spouse has been reported to be a prisoner of war or missing on public service.

History of Fam §5.103: Acts 1997, 75th Leg., ch. 7, §1, eff. April 17, 1997. Amended by Acts 2001, 77th Leg., ch. 217, §28, eff. Sept. 1, 2001. Source: Former Fam §§5.83(b), 5.831(b), 5.85(b), 5.87(b).

FAM §5.103. TIME FOR FILING PETITION

Section 5.103 below is effective for proceedings in which original petitions were filed before Sept. 1, 2001.

The petitioning spouse may file the petition in a court of the county in which any portion of the property is located not earlier than the 60th day after the date of the occurrence of an event described by Sections 5.101(1)-(4) and 5.102(1)-(4) or not less than six months after the date the other spouse has been reported to be a prisoner of war or missing on public service.

FAM §5.104. APPOINTMENT OF ATTORNEY

(a) Except as provided by Subsection (b), the court may appoint an attorney in a suit filed under this subchapter for the respondent.

(b) The court shall appoint an attorney in a suit filed under this subchapter for a respondent reported to be a prisoner of war or missing on public service.

(c) The court shall allow a reasonable fee for the appointed attorney's services as a part of the costs of the suit.

History of Fam §5.104: Acts 1997, 75th Leg., ch. 7, §1, eff. April 17, 1997. Source: Former Fam §§5.83(b), 5.831(b), 5.85(b), 5.87(b).

FAM §5.105. CITATION; NOTICE OF HEARING

Citation and notice of hearing for a suit filed as provided by this subchapter shall be issued and served in the manner provided in Subchapter D, Chapter 3.

History of Fam §5.105: Acts 1997, 75th Leg., ch. 7, §1, eff. April 17, 1997. Source: Former Fam §§5.83(b), 5.831(b), 5.85(b), 5.87(b).

FAM §5.106. COURT ORDER

(a) After notice and hearing, the court shall render an order the court deems just and equitable with respect to the sale, conveyance, or encumbrance of a separate property homestead.

(b) After hearing the evidence, the court, on terms the court deems just and equitable, shall render an order describing or defining the community property at issue that will be subject to the management, control, and disposition of each spouse during marriage.

(c) The court may:

(1) impose any conditions and restrictions the court deems necessary to protect the rights of the respondent;

(2) require a bond conditioned on the faithful administration of the property; and

(3) require payment to the registry of the court of all or a portion of the proceeds of the sale of the property to be disbursed in accordance with the court's further directions.

History of Fam §5.106: Acts 1997, 75th Leg., ch. 7, §1, eff. April 17, 1997. Source: Former Fam §§5.83(c), 5.831(c), 5.85(c), 5.87(c).

FAM §5.107. RENUMBERED

Renumbered as §5.003 by Acts 2001, 77th Leg., ch. 217, §29, eff. Sept. 1, 2001.

FAM §5.108. REMEDIES & POWERS CUMULATIVE

The remedies and the powers of a spouse provided by this subchapter are cumulative of the other rights, powers, and remedies afforded the spouses by law.

History of Fam §5.108: Acts 1997, 75th Leg., ch. 7, §1, eff. April 17, 1997. Source: Former Fam §5.86.

SUBTITLE C. DISSOLUTION OF MARRIAGE

CHAPTER 6. SUIT FOR DISSOLUTION OF MARRIAGE

Subchapter A. Grounds for Divorce & Defenses

Subchapter B. Grounds for Annulment

Subchapter C. Declaring a Marriage Void

Subchapter D. Jurisdiction, Venue, & Residence Qualifications

Subchapter E. Filing Suit

Subchapter F. Temporary Orders

SUBCHAPTER A. GROUNDS FOR DIVORCE & DEFENSES

FAM §6.001. INSUPPORTABILITY

On the petition of either party to a marriage, the court may grant a divorce without regard to fault if the marriage has become insupportable because of discord or conflict of personalities that destroys the legitimate ends of the marital relationship and prevents any reasonable expectation of reconciliation.

History of Fam §6.001: Acts 1997, 75th Leg., ch. 7, §1, eff. April 17, 1997. Source: Former Fam §3.01.

Waite v. Waite, 64 S.W.3d 217, 221 (Tex.App.—Houston [14th Dist.] 2001, pet. denied). Husband "asserts that any determination by the trial court of what constitutes the 'legitimate ends of marriage' or the reasonable expectation of 'reconciliation' necessarily involves a religious determination [and therefore violates the Establishment Clause of the U.S. Constitution]. ... We believe, as was true in 1888, that the trial court is not being asked to make a religious determination, but rather to determine whether the continuance of the marriage relation has been rendered intolerable to the other party, and productive of no possible benefit to society. The Texas legislature could rationally conclude that public policy requires an accommodation to the unfortunate reality that a marital relationship may terminate without regard to the fault of either marital partner, and that such a relationship should therefore be dissolvable in law upon a judicial determination that the marriage has become insupportable."

In re Marriage of Richards, 991 S.W.2d 32, 37-38 (Tex.App.—Amarillo 1999, pet. dism'd). The insupportability "ground, also known as no-fault divorce ... has three elements. They are 1) that the marriage has become insupportable because of discord or conflict, 2) that discord or conflict destroys the legitimate ends of the marriage, and 3) there is no reasonable expectation of reconciliation. There is nothing in the language of the statute to support the conclusion that these are not questions of fact. [¶] Even assuming, arguendo, that the trial court's statement that there is 'no defense' to a petition for divorce on the ground of insupportability were a correct statement of the law, that would not relieve the petitioner of his duty to establish the statutory elements with adequate evidence. Any attempt to determine those factual issues without giving [appellant] an opportunity to respond would violate due process. ... While the adoption of 'no-fault' divorce dispenses with any burden to establish the source of the conflict rendering the marriage insupportable, it does not relieve the petitioner of the burden to establish the existence of the statutory elements."

Clay v. Clay, 550 S.W.2d 730, 733-34 (Tex.App.—Houston [1st Dist.] 1977, no writ). "The jury, or the trial court when acting as a fact finder, is not concerned with the fault of the parties. While a divorce granted under the authority given in §3.01 [now §6.001] is popularly termed a 'no fault' divorce it is in fact a divorce which the court is authorized to grant without regard to fault."

Baxla v. Baxla, 522 S.W.2d 736, 738 (Tex.App.—Dallas 1975, no writ), *overruled on other grounds*, ***Eggemeyer v. Eggemeyer***, 554 S.W.2d 137 (Tex.1977). "'[T]he prima facie case for dissolution should be satisfied by the declaration of petitioner that he or she sincerely believes that the marriage has irreparably broken down. Courtroom questions are expected to be brief and would go directly to petitioner's state of mind. ... Upon such testimony, dissolution should ordinarily be granted, unless the judge detects hesitancy on the part of the petitioner about the possibility of saving the marriage. In that case the judge may refer the spouses to conciliation counseling.'"

Cusack v. Cusack, 491 S.W.2d 714, 717 (Tex.App.—Corpus Christi 1973, writ dism'd). "It is not incumbent upon the plaintiff who brings the divorce action upon the ground of insupportability to show any misconduct on the part of the defendant, but it is only incumbent upon that spouse to establish by the evidence that a state of insupportability exists regardless of whether it is anyone's or no one's fault. *At 720:* The term 'insupportable' has been defined by our appellate courts on many occasions as 'unendurable, insufferable, intolerable.'"

FAM §6.002. CRUELTY

The court may grant a divorce in favor of one spouse if the other spouse is guilty of cruel treatment toward the complaining spouse of a nature that renders further living together insupportable.

History of Fam §6.002: Acts 1997, 75th Leg., ch. 7, §1, eff. April 17, 1997. Source: Former Fam §3.02.

Henry v. Henry, 48 S.W.3d 468, 473-74 (Tex.App.—Houston [14th Dist.] 2001, no pet.). "To constitute cruel treatment, the conduct of the accused party must rise to such a level as to render the couples' living together insupportable. 'Insupportable' in this context means 'incapable of being borne, unendurable, insufferable, intolerable.' Mere trivial matters or disagreements do not justify the granting of divorce for cruel treatment. Acts occurring after separation can support a finding of cruel treatment."

Brown v. Brown, 704 S.W.2d 528, 529 (Tex.App.—Amarillo 1986, no writ). Cruelty is defined as "willful and persistent infliction of unnecessary suffering, whether in realization or apprehension, whether of mind or body and as acts that endanger or threaten life, limb or health of the aggrieved party and inflict mental anguish."

Caywood v. Caywood, 290 S.W. 889, 891 (Tex. App.—El Paso 1927, no writ). "The cruel treatment given in the statute as one of the grounds for divorce has often been held to include injury to the feelings and sensibilities as well as physical injuries actually inflicted or threatened. It includes outrages upon the feelings, inflicting mental pain or anguish; it includes a series of studied vexations and deliberate insults and provocations."

FAM §6.003. ADULTERY

The court may grant a divorce in favor of one spouse if the other spouse has committed adultery.

History of Fam §6.003: Acts 1997, 75th Leg., ch. 7, §1, eff. April 17, 1997. Source: Former Fam §3.03.

Bell v. Bell, 540 S.W.2d 432, 435 (Tex.App.—Houston [1st Dist.] 1976, no writ). "The ground is not limited to adultery committed before the separation of the parties. [¶] 'Adultery,' as used in a divorce proceeding, means the voluntary sexual intercourse of a married person with one not the husband or wife of the offender."

FAM §6.004. CONVICTION OF FELONY

(a) The court may grant a divorce in favor of one spouse if during the marriage the other spouse:

(1) has been convicted of a felony;

(2) has been imprisoned for at least one year in the state penitentiary, a federal penitentiary, or the penitentiary of another state; and

(3) has not been pardoned.

(b) The court may not grant a divorce under this section against a spouse who was convicted on the testimony of the other spouse.

History of Fam §6.004: Acts 1997, 75th Leg., ch. 7, §1, eff. April 17, 1997. Source: Former Fam §3.04.

FAM §6.005. ABANDONMENT

The court may grant a divorce in favor of one spouse if the other spouse:

(1) left the complaining spouse with the intention of abandonment; and

(2) remained away for at least one year.

History of Fam §6.005: Acts 1997, 75th Leg., ch. 7, §1, eff. April 17, 1997. Source: Former Fam §3.05.

FAM §6.006. LIVING APART

The court may grant a divorce in favor of either spouse if the spouses have lived apart without cohabitation for at least three years.

History of Fam §6.006: Acts 1997, 75th Leg., ch. 7, §1, eff. April 17, 1997. Source: Former Fam §3.06.

FAM §6.007. CONFINEMENT IN MENTAL HOSPITAL

The court may grant a divorce in favor of one spouse if at the time the suit is filed:

(1) the other spouse has been confined in a state mental hospital or private mental hospital, as defined in Section 571.003, Health and Safety Code, in this state or another state for at least three years; and

(2) it appears that the hospitalized spouse's mental disorder is of such a degree and nature that adjustment

is unlikely or that, if adjustment occurs, a relapse is probable.

History of Fam §6.007: Acts 1997, 75th Leg., ch. 7, §1, eff. April 17, 1997. Source: Former Fam §3.07.

FAM §6.008. DEFENSES

(a) The defenses to a suit for divorce of recrimination and adultery are abolished.

(b) Condonation is a defense to a suit for divorce only if the court finds that there is a reasonable expectation of reconciliation.

History of Fam §6.008: Acts 1997, 75th Leg., ch. 7, §1, eff. April 17, 1997. Source: Former Fam §3.08.

Cusack v. Cusack, 491 S.W.2d 714, 718 (Tex.App.—Corpus Christi 1973, writ dism'd). "Adultery is no longer a bar to the granting of a divorce. It is not a defense in an action for divorce where insupportability is alleged as a ground therefor. Therefore, the matter of [husband's] adultery, if any, was irrelevant and immaterial to the divorce action brought by [husband]."

Sections 6.009-6.100 reserved for expansion

SUBCHAPTER B. GROUNDS FOR ANNULMENT

FAM §6.101. ANNULMENT OF MARRIAGE OF PERSON UNDER AGE 14

(a) The court may grant an annulment of a licensed marriage of a person under 14 years of age unless a court order has been obtained as provided in Subchapter B, Chapter 2.

(b) A petition for annulment under this section may be filed by a next friend for the benefit of a person under 14 years of age or on the petition of the parent or the judicially designated managing conservator or guardian, whether an individual, authorized agency, or court, of the person.

(c) A suit by a parent, managing conservator, or guardian of the person may be brought at any time before the person is 14 years of age.

(d) A suit under this section to annul the marriage of a person 14 years of age or older that was entered into before the person was 14 years of age is barred unless the suit is filed within the later of:

(1) 90 days after the date the petitioner knew or should have known of the marriage; or

(2) 90 days after the date of the 14th birthday of the underage party.

History of Fam §6.101: Acts 1997, 75th Leg., ch. 7, §1, eff. April 17, 1997. Amended by Acts 1997, 75th Leg., ch. 1362, §3, eff. Sept. 1, 1997. Source: Former Fam §2.41(a).

FAM §6.102. ANNULMENT OF MARRIAGE OF PERSON UNDER AGE 18

(a) The court may grant an annulment of a licensed or informal marriage of a person 14 years of age or older but under 18 years of age that occurred without parental consent or without a court order as provided by Subchapters B and E, Chapter 2.

(b) A petition for annulment under this section may be filed by:

(1) a next friend for the benefit of the underage party;

(2) a parent; or

(3) the judicially designated managing conservator or guardian of the person of the underage party, whether an individual, authorized agency, or court.

(c) A suit filed under this subsection by a next friend is barred unless it is filed within 90 days after the date of the marriage.

History of Fam §6.102: Acts 1997, 75th Leg., ch. 7, §1, eff. April 17, 1997. Source: Former Fam §2.41(b).

FAM §6.103. UNDERAGE ANNULMENT BARRED BY ADULTHOOD

A suit to annul a marriage may not be filed under Section 6.101 or 6.102 by a parent, managing conservator, or guardian of a person after the 18th birthday of the person.

History of Fam §6.103: Acts 1997, 75th Leg., ch. 7, §1, eff. April 17, 1997. Source: Former Fam §2.41(a), (b).

FAM §6.104. DISCRETIONARY ANNULMENT OF UNDERAGE MARRIAGE

(a) An annulment under Section 6.101 or 6.102 of a marriage may be granted at the discretion of the court sitting without a jury.

(b) In exercising its discretion, the court shall consider the pertinent facts concerning the welfare of the parties to the marriage, including whether the female is pregnant.

History of Fam §6.104: Acts 1997, 75th Leg., ch. 7, §1, eff. April 17, 1997. Source: Former Fam §2.41(c).

FAM §6.105. UNDER INFLUENCE OF ALCOHOL OR NARCOTICS

The court may grant an annulment of a marriage to a party to the marriage if:

(1) at the time of the marriage the petitioner was under the influence of alcoholic beverages or narcotics

and as a result did not have the capacity to consent to the marriage; and

(2) the petitioner has not voluntarily cohabited with the other party to the marriage since the effects of the alcoholic beverages or narcotics ended.

History of Fam §6.105: Acts 1997, 75th Leg., ch. 7, §1, eff. April 17, 1997. Source: Former Fam §2.42.

FAM §6.106. IMPOTENCY

The court may grant an annulment of a marriage to a party to the marriage if:

(1) either party, for physical or mental reasons, was permanently impotent at the time of the marriage;

(2) the petitioner did not know of the impotency at the time of the marriage; and

(3) the petitioner has not voluntarily cohabited with the other party since learning of the impotency.

History of Fam §6.106: Acts 1997, 75th Leg., ch. 7, §1, eff. April 17, 1997. Source: Former Fam §2.43.

FAM §6.107. FRAUD, DURESS, OR FORCE

The court may grant an annulment of a marriage to a party to the marriage if:

(1) the other party used fraud, duress, or force to induce the petitioner to enter into the marriage; and

(2) the petitioner has not voluntarily cohabited with the other party since learning of the fraud or since being released from the duress or force.

History of Fam §6.107: Acts 1997, 75th Leg., ch. 7, §1, eff. April 17, 1997. Source: Former Fam §2.44.

Coulter v. Melady, 489 S.W.2d 156, 158 (Tex. App.—Texarkana 1972, writ ref'd n.r.e.). "Want of consent to marriage, standing alone, is not listed in the Family Code as a cause that renders a marriage either void or voidable. Nevertheless this court is persuaded that free consent and agreement of the parties is essential to a valid ceremonial marriage. ... A party's knowing compliance with the Code's requirements ... evidences voluntary consent to marriage and by force of law is conclusive that such party voluntarily consented. And such marriage may be annulled only when it is judicially ascertained to be void or voidable for a reason listed in the statutes."

FAM §6.108. MENTAL INCAPACITY

(a) The court may grant an annulment of a marriage to a party to the marriage on the suit of the party or the party's guardian or next friend, if the court finds it to be in the party's best interest to be represented by a guardian or next friend, if:

(1) at the time of the marriage the petitioner did not have the mental capacity to consent to marriage or to understand the nature of the marriage ceremony because of a mental disease or defect; and

(2) since the marriage ceremony, the petitioner has not voluntarily cohabited with the other party during a period when the petitioner possessed the mental capacity to recognize the marriage relationship.

(b) The court may grant an annulment of a marriage to a party to the marriage if:

(1) at the time of the marriage the other party did not have the mental capacity to consent to marriage or to understand the nature of the marriage ceremony because of a mental disease or defect;

(2) at the time of the marriage the petitioner neither knew nor reasonably should have known of the mental disease or defect; and

(3) since the date the petitioner discovered or reasonably should have discovered the mental disease or defect, the petitioner has not voluntarily cohabited with the other party.

History of Fam §6.108: Acts 1997, 75th Leg., ch. 7, §1, eff. April 17, 1997. Source: Former Fam §2.45.

FAM §6.109. CONCEALED DIVORCE

(a) The court may grant an annulment of a marriage to a party to the marriage if:

(1) the other party was divorced from a third party within the 30-day period preceding the date of the marriage ceremony;

(2) at the time of the marriage ceremony the petitioner did not know, and a reasonably prudent person would not have known, of the divorce; and

(3) since the petitioner discovered or a reasonably prudent person would have discovered the fact of the divorce, the petitioner has not voluntarily cohabited with the other party.

(b) A suit may not be brought under this section after the first anniversary of the date of the marriage.

History of Fam §6.109: Acts 1997, 75th Leg., ch. 7, §1, eff. April 17, 1997. Source: Former Fam §2.46.

FAM §6.110. MARRIAGE LESS THAN 72 HOURS AFTER ISSUANCE OF LICENSE

(a) The court may grant an annulment of a marriage to a party to the marriage if the marriage ceremony took place in violation of Section 2.204 during the 72-hour period immediately following the issuance of the marriage license.

(b) A suit may not be brought under this section after the 30th day after the date of the marriage.

History of Fam §6.110: Acts 1997, 75th Leg., ch. 7, §1, eff. April 17, 1997. Source: Former Fam §2.48.

FAM §6.111. DEATH OF PARTY TO VOIDABLE MARRIAGE

A marriage subject to annulment may not be challenged in a proceeding instituted after the death of either party to the marriage.

History of Fam §6.111: Acts 1997, 75th Leg., ch. 7, §1, eff. April 17, 1997. Source: Former Fam §2.47

Sections 6.112-6.200 reserved for expansion

SUBCHAPTER C. DECLARING A MARRIAGE VOID

FAM §6.201. CONSANGUINITY

A marriage is void if one party to the marriage is related to the other as:

(1) an ancestor or descendant, by blood or adoption;

(2) a brother or sister, of the whole or half blood or by adoption;

(3) a parent's brother or sister, of the whole or half blood or by adoption; or

(4) a son or daughter of a brother or sister, of the whole or half blood or by adoption.

History of Fam §6.201: Acts 1997, 75th Leg., ch. 7, §1, eff. April 17, 1997. Source: Former Fam §2.21.

FAM §6.202. MARRIAGE DURING EXISTENCE OF PRIOR MARRIAGE

(a) A marriage is void if entered into when either party has an existing marriage to another person that has not been dissolved by legal action or terminated by the death of the other spouse.

(b) The later marriage that is void under this section becomes valid when the prior marriage is dissolved if, after the date of the dissolution, the parties have lived together as husband and wife and represented themselves to others as being married.

History of Fam §6.202: Acts 1997, 75th Leg., ch. 7, §1, eff. April 17, 1997. Source: Former Fam §2.22.

Loera v. Loera, 815 S.W.2d 910, 911 (Tex.App.—Corpus Christi 1991, no writ). The most recent marriage "places the burden of proof on appellee to establish 1) the prior marriage and 2) its continuing validity at the time of the subsequent marriage. Because the presumption is, in itself, considered evidence, the party attacking the validity of the marriage has a burden to 'introduce sufficient evidence, standing alone, to negate the dissolution of the prior marriage.'"

FAM §6.203. CERTAIN VOID MARRIAGES VALIDATED

Except for a marriage that would have been void under Section 6.201, a marriage that was entered into before January 1, 1970, in violation of the prohibitions of Article 496, Penal Code of Texas, 1925, is validated from the date the marriage commenced if the parties continued until January 1, 1970, to live together as husband and wife and to represent themselves to others as being married.

History of Fam §6.203: Acts 1997, 75th Leg., ch. 7, §1, eff. April 17, 1997. Source: Former Fam §2.23.

Sections 6.204-6.300 reserved for expansion

SUBCHAPTER D. JURISDICTION, VENUE, & RESIDENCE QUALIFICATIONS

FAM §6.301. GENERAL RESIDENCY RULE FOR DIVORCE SUIT

A suit for divorce may not be maintained in this state unless at the time the suit is filed either the petitioner or the respondent has been:

(1) a domiciliary of this state for the preceding six-month period; and

(2) a resident of the county in which the suit is filed for the preceding 90-day period.

History of Fam §6.301: Acts 1997, 75th Leg., ch. 7, §1, eff. April 17, 1997. Source: Former Fam §3.21.

Vickery v. Commission for Lawyer Discipline, 5 S.W.3d 241, 263 (Tex.App.—Houston [14th Dist.] 1999, pet. denied). "In a suit for divorce, residency requires 'actual, physical, continuous living in the county of suit by one of the parties for the time specified [by §3.21, now §6.301], coupled with a good-faith intent to make that county home.'"

Cook v. Mayfield, 886 S.W.2d 840, 841 (Tex.App.—Waco 1994, orig. proceeding). "The residency requirement of §3.21 [now §6.301] does not deal with jurisdiction or the right to bring suit. It deals with the right to maintain suit. A plea in abatement is the proper vehicle to challenge residency. [Relator] argues that, should relief not be granted, [his wife] will have satisfied the residency requirements by the time an ordinary appeal could be perfected and his complaint will then be moot. Thus, he argues that he has no adequate remedy at law. We agree." Held: Mandamus is appropriate.

Dokmanovic v. Schwarz, 880 S.W.2d 272, 277 (Tex.App.—Houston [14th Dist.] 1994, no writ). "[A]dmissions in trial pleadings are considered judicial admissions in the case in which the pleading is filed and no proof is required of the admitted fact. [Husband] admitted in his petition that he satisfied the residency requirement of §3.21 [now §6.301], and thus, he may not now challenge the evidence as insufficient to show that the requirements of §3.21 were met. ... We find these judicial admissions more than sufficient evidence of residency."

Harmon v. Harmon, 879 S.W.2d 213, 216 (Tex. App.—Houston [14th Dist.] 1994, writ denied). "Section 3.21's [now §6.301's] residency requirements are not *jurisdictional*. Rather, they establish the qualifications of the parties necessary for a plaintiff to bring suit. As such, a judgment based on false testimony of residency would not be void and subject to collateral attack, but merely voidable by direct appeal or suitable equitable proceeding."

McCaskill v. McCaskill, 761 S.W.2d 470, 473 (Tex. App.—Corpus Christi 1988, writ denied). "Though not jurisdictional, the residency requirement protects the interests of the State as well as the parties, and cannot be waived by the parties."

Whiteman v. Whiteman, 682 S.W.2d 357, 358 (Tex. App.—Dallas 1984, no writ). "Where ... a petitioner has not met the residency requirement in §3.21 [now §6.301] when the original petition is filed, and subsequently the petitioner files an amended petition after meeting the requirement, the filing of the amended petition constitutes the filing of a new suit."

Beavers v. Beavers, 543 S.W.2d 720, 721 (Tex. App.—Waco 1976, no writ). "A mere constructive residence will not satisfy [§3.21, now §6.301]. ... Of course, the continuity of residence is not broken by a simple, temporary absence from the county."

Lutes v. Lutes, 538 S.W.2d 256, 258 (Tex.App.—Houston [14th Dist.] 1976, no writ). "The residence requirements of §3.21 [now §6.301] are satisfied if either the petitioner or respondent has been a domiciliary of Texas for the preceding six months and a resident of the county in which the suit is filed for the preceding 90 days. Thus the petitioner may now bring suit in either the county of his residence or in that of the respondent's. But the choice of in which of those counties the suit is to be filed is still given to the petitioner."

Stacy v. Stacy, 480 S.W.2d 479, 482 (Tex.App.—Waco 1972, no writ). "[A] temporary absence from the state or county of a Plaintiff who is an inhabitant of the state during the six months next preceding the filing of his petition for divorce [does] not ... affect his right to maintain his suit for divorce."

FAM §6.302. SUIT FOR DIVORCE BY NONRESIDENT SPOUSE

If one spouse has been a domiciliary of this state for at least the last six months, a spouse domiciled in another state or nation may file a suit for divorce in the county in which the domiciliary spouse resides at the time the petition is filed.

History of Fam §6.302: Acts 1997, 75th Leg., ch. 7, §1, eff. April 17, 1997. Source: Former Fam §3.24.

FAM §6.303. ABSENCE ON PUBLIC SERVICE

Time spent by a Texas domiciliary outside this state or outside the county of residence of the domiciliary while in the service of the armed forces or other service of the United States or of this state is considered residence in this state and in that county.

History of Fam §6.303: Acts 1997, 75th Leg., ch. 7, §1, eff. April 17, 1997. Source: Former Fam §3.22.

FAM §6.304. ARMED FORCES PERSONNEL NOT PREVIOUSLY RESIDENTS

A person not previously a resident of this state who is serving in the armed forces of the United States and has been stationed at one or more military installations in this state for at least the last six months and at a military installation in a county of this state for at least the last 90 days is considered to be a Texas domiciliary and a resident of that county for those periods for the purpose of filing suit for dissolution of a marriage.

History of Fam §6.304: Acts 1997, 75th Leg., ch. 7, §1, eff. April 17, 1997. Source: Former Fam §3.23.

Fox v. Fox, 559 S.W.2d 407, 410 (Tex.App.—Austin 1977, no writ). "Divorce jurisdiction is extended to Texas courts regarding military personnel stationed in the state meeting certain requirements, pursuant to ... §3.23 [now §6.304]. Even though the spouses are domiciled in different states, a Texas court may grant an *ex parte* divorce under [§3.23] if one of the parties falls within the statute."

FAM §6.305. ACQUIRING JURISDICTION OVER NONRESIDENT RESPONDENT

(a) If the petitioner in a suit for dissolution of a marriage is a resident or a domiciliary of this state at the time the suit for dissolution is filed, the court may exercise personal jurisdiction over the respondent or over the respondent's personal representative although the respondent is not a resident of this state if:

(1) this state is the last marital residence of the petitioner and the respondent and the suit is filed before the second anniversary of the date on which marital residence ended; or

(2) there is any basis consistent with the constitutions of this state and the United States for the exercise of the personal jurisdiction.

(b) A court acquiring jurisdiction under this section also acquires jurisdiction over the respondent in a suit affecting the parent-child relationship.

History of Fam §6.305: Acts 1997, 75th Leg., ch. 7, §1, eff. April 17, 1997. Source: Former Fam §3.26.

Dawson-Austin v. Austin, 968 S.W.2d 319, 326 (Tex.1998). "The United States Constitution permits 'a state court [to] take personal jurisdiction over a defendant only if it has some minimum, purposeful contacts with the state, and the exercise of jurisdiction will not offend traditional notions of fair play and substantial justice.' *At 327:* In the present case, the location in Texas of property that either is or is claimed to be part of the marital estate does not supply the minimum contacts required for the court to exercise jurisdiction over [the wife]. ... We do not believe that one spouse may leave the other, move to another state in which neither has ever lived, buy a home or open a bank account or store a stock certificate there, and by those unilateral actions, and nothing more, compel the other spouse to litigate their divorce in the new domicile consistent with due process. One spouse cannot, solely by actions in which the other spouse is not involved, create the contacts between a state and the other spouse necessary for jurisdiction over a divorce action."

Goodenbour v. Goodenbour, 64 S.W.3d 69, 76-77 (Tex.App.—Austin 2001, pet. denied). "In applying the term 'last marital residence,' we should acknowledge that more and more frequently one spouse may, by choice or necessity, work in a state or country apart from the family unit for a period of time. A work separation, where spouses live apart to pursue professional opportunities, must be distinguished from a marital separation when spouses have decided to dissolve their marriage. Much as a military member may be on temporary assignment elsewhere, one spouse may, for a time, pursue a work assignment away from the other family members. The family decision to endure a work separation may include consideration of what schooling or other opportunities are best for the children. Because the family has made the decision to remain an intact unit, the fact that the spouses live apart does not mean that a marital residence no longer exists. As long as the parties choose to maintain a marriage, there will be a marital residence somewhere."

Reynolds v. Reynolds, 2 S.W.3d 429, 431 (Tex. App.—Houston [1st Dist.] 1999, no pet.). "The rule generally followed as to jurisdiction over nonresidents is that due process requires a nonresident have certain minimum contacts with Texas such that the maintenance of the suit does not offend traditional notions of fair play and substantial justice. ... A single act can support jurisdiction as long as there is a substantial connection with the forum state. A single act or occasional acts may be insufficient to establish jurisdiction if the nature, quality, and circumstances surrounding their commission only create an attenuated connection with the state, diminishing reasonable forseeability of litigation in the forum state. [¶] The evidence showed [husband] and [wife] resided in Texas from 1981 until 1993 when they separated. After [husband] moved to Colorado, he continued to send money to [wife] for the mortgage payments on their home in Texas. ... He also sent payments to State Farm Insurance Company to pay for the car insurance on [wife's] car in Texas. ... At least through August 1995, [wife] continued to receive [husband's] mail at their home in Texas. We hold [husband's] minimum contacts were such that he should not have been surprised to be called into a Texas court for divorce proceedings, including a division of marital property incident to that proceeding."

Bloom v. Bloom, 935 S.W.2d 942, 948 (Tex.App.—San Antonio 1996, no writ). Wife "does not contest the trial court's subject matter jurisdiction over the divorce proceeding. She does, however, contend that the trial court lacked subject matter jurisdiction to determine child visitation and custody, child support, and the division of marital property. What [wife] fails to recognize is that the two are inextricably interrelated. The trial court acquires subject matter jurisdiction over a divorce proceeding if the suit is filed by a qualified resident, 'this state is the last marital residence of the petitioner and the respondent,' and 'the suit is commenced within two years after the date on which the marital residence ended.' And, once the trial court acquires subject matter jurisdiction in this manner, it 'shall' divide the community estate. Additionally, a trial court that obtains subject matter jurisdiction under §3.26(a) [now §6.305], 'also acquires jurisdiction over the respondent in a [SAPCR],' including jurisdiction 'to make a child custody determination by initial decree ... if ... this state ... is the home state of the child on the date of the commencement of the proceeding....'"

Hoffman v. Hoffman, 821 S.W.2d 3, 5 (Tex.App.—Fort Worth 1992, no writ). "Where the trial court in a divorce proceeding has no personal jurisdiction over the respondent, the trial court has the jurisdiction to grant the divorce, but not to determine the managing conservatorship of children or divide property outside the State of Texas. It may also lack jurisdiction to divide property within the state."

Cossey v. Cossey, 602 S.W.2d 591, 595 (Tex.App.—Waco 1980, no writ). "The term 'marital cohabitation' as used in ... §3.26(a)(1) [now "marital residence" under §6.305(a)(1)] has not been defined by the courts. It has been suggested that at a minimum it should require the establishment of 'a permanent place of abode' by the spouses. It would certainly require more than occasional visits by one spouse with the other and their children at the other's place of residence during marital separation coupled with submission of the parties to marriage counseling during the visits in an attempt to reconcile their problems...."

FAM §6.306. JURISDICTION TO ANNUL MARRIAGE

(a) A suit for annulment of a marriage may be maintained in this state only if the parties were married in this state or if either party is domiciled in this state.

(b) A suit for annulment is a suit in rem, affecting the status of the parties to the marriage.

History of Fam §6.306: Acts 1997, 75th Leg., ch. 7, §1, eff. April 17, 1997. Source: Former Fam §3.25.

FAM §6.307. JURISDICTION TO DECLARE MARRIAGE VOID

(a) Either party to a marriage made void by this chapter may sue to have the marriage declared void, or the court may declare the marriage void in a collateral proceeding.

(b) The court may declare a marriage void only if:

(1) the purported marriage was contracted in this state; or

(2) either party is domiciled in this state.

(c) A suit to have a marriage declared void is a suit in rem, affecting the status of the parties to the purported marriage.

History of Fam §6.307: Acts 1997, 75th Leg., ch. 7, §1, eff. April 17, 1997. Source: Former Fam §§2.24, 3.25.

FAM §6.308. EXERCISING PARTIAL JURISDICTION

(a) A court in which a suit for dissolution of a marriage is filed may exercise its jurisdiction over those portions of the suit for which it has authority.

(b) The court's authority to resolve the issues in controversy between the parties may be restricted because the court lacks:

(1) the required personal jurisdiction over a nonresident party in a suit for dissolution of the marriage;

(2) the required jurisdiction under Chapter 152; or

(3) the required jurisdiction under Chapter 159.

History of Fam §6.308: Acts 1997, 75th Leg., ch. 7, §1, eff. April 17, 1997.

Dawson-Austin v. Austin, 968 S.W.2d 319, 324 (Tex.1998). "The cases that hold adjudication of divorce and division of the marital estate to be non-severable claims all do so in the context of Rules 41 (Misjoinder and Non-Joinder of Parties), 174 (Consolidation; Separate Trials), and 320 (Motion [for New Trial] and Action of Court Thereon). [¶] No case holds that claims of divorce and division of property do not involve severable *jurisdictional* issues. The United States Supreme Court recognized long ago that a court could have jurisdiction to grant a divorce—an adjudication of parties' status—without having jurisdiction to divide their property—an adjudication of parties' rights." (Internal quotations omitted.)

Boots v. Lopez, 6 S.W.3d 292, 294 (Tex.App.—Houston [14th Dist.] 1999, pet. denied). Husband "correctly points out that §6.308 ... allows the trial court to exercise partial jurisdiction over those portions of the suit for which it has authority. However, we note the language of the statute is discretionary, not mandatory. The statute provides that the trial court *may* exercise its jurisdiction. Thus, it was within the trial court's discretion whether to exercise partial jurisdiction over this case."

Sections 6.309-6.400 reserved for expansion

SUBCHAPTER E. FILING SUIT

FAM §6.401. CAPTION

(a) Pleadings in a suit for divorce or annulment shall be styled "In the Matter of the Marriage of __________ and __________."

(b) Pleadings in a suit to declare a marriage void shall be styled "A Suit To Declare Void the Marriage of __________ and __________."

History of Fam §6.401: Acts 1997, 75th Leg., ch. 7, §1, eff. April 17, 1997. Source: Former Fam §3.51.

FAM §6.402. PLEADINGS

(a) A petition in a suit for dissolution of a marriage is sufficient without the necessity of specifying the underlying evidentiary facts if the petition alleges the grounds relied on substantially in the language of the statute.

(b) Allegations of grounds for relief, matters of defense, or facts relied on for a temporary order that are stated in short and plain terms are not subject to special exceptions because of form or sufficiency.

(c) The court shall strike an allegation of evidentiary fact from the pleadings on the motion of a party or on the court's own motion.

History of Fam §6.402: Acts 1997, 75th Leg., ch. 7, §1, eff. April 17, 1997. Source: Former Fam §3.52.

In re Marriage of Richards, 991 S.W.2d 32, 36 (Tex.App.—Amarillo 1999, pet. dism'd). "The thrust of [wife's] argument is that [§6.402(b)] denies her a 'legal and factual test of the petitioner's pleadings before trial, [therefore] the respondent is denied honest and fair adjudication of her defense that the petitioner's facts do not support his allegations.' [¶] [Wife] presents no argument showing that she could not obtain the facts necessary for her defense through discovery, or that summary judgment did not provide an adequate method to avoid the burdens of trial if the facts did not support the action asserted. Because these procedures were available to her, §6.402 neither denies her access to the courts of this state or deprives her of equal protection of the laws."

FAM §6.403. ANSWER

The respondent in a suit for dissolution of a marriage is not required to answer on oath or affirmation.

History of Fam §6.403: Acts 1997, 75th Leg., ch. 7, §1, eff. April 17, 1997. Source: Former Fam §3.53.

Harmon v. Harmon, 879 S.W.2d 213, 215 (Tex. App.—Houston [14th Dist.] 1994, writ denied). "Since [husband] did not answer, this was a *noncontested* case, and [husband] was vulnerable to a default judgment. [Husband] was not entitled notice of a trial setting. [¶] [Husband] contends that the case was 'contested' until the 60-day waiting period required by §3.60 [now §6.702] had elapsed. We disagree. ... It is true that the 60-day statutory waiting period precluded a divorce judgment, default or otherwise, from being rendered.... But this does not mean that the case was 'contested' for purposes of [TRCP] 245. The case became *non*contested when [husband] failed to answer."

Considine v. Considine, 726 S.W.2d 253, 254 (Tex. App.—Austin 1987, no writ). "In the usual case, the defendant who fails to file an answer is said to confess to the facts properly pleaded in the petition. In such a case, the non-answering defendant cannot mount an evidentiary attack against the judgment on motion for new trial or on appeal. [¶] In a divorce case, however, the petition is not taken as confessed for want of an answer. Even if the respondent fails to file an answer, the petitioner must adduce proof to support the material allegations in the petition. Accordingly, the judgment of divorce is subject to an evidentiary attack on motion for new trial and appeal. [¶] This Court knows of no Family Code provision relating to modification of prior orders that is comparable to §3.53 [now §6.403]. Reason suggests, nonetheless, that the same policy considerations underlying [§3.53], applicable to original divorce judgments appointing conservators and setting support for and access to children, should also obtain in ... proceedings to modify like provisions in prior orders. We note that before provisions relating to conservatorship, possession, and support in prior orders may be modified, the court must conduct a hearing. A 'hearing,' in this context, implies the admission and consideration of proof—the opposite of taking allegations of the motion for modification 'as confessed for want of an answer.' We conclude that the allegations in the motion to modify may not be taken as confessed for want of an answer. As a result, in a case of default by the respondent, the movant must prove up the required allegations of the motion to modify."

FAM §6.4035. WAIVER OF SERVICE

(a) A party to a suit for the dissolution of a marriage may waive the issuance or service of process after the suit is filed by filing with the clerk of the court in which the suit is filed the waiver of the party acknowledging receipt of a copy of the filed petition.

(b) The waiver must contain the mailing address of the party who executed the waiver.

(c) The waiver must be sworn but may not be sworn before an attorney in the suit.

(d) The Texas Rules of Civil Procedure do not apply to a waiver executed under this section.

History of Fam §6.4035: Acts 1997, 75th Leg., ch. 614, §1, eff. Sept. 1, 1997.

FAM §6.404. STATEMENT ON ALTERNATE DISPUTE RESOLUTION

(a) A party to a proceeding under this title shall include in the first pleading filed by the party in the proceeding the following statement:

"I AM AWARE THAT IT IS THE POLICY OF THE STATE OF TEXAS TO PROMOTE THE AMICABLE AND NONJUDICIAL SETTLEMENT OF DISPUTES INVOLVING CHILDREN AND FAMILIES. I AM AWARE OF ALTERNATIVE DISPUTE RESOLUTION METHODS, INCLUDING MEDIATION. WHILE I RECOGNIZE THAT ALTERNATIVE DISPUTE RESOLUTION IS AN ALTERNATIVE TO AND NOT A SUBSTITUTE FOR A TRIAL AND THAT THIS CASE MAY BE TRIED IF IT IS NOT SETTLED, I REPRESENT TO THE COURT THAT I WILL ATTEMPT IN GOOD FAITH TO RESOLVE BEFORE FINAL TRIAL CONTESTED ISSUES IN THIS CASE BY ALTERNATIVE DISPUTE RESOLUTION WITHOUT THE NECESSITY OF COURT INTERVENTION."

(b) The statement prescribed by Subsection (a) must be prominently displayed in boldfaced type or capital letters or be underlined and be signed by the party.

(c) The statement prescribed by Subsection (a) is not required for:

(1) a pleading in which citation on all respondents entitled to service of citation is requested, issued, and given by publication;

(2) a motion or pleading that seeks a protective order as provided by Title 4; or

(3) a special appearance under Rule 120a, Texas Rules of Civil Procedure.

History of Fam §6.404: Acts 1997, 75th Leg., ch. 7, §1, eff. April 17, 1997. Amended by Acts 1997, 75th Leg., ch. 937, §1, eff. Sept. 1, 1997; Acts 1999, 76th Leg., ch. 178, §1 (eff. Aug. 30, 1999), ch. 62, §6.03 (eff. Sept. 1, 1999). Source: Former Fam §3.522[A*].

FAM §6.405. PROTECTIVE ORDER

(a) The petition in a suit for dissolution of a marriage must state whether a protective order under Title 4 is in effect or if an application for a protective order is pending with regard to the parties to the suit.

(b) The petitioner shall attach to the petition a copy of each protective order issued under Title 4 in which one of the parties to the suit was the applicant and the other party was the respondent without regard to the date of the order. If a copy of the protective order is not available at the time of filing, the petition must state that a copy of the order will be filed with the court before any hearing.

History of Fam §6.405: Acts 1997, 75th Leg., ch. 7, §1, eff. April 17, 1997. Amended by Acts 1999, 76th Leg., ch. 62, §6.04, eff. Sept. 1, 1999. Source: Former Fam §3.522[B*].

FAM §6.406. MANDATORY JOINDER OF SUIT AFFECTING PARENT-CHILD RELATIONSHIP

(a) The petition in a suit for dissolution of a marriage shall state whether there are children born or adopted of the marriage who are under 18 years of age or who are otherwise entitled to support as provided by Chapter 154.

(b) If the parties are parents of a child, as defined by Section 101.003, and the child is not under the continuing jurisdiction of another court as provided by Chapter 155, the suit for dissolution of a marriage must include a suit affecting the parent-child relationship under Title 5.

History of Fam §6.406: Acts 1997, 75th Leg., ch. 7, §1, eff. April 17, 1997. Source: Former Fam §3.55(a), (b).

Osteen v. Osteen, 999 S.W.2d 28, 29 (Tex.App.—Houston [14th Dist.] 1999, no pet.). "If there are children of the marriage, and the children are not under the continuing jurisdiction of any other court, the code requires the suit for divorce to include a [SAPCR]. However, if a [SAPCR] is filed separately from a suit for divorce, the district court that handles the divorce action will acquire dominant jurisdiction over the parent-child suit."

In re Marriage of Morales, 968 S.W.2d 508, 511 (Tex.App.—Corpus Christi 1998, no pet.). "A divorce case involving children of the marriage actually constitutes two separate and distinct lawsuits. Thus, when the parties to a divorce action are *parents* of a child, the suit for dissolution of the marriage must include a [SAPCR] under Title 5."

FAM §6.407. TRANSFER OF SUIT AFFECTING PARENT-CHILD RELATIONSHIP TO DIVORCE COURT

(a) If a suit affecting the parent-child relationship is pending at the time the suit for dissolution of a marriage is filed, the suit affecting the parent-child relationship shall be transferred as provided by Section 103.002 to the court in which the suit for dissolution is filed.

(b) If the parties are parents of a child, as defined by Section 101.003, and the child is under the continuing jurisdiction of another court under Chapter 155, either party to the suit for dissolution of a marriage may move that court for transfer of the suit affecting the parent-child relationship to the court having jurisdiction of the suit for dissolution. The court with continuing jurisdiction shall transfer the proceeding as provided by Chapter 155. On the transfer of the proceedings, the court with jurisdiction of the suit for dissolution of a marriage shall consolidate the two causes of action.

(c) After transfer of a suit affecting the parent-child relationship as provided in Chapter 155, the court with jurisdiction of the suit for dissolution of a marriage has jurisdiction to render an order in the suit affecting the parent-child relationship as provided by Title 5.

History of Fam §6.407: Acts 1997, 75th Leg., ch. 7, §1, eff. April 17, 1997. Source: Former Fam §3.55(b), (c), (d).

Neal v. Avey, 853 S.W.2d 707, 709 (Tex.App.—Houston [14th Dist.] 1993, writ denied). "If the children are under the continuing jurisdiction of a court under a parent-child suit, §3.55(c) [now §6.407] allows either of the parties to the divorce to move the court where the parent-child suit is pending for transfer of that suit to the court having jurisdiction of the divorce. Upon proper motion and showing that venue is proper in another county, this transfer is mandatory."

Garza v. Texas DHS, 757 S.W.2d 44, 46-47 (Tex.App.—San Antonio 1988, writ denied). The trial court has discretion to deny a motion to transfer when the mandatory transfer provisions are abused.

Ortiz v. Aranda, 716 S.W.2d 692, 693 (Tex.App.—Corpus Christi 1986, no writ). "The suit for divorce was filed in the 225th District Court and the motion to modify child custody was filed in the 150th District Court. The 150th District Court was the court of continuing jurisdiction over the child.... The motion to modify stated that a divorce action had been filed, and requested the 150th District Court to consolidate the two actions. Neither an order of transfer nor an order of consolidation is in the record. [¶] [T]he decree of divorce ... was entered by the 225th District Court.... [¶] We have determined ... that the divorce decree is void insofar as it purports to modify the conservatorship of the child. The decree recites on its face that it was entered by the 225th District Court, and the record contains no transfer of the modification action from the 150th District Court as required by ... §3.55(c) [now §6.407]."

In re Marriage of Allen, 593 S.W.2d 133, 138 (Tex. App.—Amarillo 1979, no writ). Wife's "final contention is that the provisions of §11.06(c) [now §155.202(b)] justify the refusal of the Lubbock court to transfer the case and give validity to its refusal to do so. The section in question permits transfer of a parent-child relationship suit to another court '[f]or the convenience of the parties ... and in the interest of justice.' We do not perceive how a provision permitting a discretionary transfer could validate an order refusing a mandatory transfer. In any event, a provision for transfer for the convenience of parties and in the interest of justice cannot override a mandatory transfer provision such as §3.55(c) [now §6.407]."

FAM §6.408. SERVICE OF CITATION

Citation on the filing of an original petition in a suit for dissolution of a marriage shall be issued and served as in other civil cases. Citation may also be served on any other person who has or who may assert an interest in the suit for dissolution of the marriage.

History of Fam §6.408: Acts 1997, 75th Leg., ch. 7, §1, eff. April 17, 1997.

Ackerly v. Ackerly, 13 S.W.3d 454, 457-58 (Tex. App.—Corpus Christi 2000, no pet.). "In the present case [involving a motion for reduction to money judgment under §9.010], the record contains no indication of service by citation. The docket sheet reflects no citation was ever issued, served, or returned for filing with the court. The only indication of any notice to appellant is a 'Certificate of Service' in the motion, which was signed by counsel, and states, 'this will certify that a copy of the above and foregoing has been mailed to Respondent at his last known address on this 26 day of June, 1998.' This notice does not comply with the citation requirements set forth in the [TRCP]. Therefore, the default judgment is not supported by proper service of process."

Avila v. Avila, 843 S.W.2d 280, 281 (Tex.App.—El Paso 1992, no writ). "There are no presumptions in favor of valid issuance, service and return of citation in this situation. Moreover, failure to affirmatively show strict compliance with the [TRCP] renders the attempted service of process invalid and of no effect."

FAM §6.409. CITATION BY PUBLICATION

(a) Citation in a suit for dissolution of a marriage may be by publication as in other civil cases, except that notice shall be published one time only.

(b) The notice shall be sufficient if given in substantially the following form:

"STATE OF TEXAS

To (name of person to be served with citation), and to all whom it may concern (if the name of any person to be served with citation is unknown), Respondent(s),

"You have been sued. You may employ an attorney. If you or your attorney do not file a written answer with the clerk who issued this citation by 10 a.m. on the Monday next following the expiration of 20 days after you were served this citation and petition, a default judgment may be taken against you. The petition of ____________, Petitioner, was filed in the Court of ____________ County, Texas, on the ______ day of __________, against __________, Respondent(s), numbered ______, and entitled 'In the Matter of Marriage of ___________ and ____________. The suit requests ___________ (statement of relief sought).'

"The Court has authority in this suit to enter any judgment or decree dissolving the marriage and providing for the division of property that will be binding on you.

"Issued and given under my hand and seal of said Court at __________, Texas, this the ______ day of __________, ______.

"..............................

Clerk of the __________ Court of

____________ County, Texas

By _______, Deputy."

(c) The form authorized in this section and the form authorized by Section 102.010 may be combined in appropriate situations.

(d) If the citation is for a suit in which a parent-child relationship does not exist, service by publication may be completed by posting the citation at the courthouse door for seven days in the county in which the suit is filed.

(e) If the petitioner or the petitioner's attorney of record makes an oath that no child presently under 18 years of age was born or adopted by the spouses and that no appreciable amount of property was accumulated by the spouses during the marriage, the court may dispense with the appointment of an attorney ad litem. In a case in which citation was by publication, a statement of the evidence, approved and signed by the judge, shall be filed with the papers of the suit as a part of the record.

History of Fam §6.409: Acts 1997, 75th Leg., ch. 7, §1, eff. April 17, 1997. Source: Former Fam §3.521.

In re A.Y., 16 S.W.3d 387, 389 (Tex.App.—El Paso 2000, no pet.). "The Family Code allows for citation by publication as in other civil cases. Therefore, the Rules of Civil Procedure apply and Rule 116 makes citation by publication proper if published in the county where suit is pending."

Sections 6.410-6.500 reserved for expansion

SUBCHAPTER F. TEMPORARY ORDERS

FAM §6.501. TEMPORARY RESTRAINING ORDER

(a) After the filing of a suit for dissolution of a marriage, on the motion of a party or on the court's own motion, the court may grant a temporary restraining order without notice to the adverse party for the preservation of the property and for the protection of the parties as necessary, including an order prohibiting one or both parties from:

(1) intentionally communicating by telephone or in writing with the other party by use of vulgar, profane, obscene, or indecent language or in a coarse or offensive manner, with intent to annoy or alarm the other;

(2) threatening the other, by telephone or in writing, to take unlawful action against any person, intending by this action to annoy or alarm the other;

(3) placing a telephone call, anonymously, at an unreasonable hour, in an offensive and repetitious manner, or without a legitimate purpose of communication with the intent to annoy or alarm the other;

(4) intentionally, knowingly, or recklessly causing bodily injury to the other or to a child of either party;

(5) threatening the other or a child of either party with imminent bodily injury;

(6) intentionally, knowingly, or recklessly destroying, removing, concealing, encumbering, transferring, or otherwise harming or reducing the value of the property of the parties or either party with intent to obstruct the authority of the court to order a division of the estate of the parties in a manner that the court deems just and right, having due regard for the rights of each party and any children of the marriage;

(7) intentionally falsifying a writing or record relating to the property of either party;

(8) intentionally misrepresenting or refusing to disclose to the other party or to the court, on proper request, the existence, amount, or location of any property of the parties or either party;

(9) intentionally or knowingly damaging or destroying the tangible property of the parties or either party; or

(10) intentionally or knowingly tampering with the tangible property of the parties or either party and causing pecuniary loss or substantial inconvenience to the other.

(b) A temporary restraining order under this subchapter may not include a provision:

(1) the subject of which is a requirement, appointment, award, or other order listed in Section 64.104, Civil Practice and Remedies Code; or

(2) that:

(A) excludes a spouse from occupancy of the residence where that spouse is living except as provided in a protective order made in accordance with Title 4;

(B) prohibits a party from spending funds for reasonable and necessary living expenses; or

(C) prohibits a party from engaging in acts reasonable and necessary to conduct that party's usual business and occupation.

History of Fam §6.501: Acts 1997, 75th Leg., ch. 7, §1, eff. April 17, 1997. Amended by Acts 1999, 76th Leg., ch. 1081, §6, eff. Sept. 1, 1999. Source: Former Fam §3.58(a), (b).

FAM §6.502. TEMPORARY INJUNCTION & OTHER TEMPORARY ORDERS

(a) While a suit for dissolution of a marriage is pending and on the motion of a party or on the court's own motion after notice and hearing, the court may render an appropriate order, including the granting of a temporary injunction for the preservation of the property and protection of the parties as deemed necessary and equitable and including an order directed to one or both parties:

(1) requiring a sworn inventory and appraisement of the real and personal property owned or claimed by the parties and specifying the form, manner, and substance of the inventory and appraisal and list of debts and liabilities;

(2) requiring payments to be made for the support of either spouse;

(3) requiring the production of books, papers, documents, and tangible things by a party;

(4) ordering payment of reasonable attorney's fees and expenses;

(5) appointing a receiver for the preservation and protection of the property of the parties;

(6) awarding one spouse exclusive occupancy of the residence during the pendency of the case;

(7) prohibiting the parties, or either party, from spending funds beyond an amount the court determines to be for reasonable and necessary living expenses;

(8) awarding one spouse exclusive control of a party's usual business or occupation; or

(9) prohibiting an act described by Section 6.501(a).

E (b) Not later than the 30th day after the date a receiver is appointed under Subsection (a)(5), the receiver shall give notice of the appointment to each lienholder of any property under the receiver's control.

History of Fam §6.502: Acts 1997, 75th Leg., ch. 7, §1, eff. April 17, 1997. Amended by Acts 2001, 77th Leg., ch. 695, §1, eff. Sept. 1, 2001. Source: Former Fam §§3.58(c), 3.59.

Generally

Post v. Garza, 867 S.W.2d 88, 90 (Tex.App.—Corpus Christi 1993, orig. proceeding). Section 3.58(c), now §6.502, "requires notice and a hearing before the court may award [a temporary order]. This requirement of a hearing implies that the opposing spouse will be afforded the normal right to participate in an *adversarial* hearing, rather than merely the right to be present as a spectator at an *ex parte* hearing. In the present case, the trial court's refusal to allow [husband] to participate through cross-examination and the presentation of his own evidence amounted to a clear abuse of discretion and a violation of his due process right to be heard."

Commonwealth Mortg. Corp. v. Wadkins, 709 S.W.2d 679, 680 (Tex.App.—Houston [14th Dist.] 1985, no writ). "The language of the statute clearly indicates the temporary orders are limited to orders directed to one or both 'parties.' 'Parties' in the context of §3.58 [now §6.502] means spouses."

Mussina v. Morton, 657 S.W.2d 871, 872 (Tex. App.—Houston [1st Dist.] 1983, no writ). This appeal questions the authority of a domestic relations court in a divorce proceeding to issue a temporary injunction and to appoint a receiver to protect against foreclosure by a third party. *At 873:* "The purpose of a temporary injunction is to preserve the status quo of the subject matter pending a trial on the merits. An applicant for a temporary injunction has the burden of showing his probable right of recovery in a trial on the merits and probable injury in the interim if the injunction is not granted. *At 874:* [T]he institution of the divorce proceedings [does] not preclude [the assertion of] foreclosure remedies available...."

Wells v. Wells, 539 S.W.2d 220, 222 (Tex.App.—Houston [1st Dist.] 1976, writ dism'd). "The trial court in a divorce proceeding is authorized by statute to grant temporary relief as it may deem necessary and equitable with respect to the parties and their property. The order in question recited that its provisions were necessary and equitable for the preservation of the parties' rights. This was sufficient compliance with [TRCP] 683, ... requiring that every injunctive order set forth the reasons for its issuance."

Brunell v. Brunell, 494 S.W.2d 621, 623-24 (Tex. App.—Dallas 1973, no writ). "[P]ayments of temporary alimony have been held not to be violative of the public policy of Texas. [T]he court [has stated the following]: 'Alimony is not in the nature of a debt for the collection of which an execution may issue but it is a duty and the order for such may be enforced by contempt proceedings.'"

Attorney Fees

Herschberg v. Herschberg, 994 S.W.2d 273, 279 (Tex.App.—Corpus Christi 1999, no pet.). "With regard to attorney's fees, there is no specific guidance in §6.502 to suggest how the amount of expected attorney's fees is to be calculated. We conclude that, as with temporary support, the award of temporary attorney's fees must be based on the needs of the applicant as weighed against the ability of the opposing party to pay such fees. [¶] The danger to be guarded against is that the spouse in control and possession of the bulk of the marital estate will use that control to his or her advantage in the adversary process, leaving the other spouse with inferior representation and at a disadvantage with regard to the division of property. Moreover, unlike an ordinary trial in which there is no community of interest between the litigants, in a divorce proceeding the funds which assist one party are often drawn from the community interest to which the other party has an equal right. [¶] Because of the uncertainties of future litigation and of the legal and factual issues that may arise, temporary orders are only an estimate of the actual attorney's fees and costs. As long as there is a credible showing of the need for attorney's fees in the amount requested and the ability of the opposing spouse to meet that need, the trial court has authority by temporary orders to require the payment of such fees. However, the trial court may not make the opposing party destitute in order to pay the applicant's support and fees."

Ex parte Kimsey, 915 S.W.2d 523, 525 (Tex.App.—El Paso 1995, orig. proceeding). "Section 3.58 [now §6.502] allows the trial court to order the payment of reasonable interim attorney's fees. ... Thus, it is clear that Relator can be punished by contempt for his violation of the trial court's temporary order requiring him to pay sums into the registry of the court for the payment of attorney's fees."

Inventory

Ismail v. Ismail, 702 S.W.2d 216, 224 (Tex.App.—Houston [1st Dist.] 1985, writ ref'd n.r.e.). "The Family Code provides that the trial court may issue temporary orders requiring either party to file a sworn inventory. If a party fails to comply with a temporary order, the party may be punished under the court's contempt power. We hold that the request for an inventory in a divorce case is a specie of discovery, and that the sanctions provided for in [TRCP] 215, as well as those granted in §3.58(c)(1) [now §6.502(1)], are available to the trial court to punish or secure compliance with its order to furnish an inventory."

Receiver

Mallou v. Payne & Vendig, 750 S.W.2d 251, 254-55 (Tex.App.—Dallas 1988, writ denied). "Under §3.58(h)(3) [now §6.502(5)], the trial court may appoint a receiver for the preservation and protection of the property of the parties. 'Parties' in the context of §3.58 *means the spouses*. 'Parties' does not include third-party creditors.... The family courts do not have unbridled discretion in appointing a receiver. As this court has stated previously: 'In recognition of the fact that appointment of a receiver without notice is one of the most drastic actions known to law or equity and should be exercised with extreme caution and only where great emergency or imperative necessity requires it, our courts have uniformly been reluctant to grant such harsh relief.' The appointment of a receiver is disfavored in the law and is only permitted if it is conclusively shown that: (1) the property is in danger of being lost, removed, or materially injured; (2) the trial court considered other available options; and (3) from the evidence before it, the trial court concluded that a less harsh remedy was unavailable."

Readhimer v. Readhimer, 728 S.W.2d 872, 873-74 (Tex.App.—Houston [1st Dist.] 1987, no writ). "Unlike receiverships authorized by the [CPRC], the [Family Code] does not set out the predicate necessary to support a receivership order. This Court is aware of cases reciting that, in a divorce case, the court may appoint a receiver without any showing that the property is in danger of being lost, removed, or materially injured. The better rule, however, would require a showing that the parties' property was in danger and that a less harsh remedy was unavailable before a receiver is appointed. It certainly would require some evidence and a record demonstrating the options that the court could or did consider. [¶] We conclude that the family district courts do not have unbridled discretion. A receiver is not appointed for the benefit of the applicant, but to receive and preserve the property for the benefit of all parties interested therein. [¶] We hold that the trial court abused its discretion in appointing a receiver because there was no evidence showing that a receivership was necessary for the preservation and protection of the property."

Spousal Support

Ex parte Hall, 854 S.W.2d 656, 658 (Tex.1993). "The temporary support order in this case was issued solely on the basis of the parties' prenuptial agreement and not on the authority of the Family Code. ... For this reason the trial court did not consider it necessary to complete the hearing required by statute before granting temporary support. It did not determine whether the spousal support ordered was 'necessary and equitable', as required by ... §3.58(c) [now §6.502], nor whether the temporary child support was 'for the safety and welfare of the child', as required by ... §11.11(a) [now §105.001]. It did not take into account the guidelines and factors required for setting child support. ... It calculated the arrearage due without any evidentiary basis. Under these circumstances, the temporary support order was not enforceable by contempt."

Herschberg v. Herschberg, 994 S.W.2d 273, 278 (Tex.App.—Corpus Christi 1999, no pet.). "[T]emporary support pending divorce has for its purpose the maintenance of the family until the final decree. It is not a property right, but is to be determined by the consideration of the needs of the applicant. Therefore, temporary support should be awarded based on considerations of both the degree to which the applicant is destitute of means to pay for his or her necessities during the pendency of the suit, and the ability of the requested spouse to pay. [¶] [T]emporary support is only meant to pay for necessary expenses. Therefore, it is not proper to use a temporary support order to make an interim division of the property or to equalize the standard of living for each party pending a final division."

Grossnickle v. Grossnickle, 935 S.W.2d 830, 848 (Tex.App.—Texarkana 1996, writ denied). "Temporary spousal support ends when the divorce is final. A trial court may properly award temporary spousal support pending an appeal of a divorce. [H]owever, [wife] did not appeal the divorce itself, so she was not entitled to spousal support during the appeal on other issues."

FAM §6.503. AFFIDAVIT, VERIFIED PLEADING, & BOND NOT REQUIRED

(a) A temporary restraining order or temporary injunction under this subchapter:

(1) may be granted without an affidavit or a verified pleading stating specific facts showing that immediate and irreparable injury, loss, or damage will result before notice can be served and a hearing can be held; and

(2) need not:

(A) define the injury or state why it is irreparable;

(B) state why the order was granted without notice; or

(C) include an order setting the suit for trial on the merits with respect to the ultimate relief sought.

(b) In a suit for dissolution of a marriage, the court may dispense with the issuance of a bond between the spouses in connection with temporary orders for the protection of the parties and their property.

History of Fam §6.503: Acts 1997, 75th Leg., ch. 7, §1, eff. April 17, 1997. Source: Former Fam §3.58(d), (e).

FAM §6.504. PROTECTIVE ORDERS

On the motion of a party to a suit for dissolution of a marriage, the court may render a protective order as provided by Subtitle B, Title 4.

History of Fam §6.504: Acts 1997, 75th Leg., ch. 7, §1, eff. April 17, 1997. Amended by Acts 1997, 75th Leg., ch. 1193, §1, eff. Sept. 1, 1997. Source: Former Fam §3.581.

FAM §6.505. COUNSELING

(a) While a divorce suit is pending, the court may direct the parties to counsel with a person named by the court.

(b) The person named by the court to counsel the parties shall submit a written report to the court and to the parties before the final hearing. In the report, the counselor shall give only an opinion as to whether there exists a reasonable expectation of reconciliation of the parties and, if so, whether further counseling would be beneficial. The sole purpose of the report is to aid the court in determining whether the suit for divorce should be continued pending further counseling.

(c) A copy of the report shall be furnished to each party.

(d) If the court believes that there is a reasonable expectation of the parties' reconciliation, the court may by written order continue the proceedings and direct the parties to a person named by the court for further counseling for a period fixed by the court not to exceed 60 days, subject to any terms, conditions, and limitations the court considers desirable. In ordering counseling, the court shall consider the circumstances of the parties, including the needs of the parties' family and the availability of counseling services. At the expiration of the period specified by the court, the counselor to whom the parties were directed shall report to the court whether the parties have complied with the court's order. Thereafter, the court shall proceed as in a divorce suit generally.

(e) If the court orders counseling under this section and the parties to the marriage are the parents of a child under 18 years of age born or adopted during the marriage, the counseling shall include counseling on issues that confront children who are the subject of a suit affecting the parent-child relationship.

History of Fam §6.505: Acts 1997, 75th Leg., ch. 7, §1, eff. April 17, 1997. Amended by Acts 1997, 75th Leg., ch. 1325, §1, eff. Sept. 1, 1997. Source: Former Fam §3.54(a)-(c).

Philp v. Philp, 516 S.W.2d 294, 295 (Tex.App.—Waco 1974, no writ). Section 3.54, now §6.505, "provides that the trial court may in its discretion direct the parties to a divorce suit to counsel, and if the court is of the opinion there exists a reasonable expectation of the parties reconciliation the court may continue the proceedings for counseling. [¶] [Husband] testified the marriage was insupportable; that if the divorce was denied he would never go back to his wife; ... that he was unwilling to see a marriage counselor; ... that the marriage was impossible; that the marriage developed a sickness from which it could not recover; ... that he only stayed with his wife as long as he did because of the son; ... that he dreaded the thought of going home because it was the most unpleasant and most uncomfortable place there was. [¶] We cannot say the trial court abused its discretion in not ordering counseling, or in not continuing the case for counseling."

FAM §6.506. CONTEMPT

The violation of a temporary restraining order, temporary injunction, or other temporary order issued under this subchapter is punishable as contempt.

History of Fam §6.506: Acts 1997, 75th Leg., ch. 7, §1, eff. April 17, 1997. Source: Former Fam §3.58(f).

Ex parte Hall, 854 S.W.2d 656, 658 (Tex.1993). "An order requiring temporary support payments is enforceable by contempt."

Ex parte Threet, 333 S.W.2d 361, 362 (Tex.1960). Relator "has been held in contempt by a district court for refusing to make support payments [in accordance with a temporary order] pending a divorce action. [Relator] denied that he had been married, and here contends that the district court was without power to require such payments because there was no evidence introduced at the hearing that there had ever been any marriage. *At 363-64:* A valid marriage is a prerequisite to a support order in an action for divorce. The existence of the marriage must be admitted or shown before such a decree or order properly can be made. Where the marriage is denied, as it was here, the marriage must be at least tentatively established. Stated differently, when the marriage is put in issue, the burden is upon the party seeking support to establish at least a prima facie case of marriage."

Ex parte Kimsey, 915 S.W.2d 523, 525 (Tex.App.—El Paso 1995, orig. proceeding). Section 3.58(f), now §6.506, "allows the trial court to punish by contempt the violation of any temporary order. Thus, it is clear that Relator can be punished by contempt for his violation of the trial court's temporary order requiring him to pay sums into the registry of the court for the payment of attorney's fees. The question remains, however, whether that punishment can take the form of imprisonment in light of Article I, §18 of the Texas Constitution. [¶] While the constitution clearly prohibits imprisonment for debt, the courts have consistently recognized that obligations incurred for the support of children and spouses do not constitute a debt. *At 526:* Thus, an order of contempt arising from the failure to pay those obligations may be enforced by incarceration without running afoul of the constitutional prohibition."

FAM §6.507. INTERLOCUTORY APPEAL

An order under this subchapter, except an order appointing a receiver, is not subject to interlocutory appeal.

History of Fam §6.507: Acts 1997, 75th Leg., ch. 7, §1, eff. April 17, 1997. Source: Former Fam §3.58(g).

Sections 6.508-6.600 reserved for expansion

SUBCHAPTER G. ALTERNATIVE DISPUTE RESOLUTION

FAM §6.601. ARBITRATION PROCEDURES

(a) On written agreement of the parties, the court may refer a suit for dissolution of a marriage to arbitration. The agreement must state whether the arbitration is binding or nonbinding.

(b) If the parties agree to binding arbitration, the court shall render an order reflecting the arbitrator's award.

History of Fam §6.601: Acts 1997, 75th Leg., ch. 7, §1, eff. April 17, 1997.

In re Cartwright, ___ S.W.3d ___ (Tex.App.—Houston [1st Dist.] 2002, n.p.h.) (No. 01-01-00948-CV; 4-4-02). "We agree with [***Cooper v. Bushong***, 10 S.W.3d 20 (Tex.App.—Austin 1999, pet. denied)], that if, in a family law case, an arbitration is binding, ... it is appropriate to follow the [Texas Arbitration Act]. [¶] The TAA does not exclude family law claims from its coverage. Therefore, the TAA applies to Family Code arbitration if the arbitration agreement specifies that the arbitration is binding. However, the TAA, by its own terms, cannot apply to non-binding Family Code arbitration. The TAA necessarily contemplates that the arbitration award be binding and makes no provision for a non-binding arbitration procedure. At most, those provisions in the TAA that may be applied to non-binding arbitration should be used as guidelines for the arbitration, not as controlling law."

FAM §6.602. MEDIATION PROCEDURES

(a) On the written agreement of the parties or on the court's own motion, the court may refer a suit for dissolution of a marriage to mediation.

(b) A mediated settlement agreement is binding on the parties if the agreement:

(1) provides, in a prominently displayed statement that is in boldfaced type or capital letters or underlined, that the agreement is not subject to revocation;

(2) is signed by each party to the agreement; and

(3) is signed by the party's attorney, if any, who is present at the time the agreement is signed.

(c) If a mediated settlement agreement meets the requirements of this section, a party is entitled to judgment on the mediated settlement agreement notwithstanding Rule 11, Texas Rules of Civil Procedure, or another rule of law.

(d) A party may at any time prior to the final mediation order file a written objection to the referral of a suit for dissolution of a marriage to mediation on the basis of family violence having been committed against the objecting party by the other party. After an objection is filed, the suit may not be referred to mediation unless, on the request of the other party, a hearing is held and the court finds that a preponderance of the evidence does not support the objection. If the suit is referred to mediation, the court shall order appropriate measures be taken to ensure the physical and emotional safety of the party who filed the objection. The order shall provide that the parties not be required to have face-to-face contact and that the parties be placed in separate rooms during mediation.

History of Fam §6.602: Acts 1997, 75th Leg., ch. 7, §1, eff. April 17, 1997. Amended by Acts 1999, 76th Leg., ch. 1351, §1 (eff. Sept. 1, 1999), ch. 178, §2 (eff. Aug. 30, 1999).

Boyd v. Boyd, 67 S.W.3d 398, 403 (Tex.App.—Fort Worth 2002, n.p.h.). "We hold that the phrase 'notwithstanding rule 11 or another rule of law' does not require a trial court to enforce a mediated settlement agreement simply because it complies with §6.602(b), irrespective of what the agreement provides for or how it was procured."

Cayan v. Cayan, 38 S.W.3d 161, 165 (Tex.App.—Houston [14th Dist.] 2000, pet. denied). Section 6.602 "provides that where a mediated settlement agreement meets its requirements: (1) the agreement 'is binding on the parties'; and (2) a party is 'entitled to judgment on the … agreement *notwithstanding [TRCP] Rule 11, or another rule of law*.' … The plain meaning of §6.602 could hardly be more clear: a §6.602 agreement is binding, *i.e.*, irrevocable, and a party to one is entitled to judgment based on the agreement. Because [Family Code] §7.006(a) expressly recognizes that a settlement agreement can be made binding before rendition of the divorce under another rule of law, and because §6.602 expressly entitles a party to a §6.602 agreement to judgment notwithstanding other law, we interpret §6.602 simply as an exception to §7.006(a) whereby parties to a divorce may elect to make their agreement binding as of the time of its execution rather than at the subsequent time the divorce is rendered. *At 166:* [S]ection 6.602 reflects that when the Legislature enacted that section, it definitely and deliberately created a procedural shortcut for enforcement of mediated settlement agreements in divorce cases. … We are similarly persuaded that §6.602 is also an exception to §7.001 and §7.006 in allowing a judgment to be entered on a §6.602 agreement without a determination by the trial court that the terms of the agreement are just and right. Importantly, however, §6.602 cannot be imposed on parties against their wishes. Rather, they remain free to enter mediated settlement agreements that do not fall within §6.602 and, in fact, must take affirmative steps to qualify for §6.602 treatment."

In re Kasschau, 11 S.W.3d 305, 311 (Tex.App.—Houston [14th Dist.] 1999, orig. proceeding). "While we find the court's refusal to enter judgment on the mediated settlement agreement is a proper subject for mandamus, we conclude that the trial court did not violate a ministerial duty in this case. [¶] First, as noted, §6.602 and §153.0071 … provide that 'a party is entitled to judgment' on a mediated settlement agreement if certain requirements of those statutes are met. Where, as here, the legislature has not defined the terms in the statute, we must apply their ordinary meaning. 'Entitle' means in part 'to grant a legal right to or qualify for.' That a party has a 'right to' judgment, or 'qualifies for' judgment on a mediated settlement agreement does not deprive the court of discretion to review an agreement before entering judgment. … A court's duty to enter judgment on a settlement agreement becomes ministerial only after it has first rendered judgment on that agreement."

FAM §6.603. COLLABORATIVE LAW

E *Section 6.603 below is effective for actions commenced on or after Sept. 1, 2001, or actions commenced before Sept. 1, 2001 if the trial had not begun before that date.*

(a) On a written agreement of the parties and their attorneys, a dissolution of marriage proceeding may be conducted under collaborative law procedures.

(b) Collaborative law is a procedure in which the parties and their counsel agree in writing to use their best efforts and make a good faith attempt to resolve their dissolution of marriage dispute on an agreed basis without resorting to judicial intervention except to have the court approve the settlement agreement, make the legal pronouncements, and sign the orders required by law to effectuate the agreement of the parties as the court determines appropriate. The parties' counsel may not serve as litigation counsel except to ask the court to approve the settlement agreement.

(c) A collaborative law agreement must include provisions for:

(1) full and candid exchange of information between the parties and their attorneys as necessary to make a proper evaluation of the case;

(2) suspending court intervention in the dispute while the parties are using collaborative law procedures;

(3) hiring experts, as jointly agreed, to be used in the procedure;

(4) withdrawal of all counsel involved in the collaborative law procedure if the collaborative law procedure does not result in settlement of the dispute; and

(5) other provisions as agreed to by the parties consistent with a good faith effort to collaboratively settle the matter.

(d) Notwithstanding Rule 11, Texas Rules of Civil Procedure, or another rule or law, a party is entitled to judgment on a collaborative law settlement agreement if the agreement:

(1) provides, in a prominently displayed statement that is boldfaced, capitalized, or underlined, that the agreement is not subject to revocation; and

(2) is signed by each party to the agreement and the attorney of each party.

(e) Subject to Subsection (g), a court that is notified 30 days before trial that the parties are using collaborative law procedures to attempt to settle a dispute may not, until a party notifies the court that the collaborative law procedures did not result in a settlement:

(1) set a hearing or trial in the case;

(2) impose discovery deadlines;

(3) require compliance with scheduling orders; or

(4) dismiss the case.

(f) The parties shall notify the court if the collaborative law procedures result in a settlement. If they do not, the parties shall file:

(1) a status report with the court not later than the 180th day after the date of the written agreement to use the procedures; and

(2) a status report on or before the first anniversary of the date of the written agreement to use the procedures, accompanied by a motion for continuance that the court shall grant if the status report indicates the desire of the parties to continue to use collaborative law procedures.

(g) If the collaborative law procedures do not result in a settlement on or before the second anniversary of the date that the suit was filed, the court may:

(1) set the suit for trial on the regular docket; or

(2) dismiss the suit without prejudice.

History of Fam §6.603: Enacted by Acts 2001, 77th Leg., ch. 1022, §1, eff. Sept. 1, 2001.

Sections 6.604-6.700 reserved for expansion

SUBCHAPTER H. TRIAL & APPEAL

FAM §6.701. FAILURE TO ANSWER

In a suit for divorce, the petition may not be taken as confessed if the respondent does not file an answer.

History of Fam §6.701: Acts 1997, 75th Leg., ch. 7, §1, eff. April 17, 1997. Source: Former Fam §3.53.

Osteen v. Osteen, 38 S.W.3d 809, 814 (Tex.App.—Houston [14th Dist.] 2001, no pet.). "[T]he general rule regarding the scope of the allegations in a petition deemed admitted by a failure to answer in a divorce proceeding is limited by §6.701.... In a divorce case ... even if the respondent fails to file an answer, the petitioner must adduce proof to support the *material* allegations in the petition. Accordingly, a default judgment of divorce is subject to an evidentiary attack on motion for new trial and appeal."

Morris v. Morris, 717 S.W.2d 189, 190 (Tex.App.—Austin 1986, no writ). Husband's "failure to appear or answer is taken as an admission of the allegations in [wife's] petition regarding residence and domicile."

FAM §6.702. WAITING PERIOD

(a) The court may not grant a divorce before the 60th day after the date the suit was filed. A decree rendered in violation of this subsection is not subject to collateral attack.

(b) A waiting period is not required before a court may grant an annulment or declare a marriage void other than as required in civil cases generally.

History of Fam §6.702: Acts 1997, 75th Leg., ch. 7, §1, eff. April 17, 1997. Source: Former Fam §3.60.

Harmon v. Harmon, 879 S.W.2d 213, 215 (Tex. App.—Houston [14th Dist.] 1994, writ denied). "[T]he 60-day statutory waiting period preclude[s] a divorce judgment, default or otherwise, from being rendered...."

In re Marriage of Gillman, 507 S.W.2d 610, 611 (Tex.App.—Amarillo 1974, writ dism'd). "It is [wife's] basic contention ... that the court erred in overruling the motion to vacate because the record shows that the order ..., purporting to be a final judgment of divorce, was signed and entered on the same day that the divorce petition was filed in violation of §3.60 [now §6.702] and thus was null and void. *At 612:* [R]espondent's motion to vacate is a collateral attack upon the divorce decree. [¶] We hold that this collateral attack is precluded by the provision contained in the second sentence of §3.60 which in effect states that although a divorce is granted before sixty days have elapsed since the suit was filed, the decree is not subject to collateral attack. In the light of this statutory declaration of public policy, we hold that the non-compliance with the waiting period provision of §3.60 was procedural, not jurisdictional. Thus, such matter could only be challenged or corrected by direct appeal. [¶] Predicated upon this view of §3.60, it is clear that the trial court was without jurisdiction to deny the motion to vacate. The appropriate disposition was a dismissal rather than a denial upon consideration of the merits."

FAM §6.703. JURY

In a suit for dissolution of a marriage, either party may demand a jury trial unless the action is a suit to annul an underage marriage under Section 6.101 or 6.102.

History of Fam §6.703: Acts 1997, 75th Leg., ch. 7, §1, eff. April 17, 1997. Source: Former Fam §3.61.

In re Marriage of Richards, 991 S.W.2d 32, 36-38 (Tex.App.—Amarillo 1999, pet. dism'd). "We initially note §6.703 ... expressly provides that in a suit of this type, 'either party may demand a jury trial.' [Husband argues] that under the statute, there were no questions of material fact for resolution by the jury. We disagree. [¶] We begin with the language of the governing statute. The insupportability ground of divorce is set out in [Family Code] §6.001.... This ground, also known as no-fault divorce, has three elements. They are 1) that the marriage has become insupportable because of discord or conflict, 2) that discord or conflict destroys the legitimate ends of the marriage, and 3) there is no reasonable expectation of reconciliation. There is nothing in the language of the statute to support the conclusion that these are not questions of fact. [¶] Any attempt to determine those factual issues without giving [wife] an opportunity to respond would violate due process. ... While the adoption of 'no-fault' divorce dispenses with any burden to establish the source of the conflict rendering the marriage insupportable, it does not relieve the petitioner of the burden to establish the existence of the statutory elements. Therefore, at the time of [wife's] jury demand, there were questions of material fact to be resolved and it was error to deny her request."

Marr v. Marr, 905 S.W.2d 331, 333-34 (Tex.App.—Waco 1995, no writ). "Parties to divorce proceedings are entitled to a jury trial upon proper request; the jury alone decides whether contested assets will be characterized as either community or separate; and, while the question of a just and right division of the marital estate rests solely within the sound discretion of the court, the jury's findings on the factual issues underlying the division of the marital estate, including the valuation of the assets, are conclusive."

FAM §6.704. TESTIMONY OF HUSBAND OR WIFE

(a) In a suit for dissolution of a marriage, the husband and wife are competent witnesses for and against each other. A spouse may not be compelled to testify as to a matter that will incriminate the spouse.

(b) If the husband or wife testifies, the court or jury trying the case shall determine the credibility of the witness and the weight to be given the witness's testimony.

History of Fam §6.704: Acts 1997, 75th Leg., ch. 7, §1, eff. April 17, 1997. Source: Former Fam §3.62.

FAM §6.705. TESTIMONY BY MARRIAGE COUNSELOR

(a) The report by the person named by the court to counsel the parties to a suit for divorce may not be admitted as evidence in the suit.

(b) The person named by the court to counsel the parties is not competent to testify in any suit involving the parties or their children.

(c) The files, records, and other work products of the counselor are privileged and confidential for all purposes and may not be admitted as evidence in any suit involving the parties or their children.

History of Fam §6.705: Acts 1997, 75th Leg., ch. 7, §1, eff. April 17, 1997. Source: Former Fam §3.54(b), (d).

FAM §6.706. CHANGE OF NAME

(a) In a decree of divorce or annulment, the court shall change the name of a party specifically requesting the change to a name previously used by the party unless the court states in the decree a reason for denying the change of name.

(b) The court may not deny a change of name solely to keep the last name of family members the same.

(c) A change of name does not release a person from liability incurred by the person under a previous name or defeat a right the person held under a previous name.

(d) A person whose name is changed under this section may apply for a change of name certificate from the clerk of the court as provided by Section 45.106.

History of Fam §6.706: Acts 1997, 75th Leg., ch. 7, §1, eff. April 17, 1997. Source: Former Fam §3.64.

Fly v. Fly, 590 S.W.2d 179, 182 (Tex.App.—Corpus Christi 1979, no writ). Section 3.64, now §6.706, "permits a trial court to change the name of either party specifically requesting such change. The court has considerable discretion and may change the name of either party who prays for the name change. Here, the record shows that the wife did not make such a request and although the husband had petitioned the name change, the wife had not consented thereto. Therefore, the trial court erred in changing her name without her request or consent."

FAM §6.707. TRANSFERS & DEBTS PENDING DECREE

(a) A transfer of real or personal community property or a debt incurred by a spouse while a suit for divorce or annulment is pending that subjects the other spouse or the community property to liability is void with respect to the other spouse if the transfer was made or the debt incurred with the intent to injure the rights of the other spouse.

(b) A transfer or debt is not void if the person dealing with the transferor or debtor spouse did not have notice of the intent to injure the rights of the other spouse.

(c) The spouse seeking to void a transfer or debt incurred while a suit for divorce or annulment is pending has the burden of proving that the person dealing with the transferor or debtor spouse had notice of the intent to injure the rights of the spouse seeking to void the transaction.

History of Fam §6.707: Acts 1997, 75th Leg., ch. 7, §1, eff. April 17, 1997. Source: Former Fam §3.57.

Thomas v. Casale, 924 S.W.2d 433, 438 (Tex. App.—Fort Worth 1996, writ denied). "Although the trial court easily may have speculated that [mistress], living with [wife's] husband and having just gone through her own divorce, was a willing participant in a plan to defraud [wife] of a share of community funds, neither suspicion nor conjecture equates to proof by a preponderance of the evidence."

Estate of Korzekwa v. Prudential Ins. Co., 669 S.W.2d 775, 777 (Tex.App.—San Antonio 1984, writ dism'd). "It is undisputed that the life insurance policy in question was community property. ... The named insured has the right to designate the beneficiary under the insurance policy. In the instant case, the questioned change of the designated beneficiary occurred during the pendency of the divorce proceedings. ... Appellant seeks to void the change of beneficiary, but failed to discharge her burden to show that ... the prevailing last beneficiary, had notice of any intent to injure [appellant's] community property rights. Therefore, under the provisions of §3.57 [now §6.707], the transfer or change of beneficiary under the subject life insurance policy is not void."

FAM §6.708. COSTS

(a) In a suit for dissolution of a marriage, the court as it considers reasonable may award costs to a party. Costs may not be adjudged against a party against whom a divorce is granted for confinement in a mental hospital under Section 6.007.

(b) The expenses of counseling may be taxed as costs against either or both parties.

History of Fam §6.708: Acts 1997, 75th Leg., ch. 7, §1, eff. April 17, 1997. Source: Former Fam §§3.54(e), 3.65.

Pletcher v. Goetz, 9 S.W.3d 442, 448 (Tex.App.—Fort Worth 1999, pet. denied). "Costs generally refer to 'fees and charges required by law to be paid to the courts or some of their officers, the amount of which is fixed by statute or the court's rules.' Although §6.708 clearly allows expenses of counseling to be taxed as costs, there is no indication that the legislature intended attorney's fees to also be taxed as costs. Certainly, had there been such an intent, the legislature could have easily said so."

Farley v. Farley, 930 S.W.2d 208, 213 (Tex.App.—Eastland 1996, no writ). "The award of costs in a suit for divorce is a matter within the discretion of the trial court. *At 214:* While [wife's] testimony is some evidence that fees were paid to the expert witness and to her attorney, we hold that the evidence is insufficient to show the reasonableness of those fees. It is within the trial court's discretion to award such fees; but, when awarded, the evidence must be factually sufficient to support a finding that the fees are reasonable. Contrary to [wife's] position, such information cannot be supplied by resort to [CPRC] §38.001 et seq. because actions for divorce are not one of the enumerated actions covered by Chapter 38. [¶] The trial court did not abuse its discretion in deciding to award attorney's fees and expert witness fees. However, we reverse and remand that portion of the judgment pertaining to the amount of those fees so that the trial court might determine and set apart the amount of such fees."

Hirczy v. Hirczy, 838 S.W.2d 783, 786 (Tex.App.—Corpus Christi 1992, writ denied). "The trial court has discretion to tax reasonable attorney's fees as costs in divorce cases, if the awarded party pleaded for them, the parties tried the issue by consent, or the losing party waived the issue."

Mattox v. Buentello, 800 S.W.2d 320, 328 (Tex. App.—Corpus Christi 1990, no writ). "In a suit for divorce, the court may award costs, including attorney's fees, to any party as it deems reasonable. Before the court can award attorney's fees in a divorce action, however, the existence of a marriage relationship must be proven."

In re Marriage of Parr, 543 S.W.2d 433, 435 (Tex. App.—Corpus Christi 1976, no writ). "A husband may be liable for the attorney's fees of the wife when the suit is dismissed and no final decree of divorce is awarded. Under §3.65 [now §6.708] a divorce court may award costs to any party as it deems reasonable. ... [I]n situations where there is no reconciliation between the parties but the divorce is dismissed for some other reason ..., it is entirely proper for the trial court to award reasonable attorney's fees against the husband concurrent with its dismissal of the suit."

Currie v. Currie, 518 S.W.2d 386, 391 (Tex.App.—San Antonio 1974, writ dism'd). "There is no statutory authority under which a party may recover her expenses for witness fees unless same be incident to attorney's fees.'"

FAM §6.709. TEMPORARY ORDERS DURING APPEAL

(a) Not later than the 30th day after the date an appeal is perfected, on the motion of a party or on the court's own motion, after notice and hearing, the trial court may render a temporary order necessary for the preservation of the property and for the protection of the parties during the appeal, including an order to:

(1) require the support of either spouse;

(2) require the payment of reasonable attorney's fees and expenses;

(3) appoint a receiver for the preservation and protection of the property of the parties; or

(4) award one spouse exclusive occupancy of the parties' residence pending the appeal.

(b) The trial court retains jurisdiction to enforce a temporary order under this section unless the appellate court, on a proper showing, supersedes the trial court's order.

History of Fam §6.709: Acts 1997, 75th Leg., ch. 7, §1, eff. April 17, 1997. Source: Former Fam §3.58(h), (i).

McAlister v. McAlister, ___ S.W.3d ___ (Tex. App.—San Antonio 2002, n.p.h.) (No. 04-00-00604-CV; 1-16-02). Although husband argues that §6.709 "does not afford the court authority to make such orders retroactive to the date of the decree, we find no such limitation in the Code. Such an interpretation could hamstring both the court and the appellant during the time of post-decree hearings and the appeal thereby abrogating the legislature's intent to maintain the status quo and provide for spousal and child support, as necessary, during the appeal. We find that the trial court has the authority under §6.709 to issue post-judgment temporary orders retroactive to the decree. We further find that where such orders are in place, the acceptance of the benefits doctrine does not apply.

In re Boyd, 34 S.W.3d 708, 710-11 (Tex.App.—Fort Worth 2000, orig. proceeding). "The clear intent of [§6.709] is to extend the power of the trial court to enter temporary orders after an appeal has been perfected to preserve the community property and protect the parties, when such relief has not been ordered in the original decree. As the statute's language expressly states, however, the time within which the trial court must act is 'the 30th day after the date an appeal is perfected.'"

Herschberg v. Herschberg, 994 S.W.2d 273, 277 (Tex.App.—Corpus Christi 1999, no pet.). "[T]he majority of the courts of appeals to examine whether a spouse is entitled to temporary support on appeal under [Fam. Code] §3.58(h) [now §6.709], have concluded that it is irrelevant that neither spouse has challenged the underlying divorce and that the property division is the only issue on appeal." *See* ***In re Marriage of Joiner***, 755 S.W.2d 496, 499 (Tex.App.—Amarillo 1988, no writ); ***Eikenhorst v. Eikenhorst***, 746 S.W.2d 882, 891 (Tex.App.—Houston [1st Dist.] 1988, no writ). *But see* ***Grossnickle v. Grossnickle***, 935 S.W.2d 830, 848 (Tex.App.—Texarkana 1996, writ denied) (temporary spousal support not permitted if neither party appeals the divorce itself).

Ex parte Oliver, 736 S.W.2d 277, 279 (Tex.App.—Fort Worth 1987, orig. proceeding). "[T]he purpose of the adoption of §3.58(h) [now §6.709] was to extend the authority of the trial court to order support after an appeal had been perfected, when such support had not been ordered in the original decree. We find no indication that the section was intended to deprive the trial court of its recognized authority to order, in the divorce decree, temporary support pending appeal."

FAM §6.710. COPY OF DECREE

The clerk of the court shall mail a copy of the final decree of dissolution of a marriage to the party who waived service of process under Section 6.4035 by mailing the copy of the decree to the party at the mailing address contained in the waiver or to the office of the party's attorney of record.

History of Fam §6.710: Acts 1997, 75th Leg., ch. 614, §2, eff. Sept. 1, 1997.

FAM §6.711. FINDINGS OF FACT & CONCLUSIONS OF LAW

E *Section 6.711 below is effective for suits for dissolution of marriage pending on or filed on or after Sept. 1, 2001.*

(a) In a suit for dissolution of a marriage in which the court has rendered a judgment dividing the estate of the parties, on request by a party, the court shall state in writing its findings of fact and conclusions of law concerning:

(1) the characterization of each party's assets, liabilities, claims, and offsets on which disputed evidence has been presented; and

(2) the value or amount of the community estate's assets, liabilities, claims, and offsets on which disputed evidence has been presented.

(b) A request for findings of fact and conclusions of law under this section must conform to the Texas Rules of Civil Procedure.

History of Fam §6.711: Enacted by Acts 2001, 77th Leg., ch. 297, §1, eff. Sept. 1, 2001.

Sections 6.712-6.800 reserved for expansion

SUBCHAPTER I. REMARRIAGE

FAM §6.801. REMARRIAGE

(a) Except as otherwise provided by this subchapter, neither party to a divorce may marry a third party before the 31st day after the date the divorce is decreed.

(b) The former spouses may marry each other at any time.

History of Fam §6.801: Acts 1997, 75th Leg., ch. 7, §1, eff. April 17, 1997. Source: Former Fam §3.66(a), (b).

Herschberg v. Herschberg, 994 S.W.2d 273, 276-77 (Tex.App.—Corpus Christi 1999, no pet.). "We agree with [ex-husband] that the parties are actually divorced as of the date that the trial judge orally pronounces them divorced from the bench, absent some challenge to that decree on appeal. Thirty days after that decree, they are each then free to remarry someone else. [¶] Therefore, although the division of the community estate may be reversed and remanded on appeal, the marital status of the parties is not extended beyond the date of the original decree of divorce, and the nature and extent of their community property is fixed as of that date. A remand merely for division of the property ... does not prolong the marriage relationship until the decree is final after the remand."

Galbraith v. Galbraith, 619 S.W.2d 238, 240 (Tex. App.—Texarkana 1981, no writ). "Appellant's first two points of error urge that the undisputed evidence established that appellee's marriage to him prior to the expiration of the 30-day waiting period prescribed by §3.66 [now §6.801] constituted an impediment to their marriage which rendered it voidable and subject to annulment. These points are overruled. The evidence shows, and the trial court here found as a fact, that a non-interlocutory oral pronouncement of a judgment of divorce was made by the trial court in appellee's divorce on March 12, 1976, more than 30 days prior to her marriage to appellant. Although the written decree was not signed until March 24, 1976, the divorce was fully effective for all purposes, except calculation of the times for appeal, at the time it was pronounced from the bench."

FAM §6.802. WAIVER OF PROHIBITION AGAINST REMARRIAGE

For good cause shown the court may waive the prohibition against remarriage provided by this subchapter as to either or both spouses if a record of the proceedings is made and preserved or if findings of fact and conclusions of law are filed by the court.

History of Fam §6.802: Acts 1997, 75th Leg., ch. 7, §1, eff. April 17, 1997. Source: Former Fam §3.66(c).

CHAPTER 7. AWARD OF MARITAL PROPERTY

FAM §7.001. GENERAL RULE OF PROPERTY DIVISION

In a decree of divorce or annulment, the court shall order a division of the estate of the parties in a manner that the court deems just and right, having due regard for the rights of each party and any children of the marriage.

History of Fam §7.001: Acts 1997, 75th Leg., ch. 7, §1, eff. April 17, 1997. Source: Former Fam §3.63(a).

Generally

Dawson-Austin v. Austin, 968 S.W.2d 319, 324 (Tex.1998). "It is well settled in this State that the division of a marital estate is not a claim severable from the rest of a divorce proceeding. [¶] The cases that hold adjudication of divorce and division of the marital estate to be non-severable claims all do so in the context of Rules 41 (Misjoinder and Non-Joinder of Parties), 174 (Consolidation; Separate Trials), and 320 (Motion [for New Trial] and Action of Court Thereon). [¶] No case holds that claims of divorce and division of property do not involve severable *jurisdictional* issues. The United States Supreme Court recognized long ago that a court could have jurisdiction to grant a divorce—an adjudication of parties' status—without having jurisdiction to divide their property—an adjudication of parties' rights."

In re Edwards, ___ S.W.3d ___ (Tex.App.—Texarkana 2002, n.p.h.) (No. 06-00-00130-CV; 4-11-02). Section 7.001 "gives the trial court broad authority to divide the marital estate in a manner it deems just and right. That authority sometimes includes the power to appoint a receiver. The appointment of a receiver is left to the trial court's sound discretion. [¶] 'In recognition of the fact that appointment of a receiver without notice is one of the most drastic actions known to law or equity and should be exercised with extreme caution and only where great emergency or imperative necessity requires it, our courts have uniformly been reluctant to grant such harsh relief.' Judicial seizure and court management of any asset should be a last resort. [¶] It appears from the record before this court the trial court's practice is to appoint a receiver when the parties cannot reach an agreement on the division of property. Such a practice constitutes an abuse of discretion insofar as it does not ... determine what can be partitioned in kind between the parties and, if necessary to achieve a just and right division, appoint a receiver to dispose of the remainder."

Workings v. Workings, 700 S.W.2d 251, 253 (Tex. App.—Dallas 1985, no writ). "[B]ecause of the trial court's duty under §3.63 [now §7.001] to divide the estate of the parties in a divorce action, the trial court may construe the pleadings pertaining to the division of property more liberally than in other civil cases. Thus, a prayer for general relief, at least in the absence of a special exception, entitles a petitioner in a divorce action to 'her proven rights, insofar as the laws of this state entitled the court to award them.'"

Rodriguez v. Rodriguez, 616 S.W.2d 383, 384 (Tex.App.—Houston [14th Dist.] 1981, no writ). "[W]here a divorce suit is submitted to the jury, the verdict as to dividing the estate of the spouses is advisory only and trial court may in its discretion disregard jury findings and divide the property in such manner as seems just and right under facts as they appear to the court."

In re Marriage of Johnson, 595 S.W.2d 900, 902 (Tex.App.—Amarillo 1980, writ dism'd). "In divorce cases, a decree failing to dispose of the property of the parties is interlocutory and, thus, not appealable. It is immaterial whether the trial court reserved the property issues for future determination or served them and purported to enter a final judgment on other issues. The judgment remains interlocutory...."

"Estate of the Parties"

Cameron v. Cameron, 641 S.W.2d 210, 213 (Tex. 1982). Section 3.63, now §7.001, "does not provide authority for the transmutation of one spouse's separate property into the other spouse's separate property. Allowing a trial court to divest separate property from one spouse and award it to the other spouse as part of the latter's separate estate would impermissibly enlarge the exclusive constitutional definition of separate property. [¶] [T]he statutory construction of §3.63 ... does not imbue our courts with the authority to divest separate property."

Wilkerson v. Wilkerson, 992 S.W.2d 719, 722 (Tex. App.—Austin 1999, no pet.). "Section 7.001 ... provides that a divorce decree 'shall order a division of the estate of the parties in a manner that the court deems just and right.' The 'estate of the parties' has been construed to mean only the parties' community property." *See also* ***Siefkas v. Siefkas***, 902 S.W.2d 72, 77 (Tex. App.—El Paso 1995, no writ).

Factors—Generally

Murff v. Murff, 615 S.W.2d 696, 699 (Tex.1981). "[T]he trial court may consider such factors as the spouses' capacities and abilities, benefits which the party not at fault would have derived from continuation of the marriage, business opportunities, education, relative physical conditions, relative financial condition and obligations, disparity of ages, size of separate estates, and the nature of the property. We believe that the consideration of such factors by the trial court is proper in making a 'just and right' division of the property. Likewise, the consideration of a disparity in earning capacities or of incomes is proper and need not be limited by 'necessitous' circumstances."

Young v. Young, 609 S.W.2d 758, 760 (Tex.1980). "Section 3.63 [now §7.001] specifically authorizes the trial court to have 'due regard for the rights of each party and any children of the marriage' in the just and right division of the estate of the parties. [Respondent] contends that his son's support is a 'need' and not a 'right' and hence should not be considered in the property division. We hold that an unmarried disabled adult child's right to support corresponds to his parents' duty to support and is entitled to recognition under §3.63."

Walker v. Walker, 527 S.W.2d 200, 203 (Tex.App.—Fort Worth 1975, no writ). "[D]ivision of the property must take into consideration all the equities, the nature of the property, the debts secured by liens on property awarded to each, the liabilities, and the ability of the parties to manage the property that is encumbered in order that the property will not be lost to both spouses by foreclosure. Such division must be done in subordination to the rights of creditors."

Waggener v. Waggener, 460 S.W.2d 251, 253 (Tex. App.—Dallas 1970, no writ). "The points of inquiry upon which evidence should be accepted and tested by a trial court in making its decision as to equitable division of the property to be divided ... include (1) the nature of the property; (2) the relative rights of the parties and the children; (3) the condition of the parties and their ability to make a living; (4) the earning power, business opportunities, capacities, and abilities of the parties; and (5) the benefit which a spouse not at fault would have derived from the estate of the other spouse through a continuance of the marriage."

Factors—Alimony

Benedict v. Benedict, 542 S.W.2d 692, 699 (Tex. App.—Fort Worth 1976, writ dism'd). "Essentially the law is that the courts are not authorized to decree an award of permanent alimony for the support of the divorced wife because to do so would be to contradict the public policy of the state; however, an award is not alimony ... where in the property settlement provisions of a divorce decree one of the parties is required to make payments to the other after the divorce and the payments are *referable to any property that either spouse may have owned or claimed at time of the decree* which is part of the existing property which the court apportions."

Garrett v. Garrett, 534 S.W.2d 381, 382 (Tex. App.—Houston [1st Dist.] 1976, no writ). "The trial court may require one party to make monetary payments to the other party after divorce, and such payments are not construed to be in the nature of permanent alimony if they are referable to any property which either spouse may have owned or claimed. ... 'So long as the division was referable to the rights and equities of the parties in and to the properties at the time of dissolution of the marriage, such division should not be regarded as an allowance of permanent alimony....'"

Factors—Attorney Fees

Carle v. Carle, 234 S.W.2d 1002, 1005 (Tex.1950). "The attorney's fee is but a factor to be considered by the court in making an equitable division of the estate, considering the conditions and needs of the parties and all of the surrounding circumstances."

Grossnickle v. Grossnickle, 935 S.W.2d 830, 846-47 (Tex.App.—Texarkana 1996, writ denied). "The trial court has great discretion in deciding whether to award attorney's fees to either party and in determining the amount of attorney's fees to be so awarded. This same principle applies to whether the trial court should consider a party's payment of attorney's fees out of community funds in the division of the property. Because the award of attorney's fees in a divorce case can be part of the property division, the trial court can award them to either party, regardless who is successful in the trial court or on appeal. [¶] The allocation of attorney's fees is a factor to be considered by the court in making an equitable division of the community estate. Prior payments out of the community estate to attorneys in the divorce action are likewise to be taken into account in the division of the marital estate. Those payments must necessarily come from the community, because the trial court has no authority to direct one party to expend separate property funds on the other's behalf for such fees, because the sole authority of a trial court to require payment of attorney's fees lies in the court's authority to divide the marital estate."

Factors—Fault

Young v. Young, 609 S.W.2d 758, 762 (Tex.1980). "Both the Legislature and the courts have traditionally considered [cruelty, adultery, and desertion] to be 'fault.' In this situation, we agree with the trial court that fault may be a consideration to be weighed in the division of property. This does not mean that fault must be considered in all cases where a divorce is granted on fault grounds. Our holding is that it may be considered."

Phillips v. Phillips, ___ S.W.3d ___ (Tex.App.—Beaumont 2002, n.p.h.) (No. 09-01-346-CV; 5-2-02). "[W]hen dissolution of marriage is sought solely on the ground of insupportability, evidence of 'fault' becomes irrelevant as an analytical construct and may not be considered by the trial court in its 'just and right' division of the community estate."

Factors—Reimbursement

Schlueter v. Schlueter, 975 S.W.2d 584, 589 (Tex. 1998). "Trial courts also have wide discretion and are allowed to take many factors into consideration in making a just and right division, including wasting of community assets. This too allows injured spouses ... to recover her appropriate share of not only that property existing in the community at the time of divorce, but also that which was improperly depleted from the community estate."

Horlock v. Horlock, 533 S.W.2d 52, 60-61 (Tex. App.—Houston [14th Dist.] 1975, writ dism'd). "The right of reimbursement is an equitable right. It may be considered by the trial court in the division of the properties of the parties. ... The debt structure of the assets of the parties and the necessity of the renegotiation of numerous short term debts by the husband, as well as the extensive contingent liability imposed upon the husband, are equities to be considered by the trial court in dividing the parties' properties. In exercising its equitable powers, the court may consider the fact that the parties' estate primarily consists of equitable interests in real property, much of which is unimproved, and the fact that the prevailing economic conditions constitute a threat to the community estate as an entirety."

Factors—Tax Liability

Grossnickle v. Grossnickle, 935 S.W.2d 830, 847-48 (Tex.App.—Texarkana 1996, writ denied). "A trial court can appropriately consider the tax liability for the sale of capital assets that *has been realized* by the parties at the time of the divorce, *i.e.*, existing tax liabilities. However, where the question of future taxation arises, a trial court errs in allowing a credit for a future tax figure that must be derived from speculation or surmise. ... The tax rate would depend upon the tax bracket of the taxpayer at that time and also the income tax law in effect at that time. This approach would be analogous to allowing a discounted value on every piece of property because there might be future tax consequences if sold at a profit. The trial court did not abuse its discretion by failing to consider potential tax liability which might be incurred when the assets are withdrawn."

Baccus v. Baccus, 808 S.W.2d 694, 700 (Tex.App.—Beaumont 1991, no writ). "[T]ax consequences stemming from the division of property as well as any unpaid tax liabilities are proper factors to be considered by the trial court in deriving at a fair and just division of the community properties. Furthermore, it is reversible error for a court to refuse to consider tax liability, particularly when it is substantial and one of the spouses is without means to pay the obligation."

Able v. Able, 725 S.W.2d 778, 780 (Tex.App.—Houston [14th Dist.] 1987, writ ref'd n.r.e.). "While a tax is technically not a debt and a court has no power to relieve either party of personal liability to the taxing authority, in dividing property between spouses a court may take the tax liability into consideration and may even require one party to assume the other's liability or require reimbursement for taxes paid."

Factors—Torts

Schlueter v. Schlueter, 975 S.W.2d 584, 585 (Tex.1998). "Because a wronged spouse has an adequate remedy for fraud on the community through the 'just and right' property division upon divorce, we hold that there is no independent tort cause of action between spouses for damages to the community estate."

Twyman v. Twyman, 855 S.W.2d 619, 625 (Tex. 1993). "[A] spouse should not be allowed to recover tort damages and a disproportionate division of the community estate based on the same conduct. Therefore, when a factfinder awards tort damages to a divorcing spouse, the court may not consider the same tortious acts when dividing the marital estate. [A]n award for tortious conduct does not replace an analysis of the remaining factors to be considered when the trial court divides the marital estate. The court may still award a disproportionate division of property for reasons other than the tortious conduct. To avoid the potential problem of double recovery, the factfinder should consider the damages awarded in the tort action when dividing the parties' property. If a jury is used to render an advisory division of the parties' estate, the judge should limit, by appropriate instruction, the jury's consideration of the alleged tortious acts and later consider the award of damages in determining a just and right division of the marital estate."

Failure to Divide

Phillips v. Phillips, 951 S.W.2d 955, 957 (Tex. App.—Waco 1997, no pet.). "[W]here ... a divorce decree fails to provide for a division of community property, the husband and wife become tenants-in-common or joint owners thereof."

In re Marriage of Johnson, 595 S.W.2d 900, 902 (Tex.App.—Amarillo 1980, writ dism'd). "In divorce cases, a decree failing to dispose of the property of the parties is interlocutory and, thus, not appealable. It is immaterial whether the trial court reserved the property issues for future determination or served them and purported to enter a final judgment on other issues. The judgment remains interlocutory...."

Mischaracterization

Tate v. Tate, 51 S.W.3d 1 (Tex.App.—El Paso 2000, no pet.). "If property is mischaracterized and the mischaracterization affects the just and right division of the community estate, we must remand the entire community division. If the mischaracterization has a *de minimus* effect on the division, then there has been no showing of an abuse of discretion. It is only when the court mistakenly characterizes property that is of such magnitude that it materially affects the just and right division of the community estate that reversible error is demonstrated."

Butler v. Butler, 975 S.W.2d 765, 767 (Tex. App.—Corpus Christi 1998, no pet.). "The trial court's mischaracterization of property will require a reversal only if we determine that the division of the property made was, because of the legal error upon which it was based, so unfair as to constitute an abuse of discretion. In other words, [husband] must show that, due to the trial court's legal error, the division of the property was so disproportionate as to be manifestly unfair. Furthermore, [husband] must show that the trial court would have probably made a different division of the property if it had been properly characterized."

Partition in Kind

Hailey v. Hailey, 331 S.W.2d 299, 302-03 (Tex. 1960). "[T]he statute puts the duty on the trial court to make a partition of the community property whenever the pleadings of either party show the existence of such property. The trial court shall consider all the facts and circumstances shown by the evidence and then partition the community property, both personal and real estate, in such manner as may be just and right. ... The trial court has the duty to determine if the community property is subject to partition in kind. If he determines that it is then he shall equitably divide the community property between the parties. If it is not subject to partition in kind the trial court can appoint a receiver and order so much of the property as is incapable of partition to be sold and the proceeds divided between the parties in such portions as, in the discretion of the court, may be a just, fair and equitable partition, having in mind the rights of the parties and the children."

Cecola v. Ruley, 12 S.W.3d 848, 853 (Tex.App.—Texarkana 2000, no pet.). "Whether a piece of land can fairly be partitioned in kind is a question of fact for the court or jury to decide. The law favors partition in kind over partition by sale. Therefore, at trial the burden of proof falls on the party opposing partitioning in kind and seeking a partition by sale. *At 855:* If the property can be divided in kind without materially impairing its value, a sale will not be ordered, but when dividing the land into parcels causes its value to be substantially less than its value when whole, the rights of the owners are substantially prejudiced. Substantial economic loss is one of the significant factors that would warrant a sale in lieu of a partition in kind. ... [T]he trial court expressed a concern as to whether the property could be divided into parts of equal value. This is a proper concern and another significant factor in determining whether a partition could be fair and equitable, but even if the two parts are divided into equal value, if the value as a part of the larger tract has been greatly diminished, this also should be considered in determining whether or not a division in kind would be fair and equitable."

Walston v. Walston, 971 S.W.2d 687, 692-93 (Tex. App.—Waco 1998, pet. denied). "In determining if property is subject to division in kind the trial court should consider the 'nature and type of particular property involved and the relative conditions, circumstances, capabilities and experience of the parties.' These factors are also considered when the trial court must decide whether to divide community property by awarding a money judgment to one party and community assets to the other party, instead of dividing the community property in kind. Moreover, §3.63 [now §7.001] authorizes the trial court to appoint a receiver for selling property as necessary to carry out the trial court's orders and judgments."

Simpson v. Simpson, 727 S.W.2d 662, 663 (Tex. App.—Dallas 1987, no writ). "The award of a money judgment is one manner and method of dividing property in a divorce proceeding."

Valuation

Grossnickle v. Grossnickle, 935 S.W.2d 830, 842 (Tex.App.—Texarkana 1996, writ denied). "[W]hether an appraisal is near enough in time to the date of the divorce to be considered in determining the value of the property in question for purpose of the property division is generally left to the discretion of the trial court."

Parker v. Parker, 897 S.W.2d 918, 932 (Tex.App.—Fort Worth 1995, writ denied), *overruled on other grounds*, ***Formosa Plastics Corp. v. Presidio Eng'rs & Contractors, Inc.***, 960 S.W.2d 41 (Tex.1998). "[W]e hold the determination of whether to use the time of the divorce or the time of the division as the valuation date of an asset when the divorce and division of the property occur at different dates is in fact so specific that it should be left to the discretion of the trial judge to avoid the inequities that could result by making a bright line rule."

Martin v. Martin, 797 S.W.2d 347, 351 (Tex.App.—Texarkana 1990, no writ). "A division of property based on values that were not in evidence is an abuse of discretion."

Archambault v. Archambault, 763 S.W.2d 50, 51 (Tex.App.—Beaumont 1988, no writ). "If the trial court treated the jury's findings of market value as advisory, this was error. ... A jury's determination of value is binding upon the trial court."

Finn v. Finn, 658 S.W.2d 735, 746 (Tex.App.—Dallas 1983, writ ref'd n.r.e.). "We find that the denial of discovery was such a denial of the rights of the wife as was reasonably calculated to cause and probably did cause the rendition of an improper judgment. The husband's interest in the firm was a major asset of the community estate. Lack of this discovery left the trial court's valuation of this asset without proper support in the evidence. Since this interest is the largest item of the community estate, and its value was the principal contested issue at the trial with respect to the division of the property of the parties, we conclude that without a proper valuation the trial court could not properly exercise its discretion in making a 'just and right' division within §3.63 [now §7.001]."

Standard of Review

Evans v. Evans, 14 S.W.3d 343, 345-46 (Tex.App.—Houston [14th Dist.] 2000, no pet.). "To disturb a trial court's division of property..., the appellant must show the trial court clearly abused its discretion by a division ... that is manifestly unjust and unfair. In making this determination, we look to whether the trial court acted arbitrarily or unreasonably, without reference to any guiding rules and principles. Our analysis focuses on a two-pronged inquiry: *(1) Did the trial court have sufficient information upon which to exercise its discretion?;* and *(2) Did the trial court abuse its discretion by causing the property division ... to be manifestly unjust or unfair?* A trial court abuses its discretion when it rules without supporting evidence."

Robles v. Robles, 965 S.W.2d 605, 621 (Tex.App.—Houston [1st Dist.] 1998, pet. denied). "The role of an appellate court is only to determine whether the trial court abused its discretion in its disposition of the community property and an appellate court does not have the authority to render judgment dividing the marital property. We presume the trial court exercised its discretion properly."

A FAM §7.002. DIVISION OF PROPERTY UNDER SPECIAL CIRCUMSTANCES

In addition to the division of the estate of the parties required by Section 7.001, in a decree of divorce or annulment the court shall order a division of the following real and personal property, wherever situated, in a manner that the court deems just and right, having due regard for the rights of each party and any children of the marriage:

(1) property that was acquired by either spouse while domiciled in another state and that would have been community property if the spouse who acquired the property had been domiciled in this state at the time of the acquisition; or

(2) property that was acquired by either spouse in exchange for real or personal property and that would have been community property if the spouse who acquired the property so exchanged had been domiciled in this state at the time of its acquisition.

History of Fam §7.002: Acts 1997, 75th Leg., ch. 7, §1, eff. April 17, 1997. Amended by Acts 1999, 76th Leg., ch. 692, §4, eff. Sept. 1, 1999; Acts 2001, 77th Leg., ch. 838, §4, eff. Sept. 1, 2001. Source: Former Fam §3.63(b).

Cayan v. Cayan, 38 S.W.3d 161, 164 (Tex.App.—Houston [14th Dist.] 2000, pet. denied). "In a final decree of divorce, a trial court is generally required to order a division of the community and quasi-community property that the court deems 'just and right.'"

Dawson-Austin v. Austin, 920 S.W.2d 776, 789-90 (Tex.App.—Dallas 1996), *rev'd on other grounds*, 968 S.W.2d 319 (Tex.1998). "Husband asserts that §3.63(b) [now §7.002] operates as a comprehensive choice-of-law provision in property characterization issues. He argues that §3.63(b)(1) should be read as providing that the characterization of property is dependent solely on Texas law. Under Husband's interpretation of §3.63(b), if property is characterized as community property in the residential state of the acquiring party but would have been separate property if the parties had resided in Texas, then in a divorce proceeding in a Texas court, the property will be classified as separate property. [¶] We disagree with Husband's sweeping interpretation of §3.63(b). The statute by its terms acts only *to expand, not restrict, the definition of community property*. Nothing in the legislative history of the statute or the development of the law in this area suggests that §3.63(b) was intended to expand the definition of separate property and thus restrict the extent of community property. Even the popular name for the statute, the 'quasi-community' statute, suggests that it is intended to expand the definition of community property. If the legislature had intended for the statute to be a comprehensive choice-of-law provision, it would not have phrased the statute as an expanded definition of community property."

Ismail v. Ismail, 702 S.W.2d 216, 219 (Tex.App.—Houston [1st Dist.] 1985, writ ref'd n.r.e.). "The quasi-community property statute does not expressly limit its reach to situations where *both* spouses have migrated from a common law jurisdiction to Texas. [¶] We conclude that §3.63(b) [now §7.002] applies in the division of migratory spouses' property regardless of the nature of the previous domicile's legal system. [¶] The [husband] also argues that the statute should not be applied where only one spouse migrates to Texas. *At 221:* The real property that is the subject of this appeal is located in Texas. Texas follows the general rule that marital rights of spouses in real property are determined by the law of the place where the land is situated. Additionally, the [husband] ... has had other significant continuous business and personal contacts with Texas.... Thus, from a due process perspective, [husband's] contacts with Texas, when coupled with Texas' interest in protecting the migrant spouse in this case, warrant application of Texas law to the division of the Texas property. [¶] Also, we should not interpret the language of ***Cameron*** [***v. Cameron***, 641 S.W.2d (Tex. 1982)] to hold that in *every* case where a party receives less in the Texas community property division than he or she would have received under the system of the previous domicile, the party has been deprived of due process. Clearly, where the Texas division of property approximates what another domicile's law requires, the non-migrant spouse may not complain of divestment of 'separate' property. But neither can the appellant in this case complain of an unconstitutional divestment of 'separate' property under our state's constitution when, through his extensive contacts with this state, and through his personal appearance in this litigation, he has implicitly consented to Texas courts' exercising their jurisdiction in equitably dividing the marital property. *At 222:* In his second point of error, the [husband] argues that the trial court erred in deciding this case under Texas law.... Property acquired by a spouse when domiciled in another jurisdiction was, under pre-***Cameron*** common law, characterized according to the previous domicile's laws. [¶] The enactment of §3.63(b), however, obviates the need to apply this anachronistic conflict-of-laws principle."

FAM §7.003. DISPOSITION OF RETIREMENT & EMPLOYMENT BENEFITS & OTHER PLANS

In a decree of divorce or annulment, the court shall determine the rights of both spouses in a pension, retirement plan, annuity, individual retirement account, employee stock option plan, stock option, or other form of savings, bonus, profit-sharing, or other employer plan or financial plan of an employee or a participant, regardless of whether the person is self-employed, in the nature of compensation or savings.

History of Fam §7.003: Acts 1997, 75th Leg., ch. 7, §1, eff. April 17, 1997. Source: Former Fam §3.633(a).

Generally

Boggs v. Boggs, 520 U.S. 833, 835-36 117 S.Ct. 1754, 1758 (1997). "We consider whether the [ERISA] pre-empts a state law allowing a nonparticipant spouse to transfer by testamentary instrument an interest in undistributed pension plan benefits. Given the pervasive significance of pension plans in the national economy, the congressional mandate for their uniform and comprehensive regulation, and the fundamental importance of community property law in defining the marital partnership in a number of States, the question is of undoubted importance. We hold ERISA pre-empts the state law."

Cearley v. Cearley, 544 S.W.2d 661, 662 (Tex.1976). "Despite an earlier view that retirement and pension plans were gifts bestowed by benevolent employers on retiring employees, they are now regarded as a mode of employee compensation earned during a given period of employment. [¶] It is now well established that matured private retirement, annuity, and pension benefits earned by either spouse during the marital relationship are part of the community estate and thus subject to division upon dissolution of the marriage."

McClary v. Thompson, 65 S.W.3d 829, 836 (Tex. App.—Fort Worth 2002, pet. denied). Although we agree with ***Dewey v. Dewey***, 745 S.W.2d 514 (Tex.App.—Corpus Christi 1988, writ denied) "that the inception-of-title rule has no application in the context of retirement benefits, the fact is that whether we characterize the Texas rule as one of apportionment or inception-of-title, the result is the same, i.e., apportionment. Therefore, we reject [wife]'s argument that the character of the entire retirement account must be determined based on the inception-of-title rule. We conclude that, under either theory, the contributions and interest earned during the marriage constituted community property."

In re Marriage of Reinauer, 946 S.W.2d 853, 857 (Tex.App.—Amarillo 1997, writ denied). "[R]etirement pay ... connotes an earned property right that accrued by reason of years of service or deferred compensation earned during each month of service. In other words, the payment must, at the very least, be a form of compensation accruing to the individual due to his years of service with the employer. Discretionary payments made for purposes other than as compensation earned during an employee's tenure do not satisfy these criteria and, thus, are not retirement pay or benefits. Nor do mere gratuities or gifts from one's employer satisfy the requisite criteria."

Sutherland v. Cobern, 843 S.W.2d 127, 131 (Tex. App.—Texarkana 1992, writ denied). "Generally, the value of community assets, such as retirement benefits, are to be evaluated at the time of divorce, and subsequent increases in value are separate property. Cost of living increases, however, are not the result of any post-divorce labor, but rather a means of offsetting the otherwise declining value of retirement benefits after they become fixed. Ordinarily, post-divorce cost of living increases in military retirement pay are rights accrued along with the retirement benefits during marriage and, thus, are community property subject to division."

Dividing Defined Benefits Plans

Berry v. Berry, 647 S.W.2d 945, 946 (Tex.1983). "***Taggart*** only held that the divorced wife 'owned as her part of the community estate a share in the contingent right to military benefits even though that right had not matured at the time of the divorce.' ... We did not, however, determine whether the community's interest in retirement benefits should be valued as of the date of divorce, as opposed to the time the benefits were actually received. *At 947:* Retirement and pension benefits are a mode of employee compensation. It is clear from the record in this case that twelve additional years of work following divorce, which included some twelve to fourteen pay raises, plus union contract negotiations for an improved benefits plan, brought about the increase in retirement benefits paid to [husband]. These post-divorce increases cannot be awarded to [wife], for to do so would invade [husband's] separate property, which cannot be done. [¶] We are not to be understood as overruling ***Taggart v. Taggart*** or disapproving of its progeny insofar as those opinions approve an apportionment formula for determining the *extent* of the community interest in retirement benefits. When the value of such benefits is in issue, however, the benefits are to be apportioned to the spouses based upon the value of the community's interest at the time of divorce."

Taggart v. Taggart, 552 S.W.2d 422, 423 (Tex. 1977). "[R]etirement benefits are subject to division as vested contingent community property rights even though the present right has not fully matured. [¶] [W]e hold that [wife] owned as her part of the community estate a share in the contingent right to military benefits even though that right had not matured at the time of the divorce. It appears, however, that the trial court did not make the correct computation of her fractional interest. *At 424:* The trial court computed [wife's] one-half interest in [husband's] retirement benefits upon the basis of his twenty years of service as a member of the regular Navy. At the end of the twenty years, he was not entitled to receive any retirement benefits based upon his term of service, because he had to serve in the Fleet Reserve for an additional ten years. It was, therefore, his three hundred and sixty months of service that entitled him to the retirement benefits. According to the undisputed evidence, [the couple's] marriage coincided with his service in the Navy for a period of two hundred and forty-six months. The correct computation of [wife's] vested interest is that she was entitled only to one-half of 246/360th's of the retirement pay."

Limbaugh v. Limbaugh, 71 S.W.3d 1, 16 n.12 (Tex. App.—Houston [1st Dist.] 2002, n.p.h.). "Under ***Taggart***, the community interest in a fully matured retirement plan is calculated by dividing the number of months the parties were married during the employee spouse's employment by the total number of months of service of the employee spouse. The resulting percentage represents the community estate's interest in the retirement benefits. ***Berry*** applies in those cases where the employee spouse's service will continue after the divorce. In this situation, the community interest is determined as of the time of divorce. The ***Berry*** formula prevents a divorce court from awarding the non-employee spouse any portion of a post-divorce increase in retirement attributable to raises, promotions, services rendered or contributions as such an increase would be the employee spouse's separate property. Conversely, a divorce court may award the non-employee spouse her respective share of any post-divorce cost-of-living increase in the retirement benefit."

Albrecht v. Albrecht, 974 S.W.2d 262, 263-64 (Tex. App.—San Antonio 1998, no pet.). "The formulas for apportioning retirement benefits differ depending on whether the value of the pension plan is at issue. The formula used when the value of the pension plan *is not in issue* was set out in ***Taggart*** as follows:

½ × ((# years of service while married) ÷ (# years of service at retirement)) × value of accrued benefit at date of retirement = non-employee spouse's share

This formula is called the ***Taggart*** formula. The formula was used by the Supreme Court of Texas to determine the non-employee spouse's community interest in military retirement benefits. [¶] When the value of the plan *is in issue*, the following formula is used:

½ × ((# years married under pension plan) ÷ (# years employed under plan as of date of divorce)) × value of plan on date of divorce = non-employee spouse's share

This formula is called the ***Berry*** formula."

Dividing Defined Contribution Plans

Smith v. Smith, 22 S.W.3d 140, 148-49 (Tex.App.—Houston [14th Dist.] 2000, no pet.). Husband "argues on appeal that the trial court used the ***Berry/Taggart/Cearley*** method to allocate the community and separate portions of the stock ownership plan account and that this method was an incorrect application of the law. [Husband] argues that the ***Berry / Taggart / Cearley*** formula applies to a 'defined benefits' plan and is inapplicable to determine the community interest in 'defined contribution plans,' such as the plan here at issue. A defined benefit plan—such as the plans in ***Berry***, ***Taggart***, and ***Cearley***—promises employees a monthly benefit beginning at retirement. The benefit is based on the number of years of service the employee has at the time of retirement, along with other factors such as age and salary history. [¶] The proper value of a defined contribution plan, on the other hand, is not difficult to determine. An employee participating in a defined contribution has a separate account similar to a savings account into which the employee and employer make contributions. The value of this account can be readily ascertained at any time by simply looking at the account. Thus, in order to determine the community interest in a defined contribution plan, courts subtract the value of the plan at the time of marriage from the value of the plan at the time of divorce. [¶] We agree with [husband] that application the ***Berry/Taggart/Cearley*** formula would have been incorrect. The trial court should have determined the community formula by subtracting the account balance at marriage ... from the account balance at divorce ... to determine the community's portion, or that portion accumulated during marriage." *See also* ***Reiss v. Reiss***, 40 S.W.3d 605, 608 n.2 (Tex.App.—Houston [1st Dist.] 2001, pet. granted, argued 4-24-02); ***Pelzig v. Berkebile***, 931 S.W.2d 398, 402 (Tex. App.—Corpus Christi 1996, no writ).

Hatteberg v. Hatteberg, 933 S.W.2d 522, 530-31 (Tex.App.—Houston [1st Dist.] 1994, no writ). "An employee participating in a defined contribution plan has an individual account. Benefits are based solely on the contents of this account. The value of this account can be ascertained at any time before retirement simply by looking at the account. An employee in a defined benefit plan is promised a monthly benefit commencing at retirement. The benefit is calculated based on years of service, age of the employee, salary, and any other plan-specific factors. [¶] [Wife] argues that ***Berry*** is not applicable to this case because it applies only to defined benefit plans, and the plan at issue is a defined contribution plan. ... [Wife] argues that ... the proper calculation should be to subtract the value of the plan before marriage from the value of the plan upon divorce to find the community interest. [¶] We agree that ***Berry*** does not apply to this situation. ***Berry*** addresses only the apportionment of benefits, not contributions. The value of this plan is easily ascertained without resort to the ***Berry*** formula, which was developed in response to less readily ascertainable values of future benefits."

Military Retirement Benefits

Mansell v. Mansell, 490 U.S. 581, 588-89, 109 S.Ct. 2023, 2028-29 (1989). Section 1408(c)(1) of the Former Spouses' Protection Act "affirmatively grants state courts the power to divide military retirement pay, yet its language is both precise and limited. It provides that 'a court may treat disposable retired or retainer pay ... either as property solely of the member or as property of the member and his spouse in accordance with the law of the jurisdiction of such court.' The Act's definitional section specifically defines the term 'disposable retired or retainer pay' to exclude, *inter alia*, military retirement pay waived in order to receive veterans' disability payments. Thus, under the Act's plain and precise language, state courts have been granted the authority to treat disposable retired pay as community property; they have not been granted the authority to treat total retired pay as community property."

Havlen v. McDougall, 22 S.W.3d 343, 345 (Tex. 2000). "[I]n 1981, the United States Supreme Court [in ***McCarty v. McCarty***, 453 U.S. 210, 232, 101 S.Ct. 2728 (1981)] held that federal military pension law prohibited state courts from dividing military retirement benefits.... [¶] Congress reacted to ***McCarty*** by enacting legislation, [Uniformed Services Former Spouses Protection Act], that reversed ***McCarty***'s effect and once again allowed state courts to treat military retirement pay as marital property subject to division under state law. Congress set June 25, 1981, the day before the ***McCarty*** decision, to begin the period in which military retirement benefits could be divided under the new legislation. *At 346:* Subsequently, in 1990, Congress amended the Act to limit the power of state courts that were abusing the original act by reopening finalized divorces from the pre-***McCarty*** period. [¶] The sole question we consider today is whether a court may divide military benefits as community property in a former spouse's partition suit when a final divorce decree issued before June 25, 1981, did not divide or reserve jurisdiction to divide those benefits. We hold that it may not. [¶] [Wife] argues that the operation of Texas law, which converts an undivided asset such as military retirement pay into a tenancy in common, is sufficient to 'treat' [*i.e.*, divide] the asset for the Act's purposes. We disagree. *At 347:* The 1990 Amendment provides that the 'final decree' must treat or reserve jurisdiction to treat the military retirement benefits. ... The court of appeals did not consider that the Amendment expressly requires that *the decree* itself treat the asset. The Amendment does not provide any other way to treat an asset. Therefore, because the decree itself does not treat or reserve jurisdiction to treat the military benefits, they are not subject to subsequent partition."

Koepke v. Koepke, 732 S.W.2d 299, 299 (Tex. 1987). "The divorce decree was rendered after the decision in ***McCarty***..., but before the effective date of the Uniformed Services Former Spouses Protection Act [USFSPA], 10 U.S.C. §1408 (February 1, 1983). *At 300:* Since the enactment of USFSPA, we have approved partition as a means to remedy certain injustices caused by ***McCarty***. Partition, however, has been limited to those post-***McCarty*** divorce decrees which did not expressly award the military retirement benefits to the serviceman. The express award of retirement benefits in a divorce decree operates as a bar to any subsequent partition suit under principles of res judicata. [¶] The court of appeals in the present case attempts to [hold] that the following language constitutes an express award of the military retirement benefits: 'All relief requested in this case and not expressly granted herein be and is hereby denied.' To construe this language, the court of appeals looked behind the judgment to the pleadings of the former wife which purportedly sought part of the military retirement benefits. The court of appeals then deduced that the failure to award the former wife a share of the military retirement benefits must have been an award of such benefits to the former serviceman/husband because a judgment which incorporates the above language 'expressly disposes of all parties and issues in the case'.... [¶] The divorce decree does not expressly award the military retirement benefits to the former serviceman/husband. The court of appeals' application of the doctrine of res judicata to bar this partition suit is erroneous...."

Grier v. Grier, 731 S.W.2d 931, 932 (Tex.1987). "We hold that in apportioning military retirement benefits upon the dissolution of a marriage, the valuation of the community's interest in such benefits is to be based on the retirement pay which corresponds to the rank actually held by the service spouse on the date of the divorce."

Ex parte Johnson, 591 S.W.2d 453, 454 (Tex. 1979). "We hold that [disability compensation benefits from the Veterans' Administration for service-connected disabilities authorized by Title 38 of the United States Code] are not to be treated as 'property' and future benefits are not subject to division upon divorce as property."

Perez v. Perez, 587 S.W.2d 671, 672 (Tex.1979). Wife "asserts that [husband's] military readjustment benefits are analogous to military retirement benefits. She argues that readjustment benefits are a property right earned during active service and, like retirement benefits earned during marriage, constitute community property. We disagree. The legislative history of the federal statute indicates a Congressional intent to provide a non-earned gratuity. *At 673:* The separate property of a spouse consists of property owned or claimed by the spouse before marriage; the property acquired by the spouse during marriage by gift, devise, or descent; and the recovery for personal injuries sustained by the spouse during the marriage, except any recovery for loss of earning capacity during marriage. It is apparent that readjustment benefits were bestowed by Congress upon an involuntarily released member of the Army Reserve as an unearned gratuity; and that to classify these benefits as a gift under Texas property rules comports with stated federal objectives."

Cearley v. Cearley, 544 S.W.2d 661, 665-66 (Tex. 1976). "Although a serviceman's military pension is not payable before the date of its maturity, it is not 'earned' on that day. Rather it is a form of deferred compensation which is earned during each month of his military service. The portion that he earned during the months of coverture became contingent earnings of the community which may or may not bloom into full maturity at some future date. We hold that such rights, prior to accrual and maturity, constitute a contingent interest in property and a community asset subject to consideration along with other property in the division of the estate of the parties under §3.63 [now §7.001]. [¶] The administration of justice will best be served if contingent interests in retirement benefits are settled at the time of the divorce, even though it may be necessary in many instances for the judgment to make the apportionment to the nonretiring spouse effective if, as, and when the benefits are received by the retiring spouse. We approve this method of apportionment and award of contingent interests in military retirement benefits because of the uncertainties affecting the accrual and maturity of such benefits. This method will forego the difficulty of computing a present value and will fairly divide the risk that the pension may fail to mature."

Bloomer v. Bloomer, 927 S.W.2d 118, 120 (Tex. App.—Houston [1st Dist.] 1996, writ denied). "[M]ilitary retirement benefits for *active duty* personnel are in effect based on the number of months served, as long as the retiree has the minimum number of years of service, *i.e.*, 20 years. Military retirement benefits for *reserve* personnel, however, are based on the total number of points the retiree accumulated during reserve duty, as long as the retiree accumulated at least 20 years in which at least 50 or more points were earned.

Depending on how active a reservist is, the reservist could accumulate more points before marriage than are accumulated during marriage, even though the reservist has spent more calendar time as a married reservist than as an unmarried one. *At 121:* The trial court should have characterized [husband's] military retirement benefits by comparing his points accrued while married to the total accrued points, *i.e.*, 906/3385, or 26.77 percent. It was this 26.77 percent of [husband's] military retirement benefits that was subject to a just-and-right division. The remaining 73.23 percent was his separate property and was not subject to division."

Marsh v. Wallace, 924 S.W.2d 423, 425 (Tex.App.—Austin 1996, no writ). Husband "complains that the trial court erred in concluding that the [Special Separation Benefit] payment he received pursuant to [10 U.S.C.] §1174a was retirement pay and therefore divisible under the parties' divorce decree. *At 426:* SSB payments are designed to 'assist separating personnel *and their families*'. They differ from payments made upon involuntary severance from the military. In consideration of receiving an SSB payment, one voluntarily elects to separate from active duty. [¶] By its nature, an SSB payment resembles a buy-out of the service member's investment in military retirement, a sort of lump sum settlement, even though the retirement is not yet vested, in order to encourage the member's voluntary early separation from service. The recipient who reenlists and later becomes eligible for retirement has in effect received a prepayment on retirement pay because the retirement benefits are reduced by the amount of the SSB payment. Thus, one can wait to receive regular retirement benefits or opt out in favor of an SSB payment, but not both. As one court explained, an 'SSB payment [is] either retirement proceeds or a payment in lieu of retirement benefits.' *At 427:* We do not agree with an analysis which would allow one former spouse to retain all the compensation by unilaterally altering a retirement plan asset in which the other former spouse has a court-decreed interest. ... Therefore, we hold that the trial court did not err in holding that [husband's] SSB payment was retirement pay in which [wife] was entitled to share under the divorce decree."

Wallace v. Fuller, 832 S.W.2d 714, 716 (Tex.App.—Austin 1992, no writ). Husband contends "that the Former Spouses' Protection Act precludes a state court's authority to divide his military disability benefits. [Husband] argues that the Act expressly subjects disposable retired pay to state marital property laws but excludes military disability benefits from such treatment....... We agree that the Act's definition of disposable retired pay does not include the military disability benefits at issue in this case. The question then presented is whether Texas courts may treat as community property *only* disposable retired pay, as that term is defined in the Act. *At 718:* According to ***Mansell***, state courts have authority to treat only 'disposable retired pay' as marital property. Because the Act excludes both Chapter 61 disability benefits and veterans' disability benefits from its definition of 'disposable retired pay' we are unable to avoid the applicability of ***Mansell's*** preemption doctrine. By definition, the military disability pay at issue today is not disposable retired pay. ***Mansell*** ... supports [husband's] position that a state court lacks the authority to treat military disability benefits as community property subject to division in a partition proceeding."

Gallegos v. Gallegos, 788 S.W.2d 158, 160 (Tex. App.—San Antonio 1990, no writ). The husband "received V.A. Disability benefits and waived a like portion of his retirement pay. Following the holding of ***Mansell***, we hold that state courts do not have the power to treat military retirement pay that has been waived in order to receive V.A. Disability benefits as property divisible upon divorce. As a result, that portion of [husband's] retirement benefit, which was waived by the [husband] in order to receive V.A. Disability benefits, was not divisible by the court and doing so was error. [¶] [Husband also] contends that the trial court erred in awarding [wife] an interest in that portion of [husband's] military retirement pay which was subjected to a partial defeasance because of [husband's] Civil Service employment. *At 161:* The [husband] contends, and we agree, that §5532 of Title 5 U.S.C. requires the reduction of a retired officer's retired pay in order for him to receive the full pay of his Civil Service position. As with military retirement benefits, the Act specifically defines the term 'disposable retired or retainer pay' to include 'amounts waived in order to receive compensation under Title 5....' [T]herefore, we hold that the court was without authority to divide that portion of [husband's] retirement pay that was reduced in order for him to receive the full pay of his Civil Service position, as the amount waived in order to receive compensation under 5 U.S.C. §5532 must first be deducted to determine the 'disposable retired or retainer pay.' Only after such deductions are made may the court determine what portion of [husband's] retirement pay is community property."

Railroad Retirement

Eichelberger v. Eichelberger, 582 S.W.2d 395, 401 (Tex.1979). "[B]enefits payable under the Railroad Retirement Act and the expectation of ultimately receiving future benefits under the Act are not subject to division by a state court as 'property' upon divorce. [S]tate courts in community property states may not 'anticipate' such benefits by awarding upon divorce such other property of the parties that would compensate the non-employee spouse for the denied benefits in the retirement." *See also* ***Hisquierdo v. Hisquierdo***, 439 U.S. 572, 584-85, 99 S.Ct. 802, 810 (1979).

Stock Options

Charriere v. Charriere, 7 S.W.3d 217, 220 (Tex. App.—Dallas 1999, no pet.). "In Texas, a spouse is entitled to a division of property owned by the community at the time of divorce. In this case, there is no question that [wife] received the stock options during marriage, that she had the right to exercise them during marriage, and that the community therefore owned them at the time of divorce. Under these circumstances, we conclude the options were properly classified as community property and the trial court did not err in dividing them as part of the community estate. *At 221-22:* We ... reject [wife's] suggestion that we analogize the stock options to retirement benefits and, as with retirement benefits, allocate them proportionally between the parties on a 'time rule' basis. In our view, this analogy is unwarranted. This case involves a stock option plan, not retirement benefits. Unlike retirement benefits, the stock options in this case are not benefits earned over the entire period of [wife's] employment; to the contrary, *they have already been earned*. Because their value is fixed and cannot be changed except by market forces, we conclude (1) the options are distinguishable from retirement benefits, and (2) treating them the same would therefore be improper." *See also* ***Boyd v. Boyd***, 67 S.W.3d 398, 411-12 (Tex.App.—Fort Worth 2002, n.p.h.). See Annotation in Fam §3.002

FAM §7.004. DISPOSITION OF RIGHTS IN INSURANCE

In a decree of divorce or annulment, the court shall specifically divide or award the rights of each spouse in an insurance policy.

History of Fam §7.004: Acts 1997, 75th Leg., ch. 7, §1, eff. April 17, 1997. Source: Former Fam §3.632(a).

FAM §7.005. INSURANCE COVERAGE NOT SPECIFICALLY AWARDED

(a) If in a decree of divorce or annulment the court does not specifically award all of the rights of the spouses in an insurance policy other than life insurance in effect at the time the decree is rendered, the policy remains in effect until the policy expires according to the policy's own terms.

(b) The proceeds of a valid claim under the policy are payable as follows:

(1) if the interest in the property insured was awarded solely to one former spouse by the decree, to that former spouse;

(2) if an interest in the property insured was awarded to each former spouse, to those former spouses in proportion to the interests awarded; or

(3) if the insurance coverage is directly related to the person of one of the former spouses, to that former spouse.

(c) The failure of either former spouse to change the endorsement on the policy to reflect the distribution of proceeds established by this section does not relieve the insurer of liability to pay the proceeds or any other obligation on the policy.

(d) This section does not affect the right of a former spouse to assert an ownership interest in an undivided life insurance policy, as provided by Subchapter D, Chapter 9.

History of Fam §7.005: Acts 1997, 75th Leg., ch. 7, §1, eff. April 17, 1997. Source: Former Fam §3.632(d), (e).

FAM §7.006. AGREEMENT INCIDENT TO DIVORCE OR ANNULMENT

(a) To promote amicable settlement of disputes in a suit for divorce or annulment, the spouses may enter into a written agreement concerning the division of the property and the liabilities of the spouses and maintenance of either spouse. The agreement may be revised or repudiated before rendition of the divorce or annulment unless the agreement is binding under another rule of law.

(b) If the court finds that the terms of the written agreement in a divorce or annulment are just and right, those terms are binding on the court. If the court approves the agreement, the court may set forth the agreement in full or incorporate the agreement by reference in the final decree.

(c) If the court finds that the terms of the written agreement in a divorce or annulment are not just and right, the court may request the spouses to submit a revised agreement or may set the case for a contested hearing.

History of Fam §7.006: Acts 1997, 75th Leg., ch. 7, §1, eff. April 17, 1997. Source: Former Fam §3.631.

Buys v. Buys, 924 S.W.2d 369, 372 (Tex.1996). "The rules of contract law govern the construction of a property settlement agreement incorporated into a divorce decree. If the agreement is worded so that we can give it a certain or definite legal meaning, it is not ambiguous and we construe it as a matter of law."

McGoodwin v. McGoodwin, 671 S.W.2d 880, 881 (Tex.1984). "Does a divorce decree that approves a property settlement agreement by which the husband agrees to pay a sum of money as consideration for the wife's interest in a particular piece of real estate imply a vendor's lien in favor of the wife? *At 882:* Established Texas law holds that when no express lien is reserved in a deed and the purchase money is not paid, a lien nevertheless arises by implication in favor of the vendor to secure payment of the purchase money. [¶] Because the purchase money was not paid at the time of the divorce decree, a vendor's lien arose in [wife]'s favor.... This purchase money lien is superior to [husband's] claim of homestead."

Cayan v. Cayan, 38 S.W.3d 161, 164-65 (Tex.App.—Houston [14th Dist.] 2000, pet. denied). "Where parties enter into an agreement concerning the division of their property, the agreement may be revised or repudiated before rendition of the divorce '*unless the agreement is binding under another rule of law*.' If the court finds that the terms of a property division agreement are just and right, those terms are binding on the court; if not, the court may request the parties to submit a revised agreement or may set the case for a contested hearing. Once a court renders judgment on a settlement agreement, consent to the agreement cannot be revoked. [¶] Because §7.006(a) expressly recognizes that a settlement agreement can be made binding before rendition of the divorce under another rule of law, and because §6.602 expressly entitles a party to a §6.602 agreement to judgment notwithstanding other law, we interpret §6.602 simply as an exception to §7.006(a) whereby parties to a divorce may elect to make their agreement binding as of the time of its execution rather than at the subsequent time the divorce is rendered."

Vickery v. Commission for Lawyer Discipline, 5 S.W.3d 241, 262 (Tex.App.—Houston [14th Dist.] 1999, pet denied). "The Family Code allows for agreed divorces when the parties enter into a written agreement concerning the division of property and the liabilities of the spouses. A property division may be set aside, however, where the agreement is induced by fraud. Therefore, ... when a property division has been induced by fraud, the divorce cannot be agreed."

Wilson v. Uzzel, 953 S.W.2d 384, 388 (Tex.App.—El Paso 1997, no writ). "Divorcing couples may enter into agreements to facilitate property division. These agreements are considered contracts and their legal force and meaning are governed by contract law. Upon approval, the court may include the agreement in the divorce decree.... When so included, the decree becomes a consent judgment, subject to the same degree of finality and binding force as a judgment rendered in an adversary proceeding. Principles of collateral estoppel and res judicata therefore apply."

Keim v. Anderson, 943 S.W.2d 938, 946 (Tex. App.—El Paso 1997, no writ). "A final judgment founded upon a settlement agreement must be in strict compliance with the agreement. The trial court has no power to supply terms, provisions, or conditions not previously agreed to by the parties. It can merely approve or reject the agreement. If an appellate court determines that the decree contains terms and provisions dividing the community property that were never agreed to by the parties, it must reverse the judgment and remand the cause. On the other hand, when the record reflects a clerical variance between a judgment announced in open court and the judgment eventually signed by the trial judge, the appellate court can modify the judgment to correct the mistake."

Cavazos v. Cavazos, 941 S.W.2d 211, 214 (Tex. App.—Corpus Christi 1996, writ denied). "Under rules of contract construction, in order for a document to be considered part of a signed contract, it must be signed or referred to in the signed contract. [The addendum] was not signed and it was not referenced either in the decree or the [Marital Property] Agreement. The mere fact that [the addendum], at some point became attached to the court documents, does not make it a part of the Agreement."

Fryman v. Fryman, 926 S.W.2d 602, 603 (Tex. App.—Fort Worth 1996, writ denied). Wife "appeals a declaratory judgment which terminated contractual alimony provided in an agreement incident to her divorce from [husband]. [Wife] claims that: the automatic alimony termination provision is contrary to public policy and, therefore, void.... [¶] [Husband] agreed to pay [wife] $1,000 per month in contractual alimony on the condition that the alimony would be terminated upon [wife's] remarriage, [wife's] or [husband's] death, [husband's] disability, or [wife's] filing 'on her behalf or on behalf of the children any modification suit concerning' child support, conservatorship, or visitation. *At 605:* [Husband] points out that the [agreement incident to divorce] does not prevent the trial court from entering any order in the best interest of the children and that, strictly construed, the AID does not impede the trial court's authority. However, the AID penalizes [wife] for merely *asking* the trial court to enter an order based upon the best interest of the children and therefore, indirectly, limits the trial court's ability by providing [wife] with a significant financial incentive to protect the status quo. *At 606:* We conclude, therefore, that [wife's] contention that the termination provision of the AID is against public policy is correct...."

Clanin v. Clanin, 918 S.W.2d 673, 676-77 (Tex. App.—Fort Worth 1996, no writ). "An agreement for judgment will not be enforced unless the agreement is reduced to writing, signed and filed with the papers as part of the record, or unless it is made in open court and entered of record. Compliance with the 'open court and entered of record' portion of Rule 11 satisfies ... §3.631 [now §7.006] requirement of written agreements in divorce cases. This is so because the sworn testimony of the parties given to the court reporter in open court memorializes the parties' consent and can also be reduced to writing. Therefore, this procedure has the same legal effect as a written agreement signed by the parties and, in fact, results in a written agreement that meets the requirements of ... §3.631 for agreements in divorce cases to be in writing."

Delaup v. Delaup, 917 S.W.2d 411, 413-14 (Tex. App.—Houston [14th Dist.] 1996, no writ). "[A] divorce agreement made in open court by the parties and entered of record pursuant to Rule 11 has the same legal effect as a written agreement signed by the parties, and results in a written agreement that meets the requirements of §3.631 [now §7.006]. [T]he court reporter's transcription results in a written agreement. ... Although the agreement was orally dictated to the court, the record of the agreement insures that the details of the agreement will always be available for the parties to review, thus denying a party the opportunity to fraudulently exploit its terms as can occur with an oral agreement not entered of record in open court."

Dechon v. Dechon, 909 S.W.2d 950, 960 (Tex. App.—El Paso 1995, no writ). The "peculiarities of agreements incident to divorce and the final decrees incorporating them provide a party with a wide variety of remedies. In some instances, a suit for breach of contract is appropriate, particularly in the child support arena, such as where the parties contractually agree that one of the parents will provide for a college education. Typical enforcement remedies such as contempt are useless in such situations and recovery may be obtained only through suit on the contract inasmuch as the court cannot enforce by contempt that which it has no authority to order. Since a court cannot order support for a non-disabled child past the age of majority, agreements for on-going support past that age are not enforceable by contempt. A similar result occurs with contractual alimony obligations. Child support is more likely to be recovered through contempt actions rather than contract actions, although there are a number of instances in which the downward modification of support has led to a breach of contract action by the obligee against the obligor to recover the contractual support lost as a result of the modification ordered by the court."

FAM §7.007. DISPOSITION OF CLAIM FOR ECONOMIC CONTRIBUTION OR CLAIM FOR REIMBURSEMENT

E *Section 7.007 below is effective for suits for dissolution of marriage or annulments pending on or filed on or after Sept. 1, 2001.*

(a) In a decree of divorce or annulment, the court shall determine the rights of both spouses in a claim for economic contribution as provided by Subchapter E, Chapter 3, and in a manner that the court considers just and right, having due regard for the rights of each party and any children of the marriage, shall:

(1) order a division of a claim for economic contribution of the community marital estate to the separate marital estate of one of the spouses;

(2) order that a claim for an economic contribution by one separate marital estate of a spouse to the

community marital estate of the spouses be awarded to the owner of the contributing separate marital estate; and

(3) order that a claim for economic contribution of one separate marital estate in the separate marital estate of the other spouse be awarded to the owner of the contributing marital estate.

(b) In a decree of divorce or annulment, the court shall determine the rights of both spouses in a claim for reimbursement as provided by Subchapter E, Chapter 3, and shall apply equitable principles to:

(1) determine whether to recognize the claim after taking into account all the relative circumstances of the spouses; and

(2) order a division of the claim for reimbursement, if appropriate, in a manner that the court considers just and right, having due regard for the rights of each party and any children of the marriage.

History of Fam §7.007: Enacted by Acts 2001, 77th Leg., ch. 838, §5, eff. Sept. 1, 2001.

CHAPTER 8. MAINTENANCE

E

SUBCHAPTER A. GENERAL PROVISIONS

A

FAM §8.001. DEFINITIONS

In this chapter:

(1) "Maintenance" means an award in a suit for dissolution of a marriage of periodic payments from the future income of one spouse for the support of the other spouse.

E (2) "Notice of application for a writ of withholding" means the document delivered to an obligor and filed with the court as required by this chapter for the nonjudicial determination of arrears and initiation of withholding for spousal maintenance.

E (3) "Obligee" means a person entitled to receive payments under the terms of an order for spousal maintenance.

E (4) "Obligor" means a person required to make periodic payments under the terms of an order for spousal maintenance.

E (5) "Writ of withholding" means the document issued by the clerk of a court and delivered to an employer, directing that earnings be withheld for payment of spousal maintenance as provided by this chapter.

History of Fam §8.001: Acts 1997, 75th Leg., ch. 7, §1, eff. April 17, 1997. Amended by Acts 2001, 77th Leg., ch. 807, §1, eff. Sept. 1, 2001. Subchapter enacted by Acts 2001, 77th Leg., ch. 807, §1, eff. Sept. 1, 2001. Source: Former Fam §3.9601.

Sections 8.002-8.050 reserved for expansion

E

SUBCHAPTER B. COURT-ORDERED MAINTENANCE

A

FAM §8.051. ELIGIBILITY FOR MAINTENANCE; COURT ORDER

In a suit for dissolution of a marriage or in a proceeding for maintenance in a court with personal jurisdiction over both former spouses following the dissolution of their marriage by a court that lacked personal jurisdiction over an absent spouse, the court may order maintenance for either spouse only if:

(1) the spouse from whom maintenance is requested was convicted of or received deferred adjudication for a criminal offense that also constitutes an act of family violence under Title 4 and the offense occurred:

(A) within two years before the date on which a suit for dissolution of the marriage is filed; or

(B) while the suit is pending; or

A (2) the duration of the marriage was 10 years or longer, the spouse seeking maintenance lacks sufficient property, including property distributed to the spouse under this code, to provide for the spouse's minimum reasonable needs, as limited by Section 8.054, and the spouse seeking maintenance:

(A) is unable to support himself or herself through appropriate employment because of an incapacitating physical or mental disability;

(B) is the custodian of a child who requires substantial care and personal supervision because a physical or mental disability makes it necessary, taking into consideration the needs of the child, that the spouse not be employed outside the home; or

A (C) clearly lacks earning ability in the labor market adequate to provide support for the spouse's minimum reasonable needs, as limited by Section 8.054.

History of Fam §8.051: Acts 1997, 75th Leg., ch. 7, §1, eff. April 17, 1997. Amended by Acts 1999, 76th Leg., ch. 304, §1 (eff. Sept. 1, 1999), ch. 62, §6.05 (eff. Sept. 1, 1999). Renumbered from §8.002 and amended by Acts 2001, 77th Leg., ch. 807, §1, eff. Sept. 1, 2001. Source: Former Fam §3.9602.

Pickens v. Pickens, 62 S.W.3d 212, 215-16 (Tex. App.—Dallas 2001, pet. denied). "We find no authority directly addressing the quantum of evidence required to prove incapacity in a spousal maintenance action. ... Husband reason[s] that because spousal maintenance is designed to replace earned income, we should consider the evidence required to receive workers' compensation benefits, or federal social security disability benefits. Under both of these statutes, medical evidence is required to establish an impairment or disability. However, for both workers' compensation and federal disability, the requirement of medical evidence is statutory. There is no such statutory requirement found in the spousal maintenance provisions of the family code. If the legislature had intended to restrict eligibility for spousal maintenance by requiring a spouse to present medical evidence to prove his or her disability, it could easily have done so. [¶] Absent a statutory requirement to the contrary, testimony on incapacity need not be limited to experts; a fact finder may reasonably infer incapacity from circumstantial evidence or the competent testimony of lay witnesses. The question of the extent and duration of incapacity is an issue that can be answered by lay opinion and does not require medical testimony. In fact, the testimony of the injured party will support a finding of incapacity even if directly contradicted by expert medical testimony."

Alexander v. Alexander, 982 S.W.2d 116, 119 (Tex. App.—Houston [1st Dist.] 1998, no pet.). "To be eligible for spousal support, [wife] must have shown she clearly lacks earning ability adequate to provide for her reasonable needs. She must also have overcome the presumption against spousal support by showing she had diligently sought suitable employment or, during the time she and [her husband] were separated and the divorce action was pending, sought to develop skills necessary to allow her to be self-supporting."

In re Marriage of Hale, 975 S.W.2d 694, 698 (Tex. App.—Texarkana 1998, no pet.). "The term 'minimum reasonable needs' is not defined by statute, and there appear to be no cases defining the term. Deciding what the minimum reasonable need is for a particular individual or family is a fact-specific determination that ordinarily should be made by the trial court. [¶] We cannot accept the proposition that the federal minimum wage statute, as a matter of law, dictates what amount will provide the 'minimum reasonable needs' of an individual or family. Indeed, it is common knowledge that the minimum wage, standing alone, is usually inadequate to support a family. We are unwilling to hold that the minimum wage is adequate in every case."

DuBois v. DuBois, 956 S.W.2d 607, 612 (Tex.App.—Tyler 1997, no pet.). "[T]here was evidence that [husband] had paid [wife] $500.00 per month in temporary support for five months. There was also testimony that [wife] had received $7,400.00 in cash and approximately $18,000.00 in benefits from [husband's] retirement plan in property settlement. [Wife] admitted that she was a certified teacher, that she was currently looking for a position in surrounding school districts, and that she was willing to move to another community in order to be gainfully employed. … Based upon the evidence adduced at trial, the trial court did not abuse its discretion in denying spousal maintenance for [wife]."

Ⓐ FAM §8.052. FACTORS IN DETERMINING MAINTENANCE

A court that determines that a spouse is eligible to receive maintenance under this chapter shall determine the nature, amount, duration, and manner of periodic payments by considering all relevant factors, including:

(1) the financial resources of the spouse seeking maintenance, including the community and separate property and liabilities apportioned to that spouse in the dissolution proceeding, and that spouse's ability to meet the spouse's needs independently;

(2) the education and employment skills of the spouses, the time necessary to acquire sufficient education or training to enable the spouse seeking maintenance to find appropriate employment, the availability of that education or training, and the feasibility of that education or training;

(3) the duration of the marriage;

(4) the age, employment history, earning ability, and physical and emotional condition of the spouse seeking maintenance;

(5) the ability of the spouse from whom maintenance is requested to meet that spouse's personal needs and to provide periodic child support payments, if applicable, while meeting the personal needs of the spouse seeking maintenance;

(6) acts by either spouse resulting in excessive or abnormal expenditures or destruction, concealment, or fraudulent disposition of community property, joint tenancy, or other property held in common;

(7) the comparative financial resources of the spouses, including medical, retirement, insurance, or other benefits, and the separate property of each spouse;

(8) the contribution by one spouse to the education, training, or increased earning power of the other spouse;

(9) the property brought to the marriage by either spouse;

(10) the contribution of a spouse as homemaker;

(11) marital misconduct of the spouse seeking maintenance; and

(12) the efforts of the spouse seeking maintenance to pursue available employment counseling as provided by Chapter 304, Labor Code.

History of Fam §8.052: Acts 1997, 75th Leg., ch. 7, §1, eff. April 17, 1997. Renumbered from §8.003 by Acts 2001, 77th Leg., ch. 807, §1, eff. Sept. 1, 2001. Source: Former Fam §3.9603.

Ⓐ FAM §8.053. PRESUMPTION

(a) Except as provided by Subsection (b), it is presumed that maintenance is not warranted unless the spouse seeking maintenance has exercised diligence in:

(1) seeking suitable employment; or

(2) developing the necessary skills to become self-supporting during a period of separation and during the time the suit for dissolution of the marriage is pending.

(b) This section does not apply to a spouse who is not able to satisfy the presumption in Subsection (a) because of an incapacitating physical or mental disability.

History of Fam §8.053: Acts 1997, 75th Leg., ch. 7, §1, eff. April 17, 1997. Renumbered from §8.004 by Acts 2001, 77th Leg., ch. 807, §1, eff. Sept. 1, 2001. Source: Former Fam §3.9604.

A FAM §8.054. DURATION OF MAINTENANCE ORDER

(a) Except as provided by Subsection (b), a court:

(1) may not order maintenance that remains in effect for more than three years after the date of the order; and

(2) shall limit the duration of a maintenance order to the shortest reasonable period that allows the spouse seeking maintenance to meet the spouse's minimum reasonable needs by obtaining appropriate employment or developing an appropriate skill, unless the ability of the spouse to provide for the spouse's minimum reasonable needs through employment is substantially or totally diminished because of:

(A) physical or mental disability;

(B) duties as the custodian of an infant or young child; or

(C) another compelling impediment to gainful employment.

A (b) If a spouse seeking maintenance is unable to support himself or herself through appropriate employment because of an incapacitating physical or mental disability, the court may order maintenance for an indefinite period for as long as the disability continues. The court may order periodic review of its order, on the request of either party or on its own motion, to determine whether the disability is continuing. The continuation of spousal maintenance under these circumstances is subject to a motion to modify as provided by Section 8.057.

History of Fam §8.054: Acts 1997, 75th Leg., ch. 7, §1, eff. April 17, 1997. Renumbered from §8.005 and amended by Acts 2001, 77th Leg., ch. 807, §1, eff. Sept. 1, 2001. Source: Former Fam §3.9605.

A FAM §8.055. AMOUNT OF MAINTENANCE

(a) A court may not order maintenance that requires an obligor to pay monthly more than the lesser of:

(1) $2,500; or

(2) 20 percent of the spouse's average monthly gross income.

(b) The court shall set the amount that an obligor is required to pay in a maintenance order to provide for the minimum reasonable needs of the obligee, considering employment or property received in the dissolution of the marriage or otherwise owned by the obligee that contributes to the minimum reasonable needs of the obligee.

(c) Department of Veterans Affairs service-connected disability compensation, social security benefits and disability benefits, and workers' compensation benefits are excluded from maintenance.

History of Fam §8.055: Acts 1997, 75th Leg., ch. 7, §1, eff. April 17, 1997. Renumbered from §8.006 and amended by Acts 2001, 77th Leg., ch. 807, §1, eff. Sept. 1, 2001. Source: Former Fam §3.9606.

A FAM §8.056. TERMINATION

(a) The obligation to pay future maintenance terminates on the death of either party or on the remarriage of the obligee.

(b) After a hearing, the court shall terminate the maintenance order if the obligee cohabits with another person in a permanent place of abode on a continuing, conjugal basis.

History of Fam §8.056: Acts 1997, 75th Leg., ch. 7, §1, eff. April 17, 1997. Renumbered from §8.007 and amended by Acts 2001, 77th Leg., ch. 807, §1, eff. Sept. 1, 2001. Source: Former Fam §3.9607.

A FAM §8.057. MODIFICATION OF MAINTENANCE ORDER

(a) The amount of maintenance specified in a court order or the portion of a decree that provides for the support of a former spouse may be reduced by the filing of a motion in the court that originally rendered the order. A party affected by the order or the portion of the decree to be modified may file the motion.

(b) Notice of a motion to modify maintenance and the response, if any, are governed by the Texas Rules of Civil Procedure applicable to the filing of an original lawsuit. Notice must be given by service of citation, and a response must be in the form of an answer due on or before 10 a.m. of the first Monday after 20 days after the date of service. A court shall set a hearing on the motion in the manner provided by Rule 245, Texas Rules of Civil Procedure.

(c) After a hearing, the court may modify an original or modified order or portion of a decree providing for maintenance on a proper showing of a material and substantial change in circumstances of either party.

The court shall apply the modification only to payment accruing after the filing of the motion to modify.

(d) A loss of employment or circumstances that render a former spouse unable to support himself or herself through appropriate employment by reason of incapacitating physical or mental disability that occur after the divorce or annulment are not grounds for the institution of spousal maintenance for the benefit of the former spouse.

History of Fam §8.057: Acts 1997, 75th Leg., ch. 7, §1, eff. April 17, 1997. Renumbered from §8.008 by Acts 2001, 77th Leg., ch. 807, §1, eff. Sept. 1, 2001. Source: Former Fam §3.9608

E FAM §8.058. MAINTENANCE ARREARAGES

A spousal maintenance payment not timely made constitutes an arrearage.

History of Fam §8.058: Enacted by Acts 2001, 77th Leg., ch. 807, §1, eff. Sept. 1, 2001.

A FAM §8.059. ENFORCEMENT OF MAINTENANCE ORDER

(a) The court may enforce by contempt the court's maintenance order or an agreement for the payment of maintenance voluntarily entered into between the parties and approved by the court.

A (b) On the suit to enforce by an obligee, the court may render judgment against a defaulting party for the amount of arrearages after notice by service of citation, answer, if any, and a hearing finding that the defaulting party has failed or refused to carry out the terms of the order. The judgment may be enforced by any means available for the enforcement of judgment for debts.

(c) It is an affirmative defense to an allegation of contempt of court or the violation of a condition of probation requiring payment of court-ordered maintenance that the obligor:

(1) lacked the ability to provide maintenance in the amount ordered;

(2) lacked property that could be sold, mortgaged, or otherwise pledged to raise the funds needed;

(3) attempted unsuccessfully to borrow the needed funds; and

(4) did not know of a source from which the money could have been borrowed or otherwise legally obtained.

(d) The issue of the existence of an affirmative defense does not arise unless evidence is admitted supporting the defense. If the issue of the existence of an affirmative defense arises, an obligor must prove the affirmative defense by a preponderance of the evidence.

E (e) A court may enforce an order for spousal maintenance under this chapter by ordering garnishment of the obligor's wages or by any other means available under this section.

History of Fam §8.059: Acts 1997, 75th Leg., ch. 7, §1, eff. April 17, 1997. Renumbered from §8.009 and amended by Acts 2001, 77th Leg., ch. 807, §1, eff. Sept. 1, 2001. Source: Former Fam §3.9609.

A FAM §8.060. PUTATIVE SPOUSE

In a suit to declare a marriage void, a putative spouse who did not have knowledge of an existing impediment to a valid marriage may be awarded maintenance if otherwise qualified to receive maintenance under this chapter.

History of Fam §8.060: Acts 1997, 75th Leg., ch. 7, §1, eff. April 17, 1997. Renumbered from §8.010 by Acts 2001, 77th Leg., ch. 807, §1, eff. Sept. 1, 2001. Source: Former Fam §3.9610.

A FAM §8.061. UNMARRIED COHABITANTS

An order for maintenance is not authorized between unmarried cohabitants under any circumstances.

History of Fam §8.061: Acts 1997, 75th Leg., ch. 7, §1, eff. April 17, 1997. Renumbered from §8.011 by Acts 2001, 77th Leg., ch. 807, §1, eff. Sept. 1, 2001. Source: Former Fam §3.9611.

Sections 8.062-8.100 reserved for expansion

E SUBCHAPTER C. INCOME WITHHOLDING

E FAM §8.101. INCOME WITHHOLDING; GENERAL RULE

(a) In a proceeding in which periodic payments of spousal maintenance are ordered, modified, or enforced, the court may order that income be withheld from the disposable earnings of the obligor as provided by this chapter.

(b) This subchapter does not apply to contractual alimony or spousal maintenance, regardless of whether the alimony or maintenance is taxable, unless:

(1) the contract specifically permits income withholding; or

(2) the alimony or maintenance payments are not timely made under the terms of the contract.

(c) An order or writ of withholding for spousal maintenance may be combined with an order or writ of withholding for child support only if the obligee has been appointed managing conservator of the child for whom the child support is owed and is the conservator with whom the child primarily resides.

(d) An order or writ of withholding that combines withholding for spousal maintenance and child support must:

(1) require that the withheld amounts be paid to the appropriate place of payment under Section 154.004;

(2) be in the form prescribed by the Title IV-D agency under Section 158.106;

(3) clearly indicate the amounts withheld that are to be applied to current spousal maintenance and to any maintenance arrearages; and

(4) subject to the maximum withholding allowed under Section 8.106, order that withheld income be applied in the following order of priority:

(A) current child support;

(B) current spousal maintenance;

(C) child support arrearages; and

(D) spousal maintenance arrearages.

(e) Garnishment for the purposes of spousal maintenance does not apply to unemployment insurance benefit payments.

History of Fam §8.101: Enacted by Acts 2001, 77th Leg., ch. 807, §1, eff. Sept. 1, 2001.

Ⓔ FAM §8.102. WITHHOLDING FOR ARREARAGES IN ADDITION TO CURRENT SPOUSAL MAINTENANCE

(a) The court may order that, in addition to income withheld for current spousal maintenance, income be withheld from the disposable earnings of the obligor to be applied toward the liquidation of any arrearages.

(b) The additional amount withheld to be applied toward arrearages must be whichever of the following amounts will discharge the arrearages in the least amount of time:

(1) an amount sufficient to discharge the arrearages in not more than two years; or

(2) 20 percent of the amount withheld for current maintenance.

History of Fam §8.102: Enacted by Acts 2001, 77th Leg., ch. 807, §1, eff. Sept. 1, 2001.

Ⓔ FAM §8.103. WITHHOLDING FOR ARREARAGES WHEN CURRENT MAINTENANCE IS NOT DUE

A court may order income withholding to be applied toward arrearages in an amount sufficient to discharge those arrearages in not more than two years if current spousal maintenance is no longer owed.

History of Fam §8.103: Enacted by Acts 2001, 77th Leg., ch. 807, §1, eff. Sept. 1, 2001.

Ⓔ FAM §8.104. WITHHOLDING TO SATISFY JUDGMENT FOR ARREARAGES

The court, in rendering a cumulative judgment for arrearages, may order that a reasonable amount of income be withheld from the disposable earnings of the obligor to be applied toward the satisfaction of the judgment.

History of Fam §8.104: Enacted by Acts 2001, 77th Leg., ch. 807, §1, eff. Sept. 1, 2001.

Ⓔ FAM §8.105. PRIORITY OF WITHHOLDING

An order or writ of withholding under this chapter has priority over any garnishment, attachment, execution, or other order affecting disposable earnings, except for an order or writ of withholding for child support under Chapter 158.

History of Fam §8.105: Enacted by Acts 2001, 77th Leg., ch. 807, §1, eff. Sept. 1, 2001.

Ⓔ FAM §8.106. MAXIMUM AMOUNT WITHHELD FROM EARNINGS

An order or writ of withholding must direct that an obligor's employer withhold from the obligor's disposable earnings the lesser of:

(1) the amount specified in the order or writ; or

(2) an amount that, when added to the amount of income being withheld by the employer for child support, is equal to 50 percent of the obligor's disposable earnings.

History of Fam §8.106: Enacted by Acts 2001, 77th Leg., ch. 807, §1, eff. Sept. 1, 2001.

Ⓔ FAM §8.107. ORDER OR WRIT BINDING ON EMPLOYER DOING BUSINESS IN THIS STATE

An order or writ of withholding issued under this chapter and delivered to an employer doing business in this state is binding on the employer without regard to whether the obligor resides or works outside this state.

History of Fam §8.107: Enacted by Acts 2001, 77th Leg., ch. 807, §1, eff. Sept. 1, 2001.

Ⓔ FAM §8.108. VOLUNTARY WRIT OF WITHHOLDING BY OBLIGOR

(a) An obligor may file with the clerk of the court a notarized or acknowledged request signed by the obligor and the obligee for the issuance and delivery to the obligor's employer of a writ of withholding. The obligor may file the request under this section regardless of whether a writ or order has been served on any party or whether the obligor owes arrearages.

(b) On receipt of a request under this section, the clerk shall issue and deliver a writ of withholding in the manner provided by this subchapter.

(c) An employer who receives a writ of withholding issued under this section may request a hearing in the same manner and according to the same terms provided by Section 8.205.

(d) An obligor whose employer receives a writ of withholding issued under this section may request a hearing in the manner provided by Section 8.258.

(e) An obligee may contest a writ of income withholding issued under this section by requesting, not later than the 180th day after the date on which the obligee discovers that the writ was issued, a hearing to be conducted in the manner provided by Section 8.258 for a hearing on a motion to stay.

(f) A writ of withholding under this section may not reduce the total amount of spousal maintenance, including arrearages, owed by the obligor.

History of Fam §8.108: Enacted by Acts 2001, 77th Leg., ch. 807, §1, eff. Sept. 1, 2001.

Sections 8.109-8.150 reserved for expansion

E SUBCHAPTER D. PROCEDURE

E FAM §8.151. TIME LIMIT

The court may issue an order or writ for withholding under this chapter at any time before all spousal maintenance and arrearages are paid.

History of Fam §8.151: Enacted by Acts 2001, 77th Leg., ch. 807, §1, eff. Sept. 1, 2001.

E FAM §8.152. CONTENTS OF ORDER OF WITHHOLDING

(a) An order of withholding must state:

(1) the style, cause number, and court having jurisdiction to enforce the order;

(2) the name, address, and, if available, the social security number of the obligor;

(3) the amount and duration of the spousal maintenance payments, including the amount and duration of withholding for arrearages, if any; and

(4) the name, address, and, if available, the social security number of the obligee.

(b) The order for withholding must require the obligor to notify the court promptly of any material change affecting the order, including a change of employer.

(c) On request by an obligee, the court may exclude from an order of withholding the obligee's address and social security number if the obligee or a member of the obligee's family or household is a victim of family violence and is the subject of a protective order to which the obligor is also subject. On granting a request under this subsection, the court shall order the clerk to:

(1) strike the address and social security number required by Subsection (a) from the order or writ of withholding; and

(2) maintain a confidential record of the obligee's address and social security number to be used only by the court.

History of Fam §8.152: Enacted by Acts 2001, 77th Leg., ch. 807, §1, eff. Sept. 1, 2001.

E FAM §8.153. REQUEST FOR ISSUANCE OF ORDER OR WRIT OF WITHHOLDING

An obligor or obligee may file with the clerk of the court a request for issuance of an order or writ of withholding.

History of Fam §8.153: Enacted by Acts 2001, 77th Leg., ch. 807, §1, eff. Sept. 1, 2001.

E FAM §8.154. ISSUANCE & DELIVERY OF ORDER OR WRIT OF WITHHOLDING

(a) On receipt of a request for issuance of an order or writ of withholding, the clerk of the court shall deliver a certified copy of the order or writ to the obligor's current employer or to any subsequent employer of the obligor. The clerk shall attach a copy of Subchapter E to the order or writ.

(b) Not later than the fourth working day after the date the order is signed or the request is filed, whichever is later, the clerk shall issue and deliver the certified copy of the order or writ by:

(1) certified or registered mail, return receipt requested, to the employer; or

(2) service of citation to:

(A) the person authorized to receive service of process for the employer in civil cases generally; or

(B) a person designated by the employer by written notice to the clerk to receive orders or notices of income withholding.

History of Fam §8.154: Enacted by Acts 2001, 77th Leg., ch. 807, §1, eff. Sept. 1, 2001.

Sections 8.155-8.200 reserved for expansion

SUBCHAPTER E. RIGHTS & DUTIES OF EMPLOYER

FAM §8.201. ORDER OR WRIT BINDING ON EMPLOYER

(a) An employer required to withhold income from earnings under this chapter is not entitled to notice of the proceedings before the order of withholding is rendered or writ of withholding is issued.

(b) An order or writ of withholding is binding on an employer regardless of whether the employer is specifically named in the order or writ.

History of Fam §8.201: Enacted by Acts 2001, 77th Leg., ch. 807, §1, eff. Sept. 1, 2001.

FAM §8.202. EFFECTIVE DATE & DURATION OF INCOME WITHHOLDING

An employer shall begin to withhold income in accordance with an order or writ of withholding not later than the first pay period after the date the order or writ was delivered to the employer. The employer shall continue to withhold income as required by the order or writ as long as the obligor is employed by the employer.

History of Fam §8.202: Enacted by Acts 2001, 77th Leg., ch. 807, §1, eff. Sept. 1, 2001.

FAM §8.203. REMITTING WITHHELD PAYMENTS

(a) The employer shall remit to the person or office named in the order or writ of withholding the amount of income withheld from an obligor on each pay date. The remittance must include the date on which the income withholding occurred.

(b) The employer shall include with each remittance:

(1) the cause number of the suit under which income withholding is required;

(2) the payor's name; and

(3) the payee's name, unless the remittance is made by electronic funds transfer.

History of Fam §8.203: Enacted by Acts 2001, 77th Leg., ch. 807, §1, eff. Sept. 1, 2001.

FAM §8.204. EMPLOYER MAY DEDUCT FEE FROM EARNINGS

An employer may deduct an administrative fee of not more than $5 each month from the obligor's disposable earnings in addition to the amount withheld as spousal maintenance.

History of Fam §8.204: Enacted by Acts 2001, 77th Leg., ch. 807, §1, eff. Sept. 1, 2001.

FAM §8.205. HEARING REQUESTED BY EMPLOYER

(a) Not later than the 20th day after the date an order or writ of withholding is delivered to an employer, the employer may file with the court a motion for a hearing on the applicability of the order or writ to the employer.

(b) The hearing under this section must be held on or before the 15th day after the date the motion is made.

(c) An order or writ of withholding is binding and the employer shall continue to withhold income and remit the amount withheld pending further order of the court.

History of Fam §8.205: Enacted by Acts 2001, 77th Leg., ch. 807, §1, eff. Sept. 1, 2001.

FAM §8.206. LIABILITY & OBLIGATION OF EMPLOYER FOR PAYMENTS

(a) An employer who complies with an order or writ of withholding under this chapter is not liable to the obligor for the amount of income withheld and remitted as required by the order or writ.

(b) An employer who receives, but does not comply with, an order or writ of withholding is liable to:

(1) the obligee for any amount of spousal maintenance not paid in compliance with the order or writ;

(2) the obligor for any amount withheld from the obligor's disposable earnings, but not remitted to the obligee; and

(3) the obligee or obligor for reasonable attorney's fees and court costs incurred in recovering an amount described by Subdivision (1) or (2).

(c) An employer shall comply with an order of withholding for spousal maintenance or alimony issued in another state that appears regular on its face in the same manner as an order issued by a tribunal of this state. The employer shall notify the employee of the order and comply with the order in the manner provided by Subchapter F, Chapter 159, with respect to an order of withholding for child support issued by another state. The employer may contest the order of withholding in the manner provided by that subchapter with respect to an order of withholding for child support issued by another state.

History of Fam §8.206: Enacted by Acts 2001, 77th Leg., ch. 807, §1, eff. Sept. 1, 2001.

E **FAM §8.207. EMPLOYER RECEIVING MULTIPLE ORDERS OR WRITS**

(a) An employer who receives more than one order or writ of withholding to withhold income from the same obligor shall withhold the combined amounts due under each order or writ unless the combined amounts due exceed the maximum total amount of allowed income withholding under Section 8.106.

(b) If the combined amounts to be withheld under multiple orders or writs for the same obligor exceed the maximum total amount of allowed income withholding under Section 8.106, the employer shall pay, until that maximum is reached, in the following order of priority:

(1) an equal amount toward current child support owed by the obligor in each order or writ until the employer has complied fully with each current child support obligation;

(2) an equal amount toward current maintenance owed by the obligor in each order or writ until the employer has complied fully with each current maintenance obligation;

(3) an equal amount toward child support arrearages owed by the obligor in each order or writ until the employer has complied fully with each order or writ for child support arrearages; and

(4) an equal amount toward maintenance arrearages owed by the obligor in each order or writ until the employer has complied fully with each order or writ for spousal maintenance arrearages.

History of Fam §8.207: Enacted by Acts 2001, 77th Leg., ch. 807, §1, eff. Sept. 1, 2001.

E **FAM §8.208. EMPLOYER'S LIABILITY FOR DISCRIMINATORY HIRING OR DISCHARGE**

(a) An employer may not use an order or writ of withholding as grounds in whole or part for the termination of employment of, or for any other disciplinary action against, an employee.

(b) An employer may not refuse to hire an employee because of an order or writ of withholding.

(c) An employer who intentionally discharges an employee in violation of this section is liable to that employee for current wages, other employment benefits, and reasonable attorney's fees and court costs incurred in enforcing the employee's rights.

(d) In addition to liability imposed under Subsection (c), the court shall order with respect to an employee whose employment was suspended or terminated in violation of this section appropriate injunctive relief, including reinstatement of:

(1) the employee's position with the employer; and

(2) fringe benefits or seniority lost as a result of the suspension or termination.

(e) An employee may bring an action to enforce the employee's rights under this section.

History of Fam §8.208: Enacted by Acts 2001, 77th Leg., ch. 807, §1, eff. Sept. 1, 2001.

E **FAM §8.209. PENALTY FOR NONCOMPLIANCE**

(a) In addition to the civil remedies provided by this subchapter or any other remedy provided by law, an employer who knowingly violates this chapter by failing to withhold income for spousal maintenance or to remit withheld income in accordance with an order or writ of withholding issued under this chapter commits an offense.

(b) An offense under this section is punishable by a fine not to exceed $200 for each violation.

History of Fam §8.209: Enacted by Acts 2001, 77th Leg., ch. 807, §1, eff. Sept. 1, 2001.

E **FAM §8.210. NOTICE OF TERMINATION OF EMPLOYMENT & OF NEW EMPLOYMENT**

(a) An obligor who terminates employment with an employer who has been withholding income and the obligor's employer shall each notify the court and the obligee of:

(1) the termination of employment not later than the seventh day after the date of termination;

(2) the obligor's last known address; and

(3) the name and address of the obligor's new employer, if known.

(b) The obligor shall inform a subsequent employer of the order or writ of withholding after obtaining employment.

History of Fam §8.210: Enacted by Acts 2001, 77th Leg., ch. 807, §1, eff. Sept. 1, 2001.

Sections 8.211-8.250 reserved for expansion

E **SUBCHAPTER F. WRIT OF WITHHOLDING ISSUED BY CLERK**

E **FAM §8.251. NOTICE OF APPLICATION FOR WRIT OF WITHHOLDING; FILING**

(a) An obligor or obligee may file a notice of application for a writ of withholding if income withholding was not ordered at the time spousal maintenance was ordered.

(b) The obligor or obligee may file the notice of application for a writ of withholding in the court that ordered the spousal maintenance under Subchapter B.

History of Fam §8.251: Enacted by Acts 2001, 77th Leg., ch. 807, §1, eff. Sept. 1, 2001.

E FAM §8.252. CONTENTS OF NOTICE OF APPLICATION FOR WRIT OF WITHHOLDING

The notice of application for a writ of withholding must be verified and:

(1) state the amount of monthly maintenance due, including the amount of arrearages or anticipated arrearages, and the amount of disposable earnings to be withheld under a writ of withholding;

(2) state that the withholding applies to each current or subsequent employer or period of employment;

(3) state that the obligor's employer will be notified to begin the withholding if the obligor does not contest the withholding on or before the 10th day after the date the obligor receives the notice;

(4) describe the procedures for contesting the issuance and delivery of a writ of withholding;

(5) state that the obligor will be provided an opportunity for a hearing not later than the 30th day after the date of receipt of the notice of contest if the obligor contests the withholding;

(6) state that the sole ground for successfully contesting the issuance of a writ of withholding is a dispute concerning the identity of the obligor or the existence or amount of the arrearages;

(7) describe the actions that may be taken if the obligor contests the notice of application for a writ of withholding, including the procedures for suspending issuance of a writ of withholding; and

(8) include with the notice a suggested form for the motion to stay issuance and delivery of the writ of withholding that the obligor may file with the clerk of the appropriate court.

History of §8.252: Enacted by Acts 2001, 77th Leg., ch. 807, §1, eff. Sept. 1, 2001.

E FAM §8.253. INTERSTATE REQUEST FOR WITHHOLDING

(a) The registration of a foreign order that provides for spousal maintenance or alimony as provided in Chapter 159 is sufficient for filing a notice of application for a writ of withholding.

(b) The notice must be filed with the clerk of the court having venue as provided in Chapter 159.

(c) The notice of application for a writ of withholding may be delivered to the obligor at the same time that an order is filed for registration under Chapter 159.

History of Fam §8.253: Enacted by Acts 2001, 77th Leg., ch. 807, §1, eff. Sept. 1, 2001.

E FAM §8.254. ADDITIONAL ARREARAGES

If the notice of application for a writ of withholding states that the obligor has failed to pay more than one spousal maintenance payment according to the terms of the spousal maintenance order, the writ of withholding may include withholding for arrearages that accrue between the filing of the notice and the date of the hearing or the issuance of the writ.

History of Fam §8.254: Enacted by Acts 2001, 77th Leg., ch. 807, §1, eff. Sept. 1, 2001.

E FAM §8.255. DELIVERY OF NOTICE OF APPLICATION FOR WRIT OF WITHHOLDING; TIME OF DELIVERY

(a) The party who files a notice of application for a writ of withholding shall deliver the notice to the obligor by:

(1) first-class or certified mail, return receipt requested, addressed to the obligor's last known address or place of employment; or

(2) service of citation as in civil cases generally.

(b) If the notice is delivered by mail, the party who filed the notice shall file with the court a certificate stating the name, address, and date the party mailed the notice.

(c) The notice is considered to have been received by the obligor:

(1) on the date of receipt, if the notice was mailed by certified mail;

(2) on the 10th day after the date the notice was mailed, if the notice was mailed by first-class mail; or

(3) on the date of service, if the notice was delivered by service of citation.

History of Fam §8.255: Enacted by Acts 2001, 77th Leg., ch. 807, §1, eff. Sept. 1, 2001.

E FAM §8.256. MOTION TO STAY ISSUANCE OF WRIT OF WITHHOLDING

(a) The obligor may stay issuance of a writ of withholding by filing a motion to stay with the clerk of the court not later than the 10th day after the date the notice of application for a writ of withholding was received.

(b) The grounds for filing a motion to stay issuance are limited to a dispute concerning the identity of the obligor or the existence or the amount of the arrearages.

(c) The obligor shall verify that the statements of fact in the motion to stay issuance of the writ are correct.

History of Fam §8.256: Enacted by Acts 2001, 77th Leg., ch. 807, §1, eff. Sept. 1, 2001.

E FAM §8.257. EFFECT OF FILING MOTION TO STAY

If the obligor files a motion to stay as provided by Section 8.256, the clerk of the court may not deliver the writ of withholding to the obligor's employer before a hearing is held.

History of Fam §8.257: Enacted by Acts 2001, 77th Leg., ch. 807, §1, eff. Sept. 1, 2001.

E FAM §8.258. HEARING ON MOTION TO STAY

(a) If the obligor files a motion to stay as provided by Section 8.256, the court shall set a hearing on the motion and the clerk of the court shall notify the obligor and obligee of the date, time, and place of the hearing.

(b) The court shall hold a hearing on the motion to stay not later than the 30th day after the date the motion was filed unless the obligor and obligee agree and waive the right to have the motion heard within 30 days.

(c) After the hearing, the court shall:

(1) render an order for income withholding that includes a determination of any amount of arrearages; or

(2) grant the motion to stay.

History of Fam §8.258: Enacted by Acts 2001, 77th Leg., ch. 807, §1, eff. Sept. 1, 2001.

E FAM §8.259. SPECIAL EXCEPTIONS

(a) A defect in a notice of application for a writ of withholding is waived unless the respondent specially excepts in writing and cites with particularity the alleged defect, obscurity, or other ambiguity in the notice.

(b) A special exception under this section must be heard by the court before hearing the motion to stay issuance.

(c) If the court sustains an exception, the court shall provide the party filing the notice an opportunity to refile and shall continue the hearing to a specified date without requiring additional service.

History of Fam §8.259: Enacted by Acts 2001, 77th Leg., ch. 807, §1, eff. Sept. 1, 2001.

E FAM §8.260. WRIT OF WITHHOLDING AFTER ARREARAGES ARE PAID

(a) The court may not refuse to order withholding solely on the basis that the obligor paid the arrearages after the obligor received the notice of application for a writ of withholding.

(b) The court shall order that a reasonable amount of income be withheld and applied toward the liquidation of arrearages, even though a judgment confirming arrearages was rendered against the obligor.

History of Fam §8.260: Enacted by Acts 2001, 77th Leg., ch. 807, §1, eff. Sept. 1, 2001.

E FAM §8.261. REQUEST FOR ISSUANCE & DELIVERY OF WRIT OF WITHHOLDING

(a) If a notice of application for a writ of withholding is delivered and the obligor does not file a motion to stay within the time provided by Section 8.256, the party who filed the notice shall file with the clerk of the court a request for issuance of the writ of withholding stating the amount of current spousal maintenance, the amount of arrearages, and the amount to be withheld from the obligor's income.

(b) The party who filed the notice may not file a request for issuance before the 11th day after the date the obligor received the notice of application for a writ of withholding.

History of Fam §8.261: Enacted by Acts 2001, 77th Leg., ch. 807, §1, eff. Sept. 1, 2001.

E FAM §8.262. ISSUANCE & DELIVERY OF WRIT OF WITHHOLDING

The clerk of the court shall, on the filing of a request for issuance of a writ of withholding, issue and deliver the writ as provided by Subchapter D not later than the second working day after the date the request is filed. The clerk shall charge a fee in the amount of $15 for issuing the writ of withholding.

History of Fam §8.262: Enacted by Acts 2001, 77th Leg., ch. 807, §1, eff. Sept. 1, 2001.

E FAM §8.263. CONTENTS OF WRIT OF WITHHOLDING

A writ of withholding must direct that an obligor's employer or a subsequent employer withhold from the obligor's disposable earnings an amount for current spousal maintenance and arrearages consistent with this chapter.

History of Fam §8.263: Enacted by Acts 2001, 77th Leg., ch. 807, §1, eff. Sept. 1, 2001.

FAM §8.264. EXTENSION OF REPAYMENT SCHEDULE BY PARTY; UNREASONABLE HARDSHIP

A party who files a notice of application for a writ of withholding and who determines that the schedule for repaying arrearages would cause unreasonable hardship to the obligor or the obligor's family may extend the payment period in the writ.

History of Fam §8.264: Enacted by Acts 2001, 77th Leg., ch. 807, §1, eff. Sept. 1, 2001.

FAM §8.265. REMITTANCE OF AMOUNT TO BE WITHHELD

The obligor's employer shall remit the amount withheld to the person or office named in the writ on each pay date and shall include with the remittance the date on which the withholding occurred.

History of Fam §8.265: Enacted by Acts 2001, 77th Leg., ch. 807, §1, eff. Sept. 1, 2001.

FAM §8.266. FAILURE TO RECEIVE NOTICE OF APPLICATION FOR WRIT OF WITHHOLDING

(a) Not later than the 30th day after the date of the first pay period after the date the obligor's employer receives a writ of withholding, the obligor may file an affidavit with the court stating that:

(1) the obligor did not timely file a motion to stay because the obligor did not receive the notice of application for a writ of withholding; and

(2) grounds exist for a motion to stay.

(b) The obligor may:

(1) file with the affidavit a motion to withdraw the writ of withholding; and

(2) request a hearing on the applicability of the writ.

(c) Income withholding may not be interrupted until after the hearing at which the court renders an order denying or modifying withholding.

History of Fam §8.266: Enacted by Acts 2001, 77th Leg., ch. 807, §1, eff. Sept. 1, 2001.

FAM §8.267. ISSUANCE & DELIVERY OF WRIT OF WITHHOLDING TO SUBSEQUENT EMPLOYER

(a) After the clerk of the court issues a writ of withholding, a party authorized to file a notice of application for a writ of withholding under this subchapter may deliver a copy of the writ to a subsequent employer of the obligor by certified mail.

(b) Except as provided by an order under Section 8.152, the writ of withholding must include the name, address, and signature of the party and clearly indicate that the writ is being issued to a subsequent employer.

(c) The party shall file:

(1) a copy of the writ of withholding with the clerk not later than the third working day after the date of delivery of the writ to the subsequent employer; and

(2) the postal return receipt from the delivery to the subsequent employer not later than the third working day after the date the party receives the receipt.

(d) The party shall pay the clerk a fee in the amount of $15 for filing the copy of the writ.

History of Fam §8.267: Enacted by Acts 2001, 77th Leg., ch. 807, §1, eff. Sept. 1, 2001.

Sections 8.268-8.300 reserved for expansion

SUBCHAPTER G. MODIFICATION, REDUCTION, OR TERMINATION OF WITHHOLDING

FAM §8.301. AGREEMENT BY PARTIES REGARDING AMOUNT OR DURATION OF WITHHOLDING

(a) An obligor and obligee may agree to reduce or terminate income withholding for spousal maintenance on the occurrence of any contingency stated in the order.

(b) The obligor and obligee may file a notarized or acknowledged request with the clerk of the court under Section 8.108 for a revised writ of withholding or notice of termination of withholding.

(c) The clerk shall issue and deliver to the obligor's employer a writ of withholding that reflects the agreed revision or a notice of termination of withholding.

(d) An agreement by the parties under this section does not modify the terms of an order for spousal maintenance.

History of Fam §8.301: Enacted by Acts 2001, 77th Leg., ch. 807, §1, eff. Sept. 1, 2001.

FAM §8.302. MODIFICATIONS TO OR TERMINATION OF WITHHOLDING IN VOLUNTARY WITHHOLDING CASES

(a) If an obligor initiates voluntary withholding under Section 8.108, the obligee may file with the clerk of the court a notarized request signed by the obligor and the obligee for the issuance and delivery to the obligor of:

(1) a modified writ of withholding that reduces the amount of withholding; or

(2) a notice of termination of withholding.

(b) On receipt of a request under this section, the clerk shall issue and deliver a modified writ of withholding or notice of termination in the manner provided by Section 8.301.

(c) The clerk may charge a fee in the amount of $15 for issuing and delivering the modified writ of withholding or notice of termination.

(d) An obligee may contest a modified writ of withholding or notice of termination issued under this section by requesting a hearing in the manner provided by Section 8.258 not later than the 180th day after the date the obligee discovers that the writ or notice was issued.

History of Fam §8.302: Enacted by Acts 2001, 77th Leg., ch. 807, §1, eff. Sept. 1, 2001.

E FAM §8.303. TERMINATION OF WITHHOLDING IN MANDATORY WITHHOLDING CASES

(a) An obligor for whom withholding for maintenance owed or withholding for maintenance and child support owed is mandatory may file a motion to terminate withholding. On a showing by the obligor that the obligor has complied fully with the terms of the maintenance or child support order, as applicable, the court shall render an order for the issuance and delivery to the obligor of a notice of termination of withholding.

(b) The clerk shall issue and deliver the notice of termination ordered under this section to the obligor.

(c) The clerk may charge a fee in the amount of $15 for issuing and delivering the notice.

History of Fam §8.303: Enacted by Acts 2001, 77th Leg., ch. 807, §1, eff. Sept. 1, 2001.

E FAM §8.304. DELIVERY OF ORDER OF REDUCTION OR TERMINATION OF WITHHOLDING

Any person may deliver to the obligor's employer a certified copy of an order that reduces the amount of spousal maintenance to be withheld or terminates the withholding.

History of Fam §8.304: Enacted by Acts 2001, 77th Leg., ch. 807, §1, eff. Sept. 1, 2001.

E FAM §8.305. LIABILITY OF EMPLOYERS

The provisions of this chapter regarding the liability of employers for withholding apply to an order that reduces or terminates withholding.

History of Fam §8.305: Enacted by Acts 2001, 77th Leg., ch. 807, §1, eff. Sept. 1, 2001.

CHAPTER 9. POST-DECREE PROCEEDINGS

SUBCHAPTER A. SUIT TO ENFORCE DECREE

FAM §9.001. ENFORCEMENT OF DECREE

(a) A party affected by a decree of divorce or annulment providing for a division of property as provided by Chapter 7 may request enforcement of that decree by filing a suit to enforce as provided by this chapter in the court that rendered the decree.

(b) Except as otherwise provided in this chapter, a suit to enforce shall be governed by the Texas Rules of Civil Procedure applicable to the filing of an original lawsuit.

(c) A party whose rights, duties, powers, or liabilities may be affected by the suit to enforce is entitled to receive notice by citation and shall be commanded to appear by filing a written answer. Thereafter, the proceedings shall be as in civil cases generally.

History of Fam §9.001: Acts 1997, 75th Leg., ch. 7, §1, eff. April 17, 1997. Source: Former Fam §3.70(a), (b).

Brown v. Fullenweider, 52 S.W.3d 169, 170-71 (Tex. 2001). "The question in this case is whether a party's attorney may file a motion under [§9.001] to collect fees from his own client. [¶] [T]he obvious purpose of former §§3.70-3.77..., currently §§9.001-9.014, was to provide an expeditious procedure for enforcing and clarifying property divisions in divorce decrees. ... Suffice it to say that none [of the sections] contemplates that such proceedings would involve any issues other than those related to the division of a marital estate. An attorney's claim against his client for fees is not such an issue. It is wholly implausible that the Legislature intended to deny an attorney and client the right to trial by jury in a dispute over fees related to a divorce proceeding." *See also* ***Stewart v. Stine***, 57 S.W.3d 94, 101-02 (Tex.App.—Fort Worth 2001, no pet.).

FAM §9.002. CONTINUING AUTHORITY TO ENFORCE DECREE

The court that rendered the decree of divorce or annulment retains the power to enforce the property division as provided by Chapter 7.

History of Fam §9.002: Acts 1997, 75th Leg., ch. 7, §1, eff. April 17, 1997. Source: Former Fam §3.70(c).

Beach v. Beach, 912 S.W.2d 345, 348 (Tex.App.—Houston [14th Dist.] 1995, no writ). "After rendition of a divorce decree, the trial court retains the power to enforce the property division. A court order or property division may be enforced by filing a motion in the court that rendered the decree by any party affected by the order or decree."

Dechon v. Dechon, 909 S.W.2d 950, 955 (Tex. App.—El Paso 1995, no writ). "A trial court has inherent power to clarify or enforce its previously entered decree. Such jurisdiction encompasses both subject-matter jurisdiction to adjudicate the dispute and personal jurisdiction over the parties originally affected by the decree."

FAM §9.003. FILING DEADLINES

(a) A suit to enforce the division of tangible personal property in existence at the time of the decree of divorce or annulment must be filed before the second anniversary of the date the decree was signed or becomes final after appeal, whichever date is later, or the suit is barred.

(b) A suit to enforce the division of future property not in existence at the time of the original decree must be filed before the second anniversary of the date the right to the property matures or accrues or the decree becomes final, whichever date is later, or the suit is barred.

History of Fam §9.003: Acts 1997, 75th Leg., ch. 7, §1, eff. April 17, 1997. Source: Former Fam §3.70(c).

Generally

Jenkins v. Jenkins, 991 S.W.2d 440, 445 (Tex. App.—Fort Worth 1999, pet. denied). Section "9.003(b)'s two-year statute of limitations does not apply to this case because the [Bankruptcy] Trustee did not seek to compel a *division* of property via his motion to enforce. A division of property was unnecessary, because the divorce decree awarded [wife] a specific amount of alimony. The Trustee merely sought a money judgment for alimony awarded but not paid.... Because the Trustee sought a reduction of the specific monetary award in the AID to judgment, rather than a division of property, the Trustee's claim is not governed by §9.003(b)."

Dechon v. Dechon, 909 S.W.2d 950, 961 (Tex. App.—El Paso 1995, no writ). Section 3.70(c), now §9.003 "makes little sense unless it applies to all methods of enforcement under Subchapter [A]. We decline to carve exceptions depending on the method of enforcement sought. [W]e note that while clarification is a remedy, it is in fact a prerequisite to enforcement rather than a method of enforcement. A period of several years may pass before a litigant recognizes the necessity for a clarification proceeding. *At 962:* [W]e apply no statute of limitations to the clarification procedure itself. It does apply, however, to the enforcement process once clarification is obtained."

Carter v. Charles, 853 S.W.2d 667, 672 (Tex.App.—Houston [14th Dist.] 1993, no writ). The "§3.70 [now §9.003] limitations period applies to *personal* property, not real property."

§9.003(a)

Arnold v. Eaton, 910 S.W.2d 181, 183 (Tex.App.—Eastland 1995, no writ). Husband "argues that appellee's motion to enforce the property award [from the prior divorce] was barred by the limitations period in §3.70(c) [now §9.003(a)]. The original divorce decree awarded appellee a debt of $ 20,000.00 and secured that debt by a lien. Appellee's suit for enforcement sought to reduce the unpaid debt to a money judgment. Neither the debt nor the lien is tangible personal property."

§9.003(b)

Chavez v. Chavez, 12 S.W.3d 563, 564-65 (Tex. App.—San Antonio 1999, no pet.). "The proceeds from the sale of the stock constituted property not in existence at the time of the divorce decree, or future property. The statute of limitations for enforcing the division of future property is two years from the date the right to the property matures or accrues or the decree becomes final. [Husband] contends that his bankruptcy discharge date serves as the first date upon which he could be charged with failing to follow the court's order. [¶] The divorce decree does not specify when [husband] was required to sell the stock. Instead, the decree specifies when [husband] was required to deliver the proceeds of the sale of the stock; *i.e.*, 'within ten days of the receipt of said proceeds of said stock.' As a result, the first date [husband] could be charged with contempt was the eleventh day after the sale of the stock.... Based on this date, the statute of limitations would have run ... unless the discovery rule applies."

In re Marriage of Reinauer, 946 S.W.2d 853, 859-60 (Tex.App.—Amarillo 1997, writ denied). "At the time the ... Decree was signed, the [spouses'] interests in the military retirement benefits had yet to mature. Nonetheless, the interests were not mere expectancies but contingent interests in future property, or choses-in-action. Given this, [wife] was entitled to enforce their division at any time within two years after her ex-husband's interests matured."

FAM §9.004. APPLICABILITY TO UNDIVIDED PROPERTY

The procedures and limitations of this subchapter do not apply to existing property not divided on divorce, which are governed by Subchapter C and by the rules applicable to civil cases generally.

History of Fam §9.004: Acts 1997, 75th Leg., ch. 7, §1, eff. April 17, 1997. Source: Former Fam §3.70(d).

FAM §9.005. NO JURY

A party may not demand a jury trial if the procedures to enforce a decree of divorce or annulment provided by this subchapter are invoked.

History of Fam §9.005: Acts 1997, 75th Leg., ch. 7, §1, eff. April 17, 1997. Source: Former Fam §3.70(e).

FAM §9.006. ENFORCEMENT OF DIVISION OF PROPERTY

(a) Except as provided by this subchapter and by the Texas Rules of Civil Procedure, the court may render further orders to enforce the division of property made in the decree of divorce or annulment to assist in the implementation of or to clarify the prior order.

(b) The court may specify more precisely the manner of effecting the property division previously made if the substantive division of property is not altered or changed.

(c) An order of enforcement does not alter or affect the finality of the decree of divorce or annulment being enforced.

History of Fam §9.006: Acts 1997, 75th Leg., ch. 7, §1, eff. April 17, 1997. Source: Former Fam §3.71(a).

Ex parte Gorena, 595 S.W.2d 841, 844 (Tex.1979). "Despite the fact that a judgment has its genesis in an agreement between the parties, the judgment itself has an independent status. Once the agreement of the parties has been approved by the court and made a part of its judgment, the agreement is no longer merely a contract between private individuals but is the judgment of the court. [¶] 'The fact that a judgment is rendered by consent gives it neither less nor greater force or effect than it would have had it been rendered after protracted litigation....' Thus, in suits to enforce agreed judgments, parties may not raise contractual defenses because such defenses constitute impermissible collateral attacks on the prior judgments."

Wright v. Eckhardt, 32 S.W.3d 891, 894 (Tex. App.—Corpus Christi 2000, no pet.). The Family Code "provides at least two circumstances in which the trial court may issue orders clarifying the decree. [¶] Under §9.006 ..., the court may render 'further orders to enforce the division of property made in the decree of divorce ... to assist in the implementation of or to clarify the prior order.' The court may specify more precisely the manner of effecting the property division previously made if the substantive division of property is not altered or changed. The trial court may also clarify the decree [under §9.008] on a finding by the court that the original form of the division of property is not specific enough to be enforceable by contempt. [¶] [Wife] alleges that the trial court erred by finding that the divorce decree's division of property was not specific enough to be enforceable by contempt. We disagree with [wife] that the trial court made such an implied finding, and we do not agree that such a finding is required under §9.006...."

Kimsey v. Kimsey, 965 S.W.2d 690, 694-95 (Tex. App.—El Paso 1998, pet. denied). "When a divorce decree is not a consent decree or agreed judgment, the normal rules applicable to the construction of judgments apply to its interpretation. Thus, where a decree is unambiguous, the trial court has no authority to issue an order altering or modifying the original disposition of property. If the property division in the original divorce decree is ambiguous, however, or not specific enough to be enforceable by contempt, the court may enter a clarifying order to enforce compliance with the original division of property. While the Family Code authorizes the trial court to clarify its judgment, it does not prohibit our review of Wife's complaints that the judgment is vague and unenforceable, nor is there any authority which suggests that an enforcement action is a prerequisite to raising a complaint on appeal."

Sharman v. Schuble, 846 S.W.2d 574, 575 (Tex. App.—Houston [14th Dist.] 1993, orig. proceeding). "The divorce decree stated that the net proceeds from the sale would be distributed equally to the parties '*at the time of closing.*' [The] trial court's lack the authority to change the property division contained in a final divorce decree. By retaining possession of these funds, the trial court has clearly departed from the terms of the divorce decree. *At 576:* By retaining the proceeds in the registry, the trial court has effectively attached the relator's property. A writ of attachment is generally unavailable in claims for unliquidated debts. ... The trial court abused its discretion by refusing to distribute these funds in accordance with the terms of the divorce decree."

Bowden v. Knowlton, 734 S.W.2d 206, 208 (Tex. App.—Houston [1st Dist.] 1987, no writ). The wife "sought to impress an equitable lien on the [husband's] residence, and thus, her action was for aid in the enforcement of the decree, which was maintainable under the provisions of §3.71 [now §9.006]. That section authorizes the court to 'specify more precisely the manner of effecting the property division previously made if the substantive division of property is not altered or changed.' Here, the relief sought by the [wife] did not contemplate any changes in the actual, substantive division of the property. [¶] [A] divorce court may impose an equitable lien against the property of a spouse to secure that spouse's obligation to pay a monetary award that represents the consideration for the other spouse's relinquishment of his or her interest in the marital estate. Indeed, it has been held that a vendor's lien arises by implication when one spouse agrees to pay a sum of money as consideration for the other spouse's interest in a particular piece of property. We hold that the trial court had the authority, in aid of the enforcement of its monetary award, to impose a lien on the [husband's] residence."

FAM §9.007. LIMITATION ON POWER OF COURT TO ENFORCE

(a) A court may not amend, modify, alter, or change the division of property made or approved in the decree of divorce or annulment. An order to enforce the division is limited to an order to assist in the implementation of or to clarify the prior order and may not alter or change the substantive division of property.

(b) An order under this section that amends, modifies, alters, or changes the actual, substantive division of property made or approved in a final decree of divorce or annulment is beyond the power of the divorce court and is unenforceable.

(c) The power of the court to render further orders to assist in the implementation of or to clarify the property division is abated while an appellate proceeding is pending.

History of Fam §9.007: Acts 1997, 75th Leg., ch. 7, §1, eff. April 17, 1997. Source: Former Fam §3.71.

Bishop v. Bishop, ___ S.W.3d ___ (Tex.App.—San Antonio 2002, n.p.h.) (No. 04-01-00292-CV; 2-13-02). "We hold that the decree disposed of the residence. The decree disposed of the house by: (1) awarding [wife] the exclusive right to enjoy the use and possession of the premises; (2) providing for the sale of the house at a mutually agreed upon time and price; and (3) providing for a distribution of the net proceeds to [wife] and [husband] depending on the year of the sale or on the amount of years paid on the mortgage by each of the parties. We also hold that the decree is not ambiguous. The decree does not require an immediate sale and, in fact, contemplates years before a sale will occur. A change in the circumstances of the parties after the divorce does not create an ambiguity. Because the decree disposes of the residence and the provisions of the decree dealing with the residence are not ambiguous, the trial court did not have the power to change, amend, modify or alter the decree."

English v. English, 44 S.W.3d 102, 106 (Tex.App.—Houston [14th Dist.] 2001, no pet.). "Looking at the plain language of [§9.007(c)], the provision deals with *further* orders or clarification. It stands to reason there must first be a decree of divorce or annulment. Without an existing decree, there was nothing to appeal. A *further* order requires a prior order or decree. After an initial decree containing a property division, the trial court is legislatively restrained from rendering further orders to assist in the implementation or clarification of the property division pending appeal. The power of the court to do so is abated. The plain statutory language does not stay, supersede or otherwise inhibit the finality of the decree, absent a supersedeas bond. Similarly, the plain language is directed at the power of the court, not the obligations and responsibilities of the parties. Under the statute, the trial court is prohibited from implementing and clarifying the property division by way of further order. However, neither the parties nor the ministerial act of execution of the judgment are proscribed."

FAM §9.008. CLARIFICATION ORDER

(a) On the request of a party or on the court's own motion, the court may render a clarifying order before a motion for contempt is made or heard, in conjunction with a motion for contempt or on denial of a motion for contempt.

(b) On a finding by the court that the original form of the division of property is not specific enough to be enforceable by contempt, the court may render a clarifying order setting forth specific terms to enforce compliance with the original division of property.

(c) The court may not give retroactive effect to a clarifying order.

(d) The court shall provide a reasonable time for compliance before enforcing a clarifying order by contempt or in another manner.

History of Fam §9.008: Acts 1997, 75th Leg., ch. 7, §1, eff. April 17, 1997. Source: Former Fam §3.72.

In re Marriage of Alford, 40 S.W.3d 187, 189-90 (Tex.App.—Texarkana 2001, no pet.). The question is "whether the trial court had to hold a trial on the merits before issuing [a clarification order under §9.008]. We hold it did not. [¶] A party affected by a divorce decree that provides for a division of property may request enforcement of the decree by filing suit in the court that rendered the decree. Such a suit is governed by the Texas Rules of Civil Procedure, except as otherwise provided in Chapter 9, and any affected party is entitled to be served with notice and to file an answer. Thereafter, the proceedings are conducted as in civil cases generally, except that the parties are not entitled to a jury trial. [¶] Under §9.008(a), however, the trial court may render a clarifying order on the request of a party or on its own motion. Thus, §9.008(a) comes under the 'except as otherwise provided' provision of §9.001(b)."

Zeolla v. Zeolla, 15 S.W.3d 239, 242 (Tex.App.—Houston [14th Dist.] 2000, pet. denied). Husband "argues the clarifying order does not comply with ... §9.008(c) because its requirement that he pay $8,307.27 in past due benefits produces a retroactive effect. ... For context, this subsection is obviously within ... §9.008. This entire section deals with clarification in aid of contempt enforcement. Subsections (a), (b) and (d) all specifically speak in terms of contempt. Appellant argues §9.008(c) out of context. Although subsection (c) does not specifically mention contempt, viewed in context we hold all subsections of 9.008 are in conjunction with contempt. Therefore a court may not give retroactive effect to a clarifying order in such a way as to subject a party immediately to contempt. 'The court shall provide a reasonable time for compliance before enforcing a clarifying order by contempt or in another manner.'"

Wilson v. Uzzel, 953 S.W.2d 384, 391 (Tex.App.—El Paso 1997, no writ). "Section 3.72(b) [now §9.008] empowered a trial court to issue a clarifying order to effectuate the division of property in those situations where the decree was ambiguous or not sufficiently specific to enforce by contempt. However, the order could not amend, modify, alter, or change the actual substantive division of property."

Pierce v. Pierce, 850 S.W.2d 675, 679 (Tex.App.—El Paso 1993, writ denied). "Clarification orders may only be made upon 'a finding by the court that the original form of the division of property is not specific enough to be enforceable by contempt.' That means that a clarification order must be based on a finding, express or implied, that the provision dividing the property is so unspecific or ambiguous that it could not be enforced by a contempt proceeding."

Traylor v. Traylor, 789 S.W.2d 701, 703 (Tex. App.—Texarkana 1990, no writ). "We ... look at [§3.72, now §9.008] in its entirety to determine to what type of proceeding the Legislature intended the clarifying orders to apply. [¶] Subsections (a) and (b) of §3.72 contain language limiting them to contempt proceedings. The first sentence in Subsection (c) does not expand on their purpose but provides that these orders will not be given retroactive effect. The purpose of the last sentence is to provide for a reasonable time before enforcement of a clarification order. In addition to mentioning enforcement by contempt, this sentence does mention enforcement in another manner. Section 3.72 was intended to apply to property divisions enforceable by contempt. It does not prohibit another method of enforcement after the clarification order is entered. However, the language of §3.72 is not broad enough to apply to a provision in an agreement incident to divorce that could not be enforced by contempt and which could not have been ordered by the court as a part of the division of the community property."

FAM §9.009. DELIVERY OF PROPERTY

To enforce the division of property made in a decree of divorce or annulment, the court may make an order to deliver the specific existing property awarded, without regard to whether the property is of especial value, including an award of an existing sum of money or its equivalent.

History of Fam §9.009: Acts 1997, 75th Leg., ch. 7, §1, eff. April 17, 1997. Source: Former Fam §3.73.

Burton v. Burton, 734 S.W.2d 727, 729 (Tex.App.—Waco 1987, no writ). "The provisions of §§3.71(a) [now §9.006] and 3.73 [now §9.009] clearly authorize the court to enforce a property division by ordering the delivery of existing personal property from one party affected by the divorce decree to another party. The question is whether the court can take this action on its own motion or must await the filing of a motion to enforce under §3.70(a) [now §9.001]. The language of these sections does not expressly prohibit the court from acting on its own motion, and this court will not judicially add such a limitation."

FAM §9.010. REDUCTION TO MONEY JUDGMENT

(a) If a party fails to comply with a decree of divorce or annulment and delivery of property awarded in the decree is no longer an adequate remedy, the court may render a money judgment for the damages caused by that failure to comply.

(b) If a party did not receive payments of money as awarded in the decree of divorce or annulment, the court may render judgment against a defaulting party for the amount of unpaid payments to which the party is entitled.

(c) The remedy of a reduction to money judgment is in addition to the other remedies provided by law.

(d) A money judgment rendered under this section may be enforced by any means available for the enforcement of judgment for debt.

History of Fam §9.010: Acts 1997, 75th Leg., ch. 7, §1, eff. April 17, 1997. Source: Former Fam §3.74.

Ackerly v. Ackerly, 13 S.W.3d 454, 457 (Tex.App.—Corpus Christi 2000, no pet.). "Notably, §9.010 does not specify it is not governed by the rules of civil procedure. Accordingly, pursuant to §9.001(b), the rules which govern a motion for reduction to money judgment are the [TRCP] applicable to the filing of an original lawsuit, and not the rules which apply to the filing of a motion (i.e., rules 21 and 21a). Furthermore, any party affected by the motion is entitled to notice by citation. [¶] Because the motion for reduction to money judgment is a separate action, the trial court's judgment in this case, rendered in the absence of an answer or an appearance, is a default judgment. A default judgment is improper against a defendant who has not been served in strict compliance with the law."

Bowden v. Knowlton, 734 S.W.2d 206, 208 (Tex. App.—Houston [1st Dist.] 1987, no writ). Wife "was entitled to seek a money judgment under §3.74 [now §9.010] for the damages allegedly caused by the [husband's] failure to comply with the terms of the divorce decree. We hold that the limitation period specified in §3.70(c) [now §9.003] did not apply to relief sought under this section." *See also* ***Jenkins v. Jenkins***, 991 S.W.2d 440, 445 (Tex.App.—Fort Worth 1999, pet. denied).

FAM §9.011. RIGHT TO FUTURE PROPERTY

(a) The court may, by any remedy provided by this chapter, enforce an award of the right to receive installment payments or a lump-sum payment due on the maturation of an existing vested or nonvested right to be paid in the future.

(b) The subsequent actual receipt by the non-owning party of property awarded to the owner in a decree of divorce or annulment creates a fiduciary obligation in favor of the owner and imposes a constructive trust on the property for the benefit of the owner.

History of Fam §9.011: Acts 1997, 75th Leg., ch. 7, §1, eff. April 17, 1997. Source: Former Fam §3.75.

Schneider v. Schneider, 5 S.W.3d 925, 930 (Tex. App.—Austin 1999, no pet.). "The Texas statute [husband] cites in support of imposing a constructive trust in this situation states that the subsequent actual receipt by the non-owning party of property awarded to the owner in a divorce decree creates a fiduciary obligation and imposes a constructive trust. Here [wife] has not actually received any Plan benefits. In fact, in the event the Air Force eventually recognizes the court-ordered division, or should [wife] not survive [husband], she will never actually receive 100% of the benefits. The entire controversy surrounding the Plan is contingent on the occurrence of future events, and a constructive trust may not be necessary in the end to carry out the court's intent. Thus, we conclude that the trial court did not act in an unreasonable and arbitrary manner or without reference to any guiding principles when it declined to impose the equitable remedy of a constructive trust on possible future Plan disbursements."

Jeffcoat v. Jeffcoat, 886 S.W.2d 567, 570 (Tex. App.—Beaumont 1994, no writ). "The constructive trustee provision was a correct means or manner in which the divorce judge sought properly to insure a just and right partition [of future payments from appellant's pension plan]. Section 3.75 [now §9.011] provides that installment payments or a lump-sum payment to be made and paid in the future may properly be enforced by the remedies provided in the relevant subchapter."

FAM §9.012. CONTEMPT

(a) The court may enforce by contempt an order requiring delivery of specific property or an award of a right to future property.

(b) The court may not enforce by contempt an award in a decree of divorce or annulment of a sum of money payable in a lump sum or in future installment payments in the nature of debt, except for:

(1) a sum of money in existence at the time the decree was rendered; or

(2) a matured right to future payments as provided by Section 9.011.

(c) This subchapter does not detract from or limit the general power of a court to enforce an order of the court by appropriate means.

History of Fam §9.012: Acts 1997, 75th Leg., ch. 7, §1, eff. April 17, 1997. Source: Former Fam §3.76.

Ex parte Goad, 690 S.W.2d 894, 896 (Tex.1985). Wife "asserts that §3.70(c) [now §9.003] cannot operate to invalidate the judgment because her original motion for contempt was filed prior to the effective date of the statute. We agree with [wife]. Her former husband is not entitled to a retroactive application of the two year limitation period." *But see* ***Burton***, below.

Burton v. Burton, 734 S.W.2d 727, 729 (Tex.App.—Waco 1987, no writ). "The two-year limitation in §3.70(c) [now §9.003] does not expressly apply to motions for contempt under §3.76 [now §9.012], and this court will not add that limitation." *But see* ***Gonzales***, below.

Gonzales v. Gonzales, 728 S.W.2d 446, 447 n.1 (Tex.App.—San Antonio 1987, no writ). Section 3.70(c), now §9.003, "refers only to a limitation on motions for enforcement. However, our Supreme Court has interpreted that statute to bar contempt motions filed pursuant to … §3.76 [now §9.012]. By analogy, we conclude that the limitations period applies to all of the provisions of … Subchapter D, *Enforcement*." *But see* ***Burton***, above.

FAM §9.013. COSTS

The court may award costs in a proceeding to enforce a property division under this subchapter as in other civil cases.

History of Fam §9.013: Acts 1997, 75th Leg., ch. 7, §1, eff. April 17, 1997. Source: Former Fam §3.77.

FAM §9.014. ATTORNEY'S FEES

The court may award reasonable attorney's fees as costs in a proceeding under this subchapter. The court may order the attorney's fees to be paid directly to the attorney, who may enforce the order for fees in the attorney's own name by any means available for the enforcement of a judgment for debt.

History of Fam §9.014: Acts 1997, 75th Leg., ch. 7, §1, eff. April 17, 1997. Source: Former Fam §3.77.

Schneider v. Schneider, 5 S.W.3d 925, 930 (Tex. App.—Austin 1999, no pet.). "Section 9.014 … provides that '[t]he court *may* award reasonable attorney's fees as costs in a proceeding under this chapter.' This statute does not entitle either party to attorney's fees; rather, it merely permits the court to award them. The decision to grant or deny attorney's fees under this statute is reviewed for an abuse of discretion. To prevail on this issue, [husband] must prove that the trial court acted without reference to any guiding principles when it refused to award him attorney's fees."

Jenkins v. Jenkins, 991 S.W.2d 440, 450 (Tex. App.—Fort Worth 1999, pet. denied). Section 9.014 "provides that a trial court 'may award reasonable attorney's fees as costs in a proceeding under this subchapter.' The statute does not require [wife] to have 'prevailed' on her claims against [husband]; it simply requires the fee award to be reasonable under the circumstances of this case. However, when a trial court awards attorney's fees to the nonprevailing party in a family law matter, the court must state on the record or in its judgment the good cause substantiating the award."

Sections 9.015-9.100 reserved for expansion

SUBCHAPTER B. POST-DECREE QUALIFIED DOMESTIC RELATIONS ORDER

FAM §9.101. JURISDICTION FOR QUALIFIED DOMESTIC RELATIONS ORDER

(a) Notwithstanding any other provision of this chapter, the court that rendered a final decree of divorce or annulment or another final order dividing property under this title retains continuing, exclusive jurisdiction to render an enforceable qualified domestic relations order or similar order permitting payment of pension, retirement plan, or other employee benefits divisible under the law of this state or of the United States to an alternate payee or other lawful payee.

(b) Unless prohibited by federal law, a suit seeking a qualified domestic relations order or similar order under this section applies to a previously divided pension, retirement plan, or other employee benefit divisible under the law of this state or of the United States, whether the plan or benefit is private, state, or federal.

History of Fam §9.101: Acts 1997, 75th Leg., ch. 7, §1, eff. April 17, 1997. Source: Former Fam §3.711(a), (b).

Dechon v. Dechon, 909 S.W.2d 950, 961 n.9 (Tex. App.—El Paso 1995, no writ). Section 3.711, now §9.101, "confers upon the trial court continuing jurisdiction to enter orders necessary to amend or correct qualified domestic relations orders in order to ensure they are qualified and enforceable. We liken this provision to §3.72 [now §9.008] clarification orders, as they both constitute prerequisites to enforcement rather than methods of enforcement."

FAM §9.102. PROCEDURE

(a) A party to a decree of divorce or annulment may petition the court for a qualified domestic relations order or similar order.

(b) Except as otherwise provided by this code, a petition under this subchapter is governed by the Texas Rules of Civil Procedure that apply to the filing of an original lawsuit.

(c) Each party whose rights may be affected by the petition is entitled to receive notice by citation and shall be commanded to appear by filing a written answer.

(d) The proceedings shall be conducted in the same manner as civil cases generally.

History of Fam §9.102: Acts 1997, 75th Leg., ch. 7, §1, eff. April 17, 1997. Source: Former Fam §3.711(d).

FAM §9.103. PRIOR FAILURE TO RENDER QUALIFIED DOMESTIC RELATIONS ORDER

A party may petition a court to render a qualified domestic relations order or similar order if the court that rendered a final decree of divorce or annulment or another final order dividing property under this chapter did not provide a qualified domestic relations order or similar order permitting payment of benefits to an alternate payee or other lawful payee.

History of Fam §9.103: Acts 1997, 75th Leg., ch. 7, §1, eff. April 17, 1997. Source: Former Fam §3.711(a).

FAM §9.104. DEFECTIVE PRIOR DOMESTIC RELATIONS ORDER

If a plan administrator or other person acting in an equivalent capacity determines that a domestic relations order does not satisfy the requirements of a qualified domestic relations order or similar order, the court retains continuing, exclusive jurisdiction over the parties and their property to the extent necessary to render a qualified domestic relations order.

History of Fam §9.104: Acts 1997, 75th Leg., ch. 7, §1, eff. April 17, 1997. Source: Former Fam §3.711(c).

FAM §9.105. LIBERAL CONSTRUCTION

The court shall liberally construe this subchapter to effect payment of retirement benefits that were divided by a previous decree that failed to contain a qualified domestic relations order or similar order or that contained an order that failed to meet the requirements of a qualified domestic relations order or similar order.

History of Fam §9.105: Acts 1997, 75th Leg., ch. 7, §1, eff. April 17, 1997. Source: Former Fam §3.711(e).

Arena v. Arena, 822 S.W.2d 645, 649 (Tex.App.—Fort Worth 1991, no writ). "The domestic relations order issued by the trial court in this case recognized [wife's] right to receive the vested policy benefits. The Decree of Divorce specifically identifies the name of the participant, [husband], and the beneficiary, [wife]; in addition, it provides the name and address of [wife's] attorney. The decree specifically identifies five separate benefit plans under which [wife] will be the beneficiary. The domestic relations order also states the amount of each plan and that [wife] will be entitled to the entire vested portion of each. Because the Decree of Divorce includes all of the information required by the [ERISA] statute and does not involve any of the prohibitions, the decree is deemed a QDRO."

Sections 9.106-9.200 reserved for expansion

SUBCHAPTER C. POST-DECREE DIVISION OF PROPERTY

FAM §9.201. PROCEDURE FOR DIVISION OF CERTAIN PROPERTY NOT DIVIDED ON DIVORCE OR ANNULMENT

(a) Either former spouse may file a suit as provided by this subchapter to divide property not divided or awarded to a spouse in a final decree of divorce or annulment.

(b) Except as otherwise provided by this subchapter, the suit is governed by the Texas Rules of Civil Procedure applicable to the filing of an original lawsuit.

History of Fam §9.201: Acts 1997, 75th Leg., ch. 7, §1, eff. April 17, 1997. Source: Former Fam §3.90(a), (b).

McLaurin v. McLaurin, 968 S.W.2d 947, 949 n.2 (Tex.App.—Texarkana 1998, no pet.). "If the language of the decree does not encompass all of the community property, the ex-husband and ex-wife still hold the undivided property as joint owners, and an original suit for partition of the property is now brought under §3.90 [now §9.201]."

Burgess v. Easley, 893 S.W.2d 87, 90 (Tex.App.—Dallas 1994, no writ). "In an action brought under §3.90 [now §9.201], a trial court presumes property owned by either spouse during or at dissolution of marriage is community property. [Husband's] burden to rebut this presumption is to prove by clear and convincing evidence that the property was his separate property, that he did not own the property during marriage, or that he got the property during marriage by gift, devise, or descent. The trial court's task is to determine when [husband's] rights in the property vested and whether he and [wife] were married at that time or whether the acquisition was by gift, devise, or descent. As a matter of law, the property in this case would not be community property if [husband] and [wife] were not married when his rights vested."

FAM §9.202. LIMITATIONS

(a) A suit under this subchapter must be filed before the second anniversary of the date a former spouse unequivocally repudiates the existence of the ownership interest of the other former spouse and communicates that repudiation to the other former spouse.

(b) The two-year limitations period is tolled for the period that a court of this state does not have jurisdiction over the former spouses or over the property.

History of Fam §9.202: Acts 1997, 75th Leg., ch. 7, §1, eff. April 17, 1997. Source: Former Fam §3.90(c).

Mayes v. Stewart, 11 S.W.3d 440, 457 (Tex.App.—Houston [14th Dist.] 2000, pet. denied). "Section 9.202 does not apply to suits to partition under Texas Property Code §23.001. The '*right to partition is absolute.*' Similarly, nothing in §9.202 suggests that it applies to tort claims against third parties."

Sagester v. Waltrip, 970 S.W.2d 767, 769 (Tex. App.—Austin 1998, pet. denied). "The statutes of limitations on divorce-related partition suits are triggered by repudiation of a claim of entitlement to a share of the undivided community property. The Texas Family Code requires that all suits to divide property not divided or awarded to a spouse in a final decree of divorce be brought within two years of the date one former spouse notifies the other former spouse that he or she *unequivocally* repudiates that other spouse's ownership interest. A four-year statute of limitations applies to all cases not involving real property that do not have a shorter limitations period applicable. In partition suits not subject to the Family Code provision, the trigger for the running of the four-year limitations period is unequivocal repudiation. Absent unequivocal repudiation, the partition suit can be filed long after the divorce. [¶] This appeal turns on whether [husband's] general denial ... is, as a matter of law, sufficient repudiation of [wife's] claim to trigger the running of the statutes of limitations periods. [¶] We find no authority for the proposition that a general denial combined with mere failure to share benefits for twenty years proves, as a matter of law, unequivocal repudiation. [¶] A general denial is, at most, an equivocal repudiation. [Husband's] pleading and [wife's] knowledge that she was not receiving benefits do not signify, as a matter of law, an unequivocal repudiation of [wife's] claim."

Phillips v. Phillips, 951 S.W.2d 955, 957 (Tex. App.—Waco 1997, no pet.). "Even if §3.90 [now §9.202] applied to bar an enforcement action under the Family Code, that section would not operate to bar an otherwise valid partition under the Property Code [§23.001]. The *right to partition is absolute*."

Carter v. Charles, 853 S.W.2d 667, 671 (Tex.App.—Houston [14th Dist.] 1993, no writ). "For this statute to apply, [movant] must show that (1) the property sued upon was not divided or awarded in a final decree of divorce, (2) [movant] repudiated [non-movant's] ownership interest in the property, (3) [movant's] repudiation was unequivocal, and (4) that unequivocal repudiation was communicated to [non-movant]."

FAM §9.203. DIVISION OF UNDIVIDED ASSETS WHEN PRIOR COURT HAD JURISDICTION

(a) If a court of this state failed to dispose of property subject to division in a final decree of divorce or annulment even though the court had jurisdiction over the spouses or over the property, the court shall divide the property in a manner that the court deems just and right, having due regard for the rights of each party and any children of the marriage.

(b) If a final decree of divorce or annulment rendered by a court in another state failed to dispose of property subject to division under the law of that state even though the court had jurisdiction to do so, a court of this state shall apply the law of the other state regarding undivided property as required by Section 1, Article IV, United States Constitution (the full faith and credit clause), and enabling federal statutes.

History of Fam §9.203: Acts 1997, 75th Leg., ch. 7, §1, eff. April 17, 1997. Source: Former Fam §3.91.

Forgason v. Forgason, 911 S.W.2d 893, 895-96 (Tex. App.—Amarillo 1995, writ denied). "[T]he authority under §3.91 [now §9.203] to 'divide' property is the authority to effect its partition. In partitioning the asset among the ex-spouses, it does not divest either of title. Rather, it 'dissolves the tenancy in common,' ... and apportions the asset among the tenants. It does not legally divest anyone of title to the asset. [¶] It directs the trial court to divide the subject asset in a 'just and right' manner. That standard implicitly encompasses the power to divide in less than an equal way. Depending upon the facts of each case, the court may validly apportion some, all or none of the asset to any particular party."

In re Marriage of Moore, 890 S.W.2d 821, 840 (Tex.App.—Amarillo 1994, no writ). "If the language of the decree does not encompass all of the community property, the ex-husband and ex-wife still hold the undivided property as joint owners. [T]he trial court is to divide the undisposed of property in a manner that it deems just and right. The trial judge is no longer required by the tenets of property law to make an equal division based on each party's undivided one-half interest, rather, he is to consider 'the rights of each party and any children of the marriage' in making his division."

FAM §9.204. DIVISION OF UNDIVIDED ASSETS WHEN PRIOR COURT LACKED JURISDICTION

(a) If a court of this state failed to dispose of property subject to division in a final decree of divorce or annulment because the court lacked jurisdiction over a spouse or the property, and if that court subsequently acquires the requisite jurisdiction, that court may divide the property in a manner that the court deems just and right, having due regard for the rights of each party and any children of the marriage.

(b) If a final decree of divorce or annulment rendered by a court in another state failed to dispose of property subject to division under the law of that state because the court lacked jurisdiction over a spouse or the property, and if a court of this state subsequently acquires the requisite jurisdiction over the former spouses or over the property, the court in this state may divide the property in a manner that the court deems just and right, having due regard for the rights of each party and any children of the marriage.

History of Fam §9.204: Acts 1997, 75th Leg., ch. 7, §1, eff. April 17, 1997. Source: Former Fam §3.92.

FAM §9.205. ATTORNEY'S FEES

In a proceeding to divide property previously undivided in a decree of divorce or annulment as provided by this subchapter, the court may award reasonable attorney's fees as costs. The court may order the attorney's fees to be paid directly to the attorney, who may enforce the order in the attorney's own name by any means available for the enforcement of a judgment for debt.

History of Fam §9.205: Acts 1997, 75th Leg., ch. 7, §1, eff. April 17, 1997. Source: Former Fam §3.93.

Burgess v. Easley, 893 S.W.2d 87, 91 (Tex.App.—Dallas 1994, no writ). "A trial court may award reasonable attorneys fees in a suit to partition property that a court did not divide in a divorce proceeding. Such an award of attorneys fees is within the trial court's sound discretion."

Sections 9.206-9.300 reserved for expansion

SUBCHAPTER D. DISPOSITION OF UNDIVIDED BENEFICIAL INTEREST

FAM §9.301. PRE-DECREE DESIGNATION OF EX-SPOUSE AS BENEFICIARY OF LIFE INSURANCE

(a) If a decree of divorce or annulment is rendered after an insured has designated the insured's spouse as a beneficiary under a life insurance policy in force at the time of rendition, a provision in the policy in favor of the insured's former spouse is not effective unless:

(1) the decree designates the insured's former spouse as the beneficiary;

(2) the insured redesignates the former spouse as the beneficiary after rendition of the decree; or

(3) the former spouse is designated to receive the proceeds in trust for, on behalf of, or for the benefit of a child or a dependent of either former spouse.

(b) If a designation is not effective under Subsection (a), the proceeds of the policy are payable to the named alternative beneficiary or, if there is not a named alternative beneficiary, to the estate of the insured.

(c) An insurer who pays the proceeds of a life insurance policy issued by the insurer to the beneficiary under a designation that is not effective under Subsection (a) is liable for payment of the proceeds to the person or estate provided by Subsection (b) only if:

(1) before payment of the proceeds to the designated beneficiary, the insurer receives written notice at the home office of the insurer from an interested person that the designation is not effective under Subsection (a); and

(2) the insurer has not interpleaded the proceeds into the registry of a court of competent jurisdiction in accordance with the Texas Rules of Civil Procedure.

History of Fam §9.301: Acts 1997, 75th Leg., ch. 7, §1, eff. April 17, 1997. Source: Former Fam §3.632(b), (c).

Egelhoff v. Egelhoff, 532 U.S. 141, 121 S.Ct. 1322, 1325-26 (2001). See Annotation in Fam §9.302.

Barnett v. Barnett, 67 S.W.3d 107, 121 (Tex.2001). Had decedent husband "survived until divorce proceedings were concluded, [respondent wife] could have obtained a decree that qualified as a QDRO under ERISA. That decree would have effected a fair and just property division and could have dealt directly with the Prudential life insurance policy. Because [decedent husband] did not survive, [respondent wife] is relegated to a claim for constructive fraud on the community. Although preemption might result in an anomaly in this case, the reasoning in United States Supreme Court's decision *Egelhoff* compels us to conclude that [respondent wife]'s claim is based on state law that has a connection with an ERISA plan and is accordingly preempted. *At 126:* We conclude that fraud on the community, absent actual common-law fraud, is the type of claim that Congress intended to preempt under ERISA and that fraud on the community has no counterpart in federal common law. ... Accordingly, we hold that [respondent wife's] claim for constructive fraud on the community and her corresponding claim for a constructive trust are preempted by ERISA."

Sever v. Massachusetts Mut. Life Ins. Co., 944 S.W.2d 486, 490 (Tex.App.—Amarillo 1997, writ denied). "Section 3.632 [now §9.301] does not prescribe the procedure or method by which a beneficiary redesignation must be made. Because articles 3.49-1 and 3.48 of the Insurance Code and §3.632 of the Family Code, both cover designations of beneficiaries of insurance policies, they are in *pari materia* and must be read and considered together. [¶] Because the decree of divorce did not designate [ex-wife] as the beneficiary of the policy, or designate [ex-wife] to receive the proceeds in trust for or on behalf of [her daughter], by operation of law, the initial designation of [ex-wife] as the beneficiary was ineffective under §3.632(b) unless [ex-husband] effectively redesignated [her] as the beneficiary after the divorce. [¶] Upon the rendition of the decree of divorce, the designation of [ex-wife] was rendered ineffective by operation of law. Because a secondary beneficiary was not designated, the policy proceeds were payable to [ex-husband's] estate. To alter this disposition, a change or redesignation was required by the policy and permissive under article 3.49-1, §2 of the Insurance Code and §3.632 of the Family Code. [¶] Because §3.632 does not prescribe a specific method to redesignate a former spouse, the provisions of the policy and article 3.49-1 requiring that a beneficiary designation be in writing, are controlling."

Hunt v. Jefferson-Pilot Life Ins. Co., 900 S.W.2d 453, 456 (Tex.App.—Fort Worth 1995, writ denied). Section 3.632(c), now §9.301(c), "is an express limitation on the liability of an insurance company that pays the proceeds of a policy to the designated beneficiary. [¶] We find that any constructive notice the insurance company might have had upon receipt of the divorce decree does not constitute written notice under the Family Code or the Insurance Code."

In re Group Life Ins. Proceeds of Mallory, 872 S.W.2d 800, 803 (Tex.App.—Amarillo 1994, no writ). If "the beneficiary designation of a former spouse is rendered ineffective by virtue of §3.632 [now §9.301] the proceeds must be paid to the alternate beneficiary named in the policy, if any."

FAM §9.302. PRE-DECREE DESIGNATION OF EX-SPOUSE AS BENEFICIARY IN RETIREMENT BENEFITS & OTHER FINANCIAL PLANS

(a) If a decree of divorce or annulment is rendered after a spouse, acting in the capacity of a participant, annuitant, or account holder, has designated the other spouse as a beneficiary under an individual retirement account, employee stock option plan, stock option, or other form of savings, bonus, profit-sharing, or other employer plan or financial plan of an employee or a participant in force at the time of rendition, the designating provision in the plan in favor of the other former spouse is not effective unless:

(1) the decree designates the other former spouse as the beneficiary;

(2) the designating former spouse redesignates the other former spouse as the beneficiary after rendition of the decree; or

(3) the other former spouse is designated to receive the proceeds or benefits in trust for, on behalf of, or for the benefit of a child or dependent of either former spouse.

(b) If a designation is not effective under Subsection (a), the benefits or proceeds are payable to the named alternative beneficiary or, if there is not a named alternative beneficiary, to the designating former spouse.

(c) A business entity, employer, pension trust, insurer, financial institution, or other person obligated to pay retirement benefits or proceeds of a financial plan covered by this section who pays the benefits or proceeds to the beneficiary under a designation of the other former spouse that is not effective under Subsection (a) is liable for payment of the benefits or proceeds to the person provided by Subsection (b) only if:

(1) before payment of the benefits or proceeds to the designated beneficiary, the payor receives written notice at the home office or principal office of the payor from an interested person that the designation of the beneficiary or fiduciary is not effective under Subsection (a); and

(2) the payor has not interpleaded the benefits or proceeds into the registry of a court of competent jurisdiction in accordance with the Texas Rules of Civil Procedure.

(d) This section does not affect the right of a former spouse to assert an ownership interest in an undivided pension, retirement, annuity, or other financial plan described by this section as provided by this subchapter.

(e) This section does not apply to the disposition of a beneficial interest in a retirement benefit or other financial plan of a public retirement system as defined by Section 802.001, Government Code.

History of Fam §9.302: Acts 1997, 75th Leg., ch. 7, §1, eff. April 17, 1997. Source: Former Fam §3.633(b)-(e).

Egelhoff v. Egelhoff, 532 U.S. 141, 143 121 S.Ct. 1322, 1325-26 (2001). "A Washington statute provides that the designation of a spouse as the beneficiary of a nonprobate asset is revoked automatically upon divorce. We are asked to decide whether [ERISA] preempts that statute to the extent it applies to ERISA plans. We hold that it does. *At 147-48, 1327-28:* [P]etitioner argues that the Washington statute has an impermissible connection with ERISA plans. We agree. The statute binds ERISA plan administrators to a particular choice of rules for determining beneficiary status. The administrators must pay benefits to the beneficiaries chosen by state law, rather than to those identified in the plan documents. The statute thus implicates an area of core ERISA concern. ... [U]nlike generally applicable laws regulating 'areas where ERISA has nothing to say,' which we have upheld notwithstanding their incidental effect on ERISA plans, this statute governs the payment of benefits, a central matter of plan administration. [¶] The Washington statute also has a prohibited connection with ERISA plans because it interferes with nationally uniform plan administration. Uniformity is impossible, ... if plans are subject to different legal obligations in different States. [¶] The Washington statute at issue here poses precisely that threat. Plan administrators cannot make payments simply by identifying the beneficiary specified by the plan documents. Instead they must familiarize themselves with state statutes so that they can determined whether the named beneficiary's status has been 'revoked' by operation of law." *See also* ***Metropolitan Life Ins. Co. v. Marsh***, 119 F.3d 415, 420 (6th Cir.1997).

Heggy v. American Trading Employee Retirement Account Plan, 56 S.W.3d 280, 285 (Tex.App.—Houston [14th Dist.] 2001, no pet.) "Following ... the guidance provided by ***Egelhoff***, we hold that ERISA §1104(a)(1)(D) exclusively controls the designation of plan beneficiaries. Accordingly, [wife]'s purported waiver of [husband]'s pension benefits, as provided in the divorce decree, is not effective. *At n.3:* We recognize that our holding today conflicts with prior holdings of our sister courts [***Weaver v. Keen***, 43 S.W.3d 537, 538 (Tex.App.—Waco 2001, pet. granted, argument set for 10-4-02), and ***Emmens v. Johnson***, 923 S.W.2d 705, 707-08 (Tex. App.—Houston [1st Dist.] 1996, writ denied)] on the same issue. However, because these holdings rely on the Fifth Circuit's reasoning..., we respectfully decline to follow them."

Chapters 10-30 blank

FAMILY CODE—TITLE 2
CHILD IN RELATION TO THE FAMILY
TABLE OF CONTENTS

TITLE 2. CHILD IN RELATION TO THE FAMILY

FAMILY CODE—TITLE 2

CHILD IN RELATION TO THE FAMILY

TITLE 2

TITLE 2. CHILD IN RELATION TO THE FAMILY

SUBTITLE A. LIMITATIONS OF MINORITY

CHAPTER 31. REMOVAL OF DISABILITIES OF MINORITY

FAM §31.001. REQUIREMENTS

(a) A minor may petition to have the disabilities of minority removed for limited or general purposes if the minor is:

(1) a resident of this state;

(2) 17 years of age, or at least 16 years of age and living separate and apart from the minor's parents, managing conservator, or guardian; and

(3) self-supporting and managing the minor's own financial affairs.

(b) A minor may file suit under this chapter in the minor's own name. The minor need not be represented by next friend.

History of Fam §31.001: Acts 1995, 74th Leg., ch. 20, §1, eff. April 20, 1995. Source: Former Fam §31.01(a), (c).

FAM §31.002. REQUISITES OF PETITION; VERIFICATION

(a) The petition for removal of disabilities of minority must state:

(1) the name, age, and place of residence of the petitioner;

(2) the name and place of residence of each living parent;

(3) the name and place of residence of the guardian of the person and the guardian of the estate, if any;

(4) the name and place of residence of the managing conservator, if any;

(5) the reasons why removal would be in the best interest of the minor; and

(6) the purposes for which removal is requested.

(b) A parent of the petitioner must verify the petition, except that if a managing conservator or guardian of the person has been appointed, the petition must be verified by that person. If the person who is to verify the petition is unavailable or that person's whereabouts are unknown, the guardian ad litem shall verify the petition.

History of Fam §31.002: Acts 1995, 74th Leg., ch. 20, §1, eff. April 20, 1995. Source: Former Fam §31.02(a), (c).

FAM §31.003. VENUE

The petitioner shall file the petition in the county in which the petitioner resides.

History of Fam §31.003: Acts 1995, 74th Leg., ch. 20, §1, eff. April 20, 1995. Source: Former Fam §31.03(a).

FAM §31.004. GUARDIAN AD LITEM

The court shall appoint a guardian ad litem to represent the interest of the petitioner at the hearing.

History of Fam §31.004: Acts 1995, 74th Leg., ch. 20, §1, eff. April 20, 1995. Source: Former Fam §31.04.

FAM §31.005. ORDER

The court by order, or the Texas Supreme Court by rule or order, may remove the disabilities of minority of a minor, including any restriction imposed by Chapter 32, if the court or the Texas Supreme Court finds the removal to be in the best interest of the petitioner. The order or rule must state the limited or general purposes for which disabilities are removed.

History of Fam §31.005: Acts 1995, 74th Leg., ch. 20, §1, eff. April 20, 1995. Amended by Acts 1999, 76th Leg., ch. 1303, §1, eff. Sept. 1, 1999. Source: Former Fam §31.06.

A FAM §31.006. EFFECT OF GENERAL REMOVAL

Except for specific constitutional and statutory age requirements, a minor whose disabilities are removed for general purposes has the capacity of an adult, including the capacity to contract. Except as provided by federal law, all educational rights accorded to the parent of a student, including the right to make education decisions under Section 151.003(a)(10), transfer to the minor whose disabilities are removed for general purposes.

History of Fam §31.006: Acts 1995, 74th Leg., ch. 20, §1, eff. April 20, 1995. Amended by Acts 2001, 77th Leg., ch. 767, §9, eff. June 13, 2001. Source: Former Fam §31.07.

FAM §31.007. REGISTRATION OF ORDER OF ANOTHER STATE OR NATION

(a) A nonresident minor who has had the disabilities of minority removed in the state of the minor's residence may file a certified copy of the order removing disabilities in the deed records of any county in this state.

(b) When a certified copy of the order of a court of another state or nation is filed, the minor has the capacity of an adult, except as provided by Section 31.006 and by the terms of the order.

History of Fam §31.007: Acts 1995, 74th Leg., ch. 20, §1, eff. April 20, 1995. Source: Former Fam §31.08.

CHAPTER 32. CONSENT TO TREATMENT OF CHILD BY NON-PARENT OR CHILD

SUBCHAPTER A. CONSENT TO MEDICAL, DENTAL, PSYCHOLOGICAL, & SURGICAL TREATMENT

FAM §32.001. CONSENT BY NON-PARENT

(a) The following persons may consent to medical, dental, psychological, and surgical treatment of a child when the person having the right to consent as otherwise provided by law cannot be contacted and that person has not given actual notice to the contrary:

(1) a grandparent of the child;

(2) an adult brother or sister of the child;

(3) an adult aunt or uncle of the child;

(4) an educational institution in which the child is enrolled that has received written authorization to consent from a person having the right to consent;

(5) an adult who has actual care, control, and possession of the child and has written authorization to consent from a person having the right to consent;

(6) a court having jurisdiction over a suit affecting the parent-child relationship of which the child is the subject;

(7) an adult responsible for the actual care, control, and possession of a child under the jurisdiction of a juvenile court or committed by a juvenile court to the care of an agency of the state or county; or

(8) a peace officer who has lawfully taken custody of a minor, if the peace officer has reasonable grounds to believe the minor is in need of immediate medical treatment.

(b) The Texas Youth Commission may consent to the medical, dental, psychological, and surgical treatment of a child committed to it under Title 3 when the person having the right to consent has been contacted and that person has not given actual notice to the contrary.

(c) This section does not apply to consent for the immunization of a child.

(d) A person who consents to the medical treatment of a minor under Subsection (a)(7) or (8) is immune from liability for damages resulting from the examination or treatment of the minor, except to the extent of the person's own acts of negligence. A physician or dentist licensed to practice in this state, or a hospital or medical facility at which a minor is treated is immune from liability for damages resulting from the examination or treatment of a minor under this section, except to the extent of the person's own acts of negligence.

History of Fam §32.001: Acts 1995, 74th Leg., ch. 20, §1, eff. April 20, 1995. Amended by Acts 1995, 74th Leg., ch. 751, §5, eff. Sept. 1, 1995. Source: Former Fam §35.01.

See also 37 TAC §91.81.

FAM §32.002. CONSENT FORM

☠ *Acts 1995, 74th Leg., ch. 123, §4, effective Aug. 28, 1995 amended former Family Code §35.02 without reference to the conflicting repealer made by Acts 1995, 74th Leg., ch. 20, §2(1), effective April 20, 1995.*

(a) Consent to medical treatment under this subchapter must be in writing, signed by the person giving consent, and given to the doctor, hospital, or other medical facility that administers the treatment.

(b) The consent must include:

(1) the name of the child;

(2) the name of one or both parents, if known, and the name of any managing conservator or guardian of the child;

(3) the name of the person giving consent and the person's relationship to the child;

(4) a statement of the nature of the medical treatment to be given; and

(5) the date the treatment is to begin.

History of Fam §32.002: Acts 1995, 74th Leg., ch. 20, §1, eff. April 20, 1995. Amended by Acts 1995, 74th Leg., ch. 123, §4, eff. Sept. 1, 1995. Source: Former Fam §35.02.

FAM §32.003. CONSENT TO TREATMENT BY CHILD

(a) A child may consent to medical, dental, psychological, and surgical treatment for the child by a licensed physician or dentist if the child:

(1) is on active duty with the armed services of the United States of America;

(2) is:

(A) 16 years of age or older and resides separate and apart from the child's parents, managing conservator, or guardian, with or without the consent of the parents, managing conservator, or guardian and regardless of the duration of the residence; and

(B) managing the child's own financial affairs, regardless of the source of the income;

(3) consents to the diagnosis and treatment of an infectious, contagious, or communicable disease that is required by law or a rule to be reported by the licensed physician or dentist to a local health officer or the Texas Department of Health, including all diseases within the scope of Section 81.041, Health and Safety Code;

(4) is unmarried and pregnant and consents to hospital, medical, or surgical treatment, other than abortion, related to the pregnancy;

(5) consents to examination and treatment for drug or chemical addiction, drug or chemical dependency, or any other condition directly related to drug or chemical use; or

A *Subsection (6) below is effective for motions or other requests for relief made in parentage or paternity proceedings commenced on or after June 14, 2001.*

(6) is unmarried, is the parent of a child, and has actual custody of his or her child and consents to medical, dental, psychological, or surgical treatment for the child.

Subsection (6) below is effective for motions or other requests for relief made in parentage or paternity proceedings commenced before June 14, 2001.

(6) is unmarried and has actual custody of the child's biological child and consents to medical, dental, psychological, or surgical treatment for the child.

(b) Consent by a child to medical, dental, psychological, and surgical treatment under this section is not subject to disaffirmance because of minority.

(c) Consent of the parents, managing conservator, or guardian of a child is not necessary in order to authorize hospital, medical, surgical, or dental care under this section.

(d) A licensed physician, dentist, or psychologist may, with or without the consent of a child who is a patient, advise the parents, managing conservator, or guardian of the child of the treatment given to or needed by the child.

(e) A physician, dentist, psychologist, hospital, or medical facility is not liable for the examination and treatment of a child under this section except for the provider's or the facility's own acts of negligence.

(f) A physician, dentist, psychologist, hospital, or medical facility may rely on the written statement of the child containing the grounds on which the child has capacity to consent to the child's medical treatment.

History of Fam §32.003: Acts 1995, 74th Leg., ch. 20, §1, eff. April 20, 1995. Amended by Acts 1995, 74th Leg., ch. 751, §6, eff. Sept. 1, 1995; Acts 2001, 77th Leg., ch. 821, §2.01, eff. June 14, 2001. Source: Former Fam §35.03(a)-(f).

See also 25 TAC §§97.1-97.13, 97.91, 97.92, 97.101, 97.102, 97.131-97.146.

FAM §32.004. CONSENT TO COUNSELING

(a) A child may consent to counseling for:

(1) suicide prevention;

(2) chemical addiction or dependency; or

(3) sexual, physical, or emotional abuse.

(b) A licensed or certified physician, psychologist, counselor, or social worker having reasonable grounds to believe that a child has been sexually, physically, or emotionally abused, is contemplating suicide, or is suffering from a chemical or drug addiction or dependency may:

(1) counsel the child without the consent of the child's parents or, if applicable, managing conservator or guardian;

(2) with or without the consent of the child who is a client, advise the child's parents or, if applicable, managing conservator or guardian of the treatment given to or needed by the child; and

(3) rely on the written statement of the child containing the grounds on which the child has capacity to consent to the child's own treatment under this section.

(c) Unless consent is obtained as otherwise allowed by law, a physician, psychologist, counselor, or social worker may not counsel a child if consent is prohibited by a court order.

(d) A physician, psychologist, counselor, or social worker counseling a child under this section is not liable for damages except for damages resulting from the person's negligence or wilful misconduct.

(e) A parent, or, if applicable, managing conservator or guardian, who has not consented to counseling treatment of the child is not obligated to compensate a physician, psychologist, counselor, or social worker for counseling services rendered under this section.

History of Fam §32.004: Acts 1995, 74th Leg., ch. 20, §1, eff. April 20, 1995. Source: Former Fam §35.03(g).

FAM §32.005. EXAMINATION WITHOUT CONSENT OF ABUSE OR NEGLECT OF CHILD

(a) Except as provided by Subsection (c), a physician, dentist, or psychologist having reasonable grounds to believe that a child's physical or mental condition has been adversely affected by abuse or neglect may examine the child without the consent of the child, the child's parents, or other person authorized to consent to treatment under this subchapter.

(b) An examination under this section may include X-rays, blood tests, photographs, and penetration of tissue necessary to accomplish those tests.

(c) Unless consent is obtained as otherwise allowed by law, a physician, dentist, or psychologist may not examine a child:

(1) 16 years of age or older who refuses to consent; or

(2) for whom consent is prohibited by a court order.

(d) A physician, dentist, or psychologist examining a child under this section is not liable for damages except for damages resulting from the physician's or dentist's negligence.

History of Fam §32.005: Acts 1995, 74th Leg., ch. 20, §1, eff. April 20, 1995. Amended by Acts 1997, 75th Leg., ch. 575, §1, eff. Sept. 1, 1997. Source: Former Fam §35.04.

Sections 32.006-32.100 reserved for expansion

SUBCHAPTER B. IMMUNIZATION

FAM §32.101. WHO MAY CONSENT TO IMMUNIZATION OF CHILD

(a) In addition to persons authorized to consent to immunization under Chapter 151 and Chapter 153, the following persons may consent to the immunization of a child:

(1) a guardian of the child; and

(2) a person authorized under the law of another state or a court order to consent for the child.

(b) If the persons listed in Subsection (a) are not available and the authority to consent is not denied under Subsection (c), consent to the immunization of a child may be given by:

(1) a grandparent of the child;

(2) an adult brother or sister of the child;

(3) an adult aunt or uncle of the child;

(4) a stepparent of the child;

(5) an educational institution in which the child is enrolled that has written authorization to consent for the child from a parent, managing conservator, guardian, or other person who under the law of another state or a court order may consent for the child;

(6) another adult who has actual care, control, and possession of the child and has written authorization to consent for the child from a parent, managing conservator, guardian, or other person who, under the law of another state or a court order, may consent for the child;

(7) a court having jurisdiction of a suit affecting the parent-child relationship of which the minor is the subject;

(8) an adult having actual care, control, and possession of the child under an order of a juvenile court or by commitment by a juvenile court to the care of an agency of the state or county; or

(9) an adult having actual care, control, and possession of the child as the child's primary caregiver.

(c) A person otherwise authorized to consent under Subsection (a) may not consent for the child if the person has actual knowledge that a parent, managing conservator, guardian of the child, or other person who under the law of another state or a court order may consent for the child:

(1) has expressly refused to give consent to the immunization;

(2) has been told not to consent for the child; or

(3) has withdrawn a prior written authorization for the person to consent.

(d) The Texas Youth Commission may consent to the immunization of a child committed to it if a parent, managing conservator, or guardian of the minor or other person who, under the law of another state or court order, may consent for the minor has been contacted and:

(1) refuses to consent; and

(2) does not expressly deny to the Texas Youth Commission the authority to consent for the child.

(e) A person who consents under this section shall provide the health care provider with sufficient and accurate health history and other information about the minor for whom the consent is given and, if necessary, sufficient and accurate health history and information about the minor's family to enable the person who may consent to the minor's immunization and the health care provider to determine adequately the risks and benefits inherent in the proposed immunization and to determine whether immunization is advisable.

(f) Consent to immunization must meet the requirements of Section 32.002(a).

History of Fam §32.101: Acts 1995, 74th Leg., ch. 20, §1, eff. April 20, 1995. Amended by Acts 1995, 74th Leg., ch. 123, eff. Aug. 28, 1995; Acts 1997, 75th Leg., ch. 165, §7.09(a), eff. Sept. 1, 1997; Acts 1999, 76th Leg., ch. 62, §6.02, eff. Sept. 1, 1999. Source: Former Fam §35.011.

FAM §32.102. INFORMED CONSENT TO IMMUNIZATION

(a) A person authorized to consent to the immunization of a child has the responsibility to ensure that the consent, if given, is an informed consent. The person authorized to consent is not required to be present when the immunization of the child is requested if a consent form that meets the requirements of Section 32.002 has been given to the health care provider.

(b) The responsibility of a health care provider to provide information to a person consenting to immunization is the same as the provider's responsibility to a parent.

(c) As part of the information given in the counseling for informed consent, the health care provider shall provide information to inform the person authorized to consent to immunization of the procedures available under the National Childhood Vaccine Injury Act of 1986 (42 U.S.C. Section 300aa-1 et seq.) to seek possible recovery for unreimbursed expenses for certain injuries arising out of the administration of certain vaccines.

History of Fam §32.102: Acts 1995, 74th Leg., ch. 20, §1, eff. April 20, 1995. Renumbered from §32.103 and amended by Acts 1997, 75th Leg., ch. 165, §7.09(b), (d), eff. Sept. 1, 1997. Source: Former Fam §35.013.

FAM §32.103. LIMITED LIABILITY FOR IMMUNIZATION

(a) In the absence of wilful misconduct or gross negligence, a health care provider who accepts the health history and other information given by a person who is delegated the authority to consent to the immunization of a child during the informed consent counseling is not liable for an adverse reaction to an immunization or for other injuries to the child resulting from factual errors in the health history or information given by the person to the health care provider.

(b) A person consenting to immunization of a child, a physician, nurse, or other health care provider, or a public health clinic, hospital, or other medical facility is not liable for damages arising from an immunization administered to a child authorized under this subchapter except for injuries resulting from the person's or facility's own acts of negligence.

History of Fam §32.103: Acts 1995, 74th Leg., ch. 20, §1, eff. April 20, 1995. Renumbered from §32.104 by Acts 1997, 75th Leg., ch. 165, §7.09(e), eff. Sept. 1, 1997. Source: Former Fam §35.014.

FAM §32.104. RENUMBERED

Renumbered as §32.103 by Acts 1997, 75th Leg., ch. 165, §7.09(e), eff. Sept. 1, 1997.

FAM §32.105. REPEALED

Repealed by Acts 1997, 75th Leg., ch. 165, §7.09(c), eff. Sept. 1, 1997.

Sections 32.106-32.200 reserved for expansion

SUBCHAPTER C. MISCELLANEOUS PROVISIONS

FAM §32.201. EMERGENCY SHELTER FOR MINOR MOTHERS

(a) An emergency shelter facility may provide shelter and care to a minor mother who is the sole financial support of her child or children.

(b) An emergency shelter facility may provide shelter or care only during an emergency constituting an immediate danger to the physical health or safety of the minor mother or her child or children.

(c) Shelter or care provided under this section may not be provided after the 15th day after the date the shelter or care is commenced unless:

(1) the facility receives consent to continue services from a parent or guardian of the minor mother; or

(2) the minor mother has qualified for Aid to Families with Dependent Children under Chapter 31, Human Resources Code, and is on the waiting list for housing assistance.

History of Fam §32.201: Acts 1995, 74th Leg., ch. 20, §1, eff. April 20, 1995. Source: Former Fam §35.05.

FAM §32.241. REPEALED

Repealed by Acts 1997, 75th Leg., ch. 165, §7.10(c), eff. Sept. 1, 1997.

CHAPTER 33. NOTICE OF ABORTION

FAM §33.001. DEFINITIONS

In this chapter:

(1) "Abortion" means the use of any means to terminate the pregnancy of a female known by the attending physician to be pregnant, with the intention that the termination of the pregnancy by those means will with reasonable likelihood cause the death of the fetus. This definition, as applied in this chapter, applies only to an unemancipated minor known by the attending physician to be pregnant and may not be construed to limit a minor's access to contraceptives.

(2) "Fetus" means an individual human organism from fertilization until birth.

(3) "Guardian" means a court-appointed guardian of the person of the minor.

(4) "Physician" means an individual licensed to practice medicine in this state.

(5) "Unemancipated minor" includes a minor who:

(A) is unmarried; and

(B) has not had the disabilities of minority removed under Chapter 31.

History of Fam §33.001: Acts 1999, 76th Leg., ch. 395, §1, eff. Sept. 1, 1999.

FAM §33.002. PARENTAL NOTICE

(a) A physician may not perform an abortion on a pregnant unemancipated minor unless:

(1) the physician performing the abortion gives at least 48 hours actual notice, in person or by telephone, of the physician's intent to perform the abortion to:

(A) a parent of the minor, if the minor has no managing conservator or guardian; or

(B) a court-appointed managing conservator or guardian;

(2) the judge of a court having probate jurisdiction, the judge of a county court at law, the judge of a district court, including a family district court, or a court of appellate jurisdiction issues an order authorizing the minor to consent to the abortion as provided by Section 33.003 or 33.004;

(3) a probate court, county court at law, district court, including a family district court, or court of appeals, by its inaction, constructively authorizes the minor to consent to the abortion as provided by Section 33.003 or 33.004; or

(4) the physician performing the abortion:

(A) concludes that on the basis of the physician's good faith clinical judgment, a condition exists that complicates the medical condition of the pregnant minor and necessitates the immediate abortion of her pregnancy to avert her death or to avoid a serious risk of substantial and irreversible impairment of a major bodily function; and

(B) certifies in writing to the Texas Department of Health and in the patient's medical record the medical indications supporting the physician's judgment that the circumstances described by Paragraph (A) exist.

(b) If a person to whom notice may be given under Subsection (a)(1) cannot be notified after a reasonable effort, a physician may perform an abortion if the physician gives 48 hours constructive notice, by certified mail, restricted delivery, sent to the last known address, to the person to whom notice may be given under Subsection (a)(1). The period under this subsection begins when the notice is mailed. If the person required to be notified is not notified within the 48-hour period, the abortion may proceed even if the notice by mail is not received.

(c) The requirement that 48 hours actual notice be provided under this section may be waived by an affidavit of:

(1) a parent of the minor, if the minor has no managing conservator or guardian; or

(2) a court-appointed managing conservator or guardian.

(d) A physician may execute for inclusion in the minor's medical record an affidavit stating that, according to the best information and belief of the physician, notice or constructive notice has been provided as required by this section. Execution of an affidavit under this subsection creates a presumption that the requirements of this section have been satisfied.

(e) The Texas Department of Health shall prepare a form to be used for making the certification required by Subsection (a)(4).

A (f) A certification required by Subsection (a)(4) is confidential and privileged and is not subject to disclosure under Chapter 552, Government Code, or to discovery, subpoena, or other legal process. Personal or identifying information about the minor, including her name, address, or social security number, may not be included in a certification under Subsection (a)(4). The physician must keep the medical records on the minor in compliance with the rules adopted by the Texas State Board of Medical Examiners under Section 153.003, Occupations Code.

(g) A physician who intentionally performs an abortion on a pregnant unemancipated minor in violation of this section commits an offense. An offense under this subsection is punishable by a fine not to exceed $10,000. In this subsection, "intentionally" has the meaning assigned by Section 6.03(a), Penal Code.

(h) It is a defense to prosecution under this section that the minor falsely represented her age or identity to the physician to be at least 18 years of age by displaying an apparently valid governmental record of identification such that a reasonable person under similar circumstances would have relied on the representation. The defense does not apply if the physician is shown to have had independent knowledge of the minor's actual age or identity or failed to use due diligence in determining the minor's age or identity. In this subsection, "defense" has the meaning and application assigned by Section 2.03, Penal Code.

(i) In relation to the trial of an offense under this section in which the conduct charged involves a conclusion made by the physician under Subsection (a)(4), the defendant may seek a hearing before the Texas State Board of Medical Examiners on whether the physician's conduct was necessary to avert the death of the minor or to avoid a serious risk of substantial and irreversible impairment of a major bodily function. The findings of the Texas State Board of Medical Examiners under this subsection are admissible on that issue in the trial of the defendant. Notwithstanding any other reason for a continuance provided under the Code of Criminal Procedure or other law, on motion of the defendant, the court shall delay the beginning of the trial for not more than 30 days to permit a hearing under this subsection to take place.

History of Fam §33.002: Acts 1999, 76th Leg., ch. 395, §1, eff. Sept. 1, 1999. Amended by Acts 2001, 77th Leg., ch. 1420, §14.741, eff. Sept. 1, 2001.

See also 22 TAC §165.1, 25 TAC §139.50.

FAM §33.003. JUDICIAL APPROVAL

(a) A pregnant minor who wishes to have an abortion without notification to one of her parents, her managing conservator, or her guardian may file an application for a court order authorizing the minor to consent to the performance of an abortion without notification to either of her parents or a managing conservator or guardian.

(b) The application may be filed in any county court at law, court having probate jurisdiction, or district court, including a family district court, in this state.

(c) The application must be made under oath and include:

(1) a statement that the minor is pregnant;

(2) a statement that the minor is unmarried, is under 18 years of age, and has not had her disabilities removed under Chapter 31;

(3) a statement that the minor wishes to have an abortion without the notification of either of her parents or a managing conservator or guardian; and

(4) a statement as to whether the minor has retained an attorney and, if she has retained an attorney, the name, address, and telephone number of her attorney.

(d) The clerk of the court shall deliver a courtesy copy of the application made under this section to the judge who is to hear the application.

(e) The court shall appoint a guardian ad litem for the minor. If the minor has not retained an attorney, the court shall appoint an attorney to represent the minor. If the guardian ad litem is an attorney admitted to the practice of law in this state, the court may appoint the guardian ad litem to serve as the minor's attorney.

(f) The court may appoint to serve as guardian ad litem:

(1) a person who may consent to treatment for the minor under Sections 32.001(a)(1)-(3);

A (2) a psychiatrist or an individual licensed or certified as a psychologist under Chapter 501, Occupations Code;

(3) an appropriate employee of the Department of Protective and Regulatory Services;

(4) a member of the clergy; or

(5) another appropriate person selected by the court.

(g) The court shall fix a time for a hearing on an application filed under Subsection (a) and shall keep a record of all testimony and other oral proceedings in the action. The court shall enter judgment on the application immediately after the hearing is concluded.

FAM §33.003

(h) The court shall rule on an application submitted under this section and shall issue written findings of fact and conclusions of law not later than 5 p.m. on the second business day after the date the application is filed with the court. On request by the minor, the court shall grant an extension of the period specified by this subsection. If a request for an extension is made, the court shall rule on an application and shall issue written findings of fact and conclusions of law not later than 5 p.m. on the second business day after the date the minor states she is ready to proceed to hearing. If the court fails to rule on the application and issue written findings of fact and conclusions of law within the period specified by this subsection, the application is deemed to be granted and the physician may perform the abortion as if the court had issued an order authorizing the minor to consent to the performance of the abortion without notification under Section 33.002. Proceedings under this section shall be given precedence over other pending matters to the extent necessary to assure that the court reaches a decision promptly.

(i) The court shall determine by a preponderance of the evidence whether the minor is mature and sufficiently well informed to make the decision to have an abortion performed without notification to either of her parents or a managing conservator or guardian, whether notification would not be in the best interest of the minor, or whether notification may lead to physical, sexual, or emotional abuse of the minor. If the court finds that the minor is mature and sufficiently well informed, that notification would not be in the minor's best interest, or that notification may lead to physical, sexual, or emotional abuse of the minor, the court shall enter an order authorizing the minor to consent to the performance of the abortion without notification to either of her parents or a managing conservator or guardian and shall execute the required forms.

(j) If the court finds that the minor does not meet the requirements of Subsection (i), the court may not authorize the minor to consent to an abortion without the notification authorized under Section 33.002(a)(1).

(k) The court may not notify a parent, managing conservator, or guardian that the minor is pregnant or that the minor wants to have an abortion. The court proceedings shall be conducted in a manner that protects the anonymity of the minor. The application and all other court documents pertaining to the proceedings are confidential and privileged and are not subject to disclosure under Chapter 552, Government Code, or to discovery, subpoena, or other legal process. The minor may file the application using a pseudonym or using only her initials.

(*l*) An order of the court issued under this section is confidential and privileged and is not subject to disclosure under Chapter 552, Government Code, or discovery, subpoena, or other legal process. The order may not be released to any person but the pregnant minor, the pregnant minor's guardian ad litem, the pregnant minor's attorney, another person designated to receive the order by the minor, or a governmental agency or attorney in a criminal or administrative action seeking to assert or protect the interest of the minor. The supreme court may adopt rules to permit confidential docketing of an application under this section.

(m) The clerk of the supreme court shall prescribe the application form to be used by the minor filing an application under this section.

(n) A filing fee is not required of and court costs may not be assessed against a minor filing an application under this section.

History of Fam §33.003: Acts 1999, 76th Leg., ch. 395, §1, eff. Sept. 1, 1999. Amended by Acts 2001, 77th Leg., ch. 1420, §14.742, eff. Sept. 1, 2001.

See also Parental Notification Rules, p. 1148.

Generally

In re Jane Doe 1 (I), 19 S.W.3d 249, 255 (Tex. 2000). "When a minor files such an application, the court 'shall determine by a preponderance of the evidence' whether: [1] The minor is 'mature and sufficiently well informed to make the decision to have an abortion performed without notification to either of her parents;' or [2] Notification would not be in the best interest of the minor; or [3] Notification may lead to physical, sexual, or emotional abuse of the minor. If the court makes any of these determinations, the court '*shall* enter an order authorizing the minor to consent to the performance of the abortion without notification to either of her parents....' Because the Legislature used the imperative word 'shall,' we conclude that when a minor meets the statutory threshold, the trial court must grant the application."

Findings of Fact

In re Jane Doe 10, ___ S.W.3d ___ (Tex.2002) (No. 02-0376; 4-29-02). "Fact findings are necessary to demonstrate the trial court's careful consideration of each ground asserted for bypass, and particularized findings are essential to meaningful appellate review, at least when credibility or maturity concerns are involved. … 'The mere fact that the trial court has checked a box on a form does not demonstrate that it has given the careful consideration necessary for such a significant decision.' Because a remand for the trial court to make fact findings is inconsistent with the expedited nature of these proceedings, it is essential that trial courts make fact findings with regard to each ground asserted for bypass. Accordingly, we renew our admonishments to the trial courts to heed the Legislature's mandate and issue fact findings and conclusions of law with regard to each ground asserted for a judicial bypass and to issue particularized findings at least when credibility or maturity issues are involved."

"Mature and Sufficiently Well Informed"

In re Jane Doe 1 (II), 19 S.W.3d 346, 359 (Tex. 2000). "When we wrote … that a minor must have considered the 'benefits, risks, and consequences' of the various options, we did not intend to suggest that trial courts should create checklists that a minor must recite in order to establish that she has thoughtfully considered her options. That a minor does not share the court's views about what the benefits of her alternatives might be does not mean that she has not thoughtfully considered her options or acquired sufficient information about them. … Instead, the focus of the inquiry is whether the minor has thoughtfully considered her alternatives, and 'the examining court must weigh her situation not against the ideal but against a standard of basic understanding of her situation, her choices, and her options.' [¶] The concept of 'benefits' is inherently subjective; what one person may consider a benefit, another may not. That Doe does not accept and pursue the alternate benefits to abortion does not mean that she has not given those alternatives thoughtful consideration. Moreover, even though there may be generally recognized benefits to an alternative, those benefits must be considered in light of the minor's particular situation. *At 360:* Doe did not seek information or counseling from anyone who would be against her having an abortion. [The] dissent [argues] that her failure to do so supports the trial court's finding that she was not sufficiently well informed. [A] minor is not required to seek information from any particular group or viewpoint so long as 'she has obtained information on the relevant considerations from reliable sources of her choosing that enable her to make a thoughtful and informed decision.'"

In re Jane Doe 1 (I), 19 S.W.3d 249, 255 (Tex. 2000). A "minor is 'mature and sufficiently well informed to make the decision to have an abortion without notification to either of her parents' when the evidence demonstrates that the minor is capable of reasoned decision-making and that her decision is not the product of impulse, but is based upon careful consideration of the various options available to her and the benefits, risks, and consequences of those options. *At 256-57*: Obviously, whether a minor is mature and sufficiently well informed is a highly individualized decision that must take into account the diverse background and circumstances of each applicant for waiver of parental notification. [¶] In order to establish that she is sufficiently well informed the minor must make, at a minimum three showings. [¶] First, she must show that she has obtained information from a health-care professional about the health risks associated with an abortion and that she understands those risks. [¶] Second, she must show that she understands the alternatives to abortion and their implications. [¶] Third, she must show that she is also aware of the emotional and psychological aspects of undergoing an abortion, which can be significant if not severe for some women. She must also show that she has considered how this decision might affect her family relations. [¶] A determination of maturity necessarily involves more trial court discretion. [¶] A minor who can show that she is sufficiently well informed may also establish in the process that she is mature. In making a determination of maturity, there are, however, some criteria that should not be relied upon as conclusively showing immaturity. The United States Supreme Court has said that one of those is the fact, standing alone, that the pregnant female is a minor. That Court has also admonished that states and courts 'may not make a blanket determination that all minors … are too immature to make this decision or that an abortion never may be in the minor's best interests without parental approval.' A child's age, educational background or grades in school, while indicative of some level of maturity, are not conclusive on the issue of maturity. Nor is participation in extra-curricular activities. It should also go without saying that a minor's socio-economic status should not bear on the decision."

"Best Interest"

In re Jane Doe 2, 19 S.W.3d 278, 282 (Tex.2000). "To determine whether notification would not be in the minor's best interests, the trial court should weigh the advantages and disadvantages of parental notification in the minor's specific situation. Although the best interests determination necessarily involves evaluating whether notification could lead to abuse of the minor, that the Legislature included the potential for abuse as a separate reason for granting a bypass makes it clear that the best interests determination encompasses a broader concern for the minor's welfare. In ***Holley v. Adams***, we developed a list of non-exhaustive factors for determining a minor's best interests. Four of these factors are relevant when adapted to the parental notification context, and a trial court should consider them in determining best interests: (1) the minor's emotional or physical needs; (2) the possibility of emotional or physical danger to the minor; (3) the stability of the minor's home and whether notification would cause serious and lasting harm to the family structure; and (4) the relationship between the parent and the minor and the effect of notification on that relationship. An additional factor that courts in other jurisdictions have considered is whether notification may lead the parents to withdraw emotional and financial support from the minor. This list is not exhaustive, and in making the best-interests determination the trial court should consider all relevant circumstances. We note, however, that a minor's generalized fear of telling her parents does not, by itself, establish that notification would not be in the minor's best interests. [¶] Also, as with the maturity determination, meaningful appellate review is possible only if the trial court makes specific findings about its determination that the minor has not shown that notification is not in her best interests. Similarly, if the trial court's determination depends on its assessment of the minor's credibility, it should make specific findings on that issue."

"Abuse"

In re Jane Doe 2, 19 S.W.3d 278, 283 (Tex.2000). "[T]he trial court must determine whether, based on all the evidence presented at the subsequent hearing, a *preponderance* of the evidence supports a finding that notification *may* lead to abuse. For meaningful appellate review the trial court must make specific findings concerning the potential for abuse. Similarly, if the trial court determines that the minor's testimony about potential abuse is not credible, it should also make specific findings in that regard."

Hearing

In re Jane Doe 4, 19 S.W.3d 322, 325 (Tex.2000). "[B]ecause trial courts can view a witness's demeanor, they are given great latitude in believing or disbelieving a witness's testimony, particularly when the witness is interested in the outcome. Acting as factfinder, a trial judge can, therefore, reject the uncontroverted testimony of an interested witness unless it is readily controvertible, it is clear, positive, direct, and there are no circumstances tending to discredit or impeach it. The readily-controvertible prong of this test is not applicable to a parental notification proceeding under Chapter 33. Because the hearing is unopposed, the minor's testimony will rarely, if ever, be readily controvertible. The other parts of this test, however, apply to a notification proceeding as they would in any other proceeding in which the trial court acts as a factfinder."

FAM §33.004. APPEAL

(a) A minor whose application under Section 33.003 is denied may appeal to the court of appeals having jurisdiction over civil matters in the county in which the application was filed. On receipt of a notice of appeal, the clerk of the court that denied the application shall deliver a copy of the notice of appeal and record on appeal to the clerk of the court of appeals. On receipt of the notice and record, the clerk of the court of appeals shall place the appeal on the docket of the court.

(b) The court of appeals shall rule on an appeal under this section not later than 5 p.m. on the second business day after the date the notice of appeal is filed with the court that denied the application. On request by the minor, the court shall grant an extension of the period specified by this subsection. If a request for an extension is made, the court shall rule on the appeal not later than 5 p.m. on the second business day after the date the minor states she is ready to proceed. If the court of appeals fails to rule on the appeal within the period specified by this subsection, the appeal is deemed to be granted and the physician may perform the abortion as if the court had issued an order authorizing the minor to consent to the performance of the abortion without notification under Section 33.002. Proceedings under this section shall be given precedence over other pending matters to the extent necessary to assure that the court reaches a decision promptly.

(c) A ruling of the court of appeals issued under this section is confidential and privileged and is not subject to disclosure under Chapter 552, Government Code, or discovery, subpoena, or other legal process. The ruling may not be released to any person but the pregnant minor, the pregnant minor's guardian ad litem, the pregnant minor's attorney, another person designated to receive the ruling by the minor, or a governmental agency or attorney in a criminal or administrative action seeking to assert or protect the interest of the minor. The supreme court may adopt rules to permit confidential docketing of an appeal under this section.

(d) The clerk of the supreme court shall prescribe the notice of appeal form to be used by the minor appealing a judgment under this section.

(e) A filing fee is not required of and court costs may not be assessed against a minor filing an appeal under this section.

(f) An expedited confidential appeal shall be available to any pregnant minor to whom a court of appeals denies an order authorizing the minor to consent to the performance of an abortion without notification to either of her parents or a managing conservator or guardian.

History of Fam §33.004: Acts 1999, 76th Leg., ch. 395, §1, eff. Sept. 1, 1999. See also Parental Notification Rules, p. 1148.

Generally

In re Jane Doe 2, 19 S.W.3d 278, 283 (Tex.2000). "That we have provided trial courts forms for making findings of fact and conclusions of law should not prevent them from making the specific findings we require for the maturity, best interests, and potential abuse determinations. These forms are analogous to our forms allowing minors to check off that they have satisfied one or more of the statutory requirements. A minor's testimony merely parroting the language on the form is not sufficient for a judicial bypass without testimony regarding her specific circumstances. Likewise, the mere fact that the trial court has checked a box on a form does not demonstrate that it has given the careful consideration necessary for such a significant decision. Moreover, the form itself contemplates more specificity, as it includes a place for comments under each of the three statutory requirements, in which the trial court can and should detail its findings."

"Mature and Sufficiently Well Informed"

In re Jane Doe 1 (II), 19 S.W.3d 346, 356-57 (Tex.2000). "[A] minor ... who is appealing the denial of her application under the first prong of [§33.003(i)], only needs to conclusively refute the trial court's actual findings. Because the trial court found as fact that Doe was not sufficiently well informed, for us to grant her application the record must establish the converse as a matter of law. But the trial court's failure to find that Doe was not mature does not require her to conclusively establish her maturity to prevail on appeal. This distinction is, perhaps, unique to proceedings under this statute, but the statutory scheme in place requires it, as well as the Parental Notification Rules this Court adopted under the statute. [¶] This statutory scheme requires both a timely and complete judgment to support the denial of a minor's bypass application. First, if the trial court does not hold a hearing or rule on a minor's application within the statutory time limits, the application is granted as a matter of law. In addition, if the trial court holds a hearing and denies an application within the allotted time, but does not also issue written findings of fact and conclusions of law, the application is deemed granted, thereby implying findings contrary to the trial court's judgment. [¶] A trial court that fails to make a finding on one of the two elements of the first statutory prong does not run afoul of these requirements because a negative finding on only one element supports denial of the minor's application. But because the minor must establish both elements to succeed, an appellate court that determines that the minor conclusively established the element on which the trial court based its denial must confront the effect of the trial court's failure to make a finding on the other element. This failure to find creates uncertainty, because it could reflect either that the minor met her burden of proof on that element or that she did not. By providing that an application is deemed granted if a trial court fails to make required findings, the statute indicates that we must resolve this uncertainty in the minor's favor if she has put on evidence of the element the trial court did not find. Additionally, it is contrary to the expedited nature of these proceedings to require a remand when the trial court fails to issue particular findings. ... For these reasons, an omitted element should be deemed to have been found in the minor's favor if there is some evidence to support the finding."

In re Jane Doe 1 (I), 19 S.W.3d 249, 253 (Tex. 2000). "[I]n determining whether a minor is 'mature and sufficiently well informed,' the trial court is not to weigh policy considerations; it simply makes a factual determination. When the trial court acts primarily as a factfinder, appellate courts normally review its determinations under the legal and factual sufficiency standards. We therefore apply that standard of review to this appeal."

"Best Interest"

In re Jane Doe 2, 19 S.W.3d 278, 281 (Tex.2000). "[A]n appellate court should review a trial court's determination regarding whether notification is in the minor's best interests under the abuse of discretion standard. Unlike the 'mature and sufficiently well informed' determination, in which the trial court is solely making factual findings, determining the minor's best interests requires the trial court to balance the possible benefits and detriments to the minor in notifying her parents. This type of balancing necessarily involves the exercise of judicial discretion and should be reviewed on that basis."

FAM §33.005. AFFIDAVIT OF PHYSICIAN

(a) A physician may execute for inclusion in the minor's medical record an affidavit stating that, after reasonable inquiry, it is the belief of the physician that:

(1) the minor has made an application or filed a notice of an appeal with a court under this chapter;

(2) the deadline for court action imposed by this chapter has passed; and

(3) the physician has been notified that the court has not denied the application or appeal.

(b) A physician who in good faith has executed an affidavit under Subsection (a) may rely on the affidavit and may perform the abortion as if the court had issued an order granting the application or appeal.

History of Fam §33.005: Acts 1999, 76th Leg., ch. 395, §1, eff. Sept. 1, 1999.

FAM §33.006. GUARDIAN AD LITEM IMMUNITY

A guardian ad litem appointed under this chapter and acting in the course and scope of the appointment is not liable for damages arising from an act or omission of the guardian ad litem committed in good faith. The immunity granted by this section does not apply if the conduct of the guardian ad litem is committed in a manner described by Sections 107.003(b)(1)-(4).

History of Fam §33.006: Acts 1999, 76th Leg., ch. 395, §1, eff. Sept. 1, 1999.

FAM §33.007. COSTS PAID BY STATE

(a) A court acting under Section 33.003 or 33.004 may issue an order requiring the state to pay:

(1) the cost of any attorney ad litem and any guardian ad litem appointed for the minor;

(2) notwithstanding Sections 33.003(n) and 33.004(e), the costs of court associated with the application or appeal; and

(3) any court reporter's fees incurred.

(b) An order issued under Subsection (a) must be directed to the comptroller, who shall pay the amount ordered from funds appropriated to the Texas Department of Health.

History of Fam §33.007: Acts 1999, 76th Leg., ch. 395, §1, eff. Sept. 1, 1999.

FAM §33.008. PHYSICIAN'S DUTY TO REPORT ABUSE OF A MINOR; INVESTIGATION & ASSISTANCE

(a) A physician who has reason to believe that a minor has been or may be physically or sexually abused by a person responsible for the minor's care, custody, or welfare, as that term is defined by Section 261.001, shall immediately report the suspected abuse to the Department of Protective and Regulatory Services and shall refer the minor to the department for services or intervention that may be in the best interest of the minor.

(b) The Department of Protective and Regulatory Services shall investigate suspected abuse reported under this section and, if appropriate, shall assist the minor in making an application with a court under Section 33.003.

History of Fam §33.008: Acts 1999, 76th Leg., ch. 395, §1, eff. Sept. 1, 1999.

FAM §33.009. OTHER REPORTS OF SEXUAL ABUSE OF A MINOR

A court or the guardian ad litem or attorney ad litem for the minor shall report conduct reasonably believed to violate Section 22.011, 22.021, or 25.02, Penal Code, based on information obtained during a confidential court proceeding held under this chapter to:

(1) any local or state law enforcement agency;

(2) the Department of Protective and Regulatory Services, if the alleged conduct involves a person responsible for the care, custody, or welfare of the child;

(3) the state agency that operates, licenses, certifies, or registers the facility in which the alleged conduct occurred, if the alleged conduct occurred in a facility operated, licensed, certified, or registered by a state agency; or

(4) an appropriate agency designated by the court.

History of Fam §33.009: Acts 1999, 76th Leg., ch. 395, §1, eff. Sept. 1, 1999.

FAM §33.010. CONFIDENTIALITY

Notwithstanding any other law, information obtained by the Department of Protective and Regulatory Services or another entity under Section 33.008 or 33.009 is confidential except to the extent necessary to prove a violation of Section 22.011, 22.021, or 25.02, Penal Code.

History of Fam §33.010: Acts 1999, 76th Leg., ch. 395, §1, eff. Sept. 1, 1999.

FAM §33.011. INFORMATION RELATING TO JUDICIAL BYPASS

The Texas Department of Health shall produce and distribute informational materials that explain the rights of a minor under this chapter. The materials must explain the procedures established by Sections 33.003 and 33.004 and must be made available in English and in Spanish. The material provided by the department shall also provide information relating to alternatives to abortion and health risks associated with abortion.

History of Fam §33.011: Acts 1999, 76th Leg., ch. 395, §1, eff. Sept. 1, 1999.

Chapters 34-40 reserved for expansion

SUBTITLE B. PARENTAL LIABILITY

CHAPTER 41. LIABILITY OF PARENTS FOR CONDUCT OF CHILD

FAM §41.001. LIABILITY

A parent or other person who has the duty of control and reasonable discipline of a child is liable for any property damage proximately caused by:

A *Subsections (1) & (2) below are effective for property damage that occurs on or after Sept. 1, 2001.*

(1) the negligent conduct of the child if the conduct is reasonably attributable to the negligent failure of the parent or other person to exercise that duty; or

(2) the wilful and malicious conduct of a child who is at least 10 years of age but under 18 years of age.

Subsections (1) & (2) below were effective for property damage that occurred before Sept. 1, 2001.

(1) the negligent conduct of the child if the conduct is reasonably attributable to the negligent failure of the parent or other persons to exercise that duty; or

(2) the wilful and malicious conduct of a child who is at least 12 years of age but under 18 years of age.

History of Fam §41.001: Acts 1995, 74th Leg., ch. 20, §1, eff. April 20, 1995. Amended by Acts 2001, 77th Leg., ch. 587, §1, eff. Sept. 1, 2001. Source: Former Fam §33.01.

Isbell v. Ryan, 983 S.W.2d 335, 339 (Tex.App.—Houston [14th Dist.] 1998, no pet.). "As a general rule, defendants have no duty to prevent the criminal acts of a third party who does not act under defendants' supervision or control. This general rule does not apply in situations where a special relationship exists between the actor and the third person. One such exception to the rule is the parent-child relationship."

Prather v. Brandt, 981 S.W.2d 801, 806-07 (Tex. App.—Houston [1st Dist.] 1998, pet. denied). "As a general rule, minors are civilly liable for their own torts. A parent may be liable if the parent negligently allows his child to act in a manner likely to harm another, if he gives his child a dangerous instrumentality, or if he does not restrain a child known to have dangerous tendencies. A parent's duty to protect third parties from his child's acts depends on whether the injury to the third party is foreseeable. Foreseeability is evaluated by looking at the parent's knowledge of, consent to, or participation in the child's activity."

Kovar v. Krampitz, 941 S.W.2d 249, 255 (Tex. App.—Houston [14th Dist.] 1996, no writ). "[P]arents are not liable for the actions of a child 18-years-of age or older."

Williams v. Lavender, 797 S.W.2d 410, 412 (Tex. App.—Fort Worth 1990, writ denied). "While [appellee] is correct that the purpose of the statute is to protect and compensate property owners from the willful and malicious destruction of their property by minors, still, the statute expressly recognizes that a child between the ages of twelve and eighteen is capable of willful and malicious conduct. Therefore, it cannot be said that as a matter of law a minor who is fourteen years old cannot form the necessary malicious intent to warrant recovery of exemplary damages."

Amarillo Nat'l Bank v. Terry, 658 S.W.2d 702, 704 (Tex.App.—Amarillo 1983, no writ). "By the terms of the statute, liability is imposed on the parent or other person for 'property damage.' [T]he legislative intent 'is to protect and compensate property owners from the wilful and malicious *destruction* of their property by minors.' But, giving the phrase the meaning in which it is ordinarily understood, there was no property damage proximately caused by the unauthorized withdrawals of money, for there was no damage inflicted on, much less a destruction of, the money the bank lost. Instead, the bank suffered only an economic loss and, therefore, the bank was not caused property damage within the meaning of the statute."

FAM §41.002. LIMIT OF DAMAGES

Recovery for damage caused by wilful and malicious conduct is limited to actual damages, not to exceed $25,000 per occurrence, plus court costs and reasonable attorney's fees.

History of Fam §41.002: Acts 1995, 74th Leg., ch. 20, §1, eff. April 20, 1995. Amended by Acts 1997, 75th Leg., ch. 783, §1, eff. Sept. 1, 1997. Source: Former Fam §33.02.

FAM §41.0025. LIABILITY FOR PROPERTY DAMAGE TO AN INN OR HOTEL

(a) Notwithstanding Section 41.002, recovery of damages by an inn or hotel for wilful and malicious conduct is limited to actual damages, not to exceed $25,000 per occurrence, plus court costs and reasonable attorney's fees.

(b) In this section "occurrence" means one incident on a single day in one hotel room. The term does not include incidents in separate rooms or incidents that occur on different days.

History of Fam §41.0025: Acts 1997, 75th Leg., ch. 40, §1, eff. Sept. 1, 1997.

FAM §41.003. VENUE

A suit as provided by this chapter may be filed in the county in which the conduct of the child occurred or in the county in which the defendant resides.

History of Fam §41.003: Acts 1995, 74th Leg., ch. 20, §1, eff. April 20, 1995. Source: Former Fam §33.03.

CHAPTER 42. CIVIL LIABILITY FOR INTERFERENCE WITH POSSESSORY INTEREST IN CHILD

FAM §42.001. DEFINITIONS

In this chapter:

(1) "Order" means a temporary or final order of a court of this state or another state or nation.

(2) "Possessory right" means a court-ordered right of possession of or access to a child, including conservatorship, custody, and visitation.

History of Fam §42.001: Acts 1995, 74th Leg., ch. 20, §1, eff. April 20, 1995. Source: Former Fam §36.01.

FAM §42.002. LIABILITY FOR INTERFERENCE WITH POSSESSORY RIGHT

(a) A person who takes or retains possession of a child or who conceals the whereabouts of a child in violation of a possessory right of another person may be liable for damages to that person.

(b) A possessory right is violated by the taking, retention, or concealment of a child at a time when another person is entitled to possession of or access to the child.

History of Fam §42.002: Acts 1995, 74th Leg., ch. 20, §1, eff. April 20, 1995. Source: Former Fam §36.02(a), (b).

FAM §42.003. AIDING OR ASSISTING INTERFERENCE WITH POSSESSORY RIGHT

(a) A person who aids or assists in conduct for which a cause of action is authorized by this chapter is jointly and severally liable for damages.

(b) A person who was not a party to the suit in which an order was rendered providing for a possessory right is not liable unless the person at the time of the violation:

(1) had actual notice of the existence and contents of the order; or

(2) had reasonable cause to believe that the child was the subject of an order and that the person's actions were likely to violate the order.

History of Fam §42.003: Acts 1995, 74th Leg., ch. 20, §1, eff. April 20, 1995. Source: Former Fam §36.02(c), (d).

Black v. Jackson, ___ S.W.3d ___ (Tex.App.—Tyler 2002, n.p.h.) (No. 12-01-00187-CV; 2-28-02). Plaintiff "alleged that [her brother-in-law] and [sister] interfered with her possessory interest in Stacy, her minor daughter, and that such interference violated §42.003. An examination of her pleadings, however, reveals that [plaintiff] did not allege that either [defendant] assisted anyone who took, retained, or concealed Stacy while [plaintiff] was entitled to possession or access. Instead, she complained of acts she described as slander, harassment, and endangerment resulting from the dissolution of her family unit. Section 42.003 relates solely to physical interference with possession and not to the type of conduct alleged in [plaintiff's] pleadings. Therefore, an allegation of physical interference is indispensable to a claim under §42.003. By her failure to allege that [defendants] committed any act prohibited by that section, [plaintiff] has failed to state a cause of action against them for violation of §42.003."

A. H. Belo Corp. v. Corcoran, 52 S.W.3d 375, 382 (Tex.App.—Houston [1st Dist.] 2001, pet. denied). "There is nothing in §42.003 or the case law to indicate ... an affirmative duty [to reveal the whereabouts of abducted children] by all who have any knowledge of an abducted child's whereabouts."

Weirich v. Weirich, 833 S.W.2d 942, 945 (Tex. 1992). "[I]n order to hold [defendant] directly liable under §36.02(a) [now §42.003(a)], [plaintiff] had to have given her the notice required by §36.07(a) [§42.003(b)(1)]."

FAM §42.004. REPEALED

Repealed by Acts 1999, 76th Leg., ch. 437, §2, eff. Sept. 1, 1999.

FAM §42.005. VENUE

A suit may be filed in a county in which:

(1) the plaintiff resides;

(2) the defendant resides;

(3) a suit affecting the parent-child relationship as provided by Chapter 102 may be brought, concerning the child who is the subject of the court order; or

(4) a court has continuing, exclusive jurisdiction as provided by Chapter 155.

History of Fam §42.005: Acts 1995, 74th Leg., ch. 20, §1, eff. April 20, 1995. Source: Former Fam §36.05.

FAM §42.006. DAMAGES

(a) Damages may include:

(1) the actual costs and expenses incurred, including attorney's fees, in:

(A) locating a child who is the subject of the order;

(B) recovering possession of the child if the petitioner is entitled to possession; and

(C) enforcing the order and prosecuting the suit; and

(2) mental suffering and anguish incurred by the plaintiff because of a violation of the order.

(b) A person liable for damages who acted with malice or with an intent to cause harm to the plaintiff may be liable for exemplary damages.

History of Fam §42.006: Acts 1995, 74th Leg., ch. 20, §1, eff. April 20, 1995. Amended by Acts 1995, 74th Leg., ch. 751, §7, eff. Sept. 1, 1995. Source: Former Fam §36.03.

Smith v. Smith, 720 S.W.2d 586, 601 (Tex.App.—Houston [1st Dist.] 1986, no writ). "We hold that 'actual costs and expenses', as used in §36.03 [now §42.006], includes prospective costs and expenses that are supported by the evidence."

FAM §42.007. AFFIRMATIVE DEFENSE

The defendant may plead as an affirmative defense that the defendant acted in violation of the order with the express consent of the plaintiff.

History of Fam §42.007: Acts 1995, 74th Leg., ch. 20, §1, eff. April 20, 1995. Amended by Acts 1999, 76th Leg., ch. 437, §1, eff. Sept. 1, 1999. Source: Former Fam §36.04.

FAM §42.008. REMEDIES NOT AFFECTED

This chapter does not affect any other civil or criminal remedy available to any person, including the child, for interference with a possessory right, nor does it affect the power of a parent to represent the interest of a child in a suit filed on behalf of the child.

History of Fam §42.008: Acts 1995, 74th Leg., ch. 20, §1, eff. April 20, 1995. Source: Former Fam §36.06.

FAM §42.009. FRIVOLOUS SUIT

A person sued for damages as provided by this chapter is entitled to recover attorney's fees and court costs if:

(1) the claim for damages is dismissed or judgment is awarded to the defendant; and

(2) the court or jury finds that the claim for damages is frivolous, unreasonable, or without foundation.

History of Fam §42.009: Acts 1995, 74th Leg., ch. 20, §1, eff. April 20, 1995. Source: Former Fam §36.08.

Chapters 43-44 reserved for expansion

SUBTITLE C. CHANGE OF NAME

CHAPTER 45. CHANGE OF NAME

Subchapter A. Change of Name of Child

SUBCHAPTER A. CHANGE OF NAME OF CHILD

FAM §45.001. WHO MAY FILE; VENUE

A parent, managing conservator, or guardian of a child may file a petition requesting a change of name of the child in the county where the child resides.

History of Fam §45.001: Acts 1995, 74th Leg., ch. 20, §1, eff. April 20, 1995. Source: Former Fam §32.01, 32.02(a).

In re Hathcox, 981 S.W.2d 422, 426 n.2 (Tex.App.—Texarkana 1998, no pet.). "The child in this case ... turned age 18.... Because that child can now petition to use any name he desires, [the father] has no legally protected interest in having his child bear his surname and this issue is moot."

In re J.K., 922 S.W.2d 220, 222 (Tex.App.—San Antonio 1996, no writ). "The Family Code sections provide the sole method by which a name change for a minor may be accomplished."

FAM §45.002. REQUIREMENTS OF PETITION

(a) A petition to change the name of a child must be verified and include:

(1) the present name and place of residence of the child;

(2) the reason a change of name is requested;

(3) the full name requested for the child; and

(4) whether the child is subject to the continuing exclusive jurisdiction of a court under Chapter 155.

(b) If the child is 10 years of age or older, the child's written consent to the change of name must be attached to the petition.

History of Fam §45.002: Acts 1995, 74th Leg., ch. 20, §1, eff. April 20, 1995. Amended by Acts 1999, 76th Leg., ch. 1390, §1, eff. Sept. 1, 1999. Source: Former Fam §32.02.

FAM §45.003. CITATION

(a) The following persons are entitled to citation in a suit under this subchapter:

(1) a parent of the child whose parental rights have not been terminated;

(2) any managing conservator of the child; and

(3) any guardian of the child.

(b) Citation must be issued and served in the same manner as under Chapter 102.

History of Fam §45.003: Acts 1995, 74th Leg., ch. 20, §1, eff. April 20, 1995. Source: Former Fam §32.03.

FAM §45.004. ORDER

(a) The court may order the name of a child changed if the change is in the best interest of the child.

(b) If the child is subject to the continuing jurisdiction of a court under Chapter 155, the court shall send a copy of the order to the central record file as provided in Chapter 108.

History of Fam §45.004: Acts 1995, 74th Leg., ch. 20, §1, eff. April 20, 1995. Source: Former Fam §32.04.

In re Guthrie, 45 S.W.3d 719, 723-24 (Tex.App.—Dallas 2001, pet. denied). "A father has no constitutional right to have his children bear his last name. The only protectable interest a father has in a child's name recognized by Texas courts is when the mother attempts to change the child's surname from the father's. [¶] The standards for changing the name of a minor are controlled by the Texas Family Code.... The general rule is that courts will exercise the power to change a child's name reluctantly and only when the substantial welfare of the child requires it. A parent's interest and desire is only a secondary consideration. Texas has no statute giving the right to name a child to either parent. However, the name chosen by one of the parents will not be changed unless the dissident parent shows a good reason for such change. *At 725-26:* Therefore, we consider the factors that address the best interest of the child, not the needs of a particular parent, or customs or traditions that reflect a constitutionally prohibited inequality [such as giving preference to one parent's name over another on the basis of whether the parent is the father or mother]. Factors that have been considered proper in a best interest test are: [1] whether the changed name or the present name would best avoid embarrassment, inconvenience, or confusion for the custodial parent or the child; [2] whether it would be more convenient or easier for the child to have the same name as or a different name from the custodial parent, either the changed name or the present name; [3] whether the changed name or the present name would help identify the child as part of a family unit; [4] the length of time the surname has been used; parental misconduct, such as support or nonsupport or maintaining or failing to maintain contact with the child; [5] the degree of community respect associated with the present or changed name; [6] whether the change will positively or adversely affect the bond between the child and either parent or the parents' families; [7] any delay in requesting or objecting to name change; [8] the preferences of the child; [9] the age and maturity of the child; [10] when the child maintains the mother's surname, assurances by the mother that she would not change her name if she married or remarried; [11] whether the parent seeking the change is motivated by an attempt to alienate the child from the other parent."

G.K. v. K.A., 936 S.W.2d 70, 73 (Tex.App.—Austin 1996, writ denied). "The court has wide discretion in determining whether it is in the child's best interest to grant or deny an application for name change."

In re J.K., 922 S.W.2d 220, 222 (Tex.App.—San Antonio 1996, no writ). "A parent's interest and desire is only a secondary consideration. The name chosen by one parent should be changed only if the other parent provides sound reasoning why the given name would be detrimental to the child."

Brown v. Carroll, 683 S.W.2d 61, 63 (Tex.App.—Tyler 1984, no writ). "[T]he children's preference is not controlling in determining whether it is in their best interest to allow a name change."

FAM §45.005. LIABILITIES & RIGHTS UNAFFECTED

A change of name does not:

(1) release a child from any liability incurred in the child's previous name; or

(2) defeat any right the child had in the child's previous name.

History of Fam §45.005: Acts 1995, 74th Leg., ch. 20, §1, eff. April 20, 1995. Source: Former Fam §32.05.

Sections 45.006-45.100 reserved for expansion

SUBCHAPTER B. CHANGE OF NAME OF ADULT

FAM §45.101. WHO MAY FILE; VENUE

An adult may file a petition requesting a change of name in the county of the adult's place of residence.

History of Fam §45.101: Acts 1995, 74th Leg., ch. 20, §1, eff. April 20, 1995. Source: Former Fam §32.21(a).

In re Erickson, 547 S.W.2d 357, 359 (Tex.App.—Houston [14th Dist.] 1977, no writ). "An application for a change of name by an adult is controlled by §§32.21 and 32.22 [now ch. 45], which does *not* require the spouse, or anyone else, be made a party. ... Generally, the grant of an application for change of name is a matter of judicial discretion and should be granted unless there exists some wrongful, fraudulent, or capricious purpose."

FAM §45.102. REQUIREMENTS OF PETITION

(a) A petition to change the name of an adult must be verified and include:

(1) the present name and place of residence of the petitioner;

(2) the full name requested for the petitioner;

(3) the reason the change in name is requested; and

(4) whether the petitioner has been the subject of a final felony conviction.

(b) The petition must include each of the following or a reasonable explanation why the required information is not included:

(1) the petitioner's:

(A) full name;

(B) sex;

(C) race;

(D) date of birth;

(E) driver's license number for any driver's license issued in the 10 years preceding the date of the petition;

(F) social security number; and

(G) assigned FBI number, state identification number, if known, or any other reference number in a criminal history record system that identifies the petitioner;

(2) any offense above the grade of Class C misdemeanor for which the petitioner has been charged; and

(3) the case number and the court if a warrant was issued or a charging instrument was filed or presented for an offense listed in Subsection (b)(2).

History of Fam §45.102: Acts 1995, 74th Leg., ch. 20, §1, eff. April 20, 1995. Source: Former Fam §32.21(a), (b).

FAM §45.103. ORDER

(a) The court shall order a change of name under this subchapter for a person other than a person with a final felony conviction if the change is in the interest or to the benefit of the petitioner and in the interest of the public.

(b) A court may order a change of name under this subchapter for a person with a final felony conviction if, in addition to the requirements of Subsection (a), the person has:

(1) received a certificate of discharge by the pardons and paroles division of the Texas Department of Criminal Justice or completed a period of probation ordered by a court and not less than two years have passed from the date of the receipt of discharge or completion of probation; or

(2) been pardoned.

History of Fam §45.103: Acts 1995, 74th Leg., ch. 20, §1, eff. April 20, 1995. Source: Former Fam §32.22.

In re Dickey, 919 S.W.2d 790, 791 (Tex.App.—Texarkana 1996, no writ). "[Petitioner] contends on appeal that the prohibition in the statute against name changes for persons convicted of a felony refers only to felonies occurring within the State of Texas. We disagree. To limit the restrictions on name changes for felons only to convictions in Texas would subvert the purpose of the statute, *viz*, to protect the legitimate governmental interest of being able to identify persons sought on warrant and detainer and to preserve the criminal history of felons."

In re Erickson, 547 S.W.2d 357, 359 (Tex.App.—Houston [14th Dist.] 1977, no writ). "Generally, the grant of an application for change of name is a matter of judicial discretion and should be granted unless there exists some wrongful, fraudulent, or capricious purpose. [¶] It is enough that for her own proper reasons, appellant conscientiously feels the necessity of being known and referred to by her previous name. To deny her this right would be a violation of equal protection under the law by creating an invalid classification based on sex. [¶] We would not like to be understood as holding that a person has the absolute right to change his name by court order. Although the petitioner is ordinarily the only party before the court, the trial judge may appropriately inquire into matters, other than sex, which would authorize him to refuse to give legal sanction to a change of name."

FAM §45.104. LIABILITIES & RIGHTS UNAFFECTED

A change of name under this subchapter does not release a person from liability incurred in that person's previous name or defeat any right the person had in the person's previous name.

History of Fam §45.104: Acts 1995, 74th Leg., ch. 20, §1, eff. April 20, 1995. Source: Former Fam §32.23.

FAM §45.105. CHANGE OF NAME IN DIVORCE SUIT

(a) On the final disposition of a suit for divorce, for annulment, or to declare a marriage void, the court shall enter a decree changing the name of a party specially praying for the change to a prior used name unless the court states in the decree a reason for denying the change of name. The court may not deny a change of name solely to keep last names of family members the same.

(b) A person whose name is changed under this section may apply for a change of name certificate from the clerk of the court as provided by Section 45.106.

History of Fam §45.105: Acts 1997, 75th Leg., ch. 165, §7.10(a), eff. Sept. 1, 1997.

FAM §45.106. CHANGE OF NAME CERTIFICATE

(a) A person whose name is changed under Section 6.706 or 45.105 may apply to the clerk of the court ordering the name change for a change of name certificate.

(b) A certificate under this section is a one-page document that includes:

(1) the name of the person before the change of name was ordered;

(2) the name to which the person's name was changed by the court;

(3) the date on which the name change was made;

(4) the person's social security number and driver's license number, if any;

(5) the name of the court in which the name change was ordered; and

(6) the signature of the clerk of the court that issued the certificate.

(c) An applicant for a certificate under this section shall pay a $10 fee to the clerk of the court for issuance of the certificate.

(d) A certificate under this section constitutes proof of the change of name of the person named in the certificate.

History of Fam §45.106: Acts 1997, 75th Leg., ch. 165, §7.10(a), eff. Sept. 1, 1997. Amended by Acts 1999, 76th Leg., ch. 62, §6.06, eff. Sept. 1, 1999.

FAMILY CODE—TITLE 3
JUVENILE JUSTICE CODE
TABLE OF CONTENTS

TITLE 3. JUVENILE JUSTICE CODE

FAMILY CODE—TITLE 3
JUVENILE JUSTICE CODE
TABLE OF CONTENTS

TABLE OF CONTENTS

FAMILY CODE—TITLE 3
JUVENILE JUSTICE CODE

TITLE 3

TITLE 3. JUVENILE JUSTICE CODE

CHAPTER 51. GENERAL PROVISIONS

FAM §51.01. PURPOSE & INTERPRETATION

This title shall be construed to effectuate the following public purposes:

(1) to provide for the protection of the public and public safety;

(2) consistent with the protection of the public and public safety:

(A) to promote the concept of punishment for criminal acts;

(B) to remove, where appropriate, the taint of criminality from children committing certain unlawful acts; and

(C) to provide treatment, training, and rehabilitation that emphasizes the accountability and responsibility of both the parent and the child for the child's conduct;

(3) to provide for the care, the protection, and the wholesome moral, mental, and physical development of children coming within its provisions;

(4) to protect the welfare of the community and to control the commission of unlawful acts by children;

(5) to achieve the foregoing purposes in a family environment whenever possible, separating the child from the child's parents only when necessary for the child's welfare or in the interest of public safety and when a child is removed from the child's family, to give the child the care that should be provided by parents; and

(6) to provide a simple judicial procedure through which the provisions of this title are executed and enforced and in which the parties are assured a fair hearing and their constitutional and other legal rights recognized and enforced.

History of Fam §51.01: Acts 1973, 63rd Leg., ch. 544, §1, eff. Sept. 1, 1973. Amended by Acts 1995, 74th Leg., ch. 262, §2, eff. Jan. 1, 1996.

FAM §51.02. DEFINITIONS

In this title:

(1) "Aggravated controlled substance felony" means an offense under Subchapter D, Chapter 481, Health and Safety Code, that is punishable by:

(A) a minimum term of confinement that is longer than the minimum term of confinement for a felony of the first degree; or

(B) a maximum fine that is greater than the maximum fine for a felony of the first degree.

(2) "Child" means a person who is:

(A) ten years of age or older and under 17 years of age; or

(B) seventeen years of age or older and under 18 years of age who is alleged or found to have engaged in delinquent conduct or conduct indicating a need for supervision as a result of acts committed before becoming 17 years of age.

(3) "Custodian" means the adult with whom the child resides.

(4) "Guardian" means the person who, under court order, is the guardian of the person of the child or the public or private agency with whom the child has been placed by a court.

(5) "Judge" or "juvenile court judge" means the judge of a juvenile court.

(6) "Juvenile court" means a court designated under Section 51.04 of this code to exercise jurisdiction over proceedings under this title.

(7) "Law-enforcement officer" means a peace officer as defined by Article 2.12, Code of Criminal Procedure.

(8) "Nonoffender" means a child who:

(A) is subject to jurisdiction of a court under abuse, dependency, or neglect statutes under Title 5 for reasons other than legally prohibited conduct of the child; or

(B) has been taken into custody and is being held solely for deportation out of the United States.

A *Subsection (9) below is effective for motions or other requests for relief made in parentage or paternity proceedings commenced on or after June 14, 2001.*

(9) "Parent" means the mother or the father of a child, but does not include a parent whose parental rights have been terminated.

Subsection (9) below is effective for motions or other requests for relief made in parentage or paternity proceedings commenced before June 14, 2001.

(9) "Parent" means the mother, the father whether or not the child is legitimate, or an adoptive parent, but does not include a parent whose parental rights have been terminated.

(10) "Party" means the state, a child who is the subject of proceedings under this subtitle, or the child's parent, spouse, guardian, or guardian ad litem.

(11) "Prosecuting attorney" means the county attorney, district attorney, or other attorney who regularly serves in a prosecutory capacity in a juvenile court.

A *Subsection (12) below is effective for criminal conduct that occurs on or after Sept. 1, 2001.*

(12) "Referral to juvenile court" means the referral of a child or a child's case to the office or official, including an intake officer or probation officer, designated by the juvenile board to process children within the juvenile justice system.

Subsection (12) below is effective for criminal conduct in which any element of the conduct occurred before Sept. 1, 2001.

(12) "Referral to juvenile court" means the referral of a child or a child's case to the office or official, including an intake officer or probation officer, designated by the juvenile court to process children within the juvenile justice system.

(13) "Secure correctional facility" means any public or private residential facility, including an alcohol or other drug treatment facility, that:

(A) includes construction fixtures designed to physically restrict the movements and activities of juveniles or other individuals held in lawful custody in the facility; and

(B) is used for the placement of any juvenile who has been adjudicated as having committed an offense, any nonoffender, or any other individual convicted of a criminal offense.

(14) "Secure detention facility" means any public or private residential facility that:

(A) includes construction fixtures designed to physically restrict the movements and activities of juveniles or other individuals held in lawful custody in the facility; and

(B) is used for the temporary placement of any juvenile who is accused of having committed an offense, any nonoffender, or any other individual accused of having committed a criminal offense.

(15) "Status offender" means a child who is accused, adjudicated, or convicted for conduct that would not, under state law, be a crime if committed by an adult, including:

(A) truancy under Section 51.03(b)(2);

(B) running away from home under Section 51.03(b)(3);

(C) a fineable only offense under Section 51.03(b)(1) transferred to the juvenile court under Section 51.08(b), but only if the conduct constituting the offense would not have been criminal if engaged in by an adult;

(D) failure to attend school under Section 25.094, Education Code;

(E) a violation of standards of student conduct as described by Section 51.03(b)(5);

(F) a violation of a juvenile curfew ordinance or order;

(G) a violation of a provision of the Alcoholic Beverage Code applicable to minors only; or

(H) a violation of any other fineable only offense under Section 8.07(a)(4) or (5), Penal Code, but only if the conduct constituting the offense would not have been criminal if engaged in by an adult.

(16) "Traffic offense" means:

(A) a violation of a penal statute cognizable under Chapter 729, Transportation Code, except for:

(i) conduct constituting an offense under Section 550.021, Transportation Code;

(ii) conduct constituting an offense punishable as a Class B misdemeanor under Section 550.022, Transportation Code; or

(iii) conduct constituting an offense punishable as a Class B misdemeanor under Section 550.024, Transportation Code; or

(B) a violation of a motor vehicle traffic ordinance of an incorporated city or town in this state.

(17) "Valid court order" means a court order entered under Section 54.04 concerning a child adjudicated to have engaged in conduct indicating a need for supervision as a status offender.

History of Fam §51.02: Acts 1973, 63rd Leg., ch. 544, §1, eff. Sept. 1, 1973. Amended by Acts 1975, 64th Leg., ch. 693, §1, eff. Sept. 1, 1975; Acts 1995, 74th Leg., ch. 262, §3, eff. Jan. 1, 1996; Acts 1997, 75th Leg., ch. 165, §§6.06, 30.182 (eff. Sept. 1, 1997), ch. 822, §2 (eff. Sept. 1, 1997), ch. 1013, §13 (eff. Sept. 1, 1997), ch. 1086, §§41, 47 (eff. Sept. 1, 1997); Acts 2001, 77th Leg., ch. 821, §2.02 (eff. June 14, 2001), ch. 1297, §1 (eff. Sept. 1, 2001).

FAM §51.03. DELINQUENT CONDUCT; CONDUCT INDICATING A NEED FOR SUPERVISION

A *Subsection (a) below is effective for criminal conduct that occurs on or after Sept. 1, 2001.*

(a) Delinquent conduct is:

(1) conduct, other than a traffic offense, that violates a penal law of this state or of the United States punishable by imprisonment or by confinement in jail;

(2) conduct that violates a lawful order of a municipal court or justice court under circumstances that would constitute contempt of that court;

(3) conduct that violates Section 49.04, 49.05, 49.06, 49.07, or 49.08, Penal Code; or

(4) conduct that violates Section 106.041, Alcoholic Beverage Code, relating to driving under the influence of alcohol by a minor (third or subsequent offense).

Subsection (a) below is effective for criminal conduct in which any element of the conduct occurred before Sept. 1, 2001.

(a) Delinquent conduct is:

(1) conduct, other than a traffic offense, that violates a penal law of this state or of the United States punishable by imprisonment or by confinement in jail;

(2) conduct that violates a reasonable and lawful order of a juvenile court entered under Section 54.04 or 54.05 of this code, except an order prohibiting the following conduct:

(A) a violation of the penal laws of this state of the grade of misdemeanor that is punishable by fine only or a violation of the penal ordinances of any political subdivision of this state;

(B) the unexcused voluntary absence of a child from school; or

(C) the voluntary absence of a child from his home without the consent of his parent or guardian for a substantial length of time or without intent to return;

(3) conduct that violates a lawful order of a municipal court or justice court under circumstances that would constitute contempt of that court;

(4) conduct that violates Section 49.04, 49.05, 49.06, 49.07, or 49.08, Penal Code; or

(5) conduct that violates Section 106.041, Alcoholic Beverage Code, relating to driving under the influence of alcohol by a minor (third or subsequent offense).

(b) Conduct indicating a need for supervision is:

A *Subsections (1) through (3) below are effective for children alleged to have engaged in conduct that occurs on or after Sept. 1, 2001.*

(1) subject to Subsection (f), conduct, other than a traffic offense, that violates:

(A) the penal laws of this state of the grade of misdemeanor that are punishable by fine only; or

(B) the penal ordinances of any political subdivision of this state;

(2) the absence of a child on 10 or more days or parts of days within a six-month period in the same school year or on three or more days or parts of days within a four-week period from school;

(3) the voluntary absence of a child from the child's home without the consent of the child's parent or guardian for a substantial length of time or without intent to return;

Subsections (1) through (3) below are effective for children alleged to have engaged in conduct in which every element of the conduct occurred before Sept. 1, 2001.

(1) subject to Subsection (f) of this section, conduct, other than a traffic offense, that violates:

FAM §51.03

(A) the penal laws of this state of the grade of misdemeanor that are punishable by fine only; or

(B) the penal ordinances of any political subdivision of this state;

(2) the unexcused voluntary absence of a child on 10 or more days or parts of days within a six-month period or three or more days or parts of days within a four-week period from school without the consent of his parents;

(3) the voluntary absence of a child from his home without the consent of his parent or guardian for a substantial length of time or without intent to return;

(4) conduct prohibited by city ordinance or by state law involving the inhalation of the fumes or vapors of paint and other protective coatings or glue and other adhesives and the volatile chemicals itemized in Section 484.002, Health and Safety Code;

(5) an act that violates a school district's previously communicated written standards of student conduct for which the child has been expelled under Section 37.007(c), Education Code; or

(6) conduct that violates a reasonable and lawful order of a court entered under Section 264.305.

(c) Nothing in this title prevents criminal proceedings against a child for perjury.

A *Subsections (d) through (g) below are effective for children alleged to have engaged in conduct that occurs on or after Sept. 1, 2001.*

(d) It is an affirmative defense to an allegation of conduct under Subsection (b)(2) that one or more of the absences required to be proven under that subsection have been excused by a school official or should be excused by the court or that one of the absences was involuntary. The burden is on the respondent to show by a preponderance of the evidence that the absence has been or should be excused or that the absence was involuntary. A decision by the court to excuse an absence for purposes of this subsection does not affect the ability of the school district to determine whether to excuse the absence for another purpose.

(e) For the purposes of Subsection (b)(3), "child" does not include a person who is married, divorced, or widowed.

(f) Except as provided by Subsection (g), conduct described under Subsection (b)(1), other than conduct that violates Section 49.02, Penal Code, prohibiting public intoxication, does not constitute conduct indicating a need for supervision unless the child has been referred to the juvenile court under Section 51.08(b).

E (g) In a county with a population of less than 100,000, conduct described by Subsection (b)(1)(A) that violates Section 25.094, Education Code, is conduct indicating a need for supervision.

Subsections (d) through (f) below are effective for children alleged to have engaged in conduct in which every element of the conduct occurred before Sept. 1, 2001.

(d) For the purpose of Subsection (b)(2) of this section an absence is excused when the absence results from:

(1) illness of the child;

(2) illness or death in the family of the child;

(3) quarantine of the child and family;

(4) weather or road conditions making travel dangerous;

(5) an absence approved by a teacher, principal, or superintendent of the school in which the child is enrolled; or

(6) circumstances found reasonable and proper.

(e) For the purposes of Subdivisions (2) and (3) of Subsection (b) of this section, "child" does not include a person who is married, divorced, or widowed.

(f) Conduct described under Subsection (b)(1) of this section, other than conduct that violates Section 49.02, Penal Code, prohibiting public intoxication, does not constitute conduct indicating a need for supervision unless the child has been referred to the juvenile court under Section 51.08(b) of this code.

History of Fam §51.03: Acts 1973, 63rd Leg., ch. 544, §1, eff. Sept. 1, 1973. Amended by Acts 1975, 64th Leg., ch. 693, §§2 to 4, eff. Sept. 1, 1975; Acts 1977, 65th Leg., ch. 340, §1, eff. June 6, 1977; Acts 1987, 70th Leg., ch. 511, §1 (eff. Sept. 1, 1987), ch. 924, §1 (eff. Sept. 1, 1987), ch. 955, §1 (eff. June 19, 1987), ch. 1040, §20 (eff. Sept. 1, 1987), ch. 1099, §48 (eff. Sept. 1, 1987); Acts 1989, 71st Leg., ch. 1100, §3.02 (eff. Aug. 28, 1989), ch. 1245, §§1, 4 (eff. Sept. 1, 1989); Acts 1991, 72nd Leg., ch. 14, §284(35) (eff. Sept. 1, 1991), ch. 16, §7.02 (eff. Aug. 26, 1991), ch. 169, §1 (eff. Sept. 1, 1991); Acts 1993, 73rd Leg., ch. 46, §1, eff. Sept. 1, 1993; Acts 1995, 74th Leg., ch. 76, §14.30 (eff. Sept. 1, 1995), ch. 262, §4 (eff. Jan. 1, 1996); Acts 1997, 75th Leg., ch. 165, §6.07 (eff. Sept. 1, 1997), ch. 1013, §14 (eff. Sept. 1, 1997), ch. 1015, §15 (eff. June 19, 1997), ch. 1086, §1 (eff. Sept. 1, 1997); Acts 2001, 77th Leg., ch. 1297, §2 (eff. Sept. 1, 2001), ch. 1514, §11 (eff. Sept. 1, 2001).

FAM §51.031. HABITUAL FELONY CONDUCT

(a) Habitual felony conduct is conduct violating a penal law of the grade of felony, other than a state jail felony, if:

(1) the child who engaged in the conduct has at least two previous final adjudications as having engaged

in delinquent conduct violating a penal law of the grade of felony;

(2) the second previous final adjudication is for conduct that occurred after the date the first previous adjudication became final; and

(3) all appeals relating to the previous adjudications considered under Subdivisions (1) and (2) have been exhausted.

(b) For purposes of this section, an adjudication is final if the child is placed on probation or committed to the Texas Youth Commission.

(c) An adjudication based on conduct that occurred before January 1, 1996, may not be considered in a disposition made under this section.

History of Fam §51.031: Acts 1995, 74th Leg., ch. 262, §5, eff. Jan. 1, 1996. Amended by Acts 1997, 75th Leg., ch. 1086, §2, eff. Sept. 1, 1997.

FAM §51.04. JURISDICTION

A *Subsection (a) below is effective for children alleged to have engaged in conduct that occurs on or after Sept. 1, 2001.*

(a) This title covers the proceedings in all cases involving the delinquent conduct or conduct indicating a need for supervision engaged in by a person who was a child within the meaning of this title at the time the person engaged in the conduct, and, except as provided by Subsection (h), the juvenile court has exclusive original jurisdiction over proceedings under this title.

Subsection (a) below is effective for children alleged to have engaged in conduct in which every element of the conduct occurred before Sept. 1, 2001.

(a) This title covers the proceedings in all cases involving the delinquent conduct or conduct indicating a need for supervision engaged in by a person who was a child within the meaning of this title at the time he engaged in the conduct, and the juvenile court has exclusive original jurisdiction over proceedings under this title.

(b) In each county, the county's juvenile board shall designate one or more district, criminal district, domestic relations, juvenile, or county courts or county courts at law as the juvenile court, subject to Subsections (c) and (d) of this section.

(c) If the county court is designated as a juvenile court, at least one other court shall be designated as the juvenile court. A county court does not have jurisdiction of a proceeding involving a petition approved by a grand jury under Section 53.045 of this code.

(d) If the judge of a court designated in Subsection (b) or (c) of this section is not an attorney licensed in this state, there shall also be designated an alternate court, the judge of which is an attorney licensed in this state.

(e) A designation made under Subsection (b) or (c) of this section may be changed from time to time by the authorized boards or judges for the convenience of the people and the welfare of children. However, there must be at all times a juvenile court designated for each county. It is the intent of the legislature that in selecting a court to be the juvenile court of each county, the selection shall be made as far as practicable so that the court designated as the juvenile court will be one which is presided over by a judge who has a sympathetic understanding of the problems of child welfare and that changes in the designation of juvenile courts be made only when the best interest of the public requires it.

(f) If the judge of the juvenile court or any alternate judge named under Subsection (b) or (c) is not in the county or is otherwise unavailable, any magistrate may make a determination under Section 53.02(f) or may conduct the detention hearing provided for in Section 54.01.

A *Subsection (g) below is effective for criminal conduct that occurs on or after Sept. 1, 2001.*

(g) The juvenile board may appoint a referee to make determinations under Section 53.02(f) or to conduct hearings under this title. The referee shall be an attorney licensed to practice law in this state and shall comply with Section 54.10. Payment of any referee services shall be provided from county funds.

Subsection (g) below is effective for criminal conduct in which any element of the conduct occurred before Sept. 1, 2001.

(g) The juvenile board, or if there is no juvenile board, the juvenile court, may appoint a referee to make determinations under Section 53.02(f) or to conduct hearings under this title. The referee shall be an attorney licensed to practice law in this state and shall comply with Section 54.10. Payment of any referee services shall be provided from county funds.

E *Subsection (h) below is effective for children alleged to have engaged in conduct that occurs on or after Sept. 1, 2001.*

(h) In a county with a population of less than 100,000, the juvenile court has concurrent jurisdiction with the justice and municipal courts over conduct engaged in by a child that violates Section 25.094, Education Code.

History of Fam §51.04: Acts 1973, 63rd Leg., ch. 544, §1, eff. Sept. 1, 1973. Amended by Acts 1975, 64th Leg., ch. 514, §1 (eff. June 19, 1975), ch. 693, §§5 - 7 (eff. Sept. 1, 1975); Acts 1977, 65th Leg., ch. 411, §1, eff. June 15, 1977; Acts 1987, 70th Leg., ch. 385, §1, eff. Sept. 1, 1987; Acts 1993, 73rd Leg., ch. 168, §4, eff. Aug. 30, 1993; Acts 1999, 76th Leg., ch. 232, §2, eff. Sept. 1, 1999; Acts 2001, 77th Leg., ch. 1297, §3 (eff. Sept. 1, 2001), ch. 1514, §12 (eff. Sept. 1, 2001).

FAM §51.041. JURISDICTION AFTER APPEAL

Ⓐ *Section 51.041 below is effective for criminal conduct that occurs on or after Sept. 1, 2001.*

(a) The court retains jurisdiction over a person, without regard to the age of the person, for conduct engaged in by the person before becoming 17 years of age if, as a result of an appeal by the person under Chapter 56 or under Article 44.47, Code of Criminal Procedure, of an order of the court, the order is reversed or modified and the case remanded to the court by the appellate court.

Ⓔ (b) If the respondent is at least 18 years of age when the order of remand from the appellate court is received by the juvenile court, the juvenile court shall proceed as provided by Sections 54.02(o)-(r) for the detention of a person at least 18 years of age in discretionary transfer proceedings. Pending retrial of the adjudication or transfer proceeding, the juvenile court may:

(1) order the respondent released from custody;

(2) order the respondent detained in a juvenile detention facility; or

(3) set bond and order the respondent detained in a county adult facility if bond is not made.

History of Fam §51.041: Acts 1995, 74th Leg., ch. 262, §6, eff. Jan. 1, 1996. Amended by Acts 2001, 77th Leg., ch. 1297, §4, eff. Sept. 1, 2001.

FAM §51.041. JURISDICTION AFTER APPEAL

Section 51.041 below is effective for criminal conduct in which any element of the conduct occurred before Sept. 1, 2001.

The court retains jurisdiction over a person, without regard to the age of the person, for conduct engaged in by the person before becoming 17 years of age if, as a result of an appeal by the person under Chapter 56 of an order of the court, the order is reversed or modified and the case remanded to the court by the appellate court.

FAM §51.0411. JURISDICTION FOR TRANSFER OR RELEASE HEARING

The court retains jurisdiction over a person, without regard to the age of the person, who is referred to the court under Section 54.11 for transfer to the Texas Department of Criminal Justice or release under supervision.

History of Fam §51.0411: Acts 1997, 75th Leg., ch. 1086, §3, eff. June 19, 1997.

FAM §51.0412. JURISDICTION OVER INCOMPLETE PROCEEDINGS

Ⓔ *Section 51.0412 below is effective for criminal conduct that occurs on or after Sept. 1, 2001.*

The court retains jurisdiction over a person, without regard to the age of the person, who is a respondent in an adjudication proceeding, a disposition proceeding, or a proceeding to modify disposition if:

(1) the petition or motion to modify was filed while the respondent was younger than 18 years of age;

(2) the proceeding is not complete before the respondent becomes 18 years of age; and

(3) the court enters a finding in the proceeding that the prosecuting attorney exercised due diligence in an attempt to complete the proceeding before the respondent became 18 years of age.

History of Fam §51.0412: Enacted by Acts 2001, 77th Leg., ch. 1297, §5, eff. Sept. 1, 2001.

FAM §51.042. OBJECTION TO JURISDICTION BECAUSE OF AGE OF THE CHILD

(a) A child who objects to the jurisdiction of the court over the child because of the age of the child must raise the objection at the adjudication hearing or discretionary transfer hearing, if any.

(b) A child who does not object as provided by Subsection (a) waives any right to object to the jurisdiction of the court because of the age of the child at a later hearing or on appeal.

History of Fam §51.042: Acts 1995, 74th Leg., ch. 262, §6, eff. Jan. 1, 1996.

FAM §51.045. JURIES IN COUNTY COURTS AT LAW

If a provision of this title requires a jury of 12 persons, that provision prevails over any other law that limits the number of members of a jury in a particular county court at law. The state and the defense are entitled to the same number of peremptory challenges allowed in a district court.

History of Fam §51.045: Acts 1987, 70th Leg., ch. 385, §2, eff. Sept. 1, 1987.

FAM §51.05. COURT SESSIONS & FACILITIES

(a) The juvenile court shall be deemed in session at all times. Suitable quarters shall be provided by the commissioners court of each county for the hearing of cases and for the use of the judge, the probation officer, and other employees of the court.

(b) The juvenile court and the juvenile board shall report annually to the commissioners court on the suitability of the quarters and facilities of the juvenile court and may make recommendations for their improvement.

History of Fam §51.05: Acts 1973, 63rd Leg., ch. 544, §1, eff. Sept. 1, 1973. Amended by Acts 1975, 64th Leg., ch. 693, §8, eff. Sept. 1, 1975.

FAM §51.06. VENUE

(a) A proceeding under this title shall be commenced in

(1) the county in which the alleged delinquent conduct or conduct indicating a need for supervision occurred; or

(2) the county in which the child resides at the time the petition is filed, but only if:

(A) the child was under probation supervision in that county at the time of the commission of the delinquent conduct or conduct indicating a need for supervision;

(B) it cannot be determined in which county the delinquent conduct or conduct indicating a need for supervision occurred; or

(C) the county in which the child resides agrees to accept the case for prosecution, in writing, prior to the case being sent to the county of residence for prosecution.

(b) An application for a writ of habeas corpus brought by or on behalf of a person who has been committed to an institution under the jurisdiction of the Texas Youth Commission and which attacks the validity of the judgment of commitment shall be brought in the county in which the court that entered the judgment of commitment is located.

History of Fam §51.06: Acts 1973, 63rd Leg., ch. 544, §1, eff. Sept. 1, 1973. Amended by Acts 1983, 68th Leg., ch. 44, art. 1, §1, eff. April 26, 1983; Acts 1995, 74th Leg., ch. 262, §7, eff. Jan. 1, 1996; Acts 1999, 76th Leg., ch. 488, §1, eff. Sept. 1, 1999.

FAM §51.07. TRANSFER TO ANOTHER COUNTY

(a) When a child has been found to have engaged in delinquent conduct or conduct indicating a need for supervision under Section 54.03 of this code, the juvenile court, with the consent of the child and appropriate adult given in accordance with Section 51.09 of this code, may transfer the case and transcripts of records and documents to the juvenile court of the county where the child resides for disposition of the case under Section 54.04 of this code.

(b) When a child who is on probation moves with his family from one county to another, the juvenile court may transfer the case to the juvenile court in the county of the child's new residence if the transfer is in the best interest of the child. In all other cases of transfer, consent of the receiving court is required. The transferring court shall forward transcripts of records and documents in the case to the judge of the receiving court.

History of Fam §51.07: Acts 1973, 63rd Leg., ch. 544, §1, eff. Sept. 1, 1973.

FAM §51.08. TRANSFER FROM CRIMINAL COURT

(a) If the defendant in a criminal proceeding is a child who is charged with an offense other than perjury, a traffic offense, a misdemeanor punishable by fine only other than public intoxication, or a violation of a penal ordinance of a political subdivision, unless he has been transferred to criminal court under Section 54.02 of this code, the court exercising criminal jurisdiction shall transfer the case to the juvenile court, together with a copy of the accusatory pleading and other papers, documents, and transcripts of testimony relating to the case, and shall order that the child be taken to the place of detention designated by the juvenile court, or shall release him to the custody of his parent, guardian, or custodian, to be brought before the juvenile court at a time designated by that court.

(b) A court in which there is pending a complaint against a child alleging a violation of a misdemeanor offense punishable by fine only other than a traffic offense or public intoxication or a violation of a penal ordinance of a political subdivision other than a traffic offense:

Ⓐ *Subsection (1) below is effective for criminal conduct that occurs on or after Sept. 1, 2001.*

(1) except as provided by Subsection (d), shall waive its original jurisdiction and refer a child to juvenile court if the child has previously been convicted of:

(A) two or more misdemeanors punishable by fine only other than a traffic offense or public intoxication;

(B) two or more violations of a penal ordinance of a political subdivision other than a traffic offense; or

(C) one or more of each of the types of misdemeanors described in Paragraph (A) or (B) of this subdivision; and

Subsection (1) below is effective for criminal conduct in which any element of the conduct occurred before Sept. 1, 2001.

(1) shall waive its original jurisdiction and refer a child to juvenile court if the child has previously been convicted of:

(A) two or more misdemeanors punishable by fine only other than a traffic offense or public intoxication;

(B) two or more violations of a penal ordinance of a political subdivision other than a traffic offense; or

(C) one or more of each of the types of misdemeanors described in Paragraph (A) or (B) of this subdivision; and

(2) may waive its original jurisdiction and refer a child to juvenile court if the child:

(A) has not previously been convicted of a misdemeanor punishable by fine only other than a traffic offense or public intoxication or a violation of a penal ordinance of a political subdivision other than a traffic offense; or

(B) has previously been convicted of fewer than two misdemeanors punishable by fine only other than a traffic offense or public intoxication or two violations of a penal ordinance of a political subdivision other than a traffic offense.

(c) A court in which there is pending a complaint against a child alleging a violation of a misdemeanor offense punishable by fine only other than a traffic offense or public intoxication or a violation of a penal ordinance of a political subdivision other than a traffic offense shall notify the juvenile court of the county in which the court is located of the pending complaint and shall furnish to the juvenile court a copy of the final disposition of any matter for which the court does not waive its original jurisdiction under Subsection (b) of this section.

E *Subsection (d) below is effective for criminal conduct that occurs on or after Sept. 1, 2001.*

(d) A court that has implemented a juvenile case manager program under Article 45.054, Code of Criminal Procedure, may, but is not required to, waive its original jurisdiction under Subsection (b)(1).

History of Fam §51.08: Acts 1973, 63rd Leg., ch. 544, §1, eff. Sept. 1, 1973. Amended by Acts 1987, 70th Leg., ch. 1040, §21, eff. Sept. 1, 1987; Acts 1989, 71st Leg., ch. 1245, §2, eff. Sept. 1, 1989; Acts 1991, 72nd Leg., ch. 169, §2, eff. Sept. 1, 1991; Acts 2001, 77th Leg., ch. 1297, §6, eff. Sept. 1, 2001.

FAM §51.09. WAIVER OF RIGHTS

Unless a contrary intent clearly appears elsewhere in this title, any right granted to a child by this title or by the constitution or laws of this state or the United States may be waived in proceedings under this title if:

(1) the waiver is made by the child and the attorney for the child;

(2) the child and the attorney waiving the right are informed of and understand the right and the possible consequences of waiving it;

(3) the waiver is voluntary; and

(4) the waiver is made in writing or in court proceedings that are recorded.

History of Fam §51.09: Acts 1973, 63rd Leg., ch. 544, §1, eff. Sept. 1, 1973. Amended by Acts 1975, 64th Leg., ch. 693, §9, eff. Sept. 1, 1975; Acts 1989, 71st Leg., ch. 84, §1, eff. Sept. 1, 1989; Acts 1991, 72nd Leg., ch. 64, §1 (eff. Sept. 1, 1991), ch. 429, §1 (eff. Sept. 1, 1991), ch. 557, §1 (eff. Sept. 1, 1991), ch. 593, §1 (eff. Aug. 26, 1991); Acts 1995, 74th Leg., ch. 262, §§8, 9, eff. Jan. 1, 1996; Acts 1997, 75th Leg., ch. 1086, §4, eff. Sept. 1, 1997.

FAM §51.095. ADMISSIBILITY OF A STATEMENT OF A CHILD

(a) Notwithstanding Section 51.09, the statement of a child is admissible in evidence in any future proceeding concerning the matter about which the statement was given if:

(1) the statement is made in writing under a circumstance described by Subsection (d) and:

(A) the statement shows that the child has at some time before the making of the statement received from a magistrate a warning that:

(i) the child may remain silent and not make any statement at all and that any statement that the child makes may be used in evidence against the child;

(ii) the child has the right to have an attorney present to advise the child either prior to any questioning or during the questioning;

(iii) if the child is unable to employ an attorney, the child has the right to have an attorney appointed to counsel with the child before or during any interviews with peace officers or attorneys representing the state; and

(iv) the child has the right to terminate the interview at any time;

(B) and:

(i) the statement must be signed in the presence of a magistrate by the child with no law enforcement officer or prosecuting attorney present, except that a magistrate may require a bailiff or a law enforcement officer if a bailiff is not available to be present if the magistrate determines that the presence of the bailiff or law enforcement officer is necessary for the personal safety of the magistrate or other court personnel, provided that the bailiff or law enforcement officer may not carry a weapon in the presence of the child; and

(ii) the magistrate must be fully convinced that the child understands the nature and contents of the statement and that the child is signing the same voluntarily, and if a statement is taken, the magistrate must sign a written statement verifying the foregoing requisites have been met;

(C) the child knowingly, intelligently, and voluntarily waives these rights before and during the making of the statement and signs the statement in the presence of a magistrate; and

(D) the magistrate certifies that the magistrate has examined the child independent of any law enforcement officer or prosecuting attorney, except as required to ensure the personal safety of the magistrate or other court personnel, and has determined that the child understands the nature and contents of the statement and has knowingly, intelligently, and voluntarily waived these rights;

A *Subsection (2) below is effective for criminal conduct that occurs on or after Sept. 1, 2001.*

(2) the statement is made orally and the child makes a statement of facts or circumstances that are found to be true and tend to establish the child's guilt, such as the finding of secreted or stolen property, or the instrument with which the child states the offense was committed;

Subsection (2) below is effective for criminal conduct in which any element of the conduct occurred before Sept. 1, 2001.

(2) the statement is made orally and the child makes a statement of facts or circumstances that are found to be true, which conduct tends to establish the child's guilt, such as the finding of secreted or stolen property, or the instrument with which the child states the offense was committed;

(3) the statement was res gestae of the delinquent conduct or the conduct indicating a need for supervision or of the arrest;

(4) the statement is made:

(A) in open court at the child's adjudication hearing;

(B) before a grand jury considering a petition, under Section 53.045, that the child engaged in delinquent conduct; or

(C) at a preliminary hearing concerning the child held in compliance with this code, other than at a detention hearing under Section 54.01; or

(5) the statement is made orally under a circumstance described by Subsection (d) and the statement is recorded by an electronic recording device, including a device that records images, and:

(A) before making the statement, the child is given the warning described by Subdivision (1)(A) by a magistrate, the warning is a part of the recording, and the child knowingly, intelligently, and voluntarily waives each right stated in the warning;

(B) the recording device is capable of making an accurate recording, the operator of the device is competent to use the device, the recording is accurate, and the recording has not been altered;

(C) each voice on the recording is identified; and

(D) not later than the 20th day before the date of the proceeding, the attorney representing the child is given a complete and accurate copy of each recording of the child made under this subdivision.

(b) This section and Section 51.09 do not preclude the admission of a statement made by the child if:

(1) the statement does not stem from interrogation of the child under a circumstance described by Subsection (d); or

(2) without regard to whether the statement stems from interrogation of the child under a circumstance described by Subsection (d), the statement is voluntary and has a bearing on the credibility of the child as a witness.

(c) An electronic recording of a child's statement made under Subsection (a)(5) shall be preserved until all juvenile or criminal matters relating to any conduct referred to in the statement are final, including the exhaustion of all appeals, or barred from prosecution.

(d) Subsections (a)(1) and (a)(5) apply to the statement of a child made:

(1) while the child is in a detention facility or other place of confinement;

(2) while the child is in the custody of an officer; or

(3) during or after the interrogation of the child by an officer if the child is in the possession of the Department of Protective and Regulatory Services and is suspected to have engaged in conduct that violates a penal law of this state.

Ⓐ (e) A juvenile law referee or master may perform the duties imposed on a magistrate under this section without the approval of the juvenile court if the juvenile board of the county in which the statement of the child is made has authorized a referee or master to perform the duties of a magistrate under this section.

History of Fam §51.095: Acts 1997, 75th Leg., ch. 1086, §4, eff. Sept. 1, 1997. Amended by Acts 1999, 76th Leg., ch. 982, §1 (eff. Sept. 1, 1999), ch. 1477, §1 (eff. Sept. 1, 1999); Acts 2001, 77th Leg., ch. 1297, §7 (eff. Sept. 1, 2001), ch. 1420, §21.001(29), eff. Sept. 1, 2001.

FAM §51.10. RIGHT TO ASSISTANCE OF ATTORNEY; COMPENSATION

(a) A child may be represented by an attorney at every stage of proceedings under this title, including:

(1) the detention hearing required by Section 54.01 of this code;

(2) the hearing to consider transfer to criminal court required by Section 54.02 of this code;

(3) the adjudication hearing required by Section 54.03 of this code;

(4) the disposition hearing required by Section 54.04 of this code;

(5) the hearing to modify disposition required by Section 54.05 of this code;

(6) hearings required by Chapter 55 of this code;

(7) habeas corpus proceedings challenging the legality of detention resulting from action under this title; and

(8) proceedings in a court of civil appeals or the Texas Supreme Court reviewing proceedings under this title.

(b) The child's right to representation by an attorney shall not be waived in:

(1) a hearing to consider transfer to criminal court as required by Section 54.02 of this code;

(2) an adjudication hearing as required by Section 54.03 of this code;

(3) a disposition hearing as required by Section 54.04 of this code;

(4) a hearing prior to commitment to the Texas Youth Commission as a modified disposition in accordance with Section 54.05(f) of this code; or

(5) hearings required by Chapter 55 of this code.

(c) If the child was not represented by an attorney at the detention hearing required by Section 54.01 of this code and a determination was made to detain the child, the child shall immediately be entitled to representation by an attorney. The court shall order the retention of an attorney according to Subsection (d) or appoint an attorney according to Subsection (f).

(d) The court shall order a child's parent or other person responsible for support of the child to employ an attorney to represent the child, if:

(1) the child is not represented by an attorney;

(2) after giving the appropriate parties an opportunity to be heard, the court determines that the parent or other person responsible for support of the child is financially able to employ an attorney to represent the child; and

(3) the child's right to representation by an attorney:

(A) has not been waived under Section 51.09 of this code; or

(B) may not be waived under Subsection (b) of this section.

Ⓐ *Subsection (e) below is effective for criminal conduct that occurs on or after Sept. 1, 2001.*

(e) The court may enforce orders under Subsection (d) by proceedings under Section 54.07 or by appointing counsel and ordering the parent or other person responsible for support of the child to pay a reasonable attorney's fee set by the court. The order may be enforced under Section 54.07.

Subsection (e) below is effective for criminal conduct in which any element of the conduct occurred before Sept. 1, 2001.

(e) The court may enforce orders under Subsection (c) of this section by proceedings under Section 54.07 of this code or by appointing counsel and ordering the parent or other person responsible for support of the child to pay a reasonable attorney's fee set by the court. The order may be enforced under Section 54.07 of this code.

(f) The court shall appoint an attorney to represent the interest of a child entitled to representation by an attorney, if:

(1) the child is not represented by an attorney;

(2) the court determines that the child's parent or other person responsible for support of the child is

FAM §51.095

financially unable to employ an attorney to represent the child; and

(3) the child's right to representation by an attorney:

(A) has not been waived under Section 51.09 of this code; or

(B) may not be waived under Subsection (b) of this section.

(g) The juvenile court may appoint an attorney in any case in which it deems representation necessary to protect the interests of the child.

(h) Any attorney representing a child in proceedings under this title is entitled to 10 days to prepare for any adjudication or transfer hearing under this title.

(i) Except as provided in Subsection (d) of this section, an attorney appointed under this section to represent the interests of a child shall be paid from the general fund of the county in which the proceedings were instituted according to the schedule in Article 26.05 of the Texas Code of Criminal Procedure, 1965. For this purpose, a bona fide appeal to a court of civil appeals or proceedings on the merits in the Texas Supreme Court are considered the equivalent of a bona fide appeal to the Texas Court of Criminal Appeals.

History of Fam §51.10: Acts 1973, 63rd Leg., ch. 544, §1, eff. Sept. 1, 1973. Amended by Acts 1983, 68th Leg., ch. 44, art. 1, §2, eff. April 26, 1983; Acts 1995, 74th Leg., ch. 262, §11, eff. Jan. 1, 1996; Acts 2001, 77th Leg., ch. 1297, §8, eff. Sept. 1, 2001.

FAM §51.101[A*]. APPOINTMENT OF ATTORNEY & CONTINUATION OF REPRESENTATION

In 2001, the Legislature enacted two sections 51.101. Section 51.101 below was enacted by ch. 1297, §9, 77th Leg., effective Sept. 1, 2001. The [A] has been added by the editor to distinguish this section 51.101 from the other, which is marked with [B*]. In 2003, the Legislature is expected to correct the duplicate numbering. Section 51.101[A*] below is effective for criminal conduct that occurs on or after Sept. 1, 2001.*

(a) If an attorney is appointed at the initial detention hearing and the child is detained, the attorney shall continue to represent the child until the case is terminated, the family retains an attorney, or a new attorney is appointed by the juvenile court. Release of the child from detention does not terminate the attorney's representation.

(b) If there is an initial detention hearing without an attorney and the child is detained, the attorney appointed under Section 51.10(c) shall continue to represent the child until the case is terminated, the family retains an attorney, or a new attorney is appointed by the juvenile court. Release of the child from detention does not terminate the attorney's representation.

(c) The juvenile court shall determine, on the filing of a petition, whether the child's family is indigent if:

(1) the child is released by intake;

(2) the child is released at the initial detention hearing; or

(3) the case was referred to the court without the child in custody.

(d) A juvenile court that makes a finding of indigence under Subsection (c) shall appoint an attorney to represent the child on or before the fifth working day after the date the petition for adjudication or discretionary transfer hearing was served on the child. An attorney appointed under this subsection shall continue to represent the child until the case is terminated, the family retains an attorney, or a new attorney is appointed by the juvenile court.

(e) The juvenile court shall determine whether the child's family is indigent if a motion or petition is filed under Section 54.05 seeking to modify disposition by committing the child to the Texas Youth Commission or placing the child in a secure correctional facility. A court that makes a finding of indigence shall appoint an attorney to represent the child on or before the fifth working day after the date the petition or motion has been filed. An attorney appointed under this subsection shall continue to represent the child until the court rules on the motion or petition, the family retains an attorney, or a new attorney is appointed.

History of Fam §51.101[A*]: Enacted by Acts 2001, 77th Leg., ch. 1297, §9, eff. Sept. 1, 2001.

FAM §51.101[B*]. APPOINTMENT OF COUNSEL PLAN

In 2001, the Legislature enacted two sections 51.101. Section 51.101 below was enacted by ch. 906, §11, 77th Leg., effective Jan. 1, 2002. The [B] has been added by the editor to distinguish this section 51.101 from the other, which is marked with [A*]. In 2003, the Legislature is expected to correct the duplicate numbering. Section 51.101[B*] below is effective for children taken into custody for conduct alleged to have occurred on or after Jan. 1, 2002.*

(a) The juvenile board in each county shall adopt a plan that:

(1) specifies the qualifications necessary for an attorney to be included on an appointment list from which attorneys are appointed to represent children in proceedings under this title; and

(2) establishes procedures for:

(A) including attorneys on the appointment list and removing attorneys from the list; and

(B) appointing attorneys from the appointment list to individual cases.

(b) A plan adopted under Subsection (a) must:

(1) to the extent practicable, comply with the requirements of Article 26.04, Code of Criminal Procedure, except that:

(A) the income and assets of the child's parent or other person responsible for the child's support must be used in determining whether the child is indigent; and

(B) any alternative plan for appointing counsel is established by the juvenile board in the county; and

(2) recognize the differences in qualifications and experience necessary for appointments to cases in which:

(A) the allegation is:

(i) conduct indicating a need for supervision;

(ii) delinquent conduct, and commitment to the Texas Youth Commission is not an authorized disposition; or

(iii) delinquent conduct, and commitment to the Texas Youth Commission without a determinate sentence is an authorized disposition;

(B) determinate sentence proceedings have been initiated; or

(C) proceedings for discretionary transfer to criminal court have been initiated.

History of Fam §51.101[B*]: Enacted by Acts 2001, 77th Leg., ch. 906, §11, eff. Jan. 1, 2002.

FAM §51.11. GUARDIAN AD LITEM

(a) If a child appears before the juvenile court without a parent or guardian, the court shall appoint a guardian ad litem to protect the interests of the child. The juvenile court need not appoint a guardian ad litem if a parent or guardian appears with the child.

(b) In any case in which it appears to the juvenile court that the child's parent or guardian is incapable or unwilling to make decisions in the best interest of the child with respect to proceedings under this title, the court may appoint a guardian ad litem to protect the interests of the child in the proceedings.

(c) An attorney for a child may also be his guardian ad litem. A law-enforcement officer, probation officer, or other employee of the juvenile court may not be appointed guardian ad litem.

History of Fam §51.11: Acts 1973, 63rd Leg., ch. 544, §1, eff. Sept. 1, 1973.

FAM §51.115. ATTENDANCE AT HEARING: PARENT OR OTHER GUARDIAN

(a) Each parent of a child, each managing and possessory conservator of a child, each court-appointed custodian of a child, and a guardian of the person of the child shall attend each hearing affecting the child held under:

(1) Section 54.02 (waiver of jurisdiction and discretionary transfer to criminal court);

(2) Section 54.03 (adjudication hearing);

(3) Section 54.04 (disposition hearing);

(4) Section 54.05 (hearing to modify disposition); and

(5) Section 54.11 (release or transfer hearing).

(b) Subsection (a) does not apply to:

(1) a person for whom, for good cause shown, the court waives attendance;

(2) a person who is not a resident of this state; or

(3) a parent of a child for whom a managing conservator has been appointed and the parent is not a conservator of the child.

(c) A person required under this section to attend a hearing is entitled to reasonable written or oral notice that includes a statement of the place, date, and time of the hearing and that the attendance of the person is required. The notice may be included with or attached to any other notice required by this chapter to be given the person. Separate notice is not required for a disposition hearing that convenes on the adjournment of an adjudication hearing. If a person required under this section fails to attend a hearing, the juvenile court may proceed with the hearing.

(d) A person who is required by Subsection (a) to attend a hearing, who receives the notice of the hearing, and who fails to attend the hearing may be punished by the court for contempt by a fine of not less than $100 and not more than $1,000. In addition to or in lieu of contempt, the court may order the person to receive counseling or to attend an educational course on the duties and responsibilities of parents and skills and techniques in raising children.

History of Fam §51.115: Acts 1995, 74th Leg., ch. 262, §10, eff. Jan. 1, 1996.

FAM §51.116. RIGHT TO REEMPLOYMENT

(a) An employer may not terminate the employment of a permanent employee because the employee is required under Section 51.115 to attend a hearing.

(b) An employee whose employment is terminated in violation of this section is entitled to return to the same employment that the employee held when notified of the hearing if the employee, as soon as practical after the hearing, gives the employer actual notice that the employee intends to return.

(c) A person who is injured because of a violation of this section is entitled to reinstatement to the person's former position and to damages, but the damages may not exceed an amount equal to six months' compensation at the rate at which the person was compensated when required to attend the hearing.

(d) The injured person is also entitled to reasonable attorney's fees in an amount approved by the court.

(e) It is a defense to an action brought under this section that the employer's circumstances changed while the employee attended the hearing so that reemployment was impossible or unreasonable. To establish a defense under this subsection, an employer must prove that the termination of employment was because of circumstances other than the employee's attendance at the hearing.

History of Fam §51.116: Acts 1995, 74th Leg., ch. 262, §10, eff. Jan. 1, 1996.

FAM §51.12. PLACE & CONDITIONS OF DETENTION

(a) Except as provided by Subsection (h), a child may be detained only in a:

(1) juvenile processing office in compliance with Section 52.025;

Ⓐ *Subsection (2) below is effective for children alleged to have engaged in conduct that occurs on or after Sept. 1, 2001.*

(2) place of nonsecure custody in compliance with Article 45.058, Code of Criminal Procedure;

Subsection (2) below is effective for children alleged to have engaged in conduct in which every element of the conduct occurred before Sept. 1, 2001.

(2) place of nonsecure custody in compliance with Section 52.027;

(3) certified juvenile detention facility that complies with the requirements of Subsection (f);

(4) secure detention facility as provided by Subsection (j); or

(5) county jail or other facility as provided by Subsection (*l*).

Ⓐ *Subsections (b) & (c) below are effective for criminal conduct that occurs on or after Sept. 1, 2001.*

(b) The proper authorities in each county shall provide a suitable place of detention for children who are parties to proceedings under this title, but the juvenile board shall control the conditions and terms of detention and detention supervision and shall permit visitation with the child at all reasonable times.

(c) In each county, each judge of the juvenile court and a majority of the members of the juvenile board shall personally inspect the juvenile pre-adjudication secure detention facilities and any public or private juvenile secure correctional facilities used for post-adjudication confinement that are located in the county and operated under authority of the juvenile board at least annually and shall certify in writing to the authorities responsible for operating and giving financial support to the facilities and to the Texas Juvenile Probation Commission that they are suitable or unsuitable for the detention of children in accordance with:

(1) the requirements of Subsections (a), (f), and (g); and

(2) minimum professional standards for the detention of children in pre-adjudication or post-adjudication secure confinement promulgated by the Texas Juvenile Probation Commission or, at the election of the juvenile board, the current standards promulgated by the American Correctional Association.

Subsections (b) & (c) below are effective for criminal conduct in which any element of the conduct occurred before Sept. 1, 2001.

(b) The proper authorities in each county shall provide a suitable place of detention for children who are parties to proceedings under this title, but the juvenile court shall control the conditions and terms of detention and detention supervision and shall permit visitation with the child at all reasonable times.

(c) In each county, each judge of the juvenile court and the members of the juvenile board shall personally inspect the juvenile pre-adjudication secure detention facilities and any public or private juvenile secure correctional facilities used for post-adjudication confinement that are located in the county and operated under authority of the juvenile board at least annually and shall certify in writing to the authorities responsible for operating and giving financial support to the facilities and to the Texas Juvenile Probation Commission that they are suitable or unsuitable for the detention of children in accordance with:

(1) the requirements of Subsections (a), (f), and (g); and

(2) minimum professional standards for the detention of children in pre-adjudication or post-adjudication secure confinement promulgated by the Texas Juvenile Probation Commission or, at the election of the juvenile board, the current standards promulgated by the American Correctional Association.

(d) Except as provided by Subsections (j) and (*l*), a child may not be placed in a facility that has not been certified under Subsection (c) as suitable for the detention of children and registered under Subsection (i). Except as provided by Subsections (j) and (*l*), a child detained in a facility that has not been certified under Subsection (c) as suitable for the detention of children or that has not been registered under Subsection (i) shall be entitled to immediate release from custody in that facility.

(e) If there is no certified place of detention in the county in which the petition is filed, the designated place of detention may be in another county.

(f) A child detained in a building that contains a jail, lockup, or other place of secure confinement, including an alcohol or other drug treatment facility, shall be separated by sight and sound from adults detained in the same building. Children and adults are separated by sight and sound only if they are unable to see each other and conversation between them is not possible. The separation must extend to all areas of the facility, including sally ports and passageways, and those areas used for admission, counseling, sleeping, toileting, showering, dining, recreational, educational, or vocational activities, and health care. The separation may be accomplished through architectural design.

(g) Except for a child detained in a juvenile processing office, a place of nonsecure custody, a secure detention facility as provided by Subsection (j), or a facility as provided by Subsection (*l*), a child detained in a building that contains a jail or lockup may not have any contact with:

(1) part-time or full-time security staff, including management, who have contact with adults detained in the same building; or

(2) direct-care staff who have contact with adults detained in the same building.

(h) This section does not apply to a person:

(1) after transfer to criminal court for prosecution under Section 54.02; or

(2) who is at least 17 years of age and who has been taken into custody after having:

(A) escaped from a juvenile facility operated by or under contract with the Texas Youth Commission; or

(B) violated a condition of release under supervision of the Texas Youth Commission.

(i) Except for a facility operated or certified by the Texas Youth Commission or a facility as provided by Subsection (*l*), a governmental unit or private entity that operates or contracts for the operation of a juvenile pre-adjudication secure detention facility or a juvenile post-adjudication secure correctional facility in this state shall:

(1) register the facility annually with the Texas Juvenile Probation Commission; and

(2) adhere to all applicable minimum standards for the facility.

(j) After being taken into custody, a child may be detained in a secure detention facility until the child is released under Section 53.01, 53.012, or 53.02 or until a detention hearing is held under Section 54.01(a), regardless of whether the facility has been certified under Subsection (c), if:

(1) a certified juvenile detention facility is not available in the county in which the child is taken into custody;

(2) the detention facility complies with:

(A) the short-term detention standards adopted by the Texas Juvenile Probation Commission; and

(B) the requirements of Subsection (f); and

(3) the detention facility has been designated by the county juvenile board for the county in which the facility is located.

(k) If a child who is detained under Subsection (j) or (*l*) is not released from detention at the conclusion of the detention hearing for a reason stated in Section 54.01(e), the child may be detained after the hearing only in a certified juvenile detention facility.

(*l*) A child who is taken into custody and required to be detained under Section 53.02(f) may be detained in a county jail or other facility until the child is released under Section 53.02(f) or until a detention hearing is held as required by Section 54.01(p), regardless of whether the facility complies with the requirements of this section, if:

(1) a certified juvenile detention facility or a secure detention facility described by Subsection (j) is not available in the county in which the child is taken into custody or in an adjacent county;

(2) the facility has been designated by the county juvenile board for the county in which the facility is located;

(3) the child is separated by sight and sound from adults detained in the same facility through architectural design or time-phasing;

(4) the child does not have any contact with management or direct-care staff that has contact with adults detained in the same facility on the same work shift;

(5) the county in which the child is taken into custody is not located in a metropolitan statistical area as designated by the United States Bureau of the Census; and

A *Subsection (6) below is effective for criminal conduct that occurs on or after Sept. 1, 2001.*

(6) each judge of the juvenile court and a majority of the members of the juvenile board of the county in which the child is taken into custody have personally inspected the facility at least annually and have certified in writing to the Texas Juvenile Probation Commission that the facility complies with the requirements of Subdivisions (3) and (4).

Subsection (6) below is effective for criminal conduct in which any element of the conduct occurred before Sept. 1, 2001.

(6) each judge of the juvenile court and the members of the juvenile board of the county in which the child is taken into custody have personally inspected the facility at least annually and have certified in writing to the Texas Juvenile Probation Commission that the facility complies with the requirements of Subdivisions (3) and (4).

History of Fam §51.12: Acts 1973, 63rd Leg., ch. 544, §1, eff. Sept. 1, 1973. Amended by Acts 1975, 64th Leg., ch. 693, §§10, 11, eff. Sept. 1, 1975; Acts 1985, 69th Leg., ch. 293, §1, eff. Aug. 26, 1985; Acts 1987, 70th Leg., ch. 149, §31, eff. Sept. 1, 1987; Acts 1995, 74th Leg., ch. 262, §12, eff. Jan. 1, 1996; Acts 1997, 75th Leg., ch. 772, §1 (eff. Sept. 1, 1997), ch. 1374, §1 (eff. Sept. 1, 1997); Acts 1999, 76th Leg., ch. 62, §6.07 (eff. Sept. 1, 1999), ch. 232, §3 (eff. Sept. 1, 1999), ch. 1477, §2 (eff. Sept. 1, 1999); Acts 2001, 77th Leg., ch. 1297, §10 (eff. Sept. 1, 2001), ch. 1514, §13 (eff. Sept. 1, 2001).

FAM §51.13. EFFECT OF ADJUDICATION OR DISPOSITION

(a) Except as provided by Subsection (d), an order of adjudication or disposition in a proceeding under this title is not a conviction of crime. Except as provided by Chapter 841, Health and Safety Code, an order of adjudication or disposition does not impose any civil disability ordinarily resulting from a conviction or operate to disqualify the child in any civil service application or appointment.

(b) The adjudication or disposition of a child or evidence adduced in a hearing under this title may be used only in subsequent:

(1) proceedings under this title in which the child is a party;

(2) sentencing proceedings in criminal court against the child to the extent permitted by the Texas Code of Criminal Procedure, 1965; or

(3) civil commitment proceedings under Chapter 841, Health and Safety Code.

(c) A child may not be committed or transferred to a penal institution or other facility used primarily for the execution of sentences of persons convicted of crime, except:

(1) for temporary detention in a jail or lockup pending juvenile court hearing or disposition under conditions meeting the requirements of Section 51.12 of this code;

(2) after transfer for prosecution in criminal court under Section 54.02 of this code; or

(3) after transfer from the Texas Youth Commission under Section 61.084, Human Resources Code.

(d) An adjudication under Section 54.03 that a child engaged in conduct that occurred on or after January 1, 1996, and that constitutes a felony offense resulting in commitment to the Texas Youth Commission under Section 54.04(d)(2), (d)(3), or (m) or 54.05(f) is a final felony conviction only for the purposes of Sections 12.42(a)–(c) and (e), Penal Code.

History of Fam §51.13: Acts 1973, 63rd Leg., ch. 544, §1, eff. Sept. 1, 1973. Amended by Acts 1987, 70th Leg., ch. 385, §3, eff. Sept. 1, 1987; Acts 1993, 73rd Leg., ch. 799, §1, eff. June 18, 1993; Acts 1995, 74th Leg., ch. 262, §13, eff. Jan. 1, 1996; Acts 1997, 75th Leg., ch. 1086, §5, eff. Sept. 1, 1997; Acts 1999, 76th Leg., ch. 1188, §4.02, eff. Sept. 1, 1999.

FAM §§51.14, 51.15. REPEALED

Repealed by Acts 1995, 74th leg., ch. 262, §100(A), eff. Jan. 1, 1996.

FAM §51.151. POLYGRAPH EXAMINATION

If a child is taken into custody under Section 52.01 of this code, a person may not administer a polygraph examination to the child without the consent of the child's attorney or the juvenile court unless the child is transferred to criminal court for prosecution under Section 54.02 of this code.

History of Fam §51.151: Acts 1987, 70th Leg., ch. 708, §1, eff. Sept. 1, 1987.

FAM §51.16. REPEALED

Repealed by Acts 1995, 74th leg., ch. 262, §100(A), eff. Jan. 1, 1996.

FAM §51.17. PROCEDURE & EVIDENCE

(a) Except for the burden of proof to be borne by the state in adjudicating a child to be delinquent or in need of supervision under Section 54.03(f) or otherwise when in conflict with a provision of this title, the Texas Rules of Civil Procedure govern proceedings under this title.

(b) Discovery in a proceeding under this title is governed by the Code of Criminal Procedure and by case decisions in criminal cases.

(c) Except as otherwise provided by this title, the Texas Rules of Evidence applicable to criminal cases and Chapter 38, Code of Criminal Procedure, apply in a judicial proceeding under this title.

History of Fam §51.17: Acts 1973, 63rd Leg., ch. 544, §1, eff. Sept. 1, 1973. Amended by Acts 1995, 74th Leg., ch. 262, §14, eff. Jan. 1, 1996; Acts 1999, 76th Leg., ch. 1477, §3, eff. Sept. 1, 1999.

FAM §51.18. ELECTION BETWEEN JUVENILE COURT & ALTERNATE JUVENILE COURT

(a) This section applies only to a child who has a right to a trial before a juvenile court the judge of which is not an attorney licensed in this state.

(b) On any matter that may lead to an order appealable under Section 56.01 of this code, a child may be tried before either the juvenile court or the alternate juvenile court.

(c) The child may elect to be tried before the alternate juvenile court only if the child files a written notice with that court not later than 10 days before the date of the trial. After the notice is filed, the child may be tried only in the alternate juvenile court. If the child does not file a notice as provided by this subsection, the child may be tried only in the juvenile court.

(d) If the child is tried before the juvenile court, the child is not entitled to a trial de novo before the alternate juvenile court.

(e) The child may appeal any order of the juvenile court or alternate juvenile court only as provided by Section 56.01 of this code.

History of Fam §51.18: Acts 1977, 65th Leg., ch. 411, §2, eff. June 15, 1977. Amended by Acts 1993, 73rd Leg., ch. 168, §3, eff. Aug. 30, 1993.

FAM §51.19. LIMITATION PERIODS

(a) The limitation periods and the procedures for applying the limitation periods under Chapter 12, Code of Criminal Procedure, and other statutory law apply to proceedings under this title.

(b) For purposes of computing a limitation period, a petition filed in juvenile court for a transfer or an adjudication hearing is equivalent to an indictment or information and is treated as presented when the petition is filed in the proper court.

(c) The limitation period is two years for an offense or conduct that is not given a specific limitation period under Chapter 12, Code of Criminal Procedure, or other statutory law.

History of Fam §51.19: Acts 1997, 75th Leg., ch. 1086, §6, eff. Sept. 1, 1997.

FAM §51.20. PHYSICAL OR MENTAL EXAMINATION

A (a) At any stage of the proceedings under this title, the juvenile court may order a child who is referred to the juvenile court or who is alleged by a petition or found to have engaged in delinquent conduct or conduct indicating a need for supervision to be examined by the local mental health or mental retardation authority or another appropriate expert, including a physician, psychiatrist, or psychologist.

(b) If, after conducting an examination of a child ordered under Subsection (a) and reviewing any other relevant information, there is reason to believe that the child has a mental illness or mental retardation, the probation department shall refer the child to the local mental health or mental retardation authority for evaluation and services, unless the prosecuting attorney has filed a petition under Section 53.04.

History of Fam §51.20: Acts 1999, 76th Leg., ch. 1477, §4, eff. Sept. 1, 1999. Amended by Acts 2001, 77th Leg., ch. 828, §5(a), eff. Sept. 1, 2001.

CHAPTER 52. PROCEEDINGS BEFORE & INCLUDING REFERRAL TO JUVENILE COURT

FAM §52.01. TAKING INTO CUSTODY; ISSUANCE OF WARNING NOTICE

(a) A child may be taken into custody:

(1) pursuant to an order of the juvenile court under the provisions of this subtitle*;

(2) pursuant to the laws of arrest;

(3) by a law-enforcement officer, including a school district peace officer commissioned under Section 37.081, Education Code, if there is probable cause to believe that the child has engaged in:

(A) conduct that violates a penal law of this state or a penal ordinance of any political subdivision of this state; or

(B) delinquent conduct or conduct indicating a need for supervision;

(4) by a probation officer if there is probable cause to believe that the child has violated a condition of probation imposed by the juvenile court; or

(5) pursuant to a directive to apprehend issued as provided by Section 52.015.

(b) The taking of a child into custody is not an arrest except for the purpose of determining the validity of taking him into custody or the validity of a search under the laws and constitution of this state or of the United States.

A *Subsections (c) & (d) below are effective for criminal conduct that occurs on or after Sept. 1, 2001.*

(c) A law-enforcement officer authorized to take a child into custody under Subdivisions (2) and (3) of Subsection (a) of this section may issue a warning notice to the child in lieu of taking the child into custody if:

(1) guidelines for warning disposition have been issued by the law-enforcement agency in which the officer works;

(2) the guidelines have been approved by the juvenile court of the county in which the disposition is made;

(3) the disposition is authorized by the guidelines;

(4) the warning notice identifies the child and describes the child's alleged conduct;

(5) a copy of the warning notice is sent to the child's parent, guardian, or custodian as soon as practicable after disposition; and

(6) a copy of the warning notice is filed with the law-enforcement agency and the office or official designated by the juvenile board.

(d) A warning notice filed with the office or official designated by the juvenile board may be used as the basis of further action if necessary.

Subsections (c) & (d) below are effective for criminal conduct in which any element of the conduct occurred before Sept. 1, 2001.

(c) A law-enforcement officer authorized to take a child into custody under Subdivisions (2) and (3) of Subsection (a) of this section may issue a warning notice to the child in lieu of taking him into custody if:

(1) guidelines for warning disposition have been issued by the law-enforcement agency in which the officer works;

(2) the guidelines have been approved by the juvenile court of the county in which the disposition is made;

(3) the disposition is authorized by the guidelines;

(4) the warning notice identifies the child and describes his alleged conduct;

(5) a copy of the warning notice is sent to the child's parent, guardian, or custodian as soon as practicable after disposition; and

(6) a copy of the warning notice is filed with the law-enforcement agency and the office or official designated by the juvenile court.

(d) A warning notice filed with the office or official designated by the juvenile court may be used as the basis of further action if necessary.

* As enrolled, probably should read "this title."

History of Fam §52.01: Acts 1973, 63rd Leg., ch. 544, §1, eff. Sept. 1, 1973. Amended by Acts 1993, 73rd Leg., ch. 115, §2, eff. May 11, 1993; Acts 1995, 74th Leg., ch. 262, §15, eff. Jan. 1, 1996; Acts 1997, 75th Leg., ch. 165, §6.08, eff. Sept. 1, 1997; Acts 2001, 77th Leg., ch. 1297, §11, eff. Sept. 1, 2001.

FAM §52.015. DIRECTIVE TO APPREHEND

(a) On the request of a law-enforcement or probation officer, a juvenile court may issue a directive to apprehend a child if the court finds there is probable cause to take the child into custody under the provisions of this title.

(b) On the issuance of a directive to apprehend, any law-enforcement or probation officer shall take the child into custody.

(c) An order under this section is not subject to appeal.

History of Fam §52.015: Acts 1995, 74th Leg., ch. 262, §16, eff. Jan. 1, 1996.

FAM §52.02. RELEASE OR DELIVERY TO COURT

(a) Except as provided by Subsection (c), a person taking a child into custody, without unnecessary delay and without first taking the child to any place other than a juvenile processing office designated under Section 52.025, shall do one of the following:

(1) release the child to a parent, guardian, custodian of the child, or other responsible adult upon that person's promise to bring the child before the juvenile court as requested by the court;

A *Subsections (2) & (3) below are effective for criminal conduct that occurs on or after Sept. 1, 2001.*

(2) bring the child before the office or official designated by the juvenile board if there is probable cause to believe that the child engaged in delinquent conduct or conduct indicating a need for supervision;

(3) bring the child to a detention facility designated by the juvenile board;

Subsections (2) & (3) below are effective for criminal conduct in which any element of the conduct occurred before Sept. 1, 2001.

(2) bring the child before the office or official designated by the juvenile court if there is probable cause to believe that the child engaged in delinquent conduct or conduct indicating a need for supervision;

(3) bring the child to a detention facility designated by the juvenile court;

(4) bring the child to a secure detention facility as provided by Section 51.12(j);

(5) bring the child to a medical facility if the child is believed to suffer from a serious physical condition or illness that requires prompt treatment; or

(6) dispose of the case under Section 52.03.

A *Subsection (b) below is effective for criminal conduct that occurs on or after Sept. 1, 2001.*

(b) A person taking a child into custody shall promptly give notice of the person's action and a statement of the reason for taking the child into custody, to:

(1) the child's parent, guardian, or custodian; and

(2) the office or official designated by the juvenile board.

Subsection (b) below is effective for criminal conduct in which any element of the conduct occurred before Sept. 1, 2001.

(b) A person taking a child into custody shall promptly give notice of his action and a statement of the reason for taking the child into custody, to:

(1) the child's parent, guardian, or custodian; and

(2) the office or official designated by the juvenile court.

(c) A person who takes a child into custody and who has reasonable grounds to believe that the child has been operating a motor vehicle in a public place while having any detectable amount of alcohol in the child's system may, before complying with Subsection (a):

(1) take the child to a place to obtain a specimen of the child's breath or blood as provided by Chapter 724, Transportation Code; and

(2) perform intoxilyzer processing and videotaping of the child in an adult processing office of a law enforcement agency.

(d) Notwithstanding Section 51.09(a), a child taken into custody as provided by Subsection (c) may submit to the taking of a breath specimen or refuse to submit to the taking of a breath specimen without the concurrence of an attorney, but only if the request made of the child to give the specimen and the child's response to that request is videotaped. A videotape made under this subsection must be maintained until the disposition of any proceeding against the child relating to the arrest is final and be made available to an attorney representing the child during that period.

History of Fam §52.02: Acts 1973, 63rd Leg., ch. 544, §1, eff. Sept. 1, 1973. Amended by Acts 1991, 72nd Leg., ch. 495, §1, eff. Sept. 1, 1991; Acts 1997, 75th Leg., ch. 1013, §15 (eff. Sept. 1, 1997), ch. 1374, §2 (eff. Sept. 1, 1997); Acts 1999, 76th Leg., ch. 62, §6.08 (eff. Sept. 1, 1999), ch. 1477, §5 (eff. Sept. 1, 1999); Acts 2001, 77th Leg., ch. 1297, §12, eff. Sept. 1, 2001.

FAM §52.025. DESIGNATION OF JUVENILE PROCESSING OFFICE

A *Subsection (a) below is effective for criminal conduct that occurs on or after Sept. 1, 2001.*

(a) The juvenile board may designate an office or a room, which may be located in a police facility or sheriff's offices, as the juvenile processing office for the temporary detention of a child taken into custody under Section 52.01. The office may not be a cell or holding facility used for detentions other than detentions under this section. The juvenile board by written order may prescribe the conditions of the designation and limit the activities that may occur in the office during the temporary detention.

Subsection (a) below is effective for criminal conduct in which any element of the conduct occurred before Sept. 1, 2001.

(a) The juvenile court may designate an office or a room, which may be located in a police facility or sheriff's offices, as the juvenile processing office for the temporary detention of a child taken into custody under Section 52.01 of this code. The office may not be a cell or holding facility used for detentions other than detentions under this section. The juvenile court by written order may prescribe the conditions of the designation and limit the activities that may occur in the office during the temporary detention.

(b) A child may be detained in a juvenile processing office only for:

(1) the return of the child to the custody of a person under Section 52.02(a)(1);

(2) the completion of essential forms and records required by the juvenile court or this title;

(3) the photographing and fingerprinting of the child if otherwise authorized at the time of temporary detention by this title;

(4) the issuance of warnings to the child as required or permitted by this title; or

(5) the receipt of a statement by the child under Section 51.095(a)(1), (2), (3), or (5).

(c) A child may not be left unattended in a juvenile processing office and is entitled to be accompanied by the child's parent, guardian, or other custodian or by the child's attorney.

(d) A child may not be detained in a juvenile processing office for longer than six hours.

History of Fam §52.025: Acts 1991, 72nd Leg., ch. 495, §2, eff. Sept. 1, 1991. Amended by Acts 1997, 75th Leg., ch. 1086, §48, eff. Sept. 1, 1997; Acts 2001, 77th Leg., ch. 1297, §13, eff. Sept. 1, 2001.

FAM §52.026. RESPONSIBILITY FOR TRANSPORTING JUVENILE OFFENDERS

(a) It shall be the duty of the law enforcement officer who has taken a child into custody to transport the child to the appropriate detention facility if the child is not released to the parent, guardian, or custodian of the child.

(b) If the juvenile detention facility is located outside the county in which the child is taken into custody, it shall be the duty of the law enforcement officer who has taken the child into custody or, if authorized by the commissioners court of the county, the sheriff of that county to transport the child to the appropriate juvenile detention facility unless the child is:

(1) detained in a secure detention facility under Section 51.12(j); or

(2) released to the parent, guardian, or custodian of the child.

(c) On adoption of an order by the juvenile board and approval of the juvenile board's order by record vote of the commissioners court, it shall be the duty of the sheriff of the county in which the child is taken into custody to transport the child to and from all scheduled juvenile court proceedings and appearances and other activities ordered by the juvenile court.

History of Fam §52.026: Acts 1993, 73rd Leg., ch. 411, §1, eff. Aug. 30, 1993. Amended by Acts 1997, 75th Leg., ch. 1374, §3, eff. Sept. 1, 1997; Acts 1999, 76th Leg., ch. 62, §6.09 (eff. Sept. 1, 1999), ch. 1082, §1 (eff. June 18, 1999).

FAM §52.027. REPEALED

Repealed by Acts 2001, 77th Leg., ch. 1514, §19(b) (eff. Sept. 1, 2001), ch. 1297, §14 (eff. Sept. 1, 2001).

FAM §52.027. CHILDREN TAKEN INTO CUSTODY FOR TRAFFIC OFFENSES, OTHER FINEABLE ONLY OFFENSES, OR AS A STATUS OFFENDER

☠ *Section 52.027 below was repealed by Acts 2001, 77th Leg., ch. 1514, §19(b), effective Sept. 1, 2001, without reference to the conflicting amendments made by Acts 2001, 77th Leg., ch. 1297, §14, effective Sept. 1, 2001, which have been included and marked accordingly. Unless otherwise indicated, section 52.057 below is effective for children alleged to have engaged in conduct in which every element of the conduct occurred before Sept. 1, 2001.*

(a) A child may be released to the child's parent, guardian, custodian, or other responsible adult as provided in Section 52.02(a)(1) if the child is taken into custody:

(1) for an offense that a justice or municipal court has jurisdiction of under Article 4.11 or 4.14, Code of Criminal Procedure, other than public intoxication; or

(2) as a status offender or nonoffender.

(b) A child described by Subsection (a) must be taken only to a place previously designated by the head of the law enforcement agency with custody of the child as an appropriate place of nonsecure custody for children unless the child:

(1) is released under Section 52.02(a)(1);

(2) is taken before a municipal court or justice court; or

(3) for truancy or running away, is taken to a juvenile detention facility, or a secure detention facility, as

authorized by Sections 51.12(a)(3) and (4), respectively, for the detention of the child as provided by Section 54.011.

(c) A place of nonsecure custody for children must be an unlocked, multipurpose area. A lobby, office, or interrogation room is suitable if the area is not designated, set aside, or used as a secure detention area and is not part of a secure detention area. A place of nonsecure custody may be a juvenile processing office designated under Section 52.025 if the area is not locked when it is used as a place of nonsecure custody.

(d) The following procedures shall be followed in a place of nonsecure custody for children:

(1) a child may not be secured physically to a cuffing rail, chair, desk, or other stationary object;

(2) the child may be held in the nonsecure facility only long enough to accomplish the purpose of identification, investigation, processing, release to parents, or the arranging of transportation to the appropriate juvenile court, juvenile detention facility, secure detention facility, municipal court, or justice court;

(3) residential use of the area is prohibited; and

(4) the child shall be under continuous visual supervision by a law enforcement officer or facility staff person during the time the child is in nonsecure custody.

(e) Notwithstanding any other provision of this section, a child may not, under any circumstances, be detained in a place of nonsecure custody for more than six hours.

Ⓐ *Subsection (f) below is effective for criminal conduct that occurs on or after Sept. 1, 2001.*

(f) A child taken into custody for an offense that a justice or municipal court has jurisdiction of under Article 4.11 or 4.14, Code of Criminal Procedure, other than public intoxication, may be presented or detained in a detention facility designated by the juvenile board under Section 52.02(a)(3) only if:

(1) the child's non-traffic case is transferred to the juvenile court by a municipal court or justice court under Section 51.08(b); or

(2) the child is referred to the juvenile court by a municipal court or justice court for contempt of court under Subsection (h).

Subsection (f) below is effective for criminal conduct in which any element of the conduct occurred before Sept. 1, 2001.

(f) A child taken into custody for an offense that a justice or municipal court has jurisdiction of under Article 4.11 or 4.14, Code of Criminal Procedure, other than public intoxication, may be presented or detained in a detention facility designated by the juvenile court under Section 52.02(a)(3) only if:

(1) the child's non-traffic case is transferred to the juvenile court by a municipal court or justice court under Section 51.08(b); or

(2) the child is referred to the juvenile court by a municipal court or justice court for contempt of court under Subsection (h).

(g) A law enforcement officer may issue a field release citation, as provided by Article 14.06, Code of Criminal Procedure, in place of taking a child into custody for a traffic offense or an offense, other than public intoxication, punishable by fine only.

Ⓐ (h) Repealed by Acts 2001, 77th Leg., ch. 1297, §71(1), eff. Sept. 1, 2001.

Subsection (h) below is effective for criminal conduct in which any element of the conduct occurred before Sept. 1, 2001.

(h) If a child intentionally or knowingly fails to obey a lawful order of disposition after an adjudication of guilt of an offense that a justice or municipal court has jurisdiction of under Article 4.11 or 4.14, Code of Criminal Procedure, the municipal court or justice court may:

(1) except as provided by Subsection (j), hold the child in contempt of the municipal court or justice court order and order the child to pay a fine not to exceed $500; or

(2) refer the child to the appropriate juvenile court for delinquent conduct for contempt of the municipal court or justice court order.

Ⓐ *Subsection (i) below is effective for criminal conduct that occurs on or after Sept. 1, 2001.*

(i) In this section, "child" means a person who is at least 10 years of age and younger than 17 years of age and who is charged with or convicted of an offense that a justice or municipal court has jurisdiction of under Article 4.11 or 4.14, Code of Criminal Procedure, other than public intoxication.

Subsection (i) below is effective for criminal conduct in which any element of the conduct occurred before Sept. 1, 2001.

(i) In this section, "child" means a person who:

FAM CH. 52

(1) is at least 10 years of age and younger than 17 years of age and who is charged with or convicted of an offense that a justice or municipal court has jurisdiction of under Article 4.11 or 4.14, Code of Criminal Procedure, other than public intoxication; or

(2) is at least 10 years of age and younger than 18 years of age and who:

(A) is a status offender and was taken into custody as a status offender for conduct engaged in before becoming 17 years of age; or

(B) is a nonoffender and became a nonoffender before becoming 17 years of age.

A (j) Repealed by Acts 2001, 77th Leg., ch. 1297, §71(1), eff. Sept. 1, 2001.

Subsection (j) below is effective for criminal conduct in which any element of the conduct occurred before Sept. 1, 2001.

(j) A municipal or justice court may not order a child to a term of confinement or imprisonment for contempt of a municipal or justice court order under Subsection (h).

FAM §52.028. REPEALED

Repealed by Acts 2001, 77th Leg., ch. 1514, §19(b), eff. Sept. 1, 2001.

FAM §52.028. CHILDREN TAKEN INTO CUSTODY FOR VIOLATION OF JUVENILE CURFEW ORDINANCE OR ORDER

Section 52.028 below is effective for children alleged to have engaged in conduct in which every element of the conduct occurred before Sept. 1, 2001.

(a) A peace officer taking into custody a person under 17 years of age for violation of a juvenile curfew ordinance of a municipality or order of the commissioners court of a county shall, without unnecessary delay:

(1) release the person to the person's parent, guardian, or custodian;

(2) take the person before a municipal or justice court to answer the charge; or

(3) take the person to a place designated as a juvenile curfew processing office by the head of the law enforcement agency having custody of the person.

(b) A juvenile curfew processing office must observe the following procedures:

(1) the office must be an unlocked, multipurpose area that is not designated, set aside, or used as a secure detention area or part of a secure detention area;

(2) the person may not be secured physically to a cuffing rail, chair, desk, or stationary object;

(3) the person may not be held longer than necessary to accomplish the purposes of identification, investigation, processing, release to parents, guardians, or custodians, and arrangement of transportation to school or court;

(4) a juvenile curfew processing office may not be designated or intended for residential purposes;

(5) the person must be under continuous visual supervision by a peace officer or other person during the time the person is in the juvenile curfew processing office; and

(6) a person may not be held in a juvenile curfew processing office for more than six hours.

(c) A place designated under this section as a juvenile curfew processing office is not subject to the approval of the juvenile board having jurisdiction where the governmental entity is located.

FAM §52.03. DISPOSITION WITHOUT REFERRAL TO COURT

(a) A law-enforcement officer authorized by this title to take a child into custody may dispose of the case of a child taken into custody without referral to juvenile court, if:

(1) guidelines for such disposition have been adopted by the juvenile board of the county in which the disposition is made as required by Section 52.032;

(2) the disposition is authorized by the guidelines; and

(3) the officer makes a written report of the officer's disposition to the law-enforcement agency, identifying the child and specifying the grounds for believing that the taking into custody was authorized.

(b) No disposition authorized by this section may involve:

(1) keeping the child in law-enforcement custody; or

(2) requiring periodic reporting of the child to a law-enforcement officer, law-enforcement agency, or other agency.

(c) A disposition authorized by this section may involve:

(1) referral of the child to an agency other than the juvenile court;

(2) a brief conference with the child and his parent, guardian, or custodian; or

(3) referral of the child and the child's parent, guardian, or custodian for services under Section 264.302.

A *Subsection (d) below is effective for criminal conduct that occurs on or after Sept. 1, 2001.*

(d) Statistics indicating the number and kind of dispositions made by a law-enforcement agency under the authority of this section shall be reported at least annually to the office or official designated by the juvenile board, as ordered by the court.

Subsection (d) below is effective for criminal conduct in which any element of the conduct occurred before Sept. 1, 2001.

(d) Statistics indicating the number and kind of dispositions made by a law-enforcement agency under the authority of this section shall be reported at least annually to the office or official designated by the juvenile court, as ordered by the court.

History of Fam §52.03: Acts 1973, 63rd Leg., ch. 544, §1, eff. Sept. 1, 1973. Amended by Acts 1995, 74th Leg., ch. 262, §18, eff. Jan. 1, 1996; Acts 1999, 76th Leg., ch. 48, §1, eff. Sept. 1, 1999; Acts 2001, 77th Leg., ch. 1297, §15, eff. Sept. 1, 2001.

FAM §52.03

FAM §52.031. FIRST OFFENDER PROGRAM

(a) A juvenile board may establish a first offender program under this section for the referral and disposition of children taken into custody for:

(1) conduct indicating a need for supervision; or

(2) delinquent conduct other than conduct that constitutes:

(A) a felony of the first, second, or third degree, an aggravated controlled substance felony, or a capital felony; or

(B) a state jail felony or misdemeanor involving violence to a person or the use or possession of a firearm, illegal knife, or club, as those terms are defined by Section 46.01, Penal Code, or a prohibited weapon, as described by Section 46.05, Penal Code.

(b) Each juvenile board in the county in which a first offender program is established shall designate one or more law enforcement officers and agencies, which may be law enforcement agencies, to process a child under the first offender program.

(c) The disposition of a child under the first offender program may not take place until guidelines for the disposition have been adopted by the juvenile board of the county in which the disposition is made as required by Section 52.032.

(d) A law enforcement officer taking a child into custody may refer the child to the law enforcement officer or agency designated under Subsection (b) for disposition under the first offender program and not refer the child to juvenile court only if:

(1) the child has not previously been adjudicated as having engaged in delinquent conduct;

(2) the referral complies with guidelines for disposition under Subsection (c); and

(3) the officer reports in writing the referral to the agency, identifying the child and specifying the grounds for taking the child into custody.

(e) A child referred for disposition under the first offender program may not be detained in law enforcement custody.

(f) The parent, guardian, or other custodian of the child must receive notice that the child has been referred for disposition under the first offender program. The notice must:

(1) state the grounds for taking the child into custody;

(2) identify the law enforcement officer or agency to which the child was referred;

(3) briefly describe the nature of the program; and

(4) state that the child's failure to complete the program will result in the child being referred to the juvenile court.

(g) The child and the parent, guardian, or other custodian of the child must consent to participation by the child in the first offender program.

(h) Disposition under a first offender program may include:

(1) voluntary restitution by the child or the parent, guardian, or other custodian of the child to the victim of the conduct of the child;

(2) voluntary community service restitution by the child;

(3) educational, vocational training, counseling, or other rehabilitative services; and

(4) periodic reporting by the child to the law enforcement officer or agency to which the child has been referred.

(i) The case of a child who successfully completes the first offender program is closed and may not be referred to juvenile court, unless the child is taken into custody under circumstances described by Subsection (j)(3).

(j) The case of a child referred for disposition under the first offender program shall be referred to juvenile court if:

(1) the child fails to complete the program;

(2) the child or the parent, guardian, or other custodian of the child terminates the child's participation in the program before the child completes it; or

(3) the child completes the program but is taken into custody under Section 52.01 before the 90th day after the date the child completes the program for conduct other than the conduct for which the child was referred to the first offender program.

(k) A statement made by a child to a person giving advice or supervision or participating in the first offender program may not be used against the child in any proceeding under this title or any criminal proceeding.

(*l*) The law enforcement agency must report to the juvenile board in December of each year the following:

(1) the last known address of the child, including the census tract;

(2) the gender and ethnicity of the child referred to the program; and

(3) the offense committed by the child.

History of Fam §52.031: Acts 1995, 74th Leg., ch. 262, §19, eff. Jan. 1, 1996. Amended by Acts 1999, 76th Leg., ch. 48, §2, eff. Sept. 1, 1999.

FAM §52.032. INFORMAL DISPOSITION GUIDELINES

The juvenile board of each county, in cooperation with each law enforcement agency in the county, shall adopt guidelines for the disposition of a child under Section 52.03 or 52.031. The guidelines adopted under this section shall not be considered mandatory.

History of Fam §52.032: Acts 1999, 76th Leg., ch. 48, §3, eff. Sept. 1, 1999.

FAM §52.04. REFERRAL TO JUVENILE COURT; NOTICE TO PARENTS

A *Subsections (a) through (c) below are effective for criminal conduct that occurs on or after Sept. 1, 2001, and the heading above is effective for referrals based on conduct that occurs on or after Sept. 1, 2001.*

(a) The following shall accompany referral of a child or a child's case to the office or official designated by the juvenile board or be provided as quickly as possible after referral:

(1) all information in the possession of the person or agency making the referral pertaining to the identity of the child and the child's address, the name and address of the child's parent, guardian, or custodian, the names and addresses of any witnesses, and the child's present whereabouts;

(2) a complete statement of the circumstances of the alleged delinquent conduct or conduct indicating a need for supervision;

(3) when applicable, a complete statement of the circumstances of taking the child into custody; and

(4) when referral is by an officer of a law-enforcement agency, a complete statement of all prior contacts with the child by officers of that law-enforcement agency.

(b) The office or official designated by the juvenile board may refer the case to a law-enforcement agency for the purpose of conducting an investigation to obtain necessary information.

(c) If the office of the prosecuting attorney is designated by the juvenile court to conduct the preliminary investigation under Section 53.01, the referring entity shall first transfer the child's case to the juvenile probation department for statistical reporting purposes only. On the creation of a statistical record or file for the case, the probation department shall within three business days forward the case to the prosecuting attorney for review under Section 53.01.

E *Subsection (d) below is effective for referrals based on conduct that occurs on or after Sept. 1, 2001.*

(d) On referral of the case of a child who has not been taken into custody to the office or official designated by the juvenile court, the office or official designated by the juvenile court shall promptly give notice of the referral and a statement of the reason for the referral to the child's parent, guardian, or custodian.

History of Fam §52.04: Acts 1973, 63rd Leg., ch. 544, §1, eff. Sept. 1, 1973. Amended by Acts 1997, 75th Leg., ch. 1091, §1, eff. June 19, 1997; Acts 2001, 77th Leg., ch. 1297, §16 (eff. Sept. 1, 2001), ch. 136, §§1, 2 (eff. Sept. 1, 2001).

FAM §52.04. REFERRAL TO JUVENILE COURT

Section 52.04 below is effective for criminal conduct in which any element of the conduct occurred before Sept. 1, 2001, and the heading above is effective for referrals based on conduct that occurred before Sept. 1, 2001.

(a) The following shall accompany referral of a child or a child's case to the office or official designated by the juvenile court or be provided as quickly as possible after referral:

(1) all information in the possession of the person or agency making the referral pertaining to the identity of the child and his address, the name and address of the child's parent, guardian, or custodian, the names and addresses of any witnesses, and the child's present whereabouts;

(2) a complete statement of the circumstances of the alleged delinquent conduct or conduct indicating a need for supervision;

(3) when applicable, a complete statement of the circumstances of taking the child into custody; and

(4) when referral is by an officer of a law-enforcement agency, a complete statement of all prior contacts with the child by officers of that law-enforcement agency.

(b) The office or official designated by the juvenile court may refer the case to a law-enforcement agency for the purpose of conducting an investigation to obtain necessary information.

(c) If the office of the prosecuting attorney is designated by the juvenile court to conduct the preliminary investigation under Section 53.01, the referring entity shall first transfer the child's case to the juvenile probation department for statistical reporting purposes only. On the creation of a statistical record or file for the case, the probation department shall within three business days forward the case to the prosecuting attorney for review under Section 53.01.

FAM §52.041

FAM §52.041. REFERRAL OF CHILD TO JUVENILE COURT AFTER EXPULSION

(a) A school district that expels a child shall refer the child to juvenile court in the county in which the child resides.

(b) The board of the school district or a person designated by the board shall deliver a copy of the order expelling the student and any other information required by Section 52.04 on or before the second working day after the date of the expulsion hearing to the authorized officer of the juvenile court.

A *Subsections (c) & (d) below are effective for criminal conduct that occurs on or after Sept. 1, 2001.*

(c) Within five working days of receipt of an expulsion notice under this section by the office or official designated by the juvenile board, a preliminary investigation and determination shall be conducted as required by Section 53.01.

(d) The office or official designated by the juvenile board shall within two working days notify the school district that expelled the child if:

Subsections (c) & (d) below are effective for criminal conduct in which any element of the conduct occurred before Sept. 1, 2001.

(c) Within five working days of receipt of an expulsion notice under this section by the office or official designated by the juvenile court, a preliminary investigation and determination shall be conducted as required by Section 53.01.

(d) The office or official designated by the juvenile court shall within two working days notify the school district that expelled the child if:

(1) a determination was made under Section 53.01 that the person referred to juvenile court was not a child within the meaning of this title;

(2) a determination was made that no probable cause existed to believe the child engaged in delinquent conduct or conduct indicating a need for supervision;

(3) no deferred prosecution or formal court proceedings have been or will be initiated involving the child;

(4) the court or jury finds that the child did not engage in delinquent conduct or conduct indicating a need for supervision and the case has been dismissed with prejudice; or

(5) the child was adjudicated but no disposition was or will be ordered by the court.

(e) In any county where a juvenile justice alternative education program is operated, no student shall be expelled without written notification by the board of the school district or its designated agent to the juvenile board's designated representative. The notification shall be made not later than two business days following the board's determination that the student is to be expelled. Failure to timely notify the designated representative of the juvenile board shall result in the child's duty to continue attending the school district's educational program, which shall be provided to that child until such time as the notification to the juvenile board's designated representative is properly made.

History of Fam §52.041: Acts 1995, 74th Leg., ch. 262, §20, eff. Jan. 1, 1996. Amended by Acts 1997, 75th Leg., ch. 1015, §16, eff. June 19, 1997; Acts 2001, 77th Leg., ch. 1297, §17, eff. Sept. 1, 2001.

CHAPTER 53. PROCEEDINGS PRIOR TO JUDICIAL PROCEEDINGS

FAM §53.01. PRELIMINARY INVESTIGATION & DETERMINATIONS; NOTICE TO PARENTS

A *Subsection (a) below is effective for criminal conduct that occurs on or after Sept. 1, 2001.*

(a) On referral of a person believed to be a child or on referral of the person's case to the office or official designated by the juvenile board, the intake officer, probation officer, or other person authorized by the court shall conduct a preliminary investigation to determine whether:

(1) the person referred to juvenile court is a child within the meaning of this title; and

(2) there is probable cause to believe the person engaged in delinquent conduct or conduct indicating a need for supervision.

Subsection (a) below is effective for criminal conduct in which any element of the conduct occurred before Sept. 1, 2001.

(a) On referral of a person believed to be a child or on referral of the person's case to the office or official designated by the juvenile court, the intake officer, probation officer, or other person authorized by the court shall conduct a preliminary investigation to determine whether:

(1) the person referred to juvenile court is a child within the meaning of this title; and

(2) there is probable cause to believe the person engaged in delinquent conduct or conduct indicating a need for supervision.

(b) If it is determined that the person is not a child or there is no probable cause, the person shall immediately be released.

A *Subsection (c) below is effective for criminal conduct that occurs on or after Sept. 1, 2001.*

(c) When custody of a child is given to the office or official designated by the juvenile board, the intake officer, probation officer, or other person authorized by the court shall promptly give notice of the whereabouts of the child and a statement of the reason the child was taken into custody to the child's parent, guardian, or custodian unless the notice given under Section 52.02(b) provided fair notice of the child's present whereabouts.

Subsection (c) below is effective for criminal conduct in which any element of the conduct occurred before Sept. 1, 2001.

(c) When custody of a child is given to the office or official designated by the juvenile court, the intake officer, probation officer, or other person authorized by the court shall promptly give notice of the whereabouts of the child and a statement of the reason he was taken into custody to the child's parent, guardian, or custodian unless the notice given under Section 52.02(b) of this code provided fair notice of the child's present whereabouts.

(d) Unless the juvenile board approves a written procedure proposed by the office of prosecuting attorney and chief juvenile probation officer which provides otherwise, if it is determined that the person is a child and, regardless of a finding of probable cause, or a lack thereof, there is an allegation that the child engaged in delinquent conduct of the grade of felony, or conduct constituting a misdemeanor offense involving violence to a person or the use or possession of a firearm, illegal knife, or club, as those terms are defined by Section 46.01, Penal Code, or prohibited weapon, as described by Section 46.05, Penal Code, the case shall be promptly forwarded to the office of the prosecuting attorney, accompanied by:

(1) all documents that accompanied the current referral; and

(2) a summary of all prior referrals of the child to the juvenile court, juvenile probation department, or a detention facility.

(e) If a juvenile board adopts an alternative referral plan under Subsection (d), the board shall register the plan with the Texas Juvenile Probation Commission.

(f) A juvenile board may not adopt an alternate referral plan that does not require the forwarding of a child's case to the prosecuting attorney as provided by Subsection (d) if probable cause exists to believe that the child engaged in delinquent conduct that violates Section 19.03, Penal Code (capital murder), or Section 19.02, Penal Code (murder).

History of Fam §53.01: Acts 1973, 63rd Leg., ch. 544, §1, eff. Sept. 1, 1973. Amended by Acts 1995, 74th Leg., ch. 262, §21, eff. Jan. 1, 1996; Acts 1997, 75th Leg., ch. 1374, §5, eff. Sept. 1, 1997; Acts 2001, 77th Leg., ch. 1297, §18, eff. Sept. 1, 2001.

FAM §53.012. REVIEW BY PROSECUTOR

(a) The prosecuting attorney shall promptly review the circumstances and allegations of a referral made under Section 53.01 for legal sufficiency and the desirability of prosecution and may file a petition without regard to whether probable cause was found under Section 53.01.

(b) If the prosecuting attorney does not file a petition requesting the adjudication of the child referred to the prosecuting attorney, the prosecuting attorney shall:

(1) terminate all proceedings, if the reason is for lack of probable cause; or

(2) return the referral to the juvenile probation department for further proceedings.

(c) The juvenile probation department shall promptly refer a child who has been returned to the department under Subsection (b)(2) and who fails or refuses to participate in a program of the department to the prosecuting attorney for review of the child's case and determination of whether to file a petition.

History of Fam §53.012: Acts 1995, 74th Leg., ch. 262, §22, eff. Jan. 1, 1996.

FAM §53.013. PROGRESSIVE SANCTIONS PROGRAM

(a) Each juvenile board may adopt a progressive sanctions program using the guidelines for progressive sanctions in Chapter 59.

(b) A juvenile court or probation department that deviates from the guidelines under Section 59.003 shall state in writing the reasons for the deviation and submit the statement to the juvenile board regardless of whether the juvenile board has adopted a progressive sanctions program.

History of Fam §53.013: Acts 1995, 74th Leg., ch. 262, §22, eff. Jan. 1, 1996. Amended by Acts 1997, 75th Leg., ch. 1086, §7, eff. Sept. 1, 1997.

FAM §53.02. RELEASE FROM DETENTION

(a) If a child is brought before the court or delivered to a detention facility as authorized by Sections 51.12(a)(3) and (4), the intake or other authorized officer of the court shall immediately make an investigation and shall release the child unless it appears that his detention is warranted under Subsection (b). The release may be conditioned upon requirements reasonably necessary to insure the child's appearance at later proceedings, but the conditions of the release must be in writing and filed with the office or official designated by the court and a copy furnished to the child.

(b) A child taken into custody may be detained prior to hearing on the petition only if:

(1) the child is likely to abscond or be removed from the jurisdiction of the court;

(2) suitable supervision, care, or protection for the child is not being provided by a parent, guardian, custodian, or other person;

(3) the child has no parent, guardian, custodian, or other person able to return the child to the court when required;

(4) the child may be dangerous to himself or herself or the child may threaten the safety of the public if released;

(5) the child has previously been found to be a delinquent child or has previously been convicted of a penal offense punishable by a term in jail or prison and is likely to commit an offense if released; or

(6) the child's detention is required under Subsection (f).

(c) If the child is not released, a request for detention hearing shall be made and promptly presented to the court, and an informal detention hearing as provided in Section 54.01 of this code shall be held promptly, but not later than the time required by Section 54.01 of this code.

(d) A release of a child to an adult under Subsection (a) must be conditioned on the agreement of the adult to be subject to the jurisdiction of the juvenile court and to an order of contempt by the court if the adult, after notification, is unable to produce the child at later proceedings.

(e) Unless otherwise agreed in the memorandum of understanding under Section 37.011, Education Code, in a county with a population greater than 125,000, if a child being released under this section is expelled under Section 37.007, Education Code, the release shall be conditioned on the child's attending a juvenile justice alternative education program pending a deferred prosecution or formal court disposition of the child's case.

(f) A child who is alleged to have engaged in delinquent conduct and to have used, possessed, or exhibited a firearm, as defined by Section 46.01, Penal Code, in the commission of the offense shall be detained until the child is released at the direction of the judge of the juvenile court, a substitute judge authorized by Section 51.04(f), or a referee appointed under Section 51.04(g), including an oral direction by telephone, or until a detention hearing is held as required by Section 54.01.

History of Fam §53.02: Acts 1973, 63rd Leg., ch. 544, §1, eff. Sept. 1, 1973. Amended by Acts 1979, 66th Leg., ch. 518, §1, eff. June 11, 1979; Acts 1981, 67th Leg., ch. 115, §1, eff. Aug. 31, 1981; Acts 1995, 74th Leg., ch. 262, §23, eff. Jan. 1, 1996; Acts 1997, 75th Leg., ch. 1015, §17 (eff. June 19, 1997), ch. 1374, §6 (eff. Sept. 1, 1997); Acts 1999, 76th Leg., ch. 232, §1, eff. Sept. 1, 1999.

FAM §53.03. DEFERRED PROSECUTION

(a) Subject to Subsections (e) and (g), if the preliminary investigation required by Section 53.01 of this code results in a determination that further proceedings in the case are authorized, the probation officer or other designated officer of the court, subject to the direction of the juvenile court, may advise the parties for a reasonable period of time not to exceed six months concerning deferred prosecution and rehabilitation of a child if:

(1) deferred prosecution would be in the interest of the public and the child;

(2) the child and his parent, guardian, or custodian consent with knowledge that consent is not obligatory; and

(3) the child and his parent, guardian, or custodian are informed that they may terminate the deferred prosecution at any point and petition the court for a court hearing in the case.

(b) Except as otherwise permitted by this title, the child may not be detained during or as a result of the deferred prosecution process.

(c) An incriminating statement made by a participant to the person giving advice and in the discussions or conferences incident thereto may not be used against the declarant in any court hearing.

(d) The court may adopt a fee schedule for deferred prosecution services and rules for the waiver of a fee for financial hardship in accordance with guidelines that the Texas Juvenile Probation Commission shall provide. The maximum fee is $15 a month. If the court adopts a schedule and rules for waiver, the probation officer or other designated officer of the court shall collect the fee authorized by the schedule from the parent, guardian, or custodian of a child for whom a deferred prosecution is authorized under this section or waive the fee in accordance with the rules adopted by the court. The officer shall deposit the fees received under this section in the county treasury to the credit of a special fund that may be used only for juvenile probation or community-based juvenile corrections services or facilities in which a juvenile may be required to live while under court supervision. If the court does not adopt a schedule and rules for waiver, a fee for deferred prosecution services may not be imposed.

(e) A prosecuting attorney may defer prosecution for any child. A probation officer or other designated officer of the court:

(1) may not defer prosecution for a child for a case that is required to be forwarded to the prosecuting attorney under Section 53.01(d); and

(2) may defer prosecution for a child who has previously been adjudicated for conduct that constitutes a felony only if the prosecuting attorney consents in writing.

(f) The probation officer or other officer designated by the court supervising a program of deferred prosecution for a child under this section shall report to the juvenile court any violation by the child of the program.

(g) Prosecution may not be deferred for a child alleged to have engaged in conduct that:

(1) is an offense under Section 49.04, 49.05, 49.06, 49.07, or 49.08, Penal Code; or

(2) is a third or subsequent offense under Section 106.04 or 106.041, Alcoholic Beverage Code.

(h) If the child is alleged to have engaged in delinquent conduct or conduct indicating a need for supervision that violates Section 28.08, Penal Code, deferred prosecution under this section may include:

(1) voluntary attendance in a class with instruction in self-responsibility and empathy for a victim of an offense conducted by a local juvenile probation department, if the class is available; and

(2) voluntary restoration of the property damaged by the child by removing or painting over any markings

made by the child, if the owner of the property consents to the restoration.

History of Fam §53.03: Acts 1973, 63rd Leg., ch. 544, §1, eff. Sept. 1, 1973. Amended by Acts 1983, 68th Leg., ch. 565, §1, eff. Sept. 1, 1983; Acts 1987, 70th Leg., ch. 1040, §22, eff. Sept. 1, 1987; Acts 1995, 74th Leg., ch. 262, §24, eff. Jan. 1, 1996; Acts 1997, 75th Leg., ch. 593, §6 (eff. Sept. 1, 1997), ch. 1013, §16 (eff. Sept. 1, 1997); Acts 1999, 76th Leg., ch. 62, §19.01(17), eff. Sept. 1, 1999.

FAM §53.035. GRAND JURY REFERRAL

(a) The prosecuting attorney may, before filing a petition under Section 53.04, refer an offense to a grand jury in the county in which the offense is alleged to have been committed.

(b) The grand jury has the same jurisdiction and powers to investigate the facts and circumstances concerning an offense referred to the grand jury under this section as it has to investigate other criminal activity.

(c) If the grand jury votes to take no action on an offense referred to the grand jury under this section, the prosecuting attorney may not file a petition under Section 53.04 concerning the offense unless the same or a successor grand jury approves the filing of the petition.

(d) If the grand jury votes for approval of the prosecution of an offense referred to the grand jury under this section, the prosecuting attorney may file a petition under Section 53.04.

(e) The approval of the prosecution of an offense by a grand jury under this section does not constitute approval of a petition by a grand jury for purposes of Section 53.045.

History of Fam §53.035: Acts 1999, 76th Leg., ch. 1477, §6, eff. Sept. 1, 1999.

FAM §53.04. COURT PETITION; ANSWER

(a) If the preliminary investigation, required by Section 53.01 of this code results in a determination that further proceedings are authorized and warranted, a petition for an adjudication or transfer hearing of a child alleged to have engaged in delinquent conduct or conduct indicating a need for supervision may be made as promptly as practicable by a prosecuting attorney who has knowledge of the facts alleged or is informed and believes that they are true.

(b) The proceedings shall be styled "In the matter of _______________."

(c) The petition may be on information and belief.

(d) The petition must state:

(1) with reasonable particularity the time, place, and manner of the acts alleged and the penal law or standard of conduct allegedly violated by the acts;

(2) the name, age, and residence address, if known, of the child who is the subject of the petition;

(3) the names and residence addresses, if known, of the parent, guardian, or custodian of the child and of the child's spouse, if any;

(4) if the child's parent, guardian, or custodian does not reside or cannot be found in the state, or if their places of residence are unknown, the name and residence address of any known adult relative residing in the county or, if there is none, the name and residence address of the known adult relative residing nearest to the location of the court; and

(5) if the child is alleged to have engaged in habitual felony conduct, the previous adjudications in which the child was found to have engaged in conduct violating penal laws of the grade of felony.

(e) An oral or written answer to the petition may be made at or before the commencement of the hearing. If there is no answer, a general denial of the alleged conduct is assumed.

History of Fam §53.04: Acts 1973, 63rd Leg., ch. 544, §1, eff. Sept. 1, 1973. Amended by Acts 1995, 74th Leg., ch. 262, §25, eff. Jan. 1, 1996.

FAM §53.045. VIOLENT OR HABITUAL OFFENDERS

A *Subsection (a) below is effective for criminal conduct that occurs on or after Sept. 1, 2001.*

(a) Except as provided by Subsection (e), the prosecuting attorney may refer the petition to the grand jury of the county in which the court in which the petition is filed presides if the petition alleges that the child engaged in delinquent conduct that constitutes habitual felony conduct as described by Section 51.031 or that included the violation of any of the following provisions:

(1) Section 19.02, Penal Code (murder);

(2) Section 19.03, Penal Code (capital murder);

E (3) Section 19.04, Penal Code (manslaughter);

(4) Section 20.04, Penal Code (aggravated kidnapping);

(5) Section 22.011, Penal Code (sexual assault) or Section 22.021, Penal Code (aggravated sexual assault);

(6) Section 22.02, Penal Code (aggravated assault);

(7) Section 29.03, Penal Code (aggravated robbery);

(8) Section 22.04, Penal Code (injury to a child, elderly individual, or disabled individual), if the offense is punishable as a felony, other than a state jail felony;

(9) Section 22.05(b), Penal Code (felony deadly conduct involving discharging a firearm);

(10) Subchapter D, Chapter 481, Health and Safety Code, if the conduct constitutes a felony of the first degree or an aggravated controlled substance felony (certain offenses involving controlled substances);

(11) Section 15.03, Penal Code (criminal solicitation);

(12) Section 21.11(a)(1), Penal Code (indecency with a child);

(13) Section 15.031, Penal Code (criminal solicitation of a minor);

(14) Section 15.01, Penal Code (criminal attempt), if the offense attempted was an offense under Section 19.02, Penal Code (murder), or Section 19.03, Penal Code (capital murder), or an offense listed by Section 3g(a)(1), Article 42.12, Code of Criminal Procedure;

(15) Section 28.02, Penal Code (arson), if bodily injury or death is suffered by any person by reason of the commission of the conduct; or

E (16) Section 49.08, Penal Code (intoxication manslaughter).

Subsection (a) below is effective for criminal conduct in which any element of the conduct occurred before Sept. 1, 2001.

(a) Except as provided by Subsection (e), the prosecuting attorney may refer the petition to the grand jury of the county in which the court in which the petition is filed presides if the petition alleges that the child engaged in delinquent conduct that constitutes habitual felony conduct as described by Section 51.031 or that included the violation of any of the following provisions:

(1) Section 19.02, Penal Code (murder);

(2) Section 19.03, Penal Code (capital murder);

(3) Section 20.04, Penal Code (aggravated kidnapping);

(4) Section 22.011, Penal Code (sexual assault) or Section 22.021, Penal Code (aggravated sexual assault);

(5) Section 22.02, Penal Code (aggravated assault);

(6) Section 29.03, Penal Code (aggravated robbery);

(7) Section 22.04, Penal Code (injury to a child, elderly individual, or disabled individual), if the offense is punishable as a felony, other than a state jail felony;

(8) Section 22.05(b), Penal Code (felony deadly conduct involving discharging a firearm);

(9) Subchapter D, Chapter 481, Health and Safety Code, if the conduct constitutes a felony of the first degree or an aggravated controlled substance felony (certain offenses involving controlled substances);

(10) Section 15.03, Penal Code (criminal solicitation);

(11) Section 21.11(a)(1), Penal Code (indecency with a child);

(12) Section 15.031, Penal Code (criminal solicitation of a minor);

(13) Section 15.01, Penal Code (criminal attempt), if the offense attempted was an offense under Section 19.02, Penal Code (murder) or Section 19.03, Penal Code (capital murder), or an offense listed by Section 3g(a)(1), Article 42.12, Code of Criminal Procedure; or

(14) Section 28.02, Penal Code (arson), if bodily injury or death is suffered by any person by reason of the commission of the conduct.

(b) A grand jury may approve a petition submitted to it under this section by a vote of nine members of the grand jury in the same manner that the grand jury votes on the presentment of an indictment.

(c) The grand jury has all the powers to investigate the facts and circumstances relating to a petition submitted under this section as it has to investigate other criminal activity but may not issue an indictment unless the child is transferred to a criminal court as provided by Section 54.02 of this code.

(d) If the grand jury approves of the petition, the fact of approval shall be certified to the juvenile court, and the certification shall be entered in the record of the case. For the purpose of the transfer of a child to the Texas Department of Corrections as provided by Section 61.084(c), Human Resources Code, a juvenile court petition approved by a grand jury under this section is an indictment presented by the grand jury.

(e) The prosecuting attorney may not refer a petition that alleges the child engaged in conduct that violated Section 22.011(a)(2), Penal Code, or Sections 22.021(a)(1)(B) and (2)(B), Penal Code, unless the child is more than three years older than the victim of the conduct.

FAM §53.045

History of Fam §53.045: Acts 1987, 70th Leg., ch. 385, §7, eff. Sept. 1, 1987. Amended by Acts 1991, 72nd Leg., ch. 574, §1, eff. Sept. 1, 1991; Acts 1995, 74th Leg., ch. 262, §§26, 27, eff. Jan. 1, 1996; Acts 1997, 75th Leg., ch. 1086, §8, eff. Sept. 1, 1997; Acts 2001, 77th Leg., ch. 1297, §19, eff. Sept. 1, 2001.

FAM §53.05. TIME SET FOR HEARING

(a) After the petition has been filed, the juvenile court shall set a time for the hearing.

(b) The time set for the hearing shall not be later than 10 working days after the day the petition was filed if:

(1) the child is in detention; or

(2) the child will be taken into custody under Section 53.06(d) of this code.

History of Fam §53.05: Acts 1973, 63rd Leg., ch. 544, §1, eff. Sept. 1, 1973. Amended by Acts 1995, 74th Leg., ch. 262, §28, eff. Jan. 1, 1996.

FAM §53.06. SUMMONS

(a) The juvenile court shall direct issuance of a summons to:

(1) the child named in the petition;

(2) the child's parent, guardian, or custodian;

(3) the child's guardian ad litem; and

(4) any other person who appears to the court to be a proper or necessary party to the proceeding.

(b) The summons must require the persons served to appear before the court at the time set to answer the allegations of the petition. A copy of the petition must accompany the summons.

(c) The court may endorse on the summons an order directing the person having the physical custody or control of the child to bring the child to the hearing. A person who violates an order entered under this subsection may be proceeded against under Section 53.08 or 54.07 of this code.

(d) If it appears from an affidavit filed or from sworn testimony before the court that immediate detention of the child is warranted under Section 53.02(b) of this code, the court may endorse on the summons an order that a law-enforcement officer shall serve the summons and shall immediately take the child into custody and bring him before the court.

(e) A party, other than the child, may waive service of summons by written stipulation or by voluntary appearance at the hearing.

History of Fam §53.06: Acts 1973, 63rd Leg., ch. 544, §1, eff. Sept. 1, 1973. Amended by Acts 1995, 74th Leg., ch. 262, §29, eff. Jan. 1, 1996.

FAM §53.07. SERVICE OF SUMMONS

(a) If a person to be served with a summons is in this state and can be found, the summons shall be served upon him personally at least two days before the day of the adjudication hearing. If he is in this state and cannot be found, but his address is known or can with reasonable diligence be ascertained, the summons may be served on him by mailing a copy by registered or certified mail, return receipt requested, at least five days before the day of the hearing. If he is outside this state but he can be found or his address is known, or his whereabouts or address can with reasonable diligence be ascertained, service of the summons may be made either by delivering a copy to him personally or mailing a copy to him by registered or certified mail, return receipt requested, at least five days before the day of the hearing.

(b) The juvenile court has jurisdiction of the case if after reasonable effort a person other than the child cannot be found nor his post-office address ascertained, whether he is in or outside this state.

(c) Service of the summons may be made by any suitable person under the direction of the court.

(d) The court may authorize payment from the general funds of the county of the costs of service and of necessary travel expenses incurred by persons summoned or otherwise required to appear at the hearing.

(e) Witnesses may be subpoenaed in accordance with the Texas Code of Criminal Procedure, 1965.

History of Fam §53.07: Acts 1973, 63rd Leg., ch. 544, §1, eff. Sept. 1, 1973.

FAM §53.08. WRIT OF ATTACHMENT

(a) The juvenile court may issue a writ of attachment for a person who violates an order entered under Section 53.06(c).

(b) A writ of attachment issued under this section is executed in the same manner as in a criminal proceeding as provided by Chapter 24, Code of Criminal Procedure.

History of Fam §53.08: Acts 1995, 74th Leg., ch. 262, §30, eff. Jan. 1, 1996.

CHAPTER 54. JUDICIAL PROCEEDINGS

FAM §54.01. DETENTION HEARING

(a) Except as provided by Subsection (p), if the child is not released under Section 53.02, a detention hearing without a jury shall be held promptly, but not later than the second working day after the child is taken into custody; provided, however, that when a child is detained on a Friday or Saturday, then such detention hearing shall be held on the first working day after the child is taken into custody.

(b) Reasonable notice of the detention hearing, either oral or written, shall be given, stating the time, place, and purpose of the hearing. Notice shall be given to the child and, if they can be found, to his parents, guardian, or custodian. Prior to the commencement of the hearing, the court shall inform the parties of the child's right to counsel and to appointed counsel if they are indigent and of the child's right to remain silent with respect to any allegations of delinquent conduct or conduct indicating a need for supervision.

(c) At the detention hearing, the court may consider written reports from probation officers, professional court employees, or professional consultants in addition to the testimony of witnesses. Prior to the detention hearing, the court shall provide the attorney for the child with access to all written matter to be considered by the court in making the detention decision. The court may order counsel not to reveal items to the child or his parent, guardian, or guardian ad litem if such disclosure would materially harm the treatment and rehabilitation of the child or would substantially decrease the likelihood of receiving information from the same or similar sources in the future.

(d) A detention hearing may be held without the presence of the child's parents if the court has been unable to locate them. If no parent or guardian is present, the court shall appoint counsel or a guardian ad litem for the child.

(e) At the conclusion of the hearing, the court shall order the child released from detention unless it finds that:

(1) he is likely to abscond or be removed from the jurisdiction of the court;

(2) suitable supervision, care, or protection for him is not being provided by a parent, guardian, custodian, or other person;

(3) he has no parent, guardian, custodian, or other person able to return him to the court when required;

(4) he may be dangerous to himself or may threaten the safety of the public if released; or

(5) he has previously been found to be a delinquent child or has previously been convicted of a penal offense punishable by a term in jail or prison and is likely to commit an offense if released.

(f) Unless otherwise agreed in the memorandum of understanding under Section 37.011, Education Code, a release may be conditioned on requirements reasonably necessary to insure the child's appearance at later proceedings, but the conditions of the release must be in writing and a copy furnished to the child. In a county with a population greater than 125,000, if a child being released under this section is expelled under Section 37.007, Education Code, the release shall be conditioned on the child's attending a juvenile justice alternative education program pending a deferred prosecution or formal court disposition of the child's case.

FAM §54.01

(g) No statement made by the child at the detention hearing shall be admissible against the child at any other hearing.

(h) A detention order extends to the conclusion of the disposition hearing, if there is one, but in no event for more than 10 working days. Further detention orders may be made following subsequent detention hearings. The initial detention hearing may not be waived but subsequent detention hearings may be waived in accordance with the requirements of Section 51.09. Each subsequent detention order shall extend for no more than 10 working days, except that in a county that does not have a certified juvenile detention facility, as described by Section 51.12(a)(3), each subsequent detention order shall extend for no more than 15 working days.

(i) A child in custody may be detained for as long as 10 days without the hearing described in Subsection (a) of this section if:

(1) a written request for shelter in detention facilities pending arrangement of transportation to his place of residence in another state or country or another county of this state is voluntarily executed by the child not later than the next working day after he was taken into custody;

(2) the request for shelter contains:

(A) a statement by the child that he voluntarily agrees to submit himself to custody and detention for a period of not longer than 10 days without a detention hearing;

(B) an allegation by the person detaining the child that the child has left his place of residence in another state or country or another county of this state, that he is in need of shelter, and that an effort is being made to arrange transportation to his place of residence; and

(C) a statement by the person detaining the child that he has advised the child of his right to demand a detention hearing under Subsection (a) of this section; and

(3) the request is signed by the juvenile court judge to evidence his knowledge of the fact that the child is being held in detention.

(j) The request for shelter may be revoked by the child at any time, and on such revocation, if further detention is necessary, a detention hearing shall be held not later than the next working day in accordance with Subsections (a) through (g) of this section.

(k) Notwithstanding anything in this title to the contrary, the child may sign a request for shelter without the concurrence of an adult specified in Section 51.09 of this code.

A *Subsection (l) below is effective for criminal conduct that occurs on or after Sept. 1, 2001.*

(*l*) The juvenile board may appoint a referee to conduct the detention hearing. The referee shall be an attorney licensed to practice law in this state. Such payment or additional payment as may be warranted for referee services shall be provided from county funds. Before commencing the detention hearing, the referee shall inform the parties who have appeared that they are entitled to have the hearing before the juvenile court judge or a substitute judge authorized by Section 51.04(f). If a party objects to the referee conducting the detention hearing, an authorized judge shall conduct the hearing within 24 hours. At the conclusion of the hearing, the referee shall transmit written findings and recommendations to the juvenile court judge or substitute judge. The juvenile court judge or substitute judge shall adopt, modify, or reject the referee's recommendations not later than the next working day after the day that the judge receives the recommendations. Failure to act within that time results in release of the child by operation of law. A recommendation that the child be released operates to secure the child's immediate release, subject to the power of the juvenile court judge or substitute judge to reject or modify that recommendation. The effect of an order detaining a child shall be computed from the time of the hearing before the referee.

Subsection (l) below is effective for criminal conduct in which any element of the conduct occurred before Sept. 1, 2001.

(*l*) The juvenile board or, if there is none, the juvenile court, may appoint a referee to conduct the detention hearing. The referee shall be an attorney licensed to practice law in this state. Such payment or additional payment as may be warranted for referee services shall be provided from county funds. Before commencing the detention hearing, the referee shall inform the parties who have appeared that they are entitled to have the hearing before the juvenile court judge or a substitute judge authorized by Section 51.04(f) of this code. If a party objects to the referee conducting the detention hearing, an authorized judge shall conduct the hearing within 24 hours. At the conclusion of the hearing, the referee shall transmit written findings and recommendations to the juvenile court judge or substitute judge. The juvenile court judge or substitute judge shall adopt, modify, or reject the referee's recommendations not later than the next working day after the day that the judge receives the recommendations. Failure to act within that time results in release of the child by operation of law. A recommendation that the child be released operates to secure his immediate release, subject to the power of the juvenile court judge or substitute judge to reject or modify that recommendation. The effect of an order detaining a child shall be computed from the time of the hearing before the referee.

(m) The detention hearing required in this section may be held in the county of the designated place of detention where the child is being held even though the designated place of detention is outside the county of residence of the child or the county in which the alleged delinquent conduct or conduct indicating a need for supervision occurred.

(n) An attorney appointed by the court under Section 51.10(c) because a determination was made under this section to detain a child who was not represented by an attorney may request on behalf of the child and is entitled to a de novo detention hearing under this section. The attorney must make the request not later than the 10th working day after the date the attorney is appointed. The hearing must take place not later than the second working day after the date the attorney filed a formal request with the court for a hearing.

(o) The court or referee shall find whether there is probable cause to believe that a child taken into custody without an arrest warrant or a directive to apprehend has engaged in delinquent conduct or conduct indicating a need for supervision. The court or referee must make the finding within 48 hours, including weekends and holidays, of the time the child was taken into custody. The court or referee may make the finding on any reasonably reliable information without regard to admissibility of that information under the Texas Rules of Criminal Evidence. A finding of probable cause is required to detain a child after the 48th hour after the time the child was taken into custody. If a court or referee finds probable cause, additional findings of probable cause are not required in the same cause to authorize further detention.

(p) If a child is detained in a county jail or other facility as provided by Section 51.12(*l*) and the child is not released under Section 53.02(f), a detention hearing without a jury shall be held promptly, but not later than the 24th hour, excluding weekends and holidays, after the time the child is taken into custody.

A (q) If a child has not been released under Section 53.02 or this section and a petition has not been filed under Section 53.04 concerning the child, the court shall order the child released from detention not later than:

(1) the 30th working day after the date the initial detention hearing is held, if the child is alleged to have engaged in conduct constituting a capital felony, an aggravated controlled substance felony, or a felony of the first degree; or

(2) the 15th working day after the date the initial detention hearing is held, if the child is alleged to have engaged in conduct constituting an offense other than an offense listed in Subdivision (1).

History of Fam §54.01: Acts 1973, 63rd Leg., ch. 544, §1, eff. Sept. 1, 1973. Amended by Acts 1975, 64th Leg., ch. 693, §§14, 15, eff. Sept. 1, 1975; Acts 1979, 66th Leg., ch. 518, §2, eff. June 11, 1979; Acts 1995, 74th Leg., ch. 262, §31, eff. Jan. 1, 1996; Acts 1997, 75th Leg., ch. 922, §1 (eff. Sept. 1, 1997), ch. 1015, §18 (eff. June 19, 1997), ch. 1086, §9 (eff. Sept. 1, 1997); Acts 1999, 76th Leg., ch. 232, §4 (eff. Sept. 1, 1999), ch. 1477, §7 (eff. Sept. 1, 1999); Acts 2001, 77th Leg., ch. 1297, §20 (eff. Sept. 1, 2001), ch. 1420, §21.001(30) (eff. Sept. 1, 2001).

FAM §54.011. DETENTION HEARINGS FOR STATUS OFFENDERS & NONOFFENDERS

(a) The detention hearing for a status offender or nonoffender who has not been released administratively under Section 53.02 shall be held before the 24th hour after the time the child arrived at a detention facility, excluding hours of a weekend or a holiday. Except as otherwise provided by this section, the judge or referee conducting the detention hearing shall release the status offender or nonoffender from secure detention.

(b) The judge or referee may order a child in detention accused of the violation of a valid court order as defined by Section 51.02 detained not longer than 72 hours after the time the detention order was entered, excluding weekends and holidays, if:

(1) the judge or referee finds at the detention hearing that there is probable cause to believe the child violated the valid court order; and

(2) the detention of the child is justified under Section 54.01(e)(1), (2), or (3).

(c) Except as provided by Subsection (d), a detention order entered under Subsection (b) may be extended for one additional 72-hour period, excluding weekends and holidays, only on a finding of good cause by the juvenile court.

(d) A detention order for a child under this section may be extended on the demand of the child's attorney only to allow the time that is necessary to comply with the requirements of Section 51.10(h), entitling the attorney to 10 days to prepare for an adjudication hearing.

(e) A status offender may be detained for a necessary period, not to exceed five days, to enable the child's return to the child's home in another state under Chapter 60.

History of Fam §54.011: Acts 1995, 74th Leg., ch. 262, §32, eff. Jan. 1, 1996. Amended by Acts 1997, 75th Leg., ch. 1374, §7, eff. Sept. 1, 1997.

FAM §54.012. INTERACTIVE VIDEO RECORDING OF DETENTION HEARING

(a) A detention hearing under Section 54.01, other than the first detention hearing, may be held using interactive video equipment if:

(1) the child and the child's attorney agree to the video hearing; and

(2) the parties to the proceeding have the opportunity to cross-examine witnesses.

(b) A detention hearing may not be held using video equipment unless the video equipment for the hearing provides for a two-way communication of image and sound among the child, the court, and other parties at the hearing.

(c) A recording of the communications shall be made. The recording shall be preserved until the earlier of:

(1) the 91st day after the date on which the recording is made if the child is alleged to have engaged in conduct constituting a misdemeanor;

(2) the 120th day after the date on which the recording is made if the child is alleged to have engaged in conduct constituting a felony; or

(3) the date on which the adjudication hearing ends.

(d) An attorney for the child may obtain a copy of the recording on payment of the reasonable costs of reproducing the copy.

History of Fam §54.012: Acts 1995, 74th Leg., ch. 262, §33, eff. Jan. 1, 1996.

FAM §54.02. WAIVER OF JURISDICTION & DISCRETIONARY TRANSFER TO CRIMINAL COURT

(a) The juvenile court may waive its exclusive original jurisdiction and transfer a child to the appropriate district court or criminal district court for criminal proceedings if:

(1) the child is alleged to have violated a penal law of the grade of felony;

(2) the child was:

(A) 14 years of age or older at the time he is alleged to have committed the offense, if the offense is a capital felony, an aggravated controlled substance felony, or a felony of the first degree, and no adjudication hearing has been conducted concerning that offense; or

(B) 15 years of age or older at the time the child is alleged to have committed the offense, if the offense is a felony of the second or third degree or a state jail felony, and no adjudication hearing has been conducted concerning that offense; and

(3) after a full investigation and a hearing, the juvenile court determines that there is probable cause to believe that the child before the court committed the offense alleged and that because of the seriousness of the offense alleged or the background of the child the welfare of the community requires criminal proceedings.

(b) The petition and notice requirements of Sections 53.04, 53.05, 53.06, and 53.07 of this code must be satisfied, and the summons must state that the hearing is for the purpose of considering discretionary transfer to criminal court.

(c) The juvenile court shall conduct a hearing without a jury to consider transfer of the child for criminal proceedings.

(d) Prior to the hearing, the juvenile court shall order and obtain a complete diagnostic study, social evaluation, and full investigation of the child, his circumstances, and the circumstances of the alleged offense.

(e) At the transfer hearing the court may consider written reports from probation officers, professional court employees, or professional consultants in addition to the testimony of witnesses. At least one day prior to the transfer hearing, the court shall provide the attorney for the child with access to all written matter to be considered by the court in making the transfer decision. The court may order counsel not to reveal items to the child or his parent, guardian, or guardian ad litem if such disclosure would materially harm the treatment and rehabilitation of the child or would substantially decrease the likelihood of receiving information from the same or similar sources in the future.

(f) In making the determination required by Subsection (a) of this section, the court shall consider, among other matters:

(1) whether the alleged offense was against person or property, with greater weight in favor of transfer given to offenses against the person;

(2) the sophistication and maturity of the child;

(3) the record and previous history of the child; and

(4) the prospects of adequate protection of the public and the likelihood of the rehabilitation of the child by use of procedures, services, and facilities currently available to the juvenile court.

(g) If the petition alleges multiple offenses that constitute more than one criminal transaction, the juvenile court shall either retain or transfer all offenses relating to a single transaction. A child is not subject to criminal prosecution at any time for any offense arising out of a criminal transaction for which the juvenile court retains jurisdiction.

(h) If the juvenile court waives jurisdiction, it shall state specifically in the order its reasons for waiver and certify its action, including the written order and findings of the court, and shall transfer the person to the appropriate court for criminal proceedings and cause the results of the diagnostic study of the person ordered under Subsection (d), including psychological information, to be transferred to the appropriate criminal prosecutor. On transfer of the person for criminal proceedings, the person shall be dealt with as an adult and in accordance with the Code of Criminal Procedure. The transfer of custody is an arrest.

(i) A waiver under this section is a waiver of jurisdiction over the child and the criminal court may not remand the child to the jurisdiction of the juvenile court.

(j) The juvenile court may waive its exclusive original jurisdiction and transfer a person to the appropriate district court or criminal district court for criminal proceedings if:

(1) the person is 18 years of age or older;

(2) the person was:

(A) 10 years of age or older and under 17 years of age at the time the person is alleged to have committed a capital felony or an offense under Section 19.02, Penal Code;

(B) 14 years of age or older and under 17 years of age at the time the person is alleged to have committed an aggravated controlled substance felony or a felony of the first degree other than an offense under Section 19.02, Penal Code; or

(C) 15 years of age or older and under 17 years of age at the time the person is alleged to have committed a felony of the second or third degree or a state jail felony;

(3) no adjudication concerning the alleged offense has been made or no adjudication hearing concerning the offense has been conducted;

(4) the juvenile court finds from a preponderance of the evidence that:

(A) for a reason beyond the control of the state it was not practicable to proceed in juvenile court before the 18th birthday of the person; or

(B) after due diligence of the state it was not practicable to proceed in juvenile court before the 18th birthday of the person because:

(i) the state did not have probable cause to proceed in juvenile court and new evidence has been found since the 18th birthday of the person;

(ii) the person could not be found; or

(iii) a previous transfer order was reversed by an appellate court or set aside by a district court; and

(5) the juvenile court determines that there is probable cause to believe that the child before the court committed the offense alleged.

(k) The petition and notice requirements of Sections 53.04, 53.05, 53.06, and 53.07 of this code must be satisfied, and the summons must state that the hearing is for the purpose of considering waiver of jurisdiction under Subsection (j) of this section.

(*l*) The juvenile court shall conduct a hearing without a jury to consider waiver of jurisdiction under Subsection (j) of this section.

(m) Notwithstanding any other provision of this section, the juvenile court shall waive its exclusive original jurisdiction and transfer a child to the appropriate district court or criminal court for criminal proceedings if:

(1) the child has previously been transferred to a district court or criminal district court for criminal proceedings under this section, unless:

(A) the child was not indicted in the matter transferred by the grand jury;

(B) the child was found not guilty in the matter transferred;

(C) the matter transferred was dismissed with prejudice; or

(D) the child was convicted in the matter transferred, the conviction was reversed on appeal, and the appeal is final; and

(2) the child is alleged to have violated a penal law of the grade of felony.

(n) A mandatory transfer under Subsection (m) may be made without conducting the study required in discretionary transfer proceedings by Subsection (d). The requirements of Subsection (b) that the summons state that the purpose of the hearing is to consider discretionary transfer to criminal court does not apply to a transfer proceeding under Subsection (m). In a proceeding under Subsection (m), it is sufficient that the summons provide fair notice that the purpose of the hearing is to consider mandatory transfer to criminal court.

(o) If a respondent is taken into custody for possible discretionary transfer proceedings under Subsection (j), the juvenile court shall hold a detention hearing in the same manner as provided by Section 54.01, except that the court shall order the respondent released unless it finds that the respondent:

(1) is likely to abscond or be removed from the jurisdiction of the court;

(2) may be dangerous to himself or herself or may threaten the safety of the public if released; or

(3) has previously been found to be a delinquent child or has previously been convicted of a penal offense punishable by a term of jail or prison and is likely to commit an offense if released.

(p) If the juvenile court does not order a respondent released under Subsection (o), the court shall, pending the conclusion of the discretionary transfer hearing, order that the respondent be detained in:

(1) a certified juvenile detention facility as provided by Subsection (q); or

(2) an appropriate county facility for the detention of adults accused of criminal offenses.

(q) The detention of a respondent in a certified juvenile detention facility must comply with the detention requirements under this title, except that, to the extent practicable, the person shall be kept separate from children detained in the same facility.

(r) If the juvenile court orders a respondent detained in a county facility under Subsection (p), the county sheriff shall take custody of the respondent under the juvenile court's order. The juvenile court shall set or deny bond for the respondent as required by the Code of Criminal Procedure and other law applicable to the pretrial detention of adults accused of criminal offenses.

History of Fam §54.02: Acts 1973, 63rd Leg., ch. 544, §1, eff. Sept. 1, 1973. Amended by Acts 1975, 64th Leg., ch. 693, §16, eff. Sept. 1, 1975; Acts 1987, 70th Leg., ch. 140, §§1 - 3, eff. Sept. 1, 1987; Acts 1995, 74th Leg., ch. 262, §34, eff. Jan. 1, 1996; Acts 1999, 76th Leg., ch. 1477, §8, eff. Sept. 1, 1999.

FAM §54.021. JUSTICE OR MUNICIPAL COURT: TRUANCY

(a) The juvenile court may waive its exclusive original jurisdiction and transfer a child to an appropriate justice or municipal court, with the permission of the justice or municipal court, for disposition in the manner provided by Subsection (b) of this section if the child is alleged to have engaged in conduct described in Section 51.03(b)(2) of this code. A waiver of jurisdiction under this subsection may be for an individual case or for all cases in which a child is alleged to have engaged in conduct described in Section 51.03(b)(2) of this code. The waiver of a juvenile court's exclusive original jurisdiction for all cases in which a child is alleged to have engaged in conduct described in Section 51.03(b)(2) of this code is effective for a period of one year.

Ⓐ *Subsections (b) & (c) below are effective for children alleged to have engaged in conduct that occurs on or after Sept. 1, 2001.*

(b) A justice or municipal court may exercise jurisdiction over a person alleged to have engaged in conduct indicating a need for supervision by engaging in conduct described in Section 51.03(b)(2) in a case where:

(1) the juvenile court has waived its original jurisdiction under this section; and

(2) a complaint is filed by the appropriate authority in the justice or municipal court charging an offense under Section 25.094, Education Code.

Ⓔ (c) A proceeding in a justice or municipal court on a complaint charging an offense under Section 25.094, Education Code, is governed by Chapter 45, Code of Criminal Procedure.

Ⓐ (c) to (h) Repealed by Acts 2001, 77th Leg., ch. 1514, §19(b), eff. Sept. 1, 2001.

Subsections (b) through (h) below are effective for children alleged to have engaged in conduct in which every element of the conduct occurred before Sept. 1, 2001.

(b) A justice or municipal court may exercise jurisdiction over a person alleged to have engaged in conduct indicating a need for supervision by engaging in conduct described in Section 51.03(b)(2) in a case where the juvenile court has waived its original jurisdiction under this section. A justice or municipal court may exercise jurisdiction under this section without regard to whether the justice of the peace or municipal judge for the court is a licensed attorney or the hearing for a case is before a jury consisting of six persons.

(c) On a finding that a person has engaged in conduct described by Section 51.03(b)(2) or conduct that violates Section 25.094, Education Code, the justice or municipal court shall enter an order appropriate to the nature of the conduct.

(d) On a finding by the justice or municipal court that the person has engaged in truant conduct described in Section 51.03(b)(2) or conduct that violates Section 25.094, Education Code, the court has jurisdiction to enter an order that includes one or more of the following provisions requiring that:

(1) the person do either or both of the following:

(A) attend a preparatory class for the high school equivalency examination provided under Section 7.111, Education Code, if the court determines that the person is too old to do well in a formal classroom environment; or

(B) if the person is at least 16 years of age, take the high school equivalency examination provided under Section 7.111, Education Code;

(2) the person attend a special program that the court determines to be in the best interests of the person, including:

(A) an alcohol and drug abuse program;

(B) rehabilitation;

(C) counseling, including self-improvement counseling;

(D) training in self-esteem and leadership;

(E) work and job skills training;

(F) training in parenting, including parental responsibility;

(G) training in manners;

(H) training in violence avoidance;

(I) sensitivity training; and

(J) training in advocacy and mentoring;

(3) the person and the person's parents, managing conservator, or guardian attend a class for students at risk of dropping out of school designed for both the person and the person's parents, managing conservator, or guardian;

(4) the person complete reasonable community service requirements;

(5) the person's driver's license be suspended in the manner provided by Section 54.042;

(6) the person attend school without unexcused absences; or

(7) the person participate in a tutorial program provided by the school attended by the person in the academic subjects in which the person is enrolled for a total number of hours ordered by the court.

(e) An order under Subsection (d)(3) that requires the parent, managing conservator, or guardian of a person to attend a class for students at risk of dropping out of school is enforceable in the justice court by contempt.

(f) A school attendance officer may refer a person alleged to have engaged in conduct described in Section 51.03(b)(2) of this code to a justice court in the county where the person resides or where the person's school is located or to a municipal court of the municipality where the person resides or where the person's school is located if the juvenile court having exclusive original jurisdiction has waived its jurisdiction as provided by Subsection (a) of this section for all cases involving conduct described by Section 51.03(b)(2) of this code.

(g) A court having jurisdiction under this section shall endorse on the summons issued to the parent, guardian, or custodian of the person who is the subject of the hearing an order directing the parent, guardian, or custodian to appear personally at the hearing and directing the person having custody of the person to bring the person to the hearing.

(h) A person commits an offense if the person is a parent, guardian, or custodian who fails to attend a hearing under this section after receiving notice under Subsection (g) of this section that the person's attendance was required. An offense under this subsection is a Class C misdemeanor.

History of Fam §54.021: Acts 1991, 72nd Leg., ch. 741, §1, eff. Sept. 1, 1991. Amended by Acts 1993, 73rd Leg., ch. 358, §1, eff. Sept. 1, 1993; Acts 1995, 74th Leg., ch. 260, §24 (eff. May 30, 1995), ch. 262, §35 (eff. Jan. 1, 1996); Acts 1997,

75th Leg., ch. 865, §1, eff. Sept. 1, 1997; Acts 1999, 76th Leg., ch. 76, §2, eff. Sept. 1, 1999; Acts 2001, 77th Leg., ch. 1514, §§14, 19(b), eff. Sept. 1, 2001.

FAM §54.022. REPEALED

Repealed by Acts 2001, 77th Leg., ch. 1514, §19(b) (eff. Sept. 1, 2001), ch. 1297, §71(2) (eff. Sept. 1, 2001).

FAM §54.022. JUSTICE OR MUNICIPAL COURT: CERTAIN MISDEMEANORS

Section 54.022 below is effective for children alleged to have engaged in conduct in which every element of the conduct occurred before Sept. 1, 2001.

(a) On a finding by a justice or municipal court that a child committed an offense that the court has jurisdiction of under Article 4.11 or 4.14, Code of Criminal Procedure, other than a traffic offense or public intoxication, the court has jurisdiction to enter an order:

(1) referring the child or the child's parents, managing conservators, or guardians for services under Section 264.302;

(2) requiring that the child attend a special program that the court determines to be in the best interest of the child and, if the program involves the expenditure of county funds, that is approved by the county commissioners court, including a rehabilitation, counseling, self-esteem and leadership, work and job skills training, job interviewing and work preparation, self-improvement, parenting, manners, violence avoidance, tutoring, sensitivity training, parental responsibility, community service, restitution, advocacy, or mentoring program; or

(3) if the court finds the parent, managing conservator, or guardian, by act or omission, contributed to, caused, or encouraged the child's conduct, requiring that the child's parent, managing conservator, or guardian do any act or refrain from doing any act that the court determines will increase the likelihood that the child will comply with the orders of the court and that is reasonable and necessary for the welfare of the child, including:

(A) attend a parenting class or parental responsibility program; and

(B) attend the child's school classes or functions.

(b) The justice or municipal court may order the parents, managing conservator, or guardian of a child required to attend a program under Subsection (a) to pay an amount not greater than $100 to pay for the costs of the program.

(c) A justice or municipal court may require a child, parent, managing conservator, or guardian required to attend a program, class, or function under this section to submit proof of attendance to the court.

(d) A justice or municipal court shall endorse on the summons issued to a parent, managing conservator, or a guardian an order to appear personally at the hearing with the child. The summons must include a warning that the failure of the parent, managing conservator, or guardian to appear may be punishable as a Class C misdemeanor.

(e) An order under this section involving a child is enforceable under Section 51.03(a)(3) by referral to the juvenile court.

(f) A person commits an offense if the person is a parent, managing conservator, or guardian who fails to attend a hearing under this section after receiving an order under Subsection (d). An offense under this subsection is a Class C misdemeanor.

(g) Any other order under this section is enforceable by the justice or municipal court by contempt.

FAM §54.023. JUSTICE OR MUNICIPAL COURT: ENFORCEMENT

E *Section 54.023 below is effective for criminal conduct that occurs on or after Sept. 1, 2001.*

(a) If a child intentionally or knowingly fails to obey a lawful order of disposition after an adjudication of guilt of an offense that a justice or municipal court has jurisdiction of under Article 4.11 or 4.14, Code of Criminal Procedure, the justice or municipal court may:

(1) refer the child to the appropriate juvenile court for delinquent conduct for contempt of the justice or municipal court order; or

(2) retain jurisdiction of the case and:

(A) hold the child in contempt of the justice or municipal court order and impose a fine not to exceed $500;

(B) order the child to be held in a place of nonsecure custody designated under Section 52.027 for a single period not to exceed six hours; or

(C) order the Department of Public Safety to suspend the driver's license or permit of the child or, if the child does not have a license or permit, to deny the issuance of a license or permit to the child and, if the child has a continuing obligation under the court's order, require that the suspension or denial be effective until the child fully discharges the obligation.

(b) A court that orders suspension or denial of a child's driver's license or permit shall notify the Department of Public Safety on receiving proof that the child has fully complied with the orders of the court.

(c) A justice or municipal court may hold a person in contempt and impose a remedy authorized by Subsection (a)(2) if:

(1) the person as a child was placed under an order of the justice or municipal court;

(2) the person failed to obey the order while the person was 17 years of age or older; and

(3) the failure to obey occurred under circumstances that constitute contempt of court.

(d) A justice or municipal court may hold a person in contempt and impose a remedy authorized by Subsection (a)(2) if the person, while younger than 17 years of age, engaged in conduct in contempt of an order of the justice or municipal court but contempt proceedings could not be held before the child's 17th birthday.

(e) A justice or municipal court may not order a child to a term of confinement or imprisonment for contempt of a justice or municipal court order under this section.

(f) A justice or municipal court may not refer a child who violates a court order while 17 years of age or older to a juvenile court for delinquency proceedings for contempt of court.

History of Fam §54.023: Enacted by Acts 2001, 77th Leg., ch. 1297, §21, eff. Sept. 1, 2001.

FAM §54.03. ADJUDICATION HEARING

(a) A child may be found to have engaged in delinquent conduct or conduct indicating a need for supervision only after an adjudication hearing conducted in accordance with the provisions of this section.

(b) At the beginning of the adjudication hearing, the juvenile court judge shall explain to the child and his parent, guardian, or guardian ad litem:

(1) the allegations made against the child;

(2) the nature and possible consequences of the proceedings, including the law relating to the admissibility of the record of a juvenile court adjudication in a criminal proceeding;

(3) the child's privilege against self-incrimination;

(4) the child's right to trial and to confrontation of witnesses;

(5) the child's right to representation by an attorney if he is not already represented; and

(6) the child's right to trial by jury.

A *Subsection (c) below is effective for criminal conduct that occurs on or after Sept. 1, 2001.*

(c) Trial shall be by jury unless jury is waived in accordance with Section 51.09. If the hearing is on a petition that has been approved by the grand jury under Section 53.045, the jury must consist of 12 persons and be selected in accordance with the requirements in criminal cases. Jury verdicts under this title must be unanimous.

Subsection (c) below is effective for criminal conduct in which any element of the conduct occurred before Sept. 1, 2001.

(c) Trial shall be by jury unless jury is waived in accordance with Section 51.09 of this code. If the hearing is on a petition that has been approved by the grand jury under Section 53.045 of this code, the jury must consist of 12 persons. Jury verdicts under this title must be unanimous.

(d) Except as provided by Section 54.031, only material, relevant, and competent evidence in accordance with the Texas Rules of Evidence applicable to criminal cases and Chapter 38, Code of Criminal Procedure, may be considered in the adjudication hearing. Except in a detention or discretionary transfer hearing, a social history report or social service file shall not be viewed by the court before the adjudication decision and shall not be viewed by the jury at any time.

(e) A child alleged to have engaged in delinquent conduct or conduct indicating a need for supervision need not be a witness against nor otherwise incriminate himself. An extrajudicial statement which was obtained without fulfilling the requirements of this title or of the constitution of this state or the United States, may not be used in an adjudication hearing. A statement made by the child out of court is insufficient to support a finding of delinquent conduct or conduct indicating a need for supervision unless it is corroborated in whole or in part by other evidence. An adjudication of delinquent conduct or conduct indicating a need for supervision cannot be had upon the testimony of an accomplice unless corroborated by other evidence tending to connect the child with the alleged delinquent conduct or conduct indicating a need for supervision; and the corroboration is not sufficient if it merely shows the commission of the alleged conduct. Evidence illegally seized or obtained is inadmissible in an adjudication hearing.

(f) At the conclusion of the adjudication hearing, the court or jury shall find whether or not the child has engaged in delinquent conduct or conduct indicating a need for supervision. The finding must be based on competent evidence admitted at the hearing. The child shall be presumed to be innocent of the charges against the child and no finding that a child has engaged in delinquent conduct or conduct indicating a need for supervision may be returned unless the state has proved such beyond a reasonable doubt. In all jury cases the jury will be instructed that the burden is on the state to prove that a child has engaged in delinquent conduct or is in need of supervision beyond a reasonable doubt. A child may be adjudicated as having engaged in conduct constituting a lesser included offense as provided by Articles 37.08 and 37.09, Code of Criminal Procedure.

(g) If the court or jury finds that the child did not engage in delinquent conduct or conduct indicating a need for supervision, the court shall dismiss the case with prejudice.

(h) If the finding is that the child did engage in delinquent conduct or conduct indicating a need for supervision, the court or jury shall state which of the allegations in the petition were found to be established by the evidence. The court shall also set a date and time for the disposition hearing.

(i) In order to preserve for appellate or collateral review the failure of the court to provide the child the explanation required by Subsection (b), the attorney for the child must comply with Rule 52(a), Texas Rules of Appellate Procedure, before testimony begins or, if the adjudication is uncontested, before the child pleads to the petition or agrees to a stipulation of evidence.

(j) When the state and the child agree to the disposition of the case, in whole or in part, the prosecuting attorney shall inform the court of the agreement between the state and the child. The court shall inform the child that the court is not required to accept the agreement. The court may delay a decision on whether to accept the agreement until after reviewing a report filed under Section 54.04(b). If the court decides not to accept the agreement, the court shall inform the child of the court's decision and give the child an opportunity to withdraw the plea or stipulation of evidence. If the court rejects the agreement, no document, testimony, or other evidence placed before the court that relates to the rejected agreement may be considered by the court in a subsequent hearing in the case. A statement made by the child before the court's rejection of the agreement to a person writing a report to be filed under Section 54.04(b) may not be admitted into evidence in a subsequent hearing in the case. If the court accepts the agreement, the court shall make a disposition in accordance with the terms of the agreement between the state and the child.

History of Fam §54.03: Acts 1973, 63rd Leg., ch. 544, §1, eff. Sept. 1, 1973. Amended by Acts 1975, 64th Leg., ch. 693, §17, eff. Sept. 1, 1975; Acts 1979, 66th Leg., ch. 514, §1, eff. Aug. 27, 1979; Acts 1985, 69th Leg., ch. 590, §2, eff. Sept. 1, 1985; Acts 1987, 70th Leg., ch. 385, §8 (eff. Sept. 1, 1987), ch. 386, §3 (eff. Sept. 1, 1987); Acts 1995, 74th Leg., ch. 262, §37, eff. Jan. 1, 1996; Acts 1997, 75th Leg., ch. 1086, §10, eff. Sept. 1, 1997; Acts 1999, 76th Leg., ch. 1477, §9, eff. Sept. 1, 1999; Acts 2001, 77th Leg., ch. 1297, §22, eff. Sept. 1, 2001.

FAM §54.031. HEARSAY STATEMENT OF CHILD ABUSE VICTIM

(a) This section applies to a hearing under this title in which a child is alleged to be a delinquent child on the basis of a violation of any of the following provisions of the Penal Code, if a child 12 years of age or younger is the alleged victim of the violation:

(1) Chapter 21 (Sexual Offenses) or 22 (Assaultive Offenses);

(2) Section 25.02 (Prohibited Sexual Conduct); or

(3) Section 43.25 (Sexual Performance by a Child).

(b) This section applies only to statements that describe the alleged violation that:

(1) were made by the child who is the alleged victim of the violation; and

(2) were made to the first person, 18 years of age or older, to whom the child made a statement about the violation.

(c) A statement that meets the requirements of Subsection (b) of this section is not inadmissible because of the hearsay rule if:

(1) on or before the 14th day before the date the hearing begins, the party intending to offer the statement:

(A) notifies each other party of its intention to do so;

(B) provides each other party with the name of the witness through whom it intends to offer the statement; and

(C) provides each other party with a written summary of the statement;

(2) the juvenile court finds, in a hearing conducted outside the presence of the jury, that the statement is reliable based on the time, content, and circumstances of the statement; and

(3) the child who is the alleged victim testifies or is available to testify at the hearing in court or in any other manner provided by law.

History of Fam §54.031: Acts 1985, 69th Leg., ch. 590, §3, eff. Sept. 1, 1985. Amended by Acts 1995, 74th Leg., ch. 76, §14.31, eff. Sept. 1, 1995.

FAM §54.032. DEFERRAL OF ADJUDICATION & DISMISSAL OF CERTAIN CASES ON COMPLETION OF TEEN COURT PROGRAM

A *Subsection (a) below is effective for children alleged to have engaged in conduct that occurs on or after Sept. 1, 2001.*

(a) A juvenile court may defer adjudication proceedings under Section 54.03 for not more than 180 days if the child:

(1) is alleged to have engaged in conduct indicating a need for supervision that violated a penal law of this state of the grade of misdemeanor that is punishable by fine only or a penal ordinance of a political subdivision of this state;

(2) waives, under Section 51.09, the privilege against self-incrimination and testifies under oath that the allegations are true;

(3) presents to the court an oral or written request to attend a teen court program; and

(4) has not successfully completed a teen court program for the violation of the same penal law or ordinance in the two years preceding the date that the alleged conduct occurred.

Subsection (a) below is effective for children alleged to have engaged in conduct that occurred before Sept. 1, 2001.

(a) A juvenile court may defer adjudication proceedings under Section 54.03 of this code for 90 days if the child:

(1) is alleged to have engaged in conduct indicating a need for supervision that violated a penal law of this state of the grade of misdemeanor that is punishable by fine only or a penal ordinance of a political subdivision of this state;

(2) waives, under Section 51.09 of this code, the privilege against self-incrimination and testifies under oath that the allegations are true;

(3) presents to the court an oral or written request to attend a teen court program; and

(4) has not successfully completed a teen court program for the violation of the same penal law or ordinance in the two years preceding the date that the alleged conduct occurred.

(b) The teen court program must be approved by the court.

A *Subsection (c) below is effective for children alleged to have engaged in conduct that occurs on or after Sept. 1, 2001.*

(c) A child for whom adjudication proceedings are deferred under Subsection (a) shall complete the teen court program not later than the 90th day after the date the teen court hearing to determine punishment is held or the last day of the deferral period, whichever date is earlier. The court shall dismiss the case with prejudice at the time the child presents satisfactory evidence that the child has successfully completed the teen court program.

Subsection (c) below is effective for children alleged to have engaged in conduct that occurred before Sept. 1, 2001.

(c) The court shall dismiss the case with prejudice at the conclusion of the deferral period if the child presents satisfactory evidence that the child has successfully completed the teen court program.

(d) A case dismissed under this section may not be part of the child's records for any purpose.

(e) The court may require a child who requests a teen court program to pay a fee not to exceed $10 that is set by the court to cover the costs of administering this section. The court shall deposit the fee in the county treasury of the county in which the court is located. A child who requests a teen court program and does not complete the program is not entitled to a refund of the fee.

(f) A court may transfer a case in which proceedings have been deferred as provided by this section to a court in a contiguous county if the court to which the case is transferred consents. A case may not be transferred unless it is within the jurisdiction of the court to which it is transferred.

(g) In addition to the fee authorized by Subsection (e), the court may require a child who requests a teen court program to pay a $10 fee to cover the cost to the teen court for performing its duties under this section.

The court shall pay the fee to the teen court program, and the teen court program must account to the court for the receipt and disbursal of the fee. A child who pays a fee under this subsection is not entitled to a refund of the fee, regardless of whether the child successfully completes the teen court program.

History of Fam §54.032: Acts 1989, 71st Leg., ch. 1031, §2, eff. Sept. 1, 1989. Amended by Acts 1995, 74th Leg., ch. 748, §1, eff. Sept. 1, 1995; Acts 2001, 77th Leg., ch. 216, §2, eff. Sept. 1, 2001.

FAM §54.033. SEXUALLY TRANSMITTED DISEASE, AIDS, & HIV TESTING

(a) A child found at the conclusion of an adjudication hearing under Section 54.03 of this code to have engaged in delinquent conduct that included a violation of Sections 21.11(a)(1), 22.011, or 22.021, Penal Code, shall undergo a medical procedure or test at the direction of the juvenile court designed to show or help show whether the child has a sexually transmitted disease, acquired immune deficiency syndrome (AIDS), human immunodeficiency virus (HIV) infection, antibodies to HIV, or infection with any other probable causative agent of AIDS. The court may direct the child to undergo the procedure or test on the court's own motion or on the request of the victim of the delinquent conduct.

(b) If the child or another person who has the power to consent to medical treatment for the child refuses to submit voluntarily or consent to the procedure or test, the court shall require the child to submit to the procedure or test.

(c) The person performing the procedure or test shall make the test results available to the local health authority. The local health authority shall be required to notify the victim of the delinquent conduct and the person found to have engaged in the delinquent conduct of the test result.

(d) The state may not use the fact that a medical procedure or test was performed on a child under this section or use the results of the procedure or test in any proceeding arising out of the delinquent conduct.

(e) Testing under this section shall be conducted in accordance with written infectious disease control protocols adopted by the Texas Board of Health that clearly establish procedural guidelines that provide criteria for testing and that respect the rights of the child and the victim of the delinquent conduct.

(f) Nothing in this section allows a court to release a test result to anyone other than a person specifically authorized under this section. Section 81.103(d), Health and Safety Code, may not be construed to allow the disclosure of test results under this section except as provided by this section.

History of Fam §54.033: Acts 1993, 73rd Leg., ch. 811, §2, eff. Sept. 1, 1993.

FAM §54.034. LIMITED RIGHT TO APPEAL: WARNING

Before the court may accept a child's plea or stipulation of evidence in a proceeding held under this title, the court shall inform the child that if the court accepts the plea or stipulation and the court makes a disposition in accordance with the agreement between the state and the child regarding the disposition of the case, the child may not appeal an order of the court entered under Section 54.03, 54.04, or 54.05, unless:

(1) the court gives the child permission to appeal; or

(2) the appeal is based on a matter raised by written motion filed before the proceeding in which the child entered the plea or agreed to the stipulation of evidence.

History of Fam §54.034: Acts 1999, 76th Leg., ch. 74, §1, eff. Sept. 1, 1999.

A FAM §54.04. DISPOSITION HEARING

(a) The disposition hearing shall be separate, distinct, and subsequent to the adjudication hearing. There is no right to a jury at the disposition hearing unless the child is in jeopardy of a determinate sentence under Subsection (d)(3) or (m), in which case, the child is entitled to a jury of 12 persons to determine the sentence.

(b) At the disposition hearing, the juvenile court may consider written reports from probation officers, professional court employees, or professional consultants in addition to the testimony of witnesses. Prior to the disposition hearing, the court shall provide the attorney for the child with access to all written matter to be considered in disposition. The court may order counsel not to reveal items to the child or the child's parent, guardian, or guardian ad litem if such disclosure would materially harm the treatment and rehabilitation of the child or would substantially decrease the likelihood of receiving information from the same or similar sources in the future.

(c) No disposition may be made under this section unless the child is in need of rehabilitation or the protection of the public or the child requires that disposition be made. If the court or jury does not so find, the court shall dismiss the child and enter a final judgment

FAM §54.032

without any disposition. No disposition placing the child on probation outside the child's home may be made under this section unless the court or jury finds that the child, in the child's home, cannot be provided the quality of care and level of support and supervision that the child needs to meet the conditions of the probation.

(d) If the court or jury makes the finding specified in Subsection (c) allowing the court to make a disposition in the case:

(1) the court or jury may, in addition to any order required or authorized under Section 54.041 or 54.042, place the child on probation on such reasonable and lawful terms as the court may determine:

(A) in the child's own home or in the custody of a relative or other fit person; or

(B) subject to the finding under Subsection (c) on the placement of the child outside the child's home, in:

(i) a suitable foster home; or

(ii) a suitable public or private institution or agency, except the Texas Youth Commission;

(2) if the court or jury found at the conclusion of the adjudication hearing that the child engaged in delinquent conduct that violates a penal law of this state or the United States of the grade of felony or, if the requirements of Subsection (s) or (t) are met, of the grade of misdemeanor, and if the petition was not approved by the grand jury under Section 53.045, the court may commit the child to the Texas Youth Commission without a determinate sentence;

(3) if the court or jury found at the conclusion of the adjudication hearing that the child engaged in delinquent conduct that included a violation of a penal law listed in Section 53.045(a) and if the petition was approved by the grand jury under Section 53.045, the court or jury may sentence the child to commitment in the Texas Youth Commission with a possible transfer to the institutional division or the pardons and paroles division of the Texas Department of Criminal Justice for a term of:

(A) not more than 40 years if the conduct constitutes:

(i) a capital felony;

(ii) a felony of the first degree; or

(iii) an aggravated controlled substance felony;

(B) not more than 20 years if the conduct constitutes a felony of the second degree; or

(C) not more than 10 years if the conduct constitutes a felony of the third degree;

(4) the court may assign the child an appropriate sanction level and sanctions as provided by the assignment guidelines in Section 59.003; or

(5) if applicable, the court or jury may make a disposition under Subsection (m).

(e) The Texas Youth Commission shall accept a person properly committed to it by a juvenile court even though the person may be 17 years of age or older at the time of commitment.

(f) The court shall state specifically in the order its reasons for the disposition and shall furnish a copy of the order to the child. If the child is placed on probation, the terms of probation shall be written in the order.

(g) If the court orders a disposition under Subsection (d)(3) or (m) and there is an affirmative finding that the defendant used or exhibited a deadly weapon during the commission of the conduct or during immediate flight from commission of the conduct, the court shall enter the finding in the order. If there is an affirmative finding that the deadly weapon was a firearm, the court shall enter that finding in the order.

(h) At the conclusion of the dispositional hearing, the court shall inform the child of:

(1) the child's right to appeal, as required by Section 56.01; and

(2) the procedures for the sealing of the child's records under Section 58.003.

(i) If the court places the child on probation outside the child's home or commits the child to the Texas Youth Commission, the court:

(1) shall include in its order its determination that:

(A) it is in the child's best interests to be placed outside the child's home;

(B) reasonable efforts were made to prevent or eliminate the need for the child's removal from the home and to make it possible for the child to return to the child's home; and

(C) the child, in the child's home, cannot be provided the quality of care and level of support and supervision that the child needs to meet the conditions of probation; and

E *Subsection (2) below is effective for court dispositions made on or after Sept. 1, 2001.*

(2) may approve an administrative body to conduct permanency hearings pursuant to 42 U.S.C. Section 675

if required during the placement or commitment of the child.

(j) If the court or jury found that the child engaged in delinquent conduct that included a violation of a penal law of the grade of felony or jailable misdemeanor, the court:

(1) shall require that the child's thumbprint be affixed to the order; and

(2) may require that a photograph of the child be attached to the order.

(k) Except as provided by Subsection (m), the period to which a court or jury may sentence a person to commitment to the Texas Youth Commission with a transfer to the Texas Department of Criminal Justice under Subsection (d)(3) applies without regard to whether the person has previously been adjudicated as having engaged in delinquent conduct.

(*l*) Except as provided by Subsection (q), a court or jury may place a child on probation under Subsection (d)(1) for any period, except that probation may not continue on or after the child's 18th birthday. Except as provided by Subsection (q), the court may, before the period of probation ends, extend the probation for any period, except that the probation may not extend to or after the child's 18th birthday.

(m) The court or jury may sentence a child adjudicated for habitual felony conduct as described by Section 51.031 to a term prescribed by Subsection (d)(3) and applicable to the conduct adjudicated in the pending case if:

(1) a petition was filed and approved by a grand jury under Section 53.045 alleging that the child engaged in habitual felony conduct; and

(2) the court or jury finds beyond a reasonable doubt that the allegation described by Subdivision (1) in the grand jury petition is true.

(n) A court may order a disposition of secure confinement of a status offender adjudicated for violating a valid court order only if:

(1) before the order is issued, the child received the full due process rights guaranteed by the Constitution of the United States or the Texas Constitution; and

(2) the juvenile probation department in a report authorized by Subsection (b):

(A) reviewed the behavior of the child and the circumstances under which the child was brought before the court;

(B) determined the reasons for the behavior that caused the child to be brought before the court; and

(C) determined that all dispositions, including treatment, other than placement in a secure detention facility or secure correctional facility, have been exhausted or are clearly inappropriate.

(o) In a disposition under this title:

(1) a status offender may not, under any circumstances, be committed to the Texas Youth Commission for engaging in conduct that would not, under state or local law, be a crime if committed by an adult;

E *Subsections (2) & (3) below are effective for court dispositions made on or after Sept. 1, 2001.*

(2) a status offender may not, under any circumstances other than as provided under Subsection (n), be placed in a post-adjudication secure correctional facility; and

(3) a child adjudicated for contempt of a justice or municipal court order may not, under any circumstances, be placed in a post-adjudication secure correctional facility or committed to the Texas Youth Commission for that conduct.

(p) Except as provided by Subsection (*l*), a court that places a child on probation under Subsection (d)(1) for conduct described by Section 54.0405(b) and punishable as a felony shall specify a minimum probation period of two years.

(q) If a court or jury sentences a child to commitment in the Texas Youth Commission under Subsection (d)(3) for a term of not more than 10 years, the court or jury may place the child on probation under Subsection (d)(1) as an alternative to making the disposition under Subsection (d)(3). The court shall prescribe the period of probation ordered under this subsection for a term of not more than 10 years. The court may, before the sentence of probation expires, extend the probationary period under Section 54.05, except that the sentence of probation and any extension may not exceed 10 years. The court may, before the child's 18th birthday, discharge the child from the sentence of probation. If a sentence of probation ordered under this subsection and any extension of probation ordered under Section 54.05 will continue after the child's 18th birthday, the court shall discharge the child from the sentence of probation on the child's 18th birthday unless the court transfers the child to an appropriate district court under Section 54.051.

(r) If the judge orders a disposition under this section and there is an affirmative finding that the victim or intended victim was younger than 17 years of age at the time of the conduct, the judge shall enter the finding in the order.

(s) The court may make a disposition under Subsection (d)(2) for delinquent conduct that violates a penal law of the grade of misdemeanor if:

(1) the child has been adjudicated as having engaged in delinquent conduct violating a penal law of the grade of misdemeanor on at least two previous occasions;

(2) of the previous adjudications, the conduct that was the basis for one of the adjudications occurred after the date of another previous adjudication; and

(3) the conduct that is the basis of the current adjudication occurred after the date of at least two previous adjudications.

E *Subsections (t) & (u) below are effective for court dispositions made on or after Sept. 1, 2001.*

(t) The court may make a disposition under Subsection (d)(2) for delinquent conduct that violates a penal law of the grade of misdemeanor if:

(1) the child has been adjudicated as having engaged in delinquent conduct violating a penal law of the grade of felony on at least one previous occasion; and

(2) the conduct that is the basis of the current adjudication occurred after the date of that previous adjudication.

(u) For the purposes of disposition under Subsection (d)(2), delinquent conduct that violates a penal law of this state of the grade of felony or misdemeanor does not include conduct that violates a lawful order of a municipal, justice, or juvenile court under circumstances that would constitute contempt of that court.

History of Fam §54.04: Acts 1973, 63rd Leg., ch. 544, §1, eff. Sept. 1, 1973. Amended by Acts 1975, 64th Leg., ch. 693, §23, eff. Sept. 1, 1975; Acts 1981, 67th Leg., ch. 394, §1, eff. Aug. 31, 1981; Acts 1983, 68th Leg., ch. 44, art. 1, §3 (eff. April 26, 1983), ch. 565, §2 (eff. Sept. 1, 1983); Acts 1987, 70th Leg., ch. 385, §9 (eff. Sept. 1, 1987), ch. 1052, §6.11 (eff. Sept. 1, 1987); Acts 1989, 71st Leg., ch. 2, §16.01(17) (eff. Aug. 28, 1989), ch. 80, §1 (eff. Sept. 1, 1989); Acts 1991, 72nd Leg., ch. 557, §2 (eff. Sept. 1, 1991), ch. 574, §2 (eff. Sept. 1, 1991), ch. 784, §8 (eff. Sept. 1, 1991); Acts 1993, 73rd Leg., ch. 1048, §1, eff. Sept. 1, 1993; Acts 1995, 74th Leg., ch. 262, §38, eff. Jan. 1, 1996; Acts 1997, 75th Leg., ch. 669, §2 (eff. Sept. 1, 1997), ch. 1086, §11 (eff. Sept. 1, 1997); Acts 1999, 76th Leg., ch. 1193, §9 (eff. Sept. 1, 1999), ch. 1415, §19 (eff. Sept. 1, 1999), ch. 1448, §1 (eff. Sept. 1, 1999), ch. 1477, §10 (eff. Sept. 1, 1999); Acts 2001, 77th Leg., ch. 1297, §23 (eff. Sept. 1, 2001), ch. 1420, §5.001, eff. Sept. 1, 2001.

FAM §54.0405. CHILD PLACED ON PROBATION FOR CONDUCT CONSTITUTING SEXUAL OFFENSE

A (a) If a court or jury makes a disposition under Section 54.04 in which a child described by Subsection (b) is placed on probation, the court:

(1) may require as a condition of probation that the child:

(A) attend psychological counseling sessions for sex offenders as provided by Subsection (e); and

(B) submit to a polygraph examination as provided by Subsection (f) for purposes of evaluating the child's treatment progress; and

E (2) shall require as a condition of probation that the child:

(A) register under Chapter 62, Code of Criminal Procedure; and

(B) submit a blood sample or other specimen to the Department of Public Safety under Subchapter G, Chapter 411, Government Code, for the purpose of creating a DNA record of the child, unless the child has already submitted the required specimen under other state law.

A (b) This section applies to a child placed on probation for conduct constituting an offense for which the child is required to register as a sex offender under Chapter 62, Code of Criminal Procedure.

(c) Psychological counseling required as a condition of probation under Subsection (a) must be with an individual or organization that:

(1) provides sex offender treatment or counseling;

(2) is specified by the local juvenile probation department supervising the child; and

(3) meets minimum standards of counseling established by the local juvenile probation department.

(d) A polygraph examination required as a condition of probation under Subsection (a) must be administered by an individual who is:

(1) specified by the local juvenile probation department supervising the child; and

A (2) licensed as a polygraph examiner under Chapter 1703, Occupations Code.

(e) A local juvenile probation department that specifies a sex offender treatment provider under Subsection (c) to provide counseling to a child shall:

(1) establish with the cooperation of the treatment provider the date, time, and place of the first counseling session between the child and the treatment provider;

(2) notify the child and the treatment provider, not later than the 21st day after the date the order making the disposition placing the child on probation under Section 54.04 becomes final, of the date, time, and place of the first counseling session between the child and the treatment provider; and

(3) require the treatment provider to notify the department immediately if the child fails to attend any scheduled counseling session.

(f) A local juvenile probation department that specifies a polygraph examiner under Subsection (d) to administer a polygraph examination to a child shall arrange for a polygraph examination to be administered to the child:

(1) not later than the 60th day after the date the child attends the first counseling session established under Subsection (e); and

(2) after the initial polygraph examination, as required by Subdivision (1), on the request of the treatment provider specified under Subsection (c).

(g) A court that requires as a condition of probation that a child attend psychological counseling under Subsection (a) may order the parent or guardian of the child to:

(1) attend four sessions of instruction with an individual or organization specified by the court relating to:

(A) sexual offenses;

(B) family communication skills;

(C) sex offender treatment;

(D) victims' rights;

(E) parental supervision; and

(F) appropriate sexual behavior; and

(2) during the period the child attends psychological counseling, participate in monthly treatment groups conducted by the child's treatment provider relating to the child's psychological counseling.

(h) A court that orders a parent or guardian of a child to attend instructional sessions and participate in treatment groups under Subsection (g) shall require:

(1) the individual or organization specified by the court under Subsection (g) to notify the court immediately if the parent or guardian fails to attend any scheduled instructional session; and

(2) the child's treatment provider specified under Subsection (c) to notify the court immediately if the parent or guardian fails to attend a session in which the parent or guardian is required to participate in a scheduled treatment group.

(i) A court that requires as a condition of probation that a child attend psychological counseling under Subsection (a) may, before the date the probation period ends, extend the probation for any additional period necessary to complete the required counseling as determined by the treatment provider, except that the probation may not be extended to a date after the date of the child's 18th birthday.

History of Fam §54.0405: Acts 1997, 75th Leg., ch. 669, §1, eff. Sept. 1, 1997. Amended by Acts 2001, 77th Leg., ch. 211, §13 (eff. Sept. 1, 2001), ch. 1420, §14.743 (eff. Sept. 1, 2001).

FAM §54.0406. CHILD PLACED ON PROBATION FOR CONDUCT INVOLVING A HANDGUN

(a) If a court or jury places a child on probation under Section 54.04(d) for conduct that violates a penal law that includes as an element of the offense the possession, carrying, using, or exhibiting of a handgun, as defined by Section 46.01, Penal Code, and if at the adjudication hearing the court or jury affirmatively finds that the child personally possessed, carried, used, or exhibited the handgun, the court shall require as a condition of probation that the child, not later than the 30th day after the date the court places the child on probation, notify the juvenile probation officer who is supervising the child of the manner in which the child acquired the handgun, including the date and place of and any person involved in the acquisition.

(b) On receipt of information described by Subsection (a), a juvenile probation officer shall promptly notify the appropriate local law enforcement agency of the information.

(c) Information provided by a child to a juvenile probation officer as required by Subsection (a) and any other information derived from that information may not be used as evidence against the child in any juvenile or criminal proceeding.

History of Fam §54.0406: Acts 1999, 76th Leg., ch. 1446, §1, eff. Sept. 1, 1999.

FAM §54.0407. CRUELTY TO ANIMALS: COUNSELING REQUIRED

E *Section 54.0407 below is effective for offenses committed on or after Sept. 1, 2001.*

If a child is found to have engaged in delinquent conduct constituting an offense under Section 42.09, Penal Code, the juvenile court shall order the child to participate in psychological counseling for a period to be determined by the court.

History of Fam §54.0407: Enacted by Acts 2001, 77th Leg., ch. 450, §2, eff. Sept. 1, 2001.

FAM §54.041. ORDERS AFFECTING PARENTS & OTHERS

(a) When a child has been found to have engaged in delinquent conduct or conduct indicating a need for supervision and the juvenile court has made a finding that the child is in need of rehabilitation or that the protection of the public or the child requires that disposition be made, the juvenile court, on notice by any reasonable method to all persons affected, may:

(1) order any person found by the juvenile court to have, by a wilful act or omission, contributed to, caused, or encouraged the child's delinquent conduct or conduct indicating a need for supervision to do any act that the juvenile court determines to be reasonable and necessary for the welfare of the child or to refrain from doing any act that the juvenile court determines to be injurious to the welfare of the child;

(2) enjoin all contact between the child and a person who is found to be a contributing cause of the child's delinquent conduct or conduct indicating a need for supervision; or

(3) after notice and a hearing of all persons affected order any person living in the same household with the child to participate in social or psychological counseling to assist in the rehabilitation of the child and to strengthen the child's family environment.

Ⓐ *Subsection (b) below is effective for criminal conduct that occurs on or after Sept. 1, 2001.*

(b) If a child is found to have engaged in delinquent conduct or conduct indicating a need for supervision arising from the commission of an offense in which property damage or loss or personal injury occurred, the juvenile court, on notice to all persons affected and on hearing, may order the child or a parent to make full or partial restitution to the victim of the offense. The program of restitution must promote the rehabilitation of the child, be appropriate to the age and physical, emotional, and mental abilities of the child, and not conflict with the child's schooling. When practicable and subject to court supervision, the court may approve a restitution program based on a settlement between the child and the victim of the offense. An order under this subsection may provide for periodic payments by the child or a parent of the child for the period specified in the order but except as provided by Subsection (h), that period may not extend past the date of the 18th birthday of the child or past the date the child is no longer enrolled in an accredited secondary school in a program leading toward a high school diploma, whichever date is later.

Subsection (b) below is effective for criminal conduct in which any element of the conduct occurred before Sept. 1, 2001.

(b) If a child is found to have engaged in delinquent conduct or conduct indicating a need for supervision arising from the commission of an offense in which property damage or loss or personal injury occurred, the juvenile court, on notice to all persons affected and on hearing, may order the child or a parent to make full or partial restitution to the victim of the offense. The program of restitution must promote the rehabilitation of the child, be appropriate to the age and physical, emotional, and mental abilities of the child, and not conflict with the child's schooling. When practicable and subject to court supervision, the court may approve a restitution program based on a settlement between the child and the victim of the offense. An order under this subsection may provide for periodic payments by the child or a parent of the child for the period specified in the order but that period may not extend past the date of the 18th birthday of the child or past the date the child is no longer enrolled in an accredited secondary school in a program leading toward a high school diploma, whichever date is later.

(c) Restitution under this section is cumulative of any other remedy allowed by law and may be used in addition to other remedies; except that a victim of an offense is not entitled to receive more than actual damages under a juvenile court order.

(d) A person subject to an order proposed under Subsection (a) of this section is entitled to a hearing on the order before the order is entered by the court.

(e) An order made under this section may be enforced as provided by Section 54.07 of this code.

Ⓐ *Subsection (f) below is effective for children alleged to have engaged in conduct that occurs on or after Sept. 1, 2001.*

(f) If a child is found to have engaged in conduct indicating a need for supervision described under Section 51.03(b)(2) or (g), the court may order the child's parents or guardians to attend a program described by

Section 25.093(f), Education Code, if a program is available.

Subsection (f) below is effective for children alleged to have engaged in conduct in which every element of the conduct occurred before Sept. 1, 2001.

(f) If a child is found to have engaged in conduct indicating a need for supervision described under Section 51.03(b)(2) of this code, the court may order the child's parents or guardians to attend a class described by Section 25.093(h), Education Code, if the school district in which the child's parents or guardians reside offers a class under that section.

(g) On a finding by the court that a child's parents or guardians have made a reasonable good faith effort to prevent the child from engaging in delinquent conduct or engaging in conduct indicating a need for supervision and that, despite the parents' or guardians' efforts, the child continues to engage in such conduct, the court shall waive any requirement for restitution that may be imposed on a parent under this section.

E *Subsection (h) below is effective for criminal conduct that occurs on or after Sept. 1, 2001.*

(h) If the juvenile court places the child on probation in a determinate sentence proceeding initiated under Section 53.045 and transfers supervision on the child's 18th birthday to a district court for placement on community supervision, the district court shall require the payment of any unpaid restitution as a condition of the community supervision. The liability of the child's parent for restitution may not be extended by transfer to a district court for supervision.

History of Fam §54.041: Acts 1975, 64th Leg., ch. 693, §18, eff. Sept. 1, 1975. Amended by Acts 1979, 66th Leg., ch. 154, §2, eff. Sept. 1, 1979; Acts 1983, 68th Leg., ch. 110, §1 (eff. Aug. 29, 1983), ch. 565, §3 (eff. Sept. 1, 1983); Acts 1989, 71st Leg., ch. 1170, §3, eff. June 16, 1989; Acts 1995, 74th Leg., ch. 262, §39, eff. Jan. 1, 1996; Acts 1997, 75th Leg., ch. 165, §6.09, eff. Sept. 1, 1997; Acts 2001, 77th Leg., ch. 1514, §24 (eff. Sept. 1, 2001), ch. 1297, §15 (eff. Sept. 1, 2001).

FAM §54.0411. JUVENILE PROBATION DIVERSION FUND

(a) If a disposition hearing is held under Section 54.04 of this code, the juvenile court, after giving the child, parent, or other person responsible for the child's support a reasonable opportunity to be heard, shall order the child, parent, or other person, if financially able to do so, to pay a fee as costs of court of $20.

(b) Orders for the payment of fees under this section may be enforced as provided by Section 54.07 of this code.

(c) An officer collecting costs under this section shall keep separate records of the funds collected as costs under this section and shall deposit the funds in the county treasury.

(d) Each officer collecting court costs under this section shall file the reports required under Article 103.005, Code of Criminal Procedure. If no funds due as costs under this section have been collected in any quarter, the report required for each quarter shall be filed in the regular manner, and the report must state that no funds due under this section were collected.

(e) The custodian of the county treasury may deposit the funds collected under this section in interest-bearing accounts. The custodian shall keep records of the amount of funds on deposit collected under this section and not later than the last day of the month following each calendar quarter shall send to the comptroller of public accounts the funds collected under this section during the preceding quarter. A county may retain 10 percent of the funds as a service fee and may retain the interest accrued on the funds if the custodian of a county treasury keeps records of the amount of funds on deposit collected under this section and remits the funds to the comptroller within the period prescribed under this subsection.

(f) Funds collected are subject to audit by the comptroller and funds expended are subject to audit by the State Auditor.

(g) The comptroller shall deposit the funds in a special fund to be known as the juvenile probation diversion fund.

(h) The legislature shall determine and appropriate the necessary amount from the juvenile probation diversion fund to the Texas Juvenile Probation Commission for the purchase of services the commission considers necessary for the diversion of any juvenile who is at risk of commitment to the Texas Youth Commission. The Texas Juvenile Probation Commission shall develop guidelines for the use of the fund. The commission may not purchase the services if a person responsible for the child's support or a local juvenile probation department is financially able to provide the services.

History of Fam §54.0411: Acts 1987, 70th Leg., ch. 1040, §23, eff. Sept. 1, 1987. Amended by Acts 1989, 71st Leg., ch. 347, §8, eff. Oct. 1, 1989.

FAM §54.042. LICENSE SUSPENSION

(a) A juvenile court, in a disposition hearing under Section 54.04, shall:

(1) order the Department of Public Safety to suspend a child's driver's license or permit, or if the child does not have a license or permit, to deny the issuance of a license or permit to the child if the court finds that the child has engaged in conduct that violates a law of this state enumerated in Section 521.342(a), Transportation Code; or

(2) notify the Department of Public Safety of the adjudication, if the court finds that the child has engaged in conduct that violates a law of this state enumerated in Section 521.372(a), Transportation Code.

(b) A juvenile court, in a disposition hearing under Section 54.04, may order the Department of Public Safety to suspend a child's driver's license or permit or, if the child does not have a license or permit, to deny the issuance of a license or permit to the child, if the court finds that the child has engaged in conduct that violates Section 28.08, Penal Code.

(c) The order under Subsection (a)(1) shall specify a period of suspension or denial that is until the child reaches the age of 19 or for a period of 365 days, whichever is longer.

(d) The order under Subsection (b) shall specify a period of suspension or denial that is:

(1) for a period not to exceed 365 days; or

(2) if the court finds the child has been previously adjudicated as having engaged in conduct violating Section 28.08, Penal Code, until the child reaches the age of 19 or for a period not to exceed 365 days, whichever is longer.

(e) A child whose driver's license or permit has been suspended or denied pursuant to this section may, if the child is otherwise eligible for, and fulfils the requirements for issuance of, a provisional driver's license or permit under Chapter 521, Transportation Code, apply for and receive an occupational license in accordance with the provisions of Subchapter L of that chapter.

(f) A juvenile court, in a disposition hearing under Section 54.04, may order the Department of Public Safety to suspend a child's driver's license or permit or, if the child does not have a license or permit, to deny the issuance of a license or permit to the child for a period not to exceed 12 months if the court finds that the child has engaged in conduct in need of supervision or delinquent conduct other than the conduct described by Subsection (a).

(g) A juvenile court that places a child on probation under Section 54.04 may require as a reasonable condition of the probation that if the child violates the probation, the court may order the Department of Public Safety to suspend the child's driver's license or permit or, if the child does not have a license or permit, to deny the issuance of a license or permit to the child for a period not to exceed 12 months. The court may make this order if a child that is on probation under this condition violates the probation. A suspension under this subsection is cumulative of any other suspension under this section.

(h) If a child is adjudicated for conduct that violates Section 49.04, 49.07, or 49.08, Penal Code, and if any conduct on which that adjudication is based is a ground for a driver's license suspension under Chapter 524 or 724, Transportation Code, each of the suspensions shall be imposed. The court imposing a driver's license suspension under this section shall credit a period of suspension imposed under Chapter 524 or 724, Transportation Code, toward the period of suspension required under this section, except that if the child was previously adjudicated for conduct that violates Section 49.04, 49.07, or 49.08, Penal Code, credit may not be given.

History of Fam §54.042: Acts 1983, 68th Leg., ch. 303, §25, eff. Jan. 1, 1984. Amended by Acts 1985, 69th Leg., ch. 629, §1, eff. Sept. 1, 1985; Acts 1991, 72nd Leg., ch. 14, §284(42) (eff. Sept. 1, 1991), ch. 784, §7 (eff. Sept. 1, 1991); Acts 1993, 73rd Leg., ch. 491, §3, eff. June 15, 1993; Acts 1995, 74th Leg., ch. 76, §14.32 (eff. Sept. 1, 1995); Acts 1995, 74th Leg., ch. 262, §40 (eff. Jan. 1, 1996); Acts 1997, 75th Leg., ch. 165, §30.183 (eff. Sept. 1, 1997), ch. 593, §3 (eff. Sept. 1, 1997), ch. 1013, §17 (eff. Sept. 1, 1997); Acts 1999, 76th Leg., ch. 62, §19.01(18), eff. Sept. 1, 1999.

FAM §54.043. MONITORING SCHOOL ATTENDANCE

If the court places a child on probation under Section 54.04(d) and requires as a condition of probation that the child attend school, the probation officer charged with supervising the child shall monitor the child's school attendance and report to the court if the child is voluntarily absent from school.

History of Fam §54.043: Acts 1993, 73rd Leg., ch. 347, §6.02, eff. Sept. 1, 1993.

FAM §54.044. COMMUNITY SERVICE

Ⓐ *Subsection (a) below is effective for criminal conduct that occurs on or after Sept. 1, 2001.*

(a) If the court places a child on probation under Section 54.04(d), the court shall require as a condition of probation that the child work a specified number of hours at a community service project approved by the court and designated by the juvenile probation department as provided by Subsection (e), unless the court determines and enters a finding on the order placing the child on probation that:

Subsection (a) below is effective for criminal conduct in which any element of the conduct occurred before Sept. 1, 2001.

(a) If the court places a child on probation under Section 54.04(d), the court shall require as a condition of probation that the child work a specified number of hours at a community service project approved by the court and designated by the juvenile board as provided by Subsection (e), unless the court determines and enters a finding on the order placing the child on probation that:

(1) the child is physically or mentally incapable of participating in the project;

(2) participating in the project will be a hardship on the child or the family of the child; or

(3) the child has shown good cause that community service should not be required.

(b) The court may also order under this section that the child's parent perform community service with the child.

(c) The court shall order that the child and the child's parent perform a total of not more than 500 hours of community service under this section.

(d) A municipality or county that establishes a program to assist children and their parents in rendering community service under this section may purchase insurance policies protecting the municipality or county against claims brought by a person other than the child or the child's parent for a cause of action that arises from an act of the child or parent while rendering community service. The municipality or county is not liable under this section to the extent that damages are recoverable under a contract of insurance or under a plan of self-insurance authorized by statute. The liability of the municipality or county for a cause of action that arises from an action of the child or the child's parent while rendering community service may not exceed $100,000 to a single person and $300,000 for a single occurrence in the case of personal injury or death, and $10,000 for a single occurrence of property damage. Liability may not extend to punitive or exemplary damages. This subsection does not waive a defense, immunity, or jurisdictional bar available to the municipality or county or its officers or employees, nor shall this section be construed to waive, repeal, or modify any provision of Chapter 101, Civil Practice and Remedies Code.

(e) For the purposes of this section, a court may submit to the juvenile probation department a list of organizations or projects approved by the court for community service. The juvenile probation department may:

(1) designate an organization or project for community service only from the list submitted by the court; and

(2) reassign or transfer a child to a different organization or project on the list submitted by the court under this subsection without court approval.

(f) A person subject to an order proposed under Subsection (a) or (b) is entitled to a hearing on the order before the order is entered by the court.

(g) On a finding by the court that a child's parents or guardians have made a reasonable good faith effort to prevent the child from engaging in delinquent conduct or engaging in conduct indicating a need for supervision and that, despite the parents' or guardians' efforts, the child continues to engage in such conduct, the court shall waive any requirement for community service that may be imposed on a parent under this section.

(h) An order made under this section may be enforced as provided by Section 54.07.

(i) In a disposition hearing under Section 54.04 in which the court finds that a child engaged in conduct violating Section 521.453, Transportation Code, the court, in addition to any other order authorized under this title and if the court is located in a municipality or county that has established a community service program, may order the child to perform eight hours of community service as a condition of probation under Section 54.04(d) unless the child is shown to have previously engaged in conduct violating Section 521.453, Transportation Code, in which case the court may order the child to perform 12 hours of community service.

History of Fam §54.044: Acts 1995, 74th Leg., ch. 262, §41, eff. Jan. 1, 1996. Amended by Acts 1997, 75th Leg., ch. 1358, §2, eff. Sept. 1, 1997; Acts 2001, 77th Leg., ch. 1297, §25, eff. Sept. 1, 2001.

FAM §54.045. ADMISSION OF UNADJUDICATED CONDUCT

(a) During a disposition hearing under Section 54.04, a child may:

(1) admit having engaged in delinquent conduct or conduct indicating a need for supervision for which the child has not been adjudicated; and

FAM §54.044

(2) request the court to take the admitted conduct into account in the disposition of the child.

(b) If the prosecuting attorney agrees in writing, the court may take the admitted conduct into account in the disposition of the child.

(c) A court may take into account admitted conduct over which exclusive venue lies in another county only if the court obtains the written permission of the prosecuting attorney for that county.

(d) A child may not be adjudicated by any court for having engaged in conduct taken into account under this section, except that, if the conduct taken into account included conduct over which exclusive venue lies in another county and the written permission of the prosecuting attorney of that county was not obtained, the child may be adjudicated for that conduct, but the child's admission under this section may not be used against the child in the adjudication.

History of Fam §54.045: Acts 1995, 74th Leg., ch. 262, §41, eff. Jan. 1, 1996.

FAM §54.046. CONDITIONS OF PROBATION FOR DAMAGING PROPERTY WITH GRAFFITI

(a) If a juvenile court places on probation under Section 54.04(d) a child adjudicated as having engaged in conduct in violation of Section 28.08, Penal Code, in addition to other conditions of probation, the court may, with consent of the owner of the property, order the child as a condition of probation to restore the property by removing or painting over any markings made by the child on the property.

(b) In addition to a condition imposed under Subsection (a), the court may require the child as a condition of probation to attend a class with instruction in self-responsibility and empathy for a victim of an offense conducted by a local juvenile probation department.

History of Fam §54.046: Acts 1997, 75th Leg., ch. 593, §7, eff. Sept. 1, 1997.

FAM §54.0461. PAYMENT OF GRAFFITI ERADICATION FEES

(a) If a child is adjudicated as having engaged in delinquent conduct that violates Section 28.08, Penal Code, the juvenile court shall order the child, parent, or other person responsible for the child's support to pay to the court a $5 graffiti eradication fee as a cost of court.

(b) The court shall deposit fees received under this section to the credit of the county graffiti eradication fund provided for under Article 102.0171, Code of Criminal Procedure.

(c) If the court finds that a child, parent, or other person responsible for the child's support is unable to pay the graffiti eradication fee required under Subsection (a), the court shall enter into the child's case records a statement of that finding. The court may waive a fee under this section only if the court makes the finding under this subsection.

History of Fam §54.0461: Acts 1999, 76th Leg., ch. 174, §1, eff. Sept. 1, 1999.

FAM §54.047. ALCOHOL RELATED OFFENSE

If the court or jury finds at an adjudication hearing for a child that the child engaged in conduct indicating a need for supervision or delinquent conduct that violates the alcohol-related offenses in Section 106.02, 106.025, 106.04, 106.05, or 106.07, Alcoholic Beverage Code, or Section 49.02, Penal Code, the court shall, subject to a finding under Section 54.04(c), order, in addition to any other order authorized by this title, that, in the manner provided by Section 106.071(d), Alcoholic Beverage Code:

(1) the child perform community service; and

(2) the child's driver's license or permit be suspended or that the child be denied issuance of a driver's license or permit.

History of Fam §54.047: Acts 1997, 75th Leg., ch. 1013, §18, eff. Sept. 1, 1997. Renumbered from §54.046 by Acts 1999, 76th Leg., ch. 62, §19.01(19), eff. Sept. 1, 1999.

FAM §54.048. RESTITUTION

E *Section 54.048 below is effective for criminal conduct that occurs on or after Sept. 1, 2001.*

(a) A juvenile court, in a disposition hearing under Section 54.04, may order restitution to be made by the child and the child's parents.

(b) This section applies without regard to whether the petition in the case contains a plea for restitution.

History of Fam §54.048: Enacted by Acts 2001, 77th Leg., ch. 1297, §26, eff. Sept. 1, 2001.

FAM §54.05. HEARING TO MODIFY DISPOSITION

(a) Any disposition, except a commitment to the Texas Youth Commission, may be modified by the juvenile court as provided in this section until:

(1) the child reaches his 18th birthday; or

(2) the child is earlier discharged by the court or operation of law.

(b) Except for a commitment to the Texas Youth Commission, all dispositions automatically terminate when the child reaches his 18th birthday.

(c) There is no right to a jury at a hearing to modify disposition.

A *Subsection (d) below is effective for criminal conduct that occurs on or after Sept. 1, 2001.*

(d) A hearing to modify disposition shall be held on the petition of the child and his parent, guardian, guardian ad litem, or attorney, or on the petition of the state, a probation officer, or the court itself. Reasonable notice of a hearing to modify disposition shall be given to all parties.

Subsection (d) below is effective for criminal conduct in which any element of the conduct occurred before Sept. 1, 2001.

(d) A hearing to modify disposition shall be held on the petition of the child and his parent, guardian, guardian ad litem, or attorney, or on the petition of the state, a probation officer, or the court itself. Reasonable notice of a hearing to modify disposition shall be given to all parties. When the petition to modify is filed under Section 51.03(a)(2) of this code, the court must hold an adjudication hearing and make an affirmative finding prior to considering any written reports under Subsection (e) of this section.

(e) After the hearing on the merits or facts, the court may consider written reports from probation officers, professional court employees, or professional consultants in addition to the testimony of other witnesses. Prior to the hearing to modify disposition, the court shall provide the attorney for the child with access to all written matter to be considered by the court in deciding whether to modify disposition. The court may order counsel not to reveal items to the child or his parent, guardian, or guardian ad litem if such disclosure would materially harm the treatment and rehabilitation of the child or would substantially decrease the likelihood of receiving information from the same or similar sources in the future.

A (f) Except as provided by Subsection (j), a disposition based on a finding that the child engaged in delinquent conduct that violates a penal law of this state or the United States of the grade of felony or, if the requirements of Subsection (k) are met, of the grade of misdemeanor, may be modified so as to commit the child to the Texas Youth Commission if the court after a hearing to modify disposition finds by a preponderance of the evidence that the child violated a reasonable and lawful order of the court. A disposition based on a finding that the child engaged in habitual felony conduct as described by Section 51.031 or in delinquent conduct that included a violation of a penal law listed in Section 53.045(a) may be modified to commit the child to the Texas Youth Commission with a possible transfer to the institutional division or the pardons and paroles division of the Texas Department of Criminal Justice for a definite term prescribed by Section 54.04(d)(3) if the original petition was approved by the grand jury under Section 53.045 and if after a hearing to modify the disposition the court finds that the child violated a reasonable and lawful order of the court.

A (g) Except as provided by Subsection (j), a disposition based solely on a finding that the child engaged in conduct indicating a need for supervision may not be modified to commit the child to the Texas Youth Commission. A new finding in compliance with Section 54.03 must be made that the child engaged in delinquent conduct that meets the requirements for commitment under Section 54.04.

A *Subsection (h) below is effective for criminal conduct that occurs on or after Sept. 1, 2001.*

(h) A hearing shall be held prior to placement in a post-adjudication secure correctional facility for a period longer than 30 days or commitment to the Texas Youth Commission as a modified disposition. In other disposition modifications, the child and the child's parent, guardian, guardian ad litem, or attorney may waive hearing in accordance with Section 51.09.

Subsection (h) below is effective for criminal conduct in which any element of the conduct occurred before Sept. 1, 2001.

(h) A hearing shall be held prior to commitment to the Texas Youth Commission as a modified disposition. In other disposition modifications, the child and the child's parent, guardian, guardian ad litem, or attorney may waive hearing in accordance with Section 51.09.

(i) The court shall specifically state in the order its reasons for modifying the disposition and shall furnish a copy of the order to the child.

(j) If, after conducting a hearing to modify disposition without a jury, the court finds by a preponderance of the evidence that a child violated a reasonable and lawful condition of probation ordered under Section 54.04(q), the court may modify the disposition to commit the child to the Texas Youth Commission under

Section 54.04(d)(3) for a term that does not exceed the original sentence assessed by the court or jury.

A *Subsection (k) below is effective for criminal conduct that occurs on or after Sept. 1, 2001.*

(k) The court may modify a disposition under Subsection (f) that is based on a finding that the child engaged in delinquent conduct that violates a penal law of the grade of misdemeanor if:

(1) the child has been adjudicated as having engaged in delinquent conduct violating a penal law of the grade of felony or misdemeanor on at least two previous occasions; and

(2) of the previous adjudications, the conduct that was the basis for one of the adjudications occurred after the date of another previous adjudication.

Subsection (j) below is effective for criminal conduct in which any element of the conduct occurred before Sept. 1, 2001.

(j) The court may modify a disposition under Subsection (f) that is based on a finding that the child engaged in delinquent conduct that violates a penal law of the grade of misdemeanor if:

(1) the child has been adjudicated as having engaged in delinquent conduct violating a penal law of the grade of felony or misdemeanor on at least two previous occasions; and

(2) of the previous adjudications, the conduct that was the basis for the adjudications occurred after the date of another previous adjudication.

History of Fam §54.05: Acts 1973, 63rd Leg., ch. 544, §1, eff. Sept. 1, 1973. Amended by Acts 1979, 66th Leg., ch. 743, §1, eff. Aug. 27, 1979; Acts 1983, 68th Leg., ch. 44, art. 1, §4, eff. April 26, 1983; Acts 1985, 69th Leg., ch. 45, §3, eff. Sept. 1, 1985; Acts 1987, 70th Leg., ch. 385, §10, eff. Sept. 1, 1987; Acts 1991, 72nd Leg., ch. 557, §3, eff. Sept. 1, 1991; Acts 1995, 74th Leg., ch. 262, §42, eff. Jan. 1, 1996; Acts 1999, 76th Leg., ch. 1448, §2 (eff. Sept. 1, 1999), ch. 1477, §11 (eff. Sept. 1, 1999); Acts 2001, 77th Leg., ch. 1297, §§27, 28 (eff. Sept. 1, 2001), ch. 1420, §5.002 (eff. Sept. 1, 2001).

FAM §54.051. TRANSFER OF DETERMINATE SENTENCE PROBATION TO APPROPRIATE DISTRICT COURT

(a) On motion of the state concerning a child who is placed on probation under Section 54.04(q) for a period, including any extension ordered under Section 54.05, that will continue after the child's 18th birthday, the juvenile court shall hold a hearing to determine whether to transfer the child to an appropriate district court or discharge the child from the sentence of probation.

(b) The hearing must be conducted before the child's 18th birthday and in the same manner as a hearing to modify disposition under Section 54.05.

(c) If, after a hearing, the court determines to discharge the child, the court shall specify a date on or before the child's 18th birthday to discharge the child from the sentence of probation.

(d) If, after a hearing, the court determines to transfer the child, the court shall transfer the child to an appropriate district court on the child's 18th birthday.

(e) A district court that exercises jurisdiction over a child transferred under Subsection (d) shall place the child on community supervision under Article 42.12, Code of Criminal Procedure, for the remainder of the child's probationary period and under conditions consistent with those ordered by the juvenile court. If a child who is placed on community supervision under this subsection violates a condition of that supervision or if the child violated a condition of probation ordered under Section 54.04(q) and that probation violation was not discovered by the state before the child's 18th birthday, the district court shall dispose of the violation of community supervision or probation, as appropriate, in the same manner as if the court had originally exercised jurisdiction over the case. The time that a child serves on probation ordered under Section 54.04(q) is the same as time served on community supervision ordered under this subsection for purposes of determining the child's eligibility for early discharge from community supervision under Section 20, Article 42.12, Code of Criminal Procedure.

(f) The juvenile court may transfer a child to an appropriate district court as provided by this section without a showing that the child violated a condition of probation ordered under Section 54.04(q).

History of Fam §54.051: Acts 1999, 76th Leg., ch. 1477, §12, eff. Sept. 1, 1999.

FAM §54.06. JUDGMENTS FOR SUPPORT

(a) At any stage of the proceeding, when a child has been placed outside the child's home, the juvenile court, after giving the parent or other person responsible for the child's support a reasonable opportunity to be heard, shall order the parent or other person to pay in a manner directed by the court a reasonable sum for the support in whole or in part of the child or the court shall waive the payment by order. The court shall order that the payment for support be made to the local juvenile

FAM §54.06

probation department to be used only for residential care and other support for the child unless the child has been committed to the Texas Youth Commission, in which case the court shall order that the payment be made to the Texas Youth Commission for deposit in a special account in the general revenue fund that may be appropriated only for the care of children committed to the commission.

(b) At any stage of the proceeding, when a child has been placed outside the child's home and the parent of the child is obligated to pay support for the child under a court order under Title 5, the juvenile court shall order that the person entitled to receive the support assign the person's right to support for the child placed outside the child's home to the local juvenile probation department to be used for residential care and other support for the child unless the child has been committed to the Texas Youth Commission, in which event the court shall order that the assignment be made to the Texas Youth Commission.

(c) A court may enforce an order for support under this section by ordering garnishment of the wages of the person ordered to pay support or by any other means available to enforce a child support order under Title 5.

(d) An order for support may be enforced as provided in Section 54.07 of this code.

(e) The court shall apply the child support guidelines under Subchapter C, Chapter 154, in an order requiring the payment of child support under this section. The court shall also require in an order to pay child support under this section that health insurance be provided for the child. Subchapter D, Chapter 154, applies to an order requiring health insurance for a child under this section.

(f) An order under this section prevails over any previous child support order issued with regard to the child to the extent of any conflict between the orders.

History of Fam §54.06: Acts 1973, 63rd Leg., ch. 544, §1, eff. Sept. 1, 1973. Amended by Acts 1983, 68th Leg., ch. 44, art. 1, §5, eff. April 26, 1983; Acts 1987, 70th Leg., ch. 1040, §24, eff. Sept. 1, 1987; Acts 1993, 73rd Leg., ch. 798, §23, eff. Sept. 1, 1993; Acts 1993, 73rd Leg., ch. 1048, §2, eff. Sept. 1, 1993; Acts 1995, 74th Leg., ch. 262, §43, eff. Jan. 1, 1996; Acts 1997, 75th Leg., ch. 165, §7.11, eff. Sept. 1, 1997.

FAM §54.061. PAYMENT OF PROBATION FEES

(a) If a child is placed on probation under Section 54.04(d)(1) of this code, the juvenile court, after giving the child, parent, or other person responsible for the child's support a reasonable opportunity to be heard, shall order the child, parent, or other person, if financially able to do so, to pay to the court a fee of not more than $15 a month during the period that the child continues on probation.

(b) Orders for the payment of fees under this section may be enforced as provided by Section 54.07 of this code.

(c) The court shall deposit the fees received under this section in the county treasury to the credit of a special fund that may be used only for juvenile probation or community-based juvenile corrections services or facilities in which a juvenile may be required to live while under court supervision.

(d) If the court finds that a child, parent, or other person responsible for the child's support is financially unable to pay the probation fee required under Subsection (a), the court shall enter into the records of the child's case a statement of that finding. The court may waive a fee under this section only if the court makes the finding under this subsection.

History of Fam §54.061: Acts 1979, 66th Leg., ch. 154, §1, eff. Sept. 1, 1979. Amended by Acts 1981, 67th Leg., ch. 617, §4, eff. Sept. 1, 1981; Acts 1987, 70th Leg., ch. 1040, §25, eff. Sept. 1, 1987; Acts 1995, 74th Leg., ch. 262, §44, eff. Jan. 1, 1996.

FAM §54.07. ENFORCEMENT OF ORDER

(a) Any order of the juvenile court may be enforced by contempt.

(b) The juvenile court may enforce its order for support or for the payment of restitution or probation fees by civil contempt proceedings after 10 days' notice to the defaulting person of his failure or refusal to carry out the terms of the order.

(c) On the motion of the juvenile court or any person or agency entitled to receive restitution or probation payments or payments for the benefit of a child, the juvenile court may render judgment against a defaulting person for any amount unpaid and owing after 10 days' notice to the defaulting person of his failure or refusal to carry out the terms of the order. The judgment may be enforced by any means available for the enforcement of judgments for other debts.

History of Fam §54.07: Acts 1973, 63rd Leg., ch. 544, §1, eff. Sept. 1, 1973. Amended by Acts 1979, 66th Leg., ch. 154, §3, eff. Sept. 1, 1979.

FAM §54.08. PUBLIC ACCESS TO COURT HEARINGS

(a) Except as provided by this section, the court shall open hearings under this title to the public unless the court, for good cause shown, determines that the public should be excluded.

(b) The court may not prohibit a person who is a victim of the conduct of a child, or the person's family, from personally attending a hearing under this title relating to the conduct by the child unless the victim or member of the victim's family is to testify in the hearing or any subsequent hearing relating to the conduct and the court determines that the victim's or family member's testimony would be materially affected if the victim or member of the victim's family hears other testimony at trial.

(c) If a child is under the age of 14 at the time of the hearing, the court shall close the hearing to the public unless the court finds that the interests of the child or the interests of the public would be better served by opening the hearing to the public.

(d) In this section, "family" has the meaning assigned by Section 71.003.

History of Fam §54.08: Acts 1973, 63rd Leg., ch. 544, §1, eff. Sept. 1, 1973. Amended by Acts 1987, 70th Leg., ch. 385, §11, eff. Sept. 1, 1987; Acts 1995, 74th Leg., ch. 262, §45, eff. Jan. 1, 1996; Acts 1997, 75th Leg., ch. 1086, §12, eff. Sept. 1, 1997.

FAM §54.09. RECORDING OF PROCEEDINGS

All judicial proceedings under this chapter except detention hearings shall be recorded by stenographic notes or by electronic, mechanical, or other appropriate means. Upon request of any party, a detention hearing shall be recorded.

History of Fam §54.09: Acts 1973, 63rd Leg., ch. 544, §1, eff. Sept. 1, 1973.

FAM §54.10. HEARINGS BEFORE REFEREE

(a) Except as provided by Subsection (e), a hearing under Section 54.03, 54.04, or 54.05, including a jury trial, a hearing under Chapter 55, including a jury trial, or a hearing under Article IV, Article V, and Article VI of the Uniform Interstate Compact on Juveniles (Chapter 60) may be held by a referee appointed in accordance with Section 51.04(g) or a master appointed under Chapter 54, Government Code, provided:

(1) the parties have been informed by the referee or master that they are entitled to have the hearing before the juvenile court judge; and

(2) after each party is given an opportunity to object, no party objects to holding the hearing before the referee or master.

(b) The determination under Section 53.02(f) whether to release a child may be made by a referee appointed in accordance with Section 51.04(g) if:

(1) the child has been informed by the referee that the child is entitled to have the determination made by the juvenile court judge or a substitute judge authorized by Section 51.04(f); or

(2) the child and the attorney for the child have in accordance with Section 51.09 waived the right to have the determination made by the juvenile court judge or a substitute judge.

(c) If a child objects to a referee making the determination under Section 53.02(f), the juvenile court judge or a substitute judge authorized by Section 51.04(f) shall make the determination.

(d) At the conclusion of the hearing or immediately after making the determination, the referee shall transmit written findings and recommendations to the juvenile court judge. The juvenile court judge shall adopt, modify, or reject the referee's recommendations not later than the next working day after the day that the judge receives the recommendations. Failure to act within that time results in release of the child by operation of law and a recommendation that the child be released operates to secure the child's immediate release subject to the power of the juvenile court judge to modify or reject that recommendation.

(e) The hearings provided by Sections 54.03, 54.04, and 54.05 may not be held before a referee if the grand jury has approved of the petition and the child is subject to a determinate sentence.

History of Fam §54.10: Acts 1975, 64th Leg., ch. 693, §19, eff. Sept. 1, 1975. Amended by Acts 1979, 66th Leg., ch. 743, §2, eff. Aug. 27, 1979; Acts 1987, 70th Leg., ch. 385, §12, eff. Sept. 1, 1987; Acts 1991, 72nd Leg., ch. 74, §1, eff. Sept. 1, 1991; Acts 1997, 75th Leg., ch. 1086, §13, eff. Sept. 1, 1997; Acts 1999, 76th Leg., ch. 232, §5 (eff. Sept. 1, 1999), ch. 1477, §13 (eff. Sept. 1, 1999).

FAM §54.11. RELEASE OR TRANSFER HEARING

(a) On receipt of a referral under Section 61.079(a), Human Resources Code, for the transfer to the institutional division of the Texas Department of Criminal Justice of a person committed to the Texas Youth Commission under Section 54.04(d)(3), 54.04(m), or 54.05(f), or on receipt of a request by the commission under Section 61.081(g), Human Resources Code, for approval of the release under supervision of a person committed to the commission under Section 54.04(d)(3), 54.04(m), or 54.05(f), the court shall set a time and place for a hearing on the release of the person.

(b) The court shall notify the following of the time and place of the hearing:

(1) the person to be transferred or released under supervision;

(2) the parents of the person;

(3) any legal custodian of the person, including the Texas Youth Commission;

(4) the office of the prosecuting attorney that represented the state in the juvenile delinquency proceedings;

(5) the victim of the offense that was included in the delinquent conduct that was a ground for the disposition, or a member of the victim's family; and

(6) any other person who has filed a written request with the court to be notified of a release hearing with respect to the person to be transferred or released under supervision.

(c) Except for the person to be transferred or released under supervision and the prosecuting attorney, the failure to notify a person listed in Subsection (b) of this section does not affect the validity of a hearing conducted or determination made under this section if the record in the case reflects that the whereabouts of the persons who did not receive notice were unknown to the court and a reasonable effort was made by the court to locate those persons.

A *Subsection (d) below is effective for criminal conduct that occurs on or after Sept. 1, 2001.*

(d) At a hearing under this section the court may consider written reports from probation officers, professional court employees, professional consultants, or employees of the Texas Youth Commission, in addition to the testimony of witnesses. At least one day before the hearing, the court shall provide the attorney for the person to be transferred or released under supervision with access to all written matter to be considered by the court.

Subsection (d) below is effective for criminal conduct in which any element of the conduct occurred before Sept. 1, 2001.

(d) At a hearing under this section the court may consider written reports from probation officers, professional court employees, or professional consultants, in addition to the testimony of witnesses. At least one day before the hearing, the court shall provide the attorney for the person to be transferred or released under supervision with access to all written matter to be considered by the court.

(e) At the hearing, the person to be transferred or released under supervision is entitled to an attorney, to examine all witnesses against him, to present evidence and oral argument, and to previous examination of all reports on and evaluations and examinations of or relating to him that may be used in the hearing.

(f) A hearing under this section is open to the public unless the person to be transferred or released under supervision waives a public hearing with the consent of his attorney and the court.

(g) A hearing under this section must be recorded by a court reporter or by audio or video tape recording, and the record of the hearing must be retained by the court for at least two years after the date of the final determination on the transfer or release of the person by the court.

(h) The hearing on a person who is referred for transfer under Section 61.079(a), Human Resources Code, shall be held not later than the 60th day after the date the court receives the referral.

(i) On conclusion of the hearing on a person who is referred for transfer under Section 61.079(a), Human Resources Code, the court may order:

(1) the return of the person to the Texas Youth Commission; or

(2) the transfer of the person to the custody of the institutional division of the Texas Department of Criminal Justice for the completion of the person's sentence.

(j) On conclusion of the hearing on a person who is referred for release under supervision under Section 61.081(f), Human Resources Code, the court may order the return of the person to the Texas Youth Commission:

(1) with approval for the release of the person under supervision; or

(2) without approval for the release of the person under supervision.

(k) In making a determination under this section, the court may consider the experiences and character of the person before and after commitment to the youth commission, the nature of the penal offense that the person was found to have committed and the manner in which the offense was committed, the abilities of the person to contribute to society, the protection of the victim of the offense or any member of the victim's family, the recommendations of the youth commission and prosecuting attorney, the best interests of the person, and any other factor relevant to the issue to be decided.

History of Fam §54.11: Acts 1987, 70th Leg., ch. 385, §13, eff. Sept. 1, 1987. Amended by Acts 1991, 72nd Leg., ch. 574, §3, eff. Sept. 1, 1991; Acts 1995, 74th Leg., ch. 262, §46, eff. Jan. 1, 1996; Acts 2001, 77th Leg., ch. 1297, §29, eff. Sept. 1, 2001.

CHAPTER 55. PROCEEDINGS CONCERNING CHILDREN WITH MENTAL ILLNESS OR MENTAL RETARDATION

SUBCHAPTER A. GENERAL PROVISIONS

FAM §55.01. MEANING OF "HAVING A MENTAL ILLNESS"

For purposes of this chapter, a child who is described as having a mental illness means a child who suffers from mental illness as defined by Section 571.003, Health and Safety Code.

History of Fam §55.01: Acts 1999, 76th Leg., ch. 1477, §14, eff. Sept. 1, 1999.

FAM §55.02. MENTAL HEALTH & MENTAL RETARDATION JURISDICTION

For the purpose of initiating proceedings to order mental health or mental retardation services for a child or for commitment of a child as provided by this chapter, the juvenile court has jurisdiction of proceedings under Subtitle C or D, Title 7, Health and Safety Code.

History of Fam §55.02: Acts 1999, 76th Leg., ch. 1477, §14, eff. Sept. 1, 1999.

FAM §55.03. STANDARDS OF CARE

(a) Except as provided by this chapter, a child for whom inpatient mental health services is ordered by a court under this chapter shall be cared for as provided by Subtitle C, Title 7, Health and Safety Code.

(b) Except as provided by this chapter, a child who is committed by a court to a residential care facility for mental retardation shall be cared for as provided by Subtitle D, Title 7, Health and Safety Code.

History of Fam §55.03: Acts 1999, 76th Leg., ch. 1477, §14, eff. Sept. 1, 1999.

FAM §55.04. RENUMBERED

Renumbered as §§55.31, 55.32 by Acts 1999, 76th Leg., ch. 1477, §14, eff. Sept. 1, 1999.

FAM §55.05. RENUMBERED

Renumbered as §55.51 by Acts 1999, 76th Leg., ch. 1477, §14, eff. Sept. 1, 1999.

Sections 55.06-55.10 reserved for expansion

SUBCHAPTER B. CHILD WITH MENTAL ILLNESS

FAM §55.11. MENTAL ILLNESS DETERMINATION; EXAMINATION

(a) On a motion by a party, the juvenile court shall determine whether probable cause exists to believe that a child who is alleged by petition or found to have engaged in delinquent conduct or conduct indicating a need for supervision has a mental illness. In making its determination, the court may:

(1) consider the motion, supporting documents, professional statements of counsel, and witness testimony; and

(2) make its own observation of the child.

(b) If the court determines that probable cause exists to believe that the child has a mental illness, the court shall temporarily stay the juvenile court proceedings and immediately order the child to be examined under Section 51.20. The information obtained from the examination must include expert opinion as to whether the child has a mental illness and whether the child meets the commitment criteria under Subtitle C, Title 7, Health and Safety Code. If ordered by the court, the information must also include expert opinion as to whether the child is unfit to proceed with the juvenile court proceedings.

(c) After considering all relevant information, including information obtained from an examination under Section 51.20, the court shall:

(1) if the court determines that evidence exists to support a finding that the child has a mental illness and that the child meets the commitment criteria under Subtitle C, Title 7, Health and Safety Code, proceed under Section 55.12; or

(2) if the court determines that evidence does not exist to support a finding that the child has a mental illness or that the child meets the commitment criteria under Subtitle C, Title 7, Health and Safety Code, dissolve the stay and continue the juvenile court proceedings.

History of Fam §55.11: Acts 1999, 76th Leg., ch. 1477, §14, eff. Sept. 1, 1999.

FAM §55.12. INITIATION OF COMMITMENT PROCEEDINGS

If, after considering all relevant information, the juvenile court determines that evidence exists to support a finding that a child has a mental illness and that the child meets the commitment criteria under Subtitle C, Title 7, Health and Safety Code, the court shall:

(1) initiate proceedings as provided by Section 55.13 to order temporary or extended mental health services, as provided in Subchapter C, Chapter 574, Health and Safety Code; or

(2) refer the child's case as provided by Section 55.14 to the appropriate court for the initiation of proceedings in that court for commitment of the child under Subchapter C, Chapter 574, Health and Safety Code.

History of Fam §55.12: Acts 1973, 63rd Leg., ch. 544, §1, eff. Sept. 1, 1973. Amended by Acts 1995, 74th Leg., ch. 262, §47, eff. May 31, 1995. Renumbered from §55.02(a) and amended by Acts 1999, 76th Leg., ch. 1477, §14, eff. Sept. 1, 1999.

FAM §55.13. COMMITMENT PROCEEDINGS IN JUVENILE COURT

(a) If the juvenile court initiates proceedings for temporary or extended mental health services under Section 55.12(1), the prosecuting attorney or the attorney for the child may file with the juvenile court an application for court-ordered mental health services under Section 574.001, Health and Safety Code. The juvenile court shall:

(1) set a date for a hearing and provide notice as required by Sections 574.005 and 574.006, Health and Safety Code; and

(2) conduct the hearing in accordance with Subchapter C, Chapter 574, Health and Safety Code.

(b) The burden of proof at the hearing is on the party who filed the application.

(c) The juvenile court shall appoint the number of physicians necessary to examine the child and to complete the certificates of medical examination for mental illness required under Section 574.009, Health and Safety Code.

(d) After conducting a hearing on an application under this section, the juvenile court shall:

(1) if the criteria under Section 574.034, Health and Safety Code, are satisfied, order temporary mental health services for the child; or

(2) if the criteria under Section 574.035, Health and Safety Code, are satisfied, order extended mental health services for the child.

History of Fam §55.13: Acts 1999, 76th Leg., ch. 1477, §14, eff. Sept. 1, 1999.

FAM §55.14. REFERRAL FOR COMMITMENT PROCEEDINGS

(a) If the juvenile court refers the child's case to the appropriate court for the initiation of commitment proceedings under Section 55.12(2), the juvenile court shall:

(1) send all papers relating to the child's mental illness to the clerk of the court to which the case is referred;

(2) send to the office of the appropriate county attorney or, if a county attorney is not available, to the office of the appropriate district attorney, copies of all papers sent to the clerk of the court under Subdivision (1); and

(3) if the child is in detention:

(A) order the child released from detention to the child's home or another appropriate place;

(B) order the child detained in an appropriate place other than a juvenile detention facility; or

(C) if an appropriate place to release or detain the child as described by Paragraph (A) or (B) is not available, order the child to remain in the juvenile detention facility subject to further detention orders of the court.

(b) The papers sent to the clerk of a court under Subsection (a)(1) constitute an application for mental health services under Section 574.001, Health and Safety Code.

History of Fam §55.14: Acts 1999, 76th Leg., ch. 1477, §14, eff. Sept. 1, 1999.

FAM §55.15. STANDARDS OF CARE; EXPIRATION OF COURT ORDER FOR MENTAL HEALTH SERVICES

If the juvenile court or a court to which the child's case is referred under Section 55.12(2) orders mental health services for the child, the child shall be cared for, treated, and released in conformity to Subtitle C, Title 7, Health and Safety Code, except:

(1) a court order for mental health services for a child automatically expires on the 120th day after the date the child becomes 18 years of age; and

(2) the administrator of a mental health facility shall notify, in writing, by certified mail, return receipt requested, the juvenile court that ordered mental health services or the juvenile court that referred the case to a court that ordered the mental health services of the intent to discharge the child at least 10 days prior to discharge.

History of Fam §55.15: Acts 1973, 63rd Leg., ch. 544, §1, eff. Sept. 1, 1973. Amended by Acts 1975, 64th Leg., ch. 693, §§20 & 21, eff. Sept. 1, 1975; Acts 1991, 72nd Leg., ch. 76, §9, eff. Sept. 1, 1991; Acts 1995, 74th Leg., ch. 262, §47, eff. May 31, 1995. Renumbered from §55.02(c) and amended by Acts 1999, 76th Leg., ch. 1477, §14, eff. Sept. 1, 1999.

FAM §55.16. ORDER FOR MENTAL HEALTH SERVICES; STAY OF PROCEEDINGS

(a) If the court to which the child's case is referred under Section 55.12(2) orders temporary or extended inpatient mental health services for the child, the court shall immediately notify in writing the referring juvenile court of the court's order for mental health services.

(b) If the juvenile court orders temporary or extended inpatient mental health services for the child or if the juvenile court receives notice under Subsection (a) from the court to which the child's case is referred, the proceedings under this title then pending in juvenile court shall be stayed.

History of Fam §55.16: Acts 1973, 63rd Leg., ch. 544, §1, eff. Sept. 1, 1973. Amended by Acts 1995, 74th Leg., ch. 262, §47, eff. May 31, 1995. Renumbered from §55.02(d) and amended by Acts 1999, 76th Leg., ch. 1477, §14, eff. Sept. 1, 1999.

FAM §55.17. MENTAL HEALTH SERVICES NOT ORDERED; DISSOLUTION OF STAY

(a) If the court to which a child's case is referred under Section 55.12(2) does not order temporary or extended inpatient mental health services for the child, the court shall immediately notify in writing the referring juvenile court of the court's decision.

(b) If the juvenile court does not order temporary or extended inpatient mental health services for the child or if the juvenile court receives notice under Subsection (a) from the court to which the child's case is referred, the juvenile court shall dissolve the stay and continue the juvenile court proceedings.

History of Fam §55.17: Acts 1999, 76th Leg., ch. 1477, §14, eff. Sept. 1, 1999.

FAM §55.18. DISCHARGE FROM MENTAL HEALTH FACILITY BEFORE REACHING 18 YEARS OF AGE

If the child is discharged from the mental health facility before reaching 18 years of age, the juvenile court may:

(1) dismiss the juvenile court proceedings with prejudice; or

(2) continue with proceedings under this title as though no order of mental health services had been made.

History of Fam §55.18: Acts 1973, 63rd Leg., ch. 544, §1, eff. Sept. 1, 1973. Amended by Acts 1995, 74th Leg., ch. 262, §47, eff. May 31, 1995. Renumbered from §55.02(e) by Acts 1999, 76th Leg., ch. 1477, §14, eff. Sept. 1, 1999.

FAM §55.19. TRANSFER TO CRIMINAL COURT ON 18TH BIRTHDAY

(a) The juvenile court shall transfer all pending proceedings from the juvenile court to a criminal court on the 18th birthday of a child for whom the juvenile court or a court to which the child's case is referred under Section 55.12(2) has ordered inpatient mental health services if:

(1) the child is not discharged or furloughed from the inpatient mental health facility before reaching 18 years of age; and

(2) the child is alleged to have engaged in delinquent conduct that included a violation of a penal law listed in Section 53.045 and no adjudication concerning the alleged conduct has been made.

(b) The juvenile court shall send notification of the transfer of a child under Subsection (a) to the inpatient mental health facility. The criminal court shall, within 90 days of the transfer, institute proceedings under Article 46.02, Code of Criminal Procedure. If those or any subsequent proceedings result in a determination that the defendant is competent to stand trial, the defendant may not receive a punishment for the delinquent conduct described by Subsection (a)(2) that results in confinement for a period longer than the maximum period of confinement the defendant could have received if the defendant had been adjudicated for the delinquent conduct while still a child and within the jurisdiction of the juvenile court.

History of Fam §55.19: Acts 1995, 74th Leg., ch. 262, §47, eff. May 31, 1995. Renumbered from §55.02(f) & (g) and amended by Acts 1999, 76th Leg., ch. 1477, §14, eff. Sept. 1, 1999.

Sections 55.20-55.30 reserved for expansion

SUBCHAPTER C. CHILD UNFIT TO PROCEED AS A RESULT OF MENTAL ILLNESS OR MENTAL RETARDATION

FAM §55.31. UNFITNESS TO PROCEED DETERMINATION; EXAMINATION

(a) A child alleged by petition or found to have engaged in delinquent conduct or conduct indicating a need for supervision who as a result of mental illness or mental retardation lacks capacity to understand the proceedings in juvenile court or to assist in the child's own defense is unfit to proceed and shall not be subjected to discretionary transfer to criminal court, adjudication, disposition, or modification of disposition as long as such incapacity endures.

(b) On a motion by a party, the juvenile court shall determine whether probable cause exists to believe that a child who is alleged by petition or who is found to have engaged in delinquent conduct or conduct indicating a need for supervision is unfit to proceed as a result of mental illness or mental retardation. In making its determination, the court may:

(1) consider the motion, supporting documents, professional statements of counsel, and witness testimony; and

(2) make its own observation of the child.

(c) If the court determines that probable cause exists to believe that the child is unfit to proceed, the court shall temporarily stay the juvenile court proceedings and immediately order the child to be examined under Section 51.20. The information obtained from the examination must include expert opinion as to whether the child is unfit to proceed as a result of mental illness or mental retardation.

(d) After considering all relevant information, including information obtained from an examination under Section 51.20, the court shall:

(1) if the court determines that evidence exists to support a finding that the child is unfit to proceed, proceed under Section 55.32; or

(2) if the court determines that evidence does not exist to support a finding that the child is unfit to proceed, dissolve the stay and continue the juvenile court proceedings.

History of Fam §55.31: Acts 1973, 63rd Leg., ch. 544, §1, eff. Sept. 1, 1973. Amended by Acts 1995, 74th Leg., ch. 262, §47, eff. May 31, 1995. Renumbered from §55.04(a) & (b) and amended by Acts 1999, 76th Leg., ch. 1477, §14, eff. Sept. 1, 1999.

FAM §55.32. HEARING ON ISSUE OF FITNESS TO PROCEED

(a) If the juvenile court determines that evidence exists to support a finding that a child is unfit to proceed as a result of mental illness or mental retardation, the court shall set the case for a hearing on that issue.

(b) The issue of whether the child is unfit to proceed as a result of mental illness or mental retardation shall be determined at a hearing separate from any other hearing.

(c) The court shall determine the issue of whether the child is unfit to proceed unless the child or the attorney for the child demands a jury before the 10th day before the date of the hearing.

(d) Unfitness to proceed as a result of mental illness or mental retardation must be proved by a preponderance of the evidence.

(e) If the court or jury determines that the child is fit to proceed, the juvenile court shall continue with proceedings under this title as though no question of fitness to proceed had been raised.

(f) If the court or jury determines that the child is unfit to proceed as a result of mental illness or mental retardation, the court shall:

(1) stay the juvenile court proceedings for as long as that incapacity endures; and

(2) proceed under Section 55.33.

(g) The fact that the child is unfit to proceed as a result of mental illness or mental retardation does not preclude any legal objection to the juvenile court proceedings which is susceptible of fair determination prior to the adjudication hearing and without the personal participation of the child.

History of Fam §55.32: Acts 1973, 63rd Leg., ch. 544, §1, eff. Sept. 1, 1973. Amended by Acts 1995, 74th Leg., ch. 262, §47, eff. May 31, 1995. Renumbered from §55.04(c) - (f) & (h) and amended by Acts 1999, 76th Leg., ch. 1477, §14, eff. Sept. 1, 1999.

FAM §55.33. PROCEEDINGS FOLLOWING FINDING OF UNFITNESS TO PROCEED

(a) If the juvenile court or jury determines under Section 55.32 that a child is unfit to proceed with the juvenile court proceedings for delinquent conduct, the court shall:

(1) if the unfitness to proceed is a result of mental illness or mental retardation:

(A) provided that the child meets the commitment criteria under Subtitle C or D, Title 7, Health and Safety Code, order the child placed with the Texas Department of Mental Health and Mental Retardation for a period of not more than 90 days, which order may not specify a shorter period, for placement in a facility designated by the department; or

(B) on application by the child's parent, guardian, or guardian ad litem, order the child placed in a private psychiatric inpatient facility for a period of not more than 90 days, which order may not specify a shorter period, but only if the placement is agreed to in writing by the administrator of the facility; or

(2) if the unfitness to proceed is a result of mental illness and the court determines that the child may be adequately treated in an alternative setting, order the child to receive treatment for mental illness on an outpatient basis for a period of not more than 90 days, which order may not specify a shorter period.

(b) If the court orders a child placed in a private psychiatric inpatient facility under Subsection (a)(1)(B), the state or a political subdivision of the state may be ordered to pay any costs associated with the child's placement, subject to an express appropriation of funds for the purpose.

History of Fam §55.33: Acts 1999, 76th Leg., ch. 1477, §14, eff. Sept. 1, 1999.

FAM §55.34. TRANSPORTATION TO & FROM FACILITY

(a) If the court issues a placement order under Section 55.33(a)(1), the court shall order the probation department or sheriff's department to transport the child to the designated facility.

(b) On receipt of a report from a facility to which a child has been transported under Subsection (a), the court shall order the probation department or sheriff's department to transport the child from the facility to the court. If the child is not transported to the court before the 11th day after the date of the court's order, an authorized representative of the facility shall transport the child from the facility to the court.

(c) The county in which the juvenile court is located shall reimburse the facility for the costs incurred in transporting the child to the juvenile court as required by Subsection (b).

History of Fam §55.34: Acts 1999, 76th Leg., ch. 1477, §14, eff. Sept. 1, 1999.

FAM §55.35. INFORMATION REQUIRED TO BE SENT TO FACILITY; REPORT TO COURT

(a) If the juvenile court issues a placement order under Section 55.33(a), the court shall order the probation department to send copies of any information in the possession of the department and relevant to the issue of the child's mental illness or mental retardation to the public or private facility or outpatient center, as appropriate.

(b) Not later than the 75th day after the date the court issues a placement order under Section 55.33(a), the public or private facility or outpatient center, as appropriate, shall submit to the court a report that:

(1) describes the treatment of the child provided by the facility or center; and

(2) states the opinion of the director of the facility or center as to whether the child is fit or unfit to proceed.

(c) The court shall provide a copy of the report submitted under Subsection (b) to the prosecuting attorney and the attorney for the child.

History of Fam §55.35: Acts 1999, 76th Leg., ch. 1477, §14, eff. Sept. 1, 1999.

FAM §55.36. REPORT THAT CHILD IS FIT TO PROCEED; HEARING ON OBJECTION

(a) If a report submitted under Section 55.35(b) states that a child is fit to proceed, the juvenile court shall find that the child is fit to proceed unless the child's attorney objects in writing or in open court not later than the second day after the date the attorney receives a copy of the report under Section 55.35(c).

(b) On objection by the child's attorney under Subsection (a), the juvenile court shall promptly hold a hearing to determine whether the child is fit to proceed, except that the hearing may be held after the date that the placement order issued under Section 55.33(a) expires. At the hearing, the court shall determine the issue of the fitness of the child to proceed unless the child or the child's attorney demands in writing a jury before the 10th day before the date of the hearing.

(c) If, after a hearing, the court or jury finds that the child is fit to proceed, the court shall dissolve the stay and continue the juvenile court proceedings as though a question of fitness to proceed had not been raised.

(d) If, after a hearing, the court or jury finds that the child is unfit to proceed, the court shall proceed under Section 55.37.

History of Fam §55.36: Acts 1999, 76th Leg., ch. 1477, §14, eff. Sept. 1, 1999.

FAM §55.37. REPORT THAT CHILD IS UNFIT TO PROCEED AS A RESULT OF MENTAL ILLNESS; INITIATION OF COMMITMENT PROCEEDINGS

If a report submitted under Section 55.35(b) states that a child is unfit to proceed as a result of mental illness and that the child meets the commitment criteria for civil commitment under Subtitle C, Title 7, Health and Safety Code, the director of the public or private facility or outpatient center, as appropriate, shall submit to the court two certificates of medical examination for mental illness. On receipt of the certificates, the court shall:

(1) initiate proceedings as provided by Section 55.38 in the juvenile court for commitment of the child under Subtitle C, Title 7, Health and Safety Code; or

(2) refer the child's case as provided by Section 55.39 to the appropriate court for the initiation of proceedings in that court for commitment of the child under Subtitle C, Title 7, Health and Safety Code.

History of Fam §55.37: Acts 1999, 76th Leg., ch. 1477, §14, eff. Sept. 1, 1999.

FAM §55.38. COMMITMENT PROCEEDINGS IN JUVENILE COURT FOR MENTAL ILLNESS

(a) If the juvenile court initiates commitment proceedings under Section 55.37(1), the prosecuting attorney may file with the juvenile court an application for court-ordered mental health services under Section 574.001, Health and Safety Code. The juvenile court shall:

(1) set a date for a hearing and provide notice as required by Sections 574.005 and 574.006, Health and Safety Code; and

(2) conduct the hearing in accordance with Subchapter C, Chapter 574, Health and Safety Code.

(b) After conducting a hearing under Subsection (a)(2), the juvenile court shall:

(1) if the criteria under Section 574.034, Health and Safety Code, are satisfied, order temporary mental health services; or

(2) if the criteria under Section 574.035, Health and Safety Code, are satisfied, order extended mental health services.

History of Fam §55.38: Acts 1999, 76th Leg., ch. 1477, §14, eff. Sept. 1, 1999.

FAM §55.39. REFERRAL FOR COMMITMENT PROCEEDINGS FOR MENTAL ILLNESS

(a) If the juvenile court refers the child's case to an appropriate court for the initiation of commitment proceedings under Section 55.37(2), the juvenile court shall:

(1) send all papers relating to the child's unfitness to proceed, including the verdict and judgment of the juvenile court finding the child unfit to proceed, to the clerk of the court to which the case is referred;

(2) send to the office of the appropriate county attorney or, if a county attorney is not available, to the office of the appropriate district attorney, copies of all papers sent to the clerk of the court under Subdivision (1); and

(3) if the child is in detention:

(A) order the child released from detention to the child's home or another appropriate place;

(B) order the child detained in an appropriate place other than a juvenile detention facility; or

(C) if an appropriate place to release or detain the child as described by Paragraph (A) or (B) is not available, order the child to remain in the juvenile detention facility subject to further detention orders of the court.

(b) The papers sent to a court under Subsection (a)(1) constitute an application for mental health services under Section 574.001, Health and Safety Code.

History of Fam §55.39: Acts 1999, 76th Leg., ch. 1477, §14, eff. Sept. 1, 1999.

FAM §55.40. REPORT THAT CHILD IS UNFIT TO PROCEED AS A RESULT OF MENTAL RETARDATION

If a report submitted under Section 55.35(b) states that a child is unfit to proceed as a result of mental retardation and that the child meets the commitment criteria for civil commitment under Subtitle D, Title 7, Health and Safety Code, the director of the residential care facility shall submit to the court an affidavit stating the conclusions reached as a result of the diagnosis. On receipt of the affidavit, the court shall:

(1) initiate proceedings as provided by Section 55.41 in the juvenile court for commitment of the child under Subtitle D, Title 7, Health and Safety Code; or

(2) refer the child's case as provided by Section 55.42 to the appropriate court for the initiation of proceedings in that court for commitment of the child under Subtitle D, Title 7, Health and Safety Code.

History of Fam §55.40: Acts 1999, 76th Leg., ch. 1477, §14, eff. Sept. 1, 1999.

FAM §55.41. COMMITMENT PROCEEDINGS IN JUVENILE COURT FOR MENTAL RETARDATION

(a) If the juvenile court initiates commitment proceedings under Section 55.40(1), the prosecuting attorney may file with the juvenile court an application for placement under Section 593.041, Health and Safety Code. The juvenile court shall:

(1) set a date for a hearing and provide notice as required by Sections 593.047 and 593.048, Health and Safety Code; and

(2) conduct the hearing in accordance with Sections 593.049–593.056, Health and Safety Code.

(b) After conducting a hearing under Subsection (a)(2), the juvenile court may order commitment of the child to a residential care facility if the commitment criteria under Section 593.052, Health and Safety Code, are satisfied.

E *Subsection (c) below is effective for criminal conduct that occurs on or after Sept. 1, 2001.*

(c) On receipt of the court's order, the Texas Department of Mental Health and Mental Retardation or the appropriate community center shall admit the child to a residential care facility.

History of Fam §55.41: Acts 1999, 76th Leg., ch. 1477, §14, eff. Sept. 1, 1999. Amended by Acts 2001, 77th Leg., ch. 1297, §30, eff. Sept. 1, 2001.

FAM §55.42. REFERRAL FOR COMMITMENT PROCEEDINGS FOR MENTAL RETARDATION

(a) If the juvenile court refers the child's case to an appropriate court for the initiation of commitment proceedings under Section 55.40(2), the juvenile court shall:

(1) send all papers relating to the child's mental retardation to the clerk of the court to which the case is referred;

(2) send to the office of the appropriate county attorney or, if a county attorney is not available, to the office of the appropriate district attorney, copies of all papers sent to the clerk of the court under Subdivision (1); and

(3) if the child is in detention:

(A) order the child released from detention to the child's home or another appropriate place;

(B) order the child detained in an appropriate place other than a juvenile detention facility; or

(C) if an appropriate place to release or detain the child as described by Paragraph (A) or (B) is not available, order the child to remain in the juvenile detention facility subject to further detention orders of the court.

(b) The papers sent to a court under Subsection (a)(1) constitute an application for placement under Section 593.041, Health and Safety Code.

History of Fam §55.42: Acts 1999, 76th Leg., ch. 1477, §14, eff. Sept. 1, 1999.

FAM §55.43. RESTORATION HEARING

(a) The prosecuting attorney may file with the juvenile court a motion for a restoration hearing concerning a child if:

(1) the child is found unfit to proceed as a result of mental illness or mental retardation; and

(2) the child:

(A) is not:

(i) ordered by a court to receive inpatient mental health services;

(ii) committed by a court to a residential care facility; or

(iii) ordered by a court to receive treatment on an outpatient basis; or

(B) is discharged or furloughed from a mental health facility or outpatient center before the child reaches 18 years of age.

(b) At the restoration hearing, the court shall determine the issue of whether the child is fit to proceed.

(c) The restoration hearing shall be conducted without a jury.

(d) The issue of fitness to proceed must be proved by a preponderance of the evidence.

(e) If, after a hearing, the court finds that the child is fit to proceed, the court shall continue the juvenile court proceedings.

(f) If, after a hearing, the court finds that the child is unfit to proceed, the court shall dismiss the motion for restoration.

History of Fam §55.43: Acts 1999, 76th Leg., ch. 1477, §14, eff. Sept. 1, 1999.

FAM §55.44. TRANSFER TO CRIMINAL COURT ON 18TH BIRTHDAY OF CHILD

(a) The juvenile court shall transfer all pending proceedings from the juvenile court to a criminal court on the 18th birthday of a child for whom the juvenile court or a court to which the child's case is referred has ordered inpatient mental health services or residential care for persons with mental retardation if:

(1) the child is not discharged or furloughed from the facility before reaching 18 years of age; and

(2) the child is alleged to have engaged in delinquent conduct that included a violation of a penal law listed in Section 53.045 and no adjudication concerning the alleged conduct has been made.

(b) The juvenile court shall send notification of the transfer of a child under Subsection (a) to the facility. The criminal court shall, before the 91st day after the date of the transfer, institute proceedings under Article 46.02, Code of Criminal Procedure. If those or any subsequent proceedings result in a determination that the defendant is competent to stand trial, the defendant may not receive a punishment for the delinquent conduct described by Subsection (a)(2) that results in confinement for a period longer than the maximum period of confinement the defendant could have received if the defendant had been adjudicated for the delinquent conduct while still a child and within the jurisdiction of the juvenile court.

History of Fam §55.44: Acts 1999, 76th Leg., ch. 1477, §14, eff. Sept. 1, 1999.

FAM §55.45. STANDARDS OF CARE; NOTICE OF RELEASE OR FURLOUGH

E *Section 55.45 below is effective for criminal conduct that occurs on or after Sept. 1, 2001.*

(a) If the juvenile court or a court to which the child's case is referred under Section 55.37(2) orders mental health services for the child, the child shall be cared for, treated, and released in accordance with Subtitle C, Title 7, Health and Safety Code, except that the administrator of a mental health facility shall notify, in writing, by certified mail, return receipt requested, the juvenile court that ordered mental health services or that referred the case to a court that ordered mental health services of the intent to discharge the child on or before the 10th day before the date of discharge.

(b) If the juvenile court or a court to which the child's case is referred under Section 55.40(2) orders the commitment of the child to a residential care facility, the child shall be cared for, treated, and released in accordance with Subtitle D, Title 7, Health and Safety

Code, except that the administrator of the residential care facility shall notify, in writing, by certified mail, return receipt requested, the juvenile court that ordered commitment of the child or that referred the case to a court that ordered commitment of the child of the intent to discharge or furlough the child on or before the 20th day before the date of discharge or furlough.

History of Fam §55.45: Enacted by Acts 2001, 77th Leg., ch. 1297, §31, eff. Sept. 1, 2001.

Sections 55.46-55.50 reserved for expansion

SUBCHAPTER D. LACK OF RESPONSIBILITY FOR CONDUCT AS A RESULT OF MENTAL ILLNESS OR MENTAL RETARDATION

FAM §55.51. LACK OF RESPONSIBILITY FOR CONDUCT DETERMINATION; EXAMINATION

(a) A child alleged by petition to have engaged in delinquent conduct or conduct indicating a need for supervision is not responsible for the conduct if at the time of the conduct, as a result of mental illness or mental retardation, the child lacks substantial capacity either to appreciate the wrongfulness of the child's conduct or to conform the child's conduct to the requirements of law.

(b) On a motion by a party in which it is alleged that a child may not be responsible as a result of mental illness or mental retardation for the child's conduct, the court shall order the child to be examined under Section 51.20. The information obtained from the examinations must include expert opinion as to whether the child is not responsible for the child's conduct as a result of mental illness or mental retardation.

(c) The issue of whether the child is not responsible for the child's conduct as a result of mental illness or mental retardation shall be tried to the court or jury in the adjudication hearing.

(d) Lack of responsibility for conduct as a result of mental illness or mental retardation must be proved by a preponderance of the evidence.

(e) In its findings or verdict the court or jury must state whether the child is not responsible for the child's conduct as a result of mental illness or mental retardation.

(f) If the court or jury finds the child is not responsible for the child's conduct as a result of mental illness or mental retardation, the court shall proceed under Section 55.52.

(g) A child found to be not responsible for the child's conduct as a result of mental illness or mental retardation shall not be subject to proceedings under this title with respect to such conduct, other than proceedings under Section 55.52.

History of Fam §55.51: Acts 1973, 63rd Leg., ch. 544, §1, eff. Sept. 1, 1973. Amended by Acts 1995, 74th Leg., ch. 262, §47, eff. May 31, 1995. Renumbered from §55.05 and amended by Acts 1999, 76th Leg., ch. 1477, §14, eff. Sept. 1, 1999.

FAM §55.52. PROCEEDINGS FOLLOWING FINDING OF LACK OF RESPONSIBILITY FOR CONDUCT

(a) If the court or jury finds that a child is not responsible for the child's conduct under Section 55.51, the court shall:

(1) if the lack of responsibility is a result of mental illness or mental retardation:

(A) provided that the child meets the commitment criteria under Subtitle C or D, Title 7, Health and Safety Code, order the child placed with the Texas Department of Mental Health and Mental Retardation for a period of not more than 90 days, which order may not specify a shorter period, for placement in a facility designated by the department; or

(B) on application by the child's parent, guardian, or guardian ad litem, order the child placed in a private psychiatric inpatient facility for a period of not more than 90 days, which order may not specify a shorter period, but only if the placement is agreed to in writing by the administrator of the facility; or

(2) if the child's lack of responsibility is a result of mental illness and the court determines that the child may be adequately treated in an alternative setting, order the child to receive treatment on an outpatient basis for a period of not more than 90 days, which order may not specify a shorter period.

(b) If the court orders a child placed in a private psychiatric inpatient facility under Subsection (a)(1)(B), the state or a political subdivision of the state may be ordered to pay any costs associated with the child's placement, subject to an express appropriation of funds for the purpose.

History of Fam §55.52: Acts 1999, 76th Leg., ch. 1477, §14, eff. Sept. 1, 1999.

FAM §55.53. TRANSPORTATION TO & FROM FACILITY

(a) If the court issues a placement order under Section 55.52(a)(1), the court shall order the probation

FAM §55.53

department or sheriff's department to transport the child to the designated facility.

(b) On receipt of a report from a facility to which a child has been transported under Subsection (a), the court shall order the probation department or sheriff's department to transport the child from the facility to the court. If the child is not transported to the court before the 11th day after the date of the court's order, an authorized representative of the facility shall transport the child from the facility to the court.

(c) The county in which the juvenile court is located shall reimburse the facility for the costs incurred in transporting the child to the juvenile court as required by Subsection (b).

History of Fam §55.53: Acts 1999, 76th Leg., ch. 1477, §14, eff. Sept. 1, 1999.

FAM §55.54. INFORMATION REQUIRED TO BE SENT TO FACILITY; REPORT TO COURT

(a) If the juvenile court issues a placement order under Section 55.52(a), the court shall order the probation department to send copies of any information in the possession of the department and relevant to the issue of the child's mental illness or mental retardation to the public or private facility or outpatient center, as appropriate.

(b) Not later than the 75th day after the date the court issues a placement order under Section 55.52(a), the public or private facility or outpatient center, as appropriate, shall submit to the court a report that:

(1) describes the treatment of the child provided by the facility or center; and

(2) states the opinion of the director of the facility or center as to whether the child is mentally ill or mentally retarded.

(c) The court shall send a copy of the report submitted under Subsection (b) to the prosecuting attorney and the attorney for the child.

History of Fam §55.54: Acts 1999, 76th Leg., ch. 1477, §14, eff. Sept. 1, 1999.

FAM §55.55. REPORT THAT CHILD IS NOT MENTALLY ILL OR MENTALLY RETARDED; HEARING ON OBJECTION

(a) If a report submitted under Section 55.54(b) states that a child does not have a mental illness or mental retardation, the juvenile court shall discharge the child unless:

(1) an adjudication hearing was conducted concerning conduct that included a violation of a penal law listed in Section 53.045(a) and a petition was approved by a grand jury under Section 53.045; and

(2) the prosecuting attorney objects in writing not later than the second day after the date the attorney receives a copy of the report under Section 55.54(c).

(b) On objection by the prosecuting attorney under Subsection (a), the juvenile court shall hold a hearing without a jury to determine whether the child has a mental illness or mental retardation and whether the child meets the commitment criteria for civil commitment under Subtitle C or D, Title 7, Health and Safety Code.

(c) At the hearing, the burden is on the state to prove by clear and convincing evidence that the child has a mental illness or mental retardation and that the child meets the commitment criteria for civil commitment under Subtitle C or D, Title 7, Health and Safety Code.

(d) If, after a hearing, the court finds that the child does not have a mental illness or mental retardation and that the child does not meet the commitment criteria under Subtitle C or D, Title 7, Health and Safety Code, the court shall discharge the child.

(e) If, after a hearing, the court finds that the child has a mental illness or mental retardation and that the child meets the commitment criteria under Subtitle C or D, Title 7, Health and Safety Code, the court shall issue an appropriate commitment order.

History of Fam §55.55: Acts 1999, 76th Leg., ch. 1477, §14, eff. Sept. 1, 1999.

FAM §55.56. REPORT THAT CHILD HAS MENTAL ILLNESS; INITIATION OF COMMITMENT PROCEEDINGS

If a report submitted under Section 55.54(b) states that a child has a mental illness and that the child meets the commitment criteria for civil commitment under Subtitle C, Title 7, Health and Safety Code, the director of the public or private facility or outpatient center, as appropriate, shall submit to the court two certificates of medical examination for mental illness. On receipt of the certificates, the court shall:

(1) initiate proceedings as provided by Section 55.57 in the juvenile court for commitment of the child under Subtitle C, Title 7, Health and Safety Code; or

(2) refer the child's case as provided by Section 55.58 to the appropriate court for the initiation of proceedings in that court for commitment of the child under Subtitle C, Title 7, Health and Safety Code.

History of Fam §55.56: Acts 1999, 76th Leg., ch. 1477, §14, eff. Sept. 1, 1999.

FAM §55.57. COMMITMENT PROCEEDINGS IN JUVENILE COURT FOR MENTAL ILLNESS

(a) If the juvenile court initiates commitment proceedings under Section 55.56(1), the prosecuting attorney may file with the juvenile court an application for court-ordered mental health services under Section 574.001, Health and Safety Code. The juvenile court shall:

(1) set a date for a hearing and provide notice as required by Sections 574.005 and 574.006, Health and Safety Code; and

(2) conduct the hearing in accordance with Subchapter C, Chapter 574, Health and Safety Code.

(b) After conducting a hearing under Subsection (a)(2), the juvenile court shall:

(1) if the criteria under Section 574.034, Health and Safety Code, are satisfied, order temporary mental health services; or

(2) if the criteria under Section 574.035, Health and Safety Code, are satisfied, order extended mental health services.

History of Fam §55.57: Acts 1999, 76th Leg., ch. 1477, §14, eff. Sept. 1, 1999.

FAM §55.58. REFERRAL FOR COMMITMENT PROCEEDINGS FOR MENTAL ILLNESS

(a) If the juvenile court refers the child's case to an appropriate court for the initiation of commitment proceedings under Section 55.56(2), the juvenile court shall:

(1) send all papers relating to the child's mental illness, including the verdict and judgment of the juvenile court finding that the child was not responsible for the child's conduct, to the clerk of the court to which the case is referred;

(2) send to the office of the appropriate county attorney or, if a county attorney is not available, to the office of the district attorney, copies of all papers sent to the clerk of the court under Subdivision (1); and

(3) if the child is in detention:

(A) order the child released from detention to the child's home or another appropriate place;

(B) order the child detained in an appropriate place other than a juvenile detention facility; or

(C) if an appropriate place to release or detain the child as described by Paragraph (A) or (B) is not available, order the child to remain in the juvenile detention facility subject to further detention orders of the court.

(b) The papers sent to a court under Subsection (a)(1) constitute an application for mental health services under Section 574.001, Health and Safety Code.

History of Fam §55.58: Acts 1999, 76th Leg., ch. 1477, §14, eff. Sept. 1, 1999.

FAM §55.59. REPORT THAT CHILD HAS MENTAL RETARDATION; INITIATION OF COMMITMENT PROCEEDINGS

If a report submitted under Section 55.54(b) states that a child has mental retardation and that the child meets the commitment criteria for civil commitment under Subtitle D, Title 7, Health and Safety Code, the director of the residential care facility shall submit to the court an affidavit stating the conclusions reached as a result of the diagnosis. On receipt of an affidavit, the juvenile court shall:

(1) initiate proceedings in the juvenile court as provided by Section 55.60 for commitment of the child under Subtitle D, Title 7, Health and Safety Code; or

(2) refer the child's case to the appropriate court as provided by Section 55.61 for the initiation of proceedings in that court for commitment of the child under Subtitle D, Title 7, Health and Safety Code.

History of Fam §55.59: Acts 1999, 76th Leg., ch. 1477, §14, eff. Sept. 1, 1999.

FAM §55.60. COMMITMENT PROCEEDINGS IN JUVENILE COURT FOR MENTAL RETARDATION

(a) If the juvenile court initiates commitment proceedings under Section 55.59(1), the prosecuting attorney may file with the juvenile court an application for placement under Section 593.041, Health and Safety Code. The juvenile court shall:

(1) set a date for a hearing and provide notice as required by Sections 593.047 and 593.048, Health and Safety Code; and

(2) conduct the hearing in accordance with Sections 593.049–593.056, Health and Safety Code.

(b) After conducting a hearing under Subsection (a)(2), the juvenile court may order commitment of the child to a residential care facility only if the commitment criteria under Section 593.052, Health and Safety Code, are satisfied.

E *Subsection (c) below is effective for criminal conduct that occurs on or after Sept. 1, 2001.*

(c) On receipt of the court's order, the Texas Department of Mental Health and Mental Retardation or the appropriate community center shall admit the child to a residential care facility.

History of Fam §55.60: Acts 1999, 76th Leg., ch. 1477, §14, eff. Sept. 1, 1999. Amended by Acts 2001, 77th Leg., ch. 1297, §32, eff. Sept. 1, 2001.

FAM §55.61. REFERRAL FOR COMMITMENT PROCEEDINGS FOR MENTAL RETARDATION

(a) If the juvenile court refers the child's case to an appropriate court for the initiation of commitment proceedings under Section 55.59(2), the juvenile court shall:

(1) send all papers relating to the child's mental retardation to the clerk of the court to which the case is referred;

(2) send to the office of the appropriate county attorney or, if a county attorney is not available, to the office of the appropriate district attorney, copies of all papers sent to the clerk of the court under Subdivision (1); and

(3) if the child is in detention:

(A) order the child released from detention to the child's home or another appropriate place;

(B) order the child detained in an appropriate place other than a juvenile detention facility; or

(C) if an appropriate place to release or detain the child as described by Paragraph (A) or (B) is not available, order the child to remain in the juvenile detention facility subject to further detention orders of the court.

(b) The papers sent to a court under Subsection (a)(1) constitute an application for placement under Section 593.041, Health and Safety Code.

History of Fam §55.61: Acts 1999, 76th Leg., ch. 1477, §14, eff. Sept. 1, 1999.

CHAPTER 56. APPEAL

FAM §56.01. RIGHT TO APPEAL

(a) An appeal from an order of a juvenile court is to a court of appeals and the case may be carried to the Texas Supreme Court by writ of error or upon certificate, as in civil cases generally.

(b) The requirements governing an appeal are as in civil cases generally. When an appeal is sought by filing a notice of appeal, security for costs of appeal, or an affidavit of inability to pay the costs of appeal, and the filing is made in a timely fashion after the date the disposition order is signed, the appeal must include the juvenile court adjudication and all rulings contributing to that adjudication. An appeal of the adjudication may be sought notwithstanding that the adjudication order was signed more than 30 days before the date the notice of appeal, security for costs of appeal, or affidavit of inability to pay the costs of appeal was filed. A motion for new trial seeking to vacate an adjudication is timely if the motion is filed not later than the 30th day after the date on which the disposition order is signed.

(c) An appeal may be taken:

(1) except as provided by Subsection (n), by or on behalf of a child from an order entered under:

(A) Section 54.03 with regard to delinquent conduct or conduct indicating a need for supervision;

(B) Section 54.04 disposing of the case;

(C) Section 54.05 respecting modification of a previous juvenile court disposition; or

(D) Chapter 55 by a juvenile court committing a child to a facility for the mentally ill or mentally retarded; or

(2) by a person from an order entered under Section 54.11(i)(2) transferring the person to the custody of the institutional division of the Texas Department of Criminal Justice.

(d) A child has the right to:

(1) appeal, as provided by this subchapter;

(2) representation by counsel on appeal; and

(3) appointment of an attorney for the appeal if an attorney cannot be obtained because of indigency.

(e) On entering an order that is appealable under this section, the court shall advise the child and the child's parent, guardian, or guardian ad litem of the child's rights listed under Subsection (d) of this section.

(f) If the child and his parent, guardian, or guardian ad litem express a desire to appeal, the attorney who represented the child before the juvenile court shall file a notice of appeal with the juvenile court and inform the court whether that attorney will handle the appeal. Counsel shall be appointed under the standards provided in Section 51.10 of this code unless the right to appeal is waived in accordance with Section 51.09 of this code.

(g) An appeal does not suspend the order of the juvenile court, nor does it release the child from the custody of that court or of the person, institution, or agency to whose care the child is committed, unless the juvenile court so orders. However, the appellate court may provide for a personal bond.

(h) If the order appealed from takes custody of the child from his parent, guardian, or custodian, the appeal has precedence over all other cases.

(i) The appellate court may affirm, reverse, or modify the judgment or order, including an order of disposition or modified disposition, from which appeal was taken. It may reverse or modify an order of disposition or modified order of disposition while affirming the juvenile court adjudication that the child engaged in delinquent conduct or conduct indicating a need for supervision. It may remand an order that it reverses or modifies for further proceedings by the juvenile court.

(j) Neither the child nor his family shall be identified in an appellate opinion rendered in an appeal or habeas corpus proceedings related to juvenile court proceedings under this title. The appellate opinion shall be styled, "In the matter of ....," identifying the child by his initials only.

(k) The appellate court shall dismiss an appeal on the state's motion, supported by affidavit showing that the appellant has escaped from custody pending the appeal and, to the affiant's knowledge, has not voluntarily returned to the state's custody on or before the 10th day after the date of the escape. The court may not dismiss an appeal, or if the appeal has been dismissed, shall reinstate the appeal, on the filing of an affidavit of an officer or other credible person showing that the appellant voluntarily returned to custody on or before the 10th day after the date of the escape.

(*l*) The court may order the child, the child's parent, or other person responsible for support of the child to pay the child's costs of appeal, including the costs of representation by an attorney, unless the court determines the person to be ordered to pay the costs is indigent.

(m) For purposes of determining indigency of the child under this section, the court shall consider the assets and income of the child, the child's parent, and any other person responsible for the support of the child.

(n) A child who enters a plea or agrees to a stipulation of evidence in a proceeding held under this title may not appeal an order of the juvenile court entered under Section 54.03, 54.04, or 54.05 if the court makes a disposition in accordance with the agreement between the state and the child regarding the disposition of the case, unless:

(1) the court gives the child permission to appeal; or

(2) the appeal is based on a matter raised by written motion filed before the proceeding in which the child entered the plea or agreed to the stipulation of evidence.

E *Subsection (o) below is effective for criminal conduct that occurs on or after Sept. 1, 2001.*

(o) This section does not limit a child's right to obtain a writ of habeas corpus.

History of Fam §56.01: Acts 1973, 63rd Leg., ch. 544, §1, eff. Sept. 1, 1973. Amended by Acts 1987, 70th Leg., ch. 385, §14, eff. Sept. 1, 1987; Acts 1991, 72nd Leg., ch. 680, §1, eff. Sept. 1, 1991; Acts 1995, 74th Leg., ch. 262, §48, eff. Jan. 1, 1996; Acts 1997, 75th Leg., ch. 1086, §15, eff. Sept. 1, 1997; Acts 1999, 76th Leg., ch. 74, §2 (eff. Sept. 1, 1999), ch. 1477, §15 (eff. Sept. 1, 1999); Acts 2001, 77th Leg., ch. 1297, §33, eff. Sept. 1, 2001.

FAM §56.02. TRANSCRIPT ON APPEAL

(a) An attorney retained to represent a child on appeal who desires to have included in the record on appeal a transcription of notes of the reporter has the responsibility of obtaining and paying for the transcription and furnishing it to the clerk in duplicate in time for inclusion in the record.

(b) The juvenile court shall order the reporter to furnish a transcription without charge to the attorney if the court finds, after hearing or on an affidavit filed by the child's parent or other person responsible for support of the child that the parent or other responsible person is unable to pay or to give security therefor.

(c) On certificate of the court that a transcription has been provided without charge, payment therefor shall be made from the general funds of the county in which the proceedings appealed from occurred.

(d) The court reporter shall report any portion of the proceedings requested by either party or directed by the court and shall report the proceedings in question and answer form unless a narrative transcript is requested.

History of Fam §56.02: Acts 1973, 63rd Leg., ch. 544, §1, eff. Sept. 1, 1973. Amended by Acts 1991, 72nd Leg., ch. 674, §1, eff. Sept. 1, 1991.

CHAPTER 57. RIGHTS OF VICTIMS

FAM §57.001. DEFINITIONS

In this chapter:

(1) "Close relative of a deceased victim" means a person who was the spouse of a deceased victim at the time of the victim's death or who is a parent or adult brother, sister, or child of the deceased victim.

(2) "Guardian of a victim" means a person who is the legal guardian of the victim, whether or not the legal relationship between the guardian and victim exists because of the age of the victim or the physical or mental incompetency of the victim.

(3) "Victim" means a person who as the result of the delinquent conduct of a child suffers a pecuniary loss or personal injury or harm.

History of Fam §57.001: Acts 1989, 71st Leg., ch. 633, §1, eff. June 14, 1989. Amended by Acts 1995, 74th Leg., ch. 262, §49, eff. Jan. 1, 1996; Acts 1997, 75th Leg., ch. 368, §1, eff. Sept. 1, 1997.

FAM §57.002. VICTIM'S RIGHTS

(a) A victim, guardian of a victim, or close relative of a deceased victim is entitled to the following rights within the juvenile justice system:

(1) the right to receive from law enforcement agencies adequate protection from harm and threats of harm arising from cooperation with prosecution efforts;

(2) the right to have the court or person appointed by the court take the safety of the victim or the victim's family into consideration as an element in determining whether the child should be detained before the child's conduct is adjudicated;

(3) the right, if requested, to be informed of relevant court proceedings, including appellate proceedings, and to be informed in a timely manner if those court proceedings have been canceled or rescheduled;

(4) the right to be informed, when requested, by the court or a person appointed by the court concerning the procedures in the juvenile justice system, including general procedures relating to:

(A) the preliminary investigation and deferred prosecution of a case; and

(B) the appeal of the case;

(5) the right to provide pertinent information to a juvenile court conducting a disposition hearing concerning the impact of the offense on the victim and the victim's family by testimony, written statement, or any other manner before the court renders its disposition;

Ⓐ (6) the right to receive information regarding compensation to victims as provided by Subchapter B, Chapter 56, Code of Criminal Procedure, including information related to the costs that may be compensated under that subchapter and the amount of compensation, eligibility for compensation, and procedures for application for compensation under that subchapter, the payment of medical expenses under Section 56.06, Code of Criminal Procedure, for a victim of a sexual assault, and when requested, to referral to available social service agencies that may offer additional assistance;

Ⓐ (7) the right to be informed, upon request, of procedures for release under supervision or transfer of the person to the custody of the pardons and paroles division of the Texas Department of Criminal Justice for parole, to participate in the release or transfer for parole process, to be notified, if requested, of the person's release, escape, or transfer for parole proceedings concerning the person, to provide to the Texas Youth Commission for inclusion in the person's file information to be considered by the commission before the release under supervision or transfer for parole of the person, and to be notified, if requested, of the person's release or transfer for parole;

(8) the right to be provided with a waiting area, separate or secure from other witnesses, including the child alleged to have committed the conduct and relatives of the child, before testifying in any proceeding concerning the child, or, if a separate waiting area is not available, other safeguards should be taken to minimize the victim's contact with the child and the child's relatives and witnesses, before and during court proceedings;

(9) the right to prompt return of any property of the victim that is held by a law enforcement agency or the attorney for the state as evidence when the property is no longer required for that purpose;

(10) the right to have the attorney for the state notify the employer of the victim, if requested, of the

necessity of the victim's cooperation and testimony in a proceeding that may necessitate the absence of the victim from work for good cause;

(11) the right to be present at all public court proceedings related to the conduct of the child as provided by Section 54.08, subject to that section; and

(12) any other right appropriate to the victim that a victim of criminal conduct has under Article 56.02, Code of Criminal Procedure.

E (b) In notifying a victim of the release or escape of a person, the Texas Youth Commission shall use the same procedure established for the notification of the release or escape of an adult offender under Article 56.11, Code of Criminal Procedure.

History of Fam §57.002: Acts 1989, 71st Leg., ch. 633, §1, eff. June 14, 1989. Amended by Acts 1995, 74th Leg., ch. 76, §5.95(110) (eff. Sept. 1, 1995), ch. 262, §50 (eff. Jan. 1, 1996); Acts 2001, 77th Leg., ch. 1034, §8, eff. Sept. 1, 2001.

FAM §57.003. DUTY OF JUVENILE BOARD

(a) The juvenile board shall ensure to the extent practicable that a victim, guardian of a victim, or close relative of a deceased victim is afforded the rights granted by Section 57.002 and, on request, an explanation of those rights.

(b) The juvenile board may designate a person to serve as victim assistance coordinator in the juvenile board's jurisdiction for victims of juvenile offenders.

(c) The victim assistance coordinator shall ensure that a victim, or close relative of a deceased victim, is afforded the rights granted victims, guardians, and relatives by Section 57.002 and, on request, an explanation of those rights. The victim assistance coordinator shall work closely with appropriate law enforcement agencies, prosecuting attorneys, the Texas Juvenile Probation Commission, and the Texas Youth Commission in carrying out that duty.

(d) The victim assistance coordinator shall ensure that at a minimum, a victim, guardian of a victim, or close relative of a deceased victim receives:

(1) a written notice of the rights outlined in Section 57.002;

(2) an application for compensation under the Crime Victims' Compensation Act (Subchapter B, Chapter 56, Code of Criminal Procedure); and

(3) a victim impact statement with information explaining the possible use and consideration of the victim impact statement at detention, adjudication, and release proceedings involving the juvenile.

(e) The victim assistance coordinator shall, on request, offer to assist a person receiving a form under Subsection (d) to complete the form.

(f) The victim assistance coordinator shall send a copy of the victim impact statement to the court conducting a disposition hearing involving the juvenile.

History of Fam §57.003: Acts 1989, 71st Leg., ch. 633, §1, eff. June 14, 1989. Amended by Acts 1995, 74th Leg., ch. 262, §51, eff. Jan. 1, 1996.

FAM §57.0031. NOTIFICATION OF RIGHTS OF VICTIMS OF JUVENILES

At the initial contact or at the earliest possible time after the initial contact between the victim of a reported crime and the juvenile probation office having the responsibility for the disposition of the juvenile, the office shall provide the victim a written notice:

(1) containing information about the availability of emergency and medical services, if applicable;

(2) stating that the victim has the right to receive information regarding compensation to victims of crime as provided by the Crime Victims' Compensation Act (Subchapter B, Chapter 56, Code of Criminal Procedure), including information about:

(A) the costs that may be compensated and the amount of compensation, eligibility for compensation, and procedures for application for compensation;

(B) the payment for a medical examination for a victim of a sexual assault; and

(C) referral to available social service agencies that may offer additional assistance;

(3) stating the name, address, and phone number of the victim assistance coordinator for victims of juveniles;

(4) containing the following statement: "You may call the crime victim assistance coordinator for the status of the case and information about victims' rights.";

(5) stating the rights of victims of crime under Section 57.002;

(6) summarizing each procedural stage in the processing of a juvenile case, including preliminary investigation, detention, informal adjustment of a case, disposition hearings, release proceedings, restitution, and appeals;

(7) suggesting steps the victim may take if the victim is subjected to threats or intimidation;

(8) stating the case number and assigned court for the case; and

(9) stating that the victim has the right to file a victim impact statement and to have it considered in juvenile proceedings.

History of Fam §57.0031: Acts 1995, 74th Leg., ch. 262, §51, eff. Jan. 1, 1996.

FAM §57.004. NOTIFICATION

A court, a person appointed by the court, or the Texas Youth Commission is responsible for notifying a victim, guardian of a victim, or close relative of a deceased victim of a proceeding under this chapter only if the victim, guardian of a victim, or close relative of a deceased victim requests the notification in writing and provides a current address to which the notification is to be sent.

History of Fam §57.004: Acts 1989, 71st Leg., ch. 633, §1, eff. June 14, 1989.

FAM §57.005. LIABILITY

The Texas Youth Commission, a juvenile board, a court, a person appointed by a court, an attorney for the state, a peace officer, or a law enforcement agency is not liable for a failure or inability to provide a right listed under Section 57.002 of this code.

History of Fam §57.005: Acts 1989, 71st Leg., ch. 633, §1, eff. June 14, 1989.

FAM §57.006. APPEAL

The failure or inability of any person to provide a right or service listed under Section 57.002 of this code may not be used by a child as a ground for appeal or for a post conviction writ of habeas corpus.

History of Fam §57.006: Acts 1989, 71st Leg., ch. 633, §1, eff. June 14, 1989.

FAM §57.007. STANDING

A victim, guardian of a victim, or close relative of a victim does not have standing to participate as a party in a juvenile proceeding or to contest the disposition of any case.

History of Fam §57.007: Acts 1989, 71st Leg., ch. 633, §1, eff. June 14, 1989.

FAM §57.008. COURT ORDER FOR PROTECTION FROM JUVENILES

(a) A court may issue an order for protection from juveniles directed against a child to protect a victim of the child's conduct who, because of the victim's participation in the juvenile justice system, risks further harm by the child.

(b) In the order, the court may prohibit the child from doing specified acts or require the child to do specified acts necessary or appropriate to prevent or reduce the likelihood of further harm to the victim by the child.

History of Fam §57.008: Acts 1995, 74th Leg., ch. 262, §52, eff. Jan. 1, 1996.

CHAPTER 58. RECORDS; JUVENILE JUSTICE INFORMATION SYSTEM

Subchapter A. Records

Subchapter B. Juvenile Justice Information System

Subchapter C. Automatic Restriction of Access to Records

Subchapter D. Local Juvenile Justice Information System

SUBCHAPTER A. RECORDS

FAM §58.001. COLLECTION OF RECORDS OF CHILDREN

(a) Law enforcement officers and other juvenile justice personnel shall collect information described by Section 58.104 as a part of the juvenile justice information system created under Subchapter B.

(b) The information is available as provided by Subchapter B.

(c) A law enforcement agency shall forward information, including fingerprints, relating to a child who has been taken into custody under Section 52.01 by the agency to the Department of Public Safety for inclusion in the juvenile justice information system created under Subchapter B, but only if the child is referred to juvenile court on or before the 10th day after the date the child is taken into custody under Section 52.01. If the child is not referred to juvenile court within that time, the law enforcement agency shall destroy all information, including photographs and fingerprints, relating to the child unless the child is placed in a first offender program under Section 52.031 or on informal disposition under Section 52.03. The law enforcement agency may not forward any information to the Department of Public Safety relating to the child while the child is in a first offender program under Section 52.031, or during the 90 days following successful completion of the program or while the child is on informal disposition under Section 52.03. Except as provided by Subsection (f), after the date the child completes an informal disposition under Section 52.03 or after the 90th day after the date the child successfully completes a first offender program under Section 52.031, the law enforcement agency shall destroy all information, including photographs and fingerprints, relating to the child.

(d) If information relating to a child is contained in a document that also contains information relating to an adult and a law enforcement agency is required to destroy all information relating to the child under this section, the agency shall alter the document so that the information relating to the child is destroyed and the information relating to the adult is preserved.

(e) The deletion of a computer entry constitutes destruction of the information contained in the entry.

(f) A law enforcement agency may maintain information relating to a child after the 90th day after the date the child successfully completes a first offender program under Section 52.031 only to determine the child's eligibility to participate in a first offender program.

History of Fam §58.001: Acts 1995, 74th Leg., ch. 262, §53, eff. Jan. 1, 1996. Amended by Acts 1997, 75th Leg., ch. 1086, §16, eff. Sept. 1, 1997; Acts 1999, 76th Leg., ch. 1477, §16, eff. Sept. 1, 1999.

FAM §58.002. PHOTOGRAPHS & FINGERPRINTS OF CHILDREN

Ⓐ *Subsections (a) & (b) below are effective for criminal conduct that occurs on or after Sept. 1, 2001.*

(a) Except as provided by Chapter 63, Code of Criminal Procedure, a child may not be photographed or fingerprinted without the consent of the juvenile court unless the child is taken into custody or referred to the juvenile court for conduct that constitutes a felony or a misdemeanor punishable by confinement in jail.

(b) On or before December 31 of each year, the head of each municipal or county law enforcement agency located in a county shall certify to the juvenile board for that county that the photographs and fingerprints required to be destroyed under Section 58.001 have been destroyed. The juvenile board shall conduct or cause to be conducted an audit of the records of the law enforcement agency to verify the destruction of the photographs and fingerprints and the law enforcement agency shall make its records available for this purpose. If the audit shows that the certification provided by the head of the law enforcement agency is false, that person is subject to prosecution for perjury under Chapter 37, Penal Code.

Subsections (a) & (b) below are effective for criminal conduct in which any element of the conduct occurred before Sept. 1, 2001.

(a) Except as provided by Chapter 79, Human Resources Code, a child may not be photographed or fingerprinted without the consent of the juvenile court unless the child is taken into custody or referred to the juvenile court for conduct that constitutes a felony or a misdemeanor punishable by confinement in jail.

(b) On or before December 31 of each year, the head of each municipal or county law enforcement agency located in a county shall certify to the juvenile board for that county that the photographs and fingerprints required to be destroyed under Section 58.001 have been destroyed. The juvenile board shall conduct an audit of the records of the law enforcement agency to verify the destruction of the photographs and fingerprints and the law enforcement agency shall make its records available for this purpose. If the audit shows that the certification provided by the head of the law enforcement agency is false, that person is subject to prosecution for perjury under Chapter 37, Penal Code.

(c) This section does not prohibit a law enforcement officer from photographing or fingerprinting a child who is not in custody if the child's parent or guardian voluntarily consents in writing to the photographing or fingerprinting of the child.

(d) This section does not apply to fingerprints that are required or authorized to be submitted or obtained for an application for a driver's license or personal identification card.

E *Subsection (e) below is effective for criminal conduct that occurs on or after Sept. 1, 2001.*

(e) This section does not prohibit a law enforcement officer from fingerprinting or photographing a child as provided by Section 58.0021.

History of Fam §58.002: Acts 1995, 74th Leg., ch. 262, §53, eff. Jan. 1, 1996. Amended by Acts 1997, 75th Leg., ch. 1086, §17, eff. Sept. 1, 1997; Acts 1999, 76th Leg., ch. 1477, §17, eff. Sept. 1, 1999; Acts 2001, 77th Leg., ch. 1297, §34, eff. Sept. 1, 2001.

FAM §58.0021. FINGERPRINTS OR PHOTOGRAPHS FOR COMPARISON IN INVESTIGATION

E *Section 58.0021 below is effective for criminal conduct that occurs on or after Sept. 1, 2001.*

(a) A law enforcement officer may take temporary custody of a child to take the child's fingerprints if:

(1) the officer has probable cause to believe that the child has engaged in delinquent conduct;

(2) the officer has investigated that conduct and has found other fingerprints during the investigation; and

(3) the officer has probable cause to believe that the child's fingerprints will match the other fingerprints.

(b) A law enforcement officer may take temporary custody of a child to take the child's photograph if:

(1) the officer has probable cause to believe that the child has engaged in delinquent conduct; and

(2) the officer has probable cause to believe that the child's photograph will be of material assistance in the investigation of that conduct.

(c) Temporary custody for the purpose described by Subsection (a) or (b):

(1) is not a taking into custody under Section 52.01; and

(2) may not be reported to the juvenile justice information system under Subchapter B.

(d) If a law enforcement officer does not take the child into custody under Section 52.01, the child shall be released from temporary custody authorized under this section as soon as the fingerprints or photographs are obtained.

(e) A law enforcement officer who under this section obtains fingerprints or photographs from a child shall:

(1) immediately destroy them if they do not lead to a positive comparison or identification; and

(2) make a reasonable effort to notify the child's parent, guardian, or custodian of the action taken.

(f) A law enforcement officer may under this section obtain fingerprints or photographs from a child at:

(1) a juvenile processing office; or

(2) a location that affords reasonable privacy to the child.

History of Fam §58.0021: Enacted by Acts 2001, 77th Leg., ch. 1297, §35, eff. Sept. 1, 2001.

FAM §58.0022. FINGERPRINTS OR PHOTOGRAPHS TO IDENTIFY RUNAWAYS

E *Section 58.0022 below is effective for criminal conduct that occurs on or after Sept. 1, 2001.*

A law enforcement officer who takes a child into custody with probable cause to believe that the child has engaged in conduct indicating a need for supervision as described by Section 51.03(b)(3) and who after reasonable effort is unable to determine the identity of the child, may fingerprint or photograph the child to establish the child's identity. On determination of the child's identity or that the child cannot be identified by the fingerprints or photographs, the law enforcement officer shall immediately destroy all copies of the fingerprint records or photographs of the child.

History of Fam §58.0022: Enacted by Acts 2001, 77th Leg., ch. 1297, §36, eff. Sept. 1, 2001.

FAM §58.003. SEALING OF RECORDS

(a) Except as provided by Subsections (b) and (c), on the application of a person who has been found to have engaged in delinquent conduct or conduct indicating a need for supervision, or a person taken into custody to determine whether the person engaged in delinquent conduct or conduct indicating a need for supervision, on the juvenile court's own motion or on receipt of a certification from the Department of Public Safety of the State of Texas that the records of a person are eligible for sealing under this section, the court shall order the sealing of the records in the case if the court finds that:

(1) two years have elapsed since final discharge of the person or since the last official action in the person's case if there was no adjudication; and

(2) since the time specified in Subdivision (1), the person has not been convicted of a felony or a misdemeanor involving moral turpitude or found to have engaged in delinquent conduct or conduct indicating a need for supervision and no proceeding is pending seeking conviction or adjudication.

(b) A court may not order the sealing of the records of a person who has received a determinate sentence for engaging in delinquent conduct that violated a penal law listed in Section 53.045 or engaging in habitual felony conduct as described by Section 51.031.

(c) Subject to Subsection (b), a court may order the sealing of records concerning a person adjudicated as having engaged in delinquent conduct that violated a penal law of the grade of felony only if:

(1) the person is 21 years of age or older;

(2) the person was not transferred by a juvenile court under Section 54.02 to a criminal court for prosecution;

(3) the records have not been used as evidence in the punishment phase of a criminal proceeding under Section 3(a), Article 37.07, Code of Criminal Procedure; and

(4) the person has not been convicted of a penal law of the grade of felony after becoming age 17.

(d) The court may grant the relief authorized in Subsection (a) at any time after final discharge of the person or after the last official action in the case if there was no adjudication. If the child is referred to the juvenile court for conduct constituting any offense and at the adjudication hearing the child is found to be not guilty of each offense alleged, the court shall immediately order the sealing of all files and records relating to the case.

(e) Reasonable notice of the hearing shall be given to:

(1) the person who made the application or who is the subject of the records named in the motion;

(2) the prosecuting attorney for the juvenile court;

(3) the authority granting the discharge if the final discharge was from an institution or from parole;

(4) the public or private agency or institution having custody of records named in the application or motion; and

(5) the law enforcement agency having custody of files or records named in the application or motion.

(f) A copy of the sealing order shall be sent to each agency or official named in the order.

(g) On entry of the order:

(1) all law enforcement, prosecuting attorney, clerk of court, and juvenile court records ordered sealed shall be sent before the 61st day after the date the order is received to the court issuing the order;

(2) all records of a public or private agency or institution ordered sealed shall be sent before the 61st day after the date the order is received to the court issuing the order;

(3) all index references to the records ordered sealed shall be deleted before the 61st day after the date the order is received, and verification of the deletion shall be sent before the 61st day after the date of the deletion to the court issuing the order;

(4) the juvenile court, clerk of court, prosecuting attorney, public or private agency or institution, and law enforcement officers and agencies shall properly reply that no record exists with respect to the person on inquiry in any matter; and

(5) the adjudication shall be vacated and the proceeding dismissed and treated for all purposes other than a subsequent capital prosecution, including the purpose of showing a prior finding of delinquent conduct, as if it had never occurred.

(h) Inspection of the sealed records may be permitted by an order of the juvenile court on the petition of the person who is the subject of the records and only by those persons named in the order.

(i) On the final discharge of a child or on the last official action in the case if there is no adjudication, the child shall be given a written explanation of the child's rights under this section and a copy of the provisions of this section.

(j) A person whose records have been sealed under this section is not required in any proceeding or in any application for employment, information, or licensing to state that the person has been the subject of a proceeding under this title and any statement that the person has never been found to be a delinquent child shall never be held against the person in any criminal or civil proceeding.

(k) A prosecuting attorney may, on application to the juvenile court, reopen at any time the files and records of a person adjudicated as having engaged in delinquent conduct that violated a penal law of the grade of felony sealed by the court under this section for the purposes of Sections 12.42(a)–(c) and (e), Penal Code.

(*l*) On the motion of a person in whose name records are kept or on the court's own motion, the court may order the destruction of records that have been sealed under this section if:

(1) the records relate to conduct that did not violate a penal law of the grade of felony or a misdemeanor punishable by confinement in jail;

(2) five years have elapsed since the person's 16th birthday; and

(3) the person has not been convicted of a felony.

(m) On request of the Department of Public Safety, a juvenile court shall reopen and allow the department to inspect the files and records of the juvenile court relating to an applicant for a license to carry a concealed handgun under Subchapter H, Chapter 411, Government Code.

(n) A record created or maintained under Article 6252–13c.1, Revised Statutes, may not be sealed under this section if the person who is the subject of the record has a continuing obligation to register under that article.

(o) An agency or official named in the order that cannot seal the records because there is incorrect or insufficient information in the order shall notify the court issuing the order before the 61st day after the date the agency or official receives the order. The court shall notify the person who made the application or who is the subject of the records named in the motion, or the attorney for that person, before the 61st day after the date the court receives the notice that the agency or official cannot seal the records because there is incorrect or insufficient information in the order.

History of Fam §58.003: Acts 1995, 74th Leg., ch. 262, §53, eff. Jan. 1, 1996. Amended by Acts 1997, 75th Leg., ch. 165, §10.05(a) (eff. Sept. 1, 1997), ch. 1086, §18 (eff. Sept. 1, 1997); Acts 1999, 76th Leg., ch. 62, §19.01(20) (eff. Sept. 1, 1999), ch. 147, §1 (eff. Sept. 1, 1999).

FAM §58.004. REPEALED

Repealed by Acts 1997, 75th Leg., ch. 1086, §49(a), eff. Sept. 1, 1997.

FAM §58.005. CONFIDENTIALITY OF RECORDS

(a) Information obtained for the purpose of diagnosis, examination, evaluation, or treatment or for making a referral for treatment of a child by a public or private agency or institution providing supervision of a child by arrangement of the juvenile court or having custody of the child under order of the juvenile court may be disclosed only to:

(1) the professional staff or consultants of the agency or institution;

(2) the judge, probation officers, and professional staff or consultants of the juvenile court;

(3) an attorney for the child;

(4) a governmental agency if the disclosure is required or authorized by law;

(5) a person or entity to whom the child is referred for treatment or services if the agency or institution disclosing the information has entered into a written confidentiality agreement with the person or entity regarding the protection of the disclosed information;

(6) the Texas Department of Criminal Justice and the Texas Juvenile Probation Commission for the purpose of maintaining statistical records of recidivism and for diagnosis and classification; or

(7) with leave of the juvenile court, any other person, agency, or institution having a legitimate interest in the proceeding or in the work of the court.

(b) This section does not apply to information collected under Section 58.104.

History of Fam §58.005: Acts 1995, 74th Leg., ch. 262, §53, eff. Jan. 1, 1996.

FAM §58.0051. INTERAGENCY SHARING OF RECORDS

(a) Within each county, a district school superintendent and the juvenile probation department may enter into a written interagency agreement to share information about juvenile offenders. The agreement must specify the conditions under which summary criminal history information is to be made available to appropriate school personnel and the conditions under which school records are to be made available to appropriate juvenile justice agencies.

(b) Information disclosed under this section by a school district must relate to the juvenile system's ability to serve, before adjudication, the student whose records are being released.

(c) A juvenile justice agency official who receives educational information under this section shall certify in writing that the institution or individual receiving the personally identifiable information has agreed not to disclose it to a third party, other than another juvenile justice agency.

(d) A juvenile justice agency that receives educational information under this section shall destroy all information when the child is no longer under the jurisdiction of a juvenile court.

History of Fam §58.0051: Acts 1999, 76th Leg., ch. 217, §1, eff. May 24, 1999.

FAM §58.006. DESTRUCTION OF CERTAIN RECORDS

The court shall order the destruction of the records relating to the conduct for which a child is taken into custody, including records contained in the juvenile justice information system, if:

(1) a determination that no probable cause exists to believe the child engaged in the conduct is made under Section 53.01 and the case is not referred to a prosecutor for review under Section 53.012; or

(2) a determination that no probable cause exists to believe the child engaged in the conduct is made by a prosecutor under Section 53.012.

History of Fam §58.006: Acts 1995, 74th Leg., ch. 262, §53, eff. Jan. 1, 1996.

FAM §58.007. PHYSICAL RECORDS OR FILES

(a) This section applies only to the inspection and maintenance of a physical record or file concerning a child and the storage of information, by electronic means or otherwise, concerning the child from which a physical record or file could be generated and does not affect the collection, dissemination, or maintenance of information as provided by Subchapter B. This section does not apply to a record or file relating to a child that is:

(1) required or authorized to be maintained under the laws regulating the operation of motor vehicles in this state;

(2) maintained by a municipal or justice court; or

(3) subject to disclosure under Chapter 62, Code of Criminal Procedure, as added by Chapter 668, Acts of the 75th Legislature, Regular Session, 1997.

(b) Except as provided by Article 15.27, Code of Criminal Procedure, the records and files of a juvenile court, a clerk of court, a juvenile probation department, or a prosecuting attorney relating to a child who is a party to a proceeding under this title are open to inspection only by:

(1) the judge, probation officers, and professional staff or consultants of the juvenile court;

(2) a juvenile justice agency as that term is defined by Section 58.101;

(3) an attorney for a party to the proceeding;

(4) a public or private agency or institution providing supervision of the child by arrangement of the juvenile court, or having custody of the child under juvenile court order; or

(5) with leave of the juvenile court, any other person, agency, or institution having a legitimate interest in the proceeding or in the work of the court.

(c) Except as provided by Subsection (d), law enforcement records and files concerning a child and information stored, by electronic means or otherwise, concerning the child from which a record or file could be generated may not be disclosed to the public and shall be:

(1) if maintained on paper or microfilm, kept separate from adult files and records;

(2) if maintained electronically in the same computer system as records or files relating to adults, be accessible under controls that are separate and distinct from controls to access electronic data concerning adults; and

(3) maintained on a local basis only and not sent to a central state or federal depository, except as provided by Subchapter B.

(d) The law enforcement files and records of a person who is transferred from the Texas Youth Commission to the institutional division or the pardons and paroles division of the Texas Department of Criminal Justice may be transferred to a central state or federal depository for adult records on or after the date of transfer.

(e) Law enforcement records and files concerning a child may be inspected by a juvenile justice agency as that term is defined by Section 58.101 and a criminal justice agency as that term is defined by Section 411.082, Government Code.

(f) If a child has been reported missing by a parent, guardian, or conservator of that child, information about the child may be forwarded to and disseminated by the Texas Crime Information Center and the National Crime Information Center.

(g) For the purpose of offering a record as evidence in the punishment phase of a criminal proceeding, a prosecuting attorney may obtain the record of a defendant's adjudication that is admissible under Section 3(a), Article 37.07, Code of Criminal Procedure, by submitting a request for the record to the juvenile court that made the adjudication. If a court receives a request from a prosecuting attorney under this subsection, the court shall, if the court possesses the requested record of adjudication, certify and provide the prosecuting attorney with a copy of the record.

(h) The juvenile court may disseminate to the public the following information relating to a child who is the subject of a directive to apprehend or a warrant of arrest and who cannot be located for the purpose of apprehension:

(1) the child's name, including other names by which the child is known;

(2) the child's physical description, including sex, weight, height, race, ethnicity, eye color, hair color, scars, marks, and tattoos;

(3) a photograph of the child; and

(4) a description of the conduct the child is alleged to have committed, including the level and degree of the alleged offense.

E *Subsection (i) below is effective for criminal conduct that occurs on or after Sept. 1, 2001.*

(i) In addition to the authority to release information under Subsection (b)(5), a juvenile probation department may release information contained in its records without leave of the juvenile court pursuant to guidelines adopted by the juvenile board.

History of Fam §58.007: Acts 1995, 74th Leg., ch. 262, §53, eff. Jan. 1, 1996. Amended by Acts 1997, 75th Leg., ch. 1086, §19 (eff. Sept. 1, 1997), ch. 1086, §20 (eff. Sept. 1, 1997); Acts 1999, 76th Leg., ch. 815, §1 (eff. June 18, 1999), ch. 1415, §20 (eff. Sept. 1, 1999), ch. 1477, §18 (eff. Sept. 1, 1999); Acts 2001, 77th Leg., ch. 1297, §37, eff. Sept. 1, 2001.

FAM §58.0071. DESTRUCTION OF CERTAIN PHYSICAL RECORDS & FILES

E *Section 58.0071 below is effective for records and files in a juvenile case destroyed on or after Sept. 1, 2001.*

(a) In this section:

(1) "Juvenile case" means:

(A) a referral for conduct indicating a need for supervision or delinquent conduct; or

(B) if a petition was filed, all charges made in the petition.

(2) "Physical records and files" include entries in a computer file or information on microfilm, microfiche, or any other electronic storage media.

(b) The custodian of physical records and files in a juvenile case may destroy the records and files if the custodian duplicates the information in the records and files in a computer file or information on microfilm, microfiche, or any other electronic storage media.

(c) The following persons may authorize, subject to Subsections (d) and (e) and any other restriction the person may impose, the destruction of the physical records and files relating to a closed juvenile case:

(1) a juvenile board in relation to the records and files in the possession of the juvenile probation department;

(2) the head of a law enforcement agency in relation to the records and files in the possession of the agency; and

(3) a prosecuting attorney in relation to the records and files in the possession of the prosecuting attorney's office.

(d) The physical records and files of a juvenile case may only be destroyed if the child who is the respondent in the case:

(1) is at least 18 years of age and:

(A) the most serious allegation adjudicated was conduct indicating a need for supervision;

(B) the most serious allegation was conduct indicating a need for supervision and there was not an adjudication; or

(C) the referral or information did not relate to conduct indicating a need for supervision or delinquent conduct and the juvenile court or the court's staff did not take action on the referral or information for that reason;

(2) is at least 21 years of age and:

(A) the most serious allegation adjudicated was delinquent conduct that violated a penal law of the grade of misdemeanor; or

(B) the most serious allegation was delinquent conduct that violated a penal law of the grade of misdemeanor or felony and there was not an adjudication; or

(3) is at least 31 years of age and the most serious allegation adjudicated was delinquent conduct that violated a penal law of the grade of felony.

(e) If a record or file contains information relating to more than one juvenile case, information relating to each case may only be destroyed if:

(1) the destruction of the information is authorized under this section; and

(2) the information can be separated from information that is not authorized to be destroyed under this section.

(f) This section does not affect the destruction of physical records and files authorized by the Texas State Library Records Retention Schedule.

History of Fam §58.0071: Enacted by Acts 2001, 77th Leg., ch. 1297, §38, eff. Sept. 1, 2001.

Sections 58.008-58.100 reserved for expansion

SUBCHAPTER B. JUVENILE JUSTICE INFORMATION SYSTEM

FAM §58.101. DEFINITIONS

In this subchapter:

(1) "Criminal justice agency" has the meaning assigned by Section 411.082, Government Code.

(2) "Department" means the Department of Public Safety of the State of Texas.

(3) "Disposition" means an action that results in the termination, transfer of jurisdiction, or indeterminate suspension of the prosecution of a juvenile offender.

A *Subsection (4) below is effective for criminal conduct that occurs on or after Sept. 1, 2001.*

(4) "Incident number" means a unique number assigned to a child during a specific custodial or detention period or for a specific referral to the office or official designated by the juvenile board, if the juvenile offender was not taken into custody before the referral.

Subsection (4) below is effective for criminal conduct in which any element of the conduct occurred before Sept. 1, 2001.

(4) "Incident number" means a unique number assigned to a child during a specific custodial or detention period or for a specific referral to the office or official designated by the juvenile court, if the juvenile offender was not taken into custody before the referral.

(5) "Juvenile justice agency" means an agency that has custody or control over juvenile offenders.

(6) "Juvenile offender" means a child who has been assigned an incident number.

(7) "State identification number" means a unique number assigned by the department to a child in the juvenile justice information system.

(8) "Uniform incident fingerprint card" means a multiple-part form containing a unique incident number with space for information relating to the conduct for which a child has been taken into custody, detained, or referred, the child's fingerprints, and other relevant information.

History of Fam §58.101: Acts 1995, 74th Leg., ch. 262, §53, eff. Jan. 1, 1996. Amended by Acts 2001, 77th Leg., ch. 1297, §39, eff. Sept. 1, 2001.

FAM §58.102. JUVENILE JUSTICE INFORMATION SYSTEM

(a) The department is responsible for recording data and maintaining a database for a computerized juvenile justice information system that serves:

(1) as the record creation point for the juvenile justice information system maintained by the state; and

(2) as the control terminal for entry of records, in accordance with federal law, rule, and policy, into the federal records system maintained by the Federal Bureau of Investigation.

(b) The department shall develop and maintain the system with the cooperation and advice of the:

(1) Texas Youth Commission;

(2) Texas Juvenile Probation Commission;

(3) Criminal Justice Policy Council; and

(4) juvenile courts and clerks of juvenile courts.

(c) The department may not collect or retain information relating to a juvenile if this chapter prohibits or restricts the collection or retention of the information.

(d) The database must contain the information required by this subchapter.

(e) The department shall designate the offense codes and has the sole responsibility for designating the state identification number for each juvenile whose name appears in the juvenile justice system.

History of Fam §58.1102: Acts 1995, 74th Leg., ch. 262, §53, eff. Jan. 1, 1996.

FAM §58.103. PURPOSE OF SYSTEM

The purpose of the juvenile justice information system is to:

(1) provide agencies and personnel within the juvenile justice system accurate information relating to children who come into contact with the juvenile justice system of this state;

(2) provide, where allowed by law, adult criminal justice agencies accurate and easily accessible information relating to children who come into contact with the juvenile justice system;

(3) provide an efficient conversion, where appropriate, of juvenile records to adult criminal records;

(4) improve the quality of data used to conduct impact analyses of proposed legislative changes in the juvenile justice system; and

(5) improve the ability of interested parties to analyze the functioning of the juvenile justice system.

History of Fam §58.103: Acts 1995, 74th Leg., ch. 262, §53, eff. Jan. 1, 1996.

FAM §58.104. TYPES OF INFORMATION COLLECTED

(a) Subject to Subsection (f), the juvenile justice information system shall consist of information relating to delinquent conduct committed by a juvenile offender that, if the conduct had been committed by an adult, would constitute a criminal offense other than an offense punishable by a fine only, including information relating to:

(1) the juvenile offender;

(2) the intake or referral of the juvenile offender into the juvenile justice system;

(3) the detention of the juvenile offender;

(4) the prosecution of the juvenile offender;

(5) the disposition of the juvenile offender's case, including the name and description of any program to which the juvenile offender is referred; and

(6) the probation or commitment of the juvenile offender.

(b) To the extent possible and subject to Subsection (a), the department shall include in the juvenile justice information system the following information for each juvenile offender taken into custody, detained, or referred under this title for delinquent conduct:

(1) the juvenile offender's name, including other names by which the juvenile offender is known;

(2) the juvenile offender's date and place of birth;

(3) the juvenile offender's physical description, including sex, weight, height, race, ethnicity, eye color, hair color, scars, marks, and tattoos;

(4) the juvenile offender's state identification number, and other identifying information, as determined by the department;

(5) the juvenile offender's fingerprints;

(6) the juvenile offender's last known residential address, including the census tract number designation for the address;

(7) the name and identifying number of the agency that took into custody or detained the juvenile offender;

(8) the date of detention or custody;

(9) the conduct for which the juvenile offender was taken into custody, detained, or referred, including level and degree of the alleged offense;

(10) the name and identifying number of the juvenile intake agency or juvenile probation office;

(11) each disposition by the juvenile intake agency or juvenile probation office;

(12) the date of disposition by the juvenile intake agency or juvenile probation office;

(13) the name and identifying number of the prosecutor's office;

(14) each disposition by the prosecutor;

(15) the date of disposition by the prosecutor;

(16) the name and identifying number of the court;

(17) each disposition by the court, including information concerning custody of a juvenile offender by a juvenile justice agency or probation;

(18) the date of disposition by the court;

(19) any commitment or release under supervision by the Texas Youth Commission;

(20) the date of any commitment or release under supervision by the Texas Youth Commission; and

(21) a description of each appellate proceeding.

(c) The department may designate codes relating to the information described by Subsection (b).

(d) The department shall designate a state identification number for each juvenile offender.

(e) This subchapter does not apply to a disposition that represents an administrative status notice of an agency described by Section 58.102(b).

(f) Records maintained by the department in the depository are subject to being sealed under Section 58.003. The department shall send to the appropriate juvenile court its certification of records that the department determines, according to the department's records, are eligible for sealing under Section 58.003(a).

History of Fam §58.104: Acts 1995, 74th Leg., ch. 262, §53, eff. Jan. 1, 1996. Amended by Acts 1997, 75th Leg., ch. 1086, §21, eff. Sept. 1, 1997.

FAM §58.105. DUTIES OF JUVENILE BOARD

Each juvenile board shall provide for:

(1) the compilation and maintenance of records and information needed for reporting information to the department under this subchapter;

(2) the transmittal to the department, in the manner provided by the department, of all records and information required by the department under this subchapter; and

(3) access by the department to inspect records and information to determine the completeness and accuracy of information reported.

History of Fam §58.105: Acts 1995, 74th Leg., ch. 262, §53, eff. Jan. 1, 1996.

FAM §58.106. CONFIDENTIALITY

(a) Except as otherwise provided by this section, information contained in the juvenile justice information system is confidential information for the use of the department and may not be disseminated by the department except:

(1) with the permission of the juvenile offender, to military personnel of this state or the United States;

(2) to a person or entity to which the department may grant access to adult criminal history records as provided by Section 411.083, Government Code;

(3) to a juvenile justice agency; and

(4) to the Criminal Justice Policy Council, the Texas Youth Commission, and the Texas Juvenile Probation Commission for analytical purposes.

(b) Subsection (a) does not apply to a document maintained by a juvenile justice agency that is the source of information collected by the department.

(c) The department may, if necessary to protect the welfare of the community, disseminate to the public the following information relating to a juvenile who has escaped from the custody of the Texas Youth Commission or from another secure detention or correctional facility:

(1) the juvenile's name, including other names by which the juvenile is known;

(2) the juvenile's physical description, including sex, weight, height, race, ethnicity, eye color, hair color, scars, marks, and tattoos;

(3) a photograph of the juvenile; and

(4) a description of the conduct for which the juvenile was committed to the Texas Youth Commission or detained in the secure detention or correctional facility, including the level and degree of the alleged offense.

(d) The department may, if necessary to protect the welfare of the community, disseminate to the public the information listed under Subsection (c) relating to a juvenile offender when notified by a law enforcement agency of this state that the law enforcement agency has been issued a directive to apprehend the offender or an arrest warrant for the offender or that the law enforcement agency is otherwise authorized to arrest the offender and that the offender is suspected of having:

(1) committed a felony offense under the following provisions of the Penal Code:

(A) Title 5;

(B) Section 29.02; or

(C) Section 29.03; and

(2) fled from arrest or apprehension for commission of the offense.

History of Fam §58.106: Acts 1995, 74th Leg., ch. 262, §53, eff. Jan. 1, 1996. Amended by Acts 1997, 75th Leg., ch. 380, §1, eff. Sept. 1, 1997; Acts 1999, 76th Leg., ch. 407, §1 (eff. Sept. 1, 1999), ch. 1477, §19 (eff. Sept. 1, 1999).

FAM §58.107. COMPATIBILITY OF DATA

Data supplied to the juvenile justice information system must be compatible with the system and must contain both incident numbers and state identification numbers.

History of Fam §58.107: Acts 1995, 74th Leg., ch. 262, §53, eff. Jan. 1, 1996.

FAM §58.108. DUTIES OF AGENCIES & COURTS

(a) A juvenile justice agency and a clerk of a juvenile court shall:

(1) compile and maintain records needed for reporting data required by the department;

(2) transmit to the department in the manner provided by the department data required by the department;

(3) give the department or its accredited agents access to the agency or court for the purpose of inspection to determine the completeness and accuracy of data reported; and

(4) cooperate with the department to enable the department to perform its duties under this chapter.

(b) A juvenile justice agency and clerk of a court shall retain documents described by this section.

History of Fam §58.108: Acts 1995, 74th Leg., ch. 262, §53, eff. Jan. 1, 1996.

FAM §58.109. UNIFORM INCIDENT FINGERPRINT CARD

(a) The department may provide for the use of a uniform incident fingerprint card in the maintenance of the juvenile justice information system.

(b) The department shall design, print, and distribute to each law enforcement agency and juvenile intake agency uniform incident fingerprint cards.

(c) The incident cards must:

(1) be serially numbered with an incident number in a manner that allows each incident of referral of a juvenile offender who is the subject of the incident fingerprint card to be readily ascertained; and

(2) be multiple-part forms that can be transmitted with the juvenile offender through the juvenile justice process and that allow each agency to report required data to the department.

(d) Subject to available telecommunications capacity, the department shall develop the capability to receive by electronic means from a law enforcement agency the information on the uniform incident fingerprint card. The information must be in a form that is compatible to the form required of data supplied to the juvenile justice information system.

History of Fam §58.109: Acts 1995, 74th Leg., ch. 262, §53, eff. Jan. 1, 1996.

FAM §58.110. REPORTING

(a) The department by rule shall develop reporting procedures that ensure that the juvenile offender processing data is reported from the time a juvenile offender is initially taken into custody, detained, or referred until the time a juvenile offender is released from the jurisdiction of the juvenile justice system.

(b) The law enforcement agency or the juvenile intake agency that initiates the entry of the juvenile offender into the juvenile justice information system for a specific incident shall prepare a uniform incident fingerprint card and initiate the reporting process for each incident reportable under this subchapter.

(c) The clerk of the court exercising jurisdiction over a juvenile offender's case shall report the disposition of the case to the department. A clerk of the court who violates this subsection commits an offense. An offense under this subsection is a Class C misdemeanor.

(d) In each county, the reporting agencies may make alternative arrangements for reporting the required information, including combined reporting or electronic reporting, if the alternative reporting is approved by the juvenile board and the department.

(e) Except as otherwise required by applicable state laws or regulations, information required by this chapter to be reported to the department shall be reported promptly. The information shall be reported not later than the 30th day after the date the information is received by the agency responsible for reporting the information, except that a juvenile offender's custody, detention, or referral without previous custody shall be reported to the department not later than the seventh day after the date of the custody, detention, or referral.

(f) Subject to available telecommunications capacity, the department shall develop the capability to receive by electronic means the information required under this section to be reported to the department. The information must be in a form that is compatible to the form required of data to be reported under this section.

History of Fam §58.110: Acts 1995, 74th Leg., ch. 262, §53, eff. Jan. 1, 1996.

FAM §58.111. LOCAL DATA ADVISORY BOARDS

The commissioners court of each county may create a local data advisory board to perform the same duties relating to the juvenile justice information system as the duties performed by a local data advisory board in relation to the criminal history record system under Article 60.09, Code of Criminal Procedure.

History of Fam §58.111: Acts 1995, 74th Leg., ch. 262, §53, eff. Jan. 1, 1996.

FAM §58.112. REPORT TO LEGISLATURE

A *Section 58.112 below is effective for criminal conduct that occurs on or after Sept. 1, 2001.*

Not later than August 15 of each year, the Texas Juvenile Probation Commission shall submit to the lieutenant governor, the speaker of the house of representatives, and the governor a report that contains the following statistical information relating to children referred to a juvenile court during the preceding year:

(1) the ages, races, and counties of residence of the children transferred to a district court or criminal district court for criminal proceedings; and

(2) the ages, races, and counties of residence of the children committed to the Texas Youth Commission, placed on probation, or discharged without any disposition.

History of Fam §58.112: Acts 1995, 74th Leg., ch. 262, §53, eff. Jan. 1, 1996. Amended by Acts 2001, 77th Leg., ch. 1297, §40, eff. Sept. 1, 2001.

FAM §58.112. REPORT TO LEGISLATURE

Section 58.112 below is effective for criminal conduct in which any element of the conduct occurred before Sept. 1, 2001.

Not later than January 15 of each year, the Criminal Justice Policy Council shall submit to the lieutenant governor, the speaker of the house of representatives, and the governor a report that contains the following statistical information relating to children referred to a juvenile court during the preceding year:

(1) the ages, races, and counties of residence of the children transferred to a district court or criminal district court for criminal proceedings; and

(2) the ages, races, and counties of residence of the children committed to the Texas Youth Commission, placed on probation, or discharged without any disposition.

FAM §58.113. WARRANTS

The department shall maintain in a computerized database that is accessible by the same entities that may access the juvenile justice information system information relating to a warrant of arrest, as that term is defined by Article 15.01, Code of Criminal Procedure, or a directive to apprehend under Section 52.015 for any child, without regard to whether the child has been taken into custody.

History of Fam §58.113: Acts 1995, 74th Leg., ch. 262, §53, eff. Jan. 1, 1996.

SUBCHAPTER C. AUTOMATIC RESTRICTION OF ACCESS TO RECORDS

E *Subchapter C below is effective for all records relating to a juvenile case on or after Sept. 1, 2001.*

E FAM §58.201. DEFINITION

In this subchapter, "department" means the Department of Public Safety of the State of Texas.

History of Fam §58.201: Enacted by Acts 2001, 77th Leg., ch. 1297, §41, eff. Sept. 1, 2001.

E FAM §58.202. EXEMPTED RECORDS

The following records are exempt from this subchapter:

(1) sex offender registration records maintained by the department or a local law enforcement agency under Chapter 62, Code of Criminal Procedure; and

(2) records relating to a criminal combination or criminal street gang maintained by the department or a local law enforcement agency under Chapter 61, Code of Criminal Procedure.

History of Fam §58.202: Enacted by Acts 2001, 77th Leg., ch. 1297, §41, eff. Sept. 1, 2001.

E FAM §58.203. CERTIFICATION

The department shall certify to the juvenile court or the juvenile probation department to which a referral was made that resulted in information being submitted to the juvenile justice information system that the records relating to a person's juvenile case are subject to automatic restriction of access if:

(1) the person is at least 21 years of age;

(2) the juvenile case did not include violent or habitual felony conduct resulting in proceedings in the juvenile court under Section 53.045;

(3) the juvenile case was not certified for trial in criminal court under Section 54.02; and

(4) the department has not received a report in its criminal history system that the person was granted deferred adjudication for or convicted of a felony or a misdemeanor punishable by confinement in jail for an offense committed after the person became 17 years of age.

History of Fam §58.203: Enacted by Acts 2001, 77th Leg., ch. 1297, §41, eff. Sept. 1, 2001.

E FAM §58.204. RESTRICTED ACCESS ON CERTIFICATION

(a) On certification of records in a case under Section 58.203, the department, except as provided by Subsection (b):

(1) may not disclose the existence of the records or any information from the records in response to an inquiry from:

(A) a law enforcement agency;

(B) a criminal or juvenile justice agency;

(C) a governmental or other agency given access to information under Chapter 411, Government Code; or

(D) any other person, agency, organization, or entity; and

(2) shall respond to a request for information about the records by stating that the records do not exist.

(b) On certification of records in a case under Section 58.203, the department may permit access to the information in the juvenile justice information system relating to the case of an individual only:

(1) by a criminal justice agency for a criminal justice purpose, as those terms are defined by Section 411.082, Government Code; or

(2) for research purposes, by the Texas Juvenile Probation Commission, the Texas Youth Commission, or the Criminal Justice Policy Council.

History of Fam §58.204: Enacted by Acts 2001, 77th Leg., ch. 1297, §41, eff. Sept. 1, 2001.

E FAM §58.205. REQUEST TO THE FEDERAL BUREAU OF INVESTIGATION ON CERTIFICATION

On certification of records in a case under Section 58.203, the department shall request the Federal Bureau of Investigation to:

(1) place the information in its files on restricted status, with access only by a criminal justice agency for a criminal justice purpose, as those terms are defined by Section 411.082, Government Code; or

(2) if the action described in Subdivision (1) is not feasible, delete all information in its database concerning the case.

History of Fam §58.205: Enacted by Acts 2001, 77th Leg., ch. 1297, §41, eff. Sept. 1, 2001.

E FAM §58.206. EFFECT OF CERTIFICATION IN RELATION TO THE PROTECTED PERSON

(a) On certification of records in a case under Section 58.203:

(1) the person who is the subject of the records is not required to state in any proceeding, except as otherwise authorized by law in a criminal proceeding in which the person is testifying as a defendant, or in any application for employment, licensing, or other public or private benefit that the person has been a respondent in a case under this title and may not be punished, by perjury prosecution or otherwise, for denying:

(A) the existence of the records; or

(B) the person's participation in a juvenile proceeding related to the records; and

(2) information from the records may not be admitted against the person who is the subject of the records in a civil or criminal proceeding except a proceeding in which a juvenile adjudication was admitted under:

(A) Section 12.42, Penal Code;

(B) Article 37.07, Code of Criminal Procedure; or

(C) as otherwise authorized by criminal procedural law.

(b) A person who is the subject of records certified under this subchapter may not waive the restricted status of the records or the consequences of the restricted status.

History of Fam §58.206: Enacted by Acts 2001, 77th Leg., ch. 1297, §41, eff. Sept. 1, 2001.

E FAM §58.207. JUVENILE COURT ORDERS ON CERTIFICATION

(a) On certification of records in a case under Section 58.203, the juvenile court shall order:

(1) that the following records relating to the case may be accessed only as provided by Section 58.204(b):

(A) if the respondent was committed to the Texas Youth Commission, records maintained by the commission;

(B) records maintained by the juvenile probation department and by any agency that provided care or custody of the child under order or arrangement of the juvenile court;

(C) records maintained by the clerk of the court;

(D) records maintained by the prosecutor's office; and

(E) records maintained by a law enforcement agency; and

(2) the juvenile probation department to make a reasonable effort to notify the person who is the subject of records for which access has been restricted of the action restricting access and the legal significance of the action for the person.

(b) On receipt of an order under Subsection (a)(1), the agency maintaining the records:

(1) may allow access only as provided by Section 58.204(b); and

(2) shall respond to a request for information about the records by stating that the records do not exist.

History of Fam §58.207: Enacted by Acts 2001, 77th Leg., ch. 1297, §41, eff. Sept. 1, 2001.

E FAM §58.208. INFORMATION TO CHILD ON DISCHARGE

On the final discharge of a child from the juvenile system or on the last official action in the case, if there is no adjudication, the appropriate juvenile justice official shall provide to the child:

(1) a written explanation of how automatic restricted access under this subchapter works; and

(2) a copy of this subchapter.

History of Fam §58.208: Enacted by Acts 2001, 77th Leg., ch. 1297, §41, eff. Sept. 1, 2001.

E FAM §58.209. INFORMATION TO CHILD BY PROBATION OFFICER OR TEXAS YOUTH COMMISSION

(a) When a child is placed on probation for an offense that may be eligible for automatic restricted access at age 21 or when a child is received by the Texas Youth Commission on an indeterminate commitment, a probation officer or an official at the Texas Youth Commission reception center, as soon as practicable, shall explain the substance of the following information to the child:

(1) if the child was adjudicated as having committed delinquent conduct for a felony or jailable misdemeanor, that the child probably has a juvenile record with the department and the Federal Bureau of Investigation;

(2) that the child's juvenile record is a permanent record that is not destroyed or erased unless the record is eligible for sealing and the child or the child's family hires a lawyer and files a petition in court to have the record sealed;

(3) that the child's juvenile record, other than treatment records made confidential by law, can be accessed by police, sheriff's officers, prosecutors, probation officers, correctional officers, and other criminal and juvenile justice officials in this state and elsewhere;

(4) that the child's juvenile record, other than treatment records made confidential by law, can be accessed by employers, educational institutions, licensing agencies, and other organizations when the child applies for employment or educational programs;

(5) if the child's juvenile record is placed on restricted access when the child becomes 21 years of age, that access will be denied to employers, educational institutions, and others except for criminal justice agencies;

(6) that to have the child's juvenile record placed on restricted access at age 21, the child must not:

(A) commit a felony or jailable misdemeanor; and

(B) receive deferred adjudication for or be convicted in adult court of a felony or jailable misdemeanor; and

(7) that restricted access does not require any action by the child or the child's family, including the filing of a petition or hiring of a lawyer, but occurs automatically at age 21 if the child does not commit a criminal offense in the future.

(b) The probation officer or Texas Youth Commission official shall:

(1) give the child a written copy of the explanation provided; and

(2) communicate the same information to at least one of the child's parents or, if none can be found, to the child's guardian or custodian.

(c) The Texas Juvenile Probation Commission and the Texas Youth Commission shall adopt rules to implement this section and to facilitate the effective explanation of the information required to be communicated by this section.

History of Fam §58.209: Enacted by Acts 2001, 77th Leg., ch. 1297, §41, eff. Sept. 1, 2001.

Ⓔ FAM §58.210. SEALING OR DESTRUCTION OF RECORDS NOT AFFECTED

(a) This subchapter does not prevent or restrict the sealing or destruction of juvenile records as authorized by law.

(b) Restricted access provided under this subchapter is in addition to sealing or destruction of juvenile records.

(c) A person who is the subject of records certified under this subchapter is entitled to access to the records for the purpose of preparing and presenting a motion to seal or destroy the records.

History of Fam §58.210: Enacted by Acts 2001, 77th Leg., ch. 1297, §41, eff. Sept. 1, 2001.

SUBCHAPTER D. LOCAL JUVENILE JUSTICE INFORMATION SYSTEM

Ⓔ *Subchapter D below is effective for criminal conduct that occurs on or after Sept. 1, 2001.*

Ⓔ FAM §58.301. DEFINITIONS

In this subchapter:

(1) "County juvenile board" means a juvenile board created under Chapter 152, Human Resources Code.

(2) "Governmental placement facility" means a juvenile residential placement facility operated by a unit of government.

(3) "Governmental service provider" means a juvenile justice service provider operated by a unit of government.

(4) "Local juvenile justice information system" means a county or multicounty computerized database of information concerning children, with data entry and access by the partner agencies that are members of the system.

(5) "Partner agency" means a governmental service provider or governmental placement facility that is required by this subchapter to be a member of a local juvenile justice information system or that has applied to be a member of a local juvenile justice information system and has been approved by the county juvenile board

or regional juvenile board committee as a member of the system.

(6) "Regional juvenile board committee" means a committee that is composed of two members from each county juvenile board in a region that comprises a multicounty local juvenile information system.

History of Fam §58.301: Enacted by Acts 2001, 77th Leg., ch. 1297, §41, eff. Sept. 1, 2001.

E FAM §58.302. PURPOSES OF SYSTEM

The purposes of a local juvenile justice information system are to:

(1) provide accurate information at the county or regional level relating to children who come into contact with the juvenile justice system;

(2) assist in the development and delivery of services to children in the juvenile justice system;

(3) assist in the development and delivery of services to children:

(A) who school officials have reasonable cause to believe have committed an offense for which a report is required under Section 37.015, Education Code; or

(B) who have been expelled, the expulsion of which school officials are required to report under Section 52.041;

(4) provide for an efficient transmission of juvenile records from justice and municipal courts to county juvenile probation departments and the juvenile court and from county juvenile probation departments and juvenile court to the state juvenile justice information system created by Subchapter B;

(5) provide efficient computerized case management resources to juvenile courts, county juvenile probation departments, and partner agencies authorized by this subchapter;

(6) provide a directory of services available to children to the partner agencies to facilitate the delivery of services to children;

(7) provide an efficient means for municipal and justice courts to report filing of charges, adjudications, and dispositions of juveniles to the juvenile court as required by Section 51.08; and

(8) provide a method for agencies to fulfill their duties under Section 58.108, including the electronic transmission of information required to be sent to the Department of Public Safety by Section 58.110(f).

History of Fam §58.302: Enacted by Acts 2001, 77th Leg., ch. 1297, §41, eff. Sept. 1, 2001.

E FAM §58.303. LOCAL JUVENILE JUSTICE INFORMATION SYSTEM

(a) Juvenile justice agencies in a county or region of this state may jointly create and maintain a local juvenile justice information system to aid in processing the cases of children under this code, to facilitate the delivery of services to children in the juvenile justice system, and to aid in the early identification of at-risk and delinquent children.

(b) A local juvenile justice information system must contain the following components:

(1) case management resources for juvenile courts, prosecuting attorneys, and county juvenile probation departments;

(2) reporting systems to fulfill statutory requirements for reporting in the juvenile justice system;

(3) service provider directories and indexes of agencies providing services to children; and

(4) victim-witness notices required under Chapter 57.

(c) A local juvenile justice information system may contain the following components:

(1) electronic filing of complaints or petitions;

(2) electronic offense and intake processing;

(3) case docket management and calendaring;

(4) communications by email or other electronic communications between partner agencies;

(5) reporting of charges filed, adjudications and dispositions of juveniles by municipal and justice courts and the juvenile court, and transfers of cases to the juvenile court as authorized or required by Section 51.08;

(6) reporting to schools under Article 15.27, Code of Criminal Procedure, by law enforcement agencies, prosecuting attorneys, and juvenile courts;

(7) records of adjudications and dispositions, including probation conditions ordered by the juvenile court; and

(8) warrant management and confirmation capabilities.

(d) Membership in a local juvenile justice information system is determined by this subchapter. Membership in a regional juvenile justice information system is determined by the regional juvenile board committee from among partner agencies that have applied for membership.

History of Fam §58.303: Enacted by Acts 2001, 77th Leg., ch. 1297, §41, eff. Sept. 1, 2001.

E FAM §58.304. TYPES OF INFORMATION CONTAINED IN A LOCAL JUVENILE INFORMATION SYSTEM

(a) Subject to Subsection (d), a local juvenile justice information system must consist of:

(1) information relating to all referrals to the juvenile court of any type, including referrals for conduct indicating a need for supervision and delinquent conduct; and

(2) information relating to:

(A) the juvenile;

(B) the intake or referral of the juvenile into the juvenile justice system for any offense or conduct;

(C) the detention of the juvenile;

(D) the prosecution of the juvenile;

(E) the disposition of the juvenile's case, including the name and description of any program to which the juvenile is referred; and

(F) the probation, placement, or commitment of the juvenile.

(b) To the extent possible and subject to Subsections (a) and (d), the local juvenile justice information system may include the following information for each juvenile taken into custody, detained, or referred under this title:

(1) the juvenile's name, including other names by which the juvenile is known;

(2) the juvenile's date and place of birth;

(3) the juvenile's physical description, including sex, weight, height, race, ethnicity, eye color, hair color, scars, marks, and tattoos;

(4) the juvenile's state identification number and other identifying information;

(5) the juvenile's fingerprints and photograph;

(6) the juvenile's last known residential address, including the census tract number designation for the address;

(7) the name, address, and phone number of the juvenile's parent, guardian, or custodian;

(8) the name and identifying number of the agency that took into custody or detained the juvenile;

(9) each date of custody or detention;

(10) a detailed description of the conduct for which the juvenile was taken into custody, detained, or referred, including the level and degree of the alleged offense;

(11) the name and identifying number of the juvenile intake agency or juvenile probation office;

(12) each disposition by the juvenile intake agency or juvenile probation office;

(13) the date of disposition by the juvenile intake agency or juvenile probation office;

(14) the name and identifying number of the prosecutor's office;

(15) each disposition by the prosecutor;

(16) the date of disposition by the prosecutor;

(17) the name and identifying number of the court;

(18) each disposition by the court, including information concerning custody of a juvenile by a juvenile justice agency or county juvenile probation department;

(19) the date of disposition by the court;

(20) any commitment or release under supervision by the Texas Youth Commission, including the date of the commitment or release; and

(21) information concerning each appellate proceeding.

(c) If the Department of Public Safety assigns a state identification number for the juvenile, the identification number shall be entered in the local juvenile information system.

(d) Information obtained for the purpose of diagnosis, examination, evaluation, or treatment or for making a referral for treatment of a child by a public or private agency or institution providing supervision of a child by arrangement of the juvenile court or having custody of the child under order of the juvenile court may not be collected under Subsection (a) or (b).

History of Fam §58.304: Enacted by Acts 2001, 77th Leg., ch. 1297, §41, eff. Sept. 1, 2001.

E FAM §58.305. PARTNER AGENCIES

(a) A local juvenile justice information system for a single county shall include the following partner agencies within that county:

(1) the juvenile court;

(2) justice of the peace and municipal courts;

(3) the county juvenile probation department;

(4) the prosecuting attorneys who prosecute juvenile cases in juvenile court, municipal court, or justice court;

(5) law enforcement agencies;

(6) each public school district in the county;

(7) governmental service providers approved by the county juvenile board; and

(8) governmental placement facilities approved by the county juvenile board.

(b) A local juvenile justice information system for a multicounty region shall include the partner agencies listed in Subsections (a)(1)-(6) for each county in the region and the following partner agencies from within the multicounty region that have applied for membership in the system and have been approved by the regional juvenile board committee:

(1) governmental service providers; and

(2) governmental placement facilities.

History of Fam §58.305: Enacted by Acts 2001, 77th Leg., ch. 1297, §41, eff. Sept. 1, 2001.

E FAM §58.306. ACCESS TO INFORMATION; LEVELS

(a) This section describes the level of access to information to which each partner agency in a local juvenile justice information system is entitled.

(b) Information is at Access Level 1 if the information relates to a child:

(1) who:

(A) a school official has reasonable grounds to believe has committed an offense for which a report is required under Section 37.015, Education Code; or

(B) has been expelled, the expulsion of which is required to be reported under Section 52.041; and

(2) who has not been charged with a fineable only offense, a status offense, or delinquent conduct.

(c) Information is at Access Level 2 if the information relates to a child who:

(1) is alleged in a justice or municipal court to have committed a fineable only offense, municipal ordinance violation, or status offense; and

(2) has not been charged with delinquent conduct or conduct indicating a need for supervision.

(d) Information is at Access Level 3 if the information relates to a child who is alleged to have engaged in delinquent conduct or conduct indicating a need for supervision.

(e) Level 1 Access is by public school districts in the county or region served by the local juvenile justice information system.

(f) Level 2 Access is by:

(1) justice of the peace courts that process juvenile cases; and

(2) municipal courts that process juvenile cases.

(g) Level 3 Access is by:

(1) the juvenile court;

(2) the prosecuting attorney;

(3) the county juvenile probation department;

(4) law enforcement agencies;

(5) governmental service providers that are partner agencies; and

(6) governmental placement facilities that are partner agencies.

(h) Access for Level 1 agencies is only to information at Level 1. Access for Level 2 agencies is only to information at Levels 1 and 2. Access for Level 3 agencies is to information at Levels 1, 2, and 3.

History of Fam §58.306: Enacted by Acts 2001, 77th Leg., ch. 1297, §41, eff. Sept. 1, 2001.

E FAM §58.307. CONFIDENTIALITY OF INFORMATION

(a) Information that is part of a local juvenile justice system is not public information and may not be released to the public, except as authorized by law.

(b) Information that is part of a local juvenile justice information system is for the professional use of the partner agencies that are members of the system and may be used only by authorized employees of those agencies to discharge duties of those agencies.

(c) Information from a local juvenile justice information system may not be disclosed to persons, agencies, or organizations that are not members of the system except to the extent disclosure is authorized or mandated by this title.

(d) Information in a local juvenile justice information system is subject to destruction, sealing, or restricted access as provided by this title.

(e) Information in a local juvenile justice information system shall be protected from unauthorized access by a system of access security and any access to information in a local juvenile information system performed by browser software shall be at the level of at least 128-bit encryption. A juvenile board or a regional juvenile board committee shall require all partner agencies to maintain security and restrict access in accordance with the requirements of this title.

History of Fam §58.307: Enacted by Acts 2001, 77th Leg., ch. 1297, §41, eff. Sept. 1, 2001.

CHAPTER 59. PROGRESSIVE SANCTIONS GUIDELINES

FAM §59.001. PURPOSES

The purposes of the progressive sanctions guidelines are to:

(1) ensure that juvenile offenders face uniform and consistent consequences and punishments that correspond to the seriousness of each offender's current offense, prior delinquent history, special treatment or training needs, and effectiveness of prior interventions;

(2) balance public protection and rehabilitation while holding juvenile offenders accountable;

(3) permit flexibility in the decisions made in relation to the juvenile offender to the extent allowed by law;

(4) consider the juvenile offender's circumstances; and

(5) improve juvenile justice planning and resource allocation by ensuring uniform and consistent reporting of disposition decisions at all levels.

History of Fam §59.01: Acts 1995, 74th Leg., ch. 262, §53, eff. Jan. 1, 1996.

FAM §59.002. SANCTION LEVEL ASSIGNMENT BY PROBATION DEPARTMENT

(a) The probation department may assign a sanction level of one to a child referred to the probation department under Section 53.012.

(b) The probation department may assign a sanction level of two to a child for whom deferred prosecution is authorized under Section 53.03.

History of Fam §59.002: Acts 1995, 74th Leg., ch. 262, §53, eff. Jan. 1, 1996.

FAM §59.003. SANCTION LEVEL ASSIGNMENT GUIDELINES

(a) Subject to Subsection (e), after a child's first commission of delinquent conduct or conduct indicating a need for supervision, the probation department or prosecuting attorney may, or the juvenile court may, in a disposition hearing under Section 54.04 or a modification hearing under Section 54.05, assign a child one of the following sanction levels according to the child's conduct:

(1) for conduct indicating a need for supervision, other than conduct described in Section 51.03(b)(5) or a Class A or B misdemeanor, the sanction level is one;

A *Subsection (2) below is effective for criminal conduct that occurs on or after Sept. 1, 2001.*

(2) for conduct indicating a need for supervision under Section 51.03(b)(5) or a Class A or B misdemeanor, other than a misdemeanor involving the use or possession of a firearm, or for delinquent conduct under Section 51.03(a)(2), the sanction level is two;

Subsection (2) below is effective for criminal conduct in which any element of the conduct occurred before Sept. 1, 2001.

(2) for conduct indicating a need for supervision under Section 51.03(b)(5) or a Class A or B misdemeanor, other than a misdemeanor involving the use or possession of a firearm, or for delinquent conduct under Section 51.03(a)(2) or (3), the sanction level is two;

(3) for a misdemeanor involving the use or possession of a firearm or for a state jail felony or a felony of the third degree, the sanction level is three;

(4) for a felony of the second degree, the sanction level is four;

(5) for a felony of the first degree, other than a felony involving the use of a deadly weapon or causing serious bodily injury, the sanction level is five;

(6) for a felony of the first degree involving the use of a deadly weapon or causing serious bodily injury, for an aggravated controlled substance felony, or for a capital felony, the sanction level is six; or

(7) for a felony of the first degree involving the use of a deadly weapon or causing serious bodily injury, for an aggravated controlled substance felony, or for a capital felony, if the petition has been approved by a grand jury under Section 53.045, or if a petition to transfer the

child to criminal court has been filed under Section 54.02, the sanction level is seven.

(b) Subject to Subsection (e), if the child subsequently is found to have engaged in delinquent conduct in an adjudication hearing under Section 54.03 or a hearing to modify a disposition under Section 54.05 on two separate occasions and each involves a violation of a penal law of a classification that is less than the classification of the child's previous conduct, the juvenile court may assign the child a sanction level that is one level higher than the previously assigned sanction level, unless the child's previously assigned sanction level is six.

Ⓐ *Subsection (c) below is effective for criminal conduct that occurs on or after Sept. 1, 2001.*

(c) Subject to Subsection (e), if the child's subsequent commission of delinquent conduct or conduct indicating a need for supervision involves a violation of a penal law of a classification that is the same as or greater than the classification of the child's previous conduct, the juvenile court may assign the child a sanction level authorized by law that is one level higher than the previously assigned sanction level.

Subsection (c) below is effective for criminal conduct in which any element of the conduct occurred before Sept. 1, 2001.

(c) Subject to Subsection (e), if the child's subsequent commission of delinquent conduct or conduct indicating a need for supervision involves a violation of a penal law of a classification that is the same as or greater than the classification of the child's previous conduct, the juvenile court may assign the child a sanction level that is one level higher than the previously assigned sanction level, unless:

(1) the child's previously assigned sanction level is five and the child has not been adjudicated for delinquent conduct;

(2) the child's previously assigned sanction level is six, unless the subsequent violation is of a provision listed under Section 53.045(a) and the petition has been approved by a grand jury under Section 53.045; or

(3) the child's previously assigned sanction level is seven.

(d) Subject to Subsection (e), if the child's previously assigned sanction level is four or five and the child's subsequent commission of delinquent conduct is of the grade of felony, the juvenile court may assign the child a sanction level that is one level higher than the previously assigned sanction level.

Ⓐ *Subsection (e) below is effective for criminal conduct that occurs on or after Sept. 1, 2001.*

(e) Except as otherwise provided by this subsection, a juvenile court or probation department that deviates from the guidelines under this section shall state in writing its reasons for the deviation and submit the statement to the juvenile board regardless of whether a progressive sanctions program has been adopted by the juvenile board. Nothing in this chapter prohibits the imposition of appropriate sanctions that are different from those provided at any sanction level. A juvenile court that makes a disposition required by this title that deviates from the guidelines under this section is not required to report the disposition as a deviation.

Subsection (e) below is effective for criminal conduct in which any element of the conduct occurred before Sept. 1, 2001.

(e) A juvenile court or probation department that deviates from the guidelines under this section shall state in writing its reasons for the deviation and submit the statement to the juvenile board regardless of whether a progressive sanctions program has been adopted by the juvenile board. Nothing in this chapter prohibits the imposition of appropriate sanctions that are different from those provided at any sanction level.

(f) The probation department may, in accordance with Section 54.05, request the extension of a period of probation specified under sanction levels one through five if the circumstances of the child warrant the extension.

(g) Before the court assigns the child a sanction level that involves the revocation of the child's probation and the commitment of the child to the Texas Youth Commission, the court shall hold a hearing to modify the disposition as required by Section 54.05.

History of Fam §59.003: Acts 1995, 74th Leg., ch. 262, §53, eff. Jan. 1, 1996. Amended by Acts 1997, 75th Leg., ch. 1015, §19 (eff. June 19, 1997), ch. 1086, §22 (eff. Sept. 1, 1997); Acts 1999, 76th Leg., ch. 1477, §20, eff. Sept. 1, 1999; Acts 2001, 77th Leg., ch. 1297, §42, eff. Sept. 1, 2001.

FAM §59.004. SANCTION LEVEL ONE

(a) For a child at sanction level one, the juvenile court or probation department may:

(1) require counseling for the child regarding the child's conduct;

(2) inform the child of the progressive sanctions that may be imposed on the child if the child continues

to engage in delinquent conduct or conduct indicating a need for supervision;

(3) inform the child's parents or guardians of the parents' or guardians' responsibility to impose reasonable restrictions on the child to prevent the conduct from recurring;

(4) provide information or other assistance to the child or the child's parents or guardians in securing needed social services;

(5) require the child or the child's parents or guardians to participate in a program for services under Section 264.302, if a program under Section 264.302 is available to the child or the child's parents or guardians;

(6) refer the child to a community-based citizen intervention program approved by the juvenile court; and

(7) release the child to the child's parents or guardians.

(b) The probation department shall discharge the child from the custody of the probation department after the provisions of this section are met.

History of Fam §59.004: Acts 1995, 74th Leg., ch. 262, §53, eff. Jan. 1, 1996. Amended by Acts 1997, 75th Leg., ch. 1086, §23, eff. Sept. 1, 1997.

FAM §59.005. SANCTION LEVEL TWO

(a) For a child at sanction level two, the juvenile court, the prosecuting attorney, or the probation department may, as provided by Section 53.03:

(1) place the child on deferred prosecution for not less than three months or more than six months;

(2) require the child to make restitution to the victim of the child's conduct or perform community service restitution appropriate to the nature and degree of harm caused and according to the child's ability;

(3) require the child's parents or guardians to identify restrictions the parents or guardians will impose on the child's activities and requirements the parents or guardians will set for the child's behavior;

(4) provide the information required under Sections 59.004(a)(2) and (4);

(5) require the child or the child's parents or guardians to participate in a program for services under Section 264.302, if a program under Section 264.302 is available to the child or the child's parents or guardians;

(6) refer the child to a community-based citizen intervention program approved by the juvenile court; and

(7) if appropriate, impose additional conditions of probation.

(b) The juvenile court or the probation department shall discharge the child from the custody of the probation department on the date the provisions of this section are met or on the child's 18th birthday, whichever is earlier.

History of Fam §59.005: Acts 1995, 74th Leg., ch. 262, §53, eff. Jan. 1, 1996. Amended by Acts 1997, 75th Leg., ch. 1086, §24, eff. Sept. 1, 1997; Acts 1999, 76th Leg., ch. 1477, §21, eff. Sept. 1, 1999.

FAM §59.006. SANCTION LEVEL THREE

(a) For a child at sanction level three, the juvenile court may:

(1) place the child on probation for not less than six months or more than 12 months;

(2) require the child to make restitution to the victim of the child's conduct or perform community service restitution appropriate to the nature and degree of harm caused and according to the child's ability;

(3) impose specific restrictions on the child's activities and requirements for the child's behavior as conditions of probation;

(4) require a probation officer to closely monitor the child's activities and behavior;

(5) require the child or the child's parents or guardians to participate in programs or services designated by the court or probation officer; and

(6) if appropriate, impose additional conditions of probation.

(b) The juvenile court shall discharge the child from the custody of the probation department on the date the provisions of this section are met or on the child's 18th birthday, whichever is earlier.

History of Fam §59.006: Acts 1995, 74th Leg., ch. 262, §53, eff. Jan. 1, 1996. Amended by Acts 1997, 75th Leg., ch. 1086, §25, eff. Sept. 1, 1997.

FAM §59.007. SANCTION LEVEL FOUR

(a) For a child at sanction level four, the juvenile court may:

A *Subsection (1) below is effective for criminal conduct that occurs on or after Sept. 1, 2001.*

(1) require the child to participate as a condition of probation for not less than three months or more than 12 months in an intensive services probation program that emphasizes frequent contact and reporting with a probation officer, discipline, intensive supervision services, social responsibility, and productive work;

Subsection (1) below is effective for criminal conduct in which any element of the conduct occurred before Sept. 1, 2001.

(1) require the child to participate as a condition of probation for not less than three months or more than 12 months in a highly intensive and regimented program that emphasizes discipline, physical fitness, social responsibility, and productive work;

(2) after release from the program described by Subdivision (1), continue the child on probation supervision for not less than six months or more than 12 months;

(3) require the child to make restitution to the victim of the child's conduct or perform community service restitution appropriate to the nature and degree of harm caused and according to the child's ability;

(4) impose highly structured restrictions on the child's activities and requirements for behavior of the child as conditions of probation;

(5) require a probation officer to closely monitor the child;

(6) require the child or the child's parents or guardians to participate in programs or services designed to address their particular needs and circumstances; and

(7) if appropriate, impose additional sanctions.

(b) The juvenile court shall discharge the child from the custody of the probation department on the date the provisions of this section are met or on the child's 18th birthday, whichever is earlier.

History of Fam §59.007: Acts 1995, 74th Leg., ch. 262, §53, eff. Jan. 1, 1996. Amended by Acts 1997, 75th Leg., ch. 1086, §26, eff. Sept. 1, 1997; Acts 2001, 77th Leg., ch. 1297, §43, eff. Sept. 1, 2001.

FAM §59.008. SANCTION LEVEL FIVE

(a) For a child at sanction level five, the juvenile court may:

(1) as a condition of probation, place the child for not less than six months or more than 12 months in a post-adjudication secure correctional facility;

(2) after release from the program described by Subdivision (1), continue the child on probation supervision for not less than six months or more than 12 months;

(3) require the child to make restitution to the victim of the child's conduct or perform community service restitution appropriate to the nature and degree of harm caused and according to the child's ability;

(4) impose highly structured restrictions on the child's activities and requirements for behavior of the child as conditions of probation;

(5) require a probation officer to closely monitor the child;

(6) require the child or the child's parents or guardians to participate in programs or services designed to address their particular needs and circumstances; and

(7) if appropriate, impose additional sanctions.

(b) The juvenile court shall discharge the child from the custody of the probation department on the date the provisions of this section are met or on the child's 18th birthday, whichever is earlier.

History of Fam §59.008: Acts 1995, 74th Leg., ch. 262, §53, eff. Jan. 1, 1996. Amended by Acts 1997, 75th Leg., ch. 1086, §27, eff. Sept. 1, 1997.

FAM §59.009. SANCTION LEVEL SIX

(a) For a child at sanction level six, the juvenile court may commit the child to the custody of the Texas Youth Commission. The commission may:

(1) require the child to participate in a highly structured residential program that emphasizes discipline, accountability, fitness, training, and productive work for not less than nine months or more than 24 months unless the commission extends the period and the reason for an extension is documented;

(2) require the child to make restitution to the victim of the child's conduct or perform community service restitution appropriate to the nature and degree of the harm caused and according to the child's ability, if there is a victim of the child's conduct;

(3) require the child and the child's parents or guardians to participate in programs and services for their particular needs and circumstances; and

(4) if appropriate, impose additional sanctions.

(b) On release of the child under supervision, the Texas Youth Commission parole programs may:

(1) impose highly structured restrictions on the child's activities and requirements for behavior of the child as conditions of release under supervision;

(2) require a parole officer to closely monitor the child for not less than six months; and

(3) if appropriate, impose any other conditions of supervision.

(c) The Texas Youth Commission may discharge the child from the commission's custody on the date the

FAM §59.007

provisions of this section are met or on the child's 19th birthday, whichever is earlier.

History of Fam §59.009: Acts 1995, 74th Leg., ch. 262, §53, eff. Jan. 1, 1996. Amended by Acts 1997, 75th Leg., ch. 1086, §28, eff. Sept. 1, 1997.

FAM §59.010. SANCTION LEVEL SEVEN

(a) For a child at sanction level seven, the juvenile court may certify and transfer the child under Section 54.02 or sentence the child to commitment to the Texas Youth Commission under Section 54.04(d)(3), 54.04(m), or 54.05(f). The commission may:

(1) require the child to participate in a highly structured residential program that emphasizes discipline, accountability, fitness, training, and productive work for not less than 12 months or more than 10 years unless the commission extends the period and the reason for the extension is documented;

(2) require the child to make restitution to the victim of the child's conduct or perform community service restitution appropriate to the nature and degree of harm caused and according to the child's ability, if there is a victim of the child's conduct;

(3) require the child and the child's parents or guardians to participate in programs and services for their particular needs and circumstances; and

(4) impose any other appropriate sanction.

(b) On release of the child under supervision, the Texas Youth Commission parole programs may:

(1) impose highly structured restrictions on the child's activities and requirements for behavior of the child as conditions of release under supervision;

(2) require a parole officer to monitor the child closely for not less than 12 months; and

(3) impose any other appropriate condition of supervision.

History of Fam §59.010: Acts 1995, 74th Leg., ch. 262, §53, eff. Jan. 1, 1996. Amended by Acts 1997, 75th Leg., ch. 1086, §29, eff. Sept. 1, 1997.

FAM §59.011. DUTY OF JUVENILE BOARD

A *Section 59.011 below is effective for criminal conduct that occurs on or after Sept. 1, 2001.*

A juvenile board shall require the juvenile probation department to report progressive sanction data electronically to the Texas Juvenile Probation Commission in the format and time frames specified by the commission.

History of Fam §59.011: Acts 1995, 74th Leg., ch. 262, §53, eff. Jan. 1, 1996. Amended by Acts 2001, 77th Leg., ch. 1297, §44, eff. Sept. 1, 2001.

FAM §59.011. DUTY OF JUVENILE BOARD

Section 59.011 below is effective for criminal conduct in which any element of the conduct occurred before Sept. 1, 2001.

A juvenile board shall prepare a report to the Texas Juvenile Probation Commission, at least quarterly on forms provided by the commission, showing the referrals, probation or progressive sanctions violations, and commitments to the Texas Youth Commission administered under this chapter according to the progressive sanctions guidelines and the reasons for any deviations from the guidelines.

FAM §59.012. REPORTS BY CRIMINAL JUSTICE POLICY COUNCIL

A *Section 59.012 below is effective for criminal conduct that occurs on or after Sept. 1, 2001.*

(a) The Criminal Justice Policy Council shall analyze trends related to juvenile referrals, compliance with the progressive sanctions guidelines, and the impact of the guidelines and related reforms on recidivism rates using standard scientific sampling or appropriate scientific methodologies to represent statewide patterns. The council shall compile other policy studies as determined by the executive director of the council or as requested by the governor, lieutenant governor, or speaker of the house of representatives to assist in policy development.

E (b) The Criminal Justice Policy Council shall report its findings and related recommendations to improve juvenile justice policies to the governor and the members of the legislature on or before January 15 of each odd-numbered year.

E (c) The Criminal Justice Policy Council may incorporate its findings and recommendations under this section into its report required under Section 413.013, Government Code.

History of Fam §59.012: Acts 1995, 74th Leg., ch. 262, §53, eff. Jan. 1, 1996. Amended by Acts 2001, 77th Leg., ch. 1297, §45, eff. Sept. 1, 2001.

FAM §59.012. REPORTS BY CRIMINAL JUSTICE POLICY COUNCIL

Section 59.012 below is effective for criminal conduct in which any element of the conduct occurred before Sept. 1, 2001.

(a) The Texas Youth Commission shall compile information, at least quarterly, showing the commitments, placements, parole releases, and revocations administered under this chapter according to the progressive sanctions guidelines and the reasons for any deviation from the guidelines.

(b) The Texas Juvenile Probation Commission and the Texas Youth Commission shall compile the information obtained under this section and Section 59.011 and submit this information to the Criminal Justice Policy Council.

(c) The Criminal Justice Policy Council shall analyze the information compiled by the Texas Juvenile Probation Commission and the Texas Youth Commission under this section and submit the council's findings and recommendations at least annually to the governor and both houses of the legislature showing the primary reasons for any deviation and the effect of the implementation of the sanctions guidelines on recidivism rates.

FAM §59.013. LIABILITY

The Texas Youth Commission, a juvenile board, a court, a person appointed by a court, an attorney for the state, a peace officer, or a law enforcement agency is not liable for a failure or inability to provide a service listed under Sections 59.004–59.010.

History of Fam §59.013: Acts 1995, 74th Leg., ch. 262, §53, eff. Jan. 1, 1996.

FAM §59.014. APPEAL

A child may not bring an appeal or a postconviction writ of habeas corpus based on:

(1) the failure or inability of any person to provide a service listed under Sections 59.004–59.010;

(2) the failure of a court or of any person to make a sanction level assignment as provided in Section 59.002 or 59.003; or

(3) a deviation from the sanction level assignment guidelines provided by this chapter; or

(4) the failure of a juvenile court or probation department to report a deviation from the guidelines as required by Section 59.003(e).

History of Fam §59.014: Acts 1995, 74th Leg., ch. 262, §53, eff. Jan. 1, 1996. Amended by Acts 1999, 76th Leg., ch. 1011, §1 (eff. Sept. 1, 1999), ch. 1477, §22 (eff. Sept. 1, 1999).

FAM §59.015. WAIVER OF SANCTIONS ON PARENTS OR GUARDIANS

On a finding by the juvenile court or probation department that a child's parents or guardians have made a reasonable good faith effort to prevent the child from engaging in delinquent conduct or engaging in conduct indicating a need for supervision and that, despite the parents' or guardians' efforts, the child continues to engage in such conduct, the court or probation department shall waive any sanction that may be imposed on the parents or guardians at any sanction level.

History of Fam §59.015: Acts 1995, 74th Leg., ch. 262, §53, eff. Jan. 1, 1996.

CHAPTER 60. UNIFORM INTERSTATE COMPACT ON JUVENILES

FAM §60.001. SHORT TITLE

This chapter may be cited as the Uniform Interstate Compact on Juveniles.

History of Fam §60.001: Acts 1995, 74th Leg., ch. 262, §53, eff. Jan. 1, 1996.

FAM §60.002. EXECUTION OF INTERSTATE COMPACT

The governor shall execute a compact on behalf of the state with any other state or states legally joining in it in substantially the following form:

INTERSTATE COMPACT ON JUVENILES

The contracting states solemnly agree:

Article I

FINDINGS AND PURPOSE

That juveniles who are not under proper supervision and control, or who have absconded, escaped, or run away are likely to endanger their own health, morals, and welfare, and the health, morals, and welfare of others. The cooperation of the states party to this compact is therefore necessary to provide for the welfare and protection of juveniles and of the public with respect to (1) cooperative supervision of delinquent juveniles on probation or parole; (2) the return, from one state to another, of delinquent juveniles who have escaped or absconded; (3) the return, from one state to another, of nondelinquent juveniles who have run away from home; and (4) additional measures for the protection of juveniles and of the public, which any two or more of the party states may find desirable to undertake cooperatively. In carrying out the provisions of this compact the party states shall be guided by the noncriminal, reformative, and protective policies which guide their laws concerning delinquent, neglected, or dependent juveniles generally. It shall be the policy of the states party to this compact to cooperate and observe their respective responsibilities for the prompt return and acceptance of juveniles and delinquent juveniles who become subject to the provisions of this compact. The provisions of this compact shall be reasonably and liberally construed to accomplish the foregoing purposes.

Article II

EXISTING RIGHTS AND REMEDIES

That all remedies and procedures provided by this compact shall be in addition to and not in substitution for other rights, remedies, and procedures, and shall not be in derogation of parental rights and responsibilities.

Article III

DEFINITIONS

That, for the purpose of this compact, "delinquent juvenile" means any juvenile who has been adjudged delinquent and who, at the time the provisions of this compact are invoked, is still subject to the jurisdiction of the court that has made such adjudication or to the jurisdiction or supervision of an agency or institution pursuant to an order of such court; "probation or parole" means any kind of conditional release of juveniles authorized under the laws of the states party hereto; "court" means any court having jurisdiction over delinquent, neglected, or dependent children; "state" means any state, territory, or possessions of the United States, the District of Columbia, and the Commonwealth of Puerto Rico; and "residence" or any variant thereof means a place at which a home or regular place of abode is maintained.

Article IV

RETURN OF RUNAWAYS

(a) That the parent, guardian, person, or agency entitled to legal custody of a juvenile who has not been adjudged delinquent but who has run away without the consent of such parent, guardian, person, or agency may petition the appropriate court in the demanding state for the issuance of a requisition for his return. The petition shall state the name and age of the juvenile, the name of the petitioner, and the basis of entitlement to the juvenile's custody, the circumstances of his running away, his location if known at the time application is made, and such other facts as may tend to show that the juvenile who has run away is endangering his own welfare or the welfare of others and is not an emancipated minor. The petition shall be verified by affidavit, shall be executed in duplicate, and shall be accompanied by two certified copies of the document or documents on which the petitioner's entitlement to the juvenile's custody is based, such as birth certificates, letters of guardianship, or custody decrees. Such further affidavits and other documents as may be deemed proper may be submitted with such petition. The judge of the court to which this application is made may hold a hearing thereon to determine whether for the purposes of this compact the petitioner is entitled to the legal custody of the juvenile, whether or not it appears that the juvenile has in fact run away without consent, whether or not he is an emancipated minor, and whether or not it is in the best interest of the juvenile to compel his return to the state. If the judge determines, either with or without a hearing, that the juvenile should be returned, he shall present to the appropriate court or to the executive authority of the state where the juvenile is alleged to be located a written requisition for the return of such juvenile. Such requisition shall set forth the name and age of the juvenile, the determination of the court that the juvenile has run away without the consent of a parent, guardian, person, or agency entitled to his legal custody, and that it is in the best interest and for the protection of such juvenile that he be returned. In the event that a proceeding for the adjudication of the juvenile as a delinquent, neglected, or dependent juvenile is pending in the court at the time when such juvenile runs away, the court may issue a requisition for the return of such juvenile upon its own motion, regardless of the consent of the parent, guardian, person, or agency entitled to legal custody, reciting therein the nature and circumstances of the pending proceeding. The requisition shall in every case be executed in duplicate and shall be signed by the judge. One copy of the requisition shall be filed with the compact administrator of the demanding state, there to remain on file subject to the provisions of law governing records of such court. Upon the receipt of a requisition demanding the return of a juvenile who has run away, the court or the executive authority to whom the requisition is addressed shall issue an order to any peace officer or other appropriate person directing him to take into custody and detain such juvenile. Such detention order must substantially recite the facts necessary to the validity of its issuance hereunder. No juvenile detained upon such order shall be delivered over to the officer whom the court demanding him shall have appointed to receive him unless he shall first be taken forthwith before a judge of a court in the state, who shall inform him of the demand made for his return, and who may appoint counsel or guardian ad litem for him. If the judge of such court shall find that the requisition is in order, he shall deliver such juvenile over to the officer whom the court demanding him shall have appointed to receive him. The judge, however, may fix a reasonable time to be allowed for the purpose of testing the legality of the proceeding.

Upon reasonable information that a person is a juvenile who has run away from another state party to this compact without the consent of a parent, guardian, person, or agency entitled to his legal custody, such juvenile may be taken into custody without a requisition and brought forthwith before a judge of the appropriate court who may appoint counsel or guardian ad litem for such juvenile and who shall determine after a hearing whether sufficient cause exists to hold the person, subject to the order of the court, for his own protection and welfare, for such a time not exceeding 90 days as will enable his return to another state party to this compact pursuant to a requisition for his return from a court of that state. If, at the time when a state seeks the return of a juvenile who has run away, there is pending in the state wherein he is found any criminal charge, or any proceeding to have him adjudicated a delinquent juvenile for an act committed in such state, or if he is suspected of having committed within such state a criminal offense or an act of juvenile delinquency, he shall not be returned without the consent of such state until discharged from prosecution or other form of proceeding, imprisonment, detention, or supervision for such offense of juvenile delinquency. The duly accredited officers of any state party to this compact, upon the establishment of their authority and the identity of the juvenile being returned, shall be permitted to transport such juvenile through any and all states party to this compact, without interference. Upon his return to the state from which he ran away, the juvenile shall be subject to such further proceedings as may be appropriate under the laws of that state.

(b) That the state to which a juvenile is returned under this article shall be responsible for payment of the transportation costs of such return.

(c) That "juvenile" as used in this article means any person who is a minor under the law of the state of residence of the parent, guardian, person, or agency entitled to the legal custody of such minor.

Article V

RETURN OF ESCAPEES AND ABSCONDERS

(a) That the appropriate person or authority from whose probation or parole supervision a delinquent juvenile has absconded or from whose institutional custody he has escaped shall present to the appropriate court or to the executive authority of the state where the delinquent juvenile is alleged to be located a written requisition for the return of such delinquent juvenile. Such requisition shall state the name and age of the delinquent juvenile, the particulars of his adjudication as a delinquent juvenile, the circumstances of the breach of the terms of his probation or parole or of his escape from an institution or agency vested with his legal custody or supervision, and the location of such delinquent juvenile, if known, at the time the requisition is made. The requisition shall be verified by affidavit, shall be executed in duplicate, and shall be accompanied by two certified copies of the judgment, formal adjudication, or order of commitment which subjects such delinquent juvenile to probation or parole or to the legal custody of the institution or agency concerned. Such further affidavits and other documents as may be deemed proper may be submitted with such requisition. One copy of the requisition shall be filed with the compact administrator of the demanding state, there to remain on file subject to the provisions of law governing records of the appropriate court. Upon the receipt of a requisition demanding the return of a delinquent juvenile who has absconded or escaped, the court or the executive authority to whom the requisition is addressed shall issue an order to any peace officer or other appropriate person directing him to take into custody and detain such delinquent juvenile. Such detention order must substantially recite the facts necessary to the validity of its issuance hereunder. No delinquent juvenile detained upon such order shall be delivered over to the officer whom the appropriate person or authority demanding him shall have appointed to receive him unless he shall first be taken forthwith before a judge of an appropriate court in the state, who shall inform him of the demand made for his return and who may appoint counsel or guardian ad litem for him. If the judge of such court shall find that the requisition is in order, he shall deliver such delinquent juvenile over to the officer whom the appropriate person or authority demanding him shall have appointed to receive him. The judge, however, may fix a reasonable time to be allowed for the purpose of testing the legality of the proceeding.

Upon reasonable information that a person is a delinquent juvenile who has absconded while on probation or parole, or escaped from an institution or agency vested with this legal custody or supervision in any state party to this compact, such person may be taken into custody in any other state party to this compact without a requisition. But in such event, he must be taken forthwith before a judge of the appropriate court, who may appoint counsel or guardian ad litem for such person and who shall determine, after a hearing, whether sufficient cause exists to hold the person subject to the order of the court for such a time, not exceeding 90 days, as will enable his detention under a detention order issued on a requisition pursuant to this article. If, at the time when a state seeks the return of a delinquent juvenile who has either absconded while on probation or parole or escaped from an institution or agency vested with his legal custody or supervision, there is pending in the state wherein he is detained any criminal charge or any proceeding to have him adjudicated a delinquent juvenile for an act committed in such state, or if he is suspected of having committed within such state a criminal offense or an act of juvenile delinquency, he shall not be returned without the consent of such state until discharged from prosecution or other form of proceeding, imprisonment, detention, or supervision for such offense of juvenile delinquency. The duly accredited officers of any state party to this compact, upon the establishment of their authority and the identity of the delinquent juvenile being returned, shall be permitted to transport such delinquent juvenile through any and all states party to this compact, without interference. Upon his return to the state from which he escaped or absconded, the delinquent juvenile shall be subject to such further proceedings as may be appropriate under the laws of that state.

(b) That the state to which a delinquent juvenile is returned under this article shall be responsible for the payment of the transportation costs of such return.

Article VI

VOLUNTARY RETURN PROCEDURE

That any delinquent juvenile who has absconded while on probation or parole, or escaped from an institution or agency vested with his legal custody or supervision in any state party to this compact, and any juvenile who has run away from any state party to this compact, who is taken into custody without a requisition in another state party to this compact under the provisions of Article IV(a) or of Article V(a), may consent to his immediate return to the state from which he absconded, escaped, or ran away. Such consent shall be given by the juvenile or delinquent juvenile and his counsel or guardian ad litem, if any, by executing or subscribing in writing, in the presence of a judge of the appropriate court, which states that the juvenile or delinquent juvenile and his counsel or guardian ad litem, if any, consent to his return to the demanding state. Before such consent shall be executed or subscribed, however, the judge, in the presence of counsel or guardian ad litem, if any, shall inform the juvenile or delinquent juvenile of his rights under this compact. When the consent has been duly executed, it shall be forwarded to and filed with the compact administrator of the state in which the court is located and the judge shall direct the officer having the juvenile or delinquent juvenile in custody to deliver him to the duly accredited officer or officers of the state demanding his return, and shall cause to be delivered to such officer or officers a copy of the consent. The court may, however, upon the request of the state to which the juvenile or delinquent juvenile is being returned, order him to return unaccompanied to such state and shall provide him with a copy of such court order; in such event a copy of the consent shall be forwarded to the compact administrator of the state to which said juvenile or delinquent juvenile is ordered to return.

Article VII

COOPERATIVE SUPERVISION
OF PROBATIONERS AND PAROLEES

(a) That the duly constituted judicial and administrative authorities of a state party to this compact (herein called "sending state") may permit any delinquent juvenile within such state, placed on probation or parole, to reside in any other state party to this compact (herein called "receiving state") while on probation or parole, and the receiving state shall accept such delinquent juvenile, if the parent, guardian, or person entitled to the legal custody of such delinquent juvenile is residing or undertakes to reside within the receiving state. Before granting such permission, opportunity shall be given to the receiving state to make such investigations as it deems necessary. The authorities of the sending state shall send to the authorities of the receiving state copies of pertinent court orders, social case studies, and all other available information which may be of value to and assist the receiving state in supervising a probationer or parolee under this compact. A receiving state, in its discretion, may agree to accept supervision of a probationer or parolee in cases where the parent, guardian, or person entitled to the legal custody of the delinquent juvenile is not a resident of the receiving state, and if so accepted the sending state may transfer supervision accordingly.

(b) That each receiving state will assume the duties of visitation and of supervision over any such delinquent juvenile and in the exercise of those duties will be governed by the same standards of visitation and supervision that prevail for its own delinquent juveniles released on probation or parole.

(c) That, after consultation between the appropriate authorities of the sending state and of the receiving state as to the desirability and necessity of returning such a delinquent juvenile, the duly accredited officers of a sending state may enter a receiving state and there apprehend and retake any such delinquent juvenile on probation or parole. For that purpose, no formalities will be required, other than establishing the authority of the officer and the identity of the delinquent juvenile to be retaken and returned. The decision of the sending state to retake a delinquent juvenile on probation or parole shall be conclusive upon and not reviewable within the receiving state, but if, at the time the sending state seeks to retake a delinquent juvenile on probation or parole, there is pending against him within the receiving state any criminal charge or any proceedings to have him adjudicated a delinquent juvenile for any act committed in such state or if he is suspected of having committed within such state a criminal offense or an act of juvenile delinquency, he shall not be returned without the consent of the receiving state until discharged from prosecution or other form of proceeding, imprisonment, detention, or supervision for such offense of juvenile delinquency. The duly accredited officers of the sending state shall be permitted to transport delinquent juveniles being so returned through any and all states party to this compact, without interference.

(d) That the sending state shall be responsible under this article for paying the costs of transporting any delinquent juvenile to the receiving state or of returning any delinquent juvenile to the sending state.

Article VIII
RESPONSIBILITY FOR COSTS

(a) That the provisions of Articles IV(b), V(b), and VII(d) of this compact shall not be construed to alter or affect any internal relationship among the departments, agencies, and officers of and in the government of a party state, or between a party state and its subdivisions, as to the payment of costs, or responsibilities therefor.

(b) That nothing in this compact shall be construed to prevent any party state or subdivision thereof from asserting any right against any person, agency, or other entity in regard to costs for which such party state or subdivision thereof may be responsible pursuant to Articles IV(b), V(b), or VII(d) of this compact.

Article IX
DETENTION PRACTICES

That, to every extent possible, it shall be the policy of states party to this compact that no juvenile or delinquent juvenile shall be placed or detained in any prison, jail, or lockup nor be detained or transported in association with criminal, vicious, or dissolute persons.

Article X
SUPPLEMENTARY AGREEMENTS

That the duly constituted administrative authorities of a state party to this compact may enter into supplementary agreements with any other state or states party hereto for the cooperative care, treatment, and rehabilitation of delinquent juveniles whenever they shall find that such agreements will improve the facilities or programs available for such care, treatment, and rehabilitation. Such care, treatment, and rehabilitation may be provided in an institution located within any state entering into such supplementary agreement. Such supplementary agreements shall (1) provide the rates to be paid for the care, treatment, and custody of such delinquent juveniles, taking into consideration the character of facilities, services, and subsistence furnished; (2) provide that the delinquent juvenile shall be given a court hearing prior to his being sent to another state for care, treatment, and custody; (3) provide that the state receiving such a delinquent juvenile in one of its institutions shall act solely as agent for the state sending such delinquent juvenile; (4) provide that the sending state shall at all times retain jurisdiction over delinquent juveniles sent to an institution in another state; (5) provide for reasonable inspection of such institutions by the sending state; (6) provide that the consent of the parent, guardian, person, or agency entitled to the legal custody of said delinquent juvenile shall be secured prior to his being sent to another state; and (7) make provision for such other matters and details as shall be necessary to protect the rights and equities of such delinquent juveniles and of the co-operating states.

Article XI

ACCEPTANCE OF FEDERAL AND OTHER AID

That any state party to this compact may accept any and all donations, gifts, and grants of money, equipment, and services from the federal or any local government, or any agency thereof and from any person, firm, or corporation, for any of the purposes and functions of this compact, and may receive and utilize the same, subject to the terms, conditions, and regulations governing such donations, gifts, and grants.

Article XII

COMPACT ADMINISTRATORS

That the governor of each state party to this compact shall designate an officer who, acting jointly with like officers of other party states, shall promulgate rules and regulations to carry out more effectively the terms and provisions of this compact.

Article XIII

EXECUTION OF COMPACT

That this compact shall become operative immediately upon its execution by any state as between it and any other state or states so executing. When executed it shall have the full force and effect of law within such state, the form or execution to be in accordance with the laws of the executing state.

Article XIV

RENUNCIATION

That this compact shall continue in force and remain binding upon each executing state until renounced by it. Renunciation of this compact shall be by the same authority which executed it, by sending six months notice in writing of its intention to withdraw from the compact to the other states party hereto. The duties and obligations of a renouncing state under Article VII hereof shall continue as to parolees and probationers residing therein at the time of withdrawal until retaken or finally discharged. Supplementary agreements entered into under Article X hereof shall be subject to renunciation as provided by such supplementary agreements, and shall not be subject to the six months renunciation notice of the present article.

Article XV

SEVERABILITY

That the provisions of this compact shall be severable and if any phrase, clause, sentence, or provision of this compact is declared to be contrary to the constitution of any participating state or of the United States or the applicability thereof to any government, agency, person, or circumstance is held invalid, the validity of the remainder of this compact and the applicability thereof to any government, agency, person, or circumstances shall not be affected thereby. If this compact shall be held contrary to the constitution of any state participating therein, the compact shall remain in full force and effect as to the remaining states and in full force and effect as to the state affected as to all severable matters.

History of Fam §60.002: Acts 1995, 74th Leg., ch. 262, §53, eff. Jan. 1, 1996.

FAM §60.003. EXECUTION OF ADDITIONAL ARTICLE

The governor shall also execute on the behalf of the state with any other state or states legally joining in it, an additional article to the Interstate Compact on Juveniles in substantially the following form:

Article XVI

ADDITIONAL ARTICLE

That this article shall provide additional remedies, and shall be binding only as among and between those party states which specifically execute the same.

For the purposes of this article, "child," as used herein, means any minor within the jurisdictional age limits of any court in the home state.

When any child is brought before a court of a state of which such child is not a resident, and such state is willing to permit such child's return to the home state of such child, such home state, upon being so advised by the state in which such proceeding is pending, shall immediately institute proceedings to determine the residence and jurisdictional facts as to such child in such home state, and upon finding that such child is in fact a resident of said state and subject to the jurisdiction of the court thereof shall within five days authorize the return of such child to the home state, and to the parent or custodial agency legally authorized to accept such custody in such home state, and at the expense of such home state, to be paid from such funds as such home state may procure, designate, or provide, prompt action being of the essence.

History of Fam §60.003: Acts 1995, 74th Leg., ch. 262, §53, eff. Jan. 1, 1996.

FAM §60.004. EXECUTION OF AMENDMENT

The governor shall also execute on the behalf of the state with any other state or states legally joining in it, an amendment to the Interstate Compact on Juveniles in substantially the following form:

RENDITION AMENDMENT

(a) This amendment shall provide additional remedies, and shall be binding only as among and between those party states which specifically execute the same.

(b) All provisions and procedures of Articles V and VI of the Interstate Compact on Juveniles shall be construed to apply to any juvenile charged with being a delinquent by reason of a violation of any criminal law. Any juvenile charged with being a delinquent by reason of violating any criminal law shall be returned to the requesting state upon a requisition to the state where the juvenile may be found. A petition in such case shall be filed in a court of competent jurisdiction in the requesting state where the violation of criminal law is alleged to have been committed. The petition may be filed regardless of whether the juvenile has left the state before or after the filing of the petition. The requisition described in Article V of the compact shall be forwarded by the judge of the court in which the petition has been filed.

History of Fam §60.004: Acts 1995, 74th Leg., ch. 262, §53, eff. Jan. 1, 1996.

FAM §60.005. JUVENILE COMPACT ADMINISTRATOR

Under the compact, the governor may designate an officer as the compact administrator. The administrator, acting jointly with like officers of other party states, shall adopt regulations to carry out more effectively the terms of the compact. The compact administrator serves at the pleasure of the governor. The compact administrator shall cooperate with all departments, agencies, and officers of and in the government of this state and its subdivisions in facilitating the proper administration of the compact or of a supplementary agreement entered into by this state.

History of Fam §60.005: Acts 1995, 74th Leg., ch. 262, §53, eff. Jan. 1, 1996.

FAM §60.006. SUPPLEMENTARY AGREEMENTS

A compact administrator may make supplementary agreements with appropriate officials of other states pursuant to the compact. If a supplementary agreement requires or contemplates the use of an institution or facility of this state or requires or contemplates the provision of a service of this state, the supplementary agreement has no force or effect until approved by the head of the department or agency under whose jurisdiction the institution is operated, or whose department or agency is charged with performing the service.

History of Fam §60.006: Acts 1995, 74th Leg., ch. 262, §53, eff. Jan. 1, 1996.

FAM §60.007. FINANCIAL ARRANGEMENTS

The compact administrator may make or arrange for the payments necessary to discharge the financial obligations imposed upon this state by the compact or by a supplementary agreement made under the compact, subject to legislative appropriations.

History of Fam §60.007: Acts 1995, 74th Leg., ch. 262, §53, eff. Jan. 1, 1996.

FAM §60.008. ENFORCEMENT

The courts, departments, agencies, and officers of this state and its subdivisions shall enforce this compact and shall do all things appropriate to effectuate its purposes and intent which are within their respective jurisdictions.

History of Fam §60.008: Acts 1995, 74th Leg., ch. 262, §53, eff. Jan. 1, 1996.

FAM §60.009. ADDITIONAL PROCEDURES NOT PRECLUDED

In addition to the procedures provided in Articles IV and VI of the compact for the return of a runaway juvenile, the particular states, the juvenile, or his parents, the courts, or other legal custodian involved may agree upon and adopt any plan or procedure legally authorized under the laws of this state and the other respective party states for the return of the runaway juvenile.

History of Fam §60.009: Acts 1995, 74th Leg., ch. 262, §53, eff. Jan. 1, 1996.

Chapters 61-70 blank

FAMILY CODE—TITLE 4
PROTECTIVE ORDERS & FAMILY VIOLENCE
TABLE OF CONTENTS

TITLE 4

FAMILY CODE—TITLE 4
PROTECTIVE ORDERS & FAMILY VIOLENCE
TABLE OF CONTENTS

TITLE 4

TITLE 4. PROTECTIVE ORDERS & FAMILY VIOLENCE

SUBTITLE A. GENERAL PROVISIONS

CHAPTER 71. DEFINITIONS

FAM §71.001. APPLICABILITY OF DEFINITIONS

(a) Definitions in this chapter apply to this title.

(b) If, in another part of this title, a term defined by this chapter has a meaning different from the meaning provided by this chapter, the meaning of that other provision prevails.

(c) Except as provided by this chapter, the definitions in Chapter 101 apply to terms used in this title.

History of Fam §71.001: Acts 1997, 75th Leg., ch. 34, §1, eff. May 5, 1997. Source: Former Fam §71.01(a).

FAM §71.002. COURT

"Court" means the district court, court of domestic relations, juvenile court having the jurisdiction of a district court, statutory county court, constitutional county court, or other court expressly given jurisdiction under this title.

History of Fam §71.002: Acts 1997, 75th Leg., ch. 34, §1, eff. May 5, 1997. Amended by Acts 1997, 75th Leg., ch. 1220, §1, eff. Sept. 1, 1997. Source: Former Fam §71.01(b)(1).

Williams v. Williams, 19 S.W.3d 544, 547-48 (Tex. App.—Fort Worth 2000, pet. denied). "For purposes of family violence protective orders, the legislature defines 'court' as a district court, court of domestic relations, juvenile court having the jurisdiction of a district court, statutory county court, constitutional county court, or other court expressly given jurisdiction under this title. In contrast, the word 'jury' and the phrase 'trier of fact' do not appear in chapters seventy-one through eighty-five. The statutory definition of 'court' and the legislature's omission of 'jury' and 'trier of fact,' make clear that the legislature intended that courts, not juries, have the responsibility of making the findings necessary for the issuance of a family violence protective order. We must presume that words excluded from the statute were excluded purposely by the legislature. It is not possible to comply with the statutory requirement to hold a hearing within fourteen days, yet also comply with the rule that requires filing of a written request for a jury trial thirty days in advance."

E FAM §71.0021. DATING VIOLENCE

(a) "Dating violence" means an act by an individual that is against another individual with whom that person has or has had a dating relationship and that is intended to result in physical harm, bodily injury, assault, or sexual assault or that is a threat that reasonably places the individual in fear of imminent physical harm, bodily injury, assault, or sexual assault, but does not include defensive measures to protect oneself.

(b) For purposes of this title, "dating relationship" means a relationship between individuals who have or have had a continuing relationship of a romantic or intimate nature. The existence of such a relationship shall be determined based on consideration of:

(1) the length of the relationship;

(2) the nature of the relationship; and

(3) the frequency and type of interaction between the persons involved in the relationship.

(c) A casual acquaintanceship or ordinary fraternization in a business or social context does not constitute a "dating relationship" under Subsection (b).

History of Fam §71.0021: Enacted by Acts 2001, 77th Leg., ch. 91, §1, eff. Sept. 1, 2001.

FAM §71.003. FAMILY

A *Section 71.003 below is effective for motions or other requests for relief made in parentage or paternity proceedings commenced on or after June 14, 2001.*

"Family" includes individuals related by consanguinity or affinity, as determined under Sections 573.022 and 573.024, Government Code, individuals who are former spouses of each other, individuals who are the parents of the same child, without regard to marriage, and a foster child and foster parent, without regard to whether those individuals reside together.

History of Fam §71.003: Acts 1997, 75th Leg., ch. 34, §1, eff. May 5, 1997. Amended by Acts 2001, 77th Leg., ch. 821, §2.03, eff. June 14, 2001. Source: Former Fam §71.01(b)(3).

James v. Hubbard, 21 S.W.3d 558, 561 (Tex.App.—San Antonio 2000, no pet.). "'Family' includes relationships established by marriage such as in-laws, as determined by §573.024 of the Government Code. Divorce terminates family relationships established by marriage. Thus, by operation of law, had [husband] and [ex-wife] been divorced then [ex-wife's mother] would not have been entitled to this protective order against the [husband]."

FAM §71.003. FAMILY

Section 71.003 below is effective for motions or other requests for relief made in parentage or paternity proceedings commenced before June 14, 2001.

"Family" includes individuals related by consanguinity or affinity, as determined under Sections 573.022 and 573.024, Government Code, individuals who are former spouses of each other, individuals who are the biological parents of the same child, without regard to marriage, and a foster child and foster parent, without regard to whether those individuals reside together.

FAM §71.004. FAMILY VIOLENCE

"Family violence" means:

(1) an act by a member of a family or household against another member of the family or household that is intended to result in physical harm, bodily injury, assault, or sexual assault or that is a threat that reasonably places the member in fear of imminent physical harm, bodily injury, assault, or sexual assault, but does not include defensive measures to protect oneself;

Ⓐ (2) abuse, as that term is defined by Sections 261.001(1)(C), (E), and (G), by a member of a family or household toward a child of the family or household; or

Ⓔ (3) dating violence, as that term is defined by Section 71.0021.

History of Fam §71.004: Acts 1997, 75th Leg., ch. 34, §1, eff. May 5, 1997. Amended by Acts 2001, 77th Leg., ch. 91, §2, eff. Sept. 1, 2001. Source: Former Fam §71.01(b)(2).

FAM §71.003

Ex parte Arenivas, 6 S.W.3d 631, 635-36 (Tex. App.—El Paso 1999, no pet.). "[T]he elements of [defendant's] contempt conviction are: (1) [Defendant], as a member of a family or household; (2) committed an act against another member of the same family or household; (3) that was intended to result in physical harm, bodily injury, or assault; (4) while knowing that this conduct is a violation of the court order. The indictment alleged in the first count that [defendant] committed injury to a child by intentionally or knowingly causing bodily injury to ... a child younger than fourteen years of age. In the second count, it alleged that [defendant] recklessly or with criminal negligence caused bodily injury to [the child]. Pursuant to the relevant portion of §22.04 of the Penal Code, the elements of injury to a child are: (1) intentionally, knowingly, recklessly, or with criminal negligence, by act, causing bodily injury to a child. Even though the 'knowing' culpable mental state and assaultive elements are the same in each offense, the injury to a child offense requires that the State prove that the victim is younger than fourteen years of age, an element not found in the contempt offense. Likewise, the contempt offense requires the movant to prove elements not found in the criminal offense, namely, that both the actor and victim are members of the same family or household and that the actor knew his conduct violated the court order. Accordingly, ... the two offenses are not the same, and therefore, the injury to a child prosecution is not jeopardy barred."

FAM §71.005. HOUSEHOLD

"Household" means a unit composed of persons living together in the same dwelling, without regard to whether they are related to each other.

History of Fam §71.005: Acts 1997, 75th Leg., ch. 34, §1, eff. May 5, 1997. Source: Former Fam §71.01(b)(5).

FAM §71.006. MEMBER OF A HOUSEHOLD

"Member of a household" includes a person who previously lived in a household.

History of Fam §71.006: Acts 1997, 75th Leg., ch. 34, §1, eff. May 5, 1997. Source: Former Fam §71.01(b)(4), (6).

FAM §71.007. PROSECUTING ATTORNEY

"Prosecuting attorney" means the attorney, determined as provided in this title, who represents the state in a district or statutory county court in the county in which venue of the application for a protective order is proper.

History of Fam §71.007: Acts 1997, 75th Leg., ch. 34, §1, eff. May 5, 1997.

FAM §71.008. REPEALED

Repealed by Acts 2001, 77th Leg., ch. 48, §2, eff. Sept. 1, 2001.

FAM §71.008. PROTECTIVE ORDER FROM ANOTHER JURISDICTION

Section 71.008 below is effective for actions to enforce foreign protective orders filed before Sept. 1, 2001.

"Protective order from another jurisdiction" means a protective order rendered by a military court or a court of another state, tribe, or territory related to protecting an individual from domestic or family violence and that meets the following requirements:

(1) the order is rendered by a court that has jurisdiction over the parties and the matter under the law of the military, state, tribe, or territory; and

(2) the respondent is given notice and an opportunity to be heard consistent with due process either:

(A) before the date the order was rendered; or

(B) in the case of an ex parte order, within the time required by the jurisdiction rendering the order after the date the order is rendered, but not later than a reasonable time.

Chapters 72-80 blank

SUBTITLE B. PROTECTIVE ORDERS

CHAPTER 81. GENERAL PROVISIONS

FAM §81.001. ENTITLEMENT TO PROTECTIVE ORDER

A court shall render a protective order as provided by Section 85.001(b) if the court finds that family violence has occurred and is likely to occur in the future.

History of Fam §81.001: Acts 1997, 75th Leg., ch. 34, §1, eff. May 5, 1997. Source: Former Fam §71.10(a), (b).

FAM §81.002. NO FEE FOR APPLICANT

An applicant for a protective order or an attorney representing an applicant may not be assessed a fee, cost, charge, or expense by a district or county clerk of the court or a sheriff, constable, or other public official or employee in connection with the filing, serving, or entering of a protective order or for any other service described by this subsection, including:

(1) a fee to dismiss, modify, or withdraw a protective order;

(2) a fee for certifying copies;

(3) a fee for comparing copies to originals;

(4) a court reporter fee;

(5) a judicial fund fee;

(6) a fee for any other service related to a protective order; or

(7) a fee to transfer a protective order.

History of Fam §81.002: Acts 1997, 75th Leg., ch. 34, §1, eff. May 5, 1997. Amended by Acts 1997, 75th Leg., ch. 1193, §3, eff. Sept. 1, 1997. Source: Former Fam §71.041(a).

FAM §81.003. FEES & COSTS PAID BY PARTY FOUND TO HAVE COMMITTED FAMILY VIOLENCE

(a) Except on a showing of good cause or of the indigence of a party found to have committed family violence, the court shall require in a protective order that the party against whom the order is rendered pay the $16 protective order fee, the standard fees charged by the clerk of the court in a general civil proceeding for the cost of serving the order, the costs of court, and all other fees, charges, or expenses incurred in connection with the protective order.

(b) The court may order a party against whom an agreed protective order is rendered under Section 85.005 to pay the fees required in Subsection (a).

History of Fam §81.003: Acts 1997, 75th Leg., ch. 34, §1, eff. May 5, 1997. Amended by Acts 1997, 75th Leg., ch. 1193, §4, eff. Sept. 1, 1997. Source: Former Fam §71.041(b).

FAM §81.004. CONTEMPT FOR NONPAYMENT OF FEE

(a) A party who is ordered to pay fees and costs and who does not pay before the date specified by the order may be punished for contempt of court as provided by Section 21.002, Government Code.

(b) If a date is not specified by the court under Subsection (a), payment of costs is required before the 60th day after the date the order was rendered.

History of Fam §81.004: Acts 1997, 75th Leg., ch. 34, §1, eff. May 5, 1997. Amended by Acts 1997, 75th Leg., ch. 1193, §5, eff. Sept. 1, 1997. Source: Former Fam §71.041(c).

FAM §81.005. ATTORNEY'S FEES

(a) The court may assess reasonable attorney's fees against the party found to have committed family violence or a party against whom an agreed protective order is rendered under Section 85.005 as compensation for the services of a private or prosecuting attorney or an attorney employed by the Department of Protective and Regulatory Services.

(b) In setting the amount of attorney's fees, the court shall consider the income and ability to pay of the person against whom the fee is assessed.

History of Fam §81.005: Acts 1997, 75th Leg., ch. 34, §1, eff. May 5, 1997. Amended by Acts 1997, 75th Leg., ch. 1193, §6, eff. Sept. 1, 1997. Source: Former Fam §71.041(d).

FAM §81.006. PAYMENT OF ATTORNEY'S FEES

The amount of fees collected under this chapter as compensation for the fees:

(1) of a private attorney shall be paid to the private attorney who may enforce the order for fees in the attorney's own name;

(2) of a prosecuting attorney shall be paid to the credit of the county fund from which the salaries of the employees of the prosecuting attorney are paid or supplemented; and

(3) of an attorney employed by the Department of Protective and Regulatory Services shall be deposited in the general revenue fund to the credit of the Department of Protective and Regulatory Services.

History of Fam §81.006: Acts 1997, 75th Leg., ch. 34, §1, eff. May 5, 1997. Source: Former Fam §71.041(d).

FAM §81.007. PROSECUTING ATTORNEY

(a) The county attorney or the criminal district attorney is the prosecuting attorney responsible for filing applications under this subtitle unless the district attorney assumes the responsibility by giving notice of that assumption to the county attorney.

(b) The prosecuting attorney responsible for filing an application under this subtitle shall provide notice of that responsibility to all law enforcement agencies in the jurisdiction of the prosecuting attorney.

(c) The prosecuting attorney shall comply with Article 5.06, Code of Criminal Procedure, in filing an application under this subtitle.

History of Fam §81.007: Acts 1997, 75th Leg., ch. 34, §1, eff. May 5, 1997. Source: Former Fam §71.04(c).

Striedel v. Striedel, 15 S.W.3d 163, 167 (Tex.App.—Corpus Christi 2000, no pet.). "[W]e express our concern regarding the trial court's failure to give consideration to the appointment of counsel for [respondent]. In this case, [respondent] filed an affidavit of indigency. Attorney for [applicant] objected to further consideration because this was a civil, not criminal proceeding. *At 167 n.2:* We note that, unlike any other 'civil' proceeding in which injunctive relief is sought, a petitioner for a protective order is statutorily guaranteed counsel. Moreover, the statute specifically states that 'The county attorney or the criminal district attorney is the prosecuting attorney responsible for filing applications under this subtitle....' Examining the nature of a protective order, the method by which it is prosecuted, the sanctioned deprivations of liberty and property which are possible pursuant to such an order, and the possibility of incarceration, we believe the proceeding is quasi-criminal in its nature."

FAM §81.0075. REPRESENTATION BY PROSECUTING ATTORNEY IN CERTAIN SUBSEQUENT ACTIONS

A prosecuting attorney who represents a party in a proceeding under this subtitle is not precluded from representing the Department of Protective and Regulatory Services in a subsequent action involving the party.

History of Fam §81.0075: Acts 1997, 75th Leg., ch. 1193, §7, eff. Sept. 1, 1997.

FAM §81.008. RELIEF CUMULATIVE

Except as provided by this subtitle, the relief and remedies provided by this subtitle are cumulative of other relief and remedies provided by law.

History of Fam §81.008: Acts 1997, 75th Leg., ch. 34, §1, eff. May 5, 1997. Source: Former Fam §71.19.

CHAPTER 82. APPLYING FOR PROTECTIVE ORDER

Subchapter A. Application for Protective Order

Subchapter B. Pleadings by Respondent

Subchapter C. Notice of Application for Protective Order

FAM §81.006

SUBCHAPTER A. APPLICATION FOR PROTECTIVE ORDER

FAM §82.001. APPLICATION

A proceeding under this subtitle is begun by filing "An Application for a Protective Order" with the clerk of the court.

History of Fam §82.001: Acts 1997, 75th Leg., ch. 34, §1, eff. May 5, 1997. Source: Former Fam §§71.02, 71.04(a).

A FAM §82.002. WHO MAY FILE APPLICATION

(a) With regard to family violence under Section 71.004(1) or (2), an adult member of the family or household may file an application for a protective order to protect the applicant or any other member of the applicant's family or household.

E (b) With regard to family violence under Section 71.004(3), an application for a protective order to protect the applicant may be filed by an adult member of the dating relationship.

E (c) Any adult may apply for a protective order to protect a child from family violence.

(d) In addition, an application may be filed for the protection of any person alleged to be a victim of family violence by:

(1) a prosecuting attorney; or

(2) the Department of Protective and Regulatory Services.

(e) The person alleged to be the victim of family violence in an application filed under Subsection (c) or (d) is considered to be the applicant for a protective order under this subtitle.

History of Fam §82.002: Acts 1997, 75th Leg., ch. 34, §1, eff. May 5, 1997. Amended by Acts 1997, 75th Leg., ch. 1193, §8, eff. Sept. 1, 1997; Acts 2001, 77th Leg., ch. 91, §3, eff. Sept. 1, 2001. Source: Former Fam §71.04(b).

See also 40 TAC §705.3102.

FAM §82.003. VENUE

An application may be filed in:

(1) the county in which the applicant resides; or

(2) the county in which the respondent resides.

History of Fam §82.003: Acts 1997, 75th Leg., ch. 34, §1, eff. May 5, 1997. Source: Former Fam §71.03.

Magill v. Sheffield, 612 S.W.2d 677, 679 (Tex. App.—Dallas 1981, writ ref'd n.r.e.). A "proceeding for protective orders brought under [Title 4] is an independent remedy which is not limited to the court having continuing jurisdiction. *At 681:* We recognize that a proceeding seeking to deny a parent access to his child and authorize another person to have possession is, in a broad sense, one which affects the parent-child relationship. Nevertheless, the legislature, by enacting [T]itle 4, has expressly provided an independent remedy for protective orders in addition to the remedies available under [T]itle 2. Except with respect to temporary ex parte orders, the legislature has limited the court's authority to orders that do not conflict with any order of a court of continuing jurisdiction. Any potential conflict of jurisdiction, therefore, is minimized. It might be advisable to insert in [T]itle 4 a provision authorizing the court to transfer the proceeding to the court of continuing jurisdiction, rather than to consider the respondent's plea of privilege, but we find no authority for such a transfer in the Code as it stands. Any argument, in this respect, therefore, must be addressed to the legislature rather than to the courts."

FAM §82.004. CONTENTS OF APPLICATION

An application must state:

(1) the name and county of residence of each applicant;

A *Subsection (2) below is effective for applications for protective orders filed on or after Sept. 1, 2001.*

(2) the name and county of residence of each individual alleged to have committed family violence;

Subsection (2) below is effective for applications for protective orders filed before Sept. 1, 2001.

(2) the name, address, and county of residence of each individual alleged to have committed family violence;

(3) the relationships between the applicants and the individual alleged to have committed family violence; and

(4) a request for one or more protective orders.

History of Fam §82.004: Acts 1997, 75th Leg., ch. 34, §1, eff. May 5, 1997. Amended by Acts 2001, 77th Leg., ch. 296, §1, eff. Sept. 1, 2001. Source: Former Fam §71.05(a).

FAM §82.005. APPLICATION FILED DURING SUIT FOR DISSOLUTION OF MARRIAGE OR SUIT AFFECTING PARENT-CHILD RELATIONSHIP

A person who wishes to apply for a protective order with respect to the person's spouse and who is a party to a suit for the dissolution of a marriage or a suit affecting the parent-child relationship that is pending in a court must file the application as required by Subchapter D, Chapter 85.

History of Fam §82.005: Acts 1997, 75th Leg., ch. 34, §1, eff. May 5, 1997. Amended by Acts 1997, 75th Leg., ch. 1193, §9, eff. Sept. 1, 1997. Source: Former Fam §71.06.

Ruiz v. Ruiz, 946 S.W.2d 123, 124 (Tex.App.—El Paso 1997, no writ). Section 71.06(a), now §82.005, "requires that protective orders be issued under §3.581 [now §6.504] if a divorce is pending. ... Absent action by the legislature, the method for seeking review of a protective order entered during pendency of a divorce is mandamus."

FAM §82.006. APPLICATION FILED AFTER DISSOLUTION OF MARRIAGE

If an applicant for a protective order is a former spouse of the individual alleged to have committed family violence, the application must include:

(1) a copy of the decree dissolving the marriage; or

(2) a statement that the decree is unavailable to the applicant and that a copy of the decree will be filed with the court before the hearing on the application.

History of Fam §82.006: Acts 1997, 75th Leg., ch. 34, §1, eff. May 5, 1997. Source: Former Fam §71.05(c).

FAM §82.007. APPLICATION FILED FOR CHILD SUBJECT TO CONTINUING JURISDICTION

An application that requests a protective order for a child who is subject to the continuing exclusive jurisdiction of a court under Title 5 or alleges that a child who is subject to the continuing exclusive jurisdiction of a court under Title 5 has committed family violence must include:

(1) a copy of each court order affecting the conservatorship, support, and possession of or access to the child; or

(2) a statement that the orders affecting the child are unavailable to the applicant and that a copy of the orders will be filed with the court before the hearing on the application.

History of Fam §82.007: Acts 1997, 75th Leg., ch. 34, §1, eff. May 5, 1997. Source: Former Fam §71.05(d).

FAM §82.008. APPLICATION FILED AFTER EXPIRATION OF FORMER PROTECTIVE ORDER

(a) An application for a protective order that is filed after a previously rendered protective order has expired must include:

(1) a copy of the expired protective order attached to the application or, if a copy of the expired protective order is unavailable, a statement that the order is unavailable to the applicant and that a copy of the order will be filed with the court before the hearing on the application;

(2) a description of either:

(A) the violation of the expired protective order, if the application alleges that the respondent violated the expired protective order by committing an act prohibited by that order before the order expired; or

(B) the threatened harm that reasonably places the applicant in fear of imminent physical harm, bodily injury, assault, or sexual assault; and

(3) if a violation of the expired order is alleged, a statement that the violation of the expired order has not been grounds for any other order protecting the applicant that has been issued or requested under this subtitle.

(b) The procedural requirements for an original application for a protective order apply to a protective order requested under this section.

History of Fam §82.008: Acts 1997, 75th Leg., ch. 34, §1, eff. May 5, 1997. Amended by Acts 1999, 76th Leg., ch. 1160, §1, eff. Sept. 1, 1999. Source: Former Fam §71.05(f), (g).

FAM §82.0085. APPLICATION FILED BEFORE EXPIRATION OF PREVIOUSLY RENDERED PROTECTIVE ORDER

(a) If an application for a protective order alleges that an unexpired protective order applicable to the respondent is due to expire not later than the 30th day after the date the application was filed, the application for the subsequent protective order must include:

(1) a copy of the previously rendered protective order attached to the application or, if a copy of the previously rendered protective order is unavailable, a statement that the order is unavailable to the applicant and that a copy of the order will be filed with the court before the hearing on the application; and

(2) a description of the threatened harm that reasonably places the applicant in fear of imminent physical harm, bodily injury, assault, or sexual assault.

(b) The procedural requirements for an original application for a protective order apply to a protective order requested under this section.

History of Fam §82.0085: Acts 1999, 76th Leg., 1160, §2, eff. Sept. 1, 1999.

FAM §82.009. APPLICATION FOR TEMPORARY EX PARTE ORDER

An application that requests the issuance of a temporary ex parte order under Chapter 83 must:

(1) contain a detailed description of the facts and circumstances concerning the alleged family violence and the need for the immediate protective order; and

(2) be signed by each applicant under an oath that the facts and circumstances contained in the application are true to the best knowledge and belief of each applicant.

History of Fam §82.009: Acts 1997, 75th Leg., ch. 34, §1, eff. May 5, 1997. Source: Former Fam §71.05(e).

Sections 82.010-82.020 reserved for expansion

SUBCHAPTER B. PLEADINGS BY RESPONDENT

FAM §82.021. ANSWER

A respondent to an application for a protective order who is served with notice of an application for a protective order may file an answer at any time before the hearing. A respondent is not required to file an answer to the application.

History of Fam §82.021: Acts 1997, 75th Leg., ch. 34, §1, eff. May 5, 1997. Source: Former Fam §71.08.

FAM §82.022. REQUEST BY RESPONDENT FOR PROTECTIVE ORDER

To apply for a protective order, a respondent to an application for a protective order must file a separate application.

History of Fam §82.022: Acts 1997, 75th Leg., ch. 34, §1, eff. May 5, 1997. Source: Former Fam §71.121(a).

Sections 82.023-82.040 reserved for expansion

SUBCHAPTER C. NOTICE OF APPLICATION FOR PROTECTIVE ORDER

FAM §82.041. CONTENTS OF NOTICE OF APPLICATION

(a) A notice of an application for a protective order must:

(1) be styled "The State of Texas";

(2) be signed by the clerk of the court under the court's seal;

(3) contain the name and location of the court;

(4) show the date the application was filed;

(5) show the date notice of the application for a protective order was issued;

(6) show the date, time, and place of the hearing;

(7) show the file number;

(8) show the name of each applicant and each person alleged to have committed family violence;

(9) be directed to each person alleged to have committed family violence;

(10) show the name and address of the attorney for the applicant or the mailing address of the applicant, if the applicant is not represented by an attorney; and

(11) contain the address of the clerk of the court.

(b) The notice of an application for a protective order must state: "An application for a protective order has been filed in the court stated in this notice alleging that you have committed family violence. You may employ an attorney to defend you against this allegation. You or your attorney may, but are not required to, file a written answer to the application. Any answer must be filed before the hearing on the application. If you receive this notice within 48 hours before the time set for the hearing, you may request the court to reschedule the hearing not later than 14 days after the date set for the hearing. If you do not attend the hearing, a default judgment may be taken and a protective order may be issued against you."

History of Fam §82.041: Acts 1997, 75th Leg., ch. 34, §1, eff. May 5, 1997. Amended by Acts 1997, 75th Leg., ch. 1193, §10, eff. Sept. 1, 1997. Source: Former Fam §71.07(d), (e).

FAM §82.042. ISSUANCE OF NOTICE OF APPLICATION

(a) On the filing of an application, the clerk of the court shall issue a notice of an application for a protective order and deliver the notice as directed by the applicant.

(b) On request by the applicant, the clerk of the court shall issue a separate or additional notice of an application for a protective order.

History of Fam §82.042: Acts 1997, 75th Leg., ch. 34, §1, eff. May 5, 1997. Source: Former Fam §71.07(b), (c).

FAM §82.043. SERVICE OF NOTICE OF APPLICATION

(a) Each respondent to an application for a protective order is entitled to service of notice of an application for a protective order.

(b) An applicant for a protective order shall furnish the clerk with a sufficient number of copies of the application for service on each respondent.

(c) Notice of an application for a protective order must be served in the same manner as citation under the Texas Rules of Civil Procedure, except that service by publication is not authorized.

(d) Service of notice of an application for a protective order is not required before the issuance of a temporary ex parte order under Chapter 83.

(e) The requirements of service of notice under this subchapter do not apply if the application is filed as a motion in a suit for dissolution of a marriage. Notice for the motion is given in the same manner as any other motion in a suit for dissolution of a marriage.

History of Fam §82.043: Acts 1997, 75th Leg., ch. 34, §1, eff. May 5, 1997. Source: Former Fam §§71.06(e), 71.07(a), (f)-(h).

CHAPTER 83. TEMPORARY EX PARTE ORDERS

FAM §83.001. REQUIREMENTS FOR TEMPORARY EX PARTE ORDER

A (a) If the court finds from the information contained in an application for a protective order that there is a clear and present danger of family violence, the court, without further notice to the individual alleged to have committed family violence and without a hearing, may enter a temporary ex parte order for the protection of the applicant or any other member of the family or household of the applicant.

(b) In a temporary ex parte order, the court may direct a respondent to do or refrain from doing specified acts.

History of Fam §83.001: Acts 1997, 75th Leg., ch. 34, §1, eff. May 5, 1997. Amended by Acts 2001, 77th Leg., ch. 91, §4, eff. Sept. 1, 2001. Source: Former Fam §71.15(a).

FAM §83.002. DURATION OF ORDER; EXTENSION

(a) A temporary ex parte order is valid for the period specified in the order, not to exceed 20 days.

(b) On the request of an applicant or on the court's own motion, a temporary ex parte order may be extended for additional 20-day periods.

History of Fam §83.002: Acts 1997, 75th Leg., ch. 34, §1, eff. May 5, 1997. Source: Former Fam §71.15(b), (c).

FAM §83.003. BOND NOT REQUIRED

The court, at the court's discretion, may dispense with the necessity of a bond for a temporary ex parte order.

History of Fam §83.003: Acts 1997, 75th Leg., ch. 34, §1, eff. May 5, 1997. Source: Former Fam §71.15(d).

A FAM §83.004. MOTION TO VACATE

Any individual affected by a temporary ex parte order may file a motion at any time to vacate the order. On the filing of the motion to vacate, the court shall set a date for hearing the motion as soon as possible.

History of Fam §83.004: Acts 1997, 75th Leg., ch. 34, §1, eff. May 5, 1997. Amended by Acts 2001, 77th Leg., ch. 91, §5, eff. Sept. 1, 2001. Source: Former Fam §71.15(e).

FAM §83.005. CONFLICTING ORDERS

During the time the order is valid, a temporary ex parte order prevails over any other court order made under Title 5 to the extent of any conflict between the orders.

History of Fam §83.005: Acts 1997, 75th Leg., ch. 34, §1, eff. May 5, 1997. Amended by Acts 1997, 75th Leg., ch. 1193, §11, eff. Sept. 1, 1997. Source: Former Fam §71.15(f).

FAM §83.006. EXCLUSION OF PARTY FROM RESIDENCE

(a) Subject to the limitations of Section 85.021(2), a person may only be excluded from the occupancy of the person's residence by a temporary ex parte order under this chapter if the applicant:

(1) files a sworn affidavit that provides a detailed description of the facts and circumstances requiring the exclusion of the person from the residence; and

(2) appears in person to testify at a temporary ex parte hearing to justify the issuance of the order without notice.

(b) Before the court may render a temporary ex parte order excluding a person from the person's residence, the court must find from the required affidavit and testimony that:

(1) the applicant requesting the excluding order either resides on the premises or has resided there within 30 days before the date the application was filed;

(2) the person to be excluded has within the 30 days before the date the application was filed committed family violence against a member of the household; and

(3) there is a clear and present danger that the person to be excluded is likely to commit family violence against a member of the household.

History of Fam §83.006: Acts 1997, 75th Leg., ch. 34, §1, eff. May 5, 1997. Source: Former Fam §71.15(g), (h).

FAM §83.007. RECESS OF HEARING TO CONTACT RESPONDENT

The court may recess the hearing on a temporary ex parte order to contact the respondent by telephone and provide the respondent the opportunity to be present when the court resumes the hearing. Without regard to whether the respondent is able to be present at the hearing, the court shall resume the hearing before the end of the working day.

History of Fam §83.007: Acts 1997, 75th Leg., ch. 34, §1, eff. May 5, 1997. Source: Former Fam §71.15(j).

CHAPTER 84. HEARING

FAM §84.001. TIME SET FOR HEARING

(a) On the filing of an application for a protective order, the court shall set a date and time for the hearing unless a later date is requested by the applicant. Except as provided by Section 84.002, the court may not set a date later than the 14th day after the date the application is filed.

(b) The court may not delay a hearing on an application in order to consolidate it with a hearing on a subsequently filed application.

History of Fam §84.001: Acts 1997, 75th Leg., ch. 34, §1, eff. May 5, 1997. Source: Former Fam §§71.09(a), 71.121(c).

Martinez v. Martinez, 52 S.W.3d 429, 432-33 (Tex.App.—Fort Worth 2001, pet. denied). Husband "asked for and received a continuance on the protective order hearing on the same day he filed his deposition notice and production request. As a result, [wife] was forced to wait an additional fifteen days for her final protective order hearing, instead of the maximum fourteen additional days. As the State points out, during this time the temporary protective order remained in effect but only for a portion of the time. It expired on May 3, 2000, even though the hearing was rescheduled to May 10. Because of the continuance, [wife] showed particular, demonstrable injury because she was unprotected for seven days before the hearing. And even while in effect, a temporary protective order is not a criminally enforceable order as is a final protective order after hearing. The basis for the continuance was solely to accommodate [husband]'s discovery requests. The need to conduct discovery is not one of the statutory bases to continue a protective order hearing. Thus, the associate judge erred when it granted [husband]'s motion for continuance."

FAM §84.002. EXTENDED TIME FOR HEARING IN DISTRICT COURT IN CERTAIN COUNTIES

(a) On the request of the prosecuting attorney in a county with a population of more than 1.5 million or in a county in a judicial district that is composed of more than one county, the district court shall set the hearing on a date and time not later than 20 days after the date the application is filed or 20 days after the date a request is made to reschedule a hearing under Section 84.003.

(b) The district court shall grant the request of the prosecuting attorney for an extended time in which to hold a hearing on a protective order either on a case-by-case basis or for all cases filed under this subtitle.

History of Fam §84.002: Acts 1997, 75th Leg., ch. 34, §1, eff. May 5, 1997. Amended by Acts 1997, 75th Leg., ch. 1193, §12, eff. Sept. 1, 1997. Source: Former Fam §71.09(d).

FAM §84.003. HEARING RESCHEDULED FOR FAILURE OF SERVICE

(a) If a hearing set under this chapter is not held because of the failure of a respondent to receive service of notice of an application for a protective order, the applicant may request the court to reschedule the hearing.

(b) Except as provided by Section 84.002, the date for a rescheduled hearing shall be not later than 14 days after the date the request is made.

History of Fam §84.003: Acts 1997, 75th Leg., ch. 34, §1, eff. May 5, 1997. Source: Former Fam §71.09(c).

FAM §84.004. HEARING RESCHEDULED FOR INSUFFICIENT NOTICE

(a) If a respondent receives service of notice of an application for a protective order within 48 hours before the time set for the hearing, on request by the respondent, the court shall reschedule the hearing for a date not later than 14 days after the date set for the hearing.

(b) The respondent is not entitled to additional service for a hearing rescheduled under this section.

History of Fam §84.004: Acts 1997, 75th Leg., ch. 34, §1, eff. May 5, 1997. Source: Former Fam §71.09(b).

FAM §84.005. LEGISLATIVE CONTINUANCE

If a proceeding for which a legislative continuance is sought under Section 30.003, Civil Practice and Remedies Code, includes an application for a protective order, the continuance is discretionary with the court.

History of Fam §84.005: Acts 1999, 76th Leg., ch. 62, §6.10(a), eff. Sept. 1, 1999.

CHAPTER 85. ISSUANCE OF PROTECTIVE ORDER

SUBCHAPTER A. FINDINGS & ORDERS

FAM §85.001. REQUIRED FINDINGS & ORDERS

(a) At the close of a hearing on an application for a protective order, the court shall find whether:

(1) family violence has occurred; and

(2) family violence is likely to occur in the future.

(b) If the court finds that family violence has occurred and that family violence is likely to occur in the future, the court:

(1) shall render a protective order as provided by Section 85.022 applying only to a person found to have committed family violence; and

A (2) may render a protective order as provided by Section 85.021 applying to both parties that is in the best interest of the person protected by the order or member of the family or household of the person protected by the order.

(c) A protective order that requires the first applicant to do or refrain from doing an act under Section 85.022 shall include a finding that the first applicant has committed family violence and is likely to commit family violence in the future.

History of Fam §85.001: Acts 1997, 75th Leg., ch. 34, §1, eff. May 5, 1997. Amended by Acts 2001, 77th Leg., ch. 91, §6, eff. Sept. 1, 2001. Source: Former Fam §§71.10(a), (b), 71.121(d).

Cooke v. Cooke, 65 S.W.3d 785, 788 (Tex.App.—Dallas 2001, no pet.). "[W]e hold a protective order rendered pursuant to the family code is a final, appealable order as long as it disposes of all parties and all issues." *See also* ***Kelt v. Kelt***, 67 S.W.3d 364, 366 (Tex.App.—Waco 2001, no pet.) (reversing ***Normand v. Fox***, 940 S.W.2d 401 (Tex.App.—Waco 1997, no. pet.), which held protective orders were not final, appealable orders); ***Winsett v. Edgar***, 22 S.W.3d 509, 510 (Tex.App.—Fort Worth 2000, no pet.); ***James v. Hubbard***, 985 S.W.2d 516, 517 (Tex.App.—San Antonio 1998, no pet.).

Williams v. Williams, 19 S.W.3d 544, 546-47 (Tex. App.—Fort Worth 2000, pet. denied). Respondent "contends that a party against whom an application for a protective order has been filed is entitled to have a jury, not the court, determine whether family violence has occurred and whether it is likely to occur in the future. [¶] Because §§81.001 and 85.001(a) are clear and unambiguous, we are bound to enforce their provisions as written. Section 85.001(a), entitled 'Required Findings and Orders,' states that the *court* shall determine whether family violence has occurred and whether it is likely to occur in the future. Section 81.001 provides that the *court* shall render a protective order if the *court* finds that family violence has occurred and is likely to occur in the future. A 'court' is '[a]n organ of the government, belonging to the judicial department, whose function is the application of the laws to controversies brought before it and the public administration of justice.' In law, the words 'court' and 'judge' are frequently used in statutes as synonymous terms. Statutes are presumed to have been enacted by the legislature with complete knowledge of existing law and with reference to it. Here, the legislature's intent to designate the court as sole fact finder is evident from the plain and common meaning of the language used in the statutes."

Striedel v. Striedel, 15 S.W.3d 163, 166 (Tex.App.—Corpus Christi 2000, no pet.). "General principles of due process dictate that a litigant has a right to be heard and that the court must protect that right. The opportunity to be heard and present evidence must generally amount to more than a cursory opportunity to cross-examine the other party's witnesses. A trial court is vested with broad discretion regarding the admission and presentation of evidence. However, fundamental fairness dictates that a party not be arbitrarily deprived of the right to offer any evidence. [¶] In this instance, the trial court denied [respondent] any opportunity to present evidence, despite the fact that he affirmatively stated his ability and willingness to do so. The deprivation is particularly egregious because the issuance of the protective order may have a substantial effect on appellant's liberty in the future. Moreover, we are not convinced that the record developed prior to the premature conclusion of the hearing would adequately support issuing the protective order. … While it is true that [applicant] testified that violence ensued at the close of this meeting, the trial court was obligated to allow [respondent] an opportunity to present his evidence as to that occurrence as well as the probability of future violence. By depriving [respondent] of that opportunity, the trial court abused its discretion."

FAM §85.002. EXCEPTION FOR VIOLATION OF EXPIRED PROTECTIVE ORDER

If the court finds that a respondent violated a protective order by committing an act prohibited by the order as provided by Section 85.022, that the order was in effect at the time of the violation, and that the order has expired after the date that the violation occurred, the court, without the necessity of making the findings described by Section 85.001(a), shall render a protective order as provided by Section 85.022 applying only to the respondent and may render a protective order as provided by Section 85.021.

History of Fam §85.002: Acts 1997, 75th Leg., ch. 34, §1, eff. May 5, 1997. Amended by Acts 1997, 75th Leg., ch. 1193, §13, eff. Sept. 1, 1997. Source: Former Fam §71.10(c).

FAM §85.003. SEPARATE PROTECTIVE ORDERS REQUIRED

(a) A court that renders separate protective orders that apply to both parties and require both parties to do or refrain from doing acts under Section 85.022 shall render two distinct and separate protective orders in two separate documents that reflect the appropriate conditions for each party.

(b) A court that renders protective orders that apply to both parties and require both parties to do or refrain from doing acts under Section 85.022 shall render the protective orders in two separate documents. The court shall provide one of the documents to the applicant and the other document to the respondent.

(c) A court may not render one protective order under Section 85.022 that applies to both parties.

History of Fam §85.003: Acts 1997, 75th Leg., ch. 34, §1, eff. May 5, 1997. Source: Former Fam §71.121(a), (e), (f).

In re Salgado, 53 S.W.3d 752, 763 (Tex.App.—El Paso 2001, no pet.). "Chapter 81 does not define residency of a child applicant for purposes of establishing venue under §82.003. In determining the elements of residence, we look for guidance to cases construing residency in various contexts. The Supreme Court has articulated the elements of residency under the general civil venue statute: (1) a fixed place of abode within the possession of the party; (2) occupied or intended to be occupied consistently over a substantial period of time; (3) which is permanent rather than temporary. An element of permanency is necessary before a party can be considered a resident of a particular county."

FAM §85.004. PROTECTIVE ORDER IN SUIT FOR DISSOLUTION OF MARRIAGE

A protective order in a suit for dissolution of a marriage must be in a separate document entitled "PROTECTIVE ORDER."

History of Fam §85.004: Acts 1997, 75th Leg., ch. 34, §1, eff. May 5, 1997. Source: Former Fam §71.06(f).

In re Edwards, ___ S.W.3d ___ (Tex.App.—Texarkana 2002, n.p.h.) (No. 06-00-00130-CV; 4-11-02). Petitioner "contends the Protective Order incorporated in the divorce decree is unenforceable because it does not comply with [§85.004]. [Petitioner] does not cite any authority for her theory that incorporating the Protective Order in the divorce decree renders it unenforceable, and our research reveals no such authority either in caselaw or in the Texas Family Code. Such a harsh outcome is inconsistent with the Legislature's intent of preventing family violence."

FAM §85.005. AGREED ORDER

(a) To facilitate settlement, the parties to a proceeding may agree in writing to the terms of a protective order as provided by Section 85.021. An agreement under this subsection is subject to the approval of the court.

(b) To facilitate settlement, a respondent may agree in writing to the terms of a protective order as provided by Section 85.022, subject to the approval of the court. The court may not approve an agreement that requires the applicant to do or refrain from doing an act under Section 85.022.

(c) If the court approves an agreement between the parties, the court shall render an agreed protective order that is in the best interest of the applicant, the family or household, or a member of the family or household.

(d) An agreed protective order is not enforceable as a contract.

(e) An agreed protective order expires on the date the court order expires.

History of Fam §85.005: Acts 1997, 75th Leg., ch. 34, §1, eff. May 5, 1997. Source: Former Fam §§71.10(d), 71.12(a), (b), (d), (e).

Moreno v. Moore, 897 S.W.2d 439, 442 (Tex.App.—Corpus Christi 1995, no writ). "In the instant case, the mutual protective order did not include an agreement of the parties pursuant to §71.12(a) [now §85.005]. Further, the record does not show that the parties entered into an agreement as described by §71.12(a). The parties' failure to comply with §71.12(a) prevented the trial court from entering a single protective order that applied to both of them. Thus, [applicant] had to file a *separate* application for a protective order if he wanted to receive a protective order against [respondent]. Since [applicant] did not file any pleadings requesting a protective order, the trial court was without authority to enter that part of the mutual protective order which granted [applicant] a protective order against [respondent]."

FAM §85.006. DEFAULT ORDER

(a) A court may render a protective order that is binding on a respondent who does not attend a hearing if the respondent received service of the application and notice of the hearing.

(b) If the court reschedules the hearing under Chapter 84, a protective order may be rendered if the respondent does not attend the rescheduled hearing.

History of Fam §85.006: Acts 1997, 75th Leg., ch. 34, §1, eff. May 5, 1997. Source: Former Fam §71.09(e).

FAM §85.007. CONFIDENTIALITY OF CERTAIN INFORMATION

Ⓐ (a) On request by a person protected by an order or member of the family or household of a person protected by an order, the court may exclude from a protective order the address and telephone number of:

(1) a person protected by the order, in which case the order shall state the county in which the person resides;

(2) the place of employment or business of a person protected by the order; or

(3) the child-care facility or school a child protected by the order attends or in which the child resides.

(b) On granting a request for confidentiality under this section, the court shall order the clerk to:

(1) strike the information described by Subsection (a) from the public records of the court; and

(2) maintain a confidential record of the information for use only by the court.

History of Fam §85.007: Acts 1997, 75th Leg., ch. 34, §1, eff. May 5, 1997. Amended by Acts 2001, 77th Leg., ch. 91, §7, eff. Sept. 1, 2001. Source: Former Fam §71.111.

Patton v. State, 835 S.W.2d 684, 688-89 (Tex. App.—Dallas 1992, no writ). "The undisputed evidence shows that Husband and Wife agreed to the protective order that was entered. Wife testified that Husband's attorney drafted the protective order. The protective order restrained both parties from committing certain acts for one year. When this point was argued to the trial court, the court stated that this was a mutual protective order and that the court, therefore, would infer that the parties agreed to omit the address of Wife's place of employment or business. This was a reasonable inference from the evidence presented at trial. We find nothing in §71.111 [now §85.007] or any other section of the Texas Family Code that requires the protective order to affirmatively state that certain information has been omitted from the order pursuant to §71.111(a)(2). We conclude that the address of Wife's place of employment was properly omitted from the agreed protective order pursuant to §71.111(a)(2)...."

FAM §85.008. REPEALED

Repealed by Acts 1997, 75th Leg., ch. 1193, §24, eff. Sept. 1, 1997.

FAM §85.009. ORDER VALID UNTIL SUPERSEDED

A protective order rendered under this chapter is valid and enforceable pending further action by the court that rendered the order until the order is properly superseded by another court with jurisdiction over the order.

History of Fam §85.009: Acts 1997, 75th Leg., ch. 34, §1, eff. May 5, 1997. Source: Former Fam §71.06(c).

In re Salgado, 53 S.W.3d 752, 761 (Tex.App.—El Paso 2001, no pet.). "Section 83.005 expressly provides that a temporary ex parte order—issued without notice or hearing—prevails to the extent of any conflict with an order issued under Title 5. Title 4 does not currently contain a similar provision to resolve conflicts between protective orders—issued after notice and hearing—and other existing orders. If, however, a protective order affects a party's right of possession of or access to a child, the court may transfer the protective order to the court of continuing, exclusive jurisdiction if the court finds that the transfer is in the interest of justice or for the safety or convenience of a party or witness. The transfer may be made on the court's own motion or on the motion of a party. Given these provisions, the Legislature obviously anticipated that a protective order may conflict with a valid pre-existing custody order."

Sections 85.010-85.020 reserved for expansion

SUBCHAPTER B. CONTENTS OF PROTECTIVE ORDER

FAM §85.021. REQUIREMENTS OF ORDER APPLYING TO ANY PARTY

In a protective order, the court may:

(1) prohibit a party from:

(A) removing a child who is a member of the family or household from:

(i) the possession of a person named in the order; or

(ii) the jurisdiction of the court; or

(B) transferring, encumbering, or otherwise disposing of property, other than in the ordinary course of business, that is mutually owned or leased by the parties;

(2) grant exclusive possession of a residence to a party and, if appropriate, direct one or more parties to vacate the residence if the residence:

(A) is jointly owned or leased by the party receiving exclusive possession and a party being denied possession;

(B) is owned or leased by the party retaining possession; or

(C) is owned or leased by the party being denied possession and that party has an obligation to support the party or a child of the party granted possession of the residence;

(3) provide for the possession of and access to a child of a party if the person receiving possession of or access to the child is a parent of the child;

(4) require the payment of support for a party or for a child of a party if the person required to make the payment has an obligation to support the other party or the child; or

(5) award to a party the use and possession of specified property that is community property or jointly owned or leased property.

History of Fam §85.021: Acts 1997, 75th Leg., ch. 34, §1, eff. May 5, 1997. Source: Former Fam §71.11(a)(1)-(4), (6).

FAM §85.022. REQUIREMENTS OF ORDER APPLYING TO PERSON WHO COMMITTED FAMILY VIOLENCE

(a) In a protective order, the court may order the person found to have committed family violence to:

(1) complete a battering intervention and prevention program as provided by Article 42.141, Code of Criminal Procedure, and that meets the guidelines adopted by the community justice assistance division of the Texas Department of Criminal Justice if a program is available;

(2) counsel with a social worker, family service agency, physician, psychologist, licensed therapist, or licensed professional counselor if a program under Subdivision (1) is not available; or

(3) perform acts specified by the court that the court determines are necessary or appropriate to prevent or reduce the likelihood of family violence.

A (b) In a protective order, the court may prohibit the person found to have committed family violence from:

(1) committing family violence;

(2) communicating:

(A) directly with a person protected by an order or a member of the family or household of a person protected by an order, in a threatening or harassing manner;

(B) a threat through any person to a person protected by an order or a member of the family or household of a person protected by an order; and

(C) if the court finds good cause, in any manner with a person protected by an order or a member of the family or household of a person protected by an order, except through the party's attorney or a person appointed by the court;

(3) going to or near the residence or place of employment or business of a person protected by an order or a member of the family or household of a person protected by an order;

(4) going to or near the residence, child-care facility, or school a child protected under the order normally attends or in which the child normally resides;

(5) engaging in conduct directed specifically toward a person who is a person protected by an order or a member of the family or household of a person protected by an order, including following the person, that is reasonably likely to harass, annoy, alarm, abuse, torment, or embarrass the person; and

E (6) possessing a firearm, unless the person is a peace officer, as defined by Section 1.07, Penal Code, actively engaged in employment as a sworn, full-time paid employee of a state agency or political subdivision.

(c) In an order under Subsection (b)(3) or (4), the court shall specifically describe each prohibited location and the minimum distances from the location, if any, that the party must maintain. This subsection does not apply to an order in which Section 85.007 applies.

(d) In a protective order, the court may suspend a license to carry a concealed handgun issued under Section 411.177, Government Code, that is held by a person found to have committed family violence.

E (e) In this section, "firearm" has the meaning assigned by Section 46.01, Penal Code.

History of Fam §85.022: Acts 1997, 75th Leg., ch. 34, §1, eff. May 5, 1997. Amended by Acts 1997, 75th Leg., ch. 1193, §14, eff. Sept. 1, 1997; Acts 1999, 76th Leg., ch. 1412, §3, 77th Leg., eff. Sept. 1, 1999; Acts 2001, 77th Leg., ch. 91, §8 (eff. Sept. 1, 2001), ch. 23, §3 (eff. Sept. 1, 2001). Source: Former Fam §71.11(a)(5), (7), (b), (c).

Collins v. State, 955 S.W.2d 464, 466 (Tex.App.—Fort Worth 1997, no pet.). "We disagree with [respondent] that a §71.11 [now §85.022] order prohibiting a person from going to or near the residence or place of employment or business of another person must describe both a location *and* a minimum distance. *At 467:* By its plain meaning, the section only requires that a distance be set out by the court *if there is one*. We see no requirement that a distance always be set out, nor do we see any absurdity in such an interpretation of the provision. [¶] Moreover, it is not necessary that the underlying protective order be specific enough to support a judgment of contempt; it is only necessary that it be specific enough to meet the normal requirements of specificity that attach to allegations of culpable conduct."

FAM §85.023. EFFECT ON PROPERTY RIGHTS

A protective order or an agreement approved by the court under this subtitle does not affect the title to real property.

History of Fam §85.023: Acts 1997, 75th Leg., ch. 34, §1, eff. May 5, 1997. Source: Former Fam §71.11(d).

FAM §85.024. ENFORCEMENT OF COUNSELING REQUIREMENT

(a) A person found to have engaged in family violence who is ordered to attend a program or counseling under Section 85.022(a)(1) or (2) shall file with the court an affidavit before the 60th day after the date the order was rendered stating either that the person has begun the program or counseling or that a program or counseling is not available within a reasonable distance from the person's residence. A person who files an affidavit that the person has begun the program or counseling shall file with the court before the date the protective order expires a statement that the person completed the program or counseling not later than the 30th day before the expiration date of the protective order. An affidavit under this subsection must be accompanied by a letter, notice, or certificate from the program or counselor that verifies the person's completion of the program or counseling. A person who fails to comply with this subsection may be punished for contempt of court under Section 21.002, Government Code.

(b) A protective order under Section 85.022 must specifically advise the person subject to the order of the requirement of this section and the possible punishment if the person fails to comply with the requirement.

History of Fam §85.024: Acts 1997, 75th Leg., ch. 34, §1, eff. May 5, 1997. Amended by Acts 1997, 75th Leg., ch. 1193, §15, eff. Sept. 1, 1997. Source: Former Fam §71.11(i).

FAM §85.025. DURATION OF PROTECTIVE ORDER

(a) Except as provided by Subsection (b) or (c), an order under this subtitle is effective:

(1) for the period stated in the order, not to exceed two years; or

(2) if a period is not stated in the order, until the second anniversary of the date the order was issued.

(b) A person who is the subject of a protective order may file a motion not earlier than the first anniversary of the date on which the order was rendered requesting that the court review the protective order and determine whether there is a continuing need for the order. After a hearing on the motion, if the court finds there is a continuing need for the protective order, the protective order remains in effect until the date the order expires under this section. If the court finds there is no continuing need for the protective order, the court shall order that the protective order expires on a date set by the court.

(c) If a person who is the subject of a protective order is confined or imprisoned on the date the protective order would expire under Subsection (a), the period for which the order is effective is extended, and the order expires on the first anniversary of the date the person is released from confinement or imprisonment.

History of Fam §85.025: Acts 1997, 75th Leg., ch. 34, §1, eff. May 5, 1997. Amended by Acts 1999, 76th Leg., ch. 1160, §3, eff. Sept. 1, 1999. Source: Former Fam §71.13.

FAM §85.026. WARNING ON PROTECTIVE ORDER

A (a) Each protective order issued under this subtitle, including a temporary ex parte order, must contain the following prominently displayed statements in boldfaced type, capital letters, or underlined:

"A PERSON WHO VIOLATES THIS ORDER MAY BE PUNISHED FOR CONTEMPT OF COURT BY A FINE OF AS MUCH AS $500 OR BY CONFINEMENT IN JAIL FOR AS LONG AS SIX MONTHS, OR BOTH.

"NO PERSON, INCLUDING A PERSON WHO IS PROTECTED BY THIS ORDER, MAY GIVE PERMISSION TO ANYONE TO IGNORE OR VIOLATE ANY PROVISION OF THIS ORDER. DURING THE TIME IN WHICH THIS ORDER IS VALID, EVERY PROVISION OF THIS ORDER IS IN FULL FORCE AND EFFECT UNLESS A COURT CHANGES THE ORDER.

"IT IS UNLAWFUL FOR ANY PERSON, OTHER THAN A PEACE OFFICER, AS DEFINED BY SECTION 1.07, PENAL CODE, ACTIVELY ENGAGED IN EMPLOYMENT AS A SWORN, FULL-TIME PAID EMPLOYEE OF A STATE AGENCY OR POLITICAL SUBDIVISION, WHO IS SUBJECT TO A PROTECTIVE ORDER TO POSSESS A FIREARM OR AMMUNITION."

(b) Each protective order issued under this subtitle, except for a temporary ex parte order, must contain the following prominently displayed statement in boldfaced type, capital letters, or underlined:

"A VIOLATION OF THIS ORDER BY COMMISSION OF AN ACT PROHIBITED BY THE ORDER MAY BE PUNISHABLE BY A FINE OF AS MUCH AS $4,000 OR BY CONFINEMENT IN JAIL FOR AS LONG AS ONE YEAR, OR BOTH. AN ACT THAT RESULTS IN FAMILY VIOLENCE MAY BE PROSECUTED AS A SEPARATE MISDEMEANOR OR FELONY OFFENSE. IF THE ACT IS PROSECUTED AS A SEPARATE FELONY OFFENSE, IT IS PUNISHABLE BY CONFINEMENT IN PRISON FOR AT LEAST TWO YEARS."

Subsection (c) below was amended by Acts 1999, 76th Leg., ch. 178, §3, effective Aug. 30, 1999, without reference to the conflicting deletion made by Acts 1999, 76th Leg., ch. 1160, §4, effective Sept. 1, 1999. Subsection (c) below is effective for agreements, statements, or notices executed on or after Aug. 30, 1999.

(c) Each protective order issued under this subtitle, including a temporary ex parte order, must contain the following prominently displayed statement in boldfaced type, capital letters, or underlined:

"NO PERSON, INCLUDING A PERSON WHO IS PROTECTED BY THIS ORDER, MAY GIVE PERMISSION TO ANYONE TO IGNORE OR VIOLATE ANY PROVISION OF THIS ORDER. DURING THE TIME IN WHICH THIS ORDER IS VALID, EVERY PROVISION OF THIS ORDER IS IN FULL FORCE AND EFFECT UNLESS A COURT CHANGES THE ORDER."

Subsection (c) below was deleted by Acts 1999, 76th Leg., ch. 1160, §4, effective Sept. 1, 1999, without reference to the conflicting amendment made by Acts 1999, 76th Leg., ch. 178, §3, effective Aug. 30, 1999. Subsection (c) below is effective for agreements, statements, or notices executed before Aug. 30, 1999, and for protective orders issued before Sept. 1, 1999.

(c) Each protective order issued under this subtitle, except for a temporary ex parte order, must contain the following printed statement in bold faced type or capital letters:

"NO PERSON, INCLUDING A PERSON WHO IS PROTECTED BY THIS ORDER, MAY GIVE PERMISSION TO ANYONE TO IGNORE OR VIOLATE ANY PROVISION OF THIS ORDER. DURING THE TIME IN WHICH THIS ORDER IS VALID, EVERY PROVISION OF THIS ORDER IS IN FULL FORCE AND EFFECT UNLESS A COURT CHANGES THE ORDER."

History of Fam §85.026: Acts 1997, 75th Leg., ch. 34, §1, eff. May 5, 1997. Amended by Acts 1999, 76th Leg., ch. 1160, §4 (eff. Sept. 1, 1999), ch. 178, §3 (eff. Aug. 30, 1999); Acts 2001, 77th Leg., ch. 23, §5, eff. Sept. 1, 2001. Source: Former Fam §71.16.

Sections 85.027-85.040 reserved for expansion

SUBCHAPTER C. DELIVERY OF PROTECTIVE ORDER

FAM §85.041. DELIVERY TO RESPONDENT

(a) A protective order rendered under this subtitle shall be:

(1) delivered to the respondent as provided by Rule 21a, Texas Rules of Civil Procedure;

(2) served in the same manner as a writ of injunction; or

(3) served in open court at the close of the hearing as provided by this section.

(b) The court shall serve an order in open court to a respondent who is present at the hearing by giving to the respondent a copy of the order, reduced to writing and signed by the judge or master. A certified copy of the signed order shall be given to the applicant at the time the order is given to the respondent. If the applicant is not in court at the conclusion of the hearing, the clerk of the court shall mail a certified copy of the order to the applicant not later than the third business day after the date the hearing is concluded.

(c) If the order has not been reduced to writing, the court shall give notice orally to a respondent who is present at the hearing of the part of the order that contains prohibitions under Section 85.022 or any other part of the order that contains provisions necessary to prevent further family violence. The clerk of the court shall mail a copy of the order to the respondent and a certified copy of the order to the applicant not later than the third business day after the date the hearing is concluded.

(d) If the respondent is not present at the hearing and the order has been reduced to writing at the conclusion of the hearing, the clerk of the court shall immediately provide a certified copy of the order to the applicant and mail a copy of the order to the respondent not later than the third business day after the date the hearing is concluded.

History of Fam §85.041: Acts 1997, 75th Leg., ch. 34, §1, eff. May 5, 1997. Source: Former Fam §71.17(a)-(d).

FAM §85.042. DELIVERY OF ORDER TO OTHER PERSONS

A *Subsection (a) below is effective for protective orders issued or modified on or after Sept. 1, 2001.*

(a) The clerk of the court issuing an original or modified protective order under this subtitle shall send a copy of the order, along with the information provided by the applicant or the applicant's attorney that is required under Section 411.042(b)(6), Government Code, to the chief of police of the municipality in which the person protected by the order resides, if the person resides in a municipality, or to the appropriate constable and the sheriff of the county in which the person resides, if the person does not reside in a municipality.

Subsection (a) below is effective for protective orders issued or modified before Sept. 1, 2001.

(a) The clerk of the court issuing an original or modified protective order under this subtitle shall send a copy of the order, along with the information provided by the applicant or the applicant's attorney that is required under Section 411.042(b)(5), Government Code, to the chief of police of the municipality in which the member of the family or household protected by the order resides, if the person resides in a municipality, or to the appropriate constable and the sheriff of the county in which the person resides, if the person does not reside in a municipality. The chief of police or constable and sheriff shall enter the information into the statewide law enforcement information system.

(b) If a protective order made under this chapter prohibits a respondent from going to or near a child-care facility or school, the clerk of the court shall send a copy of the order to the child-care facility or school.

(c) The clerk of a court that vacates an original or modified protective order under this subtitle shall notify the chief of police or constable and sheriff who received a copy of the original or modified order that the order is vacated.

(d) The applicant or the applicant's attorney shall provide to the clerk of the court:

(1) the name and address of each law enforcement agency, child-care facility, and school to which the clerk is required to mail a copy of the order under this section; and

A *Subsection (2) below is effective for protective orders issued or modified on or after Sept. 1, 2001.*

(2) any other information required under Section 411.042(b)(6), Government Code.

Subsection (2) below is effective for protective orders issued or modified before Sept. 1, 2001.

(2) any other information required under Section 411.042(b)(5), Government Code.

FAM §85.041

(e) The clerk of the court issuing an original or modified protective order under Section 85.022 that suspends a license to carry a concealed handgun shall send a copy of the order to the appropriate division of the Department of Public Safety at its Austin headquarters. On receipt of the order suspending the license, the department shall:

(1) record the suspension of the license in the records of the department;

(2) report the suspension to local law enforcement agencies, as appropriate; and

(3) demand surrender of the suspended license from the license holder.

History of Fam §85.042: Acts 1997, 75th Leg., ch. 34, §1, eff. May 5, 1997. Amended by Acts 1997, 75th Leg., ch. 614, §3, eff. Sept. 1, 1997; Acts 1999, 76th Leg., ch. 1412, §4, eff. Sept. 1, 1999; Acts 2001, 77th Leg., ch. 91, §9 (eff. Sept. 1, 2001), ch. 35, §1 (eff. Sept. 1, 2001). Source: Former Fam §71.17(e)-(g).

See also 37 TAC §§27.71-27.76.

Sections 85.043-85.060 blank

SUBCHAPTER D. RELATIONSHIP BETWEEN PROTECTIVE ORDER & SUIT FOR DISSOLUTION OF MARRIAGE & SUIT AFFECTING PARENT-CHILD RELATIONSHIP

FAM §85.061. DISMISSAL OF APPLICATION PROHIBITED; SUBSEQUENTLY FILED SUIT FOR DISSOLUTION OF MARRIAGE OR SUIT AFFECTING PARENT-CHILD RELATIONSHIP

If an application for a protective order is pending, a court may not dismiss the application or delay a hearing on the application on the grounds that a suit for dissolution of marriage or suit affecting the parent-child relationship is filed after the date the application was filed.

History of Fam §85.061: Acts 1997, 75th Leg., ch. 1193, §16, eff. Sept. 1, 1997.

FAM §85.062. APPLICATION FILED WHILE SUIT FOR DISSOLUTION OF MARRIAGE OR SUIT AFFECTING PARENT-CHILD RELATIONSHIP PENDING

(a) If a suit for dissolution of a marriage or suit affecting the parent-child relationship is pending, a party to the suit may apply for a protective order against another party to the suit by filing an application:

(1) in the court in which the suit is pending; or

(2) in a court in the county in which the applicant resides if the applicant resides outside the jurisdiction of the court in which the suit is pending.

(b) An applicant subject to this section shall inform the clerk of the court that renders a protective order that a suit for dissolution of a marriage or a suit affecting the parent-child relationship is pending in which the applicant is party.

(c) If a final protective order is rendered by a court other than the court in which a suit for dissolution of a marriage or a suit affecting the parent-child relationship is pending, the clerk of the court that rendered the protective order shall:

(1) inform the clerk of the court in which the suit is pending that a final protective order has been rendered; and

(2) forward a copy of the final protective order to the court in which the suit is pending.

(d) A protective order rendered by a court in which an application is filed under Subsection (a)(2) is subject to transfer under Section 85.064.

History of Fam §85.062: Acts 1997, 75th Leg., ch. 1193, §16, eff. Sept. 1, 1997.

FAM §85.063. APPLICATION FILED AFTER FINAL ORDER RENDERED IN SUIT FOR DISSOLUTION OF MARRIAGE OR SUIT AFFECTING PARENT-CHILD RELATIONSHIP

(a) If a final order has been rendered in a suit for dissolution of marriage or suit affecting the parent-child relationship, an application for a protective order by a party to the suit against another party to the suit filed after the date the final order was rendered, and that is:

(1) filed in the county in which the final order was rendered, shall be filed in the court that rendered the final order; and

(2) filed in another county, shall be filed in a court having jurisdiction to render a protective order under this subtitle.

(b) A protective order rendered by a court in which an application is filed under Subsection (a)(2) is subject to transfer under Section 85.064.

History of Fam §85.063: Acts 1997, 75th Leg., ch. 1193, §16, eff. Sept. 1, 1997.

Cooke v. Cooke, 65 S.W.3d 785, 790 (Tex.App.—Dallas 2001, no pet.). Section 85.063 "requires that all applications for protective orders involving parties to a prior divorce action must be filed in the court that rendered the final divorce decree. The plain language of the statute requires the application to be *filed* in the same court as the prior proceeding. However, the statute does not prohibit the transfer or reassignment of the case. The statute also does not require the protective order to actually be heard and ruled upon by the original divorce court."

FAM §85.064. TRANSFER OF PROTECTIVE ORDER

(a) If a protective order was rendered before the filing of a suit for dissolution of marriage or suit affecting the parent-child relationship or while the suit is pending as provided by Section 85.062, the court that rendered the order may, on the motion of a party or on the court's own motion, transfer the protective order to the court having jurisdiction of the suit if the court makes the finding prescribed by Subsection (c).

(b) If a protective order that affects a party's right to possession of or access to a child is rendered after the date a final order was rendered in a suit affecting the parent-child relationship, on the motion of a party or on the court's own motion, the court may transfer the protective order to the court of continuing, exclusive jurisdiction if the court makes the finding prescribed by Subsection (c).

(c) A court may transfer a protective order under this section if the court finds that the transfer is:

(1) in the interest of justice; or

(2) for the safety or convenience of a party or a witness.

(d) The transfer of a protective order under this section shall be conducted according to the procedures provided by Section 155.207.

(e) Except as provided by Section 81.002, the fees or costs associated with the transfer of a protective order shall be paid by the movant.

History of Fam §85.064: Acts 1997, 75th Leg., ch. 1193, §16, eff. Sept. 1, 1997.

In re Salgado, 53 S.W.3d 752, 764 (Tex.App.—El Paso 2001, pet. denied). "Relying upon TRCP 87, [relator's father] assigns error to the trial court's failure to conduct a separate hearing on his motion to transfer venue. Because we have not been provided with a reporter's record of any of the proceedings, we cannot ascertain whether a separate hearing was even requested, much less that the request was denied. Further, we question whether Rule 87 applies to a motion to transfer venue in this context."

FAM §85.065. EFFECT OF TRANSFER

(a) A protective order transferred under Section 85.064 has the same effect as if the order remained in the court that rendered the order. The protective order may be enforced by the court that receives the order in the same manner as if the court originally rendered the order.

(b) A protective order that is transferred is enforceable by contempt or by any other means by which the court that rendered the order could enforce the order. The court that receives the protective order may punish a violation of the order regardless of whether the violation occurred before or after the date of the transfer.

(c) A protective order that is transferred is subject to modification by the court that receives the order to the same extent modification is permitted under Chapter 87 by a court that rendered the order.

History of Fam §85.065: Acts 1997, 75th Leg., ch. 1193, §16, eff. Sept. 1, 1997.

CHAPTER 86. LAW ENFORCEMENT DUTIES RELATING TO PROTECTIVE ORDERS

FAM §86.001. ADOPTION OF PROCEDURES BY LAW ENFORCEMENT AGENCY

(a) To ensure that law enforcement officers responding to calls are aware of the existence and terms of protective orders issued under this subtitle, each law enforcement agency shall establish procedures in the agency to provide adequate information or access to information for law enforcement officers of the names of each person protected by an order issued under this subtitle and of each person against whom protective orders are directed.

(b) A law enforcement agency may enter a protective order in the agency's computer records of outstanding warrants as notice that the order has been issued and is currently in effect. On receipt of notification by a clerk of court that the court has vacated or dismissed an order, the law enforcement agency shall remove the order from the agency's computer record of outstanding warrants.

History of Fam §86.001: Acts 1997, 75th Leg., ch. 34, §1, eff. May 5, 1997. Source: Former Fam §71.18(a), (b).

FAM §85.063

FAM §86.0011. DUTY TO ENTER INFORMATION INTO STATEWIDE LAW ENFORCEMENT INFORMATION SYSTEM

E *Section 86.0011 below is effective for protective orders issued or modified on or after Sept. 1, 2001.*

On receipt of an original or modified protective order from the clerk of the issuing court, a law enforcement agency shall immediately, but not later than the 10th day after the date the order is received, enter the information required by Section 411.042(b)(6), Government Code, into the statewide law enforcement information system maintained by the Department of Public Safety.

History of Fam §86.0011: Enacted by Acts 2001, 77th Leg., ch. 35, §2, eff. Sept. 1, 2001.

FAM §86.002. DUTY TO PROVIDE INFORMATION TO FIREARMS DEALERS

(a) On receipt of a request for a law enforcement information system record check of a prospective transferee by a licensed firearms dealer under the Brady Handgun Violence Prevention Act, 18 U.S.C. Section 922, the chief law enforcement officer shall determine whether the Department of Public Safety has in the department's law enforcement information system a record indicating the existence of an active protective order directed to the prospective transferee.

(b) If the department's law enforcement information system indicates the existence of an active protective order directed to the prospective transferee, the chief law enforcement officer shall immediately advise the dealer that the transfer is prohibited.

History of Fam §86.002: Acts 1997, 75th Leg., ch. 34, §1, eff. May 5, 1997. Source: Former Fam §71.18(c)[A*].

FAM §86.003. COURT ORDER FOR LAW ENFORCEMENT ASSISTANCE UNDER TEMPORARY ORDER

On request by an applicant obtaining a temporary ex parte protective order that excludes the respondent from the respondent's residence, the court granting the temporary order shall render a written order to the sheriff, constable, or chief of police to provide a law enforcement officer from the department of the chief of police, constable, or sheriff to:

(1) accompany the applicant to the residence covered by the order;

(2) inform the respondent that the court has ordered that the respondent be excluded from the residence;

(3) protect the applicant while the applicant takes possession of the residence; and

(4) protect the applicant if the respondent refuses to vacate the residence while the applicant takes possession of the applicant's necessary personal property.

History of Fam §86.003: Acts 1997, 75th Leg., ch. 34, §1, eff. May 5, 1997. Amended by Acts 1997, 75th Leg., ch. 852, §1, eff. June 18. 1997. Source: Former Fam §71.18(c)[B*].

FAM §86.004. COURT ORDER FOR LAW ENFORCEMENT ASSISTANCE UNDER FINAL ORDER

On request by an applicant obtaining a final protective order that excludes the respondent from the respondent's residence, the court granting the final order shall render a written order to the sheriff, constable, or chief of police to provide a law enforcement officer from the department of the chief of police, constable, or sheriff to:

(1) accompany the applicant to the residence covered by the order;

(2) inform the respondent that the court has ordered that the respondent be excluded from the residence;

(3) protect the applicant while the applicant takes possession of the residence and the respondent takes possession of the respondent's necessary personal property; and

(4) if the respondent refuses to vacate the residence:

(A) remove the respondent from the residence; and

(B) arrest the respondent for violating the court order.

History of Fam §86.004: Acts 1997, 75th Leg., ch. 34, §1, eff. May 5, 1997. Amended by Acts 1997, 75th Leg., ch. 852, §2, eff. June 18, 1997. Source: Former Fam §71.18(d).

FAM §86.005. PROTECTIVE ORDER FROM ANOTHER JURISDICTION

A *Section 86.005 below is effective for actions to enforce foreign protective orders filed on or after Sept. 1, 2001.*

To ensure that law enforcement officers responding to calls are aware of the existence and terms of a protective order from another jurisdiction, each law enforcement agency shall establish procedures in the agency to provide adequate information or access to information for law enforcement officers regarding the name of each person protected by an order rendered in another jurisdiction and of each person against whom the protective order is directed.

History of Fam §86.005: Acts 1997, 75th Leg., ch. 1193, §17, eff. Sept. 1, 1997. Amended by Acts 2001, 77th Leg., ch. 48, §1, eff. Sept. 1, 2001.

FAM §86.005. PROTECTIVE ORDER FROM ANOTHER JURISDICTION

Section 86.005 below is effective for actions to enforce foreign protective orders filed before Sept. 1, 2001.

(a) To ensure that law enforcement officers responding to calls are aware of the existence and terms of a protective order from another jurisdiction, each law enforcement agency shall establish procedures in the agency to provide adequate information or access to information for law enforcement officers regarding the name of each person protected by an order rendered in another jurisdiction and of each person against whom the protective order is directed.

(b) Unless a law enforcement officer knows that the protective order has expired, the officer shall rely on:

(1) a copy of a protective order from another jurisdiction that has been provided to the officer by any source; and

(2) the statement by a person protected by the order that the order remains in effect.

(c) A law enforcement officer acting in good faith is not subject to civil or criminal liability for any action arising in connection with the enforcement of a protective order issued in another jurisdiction that a court later determines was not entitled to full faith and credit under Chapter 88.

FAM §86.005

CHAPTER 87. MODIFICATION OF PROTECTIVE ORDERS

FAM §87.001. MODIFICATION OF PROTECTIVE ORDER

On the motion of any party, the court, after notice and hearing, may modify an existing protective order to:

(1) exclude any item included in the order; or

(2) include any item that could have been included in the order.

History of Fam §87.001: Acts 1997, 75th Leg., ch. 34, §1, eff. May 5, 1997. Source: Former Fam §71.14(a).

FAM §87.002. MODIFICATION MAY NOT EXTEND DURATION OF ORDER

A protective order may not be modified to extend the period of the order's validity beyond the second anniversary of the date the original order was rendered or beyond the date the order expires under Section 85.025(c), whichever date occurs later.

History of Fam §87.002: Acts 1997, 75th Leg., ch. 34, §1, eff. May 5, 1997. Amended by Acts 1999, 76th Leg., ch. 1160, §5, eff. Sept. 1, 1999. Source: Former Fam §71.14(b).

FAM §87.003. NOTIFICATION OF MOTION TO MODIFY

Notice of a motion to modify a protective order is sufficient if delivery of the motion is attempted on the respondent at the respondent's last known address by registered or certified mail as provided by Rule 21a, Texas Rules of Civil Procedure.

History of Fam §87.003: Acts 1997, 75th Leg., ch. 34, §1, eff. May 5, 1997. Source: Former Fam §71.14(c).

FAM §87.004. CHANGE OF ADDRESS OR TELEPHONE NUMBER

(a) If a protective order contains the address or telephone number of a person protected by the order, of the place of employment or business of the person, or of the child-care facility or school of a child protected by the order and that information is not confidential under Section 85.007, the person protected by the order may file a notification of change of address or telephone number with the court that rendered the order to modify the information contained in the order.

(b) The clerk of the court shall attach the notification of change to the protective order and shall deliver a copy of the notification to the respondent by registered or certified mail as provided by Rule 21a, Texas Rules of Civil Procedure.

(c) The filing of a notification of change of address or telephone number and the attachment of the notification to a protective order does not affect the validity of the order.

History of Fam §87.004: Acts 1997, 75th Leg., ch. 1193, §18, eff. Sept. 1, 1997.

CHAPTER 88. UNIFORM INTERSTATE ENFORCEMENT OF PROTECTIVE ORDERS ACT

A *Chapter 88 below is effective for actions to enforce foreign protective orders filed on or after Sept. 1, 2001.*

Editor's note: Changes have been made to the official comments to reflect the Texas Legislature's omission of sections and changing section numbers. The full uniform act and official comments can be found at http://www.nccusl.org.

Official Prefatory Comment

I. Introduction

The Uniform Interstate Enforcement of Domestic-Violence Protection Orders Act ("the Act") provides a uniform mechanism for the interstate enforcement of domestic-violence protection orders. The need for such a mechanism is founded on the widespread understanding that States have not consistently or effectively enforced domestic-violence protection orders issued by other States. The Act, therefore, has two main purposes. First, it defines the meaning of interstate enforcement in the context of the enforcement of domestic-violence protection orders. Second, it establishes uniform procedures for the effective interstate enforcement of domestic-violence protection orders.

Many States, recognizing the severity of the problems regarding the interstate enforcement of domestic-violence protection orders, have enacted legislation requiring their courts to enforce the domestic-violence protection orders of other States. Many of these statutes, however, while mandating enforcement, are either silent or ambiguous regarding several important questions that must be answered in order to establish an effective system for the interstate enforcement of these orders. The Congress of the United States, as well, has enacted legislation requiring interstate enforcement of domestic-violence protection orders, but this legislation is also silent or ambiguous regarding these important questions.

First, many of the existing statutes do not sufficiently explain the core requirements of interstate enforcement of protection orders. For example, many of the state statutes, and the federal legislation, require courts and law enforcement officers to enforce the orders of other States as if they were the protection orders of the enforcing State. This provision, however, does not answer the question of whether state courts and officers are required to enforce provisions of foreign protection orders that would not be authorized by the law of the enforcing State. This question, and others, must be answered if there is to be effective uniform enforcement of protection orders. Second, many of the existing statutes do not specify the procedures state courts and officers must follow in enforcing foreign protection orders. For example, many of the statutes are silent on whether individuals seeking the enforcement of a protection order must register or file the order with the enforcing State before action can be taken on their behalf. This Act resolves the issues left unanswered in existing legislation and provides a uniform scheme for enforcement of these orders.

II. The Requirements of Interstate Enforcement

The Act first defines what it means to accord interstate enforcement to domestic-violence protection orders. These orders must be enforced if the issuing tribunals had jurisdiction over both the parties and the matter under the law of the issuing State and if the individuals against whom the order is enforced were given reasonable notice and had an opportunity to be heard consistent with the right to due process. If the order was obtained ex parte, this notice and opportunity to be heard must be provided within a reasonable time.

The Act makes it clear that all the terms of the orders of the issuing States must be enforced, including terms that provide relief that the courts of the enforcing State would lack power to provide. The Act also provides that all protection orders that both recognize the standing of the protected individual to seek enforcement of the order and satisfy the criteria of validity established by the Act must be enforced. In addition, provisions of protection orders governing custody and visitation matters are enforceable under this Act. Terms that concern support are not. [Editor's note: The Texas Legislature's enactment of the UIEDVPOA allows for enforcement of support.] The terms of mutual protection orders which favor of a respondent are also not enforceable if they were not issued in response to a written pleading filed by the respondent and if the issuing tribunal did not make specific findings in favor of the respondent.

III. Enforcement Procedures

The Act also provides uniform procedures for the interstate enforcement of domestic-violence protection orders. The Act envisions that the enforcement of foreign protection orders will require law enforcement officers of enforcing States to rely on probable cause judgments that a valid order exists and has been violated. The Act, however, provides that if a protected individual can provide direct proof of the existence of a facially valid order, by, for example, presenting a paper copy or through an electronic registry, probable cause is conclusively established. If no such proof is forthcoming, the Act provides that if officers, relying on the totality of the circumstances, determine that there is probable cause to believe that a valid protection order exists and has been violated, the order will be enforced. The individual against whom the order is enforced will have sufficient opportunity to demonstrate that the order is invalid when the case is brought before the enforcing tribunal. Law enforcement officers, as well as other government agents, will be encouraged to rely on probable cause judgments by the Act's inclusion of an immunity provision, protecting agents of the government acting in good faith.

The Act does not require individuals seeking the enforcement of a protection order to register or file the order with the enforcing State. The Act does, however, include an optional registration process. This process permits individuals to register a protection order by presenting a copy of the order to a responsible state agency or any state officer or agency. The copy presented must be certified by the issuing State. The purpose of these procedures is to make it as easy as possible for the protected individual to register the protection order and thus facilitate its enforcement.

E FAM §88.001. SHORT TITLE

This chapter may be cited as the Uniform Interstate Enforcement of Domestic Violence Protection Orders Act.

History of Fam §88.001: Enacted by Acts 2001, 77th Leg., ch. 48, §2, eff. Sept. 1, 2001.

History of Former Fam §88.001: Acts 1997, 75th Leg., ch. 1193, §19, eff. Sept. 1, 1997. Deleted by Acts 2001, 77th Leg., ch. 48, §2, eff. Sept. 1, 2001.

E FAM §88.002. DEFINITIONS

In this chapter:

(1) "Foreign protective order" means a protective order issued by a tribunal of another state.

(2) "Issuing state" means the state in which a tribunal issues a protective order.

(3) "Mutual foreign protective order" means a foreign protective order that includes provisions issued in favor of both the protected individual seeking enforcement of the order and the respondent.

(4) "Protected individual" means an individual protected by a protective order.

(5) "Protective order" means an injunction or other order, issued by a tribunal under the domestic violence or family violence laws or another law of the issuing state, to prevent an individual from engaging in violent or threatening acts against, harassing, contacting or communicating with, or being in physical proximity to another individual.

(6) "Respondent" means the individual against whom enforcement of a protective order is sought.

(7) "State" means a state of the United States, the District of Columbia, the Commonwealth of Puerto Rico, the United States Virgin Islands, or a territory or insular possession subject to the jurisdiction of the United States. The term includes a military tribunal of

the United States, an Indian tribe or band, and an Alaskan native village that has jurisdiction to issue protective orders.

(8) "Tribunal" means a court, agency, or other entity authorized by law to issue or modify a protective order.

History of Fam §88.002: Enacted by Acts 2001, 77th Leg., ch. 48, §2, eff. Sept. 1, 2001.

History of Former Fam §88.002: Acts 1997, 75th Leg., ch. 1193, §19, eff. Sept. 1, 1997. Deleted by Acts 2001, 77th Leg., ch. 48, §2, eff. Sept. 1, 2001.

Official Comment

The term "protection order" includes only those orders issued under the domestic-violence or family-violence laws of the issuing State. Protection orders issued outside of the domestic or family violence context are not enforceable under the provisions of this Act. The scope of enforceable protection orders is further limited by the provisions of Section 2(b) and (d). In addition, the term "protection order" includes an order modifying a previous order. Thus, a modified order, is enforceable, under the Act, in the same manner as a newly issued order.

The term "mutual protection orders" refers to protection orders in which an issuing State includes provisions protecting both parties. Enforcement of these foreign protection orders is governed by Section 88.003(g).

The Violence Against Women Act, 18 U.S.C. Sec. 2265, requires that States accord full faith and credit to tribal protection orders. Like state orders, tribal orders must satisfy the criteria for validity, as defined in Section 2(e), in order to qualify for interstate enforcement across state or tribal lines.

The Act uses the term "tribunal," rather than "court," in order to accommodate States that rely upon administrative or other entities to issue or modify protection orders.

E FAM §88.003. JUDICIAL ENFORCEMENT OF ORDER

(a) A tribunal of this state shall enforce the terms of a foreign protective order, including a term that provides relief that a tribunal of this state would not have power to provide but for this section. The tribunal shall enforce the order regardless of whether the order was obtained by independent action or in another proceeding, if the order is an order issued in response to a complaint, petition, or motion filed by or on behalf of an individual seeking protection. In a proceeding to enforce a foreign protective order, the tribunal shall follow the procedures of this state for the enforcement of protective orders.

(b) A tribunal of this state shall enforce the provisions of the foreign protective order that govern the possession of and access to a child if the provisions were issued in accordance with the jurisdictional requirements governing the issuance of possession and access orders in the issuing state.

(c) A tribunal of this state may enforce a provision of the foreign protective order relating to child support if the order was issued in accordance with the jurisdictional requirements of Chapter 159 and the federal Full Faith and Credit for Child Support Orders Act, 28 U.S.C. Section 1738B, as amended.

(d) A foreign protective order is valid if the order:

(1) names the protected individual and the respondent;

(2) is currently in effect;

(3) was rendered by a tribunal that had jurisdiction over the parties and the subject matter under the law of the issuing state; and

(4) was rendered after the respondent was given reasonable notice and an opportunity to be heard consistent with the right to due process, either:

(A) before the tribunal issued the order; or

(B) in the case of an ex parte order, within a reasonable time after the order was rendered.

(e) A protected individual seeking enforcement of a foreign protective order establishes a prima facie case for its validity by presenting an order that is valid on its face.

(f) It is an affirmative defense in an action seeking enforcement of a foreign protective order that the order does not meet the requirements for a valid order under Subsection (d).

(g) A tribunal of this state may enforce the provisions of a mutual foreign protective order that favor a respondent only if:

(1) the respondent filed a written pleading seeking a protective order from the tribunal of the issuing state; and

(2) the tribunal of the issuing state made specific findings in favor of the respondent.

History of Fam §88.003: Enacted by Acts 2001, 77th Leg., ch. 48, §2, eff. Sept. 1, 2001.

History of Former Fam §88.003: Acts 1997, 75th Leg., ch. 1193, §19, eff. Sept. 1, 1997. Deleted by Acts 2001, 77th Leg., ch. 48, §2, eff. Sept. 1, 2001.

Official Comment

Subsection (a) implements the core purpose of the Act. Effective intestate enforcement of protection orders is founded on the principle that enforcing States must enforce all the substantive terms of a foreign protection order, including terms that provide relief that a tribunal of the enforcing State would lack power to provide, but for this Act. This provision means that the tribunals of enforcing States must enforce the specific terms of a foreign protection order even if their state law would not allow the relief in question. For example, if the law of the issuing State provides that a court may issue a protection order including terms that concern the possession of property, e.g., an order giving the protected individual possession of the family automobile, but the law of the enforcing State does not authorize such substantive relief, the tribunal of the enforcing State must enforce the order in its entirety. To give another example, if the law of the issuing State allows protection orders to remain effective for a longer period than is allowed by the enforcing State, the tribunal of the enforcing State should enforce the order for the time specified in the order of the issuing State. In a proceeding to enforce the substantive terms of the foreign protection order, however, the court of the enforcing State shall follow its own procedures.

Subsection (a) provides that any person authorized by the law of the enforcing State to seek enforcement of a protection order may seek enforcement of valid foreign protection order in the enforcing State. This provision recognizes that States frequently authorize public agencies and officers, such as a local prosecutor, to bring enforcement actions on behalf of a protected individual. The Act, however, in recognizing the importance of these agencies and officers, should not be interpreted to mean that States, and their agencies and officers, are required to bring these actions when possible. This subsection further provides that only protection orders that were issued in response to a complaint, petition, or motion filed by or on behalf of an individual seeking protection can be enforced under this Act; orders issued sua sponte are not enforceable under this Act.

...

Subsections (b) and (c) further define the scope of enforceable protection orders under the Act. Subsection (b) provides that the provisions of protection orders that govern custody and visitation rights must be enforced. Enforcement of these provisions is essential because, first, the award of custody is often essential for the protection of children from potential violence, and, second, because the protected individual will not seek a safe distance from a threatening individual if custody of a child is jeopardized. These provisions may only be enforced, however, if they were issued in accordance with the jurisdictional requirements for the issuance of all custody and visitation orders, contained, depending on the State, either in the Uniform Child Custody Jurisdiction Act or the Uniform Child Custody Jurisdiction and Enforcement Act, and the federal Parental Kidnapping Prevention Act. This Act, however, does not provide for the enforcement of orders governing custody and visitation rights that are not included in a protection order.

...

Subsection (d) requires that, to be valid for the purpose of enforcement under this Act, a foreign protection order must be "currently in effect." This provision includes orders that have been modified; the modified order is the one currently in effect. While the Act requires that a foreign protection order, to be valid, identify the protected individual and respondent, merely technical errors, such as an incorrect spelling of a name, should not preclude enforcement of the order. The question of the validity of an order is a question of law for the court of the enforcing State. Once an order is adjudged valid, the proceeding shall be governed by the established procedures of the enforcing State.

The respondent's constitutional right to due process is protected by the opportunity to raise defenses in the enforcement proceeding, as provided in subsection (f). If, for example, the respondent was not provided with reasonable notice and opportunity to be heard by the tribunal of the State issuing the protection order, the enforcing tribunal may not enforce the order. Thus, the interstate enforcement of a valid foreign protection order, even without a prior hearing, does not deprive the respondent of any rights to due process because the respondent was provided with reasonable notice and opportunity to be heard when the order was issued.

The enforcement mechanisms established by the Act do not require the presentation by the protected individual of an authenticated copy of the foreign protection order. While States, as required by the Constitution and federal statutes that articulate authentication requirements, including 28 U.S.C. Sec. 1738, must accord properly authenticated foreign judgments full faith and credit enforcement, they may choose to enforce foreign orders they would not be required to enforce under the provisions of the Constitution or other federal law. By adopting this Act, States have chosen to give that extra measure of full faith and credit to foreign protection orders.

In addition, in recent years, particularly with regard to the enforcement of domestic relations orders, the federal government has employed the power granted to it by Article IV, Sec. 1 of the Constitution of the United States to prescribe the manner in which States give full faith and credit to the acts, records, and proceedings of other States to require States to enforce foreign orders in circumstances in which States have traditionally been reluctant to render such enforcement. For example, the federal Parental Kidnapping Prevention Act, 28 U.S.C. Sec. 1738a, requires greater interstate enforcement of child custody orders and the federal Personal Responsibility and Work Opportunity Reconciliation Act, 110 Stat. 2105 (1996), requires that States, in order to facilitate the enforcement of support orders, adopt the provisions of the Uniform Interstate Family Support Act. The Violence Against Women Act extends the principle of these laws to the subject of the interstate enforcement of domestic-violence protection orders.

Subsection (g), adapted from the federal Violence Against Women Act, 18 U.S.C. Sec. 2265(c), addresses the enforcement of mutual foreign protection orders, which contain provisions protecting both the protected individual and the respondent. Provisions of a mutual foreign protection order issued in favor of the respondent will not be enforced without proof that the respondent filed a written pleading seeking a protection order. If a respondent can prove that he or she made a specific request for relief and that the issuing tribunal made specific findings that the respondent was entitled to the requested relief, the protection orders will be enforced against the protected individual.

In order to facilitate the interstate enforcement of foreign protection orders, States should strongly consider requiring tribunals that issue protection orders to state clearly that these orders are entitled to interstate enforcement under both federal and state law. Such enforcement would also be greatly facilitated if issuing States provided each protected individual with a certified copy of the protection order. In addition, States should consider adopting a standard certification or confirmation form stating the protection order issued by their tribunals satisfies the criteria of validity articulated in subsection (e), thus qualifying the protection order for interstate enforcement. Use of the following certification form is recommended.

________________ (Name),	:	IN THE ________________ COURT OF
Plaintiff	:	____________ (County/Judicial District)
	:	____________ (State/Territory)
vs.	:	CIVIL ACTION – LAW
	:	PROTECTION/RESTRAINING ORDER
________________ (Name),	:	
Defendant	:	Docket No. ______________, 200____

Certification of Protection/Restraining Order

It is hereby certified that the attached is a true and correct copy of the order entered in the above-captioned action on ________________ (date) and that the original of the attached order was duly executed by the judicial authority whose signature appears thereon. The order expires on ____________ (date).

The order is: [ ] a civil protection/restraining order
OR [ ] a criminal protection/restraining order, that recognizes the standing of the plaintiff to seek enforcement of the order

It is further certified that:

(a) the issuing court determined that it had jurisdiction over the parties and the subject matter under the laws of ________________ (state or Indian tribe).

(b) the defendant was given reasonable notice and had opportunity to be heard before this order was issued; or if the order was issued ex parte, the defendant was given notice and had opportunity to be heard after the order was issued, consistent with the rights of the defendant to due process.

(c) the order was otherwise issued in accordance with the requirements of the Uniform Interstate Enforcement of Domestic-Violence Protection Orders Act, and the Violence Against Women Act, 18 U.S.C. §2265.

For custody and visitation orders:

the order was issued in accordance with the requirements of the Uniform Child Custody Jurisdiction Act or the Uniform Child Custody Jurisdiction and Enforcement Act of this state/territory and is consistent with the provisions of the Parental Kidnapping Prevention Act. 28 U.S.C. §1738a.

The attached order shall be presumed to be valid and enforceable in this and other jurisdictions.

Signature of Clerk of Court or other authorized official: ________________
Judicial District: ________________ Address ________________
Phone: ____________ Fax: ____________ Date: ____________
Seal:

E FAM §88.004. NONJUDICIAL ENFORCEMENT OF ORDER

(a) A law enforcement officer of this state, on determining that there is probable cause to believe that a valid foreign protective order exists and that the order has been violated, shall enforce the foreign protective

FAM §88.004

order as if it were an order of a tribunal of this state. A law enforcement officer has probable cause to believe that a foreign protective order exists if the protected individual presents a foreign protective order that identifies both the protected individual and the respondent and on its face, is currently in effect.

(b) For the purposes of this section, a foreign protective order may be inscribed on a tangible medium or may be stored in an electronic or other medium if it is retrievable in a perceivable form. Presentation of a certified copy of a protective order is not required for enforcement.

(c) If a protected individual does not present a foreign protective order, a law enforcement officer may determine that there is probable cause to believe that a valid foreign protective order exists by relying on any relevant information.

(d) A law enforcement officer of this state who determines that an otherwise valid foreign protective order cannot be enforced because the respondent has not been notified or served with the order shall inform the respondent of the order and make a reasonable effort to serve the order on the respondent. After informing the respondent and attempting to serve the order, the officer shall allow the respondent a reasonable opportunity to comply with the order before enforcing the order.

(e) The registration or filing of an order in this state is not required for the enforcement of a valid foreign protective order under this chapter.

History of Fam §88.004: Enacted by Acts 2001, 77th Leg., ch. 48, §2, eff. Sept. 1, 2001.

History of Former Fam §88.004: Acts 1997, 75th Leg., ch. 1193, §19, eff. Sept. 1, 1997. Deleted by Acts 2001, 77th Leg., ch. 48, §2, eff. Sept. 1, 2001.

Official Comment

The enforcement procedures in subsections (a)-(c) rely on the sound exercise of the judgment of law enforcement officers to determine whether there exists probable cause to believe that a valid foreign protection order exists and has been violated. These procedures anticipate that there will be many instances in which the protected individual does not have, or cannot, under the circumstances, produce a paper copy of the foreign protection order. Subsections (a) and (b) establish a per se rule for determining probable cause of the existence of an order. If the protected individual presents, whether by providing a paper copy (which need not be certified) of a protection order or through an electronic medium, such as access to a state registry of orders, proof of a facially valid order, the order should be enforced. In determining whether there is proof of a facially valid order, a law enforcement officer, where possible, may, and, indeed, should, search, using an electronic or other medium, a state or federal registry of orders.

Subsection (c) concerns the circumstance in which the protected individual cannot present direct proof of the protection order. In this situation, law enforcement officers are expected to obtain information from all available sources, including interviewing the parties and contacting other law enforcement agencies, to determine whether there is a valid protection order in effect. If the officer finds, after considering the totality of the circumstances, that there is probable cause to believe that a valid foreign protection order exists and has been violated, he or she should enforce the order. This probable cause determination must meet the constitutional standards for determining probable cause. If it is later determined that no such order was in place or the order was otherwise unenforceable, law enforcement agencies, officers, or other state officials will be protected by the immunity provision of Section 88.006 for actions taken in good faith.

Subsection (d) provides that if a law enforcement officer discovers in the course of a probable cause investigation that the respondent has not been notified of the issuance of or served with an otherwise valid foreign protection order, the officer must then inform the respondent of the terms and conditions of the protection order and make a reasonable effort to serve the order upon the respondent. The respondent must be allowed a reasonable opportunity to comply with the order before the order is enforced.

Subsection (e) makes clear that, if a State either adopts its own process for the registration or filing of foreign protection orders or adopts the process provided in Section 5, the State shall not require the registration or filing of a foreign protection order for enforcement.

E FAM §88.005. REGISTRATION OF ORDER

(a) An individual may register a foreign protective order in this state. To register a foreign protective order, an individual shall:

(1) present a certified copy of the order to a sheriff, constable, or chief of police responsible for the registration of orders in the local computer records and in the statewide law enforcement system maintained by the Texas Department of Public Safety; or

(2) present a certified copy of the order to the Department of Public Safety and request that the order be registered in the statewide law enforcement system maintained by the Department of Public Safety.

(b) On receipt of a foreign protective order, the agency responsible for the registration of protective orders shall register the order in accordance with this section and furnish to the individual registering the order a certified copy of the registered order.

(c) The agency responsible for the registration of protective orders shall register a foreign protective order on presentation of a copy of a protective order that has been certified by the issuing state. A registered foreign protective order that is inaccurate or not currently in effect shall be corrected or removed from the registry in accordance with the law of this state.

(d) An individual registering a foreign protective order shall file an affidavit made by the protected individual that, to the best of the protected individual's knowledge, the order is in effect.

(e) A foreign protective order registered under this section may be entered in any existing state or federal registry of protective orders, in accordance with state or federal law.

(f) A fee may not be charged for the registration of a foreign protective order.

History of Fam §88.005: Enacted by Acts 2001, 77th Leg., ch. 48, §2, eff. Sept. 1, 2001.

Official Comment

While the management of state registries is purely governed by state law, in implementing a registration system, however, enforcing States should strongly consider keeping these protection orders under seal. The purpose of more effectively protecting victims of domestic violence will be undermined if respondents can use the process of registration to locate the very people who are trying to escape from them. In addition, the federal Violence Against Women Act, as amended by the Violence Against Women Act of 2000 (Pub. L No.106-386), prohibits States that provide for the registration or filing of orders from, without the permission of the individual registering or filing the order, notifying other States of the registration or filing of the order.

Subsection (a) provides that any person, including a potential respondent, may register foreign protection orders. This reason behind this provision is to ensure that all parties have the opportunity to provide relevant information to the State. Orders, for example, may be modified with custody arrangements. Subsection (a) also requires that a person seeking to register a foreign protection order must present a certified copy of that order. The copy must be a writing on paper, thus exempting this requirement from the provisions of the Uniform Electronic Transactions Act.

Subsection (c) provides that if the State has registered orders that are no longer in effect or are inaccurate, these orders must be removed from the registry or, in the case of error, corrected. The precise method of how state and federal registries manage their registries, including the deletion of inaccurate information, is governed by each government's law regarding the management of records.

If an order is registered under this section, the individual who registered the order is expected to inform the enforcing State of any modifications to the registered protection order.

Subsection (f) is bracketed because some States may wish to charge a fee for registration.

E FAM §88.006. IMMUNITY

A state or local governmental agency, law enforcement officer, prosecuting attorney, clerk of court, or any state or local governmental official acting in an official capacity is immune from civil and criminal liability for an act or omission arising from the registration or enforcement of a foreign protective order or the detention or arrest of a person alleged to have violated a foreign protective order if the act or omission was done in good faith in an effort to comply with this chapter.

History of Fam §88.006: Enacted by Acts 2001, 77th Leg., ch. 48, §2, eff. Sept. 1, 2001.

Official Comment

This immunity provision includes States, state and local governmental agencies, and all state and local government officials acting in their official capacity in order to prevent those seeking the imposition of criminal and civil liability for acts or omissions done in good faith in an effort to comply with the provisions of this Act from circumventing this immunity provision. The necessity for a generous immunity provision for the enforcement of foreign protection orders does not preclude state and local governments from using personnel and other internal sanctions in order to prevent and punish actions that, in the absence of this immunity provision, would have rendered the government agencies, officers, or officials civilly or criminally liable.

E FAM §88.007. OTHER REMEDIES

A protected individual who pursues a remedy under this chapter is not precluded from pursuing other legal or equitable remedies against the respondent.

History of Fam §88.007: Enacted by Acts 2001, 77th Leg., ch. 48, §2, eff. Sept. 1, 2001.

Official Comment

This section clarifies that the protection orders enforced under the Act are not the only means of protection available to victims of domestic violence. Other legal remedies, such as tort actions and criminal prosecution, are left undisturbed by this Act.

E FAM §88.008. UNIFORMITY OF APPLICATION & CONSTRUCTION

In applying and construing this chapter, consideration shall be given to the need to promote uniformity of the law with respect to its subject matter among the states that enact the Uniform Interstate Enforcement of Domestic Violence Protection Orders Act.

History of Fam §88.008: Enacted by Acts 2001, 77th Leg., ch. 48, §2, eff. Sept. 1, 2001.

CHAPTER 88. PROTECTIVE ORDER FROM ANOTHER JURISDICTION

Chapter 88 below is effective for actions to enforce foreign protective orders filed before Sept. 1, 2001.

FAM §88.001. FULL FAITH & CREDIT OF PROTECTIVE ORDER FROM ANOTHER JURISDICTION

(a) Except as provided by Subsection (b), a protective order from another jurisdiction shall be accorded full faith and credit by the courts of this state and enforced as if the order were rendered by a court in this state.

(b) A protective order from another jurisdiction rendered against both the applicant and respondent is not enforceable against the applicant in this state unless:

(1) the respondent filed a cross or counter petition, complaint, or other written pleading seeking a protective order against the applicant; and

(2) the issuing court determined that each party was entitled to a protective order.

FAM §88.002. PRESUMPTION OF VALIDITY

A protective order from another jurisdiction is presumed to be valid if the order appears authentic on the order's face.

FAM §88.003. AFFIRMATIVE DEFENSE

It is an affirmative defense in any action seeking enforcement of a protective order rendered in another jurisdiction that the respondent was not given reasonable notice and an opportunity to be heard consistent with due process either:

(1) before the date the order was rendered; or

(2) in the case of an ex parte order, within the time required by the jurisdiction rendering the order after the date the order was rendered, but not later than a reasonable time.

FAM §88.004. ENFORCEMENT OF AN ORDER

A protective order from another jurisdiction may be enforced even if the order is not entered into the state law enforcement information system maintained by the Department of Public Safety.

SUBTITLE C. REPORTING FAMILY VIOLENCE

CHAPTER 91. REPORTING FAMILY VIOLENCE

FAM §91.001. DEFINITIONS

In this subtitle:

(1) "Family violence" has the meaning assigned by Section 71.004.

(2) "Medical professional" means a licensed doctor, nurse, physician assistant, or emergency medical technician.

History of Fam §91.001: Acts 1997, 75th Leg., ch. 34, §1, eff. May 5, 1997. Source: Former Fam §73.01.

FAM §91.002. REPORTING BY WITNESSES ENCOURAGED

A person who witnesses family violence is encouraged to report the family violence to a local law enforcement agency.

History of Fam §91.002: Acts 1997, 75th Leg., ch. 34, §1, eff. May 5, 1997. Source: Former Fam §73.02.

FAM §91.003. INFORMATION PROVIDED BY MEDICAL PROFESSIONALS

A medical professional who treats a person for injuries that the medical professional has reason to believe were caused by family violence shall:

(1) immediately provide the person with information regarding the nearest family violence shelter center;

(2) document in the person's medical file:

(A) the fact that the person has received the information provided under Subdivision (1); and

(B) the reasons for the medical professional's belief that the person's injuries were caused by family violence; and

(3) give the person a written notice in substantially the following form, completed with the required information, in both English and Spanish:

"NOTICE TO ADULT VICTIMS OF FAMILY VIOLENCE

"It is a crime for any person to cause you any physical injury or harm even if that person is a member or former member of your family or household.

"You may report family violence to a law enforcement officer by calling the following telephone numbers:_______________.

"If you, your child, or any other household resident has been injured or if you feel you are going to be in danger after a law enforcement officer investigating family violence leaves your residence or at a later time, you have the right to:

"Ask the local prosecutor to file a criminal complaint against the person committing family violence; and

"Apply to a court for an order to protect you. You may want to consult with a legal aid office, a prosecuting attorney, or a private attorney. A court can enter an order that:

"(1) prohibits the abuser from committing further acts of violence;

"(2) prohibits the abuser from threatening, harassing, or contacting you at home;

"(3) directs the abuser to leave your household; and

"(4) establishes temporary custody of the children or any property.

"A VIOLATION OF CERTAIN PROVISIONS OF COURT-ORDERED PROTECTION MAY BE A FELONY.

"CALL THE FOLLOWING VIOLENCE SHELTERS OR SOCIAL ORGANIZATIONS IF YOU NEED PROTECTION: _______________."

History of Fam §91.003: Acts 1997, 75th Leg., ch. 34, §1, eff. May 5, 1997. Source: Former Fam §73.03.

FAM §91.004. APPLICATION OF SUBTITLE

This subtitle does not affect a duty to report child abuse under Chapter 261.

History of Fam §91.004: Acts 1997, 75th Leg., ch. 34, §1, eff. May 5, 1997. Source: Former Fam §73.05.

CHAPTER 92. IMMUNITY

FAM §92.001. IMMUNITY

(a) Except as provided by Subsection (b), a person who reports family violence under Section 91.002 or provides information under Section 91.003 is immune from civil liability that might otherwise be incurred or imposed.

(b) A person who reports the person's own conduct or who otherwise reports family violence in bad faith is not protected from liability under this section.

History of Fam §92.001: Acts 1997, 75th Leg., ch. 34, §1, eff. May 5, 1997. Source: Former Fam §73.04.

Chapters 93-99 blank

Family Code—Title 5
The Parent-Child Relationship & the SAPCR
Table of Contents

Title 5. The Parent-Child Relationship & the Suit Affecting the Parent-Child Relationship
Subtitle A. General Provisions

TABLE OF CONTENTS

TABLE OF CONTENTS

FAMILY CODE—TITLE 5
THE PARENT-CHILD RELATIONSHIP & THE SAPCR
TABLE OF CONTENTS

TITLE 5

TABLE OF CONTENTS

TABLE OF CONTENTS

TABLE OF CONTENTS

TABLE OF CONTENTS

TABLE OF CONTENTS

TABLE OF CONTENTS

Table of Contents

TITLE 5. THE PARENT-CHILD RELATIONSHIP & THE SUIT AFFECTING THE PARENT-CHILD RELATIONSHIP

SUBTITLE A. GENERAL PROVISIONS

CHAPTER 101. DEFINITIONS

FAM §101.001. APPLICABILITY OF DEFINITIONS

(a) Definitions in this subchapter* apply to this title.

(b) If, in another part of this title, a term defined by this chapter has a meaning different from the meaning provided by this chapter, the meaning of that other provision prevails.

* Editor's note: This should probably be "chapter." ***Hughey v. Hughey***, 923 S.W.2d 778, 780 n.7 (Tex.App.—Tyler 1996, writ denied).

History of Fam §101.001: Acts 1995, 74th Leg., ch. 20, §1, eff. April 20, 1995. Source: Former Fam §11.01.

FAM §101.0010. ACKNOWLEDGED FATHER

E *Section 101.0010 below is effective for motions or other requests for relief made in parentage or paternity proceedings commenced on or after June 14, 2001.*

"Acknowledged father" means a man who has established a father-child relationship under Chapter 160.

History of Fam §101.0010: Enacted by Acts 2001, 77th Leg., ch. 821, §2.04, eff. June 14, 2001.

FAM §101.0011. ADMINISTRATIVE WRIT OF WITHHOLDING

"Administrative writ of withholding" means the document issued by the Title IV-D agency and delivered to an employer directing that earnings be withheld for payment of child support as provided by Chapter 158.

History of Fam §101.0011: Acts 1997, 75th Leg., ch. 911, §5, eff. Sept. 1, 1997.

FAM §101.0015. ALLEGED FATHER

E *Section 101.0015 below is effective for motions or other requests for relief made in parentage or paternity proceedings commenced on or after June 14, 2001.*

(a) "Alleged father" means a man who alleges himself to be, or is alleged to be, the genetic father or a possible genetic father of a child, but whose paternity has not been determined.

(b) The term does not include:

(1) a presumed father;

(2) a man whose parental rights have been terminated or declared to not exist; or

(3) a male donor.

History of Fam §101.0015: Enacted by Acts 2001, 77th Leg., ch. 821, §2.04, eff. June 14, 2001.

FAM §101.002. AUTHORIZED AGENCY

"Authorized agency" means a public social agency authorized to care for children, including the Texas Department of Protective and Regulatory Services.

History of Fam §101.002: Acts 1995, 74th Leg., ch. 20, §1, eff. April 20, 1995. Source: Former Fam §11.01(7).

FAM §101.0021. BUREAU OF VITAL STATISTICS

"Bureau of vital statistics" means the bureau of vital statistics of the Texas Department of Health.

History of Fam §101.0021: Acts 1999, 76th Leg., ch. 556, §1, eff. Sept. 1, 1999.

FAM §101.003. CHILD OR MINOR; ADULT

(a) "Child" or "minor" means a person under 18 years of age who is not and has not been married or who has not had the disabilities of minority removed for general purposes.

(b) In the context of child support, "child" includes a person over 18 years of age for whom a person may be obligated to pay child support.

(c) "Adult" means a person who is not a child.

History of Fam §101.003: Acts 1995, 74th Leg., ch. 20, §1, eff. April 20, 1995. Source: Former Fam §11.01(1).

In re M.J.M.L., 31 S.W.3d 347, 351 (Tex.App.—San Antonio 2000, pet. denied). Defendant "argues that the trial court could not consider any evidence of conduct which may have occurred before the child was born, referring us to the definition of 'child' in §101.003 of the code. [Defendant] asserts that this definition of child precludes consideration of events which occurred before a child was born. However, no court has held, and we do not find that the statutory definition of 'child' conflicts with a definition of a course of conduct endangering a child which incorporates conduct occurring before and after a child's birth."

FAM §101.004. CHILD SUPPORT AGENCY

"Child support agency" means:

(1) the Title IV-D agency;

(2) a county or district attorney or any other county officer or county agency that executes a cooperative agreement with the Title IV-D agency to provide child support services under Part D of Title IV of the federal Social Security Act (42 U.S.C. Section 651 et seq.) and Chapter 231; or

(3) a domestic relations office.

History of Fam §101.004: Acts 1995, 74th Leg., ch. 20, §1, eff. April 20, 1995. Source: Former Fam §14.80(3).

FAM §101.005. CHILD SUPPORT REVIEW OFFICER

"Child support review officer" means an individual designated and trained by a child support agency to conduct reviews under this title.

History of Fam §101.005: Acts 1995, 74th Leg., ch. 20, §1, eff. April 20, 1995. Amended by Acts 1995, 74th Leg., ch. 341, §2.01, eff. Sept. 1, 1995. Source: Former Fam §14.80(7).

FAM §101.006. CHILD SUPPORT SERVICES

"Child support services" means administrative or court actions to:

(1) establish paternity;

(2) establish, modify, or enforce child support or medical support obligations;

(3) locate absent parents; or

(4) cooperate with other states in these actions and any other action authorized or required under Part D of Title IV of the federal Social Security Act (42 U.S.C. Section 651 et seq.) or Chapter 231.

History of Fam §101.006: Acts 1995, 74th Leg., ch. 20, §1, eff. April 20, 1995. Source: Former Fam §14.80(4).

FAM §101.007. CLEAR & CONVINCING EVIDENCE

"Clear and convincing evidence" means the measure or degree of proof that will produce in the mind of the trier of fact a firm belief or conviction as to the truth of the allegations sought to be established.

History of Fam §101.007: Acts 1995, 74th Leg., ch. 20, §1, eff. April 20, 1995. Source: Former Fam §11.15(c).

In re G.M., 596 S.W.2d 846, 847 (Tex.1980). Clear and convincing "is an intermediate standard, falling between the preponderance standard of ordinary civil proceedings and the reasonable doubt standard of criminal proceedings."

Meadows v. Green, 524 S.W.2d 509, 510 (Tex. 1975). "[T]he Court of Civil Appeals has sought to apply a third standard of reviewing the evidence presented at trial—the 'clear and convincing' standard. In Texas there are but two standards by which evidence is reviewed: factual sufficiency and legal sufficiency. The requirement of clear and convincing evidence is merely another method of stating that a cause of action must be supported by factually sufficient evidence."

In re S.F., 32 S.W.3d 318, 321 (Tex.App.—San Antonio 2000, no pet.). "This intermediate standard colors our review of the factual sufficiency of the evidence in a termination case. Applying this standard to our review of a trial judge's findings, we ask whether sufficient evidence was presented to produce in the mind of a rational fact finder a 'firm belief or conviction as to the truth of the allegations sought to be established.'" *See also* ***Ybarra v. Texas DHS***, 869 S.W.2d 574, 579-80 (Tex.App.—Corpus Christi 1993, no writ). *But see* ***In re King***, below; ***In re J.R.***, 991 S.W.2d 318, 320 (Tex. App.—Fort Worth 1999, no pet.).

In re King, 15 S.W.3d 272, 275 (Tex.App.—Texarkana 2000, pet. denied). The "courts of appeals have disagreed on whether this intermediate standard of proof requires the application of a corresponding intermediate standard of appellate review. [W]e reassert our position that the clear and convincing standard of proof at the trial court level does not alter the fundamental standards of appellate review." *See also* ***In re J.R.***, 991 S.W.2d 318, 320 (Tex.App.—Fort Worth 1999, no pet.). *But see* ***In re S.F.***, above; ***Ybarra v. Texas DHS***, 869 S.W.2d 574, 579-80 (Tex.App.—Corpus Christi 1993, no writ).

FAM §101.008. COURT

"Court" means the district court, juvenile court having the same jurisdiction as a district court, or other court expressly given jurisdiction of a suit affecting the parent-child relationship.

History of Fam §101.008: Acts 1995, 74th Leg., ch. 20, §1, eff. April 20, 1995. Source: Former Fam §11.01(2).

FAM §101.009. DANGER TO PHYSICAL HEALTH OR SAFETY OF CHILD

"Danger to the physical health or safety of a child" includes exposure of the child to loss or injury that jeopardizes the physical health or safety of the child without regard to whether there has been an actual prior injury to the child.

History of Fam §101.009: Acts 1995, 74th Leg., ch. 20, §1, eff. April 20, 1995. Source: Former Fam §17.001.

FAM §101.010. DISPOSABLE EARNINGS

"Disposable earnings" means the part of the earnings of an individual remaining after the deduction from those earnings of any amount required by law to be withheld, union dues, nondiscretionary retirement contributions, and medical, hospitalization, and disability insurance coverage for the obligor and the obligor's children.

History of Fam §101.010: Acts 1995, 74th Leg., ch. 20, §1, eff. April 20, 1995. Source: Former Fam §14.30(a)(2).

FAM §101.011. EARNINGS

"Earnings" means a payment to or due an individual, regardless of source and how denominated. The term includes a periodic or lump-sum payment for:

(1) wages, salary, compensation received as an independent contractor, overtime pay, severance pay, commission, bonus, and interest income;

(2) payments made under a pension, an annuity, workers' compensation, and a disability or retirement program; and

(3) unemployment benefits.

History of Fam §101.011: Acts 1995, 74th Leg., ch. 20, §1, eff. April 20, 1995. Amended by Acts 1997, 75th Leg., ch. 911, §1, eff. Sept. 1, 1997. Source: Former Fam §14.30(a)(1).

FAM §101.012. EMPLOYER

"Employer" means a person, corporation, partnership, workers' compensation insurance carrier, governmental entity, the United States, or any other entity that pays or owes earnings to an individual. The term includes, for the purposes of enrolling dependents in a group health insurance plan, a union, trade association, or other similar organization.

History of Fam §101.012: Acts 1995, 74th Leg., ch. 20, §1, eff. April 20, 1995. Amended by Acts 1995, 74th Leg., ch. 341, §4.02, eff. Sept. 1, 1995; Acts 1997, 75th Leg., ch. 911, §2, eff. Sept. 1, 1997. Source: Former Fam §14.30(a)(3).

FAM §101.0125. FAMILY VIOLENCE

"Family violence" has the meaning assigned by Section 71.004.

History of Fam §101.0125: Acts 1999, 76th Leg., ch. 787, §1, eff. Sept. 1, 1999.

FAM §101.013. FILED

"Filed" means officially filed with the clerk of the court.

History of Fam §101.013: Acts 1995, 74th Leg., ch. 20, §1, eff. April 20, 1995.

FAM §101.014. GOVERNMENTAL ENTITY

"Governmental entity" means the state, a political subdivision of the state, or an agency of the state.

History of Fam §101.014: Acts 1995, 74th Leg., ch. 20, §1, eff. April 20, 1995. Source: Former Fam §11.01(8).

FAM §101.015. HEALTH INSURANCE

A *Section 101.015 below is effective for SAPCRs commenced on or after Sept. 1, 2001.*

"Health insurance" means insurance coverage that provides basic health care services, including usual physician services, office visits, hospitalization, and laboratory, X-ray, and emergency services, that may be provided through a health maintenance organization or other private or public organization, other than medical assistance under Chapter 32, Human Resources Code.

History of Fam §101.015: Acts 1995, 74th Leg., ch. 20, §1, eff. April 20, 1995. Amended by Acts 2001, 77th Leg., ch. 1023, §1, eff. Sept. 1, 2001. Source: Former Fam §14.061(d).

FAM §101.015. HEALTH INSURANCE

Section 101.015 below is effective for SAPCRs commenced before Sept. 1, 2001.

"Health insurance" means insurance coverage that provides basic health care services, including usual physician services, office visits, hospitalization, and laboratory, X-ray, and emergency services, that may be provided through a health maintenance organization or other private or public organization.

FAM §101.016. JOINT MANAGING CONSERVATORSHIP

"Joint managing conservatorship" means the sharing of the rights and duties of a parent by two parties, ordinarily the parents, even if the exclusive right to make certain decisions may be awarded to one party.

History of Fam §101.016: Acts 1995, 74th Leg., ch. 20, §1, eff. April 20, 1995. Source: Former Fam §14.021(b).

FAM §101.0161. JUDICIAL WRIT OF WITHHOLDING

"Judicial writ of withholding" means the document issued by the clerk of a court and delivered to an employer directing that earnings be withheld for payment of child support as provided by Chapter 158.

History of Fam §101.0161: Acts 1997, 75th Leg., ch. 911, §5, eff. Sept. 1, 1997.

FAM §101.017. LICENSED CHILD PLACING AGENCY

"Licensed child placing agency" means a person, private association, or corporation approved by the Department of Protective and Regulatory Services to place children for adoption through a license, certification, or other means.

History of Fam §101.017: Acts 1995, 74th Leg., ch. 20, §1, eff. April 20, 1995. Source: Former Fam §11.01(7); former Hum. Res. Code §42.002(12).

FAM §101.018. LOCAL REGISTRY

"Local registry" means an agency or entity operated under the authority of a district clerk, county government, juvenile board, juvenile probation office, domestic relations office, or other county agency or entity that serves a county or a court that has jurisdiction under this title and that:

(1) receives child support payments;

(2) maintains records of child support payments;

(3) distributes child support payments as required by law; and

(4) maintains custody of official child support payment records.

History of Fam §101.018: Acts 1995, 74th Leg., ch. 20, §1, eff. April 20, 1995. Source: Former Fam §11.01(11).

FAM §101.019. MANAGING CONSERVATORSHIP

"Managing conservatorship" means the relationship between a child and a managing conservator appointed by court order.

History of Fam §101.019: Acts 1995, 74th Leg., ch. 20, §1, eff. April 20, 1995. Source: Former Fam §11.01(6).

FAM §101.020. MEDICAL SUPPORT

"Medical support" means periodic payments or a lump-sum payment made under an order to cover medical expenses, including health insurance coverage, incurred for the benefit of a child.

History of Fam §101.020: Acts 1995, 74th Leg., ch. 20, §1, eff. April 20, 1995. Amended by Acts 1997, 75th Leg., ch. 911, §3, eff. Sept. 1, 1997. Source: Former Fam §14.80(5).

FAM §101.0201. NOTICE OF APPLICATION FOR JUDICIAL WRIT OF WITHHOLDING

"Notice of application for judicial writ of withholding" means the document delivered to an obligor and filed with the court as required by Chapter 158 for the nonjudicial determination of arrears and initiation of withholding.

History of Fam §101.0201: Acts 1997, 75th Leg., ch. 911, §5, eff. Sept. 1, 1997.

FAM §101.021. OBLIGEE

"Obligee" means a person or entity entitled to receive payments of child support, including an agency of this state or of another jurisdiction to which a person has assigned the person's right to support.

History of Fam §101.021: Acts 1995, 74th Leg., ch. 20, §1, eff. April 20, 1995. Amended by Acts 1999, 76th Leg., ch. 556, §1, eff. Sept. 1, 1999. Source: Former Fam §11.01(10).

FAM §101.022. OBLIGOR

"Obligor" means a person required to make payments under the terms of a support order for a child.

History of Fam §101.022: Acts 1995, 74th Leg., ch. 20, §1, eff. April 20, 1995. Source: Former Fam §11.01(9).

FAM §101.023. ORDER

"Order" means a final order unless identified as a temporary order or the context clearly requires a different meaning. The term includes a decree and a judgment.

History of Fam §101.023: Acts 1995, 74th Leg., ch. 20, §1, eff. April 20, 1995.

FAM §101.024. PARENT

Ⓐ *Section 101.024 below is effective for motions or other requests for relief made in parentage or paternity proceedings commenced on or after June 14, 2001.*

"Parent" means the mother, a man presumed to be the father, a man legally determined to be the father, a man who has been adjudicated to be the father by a court of competent jurisdiction, a man who has acknowledged his paternity under applicable law, or an adoptive mother or father. The term does not include a parent as to whom the parent-child relationship has been terminated.

History of Fam §101.024: Acts 1995, 74th Leg., ch. 20, §1, eff. April 20, 1995. Amended by Acts 1999, 76th Leg., ch. 556, §1, eff. Sept. 1, 1999; Acts 2001, 77th Leg., ch. 821, §2.05, eff. June 14, 2001. Source: Former Fam §11.01(3).

In re M.L.P.J., 16 S.W.3d 45, 48 (Tex.App.—Eastland 2000, pet. denied). "[W]e are asked to extend the doctrine of equitable adoption into an area governed by the Family Code. [Section] 154.001(a) authorizes a court to order 'either or both parents' to support a child in the manner specified in the order. ... We hold that the doctrine of equitable adoption is inapplicable to this case. Therefore, ... [mother's ex-husband] does not fit the strict definition of 'Parent' within the Family Code because he did not formally adopt the child."

In re Lambert, 993 S.W.2d 123, 129 (Tex.App.—San Antonio 1999, orig. proceeding). "The [natural parents] ceased to be [child's] parents for purposes of the Texas Family Code upon the rendition of the termination decree, and they ceded the role of acting as parents when they released [child's] physical custody to the [adopting parents] the day after her birth."

McGee v. McGee, 936 S.W.2d 360, 369 n.1 (Tex. App.—Waco 1996, writ denied). "We recognize that the Family Code contains a definition of 'parent.' However, we do not believe that this definition controls the application of the doctrine of parental immunity. Sometimes the word 'parent' in a statute includes one who merely occupies the position of a parent."

Hopper v. Brittain, 612 S.W.2d 636, 639 (Tex. App.—Houston [14th Dist.] 1981, no writ). "[T]o have a parent-child relationship one party must be a 'parent' as defined in §11.01(3) [now §101.024]. If this requirement is not met no such relationship may exist no matter how much natural love and affection is shown to exist."

FAM §101.024. PARENT

Section 101.024 below is effective for motions or other requests for relief made in parentage or paternity proceedings commenced before June 14, 2001.

"Parent" means the mother, a man presumed to be the biological father, a man legally determined to be the biological father, a man who has been adjudicated to be the biological father by a court of competent jurisdiction, or an adoptive mother or father. The term does not include a parent as to whom the parent-child relationship has been terminated.

FAM §101.025. PARENT-CHILD RELATIONSHIP

Ⓐ *Section 101.025 below is effective for motions or other requests for relief made in parentage or paternity proceedings commenced on or after June 14, 2001.*

"Parent-child relationship" means the legal relationship between a child and the child's parents as provided by Chapter 160. The term includes the mother and child relationship and the father and child relationship.

History of Fam §101.025: Acts 1995, 74th Leg., ch. 20, §1, eff. April 20, 1995. Amended by Acts 2001, 77th Leg., ch. 821, §2.06, eff. June 14, 2001. Source: Former Fam §11.01(4).

FAM §101.025. PARENT-CHILD RELATIONSHIP

Section 101.025 below is effective for motions or other requests for relief made in parentage or paternity proceedings commenced before June 14, 2001.

"Parent-child relationship" means the legal relationship between a child and the child's biological or adoptive parents as provided by Chapter 151. The term includes the mother and child relationship and the father and child relationship.

FAM §101.026. RENDER

"Render" means the pronouncement by a judge of the court's ruling on a matter. The pronouncement may be made orally in the presence of the court reporter or in writing, including on the court's docket sheet or by a separate written instrument.

History of Fam §101.026: Acts 1995, 74th Leg., ch. 20, §1, eff. April 20, 1995.

FAM §101.027. PARENT LOCATOR SERVICE

"Parent locator service" means the service established under 42 U.S.C. Section 653.

History of Fam §101.027: Acts 1995, 74th Leg., ch. 20, §1, eff. April 20, 1995. Source: Former Fam §15.051(a).

FAM §101.028. SCHOOL

"School" means a primary or secondary school in which a child is enrolled or, if the child is not enrolled in a primary or secondary school, the public school district in which the child primarily resides.

History of Fam §101.028: Acts 1995, 74th Leg., ch. 20, §1, eff. April 20, 1995. Source: Former Fam §14.033(a).

FAM §101.029. STANDARD POSSESSION ORDER

"Standard possession order" means an order that provides a parent with rights of possession of a child in accordance with the terms and conditions of Subchapter F, Chapter 153.

History of Fam §101.029: Acts 1995, 74th Leg., ch. 20, §1, eff. April 20, 1995. Source: Former Fam §14.033(a)(2).

FAM §101.030. STATE

"State" means a state of the United States, the District of Columbia, the Commonwealth of Puerto Rico, or a territory or insular possession subject to the jurisdiction of the United States. The term includes an Indian tribe and a foreign jurisdiction that has established procedures for rendition and enforcement of an order that are substantially similar to the procedures of this title.

History of Fam §101.030: Acts 1995, 74th Leg., ch. 20, §1, eff. April 20, 1995. Source: Former Fam §§14.80(6), 21.01(19).

FAM §101.0301. STATE CASE REGISTRY

"State case registry" means the registry established and operated by the Title IV-D agency under 42 U.S.C. Section 654a that has responsibility for maintaining records with respect to child support orders in all Title IV-D cases and in all other cases in which a support order is rendered or modified under this title on or after October 1, 1998.

History of Fam §101.0301: Acts 1997, 75th Leg., ch. 911, §5, eff. Sept. 1, 1997.

FAM §101.0302. STATE DISBURSEMENT UNIT

"State disbursement unit" means the unit established and operated by the Title IV-D agency under 42 U.S.C. Section 654b that has responsibility for receiving, distributing, maintaining, and furnishing child support payments and records on or after October 1, 1999.

History of Fam §101.0302: Acts 1999, 76th Leg., ch. 556, §1, eff. Sept. 1, 1999.

FAM §101.031. SUIT

"Suit" means a suit affecting the parent-child relationship.

History of Fam §101.031: Acts 1995, 74th Leg., ch. 20, §1, eff. April 20, 1995.

In re Lambert, 993 S.W.2d 123, 128 (Tex.App.—San Antonio 1999, orig. proceeding). "Suit ... means a suit affecting the parent-child relationship or, in common parlance, a SAPCR." (Internal quotations omitted.)

FAM §101.032. SUIT AFFECTING THE PARENT-CHILD RELATIONSHIP

(a) "Suit affecting the parent-child relationship" means a suit filed as provided by this title in which the appointment of a managing conservator or a possessory conservator, access to or support of a child, or establishment or termination of the parent-child relationship is requested.

(b) The following are not suits affecting the parent-child relationship:

(1) a habeas corpus proceeding under Chapter 157;

(2) a proceeding filed under Chapter 159 to determine parentage or to establish, enforce, or modify child support, whether this state is acting as the initiating or responding state; and

(3) a proceeding under Title 2.

History of Fam §101.032: Acts 1995, 74th Leg., ch. 20, §1, eff. April 20, 1995. Source: Former Fam §11.01(5).

Martin v. Martin, 776 S.W.2d 572, 574 (Tex.1989). A "suit to modify access rights constitutes a §11.01(5) [now §101.032] [SAPCR]."

Leonard v. Paxson, 654 S.W.2d 440, 441 (Tex. 1983). Plaintiff "instituted a proceeding to modify the child support provisions of the divorce decree. [¶] The question before us is whether the proceeding ... is a [SAPCR] under §11.01(5) [now §101.032]. We conclude that it is...."

Office of Attorney Gen. v. Carter, 977 S.W.2d 159, 162 (Tex.App.—Houston [14th Dist.] 1998, no pet.). "A proceeding filed under UIFSA [Family Code, ch. 159] is not a SAPCR."

Flores v. Melo-Palacios, 921 S.W.2d 399, 403 (Tex. App.—Corpus Christi 1996, writ denied). "The imposition of child support obligations is included within a [SAPCR]."

Little v. McAninch, 896 S.W.2d 199, 201 (Tex. App.—Houston [1st Dist.] 1994, writ denied). "The establishment of a parent-child relationship and the imposition of child support obligations are included within a '[SAPCR].'"

Urbish v. James, 688 S.W.2d 230, 234 (Tex.App.—Houston [14th Dist.] 1985, no writ). "The personal injury suit brought by [mother on behalf of son] is not a [SAPCR] brought under Subtitle A of Title 2 [now Title 5]."

Magill v. Sheffield, 612 S.W.2d 677, 680 (Tex. App.—Dallas 1981, no writ). "[N]ot every proceeding concerning possession or support of a child is a [SAPCR] subject to the continuing jurisdiction of the divorce court within §11.05 [now §101.032]. It must actually be brought under subtitle A of [T]itle 2 [now Title 5] of the Code."

Garza v. Schilling, 576 S.W.2d 147, 150 (Tex. App.—Corpus Christi 1978, no writ). "'Access to', as used in [§11.01(5), now §101.032(a)], is limited to a suit brought for determination of the legal right of access to a child rather than to enforce a right of possession under a court order or by virtue of parental rights as enumerated in ... §12.04 [now §151.001]."

Adwan v. Adwan, 538 S.W.2d 192, 194 (Tex.App.—Dallas 1976, no writ). A SAPCR "may be brought only on statutory grounds."

FAM §101.033. TITLE IV-D AGENCY

"Title IV-D agency" means the state agency designated under Chapter 231 to provide services under Part D of Title IV of the federal Social Security Act (42 U.S.C. Section 651 et seq.).

History of Fam §101.033: Acts 1995, 74th Leg., ch. 20, §1, eff. April 20, 1995. Source: Former Fam §14.80(2); former Hum. Res. Code §76.001.

FAM §101.034. TITLE IV-D CASE

"Title IV-D case" means an action in which services are provided by the Title IV-D agency under Part D, Title IV, of the federal Social Security Act (42 U.S.C. Section 651 et seq.), relating to the location of an absent parent, determination of parentage, or establishment, modification, or enforcement of a child support or medical support obligation.

History of Fam §101.034: Acts 1995, 74th Leg., ch. 20, §1, eff. April 20, 1995. Amended by Acts 1997, 75th Leg., ch. 911, §4, eff. Sept. 1, 1997. Source: Former Fam §14.80(2).

FAM §101.035. TRIBUNAL

"Tribunal" means a court, administrative agency, or quasi-judicial entity of a state authorized to establish, enforce, or modify support orders or to determine parentage.

History of Fam §101.035: Acts 1995, 74th Leg., ch. 20, §1, eff. April 20, 1995. Source: Former Fam §21.01(22).

CHAPTER 102. FILING SUIT

FAM §102.001. SUIT AUTHORIZED; SCOPE OF SUIT

(a) A suit may be filed as provided in this title.

(b) One or more matters covered by this title may be determined in the suit. The court, on its own motion, may require the parties to replead in order that any issue affecting the parent-child relationship may be determined in the suit.

History of Fam §102.001: Acts 1995, 74th Leg., ch. 20, §1, eff. April 20, 1995. Source: Former Fam §11.02.

FAM §102.002. COMMENCEMENT OF SUIT

An original suit begins by the filing of a petition as provided by this chapter.

History of Fam §102.002: Acts 1995, 74th Leg., ch. 20, §1, eff. April 20, 1995. Source: Former Fam §11.07(a).

FAM §102.003. GENERAL STANDING TO FILE SUIT

(a) An original suit may be filed at any time by:

(1) a parent of the child;

(2) the child through a representative authorized by the court;

(3) a custodian or person having the right of visitation with or access to the child appointed by an order of a court of another state or country;

(4) a guardian of the person or of the estate of the child;

(5) a governmental entity;

(6) an authorized agency;

(7) a licensed child placing agency;

A *Subsection (8) below is effective for motions or other requests for relief made in parentage or paternity proceedings commenced on or after June 14, 2001.*

(8) a man alleging himself to be the father of a child filing in accordance with Chapter 160, subject to the limitations of that chapter, but not otherwise;

Subsection (8) below is effective for motions or other requests for relief made in parentage or paternity proceedings commenced before June 14, 2001.

(8) a man alleging himself to be the biological father of a child filing in accordance with Chapter 160, subject to the limitations of Section 160.101, but not otherwise;

(9) a person, other than a foster parent, who has had actual care, control, and possession of the child for at least six months ending not more than 90 days preceding the date of the filing of the petition;

(10) a person designated as the managing conservator in a revoked or unrevoked affidavit of relinquishment under Chapter 161 or to whom consent to adoption has been given in writing under Chapter 162;

(11) a person with whom the child and the child's guardian, managing conservator, or parent have resided for at least six months ending not more than 90 days preceding the date of the filing of the petition if the child's guardian, managing conservator, or parent is deceased at the time of the filing of the petition;

(12) a person who is the foster parent of a child placed by the Department of Protective and Regulatory Services in the person's home for at least 12 months ending not more than 90 days preceding the date of the filing of the petition; or

(13) a person who is a relative of the child within the third degree by consanguinity, as determined by Chapter 573, Government Code, if the child's parents are deceased at the time of the filing of the petition.

(b) In computing the time necessary for standing under Subsections (a)(9), (11), and (12), the court may not require that the time be continuous and uninterrupted but shall consider the child's principal residence during the relevant time preceding the date of commencement of the suit.

History of Fam §102.003: Acts 1995, 74th Leg., ch. 20, §1, eff. April 20, 1995. Amended by Acts 1995, 74th Leg., ch. 751, §8, eff. Sept. 1, 1995; Acts 1997, 75th Leg., ch. 575, §3, eff. Sept. 1, 1997; Acts 1999, 76th Leg., ch. 1390, §2 (eff. Sept. 1, 1999), ch. 1048, §1 (eff. June 18, 1999); Acts 2001, 77th Leg., ch. 821, §2.07, eff. June 14, 2001. Source: Former Fam §11.03(a).

Texas DPRS v. Sherry, 46 S.W.3d 857, 861 (Tex.2001). "[M]ere 'legal residence' is not sufficient to satisfy the 'have resided' requirement in [§102.003(a)(11)]. Although the law sometimes gives a technical meaning to the noun 'residence,' it does not similarly interpret the verb 'resided,' and there is no indication that the Legislature meant anything more than the usual meaning of those words. We thus read 'have resided' to mean living together in the same household."

Jones v. Fowler, 969 S.W.2d 429, 433 (Tex.1998). "[T]he Legislature did not intend a substantive change when it deleted 'immediately' from 'immediately preceding' in §102.003(9).... Because [plaintiff] does not meet the custody, control, and possession requirements of this section, we hold that she does not have standing to seek visitation rights with the child."

Doncer v. Dickerson, ___ S.W.3d ___ (Tex.App.—El Paso 2002, n.p.h.) (No. 08-00-00298-CV; 5-9-02). "Subsection 102.003(a)(11) was designed as a 'stepparent' statute, affording standing to, among others, a stepparent who helps raise a child when the stepparent's spouse—one of the child's parents—dies. A traditional application would indicate that upon the death of the mother, as a sole managing conservator of the child, her current husband would have standing. [Stepmother] contends this section should apply equally to the surviving spouse of the parent who, as a joint managing conservator of the child, does not have *de jure* primary possession but has *de facto* possession for approximately 50 percent of the time." The court agreed.

Office of Attorney Gen. v. Carter, 977 S.W.2d 159, 162 (Tex.App.—Houston [14th Dist.] 1998, no pet.). "Section 102.003(9) determines who has general standing to file suit in a [SAPCR]."

Rivera v. Office of Attorney Gen., 960 S.W.2d 280, 281 (Tex.App.—Houston [1st Dist.] 1997, no pet.). "The attorney general has independent standing to bring a [SAPCR]."

In re Garcia, 944 S.W.2d 725, 727 (Tex.App.—Amarillo 1997, no writ). "[T]he trial court correctly dismissed the [plaintiffs'] suit with prejudice when they failed to evince they had actual care, control, and possession of the child for six consecutive months preceding the filing of their petition."

In re A.L.J., 929 S.W.2d 467, 471 (Tex.App.—Tyler 1996, writ denied). "Under Texas statutory law, a parent of a child has standing to establish paternity."

T.W.E. v. K.M.E., 828 S.W.2d 806, 808 (Tex.App.—San Antonio 1992, no writ). "The plain purpose of paragraph (a)(8) [now §102.003(a)(9)] is to create standing for those who have developed and maintained a relationship with a child over time. Six months is, in the judgment of the legislature, the minimum span of time needed to develop a significant relationship for purposes of standing to seek custody. [¶] It would not serve the purposes of the statute to allow a brief, involuntary interruption in actual possession to destroy a putative father's standing to counterclaim for custody of a child whom all the world has considered for six years to be his own. If the three weeks' interruption in this case—which happened because [mother] abruptly left home with the child—destroys [putative father's] standing, we see no reason why three days' interruption by one party's unilateral act would not do the same thing. We cannot attribute such an intention to the legislature."

FAM §102.004. STANDING FOR GRANDPARENT

(a) In addition to the general standing to file suit provided by Section 102.003(13), a grandparent may file an original suit requesting managing conservatorship if there is satisfactory proof to the court that:

(1) the order requested is necessary because the child's present environment presents a serious question concerning the child's physical health or welfare; or

(2) both parents, the surviving parent, or the managing conservator or custodian either filed the petition or consented to the suit.

(b) An original suit requesting possessory conservatorship may not be filed by a grandparent or other person. However, the court may grant a grandparent or other person deemed by the court to have had substantial past contact with the child leave to intervene in a pending suit filed by a person authorized to do so under this subchapter.*

(c) Access to a child by a grandparent is governed by the standards established by Chapter 153.

* Editor's note: This should probably be "chapter."

History of Fam §102.004: Acts 1995, 74th Leg., ch. 20, §1, eff. April 20, 1995. Amended by Acts 1999, 76th Leg., ch. 1048, §2, eff. June 19, 1999. Source: Former Fam §11.03(b), (c).

Mendez v. Brewer, 626 S.W.2d 498, 499-500 (Tex. 1982). TRCP 60 "provides in part that any party may intervene, subject to being stricken by the court for sufficient cause on the motion of the opposite party. [¶] The intervenor bears the burden to show a justiciable interest, legal or equitable, in the lawsuit. The only relationship the [foster parents] had with [child] was as agent for the [TDHR, now DPRS] under the written contract to provide foster home care for [child]. The [foster parents] admitted that the contract expressly provided that the [TDHR, now DPRS], as temporary managing conservator of the child, retained the absolute right to remove the child for any of several reasons: to place it with another family, to return the child to his home, or to have the child adopted by other persons. [¶] The sole interest alleged by the [foster parents] in their petition in intervention was their wish to adopt the child if the parent-child relationship with the [biological parents] was terminated.... We do not believe this was sufficient standing to entitle them to join in this suit...."

In re R.D.Y., 51 S.W.3d 314, 325 (Tex.App.—Houston [1st Dist.] 2001, no pet.). "A suit requesting managing conservatorship may be filed by a grandparent as necessary when 'the child's present environment presents a serious question concerning the child's physical health or welfare.' The court must make a threshold finding of serious and immediate concern for the welfare of the child based upon a preponderance of the evidence before grandparents will have the right to sue for custody. [A] child must be in imminent danger of physical or emotional harm for there to be a serious question concerning the child's physical health or welfare."

In re M.A.M., 35 S.W.3d 788, 790 (Tex.App.—Beaumont 2001, no pet.). "The qualifying phrase, 'deemed by the court to have had substantial past contact with the child,' modifies 'other person,' not 'grandparent or other person.' Section 102.004(b) recognizes two classes of persons: 1) grandparents, and 2) other persons deemed by the court to have had substantial past contact with the child. As [intervenor] is indisputably the biological maternal grandmother of [the child], no finding of substantial past contact with [the child] was required for her to satisfy the standing requirement of §102.004(b)."

In re M.T., 21 S.W.3d 925, 926 (Tex.App.—Beaumont 2000, no pet.). "There is a distinction between bringing an original suit and intervening in an existing suit. *At 927:* A party who does not qualify to initiate a [SAPCR] may be permitted to intervene in a suit filed by a qualified party." *See also* ***In re A.M.***, 60 S.W.3d 166, 168-69 (Tex.App.—Houston [1st Dist.] 2001, no pet.).

In re Hidalgo, 938 S.W.2d 492, 496 (Tex.App.—Texarkana 1996, no writ). "Subdivision (b) states that the court may permit a grandparent or other person with substantial past contact to *intervene* in a pending suit filed 'under this subchapter.' The subchapter pertains to suits seeking managing conservatorship as well as those seeking possessory conservatorship."

Segovia-Slape v. Paxson, 893 S.W.2d 694, 696 (Tex.App.—El Paso 1995, orig. proceeding). Section 102.004 "clearly adopts the rule that an intervenor need not be capable of prosecuting the SAPCR in her own right. Furthermore, this relaxed standing rule promotes the overriding policy in all SAPCR suits, that of protecting the best interest of the child. Therefore, it is clear that persons who can demonstrate sufficient interest in the child can intervene in a divorce proceeding in which managing conservatorship is in issue, even if they cannot institute an original SAPCR."

Von Behren v. Von Behren, 800 S.W.2d 919, 921 (Tex.App.—San Antonio 1990, writ denied). Grandparent "alleges that satisfactory proof is equivalent to a probable cause or reasonable person standard, a lower quantity than preponderance of the evidence. ... Section 11.03(a) [now §102.003(a)] now provides a list of persons who automatically have standing to bring an original suit whereas §11.03(b) [§102.004] is limited to emergency situations. The limiting requirement of an emergency is designed to strike a balance between those grandparents or other friends or relatives, who undertake a rescue mission and those who are just out to do a little officious intermeddling to correct the unsatisfactory childrearing methods of the younger generation. Therefore, the non-parent or grandparent does not have standing automatically by virtue of the relationship that exists with the child, but must show satisfactory proof that the child's environment with the parent or parents presents a serious and immediate question concerning the welfare of the child."

FAM §102.005. STANDING TO REQUEST TERMINATION & ADOPTION

An original suit requesting only an adoption or for termination of the parent-child relationship joined with a petition for adoption may be filed by:

(1) a stepparent of the child;

(2) an adult who, as the result of a placement for adoption, has had actual possession and control of the child at any time during the 30-day period preceding the filing of the petition;

(3) an adult who has had actual possession and control of the child for not less than two months during the three-month period preceding the filing of the petition; or

(4) another adult whom the court determines to have had substantial past contact with the child sufficient to warrant standing to do so.

History of Fam §102.005: Acts 1995, 74th Leg., ch. 20, §1, eff. April 20, 1995. Source: Former Fam §11.03(d).

Rodarte v. Cox, 828 S.W.2d 65, 69-70 (Tex.App.—Tyler 1991, writ denied). "Other subsections of 11.03 [now §§102.003 & 102.004] require 'possession and control' of a child in order to bring [SAPCR]. However, §11.03(d)(4) [now §102.005(4)] requires only that the petitioner be an adult whom the judge determines 'to have had sufficient past contact with the child to warrant standing to do so.' We do not agree with the [parents] that 'substantial contact' necessarily requires control."

FAM §102.006. LIMITATIONS ON STANDING

(a) Except as provided by Subsection (b), if the parent-child relationship between the child and every living parent of the child has been terminated, an original suit may not be filed by:

(1) a former parent whose parent-child relationship with the child has been terminated by court order;

A *Subsections (2) & (3) below are effective for motions or other requests for relief made in parentage or paternity proceedings commenced on or after June 14, 2001.*

(2) the father of the child; or

(3) a family member or relative by blood, adoption, or marriage of either a former parent whose parent-child relationship has been terminated or of the father of the child.

Subsections (2) & (3) below are effective for motions or other requests for relief made in parentage or paternity proceedings commenced before June 14, 2001.

(2) the biological father of the child; or

(3) a family member or relative by blood, adoption, or marriage of either a former parent whose parent-child

FAM §102.004

relationship has been terminated or of the biological father of the child.

(b) The limitations on filing suit imposed by this section do not apply to a person who:

(1) has a continuing right to possession of or access to the child under an existing court order; or

(2) has the consent of the child's managing conservator, guardian, or legal custodian to bring the suit.

History of Fam §102.006: Acts 1995, 74th Leg., ch. 20, §1, eff. April 20, 1995. Amended by Acts 2001, 77th Leg., ch. 821, §2.08, eff. June 14, 2001. Source: Former Fam §11.03(g), (h).

FAM §102.007. STANDING OF TITLE IV-D AGENCY

In providing services authorized by Chapter 231, the Title IV-D agency or a political subdivision contracting with the attorney general to provide Title IV-D services under this title may file a child support action authorized under this title, including a suit for modification or a motion for enforcement.

History of Fam §102.007: Acts 1995, 74th Leg., ch. 20, §1, eff. April 20, 1995. Amended by Acts 1995, 74th Leg., ch. 341, §2.02, eff. Sept. 1, 1995. Source: Former Fam §11.03(i).

In re Vega, 10 S.W.3d 720, 722 (Tex.App.—Amarillo 1999, no pet.). "[T]he Attorney General has standing to file a child support action pursuant to §102.007...."

FAM §102.008. CONTENTS OF PETITION

(a) The petition and all other documents in a proceeding filed under this title, except a suit for adoption of an adult, shall be entitled "In the interest of __________, a child." In a suit in which adoption of a child is requested, the style shall be "In the interest of a child."

A *Subsection (b) below is effective for petitions in SAPCRs filed on or after Sept. 1, 2001.*

(b) The petition must include:

(1) a statement that the court in which the petition is filed has continuing, exclusive jurisdiction or that no court has continuing jurisdiction of the suit;

(2) the name and date of birth of the child, except that if adoption of a child is requested, the name of the child may be omitted;

(3) the full name of the petitioner and the petitioner's relationship to the child or the fact that no relationship exists;

(4) the names of the parents, except in a suit in which adoption is requested;

(5) the name of the managing conservator, if any, or the child's custodian, if any, appointed by order of a court of another state or country;

(6) the names of the guardians of the person and estate of the child, if any;

(7) the names of possessory conservators or other persons, if any, having possession of or access to the child under an order of the court;

(8) the name of an alleged father of the child or a statement that the identity of the father of the child is unknown;

(9) a full description and statement of value of all property owned or possessed by the child;

(10) a statement describing what action the court is requested to take concerning the child and the statutory grounds on which the request is made; and

(11) any other information required by this title.

Subsection (b) below is effective for petitions in SAPCRs filed before Sept. 1, 2001.

(b) The petition must include:

(1) a statement that the court in which the petition is filed has continuing, exclusive jurisdiction or that no court has continuing jurisdiction of the suit;

(2) the name, sex, place and date of birth, and place of residence of the child, except that if adoption of a child is requested, the name of the child may be omitted;

(3) the full name, age, and place of residence of the petitioner and the petitioner's relationship to the child or the fact that no relationship exists;

(4) the names, ages, and place of residence of the parents, except in a suit in which adoption is requested;

(5) the name and place of residence of the managing conservator, if any, or the child's custodian, if any, appointed by order of a court of another state or country;

(6) the names and places of residence of the guardians of the person and estate of the child, if any;

(7) the names and places of residence of possessory conservators or other persons, if any, having possession of or access to the child under an order of the court;

(8) the name and place of residence of an alleged father of the child or a statement that the identity of the father of the child is unknown;

(9) a full description and statement of value of all property owned or possessed by the child;

(10) a statement describing what action the court is requested to take concerning the child and the statutory grounds on which the request is made; and

(11) any other information required by this title.

History of Fam §102.008: Acts 1995, 74th Leg., ch. 20, §1, eff. April 20, 1995. Amended by Acts 2001, 77th Leg., ch. 296, §2, eff. Sept. 1, 2001. Source: Former Fam §11.08(a), (b).

Dohrn v. Delgado, 941 S.W.2d 244, 248 (Tex.App.—Corpus Christi 1996, orig. proceeding). "[W]e indulge a liberal construction of pleadings and pre-trial procedures in [SAPCRs], and technical rules of pleading and practice need not be strictly followed. The [SAPCR] petition need not specifically name the section of the Family Code on which the petitioner relies, as long as it makes the necessary allegations to support the relief afforded by that section."

FAM §102.0085. STATEMENT ON ALTERNATIVE DISPUTE RESOLUTION

(a) A party to a proceeding brought under this title shall include in the first pleading filed by the party in the proceeding the following statement:

"I AM AWARE THAT IT IS THE POLICY OF THE STATE OF TEXAS TO PROMOTE THE AMICABLE AND NONJUDICIAL SETTLEMENT OF DISPUTES INVOLVING CHILDREN AND FAMILIES. I AM AWARE OF ALTERNATIVE DISPUTE RESOLUTION METHODS, INCLUDING MEDIATION. WHILE I RECOGNIZE THAT ALTERNATIVE DISPUTE RESOLUTION IS AN ALTERNATIVE TO AND NOT A SUBSTITUTE FOR A TRIAL AND THAT THIS CASE MAY BE TRIED IF IT IS NOT SETTLED, I REPRESENT TO THE COURT THAT I WILL ATTEMPT IN GOOD FAITH TO RESOLVE BEFORE FINAL TRIAL CONTESTED ISSUES IN THIS CASE BY ALTERNATIVE DISPUTE RESOLUTION WITHOUT THE NECESSITY OF COURT INTERVENTION."

(b) The statement required by Subsection (a) must be prominently displayed in boldfaced type or capital letters or be underlined and be signed by the party.

(c) The statement in Subsection (a) is not required for:

(1) a pleading in which citation on all respondents entitled to service of citation is requested, issued, and given by publication;

(2) a motion or pleading that seeks relief under Section 105.001(c), Subchapter H, Chapter 157, or Chapter 262; or

(3) a special appearance under Rule 120A, Texas Rules of Civil Procedure.

History of Fam §102.0085: Acts 1995, 74th Leg., ch. 751, §9, eff. Sept. 1, 1995. Amended by Acts 1997, 75th Leg., ch. 937, §2, eff. Sept. 1, 1997; Acts 1999, 76th Leg., ch. 178, §4 (eff. Aug. 30, 1999), ch. 62, §6.11 (eff. Sept. 1, 1999).

FAM §102.009. SERVICE OF CITATION

(a) Except as provided by Subsection (b), the following are entitled to service of citation on the filing of a petition in an original suit:

(1) a managing conservator;

(2) a possessory conservator;

(3) a person having possession of or access to the child under an order;

(4) a person required by law or by order to provide for the support of the child;

(5) a guardian of the person of the child;

(6) a guardian of the estate of the child;

(7) each parent as to whom the parent-child relationship has not been terminated or process has not been waived under Chapter 161;

(8) an alleged father, unless there is attached to the petition an affidavit of waiver of interest in a child executed by the alleged father as provided by Chapter 161 or unless the petitioner has complied with the provisions of Section 161.002(b)(2) or (b)(3);

A *Subsection (9) below is effective for motions or other requests for relief made in parentage or paternity proceedings commenced on or after June 14, 2001.*

(9) a man who has filed a notice of intent to claim paternity as provided by Chapter 160;

Subsection (9) below is effective for motions or other requests for relief made in parentage or paternity proceedings commenced before June 14, 2001.

(9) a man who has filed a notice of intent to claim paternity as provided by Subchapter D, Chapter 160;

(10) the Department of Protective and Regulatory Services, if the petition requests that the department be appointed as managing conservator of the child; and

(11) the Title IV-D agency, if the petition requests the termination of the parent-child relationship and support rights have been assigned to the Title IV-D agency under Chapter 231.

(b) Citation may be served on any other person who has or who may assert an interest in the child.

(c) Citation on the filing of an original petition in a suit shall be issued and served as in other civil cases.

(d) If the petition requests the establishment, modification, or enforcement of a support right assigned to the Title IV-D agency under Chapter 231 or the rescission of a voluntary acknowledgment of paternity under Chapter 160, notice shall be given to the Title IV-D agency in a manner provided by Rule 21a, Texas Rules of Civil Procedure.

History of Fam §102.009: Acts 1995, 74th Leg., ch. 20, §1, eff. April 20, 1995. Amended by Acts 1995, 74th Leg., ch. 751, §10, eff. Sept. 1, 1995; Acts 1997, 75th Leg., ch. 561, §1 (eff. Sept. 1, 1997), ch. 599, §1 (eff. Sept. 1, 1997); Acts 1999, 76th Leg., ch. 556, §2 (eff. Sept. 1, 1999), ch. 62, §6.12 (eff. Sept. 1, 1999); Acts 2001, 77th Leg., ch. 821, §2.09, eff. June 14, 2001. Source: Former Fam §11.09(a)-(c), (f).

Texas DPRS v. Sherry, 46 S.W.3d 857, 860 (Tex. 2001). "Section 102.009 identifies those persons entitled to be served with citation in a SAPCR and includes 'an alleged father.' When the Attorney General filed the 1993 paternity suit, he alleged in the pleadings that [initially alleged father] was [child's] father. The Attorney General did not allege that [plaintiff] was [child's] father. Thus, [initially alleged father] was the only 'alleged father,' as the term is used in the statute, who was entitled to notice. *At 861:* [Section 102.009(b)] does not require service ...; it merely allows voluntary service by the plaintiff or at the court's discretion."

In re K.M.S., 68 S.W.3d 61, 68 (Tex.App.—Dallas 2001, no pet.). "Implicit in [managing conservator's] testimony is that [petitioner] told [managing conservator's] mother and [managing conservator] that he believed he was [the child's] father. Thus, [managing conservator] had notice that [petitioner] claimed to be [child's] father. Knowing that [petitioner] was an alleged father, [managing conservator] was required by ... §102.009(a)(8) to serve [petitioner] with his petition to establish paternity. *At 69:* Although not clearly stated, it appears the supreme court's opinion [in ***Texas DPRS v. Sherry***], defines 'alleged father' under §102.009(a)(8) to mean a man alleged in a petition in a SAPCR to be the biological father. The supreme court's reason for choosing to define 'alleged father' is unclear. *At 70-71:* Clearly, the purpose of requiring service on the laundry list of persons entitled to service under §102.009(a) is to require the petitioner of a SAPCR to give notice to anyone who may have a legal interest in the child. The supreme court's restrictive definition of 'alleged father' would encourage deception. [¶] Accordingly, we decline to follow the supreme court's apparent definition of 'alleged father' as being a man alleged in a formal pleading filed in that case to be the father because: (a) it is dicta; (b) the sole authority it cites for the definition fails to support such a definition and is irrelevant to the issue; and (c) in instances where there is more than one man who believes himself to be the father of the child, it would encourage races to the courthouse to establish paternity without notice to the other men who have informed the petitioner of their claim to paternity of the child. We conclude the better construction is to interpret 'alleged father' ... to include a man who has informed the petitioner, either formally through service of process or informally by other means of communication, of his belief that he is the biological father of the child."

Bowers v. Matula, 943 S.W.2d 536, 538 (Tex.App.—Houston [1st Dist] 1997, no writ). Maternal grandparents "filed this lawsuit requesting reasonable access to the grandchild. The [managing conservators] answered, and on the same date, filed a separate lawsuit for termination of the parents' rights and for adoption. No notice was given to the [grandparents], nor was it required."

Roberson v. Pickett, 900 S.W.2d 112, 116 (Tex. App.—Houston [14th Dist.] 1995, no writ). "The issue presented ... is whether the statute intends for a person who has asserted an interest in a child by filing suit but has yet to have that right recognized is entitled to mandatory service. By filing suit to establish the relationship, the person moves from the group of those who have or may assert an interest who are not entitled to mandatory service to the group of those who are entitled to mandatory service. [A] person who has filed suit seeking guardianship fits within the meaning of guardian of the person or estate under §§11.09(a)(5) [now §102.009(a)(5)] and (a)(6) [now §102.009(a)(6)]."

Young v. Young, 693 S.W.2d 696, 698 (Tex.App.—Houston [[14th Dist.] 1985, writ dism'd). "Section 11.09(a) [now §102.009(a)] does not specifically list 'grandparents' as being entitled to service in a [SAPCR]."

Grasz v. Grasz, 608 S.W.2d 356, 357-58 (Tex.App.—Dallas 1980, no writ). "Formal citation and notice are not synonymous, and mere notice that one has been sued does not obligate the defendant to appear and answer."

FAM §102.010. SERVICE OF CITATION BY PUBLICATION

(a) Citation may be served by publication as in other civil cases to persons entitled to service of citation who cannot be notified by personal service or registered or certified mail and to persons whose names are unknown.

(b) Citation by publication shall be published one time. If the name of a person entitled to service of citation is unknown, the notice to be published shall be addressed to "All Whom It May Concern." One or more causes to be heard on a certain day may be included in one notice and hearings may be continued from time to time without further notice.

(c) Citation by publication shall be sufficient if given in substantially the following form:

"STATE OF TEXAS

To (names of persons to be served with citation) and to all whom it may concern (if the name of any person to be served with citation is unknown), Respondent(s),

"You have been sued. You may employ an attorney. If you or your attorney do (does) not file a written answer with the clerk who issued this citation by 10 a.m. on the Monday next following the expiration of 20 days after you were served this citation and petition, a default judgment may be taken against you. The petition of ______________, Petitioner, was filed in the Court of ______________ County, Texas, on the ___ day of __________, _____, against __________, Respondent(s), numbered _____, and entitled "In the interest of _________, a child (or children).' The suit requests (statement of relief requested, e.g., "terminate the parent-child relationship'). The date and place of birth of the child (children) who is (are) the subject of the suit: ______________.

"The court has authority in this suit to render an order in the child's (children's) interest that will be binding on you, including the termination of the parent-child relationship, the determination of paternity, and the appointment of a conservator with authority to consent to the child's (children's) adoption.

"Issued and given under my hand and seal of the Court at __________, Texas, this the ___ day of _______, ____.

"________________________

Clerk of the District Court of

__________ County, Texas.

By ______________, Deputy."

History of Fam §102.010: Acts 1995, 74th Leg., ch. 20, §1, eff. April 20, 1995. Source: Former Fam §11.09(d), (e).

In re A.Y., 16 S.W.3d 387, 388-89 (Tex.App.—El Paso 2000, no pet.). "When a statute directs that citation by publication be issued or served as in other civil cases, the requisites of the Rules of Civil Procedure govern, unless the statute expressly provides otherwise."

Rider v. Farris, 718 S.W.2d 883, 884 (Tex.App.—Beaumont 1986, writ dism'd). Mother "was cited by publication on or after July 8, 1985, and the judgment appointing the [plaintiffs] managing conservators was signed July 24, 1985. Therefore, [mother] was given no more than 16 days notice, whereas, by law, she was entitled to at least 20 days notice prior to hearing. Therefore, the judgment signed July 24, 1985, was void for want of personal jurisdiction over [mother]."

Wiebusch v. Wiebusch, 636 S.W.2d 540, 541-42 (Tex.App.—San Antonio 1982, no writ). "The requirements of §11.09(d) [now §102.010] comport with those of [TRCP] 114, which mandates that, in addition to certain other matters, the citation by publication shall contain 'a brief statement of the nature of the suit.' Thus, notice of the nature of the suit is essential to a valid citation by publication. [¶] Since authority for citation by publication comes solely from the statutes, enactments authorizing the mode of service are strictly construed; and when a statute provides for constructive service in a given case, the method prescribed is exclusive and admits of no substitute."

FAM §102.011. ACQUIRING JURISDICTION OVER NONRESIDENT

(a) The court may exercise status or subject matter jurisdiction over the suit as provided by Chapter 152.

(b) The court may also exercise personal jurisdiction over a person on whom service of citation is required or over the person's personal representative, although the person is not a resident or domiciliary of this state, if:

(1) the person is personally served with citation in this state;

(2) the person submits to the jurisdiction of this state by consent, by entering a general appearance, or by filing a responsive document having the effect of waiving any contest to personal jurisdiction;

(3) the child resides in this state as a result of the acts or directives of the person;

(4) the person resided with the child in this state;

(5) the person resided in this state and provided prenatal expenses or support for the child;

(6) the person engaged in sexual intercourse in this state and the child may have been conceived by that act of intercourse;

(7) the person registered with the paternity registry maintained by the bureau of vital statistics as provided by Chapter 160; or

(8) there is any basis consistent with the constitutions of this state and the United States for the exercise of the personal jurisdiction.

History of Fam §102.011: Acts 1995, 74th Leg., ch. 20, §1, eff. April 20, 1995. Amended by Acts 1997, 75th Leg., ch. 561, §2, eff. Sept. 1, 1997. Source: Former Fam §11.051.

In re S.A.V., 837 S.W.2d 80, 83 (Tex.1992). "Claims for child support and visitation expenses are like claims for debt in that they seek a personal judgment establishing a direct obligation to pay money. Therefore, a valid judgment for child support or visitation expenses may be rendered only by a court having jurisdiction over the person of the defendant. *At 84:* A 'custody determination' means a court decision providing for the custody of a child, including visitation rights. Unlike adjudications of child support and visitation expense, custody determinations are status adjudications not dependent upon personal jurisdiction over the parents. [¶] Generally, a family relationship is among those matters in which the forum state has such a strong interest that its courts may reasonably make an adjudication affecting that relationship even though one of the parties to the relationship may have had no personal contacts with the forum state. Consequently, due process permits adjudication of the custody and visitation of a child residing in the forum state without a showing of 'minimum contacts' on the part of the nonresident parent."

In re Gonzalez, 993 S.W.2d 147, 151-52 (Tex. App.—San Antonio 1999, no pet.). "It is undisputed that personal service was effected on [father] when his plane touched down in Texas to refuel. The Family Code provides that a court may exercise jurisdiction over a nonresident if he was personally served in this state."

Flores v. Melo-Palacios, 921 S.W.2d 399, 404 (Tex. App.—Corpus Christi 1996, writ denied). "[T]he status or subject matter jurisdiction permitted by §11.051 [now §102.011] for [SAPCRs] is merely an alternative means of obtaining jurisdiction when the court is unable to obtain personal jurisdiction over the nonresident party. There is simply no requirement that there be both status and personal jurisdiction before a court may entertain a suit for child support."

Phillips v. Phillips, 826 S.W.2d 746, 748 (Tex. App.—Houston [14th Dist.] 1992, no writ). "Federal constitutional requirements of due process limit the power of the state to assert personal jurisdiction over a nonresident defendant.... Regarding the due process requirements, the United States Supreme Court has established a two-prong test: (1) whether the nonresident defendant has purposely established minimum contacts with the forum state; and (2) if so, whether the exercise of jurisdiction comports with fair play and substantial justice."

Williams v. Knott, 690 S.W.2d 605, 606 (Tex.App.—Austin 1985, no writ). "The Supreme Court of the United States has noted that the minimum contacts standard 'cannot accommodate some necessary litigation,' and recognized the need for exceptions, such as status adjudication. Special jurisdictional principles thereby apply to status adjudications like custody. *At 607:* There exists little case authority involving termination of parental rights when the respondent is a nonresident of Texas. There is authority, however, to the effect that a termination proceeding is a status determination which does not require personal jurisdiction over a nonresident respondent."

In re R.L., 622 S.W.2d 660, 663 (Tex.App.—Fort Worth 1981, no writ). "The trial court was justified in concluding from the testimony that the children were conceived and born in Texas, thus providing the necessary minimal contacts to support jurisdiction in Texas over the non-resident who is alleged to be a legal parent of those children."

Cossey v. Cossey, 602 S.W.2d 591, 595-96 (Tex. App.—Waco 1980, no writ). "Our record conclusively shows that Texas was the last state of marital cohabitation between [the couple], that [plaintiff's] suit was commenced within two years after the date on which cohabitation ended, and that [defendant] resided with the children in Texas for almost five years. Those facts satisfy the minimum contact requirements of ... §3.26(a)(1) [now Family Code §6.305] and §11.051(3) [now §102.011(b)(4)] for Texas to exercise long-arm jurisdiction over [defendant] on all aspects of the present suit. However, those contacts alone do not mandate the assumption of jurisdiction under the record. [N]otwithstanding satisfaction of the minimum contacts necessary for long-arm jurisdiction over the nonresident, federal constitutional due process requires that the assumption of jurisdiction by the forum state must not offend traditional notions of fair play and substantial justice, consideration being given to the quality, nature, and extent of the activity in the forum state, the relative convenience of the parties, the benefits and protection of the laws of the forum state afforded the parties, and the basic equities of the situation." (Internal quotations omitted.)

Bergdoll v. Whitley, 598 S.W.2d 932, 934-35 (Tex. App.—Austin 1980, no writ). "Section 11.051 [now §102.011] authorizes personal jurisdiction over a nonresident defendant in matters affecting the parent-child relationship if, among other things, the child is conceived in this state or resides here as a result of acts or directives or with the approval of the non-resident parent. However, this statute must be read as implicitly requiring, in addition, basic 'minimum contacts' with the state of Texas by the non-resident parent. If such 'minimum contacts' are not present, jurisdiction assumed thereunder would not withstand constitutional attack. [¶] The defendant must have performed some act by which he purposefully avails himself of the privilege of conducting activities within the forum state, thus invoking the benefits and protections of its laws."

FAM §102.012. EXERCISING PARTIAL JURISDICTION

(a) A court in which a suit is filed may exercise its jurisdiction over those portions of the suit for which it has authority.

(b) The court's authority to resolve all issues in controversy between the parties may be restricted because the court lacks:

(1) the required personal jurisdiction over a nonresident party;

(2) the required jurisdiction under Chapter 152; or

(3) the required jurisdiction under Chapter 159.

(c) If a provision of Chapter 152 or Chapter 159 expressly conflicts with another provision of this title and the conflict cannot be reconciled, the provision of Chapter 152 or Chapter 159 prevails.

(d) In exercising jurisdiction, the court shall seek to harmonize the provisions of this code, the federal Parental Kidnapping Prevention Act (28 U.S.C. Section 1738A), and the federal Full Faith and Credit for Child Support Order Act (28 U.S.C. Section 1738B).

History of Fam §102.012: Acts 1995, 74th Leg., ch. 20, §1, eff. April 20, 1995. Amended by Acts 1999, 76th Leg., ch. 62, §6.13, eff. Sept. 1, 1999.

See also Fam. Code §6.308.

FAM §102.013. DOCKETING REQUIREMENTS

(a) In a suit for modification or a motion for enforcement, the clerk shall file the petition or motion and all related papers under the same docket number as the prior proceeding without additional letters, digits, or special designations.

(b) If a suit requests the adoption of a child, the clerk shall file the suit and all other papers relating to the suit in a new file having a new docket number.

E *Subsection (c) below is effective for modification or enforcement proceedings commenced on or after Sept. 1, 2001.*

(c) In a suit to determine parentage under this title in which the court has rendered an order relating to an earlier born child of the same parents, the clerk shall file the suit and all other papers relating to the suit under the same docket number as the prior parentage action. For all other purposes, including the assessment of fees and other costs, the suit is a separate suit.

History of Fam §102.013: Acts 1995, 74th Leg., ch. 20, §1, eff. April 20, 1995. Amended by Acts 2001, 77th Leg., ch. 1023, §2, eff. Sept. 1, 2001. Source: Former Fam §11.07(c).

CHAPTER 103. VENUE & TRANSFER OF ORIGINAL PROCEEDINGS

FAM §103.001. VENUE FOR ORIGINAL SUIT

(a) Except as otherwise provided by this title, an original suit shall be filed in the county where the child resides, unless:

(1) another court has continuing exclusive jurisdiction under Chapter 155; or

(2) venue is fixed in a suit for dissolution of a marriage under Subchapter D, Chapter 6.

(b) A suit in which adoption is requested may be filed in the county where the child resides or in the county where the petitioners reside.

(c) A child resides in the county where the child's parents reside or the child's parent resides, if only one parent is living, except that:

(1) if a guardian of the person has been appointed by order of a county or probate court and a managing conservator has not been appointed, the child resides in the county where the guardian of the person resides;

(2) if the parents of the child do not reside in the same county and if a managing conservator, custodian, or guardian of the person has not been appointed, the child resides in the county where the parent having actual care, control, and possession of the child resides;

(3) if the child is in the care and control of an adult other than a parent and a managing conservator, custodian, or guardian of the person has not been appointed, the child resides where the adult having actual care, control, and possession of the child resides;

(4) if the child is in the actual care, control, and possession of an adult other than a parent and the whereabouts of the parent and the guardian of the person is unknown, the child resides where the adult having actual possession, care, and control of the child resides;

(5) if the person whose residence would otherwise determine venue has left the child in the care and control of the adult, the child resides where that adult resides;

(6) if a guardian or custodian of the child has been appointed by order of a court of another state or country, the child resides in the county where the guardian or custodian resides if that person resides in this state; or

(7) if it appears that the child is not under the actual care, control, and possession of an adult, the child resides where the child is found.

History of Fam §103.001: Acts 1995, 74th Leg., ch. 20, §1, eff. April 20, 1995. Amended by Acts 1999, 76th Leg., ch. 62, §6.14, eff. Sept. 1, 1999. Source: Former Fam §11.04.

In re S.D., 980 S.W.2d 758, 760-61 (Tex.App.—San Antonio 1998, pet. denied). "Normally, children reside where their parents reside. … Texas law is clear that an element of permanency is necessary before a party can be considered a resident of a particular county."

McManus v. Wilborn, 932 S.W.2d 662, 665 (Tex. App.—Houston [14th Dist.] 1996, orig. proceeding). "[A]ny broad characterization that Chapters 103 and 155 derive from §11.06 is incorrect. Further, we find it impossible to harmonize the two chapters except in the narrow area of procedures for transfer. *At 666:* [For] original [SAPCRs], we hold that §103.001 establishes venue in an original suit. Sections 155.201-155.203 are not applicable to original suits under the incorporation clause of §103.002(c)."

Arteaga v. Texas DPRS, 924 S.W.2d 756, 762 (Tex. App.—Austin 1996, writ denied). "The venue statute comes into play only after the trial court has determined that Texas courts have jurisdiction over the custody dispute."

Pratt v. Texas DHR, 614 S.W.2d 490, 493 (Tex. App.—Amarillo 1981, writ ref'd n.r.e.). "We construe §11.04(c)(4)(C) [now §103.001(c)(4)] to mean care and control of the child when the motion to transfer is heard and not at some earlier time."

FAM §103.002. TRANSFER OF ORIGINAL PROCEEDINGS WITHIN STATE

(a) If venue of a suit is improper in the court in which an original suit is filed and no other court has continuing, exclusive jurisdiction of the suit, on the timely motion of a party other than the petitioner, the court shall transfer the proceeding to the county where venue is proper.

(b) On a showing that a suit for dissolution of the marriage of the child's parents has been filed in another court, a court in which a suit is pending shall transfer the proceedings to the court where the dissolution of the marriage is pending.

(c) The procedures in Chapter 155 apply to a transfer of:

(1) an original suit under this section; or

(2) a suit for modification or a motion for enforcement under this title.

History of Fam §103.002: Acts 1995, 74th Leg., ch. 20, §1, eff. April 20, 1995. Source: Former Fam §11.06(a), (c).

FAM §103.003. TRANSFER OF ORIGINAL SUIT WITHIN STATE WHEN PARTY OR CHILD RESIDES OUTSIDE STATE

(a) A court of this state in which an original suit is filed or in which a suit for child support is filed under Chapter 159 shall transfer the suit to the county of residence of the party who is a resident of this state if all other parties and children affected by the proceedings reside outside this state.

(b) If one or more of the parties affected by the suit reside outside this state and if more than one party or one or more children affected by the proceeding reside in this state in different counties, the court shall transfer the suit according to the following priorities:

(1) to the court of continuing, exclusive jurisdiction, if any;

(2) to the county of residence of the child, if applicable, provided that:

(A) there is no court of continuing, exclusive jurisdiction; or

(B) the court of continuing, exclusive jurisdiction finds that neither a party nor a child affected by the proceeding resides in the county of the court of continuing jurisdiction; or

(3) if Subdivisions (1) and (2) are inapplicable, to the county most appropriate to serve the convenience of the resident parties, the witnesses, and the interest of justice.

(c) If a transfer of an original suit or suit for child support under Chapter 159 is sought under this section, Chapter 155 applies to the procedures for transfer of the suit.

History of Fam §103.003: Acts 1995, 74th Leg., ch. 20, §1, eff. April 20, 1995. Source: Former Fam §11.061.

CHAPTER 104. EVIDENCE

FAM §104.001. RULES OF EVIDENCE

Except as otherwise provided, the Texas Rules of Civil Evidence apply as in other civil cases.

History of Fam §104.001: Acts 1995, 74th Leg., ch. 20, §1, eff. April 20, 1995. Source: Former Fam §11.14(e).

FAM §104.002. PRERECORDED STATEMENT OF CHILD

If a child 12 years of age or younger is alleged in a suit under this title to have been abused, the recording of an oral statement of the child recorded prior to the proceeding is admissible into evidence if:

(1) no attorney for a party was present when the statement was made;

(2) the recording is both visual and aural and is recorded on film or videotape or by other electronic means;

(3) the recording equipment was capable of making an accurate recording, the operator was competent, and the recording is accurate and has not been altered;

(4) the statement was not made in response to questioning calculated to lead the child to make a particular statement;

(5) each voice on the recording is identified;

(6) the person conducting the interview of the child in the recording is present at the proceeding and available to testify or be cross-examined by either party; and

(7) each party is afforded an opportunity to view the recording before it is offered into evidence.

History of Fam §104.002: Acts 1995, 74th Leg., ch. 20, §1, eff. April 20, 1995. Source: Former Fam §11.21(a), (b).

In re R.V., 977 S.W.2d 777, 781 (Tex.App.—Fort Worth 1998, no pet.). "[A]n exception to the right of face-to-face confrontation exists when the State shows that a special procedure is necessary to protect child witnesses from the trauma of testifying in court. [¶] The determination of whether such alternative forms of testimony [such as one-way, closed-circuit television] are necessary should be made on a case-by-case basis. In making such a determination, courts should consider whether: (1) use of a video is necessary to protect the welfare of the child; (2) the trauma to the child comes from exposure to the abuser, rather than from the courtroom generally; and (3) the emotional distress to the child would be more than minimal."

James v. Texas DHS, 836 S.W.2d 236, 239-41 (Tex. App.—Texarkana 1992, no writ). "By prohibiting leading questions in cases governed by §11.21(b)(4) [now §104.002(4)], the legislative branch adopted the common-law rule insofar as the uncross-examined videotaped testimony of children under the age of twelve is concerned. Under the strictures of … §11.21, questions directed to a child must be open-ended and not suggestive of a response. We conclude that the videotape with these children's statements should have been excluded because the questioning was calculated to lead the children to a particular statement. The questioning itself was generally leading. In addition, [interviewer's] nonverbal communication, such as her approving, affectionate pats in response to desired answers and her active, demonstrative use of the dolls, coupled with her argumentative refusal to accept undesired answers, contributed to making a particular statement. Thus, the statement should not have been admitted as evidence."

FAM §104.003. PRERECORDED VIDEOTAPED TESTIMONY OF CHILD

(a) The court may, on the motion of a party to the proceeding, order that the testimony of the child be taken outside the courtroom and be recorded for showing in the courtroom before the court, the finder of fact, and the parties to the proceeding.

(b) Only an attorney for each party, an attorney ad litem for the child or other person whose presence would contribute to the welfare and well-being of the child, and persons necessary to operate the equipment may be present in the room with the child during the child's testimony.

(c) Only the attorneys for the parties may question the child.

(d) The persons operating the equipment shall be placed in a manner that prevents the child from seeing or hearing them.

(e) The court shall ensure that:

(1) the recording is both visual and aural and is recorded on film or videotape or by other electronic means;

(2) the recording equipment was capable of making an accurate recording, the operator was competent, and the recording is accurate and is not altered;

(3) each voice on the recording is identified; and

(4) each party to the proceeding is afforded an opportunity to view the recording before it is shown in the courtroom.

History of Fam §104.003: Acts 1995, 74th Leg., ch. 20, §1, eff. April 20, 1995. Source: Former Fam §11.21(d).

FAM §104.004. REMOTE TELEVISED BROADCAST OF TESTIMONY OF CHILD

(a) If in a suit a child 12 years of age or younger is alleged to have been abused, the court may, on the motion of a party to the proceeding, order that the testimony of the child be taken in a room other than the courtroom and be televised by closed-circuit equipment in the courtroom to be viewed by the court and the parties.

(b) The procedures that apply to prerecorded videotaped testimony of a child apply to the remote broadcast of testimony of a child.

History of Fam §104.004: Acts 1995, 74th Leg., ch. 20, §1, eff. April 20, 1995. Source: Former Fam §11.21(c).

FAM §104.005. SUBSTITUTION FOR IN-COURT TESTIMONY OF CHILD

(a) If the testimony of a child is taken as provided by this chapter, the child may not be compelled to testify in court during the proceeding.

(b) The court may allow the testimony of a child of any age to be taken in any manner provided by this chapter if the child, because of a medical condition, is incapable of testifying in open court.

History of Fam §104.005: Acts 1995, 74th Leg., ch. 20, §1, eff. April 20, 1995. Amended by Acts 1995, 74th Leg., ch. 751, §11, eff. Sept. 1, 1995. Source: Former Fam §11.21(e).

FAM §104.006. HEARSAY STATEMENT OF CHILD ABUSE VICTIM

In a suit affecting the parent-child relationship, a statement made by a child 12 years of age or younger that describes alleged abuse against the child, without regard to whether the statement is otherwise inadmissible as hearsay, is admissible as evidence if, in a hearing conducted outside the presence of the jury, the court finds that the time, content, and circumstances of the statement provide sufficient indications of the statement's reliability and:

(1) the child testifies or is available to testify at the proceeding in court or in any other manner provided for by law; or

(2) the court determines that the use of the statement in lieu of the child's testimony is necessary to protect the welfare of the child.

History of Fam §104.006: Acts 1997, 75th Leg., ch. 575, §4, eff. Sept. 1, 1997.

CHAPTER 105. SETTINGS, HEARINGS, & ORDERS

FAM §105.001. TEMPORARY ORDERS BEFORE FINAL ORDER

(a) In a suit, the court may make a temporary order, including the modification of a prior temporary order, for the safety and welfare of the child, including an order:

(1) for the temporary conservatorship of the child;

(2) for the temporary support of the child;

(3) restraining a party from molesting or disturbing the peace of the child or another party;

(4) prohibiting a person from removing the child beyond a geographical area identified by the court; or

(5) for payment of reasonable attorney's fees and expenses.

(b) Except as provided by Subsection (c), temporary restraining orders and temporary injunctions under this section shall be granted without the necessity of an affidavit or verified pleading stating specific facts showing that immediate and irreparable injury, loss, or damage will result before notice can be served and a hearing can be held. Except as provided by Subsection (h), an order may not be rendered under Subsection (a)(1), (2), or (5) except after notice and a hearing. A temporary restraining order or temporary injunction granted under this section need not:

(1) define the injury or state why it is irreparable;

(2) state why the order was granted without notice; or

(3) include an order setting the cause for trial on the merits with respect to the ultimate relief requested.

(c) Except on a verified pleading or an affidavit in accordance with the Texas Rules of Civil Procedure, an order may not be rendered:

(1) attaching the body of the child;

(2) taking the child into the possession of the court or of a parent designated by the court; or

(3) excluding a parent from possession of or access to a child.

(d) In a suit, the court may dispense with the necessity of a bond in connection with temporary orders on behalf of the child.

(e) Temporary orders rendered under this section are not subject to interlocutory appeal.

(f) The violation of a temporary restraining order, temporary injunction, or other temporary order rendered under this section is punishable by contempt and the order is subject to and enforceable under Chapter 157.

(g) The rebuttable presumptions established in favor of the application of the guidelines for a child support order and for the standard possession order under Chapters 153 and 154 apply to temporary orders. The presumptions do not limit the authority of the court to render other temporary orders.

(h) An order under Subsection (a)(1) may be rendered without notice and an adversary hearing if the order is an emergency order sought by a governmental entity under Chapter 262.

History of Fam §105.001: Acts 1995, 74th Leg., ch. 20, §1, eff. April 20, 1995. Amended by Acts 1997, 75th Leg., ch. 575, §5, eff. Sept. 1, 1997; Acts 1999, 76th Leg., ch. 1390, §3, eff. Sept. 1, 1999. Source: Former Fam §§11.11(a)-(d), (g), (h), 14.033(*l*), 14.055(e).

Grigsby v. Coker, 904 S.W.2d 619, 620 (Tex.1995). "Gag orders in civil judicial proceedings are valid only when an imminent and irreparable harm to the judicial process will deprive litigants of a just resolution of their dispute, and the judicial action represents the least restrictive means to prevent that harm. *At 621:* While §11.11 [now §105.001] does give trial courts broad powers in family cases, it does not authorize them to invade constitutional guarantees. The trial court here could have adopted [a gag] order [that was less restrictive], but it failed to do so. This was a clear abuse of discretion. [¶] The faults in this gag order are likely a function of the procedure, or lack of procedure, used in adopting it: no formal motion, no prior notice, and no formal hearing or evidence. There is no indication that exigent circumstances warranted an abbreviation in procedures authorized by §11.11, when seven weeks passed between the date the trial court stated it would issue a gag order and the date the order was signed."

Ex parte Hall, 854 S.W.2d 656, 658 (Tex.1993). "The temporary support order in this case was issued solely on the basis of the parties' prenuptial agreement and not on the authority of the Family Code. ... For this reason the trial court did not consider it necessary to complete the hearing required by statute before granting temporary support. It did not determine whether the spousal support ordered was 'necessary and equitable', as required by ... §3.58(c) [now Family Code §6.502], nor whether the temporary child support was 'for the safety and welfare of the child', as required by ... §11.11(a) [now §105.001(a)(2)]. It did not take into account the guidelines and factors required for setting child support. ... It calculated the arrearage due without any evidentiary basis. Under these circumstances, the temporary support order was not enforceable by contempt."

In re Aubin, 29 S.W.3d 199, 203-04 (Tex.App.—Beaumont 2000, orig. proceeding). "The Family Code authorizes the trial court to enter temporary orders for the safety and welfare of the children. The strong presumption in favor of parental custody requires that the nonparent seeking custody affirmatively prove by a preponderance of the evidence that appointment of the parent as managing conservator would significantly impair the child, either physically or emotionally. [¶] Absent a finding, supported by evidence, that the safety and welfare of the children is significantly impaired by the denial of the [nonparents'] visitation, [mother's] decision regarding whether the children will have any contact with the [nonparents] is an exercise of her fundamental right as a parent. That right is shielded from judicial interference by the Due Process clause of the United States Constitution. Section 105.001, is unconstitutional as applied to [mother] in the trial court's ... temporary restraining orders and ... temporary order. The trial court clearly abused its discretion in appointing [nonparents] as temporary possessory conservators."

Dohrn v. Delgado, 941 S.W.2d 244, 249 (Tex.App.—Corpus Christi 1996, orig. proceeding). "[A]lthough §§105.001(b) & (c) generally eliminate the need for sworn pleadings for a temporary restraining order, they specifically require that a TRO which excludes a parent from possession of or access to a child be based on a verified pleading or affidavit stating specific facts showing that immediate and irreparable injury, loss, or damage will result before notice can be served and a hearing held."

Morse v. Baker-Olsen, 929 S.W.2d 659, 661-62 (Tex.App.—Houston [14th Dist.] 1996, orig. proceeding). Section 105.001 "primarily concerns the entry of orders for the child's welfare and protection. If we were to hold this section does not apply after the entry of a final decree of divorce or other final order, the trial court would have no authority to enter a post-judgment temporary order affecting a child's safety and welfare. Therefore, we decline relator's invitation to construe §105.001 as applicable only to cases where no final judgment has yet been rendered. *At 662 n.2:* Although there is no authority preventing issuance of a temporary injunction in situations where a parent tries to move to another geographical area, we believe there is potential for abuse if the trial court does not hold a hearing in a timely fashion following the issuance of the temporary injunction. The Family Code does not require a temporary injunction to include a date for the hearing on the ultimate relief requested."

Hughey v. Hughey, 923 S.W.2d 778, 780 (Tex. App.—Tyler 1996, writ denied). "Section 105.001(e), which precludes the interlocutory appeal of temporary orders, likewise applies to temporary orders rendered under Chapter 156."

Smelscer v. Smelscer, 901 S.W.2d 708, 711 n.4 (Tex.App.—El Paso 1995, no writ). "Once a trial court in which parties initiate divorce proceedings ... acquires jurisdiction over the minor children of the marriage and enters temporary orders concerning their custody, such orders survive any subsequent dismissal of the underlying divorce action and continue in effect until a court of competent jurisdiction modifies them or provides for permanent custody of the children."

FAM §105.002. JURY

(a) Except as provided by Subsection (b), a party may demand a jury trial.

(b) A party may not demand a jury trial in:

(1) a suit in which adoption is sought, including a trial on the issue of denial or revocation of consent to the adoption by the managing conservator; or

A *Subsection (2) below is effective for motions or other requests for relief made in parentage or paternity proceedings commenced on or after June 14, 2001.*

(2) a suit to adjudicate parentage under Chapter 160.

Subsection (2) below is effective for motions or other requests for relief made in parentage or paternity proceedings commenced before June 14, 2001.

(2) a suit to determine parentage under Chapter 160.

(c) In a jury trial:

(1) a party is entitled to a verdict by the jury on the issues of:

(A) the appointment of a managing conservator;

(B) the appointment of joint managing conservators;

(C) the appointment of a possessory conservator; and

(D) the determination of the primary residence of the child;

(2) a party is not entitled to a jury verdict on the issues of:

(A) child support;

(B) a specific term or condition of possession of or access to the child; or

(C) any right or duty of a possessory or managing conservator, other than the issue of primary residence determined under Subdivision (1)(D); and

(3) the court may submit to the jury an issue described by Subdivision (2).

(d) The court may not contravene a jury verdict on an issue submitted under Subsection (c)(1). A jury verdict on an issue submitted under Subsection (c)(3) is advisory only.

History of Fam §105.002: Acts 1995, 74th Leg., ch. 20, §1, eff. April 20, 1995. Amended by Acts 1995, 74th Leg., ch. 751, §12, eff. Sept. 1, 1995; Acts 1997, 75th Leg., ch. 180, §1, eff. Sept. 1, 1997; Acts 1999, 76th Leg., ch. 556, §3, eff. Sept. 1, 1999; Acts 2001, 77th Leg., ch. 821, §2.10, 77th Leg., eff. June 14, 2001. Source: Former Fam §11.13.

Lenz v. Lenz, ___ S.W.3d ___ (Tex.2002) (No. 01-0232; 6-6-02). Section "105.002(d) restricts the trial court's power to 'contravene a jury verdict' on the issue of primary residence. Therefore, [mother] is correct that the statute's plain language means that she was entitled to a jury verdict in this case, and the trial court was not authorized to contravene that verdict by imposing an additional geographical restriction."

Ex parte Sproull, 815 S.W.2d 250, 250 (Tex.1991). "An alleged contemnor has a constitutional right to a jury trial on a 'serious' charge of criminal contempt. A charge for which confinement may exceed six months is serious."

Martin v. Martin, 776 S.W.2d 572, 574 (Tex.1989). "The grant of a jury trial in §11.13(a) [now §105.002(a)] is limited by §11.13(b) [now §105.002(b)]; accordingly, as the court determines appropriate it may grant or refuse a jury trial in actions concerning the modification of specific details of administering a prior divorce decree. Inasmuch as the trial court determines the conditions of access, it is not reversible error to refuse a jury trial in actions involving only the modification of the conditions of access or the threshold requirements for the conditions of access."

In re Walters, 39 S.W.3d 280, 290 (Tex.App.—Texarkana 2001, no pet.). Section "105.002(c)(1) entitles a party to a jury verdict on issues of the appointment of a managing conservator, joint managing conservators, or possessory conservators, and the determination of the child's primary residence. A party is not entitled to a jury verdict on the issues of child support, a specific term or condition of possession of or access to the child, or a right or duty of a possessory or managing conservator. The trial court may nevertheless submit an issue to the jury on these issues."

In re Rodriguez, 940 S.W.2d 265, 271 (Tex.App.—San Antonio 1997, writ denied). A jury's custody "determination is binding on the trial court if it is supported by the evidence. The jury's decision is also entitled to substantial deference.... We are not permitted to act, and will not act, as a second jury; accordingly, we do not pass upon the credibility of the witnesses or otherwise substitute our judgment for that of the jury."

Varner v. Howe, 860 S.W.2d 458, 465 (Tex.App.—El Paso 1993, no writ). "The ultimate determination of child support is for the court—if an issue on child support is submitted to the jury, the jury's answer is merely advisory and need not be followed by the court. Here, although the trial judge indicated prior to submission of the case to the jury that he intended to follow the jury finding, it was still a decision that was within his discretion."

FAM §105.003. PROCEDURE FOR CONTESTED HEARING

(a) Except as otherwise provided by this title, proceedings shall be as in civil cases generally.

(b) On the agreement of all parties to the suit, the court may limit attendance at the hearing to only those persons who have a direct interest in the suit or in the work of the court.

(c) A record shall be made as in civil cases generally unless waived by the parties with the consent of the court.

(d) When information contained in a report, study, or examination is before the court, the person making the report, study, or examination is subject to both direct examination and cross-examination as in civil cases generally.

(e) The hearing may be adjourned from time to time.

History of Fam §105.003: Acts 1995, 74th Leg., ch. 20, §1, eff. April 20, 1995. Source: Former Fam §11.14(a), (b), (d), (f), (g).

Author's Comment: Although many jurisdictions do not provide for the making of a record at a temporary hearing in front of an associate judge, this practice constitutes error in SAPCR suits unless waived as provided by 105.003(c).

Stubbs v. Stubbs, 685 S.W.2d 643, 645 (Tex.1985). In a SAPCR, "all oral testimony must be recorded. It is the responsibility of the trial judge to see that the court reporter performs this duty."

Rogers v. Rogers, 561 S.W.2d 172, 173-74 (Tex. 1978). Section 11.14(d), now §105.003(c), "requires that a record be made in all [SAPCRs] unless waived by the parties with the consent of the court. This provision places a duty on the court to make a record of the proceedings. [¶] '[I]f an appellant exercises due diligence and through no fault of his own is unable to obtain a proper record of the evidence introduced, this may require a new trial where his right to have the case reviewed on appeal can be preserved in no other way.'"

In re Vega, 10 S.W.3d 720, 722 (Tex.App.—Amarillo 1999, no pet.). "The order here contains a recitation that a 'record of the proceedings was waived.' However, where ... a party is not present nor represented by counsel at the hearing, the making of record cannot be waived as to the absent party and a trial court commits error in consenting to the waiver of a record."

G.S.K. v. T.K.N., 940 S.W.2d 797, 799 (Tex.App.—El Paso 1997, no writ). "[I]n a [SAPCR], failure to provide a statement of facts in violation of [§105.003(c)] constitutes error on the face of the record requiring reversal. [T]his provision places an affirmative duty on the court to make a record of the proceedings. We find no suggestion that this duty may be waived upon consent of only those parties present in the courtroom at the time of hearing, and indeed such an interpretation would subvert the purposes of requiring a record."

Walker v. Stefanic, 898 S.W.2d 347, 349 (Tex. App.—San Antonio 1995, no writ). "The trial judge is ultimately responsible to see that a record is made of the proceedings, including all testimony. The failure to make a record of proceedings involving custody of a minor child constitutes error on the face of the record. [¶] We are concerned that this duty to preserve may be routinely ignored in those courts utilizing electronic tape recordings. The record reflects that the family law master, operating under budget constraints, exhausts his tape supply within three months, and therefore, permits the court recorder to erase previously-recorded proceedings at three-month intervals in order to replenish the tape supply. The duty to preserve the record, however, is not diminished by use of an alternative form of recordation. Neither can it be eviscerated by budget constraints. We strongly recommend that all courts utilizing electronic tape recorders take such steps as are necessary to insure that electronically-recorded statements of facts are preserved for three years, as required by [Government Code] §52.046...."

Henning v. Henning, 889 S.W.2d 611, 613 (Tex. App.—Houston [14th Dist.] 1994, writ denied). Appellant "concedes she waived the presence of a court reporter, but insists she did not waive her right to a record. However, even when there is no express waiver, the absence of a record does not warrant reversal unless appellant shows the record's absence is not a result of her own negligence or lack of due diligence. Section 11.14(d) [now §105.003(c)] has been clarified by case law to require a showing of diligence and responsibility on behalf of the complaining party to be certain a record is made. [U]nder §11.14(d), [a] party may waive the making of a record by express written agreement, or by not objecting to the lack of record during the hearing. Where there is no default by a party and the complaining party is present at the hearing, §11.14(d) requires a timely objection by counsel, without which he is deemed to have waived the making of a record. [S]ection 11.14(d) ... does not deny a party's right to a record, but merely prevents one from lying behind the log. When a party is present before the court, due diligence must be exercised in seeking a record. There is no requirement that a waiver of the record be made in writing." (Internal quotations omitted.) *But see **Ex parte Juarez***, below.

Ex parte Juarez, 665 S.W.2d 200, 201 (Tex.App.—San Antonio 1984, orig. proceeding). "The language of §11.14(d) [now §105.003] is mandatory and requires a record whether requested or not. ... A mere showing that relator was present at the hearing and that he failed to object to the absence of a court reporter is not a showing that he waived his right to a statement of facts and that the court consented to this waiver. It is not the relator's burden to request a record. Section 11.14(d) requires that a record automatically be made in parent-child relationship matters *unless* the parties waive it *and* the court consents to that waiver." *But see **Henning***, above.

Kates v. Smith, 556 S.W.2d 630, 631 (Tex.App.—Texarkana 1977, orig. proceeding). "The provisions of the Texas Family Code make it mandatory that parties have the opportunity to examine and cross-examine any person making an investigation or report which is considered by the court in a [SAPCR]. *At 632:* To deny a party the opportunity to examine or cross-examine the author of such a report deprives that party of a valuable right to deny, contradict or overcome by other evidence the matters contained in the report. Even if it can be said in such a case that the court's decision would have been the same without considering the report, the aggrieved party still has been deprived of information possibly valuable to him and has been denied the opportunity to properly present his case both in the trial court and in the appellate court."

FAM §105.004. PREFERENTIAL SETTING

After a hearing, the court may:

(1) grant a motion filed by a party or the attorney or guardian ad litem for the child for a preferential setting for a trial on the merits; and

(2) give precedence to that hearing over other civil cases if the court finds that the delay created by ordinary scheduling practices will unreasonably affect the best interest of the child.

History of Fam §105.004: Acts 1995, 74th Leg., ch. 20, §1, eff. April 20, 1995. Source: Former Fam §11.14(i).

FAM §105.005. FINDINGS

Except as otherwise provided by this title, the court's findings shall be based on a preponderance of the evidence.

History of Fam §105.005: Acts 1995, 74th Leg., ch. 20, §1, eff. April 20, 1995. Source: Former Fam §11.15(a).

FAM §105.006. CONTENTS OF FINAL ORDER

A *Subsection (a) below is effective for SAPCRs filed on or after Sept. 1, 2001.*

(a) A final order, other than in a proceeding under Chapter 161 or 162, must contain:

Subsection (a) below is effective for SAPCRs filed before Sept. 1, 2001.

(a) A final order must contain:

(1) the social security number and driver's license number of each party to the suit, including the child, except that the child's social security number or driver's license number is not required if the child has not been assigned a social security number or driver's license number; and

(2) each party's current residence address, mailing address, home telephone number, name of employer, address of employment, and work telephone number, except as provided by Subsection (c).

(b) Except as provided by Subsection (c), the court shall order each party to inform each other party, the court that rendered the order, and the state case registry under Chapter 234 of an intended change in any of the information required by this section as long as any person, as a result of the order, is under an obligation to pay child support or is entitled to possession of or access to a child. The court shall order that notice of the intended change be given at the earlier of:

(1) the 60th day before the date the party intends to make the change; or

(2) the fifth day after the date that the party knew of the change, if the party did not know or could not have known of the change in sufficient time to comply with Subdivision (1).

(c) If a court finds after notice and hearing that requiring a party to provide the information required by this section to another party is likely to cause the child or a conservator harassment, abuse, serious harm, or injury, the court may:

(1) order the information not to be disclosed to another party; or

(2) render any other order the court considers necessary.

(d) An order in a suit that orders child support or possession of or access to a child must contain the following prominently displayed statement in boldfaced type, capital letters, or underlined:

"FAILURE TO OBEY A COURT ORDER FOR CHILD SUPPORT OR FOR POSSESSION OF OR ACCESS TO A CHILD MAY RESULT IN FURTHER LITIGATION TO ENFORCE THE ORDER, INCLUDING CONTEMPT OF COURT. A FINDING OF CONTEMPT MAY BE PUNISHED BY CONFINEMENT IN JAIL FOR UP TO SIX MONTHS, A FINE OF UP TO $500 FOR EACH VIOLATION, AND A MONEY JUDGMENT FOR PAYMENT OF ATTORNEY'S FEES AND COURT COSTS."

"FAILURE OF A PARTY TO MAKE A CHILD SUPPORT PAYMENT TO THE PLACE AND IN THE MANNER REQUIRED BY A COURT ORDER MAY RESULT IN THE PARTY NOT RECEIVING CREDIT FOR MAKING THE PAYMENT."

"FAILURE OF A PARTY TO PAY CHILD SUPPORT DOES NOT JUSTIFY DENYING THAT PARTY COURT-ORDERED POSSESSION OF OR ACCESS TO A CHILD. REFUSAL BY A PARTY TO ALLOW POSSESSION OF OR ACCESS TO A CHILD DOES NOT JUSTIFY FAILURE TO PAY COURT-ORDERED CHILD SUPPORT TO THAT PARTY."

(e) Except as provided by Subsection (c), an order in a suit that orders child support or possession of or access to a child must also contain the following prominently displayed statement in boldfaced type, capital letters, or underlined:

"EACH PERSON WHO IS A PARTY TO THIS ORDER IS ORDERED TO NOTIFY EACH OTHER PARTY, THE COURT, AND THE STATE CASE REGISTRY OF ANY CHANGE IN THE PARTY'S CURRENT RESIDENCE ADDRESS, MAILING ADDRESS, HOME TELEPHONE NUMBER, NAME OF EMPLOYER, ADDRESS OF EMPLOYMENT, DRIVER'S LICENSE NUMBER, AND WORK TELEPHONE NUMBER. THE PARTY IS ORDERED TO GIVE NOTICE OF AN INTENDED CHANGE IN ANY OF THE REQUIRED INFORMATION TO EACH OTHER PARTY, THE COURT, AND THE STATE CASE REGISTRY ON OR BEFORE THE 60TH DAY BEFORE THE INTENDED CHANGE. IF THE PARTY DOES NOT KNOW OR COULD NOT HAVE KNOWN OF THE CHANGE IN SUFFICIENT TIME TO PROVIDE 60-DAY NOTICE, THE PARTY IS ORDERED TO GIVE NOTICE OF THE CHANGE ON OR BEFORE THE FIFTH DAY AFTER THE DATE THAT THE PARTY KNOWS OF THE CHANGE.

"THE DUTY TO FURNISH THIS INFORMATION TO EACH OTHER PARTY, THE COURT, AND THE STATE CASE REGISTRY CONTINUES AS LONG AS ANY PERSON, BY VIRTUE OF THIS ORDER, IS UNDER AN OBLIGATION TO PAY CHILD SUPPORT OR ENTITLED TO POSSESSION OF OR ACCESS TO A CHILD.

"FAILURE BY A PARTY TO OBEY THE ORDER OF THIS COURT TO PROVIDE EACH OTHER PARTY, THE COURT, AND THE STATE CASE REGISTRY WITH THE CHANGE IN THE REQUIRED INFORMATION MAY RESULT IN FURTHER LITIGATION TO ENFORCE THE ORDER, INCLUDING CONTEMPT OF COURT. A FINDING OF CONTEMPT MAY BE PUNISHED BY CONFINEMENT IN JAIL FOR UP TO SIX MONTHS, A FINE OF UP TO $500 FOR EACH VIOLATION, AND A MONEY JUDGMENT FOR PAYMENT OF ATTORNEY'S FEES AND COURT COSTS."

(f) Except for an action in which contempt is sought, in any subsequent child support enforcement action, the court may, on a showing that diligent effort has been made to determine the location of a party, consider due process requirements for notice and service of process to be met with respect to that party on delivery of written notice to the most recent residential or employer address filed by that party with the court and the state case registry.

(g) The Title IV-D agency shall promulgate and provide forms for a party to use in reporting to the court and, when established, to the state case registry under Chapter 234 the information required under this section.

(h) The court may include in a final order in a suit in which a party to the suit makes an allegation of child abuse or neglect a finding on whether the party who made the allegation knew that the allegation was false. This finding shall not constitute collateral estoppel for any criminal proceeding. The court may impose on a party found to have made a false allegation of child abuse or neglect any civil sanction permitted under law, including attorney's fees, costs of experts, and any other costs.

History of Fam §105.006: Acts 1995, 74th Leg., ch. 20, §1, eff. April 20, 1995. Amended by Acts 1995, 74th Leg., ch. 751, §§13, 128, eff. Sept. 1, 1995; Acts 1997, 75th Leg., ch. 786, §1 (eff. Sept. 1, 1997), ch. 911, §6 (eff. Sept. 1, 1997); Acts 1999, 76th Leg., ch. 178, §5 (eff. Aug. 30, 1999), ch. 62, §19.01(21) (eff. Sept. 1, 1999); Acts 2001, 77th Leg., ch. 133, §1, eff. Sept. 1, 2001. Source: Former Fam §11.155.

FAM §105.007. COMPLIANCE WITH ORDER REQUIRING NOTICE OF CHANGE OF REQUIRED INFORMATION

(a) A party shall comply with the order by giving written notice to each other party of an intended change in the party's current residence address, mailing address, home telephone number, name of employer, address of employment, and work telephone number.

(b) The party must give written notice by registered or certified mail of an intended change in the required information to each other party on or before the 60th day before the change is made. If the party does not know or could not have known of the change in sufficient time to provide 60-day notice, the party shall provide the written notice of the change on or before the fifth day after the date that the party knew of the change.

(c) The court may waive the notice required by this section on motion by a party if it finds that the giving of notice of a change of the required information would be likely to expose the child or the party to harassment, abuse, serious harm, or injury.

History of Fam §105.007: Acts 1995, 74th Leg., ch. 20, §1, eff. April 20, 1995. Amended by Acts 1995, 74th Leg., ch. 751, §14, eff. Sept. 1, 1995. Source: Former Fam §14.045(a), (b).

FAM §105.008. RECORD OF SUPPORT ORDER FOR STATE CASE REGISTRY

(a) The clerk of the court shall provide the state case registry with a record of a court order for child support as required by procedures adopted under Section 234.003. The record of an order shall include information provided by the parties on a form developed by the Title IV-D agency. The form shall be completed by the petitioner and submitted to the clerk at the time the order is filed for record.

(b) To the extent federal funds are available, the Title IV-D agency shall reimburse the clerk of the court for the costs incurred in providing the record of support order required under this section.

History of Fam §105.008: Acts 1997, 75th Leg., ch. 911, §7, eff. Sept. 1, 1997.

FAM §105.009. PARENT EDUCATION & FAMILY STABILIZATION COURSE

(a) In a suit affecting the parent-child relationship, including an action to modify an order in a suit affecting the parent-child relationship providing for possession of or access to a child, the court may order the parties to the suit to attend a parent education and family stabilization course if the court determines that the order is in the best interest of the child.

(b) The parties to the suit may not be required to attend the course together. The court, on its own motion or the motion of either party, may prohibit the parties from taking the course together if there is a history of family violence in the marriage.

(c) A course under this section must be at least four hours, but not more than 12 hours, in length and be designed to educate and assist parents with regard to the consequences of divorce on parents and children. The course must include information on the following issues:

(1) the emotional effects of divorce on parents;

(2) the emotional and behavioral reactions to divorce by young children and adolescents;

(3) parenting issues relating to the concerns and needs of children at different development stages;

(4) stress indicators in young children and adolescents;

(5) conflict management;

(6) family stabilization through development of a coparenting relationship;

(7) the financial responsibilities of parenting;

(8) family violence, spousal abuse, and child abuse and neglect; and

(9) the availability of community services and resources.

(d) A course may not be designed to provide individual mental health therapy or individual legal advice.

(e) A course satisfies the requirements of this section if it is offered by:

(1) a mental health professional who has at least a master's degree with a background in family therapy or parent education; or

(2) a religious practitioner who performs counseling consistent with the laws of this state or another person designated as a program counselor by a church or religious institution if the litigant so chooses.

(f) Information obtained in a course or a statement made by a participant to a suit during a course may not be considered in the adjudication of the suit or in any subsequent legal proceeding. Any report that results from participation in the course may not become a record in the suit unless the parties stipulate to the record in writing.

(g) The court may take appropriate action with regard to a party who fails to attend or complete a course ordered by the court under this section, including holding the party in contempt of court, striking pleadings, or invoking any sanction provided by Rule 215, Texas Rules of Civil Procedure. The failure or refusal by a party to attend or complete a course required by this section may not delay the court from rendering a judgment in a suit affecting the parent-child relationship.

(h) The course required under this section may be completed by:

(1) personal instruction;

(2) videotape instruction;

(3) instruction through an electronic medium; or

(4) a combination of those methods.

(i) On completion of the course, the course provider shall issue a certificate of completion to each participant. The certificate must state:

(1) the name of the participant;

(2) the name of the course provider;

(3) the date the course was completed; and

(4) whether the course was provided by:

(A) personal instruction;

(B) videotape instruction;

(C) instruction through an electronic medium; or

(D) a combination of those methods.

(j) The county clerk in each county may establish a registry of course providers in the county and a list of locations at which courses are provided. The clerk shall include information in the registry identifying courses that are offered on a sliding fee scale or without charge.

(k) The court may not order the parties to a suit to attend a course under this section if the parties cannot afford to take the course. If the parties cannot afford to take a course, the court may direct the parties to a course that is offered on a sliding fee scale or without charge, if a course of that type is available. A party to a suit may not be required to pay more than $100 to attend a course ordered under this section.

(*l*) A person who has attended a course under this section may not be required to attend the course more than twice before the fifth anniversary of the date the person completes the course for the first time.

History of Fam §105.009: Acts 1999, 76th Leg., ch. 946, §1, eff. Sept. 1, 1999.

CHAPTER 106. COSTS & ATTORNEY'S FEES

§106.001 Costs
§106.002 Attorney's Fees

FAM §106.001. COSTS

The court may award costs in a suit or motion under this title and in a habeas corpus proceeding.

History of Fam §106.001: Acts 1995, 74th Leg., ch. 20, §1, eff. April 20, 1995. Amended by Acts 1997, 75th Leg., ch. 15, §1, eff. Sept. 1, 1997. Source: Former Fam §11.18(a).

Carlson v. Carlson, 983 S.W.2d 304, 308 (Tex. App.—Houston [1st Dist.] 1998, no pet.). "Under the Family Code, the award of costs and attorney's fees is within the discretion of the trial court."

Ex parte Williams, 866 S.W.2d 751, 753 (Tex. App.—Houston [1st Dist.] 1993, orig. proceeding). "'Costs' usually refer to fees and charges required by law to be paid to the courts or some of their officers, the amount of which is fixed by statute or the court's rules e.g. filing and service fees."

FAM §106.002. ATTORNEY'S FEES

(a) In a suit under this title, the court may order reasonable attorney's fees as costs and order the fees to be paid directly to an attorney.

(b) An award of attorney's fees may be enforced in the attorney's name by any means available for the enforcement of a judgment for debt.

History of Fam §106.002: Acts 1995, 74th Leg., ch. 20, §1, eff. April 20, 1995. Amended by Acts 1997, 75th Leg., ch. 15, §2, eff. Sept. 1, 1997. Source: Former Fam §§11.18(a), 11.22(j).

Author's Comment: "Suit is defined" as a SAPCR—habeas corpus is not a SAPCR. See Fam. Code §101.032.

Pletcher v. Goetz, 9 S.W.3d 442, 448 (Tex.App.—Fort Worth 1999, pet. denied). "The [F]amily [C]ode expressly provides for recovery of attorney's fees in two limited circumstances: (1) proceedings affecting the parent-child relationship and (2) post-divorce petitions to divide property."

Nordstrom v. Nordstrom, 965 S.W.2d 575, 583 (Tex. App.—Houston [1st Dist.] 1997, pet. denied). "The award of attorney's fees in a [SAPCR] is within the sound discretion of the trial court. Deciding which litigant is a 'successful party' is often a difficult task in family law cases. In some instances, attorney's fees may be awarded as costs even against the successful party if based on the best interest of the child."

Farish v. Farish, 921 S.W.2d 538, 546 (Tex.App.—Beaumont 1996, no writ). "In order to be entitled to a discretionary award of attorney's fees in a child support case, a party must file with the court an affirmative pleading requesting them unless the issue is waived or tried by consent."

Capellen v. Capellen, 888 S.W.2d 539, 545 (Tex. App.—El Paso 1994, writ denied). "In cases involving both the division of community property and the parent-child relationship, the court may, within its discretionary powers, award reasonable attorney's fees either as a part of a just and fair division of such property or as costs in the SAPCR proceeding, or may allocate the attorney's fees award between the two categories as the facts may warrant."

Sullivan v. Deguerin, Dickson & Szekely, 786 S.W.2d 59, 61 (Tex.App.—Houston [1st Dist.] 1990, no writ). "[A]n award of attorneys' fees is an issue severable from the remainder of a judgment in a [SAPCR]."

Billeaud v. Billeaud, 697 S.W.2d 652, 655 (Tex. App.—Houston [1st Dist.] 1985, no writ). "Since 1981, ... §11.18(a) [now §106.002] does not require a family court judgment to state good cause for adjudging costs against the successful party as is required in other civil cases. By deleting that portion of the statute which required costs to be assessed 'as in other civil cases,' the legislature recognized the difficulty of deciding, in family cases, which party is successful."

Havis v. Havis, 657 S.W.2d 921, 924 (Tex.App.—Corpus Christi 1983, writ dism'd). "The trial court is not bound by a jury finding as to attorney's fees under the Texas Family Code."

Autry v. Autry, 646 S.W.2d 586, 589 (Tex.App.—Tyler 1983, no writ). "Section 11.18(a) [now §106.002] does not create a new cause of action for attorney's fees."

Drexel v. McCutcheon, 604 S.W.2d 430, 435 (Tex. App.—Waco 1980, no writ). Under §11.18(a), now §106.002, "an award of attorney's fees for services rendered at the instance of the custodial parent in defending an action for change of custody may be allowed, even though the defense was unsuccessful, if the record properly establishes that the services of the attorney were necessary legal services rendered and performed for the benefit of the child."

CHAPTER 107. SPECIAL APPOINTMENTS & SOCIAL STUDIES

Subchapter A. Guardian Ad Litem Representation

Subchapter B. Attorney Ad Litem

Subchapter C. Other Court Appointments

Subchapter D. Social Study

SUBCHAPTER A. GUARDIAN AD LITEM REPRESENTATION

FAM §107.001. APPOINTMENT OF GUARDIAN AD LITEM

(a) In a suit in which termination of the parent-child relationship is requested, the court or an associate judge shall appoint a guardian ad litem to represent the interests of the child immediately after the filing of the petition but before the full adversary hearing to ensure adequate representation of the child, unless:

(1) the child is a petitioner;

(2) an attorney ad litem has been appointed for the child; or

(3) the court or an associate judge finds that the interests of the child will be represented adequately by a party to the suit and are not adverse to that party.

(b) In a suit filed by a governmental entity in which the entity requests the termination of the parent-child relationship or to be named conservator of a child, the court or an associate judge shall appoint a guardian ad litem to represent the best interests of the child immediately after the filing of the petition but before the full adversary hearing to ensure adequate representation of the child.

(c) In any other suit, the court or an associate judge may appoint a guardian ad litem.

(d) A guardian ad litem appointed under this section may be an attorney, a volunteer advocate appointed under Section 107.031, or another adult having the competence, training, and expertise determined by the court to be sufficient to represent the best interests of the child.

(e) The managing conservator may be appointed guardian ad litem if the managing conservator:

(1) is not a parent of the child or a person petitioning for adoption of the child; and

(2) has no personal interest in the suit.

(f) A guardian ad litem shall be appointed to represent any other person entitled to service of citation under this code if the person is incompetent or a child, unless the person has executed an affidavit of relinquishment of parental rights or an affidavit of waiver of interest in child containing a waiver of service of citation.

History of Fam §107.001: Acts 1995, 74th Leg., ch. 20, §1, eff. April 20, 1995. Amended by Acts 1995, 74th Leg., ch. 751, §15, eff. Sept. 1, 1995; Acts 1997, 75th Leg., ch. 1294, §1, eff. Sept. 1, 1997. Source: Former Fam §11.10(a), (b)(1).

In re M.D.S., 1 S.W.3d 190, 195 (Tex.App.—Amarillo 1999, no pet.). "The provisions of §107.001(a) are mandatory. A trial court's failure to comply with §107.001(a) is reversible error and cannot be treated as harmless because of the serious nature of termination proceedings. *At 196:* [I]n the absence of proof or a record specifying otherwise, when the trial court's judgment or its findings of fact in support of the judgment contain the finding that no guardian ad litem or attorney ad litem was necessary because a party to the suit adequately represented the interests of the child and their interests were not adverse, the trial court complied with the mandatory provisions of §107.001(a)."

Ray v. Burns, 832 S.W.2d 431, 435 (Tex.App.—Waco 1992, no writ). "Appointment of a guardian ad litem is not required ... when termination of parental rights is not involved."

Pleasant Hills Children's Home, Inc. v. Nida, 596 S.W.2d 947, 951 (Tex.App.—Fort Worth 1980, no writ). "The guardian ad litem contemplated by §11.10(a) [now §107.001] is intended to represent the interests of minor children with respect to the termination of their parent-child relationship, and no more. ... A guardian can (1) prosecute an appeal from the trial court in which the guardian was appointed, (2) remove, under the proper circumstances, a suit to federal court from state court, and (3) initiate an extraordinary proceeding, such as a writ of mandamus or prohibition, on behalf of a minor for whom the guardian ad litem was appointed to represent. However, none of these actions involve the institution of a new lawsuit, in a different court, grounded on an independent cause of action."

FAM §107.002. POWERS & DUTIES OF GUARDIAN AD LITEM

(a) A guardian ad litem appointed under this subchapter is not a party to the suit but may:

(1) conduct an investigation to the extent that the guardian ad litem considers necessary to determine the best interest of the child for whom the guardian is appointed; and

(2) obtain and review copies of the child's relevant medical, psychological, and school records.

(b) A guardian ad litem appointed under this subchapter shall, within a reasonable time after the appointment, interview:

(1) the child, if the child is four years of age or older; and

(2) each individual that the guardian ad litem considers likely to have significant knowledge of the child's history and condition.

(c) A guardian ad litem appointed under this subchapter is not a party to the suit but is entitled to:

(1) receive a copy of each pleading or other paper filed with the court in the case in which the guardian ad litem is appointed;

(2) receive notice of each hearing in the case;

(3) participate in case staffings by an authorized agency concerning the child;

(4) attend all legal proceedings in the case but may not call or question a witness unless the ad litem is a licensed attorney;

(5) review and sign or decline to sign any agreed order affecting the child; and

(6) testify in court, except as provided by Subsection (d), regarding the recommendations concerning the actions that the guardian ad litem considers to be in the best interest of the child, including giving reasons for the guardian ad litem's opposition if the guardian ad litem does not agree to the terms of a proposed order.

(d) An attorney who is appointed as attorney ad litem and guardian ad litem for a child may not testify under Subsection (c)(6).

(e) An attorney who is appointed as attorney ad litem and guardian ad litem for a child shall:

(1) become familiar with the American Bar Association's standards of practice for lawyers who represent children in abuse and neglect cases; and

(2) comply with the requirements of the Texas Disciplinary Rules of Professional Conduct.

(f) An attorney who is appointed as attorney ad litem and guardian ad litem for a child and who determines that a conflict exists by performing both roles shall:

(1) withdraw as the child's guardian ad litem;

(2) continue to serve as the child's attorney ad litem; and

(3) request appointment of a new guardian ad litem for the child without revealing the reason a new appointment is required.

History of Fam §107.002: Acts 1995, 74th Leg., ch. 20, §1, eff. Sept. 1, 1995. Amended by Acts 1995, 74th Leg., ch. 943, §10, eff. Sept. 1, 1995; Acts 1997, 75th Leg., ch. 1294, §2, eff. Sept. 1, 1997.

FAM §107.003. IMMUNITY

(a) A guardian ad litem appointed under this subchapter is not liable for civil damages arising from a recommendation made or an opinion given in the capacity of guardian ad litem.

(b) Subsection (a) does not apply to a recommendation or opinion that is:

(1) wilfully wrongful;

(2) given with conscious indifference or reckless disregard to the safety of another;

(3) given in bad faith or with malice; or

(4) grossly negligent.

History of Fam §107.003: Acts 1997, 75th Leg., ch. 1294, §3, eff. Sept. 1, 1997.

History of Former Fam §107.003: Acts 1995, 74th Leg., ch. 20, §1, eff. April 20, 1995. Renumbered as §107.015 by Acts 1995, 74th Leg., ch. 75, §15, eff. Sept. 1, 1995.

Delcourt v. Silverman, 919 S.W.2d 777, 781 (Tex. App.—Houston [14th Dist.] 1996, writ denied). "When judges delegate their authority or appoint others to perform services for the court, the judicial immunity that attaches to the judge may follow the delegation or appointment. *At 786:* Based upon our review of the available case law, we hold that a guardian ad litem appointed under §11.10 [now §107.001] is absolutely immune from liability for his or her actions taken pursuant to and within the scope of their appointment, provided that the appointment contemplates the ad litem acting as an extension of the court. [¶] To be entitled to summary judgment in this case, [guardian ad litem] had to prove as a matter of law that: (1) the appointment contemplated she act as an extension or arm of the court; and (2) she did not depart from the scope of the appointment."

FAM §§107.004, 107.005. RENUMBERED

Renumbered as §§107.031 & 107.051 by Acts 1995, 74th Leg., ch. 751, §15, eff. Sept. 1, 1995.

FAM §107.006. GUARDIAN AD LITEM & ATTORNEY AD LITEM POOL; QUALIFICATIONS

(a) The local administrative district judge in each county in a Department of Protective and Regulatory Services region for child protective services that contains a county having a population of 2.8 million or more shall establish a pool from which guardians ad litem and attorneys ad litem are appointed for proceedings in the district courts of the county. A local administrative district judge in any other county may establish a pool from which guardians ad litem and attorneys ad litem are appointed for proceedings in the district courts of that county. To be eligible for a pool established under this subsection, a person must:

(1) complete training approved by the State Bar of Texas in family law and the responsibilities of ad litems;

(2) complete as part of the person's annual continuing legal education requirement not fewer than three hours in family law issues; and

(3) meet other requirements established by the local administrative district judge.

(b) Before appointment as a guardian ad litem or an attorney ad litem, the person must have read, acknowledged by signing, and filed with the local administrative judge a written statement prepared by the local administrative district judge that lists the responsibilities of an ad litem, some or all of which may be appropriate to the person's specific case. The court shall retain a copy of the acknowledgment for two years. To continue to receive appointments under this section, the person must execute a new statement at least every two years.

(c) A party to a proceeding in which a person is appointed as a guardian ad litem or an attorney ad litem may object to appointment of the person at any time before the date of the trial of the proceeding. A party may object under this subsection by filing a written motion stating the grounds and facts on which the party believes that the person appointed lacks objectivity or is failing to fulfill the person's responsibilities as an ad litem as outlined in the written statement of ad litem responsibilities. The court shall promptly rule on an objection raised under this subsection and shall order the removal of the guardian ad litem or attorney ad litem if the court finds that the objection is justifiable.

(d) A person appointed as a guardian ad litem or attorney ad litem shall complete and submit to the court a voucher or claim for payment that includes the fees charged and hours worked by the ad litem. Information submitted under this section is subject to disclosure under Chapter 552, Government Code.

(e) The Bureau of Vital Statistics may compile information submitted under Subsection (d) for a county that maintains that information on an electronic database. On the request of the bureau, the county shall provide the information. Information compiled by the bureau under this section shall be made available to the Department of Protective and Regulatory Services.

History of Fam §107.006: Acts 1995, 74th Leg., ch. 943, §11, eff. Sept. 1, 1995. Amended by Acts 1997, 75th Leg., ch. 1294, §4, eff. Sept. 1, 1997.

Gonzalez v. Gonzalez, 26 S.W.3d 657, 659 (Tex. App.—San Antonio 2000, no pet.). "While §107.006(c) authorizes an ad litem's removal, it also makes clear that such removal is strictly within the discretion of the trial court."

Sections 107.007-107.010 reserved for expansion

SUBCHAPTER B. ATTORNEY AD LITEM

FAM §107.011. DISCRETIONARY APPOINTMENT OF ATTORNEY AD LITEM

(a) An associate judge shall recommend the appointment of an attorney ad litem for any party in a case in which the associate judge deems representation necessary to protect the interests of the child who is the subject matter of the suit.

(b) The court shall appoint an attorney ad litem for any party in a case in which the court deems representation necessary to protect the interests of the child who is the subject matter of the suit.

History of Fam §107.011: Acts 1995, 74th Leg., ch. 20, §1, eff. April 20, 1995. Renumbered from §107.002(a), (b) by Acts 1995, 74th Leg., ch. 751, §15, eff. Sept. 1, 1995. Source: Former Fam §11.10(b)(2), (c).

Samara v. Samara, 52 S.W.3d 455, 457-58 (Tex. App.—Houston [1st Dist.] 2001, pet. denied). "The judge's order allowing [guardian ad litem] to hire [an attorney] had the same effect as if the judge had appointed [an attorney] to represent the children. No statute expressly allows a judge to appoint an attorney for a guardian ad litem. Moreover, courts do not have inherent power to do so. If [guardian ad litem] needed legal advice to protect the children's interests, she should have consulted ... the attorney ad litem. If dissatisfied with [attorney ad litem], [guardian ad litem] should have requested a different attorney ad litem or resigned and requested the judge to appoint an attorney as guardian ad litem."

Gonzalez v. Gonzalez, 26 S.W.3d 657, 658 (Tex. App.—San Antonio 2000, no pet.). "While §107.011(b) does not specifically authorize the trial court to appoint an attorney ad litem without a hearing, it certainly does not require the trial court to conduct a hearing. We have been unable to locate a single case, published or unpublished, interpreting §107.011(b) to require an evidentiary hearing before an attorney ad litem can be appointed. [¶] Following the rules of strict statutory construction, we must assume that if a hearing was necessary under §107.011(b) to protect the interests of the parties, the family code would have required it."

L.P.D. v. R.C, 959 S.W.2d 728, 731 (Tex.App.—Austin 1998, pet. denied). "When there is no person before the court who has had care and custody of the child, or understands the child's interests through another relationship, or even professes to have met the child, we hold the presumption that the party bringing suit will adequately represent the child's interest has been rebutted as a matter of law. There was simply no party present at this proceeding who could satisfy the Family Code's concern that the interests of the child would be adequately represented. We therefore hold that the trial court abused its discretion in not ordering an attorney ad litem to represent the child's interests."

FAM §107.012. MANDATORY APPOINTMENT OF ATTORNEY AD LITEM FOR CHILD

In a suit filed by a governmental entity requesting termination of the parent-child relationship or to be named conservator of a child, the court shall appoint an attorney ad litem to represent the interests of the child immediately after the filing, but before the full adversary hearing, to ensure adequate representation of the child.

History of Fam §107.012: Acts 1995, 74th Leg., ch. 20, §1. Renumbered from §107.002(c) by Acts 1995, 74th Leg., ch. 751, §15, eff. Sept. 1, 1995. Source: Former Fam §11.10(d).

FAM §107.013. MANDATORY APPOINTMENT OF ATTORNEY AD LITEM FOR PARENT

(a) In a suit in which termination of the parent-child relationship is requested, the court shall appoint an attorney ad litem to represent the interests of:

(1) an indigent parent of the child who responds in opposition to the termination;

(2) a parent served by citation by publication;

A *Subsections (3) & (4) below are effective for motions or other requests for relief made in parentage or paternity proceedings commenced on or after June 14, 2001.*

(3) an alleged father who failed to register with the registry under Chapter 160 and whose identity or location is unknown; and

(4) an alleged father who registered with the paternity registry under Chapter 160, but the petitioner's attempt to personally serve citation at the address provided to the registry and at any other address for the alleged father known by the petitioner has been unsuccessful.

Subsections (3) & (4) below are effective for motions or other requests for relief made in parentage or paternity proceedings commenced before June 14, 2001.

(3) an alleged father who failed to register with the registry under Subchapter D, Chapter 160, and whose identity or location is unknown; and

(4) an alleged father who registered with the paternity registry under Subchapter D, Chapter 160, but the petitioner's attempt to personally serve citation at the address provided to the registry and at any other address for the alleged father known by the petitioner has been unsuccessful.

(b) If both parents of the child are entitled to the appointment of an attorney ad litem under this section and the court finds that the interests of the parents are not in conflict, the court may appoint a single attorney ad litem to represent the interests of both parents.

History of Fam §107.013: Acts 1995, 74th Leg., ch. 20, §1, eff. April 20, 1995. Renumbered from §107.002(d) by Acts 1995, 74th Leg., ch. 751, §15, eff. Sept. 1, 1995. Amended by Acts 1997, 75th Leg., ch. 561, §3, eff. Sept. 1, 1997; Acts 2001, 77th Leg., ch. 821, §2.11, eff. June 14, 2001. Source: Former Fam §11.10(d).

In re R.D.Y., 51 S.W.3d 314, 325 (Tex.App.—Houston [1st Dist.] 2001, pet. denied). "The fact that Mother is presently receiving a governmental entitlement based upon indigency is prima facie evidence that Mother is indigent."

In re M.J.M.L., 31 S.W.3d 347, 354 (Tex.App.—San Antonio 2000, pet. denied). "Complete failure of a trial court to appoint counsel for indigent parents constitutes reversible error. However, the Legislature did not set forth any time frame or procedure by which trial courts must appoint counsel. [¶] While we recognize that involuntary termination of parental rights statutes must be strictly construed in favor of parents, it is a well established canon of statutory construction that every word excluded from a statute is presumed to be excluded for a purpose. The more open-ended language of §107.013(a)(1) directly contrasts with [Family Code §107.012] which mandates the appointment of an attorney ad litem for children involved in termination proceedings 'immediately after the filing [of the suit], but before the full adversary hearing.' Presumably, if the Legislature wished to impose a similar deadline for appointment of counsel for indigent parents, it would have done so. We decline to read such a deadline into the statute. The appointment of counsel six months after the case began was not in itself a violation of §107.013(a)(1)." *See also* ***In re J.R.P.***, 55 S.W.2d 147, 150 (Tex.App.—Corpus Christi 2001, pet. denied).

In re T.V., 8 S.W.3d 448, 449 (Tex.App.—Waco 1999, no pet.). "The statute regarding appointment of counsel for indigent parents does not expressly provide for representation on appeal. However, we believe the rights would not be adequately protected if an indigent parent, whose parental rights were in jeopardy of being terminated, was required to pursue an appeal without an attorney."

Ybarra v. Texas DHS, 869 S.W.2d 574, 580 (Tex. App.—Corpus Christi 1993, no writ). "Indigent parents are entitled to appointed counsel in termination proceedings under the terms of the Family Code. The Code does not specify any particular procedure for obtaining counsel under that section. However, the trial court did not err in failing to appoint counsel under these circumstances: [parent] did not request appointed counsel and was represented by retained counsel at trial."

FAM §107.0135. APPOINTMENT OF ATTORNEY AD LITEM NOT REQUIRED; CERTAIN CASES

A court is not required to appoint an attorney ad litem in a proceeding in which:

(1) a suit for the dissolution of a marriage is uncontested; or

(2) the issues of possession of and access to a child are agreed to by both parents.

History of Fam §107.0135: Acts 1997, 75th Leg., ch. 1294, §5, eff. Sept. 1, 1997. Amended by Acts 1999, 76th Leg., ch. 1390, §4 (eff. Sept. 1, 1999), ch. 62, §6.15 (eff. Sept. 1, 1999). Source: Former Fam §107.002(e).

FAM §107.014. POWERS & DUTIES OF ATTORNEY AD LITEM FOR CHILD

(a) An attorney ad litem appointed under this subchapter to represent a child:

(1) shall investigate to the extent the attorney ad litem considers appropriate to determine the facts of the case;

(2) shall obtain and review copies of all of the child's relevant medical, psychological, and school records;

(3) may call, examine, or cross-examine witnesses; and

(4) shall become familiar with the American Bar Association's standards of practice for lawyers who represent children in abuse and neglect cases.

(b) An attorney ad litem appointed to represent a child shall within a reasonable time after the appointment:

(1) interview the child if the child is four years of age or older;

(2) interview individuals with significant knowledge of the child's history and condition, including the child's foster parents; and

(3) interview all parties to the suit.

History of Fam §107.014: Acts 1995, 74th Leg., ch. 751, §15, eff. Sept. 1, 1995. Amended by Acts 1997, 75th Leg., ch. 650, §1, eff. Sept. 1, 1997; Acts 1999, 76th Leg., ch. 1390, §5 (eff. Sept. 1, 1999), ch. 1515, §1 (eff. Sept. 1, 1999).

In re AWT, 61 S.W.3d 87, 88 (Tex.App.—Amarillo 2001, no pet.). We address whether "appellate counsel may file an ***Anders*** brief in a civil proceeding. Historically, the use of such briefs have been limited to appeals arising from criminal convictions. [¶] The rationale underlying ***Anders*** is no less applicable to a civil matter in which counsel has been appointed to represent the appellant. Counsel remains obligated to zealously pursue the rights and interests of his client. Yet, that obligation does not include the task of arguing the frivolous. Indeed, to press a frivolous appeal would be to violate not only rules of discipline applicable to attorneys, but also the rules of appellate procedure. To strike a balance between these competing duties, we see no reason why the procedure utilized in ***Anders v. California*** and its progeny should not be available to appointed counsel faced with the prospect of conducting a meritless appeal, irrespective of whether the appeal involves a criminal or civil matter." *See also* ***In re E.L.Y.***, 69 S.W.3d 838, 841 (Tex.App.—Waco 2002, n.p.h.).

Author's Comment: An Anders brief allows appointed counsel to withdraw from an appeal that counsel believes is frivolous. ***In re D.A.S.***, 973 S.W.2d 296, 297 (Tex.1998). Before requesting permission to withdraw, counsel must master the trial record, thoroughly research the law, and exercise judgment in identifying the arguments that may be advanced on appeal. *Id.* If, after a conscientious review of the record, counsel concludes that the case is wholly frivolous, he or she may so advise the court of appeals and request permission to withdraw. *Id.* To make such a request, counsel must file a brief with the court referring to anything in the record that might arguably support the appeal. *Id.*

In re D.L.B., 943 S.W.2d 175, 180 (Tex.App.—San Antonio 1997, no writ). "We do not support [parents'] position that an attorney ad litem is required to choose a position to advocate, even when unable to determine what the child's wishes are. We also do not agree that where the potential adoptive parents are also the managing conservators of the child, the attorney ad litem is required to advocate a position based on the direction of the legal guardians of the child. This would obviously result in a unfair advantage to the managing conservators. ... If, however, the attorney ad litem is able to determine a clear position that should be taken for the child, that position should be advocated."

FAM §107.015. ATTORNEY AD LITEM FEES

(a) An attorney appointed to represent a child or parent as authorized by this subchapter is entitled to reasonable fees and expenses in the amount set by the court to be paid by the parents of the child unless the parents are indigent.

(b) If the court or associate judge determines that one or more of the parties are able to defray the costs of an attorney ad litem's fees and expenses as determined by the reasonable and customary fees for similar services in the county of jurisdiction, the fees and expenses may be ordered paid by one or more of those parties, or the court or associate judge may order one or more of those parties, prior to final hearing, to pay the sums into the registry of the court or into an account authorized by the court for the use and benefit of the attorney ad litem on order of the court. The sums may be taxed as costs to be assessed against one or more of the parties.

(c) If indigency of the parents is shown, an attorney appointed to represent a child or parent in a suit to terminate the parent-child relationship shall be paid from the general funds of the county according to the fee schedule that applies to an attorney appointed to represent a child in a suit under Title 3 as provided by Chapter 51. The court may not award attorney ad litem fees under this chapter against the state, a state agency, or a political subdivision of the state except as provided by this subsection.

History of Fam §107.015: Acts 1995, 74th Leg., ch. 20, §1. Renumbered from §107.003 by Acts 1995, 74th Leg., ch. 751, §15, eff. Sept. 1, 1995. Amended by Acts 1999, 76th Leg., ch. 1390, §6, eff. Sept. 1, 1999. Source: Former Fam §11.10(a), (e).

Brownsville-Valley Reg'l Med. Ctr., Inc. v. Gamez, 894 S.W.2d 753, 754 (Tex.1995). We hold that "it is an abuse of discretion for a trial court to award ad litem fees for services performed after resolution of the conflict of interest which gave rise to the appointment."

In re R.D.Y., 51 S.W.3d 314, 325 (Tex.App.—Houston [1st Dist.] 2001, pet. denied). See Annotation in FAM §107.013.

Gonzalez v. Gonzalez, 26 S.W.3d 657, 659 (Tex. App.—San Antonio 2000, no pet.). Father "contends that the trial court erred in awarding attorney ad litem fees without submitting the issue to the jury. *At 660:* Because [§107.015] expressly provides that the trial court shall set the amount of attorney ad litem fees, the trial court did not err in refusing to submit the issue of ad litem fees to the jury."

Harris Cty. Children Protective Servs. v. Richker, 2 S.W.3d 741, 743 (Tex.App.—Houston [14th Dist.] 1999, no pet.). "Generally, the State of Texas and its agencies cannot be liable for damages absent legislative consent to sue the state. This rule has been applied to preclude liability for attorney fees. Any waiver of sovereign immunity must be by clear and unambiguous language. [¶] [Section 107.015(a)] clearly waives immunity for the county. [¶] The next issue, then, is whether HCCPS is an arm of the county. *At 744:* We hold that HCCPS is an arm of the state and not the county, and therefore, §107.015(c) ... is not a clear waiver of immunity as to HCCPS."

In re Texas DPRS, 990 S.W.2d 848, 851 (Tex.App.—Amarillo 1999, orig. proceeding). Section 107.015(b) is "an instruction as to the manner by which the trial court can direct the non-indigent parent or parents to pay ad litem fees it assesses. Viewed in that light, it authorizes the trial court to assess the fees against one or both parents and to order the payment of the fees prior to final hearing into the registry of the court or into an account authorized by the court or it may defer payment of the fees until the final hearing."

Moore v. Moore, 898 S.W.2d 355, 359 (Tex.App.—San Antonio 1995, no writ). "An attorney appointed to represent a child or parent is authorized ... to be entitled to a reasonable fee in an amount set by the court. This fee is to be assessed against one or more of the parties, especially if they are the parents of the child, unless the parents are indigent. The award of attorney's fees to the attorney ad litem in responding to this appeal is within the trial court's discretion."

FAM §107.016. CONTINUED REPRESENTATION

In a suit brought by a governmental entity seeking termination of the parent-child relationship or appointment of the entity as conservator of the child, an order appointing the Department of Protective and Regulatory Services as the child's managing conservator may provide for the continuation of the attorney ad litem appointment for the child for any period set by the court.

History of Fam §107.016: Acts 1995, 74th Leg., ch. 751, §15, eff. Sept. 1, 1995. Amended by Acts 1997, 75th Leg., ch. 575, §6, eff. Sept. 1, 1997.

Sections 107.017-107.030 reserved for expansion

SUBCHAPTER C. OTHER COURT APPOINTMENTS

FAM §107.031. VOLUNTEER ADVOCATES

(a) In a suit filed by a governmental entity, the court may appoint a person who has received the court's approved training and who has been certified by the court to appear at court hearings as a volunteer advocate on behalf of the child.

(b) In addition, the court may appoint a group of court-certified volunteers to serve as an administrative review board to advise the court as to the conservatorship appointment and the placement of the child by the Department of Protective and Regulatory Services or authorized agency in substitute care.

(c) A court-appointed volunteer, a board member or employee of a volunteer advocate charitable organization, or a member of an administrative review board is not liable for civil damages for a recommendation made or opinion rendered while serving or having served as a court-appointed volunteer, board member or employee of a volunteer advocate charitable organization, or member of an administrative review board under this section unless the act or failure to act is wilfully wrongful, committed with conscious indifference or reckless disregard for the safety of another, committed in bad faith or with malice, or is grossly negligent.

(d) This section does not prohibit the court from appointing as a guardian ad litem for a child under Section 107.001 a court-certified volunteer advocate appointed for the child under this section.

(e) A court-certified volunteer advocate appointed under this section for a child with a disability may be assigned to act as a surrogate parent for the child, as provided by 20 U.S.C. Section 1415(b) and its subsequent amendments, if:

(1) the child is in the conservatorship of the Department of Protective and Regulatory Services;

(2) the volunteer advocate is serving as guardian ad litem for the child; and

(3) a foster parent of the child is not acting as the child's parent under Section 29.015, Education Code.

History of Fam §107.031: Acts 1995, 74th Leg., ch. 20, §1, eff. April 20, 1995. Renumbered from §107.004 by Acts 1995, 74th Leg., ch. 751, §15, eff. Sept. 1, 1995. Amended by Acts 1997, 75th Leg., ch. 1294, §6, eff. Sept. 1, 1997; Acts 1999, 76th Leg., ch. 430, §3, eff. Sept. 1, 1999. Source: Former Fam §11.101.

Sections 107.032-107.050 reserved for expansion

SUBCHAPTER D. SOCIAL STUDY

FAM §107.051. ORDER FOR SOCIAL STUDY

(a) The court may order the preparation of a social study into the circumstances and condition of the child and of the home of any person requesting managing conservatorship or possession of the child.

A *Subsection (b) below is effective for SAPCRs filed on or after Sept. 1, 2001.*

(b) The social study may be made by a private entity, a person appointed by the court, or a state agency, including the Department of Protective and Regulatory Services if the department is a party to the suit.

Subsection (b) below is effective for SAPCRs filed before Sept. 1, 2001.

(b) The social study may be made by a state agency, including the Department of Protective and Regulatory Services, or a person appointed by the court.

A (c) In a suit in which adoption is requested or possession of or access to the child is an issue and in which the Department of Protective and Regulatory Services is not a party, the court shall appoint a private agency or another person, including a domestic relations office, to conduct the social study.

History of Fam §107.051: Acts 1995, 74th Leg., ch. 20, §1, eff. April 20, 1995. Renumbered from §107.005(a), (b) by Acts 1995, 74th Leg., ch. 751, §15, eff. Sept. 1, 1995. Amended by Acts 1999, 76th Leg., ch. 1390, §7, eff. Sept. 1, 1999; Acts 2001, 77th Leg., ch. 488, §1 (eff. June 11, 2001), ch. 133, §2 (eff. Sept. 1, 2001). Source: Former Fam §11.12(a), (b).

See also 40 TAC §§700.1715, 725.6052.

Chacon v. Chacon, 978 S.W.2d 633, 637-38 (Tex. App.—El Paso 1998, no pet.). "Generally speaking, the purpose of a social study is to interview the litigants and those individuals with knowledge of relevant facts, such as extended family members, neighbors, scout leaders, teachers, baby sitters, day-care providers, doctors, sports coaches, and other individuals who have had the opportunity to observe the parenting abilities of the litigants, the relationship between the child and the parents, the living arrangements at both households, and the plans each litigant has adopted for the day-to-day caretaking of the child. It is designed to be comparative in nature, that is to compare the circumstances and conditions of all individuals seeking managing conservatorship or possession of a child, and to make recommendations to the court regarding the best interest of the child. The Family Code does not detail the individuals to be interviewed nor the issues to be covered by the report for the simple reason that the relevant facts to be developed will largely depend on the disputed issues and the theory or theories which will be litigated. Further, because the trial court has great discretion in determining the overriding best interest of the child, the Legislature has deferred the development of appropriate standards and criteria to either the appropriate state agency or to the court itself."

Bott v. Bott, 962 S.W.2d 626, 630 (Tex.App.—Houston [14th Dist.] 1997, no pet.). Section 107.051 "vests the trial court with discretion to order a social study. [¶] Given the discretionary nature of ordering a social study, we find that waiver will … result where a party does not request an updated social study or object to the trial court's failure to order one."

Wimpey v. Wimpey, 662 S.W.2d 680, 682 (Tex. App.—Dallas 1983, no writ). "[W]e must determine whether the social study made in this case could be considered in its entirety by the judge in determining the child's best interest. We hold that the social study can be so considered. [¶] We are not to be understood as holding that the social study is binding on the trial judge but rather we are holding that the judge, in his discretion, may consider the study. Neither do we hold that a party or the judge cannot challenge the accuracy of the information contained in the social study."

FAM §107.0511. PRE-ADOPTIVE HOME SCREENING

E *Section 107.0511 below is effective for SAPCRs filed on or after Sept. 1, 2001.*

(a) In this section, "department" means the Department of Protective and Regulatory Services.

(b) A pre-adoptive home screening shall be conducted as provided by this section to evaluate each party in a proceeding described by Subsection (c) who requests termination of the parent-child relationship or an adoption.

(c) Except for a suit brought by a licensed child-placing agency or the department, the home screening under this section shall be filed in any suit for:

(1) termination of the parent-child relationship in which a person other than a parent may be appointed managing conservator of a child; or

(2) an adoption.

(d) Other than in a suit in which a licensed child-placing agency or the department is appointed managing conservator of the child, the home screening under this section must be filed with the court before the court may sign the final order for termination of the parent-child relationship.

(e) The costs of a home screening in a suit for adoption under this section shall be paid by the prospective adoptive parent.

(f) Unless otherwise agreed to by the court, the home screening under this section must comply with the minimum requirements for the screening under rules adopted by the Board of Protective and Regulatory Services.

(g) In a stepparent adoption, the pre-adoptive home screening under this section and the post-placement adoptive report under Section 107.052 may be combined.

History of Fam §107.0511: Enacted by Acts 2001, 77th Leg., ch. 133, §3, eff. Sept. 1, 2001.

See also 40 TAC §§725.6070-725.6072.

FAM §107.052. POST-PLACEMENT ADOPTIVE REPORT

A *Section 107.052 below is effective for SAPCRs filed on or after Sept. 1, 2001.*

(a) In a proceeding in which a pre-adoptive home screening is required by Section 107.0511 for an adoption, a post-placement adoptive report must be conducted and filed with the court before the court may render a final order in the adoption.

(b) Unless otherwise agreed to by the court, the post-placement adoptive report must comply with the minimum requirements for the report under rules adopted by the Board of Protective and Regulatory Services.

(c) Deleted by Acts 2001, 77th Leg., ch. 133, §4, eff. Sept. 1, 2001.

History of Fam §107.052: Acts 1995, 74th Leg., ch. 20, §1, eff. April 20, 1995. Renumbered from §107.005(c)-(e) by Acts 1995, 74th Leg., ch. 751, §15, eff. Sept. 1, 1995. Amended by Acts 2001, 77th Leg., ch. 133, §4, eff. Sept. 1, 2001. Source: Former Fam §11.12(b).

FAM §107.052. STANDARDS FOR CONDUCTING SOCIAL STUDY

Section 107.052 below is effective for SAPCRs filed before Sept. 1, 2001.

(a) The court may appoint an investigator to conduct the social study required by this section who has the qualifications established by the rules of the Department of Protective and Regulatory Services providing minimum qualifications for persons who may conduct social studies. If the Department of Protective and Regulatory Services or another governmental entity is appointed, the person who conducts the investigation and makes the report must also have those qualifications.

(b) A study made under this section shall comply with the rules of the Department of Protective and Regulatory Services establishing minimum standards, guidelines, and procedures for social studies or the criteria established by the court.

(c) The social study shall contain any history of physical, sexual, or emotional abuse suffered by the child.

FAM §107.053. PROSPECTIVE ADOPTIVE PARENTS TO RECEIVE COPY

In all adoptions a copy of the report shall be made available to the prospective adoptive parents prior to a final order of adoption.

History of Fam §107.053: Acts 1995, 74th Leg., ch. 20, §1, eff. April 20, 1995. Renumbered from §107.005(g) by Acts 1995, 74th Leg., ch. 751, §15, eff. Sept. 1, 1995. Source: Former Fam §11.12(b).

FAM §107.054. REPORT FILED WITH COURT

The agency or person making the social study shall file with the court on a date set by the court a report containing its findings and conclusions. The report shall be made a part of the record of the suit.

History of Fam §107.054: Acts 1995, 74th Leg., ch. 20, §1, eff. April 20, 1995. Renumbered from §107.005(h) by Acts 1995, 74th Leg., ch. 751, §15, eff. Sept. 1, 1995. Source: Former Fam §11.12(c).

See also 40 TAC §§700.1715, 725.6052.

Chacon v. Chacon, 978 S.W.2d 633, 636 (Tex. App.—El Paso 1998, no pet.). "The social study is to be made a part of the record in every case and need not be tendered into evidence."

FAM §107.055. INTRODUCTION OF REPORT AT TRIAL

(a) Disclosure to the jury of the contents of a report to the court of a social study is subject to the rules of evidence.

(b) In a contested case, the agency or person making the social study shall furnish copies of the report to the attorneys for the parties before the earlier of:

(1) the seventh day after the date the social study is completed; or

(2) the fifth day before the date of commencement of the trial.

(c) The court may compel the attendance of witnesses necessary for the proper disposition of the suit, including a representative of the agency making the social study, who may be compelled to testify.

History of Fam §107.055: Acts 1995, 74th Leg., ch. 20, §1, eff. April 20, 1995. Renumbered from §107.005(i)-(k) by Acts 1995, 74th Leg., ch. 751, §15, eff. Sept. 1, 1995. Source: Former Fam §§11.12(c), 11.14(c).

See also 40 TAC §§700.1715, 725.6052.

Chacon v. Chacon, 978 S.W.2d 633, 636 (Tex. App.—El Paso 1998, no pet.). "Both the statute and the case law interpreting it distinguish between a bench trial and a jury trial with regard to the use of a social study. The social study is to be made a part of the record in every case and need not be tendered into evidence. Thus, in a bench trial, the court may consider the report regardless of whether it is formally introduced into evidence. A party is entitled to call as a witness the author of the report to attack the accuracy of the information included or the conclusions drawn therefrom. However, the Legislature never intended that the trial court *sua sponte* require the author's attendance at the hearing. Only in a jury trial do the traditional rules of evidence apply."

FAM §107.056. PREPARATION FEE

If the court orders a social study to be conducted and a report to be prepared, the court shall award the agency or other person a reasonable fee for the preparation of the study that shall be taxed as costs and paid directly to the agency or other person. The person or agency may enforce the order for the fee.

History of Fam §107.056: Acts 1995, 74th Leg., ch. 20, §1, eff. April 20, 1995. Renumbered from §107.005(*l*) by Acts 1995, 74th Leg., ch. 751, §15, eff. Sept. 1, 1995. Source: Former Fam §11.18(c).

CHAPTER 108. CENTRAL RECORD FILE; VITAL STATISTICS

FAM §108.001. TRANSMITTAL OF RECORDS OF SUIT BY CLERK

(a) Except as provided by this chapter, the clerk of the court shall transmit to the bureau of vital statistics a certified record of the order rendered in a suit, together with the name and all prior names, birth date, and place of birth of the child prepared by the petitioner on a form provided by the bureau.

(b) The bureau of vital statistics shall maintain these records in a central file according to the name, birth date, and place of birth of the child, the court that rendered the order, and the docket number of the suit.

(c) Except as otherwise provided by law, the records required under this section to be maintained by the bureau of vital statistics are confidential.

History of Fam §108.001: Acts 1995, 74th Leg., ch. 20, §1, eff. April 20, 1995. Amended by Acts 1995, 74th Leg., ch. 751, §16, eff. Sept. 1, 1995; Acts 1999, 76th Leg., ch. 1390, §8, eff. Sept. 1, 1999. Source: Former Fam §11.17(a), (d).

FAM §108.002. DISSOLUTION OF MARRIAGE RECORDS MAINTAINED BY CLERK

A clerk may not transmit to the central record file the pleadings, papers, studies, and records relating to a suit for divorce or annulment or to declare a marriage void.

History of Fam §108.002: Acts 1995, 74th Leg., ch. 20, §1, eff. April 20, 1995. Source: Former Fam §11.17(b).

FAM §108.003. TRANSMITTAL OF INFORMATION REGARDING ADOPTION

(a) The clerk of a court that renders a decree of adoption shall, not later than the 10th day of the first month after the month in which the adoption is rendered, transmit to the central registry of the bureau of vital statistics certified report of adoption that includes:

(1) the name of the adopted child after adoption as shown in the adoption order;

(2) the birth date of the adopted child;

(3) the docket number of the adoption suit;

(4) the identity of the court rendering the adoption;

(5) the date of the adoption order;

(6) the name and address of each parent, guardian, managing conservator, or other person whose consent to adoption was required or waived under Chapter 162, or whose parental rights were terminated in the adoption suit;

(7) the identity of the licensed child placing agency, if any, through which the adopted child was placed for adoption; and

(8) the identity, address, and telephone number of the registry through which the adopted child may register as an adoptee.

(b) Except as otherwise provided by law, for good cause shown, or on an order of the court that granted the adoption or terminated the proceedings under Section 155.001, the records concerning a child maintained by the district clerk after rendition of a decree of adoption, the records of a child-placing agency that has ceased operations, and the records required under this section to be maintained by the bureau of vital statistics are confidential, and no person is entitled to access to or information from these records.

History of Fam §108.003: Acts 1995, 74th Leg., ch. 20, §1, eff. April 20, 1995. Amended by Acts 1995, 74th Leg., ch. 751, §17, eff. Sept. 1, 1995; Acts 1999, 76th Leg., ch. 1390, §9 (eff. Sept. 1, 1999), ch. 62, §6.16 (eff. Sept. 1, 1999). Source: Former Fam §11.17(b); former Hum. Res. Code §§49.003(d), 49.005(d).

See also 25 TAC §181.31.

FAM §108.004. TRANSMITTAL OF FILES ON LOSS OF JURISDICTION

On the loss of jurisdiction of a court under Chapter 155, the clerk of the court shall transmit to the central registry of the bureau of vital statistics a certified record, on a form provided by the bureau, stating that jurisdiction has been lost, the reason for the loss of jurisdiction, and the name and all previous names, date of birth, and place of birth of the child.

History of Fam §108.004: Acts 1995, 74th Leg., ch. 20, §1, eff. April 20, 1995. Amended by Acts 1995, 74th Leg., ch. 751, §18, eff. Sept. 1, 1995. Source: Former Fam §11.17(b).

FAM §108.005. ADOPTION RECORDS RECEIVED BY BUREAU OF VITAL STATISTICS

Section 108.005 below was repealed by Acts 1995, 74th Leg., ch. 968, §11, effective Sept. 1, 1995, without reference to the conflicting amendment by Acts 1995, 74th Leg., ch. 751, §19, effective Sept. 1, 1995.

(a) When the bureau of vital statistics receives a record from the district clerk showing that continuing, exclusive jurisdiction of a child has been lost due to the adoption of the child, the bureau shall close the records concerning that child.

(b) An inquiry concerning a child who has been adopted shall be handled as though the child had not previously been the subject of a suit affecting the parent-child relationship.

History of Fam §108.005: Acts 1995, 74th Leg., ch. 20, §1, eff. April 20, 1995. Amended by Acts 1995, 74th Leg., ch. 751, §19 (eff. Sept. 1, 1995), and repealed by ch. 968, §11 (eff. Sept. 1, 1995); Acts 1999, 76th Leg., ch. 1390, §10, eff. Sept. 1, 1999. Source: Former Fam §11.17(b).

FAM §108.006. FEES

(a) The bureau of vital statistics may charge a reasonable fee to cover the cost of determining and sending information concerning the identity of the court with continuing, exclusive jurisdiction.

(b) On the filing of a suit requesting the adoption of a child, the clerk of the court shall collect an additional fee of $15.

(c) The clerk shall send the fees collected under Subsection (b) to the bureau of vital statistics for deposit in a special fund in the state treasury from which the legislature may appropriate money only to operate and maintain the central file and central registry of the bureau.

(d) The receipts from the fees charged under Subsection (a) shall be deposited in a financial institution as determined by the director of the bureau of vital statistics and withdrawn as necessary for the sole purpose of operating and maintaining the central record file.

History of Fam §108.006: Acts 1995, 74th Leg., ch. 20, §1, eff. April 20, 1995. Amended by Acts 1995, 74th Leg., ch. 751, §20, eff. Sept. 1, 1995. Source: Former Fam §§11.17(c), 11.171.

FAM §108.007. MICROFILM

(a) The bureau of vital statistics may use microfilm or other suitable means for maintaining the central record file.

(b) A certified reproduction of a document maintained by the bureau of vital statistics is admissible in evidence as the original document.

History of Fam §108.007: Acts 1995, 74th Leg., ch. 20, §1, eff. April 20, 1995. Amended by Acts 1995, 74th Leg., ch. 751, §21, eff. Sept. 1, 1995. Source: Former Fam §11.17(e).

FAM §108.008. FILING INFORMATION AFTER DETERMINATION OF PATERNITY

(a) On a determination of paternity, the petitioner shall provide the clerk of the court in which the order was rendered the information necessary to prepare the report of determination of paternity. The clerk shall:

(1) prepare the report on a form provided by the Bureau of Vital Statistics; and

(2) complete the report immediately after the order becomes final.

(b) On completion of the report, the clerk of the court shall forward to the state registrar a report for each order that became final in that court.

History of Fam §108.008: Acts 1995, 74th Leg., ch. 20, §1, eff. April 20, 1995. Amended by Acts 1999, 76th Leg., ch. 556, §4, eff. Sept. 1, 1999. Source: Former Fam §13.43(a)-(c).

FAM §108.009. BIRTH CERTIFICATE

A *Subsection (a) below is effective for motions or other requests for relief made in parentage or paternity proceedings commenced on or after June 14, 2001.*

(a) The state registrar shall substitute a new birth certificate for the original based on the order in accordance with laws or rules that permit the correction or substitution of a birth certificate for an adopted child or a child whose parents marry each other subsequent to the birth of the child.

Subsection (a) below is effective for motions or other requests for relief made in parentage or paternity proceedings commenced before June 14, 2001.

(a) The state registrar shall substitute a new birth certificate for the original based on the order in accordance with laws or rules that permit the correction or substitution of birth certificates for adopted children or children presumed to be biological children by the subsequent marriage of their parents.

(b) The new certificate may not show that the father and child relationship was established after the child's birth but may show the child's actual place and date of birth.

History of Fam §108.009: Acts 1995, 74th Leg., ch. 20, §1, eff. April 20, 1995. Amended by Acts 2001, 77th Leg., ch. 821, §2.12, eff. June 14, 2001. Source: Former Fam §13.43(e), (f).

See also 25 TAC 181.8.

FAM §108.110. RELEASE OF INFORMATION BY BUREAU OF VITAL STATISTICS

(a) The bureau of vital statistics shall provide to the Department of Protective and Regulatory Services:

(1) adoption information as necessary for the department to comply with federal law or regulations regarding the compilation or reporting of adoption information to federal officials; and

(2) other information as necessary for the department to administer its duties.

(b) The bureau may release otherwise confidential information from the bureau's central record files to another governmental entity that has a specific need for the information and maintains appropriate safeguards to prevent further dissemination of the information.

History of Fam §108.110: Acts 1999, 76th Leg., ch. 1390, §11, eff. Sept. 1, 1999.

CHAPTER 109. APPEALS

FAM §109.001. TEMPORARY ORDERS DURING PENDENCY OF APPEAL

(a) Not later than the 30th day after the date an appeal is perfected, on the motion of any party or on the court's own motion and after notice and hearing, the court may make any order necessary to preserve and protect the safety and welfare of the child during the pendency of the appeal as the court may deem necessary and equitable. In addition to other matters, an order may:

(1) appoint temporary conservators for the child and provide for possession of the child;

(2) require the temporary support of the child by a party;

(3) restrain a party from molesting or disturbing the peace of the child or another party;

(4) prohibit a person from removing the child beyond a geographical area identified by the court;

(5) require payment of reasonable attorney's fees and expenses; or

(6) suspend the operation of the order or judgment that is being appealed.

(b) A court retains jurisdiction to enforce its orders rendered under this section unless the appellate court, on a proper showing, supersedes the court's order.

(c) A temporary order rendered under this section is not subject to interlocutory appeal.

E *Subsection (d) below is effective for appeals in SAPCRs pending on or commenced on or after Sept. 1, 2001.*

(d) The court may not suspend under Subsection (a)(6) the operation of an order or judgment terminating the parent-child relationship in a suit brought by the state or a political subdivision of the state permitted by law to bring the suit.

History of Fam §109.001: Acts 1995, 74th Leg., ch. 20, §1, eff. April 20, 1995. Amended by Acts 2001, 77th Leg., ch. 539, §1, eff. Sept. 1, 2001. Source: Former Fam §11.11(e)-(g).

Dancy v. Daggett, 815 S.W.2d 548, 549 (Tex.1991). We hold that "mandamus is an appropriate remedy ... since the trial court's issuance of temporary orders is not subject to interlocutory appeal."

In re Gonzalez, 981 S.W.2d 313, 314 (Tex.App.—San Antonio 1998, pet. denied). In §109.001, "if the trial court has the authority to *suspend* an order or judgment that is being appealed, the court has jurisdiction to *enforce* an order or judgment that is being appealed. While this provision might appear to empower the court to act only within a 30-day window after an appeal is perfected, the [Family] Code clearly indicates in §109.001 that the court retains jurisdiction beyond 30 days even where the merits of the order is under appeal. [¶] We interpret [§109.001(b)'s] language to mean that the trial court retains jurisdiction to enforce temporary orders for child support whenever the payor-parent fails to pay."

Hudson v. Markum, 931 S.W.2d 336, 338 (Tex. App.—Dallas 1996, no writ). "The Family Code treats a motion to modify as an original proceeding. It is not a temporary order as contemplated by §11.11(e) [now §109.001].

FAM §109.002. APPEAL

A (a) An appeal from a final order rendered in a suit, when allowed under this section or under other provisions of law, shall be as in civil cases generally. An appeal in a suit in which termination of the parent-child relationship is in issue shall be given precedence over other civil cases and shall be accelerated by the appellate courts. The procedures for an accelerated appeal under the Texas Rules of Appellate Procedure apply to an appeal in which the termination of the parent-child relationship is in issue.

(b) An appeal may be taken by any party to a suit from a final order rendered under this title.

A (c) An appeal from a final order, with or without a supersedeas bond, does not suspend the order unless suspension is ordered by the court rendering the order. The appellate court, on a proper showing, may permit the order to be suspended, unless the order provides for the termination of the parent-child relationship in a suit brought by the state or a political subdivision of the state permitted by law to bring the suit.

(d) On the motion of the parties or on the court's own motion, the appellate court in its opinion may identify the parties by fictitious names or by their initials only.

History of Fam §109.002: Acts 1995, 74th Leg., ch. 20, §1, eff. April 20, 1995. Amended by Acts 1999, 76th Leg., ch. 62, §6.17, eff. Sept. 1, 1999; Acts 2001, 77th Leg., ch. 421, §1 (eff. Sept. 1, 2001), ch. 539, §2 (eff. Sept. 1, 2001). Source: Former Fam §11.19.

In re Gonzalez, 981 S.W.2d 313, 314-15 (Tex. App.—San Antonio 1998, pet. denied). "[N]either the trial court nor this court has suspended enforcement of the orders awarding [appellant] child support. Because the court's orders have not been suspended, the trial court has the authority to reduce arrearages due by virtue of its previous orders to a money judgment."

In re N.J.G., 980 S.W.2d 764, 766-67 (Tex.App.—San Antonio 1998, no pet.). "The Texas Family Code permits a party to appeal a final order in a [SAPCR]. To be final, a judgment must determine the rights of the parties and dispose of all the issues involved so no future action will be necessary in order to settle and determine the case. A judgment is interlocutory when it determines less than all issues as to all parties thereby leaving something to be determined and adjudicated by the court in disposing of the parties and their rights. Accordingly, an order is interlocutory if it leaves open the issue of permanent conservatorship." (Internal quotations omitted.)

Aguirre v. Texas DPRS, 917 S.W.2d 462, 465 (Tex.App.—Austin 1996, no writ). Section 11.19, now §109.002, "which provides that appeals from suits terminating the parent-child relationship are allowed 'as in civil cases generally,' does not authorize the appeal of interlocutory orders terminating the parent-child relationship."

In re Hall, 871 S.W.2d 251, 252 (Tex.App.—Amarillo 1994, no writ). There is nothing in TRCP 40(a)(2) "that supports [appellant's] understanding that security is not required in matters regarding possession and access to minor children. [¶] The Texas Family Code declares that '[a]ppeals from orders, decrees, or judgments entered in [SAPCRs] shall be as in civil cases generally.' The judgment in the present case is one affecting the parent-child relationship and we can find no reason to treat this cause any differently than other civil cases. We find nothing in the law that would excuse security for costs on appeal in this instance."

Mierické v. Lemoine, 786 S.W.2d 810, 811 (Tex. App.—Dallas 1990, orig. proceeding). "The award of attorney's fees and costs is generally appealable."

FAM §109.003. PAYMENT FOR STATEMENT OF FACTS

A (a) If the party requesting a statement of facts in an appeal of a suit has filed an affidavit stating the party's inability to pay costs as provided by Rule 20, Texas Rules of Appellate Procedure, and the affidavit is approved by the trial court, the trial court may order the county in which the trial was held to pay the costs of preparing the statement of facts.

(b) Nothing in this section shall be construed to permit an official court reporter to be paid more than once for the preparation of the statement of facts.

History of Fam §109.003: Acts 1995, 74th Leg., ch. 20, §1, eff. April 20, 1995. Amended by Acts 1995, 74th Leg., ch. 472, §1, eff. Sept. 1, 1995; Acts 2001, 77th Leg., ch. 1420, §5.0025, eff. Sept. 1, 2001. Source: Former Fam §11.191.

CHAPTER 110. COURT FEES

FAM §110.001. GENERAL RULE

Except as provided by this chapter, fees in a matter covered by this title shall be as in civil cases generally.

History of Fam §110.001: Acts 1995, 74th Leg., ch. 20, §1, eff. April 20, 1995.

FAM §110.002. FILING FEES & DEPOSITS

(a) The clerk of the court may collect a filing fee of $15 in a suit for filing:

(1) a suit for modification;

(2) a motion for enforcement;

(3) a notice of application for judicial writ of withholding;

(4) a motion to transfer.

(5) a petition for license suspension; or

(6) a motion to revoke a stay of license suspension.

(b) No other filing fee may be collected or required for an action described in this section.

(c) The clerk may collect a deposit as in other cases, in the amount set by the clerk for payment of expected costs and other expenses arising in the proceeding.

History of Fam §110.002: Acts 1995, 74th Leg., ch. 20, §1, eff. April 20, 1995. Amended by Acts 1997, 75th Leg., ch. 911, §8 (eff. Sept. 1, 1997), ch. 976, §6 (eff. Sept. 1, 1997). Source: Former Fam §14.13.

FAM §110.003. NO SEPARATE OR ADDITIONAL FILING FEE

The clerk of the court may not require:

(1) a separate filing fee in a suit joined with a suit for dissolution of marriage under Title 1; or

(2) an additional filing fee if more than one form of relief is requested in a suit.

History of Fam §110.003: Acts 1995, 74th Leg., ch. 20, §1, eff. April 20, 1995. Source: Former Fam §11.18(b).

FAM §110.004. FEE FOR ISSUING & DELIVERING WITHHOLDING ORDER OR WRIT

The clerk of the court may charge a reasonable fee, not to exceed $15, for each order or writ of income withholding issued by the clerk and delivered to an employer.

History of Fam §110.004: Acts 1995, 74th Leg., ch. 20, §1, eff. April 20, 1995. Amended by Acts 1997, 75th Leg., ch. 911, §9, eff. Sept. 1, 1997. Source: Former Fam §§14.43(i), 14.45(h).

FAM §110.005. TRANSFER FEE

(a) The fee for filing a transferred case is $45 payable to the clerk of the court to which the case is transferred. No portion of this fee may be sent to the state.

(b) A party may not be assessed any other fee, cost, charge, or expense by the clerk of the court or other public official in connection with filing of the transferred case.

(c) The fee limitation in this section does not affect a fee payable to the court transferring the case.

History of Fam §110.005: Acts 1995, 74th Leg., ch. 20, §1, eff. April 20, 1995. Source: Former Fam §11.06(*l*).

FAM §110.006. DOMESTIC RELATIONS OFFICE FEES

If an administering entity of a domestic relations office adopts an initial operations fee under Section 203.005(a)(1) or an initial child support service fee under Section 203.005(a)(2), the clerk of the court shall collect the fee at the time the suit is filed and send the fee to the domestic relations office.

History of Fam §110.006: Acts 1997, 75th Leg., ch. 702, §1, eff. Sept. 1, 1997. Amended by Acts 1999, 76th Leg., ch. 556, §5, eff. Sept. 1, 1999.

CHAPTER 111. GUIDELINES FOR POSSESSION & CHILD SUPPORT

FAM §111.001. REVIEW OF GUIDELINES

(a) Prior to each regular legislative session, the standing committees of each house of the legislature having jurisdiction over family law issues shall review and, if necessary, recommend revisions to the guidelines for possession of and access to a child under Chapter 153 and for support of a child under Chapter 154. The committee shall report the results of the review and shall include any recommended revisions in the committee's report to the legislature.

(b) Not later than December 1 of each even-numbered year, the Title IV-D agency shall submit a report to the standing committees of each house of the legislature having jurisdiction over family law issues for use by the committee in conducting the review required by Subsection (a). The report must contain:

(1) economic data obtained from the United States Department of Agriculture on the cost of raising children;

(2) an analysis of case data on the application of and deviations from the child support guidelines; and

(3) a summary of any federal legislation enacted since the date of the last review.

History of Fam §111.001: Acts 1995, 74th Leg., ch. 20, §1, eff. April 20, 1995. Amended by Acts 1999, 76th Leg., ch. 556, §6, eff. Sept. 1, 1999. Source: Former Fam §§14.03(j), 14.05(h), (i).

FAM §111.002. GUIDELINES SUPERSEDE COURT RULES

(a) The guidelines in this title supersede local court rules and rules of the supreme court that conflict with the guidelines.

(b) Notwithstanding other law, the guidelines may not be repealed or modified by a rule adopted by the supreme court.

History of Fam §111.002: Acts 1995, 74th Leg., ch. 20, §1, eff. April 20, 1995. Source: Former Fam §§14.032(e), (f), 14.052(c), (d).

FAM §111.003. POSTING GUIDELINES

A copy of the guidelines for possession of and access to a child under Chapter 153 and a copy of the guidelines for the support of a child under Chapter 154 shall be prominently displayed at or near the entrance to the courtroom of every court having jurisdiction of a suit.

History of Fam §111.003: Acts 1995, 74th Leg., ch. 20, §1, eff. April 20, 1995. Source: Former Fam §§14.033(p), 14.058.

Chapters 112-150 reserved for expansion

SUBTITLE B. SUITS AFFECTING THE PARENT-CHILD RELATIONSHIP

CHAPTER 151. RIGHTS & DUTIES IN PARENT-CHILD RELATIONSHIP

Ⓐ *The heading for Chapter 151 above is effective for motions or other requests for relief made in parentage or paternity proceedings commenced on or after June 14, 2001.*

CHAPTER 151. THE PARENT-CHILD RELATIONSHIP

The heading for Chapter 151 above is effective for motions or other requests for relief made in parentage or paternity proceedings commenced before June 14, 2001.

FAM §151.001. RIGHTS & DUTIES OF PARENT

Ⓐ *Section 151.001 below is effective for motions or other requests for relief made in parentage or paternity proceedings commenced on or after June 14, 2001.*

(a) A parent of a child has the following rights and duties:

(1) the right to have physical possession, to direct the moral and religious training, and to establish the residence of the child;

(2) the duty of care, control, protection, and reasonable discipline of the child;

(3) the duty to support the child, including providing the child with clothing, food, shelter, medical and dental care, and education;

(4) the duty, except when a guardian of the child's estate has been appointed, to manage the estate of the child, including the right as an agent of the child to act in relation to the child's estate if the child's action is

required by a state, the United States, or a foreign government;

A (5) except as provided by Section 264.0111, the right to the services and earnings of the child;

(6) the right to consent to the child's marriage, enlistment in the armed forces of the United States, medical and dental care, and psychiatric, psychological, and surgical treatment;

(7) the right to represent the child in legal action and to make other decisions of substantial legal significance concerning the child;

(8) the right to receive and give receipt for payments for the support of the child and to hold or disburse funds for the benefit of the child;

(9) the right to inherit from and through the child;

(10) the right to make decisions concerning the child's education; and

(11) any other right or duty existing between a parent and child by virtue of law.

(b) The duty of a parent to support his or her child exists while the child is an unemancipated minor and continues as long as the child is fully enrolled in an accredited secondary school in a program leading toward a high school diploma until the end of the school year in which the child graduates.

(c) A parent who fails to discharge the duty of support is liable to a person who provides necessaries to those to whom support is owed.

(d) The rights and duties of a parent are subject to:

(1) a court order affecting the rights and duties;

(2) an affidavit of relinquishment of parental rights; and

(3) an affidavit by the parent designating another person or agency to act as managing conservator.

History of Fam §151.001: Acts 1995, 74th Leg., ch. 20, §1, eff. April 20, 1995. Amended by Acts 1995, 74th Leg., ch. 751, §23, eff. Sept. 1, 1995. Amended by Acts 2001, 77th Leg., ch. 509, §2, eff. Sept. 1, 2001. Renumbered from §151.003 and amended by Acts 2001, 77th Leg., ch. 821, §2.13, eff. June 14, 2001.

History of Former Fam §151.001: Acts 1995, 74th Leg., ch. 20, §1, eff. April 20, 1995. Deleted by Acts 2001, 77th Leg., ch. 821, §2.13, eff. June 14, 2001. Source: Former Fam §§4.02, 12.04.

Patterson v. Planned Parenthood, Inc., 971 S.W.2d 439, 446 (Tex.1998). "[O]nly the parents or guardians of a minor may represent their legal interests."

Harrington v. State, 547 S.W.2d 621, 624 (Tex. Crim.App.1977). "It is the duty of *each* parent to support his or her minor children. The fact that a father might entrust the care of his child to his wife or some other person does not relieve him of his responsibility to see that his child is properly cared for unless it is shown that some other person had *sole* and *exclusive* care, custody, and control of the minor child."

HCA, Inc. v. Miller, 36 S.W.3d 187, 193 (Tex. App.—Houston [14th Dist.] 2000, pet. granted, argued 4-30-02). "In Texas, the Legislature has expressly given parents a right to withhold medical treatment, urgently needed or not, for a child whose medical condition is certifiably terminal, but it has not extended that right to the parents of children with non-terminal impairments, deformities, or disabilities, regardless of their severity. *At 194:* In light of the high value our law places on preserving human life, and especially on protecting the life and well-being of minors, we perceive no legal basis or other rationale for concluding that Texas law gives parents a common law right to withhold urgently needed life-sustaining medical treatment from children in circumstances in which the Act does not apply. Moreover, in Texas, a child born alive after a premature birth (or abortion) is entitled to the same rights as are granted by the State to any other child born alive after normal gestation."

Bailey v. Bailey, 987 S.W.2d 206, 209 (Tex.App.—Amarillo 1999, no pet.). "[T]he scope of the duty to support was, and is, quite plenary. [I]t encompasses the rather boundless task of maintaining and educating, which at a minimum obligates the parents to provide the child those things necessary in sickness and health, such as clothing, food, shelter, medical and dental attention, and education."

In re Marriage of Jones, 983 S.W.2d 377, 381 (Tex. App.—Houston [14th Dist.] 1999), *rev'd on other grounds*, 35 S.W.3d 620 (Tex.2000). "The Legislature has ... made it clear that as between parent and child, the *parent* is responsible for making decisions relating to the child's welfare. This responsibility, of course, extends to any parent ... who is appointed as either joint or sole managing conservator of the child."

Farish v. Farish, 982 S.W.2d 623, 628 (Tex.App.—Houston [1st Dist.] 1998, no pet.). "A child's right to be supported by his or her parents is a moral and legal right the nature of which does not change upon remarriage by one or both of the parents."

Office of Attorney Gen. v. Carter, 977 S.W.2d 159, 160-61 (Tex.App.—Houston [14th Dist.] 1998, no pet.).

"A support claim is like a claim for debt in that it seeks a personal judgment establishing a direct obligation to pay money. Each parent is obligated to support his or her child during the period of the child's minority, and is liable to *any person* who provides necessaries for that child. This duty is imposed at the birth of the child, and is not altered merely because the parents subsequently get divorced. Thus, *any person*, including the other parent, who provides necessaries for that child *may bring suit* to recover from a parent who fails to discharge that duty of support."

In re B.T., 954 S.W.2d 44, 49 (Tex.App.—San Antonio 1997, writ denied). Section 151.001(a)(3) "makes it clear that a parent has a duty to support his child. This duty of support exists regardless of whether a parent is court-ordered to support the child or not. [O]ccasional gifts are insufficient to fulfill a parent's obligation of support."

R.W. v. Texas DPRS, 944 S.W.2d 437, 439-40 (Tex. App.—Houston [14th Dist.] 1997, no writ). "Under the Texas Family Code, a presumed father is treated the same as all other parents, natural or adoptive. Just like all other parents, [presumed father] shouldered the duty to support the child, including providing the child with clothing, food, shelter, medical and dental care, and education and the duty of care, control, protection, and reasonable discipline of the child. And just like all other parents, these duties arose long before [presumed father] filed his voluntary statement of paternity and without regard to any adjudication by a court establishing his parentage. The duty existed from the moment [presumed father], by his actions, recognized the child as his own." (Internal quotations omitted.)

Rodriguez v. Spencer, 902 S.W.2d 37, 40-41 (Tex. App.—Houston [1st Dist.] 1995, no writ). Section 12.04, now §151.001(a)(2), "is limited to the parent-child relationship, not the parent-third party relationship. [T]he cases applying §12.04 have done so only when a parent faces criminal liability for acts or omissions toward his or her own child. [S]ection 12.04 does not establish a parent's duty to control or discipline children for the benefit of third parties."

Munoz v. II Jaz Inc., 863 S.W.2d 207, 209-210 (Tex. App.—Houston [14th Dist.] 1993, no writ). Section 12.04(7), now §151.001(a)(7), "which empowers a parent to make legal decisions concerning their child, does not give parents the power to waive a child's cause of action for personal injuries. Such an interpretation of the statute would be against the public policy to protect minor children."

Klise v. Klise, 678 S.W.2d 545, 547 (Tex.App.—Houston [14th Dist.] 1984, no writ). Section 4.02, now §151.001, "does not require that the parents make mathematically equal contributions for the support of their children. It only provides that each parent has the equal obligation, in accordance with their respective ability, to contribute money or services to support and maintain the children. The fact that the parties have independent earning capacities is *not* to be included in this determination."

Woodruff v. Woodruff, 487 S.W.2d 791, 793 (Tex. App.—Texarkana 1972, no writ). "While ... each spouse has the duty to support his or her minor children, ... such support is for necessities. The necessities of life ordinarily include food, clothing, shelter and medical attention. A college or university education is not a general necessity, but is a special advantage."

FAM §151.001. RELATION OF CHILD TO MOTHER & FATHER

Section 151.001 below is effective for motions or other requests for relief made in parentage or paternity proceedings commenced before June 14, 2001.

(a) The parent-child relationship may be established between a child and:

(1) the biological mother by proof of her having given birth to the child;

(2) the biological father as provided by this code; and

(3) an adoptive parent by proof of adoption.

(b) The parent-child relationship extends equally to every child and parent regardless of the marital status of the parents.

Holick v. Smith, 685 S.W.2d 18, 20 (Tex.1985). "The natural right existing between parents and their children is of constitutional dimensions. Indeed, involuntary termination of parental rights involves fundamental constitutional rights. This natural parental right has been characterized as essential, a basic civil right of man, and far more precious than property rights." (Internal quotations omitted.)

FAM §151.002. PRESUMPTION OF PATERNITY

Section 151.002 below is effective for motions or other requests for relief made in parentage or paternity proceedings commenced before June 14, 2001.

(a) A man is presumed to be the biological father of a child if:

(1) he and the child's biological mother are or have been married to each other and the child is born during the marriage or not more than 300 days after the date the marriage terminated by death, annulment, or divorce or by having been declared void;

(2) before the child's birth, he and the child's biological mother attempted to marry each other by a marriage in apparent compliance with law, although the attempted marriage is or could be declared void, and the child is born during the attempted marriage or not more than 300 days after the date the attempted marriage terminated by death, annulment, or divorce or by having been declared void; or

(3) after the child's birth, he and the child's biological mother have married or attempted to marry each other by a marriage in apparent compliance with law, although the attempted marriage is or could be declared void or voided by annulment, and:

(A) he has filed a written acknowledgment of his paternity of the child under Chapter 160;

(B) he consents in writing to be named and is named as the child's father on the child's birth certificate; or

(C) he is obligated to support the child under a written voluntary promise or by court order.

(b) A presumption under this section may be rebutted as provided by Section 160.110.

Attorney Gen. v. Lavan, 833 S.W.2d 952, 954 (Tex.1992). Nothing in the Family Code "expressly prohibits the State from bringing a claim under chapter 12 [now chapter 151] to disestablish the paternity of a presumed father in the same suit in which it brings a claim under chapter 13 [now chapter 160] to establish paternity in an alleged biological father. To allow both claims in this case to be joined in one suit advances the best interest of the child by eliminating any period of time a child would be left without the benefit of a legal father."

In re S.C.V., 750 S.W.2d 762, 764 (Tex.1988). "A blood test which positively excludes the alleged father is clear and convincing evidence of non-paternity."

In re A.L.J., 929 S.W.2d 467, 473 (Tex.App.—Tyler 1996, writ denied). Mother "argues that the termination of a parent-child relationship between a child and a presumed father who has been judicially declared the biological father opens the door for another man to be declared the biological father. We reject this reasoning. The Family Code simply provides that a man is presumed to be the biological father of a child if the child is born during the marriage of the man and the biological mother."

Yavapai-Apache Tribe v. Mejia, 906 S.W.2d 152, 175 n.15 (Tex.App.—Houston [14th Dist.] 1995, orig. proceeding). "White is listed as the father of [the children] on their birth certificates. Because there is nothing in the record to show that White consented in writing to having his name placed on the birth certificates, he cannot be presumed to be the father under §12.02(a)(4) [now §151.002(a)(3)(B)] of the Texas Family Code. However, we do view the fact that he is listed on the birth certificates as more evidence that White did acknowledge his paternity of [the children] early on, and should not be excluded from the definition of 'parent' contained in the [Indian Child Welfare Act]."

Attorney Gen. v. Ridge, 773 S.W.2d 645, 648-49 (Tex.App.—San Antonio 1989, writ denied). "A child is rebuttably presumed to be the legitimate child of a man if the child is born during the marriage. [¶] No Texas courts have ruled directly on a child's right to file a paternity suit against an alleged father where a previous agreement of nonpaternity was approved in a prior agreed divorce decree. [¶] While this divorce decree was res judicata as to the husband-wife parties, we hold that the ... decree of divorce was not res judicata as to the issue of paternity brought in this case by the child (through attorney general as next friend) because the child was not a party to the ... divorce proceedings. In a personal action, the judgment is conclusive only upon those persons who are named as parties or whose interests are represented by a party of record. A review of the ... divorce record shows that the child was not named in the petitioner's ... pleadings as a party. Neither the petitioner nor respondent purported to represent the child as his or her next friend and no guardian ad litem was appointed."

FAM §151.003. RIGHTS & DUTIES OF PARENT

Section 151.003 below is effective for motions or other requests for relief made in parentage or paternity proceedings commenced before June 14, 2001.

(a) A parent of a child has the following rights and duties:

(1) the right to have physical possession, to direct the moral and religious training, and to establish the residence of the child;

(2) the duty of care, control, protection, and reasonable discipline of the child;

(3) the duty to support the child, including providing the child with clothing, food, shelter, medical and dental care, and education;

(4) the duty, except when a guardian of the child's estate has been appointed, to manage the estate of the child, including the right as an agent of the child to act in relation to the child's estate if the child's action is required by a state, the United States, or a foreign government;

(5) the right to the services and earnings of the child;

(6) the right to consent to the child's marriage, enlistment in the armed forces of the United States, medical and dental care, and psychiatric, psychological, and surgical treatment;

(7) the right to represent the child in legal action and to make other decisions of substantial legal significance concerning the child;

(8) the right to receive and give receipt for payments for the support of the child and to hold or disburse funds for the benefit of the child;

(9) the right to inherit from and through the child;

(10) the right to make decisions concerning the child's education; and

(11) any other right or duty existing between a parent and child by virtue of law.

(b) The duty of a parent to support his or her child exists while the child is an unemancipated minor and continues as long as the child is fully enrolled in an accredited secondary school in a program leading toward a high school diploma until the end of the school year in which the child graduates.

(c) A parent who fails to discharge the duty of support is liable to a person who provides necessaries to those to whom support is owed.

(d) The rights and duties of a parent are subject to:

(1) a court order affecting the rights and duties;

(2) an affidavit of relinquishment of parental rights; and

(3) an affidavit by the parent designating another person or agency to act as managing conservator.

FAM §151.002. RIGHTS OF A LIVING CHILD AFTER AN ABORTION OR PREMATURE BIRTH

A *Section 151.002 below is effective for motions or other requests for relief made in parentage or paternity proceedings commenced on or after June 14, 2001.*

(a) A living human child born alive after an abortion or premature birth is entitled to the same rights, powers, and privileges as are granted by the laws of this state to any other child born alive after the normal gestation period.

(b) In this code, "born alive" means the complete expulsion or extraction from its mother of a product of conception, irrespective of the duration of pregnancy, which, after such separation, breathes or shows any other evidence of life such as beating of the heart, pulsation of the umbilical cord, or definite movement of voluntary muscles, whether or not the umbilical cord has been cut or the placenta is attached. Each product of the birth is considered born alive.

History of Fam §151.002: Acts 1995, 74th Leg., ch. 20, §1, eff. April 20, 1995. Renumbered from §151.004 by Acts 2001, 77th Leg., ch. 821, §2.13, eff. June 14, 2001.

History of Former Fam §151.002: Acts 1995, 74th Leg., ch. 20, §1, eff. April 20, 1995. Deleted by Acts 2001, 77th Leg., ch. 821, §2.13, eff. June 14, 2001. Source: Former Fam §12.05.

FAM §151.004. RIGHTS OF A LIVING CHILD AFTER AN ABORTION OR PREMATURE BIRTH

Section 151.004 below is effective for motions or other requests for relief made in parentage or paternity proceedings commenced before June 14, 2001.

(a) A living human child born alive after an abortion or premature birth is entitled to the same rights, powers, and privileges as are granted by the laws of this state to any other child born alive after the normal gestation period.

(b) In this code, "born alive" means the complete expulsion or extraction from its mother of a product of conception, irrespective of the duration of pregnancy, which, after such separation, breathes or shows any other evidence of life such as beating of the heart, pulsation of the umbilical cord, or definite movement of voluntary muscles, whether or not the umbilical cord has been cut or the placenta is attached. Each product of the birth is considered born alive.

FAM §151.003. LIMITATION ON STATE AGENCY ACTION

A *Section 151.003 below is effective for motions or other requests for relief made in parentage or paternity proceedings commenced on or after June 14, 2001.*

A state agency may not adopt rules or policies or take any other action that violates the fundamental right and duty of a parent to direct the upbringing of the parent's child.

History of Fam §151.003: Acts 1999, 76th Leg., ch. 62, §6.18(a), eff. Sept. 1, 1999. Renumbered from §151.005 by Acts 2001, 77th Leg., ch. 821, §2.13, eff. June 14, 2001.

History of Former Fam §151.003: Acts 1995, 74th Leg., ch. 20, §1, eff. April 20, 1995. Amended by Acts 1995, 74th Leg., ch. 751, §23, eff. Sept. 1, 1995; Acts 2001, 77th Leg., ch. 509, §2, eff. Sept. 1, 2001. Renumbered as §151.001 by Acts 2001, 77th Leg., ch. 821, §2.13, eff. June 14, 2001.

FAM §151.005. LIMITATION ON STATE AGENCY ACTION

Section 151.005 below is effective for motions or other requests for relief made in parentage or paternity proceedings commenced before June 14, 2001.

A state agency may not adopt rules or policies or take any other action that violates the fundamental right and duty of a parent to direct the upbringing of the parent's child.

FAM §§151.004, 151.005. RENUMBERED

Renumbered as §§151.002 & 151.003 by Acts 2001, 77th Leg., ch. 821, §2.13, eff. June 14, 2001.

Sections 151.006-151.100 reserved for expansion

FAM §§151.101 TO 151.103. DELETED

Deleted by Acts 2001, 77th Leg., ch. 821, §2.13, eff. June 14, 2001.
See also Family Code §§160.701-160.707.

SUBCHAPTER B. ASSISTED CONCEPTION

Subchapter B below is effective for motions or other requests for relief made in parentage or paternity proceedings commenced before June 14, 2001.

FAM §151.101. ARTIFICIAL INSEMINATION

(a) If a husband consents to the artificial insemination of his wife, any resulting child is the child of both of them. The consent must be in writing and must be acknowledged.

(b) If a woman is artificially inseminated, the resulting child is not the child of the donor unless he is the husband.

History of Fam §151.101: Acts 1995, 74th Leg., ch. 20, §1, eff. April 20, 1995. Deleted by Acts 2001, 77th Leg., ch. 821, §2.13, eff. June 14, 2001. Source: Former Fam §12.03.

In re O.G.M., 988 S.W.2d 473, 477 (Tex.App.—Houston [1st Dist.] 1999, pet. dism'd). "The legislative history of §151.101 does not make any reference to the *in vitro* fertilization procedure. Webster's dictionary defines artificial insemination as the introduction of semen into the uterus or oviduct by other than natural means. The *in vitro* fertilization procedure which produced [their child] involved removing ova from [mother], fertilizing her ova with [her former husband's] semen in a lab procedure, freezing a portion of the resulting pre-embryos, and later implanting a pre-embryo into [mother's] uterus. [Mother] does not cite any authority holding that IVF is the same as artificial insemination. We find Family Code §151.101 entitled 'Artificial Insemination' inapplicable to the facts of this case. *At 477 n.8:* We note that legislature set out the parental rights to children born through IVF from oocyte or embryo donations."

K.B. v. N.B., 811 S.W.2d 634, 637 (Tex.App.—San Antonio 1991, writ denied). "In view of §12.03 [now §151.101's] clear requirement of a writing, we cannot accept the wife's suggestion that oral consent, without more, suffices."

FAM §151.102. OOCYTE DONATION

(a) If a husband consents to provide sperm to fertilize a donor oocyte by in vitro fertilization or other assisted reproductive techniques and the wife consents to have a donor oocyte that has been fertilized with her husband's sperm, pursuant to his consent, placed in her uterus, a resulting child is the child of both of them. The consent of each must be in writing.

(b) If a donor oocyte that has been fertilized with her husband's sperm implants in a wife's uterus, a resulting child is not the child of the donor of the oocyte.

History of Fam §151.102: Acts 1995, 74th Leg., ch. 20, §1, eff. April 20, 1995. Deleted by Acts 2001, 77th Leg., ch. 821, §2.13, eff. June 14, 2001. Source: Former Fam §12.03A.

FAM §151.103. EMBRYO DONATION

(a) If, with the consent of the husband and the wife, a donated preimplantation embryo implants in the uterus of the wife, a resulting child is the child of both of them. The consent must be in writing.

(b) If, with the consent of the husband and the wife, a donated preimplantation embryo implants in the uterus of the wife, a resulting child is not the child of the donor or donors of the preimplantation embryo.

(c) Subsections (a) and (b) apply whether the donated preimplantation embryo is the result of separate egg and sperm donations or the result of donation of an embryo created for the purpose of assisting the reproduction of the donating couple.

History of Fam §151.103: Acts 1995, 74th Leg., ch. 20, §1, eff. April 20, 1995. Deleted by Acts 2001, 77th Leg., ch. 821, §2.13, eff. June 14, 2001. Source: Former Fam §12.03B.

CHAPTER 152. UNIFORM CHILD CUSTODY JURISDICTION & ENFORCEMENT ACT

Editor's note: Changes have been made to the official comments to reflect the Texas Legislature's omission of sections and changing section numbers. The full uniform act and official comments can be found at http://www.nccusl.org.

Official Prefatory Note

This Act, the Uniform Child Custody Jurisdiction and Enforcement Act (UCCJEA), revisits the problem of the interstate child almost thirty years after the Conference promulgated the Uniform Child Custody Jurisdiction Act (UCCJA). The UCCJEA accomplishes two major purposes.

First, it revises the law on child custody jurisdiction in light of federal enactments and almost thirty years of inconsistent case law. Article 2 of this Act provides clearer standards for which States can exercise original jurisdiction over a child custody determination. It also, for the first time, enunciates a standard of continuing jurisdiction and clarifies modification jurisdiction. Other aspects of the article harmonize the law on simultaneous proceedings, clean hands, and forum non conveniens.

Second, this Act provides in Article 3 for a remedial process to enforce interstate child custody and visitation determinations. In doing so, it brings a uniform procedure to the law of interstate enforcement that is currently producing inconsistent results. In many respects, this Act accomplishes for custody and visitation determinations the same uniformity that has occurred in interstate child support with the promulgation of the Uniform Interstate Family Support Act (UIFSA).

Revision of Uniform Child Custody Jurisdiction Act

The UCCJA was adopted as law in all 50 States, the District of Columbia, and the Virgin Islands. A number of adoptions, however, significantly departed from the original text. In addition, almost thirty years of litigation since the promulgation of the UCCJA produced substantial inconsistency in interpretation by state courts. As a result, the goals of the UCCJA were rendered unobtainable in many cases.

In 1980, the federal government enacted the Parental Kidnapping Prevention Act (PKPA), 28 U.S.C. §1738A, to address the interstate custody jurisdictional problems that continued to exist after the adoption of the UCCJA. The PKPA mandates that state authorities give full faith and credit to other states' custody determinations, so long as those determinations were made in conformity with the provisions of the PKPA. The PKPA provisions regarding bases for jurisdiction, restrictions on modifications, preclusion of simultaneous proceedings, and notice requirements are similar to those in the UCCJA. There are, however, some significant differences. For example, the PKPA authorizes continuing exclusive jurisdiction in the original decree State so long as one parent or the child remains there and that State has continuing jurisdiction under its own law. The UCCJA did not directly address this issue. To further complicate the process, the PKPA partially incorporates state UCCJA law in its language. The relationship between these two statutes became "technical enough to delight a medieval property lawyer." Homer H. Clark, *Domestic Relations* §12.5 at 494 (2d ed. 1988).

As documented in an extensive study by the American Bar Association's Center on Children and the Law, *Obstacles to the Recovery and Return of Parentally Abducted Children* (1993) (*Obstacles Study*), inconsistency of interpretation of the UCCJA and the technicalities of applying the PKPA, resulted in a loss of uniformity among the States. The Obstacles Study suggested a number of amendments which would eliminate the inconsistent state interpretations and harmonize the UCCJA with the PKPA.

The revisions of the jurisdictional aspects of the UCCJA eliminate the inconsistent state interpretations and can be summarized as follows:

1. Home state priority. The PKPA prioritizes "home state" jurisdiction by requiring that full faith and credit cannot be given to a child custody determination by a State that exercises initial jurisdiction as a "significant connection state" when there is a "home State." Initial custody determinations based on "significant connections" are not entitled to PKPA enforcement unless there is no home State. The UCCJA, however, specifically authorizes four independent bases of jurisdiction without prioritization. Under the UCCJA, a significant connection custody determination may have to be enforced even if it would be denied enforcement under the PKPA. The UCCJEA prioritizes home state jurisdiction in Section 201.

2. Clarification of emergency jurisdiction. There are several problems with the current emergency jurisdiction provision of the UCCJA §3(a)(3). First, the language of the UCCJA does not specify that emergency jurisdiction may be exercised only to protect the child on a temporary basis until the court with appropriate jurisdiction issues a permanent order. Some courts have interpreted the UCCJA language to so provide. Other courts, however, have held that there is no time limit on a custody determination based on emergency jurisdiction. Simultaneous proceedings and conflicting custody orders have resulted from these different interpretations.

Second, the emergency jurisdiction provisions predated the widespread enactment of state domestic violence statutes. Those statutes are often invoked to keep one parent away from the other parent and the children when there is a threat of violence. Whether these situations are sufficient to invoke the emergency jurisdiction provision of the UCCJA has been the subject of some confusion since the emergency jurisdiction provision does not specifically refer to violence directed against the parent of the child or against a sibling of the child.

The UCCJEA contains a separate section on emergency jurisdiction at Section 204 which addresses these issues.

3. Exclusive continuing jurisdiction for the State that entered the decree. The failure of the UCCJA to clearly enunciate that the decree-granting State retains exclusive continuing jurisdiction to modify a decree has resulted in two major problems. First, different interpretations of the UCCJA on continuing jurisdiction have produced conflicting custody decrees. States also have different interpretations as to how long continuing jurisdiction lasts. Some courts have held that modification jurisdiction continues until the last contestant leaves the State, regardless of how many years the child has lived outside the State or how tenuous the child's connections to the State have become. Other courts have held that continuing modification jurisdiction ends as soon as the child has established a new home State, regardless of how significant the child's connections to the decree State remain. Still other States distinguish between custody orders and visitation orders. This divergence of views leads to simultaneous proceedings and conflicting custody orders.

The second problem arises when it is necessary to determine whether the State with continuing jurisdiction has relinquished it. There should be a clear basis to determine when that court has relinquished jurisdiction. The UCCJA provided no guidance on this issue. The ambiguity regarding whether a court has declined jurisdiction can result in one court improperly exercising jurisdiction because it erroneously believes that the other court has declined jurisdiction. This caused simultaneous proceedings and conflicting custody orders. In addition, some courts have declined jurisdiction after only informal contact between courts with no opportunity for the parties to be heard. This raised significant due process concerns. The UCCJEA addresses these issues in Sections 110, 202, and 206.

4. Specification of what custody proceedings are covered. The definition of custody proceeding in the UCCJA is ambiguous. States have rendered conflicting decisions regarding certain types of proceedings. There is no general agreement on whether the UCCJA applies to neglect, abuse, dependency, wardship, guardianship, termination of parental rights, and protection from domestic violence proceedings. The UCCJEA includes a sweeping definition that, with the exception of adoption, includes virtually all cases that can involve custody of or visitation with a child as a "custody determination."

5. Role of "Best Interests." The jurisdictional scheme of the UCCJA was designed to promote the best interests of the children whose custody was at issue by discouraging parental abduction and providing that, in general, the State with the closest connections to, and the most evidence regarding, a child should decide that child's custody. The "best interest" language in the jurisdictional sections of the UCCJA was not intended to be an invitation to address the merits of the custody dispute in the jurisdictional determination or to otherwise provide that "best interests" considerations should override jurisdictional determinations or provide an additional jurisdictional basis.

The UCCJEA eliminates the term "best interests" in order to clearly distinguish between the jurisdictional standards and the substantive standards relating to custody and visitation of children.

6. Other changes. This draft also makes a number of additional amendments to the UCCJA. Many of these changes were made to harmonize the provisions of this Act with those of the Uniform Interstate Family Support Act. One of the policy bases underlying this Act is to make uniform the law of interstate family proceedings to the extent possible, given the very different jurisdictional foundations. It simplifies the life of the family law practitioner when the same or similar provisions are found in both Acts.

Enforcement Provisions

One of the major purposes of the revision of the UCCJA was to provide a remedy for interstate visitation and custody cases. As with child support, state borders have become one of the biggest obstacles to enforcement of custody and visitation orders. If either parent leaves the State where the custody determination was made, the other parent faces considerable difficulty in enforcing the visitation and custody provisions of the decree. Locating the child, making service of process, and preventing adverse modification in a new forum all present problems.

There is currently no uniform method of enforcing custody and visitation orders validly entered in another State. As documented by the *Obstacles Study*, despite the fact that both the UCCJA and the PKPA direct the enforcement of visitation and custody orders entered in accordance with mandated jurisdictional prerequisites and due process, neither act provides enforcement procedures or remedies.

As the *Obstacles Study* pointed out, the lack of specificity in enforcement procedures has resulted in the law of enforcement evolving differently in different jurisdictions. In one State, it might be common practice to file a Motion to Enforce or a Motion to Grant Full Faith and Credit to initiate an enforcement proceeding. In another State, a Writ of Habeas Corpus or a Citation for Contempt might be commonly used. In some States, Mandamus and Prohibition also may be utilized. All of these enforcement procedures differ from jurisdiction to jurisdiction. While many States tend to limit considerations in enforcement proceedings to whether the court which issued the decree had jurisdiction to make the custody determination, others broaden the considerations to scrutiny of whether enforcement would be in the best interests of the child.

Lack of uniformity complicates the enforcement process in several ways: (1) It increases the costs of the enforcement action in part because the services of more than one lawyer may be required – one in the original forum and one in the State where enforcement is sought; (2) It decreases the certainty of outcome; (3) It can turn enforcement into a long and drawn out procedure. A parent opposed to the provisions of a visitation determination may be able to delay implementation for many months, possibly even years, thereby frustrating not only the other parent, but also the process that led to the issuance of the original court order.

The provisions of Article 3 provide several remedies for the enforcement of a custody determination. First, there is a simple procedure for registering a custody determination in another State. This will allow a party to know in advance whether that State will recognize the party's custody determination. This is extremely important in estimating the risk of the child's non-return when the child is sent on visitation. The provision should prove to be very useful in international custody cases.

Second, the Act provides a swift remedy along the lines of habeas corpus. Time is extremely important in visitation and custody cases. If visitation rights cannot be enforced quickly, they often cannot be enforced at all. This is particularly true if there is a limited time within which visitation can be exercised such as may be the case when one parent has been granted visitation during the winter or spring holiday period. Without speedy consideration and resolution of the enforcement of such visitation rights, the ability to visit may be lost entirely. Similarly, a custodial parent visitation extension will infringe on the school year. A swift enforcement mechanism is desirable for violations of both custody and visitation provisions.

The scope of the enforcing court's inquiry is limited to the issue of whether the decree court had jurisdiction and complied with due process in rendering the original custody decree. No further inquiry is necessary because neither Article 2 nor the PKPA allows an enforcing court to modify a custody determination.

Third, the enforcing court will be able to utilize an extraordinary remedy. If the enforcing court is concerned that the parent, who has physical custody of the child, will flee or harm the child, a warrant to take physical possession of the child is available.

Finally, there is a role for public authorities, such as prosecutors, in the enforcement process. Their involvement will encourage the parties to abide by the terms of the custody determination. If the parties know that public authorities and law enforcement officers are available to help in securing compliance with custody determinations, the parties may be deterred from interfering with the exercise of rights established by court order.

The involvement of public authorities will also prove more effective in remedying violations of custody determinations. Most parties do not have the resources to enforce a custody determination in another jurisdiction. The availability of the public authorities as an enforcement agency will help ensure that this remedy can be made available regardless of income level. In addition, the public authorities may have resources to draw on that are unavailable to the average litigant.

This Act does not authorize the public authorities to be involved in the action leading up to the making of the custody determination, except when requested by the court, when there is a violation of the Hague Convention on the Civil Aspects of International Child Abduction, or when the person holding the child has violated a criminal statute. The Act does not mandate that public authorities be involved in all cases. Not all States, or local authorities, have the funds necessary for an effective custody and visitation enforcement program.

SUBCHAPTER A. APPLICATION & CONSTRUCTION

FAM §152.001. APPLICATION & CONSTRUCTION

This chapter shall be applied and construed to promote the uniformity of the law among the states that enact it.

History of Fam §152.001: Acts 1995, 74th Leg., ch. 20, §1, eff. April 20, 1995. Renumbered from §152.001(a)(9), (b) by Acts 1999, 76th Leg., ch. 34, §1, eff. Sept. 1, 1999. Source: Former Fam §11.51.

McGuire v. McGuire, 18 S.W.3d 801, 806 (Tex. App.—El Paso 2000, no pet.). "[C]ase law under the former Texas version of the Uniform Child Custody Jurisdiction Act regarding continuing jurisdiction will have little, if any, precedent value under the new act." (Internal quotations omitted.)

FAM §152.002. CONFLICTS BETWEEN PROVISIONS

If a provision of this chapter conflicts with a provision of this title or another statute or rule of this state and the conflict cannot be reconciled, this chapter prevails.

History of Fam §152.002: Acts 1999, 76th Leg., ch. 34, §1, eff. Sept. 1, 1999.

In re Bellamy, 67 S.W.3d 482, 484 (Tex.App.—Texarkana 2002, n.p.h.). "[W]e find that §§152.202 and 155.003(b)(1) conflict in this case. When a provision of Chapter 152 conflicts with another provision of the Family Code or another statute or rule of Texas and the conflict cannot be reconciled, Chapter 152 prevails. Under the UCCJEA, Texas retains jurisdiction even if Texas is no longer the home state of the child or of the custodial parent, so long as there is a significant connection with this state."

FAM §§152.003 TO 152.025. DELETED

Deleted by Acts 1999, 76th Leg., ch. 34, §1, eff. Sept. 1, 1999.

Sections 152.003-152.100 reserved for expansion

SUBCHAPTER B. GENERAL PROVISIONS

FAM §152.101. SHORT TITLE

This chapter may be cited as the Uniform Child Custody Jurisdiction and Enforcement Act.

History of Fam §152.101: Acts 1995, 74th Leg., ch. 20, §1, eff. April 20, 1995. Renumbered from §152.025 by Acts 1999, 76th Leg., ch. 34, §1, eff. Sept. 1, 1999. Source: Former Fam §11.75.

Official Comment

Section 1 of the UCCJA was a statement of the purposes of the Act. Although extensively cited by courts, it was eliminated because Uniform Acts no longer contain such a section. Nonetheless, this Act should be interpreted according to its purposes which are to:

(1) Avoid jurisdictional competition and conflict with courts of other States in matters of child custody which have in the past resulted in the shifting of children from State to State with harmful effects on their well-being;

(2) Promote cooperation with the courts of other States to the end that a custody decree is rendered in that State which can best decide the case in the interest of the child;

(3) Discourage the use of the interstate system for continuing controversies over child custody;

(4) Deter abductions of children;

(5) Avoid relitigation of custody decisions of other States in this State; and

(6) Facilitate the enforcement of custody decrees of other States.

FAM §152.102. DEFINITIONS

In this chapter:

(1) "Abandoned" means left without provision for reasonable and necessary care or supervision.

(2) "Child" means an individual who has not attained 18 years of age.

(3) "Child custody determination" means a judgment, decree, or other order of a court providing for legal custody, physical custody, or visitation with respect to a child. The term includes permanent, temporary, initial, and modification orders. The term does not include an order relating to child support or another monetary obligation of an individual.

(4) "Child custody proceeding" means a proceeding in which legal custody, physical custody, or visitation with respect to a child is an issue. The term includes a proceeding for divorce, separation, neglect, abuse, dependency, guardianship, paternity, termination of parental rights, and protection from domestic violence in

which the issue may appear. The term does not include a proceeding involving juvenile delinquency, contractual emancipation, or enforcement under Subchapter D.

(5) "Commencement" means the filing of the first pleading in a proceeding.

(6) "Court" means an entity authorized under the law of a state to establish, enforce, or modify a child custody determination.

(7) "Home state" means the state in which a child lived with a parent or a person acting as a parent for at least six consecutive months immediately before the commencement of a child custody proceeding. In the case of a child less than six months of age, the term means the state in which the child lived from birth with a parent or a person acting as a parent. A period of temporary absence of a parent or a person acting as a parent is part of the period.

(8) "Initial determination" means the first child custody determination concerning a particular child.

(9) "Issuing court" means the court that makes a child custody determination for which enforcement is sought under this chapter.

(10) "Issuing state" means the state in which a child custody determination is made.

(11) "Legal custody" means the managing conservatorship of a child.

(12) "Modification" means a child custody determination that changes, replaces, supersedes, or is otherwise made after a previous determination concerning the same child, whether or not it is made by the court that made the previous determination.

(13) "Person acting as a parent" means a person, other than a parent, who:

(A) has physical custody of the child or has had physical custody for a period of six consecutive months, including any temporary absence, within one year immediately before the commencement of a child custody proceeding; and

(B) has been awarded legal custody by a court or claims a right to legal custody under the law of this state.

(14) "Physical custody" means the physical care and supervision of a child.

(15) "Tribe" means an Indian tribe or band, or Alaskan Native village, that is recognized by federal law or formally acknowledged by a state.

(16) "Visitation" means the possession of or access to a child.

(17) "Warrant" means an order issued by a court authorizing law enforcement officers to take physical custody of a child.

History of Fam §152.102: Acts 1995, 74th Leg., ch. 20, §1, eff. April 20, 1995. Renumbered from §152.002 by Acts 1999, 76th Leg., ch. 34, §1, eff. Sept. 1, 1999. Source: Former Fam §11.52.

Official Comment

The UCCJA did not contain a definition of "child." The definition here is taken from the PKPA.

The definition of "child-custody determination" now closely tracks the PKPA definition. It encompasses any judgment, decree or other order which provides for the custody of, or visitation with, a child, regardless of local terminology, including such labels as "managing conservatorship" or "parenting plan."

The definition of "child-custody proceeding" has been expanded from the comparable definition in the UCCJA. These listed proceedings have generally been determined to be the type of proceeding to which the UCCJA and PKPA are applicable. The list of examples removes any controversy about the types of proceedings where a custody determination can occur. Proceedings that affect access to the child are subject to this Act. The inclusion of proceedings related to protection from domestic violence is necessary because in some States domestic violence proceedings may affect custody of and visitation with a child. Juvenile delinquency or proceedings to confer contractual rights are not "custody proceedings" because they do not relate to civil aspects of access to a child. While a determination of paternity is covered under the Uniform Interstate Family Support Act, the custody and visitation aspects of paternity cases are custody proceedings. Cases involving the Hague Convention on the Civil Aspects of International Child Abduction have not been included at this point because custody of the child is not determined in a proceeding under the International Child Abductions Remedies Act. Those proceedings are specially included in the Article 3 enforcement process.

"Commencement" has been included in the definitions as a replacement for the term "pending" found in the UCCJA. Its inclusion simplifies some of the simultaneous proceedings provisions of this Act.

The definition of "home State" has been reworded slightly. No substantive change is intended from the UCCJA.

The term "issuing State" is borrowed from UIFSA. In UIFSA, it refers to the court that issued the support or parentage order. Here, it refers to the State, or the court, which made the custody determination that is sought to be enforced. It is used primarily in Article 3.

[This paragraph is commenting on §102(12) of the UCCJEA, which the Texas Legislature did not enact.] The term "person" has been added to ensure that the provisions of this Act apply when the State is the moving party in a custody proceeding or has legal custody of a child. The definition of "person" is the one that is mandated for all Uniform Acts.

The term "person acting as a parent" has been slightly redefined. It has been broadened from the definition in the UCCJA to include a person who has acted as a parent for a significant period of time prior to the filing of the custody proceeding as well as a person who currently has physical custody of the child. In addition, a person acting as a parent must either have legal custody or claim a right to legal custody under the law of this State. The reference to the law of this State means that a court determines the issue of whether someone is a "person acting as a parent" under its own law. This reaffirms the traditional view that a court in a child custody case applies its own substantive law. The court does not have to undertake a choice-of-law analysis to determine whether the individual who is claiming to be a person acting as a parent has standing to seek custody of the child.

The definition of "tribe" is the one mandated for use in Uniform Acts. Should a State choose to apply this Act to tribal adjudications, this definition should be enacted as well as the entirety of Section 104.

The term "contestant" as has been omitted from this revision. It was defined in the UCCJA §2(1) as "a person, including a parent, who claims a right to custody or visitation rights with respect to a child." It seems to have served little purpose over the years, and whatever function it once had has been subsumed by state laws on who has standing to seek custody of or visitation with a child. In addition UCCJA §2(5) which defined "decree" and "custody decree" has been eliminated as duplicative of the definition of "custody determination."

FAM §152.103. PROCEEDINGS GOVERNED BY OTHER LAW

This chapter does not govern an adoption proceeding or a proceeding pertaining to the authorization of emergency medical care for a child.

History of Fam §152.103: Acts 1999, 76th Leg., ch. 34, §1, eff. Sept. 1, 1999.

Official Comment

Two proceedings are governed by other acts. Adoption cases are excluded from this Act because adoption is a specialized area which is thoroughly covered by the Uniform Adoption Act (UAA) (1994). Most States either will adopt that Act or will adopt the jurisdictional provisions of that Act. Therefore the jurisdictional provisions governing adoption proceeding are generally found elsewhere.

However, there are likely to be a number of instances where it will be necessary to apply this Act in an adoption proceeding. For example, if a State adopts the UAA then Section 3-101 of the Act specifically refers in places to the Uniform Child Custody Jurisdiction Act which will become a reference to this Act. Second, the UAA requires that if an adoption is denied or set aside, the court is to determine the child's custody. UAA §3-704. Those custody proceedings would be subject to this Act. See Joan Heifetz Hollinger, The Uniform Adoption Act: Reporter's Ruminations, 30 Fam.L.Q. 345 (1996).

Children that are the subject of interstate placements for adoption or foster care are governed by the Interstate Compact on the Placement of Children (ICPC). The UAA §2-107 provides that the provisions of the compact, although not jurisdictional, supply the governing rules for all children who are subject to it. As stated in the Comments to that section: "Once a court exercises jurisdiction, the ICPC helps determine the legality of an interstate placement." For a discussion of the relationship between the UCCJA and the ICPC see *J.D.S. v. Franks*, 893 P.2d 732 (Ariz. 1995).

Proceedings pertaining to the authorization of emergency medical care for children are outside the scope of this Act since they are not custody determinations. All States have procedures which allow the State to temporarily supersede parental authority for purposes of emergency medical procedures. Those provisions will govern without regard to this Act.

FAM §152.104. APPLICATION TO INDIAN TRIBES

(a) A child custody proceeding that pertains to an Indian child as defined in the Indian Child Welfare Act of 1978 (25 U.S.C. Section 1901 et seq.) is not subject to this chapter to the extent that it is governed by the Indian Child Welfare Act.

(b) A court of this state shall treat a tribe as if it were a state of the United States for the purpose of applying this subchapter and Subchapter C.

(c) A child custody determination made by a tribe under factual circumstances in substantial conformity with the jurisdictional standards of this chapter must be recognized and enforced under Subchapter D.

History of Fam §152.104: Acts 1999, 76th Leg., ch. 34, §1, eff. Sept. 1, 1999.

Official Comment

This section allows States the discretion to extend the terms of this Act to Indian tribes by removing the brackets. The definition of "tribe" is found at Section 102(16). This Act does not purport to legislate custody jurisdiction for tribal courts. However, a Tribe could adopt this Act as enabling legislation by simply replacing references to "this State" with "this Tribe."

Subsection (a) is not bracketed. If the Indian Child Welfare Act requires that a case be heard in tribal court, then its provisions determine jurisdiction.

FAM §152.105. INTERNATIONAL APPLICATION OF CHAPTER

(a) A court of this state shall treat a foreign country as if it were a state of the United States for the purpose of applying this subchapter and Subchapter C.

(b) Except as otherwise provided in Subsection (c), a child custody determination made in a foreign country under factual circumstances in substantial conformity with the jurisdictional standards of this chapter must be recognized and enforced under Subchapter D.

(c) A court of this state need not apply this chapter if the child custody law of a foreign country violates fundamental principles of human rights.

History of Fam §152.105: Acts 1995, 74th Leg., ch. 20, §1, eff. April 20, 1995. Renumbered from §152.023 by Acts 1999, 76th Leg., ch. 34, §1, eff. Sept. 1, 1999. Source: Former Fam §11.73.

Official Comment

The provisions of this Act have international application to child custody proceedings and determinations of other countries. Another country will be treated as if it were a State of the United States for purposes of applying Articles 1 and 2 of this Act. Custody determinations of other countries will be enforced if the facts of the case indicate that jurisdiction was in substantial compliance with the requirements of this Act.

In this section, the term "child-custody determination" should be interpreted to include proceedings relating to custody or analogous institutions of the other country. See generally, Article 3 of The Hague Convention on Jurisdiction, Applicable Law, Recognition, Enforcement and Co-operation in Respect of Parental Responsibility and Measures for the Protection of Children. 35 I.L.M. 1391 (1996).

A court of this State may refuse to apply this Act when the child custody law of the other country violates basic principles relating to the protection of human rights and fundamental freedoms. The same concept is found in Section 20 of the Hague Convention on the Civil Aspects of International Child Abduction (return of the child may be refused if this would not be permitted by the fundamental principles of the requested State relating to the protection of human rights and fundamental freedoms). In applying subsection (c), the court's scrutiny should be on the child custody law of the foreign country and not on other aspects of the other legal system. This Act takes no position on what laws relating to child custody would violate fundamental freedoms. While the provision is a traditional one in international agreements, it is invoked only in the most egregious cases.

This section is derived from Section 23 of the UCCJA.

FAM §152.106. EFFECT OF CHILD CUSTODY DETERMINATION

A child custody determination made by a court of this state that had jurisdiction under this chapter binds all persons who have been served in accordance with the laws of this state or notified in accordance with Section 152.108 or who have submitted to the jurisdiction of the court and who have been given an opportunity to be heard. As to those persons, the determination is conclusive as to all decided issues of law and fact except to the extent the determination is modified.

History of Fam §152.106: Acts 1995, 74th Leg., ch. 20, §1, eff. April 20, 1995. Renumbered from §152.012 by Acts 1999, 76th Leg., ch. 34, §1, eff. Sept. 1, 1999. Source: Former Fam §11.62.

Official Comment

No substantive changes have been made to this section which was Section 12 of the UCCJA.

FAM §152.107. PRIORITY

If a question of existence or exercise of jurisdiction under this chapter is raised in a child custody proceeding, the question, upon request of a party, must be given priority on the calendar and handled expeditiously.

History of Fam §152.107: Acts 1995, 74th Leg., ch. 20, §1, eff. April 20, 1995. Renumbered from §152.024 by Acts 1999, 76th Leg., ch. 34, §1, eff. Sept. 1, 1999. Source: Former Fam §11.74.

Official Comment

No substantive change was made to this section which was Section 24 of the UCCJA. The section is placed toward the beginning of Article 1 to emphasize its importance.

The language change from "case" to "question" is intended to clarify that it is the jurisdictional issue which must be expedited and not the entire custody case. Whether the entire custody case should be given priority is a matter of local law.

FAM §152.108. NOTICE TO PERSONS OUTSIDE STATE

(a) Notice required for the exercise of jurisdiction when a person is outside this state may be given in a manner prescribed by the law of this state for service of process or by the law of the state in which the service is made. Notice must be given in a manner reasonably calculated to give actual notice but may be by publication if other means are not effective.

(b) Proof of service may be made in the manner prescribed by the law of this state or by the law of the state in which the service is made.

(c) Notice is not required for the exercise of jurisdiction with respect to a person who submits to the jurisdiction of the court.

History of Fam §152.108: Acts 1995, 74th Leg., ch. 20, §1, eff. April 20, 1995. Amended by Acts 1999, 76th Leg., ch. 178, §6, eff. Aug. 30, 1999. Renumbered from §152.005 and amended by Acts 1999, 76th Leg., ch. 34, §1, eff. Sept. 1, 1999. Source: Former Fam §11.55.

Official Comment

This section authorizes notice and proof of service to be made by any method allowed by either the State which issues the notice or the State where the notice is received. This eliminates the need to specify the type of notice in the Act and therefore the provisions of Section 5 of the UCCJA which specified how notice was to be accomplished were eliminated. The change reflects an approach in this Act to use local law to determine many procedural issues. Thus, service by facsimile is permissible if allowed by local rule in either State. In addition, where special service or notice rules are available for some procedures, in either jurisdiction, they could be utilized under this Act. For example, if a case involves domestic violence and the statute of either State would authorize notice to be served by a peace officer, such service could be used under this Act.

Although Section 105 requires foreign countries to be treated as States for purposes of this Act, attorneys should be cautioned about service and notice in foreign countries. Countries have their own rules on service which must usually be followed. Attorneys should consult the Hague Convention on the Service Abroad of Judicial and Extrajudicial Documents in Civil or Commercial Matters, 20 U.S.T. 36, T.I.A.S. 6638 (1965).

FAM §152.109. APPEARANCE & LIMITED IMMUNITY

(a) A party to a child custody proceeding, including a modification proceeding, or a petitioner or respondent in a proceeding to enforce or register a child custody determination, is not subject to personal jurisdiction in this state for another proceeding or purpose solely by reason of having participated, or of having been physically present for the purpose of participating, in the proceeding.

(b) A person who is subject to personal jurisdiction in this state on a basis other than physical presence is not immune from service of process in this state. A party present in this state who is subject to the jurisdiction of another state is not immune from service of process allowed under the laws of that state.

(c) The immunity granted by Subsection (a) does not extend to civil litigation based on acts unrelated to the participation in a proceeding under this chapter committed by an individual while present in this state.

History of Fam §152.109: Acts 1999, 76th Leg., ch. 34, §1, eff. Sept. 1, 1999.

Official Comment

This section establishes a general principle that participation in a custody proceeding does not, by itself, give the court jurisdiction over any issue for which personal jurisdiction over the individual is required. The term "participate" should be read broadly. For example, if jurisdiction is proper under Article 2, a respondent in an original custody determination, or a party in a modification determination, should be able to request custody without this constituting the seeking of affirmative relief that would waive personal jurisdictional objections. Once jurisdiction is proper under Article 2, a party should not be placed in the dilemma of choosing between seeking custody or protecting a right not to be subject to a monetary judgment by a court with no other relationship to the party.

This section is comparable to the immunity provision of UIFSA §314. A party who is otherwise not subject to personal jurisdiction can appear in a custody proceeding or an enforcement action without being subject to the general jurisdiction of the State by virtue of the appearance. However, if the petitioner would otherwise be subject to the jurisdiction of the State, appearing in a custody proceeding or filing an enforcement proceeding will not provide immunity. Thus, if the non-custodial parent moves from the State that decided the custody determination, that parent is still subject to the state's jurisdiction for enforcement of child support if the child or an individual obligee continues to reside there. See also UIFSA §205. If the non-custodial parent returns to enforce the visitation aspects of the custody determination, the State can utilize any appropriate means to collect the back-due child support. However, the situation is different if both parties move from State A after the determination, with the custodial parent and the child establishing a new home State in State B, and the non-custodial parent moving to State C. The non-custodial parent is not, at this point, subject to the jurisdiction of State B for monetary matters. See also *Kulko v. Superior Court*, 436 U.S. 84 (1978). If the non-custodial parent comes into State B to enforce the visitation aspects of the determination, the non-custodial parent is not subject to the jurisdiction of State B for those proceedings and issues requiring personal jurisdiction by filing the enforcement action.

A party also is immune from service of process during the time in the State for an enforcement action except for those claims for which jurisdiction could be based on contacts other than mere physical presence. Thus, when the non-custodial parent comes into State B to enforce the visitation aspects of the decree, State B cannot acquire jurisdiction over the child support aspects of the decree by serving the non-custodial parent in the State. Cf. UIFSA §611 (personally serving the obligor in the State of the residence of the obligee is not by itself a sufficient jurisdictional basis to authorize a modification of child support). However, a party who is in this State and subject to the jurisdiction of another State may be served with process to appear in that State, if allowable under the laws of that State.

As the Comments to UIFSA §314 note, the immunity provided by this section is limited. It does not provide immunity for civil litigation unrelated to the enforcement action. For example, a party to an enforcement action is not immune from service regarding a claim that involves an automobile accident occurring while the party is in the State.

FAM §152.110. COMMUNICATION BETWEEN COURTS

(a) In this section, "record" means information that is inscribed on a tangible medium or that is stored in an electronic or other medium and is retrievable in perceivable form.

(b) A court of this state may communicate with a court in another state concerning a proceeding arising under this chapter.

(c) The court may allow the parties to participate in the communication. If the parties are not able to participate in the communication, they must be given the opportunity to present facts and legal arguments before a decision on jurisdiction is made.

E (d) If proceedings involving the same parties are pending simultaneously in a court of this state and a court of another state, the court of this state shall inform the other court of the simultaneous proceedings. The court of this state shall request that the other court hold the proceeding in that court in abeyance until the court in this state conducts a hearing to determine whether the court has jurisdiction over the proceeding.

A (e) Communication between courts on schedules, calendars, court records, and similar matters may occur without informing the parties. A record need not be made of the communication.

A (f) Except as otherwise provided in Subsection (e), a record must be made of any communication under this section. The parties must be informed promptly of the communication and granted access to the record.

History of Fam §152.110: Acts 1999, 76th Leg., ch. 34, §1, eff. Sept. 1, 1999. Amended by Acts 2001, 77th Leg., ch. 329, §1, eff. May 25, 2001.

Official Comment

This section emphasizes the role of judicial communications. It authorizes a court to communicate concerning any proceeding arising under this Act. This includes communication with foreign tribunals and tribal courts. Communication can occur in many different ways such as by telephonic conference and by on-line or other electronic communication. The Act does not preclude any method of communication and recognizes that there will be increasing use of modern communication techniques.

Communication between courts is required under Sections 204, 206, and 306 and strongly suggested in applying Section 207. Apart from those sections, there may be less need under this Act for courts to communicate concerning jurisdiction due to the prioritization of home state jurisdiction. Communication is authorized, however, whenever the court finds it would be helpful. The court may authorize the parties to participate in the communication. However, the Act does not mandate participation. Communication between courts is often difficult to schedule and participation by the parties may be impractical. Phone calls often have to be made after-hours or whenever the schedules of judges allow.

This section does require that a record be made of the conversation and that the parties have access to that record in order to be informed of the content of the conversation. The only exception to this requirement is when the communication involves relatively inconsequential matters such as scheduling, calendars, and court records. Included within this latter type of communication would be matters of cooperation between courts under Section 112. A record includes notes or transcripts of a court reporter who listened to a conference call between the courts, an electronic recording of a telephone call, a memorandum or an electronic record of the communication between the courts, or a memorandum or an electronic record made by a court after the communication.

The second sentence of subsection (c) protects the parties against unauthorized ex parte communications. The parties' participation in the communication may amount to a hearing if there is an opportunity to present facts and jurisdictional arguments. However, absent such an opportunity, the participation of the parties should not to be considered a substitute for a hearing and the parties must be given an opportunity to fairly and fully present facts and arguments on the jurisdictional issue before a determination is made. This may be done through a hearing or, if appropriate, by affidavit or memorandum. The court is expected to set forth the basis for its jurisdictional decision, including any court-to-court communication which may have been a factor in the decision.

FAM §152.111. TAKING TESTIMONY IN ANOTHER STATE

(a) In addition to other procedures available to a party, a party to a child custody proceeding may offer testimony of witnesses who are located in another state, including testimony of the parties and the child, by deposition or other means allowed in this state for testimony taken in another state. The court on its own motion may order that the testimony of a person be taken in another state and may prescribe the manner in which and the terms upon which the testimony is taken.

(b) A court of this state may permit an individual residing in another state to be deposed or to testify by telephone, audiovisual means, or other electronic means before a designated court or at another location in that state. A court of this state shall cooperate with courts of other states in designating an appropriate location for the deposition or testimony.

(c) Documentary evidence transmitted from another state to a court of this state by technological means that do not produce an original writing may not be excluded from evidence on an objection based on the means of transmission.

History of Fam §152.111: Acts 1995, 74th Leg., ch. 20, §1, eff. April 20, 1995. Renumbered from §152.018 by Acts 1999, 76th Leg., ch. 34, §1, eff. Sept. 1, 1999. Source: Former Fam §11.68.

Official Comment

No substantive changes have been made to subsection (a) which was Section 18 of the UCCJA.

Subsections (b) and (c) merely provide that modern modes of communication are permissible in the taking of testimony and the transmittal of documents. See also UIFSA §316.

FAM §152.112. COOPERATION BETWEEN COURTS; PRESERVATION OF RECORDS

(a) A court of this state may request the appropriate court of another state to:

(1) hold an evidentiary hearing;

(2) order a person to produce or give evidence pursuant to procedures of that state;

(3) order that an evaluation be made with respect to the custody of a child involved in a pending proceeding;

(4) forward to the court of this state a certified copy of the transcript of the record of the hearing, the evidence otherwise presented, and any evaluation prepared in compliance with the request; and

(5) order a party to a child custody proceeding or any person having physical custody of the child to appear in the proceeding with or without the child.

(b) Upon request of a court of another state, a court of this state may hold a hearing or enter an order described in Subsection (a).

(c) Travel and other necessary and reasonable expenses incurred under Subsections (a) and (b) may be assessed against the parties according to the law of this state.

(d) A court of this state shall preserve the pleadings, orders, decrees, records of hearings, evaluations, and other pertinent records with respect to a child custody proceeding until the child attains 18 years of age. Upon appropriate request by a court or law enforcement official of another state, the court shall forward a certified copy of those records.

History of Fam §152.112: Acts 1995, 74th Leg., ch. 20, §1, eff. April 20, 1995. Renumbered from §§152.019-.021 by Acts 1999, 76th Leg., ch. 34, §1, eff. Sept. 1, 1999. Source: Former Fam §§11.69-.71.

Official Comment

This section is the heart of judicial cooperation provision of this Act. It provides mechanisms for courts to cooperate with each other in order to decide cases in an efficient manner without causing undue expense to the parties. Courts may request assistance from courts of other States and may assist courts of other States.

The provision on the assessment of costs for travel provided in the UCCJA §19 has been changed. The UCCJA provided that the costs may be assessed against the parties or the State or county. Assessment of costs against a government entity in a case where the government is not involved is inappropriate and therefore that provision has been removed. In addition, if the State is involved as a party, assessment of costs and expenses against the State must be authorized by other law. It should be noted that the term "expenses" means out-of-pocket costs. Overhead costs should not be assessed as expenses.

No other substantive changes have been made. The term "social study" as used in the UCCJA was replaced with the modern term: "custody evaluation." The Act does not take a position on the admissibility of a custody evaluation that was conducted in another State. It merely authorizes a court to seek assistance of, or render assistance to, a court of another State.

This section combines the text of Sections 19-22 of the UCCJA.

Sections 152.113-152.200 reserved for expansion

SUBCHAPTER C. JURISDICTION

FAM §152.201. INITIAL CHILD CUSTODY JURISDICTION

(a) Except as otherwise provided in Section 152.204, a court of this state has jurisdiction to make an initial child custody determination only if:

(1) this state is the home state of the child on the date of the commencement of the proceeding, or was the home state of the child within six months before the commencement of the proceeding and the child is absent from this state but a parent or person acting as a parent continues to live in this state;

(2) a court of another state does not have jurisdiction under Subdivision (1), or a court of the home state of the child has declined to exercise jurisdiction on the ground that this state is the more appropriate forum under Section 152.207 or 152.208, and:

(A) the child and the child's parents, or the child and at least one parent or a person acting as a parent, have a significant connection with this state other than mere physical presence; and

(B) substantial evidence is available in this state concerning the child's care, protection, training, and personal relationships;

(3) all courts having jurisdiction under Subdivision (1) or (2) have declined to exercise jurisdiction on the ground that a court of this state is the more appropriate forum to determine the custody of the child under Section 152.207 or 152.208; or

(4) no court of any other state would have jurisdiction under the criteria specified in Subdivision (1), (2), or (3).

(b) Subsection (a) is the exclusive jurisdictional basis for making a child custody determination by a court of this state.

(c) Physical presence of, or personal jurisdiction over, a party or a child is not necessary or sufficient to make a child custody determination.

History of Fam §152.201: Acts 1995, 74th Leg., ch. 20, §1, eff. April 20, 1995. Amended by Acts 1995, 74th Leg., ch. 751, §24, eff. Sept. 1, 1995; Acts 1997, 75th Leg., ch. 575, §7, eff. Sept. 1, 1997. Renumbered from §152.003 and amended by Acts 1999, 76th Leg., ch. 34, §1, eff. Sept. 1, 1999. Source: Former Fam §11.53.

In re McCoy, 52 S.W.3d 297, 306 (Tex.App.—Corpus Christi 2001, orig. proceeding). "We hold the 'date of commencement of the proceeding,' for purposes of

§152.201, must be the date of commencement of a proceeding in a *Texas* court. We find no provision that would allow the date of commencement to somehow 'relate back' to the date that either [husband] filed suit in Qatar, or the date [wife] filed suit in Arkansas."

Official Comment

This section provides mandatory jurisdictional rules for the original child custody proceeding. It generally continues the provisions of the UCCJA §3. However, there have been a number of changes to the jurisdictional bases.

1. Home state jurisdiction. The jurisdiction of the home State has been prioritized over other jurisdictional bases. Section 3 of the UCCJA provided four independent and concurrent bases of jurisdiction. The PKPA provides that full faith and credit can only be given to an initial custody determination of a "significant connection" State when there is no home State. This Act prioritizes home state jurisdiction in the same manner as the PKPA thereby eliminating any potential conflict between the two acts.

The six-month extended home state provision of subsection (a)(1) has been modified slightly from the UCCJA. The UCCJA provided that home state jurisdiction continued for six months when the child had been removed by a person seeking the child's custody or for other reasons and a parent or a person acting as a parent continues to reside in the home State. Under this Act, it is no longer necessary to determine why the child has been removed. The only inquiry relates to the status of the person left behind. This change provides a slightly more refined home state standard than the UCCJA or the PKPA, which also requires a determination that the child has been removed "by a contestant or for other reasons." The scope of the PKPA's provision is theoretically narrower than this Act. However, the phrase "or for other reasons" covers most fact situations where the child is not in the home State and, therefore, the difference has no substantive effect.

In another sense, the six-month extended home state jurisdiction provision in this Act is narrower than the comparable provision in the PKPA. The PKPA's definition of extended home State is more expansive because it applies whenever a "contestant" remains in the home State. That class of individuals has been eliminated in this Act. This Act retains the original UCCJA classification of "parent or person acting as parent" to define who must remain for a State to exercise the six-month extended home state jurisdiction. This eliminates the undesirable jurisdictional determinations which would occur as a result of differing state substantive laws on visitation involving grandparents and others. For example, if State A's law provided that grandparents could obtain visitation with a child after the death of one of the parents, then the grandparents, who would be considered "contestants" under the PKPA, could file a proceeding within six months after the remaining parent moved and have the case heard in State A. However, if State A did not provide that grandparents could seek visitation under such circumstances, the grandparents would not be considered "contestants" and State B where the child acquired a new home State would provide the only forum. This Act bases jurisdiction on the parent and child or person acting as a parent and child relationship without regard to grandparents or other potential seekers of custody or visitation. There is no conflict with the broader provision of the PKPA. The PKPA in §(c)(1) authorizes States to narrow the scope of their jurisdiction.

2. Significant connection jurisdiction. This jurisdictional basis has been amended in four particulars from the UCCJA. First, the "best interest" language of the UCCJA has been eliminated. This phrase tended to create confusion between the jurisdictional issue and the substantive custody determination. Since the language was not necessary for the jurisdictional issue, it has been removed.

Second, the UCCJA based jurisdiction on the presence of a significant connection between the child and the child's parents or the child and at least one contestant. This Act requires that the significant connections be between the child, the child's parents or the child and a person acting as a parent.

Third, a significant connection State may assume jurisdiction only when there is no home State or when the home State decides that the significant connection State would be a more appropriate forum under Section 207 or 208. Fourth, the determination of significant connections has been changed to eliminate the language of "present or future care." The jurisdictional determination should be made by determining whether there is sufficient evidence in the State for the court to make an informed custody determination. That evidence might relate to the past as well as to the "present or future."

Emergency jurisdiction has been moved to a separate section. This is to make it clear that the power to protect a child in crisis does not include the power to enter a permanent order for that child except as provided by that section.

Paragraph (a)(3) provides for jurisdiction when all States with jurisdiction under paragraphs (a)(1) and (2) determine that this State is a more appropriate forum. The determination would have to be made by all States with jurisdiction under subsection (a)(1) and (2). Jurisdiction would not exist under this paragraph because the home State determined it is a more appropriate place to hear the case if there is another State that could exercise significant connection jurisdiction under subsection (a)(2).

Paragraph (a)(4) retains the concept of jurisdiction by necessity as found in the UCCJA and in the PKPA. This default jurisdiction only occurs if no other State would have jurisdiction under subsections (a)(1) through (a)(3).

Subsections (b) and (c) clearly State the relationship between jurisdiction under this Act and other forms of jurisdiction. Personal jurisdiction over, or the physical presence of, a parent or the child is neither necessary nor required under this Act. In other words neither minimum contacts nor service within the State is required for the court to have jurisdiction to make a custody determination. Further, the presence of minimum contacts or service within the State does not confer jurisdiction to make a custody determination. Subject to Section 204, satisfaction of the requirements of subsection (a) is mandatory.

The requirements of this section, plus the notice and hearing provisions of the Act, are all that is necessary to satisfy due process. This Act, like the UCCJA and the PKPA is based on Justice Frankfurter's concurrence in *May v. Anderson*, 345 U.S. 528 (1953). As pointed out by Professor Bodenheimer, the reporter for the UCCJA, no "workable interstate custody law could be built around [Justice] Burton's plurality opinion ...." Bridgette Bodenheimer, The Uniform Child Custody Jurisdiction Act: A Legislative Remedy for Children Caught in the Conflict of Laws, 22 Vand.L.Rev. 1207, 1233 (1969). It should also be noted that since jurisdiction to make a child custody determination is subject matter jurisdiction, an agreement of the parties to confer jurisdiction on a court that would not otherwise have jurisdiction under this Act is ineffective.

FAM §152.202. EXCLUSIVE CONTINUING JURISDICTION

(a) Except as otherwise provided in Section 152.204, a court of this state which has made a child custody determination consistent with Section 152.201 or 152.203 has exclusive continuing jurisdiction over the determination until:

(1) a court of this state determines that neither the child, nor the child and one parent, nor the child and a person acting as a parent, have a significant connection with this state and that substantial evidence is no longer available in this state concerning the child's care, protection, training, and personal relationships; or

(2) a court of this state or a court of another state determines that the child, the child's parents, and any person acting as a parent do not presently reside in this state.

(b) A court of this state which has made a child custody determination and does not have exclusive, continuing jurisdiction under this section may modify that determination only if it has jurisdiction to make an initial determination under Section 152.201.

History of Fam §152.202: Acts 1995, 74th Leg., ch. 20, §1, eff. April 20, 1995. Amended by Acts 1995, 74th Leg., ch. 751, §24, eff. Sept. 1, 1995; Acts 1997, 75th

Leg., ch. 575, §7, eff. Sept. 1, 1997. Renumbered from §152.003(d) by Acts 1999, 76th Leg., ch. 34, §1, eff. Sept. 1, 1999. Source: Former Fam §11.53.

In re Bellamy, 67 S.W.3d 482, 484-85 (Tex.App.—Texarkana 2002, n.p.h.). "[W]e find that §§152.202 and 155.003(b)(1) conflict in this case. When a provision of Chapter 152 conflicts with another provision of the Family Code or another statute or rule of Texas and the conflict cannot be reconciled, Chapter 152 prevails. Under the UCCJEA, Texas retains jurisdiction even if Texas is no longer the home state of the child or of the custodial parent, so long as there is a significant connection with this state. [Mother] contends that, because most of the exhibits admitted into evidence by [father] were from Louisiana, this shows substantial evidence is no longer available in Texas. [Section 152.202(a)(1)] allows Texas to maintain jurisdiction so long as there is substantial evidence relating to [child]'s care, protection, training, and personal relationships in Texas. Just because evidence is introduced from other states does not mean substantial evidence in Texas is lacking."

Official Comment

This is a new section addressing continuing jurisdiction. Continuing jurisdiction was not specifically addressed in the UCCJA. Its absence caused considerable confusion, particularly because the PKPA, §1738(d), requires other States to give Full Faith and Credit to custody determinations made by the original decree State pursuant to the decree State's continuing jurisdiction so long as that State has jurisdiction under its own law and remains the residence of the child or any contestant.

This section provides the rules of continuing jurisdiction and borrows from UIFSA as well as recent UCCJA case law. The continuing jurisdiction of the original decree State is exclusive. It continues until one of two events occurs:

1. If a parent or a person acting as a parent remains in the original decree State, continuing jurisdiction is lost when neither the child, the child and a parent, nor the child and a person acting as a parent continue to have a significant connection with the original decree State and there is no longer substantial evidence concerning the child's care, protection, training and personal relations in that State. In other words, even if the child has acquired a new home State, the original decree State retains exclusive, continuing jurisdiction, so long as the general requisites of the "substantial connection" jurisdiction provisions of Section 201 are met. If the relationship between the child and the person remaining in the State with exclusive, continuing jurisdiction becomes so attenuated that the court could no longer find significant connections and substantial evidence, jurisdiction would no longer exist.

The use of the phrase "a court of this State" under subsection (a)(1) makes it clear that the original decree State is the sole determinant of whether jurisdiction continues. A party seeking to modify a custody determination must obtain an order from the original decree State stating that it no longer has jurisdiction.

2. Continuing jurisdiction is lost when the child, the child's parents, and any person acting as a parent no longer reside in the original decree State. The exact language of subparagraph (a)(2) was the subject of considerable debate. Ultimately the Conference settled on the phrase that "a court of this State or a court of another State determines that the child, the child's parents, and any person acting as a parent do not presently reside in this State" to determine when the exclusive, continuing jurisdiction of a State ended. The phrase is meant to be identical in meaning to the language of the PKPA which provides that full faith and credit is to be given to custody determinations made by a State in the exercise of its continuing jurisdiction when that "State remains the residence of …." The phrase is also the equivalent of the language "continues to reside" which occurs in UIFSA §205(a)(1) to determine the exclusive, continuing jurisdiction of the State that made a support order. The phrase "remains the residence of" in the PKPA has been the subject of conflicting case law. It is the intention of this Act that paragraph (a)(2) of this section means that the named persons no longer continue to actually live within the State. Thus, unless a modification proceeding has been commenced, when the child, the parents, and all persons acting as parents physically leave the State to live elsewhere, the exclusive, continuing jurisdiction ceases.

The phrase "do not presently reside" is not used in the sense of a technical domicile. The fact that the original determination State still considers one parent a domiciliary does not prevent it from losing exclusive, continuing jurisdiction after the child, the parents, and all persons acting as parents have moved from the State.

If the child, the parents, and all persons acting as parents have all left the State which made the custody determination prior to the commencement of the modification proceeding, considerations of waste of resources dictate that a court in State B, as well as a court in State A, can decide that State A has lost exclusive, continuing jurisdiction.

The continuing jurisdiction provisions of this section are narrower than the comparable provisions of the PKPA. That statute authorizes continuing jurisdiction so long as any "contestant" remains in the original decree State and that State continues to have jurisdiction under its own law. This Act eliminates the contestant classification. The Conference decided that a remaining grandparent or other third party who claims a right to visitation, should not suffice to confer exclusive, continuing jurisdiction on the State that made the original custody determination after the departure of the child, the parents and any person acting as a parent. The significant connection to the original decree State must relate to the child, the child and a parent, or the child and a person acting as a parent. This revision does not present a conflict with the PKPA. The PKPA's reference in §1738(d) to §1738(c)(1) recognizes that States may narrow the class of cases that would be subject to exclusive, continuing jurisdiction. However, during the transition from the UCCJA to this Act, some States may continue to base continuing jurisdiction on the continued presence of a contestant, such as a grandparent. The PKPA will require that such decisions be enforced. The problem will disappear as States adopt this Act to replace the UCCJA.

Jurisdiction attaches at the commencement of a proceeding. If State A had jurisdiction under this section at the time a modification proceeding was commenced there, it would not be lost by all parties moving out of the State prior to the conclusion of proceeding. State B would not have jurisdiction to hear a modification unless State A decided that State B was more appropriate under Section 207.

Exclusive, continuing jurisdiction is not reestablished if, after the child, the parents, and all persons acting as parents leave the State, the non-custodial parent returns. As subsection (b) provides, once a State has lost exclusive, continuing jurisdiction, it can modify its own determination only if it has jurisdiction under the standards of Section 201. If another State acquires exclusive continuing jurisdiction under this section, then its orders cannot be modified even if this State has once again become the home State of the child.

In accordance with the majority of UCCJA case law, the State with exclusive, continuing jurisdiction may relinquish jurisdiction when it determines that another State would be a more convenient forum under the principles of Section 207.

FAM §152.203. JURISDICTION TO MODIFY DETERMINATION

Except as otherwise provided in Section 152.204, a court of this state may not modify a child custody determination made by a court of another state unless a court of this state has jurisdiction to make an initial determination under Section 152.201(a)(1) or (2) and:

(1) the court of the other state determines it no longer has exclusive continuing jurisdiction under Section 152.202 or that a court of this state would be a more convenient forum under Section 152.207; or

(2) a court of this state or a court of the other state determines that the child, the child's parents, and any person acting as a parent do not presently reside in the other state.

History of Fam §152.203: Acts 1995, 74th Leg., ch. 20, §1, eff. April 20, 1995. Amended by Acts 1995, 74th Leg., ch. 751, §24, eff. Sept. 1, 1995; Acts 1997, 75th Leg., ch. 575, §7, eff. Sept. 1, 1997. Renumbered from §152.003(d) by Acts 1999, 76th Leg., ch. 34, §1, eff. Sept. 1, 1999. Source: Former Fam §11.64.

Official Comment

This section complements Section 202 and is addressed to the court that is confronted with a proceeding to modify a custody determination of another State. It prohibits a court from modifying a custody determination made consistently with this Act by a court in another State unless a court of that State determines that it no longer has exclusive, continuing jurisdiction under Section 202 or that this State would be a more convenient forum under Section 207. The modification State is not authorized to determine that the original decree State has lost its jurisdiction. The only exception is when the child, the child's parents, and any person acting as a parent do not presently reside in the other State. In other words, a court of the modification State can determine that all parties have moved away from the original State. The court of the modification State must have jurisdiction under the standards of Section 201.

FAM §152.204. TEMPORARY EMERGENCY JURISDICTION

(a) A court of this state has temporary emergency jurisdiction if the child is present in this state and the child has been abandoned or it is necessary in an emergency to protect the child because the child, or a sibling or parent of the child, is subjected to or threatened with mistreatment or abuse.

(b) If there is no previous child custody determination that is entitled to be enforced under this chapter and a child custody proceeding has not been commenced in a court of a state having jurisdiction under Sections 152.201 through 152.203, a child custody determination made under this section remains in effect until an order is obtained from a court of a state having jurisdiction under Sections 152.201 through 152.203. If a child custody proceeding has not been or is not commenced in a court of a state having jurisdiction under Sections 152.201 through 152.203, a child custody determination made under this section becomes a final determination, if it so provides and this state becomes the home state of the child.

(c) If there is a previous child custody determination that is entitled to be enforced under this chapter, or a child custody proceeding has been commenced in a court of a state having jurisdiction under Sections 152.201 through 152.203, any order issued by a court of this state under this section must specify in the order a period that the court considers adequate to allow the person seeking an order to obtain an order from the state having jurisdiction under Sections 152.201 through 152.203. The order issued in this state remains in effect until an order is obtained from the other state within the period specified or the period expires.

(d) A court of this state which has been asked to make a child custody determination under this section, upon being informed that a child custody proceeding has been commenced in or a child custody determination has been made by a court of a state having jurisdiction under Sections 152.201 through 152.203, shall immediately communicate with the other court. A court of this state which is exercising jurisdiction pursuant to Sections 152.201 through 152.203, upon being informed that a child custody proceeding has been commenced in or a child custody determination has been made by a court of another state under a statute similar to this section shall immediately communicate with the court of that state to resolve the emergency, protect the safety of the parties and the child, and determine a period for the duration of the temporary order.

History of Fam §152.204: Acts 1995, 74th Leg., ch. 20, §1, eff. April 20, 1995. Amended by Acts 1995, 74th Leg., ch. 751, §24, eff. Sept. 1, 1995; Acts 1997, 75th Leg., ch. 575, §7, eff. Sept. 1, 1997. Renumbered from §152.003(e) by Acts 1999, 76th Leg., ch. 34, §1, eff. Sept. 1, 1999.

Official Comment

The provisions of this section are an elaboration of what was formerly Section 3(a)(3) of the UCCJA. It remains, as Professor Bodenheimer's comments to that section noted, "an extraordinary jurisdiction reserved for extraordinary circumstances."

This section codifies and clarifies several aspects of what has become common practice in emergency jurisdiction cases under the UCCJA and PKPA. First, a court may take jurisdiction to protect the child even though it can claim neither home State nor significant connection jurisdiction. Second, the duties of States to recognize, enforce and not modify a custody determination of another State do not take precedence over the need to enter a temporary emergency order to protect the child. Third, a custody determination made under the emergency jurisdiction provisions of this section is a temporary order. The purpose of the order is to protect the child until the State that has jurisdiction under Sections 201-203 enters an order.

Under certain circumstances, however, subsection (b) provides that an emergency custody determination may become a final custody determination. If there is no existing custody determination, and no custody proceeding is filed in a State with jurisdiction under Sections 201-203, an emergency custody determination made under this section becomes a final determination, if it so provides, when the State that issues the order becomes the home State of the child.

Subsection (c) is concerned with the temporary nature of the order when there exists a prior custody order that is entitled to be enforced under this Act or when a subsequent custody proceeding is filed in a State with jurisdiction under Sections 201- 203. Subsection (c) allows the temporary order to remain in effect only so long as is necessary for the person who obtained the determination under this section to present a case and obtain an order from the State with jurisdiction under Sections 201-203. That time period must be specified in the order. If there is an existing order by a State with jurisdiction under Sections 201-203, that order need not be reconfirmed. The temporary emergency determination would lapse by its own terms at the end of the specified period or when an order is obtained from the court with jurisdiction under Sections 202-203. The court with appropriate jurisdiction also may decide, under the provisions of 207, that the court that entered the emergency order is in a better position to address the safety of the person who obtained the emergency order, or the child, and decline jurisdiction under Section 207.

Any hearing in the State with jurisdiction under Sections 201-203 on the temporary emergency determination is subject to the provisions of Sections 111 and 112. These sections facilitate the presentation of testimony and evidence taken out of State. If there is a concern that the person obtaining the temporary emergency determination under this section would be in danger upon returning to the State with jurisdiction under Sections 201-203, these provisions should be used.

Subsection (d) requires communication between the court of the State that is exercising jurisdiction under this section and the court of another State that is exercising jurisdiction under Sections 201-203. The pleading rules of Section 209 apply fully to determinations made under this section. Therefore, a person seeking a temporary emergency custody determination is required to inform the court pursuant to Section 209(d) of any proceeding concerning the child that has been commenced elsewhere. The person commencing the custody proceeding under Sections 201-203 is required under Section 209(a) to inform the court about the temporary emergency proceeding. These pleading requirements are to be strictly followed so that the courts are able to resolve the emergency, protect the safety of the parties and the child, and determine a period for the duration of the temporary order.

Relationship to the PKPA. The definition of emergency has been modified to harmonize it with the PKPA. The PKPA's definition of emergency jurisdiction does not use the term "neglect." It defines an emergency as "mistreatment or abuse." Therefore "neglect" has been eliminated as a basis for the assumption of temporary emergency jurisdiction. Neglect is so elastic a concept that it could justify taking emergency jurisdiction in a wide variety of cases. Under the PKPA, if a State exercised temporary emergency jurisdiction based on a finding that the child was neglected without a finding of mistreatment or abuse, the order would not be entitled to federal enforcement in other States.

Relationship to Protective Order Proceedings. The UCCJA and the PKPA were enacted long before the advent of state procedures on the use of protective orders to alleviate problems of domestic violence. Issues of custody and visitation often arise within the context of protective order proceedings since the protective order is often invoked to keep one parent away from the other parent and the children when there is a threat of violence. This Act recognizes that a protective order proceeding will often be the procedural vehicle for invoking jurisdiction by authorizing a court to assume temporary emergency jurisdiction when the child's parent or sibling has been subjected to or threatened with mistreatment or abuse.

In order for a protective order that contains a custody determination to be enforceable in another State it must comply with the provisions of this Act and the PKPA. Although the Violence Against Women's Act (VAWA), 18 U.S.C. §2265, does provide an independent basis for the granting of full faith and credit to protective orders, it expressly excludes "custody" orders from the definition of "protective order," 22 U.S.C. §2266.

Many States authorize the issuance of protective orders in an emergency without notice and hearing. This Act does not address the propriety of that procedure. It is left to local law to determine the circumstances under which such an order could be issued, and the type of notice that is required, in a case without an interstate element. However, an order issued after the assumption of temporary emergency jurisdiction is entitled to interstate enforcement and nonmodification under this Act and the PKPA only if there has been notice and a reasonable opportunity to be heard as set out in Section 205. Although VAWA does require that full faith and credit be accorded to ex parte protective orders if notice will be given and there will be a reasonable opportunity to be heard, it does not include a "custody" order within the definition of "protective order."

VAWA does play an important role in determining whether an emergency exists. That Act requires a court to give full faith and credit to a protective order issued in another State if the order is made in accordance with the VAWA. This would include those findings of fact contained in the order. When a court is deciding whether an emergency exists under this section, it may not relitigate the existence of those factual findings.

FAM §152.205. NOTICE; OPPORTUNITY TO BE HEARD; JOINDER

(a) Before a child custody determination is made under this chapter, notice and an opportunity to be heard in accordance with the standards of Section 152.108 must be given to all persons entitled to notice under the law of this state as in child custody proceedings between residents of this state, any parent whose parental rights have not been previously terminated, and any person having physical custody of the child.

(b) This chapter does not govern the enforceability of a child custody determination made without notice or an opportunity to be heard.

(c) The obligation to join a party and the right to intervene as a party in a child custody proceeding under this chapter are governed by the law of this state as in child custody proceedings between residents of this state.

History of Fam §152.205: Acts 1995, 74th Leg., ch. 20, §1, eff. April 20, 1995. Renumbered from §§152.004, 152.010 by Acts 1999, 76th Leg., ch. 34, §1, eff. Sept. 1, 1999. Source: Former Fam §§11.54, 11.60.

Official Comment

This section generally continues the notice provisions of the UCCJA. However, it does not attempt to dictate who is entitled to notice. Local rules vary with regard to persons entitled to seek custody of a child. Therefore, this section simply indicates that persons entitled to seek custody should receive notice but leaves the rest of the determination to local law. Parents whose parental rights have not been previously terminated and persons having physical custody of the child are specifically mentioned as persons who must be given notice. The PKPA, §1738A(e), requires that they be given notice in order for the custody determination to be entitled to full faith and credit under that Act.

State laws also vary with regard to whether a court has the power to issue an enforceable temporary custody order without notice and hearing in a case without any interstate element. Such temporary orders may be enforceable, as against due process objections, for a short period of time if issued as a protective order or a temporary restraining order to protect a child from harm. Whether such orders are enforceable locally is beyond the scope of this Act. Subsection (b) clearly provides that the validity of such orders and the enforceability of such orders is governed by the law which authorizes them and not by this Act. An order is entitled to interstate enforcement and nonmodification under this Act only if there has been notice and an opportunity to be heard. The PKPA, §1738A(e), also requires that a custody determination is entitled to full faith and credit only if there has been notice and an opportunity to be heard.

Rules requiring joinder of people with an interest in the custody of and visitation with a child also vary widely throughout the country. The UCCJA has a separate section on joinder of parties which has been eliminated. The issue of who is entitled to intervene and who must be joined in a custody proceeding is to be determined by local state law.

A sentence of the UCCJA §4 which indicated that persons outside the State were to be given notice and an opportunity to be heard in accordance with the provision of that Act has been eliminated as redundant.

FAM §152.206. SIMULTANEOUS PROCEEDINGS

(a) Except as otherwise provided in Section 152.204, a court of this state may not exercise its jurisdiction under this subchapter if, at the time of the commencement of the proceeding, a proceeding concerning the custody of the child has been commenced in a court of another state having jurisdiction substantially in conformity with this chapter, unless the proceeding has been terminated or is stayed by the court of the other state because a court of this state is a more convenient forum under Section 152.207.

(b) Except as otherwise provided in Section 152.204, a court of this state, before hearing a child custody proceeding, shall examine the court documents and other information supplied by the parties pursuant to Section 152.209. If the court determines that a child custody proceeding has been commenced in a court in another state having jurisdiction substantially in accordance with this chapter, the court of this state shall stay its proceeding and communicate with the court of the other state. If the court of the state having jurisdiction substantially in accordance with this chapter does not determine that the court of this state is a more appropriate forum, the court of this state shall dismiss the proceeding.

(c) In a proceeding to modify a child custody determination, a court of this state shall determine whether a proceeding to enforce the determination has been commenced in another state. If a proceeding to enforce a child custody determination has been commenced in another state, the court may:

(1) stay the proceeding for modification pending the entry of an order of a court of the other state enforcing, staying, denying, or dismissing the proceeding for enforcement;

(2) enjoin the parties from continuing with the proceeding for enforcement; or

(3) proceed with the modification under conditions it considers appropriate.

History of Fam §152.206: Acts 1995, 74th Leg., ch. 20, §1, eff. April 20, 1995. Renumbered from §152.006 by Acts 1999, 76th Leg., ch. 34, §1, eff. Sept. 1, 1999. Source: Former Fam §11.56.

Official Comment

This section represents the remnants of the simultaneous proceedings provision of the UCCJA §6. The problem of simultaneous proceedings is no longer a significant issue. Most of the problems have been resolved by the prioritization of home state jurisdiction under Section 201; the exclusive, continuing jurisdiction provisions of Section 202; and the prohibitions on modification of Section 203. If there is a home State, there can be no exercise of significant connection jurisdiction in an initial child custody determination and, therefore, no simultaneous proceedings. If there is a State of exclusive, continuing jurisdiction, there cannot be another State with concurrent jurisdiction and, therefore, no simultaneous proceedings. Of course, the home State, as well as the State with exclusive, continuing jurisdiction, could defer to another State under Section 207. However, that decision is left entirely to the home State or the State with exclusive, continuing jurisdiction.

Under this Act, the simultaneous proceedings problem will arise only when there is no home State, no State with exclusive, continuing jurisdiction and more than one significant connection State. For those cases, this section retains the "first in time" rule of the UCCJA. Subsection (b) retains the UCCJA's policy favoring judicial communication. Communication between courts is required when it is determined that a proceeding has been commenced in another State.

Subsection (c) concerns the problem of simultaneous proceedings in the State with modification jurisdiction and enforcement proceedings under Article 3. This section authorizes the court with exclusive, continuing jurisdiction to stay the modification proceeding pending the outcome of the enforcement proceeding, to enjoin the parties from continuing with the enforcement proceeding, or to continue the modification proceeding under such conditions as it determines are appropriate. The court may wish to communicate with the enforcement court. However, communication is not mandatory. Although the enforcement State is required by the PKPA to enforce according to its terms a custody determination made consistently with the PKPA, that duty is subject to the decree being modified by a State with the power to do so under the PKPA. An order to enjoin the parties from enforcing the decree is the equivalent of a temporary modification by a State with the authority to do so. The concomitant provision addressed to the enforcement court is Section 306 of this Act. That section requires the enforcement court to communicate with the modification court in order to determine what action the modification court wishes the enforcement court to take.

The term "pending" that was utilized in the UCCJA section on simultaneous proceeding has been replaced. It has caused considerable confusion in the case law. It has been replaced with the term "commencement of the proceeding" as more accurately reflecting the policy behind this section. The latter term is defined in Section 102(5).

FAM §152.207. INCONVENIENT FORUM

(a) A court of this state which has jurisdiction under this chapter to make a child custody determination may decline to exercise its jurisdiction at any time if it determines that it is an inconvenient forum under the circumstances and that a court of another state is a more appropriate forum. The issue of inconvenient forum may be raised upon motion of a party, the court's own motion, or request of another court.

(b) Before determining whether it is an inconvenient forum, a court of this state shall consider whether it is appropriate for a court of another state to exercise jurisdiction. For this purpose, the court shall allow the parties to submit information and shall consider all relevant factors, including:

(1) whether domestic violence has occurred and is likely to continue in the future and which state could best protect the parties and the child;

(2) the length of time the child has resided outside this state;

(3) the distance between the court in this state and the court in the state that would assume jurisdiction;

(4) the relative financial circumstances of the parties;

(5) any agreement of the parties as to which state should assume jurisdiction;

(6) the nature and location of the evidence required to resolve the pending litigation, including testimony of the child;

(7) the ability of the court of each state to decide the issue expeditiously and the procedures necessary to present the evidence; and

(8) the familiarity of the court of each state with the facts and issues in the pending litigation.

(c) If a court of this state determines that it is an inconvenient forum and that a court of another state is a more appropriate forum, the court shall stay the proceedings upon condition that a child custody proceeding be promptly commenced in another designated state and may impose any other condition the court considers just and proper.

(d) A court of this state may decline to exercise its jurisdiction under this chapter if a child custody determination is incidental to an action for divorce or another proceeding while still retaining jurisdiction over the divorce or other proceeding.

History of Fam §152.207: Acts 1995, 74th Leg., ch. 20, §1, eff. April 20, 1995. Amended by Acts 1997, 75th Leg., ch. 15, §3, eff. Sept. 1, 1997. Renumbered from §152.007 by Acts 1999, 76th Leg., ch. 34, §1, eff. Sept. 1, 1999. Source: Former Fam §11.57.

Official Comment

This section retains the focus of Section 7 of the UCCJA. It authorizes courts to decide that another State is in a better position to make the custody determination, taking into consideration the relative circumstances of the parties. If so, the court may defer to the other State.

The list of factors that the court may consider has been updated from the UCCJA. The list is not meant to be exclusive. Several provisions require comment. Subparagraph (1) is concerned specifically with domestic violence and other matters affecting the health and safety of the parties. For this purpose, the court should determine whether the parties are located in different States because one party is a victim of domestic violence or child abuse. If domestic violence or child abuse has occurred, this factor authorizes the court to consider which State can best protect the victim from further violence or abuse.

In applying subparagraph (3), courts should realize that distance concerns can be alleviated by applying the communication and cooperation provisions of Sections 111 and 112.

In applying subsection (7) on expeditious resolution of the controversy, the court could consider the different procedural and evidentiary laws of the two States, as well as the flexibility of the court dockets. It also should consider the ability of a court to arrive at a solution to all the legal issues surrounding the family. If one State has jurisdiction to decide both the custody and support issues, it would be desirable to determine that State to be the most convenient forum. The same is true when children of the same family live in different States. It would be inappropriate to require parents to have custody proceedings in several States when one State could resolve the custody of all the children.

Before determining whether to decline or retain jurisdiction, the court of this State may communicate, in accordance with Section 110, with a court of another State and exchange information pertinent to the assumption of jurisdiction by either court.

There are two departures from Section 7 of the UCCJA. First, the court may not simply dismiss the action. To do so would leave the case in limbo. Rather the court shall stay the case and direct the parties to file in the State that has been found to be the more convenient forum. The court is also authorized to impose any other conditions it considers appropriate. This might include the issuance of temporary custody orders during the time necessary to commence a proceeding in the designated State, dismissing the case if the custody proceeding is not commenced in the other State or resuming jurisdiction if a court of the other State refuses to take the case.

Second, UCCJA, §7(g) which allowed the court to assess fees and costs if it was a clearly inappropriate court, has been eliminated. If a court has jurisdiction under this Act, it could not be a clearly inappropriate court.

FAM §152.208. JURISDICTION DECLINED BY REASON OF CONDUCT

(a) Except as otherwise provided in Section 152.204 or other law of this state, if a court of this state has jurisdiction under this chapter because a person seeking to invoke its jurisdiction has engaged in unjustifiable conduct, the court shall decline to exercise its jurisdiction unless:

(1) the parents and all persons acting as parents have acquiesced in the exercise of jurisdiction;

(2) a court of the state otherwise having jurisdiction under Sections 152.201 through 152.203 determines that this state is a more appropriate forum under Section 152.207; or

(3) no court of any other state would have jurisdiction under the criteria specified in Sections 152.201 through 152.203.

(b) If a court of this state declines to exercise its jurisdiction pursuant to Subsection (a), it may fashion an appropriate remedy to ensure the safety of the child and prevent a repetition of the unjustifiable conduct, including staying the proceeding until a child custody proceeding is commenced in a court having jurisdiction under Sections 152.201 through 152.203.

(c) If a court dismisses a petition or stays a proceeding because it declines to exercise its jurisdiction pursuant to Subsection (a), it shall assess against the party seeking to invoke its jurisdiction necessary and reasonable expenses including costs, communication expenses, attorney's fees, investigative fees, expenses for witnesses, travel expenses, and child care during the course of the proceedings, unless the party from whom fees are sought establishes that the assessment would be clearly inappropriate. The court may not assess fees, costs, or expenses against this state unless authorized by law other than this chapter.

History of Fam §152.208: Acts 1995, 74th Leg., ch. 20, §1, eff. April 20, 1995. Renumbered from §152.008 by Acts 1999, 76th Leg., ch. 34, §1, eff. Sept. 1, 1999. Source: Former Fam §11.58.

Official Comment

The "Clean Hands" section of the UCCJA has been truncated in this Act. Since there is no longer a multiplicity of jurisdictions which could take cognizance of a child-custody proceeding, there is less of a concern that one parent will take the child to another jurisdiction in an attempt to find a more favorable forum. Most of the jurisdictional problems generated by abducting parents should be solved by the prioritization of home State in Section 201; the exclusive, continuing jurisdiction provisions of Section 202; and the ban on modification in Section 203. For example, if a parent takes the child from the home State and seeks an original custody determination elsewhere, the stay-at-home parent has six months to file a custody petition under the extended home state jurisdictional provision of Section 201, which will ensure that the case is retained in the home State. If a petitioner for a modification determination takes the child from the State that issued the original custody determination, another State cannot assume jurisdiction as long at the first State exercises exclusive, continuing jurisdiction.

Nonetheless, there are still a number of cases where parents, or their surrogates, act in a reprehensible manner, such as removing, secreting, retaining, or restraining the child. This section ensures that abducting parents will not receive an advantage for their unjustifiable conduct. If the conduct that creates the jurisdiction is unjustified, courts must decline to exercise jurisdiction that is inappropriately invoked by one of the parties. For example, if one parent abducts the child pre-decree and establishes a new home State, that jurisdiction will decline to hear the case. There are exceptions. If the other party has acquiesced in the court's jurisdiction, the court may hear the case. Such acquiescence may occur by filing a pleading submitting to the jurisdiction, or by not filing in the court that would otherwise have jurisdiction under this Act. Similarly, if the court that would have jurisdiction finds that the court of this State is a more appropriate forum, the court may hear the case.

This section applies to those situations where jurisdiction exists because of the unjustified conduct of the person seeking to invoke it. If, for example, a parent in the State with exclusive, continuing jurisdiction under Section 202 has either restrained the child from visiting with the other parent, or has retained the child after visitation, and seeks to modify the decree, this section in inapplicable. The conduct of restraining or retaining the child did not create jurisdiction. Jurisdiction existed under this Act without regard to the parent's conduct. Whether a court should decline to hear the parent's request to modify is a matter of local law.

The focus in this section is on the unjustified conduct of the person who invokes the jurisdiction of the court. A technical illegality or wrong is insufficient to trigger the applicability of this section. This is particularly important in cases involving domestic violence and child abuse. Domestic violence victims should not be charged with unjustifiable conduct for conduct that occurred in the process of fleeing domestic violence, even if their conduct is technically illegal. Thus, if a parent flees with a child to escape domestic violence and in the process violates a joint custody decree, the case should not be automatically dismissed under this section. An inquiry must be made into whether the flight was justified under the circumstances of the case. However, an abusive parent who seizes the child and flees to another State to establish jurisdiction has engaged in unjustifiable conduct and the new State must decline to exercise jurisdiction under this section.

Subsection (b) authorizes the court to fashion an appropriate remedy for the safety of the child and to prevent a repetition of the unjustified conduct. Thus, it would be appropriate for the court to notify the other parent and to provide for foster care for the child until the child is returned to the other parent. The court could also stay the proceeding and require that a custody proceeding be instituted in another State that would have jurisdiction under this Act. It should be noted that the court is not making a forum non conveniens analysis in this section. If the conduct is unjustifiable, it must decline jurisdiction. It may, however, retain jurisdiction until a custody proceeding is commenced in the appropriate tribunal if such retention is necessary to prevent a repetition of the wrongful conduct or to ensure the safety of the child.

The attorney's fee standard for this section is patterned after the International Child Abduction Remedies Act, 42 U.S.C. §11607(b)(3). The assessed costs and fees are to be paid to the respondent who established that jurisdiction was based on unjustifiable conduct.

FAM §152.209. INFORMATION TO BE SUBMITTED TO COURT

(a) Except as provided by Subsection (e), in a child custody proceeding, each party, in its first pleading or in an attached affidavit, shall give information, if reasonably ascertainable, under oath as to the child's present address or whereabouts, the places where the child has lived during the last five years, and the names and present addresses of the persons with whom the child has lived during that period. The pleading or affidavit must state whether the party:

(1) has participated, as a party or witness or in any other capacity, in any other proceeding concerning the custody of or visitation with the child and, if so, identify the court, the case number, and the date of the child custody determination, if any;

(2) knows of any proceeding that could affect the current proceeding, including proceedings for enforcement and proceedings relating to domestic violence, protective orders, termination of parental rights, and adoptions and, if so, identify the court, the case number, and the nature of the proceeding; and

(3) knows the names and addresses of any person not a party to the proceeding who has physical custody of the child or claims rights of legal custody or physical custody of, or visitation with, the child and, if so, the names and addresses of those persons.

(b) If the information required by Subsection (a) is not furnished, the court, upon motion of a party or its own motion, may stay the proceeding until the information is furnished.

(c) If the declaration as to any of the items described in Subsections (a)(1) through (3) is in the affirmative, the declarant shall give additional information under oath as required by the court. The court may examine the parties under oath as to details of the information furnished and other matters pertinent to the court's jurisdiction and the disposition of the case.

(d) Each party has a continuing duty to inform the court of any proceeding in this or any other state that could affect the current proceeding.

(e) If a party alleges in an affidavit or a pleading under oath that the health, safety, or liberty of a party or child would be jeopardized by disclosure of identifying information, the information must be sealed and may not be disclosed to the other party or the public unless the court orders the disclosure to be made after a hearing in which the court takes into consideration the health, safety, or liberty of the party or child and determines that the disclosure is in the interest of justice.

History of Fam §152.209: Acts 1995, 74th Leg., ch. 20, §1, eff. April 20, 1995. Renumbered from §152.009 by Acts 1999, 76th Leg., ch. 34, §1, eff. Sept. 1, 1999. Source: Former Fam §11.59.

Official Comment

The pleading requirements from Section 9 of the UCCJA are generally carried over into this Act. However, the information is made subject to local law on the protection of names and other identifying information in certain cases. A number of States have enacted laws relating to the protection of victims in domestic violence and child abuse cases which provide for the confidentiality of victims names, addresses, and other information. These procedures must be followed if the child-custody proceeding of the State requires their applicability. See also, e.g., California Family Law Code §3409(a). If a State does not have local law that provides for protecting names and addresses, then subsection (e) or a similar provision should be adopted. Subsection (e) is based on the National Council of Juvenile and Family Court Judge's, Model Code on Domestic and Family Violence §304(c). There are other models to choose from, in particular UIFSA §312.

In subsection (a)(2), the term "proceedings" should be read broadly to include more than custody proceedings. Thus, if one parent was being criminally prosecuted for child abuse or custodial interference, those proceedings should be disclosed. If the child is subject to the Interstate Compact on the Placement of Children, facts relating to compliance with the Compact should be disclosed in the pleading or affidavit.

Subsection (b) has been added. It authorizes the court to stay the proceeding until the information required in subsection (a) has been disclosed, although failure to provide the information does not deprive the court of jurisdiction to hear the case. This follows the majority of jurisdictions which held that failure to comply with the pleading requirements of the UCCJA did not deprive the court of jurisdiction to make a custody determination.

FAM §152.210. APPEARANCE OF PARTIES & CHILD

(a) In a child custody proceeding in this state, the court may order a party to the proceeding who is in this state to appear before the court in person with or without the child. The court may order any person who is in this state and who has physical custody or control of the child to appear in person with the child.

(b) If a party to a child custody proceeding whose presence is desired by the court is outside this state, the court may order that a notice given pursuant to Section 152.108 include a statement directing the party to appear in person with or without the child and informing the party that failure to appear may result in a decision adverse to the party.

(c) The court may enter any orders necessary to ensure the safety of the child and of any person ordered to appear under this section.

(d) If a party to a child custody proceeding who is outside this state is directed to appear under Subsection (b) or desires to appear personally before the court with or without the child, the court may require another party to pay reasonable and necessary travel and other expenses of the party so appearing and of the child.

History of Fam §152.210: Acts 1995, 74th Leg., ch. 20, §1, eff. April 20, 1995. Renumbered from §152.011 by Acts 1999, 76th Leg., ch. 34, §1, eff. Sept. 1, 1999. Source: Former Fam §11.61.

Official Comment

No major changes have been made to this section which was Section 11 of the UCCJA. Language was added to subsection (a) to authorize the court to require a non-party who has physical custody of the child to produce the child.

Subsection (c) authorizes the court to enter orders providing for the safety of the child and the person ordered to appear with the child. If safety is a major concern, the court, as an alternative to ordering a party to appear with the child, could order and arrange for the party's testimony to be taken in another State under Section 111. This alternative might be important when there are safety concerns regarding requiring victims of domestic violence or child abuse to travel to the jurisdiction where the abuser resides.

Sections 152.211-152.300 reserved for expansion

SUBCHAPTER D. ENFORCEMENT

FAM §152.301. DEFINITIONS

In this subchapter:

(1) "Petitioner" means a person who seeks enforcement of an order for return of a child under the Hague Convention on the Civil Aspects of International Child Abduction or enforcement of a child custody determination.

(2) "Respondent" means a person against whom a proceeding has been commenced for enforcement of an order for return of a child under the Hague Convention on the Civil Aspects of International Child Abduction or enforcement of a child custody determination.

History of Fam §152.301: Acts 1999, 76th Leg., ch. 34, §1, eff. Sept. 1, 1999.

Official Comment

For purposes of this article, "petitioner" and "respondent" are defined. The definitions clarify certain aspects of the notice and hearing sections.

FAM §152.302. ENFORCEMENT UNDER HAGUE CONVENTION

Under this subchapter a court of this state may enforce an order for the return of the child made under the Hague Convention on the Civil Aspects of International Child Abduction as if it were a child custody determination.

History of Fam §152.302: Acts 1999, 76th Leg., ch. 34, §1, eff. Sept. 1, 1999.

Official Comment

This section applies the enforcement remedies provided by this article to orders requiring the return of a child issued under the authority of the International Child Abduction Remedies Act (ICARA), 42 U.S.C. §11601 et seq., implementing the Hague Convention on the Civil Aspects of International Child Abduction. Specific mention of ICARA proceedings is necessary because they often occur prior to any formal custody determination. However, the need for a speedy enforcement remedy for an order to return the child is just as necessary.

FAM §152.303. DUTY TO ENFORCE

(a) A court of this state shall recognize and enforce a child custody determination of a court of another state if the latter court exercised jurisdiction in substantial conformity with this chapter or the determination was made under factual circumstances meeting the jurisdictional standards of this chapter and the determination has not been modified in accordance with this chapter.

(b) A court of this state may utilize any remedy available under other law of this state to enforce a child custody determination made by a court of another state. The remedies provided in this subchapter are cumulative and do not affect the availability of other remedies to enforce a child custody determination.

History of Fam §152.303: Acts 1999, 76th Leg., ch. 34, §1, eff. Sept. 1, 1999.

Official Comment

This section is based on Section 13 of the UCCJA which contained the basic duty to enforce. The language of the original section has been retained and the duty to enforce is generally the same.

Enforcement of custody determinations of issuing States is also required by federal law in the PKPA, 28 U.S.C. §1738A(a). The changes made in Article 2 of this Act now make a State's duty to enforce and not modify a child custody determination of another State consistent with the enforcement and nonmodification provisions of the PKPA. Therefore custody determinations made by a State pursuant to the UCCJA that would be enforceable under the PKPA will generally be enforced under this Act. However, if a State custody determination made pursuant to the UCCJA would not be enforceable under the PKPA, it will also not be enforceable under this Act. Thus a custody determination made by a "significant connection" jurisdiction when there is a home State is not enforceable under the PKPA regardless of whether a proceeding was ever commenced in the home

State. Even though such a determination would be enforceable under the UCCJA with its four concurrent bases of jurisdiction, it would not be enforceable under this Act. This carries out the policy of the PKPA of strongly discouraging a State from exercising its concurrent "significant connection" jurisdiction under the UCCJA when another State could exercise "home state" jurisdiction.

This section also incorporates the concept of Section 15 of the UCCJA to the effect that a custody determination of another State will be enforced in the same manner as a custody determination made by a court of this State. Whatever remedies are available to enforce a local determination can be utilized to enforce a custody determination of another State. However, it remains a custody determination of the State that issued it. A child-custody determination of another State is not subject to modification unless the State would have jurisdiction to modify the determination under Article 2.

The remedies provided by this article for the enforcement of a custody determination will normally be used. This article does not detract from other remedies available under other local law. There is often a need for a number of remedies to ensure that a child-custody determination is obeyed. If other remedies would easily facilitate enforcement, they are still available. The petitioner, for example, can still cite the respondent for contempt of court or file a tort claim for intentional interference with custodial relations if those remedies are available under local law.

FAM §152.304. TEMPORARY VISITATION

(a) A court of this state which does not have jurisdiction to modify a child custody determination may issue a temporary order enforcing:

(1) a visitation schedule made by a court of another state; or

(2) the visitation provisions of a child custody determination of another state that does not provide for a specific visitation schedule.

(b) If a court of this state makes an order under Subsection (a)(2), the court shall specify in the order a period that it considers adequate to allow the petitioner to obtain an order from a court having jurisdiction under the criteria specified in Subchapter C. The order remains in effect until an order is obtained from the other court or the period expires.

History of Fam §152.304: Acts 1999, 76th Leg., ch. 34, §1, eff. Sept. 1, 1999.

Official Comment

This section authorizes a court to issue a temporary order if it is necessary to enforce visitation rights without violating the rules on nonmodification contained in Section 303. Therefore, if there is a visitation schedule provided in the custody determination that was made in accordance with Article 2, a court can issue an order under this section implementing the schedule. An implementing order may include make-up or substitute visitation.

A court may also issue a temporary order providing for visitation if visitation was authorized in the custody determination, but no specific schedule was included in the custody determination. Such an order could include a substitution of a specific visitation schedule for "reasonable and seasonable."

However, a court may not, under subsection (a)(2) provide for a permanent change in visitation. Therefore, requests for a permanent change in the visitation schedule must be addressed to the court with exclusive, continuing jurisdiction under Section 202 or modification jurisdiction under Section 203. As under Section 204, subsection (b) of this section requires that the temporary visitation order stay in effect only long enough to allow the person who obtained the order to obtain a permanent modification in the State with appropriate jurisdiction under Article 2.

FAM §152.305. REGISTRATION OF CHILD CUSTODY DETERMINATION

(a) A child custody determination issued by a court of another state may be registered in this state, with or without a simultaneous request for enforcement, by sending to the appropriate court in this state:

(1) a letter or other document requesting registration;

(2) two copies, including one certified copy, of the determination sought to be registered and a statement under penalty of perjury that to the best of the knowledge and belief of the person seeking registration the order has not been modified; and

(3) except as otherwise provided in Section 152.209, the name and address of the person seeking registration and any parent or person acting as a parent who has been awarded custody or visitation in the child custody determination sought to be registered.

(b) On receipt of the documents required by Subsection (a), the registering court shall:

(1) cause the determination to be filed as a foreign judgment, together with one copy of any accompanying documents and information, regardless of their form; and

(2) serve notice upon the persons named pursuant to Subsection (a)(3) and provide them with an opportunity to contest the registration in accordance with this section.

(c) The notice required by Subsection (b)(2) must state that:

(1) a registered determination is enforceable as of the date of the registration in the same manner as a determination issued by a court of this state;

(2) a hearing to contest the validity of the registered determination must be requested within 20 days after service of notice; and

(3) failure to contest the registration will result in confirmation of the child custody determination and preclude further contest of that determination with respect to any matter that could have been asserted.

(d) A person seeking to contest the validity of a registered order must request a hearing within 20 days after service of the notice. At that hearing, the court shall confirm the registered order unless the person contesting registration establishes that:

(1) the issuing court did not have jurisdiction under Subchapter C;

(2) the child custody determination sought to be registered has been vacated, stayed, or modified by a court having jurisdiction to do so under Subchapter C; or

(3) the person contesting registration was entitled to notice, but notice was not given in accordance with the standards of Section 152.108, in the proceedings before the court that issued the order for which registration is sought.

(e) If a timely request for a hearing to contest the validity of the registration is not made, the registration is confirmed as a matter of law and the person requesting registration and all persons served must be notified of the confirmation.

(f) Confirmation of a registered order, whether by operation of law or after notice and hearing, precludes further contest of the order with respect to any matter that could have been asserted at the time of registration.

History of Fam §152.305: Acts 1995, 74th Leg., ch. 20, §1, eff. April 20, 1995. Renumbered from §§152.014 by Acts 1999, 76th Leg., ch. 34, §1, eff. Sept. 1, 1999. Source: Former Fam §11.66.

Official Comment

The remainder of this article provides enforcement mechanisms for interstate child custody determinations.

This section authorizes a simple registration procedure that can be used to predetermine the enforceability of a custody determination. It parallels the process in UIFSA for the registration of child support orders. It should be as much of an aid to pro se litigants as the registration procedure of UIFSA.

A custody determination can be registered without any accompanying request for enforcement. This may be of significant assistance in international cases. For example, the custodial parent under a foreign custody order can receive an advance determination of whether that order would be recognized and enforced before sending the child to the United States for visitation. Article 26 of the 1996 Hague Convention on Jurisdiction, Applicable Law, Recognition and Cooperation in Respect of Parental Responsibility and Measures for the Protection of Children, 35 I.L.M. 1391 (1996), requires those States which accede to the Convention to provide such a procedure.

FAM §152.306. ENFORCEMENT OF REGISTERED DETERMINATION

(a) A court of this state may grant any relief normally available under the law of this state to enforce a registered child custody determination made by a court of another state.

(b) A court of this state shall recognize and enforce, but may not modify, except in accordance with Subchapter C, a registered child custody determination of a court of another state.

History of Fam §152.306: Acts 1995, 74th Leg., ch. 20, §1, eff. April 20, 1995. Renumbered from §152.015 by Acts 1999, 76th Leg., ch. 34, §1, eff. Sept. 1, 1999. Source: Former Fam §11.65.

Official Comment

A registered child-custody determination can be enforced as if it was a child-custody determination of this State. However, it remains a custody determination of the State that issued it. A registered custody order is not subject to modification unless the State would have jurisdiction to modify the order under Article 2.

FAM §152.307. SIMULTANEOUS PROCEEDINGS

If a proceeding for enforcement under this subchapter is commenced in a court of this state and the court determines that a proceeding to modify the determination is pending in a court of another state having jurisdiction to modify the determination under Subchapter C, the enforcing court shall immediately communicate with the modifying court. The proceeding for enforcement continues unless the enforcing court, after consultation with the modifying court, stays or dismisses the proceeding.

History of Fam §152.307: Acts 1995, 74th Leg., ch. 20, §1, eff. April 20, 1995. Renumbered from §152.006 by Acts 1999, 76th Leg., ch. 34, §1, eff. Sept. 1, 1999. Source: Former Fam §11.56.

Official Comment

The pleading rules of Section 308, require the parties to disclose any pending proceedings. Normally, an enforcement proceeding will take precedence over a modification action since the PKPA requires enforcement of child custody determinations made in accordance with its terms. However, the enforcement court must communicate with the modification court in order to avoid duplicative litigation. The courts might decide that the court with jurisdiction under Article 2 shall continue with the modification action and stay the enforcement proceeding. Or they might decide that the enforcement proceeding shall go forward. The ultimate decision rests with the court having exclusive, continuing jurisdiction under Section 202, or if there is no State with exclusive, continuing jurisdiction, then the decision rests with the State that would have jurisdiction to modify under Section 203. Therefore, if that court determines that the enforcement proceeding should be stayed or dismissed, the enforcement court should stay or dismiss the proceeding. If the enforcement court does not do so, the court with exclusive, continuing jurisdiction under Section 202, or with modification jurisdiction under Section 203, could enjoin the parties from continuing with the enforcement proceeding.

FAM §152.308. EXPEDITED ENFORCEMENT OF CHILD CUSTODY DETERMINATION

(a) A petition under this subchapter must be verified. Certified copies of all orders sought to be enforced and of any order confirming registration must be attached to the petition. A copy of a certified copy of an order may be attached instead of the original.

(b) A petition for enforcement of a child custody determination must state:

(1) whether the court that issued the determination identified the jurisdictional basis it relied upon in exercising jurisdiction and, if so, what the basis was;

(2) whether the determination for which enforcement is sought has been vacated, stayed, or modified by a court whose decision must be enforced under this chapter and, if so, identify the court, the case number, and the nature of the proceeding;

(3) whether any proceeding has been commenced that could affect the current proceeding, including proceedings relating to domestic violence, protective orders, termination of parental rights, and adoptions

and, if so, identify the court, the case number, and the nature of the proceeding;

(4) the present physical address of the child and the respondent, if known;

(5) whether relief in addition to the immediate physical custody of the child and attorney's fees is sought, including a request for assistance from law enforcement officials and, if so, the relief sought; and

(6) if the child custody determination has been registered and confirmed under Section 152.305, the date and place of registration.

(c) Upon the filing of a petition, the court shall issue an order directing the respondent to appear in person with or without the child at a hearing and may enter any order necessary to ensure the safety of the parties and the child. The hearing must be held on the next judicial day after service of the order unless that date is impossible. In that event, the court shall hold the hearing on the first judicial day possible. The court may extend the date of hearing at the request of the petitioner.

(d) An order issued under Subsection (c) must state the time and place of the hearing and advise the respondent that at the hearing the court will award the petitioner immediate physical custody of the child and order the payment of fees, costs, and expenses under Section 152.312, and may schedule a hearing to determine whether further relief is appropriate, unless the respondent appears and establishes that:

(1) the child custody determination has not been registered and confirmed under Section 152.305 and that:

(A) the issuing court did not have jurisdiction under Subchapter C;

(B) the child custody determination for which enforcement is sought has been vacated, stayed, or modified by a court having jurisdiction to do so under Subchapter C; or

(C) the respondent was entitled to notice, but notice was not given in accordance with the standards of Section 152.108, in the proceedings before the court that issued the order for which enforcement is sought; or

(2) the child custody determination for which enforcement is sought was registered and confirmed under Section 152.305, but has been vacated, stayed, or modified by a court of a state having jurisdiction to do so under Subchapter C.

History of Fam §152.308: Acts 1999, 76th Leg., ch. 34, §1, eff. Sept. 1, 1999.

Official Comment

This section provides the normal remedy that will be used in interstate cases: the production of the child in a summary, remedial process based on habeas corpus.

The petition is intended to provide the court with as much information as possible. Attaching certified copies of all orders sought to be enforced allows the court to have the necessary information. Most of the information relates to the permissible scope of the court's inquiry. The petitioner has the responsibility to inform the court of all proceedings that would affect the current enforcement action. Specific mention is made of certain proceedings to ensure that they are disclosed. A "procedure relating to domestic violence" includes not only protective order proceedings but also criminal prosecutions for child abuse or domestic violence.

The order requires the respondent to appear at a hearing on the next judicial day. The term "next judicial day" in this section means the next day when a judge is at the courthouse. At the hearing, the court will order the child to be delivered to the petitioner unless the respondent is prepared to assert that the issuing State lacked jurisdiction, that notice was not given in accordance with Section 108, or that the order sought to be enforced has been vacated, modified, or stayed by a court with jurisdiction to do so under Article 2. The court is also to order payment of the fees and expenses set out in Section 312. The court may set another hearing to determine whether additional relief available under this state's law should be granted.

If the order has been registered and confirmed in accordance with Section 304, the only defense to enforcement is that the order has been vacated, stayed or modified since the registration proceeding by a court with jurisdiction to do so under Article 2.

FAM §152.309. SERVICE OF PETITION & ORDER

Except as otherwise provided in Section 152.311, the petition and order must be served, by any method authorized by the law of this state, upon the respondent and any person who has physical custody of the child.

History of Fam §152.309: Acts 1999, 76th Leg., ch. 34, §1, eff. Sept. 1, 1999.

Official Comment

In keeping with other sections of this Act, the question of how the petition and order should be served is left to local law.

FAM §152.310. HEARING & ORDER

(a) Unless the court issues a temporary emergency order pursuant to Section 152.204, upon a finding that a petitioner is entitled to immediate physical custody of the child, the court shall order that the petitioner may take immediate physical custody of the child unless the respondent establishes that:

(1) the child custody determination has not been registered and confirmed under Section 152.305 and that:

(A) the issuing court did not have jurisdiction under Subchapter C;

(B) the child custody determination for which enforcement is sought has been vacated, stayed, or modified by a court of a state having jurisdiction to do so under Subchapter C; or

(C) the respondent was entitled to notice, but notice was not given in accordance with the standards of Section 152.108, in the proceedings before the court that issued the order for which enforcement is sought; or

(2) the child custody determination for which enforcement is sought was registered and confirmed under Section 152.305 but has been vacated, stayed, or modified by a court of a state having jurisdiction to do so under Subchapter C.

(b) The court shall award the fees, costs, and expenses authorized under Section 152.312 and may grant additional relief, including a request for the assistance of law enforcement officials, and set a further hearing to determine whether additional relief is appropriate.

(c) If a party called to testify refuses to answer on the ground that the testimony may be self-incriminating, the court may draw an adverse inference from the refusal.

(d) A privilege against disclosure of communications between spouses and a defense of immunity based on the relationship of husband and wife or parent and child may not be invoked in a proceeding under this subchapter.

History of Fam §152.310: Acts 1999, 76th Leg., ch. 34, §1, eff. Sept. 1, 1999.

Official Comment

The scope of inquiry for the enforcing court is quite limited. Federal law requires the court to enforce the custody determination if the issuing state's decree was rendered in compliance with the PKPA. 28 U.S.C. §1738A(a). This Act requires enforcement of custody determinations that are made in conformity with Article 2's jurisdictional rules.

The certified copy, or a copy of the certified copy, of the custody determination entitling the petitioner to the child is prima facie evidence of the issuing court's jurisdiction to enter the order. If the order is one that is entitled to be enforced under Article 2 and if it has been violated, the burden shifts to the respondent to show that the custody determination is not entitled to enforcement.

It is a defense to enforcement that another jurisdiction has issued a custody determination that is required to be enforced under Article 2. An example is when one court has based its original custody determination on the UCCJA §3(a)(2) (significant connections) and another jurisdiction has rendered an original custody determination based on the UCCJA §3(a)(1) (home State). When this occurs, Article 2 of this Act, as well as the PKPA, mandate that the home state determination be enforced in all other States, including the State that rendered the significant connections determination.

Lack of notice in accordance with Section 108 by a person entitled to notice and opportunity to be heard at the original custody determination is a defense to enforcement of the custody determination. The scope of the defense under this Act is the same as the defense would be under the law of the State that issued the notice. Thus, if the defense of lack of notice would not be available under local law if the respondent purposely hid from the petitioner, took deliberate steps to avoid service of process or elected not to participate in the initial proceedings, the defense would also not be available under this Act.

There are no other defenses to an enforcement action. If the child would be endangered by the enforcement of a custody or visitation order, there may be a basis for the assumption of emergency jurisdiction under Section 204 of this Act. Upon the finding of an emergency, the court issues a temporary order and directs the parties to proceed either in the court that is exercising continuing jurisdiction over the custody proceeding under Section 202, or the court that would have jurisdiction to modify the custody determination under Section 203.

The court shall determine at the hearing whether fees should be awarded under Section 312. If so, it should order them paid. The court may determine if additional relief is appropriate, including requesting law enforcement officers to assist the petitioner in the enforcement of the order. The court may set a hearing to determine whether further relief should be granted.

The remainder of this section is derived from UIFSA §316 with regard to the privilege of self-incrimination, spousal privileges, and immunities. It is included to keep parallel the procedures for child support and child custody proceedings to the extent possible.

FAM §152.311. WARRANT TO TAKE PHYSICAL CUSTODY OF CHILD

(a) Upon the filing of a petition seeking enforcement of a child custody determination, the petitioner may file a verified application for the issuance of a warrant to take physical custody of the child if the child is imminently likely to suffer serious physical harm or be removed from this state.

(b) If the court, upon the testimony of the petitioner or other witness, finds that the child is imminently likely to suffer serious physical harm or be removed from this state, it may issue a warrant to take physical custody of the child. The petition must be heard on the next judicial day after the warrant is executed unless that date is impossible. In that event, the court shall hold the hearing on the first judicial day possible. The application for the warrant must include the statements required by Section 152.308(b).

(c) A warrant to take physical custody of a child must:

(1) recite the facts upon which a conclusion of imminent serious physical harm or removal from the jurisdiction is based;

(2) direct law enforcement officers to take physical custody of the child immediately; and

(3) provide for the placement of the child pending final relief.

(d) The respondent must be served with the petition, warrant, and order immediately after the child is taken into physical custody.

(e) A warrant to take physical custody of a child is enforceable throughout this state. If the court finds on the basis of the testimony of the petitioner or other witness that a less intrusive remedy is not effective, it may authorize law enforcement officers to enter private property to take physical custody of the child. If required by exigent circumstances of the case, the court may authorize law enforcement officers to make a forcible entry at any hour.

(f) The court may impose conditions upon placement of a child to ensure the appearance of the child and the child's custodian.

History of Fam §152.311: Acts 1999, 76th Leg., ch. 34, §1, eff. Sept. 1, 1999.

Official Comment

The section provides a remedy for emergency situations where there is a reason to believe that the child will suffer imminent, serious physical harm or be removed from the jurisdiction once the respondent learns that the petitioner has filed an enforcement proceeding. If the court finds such harm exists, it should temporarily waive the notice requirements and issue a warrant to take physical custody of the child. Immediately after the warrant is executed, the respondent is to receive notice of the proceedings.

The term "harm" cannot be totally defined and, as in the issuance of temporary retraining orders, the appropriate issuance of a warrant is left to the circumstances of the case. Those circumstances include cases where the respondent is the subject of a criminal proceeding as well as situations where the respondent is secreting the child in violation of a court order, abusing the child, a flight risk and other circumstances that the court concludes make the issuance of notice a danger to the child. The court must hear the testimony of the petitioner or another witness prior to issuing the warrant. The testimony may be heard in person, via telephone, or by any other means acceptable under local law. The court must State the reasons for the issuance of the warrant. The warrant can be enforced by law enforcement officers wherever the child is found in the State. The warrant may authorize entry upon private property to pick up the child if no less intrusive means are possible. In extraordinary cases, the warrant may authorize law enforcement to make a forcible entry at any hour.

The warrant must provide for the placement of the child pending the determination of the enforcement proceeding. Since the issuance of the warrant would not occur absent a risk of serious harm to the child, placement cannot be with the respondent. Normally, the child would be placed with the petitioner. However, if placement with the petitioner is not indicated, the court can order any other appropriate placement authorized under the laws of the court's State. Placement with the petitioner may not be indicated if there is a likelihood that the petitioner also will flee the jurisdiction. Placement with the petitioner may not be practical if the petitioner is proceeding through an attorney and is not present before the court.

This section authorizes the court to utilize whatever means are available under local law to ensure the appearance of the petitioner and child at the enforcement hearing. Such means might include cash bonds, a surrender of a passport, or whatever the court determines is necessary.

FAM §152.312. COSTS, FEES, & EXPENSES

(a) The court shall award the prevailing party, including a state, necessary and reasonable expenses incurred by or on behalf of the party, including costs, communication expenses, attorney's fees, investigative fees, expenses for witnesses, travel expenses, and child care during the course of the proceedings, unless the party from whom fees or expenses are sought establishes that the award would be clearly inappropriate.

(b) The court may not assess fees, costs, or expenses against a state unless authorized by law other than this chapter.

History of Fam §152.312: Acts 1999, 76th Leg., ch. 34, §1, eff. Sept. 1, 1999.

Official Comment

This section is derived from the International Child Abduction Remedies Act, 42 U.S.C. §11607(b)(3). Normally the court will award fees and costs against the non-prevailing party. Included as expenses are the amount of investigation fees incurred by private persons or by public officials as well as the cost of child placement during the proceedings.

The non-prevailing party has the burden of showing that such an award would be clearly inappropriate. Fees and costs may be inappropriate if their payment would cause the parent and child to seek public assistance.

This section implements the policies of Section 8(c) of Pub.L. 96-611 (part of the PKPA) which provides that:

In furtherance of the purposes of section 1738A of title 28, United States Code [this section], as added by subsection (a) of this section, State courts are encouraged to –

(2) award to the person entitled to custody or visitation pursuant to a custody determination which is consistent with the provisions of such section 1738A [this section], necessary travel expenses, attorneys' fees, costs of private investigations, witness fees or expenses, and other expenses incurred in connection with such custody determination ....

The term "prevailing party" is not given a special definition for this Act. Each State will apply its own standard.

Subsection (b) was added to ensure that this section would not apply to the State unless otherwise authorized. The language is taken from UIFSA §313 (court may assess costs against obligee or support enforcement agency only if allowed by local law).

FAM §152.313. RECOGNITION & ENFORCEMENT

A court of this state shall accord full faith and credit to an order issued by another state and consistent with this chapter which enforces a child custody determination by a court of another state unless the order has been vacated, stayed, or modified by a court having jurisdiction to do so under Subchapter C.

History of Fam §152.313: Acts 1995, 74th Leg., ch. 20, §1, eff. April 20, 1995. Renumbered from §152.013 by Acts 1999, 76th Leg., ch. 34, §1, eff. Sept. 1, 1999. Source: Former Fam §11.63.

Official Comment

The enforcement order, to be effective, must also be enforced by other States. This section requires courts of this State to enforce and not modify enforcement orders issued by other States when made consistently with the provisions of this Act.

FAM §152.314. APPEALS

An appeal may be taken from a final order in a proceeding under this subchapter in accordance with expedited appellate procedures in other civil cases. Unless the court enters a temporary emergency order under Section 152.204, the enforcing court may not stay an order enforcing a child custody determination pending appeal.

History of Fam 152.314: Acts 1999, 76th Leg., ch. 34, §1, eff. Sept. 1, 1999.

Official Comment

The order may be appealed as an expedited civil matter. An enforcement order should not be stayed by the court. Provisions for a stay would defeat the purpose of having a quick enforcement procedure. If there is a risk of serious mistreatment or abuse to the child, a petition to assume emergency jurisdiction must be filed under Section 204. This section leaves intact the possibility of obtaining an extraordinary remedy such as mandamus or prohibition from an appellate court to stay the court's enforcement action. In many States, it is not possible to limit the constitutional authority of appellate courts to issue a stay. However, unless the information before the appellate panel indicates that emergency jurisdiction would be assumed under Section 204, there is no reason to stay the enforcement of the order pending appeal.

FAM §152.315. ROLE OF PROSECUTOR OR PUBLIC OFFICIAL

(a) In a case arising under this chapter or involving the Hague Convention on the Civil Aspects of International Child Abduction, the prosecutor or other appropriate public official may take any lawful action, including resorting to a proceeding under this subchapter or any other available civil proceeding to locate a child, obtain the return of a child, or enforce a child custody determination if there is:

(1) an existing child custody determination;

(2) a request to do so from a court in a pending child custody proceeding;

(3) a reasonable belief that a criminal statute has been violated; or

(4) a reasonable belief that the child has been wrongfully removed or retained in violation of the Hague Convention on the Civil Aspects of International Child Abduction.

(b) A prosecutor or appropriate public official acting under this section acts on behalf of the court and may not represent any party.

History of Fam §152.315: Acts 1999, 76th Leg., ch. 34, §1, eff. Sept. 1, 1999.

Official Comment

Sections 315-317 are derived from the recommendations of the *Obstacles Study* that urge a role for public authorities in civil enforcement of custody and visitation determinations. One of the basic policies behind this approach is that, as is the case with child support, the involvement of public authorities will encourage the parties to abide by the terms of the court order. The prosecutor usually would be the most appropriate public official to exercise authority under this section. However, States may locate the authority described in the section in the most appropriate public office for their governmental structure. The authority could be, for example, the Friend of the Court Office or the Attorney General. If the parties know that prosecutors and law enforcement officers are available to help secure the return of a child, the parties may be deterred from interfering with the exercise of rights established by court order.

The use of public authorities should provide a more effective method of remedying violations of the custody determination. Most parties do not have the resources to enforce a custody determination in another jurisdiction. The availability of the prosecutor or other government official as an enforcement agency will help ensure that remedies of this Act can be made available regardless of income level. In addition, the prosecutor may have resources to draw on that are unavailable to the average litigant.

The role of the public authorities should generally not begin until there is a custody determination that is sought to be enforced. The Act does not authorize the public authorities to be involved in the action leading up to the making of the custody determination, except when requested by the court, when there is a violation the Hague Convention on the Civil Aspects of International Child Abduction, or when the person holding the child has violated a criminal statute. This Act does not mandate that the public authorities be involved in all cases referred to it. There is only so much time and money available for enforcement proceedings. Therefore, the public authorities eventually will develop guidelines to determine which cases will receive priority.

The use of civil procedures instead of, or in addition to, filing and prosecuting criminal charges enlarges the prosecutor's options and may provide a more economical and less disruptive means of solving problems of criminal abduction and retention. With the use of criminal proceedings alone, the procedure may be inadequate to ensure the return of the child. The civil options would permit the prosecutor to resolve that recurring and often frustrating problem.

A concern was expressed about whether allowing the prosecutor to use civil means as a method of settling a child abduction violated either DR 7-105(A) of the Code of Professional Responsibility or Model Rule of Professional Responsibility 4.4. Both provisions either explicitly or implicitly disapprove of a lawyer threatening criminal action to gain an advantage in a civil case. However, the prohibition relates to threats that are solely to gain an advantage in a civil case. If the prosecutor has a good faith reason for pursuing the criminal action, there is no ethical violation. See also *Committee on Legal Ethics v. Printz*, 416 S.E. 2d 720 (W.Va. 1992) (lawyer can threaten to press criminal charges against a client's former employee unless employee made restitution).

It must be emphasized that the public authorities do not become involved in the merits of the case. They are authorized only to locate the child and enforce the custody determination. The public authority is authorized by this section to utilize any civil proceeding to secure the enforcement of the custody determination. In most jurisdictions, that would be a proceeding under this Act. If the prosecutor proceeds pursuant to this Act, the prosecutor is subject to its provisions. There is nothing in this Act that would prevent a State from authorizing the prosecutor or other public official to use additional remedies beyond those provided in this Act.

The public authority does not represent any party to the custody determination. It acts as a "friend of the court." Its role is to ensure that the custody determination is enforced.

Sections 315-317 are limited to cases covered by this Act, i.e. interstate cases. However, States may, if they wish, extend this part of the Act to intrastate cases.

It should also be noted that the provisions of this section relate to the civil enforcement of child custody determinations. Nothing in this section is meant to detract from the ability of the prosecutor to use criminal provisions in child abduction cases.

FAM §152.316. ROLE OF LAW ENFORCEMENT

At the request of a prosecutor or other appropriate public official acting under Section 152.315, a law enforcement officer may take any lawful action reasonably necessary to locate a child or a party and assist a prosecutor or appropriate public official with responsibilities under Section 152.315.

History of Fam §152.316: Acts 1999, 76th Leg., ch. 34, §1, eff. Sept. 1, 1999.

Official Comment

This section authorizes law enforcement officials to assist in locating a child and enforcing a custody determination when requested to do so by the public authorities. It is to be read as an enabling provision. Whether law enforcement officials have discretion in responding to a request by the prosecutor or other public official is a matter of local law.

FAM §152.317. COSTS & EXPENSES

If the respondent is not the prevailing party, the court may assess against the respondent all direct expenses and costs incurred by the prosecutor or other appropriate public official and law enforcement officers under Section 152.315 or 152.316.

History of Fam §152.317: Acts 1999, 76th Leg., ch. 34, §1, eff. Sept. 1, 1999.

Official Comment

One of the major problems of utilizing public officials to locate children and enforce custody and visitation determinations is cost. This section authorizes the prosecutor and law enforcement to recover costs against the non-prevailing party. The use of the term "direct" indicates that overhead is not a recoverable cost. This section cannot be used to recover the value of the time spent by the public authorities' attorneys.

CHAPTER 153. CONSERVATORSHIP, POSSESSION, & ACCESS

Subchapter A. General Provisions

SUBCHAPTER A. GENERAL PROVISIONS

FAM §153.001. PUBLIC POLICY

(a) The public policy of this state is to:

(1) assure that children will have frequent and continuing contact with parents who have shown the ability to act in the best interest of the child;

(2) provide a safe, stable, and nonviolent environment for the child; and

(3) encourage parents to share in the rights and duties of raising their child after the parents have separated or dissolved their marriage.

(b) A court may not render an order that conditions the right of a conservator to possession of or access to a child on the payment of child support.

History of Fam §153.001: Acts 1995, 74th Leg., ch. 20, §1, eff. April 20, 1995. Amended by Acts 1995, 74th Leg., ch. 751, §25, eff. Sept. 1, 1995; Acts 1999, 76th Leg., ch. 787, §2, eff. Sept. 1, 1999. Source: Former Fam §14.021(a).

Hann v. Texas DPRS, 969 S.W.2d 77, 83 (Tex. App.—El Paso 1998, pet. denied). "Because the relationship between a parent and child is one of constitutional dimensions, we must recognize the presumption that the best interest of the child will be served by preserving the parent-child relationship. [¶] The need for permanence is the paramount consideration for the child's present and future physical and emotional needs. The goal of establishing a stable, permanent home for a child is a compelling interest of the government."

FAM §153.002. BEST INTEREST OF CHILD

The best interest of the child shall always be the primary consideration of the court in determining the issues of conservatorship and possession of and access to the child.

History of Fam §153.002: Acts 1995, 74th Leg., ch. 20, §1, eff. April 20, 1995. Source: Former Fam §14.07(a).

Troxel v. Granville, 530 U.S. 57, 68, 120 S.Ct. 2054, 2061 (2000). "[T]here is a presumption that fit parents act in the best interests of their children."

Gillespie v. Gillespie, 644 S.W.2d 449, 451 (Tex. 1982). "The trial court is given wide latitude in determining the best interests of a minor child. The judgment of the trial court will be reversed only when it appears from the record as a whole that the court has abused its discretion."

Holley v. Adams, 544 S.W.2d 367, 371-72 (Tex. 1976). "An extended number of factors have been considered by the courts in ascertaining the best interest of the child. Included among these are the following: (A) the desires of the child; (B) the emotional and physical needs of the child now and in the future; (C) the emotional and physical danger to the child now and in the future; (D) the parental abilities of the individuals seeking custody; (E) the programs available to assist these individuals to promote the best interest of the child; (F) the plans for the child by these individuals or by the agency seeking custody; (G) the stability of the home or proposed placement; (H) the acts or omissions of the parent which may indicate that the existing parent-child relationship is not a proper one; and (I) any excuse for the acts or omissions of the parent. This listing is by no means exhaustive, but does indicate a number of considerations which either have been or would appear to be pertinent."

Bukovich v. Bukovich, 399 S.W.2d 528, 529 (Tex. 1966). "The controlling considerations are those changes of conditions affecting the welfare of the child. The desires, acts and claims of the respective parents are secondary considerations and material only as they bear upon the question of the best interest of the child."

In re Edwards, ___ S.W.3d ___ (Tex.App.—Texarkana 2002, n.p.h.) (No. 06-00-00130-CV; 4-11-02). "A trial court does not err in considering the role grandparents or other family members will play in a child's life in determining the best interest of the child."

E.C. v. Graydon, 28 S.W.3d 825, 828-29 (Tex.App.—Corpus Christi 2000, no pet.). "The trial court's judgment regarding what serves the best interest of the children with regard to child support and visitation, specifically the establishment of terms and conditions of the conservatorship, is a discretionary function of the trial court and will only be reversed upon a determination that the trial court has abused its discretion. This is because the trial court is in the best position to observe the demeanor and personalities of the witnesses and can feel forces, powers, and influences that cannot be discerned by merely reading the record. The test for abuse of discretion is whether the trial court acted without reference to any guiding rules or principles; in other words, whether the act was arbitrary or unreasonable."

In re Macalik, 13 S.W.3d 43, 45 (Tex.App.—Texarkana 1999, no pet.). "[I]n [SAPCRs], when the best interest of the child is always the overriding consideration, technical rules of pleading and practice are of little importance, and fair notice is afforded when the pleadings generally invoke the court's jurisdiction over custody and control of the children."

Fair v. Davis, 787 S.W.2d 422, 428-29 (Tex.App.—Dallas 1990, no writ). "*[W]eighing or taking into account* 'best interest' is different from requiring an affirmative finding of 'best interest.' Some courts have included 'best interests' as an element to be established in modifying visitation. We do not find a statutory requirement to do so. ... We hold that the requirement to *consider* best interest under §14.07(a) [now §153.002] is an instruction to give *deliberate thought to and weigh* all facts and circumstances that bear directly or indirectly on a child, including but not limited to, present or future physical, mental, emotional, educational, social, disciplinary and moral welfare, well-being, stability, and developmental needs. Likewise a finding of positive improvement is not a requirement under this section of the code."

O. v. P., 560 S.W.2d 122, 127 (Tex.App.—Fort Worth 1977, no writ). "The law in Texas is clear that the custody of two or more children of a marriage should not be divided, except for clear and compelling reasons. In the absence of such clear and compelling reasons, children should be raised with their brother(s) and/or sister(s)."

FAM §153.003. NO DISCRIMINATION BASED ON SEX OR MARITAL STATUS

The court shall consider the qualifications of the parties without regard to their marital status or to the sex of the party or the child in determining:

(1) which party to appoint as sole managing conservator;

(2) whether to appoint a party as joint managing conservator; and

(3) the terms and conditions of conservatorship and possession of and access to the child.

History of Fam §153.003: Acts 1995, 74th Leg., ch. 20, §1, eff. April 20, 1995. Source: Former Fam §§14.01(c)(1), 14.032(d).

In re McLean, 725 S.W.2d 696, 698 (Tex.1987). "The state no doubt has a significant interest in protecting the welfare of a child born to a mother not married to the child's father. [¶] Nevertheless, the state's interest can be protected without discriminating solely on the basis of sex. The state goal of protecting children's welfare is better served by keying that interest to the father's relationship to the child. A father who steps forward, willing and able to shoulder the responsibilities of raising a child should not be required to meet a higher burden of proof solely because he is male."

Dennis v. Smith, 962 S.W.2d 67, 69-70 (Tex.App.—Houston [1st Dist.] 1997, pet. denied). "[S]ex discrimination is now illegal. That is a major reason why we have a joint managing conservator statute today. The law no longer presumes that the mother is the better parent to raise the child. ... Thus, just as there is no longer a presumption that the mother should raise the child, there is no presumption that the conservator with the longer period of possession should decide where a child lives or goes to school. The issue is not, is someone being made a nanny? The issue is, what is in the child's best interest?"

Tye v. Tye, 532 S.W.2d 124, 127 (Tex.App.—Corpus Christi 1975, no writ). "In awarding custody of a minor child in a divorce proceeding the courts of this State may not indulge any preference towards the mother."

FAM §153.004. HISTORY OF DOMESTIC VIOLENCE

(a) In determining whether to appoint a party as a sole or joint managing conservator, the court shall consider evidence of the intentional use of abusive physical force by a party against the party's spouse, a parent of the child, or any person younger than 18 years of age committed within a two-year period preceding the filing of the suit or during the pendency of the suit.

Ⓐ (b) The court may not appoint joint managing conservators if credible evidence is presented of a history or pattern of past or present child neglect, or physical or sexual abuse by one parent directed against the other parent, a spouse, or a child, including a sexual assault in violation of Section 22.011 or 22.021, Penal Code, that results in the other parent becoming pregnant with the child. A history of sexual abuse includes a sexual assault that results in the other parent becoming pregnant with the child, regardless of the prior relationship of the parents. It is a rebuttable presumption that the appointment of a parent as the sole managing conservator of a child or as the conservator who has the exclusive right to determine the primary residence of a child is not in the best interest of the child if credible evidence is presented of a history or pattern of past or present child neglect, or physical or sexual abuse by that parent directed against the other parent, a spouse, or a child.

(c) The court shall consider the commission of family violence in determining whether to deny, restrict, or limit the possession of a child by a parent who is appointed as a possessory conservator.

(d) The court may not allow a parent to have access to a child for whom it is shown by a preponderance of the evidence that there is a history or pattern of committing family violence during the two years preceding the date of the filing of the suit or during the pendency of the suit, unless the court:

(1) finds that awarding the parent access to the child would not endanger the child's physical health or emotional welfare and would be in the best interest of the child; and

(2) renders a possession order that is designed to protect the safety and well-being of the child and any other person who has been a victim of family violence committed by the parent and that may include a requirement that:

(A) the periods of access be continuously supervised by an entity or person chosen by the court;

(B) the exchange of possession of the child occur in a protective setting;

(C) the parent abstain from the consumption of alcohol or a controlled substance, as defined by Chapter 481, Health and Safety Code, within 12 hours prior to or during the period of access to the child; or

(D) the parent attend and complete a battering intervention and prevention program as provided by Article 42.141, Code of Criminal Procedure, or, if such a program is not available, complete a course of treatment under Section 153.010.

E *Subsection (e) below is effective for SAPCR orders rendered on or after Sept. 1, 2001.*

(e) It is a rebuttable presumption that it is not in the best interest of a child for a parent to have unsupervised visitation with the child if credible evidence is presented of a history or pattern of past or present child neglect or physical or sexual abuse by that parent directed against the other parent, a spouse, or a child.

History of Fam §153.004: Acts 1995, 74th Leg., ch. 20, §1, eff. April 20, 1995. Amended by Acts 1999, 76th Leg., ch. 774, §1 (eff. Sept. 1, 1999), ch. 787, §3 (eff. Sept. 1, 1999); Acts 2001, 77th Leg., ch. 586, §1, eff. Sept. 1, 2001. Source: Former Fam §§14.01(c)(2), 14.021(h), 14.03(d), (e)(3).

Pena v. Pena, 8 S.W.3d 639, 639 (Tex.1999). Wife "argues that she presented 'credible evidence' of a 'history or pattern' of domestic violence, and thus that the trial court could not appoint joint managing conservators under §153.004(b). In affirming the trial court's judgment, the court of appeals correctly recited that the trial court is vested with wide discretion in determining custody issues. However, we disapprove of the following language in the court of appeals' opinion: 'In the present case, the two hitting incidents left [wife] with a black eye each time. However, [wife's] testimony only vaguely connects the two hitting incidents as both having been precipitated by arguments over [husband's] ex-wife and daughters. We do not know who initiated the arguments, whether the hittings were provoked in any manner, or what other factors may have contributed to either or both incidents, or any other relevant details that may show a relationship, connection or predictable pattern of physical abuse.' These considerations are not relevant to determining whether there was physical abuse or a history or pattern of domestic violence under the statute." (Internal quotations omitted.)

Lewelling v. Lewelling, 796 S.W.2d 164, 168 (Tex. 1990). Section 153.004 "creates a preference that the non-violent parent, rather than the violent parent, be appointed managing conservator. Thus, in a custody dispute between two parents, §14.01(c)(2) [now §153.004(a)] allows evidence of spousal abuse to be considered only as a factor that weighs heavily against the abusive parent; such evidence does not weigh against the abused. As the abuser cannot take advantage of his acts of abuse in a custody battle with the abused, so the abuser's parents also may not benefit from that abuse. While expressing continued concern for the best interest of the child, the Legislature has also determined that removing a child from a parent simply because she has suffered physical abuse at the hands of her spouse is not in the best interest of our state."

In re M.R., 975 S.W.2d 51, 53-54 (Tex.App.—San Antonio 1998, pet. denied). Unmarried father "asserts that §153.004(a) does not mandate admission of evidence of violence because that provision applies only to violence committed by one spouse against another. [W]e believe that the statute, when construed as a whole and with the rest of the family code, cannot be interpreted so narrowly. [¶] We can think of no reason why the state legislature would believe it appropriate to exclude evidence of abuse between unmarried parents when determining who is to be a child's sole managing conservator, but allow evidence of such abuse when determining whether to appoint joint managing conservators or whether to limit the access of a possessory conservator. Since the ultimate question in each instance is who is to have possession of the child, the same evidence would always be relevant."

FAM §153.005. APPOINTMENT OF SOLE OR JOINT MANAGING CONSERVATOR

(a) In a suit, the court may appoint a sole managing conservator or may appoint joint managing conservators. If the parents are or will be separated, the court shall appoint at least one managing conservator.

(b) A managing conservator must be a parent, a competent adult, an authorized agency, or a licensed child-placing agency.

History of Fam §153.005: Acts 1995, 74th Leg., ch. 20, §1, eff. April 20, 1995. Source: Former Fam §14.01(a).

Brook v. Brook, 881 S.W.2d 297, 298 (Tex.1994). "A nonparent may be named sole managing conservator, and joint custody is permitted between two nonparents or between a parent and nonparent."

Martinez v. Molinar, 953 S.W.2d 399, 403 (Tex. App.—El Paso 1997, no writ). "The matter of determining who should be appointed managing conservator of [the child] was addressed to the sound discretion of the trial judge as the trier of fact. The trial judge was in a better position to determine what will be in the best interest of [the child] since he faced the parties and their witnesses, observed their demeanor, and had the opportunity to evaluate the claims made by each parent. His judgment will not be disturbed on appeal unless there has been a clear abuse of discretion. The test for abuse of discretion in custody matters is whether the trial court acted without reference to any guiding rules or principles."

FAM §153.006. APPOINTMENT OF POSSESSORY CONSERVATOR

(a) If a managing conservator is appointed, the court may appoint one or more possessory conservators.

(b) The court shall specify the rights and duties of a person appointed possessory conservator.

(c) The court shall specify and expressly state in the order the times and conditions for possession of or access to the child, unless a party shows good cause why specific orders would not be in the best interest of the child.

History of Fam §153.006: Acts 1995, 74th Leg., ch. 20, §1, eff. April 20, 1995. Source: Former Fam §14.03(a), (c).

In re A.P.S., 54 S.W.3d 493, 499 (Tex.App.—Texarkana 2001, no pet.). "Although a judge can rightfully restrict the conditions of the environment in which a parent's visitation will take place, we respectfully disagree ... that giving total discretion, unenforceable by contempt, to one conservator constitutes a mere restriction on the conditions of visitation. [¶] Because the order in the present case could effectively deny [respondent] access to the children, because complete denial was not shown to be in the children's best interests, and because [petitioner] did not show good cause why specific orders were inappropriate, the trial court is required to fashion an order that specifically articulates the times and conditions of [respondent's] access to the children."

Hopkins v. Hopkins, 853 S.W.2d 134, 137 (Tex. App.—Corpus Christi 1993, no writ). "The Family Code ... gives trial courts only two options after appointing one parent sole managing conservator. If the trial court finds that the best interest of the child is served by granting the other parent possession of or access to the child, then it has no discretion and *must* appoint that parent a possessory conservator. If the trial court finds that it is *not* in the best interest of the child for the other parent to have possession of or access to the child and additionally finds that such possession of or access to the child would endanger the physical or emotional welfare of the child, then the court has discretion to either appoint or refuse to appoint that parent as a possessory conservator. *At 138:* [I]f the trial court *refuses* to appoint the parent a possessory conservator, it can do so only after finding neither possession nor access to be in the child's best interest and additionally finding that parental possession or access would endanger the physical or emotional welfare of the child. These findings preclude the trial court granting the parent any possession of or access to the child, whether supervised or not."

Beaupre v. Beaupre, 700 S.W.2d 353, 355 (Tex. App.—Fort Worth 1985, writ dism'd). "[W]hen a divorce decree appoints a possessory conservator and neither denies visitation nor provides for the same, the possessory conservator has the right of reasonable visitation. Although ... §14.03(a) [now §153.006] provides that the times and conditions for access to the child must be specific and expressly stated in the order unless either party shows good cause why specific orders would not be in the best interest of the child, it has been held that the provision of reasonable visitation rights, without specification, does not constitute reversible error."

FAM §153.007. AGREEMENT CONCERNING CONSERVATORSHIP

(a) To promote the amicable settlement of disputes between the parties to a suit, the parties may enter into a written agreement containing provisions for conservatorship and possession of the child and for modification of the agreement, including variations from the standard possession order.

(b) If the court finds that the agreement is in the child's best interest, the court shall render an order in accordance with the agreement.

(c) Terms of the agreement contained in the order or incorporated by reference regarding conservatorship or support of or access to a child in an order may be enforced by all remedies available for enforcement of a judgment, including contempt, but are not enforceable as a contract.

(d) If the court finds the agreement is not in the child's best interest, the court may request the parties to submit a revised agreement or the court may render an order for the conservatorship and possession of the child.

History of Fam §153.007: Acts 1995, 74th Leg., ch. 20, §1, eff. April 20, 1995. Amended by Acts 1995, 74th Leg., ch. 751, §26, eff. Sept. 1, 1995. Source: Former Fam §14.06.

Cross-reference: Fam. Code §§153.133, 153.255, 154.124.

Ex parte Gorena, 595 S.W.2d 841, 844 (Tex.1979). "Despite the fact that a judgment has its genesis in an agreement between the parties, the judgment itself has an independent status. Once the agreement of the parties has been approved by the court and made a part of its judgment, the agreement is no longer merely a contract between private individuals but is the judgment of the court."

Ex parte Jones, 358 S.W.2d 370, 375 (Tex.1962), *overruled on other grounds*, ***Ex Parte Gorena***, 595 S.W.2d 841 (Tex.1979). "Upon the face of the judgment, [it] appears that the provisions relating to the agreement to construct the residence and convey the property to Trustees for the benefit of the minor children are based entirely upon the terms of the settlement agreement between the parties. This agreed judgment must be interpreted as if it were a contract between the parties and the interpretation thereof is governed by the laws relating to contracts, rather than laws relating to judgments."

Stein v. Stein, 868 S.W.2d 902, 903 (Tex.App.—Houston [14th Dist.] 1994, no writ). "[A] party may revoke its consent to a settlement agreement any time before judgment is rendered. Without consent, the judgment is void. [¶] Generally, an order is valid when orally pronounced from the bench in open court, and 'rendition' occurs when the trial court officially announces its decision, either orally in open court, or by a memorandum filed by the clerk of the court. Thus, if the parties ... had been before a trial judge in district court, the judgment pronounced from the bench would have been a rendition, and the signing of the settlement agreement would have been 'entry' of judgment, a purely ministerial act."

McLendon v. McLendon, 847 S.W.2d 601, 608 (Tex. App.—Dallas 1992, writ denied). "The court reporter's transcription of the dictated agreement results in a written agreement, and the sworn testimony of the parties given to the court reporter in open court memorializes the parties' consent and can also be reduced to writing. We hold that this procedure has the same legal effect as a written agreement signed by the parties and, in fact, results in a written agreement that meets the requirements of §§3.631 [now §7.006], 14.06 [now §§153.007 & 154.124], and 14.021 [now §153.133]."

Hill v. Hill, 819 S.W.2d 570, 572-73 (Tex.App.—Dallas 1991, writ denied). "Child-support agreements require different consideration from property-settlement agreements, which are construed under the law of contracts. In property-settlement agreements, finality is critical. The parties must be able to prove title to the property in order to mortgage, sell, lease, or otherwise utilize their property. No such considerations inhere in child-support agreements; there, the State's interest in the continuing welfare of the children outweighs the parents' interest in having an established, permanent level of support payments. [¶] [A]n interpretation of an agreement that would, as a practical matter, nullify Wife's ability to seek an increase in child support is against public policy. Child-support agreements are not like other long-term contracts where the parties assume the risk of changes in the economy and in the cost of the product. Child-support payments are for the benefit of the children, not the parents, and child-support agreements are structured to fairly provide for the 'best interests' of the children, not so that one party or another can make a profit. When the economy changes or when special circumstances arise so that the best interests of the children require larger support payments, the courts must be able to order an effective increase in the payments without regard to any 'contracts' between the parties. [¶] When the parties draft child-support agreements, they cannot agree to prohibit the intervention of the courts required by the Family Code as necessary to protect the children. Thus, the parties may agree to do more than the court would require to provide for the best interest of the children, but they cannot agree to do less. Therefore, when the court decreases the amount of court-ordered child support, the paid spouse may enforce the higher amount of child support agreed to in the support agreement because the paying spouse has obligated himself to do more than the court requires. However, when the court requires more than was agreed to in the support agreement, the paying spouse must pay the increased amount and cannot rely on an agreement that permits him to do less."

K.D.B. v. C.B.B., 688 S.W.2d 684, 686-87 (Tex. App.—Tyler 1985, writ dism'd). Section 14.06, now §153.007, "is the sole provision in the Texas Family Code addressing agreements of parties related to issues of conservatorship and support. ... If in a trial judge's perception, the agreement between divorcing parents for conservatorship and support of the children of the marriage 'is not in the child's best interest,' what is the judge authorized to do when he is conducting an uncontested hearing on a petition for divorce in which suit such issues have been resolved by written agreement before trial, and the petitioner is the only party present before the court? Such question calls for an interpretation of the second alternative provided by that portion of §14.06(b), ... reading, 'or the court may make orders for the conservatorship and support of the child.' [W]e construe the quoted provisions to mean simply that a trial judge is not bound by the agreement of the parents when he concludes that such agreement is not in a child's best interest. This is not to say, however, that being of such a mind, the trial judge can summarily, and without affording the parties a reasonable opportunity to present evidence relevant to a proper determination of the issues, proceed in a noncontested hearing, as here, to decree that the absent spouse pay child support in a sum certain periodically contrary to the terms of the agreement. Any other construction of subsection (b) would void the statute under Article I §19 of the Texas Constitution and the Due Process Clause of the U.S. Constitution."

Kibby v. Langley, 612 S.W.2d 718, 721 (Tex.App.—Dallas 1981, no writ). "[W]hen an 'amicable settlement' of a modification motion is reached by the parties affected, and the court concurs therein as authorized by §14.06 [now §153.007], neither party may complain of his, or her, own act or the modification order resulting therefrom because the child's best interests are not to be subjected to such caprice."

Taft v. Johnson, 553 S.W.2d 408, 410-11 (Tex. App.—El Paso 1977, writ ref'd n.r.e.). "We do not believe a pleading signed by counsel for one party is a written agreement entered into by the parties, as required by §14.06 [now §153.007]. ... There is absolutely no language in the decree of divorce that the Court had considered any written agreement as to conservatorship of the child, or that such conservatorship should be changed upon restoration of [possessory conservator's] health. Certainly, the Court did not order any such change to be carried out by the parties at such time as [possessory conservator] regained her good health. [¶] We find no conflict between §11.13 [now §105.002], which provides for a jury trial in [SAPCRs], and §14.06, which gives the Court the right to approve and order enforcement of written agreements as to conservatorship and support of a child. Section 14.06 applies where the parties are in agreement, while §11.13 applies where the parties cannot agree and desire to have a jury decide their dispute. But if the parties are in agreement about conservatorship and support, that agreement must be in writing in language which is clear and unambiguous so that the trial Court may approve the agreement and order that it be performed by the parties, and they may do so without further dispute as to their respective duties and obligations."

Radtke v. Radtke, 521 S.W.2d 749, 751 (Tex.App.—Houston [14th Dist.] 1975, no writ). "The burden of showing a change of conditions affecting the welfare of the child is the burden to show that the interests would be best served by a change of custody. ... Normally, there will be no conflict between findings of material changes in conditions and the best interests of a child. However, where a conflict exists, it is the latter question which governs. The parties' stipulation in an agreement that a child's election will constitute a material change in conditions is, therefore, not binding upon the court. It is the duty and responsibility of the court to determine whether the agreement sought to be enforced will serve the best interests of the child."

FAM §153.0071. ALTERNATE DISPUTE RESOLUTION PROCEDURES

(a) On written agreement of the parties, the court may refer a suit affecting the parent-child relationship to arbitration. The agreement must state whether the arbitration is binding or non-binding.

(b) If the parties agree to binding arbitration, the court shall render an order reflecting the arbitrator's award unless the court determines at a non-jury hearing that the award is not in the best interest of the child. The burden of proof at a hearing under this subsection is on the party seeking to avoid rendition of an order based on the arbitrator's award.

(c) On the written agreement of the parties or on the court's own motion, the court may refer a suit affecting the parent-child relationship to mediation.

(d) A mediated settlement agreement is binding on the parties if the agreement:

(1) provides, in a prominently displayed statement that is in boldfaced type or capital letters or underlined, that the agreement is not subject to revocation;

(2) is signed by each party to the agreement; and

(3) is signed by the party's attorney, if any, who is present at the time the agreement is signed.

(e) If a mediated settlement agreement meets the requirements of Subsection (d), a party is entitled to judgment on the mediated settlement agreement notwithstanding Rule 11, Texas Rules of Civil Procedure, or another rule of law.

(f) A party may at any time prior to the final mediation order file a written objection to the referral of a suit affecting the parent-child relationship to mediation on the basis of family violence having been committed by another party against the objecting party or a child who is the subject of the suit. After an objection is filed, the suit may not be referred to mediation unless, on the request of a party, a hearing is held and the court finds that a preponderance of the evidence does not support the objection. If the suit is referred to mediation, the court shall order appropriate measures be taken to ensure the physical and emotional safety of the party who filed the objection. The order shall provide that the parties not be required to have face-to-face contact and that the parties be placed in separate rooms during mediation. This subsection does not apply to suits filed under Chapter 262.

History of Fam §153.0071: Acts 1995, 74th Leg., ch. 751, §27, eff. Sept. 1, 1995. Amended by Acts 1997, 75th Leg., ch. 937, §3, eff. Sept. 1, 1997; Acts 1999, 76th Leg., ch. 178, §7 (eff. Aug. 30, 1999), ch. 1351, §2 (eff. Sept. 1, 1999).

In re Kasschau, 11 S.W.3d 305, 311-12 (Tex.App.—Houston [14th Dist.] 1999, orig. proceeding). "[S]ections 6.602 and 153.0071 ... provide that 'a party is entitled to judgment' on a mediated settlement agreement if certain requirements of those statutes are met. Where ... the legislature has not defined the terms in the statute, we must apply their ordinary meaning. 'Entitle' means in part 'to grant a legal right to or qualify for.' That a party has a 'right to' judgment, or 'qualifies for' judgment on a mediated settlement agreement does not deprive the court of discretion to review an agreement before entering judgment. [W]hile ***Alvarez*** precludes a party from revoking consent to a mediated settlement agreement that complies with §153.0071, it does not hold that the court's duty to enter judgment on such an agreement is ministerial. A court's duty to enter judgment on a settlement agreement becomes ministerial only after it has first rendered judgment on that agreement. Here, the trial court approved the settlement agreement, but never rendered judgment on the agreement. As a result, the court had no ministerial duty to enter judgment and thus, did not violate such a duty."

Cooper v. Bushong, 10 S.W.3d 20, 26 n.12 (Tex. App.—Austin 1999, pet. denied). "[T]he court is not bound by the arbitrator's award if the award is not in the best interest of the child."

Alvarez v. Reiser, 958 S.W.2d 232, 234 (Tex.App.—Eastland 1997, pet. denied). "Under the language of subsections d and e, mediated settlement agreements complying with §153.0071 are binding, and a party to such an agreement is entitled to a judgment. Unilateral withdrawal of consent does not negate the enforceability of the agreement, and a separate suit for enforcement of a contract is not necessary."

Davis v. Wickham, 917 S.W.2d 414, 416-17 (Tex. App.—Houston [14th Dist.] 1996, no writ). "Because a mediated settlement agreement is enforceable under contract law, the same procedures used to enforce and enter judgment on other contracts should apply to mediated settlement agreements. [¶] The only methods existing under the rules of civil procedure to enforce a contract and obtain a judgment are: (1) summary judgment proceedings, if no fact issue exists; and (2) trial, jury or non-jury, if a fact issue exists. A trial court may enter a judgment on a mediated settlement agreement where one of the parties contests his intent to be bound only by following one of these vehicles set out in the rules of civil procedure."

In re Marriage of Banks, 887 S.W.2d 160, 163 (Tex. App.—Texarkana 1994, no writ). "A party who has reached a settlement agreement disposing of a dispute through alternative dispute resolution procedures may not unilaterally repudiate the agreement. If voluntary agreements reached through mediation were nonbinding, many positive efforts to amicably settle differences would be for naught. In order to effect the purposes of mediation and other alternative dispute resolution mechanisms, settlement agreements must be treated like other contracts reached after arm's length negotiations. [¶] No party to a dispute can be forced to settle the conflict outside of court; but if a voluntary agreement that disposes of the agreement is reached, the parties should be required to honor the agreement."

FAM §153.0072. COLLABORATIVE LAW

E *Section 153.0072 below is effective for actions commenced on or after Sept. 1, 2001, or for actions commenced before Sept. 1, 2001 if the trial had not begun before that date.*

(a) On a written agreement of the parties and their attorneys, a suit affecting the parent-child relationship may be conducted under collaborative law procedures.

(b) Collaborative law is a procedure in which the parties and their counsel agree in writing to use their best efforts and make a good faith attempt to resolve the suit affecting the parent-child relationship on an agreed basis without resorting to judicial intervention except to have the court approve the settlement agreement, make the legal pronouncements, and sign the orders required by law to effectuate the agreement of the parties as the court determines appropriate. The parties' counsel may not serve as litigation counsel except to ask the court to approve the settlement agreement.

(c) A collaborative law agreement must include provisions for:

(1) full and candid exchange of information between the parties and their attorneys as necessary to make a proper evaluation of the case;

(2) suspending court intervention in the dispute while the parties are using collaborative law procedures;

(3) hiring experts, as jointly agreed, to be used in the procedure;

(4) withdrawal of all counsel involved in the collaborative law procedure if the collaborative law procedure does not result in settlement of the dispute; and

(5) other provisions as agreed to by the parties consistent with a good faith effort to collaboratively settle the matter.

(d) Notwithstanding Rule 11, Texas Rules of Civil Procedure, or another rule or law, a party is entitled to judgment on a collaborative law settlement agreement if the agreement:

(1) provides, in a prominently displayed statement that is boldfaced, capitalized, or underlined, that the agreement is not subject to revocation; and

(2) is signed by each party to the agreement and the attorney of each party.

(e) Subject to Subsection (g), a court that is notified 30 days before trial that the parties are using collaborative law procedures to attempt to settle a dispute may not, until a party notifies the court that the collaborative law procedures did not result in a settlement:

(1) set a hearing or trial in the case;

(2) impose discovery deadlines;

(3) require compliance with scheduling orders; or

(4) dismiss the case.

(f) The parties shall notify the court if the collaborative law procedures result in a settlement. If they do not, the parties shall file:

(1) a status report with the court not later than the 180th day after the date of the written agreement to use the procedures; and

(2) a status report on or before the first anniversary of the date of the written agreement to use the procedures, accompanied by a motion for continuance that the court shall grant if the status report indicates the desire of the parties to continue to use collaborative law procedures.

(g) If the collaborative law procedures do not result in a settlement on or before the second anniversary of the date that the suit was filed, the court may:

(1) set the suit for trial on the regular docket; or

(2) dismiss the suit without prejudice.

History of Fam §153.0072: Enacted by Acts 2001, 77th Leg., ch. 1022, §2, eff. Sept 1, 2001.

A FAM §153.008. CHILD'S CHOICE OF MANAGING CONSERVATOR

If the child is 12 years of age or older, the child may, by writing filed with the court, choose the managing conservator, subject to the approval of the court.

History of Fam §153.008: Acts 1995, 74th Leg., ch. 20, §1, eff. April 20, 1995. Amended by Acts 1999, 76th Leg., ch. 1390, §12, eff. Sept. 1, 1999; Acts 2001, 77th Leg., ch. 1289, §1, eff. Sept. 1, 2001. Source: Former Fam §14.07(a).

Dohrn v. Delgado, 941 S.W.2d 244, 246 n.2 (Tex. App.—Corpus Christi 1996, no writ). "While it is true that ... §153.008 allows a child twelve years of age or older, subject to court approval, to choose their [sic] managing conservator, the statute presupposes a choice among persons who would otherwise qualify to be appointed managing conservator. We do not read §153.008 to provide an independent basis to appoint a managing conservator who would not otherwise qualify as such, merely because the child chooses him. Accordingly, a nonparent seeking appointment as managing conservator must still prove the elements listed in §153.131 in order to prevail over the child's surviving parent in a custody dispute."

In re Galliher, 546 S.W.2d 665, 667 (Tex.App.—Beaumont 1977, no writ). "[T]he child's preference is subject always to the discharge of the court's primary obligation of determining what is to the best interest of the child. If, from a consideration of the record as a whole, including the child's preference, the court should determine that it is to the best interest of the child that the court approve the designation, it will be given effect; otherwise, it may be ignored. In no event is such designation absolute or controlling."

FAM §153.009. INTERVIEW OF CHILD IN CHAMBERS

(a) In a nonjury trial the court may interview the child in chambers to determine the child's wishes as to conservatorship.

A (b) When the issue of managing conservatorship is contested, on the application of a party, the court shall interview a child 12 years of age or older and may interview a child under 12 years of age. Interviewing a child does not diminish the discretion of the court.

(c) The court may permit the attorney for a party or the attorney ad litem for the child to be present at the interview.

A (d) On the motion of a party or on the court's own motion, the court shall cause a record of the interview to be made when the child is 12 years of age or older. A record of the interview shall be part of the record in the case.

History of Fam §153.009: Acts 1995, 74th Leg., ch. 20, §1, eff. April 20, 1995. Amended by Acts 1997, 75th Leg., ch. 781, §1, eff. Sept. 1, 1997; Acts 2001, 77th Leg., ch. 1289, §2, eff. Sept. 1, 2001. Source: Former Fam §14.07(c).

FAM §153.010. ORDER FOR FAMILY COUNSELING

(a) If the court finds at the time of a hearing that the parties have a history of conflict in resolving an issue of conservatorship or possession of or access to the child, the court may order a party to:

(1) participate in counseling with a mental health professional who:

(A) has a background in family therapy;

(B) has a mental health license that requires as a minimum a master's degree; and

(C) has training in domestic violence if the court determines that the training is relevant to the type of counseling needed; and

(2) pay the cost of counseling.

(b) If a person possessing the requirements of Subsection (a)(1) is not available in the county in which the court presides, the court may appoint a person the court believes is qualified to conduct the counseling ordered under Subsection (a).

History of Fam §153.010: Acts 1995, 74th Leg., ch. 20, §1, eff. April 20, 1995. Amended by Acts 1997, 75th Leg., ch. 645, §1, eff. Sept. 1, 1997. Source: Former Fam §14.03(h).

FAM §153.011. SECURITY BOND

If the court finds that a person who has a possessory interest in a child may violate the court order relating to the interest, the court may order the party to execute a bond or deposit security. The court shall set the amount and condition the bond or security on compliance with the order.

History of Fam §153.011: Acts 1995, 74th Leg., ch. 20, §1, eff. April 20, 1995. Source: Former Fam §14.03(i).

FAM §153.012. RIGHT TO PRIVACY; DELETION OF PERSONAL INFORMATION IN RECORDS

The court may order the custodian of records to delete all references in the records to the place of residence of either party appointed as a conservator of the child before the release of the records to another party appointed as a conservator.

History of Fam §153.012: Acts 1995, 74th Leg., ch. 20, §1, eff. April 20, 1995. Source: Former Fam §14.04(c).

FAM §153.013. FALSE REPORT OF CHILD ABUSE

(a) If a party to a pending suit affecting the parent-child relationship makes a report alleging child abuse by another party to the suit that the reporting party knows lacks a factual foundation, the court shall deem the report to be a knowingly false report.

(b) Evidence of a false report of child abuse is admissible in a suit between the involved parties regarding the terms of conservatorship of a child.

(c) If the court makes a finding under Subsection (a), the court shall impose a civil penalty not to exceed $500.

History of Fam §153.013: Acts 1995, 74th Leg., ch. 751, §28, eff. Sept. 1, 1995. Amended by Acts 1997, 75th Leg., ch. 786, §2, eff. Sept. 1, 1997. Source: Former Fam §34.031(b).

E

FAM §153.014. VISITATION CENTERS & VISITATION EXCHANGE FACILITIES

A county may establish a visitation center or a visitation exchange facility for the purpose of facilitating the terms of a court order providing for the possession of or access to a child.

History of Fam §153.014: Enacted by Acts 2001, 77th Leg., ch. 577, §1, eff. June 11, 2001.

See also http://www.sbotfam.org/visitation centers.pdf

Sections 153.015-153.070 reserved for expansion

SUBCHAPTER B. PARENT APPOINTED AS CONSERVATOR: IN GENERAL

FAM §153.071. COURT TO SPECIFY RIGHTS & DUTIES OF PARENT APPOINTED A CONSERVATOR

If both parents are appointed as conservators of the child, the court shall specify the rights and duties of a parent that are to be exercised:

(1) by each parent independently;

(2) by the joint agreement of the parents; and

(3) exclusively by one parent.

History of Fam §153.071: Acts 1995, 74th Leg., ch. 20, §1, eff. April 20, 1995. Source: Former Fam §14.02(a).

FAM §153.072. WRITTEN FINDING REQUIRED TO LIMIT PARENTAL RIGHTS & DUTIES

The court may limit the rights and duties of a parent appointed as a conservator if the court makes a written finding that the limitation is in the best interest of the child.

History of Fam §153.072: Acts 1995, 74th Leg., ch. 20, §1, eff. April 20, 1995. Source: Former Fam §14.02(b).

FAM §153.073. RIGHTS OF PARENT AT ALL TIMES

(a) Unless limited by court order, a parent appointed as a conservator of a child has at all times the right:

(1) as specified by court order:

(A) to receive information from the other parent concerning the health, education, and welfare of the child; and

(B) to confer with the other parent to the extent possible before making a decision concerning the health, education, and welfare of the child;

(2) of access to medical, dental, psychological, and educational records of the child;

(3) to consult with a physician, dentist, or psychologist of the child;

(4) to consult with school officials concerning the child's welfare and educational status, including school activities;

(5) to attend school activities;

(6) to be designated on the child's records as a person to be notified in case of an emergency;

(7) to consent to medical, dental, and surgical treatment during an emergency involving an immediate danger to the health and safety of the child; and

(8) to manage the estate of the child to the extent the estate has been created by the parent or the parent's family.

(b) The court shall specify in the order the rights that a parent retains at all times.

History of Fam §153.073: Acts 1995, 74th Leg., ch. 20, §1, eff. April 20, 1995. Amended by Acts 1995, 74th Leg., ch. 751, §29, eff. Sept. 1, 1995. Source: Former Fam §14.02(a), (b)(2).

Abrams v. Jones, 35 S.W.3d 620, 624 (Tex.2000). "We interpret §153.073 to ensure that a court may grant a parent who is divorced and who has been named a conservator the same rights of access to his or her child's psychological records as a parent who is not divorced. We do not interpret §153.073 to override the provisions of chapter 611 of the Health and Safety Code that specifically address parents' rights to the mental health records of their children. The legislative history of §153.073 indicates that it was enacted to equalize the rights of nonmanaging-conservator parents in comparison to managing-conservator parents. The Legislature did not intend in §153.073 to give greater rights to divorced parents than to parents who are not divorced."

HCA, Inc. v. Miller, 36 S.W.3d 187, 191 (Tex. App.—Houston [14th Dist.] 2000, pet. granted, argued 4-3-02). "[U]nless a child's need for life-sustaining medical treatment is too urgent for consent to be obtained from a parent or other person with legal authority (the 'emergency exception'), a doctor's treatment of the child without such consent is actionable even if the condition requiring treatment would eventually be life-threatening and the treatment is otherwise provided without negligence."

FAM §153.074. RIGHTS & DUTIES DURING PERIOD OF POSSESSION

Unless limited by court order, a parent appointed as a conservator of a child has the following rights and duties during the period that the parent has possession of the child:

(1) the duty of care, control, protection, and reasonable discipline of the child;

(2) the duty to support the child, including providing the child with clothing, food, shelter, and medical and dental care not involving an invasive procedure;

(3) the right to consent for the child to medical and dental care not involving an invasive procedure;

(4) the right to consent for the child to medical, dental, and surgical treatment during an emergency involving immediate danger to the health and safety of the child; and

(5) the right to direct the moral and religious training of the child.

History of Fam §153.074: Acts 1995, 74th Leg., ch. 20, §1, eff. April 20, 1995. Amended by Acts 1995, 74th Leg., ch. 751, §30, eff. Sept. 1, 1995. Source: Former Fam §14.02(b)(1).

FAM §153.075. DUTIES OF PARENT NOT APPOINTED CONSERVATOR

The court may order a parent not appointed as a managing or a possessory conservator to perform other parental duties, including paying child support.

History of Fam §153.075: Acts 1995, 74th Leg., ch. 20, §1, eff. April 20, 1995. Source: Former Fam §14.03(d).

FAM §153.076. PARENTS' DUTY TO PROVIDE INFORMATION

(a) If both parents are appointed as conservators of the child, the court shall order that each parent has a duty to inform the other parent in a timely manner of significant information concerning the health, education, and welfare of the child.

(b) If both parents are appointed as conservators of a child, the court shall order that each parent has the duty to inform the other parent if the parent resides with for at least 30 days, marries, or intends to marry a person who the parent knows:

(1) is registered as a sex offender under Chapter 62, Code of Criminal Procedure, as added by Chapter 668, Acts of the 75th Legislature, Regular Session, 1997; or

(2) is currently charged with an offense for which on conviction the person would be required to register under that chapter.

(c) The notice required to be made under Subsection (b) must be made as soon as practicable but not later than the 40th day after the date the parent begins to reside with the person or the 10th day after the date the marriage occurs, as appropriate. The notice must include a description of the offense that is the basis of the person's requirement to register as a sex offender or of the offense with which the person is charged.

(d) A person commits an offense if the person fails to provide notice in the manner required by Subsections (b) and (c). An offense under this subsection is a Class C misdemeanor.

History of Fam §153.076: Acts 1995, 74th Leg., ch. 751, §31, eff. Sept. 1, 1995. Amended by Acts 1999, 76th Leg., ch. 330, §1, eff. Sept. 1, 1999. Source: Former Fam §14.02(a).

Hodgson v. Minnesota, 497 U.S. 417, 450, 110 S.Ct. 2926, 2945 (1990). "It is equally clear that the requirement that both parents be notified ... does not reasonably further any legitimate state interest. ... A statute requiring two-parent notification would not further any state interest in those instances. *At 452, 2946:* The second parent may well have an interest in the minor's abortion decision, making full communication among all members of a family desirable in some cases, but such communication may not be decreed by the State. The State has no more interest in requiring all family members to talk with one another than it has in requiring certain of them to live together."

In re Doe 3, 19 S.W.3d 300, 320 (Tex.2000). "The constitutionality of §153.076 if applied in parental notification matters is questionable in light of ***Hodgson v. Minnesota***, 497 U.S. 417, 450-52, 110 S.Ct. 2926, 111 L.Ed.2d 344 (1990)."

Sections 153.077-153.130 reserved for expansion

SUBCHAPTER C. PARENT APPOINTED AS SOLE OR JOINT MANAGING CONSERVATOR

FAM §153.131. PRESUMPTION THAT PARENT TO BE APPOINTED MANAGING CONSERVATOR

(a) Subject to the prohibition in Section 153.004, unless the court finds that appointment of the parent or parents would not be in the best interest of the child because the appointment would significantly impair the child's physical health or emotional development, a parent shall be appointed sole managing conservator or both parents shall be appointed as joint managing conservators of the child.

(b) It is a rebuttable presumption that the appointment of the parents of a child as joint managing conservators is in the best interest of the child. A finding of a history of family violence involving the parents of a child removes the presumption under this subsection.

History of Fam §153.131: Acts 1995, 74th Leg., ch. 20, §1, eff. April 20, 1995. Amended by Acts 1995, 74th Leg., ch. 751, §32, eff. Sept. 1, 1995; Acts 1997, 75th Leg., ch. 1193, §20, eff. Sept. 1, 1997. Source: Former Fam §14.01(b)(1).

In re V.L.K., 24 S.W.3d 338, 343 (Tex.2000). "A natural parent has the benefit of the parental presumption in an original proceeding, and the nonparent seeking conservatorship has a higher burden. However, the Legislature did not impose different burdens on parents and nonparents in modification suits."

Brook v. Brook, 881 S.W.2d 297, 298 (Tex.1994). "[W]e are concerned with the type of finding required for appointment of a parent and a nonparent to be joint managing conservators under §14.01(b)(1) [now §153.131]. [¶] A nonparent may be named sole managing conservator, and joint custody is permitted between two nonparents or between a parent and nonparent. Before a nonparent may be appointed as sole managing conservator or two nonparents as joint managing conservators, however, a higher standard must be satisfied, requiring proof that appointment of the parent or parents would significantly impair the child's health or development. *At 299:* In accordance with this view, §14.01(b)(1) [now §153.131] has been held to apply only to those situations in which a nonparent seeks custody in lieu of a natural parent."

Lewelling v. Lewelling, 796 S.W.2d 164, 167 (Tex. 1990). "It is no longer adequate to offer evidence that the nonparent would be a better custodian of the child. Under §14.01 [now §153.131], the nonparent must affirmatively prove by a preponderance of the evidence that appointment of the parent as managing conservator would *significantly impair* the child, either physically or emotionally. This statute thus requires the nonparent to offer evidence of specific actions or omissions of the parent that demonstrate an award of custody to the parent would result in physical or emotional harm to the child."

Mumma v. Aguirre, 364 S.W.2d 220, 221 (Tex. 1963). "There is a presumption that the interests of a young child are best served by award of its custody to its natural parents. The presumption is based upon a logical belief that the ties of the natural relationship of parent and child ordinarily furnish strong assurance of genuine efforts on the part of the custodians to provide the child with the best care and opportunities possible and, as well, the best atmosphere for the mental, moral and emotional development of the child."

In re De La Pena, 999 S.W.2d 521, 527-28 (Tex. App.—El Paso 1999, no pet.). "For the court to award managing conservatorship to a nonparent under §153.131, the nonparent must prove by a preponderance of credible evidence that appointing the parent as a managing conservator would result in serious physical or emotional harm to the child. There must be evidence to support the logical inference that some specific, identifiable behavior or conduct of the parent will probably cause that harm. This link between the parent's conduct and harm to the child may not be based on evidence which merely raises a surmise or speculation of possible harm. When a nonparent and a parent are both seeking managing conservatorship, 'close calls' go to the parent. *At 535:* To hold otherwise would permit the court to apply the presumption in appointing the parent a joint managing conservator but nevertheless choose the primary residence of the child on the basis of a heads-up best interest test, with the court determining which of the parties is the 'better' choice. This results in the appointment of a parent as a managing conservator in name only, a paper title which eviscerates the purpose of the statute."

In re A.D.H., 979 S.W.2d 445, 447 (Tex.App.—Beaumont 1998, no pet.). "Although the parental presumption is a factor to consider, it does not take precedence ... over the requirements of modification as set out in ... §156.202."

Doyle v. Doyle, 955 S.W.2d 478, 481-82 (Tex.App.—Austin 1997, no pet.). "Even though the Family Code created a presumption that the appointment of joint managing conservators is in a child's best interest where feasible, the matter of determining whether that presumption has been rebutted is addressed to the sound discretion of the trial judge as the trier of fact. ... In custody matters, where personal observation and evaluation of the parties and their claims is so valuable, we give great deference to the trial court's judgment. We will set aside that judgment only if the trial court acted without reference to any guiding rules or principles."

Dohrn v. Delgado, 941 S.W.2d 244, 246 n.2 (Tex. App.—Corpus Christi 1996, no writ). "While it is true that ... §153.008, allows a child twelve years of age or older, subject to court approval, to choose their managing conservator, the statute presupposes a choice among persons who would otherwise qualify to be appointed managing conservator. We do not read §153.008 to provide an independent basis to appoint a managing conservator who would not otherwise qualify as such, merely because the child chooses him. Accordingly, a nonparent seeking appointment as managing conservator must still prove the elements listed in §153.131 in order to prevail over the child's surviving parent in a custody dispute."

In re Rodriguez, 940 S.W.2d 265, 271 (Tex.App.—San Antonio 1997, writ denied). "Significantly, a jury's custody's determination is binding on the trial court if it is supported by the evidence. The jury's decision is also entitled to substantial deference in this court.... *At 272:* In sum, Texas law permits naming a non-parent as a child's managing conservator even when both biological parents' rights have not been terminated but only if the appointment of the parent would not be in the child's best interest, because it would significantly impair the child's physical health or emotional development; it entrusts juries with these difficult issues; and it prohibits this court from setting aside the jury's verdict if there is legally and factually sufficient evidence to support it." (Internal quotations omitted.)

In re Hidalgo, 938 S.W.2d 492, 496-97 (Tex.App.—Texarkana 1996, no writ). "The fact that a contesting third party would be a *better* custodian is not sufficient to rebut the parental presumption absent a showing of some impairment. Moreover, the cases require a nonparent to show specific acts or omissions of the parent that demonstrate a significant impairment."

Neely v. Neely, 698 S.W.2d 758, 759 (Tex.App.—Austin 1985, no writ). Section 14.01(b), now §153.131, "requires that the trial court, in a [SAPCR], appoint a parent as managing conservator unless such appointment is *not* in the child's best interest. The party seeking to avoid the presumption's effects must first produce evidence to overcome it. In our view, the production of evidence relating only to the positive benefits of appointing the non-parent will not rebut the presumption."

FAM §153.132. RIGHTS & DUTIES OF PARENT APPOINTED SOLE MANAGING CONSERVATOR

Unless limited by court order, a parent appointed as sole managing conservator of a child has the rights and duties provided by Subchapter B and the following exclusive rights:

(1) the right to establish the primary residence of the child;

(2) the right to consent to medical, dental, and surgical treatment involving invasive procedures, and to consent to psychiatric and psychological treatment;

(3) the right to receive and give receipt for periodic payments for the support of the child and to hold or disburse these funds for the benefit of the child;

(4) the right to represent the child in legal action and to make other decisions of substantial legal significance concerning the child;

(5) the right to consent to marriage and to enlistment in the armed forces of the United States;

(6) the right to make decisions concerning the child's education;

(7) the right to the services and earnings of the child; and

(8) except when a guardian of the child's estate or a guardian or attorney ad litem has been appointed for the child, the right to act as an agent of the child in relation to the child's estate if the child's action is required by a state, the United States, or a foreign government.

History of Fam §153.132: Acts 1995, 74th Leg., ch. 20, §1, eff. April 20, 1995. Amended by Acts 1995, 74th Leg., ch. 751, §33, eff. Sept. 1, 1995. Source: Former Fam §14.02(b)(3).

In re J.E.P., 49 S.W.3d 380, 385 (Tex.App.—Fort Worth 2000, no pet.). "[T]he rights granted exclusively to a sole managing conservator under §153.132 do not include the right to have periods of possession in excess of those granted to the possessory conservator, nor do they include the right to weekend possession of the child. While a managing conservator must necessarily enjoy sufficient access to and possession of the child to enable him to fully realize his rights and perform his duties, Father has made no allegation here that a Monday through Friday schedule deprives him of this opportunity. [A] court is given discretion to deviate from standard possession terms, which provide only for 'reasonable minimum possession of a child for a parent named as a possessory conservator,' if it determines that an application of the standard order would be unworkable or inappropriate under the circumstances. Most important is the trial court's determination of what arrangement is in the best interest of the child. [¶] The only exclusive right previously held by Father that the court granted to Mother in the Order was the 'exclusive right to determine where the parties' two minor children attend school whether public or private.' In view of the fact that the family code gives courts the discretion to limit the rights ordinarily held by a sole managing conservator and to expressly grant rights to the possessory conservator, we hold that this change alone is not the sort of drastic modification of the functions of the sole managing conservator that would create a de facto change in conservatorship. Contrary to Father's assertion that he has been 'effectively deprived ... of any meaningful function as managing conservator,' he retains all of the other rights granted to him in the original decree and set out in §153.132, rights that are the very essence of the "function" of a sole managing conservator."

In re Macalik, 13 S.W.3d 43, 46 (Tex.App.—Texarkana 1999, no pet.). The court modified provisions of custody determination by removing requirement that possessory conservator must take the children to managing conservator's church when he has possession of them. Managing conservator "contends that the provision about church attendance violates her right to determine the religious training for her children which is granted by ... §153.132. We disagree. That section does not contain any provision concerning religious training. Moreover, §153.132 prescribes the rights of sole managing conservators, '*[u]nless limited by court order.*'"

Lueg v. Lueg, 976 S.W.2d 308, 313 (Tex.App.—Corpus Christi 1998, pet. denied). "Section 153.132 ... provides that a sole managing conservator has the exclusive right to receive and give receipt for child support payments and to hold or disburse these funds for the benefit of the child. No such right is expressly ascribed to the possessory conservator. We therefore hold that the [F]amily [C]ode does not contemplate a sole managing conservator paying child support to a possessory conservator."

Enochs v. Brown, 872 S.W.2d 312, 316 (Tex.App.—Austin 1994, no writ). Sole managing conservator settled with tortfeasor for injuries to son. "While [possessory conservator] may challenge the trial court's discretion in its apportionment of the settlement proceeds, he has no standing to challenge the validity or interpretation of the fee contract between [son] and [son's attorney]. [Sole managing conservator] was, and is, the sole managing conservator. The Family Code delegates to the sole managing conservator the exclusive right to represent a child in a legal action and to make substantial legal decisions."

Rodriguez v. Lutheran Social Servs., 814 S.W.2d 153, 154 (Tex.App.—San Antonio 1991, writ denied). "A managing conservator, not the parent of the child in question, is empowered to consent to an adoption of a child if the parent-child relationship between the parent and child has been terminated."

FAM §153.133. AGREEMENT FOR JOINT MANAGING CONSERVATORSHIP

(a) If a written agreement of the parents is filed with the court, the court shall render an order appointing the parents as joint managing conservators only if the agreement:

(1) designates the conservator who has the exclusive right to establish the primary residence of the child and:

(A) establishes, until modified by further order, the geographic area within which the conservator shall maintain the child's primary residence; or

(B) specifies that the conservator may establish the child's primary residence without regard to geographic location;

(2) specifies the rights and duties of each parent regarding the child's physical care, support, and education;

(3) includes provisions to minimize disruption of the child's education, daily routine, and association with friends;

(4) allocates between the parents, independently, jointly, or exclusively, all of the remaining rights and duties of a parent provided by Chapter 151;

(5) is voluntarily and knowingly made by each parent and has not been repudiated by either parent at the time the order is rendered; and

(6) is in the best interest of the child.

(b) The agreement may contain an alternative dispute resolution procedure that the parties agree to use before requesting enforcement or modification of the terms and conditions of the joint conservatorship through litigation, except in an emergency.

History of Fam §153.133: Acts 1995, 74th Leg., ch. 20, §1, eff. April 20, 1995. Amended by Acts 1999, 76th Leg., ch. 936, §1, eff. Sept. 1, 1999. Source: Former Fam §14.021(c), (d).

Albrecht v. Albrecht, 974 S.W.2d 262, 265 (Tex. App.—San Antonio 1998, no pet.). See Annotation in FAM §153.136.

McLendon v. McLendon, 847 S.W.2d 601, 608 (Tex. App.—Dallas 1992, writ denied). "We note that [TRCP 11] itself equates a written agreement with the 'open court and entered of record' portion of rule 11. Both alternatives attain the purpose of the rule, which is to memorialize the terms of the agreement reached by the litigants. The court reporter's transcription of the dictated agreement results in a written agreement, and the sworn testimony of the parties given to the court reporter in open court memorializes the parties' consent and can also be reduced to writing. We hold that this procedure has the same legal effect as a written agreement signed by the parties and, in fact, results in a written agreement that meets the requirements of §§3.631 [now §7.006], 14.06 [now §§153.007 & 154.124], and 14.021 [now §153.133] of the Family Code."

FAM §153.134. COURT-ORDERED JOINT CONSERVATORSHIP

(a) If a written agreement of the parents is not filed with the court, the court may render an order appointing the parents joint managing conservators only if the appointment is in the best interest of the child, considering the following factors:

(1) whether the physical, psychological, or emotional needs and development of the child will benefit from the appointment of joint managing conservators;

(2) the ability of the parents to give first priority to the welfare of the child and reach shared decisions in the child's best interest;

(3) whether each parent can encourage and accept a positive relationship between the child and the other parent;

(4) whether both parents participated in child rearing before the filing of the suit;

(5) the geographical proximity of the parents' residences;

(6) if the child is 12 years of age or older, the child's preference, if any, regarding the appointment of joint managing conservators; and

(7) any other relevant factor.

(b) In rendering an order appointing joint managing conservators, the court shall:

(1) designate the conservator who has the exclusive right to determine the primary residence of the child and:

(A) establish, until modified by further order, a geographic area consisting of the county in which the child is to reside and any contiguous county thereto within which the conservator shall maintain the child's primary residence; or

(B) specify that the conservator may determine the child's primary residence without regard to geographic location;

(2) specify the rights and duties of each parent regarding the child's physical care, support, and education;

(3) include provisions to minimize disruption of the child's education, daily routine, and association with friends;

(4) allocate between the parents, independently, jointly, or exclusively, all of the remaining rights and duties of a parent as provided by Chapter 151; and

(5) if feasible, recommend that the parties use an alternative dispute resolution method before requesting enforcement or modification of the terms and conditions of the joint conservatorship through litigation, except in an emergency.

History of Fam §153.134: Acts 1995, 74th Leg., ch. 20, §1, eff. April 20, 1995. Amended by Acts 1999, 76th Leg., ch. 936, §2, eff. Sept. 1, 1999. Source: Former Fam §14.021(e), (f).

Lenz v. Lenz, 40 S.W.3d 111, 118 n.3 (Tex.App.—San Antonio 2000), *rev'd on other grounds*, ___ S.W.3d ___ (Tex.2002) (No. 01-0232; 6-6-02). "We find no merit to [primary custodial parent's] claim that the trial court's action infringes on her U.S. Constitutional right to travel. This right embraces three different components: the right to enter and leave another State; the right to be treated as a welcome visitor while temporarily present in another State; and, for those travelers who elect to become permanent residents, the right to be treated like other citizens of that State. Because the trial court's order in no way affects [primary custodial parent's] ability to return to Germany, the trial court's order does not interfere with: (1) her right to enter and leave another State; (2) her right to be treated as a welcome visitor in another State; or (3) her right to be treated like any other citizen of Texas who voluntarily subjects herself to the jurisdiction of the court system by filing a divorce proceeding. Section 153.134 requires a court to include certain provisions in its order appointing joint managing conservators. One of those essential provisions concerns residence: the order must either establish the county of the child's residence or designate the conservator who has the exclusive right to determine the child's primary residence. That the order must include a residence provision, however, does not affect a party's right to have the primary residence issue determined by a jury. Section 153.134 required the trial court to include a residence provision in its order, but in this case that provision had to be in accord with the jury's verdict giving [mother] the exclusive right to determine her children's primary residence."

Jenkins v. Jenkins, 16 S.W.3d 473, 482-83 (Tex. App.—El Paso 2000, no pet.). Section 153.134 "is mandatory, but it is only mandatory in the sense that any order entered by the trial court appointing a joint managing conservatorship must contain language delineating the various rights and duties of the conservators listed under §153.134(b). The list of rights and duties is not exclusive, nor does it define how the trial court shall assign or implement those rights and duties. The trial court retains broad discretion in crafting the rights and duties of each conservators so as to effectuate the best interest of the child."

Bailey v. Bailey, 987 S.W.2d 206, 210 (Tex.App.—Amarillo 1999, no pet.). "Section 153.134(b)(2) of the Family Code obligates the court to 'specify the rights and duties of each parent regarding the child's physical care, support, and education' when it appoints both parents as joint conservators. We have been cited to no limitation upon the manner in which the court may parcel those rights. [I]t is obvious that the legislature both contemplated and acquiesced in the likelihood that the rights over the child could be exercised jointly."

In re Marriage of Bertram, 981 S.W.2d 820, 825 (Tex.App.—Texarkana 1998, no pet.). "The trial court must consider several factors in weighing the appointment of joint managing conservators. These factors are: benefits to the child, the cooperative decision-making ability of the parents, geographical proximity, the parents' ability to promote a positive relationship with the other parent, the parents' prior child-rearing participation, and any other relevant factor. These factors are reviewed to determine whether the presumption in favor of joint managing conservatorship has been rebutted."

Ray v. Burns, 832 S.W.2d 431, 437-38 (Tex.App.—Waco 1992, no writ). "That the court omitted from the order appointing joint managing conservators provisions required by §14.021(f) [now §153.134(b)] does not make the order void. Any error resulting from the omission of a required provision is harmless, and [possessory conservator] does not allege that she has been harmed by the omission. Because the trial court has continuing jurisdiction over [child's] conservatorship and because possessory orders are interlocutory, [possessory conservator] can request the trial court to modify the order to include any omitted provision. Furthermore, she can request the court to enter a standard order and, if the court refuses to do so, she can then appeal the denial."

FAM §153.135. EQUAL POSSESSION NOT REQUIRED

Joint managing conservatorship does not require the award of equal or nearly equal periods of physical possession of and access to the child to each of the joint conservators.

History of Fam §153.135: Acts 1995, 74th Leg., ch. 20, §1, eff. April 20, 1995. Source: Former Fam §14.021(b).

Norris v. Norris, 56 S.W.3d 333, 346 (Tex.App.—El Paso 2001, no pet.). "The modification order substantially expanded [father's] possession of the children from the minimum amount agreed upon at the time of the divorce. We would be hard pressed to conclude that the trial court's ruling was made without reference to any guiding rules and principles given a statutory provision expressly mandating that equal possession is not required."

Albrecht v. Albrecht, 974 S.W.2d 262, 265 (Tex. App.—San Antonio 1998, no pet.). "Equal time between parents is neither recommended nor prohibited."

FAM §153.136. COURT DESIGNATION OF PRIMARY PHYSICAL RESIDENCE

If joint managing conservatorship is ordered, the best interest of the child ordinarily requires the court to designate a primary physical residence for the child.

History of Fam §153.136: Acts 1995, 74th Leg., ch. 20, §1, eff. April 20, 1995. Source: Former Fam §14.021(b).

Albrecht v. Albrecht, 974 S.W.2d 262, 265 (Tex. App.—San Antonio 1998, no pet.). "In joint managing conservatorship, one parent is usually given slightly greater powers than the other parent. In particular, §153.136 directs the court to designate the conservator who has the right to designate the child's primary physical residence. Slightly greater power, however, does not necessarily require the court to give one parent more time with the child than the other parent. As a minimum, the parent without the power to designate the child's primary residence is entitled to the time specified in the standard possession order."

Weldon v. Weldon, 968 S.W.2d 515, 516 n.2 (Tex. App.—Texarkana 1998, no pet.). "Even though the standard possession order under §153.316 sets out the possessory rights of the possessory conservator, the Section applies to joint managing conservators not awarded primary physical residence of the child pursuant to … §153.137."

FAM §153.137. GUIDELINES FOR THE POSSESSION OF CHILD BY PARENT NAMED AS JOINT MANAGING CONSERVATOR

The standard possession order provided by Subchapter F constitutes a presumptive minimum amount of time for possession of a child by a parent named as a joint managing conservator who is not awarded the primary physical residence of the child in a suit.

History of Fam §153.137: Acts 1995, 74th Leg., ch. 20, §1, eff. April 20, 1995. Source: Former Fam §14.034.

Weldon v. Weldon, 968 S.W.2d 515, 516 n.2 (Tex. App.—Texarkana 1998, no pet.). See Annotation in FAM §153.136.

FAM §153.138. CHILD SUPPORT ORDER AFFECTING JOINT CONSERVATORS

The appointment of joint managing conservators does not impair or limit the authority of the court to order a joint managing conservator to pay child support to another joint managing conservator.

History of Fam §153.138: Acts 1995, 74th Leg., ch. 20, §1, eff. April 20, 1995. Source: Former Fam §14.021(g).

FAM §153.139. REPEALED

Repealed by Acts 1997, 75th Leg., ch. 561, §30, eff. Sept. 1, 1997.

Sections 153.140-153.190 reserved for expansion

SUBCHAPTER D. PARENT APPOINTED AS POSSESSORY CONSERVATOR

FAM §153.191. PRESUMPTION THAT PARENT TO BE APPOINTED POSSESSORY CONSERVATOR

The court shall appoint as a possessory conservator a parent who is not appointed as a sole or joint managing conservator unless it finds that the appointment is not in the best interest of the child and that parental possession or access would endanger the physical or emotional welfare of the child.

History of Fam §153.191: Acts 1995, 74th Leg., ch. 20, §1, eff. April 20, 1995. Source: Former Fam §14.03(d).

In re Walters, 39 S.W.3d 280, 286-87 (Tex.App.—Texarkana 2001, no pet.). "Reading §153.191 in conjunction with §153.193, when a trial court appoints a parent possessory conservator, it can conclude that unrestricted possession would endanger the physical or emotional welfare of the child, but that restricted possession or access would not. The court can also conclude that access would not endanger the physical or emotional welfare of the child, but that access is not in the best interest of the child. It cannot conclude, however, that access, even restricted access, would endanger the physical or emotional welfare of the child, because such a conclusion would prevent the trial court from appointing the parent possessory conservator. [¶] Therefore, a trial court has two options regarding possession and access when it appoints a parent possessory conservator and decides that the standard possession order is not in the best interest of the child: (1) fashion an order that restricts possession or access so as to eliminate any danger to the physical or emotional welfare of the child; or (2) deny that parent possession and access. However, because appointment of a parent as possessory conservator implies a finding that access by that parent will not endanger the physical or emotional welfare of the child, complete denial of access is limited to those situations in which the parent's access will not endanger the physical or emotional welfare of the child, but is not in the best interest of the child."

Hopkins v. Hopkins, 853 S.W.2d 134, 138 (Tex. App.—Corpus Christi 1993, no writ). "The trial court's judgment grants [father] some access to the children, indicating that the trial court found limited, supervised access to be in the best interest of the children. This finding alone is sufficient to compel the trial court to appoint [father] possessory conservator under … §14.03(d) [now §153.191]."

FAM §153.192. RIGHTS & DUTIES OF PARENT APPOINTED POSSESSORY CONSERVATOR

(a) Unless limited by court order, a parent appointed as possessory conservator of a child has the rights and duties provided by Subchapter B and any other right or duty expressly granted to the possessory conservator in the order.

(b) In ordering the terms and conditions for possession of a child by a parent appointed possessory conservator, the court shall be guided by the guidelines in Subchapter E.

History of Fam §153.192: Acts 1995, 74th Leg., ch. 20, §1, eff. April 20, 1995. Source: Former Fam §§14.03(b), 14.04.

Lueg v. Lueg, 976 S.W.2d 308, 313 (Tex.App.—Corpus Christi 1998, pet. denied). "While the [F]amily [C]ode does authorize a court to order either parent or both to support a child 'in the manner authorized by the order,' the specific rights and duties assigned to sole managing conservators differ form those assigned to possessory conservators. Section 153.132 ... provides that a sole managing conservator has the exclusive right to receive and give receipt for child support payments and to hold or disburse these funds for the benefit of the child. No such right is expressly ascribed to the possessory conservator. We therefore hold that the [F]amily [C]ode does not contemplate a sole managing conservator paying child support to a possessory conservator."

MacCallum v. MacCallum, 801 S.W.2d 579, 586 (Tex.App.—Corpus Christi 1990, writ denied). Father "complains that the court erred in ordering that he not allow either of the children to operate farm equipment or in any way be involved in the mixing or application of herbicides, pesticides or other farm chemicals during any period of visitation until the children are at least fourteen years of age. *At 587:* From the evidence adduced, the trial court could have reasonably concluded that the operation of farm equipment and the handling of chemicals before the boys reached the age of fourteen years was not in the best interest of the minor children. The condition does not violate the rights and duties of a possessory conservator because §14.04 [now §153.192] of the Family Code provides and contemplates for limitations on those rights and duties."

Beaupre v. Beaupre, 700 S.W.2d 353, 355 (Tex. App.—Fort Worth 1985, writ dism'd). "Since ... §14.04 [now §153.192], in providing for the rights, privileges, duties, and powers of the possessory conservator, presupposes the right of possession on the part of the possessory conservator, we hold that when a divorce decree appoints a possessory conservator and neither denies visitation nor provides for the same, the possessory conservator has the right of reasonable visitation. Although ... §14.03(a) [now §153.006] provides that the times and conditions for access to the child must be specific and expressly stated in the order unless either party shows good cause why specific orders would not be in the best interest of the child, it has been held that the provision of reasonable visitation rights, without specification, does not constitute reversible error."

Fergus v. Fergus, 547 S.W.2d 51, 53 (Tex.App.—Eastland 1977, no writ). "The appointment of [mother] as 'possessory conservator' gave her the rights, privileges, duties, and powers contained in §14.04 [now §153.192]. The judgment contained no limitation nor granted any additional rights, privileges, duties, or powers as contemplated by §14.04. The court did not commit error in failing to list in the judgment the rights, privileges, duties, and powers given the possessory conservator in §14.04."

FAM §153.193. MINIMAL RESTRICTION ON PARENT'S POSSESSION OR ACCESS

The terms of an order that denies possession of a child to a parent or imposes restrictions or limitations on a parent's right to possession of or access to a child may not exceed those that are required to protect the best interest of the child.

History of Fam §153.193: Acts 1995, 74th Leg., ch. 20, §1, eff. April 20, 1995. Source: Former Fam §14.03(d).

In re Walters, 39 S.W.3d 280, 286 n.2 (Tex.App.—Texarkana 2001, no pet.). "By its terms, §153.193 allows for either a denial of possession or a restriction or limitation on possession or access. The Legislature could have used the words 'denies a parent's right to possession of or access to a child' in §153.193, but did not. Arguably, therefore, the statute does not envision a complete denial of parental access in any situation. It must be remembered, however, that the best interest of the child is always the primary consideration in determining issues of possession and access. Therefore, a severe restriction or limitation, even one that amounts to a denial of access, if permissible if it is in the best interest of the child."

Roosth v. Roosth, 889 S.W.2d 445, 451 (Tex.App.—Houston [14th Dist.] 1994, writ denied). "Because the trial court granted [father] status as a possessory conservator, the trial court must have implicitly found that [father's] possession or access to the children would *not* endanger the physical or emotional welfare of the children. Limitations upon [father's] right to possession of or access to the children may not exceed that required to protect the children's best interest."

Sections 153.194-153.250 reserved for expansion

SUBCHAPTER E. GUIDELINES FOR THE POSSESSION OF A CHILD BY A PARENT NAMED AS POSSESSORY CONSERVATOR

FAM §153.251. POLICY & GENERAL APPLICATION OF GUIDELINES

(a) The guidelines established in the standard possession order are intended to guide the courts in ordering the terms and conditions for possession of a child by a parent named as a possessory conservator or as the minimum possession for a joint managing conservator.

(b) It is the policy of this state to encourage frequent contact between a child and each parent for periods of possession that optimize the development of a close and continuing relationship between each parent and child.

(c) It is preferable for all children in a family to be together during periods of possession.

(d) The standard possession order is designed to apply to a child three years of age or older.

History of Fam §153.251: Acts 1995, 74th Leg., ch. 20, §1, eff. April 20, 1995. Source: Former Fam §14.032(a).

E.C. v. Graydon, 28 S.W.3d 825, 829-30 (Tex.App.—Corpus Christi 2000, no pet.). "[T]he standard possession order serves as a tool for determining possession, and the court has the ability to alter the terms when it is in the best interest of the child and devise a possession order that is suitable for the custody situation at issue."

In re C.B.M., 14 S.W.3d 855, 860 (Tex.App.—Beaumont 2000, no pet.). "At the time the trial court entered its order, the child was under three. Consequently, the standard guidelines had no application."

Prause v. Wilder, 820 S.W.2d 386, 387 (Tex.App.—Texarkana 1991, no writ). "There is ... a rebuttable presumption that the standard order provides a reasonable minimum visitation and that it is in the best interests of the child. However, the primary consideration of the court in determining the questions of managing conservatorship, possession, and support of and access to a child shall be the best interests of the child. The movant has the burden to establish that the proposed modification is in the best interests of the child."

FAM §153.252. REBUTTABLE PRESUMPTION

In a suit, there is a rebuttable presumption that the standard possession order in Subchapter F:

(1) provides reasonable minimum possession of a child for a parent named as a possessory conservator or joint managing conservator; and

(2) is in the best interest of the child.

History of Fam §153.252: Acts 1995, 74th Leg., ch. 20, §1, eff. April 20, 1995. Source: Former Fam §14.033(k).

FAM §153.253. STANDARD POSSESSION ORDER INAPPROPRIATE OR UNWORKABLE

The court shall render an order that grants periods of possession of the child as similar as possible to those provided by the standard possession order if the work schedule or other special circumstances of the managing conservator, the possessory conservator, or the child, or the year-round school schedule of the child, make the standard order unworkable or inappropriate.

History of Fam §153.253: Acts 1995, 74th Leg., ch. 20, §1, eff. April 20, 1995. Source: Former Fam §14.033(k), (m).

In re J.E.P., 49 S.W.3d 380, 385 (Tex.App.—Fort Worth 2000, no pet.). "[A] court is given discretion to deviate from standard possession terms, which provide only for 'reasonable *minimum* possession of a child for a parent named as a possessory conservator,' if it determines that an application of the standard order would be unworkable or inappropriate under the circumstances. Most important is the trial court's determination of what arrangement is in the best interest of the child."

FAM §153.254. CHILD LESS THAN THREE YEARS OF AGE

(a) The court shall render an order appropriate under the circumstances for possession of a child less than three years of age.

(b) The court shall render a prospective order to take effect on the child's third birthday, which presumptively will be the standard possession order.

History of Fam §153.254: Acts 1995, 74th Leg., ch. 20, §1, eff. April 20, 1995. Source: Former Fam §14.032(b).

In re Bertram, 981 S.W.2d 820, 828-29 (Tex.App.—Texarkana 1998, no pet.). "Section 153.254(a) ... provides that when a child is less than three years of age, the court shall render an appropriate order under the circumstances for possession of the child. This section suggests that the trial court is not bound by the guidelines when the children are under three years of age. ... Section 153.254(b) provides that, at the same time, the trial court shall render a prospective order to take effect on the child's third birthday, which presumptively shall be the standard possession order. [¶] The judgment in the present case does not speak in terms of a prospective order to take effect after the children's third birthday. But because the order attempts to cover matters involving attendance at school, which is not applicable at this time, and situations in which the parents reside 100 miles or less apart, which is not the situation at this time, it can be assumed that this order was intended to apply after the children's third birthday. Thus, the presumptive application of the standard possession order should be applied for the time after the children reach their third birthday."

FAM §153.255. AGREEMENT

The court may render an order for periods of possession of a child that vary from the standard possession order based on the agreement of the parties.

History of Fam §153.255: Acts 1995, 74th Leg., ch. 20, §1, eff. April 20, 1995. Source: Former Fam §14.033(n).

FAM §153.256. FACTORS FOR COURT TO CONSIDER

In ordering the terms of possession of a child under an order other than a standard possession order, the court shall be guided by the guidelines established by the standard possession order and may consider:

(1) the age, developmental status, circumstances, needs, and best interest of the child;

(2) the circumstances of the managing conservator and of the parent named as a possessory conservator; and

(3) any other relevant factor.

History of Fam §153.256: Acts 1995, 74th Leg., ch. 20, §1, eff. April 20, 1995. Amended by Acts 1995, 74th Leg., ch. 751, §35, eff. Sept. 1, 1995. Source: Former Fam §14.032(c).

Welsh v. Welsh, 905 S.W.2d 615, 619 (Tex.App.—Houston [14th Dist.] 1995, writ denied). Possessory conservator "places great emphasis on the word 'shall' in this statute, arguing in effect that the standard possession is a mandatory order. We find it clear from the language of the statute itself that the mandatory 'shall' is used in conjunction with the word 'guide,' thus indicating that the standard order is intended only as that, a guide by which the trial court determines an appropriate order for the parties before it. [Possessory conservator] correctly concludes that the standard order provides the reasonable minimum possession of a child. Moreover, courts will uphold such orders based on the presumption that it is in the best interest of the child or children. The standard possession order, however, is not mandatory in every case."

FAM §153.257. MEANS OF TRAVEL

In an order providing for the terms and conditions of possession of a child, the court may restrict the means of travel of the child by a legal mode of transportation only after a showing of good cause contained in the record and a finding by the court that the restriction is in the best interest of the child. The court shall specify the duties of the conservators to provide transportation to and from the transportation facilities.

History of Fam §153.257: Acts 1995, 74th Leg., ch. 20, §1, eff. April 20, 1995. Source: Former Fam §14.033(h).

FAM §153.258. REQUEST FOR FINDINGS WHEN ORDER VARIES FROM STANDARD ORDER

Without regard to Rules 296 through 299, Texas Rules of Civil Procedure, in all cases in which possession of a child by a parent is contested and the possession of the child varies from the standard possession order, on written request made or filed with the court not later than 10 days after the date of the hearing or on oral request made in open court during the hearing, the court shall state in the order the specific reasons for the variance from the standard order.

History of Fam §153.258: Acts 1995, 74th Leg., ch. 20, §1, eff. April 20, 1995. Source: Former Fam §14.033(k).

Jacobs v. Dobrei, 991 S.W.2d 462, 464 (Tex.App.—Dallas 1999, no pet.). "On timely request, a trial court's order must state its specific reason for varying from the standard possession. *At 464 n.2:* [W]e apply the same standard of review when a party fails to request specific reasons for the variance under §153.258 as when a party fails to make a request for findings of fact under rules 296 through 299." *See also* ***In re T.J.S.***, 71 S.W.3d 452, 459 (Tex.App.—Waco 2002, n.p.h.).

Gray v. Gray, 971 S.W.2d 212, 216 (Tex.App.—Beaumont 1998, no pet.). The mother's brief confuses "the requirements of §153.258 and a request for findings of fact and conclusions of law under the [TRCPs]. As we appreciate the language of §153.258, the trial court is directed to include, *in the modification order itself*, its reasons for deviating from standard possession order language. In the instant case, written findings of fact are indeed present in the record before us, albeit not in the order itself. Additionally, as set out above, the trial judge provided the parties with a lengthy verbal explanation for ruling as he did. *At 217:* [T]he written findings and the verbal explanation combined to eliminate any 'guessing game' on the part of either party with regard to reasons for deviating from the standard possession order. Any error in not specifying said reasons in the modification order itself is entirely harmless."

Voros v. Turnage, 849 S.W.2d 353, 354 (Tex.App.—Houston [1st Dist.] 1992, no writ). "If the judge orders less time of possession than the guidelines require, she shall, upon timely request, state in the order the specific reasons for all deviations from the standard possession order. This requirement in §14.033(k) [now §153.258] is mandatory."

Ray v. Burns, 832 S.W.2d 431, 437 (Tex.App.—Waco 1992, no writ). "Because [child] was under three years of age when the order was entered, the court could deviate from the standard terms of possession without listing its reasons in the order."

Sections 153.259-153.310 reserved for expansion

SUBCHAPTER F. STANDARD POSSESSION ORDER

FAM §153.311. MUTUAL AGREEMENT OR SPECIFIED TERMS FOR POSSESSION

The court shall specify in a standard possession order that the parties may have possession of the child at times mutually agreed to in advance by the parties and, in the absence of mutual agreement, shall have possession of the child under the specified terms set out in the standard order.

History of Fam §153.311: Acts 1995, 74th Leg., ch. 20, §1, eff. April 20, 1995. Source: Former Fam §14.033(b).

FAM §153.312. PARENTS WHO RESIDE 100 MILES OR LESS APART

(a) If the possessory conservator resides 100 miles or less from the primary residence of the child, the possessory conservator shall have the right to possession of the child as follows:

(1) on weekends beginning at 6 p.m. on the first, third, and fifth Friday of each month and ending at 6 p.m. on the following Sunday or, at the possessory conservator's election made before or at the time of the rendition of the original or modification order, and as specified in the original or modification order, beginning at the time the child's school is regularly dismissed and ending at 6 p.m. on the following Sunday; and

(2) on Wednesdays of each week during the regular school term beginning at 6 p.m. and ending at 8 p.m., or, at the possessory conservator's election made before or at the time of the rendition of the original or modification order, and as specified in the original or modification order, beginning at the time the child's school is regularly dismissed and ending at the time the child's school resumes, unless the court finds that visitation under this subdivision is not in the best interest of the child.

(b) The following provisions govern possession of the child for vacations and certain specific holidays and supersede conflicting weekend or Wednesday periods of possession. The possessory conservator and the managing conservator shall have rights of possession of the child as follows:

(1) the possessory conservator shall have possession in even-numbered years, beginning at 6 p.m. on the day the child is dismissed from school for the school's spring vacation and ending at 6 p.m. on the day before school resumes after that vacation, and the managing conservator shall have possession for the same period in odd-numbered years;

(2) if a possessory conservator:

(A) gives the managing conservator written notice by April 1 of each year specifying an extended period or periods of summer possession, the possessory conservator shall have possession of the child for 30 days beginning not earlier than the day after the child's school is dismissed for the summer vacation and ending not later than seven days before school resumes at the end of the summer vacation, to be exercised in not more than two separate periods of at least seven consecutive days each; or

(B) does not give the managing conservator written notice by April 1 of each year specifying an extended period or periods of summer possession, the possessory conservator shall have possession of the child for 30 consecutive days beginning at 6 p.m. on July 1 and ending at 6 p.m. on July 31;

(3) if the managing conservator gives the possessory conservator written notice by April 15 of each year, the managing conservator shall have possession of the child on any one weekend beginning Friday at 6 p.m. and ending at 6 p.m. on the following Sunday during one period of possession by the possessory conservator under Subdivision (2), provided that the managing conservator picks up the child from the possessory conservator and returns the child to that same place; and

(4) if the managing conservator gives the possessory conservator written notice by April 15 of each year

or gives the possessory conservator 14 days' written notice on or after April 16 of each year, the managing conservator may designate one weekend beginning not earlier than the day after the child's school is dismissed for the summer vacation and ending not later than seven days before school resumes at the end of the summer vacation, during which an otherwise scheduled weekend period of possession by the possessory conservator will not take place, provided that the weekend designated does not interfere with the possessory conservator's period or periods of extended summer possession or with Father's Day if the possessory conservator is the father of the child.

History of Fam §153.312: Acts 1995, 74th Leg., ch. 20, §1, eff. April 20, 1995. Amended by Acts 1997, 75th Leg., ch. 802, §1, eff. Sept. 1, 1997; Acts 1999, 76th Leg., ch. 236, §1, eff. Sept. 1, 1999. Source: Former Fam §14.033(c), (e)(4)-(7).

FAM §153.313. PARENTS WHO RESIDE OVER 100 MILES APART

If the possessory conservator resides more than 100 miles from the residence of the child, the possessory conservator shall have the right to possession of the child as follows:

(1) either regular weekend possession beginning on the first, third, and fifth Friday as provided under the terms applicable to parents who reside 100 miles or less apart or not more than one weekend per month of the possessory conservator's choice beginning at 6 p.m. on the day school recesses for the weekend and ending at 6 p.m. on the day before school resumes after the weekend, provided that the possessory conservator gives the managing conservator 14 days' written or telephonic notice preceding a designated weekend, and provided that the possessory conservator elects an option for this alternative period of possession by written notice given to the managing conservator within 90 days after the parties begin to reside more than 100 miles apart, as applicable;

(2) each year beginning on the day the child is dismissed from school for the school's spring vacation and ending at 6 p.m. on the day before school resumes after that vacation;

(3) if the possessory conservator:

(A) gives the managing conservator written notice by April 1 of each year specifying an extended period or periods of summer possession, the possessory conservator shall have possession of the child for 42 days beginning not earlier than the day after the child's school is dismissed for the summer vacation and ending not later than seven days before school resumes at the end of the summer vacation, to be exercised in not more than two separate periods of at least seven consecutive days each; or

(B) does not give the managing conservator written notice by April 1 of each year specifying an extended period or periods of summer possession, the possessory conservator shall have possession of the child for 42 consecutive days beginning at 6 p.m. on June 15 and ending at 6 p.m. on July 27;

(4) if the managing conservator gives the possessory conservator written notice by April 15 of each year the managing conservator shall have possession of the child on one weekend beginning Friday at 6 p.m. and ending at 6 p.m. on the following Sunday during one period of possession by the possessory conservator under Subdivision (3), provided that if a period of possession by the possessory conservator exceeds 30 days, the managing conservator may have possession of the child under the terms of this subdivision on two nonconsecutive weekends during that time period, and further provided that the managing conservator picks up the child from the possessory conservator and returns the child to that same place; and

(5) if the managing conservator gives the possessory conservator written notice by April 15 of each year, the managing conservator may designate 21 days beginning not earlier than the day after the child's school is dismissed for the summer vacation and ending not later than seven days before school resumes at the end of the summer vacation, to be exercised in not more than two separate periods of at least seven consecutive days each, during which the possessory conservator may not have possession of the child, provided that the period or periods so designated do not interfere with the possessory conservator's period or periods of extended summer possession or with Father's Day if the possessory conservator is the father of the child.

History of Fam §153.313: Acts 1995, 74th Leg., ch. 20, §1, eff. April 20, 1995. Amended by Acts 1995, 74th Leg., ch. 751, §36, eff. Sept. 1, 1995; Acts 1999, 76th Leg., ch. 236, §2, eff. Sept. 1, 1999. Source: Former Fam §14.033(f).

FAM §153.314. HOLIDAY POSSESSION UNAFFECTED BY DISTANCE PARENTS RESIDE APART

The following provisions govern possession of the child for certain specific holidays and supersede conflicting weekend or Wednesday periods of possession without regard to the distance the parents reside apart. The possessory conservator and the managing conservator shall have rights of possession of the child as follows:

(1) the possessory conservator shall have possession of the child in even-numbered years beginning at 6 p.m. on the day the child is dismissed from school for the Christmas school vacation and ending at noon on December 26, and the managing conservator shall have possession for the same period in odd-numbered years;

(2) the possessory conservator shall have possession of the child in odd-numbered years beginning at noon on December 26 and ending at 6 p.m. on the day before school resumes after that vacation, and the managing conservator shall have possession for the same period in even-numbered years;

(3) the possessory conservator shall have possession of the child in odd-numbered years, beginning at 6 p.m. on the day the child is dismissed from school before Thanksgiving and ending at 6 p.m. on the following Sunday, and the managing conservator shall have possession for the same period in even-numbered years;

(4) the parent not otherwise entitled under this standard order to present possession of a child on the child's birthday shall have possession of the child beginning at 6 p.m. and ending at 8 p.m. on that day, provided that the parent picks up the child from the residence of the conservator entitled to possession and returns the child to that same place;

(5) if a conservator, the father shall have possession of the child beginning at 6 p.m. on the Friday preceding Father's Day and ending on Father's Day at 6 p.m., provided that, if he is not otherwise entitled under this standard order to present possession of the child, he picks up the child from the residence of the conservator entitled to possession and returns the child to that same place; and

(6) if a conservator, the mother shall have possession of the child beginning at 6 p.m. on the Friday preceding Mother's Day and ending on Mother's Day at 6 p.m., provided that, if she is not otherwise entitled under this standard order to present possession of the child, she picks up the child from the residence of the conservator entitled to possession and returns the child to that same place.

History of Fam §153.314: Acts 1995, 74th Leg., ch. 20, §1, eff. April 20, 1995. Source: Former Fam §14.033(e)(1)-(3), (8)-(10), (f)(2).

FAM §153.315. WEEKEND POSSESSION EXTENDED BY HOLIDAY

(a) If a weekend period of possession of the possessory conservator coincides with a school holiday during the regular school term or with a federal, state, or local holiday during the summer months in which school is not in session, the weekend possession shall end at 6 p.m. on a Monday holiday or school holiday or shall begin at 6 p.m. Thursday for a Friday holiday or school holiday, as applicable.

(b) At the possessory conservator's election, made before or at the time of the rendition of the original or modification order, and as specified in the original or modification order, periods of possession extended by a holiday may begin at the time the child's school is regularly dismissed.

History of Fam §153.315: Acts 1995, 74th Leg., ch. 20, §1, eff. April 20, 1995. Source: Former Fam §14.033(d).

FAM §153.316. GENERAL TERMS & CONDITIONS

The court shall order the following general terms and conditions of possession of a child to apply without regard to the distance between the residence of a parent and the child:

(1) the managing conservator shall surrender the child to the possessory conservator at the beginning of each period of the possessory conservator's possession at the residence of the managing conservator;

(2) if the possessory conservator elects to begin a period of possession at the time the child's school is regularly dismissed, the managing conservator shall surrender the child to the possessory conservator at the beginning of each period of possession at the school in which the child is enrolled;

(3) the possessory conservator shall be ordered to do one of the following:

(A) the possessory conservator shall surrender the child to the managing conservator at the end of each period of possession at the residence of the possessory conservator; or

(B) the possessory conservator shall return the child to the residence of the managing conservator at the end of each period of possession, except that the order shall provide that the possessory conservator shall surrender the child to the managing conservator at the end of each period of possession at the residence of the possessory conservator if:

(i) at the time the original order or a modification of an order establishing terms and conditions of possession or access the possessory conservator and the managing conservator lived in the same county, the possessory conservator's county of residence remains the same after the rendition of the order, and the managing conservator's county of residence changes, effective on the date of the change of residence by the managing conservator; or

(ii) the possessory conservator and managing conservator lived in the same residence at any time during a six-month period preceding the date on which a suit for dissolution of the marriage was filed and the possessory conservator's county of residence remains the same and the managing conservator's county of residence changes after they no longer live in the same residence, effective on the date the order is rendered;

(4) if the possessory conservator elects to end a period of possession at the time the child's school resumes, the possessory conservator shall surrender the child to the managing conservator at the end of each period of possession at the school in which the child is enrolled;

(5) each conservator shall return with the child the personal effects that the child brought at the beginning of the period of possession;

(6) either parent may designate a competent adult to pick up and return the child, as applicable; a parent or a designated competent adult shall be present when the child is picked up or returned;

(7) a parent shall give notice to the person in possession of the child on each occasion that the parent will be unable to exercise that parent's right of possession for a specified period;

(8) written notice shall be deemed to have been timely made if received or postmarked before or at the time that notice is due; and

(9) if a conservator's time of possession of a child ends at the time school resumes and for any reason the child is not or will not be returned to school, the conservator in possession of the child shall immediately notify the school and the other conservator that the child will not be or has not been returned to school.

History of Fam §153.316: Acts 1995, 74th Leg., ch. 20, §1, eff. April 20, 1995. Amended by Acts 1995, 74th Leg., ch. 751, §37, eff. Sept. 1, 1995; Acts 1997, 75th Leg., ch. 9, §1, eff. Sept. 1, 1997. Source: Former Fam §14.033(g).

Weldon v. Weldon, 968 S.W.2d 515, 516 n.2 (Tex. App.—Texarkana 1998, no pet.). "Even though the standard possession order under §153.316 sets out the possessory rights of the possessory conservator, the Section applies to joint managing conservators not awarded primary physical residence of the child pursuant to ... §153.137."

FAM §153.317. ALTERNATIVE POSSESSION TIMES

If a child is enrolled in school and the possessory conservator elects before or at the time of the rendition of the original or modification order, the standard order must expressly provide that the possessory conservator's period of possession shall begin or end, or both, at a different time expressly set in the standard order under and within the range of alternative times provided by one or both of the following subdivisions:

(1) instead of a period of possession by a possessory conservator beginning at 6 p.m. on the day school recesses, the period of possession may be set in the standard possession order to begin at the time the child's school is regularly dismissed or at any time between the time the child's school is regularly dismissed and 6 p.m.; and

(2) except for Wednesday evening possession, instead of a period of possession by a possessory conservator ending at 6 p.m. on the day before school resumes, the period of possession may be set in the standard order to end at the time school resumes.

History of Fam §153.317: Acts 1995, 74th Leg., ch. 20, §1, eff. April 20, 1995. Amended by Acts 1997, 75th Leg., ch. 9, §1, eff. Sept. 1, 1997. Source: Former Fam §14.033(i).

In re Davis, 30 S.W.3d 609, 612 (Tex.App.—Texarkana 2000, no pet.). "The former version of the statute provided that the visitation *may* expressly provide for the Monday morning surrender. The present version provides that the visitation *must* expressly provide such language on request of the possessory conservator. [¶] [T]he question is whether a party seeking a modified visitation order must first comply with §156.301 before the court is required to apply the mandatory election language of §153.317 and order surrender of a child after visitation as provided under the present version of the standard possession statutes. *At 613:* [I]n order to read these statutory provisions in harmony with each other, we conclude that a movant must first meet the requirements of §156.301. If the movant does so successfully and makes the requisite election, then the trial court is required to provide visitation as set out by §153.317."

Weldon v. Weldon, 968 S.W.2d 515, 518 (Tex. App.—Texarkana 1998, no pet.). "Use of the word 'may' in a statute shows that the provision is directory and not mandatory. The legislature chose to use the word 'may' in this section regarding alternative possession times in original orders and orders on modification. Had the legislature intended to make the section mandatory at the time, it would have used 'shall,' as it did in §153.316, setting out similar terms in standard possession orders, or 'must,' as it did in the revised §153.317. We must presume that all words chosen by the legislature were used for a purpose. This is true despite the legislature's subsequent revision of the statute. A trial judge rules on a statute that is in effect at the time of the case and is not in the position of predicting future changes by the legislature."

Sections 153.318-153.370 reserved for expansion

SUBCHAPTER G. APPOINTMENT OF NONPARENT AS CONSERVATOR

FAM §153.371. RIGHTS & DUTIES OF NONPARENT APPOINTED AS SOLE MANAGING CONSERVATOR

Unless limited by court order or other provisions of this chapter, a nonparent, licensed child-placing agency, or authorized agency appointed as a managing conservator of the child has the following rights and duties:

(1) the right to have physical possession and to direct the moral and religious training of the child;

(2) the duty of care, control, protection, and reasonable discipline of the child;

(3) the duty to provide the child with clothing, food, shelter, education, and medical, psychological, and dental care;

(4) the right to consent for the child to medical, psychiatric, psychological, dental, and surgical treatment and to have access to the child's medical records;

(5) the right to receive and give receipt for payments for the support of the child and to hold or disburse funds for the benefit of the child;

(6) the right to the services and earnings of the child;

(7) the right to consent to marriage and to enlistment in the armed forces of the United States;

(8) the right to represent the child in legal action and to make other decisions of substantial legal significance concerning the child;

(9) except when a guardian of the child's estate or a guardian or attorney ad litem has been appointed for the child, the right to act as an agent of the child in relation to the child's estate if the child's action is required by a state, the United States, or a foreign government;

(10) the right to establish the primary residence of the child and to make decisions regarding the child's education; and

(11) if the parent-child relationship has been terminated with respect to the parents, or only living parent, or if there is no living parent, the right to consent to the adoption of the child and to make any other decision concerning the child that a parent could make.

History of Fam §153.371: Acts 1995, 74th Leg., ch. 20, §1, eff. April 20, 1995. Amended by Acts 1995, 74th Leg., ch. 751, §34, eff. Sept. 1, 1995; Acts 1999, 76th Leg., ch. 949, §1, eff. Sept. 1, 1999. Source: Former Fam §14.02(c).

In re V.L.K., 24 S.W.3d 338, 340 n.1 (Tex.2000). "A managing conservator has the right to establish the child's residence and has primary custody of the child."

Office of Attorney Gen. v. Carter, 977 S.W.2d 159, 162 n.3 (Tex.App.—Houston [14th Dist.] 1998, no pet.). "Unless a grandparent has a legal obligation to care for the grandchild, as a legal custodian or legal guardian, the grandparent has no legal duty to spend the money received under a support order for the child's care."

Harris Cty. Child Welfare Unit v. Caloudas, 590 S.W.2d 596, 599 (Tex.App.—Houston [1st Dist.] 1979, no writ). "[W]ith the enactment of the Texas Family Code, the rights, privileges, duties and responsibilities of agencies and persons dealing with minor children have been set out and defined in minute detail. No distinction is made between an authorized agency and a person."

FAM §153.372. NONPARENT APPOINTED AS JOINT MANAGING CONSERVATOR

(a) A nonparent, authorized agency, or licensed child-placing agency appointed as a joint managing conservator may serve in that capacity with either another nonparent or with a parent of the child.

(b) The procedural and substantive standards regarding an agreed or court-ordered joint managing conservatorship provided by Subchapter C apply to a nonparent joint managing conservator.

History of Fam §153.372: Acts 1995, 74th Leg., ch. 20, §1, eff. April 20, 1995. Source: Former Fam §14.021(j).

In re De La Pena, 999 S.W.2d 521, 534-35 (Tex. App.—El Paso 1999, no pet.). "If the right of primary possession is at the very core of managing conservatorship, it appears to us that the parental presumption must apply here as well. Section 153.372(b) provides that the procedural and substantive standards regarding a court-ordered joint managing conservatorship provided by Subchapter C of [Chapter 153] apply to a nonparent joint managing conservator. The very first section of Subchapter C contains the parental presumption. Accordingly, we conclude that as between a parent and nonparent, unless the court finds that appointment of the parent would not be in the best interest of the child because it would significantly impair the child's physical health or emotional development, the parent shall be appointed sole managing conservator or the parent and nonparent shall be appointed joint managing conservators. If the court chooses the latter, the parent shall be awarded primary possession unless such an order would not be in the best interest of the child because it would significantly impair the child's physical health or emotional development. To hold otherwise would permit the court to apply the presumption in appointing the parent a joint managing conservator but nevertheless choose the primary residence of the child on the basis of a heads-up best interest test, with the court determining which of the parties is the 'better' choice. This results in the appointment of a parent as a managing conservator in name only, a paper title which eviscerates the purpose of the statute."

FAM §153.3721. ACCESS TO CERTAIN RECORDS BY NONPARENT JOINT MANAGING CONSERVATOR

Unless limited by court order or other provisions of this chapter, a nonparent joint managing conservator has the right of access to the medical records of the child, without regard to whether the right is specified in the order.

History of Fam §153.3721: Acts 1999, 76th Leg., ch. 949, §2, eff. Sept. 1, 1999.

FAM §153.373. VOLUNTARY SURRENDER OF POSSESSION REBUTS PARENTAL PRESUMPTION

The presumption that a parent should be appointed or retained as managing conservator of the child is rebutted if the court finds that:

(1) the parent has voluntarily relinquished actual care, control, and possession of the child to a nonparent, licensed child-placing agency, or authorized agency for a period of one year or more, a portion of which was within 90 days preceding the date of intervention in or filing of the suit; and

(2) the appointment of the nonparent or agency as managing conservator is in the best interest of the child.

History of Fam §153.373: Acts 1995, 74th Leg., ch. 20, §1, eff. April 20, 1995. Source: Former Fam §14.01(b)(2).

FAM §153.374. DESIGNATION OF MANAGING CONSERVATOR IN AFFIDAVIT OF RELINQUISHMENT

(a) A parent may designate a competent person, authorized agency, or licensed child-placing agency to serve as managing conservator of the child in an unrevoked or irrevocable affidavit of relinquishment of parental rights executed as provided by Chapter 161.

(b) The person or agency designated to serve as managing conservator shall be appointed managing conservator unless the court finds that the appointment would not be in the best interest of the child.

History of Fam §153.374: Acts 1995, 74th Leg., ch. 20, §1, eff. April 20, 1995. Amended by Acts 1995, 74th Leg., ch. 751, §38, eff. Sept. 1, 1995. Source: Former Fam §14.01(d).

FAM §153.375. ANNUAL REPORT BY NONPARENT MANAGING CONSERVATOR

(a) A nonparent appointed as a managing conservator of a child shall each 12 months after the appointment file with the court a report of facts concerning the child's welfare, including the child's whereabouts and physical condition.

(b) The report may not be admitted in evidence in a subsequent suit.

History of Fam §153.375: Acts 1995, 74th Leg., ch. 20, §1, eff. April 20, 1995. Source: Former Fam §14.01(e).

FAM §153.376. RIGHTS & DUTIES OF NONPARENT POSSESSORY CONSERVATOR

(a) Unless limited by court order or other provisions of this chapter, a nonparent, licensed child-placing agency, or authorized agency appointed as a possessory conservator has the following rights and duties during the period of possession:

(1) the duty of care, control, protection, and reasonable discipline of the child;

(2) the duty to provide the child with clothing, food, and shelter; and

(3) the right to consent to medical, dental, and surgical treatment during an emergency involving an immediate danger to the health and safety of the child.

(b) A nonparent possessory conservator has any other right or duty specified in the order.

History of Fam §153.376: Acts 1995, 74th Leg., ch. 20, §1, eff. April 20, 1995. Source: Former Fam §14.04(a), (b).

FAM §153.377. ACCESS TO CHILD'S RECORDS

A nonparent possessory conservator has the right of access to medical, dental, psychological, and educational records of the child to the same extent as the managing conservator, without regard to whether the right is specified in the order.

History of Fam §153.377: Acts 1995, 74th Leg., ch. 20, §1, eff. April 20, 1995. Source: Former Fam §14.04(c).

Sections 153.378-153.430 reserved for expansion

SUBCHAPTER H. RIGHTS OF GRANDPARENT

FAM §153.431. GRANDPARENTAL APPOINTMENT AS MANAGING CONSERVATORS

If the parents are deceased, the grandparents may be considered for appointment as managing conservators, but consideration does not alter or diminish the discretionary power of the court.

History of Fam §153.431: Acts 1995, 74th Leg., ch. 20, §1, eff. April 20, 1995. Source: Former Fam §14.07(b).

FAM §153.432. SUIT FOR ACCESS

(a) A biological or adoptive grandparent may request access to a grandchild by filing:

(1) an original suit; or

(2) a suit for modification as provided by Chapter 156.

(b) A grandparent may request access to a grandchild in a suit filed for the sole purpose of requesting the relief, without regard to whether the appointment of a managing conservator is an issue in the suit.

History of Fam §153.432: Acts 1995, 74th Leg., ch. 20, §1, eff. April 20, 1995. Source: Former Fam §14.03(e), (f)(1), (3).

Troxel v. Granville, 530 U.S. 57, 70, 120 S.Ct. 2054, 2062 (2000). See Annotation in FAM §153.433.

FAM §153.433. POSSESSION OF & ACCESS TO GRANDCHILD

The court shall order reasonable access to a grandchild by a grandparent if:

(1) at the time the relief is requested, at least one biological or adoptive parent of the child has not had that parent's parental rights terminated; and

(2) access is in the best interest of the child, and at least one of the following facts is present:

(A) the grandparent requesting access to the child is a parent of a parent of the child and that parent of the child has been incarcerated in jail or prison during the three-month period preceding the filing of the petition or has been found by a court to be incompetent or is dead;

(B) the parents of the child are divorced or have been living apart for the three-month period preceding the filing of the petition or a suit for the dissolution of the parents' marriage is pending;

(C) the child has been abused or neglected by a parent of the child;

(D) the child has been adjudicated to be a child in need of supervision or a delinquent child under Title 3;

(E) the grandparent requesting access to the child is the parent of a person whose parent-child relationship with the child has been terminated by court order; or

(F) the child has resided with the grandparent requesting access to the child for at least six months within the 24-month period preceding the filing of the petition.

History of Fam §153.433: Acts 1995, 74th Leg., ch. 20, §1, eff. April 20, 1995. Amended by Acts 1997, 75th Leg., ch. 1397, §1, eff. Sept. 1, 1997. Source: Former Fam §14.03(e).

Troxel v. Granville, 530 U.S. 57, 70, 120 S.Ct. 2054, 2062 (2000). "In an ideal world, parents might always seek to cultivate the bonds between grandparents and their grandchildren. Needless to say, however, our world is far from perfect, and in it the decision whether such an intergenerational relationship would be beneficial in any specific case is for the parent to make in the first instance. And, if a fit parent's decision of the kind at issue here becomes subject to judicial review, the court must accord at least some special weight to the parent's own determination. *At 72-73, 2064:* [T]he Due Process Clause does not permit a State to infringe on the fundamental right of parents to make child rearing decisions simply because a state judge believes a 'better' decision could be made. Neither the Washington nonparental visitation statute generally–which places no limits on either the persons who may petition for visitation or the circumstances in which such a petition may be granted—nor the Superior Court in this specific case required anything more. [¶] [W]e do not consider the primary constitutional question passed on by the Washington Supreme Court—whether the Due Process Clause requires all nonparental visitation statutes to include a showing

FAM §153.433

of harm or potential harm to the child as a condition precedent to granting visitation [in an original action] ... Because much state-court adjudication in this context occurs on a case-by-case basis, we would be hesitant to hold that specific nonparental visitation statutes violate the Due Process Clause as a per se matter."

Roby v. Adams, 68 S.W.3d 822, 827-28 (Tex.App.—El Paso 2002, n.p.h.). "This Court is aware of ... ***Lilley v. Lilley***, 43 S.W.3d 703 (Tex.App.—Austin 2001, no pet.). In ***Lilley***, the Court found it dispositive that the parent had testified that it was in the best interest of her child to have visitation with the grandparent and that the parent had taken inconsistent positions on the grandparent's access to the child. The facts of our case are distinguishable in that [father] never declared it would be in the best interest of his children to allow the [grandparents] access to the children and [father] was consistent in his position on the [grandparents]' access to them. Furthermore, the holding in ***Lilley*** appears to place the burden of persuasion upon the parent to prove the best interest of the child. This goes against the presumption so strongly enunciated in ***Troxel***, that a fit parent acts in the best interest of his or her child. A grandparent seeking access under ... §153.433 has the burden to overcome the presumption that a fit parent acts in the best interest of the parent's child in order to establish the 'best interest of the child' prong of the statute."

Lilley v. Lilley, 43 S.W.3d 703, 712 (Tex.App.—Austin 2001, no pet.). "Section 153.433 ... is not 'breathtakingly broad,' as was the Washington statute in ***Troxel***. Section 153.433 allows only grandparents, under particular circumstances, to petition for access to a child, provided it is in the child's best interest. The Texas grandparent access statute has already been examined and held to be constitutional." *See also* ***Deweese v. Crawford***, below.

E.C. v. Graydon, 28 S.W.3d 825, 831-32 (Tex.App.—Corpus Christi 2000, no pet.). "The [F]amily [C]ode, in §153.433, only allows a trial court to grant a grandparent reasonable access to, not possession of, a grandchild. [¶] The [F]amily [C]ode does not define the terms 'possession' and 'access.' When a statute does not define a term, we apply the term's ordinary meaning. [¶] A person with rights of 'access to' children may approach them, communicate with them and visit with them, but may not take possession or control of the children away from the managing conservator. A person with rights to 'possession of' children may exercise possession and control of the children, to the exclusion of all other persons including the managing conservator, during periods of possession. A person with rights of possession of children also has rights and responsibilities toward their care and behavior."

In re Webster, 982 S.W.2d 526, 528 (Tex.App.—Amarillo 1998, no pet.). Grandmother "asserts the trial court abused its discretion in granting access to [child] only at the discretion of the [DPRS]. We agree. [¶] Here, because the court's amended decree delegated its discretionary authority to determine reasonable access to [the child] to the [DPRS] at the times and on the dates to be set by the [DPRS], we conclude that it was an improper delegation of judicial power."

Bowers v. Matula, 943 S.W.2d 536, 539 (Tex. App.—Houston [1st Dist.] 1997, no writ). "[T]he plain meaning of the phrase 'at the time relief is requested' is the time a petition is filed requesting access. This is the time standing is determined for purposes of grandparent requests for access."

Blalock v. Blalock, 559 S.W.2d 442, 443 (Tex. App.—Houston [14th Dist.] 1977, no writ). "The grandparents' ... acquisition of access rights did not serve to create a general duty to support the children. Undoubtedly, possessory conservators are required to provide for a child during the period of possession, but their duties are limited to that period. [¶] [A]ppointment as a possessory conservator of a child does not create a general obligation to support the child...."

Deweese v. Crawford, 520 S.W.2d 522, 526 (Tex. App—Houston [14th Dist.] 1975, writ ref'd n.r.e.), *overruled on other grounds*, ***Cherne Indus., Inc. v. Magallanes***, 763 S.W.2d 768 (Tex.1989). "We reject [grandparents'] constitutional attack on the grandparents' visitation provision of the Family Code. We recognize that it might be generally said that the state may not constitutionally interfere with the natural liberty of parents to direct the upbringing of their children. We further recognize that while it is desirable that the ties of affection that nature creates between grandparents and their grandchildren be strengthened and unceasing, if there is a conflict, the father or the mother should be the judge. Judicial enforcement of such visitation rights might divide parental authority and bring the child into the midst of conflict and cause ill feeling between the parent and the grandparents. However, other circumstances may justify judicial intervention. Visitation privileges may be incident to a divorce proceeding wherein the parents consented or acquiesced in such visitation. The custodial parent may have voluntarily involved the grandparent in the upbringing of the child. In the final analysis, the question before the court will always be the *best interest* of the children involved. Keeping this in mind, the court can best determine to deny visitation rights in the best interest of the children where such would be damaging and disruptive and to allow such rights where it would be more harmful to do otherwise. The state has sufficient interest in the family relationship to permit legislation in this area."

FAM §153.434. LIMITATION ON RIGHT TO REQUEST ACCESS

A biological or adoptive grandparent may not request possession of or access to a grandchild if:

(1) each of the biological parents of the grandchild has:

(A) died;

(B) had the person's parental rights terminated; or

(C) executed an affidavit of waiver of interest in child or an affidavit of relinquishment of parental rights under Chapter 161 and the affidavit designates an authorized agency, licensed child-placing agency, or person other than the child's stepparent as the managing conservator of the child; and

(2) the grandchild has been adopted, or is the subject of a pending suit for adoption, by a person other than the child's stepparent.

History of Fam §153.434: Acts 1995, 74th Leg., ch. 20, §1, eff. April 20, 1995. Amended by Acts 1997, 75th Leg., ch. 561, §4, eff. Sept. 1, 1997; Acts 1999, 76th Leg., ch. 1390, §13, eff. Sept. 1, 1999. Source: Former Fam §14.03(g).

CHAPTER 154. CHILD SUPPORT

SUBCHAPTER A. COURT-ORDERED CHILD SUPPORT

FAM §154.001. SUPPORT OF CHILD

(a) The court may order either or both parents to support a child in the manner specified by the order:

(1) until the child is 18 years of age or until graduation from high school, whichever occurs later;

(2) until the child is emancipated through marriage, through removal of the disabilities of minority by court order, or by other operation of law;

(3) until the death of the child; or

(4) if the child is disabled as defined in this chapter, for an indefinite period.

(b) The court may order either or both parents to make periodic payments for the support of a child in a proceeding in which the Department of Protective and Regulatory Services is named temporary managing conservator. In a proceeding in which the Department of Protective and Regulatory Services is named permanent managing conservator of a child whose parents' rights have not been terminated, the court shall order each parent that is financially able to make periodic payments for the support of the child.

(c) In a Title IV-D case, if neither parent has physical possession or conservatorship of the child, the court may render an order providing that a nonparent or agency having physical possession may receive, hold, or disburse child support payments for the benefit of the child.

History of Fam §154.001: Acts 1995, 74th Leg., ch. 20, §1, eff. April 20, 1995. Amended by Acts 1995, 74th Leg., ch. 751, §39, eff. Sept. 1, 1995; Acts 1999, 76th Leg., ch. 556, §8, eff. Sept. 1, 1999. Source: Former Fam §14.05(a), (b), (d).

Rodriguez v. Rodriguez, 860 S.W.2d 414, 415 (Tex. 1993). "A trial court has discretion to set child support within the parameters established by the child support guidelines set forth in the [Family] Code. A trial court's decision in this regard will not be overturned unless a clear abuse of discretion is shown."

In re M.L.P.J., 16 S.W.3d 45, 47 (Tex.App.—Eastland 2000, pet. denied). "From its beginnings, the doctrine of adoption by estoppel has been used only 'to preclude adoptive parents and their privies' from asserting that the child seeking to inherit was not the adopted child of the deceased. *At 48:* [W]e are asked to extend the doctrine of equitable adoption into an area governed by the Family Code. [Section] 154.001(a) authorizes a court to order 'either or both parents' to support a child in the manner specified in the order. Section 101.024 defines a 'Parent' as: [T]he mother, a man presumed to be the biological father, a man legally determined to be the biological father, a man who has been adjudicated to be the biological father by a court of competent jurisdiction, or an adoptive mother or father. [¶] We hold that the doctrine of equitable adoption is inapplicable to this case. [Alleged father] does not fit the strict definition of 'Parent' within the Family Code because he did not formally adopt the child. The trial court erred in ordering [alleged father] to pay child support and to provide health insurance for the child."

Bailey v. Bailey, 987 S.W.2d 206, 209 (Tex.App.—Amarillo 1999, no pet.). "By using the phrase 'in the manner specified by the order,' the [L]egislature implicitly granted the trial judge leeway in determining the manner in which support is to be used. [¶] So long as the manner specified by the court rationally comports with the purpose of child support, we are hard-pressed to say that the court exceeded the grant of authority implicit in §154.001(a) and abused its discretion."

In re Marriage of Driver, 895 S.W.2d 875, 876 (Tex. App.—Texarkana 1995, no writ). "A trial court has broad discretion to set child support within the statutory limits of the Family Code. We will not disturb that decision unless it constitutes a clear abuse of discretion. In determining whether a trial court has abused its discretion, we look to see whether it acted arbitrarily or unreasonably and without reference to guiding rules or principles."

In re R.R.F., 846 S.W.2d 65, 68 (Tex.App.—Corpus Christi 1992, writ denied). "The child support order includes within it an implicit finding that the obligor has the means to pay the amount ordered."

Gross v. Gross, 808 S.W.2d 215, 218 (Tex.App.—Houston [14th Dist.] 1991, no writ). "The court may order support for an indefinite period if the child is mentally or physically disabled."

FAM §154.002. CHILD SUPPORT THROUGH HIGH SCHOOL GRADUATION

(a) If the child is fully enrolled in an accredited secondary school in a program leading toward a high school diploma or enrolled in courses for joint high school and junior college credit pursuant to Section 130.008, Education Code, the court may render an original support order or modify an existing order providing child support past the 18th birthday of the child.

(b) The request for a support order through high school graduation may be filed before or after the child's 18th birthday.

(c) The order for periodic support may provide that payments continue through the end of the month in which the child graduates.

History of Fam §154.002: Acts 1995, 74th Leg., ch. 20, §1, eff. April 20, 1995. Amended by Acts 1999, 76th Leg., ch. 506, §1, eff. Aug. 30, 1999. Source: Former Fam §14.05(a).

In re J.A.B., 13 S.W.3d 813, 816 (Tex.App.—Fort Worth 2000, no pet.). "We find no binding authority for the proposition that a child must be 'participating' in high school or its equivalent in order to be considered 'fully enrolled.' This court has determined that it would be unjust 'to establish an arbitrary number of hours in which a student must be enlisted in order [to be] deemed fully enrolled.' [W]e recognized that the intent of the legislature in allowing for child support after the child's eighteenth birthday was 'to require a father to aid in the support of his child, even if that child is over the age of eighteen, so long as that child was *actively participating* in studies which would lead to a high school diploma.' We held, however, that a child enrolled in a single correspondence course worth one credit hour was 'fully enrolled,' when that was the only course required for her to graduate. [¶] Implicit in the legislature's intent is its overriding concern that the child's participation be under appropriate supervision to ensure that it is an effective course of study. [¶] Supervision requires not only classroom teachers or course instructors, but also parents. A primary duty of a parent is to support the child, and this duty, according to the Family Code, includes providing the child with an education. The fact that the child ... has accumulated too many unexcused absences to receive credit in four of six courses, in and of itself, does not determine that the child is not 'fully enrolled.' 'Full enrollment' does not require the child to make a good faith effort to attend school and pass, rather, it requires that a child's name appear on the rolls of the school district, that the child be registered for the normal number of classes, and that he has not been withdrawn or expelled. It may also require both parents to participate actively in their duties to support and educate the child, and when necessary, to supervise the child's attendance."

Crocker v. Attorney Gen., 3 S.W.3d 650, 652-54 (Tex.App.—Austin 1999, no pet.). "The general language the legislature used in subsection (b) to refer to the manner of seeking child support covers both a motion to modify and an original proceeding seeking support. We therefore conclude that the Family Code confers jurisdiction on the trial court to order support for a child who is enrolled in high school after he turns eighteen, and that this jurisdiction is invoked by a motion to modify filed after the child's eighteenth birthday. [¶] The intent of §154.002(a) is to require a parent to help support his child, even if the child is over eighteen years of age, so long as that child is actively participating in studies that would lead to a high school diploma. We analyze whether [child] is fully enrolled, not on the basis of how many hours of class he is taking, but on how many hours he would be required to take if seeking to graduate.... Although [child] could theoretically have graduated in less than four years by not participating in the jobs program, a curriculum that is adapted to his particular educational needs does not disqualify him from being fully enrolled."

In re A.B., 994 S.W.2d 229, 231-32 (Tex.App.—Eastland 1999, pet. denied). "The fact that [child] was failing a majority of her classes does not determine whether she is fully enrolled. To hold otherwise would require courts to make a highly-subjective determination in each case. A student might fail despite his or her best efforts because he or she has a learning disability or other personal problems. One court might find full enrollment in facts under which another court would not. Under an 'active participation' analysis, the trial court could relieve a parent of his or her support obligation if a student who turned 18 began to make failing grades, unless the parent seeking to enforce the obligation could prove that the decrease in grades was despite the student's best efforts. The plain language of the statute and of the agreed order does not require [child] to make a 'good faith effort' to attend school and pass her classes. When she is enrolled in school and registered for classes, [child] is 'fully enrolled.' [¶] The purpose of the language in the agreed order, like the purpose of the statute, is to encourage [child] to pursue her education. To achieve that end, we hold that [child] is 'fully enrolled in an accredited secondary school program' when her name appears on the rolls of the school district and when she is registered for the normal number of classes and has not been expelled."

Ewing v. Holt, 835 S.W.2d 274, 275-76 (Tex.App.—Fort Worth 1992, no writ). "The intent of the [L]egislature in passage of this statute was to require a [obligor] to aid in the support of his child, even if that child is over the age of eighteen, so long as that child was actively participating in studies which would lead to a high school diploma. While agreeing with [obligor] that enrollment in a correspondence course for one credit hour seems at first glance not to be 'fully enrolled,' we are unable to specifically enumerate how many hours [child] would be required to take in order that she might be 'fully enrolled.' Instead, we prefer to analyze this issue on the basis of how many hours she would be required to take if seeking to graduate. [¶] In the present case, [child] presumably only needed one credit to graduate and therefore was as fully enrolled as necessary to receive a high school diploma. Had [child] needed two credits to graduate yet was only enrolled in a course for one credit which did not require full commitment of her time, we would not consider such to be full enrollment. [¶] We are not inclined to establish an arbitrary number of hours in which a student must be enlisted in order that she be deemed 'fully enrolled.' We believe that such an arbitrary finding would be unjust in the present case in that it would require [child] to choose to either forego support from her father or take a heavier academic load than is required for her graduation. In the case before us, we hold that [child] was fully enrolled in that she was taking the maximum load required for graduation from high school. *At 275 n.1:* We interpret 14.05(a) [now §154.002] similarly to 14.08(c)(2) [now §156.401] on the point of retroactive compensation; therefore, when extending child support beyond the child's eighteenth birthday under 14.05(a), the existing order may be modified only prospectively from the earlier of the date of service of process or the appearance date on the motion."

In re Frost, 815 S.W.2d 890, 892-93 (Tex.App.—Amarillo 1991, no writ). "[T]he crux of [obligor's] attack must be that [child's] enrollment in the [ACCESS program at Amarillo College] does not constitute full enrollment in an accredited secondary school within the purview of the statute. [¶] [T]he obvious intent of the [L]egislature was to require a father to aid in the support of his child, even if that child is over eighteen years of age, so long as that child was actively participating in studies which would lead to a high school diploma. ... [I]mplicit in the legislature's intent was its overriding concern that the child's participation be under supervision which would ensure that it would be a proper and effective course of study accomplished in accordance with established educational precepts. [¶] The only place [child] could obtain the educational supervision to meet his special needs was in the ACCESS program. Although his studies will not actually take place within the physical confines of Amarillo High School, his enrollment in the program was approved by the principal of the school. That approval, coupled with the commitment to review [child's] record at Amarillo College and to award a diploma upon a successful completion of the ACCESS program, constitutes a sufficient constructive compliance with the obvious legislative intent to encourage minors to complete their high school education and to do so under proper educational supervision."

FAM §154.003. MANNER OF PAYMENT

The court may order that child support be paid by:

(1) periodic payments;

(2) a lump-sum payment;

(3) an annuity purchase;

(4) the setting aside of property to be administered for the support of the child as specified in the order; or

(5) any combination of periodic payments, lump-sum payments, annuity purchases, or setting aside of property.

History of Fam §154.003: Acts 1995, 74th Leg., ch. 20, §1, eff. April 20, 1995. Source: Former Fam §14.05(a).

In re Marriage of Thurmond, 888 S.W.2d 269, 275 n.5 (Tex.App.—Amarillo 1994, writ denied). "[T]he trial court could set aside [obligor's] separate property to be administered for the support of the child."

Fanning v. Fanning, 828 S.W.2d 135, 147 (Tex. App.—Waco 1992), *rev'd in part on other grounds*, 847 S.W.2d 225 (Tex.1993). "Separate property may ... be set aside to assure compliance with an order for child support."

FAM §154.004. PLACE OF PAYMENT

(a) The court shall order the payment of child support to a local registry, the Title IV-D agency, or the state disbursement unit, as provided by Chapter 234, as added by Chapter 911, Acts of the 75th Legislature, Regular Session, 1997.

(b) In a Title IV-D case, the court or the Title IV-D agency shall order that income withheld for child support be paid:

(1) to the Title IV-D agency through a local registry, which shall forward the payment to the Title IV-D agency;

(2) to the Title IV-D agency; or

(3) to the state disbursement unit.

History of Fam §154.004: Acts 1995, 74th Leg., ch. 20, §1, eff. April 20, 1995. Amended by Acts 1999, 76th Leg., ch. 556, §9, eff Sept. 1, 1999. Source: Former Fam §14.0503.

FAM §154.005. PAYMENTS OF SUPPORT OBLIGATION BY TRUST

(a) The court may order the trustees of a spendthrift or other trust to make disbursements for the support of a child to the extent the trustees are required to make payments to a beneficiary who is required to make child support payments as provided by this chapter.

(b) If disbursement of the assets of the trust is discretionary, the court may order child support payments from the income of the trust but not from the principal.

History of Fam §154.005: Acts 1995, 74th Leg., ch. 20, §1, eff. April 20, 1995. Source: Former Fam §14.05(c).

Kolpack v. Torres, 829 S.W.2d 913, 916 (Tex. App.—Corpus Christi 1992, writ denied). "We do not find a provision in the Family Code that would place a duty on a discretionary trust to support its beneficiary-parent's child. The only provision in the Family Code relating directly to trusts is §14.05(c) [now §154.005], which we interpret allows a court to order a trustee to disburse income from a discretionary trust, to the extent that the trustee is required to make payments to a beneficiary who is required to make support payments under this section. [¶] The discretionary trust under §14.05(c) may be ordered by the trial court to make disbursements for child support if the beneficiary-parent is first obligated to the amount of child support."

Robinson v. Robinson, 694 S.W.2d 569, 572 (Tex. App.—Corpus Christi 1985, no writ). "[B]efore the trial court could have ordered pursuant to ... §14.05(c) [now §154.005] that the trustees make disbursement for child support, [obligor], the trust beneficiary/parent, must have first been ordered by the trial court to make the child support payment or payments."

In re Marriage of Long, 542 S.W.2d 712, 719 (Tex. App.—Texarkana 1976, no writ). "[T]he court must first order the trust beneficiary-parent to make the child support payment or payments, after which it may then order the trustees to make disbursement for the support of the child."

Prewitt v. Smith, 528 S.W.2d 893, 896 (Tex.App.—Austin 1975, no writ). "[T]he provisions of §14.05(c) [now §154.005] are limited to 'spendthrift or other trust' of like nature and have no application to funds of public retirement system held by state officials for the benefit of members of the System. ... Funds of a retirement system are part of a member's compensation or wages which are not subject to garnishment."

FAM §154.006. TERMINATION OF DUTY OF SUPPORT

(a) Unless otherwise agreed in writing or expressly provided in the order or as provided by Subsection (b), the child support order terminates on the marriage of the child, removal of the child's disabilities for general purposes, or death of the child or a parent ordered to pay child support.

(b) Unless a nonparent or agency has been appointed conservator of the child under Chapter 153, the order for current child support, and any provision relating to conservatorship, possession, or access terminates on the marriage or remarriage of the obligor and obligee to each other.

History of Fam §154.006: Acts 1995, 74th Leg., ch. 20, §1, eff. April 20, 1995. Amended by Acts 1999, 76th Leg., ch. 556, §9, eff. Sept. 1, 1999. Source: Former Fam §14.05(d).

De La Garza v. Salazar, 851 S.W.2d 380, 382 (Tex. App.—San Antonio 1993, no writ). "Under §14.05(d) [now §154.006], a decree may provide that the support-paying parent's death will not terminate the support obligation."

Fanning v. Fanning, 828 S.W.2d 135, 151 (Tex. App.—Waco 1992), *rev'd in part on other grounds*, 847 S.W.2d 225 (Tex.1993). Section 14.05(d) [now §154.006] "impliedly authorizes the court to make provisions for child support an obligation of the obligor's estate."

Laird v. Swor, 737 S.W.2d 601, 603 (Tex.App.—Beaumont 1987, no writ). "The fact that the minor daughter later divorced and returned to her mother would not, we think, cancel her emancipation."

Fernandez v. Fernandez, 717 S.W.2d 781, 782-83 (Tex.App.—El Paso 1986, writ dism'd). "Should [a minor's] marriage, which consisted of living with a husband for sixty days resulting in annulment of the marriage, forever free the natural father of any support obligation? [¶] [T]he annulment of the [father's] minor daughter reinstated her minority and, also, reinstated [father's] duty of support as provided in the previous court orders."

FAM §154.007. ORDER TO WITHHOLD CHILD SUPPORT FROM INCOME

(a) In a proceeding in which periodic payments of child support are ordered, modified, or enforced, the court or Title IV-D agency shall order that income be withheld from the disposable earnings of the obligor as provided by Chapter 158.

(b) If the court does not order income withholding, an order for support must contain a provision for income withholding to ensure that withholding may be effected if a delinquency occurs.

(c) A child support order must be construed to contain a withholding provision even if the provision has been omitted from the written order.

(d) If the order was rendered or last modified before January 1, 1987, the order is presumed to contain a provision for income withholding procedures to take effect in the event a delinquency occurs without further amendment to the order or future action by the court.

History of Fam §154.007: Acts 1995, 74th Leg., ch. 20, §1, eff. April 20, 1995. Amended by Acts 1997, 75th Leg., ch. 911, §10, eff. Sept. 1, 1997. Source: Former Fam §14.05(e).

FAM §154.008. PROVISION FOR MEDICAL SUPPORT

A *Section 154.008 below is effective for SAPCRs commenced on or after Sept. 1, 2001.*

The court shall order medical support for the child as provided by Subchapters B and D.

History of Fam §154.008: Acts 1995, 74th Leg., ch. 20, §1, eff. April 20, 1995. Amended by Acts 2001, 77th Leg., ch. 1023, §3, eff. Sept. 1, 2001. Source: Former Fam §14.061(a).

FAM §154.008. PROVISION FOR HEALTH INSURANCE COVERAGE

Section 154.008 below is effective for SAPCRs commenced before Sept. 1, 2001.

The court shall order health insurance coverage for the child as provided by Subchapters B and D.

FAM §154.009. RETROACTIVE CHILD SUPPORT

(a) The court may order a parent to pay retroactive child support if the parent:

(1) has not previously been ordered to pay support for the child; and

(2) was not a party to a suit in which support was ordered.

(b) In ordering retroactive child support, the court shall apply the child support guidelines provided by this chapter.

(c) Unless the Title IV-D agency is a party to an agreement concerning support or purporting to settle past, present, or future support obligations by prepayment or otherwise, an agreement between the parties does not reduce or terminate retroactive support that the agency may request.

E *Subsections (d) & (e) below are effective for SAPCRs commenced on or after Sept. 1, 2001.*

(d) Notwithstanding Subsection (a), the court may order a parent subject to a previous child support order to pay retroactive child support if:

(1) the previous child support order terminated as a result of the marriage or remarriage of the child's parents;

(2) the child's parents separated after the marriage or remarriage; and

(3) a new child support order is sought after the date of the separation.

(e) In rendering an order under Subsection (d), the court may order retroactive child support back to the date of the separation of the child's parents.

History of Fam §154.009: Acts 1995, 74th Leg., ch. 20, §1, eff. April 20, 1995. Amended by Acts 2001, 77th Leg., ch. 1023, §4, eff. Sept. 1, 2001. Source: Former Fam §14.062.

FAM §154.010. NO DISCRIMINATION BASED ON MARITAL STATUS OF PARENTS OR SEX

The amount of support ordered for the benefit of a child shall be determined without regard to:

(1) the sex of the obligor, obligee, or child; or

(2) the marital status of the parents of the child.

History of Fam §154.010: Acts 1995, 74th Leg., ch. 20, §1, eff. April 20, 1995. Source: Former Fam §§14.05(g), 14.053(i).

FAM §154.011. SUPPORT NOT CONDITIONED ON POSSESSION OR ACCESS

A court may not render an order that conditions the payment of child support on whether a managing conservator allows a possessory conservator to have possession of or access to a child.

History of Fam §154.011: Acts 1995, 74th Leg., ch. 751, §40, eff. Sept. 1, 1995.

Seidel v. Seidel, 10 S.W.3d 365, 369 (Tex.App.—Dallas 1999, no pet.). "An order which makes one parent's visitation rights with the child contingent upon their timely payment of child support is 'coercive' and 'operatively null and void.' [¶] [S]ection 154.011 prohibits the trial court from rendering an order which provides for the release of the domicile restrictions imposed by the divorce decree on [wife] and the children in the event [obligor] is deficient in the payment of the $38,000 child support judgment."

FAM §154.012. SUPPORT PAID IN EXCESS OF SUPPORT ORDER

A *Section 154.012 below is effective for modification or enforcement proceedings commenced on or after Sept. 1, 2001.*

(a) If an obligor is not in arrears and the obligor's child support obligation has terminated, the obligee shall return to the obligor a child support payment made by the obligor that exceeds the amount of support ordered, regardless of whether the payment was made before, on, or after the date the child support obligation terminated.

(b) An obligor may file a suit to recover a child support payment under Subsection (a). If the court finds that the obligee failed to return a child support payment under Subsection (a), the court shall order the obligee to pay to the obligor attorney's fees and all court costs in addition to the amount of support paid after the date the child support order terminated. For good cause shown, the court may waive the requirement that the obligee pay attorney's fees and costs if the court states the reasons supporting that finding.

History of Fam §154.012: Acts 1999, 76th Leg., ch. 363, §1, eff. Sept. 1, 1999. Amended by Acts 2001, 77th Leg., ch. 1023, §5, eff. Sept. 1, 2001.

FAM §154.012. SUPPORT PAID AFTER TERMINATION OF SUPPORT ORDER

Section 154.012 below is effective for modification or enforcement proceedings commenced before Sept. 1, 2001.

(a) If the obligor is not in arrears, an obligee shall return to an obligor a child support payment made by the obligor after the date the child support order has terminated.

(b) An obligor may file a suit to recover a child support payment under Subsection (a). If the court finds that the obligee failed to return a child support payment under Subsection (a), the court shall order the obligee to pay to the obligor attorney's fees and all court costs in addition to the amount of support paid after the date the child support order terminated. For good cause shown, the court may waive the requirement that the obligee pay attorney's fees and costs if the court states the reasons supporting that finding.

FAM §154.013[A*]. CONTINUATION OF DUTY TO PAY SUPPORT AFTER DEATH OF OBLIGEE

E *In 2001, the Legislature enacted two sections 154.013. Section 154.013 below was enacted by Acts 2001, 77th Leg., ch. 1023, §6, effective Sept. 1, 2001. The [A*] has been added by the editor to distinguish this section 154.013 from the other, which is marked with [B*]. In 2003, the Legislature is expected to correct the duplicate numbering. Section 154.013[A*] below is effective for modification or enforcement proceedings commenced on or after Sept. 1, 2001.*

(a) A child support obligation does not terminate on the death of the obligee but continues as an obligation to the child named in the support order, as required by this section.

(b) Notwithstanding any provision of the Probate Code, a child support payment held by the Title IV-D agency, a local registry, or the state disbursement unit or any uncashed check or warrant representing a child support payment made before, on, or after the date of death of the obligee shall be paid proportionately for the benefit of each surviving child named in the support order and not to the estate of the obligee. The payment is free of any creditor's claim against the deceased obligee's estate and may be disbursed as provided by Subsection (c).

(c) On the death of the obligee, current child support owed by the obligor for the benefit of the child or any amount described by Subsection (b) shall be paid to:

(1) a person, other than a parent, who is appointed as managing conservator of the child;

(2) a person, including the obligor, who has assumed actual care, control, and possession of the child, if a managing conservator or guardian of the child has not been appointed;

(3) the county clerk, as provided by Section 887, Texas Probate Code, in the name of and for the account of the child for whom the support is owed;

(4) a guardian of the child appointed under Chapter XIII, Texas Probate Code, as provided by that code; or

(5) the surviving child, if the child is an adult or has otherwise had the disabilities of minority removed.

(d) On presentation of the obligee's death certificate, the court shall render an order directing payment of child support paid but not disbursed to be made as provided by Subsection (c). A copy of the order shall be provided to:

(1) the obligor;

(2) as appropriate:

(A) the person having actual care, control, and possession of the child;

(B) the county clerk; or

(C) the managing conservator or guardian of the child, if one has been appointed;

(3) the local registry or state disbursement unit and, if appropriate, the Title IV-D agency; and

(4) the child named in the support order, if the child is an adult or has otherwise had the disabilities of minority removed.

(e) The order under Subsection (d) must contain:

(1) a statement that the obligee is deceased and that child support amounts otherwise payable to the obligee shall be paid for the benefit of a surviving child named in the support order as provided by Subsection (c);

(2) the name and age of each child named in the support order; and

(3) the name and mailing address of, as appropriate:

(A) the person having actual care, control, and possession of the child;

(B) the county clerk; or

(C) the managing conservator or guardian of the child, if one has been appointed.

(f) On receipt of the order required under this section, the local registry, state disbursement unit, or Title IV-D agency shall disburse payments as required by the order.

History of Fam §154.013[A*]: Enacted by Acts 2001, 77th Leg., ch. 1023, §6, eff. Sept. 1, 2001.

FAM §154.013[B*]. PAYMENTS IN EXCESS OF COURT-ORDERED AMOUNT

☠ E *In 2001, the Legislature enacted two sections 154.013. Section 154.013 below was enacted by Acts 2001, 77th Leg., ch. 1491, §2(a), effective Sept. 1, 2001. The [B*] has been added by the editor to distinguish this section 154.013 from the other, which is marked with [A*]. In 2003, the Legislature is expected to correct the duplicate numbering. Section 154.013[B*] below is effective for child support payments made on or after Sept. 1, 2001.*

(a) If a child support agency or local child support registry receives from an obligor who is not in arrears a child support payment in an amount that exceeds the court-ordered amount, the agency or registry, to the extent possible, shall give effect to any expressed intent of the obligor for the application of the amount that exceeds the court-ordered amount.

(b) If the obligor does not express an intent for the application of the amount paid in excess of the court-ordered amount, the agency or registry shall:

(1) credit the excess amount to the obligor's future child support obligation; and

(2) promptly disburse the excess amount to the obligee.

(c) This section does not apply to an obligee who is a recipient of public assistance under Chapter 31, Human Resources Code.

History of Fam §154.013[B*]: Enacted by Acts 2001, 77th Leg., ch. 1491, §2(a), eff. Sept. 1, 2001.

Sections 154.014-154.060 reserved for expansion

SUBCHAPTER B. COMPUTING NET RESOURCES AVAILABLE FOR PAYMENT OF CHILD SUPPORT

FAM §154.061. COMPUTING NET MONTHLY INCOME

(a) Whenever feasible, gross income should first be computed on an annual basis and then should be recalculated to determine average monthly gross income.

(b) The Title IV-D agency shall annually promulgate tax charts to compute net monthly income, subtracting from gross income social security taxes and federal income tax withholding for a single person claiming one personal exemption and the standard deduction.

History of Fam §154.061: Acts 1995, 74th Leg., ch. 20, §1, eff. April 20, 1995. Source: Former Fam §14.053(a), (h).

Wilemon v. Wilemon, 930 S.W.2d 290, 293 (Tex. App.—Waco 1996, no writ). "In ordering child support payments, the trial court is to base the amount on the net resources of the parties and other applicable factors listed in the Family Code."

Wright v. Wright, 867 S.W.2d 807, 814 (Tex.App.—El Paso 1993, writ denied). Obligor argues that §14.053(h), now §154.061, is "inconsistent with §14.053(b) [now §154.062] in that it does not allow a deduction of health insurance costs from gross income in calculating net income. A careful reading of that statute, however, demonstrates that the purpose of [§14.053(h)] is to assist the courts in calculating the amount of deductions from gross income for taxes and social security to determine the obligor's net income as a single person claiming one personal exemption. Since many obligors may elect not to file their tax returns as single persons with one exemption, these charts serve as an aid in making the calculations for the courts. The net income calculation in [§14.053(h)] is not the same as the net resources calculation in [§14.053(b)]. Moreover, the 'Instructions for Use' included in the [§14.053(h)] tax charts clearly indicate that additional steps are required, after calculating net income, to determine net resources."

OFFICE OF THE ATTORNEY GENERAL 2002 TAX CHARTS

Pursuant to §154.061(b) of the Texas Family Code, the Attorney General of Texas, as the Title IV-D agency, has promulgated the following tax charts for 2002 to assist courts in establishing the amount of a child support order. These tax charts are applicable to employed and self-employed persons in computing net monthly income.

INSTRUCTIONS FOR USE

To use these tables, first compute the obligor's annual gross income. Then recompute to determine the obligor's average monthly gross income. These tables provide a method for calculating "monthly net income" for child support purposes, subtracting from monthly gross income the social security taxes and the federal income tax withholding for a single person claiming one personal exemption and the standard deduction.

Thereafter, in many cases the guidelines call for a number of additional steps to complete the necessary calculations. For example, §§154.061 - 154.068 provide for appropriate additions to "income" as that term is defined for federal income tax purposes, and for certain subtractions from monthly net income, in order to arrive at the net resources of the obligor available for child support purposes. Computation of the obligee's net resources should follow similar steps.

EMPLOYED PERSONS 2002 TAX CHART

Monthly Gross Wages	Social Security Taxes		Federal Income Taxes**	Net Monthly Income
	Old-Age, Survivors & Disability Insurance Taxes (6.2%)*	Hospital (Medicare) Insurance Taxes (1.45%)*		
$100.00	$6.20	$1.45	$0.00	$92.35
$200.00	$12.40	$2.90	$0.00	$184.70
$300.00	$18.60	$4.35	$0.00	$277.05
$400.00	$24.80	$5.80	$0.00	$369.40
$500.00	$31.00	$7.25	$0.00	$461.75
$600.00	$37.20	$8.70	$0.00	$554.10
$700.00	$43.40	$10.15	$5.83	$640.62
$800.00	$49.60	$11.60	$15.83	$722.97
$900.00	$55.80	$13.05	$25.83	$805.32
$1,000.00	$62.00	$14.50	$35.83	$887.67
$1,100.00	$68.20	$15.95	$45.83	$970.02
$1,200.00	$74.40	$17.40	$58.75	$1,049.45
$1,300.00	$80.60	$18.85	$73.75	$1,126.80
$1,400.00	$86.80	$20.30	$88.75	$1,204.15
$1,500.00	$93.00	$21.75	$103.75	$1,281.50
$1,600.00	$99.20	$23.20	$118.75	$1,358.85
$1,700.00	$105.40	$24.65	$133.75	$1,436.20
$1,800.00	$111.60	$26.10	$148.75	$1,513.55
$1,900.00	$117.80	$27.55	$163.75	$1,590.90
$2,000.00	$124.00	$29.00	$178.75	$1,668.25
$2,100.00	$130.20	$30.45	$193.75	$1,745.60
$2,200.00	$136.40	$31.90	$208.75	$1,822.95
$2,300.00	$142.60	$33.35	$223.75	$1,900.30

EMPLOYED PERSONS 2002 TAX CHART				
Monthly Gross Wages	Social Security Taxes		Federal Income Taxes**	Net Monthly Income
	Old-Age, Survivors & Disability Insurance Taxes (6.2%)*	Hospital (Medicare) Insurance Taxes (1.45%)*		
$2,400.00	$148.80	$34.80	$238.75	$1,977.65
$2,500.00	$155.00	$36.25	$253.75	$2,055.00
$2,600.00	$161.20	$37.70	$268.75	$2,132.35
$2,700.00	$167.40	$39.15	$283.75	$2,209.70
$2,800.00	$173.60	$40.60	$298.75	$2,287.05
$2,900.00	$179.80	$42.05	$313.75	$2,364.40
$3,000.00	$186.00	$43.50	$332.25	$2,438.25
$3,100.00	$192.20	$44.95	$359.25	$2,503.60
$3,200.00	$198.40	$46.40	$386.25	$2,568.95
$3,300.00	$204.60	$47.85	$413.25	$2,634.30
$3,400.00	$210.80	$49.30	$440.25	$2,699.65
$3,500.00	$217.00	$50.75	$467.25	$2,765.00
$3,600.00	$223.20	$52.20	$494.25	$2,830.35
$3,700.00	$229.40	$53.65	$521.25	$2,895.70
$3,800.00	$235.60	$55.10	$548.25	$2,961.05
$3,900.00	$241.80	$56.55	$575.25	$3,026.40
$4,000.00	$248.00	$58.00	$602.25	$3,091.75
$4,250.00	$263.50	$61.63	$669.75	$3,255.12
$4,500.00	$279.00	$65.25	$737.25	$3,418.50
$4,750.00	$294.50	$68.88	$804.75	$3,581.87
$5,000.00	$310.00	$72.50	$872.25	$3,745.25
$5,250.00	$325.50	$76.13	$939.75	$3,908.62
$5,500.00	$341.00	$79.75	$1,007.25	$4,072.00
$5,750.00	$356.50	$83.38	$1,074.75	$4,235.37
$6,000.00	$372.00	$87.00	$1,142.25	$4,398.75
$6,250.00	$387.50	$90.63	$1,209.75	$4,562.12
$6,500.00	$403.00	$94.25	$1,283.75	$4,719.00
$6,750.00	$418.50	$97.88	$1,358.75	$4,874.87
$7,000.00	$434.00	$101.50	$1,433.75	$5,030.75
$7,500.00	$438.65***	$108.75	$1,583.75	$5,368.85
$8,000.00	$438.65	$116.00	$1,733.75	$5,711.60
$8,500.00	$438.65	$123.25	$1,883.75	$6,054.35
$9,000.00	$438.65	$130.50	$2,033.75	$6,397.10
$9,500.00	$438.65	$137.75	$2,183.75	$6,739.85
$10,000.00	$438.65	$145.00	$2,333.75	$7,082.60
$10,500.00	$438.65	$152.25	$2,483.75	$7,425.35
$11,000.00	$438.65	$159.50	$2,633.75	$7,768.10

EMPLOYED PERSONS 2002 TAX CHART

Monthly Gross Wages	Social Security Taxes		Federal Income Taxes**	Net Monthly Income
	Old-Age, Survivors & Disability Insurance Taxes (6.2%)*	Hospital (Medicare) Insurance Taxes (1.45%)*		
$11,500.00	$438.65	$166.75	$2,785.25	$8,109.35
$12,000.00	$438.65	$174.00	$2,938.25	$8,449.10
$12,500.00	$438.65	$181.25	$3,098.63	$8,781.47
$13,000.00	$438.65	$188.50	$3,277.13	$9,095.72
$13,500.00	$438.65	$195.75	$3,455.63	$9,409.97
$14,000.00	$438.65	$203.00	$3,635.88	$9,722.47
$14,500.00	$438.65	$210.25	$3,814.38	$10,036.72
$15,000.00	$438.65	$217.50	$3,994.63	$10,349.22

FOOTNOTES TO EMPLOYED PERSONS 2002 TAX CHART:

* An employed person not subject to the Old-age, Survivors and Disability Insurance/Hospital (Medicare) Insurance taxes will be allowed the reductions reflected in these columns, unless it is shown that such person has no similar contributory plan such as teacher retirement, federal railroad retirement, federal civil service retirement, etc.

** These amounts represent one-twelfth (1/12th) of the annual Federal income tax calculated for a single taxpayer claiming one personal exemption ($3,000.00, subject to reduction in certain cases, as described in the next paragraph of this footnote) and taking the standard deduction ($4,700.00).

For a single taxpayer with an adjusted gross income in excess of $137,300.00, the deduction for the personal exemption is reduced by two percent (2%) for each $2,500.00 or fraction thereof by which adjusted gross income exceeds $137,300.00. The reduction is completed (*i.e.*, the deduction for the personal exemption is eliminated) for adjusted gross income in excess of $259,800.00. In no case is the deduction for the personal exemption reduced by more than 100%. For example, monthly gross wages of $12,000.00 times 12 months equals $144,000.00. The excess over $137,300.00 is $6,700.00. $6,700.00 divided by $2,500.00 equals 2.68. The 2.68 amount is rounded up to 3. The reduction percentage is 6% (3 x 2% = 6%). The $3,000.00 deduction for one personal exemption is reduced by $180.00 ($3,000.00 x 6% = $180.00) to $2,820.00 ($3,000.00 - $180.00 = $2,820.00).

*** For annual gross wages above $84,900.00, this amount represents a monthly average of the Old-Age, Survivors and Disability Insurance tax based on the 2002 maximum Old-Age, Survivors and Disability Insurance tax of $5,263.80 per person (6.2% of the first $84,900.00 of annual gross wages equals $5,263.80). One-twelfth (1/12th) of $5,263.80 equals $438.65.

REFERENCES RELATING TO EMPLOYED PERSONS 2002 TAX CHART:

1 **Old-Age, Survivors and Disability Insurance Tax**
- (a) **Contribution Base**
  - (1) Social Security Administration's notice dated October 19, 2001, and appearing in 66 Fed. Reg. 54,047 (October 25, 2001)
  - (2) Section 3121(a) of the Internal Revenue Code of 1986, as amended (26 U.S.C. §3121(a))
  - (3) Section 230 of the Social Security Act, as amended (42 U.S.C. §430)
- (b) **Tax Rate**
  - (1) Section 3101(a) of the Internal Revenue Code of 1986, as amended (26 U.S.C. §3101(a))

2 **Hospital (Medicare) Insurance Tax**
- (a) **Contribution Base**
  - (1) Section 3121(a) of the Internal Revenue Code of 1986, as amended (26 U.S.C. §3121(a))
  - (2) Omnibus Budget Reconciliation Act of 1993, Pub. L. No. 103-66, §13207, 107 Stat. 312, 467-69 (1993)
- (b) **Tax Rate**
  - (1) Section 3101(b) of the Internal Revenue Code of 1986, as amended (26 U.S.C. §3101(b))

3 **Federal Income Tax**
- (a) **Inflation Adjusted Tax Rate Table for 2002 for Single Taxpayers**
  - (1) Revenue Procedure 2001-59 Section 3.01, Table 3, which appears in Internal Revenue Bulletin 2001-52, dated December 26, 2001
  - (2) Section 1(c) and (f) of the Internal Revenue Code of 1986, as amended (26 U.S.C. §1(c) and (f))
- (b) **Standard Deduction**
  - (1) Revenue Procedure 2001-59, Section 3.07(1), which appears in Internal Revenue Bulletin 2001-52, dated December 26, 2001
  - (2) Section 63(c) of the Internal Revenue Code of 1986, as amended (26 U.S.C. §63(c))
- (c) **Personal Exemption**
  - (1) Revenue Procedure 2001-59, Section 3.11, which appears in Internal Revenue Bulletin 2001-52, dated December 26, 2001
  - (2) Section 151(d) of the Internal Revenue Code of 1986, as amended (26 U.S.C. §151(d))

SELF-EMPLOYED PERSONS 2002 TAX CHART				
Monthly Net Earnings From Self-Employment*	Social Security Taxes		Federal Income Taxes***	Net Monthly Income
	Old-Age, Survivors & Disability Insurance Taxes (12.4%)**	Hospital (Medicare) Insurance Taxes (2.9%)**		
$100.00	$11.45	$2.68	$0.00	$85.87
$200.00	$22.90	$5.36	$0.00	$171.74
$300.00	$34.35	$8.03	$0.00	$257.62
$400.00	$45.81	$10.71	$0.00	$343.48
$500.00	$57.26	$13.39	$0.00	$429.35
$600.00	$68.71	$16.07	$0.00	$515.22
$700.00	$80.16	$18.75	$0.89	$600.20
$800.00	$91.61	$21.43	$10.18	$676.78
$900.00	$103.06	$24.10	$19.48	$753.36
$1,000.00	$114.51	$26.78	$28.77	$829.94
$1,100.00	$125.97	$29.46	$38.06	$906.51
$1,200.00	$137.42	$32.14	$47.36	$983.08
$1,300.00	$148.87	$34.82	$59.97	$1,056.34
$1,400.00	$160.32	$37.49	$73.91	$1,128.28
$1,500.00	$171.77	$40.17	$87.85	$1,200.21
$1,600.00	$183.22	$42.85	$101.79	$1,272.14
$1,700.00	$194.67	$45.53	$115.73	$1,344.07
$1,800.00	$206.13	$48.21	$129.68	$1,415.98
$1,900.00	$217.58	$50.88	$143.62	$1,487.92
$2,000.00	$229.03	$53.56	$157.56	$1,559.85
$2,100.00	$240.48	$56.24	$171.50	$1,631.78
$2,200.00	$251.93	$58.92	$185.44	$1,703.71
$2,300.00	$263.38	$61.60	$199.38	$1,775.64
$2,400.00	$274.83	$64.28	$213.32	$1,847.57
$2,500.00	$286.29	$66.95	$227.26	$1,919.50
$2,600.00	$297.74	$69.63	$241.20	$1,991.43
$2,700.00	$309.19	$72.31	$255.14	$2,063.36
$2,800.00	$320.64	$74.99	$269.08	$2,135.29
$2,900.00	$332.09	$77.67	$283.02	$2,207.22
$3,000.00	$343.54	$80.34	$296.96	$2,279.16
$3,100.00	$354.99	$83.02	$310.90	$2,351.09
$3,200.00	$366.44	$85.70	$325.21	$2,422.65
$3,300.00	$377.90	$88.38	$350.30	$2,483.42
$3,400.00	$389.35	$91.06	$375.40	$2,544.19
$3,500.00	$400.80	$93.74	$400.49	$2,604.97
$3,600.00	$412.25	$96.41	$425.58	$2,665.76

SELF-EMPLOYED PERSONS 2002 TAX CHART				
Monthly Net Earnings From Self-Employment*	Social Security Taxes		Federal Income Taxes***	Net Monthly Income
	Old-Age, Survivors & Disability Insurance Taxes (12.4%)**	Hospital (Medicare) Insurance Taxes (2.9%)**		
$3,700.00	$423.70	$99.09	$450.67	$2,726.54
$3,800.00	$435.15	$101.77	$475.77	$2,787.31
$3,900.00	$446.60	$104.45	$500.86	$2,848.09
$4,000.00	$458.06	$107.13	$525.95	$2,908.86
$4,250.00	$486.68	$113.82	$588.68	$3,060.82
$4,500.00	$515.31	$120.52	$651.41	$3,212.76
$4,750.00	$543.94	$127.21	$714.14	$3,364.71
$5,000.00	$572.57	$133.91	$776.88	$3,516.64
$5,250.00	$601.20	$140.60	$839.61	$3,668.59
$5,500.00	$629.83	$147.30	$902.34	$3,820.53
$5,750.00	$658.46	$153.99	$965.07	$3,972.48
$6,000.00	$687.08	$160.69	$1,027.80	$4,124.43
$6,250.00	$715.71	$167.38	$1,090.53	$4,276.38
$6,500.00	$744.34	$174.08	$1,153.26	$4,428.32
$6,750.00	$772.97	$180.78	$1,215.99	$4,580.26
$7,000.00	$801.60	$187.47	$1,285.39	$4,725.54
$7,500.00	$858.86	$200.86	$1,424.79	$5,015.49
$8,000.00	$877.30****	$214.25	$1,570.02	$5,338.43
$8,500.00	$877.30	$227.64	$1,718.01	$5,677.05
$9,000.00	$877.30	$241.03	$1,866.00	$6,015.67
$9,500.00	$877.30	$254.42	$2,013.99	$6,354.29
$10,000.00	$877.30	$267.82	$2,161.98	$6,692.90
$10,500.00	$877.30	$281.21	$2,309.97	$7,031.52
$11,000.00	$877.30	$294.60	$2,457.97	$7,370.13
$11,500.00	$877.30	$307.99	$2,605.96	$7,708.75
$12,000.00	$877.30	$321.38	$2,753.95	$8,047.37
$12,500.00	$877.30	$334.77	$2,906.44	$8,381.49
$13,000.00	$877.30	$348.16	$3,057.43	$8,717.11
$13,500.00	$877.30	$361.55	$3,233.58	$9,027.57
$14,000.00	$877.30	$374.94	$3,411.48	$9,336.28
$14,500.00	$877.30	$388.33	$3,587.64	$9,646.73
$15,000.00	$877.30	$401.72	$3,765.55	$9,955.43

FOOTNOTES TO SELF-EMPLOYED PERSONS 2001 TAX CHART:

* Determined without regard to Section 1402(a)(12) of the Internal Revenue Code of 1986, as amended (26 U.S.C.) (the "Code").

** In calculating each of the Old-Age, Survivors and Disability Insurance tax and the Hospital (Medicare) Insurance tax, net earnings from self-employment are reduced by the deduction under Section 1402(a)(12) of the Code. The deduction under Section 1402(a)(12) of the Code is equal to net earnings from self-employment (determined without regard to Section 1402(a)(12) of the Code) multiplied by one-half (1/2) of the sum of the Old-Age, Survivors and Disability

Insurance tax rate (12.4%) and the Hospital (Medicare) Insurance tax rate (2.9%). The sum of these rates is 15.3% (12.4% + 2.9% = 15.3%). One-half (1/2) of the combined rate is 7.65% (15.3% x 1/2 = 7.65%). The deduction can be computed by multiplying the net earnings from self-employment (determined without regard to Section 1402(a)(12) of the Code) by 92.35%. This gives the same deduction as multiplying the net earnings from self-employment (determined without regard to Section 1402(a)(12) of the Code) by 7.65% and then subtracting the result.

For example, the Social Security taxes imposed on monthly net earnings from self-employment (determined without regard to Section 1402(a)(12) of the Code) of $2,500.00 are calculated as follows:

(i) Old-Age, Survivors and Disability Insurance Taxes:

$2,500.00 x 92.35% x 12.4% = $286.29

(ii) Hospital (Medicare) Insurance Taxes:

$2,500.00 x 92.35% x 2.9% = $66.95

*** These amounts represent one-twelfth (1/12th) of the annual Federal income tax calculated for a single taxpayer claiming one personal exemption ($3,000.00, subject to reduction in certain cases, as described below in this footnote) and taking the standard deduction ($4,700.00).

In calculating the annual Federal income tax, gross income is reduced by the deduction under Section 164(f) of the Code. The deduction under Section 164(f) of the Code is equal to one-half (1/2) of the self-employment taxes imposed by Section 1401 of the Code for the taxable year. For example, monthly net earnings from self-employment of $12,500.00 times 12 months equals $150,000.00. The Old-Age, Survivors and Disability Insurance taxes imposed by Section 1401 of the Code for the taxable year equal $10,527.60 ($84,900.00 x 12.4% = $10,527.60). The Hospital (Medicare) Insurance taxes imposed by Section 1401 of the Code for the taxable year equal $4,017.23 ($150,000.00 x .9235 x 2.9% = $4,017.23). The sum of the taxes imposed by Section 1401 of the Code for the taxable year equals $14,544.83 ($10,527.60 + $4,017.23 = $14,544.83). The deduction under Section 164(f) of the Code is equal to one-half (1/2) of $14,544.83 or $7,272.42.

For a single taxpayer with an adjusted gross income in excess of $137,300.00, the deduction for the personal exemption is reduced by two percent (2%) for each $2,500.00 or fraction thereof by which adjusted gross income exceeds $137,300.00. The reduction is completed (*i.e.*, the deduction for the personal exemption is eliminated) for adjusted gross income in excess of $259,800.00. In no case is the deduction for the personal exemption reduced by more than 100%. For example, monthly net earnings from self-employment of $12,500.00 times 12 months equals $150,000.00. The $150,000.00 amount is reduced by $7,272.42 (*i.e.*, the deduction under Section 164(f) of the Code—see the immediately preceding paragraph of this footnote for the computation) to arrive at adjusted gross income of $142,727.58. The excess over $137,300.00 is $5,427.58. $5,427.58 divided by $2,500.00 equals 2.17. The 2.17 amount is rounded up to 3. The reduction percentage is 6% (3 x 2% = 6%). The $3,000.00 deduction for one personal exemption is reduced by $180.00 ($3,000.00 x 6% = $180.00) to $2,820.00 ($3,000.00 - $180.0 = $2,820.00).

**** For annual net earnings from self-employment (determined with regard to Section 1402(a)(12) of the Code) above $84,900.00, this amount represents a monthly average of the Old-Age, Survivors and Disability Insurance tax based on the 2002 maximum Old-Age, Survivors and Disability Insurance tax of $10,527.60 per person (12.4% of the first $84,900.00 of net earnings from self-employment (determined with regard to Section 1402(a)(12) of the Code) equals $10,527.60). One-twelfth (1/12th) of $10,527.60 equals $877.30.

REFERENCES RELATING TO SELF-EMPLOYED PERSONS 2002 TAX CHART:

1 **Old-Age, Survivors and Disability Insurance Tax**

(a) **Contribution Base**

(1) Social Security Administration's notice dated October 19, 2001, and appearing in 66 Fed. Reg. 54,047 (October 25, 2001)

(2) Section 1402(b) of the Internal Revenue Code of 1986, as amended (26 U.S.C. §1402(b))

(3) Section 230 of the Social Security Act, as amended (42 U.S.C. §430)

(b) **Tax Rate**

(1) Section 1401(a) of the Internal Revenue Code of 1986, as amended (26 U.S.C. §1401(a))

(c) **Deduction Under Section 1402(a)(12)**

(1) Section 1402(a)(12) of the Internal Revenue Code of 1986, as amended (26 U.S.C. §1402(a)(12))

2. **Hospital (Medicare) Insurance Tax**

(a) **Contribution Base**

(1) Section 1402(b) of the Internal Revenue Code of 1986, as amended (26 U.S.C. §1402(b))

(2) Omnibus Budget Reconciliation Act of 1993, Pub. L. No. 103-66, §13207, 107 Stat. 312, 467-69 (1993)

(b) **Tax Rate**

(1) Section 1401(b) of the Internal Revenue Code of 1986, as amended (26 U.S.C. §1401(b))

(c) **Deduction Under Section 1402(a)(12)**

(1) Section 1402(a)(12) of the Internal Revenue Code of 1986, as amended (26 U.S.C. §1402(a)(12))

3. **Federal Income Tax**

(a) **Inflation Adjusted Tax Rate Table for 2002 for Single Taxpayers**

(1) Revenue Procedure 2001-59, Section 3.01, Table 3, which appears in Internal Revenue Bulletin 2001-52, dated December 26, 2001

(2) Section 1(c) and (f) of the Internal Revenue Code of 1986, as amended (26 U.S.C. §1(c) and (f))

(b) **Standard Deduction**

(1) Revenue Procedure 2001-59, Section 3.07(1), which appears in Internal Revenue Bulletin 2001-52, dated December 26, 2001

(2) Section 63(c) of the Internal Revenue Code of 1986, as amended (26 U.S.C. §63(c))

(c) **Personal Exemption**

(1) Revenue Procedure 2001-59, Section 3.11, which appears in Internal Revenue Bulletin 2001-52, dated December 26, 2001

(2) Section 151(d) of the Internal Revenue Code of 1986, as amended (26 U.S.C. §151(d))

(d) **Deduction Under Section 164(f)**

(1) Section 164(f) of the Internal Revenue Code of 1986, as amended (26 U.S.C. §164(f))

FAM §154.062. NET RESOURCES

(a) The court shall calculate net resources for the purpose of determining child support liability as provided by this section.

(b) Resources include:

(1) 100 percent of all wage and salary income and other compensation for personal services (including commissions, overtime pay, tips, and bonuses);

(2) interest, dividends, and royalty income;

(3) self-employment income;

(4) net rental income (defined as rent after deducting operating expenses and mortgage payments, but not including noncash items such as depreciation); and

(5) all other income actually being received, including severance pay, retirement benefits, pensions, trust income, annuities, capital gains, social security benefits, unemployment benefits, disability and workers' compensation benefits, interest income from notes regardless of the source, gifts and prizes, spousal maintenance, and alimony.

(c) Resources do not include:

(1) return of principal or capital;

(2) accounts receivable; or

(3) benefits paid in accordance with aid for families with dependent children.

(d) The court shall deduct the following items from resources to determine the net resources available for child support:

(1) social security taxes;

(2) federal income tax based on the tax rate for a single person claiming one personal exemption and the standard deduction;

(3) state income tax;

(4) union dues; and

(5) expenses for health insurance coverage for the obligor's child.

History of Fam §154.062: Acts 1995, 74th Leg., ch. 20, §1, eff. April 20, 1995. Amended by Acts 1995, 74th Leg., ch. 751, §41, eff. Sept. 1, 1995. Source: Former Fam §14.053(b).

Norris v. Norris, 56 S.W.3d 333, 340 (Tex.App.—El Paso 2001, no pet.). "[W]hile it would be preferable for a trial court to find specific sums for net resources in the normal wage earner's or salaried person's case, where a person's income and net resources vary a great deal from month to month, it may only be possible to state a range of net resources. This is not prohibited provided the range is supported by the evidence."

In re S.B.C., 952 S.W.2d 15, 18 (Tex.App.—San Antonio 1997, no writ). "[T]he duty to pay support is not limited to an obligor's ability to pay from current earnings, but also extends to his or her financial ability to pay from any and all sources that might be available. *At 19:* Because courts may look to assets other than income when determining whether an obligor can reasonably afford the ordered child support, and a court may look to earning potential upon a finding of intentional unemployment, it was reasonable for the trial court ... to conclude that in light of his education, work experience, and ability to either sell or use his house as an income-producing asset, [obligor] could reasonably afford to pay the existing support order."

Farish v. Farish, 921 S.W.2d 538, 543 (Tex.App.—Beaumont 1996, no writ). Section 14.053(b) [now §154.062(c)(1)] "excludes 'return of principal or capital' from net resources. ... Rather than referring to proceeds from the sale of assets or to capital gains on the sale of those assets, the phrase refers to the return of principal or capital on a note, which is not a net resource for child support purposes. [¶] The Texas Family Code does not exclude capital gains from the definition of 'net resources.' Indeed, capital gains are specifically included in ... 14.053(b). Moreover, the Code provides in §14.053(e) [now §154.123] that the court may consider any additional factors that increase or decrease the ability of the obligor to make child support payments."

In re Striegler, 915 S.W.2d 629, 636 (Tex.App.—Amarillo 1996, writ denied). Obligor "contends the trial court erred in failing to reduce his net resources by the amount of his long-term mortgage payments on income-producing real property. *At 638:* While §14.053(b) [now §154.062] does not expressly allow reduction of an obligor's net resources by long-term mortgage payments on income producing real property, ... we do note that [§14.053(c), now §154.065] allows an obligor to deduct ordinary and necessary expenses from self-employment income. However, we do not need to consider its applicability to [obligor's] capital investments. Considering [obligor's] overall financial resources, his earning potential, the latitude given the trial judge by the 'additional factors' provision of the statute, and the standard by which we review the trial court's decision, we find that court did not abuse its discretion in making that decision."

FAM §154.063. PARTY TO FURNISH INFORMATION

The court shall require a party to:

(1) furnish information sufficient to accurately identify that party's net resources and ability to pay child support; and

(2) produce copies of income tax returns for the past two years, a financial statement, and current pay stubs.

History of Fam §154.063: Acts 1995, 74th Leg., ch. 20, §1, eff. April 20, 1995. Source: Former Fam §14.053(g).

Powell v. Swanson, 893 S.W.2d 161, 164-65 (Tex. App.—Houston [1st Dist.] 1995, no writ). Obligee "timely and properly requested [obligor's] tax returns for 1991 and 1992. Before trial, [obligor] produced only his 1991 return. [¶] In this case, production of tax returns is of particular importance. [Obligor] is self-employed; he owns a day care center and various rental properties. Without the tax returns, both [obligee] and the court are unable to properly evaluate [obligor's] net resources. The trial court erred in failing to compel production of [obligor's] 1992 income tax return."

Stocker v. Magera, 807 S.W.2d 753, 754 (Tex. App.—Texarkana 1990, writ denied). Section 14.053(g), now §154.063, "provides that the court *shall* require the parties to furnish sufficient information to enable it to accurately identify their net resources and abilities to provide child support. Inasmuch as this provision is mandatory, the trial court erred in failing to require that such information be furnished."

FAM §154.064. MEDICAL SUPPORT FOR CHILD PRESUMPTIVELY PROVIDED BY OBLIGOR

Ⓐ *Section 154.064 below is effective for SAPCRs commenced on or after Sept. 1, 2001.*

The guidelines for support of a child are based on the assumption that the court will order the obligor to provide medical support for the child in addition to the amount of child support calculated in accordance with those guidelines.

History of Fam §154.064: Acts 1995, 74th Leg., ch. 20, §1, eff. April 20, 1995. Amended by Acts 2001, 77th Leg., ch. 1023, §7, eff. Sept. 1, 2001. Source: Former Fam §14.053(d).

Kish v. Kole, 874 S.W.2d 835, 837 (Tex.App.—Beaumont 1994, no writ). Obligor argues that the judgment should have allowed "an offset against the child support for the health insurance coverage paid by [obligor] for the minor child. We note that [obligor] pays approximately $60.00 per month for medical insurance for the minor child. The court is required to order that health insurance be provided for the child, in this case by the [obligor]. This is in addition to the child support ordered by the court."

De La Garza v. Salazar, 851 S.W.2d 380, 382 (Tex. App.—San Antonio 1993, no writ). Obligor "complains that the court improperly ordered him to provide health insurance in the future without regard to his future employment or the availability of insurance. We reject this argument. The [F]amily [C]ode contemplates that the court will order health insurance for the child. Trial courts need not anticipate and provide for all possible changes in the parties' circumstances; they must establish the rights and duties of the parties based on the evidence at trial. The [F]amily [C]ode recognizes that a party's circumstances may change. When that happens, he must bring a motion to modify…."

Stocker v. Magera, 807 S.W.2d 753, 755 (Tex. App.—Texarkana 1990, writ denied). "Another question presented on this appeal concerns [mother's] claim that the trial court erred in setting an amount of child support 'plus medical insurance.' Under … §14.053(d) [now §154.064], the guidelines assume that the court will order the obligor to provide health insurance coverage in addition to the amount of child support calculated pursuant to the guidelines. It appears that the trial court has strictly complied with this provision by calculating the amount of support and additionally requiring that [father] provide health insurance coverage."

FAM §154.064. HEALTH INSURANCE FOR CHILD PRESUMPTIVELY PROVIDED BY OBLIGOR

Section 154.064 below is effective for SAPCRs commenced before Sept. 1, 2001.

The guidelines for support of a child are based on the assumption that the court will order the obligor to provide health insurance coverage for the child in addition to the amount of child support calculated in accordance with those guidelines.

FAM §154.065. SELF-EMPLOYMENT INCOME

(a) Income from self-employment, whether positive or negative, includes benefits allocated to an individual from a business or undertaking in the form of a proprietorship, partnership, joint venture, close corporation, agency, or independent contractor, less ordinary and necessary expenses required to produce that income.

(b) In its discretion, the court may exclude from self-employment income amounts allowable under federal income tax law as depreciation, tax credits, or any other business expenses shown by the evidence to be inappropriate in making the determination of income available for the purpose of calculating child support.

History of Fam §154.065: Acts 1995, 74th Leg., ch. 20, §1, eff. April 20, 1995. Source: Former Fam §14.053(c).

Powell v. Swanson, 893 S.W.2d 161, 164 (Tex. App.—Houston [1st Dist.] 1995, no writ). Obligee "contends that the deduction of business depreciation from [obligee's] adjusted gross income was erroneous. ... The Family Code provides that the trial court may decline deduction of depreciation if the evidence shows that the deduction is 'inappropriate to the determination of income for the purpose of calculating child support.' 'Net rental income' is defined in ... §14.053(b) [now §154.062] as 'rent after deducting operating expenses and mortgage payments, but not including noncash items such as depreciation.' We interpret these two sections to mean that depreciation is not to be included in the calculation of net rental income for the purpose of determining child support. [Obligor's] adjusted gross income should have been increased by the amount of the depreciation deducted from [obligor's] gross income on his federal income tax return."

FAM §154.066. INTENTIONAL UNEMPLOYMENT OR UNDEREMPLOYMENT

If the actual income of the obligor is significantly less than what the obligor could earn because of intentional unemployment or underemployment, the court may apply the support guidelines to the earning potential of the obligor.

History of Fam §154.066: Acts 1995, 74th Leg., ch. 20, §1, eff. April 20, 1995. Source: Former Fam §14.053(f).

DuBois v. DuBois, 956 S.W.2d 607, 610 (Tex. App.—Tyler 1997, no pet.). "The Family Code fails to define 'intentional underemployment or unemployment,' and there is an absence of caselaw illuminating the utilization of §154.066. The traditional interpretation, however, requires a finding that the reduction in income must have been effectuated with a design to reduce the child support payments. Thus, in order for a court to find that a parent is intentionally underemployed or unemployed under §154.066, there must be evidence that the parent reduced his income for the purpose of decreasing his child support payments. There is no presumption that simply because a parent is no longer as lucratively employed as he was during his marriage, he is intentionally underemployed or unemployed. The requisite intent or lack thereof, however, may be inferred from such circumstances as the parent's education, economic adversities and business reversals, business background, and earning potential. In addition, we must be cognizant of a parent's right as a citizen to the pursuit of happiness and to the freedom to live where he chooses. And it is axiomatic that although a parent's financial support of his children is of prime importance, so too is his physical presence in their lives."

In re Marriage of Hamer, 906 S.W.2d 263, 267 (Tex.App.—Amarillo 1995, no writ). "That [obligor] may have sought to better his lot did not entitle him to do so at the expense of his children. Indeed, statute empowers the court to determine his net resources in relation to his earning potential rather than actual earnings. Since the [obligor] voluntarily ended prior employment, took lesser paying jobs, and opted to remain in the lesser paying jobs despite the needs of his offspring, the trial court was entitled to assess his income based on his earning potential."

Roosth v. Roosth, 889 S.W.2d 445, 454 (Tex.App.—Houston [14th Dist.] 1994, writ denied). "The finding that [obligor] chose to live off the gifts of his father-in-law is related to this finding of intentional unemployment. While this factor is not among the listed factors a judge can consider in varying from the standard guidelines, §14.054 [now §154.123] provides that the court can consider 'all relevant factors,' and is not limited to the enumerated factors. Therefore, we find no abuse of discretion in the trial court's consideration of [obligor's] unemployment and underemployment."

Starck v. Nelson, 878 S.W.2d 302, 307 (Tex.App.—Corpus Christi 1994, no writ). "The Family Code permits a finding that an obligor is intentionally underemployed and if such a finding is made permits the court to assess child support based on earning potential. The Code does not define intentional underemployment, however, intentional underemployment must require a voluntary choice by the obligor. In this case, there is no evidence that [obligor] voluntarily changed jobs to accept a position that paid less. The undisputed testimony is that he has been involuntarily terminated from three positions and that since 1986 he has voluntarily left only one position. The single, voluntary job change was to accept a position in mall management. There is no evidence to support a finding of intentional underemployment."

FAM §154.067. DEEMED INCOME

(a) When appropriate, in order to determine the net resources available for child support, the court may assign a reasonable amount of deemed income attributable to assets that do not currently produce income. The court shall also consider whether certain property that is not producing income can be liquidated without an unreasonable financial sacrifice because of cyclical or other market conditions. If there is no effective market for the property, the carrying costs of such an investment, including property taxes and note payments, shall be offset against the income attributed to the property.

(b) The court may assign a reasonable amount of deemed income to income-producing assets that a party has voluntarily transferred or on which earnings have intentionally been reduced.

History of Fam §154.067: Acts 1995, 74th Leg., ch. 20, §1, eff. April 20, 1995. Source: Former Fam §14.053(e).

Roosth v. Roosth, 889 S.W.2d 445, 455 (Tex.App.—Houston [14th Dist.] 1994, writ denied). Obligor's "inventory ... indicates an ownership interest in four real estate rental partnerships and an interest in four oil & gas production partnerships. ... Although his income tax records indicate some distributions, [obligor] contended he did not physically receive cash distributions. Instead, [obligor] maintained that these distributions went directly to pay off tax liabilities. [¶] Section 14.053(e) [now §154.067] allows a trial court to assign a reasonable amount of income attributable to assets that do not currently produce income. Furthermore, the duty to support is not limited to a parent's ability to pay from current earnings, but extends to his financial ability to pay from any and all available sources. Based on the evidence, we find no abuse of discretion by the trial court in requiring [obligor] to pay $3,000.00 per month in child support." (Internal quotations omitted.)

FAM §154.068. WAGE & SALARY PRESUMPTION

In the absence of evidence of the wage and salary income of a party, the court shall presume that the party has wages or salary equal to the federal minimum wage for a 40-hour week.

History of Fam §154.068: Acts 1995, 74th Leg., ch. 20, §1, eff. April 20, 1995. Source: Former Fam §14.053(k).

In re A.P., 46 S.W.3d 347, 349-50 (Tex.App.—Corpus Christi 2001, no pet.). "The retroactive child support was calculated under the minimum wage presumption set forth in the [F]amily [C]ode. [Obligor] asserts that because he is in prison, he could not have earned even the minimum wage. There is no legal presumption that an inmate has no assets; incarceration alone does not rebut the minimum wage presumption."

In re Moss, 887 S.W.2d 186, 188 (Tex.App.—Texarkana 1994, no writ). "The only evidence relating to the mother's income was the categorical statement by the father that he did not know where she worked and no idea how much money she made. No findings in support of the child support order were requested. [¶] In this situation, the trial court should apply the statutory presumption set forth in ... §14.053(k) [now §154.068] and set child support accordingly. When evidence is insufficient to determine actual income, the court is required to apply the federal minimum wage ... to a forty-hour week."

In re Martin, 881 S.W.2d 531, 536-37 (Tex.App.—Texarkana 1994, writ denied). "There is conflicting evidence about the extent of his liabilities. In the absence of sufficient evidence to determine the wages and salary income of the obligor, the trial court applies the presumption that they have wages or salary equal to the prevailing federal minimum wage for a forty-hour week. Proof that [obligor] was temporarily unemployed, when set against his testimony that he had been gainfully employed for several years and had prospects for future work, does not create a situation in which no obligation may be imposed. Based on his testimony about his previous earning ability and income, and in the absence of any evidence that he is unemployable, there is at least some evidence to support the trial court's setting of child support based on the federal minimum wage."

FAM §154.069. NET RESOURCES OF SPOUSE

(a) The court may not add any portion of the net resources of a spouse to the net resources of an obligor or obligee in order to calculate the amount of child support to be ordered.

(b) The court may not subtract the needs of a spouse, or of a dependent of a spouse, from the net resources of the obligor or obligee.

History of Fam §154.069: §14.056(c) by Acts 1995, 74th Leg., ch. 20, §1, eff. April 20, 1995. Source: Former Fam §14.056(c).

Starck v. Nelson, 878 S.W.2d 302, 305-06 (Tex. App.—Corpus Christi 1994, no writ). The obligor "claims that the trial court erred because it considered [his new] wife's income. ... [T]he court did not use [his new] wife's income to calculate [his] net resources; however, the court considered [his] remarriage in deviating from child support guidelines. The trial court found that [his new] wife's contribution to their joint living expenses enabled [obligor] to pay more child support than if he were solely responsible for his living expenses. [¶] The precise language of [§14.056(c), now §154.069] does not prohibit the trial court's action in this case. [However, permitting] the court to deviate from child support guidelines because the obligor's new spouse contributes to their joint living expenses allows the court to do indirectly what the statute directly prohibits." Thus, trial court should not have considered obligor's new wife's income.

FAM §154.070. CHILD SUPPORT RECEIVED BY OBLIGOR

In a situation involving multiple households due child support, child support received by an obligor shall be added to the obligor's net resources to compute the net resources before determining the child support credit or applying the percentages in the multiple household table in this chapter.

History of Fam §154.070: Acts 1995, 74th Leg., ch. 20, §1, eff. April 20, 1995. Source: Former Fam §14.055(i).

Sections 154.071-154.120 reserved for expansion

SUBCHAPTER C. CHILD SUPPORT GUIDELINES

FAM §154.121. GUIDELINES FOR THE SUPPORT OF A CHILD

The child support guidelines in this subchapter are intended to guide the court in determining an equitable amount of child support.

History of Fam §154.121: Acts 1995, 74th Leg., ch. 20, §1, eff. April 20, 1995. Source: Former Fam §14.052(a).

In re Striegler, 915 S.W.2d 629, 639 (Tex.App.—Amarillo 1996, writ denied). "[E]ach spouse has a duty to support his or her minor children. That obligation corresponds in large measure to the parent's financial ability and earning potential. The guidelines found in Chapter 14 [now Chapter 154] are intended to guide the courts in determining what is an equitable amount of child support, and the trial court is given broad discretion in assessing child support payments."

FAM §154.122. APPLICATION OF GUIDELINES REBUTTABLY PRESUMED IN BEST INTEREST OF CHILD

(a) The amount of a periodic child support payment established by the child support guidelines in effect in this state at the time of the hearing is presumed to be reasonable, and an order of support conforming to the guidelines is presumed to be in the best interest of the child.

(b) A court may determine that the application of the guidelines would be unjust or inappropriate under the circumstances.

History of Fam §154.122: Acts 1995, 74th Leg., ch. 20, §1, eff. April 20, 1995. Source: Former Fam §§14.05(j), 14.055(a).

FAM §154.123. ADDITIONAL FACTORS FOR COURT TO CONSIDER

(a) The court may order periodic child support payments in an amount other than that established by the guidelines if the evidence rebuts the presumption that application of the guidelines is in the best interest of the child and justifies a variance from the guidelines.

(b) In determining whether application of the guidelines would be unjust or inappropriate under the circumstances, the court shall consider evidence of all relevant factors, including:

(1) the age and needs of the child;

(2) the ability of the parents to contribute to the support of the child;

(3) any financial resources available for the support of the child;

(4) the amount of time of possession of and access to a child;

(5) the amount of the obligee's net resources, including the earning potential of the obligee if the actual income of the obligee is significantly less than what the obligee could earn because the obligee is intentionally unemployed or underemployed and including an increase or decrease in the income of the obligee or income that may be attributed to the property and assets of the obligee;

(6) child care expenses incurred by either party in order to maintain gainful employment;

(7) whether either party has the managing conservatorship or actual physical custody of another child;

(8) the amount of alimony or spousal maintenance actually and currently being paid or received by a party;

(9) the expenses for a son or daughter for education beyond secondary school;

(10) whether the obligor or obligee has an automobile, housing, or other benefits furnished by his or her employer, another person, or a business entity;

(11) the amount of other deductions from the wage or salary income and from other compensation for personal services of the parties;

(12) provision for health care insurance and payment of uninsured medical expenses;

(13) special or extraordinary educational, health care, or other expenses of the parties or of the child;

(14) the cost of travel in order to exercise possession of and access to a child;

(15) positive or negative cash flow from any real and personal property and assets, including a business and investments;

(16) debts or debt service assumed by either party; and

(17) any other reason consistent with the best interest of the child, taking into consideration the circumstances of the parents.

History of Fam §154.123: Acts 1995, 74th Leg., ch. 20, §1, eff. April 20, 1995. Source: Former Fam §§14.052(b), 14.054.

Rodriguez v. Rodriguez, 860 S.W.2d 414, 417 (Tex. 1993). "The factors listed in §14.052(b) [now §154.123(b)(1)-(4)] and §14.054 [now §154.123(5)-(17)] provide bases for variance from strict application of the percentage guidelines, but only apply to the first $4,000 [now $6,000] of net resources."

Sanchez v. Sanchez, 915 S.W.2d 99, 102-03 (Tex. App.—San Antonio 1996, no writ). "The Texas Family Code permits the court to render a final determination of support outside the range recommended by the guidelines if other relevant factors justify such a variance. Expressly included in the factors the court must consider in making its final determination are whether either party has the managing conservatorship or actual physical custody of another child and debts or debt service assumed by either party. Thus, consideration of the amount of debt service assumed by the [father] and the split custody of the children are expressly authorized by §14.054 [now §154.123]. Since the note payments would clearly increase the amount of resources available to the [mother], while decreasing the amount of resources available to the [father], it cannot be said that considering the note payment to be a relevant factor is without reference to any guiding rules and principles. Although it is not a factor expressly listed in §14.054, it is clear that the list is not exclusive and the court may consider any factor it deems relevant."

Belcher v. Belcher, 808 S.W.2d 202, 208 (Tex. App.—El Paso 1991, no writ), *overruled on other grounds,* ***Rodriguez v. Rodriguez***, 860 S.W.2d 414 (Tex. 1993). "[W]e believe the intent of the legislature in enacting §14.054(1) [now §154.123(5)] was to prevent an obligee from intentionally remaining unemployed or underemployed in order to gain an increase in child support, not to prevent an obligee from seeking to improve him or herself educationally so that he or she can hold a better or a permanent job. [Mother's] circumstances are distinguishable from a situation in which a woman decides on her own that her children need a full-time mother and quits working. Her unemployment was for a finite period of short duration while she completed her education which would presumably enable her to obtain steady and permanent employment. The evidence shows that she intended to maintain a full-time job as soon as she received her teaching certificate."

In re Marriage of Edwards, 804 S.W.2d 653, 657 (Tex.App.—Amarillo 1991, no writ). "In affirming the court master's findings, the court adjudged that the reason the ordered amount varied from the percentage guidelines 'because of the [voluntary] support provided by [father] in addition to the ordered support.' [¶] Although the reason given by the trial court is not expressly prohibited by statute, it clearly is neither a need of the child at the time of the order as required by §14.055(c) [now §154.126], nor a factor listed in §14.052(b) [now §154.123]. Indeed, the reason given cannot be a cause to increase the amount of an existing child support order. [¶] It follows that the history of voluntary support provided in excess of the amount ordered is not a proper basis upon which the trial court may vary the percentage guidelines. Variance from the guidelines predicated on this factor is such a gross and prejudicial error of law as to constitute an abuse of discretion."

FAM §154.124. AGREEMENT CONCERNING SUPPORT

(a) To promote the amicable settlement of disputes between the parties to a suit, the parties may enter into a written agreement containing provisions for support of the child and for modification of the agreement, including variations from the child support guidelines provided by Subchapter C.

(b) If the court finds that the agreement is in the child's best interest, the court shall render an order in accordance with the agreement.

(c) Terms of the agreement in the order may be enforced by all remedies available for enforcement of a judgment, including contempt, but are not enforceable as contract terms unless provided by the agreement.

(d) If the court finds the agreement is not in the child's best interest, the court may request the parties to submit a revised agreement or the court may render an order for the support of the child.

History of Fam §154.124: Acts 1995, 74th Leg., ch. 20, §1, eff. April 20, 1995. Source: Former Fam §§14.053(j), 14.06.

Bruni v. Bruni, 924 S.W.2d 366, 367-68 (Tex.1996). "[T]he Family Code authorizes court-ordered child support only until a child is eighteen years old. The parties' agreement that [father] provide support for their children until age twenty-one is enforceable as a contract only if their agreement so provides. If so, [father's] support obligation for children over eighteen may be enforced by ordinary processes of law. [¶] Section 14.06(d) [now §154.124(c)] requires that the agreement on support, not the trial court's order, provide for enforceability as a contract. ... When there is no separate written agreement and the trial court's order is the only written manifestation of the parties' agreement on support, ***Elfeldt*** [***v. Elfeldt***, 730 S.W.2d 657, 658 (Tex.1987)] requires that the trial court's order provide for enforceability. ***Elfeldt*** does not require the trial court's order to provide for enforceability if the parties' written agreement reflected in the order provides for enforceability as a contract. [¶] Here, the parties' 1975 agreement specifically provides that it *survives* the court's judgment, the divorce decree, and is *binding* on the parties, their heirs, and their representatives, if the trial court approved the agreement and incorporated it into the decree. Section 14.06(d) does not require any 'magic words' providing for enforceability. We hold that this language expresses the parties' intent that the 1975 agreement, including the child support obligations, be enforced as a contract once approved and incorporated into the divorce decree."

In re D.S., ___ S.W.3d ___ (Tex.App.—Houston [14th Dist.] 2002, n.p.h.) (No. 14-00-01457-CV; 2-28-02). "Although a court may not arbitrarily impose automatic or formula increases in child support, if the parties agree on an automatic increase in child support upon the occurrence of a certain event, and the court has found that the agreement is in the best interest of the child, the parties may be ordered to perform in accordance with that agreement; and compliance may be enforced by all available remedies." ***See also Cisneros v. Cisneros***, 787 S.W.2d 550, 552-52 (Tex.App.—El Paso 1990, no writ).

McLendon v. McLendon, 847 S.W.2d 601, 608 (Tex. App.—Dallas 1992, writ denied). "We note that [TRCP 11] itself equates a written agreement with the 'open court and entered of record' portion of rule 11. Both alternatives attain the purpose of the rule, which is to memorialize the terms of the agreement reached by the litigants. The court reporter's transcription of the dictated agreement results in a written agreement, and the sworn testimony of the parties given to the court reporter in open court memorializes the parties' consent and can also be reduced to writing. We hold that this procedure has the same legal effect as a written agreement signed by the parties and, in fact, results in a written agreement that meets the requirements of ... §14.06 [now §154.124]."

In re Marriage of Edwards, 804 S.W.2d 653, 655 (Tex.App.—Amarillo 1991, no writ). "[A]lthough the contractual agreement of [the spouses] is incorporated in the decree of divorce pursuant to §14.06 [now §154.124], that section's provisions do not extinguish or limit the court's power to modify the support order to provide for the best interest of the child. Consequently, the trial court had the power to modify the child support provisions incorporated into the decree of divorce."

K.D.B. v. C.B.B., 688 S.W.2d 684, 686-87 (Tex. App.—Tyler 1985, writ dism'd). "If in a trial judge's perception, the agreement between divorcing parents for ... support of the children of the marriage 'is not in the child's best interest,' what is the judge authorized to do when he is conducting an uncontested hearing on a petition for divorce in which suit such issues have been resolved by written agreement before trial, and the petitioner is the only party present before the court? Such question calls for an interpretation of the second alternative provided by that portion of §14.06(b) [now §154.124] reading, 'or the court may make orders for the ... support of the child.' Applying the standards of the Code Construction Act..., we construe the quoted provisions to mean simply that a trial judge is not bound by the agreement of the parents when he concludes that such agreement is not in a child's best interest. This is not to say, however, that being of such a mind, the trial judge can summarily, and without affording the parties a reasonable opportunity to present evidence relevant to a proper determination of the issues, proceed in a noncontested hearing, as here, to decree that the absent spouse pay child support in a sum certain periodically contrary to the terms of the agreement."

Dorshaw v. Dorshaw, 635 S.W.2d 783, 785 (Tex. App.—Corpus Christi 1982, no writ). "It appears to us that the adoption by the Legislature of the Family Code mandates a holding on our part that, in a situation such as this, the consent of the parties is no longer a prerequisite to the modification of a child support agreement. Specifically, we refer to §14.06(d) [now §154.124(c)] wherein it is stated that the terms of a child support agreement are not enforceable as a contract unless the agreement so provides. No such provision exists in the agreement before us. We interpret §14.06(d) to mean that unless the parties stipulate that the agreement is to survive the judgment and be enforceable as a contract, contract law no longer governs."

FAM §154.125. APPLICATION OF GUIDELINES TO NET RESOURCES OF $6,000 OR LESS

(a) The guidelines for the support of a child in this section are specifically designed to apply to situations in which the obligor's monthly net resources are $6,000 or less.

(b) If the obligor's monthly net resources are $6,000 or less, the court shall presumptively apply the following schedule in rendering the child support order:

CHILD SUPPORT GUIDELINES	
Based on the monthly net resources of the obligor	
1 child	20% of Obligor's Net Resources
2 children	25% of Obligor's Net Resources
3 children	30% of Obligor's Net Resources
4 children	35% of Obligor's Net Resources
5 children	40% of Obligor's Net Resources
6+ children	Not less than the amount for 5 children

History of Fam §154.125: Acts 1995, 74th Leg., ch. 20, §1, eff. April 20, 1995. Source: Former Fam §14.055(a), (b).

Escue v. Escue, 810 S.W.2d 845, 847 (Tex.App.—Texarkana 1991, no writ). Section 14.055(a), now §154.125, "creates a rebuttable presumption that an order for periodic child support payments established by the [child support guidelines] is reasonable and in the best interest of the child[.] *At 848:* The reference to the number of children in the guidelines is to the number of children involved in the particular suit before the court, not the obligor's total offspring."

FAM §154.126. APPLICATION OF GUIDELINES TO NET RESOURCES OF MORE THAN $6,000 MONTHLY

(a) If the obligor's net resources exceed $6,000 per month, the court shall presumptively apply the percentage guidelines to the first $6,000 of the obligor's net resources. Without further reference to the percentage recommended by these guidelines, the court may order additional amounts of child support as appropriate, depending on the income of the parties and the proven needs of the child.

(b) The proper calculation of a child support order that exceeds the presumptive amount established for the first $6,000 of the obligor's net resources requires that the entire amount of the presumptive award be subtracted from the proven total needs of the child. After the presumptive award is subtracted, the court shall allocate between the parties the responsibility to meet the additional needs of the child according to the circumstances of the parties. However, in no event may the obligor be required to pay more child support than the greater of the presumptive amount or the amount equal to 100 percent of the proven needs of the child.

History of Fam §154.126: Acts 1995, 74th Leg., ch. 20, §1, eff. April 20, 1995. Source: Former Fam §14.055(c).

Rodriguez v. Rodriguez, 860 S.W.2d 414, 417 n.3 (Tex.1993). We conclude "that 'needs of the child' includes more than the bare necessities of life, but is not determined by the parents' ability to pay or the lifestyle of the family. In determining the needs of the child, we direct courts to continue to follow the paramount guiding principle: *the best interest of the child.*"

In re Gonzalez, 993 S.W.2d 147, 154 (Tex.App.—San Antonio 1999, no pet.). "If the court orders additional child support beyond the presumptive amount, the court must make a written finding regarding the specific reasons for deviating from the guidelines."

Nordstrom v. Nordstrom, 965 S.W.2d 575, 579 n.4 (Tex.App.—Houston [1st Dist.] 1997, pet. denied). Based on the clear language of §154.126, "we hold that 'income of the parties' and 'proven needs of the child' are the only factors to be considered in awarding additional support over the presumptive amount for an obligor with over $6,000 in monthly net resources. *At 581:* Notwithstanding the needs [obligee] may have proven, §154.126 vests the court with the *discretion* to award additional amounts. It *mandates* only that the court consider the needs of the child and the parties' income in arriving at that decision, and that the amount allocated to the obligor not exceed the proven needs of the child. Therefore, even if [obligee] did conclusively prove the needs of the child, it was within the court's discretion to refuse to award additional support."

Scott v. Younts, 926 S.W.2d 415, 422 (Tex.App.—Corpus Christi 1996, writ denied). "We do not now state that 'needs of the child' can encompass even the most extravagant demands. We are reluctant to recognize a child's need for a special pet as a compelling justification to increase support above the presumptive guidelines without some evidence. [¶] However, given the broad discretion allowed to courts to determine the needs of the child, we cannot conclude that the court abused its discretion in setting the support order at $2500. Clearly, the evidence on the current expenses for the child amounted to $2067. Adding expenses for private school ($250 per month), extracurricular activities ($200 per month), and summer camp ($200 per month), the proven needs of the child exceed $2700. Although these items are not bare necessities, we cannot say that they are contrary to the best interests of the child."

Zajac v. Penkava, 924 S.W.2d 405, 410 (Tex.App.—San Antonio 1996, no writ). "We conclude from the argument in his brief that his specific complaint is the failure of the trial court to file findings of the calculations made under the provisions of §14.055(c) [now §154.126(b)]. There is no statutory requirement that the calculations be included in the findings. The only requirement is that, after the calculations are made, the court should allocate between the parties, according to their circumstances, the responsibility to meet the additional needs of the children, and the obligor may not be required to pay more than 100 percent of the proven needs."

FAM §154.127. PARTIAL TERMINATION OF SUPPORT OBLIGATION

A child support order for more than one child shall provide that, on the termination of support for a child, the level of support for the remaining child or children is in accordance with the child support guidelines.

History of Fam §154.127: Acts 1995, 74th Leg., ch. 20, §1, eff. April 20, 1995. Source: Former Fam §14.055(d).

FAM §154.128. COMPUTING SUPPORT FOR CHILDREN IN MORE THAN ONE HOUSEHOLD

(a) In applying the child support guidelines for an obligor who has children in more than one household, the court shall apply the percentage guidelines in this subchapter by making the following computation:

(1) determine the amount of child support that would be ordered if all children whom the obligor has the legal duty to support lived in one household by applying the schedule in this subchapter;

(2) compute a child support credit for the obligor's children who are not before the court by dividing the amount determined under Subdivision (1) by the total number of children whom the obligor is obligated to support and multiplying that number by the number of the obligor's children who are not before the court;

(3) determine the adjusted net resources of the obligor by subtracting the child support credit computed under Subdivision (2) from the net resources of the obligor; and

(4) determine the child support amount for the children before the court by applying the percentage guidelines for one household for the number of children of the obligor before the court to the obligor's adjusted net resources.

(b) For the purpose of determining a child support credit, the total number of an obligor's children includes the children before the court for the establishment or modification of a support order and any other children, including children residing with the obligor, whom the obligor has the legal duty of support.

(c) The child support credit with respect to children for whom the obligor is obligated by an order to pay support is computed, regardless of whether the obligor is delinquent in child support payments, without regard to the amount of the order.

History of Fam §154.128: Acts 1995, 74th Leg., ch. 20, §1, eff. April 20, 1995. Source: Former Fam §14.055(f)-(h).

FAM §154.129. ALTERNATIVE METHOD OF COMPUTING SUPPORT FOR CHILDREN IN MORE THAN ONE HOUSEHOLD

In lieu of performing the computation under the preceding section, the court may determine the child support amount for the children before the court by applying the percentages in the table below to the obligor's net resources:

MULTIPLE FAMILY ADJUSTED GUIDELINES (% OF NET RESOURCES)

		Number of children before the court						
		1	2	3	4	5	6	7
Number of other children for whom the obligor has a duty of support	0	20.00	25.00	30.00	35.00	40.00	40.00	40.00
	1	17.50	22.50	27.38	32.20	37.33	37.71	38.00
	2	16.00	20.63	25.20	30.33	35.43	36.00	36.44
	3	14.75	19.00	24.00	29.00	34.00	34.67	35.20
	4	13.60	18.33	23.14	28.00	32.89	33.60	34.18
	5	13.33	17.86	22.50	27.22	32.00	32.73	33.33
	6	13.14	17.50	22.00	26.60	31.27	32.00	32.62
	7	13.00	17.22	21.60	26.09	30.67	31.38	32.00

History of Fam §154.129: Acts 1995, 74th Leg., ch. 20, §1, eff. April 20, 1995. Source: Former Fam §14.055(j).

In re Hidalgo, 938 S.W.2d 492, 498 (Tex.App.—Texarkana 1996, no writ). "The court is to presumptively apply a schedule set out in §154.125, which provides that child support should be set for one child at twenty percent of the obligor's net resources. [¶] That amount, however, is to be reduced when the obligor has children residing in more than one household. Sections 154.128 and 154.129 of the Act set out two alternative methods of computing support when the obligor has children in more than one household. [Obligor] has three children including [the appellant's child]. Pursuant to §154.129, the percentage of net income to be applied when the obligor has one child before the court and two other children in another household is sixteen percent. If the amount of support ordered varies from the amount computed by applying the guidelines, the trial court must enter findings to support its ruling."

FAM §154.130. FINDINGS IN CHILD SUPPORT ORDER

(a) Without regard to Rules 296 through 299, Texas Rules of Civil Procedure, in rendering an order of child support, the court shall make the findings required by Subsection (b) if:

(1) a party files a written request with the court not later than 10 days after the date of the hearing;

(2) a party makes an oral request in open court during the hearing; or

(3) the amount of child support ordered by the court varies from the amount computed by applying the percentage guidelines.

(b) If findings are required by this section, the court shall state whether the application of the guidelines would be unjust or inappropriate and shall state the following in the child support order:

"(1) the monthly net resources of the obligor per month are $_______;

"(2) the monthly net resources of the obligee per month are $_______;

"(3) the percentage applied to the obligor's net resources for child support by the actual order rendered by the court is _______%;

"(4) the amount of child support if the percentage guidelines are applied to the first $6,000 of the obligor's net resources is $_______;

"(5) if applicable, the specific reasons that the amount of child support per month ordered by the court varies from the amount stated in Subdivision (4) are: _______; and

"(6) if applicable, the obligor is obligated to support children in more than one household, and:

"(A) the number of children before the court is _______;

"(B) the number of children not before the court residing in the same household with the obligor is _______; and

"(C) the number of children not before the court for whom the obligor is obligated by a court order to pay support, without regard to whether the obligor is delinquent in child support payments, and who are not counted under Paragraph (A) or (B) is _______."

E *Subsection (c) below is effective for SAPCRs commenced on or after Sept. 1, 2001.*

(c) The application of the guidelines under Section 154.129 does not constitute a variance from the child support guidelines requiring specific findings by the court under this section.

History of Fam §154.130: Acts 1995, 74th Leg., ch. 20, §1, eff. April 20, 1995. Amended by Acts 2001, 77th Leg., ch. 1023, §8, eff. Sept. 1, 2001. Source: Former Fam §14.057.

Rodriguez v. Rodriguez, 860 S.W.2d 414, 418 n.4 (Tex.1993). "Section 14.057 [now §154.130] requires a trial court to make findings of fact of its reasons for varying from the percentage guidelines; it does not require a trial court to make findings regarding its basis for the presumptive percentage award. We do not add such a requirement here. We note only that we do not have the benefit of any explanation by the trial court for determining what portion of its award out of the first $4,000 [now $6,000] of net resources are based on the needs of the child. It obviously would be helpful for appellate review of child support awards, when the obligor's net resources exceed [$6,000] per month, to have the benefit of the trial court's findings concerning the basis for the presumptive percentage award, and we commend this practice to our trial courts."

In re Guthrie, 45 S.W.3d 719, 723 (Tex.App.—Dallas 2001, pet. denied). "Retroactive support concerns payment of child support for a period before a child support order. Section 154.130 is directed to the setting of monthly support. Therefore, the refusal to award any retroactive support does not constitute a deviation from the guidelines such that a statutory finding is required."

Hatteberg v. Hatteberg, 933 S.W.2d 522, 528 (Tex.App.—Houston [1st Dist.] 1994, no writ). Obligee "argues that whether or not a party requests specific child support findings, a trial court is required to make the findings when the amount awarded varies from the amount computed by applying the Family Code's percentage guidelines. Under ... §14.057(b) [now §154.130(b)(3)], the trial court is required to find that the application of the statutory percentage guidelines would be unjust or inappropriate, and make the same five findings required by [§14.057(a)], in any [SAPCR] in which the amount of child support ordered by the court varies from the amount computed by applying the guidelines contained in §14.055 [now §154.125]."

Zajac v. Penkava, 924 S.W.2d 405, 410 (Tex.App.—San Antonio 1996, no writ). "Points of error seven and eight complain that the trial court did not file the findings required by ... §14.057 [now §154.130] in the child support order. The trial judge substantially complied with the statute by making the required findings in two separate documents which were subsequently filed with the papers in the case."

Starck v. Nelson, 878 S.W.2d 302, 306-07 (Tex. App.—Corpus Christi 1994, no writ). Obligor "complains that the trial court erred by entering a child support order that deviates from child support guidelines without making the necessary findings that the application of the child support guidelines would be unjust or inappropriate as required by §14.057(b) [now §154.130]. [Obligor] never brought the absence of §14.057(b) [now §154.130(b)] required findings to the trial court's attention. Although the statute requires the court to make such a finding without requiring the procedures set out in [TRCPs] 296-299, we hold that [obligor's] failure to bring that requirement to the court's attention constitutes a waiver of that complaint."

FAM §154.131. RETROACTIVE CHILD SUPPORT

A *Section 154.131 below is effective for SAPCRs commenced on or after Sept. 1, 2001, and for suits for child support or motions to enforce child support filed on or after Sept. 1, 2001.*

(a) The child support guidelines are intended to guide the court in determining the amount of retroactive child support, if any, to be ordered.

(b) In ordering retroactive child support, the court shall consider the net resources of the obligor during the relevant time period and whether:

A *Subsections (1) & (2) below are effective for motions or other requests for relief made in parentage or paternity proceedings commenced on or after June 14, 2001.*

(1) the mother of the child had made any previous attempts to notify the obligor of his paternity or probable paternity;

(2) the obligor had knowledge of his paternity or probable paternity;

(3) the order of retroactive child support will impose an undue financial hardship on the obligor or the obligor's family; and

(4) the obligor has provided actual support or other necessaries before the filing of the action.

E (c) It is presumed that a court order limiting the amount of retroactive child support to an amount that does not exceed the total amount of support that would have been due for the four years preceding the date the petition seeking support was filed is reasonable and in the best interest of the child.

E (d) The presumption created under this section may be rebutted by evidence that the obligor:

(1) knew or should have known that the obligor was the father of the child for whom support is sought; and

(2) sought to avoid the establishment of a support obligation to the child.

E (e) An order under this section limiting the amount of retroactive support does not constitute a variance from the guidelines requiring the court to make specific findings under Section 154.130.

History of Fam §154.131: Acts 1995, 74th Leg., ch. 20, §1, eff. April 20, 1995. Amended by Acts 2001, 77th Leg., ch. 329, §1 (eff. Sept. 1, 2001), ch. 821, §2.14 (eff. June 14, 2001), ch. 1023, §9 (eff. Sept. 1, 2001). Source: Former Fam §14.053(*l*).

In re Valadez, 980 S.W.2d 910, 913 (Tex.App.—Corpus Christi 1998, no pet.). "Regarding retroactive child support, §154.131(a) states, '[t]he child support guidelines are intended *to guide the court* in determining the amount of retroactive child support, if any, to be ordered.' We agree with our sister courts that the guidelines are just that when applied to retroactive support; they are not mandatory, and §§154.130(a)(3) & (b) requiring the court to specify why they are not being followed does not apply. [¶] 'Retroactive child support' is a repayment of monies expended for the care of the child in the past. It represents funds the nonsupporting parent owed to the child, as well as funds owed the supporting parent to discharge his or her proportionate duty of financial support to the child. In awarding retroactive support a trial court considers not only the support the errant parent should have provided to the child, but also the right to reimbursement afforded someone who has supported the child in the meantime. [¶] We hold a trial court has discretion in deciding whether to award retroactive child support and in deciding the amount of the award. Accordingly we will not reverse the trial court's judgment absent an abuse of discretion." *See also* ***Garza v. Blanton***, 55 S.W.3d 708, 710 (Tex.App.—Corpus Christi 2001, no pet.).

Nordstrom v. Nordstrom, 965 S.W.2d 575, 582 n.7 (Tex.App.—Houston [1st Dist.] 1997, pet. denied). "Because we find that the trial court did not abuse its discretion in refusing to award the retroactive modification, we do not decide whether §154.131 is applicable in claims for retroactive *modification*, as opposed to a trial court's decision to make an *initial* retroactive award of child support against an obligor not subject to an existing support order."

FAM §154.131. APPLICATION OF GUIDELINES TO RETROACTIVE SUPPORT

Section 154.131 below is effective for SAPCRs commenced before Sept. 1, 2001, and for suits for child support or motions to enforce child support filed before Sept. 1, 2001.

(a) The child support guidelines are intended to guide the court in determining the amount of retroactive child support, if any, to be ordered.

(b) In ordering retroactive child support, the court shall consider the net resources of the obligor during the relevant time period and whether:

Subsections (1) & (2) below are effective for motions or other requests for relief made in parentage or paternity proceedings commenced before June 14, 2001.

(1) the mother of the child had made any previous attempts to notify the biological father of his paternity or probable paternity;

(2) the biological father had knowledge of his paternity or probable paternity;

(3) the order of retroactive child support will impose an undue financial hardship on the obligor or the obligor's family; and

(4) the obligor has provided actual support or other necessaries before the filing of the action.

FAM §154.132. APPLICATION OF GUIDELINES TO CHILDREN OF CERTAIN DISABLED OBLIGORS

In applying the child support guidelines for an obligor who has a disability and who is required to pay support for a child who receives benefits as a result of the obligor's disability, the court shall apply the guidelines by determining the amount of child support that would be ordered under the child support guidelines and subtracting from that total the amount of benefits or the value of the benefits paid to or for the child as a result of the obligor's disability.

History of Fam §154.132: Acts 1999, 76th Leg., ch. 891, §1, eff. Sept. 1, 1999.

E FAM §154.133. APPLICATION OF GUIDELINES TO CHILDREN OF OBLIGORS RECEIVING SOCIAL SECURITY

In applying the child support guidelines for an obligor who is receiving social security old age benefits and who is required to pay support for a child who receives benefits as a result of the obligor's receipt of social security old age benefits, the court shall apply the guidelines by determining the amount of child support that would be ordered under the child support guidelines and subtracting from that total the amount of benefits or the value of the benefits paid to or for the child as a result of the obligor's receipt of social security old age benefits.

History of Fam §154.133: Enacted by Acts 2001, 77th Leg., ch. 544, §1, eff. Sept. 1, 2001.

Sections 154.134-154.180 reserved for expansion

SUBCHAPTER D. MEDICAL SUPPORT FOR CHILD

FAM §154.181. MEDICAL SUPPORT ORDER

A (a) In a suit affecting the parent-child relationship or in a proceeding under Chapter 159, the court shall render an order for the medical support of the child as provided by this section and Section 154.182.

E (b) Before a hearing on temporary orders or a final order, if no hearing on temporary orders is held, the court shall require the parties to the proceedings to disclose in a pleading or other statement:

(1) if private health insurance is in effect for the child, the identity of the insurance company providing the coverage, the policy number, which parent is responsible for payment of any insurance premium for the coverage, whether the coverage is provided through a parent's employment, and the cost of the premium; or

(2) if private health insurance is not in effect for the child, whether:

(A) the child is receiving medical assistance under Chapter 32, Human Resources Code;

(B) the child is receiving health benefits coverage under the state child health plan under Chapter 62, Health and Safety Code, and the cost of any premium; and

(C) either parent has access to private health insurance at reasonable cost to that parent.

E (c) In rendering temporary orders, the court shall, except for good cause shown, order that any health insurance coverage in effect for the child continue in effect pending the rendition of a final order, except that the court may not require the continuation of any health insurance that is not available to the parent at reasonable cost. If there is no health insurance coverage in effect for the child or if the insurance in effect is not available at a reasonable cost and the child is not receiving medical assistance under Chapter 32, Human Resources Code, or coverage under the state child health plan under Chapter 62, Health and Safety Code, the court shall, except for good cause shown, order health care coverage for the child as provided under Section 154.182.

E (d) Except for good cause shown, on rendering a final order the court shall require the parent ordered to provide health care coverage for the child as provided under Section 154.182 to produce evidence to the court's satisfaction that the parent has applied for or secured health insurance or has otherwise taken necessary action to provide for health care coverage for the child, as ordered by the court.

E (e) In this section, "reasonable cost" means the cost of a health insurance premium that does not exceed 10 percent of the responsible parent's net income in a month.

History of Fam §154.181: Acts 1995, 74th Leg., ch. 20, §1, eff. April 20, 1995. Amended by Acts 2001, 77th Leg., ch. 449, §1, eff. June 5, 2001. Source: Former Fam §14.061.

De La Garza v. Salazar, 851 S.W.2d 380, 382 (Tex. App.—San Antonio 1993, no writ). Obligor "complains that the court improperly ordered him to provide health insurance in the future without regard to his future employment or the availability of insurance. We reject this argument. The [F]amily [C]ode contemplates that the court will order health insurance for the child. Trial courts need not anticipate and provide for all possible changes in the parties' circumstances; they must establish the rights and duties of the parties based on the evidence at trial."

FAM §154.182. HEALTH INSURANCE

(a) The court shall consider the cost and quality of health insurance coverage available to the parties and shall give priority to health insurance coverage available through the employment of one of the parties.

A (b) In determining the manner in which health insurance for the child is to be ordered, the court shall render its order in accordance with the following priorities, unless a party shows good cause why a particular order would not be in the best interest of the child:

(1) if health insurance is available for the child through the obligor's employment or membership in a union, trade association, or other organization at reasonable cost to the obligor, the court shall order the obligor to include the child in the obligor's health insurance;

(2) if health insurance is not available for the child through the obligor's employment but is available for the child at a reasonable cost through the obligee's employment or membership in a union, trade association, or other organization, the court may order the obligee to provide health insurance for the child, and, in such event, shall order the obligor to pay additional child support to be withheld from earnings under Chapter 158 to the obligee for the actual cost of the health insurance for the child;

(3) if health insurance is not available for the child under Subdivision (1) or (2), the court shall order the obligor to provide health insurance for the child if the court finds that health insurance is available to the obligor for the child from another source and at reasonable cost;

(4) if neither parent has access to private health insurance at a reasonable cost, the court shall order that the custodial parent or, to the extent permitted by law, the noncustodial parent immediately apply on behalf of the child for participation in a medical assistance program under Chapter 32, Human Resources Code, or the state child health plan under Chapter 62, Health and Safety Code, and that the obligor pay additional child support, to be withheld from income under Chapter 158, to the obligee for the actual cost of participation of the child in such program; or

(5) if health coverage is not available for the child under Subdivision (1), (2), (3), or (4), the court shall order the obligor to pay the obligee, in addition to any amount ordered under the guidelines for child support, a reasonable amount each month as medical support for the child to be withheld from earnings under Chapter 158.

A (c) In this section, "reasonable cost" has the meaning assigned by Section 154.181(e).

History of Fam §154.182: Acts 1995, 74th Leg., ch. 20, §1, eff. April 20, 1995. Amended by Acts 1997, 75th Leg., ch. 550, §2, eff. June 2, 1997; Acts 2001, 77th Leg., ch. 449, §2, eff. June 5, 2001. Source: Former Fam §14.061(a), (b).

See also 28 TAC §§21.2001-21.2011.

Kish v. Kole, 874 S.W.2d 835, 837 (Tex.App.—Beaumont 1994, no writ). Obligor "attacks the trial court judgment for not allowing an offset against the child support for the health insurance coverage paid by [obligor] for the minor child. We note that [obligor] pays approximately $60.00 per month for medical insurance for the minor child. The court is required to order that health insurance be provided for the child, in this case by the [obligor]. This is in addition to the child support ordered by the court."

Voros v. Turnage, 856 S.W.2d 759, 763-64 (Tex. App.—Houston [1st Dist.] 1993, writ denied). "The original divorce decree did not require insurance for the children. The Family Code now requires medical insurance as part of the child support obligation. [O]bligor claims §14.061 [now §154.182] creates a rebuttable presumption that the obligor provide the insurance through his employer. He argues that when an obligor offers insurance coverage in complete compliance with state and federal guidelines, as he did, the trial judge must accept that offer. [¶] [U]nlike language in other sections of the Family Code, §14.061 does not create a rebuttable presumption requiring the judge to accept the obligor's offer of insurance when other alternatives are available. Section 14.061(a) requires a judge to 'consider' the costs and benefits and to 'give priority' to employer plans, but section (b)(1) provides merely that a judge 'may' order insurance through the obligor's employer, not that she must require employer coverage."

FAM §154.183. HEALTH INSURANCE ADDITIONAL SUPPORT DUTY OF OBLIGOR

(a) An amount that an obligor is required to pay for health insurance for the child:

(1) is in addition to the amount that the obligor is required to pay for child support under the guidelines for child support;

(2) is a child support obligation; and

(3) may be enforced as a child support obligation.

(b) If the court finds and states in the child support order that the obligee will maintain health insurance coverage for the child at the obligee's expense, the court may increase the amount of child support to be paid by the obligor in an amount not exceeding the total expense to the obligee for maintaining health insurance coverage.

(c) As additional child support, the court shall allocate between the parties, according to their circumstances, the reasonable and necessary health care expenses of a child that are not reimbursed by health insurance.

History of Fam §154.183: Acts 1995, 74th Leg., ch. 20, §1, eff. April 20, 1995. Source: Former Fam §§14.053(d), 14.061(c).

Wright v. Wright, 867 S.W.2d 807, 814 (Tex.App.—El Paso 1993, writ denied). "The language in §14.053(d) [now §154.183(c)] provides that 'the court will order the obligor to provide health insurance coverage for the child subject of the suit in addition to the amount of child support calculated pursuant to these guidelines.' We do not interpret that language to mean that the costs of such insurance can not be subtracted from the obligor's gross income to determine the amount of support due. The insurance costs paid by the obligor are to be paid in addition to the child support ordered by the trial court, in that the insurance costs are a separate obligation, not included within the amount of the child support ordered. [¶] In the present case, [obligor] was ordered to pay $618 per month in support. He was also ordered to maintain and pay for hospitalization insurance for the children. These insurance costs are not part of the $618; they are a separate obligation."

Stocker v. Magera, 807 S.W.2d 753, 755 (Tex. App.—Texarkana 1990, writ denied). "Another question presented on this appeal concerns [obligee's] claim that the trial court erred in setting an amount of child support 'plus medical insurance.' Under ... §14.053(d) [now §154.183(c)], the guidelines assume that the court will order the obligor to provide health insurance coverage in addition to the amount of child support calculated pursuant to the guidelines. It appears that the trial court has strictly complied with this provision by calculating the amount of support and additionally requiring that [obligor] provide health insurance coverage. [Obligee] shows no error in this regard."

FAM §154.184. EFFECT OF ORDER

(a) Receipt of a medical support order requiring that health insurance be provided for a child shall be considered a change in the family circumstances of the employee or member, for health insurance purposes, equivalent to the birth or adoption of a child.

(b) If the employee or member is eligible for dependent health coverage, the employer shall automatically enroll the child for the first 31 days after the receipt of the order or notice of the medical support order under Section 154.186 on the same terms and conditions as apply to any other dependent child.

(c) The employer shall notify the insurer of the automatic enrollment.

(d) During the 31-day period, the employer and insurer shall complete all necessary forms and procedures to make the enrollment permanent or shall report in accordance with this subchapter the reasons the coverage cannot be made permanent.

History of Fam §154.184: Acts 1995, 74th Leg., ch. 20, §1, eff. April 20, 1995. Amended by Acts 1995, 74th Leg., ch. 341, §4.03, eff. Sept. 1, 1995; Acts 1997, 75th Leg., ch. 911, §11, eff. Sept. 1, 1997. Source: Former Fam §14.061(r).

FAM §154.185. PARENT TO FURNISH INFORMATION

A *Section 154.185 below is effective for modification or enforcement proceedings commenced on or after Sept. 1, 2001.*

(a) The court shall order a parent providing health insurance to furnish to either the obligee, obligor, or child support agency the following information not later than the 30th day after the date the notice of rendition of the order is received:

(1) the social security number of the parent;

(2) the name and address of the parent's employer;

(3) whether the employer is self-insured or has health insurance available;

(4) proof that health insurance has been provided for the child;

(5) if the employer has health insurance available, the name of the health insurance carrier, the number of the policy, a copy of the policy and schedule of benefits, a health insurance membership card, claim forms, and any other information necessary to submit a claim; and

(6) if the employer is self-insured, a copy of the schedule of benefits, a membership card, claim forms, and any other information necessary to submit a claim.

(b) The court shall also order a parent providing health insurance to furnish the obligor, obligee, or child support agency with additional information regarding health insurance coverage not later than the 15th day after the date the information is received by the parent.

History of Fam §154.185: Acts 1995, 74th Leg., ch. 20, §1, eff. April 20, 1995. Amended by Acts 2001, 77th Leg., ch. 1023, §10, eff. Sept. 1, 2001. Source: Former Fam §14.061(e), (f).

FAM §154.185. PARENT TO FURNISH INFORMATION

Section 154.185 below is effective for modification or enforcement proceedings commenced before Sept. 1, 2001.

(a) The court shall order a parent providing health insurance to furnish to either the obligee, obligor, local domestic relations office, or Title IV-D agency the following information not later than the 30th day after the date the notice of rendition of the order is received:

(1) the social security number of the parent;

(2) the name and address of the parent's employer;

(3) whether the employer is self-insured or has health insurance available;

(4) proof that health insurance has been provided for the child;

(5) if the employer has health insurance available, the name of the health insurance carrier, the number of the policy, a copy of the policy and schedule of benefits, a health insurance membership card, claim forms, and any other information necessary to submit a claim; and

(6) if the employer is self-insured, a copy of the schedule of benefits, a membership card, claim forms, and any other information necessary to submit a claim.

(b) The court shall also order a parent providing health insurance to furnish the obligor, obligee, local domestic relations office, or Title IV-D agency with additional information regarding health insurance coverage not later than the 15th day after the date the information is received by the parent.

FAM §154.186. NOTICE TO EMPLOYER CONCERNING MEDICAL SUPPORT

The obligee, obligor, or a child support agency may send to the employer a copy of the order requiring an employee to provide health insurance coverage for a child or may include notice of the medical support order in an order or writ of withholding sent to the employer in accordance with Chapter 158.

History of Fam §154.186: Acts 1995, 74th Leg., ch. 20, §1, eff. April 20, 1995. Amended by Acts 1995, 74th Leg., ch. 341, §4.04, eff. Sept. 1, 1995; Acts 1997, 75th Leg., ch. 911, §12, eff. Sept. 1, 1997. Source: Former Fam §14.061(g).

FAM §154.187. DUTIES OF EMPLOYER

(a) An order or notice under this subchapter to an employer directing that health insurance coverage be provided to a child of an employee or member is binding on a current or subsequent employer on receipt without regard to the date the order was rendered. If the employee or member is eligible for dependent health coverage for the child, the employer shall immediately enroll the child in a health insurance plan regardless of whether the employee is enrolled in the plan. If dependent coverage is not available to the employee or member through the employer's health insurance plan or enrollment cannot be made permanent or if the employer is not responsible or otherwise liable for providing such coverage, the employer shall provide notice to the sender in accordance with Subsection (c).

(b) If additional premiums are incurred as a result of adding the child to the health insurance plan, the employer shall deduct the health insurance premium from the earnings of the employee in accordance with Chapter 158 and apply the amount withheld to payment of the insurance premium.

(c) An employer who has received an order or notice under this subchapter shall provide to the sender, by first class mail not later than the 30th day after the date the employer receives the order or notice, a statement that the child:

(1) has been enrolled in a health insurance plan; or

(2) cannot be enrolled or cannot be enrolled permanently in a health insurance plan and provide the reason why coverage or permanent coverage cannot be provided.

(d) If the employee ceases employment or if the health insurance coverage lapses, the employer shall provide to the sender, by first class mail not later than the 15th day after the date of the termination of employment or the lapse of the coverage, notice of the termination or lapse and of the availability of any conversion privileges.

(e) On request, the employer shall release to the sender information concerning the available health insurance coverage, including the name of the health insurance carrier, the policy number, a copy of the policy and schedule of benefits, a health insurance membership card, and claim forms.

(f) In this section, "sender" means the person sending the order under Section 154.186.

(g) An employer who fails to enroll a child, fails to withhold or remit premiums or cash medical support, or discriminates in hiring or employment on the basis of a medical support order shall be subject to the penalties and fines in Subchapter C, Chapter 158.

History of Fam §154.187: Acts 1995, 74th Leg., ch. 20, §1, eff. April 20, 1995. Amended by Acts 1995, 74th Leg., ch. 341, §4.05, eff. Sept. 1, 1995; Acts 1997, 75th Leg., ch. 911, §13, eff. Sept. 1, 1997. Source: Former Fam §14.061(h)-(k), (p).

FAM §154.188. FAILURE TO PROVIDE REQUIRED HEALTH INSURANCE

A *Section 154.188 below is effective for actions to enforce medical support orders commenced on or after Sept. 1, 2001.*

A parent ordered to provide health insurance who fails to do so is liable for:

(1) necessary medical expenses of the child, without regard to whether the expenses would have been paid if health insurance had been provided; and

E (2) the cost of health insurance premiums or contributions, if any, paid on behalf of the child.

History of Fam §154.188: Acts 1995, 74th Leg., ch. 20, §1, eff. April 20, 1995. Amended by Acts 2001, 77th Leg., ch. 295, §1, eff. Sept. 1, 2001. Source: Former Fam §14.061(*l*).

FAM §154.188. FAILURE TO PROVIDE REQUIRED HEALTH INSURANCE

Section 154.188 below is effective for actions to enforce medical support orders commenced before Sept. 1, 2001.

A parent ordered to provide health insurance who fails to do so is liable for necessary medical expenses of the child, without regard to whether the expenses would have been paid if health insurance had been provided.

FAM §154.189. NOTICE OF TERMINATION OR LAPSE OF INSURANCE COVERAGE

(a) An obligor ordered to provide health insurance coverage for a child must notify the obligee and any child support agency enforcing a support obligation against the obligor of the:

(1) termination or lapse of health insurance coverage for the child not later than the 15th day after the date of a termination or lapse; and

(2) availability of additional health insurance to the obligor for the child after a termination or lapse of coverage not later than the 15th day after the date the insurance becomes available.

(b) If termination of coverage results from a change of employers, the obligor, the obligee, or the child support agency may send the new employer a copy of the order requiring the employee to provide health insurance for a child or notice of the medical support order as provided by this subchapter.

History of Fam §154.189: Acts 1995, 74th Leg., ch. 20, §1, eff. April 20, 1995. Amended by Acts 1997, 75th Leg., ch. 911, §14, eff. Sept. 1, 1997. Source: Former Fam §14.061(m).

FAM §154.190. REENROLLING CHILD FOR INSURANCE COVERAGE

After health insurance has been terminated or has lapsed, an obligor ordered to provide health insurance coverage for the child must enroll the child in a health insurance plan at the next available enrollment period.

History of Fam §154.190: Acts 1995, 74th Leg., ch. 20, §1, eff. April 20, 1995. Source: Former Fam §14.061(m).

FAM §154.191. REMEDY NOT EXCLUSIVE

(a) This subchapter does not limit the rights of the obligor, obligee, local domestic relations office, or Title IV-D agency to enforce, modify, or clarify the medical support order.

(b) This subchapter does not limit the authority of the court to render or modify a medical support order containing a provision for payment of uninsured health expenses, health care costs, or health insurance premiums that are in addition to and inconsistent with this subchapter.

History of Fam §154.191: Acts 1995, 74th Leg., ch. 20, §1, eff. April 20, 1995. Source: Former Fam §14.061(n), (o).

Wright v. Wright, 867 S.W.2d 807, 813 (Tex.App.—El Paso 1993, writ denied). Section 14.061(o), now §154.191(b), "does not mandate an apportionment of uninsured medical expenses.... [¶] Section 14.061(o) leaves the issue of uncovered medical expenses to the discretion of the court, and as discussed above, the court's decision will be disturbed only if it acted without reference to guiding rules and principles. In the instant case, there was evidence before the trial court, in the form of testimony of both parties, that the parties wished to abide by the guidelines as found in the Texas Family Code. We find that the trial court properly exercised its discretion in refusing to provide for the payment of uninsured medical expenses, as payment of such is left to the sound discretion of the trial court pursuant to §14.061(o)."

FAM §154.192. CANCELLATION OR ELIMINATION OF INSURANCE COVERAGE FOR CHILD

(a) Unless the employee or member ceases to be eligible for dependent coverage, or the employer has eliminated dependent health coverage for all of the employer's employees or members, the employer may not cancel or eliminate coverage of a child enrolled under this subchapter until the employer is provided satisfactory written evidence that:

(1) the court order or administrative order requiring the coverage is no longer in effect; or

(2) the child is enrolled in comparable health insurance coverage or will be enrolled in comparable coverage that will take effect not later than the effective date of the cancellation or elimination of the employer's coverage.

History of Fam §154.192: Acts 1995, 74th Leg., ch. 20, §1, eff. April 20, 1995. Amended by Acts 1995, 74th Leg., ch. 341, §4.06, eff. Sept. 1, 1995. Source: Former Fam §14.061(q).

FAM §154.193. MEDICAL SUPPORT ORDER NOT QUALIFIED

(a) If a plan administrator or other person acting in an equivalent position determines that a medical support order issued under this subchapter does not qualify for enforcement under federal law, the tribunal may, on its own motion or the motion of a party, render an order that qualifies for enforcement under federal law.

(b) The procedure for filing a motion for enforcement of a final order applies to a motion under this section. Service of citation is not required, and a person is not entitled to a jury in a proceeding under this section.

(c) The employer or plan administrator is not a necessary party to a proceeding under this section.

History of Fam §154.193: Acts 1997, 75th Leg., ch. 911, §15, eff. Sept. 1, 1997.

Sections 154.194-154.240 reserved for expansion

SUBCHAPTER E. LOCAL CHILD SUPPORT REGISTRY

FAM §154.241. LOCAL REGISTRY

(a) A local registry shall receive a court-ordered child support payment or a payment otherwise authorized by law and shall forward the payment, as appropriate, to the Title IV-D agency, local domestic relations office, or obligee within two working days after the date the local registry receives the payment.

(b) A local registry may not require an obligor, obligee, or other party or entity to furnish a certified copy of a court order as a condition of processing child support payments and shall accept as sufficient authority to process the payments a photocopy, facsimile copy, or conformed copy of the court's order.

(c) A local registry shall include with each payment it forwards to the Title IV-D agency the date it received the payment and the withholding date furnished by the employer.

(d) A local registry shall accept child support payments made by personal check, money order, or cashier's check. A local registry may refuse payment by personal check if a pattern of abuse regarding the use of personal checks has been established. Abuse includes checks drawn on insufficient funds, abusive or offensive language written on the check, intentional mutilation of the instrument, or other actions that delay or disrupt the registry's operation.

(e) Subject to Section 154.004, at the request of an obligee, a local registry shall redirect and forward a child support payment to an address and in care of a person or entity designated by the obligee. A local registry may require that the obligee's request be in writing or be made on a form provided by the local registry for that purpose, but may not charge a fee for receiving the request or redirecting the payments as requested.

History of Fam §154.241: Acts 1995, 74th Leg., ch. 20, §1, eff. April 20, 1995. Amended by Acts 1995, 74th Leg., ch. 751, §42, eff. Sept. 1, 1995. Source: Former Fam §14.0501.

FAM §154.242. PAYMENT OR TRANSFER OF CHILD SUPPORT PAYMENTS BY ELECTRONIC FUNDS TRANSFER

(a) A child support payment may be made by electronic funds transfer to:

(1) the Title IV-D agency;

(2) a local registry if the registry agrees to accept electronic payment; or

(3) the state disbursement unit.

(b) A local registry may transmit child support payments to the Title IV-D agency by electronic funds transfer. Unless support payments are required to be made to the state disbursement unit, an obligor may make payments, with the approval of the court entering the order, directly to the bank account of the obligee by electronic transfer and provide verification of the deposit to the local registry. A local registry in a county that makes deposits into personal bank accounts by electronic funds transfer as of April 1, 1995, may transmit a child support payment to an obligee by electronic funds transfer if the obligee maintains a bank account and provides the local registry with the necessary bank account information to complete electronic payment.

History of Fam §154.242: Acts 1995, 74th Leg., ch. 20, §1, eff. April 20, 1995. Amended by Acts 1995, 74th Leg., ch. 597, §1, eff. Jan. 1, 1996; Acts 1997, 75th Leg., ch. 702, §2 (eff. Jan. 1, 1998), ch. 1053, §2 (eff. Sept. 1, 1997); Acts 1999, 76th Leg., ch. 556, §10, eff. Sept. 1, 1999. Source: Former Fam §14.0502.

FAM 154.243. PRODUCTION OF CHILD SUPPORT PAYMENT RECORD

The Title IV-D agency, a local registry, or the state disbursement unit may comply with a subpoena or other order directing the production of a child support payment record by sending a certified copy of the record or an affidavit regarding the payment record to the court that directed production of the record.

History of Fam §154.243: Acts 1995, 74th Leg., ch. 20, §1, eff. April 20, 1995. Amended by Acts 1999, 76th Leg., ch. 556, §10, eff. Sept. 1, 1999. Source: Former Fam §14.0504.

Sections 154.244-154.300 reserved for expansion

SUBCHAPTER F. SUPPORT FOR A MINOR OR ADULT DISABLED CHILD

FAM §154.301. DEFINITIONS

In this subchapter:

(1) "Adult child" means a child 18 years of age or older.

(2) "Child" means a son or daughter of any age.

History of Fam §154.301: Acts 1995, 74th Leg., ch. 20, §1, eff. April 20, 1995. Source: Former Fam §14.051(a).

FAM §154.302. COURT-ORDERED SUPPORT FOR DISABLED CHILD

(a) The court may order either or both parents to provide for the support of a child for an indefinite period and may determine the rights and duties of the parents if the court finds that:

(1) the child, whether institutionalized or not, requires substantial care and personal supervision because of a mental or physical disability and will not be capable of self-support; and

(2) the disability exists, or the cause of the disability is known to exist, on or before the 18th birthday of the child.

(b) A court that orders support under this section shall designate a parent of the child or another person having physical custody or guardianship of the child under a court order to receive the support for the child. The court may designate a child who is 18 years of age or older to receive the support directly.

History of Fam §154.302: Acts 1995, 74th Leg., ch. 20, §1, eff. April 20, 1995. Amended by Acts 1997, 75th Leg., ch. 1173, §1, eff. Sept. 1, 1997. Source: Former Fam §14.051(b).

Worford v. Stamper, 801 S.W.2d 108, 108 (Tex. 1990). "Under the original divorce decree, [obligor] was ordered to pay $180 per month in child support until his son, ... reached the age of eighteen. [Son] was five years old at the time of the divorce. [¶] [Obligee] filed a motion to modify the 1975 order in June 1986, requesting that the child support payments be increased and continued past the age of eighteen. It was undisputed by the parties that [son] would be unable to support himself after the age of eighteen due to various physical and mental handicaps. When [son] was fifteen years old, his developmental levels were between three and five years. His speech is unintelligible except to those closest to him and familiar with his responses. [Son] also suffers from a dentofacial deformity which makes it difficult for him to chew his food and maintain proper hygiene. *At 109:* The trial court entered a final modification order ..., increasing [obligor's] child support payments to $1350 per month and extending such payments beyond [son's] eighteenth birthday. *At 110:* Based upon [obligor's] net income and the special needs of the child in this case, we hold that the trial court did not abuse its discretion by entering an order of child support in the amount of $1350 per month."

Garland v. Garland, 868 S.W.2d 847, 849-50 (Tex. App.—Dallas 1993, no writ). Obligee argues that §14.051(b), now §154.302(a), "vests in the family district court the power to determine [child's] guardianship. The language of §14.051(b) grants the family district court continuing jurisdiction to enter orders relating to the support of the child only. Section 14.051(b) allows a family district court to order support for a disabled adult child, but, as recently reinforced by the legislature, any guardianship of that adult child must first be filed in the statutory probate court. We note that the probate code, as amended, allows a statutory probate court to transfer the guardianship of the person of a minor, but not an 'adult child,' to a court of continuing jurisdiction, such as a family district court. [Child] is not a minor. [¶] For these reasons, this Court holds that a family district court's continuing jurisdiction over support of a disabled adult child does not vest that court with jurisdiction to grant or deny a guardianship of that adult child's estate. Guardianship of the person or the estate of an adult child in Dallas County must first be filed in a statutory probate court."

FAM §154.303. STANDING TO SUE

(a) A suit provided by this subchapter may be filed only by:

(1) a parent of the child or another person having physical custody or guardianship of the child under a court order; or

(2) the child if the child:

(A) is 18 years of age or older;

(B) does not have a mental disability; and

(C) is determined by the court to be capable of managing the child's financial affairs.

(b) The parent, the child, if the child is 18 years of age or older, or other person may not transfer or assign the cause of action to any person, including a governmental or private entity or agency, except for an assignment made to the Title IV-D agency.

History of Fam §154.303: Acts 1995, 74th Leg., ch. 20, §1, eff. April 20, 1995. Amended by Acts 1997, 75th Leg., ch. 1173, §2, eff. Sept. 1, 1997. Source: Former Fam §14.051(c).

FAM §154.304. GENERAL PROCEDURE

Except as otherwise provided by this subchapter, the substantive and procedural rights and remedies in a suit affecting the parent-child relationship relating to the establishment, modification, or enforcement of a child support order apply to a suit filed and an order rendered under this subchapter.

History of Fam §154.304: Acts 1995, 74th Leg., ch. 20, §1, eff. April 20, 1995. Source: Former Fam §14.051(i).

FAM §154.305. SPECIFIC PROCEDURES

(a) A suit under this subchapter may be filed:

(1) regardless of the age of the child; and

(2) as an independent cause of action or joined with any other claim or remedy provided by this code.

(b) If no court has continuing, exclusive jurisdiction of the child, an action under this subchapter may be filed as an original suit affecting the parent-child relationship.

(c) If there is a court of continuing, exclusive jurisdiction, an action under this subchapter may be filed as a suit for modification as provided by Chapter 156.

History of Fam §154.305: Acts 1995, 74th Leg., ch. 20, §1, eff. April 20, 1995. Source: Former Fam §14.051(d)-(f).

FAM §154.306. AMOUNT OF SUPPORT AFTER AGE 18

In determining the amount of support to be paid after a child's 18th birthday, the specific terms and conditions of that support, and the rights and duties of both parents with respect to the support of the child, the court shall determine and give special consideration to:

(1) any existing or future needs of the adult child directly related to the adult child's mental or physical disability and the substantial care and personal supervision directly required by or related to that disability;

(2) whether the parent pays for or will pay for the care or supervision of the adult child or provides or will provide substantial care or personal supervision of the adult child;

(3) the financial resources available to both parents for the support, care, and supervision of the adult child; and

(4) any other financial resources or other resources or programs available for the support, care, and supervision of the adult child.

History of Fam §154.306: Acts 1995, 74th Leg., ch. 20, §1, eff. April 20, 1995. Source: Former Fam §14.051(g).

FAM §154.307. MODIFICATION & ENFORCEMENT

An order provided by this subchapter may contain provisions governing the rights and duties of both parents with respect to the support of the child and may be modified or enforced in the same manner as any other order provided by this title.

History of Fam §154.307: Acts 1995, 74th Leg., ch. 20, §1, eff. April 20, 1995. Source: Former Fam §14.051(h).

FAM §154.308. REMEDY NOT EXCLUSIVE

(a) This subchapter does not affect a parent's:

(1) cause of action for the support of a disabled child under any other law; or

(2) ability to contract for the support of a disabled child.

(b) This subchapter does not affect the substantive or procedural rights or remedies of a person other than a parent, including a governmental or private entity or agency, with respect to the support of a disabled child under any other law.

History of Fam §154.308: Acts 1995, 74th Leg., ch. 20, §1, eff. April 20, 1995. Source: Former Fam §14.051(j), (k).

FAM §154.309. POSSESSION OF OR ACCESS TO ADULT DISABLED CHILD

(a) A court may render an order for the possession of or access to an adult disabled child that is appropriate under the circumstances.

(b) Possession of or access to an adult disabled child is enforceable in the manner provided by Chapter 157. An adult disabled child may refuse possession or access if the adult disabled child is mentally competent.

(c) A court that obtains continuing, exclusive jurisdiction of a suit affecting the parent-child relationship involving a disabled person who is a child retains continuing, exclusive jurisdiction of subsequent proceedings involving the person, including proceedings after the person is an adult.

History of Fam §154.309: Acts 1995, 74th Leg., ch. 751, §43, eff. Sept. 1, 1995.

CHAPTER 155. CONTINUING, EXCLUSIVE JURISDICTION; TRANSFER

SUBCHAPTER A. CONTINUING, EXCLUSIVE JURISDICTION

FAM §155.001. ACQUIRING CONTINUING, EXCLUSIVE JURISDICTION

(a) Except as otherwise provided by this section, a court acquires continuing, exclusive jurisdiction over the matters provided for by this title in connection with a child on the rendition of a final order.

(b) The following final orders do not create continuing, exclusive jurisdiction in a court:

(1) a voluntary or involuntary dismissal of a suit affecting the parent-child relationship;

Ⓐ *Subsection (2) below is effective for motions or other requests for relief made in parentage or paternity proceedings commenced on or after June 14, 2001.*

(2) in a suit to determine parentage, a final order finding that an alleged or presumed father is not the father of the child, except that the jurisdiction of the court is not affected if the child was subject to the jurisdiction of the court or some other court in a suit affecting the parent-child relationship before the commencement of the suit to adjudicate parentage; and

Subsection (2) below is effective for motions or other requests for relief made in parentage or paternity proceedings commenced before June 14, 2001.

(2) in a suit to determine parentage, a final order finding that an alleged or presumed father is not the biological father of the child, except that the jurisdiction of the court is not affected if the child was subject to the jurisdiction of the court or some other court in a suit affecting the parent-child relationship before the commencement of the suit to determine parentage; and

(3) a final order of adoption, after which a subsequent suit affecting the child must be commenced as though the child had not been the subject of a suit for adoption or any other suit affecting the parent-child relationship before the adoption.

(c) If a court of this state has acquired continuing, exclusive jurisdiction, no other court of this state has jurisdiction of a suit with regard to that child except as provided by this chapter or Chapter 262.

(d) Unless a final order has been rendered by a court of continuing, exclusive jurisdiction, a subsequent suit shall be commenced as an original proceeding.

History of Fam §155.001: Acts 1995, 74th Leg., ch. 20, §1, eff. April 20, 1995. Amended by Acts 1999, 76th Leg., ch. 62, §6.19, eff. Sept. 1, 1999; Acts 2001, 77th Leg., ch. 821, §2.15, eff. June 14, 2001. Source: Former Fam §11.05(a), (b), (d), (e).

Alexander v. Russell, 699 S.W.2d 209, 210 (Tex. 1985). "Section 11.06 [now §155.204] requires a timely motion by any party to the suit to transfer the proceedings. Absent a motion and order of transfer, the 243rd District Court retained exclusive jurisdiction. Despite what the conservatorship order says about the 327th District Court having jurisdiction, there is no order transferring the cause to the 327th District Court. Thus, the 243rd District Court retained jurisdiction. Any attempted transfer of this cause to the 327th District Court was not for a reason authorized under §11.06 and therefore the judge had no authority to transfer the cause. If the judge of the 243rd District Court found it necessary to recuse himself, the proper procedure was to have another district judge preside in the 243rd District Court, not to transfer the cause."

Ramsey v. Ramsey, 19 S.W.3d 548, 554 n.7 (Tex. App.—Austin 2000, no pet.). "It is worth noting that while, standing alone, §155.001 may appear to establish by its strong language a rigid jurisdictional rule, the statutory scheme surrounding that provision reveals that it is designed to operate more in the nature of dominant jurisdiction or venue, rather than true jurisdiction. For instance, on a showing that a suit for divorce has been filed in another court, the court having continuing, exclusive jurisdiction of a [SAPCR] *must* transfer the SAPCR proceedings to the divorce court. The task of transferring the case is a mandatory, ministerial duty. [¶] Additionally, if the court in which the divorce is pending renders a final judgment after being led by the bureau of vital statistics to believe erroneously that no court of continuing, exclusive jurisdiction existed, the first court is deemed to have lost its jurisdiction, and the divorce decree of the second court is enforceable—child custody and support issues included. This same policy is implicated in this case, although here the erroneous information was supplied by the parties, rather than the bureau of vital statistics. [¶] In light of these provisions, we believe that the scheme employed by §155.001 does not concern true *jurisdiction*, in the strictest sense of the word. Rather, it is more comparable to dominant jurisdiction or the rules of venue."

Fleming v. Easton, 998 S.W.2d 252, 255 (Tex. App.—Dallas 1999, no pet.). "Because [mother's] claims involve matters pertaining to the parent-child relationship between [father] and their child, the district court that had previously acquired jurisdiction over the child through [the couple's] divorce action, retains continuing and exclusive jurisdiction to decide these issues. [¶] The district court's acquisition of jurisdiction over the [P-C] issues in this case preceded any jurisdiction that could have been acquired by the probate court. This case is distinguishable, therefore, from those in which the probate court acquired dominant jurisdiction by virtue of the administration of the estate being the 'first filed action.' Because jurisdiction vested in the district court before the probate court acquired jurisdiction over [father's] estate, the probate court would have had to *divest* the district court of its jurisdiction before deciding this case. We see nothing in the record to indicate that a transfer or other form of permissible divestiture took place. [¶] Furthermore, we have found no authority that would automatically divest the district court of its jurisdiction over the parent-child relationship upon [father's] death. Indeed, previously decided cases clearly indicate that the district court's continuing jurisdiction over the issues in this case was not affected by [father's] death."

Garland v. Garland, 868 S.W.2d 847, 849 (Tex. App.—Dallas 1993, no writ). Mother argues that §11.05(a), now §155.001, vests "concurrent jurisdiction in the family court over [son's] guardianship proceeding. The term 'child' as used in §11.05(a) ... is defined in §11.01(1) [now §101.003] as 'a person under 18 years of age who is not and has not been married or who has not had his disabilities of minority removed for general purposes.' In this case, [son] was twenty-two years old at the time the application for guardianship was filed. Because [son] was twenty-two years old, he was not a 'child' as defined in §11.01(1). Since he was not a child as defined by the statute, §11.05(a) [does] not apply."

Ex parte Holland, 807 S.W.2d 827, 827 (Tex.App.—Dallas 1991, writ dism'd). "Husband contends that the [contempt] order is void because the visiting judge who signed it was without authority to preside in the contempt proceeding. *At 829:* Under §11.05(a) [now §155.001], when a court acquires jurisdiction of a [SAPCR], it retains continuing, exclusive jurisdiction of various subsequent suits in connection with the child. Contempt proceedings brought to enforce child support obligations fall within this continuing jurisdiction. Thus we must consider whether, because of this continuing jurisdiction, [the visiting judge] retained jurisdiction to enter the ... order of contempt and commitment. [¶] Opinions construing orders of assignment in non-family law matters and cases under the [F]amily [C]ode have distinguished between an individual judge's authority and the jurisdiction of the court in which he is sitting. *At 830:* [W]e conclude that the trial court's continuing jurisdiction in family law matters vested no jurisdiction in [the visiting judge] that was independent of the ... order of assignment. Nor did the court's continuing jurisdiction extend the duration of his authority under that assignment. [The visiting judge's] assignment expired with the expiration of his plenary power.... Absent a new assignment, he was without authority to preside in the contempt proceedings leading to the ... order of contempt and commitment."

Creavin v. Moloney, 773 S.W.2d 698, 702 (Tex. App.—Corpus Christi 1989, writ denied). "In the instant case, the Pennsylvania court entered a decree of divorce, but failed to enter any judgment regarding the parent-child relationship. No final order has been entered regarding the parent-child relationship in the Pennsylvania court.... Moreover, neither the child nor the parties presently reside in Pennsylvania, but each maintains their principal residence outside of that state. [¶] We conclude, therefore, that the Pennsylvania court which entered the decree of divorce no longer has jurisdiction to modify that decree on any matter affecting the parent-child relationship. Further, we conclude that insofar as the Texas court has jurisdiction over the causes of action, a subsequent suit could be commenced as an original proceeding in the Texas courts."

Ault v. Mulanax, 724 S.W.2d 824, 830 (Tex.App.—Texarkana 1986, no writ). "In the event that two different courts have a divorce action pending which include the parent-child relationship or two courts have matters which involve only the parent-child relationship, then when the court having dominant jurisdiction renders a final decree, the jurisdiction of the other court will terminate. When a final decree is entered by a court, it acquires continuing, exclusive jurisdiction pursuant to Section 11.05(e) [now §155.001]. This section further provides that a voluntary dismissal of a [SAPCR] prior to a final decree terminates all the jurisdiction of the court, and that unless a final decree has been entered by a court of continuing, exclusive jurisdiction, a subsequent suit shall be commenced as an original proceeding."

Crockett v. Crockett, 589 S.W.2d 759, 763 (Tex. App.—Dallas 1979, writ ref'd n.r.e.). Father "claims that the Ohio court which rendered the divorce decree has continuing and exclusive jurisdiction over all [SAPCRs], including modification of support and visitation. On the other hand, [mother] argues that 'continuing jurisdiction,' as defined in §11.05 [now §§155.001, 155.002], relates only to Texas courts and has no extraterritorial effect. [¶] We ... hold that §11.05(a), when it mentions 'continuing jurisdiction,' refers only to courts within the State of Texas and has no extraterritorial application."

Ex parte Pepper, 544 S.W.2d 836, 839 (Tex.App.—Amarillo 1976), *writ dism'd*, 548 S.W.2d 884 (Tex.1977). "The paternal grandparents, possessing the order for visitation with the children, were given notice of the adoption proceedings. The final decree of adoption reserved no rights to them. The legal effect of the adoption decree was to end the trial court's continuing jurisdiction over the preadoption proceedings, §11.05(b) [now §155.001(b)(3)], and, except for the children's right to inherit from their natural parents, to sever old legal ties and to create new legal relationships. Accordingly, the prior order for grandparental visitation ceased to have any legal effect upon entry of the final decree of adoption."

FAM §155.002. RETAINING CONTINUING, EXCLUSIVE JURISDICTION

Except as otherwise provided by this subchapter, a court with continuing, exclusive jurisdiction retains jurisdiction of the parties and matters provided by this title.

History of Fam §155.002: Acts 1995, 74th Leg., ch. 20, §1, eff. April 20, 1995. Amended by Acts 1999, 76th Leg., ch. 62, §6.20, eff. Sept. 1, 1999. Source: Former Fam §11.05(a).

Hudson v. Markum, 931 S.W.2d 336, 337 (Tex. App.—Dallas 1996, no writ). "A [SAPCR] includes a suit to determine paternity. A motion to modify child support is also a '[SAPCR].' A child support order 'may be modified only by the filing of a motion in the court having continuing, exclusive jurisdiction of the [SAPCR] as provided by §11.05 [now §156.002] of this code.' *At 338:* No one contests the trial court's jurisdiction to decide the paternity and support of the child who is the subject of this suit. Once the trial court decided the paternity and support of the child, it acquired continuing jurisdiction over the parent-child relationship. It retained continuing, exclusive jurisdiction to hear a new proceeding affecting that relationship."

Welsh v. Welsh, 905 S.W.2d 615, 616-17 (Tex. App.—Houston [14th Dist.] 1995, writ denied). Plaintiff argues "that the case was transferred to an Impact Court in violation of the Family Code's specific provisions concerning how and when a case may be transferred to another court. Challenges to impact courts have arisen in numerous contexts, most frequently in criminal cases in which an appellant is contesting the legitimacy of the court itself. Such cases have been routinely resolved in favor of the legitimacy of these courts. ... All of these cases are resolved on the basis of the constitutional provision that authorizes district judges to hold court for each other when they deem it expedient. Out of this constitutional language comes the authorization for one district judge to try cases for another district judge, 'in the same court at the same time, each occupying a different courtroom.' These principles bear out [defendant's] contention that the Impact Court is a type of derivative court, a court acting as the 328th but with a different judge and in a different courtroom. [¶] All the documentation in the record, in addition to the caselaw resolving questions concerning impact courts, leads to the conclusion that this cause remained in the appropriate court, the 328th, the court of continuing jurisdiction."

Lewis v. McCoy, 747 S.W.2d 48, 49 (Tex.App.—El Paso 1988, orig. proceeding). "What happens to the court's jurisdiction and order as to custody when the mother dies? In ***Greene v. Schuble***, 654 S.W.2d 436 (Tex.1983), the majority of the Court, in a mandamus proceeding, agreed that upon the death of the managing conservator the divorce decree no longer constituted a valid order governing possession of the child. *At 50:* We do not read the majority opinion in ***Greene v. Schuble***, ... to hold that the death of the managing conservator terminates the jurisdiction of the court which appointed the conservator. ... Since the Dallas County District Court originally had jurisdiction and the death of the managing conservator did not terminate that jurisdiction, another court could not obtain jurisdiction without a transfer order. This would include a probate court where an application was filed for appointment of a temporary guardian. [¶] We conclude that the Dallas County District Court had continuing jurisdiction to name a managing conservator for [the minor child] after her mother died." *See also* ***Dohrn v. Delgado***, 941 S.W.2d 244, 248 (Tex.App.—Corpus Christi 1996, no writ) (death of one of the parties to a divorce decree does not terminate the continuing jurisdiction of the court rendering the decree over the children, if any, who are still subject to further orders and supervision by the court as long as they are minors).

FAM §155.003. EXERCISE OF CONTINUING, EXCLUSIVE JURISDICTION

(a) Except as otherwise provided by this section, a court with continuing, exclusive jurisdiction may exercise its jurisdiction to modify its order regarding managing conservatorship, possessory conservatorship, possession of and access to the child, and support of the child.

(b) A court of this state may not exercise its continuing, exclusive jurisdiction to modify managing conservatorship if:

(1) the child's home state is other than this state; or

(2) modification is precluded by Chapter 152.

(c) A court of this state may not exercise its continuing, exclusive jurisdiction to modify possessory conservatorship or possession of or access to a child if:

(1) the child's home state is other than this state and all parties have established and continue to maintain their principal residence outside this state; or

(2) each individual party has filed written consent with the tribunal of this state for a tribunal of another state to modify the order and assume continuing, exclusive jurisdiction of the suit.

(d) A court of this state may not exercise its continuing, exclusive jurisdiction to modify its child support order if modification is precluded by Chapter 159.

History of Fam §155.003: Acts 1995, 74th Leg., ch. 20, §1, eff. April 20, 1995. Source: Former Fam §11.05(g).

In re Bellamy, 67 S.W.3d 482, 484 (Tex.App.—Texarkana 2002, n.p.h.). "[W]e find that §§152.202 and 155.003(b)(1) conflict in this case. When a provision of Chapter 152 conflicts with another provision of the Family Code or another statute or rule of Texas and the conflict cannot be reconciled, Chapter 152 prevails. Under the UCCJEA, Texas retains jurisdiction even if Texas is no longer the home state of the child or of the custodial parent, so long as there is a significant connection with this state."

FAM §155.004. LOSS OF CONTINUING, EXCLUSIVE JURISDICTION

(a) A court of this state loses its continuing, exclusive jurisdiction to modify its order if:

(1) an order of adoption is rendered after the court acquires continuing, exclusive jurisdiction of the suit;

(2) the parents of the child have remarried each other after the dissolution of a previous marriage between them and file a suit for the dissolution of their subsequent marriage combined with a suit affecting the parent-child relationship as if there had not been a prior court with continuing, exclusive jurisdiction over the child; or

(3) another court assumed jurisdiction over a suit and rendered a final order based on incorrect information received from the bureau of vital statistics that there was no court of continuing, exclusive jurisdiction.

(b) This section does not affect the power of the court to enforce its order for a violation that occurred before the time continuing, exclusive jurisdiction was lost under this section.

History of Fam §155.004: Acts 1995, 74th Leg., ch. 20, §1, eff. April 20, 1995. Amended by Acts 1997, 75th Leg., ch. 575, §8, eff. Sept. 1, 1997. Source: Former Fam §11.05(b), (f), (g).

FAM §155.005. JURISDICTION PENDING TRANSFER

(a) During the transfer of a suit from a court with continuing, exclusive jurisdiction, the transferring court retains jurisdiction to render temporary orders.

(b) The jurisdiction of the transferring court terminates on the docketing of the case in the transferee court.

History of Fam §155.005: Acts 1995, 74th Leg., ch. 20, §1, eff. April 20, 1995. Source: Former Fam §11.05(h).

Bigham v. Dempster, 901 S.W.2d 424, 430 (Tex. 1995). Mother argues "a number of the Family Code transfer provisions ... require that docketing occur only after the full file of original documents or certified copies have been supplied *by the transferring clerk*, and that certified copies from parties, as from [father] here, may not be the basis for 'docketing.' She urges we must read these provisions into the definition of 'docketing' for §11.05(h) [now §155.005(b)]. [¶] We cannot agree that the jurisdiction of the court turns on whether, or with what diligence, a clerk performs a ministerial duty to forward court documents. The Family Code places a ministerial duty on both the judge and the clerk of the transferring court to expedite the transfer of records to the transferee court. *At 431:* The definition of 'docketing' should be consistent with this purpose of expediting the transfer process. We conclude that a transfer case is 'docketed' when the traditional legal meaning of the event has occurred, rather than when all certified document copies have been ministerially sent (expressly by the clerk, not someone else) or other limitations urged by [mother] have been met."

Sections 155.006-155.100 reserved for expansion

SUBCHAPTER B. IDENTIFICATION OF COURT OF CONTINUING, EXCLUSIVE JURISDICTION

FAM §155.101. REQUEST FOR IDENTIFICATION OF COURT OF CONTINUING, EXCLUSIVE JURISDICTION

(a) The petitioner or the court shall request from the bureau of vital statistics identification of the court that last had continuing, exclusive jurisdiction of the child in a suit unless:

(1) the petition alleges that no court has continuing, exclusive jurisdiction of the child and the issue is not disputed by the pleadings; or

(2) the petition alleges that the court in which the suit or petition to modify has been filed has acquired and retains continuing, exclusive jurisdiction of the child as the result of a prior proceeding and the issue is not disputed by the pleadings.

(b) The bureau of vital statistics shall, on the written request of the court, an attorney, or a party:

(1) identify the court that last had continuing, exclusive jurisdiction of the child in a suit and give the docket number of the suit; or

(2) state that the child has not been the subject of a suit.

(c) The child shall be identified in the request by name, birthdate, and place of birth.

(d) The bureau of vital statistics shall transmit the information not later than the 10th day after the date on which the request is received.

History of Fam §155.101: Acts 1995, 74th Leg., ch. 20, §1, eff. April 20, 1995. Amended by Acts 1995, 74th Leg., ch. 751, §44, eff. Sept. 1, 1995; Acts 1999, 76th Leg., ch. 178, §8, eff. Aug. 30, 1999. Source: Former Fam §11.071(a), (b).

In re M.R.M., 807 S.W.2d 779, 783 (Tex.App.—Houston [14th Dist.] 1991, writ denied). Father "contends the court erred when it failed to dismiss this suit without prejudice since 'it discovered another court was the court of continuing jurisdiction.' [¶] The petition filed by the Harris County Children's Protective Services specifically alleged that no other court had continuing jurisdiction. Both [mother] and the attorney ad litem for the children filed general denials. Furthermore, [father's] attorney appeared in this cause and never contested the transfer. We find that the issue of continuing jurisdiction was not disputed in the pleadings and, therefore, the Harris County Children's Protective Service was not required to make a request to the Texas Department of Human Services. Thus, the court did not err in refusing to dismiss this suit."

Crockett v. Crockett, 589 S.W.2d 759, 764 (Tex. App.—Dallas 1979, writ ref'd n.r.e.). Section 11.071, now §155.101, "provides the procedure by which a court of continuing jurisdiction is to be identified. The petitioner or the court is to request from the State Department of Public Welfare [now the Bureau of Vital Statistics] the identification of the court of continuing jurisdiction if a question exists whether any court has continuing jurisdiction. Obviously, the legislature did not expect the State Department of Public Welfare to maintain records on out-of-state courts having jurisdiction over every child that comes into Texas or every child that might be the subject of a [Texas SAPCR]. It is ridiculous to assume that the legislature would have enacted a system which would require the courts to perform these useless acts. Thus, the only reasonable context in which the term 'continuing jurisdiction' can be read is as applying exclusively to Texas courts."

Brown v. Brown, 555 S.W.2d 784, 786 (Tex.App.—El Paso 1977, no writ). "But §11.071(a)(1) [now §155.101(a)(1)] requires information from the State Department of Public Welfare [now the Bureau of Vital Statistics] unless 'the issue is not disputed by the pleadings.' We conclude that when [father] alleged that another Court had granted custody of the minor child to the mother, the issue of continuing jurisdiction was raised, and such pleading disputed the prior allegation that no other Court had continuing jurisdiction. *At 787:* Thus, we conclude that [father's] own pleadings did dispute the allegation of no other Court having continuing jurisdiction. In such instance, it was incumbent upon him or the Court to obtain information from [the Bureau of Vital Statistics] as to the identity of the Court having continuing jurisdiction, and any order entered in the absence of such information is voidable."

FAM §155.102. DISMISSAL

If a court in which a suit is filed determines that another court has continuing, exclusive jurisdiction of the child, the court in which the suit is filed shall dismiss the suit without prejudice.

History of Fam §155.102: Acts 1995, 74th Leg., ch. 20, §1, eff. April 20, 1995. Source: Former Fam §11.071(d).

Counts v. Counts, 560 S.W.2d 186, 188 (Tex.App.—Dallas 1977, no writ). Section 11.071(d), now §155.102, provides "that if the court in which a [SAPCR] petition is filed ... determines that another court has continuing jurisdiction, which factual determination was made here, then the court should dismiss the suit without prejudice. In this case, the issue with respect to the jurisdiction of the Dallas court was ... challenged by [mother's] motion to dismiss, attaching copies of a certified order of the Schleicher court clearly showing that the Schleicher court was the court with continuing jurisdiction of the parent-child relationship. When the welfare department sent its erroneous report to the contrary, an obvious conflict in the evidence was presented which [mother] attempted to resolve by requesting the welfare department to recheck its records. This recheck of the records of the welfare department resulted in a corrected report reflecting the Schleicher court as the court with continuing jurisdiction of the parent-child relationship. Thus, in our opinion, the Dallas court acted properly in dismissing the suit and preventing the unseemly conflict between two courts.... Accordingly, we hold that once the Dallas court was informed by the welfare department that the Schleicher County Court had continuing exclusive jurisdiction over the minor child, whether it be a first report or an amended one, it had the duty to dismiss the case without prejudice."

FAM §155.103. RELIANCE ON BUREAU OF VITAL STATISTICS INFORMATION

(a) A court shall have jurisdiction over a suit if it has been, correctly or incorrectly, informed by the bureau of vital statistics that the child has not been the subject of a suit and the petition states that no other court has continuing, exclusive jurisdiction over the child.

(b) If the bureau of vital statistics notifies the court that the bureau has furnished incorrect information regarding the existence of another court with continuing, exclusive jurisdiction before the rendition of a final order, the provisions of this chapter apply.

History of Fam §155.103: Acts 1995, 74th Leg., ch. 20, §1, eff. April 20, 1995. Amended by Acts 1995, 74th Leg., ch. 751, §45, eff. Sept. 1, 1995. Source: Former Fam §11.05(c).

FAM §155.104. VOIDABLE ORDER

(a) If a request for information from the bureau of vital statistics relating to the identity of the court having continuing, exclusive jurisdiction of the child has been made under this subchapter, a final order, except an order of dismissal, may not be rendered until the information is filed with the court.

(b) If a final order is rendered in the absence of the filing of the information from the bureau of vital statistics, the order is voidable on a showing that a court other than the court that rendered the order had continuing, exclusive jurisdiction.

History of Fam §155.104: Acts 1995, 74th Leg., ch. 20, §1, eff. April 20, 1995. Amended by Acts 1995, 74th Leg., ch. 751, §46, eff. Sept. 1, 1995. Source: Former Fam §11.071(c).

Sections 155.105-155.200 reserved for expansion

SUBCHAPTER C. TRANSFER OF CONTINUING, EXCLUSIVE JURISDICTION

FAM §155.201. MANDATORY TRANSFER

(a) On a showing that a suit for dissolution of the marriage of the child's parents has been filed in another court, the court having continuing, exclusive jurisdiction of a suit affecting the parent-child relationship shall transfer the proceedings to the court in which the dissolution of the marriage is pending.

(b) If a suit to modify or a motion to enforce an order is filed in the court having continuing, exclusive jurisdiction of a suit, on the timely motion of a party the court shall transfer the proceeding to another county in this state if the child has resided in the other county for six months or longer.

(c) If a suit to modify or a motion to enforce an order is pending at the time a subsequent suit to modify or motion to enforce is filed, the court may transfer the proceeding as provided by Subsection (b) only if the court could have transferred the proceeding at the time the first motion or suit was filed.

History of Fam §155.201: Acts 1995, 74th Leg., ch. 20, §1, eff. April 20, 1995. Amended by Acts 1999, 76th Leg., ch. 1135, §1, eff. Sept. 1, 1999. Source: Former Fam §11.06(b), (c).

Tippy v. Walker, 865 S.W.2d 928, 929 (Tex.1993). "This petition for writ of mandamus raises the issue of whether the six months residency period for mandatory transfer of venue in child custody modification motions under ... §11.06(b) [now §155.201(b)] only begins to run after the original custody decree is signed, or at the earlier date when the child's actual residency in the different county begins. Here the facts are that although the child had continuous residency with the mother in Harris County for fifteen months prior to her filing of the motion to transfer venue, the motion was filed less than six months after Judge Walker actually signed the original final custody order. [¶] The respondent and real party in interest have had notice and opportunity to respond, but have offered no argument beyond that advanced in the trial court—that the six months only begins to run after the decree is finally signed. We previously *implicitly* held that residency runs from the earlier date in holding that transfer was mandatory in ***Arias v. Spector***, 623 S.W.2d 312 (Tex.1981). In our computation in ***Arias*** we included part of the pre-judgment residency period to reach the required total residency then specified in §11.06(b). We now make that implicit holding explicit."

Proffer v. Yates, 734 S.W.2d 671, 672 (Tex.1987). "The writ of mandamus has been available to compel mandatory transfer in [SAPCRs] for a number of years. *At 673:* Transfer of a case to a county where the child has resided for more than six months is a mandatory ministerial duty under §11.06(b) [now §155.201(b)]. And remedy by appeal, though available, is frequently inadequate to protect the rights of parents and children to a trial in a particular venue. Parents and children who have a right under the mandatory venue provisions to venue in a particular county should not be forced to go through a trial that is for naught. Justice demands a speedy resolution of child custody and child support issues."

Leonard v. Paxson, 654 S.W.2d 440, 441 (Tex. 1983). "The venue provisions of the Family Code remove [SAPCRs] from the operation of the general venue statute and the transfer provisions set forth in §11.06(b) [now §155.201] supplant the [TRCPs] governing pleas of privilege. Section 11.01(5) [now §101.032] defines a [SAPCR] as, among other things, 'a suit ... in which ... support of a child ... is sought.' [Mother's] motion, which seeks modification of [a Texas child support order], is clearly a '[SAPCR].'"

Seay v. Valderas, 643 S.W.2d 395, 396 (Tex.1982). Section 11.06(b), now §155.201(b), "provides that on a timely motion of any party, and a showing that venue is proper in another county, the court shall transfer the proceeding to the county where venue is proper. ... This Court has held this section is mandatory."

Cassidy v. Fuller, 568 S.W.2d 845, 847 (Tex.1978). "[W]e hold that §11.06(b) [now §155.201(b)] is mandatory in its provision that '... the court, on the timely motion of any party, and on a showing that venue is proper in another county ... *shall* transfer the proceeding to the county where venue is proper....' While the use of the word 'shall' is not necessarily determinative that a statute is mandatory, it clearly was so intended here. Immediately following in §11.06(b) is the further provision [now §155.202(a)] that the court 'may' deny the motion (for a change of venue where the child resides in another county) if it is shown that the child has not resided in such county for at least six months. The mandatory provisions of the statute are invoked here by the motion to transfer the proceeding to Clay County where it is undisputed that the two children of the marriage, together with ... their appointed managing conservator, have resided more than six months." *See also* ***Brod v. Baker***, 591 S.W.2d 457, 458 (Tex.1979).

FAM §155.202. DISCRETIONARY TRANSFER

(a) If the basis of a motion to transfer a proceeding under this subchapter is that the child resides in another county, the court may deny the motion if it is shown that the child has resided in that county for less than six months at the time the proceeding is commenced.

(b) For the convenience of the parties and witnesses and in the interest of justice, the court, on the timely motion of a party, may transfer the proceeding to a proper court in another county in the state.

History of Fam §155.202: Acts 1995, 74th Leg., ch. 20, §1, eff. April 20, 1995. Source: Former Fam §11.06(b), (d).

Hathorn v. Sivers, 962 S.W.2d 284, 286 n.3 (Tex. App.—Houston [14th Dist.] 1998, no writ). "When the Texas Legislature revised the Texas Family Code in 1995, §11.06(d) became §155.202(b). When it was renumbered, the text did not change. We recognize that former §11.06(d) and §155.202(b) refer to transfers to other counties in the state, not intra-county transfers. The case law, however, refers to these sections of the Family Code when dealing with intra-county transfers. We see no reason to treat intra-county transfers differently, and therefore find §155.202(b) is applicable to this case. *At 287:* In this case, [mother's] motion specifically stated that the transfer was sought because she believed 'that the matters at hand may be handled more expeditiously for the parties and for the District Court, if this case is transferred to the county court.' We find that this is simply another way of stating that the request is for the convenience of the parties and in the interest of justice, a reason specifically authorizing transfers under §155.202 of the Family Code for discretionary transfers. Thus, ... we hold that the transfer to the county court at law was appropriate under §155.202(b) because there was a proper motion and order."

FAM §155.203. DETERMINING COUNTY OF CHILD'S RESIDENCE

In computing the time during which the child has resided in a county, the court may not require that the period of residence be continuous and uninterrupted but shall look to the child's principal residence during the six-month period preceding the commencement of the suit.

History of Fam §155.203: Acts 1995, 74th Leg., ch. 20, §1, eff. April 20, 1995. Source: Former Fam §11.06(b).

FAM §155.204. PROCEDURE FOR TRANSFER

(a) Except as provided by Section 262.203, a motion to transfer by a petitioner or movant is timely if it is made at the time the initial pleadings are filed. A motion to transfer by another party is timely if it is made on or before the first Monday after the 20th day after the date of service of citation or notice of the suit or before the commencement of the hearing, whichever is sooner. If a timely motion to transfer has been filed and no controverting affidavit is filed within the period allowed for its filing, the proceeding shall be transferred promptly without a hearing to the proper court.

(b) On or before the first Monday after the 20th day after the date of notice of a motion to transfer is served, a party desiring to contest the motion must file a controverting affidavit denying that grounds for the transfer exist.

(c) If a controverting affidavit contesting the motion to transfer is filed, each party is entitled to notice not less than 10 days before the date of the hearing on the motion to transfer.

(d) Only evidence pertaining to the transfer may be taken at the hearing.

(e) An order transferring or refusing to transfer the proceeding is not subject to interlocutory appeal.

(f) If a transfer order has been rendered by a court exercising jurisdiction under Chapter 262, a party may file the transfer order with the clerk of the court of continuing, exclusive jurisdiction. On receipt and without a hearing, the clerk of the court of continuing, exclusive jurisdiction shall transfer the files as provided by this subchapter.

History of Fam §155.204: Acts 1995, 74th Leg., ch. 20, §1, eff. April 20, 1995. Amended by Acts 1999, 76th Leg., ch. 1150, §1 (eff. Sept. 1, 1999), ch. 1390, §14 (eff. Sept. 1, 1999). Source: Former Fam §11.06(f)-(i).

Alexander v. Russell, 699 S.W.2d 209, 210 (Tex. 1985). "Section 11.06 [now §155.204] requires a timely motion by any party to the suit to transfer the proceedings. Absent a motion and order of transfer, the 243rd District Court retained exclusive jurisdiction. Despite what the conservatorship order says about the 327th District Court having jurisdiction, there is no order transferring the cause to the 327th District Court. Thus, the 243rd District Court retained jurisdiction. Any attempted transfer of this cause to the 327th District

Court was not for a reason authorized under §11.06 and therefore the judge had no authority to transfer the cause. If the judge of the 243rd District Court found it necessary to recuse himself, the proper procedure was to have another district judge preside in the 243rd District Court, not to transfer the cause."

In re S.G.S., 53 S.W.3d 848, 851 (Tex.App.—Fort Worth 2001, no pet.). Wife argues that husband's "motion to transfer was untimely because he did not move to transfer jurisdiction ... when he filed a proposed agreed order to modify their divorce decree to award [husband] 100% of the [bank] account. [Wife] contends that [husband's] filing of the proposed agreed order is the 'initial pleading' under §155.204(a). Thus, she argues that [husband], as the petitioner or movant, was required to file his motion to transfer venue then. [¶] Section 155.204(a), however, applies only to [SAPCRs]. Unlike [wife]'s ... petition that sought to modify the children's visitation schedules, [husband]'s ... proposed order sought only to modify their property settlement. Therefore, his proposed order was not a [SAPCR] and he was not required to file his transfer motion when he filed the proposed order."

Bollard v. Berchelmann, 921 S.W.2d 861, 864 (Tex. App.—San Antonio 1996, no writ). "A motion to modify a [SAPCR] must be filed in the court of continuing, exclusive jurisdiction; but, upon '*timely* motion of a party the court shall transfer the proceeding to another county in this state if the child has resided in the other county for six months or longer.' The timeliness of a motion depends upon whether the movant is a petitioner or 'other party'.... *At 865:* As [child's] biological mother, [mother] had standing to file a motion to modify. Although she could have filed an intervention under [TRCP] 60, she could also become a plaintiff or petitioner by adding her name to an amended petition. In this case, [mother] was not required to intervene because she had no interests adverse to that of her parents; they agreed that [mother] should be named as one of three joint managing conservators. *At 866:* Section 155.204 ... does not distinguish between petitioners and counter-petitioners. Instead, '[a] motion to transfer by a petitioner or movant is timely if it is made at the time *the initial pleadings* are filed.' ... Because [mother] joined the suit as a counter-petitioner, and on the same day filed her motion to transfer, her motion was timely."

FAM §155.205. TRANSFER OF CHILD SUPPORT REGISTRY

A *Section 155.205 below is effective for modification or enforcement proceedings commenced on or after Sept. 1, 2001.*

(a) On rendition of an order transferring continuing, exclusive jurisdiction to another court, the transferring court shall also order that all future payments of child support be made to the local registry of the transferee court or, if payments have previously been directed to the state disbursement unit, to the state disbursement unit.

(b) The transferring court's local registry or the state disbursement unit shall continue to receive, record, and forward child support payments to the payee until it receives notice that the transferred case has been docketed by the transferee court.

(c) After receiving notice of docketing from the transferee court, the transferring court's local registry shall send a certified copy of the child support payment record to the clerk of the transferee court and shall forward any payments received to the transferee court's local registry or to the state disbursement unit, as appropriate.

History of Fam §155.205: Acts 1995, 74th Leg., ch. 20, §1, eff. April 20, 1995. Amended by Acts 1999, 76th Leg., ch. 556, §11, eff. Sept. 1, 1999; Acts 2001, 77th Leg., ch. 1023, §11, eff. Sept. 1, 2001. Source: Former Fam §§11.05(h), 11.06(j).

FAM §155.205. TRANSFER OF CHILD SUPPORT REGISTRY

Section 155.205 below is effective for modification or enforcement proceedings commenced before Sept. 1, 2001.

(a) On rendition of an order transferring continuing, exclusive jurisdiction to another court, the transferring court shall also order that all future payments of child support be made to the local registry of the transferee court, the Title IV-D agency, or the state disbursement unit.

(b) The transferring court's local registry, the Title IV-D agency, or the state disbursement unit shall continue to receive, record, and forward child support payments to the payee until it receives notice that the transferred case has been docketed by the transferee court.

(c) After receiving notice of docketing from the transferee court, the transferring court's local registry shall send a certified copy of the child support payment record to the clerk of the transferee court and shall forward any payments received to the transferee court's local registry.

FAM §155.206. EFFECT OF TRANSFER

(a) A court to which a transfer is made becomes the court of continuing, exclusive jurisdiction and all proceedings in the suit are continued as if it were brought there originally.

(b) A judgment or order transferred has the same effect and shall be enforced as if originally rendered in the transferee court.

(c) The transferee court shall enforce a judgment or order of the transferring court by contempt or by any other means by which the transferring court could have enforced its judgment or order. The transferee court shall have the power to punish disobedience of the transferring court's order, whether occurring before or after the transfer, by contempt.

(d) After the transfer, the transferring court does not retain jurisdiction of the child who is the subject of the suit, nor does it have jurisdiction to enforce its order for a violation occurring before or after the transfer of jurisdiction.

History of Fam §155.206: Acts 1995, 74th Leg., ch. 20, §1, eff. April 20, 1995. Source: Former Fam §11.06(k).

Seay v. Valderas, 643 S.W.2d 395, 396 (Tex.1982). "Almost three months [after the initial transfer order was rendered,] Judge Valderas rendered an order vacating [that transfer order]. Judge Valderas ordered the clerk of the court in Comanche County to immediately return to Tarrant County the complete files in the case. *At 397:* Once a court has transferred a case it looses jurisdiction of the child. ... Although a transfer order is an interlocutory order, it is final as to the transferring judge once the judge loses plenary power over the order. [¶] Judge Valderas had no authority to exercise control over the [SAPCR] [by rendering a later order vacating the transfer order]."

Ex parte Barnett, 600 S.W.2d 252, 255 (Tex.1980). "It would indeed be anomalous to permit courts to enforce by contempt proceedings the orders of another court in the circumstances described, but not permit the transferee court to enforce the orders of the transferring court in the face of the legislative intent clearly manifested in the Family Code that the new 'court of continuing jurisdiction' decide all matters relating to the subject matter of the case transferred. We hold that the district court of Collin County is empowered under the provisions of the Family Code to hear and decide pending and new contempt proceedings arising from the alleged failure to comply with orders of the transferring district court of Dallas County, regardless of whether all or some of the alleged contemptuous acts were committed before the transfer of the cause to the transferee court."

Wilemon v. Wilemon, 930 S.W.2d 290, 292 (Tex. App.—Waco 1996, no writ). "The Family Code mandates that a court exercising continuing exclusive jurisdiction over a SAPCR is mandatorily required to transfer any subsequent SAPCR to the county where the child at issue has resided for six months or more. In the present case, the 330th District Court of Dallas County was the proper court of continuing and exclusive jurisdiction.... Consequently, when [mother] filed her Motion to Transfer, which she properly supported with affidavit proof that the child had resided in Navarro County for six months or more, the 330th District Court was required to transfer not only [mother's] modification suit, but also its continuing exclusive jurisdiction over all suits affecting the [parties'] child, to the 13th District Court of Navarro County."

FAM §155.207. TRANSFER OF COURT FILES

(a) On rendition of an order of transfer, the clerk of the court transferring a proceeding shall send to the proper court in the county to which transfer is being made:

A *Subsection (1) below is effective for modification or enforcement proceedings commenced on or after Sept. 1, 2001.*

(1) the complete files in all matters affecting the child in any pending proceeding;

Subsection (1) below is effective for modification or enforcement proceedings commenced before Sept. 1, 2001.

(1) the complete files in all matters affecting the child;

(2) certified copies of all entries in the minutes;

(3) a certified copy of any order of dissolution of marriage rendered in a suit joined with the suit affecting the parent-child relationship; and

(4) a certified copy of each order rendered.

(b) The clerk of the transferring court shall keep a copy of the transferred files. If the transferring court retains jurisdiction of another child who was the subject of the suit, the clerk shall send a copy of the complete files to the court to which the transfer is made and shall keep the original files.

A *Subsections (c) & (d) below are effective for modification or enforcement proceedings commenced on or after Sept. 1, 2001.*

(c) On receipt of the files, documents, and orders from the transferring court, the clerk of the transferee court shall docket the suit and shall notify all parties, the clerk of the transferring court, and, if appropriate, the transferring court's local registry that the suit has been docketed.

(d) The clerk of the transferring court shall send a certified copy of the order directing payments to the transferee court, to any party or employer affected by that order, and, if appropriate, to the local registry of the transferee court.

Subsections (c) & (d) below are effective for modification or enforcement proceedings commenced before Sept. 1, 2001.

(c) On receipt of the files, documents, and orders from the transferring court, the clerk of the transferee court shall docket the suit and shall notify all parties, the clerk of the transferring court, and the transferring court's local registry that the suit has been docketed.

(d) The clerk of the transferring court shall send a certified copy of the order directing payments to the transferee court, to any party or employer affected by that order, and to the local registry of the transferee court.

History of Fam §155.207: Acts 1995, 74th Leg., ch. 20, §1, eff. April 20, 1995. Amended by Acts 2001, 77th Leg., ch. 1023, §12, eff. Sept. 1, 2001. Source: Former Fam §11.06(j), (m).

Bigham v. Dempster, 901 S.W.2d 424, 430 (Tex. 1995). "We cannot agree that the jurisdiction of the court turns on whether, or with what diligence, a clerk performs a ministerial duty to forward court documents. ... Section 11.06(j) [now §155.207] provides '[t]he court transferring a proceeding *shall send* to the proper court in the county to which transfer is made *the complete files* in all matters *affecting the child*, certified copies of all entries in the minutes,' and other specifically designated records. Although it refers to the receipt of all files, the apparent purpose of §11.06(m) [now §155.207(c)] is not to delay jurisdiction in the transferee court until it receives all files, but to require the clerk of the transferee court to declare the suit docketed after all files have been received. *At 431:* The term 'docketed' in our jurisprudence has the connotation not only of the clerk's formally placing the case on the list of cases pending in the court, but also of notice that the court is ready to act on the matter, to take jurisdiction over it. ... The rule is that the case is docketed when the court to which it is transferred has received a certified copy of the transfer order and asserts jurisdiction, or when all files have been transferred, whichever occurs first."

Ex parte Barnett, 600 S.W.2d 252, 254 (Tex.1980). "When a transfer is ordered, the transferring court, except when it retains jurisdiction of another child, sends 'the complete files in all matters affecting the child' and certified copies of entries in the minutes and of the decree of divorce to the transferee court."

Sections 155.208-155.300 reserved for expansion

SUBCHAPTER D. TRANSFER OF PROCEEDINGS WITHIN THE STATE WHEN PARTY OR CHILD RESIDES OUTSIDE THE STATE

FAM §155.301. AUTHORITY TO TRANSFER

(a) A court of this state with continuing, exclusive jurisdiction over a suit or an action for child support under Chapter 159 shall transfer the proceeding to the county of residence of the resident party if one party is a resident of this state and all other parties including the child or all of the children affected by the proceedings reside outside this state.

(b) If one or more of the parties affected by the proceedings reside outside the state and if more than one party or one or more children affected by the proceeding reside in this state in different counties, the court shall transfer the proceeding according to the following priorities:

(1) to the court of continuing, exclusive jurisdiction, if any;

(2) to the county of residence of the child, if applicable, provided that:

(A) Subdivision (1) is inapplicable; or

(B) the court of continuing, exclusive jurisdiction finds that neither a party nor a child affected by the proceeding resides in the county of the court of continuing, exclusive jurisdiction; or

(3) if Subdivisions (1) and (2) are inapplicable, to the county most appropriate to serve the convenience of the resident parties, the witnesses, and the interest of justice.

(c) If a transfer of continuing, exclusive jurisdiction is sought under this section, the procedures for determining and effecting a transfer of proceedings provided by this chapter apply.

History of Fam §155.301: Acts 1995, 74th Leg., ch. 20, §1, eff. April 20, 1995. Source: Former Fam §11.061.

CHAPTER 156. MODIFICATION

SUBCHAPTER A. GENERAL PROVISIONS

FAM §156.001. ORDERS SUBJECT TO MODIFICATION

A court with continuing, exclusive jurisdiction may modify an order that provides for the conservatorship, support, or possession of and access to a child.

History of Fam §156.001: Acts 1995, 74th Leg., ch. 20, §1, eff. April 20, 1995. Source: Former Fam §§11.05(g), 14.08(a).

Broyles v. Ashworth, 782 S.W.2d 31, 34 (Tex. App.—Fort Worth 1989, orig. proceeding). "The trial court is without authority to amend an order designating managing conservators in the absence of the filing of a motion to modify."

Rogers v. Griffin, 774 S.W.2d 706, 707 (Tex.App.—Texarkana 1989, no writ). "A court order that provides for the support of a child may be modified *only* by filing a motion in the court having continuing, exclusive jurisdiction of the [SAPCR]. Parents do not have the authority to reduce or modify court-ordered child support provisions without express court approval; such agreements violate public policy and are unenforceable."

FAM §156.002. WHO CAN FILE

(a) A party affected by an order may file a suit for modification in the court with continuing, exclusive jurisdiction.

(b) A person or entity who, at the time of filing, has standing to sue under Chapter 102 may file a suit for modification in the court with continuing, exclusive jurisdiction.

History of Fam §156.002: Acts 1995, 74th Leg., ch. 20, §1, eff. April 20, 1995. Source: Former Fam §§11.03(f), 14.08(a).

Hudson v. Markum, 931 S.W.2d 336, 338 n.5 (Tex. App.—Dallas 1996, no writ). "We note that the recodification of §14.08 [now §156.002] refers to 'a suit for modification' rather than 'a motion to modify.' This change emphasizes that the legislature intends the trial courts to continue to treat motions to modify as original lawsuits."

McDuffie v. Blassingame, 883 S.W.2d 329, 334 (Tex.App.—Amarillo 1994, writ denied). "The Texas Family Code provides that an order setting the terms and conditions for conservatorship of, support of, or access to a child may be modified by filing a motion in the court having continuing, exclusive jurisdiction of the [SAPCR]. The Family Code also provides that any party affected by the prior decree may file such a motion. Furthermore, in determining the jurisdiction of the trial court, allegations made in good faith in the petition are determinative of the cause of action."

FAM §156.003. NOTICE

A party whose rights and duties may be affected by a suit for modification is entitled to receive notice by service of citation.

History of Fam §156.003: Acts 1995, 74th Leg., ch. 20, §1, eff. April 20, 1995. Amended by Acts 1999, 76th Leg., ch. 178, §9, eff. Aug. 30, 1999. Source: Former Fam §§11.08(c), 14.08(b).

FAM §156.004. PROCEDURE

The Texas Rules of Civil Procedure applicable to the filing of an original lawsuit apply to a suit for modification under this chapter.

History of Fam §156.004: Acts 1995, 74th Leg., ch. 20, §1, eff. April 20, 1995. Source: Former Fam §14.08(b).

FAM §156.005. FRIVOLOUS FILING OF SUIT FOR MODIFICATION

If the court finds that a suit for modification is filed frivolously or is designed to harass a party, the court shall tax attorney's fees as costs against the offending party.

History of Fam §156.005: Acts 1995, 74th Leg., ch. 20, §1, eff. April 20, 1995. Source: Former Fam §14.082.

Warchol v. Warchol, 853 S.W.2d 165, 170 (Tex. App.—Beaumont 1993, no writ). "In determining whether the trial court abused its discretion in awarding attorney's fees we must look to the evidence presented, as well as evidence not presented. We do find evidence in the record that the child did not want to leave her mother to live with the father. We find no corroborating evidence supporting the contention that the child should live with the father and be taken away from the mother. Also lacking is evidence of [father's] stable living conditions, that [father] could care for the child on a daily basis, that the [father] had plans or routines for the child, nor was there evidence of any support persons available to assist the father in the care of the child. [Father] did take the child to a local psychiatrist ... but offered no testimony from [the doctor]. [¶] [Father] has failed to show this Court any abuse of trial court discretion regarding the award of $5,000 attorney's fees."

FAM §156.006. TEMPORARY ORDERS

(a) Except as provided by Subsection (b), the court may render a temporary order in a suit for modification.

(A) (b) While a suit for modification is pending, the court may not render a temporary order that has the effect of changing the designation of the person who has the exclusive right to determine the primary residence of the child under the final order unless:

(1) the order is necessary because the child's present living environment may endanger the child's physical health or significantly impair the child's emotional development;

(2) the person designated in the final order has voluntarily relinquished the primary care and possession of the child for more than six months and the temporary order is in the best interest of the child; or

(3) the child is 12 years of age or older and has filed with the court in writing the name of the person who is the child's preference to have the exclusive right to determine the primary residence of the child and the temporary order designating that person is in the best interest of the child.

History of Fam §156.006: Acts 1995, 74th Leg., ch. 20, §1, eff. April 20, 1995. Amended by Acts 1999, 76th Leg., ch. 1390, §15, eff. Sept. 1, 1999; Acts 2001, 77th Leg., ch. 1289, §3, eff. Sept. 1, 2001. Source: Former Fam §§11.11(a), 14.08(g).

Saxton v. Daggett, 864 S.W.2d 729, 736 (Tex. App.—Houston [1st Dist.] 1993, orig. proceeding). "Temporary orders under §11.11(a) [now §156.006] are not appealable. Mandamus is the appropriate remedy to attack the issuance of temporary orders...."

Bolden v. Clapp, 751 S.W.2d 674, 676 (Tex.App.—Tyler 1988, orig. proceeding). "The question of law involved is what constitutes voluntary relinquishment of actual care, control, and possession so as to satisfy the requirement of §14.08(g)(2) [now §156.006(b)(2)] and thus empowering the trial court to enter temporary orders. [Mother] contends that relinquishment is the equivalent of abandonment and analogizes the requirements of §14.08(g)(2) to those for involuntary termination of parental rights under §15.02 [now §161.001]. That analogy is inapt. The statutes differ in their provisions and their purposes. *At 677:* We believe §14.08(g)(2) requires something less than the showing required by §15.02. Since the consequences of an action or order under Chapter 14 are not as far-reaching, irrevocable and complete, we conclude that a lesser showing satisfies the voluntary relinquishment requirement of section 14.08(g)(2)."

Sections 156.007-156.100 reserved for expansion

Ⓐ SUBCHAPTER B. MODIFICATION OF CONSERVATORSHIP, POSSESSION & ACCESS, OR DETERMINATION OF RESIDENCE

Ⓐ FAM §156.101. GROUNDS FOR MODIFICATION OF ORDER ESTABLISHING CONSERVATORSHIP OR POSSESSION & ACCESS

The court may modify an order or portion of a decree that provides for the appointment of a conservator of a child, that provides the terms and conditions of conservatorship, or that provides for the possession of or access to a child if modification would be in the best interest of the child and:

(1) the circumstances of the child, a conservator, or other party affected by the order have materially and substantially changed since the date of the rendition of the order;

(2) the child is at least 12 years of age and has filed with the court, in writing, the name of the conservator who is the child's preference to have the exclusive right to determine the primary residence of the child; or

Ⓔ *Subsection (3) below is effective for actions to modify an order in a SAPCR pending on or filed on or after Sept. 1, 2001.*

(3) the conservator who has the exclusive right to establish the primary residence of the child has voluntarily relinquished the primary care and possession of the child to another person for at least six months.

History of Fam §156.101: Acts 1995, 74th Leg., ch. 20, §1, eff. April 20, 1995. Amended by Acts 1995, 74th Leg., ch. 751, §47, eff. Sept. 1, 1995; Acts 1999, 76th Leg., ch. 1390, §16, eff. Sept. 1, 1999; Acts 2001, 77th Leg., ch. 1289, §§4, 5, eff. Sept. 1, 2001. Source: Former Fam §14.08(c)(1), (g)(3).

Lenz v. Lenz, ___ S.W.3d ___ (Tex.2002) (No. 01-0232; 6-6-02). "The Legislature has made clear that 'the best interest of the child shall always be the primary consideration of the court in determining the issues of conservatorship and possession of and access to the child.' Yet, the Family Code does not elaborate on the specific requirements for modification in the residency-restriction context, and we have no specific statute governing residency restrictions or their removal for purposes of relocation. Neither have Texas courts articulated any specific standards to apply in this context. Nonetheless, the Legislature has provided a basic framework upon which we may build guidelines for reviewing a modification that removes a residency restriction for purposes of relocation. Family Code 153.001 outlines this framework by pronouncing our public policy for all suits affecting the parent-child relationship.... We must endeavor to give meaning to these public policy imperatives as we interpret the Family Code modification standards in the relocation context."

In re Ferguson, 927 S.W.2d 766, 768-69 (Tex. App.—Texarkana 1996, no writ). "If a nonparent rebuts the presumption in the original custody determination, the parents in a subsequent modification proceeding must meet the requirements for a change of custody set out in ... §156.101."

In re Marriage of Chandler, 914 S.W.2d 252, 254, (Tex.App.—Amarillo 1996, no writ). "Though now creatures of statute, the elements expressed in §14.08(c) [now §§156.101, 156.103, 156.104, 156.301, 156.401] went undefined by the legislature. So, courts have been left to develop a body of common law construing them. For instance, they recognize that not every changed circumstance warrants modification. Yet, many deem changes which may injuriously affect the child's best interest sufficient to require modification. Those include, among other things, remarriage by a parent, poisoning the child's mind against a parent, or mistreatment of the child by a parent or step-parent. [¶] Additionally, the state maintains a paramount interest in fostering a stable home environment for children. To bolster this interest, jurists also hold that repeated changes in the child's home environment supply ground for redesignating managing conservators. [¶] Similarly, a course of conduct pursued by the manager which hampers the ward's opportunities to favorably associate with the other parent may also suffice."

Considine v. Considine, 726 S.W.2d 253, 255 (Tex. App.—Austin 1987, no writ). "To prove that a material change of circumstance has occurred, the movant must demonstrate what conditions existed at the time of the entry of the prior order. Once such conditions have been established, movant must show what material changes have occurred in the intervening period."

Guy v. Stubberfield, 666 S.W.2d 176, 180 (Tex. App.—Dallas 1983, no writ). "[T]he record reflects that the relationship between [father] and [mother] had become strained and that in February, 1982, [mother] decided to use [father's] paternal love for [child] as a weapon in the dispute by denying him access to their child even though the legitimation decree named [father] as possessory conservator with certain limited rights to possession. Thus, the evidence established that [child] was used by the managing conservator, [mother], as a pawn in a dispute with the child's father that arose concerning [child]. Therefore, there is evidence that the managing conservator, [mother], was the person responsible for the deprivation of a custody arrangement beneficial to the child and that [mother] continued to act so as to deprive the child of that beneficial arrangement through her position as managing conservator until time of trial. Accordingly, we hold that the evidence raised a fact issue as to whether retention of [mother] as managing conservator would be injurious to the child's welfare."

A FAM §156.102. MODIFICATION OF EXCLUSIVE RIGHT TO DETERMINE PRIMARY RESIDENCE OF CHILD WITHIN ONE YEAR OF ORDER

(a) If a suit seeking to modify the designation of the person having the exclusive right to determine the primary residence of a child is filed not later than one year after the date of rendition of the order, the person filing the suit shall execute and attach an affidavit as provided by Subsection (b).

(b) The affidavit must contain, along with supporting facts, at least one of the following allegations:

(1) that the child's present environment may endanger the child's physical health or significantly impair the child's emotional development;

(2) that the person who has the exclusive right to determine the primary residence of the child is the person seeking or consenting to the modification and the modification is in the best interest of the child; or

(3) that the person who has the exclusive right to determine the primary residence of the child has voluntarily relinquished the primary care and possession of the child for at least six months and the modification is in the best interest of the child.

(c) The court shall deny the relief sought and refuse to schedule a hearing for modification under this section unless the court determines, on the basis of the affidavit, that facts adequate to support an allegation listed in Subsection (b) are stated in the affidavit. If the court determines that the facts stated are adequate to support an allegation, the court shall set a time and place for the hearing.

History of Fam §156.102: Acts 1995, 74th Leg., ch. 20, §1, eff. April 20, 1995. Amended by Acts 2001, 77th Leg., ch. 1289, §6, eff. Sept. 1, 2001. Source: Former Fam §14.08(d), (e).

Mobley v. Mobley, 684 S.W.2d 226, 229 (Tex.App.—Fort Worth 1985, writ dism'd). "It is obvious that the intention of the Legislature in putting §14.08(d) [now §156.102(a)] in the Family Code was to assure stability to the provision for custody of divorced parents and to prevent the custody award from being relitigated within a short period of time, except in cases involving the children's physical health and emotional development. Therefore, §14.08(e) [now §156.102(c)] requires that an initial determination be made by the court as to whether the facts sworn to in the affidavit supporting the motion to modify justify a hearing. [¶]To be entitled to have the motion set for a hearing in the instant case, [mother] had to state adequate facts to support the allegation that the child's physical health *may* be endangered or his emotional development significantly impaired. The facts alleged had to be sufficient to show the *possibility* of harm rather than the existence of harm."

Dunker v. Dunker, 659 S.W.2d 106, 109 (Tex. App.—Houston [14th Dist.] 1983, no writ). Mother "contends that the trial court erred … in allowing any hearing on the modification without the sworn affidavit required in … §14.08(d) [now §156.102(a)]. In this case, the motion to modify was filed by the [father] less than one year from the date of the original divorce. This motion cited the [mother] for contempt and requested a modification of visitation. An amended motion to modify was filed shortly thereafter. Within a short period of time, the [mother] responded by Original Answer and requested a transfer of the hearing to the State of Indiana. Later, still within one year, the [mother] filed a motion to modify with an affidavit attached which, among other statements, states that 'a co or joint managing conservator situation is not a viable or workable arrangement because of the child's age and the distance involved'. With the pleadings, the case was set for a hearing and the [father] was appointed the managing conservator. We feel that the requirement of the affidavit is designed not only to prevent relitigation within a short period of time after the divorce but, where both parties seek modification of the original order, it is also within the discretion of the trial court to set the modification application for a hearing. The two motions raised the same issues; [mother] sought the very opposite relief sought by [father]. The courts are given wide discretion in such proceedings. [Mother's] contention on this point of error cannot be sustained...."

Jilek v. Chatman, 613 S.W.2d 558, 559-60 (Tex. App.—Beaumont 1981, no writ). "The proper procedure to be followed upon the filing of a motion pursuant to §14.08(d) [now §156.102(a)] is to present the motion to the trial court immediately upon the filing of such motion and obtain a date for hearing. This will enable the court to make the determination of the adequacy of the contents of the required affidavit. If such presentment is not made, a hearing date, based upon emergency conditions affecting the child, will not and cannot be made. In the absence of any such presentment to the trial court within the one year period following the initial custody order, we hold that such motion then can be set for hearing, and a hearing can be had thereon as if it was a motion to modify under any other relevant section of the Family Code which does not require the §14.08(d) affidavit. Under the facts of this case, we hold [mother's] motion to modify, which was set for hearing and actually was heard four months after the expiration of one year following the original custody order, could properly be heard by the trial court."

DeLeon v. Periman, 530 S.W.2d 174, 176 (Tex. App.—Amarillo 1975, orig. proceeding). "It is to be noticed that ... the [L]egislature specified that the court *shall* deny a §14.08(d) [now §156.102(a)] motion unless the court determines that the attached affidavit expresses adequate facts to support his allegation, in which event the court *shall* schedule a hearing. [¶] Considering the nature and object of the parent-child relationship legislation and the effect thereon of contrasting consequences that flow from the mandatory or directory construction given the word 'shall' as used in §14.08(e) [now §156.102(c)], it is evident that the legislature intended to use the word in the mandatory sense. ... Obviously, then, the legislature intended, and we hold, that upon presentation of a §14.08(d) motion filed in the court of continuing jurisdiction, the judge is required to entertain the motion and to seasonably either deny the motion and refuse to schedule a hearing or, if the affidavit be deemed adequate, schedule a hearing on its merits."

FAM §156.103. INCREASED EXPENSES BECAUSE OF CHANGE OF RESIDENCE

E *Section 156.103 below is effective for actions to modify an order in a SAPCR pending on or filed on or after Sept. 1, 2001.*

(a) If a change of residence results in increased expenses for a party having possession of or access to a child, the court may render appropriate orders to allocate those increased expenses on a fair and equitable basis, taking into account the cause of the increased expenses and the best interest of the child.

(b) The payment of increased expenses by the party whose residence is changed is rebuttably presumed to be in the best interest of the child.

(c) The court may render an order without regard to whether another change in the terms and conditions for the possession of or access to the child is made.

History of Fam §156.103: Enacted by Acts 2001, 77th Leg., ch. 1289, §7, eff. Sept. 1, 2001.

History of Former Fam §156.103: Acts 1995, 74th Leg., ch. 20, §1, eff. April 20, 1995. Deleted by Acts 2001, 77th Leg., ch. 1289, §7, eff. Sept. 1, 2001. Source: Former Fam §14.08(c)(4).

FAM §156.104. MODIFICATION OF ORDER ON CONVICTION FOR CHILD ABUSE; PENALTY

E *Section 156.104 below is effective for actions to modify an order in a SAPCR pending on or filed on or after Sept. 1, 2001.*

(a) Except as provided by Section 156.1045, the conviction of a conservator, or an order deferring adjudication with regard to the conservator, for an offense involving the abuse of a child under Section 21.11, 22.011, or 22.021, Penal Code, is a material and substantial change of circumstances sufficient to justify a temporary order and modification of an existing court order or portion of a decree that provides for the appointment of a conservator or that sets the terms and conditions of conservatorship or for the possession of or access to a child.

(b) A person commits an offense if the person files a suit to modify an order or portion of a decree based on the grounds permitted under Subsection (a) and the person knows that the person against whom the motion is filed has not been convicted of an offense, or received deferred adjudication for an offense, under Section 21.11, 22.011, or 22.021, Penal Code. An offense under this subsection is a Class B misdemeanor.

History of Fam §156.104: Enacted by Acts 2001, 77th Leg., ch. 1289, §8, eff. Sept. 1, 2001.

History of Former Fam §156.104: Acts 1995, 74th Leg., ch. 20, §1, eff. April 20, 1995. Deleted by Acts 2001, 77th Leg., ch. 1289, §8, eff. Sept. 1, 2001. Source: Former Fam §§14.021(g), 14.08(c)(5).

FAM §156.1045. MODIFICATION OF ORDER ON CONVICTION FOR FAMILY VIOLENCE

Ⓔ *Section 156.1045 below is effective for actions to modify an order in a SAPCR pending on or filed on or after Sept. 1, 2001.*

(a) The conviction or an order deferring adjudication of a person who is a possessory conservator or a sole or joint managing conservator for an offense involving family violence is a material and substantial change of circumstances sufficient to justify a temporary order and modification of an existing court order or portion of a decree that provides for the appointment of a conservator or that sets the terms and conditions of conservatorship or for the possession of or access to a child to conform the order to the requirements of Section 153.004(d).

(b) A person commits an offense if the person files a suit to modify an order or portion of a decree based on the grounds permitted under Subsection (a) and the person knows that the person against whom the motion is filed has not been convicted of an offense, or received deferred adjudication for an offense, involving family violence. An offense under this subsection is a Class B misdemeanor.

History of Fam §156.1045: Enacted by Acts 2001, 77th Leg., ch. 1289, §9, eff. Sept. 1, 2001.

FAM §156.105. REPEALED

Repealed by Acts 2001, 77th Leg., ch. 1289, §12(1), eff. Sept. 1, 2001.

Sections 156.106-156.200 reserved for expansion

FAM §§156.201 TO 156.203. REPEALED

Repealed by Acts 2001, 77th Leg., ch. 1289, §12(2), eff. Sept. 1, 2001.

Sections 156.204-156.300 reserved for expansion

FAM §§156.301 TO 156.304. REPEALED

Repealed by Acts 2001, 77th Leg., ch. 1289, §12(2), eff. Sept. 1, 2001.

Sections 156.305-156.400 reserved for expansion

SUBCHAPTER E. MODIFICATION OF CHILD SUPPORT

FAM §156.401. GROUNDS FOR MODIFICATION OF CHILD SUPPORT

(a) Except as provided by Subsection (b), the court may modify an order that provides for the support of a child if:

(1) the circumstances of the child or a person affected by the order have materially and substantially changed since the date of the order's rendition; or

(2) it has been three years since the order was rendered or last modified and the monthly amount of the child support award under the order differs by either 20 percent or $100 from the amount that would be awarded in accordance with the child support guidelines.

(b) A support order may be modified only as to obligations accruing after the earlier of:

(1) the date of service of citation; or

(2) an appearance in the suit to modify.

(c) An order of joint conservatorship, in and of itself, does not constitute grounds for modifying a support order.

(d) Release of a child support obligor from incarceration is a material and substantial change in circumstances for purposes of Subsection (a)(1) if the obligor's child support obligation was abated, reduced, or suspended during the period of the obligor's incarceration.

History of Fam §156.401: Acts 1995, 74th Leg., ch. 20, §1, eff. April 20, 1995. Amended by Acts 1997, 75th Leg., ch. 911, §16, eff. Sept. 1, 1997; Acts 1999, 76th Leg., ch. 43, §1, eff. Sept. 1, 1999. Source: Former Fam §§14.021(g), 14.08(c)(2).

In re H.S.N., 69 S.W.3d 829, 833 (Tex.App.—Corpus Christi 2002, n.p.h.). "The purpose of allowing child support to be modified retroactive to the date of the original request is to remove any motive on the part of the obligor to engage in delay tactics."

Friermood v. Friermood, 25 S.W.3d 758, 760 (Tex.App.—Houston [14th Dist.] 2000, no pet.). "A child support order not in compliance with guidelines does not in and of itself establish material and substantial change in circumstances warranting modification."

Willis v. Willis, 826 S.W.2d 700, 702 (Tex.App.—Houston [14th Dist.] 1992, no writ). "Child support payments may not be modified once they have accrued. A support order may be modified only as to subsequent child support obligations. A trial court may also retroactively modify support obligations which have accrued *since the filing of the motion to modify*. Here, the trial court abused its discretion by ordering the modification of child support obligations which accrued prior to the filing of the agreed motion to modify. The trial court was without authority to approve the agreed motion and to enforce the payment of the accrued child support."

Penick v. Penick, 780 S.W.2d 407, 408 (Tex.App.—Texarkana 1989, writ denied). Section 14.08(c)(2), now §156.401, "provides that a support order may be modified if the circumstances 'of the child or a person affected by the order ... have materially and substantially changed' since the order's entry. To determine if the required change has occurred, the court must compare the financial circumstances of the children and the affected parties at the time the order was entered with their circumstances at the time the modification is sought." *See also* ***In re D.S.***, ___ S.W.3d ___ (Tex. App.—Houston [14th Dist.] 2002, n.p.h.) (No. 14-00-01457-CV; 2-28-02).

FAM §156.402. EFFECT OF GUIDELINES

(a) The court may consider the child support guidelines for single and multiple families under Chapter 154 to determine whether there has been a material or substantial change of circumstances under this chapter that warrants a modification of an existing child support order if the modification is in the best interest of the child.

(b) If the amount of support contained in the order does not substantially conform with the guidelines for single and multiple families under Chapter 154, the court may modify the order to substantially conform with the guidelines if the modification is in the best interest of the child. A court may consider other relevant evidence in addition to the factors listed in the guidelines.

History of Fam §156.402: Acts 1995, 74th Leg., ch. 20, §1, eff. April 20, 1995. Amended by Acts 1999, 76th Leg., ch. 556, §12 (eff. Sept. 1, 1999), ch. 62, §6.22 (eff. Sept. 1, 1999). Source: Former Fam §14.056(a), (b).

Scott v. Younts, 926 S.W.2d 415, 418-19 (Tex. App.—Corpus Christi 1996, writ denied). "In determining whether a material and substantial change in circumstances warrants a modification, courts may refer to the child support guidelines listed elsewhere in the Code. The Code also specifically prevents courts from considering certain things as grounds for modification: namely, any increase in needs, standard of living or lifestyle of obligee, any history of voluntarily provided support, and net resources of new spouses. [¶] The 'guidelines' referred to in §14.056 [now §156.402] instruct the courts to consider various factors when ordering child support, based in part on the net resources and abilities of the parties, as well as the needs of the child. A court may deviate from the guidelines when their application would be inappropriate or unjust under the circumstances."

FAM §156.403. VOLUNTARY ADDITIONAL SUPPORT

A history of support voluntarily provided in excess of the court order does not constitute cause to increase the amount of an existing child support order.

History of Fam §156.403: Acts 1995, 74th Leg., ch. 20, §1, eff. April 20, 1995. Source: Former Fam §14.056(b).

FAM §156.404. NET RESOURCES OF NEW SPOUSE

(a) The court may not add any portion of the net resources of a new spouse to the net resources of an obligor or obligee in order to calculate the amount of child support to be ordered in a suit for modification.

(b) The court may not subtract the needs of a new spouse, or of a dependent of a new spouse, from the net resources of the obligor or obligee in a suit for modification.

History of Fam §156.404: Acts 1995, 74th Leg., ch. 20, §1, eff. April 20, 1995. Source: Former Fam §14.056(c).

Starck v. Nelson, 878 S.W.2d 302, 305-06 (Tex. App.—Corpus Christi 1994, no writ). "[T]he court did not use [obligor's] wife's income to calculate [obligor's] net resources; however, the court considered [obligor's] remarriage in deviating from child support guidelines. The trial court found that [obligor's] wife's contribution to their joint living expenses enabled [obligor] to pay more child support than if he were solely responsible for his living expenses. [¶] The precise language of [§14.056(c), now §156.404(a)] does not prohibit the trial court's action in this case. ... The language of §14.056(c), and the definition of net resources in §14.053(b) [now §154.062] indicate that the legislature was attempting to design a neutral scheme that would be unaffected by the remarriage of the child support obligor, either for the purpose of increasing or decreasing child support. The Code permits consideration of additional factors in §14.053(e) [now §154.067] and provides a list of evidentiary factors in §14.054 [now §154.123] which allow the court to set child support either within or outside the range recommended if relevant factors, other than the guidelines, justify a variance; the list of factors is extensive, but not exclusive. ... All three provisions should be read together and construed harmoniously if possible. Permitting the court to deviate from child support guidelines because the obligor's new spouse contributes to their joint living expenses allows the court to do indirectly what the statute directly prohibits."

FAM §156.405. CHANGE IN LIFESTYLE

An increase in the needs, standard of living, or lifestyle of the obligee since the rendition of the existing order does not warrant an increase in the obligor's child support obligation.

History of Fam §156.405: Acts 1995, 74th Leg., ch. 20, §1, eff. April 20, 1995. Source: Former Fam §14.056(c).

Scott v. Younts, 926 S.W.2d 415, 422-23 (Tex. App.—Corpus Christi 1996, writ denied). Father "contends that the court erroneously relied on changes in the lifestyle and needs of the mother in setting the support award, contrary to the direction of the Family Code. [¶] We find nothing in the record or in the court's findings to substantiate this point. All the evidence presented suggested that [mother's] lifestyle had actually become more restrained as a result of losing her job and the resulting dwindling of her savings. ... The evidence actually illustrated the standard of living and lifestyle of [mother] had declined. Therefore, any findings in this regard do not conflict with §14.056(c) [now §156.405]."

FAM §156.406. USE OF GUIDELINES FOR CHILDREN IN MORE THAN ONE HOUSEHOLD

In applying the child support guidelines in a suit under this subchapter, if the obligor has the duty to support children in more than one household, the court shall apply the percentage guidelines for multiple families under Chapter 154.

History of Fam §156.406: Acts 1995, 74th Leg., ch. 20, §1, eff. April 20, 1995. Amended by Acts 1999, 76th Leg., ch. 556, §13 (eff. Sept. 1, 1999), ch. 62, §6.23 (eff. Sept. 1, 1999). Source: Former Fam §14.056(d).

FAM §156.407. ASSIGNMENT OF CHILD SUPPORT RIGHT

A notice of assignment filed under Chapter 231 does not constitute a modification of an order to pay child support.

History of Fam §156.407: Acts 1995, 74th Leg., ch. 20, §1, eff. April 20, 1995. Source: Former Fam §14.08(h).

FAM §156.408. MODIFICATION OF SUPPORT ORDER RENDERED BY ANOTHER STATE

(a) Unless both parties and the child reside in this state, a court of this state may modify an order of child support rendered by an appropriate tribunal of another state only as provided by Chapter 159.

A *Subsection (b) below is effective for modification or enforcement proceedings commenced on or after Sept. 1, 2001.*

(b) If both parties and the child reside in this state, a court of this state may modify an order of child support rendered by an appropriate tribunal of another state after registration of the order as provided by Chapter 159.

Subsection (b) below is effective for modification or enforcement proceedings commenced before Sept. 1, 2001.

(b) If both parties and the child reside in this state, a court of this state may modify an order of child support rendered by an appropriate tribunal of another state and any aspect of conservatorship as provided by this chapter without reference to Chapter 159.

History of Fam §156.408: Acts 1995, 74th Leg., ch. 20, §1, eff. April 20, 1995. Amended by Acts 2001, 77th Leg., ch. 1023, §13, eff. Sept. 1, 2001.

FAM §156.409. CHANGE IN PHYSICAL POSSESSION

A (a) If the sole managing conservator of a child or the joint managing conservator who has the exclusive right to determine the primary residence of the child has voluntarily relinquished the primary care and possession of the child to another person for at least six months, the court may modify an order providing for the support of the child to provide that the other person having physical possession of the child shall have the right to receive and give receipt for payments of support for the child and to hold or disburse money for the benefit of the child.

E *Subsection (b) below is effective for modification or enforcement proceedings commenced on or after Sept. 1, 2001.*

(b) Notice of a motion for modification under this section may be served in the manner for serving a notice under Section 157.065.

History of Fam §156.409: Acts 1999, 76th Leg., ch. 556, §14, eff. Sept. 1, 1999. Amended by Acts 2001, 77th Leg., ch. 1289, §10 (eff. Sept. 1, 2001), ch. 1023, §14 (eff. Sept. 1, 2001).

CHAPTER 157. ENFORCEMENT

Subchapter A. Pleadings & Defenses

SUBCHAPTER A. PLEADINGS & DEFENSES

FAM §157.001. MOTION FOR ENFORCEMENT

(a) A motion for enforcement as provided in this chapter may be filed to enforce a final order for conservatorship, child support, possession of or access to a child, or other provisions of a final order.

(b) The court may enforce by contempt a final order for possession of and access to a child as provided in this chapter.

(c) The court may enforce a final order for child support as provided in this chapter or Chapter 158.

(d) A motion for enforcement shall be filed in the court of continuing, exclusive jurisdiction.

History of Fam §157.001: Acts 1995, 74th Leg., ch. 20, §1, eff. April 20, 1995. Source: Former Fam §§14.30(b), 14.31, 14.40(a), 14.50(a).

Ex parte Hightower, 877 S.W.2d 17, 21 (Tex. App.—Dallas 1994, orig. proceeding). Section 157.001 "does not provide statutory support for enforcement of the ad litem's unpaid fees by contempt."

FAM §157.002. CONTENTS OF MOTION

(a) A motion for enforcement must, in ordinary and concise language:

(1) identify the provision of the order allegedly violated and sought to be enforced;

(2) state the manner of the respondent's alleged noncompliance;

(3) state the relief requested by the movant; and

(4) contain the signature of the movant or the movant's attorney.

(b) A motion for enforcement of child support:

(1) must include the amount owed as provided in the order, the amount paid, and the amount of arrearages;

(2) if contempt is requested, must include the portion of the order allegedly violated and, for each date of alleged contempt, the amount due and the amount paid, if any;

(3) may include as an attachment a copy of a record of child support payments maintained by the Title IV-D registry or a local registry; and

(4) if the obligor owes arrearages for a child receiving assistance under Part A of Title IV of the federal Social Security Act (42 U.S.C. Section 601 et seq.), may include a request that:

(A) the obligor pay the arrearages in accordance with a plan approved by the court; or

(B) if the obligor is already subject to a plan and is not incapacitated, the obligor participate in work activities, as defined under 42 U.S.C. Section 607(d), that the court determines appropriate.

(c) A motion for enforcement of the terms and conditions of conservatorship or possession of or access to a child must include the date, place, and, if applicable, the time of each occasion of the respondent's failure to comply with the order.

(d) The movant is not required to plead that the underlying order is enforceable by contempt to obtain other appropriate enforcement remedies.

(e) The movant may allege repeated past violations of the order and that future violations of a similar nature may occur before the date of the hearing.

History of Fam §157.002: Acts 1995, 74th Leg., ch. 20, §1, eff. April 20, 1995. Amended by Acts 1997, 75th Leg., ch. 911, §17, eff. Sept. 1, 1997. Source: Former Fam §§14.311(a)-(e), 14.312.

In re Taylor, 28 S.W.3d 240, 248 (Tex.App.—Waco 2000, orig. proceeding). Relator's "motion refers to the specific provisions of the decree which [alleged contemnor] violated. ... He asks that [the court] hold [alleged contemnor] in contempt of court for these alleged violations. He signed the motion. Thus, the motion satisfies §157.002(a). Because the motion was properly filed, [the court] has a ministerial duty to consider the motion and rule on it."

FAM §157.003. JOINDER OF CLAIMS & REMEDIES; NO ELECTION OF REMEDIES

(a) A party requesting enforcement may join in the same proceeding any claim and remedy provided for in this chapter, other provisions of this title, or other rules of law.

(b) A motion for enforcement does not constitute an election of remedies that limits or precludes:

(1) the use of any other civil or criminal proceeding to enforce a final order; or

(2) a suit for damages under Chapter 42.

History of Fam §157.003: Acts 1995, 74th Leg., ch. 20, §1, eff. April 20, 1995. Amended by Acts 1999, 76th Leg., ch. 62, §6.24, eff. Sept. 1, 1999. Source: Former Fam §§14.30(d), 14.313(a), 14.33(d).

Ex parte Suter, 920 S.W.2d 685, 687 (Tex.App.—Houston [1st Dist.] 1995, orig. proceeding). "It is permissible to join several allegations of contemptuous conduct in one pleading. However, where the contemptuous acts are treated as separate offenses and where no more than a six-month sentence is imposed for any single offense, which would normally be a petty offense triable without a jury, if the sentences are aggregated so as to run consecutively rather than concurrently (thus extending the jail term beyond that allowable for a petty criminal offense) the relator must be afforded a trial by jury, unless he waives it."

FAM §157.004. TIME LIMITATIONS; ENFORCEMENT OF POSSESSION

The court retains jurisdiction to render a contempt order for failure to comply with the order of possession and access if the motion for enforcement is filed not later than the sixth month after the date:

(1) the child becomes an adult; or

(2) on which the right of possession and access terminates under the order or by operation of law.

History of Fam §157.004: Acts 1995, 74th Leg., ch. 20, §1, eff. April 20, 1995. Source: Former Fam §14.50(b).

FAM §157.005. TIME LIMITATIONS; ENFORCEMENT OF CHILD SUPPORT

(a) The court retains jurisdiction to render a contempt order for failure to comply with the child support order if the motion for enforcement is filed not later than the sixth month after the date:

(1) the child becomes an adult; or

(2) on which the child support obligation terminates under the order or by operation of law.

(b) The court retains jurisdiction to confirm the total amount of child support arrearages and render judgment for past-due child support until the date all current child support and medical support and child support arrearages, including interest and any applicable fees and costs, have been paid.

History of Fam §157.005: Acts 1995, 74th Leg., ch. 20, §1, eff. April 20, 1995. Amended by Acts 1999, 76th Leg., ch. 556, §15, eff. Sept. 1, 1999. Source: Former Fam §§14.40(b), 14.41(b).

In re W.J.S., 35 S.W.3d 274, 276 (Tex.App.—Houston [14th Dist.] 2000, no pet.). "The Family Code vests continuing, exclusive jurisdiction with the trial court that renders a final order in connection with a child. … Among the powers the court retains is the power to 'render a contempt order' against a defaulting parent and the power to 'confirm the total amount of child support arrearages and render judgment for past-due child support.' Put more simply, in Texas, the court that enters a support order retains jurisdiction to enforce that order, including the power to hold a non-complying party in contempt and the power to reduce accrued, unpaid child support to a money judgment which can be enforced in Texas or elsewhere."

In re Dickinson, 829 S.W.2d 919, 921 (Tex.App.—Amarillo 1992, no writ). "Section 14.40(b) [now §157.005] provides a definitive time within which the liability created by the divorce decree may be enforced by contempt proceedings. It does not affect substantive rights; it merely affects the remedy by defining the limitation period within which the substantive right created by the divorce decree or other pertinent order of the court pertaining to child support may be enforced by contempt proceedings." *See also* ***In re S.C.S.***, 48 S.W.3d 831, 834 (Tex.App.—Houston [14th Dist.] 2001, no pet.) (§157.005 is not a statute of limitation; rather, it addresses how long a court has jurisdiction to enforce its orders).

Sandford v. Sandford, 732 S.W.2d 449, 451 (Tex. App.—Dallas 1987, no writ). Section 14.41(b), now §157.005, "is a substantive limitation upon the power of the court to act which need not be pleaded as an affirmative defense."

FAM §157.006. AFFIRMATIVE DEFENSE TO MOTION FOR ENFORCEMENT

(a) The issue of the existence of an affirmative defense to a motion for enforcement does not arise unless evidence is admitted supporting the defense.

(b) The respondent must prove the affirmative defense by a preponderance of the evidence.

History of Fam §157.006: Acts 1995, 74th Leg., ch. 20, §1, eff. April 20, 1995. Source: Former Fam §§14.40(h), 14.50(e).

FAM §157.007. AFFIRMATIVE DEFENSE TO MOTION FOR ENFORCEMENT OF POSSESSION OR ACCESS

(a) The respondent may plead as an affirmative defense to contempt for failure to comply with an order for possession or access to a child that the movant voluntarily relinquished actual possession and control of the child.

(b) The voluntary relinquishment must have been for the time encompassed by the court-ordered periods during which the respondent is alleged to have interfered.

History of Fam §157.007: Acts 1995, 74th Leg., ch. 20, §1, eff. April 20, 1995. Source: Former Fam §14.50(c).

Ex parte Rosser, 899 S.W.2d 382, 385 (Tex.App.—Houston [14th Dist.] 1995, orig. proceeding). "[T]he involuntary inability to comply with an order is a valid defense to contempt, for one's noncompliance cannot have been willful if the failure to comply was involuntary. Although the inability to comply defense technically rebuts the willfulness element of contempt liability, the relator nevertheless bears the burden to conclusively establish his inability to comply. [¶] All of the evidence ... indicates that [father] encouraged the visitation and did what he could to convince [daughter] to see her mother. The testimony ... shows that [daughter] steadfastly refused to go and threatened to run away if she was forced to visit her mother. *At 386:* Within the spectrum of visitation disputes, there may be instances in which: (1) a parent actively discourages or impedes visitation; (2) a parent passively fails to insist that a child comply with visitation; or (3) a parent is legitimately unable to compel a child to comply with visitation. We believe that the defense of involuntary inability to comply applies only to the third alternative, and not the first two." *But see* ***Morgan***, below.

Ex parte Morgan, 886 S.W.2d 829, 832 (Tex.App.—Amarillo 1994, orig. proceeding). "Under the law, and this court order, [father] was entitled to possession of the children during specified visitation periods. [Mother] would be subject to contempt proceedings if she overtly or covertly sought to impede [father's] taking possession of the children for his visitation. However, in this case, the trial judge did not find that she acted in such a manner. Rather, his finding was that [mother's] passive conduct amounted to a denial of visitation. The evidence shows that [mother] did have the children and their baggage present at the agreed location for [father] to take possession of them. Under this record, [mother's] passivity was not punishable by contempt. [¶] We reiterate, however, that if the evidence in such a proceeding shows that a parent has encouraged minor children to resist court ordered visitation with the other parent, the line has been crossed between passivity, which is not punishable by contempt, and overt conduct, which would be punishable." *But see* ***Rosser***, above.

FAM §157.008. AFFIRMATIVE DEFENSE TO MOTION FOR ENFORCEMENT OF CHILD SUPPORT

(a) An obligor may plead as an affirmative defense in whole or in part to a motion for enforcement of child support that the obligee voluntarily relinquished to the obligor actual possession and control of a child.

(b) The voluntary relinquishment must have been for a time period in excess of any court-ordered periods of possession of and access to the child and actual support must have been supplied by the obligor.

(c) An obligor may plead as an affirmative defense to an allegation of contempt or of the violation of a condition of community service requiring payment of child support that the obligor:

(1) lacked the ability to provide support in the amount ordered;

(2) lacked property that could be sold, mortgaged, or otherwise pledged to raise the funds needed;

(3) attempted unsuccessfully to borrow the funds needed; and

(4) knew of no source from which the money could have been borrowed or legally obtained.

(d) An obligor who has provided actual support to the child during a time subject to an affirmative defense under this section may request reimbursement for that support as a counterclaim or offset against the claim of the obligee.

(e) An action against the obligee for support supplied to a child is limited to the amount of periodic payments previously ordered by the court.

History of Fam §157.008: Acts 1995, 74th Leg., ch. 20, §1, eff. April 20, 1995. Source: Former Fam §§14.40(c), (g), 14.41(c).

Ex parte Rojo, 925 S.W.2d 654, 655 (Tex.1996). "A person cannot be incarcerated indefinitely for civil contempt if he or she does not have the ability to perform the condition required for release. Civil contempt is coercive, and is based on the notion that the contemnor carries the keys of his prison in his own pocket. *At 656:* [Relator's] ex-wife argues that he should have sought a regular job that would have paid more than the meager sums he was netting with his duct-cleaning business. This factor, while possibly relevant to the criminal contempt sanction, does not bear on the question of whether [relator] had the ability, when the trial court committed him, to purge himself of the civil contempt." (Internal quotations omitted.)

Ex parte Roosth, 881 S.W.2d 300, 300-01 (Tex. 1994). "Due process requires that an alleged criminal contemnor not shoulder the burden of persuasion to disprove an element of the offense of contempt. However, whether ability to pay court-ordered child support is an element of the offense of contempt, or is instead an affirmative defense to that charge, is a question left to state law. In Texas, inability to pay child support is an affirmative defense to the offense of contempt that must be proved by a preponderance of the evidence. The burden of proof and evidentiary standard imposed by the trial court under §14.40(g), (h) [now §§157.006, 157.008] are consistent with due process."

Curtis v. Curtis, 11 S.W.3d 466, 472 (Tex.App.—Tyler 2000, no pet.). Obligee "had the burden of establishing the arrearage, *i.e.*, the difference between the payments made by [obligor] and the payments required under the divorce decree. Thereafter, [obligor] had the burden of establishing 'excess possession' and any amount of 'actual support' during periods of excess possession."

Ex parte Robertson, 880 S.W.2d 803, 803 (Tex. App.—Houston [1st Dist.] 1994, orig. proceeding). "A relator's current inability to pay does not affect his obligation to serve the criminal contempt portion of his sentence. The relator's current inability to pay the arrearage is therefore no defense to the criminal contempt."

Buzbee v. Buzbee, 870 S.W.2d 335, 339 (Tex.App.—Waco 1994, no writ). "By the plain language of the statute, the plaintiff in the action has the burden of proving the dollar amount of the difference between payments made and the payments required by the terms of a child-support order. The obligor then has the burden of establishing any amounts claimed as an offset against the arrearage. Under §14.41(c) [now §157.008], the amount of offset is limited to the amount of 'actual support' during periods of 'excess' possession. Therefore, the [obligee] had the initial burden of establishing the amount of [obligor's] child-support arrearage. After this amount is established, [obligor] had the burden of establishing 'excess' possession and the amount of 'actual support.' *At 340-41:* By the plain language of the statute, the party claiming the benefit of the section must prove (1) that he had possession of the child for periods in excess of the court-ordered periods of possession (2) during which he incurred expenses for actual support of the child. Thus, to gain a credit against the arrearage, [obligor] was required to provide the court with some evidence of his expenditures on the child."

Ex parte Bregenzer, 802 S.W.2d 884, 887 (Tex. App.—Houston [1st Dist.] 1991, orig. proceeding). "Although relator argues to the contrary, we conclude, under the circumstances, that relator's wife was a potential lender. Relator has not met his burden of conclusively proving his present inability to pay the child support arrearage, because he did not establish he had requested a loan from his wife and been denied."

Sections 157.009-157.060 reserved for expansion

SUBCHAPTER B. PROCEDURE

FAM §157.061. SETTING HEARING

(a) On filing a motion for enforcement requesting contempt, the court shall set the date, time, and place of the hearing and order the respondent to personally appear and respond to the motion.

(b) If the motion for enforcement does not request contempt, the court shall set the motion for hearing on the request of a party.

(c) The court shall give preference to a motion for enforcement of child support in setting a hearing date and may not delay the hearing because a suit for modification of the order requested to be enforced has been or may be filed.

History of Fam §157.061: Acts 1995, 74th Leg., ch. 20, §1, eff. April 20, 1995. Source: Former Fam §§14.314(a), 14.32(d).

In re Taylor, 39 S.W.3d 406, 413 (Tex.App.—Waco 2001, orig. proceeding). "The provisions which govern notice of and appearance at hearings in which contempt is a requested remedy are found in §§105.006(f), 157.061(a), 157.062(a), 157.065, 157.066, 157.114, and 157.115.... These provisions read together require the following: (a) The court shall set a hearing date, and shall order the respondent to personally appear at the hearing and respond to the motion. This frequently is in the form of a 'show cause' order[;] (b) The movant should give written notice to the respondent of the date, time, and place of hearing, and a copy of the motion should be attached. The notice should be served at least ten days before the hearing [and;] (c) Although the notice may be sent by certified, if the respondent fails to appear, there is little remedy other than a resetting of the hearing. Therefore, the notice should be served in person on the respondent, after which if the respondent fails to appear, the court may not hold the respondent in contempt, but may render a default judgment in favor of movant, and order a capias to be issued for the arrest of the respondent."

FAM §157.062. NOTICE OF HEARING

(a) The notice of hearing must include the date, time, and place of the hearing.

(b) The notice of hearing need not repeat the allegations contained in the motion for enforcement.

(c) Notice of hearing on a motion for enforcement of an existing order providing for child support or possession of or access to a child shall be given to the respondent by personal service of a copy of the motion and notice not later than the 10th day before the date of the hearing.

(d) If a motion for enforcement is joined with another claim:

(1) the hearing may not be held before 10 a.m. on the first Monday after the 20th day after the date of service; and

(2) the provisions of the Texas Rules of Civil Procedure applicable to the filing of an original lawsuit apply.

History of Fam §157.062: Acts 1995, 74th Leg., ch. 20, §1, eff. April 20, 1995. Amended by Acts 1995, 74th Leg., ch. 751, §49, eff. Sept. 1, 1995. Source: Former Fam §§14.314(a), (b), 14.315(b), (c).

In re Taylor, 39 S.W.3d 406, 413 (Tex.App.—Waco 2001, orig. proceeding). See Annotation in Fam §157.061.

In re Aguilera, 37 S.W.3d 43, 53 (Tex.App.—El Paso 2000, orig. proceeding). "The failure to give the notice required by §157.062 does not render the proceeding void unless the lack of notice amounts to a denial of constitutional due process. *At 54:* When an obligor who has been personally served fails to appear, the court may not hold the obligor in contempt but may ... issue a capias for his arrest. While finding the obligor in contempt on less than ten days' notice violates due process, there is no constitutional prohibition against compelling him to appear pursuant to the show cause order even if he has not been provided with the requisite notice. ... Relator did not have the option of ignoring the show cause order as he might ignore citation in a civil suit because he is commanded by the court to appear, and if he ignores the command he may be brought in under a capias."

In re Hathcox, 981 S.W.2d 422, 425 (Tex.App.—Texarkana 1998, no pet.). "The obvious purpose of §157.062(d) is to allow a respondent extra time to answer and prepare for a hearing when a new claim has been joined with a motion for enforcement. [Petitioner's] argument that §157.062(d) applies only to original proceedings would defeat this purpose and would allow a petitioner to file only an original motion for enforcement of a support order and then amend that original motion to add new claims and avoid completely the additional time for answer and hearing provided by §157.062(d). We do not believe the legislature intended such a result."

Crawford v. Gardner, 690 S.W.2d 296, 297 (Tex. App.—Dallas 1985, no writ). "[T]he constitutional protections necessary in a proceeding based on a motion for contempt are not required in a proceeding that results solely in an order which reduces child support arrearage to money judgment.... [¶] Because [obligor] was not entitled to such constitutional protections, trial court did not err in rendering its money judgment award without greater notice than was afforded to [obligor] and the trial court's money judgment award is not void."

Ex parte Boyle, 545 S.W.2d 25, 27 (Tex.App.—Houston [1st Dist.] 1976, orig. proceeding). "The holding of a contempt hearing within less than ten days from the date of service of a show cause order is a procedural irregularity only. The court does not lack jurisdiction because the hearing was held within less than ten days. On the other hand, holding the hearing in less than ten days after service of notice may constitute a denial of due process. No clear and definite line can be drawn between that length of notice which will afford due process and that which will not. Each case must be evaluated on its own facts."

FAM §157.063. APPEARANCE

A party makes a general appearance for all purposes in an enforcement proceeding if:

(1) the party appears at the hearing or is present when the case is called; and

(2) the party does not object to the court's jurisdiction or the form or manner of the notice of hearing.

History of Fam §157.063: Acts 1995, 74th Leg., ch. 20, §1, eff. April 20, 1995. Source: Former Fam §14.314(c).

FAM §157.064. SPECIAL EXCEPTION

(a) If a respondent specially excepts to the motion for enforcement or moves to strike, the court shall rule on the exception or the motion to strike before it hears the motion for enforcement.

(b) If an exception is sustained, the court shall give the movant an opportunity to replead and continue the hearing to a designated date and time without the requirement of additional service.

History of Fam §157.064: Acts 1995, 74th Leg., ch. 20, §1, eff. April 20, 1995. Source: Former Fam §14.311(f).

FAM §157.065. NOTICE OF HEARING, FIRST CLASS MAIL

(a) If a party has been ordered under Chapter 105 to provide the court and the state case registry with the party's current mailing address, notice of a motion for enforcement may be served by mailing a copy of the notice to the respondent, together with a copy of the motion, by first class mail to the last mailing address of the respondent on file with the court and the registry.

(b) The notice may be sent by the clerk of the court, the movant's attorney, or any person entitled to the address information as provided in Chapter 105.

(c) A person who sends the notice shall file of record a certificate of service showing the date of mailing and the name of the person who sent the notice.

(d) Repealed by Acts 1997, 75th Leg., ch. 911, Sec. 97(a), eff. Sept. 1, 1997.

History of Fam §157.065: Acts 1995, 74th Leg., ch. 20, §1, eff. April 20, 1995. Amended by Acts 1997, 75th Leg., ch. 911, §18, eff. Sept. 1, 1997. Source: Former Fam §14.314(c).

FAM §157.066. FAILURE TO APPEAR

If a respondent who has been personally served with notice to appear at a hearing does not appear at the designated time, place, and date to respond to a motion for enforcement of an existing court order, regardless of whether the motion is joined with other claims or remedies, the court may not hold the respondent in contempt but may, on proper proof, grant a default judgment for the relief sought and issue a capias for the arrest of the respondent.

History of Fam §157.066: Acts 1995, 74th Leg., ch. 20, §1, eff. April 20, 1995. Amended by Acts 1995, 74th Leg., ch. 751, §50, eff. Sept. 1, 1995. Source: Former Fam §14.317(a).

In re Taylor, 39 S.W.3d 406, 413-14 (Tex.App.—Waco 2001, orig. proceeding). "[A]lthough the trial court is supposed to 'order' the respondent to appear, §157.066 makes it clear that even if that is done, failure to appear is not punishable by contempt, but rather, if and only if personal service has been obtained, the court can render a default judgment and order a capias for the arrest of the respondent. If Relator wants to preserve these remedies of default judgment and a capias, it is his responsibility to obtain personal service on [respondent] of a proper notice of the hearing, and provide proof of same to the trial court."

Sections 157.067-157.100 reserved for expansion

SUBCHAPTER C. FAILURE TO APPEAR; BOND OR SECURITY

FAM §157.101. BOND OR SECURITY FOR RELEASE OF RESPONDENT

(a) When the court orders the issuance of a capias as provided in this chapter, the court shall also set an appearance bond or security, payable to the obligee or to a person designated by the court, in a reasonable amount.

(b) An appearance bond or security in the amount of $1,000 or a cash bond in the amount of $250 is presumed to be reasonable. Evidence that the respondent has attempted to evade service of process, has previously been found guilty of contempt, or has accrued arrearages over $1,000 is sufficient to rebut the presumption. If the presumption is rebutted, the court shall set a reasonable bond.

History of Fam §157.101: Acts 1995, 74th Leg., ch. 20, §1, eff. April 20, 1995. Source: Former Fam §§14.318(a), 14.32(e).

In re Clark, 977 S.W.2d 152, 155 (Tex.App.—Houston [14th Dist.] 1998, orig. proceeding). "[A]ny appeal from an order setting a bond in violation of §157.101 would be inadequate. Accordingly, we conclude that review of the trial court's orders by mandamus is appropriate. *At 156-57:* If the Legislature had not intended the factors listed in §157.101(b) to be exclusive it could have so stated in the statute. Nothing in §157.101(b) suggests the court can consider factors other than those enumerated in the statute for setting bond. The express mention or enumeration of one thing, consequence or class is equal to the express exclusion of all others. Accordingly, we conclude that the factors listed in §157.101(b) are exclusive. [¶] [T]he trial court's finding that relator has 'avoided the execution of the capias,' is *not* the same as 'attempted to evade service of process' as that phrase is used in §157.101(b). 'Service of process' generally 'signifies the delivering to or leaving [of writs complaints, summons, etc.], with the party to whom or with whom they ought to be delivered or left.' Neither the Code of Criminal Procedure nor case law requires 'service' of an arrest warrant. ... Although avoiding execution of a capias is arguably worse than avoiding service of process, the statute simply does not make the former a consideration in setting bond. Because avoiding arrest is not listed in §157.101(b) as rebuttal evidence, the trial court's finding that relator 'avoided the execution of the capias,' does not rebut the presumption in the statute that a $1,000 bond is reasonable. [¶] Likewise, the trial court's finding that relator was in arrears 'in [sic] the payment of court-ordered interim attorney's fees in excess of $1,000 does not satisfy §157.101(b). An 'arrearage' is 'money which is overdue and unpaid.' Although §157.101(b) does not specify the type of 'arrearage,' chapter 157 of the Family Code deals primarily with enforcement of child support and repeatedly refers to 'arrearages' in that context. ... Attorney's fees incurred in connection with the enforcement of child custody orders by motion or writ of habeas corpus are recoverable as costs. Such attorney's fees are plainly not 'arrearages' within the ordinary meaning of that term under §157.101(b). Thus, the trial court's finding in the underlying custody case that relator was in arrears in the payment of attorney's fees is not the same as a finding that relator accrued child support arrearages over $1,000 as required by §157.101(b) and therefore, does not rebut the presumption in that statute."

FAM §157.102. CAPIAS; DUTY OF LAW ENFORCEMENT OFFICIALS

Law enforcement officials shall treat the capias in the same manner as an arrest warrant for a criminal offense and shall enter the capias in the computer records for outstanding warrants maintained by the local police, sheriff, and Department of Public Safety. The capias shall be forwarded to and disseminated by the Texas Crime Information Center and the National Crime Information Center.

History of Fam §157.102: Acts 1995, 74th Leg., ch. 20, §1, eff. April 20, 1995. Amended by Acts 1997, 75th Leg., ch. 702, §3, eff. Sept. 1, 1997; Acts 1999, 76th Leg., ch. 556, §16, eff. Sept. 1, 1999. Source: Former Fam §14.317(d).

FAM §157.103. CAPIAS FEES

(a) The fee for issuing a capias as provided in this chapter is the same as the fee for issuance of a writ of attachment.

(b) The fee for serving a capias is the same as the fee for service of a writ in civil cases generally.

History of Fam §157.103: Acts 1995, 74th Leg., ch. 20, §1, eff. April 20, 1995. Source: Former Fam §14.317(e).

FAM §157.104. CONDITIONAL RELEASE

If the respondent is taken into custody and released on bond, the court shall condition the bond on the respondent's promise to appear in court for a hearing as required by the court without the necessity of further personal service of notice on the respondent.

History of Fam §157.104: Acts 1995, 74th Leg., ch. 20, §1, eff. April 20, 1995. Source: Former Fam §14.318(b).

FAM §157.105. RELEASE HEARING

(a) If the respondent is taken into custody and not released on bond, the respondent shall be brought before the court that issued the capias on or before the first working day after the arrest. The court shall determine whether the respondent's appearance in court at a designated time and place can be assured by a method other than by posting the bond or security previously established.

(b) If the respondent is released without posting bond or security, the court shall set a hearing on the alleged contempt at a designated date, time, and place and give the respondent notice of hearing in open court. No other notice to the respondent is required.

(c) If the court is not satisfied that the respondent's appearance in court can be assured and the respondent remains in custody, a hearing on the alleged contempt shall be held as soon as practicable, but not later than the fifth day after the date that the respondent was taken into custody, unless the respondent and the respondent's attorney waive the accelerated hearing.

History of Fam §157.105: Acts 1995, 74th Leg., ch. 20, §1, eff. April 20, 1995. Source: Former Fam §14.318(c).

FAM §157.106. CASH BOND AS SUPPORT

(a) If the respondent has posted a cash bond and is found to be in arrears in the payment of court-ordered child support, the court shall order that the proceeds of the cash bond be paid to the child support obligee or to a person designated by the court, not to exceed the amount of child support arrearages determined to exist.

(b) This section applies without regard to whether the respondent appears at the hearing.

History of Fam §157.106: Acts 1995, 74th Leg., ch. 20, §1, eff. April 20, 1995. Source: Former Fam §14.318(d).

FAM §157.107. APPEARANCE BOND OR SECURITY OTHER THAN CASH BOND AS SUPPORT

(a) If the respondent fails to appear at the hearing as directed, the court shall order that the appearance bond or security be forfeited and that the proceeds of any judgment on the bond or security, not to exceed the amount of child support arrearages determined to exist, be paid to the obligee or to a person designated by the court.

(b) The obligee may file suit on the bond.

History of Fam §157.107: Acts 1995, 74th Leg., ch. 20, §1, eff. April 20, 1995. Source: Former Fam §14.318(e).

FAM §157.108. CASH BOND AS PROPERTY OF RESPONDENT

A court shall treat a cash bond posted for the benefit of the respondent as the property of the respondent. A person who posts the cash bond does not have recourse in relation to an order regarding the bond other than against the respondent.

History of Fam §157.108: Acts 1995, 74th Leg., ch. 20, §1, eff. April 20, 1995. Source: Former Fam §14.318(f).

FAM §157.109. SECURITY FOR COMPLIANCE WITH ORDER

(a) The court may order the respondent to execute a bond or post security if the court finds that the respondent:

(1) has on two or more occasions denied possession of or access to a child who is the subject of the order; or

(2) is employed by an employer not subject to the jurisdiction of the court or for whom income withholding is unworkable or inappropriate.

(b) The court shall set the amount of the bond or security and condition the bond or security on compliance with the court order permitting possession or access or the payment of past-due or future child support.

(c) The court shall order the bond or security payable through the registry of the court:

(1) to the obligee or other person or entity entitled to receive child support payments designated by the court if enforcement of child support is requested; or

(2) to the person who is entitled to possession or access if enforcement of possession or access is requested.

History of Fam §157.109: Acts 1995, 74th Leg., ch. 20, §1, eff. April 20, 1995. Source: Former Fam §§14.42(a), 14.51(a).

In re Gonzalez, 993 S.W.2d 147, 157 (Tex.App.—San Antonio 1999, no pet.). "By its terms, [§157.109] does not require the court to make a written finding."

FAM §157.110. FORFEITURE OF SECURITY FOR FAILURE TO COMPLY WITH ORDER

(a) On the motion of a person or entity for whose benefit a bond has been executed or security deposited, the court may forfeit all or part of the bond or security deposit on a finding that the person who furnished the bond or security:

(1) has violated the court order for possession of and access to a child; or

(2) failed to make child support payments.

(b) The court shall order the registry to pay the funds from a forfeited bond or security deposit to the obligee or person or entity entitled to receive child support payments in an amount that does not exceed the child support arrearages or, in the case of possession of or access to a child, to the person entitled to possession or access.

(c) The court may order that all or part of the forfeited amount be applied to pay attorney's fees and costs incurred by the person or entity bringing the motion for contempt or motion for forfeiture.

History of Fam §157.110: Acts 1995, 74th Leg., ch. 20, §1, eff. April 20, 1995. Source: Former Fam §§14.42(b), (c), (f), 14.51(b), (c), (f).

FAM §157.111. FORFEITURE NOT DEFENSE TO CONTEMPT

The forfeiture of bond or security is not a defense in a contempt proceeding.

History of Fam §157.111: Acts 1995, 74th Leg., ch. 20, §1, eff. April 20, 1995. Source: Former Fam §§14.42(e), 14.51(e).

FAM §157.112. JOINDER OF FORFEITURE & CONTEMPT PROCEEDINGS

A motion for enforcement requesting contempt may be joined with a forfeiture proceeding.

History of Fam §157.112: Acts 1995, 74th Leg., ch. 20, §1, eff. April 20, 1995. Source: Former Fam §§14.42(d), 14.51(d).

FAM §157.113. APPLICATION OF BOND PENDING WRIT

If the obligor requests to execute a bond or to post security pending a hearing by an appellate court on a writ, the bond or security on forfeiture shall be payable to the obligee.

History of Fam §157.113: Acts 1995, 74th Leg., ch. 20, §1, eff. April 20, 1995. Source: Former Fam §§14.40(f), 14.32(e).

FAM §157.114. FAILURE TO APPEAR

The court may order a capias to be issued for the arrest of the respondent if:

(1) the motion for enforcement requests contempt;

(2) the respondent was personally served; and

(3) the respondent fails to appear.

History of Fam §157.114: Acts 1995, 74th Leg., ch. 20, §1, eff. April 20, 1995. Source: Former Fam §14.317(a).

FAM §157.115. DEFAULT JUDGMENT

(a) The court may render a default order for the relief requested if the respondent:

(1) has been personally served, has filed an answer, or has entered an appearance; and

(2) does not appear at the designated time, place, and date to respond to the motion.

(b) If the respondent fails to appear, the court may not hold the respondent in contempt but may order a capias to be issued.

History of Fam §157.115: Acts 1995, 74th Leg., ch. 20, §1, eff. April 20, 1995. Amended by Acts 1995, 74th Leg., ch. 751, §51, eff. Sept. 1, 1995. Source: Former Fam §14.317(a), (c).

Lowe v. Lowe, 971 S.W.2d 720, 723 (Tex.App.—Houston [14th Dist.] 1998, pet. denied). "Since 1939, ***Craddock*** has been the seminal case setting forth the elements of proof a defaulting party must show to obtain a new trial following a default judgment. *At 725:* Although we have found that [defendant] met the three prongs of the ***Craddock*** test, we feel obligated to note our reluctance to apply it to a [SAPCR]. We applied ***Craddock*** because, historically, that is what courts have done. But we do not think ***Craddock*** is an appropriate test for [SAPCRs]. [¶] ***Craddock*** was designed to be applied to traditional civil litigation—personal injury, products liability, consumer, and commercial litigation—in which only two competing interests—the plaintiff's and the defendant's—are involved. [I]n [a SAPCR], we have more than two interests involved, we have three interests: the mother's interests, the father's interests, and, of paramount importance, the child's interests. Under our [F]amily [C]ode, the ultimate question to ask is what is in the best interest of the child. [W]hen the ***Craddock*** test is applied, it only takes into consideration the actions of the father and/or the mother, whichever happens to be the defaulting party. ***Craddock*** does not inquire into the child's interests and leaves no maneuvering room for a judge to consider the child's interests. *At 726:* [T]he ***Craddock*** test assumes an adversarial relationship between the parties. And yet, our legislature has made great attempts to rid family law proceedings of an adversarial nature."

Sections 157.116-157.160 reserved for expansion

SUBCHAPTER D. HEARING & ENFORCEMENT ORDER

FAM §157.161. RECORD

(a) Except as provided by Subsection (b), a record of the hearing in a motion for enforcement shall be made by a court reporter or as provided by Chapter 201.

(b) A record is not required if:

(1) the parties agree to an order; or

(2) the motion does not request incarceration and the parties waive the requirement of a record at the time of hearing, either in writing or in open court, and the court approves waiver.

History of Fam §157.161: Acts 1995, 74th Leg., ch. 20, §1, eff. April 20, 1995. Source: Former Fam §14.32(b).

FAM §157.162. PROOF

(a) The movant is not required to prove that the underlying order is enforceable by contempt to obtain other appropriate enforcement remedies.

(b) A finding that the respondent is not in contempt does not preclude the court from ordering any other enforcement remedy, including rendering a money judgment, posting a bond or other security, or withholding income.

(c) A copy of the payment record attached to the motion is evidence of the facts asserted in the payment record and is admissible to show whether payments were made. The respondent may offer controverting evidence.

History of Fam §157.162: Acts 1995, 74th Leg., ch. 20, §1, eff. April 20, 1995. Source: Former Fam §§14.311(b), (c), 14.33(d).

FAM §157.163. APPOINTMENT OF ATTORNEY

(a) In a motion for enforcement or motion to revoke community service, the court must first determine whether incarceration of the respondent is a possible result of the proceedings.

(b) If the court determines that incarceration is a possible result of the proceedings, the court shall inform a respondent not represented by an attorney of the right to be represented by an attorney and, if the respondent is indigent, of the right to the appointment of an attorney.

(c) If the court determines that the respondent will not be incarcerated as a result of the proceedings, the court may require a respondent who is indigent to proceed without an attorney.

(d) If the respondent claims indigency and requests the appointment of an attorney, the court shall require the respondent to file an affidavit of indigency. The court may hear evidence to determine the issue of indigency.

(e) Except as provided by Subsection (c), the court shall appoint an attorney to represent the respondent if the court determines that the respondent is indigent.

(f) If the respondent is not in custody, an appointed attorney is entitled to not less than 10 days from the date of the attorney's appointment to respond to the movant's pleadings and prepare for the hearing.

(g) If the respondent is in custody, an appointed attorney is entitled to not less than five days from the date the respondent was taken into custody to respond to the movant's pleadings and prepare for the hearing.

(h) The court may shorten or extend the time for preparation if the respondent and the respondent's attorney sign a waiver of the time limit.

(i) The scope of the court appointment of an attorney to represent the respondent is limited to the allegation of contempt or of violation of community supervision contained in the motion for enforcement or motion to revoke community supervision.

History of Fam §157.163: Acts 1995, 74th Leg., ch. 20, §1, eff. April 20, 1995. Source: Former Fam §14.32(f).

Ex parte Acker, 949 S.W.2d 314, 316 (Tex.1997). "[S]ection 157.163 requires courts to admonish pro se litigants of their right to counsel, regardless of whether they are indigent or not."

Ex parte Keene, 909 S.W.2d 507, 507 (Tex.1995). Relator "contends that he is unlawfully confined because the trial court did not advise him of his right to counsel or of his right to appointed counsel under §14.32(f) [now §157.163]. We agree. *At 508:* In the absence of a knowing and intelligent waiver by [relator] of his right to counsel, made on the record, the trial court had no authority to hold him in contempt."

In re Aarons, 10 S.W.3d 833, 833-34 (Tex.App.—Beaumont 2000, orig. proceeding). "We hold the trial court's failure to admonish [petitioner] of his right to counsel renders void the commitment arising from the ... contempt order. [¶] The entire order, however, is not void, only the invalid portion." *See also* ***In re Chaney***, ___ S.W.3d ___ (Tex.App.—Beaumont 2001, orig. proceeding) (No. 09-01-243-CV; 8-30-01).

In re Pruitt, 6 S.W.3d 363, 365 (Tex.App.—Beaumont 1999, orig. proceeding). "Section 157.163 gives no guidelines for determining indigency. Nor does any rigid standard exist for determining indigency for the purpose of appointing counsel."

In re Castro, 998 S.W.2d 935, 937-38 (Tex.App.—Houston [1st Dist.] 1999, orig. proceeding). "In construing a statute, a court may consider, among other matters, common law. [T]he Fort Worth Court of Appeals held that a person was entitled to be advised of his right to counsel at both his contempt hearing and motion to revoke community supervision hearing. We presume the Legislature had complete knowledge of the existing law and acted with reference to it, when it passed §157.163(a)."

In re Luebe, 983 S.W.2d 889, 890 (Tex.App.—Houston [1st Dist.] 1999, orig. proceeding). "Section 157.163 gives no guidelines for determining indigency. [C]ontempt cases are considered quasi-criminal in nature, and their proceedings should conform as nearly as practicable to those in criminal cases. [¶] Whether one's relative is financially able to assist is not to be considered."

Ex parte Linder, 783 S.W.2d 754, 760 (Tex.App.—Dallas 1990, orig. proceeding). "In our view, whether a relator has knowingly and intelligently waived his right to counsel and whether the trial court complied with §14.32(f) [now §157.163] are fact questions. We conclude that if either of these grounds are urged to void a contempt order, this Court cannot review them unless relator's application for writ of habeas corpus is accompanied by a statement of facts of the hearing resulting in his or her incarceration. Further, to require the movant for contempt, in the absence of a statement of facts, to see that a court's finding of a contemnor's knowing and intelligent waiver of the right to counsel be reduced to writing and included in the appellate record impermissibly shifts the burden of proof from the relator to the respondent in a habeas corpus proceeding. *At 761:* [Section 14.32(f), now §157.163], mandating the trial court to admonish an alleged contemnor appearing pro se of his right to counsel or his right to have one appointed if he is indigent, does not require the trial court to include in its contempt order any findings on this requirement. Nor does this section address waiver of these rights to counsel."

FAM §157.164. PAYMENT OF APPOINTED ATTORNEY

(a) An attorney appointed to represent an indigent respondent is entitled to a reasonable fee for services within the scope of the appointment in the amount set by the court.

(b) The fee shall be paid from the general funds of the county according to the schedule for the compensation of counsel appointed to defend criminal defendants as provided in the Code of Criminal Procedure.

(c) For purposes of this section, a proceeding in a court of appeals or the Supreme Court of Texas is considered the equivalent of a bona fide appeal to the Texas Court of Criminal Appeals.

History of Fam §157.164: Acts 1995, 74th Leg., ch. 20, §1, eff. April 20, 1995. Source: Former Fam §14.33(b).

FAM §157.165. PROBATION OF CONTEMPT ORDER

The court may place the respondent on community supervision and suspend commitment if the court finds that the respondent is in contempt of court for failure or refusal to obey an order rendered as provided in this title.

History of Fam §157.165: Acts 1995, 74th Leg., ch. 20, §1, eff. April 20, 1995. Amended by Acts 1999, 76th Leg., ch. 62, §6.25, eff. Sept. 1, 1999. Source: Former Fam §§14.40(e)(1), 14.50(d)(1).

Ex parte Spikes, 909 S.W.2d 245, 247 (Tex.App.—Amarillo 1995, orig. proceeding). "It is our studied decision that the discretion the trial judge has to revoke the suspension of commitment for contempt and probation ordered terminates when the period of probation has expired without a motion to revoke having been filed during the period of probation, and that the contemnor cannot afterwards be committed under the prior order of contempt. Our holding of the termination of the judge's discretion under such circumstances is the same holding applicable to revocation of probation in criminal cases under similar circumstances."

Ex parte Whitehead, 908 S.W.2d 68, 70 (Tex. App.—Houston [1st Dist.] 1995, orig. proceeding). "The purpose of the compliance hearing is to determine whether the offender has complied and, if not, for commitment under the terms of the judgment—not for violating the terms of the probation. We hold that, as a general rule, failing to comply with conditions of probation does not constitute a new act of contempt. Rather, it exposes the offender to commitment for the acts adjudicated at the earlier hearing on the motion for contempt."

Ex parte Duncan, 796 S.W.2d 562, 564 (Tex.App.—Houston [1st Dist.] 1990, orig. proceeding). "Where the trial court finds that an obligor is in contempt for failure or refusal to make a payment, the trial court may suspend commitment and place the obligor on probation. This Court may order the release of a relator in a habeas corpus proceeding where the commitment, or the order on which it is based, is void."

Ex parte Mackie, 727 S.W.2d 129, 131 (Tex.App.—San Antonio 1987, orig. proceeding). "Where a person has been found to be in contempt of an order of a court and punishment has been suspended on condition of compliance with the court order, no commitment may be ordered without a subsequent hearing to determine if a breach of the condition has occurred."

FAM §157.166. CONTENTS OF ENFORCEMENT ORDER

(a) An enforcement order must include:

(1) in ordinary and concise language the provisions of the order for which enforcement was requested;

(2) the acts or omissions that are the subject of the order;

(3) the manner of the respondent's noncompliance; and

(4) the relief granted by the court.

(b) If the order imposes incarceration or a fine for criminal contempt, an enforcement order must contain findings identifying, setting out, or incorporating by reference the provisions of the order for which enforcement was requested and the date of each occasion when the respondent's failure to comply with the order was found to constitute criminal contempt.

(c) If the enforcement order imposes incarceration for civil contempt, the order must state the specific conditions on which the respondent may be released from confinement.

History of Fam §157.166: Acts 1995, 74th Leg., ch. 20, §1, eff. April 20, 1995. Amended by Acts 1999, 76th Leg., ch. 556, §17, eff. Sept. 1, 1999. Source: Former Fam §14.33(a).

Generally

In re Levingston, 996 S.W.2d 936, 938-39 (Tex. App.—Houston [14th Dist.] 1999, orig. proceeding). "The purpose of an enforcement order is to notify the offender of how he has violated its provisions and how he can purge himself of contempt, to notify the sheriff so that he can carry out enforcement, and to provide sufficient information for an adequate review. An enforcement order may comply with §157.166 ... by (1) copying into the order the provisions for which enforcement was sought; (2) attaching as an exhibit a copy of the order for which enforcement was sought and incorporating it by reference; or (3) giving the volume and page numbers in the minutes of the court where the order and its pertinent language is located. [T]hese methods are not exclusive...."

Ex parte Coleman, 864 S.W.2d 573, 576 (Tex. App.—Tyler 1993, orig. proceeding). "While §14.33(a) [now §157.166] does not prohibit stipulations in enforcement orders, it does require specificity and particularity. Thus, if a court relies upon the stipulation of parties, its order must either set out the stipulation in its entirety, or incorporate it sufficiently by reference in order to meet the requirements of [§157.166]."

Order Being Enforced

Ex parte Chambers, 898 S.W.2d 257, 260 (Tex. 1995). "A court order is insufficient to support a judgment of contempt only if its interpretation requires inferences or conclusions about which *reasonable* persons might differ. Only the existence of *reasonable* alternative constructions will prevent enforcement of the order. The order need not be full of superfluous terms and specifications adequate to counter any flight of fancy a contemnor may imagine in order to declare it vague."

Ex parte Slavin, 412 S.W.2d 43, 44 (Tex.1967). "It is an accepted rule of law that for a person to be held in contempt for disobeying a court decree, the decree must spell out the details of compliance in clear, specific and unambiguous terms so that such person will readily know exactly what duties or obligations are imposed upon him."

In re Gonzalez, 993 S.W.2d 147, 158 (Tex.App.—San Antonio 1999, no pet.). "The law views attorney fees incurred in a suit to establish paternity and to enforce the father's child support obligation as part of the child support obligation. Therefore, a parent may be held in contempt for failing to pay such attorney fees."

Ex parte Tanner, 904 S.W.2d 202, 204-05 (Tex. App.—Houston [14th Dist.] 1995, orig. proceeding). "In this case, the divorce decree ordered that 'ROBIN LEE TANNER pay to TERRI J. TANNER periodic child support' of $35.00 per week. Although providing a location or mailing address for payment might have been preferable, relator has cited no actual difficulty or confusion concerning Terri's address. ... Under these circumstances, we are not persuaded that a failure to specify a location for payment of child support rendered the divorce decree so ambiguous as to be unenforceable by contempt."

Ex parte Wessell, 807 S.W.2d 17, 20 (Tex.App.—Houston [14th Dist.] 1991, orig. proceeding). "Generally, attorneys fees awarded may not be collected through contempt proceedings. One exception to this rule, however, is the collection of attorney's fees as costs in suits to recover child support payments. This exception is based upon the public policy that parents should support their children. [¶] Attorney's fees and costs to enforce a child support obligation are of the 'same nature' as the obligation for the enforcement of which they were incurred."

Ex parte Grothe, 570 S.W.2d 183, 184 (Tex.App.—Austin 1978, orig. proceeding). "For one to be held in constructive contempt for refusing to obey an order of the court, that order '... must spell out the details of compliance in clear, specific and unambiguous terms so that such person will readily know exactly what duties or obligations are imposed upon him.' If there were an order ..., it was oral and, as a result, cannot comply with any of the requirements of ***Slavin***. It follows that the judgment of contempt for violation of the oral order..., cannot stand."

Contempt Order

Ex parte Shaklee, 939 S.W.2d 144, 145 (Tex.1997). "[T]o satisfy due process, the contempt order must clearly specify the punishment imposed by the court."

Ex parte Hall, 854 S.W.2d 656, 658 (Tex.1993). "[T]he failure to comply with an order to pay a 'debt' is not contempt punishable by imprisonment because of the prohibition of [A]rticle I, §18 of the Texas Constitution, which states: 'No person shall ever be imprisoned for debt.' Such an order may be enforced by other legal processes, such as execution or attachment of property, but not by imprisonment of the adjudicated debtor. The obligation which the law imposes on spouses to support one another and on parents to support their children is not considered a 'debt' within Article I, §18, but a legal duty arising out of the status of the parties."

Ex parte Garcia, 795 S.W.2d 740, 741 (Tex.1990). "The district court ordered relator jailed, finding that he was $4,151 in arrears. The court failed to specify, however, the time, date, and place of each occasion on which relator failed to pay such child support. [¶] Because the enforcement order does not contain the requisite specificity, it is not enforceable by contempt."

Ex parte Strickland, 723 S.W.2d 668, 669 (Tex. 1987). "Due process requires both a written judgment of contempt and a written order of commitment in order to punish a person for constructive contempt of court."

Ex parte Davila, 718 S.W.2d 281, 282 (Tex.1986). "If one punishment is assessed for multiple acts of contempt, and one of those acts is not punishable by contempt, the entire judgment is void."

Ex parte De Wees, 210 S.W.2d 145, 146-47 (Tex. 1948). "To order that one be imprisoned for an indefinite period in a civil contempt is purely a remedial measure. Its purpose is to coerce the contemnor to do an act within his or her power to perform. He must have the means by which he may purge himself of the contempt. [¶] Where it is not within the power of a person to perform the act which alone will purge him of contempt, the court is without power to imprison him for an indefinite term as punishment for an offense already committed."

Ex parte Kottwitz, 8 S.W.2d 508, 509 (Tex.1928). "It is an elementary principle of the law of contempt that the punishment must be definite, where its purpose is punishment for a past offense; and, where its purpose is to secure the compliance of some order, it must be entire, and for a time or upon condition certain, and that a judgment which is not certain as to time or condition in some manner is a void judgment. [¶] The rule is that, while a judgment for contempt, the purpose of which is to secure compliance with lawful orders of the court, need not designate the term of imprisonment in months or days, it must, like all judgments, be intelligible and certain, so that the defendant may know what is required of him; and where ... the order does not state that the commitment is until the defendant shall do or perform certain acts in compliance with the orders of the court, but simply states in indefinite language that he is committed until he purges himself of contempt, the order is too indefinite, and is void."

In re Forest, 45 S.W.3d 268, 271 n.1 (Tex.App.—Houston [1st Dist.] 2001, orig. proceeding). "Contrary to relator's assertion in his brief, the contempt order and order of commitment do not have to be signed at the same time. The Texas Family Code contemplates situations such as the one here, when a contempt order providing for incarceration is conditionally suspended, but relator is later committed to jail if he does not comply with the conditions of suspension."

Ex parte Tanner, 904 S.W.2d 202, 205 (Tex.App.—Houston [14th Dist.] 1995, orig. proceeding). "Relator contends that because the commitment order in this case did not comply with one of the three methods listed in ***Stanley***, it is void. [W]e disagree. While those methods were held to be adequate to comply with §14.33(a) [now §157.166], we have been cited no authority that they are the exclusive methods for doing so, or that paraphrasing the provisions to be enforced is not an adequate method."

Ex parte Stanley, 826 S.W.2d 772, 772-73 (Tex. App.—Dallas 1992, orig. proceeding). "An enforcement order shall contain findings setting out in ordinary and concise language the provisions of the final order, decree, or judgment a party seeks to enforce. The enforcement order may do so by: (1) copying in their entirety the provisions for which enforcement was sought; (2) attaching a copy of the order for which enforcement was sought as an exhibit and incorporating it by reference; or (3) giving the volume and page numbers in the minutes of the court where one can find the order for which enforcement was sought. The punitive portion of an enforcement order that does not comply with the statutory requirements of §14.33(a) [now §157.166] is void. [¶] The least preferable method to attempt to comply with [§157.166] is solely by reference to the volume and page of the court minutes where the order can be found. That method requires a contemnor to look beyond the face of the enforcement order itself to determine what provisions of the earlier order he violated. [¶] Typographical errors do not necessarily invalidate contempt orders. When one seeking enforcement of an earlier court order chooses to draft a contempt order referencing the earlier order solely by volume and page of the court's minutes, we hold that strict compliance with [§157.166] requires that both the volume number and the page number be accurate."

Commitment Order

Ex parte Hernandez, 827 S.W.2d 858, 858 (Tex. 1992). "A commitment order is the warrant, process or order by which a court directs a ministerial officer to take custody of a person. The order containing this directive need not take a particular form and may be a separate order issued by the court, an attachment or order issued by the clerk at the court's direction, or included in the contempt judgment. Although the form of the order is not important, the substance is. *At 859:* The contempt order does not direct the sheriff or other ministerial officer to take [contemnor] into custody and detain him under the terms of the judgment, nor does it direct the clerk to issue a written attachment or order of commitment to the proper officer. [¶] Accordingly, a majority of the Court grants the writ of habeas corpus, and orders [contemnor] discharged." *See also* ***Ex parte Ustick***, 9 S.W.3d 922, 925 (Tex.App.—Waco 2000, orig. proceeding).

Ex parte Amaya, 748 S.W.2d 224, 224-25 (Tex. 1988). "In order to satisfy due process requirements, both a written judgment of contempt and a written commitment order are necessary to imprison a person for civil constructive contempt of court. [¶] The trial court may cause a contemnor to be detained by the sheriff or other officer for a short and reasonable time while the judgment of contempt and the order of commitment are being prepared for the judge's signature. We hold that a three-day delay is not a 'short and reasonable time' while the documents are being prepared for signature. [¶] To hold otherwise would allow the trial court to place a person in jail indefinitely without any method for the prisoner to obtain his release by purging himself of the contempt and perhaps, without knowledge of why he was being held in contempt. Such proceedings would be in violation of due process."

In re Markowitz, 25 S.W.3d 1, 3 (Tex.App.—Houston [14th Dist.] 1998, orig. proceeding). "Where the court does not sign a contempt judgment coincidently with a commitment order, the commitment order must contain the elements of a contempt judgment; that is, 'the order should clearly state in what respect the court's order has been violated.'"

Right to Jury Trial

Ex parte Whitehead, 908 S.W.2d 68, 70 (Tex. App.—Houston [1st Dist.] 1995, orig. proceeding). "Another defect in the judgment is that all punishment it assesses for criminal contempt beyond 180 days is void because criminal contempt sentences of more than 180 days may not be assessed unless there was a jury trial or a jury waiver."

FAM §157.167. RESPONDENT TO PAY ATTORNEY'S FEES & COSTS

(a) If the court finds that the respondent has failed to make child support payments, the court shall order the respondent to pay the movant's reasonable attorney's fees and all court costs in addition to the arrearages.

(b) For good cause shown, the court may waive the requirement that the respondent pay attorney's fees and costs if the court states the reasons supporting that finding.

(c) Fees and costs ordered under this section may be enforced by any means available for the enforcement of child support, including contempt.

History of Fam §157.167: Acts 1995, 74th Leg., ch. 20, §1, eff. April 20, 1995. Amended by Acts 1999, 76th Leg., ch. 556, §18, eff. Sept. 1, 1999. Source: Former Fam §14.33(c).

Goudeau v. Marquez, 830 S.W.2d 681, 682 (Tex. App.—Houston [1st Dist.] 1992, no writ). Section 157.167 "requires the trial court to impose attorney's fees and court costs, provided they are reasonable, absent a specific finding that the respondent need not pay the attorney's fees or court costs. The provision is mandatory."

FAM §157.168. ADDITIONAL PERIODS OF POSSESSION OR ACCESS

(a) A court may order additional periods of possession of or access to a child to compensate for the denial of court-ordered possession or access. The additional periods of possession or access:

(1) must be of the same type and duration of the possession or access that was denied;

(2) may include weekend, holiday, and summer possession or access; and

(3) must occur on or before the second anniversary of the date the court finds that court-ordered possession or access has been denied.

(b) The person denied possession or access is entitled to decide the time of the additional possession or access, subject to the provisions of Subsection (a)(1).

History of Fam §157.168: Acts 1995, 74th Leg., ch. 751, §52, eff. Sept. 1, 1995. Amended by Acts 1997, 75th Leg., ch. 974, §1, eff. Sept. 1, 1997; Acts 1999, 76th Leg., ch. 1034, §1, eff. Sept. 1, 1999.

Sections 157.169-157.210 reserved for expansion

SUBCHAPTER E. COMMUNITY SUPERVISION

FAM §157.211. CONDITIONS OF COMMUNITY SUPERVISION

Ⓐ *Section 157.211 below is effective for orders placing a person on community supervision rendered on or after Sept. 1, 2001.*

If the court places the respondent on community supervision and suspends commitment, the terms and conditions of community supervision may include the requirement that the respondent:

(1) report to the community supervision officer as directed;

(2) permit the community supervision officer to visit the respondent at the respondent's home or elsewhere;

(3) obtain counseling on financial planning, budget management, conflict resolution, parenting skills, alcohol or drug abuse, or other matters causing the respondent to fail to obey the order;

(4) pay required child support and any child support arrearages;

(5) pay court costs and attorney's fees ordered by the court;

(6) seek employment assistance services offered by the Texas Workforce Commission under Section 302.0035, Labor Code, if appropriate; and

(7) participate in mediation or other services to alleviate conditions that prevent the respondent from obeying the court's order.

History of Fam §157.211: Acts 1995, 74th Leg., ch. 20, §1, eff. April 20, 1995. Amended by Acts 1997, 75th Leg., ch. 702, §4, eff. Sept. 1, 1997; Acts 1999, 76th Leg., ch. 946, §2, eff. Sept. 1, 1999; Acts 2001, 77th Leg., ch. 311, §1, eff. Sept. 1, 2001. Source: Former Fam §§14.40(e)(1), 14.50(d)(1).

In re Pierre, 50 S.W.3d 554, 559 (Tex.App.—El Paso 2001, orig. proceeding). "[I]n the absence of any evidence of drug abuse and any correlation to Relator's ability to comply with the clear order of support, the trial court abused its discretion by requiring Relator to submit to drug and alcohol testing and ordering him to pay for the same."

FAM §157.211. CONDITIONS OF COMMUNITY SUPERVISION

Section 157.211 below is effective for orders placing a person on community supervision rendered before Sept. 1, 2001.

If the court places the respondent on community supervision and suspends commitment, the terms and conditions of community supervision may include the requirement that the respondent:

(1) report to the community supervision and corrections department officer as directed;

(2) permit the community supervision and corrections department officer to visit the respondent at the respondent's home or elsewhere;

(3) obtain counseling on financial planning, budget management, conflict resolution, parenting skills, alcohol or drug abuse, or other matters causing the respondent to fail to obey the order;

(4) pay required child support and any child support arrearages; and

(5) pay court costs and attorney's fees ordered by the court.

FAM §157.212. TERM OF COMMUNITY SUPERVISION

The community supervision period may not exceed 10 years.

History of Fam §157.212: Acts 1995, 74th Leg., ch. 20, §1, eff. April 20, 1995. Amended by Acts 1999, 76th Leg., ch. 1313, §1, eff. Sept. 1, 1999. Source: Former Fam §§14.40(e)(2), 14.50(d)(2).

FAM §157.213. COMMUNITY SUPERVISION FEES

(a) The court may require the respondent to pay a fee to the court in an amount equal to that required of a criminal defendant subject to community supervision.

(b) The court may make payment of the fee a condition of granting or continuing community supervision.

Subsection (c) below is effective for deposits of fees paid to courts on or after Sept. 1, 2001.

(c) The court shall deposit the fees received under this subchapter as follows:

(1) if the community supervision officer is employed by a community supervision and corrections department, in the special fund of the county treasury provided by the Code of Criminal Procedure to be used for community supervision; or

(2) if the community supervision officer is employed by a domestic relations office, in one of the following funds, as determined by the office's administering entity:

(A) the general fund for the county in which the domestic relations office is located; or

(B) the office fund established by the administering entity for the domestic relations office.

Subsection (c) below is effective for deposits of fees paid to courts before Sept. 1, 2001.

(c) The court shall deposit the fees received under this subchapter in the special fund of the county treasury provided by the Code of Criminal Procedure to be used for community supervision.

History of Fam §157.213: Acts 1995, 74th Leg., ch. 20, §1, eff. April 20, 1995. Amended by Acts 2001, 77th Leg., ch. 311, §2, eff. Sept. 1, 2001. Source: Former Fam §§14.40(e)(3), 14.50(d)(3).

FAM §157.214. MOTION TO REVOKE COMMUNITY SUPERVISION

A prosecuting attorney, the Title IV-D agency, a domestic relations office, or a party affected by the order may file a verified motion alleging specifically that certain conduct of the respondent constitutes a violation of the terms and conditions of community supervision.

History of Fam §157.214: Acts 1995, 74th Leg., ch. 20, §1, eff. April 20, 1995. Amended by Acts 2001, 77th Leg., ch. 311, §3, eff. Sept. 1, 2001. Source: Former Fam §§14.40(e)(4), 14.50(d)(4).

Ex parte Cuellar, 791 S.W.2d 324, 325 (Tex.App.—Houston [14th Dist.] 1990, orig. proceeding). "The filing of a verified motion which alleges a specific and particular manner in which certain conduct constitutes a violation of the terms and conditions of probation is permitted by ... §14.40(e)(4) [now §157.214]. [¶] Nothing comes to our attention requiring the stringent specificity and particularity of ... §14.33 [now §157.166] to be extended to orders of commitment for violation of probation granted pursuant to ... §14.40 [now §157.001]. It is only necessary that the motion to revoke probation include the requisite degree of specificity and particularity prescribed by [§157.214]."

FAM §157.215. ARREST FOR ALLEGED VIOLATION OF COMMUNITY SUPERVISION

(a) If the motion to revoke community supervision alleges a prima facie case that the respondent has violated a term or condition of community supervision, the court may order the respondent's arrest by warrant.

(b) The respondent shall be brought promptly before the court ordering the arrest.

History of Fam §157.215: Acts 1995, 74th Leg., ch. 20, §1, eff. April 20, 1995. Source: Former Fam §§14.40(e)(5), 14.50(d)(5).

FAM §157.216. HEARING ON MOTION TO REVOKE COMMUNITY SUPERVISION

(a) The court shall hold a hearing without a jury on or before the first working day after the date the respondent is arrested under Section 157.215. If the court is unavailable for a hearing on that date, the hearing shall be held not later than the first working day after the date the court becomes available.

(b) The hearing under this section may not be held later than the third working day after the date the respondent is arrested.

(c) After the hearing, the court may continue, modify, or revoke the community supervision.

History of Fam §157.216: Acts 1995, 74th Leg., ch. 20, §1, eff. April 20, 1995. Source: Former Fam §§14.40(e)(6), 14.50(d)(6).

FAM §157.217. DISCHARGE FROM COMMUNITY SUPERVISION

(a) When a community supervision period has been satisfactorily completed, the court on its own motion shall discharge the respondent from community supervision.

(b) The court may discharge the respondent from community supervision on the motion of the respondent if the court finds that the respondent:

(1) has satisfactorily completed one year of community supervision; and

(2) has fully complied with the community supervision order.

History of Fam §157.217: Acts 1995, 74th Leg., ch. 20, §1, eff. April 20, 1995. Source: Former Fam §§14.40(e)(7), 14.50(d)(7).

Sections 157.218-157.260 reserved for expansion

SUBCHAPTER F. JUDGMENT & INTEREST

FAM §157.261. UNPAID CHILD SUPPORT AS JUDGMENT

(a) A child support payment not timely made constitutes a final judgment for the amount due and owing, including interest as provided in this chapter.

(b) For the purposes of this subchapter, interest begins to accrue on the date the judge signs the order for the judgment unless the order contains a statement that the order is rendered on another specific date.

History of Fam §157.261: Acts 1995, 74th Leg., ch. 20, §1, eff. April 20, 1995. Amended by Acts 1997, 75th Leg., ch. 702, §5, eff. Sept. 1, 1997. Source: Former Fam §14.41(a).

Williams v. Patton, 821 S.W.2d 141, 141 (Tex. 1991). "This case presents the question whether §14.41(a) [now §157.261] prohibits parents from settling claims for child support arrearages before the unpaid amount has been reduced to a final judgment. We hold that [§157.261] does prohibit such settlements. *At 144:* The purpose of [§157.261] is to provide a custodial parent with remedies for nonpayment of child support in addition to contempt. Once the custodial parent obtains a money judgment for the amount of arrearages, this judgment may be enforced by any means normally available to a judgment creditor. Requiring that the trial court reduce arrearages to a final judgment before the parties can enter into a settlement and release agreement shields the custodial parent from the financial pressures which frequently result when child support goes unpaid. *At 146:* Requiring that the trial court reduce arrearages to a final judgment before such agreements can be entered into protects the interests of the child by encouraging the payment of child support and protects the interests of the custodial parent by equalizing the bargaining positions of the parties."

In re J.M.T., 39 S.W.3d 234, 244 (Tex.App.—Waco 1999, no pet.). "[W]e find nothing [in the Family Code] that alleviates the need for [mother] to have pleadings to support the relief requested. [Mother] pleaded in the alternative. Only in the event that the trial court failed to terminate the parental rights of [father] did [mother] request a judgment for the arrearage. Because the trial court's judgment ordered termination, and no trial amendment was filed modifying the relief requested, [mother] has no pleading to support the entry of a judgment for the arrearage. Accordingly the trial court did not err when he refused to enter a judgment for the arrearage."

In re Dickinson, 829 S.W.2d 919, 921 (Tex.App.—Amarillo 1992, no writ). "The remedies for delinquent child support which may be pursued by an obligee of either pursuing contempt under §14.40 [now §157.001], or obtaining a judgment for arrearage under §14.41 [now §157.261], are separate and distinct. However, pursuance of the remedy of a judgment for arrearage does not exclude enforcement of the same obligation by contempt."

FAM §157.262. REDUCTION OF ARREARAGES; ABEYANCE OF ENFORCEMENT

A *Section 157.262 below is effective for modification or enforcement proceedings commenced on or after Sept. 1, 2001, and for suits for child support or motions to enforce child support filed on or after Sept. 1, 2001.*

(a) Except as provided by this section, in a contempt proceeding or in rendering a money judgment, the court may not reduce or modify the amount of child support arrearages.

(b) In an enforcement action under this chapter, the court may, with the agreement of the Title IV-D agency, hold in abeyance the enforcement of any arrearages, including interest, assigned to the Title IV-D agency under Section 231.104(a) if, for the period of the court's order of abeyance of enforcement, the obligor:

(1) timely and fully pays the obligor's current child support under a court or administrative order; and

(2) is involved in the life of the child for whom support is ordered through the exercise of the obligor's right of possession of or access to the child.

(c) If the court orders an abeyance of enforcement of arrearages under this section, the court may require the obligor to obtain counseling on parenting skills, work skills, job placement, financial planning, conflict resolution, substance abuse, or other matters causing the obligor to fail to obey the child support order.

(d) If the court finds in a subsequent hearing that the obligor has not met the conditions set by the court's order under this section, the court shall terminate the abeyance of enforcement of the arrearages.

(e) On the expiration of the child support order, the court may, with the agreement of the Title IV-D agency, reduce the amount of the arrearages assigned to the Title IV-D agency under Section 231.104(a) if the court finds that the obligor has complied with the conditions set by the court under this section.

(f) The money judgment for arrearages rendered by the court may be subject to a counterclaim or offset as provided by this subchapter.

History of Fam §157.262: Acts 1995, 74th Leg., ch. 20, §1, eff. April 20, 1995. Amended by Acts 2001, 77th Leg., ch. 1023, §15 (eff. Sept. 1, 2001), ch. 392, §3 (eff. Sept. 1, 2001). Source: Former Fam §§14.40(d), 14.41(a), (d).

Curtis v. Curtis, 11 S.W.3d 466, 473 (Tex.App.—Tyler 2000, no pet.). "As noted in §157.262(b) [now §157.262(f)], a judgment for arrearages may be subject to a counterclaim or offset. Under §157.008, [father] had the burden of proof to establish his entitlement to such an offset. Section 157.008 provides that an offset may be given when he pleads the affirmative defense of voluntary relinquishment, *i.e.*, that 'the obligee voluntarily relinquished to the obligor actual possession and control of a child.' Section 157.008(b), however, specifies that voluntary relinquishment must be for 'a time period in excess of any court-ordered periods of possession of and access to the child,' and it requires that 'actual support must have been supplied by the obligor.' Thus, to receive a credit against the arrearage, the obligor must have provided the court with 'some evidence of his expenditures on the child.'"

FAM §157.262. REDUCTION OF ARREARAGES

Section 157.262 below is effective for modification or enforcement proceedings commenced before Sept. 1, 2001, and for suits for child support or motions to enforce child support filed before Sept. 1, 2001.

(a) In a contempt proceeding or in rendering a money judgment, the court may not reduce or modify the amount of child support arrearages.

(b) The money judgment for arrearages rendered by the court may be subject to a counterclaim or offset as provided by this subchapter.

FAM §157.263. CONFIRMATION OF ARREARAGES

(a) If a motion for enforcement of child support requests a money judgment for arrearages, the court shall confirm the amount of arrearages and render one cumulative money judgment.

(b) A cumulative money judgment includes:

(1) unpaid child support not previously confirmed;

(2) the balance owed on previously confirmed arrearages or lump sum or retroactive support judgments;

(3) interest on the arrearages; and

(4) a statement that it is a cumulative judgment.

History of Fam §157.263: Acts 1995, 74th Leg., ch. 20, §1, eff. April 20, 1995. Source: Former Fam §14.41(a), (e).

In re M.C.R., 55 S.W.3d 104, 109-110 (Tex.App.—San Antonio 2001, no pet.). "[W]e find that the court had no discretion to reduce the arrearage amount by awarding half the accrued interest to the obligor. The court had a ministerial duty to confirm the amount of the arrearage plus accrued interest and render a money judgment in the total amount due and owing the obligee."

In re Dryden, 52 S.W.3d 257, 263-64 (Tex.App.—Corpus Christi 2001, orig. proceeding). "We conclude that the 'error' complained of here—the granting of a judgment for past-due child support which may be executed upon at any time as long as the judgment is unsatisfied—is not erroneous at all. Even though [judge] stated in her April 5 letter that she did not intend for [obligee] to be able to execute on the child-support-arrearage judgment so long as [obligor] complied with the repayment orders, we conclude that [judge] had no authority to preclude [obligee] from attempting to collect the judgment. [Section 157.263] imposes an affirmative, mandatory duty on the trial court to reduce a child support arrearage to a money judgment upon request. [¶] [Because it] was mandatory that [judge] confirm and render the cumulative child-support-arrearage judgment, [judge] had no authority to preclude [obligee] from attempting to collect on the judgment."

In re Gonzalez, 981 S.W.2d 313, 315 (Tex.App.—San Antonio 1998, pet. denied). "We find that by using the word 'shall' in §157.263, the Legislature intended to place the trial court under an affirmative duty."

Buzbee v. Buzbee, 870 S.W.2d 335, 340 (Tex.App.—Waco 1994, no writ). "Section 14.41(a) [now §157.263] merely directs the court to confirm the amount of child-support arrearage. Under its provisions, the trial court has no independent authority to reduce or modify the amount of child support arrearage … the judge here acts as a mere scrivener. Only after the arrearage is confirmed can the judge reduce the amount of the *judgment* to reflect offsets and counterclaims for actual support. Thus, the arrearage calculation under [§157.263] concerns only the monies paid by the obligor to the obligee. It is strictly an arithmetic procedure: What the obligor owes less what the obligor has paid." (Internal quotations omitted.)

FAM §157.264. ENFORCEMENT OF JUDGMENT

Ⓐ *Section 157.264 below is effective for modification or enforcement proceedings commenced on or after Sept. 1, 2001.*

(a) A money judgment rendered as provided in this subchapter may be enforced by any means available for the enforcement of a judgment for debts.

(b) The court may render an order requiring:

(1) that income be withheld from the disposable earnings of the obligor in an amount sufficient to discharge the judgment in not more than two years; or

(2) if the obligor is not subject to income withholding, that the obligor make periodic payments to the obligee in an amount sufficient to discharge the judgment within a reasonable time.

History of Fam §157.264: Acts 1995, 74th Leg., ch. 20, §1, eff. April 20, 1995. Amended by Acts 2001, 77th Leg., ch. 1023, §16, eff. Sept. 1, 2001. Source: Former Fam §14.41(a).

FAM §157.264. ENFORCEMENT BY INCOME WITHHOLDING

Section 157.264 below is effective for modification or enforcement proceedings commenced before Sept. 1, 2001.

A money judgment rendered as provided in this subchapter may be enforced by any means available for the enforcement of a judgment for debts and by an order requiring that income be withheld from the disposable earnings of the obligor.

FAM §157.265. ACCRUAL OF INTEREST ON CHILD SUPPORT

Ⓐ *Section 157.265 below is effective for child support due on or after Jan. 1, 2002, and for unpaid support due before Jan. 1, 2002 when the court has not confirmed arrearages and rendered judgment.*

(a) Interest accrues on the portion of delinquent child support that is greater than the amount of the monthly periodic support obligation at the rate of six percent simple interest per year from the date the support is delinquent until the date the support is paid or the arrearages are confirmed and reduced to money judgment.

(b) Interest accrues on child support arrearages that have been confirmed and reduced to money judgment as provided in this subchapter at the rate of six percent simple interest per year from the date the order is rendered until the date the judgment is paid.

(c) Interest accrues on a money judgment for retroactive or lump-sum child support at the annual rate of six percent simple interest from the date the order is rendered until the judgment is paid.

History of Fam §157.265: Acts 1995, 74th Leg., ch. 20, §1, eff. April 20, 1995. Amended by Acts 1995, 74th Leg., ch. 751, §53, eff. Sept. 1, 1995; Acts 1999, 76th Leg., ch. 943, §1, eff. Jan. 1, 2000; Acts 2001, 77th Leg., ch. 1491, §1, eff. Jan. 1, 2002. Source: Former Fam §14.34(a).

FAM §157.265. ACCRUAL OF INTEREST ON CHILD SUPPORT

Section 157.265 below is effective for money judgments for child support rendered before Jan. 1, 2002.

(a) Interest accrues on the portion of delinquent child support that is greater than the amount of the monthly periodic support obligation at the rate of 12 percent simple interest per year from the date the support is delinquent until the date the support is paid or the arrearages are confirmed and reduced to money judgment.

(b) Interest accrues on child support arrearages that have been confirmed and reduced to money judgment as provided in this subchapter at the rate of 12 percent simple interest per year from the date the order is rendered until the date the judgment is paid.

(c) Interest accrues on a money judgment for retroactive or lump-sum child support at the annual rate of 12 percent simple interest from the date the order is rendered until the judgment is paid.

FAM §157.266. DATE OF DELINQUENCY

(a) A child support payment is delinquent for the purpose of accrual of interest if the payment is not received before the 31st day after the payment date stated in the order by:

(1) the local registry, Title IV-D registry, or state disbursement unit; or

(2) the obligee or entity specified in the order, if payments are not made through a registry.

(b) If a payment date is not stated in the order, a child support payment is delinquent if payment is not received by the registry or the obligee or entity specified in the order on the date that an amount equal to the support payable for one month becomes past due.

History of Fam §157.266: Acts 1995, 74th Leg., ch. 20, §1, eff. April 20, 1995. Amended by Acts 1999, 76th Leg., ch. 943, §2, eff. Jan. 1, 2000. Source: Former Fam §14.34(b).

FAM §157.267. INTEREST ENFORCED AS CHILD SUPPORT

Accrued interest is part of the child support obligation and may be enforced by any means provided for the collection of child support.

History of Fam §157.267: Acts 1995, 74th Leg., ch. 20, §1, eff. April 20, 1995. Source: Former Fam §14.34(c).

FAM §157.268. APPLICATION OF CHILD SUPPORT PAYMENT

Child support collected shall be applied in the following order of priority:

(1) current child support;

(2) non-delinquent child support owed;

(3) interest on the principal amounts specified in Subdivisions (4) and (5);

(4) the principal amount of child support that has not been confirmed and reduced to money judgment;

(5) the principal amount of child support that has been confirmed and reduced to money judgment; and

E *Subsection (6) below is effective for modification or enforcement proceedings commenced on or after Sept. 1, 2001.*

(6) the amount of any ordered attorney's fees or costs.

History of Fam §157.268: Acts 1995, 74th Leg., ch. 20, §1, eff. April 20, 1995. Amended by Acts 2001, 77th Leg., ch. 1023, §17, eff. Sept. 1, 2001. Source: Former Fam §14.34(c).

FAM §157.269. RETENTION OF JURISDICTION

A court that renders an order providing for the payment of child support arrearages retains jurisdiction until all current support and medical support and child support arrearages, including interest and any applicable fees and costs, have been paid.

History of Fam §157.269: Acts 1995, 74th Leg., ch. 751, §54, eff. Sept. 1, 1995. Amended by Acts 1999, 76th Leg., ch. 556, §19, eff. Sept. 1, 1999.

In re Dryden, 52 S.W.3d 257, 265 (Tex.App.—Corpus Christi 2001, orig. proceeding). We "hold that §157.269 ... does not empower a trial court to modify a judgment for child support arrearage after the court's plenary power has expired."

Moore v. Brown, 993 S.W.2d 871, 874 (Tex.App.—Fort Worth 1999, pet. denied). "Nothing in §157.269 suggests that the Legislature intended to vest the trial court with *continuing, exclusive jurisdiction* to later modify an earlier judgment that awarded a specific amount of past-due child support. We must presume that in drafting a statute, the Legislature has a sound purpose for including or excluding relevant provisions. Because §157.269 does not state that the trial court maintains *continuing, exclusive jurisdiction*, we will not imply it absent clear legislative intent."

Sections 157.270-157.310 reserved for expansion

SUBCHAPTER G. CHILD SUPPORT LIEN

FAM §157.311. DEFINITIONS

A *Section 157.311 below is effective for modification or enforcement proceedings commenced on or after Sept. 1, 2001.*

In this subchapter:

(1) "Account" means:

(A) any type of a demand deposit account, checking or negotiable withdrawal order account, savings account, time deposit account, money market mutual fund account, certificate of deposit, or any other instrument of deposit in which an individual has a beneficial ownership either in its entirety or on a shared or multiple party basis, including any accrued interest and dividends; and

(B) a life insurance policy in which an individual has a beneficial ownership or liability insurance against which an individual has filed a claim or counterclaim, including for workers' compensation.

(2) "Claimant" means:

(A) the obligee or a private attorney representing the obligee;

(B) the Title IV-D agency providing child support services;

(C) a domestic relations office or local registry; or

(D) an attorney appointed as a friend of the court.

(3) "Court having continuing jurisdiction" is the court of continuing, exclusive jurisdiction in this state or a tribunal of another state having jurisdiction under the Uniform Interstate Family Support Act or a substantially similar act.

(4) "Financial institution" has the meaning assigned by 42 U.S.C. Section 669a(d)(1) and includes a depository institution, credit union, benefit association, liability or life insurance company, workers' compensation insurer, money market mutual fund, and any similar entity authorized to do business in this state.

(5) "Lien" means a child support lien issued in this or another state.

History of Fam §157.311: Acts 1995, 74th Leg., ch. 20, §1, eff. April 20, 1995. Amended by Acts 1997, 75th Leg., ch. 420, §1 (eff. Sept. 1, 1997), ch. 911, §19 (eff. Sept. 1, 1997); Acts 2001, 77th Leg., ch. 1023, §18, eff. Sept. 1, 2001. Source: Former Fam §14.971(a), (b).

FAM §157.311. DEFINITIONS

Section 157.311 below is effective for modification or enforcement proceedings commenced before Sept. 1, 2001.

In this subchapter:

(1) "Claimant" means:

(A) the obligee or a private attorney representing the obligee;

(B) the Title IV-D agency providing child support services;

(C) a domestic relations office or local registry; or

(D) an attorney appointed as a friend of the court.

(2) "Court having continuing jurisdiction" is the court of continuing, exclusive jurisdiction in this state or a tribunal of another state having jurisdiction under the Uniform Interstate Family Support Act or a substantially similar act.

(3) "Lien" means a child support lien.

FAM §157.312. GENERAL PROVISIONS

(a) A claimant may enforce child support by a lien as provided in this subchapter.

(b) The remedies provided by this subchapter do not affect the availability of other remedies provided by law.

(c) The lien is in addition to any other lien provided by law.

A *Subsection (d) below is effective for modification or enforcement proceedings commenced on or after Sept. 1, 2001.*

(d) A child support lien arises by operation of law against real and personal property of an obligor for all amounts of child support due and owing, including any accrued interest, regardless of whether the amounts have been adjudicated or otherwise determined, subject to the requirements of this subchapter for perfection of the lien.

Subsection (d) below is effective for modification or enforcement proceedings commenced before Sept. 1, 2001.

(d) A child support lien arises:

(1) by operation of law against real and personal property of an obligor for all amounts of overdue support, regardless of whether the amounts have been adjudicated or otherwise determined, subject to the requirements of this subchapter for recording and notice; or

(2) when a court having continuing jurisdiction or, in a Title IV-D case, the Title IV-D agency determines an amount of arrears owed by a child support obligor.

(e) A child support lien arising in another state may be enforced in the same manner and to the same extent as a lien arising in this state.

Ⓐ *Subsection (f) below is effective for modification or enforcement proceedings commenced on or after Sept. 1, 2001.*

(f) A foreclosure action under this subchapter is not required as a prerequisite to levy and execution on a judicial or administrative determination of arrearages as provided by Section 157.327.

Subsection (f) below is effective for modification or enforcement proceedings commenced before Sept. 1, 2001.

(f) A foreclosure action under this subchapter is not required as a prerequisite to levy and execution on a judgment or an administrative determination of arrears rendered after notice and opportunity for hearing.

History of Fam §157.312: Acts 1995, 74th Leg., ch. 20, §1, eff. April 20, 1995. Amended by Acts 1997, 75th Leg., ch. 420, §2 (eff. Sept. 1, 1997), ch. 911, §20 (eff. Sept. 1, 1997); Acts 2001, 77th Leg., ch. 1023, §19, eff. Sept. 1, 2001. Source: Former Fam §§14.971(c), (d), 14.972(d).

FAM §157.313. CONTENTS OF CHILD SUPPORT LIEN NOTICE

Ⓐ *Section 157.313 below is effective for modification or enforcement proceedings commenced on or after Sept. 1, 2001.*

(a) Except as provided by Subsection (e), a child support lien notice must contain:

(1) the name and address of the person to whom the notice is being sent;

(2) the style, docket or cause number, and identity of the tribunal of this or another state having continuing jurisdiction of the child support action and, if the case is a Title IV-D case, the case number;

(3) the full name, address, and, if known, the birth date, driver's license number, social security number, and any aliases of the obligor;

(4) the full name and, if known, social security number of the obligee;

(5) the amount of the current or prospective child support obligation, the frequency with which current or prospective child support is ordered to be paid, and the amount of child support arrearages owed by the obligor and the date of the signing of the court order, administrative order, or writ that determined the arrearages or the date and manner in which the arrearages were determined;

(6) the rate of interest specified in the court order, administrative order, or writ or, in the absence of a specified interest rate, the rate provided for by law;

(7) the name and address of the person or agency asserting the lien;

(8) the motor vehicle identification number as shown on the obligor's title if the property is a motor vehicle;

(9) a statement that the lien attaches to all nonexempt real and personal property of the obligor that is located or recorded in the state, including any property specifically identified in the notice;

(10) a statement that any ordered child support not timely paid in the future constitutes a final judgment for the amount due and owing, including interest, and accrues up to an amount that may not exceed the lien amount; and

(11) a statement that the obligor is being provided a copy of the lien notice and that the obligor may dispute the arrearage amount by filing suit under Section 157.323.

(b) A claimant may include any other information that the claimant considers necessary.

(c) The lien notice must be verified.

(d) A claimant must file a notice for each after-acquired motor vehicle.

(e) A notice of a lien for child support under this section may be in the form authorized by federal law or regulation.

History of Fam §157.313: Acts 1995, 74th Leg., ch. 20, §1, eff. April 20, 1995. Amended by Acts 1997, 75th Leg., ch. 420, §3 (eff. Sept. 1, 1997), ch. 911, §21 (eff. Sept. 1, 1997); Acts 2001, 77th Leg., ch. 1023, §20, eff. Sept. 1, 2001. Source: Former Fam §14.973.

See also 1 TAC §55.119(a).

FAM §157.313. CONTENTS OF LIEN NOTICE

Section 157.313 below is effective for modification or enforcement proceedings commenced before Sept. 1, 2001.

(a) A child support lien notice must contain:

(1) the style, docket number, and identity of the tribunal of this or another state having continuing jurisdiction of the child support action;

(2) the name, address, and, if available, the birth date, driver's license number, and social security number of the obligor;

(3) the name and social security number, if available, of the obligee and the child;

(4) the amount of child support arrearages owed by the obligor and the date of the signing of the court order, administrative order, or writ that determined the arrearages or the date and manner in which the arrearages were determined;

(5) the rate of interest specified in the court order, administrative order, or writ or, in the absence of a specified interest rate, the rate provided for by law;

(6) the name and address of the person or agency asserting the lien; and

(7) the motor vehicle identification number as shown on the obligor's title if the property is a motor vehicle.

(b) A claimant may include any other information that the claimant considers necessary.

(c) The lien notice must be verified.

(d) A claimant must file a notice for each after-acquired motor vehicle.

FAM §157.314. FILING LIEN NOTICE OR ABSTRACT OF JUDGMENT; NOTICE TO OBLIGOR

A *The heading for §157.314 above is effective for modification or enforcement proceedings commenced on or after Sept. 1, 2001.*

FAM §157.314. FILING LIEN NOTICE OR ABSTRACT OF JUDGMENT

The heading for §157.314 above is effective for modification or enforcement proceedings commenced before Sept. 1, 2001.

(a) A child support lien notice or an abstract of judgment for past due child support may be filed by the claimant with the county clerk of:

(1) any county in which the obligor is believed to own nonexempt real or personal property;

(2) the county in which the obligor resides; or

(3) the county in which the court having continuing jurisdiction has venue of the suit affecting the parent-child relationship.

A *Subsection (b) below is effective for modification or enforcement proceedings commenced on or after Sept. 1, 2001.*

(b) A child support lien notice may be filed with or delivered to the following, as appropriate:

Subsection (b) below is effective for modification or enforcement proceedings commenced before Sept. 1, 2001.

(b) A child support lien notice may be filed with:

(1) the clerk of the court in which a claim, counterclaim, or suit by, or on behalf of, the obligor, including a claim or potential right to proceeds from an estate as an heir, beneficiary, or creditor, is pending, provided that a copy of the lien is mailed to the attorney of record for the obligor, if any;

(2) an attorney who represents the obligor in a claim or counterclaim that has not been filed with a court;

(3) any other individual or organization believed to be in possession of real or personal property of the obligor; or

(4) any governmental unit or agency that issues or records certificates, titles, or other indicia of property ownership.

E *Subsections (c) & (d) below are effective for modification or enforcement proceedings commenced on or after Sept. 1, 2001.*

(c) Not later than the 21st day after the date of filing or delivering the child support lien notice, the claimant shall provide a copy of the notice to the obligor by first class or certified mail, return receipt requested, addressed to the obligor at the obligor's last known address. If another person is known to have an ownership interest in the property subject to the lien, the claimant shall provide a copy of the lien notice to that person at the time notice is provided to the obligor.

(d) If a child support lien notice is delivered to a financial institution with respect to an account of the obligor, the institution shall immediately:

(1) provide the claimant with the last known address of the obligor; and

(2) notify any other person having an ownership interest in the account that the account has been frozen in an amount not to exceed the amount of the child support arrearage identified in the notice.

History of Fam §157.314: Acts 1995, 74th Leg., ch. 20, §1, eff. April 20, 1995. Amended by Acts 1997, 75th Leg., ch. 420, §4 (eff. Sept. 1, 1997), ch. 911, §22 (eff. Sept. 1, 1997); Acts 2001, 77th Leg., ch. 1023, §21, eff. Sept. 1, 2001. Source: Former Fam §14.974.

FAM §157.3145. SERVICE ON FINANCIAL INSTITUTION

E *Section 157.3145 below is effective for modification or enforcement proceedings commenced on or after Sept. 1, 2001.*

Service of a child support lien notice on a financial institution relating to property held by the institution in the name of, or in behalf of, an obligor is governed by Section 59.008, Finance Code, if the institution is subject to that law, or may be delivered to the registered agent, the institution's main business office in this state, or another address provided by the institution under Section 231.307.

History of Fam §157.3145: Enacted by Acts 2001, 77th Leg., ch. 1023, §22, eff. Sept. 1, 2001.

FAM §157.315. RECORDING & INDEXING LIEN

A *Section 157.315 below is effective for modification or enforcement proceedings commenced on or after Sept. 1, 2001.*

(a) On receipt of a child support lien notice, the county clerk shall immediately record the notice in the county judgment records as provided in Chapter 52, Property Code.

(b) The county clerk may not charge the Title IV-D agency, a domestic relations office, a friend of the court, or any other party a fee for recording the notice of a lien. To qualify for this exemption, the lien notice must be styled "Notice of Child Support Lien" or be in the form authorized by federal law or regulation.

(c) The county clerk may not charge the Title IV-D agency, a domestic relations office, or a friend of the court a fee for recording the release of a child support lien. The lien release must be styled "Release of Child Support Lien."

History of Fam §157.315: Acts 1995, 74th Leg., ch. 20, §1, eff. April 20, 1995. Amended by Acts 1999, 76th Leg., ch. 769, §1 (eff. Sept. 1, 1999), ch. 595, §1 (eff. Sept. 1, 1999); Acts 2001, 77th Leg., ch. 1023, §23, eff. Sept. 1, 2001. Source: Former Fam §14.975.

FAM §157.315. RECORDING & INDEXING LIEN

Section 157.315 below is effective for modification or enforcement proceedings commenced before Sept. 1, 2001.

(a) On receipt of a lien notice, the county clerk shall record the notice in the county judgment records as provided in Chapter 52, Property Code.

(b) The county clerk may not charge the Title IV-D agency, a domestic relations office, a friend of the court, or any other party a fee for recording the notice of a lien. To qualify for this exemption, the lien notice must be styled "Notice of Child Support Lien."

(c) The county clerk may not charge the Title IV-D agency, a domestic relations office, or a friend of the court a fee for recording the release of a lien. The lien release must be styled "Release of Child Support Lien."

FAM §157.316. PERFECTION OF CHILD SUPPORT LIEN

A *Subsection (a) below is effective for modification or enforcement proceedings commenced on or after Sept. 1, 2001.*

(a) Except as provided by Subsection (b), a child support lien is perfected when an abstract of judgment for past due child support or a child support lien notice is filed or delivered as provided by Section 157.314.

Subsection (a) below is effective for modification or enforcement proceedings commenced before Sept. 1, 2001.

(a) Except as provided by Subsection (b), a child support lien is perfected when an abstract of judgment for past due child support or a child support lien notice is filed with the county clerk as provided by this subchapter.

(b) If a lien established under this subchapter attaches to a motor vehicle, the lien must be perfected in the manner provided by Chapter 501, Transportation Code, and the court or Title IV-D agency that rendered the order of child support shall include in the order a requirement that the obligor surrender to the court or Title IV-D agency evidence of the legal ownership of the motor vehicle against which the lien may attach. A lien against a motor vehicle under this subchapter is not perfected until the obligor's title to the vehicle has been surrendered to the court or Title IV-D agency and the Texas Department of Transportation has issued a subsequent title that discloses on its face the fact that the vehicle is subject to a child support lien under this subchapter.

History of Fam §157.316: Acts 1995, 74th Leg., ch. 20, §1, eff. April 20, 1995. Amended by Acts 1997, 75th Leg., ch. 420, §5 (eff. Sept. 1, 1997), ch. 911, §23 (eff. Sept. 1, 1997); Acts 2001, 77th Leg., ch. 1023, §23, eff. Sept. 1, 2001. Source: Former Fam §14.972(a).

See also 43 TAC §17.9.

FAM §157.317. PROPERTY TO WHICH LIEN ATTACHES

A *Subsection (a) below is effective for modification or enforcement proceedings commenced on or after Sept. 1, 2001.*

(a) A child support lien attaches to all real and personal property not exempt under the Texas Constitution or other law, including an account in a financial institution, a retirement plan, including an individual retirement account, the proceeds of a life insurance policy, a claim for negligence, personal injury, or workers' compensation, or an insurance settlement or award for the claim, due to or owned by the obligor on or after the date the lien notice or abstract of judgment is filed with the county clerk of the county in which the property is located, with the court clerk as to property or claims in litigation, or, as to property of the obligor in the possession or control of a third party, from the date the lien notice is filed with that party.

Subsection (a) below is effective for modification or enforcement proceedings commenced before Sept. 1, 2001.

(a) A child support lien attaches to all real and personal property not exempt under the Texas Constitution or other law, including a depository account in a financial institution, including a mutual fund money market account, or a retirement plan, a claim for negligence, personal injury, or workers' compensation, or an insurance award for the claim, owned by the obligor on or after the date the lien notice or abstract of judgment is filed with the county clerk of the county in which the property is located, with the court clerk as to property or claims in litigation, or, as to property of the obligor in the possession or control of a third party, from the date the lien notice is filed with that party. Service of a lien notice on a financial institution relating to property held by the financial institution in the name of or on behalf of an obligor who is a customer of the financial institution is governed by Section 59.008, Finance Code.

(b) A lien attaches to all nonhomestead real property of the obligor but does not attach to a homestead exempt under the Texas Constitution or the Property Code.

History of Fam §157.317: Acts 1995, 74th Leg., ch. 20, §1, eff. April 20, 1995. Amended by Acts 1997, 75th Leg., ch. 420, §6 (eff. Sept. 1, 1997), ch. 911, §24 (eff. Sept. 1, 1997); Acts 1999, 76th Leg., ch. 556, §20 (eff. Sept. 1, 1999), ch. 344, §7.007 (eff. Sept. 1, 1999); Acts 2001, 77th Leg., ch. 1023, §25, eff. Sept. 1, 2001. Source: Former Fam §14.972(b), (c).

FAM §157.318. DURATION & EFFECT OF CHILD SUPPORT LIEN

A *Subsections (a) & (b) below are effective for modification or enforcement proceedings commenced on or after Sept. 1, 2001.*

(a) A lien is effective until all current support and child support arrearages, including interest and any costs and reasonable attorney's fees, have been paid or the lien is otherwise released as provided by this subchapter.

(b) The lien secures payment of all child support arrearages owed by the obligor under the underlying child support order, including arrearages that accrue after the lien notice was filed or delivered as provided by Section 157.314.

Subsections (a) & (b) below are effective for modification or enforcement proceedings commenced before Sept. 1, 2001.

(a) A lien is effective until all current support and child support arrearages, including interest, have been paid or the lien is otherwise released as provided by this subchapter.

(b) The lien secures payment of all child support arrearages owed by the obligor under the underlying support order, including arrearages that accrue after the administrative or judicial determination of arrearages stated in the lien notice.

(c) The filing of a lien notice or abstract of judgment with the county clerk is a record of the notice and has the same effect as any other lien notice with respect to real property records.

History of Fam §157.318: Acts 1995, 74th Leg., ch. 20, §1, eff. April 20, 1995. Amended by Acts 1997, 75th Leg., ch. 420, §7 (eff. Sept. 1, 1997), ch. 911, §25 (eff. Sept. 1, 1997); Acts 2001, 77th Leg., ch. 1023, §26, eff. Sept. 1, 2001. Source: Former Fam §14.972(e).

FAM §157.319. EFFECT OF LIEN NOTICE

(a) If a person having actual notice of the lien possesses nonexempt personal property of the obligor that may be subject to the lien, the property may not be paid over, released, sold, transferred, encumbered, or conveyed unless:

(1) a release of lien signed by the claimant is delivered to the person in possession; or

(2) a court, after notice to the claimant and hearing, has ordered the release of the lien because arrearages do not exist.

(b) A person having notice of a child support lien who violates this section may be joined as a party to a foreclosure action under this chapter and is subject to the penalties provided by this subchapter.

E *Subsection (c) below is effective for modification or enforcement proceedings commenced on or after Sept. 1, 2001.*

(c) This section does not affect the validity or priority of a lien of a health care provider, a lien for attorney's fees, or a lien of a holder of a security interest. This section does not affect the assignment of rights or subrogation of a claim under Title XIX of the federal Social Security Act (42 U.S.C. Section 1396 et seq.), as amended.

History of Fam §157.319: Acts 1995, 74th Leg., ch. 20, §1, eff. April 20, 1995. Amended by Acts 1997, 75th Leg., ch. 420, §8 (eff. Sept. 1, 1997), ch. 911, §26 (eff. Sept. 1, 1997); Acts 2001, 77th Leg., ch. 1023, §27, eff. Sept. 1, 2001. Source: Former Fam §14.976(b).

FAM §157.320. PRIORITY OF LIEN AS TO REAL PROPERTY

(a) A lien created under this subchapter does not have priority over a lien or conveyance of an interest in the nonexempt real property recorded before the child support lien notice is recorded in the county where the real property is located.

(b) A lien created under this subchapter has priority over any lien or conveyance of an interest in the nonexempt real property recorded after the child support lien notice is recorded in the county clerk's office in the county where the property of the obligor is located.

(c) A conveyance of real property by the obligor after a lien notice has been recorded in the county where the real property is located is subject to the lien and may not impair the enforceability of the lien against the real property.

(d) A lien created under this subchapter is subordinate to a vendor's lien retained in a conveyance to the obligor.

History of Fam §157.320: Acts 1995, 74th Leg., ch. 20, §1, eff. April 20, 1995. Amended by Acts 1997, 75th Leg., ch. 911, §27, eff. Sept. 1, 1997. Source: Former Fam §§14.976(c), 14.977.

FAM §157.321. DISCRETIONARY RELEASE OF LIEN

A *Section 157.321 below is effective for modification or enforcement proceedings commenced on or after Sept. 1, 2001.*

A child support lien claimant may at any time release a lien on all or part of the property of the obligor or return seized property, without liability, if assurance of payment is considered adequate by the claimant or if the release or return will facilitate the collection of the arrearages. The release or return may not operate to prevent future action to collect from the same or other property owned by the obligor.

History of Fam §157.321: Acts 1995, 74th Leg., ch. 20, §1, eff. April 20, 1995. Amended by Acts 1997, 75th Leg., ch. 420, §9 (eff. Sept. 1, 1997), ch. 911, §28 (eff. Sept. 1, 1997); Acts 2001, 77th Leg., ch. 1023, §28, eff. Sept. 1, 2001. Source: Former Fam §14.980.

FAM §157.321. DISCRETIONARY RELEASE OF LIEN

Section 157.321 below is effective for modification or enforcement proceedings commenced before Sept. 1, 2001.

A claimant may at any time release a lien on all or part of the property of the obligor or return seized property, without liability, if assurance of payment is considered adequate by the claimant or if the release or return will facilitate the collection of the arrearages. The release or return may not operate to prevent future action to collect from the same or other property owned by the obligor.

FAM §157.322. MANDATORY RELEASE OF LIEN

A *Section 157.322 below is effective for modification or enforcement proceedings commenced on or after Sept. 1, 2001.*

(a) On payment in full of the amount of child support due, together with any costs and reasonable attorney's fees, the child support lien claimant shall execute and deliver to the obligor or the obligor's attorney a release of the child support lien.

(b) The release of the child support lien is effective when:

(1) filed with the county clerk with whom the lien notice or abstract of judgment was filed; or

(2) delivered to any other individual or organization that may have been served with a lien notice under this subchapter.

History of Fam §157.322: Acts 1995, 74th Leg., ch. 20, §1, eff. April 20, 1995. Amended by Acts 1997, 75th Leg., ch. 420, §10 (eff. Sept. 1, 1997), ch. 911, §29, 97(a) (eff. Sept. 1, 1997); Acts 2001, 77th Leg., ch. 1023, §29, eff. Sept. 1, 2001. Source: Former Fam §14.978.

See also 1 TAC §147.119(b), (c).

FAM §157.322. MANDATORY RELEASE OF LIEN

Section 157.322 below is effective for modification or enforcement proceedings commenced before Sept. 1, 2001.

(a) On payment in full of the amount of child support due, together with any costs and reasonable attorney's fees, the claimant shall execute and deliver to the obligor or the obligor's attorney a release of the child support lien.

(b) The release of lien is effective when filed with the county clerk with whom the lien notice or abstract of judgment was filed. A copy of the release of lien may be filed with any other individual or organization that may have been served with a lien notice under this subchapter.

(c) to (e) Repealed by Acts 1997, 75th Leg., ch. 911, §97(a), eff. Sept. 1, 1997.

FAM §157.323. FORECLOSURE OR SUIT TO DETERMINE ARREARAGES

Ⓐ *Subsections (a) & (b) below are effective for modification or enforcement proceedings commenced on or after Sept. 1, 2001.*

(a) In addition to any other remedy provided by law, an action to foreclose a child support lien, to dispute the amount of arrearages stated in the lien, or to resolve issues of ownership interest with respect to property subject to a child support lien may be brought in:

(1) the court in which the lien notice was filed under Section 157.314(b)(1);

(2) the district court of the county in which the property is or was located and the lien was filed; or

(3) the court of continuing jurisdiction.

(b) The procedures provided by Subchapter B apply to a foreclosure action under this section, except that a person or organization in possession of the property of the obligor or known to have an ownership interest in property that is subject to the lien may be joined as an additional respondent.

Subsections (a) & (b) below are effective for modification or enforcement proceedings commenced before Sept. 1, 2001.

(a) In addition to any other remedy provided by law, an action to foreclose a child support lien or to dispute the amount of arrearages stated in the lien may be brought in the court of continuing jurisdiction or, if there is no court of continuing jurisdiction in this state, in the district court of the county in which the property is or was located and the lien was filed.

(b) The procedures provided by Subchapter B apply to a foreclosure action under this section, except that a person or organization in possession of the property of the obligor may be joined as an additional respondent.

(c) If arrearages are owed by the obligor, the court shall:

(1) render judgment against the obligor for the amount due, plus costs and reasonable attorney's fees;

(2) order any official authorized to levy execution to satisfy the lien, costs, and attorney's fees by selling any property on which a lien is established under this subchapter; or

(3) order an individual or organization in possession of nonexempt personal property or cash owned by the obligor to dispose of the property as the court may direct.

(d) For execution and sale under this section, publication of notice is necessary only for three consecutive weeks in a newspaper published in the county where the property is located or, if there is no newspaper in that county, in the most convenient newspaper in circulation in the county.

History of Fam §157.323: Acts 1995, 74th Leg., ch. 20, §1, eff. April 20, 1995. Amended by Acts 1997, 75th Leg., ch. 420, §11 (eff. Sept. 1, 1997), ch. 911, §30 (eff. Sept. 1, 1997); Acts 2001, 77th Leg., ch. 1023, §30, eff. Sept. 1, 2001. Source: Former Fam §14.979.

FAM §157.324. LIABILITY FOR FAILURE TO COMPLY WITH ORDER OR LIEN

Ⓐ *Section 157.324 below is effective for modification or enforcement proceedings commenced on or after Sept. 1, 2001.*

A person who knowingly disposes of property subject to a child support lien, who, after a foreclosure hearing, fails to surrender on demand nonexempt personal property as directed by a court or administrative order under this subchapter, or who fails to comply with a notice of levy under this subchapter is liable to the claimant in an amount equal to the arrearages for which the lien, notice of levy, or foreclosure judgment was issued.

History of Fam §157.324: Acts 1995, 74th Leg., ch. 20, §1, eff. April 20, 1995. Amended by Acts 1997, 75th Leg., ch. 420, §12 (eff. Sept. 1, 1997), ch. 911, §31 (eff. Sept. 1, 1997); Acts 2001, 77th Leg., ch. 1023, §31, eff. Sept. 1, 2001. Source: Former Fam §14.981.

FAM §157.324. LIABILITY FOR FAILURE TO COMPLY WITH ORDER OR LIEN

Section 157.324 below is effective for modification or enforcement proceedings commenced before Sept. 1, 2001.

A person who knowingly disposes of property subject to a lien or who, after a foreclosure hearing, fails to surrender on demand nonexempt personal property as directed by a court or administrative order under this subchapter is liable to the claimant in an amount equal to the arrearages for which the foreclosure judgment was issued.

FAM §157.325. RELEASE OF EXCESS FUNDS TO DEBTOR OR OBLIGOR

A *Subsection (a) below is effective for modification or enforcement proceedings commenced on or after Sept. 1, 2001.*

(a) If a person has in the person's possession earnings, deposits, accounts, balances, or other funds or assets of the obligor, including the proceeds of a judgment or other settlement of a claim or counterclaim due to the obligor that are in excess of the amount of arrearages specified in the child support lien, the holder of the nonexempt personal property or the obligor may request that the claimant release any excess amount from the lien. The claimant shall grant the request and discharge any lien on the excess amount unless the security for the arrearages would be impaired.

Subsection (a) below is effective for modification or enforcement proceedings commenced before Sept. 1, 2001.

(a) If a person has in the person's possession earnings, deposits, accounts, or balances in excess of the amount of arrearages specified in the child support lien, the holder of the nonexempt personal property or the obligor may request that the claimant release any excess amount from the lien. The claimant shall grant the request and discharge any lien on the excess unless the security for the arrearages would be impaired.

(b) If the claimant refuses the request, the holder of the personal property or the obligor may file suit under this subchapter for an order determining the amount of arrearages and discharging excess personal property or money from the lien.

History of Fam §157.325: Acts 1995, 74th Leg., ch. 20, §1, eff. April 20, 1995. Amended by Acts 1997, 75th Leg., ch. 420, §13 (eff. Sept. 1, 1997), ch. 911, §32 (eff. Sept. 1, 1997); Acts 2001, 77th Leg., ch. 1023, §32, eff. Sept. 1, 2001. Source: Former Fam §14.982.

FAM §157.326. INTEREST OF OBLIGOR'S SPOUSE OR ANOTHER PERSON HAVING OWNERSHIP INTEREST

A *Section 157.326 below is effective for modification or enforcement proceedings commenced on or after Sept. 1, 2001.*

(a) A spouse of an obligor or another person having an ownership interest in property that is subject to a child support lien may file suit under Section 157.323 to determine the extent, if any, of the spouse's or other person's interest in real or personal property that is subject to:

(1) a lien perfected under this subchapter; or

(2) an action to foreclose under this subchapter.

(b) After notice to the obligor, the obligor's spouse, any other person alleging an ownership interest, the claimant, and the obligee, the court shall conduct a hearing and determine the extent, if any, of the ownership interest in the property held by the obligor's spouse or other person. If the court finds that:

(1) the property is the separate property of the obligor's spouse or the other person, the court shall order that the lien against the property be released and that any action to foreclose on the property be dismissed;

(2) the property is jointly owned by the obligor and the obligor's spouse, the court shall determine whether the sale of the obligor's interest in the property would result in an unreasonable hardship on the obligor's spouse or family and:

(A) if so, the court shall render an order that the obligor's interest in the property not be sold and that the lien against the property should be released; or

(B) if not, the court shall render an order partitioning the property and directing that the property be sold and the proceeds applied to the child support arrearages; or

E (3) the property is owned in part by another person, other than the obligor's spouse, the court shall render an order partitioning the property and directing that the obligor's share of the property be applied to the child support arrearages.

(c) In a proceeding under this section, the spouse or other person claiming an ownership interest in the property has the burden to prove the extent of that ownership interest.

History of Fam §157.326: Acts 1995, 74th Leg., ch. 20, §1, eff. April 20, 1995. Amended by Acts 1997, 75th Leg., ch. 420, §14 (eff. Sept. 1, 1997), ch. 911, §33 (eff. Sept. 1, 1997); Acts 2001, 77th Leg., ch. 1023, §33, eff. Sept. 1, 2001. Source: Former Fam §14.983.

FAM §157.326. INTEREST OF OBLIGOR'S SPOUSE

Section 157.326 below is effective for modification or enforcement proceedings commenced before Sept. 1, 2001.

(a) A spouse of an obligor may file an affidavit with the court of continuing jurisdiction or, if there is no court of continuing jurisdiction in this state, in the district court of the county in which the property is or was located and the lien was filed requesting that the court determine the extent, if any, of the spouse's interest in real or personal property that is subject to:

(1) a lien perfected under this subchapter; or

(2) an action to foreclose under this subchapter.

(b) After notice to the obligor, obligor's spouse, the claimant, and the obligee, the court shall conduct a hearing and determine the extent, if any, of the ownership interest in the property held by the obligor's spouse. If the court finds that:

(1) the property is the separate property of the obligor's spouse, the court shall order that the lien against the property be released and that any action to foreclose on the property be dismissed; or

(2) the property is jointly owned by the obligor and the obligor's spouse, the court shall determine whether the sale of the obligor's interest in the property would result in an unreasonable hardship on the obligor's spouse or family and:

(A) if so, the court shall render an order that the obligor's interest in the property not be sold and that the lien against the property should be released; or

(B) if not, the court shall render an order partitioning the property and directing that the property be sold and the proceeds applied to the child support arrearages.

(c) In a proceeding under this section, the spouse claiming an ownership interest in the property has the burden to prove the extent of that ownership interest.

FAM §157.327. EXECUTION & LEVY ON FINANCIAL ASSETS OF OBLIGOR

E *Section 157.327 below is effective for modification or enforcement proceedings commenced on or after Sept. 1, 2001.*

(a) Notwithstanding any other provision of law, if a judgment or administrative determination of arrearages has been rendered, a claimant may deliver a notice of levy to any financial institution possessing or controlling assets or funds owned by, or owed to, an obligor and subject to a child support lien, including a lien for child support arising in another state.

(b) The notice under this section must:

(1) identify the amount of child support arrearages owing at the time the amount of arrearages was determined; and

(2) direct the financial institution to pay to the claimant, not earlier than the 15th day or later than the 21st day after the date of delivery of the notice, an amount from the assets of the obligor or from funds due to the obligor that are held or controlled by the institution, not to exceed the amount of the child support arrearages identified in the notice, unless:

(A) the institution is notified by the claimant that the obligor has paid the arrearages or made arrangements satisfactory to the claimant for the payment of the arrearages;

(B) the obligor or another person files a suit under Section 157.323 requesting a hearing by the court; or

(C) if the claimant is the Title IV-D agency, the obligor has requested an agency review under Section 157.328.

(c) A financial institution that receives a notice of levy under this section may not close an account in which the obligor has an ownership interest, permit a withdrawal from any account the obligor owns, in whole or in part, or pay funds to the obligor so that any amount remaining in the account is less than the amount of the arrearages identified in the notice, plus any fees due to the institution and any costs of the levy identified by the claimant.

(d) A financial institution that receives a notice of levy under this section shall notify any other person having an ownership interest in an account in which the obligor has an ownership interest that the account has been levied on in an amount not to exceed the amount of the child support arrearages identified in the notice of levy.

(e) The notice of levy may be delivered to a financial institution as provided by Section 59.008, Finance Code, if the institution is subject to that law or may be delivered to the registered agent, the institution's main business office in this state, or another address provided by the institution under Section 231.307.

History of Fam §157.327: Enacted by Acts 2001, 77th Leg., ch. 1023, §34, eff. Sept. 1, 2001.

FAM §157.328. NOTICE OF LEVY SENT TO OBLIGOR

E *Section 157.328 below is effective for modification or enforcement proceedings commenced on or after Sept. 1, 2001.*

(a) At the time the notice of levy under Section 157.327 is delivered to a financial institution, the claimant shall serve the obligor with a copy of the notice.

(b) The notice of levy delivered to the obligor must inform the obligor that:

(1) the claimant will not proceed with levy if, not later than the 10th day after the date of receipt of the notice, the obligor pays in full the amount of arrearages identified in the notice or otherwise makes arrangements acceptable to the claimant for the payment of the arrearage amounts; and

(2) the obligor may contest the levy by filing suit under Section 157.323 not later than the 10th day after the date of receipt of the notice.

(c) If the claimant is the Title IV-D agency, the obligor receiving a notice of levy may request review by the agency not later than the 10th day after the date of receipt of the notice to resolve any issue in dispute regarding the existence or amount of the arrearages. The agency shall provide an opportunity for a review, by telephone conference or in person, as appropriate to the circumstances, not later than the fifth business day after the date an oral or written request from the obligor for the review is received. If the review fails to resolve any issue in dispute, the obligor may file suit under Section 157.323 for a hearing by the court not later than the fifth day after the date of the conclusion of the agency review. If the obligor fails to timely file suit, the Title IV-D agency may request the financial institution to release and remit the funds subject to levy.

(d) The notice under this section may be delivered to the last known address of the obligor by first class mail, certified mail, or registered mail.

History of Fam §157.328: Enacted by Acts 2001, 77th Leg., ch. 1023, §34, eff. Sept. 1, 2001.

FAM §157.329. NO LIABILITY FOR COMPLIANCE WITH NOTICE OF LEVY

E *Section 157.329 below is effective for modification or enforcement proceedings commenced on or after Sept. 1, 2001.*

A financial institution that possesses or has a right to an obligor's assets for which a notice of levy has been delivered and that surrenders the assets or right to assets to a child support lien claimant is not liable to the obligor or any other person for the property or rights surrendered.

History of Fam §157.329: Enacted by Acts 2001, 77th Leg., ch. 1023, §34, eff. Sept. 1, 2001.

FAM §157.330. FAILURE TO COMPLY WITH NOTICE OF LEVY

E *Section 157.330 below is effective for modification or enforcement proceedings commenced on or after Sept. 1, 2001.*

A person who possesses or has a right to property that is the subject of a notice of levy delivered to the person and who refuses to surrender the property or right to property to the claimant on demand is liable to the claimant in an amount equal to the value of the property or right to property not surrendered but that does not exceed the amount of the child support arrearages for which the notice of levy has been filed.

History of Fam §157.330: Enacted by Acts 2001, 77th Leg., ch. 1023, §34, eff. Sept. 1, 2001.

FAM §157.331. ADDITIONAL LEVY TO SATISFY ARREARAGES

E *Section 157.331 below is effective for modification or enforcement proceedings commenced on or after Sept. 1, 2001.*

If the property or right to property on which a notice of levy has been filed does not produce money sufficient to satisfy the amount of child support arrearages identified in the notice of levy, the claimant may proceed to levy on other property of the obligor until the total amount of child support due is paid.

History of Fam §157.331: Enacted by Acts 2001, 77th Leg., ch. 1023, §34, eff. Sept. 1, 2001.

Sections 157.332-157.370 reserved for expansion

SUBCHAPTER H. HABEAS CORPUS

FAM §157.371. JURISDICTION

(a) The relator may file a petition for a writ of habeas corpus in either the court of continuing, exclusive jurisdiction or in a court with jurisdiction to issue a writ of habeas corpus in the county in which the child is found.

(b) Although a habeas corpus proceeding is not a suit affecting the parent-child relationship, the court may refer to the provisions of this title for definitions and procedures as appropriate.

History of Fam §157.371: Acts 1995, 74th Leg., ch. 20, §1, eff. April 20, 1995.

FAM §157.372. RETURN OF CHILD

(a) Subject to Chapter 152 and the Parental Kidnapping Prevention Act (28 U.S.C. Section 1738A), if the right to possession of a child is governed by a court order, the court in a habeas corpus proceeding involving the right to possession of the child shall compel return of the child to the relator only if the court finds that the relator is entitled to possession under the order.

(b) If the court finds that the previous order was granted by a court that did not give the contestants reasonable notice of the proceeding and an opportunity to be heard, the court may not render an order in the habeas corpus proceeding compelling return of the child on the basis of that order.

History of Fam §157.372: Acts 1995, 74th Leg., ch. 20, §1, eff. April 20, 1995. Source: Former Fam §14.10(a), (b).

Greene v. Schuble, 654 S.W.2d 436, 437-38 (Tex. 1983). "In the absence of specific provisions to the contrary in an order establishing conservatorship, the death of the managing conservator ends the conservatorship order and it no longer constitutes a valid subsisting court order for purposes of §14.10 [now §157.372]. Subsection (e) [now §157.376] therefore applies."

Mergerson v. Daggett, 644 S.W.2d 451, 452 (Tex. 1982). Section 157.376, now §14.10(f), "applies only when the right to possession of a child is not governed by a court order. Since the ... Court had previously issued temporary orders regarding [conservatorship], ... §14.10(a) [now §157.372] applies."

Lamphere v. Chrisman, 554 S.W.2d 935, 938 (Tex. 1977). "[T]he writ [of habeas corpus] should be granted when the relator shows that he or she is entitled to custody of the child by virtue of a valid and subsisting court order. The right to possession may *not* be relitigated in the habeas corpus hearing; the relator is entitled to an issuance of the writ immediately on a showing of his or her right to custody."

In re Johnston, 957 S.W.2d 945, 947 (Tex.App.—Beaumont 1997, orig. proceeding). "Assuming that [relator] had the right of possession pursuant to the decree, the trial court was under a duty to compel the return of the children to him. Upon proof of the prior order, and in the absence of a trial court finding that there is a serious, immediate question concerning the welfare of the child, the grant of the writ of habeas corpus should be automatic, immediate, and ministerial, based upon proof of the bare legal right to possession. The motion filed by the real parties in interest does not allege there was a serious immediate question concerning the welfare of the child, nor did the trial court make such a finding. We therefore must conclude the trial court erred by failing to grant [relator's] Application for Writ of Habeas Corpus."

Huffstutlar v. Koons, 789 S.W.2d 707, 710 (Tex. App.—Dallas 1990, orig. proceeding). "There is no right to appeal from the denial of a writ of habeas corpus because the denial is not an appealable order. Thus, mandamus is the proper remedy to compel enforcement of a relator's right to possession of a child."

Alston v. Rains, 589 S.W.2d 481, 483-84 (Tex. App.—Texarkana 1979, orig. proceeding). In a suit brought under §14.10, now §157.372, "the trial court must first determine if the relator is entitled to possession of the child by virtue of a court order. If the court so finds, and unless one of the statutory exceptions listed under [§§157.372-157.376] applies, the duty of the court is to deliver immediate possession of the child to the party named in the court order."

FAM §157.373. RELATOR RELINQUISHED POSSESSION; TEMPORARY ORDERS

(a) If the relator has by consent or acquiescence relinquished actual possession and control of the child for not less than 6 months preceding the date of the filing of the petition for the writ, the court may either compel or refuse to order return of the child.

(b) The court may disregard brief periods of possession and control by the relator during the 6-month period.

(c) In a suit in which the court does not compel return of the child, the court may issue temporary orders under Chapter 105 if a suit affecting the parent-child relationship is pending and the parties have received notice of a hearing on temporary orders set for the same time as the habeas corpus proceeding.

History of Fam §157.373: Acts 1995, 74th Leg., ch. 20, §1, eff. April 20, 1995. Source: Former Fam §14.10(c).

Lewelling v. Bosworth, 840 S.W.2d 640, 644 (Tex. App.—Dallas 1992, orig. proceeding). "We note that §14.10(c) [now §157.373(a)] expressly limits the 'consent and acquiescence' exception to the period immediately *preceding* filing of the petition. The Paternal Grandparents request that we interpret this section to include a 'consent and acquiescence' exception for periods *following* the filing of the petition. We decline to interpret §14.10(c) in a fashion contrary to the unambiguous language of the statute."

FAM §157.374. WELFARE OF CHILD

Notwithstanding any other provision of this subchapter, the court may render an appropriate temporary order if there is a serious immediate question concerning the welfare of the child.

History of Fam §157.374: Acts 1995, 74th Leg., ch. 20, §1, eff. April 20, 1995. Source: Former Fam §14.10(d).

Whatley v. Bacon, 649 S.W.2d 297, 299 (Tex.1983). "[A]n order made pursuant to §14.10(c) [now §157.374] must include a court's finding of a serious and immediate question as is required by the plain language of the statute."

McElreath v. Stewart, 545 S.W.2d 955, 958 (Tex. 1977). Section 157.374 is for "a situation where the child was in imminent danger of physical or emotional harm and immediate action was necessary to protect the child."

Brown v. Dixon, 776 S.W.2d 599, 601 (Tex.App.—Tyler 1989, orig. proceeding). "Whether possession is governed by a court order or not, the issue of a serious immediate question as to the child's welfare may be determined. Such a serious, immediate question must be one in which the child is in such imminent danger of physical or emotional harm that immediate action is necessary to protect the child."

Young v. Martinez, 685 S.W.2d 361, 363 (Tex. App.—San Antonio 1984, orig. proceeding). "While we acknowledge the right of a trial court to enter temporary orders under §14.10(c) [now §157.374], such *temporary* orders should not have the force and effect of a final adjudication of custody."

FAM §157.375. IMMUNITY TO CIVIL PROCESS

(a) While in this state for the sole purpose of compelling the return of a child through a habeas corpus proceeding, the relator is not amenable to civil process and is not subject to the jurisdiction of any civil court except the court in which the writ is pending. The relator is subject to process and jurisdiction in that court only for the purpose of prosecuting the writ.

(b) A request by the relator for costs, attorney's fees, and necessary travel and other expenses under Chapter 106 or 152 is not a waiver of immunity to civil process.

History of Fam §157.375: Acts 1995, 74th Leg., ch. 20, §1, eff. April 20, 1995. Source: Former Fam §14.10(e).

FAM §157.376. NO EXISTING ORDER

(a) If the right to possession of a child is not governed by an order, the court in a habeas corpus proceeding involving the right of possession of the child:

(1) shall compel return of the child to the parent if the right of possession is between a parent and a nonparent and a suit affecting the parent-child relationship has not been filed; or

(2) may either compel return of the child or issue temporary orders under Chapter 105 if a suit affecting the parent-child relationship is pending and the parties have received notice of a hearing on temporary orders set for the same time as the habeas corpus proceeding.

(b) The court may not use a habeas corpus proceeding to adjudicate the right of possession of a child between two parents or between two or more nonparents.

History of Fam §157.376: Acts 1995, 74th Leg., ch. 20, §1, eff. April 20, 1995. Source: Former Fam §14.10(f).

Greene v. Schuble, 654 S.W.2d 436, 437-38 (Tex. 1983). "In the absence of specific provisions to the contrary in an order establishing conservatorship, the death of the managing conservator ends the conservatorship order and it no longer constitutes a valid subsisting court order for purposes of §14.10 [now §157.372]. Subsection (e) [now §157.376] therefore applies. We adhere to the rule we stated prior to the adoption of the Family Code that in the event of the death of the managing conservator, the surviving parent has a right to possession of the children, and a court may enforce this right by issuance of a writ of habeas corpus."

Sections 157.377-157.420 reserved for expansion

SUBCHAPTER I. CLARIFICATION OF ORDERS

FAM §157.421. CLARIFYING NONSPECIFIC ORDER

(a) A court may clarify an order rendered by the court in a proceeding under this title if the court finds, on the motion of a party or on the court's own motion, that the order is not specific enough to be enforced by contempt.

(b) The court shall clarify the order by rendering an order that is specific enough to be enforced by contempt.

(c) A clarified order does not affect the finality of the order that it clarifies.

History of Fam §157.421: Acts 1995, 74th Leg., ch. 20, §1, eff. April 20, 1995. Source: Former Fam §11.22(a), (b), (g).

In re Hamilton, 975 S.W.2d 758, 762 (Tex.App.—Corpus Christi 1998, pet. denied). "A clarification order is analogous to a judgment *nunc pro tunc* in that it cannot substantively change a final order. Because of the confusion between the two competing orders, [obligor] properly sought clarification to learn which order he was expected to obey. The clarification order merely states that the [original] order is effective. Because the second order was never legally effective and could not be enforced, the sole effect of the district court's clarification order was to clarify [attorney general's] obligations and correct the erroneous entry of an unenforceable order. This is not outside the power of the district court as neither order was specific enough to be enforceable until the court clarified which was, in fact, effective."

FAM §157.422. PROCEDURE

(a) The procedure for filing a motion for enforcement of a final order applies to a motion for clarification.

(b) A person is not entitled to a jury in a proceeding under this subchapter.

History of Fam §157.422: Acts 1995, 74th Leg., ch. 20, §1, eff. April 20, 1995. Source: Former Fam §11.22(h), (i).

FAM §157.423. SUBSTANTIVE CHANGE NOT ENFORCEABLE

(a) A court may not change the substantive provisions of an order to be clarified under this subchapter.

(b) A substantive change made by a clarification order is not enforceable.

History of Fam §157.423: Acts 1995, 74th Leg., ch. 20, §1, eff. April 20, 1995. Source: Former Fam §11.22(c).

In re Dryden, 52 S.W.3d 257, 263-64 (Tex.App.—Corpus Christi 2001, orig. proceeding). "The [F]amily [C]ode prohibits a court from substantively changing the provisions of an earlier order, but does not define 'substantive change.' A clarification order is analogous to a judgment *nunc pro tunc* in that it cannot substantively change a final order. Therefore, case law addressing judgments *nunc pro tunc* illuminates what constitutes an impermissible substantive change. A substantive change occurs when a judicial error is corrected because such an error results from judicial reasoning and determination. [W]hen an error results from inaccurately recording the decision of the court, the error is clerical."

Lundy v. Lundy, 973 S.W.2d 687, 688-89 (Tex. App.—Tyler 1998, pet. denied). "Although a court does retain the inherent power to clarify, interpret or enforce a provision of a divorce decree, a court may not set aside or alter a judgment after the expiration of its plenary power, and an order attempting to do so is void. A court may not change the substantive provisions of an order to be clarified, and a substantive change is not enforceable. The only basis for clarifying a prior decree is when a provision is ambiguous and non-specific. In the absence of an ambiguity, the trial court is without authority to modify the judgment."

Dickens v. Willis, 957 S.W.2d 657, 659 (Tex.App.—Austin 1997, no pet.). "The Family Code prohibits a court from substantively changing the provisions of an earlier order with a clarification order. The statute does not define substantive change, but we may look to a similar area of the law for guidance. Like clarification orders, judgments nunc pro tunc cannot substantively change a final order; therefore, case law addressing such judgments illuminates what constitutes an impermissible substantive change. A substantive change occurs when a judicial error is corrected because such an error results from judicial reasoning and determination. On the other hand, when an error results from inaccurately recording the decision of the court, the error is *clerical*. [T]he correction of a clerical error does not [a]ffect a substantive change. [¶] Whether an error is clerical or judicial is a question of law. The question, however, becomes one of law only after the trial court factually determines whether it previously rendered judgment and the judgment's contents. ... Proof of a clerical error must be clear, satisfying, and convincing. Furthermore, [t]his Court must construe the original judgment as a whole toward the end of harmonizing and giving effect to all the court has written." (Internal quotations omitted.)

FAM §157.424. RELATION TO MOTION FOR CONTEMPT

The court may render a clarification order before a motion for contempt is made or heard, in conjunction with a motion for contempt, or after the denial of a motion for contempt.

History of Fam §157.424: Acts 1995, 74th Leg., ch. 20, §1, eff. April 20, 1995. Source: Former Fam §11.22(d).

FAM §157.425. ORDER NOT RETROACTIVE

The court may not provide that a clarification order is retroactive for the purpose of enforcement by contempt.

History of Fam §157.425: Acts 1995, 74th Leg., ch. 20, §1, eff. April 20, 1995. Source: Former Fam §11.22(e).

FAM §157.426. TIME ALLOWED TO COMPLY

(a) In a clarification order, the court shall provide a reasonable time for compliance.

(b) The clarification order may be enforced by contempt after the time for compliance has expired.

History of Fam §157.426: Acts 1995, 74th Leg., ch. 20, §1, eff. April 20, 1995. Source: Former Fam §11.22(f).

CHAPTER 158. WITHHOLDING FROM EARNINGS FOR CHILD SUPPORT

Subchapter A. Income Withholding Required; General Provisions

Subchapter B. Procedure

Subchapter C. Rights & Duties of Employer

Subchapter D. Judicial Writ of Withholding Issued by Clerk

Subchapter E. Modification, Reduction, or Termination of Withholding

Subchapter F. Administrative Writ of Withholding in Title IV-D Cases

SUBCHAPTER A. INCOME WITHHOLDING REQUIRED; GENERAL PROVISIONS

FAM §158.001. INCOME WITHHOLDING; GENERAL RULE

In a proceeding in which periodic payments of child support are ordered, modified, or enforced, the court or the Title IV-D agency shall order that income be withheld from the disposable earnings of the obligor as provided by this chapter.

History of Fam §158.001: Acts 1995, 74th Leg., ch. 20, §1, eff. April 20, 1995. Amended by Acts 1997, 75th Leg., ch. 911, §34, eff. Sept. 1, 1997. Source: Former Fam §§14.05(e), 14.43(a)(1).

FAM §158.002. SUSPENSION OF INCOME WITHHOLDING

Except in a Title IV-D case, the court may provide, for good cause shown or on agreement of the parties, that the order withholding income need not be issued or delivered to an employer until:

(1) the obligor has been in arrears for an amount due for more than 30 days;

(2) the amount of the arrearages is an amount equal to or greater than the amount due for a one-month period; or

(3) any other violation of the child support order has occurred.

History of Fam §158.002: Acts 1995, 74th Leg., ch. 20, §1, eff. April 20, 1995. Amended by Acts 1997, 75th Leg., ch. 911, §35, eff. Sept. 1, 1997. Source: Former Fam §14.43(a)(2), (3).

FAM §158.003. WITHHOLDING FOR ARREARAGES IN ADDITION TO CURRENT SUPPORT

(a) In addition to income withheld for the current support of a child, income shall be withheld from the disposable earnings of the obligor to be applied toward the liquidation of any child support arrearages, including accrued interest as provided in Chapter 157.

(b) The additional amount to be withheld for arrearages shall be an amount sufficient to discharge those arrearages in not more than two years or an additional 20 percent added to the amount of the current monthly support order, whichever amount will result in the arrearages being discharged in the least amount of time.

History of Fam §158.003: Acts 1995, 74th Leg., ch. 20, §1, eff. April 20, 1995. Amended by Acts 1999, 76th Leg., ch. 556, §21, eff. Sept. 1, 1999. Source: Former Fam §14.43(d).

FAM §158.004. WITHHOLDING FOR ARREARAGES WHEN NO CURRENT SUPPORT IS DUE

If current support is no longer owed, the court or the Title IV-D agency shall order that income be withheld for arrearages, including accrued interest as provided in Chapter 157, in an amount sufficient to discharge those arrearages in not more than two years.

History of Fam §158.004: Acts 1995, 74th Leg., ch. 20, §1, eff. April 20, 1995. Amended by Acts 1999, 76th Leg., ch. 556, §22, eff. Sept. 1, 1999. Source: Former Fam §14.43(d).

FAM §158.005. WITHHOLDING TO SATISFY JUDGMENT FOR ARREARAGES

In rendering a cumulative judgment for arrearages, the court shall order that a reasonable amount of income be withheld from the disposable earnings of the obligor to be applied toward the satisfaction of the judgment.

History of Fam §158.005: Acts 1995, 74th Leg., ch. 20, §1, eff. April 20, 1995. Source: Former Fam §§14.41(a), 14.43(d).

Starck v. Nelson, 878 S.W.2d 302, 309 (Tex.App.—Corpus Christi 1994, no writ). "Disposable earnings are different and usually less than net resources."

FAM §158.0051. ORDER FOR WITHHOLDING FOR COSTS & FEES

E *Section 158.0051 below is effective for modification or enforcement proceedings commenced on or after Sept. 1, 2001.*

(a) In addition to an order for income to be withheld for child support, including child support and child support arrearages, the court may render an order that income be withheld from the disposable earnings of the obligor to be applied towards the satisfaction of any ordered attorney's fees and costs resulting from an action to enforce child support under this title.

(b) An order rendered under this section is subordinate to an order or writ of withholding for child support under this chapter and is subject to the maximum amount allowed to be withheld under Section 158.009.

(c) The court shall order that amounts withheld for fees and costs under this section be remitted directly to the person entitled to the ordered attorney's fees or costs or be paid through a local registry for disbursement to that person.

History of Fam §158.0051: Enacted by Acts 2001, 77th Leg., ch. 1023, §35, eff. Sept. 1, 2001.

FAM §158.006. INCOME WITHHOLDING IN TITLE IV-D SUITS

In a Title IV-D case, the court or the Title IV-D agency shall order that income be withheld from the disposable earnings of the obligor and may not suspend, stay, or delay issuance of the order or of a judicial or administrative writ of withholding.

History of Fam §158.006: Acts 1995, 74th Leg., ch. 20, §1, eff. April 20, 1995. Amended by Acts 1997, 75th Leg., ch. 911, §36, eff. Sept. 1, 1997. Source: Former Fam §14.43(b).

FAM §158.007. EXTENSION OF REPAYMENT SCHEDULE BY COURT OR TITLE IV-D AGENCY; UNREASONABLE HARDSHIP

If the court or the Title IV-D agency finds that the schedule for discharging arrearages would cause the obligor, the obligor's family, or children for whom support is due from the obligor to suffer unreasonable hardship, the court or agency may extend the payment period for a reasonable length of time.

History of Fam §158.007: Acts 1995, 74th Leg., ch. 20, §1, eff. April 20, 1995. Amended by Acts 1999, 76th Leg., ch. 556, §22, eff. Sept. 1, 1999. Source: Former Fam §14.43(d).

In re Chambers, 5 S.W.3d 341, 343 (Tex.App.—Texarkana 1999, no pet.). "The plain language of the statute gives the trial court discretionary power over the amount of payment. Thus, the amount of arrearage to be paid each month is determined by the court and is subject to appellate review for an abuse of discretion. [¶] The Legislature chose to write this statute to give the trial court discretion to make its decision based upon the facts of the particular case. [¶] Thus, if the trial court had facts before it from which it could conclude that a higher payment would cause the obligor to suffer an unreasonable hardship, it had the authority to extend the payment schedule. Further, the 'reasonable length of time' aspect of the statute is linked with the requirement that the amount of payment not cause an 'unreasonable hardship' upon the obligor or the obligor's family. This is a factually based question, which must be decided by each court based upon the particular case at bar."

FAM §158.008. PRIORITY OF WITHHOLDING

An order or writ of withholding has priority over any garnishment, attachment, execution, or other assignment or order affecting disposable earnings.

History of Fam §158.008: Acts 1995, 74th Leg., ch. 20, §1, eff. April 20, 1995. Source: Former Fam §14.43(k).

FAM §158.009. MAXIMUM AMOUNT WITHHELD FROM EARNINGS

An order or writ of withholding shall direct that any employer of the obligor withhold from the obligor's disposable earnings the amount specified up to a maximum amount of 50 percent of the obligor's disposable earnings.

History of Fam §158.009: Acts 1995, 74th Leg., ch. 20, §1, eff. April 20, 1995. Amended by Acts 1997, 75th Leg., ch. 911, §37, eff. Sept. 1, 1997. Source: Former Fam §14.43(f).

In re Chambers, 5 S.W.3d 341, 343 (Tex.App.—Texarkana 1999, no pet.). Section 158.009 "mandates that a court may order withholding of no more than the maximum amount of fifty percent of the obligor's disposable earnings. This Court will not impose a mandatory minimum payment as a matter of law when the Legislature has chosen not to write such a minimum into the statute and has provided other factors that must be considered in deciding the amount of monthly payments to be imposed upon the obligor."

Ruffin v. Ruffin, 753 S.W.2d 824, 827 (Tex.App.—Houston [14th Dist.] 1988, no writ). "Texas courts may order any employer of the obligor to withhold up to 50 percent of the obligor's disposable earnings toward the liquidation of any child support arrears. 'Disposable earnings' include disability benefits."

FAM §158.010. ORDER OR WRIT BINDING ON EMPLOYER DOING BUSINESS IN STATE

An order or writ of withholding issued under this chapter and delivered to an employer doing business in this state is binding on the employer without regard to whether the obligor resides or works outside this state.

History of Fam §158.010: Acts 1995, 74th Leg., ch. 20, §1, eff. April 20, 1995. Amended by Acts 1997, 75th Leg., ch. 911, §38, eff. Sept. 1, 1997. Source: Former Fam §14.43(h).

FAM §158.011. VOLUNTARY WITHHOLDING BY OBLIGOR

(a) An obligor may file with the clerk of the court a notarized or acknowledged request signed by the obligor and the obligee for the issuance and delivery to the obligor's employer of a writ of withholding. A notarized or acknowledged request may be filed under this section regardless of whether a writ or order has been served on any party or of the existence or amount of an arrearage.

(b) On receipt of a request under this section, the clerk shall issue and deliver a writ of withholding in the manner provided by this chapter.

(c) An employer that receives a writ of withholding issued under this section may request a hearing in the same manner and according to the same terms provided by Section 158.205.

(d) An obligor whose employer receives a writ of withholding issued under this section may request a hearing in the manner provided by Section 158.309.

(e) An obligee may contest a writ of withholding issued under this section by requesting, not later than the 180th day after the date on which the obligee discovers that the writ has been issued, a hearing in the manner provided by Section 158.309.

(f) A writ of withholding under this section may not reduce the total amount of child support, including arrearages, owed by the obligor.

History of Fam §158.011: Acts 1995, 74th Leg., ch. 751, §55, eff. Sept. 1, 1995. Amended by Acts 1997, 75th Leg., ch. 911, §39, eff. Sept. 1, 1997.

Sections 158.012-158.100 reserved for expansion

SUBCHAPTER B. PROCEDURE

FAM §158.101. APPLICABILITY OF PROCEDURE

Except as otherwise provided in this chapter, the procedure for a motion for enforcement of child support as provided in Chapter 157 applies to an action for income withholding.

History of Fam §158.101: Acts 1995, 74th Leg., ch. 20, §1, eff. April 20, 1995.

FAM §158.102. TIME LIMITATIONS

An order or writ for income withholding under this chapter may be issued until all current support and child support arrearages, interest, and any applicable fees and costs, including ordered attorney's fees and court costs, have been paid.

History of Fam §158.102: Acts 1995, 74th Leg., ch. 20, §1, eff. April 20, 1995. Amended by Acts 1997, 75th Leg., ch. 911, §40, eff. Sept. 1, 1997; Acts 1999, 76th Leg., ch. 556, §23, eff. Sept. 1, 1999. Source: Former Fam §14.43(r).

In re A.D., ___ S.W.3d ___ (Tex.2002) (No. 00-0337; 4-11-02). "Like an order holding the obligor in contempt, a wage-withholding order is available to remedy past violations of a support order whether or not the court has reduced the delinquent amount to a single, cumulative judgment. *At ___:* [S]tatutes providing time limits within which enforcement of an existing support liability may be effected concern the court's continuing enforcement jurisdiction and do not affect substantive rights. When the [parties] divorced in 1974, the only means available to enforce the support order were contempt and a cumulative judgment. Later, the Legislature and Texas voters added wage withholding to the court's enforcement mechanisms, and the court could have used this method to collect [obligor]'s overdue support whether or not it existed as a remedy when [obligor] failed to meet his child-support obligations. Now, the Legislature has created another enforcement method, administrative wage withholding, and has made it available regardless of how long an obligor has avoided his court-ordered support duty. The Legislature has thus elected not to reward [obligor]'s sixteen-year refusal to follow the terms of his divorce decree by forever excusing his duty to support his family. The Legislature was free to adopt new remedies for collecting delinquent child support, such as the administrative writ at issue here, and to apply those remedies in cases in which the court's enforcement power had lapsed. The administrative withholding statute, being remedial in nature, does not violate the Texas Constitution's ban on retroactive laws. *At ___ n.1:* A cumulative judgment for past-due child support increases the available enforcement methods, however, because such cumulative judgments are also enforceable 'by any means available for the enforcement of judgments for debts.'"

In re Digges, 981 S.W.2d 445, 446 n.1 (Tex.App.—San Antonio 1998, no pet.). "Section 158.102 was amended effective September 1, 1997. ... The amendments eliminated the previous four year limitations period imposed on obtaining a writ of income withholding. The amendments allow the income withholding remedy for collecting current and past due support to continue indefinitely but do not affect the four year limitations period on obtaining an arrearage judgment."

FAM §158.103. CONTENTS OF ORDER OR WRIT OF WITHHOLDING

Ⓐ *Section 158.103 below is effective for modification or enforcement proceedings commenced on or after Sept. 1, 2001.*

An order of withholding or writ of withholding issued under this chapter must contain the information required by the forms prescribed by the Title IV-D agency under Section 158.106.

History of Fam §158.103: Acts 1995, 74th Leg., ch. 20, §1, eff. April 20, 1995. Amended by Acts 1997, 75th Leg., ch. 911, §41, eff. Sept. 1, 1997; Acts 1999, 76th Leg., ch. 556, §23, eff. Sept. 1, 1999; Acts 2001, 77th Leg., ch. 1023, §36, eff. Sept. 1, 2001. Source: Former Fam §14.43(e).

FAM §158.103. CONTENTS OF ORDER OR WRIT OF WITHHOLDING

Section 158.103 below is effective for modification or enforcement proceedings commenced before Sept. 1, 2001.

An order of withholding or writ of withholding issued under this chapter must contain the information that is necessary for an employer or other entity to comply with the existing child support order, including:

(1) the style, cause number, and court having continuing jurisdiction of the suit;

(2) the name, address, and, if available, the social security number of the obligor;

(3) the amount and duration of the child support payments and medical support payments or other provisions for medical support, the amount of arrearages, accrued interest, and ordered fees and costs;

(4) the name, address, and, if available, the social security numbers of the child and the obligee;

(5) the name and address of the person or agency to whom the payments shall be made;

(6) the amount of income to be withheld and remitted; and

(7) whether the child is to be enrolled in health insurance coverage available through the obligor's employment.

FAM §158.104. REQUEST FOR ISSUANCE OF ORDER OR JUDICIAL WRIT OF WITHHOLDING

A request for issuance of an order or judicial writ of withholding may be filed with the clerk of the court by the prosecuting attorney, the Title IV-D agency, the friend of the court, a domestic relations office, the obligor, the obligee, or an attorney representing the obligee or obligor.

History of Fam §158.104: Acts 1995, 74th Leg., ch. 20, §1, eff. April 20, 1995. Amended by Acts 1997, 75th Leg., ch. 702, §6, eff. Sept. 1, 1997; Acts 1999, 76th Leg., ch. 556, §23, eff. Sept. 1, 1999. Source: Former Fam §14.43(g).

FAM §158.105. ISSUANCE & DELIVERY OF ORDER OR JUDICIAL WRIT OF WITHHOLDING

(a) On filing a request for issuance of an order or judicial writ of withholding, the clerk of the court shall cause a certified copy of the order or writ to be delivered to the obligor's current employer or to any subsequent employer of the obligor.

Ⓐ *Subsections (b) & (c) below are effective for modification or enforcement proceedings commenced on or after Sept. 1, 2001.*

(b) The clerk shall issue and mail the certified copy of the order or judicial writ not later than the fourth working day after the date the order is signed or the request is filed, whichever is later.

(c) An order or judicial writ of withholding shall be delivered to the employer by first class mail or, if requested, by certified or registered mail, return receipt requested, electronic transmission, or by service of citation to:

(1) the person authorized to receive service of process for the employer in civil cases generally; or

(2) a person designated by the employer, by written notice to the clerk, to receive orders or writs of withholding.

Subsections (b) through (d) below are effective for modification or enforcement proceedings commenced before Sept. 1, 2001.

(b) In order to inform the employer, the clerk shall attach a copy of Subchapter C to the order or writ.

(c) The clerk shall issue and mail the certified copy of the order or judicial writ not later than the fourth working day after the date the order is signed or the request is filed, whichever is later.

(d) An order or judicial writ of withholding shall be delivered to the employer by certified or registered mail, return receipt requested, electronic transmission, or by service of citation to:

(1) the person authorized to receive service of process for the employer in civil cases generally; or

(2) a person designated by the employer, by written notice to the clerk, to receive orders or writs of withholding.

History of Fam §158.105: Acts 1995, 74th Leg., ch. 20, §1, eff. April 20, 1995. Amended by Acts 1997, 75th Leg., ch. 702, §7, eff. Sept. 1, 1997; Acts 1999, 76th Leg., ch. 556, §24, eff. Sept. 1, 1999; Acts 2001, 77th Leg., ch. 1023, §37, eff. Sept. 1, 2001. Source: Former Fam §14.43(g), (h).

FAM §158.106. FORMS FOR INCOME WITHHOLDING

Ⓐ *Subsection (a) below is effective for modification or enforcement proceedings commenced on or after Sept. 1, 2001.*

(a) The Title IV-D agency shall prescribe forms as required by federal law in a standard format entitled order or notice to withhold income for child support.

Subsection (a) below is effective for modification or enforcement proceedings commenced before Sept. 1, 2001.

(a) The Title IV-D agency shall prescribe forms as authorized by federal law in a standard format entitled order or notice to withhold income for child support

(b) The Title IV-D agency shall make the appropriate forms available to obligors, obligees, domestic relations offices, friends of the court, and private attorneys.

(c) The Title IV-D agency may prescribe additional forms for the efficient collection of child support and to promote the administration of justice for all parties.

(d) The forms prescribed by the Title IV-D agency under this section may be used to request voluntary withholding under Section 158.011.

History of Fam §158.106: Acts 1995, 74th Leg., ch. 20, §1, eff. April 20, 1995. Amended by Acts 1997, 75th Leg., ch. 911, §42, eff. Sept. 1, 1997; Acts 1999, 76th Leg., ch. 556, §25, eff. Sept. 1, 1999; Acts 2001, 77th Leg., ch. 1023, §38, eff. Sept. 1, 2001. Source: Former Fam §§14.43(p), 14.44(f), 14.45(g).

See also 1 TAC §§55.111-55.119.

FAM §158.107. REPEALED

Repealed by Acts 1997, 75th Leg., ch. 911, §97(a), eff. Sept. 1, 1997.

Sections 158.108-158.200 reserved for expansion

SUBCHAPTER C. RIGHTS & DUTIES OF EMPLOYER

FAM §158.201. ORDER OR WRIT BINDING ON EMPLOYER

(a) An employer required to withhold income from earnings is not entitled to notice of the proceedings before the order is rendered or writ of withholding is issued.

(b) An order or writ of withholding is binding on an employer regardless of whether the employer is specifically named in the order or writ.

History of Fam §158.201: Acts 1995, 74th Leg., ch. 20, §1, eff. April 20, 1995. Amended by Acts 1997, 75th Leg., ch. 911, §43, eff. Sept. 1, 1997. Source: Former Fam §14.316.

FAM §158.202. EFFECTIVE DATE OF & DURATION OF WITHHOLDING

An employer shall begin to withhold income in accordance with an order or writ of withholding not later than the first pay period following the date on which the order or writ was delivered to the employer and shall continue to withhold income as required by the order or writ as long as the obligor is employed by the employer.

History of Fam §158.202: Acts 1995, 74th Leg., ch. 20, §1, eff. April 20, 1995. Amended by Acts 1997, 75th Leg., ch. 911, §44, eff. Sept. 1, 1997. Source: Former Fam §14.43(h).

FAM §158.203. REMITTING WITHHELD PAYMENTS

(a) The employer shall remit the amount to be withheld to the person or office named in the order or writ on each pay date. The payment must include the date on which the withholding occurred.

(b) For payments made by electronic funds transfer or electronic data interchange, the employer shall transmit the amount withheld not later than the second business day after the pay date.

(c) The employer shall include with each payment transmitted:

(1) the number assigned by the Title IV-D agency, if available, and the county identification number, if available;

(2) the name of the county or the county's federal information processing standard code;

(3) the cause number of the suit under which withholding is required;

(4) the payor's name and social security number; and

(5) the payee's name and, if available, social security number, unless the payment is transmitted by electronic funds transfer.

(d) In a case in which an obligor's income is subject to withholding, the employer shall remit the payment of child support directly to a local registry, the Title IV-D agency, or to the state disbursement unit.

History of Fam §158.203: Acts 1995, 74th Leg., ch. 20, §1, eff. April 20, 1995. Amended by Acts 1997, 75th Leg., ch. 702, §8, eff. Jan. 1, 1998; Acts 1999, 76th Leg., ch. 556, §26, eff. Sept. 1, 1999. Source: Former Fam §14.43(h).

FAM §158.204. EMPLOYER MAY DEDUCT FEE FROM EARNINGS

An employer may deduct an administrative fee of not more than $10 each month from the obligor's disposable earnings in addition to the amount to be withheld as child support.

History of Fam §158.204: Acts 1995, 74th Leg., ch. 20, §1, eff. April 20, 1995. Amended by Acts 1999, 76th Leg., ch. 859, §1 (eff. Sept. 1, 1999). Source: Former Fam §14.43(i).

FAM §158.205. HEARING REQUESTED BY EMPLOYER

(a) Not later than the 20th day after the date an order or writ of withholding is delivered, the employer may, as appropriate, file a motion with the court or file a request with the Title IV-D agency for a hearing on the applicability of the order or writ to the employer. The Title IV-D agency by rule shall establish procedures for an agency hearing under this section.

(b) The hearing under this section shall be held not later than the 15th day after the date the motion or request was made.

(c) An order or writ of withholding remains binding and payments shall continue to be made pending further order of the court or, in the case of an administrative writ, action of the Title IV-D agency.

History of Fam §158.205: Acts 1995, 74th Leg., ch. 20, §1, eff. April 20, 1995. Amended by Acts 1997, 75th Leg., ch. 911, §45, eff. Sept. 1, 1997. Source: Former Fam §§14.43(j), 14.43(d).

See also 1 TAC §55.115.

FAM §158.206. LIABILITY & OBLIGATION OF EMPLOYER; WORKERS' COMPENSATION CLAIMS

A *The heading above is effective for modification or enforcement proceedings commenced on or after Sept. 1, 2001.*

FAM §158.206. LIABILITY & OBLIGATION OF EMPLOYER FOR PAYMENTS

The heading above is effective for modification or enforcement proceedings commenced before Sept. 1, 2001.

(a) An employer receiving an order or a writ of withholding under this chapter, including an order or writ directing that health insurance be provided to a child, who complies with the order or writ is not liable to the obligor for the amount of income withheld and paid as required by the order or writ.

(b) An employer receiving an order or writ of withholding who does not comply with the order or writ is liable:

(1) to the obligee for the amount not paid in compliance with the order or writ, including the amount the obligor is required to pay for health insurance under Chapter 154;

(2) to the obligor for:

(A) the amount withheld and not paid as required by the order or writ; and

(B) an amount equal to the interest that accrues under Section 157.265 on the amount withheld and not paid; and

(3) for reasonable attorney's fees and court costs.

E *Subsection (c) below is effective for modification or enforcement proceedings commenced on or after Sept. 1, 2001.*

(c) If an obligor has filed a claim for workers' compensation, the obligor's employer shall send a copy of the income withholding order or writ to the insurance carrier with whom the claim has been filed in order to continue the ordered withholding of income.

History of Fam §158.206: Acts 1995, 74th Leg., ch. 20, §1, eff. April 20, 1995. Amended by Acts 1995, 74th Leg., ch. 341, §4.07, eff. Sept. 1, 1995; Acts 1997, 75th Leg., ch. 911, §46, eff. Sept. 1, 1997; Acts 1999, 76th Leg., ch. 859, §2 (eff. Sept. 1, 1999), ch. 1580, §1 (eff. Sept. 1, 1999); Acts 2001, 77th Leg., ch. 1023, §39, eff. Sept. 1, 2001. Source: Former Fam §14.43(*l*).

FAM §158.207. EMPLOYER RECEIVING MORE THAN ONE ORDER OR WRIT

(a) An employer receiving two or more orders or writs for one obligor shall comply with each order or writ to the extent possible.

(b) If the total amount due under the orders or writs exceeds the maximum amount allowed to be withheld under Section 158.009, the employer shall pay an equal amount towards the current support in each order or writ until the employer has complied fully with each current support obligation and, thereafter, equal amounts on the arrearages until the employer has complied with each order or writ, or until the maximum total amount of allowed withholding is reached, whichever occurs first.

E (c) An employer who receives more than one order or writ of withholding that combines withholding for child support and spousal maintenance as provided by Section 8.101 shall withhold income and pay the amount withheld in accordance with Section 8.207.

History of Fam §158.207: Acts 1995, 74th Leg., ch. 20, §1, eff. April 20, 1995. Amended by Acts 1997, 75th Leg., ch. 911, §47, eff. Sept. 1, 1997; Acts 2001, 77th Leg., ch. 807, §2, eff. Sept. 1, 2001. Source: Former Fam §14.43(*l*).

FAM §158.208. EMPLOYER MAY COMBINE AMOUNTS WITHHELD

An employer required to withhold from more than one obligor may combine the amounts withheld and make a single payment to each agency designated if the employer separately identifies the amount of the payment that is attributable to each obligor.

History of Fam §158.208: Acts 1995, 74th Leg., ch. 20, §1, eff. April 20, 1995. Source: Former Fam §14.43(*l*).

FAM §158.209. EMPLOYER'S PENALTY FOR DISCRIMINATORY HIRING OR DISCHARGE

(a) An employer may not use an order or writ of withholding as grounds in whole or part for the termination of employment or for any other disciplinary action against an employee.

(b) An employer may not refuse to hire an employee because of an order or writ of withholding.

(c) If an employer intentionally discharges an employee in violation of this section, the employer continues to be liable to the employee for current wages and other benefits and for reasonable attorney's fees and court costs incurred in enforcing the employee's rights as provided in this section.

(d) An action under this section may be brought by the employee, a friend of the court, the domestic relations office, or the Title IV-D agency.

History of Fam §158.209: Acts 1995, 74th Leg., ch. 20, §1, eff. April 20, 1995. Amended by Acts 1997, 75th Leg., ch. 911, §48, eff. Sept. 1, 1997. Source: Former Fam §14.43(m).

FAM §158.210. FINE FOR NONCOMPLIANCE

(a) In addition to the civil remedies provided by this subchapter or any other remedy provided by law, an employer who knowingly violates the provisions of this chapter may be subject to a fine not to exceed $200 for each occurrence in which the employer fails to:

(1) withhold income for child support as instructed in an order or writ issued under this chapter; or

(2) remit withheld income within the time required by Section 158.203 to the payee identified in the order or writ or to the state disbursement unit.

(b) A fine recovered under this section shall be paid to the county in which the obligee resides and shall be used by the county to improve child support services.

History of Fam §158.210: Acts 1995, 74th Leg., ch. 20, §1, eff. April 20, 1995. Amended by Acts 1997, 75th Leg., ch. 420, §15, eff. Sept. 1, 1997; Acts 1999, 76th Leg., ch. 556, §27, eff. Sept. 1, 1999. Source: Former Fam §14.43(n).

FAM §158.211. NOTICE OF TERMINATION OF EMPLOYMENT & OF NEW EMPLOYMENT

(a) If an obligor terminates employment with an employer who has been withholding income, both the obligor and the employer shall notify the court or the Title IV-D agency and the obligee of that fact not later than the seventh day after the date employment terminated and shall provide the obligor's last known address and the name and address of the obligor's new employer, if known.

(b) The obligor has a continuing duty to inform any subsequent employer of the order or writ of withholding after obtaining employment.

History of Fam §158.211: Acts 1995, 74th Leg., ch. 20, §1, eff. April 20, 1995. Amended by Acts 1999, 76th Leg., ch. 556, §28, eff. Sept. 1, 1999. Source: Former Fam §14.43(o).

FAM §158.212. IMPROPER PAYMENT

An employer who remits a payment to an incorrect office or person shall remit the payment to the agency or person identified in the order of withholding not later than the second business day after the date the employer receives the returned payment.

History of Fam §158.212: Acts 1999, 76th Leg., ch. 556, 29, eff. Sept. 1, 1999.

Sections 158.213-158.300 reserved for expansion

SUBCHAPTER D. JUDICIAL WRIT OF WITHHOLDING ISSUED BY CLERK

FAM §158.301. NOTICE OF APPLICATION FOR JUDICIAL WRIT OF WITHHOLDING; FILING

(a) A notice of application for judicial writ of withholding may be filed if:

(1) a delinquency occurs in child support payments in an amount equal to or greater than the total support due for one month; or

(2) income withholding was not ordered at the time child support was ordered.

(b) The notice of application for judicial writ of withholding may be filed in the court of continuing jurisdiction by:

(1) the Title IV-D agency;

(2) the attorney representing the local domestic relations office;

(3) the attorney appointed a friend of the court as provided in Chapter 202;

(4) the obligor or obligee; or

(5) a private attorney representing the obligor or obligee.

(c) The Title IV-D agency may in a Title IV-D case file a notice of application for judicial writ of withholding on request of the obligor or obligee.

History of Fam §158.301: Acts 1995, 74th Leg., ch. 20, §1, eff. April 20, 1995. Amended by Acts 1995, 74th Leg., ch. 751, §57, eff. Sept. 1, 1995; Acts 1997, 75th Leg., ch. 911, §50, eff. Sept. 1, 1997. Source: Former Fam §14.44(a).

FAM §158.302. CONTENTS OF NOTICE OF APPLICATION FOR JUDICIAL WRIT OF WITHHOLDING

The notice of application for judicial writ of withholding shall be verified and:

(1) state the amount of monthly support due, including medical support, the amount of arrearages or anticipated arrearages, including accrued interest, and the amount of wages that will be withheld in accordance with a judicial writ of withholding;

(2) state that the withholding applies to each current or subsequent employer or period of employment;

(3) state that if the obligor does not contest the withholding within 10 days after the date of receipt of the notice, the obligor's employer will be notified to begin the withholding;

(4) describe the procedures for contesting the issuance and delivery of a writ of withholding;

(5) state that if the obligor contests the withholding, the obligor will be afforded an opportunity for a hearing by the court not later than the 30th day after the date of receipt of the notice of contest;

(6) state that the sole ground for successfully contesting the issuance of a writ of withholding is a dispute concerning the identity of the obligor or the existence or amount of the arrearages, including accrued interest;

(7) describe the actions that may be taken if the obligor contests the notice of application for judicial writ of withholding, including the procedures for suspending issuance of a writ of withholding; and

(8) include with the notice a suggested form for the motion to stay issuance and delivery of the judicial writ of withholding that the obligor may file with the clerk of the appropriate court.

History of Fam §158.302: Acts 1995, 74th Leg., ch. 20, §1, eff. April 20, 1995. Amended by Acts 1997, 75th Leg., ch. 911, §51, eff. Sept. 1, 1997. Source: Former Fam §14.44(b).

See also 1 TAC §55.111.

Attorney General's Office v. Mitchell, 819 S.W.2d 556, 559-60 (Tex.App.—Dallas 1991, no writ). Appellant's "failure to *timely* seek judicial review [within ten days of the delinquency asserted to support the issuance of the writ], bars his *untimely* complaints from being heard. [¶] [A]dequacy of [appellant's] notice of his delinquency was an administrative determination reviewable by the court *only* if [appellant] timely sought judicial review, and since no review was timely sought, the determination remained effective. No jurisdiction could thereafter be conferred upon a court to review his delinquency."

FAM §158.303. INTERSTATE REQUEST FOR INCOME WITHHOLDING

(a) The registration of a foreign support order as provided in Chapter 159 is sufficient for the filing of a notice of application for judicial writ of withholding.

(b) The notice shall be filed with the clerk of the court having venue as provided in Chapter 159.

(c) Notice of application for judicial writ of withholding may be delivered to the obligor at the same time that an order is filed for registration under Chapter 159.

History of Fam §158.303: Acts 1995, 74th Leg., ch. 20, §1, eff. April 20, 1995. Amended by Acts 1995, 74th Leg., ch. 751, §58, eff. Sept. 1, 1995; Acts 1997, 75th Leg., ch. 911, §52, eff. Sept. 1, 1997. Source: Former Fam §14.44(h).

FAM §158.304. ADDITIONAL ARREARAGES

If the notice of application for judicial writ of withholding states that the obligor has repeatedly failed to pay support in accordance with the underlying support order, the judicial writ may include arrearages that accrue between the filing of the notice and the date of the hearing or the issuance of a judicial writ of withholding.

History of Fam §158.304: Acts 1995, 74th Leg., ch. 20, §1, eff. April 20, 1995. Amended by Acts 1997, 75th Leg., ch. 911, §53, eff. Sept. 1, 1997. Source: Former Fam §14.44(d).

FAM §158.305. REPEALED

Repealed by Acts 1997, 75th Leg., ch. 911, §97(a), eff. Sept. 1, 1997.

FAM §158.306. DELIVERY OF NOTICE OF APPLICATION FOR JUDICIAL WRIT OF WITHHOLDING; TIME OF DELIVERY

(a) A notice of application for judicial writ of withholding may be delivered to the obligor by:

(1) hand delivery by a person designated by the Title IV-D agency or local domestic relations office;

(2) first-class or certified mail, return receipt requested, addressed to the obligor's last known address or place of employment; or

(3) by service of citation as in civil cases generally.

(b) If the notice is delivered by mailing or hand delivery, the party who filed the notice shall file with the court a certificate stating the name, address, and date on which the mailing or hand delivery was made.

(c) Notice is considered to have been received by the obligor:

(1) if hand delivered, on the date of delivery;

(2) if mailed by certified mail, on the date of receipt;

(3) if mailed by first-class mail, on the 10th day after the date the notice was mailed; or

(4) if delivered by service of citation, on the date of service.

History of Fam §158.306: Acts 1995, 74th Leg., ch. 20, §1, eff. April 20, 1995. Amended by Acts 1997, 75th Leg., ch. 911, §54, eff. Sept. 1, 1997. Source: Former Fam §14.45(a).

FAM §158.307. MOTION TO STAY ISSUANCE OF WRIT OF WITHHOLDING

(a) The obligor may stay issuance of a judicial writ of withholding by filing a motion to stay with the clerk of court not later than the 10th day after the date the notice of application for judicial writ of withholding was received.

(b) The grounds for filing a motion to stay issuance are limited to a dispute concerning the identity of the obligor or the existence or the amount of the arrearages.

(c) The obligor shall verify that statements of fact in the motion to stay issuance of the writ are true and correct.

History of Fam §158.307: Acts 1995, 74th Leg., ch. 20, §1, eff. April 20, 1995. Amended by Acts 1997, 75th Leg., ch. 911, §55, eff. Sept. 1, 1997. Source: Former Fam §14.44(c).

FAM §158.308. EFFECT OF FILING MOTION TO STAY

The filing of a motion to stay by an obligor in the manner provided by Section 158.307 prohibits the clerk of court from delivering the judicial writ of withholding to any employer of the obligor before a hearing is held.

History of Fam §158.308: Acts 1995, 74th Leg., ch. 20, §1, eff. April 20, 1995. Amended by Acts 1997, 75th Leg., ch. 911, §56, eff. Sept. 1, 1997. Source: Former Fam §14.44(c).

FAM §158.309. HEARING ON MOTION TO STAY

(a) If a motion to stay is filed in the manner provided by Section 158.307, the court shall set a hearing on the motion and the clerk of court shall notify the obligor, obligee, or their authorized representatives, and the party who filed the application for judicial writ of withholding of the date, time, and place of the hearing.

(b) The court shall hold a hearing on the motion to stay not later than the 30th day after the date the motion was filed, except that a hearing may be held later than the 30th day after filing if both the obligor and obligee agree and waive the right to have the motion heard within 30 days.

(c) Upon hearing, the court shall:

(1) render an order for income withholding that includes a determination of the amount of child support arrearages, including medical support and interest; or

(2) grant the motion to stay.

History of Fam §158.309: Acts 1995, 74th Leg., ch. 20, §1, eff. April 20, 1995. Amended by Acts 1995, 74th Leg., ch. 751, §59, eff. Sept. 1, 1995; Acts 1997, 75th Leg., ch. 911, §57, eff. Sept. 1, 1997. Source: Former Fam §14.44(d).

FAM §158.310. SPECIAL EXCEPTIONS

(a) A defect in a notice of application for judicial writ of withholding is waived unless the respondent specially excepts in writing and cites with particularity the alleged defect, obscurity, or other ambiguity in the notice.

(b) A special exception under this section must be heard by the court before hearing the motion to stay issuance.

(c) If the court sustains an exception, the court shall provide the party filing the notice an opportunity to refile and the court shall continue the hearing to a date certain without the requirement of additional service.

History of Fam §158.310: Acts 1995, 74th Leg., ch. 20, §1, eff. April 20, 1995. Amended by Acts 1997, 75th Leg., ch. 911, §58, eff. Sept. 1, 1997. Source: Former Fam §14.44(d).

FAM §158.311. ARREARAGES

(a) Payment of arrearages after receipt of notice of application for judicial writ of withholding may not be the sole basis for the court to refuse to order withholding.

(b) The court shall order that a reasonable amount of income be withheld to be applied toward the liquidation of arrearages, even though a judgment confirming arrearages has been rendered against the obligor.

History of Fam §158.311: Acts 1995, 74th Leg., ch. 20, §1, eff. April 20, 1995. Amended by Acts 1997, 75th Leg., ch. 911, §59, eff. Sept. 1, 1997. Source: Former Fam §§14.43(a)(4), 14.44(a).

FAM §158.312. REQUEST FOR ISSUANCE & DELIVERY OF WRIT OF WITHHOLDING

(a) If a notice of application for judicial writ of withholding is delivered and a motion to stay is not filed within the time limits provided by Section 158.307, the party who filed the notice shall file with the clerk of the court a request for issuance of the writ of withholding stating the amount of current support, including medical support, the amount of arrearages, and the amount to be withheld from the obligor's income.

(b) The request for issuance may not be filed before the 11th day after the date of receipt of the notice of application for judicial writ of withholding by the obligor.

History of Fam §158.312: Acts 1995, 74th Leg., ch. 20, §1, eff. April 20, 1995. Amended by Acts 1997, 75th Leg., ch. 911, §60, eff. Sept. 1, 1997; Acts 1999, 76th Leg., ch. 307, §30, eff. Sept. 1, 1999. Source: Former Fam §14.45(a).

FAM §158.313. ISSUANCE & DELIVERY OF WRIT OF WITHHOLDING

(a) On the filing of a request for issuance of a writ of withholding, the clerk of the court shall issue the writ.

(b) The writ shall be delivered as provided by Subchapter B.

(c) The clerk shall issue and mail the writ not later than the second working day after the date the request is filed.

History of Fam §158.313: Acts 1995, 74th Leg., ch. 20, §1, eff. April 20, 1995. Source: Former Fam §14.45(a).

FAM §158.314. CONTENTS OF WRIT OF WITHHOLDING

The judicial writ of income withholding issued by the clerk must direct that the employer or a subsequent employer withhold from the obligor's disposable income for current child support, including medical support, and child support arrearages an amount that is consistent with the provisions of this chapter regarding orders of withholding.

History of Fam §158.314: Acts 1995, 74th Leg., ch. 20, §1, eff. April 20, 1995. Amended by Acts 1997, 75th Leg., ch. 911, §61, eff. Sept. 1, 1997. Source: Former Fam §14.45(b).

FAM §158.315. EXTENSION OF REPAYMENT SCHEDULE BY PARTY; UNREASONABLE HARDSHIP

If the party who filed the notice of application for judicial writ of withholding finds that the schedule for repaying arrearages would cause the obligor, the obligor's family, or the children for whom the support is due from the obligor to suffer unreasonable hardship, the party may extend the payment period in the writ.

History of Fam §158.315: Acts 1995, 74th Leg., ch. 20, §1, eff. April 20, 1995. Amended by Acts 1997, 75th Leg., ch. 911, §62, eff. Sept. 1, 1997. Source: Former Fam §14.45(c).

FAM §158.316. PAYMENT OF AMOUNT TO BE WITHHELD

The amount to be withheld shall be paid to the person or office named in the writ on each pay date and shall include with the payment the date on which the withholding occurred.

History of Fam §158.316: Acts 1995, 74th Leg., ch. 20, §1, eff. April 20, 1995. Source: Former Fam §14.45(a).

FAM §158.317. FAILURE TO RECEIVE NOTICE OF APPLICATION FOR JUDICIAL WRIT OF WITHHOLDING

(a) Not later than the 30th day after the date of the first pay period following the date of delivery of the writ of withholding to the obligor's employer, the obligor may file an affidavit with the court that a motion to stay was not timely filed because the notice of application for judicial writ of withholding was not received by the obligor and that grounds exist for a motion to stay.

(b) Concurrently with the filing of the affidavit, the obligor may file a motion to withdraw the writ of withholding and request a hearing on the applicability of the writ.

(c) Income withholding may not be interrupted until after the hearing at which the court renders an order denying or modifying withholding.

History of Fam §158.317: Acts 1995, 74th Leg., ch. 20, §1, eff. April 20, 1995. Amended by Acts 1997, 75th Leg., ch. 911, §63, eff. Sept. 1, 1997. Source: Former Fam §14.44(e).

Section 158.318 reserved for expansion

FAM §158.319. ISSUANCE & DELIVERY OF JUDICIAL WRIT OF WITHHOLDING TO SUBSEQUENT EMPLOYER

(a) After the issuance of a judicial writ of withholding by the clerk, a party authorized to file a notice of application for judicial writ of withholding under this subchapter may issue the judicial writ of withholding to a subsequent employer of the obligor by delivering to the employer by certified mail a copy of the writ.

(b) The judicial writ of withholding must include the name, address, and signature of the party and clearly indicate that the writ is being issued to a subsequent employer.

(c) The party shall file a copy of the judicial writ of withholding with the clerk not later than the third working day following delivery of the writ to the subsequent employer. The party shall pay the clerk a fee of $15 at the time the copy of the writ is filed.

(d) The party shall file the postal return receipt from the delivery to the subsequent employer not later than the third working day after the party receives the receipt.

History of Fam §158.319: Acts 1995, 74th Leg., ch. 751, §60, eff. Sept. 1, 1995. Amended by Acts 1997, 75th Leg., ch. 911, §64, eff. Sept. 1, 1997.

Sections 158.320-158.400 reserved for expansion

SUBCHAPTER E. MODIFICATION, REDUCTION, OR TERMINATION OF WITHHOLDING

FAM §158.401. MODIFICATIONS TO OR TERMINATION OF WITHHOLDING BY TITLE IV-D AGENCY

(a) The Title IV-D agency shall establish procedures for the reduction in the amount of or termination of withholding from income on the liquidation of an arrearages or the termination of the obligation of support in Title IV-D cases. The procedures shall provide that the payment of overdue support may not be used as the sole basis for terminating withholding.

(b) At the request of the Title IV-D agency, the clerk of the court shall issue a judicial writ of withholding to the obligor's employer reflecting any modification or changes in the amount to be withheld or the termination of withholding.

History of Fam §158.401: Acts 1995, 74th Leg., ch. 20, §1, eff. April 20, 1995. Amended by Acts 1997, 75th Leg., ch. 911, §65, eff. Sept. 1, 1997. Source: Former Fam §§14.43(q), 14.45(f).

FAM §158.402. AGREEMENT BY PARTIES REGARDING AMOUNT OR DURATION OF WITHHOLDING

(a) An obligor and obligee may agree on a reduction in or termination of income withholding for child support on the occurrence of one of the following contingencies stated in the order:

(1) the child becomes 18 years of age or is graduated from high school, whichever is later;

(2) the child's disabilities of minority are removed by marriage, court order, or other operation of law; or

(3) the child dies.

(b) The obligor and obligee may file a notarized or acknowledged request with the clerk of the court under Section 158.011 for a revised judicial writ of withholding, including the termination of withholding.

(c) The clerk shall issue and deliver to an employer of the obligor a judicial writ of withholding that reflects the agreed revision or termination of withholding.

(d) An agreement by the parties under this section does not modify the terms of a support order.

History of Fam §158.402: Acts 1995, 74th Leg., ch. 751, §61, eff. Sept. 1, 1995. Amended by Acts 1997, 75th Leg., ch. 911, §66, eff. Sept. 1, 1997.

FAM §158.403. MODIFICATIONS TO OR TERMINATION OF WITHHOLDING IN VOLUNTARY WITHHOLDING CASES

(a) If an obligor initiates voluntary withholding under Section 158.011, the obligee or an agency providing child support services may file with the clerk of the court a notarized request signed by the obligor and the obligee or agency, as appropriate, for the issuance and delivery to the obligor of a:

(1) modified writ of withholding that reduces the amount of withholding; or

(2) notice of termination of withholding.

(b) On receipt of a request under this section, the clerk shall issue and deliver a modified writ of withholding or notice of termination in the manner provided by Section 158.402.

(c) The clerk may charge a reasonable fee not to exceed $15 for filing the request.

(d) An obligee may contest a modified writ of withholding or notice of termination issued under this section by requesting a hearing in the manner provided by Section 158.309 not later than the 180th day after the date the obligee discovers that the writ or notice has been issued.

History of Fam §158.403: Acts 1995, 74th Leg., ch. 751, §61, eff. Sept. 1, 1995.

FAM §158.404. DELIVERY OF ORDER OF REDUCTION OR TERMINATION OF WITHHOLDING

If a court has rendered an order that reduces the amount of child support to be withheld or terminates withholding for child support, any person or governmental entity may deliver to the employer a certified copy of the order without the requirement that the clerk of the court deliver the order.

History of Fam §158.404: Acts 1995, 74th Leg., ch. 20, §1, eff. April 20, 1995. Renumbered from §158.402 by Acts 1995, 74th Leg., ch. 751, §61, eff. Sept. 1, 1995. Source: Former Fam §14.43(q).

FAM §158.405. LIABILITY OF EMPLOYERS

The provisions of this chapter regarding the liability of employers for withholding apply to an order that reduces or terminates withholding.

History of Fam §158.405: Acts 1995, 74th Leg., ch. 20, §1, eff. April 20, 1995. Renumbered from §158.403 by Acts 1995, 74th Leg., ch. 751, §61, eff. Sept. 1, 1995. Source: Former Fam §14.43(q).

Sections 158.406-158.500 blank

SUBCHAPTER F. ADMINISTRATIVE WRIT OF WITHHOLDING IN TITLE IV-D CASES

FAM §158.501. ISSUANCE OF ADMINISTRATIVE WRIT OF WITHHOLDING BY TITLE IV-D AGENCY

(a) The Title IV-D agency may initiate income withholding by issuing an administrative writ of withholding for the enforcement of an existing order as authorized by this subchapter.

(b) The Title IV-D agency is the only entity that may issue an administrative writ under this subchapter.

E *Subsection (c) below is effective for modification or enforcement proceedings commenced on or after Sept. 1, 2001.*

(c) The Title IV-D agency may use the procedures authorized by this subchapter to enforce a support order rendered by a tribunal of another state regardless of whether the order has been registered under Chapter 159.

History of Fam §158.501: Acts 1997, 75th Leg., ch. 911, §67, eff. Sept. 1, 1997. Amended by Acts 1999, 76th Leg., ch. 556, §31, eff. Sept. 1, 1999; Acts 2001, 77th Leg., ch. 1023, §40, eff. Sept. 1, 2001.

Atty. Gen. v. Redding, 60 S.W.3d 891, 895 (Tex. App.—Dallas 2001, no pet.). "Section 158.501(a) provides 'the [Attorney General] may initiate income withholding by issuing an administrative writ of withholding for the enforcement of an existing order as authorized by this subchapter.' [Obligor] asserts an 'existing order' is limited to (1) a current support order, (2) an order holding an obligor in contempt, or (3) a *judgment* confirming arrearages. [Obligor] concludes that because the trial court lost jurisdiction to enter a judgment for arrearages, and such a judgment is a prerequisite to an administrative writ for arrears, the trial court properly withdrew the writ. The Attorney General responds the definition of 'existing' order is not so limited and includes any enforceable order for support, including a child support order in which arrearages remain due. We agree with the Attorney General."

FAM §158.502. WHEN ADMINISTRATIVE WRIT OF WITHHOLDING MAY BE ISSUED

(a) An administrative writ of withholding under this subchapter may be issued by the Title IV-D agency at any time until all current support, including medical support, and child support arrearages have been paid. The writ issued under this subsection may be based on an obligation in more than one support order.

(b) The Title IV-D agency may issue an administrative writ of withholding that directs that an amount be withheld for an arrearage or adjusts the amount to be withheld for an arrearage. An administrative writ issued under this subsection may be contested as provided by Section 158.506.

Ⓐ *Subsection (c) below is effective for modification or enforcement proceedings commenced on or after Sept. 1, 2001.*

(c) The Title IV-D agency may issue an administrative writ of withholding as a reissuance of an existing withholding order on file with the court of continuing jurisdiction or a tribunal of another state. The administrative writ under this subsection is not subject to the contest provisions of Sections 158.505(a)(2) and 158.506.

Subsection (c) below is effective for modification or enforcement proceedings commenced before Sept. 1, 2001.

(c) The Title IV-D agency may issue an administrative writ of withholding as a reissuance of an existing withholding order on file with the court of continuing jurisdiction. The administrative writ under this subsection is not subject to the contest provisions of Sections 158.505(a)(2) and 158.506.

History of Fam §158.502: Acts 1997, 75th Leg., ch. 911, §67, eff. Sept. 1, 1997. Amended by Acts 1999, 76th Leg., ch. 556, §31, eff. Sept. 1, 1999; Acts 2001, 77th Leg., ch. 1023, §41, eff. Sept. 1, 2001.

In re A.D., ___ S.W.3d ___ (Tex.2002) (No. 00-0337; 4-11-02). "Like an order holding the obligor in contempt, a wage-withholding order is available to remedy past violations of a support order whether or not the court has reduced the delinquent amount to a single, cumulative judgment. *At* ___: [S]tatutes providing time limits within which enforcement of an existing support liability may be effected concern the court's continuing enforcement jurisdiction and do not affect substantive rights. When the [parties] divorced in 1974, the only means available to enforce the support order were contempt and a cumulative judgment. Later, the Legislature and Texas voters added wage withholding to the court's enforcement mechanisms, and the court could have used this method to collect [obligor]'s overdue support whether or not it existed as a remedy when [obligor] failed to meet his child-support obligations. Now, the Legislature has created another enforcement method, administrative wage withholding, and has made it available regardless of how long an obligor has avoided his court-ordered support duty. The Legislature has thus elected not to reward [obligor]'s sixteen-year refusal to follow the terms of his divorce decree by forever excusing his duty to support his family. The Legislature was free to adopt new remedies for collecting delinquent child support, such as the administrative writ at issue here, and to apply those remedies in cases in which the court's enforcement power had lapsed. The administrative withholding statute, being remedial in nature, does not violate the Texas Constitution's ban on retroactive laws. *At* ___ *n.1:* A cumulative judgment for past-due child support increases the available enforcement methods, however, because such cumulative judgments are also enforceable 'by any means available for the enforcement of judgments for debts.'"

FAM §158.503. DELIVERY OF ADMINISTRATIVE WRIT TO EMPLOYER; FILING WITH COURT

(a) An administrative writ of withholding issued under this subchapter may be delivered to an obligor, obligee, and employer by mail or by electronic transmission.

A *Subsection (b) below is effective for modification or enforcement proceedings commenced on or after Sept. 1, 2001.*

(b) Not later than the third business day after the date of delivery of the administrative writ of withholding to an employer, the Title IV-D agency shall file a copy of the writ, together with a signed certificate of service, in the court of continuing jurisdiction. The certificate of service may be signed electronically. This subsection does not apply to the enforcement under Section 158.501(c) of a support order rendered by a tribunal of another state.

Subsection (b) below is effective for modification or enforcement proceedings commenced before Sept. 1, 2001.

(b) Not later than the third business day after the date of delivery of the administrative writ of withholding to an employer, the Title IV-D agency shall file a copy of the writ, together with a signed certificate of service, in the court of continuing jurisdiction. The certificate of service may be signed electronically.

(c) The copy of the administrative writ of withholding filed with the clerk of court must include:

(1) the name, address, and signature of the authorized attorney or individual that issued the writ;

(2) the name and address of the employer served with the writ; and

(3) a true copy of the information provided to the employer.

E *Subsection (d) below is effective for Title IV-D cases filed on or after Sept. 1, 2001.*

(d) The clerk of the court may charge a reasonable fee not to exceed $15 for filing an administrative writ under this section.

History of Fam §158.503: Acts 1997, 75th Leg., ch. 911, §67, eff. Sept. 1, 1997. Amended by Acts 1999, 76th Leg., ch. 556, §32, eff. Sept. 1, 1999; Acts 2001, 77th Leg., ch. 1023, §42 (eff. Sept. 1, 2001), ch. 116, §1 (eff. Sept. 1, 2001).

FAM §158.504. CONTENTS OF ADMINISTRATIVE WRIT OF WITHHOLDING

(a) The administrative writ of withholding must be in the form prescribed by the Title IV-D agency as required by this chapter and in a standard format authorized by the United States Department of Health and Human Services.

A *Subsection (b) below is effective for modification or enforcement proceedings commenced on or after Sept. 1, 2001.*

(b) An administrative writ of withholding issued under this subchapter may contain only the information that is necessary for the employer to withhold income for child support and medical support and shall specify the place where the withheld income is to be paid.

Subsection (b) below is effective for modification or enforcement proceedings commenced before Sept. 1, 2001.

(b) An administrative writ of withholding issued under this subchapter may contain only the information that is necessary for the employer to comply with the existing support order, including the amount of current support and medical support, the amount of arrearages, accrued interest, and the amount of earnings to be withheld.

History of Fam §158.504: Acts 1997, 75th Leg., ch. 911, §67, eff. Sept. 1, 1997. Amended by Acts 1999, 76th Leg., ch. 556, §33, eff. Sept. 1, 1999; Acts 2001, 77th Leg., ch. 1023, §43, eff. Sept. 1, 2001.

FAM §158.505. NOTICE TO OBLIGOR

(a) On issuance of an administrative writ of withholding, the Title IV-D agency shall send the obligor:

A *Subsection (1) below is effective for modification or enforcement proceedings commenced on or after Sept. 1, 2001.*

(1) notice that the withholding has commenced, including, if the writ is issued as provided by Section 158.502(b), the amount of the arrearages, including accrued interest;

Subsection (1) below is effective for modification or enforcement proceedings commenced before Sept. 1, 2001.

(1) notice that the withholding has commenced;

(2) except as provided by Section 158.502(c), notice of the procedures to follow if the obligor desires to contest withholding on the grounds that the identity

of the obligor or the existence or amount of arrearages is incorrect; and

(3) a copy of the administrative writ, including the information concerning income withholding provided to the employer.

(b) The notice required under this section may be sent to the obligor by:

(1) personal delivery by a person designated by the Title IV-D agency;

(2) first-class mail or certified mail, return receipt requested, addressed to the obligor's last known address; or

(3) service of citation as in civil cases generally.

(c) Repealed by Acts 1999, 76th Leg., ch. 556, §81, eff. Sept. 1, 1999.

History of Fam §158.505: Acts 1997, 75th Leg., ch. 911, §67, eff. Sept. 1, 1997. Amended by Acts 1999, 76th Leg., ch. 556, §§34 & 81, eff Sept. 1, 1999; Acts 2001, 77th Leg., ch. 1023, §44, eff. Sept. 1, 2001.

FAM §158.506. CONTEST BY OBLIGOR TO ADMINISTRATIVE WRIT OF WITHHOLDING

(a) Except as provided by Section 158.502(c), an obligor receiving the notice under Section 158.505 may request a review by the Title IV-D agency to resolve any issue in dispute regarding the identity of the obligor or the existence or amount of arrearages. The Title IV-D agency shall provide an opportunity for a review, by telephonic conference or in person, as may be appropriate under the circumstances.

(b) After a review under this section, the Title IV-D agency may issue a new administrative writ of withholding to the employer, including a writ modifying the amount to be withheld or terminating withholding.

(c) If a review under this section fails to resolve any issue in dispute, the obligor is entitled to the remedies provided by Section 158.317 for cases in which a notice of an application for judicial writ of withholding was not received. The obligor may file a motion with the court to withdraw the administrative writ and request a hearing with the court not later than the 30th day after receiving notice of the agency's determination. Income withholding may not be interrupted pending a hearing by the court.

History of Fam §158.506: Acts 1997, 75th Leg., ch. 911, §67, eff. Sept. 1, 1997. Amended by Acts 1999, 76th Leg., ch. 556, §35, eff. Sept. 1, 1999.

FAM §158.507. ADMINISTRATIVE WRIT TERMINATING WITHHOLDING

An administrative writ to terminate withholding may be issued and delivered to an employer by the Title IV-D agency when all current support, including medical support, and child support arrearages have been paid.

History of Fam §158.507: Acts 1997, 75th Leg., ch. 911, §67, eff. Sept. 1, 1997.

FAM §158.508. REPEALED

Repealed by Acts 2001, 77th Leg., ch. 1023, §76, eff. Sept. 1, 2001.

FAM §158.508. INTERSTATE REQUEST FOR INCOME WITHHOLDING

Section 158.508 below is effective for modification or enforcement proceedings commenced before Sept. 1, 2001.

An administrative writ of withholding may be issued in a Title IV-D interstate case on registration of a foreign support order as provided in Chapter 159.

CHAPTER 159. UNIFORM INTERSTATE FAMILY SUPPORT ACT

Editor's note: Changes have been made to the official comments to reflect the Texas Legislature's omission of sections and changing section numbers. The full uniform act and official comments can be found at http://www.nccusl.org.

Official Prefatory Note

I. Background Information

Congressional legislation in 1975, 1984, 1988, and 1996 has had a major impact on state child support enforcement law. Over time Congress has mandated that, in order to be eligible for federal funding of child support enforcement programs, States must adopt child support guidelines, and establish child support enforcement procedures such as wage withholding, tax intercepts, and credit reporting. Similarly, as a practical matter federal law invaded the area of substantive rules for child support; for example, the Bradley Amendment, adopted in 1986, directs States to enact laws which prohibit retroactive reduction of a child support arrearage stemming from a court order.

To respond to these developments, in 1988 the National Conference of Commissioners on Uniform State Laws (hereafter Conference) established a Drafting Committee to review the Uniform Reciprocal Enforcement of Support Act (URESA) and its revised version (RURESA), some formulation of which had been adopted in all States, and to adopt appropriate revisions to the Uniform Act. After reviewing the congressional legislation of the 1980's and the Model Interstate Income Withholding Act (MIIWA) drafted in 1984 by the American Bar Association and the National Conference of State Legislatures, the Committee originally decided that the interstate aspects of child support enforcement could be adequately addressed by amendments to RURESA.

At the Conference's Annual Meeting in the summer of 1989, the Drafting Committee presented some limited initial changes to RURESA. After obtaining the views of numerous persons familiar with the Act, however, the Committee decided to revise it much more extensively. These changes were presented for a first reading at the Conference's 1990 Annual Meeting. Following additional extensive comments at the 1990 Annual Meeting and from numerous groups and individuals, the Drafting Committee recommended, and the Executive Committee of the Conference agreed, that final approval of the revised RURESA should be delayed until the Conference's 1992 Annual Meeting. Such a timetable coincided with the work of the U.S. Commission on Interstate Child Support. Throughout 1991 and 1992, the Drafting Committee continued to work on the Act, in conjunction with numerous knowledgeable advisors and observers, including five persons who also served as members of the U.S. Commission.

The Drafting Committee and Executive Committee determined that the Act should have a new name – the Uniform Interstate Family Support Act (UIFSA), which was intended to completely revise and replace URESA and RURESA. The Act was unanimously approved by the Uniform Law Conference in August of 1992, and officially ratified by the American Bar Association in February 1993. As of June 1, 1996, 33 States and the District of Columbia had enacted UIFSA.

Implementation of UIFSA by child support enforcement agencies throughout the nation in thousands of cases spurred requests for amendments to a limited number of provisions. A major source of these requests came from individual employers and national payroll associations. Specifically, they sought additional statutory guidance regarding direct income withholding from earnings which the original UIFSA authorized, but did not supply significant detail on its operation (only one relatively short provision controlled, Section 501). In UIFSA the Conference had established a bare legal framework for the withholding of income for child support across state lines without the necessity of involving initiating or responding tribunals or acting through a child support agency. However, employers stated that in order to act efficiently they needed additional explanation of their rights and duties upon the receipt of an out-of-state income-withholding order. Further, proposed federal legislation pending in the U.S. Congress as part of its consideration of "welfare reform" furnished another major reason to reexamine some of the terms of UIFSA.

Motivated by these developments, the Conference convened its UIFSA Oversight Committee to draft proposed amendments. Once again the Drafting Committee enlisted the volunteer assistance of a wide variety of observers, advisors, and consultants to aid in drafting the proposed amendments. Representatives of payroll associations and major employers were included in the discussions to assure that employer interests were taken into account. In this regard, the majority of employers have been very cooperative in assisting in the collection of child support. Their suggestions were centered on making their collection efforts more efficient and effective, and were not an attempt to avoid contributing to this valuable social policy. The amendments approved for incorporation into the Uniform Interstate Family Support Act (1996) were unanimously adopted by the Conference at its San Antonio, Texas, meeting in July 1996.

Shortly after the Conference adopted UIFSA 1996, the likelihood of universal acceptance of the revised Act became virtually certain. In enacting welfare reform, officially known as the Personal Responsibility and Work Opportunity Reconciliation Act of 1996, Congress mandated enactment of UIFSA in order for a State to remain eligible for the federal funding of child support enforcement, as follows:

Sec. 321. ADOPTION OF UNIFORM STATE LAWS

Section 466 (42 U.S.C. §666) is amended by adding at the end the following new subsection:

"(f) Uniform Interstate Family Support Act. – In order to satisfy section 454(20(A), on and after January 1, 1998, each State must have in effect the Uniform Interstate Family Support Act, as approved by the American Bar Association on February 9, 1993, together with any amendments officially adopted before January 1, 1998, by the National Conference of Commissioners on Uniform State Laws." P.L. 104-193, §321, 110 Stat. 2221.

A description of the major changes made to the RURESA procedure by UIFSA and the 1996 amendments to the original Act are as follows.

II. Proposed Changes

A. In General

1. TERMINOLOGY. The terminology of URESA and RURESA has been retained as much as possible to ease the transition to UIFSA, *i.e.*, "responding" and "initiating" State. One notable change is the substitution of the term "tribunal" for "court," in recognition of the fact that many States have created administrative agencies to establish, enforce, and modify child support.

2. REORGANIZATION. UIFSA is organized into a more logical and understandable order than was found in URESA and RURESA ("RURESA" hereafter will be used to refer to both versions unless they each need to be cited separately). The order in which civil and criminal proceedings are dealt with is reversed, which more accurately reflects the frequency and utility of the two proceedings. On the civil side of the docket, separate articles are created for: provisions common to all types of actions (Article 3); the establishment of support (Article 4); the enforcement of a support order of another State without registration (Article 5); the enforcement and modification of support orders after registration (Article 6); and, the determination of parentage (Article 7). In addition, new jurisdictional provisions (Article 2) establish uniform long-arm jurisdiction over nonresidents in order to facilitate one-state proceedings whenever possible. Further, the key principle of "continuing, exclusive jurisdiction" is introduced to interstate child support enforcement and modification. Finally, a method for the transition from URESA and RURESA to the new Act is provided.

3. RECIPROCITY NOT REQUIRED. The hallmark of URESA and RURESA, reciprocity of laws between States, is not required under UIFSA. Prior to the promulgation of UIFSA, all States had quite similar laws. But, UIFSA takes the position that a responding State should enforce a child support obligation irrespective of another state's law. Further, to avoid conflict between state laws UIFSA declares that URESA, RURESA and all substantially similar state laws should be recognized and enforced for purposes of interstate actions (Section 101(7), (16)). Tolerance for the laws of other States and nations in order to facilitate child support enforcement is a prime goal of the Act, which also contains provisions to help ease the transition to the new system. Finally, reciprocity continues to have an impact for international enforcement of support orders.

4. LONG-ARM JURISDICTION. The Act contains a broad provision for asserting long-arm jurisdiction to provide a tribunal in the home State of the supported family with the maximum possible opportunity to secure personal jurisdiction over an absent respondent (Section 201). This converts what otherwise would be a two-state proceeding into a one-state lawsuit. When jurisdiction over a nonresident is obtained, the tribunal may obtain evidence, provide for discovery, and elicit testimony through use of the "information route" provided (Sections 202, 316, and 318).

B. Establishing a Support Order

1. FAMILY SUPPORT. The Act may be used only for proceedings involving the support of a child or spouse of the support obligor, and not to enforce other duties such as support of a parent (Section 101(2), (18)). Under RURESA child support and spousal support were treated identically. However, spousal support is modifiable in the interstate context under UIFSA only when such a request is forwarded to the original issuing State from an initiating State (Sections 205 and 206).

2. LOCAL LAW. A somewhat complex choice of law for establishment of duties of support was provided in RURESA, *i.e.*, the law of the State where the obligor was present for the period during which support was sought. Otherwise RURESA generally referred to the law of the forum. The new Act provides that the procedures and law of the forum apply, with some significant additions or exceptions:

(a) Certain procedures are prescribed for interstate cases even if they are not consistent with local law, *i.e.*, the contents of interstate petitions (Sections 311 and 602); the nondisclosure of certain sensitive information (Section 312); authority to award fees and costs including attorney's fees (Section 313); elimination of certain testimonial immunities (Section 314); and limits on the assertion of nonparentage as a defense to support enforcement (Section 315).

(b) Visitation issues cannot be raised in child support proceedings (Section 305(d)).

(c) Special rules for the interstate transmission of evidence and discovery are added to help place the maximum amount of information before the deciding tribunal. These procedures are available even in one-state cases in which the tribunal asserts long-arm jurisdiction over a nonresident (Sections 202, 316, and 318), and may have the effect of amending local law for long-arm cases.

(d) The choice of law for the interpretation of a registered order is that the law of the issuing State governs the underlying terms of the controlling support order. One important exception exists; if there are different statutes of limitation for enforcement, the longer time limit of either the registering State or the issuing State applies (Section 604).

3. ONE-ORDER SYSTEM. Under RURESA, the majority of support proceedings were de novo. Even when an existing order of one State was "registered" in a second State, the registering State often asserted the right to modify the registered order. This meant that multiple support orders could be in effect in several States. Under UIFSA, the principle of continuing, exclusive jurisdiction aims, so far as possible, to recognize that only one valid support order may be effective at any one time. This principle is carried out in Sections 204 (rules for resolving actions pending in two or more States); 205, and 206 (rules for determining which tribunal has continuing, exclusive jurisdiction over the controlling child support order); 207 (reconciliation with orders issued before the effective date of the Act); and 208 (multiple orders for two or more families supported by the same obligor).

4. PRIVATE ATTORNEYS. In support actions, UIFSA explicitly authorizes parties to retain private legal counsel (Section 309), as well as to use the services of a state support enforcement agency (Section 307(a)). The Act expressly takes no position on whether the support enforcement agency assisting a supported family establishes an attorney-client relationship with the applicant (Section 307(c)).

5. EFFICIENCY. A number of improvements are made to RURESA to streamline interstate proceedings:

(a) Proceedings may be initiated by or referred to administrative agencies rather than to courts in those States that use those agencies to establish support orders (Section 101(22)).

(b) Initiation of an interstate case in the initiating State is expressly made ministerial rather than a matter for adjudication or review by a tribunal. Further, a party in the initiating State may file an action directly in the responding State (Section 301(c)).

(c) To facilitate efficient interstate establishment, enforcement, and modification of child support orders, forms sanctioned by the federal Office of Child Support Enforcement, Department of Health and Human Services, are available. Although developed in conjunction with the federal IV-D program, even private parties and their attorneys who are engaged in an interstate child support case are well advised to use the appropriate forms for transmission of information from the initiating to the responding State (Section 311(b)). The information in those forms is declared to be admissible evidence (Section 316(b)).

(d) Authority is provided for the transmission of information and documents through electronic and other modern means of communication (Section 316(e)).

(e) A tribunal may permit an out-of-state party or witness to be deposed or to testify by telephone conference (Section 316(f)).

(f) Tribunals are required to cooperate in the discovery process for use in a tribunal in another State (Section 318).

(g) Tribunal and a support enforcement agency providing services to a supported family must keep the parties informed about all important developments in a case (Sections 305 and 307).

(h) A registered support order is confirmed and immediately enforceable unless the respondent files a written objection within 20 days after service and sustains that objection (Sections 603 and 607).

6. INTERSTATE PARENTAGE. UIFSA authorizes establishment of parentage in an interstate proceeding, even if not coupled with a proceeding to establish support (Section 701).

C. Enforcing a Support Order

1. DIRECT ENFORCEMENT. The Act provides two direct enforcement procedures that do not require assistance from a tribunal. First, the support order may be sent directly to the obligor's employer in another State (Section 501), which triggers wage withholding by that employer without the necessity of a hearing unless the employee objects. In response to requests from major employers and national payroll associations, UIFSA 1996 greatly expands the procedure to be followed by the employer in response to an interstate request for direct income withholding. Instead of only Section 501 outlining the procedure, the directives on compliance with direct income-withholding now cover six sections (Sections 501-506).

In addition, the Act provides for direct administrative enforcement by the support enforcement agency of the obligor's State (Section 507).

2. REGISTRATION. The registration process of the Act is modeled after that procedure originated in RURESA, but is far more comprehensive. All judicial or administrative agency enforcement activity must begin with the registration of the existing support order in the responding State (Sections 601-604). However, the registered order continues to be the order of the issuing State; the role of the responding State is limited to enforcing that order except in the very limited circumstances under which modification is permitted (Sections 605-608).

D. Modifying a Support Order

1. REGISTRATION. A party (whether obligor or obligee) requesting a tribunal of another State to modify an existing child support order is first directed to follow the identical procedure for registration as when enforcement is sought. Various combination sequences are allowable: *i.e.*, registration for enforcement and later modification; or, a request for contemporaneous modification and enforcement.

2. MODIFICATION LIMITED. Under RURESA most courts held that a responding State could modify a support order for which enforcement was sought. Except for narrowly defined fact circumstances, under UIFSA the only tribunal that can modify a support order is the one having continuing, exclusive jurisdiction over the order. But, if the parties no longer reside in the issuing State, or if they agree in writing that another tribunal may assume modification jurisdiction, a tribunal with personal jurisdiction over the parties, has jurisdiction to modify (Sections 205, 206, 603(c), 609-612). Except for modification by agreement or when the parties have all moved to the same new State, the party petitioning for modification must submit himself or herself to the forum State where the respondent resides. To facilitate modification across international borders, an exception to this rule was added in 1996 for child support orders issued by foreign jurisdictions.

Two additional sections relating to modification were added by UIFSA 1996. Section 613 makes specific that which was previously only implied; when the parties and the child have moved from the issuing State and by coincidence or design the parties currently reside in the same State, that State has jurisdiction to modify the existing order and assume continuing, exclusive jurisdiction over the child support order. Section 614 continues the rule originally found in a subsection of Section 611 that the party obtaining a modification has a duty to provide notice of the new order to all interested tribunals. This stand-alone section serves to improve the organization of the Act; the new section also grants the tribunal authority to sanction a party who fails to perform this duty of notice.

E. Parentage

It was not entirely clear whether RURESA provided for an interstate determination of parentage without also requiring the establishment of support. UIFSA clearly states that interstate determination of parentage is authorized. It may be accomplished without an accompanying establishment of support, or in a contemporaneous manner to both determine parentage and establish support. The Act provides no substantive or procedural alterations to the existing law of the forum with regard to a determination of parentage.

SUBCHAPTER A. CONFLICTS BETWEEN PROVISIONS

FAM §159.001. CONFLICTS BETWEEN PROVISIONS

If a provision of this chapter conflicts with a provision of this title or another statute or rule of this state and the conflict cannot be reconciled, this chapter prevails.

History of Fam §159.001: Acts 1995, 74th Leg., ch. 20, §1, eff. April 20, 1995.

Attorney Gen. v. Litten, 999 S.W.2d 74, 77 (Tex. App.—Houston [14th Dist.] 1999, no pet.). "[T]o the extent any provision in Chapter 157 conflicts with Chapter 159, the provisions of Chapter 159 prevail. Because there is no statutory basis for applying the provisions of Chapter 157 to an action to register and enforce a foreign judgment for child support, we hold Chapter 157 is not applicable to this suit."

In re Henderson, 982 S.W.2d 566, 567 (Tex.App.—Amarillo 1998, no pet.). "[W]hen a party seeks to modify a child support order issued by another state ... the Uniform Interstate Family Support Act applies."

In re Chapman, 973 S.W.2d 346, 348 (Tex.App.—Amarillo 1998, no pet.). "In addition to the Uniform Enforcement of Foreign Judgments Act, the Uniform Interstate Family Support Act, provides the procedure for registering a foreign support order in Texas."

Sections 159.002-159.100 reserved for expansion

SUBCHAPTER B. GENERAL PROVISIONS

FAM §159.101. DEFINITIONS

In this chapter:

(1) "Child" means an individual, whether over or under the age of majority, who:

(A) is or is alleged to be owed a duty of support by the individual's parent; or

(B) is or is alleged to be the beneficiary of a support order directed to the parent.

(2) "Child support order" means a support order for a child, including a child who has attained the age of majority under the law of the issuing state.

(3) "Duty of support" means an obligation imposed or imposable by law to provide support for a child, spouse, or former spouse, including an unsatisfied obligation to provide support.

(4) "Home state" means the state in which a child lived with a parent or a person acting as parent for at least six consecutive months preceding the time of filing of a petition or a comparable pleading for support and, if a child is less than six months old, the state in which the child lived with a parent or a person acting as parent from the time of birth. A period of temporary absence of any of them is counted as part of the six-month or other period.

(5) "Income" includes earnings or other periodic entitlements to money from any source and any other property subject to withholding for support under the law of this state.

(6) "Income-withholding order" means an order or other legal process directed to an obligor's employer, as provided in Chapter 158, to withhold support from the income of the obligor.

(7) "Initiating state" means a state from which a proceeding is forwarded or in which a proceeding is filed for forwarding to a responding state under this chapter or a law or procedure substantially similar to this chapter, the Uniform Reciprocal Enforcement of Support Act, or the Revised Uniform Reciprocal Enforcement of Support Act.

(8) "Initiating tribunal" means the authorized tribunal in an initiating state.

(9) "Issuing state" means the state in which a tribunal issues a support order or renders a judgment determining parentage.

(10) "Issuing tribunal" means the tribunal that issues a support order or renders a judgment determining parentage.

(11) "Law" includes decisional and statutory law and rules and regulations having the force of law.

(12) "Obligee" means:

(A) an individual to whom a duty of support is or is alleged to be owed or in whose favor a support order has been issued or a judgment determining parentage has been rendered;

(B) a state or political subdivision to which the rights under a duty of support or support order have been assigned or that has independent claims based on financial assistance provided to an individual obligee; or

(C) an individual seeking a judgment determining parentage of the individual's child.

(13) "Obligor" means an individual or the estate of a decedent:

(A) who owes or is alleged to owe a duty of support;

(B) who is alleged but has not been adjudicated to be a parent of a child; or

(C) who is liable under a support order.

(14) "Register" means to file a support order or judgment determining parentage in the registry of foreign support orders.

(15) "Registering tribunal" means a tribunal in which a support order is registered.

(16) "Responding state" means a state in which a proceeding is filed or to which a proceeding is forwarded for filing from an initiating state under this chapter or a law or procedure substantially similar to this chapter, the Uniform Reciprocal Enforcement of Support Act, or the Revised Uniform Reciprocal Enforcement of Support Act.

(17) "Responding tribunal" means the authorized tribunal in a responding state.

(18) "Spousal support order" means a support order for a spouse or former spouse of the obligor.

(19) "State" means a state of the United States, the District of Columbia, Puerto Rico, the United States Virgin Islands, or any territory or insular possession subject to the jurisdiction of the United States. The term includes:

(A) an Indian tribe; and

(B) a foreign jurisdiction that has enacted a law or established procedures for issuance and enforcement of support orders that are substantially similar to the procedures under this chapter, the Uniform Reciprocal Enforcement of Support Act, or the Revised Uniform Reciprocal Enforcement of Support Act.

(20) "Support enforcement agency" means a public official or agency authorized to seek:

(A) enforcement of support orders or laws relating to the duty of support;

(B) establishment or modification of child support;

(C) determination of parentage; or

(D) the location of obligors or their assets.

"Support enforcement agency" does not include a domestic relations office unless that office has entered into a cooperative agreement with the Title IV-D agency to perform duties under this chapter.

(21) "Support order" means a judgment, decree, or order, whether temporary, final, or subject to modification, for the benefit of a child, a spouse, or a former spouse that provides for monetary support, health care, arrearages, or reimbursement and may include related costs and fees, interest, income withholding, attorney's fees, and other relief.

(22) "Tribunal" means a court, administrative agency, or quasi-judicial entity authorized to establish, enforce, or modify support orders or to determine parentage.

History of Fam §159.101: Acts 1995, 74th Leg., ch. 20, §1, eff. April 20, 1995. Amended by Acts 1997, 75th Leg., ch. 607, §1, eff. Sept. 1, 1997. Source: Former Fam §21.01.

Office of Attorney Gen. v. Carter, 977 S.W.2d 159, 161 (Tex.App.—Houston [14th Dist.] 1998, no pet.). "While it is true that a parent has a duty to support his or her child, under UIFSA, a nonparent seeking a support order to be established and enforced against a parent must have legal custody of the child. [T]he statute requires an 'obligor' to owe a duty of support to an 'obligee.' *At 162-63:* In this case, [grandparent] was not [child's] custodial parent or legal custodian. Thus, she was not an obligee under the statute's definition. Moreover, because [grandmother] had no right to receive support payments, she had no rights to assign to the State of Georgia's Department of Human Resources. Thus, Georgia's Department of Human Resources was not an obligee under the statute's definition. Consequently, the trial court did not err in refusing to enter a child support order for [child]. [¶] Section 102.003(9) determines who has general standing to file suit in a ['SAPCR']. A proceeding filed under UIFSA, however, is not a SAPCR. Thus, §102.003(9) does not apply in this case. *At 162 n.3:* We believe if the Texas Legislature had intended 'obligee' to include a nonparent without legal custody who is supporting the child, they would have so stated. *At 163:* We are not holding that [mother] is not liable to [grandparent] for the necessaries [grandparent] provided for [child]. However, [grandparent] may not seek support from [mother] under UIFSA because it requires that either (1) a support order exist or (2) [grandparent] have legal custody of [child]. [Grandparent] may sue [mother] to be reimbursed for the necessaries she has provided [child]. The Attorney General, however, cannot petition the trial court under UIFSA to issue a child support order withholding [mother's] income."

Official Comment

Twenty-two terms are defined in UIFSA as compared with the parallel RURESA §2, which had fourteen entries. Many crucial definitions continue to be left to local law. For example, the definitions of "child" and "child-support order" provided by subsections (1) and (2) refer to "the age of majority" without further elaboration. The exact age at which a child becomes an adult for different purposes is a matter for the law of each State, as is the age at which a parent's duty to furnish child support terminates. Similarly, a wide variety of other terms of art are implicitly left to state law. For example, subsection (21) refers inter alia to "health care, arrearages, or reimbursement." All of these terms are subject to individualized definitions on a state-by-state basis.

Subsection (3) defines "duty of support" to mean the legal obligation to provide support before it has been reduced to judgment. This broad definition includes both prospective and retrospective obligations to the extent they are imposed by the relevant state law.

In order to resolve certain conflicts in the exercise of jurisdiction, for limited purposes subsection (4) borrows the concept of the "home State of a child" from the Uniform Child Custody Jurisdiction Act (UCCJA), versions of which have been adopted in all 50 States, and incorporated into the federal Parental Kidnapping Prevention Act, 42 U.S.C. §1738A (PKPA).

Subsection (6) is written broadly so states that direct income withholding by an obligor's employer based on "other legal process," as distinguished from an order of a tribunal, may have that legal process recognized as an income-withholding order. Federal law requires that each State provide for income withholding "without the necessity of any application therefor, or for any further action by the court or other entity which issued such order…." 42 U.S.C. §666(b)(2). States have complied with this directive in a variety of ways. For example, at the time UIFSA was originally drafted New York provided a method for obtaining income withholding of court-ordered support by authorizing an attorney, clerk of court, sheriff or agent of the child support enforcement agency to serve upon the defaulting obligor's employer an "income execution for support enforcement." New York McKinney's C.P.L.R. 5241. This "other legal process" reportedly was the standard method for obtaining income withholding in that State, while the statutory provision for an income-withholding order, C.P.L.R. 5242, was rarely used by either the courts or the litigants.

Subsections (7) and (8) define "initiating State" and "initiating tribunal" similarly to RURESA §2(d). It is important to note, however, that UIFSA permits the direct filing of an interstate action in the responding State without an initial filing in an initiating tribunal. Thus, in addition to the traditional resort to a local "initiating tribunal," a petitioner in one State may seek to establish a support order in a second State by either filing in the responding state's tribunal or by directly seeking the assistance of the support enforcement agency in the second State.

The relationship between UIFSA and the prior Uniform Acts is captured in the phrasing of subsection (7), and repeated several times throughout the Act. *See, i.e.*, subsections (16) and (19). The Act declares that URESA and RURESA are compatible with UIFSA, and the new Act is designed to function with the earlier Acts without conflict. Support orders issued under one of the earlier Acts should be honored and enforced in any State with any of the three Uniform Acts. But, despite their common roots, neither URESA nor RURESA can be said to be "substantially similar" to the one-order system established in UIFSA. States enacting UIFSA are directed to accord full enforcement remedies to support orders from those States, but also to apply UIFSA restraint regarding modification, and to apply its "one-order" rule to orders from non-UIFSA States, *infra*.

The term "obligee" in subsection (12) is defined in a broad manner similar to RURESA §2(f), which is consistent with common usage. In instances of spousal support, the person owed the duty of support and the person receiving the payments are almost always the same. Use of the term is more complicated in the context of a child support order. The child is the person to whom the duty of support is owed, and therefore can be viewed as the ultimate obligee. However, "obligee" usually refers to the individual receiving the payments. While this is most commonly the custodial parent or other legal custodian, the "obligee" may be a support enforcement agency that has been assigned the right to receive support payments in order to recoup Temporary Assistance for Needy Families (TANF), 42 U.S.C. §601 et seq., formerly known as Aid to Families with Dependent Children (AFDC). Even in the absence of such an assignment, a State may have an independent statutory claim for reimbursement for general assistance provided to a spouse, a former spouse, or a child of an obligor. The Act also uses "obligee" to identify an individual who is asserting a claim for support, not just for a person whose right to support is unquestioned, presumed, or has been established in a legal action.

Subsection (13) provides the correlative definition of an "obligor," which includes an individual who is alleged to owe a duty of support as well as a person whose obligation has previously been determined.

The definitions of "responding State" and "responding tribunal" in subsections (16) and (17) accommodate the direct filing of a petition under UIFSA without the intervention of an initiating tribunal. Both definitions acknowledge the possibility that there may be a responding State or tribunal in a situation where there is no initiating State or tribunal.

Subsection (19) withdraws the requirement of reciprocity between the several States and other U.S. jurisdictions formerly demanded by RURESA and URESA. A State need not enact UIFSA for support orders issued by its tribunals to be enforced by other States. Public policy favoring such enforcement is sufficiently strong to warrant waiving any quid pro quo among the States. This provision will be mooted by the likelihood that all States will enact UIFSA by January 1, 1998, as mandated by Congress in its 1996 welfare reform. In the original promulgation of UIFSA, the language of subsection (19) was somewhat ambiguous regarding the necessity of extending reciprocity to an Indian tribe and to foreign jurisdictions. By reorganizing the statutory language, the 1996 amendment clarifies that reciprocity is not required between the several States and Indian tribes. Further, the additional language and reorganization in subsection (19)(ii) makes clear that in this instance UIFSA follows the pattern of RURESA to require that a foreign nation must have substantially similar law or procedures to either UIFSA, RURESA, or URESA (that is, reciprocity) in order for its support orders to be treated as if they had been issued by a sister State. This is sharply different from the rule for States; amended UIFSA 1996 recognizes that in international relations the concept of reciprocity is crucial to acceptance of child support orders by other nations.

Subsection (20), "Support Enforcement Agency," includes the state IV-D agency (Part IV-D, Social Security Act, 42 U.S.C. §651 et seq.), and other state or local governmental entities charged with establishing or enforcing support.

Subsection (22) introduces a completely new term, "tribunal," which replaces the term "court" used in RURESA. With the advent of federally-funded IV-D programs, a number of States have delegated various aspects of child support establishment and enforcement to quasi-judicial bodies and administrative agencies. UIFSA adopts the term "tribunal" to account for the breadth of state variations in dealing with support orders. Unless expressly noted otherwise, throughout the Act the term refers to a tribunal of the enacting State. To avoid confusion, however, when actions of tribunals of the enacting State and another State are contrasted in the same section or subsection, the phrases "tribunal of this State" and "tribunal of another State" are used for the sake of clarity.

FAM §159.102. TRIBUNAL OF STATE

The court is the tribunal of this state.

History of Fam §159.102: Acts 1995, 74th Leg., ch. 20, §1, eff. April 20, 1995. Amended by Acts 1997, 75th Leg., ch. 607, §2, eff. Sept. 1, 1997. Source: Former Fam §21.02.

Official Comment

The enacting State must identify the court, administrative agency, or the combination of those entities, which constitute the tribunal or tribunals authorized to deal with family support. In a particular State there may be several different such entities authorized to determine family support matters.

FAM §159.103. REMEDIES CUMULATIVE

Remedies provided in this chapter are cumulative and do not affect the availability of remedies under other law.

History of Fam §159.103: Acts 1995, 74th Leg., ch. 20, §1, eff. April 20, 1995. Source: Former Fam §21.03.

Official Comment

The existence of procedures for interstate establishment, enforcement, or modification of support or a determination of parentage in UIFSA does not preclude the application of the general law of the forum. Even if the parents live in different States, for example, a petitioner may decide to file an original action for child support (and most likely for other relief as well) directly in the State of residence of the respondent and proceed under that forum's generally applicable support law. In so doing, the petitioner thereby submits to the personal jurisdiction of the forum and foregoes reliance on UIFSA. Once a child support order has been issued, this option is no longer available to interstate parties. Under UIFSA, a State may not permit a party to proceed to obtain a second support order; rather, in further litigation the tribunal must apply the Act's provisions for enforcement of an existing order and limit modification to the strict standards of UIFSA.

Sections 159.104-159.200 reserved for expansion

SUBCHAPTER C. JURISDICTION

FAM §159.201. BASES FOR JURISDICTION OVER NONRESIDENT

In a proceeding to establish, enforce, or modify a support order or to determine parentage, a tribunal of this state may exercise personal jurisdiction over a nonresident individual or the individual's guardian or conservator if:

(1) the individual is personally served with citation in this state;

(2) the individual submits to the jurisdiction of this state by consent, by entering a general appearance, or by filing a responsive document having the effect of waiving any contest to personal jurisdiction;

(3) the individual resided with the child in this state;

(4) the individual resided in this state and provided prenatal expenses or support for the child;

(5) the child resides in this state as a result of the acts or directives of the individual;

(6) the individual engaged in sexual intercourse in this state and the child may have been conceived by that act of intercourse;

(7) the individual asserted parentage in the paternity registry maintained in this state by the bureau of vital statistics; or

(8) there is any other basis consistent with the constitutions of this state and the United States for the exercise of personal jurisdiction.

History of Fam §159.201: Acts 1995, 74th Leg., ch. 20, §1, eff. April 20, 1995. Amended by Acts 1997, 75th Leg., ch. 561, §5, eff. Sept. 1, 1997. Source: Former Fam §21.04.

In re Cannon, 993 S.W.2d 354, 355 n.1 (Tex.App.—San Antonio 1999, orig. proceeding). "[T]he provisions of §159.201 are almost identical to those of the Family Code's long-arm statute...."

Official Comment

Sections 201 and 202 assert what is commonly described as long-arm jurisdiction over a nonresident respondent for purposes of establishing a support order or determining parentage. Inclusion of this long-arm provision in this interstate Act is justified because residents of two separate States are involved in the litigation, both of whom are subject to the personal jurisdiction of the forum. Thus, the case has a clear interstate aspect, despite the fact that only the law of the forum State is applicable. Moreover, this is sufficient to invoke additional UIFSA provisions in an otherwise intrastate lawsuit. *See* Sections 202, 316, and 318, *infra*. The intent is to insure that every enacting State has a long-arm statute as broad as constitutionally permitted. In situations in which the long-arm statute can be satisfied, the petitioner (either the obligor or the obligee) has two options: (1) utilize the long-arm statute to obtain personal jurisdiction over the respondent; or (2) initiate a two-state action under the succeeding provisions of UIFSA seeking to establish a support order in the respondent's State of residence. Of course, a third option is available that does not implicate UIFSA; a petitioner may file a suit in the respondent's State of residence (perhaps to settle all issues between the parties in a single proceeding).

This long-arm statute applies to an order for spousal support as well as for child support. However, almost all of the specific provisions relate to child support orders or determinations of parentage. This accords with the fact that very few States have chosen to enact specific domestic relations long-arm statutes and that the focus of UIFSA is primarily on child support. Only subsections (1), (2) and (8) are applicable to an action for spousal support asserting long-arm jurisdiction over a nonresident. The first two subsections are wholly noncontroversial insofar as an assertion of personal jurisdiction is concerned. Moreover, assertion of personal jurisdiction under subsections (1), (2), or (8) will doubtless yield jurisdiction over all matters to be decided between the spouses, including division of property on divorce. Thus, the most obvious basis for asserting long-arm jurisdiction over spousal support, *i.e.*, "last matrimonial domicile," is not included in Section 201 to avoid the potential problem of another instance of bifurcated jurisdiction. That is, a situation is not created in which a tribunal is authorized to order a nonresident to pay spousal support, but may not personally bind the nonresident to a property division on divorce.

Under RURESA, multiple support orders affecting the same parties were commonplace. UIFSA creates a structure designed to provide for only one support order at a time. The new one-order regime is facilitated and combined with a broad assertion of personal jurisdiction under this long-arm provision. The frequency of a two-state procedure involving the participation of tribunals in both States should be substantially reduced by the introduction of this long-arm statute.

Subsections (1) through (8) are derived from a variety of sources, including the Uniform Parentage Act §8, Texas Family Code §102.011, and New York Family Court Act §154.

Subsection (1) codifies the holding of *Burnham v. Superior Court*, 495 U.S. 604 (1990), which reaffirms the constitutional validity of asserting personal jurisdiction based on personal service within a State.

Subsection (2) expresses the principle that a nonresident party concedes personal jurisdiction by seeking affirmative relief or by submitting to the jurisdiction by answering or entering an appearance. However, the power to assert jurisdiction over a support issue under the Act does not extend the tribunal's jurisdiction to other matters.

Subsections (3) through (6) identify specific fact situations justifying the assertion of long-arm jurisdiction over a nonresident. Each provides an appropriate affiliating nexus for such an assertion, when judged on a case-by-case basis with an eye on procedural and substantive due process. Further, each subsection does contain a possibility that an overly literal construction of the terms of the statute will overreach due process. For example, subsection (3) provides that long-arm jurisdiction to establish a support order may be asserted if "the individual resided with the child in this State." The typical scenario contemplated by the statute is that the parties lived as a family unit in the forum State, separated, and one of the parents subsequently moved to another State while the other parent and the child continued to reside in the forum. No time frame is stated for filing suit; this is based on the fact that the absent parent has a support obligation that extends for at least the minority of the child (and often longer in many States). On the other hand, suppose that the two parents and their child lived in State A for many years, and then decided to move the family to State B to seek better employment opportunities. Those opportunities did not materialize and, after several weeks or a few months of frustration with the situation, one of the parents returned with the child to State A. Under these facts a tribunal of State A may conclude it has long-arm jurisdiction to establish the support obligation of the absent parent. But, suppose that the family's sojourn in State B lasted for many years, and one parent unilaterally decides to return to State A. Many, and perhaps all, tribunals will conclude that assertion of personal jurisdiction over the absent parent immediately after the return based on subsection (3) would offend due process. The interstate provisions of UIFSA are available to the returning parent to establish child support. Note that State B will have long-arm jurisdiction to establish support under Section 201. *See also* Section 204, *infra*, for the resolution of simultaneous proceedings provided by the Act.

The factual situations catalogued in the first seven subsections are appropriate and constitutionally acceptable grounds upon which to exercise personal jurisdiction over an individual.

Finally, subsection (8) tracks the broad, catch-all provisions found in many state statutes, including California, Civ. P. Code §410.10 (1973); New York, *supra*; and Texas, *supra*. Note, however, that the California provision, standing alone, was found to be inadequate to sustain a child support order under the facts presented in *Kulko v. Superior Court of Calif.*, 436 U.S. 84 (1978).

FAM §159.202. PROCEDURE WHEN EXERCISING JURISDICTION OVER NONRESIDENT

A tribunal of this state exercising personal jurisdiction over a nonresident under Section 159.201 may apply Section 159.316 to receive evidence from another state and Section 159.318 to obtain discovery through a tribunal of another state. In all other respects, Subchapters D-H do not apply and the tribunal shall apply the procedural and substantive law of this state, including the rules on choice of law other than those established by this chapter.

History of Fam §159.202: Acts 1995, 74th Leg., ch. 20, §1, eff. April 20, 1995. Source: Former Fam §21.05.

Official Comment

Assertion of long-arm jurisdiction over a nonresident essentially results in a one-state proceeding, notwithstanding the fact that the parties reside in different States. With two exceptions, the provisions of UIFSA – labeled an interstate act – are not applicable to such a proceeding. To facilitate interstate exchange of information and to enable the nonresident to participate as fully as possible in the proceedings without the necessity of personally appearing in the forum State, Section 202 expressly incorporates two special UIFSA sections to long-arm cases. The first exception allows the tribunal to apply the special rules of evidence and procedure of Section 316 in order to facilitate decision-making when one party resides in another State, even though that party is subject to the personal jurisdiction of the tribunal. The same consideration accounts for the second exception; the two-state discovery procedures of Section 318 are applicable to a one-state proceeding when a foreign tribunal can assist in that process. In all other situations, the substantive and procedural law of the forum State applies. In sum, a one-state UIFSA case may utilize those two-state procedures which forward the interests of economy, efficiency, and fair play.

FAM §159.203. INITIATING & RESPONDING TRIBUNAL OF STATE

Under this chapter, a tribunal of this state may serve as an initiating tribunal to forward proceedings to another state and as a responding tribunal for proceedings initiated in another state.

History of Fam §159.203: Acts 1995, 74th Leg., ch. 20, §1, eff. April 20, 1995. Amended by Acts 1997, 75th Leg., ch. 607, §3, eff. Sept. 1, 1997. Source: Former Fam §21.06.

Official Comment

Sections 203 through 206 track the traditional RURESA action involving residents of separate States. In this situation the initiating State does not assert personal jurisdiction over the nonresident, but instead forwards the case to another, responding State, which has the authority to assert personal jurisdiction over its resident. This section identifies the various roles a tribunal of the forum may serve; as appropriate, it may act as either an initiating or a responding tribunal. Under UIFSA a tribunal may serve as a responding tribunal even when there is no initiating tribunal in another State. This accommodates the direct filing of an action in a responding tribunal by a nonresident.

FAM §159.204. SIMULTANEOUS PROCEEDINGS IN ANOTHER STATE

(a) A tribunal of this state may exercise jurisdiction to establish a support order if the petition or comparable pleading is filed after a pleading is filed in another state only if:

(1) the petition or comparable pleading in this state is filed before the expiration of the time allowed in the other state for filing a responsive pleading challenging the exercise of jurisdiction by the other state;

(2) the contesting party timely challenges the exercise of jurisdiction in the other state; and

(3) if relevant, this state is the home state of the child.

(b) A tribunal of this state may not exercise jurisdiction to establish a support order if the petition or comparable pleading is filed before a petition or comparable pleading is filed in another state if:

(1) the petition or comparable pleading in the other state is filed before the expiration of the time allowed in this state for filing a responsive pleading challenging the exercise of jurisdiction by this state;

(2) the contesting party timely challenges the exercise of jurisdiction in this state; and

(3) if relevant, the other state is the home state of the child.

History of Fam §159.204: Acts 1995, 74th Leg., ch. 20, §1, eff. April 20, 1995. Source: Former Fam §21.07.

Official Comment

This section is similar to Section 6 of the Uniform Child Custody Jurisdiction Act. Under the one-order system established by UIFSA, it is necessary to provide a new procedure to eliminate the multiple orders so common under RURESA and URESA. This requires cooperation between, and deference by, sister-state tribunals in order to avoid issuance of competing support orders. To this end, tribunals are expected to take an active role in seeking out information about support proceedings in other States concerning the same child. Depending on the circumstances, one or the other of two tribunals considering the same support obligation should decide to defer to the other. In this regard, UIFSA makes a significant departure from the approach adopted by the UCCJA, which chooses "first filing" as the method for resolving competing jurisdictional disputes. In the analogous situation, the federal Parental Kidnapping Prevention Act chooses the home State of the child to establish priority. Given the preemptive nature of the PKPA, and the possibility that custody and support are both involved in the case, UIFSA opts for the federal method of resolving disputes between competing jurisdictional assertions by establishing a priority for the tribunal in the child's home State. If the child has no home State, "first filing" controls.

FAM §159.205. CONTINUING, EXCLUSIVE JURISDICTION

(a) A tribunal of this state issuing a support order consistent with the law of this state has continuing, exclusive jurisdiction over a child support order:

(1) as long as this state remains the residence of the obligor, the individual obligee, or the child for whose benefit the support order is issued; or

(2) until all of the parties who are individuals have filed written consents with the tribunal of this state for a tribunal of another state to modify the order and assume continuing, exclusive jurisdiction.

(b) A tribunal of this state issuing a child support order consistent with the law of this state may not exercise its continuing jurisdiction to modify the order if the order has been modified by a tribunal of another state under a law substantially similar to this chapter.

(c) If a child support order of this state is modified by a tribunal of another state under a law substantially similar to this chapter, a tribunal of this state loses its continuing, exclusive jurisdiction with regard to prospective enforcement of the order issued in this state and may only:

(1) enforce the order that was modified as to amounts accruing before the modification;

(2) enforce nonmodifiable aspects of that order; and

(3) provide other appropriate relief for violations of that order that occurred before the effective date of the modification.

(d) A tribunal of this state shall recognize the continuing, exclusive jurisdiction of a tribunal of another state that issued a child support order under a law substantially similar to this chapter.

(e) A temporary support order issued ex parte or pending resolution of a jurisdictional conflict does not create continuing, exclusive jurisdiction in the issuing tribunal.

(f) A tribunal of this state issuing a support order consistent with the law of this state has continuing, exclusive jurisdiction over a spousal support order throughout the existence of the support obligation. A tribunal of this state may not modify a spousal support order issued by a tribunal of another state having continuing, exclusive jurisdiction over that order under the law of that state.

History of Fam §159.205: Acts 1995, 74th Leg., ch. 20, §1, eff. April 20, 1995. Amended by Acts 1997, 75th Leg., ch. 607, §4, eff. Sept. 1, 1997. Source: Former Fam §21.08.

Official Comment

This section is perhaps the most crucial provision in UIFSA. Drawing on the precedent of the federal Parental Kidnapping Prevention Act, 28 U.S.C. §1738A, the issuing tribunal retains continuing, exclusive jurisdiction over a child support order, except in very narrowly defined circumstances. As long as one of the individual parties or the child continues to reside in the issuing State, and as long as the parties do not agree to the contrary, the issuing tribunal has continuing, exclusive jurisdiction over its order – which in practical terms means that it may modify its order. The statute attempts to be even-handed – the identity of the remaining party – obligor or obligee – does not matter. If the individual parties have left the issuing State but the child remains behind, continuing, exclusive jurisdiction remains with the issuing State.

The other side of the coin follows logically. Just as subsection (a)(1) defines the retention of continuing, exclusive jurisdiction, by clear implication the subsection also defines how jurisdiction to modify may be lost. That is, if all the relevant persons – the obligor, the individual obligee, and the child – have permanently left the issuing State, the issuing State no longer has an appropriate nexus with the parties or child to justify exercise of jurisdiction to modify. Further, the issuing tribunal has no current information about the factual circumstances of anyone involved, and the taxpayers of that State have no reason to expend public funds on the process. Note, however, that the original order of the issuing tribunal remains valid and enforceable. That order is in effect not only in the issuing State and those States in which the order has been registered, but also may be registered and enforced in additional States even after the issuing State has lost its power to modify its order, see Sections 601-604 (Registration and Enforcement of Support Order), *infra*. The original order remains in effect until it is properly modified in accordance with the narrow terms of Sections 609-612 (Registration and Modification of Child Support Order), *infra*.

According to the logical implication of subsection (a)(2), the issuing State may also lose its continuing, exclusive jurisdiction to modify if the parties consent in writing for another State to assume jurisdiction to modify (even though one of the parties or the child continues to reside in the issuing State). The only statutory requirement for the parties to divest the issuing tribunal of its continuing, exclusive jurisdiction is the filing of a written agreement to that effect with that tribunal. The Drafting Committee anticipated that such an agreement would seldom occur because of the almost universal desire of each party to prefer his or her local tribunal; but, the Committee also believed that the parties should be allowed to agree upon an alternate forum if they choose to do so.

Although subsection (a) identifies the methods for the retention and the loss of continuing, exclusive jurisdiction by the issuing tribunal, it does not confer jurisdiction to modify on another tribunal. Modification requires that a tribunal have personal jurisdiction over the parties and meet other criteria as provided in Sections 609 through 614, *infra*. It should also be noted that nothing in this section is intended to deprive a tribunal which has lost continuing, exclusive jurisdiction of the power to enforce arrearages that have accrued during the existence of a valid order.

Spousal support is treated differently; the issuing tribunal retains continuing, exclusive jurisdiction over an order of spousal support throughout the entire existence of the support obligation. Sections 205(f) and 206(c) state that the procedures of UIFSA are not available to a responding tribunal to modify the existing spousal support order of the issuing State. This marks a radical departure from RURESA, which treated spousal and child support orders identically. Under UIFSA, modification of spousal support is limited to a procedure whereby an action is initiated outside of the issuing State and a tribunal in that original State modifies its order under its law. While UIFSA revises RURESA in this regard, in fact this will have a minimal effect on actual practice. Interstate modification of pure spousal support was relatively rare under RURESA, and played almost no part in the activities of support enforcement agencies.

The prohibition of modification of spousal support by a nonissuing State tribunal under UIFSA is consistent with the principle that a tribunal should apply local law to such cases to insure efficient handling and to minimize choice of law problems. Avoiding conflict of law problems is almost impossible if spousal support orders are subject to modification in a second State. For example, States take widely varying views of the effect on a spousal support order of the obligee's remarriage or nonmarital cohabitation. Making a distinction between spousal and child support is further justified because the standards for modification of child support and spousal support are very different. In most jurisdictions a dramatic improvement in the obligor's economic circumstances will have little or no relevance in an action seeking an upward modification of spousal support, while a similar change in an obligor's situation typically is the primary basis for an increase in child support. This disparity is founded on a policy choice that post-divorce success of an obligor-parent should benefit the obligor's child, but not the obligor's ex-spouse.

Finally, UIFSA does not provide for shifting the continuing, exclusive jurisdiction over a spousal-support order by mutual agreement. That procedure is limited to child support under subsection (a)(2). Note that the Act is silent rather than preclusive on the subject. If the parties wish to enter into such an agreement, it is up to the individual States to decide whether to recognize it. A waiver of continuing, exclusive jurisdiction and subsequent modification of spousal support by a tribunal of another State simply is not authorized under the auspices of UIFSA.

FAM §159.206. ENFORCEMENT & MODIFICATION OF SUPPORT ORDER BY TRIBUNAL HAVING CONTINUING JURISDICTION

(a) A tribunal of this state may serve as an initiating tribunal to request a tribunal of another state to enforce or modify a support order issued in that state.

(b) A tribunal of this state having continuing, exclusive jurisdiction over a support order may act as a responding tribunal to enforce or modify the order. If a party subject to the tribunal's continuing, exclusive jurisdiction no longer resides in the issuing state, in subsequent proceedings the tribunal may apply Section 159.316 to receive evidence from another state and Section 159.318 to obtain discovery through a tribunal of another state.

(c) A tribunal of this state that lacks continuing, exclusive jurisdiction over a spousal support order may not serve as a responding tribunal to modify a spousal support order of another state.

History of Fam §159.206: Acts 1995, 74th Leg., ch. 20, §1, eff. April 20, 1995. Source: Former Fam §21.09.

Official Comment

This section is the correlative of the continuing, exclusive jurisdiction asserted in the preceding section. Subsection (a) authorizes a tribunal of the enacting State to initiate a request for enforcement or modification to the tribunal with continuing, exclusive jurisdiction over a support order.

Subsection (b) confirms the power of the issuing tribunal to modify its child support order as the responding tribunal, provided it retains a sufficient nexus with its order. UIFSA defines that nexus as a situation in which the child or at least one of the parties continues to reside in the issuing State. Subsection (b) also makes a vital contribution to the exercise of its continuing, exclusive jurisdiction if one of the parties leaves the State after the initial order was issued. The petitioner and the absent respondent may take advantage of the special rules of evidence and discovery in order to provide the tribunal with maximum current information in a modification proceeding.

Subsection (c) is the correlative of Section 205(f), acknowledging the continuing, exclusive jurisdiction of the tribunal ordering alimony and specifically prohibiting a responding tribunal from modifying a spousal support order of another State.

FAM §159.207. RECOGNITION OF CONTROLLING CHILD SUPPORT ORDER

(a) If a proceeding is brought under this chapter and only one tribunal has issued a child support order, the order of that tribunal controls and must be so recognized.

(b) If a proceeding is brought under this chapter and two or more child support orders have been issued by tribunals of this state or another state with regard to the same obligor and child, a tribunal of this state shall apply the following rules in determining which order to recognize for purposes of continuing, exclusive jurisdiction:

(1) if only one of the tribunals would have continuing, exclusive jurisdiction under this chapter, the order of that tribunal controls and must be so recognized;

(2) if more than one of the tribunals would have continuing, exclusive jurisdiction under this chapter, an order issued by a tribunal in the current home state of the child controls and must be so recognized, but if an order has not been issued in the current home state of the child, the order most recently issued controls and must be so recognized; and

(3) if none of the tribunals would have continuing, exclusive jurisdiction under this chapter, the tribunal of this state having jurisdiction over the parties shall issue a child support order that controls and must be so recognized.

(c) If two or more child support orders have been issued for the same obligor and child and if the obligor or the individual obligee resides in this state, a party may request a tribunal of this state to determine which order controls and must be so recognized under Subsection (b). The request must be accompanied by a certified copy of every support order in effect. The requesting party shall give notice of the request to each party whose rights may be affected by the determination.

(d) The tribunal that issued the controlling order under Subsection (a), (b), or (c) is the tribunal that has continuing, exclusive jurisdiction under Section 159.205.

(e) A tribunal of this state that determines by order the identity of the controlling order under Subsection (b)(1) or (2) or that issues a new controlling order under Subsection (b)(3) shall state in that order the basis upon which the tribunal made its determination.

(f) Within 30 days after issuance of an order determining the identity of the controlling order, the party obtaining the order shall file a certified copy of it with each tribunal that issued or registered an earlier order of child support. A party who obtains the order and fails to file a certified copy is subject to appropriate sanctions by a tribunal in which the issue of failure to file arises. The failure to file does not affect the validity or enforceability of the controlling order.

History of Fam §159.207: Acts 1995, 74th Leg., ch. 20, §1, eff. April 20, 1995. Amended by Acts 1997, 75th Leg., ch. 607, §5, eff. Sept. 1, 1997. Source: Former Fam §21.10.

Official Comment

Sections 207-209 are designed to span the gulf between the one-order system created by UIFSA and the multiple-order system previously in place under RURESA and URESA. A keystone of UIFSA is to provide a transitional procedure for the eventual elimination of existing multiple support orders in an expeditious and efficient manner. But, even assuming all U.S. jurisdictions enact UIFSA, many years will pass before its one-order system will be completely in place. Multiple orders covering the same parties and child number in the tens of thousands; it can be reasonably anticipated that these orders will continue in effect far into the future. To begin the process towards a one-order system, however, this section provides a relatively simple procedure designed to identify a single viable order that will be entitled to prospective enforcement in every UIFSA State.

Subsection (a) declares that if only one child support order exists, it is to be denominated the controlling order, irrespective of when and where it was issued and whether any of the individual parties or the child continue to reside in the issuing State.

Subsection (b) establishes the priority scheme for recognition and prospective enforcement of a single order among existing multiple orders regarding the same obligor, obligee, and child. For UIFSA to function, one order must be denominated as the controlling order, and its issuing tribunal must be recognized as having continuing, exclusive jurisdiction. In choosing among existing multiple orders, none of which can be distinguished as being in conflict with the principles of UIFSA, subsection (b)(1) gives first priority to the order issued by the only tribunal that is entitled to continuing, exclusive jurisdiction under the terms of UIFSA, *i.e.*, an individual party or the child continues to reside in that State, and no other issuing State meets this criterion. If two or more tribunals would have continuing, exclusive jurisdiction under the Act, subsection (b)(2) first looks to the tribunal of the child's current home State. If that State has not issued a support order, subsection (b)(2) looks next to the order most recently issued. Finally, if none of the existing multiple orders are entitled to be denominated as the controlling order because none of the preceding priorities apply, the forum tribunal is directed to issue a new order, assuming that it has personal jurisdiction over the obligor and obligee. The new order is to be treated as the controlling order, establishing the support obligation, the nonmodifiable aspects of the support obligation, see Section 611(c), *infra*, and the issuing tribunal's continuing, exclusive jurisdiction. The rationale for creating yet another order is that there is no valid reason under UIFSA to prefer the terms of one of the multiple orders over another.

As originally promulgated, UIFSA did not come to grips with whether existing multiple orders issued by different States might be entitled to full faith and credit without regard to the determination of the controlling order under the Act. The drafters took the position that state law, however uniform, could not interfere with the ultimate interpretation of a constitutional directive. Fortunately, this question has almost certainly been mooted by the 1996 amendment to 28 U.S.C. §1738B, Full Faith and Credit for Child Support Orders. Congress adopted the terms of Section 207 of UIFSA virtually word for word in the Personal Responsibility and Work Opportunity Reconciliation Act of 1996. Pub. L. 104-193, Aug. 22, 1996, 110 Stat. 2221.

It is not altogether clear whether the terms of UIFSA apply to a strictly intrastate case; that is, a situation in which multiple child support orders have been issued by multiple tribunals of a single State and all parties and the child continue to reside in that State. This is not an uncommon situation, often traceable to the intrastate applicability of RURESA. A literal reading of the statutory language suggests the section applies. For a tribunal of the issuing State to so conclude will further the goal of the Act of identifying a single controlling order for prospective enforcement and modification. At the very least, the section provides a template for resolving such conflicts, most likely yielding a determination that the last order is the controlling order.

Subsection (c), added in 1996, clarifies that any party may request a tribunal of the forum State to identify the controlling order. That party is directed to fully inform the tribunal of all existing child support orders.

Amended subsection (d) provides that the determination of the controlling order under this section has the effect of establishing the tribunal with continuing, exclusive jurisdiction; only the order of that tribunal is entitled to prospective enforcement by a sister State. To help insure regularity, subsection (e) directs the forum tribunal to set forth the basis of its finding. Finally, the party obtaining the determination is directed by subsection (f) to notify all interested tribunals of the decision.

Section 207 presumes that a tribunal will be fully informed about all existing orders if it is requested to determine which one of the existing multiple child support orders is to be accorded prospective enforcement. If this does not occur and one or more existing orders is not considered by the tribunal, the finality of its decision is likely to turn on principles of estoppel on a case-by-case basis. Assuming that the parties were accorded notice and opportunity to be heard by the tribunal, a final decision on the subject is entitled to full faith and credit.

FAM §159.208. MULTIPLE CHILD SUPPORT ORDERS FOR TWO OR MORE OBLIGEES

In responding to multiple registrations or petitions for enforcement of two or more child support orders in effect at the same time with regard to the same obligor and different individual obligees, at least one of which was issued by a tribunal of another state, a tribunal of this state shall enforce those orders in the same manner as if the multiple orders had been issued by a tribunal of this state.

History of Fam §159.208: Acts 1995, 74th Leg., ch. 20, §1, eff. April 20, 1995. Source: Former Fam §21.11.

Official Comment

Multiple orders may involve two or more families of the same obligor. Although all such orders are entitled to enforcement, practical difficulties are often presented. For example, full enforcement of each of the multiple orders may exceed the maximum allowed for income withholding. The federal statute, 42 U.S.C. §666(b)(1), requires that to be eligible for the federal funding for enforcement, States must provide for a maximum to be withheld from earnings for child support in a percentage that may not exceed the federal consumer credit code limitations on wage garnishment, 15 U.S.C. §1673(b). In order to allocate resources between competing families, UIFSA refers to state law. The basic principle is that one or more foreign orders for the support of an out-of-state family of the obligor, and one or more orders of an in-state family, are all of equal dignity. In allocating payments to different obligees, every child support order should be treated as if it had been issued by a tribunal of the forum State.

FAM §159.209. CREDIT FOR PAYMENTS

Amounts collected and credited for a particular period under a support order issued by a tribunal of another state must be credited against the amounts accruing or accrued for the same period under a support order issued by the tribunal of this state.

History of Fam §159.209: Acts 1995, 74th Leg., ch. 20, §1, eff. April 20, 1995. Source: Former Fam §21.12.

Official Comment

This section is derived from RURESA §31 (Application of Payments). Because of the multiple orders possible under RURESA, that section was primarily concerned with insuring that payments made on a particular order were credited towards the amounts due on all other orders. For example, full payment of $300 on an order of State C earns a 100% pro tanto discharge of the current support owed on a $200 order of State A, and a 75% credit against a $400 order of State B. Crediting payments against arrears on multiple orders is more complex, and is subject to different constructions in various States. Under the one-order system of UIFSA, an obligor ultimately will be ordered to pay only one sum-certain amount for current support (a sum certain to reduce arrears, if any).

The issuing tribunal is ultimately responsible for the overall control of the enforcement methods employed and for accounting for the payments made on its order from multiple sources. Until that scheme is fully in place, however, it will be necessary to continue to mandate pro tanto credit for actual payments made against all existing orders.

Sections 159.210-159.300 reserved for expansion

SUBCHAPTER D. CIVIL PROVISIONS OF GENERAL APPLICATION

FAM §159.301. PROCEEDINGS UNDER CHAPTER

(a) Except as otherwise provided in this chapter, this subchapter applies to all proceedings under this chapter.

(b) This chapter provides for the following proceedings:

(1) establishment of an order for spousal support or child support pursuant to Section 159.401;

(2) enforcement of a support order and income-withholding order of another state without registration pursuant to Sections 159.501 through 159.507;

(3) registration of an order for spousal support or child support of another state for enforcement pursuant to Sections 159.601 through 159.608;

(4) modification of an order for child support or spousal support issued by a tribunal of this state pursuant to Sections 159.203 through 159.205;

(5) registration of an order for child support of another state for modification pursuant to Sections 159.609 through 159.614;

(6) determination of parentage pursuant to Section 159.701; and

(7) assertion of jurisdiction over nonresidents pursuant to Sections 159.201 and 159.202.

(c) An individual or a support enforcement agency may commence a proceeding authorized under this chapter by filing a petition in an initiating tribunal for forwarding to a responding tribunal or by filing a petition or a comparable pleading directly in a tribunal of another state that has or that can obtain personal jurisdiction over the respondent.

History of Fam §159.301: Acts 1995, 74th Leg., ch. 20, §1, eff. April 20, 1995. Amended by Acts 1997, 75th Leg., ch. 607, §6, eff. Sept. 1, 1997. Source: Former Fam §21.13.

Attorney Gen. v. Litten, 999 S.W.2d 74, 77 (Tex. App.—Houston [14th Dist.] 1999, no pet.). "Chapter 157 governs enforcement of final orders. Chapter 159, however, is the Texas Codification of the Uniform Interstate Family Support Act (UIFSA), and Subchapter G sets out the procedures for the registering and enforcement of a support order issued by a tribunal of another state. Section 159.301(b)(3) specifically dictates that proceedings for the registration and enforcement of a support order of another state fall under Subchapter G of Chapter 159. ... Because there is no statutory basis for applying the provisions of Chapter 157 to an action to register and enforce a foreign judgment for child support, we hold Chapter 157 is not applicable to this suit.

Official Comment

This section is a "road map" of the types of actions authorized by UIFSA. Although such a section is unusual for a Uniform Act, it is justified in this instance because the majority of those persons administering the Act are not attorneys and will doubtless find such assistance to be useful.

Subsection (a) mandates application of the general provisions of this article to all UIFSA actions.

Subsection (b) identifies the general principles and structure of the Act. Note that although orders for spousal support and child support are generally dealt with in the same manner, subsection (b)(5) implicitly restates the fact that the modification provisions are limited to child support orders, and do not apply to spousal support orders.

Subsection (c) establishes the basic two-state procedure contemplated by the Act. The initiating responding procedure is derived from the two-state procedure under RURESA. Direct filing in the responding State by an individual or a support enforcement agency without reference to an initiating State is new to this Act, however.

FAM §159.302. ACTION BY MINOR PARENT

A minor parent or a guardian or other legal representative of a minor parent may maintain a proceeding on behalf of or for the benefit of the minor's child.

History of Fam §159.302: Acts 1995, 74th Leg., ch. 20, §1, eff. April 20, 1995. Source: Former Fam §21.14.

Official Comment

This section is derived from RURESA §13. A minor parent may maintain an action under UIFSA without the appointment of a guardian ad litem, even if the law of the forum jurisdiction requires a guardian for an in-state case. If a guardian or legal representative has been appointed, he or she may act on behalf of the minor's child in seeking support.

FAM §159.303. APPLICATION OF LAW OF STATE

Except as otherwise provided in this chapter, a responding tribunal of this state shall:

(1) apply the procedural and substantive law, including the rules on choice of law, generally applicable to similar proceedings originating in this state and may exercise all powers and provide all remedies available in those proceedings; and

(2) determine the duty of support and the amount payable in accordance with the law and support guidelines of this state.

History of Fam §159.303: Acts 1995, 74th Leg., ch. 20, §1, eff. April 20, 1995. Amended by Acts 1997, 75th Leg., ch. 607, §7, eff. Sept. 1, 1997. Source: Former Fam §21.15.

Official Comment

Historically States have insisted that forum law be applied to support cases whenever possible. This continues as a key principle of UIFSA. In general, a responding tribunal has the same powers in an action involving interstate parties as it has in an intrastate case. This inevitably means that the Act is not self-contained; rather, it is supplemented by the forum's statutes and procedures governing support orders. To insure the efficient processing of the huge number of interstate support cases, it is vital that decision-makers apply familiar rules of local law to the maximum degree possible. This must be accomplished in a manner consistent with the overriding principle of UIFSA that enforcement is of the issuing tribunal's order, and that the responding State does not make the order its own as a condition of enforcing it.

FAM §159.304. DUTIES OF INITIATING TRIBUNAL

(a) On the filing of a petition authorized by this chapter, an initiating tribunal of this state shall forward three copies of the petition and its accompanying documents:

(1) to the responding tribunal or appropriate support enforcement agency in the responding state; or

(2) if the identity of the responding tribunal is unknown, to the state information agency of the responding state with a request that they be forwarded to the appropriate tribunal and that receipt be acknowledged.

(b) If a responding state has not enacted the Uniform Interstate Family Support Act or a law or procedure substantially similar to that Act, a tribunal of this state may issue a certificate or other document and make findings required by the law of the responding state. If the responding state is a foreign jurisdiction, the tribunal may specify the amount of support sought and provide other documents necessary to satisfy the requirements of the responding state.

History of Fam §159.304: Acts 1995, 74th Leg., ch. 20, §1, eff. April 20, 1995. Amended by Acts 1997, 75th Leg., ch. 607, §8, eff. Sept. 1, 1997. Source: Former Fam §21.16.

Official Comment

Under RURESA §14, the initiating tribunal was required to make a preliminary finding of the existence of a support obligation. As a practical matter, observance of this obligation was at best erratic across the nation; very often courts viewed the finding as boilerplate. By contrast, under UIFSA the role of the initiating tribunal clearly consists of the ministerial function of forwarding the documents. *See Mossburg v. Coffman*, 6 Kan. App. 2d 428, 629 P.2d 745 (1981); *Neff v. Johnson*, 391 S.W.2d 760 (Tex. Civ. App.—Houston 1965, no writ).

New subsection (b), a transition provision, facilitates interstate enforcement between UIFSA States and those URESA and RURESA States prior to the likely nationwide enactment of UIFSA by January 1, 1998. *See* P.L. 104-193, §321. Although the three uniform acts seek the same goal – interstate child support – and are compatible in the main, neither URESA nor RURESA can be said to be "substantially similar" to UIFSA. Careful reading of UIFSA reveals that an arms-length view is maintained on this topic, see Section 101(7), (16), and (19)(ii), *supra*. Exemplary of the imperfect fit between the acts is the number of complaints received during the period between the original promulgation of the Act in February 1993 and the amendments in July 1996 alleging that the elimination of the RURESA requirement for certification of a duty of support had led to serious communication problems between RURESA States and UIFSA States. Supposedly the difference in procedure and documentation required by the two acts caused a tribunal in one State or the other to refuse to enforce a child support obligation unless the paperwork conformed to its requirements or, alternatively, a tribunal refused to provide the requested documents on the basis that the law of its State did not require the production of such documents. The loser in the exercise of such hypertechnical interstate recalcitrance was the child who was due support. In response to such bureaucratic impasses, the 1996 amendment authorizes a tribunal in a UIFSA State to provide whatever documentation is required by a RURESA State to facilitate child support enforcement.

Supplying documentation required by a foreign jurisdiction that is not required by UIFSA procedure will continue to be necessary into the future. The initiating tribunal is authorized to cooperate and provide whatever information or documentation is requested by the foreign jurisdiction, *i.e.*, a statement of the amount of support being requested is required by Canadian provinces.

FAM §159.305. DUTIES & POWERS OF RESPONDING TRIBUNAL

(a) When a responding tribunal of this state receives a petition or comparable pleading from an initiating tribunal or directly under Section 159.301(c), the responding tribunal shall cause the petition or pleading to be filed and notify the petitioner where and when it was filed.

(b) A responding tribunal of this state, to the extent otherwise authorized by law, may do one or more of the following:

(1) issue or enforce a support order, modify a child support order, or render a judgment to determine parentage;

(2) order an obligor to comply with a support order and specify the amount and the manner of compliance;

(3) order income withholding;

(4) determine the amount of any arrearages and specify a method of payment;

(5) enforce orders by civil or criminal contempt, or both;

(6) set aside property for satisfaction of the support order;

(7) place liens and order execution on the obligor's property;

(8) order an obligor to keep the tribunal informed of the obligor's current residential address, telephone number, employer, address of employment, and telephone number at the place of employment;

(9) issue a bench warrant or capias for an obligor who has failed after proper notice to appear at a hearing ordered by the tribunal and enter the bench warrant or capias in any local and state computer systems for criminal warrants;

(10) order the obligor to seek appropriate employment by specified methods;

(11) award reasonable attorney's fees and other fees and costs; and

(12) grant any other available remedy.

(c) A responding tribunal of this state shall include in a support order issued under this chapter, or in the documents accompanying the order, the calculations on which the support order is based.

(d) A responding tribunal of this state may not condition the payment of a support order issued under this chapter on compliance by a party with provisions for visitation.

(e) If a responding tribunal of this state issues an order under this chapter, the tribunal shall send a copy of the order to the petitioner and the respondent and to the initiating tribunal, if any.

History of Fam §159.305: Acts 1995, 74th Leg., ch. 20, §1, eff. April 20, 1995. Amended by Acts 1997, 75th Leg., ch. 607, §9, eff. Sept. 1, 1997. Source: Former Fam §21.17.

Office of Attorney Gen. v. Carter, 977 S.W.2d 159, 161 (Tex.App.—Houston [14th Dist.] 1998, no pet.). "UIFSA ... permits a responding tribunal, upon receiving a petition from an initiating tribunal, to establish, enforce, or modify child support."

Official Comment

This section revises RURESA §§9, 18, 19, 24, 25, and 26. It contains both ministerial functions, such as those in subsection (a); judicial functions, as in subsection (b); and substantive rules applicable to interstate cases, subsections (c)-(e). Because a responding tribunal may be an administrative agency rather than a court, the Act explicitly states that a tribunal is not granted powers that it does not otherwise possess under state law. For example, authority to enforce orders by contempt often is limited to courts.

Subsection (a) eliminates the authorization of notice "by first class mail." Several reasons underlie this deletion. Originally the authorization of first class mail was intended to facilitate relatively informal notice of the issuing tribunal's action, that is, formal service of the order by an officer was not to be required. The intent was that first class mail notice would be sufficient. The deletion of specificity regarding notice is not intended to increase the burden of giving notice. Rather, the advent of a variety of swifter and perhaps even more reliable forms of notice in the modern era justifies the deletion of the first class mail requirement, which may very well be unduly restrictive. For example, many States now authorize notice by telephone facsimile (FAX), or by an express delivery company. In addition, the authorization of legal notice of at least some documents by electronic mail (email) may not be far off. Finally, authorization of notice by first class mail in UIFSA could be regarded as an undue interference with state law, something a Uniform Act should avoid.

Subsection (b)(7) purposefully avoids mention of the priority of liens issued under UIFSA. As is generally true under the Act, that priority will be determined by applicable state law concerning support liens. Subsection (b) supplies much more detail than did RURESA §§24 and 26 to make explicit the wide range of specific powers of the responding tribunal. Subsection (b)(9) replaces RURESA §16 (Jurisdiction By Arrest), which authorized the responding tribunal "to obtain the body of the obligor" if the tribunal "believes that the obligor may flee." Under UIFSA, the physical seizure of an obligor is left to the procedures available under state law in other civil cases.

Subsection (c) clarifies that the details of calculating the child support order are to be included along with the order. Local law generally requires that variation from the child support guidelines must be explained, see 42 U.S.C. §667; this requirement is extended to interstate cases.

Subsection (d) states that an interstate support order may not be conditioned on compliance with a visitation order. While this may be at variance with state law governing intrastate cases, under a UIFSA action the petitioner generally is not present before the tribunal. This distinction justifies prohibiting visitation issues from being litigated in the context of a support proceeding.

Subsection (e) introduces the policy determination that the petitioner, the respondent, and the initiating tribunal, if any, shall be kept informed about actions taken by the responding tribunal.

FAM §159.306. INAPPROPRIATE TRIBUNAL

If a petition or comparable pleading is received by an inappropriate tribunal of this state, that tribunal shall forward the pleading and accompanying documents to an appropriate tribunal in this state or another state and notify the petitioner where and when the pleading was sent.

History of Fam §159.306: Acts 1995, 74th Leg., ch. 20, §1, eff. April 20, 1995. Amended by Acts 1997, 75th Leg., ch. 607, §10, eff. Sept. 1, 1997. Source: Former Fam §21.18.

Official Comment

This section directs a tribunal receiving UIFSA documents in error to forward the original documents to their proper destination without undue delay, whether the appropriate tribunal is located in the same State or elsewhere. This section is intended to apply both to initiating and responding tribunals receiving such documents. For example, if a tribunal is inappropriately designated as the responding tribunal, it shall forward the petition to the appropriate responding tribunal wherever located, if known, and notify the initiating tribunal of its action. Such a procedure is much to be preferred to returning the documents to the initiating tribunal to begin the process anew. Cooperation of this sort will facilitate the ultimate goals of the Act.

For a full explanation regarding the deletion of the authorization of notice by first class mail, see the Comment to Section 305.

FAM §159.307. DUTIES OF SUPPORT ENFORCEMENT AGENCY

(a) A support enforcement agency of this state, on request, shall provide services to a petitioner in a proceeding under this chapter.

(b) A support enforcement agency that provides services to the petitioner as appropriate shall:

(1) take all steps necessary to enable an appropriate tribunal in this state or another state to obtain jurisdiction over the respondent;

(2) request an appropriate tribunal to set a date, time, and place for a hearing;

(3) make a reasonable effort to obtain all relevant information, including information as to income and property of the parties;

(4) not later than the second day, excluding Saturdays, Sundays, and legal holidays, after the date of receipt of a written notice from an initiating, responding, or registering tribunal, send a copy of the notice to the petitioner;

(5) not later than the second day, excluding Saturdays, Sundays, and legal holidays, after the date of receipt of a written communication from the respondent or the respondent's attorney, send a copy of the communication to the petitioner; and

(6) notify the petitioner if jurisdiction over the respondent cannot be obtained.

(c) This chapter does not create or negate a relationship of attorney and client or other fiduciary relationship between a support enforcement agency or the attorney for the agency and the individual being assisted by the agency.

History of Fam §159.307: Acts 1995, 74th Leg., ch. 20, §1, eff. April 20, 1995. Amended by Acts 1997, 75th Leg., ch. 607, §11, eff. Sept. 1, 1997. Source: Former Fam §21.19.

Official Comment

This section is derived from RURESA §§12, 18, and 19.

Subsection (a) changes the focus of RURESA §12 (Officials to Represent Obligee) from representation of an obligee to providing services to a petitioner. Care should be exercised in the use of terminology given this substantial alteration of past practice under RURESA. Not only may either the obligee or the obligor request services, but that request may be in the context of the establishment of an initial support order, enforcement or review and adjustment of an existing order, or a modification of that order (upwards or downwards). Note that the Act does not distinguish between child support and spousal support for purposes of providing services. Note also, that the services available may differ significantly; for example, modification of spousal support is limited to the issuing State, see Section 205(f), *supra*.

Subsection (b) responds to the complaint of many RURESA petitioners that they were not properly kept informed about the progress of their requests for services.

Subsection (c) explicitly states that UIFSA neither creates nor rejects the establishment of an attorney-client or fiduciary relationship between the support enforcement agency and a petitioner receiving services from that agency. This highly controversial issue is left to otherwise applicable state law.

For a full explanation regarding the deletion of the authorization of notice by first class mail, see the Comment to Section 305.

FAM §159.308. DUTY OF ATTORNEY GENERAL

If the attorney general determines that the support enforcement agency is neglecting or refusing to provide services to an individual, the attorney general may order the agency to perform its duties under this chapter or may provide those services directly to the individual.

History of Fam §159.308: Acts 1995, 74th Leg., ch. 20, §1, eff. April 20, 1995. Source: Former Fam §21.20.

Official Comment

This section continues the principle of RURESA §18(c), under which the State Attorney General, or an alternative designated by state law, is given oversight responsibility for the diligent provision of services by the support enforcement agency and the power to seek compliance with the Act.

FAM §159.309. PRIVATE COUNSEL

An individual may employ private counsel to represent the individual in proceedings authorized by this chapter.

History of Fam §159.309: Acts 1995, 74th Leg., ch. 20, §1, eff. April 20, 1995. Source: Former Fam §21.21.

Official Comment

The right of a party to retain private counsel in an action to be brought under UIFSA is explicitly recognized. RURESA's failure to clearly recognize that power led to some confusion and inconsistent decisions.

FAM §159.310. DUTIES OF STATE INFORMATION AGENCY

(a) The Title IV-D agency is the state information agency under this chapter.

(b) The state information agency shall:

(1) compile and maintain a current list, including addresses, of the tribunals in this state that have jurisdiction under this chapter and any support enforcement agencies in this state and send a copy to the state information agency of every other state;

(2) maintain a register of tribunals and support enforcement agencies received from other states;

(3) forward to the appropriate tribunal in the place in this state where the individual obligee or the obligor resides, or where the obligor's property is believed to be located, all documents concerning a proceeding under this chapter received from an initiating tribunal or the state information agency of the initiating state; and

(4) obtain information concerning the location of the obligor and the obligor's property in this state not exempt from execution, by such means as postal verification and federal or state locator services, examination of telephone directories, requests for the obligor's address from employers, and examination of governmental records, including, to the extent not prohibited by other law, those relating to real property, vital statistics, law enforcement, taxation, motor vehicles, driver's licenses, and social security.

History of Fam §159.310: Acts 1995, 74th Leg., ch. 20, §1, eff. April 20, 1995. Source: Former Fam §21.22.

Official Comment

This section, based on RURESA §17 (State Information Agency), continues the information-gathering duties of the central information agency.

Subsection (b)(4) does not provide independent access to the information sources or to the governmental documents listed. Because States have different requirements and limitations concerning such access based on differing views of the privacy interests of individual citizens, the agency is directed to use all lawful means under the relevant state law to obtain and disseminate information.

FAM §159.311. PLEADINGS & ACCOMPANYING DOCUMENTS

(a) A petitioner seeking to establish or modify a support order or to determine parentage in a proceeding under this chapter must verify the petition. Unless otherwise ordered under Section 159.312, the petition or accompanying documents must provide, so far as known, the name, residential address, and social security numbers of the obligor and the obligee and the name, sex, residential address, social security number, and date of birth of each child for whom support is sought. The petition must be accompanied by a certified copy of any support order in effect. The petition may include any other information that may assist in locating or identifying the respondent.

(b) The petition must specify the relief sought. The petition and accompanying documents must conform substantially with the requirements imposed by the forms mandated by federal law for use in cases filed by a support enforcement agency.

History of Fam §159.311: Acts 1995, 74th Leg., ch. 20, §1, eff. April 20, 1995. Source: Former Fam §21.23.

Official Comment

Derived from RURESA §11, this section establishes the basic requirements for drafting and filing interstate pleadings. Subsection (a) should be read in conjunction with Section 312, which provides for the confidentiality of certain information if disclosure is likely to result in harm to a party or a child.

Subsection (b) provides authorization for the use of the federally authorized forms promulgated in connection with the IV-D child support enforcement program and mandates substantial compliance with those forms. Although the use of other forms is not prohibited, statutory preapproval of forms that substantially conform to those sanctioned by federal law will help to standardize documents, with a concomitant improvement in the efficient processing of UIFSA actions.

FAM §159.312. NONDISCLOSURE OF INFORMATION IN EXCEPTIONAL CIRCUMSTANCES

On a finding, which may be made ex parte, that the health, safety, or liberty of a party or child would be unreasonably put at risk by the disclosure of identifying information or if an existing order so provides, a tribunal shall order that the address of the child or party or other identifying information not be disclosed in a pleading or other document filed in a proceeding under this chapter.

History of Fam §159.312: Acts 1995, 74th Leg., ch. 20, §1, eff. April 20, 1995. Source: Former Fam §21.24.

Official Comment

Public awareness of and sensitivity to the dangers of domestic violence has significantly increased since the original promulgation of URESA and RURESA. This section authorizes confidentiality in instances where there is a serious risk of domestic violence or child abduction. Although local law generally governs the conduct of the forum tribunal, state law may not provide for maintaining secrecy about the exact whereabouts of a litigant or other information ordinarily required to be disclosed under state law, *i.e.*, Social Security number of the parties or the child. If so, this provision creates a confidentiality provision which is particularly appropriate in the light of the intractable problems associated with interstate (as opposed to intrastate) childnapping.

FAM §159.313. COSTS & FEES

(a) The petitioner may not be required to pay a filing fee or other costs.

(b) If an obligee prevails, a responding tribunal may assess against an obligor filing fees, reasonable attorney's fees, other costs, and necessary travel and other reasonable expenses incurred by the obligee and the obligee's witnesses. The tribunal may not assess fees, costs, or expenses against the obligee or the support enforcement agency of either the initiating state or the responding state, except as provided by other law. Attorney's fees may be taxed as costs and may be ordered paid directly to the attorney, who may enforce the order in the attorney's own name. Payment of support owed to the obligee has priority over fees, costs, and expenses.

(c) The tribunal shall order the payment of costs and reasonable attorney's fees if it determines that a hearing was requested primarily for delay. In a proceeding pursuant to Sections 159.601 through 159.608, a hearing is presumed to have been requested primarily for delay if a registered support order is confirmed or enforced without change.

History of Fam §159.313: Acts 1995, 74th Leg., ch. 20, §1, eff. April 20, 1995. Amended by Acts 1997, 75th Leg., ch. 607, §12, eff. Sept. 1, 1997. Source: Former Fam §21.25.

Official Comment

This section is derived from RURESA §15 (Costs and Fees), which authorized fees and costs to be assessed against "the obligor." In recognition of the fact that under UIFSA either the obligor or the obligee may file suit or seek services from a support enforcement agency, subsection (a) permits either party to file without payment of a filing fee or other costs. Subsection (b), however, continues the RURESA determination that only the support obligor may be assessed the specified costs and fees.

Subsection (c) provides a sanction to deal with a frivolous contest regarding compliance with an interstate withholding order, registration of a support order, or comparable delaying tactics regarding an appropriate enforcement remedy.

FAM §159.314. LIMITED IMMUNITY OF PETITIONER

(a) Participation by a petitioner in a proceeding before a responding tribunal, whether in person, by private attorney, or through services provided by the support enforcement agency, does not confer personal jurisdiction over the petitioner in another proceeding.

(b) A petitioner is not amenable to service of civil process while physically present in this state to participate in a proceeding under this chapter.

(c) The immunity granted by this section does not extend to civil litigation based on acts unrelated to a proceeding under this chapter committed by a party while present in this state to participate in the proceeding.

History of Fam §159.314: Acts 1995, 74th Leg., ch. 20, §1, eff. April 20, 1995. Source: Former Fam §21.26.

Official Comment

This section significantly expands RURESA §32. Under subsection (a), direct or indirect participation in a UIFSA proceeding does not subject a petitioner to an assertion of personal jurisdiction over the petitioner by the forum State in other litigation between the parties. The primary object of this prohibition is to preclude joining disputes over child custody and visitation with the establishment, enforcement, or modification of child support. This prohibition strengthens the ban on visitation litigation established in Section 305(d). A petition for affirmative relief under UIFSA limits the jurisdiction of the tribunal to the boundaries of the support proceeding.

Similarly, subsection (b) grants a litigant a variety of limited immunity from service of process during the time a party is physically present in a State for a UIFSA action. The immunity provided is in no way comparable to diplomatic immunity, however, which should be clear from reading subsection (c) in conjunction with the other subsections.

Subsection (c) does not extend immunity to civil litigation unrelated to the support action which stems from contemporaneous acts committed by a party while present in the State for the support litigation. For example, a petitioner involved in an automobile accident or a contract dispute over the cost of lodging while present in the State does not have immunity from a civil suit on those issues.

FAM §159.315. NONPARENTAGE AS DEFENSE

A party whose parentage of a child has been previously determined by or under law may not plead nonparentage as a defense to a proceeding under this chapter.

History of Fam §159.315: Acts 1995, 74th Leg., ch. 20, §1, eff. April 20, 1995. Source: Former Fam §21.27.

Official Comment

Arguably this section does no more than restate the basic principle of res judicata. However, there is a great variety of state law regarding presumptions of parentage and available defenses after a prior determination of parentage. This section is intended neither to discourage nor encourage collateral attacks in situations in which the law of a foreign jurisdiction is at significant odds with local law. If a collateral attack on a parentage decree is permissible under the law of the issuing jurisdiction, such an action must be pursued in that forum and not in a UIFSA proceeding. In sum, this section mandates that a parentage decree rendered by another tribunal is not subject to collateral attack in a UIFSA proceeding. Of course, an attack on an alleged final order on a fundamental constitutional ground is permissible in the forum State, such as a denial of due process because of a failure of notice and opportunity to be heard or a lack of personal jurisdiction over a party who did not answer or appear.

Similarly, the law of the issuing State may provide for a determination of parentage based on certain specific acts of the obligor acknowledging parentage as a substitute for a decree, *i.e.*, signing the child's birth certificate or publicly acknowledging a duty of support after receiving the child into his home. UIFSA also is neutral regarding a collateral attack on such a parentage determination. The responding tribunal must give effect to such an act of acknowledgment of parentage if it is recognized as determinative in the issuing State. The consistent theme of this section is that a collateral attack cannot be made in a UIFSA proceeding.

FAM §159.316. SPECIAL RULES OF EVIDENCE & PROCEDURE

(a) The physical presence of the petitioner in a responding tribunal of this state is not required for the establishment, enforcement, or modification of a support order or the rendition of a judgment determining parentage.

(b) A verified petition, affidavit, document substantially complying with federally mandated forms, and a document incorporated by reference in the petition, affidavit, or document, not excluded under the hearsay rule if given in person, are admissible in evidence if given under oath by a party or witness residing in another state.

(c) A copy of the record of child support payments certified as a true copy of the original by the custodian of the record may be forwarded to a responding tribunal. The copy is evidence of facts asserted in it and is admissible to show whether payments were made.

(d) Copies of bills for testing for parentage and for prenatal and postnatal health care of the mother and child that are furnished to the adverse party not less than 10 days before the date of trial are admissible in evidence to prove the amount of the charges billed and that the charges were reasonable, necessary, and customary.

(e) Documentary evidence sent from another state to a tribunal of this state by telephone, telecopier, or another means that does not provide an original writing may not be excluded from evidence on an objection based on the means of transmission.

(f) In a proceeding under this chapter, a tribunal of this state may permit a party or witness residing in another state to be deposed or to testify by telephone, audiovisual means, or other electronic means at a designated tribunal or other location in that state. A tribunal of this state shall cooperate with a tribunal of another state in designating an appropriate location for the deposition or testimony.

(g) If a party called to testify at a civil hearing refuses to answer on the ground that the testimony may be self-incriminating, the trier of fact may draw an adverse inference from the refusal.

(h) A privilege against disclosure of communications between spouses does not apply in a proceeding under this chapter.

(i) The defense of immunity based on the relationship of husband and wife or parent and child does not apply in a proceeding under this chapter.

History of Fam §159.316: Acts 1995, 74th Leg., ch. 20, §1, eff. April 20, 1995. Source: Former Fam §21.28.

Official Comment

This section combines RURESA §§9, 19, 21, 22, and 23; and, provides additional innovative methods for gathering evidence in interstate cases.

Subsections (b) through (f) greatly expand on RURESA §23 (Rules of Evidence). The intent is to eliminate as many potential hearsay problems as possible in interstate litigation because the out-of-state party and that party's witnesses usually do not appear in person at the hearing.

Subsection (d) provides a simplified means for proving health care expenses related to the birth of a child. Because ordinarily these charges are not in dispute, this is designed to obviate the cost of having health care providers appear in person or of obtaining affidavits of business records from each provider.

Subsections (e) and (f) encourage tribunals and litigants to take advantage of modern methods of communication in interstate support litigation; most dramatically, the out-of-state party is authorized to testify by telephone and supply documents by fax.

Subsection (g) codifies the rule in effect in many States that in civil litigation an adverse inference may be drawn from a litigant's silence. *See, i.e., In re Matter of Joseph P.*, 487 N.Y.S.2d 685 (Fam. Ct. 1985); Pa. Cons. Stats. Ann., Tit. 23, §5104(c) (1991) and La. Rev. Stats., Tit. 9, §396(A) (1992) ("if any party refuses to submit to such tests, the court may resolve the question of paternity against such party"); 9 N.J. Stats. Ann. 17-51(d) (1991) ("refusal to submit to blood tests or genetic tests, or both, may be admitted into evidence and shall give rise to the presumption that the results of the tests would have been unfavorable to the interests of the party refusing").

FAM §159.317. COMMUNICATIONS BETWEEN TRIBUNALS

A tribunal of this state may communicate with a tribunal of another state in writing, by telephone, or by another means, to obtain information concerning the laws of that state, the legal effect of a judgment, decree, or order of that tribunal, and the status of a proceeding in the other state. A tribunal of this state may furnish similar information by similar means to a tribunal of another state.

History of Fam §159.317: Acts 1995, 74th Leg., ch. 20, §1, eff. April 20, 1995. Source: Former Fam §21.29.

Official Comment

This section is derived from UCCJA §7(d) (Inconvenient Forum), which authorizes communications between courts in order to facilitate decisions under that Act. In contrast to RURESA, broad cooperation between tribunals is permitted under UIFSA to expedite establishment and enforcement of a support order.

FAM §159.318. ASSISTANCE WITH DISCOVERY

A tribunal of this state may:

(1) request a tribunal of another state to assist in obtaining discovery; and

(2) on request, compel a person over whom the tribunal has jurisdiction to respond to a discovery order issued by a tribunal of another state.

History of Fam §159.318: Acts 1995, 74th Leg., ch. 20, §1, eff. April 20, 1995. Source: Former Fam §21.30.

Official Comment

This section takes another logical step to facilitate interstate cooperation by enlisting the power of the forum to assist a tribunal of another State with the discovery process. The grant of authority is quite broad, enabling the tribunal of the enacting State to fashion its remedies to facilitate discovery consistent with local practice.

FAM §159.319. RECEIPT & DISBURSEMENT OF PAYMENTS

A support enforcement agency or tribunal of this state shall disburse promptly any amounts received under a support order, as directed by the order. The agency or tribunal shall furnish to a requesting party or tribunal of another state a certified statement by the custodian of the record of the amounts and dates of all payments received.

History of Fam §159.319: Acts 1995, 74th Leg., ch. 20, §1, eff. April 20, 1995. Source: Former Fam §21.31.

Official Comment

The first sentence of this section is derived from RURESA §29 (Additional Duty of Initiating Court). The second sentence confirms the duty of the agency or tribunal to furnish payment information in interstate cases.

Sections 159.320-159.400 reserved for expansion

SUBCHAPTER E. ESTABLISHMENT OF SUPPORT ORDER

FAM §159.401. PETITION TO ESTABLISH SUPPORT ORDER

(a) If a support order entitled to recognition under this chapter has not been issued, a responding tribunal of this state may issue a support order if:

(1) the individual seeking the order resides in another state; or

(2) the support enforcement agency seeking the order is located in another state.

(b) The tribunal may issue a temporary child support order if:

(1) the respondent has signed a verified statement acknowledging parentage;

(2) the respondent has been determined by or under law to be the parent; or

(3) there is other clear and convincing evidence that the respondent is the child's parent.

(c) On finding, after notice and an opportunity to be heard, that an obligor owes a duty of support, the tribunal shall issue a support order directed to the obligor and may issue other orders under Section 159.305.

History of Fam §159.401: Acts 1995, 74th Leg., ch. 20, §1, eff. April 20, 1995. Source: Former Fam §21.32.

Official Comment

This section authorizes a tribunal of the responding State to issue temporary and permanent support orders binding on an obligor over whom the tribunal has personal jurisdiction. UIFSA does not permit such orders to be issued when another support order exists, thereby prohibiting a second tribunal from establishing another support order and the accompanying continuing, exclusive jurisdiction over the matter. *See* Section 205 (Continuing, Exclusive Jurisdiction) and Section 206 (Enforcement and Modification of Support Order by Tribunal Having Continuing Jurisdiction).

Sections 159.402-159.500 reserved for expansion

SUBCHAPTER F. ENFORCEMENT OF ORDER OF ANOTHER STATE WITHOUT REGISTRATION

FAM §159.501. EMPLOYER'S RECEIPT OF INCOME-WITHHOLDING ORDER OF ANOTHER STATE

An income-withholding order issued in another state may be sent to the obligor's employer under Chapter 158 without first filing a petition or comparable pleading or registering the order with a tribunal of this state.

History of Fam §159.501: Acts 1995, 74th Leg., ch. 20, §1, eff. April 20, 1995. Renumbered from §159.501(a) by Acts 1997, 75th Leg., ch. 607, §13, eff. Sept. 1, 1997. Source: Former Fam §21.33(a).

Official Comment

In 1984 Congress mandated that all States adopt procedures for enforcing income-withholding orders of sister States. As a result, the Child Support Project of the American Bar Association and the National Conference of State Legislatures promulgated a Model Interstate Income Withholding Act in 1985; however, the Model Act was not widely enacted. RURESA was silent on the subject. Direct recognition by the out-of-state obligor's employer of a withholding order issued by another State long was sought by support enforcement associations and other advocacy groups. In 1993 UIFSA recognized such a procedure.

Section 501 is deliberately written in the passive voice; the Act does not restrict who may send an income-withholding order across state lines. Although the sender will ordinarily be a child support enforcement agency or the obligee, the obligor or any other person may supply an employer with the income-withholding order. Further, "sending a copy" of a withholding order to an employer is clearly distinguishable from "service" of that order on the same employer. The latter necessarily intends to invoke the tribunal's authority only over an employer doing business in the forum State. But, for there to be valid "service" of a withholding order on an employer in another State, the tribunal must have authority to bind the employer. In most cases, this requires the assertion of the authority of a local responding tribunal in a "registration for enforcement" proceeding. The formality of "service" defeats the whole purpose of direct income withholding across state lines. This explains the deletion of the original requirement in the 1993 version of UIFSA that the income-withholding order of one State "may be sent by first class mail." In sum, the process contemplated is direct "notification" to an employer in another State of a withholding order without the involvement of initiating or responding tribunals. Therefore, receipt of a copy of a withholding order by facsimile, regular first class mail, registered or certified mail, or any other type of direct notice is sufficient to provide the requisite notice to trigger direct income withholding in the absence of a contest by the employee-obligor.

FAM §159.502. EMPLOYER'S COMPLIANCE WITH INCOME-WITHHOLDING ORDER OF ANOTHER STATE

(a) On receipt of an income-withholding order, the obligor's employer shall immediately provide a copy of the order to the obligor.

(b) The employer shall treat an income-withholding order issued in another state that appears regular on its face as if the order had been issued by a tribunal of this state.

(c) Except as otherwise provided in Subsection (d) and Section 159.503, the employer shall withhold and distribute the funds as directed in the withholding order by complying with terms of the order that specify:

(1) the duration and amount of periodic payments of current child support, stated as a sum certain;

(2) the person or agency designated to receive payments and the address to which the payments are to be forwarded;

(3) medical support, whether in the form of periodic cash payments, stated as a sum certain, or ordering the obligor to provide health insurance coverage for the child under a policy available through the obligor's employment;

(4) the amount of periodic payments of fees and costs for a support enforcement agency, the issuing tribunal, and the obligee's attorney, stated as sums certain; and

(5) the amount of periodic payments of arrearages and interest on arrearages, stated as sums certain.

(d) An employer shall comply with the law of the state of the obligor's principal place of employment for withholding from income with respect to:

(1) the employer's fee for processing an income-withholding order;

(2) the maximum amount permitted to be withheld from the obligor's income; and

(3) the times within which the employer must implement the withholding order and forward the child support payment.

History of Fam §159.502: Acts 1995, 74th Leg., ch. 20, §1, eff. April 20, 1995. Renumbered from §159.501(a) by Acts 1997, 75th Leg., ch. 607, §13, eff. Sept. 1, 1997. Source: Former Fam §21.33(a).

Official Comment

Major employers and national payroll associations urged the National Conference of Commissioners on Uniform State Laws to supply more detail regarding the rights and duties of an employer on receipt of an income-withholding order from another State. The Conference obliged with amendments to UIFSA that set forth a series of steps for the employer to track.

The employer's first step is to notify the employee of receipt of the out-of-state withholding order. If the employee disputes the validity of the withholding order, it is the employee's responsibility to take appropriate defensive measures to contest the withholding. At this point neither an initiating nor a responding tribunal is directly involved. The withholding order may have been forwarded by the obligee, the obligee's attorney, or the out-of-state IV-D agency. In fact, there is no prohibition against anyone sending a valid copy of an income-withholding order, even a stranger to the litigation, such as the child's grandparent. Subsection (a) does not specify the method for sending this relatively informal notice for direct income withholding, but rather takes a permissive view of communication notice on the assumption that an obligor will act to prevent a wrongful invasion of income not owed as current child support or arrears.

Subsection (b) directs an employer of the enacting State to recognize a withholding order of a sister State, subject to the employee's right to contest the validity of the order or its enforcement. Prior to the promulgation of UIFSA, agencies in several States adopted a procedure of sending direct withholding requests to out-of-state employers. A contemporaneous study by the federal General Accounting Office reported that employers in a second State routinely recognized withholding orders of sister States despite an apparent lack of statutory authority to do so. UIFSA marked the first official sanction of this practice. Subsection (b) does not define "regular on its face," but the term should be liberally construed, see *U.S. v. Morton*, 467 U.S. 822 (1984) ("legal process regular on its face"). The rules governing intrastate procedure and defenses for withholding orders will apply to interstate orders. Thus, subsection (a) makes clear that employers who refuse to recognize out-of-state withholding orders will be subjected to whatever remedies are otherwise available under state law.

Subsection (c) is the answer to employers' complaints that insufficient direction for action was given by the original UIFSA. Formerly the employer was merely told to "distribute the funds as directed in the withholding order." This section clarifies the terms of the out-of-state order with which the employer must strictly comply, and those terms that are subject to compliance with local law. As a general principle, an employer is directed to comply with the specific terms contained in the order, but there are exceptions. Moreover, many income-withholding orders currently do not provide the detail necessary for the employer to comply with each and every directive. Fortunately, when the long-anticipated federal forms are finally promulgated, more uniformity in the text of child support orders will eventually occur. To the extent that an order is silent, the employer is not required to respond to unstated demands of the issuing State. Formerly, employers often were so concerned about ambiguous or incomplete orders that they telephoned child support enforcement agencies in other States to attempt to understand and comply with unstated terms. Employers should not be expected to become investigators or shoulder the responsibility of learning the law of 50 States.

Subsection (c)(1) directs that the amount and duration of periodic payments of current child support must be stated in a sum certain in order to elicit compliance. The duration of the support obligation is fixed by the controlling order and should be stated in the withholding order so that the employer is informed of the date on which the withholding is anticipated to terminate. The "sum certain" requirement is crucial to facilitating the employer's compliance. An order for a "percentage of the obligor's net income," for example, does not satisfy this requirement. A State that typically issues its orders as a percentage of income is not entitled to compliance by an employer receiving an interstate income-withholding order by an employer. Such a State should revisit the issue and provide an order for a sum certain if the procedures set forth in this article are to be employed.

Subsection (c)(2) states the obvious: Necessary information must be clearly stated. For example, the destination of the payments must correspond to the destination originally designated or subsequently authorized by the issuing tribunal.

Subsection (c)(3) provides that medical support for the child must be stated either by a periodic cash payment or, alternatively, by an order directing the obligor to provide health insurance coverage from his employment. In the absence of an order for payment of a sum certain, an order for medical support as child support requires the employer to enroll the obligor's child for coverage if medical insurance is available through the obligor's employment. Failure to enroll the child should elicit, at the least, registration of the order for enforcement in the responding State, to be implemented by an order of a tribunal directing the employer to comply. Because the employer is so directed by the medical support order, enrollment of the child in the health care plan at the employee-obligor's expense is not dependent on the obligor's consent, any more than withholding a sum certain from the obligor's wages is subject to a veto. It is up to the obligor to assert any defense to prevent the employer from abiding by the medical support order.

Subsection (c)(4) identifies certain costs and fees incurred in conjunction with the support enforcement that may be added to the withholding order.

Subsection (c)(5) requires that the amount of periodic payments for arrears and interest on arrears also must be stated as a sum certain. If the one-order system is to function properly, the issuing State ultimately must be responsible to account for payments and maintain the record of arrears and interest rate on arrears. Full compliance with the support order will only be achieved when the issuing State determines that the obligation no longer exists.

Subsection (d) identifies those narrow provisions in which the law of the employee's work State, rather than the law of the issuing State, should apply. A large employer will almost certainly have a number of employees subject to income-withholding orders. From the employer's perspective, the procedural requirements for compliance should be uniform for all of those employees. Certain issues should be matters for the law of the employee's work State, such as the employer's fee for processing, the maximum amount to be withheld, and the time in which to comply. The latter necessarily includes the frequency with which income withholding must occur. This is also consistent with regard to the tax consideration imposed by choice of law considerations. The only element of the list of local law concerns identified in subsection (d) which stirred any controversy whatsoever was the fact that the maximum amount permitted to be withheld is to be subject to the law of the employee's work State. Demands of equal treatment for all citizens of the responding State and the practical concern for uniform computer programming, however, mandate this solution.

FAM §159.503. COMPLIANCE WITH MULTIPLE INCOME-WITHHOLDING ORDERS

If an obligor's employer receives multiple income-withholding orders with respect to the earnings of the same obligor, the employer satisfies the terms of the multiple orders if the employer complies with the law of the state of the obligor's principal place of employment to establish the priorities for withholding and allocating income withheld for multiple child support obligees.

History of Fam §159.503: Acts 1997, 75th Leg., ch. 607, §13, eff. Sept. 1, 1997.

Official Comment

Consistent with the Act's general problem-solving approach, the employer is directed to deal with multiple income orders for multiple families in a manner consistent with local law.

FAM §159.504. IMMUNITY FROM CIVIL LIABILITY

An employer who complies with an income-withholding order issued in another state in accordance with this subchapter is not subject to civil liability to an individual or agency with regard to the employer's withholding of child support from the obligor's income.

History of Fam §159.504: Acts 1997, 75th Leg., ch. 607, §13, eff. Sept. 1, 1997.

Official Comment

Because employer cooperation is a key element in interstate child support enforcement, it is sound policy to state explicitly that an employer who complies with the income-withholding order from another State is immune from civil liability.

FAM §159.505. PENALTIES FOR NONCOMPLIANCE

An employer who wilfully fails to comply with an income-withholding order issued by another state and received for enforcement is subject to the same penalties that may be imposed for noncompliance with an order issued by a tribunal of this state.

History of Fam §159.505: Acts 1997, 75th Leg., ch. 607, §13, eff. Sept. 1, 1997.

Official Comment

Only an employer who willfully fails to comply with an interstate order should be subject to enforcement procedures. Local law is the appropriate source for the applicable sanctions.

FAM §159.506. CONTEST BY OBLIGOR

(a) An obligor may contest the validity or enforcement of an income-withholding order issued in another state and received directly by an employer in this state in the same manner as if the order had been issued by a tribunal of this state. Section 159.604 applies to the contest.

(b) The obligor shall give notice of the contest to:

(1) a support enforcement agency providing services to the obligee;

(2) each employer that has directly received an income-withholding order; and

(3) the person or agency designated to receive payments in the income-withholding order or to the obligee, if no person or agency is designated.

History of Fam §159.506: Acts 1995, 74th Leg., ch. 20, §1, eff. April 20, 1995. Renumbered from §159.501(b) by Acts 1997, 75th Leg., ch. 607, §13, eff. Sept. 1, 1997. Source: Former Fam §21.33(b).

Official Comment

This section incorporates the law regarding defenses an alleged obligor may raise to an intrastate withholding order into the interstate context. Generally, States have accepted the IV-D requirement that the only viable defense is a "mistake of fact." 42 U.S.C. §666(b)(4)(A). This apparently includes "errors in the amount of current support owed, errors in the amount of accrued arrearage or mistaken identity of the alleged obligor" while excluding "other grounds, such as the inappropriateness of the amount of support ordered to be paid, changed financial circumstances of the obligor, or lack of visitation." H.R. Rep. No. 98-527, 98th Cong., 1st Sess. 33 (1983). The latter claims must be pursued in a separate legal action in the State having continuing, exclusive jurisdiction over the support order, not in a UIFSA proceeding.

After the employer receives a withholding order from another State, the first step is to notify the employee that income withholding for child support will begin within the time frame specified by state law, just as it would if the withholding order is received from a tribunal of the employer's State. It is the responsibility of the employee to take whatever protective measures are necessary to prevent the withholding if the employee asserts a defense.

This procedure is based on the assumption that defenses to income withholding for child support are few and far between. Experience has shown that only in a relatively few cases does an employee-obligor have a defense, *i.e.*, the child has died, another contingency ending the support has occurred, the order has been superseded, or there is a case of mistaken identity and the employee is not the obligor. An employee's complaint that "The child support is too high" must be ignored. The employee's simplest, most efficient, cost-effective method to assert a defense is probably to register the withholding order with a local tribunal and seek protection from that tribunal pending resolution of the contest. This may be accomplished through the obligor's employment of private counsel or by a request for services made to the child support enforcement agency of the responding State. In the absence of expeditious action by the employee to assert a defense and contest the request, however, the employer must begin income withholding in a timely fashion.

In contrast to the multiple-order system of RURESA, another issue the employee may raise is that the withholding order received by the employer is not based on the controlling child support order issued by the tribunal with continuing, exclusive jurisdiction, see Section 207, *supra*. Such a claim does not constitute a defense to the obligation of child support, but does put at issue the identity of the order to which the employer must respond. Clearly the employer is in no position to make such a decision. When multiple orders involve the same obligor and child, as a practical matter resort to a responding tribunal to resolve a dispute over apportionment almost certainly is necessary.

FAM §159.507. ADMINISTRATIVE ENFORCEMENT OF ORDERS

(a) A party seeking to enforce a support order or an income-withholding order, or both, issued by a tribunal of another state may send the documents required for registering the order to a support enforcement agency of this state.

(b) On receipt of the documents, the support enforcement agency, without initially seeking to register the order, shall consider and, if appropriate, use any administrative procedure authorized by the law of this state to enforce a support order or an income-withholding order, or both. If the obligor does not contest administrative enforcement, the order need not be registered. If the obligor contests the validity or administrative enforcement of the order, the support enforcement agency shall register the order under this chapter.

History of Fam §159.507: Acts 1995, 74th Leg., ch. 20, §1, eff. April 20, 1995. Renumbered from §159.502 by Acts 1997, 75th Leg., ch. 607, §13, eff. Sept. 1, 1997. Source: Former Fam §.21.34

Official Comment

This section authorizes summary enforcement of an interstate child support order through the administrative means available for intrastate orders. Under subsection (a), an interested party in another State, which necessarily may include a private attorney or a support enforcement agency, may forward a support order or income-withholding order to a support enforcement agency of the responding State. The term "responding State" in this context does not contemplate resort to a tribunal as an initial step.

Subsection (b) directs the support enforcement agency in the responding State to employ that State's regular administrative procedures to process an out-of-state order. Thus, a local employer accustomed to dealing with the local agency need not change its procedure to comply with an out-of-state order. Similarly, the administrative agency is authorized to apply its ordinary rules equally to both intrastate and interstate orders. For example, if the administrative hearing procedure must be exhausted for an intrastate order before a contesting party may seek relief in a tribunal, the same rule applies to an interstate order received for administrative enforcement. Thereafter, the order may be registered with a tribunal for enforcement if that is the next step for an intrastate order, see Sections 601-608, *infra.*

Sections 159.508-159.600 reserved for expansion

SUBCHAPTER G. ENFORCEMENT & MODIFICATION OF SUPPORT ORDER AFTER REGISTRATION

FAM §159.601. REGISTRATION OF ORDER FOR ENFORCEMENT

A support order or income-withholding order issued by a tribunal of another state may be registered in this state for enforcement.

History of Fam §159.601: Acts 1995, 74th Leg., ch. 20, §1, eff. April 20, 1995. Source: Former Fam §21.35.

Official Comment

Sections 601 through 604 greatly expand the procedure for the registration of interstate support orders available under RURESA §§35-40. The common practice under RURESA was to initiate a new suit for the establishment of a support order, even though there was an existing order for child support. That practice is specifically rejected by UIFSA. The fact that RURESA permitted (really encouraged) initiation of a new suit under those circumstances led to the multiple support order system that UIFSA is designed to eliminate.

Under the one-order system of UIFSA, only one existing order is to be enforced prospectively (if more than one child support order exists, refer to Section 207 for resolution of the conflict). Registration of that order in the responding State is the first step to enforcement by a tribunal of that State. Rather than being an optional procedure, as was the case under RURESA, registration for enforcement under UIFSA is the primary method for interstate enforcement of child support. If the prior support order has been validly issued by a tribunal with continuing, exclusive jurisdiction, see Section 205, only that order is to be prospectively enforced against the obligor in the absence of narrow, strictly-defined fact situations in which an existing order may be modified. *See* Sections 609 through 612. Until that order is modified, however, it is fully enforceable in the responding State.

Registration should be employed if the purpose is enforcement. Although registration not accompanied by a request for affirmative relief is not prohibited, the Act does not contemplate registration as serving a purpose in itself.

FAM §159.602. PROCEDURE TO REGISTER ORDER FOR ENFORCEMENT

(a) A support order or income-withholding order of another state may be registered in this state by sending to the appropriate tribunal in this state:

(1) a letter of transmittal to the tribunal requesting registration and enforcement;

(2) two copies, including one certified copy, of all orders to be registered, including any modification of an order;

(3) a sworn statement by the party seeking registration or a certified statement by the custodian of the records showing the amount of any arrearage;

(4) the name of the obligor and, if known:

A *Subsection (A) below is effective for requests for registrations of support or income-withholding orders of another state made on or after Sept. 1, 2001.*

(A) the obligor's social security number;

Subsection (A) below is effective for requests for registrations of support or income-withholding orders of another state made before Sept. 1, 2001.

(A) the obligor's address and social security number;

(B) the name and address of the obligor's employer and any other source of income of the obligor; and

(C) a description of and the location of property of the obligor in this state not exempt from execution; and

A *Subsection (5) below is effective for requests for registrations of support or income-withholding orders of another state made on or after Sept. 1, 2001.*

(5) the name of the obligee and, if applicable, the agency or person to whom support payments are to be remitted.

Subsection (5) below is effective for requests for registrations of support or income-withholding orders of another state made before Sept. 1, 2001.

(5) the name and address of the obligee and, if applicable, the agency or person to whom support payments are to be remitted.

(b) On receipt of a request for registration, the registering tribunal shall cause the order to be filed as a foreign judgment, together with one copy of the documents and information, regardless of their form.

(c) A petition or comparable pleading seeking a remedy that must be affirmatively sought under other law of this state may be filed at the same time as the request for registration or later. The pleading must specify the grounds for the remedy sought.

History of Fam §159.602: Acts 1995, 74th Leg., ch. 20, §1, eff. April 20, 1995. Amended by Acts 2001, 77th Leg., ch. 296, §3, eff. Sept. 1, 2001. Source: Former Fam §21.36.

In re Chapman, 973 S.W.2d 346, 348 (Tex.App.—Amarillo 1998, no pet.). "[T]he primary purpose for filing a foreign judgment in Texas is enforcement, and an essential prerequisite to enforcement is compliance with the provisions of the applicable uniform act. [¶] Because the procedural requirements contained in §159.602 are mandatory, the failure by [plaintiff] and/or the Attorney General to provide the required documentation is fatal to the order confirming registration…"

Official Comment

This section outlines the mechanics for registration of an interstate order. Subsection (c) warns that if a particular enforcement remedy must be specifically sought under local law, the same rule of pleading is applicable in an interstate case. The authorization of a later filing to comply with local law contemplates that interstate pleadings may be liberally amended to conform to local practice.

FAM §159.603. EFFECT OF REGISTRATION FOR ENFORCEMENT

(a) A support order or income-withholding order issued in another state is registered when the order is filed in the registering tribunal of this state.

(b) A registered order issued in another state is enforceable in the same manner and is subject to the same procedures as an order issued by a tribunal of this state.

(c) Except as otherwise provided in this subchapter, a tribunal of this state shall recognize and enforce, but may not modify, a registered order if the issuing tribunal had jurisdiction.

History of Fam §159.603: Acts 1995, 74th Leg., ch. 20, §1, eff. April 20, 1995. Source: Former Fam §21.37.

Official Comment

Subsection (a) is derived from RURESA §39(a), which stated that "filing constitutes registration." Although the registration procedure under UIFSA is nearly identical to that of RURESA, the underlying intent of registration is radically different. Under RURESA, once an order of State A was registered in State B, it became an order of the latter. Under UIFSA, the order continues to be a State A order, which is to be enforced by a State B tribunal. State B's rules of evidence and procedure apply to hearings, except as local law is supplemented or specifically superseded by the Act. The order itself remains a State A order.

Subsection (b) is derived from RURESA §40(a). RURESA specifically subjected a registered order to "proceedings for reopening, vacating, or staying as a support order of this State"; these procedures are not authorized under UIFSA. An interstate support order is to be enforced and satisfied in the same manner as if it had been issued by a tribunal of the registering State, although it remains an order of the issuing State. Conceptually, the responding State is enforcing the order of another State, not its own order.

Subsection (c) mandates enforcement of the registered order. *See* Sections 606 through 608. This is at sharp variance with the common interpretation of RURESA §40, which stated that "the registered foreign support order shall be treated in the same manner as a support order issued by a court of this State." This language was generally construed as converting the foreign order into an order of the registering State. Once the registering court concluded that it was enforcing its own order, the next logical step was to modify the order as the court deemed appropriate. This rationale resulted in yet another order in the multiple-order system. UIFSA mandates an end to this process, except as modification is authorized in this article. *See* Sections 609 through 612.

Ultimately, under UIFSA there will be only one order in existence at any one time. That order is enforceable in a responding State irrespective of whether such an order may be modified. In most instances, the support order will be subject to the continuing, exclusive jurisdiction of the issuing State. But sometimes the issuing State will have lost its authority to modify the order because neither the child nor the parties continue to reside in the issuing State. Nonetheless, the order may be registered and is fully enforceable in a responding State until the potential for modification actually occurs in accordance with the strict terms for such an action. *See* Sections 609-612.

FAM §159.604. CHOICE OF LAW

(a) The law of the issuing state governs the nature, extent, amount, and duration of current payments and other obligations of support and the payment of arrearages under the order.

(b) In a proceeding for arrearages, the statute of limitation under the laws of this state or of the issuing state, whichever statute of limitation is longer, applies.

History of Fam §159.604: Acts 1995, 74th Leg., ch. 20, §1, eff. April 20, 1995. Amended by Acts 1997, 75th Leg., ch. 607, §14, eff. Sept. 1, 1997. Source: Former Fam §21.38.

Attorney Gen. v. Litten, 999 S.W.2d 74, 77 (Tex. App.—Houston [14th Dist.] 1999, no pet.). "[I]n a proceeding to obtain a judgment for arrearages Chapter 159 requires application of the law of the state with the longer statute of limitation. … In accordance with the clear language in §159.604(b), the ten year Missouri statute of limitation applies here instead of the Texas four year limitation period provided by §157.005(b)." *See also* ***In re B.C.***, 52 S.W.3d 926, 928-29 (Tex.App.—Beaumont 2001, n.p.h.).

Official Comment

This section identifies situations in which local law is inapplicable. The basic principle of the Act is that throughout the process the controlling order remains the order of the issuing State, and that responding States only assist in the enforcement of that order. Absent a loss of continuing, exclusive jurisdiction and a subsequent modification of the order, the order never becomes an "order of the responding State." Ultimate responsibility for enforcement and final resolution of the obligor's compliance with all aspects of the support order belongs to the issuing State. Thus, calculation of whether the obligor has fully complied with the payment of current support, arrears, and interest on arrears, is the duty of the issuing State. For example, under subsection (a) the responding State must recognize and enforce an order of the issuing State for the support of a child until age 21, notwithstanding the fact that the duty of support of a child ends at age 18 under the law of the responding State. *See Gonzalez-Gongaga v. Gonzalez*, 426 So.2d 1106 (Fla. App. 1983); *Taylor v. Taylor*, 122 Cal. App. 3d 209, 175 Cal. Rptr. 716 (1981). Similarly, the law of the issuing State governs whether a payment made for the benefit of a child, such as a Social Security benefit for a child of a disabled obligor, should be credited against the obligor's child support obligation.

Subsection (b) contains another choice of law provision that may diverge from local law. In situations in which the statutes of limitation differ from State to State, the statute with the longer term is to be applied. In interstate cases, arrearages often will have accumulated over a considerable period of time before enforcement is perfected. The obligor should not gain an undue benefit from the choice of residence if the forum State has a short statute of limitations for arrearages.

FAM §159.605. NOTICE OF REGISTRATION OF ORDER

(a) When a support order or income-withholding order issued in another state is registered, the registering tribunal shall notify the nonregistering party. The notice must be accompanied by a copy of the registered order and the documents and relevant information accompanying the order.

(b) The notice must inform the nonregistering party:

(1) that a registered order is enforceable as of the date of registration in the same manner as an order issued by a tribunal of this state;

(2) that a hearing to contest the validity or enforcement of the registered order must be requested within 20 days after notice;

(3) that failure to contest the validity or enforcement of the registered order in a timely manner:

(A) will result in confirmation of the order and enforcement of the order and the alleged arrearages; and

(B) precludes further contest of that order with respect to any matter that could have been asserted; and

(4) of the amount of any alleged arrearages.

(c) On registration of an income-withholding order for enforcement, the registering tribunal shall notify the obligor's employer under Chapter 158.

History of Fam §159.605: Acts 1995, 74th Leg., ch. 20, §1, eff. April 20, 1995. Amended by Acts 1997, 75th Leg., ch. 607, §15, eff. Sept. 1, 1997. Source: Former Fam §21.39.

Official Comment

Sections 605-608 provide the procedure for the nonregistering party to contest registration of an order, either because the order is allegedly invalid, superseded, or no longer in effect, or because the enforcement remedy being sought is opposed by the nonregistering party.

This section directs that the nonregistering party be fully informed of the effect of registration. After such notice is given, absent a successful contest by the nonregistering party, the order will be confirmed and future contest will be precluded.

For a full explanation regarding the deletion of the authorization of notice by first class mail, see the Comment to Section 305. The same considerations apply to the deletion of the additional methods of notice originally prescribed in this section.

FAM §159.606. PROCEDURE TO CONTEST VALIDITY OR ENFORCEMENT OF REGISTERED ORDER

(a) A nonregistering party seeking to contest the validity or enforcement of a registered order in this state shall request a hearing within 20 days after notice of the registration. The nonregistering party may seek under Section 159.607 to:

(1) vacate the registration;

(2) assert any defense to an allegation of noncompliance with the registered order; or

(3) contest the remedies being sought or the amount of any alleged arrearages.

(b) If the nonregistering party fails to contest the validity or enforcement of the registered order in a timely manner, the order is confirmed by operation of law.

(c) If a nonregistering party requests a hearing to contest the validity or enforcement of the registered order, the registering tribunal shall schedule the matter for hearing and give notice to the parties of the date, time, and place of the hearing.

History of Fam §159.606: Acts 1995, 74th Leg., ch. 20, §1, eff. April 20, 1995. Amended by Acts 1997, 75th Leg., ch. 607, §16, eff. Sept. 1, 1997. Source: Former Fam §21.40.

Official Comment

Subsection (a) is derived in part from RURESA §40(b), under which the "obligor" was directed to contest the registration of a foreign order within a short period of time. This procedure is continued, but the terminology is changed to "nonregistering party" because either the obligor or the obligee may seek to register a foreign support order.

Moreover, subsection (a) is philosophically very different from RURESA §40, which directed that a registered order "shall be treated in the same manner as a support order issued by a court of this state." A contest of the fundamental provisions of the registered order is not permitted in the responding State. The nonregistering party must return to the issuing State to prosecute such a contest (obviously only as the law of that State permits). The procedure adopted here is akin to the prohibition found in Section 315 against asserting a nonparentage defense in a UIFSA proceeding. In short, raising a collateral issue in a UIFSA proceeding is prohibited, but no attempt is made to preclude the issue from being litigated in another, more appropriate forum if otherwise allowed by that forum.

On the other hand, the respondent may assert defenses such as "payment" or "the obligation has terminated" to allegations of past noncompliance with the registered order. Similarly, a constitutionally-based attack may always be asserted, *i.e.*, an alleged lack of personal jurisdiction over a party by the issuing tribunal. There is no defense, however, to the registration of a valid foreign support order.

Subsection (b) precludes an untimely contest of a registered support order. As noted above, the nonregistering party is free to seek redress in the issuing State from the tribunal with continuing, exclusive jurisdiction over the support order.

Subsection (c) directs that a hearing be scheduled when the nonregistering party contests some aspect of the registration. At present, federal regulations govern the allowable time frames for contesting income withholding in IV-D cases. *See* 42 U.S.C. §666(b). Additional, codification of the procedure process is unwise.

For a full explanation regarding the deletion of the authorization of notice by first class mail, see the Comment to Section 305. The same considerations apply to the deletion of the additional methods of notice originally identified in this section.

FAM §159.607. CONTEST OF REGISTRATION OR ENFORCEMENT

(a) A party contesting the validity or enforcement of a registered order or seeking to vacate the registration has the burden of proving one or more of the following defenses:

(1) the issuing tribunal lacked personal jurisdiction over the contesting party;

(2) the order was obtained by fraud;

(3) the order has been vacated, suspended, or modified by a later order;

(4) the issuing tribunal has stayed the order pending appeal;

(5) there is a defense under the law of this state to the remedy sought;

(6) full or partial payment has been made; or

(7) the statute of limitation under Section 159.604 precludes enforcement of some or all of the arrearages.

(b) If a party presents evidence establishing a full or partial defense under Subsection (a), a tribunal may stay enforcement of the registered order, continue the proceeding to permit production of additional relevant evidence, and issue other appropriate orders. An uncontested portion of the registered order may be enforced by all remedies available under the law of this state.

(c) If the contesting party does not establish a defense under Subsection (a) to the validity or enforcement of the order, the registering tribunal shall issue an order confirming the order.

History of Fam §159.607: Acts 1995, 74th Leg., ch. 20, §1, eff. April 20, 1995. Source: Former Fam §21.41.

In re Chapman, ___ S.W.3d ___ (Tex.App.—Amarillo 2001, no pet.) (No. 07-00-0079-CV; 8-16-01). Former husband "contends the trial court erred in issuing a confirming order because there was no evidence that he was given personal notice of the foreign court's hearing ..., and that [his former wife] did not produce a copy of any notice given to him. We disagree. As presented, [husband]'s point incorrectly assumes that [wife] had the burden to introduce evidence that the Minnesota court had jurisdiction over him. However, according to §159.607(a)(1), [husband] had the burden to prove that the Minnesota court did not have personal jurisdiction over him. Further, because [husband] did not establish the absence of jurisdiction by the Minnesota court, the trial court was required to issue an order confirming the order."

Official Comment

Subsection (a) places the burden on the nonregistering party to assert narrowly defined defenses to registration of a support order.

If the obligor is liable for current support, under subsection (b) the tribunal must enter an order to enforce that obligation. Proof of arrearages must result in enforcement; under the Bradley Amendment, 42 U.S.C. §666(a)(10), all States are required to treat child support payments as final judgments as they come due (or lose federal funding). Therefore, such arrearages are not subject to retroactive modification.

FAM §159.608. CONFIRMED ORDER

Confirmation of a registered order, whether by operation of law or after notice and hearing, precludes further contest of the order with respect to any matter that could have been asserted at the time of registration.

History of Fam §159.608: Acts 1995, 74th Leg., ch. 20, §1, eff. April 20, 1995. Source: Former Fam §21.42.

Official Comment

The policy determination that a foreign support order may need to be confirmed by the forum tribunal is derived from RURESA §40, which incidentally did not explain the details of the confirmation procedure. Under UIFSA, confirmation of an order may be the result of operation of law because of a failure to contest or an unsuccessful contest after a hearing. Either method precludes raising any issue that could have been asserted in a hearing. Confirmation of a foreign support order validates both the terms of the order and the asserted arrearages. *See Chapman v. Chapman*, 205 Cal. App. 3d 253, 252 Cal. Rptr. 359 (1988).

FAM §159.609. PROCEDURE TO REGISTER CHILD SUPPORT ORDER OF ANOTHER STATE FOR MODIFICATION

A party or support enforcement agency seeking to modify or to modify and enforce a child support order issued in another state shall register that order in this state in the same manner provided in Sections 159.601-159.604 if the order has not been registered. A petition for modification may be filed at the same time as a request for registration or later. The pleading must specify the grounds for modification.

History of Fam §159.609: Acts 1995, 74th Leg., ch. 20, §1, eff. April 20, 1995. Source: Former Fam §21.43.

Official Comment

Sections 609 through 614 deal with situations in which it is permissible for a registering State to modify the existing child support order of another State. A petitioner wishing to register a support order of another State for purposes of modification must conform to the general requirements for pleadings in Section 311 (Pleadings and Accompanying Documents), and follow the procedure for registration set forth in Section 602 (Procedure To Register Order for Enforcement). If the tribunal has the requisite jurisdiction over the parties as established in Section 611, modification may be sought in conjunction with registration and enforcement, or at a later date after the order has been registered, confirmed, and enforced.

FAM §159.610. EFFECT OF REGISTRATION FOR MODIFICATION

A tribunal of this state may enforce a child support order of another state registered for purposes of modification in the same manner as if the order had been issued by a tribunal of this state, but the registered order may be modified only if the requirements of Section 159.611 have been met.

History of Fam §159.610: Acts 1995, 74th Leg., ch. 20, §1, eff. April 20, 1995. Source: Former Fam §21.44.

Official Comment

An order registered for purposes of modification may be enforced in the same manner as an order registered for purposes of enforcement. But, the power of the forum tribunal to modify a child support order of another tribunal is limited by the specific factual preconditions set forth in Section 611.

FAM §159.611. MODIFICATION OF CHILD SUPPORT ORDER OF ANOTHER STATE

(a) After a child support order issued in another state has been registered in this state, the responding tribunal of this state may modify the order only if Section 159.613 does not apply and after notice and hearing the tribunal finds that:

(1) the following requirements are met:

(A) the child, the individual obligee, and the obligor do not reside in the issuing state;

(B) a petitioner who is a nonresident of this state seeks modification; and

(C) the respondent is subject to the personal jurisdiction of the tribunal of this state; or

(2) the child, or a party who is an individual, is subject to the personal jurisdiction of the tribunal of this state and all of the parties who are individuals have filed in the issuing tribunal written consents for a tribunal of this state to modify the support order and assume continuing, exclusive jurisdiction over the order; however, for the purposes of this subdivision, if the issuing state is a foreign jurisdiction that has not enacted a law or established procedures substantially similar to the procedures under this chapter, the consent otherwise required of an individual residing in this state is not required for the tribunal to assume jurisdiction to modify the child support order.

(b) Modification of a registered child support order is subject to the same requirements, procedures, and defenses that apply to the modification of an order issued by a tribunal of this state, and the order may be enforced and satisfied in the same manner.

(c) A tribunal of this state may not modify any aspect of a child support order that may not be modified under the law of the issuing state. If two or more tribunals have issued child support orders for the same obligor and child, the order that controls and must be so recognized under Section 159.207 establishes the aspects of the support order that are nonmodifiable.

(d) On issuance of an order modifying a child support order issued in another state, a tribunal of this state becomes the tribunal of continuing, exclusive jurisdiction.

Ⓐ (e) Repealed by Acts 2001, 77th Leg., ch. 1420, §5.0026, eff. Sept. 1, 2001.

History of Fam §159.611: Acts 1995, 74th Leg., ch. 20, §1, eff. April 20, 1995. Amended by Acts 1997, 75th Leg., ch. 607, §17, eff. Sept. 1, 1997; Acts 2001, 77th Leg., ch. 1420, §5.0026, eff. Sept. 1, 2001. Source: Former Fam §21.45.

Link v. Alvarado, 929 S.W.2d 674, 676 (Tex.App.—San Antonio 1996, writ dism'd). "[A] party seeking to modify a support order from another state must establish jurisdiction pursuant to the Uniform Interstate Family Support Act."

Official Comment

As long as the issuing State retains its continuing, exclusive jurisdiction over its child support order, a registering sister State is precluded from modifying that order. This is a very significant departure from the multiple-order, multiple-modification system of RURESA. However, if the issuing State no longer has a sufficient interest in the modification of its order under the factual circumstances described in this section, after registration the responding State may assume the power to modify. Note that under UIFSA a responding State does not have authority to modify a spousal support order; modification of a spousal support order is restricted to the original issuing tribunal. *See* Sections 205(f) and 206(c), *supra*.

Under the procedure established by RURESA, after a support order was registered for the purpose of enforcement it was treated as if it had originally been issued by the registering tribunal. Most States interpreted the RURESA registration provisions as also authorizing prospective modification of the registered order, see, *i.e.*, *Lagerwey v. Lagerwey*, 681 P.2d 309 (Alaska 1984); *In re Marriage of Aron*, 224 Cal. App. 3d 1086 (1990); *MacFadden v. Martini*, 119 Misc. 2d 94, 463 N.Y.S.2d 674 (1983); *Pinner v. Pinner*, 33 N.C. App. 204, 234 S.E.2d 633 (1977). In sum, by its terms RURESA contemplated the existence of multiple support orders, none of which was directly related to any of the others. Although the issuing tribunal under RURESA retained a version of continuing, exclusive jurisdiction to modify its own order, that power was not exclusive. Tribunals in other States often assumed jurisdiction to enter new orders or to modify an out-of-state support order.

Under UIFSA, registration is subdivided into distinct categories: registration for enforcement, for modification, or both. UIFSA is based on recognizing the truism that when a foreign support order is registered for enforcement, the rights of the parties affected have been previously litigated. Because the obligor already has had a day before an appropriate tribunal, an enforcement remedy may be summarily invoked. On the other hand, modification of an existing order presupposes a change in the rights of the parties. In fact, even under RURESA more elaborate procedures were required by most States prior to the issuance of a modified order. The requirements for modification of a child support order are much more explicit and restrictive under UIFSA.

Under UIFSA a tribunal may modify an existing child support order of another State only if certain quite limited conditions are met. First, the tribunal must have all the prerequisites for the exercise of personal jurisdiction required for rendition of an original support order. Second, one of the restricted fact situations described in subsection (a) must be present. This section, which is a counterpart to Section 205(b) (Continuing, Exclusive Jurisdiction), establishes the conditions under which the continuing, exclusive jurisdiction of the issuing tribunal is released. The degree to which new standards are established is illustrated by comparing UIFSA to the Uniform Child Custody Jurisdiction Act. Sections 12-14 of the UCCJA provide general principles for the judicial determination of an appropriate fact situation for subsequent modification of an existing custody order by another court. In contrast, UIFSA establishes a set of "bright line" rules which must be met before a tribunal may modify an existing child support order. The intent is to eliminate multiple support orders to the maximum extent possible consistent with the principle of continuing, exclusive jurisdiction that pervades the Act.

The UIFSA system begins with Section 205, which mandates that the continuing, exclusive jurisdiction of the issuing tribunal remains intact as long as one individual party or the child continues to reside in the issuing State, or unless the parties mutually agree to the contrary. This is also the standard for recognition of sister state custody orders under the federal Parental Kidnapping Prevention Act, 28 U.S.C. §1738A. Once every individual party and the child leave the issuing State, the continuing, exclusive jurisdiction of the issuing tribunal to modify its order terminates, although its order remains in effect and enforceable until it is modified by another tribunal with authority to do so under the Act. If and when the order is modified by a tribunal of another State, the basic principle of UIFSA is further ratified. The order of the modifying tribunal becomes the operative "controlling order" and the modifying tribunal assumes continuing, exclusive jurisdiction over the only operative child support order.

Under subsection (a)(1), the individual parties affected by the initial order must have moved from the issuing State before a tribunal in a new forum may modify. In the overwhelming majority of cases, the party seeking modification must seek that relief in a new forum, almost invariably the State of residence of the other party. This rule applies to either obligor or obligee, depending on which of those parties seeks to modify. Proof of the fact that neither individual party nor the child continues to reside in the issuing State may be made directly in the forum State; no purpose would be served by requiring the petitioner to return to the original issuing State for a document to confirm the fact that none of the relevant persons still lives there.

The policies underlying the change affected by subsection (a)(1) contemplate that the issuing State has lost continuing, exclusive jurisdiction and that the obligee may seek modification in the obligor's State of residence, or that the obligor may seek a modification in the obligee's State of residence. This restriction attempts to achieve a rough justice between the parties in the majority of cases by preventing a litigant from choosing to seek modification in a local tribunal to the marked disadvantage of the other party. For example, an obligor visiting the children at the residence of the obligee cannot be validly served with citation accompanied by a motion to modify the support order. Even though such personal service of the obligor in the obligee's home State is consistent with the jurisdictional requisites of *Burnham v. Superior Court*, 495 U.S. 604 (1990), the motion to modify does not fulfill the requirement of being brought by "a [petitioner] who is a nonresident of this State...." In short, the obligee is required to register the existing order and seek modification of that order in a State which has personal jurisdiction over the obligor other than the State of the obligee's residence. Most typically this will be the State of residence of the obligor. Similarly, fairness requires that an obligee seeking to modify or modify and enforce the existing order in the State of residence of the obligor will not be subject to a cross-motion to modify custody or visitation merely because the issuing State has lost its continuing, exclusive jurisdiction over the support order. The obligor is required to make that motion in a State other than that of his or her residence; most likely, the obligee's State of residence.

The procedure put in place by UIFSA is in marked contrast to the actual system under RURESA. The multiple-order system provided virtually no incentive for an obligor to seek to reduce an unfair or unduly burdensome child support order. Rather, the obligor typically waited for an enforcement proceeding to be filed in his State of residence and then sought modification in a forum which presented him with the "hometown advantage." Two major arguments sustain the choice of venue made by the Act. First, "jurisdiction by ambush" will be avoided. That is, personal service on either the custodial or noncustodial party found within the state borders will not yield jurisdiction to modify. Thus, parents seeking to exercise rights of visitation, delivering or picking-up the child for such visitation, or engaging in unrelated business activity in the State, will not be involuntarily subjected to protracted litigation in an inconvenient forum. The chilling effect on the exercise of parental contact with the child that the possibility of such litigation might have is avoided. Second, disputes about whether the tribunal has jurisdiction will be eliminated; submission by the petitioner to the State of residence of the respondent alleviates this issue completely.

There are two exceptions to the rule of subsection (a)(1) requiring the petitioner to be a nonresident of the forum in which modification is sought. First, under subsection (a)(2) the parties may agree that a particular forum may serve to modify the order. Second, Section 613, *infra*, applies if all parties have left the original issuing State and now reside in the same new forum State.

Subsection (a)(2), which authorizes the parties to terminate the continuing, exclusive jurisdiction of the issuing State by agreement, is based on several implicit assumptions. First, the subsection applies even if the issuing tribunal has continuing, exclusive jurisdiction because one of the parties or the child continues to reside in that State. Subsection (a)(2) also is applicable if the individual parties and the child no longer reside in the issuing State, but agree to submit the modification issue to a tribunal in the petitioner's State of residence. Also implicit in a shift of jurisdiction over the child support order is that the agreed-upon tribunal must have subject matter jurisdiction and personal jurisdiction over at least one of the parties or the child, and that the other party submits to the personal jurisdiction of that forum. In short, UIFSA does not contemplate that absent parties can agree to confer jurisdiction on a tribunal without a nexus to the parties or the child. But if the other party agrees, either the obligor or the obligee may seek assertion of jurisdiction to modify by a tribunal of the State of residence of either party. In contrast to subsection (a)(1), the written consents of the individual parties to an agreement to submit modification of child support to a tribunal of another State must be filed with the issuing tribunal. The Act does not extend discretion to refuse to yield jurisdiction to the issuing tribunal. In sum, the section contemplates that mutual agreement of the parties to submit themselves to the continuing, exclusive jurisdiction of another tribunal is sufficient to accomplish that goal.

The 1996 amendments provide a different rule if the issuing State is a foreign nation that has not enacted UIFSA or a similar statute or procedure. The policies underlying provisions of UIFSA are wholly inapplicable to a jurisdiction which is unlikely to enact the Act or even a similar act. For example, suppose the foreign jurisdiction has a prohibition against modification unless the parties actually appear before the tribunal in person. Without the amendment, an obligor who moved to the United States could have successfully warded off an attempt to modify the child support obligation in his State of residence by asserting that the obligee or child continued to reside in the foreign nation, which therefore had continuing, exclusive jurisdiction under UIFSA. This despite the fact that the issuing nation does not recognize a continuing, exclusive jurisdiction concept, and will not modify its own child support order without the obligor being physically present. Merely by refusing to agree to a modification and refusing to travel to the issuing nation, the obligor would have been able to forestall modification indefinitely. If the child support order is that of a foreign nation, the UIFSA State of residence of the obligor may adjudicate whether modification of child support is appropriate under its internal law.

Modification of child support under subsections (a)(1) and (a)(2) is distinct from custody modification under the federal Parental Kidnapping Prevention Act, 42 U.S.C. §1738A, which provides that the court of continuing, exclusive jurisdiction may "decline jurisdiction." Similar provisions are found in the UCCJA, §14. In those statutes the methodology for the declination of jurisdiction is not spelled out, but rather is left to the discretion of possibly competing courts for case-by-case determination. The privilege of declining jurisdiction, thereby creating the potential for a vacuum, is not authorized under UIFSA. Once an initial child support order is established, at all times thereafter there is an existing order in effect to be enforced. Even if the issuing tribunal no longer has continuing, exclusive jurisdiction, its order remains fully enforceable until a tribunal with modification jurisdiction issues a new order in conformance with this article.

Subsection (b) states that if the forum has modification jurisdiction because the issuing State has lost continuing, exclusive jurisdiction, the proceedings will generally follow local law with regard to modification of child support orders. However, subsection (c) prevents the modification of any final, nonmodifiable aspect of the original order. For example, if child support was ordered through age 21 in accordance with the law of the issuing State and the law of the forum State ends the support obligation at 18, modification by the forum tribunal may not affect the duration of the support order to age 21. The 1996 amendment clarifies that when multiple orders have been issued prior to the effective date of UIFSA, there will almost certainly be nonmodifiable aspects at variance from the two or more tribunals that have acted in the past. The amendment clarifies that it is the controlling order's nonmodifiable aspects that prospectively determine those issues throughout the minority of the child.

Subsection (d) provides that upon modification the new order becomes the one order to be recognized by all UIFSA States, and the issuing tribunal acquires continuing, exclusive jurisdiction.

FAM §159.612. RECOGNITION OF ORDER MODIFIED IN ANOTHER STATE

A tribunal of this state shall recognize a modification of its earlier child support order by a tribunal of another state that assumed jurisdiction under a law substantially similar to this chapter and, except as otherwise provided in this chapter, shall on request:

(1) enforce the order that was modified only as to amounts accruing before the modification;

(2) enforce only nonmodifiable aspects of the order;

(3) provide other appropriate relief only for a violation of the order that occurred before the effective date of the modification; and

(4) recognize the modifying order of the other state, on registration, for the purpose of enforcement.

History of Fam §159.612: Acts 1995, 74th Leg., ch. 20, §1, eff. April 20, 1995. Source: Former Fam §21.46.

Official Comment

Independent support orders relating to the same parties, a hallmark of RURESA, are replaced in UIFSA by deference to the support order of a sister State. This applies not just to the original order, but also to a modified child support order issued by a second State under the standards established by Section 611 (Modification of Child Support Order of Another State). For the Act to function properly, the original issuing State must recognize and defer to such a modified order, and must regard its prior order as prospectively inoperative. Because the modifying tribunal lacks the authority to direct the original issuing State to release its continuing, exclusive jurisdiction, each State must recognize this effect by enacting UIFSA.

Power is retained over post-modification by the original issuing tribunal for remedial actions directly connected to its now-modified order. A tribunal may enforce its subsequently modified order for violations of that order which occurred before the modification. Further, aspects of the original order that have become final or are not modifiable may be prospectively enforced by the issuing tribunal. For example, a contractual obligation to provide a college education trust fund for a child may be enforced under the law of the issuing State irrespective of the law of the modifying State.

FAM §159.613. JURISDICTION TO MODIFY CHILD SUPPORT ORDER OF ANOTHER STATE WHEN INDIVIDUAL PARTIES RESIDE IN THIS STATE

(a) If all of the parties who are individuals reside in this state and the child does not reside in the issuing state, a tribunal of this state has jurisdiction to enforce and to modify the issuing state's child support order in a proceeding to register that order.

(b) A tribunal of this state exercising jurisdiction under this section shall apply the provisions of Sections 159.101 through 159.209 and 159.601 through 159.614 and the procedural and substantive law of this state to the proceeding for enforcement or modification. Sections 159.301 through 159.507 and 159.701 through 159.802 do not apply.

History of Fam §159.613: Acts 1997, 75th Leg., ch. 607, §18, eff. Sept. 1, 1997.

Official Comment

The Comment to Section 611(e) in the 1992 version of UIFSA contains the following statement:

> "Finally, note that if the parties have left the issuing state and now reside in the same state, this section is not applicable. Such a fact situation does not present an interstate matter and UIFSA does not apply. Rather, the issuing state has lost its continuing, exclusive jurisdiction and the forum state, as the residence of the parties, should apply local law without regard to the interstate Act."

The intent of the Comment was to state what seemed at the time to the Drafting Committee to be obvious; an action between two citizens of the same State is not a matter for interstate concern or application. A significant number of knowledgeable commentators, however, found the statement in the Comment to be wholly inadequate. After all, the commentary is not substantive law, but rather merely expresses an interpretive opinion of the drafters of the Act. On reflection, the Drafting Committee decided that the critics were correct; the Act should deal explicitly with the possibility that the parties and the child no longer reside in the issuing State and that the individual parties have moved to the same new State. After all, there is an interstate aspect when one State purports to modify the child support order of another State. Moreover, a literal reading of the Act could yield a construction that the issuing State has lost its continuing, exclusive jurisdiction to modify, but no State is permitted under UIFSA to take its place to do so.

This section is designed to make it clear that when the issuing State no longer has continuing, exclusive jurisdiction and the obligor and obligee reside in the same State, a tribunal of that State has jurisdiction to modify the child support order and assume continuing, exclusive jurisdiction. Although the individual parties must reside in the forum State, there is no requirement that the child must also reside in the forum State (although the child must have moved from the issuing State).

Finally, because modification of the child support order when all parties reside in the forum is essentially an intrastate matter, subsection (b) withdraws authority to apply most of the substantive and procedural provisions of UIFSA, *i.e.*, those found in the Act other than in Articles 1, 2, and 6. Note, however, that the provision in Section 611(c) forbidding modification of nonmodifiable aspects of the controlling order applies. For example, the duration of the support obligation remains fixed despite the subsequent residence of all parties in a new State with a different duration of child support.

FAM §159.614. NOTICE TO ISSUING TRIBUNAL OF MODIFICATION

Within 30 days after issuance of a modified child support order, the party obtaining the modification shall file a certified copy of the order with the issuing tribunal that had continuing, exclusive jurisdiction over the earlier order and in each tribunal in which the party knows the earlier order has been registered. A party who obtains the order and fails to file a certified copy is subject to appropriate sanctions by a tribunal in which the issue of failure to file arises. The failure to file does not affect the validity or enforceability of the modified order of the new tribunal having continuing, exclusive jurisdiction.

History of Fam §159.614: Acts 1997, 75th Leg., ch. 607, §18, eff. Sept. 1, 1997.

Official Comment

This section, derived from former Section 611(e) of the 1993 version of UIFSA, is made a stand-alone provision to clarify the organization of the Act. Section 614 states a crucial proposition; the prevailing party must inform the original issuing tribunal that it has lost continuing, exclusive jurisdiction over the child support order. Thereafter, the original tribunal may not modify, or review and adjust, the amount of child support. Notice to the issuing tribunal and other affected tribunals that the former controlling order has been modified is crucial to avoid the confusion and chaos of the multiple-order system UIFSA is designed to replace.

Additionally, the 1997 amendment grants the tribunal the authority to impose sanctions on a party who fails to comply with the requirement to give notice of a modification to all interested tribunals. As originally enacted, this provision could have been regarded as hortatory because no penalty was authorized for failure to comply with the directive of the statute. The 1997 amendment not only provides discretion for sanctions as appropriate, but also states that failure to notify of a modification does not affect the validity of the modified order.

Sections 159.615-159.700 reserved for expansion

SUBCHAPTER H. DETERMINATION OF PARENTAGE

FAM §159.701. PROCEEDING TO DETERMINE PARENTAGE

(a) A tribunal of this state may serve as an initiating or responding tribunal in a proceeding brought under this chapter or a law substantially similar to this chapter, the Uniform Reciprocal Enforcement of Support Act, or the Revised Uniform Reciprocal Enforcement of Support Act to determine that the petitioner is a parent of a particular child or to determine that a respondent is a parent of that child.

(b) In a proceeding to determine parentage, a responding tribunal of this state shall apply the procedural and substantive law of this state and the rules of this state on choice of law.

History of Fam §159.701: Acts 1995, 74th Leg., ch. 20, §1, eff. April 20, 1995. Source: Former Fam §21.47.

Official Comment

This article authorizes a "pure" parentage action in the interstate context, *i.e.*, an action not joined with a claim for support. Either the mother or a man alleging to be the father of a child may bring such an action. More commonly, an action to determine parentage across state lines will also seek to establish a support order under the Act. *See* Section 401 ([Petition] to Establish Support Order).

An action to establish parentage under UIFSA is to be treated identically to such an action brought in the responding State.

Sections 159.702-159.800 reserved for expansion

SUBCHAPTER I. INTERSTATE RENDITION

FAM §159.801. GROUNDS FOR RENDITION

(a) In this subchapter, "governor" includes an individual performing the functions of governor or the executive authority of a state covered by this chapter.

(b) The governor of this state may:

(1) demand that the governor of another state surrender an individual found in the other state who is charged criminally in this state with having failed to provide for the support of an obligee; or

(2) on the demand by the governor of another state, surrender an individual found in this state who is charged criminally in the other state with having failed to provide for the support of an obligee.

(c) A provision for extradition of individuals not inconsistent with this chapter applies to the demand even if the individual whose surrender is demanded was not in the demanding state when the crime was allegedly committed and has not fled from that state.

History of Fam §159.801: Acts 1995, 74th Leg., ch. 20, §1, eff. April 20, 1995. Source: Former Fam §21.48.

Official Comment

This section tracks RURESA §5 (Interstate Rendition) with no substantive change. Virtually no controversy has been generated regarding this portion of RURESA. Arguably application of subsection (c) is problematic in situations in which the obligor neither was present in the demanding State at the time of the commission of the crime nor fled from the demanding State. The possibility that an individual may commit a crime in a State without ever being physically present there has elicited considerable discussion and some case law. *See* L. Brilmayer, "An Introduction to Jurisdiction in the American Federal System," 329-335 (1986) (discussing minimum contacts theory for criminal jurisdiction); Rotenberg, "Extraterritorial Legislative Jurisdiction and the State Criminal Law," 38 Tex. L. Rev. 763, 784-87 (1960) (due process requires that the behavior of the defendant must be predictably subject to State's criminal jurisdiction); *cf.* Ex parte Boetscher, 812 S.W.2d 600 (Tex. Crim. App. 1991) (Equal Protection Clause limits disparate treatment of nonresident defendants); *In re King*, 3 Cal.3d 226, 90 Cal. Rptr. 15, 474 P.2d 983 (1970), cert. denied 403 U.S. 931 (enhanced offense for nonresidents impacts constitutional right to travel).

FAM §159.802. CONDITIONS OF RENDITION

(a) Before making a demand that the governor of another state surrender an individual charged criminally in this state with having failed to provide for the support of an obligee, the governor may require a prosecutor of this state to demonstrate:

(1) that not less than 60 days before the date of the demand, the obligee had initiated proceedings for support under this chapter; or

(2) that initiating the proceeding would be of no avail.

(b) If, under this chapter or a law substantially similar to this chapter, the Uniform Reciprocal Enforcement of Support Act, or the Revised Uniform Reciprocal Enforcement of Support Act, the governor of another state makes a demand that the governor of this state surrender an individual charged criminally in that state with having failed to provide for the support of a child or other individual to whom a duty of support is owed, the governor may require a prosecutor to investigate the demand and report whether a proceeding for support has been initiated or would be effective. If it appears that a proceeding would be effective but has not been initiated, the governor may delay honoring the demand for a reasonable time to permit the initiation of a proceeding.

(c) If a proceeding for support has been initiated and the individual whose rendition is demanded prevails, the governor may decline to honor the demand. If the petitioner prevails and the individual whose rendition is demanded is subject to a support order, the governor may decline to honor the demand if the individual is complying with the support order.

History of Fam §159.802: Acts 1995, 74th Leg., ch. 20, §1, eff. April 20, 1995. Source: Former Fam §21.49.

Official Comment

This section tracks RURESA §6 (Conditions of Interstate Rendition) without significant change. Interstate rendition remains the last resort for support enforcement, in part because a governor may exercise considerable discretion in deciding whether to honor a demand for rendition of an obligor.

Sections 159.803-159.900 reserved for expansion

SUBCHAPTER J. MISCELLANEOUS PROVISIONS

FAM §159.901. UNIFORMITY OF APPLICATION & CONSTRUCTION

This chapter shall be applied and construed to effectuate its general purpose to make uniform the law with respect to the subject of this chapter among states enacting it.

History of Fam §159.901: Acts 1995, 74th Leg., ch. 20, §1, eff. April 20, 1995. Source: Former Fam §21.50.

FAM §159.902. SHORT TITLE

This chapter may be cited as the Uniform Interstate Family Support Act.

History of Fam §159.902: Acts 1995, 74th Leg., ch. 20, §1, eff. April 20, 1995. Source: Former Fam §21.51.

Official Comment

Renaming the Act reflects the dramatic departure from the structure of the earlier interstate reciprocal support acts, URESA and RURESA.

CHAPTER 160. UNIFORM PARENTAGE ACT

A *Chapter 160 below is effective for motions or other requests for relief made in parentage or paternity proceedings commenced on or after June 14, 2001.*

Editor's note: Changes have been made to the official comments to reflect the Texas Legislature's omission of sections and changing section numbers. The full uniform act and official comments can be found at http://www.nccusl.org.

Official Prefatory Comment

The National Conference of Commissioners on Uniform State Laws has addressed the subject of parentage throughout the 20th Century. As early as 1922, the Conference promulgated the "Uniform Illegitimacy Act," followed by the "Uniform Blood Tests To Determine Paternity Act" in 1952, the "Uniform Paternity Act" in 1960, and certain provisions in the "Uniform Probate Code" in 1969. The "Uniform Illegitimacy Act" was withdrawn by the Conference and none of the other Acts were widely adopted. As of June 1973, the Blood Tests to Determine Paternity Act had been enacted in nine States, the "Uniform Paternity Act" in four, and the "Uniform Probate Code" in five.

The most important Uniform Act addressing the special needs of the nonmarital child was the Uniform Parentage Act approved in 1973 [hereafter referred to as UPA (1973)]. As of December, 2000, UPA (1973) is in effect in 19 States stretching from Delaware to California; in addition, many other States have enacted significant portions of it. Among the many notable features of this landmark Act is the declaration of equality for all children without regard to marital status of the parents of a particular child. In addition, the Act established a set of rules for presumption of parentage, shunned the term "illegitimate," and chose instead to employ the term "child with no presumed father." The Act has contributed much to bring about a more enlightened approach to sensitive issues that can divide people of goodwill.

UPA (1973) had its genesis in a law review article, Harry D. Krause, *A Proposed Uniform Act on Legitimacy*, 44 Tex. L. Rev. 829 (1966). Professor Krause followed with a pathfinding book, Illegitimacy: Law and Social Policy (1971), and then went on to serve as the reporter for UPA (1973). When work on the Act began, the notion of substantive legal equality of children regardless of the marital status of their parents seemed revolutionary. *See* Krause, Equal Protection for the Illegitimate, 65 Mich. L. Rev. 477 (1967). Even though the Conference had put itself on record in favor of equal rights of support and inheritance in the Paternity Act and the Probate Code, the law of many States continued to differentiate very significantly in the legal treatment of marital and nonmarital children. When UPA (1973) was promulgated, the States needed new legislation on this subject because the bulk of then-current law on the subject of children born out of wedlock had already been declared to be unconstitutional by the United States Supreme Court or was subject to grave constitutional doubt.

Case law has not always reached consistent results in construing UPA (1973). Moreover, widely differing treatment on subjects not dealt with by the Act has been common. For example, California courts have held that a nonmarital father does not have standing to sue an intact family to assert his rights of fatherhood. Another UPA (1973) State, Colorado, has declared that under its state constitution the father may not be denied such rights. Texas, which has adopted many of the provisions of UPA (1973), reached a similar conclusion. Similarly, a judgment's binding effect on the child or on others seeking to claim a benefit of the judgment or to attack the judgment collaterally is confused in the case law. Adding to the confusion is the fact that UPA (1973) is entirely silent regarding the relationship between a divorce and a determination of parentage. Finally, the incredible scientific advances in parentage testing since 1973 warrant a thoroughgoing revision of the Act.

Beginning in the 1980s, States began to adopt paternity registries in an attempt to deal with the risk of a man's subsequent claim of paternity after the mother relinquishes a child for adoption. The Conference adopted the Uniform Putative and Unknown Fathers Act in 1988 to deal with the rights of such men, but UPUFA has not been enacted by any State.

In addition, in 1988, the Conference also adopted the Uniform Status of Children of Assisted Conception Act. Assisted reproduction and gestational agreements became commonplace in the 1990s, long after the promulgation of UPA (1973). The USCACA resembled a Model Act more than a Uniform Act because it provided two opposing options regarding "gestational agreements." To date, only two States have enacted USCACA, each choosing a different option. [The Texas Legislature has not enacted the USCACA.]

With the promulgation of the Uniform Parentage Act (2000), all of the earlier Uniform Acts dealing with parentage have been withdrawn by the Conference, leaving the Uniform Parentage Act (2000) as the single product of the Conference dealing with the subject. In brief outline, UPA (2000) is structured as follows:

Article 1, General Provisions, adds many new definitions to clarify this complex subject and adapt the Act to scientific developments. Article 2, Parent-Child Relationship, will look familiar to past users of UPA (1973) because it continues a number of provisions with little or no change. Article 3, Voluntary Acknowledgment of Paternity, is entirely new and is driven by federal mandates that States adopt nonjudicial means to achieve early determination of paternity. Article 4, Registry of Paternity, is entirely new and incorporates a tightly integrated registry law to deal with the rights of a man who is neither an acknowledged, presumed or adjudicated father. Article 5, Genetic Testing, comprehensively covers that subject in ten separate sections [UPA (1973) had one section on the subject]. Article 6, Proceeding to Adjudicate Parentage, is the traditional litigation section. Article 7, Child of Assisted Reproduction, recodifies USCACA (1988) without substantial change. Article 8, Gestational Agreement, also follows USCACA (1988) in large part. [The Texas Legislature did not enact Article 8, Gestational Agreements of the UPA.]

UPA (1973) contained a wide variety of other substantive provisions, such as those for setting the level of support, the enforcement of judgments, and deals with related issues such as custody. These subjects have been left out of UPA (2000) because other state law adequately provides for such matters.

Finally, Uniform Parentage Act (2000) is drafted to be consistent with the provisions of two other Uniform Acts of great significance, namely the Uniform Interstate Family Support Act [UIFSA (1996)] and the Uniform Child Custody Jurisdiction and Enforcement Act [UCCJEA (1997)].

A SUBCHAPTER A. APPLICATION & CONSTRUCTION

E FAM §160.001. APPLICATION & CONSTRUCTION

This chapter shall be applied and construed to promote the uniformity of the law among the states that enact the Uniform Parentage Act.

History of Fam §160.001: Enacted by Acts 2001, 77th Leg., ch. 821, §1.01, eff. June 14, 2001. Chapter and subchapter amended by Acts 2001, 77th Leg., ch. 821, §1.01, eff. June 14, 2001.

History of Former Fam §160.001: Acts 1995, 74th Leg., ch. 20, §1, eff. April 20, 1995. Amended by Acts 1999, 76th Leg., ch. 556, §36, eff. Sept. 1, 1999. Deleted by Acts 2001, 77th Leg., ch. 821, §1.01, eff. June 14, 2001.

E FAM §160.002. CONFLICTS BETWEEN PROVISIONS

If a provision of this chapter conflicts with another provision of this title or another state statute or rule and the conflict cannot be reconciled, this chapter prevails.

History of Fam §160.002: Enacted by Acts 2001, 77th Leg., ch. 821, §1.01, eff. June 14, 2001.

History of Former Fam §160.002: Acts 1995, 74th Leg., ch. 20, §1, eff. April 20, 1995. Amended by Acts 1999, 76th Leg., ch. 556, §81, eff. Sept. 1, 1999. Deleted by Acts 2001, 77th Leg., ch. 821, §1.01, eff. June 14, 2001. Source: Former Fam §13.01.

FAM §160.003 TO 160.007. DELETED

Deleted by Acts 2001, 77th Leg., ch. 821, §1.01, eff. June 14, 2001.

Sections 160.003-160.100 reserved for expansion

E SUBCHAPTER B. GENERAL PROVISIONS

E FAM §160.101. SHORT TITLE

This chapter may be cited as the Uniform Parentage Act.

History of Fam §160.101: Enacted by Acts 2001, 77th Leg., ch. 821, §1.01, eff. June 14, 2001.

History of Former Fam §160.101: Acts 1995, 74th Leg., ch. 20, §1, eff. April 20, 1995. Amended by Acts 1995, 74th Leg., ch. 751, §62, eff. Sept. 1, 1995; Acts 1997, 75th Leg., ch. 962, §1, eff. Sept. 1, 1997. Deleted by Acts 2001, 77th Leg., ch. 821, §1.01, eff. June 14, 2001. Source: Former Fam §12.06(a), (b).

E FAM §160.102. DEFINITIONS

In this chapter:

(1) "Adjudicated father" means a man who has been adjudicated by a court to be the father of a child.

(2) "Assisted reproduction" means a method of causing pregnancy other than sexual intercourse. The term includes:

(A) intrauterine insemination;

(B) donation of eggs;

(C) donation of embryos;

(D) in vitro fertilization and transfer of embryos; and

(E) intracytoplasmic sperm injection.

(3) "Child" means an individual of any age whose parentage may be determined under this chapter.

(4) "Commence" means to file the initial pleading seeking an adjudication of parentage in a court of this state.

(5) "Determination of parentage" means the establishment of the parent-child relationship by the signing of a valid acknowledgment of paternity under Subchapter D or by an adjudication by a court.

(6) "Donor" means an individual who produces eggs or sperm used for assisted reproduction, regardless of whether the production is for consideration. The term does not include:

(A) a husband who provides sperm or a wife who provides eggs to be used for assisted reproduction by the wife; or

(B) a woman who gives birth to a child by means of assisted reproduction.

(7) "Ethnic or racial group" means, for purposes of genetic testing, a recognized group that an individual identifies as all or part of the individual's ancestry or that is identified by other information.

(8) "Genetic testing" means an analysis of an individual's genetic markers to exclude or identify a man as the father of a child or a woman as the mother of a child. The term includes an analysis of one or more of the following:

(A) deoxyribonucleic acid; and

(B) blood-group antigens, red-cell antigens, human-leukocyte antigens, serum enzymes, serum proteins, or red-cell enzymes.

(9) "Intended parents" means individuals who enter into an agreement providing that the individuals will be the parents of a child born to a gestational mother by means of assisted reproduction, regardless of whether either individual has a genetic relationship with the child.

(10) "Man" means a male individual of any age.

(11) "Parent" means an individual who has established a parent-child relationship under Section 160.201.

(12) "Paternity index" means the likelihood of paternity determined by calculating the ratio between:

(A) the likelihood that the tested man is the father of the child, based on the genetic markers of the tested man, the mother of the child, and the child, conditioned on the hypothesis that the tested man is the father of the child; and

(B) the likelihood that the tested man is not the father of the child, based on the genetic markers of the tested man, the mother of the child, and the child, conditioned on the hypothesis that the tested man is not the father of the child and that the father of the child is of the same ethnic or racial group as the tested man.

(13) "Presumed father" means a man who, by operation of law under Section 160.204, is recognized as the

father of a child until that status is rebutted or confirmed in a judicial proceeding.

(14) "Probability of paternity" means the probability, with respect to the ethnic or racial group to which the alleged father belongs, that the alleged father is the father of the child, compared to a random, unrelated man of the same ethnic or racial group, expressed as a percentage incorporating the paternity index and a prior probability.

(15) "Record" means information that is inscribed on a tangible medium or that is stored in an electronic or other medium and is retrievable in a perceivable form.

(16) "Signatory" means an individual who authenticates a record and is bound by its terms.

(17) "Support enforcement agency" means a public official or public agency authorized to seek:

(A) the enforcement of child support orders or laws relating to the duty of support;

(B) the establishment or modification of child support;

(C) the determination of parentage;

(D) the location of child-support obligors and their income and assets; or

(E) the conservatorship of a child or the termination of parental rights.

History of Fam §160.102: Enacted by Acts 2001, 77th Leg., ch. 821, §1.01, eff. June 14, 2001.

History of Former Fam §160.102: Acts 1995, 74th Leg., ch. 20, §1, eff. April 20, 1995. Deleted by Acts 2001, 77th Leg., ch. 821, §1.01, eff. June 14, 2001. Source: Former Fam §13.02(a), (d).

Official Comment

[This paragraph comments on §102(1) of the UPA enacted by the Texas Legislature as Fam §101.0010.] Subsection (1) responds to a 1996 federal mandate encouraging States to adopt nonjudicial means to achieve an early determination of paternity. The term "acknowledged father" is given a relatively narrow meaning, rather than that previously accorded the term. Only a man who acknowledges paternity of a child in accordance with the formal requirements established in Article 3 qualifies as an "acknowledged father," which is the equivalent of an adjudication of paternity. A man who asserts paternity in an informal matter is an "alleged father" as defined in subsection (3), which is derived from the UPUFA §1(2).

[This paragraph comments on §102(3) of the UPA enacted by the Texas Legislature as Fam §101.0015.] Subsection (3) is derived from the UPUFA §1(1), although much of the terminology has been changed. Specifically, the term "putative father" has been replaced by the broader term "alleged father." According to Webster's, "putative" means "commonly accepted or supposed." Clearly, many "alleged fathers" do not fit that definition. Further, UPUFA chose the term "biological father" over more ambiguous "natural father." Because one woman may be the genetic mother of a child while another woman is the gestational mother, for consistency the term "genetic father" was substituted for "biological." No definition is supplied for "unknown father," the term being self-defining.

Subsection (4) is derived from the UCCJEA (1997) §102(5).

Subsection (7) defines the "ethnic or racial group" of the individual being tested only for purposes of the genetic testing. The genetic tests themselves do not determine the race or ethnic group of the individual; rather, for the individual who is not excluded, the race or ethnic group provided is used in the paternity calculations. This is done because the use of the race or ethnic group of the tested individual gives the most conservative calculations, that is, those most favoring non-paternity.

Subsection (8) contemplates that the genetic testing used in paternity testing is broad and includes all of the traditional genetic tests, such as blood types and HLA (Human Leukocyte Antigen), as well as newer DNA technologies. In the past the term "blood test" was commonly applied to paternity testing. However, this usage actually referred to the sample collected; in fact, the tests were genetic tests performed on blood samples. The Act uses the scientific term "deoxyribonucleic acid." This is to accommodate the changes in technology used to evaluate the DNA. Early DNA testing involved RFLP technology (Restriction Fragment Length Polymorphism), followed by PCR techniques (Polymerase Chain Reaction); these may be replaced by newer technology, such as SNP (Single Nucleotide Polymorphisms). The type of DNA technology to be employed is best left to scientific bodies, such as accreditation agencies, see Section 503(a), *infra*.

Subsection (10) is derived from the UPUFA §1(1). Defining "man" to include all male humans eliminates the connotation of adulthood, thereby satisfying the obvious need for the Act to cover under-age progenitors as well as adults. Although objection to calling a 14-year-old father a "man" was raised when UPUFA was considered by the Conference, for purposes of procreation such an individual is a man.

[This paragraph comments on §102(15) of the UPA enacted by the Texas Legislature as Fam §101.025.] Subsection (15) is derived from the UPA (1973) §1. A wide variety of the rights and duties flowing to and from parents and children are found in many other laws of this State.

Subsection (12) defines a complex concept, the "paternity index." Note that the definition includes statistical measures of the mother and tested man. The tested man may be an alleged father, or any other potential biological father. In fact, under appropriate circumstances Article 5 provides for testing without samples from the mother or the alleged father. In these cases the expert statistically reconstructs the missing potential mother or biological father from genetic testing of samples from their relatives. Therefore the definition is correct even in cases involving a missing parent.

Subsection (15) is derived from the Uniform Electronic Transactions Act §102(13), which establishes a standard for either paper or electronic record keeping.

E FAM §160.103. SCOPE OF CHAPTER; CHOICE OF LAW

(a) This chapter governs every determination of parentage in this state.

(b) The court shall apply the law of this state to adjudicate the parent-child relationship. The applicable law does not depend on:

(1) the place of birth of the child; or

(2) the past or present residence of the child.

(c) This chapter does not create, enlarge, or diminish parental rights or duties under another law of this state.

(d) This chapter does not authorize or prohibit an agreement between a woman and the intended parents of a child in which the woman relinquishes all rights as a parent of a child conceived by means of assisted reproduction and which provides that the intended parents become the parents of the child. If a birth results under a gestational agreement that is unenforceable under the law of this state, the parent-child relationship is determined as provided by Subchapter C.

History of Fam §160.103: Enacted by Acts 2001, 77th Leg., ch. 821, §1.01, eff. June 14, 2001.

History of Former Fam §160.103: Acts 1995, 74th Leg., ch. 20, §1, eff. April 20, 1995. Deleted by Acts 2001, 77th Leg., ch. 821, §1.01, eff. June 14, 2001. Source: Former Fam §13.02(a).

Official Comment

UPA (2000), in its entirety, is drafted to conform to the mandate of 42 U.S.C. §666(a)(5)(A), which requires States to provide for parentage proceedings at any time before a child attains 18 years of age on penalty of forfeiture of federal funds that subsidize child support enforcement by the State.

Subsection (b) is derived from the UIFSA (1996) §303 and UPA (1973) §8(b). This section simplifies choice of law principles; the local court is directed to apply local law. If in fact this State is an inappropriate forum, dismissal for forum non-conveniens may be appropriate.

Subsection (d) is to make clear that this Act does not affect other law of the jurisdiction on the subject of gestational agreements.

E FAM §160.104. AUTHORIZED COURTS

The following courts are authorized to adjudicate parentage under this chapter:

(1) a court with jurisdiction to hear a suit affecting the parent-child relationship under this title; or

(2) a court with jurisdiction to adjudicate parentage under another law of this state.

History of Fam §160.104: Enacted by Acts 2001, 77th Leg., ch. 821, §1.01, eff. June 14, 2001.

History of Former Fam §160.104: Acts 1995, 74th Leg., ch. 20, §1, eff. April 20, 1995. Deleted by Acts 2001, 77th Leg., ch. 821, §1.01, eff. June 14, 2001. Source: Former Fam §13.03.

Official Comment

Source: Uniform Parentage Act (1973) §8(a).

Although a proceeding to determine parentage is most often associated with an action to establish a child support order, the Act departs from the choice made by the UIFSA (1996) §102, which allows for the establishment of a child support order by an administrative agency. Insofar as establishment of parentage is concerned, UPA (2000) makes the deliberate decision to require a judicial proceeding. This decision is consistent with the practice of most States; in fact, very few States provide for the resolution of disputed paternity through administrative processes. The use of the term "tribunal, as found in UIFSA, was deliberately rejected. Joinder of a parentage proceeding with an action for divorce, annulment, separate maintenance, or child support and custody is left to state law.

E FAM §160.105. PROTECTION OF PARTICIPANTS

A proceeding under this chapter is subject to the other laws of this state governing the health, safety, privacy, and liberty of a child or any other individual who may be jeopardized by the disclosure of identifying information, including the person's address, telephone number, place of employment, and social security number and the name of the child's day-care facility and school.

History of Fam §160.105: Enacted by Acts 2001, 77th Leg., ch. 821, §1.01, eff. June 14, 2001.

History of Former Fam §160.105: Acts 1995, 74th Leg., ch. 20, §1, eff. April 20, 1995. Deleted by Acts 2001, 77th Leg., ch. 821, §1.01, eff. June 14, 2001. Source: Former Fam §13.04(a)-(e), (g).

Official Comment

Source: UCCJEA (1997) §209(e).

E FAM §160.106. DETERMINATION OF MATERNITY

The provisions of this chapter relating to the determination of paternity apply to a determination of maternity.

History of Fam §160.106: Enacted by Acts 2001, 77th Leg., ch. 821, §1.01, eff. June 14, 2001.

History of Former Fam §160.106: Acts 1995, 74th Leg., ch. 20, §1, eff. April 20, 1995. Deleted by Acts 2001, 77th Leg., ch. 821, §1.01, eff. June 14, 2001. Source: Former Fam §13.05.

Official Comment

Source: UPA (1973) §21.

This section provides for a determination of the mother-child relationship if that issue is in dispute. Except in circumstances involving immigration, cases involving disputed maternity are extraordinarily rare. Therefore, UPA (2000) is otherwise written in terms applicable to the determination of paternity. While certain provisions found in the balance of the Act do not apply in a proceeding to establish maternity, the Act continues the decision made in UPA (1973) not to burden these already complex provisions with unnecessary references to the ascertainment of maternity. Section 160.201(a) is the sole provision in the Act specifically relating to the mother-child relationship. In any given case, a judge facing a claim for the determination of the mother-child relationship should have little difficulty deciding which portions of the Act should be applied.

FAM §§160.107 TO 160.110. DELETED

Deleted by Acts 2001, 77th Leg., ch. 821, §1.01, eff. June 14, 2001.

Sections 160.107-160.200 reserved for expansion

E SUBCHAPTER C. PARENT-CHILD RELATIONSHIP

E FAM §160.201. ESTABLISHMENT OF PARENT-CHILD RELATIONSHIP

(a) The mother-child relationship is established between a woman and a child by:

(1) the woman giving birth to the child;

(2) an adjudication of the woman's maternity; or

(3) the adoption of the child by the woman.

(b) The father-child relationship is established between a man and a child by:

(1) an unrebutted presumption of the man's paternity of the child under Section 160.204;

(2) an effective acknowledgment of paternity by the man under Subchapter D, unless the acknowledgment has been rescinded or successfully challenged;

(3) an adjudication of the man's paternity;

(4) the adoption of the child by the man; or

(5) the man's consenting to assisted reproduction by his wife under Subchapter H, which resulted in the birth of the child.

History of Fam §160.201: Enacted by Acts 2001, 77th Leg., ch. 821, §1.01, eff. June 14, 2001.

History of Former Fam §160.201: Acts 1995, 74th Leg., ch. 20, §1, eff. April 20, 1995. Amended by Acts 1995, 74th Leg., ch. 751, §64, eff. Sept. 1, 1995; Acts 1999, 76th Leg., ch. 556, §37, eff. Sept. 1, 1999. Deleted by Acts 2001, 77th Leg., ch. 821, §1.01, eff. June 14, 2001. Source: Former Fam §13.21(a), (b).

Official Comment

Source: UPA (1973), §4; expanded to include all possible bases of the parent-child relationship

E FAM §160.202. NO DISCRIMINATION BASED ON MARITAL STATUS

A child born to parents who are not married to each other has the same rights under the law as a child born to parents who are married to each other.

History of Fam §160.202: Enacted by Acts 2001, 77th Leg., ch. 821, §1.01, eff. June 14, 2001.

History of Former Fam §160.202: Acts 1995, 74th Leg., ch. 20, §1, eff. April 20, 1995. Amended by Acts 1995, 74th Leg., ch. 751, §64, eff. Sept. 1, 1995; Acts 1999, 76th Leg., ch. 556, §37, eff. Sept. 1, 1999. Deleted by Acts 2001, 77th Leg., ch. 821, §1.01, eff. June 14, 2001. Source: Former Fam §13.22.

Official Comment

Source: UPA (1973) §2 and Massachusetts Gen. Laws ch. 209C, §1.

From a legal and social policy perspective, this is one of the most significant substantive provisions of the Act, reaffirming the principle that regardless of the marital status of the parents, children and parents have equal rights with respect to each other. As discussed in the Prefatory Note, U.S. Supreme Court decisions and lower federal and state court decisions require equality of treatment for a child without a presumed father with regard to most areas of substantive law.

The broad statement according equal treatment to a nonmarital child regarding his or her parents is not to be construed as eliminating all possible distinctions in all aspects of the lives of the nonmarital child and parents. For example, Uniform Probate Code (1993) §2-705(b), states that "in construing a dispositive provision of a transferor who is not a natural parent, an individual born to the natural parent is not considered a child of that parent unless the individual while a minor lived as a regular member of the household of that parent or of that parent's parent, brother, sister, spouse, or surviving spouse." In short, the UPC (1993) provides that an individual is presumed not to be included in a class gift from someone other than the child's parent unless that individual lived as a member of the parent's family during childhood. This presumed intent of the donor is rebuttable. Although this provision probably has a disproportionate effect on nonmarital children, the disparity is not based on the circumstances of birth, but rather on post-birth living conditions.

E FAM §160.203. CONSEQUENCES OF ESTABLISHMENT OF PARENTAGE

Unless parental rights are terminated, a parent-child relationship established under this chapter applies for all purposes, except as otherwise provided by another law of this state.

History of Fam §160.203: Enacted by Acts 2001, 77th Leg., ch. 821, §1.01, eff. June 14, 2001.

History of Former Fam §160.203: Acts 1995, 74th Leg., ch. 20, §1, eff. April 20, 1995. Amended by Acts 1995, 74th Leg., ch. 751, §64, eff. Sept. 1, 1995; Acts 1999, 76th Leg., ch. 556, §37, eff. Sept. 1, 1999. Deleted by Acts 2001, 77th Leg., ch. 821, §1.01, eff. June 14, 2001. Source: Former Fam §13.23.

Official Comment

Source: USCACA (1988) §10.

This section may seem to state the obvious, but both the statement and the qualifier are necessary because without this explanation a literal reading of §§160.201-160.203 could lead to erroneous statutory constructions. The basic purpose of the section is to make clear that a mother, as defined in §160.201(a), is not a parent once her parental rights have been terminated. Similarly, a man whose paternity has been established by acknowledgment or by court adjudication may subsequently have his parental rights terminated.

The qualifier, "as otherwise provided by other law of this State," is necessary because other statutes may restrict rights of a parent. For example, UPC (1993) §2-114(c) precludes a parent of a child (and the parent's family) from inheriting from the child by intestate succession "unless that natural parent has openly treated the child as his [or hers] and has not refused to support the child." Similarly, as discussed in the preceding Comment, UPC (1993) §2-705(b) affects the right of the child to take under class gifts from persons who are not the parents of the child.

E FAM §160.204. PRESUMPTION OF PATERNITY IN CONTEXT OF MARRIAGE

(a) A man is presumed to be the father of a child if:

(1) he is married to the mother of the child and the child is born during the marriage;

(2) he is married to the mother of the child and the child is born before the 301st day after the date the marriage is terminated by death, annulment, declaration of invalidity, or divorce;

(3) he married the mother of the child before the birth of the child in apparent compliance with law, even if the attempted marriage is or could be declared invalid, and the child is born during the invalid marriage or before the 301st day after the date the marriage is terminated by death, annulment, declaration of invalidity, or divorce; or

(4) he married the mother of the child after the birth of the child in apparent compliance with law, regardless of whether the marriage is or could be declared invalid, he voluntarily asserted his paternity of the child, and:

(A) the assertion is in a record filed with the bureau of vital statistics;

(B) he is voluntarily named as the child's father on the child's birth certificate; or

(C) he promised in a record to support the child as his own.

(b) A presumption of paternity established under this section may be rebutted only by an adjudication under Subchapter G.

History of Fam §160.204: Enacted by Acts 2001, 77th Leg., ch. 821, §1.01, eff. June 14, 2001.

History of Former Fam §160.204: Acts 1995, 74th Leg., ch. 20, §1, eff. April 20, 1995. Renumbered from §160.205 by Acts 1995, 74th Leg., ch. 751, §64, eff. Sept. 1, 1995. Amended by Acts 1999, 76th Leg., ch. 556, §37, eff. Sept. 1, 1999. Deleted by Acts 2001, 77th Leg., ch. 821, §1.01, eff. June 14, 2001. Source: Former Fam §13.22(a), (e).

Official Comment

Source: UPA (1973) §4.

A network of presumptions was established by UPA (1973) for application to cases in which proof of external circumstances indicate a particular man to be the probable father. The simplest of these is also the best known – birth of a child during the marriage between the mother and a man. When promulgated in 1973 the contemporaneous commentary noted that:

While perhaps no one state now includes all these presumptions in its law, the presumptions are based on existing presumptions of 'legitimacy' in state laws and do not represent a serious departure. Novel is that they have been collected under one roof. All presumptions of paternity are rebuttable in appropriate circumstances.

After some minor revision of language, UPA (2000) retains all of the original presumptions that relate to marriage. Subsection (1) deals with a child born during a marriage; subsection (2) deals with a child conceived during marriage but born after its termination; subsection (3) deals with a child conceived or born during an invalid marriage; and, subsection (4) deals with a child born before a valid or invalid marriage, accompanied by other facts indicating the husband is the father.

But, two presumptions found in UPA (1973) are not repeated in UPA (2000). Former subsection 4(4) created a presumption of paternity if a man "receives the child into his home and openly holds out the child as his natural child...." This presumption was not carried forward because genetic testing is a far better means of determining paternity. Former subsection 4(5) created a presumption of paternity if the man "acknowledges his paternity of the child in a writing filed with [named agency] [and] ... the mother ... does not dispute the acknowledgment within a reasonable time...." This presumption was eliminated because it conflicts with Article 3, Voluntary Acknowledgment of Paternity, under which a valid acknowledgment establishes paternity rather than a presumption of paternity.

Finally, UPA (1973) §4(b) has been substantially rewritten. The requirement that a presumption "may be rebutted ... only by clear and convincing evidence" was eliminated from the Act. The same fate was accorded the statement that "If two or more presumptions arise which conflict with each other, the presumption which on the facts is founded on the weightier considerations of policy and logic controls. The existence of modern genetic testing obviates this old approach to the problem of conflicting presumptions when a court is to determine paternity."

FAM §§160.205 TO 160.216 & §§160.251 TO 160.263. DELETED

Deleted by Acts 2001, 77th Leg., ch. 821, §1.01, eff. June 14, 2001.

Sections 160.205-160.300 reserved for expansion

E SUBCHAPTER D. VOLUNTARY ACKNOWLEDGMENT OF PATERNITY

Official Prefatory Comment

Voluntary acknowledgment of paternity has long been an alternative to a contested paternity suit. Under UPA (1973) §4, the inclusion of a man's name on the child's birth certificate created a presumption of paternity, which could be rebutted. A relatively recent enactment of the U.S. Congress has made necessary a fundamental change in the acknowledgment procedure. In the Personal Responsibility and Work Opportunity Reconciliation Act of 1996 (PRWORA, also known as the Welfare Reform Act) Congress conditioned federal child support enforcement funds on a requirement that a State enact laws that greatly strengthen the effect of a man's voluntary acknowledgment of paternity, 42 U.S.C. §666(a)(5)(C). In brief, a valid, unrescinded, unchallenged acknowledgment of paternity is to be considered equivalent to a judicial determination of paternity.

A comprehensive approach to comply with the congressional mandate is required because the federal act is nonspecific in many respects. Primary among the issues that Congress did not take into account was the fact that a mother who, in cooperation with the actual father of a child, seeks to have that man acknowledge paternity of the child may, in fact, be married to another man. By virtue of parentage laws that are in universal effect, including UPA (2000), the husband of the mother is the presumed father of the child, see §204, *supra*. By ignoring the real possibility that there will be both an acknowledged father and a presumed father, Congress left it to the States to sort out the difficulties inherent in such a fact situation.

Further, PRWORA does not mention that a person acknowledging parentage asserts genetic parentage of the child. Section 301 is designed to prevent circumvention of adoption laws by demanding a sworn assertion of actual parentage of the child through sexual intercourse in support of an acknowledgment under this article.

Sections 302–305 clarify that if a child who is the subject of an acknowledgment also has a presumed father, that man must cooperate by filing a denial of paternity in conjunction with the acknowledgment; if not, the document is void. If the presumed father is unwilling to cooperate, or his whereabouts are unknown, a court proceeding is necessary to resolve the issue of parentage.

Congress also directed that the acknowledgment can be "rescinded" within a particular timeframe, and subsequently can be "challenged"—without stating a timeframe. These procedures are dealt with in Sections 307–309.

E FAM §160.301. ACKNOWLEDGMENT OF PATERNITY

The mother of a child and a man claiming to be the father of the child conceived as the result of sexual intercourse with the mother may sign an acknowledgment of paternity with the intent to establish the man's paternity.

History of Fam §160.301: Enacted by Acts 2001, 77th Leg., ch. 821, §1.01, eff. June 14, 2001.

See also 1 TAC §§55.404.

Official Comment

Source: 42 U.S.C. §666(a)(5)(C).

PRWORA does not explicitly require that a man acknowledging parentage necessarily is asserting his genetic parentage of the child. In contrast, §301 prevents circumvention of adoption laws by requiring a sworn assertion of actual parentage of the child through sexual intercourse in support of an acknowledgment under this article.

E FAM §160.302. EXECUTION OF ACKNOWLEDGMENT OF PATERNITY

(a) An acknowledgment of paternity must:

(1) be in a record;

(2) be signed, or otherwise authenticated, under penalty of perjury by the mother and the man seeking to establish paternity;

(3) state that the child whose paternity is being acknowledged:

(A) does not have a presumed father or has a presumed father whose full name is stated; and

(B) does not have another acknowledged or adjudicated father;

(4) state whether there has been genetic testing and, if so, that the acknowledging man's claim of paternity is consistent with the results of the testing; and

(5) state that the signatories understand that the acknowledgment is the equivalent of a judicial adjudication of the paternity of the child and that a challenge to the acknowledgment is permitted only under limited circumstances and is barred after four years.

(b) An acknowledgment of paternity is void if it:

(1) states that another man is a presumed father of the child, unless a denial of paternity signed or otherwise authenticated by the presumed father is filed with the bureau of vital statistics;

(2) states that another man is an acknowledged or adjudicated father of the child; or

(3) falsely denies the existence of a presumed, acknowledged, or adjudicated father of the child.

(c) A presumed father may sign or otherwise authenticate an acknowledgment of paternity.

History of Fam §160.302: Enacted by Acts 2001, 77th Leg., ch. 821, §1.01, eff. June 14, 2001.

Official Comment

Source: 42 U.S.C. §666(a)(5)(C).

The federal statute cited above declares that receipt by a State of the federal subsidy for its child support enforcement program is dependent on state law providing specific procedures for voluntary acknowledgment of paternity. The principle was simple to mandate; but the application is quite complicated.

Problems most notably include fact situations in which the mother of the child is married to someone other than the man who intends to acknowledge his paternity. With an acknowledgment the child would then have both an acknowledged father and a presumed father. To deal with this circumstance, many States have passed laws allowing the presumed father to sign a denial of paternity, which must be filed as part of the acknowledgment. This Act adopts this common sense solution; otherwise the acknowledgment would have no legal consequence because it cannot affect the legal rights of the presumed father.

At least two other provisions of this section warrant special emphasis. Subsection (a)(2) requires that the acknowledgment be "signed, or otherwise authenticated, under penalty of perjury," just as income tax returns and many other government documents require. Clearly, the potential punishment for false swearing is substantial, and the benefits from avoiding the complication of requiring witnesses and a notary are significant in this context. Mandating greater formality would greatly discourage the in-hospital signatures so earnestly desired in 42 U.S.C. §666(a)(5)(C)(ii).

Similarly, in an attempt to assure full disclosure and avoid false swearing, subsection (a)(4) requires information regarding whether there has been genetic testing, and if so, confirmation of the fact that the acknowledgment is consistent with the results of that testing. This provision is designed to avoid a possible subversion of the requirements for an adoption. A would-be "father" whose parentage of a child has been excluded by genetic testing may not validly sign an acknowledgment after that fact has been established.

E FAM §160.303. DENIAL OF PATERNITY

A presumed father of a child may sign a denial of his paternity. The denial is valid only if:

(1) an acknowledgment of paternity signed or otherwise authenticated by another man is filed under Section 160.305;

(2) the denial is in a record and is signed or otherwise authenticated under penalty of perjury; and

(3) the presumed father has not previously:

(A) acknowledged paternity of the child, unless the previous acknowledgment has been rescinded under Section 160.307 or successfully challenged under Section 160.308; or

(B) been adjudicated to be the father of the child.

History of Fam §160.303: Enacted by Acts 2001, 77th Leg., ch. 821, §1.01, eff. June 14, 2001.

See also 1 TAC §55.405.

E FAM §160.304. RULES FOR ACKNOWLEDGMENT & DENIAL OF PATERNITY

(a) An acknowledgment of paternity and a denial of paternity may be contained in a single document or in different documents and may be filed separately or simultaneously. If the acknowledgment and denial are both necessary, neither document is valid until both documents are filed.

(b) An acknowledgment of paternity or a denial of paternity may be signed before the birth of the child.

(c) Subject to Subsection (a), an acknowledgment of paternity or denial of paternity takes effect on the date of the birth of the child or the filing of the document with the bureau of vital statistics, whichever occurs later.

(d) An acknowledgment of paternity or denial of paternity signed by a minor is valid if it otherwise complies with this chapter.

History of Fam §160.304: Enacted by Acts 2001, 77th Leg., ch. 821, §1.01, eff. June 14, 2001.

Official Comment

Source: 42 U.S.C. §666(a)(5)(C)(i), requiring a "simple civil process" for voluntary acknowledgment of paternity.

E FAM §160.305. EFFECT OF ACKNOWLEDGMENT OR DENIAL OF PATERNITY

(a) Except as provided by Sections 160.307 and 160.308, a valid acknowledgment of paternity filed with the bureau of vital statistics is the equivalent of an adjudication of the paternity of a child and confers on the acknowledged father all rights and duties of a parent.

(b) Except as provided by Sections 160.307 and 160.308, a valid denial of paternity filed with the bureau of vital statistics in conjunction with a valid acknowledgment of paternity is the equivalent of an adjudication of the nonpaternity of the presumed father and discharges the presumed father from all rights and duties of a parent.

History of Fam §160.305: Enacted by Acts 2001, 77th Leg., ch. 821, §1.01, eff. June 14, 2001.

Official Comment

Source: 42 U.S.C. §666(a)(5)(D)(ii), requiring that an acknowledgment of paternity be "a legal finding of Paternity," and 42 U.S.C. §666(a)(5)(M), directing that acknowledgments be "filed with the State registry of birth records…"

E FAM §160.306. FILING FEE NOT REQUIRED

The bureau of vital statistics may not charge a fee for filing an acknowledgment of paternity or denial of paternity.

History of Fam §160.306: Enacted by Acts 2001, 77th Leg., ch. 821, §1.01, eff. June 14, 2001.

FAM §160.307. PROCEEDING FOR RESCISSION

A signatory may rescind an acknowledgment of paternity or denial of paternity by commencing a proceeding to rescind before the earlier of:

(1) the 60th day after the effective date of the acknowledgment or denial, as provided by Section 160.304; or

(2) the date of the first hearing in a proceeding to which the signatory is a party before a court to adjudicate an issue relating to the child, including a proceeding that establishes child support.

History of Fam §160.307: Enacted by Acts 2001, 77th Leg., ch. 821, §1.01, eff. June 14, 2001.

Official Comment

This section reflects a decision to require a judicial adjudicatory process to rescind a voluntary acknowledgment of paternity. A federal statute, 42 U.S.C. §666(a)(5)(c)(D)(ii), mandates that in order to retain the federal child support subsidy, state law must provide signatories with a right of rescission of an acknowledgment of paternity. However, the federal statute does not prescribe the method for the rescission.

FAM §160.308. CHALLENGE AFTER EXPIRATION OF PERIOD FOR RESCISSION

(a) After the period for rescission under Section 160.307 has expired, a signatory of an acknowledgment of paternity or denial of paternity may commence a proceeding to challenge the acknowledgment or denial only on the basis of fraud, duress, or material mistake of fact. The proceeding must be commenced before the fourth anniversary of the date the acknowledgment or denial is filed with the bureau of vital statistics.

(b) A party challenging an acknowledgment of paternity or denial of paternity has the burden of proof.

(c) Notwithstanding any other provision of this chapter, a collateral attack on an acknowledgment of paternity signed under this chapter may not be maintained after the fourth anniversary of the date the acknowledgment of paternity is filed with the bureau of vital statistics.

(d) For purposes of Subsection (a), evidence that, based on genetic testing, the man who is the signatory of an acknowledgement of paternity is not rebuttably identified as the father of a child in accordance with Section 160.505 constitutes a material mistake of fact.

History of Fam §160.308: Enacted by Acts 2001, 77th Leg., ch. 821, §1.01, eff. June 14, 2001.

Official Comment

Congress also added a provision for a "challenge" of an acknowledgment of paternity after the period for rescission of a voluntary acknowledgment of paternity has elapsed. Such a collateral attack is to be limited to a challenge based on alleged "fraud, duress, or material mistake of fact," and according to 42 U.S.C. §666(a)(5)(c)(D)(iii), must be made "in court." Subsection (d) was not in the uniform act.

FAM §160.309. PROCEDURE FOR RESCISSION OR CHALLENGE

(a) Each signatory to an acknowledgment of paternity and any related denial of paternity must be made a party to a proceeding to rescind or challenge the acknowledgment or denial of paternity.

(b) For purposes of the rescission of or a challenge to an acknowledgment of paternity or denial of paternity, a signatory submits to the personal jurisdiction of this state by signing the acknowledgment or denial. The jurisdiction is effective on the filing of the document with the bureau of vital statistics.

(c) Except for good cause shown, while a proceeding is pending to rescind or challenge an acknowledgment of paternity or a denial of paternity, the court may not suspend the legal responsibilities of a signatory arising from the acknowledgment, including the duty to pay child support.

(d) A proceeding to rescind or to challenge an acknowledgment of paternity or a denial of paternity shall be conducted in the same manner as a proceeding to adjudicate parentage under Subchapter G.

(e) At the conclusion of a proceeding to rescind or challenge an acknowledgment of paternity or a denial of paternity, the court shall order the bureau of vital statistics to amend the birth record of the child, if appropriate.

History of Fam §160.309: Enacted by Acts 2001, 77th Leg., ch. 821, §1.01, eff. June 14, 2001.

Official Comment

Although the federal statute does not prescribe the method for "rescission" of an acknowledgment of paternity, it does require a proceeding in court for a subsequent "challenge." Overturning an acknowledgment of paternity is an act of significant legal consequence under either of the prescribed methods allowed. Thus, either method to dispute a prior acknowledgment should require a formal procedure because it may void an otherwise valid legal determination of the child's parentage. A procedure that allows a signatory of an acknowledgment of paternity merely to file a rescission with the state bureau of vital statistics would be an unwise policy choice. Many jurisdictions have come to the same conclusion.

FAM §160.310. RATIFICATION BARRED

A court or administrative agency conducting a judicial or administrative proceeding may not ratify an unchallenged acknowledgment of paternity.

History of Fam §160.310: Enacted by Acts 2001, 77th Leg., ch. 821, §1.01, eff. June 14, 2001.

Official Comment

Source: 42 U.S.C. §666(a)(5)(E).

FAM §160.311. FULL FAITH & CREDIT

A court of this state shall give full faith and credit to an acknowledgment of paternity or a denial of paternity that is effective in another state if the acknowledgment or denial has been signed and is otherwise in compliance with the law of the other state.

History of Fam §160.311: Enacted by Acts 2001, 77th Leg., ch. 821, §1.01, eff. June 14, 2001.

Official Comment

Source: 42 U.S.C. §666(a)(5)(C)(iv).

PRWORA requires states "to give full faith and credit to such an affidavit [of acknowledgment of paternity] signed in any other state according to its procedures." Id. And, subsection (a)(5)(D)(ii) provides that a "signed voluntary acknowledgment is considered a legal finding of paternity." In sum, federal law requires that an acknowledgment of paternity has the same status as a "judgment," 28 U.S.C. §1738, a "child custody determination," 28 U.S.C. §1738A, and a "child support order," 28 U.S.C. §1738B. This section implements these mandates.

FAM §160.312. FORMS FOR ACKNOWLEDGMENT & DENIAL OF PATERNITY

(a) To facilitate compliance with this subchapter, the bureau of vital statistics shall prescribe forms for the acknowledgment of paternity and the denial of paternity.

(b) A valid acknowledgment of paternity or denial of paternity is not affected by a later modification of the prescribed form.

History of Fam §160.312: Enacted by Acts 2001, 77th Leg., ch. 821, §1.01, eff. June 14, 2001.

Official Comment

Source: 42 U.S.C. §666(a)(5)(C)(i),(iv).

The federal Office of Child Support Enforcement has issued an Action Transmittal to all IV-D agencies specifying how to insure that the forms comply with PRWORA, OCSE-AT-98-02, Required Data Elements for Paternity Acknowledgment Affidavits, *http://www.acf.dhhs.gov/programs/cse/1998-at.htm*.

FAM §160.313. RELEASE OF INFORMATION

The bureau of vital statistics may release information relating to the acknowledgment of paternity or denial of paternity to a signatory of the acknowledgment or denial and to the courts and Title IV-D agency of this or another state.

History of Fam §160.313: Enacted by Acts 2001, 77th Leg., ch. 821, §1.01, eff. June 14, 2001.

FAM §160.314. ADOPTION OF RULES

The Title IV-D agency and the bureau of vital statistics may adopt rules to implement this subchapter.

History of Fam §160.314: Enacted by Acts 2001, 77th Leg., ch. 821, §1.01, eff. June 14, 2001.

Official Comment

States will implement voluntary acknowledgment of paternity procedures in a variety of ways, depending on local practice. This grant of rulemaking authority to carry out the provisions of this article may include electronic transmission of birth and acknowledgment data to the designated state agency.

FAM §160.315. MEMORANDUM OF UNDERSTANDING

(a) The Title IV-D agency and the bureau of vital statistics shall adopt a memorandum of understanding governing the collection and transfer of information for the voluntary acknowledgment of paternity.

(b) The Title IV-D agency and the bureau of vital statistics shall review the memorandum semiannually and renew or modify the memorandum as necessary.

History of Fam §160.315: Enacted by Acts 2001, 77th Leg., ch. 821, §1.01, eff. June 14, 2001.

FAM §160.316. SUIT TO CONTEST VOLUNTARY STATEMENT OF PATERNITY

Section 160.316 below is effective for SAPCRs commenced on or after June 14, 2001, and before Sept. 1, 2003.

(a) A man who executed a voluntary statement of paternity before September 1, 1999, and who, on the basis of that statement, is the subject of a final order declaring him to be a parent of the child who is the subject of the statement may file a suit affecting the parent-child relationship to contest the statement on the basis of fraud, duress, or material mistake of fact in the same manner that a person may contest an acknowledgment of paternity under Sections 160.308 and 160.309. For purposes of this subsection, evidence that, based on genetic testing, the man is not rebuttably identified as the father of a child in accordance with Section 160.505 constitutes a material mistake of fact.

(b) A suit filed under this section to contest a voluntary statement of paternity is not affected by an order with respect to the child that was rendered on the basis of that statement.

(c) The court, on a preliminary finding in a suit under this section that there is credible evidence of fraud, duress, or material mistake of fact regarding the execution of the voluntary statement of paternity, shall order genetic testing as provided by Subchapter F. The person contesting the voluntary statement of paternity shall pay the cost of the testing.

(d) Except as provided by Subsection (e), if the results of the genetic testing do not rebuttably identify the man as the father of the child in accordance with Section 160.505, the court shall set aside:

(1) the final order declaring the man to be a parent of the child; and

(2) any other order with respect to the child that was rendered on the basis of the voluntary statement of paternity.

(e) The court may not set aside under Subsection (d) a final order declaring a man to be a parent of a child if the man who executed the voluntary statement of paternity:

(1) executed the statement knowing that he was not the father of the child; or

(2) subsequently adopted the child.

(f) If the court sets aside a final order as provided by Subsection (d), the court shall order the bureau of vital statistics to amend the birth record of the child. The court may not as a result of the order being set aside:

(1) require an obligee to repay child support paid by the man who executed the voluntary statement of paternity; or

(2) award damages to the man who executed the voluntary statement of paternity.

(g) A suit under this section must be filed before September 1, 2003.

(h) This section expires September 1, 2004.

History of Fam §160.316: Enacted by Acts 2001, 77th Leg., ch. 821, §1.01, eff. June 14, 2001.

Sections 160.317-160.400 reserved for expansion

E SUBCHAPTER E. REGISTRY OF PATERNITY

Official Prefatory Comment

In *Stanley v. Illinois*, 405 U.S. 645 (1972), the United States Supreme Court held that an unwed father was entitled to a hearing on his fitness as a parent before his children could be taken from him in a dependency proceeding instituted by the State upon the death of the children's mother. That case on its face presented a fairly stable, although unwed, family situation, although the court did not cite that factor as the basis for its decision. The following year, the Conference promulgated the UPA (1973), §§24-25 of which dealt with notice of adoption proceedings and proceedings to terminate parental rights in a way that satisfies the *Stanley* requirements.

In Lehr v. Robertson, 463 U.S. 248 (1983), the Supreme Court upheld the constitutionality of a New York "putative father registry". The New York statute requires fathers of children born out-of-wedlock to register if they wish to be notified of a termination of parental rights or adoption proceeding. Following a series of well-publicized adoption cases wherein nonmarital fathers had not been given proper notice, legislatures began responding by enacting paternity registries similar to the New York statute. As of May, 2000, at least 28 States had enacted legislation creating paternity registries.

In the view of many commentators, the *Lehr* opinion undercut the rationale of *Stanley* by requiring affirmative action by an alleged father before he would be entitled to notice of a proceeding to terminate his parental rights. The Act excepts from registration a man who timely initiates a proceeding for paternity, notwithstanding his failure to register.

E FAM §160.401. ESTABLISHMENT OF REGISTRY

A registry of paternity is established in the bureau of vital statistics.

History of Fam §160.401: Enacted by Acts 2001, 77th Leg., ch. 821, §1.01, eff. June 14, 2001.

E FAM §160.402. REGISTRATION FOR NOTIFICATION

(a) Except as otherwise provided by Subsection (b), a man who desires to be notified of a proceeding for the adoption of or the termination of parental rights regarding a child that he may have fathered may register with the registry of paternity:

(1) before the birth of the child; or

(2) not later than the 31st day after the date of the birth of the child.

(b) A man is entitled to notice of a proceeding described by Subsection (a) regardless of whether he registers with the registry of paternity if:

(1) a father-child relationship between the man and the child has been established under this chapter or another law; or

(2) the man commences a proceeding to adjudicate his paternity before the court has terminated his parental rights.

(c) A registrant shall promptly notify the registry in a record of any change in the information provided by the registrant. The bureau of vital statistics shall incorporate all new information received into its records but is not required to affirmatively seek to obtain current information for incorporation in the registry.

History of Fam §160.402: Enacted by Acts 2001, 77th Leg., ch. 821, §1.01, eff. June 14, 2001.

Official Comment

A registry of paternity protects a claim of paternity from summary termination, but the primary advantage of such a registry is to facilitate infant adoptions through licensed agencies. By registering, a registrant insures that he will receive notice of the possible adoption of a child that he may have fathered if the birth occurs in the State of registration. In this manner, a man may seek to protect his right to assert parentage.

If a State chooses to enact subsection (b)(2), one of the major criticisms of *Lehr v. Robertson, supra*, will be eliminated. In *Lehr*, although the genetic father did not avail himself of the New York putative fathers registry, he had filed a "visitation and paternity" petition in another local court. The trial judge in the adoption proceeding knew the identity of the biological father, where he could be located, and that he was seeking to establish his paternity in another court. Nonetheless, the court granted the adoption and terminated the genetic father's parental rights without notice to him. Subsection (b)(2) exempts an alleged father from the requirement of registration if the man "commences a proceeding to adjudicate his paternity before the court has terminated his parental rights."

The act of registration submits the man to the personal jurisdiction of the tribunals of the State of registration, *see* UIFSA (1996) §201(7).

FAM §160.403. NOTICE OF PROCEEDING

Notice of a proceeding to adopt or to terminate parental rights regarding a child must be given to a registrant who has timely registered with regard to that child. Notice must be given in a manner prescribed for service of process in a civil action.

History of Fam §160.403: Enacted by Acts 2001, 77th Leg., ch. 821, §1.01, eff. June 14, 2001.

Official Comment

This section is the logical conclusion to the legal rationale for establishing a paternity registry. In an adoption of a child or termination of parental rights proceeding, the registry provides a clear procedure for resolving whether a nonmarital father intends to assert his rights with regard to the child. If he registers, termination of his rights and adoption of his child may not proceed without notice to him; this affords him the opportunity to assert his paternity and his claims for custody or visitation.

FAM §160.404. TERMINATION OF PARENTAL RIGHTS: FAILURE TO REGISTER

The parental rights of a man alleged to be the father of a child may be terminated without notice as provided by Section 161.002 if the man:

(1) did not timely register with the bureau of vital statistics; and

(2) is not entitled to notice under Section 160.402 or 161.002.

History of Fam §160.404: Enacted by Acts 2001, 77th Leg., ch. 821, §1.01, eff. June 14, 2001.

Official Comment

This section is the obverse logical conclusion to the legal rationale for establishing a paternity registry. In an infant adoption or termination of the genetic father's parental rights, the registry provides a clear procedure for resolving that a man does not intend to assert parental rights with regard to the infant. Although the registry protects a man's right to notice in a termination or adoption proceeding, his failure to register waives those rights. Thus, the registry is both a first step for claiming parental rights and the end of those rights for those individuals who do not register. If a man fails to register with the paternity registry, a termination and adoption may proceed without fear of a belated claim, most particularly a claim coming after adoptive parents have received custody of the infant. This expedited procedure greatly facilitates infant adoption, which in truth explains the existence – and popularity – of the registries and their strong support by the adoption community.

Sections 160.405-160.410 reserved for expansion

FAM §160.411. REQUIRED FORM

The bureau of vital statistics shall adopt a form for registering with the registry. The form must require the signature of the registrant. The form must state that:

(1) the form is signed under penalty of perjury;

(2) a timely registration entitles the registrant to notice of a proceeding for adoption of the child or for termination of the registrant's parental rights;

(3) a timely registration does not commence a proceeding to establish paternity;

(4) the information disclosed on the form may be used against the registrant to establish paternity;

(5) services to assist in establishing paternity are available to the registrant through the support enforcement agency;

(6) the registrant should also register in another state if the conception or birth of the child occurred in the other state;

(7) information on registries in other states is available from the bureau of vital statistics; and

(8) procedures exist to rescind the registration of a claim of paternity.

History of Fam §160.411: Enacted by Acts 2001, 77th Leg., ch. 821, §1.01, eff. June 14, 2001.

FAM §160.412. FURNISHING OF INFORMATION; CONFIDENTIALITY

(a) The bureau of vital statistics is not required to attempt to locate the mother of a child who is the subject of a registration. The bureau of vital statistics shall send a copy of the notice of the registration to a mother who has provided an address.

(b) Information contained in the registry is confidential and may be released on request only to:

(1) a court or a person designated by the court;

(2) the mother of the child who is the subject of the registration;

(3) an agency authorized by another law to receive the information;

(4) a licensed child-placing agency;

(5) a support enforcement agency;

(6) a party, or the party's attorney of record, to a proceeding under this chapter or a proceeding to adopt or to terminate parental rights regarding a child who is the subject of the registration; and

(7) the registry of paternity in another state.

History of Fam §160.412: Enacted by Acts 2001, 77th Leg., ch. 821, §1.01, eff. June 14, 2001.

FAM §160.413. OFFENSE: UNAUTHORIZED RELEASE OF INFORMATION

(a) A person commits an offense if the person intentionally releases information from the registry of paternity to another person, including an agency, that is not authorized to receive the information under Section 160.412.

(b) An offense under this section is a Class A misdemeanor.

History of Fam §160.413: Enacted by Acts 2001, 77th Leg., ch. 821, §1.01, eff. June 14, 2001.

FAM §160.414. RESCISSION OF REGISTRATION

A registrant may rescind his registration at any time by sending to the registry a rescission in a record or another manner authenticated by him and witnessed or notarized.

History of Fam §160.414: Enacted by Acts 2001, 77th Leg., ch. 821, §1.01, eff. June 14, 2001.

FAM §160.415. UNTIMELY REGISTRATION

If a man registers later than the 30th day after the date of the birth of the child, the bureau of vital statistics shall notify the registrant that the registration was not timely filed.

History of Fam §160.415: Enacted by Acts 2001, 77th Leg., ch. 821, §1.01, eff. June 14, 2001.

FAM §160.416. FEES FOR REGISTRY

(a) A fee may not be charged for filing a registration or to rescind a registration.

(b) Except as otherwise provided by Subsection (c), the bureau of vital statistics may charge a reasonable fee for making a search of the registry and for furnishing a certificate.

(c) A support enforcement agency is not required to pay a fee authorized by Subsection (b).

History of Fam §160.416: Enacted by Acts 2001, 77th Leg., ch. 821, §1.01, eff. June 14, 2001.

Sections 160.417-160.420 reserved for expansion

FAM §160.421. SEARCH OF APPROPRIATE REGISTRY

(a) If a father-child relationship has not been established under this chapter, a petitioner for the adoption of or the termination of parental rights regarding the child must obtain a certificate of the results of a search of the registry.

(b) If the petitioner for the adoption of or the termination of parental rights regarding a child has reason to believe that the conception or birth of the child may have occurred in another state, the petitioner must obtain a certificate of the results of a search of the paternity registry, if any, in the other state.

History of Fam §160.421: Enacted by Acts 2001, 77th Leg., ch. 821, §1.01, eff. June 14, 2001.

FAM §160.422. CERTIFICATE OF SEARCH OF REGISTRY

(a) The bureau of vital statistics shall furnish a certificate of the results of a search of the registry on request by an individual, a court, or an agency listed in Section 160.412(b).

(b) The certificate of the results of a search must be signed on behalf of the bureau and state that:

(1) a search has been made of the registry; and

(2) a registration containing the information required to identify the registrant:

(A) has been found and is attached to the certificate; or

(B) has not been found.

(c) A petitioner must file the certificate of the results of a search of the registry with the court before a proceeding for the adoption of or termination of parental rights regarding a child may be concluded.

(d) A search of the registry is not required if the only man alleged to be the father of the child has signed a waiver of interest in, or relinguishment* of parental rights with regard to, the child.

* Enacted as such. Should probably read "relinquishment."

History of Fam §160.422: Enacted by Acts 2001, 77th Leg., ch. 821, §1.01, eff. June 14, 2001.

FAM §160.423. ADMISSIBILITY OF CERTIFICATE

A certificate of the results of a search of the registry in this state or of a paternity registry in another state is admissible in a proceeding for the adoption of or the termination of parental rights regarding a child and, if relevant, in other legal proceedings.

History of Fam §160.423: Enacted by Acts 2001, 77th Leg., ch. 821, §1.01, eff. June 14, 2001.

Sections 160.424-160.500 reserved for expansion

SUBCHAPTER F. GENETIC TESTING

FAM §160.501. APPLICATION OF SUBCHAPTER

This subchapter governs genetic testing of an individual to determine parentage, regardless of whether the individual:

(1) voluntarily submits to testing; or

(2) is tested under an order of a court or a support enforcement agency.

History of Fam §160.501: Enacted by Acts 2001, 77th Leg., ch. 821, §1.01, eff. June 14, 2001.

Official Comment

This section is intended to avoid problems with regard to the admissibility of the result of voluntary genetic testing. Testing is often agreed upon to avoid the cost and delay engendered by requiring a proceeding be filed before the result of a genetic testing can be admitted as evidence. If the test excludes the man's paternity, an unnecessary step has been avoided.

FAM §160.502. ORDER FOR TESTING

(a) Except as otherwise provided by this subchapter and by Subchapter G, a court shall order a child and other designated individuals to submit to genetic testing if the request is made by a party to a proceeding to determine parentage.

(b) If a request for genetic testing of a child is made before the birth of the child, the court or support enforcement agency may not order in utero testing.

(c) If two or more men are subject to court-ordered genetic testing, the testing may be ordered concurrently or sequentially.

History of Fam §160.502: Enacted by Acts 2001, 77th Leg., ch. 821, §1.01, eff. June 14, 2001.

Official Comment

Source: UPA (1973) §11; 42 U.S.C. §666(a)(5)(B)(i) requiring genetic testing in certain cases.

The progress that science has made in understanding molecular genetics since the promulgation of UPA (1973) is phenomenal. Subsection (a) speaks to testing of a "designated individual" other than of the "mother, and alleged or presumed father" to take into account the fact that testing for paternity may proceed without testing the mother. Further, testing may also proceed without testing the alleged father by testing close relatives of that man. Moreover, the right of the court to order testing is not absolute; Sections 607–609 place limitations on genetic testing if the child has a presumed, acknowledged, or adjudicated father.

Subsection (b) is intended to prevent the court from ordering the mother to undergo prenatal testing, such as through amniocentesis or other in utero collection method. These procedures have a measurable risk to the life and health of both the fetus and the mother. If the mother volunteers for such testing, she may undergo prenatal sample collection for parentage determination.

Subsection (c) recognizes that multiple men may be participating in the establishment process. The laboratories prefer to evaluate all persons concurrently, as concurrent testing may prevent multiple sample collections from the child and in rare cases (such as evaluating two non-identical siblings) the laboratory can continue testing until one or both of the tested men are excluded. However, sequential testing is also acceptable.

FAM §160.503. REQUIREMENTS FOR GENETIC TESTING

(a) Genetic testing must be of a type reasonably relied on by experts in the field of genetic testing. The testing must be performed in a testing laboratory accredited by:

(1) the American Association of Blood Banks, or a successor to its functions;

(2) the American Society for Histocompatibility and Immunogenetics, or a successor to its functions; or

(3) an accrediting body designated by the federal secretary of health and human services.

(b) A specimen used in genetic testing may consist of one or more samples, or a combination of samples, of blood, buccal cells, bone, hair, or other body tissue or fluid. The specimen used in the testing is not required to be of the same kind for each individual undergoing genetic testing.

(c) Based on the ethnic or racial group of an individual, the testing laboratory shall determine the databases from which to select frequencies for use in the calculation of the probability of paternity of the individual. If there is disagreement as to the testing laboratory's choice:

(1) the objecting individual may require the testing laboratory, not later than the 30th day after the date of receipt of the report of the test, to recalculate the probability of paternity using an ethnic or racial group different from that used by the laboratory;

(2) the individual objecting to the testing laboratory's initial choice shall:

(A) if the frequencies are not available to the testing laboratory for the ethnic or racial group requested, provide the requested frequencies compiled in a manner recognized by accrediting bodies; or

(B) engage another testing laboratory to perform the calculations; and

(3) the testing laboratory may use its own statistical estimate if there is a question regarding which ethnic or racial group is appropriate and, if available, shall calculate the frequencies using statistics for any other ethnic or racial group requested.

(d) If, after recalculation using a different ethnic or racial group, genetic testing does not rebuttably identify a man as the father of a child under Section 160.505, an individual who has been tested may be required to submit to additional genetic testing.

History of Fam §160.503: Enacted by Acts 2001, 77th Leg., ch. 821, §1.01, eff. June 14, 2001.

Official Comment

Source: 42 U.S.C. §666(a)(5)(B)(i)(I)(II) and §666(a)(5)(F)(i)(I)(II),

As of December 2000, the Secretary of Health and Human Services has not officially designated any accreditation bodies as referenced in subsection (b)(3). But, Information Memorandum O.C.S.E.-IM-97-03, April 10, 1997, from the Deputy Director of the Office of Child Support Enforcement identifies the American Association of Blood Banks and American Society for Histocompatibility and Immunogenetics as meeting this requirement. The accreditation requirement assures that the testing will "be of a type reasonably relied upon by experts in the field of genetic testing."

Subsection (b) clarifies that a "specimen" suitable for genetic testing may be composed from one of a wide variety of constituent elements of "body tissue and fluids." This conforms the statutory language to biological terminology to assure common understanding between the scientific community and the legal profession. In States with statutes employing only the broad terms, bench and bar have evidenced confusion about the fact that blood, buccal cells, bone, hair, etc. are "body tissues."

Subsections (c) and (d) are designed to clarify the use of "race or ethnic group" in the paternity calculations. Generally, the individual tested provides the information regarding the ethnic or racial group to use in the calculations. These sections are designed to avoid last minute changes in the racial designation, a scientific version of "forum shopping", and to easily correct any misunderstanding about which race should be used.

FAM §160.504. REPORT OF GENETIC TESTING

(a) A report of the results of genetic testing must be in a record and signed under penalty of perjury by a designee of the testing laboratory. A report made under the requirements of this subchapter is self-authenticating.

(b) Documentation from the testing laboratory is sufficient to establish a reliable chain of custody that allows the results of genetic testing to be admissible without testimony if the documentation includes:

(1) the name and photograph of each individual whose specimens have been taken;

(2) the name of each individual who collected the specimens;

(3) the places in which the specimens were collected and the date of each collection;

(4) the name of each individual who received the specimens in the testing laboratory; and

(5) the dates the specimens were received.

History of Fam §160.504: Enacted by Acts 2001, 77th Leg., ch. 821, §1.01, eff. June 14, 2001.

Official Comment

Source: 42 U.S.C. §666(a)(5)(F) requiring genetic testing in certain cases.

Subsection (b) is designed to indicate that in civil trials only a minimal showing of reliability of the chain of custody is needed. This avoids evidentiary problems, such as arguments modeled on criminal cases in which the chain of evidence is crucial. If an element of the chain is missing, such a defect may be corrected by affidavit or other testimony as to the reliability of the sample. For example, samples from a deceased individual may be obtained from a coroner's office and a picture of the individual need not be taken. In this case, proof of the chain of custody of the body maintained by the coroner may be provided.

FAM §160.505. GENETIC TESTING RESULTS; REBUTTAL

(a) A man is rebuttably identified as the father of a child under this chapter if the genetic testing complies with this subchapter and the results disclose:

(1) that the man has at least a 99 percent probability of paternity, using a prior probability of 0.5, as calculated by using the combined paternity index obtained in the testing; and

(2) a combined paternity index of at least 100 to 1.

(b) A man identified as the father of a child under Subsection (a) may rebut the genetic testing results only by producing other genetic testing satisfying the requirements of this subchapter that:

(1) excludes the man as a genetic father of the child; or

(2) identifies another man as the possible father of the child.

(c) Except as otherwise provided by Section 160.510, if more than one man is identified by genetic testing as the possible father of the child, the court shall order each man to submit to further genetic testing to identify the genetic father.

History of Fam §160.505: Enacted by Acts 2001, 77th Leg., ch. 821, §1.01, eff. June 14, 2001.

Official Comment

Source: 42 U.S.C. §666(a)(5)(G) requiring genetic testing in certain cases.

The selection of a probability of paternity of 99.0% and a combined paternity index of 100 to 1 as the rebuttably identified man as father of the child is consistent with the year 2000 standard of practice in the genetic-testing community. Accrediting agencies require the reporting of both of these numbers. As of December, 2000, 27 States have established a presumption at less than this level. However, for several years the standard of practice in the scientific community has been 99.0%. Therefore, raising the genetic presumption to the 99.0% level should have no impact on those States. This number represents a reasonable level of testing, given the breadth of the Act and potential difficulty of working with some specimens in a probate case. It is not intended as a standard of practice for the laboratories, but as a legal presumption to satisfy the legal standard of proof. Given the rapid progress of science, it is likely that accrediting standards will rise over time. If the standard of practice becomes more strict, the newer standards will be made routine by the requirement that laboratories be accredited in order to perform testing under the Act. But, the legal significance of the genetic presumption stated in this section will be unaffected.

Genetic testing results will usually exceed the statutory minimum. During the drafting of UPA (2000) several statutory presumptions were considered, i.e., 95%, 99%, 99.9% and 99.99%. Genetic testing laboratory representatives presented quite persuasive arguments for a variety of choices. The Drafting Committee ultimately chose to settle on the 99% standard because:

(1) the 99% standard reflects the current standard of the American Association of Blood Banks (Standards for Parentage Testing Laboratories, 4th Edition 1999), and the proposed standards (5th Edition, 2001);

(2) the standards promulgated by the various accrediting bodies (American Association of Blood Banks and the American Society for Histocompatibility and Immunogenetics) will, in reality, set the benchmark for genetic testing;

(3) the 99% standard is consistent with the standards of the plurality of American jurisdictions as of December, 2000;

(4) a standard higher than 99% could cause evidentiary problems in probate proceedings because of degraded specimens. Similarly, that problem may arise in cases involving one or more missing individuals, e.g., the mother is not available, but the child and alleged father are available;

(5) the percentage is an evidentiary presumption that the respondent may always challenge by requesting a second test under Section 507; and

(6) a proceeding to adjudicate paternity is a civil action based on a preponderance of the evidence, not a criminal action based on evidence beyond reasonable doubt.

FAM §160.506. COSTS OF GENETIC TESTING

(a) Subject to the assessment of costs under Subchapter G, the cost of initial genetic testing must be advanced:

(1) by a support enforcement agency, if the agency is providing services in the proceeding;

(2) by the individual who made the request;

(3) as agreed by the parties; or

(4) as ordered by the court.

(b) In cases in which the cost of genetic testing is advanced by the support enforcement agency, the agency may seek reimbursement from a man who is rebuttably identified as the father.

History of Fam §160.506: Enacted by Acts 2001, 77th Leg., ch. 821, §1.01, eff. June 14, 2001.

Official Comment

Source: UPA (1973) §11; 42 U.S.C. §666(a)(5)(B)(ii)(I).

In general, the party seeking relief from a court must bear the cost of the initial genetic testing. The federal law mandates that the support enforcement agency pay the cost of testing, subject to recoupment. Subsection (a)(4) does present the possibility that a court might order a respondent to pay the initial cost.

E FAM §160.507. ADDITIONAL GENETIC TESTING

The court or the support enforcement agency shall order additional genetic testing on the request of a party who contests the result of the original testing. If the previous genetic testing identified a man as the father of the child under Section 160.505, the court or agency may not order additional testing unless the party provides advance payment for the testing.

History of Fam §160.507: Enacted by Acts 2001, 77th Leg., ch. 821, §1.01, eff. June 14, 2001.

Official Comment

Source: UPA (1973) §11; 42 U.S.C. §666(a)(5)(B)(ii)(II).

Obviously the opportunity for additional testing should be provided if the original testing is contested in good faith. The requirement that the contestant provide advance payment if prior testing has identified a man as the father is intended to discourage spurious contests. This section provides the most important mechanism for determining the accuracy of a paternity test. While extremely rare, even after initial tests indicate a probability of paternity greater than 99.99% it is theoretically possible that additional testing can result in exclusion of the tested man. Likewise, if there is an error in the chain of custody or testing procedures, exclusion is the expected outcome. The only way to reliably determine whether an error occurred is to obtain a second test.

E FAM §160.508. GENETIC TESTING WHEN ALL INDIVIDUALS NOT AVAILABLE

(a) Subject to Subsection (b), if a genetic testing specimen for good cause and under circumstances the court considers to be just is not available from a man who may be the father of a child, a court may order the following individuals to submit specimens for genetic testing:

(1) the parents of the man;

(2) any brothers or sisters of the man;

(3) any other children of the man and their mothers; and

(4) other relatives of the man necessary to complete genetic testing.

(b) A court may not render an order under this section unless the court finds that the need for genetic testing outweighs the legitimate interests of the individual sought to be tested.

History of Fam §160.508: Enacted by Acts 2001, 77th Leg., ch. 821, §1.01, eff. June 14, 2001.

Official Comment

In some cases, the alleged father may be unavailable for testing. Subsection (a) accommodates those cases by providing for testing of the man's relatives to establish his paternity or nonpaternity of a child. Depending on the proceeding, some of the individuals listed for testing in subsection (a) will be parties to the paternity proceeding and others will not. If an individual does not volunteer to participate in the testing and is not a party, in the absence of this provision the court would be required to decide whether it has the authority to order the testing and whether testing the objecting individual is necessary. This provision resolves the issues. Given the fact that genetic testing in the modern age is not invasive – use of the buccal swab method means that the intrusion into the privacy of the individual is relatively slight compared to the right of the child to have parentage established. Moreover, the alleged parent also has a right to have that fact determined.

Note that no provision is explicitly made for court-ordered testing of maternal relatives because the establishment of paternity by genetic testing is in no way dependent on testing the mother of the child. However, if maternity is at issue, §106, Determination of Maternity, directs that this section be construed to test the relatives of the mother.

E FAM §160.509. DECEASED INDIVIDUAL

For good cause shown, the court may order genetic testing of a deceased individual.

History of Fam §160.509: Enacted by Acts 2001, 77th Leg., ch. 821, §1.01, eff. June 14, 2001.

Official Comment

In some States, the court with jurisdiction to adjudicate parentage may lack authority to order disinterment of a deceased individual. If so, that authority is provided by this section.

E FAM §160.510. IDENTICAL BROTHERS

(a) The court may order genetic testing of a brother of a man identified as the father of a child if the man is commonly believed to have an identical brother and evidence suggests that the brother may be the genetic father of the child.

(b) If each brother satisfies the requirements of Section 160.505 for being the identified father of the child and there is not another identical brother being identified as the father of the child, the court may rely on nongenetic evidence to adjudicate which brother is the father of the child.

History of Fam §160.510: Enacted by Acts 2001, 77th Leg., ch. 821, §1.01, eff. June 14, 2001.

Official Comment

This section refers to "identical brothers" rather than "identical twins" to account for the possibility of identical triplets, etc. In some cases, non-identical brothers (and even other related men) will not be excluded after initial genetic testing. This section should not be used to resolve those cases because more sophisticated genetic testing can differentiate between non-identical siblings. If a case occurs in which, after initial testing, two men are not excluded, both men should be ordered to submit to additional testing as provided in Section 505(c) to determine which is the father. In the extremely rare case in which a competent laboratory exhausts all of its in-house testing and still cannot determine which non-identical sibling is excluded, the common practice is to provide the genetic material to another laboratory for more extensive testing to resolve the case.

Contrasting identical brothers with non-identical brothers, identical brothers can never be differentiated by additional genetic testing. This creates a completely different situation for the court. This section resolves the identical-brother conundrum as much as possible, and is designed to prevent the court from simply dismissing the case.

FAM §160.511. OFFENSE: UNAUTHORIZED RELEASE OF SPECIMEN

(a) A person commits an offense if the person intentionally releases an identifiable specimen of another person for any purpose not relevant to the parentage proceeding and without a court order or the written permission of the person who furnished the specimen.

(b) An offense under this section is a Class A misdemeanor.

History of Fam §160.511: Enacted by Acts 2001, 77th Leg., ch. 821, §1.01, eff. June 14, 2001.

Official Comment

This section seeks to protect the privacy rights of persons who are tested for a parentage determination. Although the Drafting Committee was not informed of an instance in which a paternity-testing laboratory had released samples or performed unauthorized testing, several States have proposed or passed laws regulating the "genetic privacy" of paternity tests. This section is intended to provide some guidance in this area. The term "identifiable specimen" is included, as there are beneficial uses of samples for anonymous research purposes. For example, the frequency tables used to make calculations are compiled from anonymous data and provide a more precise calculation for all persons involved in paternity testing. On occasion, a court may order the laboratory to release samples. For instance, a man who had been tested in one paternity proceeding and then dies may have his samples utilized in another paternity proceeding if a court orders testing in the second action. Courts have also ordered the release of samples when the tested man has allegedly engaged in criminal conduct. This has occurred when the alleged father has sent an imposter for sample collection. If the State pursues criminal charges, a court might order the laboratory to release the samples to a state crime laboratory for further identification and possible criminal prosecution.

The Drafting Committee was informed that in one case, a grand jury brought indictments for multiple counts of a scheme to defraud, tampering with physical evidence and perjury against the alleged father and the imposter. The results of genetic testing for paternity purposes appear to have no medical or predictive value in any other context. Thus, regulation of the paternity-test results is left to the States. In some States, the records of paternity proceedings are open, thus allowing anyone to obtain the results. A more comprehensive treatment on this subject must necessarily be left to other laws.

The control of the records is left to other state law. In some States paternity records are open to the public, and a fundamental change in handling of the records is beyond the scope of this Act. The accreditation agencies provide guidance on this subject. For example, the American Association of Blood Banks requires that accredited laboratories maintain records for at least five years. Because a laboratory performing testing under this Act should be accredited, see Section 503(a), *supra*, protection is thus provided to the tested person's records under the accreditation standards.

Sections 160.512-160.600 reserved for expansion

SUBCHAPTER G. PROCEEDING TO ADJUDICATE PARENTAGE

FAM §160.601. PROCEEDING AUTHORIZED; RULES OF PROCEDURE

(a) A civil proceeding may be maintained to adjudicate the parentage of a child.

(b) The proceeding is governed by the Texas Rules of Civil Procedure.

History of Fam §160.601: Enacted by Acts 2001, 77th Leg., ch. 821, §1.01, eff. June 14, 2001.

Official Comment

Source: UPA (1973) §14.

A determination of paternity is governed by the ordinary rules of civil procedure. The party seeking to establish paternity is entitled to full discovery, to compel the testimony of all witnesses, and to have the case tried by a preponderance of the evidence. "The equipoise of the private interests that are at stake in a paternity proceeding supports the conclusion that the standard of proof normally applied in private litigation is also appropriate for these cases." *Rivera v. Minnich*, 483 U.S. 574, 581 (1987).

A corresponding amendment to UPC §2-114 was not made until the major revision of 1990 (as further revised in 1993). By that time, it had been recognized as illogical and unjust to impose discriminatory burdens on children born out-of-wedlock who were seeking paternal inheritance. It also had been ruled unconstitutional by application of the intermediate scrutiny test formulated under the 14th Amendment. *Reed v. Campbell*, 476 U.S. 852 (1986). Moreover, by 1990 the preponderance of the evidence standard had been widely applied to determinations of paternity and probate proceedings. Against this background, UPC (1993) abandoned the clear and convincing evidence alternative for determining paternal relationships.

FAM §160.602. STANDING TO MAINTAIN PROCEEDING

Subject to Subchapter D and Sections 160.607 and 160.609, a proceeding to adjudicate parentage may be maintained by:

(1) the child;

(2) the mother of the child;

(3) a man whose paternity of the child is to be adjudicated;

(4) the support enforcement agency or another government agency authorized by other law;

(5) an authorized adoption agency or licensed child-placing agency;

(6) a representative authorized by law to act for an individual who would otherwise be entitled to maintain a proceeding but who is deceased, is incapacitated, or is a minor; or

(7) a person related within the second degree by consanguinity to the mother of the child, if the mother is deceased.

History of Fam §160.602: Enacted by Acts 2001, 77th Leg., ch. 821, §1.01, eff. June 14, 2001.

Official Comment

Source: UPA (1973) §6.

This section grants standing to a broad range of individuals and agencies to bring a parentage proceeding. But, several limitations on standing to sue are contained within the Act. Article 3 details the procedures involved in a voluntary acknowledgment of parentage. Sections 607 and 609 establish the ground rules for proceedings involving children with, and without, a presumed father. Article 8 regulates parentage determinations arising from a gestational agreement.

E FAM §160.603. NECESSARY PARTIES TO PROCEEDING

The following individuals must be joined as parties in a proceeding to adjudicate parentage:

(1) the mother of the child; and

(2) a man whose paternity of the child is to be adjudicated.

History of Fam §160.603: Enacted by Acts 2001, 77th Leg., ch. 821, §1.01, eff. June 14, 2001.

Official Comment

Source: UPA (1973) §9.

This section partially follows and partially rejects the UPA (1973) requirements regarding who must be named as parties in a parentage proceeding. First, contra to UPA (1973), the child is not a necessary party. Few States require children as necessary parties. Further, with the widespread use of DNA testing, such a requirement has outlived its usefulness. On the other hand, failure to join a child as a party may later result in a child's successful collateral attack on the original determination of paternity to be filed by the child. This subject is discussed more fully in the Comment to Section 637, *infra*.

Second, as far as can be determined, no State requires the children born to a woman during marriage to be named as parties in every divorce proceeding; and, those decrees generally serve as res judicata if a later attack on a earlier determination is mounted. Id.

E FAM §160.604. PERSONAL JURISDICTION

(a) An individual may not be adjudicated to be a parent unless the court has personal jurisdiction over the individual.

(b) A court of this state having jurisdiction to adjudicate parentage may exercise personal jurisdiction over a nonresident individual or the guardian or conservator of the individual if the conditions in Section 159.201 are satisfied.

(c) Lack of jurisdiction over one individual does not preclude the court from making an adjudication of parentage binding on another individual over whom the court has personal jurisdiction.

History of Fam §160.604: Enacted by Acts 2001, 77th Leg., ch. 821, §1.01, eff. June 14, 2001.

Official Comment

Source: UPA (1973) §6(b).

Although custody and visitation proceedings are considered to be status adjudications, and therefore do not require personal jurisdiction over both parents, subsection (a) confirms the long-standing view that paternity proceedings require personal jurisdiction.

Subsection (b) incorporates the long-arm provision for establishing personal jurisdiction over an absent respondent set forth in UIFSA (1996), which is in effect in every State.

Subsection (c) makes the best of a situation in which an adjudication will almost inevitably be incomplete because not all the necessary parties are subject to the personal jurisdiction of the court. The most likely scenario for this unfortunate circumstance is one in which the mother and alleged father of the child are subject to the court's jurisdiction, but the mother's absent husband is not. Even if the husband's whereabouts are known, if both the forum court and the court of his residence lacks jurisdiction over all three parties, there still is no court with power to bind all of them to a parentage determination.

Subsection (c) takes the common sense approach that a court should not be dissuaded from making a parentage decision, even if it cannot bind all appropriate parties. In the scenario described above, binding the mother and alleged father to a decision of the man's parentage may not technically bind the husband (the presumed father), but more than likely it will end litigation on the subject.

E FAM §160.605. VENUE

Venue for a proceeding to adjudicate parentage is in the county of this state in which:

(1) the child resides or is found;

(2) the respondent resides or is found if the child does not reside in this state; or

(3) a proceeding for probate or administration of the presumed or alleged father's estate has been commenced.

History of Fam §160.605: Enacted by Acts 2001, 77th Leg., ch. 821, §1.01, eff. June 14, 2001.

Official Comment

Source: UPA (1973) §8(c).

The venue provision provides choices proven to be reasonable and convenient since its inclusion in the 1973 Act.

E FAM §160.606. NO TIME LIMITATION: CHILD HAVING NO PRESUMED, ACKNOWLEDGED, OR ADJUDICATED FATHER

A proceeding to adjudicate the parentage of a child having no presumed, acknowledged, or adjudicated father may be commenced at any time, including after the date:

(1) the child becomes an adult; or

(2) an earlier proceeding to adjudicate paternity has been dismissed based on the application of a statute of limitation then in effect.

History of Fam §160.606: Enacted by Acts 2001, 77th Leg., ch. 821, §1.01, eff. June 14, 2001.

Official Comment

Source: UPA (1973) §§6, 7.

For a State to retain the federal child support enforcement subsidy, 42 U.S.C. 666(a)(5)(A)(i) mandates that the States must have laws to "permit the establishment of the paternity of a child at any time before the child attains 18 years of age." States have chosen a wide range of age options: age 18 (20 States), age 19 (6 States), age 20 (2 States), age 21 (10 States), age 22 (2 States), age 23 (2 States), and no limitation (9 States). Several States limit the establishment of parental rights to a shorter period.

In contrast, UPA (2000) directs that an individual whose parentage has not been determined has a civil right to determine his or her own parentage, which should not be subject to limitation except when an estate has been closed. Accordingly, this section allows a proceeding to adjudicate parentage at any time. There appear to be no reported problems encountered in States without a statute of limitations for such actions.

FAM §160.607. TIME LIMITATION: CHILD HAVING PRESUMED FATHER

(a) Except as otherwise provided by Subsection (b), a proceeding brought by a presumed father, the mother, or another individual to adjudicate the parentage of a child having a presumed father shall be commenced not later than the fourth anniversary of the date of the birth of the child.

(b) A proceeding seeking to disprove the father-child relationship between a child and the child's presumed father may be maintained at any time if the court determines that:

(1) the presumed father and the mother of the child did not live together or engage in sexual intercourse with each other during the probable time of conception; and

(2) the presumed father never openly treated the child as his own.

History of Fam §160.607: Enacted by Acts 2001, 77th Leg., ch. 821, §1.01, eff. June 14, 2001.

Official Comment

Source: UPA (1973) §6; *cf.* UPC (1993) §2-114(c).

This section deals with difficult issues. First, it fixes the right of a mother or a presumed father to challenge the presumption of his paternity established by Section 204 – a presumption based on the age-old assumption that the mother's husband is the father of a child born to her (with some additional complexities). Second, clarifying the right of a third-party male to claim paternity of a child who has an existing presumed father.

UPA (1973) §6(a) places a [five-year] limitation on the time in which a proceeding may be brought "for the purpose of declaring the non-existence of the father and child relationship presumed under [the Act]". At that time, the Comment noted that:

"Ten states have denied standing to a man claiming to be the father when the mother was married to another at the time of the child's birth. In some of these states, even though a presumed father may seek to rebut his presumed paternity, a third-party male will be denied standing to raise that same issue."

As of the year 2000, the right of an "outsider" to claim paternity of a child born to a married woman varies considerably among the States. Thirty-three States allow a man alleging himself to be the father of a child with a presumed father to rebut the marital presumption. Some States have granted this right through legislation, while in other States case law has recognized the alleged father's right to rebut the presumption and establish his paternity. In some States, there is both statutory and common law support for the standing of a man alleging himself to be the father to assert his paternity of a child born to a married woman. Finally, some States, such as California, absolutely bar a man from commencing a proceeding to establish his paternity if state law provides a statutory presumption of the paternity of another man, *see* West's Ann. Cal. Evid. Code §621, upheld in *Michael H. and Victoria D. v. Gerald D.*, 491 U.S. 110, 105 L.Ed.2d 91, 109 S.Ct. 2333 (1989).

UPA (2000) attempts to establish a middle ground on these exceedingly complex issues. Subsection (a) establishes a two-year limitation for rebutting the presumption of paternity established under Section 204 if the mother and presumed father were cohabiting at the time of conception. The presumption of paternity may be attacked by the mother, the presumed father, or a third-party male during this limited period; thereafter, the presumption is immune from attack by any of those individuals.

However, subsection (b) is open-ended if the mother did not live with the presumed father or engage in sexual intercourse with him at the probable time of conception. This distinction is based on the belief that a two-year period allows an adequate period to resolve the status of a child within the context of an intact family unit; a longer period may have severe consequences for the child in that circumstance. But, if the family is not intact and the presumed father neither cohabited with the mother at the time of conception nor treated the child as his own, the nonpaternity of the presumed father is generally assumed by all the parties as a practical matter. It is inappropriate to assume a presumption known by all those concerned to be untrue.

FAM §160.608. AUTHORITY TO DENY MOTION FOR GENETIC TESTING

(a) In a proceeding to adjudicate parentage under circumstances described by Section 160.607, a court may deny a motion for an order for the genetic testing of the mother, the child, and the presumed father if the court determines that:

(1) the conduct of the mother or the presumed father estops that party from denying parentage; and

(2) it would be inequitable to disprove the father-child relationship between the child and the presumed father.

(b) In determining whether to deny a motion for an order for genetic testing under this section, the court shall consider the best interest of the child, including the following factors:

(1) the length of time between the date of the proceeding to adjudicate parentage and the date the presumed father was placed on notice that he might not be the genetic father;

(2) the length of time during which the presumed father has assumed the role of father of the child;

(3) the facts surrounding the presumed father's discovery of his possible nonpaternity;

(4) the nature of the relationship between the child and the presumed father;

(5) the age of the child;

(6) any harm that may result to the child if presumed paternity is successfully disproved;

(7) the nature of the relationship between the child and the alleged father;

(8) the extent to which the passage of time reduces the chances of establishing the paternity of another man and a child support obligation in favor of the child; and

(9) other factors that may affect the equities arising from the disruption of the father-child relationship between the child and the presumed father or the chance of other harm to the child.

(c) In a proceeding involving the application of this section, a child who is a minor or is incapacitated must be represented by a guardian ad litem.

(d) A denial of a motion for an order for genetic testing must be based on clear and convincing evidence.

(e) If the court denies a motion for an order for genetic testing, the court shall issue an order adjudicating the presumed father to be the father of the child.

History of Fam §160.608: Enacted by Acts 2001, 77th Leg., ch. 821, §1.01, eff. June 14, 2001.

Official Comment

This section incorporates the doctrine of paternity by estoppel. The section is limited in its application to married persons and does not apply to a man in a nonmarital relationship. In appropriate circumstances, the court may deny genetic testing and find the presumed father to be the father of the child. The most common situations arise where the man has knowledge that the child of the marriage is not, or may not be, his child, but the man has affirmatively expressed his acceptance of his role as the father of the child and the mother has relied on that acceptance. Similarly, the man may have relied on the mother's acceptance of him as the father of the child and the mother is then estopped to deny the man's presumed parentage.

Subsection (b) delineates the standards for denying genetic testing. Subsection (c) requires the child to be independently represented. Subsection (d) requires an elevated standard of proof before the order for genetic testing can be denied.

Because Section 607 places a two-year limitation on challenging the presumption of parentage, the application of this section should be applied in those meritorious cases in which the best interest of the child compels the result and the conduct of the husband and wife is clear.

E FAM §160.609. TIME LIMITATION: CHILD HAVING ACKNOWLEDGED OR ADJUDICATED FATHER

(a) If a child has an acknowledged father, a signatory to the acknowledgment or denial of paternity may commence a proceeding seeking to rescind the acknowledgment or denial or to challenge the paternity of the child only within the time allowed under Section 160.307 or 160.308.

(b) If a child has an acknowledged father or an adjudicated father, an individual, other than the child, who is not a signatory to the acknowledgment or a party to the adjudication and who seeks an adjudication of paternity of the child must commence a proceeding not later than the fourth anniversary of the effective date of the acknowledgment or adjudication.

History of Fam §160.609: Enacted by Acts 2001, 77th Leg., ch. 821, §1.01, eff. June 14, 2001.

Official Comment

A two-year period is prescribed for a challenge in which the acknowledged or adjudicated father mistakenly believed himself to be the father. A similar limitation is prescribed for an individual who was not a signatory or a party to the earlier determination.

E FAM §160.610. JOINDER OF PROCEEDINGS

(a) Except as provided by Subsection (b), a proceeding to adjudicate parentage may be joined with a proceeding for adoption, termination of parental rights, possession of or access to a child, child support, divorce, annulment, or probate or administration of an estate or another appropriate proceeding.

(b) A respondent may not join a proceeding described by Subsection (a) with a proceeding to adjudicate parentage brought under Chapter 159.

History of Fam §160.610: Enacted by Acts 2001, 77th Leg., ch. 821, §1.01, eff. June 14, 2001.

Official Comment

Source: UPA (1973) §8.

Joinder of paternity proceedings with related matters is common, especially when a child support agency seeks to establish paternity and fix child support.

Subsection (b) restricts counterclaims in those instances in which an initiating State sends a paternity suit to the responding State. Because petitioner is "appearing" in the other forum, to permit counterclaims would serve as a major deterrent to bringing such proceedings. This bar does not prevent a separate action for such matters, but there must be independent jurisdiction not arising from the petitioner's appearance in the paternity proceeding.

E FAM §160.611. PROCEEDINGS BEFORE BIRTH

(a) A proceeding to determine parentage commenced before the birth of the child may not be concluded until after the birth of the child.

(b) In a proceeding described by Subsection (a), the following actions may be taken before the birth of the child:

(1) service of process;

(2) discovery; and

(3) except as prohibited by Section 160.502, collection of specimens for genetic testing.

History of Fam §160.611: Enacted by Acts 2001, 77th Leg., ch. 821, §1.01, eff. June 14, 2001.

Official Comment

This section recognizes that establishing a parental relationship as quickly as possible may be in the best interest of a child. To facilitate that process, some initial steps may be completed prior to the birth of the child.

E FAM §160.612. CHILD AS PARTY; REPRESENTATION

(a) A minor child is a permissible party, but is not a necessary party to a proceeding under this subchapter.

(b) The court shall appoint an attorney ad litem to represent a child who is a minor or is incapacitated if the child is a party or the court finds that the interests of the child are not adequately represented.

History of Fam §160.612: Enacted by Acts 2001, 77th Leg., ch. 821, §1.01, eff. June 14, 2001.

Official Comment

This section rejects UPA (1973) §9. Consistent with §603, *supra*, this Act rejects the view that the child necessarily has independent standing in a parentage proceeding. On the other hand, if the court determines that the child in fact does have a position at variance with all the other litigants, an attorney may be appointed to represent that interest.

Sections 160.613-160.620 reserved for expansion

E FAM §160.621. ADMISSIBILITY OF RESULTS OF GENETIC TESTING; EXPENSES

(a) Except as otherwise provided by Subsection (c), a report of a genetic testing expert is admissible as evidence of the truth of the facts asserted in the report. The admissibility of the report is not affected by whether the testing was performed:

(1) voluntarily or under an order of the court or a support enforcement agency; or

(2) before or after the date of commencement of the proceeding.

(b) A party objecting to the results of genetic testing may call one or more genetic testing experts to testify in person or by telephone, videoconference, deposition, or another method approved by the court. Unless otherwise ordered by the court, the party offering the testimony bears the expense for the expert testifying.

(c) If a child has a presumed, acknowledged, or adjudicated father, the results of genetic testing are inadmissible to adjudicate parentage unless performed:

(1) with the consent of both the mother and the presumed, acknowledged, or adjudicated father; or

(2) under an order of the court under Section 160.502.

(d) Copies of bills for genetic testing and for prenatal and postnatal health care for the mother and child that are furnished to the adverse party on or before the 10th day before the date of a hearing are admissible to establish:

(1) the amount of the charges billed; and

(2) that the charges were reasonable, necessary, and customary.

History of Fam §160.621: Enacted by Acts 2001, 77th Leg., ch. 821, §1.01, eff. June 14, 2001.

Official Comment

Source: 42 U.S.C. §666(a)(5)(F)(ii).

Justification for additional testing is provided by subsection (a). If the objecting party can state with specificity the grounds for rejecting a genetic test, and those grounds cannot be clarified under Article 5, retesting should be ordered. For example, if the chain of custody is seriously flawed, or the testing laboratory is not accredited, errors of this sort may be corrected by collecting new specimens and repeating the testing. Unlike the samples collected in a potential criminal proceeding which cannot be replaced, such as a blood alcohol test, the samples in a paternity proceedings remain the same no matter when, or how often, the samples are collected. Any flaw in the original test can be corrected by collection of new samples and additional testing of the individuals.

E FAM §160.622. CONSEQUENCES OF DECLINING GENETIC TESTING

(a) An order for genetic testing is enforceable by contempt.

(b) A court may adjudicate parentage contrary to the position of an individual whose paternity is being determined on the grounds that the individual declines to submit to genetic testing as ordered by the court.

(c) Genetic testing of the mother of a child is not a prerequisite to testing the child and a man whose paternity is being determined. If the mother is unavailable or declines to submit to genetic testing, the court may order the testing of the child and each man whose paternity is being adjudicated.

History of Fam §160.622: Enacted by Acts 2001, 77th Leg., ch. 821, §1.01, eff. June 14, 2001.

Official Comment

Source: UPA (1973) §10.

E FAM §160.623. ADMISSION OF PATERNITY AUTHORIZED

(a) A respondent in a proceeding to adjudicate parentage may admit to the paternity of a child by filing a pleading to that effect or by admitting paternity under penalty of perjury when making an appearance or during a hearing.

(b) If the court finds that the admission of paternity satisfies the requirements of this section and that there is no reason to question the admission, the court shall render an order adjudicating the child to be the child of the man admitting paternity.

History of Fam §160.623: Enacted by Acts 2001, 77th Leg., ch. 821, §1.01, eff. June 14, 2001.

Official Comment

Source: 42 U.S.C. 666(a)(5)(D)(i)(II).

E FAM §160.624. TEMPORARY ORDER

(a) In a proceeding under this subchapter, the court shall render a temporary order for child support for a child if the order is appropriate and the individual ordered to pay child support:

(1) is a presumed father of the child;

(2) is petitioning to have his paternity adjudicated;

(3) is identified as the father through genetic testing under Section 160.505;

(4) is an alleged father who has declined to submit to genetic testing;

(5) is shown by clear and convincing evidence to be the father of the child; or

(6) is the mother of the child.

(b) A temporary order may include provisions for the possession of or access to the child as provided by other laws of this state.

History of Fam §160.624: Enacted by Acts 2001, 77th Leg., ch. 821, §1.01, eff. June 14, 2001.

Official Comment

Source: UIFSA (1996) §401; 42 U.S.C. 666(a)(5)(J).

Sections 160.625-160.630 reserved for expansion

E FAM §160.631. RULES FOR ADJUDICATION OF PATERNITY

(a) The court shall apply the rules stated in this section to adjudicate the paternity of a child.

(b) The paternity of a child having a presumed, acknowledged, or adjudicated father may be disproved only by admissible results of genetic testing excluding that man as the father of the child or identifying another man as the father of the child.

(c) Unless the results of genetic testing are admitted to rebut other results of genetic testing, the man identified as the father of a child under Section 160.505 shall be adjudicated as being the father of the child.

(d) Unless the results of genetic testing are admitted to rebut other results of genetic testing, a man excluded as the father of a child by genetic testing shall be adjudicated as not being the father of the child.

(e) If the court finds that genetic testing under Section 160.505 does not identify or exclude a man as the father of a child, the court may not dismiss the proceeding. In that event, the results of genetic testing and other evidence are admissible to adjudicate the issue of paternity.

History of Fam §160.631: Enacted by Acts 2001, 77th Leg., ch. 821, §1.01, eff. June 14, 2001.

Official Comment

Source: UPA (1973) §14.

This section establishes the controlling supremacy of admissible genetic test results in the adjudication of paternity. Other matters such as statute of limitations, equitable estoppel and res judicata may preclude the matter from reaching trial or the court denying genetic testing. However, if test results are admissible, those results control unless other test results create a conflict rebutting the admitted results.

Paragraph (3) is included to insure that the fact a genetic test does not reach the 99% level decreed in Section 505 will not be perceived as an indicator of an exclusion of paternity. Although test results that do not reach that level do not create a presumption of paternity, the testing should be evaluated as an indicator of paternity along with the other evidence of paternity presented in the proceeding. Presumably expert testimony will be required to provide information about the measure of the weight of a test that does not achieve "at least a 99 percent probability of paternity, using a prior probability of 0.50, as calculated by using the combined paternity index obtained in the testing, and a combined paternity index of at least 100 to 1."

The inclusion of the first clause in paragraph (4) indicates that although a genetic testing exclusion of paternity can be absolute, errors (and sometimes fraud) may occur in testing. Some courts have imposed a rule that a party must first show the test is in error before ordering another test. This imposes an impossible burden because the only accurate method to show that a test is in error is to repeat the testing. Without this clause, some litigants might argue that once an exclusion is obtained it is absolute and no other test can be ordered, even when the first test is shown to be wrong.

E FAM §160.632. JURY PROHIBITED

The court shall adjudicate paternity of a child without a jury.

History of Fam §160.632: Enacted by Acts 2001, 77th Leg., ch. 821, §1.01, eff. June 14, 2001.

Official Comment

Source: 42 U.S.C. §666(a)(5)(I), requiring state law to provide that "parties to an action to establish paternity are not entitled to trial by jury…."

UPA (1973) §14[(d)] prohibited jury trials in parentage proceedings on the basis that "The use of a jury is not desirable in the emotional atmosphere of cases of this nature." Congress agreed when it enacted an effectively identical prohibition in PRWORA (1996).

E FAM §160.633. HEARINGS; INSPECTION OF RECORDS

(a) On the request of a party and for good cause shown, the court may order a proceeding under this subchapter closed to the public.

(b) A final order in a proceeding under this subchapter is available for public inspection. Other papers and records are available only with the consent of the parties or on order of the court for good cause.

History of Fam §160.633: Enacted by Acts 2001, 77th Leg., ch. 821, §1.01, eff. June 14, 2001.

Official Comment

Source: UPA (1973) §20.

UPA (1973) §20 was concerned with the privacy of the parties in a paternity proceeding and required closure of the proceedings. The high caseload and the desensitizing of such proceedings, however, lead to the conclusion that mandating closure of the proceedings is no longer appropriate.

E FAM §160.634. ORDER ON DEFAULT

The court shall issue an order adjudicating the paternity of a man who:

(1) after service of process, is in default; and

(2) is found by the court to be the father of a child.

History of Fam §160.634: Enacted by Acts 2001, 77th Leg., ch. 821, §1.01, eff. June 14, 2001.

Official Comment

Source: 42 U.S.C. 666(a)(5)(H).

E FAM §160.635. DISMISSAL FOR WANT OF PROSECUTION

The court may issue an order dismissing a proceeding commenced under this chapter for want of prosecution only without prejudice. An order of dismissal for want of prosecution purportedly with prejudice is void and has only the effect of a dismissal without prejudice.

History of Fam §160.635: Enacted by Acts 2001, 77th Leg., ch. 821, §1.01, eff. June 14, 2001.

Official Comment

A major principle of UPA (2000) – and its predecessor – is that the child's right to have a determination of paternity is fundamental. This new section confirms this right by declaring that the delinquency of another person in prosecuting such a proceeding may not permanently preclude the ultimate conclusion of that determination.

FAM §160.636. ORDER ADJUDICATING PARENTAGE; COSTS

(a) The court shall render an order adjudicating whether a man alleged or claiming to be the father is the parent of the child.

(b) An order adjudicating parentage must identify the child by name and date of birth.

(c) Except as otherwise provided by Subsection (d), the court may assess filing fees, reasonable attorney's fees, fees for genetic testing, other costs, and necessary travel and other reasonable expenses incurred in a proceeding under this subchapter. Attorney's fees awarded by the court may be paid directly to the attorney. An attorney who is awarded attorney's fees may enforce the order in the attorney's own name.

(d) The court may not assess fees, costs, or expenses against the support enforcement agency of this state or another state, except as provided by other law.

(e) On request of a party and for good cause shown, the court may order that the name of the child be changed.

(f) If the order of the court is at variance with the child's birth certificate, the court shall order the bureau of vital statistics to issue an amended birth record.

(g) On a finding of parentage, the court may order retroactive child support as provided by Chapter 154 and, on a proper showing, order a party to pay an equitable portion of all of the prenatal and postnatal health care expenses of the mother and the child.

(h) In rendering an order for retroactive child support under this section, the court shall use the child support guidelines provided by Chapter 154, together with any relevant factors.

History of Fam §160.636: Enacted by Acts 2001, 77th Leg., ch. 821, §1.01, eff. June 14, 2001.

Official Comment

Source: UIFSA (1996) §313; UPA (1973) §§15, 16; 23.

This Act differs from UPA (1973), which attempted to do more than merely establish parentage. For example, UPA (1973) §15 provided for a wide range of court orders to be made relating to the child's support, custody, guardianship, visitation privileges, as well as to the payment by the father of the mother's expenses of pregnancy and confinement. This Act leaves such matters to other state law. Only in instances where other state law is likely to be inadequate does this Act specify special treatment for litigants. For example, subsections (c) and (d) may be required because ordinary civil litigation probably does not provide for the court to apportion the costs of litigation among the parties.

FAM §160.637. BINDING EFFECT OF DETERMINATION OF PARENTAGE

(a) Except as otherwise provided by Subsection (b) or Section 160.316, a determination of parentage is binding on:

(1) all signatories to an acknowledgment or denial of paternity as provided by Subchapter D; and

(2) all parties to an adjudication by a court acting under circumstances that satisfy the jurisdictional requirements of Section 159.201.

(b) A child is not bound by a determination of parentage under this chapter unless:

(1) the determination was based on an unrescinded acknowledgment of paternity and the acknowledgment is consistent with the results of genetic testing;

(2) the adjudication of parentage was based on a finding consistent with the results of genetic testing and the consistency is declared in the determination or is otherwise shown; or

(3) the child was a party or was represented in the proceeding determining parentage by an attorney ad litem.

(c) In a proceeding to dissolve a marriage, the court is considered to have made an adjudication of the parentage of a child if the court acts under circumstances that satisfy the jurisdictional requirements of Section 159.201, and the final order:

(1) expressly identifies the child as "a child of the marriage" or "issue of the marriage" or uses similar words indicating that the husband is the father of the child; or

(2) provides for the payment of child support for the child by the husband unless paternity is specifically disclaimed in the order.

(d) Except as otherwise provided by Subsection (b), a determination of parentage may be a defense in a subsequent proceeding seeking to adjudicate parentage by an individual who was not a party to the earlier proceeding.

(e) A party to an adjudication of paternity may challenge the adjudication only under the laws of this state relating to appeal, the vacating of judgments, or other judicial review.

History of Fam §160.637: Enacted by Acts 2001, 77th Leg., ch. 821, §1.01, eff. June 14, 2001.

Official Comment

A considerable amount of litigation involves exactly who is bound and who is not bound by a final order determining parentage. This section codifies rules regarding the effect of such orders. Subsection (a) provides that, if the order is issued under standards of personal jurisdiction of the UIFSA (1996), the order is binding on all parties to the proceeding. This solves the problem of an order issued without the appropriate jurisdiction, as would be the case of a divorce based on status jurisdiction in which the court lacked the requisite personal jurisdiction over a nonresident party.

Subsection (b) partially resolves the question whether a child is bound by the terms of the order. UPA (1973) required that the child be made a party to a parentage proceeding, and be bound. However, the 1973 Act did not address whether a divorce decree had a legal impact on paternity. A majority of jurisdictions holds that the child is not bound by the divorce decree because the child was not a party to the proceeding. A minority of States holds that the child is bound by the order and that the child is in privity with the parents. In its present formulation, this subsection adopts the majority rule, which does not bind the child during minority unless the parentage order is based on genetic testing or the child was represented by an ad litem.

Subsection (c) resolves whether a divorce decree constitutes a finding of paternity. This subsection provides that a decree is a determination of paternity if the decree states that the child was born of the marriage or grants the husband visitation or custody, or orders support. This is the majority rule in American jurisprudence.

Subsection (d) gives protection to third parties who may claim benefit of an earlier determination of parentage

Finally, the section is silent on whether state IV-D agencies are bound by prior determinations of parentage. This controversial issue is left to other state law. Similarly, issues of collateral attack on final judgments are to be resolved by recourse to other state law, as in civil proceedings generally.

Sections 160.638-160.700 reserved for expansion

E SUBCHAPTER H. CHILD OF ASSISTED REPRODUCTION

Official Prefatory Comment

Medical science has developed a wide range of assisted reproductive technologies, often referred to as ARTS, which enable childless couples to become parents. Thousands of children are born in the United States each year as the result of ARTS. If a married couple uses their own eggs and sperm to conceive a child born by the wife, the parentage of the child is straightforward. The wife is the mother – by gestation and genetics, the husband is the father – by genetics and presumption, and, insofar as UPA (2000) is concerned, neither fits the definition of a "donor."

If, using assisted reproduction, a wife gives birth to a child conceived using sperm from a man other than her husband, she is the mother and her husband is the presumed father. However, the man providing the sperm might assert his biological paternity, or the husband might seek to rebut the martial presumption of paternity by proving through genetic testing that he is not the genetic father. As was the case in UPA (1973), it is necessary for UPA (2000) to establish the parentage of a child born under these circumstances.

Similarly, assisted reproduction may involve the eggs from a woman other than the wife – perhaps using the husband's sperm, perhaps not. In either event, the Act must clearly exclude the egg donor from claiming maternity. Theoretically, it is even possible that absent legislation the wife could attempt to deny maternity based on her lack of genetic relationship.

Finally, a very common ARTS procedure mixes sperm and eggs to form a pre-zygote that is then frozen for future use. If the couple later divorce or one of them dies, the disposition of these pre-zygotes can be a potential problem on which courts need guidance.

E FAM §160.701. SCOPE OF SUBCHAPTER

This subchapter applies only to a child conceived by means of assisted reproduction.

History of Fam §160.701: Enacted by Acts 2001, 77th Leg., ch. 821, §1.01, eff. June 14, 2001.

Official Comment

Article 7 applies only to children born as the result of assisted reproduction technologies; a child conceived by sexual intercourse is not covered by this article, irrespective of the alleged intent of the parties. The bracketed clause relates to gestational agreements under Article 8. If a State enacts Article 8, the brackets should be removed. If a State does not enact Article 8, the bracketed subsection should be omitted.

E FAM §160.702. PARENTAL STATUS OF DONOR

A donor is not a parent of a child conceived by means of assisted reproduction.

History of Fam §160.702: Enacted by Acts 2001, 77th Leg., ch. 821, §1.01, eff. June 14, 2001.

Official Comment

Source: UPA (1973) §5(b); USCACA (1988) §4(a).

If a child is conceived as the result of assisted reproduction, this section clarifies that a donor (whether of sperm or egg) is not a parent of the resulting child. The donor can neither sue to establish parental rights, nor be sued and required to support the resulting child. In sum, donors are eliminated from the parental equation.

UPA (2000) does not deal with many of the complex and serious legal problems raised by the practice of assisted reproduction. Issues such as ownership and disposition of embryos, regulation of the medical procedures, insurance coverage, etc., are left to other statutes or common law. Only the issue of parentage falls within the purview of this Act. This was also the case in UPA (1973), which wholly deferred speaking on the subject except to insure the husband's paternal responsibility when he gave his consent to what was then called "artificial insemination" of his wife (now known in the scientific community as "intrauterine insemination"). The commentary to UPA (1973) stated: "It was thought useful, however, to single out and cover ... at least one fact situation that occurs frequently."

UPA (2000) goes well beyond that narrow view; it governs the parentage issues in all cases in which the birth mother is also the intended mother of the child. It also insures that if the mother is a married woman, her husband will be the father of the child if he gives his consent to assisted reproduction by his wife, no matter which aspect of the technology is utilized. UPA (1973) §5(b) specified that a male donor would not be considered the father of a child born of artificial insemination if the sperm was provided to a licensed physician for use in artificial insemination of a married woman other than the donor's wife. The Act does not continue the requirement that the donor provide the sperm to a licensed physician.

This section of UPA (2000) further opts not to limit nonparenthood of a donor to situations in which the donor provides sperm for assisted reproduction by a married woman. This requirement is not realistic in light of present practices in the field of assisted reproduction. Instead, donors are to be shielded from parenthood in all situations in which either a married woman or a single woman conceives a child through assisted reproduction. If a married woman bears a child of assisted reproduction using a donor's sperm, the donor will not be the father in any event. Her husband will be the father unless and until the husband's lack of consent to the assisted reproduction is proven within two years of his learning of the birth, *see* §705, *infra*. This provides certainty of nonparentage for prospective donors. The Comment to USCACA §4(a) states that "nonparenthood is also provided for those donors who provide sperm for assisted reproduction by unmarried women." Under those circumstances—called a "relatively rare situation" in the 1988 Comment—"the child would have no legally recognized father." This result is retained in UPA (2000), although the frequency of unmarried women using assisted reproduction appears to have grown significantly since 1988.

The definition of "donor" in Section 102(8), *supra*, includes persons who provide either sperm or eggs for assisted reproduction. Thus, if a woman provides an egg for assisted reproduction that results in another woman bearing the child, the egg donor is not the child's mother. This does not create a burden on the child because §201(a)(1), *supra*, declares the general rule that the woman who gives birth to a child is that child's mother. It is clear, however, that a wife who provides eggs for her own conception and a husband who provides sperm for use by his wife in assisted reproduction are not "donors" as defined in Section 102(8).

E FAM §160.703. HUSBAND'S PATERNITY OF CHILD OF ASSISTED REPRODUCTION

If a husband provides sperm for or consents to assisted reproduction by his wife as provided by Section 160.704, he is the father of a resulting child.

History of Fam §160.703: Enacted by Acts 2001, 77th Leg., ch. 821, §1.01, eff. June 14, 2001.

Official Comment

Source: UPA (1973) §5; USCACA (1988) §§1, 3.

The presumptive paternity of the husband of a married woman who bears a child through assisted reproduction reflects a concern for the best interests of the children of assisted reproduction. Of course, a husband who provides sperm for use by his wife in assisted reproduction is the father of any resulting child born to the wife. A similar result is mandated if his sperm is not used when he consents to assisted reproduction by his wife, see §704, *infra*.

Any uncertainty concerning the identity of the father of such a child ought to be shouldered by the married woman's husband rather than by the child. Thus, the husband (but not someone acting on his behalf, such as a guardian, administrator or executor) has the obligation to file an action aimed at denying paternity through lack of consent to the assisted reproduction rather than the child or mother having an obligation to prove the husband's paternity.

By designating the husband of a woman who bears a child through assisted reproduction as the father, it is intended that he will be considered the father for purposes of any cause of action that arises before the birth of the child. Thus, for example, he would be the father under any state law authorizing a wrongful death action for the death of an unborn child during pregnancy.

E FAM §160.704. CONSENT TO ASSISTED REPRODUCTION

(a) Consent by a married woman to assisted reproduction must be in a record signed by the woman and her husband. This requirement does not apply to the donation of eggs by a married woman for assisted reproduction by another woman.

(b) Failure by the husband to sign a consent required by Subsection (a) before or after the birth of the child does not preclude a finding that the husband is the father of a child born to his wife if the wife and husband openly treated the child as their own.

History of Fam §160.704: Enacted by Acts 2001, 77th Leg., ch. 821, §1.01, eff. June 14, 2001.

Official Comment

Source: UPA (1973) §5; UPC (1993) §2-114(c).

Subsection (a) continues the requirement that the husband consent to all forms of assisted reproduction. However, the wife is exempted from obtaining her husband's consent if she is acting as an egg donor for another woman.

Subsection (b) provides that even if a husband did not consent to assisted reproduction, he may nonetheless be found to be the father of a child born through that means if he and his wife openly treat the child as their own. This principle is taken from the Uniform Probate Code (1993) section cited above, which provides that neither natural parent (nor that natural parent's kindred) inherit from or through a child unless that natural parent, mother or father, has openly treated the child as his or hers and has not refused to support the child. The latter phrase was not carried forward to subsection (b).

E FAM §160.705. LIMITATION ON HUSBAND'S DISPUTE OF PATERNITY

(a) Except as otherwise provided by Subsection (b), the husband of a wife who gives birth to a child by means of assisted reproduction may not challenge his paternity of the child unless:

(1) before the fourth anniversary of the date of learning of the birth of the child he commences a proceeding to adjudicate his paternity; and

(2) the court finds that he did not consent to the assisted reproduction before or after the birth of the child.

(b) A proceeding to adjudicate paternity may be maintained at any time if the court determines that:

(1) the husband did not provide sperm for or, before or after the birth of the child, consent to assisted reproduction by his wife;

(2) the husband and the mother of the child have not cohabited since the probable time of assisted reproduction; and

(3) the husband never openly treated the child as his own.

(c) The limitations provided by this section apply to a marriage declared invalid after assisted reproduction.

History of Fam §160.705: Enacted by Acts 2001, 77th Leg., ch. 821, §1.01, eff. June 14, 2001.

Official Comment

[References in the Official Comment below to two-year limitations on commencing paternity proceedings are four years under §160.705(a)(1), above.]

Source: USCACA (1988) §3; UPC (1993) §2-114(c).

Subsection (a) provides for a challenge to a husband's presumed paternity if the conception of the child was through assisted reproduction not consented to by the husband before or after the birth of the child. If a proceeding to establish nonpaternity is timely filed and the husband's lack of consent is demonstrated, the child will be without a legally-recognized father because the sperm donor is not the father under §702, *supra*. Because the filing of such a nonpaternity proceeding is permitted within two years of the husband's learning of the child's birth, the period of uncertainty concerning the identity of the child's father will be longer than two years in a situation in which an absent husband is not immediately made aware of the child's birth.

Subsection (b) provides an exception to the two-year time limit if the husband's sperm was not used, the couple has not cohabited since the probable time of the use of assisted reproduction, and the husband has never openly treated the child as his own.

E FAM §160.706. EFFECT OF DISSOLUTION OF MARRIAGE

(a) If a marriage is dissolved before the placement of eggs, sperm, or embryos, the former spouse is not a parent of the resulting child unless the former spouse consented in a record that if assisted reproduction were to occur after a divorce the former spouse would be a parent of the child.

(b) The consent of a former spouse to assisted reproduction may be withdrawn by that individual in a record at any time before the placement of eggs, sperm, or embryos.

History of Fam §160.706: Enacted by Acts 2001, 77th Leg., ch. 821, §1.01, eff. June 14, 2001.

Official Comment

This section is entirely new, but is derived from the policy stated in Section 707, *infra*. If there is to be no liability for a child conceived after death, then there should be no liability for a child conceived or implanted after divorce. If the wife proceeds with assisted reproduction after a divorce, the former husband is *not the legal parent* of the resulting child unless he has consented in a record to post-divorce assisted reproduction. In such a case, the child will have a legal mother under Section 201(a)(1). The child will have a genetic father, but not a legal father. Intention, rather than biology, is the controlling factor. The section is intended to encourage careful drafting of assisted reproduction agreements. The attorney and the parties themselves should discuss the issue and clarify their intent before a problem arises.

This Act does not attempt to resolve issues as to control of frozen embryos following dissolution of marriage. Those matters are left to other state laws, usually in the context of settlement of divorce and regulation of health care facilities.

E FAM §160.707. PARENTAL STATUS OF DECEASED SPOUSE

If a spouse dies before the placement of eggs, sperm, or embryos, the deceased spouse is not a parent of the resulting child unless the deceased spouse consented in a record that if assisted reproduction were to occur after death the deceased spouse would be a parent of the child.

History of Fam §160.707: Enacted by Acts 2001, 77th Leg., ch. 821, §1.01, eff. June 14, 2001.

Official Comment

Source: USCACA (1988) §4.

Absent consent in a record, the death of a spouse whose genetic material is subsequently used either in conceiving an embryo or in implanting an already existing embryo into a womb ends the potential parenthood of the deceased. This section is designed primarily to avoid the problems of intestate succession which could arise if the posthumous use of a person's genetic material could lead to the deceased being determined to be a parent. Of course, a spouse who wants to explicitly provide for such children in his or her will may do so.

CHAPTER 160. DETERMINATION OF PARENTAGE

Chapter 160 below is effective for motions or other requests for relief made in parentage or paternity proceedings commenced before June 14, 2001.

SUBCHAPTER A. GENERAL PROVISIONS

FAM §160.001. APPLICABILITY

This chapter governs a suit affecting the parent-child relationship in which the parentage of the biological mother or biological father is:

(1) sought to be adjudicated;

(2) voluntarily admitted by the putative father; or

(3) jointly acknowledged by the mother and putative father.

History of Fam §160.001: Acts 1995, 74th Leg., ch. 20, §1, eff. April 20, 1995. Amended by Acts 1999, 76th Leg., ch. 556, §36, eff. Sept. 1, 1999. Deleted by Acts 2001, 77th Leg., ch. 821, §1.01, eff. June 14, 2001.

FAM §160.002. TIME IN WHICH TO BRING SUIT TO DETERMINE PARENTAGE

(a) A suit affecting the parent-child relationship to determine parentage under Subchapter B may be brought before the birth of the child, but must be brought on or before the second anniversary of the date the child becomes an adult, or the suit is barred.

(b) This section applies to a child for whom a parentage suit was brought but dismissed because a statute of limitations of less than 18 years was then in effect.

(c) Repealed by Acts 1999, 76th Leg., ch. 556, §81, eff. Sept. 1, 1999.

History of Fam §160.002: Acts 1995, 74th Leg., ch. 20, §1, eff. April 20, 1995. Amended by Acts 1999, 76th Leg., ch. 556, §81, eff. Sept. 1, 1999. Deleted by Acts 2001, 77th Leg., ch. 821, §1.01, eff. June 14, 2001. Source: Former Fam §13.01.

In re M.W.T., 12 S.W.3d 598, 604 (Tex.App.—San Antonio 2000, pet. denied). Presumed father "claims that [mother's] claims are barred by the doctrine of laches. [C]ourts have viewed the defense of laches as not being 'available in a suit for the enforcement of a statutory legal right....' Here, [mother] seeks relief under Chapter 160.... The defense of laches is unavailable to [presumed father]."

In re A.S.L., 923 S.W.2d 814, 817 (Tex.App.—Amarillo 1996, no writ). "Sections 160.001 et seq. ... clearly authorize bringing actions through which the parentage of a child born out of wedlock may be determined and thus evinces the intent of the legislature. As we have recited above, the statutes spell out circumstances in which such a suit may be brought and circumstances in which they are time barred. Significantly, among those time-barred instances, the legislature did not include actions brought after the death of the alleged parent."

FAM §160.003. NECESSARY PARTY: REPRESENTATION OF CHILD

(a) The child is not a necessary party to a suit under this chapter.

(b) It is rebuttably presumed in a trial on the merits before a judge or jury that the interests of the child will be adequately represented by the party bringing suit to determine parentage of the child. If the court finds that the interests of the child will not be adequately represented by a party to the suit or are adverse to that party, the court shall appoint an attorney ad litem to represent the child.

(c) The child shall be represented in a settlement agreement, dismissal, or nonsuit by a guardian ad litem or an attorney ad litem appointed by the court, unless the court finds on the record that the interests of the child will be adequately represented by a party to the suit or are not adverse to that party, and that the court approves the settlement agreement, dismissal, or nonsuit.

History of Fam §160.003: Acts 1995, 74th Leg., ch. 20, §1, eff. April 20, 1995. Deleted by Acts 2001, 77th Leg., ch. 821, §1.01, eff. June 14, 2001. Source: Former Fam §13.07.

Purcell v. Bellinger, 940 S.W.2d 599, 602 (Tex. 1997). "We note that under Texas law, the Family Code provides a rebuttable presumption that 'in a trial on the merits before a judge or jury ... the interests of the child will be adequately represented by the party bringing suit to establish parentage of the child.' Unless the child rebuts this presumption, a judgment in a prior paternity action by the mother bars any subsequent suit."

L.P.D. v. R.C., 959 S.W.2d 728, 731 (Tex.App.—Austin 1998, pet. denied). "When there is no person before the court who has had care and custody of the child, or understands the child's interests through another relationship, or even professes to have met the child, we hold the presumption that the party bringing suit will adequately represent the child's interest has been rebutted as a matter of law. *At 731 n.2:* [I]t is questionable whether the statutory presumption even applies ... where judgment was had by default. The statutory presumption applies in a *trial* on the merits."

B.M.L. v. Cooper, 919 S.W.2d 855, 860-61 (Tex. App.—Austin 1996, no writ). "The Texas cases appear to favor, within reason, children having an opportunity to pursue their own interests in establishing paternity. Though Texas society also benefits by protecting citizens from repetitive and harassing lawsuits, its fiscal, emotional, and informational interests in establishing paternity can outweigh the societal interests in finality of judgments. This conclusion is more compelling as the science of blood-testing in tandem with DNA-screening becomes more precise and dispositive; the burden on alleged fathers of submitting to a second blood draw is minimal compared to the weighty burdens on children of living without knowing who their fathers are. With these added burdens, children (and their representatives) have greater incentive to pursue the suit brought explicitly for the child. Though the Family Code presumes that a statutorily authorized petitioner in a paternity suit will represent the child's interests, the balance of these burdens mandates that courts be particularly sensitive and responsive to evidence tending to rebut that presumption when considering a summary-judgment motion against the child's later suit."

FAM §160.004. TEMPORARY ORDERS

The court may render a temporary order authorized in a suit under this title, including an order for temporary support of a child, if the person ordered to pay support:

(1) is a presumed parent under Chapter 151;

(2) is an alleged father petitioning to have his paternity adjudicated or who admits paternity in pleadings filed with the court;

(3) is found by the court at the pretrial conference authorized by this chapter not to be excluded as the biological father of the child, with the court finding that at least 99 percent of the male population is excluded from being the biological father of the child; or

(4) executed a statement or acknowledgment of paternity under Subchapter C.

History of Fam §160.004: Acts 1995, 74th Leg., ch. 20, §1, eff. April 20, 1995. Amended by Acts 1999, 76th Leg., ch. 556, §36, eff. Sept. 1, 1999. Deleted by Acts 2001, 77th Leg., ch. 821, §1.01, eff. June 14, 2001. Source: Former Fam §§12.06(c), 13.04(f), 13.42(a), (d).

In re Gonzalez, 993 S.W.2d 147, 154 (Tex.App.—San Antonio 1999, no pet.). "The Family Code permits a trial court to order temporary child support in a parentage case before a final determination of parentage is made. [Alleged father] correctly observes that §160.004 says nothing about awarding retroactive support."

FAM §160.005. CONSERVATORSHIP, SUPPORT, & PAYMENTS

(a) In a suit in which a determination of parentage is sought, the court may provide for the managing and possessory conservatorship and support of and access to the child.

☠ Ⓐ *Subsection (b) below was amended by Acts 2001, 77th Leg., ch. 1023, §45, effective Sept. 1, 2001, and Acts 2001, 77th Leg., ch. 392, §2, effective Sept. 1, 2001, without reference to the conflicting deletion made by Acts 2001, 77th Leg., ch. 821, §1.01, effective June 14, 2001. To the extent of any conflict between this amendment and chapter 160 as enacted by Acts 2001, 77th Leg., ch. 821, §1.01, effective June 14, 2001, chapter 160 pre-*

vails. See also §160.002. Subsection (b) below is effective for SAPCRs commenced on or after Sept. 1, 2001, and suits for child support or motions to enforce child support filed on or after Sept. 1, 2001.

(b) Except as provided under Section 154.131, on a finding of parentage, the court may order support retroactive to the time of the birth of the child and, on a proper showing, may order a party to pay an equitable portion of all prenatal and postnatal health care expenses of the mother and child.

Subsection (b) below is effective for SAPCRs commenced before Sept. 1, 2001, and suits for child support or motions to enforce child support filed before Sept. 1, 2001.

(b) On a finding of parentage, the court may order support retroactive to the time of the birth of the child and, on a proper showing, may order a party to pay an equitable portion of all prenatal and postnatal health care expenses of the mother and child.

(c) In making an order for retroactive child support under this section, the court shall use the child support guidelines provided by Chapter 154 together with any relevant factors.

History of Fam §160.005: Acts 1995, 74th Leg., ch. 20, §1, eff. April 20, 1995. Amended by Acts 2001, 77th Leg., ch. 392, §2 (eff. Sept. 1, 2001), ch. 1023, §45 (eff. Sept. 1, 2001). Deleted by Acts 2001, 77th Leg., ch. 821, §1.01, eff. June 14, 2001. Source: Former Fam §13.42(a).

In re Gonzalez, 993 S.W.2d 147, 154 (Tex.App.—San Antonio 1999, no pet.). "Section 160.005 provides that a court may order retroactive support upon 'a finding of parentage.' ... Because the trial court clearly made a final determination of parentage at the pre-trial conference, it was authorized to award retroactive support."

In re Valadez, 980 S.W.2d 910, 912-13 (Tex.App.—Corpus Christi 1998, no pet.). "Section 160.005(b) says, 'On a finding of parentage, *the court may* order support retroactive to the time of the birth of the child....' The following subsection provides, 'In making an order for retroactive child support under this section, *the court shall use* the child support guidelines provided by Chapter 154 together with any relevant factor.' [¶] Regarding retroactive child support, §154.131(a) states, '[t]he child support guidelines are intended *to guide the court* in determining the amount of retroactive child support, if any, to be ordered.' We agree ... that the guidelines are just that when applied to retroactive support; they are not mandatory, and §154.130(a)(3) & (b) requiring the court to specify why they are not being followed does not apply."

In re S.E.W., 960 S.W.2d 954, 955 (Tex.App.—Texarkana 1998, no pet.). "The terms of [§160.005] are not mandatory, and the trial court is thus empowered to exercise its discretion in ordering an unwilling parent to pay retroactive child support and an equitable portion of other specified expenses."

FAM §160.006. FINAL ORDER REGARDING PARENTAGE

(a) On a verdict of the jury, or on a finding of the court if there is no jury, the court shall render a final order declaring whether an alleged parent is the biological parent of the child.

(b) The effect of an order declaring that an alleged parent is the biological parent of the child is to confirm or create the parent-child relationship between the parent and the child for all purposes.

(c) If parentage is established, the order shall state the name of the child.

History of Fam §160.006: Renumbered from §§13.08, 13.09, 13.43(d) by Acts 1995, 74th Leg., ch. 20, §1, eff. April 20, 1995. Deleted by Acts 2001, 77th Leg., ch. 821, §1.01, eff. June 14, 2001. Source: Former Fam §§13.08, 13.09, 13.43(d).

In re M.W.T., 12 S.W.3d 598, 601 (Tex.App.—San Antonio 2000, pet. denied). "According to [presumed father], 'no provision of the Texas Family Code authorizes a paternity action that essentially does nothing more than ratify a pre-existing presumption of paternity.' We disagree. *At 602:* Section 160.006(b) states that '[t]he effect of an order declaring that an alleged parent is the biological parent of the child is *to confirm or create* the parent-child relationship between the parent and the child for all purposes.' The plain language of the statute contemplates the possibility that an acknowledged parent-child relationship may be the subject of a judicial decree."

In re Gonzalez, 993 S.W.2d 147, 161 (Tex.App.—San Antonio 1999, no pet.). Alleged father "argues ... that the trial court was not authorized to change [daughter's] name to include [his] because she is a Mexican citizen. No authority is cited for this argument. The effect of a final judgment in a paternity case is to establish a parent-child relationship 'for all purposes.' If paternity is established, the judgment must state the name of the child."

In re J.D.G., 940 S.W.2d 246, 247-48 (Tex.App.—San Antonio 1997, no pet.). "We find no authority requiring that the court's order establishing paternity also include a finding on whether to change the surname of the child. The plain language of [§160.006(c)] requires only 'the name of the child,' which is clearly set forth in the order before us."

FAM §160.007. SUIT BARRED

(a) Except as provided by Subsection (b), a suit under this chapter with respect to a child is barred if final judgment has been rendered by a court of competent jurisdiction:

(1) adjudicating a named individual to be the biological father of the child; or

(2) terminating the parent-child relationship between the child and each living parent of the child; or

(3) granting a petition for the adoption of the child.

(b) During the pendency of an appeal or direct attack on a judgment described by Subsection (a), a suit under this chapter may be filed but shall, on motion of a party, be stayed pending the final disposition of the appeal or direct attack on the judgment.

History of Fam §160.007: Acts 1995, 74th Leg., ch. 20, §1, eff. April 20, 1995. Deleted by Acts 2001, 77th Leg., ch. 821, §1.01, eff. June 14, 2001. Source: Former Fam §13.44.

Texas DPRS v. Sherry, 46 S.W.3d 857, 860 (Tex.2001). DPRS "argues that [alleged father's] paternity suit is barred by chapter 160 ... because [child's] paternity was previously adjudicated by a court of competent jurisdiction. [Alleged father] responds that he did not receive notice of the first paternity adjudication, and that he has a constitutional right to attempt to establish his paternity. We agree with [the DPRS]. [¶] Section 160.007(a)(1) bars a paternity suit 'if final judgment has been rendered by a court of competent jurisdiction: (1) adjudicating a named individual to be the biological father of the child.' The parties do not dispute that §160.007's requirements were satisfied."

Purcell v. Bellinger, 940 S.W.2d 599, 602 (Tex. 1997). "We note that under Texas law, the Family Code provides a rebuttable presumption that 'in a trial on the merits before a judge or jury ... the interests of the child will be adequately represented by the party bringing suit to establish parentage of the child.' Unless the child rebuts this presumption, a judgment in a prior paternity action by the mother bars any subsequent suit."

Dreyer v. Greene, 871 S.W.2d 697, 697-98 (Tex. 1993). "The issue we address in this case is whether a finding in a divorce decree that the husband and wife are parents of certain children bars a later action by the children to establish that someone else is their biological father. [¶] In her divorce petition, [mother] alleged under oath that she and her husband ... were the parents of three children 'of this marriage'. [Husband] did not answer the petition, and the trial court rendered judgment by default. [¶] [Mother] contends that the trial court's findings do not bar this action by her twin sons. The finding that [husband] was the parent of the children, she argues, is not an adjudication that he is their biological father because a man can be the parent of a child without being the biological father. While this argument is certainly correct, it ignores the context of the trial court's finding in this case. The court found that [mother] and [husband] were the 'parents' of their children. It is implausible that the court would have chosen this single word to refer, without qualification or explanation, to both the biological relationship between [mother] and the children and some other relationship involving [husband]. ... We conclude that the trial court's findings constitute an adjudication that [husband] was the biological father.... Since there is no question that the trial court had jurisdiction to make this determination, it operates as a bar under §13.44 [now §160.007] to the present action."

Sections 160.008-160.100 reserved for expansion

SUBCHAPTER B. PARENTAGE SUIT

FAM §160.101. DENIAL OF PATERNITY

(a) The presumption that a man is the biological father of a child under Chapter 151 may be contested by:

(1) the biological mother of the child;

(2) a person related within the second degree of consanguinity to the biological mother of the child, if the biological mother of the child is deceased;

(3) a man presumed to be the father of the child, who may contest his own or another man's presumed paternity;

(4) a man alleging himself to be the biological father of the child; or

(5) a governmental entity, authorized agency, or a licensed child-placing agency.

(b) A contest of paternity must be raised by an express statement denying paternity of the child in a party's pleadings in the suit, without regard to whether the presumed father or biological mother is a petitioner or respondent.

(c) In a suit in which a question of paternity is raised, the court shall conduct the pretrial proceedings and order scientifically accepted paternity testing as provided by this chapter.

History of Fam §160.101: Acts 1995, 74th Leg., ch. 20, §1, eff. April 20, 1995. Amended by Acts 1995, 74th Leg., ch. 751, §62, eff. Sept. 1, 1995; Acts 1997, 75th Leg., ch. 962, §1, eff. Sept. 1, 1997. Deleted by Acts 2001, 77th Leg., ch. 821, §1.01, eff. June 14, 2001. Source: Former Fam §12.06(a), (b).

In re B.I.V., 870 S.W.2d 12, 13 (Tex.1994). Mother "brought this suit against [alleged father] to establish his paternity of her child, B.I.V. [Alleged father] moved for summary judgment on the ground that the child had a presumed father, thus barring a paternity action as a matter of law.... The court of appeals ... held as a matter of law that a paternity action could not be filed if the child had a presumed father, and thus affirmed the trial court's decision to grant [alleged father's] summary judgment. [¶] We disagree with the holding of the court of appeals. [A] claim denying a presumed father's paternity of a child [can] be raised in the same suit raising a ... claim that another man is the biological father of that child. *At 13-14 n.1:* We note that under recent amendments to §12.06(a) [now §160.101(b)], [mother] is directed to include an express statement denying the presumed father's paternity of the child in her ... pleading. We also note that [TRCP 39] governs the question of whether joinder of the presumed father in a ... suit which includes an allegation denying the presumption of paternity as well as allegations attempting to establish paternity of a putative father is required. Rule 39 states that '[a] person ... shall be joined as a party in the action if ... (2) he claims an interest relating to the subject of the action and is so situated that the disposition of the action in his absence may (i) as a practical matter impair or impede his ability to protect that interest....'"

Davis v. Davis, 521 S.W.2d 603, 608 (Tex.1975). Lord Mansfield's Rule "has never prevented proof of non-access of spouses for a determination of illegitimacy of a child born or conceived during wedlock. The exclusion has only applied to testimony by the spouses themselves. Proof of illegitimacy has been made more difficult, but there is no rule of law that prevents the fact from being shown if other evidence is available. Regarding blindfolds on triers of fact with disfavor, and finding no justification for perpetuating this decree by Lord Mansfield, we hold that testimony of non-access between man and woman is admissible from any witness knowledgeable of the fact."

FAM §160.102. ORDER FOR PARENTAGE TESTING

(a) When the respondent appears in a parentage suit, the court shall order the mother, an alleged father, and the child to submit to the taking of blood, body fluid, or tissue samples for the purpose of scientifically accepted parentage testing.

(b) If the respondent fails to appear and wholly defaults or if the allegation of parentage is admitted, the court may waive parentage testing.

History of Fam §160.102: Acts 1995, 74th Leg., ch. 20, §1, eff. April 20, 1995. Deleted by Acts 2001, 77th Leg., ch. 821, §1.01, eff. June 14, 2001. Source: Former Fam §13.02(a), (d).

Villery v. Solomon, 16 S.W.3d 106, 109 (Tex. App.—Houston [1st Dist] 2000, no pet.). "The Family Code contemplates that blood tests, for the purpose of establishing paternity, will be conducted on the mother, the alleged father, and the child. The trial court was clearly saying that it would not make any assumptions based on the DNA report in light of the facts that no expert was presented to explain the report more fully and no DNA testing was done on the alleged father. *At 110:* The trial court, as the trier of fact, was the sole judge of the credibility of the witnesses and the weight to be given to the testimony. It is clear that the results of the DNA tests were not conclusive, and the trial court did not err in refusing to make any assumptions based on the DNA report."

In re J.D.G., 940 S.W.2d 246, 249 (Tex.App.—San Antonio 1997, no writ). "We find that under the circumstances where a statement of paternity has been filed, the trial court does not abuse its discretion in denying a request for blood tests at a later date. The district court had authority to review the family law master's decision and determine that blood tests were unnecessary when there was a clear admission of paternity."

FAM §160.103. REQUIREMENTS OF TESTING

The court shall require in its order testing necessary to ascertain the possibility of an alleged father's paternity and shall require that the tests exclude at least 99 percent of the male population from the possibility of being the father of the child, except that the court shall permit the omission of any further testing if the testing has been conducted sufficiently to establish that an alleged father is not the father of the child, or if the costs of testing have reached an amount that the court determines to be the greatest amount that may reasonably be borne by one or more parties to the suit. If the appearance is before the birth of the child, the court shall order the taking of blood, body fluid, or tissue samples to be made as soon as medically practical after the birth.

History of Fam §160.103: Acts 1995, 74th Leg., ch. 20, §1, eff. April 20, 1995. Deleted by Acts 2001, 77th Leg., ch. 821, §1.01, eff. June 14, 2001. Source: Former Fam §13.02(a).

FAM §160.104. APPOINTMENT OF EXPERTS

(a) The court shall:

(1) appoint one or more experts qualified in parentage testing to perform the tests;

(2) determine the number and qualifications of the experts; and

(3) prescribe the arrangements for conducting the tests.

(b) The court may:

(1) order a reasonable fee for each court-appointed expert; and

(2) require the fee to be paid by any or all of the parties in the amounts and in the manner directed or tax all, part, or none of the fee as costs in the suit.

(c) A party may employ other experts qualified in parentage testing. The court may order blood, body fluid, or tissue samples made available to these experts if requested.

History of Fam §160.104: Acts 1995, 74th Leg., ch. 20, §1, eff. April 20, 1995. Deleted by Acts 2001, 77th Leg., ch. 821, §1.01, eff. June 14, 2001. Source: Former Fam §13.03.

State ex rel. Latty v. Owens, 893 S.W.2d 728, 731 (Tex.App.—Texarkana 1995), *rev'd on other grounds*, 907 S.W.2d 484 (Tex.1995). Alleged father contends "the paternity expert was not identified in [mother's] answers to interrogatories and that the responses were not properly verified. [¶] In response, the State first argues that the paternity testing was improperly excluded because admission of the report is not contingent upon action of a party to the suit. The State contends that the court is required to order testing and, therefore, that the expert and testing results are offered by the trial court, not by the plaintiff. *At 732*: The master appointed the expert ... and this was approved by the trial court judge.... This expert was the court's expert rather than the State's. The State was, therefore, under no duty to disclose this expert witness. The name of the court-appointed paternity test expert, along with his address and telephone number, was listed on the test results. The court ordered that a copy of the test results be given to each party and the court. The paternity testing results were improperly excluded by the trial court."

FAM §160.105. PRETRIAL CONFERENCE

(a) After completion of parentage testing, the court shall order all parties to appear, either in person or by attorney, at a pretrial conference.

(b) Either party may call a parentage testing expert to testify in person or by deposition about the expert's tests and findings.

(c) A witness at a pretrial conference is governed by the Texas Rules of Civil Evidence.

(d) A verified written report of a parentage testing expert is admissible at the pretrial conference as evidence of the truth of the matters it contains.

(e) All evidence admitted at the pretrial conference is a part of the record of the case.

(f) Parentage test results offered at a pretrial conference are admissible as evidence if the tests were conducted under a court order or by agreement without regard to whether the tests were performed before or after the filing of a suit.

History of Fam §160.105: Acts 1995, 74th Leg., ch. 20, §1, eff. April 20, 1995. Deleted by Acts 2001, 77th Leg., ch. 821, §1.01, eff. June 14, 2001. Source: Former Fam §13.04(a)-(e), (g).

Murdock v. Murdock, 811 S.W.2d 557, 559-60 (Tex. 1991). "The court of appeals implies that because [alleged father] failed to object to the trial court's failure to conduct a pretrial hearing, he waived any right to take advantage of §13.04 [now §160.105] and §13.05 [now §160.106]. We disagree. [¶] The failure to conduct a hearing has no effect on the substantive rights of either the mother or alleged father. Such motion gives the trial court the opportunity to determine if the case warrants a full trial on the merits. However, the failure to seek a pretrial conference in no way prejudices the rights of the parties. [¶] Even though the trial judge should conduct the pretrial hearing, the absence of the hearing merely means that the alleged father has lost his opportunity to seek summary dismissal of the case thereby avoiding the expense and embarrassment of a trial."

FAM §160.106. EFFECT OF PARENTAGE TESTS

(a) At the conclusion of the pretrial conference, if the court finds that the tests show by clear and convincing evidence that an alleged or presumed father is not the father of the child, the court shall dismiss with prejudice the parentage suit as to that man.

(b) If the court finds that the parentage tests do not exclude an alleged father as the father of the child, the court shall set the suit for trial.

(c) If the court finds that at least 99 percent of the male population is excluded by the tests and that an alleged father is not excluded from the possibility of being the child's father, the burden of proof at trial is on the party opposing the establishment of the alleged father's parentage.

History of Fam §160.106: Acts 1995, 74th Leg., ch. 20, §1, eff. April 20, 1995. Deleted by Acts 2001, 77th Leg., ch. 821, §1.01, eff. June 14, 2001. Source: Former Fam §13.05.

Murdock v. Murdock, 811 S.W.2d 557, 559-60 (Tex. 1991). Section 13.05, now §160.106, "imposes a duty on the trial court to conduct the pretrial conference. [T]rial judges should be mindful of this duty. Even though the trial judge should conduct the pretrial hearing, the absence of the hearing merely means that the alleged father has lost his opportunity to seek summary dismissal of the case thereby avoiding the expense and embarrassment of a trial. [¶] Section 13.05 directs the trial court to dismiss the paternity suit if the alleged father can meet the burden of establishing nonpaternity by clear and convincing evidence. [¶] The court of appeals held that the blood test evidence was inconclusive of non-paternity because [alleged father] failed to establish that the tests had been properly conducted.... [¶] The 'properly conducted' requirement is subsumed within the evidentiary predicate that must be established *prior* to the admission of the test results into evidence. Once the trial court receives blood test results into evidence, they are admitted for all relevant purposes just like any other piece of evidence. In the present case, the test results were admitted into evidence without objection. From all of the test data, it was established that there was a zero probability of paternity. Thus, [alleged father] conclusively proved that he was not the father of the child and is entitled to judgment in his favor."

In re S.C.V., 750 S.W.2d 762, 765 (Tex.1988). See Annotation in FAM §160.101.

FAM §160.107. EFFECT OF REFUSING PARENTAGE TESTING

(a) An order for parentage testing is enforceable by contempt and:

(1) if the petitioner is the mother or an alleged father and refuses to submit to parentage testing, the court may dismiss the suit; or

(2) if a party refuses to submit to court-ordered parentage testing, on proof sufficient to render a default judgment the court may resolve the question of parentage against that party.

(b) If a parent or an alleged parent refuses to submit to parentage testing, the fact of refusal may be introduced as evidence as provided by this subchapter.

History of Fam §160.107: Acts 1995, 74th Leg., ch. 20, §1, eff. April 20, 1995. Deleted by Acts 2001, 77th Leg., ch. 821, §1.01, eff. June 14, 2001. Source: Former Fam §13.02(B), (c).

County of Alameda v. Smith, 867 S.W.2d 767, 769 (Tex.1993). "Should a party refuse testing, the trial court has several pretrial options: (1) enforcement through contempt; (2) dismissal of the suit if the petitioner is the party refusing testing; or (3) court resolution against the refusing party upon sufficient proof to render a default judgment. [¶] The trial court also may allow the case to proceed to trial. If the trial court does so, '[a] party who refuses to submit to paternity testing has the burden of proving that the alleged father is not the father of the child.'"

FAM §160.108. PREFERENTIAL TRIAL SETTING

(a) In a suit provided by this chapter, after a hearing the court shall grant a motion for a preferential setting for trial on the merits filed by a party to the suit or by the attorney or guardian ad litem for the child. The court shall give precedence to that trial over other civil cases if discovery has been completed or sufficient time has elapsed since the filing of the suit for the completion of all necessary and reasonable discovery if diligently pursued.

(b) The provisions of this section regarding preferential setting apply to trial on the merits without regard to whether the suit is set for a trial before the court or before a jury.

History of Fam §160.108: Acts 1995, 74th Leg., ch. 20, §1, eff. April 20, 1995. Deleted by Acts 2001, 77th Leg., ch. 821, §1.01, eff. June 14, 2001. Source: Former Fam §11.14(j).

FAM §160.109. EVIDENCE AT TRIAL

(a) A party may call a parentage testing expert to testify at the trial in person or by deposition.

(b) A verified written report of a parentage testing expert is admissible at the trial as evidence of the truth of the matters it contains.

(c) If the parentage tests show the possibility of an alleged father's paternity, the court shall admit this evidence if offered at the trial.

(d) Parentage test results offered at the trial shall be admissible as evidence if the tests were conducted under court order or by agreement, without regard to whether the tests were performed before or after the filing of a suit.

(e) The party seeking to establish an alleged father's paternity retains the right to open and close at trial without regard to whether the court has shifted the burden of proof to the opposing party.

(f) If a copy is provided to the adverse party and to the court at the pretrial conference, submission of a copy of a medical bill for the prenatal and postnatal health care expenses of the mother and child or for charges directly related to the parentage testing constitutes a prima facie showing that the charges are reasonable, necessary, and customary and may be admitted as evidence of the truth of the matters stated in the bill.

History of Fam §160.109: Acts 1995, 74th Leg., ch. 20, §1, eff. April 20, 1995. Deleted by Acts 2001, 77th Leg., ch. 821, §1.01, eff. June 14, 2001. Source: Former Fam §13.06(a)-(c), (f), (g).

In re J.A.M., 945 S.W.2d 320, 322 (Tex.App.—San Antonio 1997, no writ). In §160.109(b) "'the legislature has made verified written reports admissible to prove the truth of their contents even if they would otherwise be inadmissible hearsay. The offering party need only offer a report that is verified, in writing, and made by a paternity testing expert; there is no need to lay the business records predicate.'"

In re Martin, 881 S.W.2d 531, 535 (Tex.App.—Texarkana 1994, writ denied). Alleged father "contends that the trial court should not have admitted the paternity test into evidence because the proof did not establish that the test excluded 95% [now 99%]of the male population as required by §13.02 [now §160.103], §13.04 [now §160.004], and §13.06 [now §160.109 & §160.110]. The only one of these statutes that involves the admission of evidence is §13.06(c). [¶] The expert's written report stated that the tests given would exclude 98.22% of the male population. ... All that was required to make the test admissible was that it show the possibility of [alleged father's] paternity. [¶] Section 13.06(c),... states that, if the paternity test shows the possibility of paternity, the court may admit the evidence. The question of whether a particular percentage of the population was excluded is used to determine whether the test data constitute a prima facie showing, thus shifting the burden of proof to the defendant."

FAM §160.110. PRESUMPTIONS; BURDEN OF PROOF

(a) In a suit in which there is a presumption of parentage under Chapter 151, the party denying a presumed father's paternity of the child has the burden of rebutting the presumption of paternity by clear and convincing evidence.

(b) If the parentage tests show the possibility of an alleged father's paternity and that at least 99 percent of the male population is excluded from the possibility of being the father, evidence of these facts constitutes a prima facie showing of an alleged father's paternity, and the party opposing the establishment of the alleged father's paternity has the burden of proving that the alleged father is not the father of the child.

(c) A party who refuses to submit to parentage testing has the burden of proving that an alleged father is not the father of the child.

(d) The court shall dismiss with prejudice a claim regarding a presumed father whose paternity is excluded by scientifically accepted paternity testing.

(e) If two or more presumptions are in conflict, the presumption that is founded on the weightier considerations of policy and logic controls. The court shall find that the weightier presumption of paternity is that of a presumed father who is not excluded as the biological father of the child by scientifically accepted paternity testing that shows that at least 99 percent of the male population is excluded.

(f) The court shall dismiss a suit contesting a presumption of paternity filed by a man who is not a presumed father, but who alleges himself to be the biological father of a child, if:

(1) the suit is filed after the second anniversary of the later of:

(A) the date of birth of the child; or

(B) the time the presumption of paternity came into existence after the child was born; and

(2) the presumed father:

(A) has resided in the same household as the child in a father-child relationship or has established a father-child relationship with the child through his other actions; and

(B) requests an order designating him as the father of the child.

(g) A suit contesting a presumption that a man is the biological father of a child may be filed at any time during the minority of the child by:

(1) the biological mother of the child;

(2) a person related within the second degree of consanguinity to the biological mother of the child, if the biological mother of the child is deceased;

(3) a presumed father; or

(4) a governmental entity, authorized agency, or licensed child-placing agency.

(h) If a presumption of paternity is rebutted, the court shall enter an order finding that the man presumed to be the father of the child is not the biological father.

History of Fam §160.110: Acts 1995, 74th Leg., ch. 20, §1, eff. April 20, 1995. Amended by Acts 1995, 74th Leg., ch. 751, §63, eff. Sept. 1, 1995; Acts 1997, 75th Leg., ch. 962, §2, eff. Sept. 1, 1997. Deleted by Acts 2001, 77th Leg., ch. 821, §1.01, eff. June 14, 2001. Source: Former Fam §§12.02(b), 13.06(c), (d).

County of Alameda v. Smith, 867 S.W.2d 767, 769 (Tex.1993). "The court of appeals [held] that although [alleged father's] refusal to submit to paternity testing shifted to him the burden of proving that he is not the child's father, the state bears the burden of coming forward with evidence sufficient to support a default judgment. [¶] [Mother] argues that the court of appeals erred in reading §13.02(b) [now §160.107(a)(2)], which allows the trial court to resolve the case on evidence sufficient to support a default judgment, into §13.06(d) [now §160.110(c)], a burden shifting provision that, at trial, shifts the burden of proof to the party refusing testing. [Mother] contends that under §13.06(d) the alleged father's failure to submit to testing shifted to him the burden of proof on the issue of paternity which effectively created a presumption of fatherhood under §13.06(d).... We agree."

Garza v. Maverick Mkt., Inc., 768 S.W.2d 273, 276 (Tex.1989). "As to what evidence is clear and convincing, a fact finder must decide that question in each case. Blood tests, if available, may help show the alleged father's paternity. Evidence of physical resemblance of the child to the alleged father, either by photographs of the child and father, or by the offer of the child itself, is also admissible to determine paternity. In addition, prior statements by the alleged father that he was the father of the child, or other admissions by him bearing on his relationship to the child may be considered. A trial court can also consider evidence of periods of conception and gestation. Whether some or all of this evidence would rise to the level of clear and convincing evidence in a particular case cannot be predicted."

In re S.C.V., 750 S.W.2d 762, 764 (Tex.1988). "A blood test which positively excludes the alleged father is clear and convincing evidence of non-paternity."

In re J.A.M., 945 S.W.2d 320, 323 (Tex.App.—San Antonio 1997, no writ). "In §160.110(b), the term 'prima facie case' is equivalent to 'rebuttable presumption.' The prima facie case established by the [genetic] tests shifts the burden to the opposing party to disprove paternity. This burden-shifting effectively creates a presumption of paternity. Because contrary evidence can overcome the test results, the presumption is rebuttable rather than conclusive. [¶] If a movant for summary judgment establishes a rebuttable presumption of the fact it needs to prove to prevail and the non-movant fails to produce controverting evidence, the movant is entitled to summary judgment. Hence, a presumption of paternity established by a genetic test is sufficient to support a summary judgment unless the opposing party has produced enough clear and convincing evidence to rebut it."

In re A.M., 936 S.W.2d 59, 62 (Tex.App.—San Antonio 1996, no writ). Section 160.110(f) "indicates that it is intended to govern limitations rather than standing. The statute speaks in terms of when a suit may be filed by an alleged biological father. This language presumes standing and focuses on the time period within which a suit may be filed. As such, §160.110(f) is a statute of limitation."

Sections 160.111-160.200 reserved for expansion

SUBCHAPTER C. ACKNOWLEDGMENT OR DENIAL OF PATERNITY

FAM §160.201. VOLUNTARY ACKNOWLEDGMENT OF PATERNITY

The mother of a child and a man claiming to be the father of the child may execute an acknowledgment of paternity as provided by this subchapter to establish the man's paternity.

History of Fam §160.201: Acts 1995, 74th Leg., ch. 20, §1, eff. April 20, 1995. Amended by Acts 1995, 74th Leg., ch. 751, §64, eff. Sept. 1, 1995; Acts 1999, 76th Leg., ch. 556, §37, eff. Sept. 1, 1999. Deleted by Acts 2001, 77th Leg., ch. 821, §1.01, eff. June 14, 2001. Source: Former Fam §13.21(a), (b).

FAM §160.202. EXECUTION OF ACKNOWLEDGMENT OF PATERNITY

(a) An acknowledgment of paternity must:

(1) be in writing;

(2) be signed by the mother and the putative father; and

(3) state whether the child whose paternity is being acknowledged has a presumed father under Section 151.002.

(b) If the mother declares in the acknowledgment that there is a presumed father of the child, the acknowledgment must be accompanied by a denial of paternity signed by the presumed father, unless the presumed father is the man who has signed the acknowledgment.

History of Fam §160.202: Acts 1995, 74th Leg., ch. 20, §1, eff. April 20, 1995. Amended by Acts 1995, 74th Leg., ch. 751, §64, eff. Sept. 1, 1995; Acts 1999, 76th Leg., ch. 556, §37, eff. Sept. 1, 1999. Deleted by Acts 2001, 77th Leg., ch. 821, §1.01, eff. June 14, 2001. Source: Former Fam §13.22.

FAM §160.203. FILING ACKNOWLEDGMENT OF PATERNITY

(a) An acknowledgment of paternity executed under this subchapter shall be filed with the bureau of vital statistics.

(b) The bureau of vital statistics may not charge a fee to file the acknowledgment.

History of Fam §160.203: Acts 1995, 74th Leg., ch. 20, §1, eff. April 20, 1995. Amended by Acts 1995, 74th Leg., ch. 751, §64, eff. Sept. 1, 1995; Acts 1999, 76th Leg., ch. 556, §37, eff. Sept. 1, 1999. Deleted by Acts 2001, 77th Leg., ch. 821, §1.01, eff. June 14, 2001. Source: Former Fam §13.23.

FAM §160.204. SIGNING OF ACKNOWLEDGMENT OR DENIAL OF PATERNITY

(a) An acknowledgment of paternity or a denial of paternity may contain the mother's signature and the putative father's signature on separate documents.

(b) An acknowledgment of paternity or a denial of paternity may be signed before the birth of the child.

(c) An adult or a minor may sign an acknowledgment of paternity or a denial of paternity.

History of Fam §160.204: Acts 1995, 74th Leg., ch. 20, §1, eff. April 20, 1995. Renumbered from §160.205 by Acts 1995, 74th Leg., ch. 751, §64, eff. Sept. 1, 1995. Amended by Acts 1999, 76th Leg., ch. 556, §37, eff. Sept. 1, 1999. Deleted by Acts 2001, 77th Leg., ch. 821, §1.01, eff. June 14, 2001. Source: Former Fam §13.22(a), (e).

FAM §160.205. EFFECT OF ACKNOWLEDGMENT OF PATERNITY

(a) Subject to the right to rescind or contest an acknowledgment of paternity under this subchapter, a signed acknowledgment of paternity filed with the bureau of vital statistics is a legal finding of paternity of a child equivalent to a judicial determination.

(b) If the mother or the man claiming to be the father falsely denies the existence of a presumed father in an acknowledgment of paternity, the acknowledgment of paternity is voidable within the time to rescind under Section 160.206.

History of Fam §160.205: Acts 1995, 74th Leg., ch. 20, §1, eff. April 20, 1995. Renumbered from §160.206 by Acts 1995, 74th Leg., ch. 751, §64, eff. Sept. 1, 1995. Amended by Acts 1999, 76th Leg., ch. 556, §37, eff. Sept. 1, 1999. Deleted by Acts 2001, 77th Leg., ch. 821, §1.01, eff. June 14, 2001. Source: Former Fam §13.24.

FAM §160.206. SUIT TO RESCIND ACKNOWLEDGMENT OR DENIAL

(a) Subject to the requirements of Subsection (b), a person who signs an acknowledgment of paternity or a denial of paternity may file a suit affecting the parent-child relationship to rescind the acknowledgment of paternity or denial of paternity.

(b) The petition to rescind an acknowledgment of paternity or a denial of paternity must be filed not later than the earlier of:

(1) the 61st day after the date the acknowledgment of paternity or denial of paternity is filed with the bureau of vital statistics; or

(2) the date of the first hearing before a tribunal to determine an issue relating to the child in which the person is a party, including a proceeding that establishes support.

(c) If a proceeding to rescind an acknowledgment of paternity or a denial of paternity is filed jointly or agreed to by all necessary parties, the court shall order the bureau of vital statistics to amend the birth record of the child by removing the father's name.

(d) If the proceeding to rescind is not agreed to by all parties, the court shall conduct a hearing in the same manner as a proceeding to determine parentage under this chapter.

History of Fam §160.206: Acts 1999, 76th Leg., ch. 556, §37, eff. Sept. 1, 1999. Former §160.206 renumbered as §160.205 by Acts 1995, 74th Leg., ch. 571, §64, eff. Sept. 1, 1995. Deleted by Acts 2001, 77th Leg., ch. 821, §1.01, eff. June 14, 2001.

FAM §160.207. SUIT TO CONTEST ACKNOWLEDGMENT OR DENIAL

(a) A person who may contest a presumption of paternity under Section 160.101 may contest an acknowledgment of paternity or a denial of paternity by filing a suit affecting the parent-child relationship. A suit to contest an acknowledgment of paternity or a denial of paternity that is filed after the time for a suit to rescind under Section 160.206 may be filed only on the basis of fraud, duress, or material mistake of fact. The party challenging the acknowledgment of paternity or the denial of paternity has the burden of proof.

(b) A suit to contest an acknowledgment of paternity or a denial of paternity shall be conducted in the same manner as a proceeding to determine parentage under this chapter.

(c) A person must bring suit to contest an acknowledgment of paternity or a denial of paternity not later than the fourth anniversary of the date the acknowledgment of paternity or the denial of paternity is filed with the bureau of vital statistics.

(d) A suit to contest an unrescinded acknowledgment of paternity may not be filed after the date a court has rendered an order, including a child support order, based on the acknowledgment of paternity.

(e) Notwithstanding any other provision of this chapter, a collateral attack on an acknowledgment of paternity executed under this subchapter may not be filed after the fourth anniversary of the date the acknowledgment of paternity is filed with the bureau of vital statistics.

History of Fam §160.207: Acts 1999, 76th Leg., ch. 556, §37, eff. Sept. 1, 1999. Deleted by Acts 2001, 77th Leg., ch. 821, §1.01, eff. June 14, 2001.

FAM §160.208. PROCEDURE FOR SUIT TO RESCIND OR CONTEST

(a) Each person who signs an acknowledgment of paternity or a denial of paternity must be made a party to a suit to rescind or contest the acknowledgment of paternity or denial of paternity.

(b) Except for good cause shown, the court may not suspend the legal responsibility of a person arising from the acknowledgment of paternity, including the duty to pay child support, while a suit is pending.

(c) On a determination of paternity or nonpaternity, the court shall order the bureau of vital statistics to amend the birth record of the child in accordance with the order of the court.

History of Fam §160.208: Acts 1999, 76th Leg., ch. 556, §37, eff. Sept. 1, 1999. Deleted by Acts 2001, 77th Leg., ch. 821, §1.01, eff. June 14, 2001.

FAM §160.209. COURT RATIFICATION

An unrescinded and uncontested acknowledgment of paternity is valid and effective without court ratification. In a judicial, administrative, or other proceeding, parentage of a child may be proved by evidence that an unrescinded and uncontested acknowledgment of paternity of the child has been filed with the bureau of vital statistics.

History of Fam §160.209: Acts 1999, 76th Leg., ch. 556, §37, eff. Sept. 1, 1999. Deleted by Acts 2001, 77th Leg., ch. 821, §1.01, eff. June 14, 2001.

FAM §160.210. FULL FAITH & CREDIT

An acknowledgment of paternity signed in another state shall be accorded full faith and credit by the courts of this state if the acknowledgment is signed in apparent compliance with the other state's law.

History of Fam §160.210: Acts 1999, 76th Leg., ch. 556, §37, eff. Sept. 1, 1999. Deleted by Acts 2001, 77th Leg., ch. 821, §1.01, eff. June 14, 2001.

FAM §160.211. VALIDATION OF EARLIER STATEMENT

A statement admitting paternity or an obligation to support a child that was signed before September 1, 1999, is valid and binding even though the statement is not executed as provided by this subchapter.

History of Fam §160.211: Acts 1999, 76th Leg., ch. 556, §37, eff. Sept. 1, 1999. Deleted by Acts 2001, 77th Leg., ch. 821, §1.01, eff. June 14, 2001.

FAM §160.212. FORMS FOR ACKNOWLEDGMENT & DENIAL OF PATERNITY

(a) The bureau of vital statistics shall prescribe forms for an acknowledgment of paternity and a denial of paternity to comply with this subchapter.

(b) The forms prescribed under this section must:

(1) contain information regarding the procedure to rescind an acknowledgment or a denial;

(2) provide that the signatures on the forms are witnessed and signed under penalty of perjury; and

(3) state whether the mother, the putative father, or the presumed father is a minor.

(c) The form for acknowledgment of paternity must inform the putative father that signing the acknowledgment of paternity with the consent of the mother:

(1) creates the parent-child relationship between him and the child;

(2) imposes upon him a legal duty to support the child; and

(3) enables a court to grant him the right of custody or visitation with the child.

(d) The form for denial of paternity must inform the man that signing the denial of paternity with the consent of the mother:

(1) legally determines his nonpaternity of the child;

(2) removes the legal duty that he support the child; and

(3) terminates his right of conservatorship or possession of or access to the child.

History of Fam §160.212: Acts 1999, 76th Leg., ch. 556, §37, eff. Sept. 1, 1999. Deleted by Acts 2001, 77th Leg., ch. 821, §1.01, eff. June 14, 2001.

FAM §160.213. VALIDITY OF FORMS

The validity of an acknowledgment of paternity or a denial of paternity is not affected by a modification of the prescribed form by the bureau of vital statistics that occurs after the acknowledgment of paternity or denial of paternity is signed if the form met the requirements of state law at the time it was signed.

History of Fam §160.213: Acts 1999, 76th Leg., ch. 556, §37, eff. Sept. 1, 1999. Deleted by Acts 2001, 77th Leg., ch. 821, §1.01, eff. June 14, 2001.

FAM §160.214. RELEASE OF INFORMATION

The bureau of vital statistics shall release information relating to the acknowledgment or denial of paternity and rescinding an acknowledgment or a denial of paternity to the Title IV-D agency and any other person authorized by law.

History of Fam §160.214: Acts 1999, 76th Leg., ch. 556, §37, eff. Sept. 1, 1999. Deleted by Acts 2001, 77th Leg., ch. 821, §1.01, eff. June 14, 2001.

FAM §160.215. ADOPTION OF RULES

The Title IV-D agency and the bureau of vital statistics may adopt rules to implement this subchapter.

History of Fam §160.215: Acts 1999, 76th Leg., ch. 556, §37, eff. Sept. 1, 1999. Deleted by Acts 2001, 77th Leg., ch. 821, §1.01, eff. June 14, 2001.

FAM §160.216. MEMORANDUM OF UNDERSTANDING

The Title IV-D agency and the bureau of vital statistics shall adopt a memorandum of understanding governing the collection and transfer of information for the voluntary acknowledgment of paternity. The Title IV-D agency and the bureau of vital statistics shall review the memorandum semiannually and renew or modify the memorandum as necessary.

History of Fam §160.216: Acts 1999, 76th Leg., ch. 556, §37, eff. Sept. 1, 1999. Deleted by Acts 2001, 77th Leg., ch. 821, §1.01, eff. June 14, 2001.

Sections 160.217-160.250 blank

SUBCHAPTER D. PATERNITY REGISTRY

FAM §160.251. PATERNITY REGISTRY; PURPOSE

(a) The bureau of vital statistics shall establish a paternity registry.

(b) The bureau of vital statistics shall administer the registry to:

(1) protect the parental rights of fathers who affirmatively assume responsibility for children they may have fathered; and

(2) expedite adoptions of children whose biological fathers are unwilling to assume responsibility for their children by registering with the registry or otherwise acknowledging their children.

(c) The registry does not relieve a mother of the obligation to identify the known father of her child.

(d) A man is not required to register with the paternity registry if he:

(1) is presumed to be the biological father of a child under Chapter 151;

(2) has been adjudicated to be the biological father of a child by a court of competent jurisdiction; or

(3) has filed an acknowledgment of paternity under Subchapter C.

History of Fam §160.251: Acts 1997, 75th Leg., ch. 561, §6, eff. Sept. 1, 1997. Amended by Acts 1999, 76th Leg., ch. 556, §38, eff. Sept. 1, 1999. Deleted by Acts 2001, 77th Leg., ch. 821, §1.01, eff. June 14, 2001.

FAM §160.252. REQUIRED INFORMATION

A man registering with the registry shall provide:

(1) the name, last known address, driver's license number, and social security number, if known, of the mother of the child;

(2) the name of the child and the location and date of birth of the child, if known, or the probable month and year of the expected birth of the child;

(3) the man's name, address, driver's license number, and social security number; and

(4) a statement in which the man claims to be the father of the child identified by the man.

History of Fam §160.252: Acts 1997, 75th Leg., ch. 561, §6, eff. Sept. 1, 1997. Deleted by Acts 2001, 77th Leg., ch. 821, §1.01, eff. June 14, 2001.

FAM §160.253. INFORMATION MAINTAINED BY REGISTRY

The registry shall record the name, address, driver's license number, and social security number of a man who claims to be the father of a child whose paternity has not been adjudicated by a court of competent jurisdiction by giving notice of intent to claim paternity, as provided by this subchapter.

History of Fam §160.253: Acts 1997, 75th Leg., ch. 561, §6, eff. Sept. 1, 1997. Deleted by Acts 2001, 77th Leg., ch. 821, §1.01, eff. June 14, 2001.

FAM §160.254. KNOWLEDGE OF PREGNANCY

(a) A person who has sexual intercourse with a person of the opposite sex is deemed to have knowledge that sexual intercourse can result in the woman's pregnancy.

(b) Except as provided by this subchapter, a man who claims to be the father of a child shall file a notice of intent to assert as provided by this subchapter his right to establish paternity of a child that may result from the sexual intercourse.

(c) Ignorance of a pregnancy is not a sufficient reason for failing to register with the registry to claim paternity of the child born of the pregnancy.

History of Fam §160.254: Acts 1997, 75th Leg., ch. 561, §6, eff. Sept. 1, 1997. Deleted by Acts 2001, 77th Leg., ch. 821, §1.01, eff. June 14, 2001.

FAM §160.2545. INFORMATION REGARDING REGISTRY, BIRTH RECORDS, & ACKNOWLEDGMENTS OF PATERNITY FILED WITH BUREAU OF VITAL STATISTICS

(a) On receipt of a request for a certificate under Section 160.260 attesting to the results of a search of the paternity registry, the bureau of vital statistics shall search:

(1) notices of intent to claim paternity filed with the registry under this subchapter;

(2) birth records maintained by the bureau;

(3) acknowledgments of paternity filed with the bureau under Subchapter C; and

(4) central file records identifying a court of continuing jurisdiction and identifying the adjudicated father, if any.

(b) The bureau shall furnish information resulting from a search under Subsection (a) to the requestor.

History of Fam §160.2545: Acts 1999, 76th Leg., ch. 556, §39, eff. Sept. 1, 1999. Deleted by Acts 2001, 77th Leg., ch. 821, §1.01, eff. June 14, 2001.

FAM §160.255. FURNISHING OF REGISTRY INFORMATION; CONFIDENTIALITY; OFFENSE

(a) If the mother's address has been provided, the registry shall send a copy of the notice of intent to claim paternity to the mother as notification that a man has registered with the paternity registry claiming to be the father of the mother's child.

(b) Information contained in the registry is confidential and may be released on request only to:

(1) a court;

(2) the mother of a child;

(3) an authorized agency;

(4) a licensed child-placing agency;

(5) an attorney at law in this state who is participating or assisting in a suit affecting the parent-child relationship, including termination of the parent-child relationship or a suit for the adoption of the child that the registrant claims to have fathered; or

(6) any other person or entity the bureau of vital statistics considers to have a legitimate interest in the information.

(c) The registry shall furnish registry information by electronic data exchange or any other means to the state's Title IV-D agency and the Department of Protective and Regulatory Services.

(d) A person commits an offense if the person intentionally and unlawfully releases information from the registry to the public or makes any other unlawful use of the information in violation of this subchapter. An offense under this subsection is a Class B misdemeanor.

History of Fam §160.255: Acts 1997, 75th Leg., ch. 561, §6, eff. Sept. 1, 1997. Deleted by Acts 2001, 77th Leg., ch. 821, §1.01, eff. June 14, 2001.

FAM §160.256. NOTICE OF INTENT TO CLAIM PATERNITY

(a) Except as provided by Subsection (d), a person may register as provided by this subchapter by filing a notice of intent to claim paternity on a form provided by the bureau of vital statistics. This form shall be signed and acknowledged before a notary public.

(b) The bureau shall make registration forms available to all:

(1) hospitals and other birthing places in this state;

(2) licensed child-placing agencies;

(3) county and district clerks;

(4) municipal clerks;

(5) justices of the peace;

(6) jails;

(7) prisons; and

(8) facilities of the Texas Department of Criminal Justice and Texas Youth Commission.

(c) A notice of intent to claim paternity may be filed before the birth of the child but may not be filed after the 30th day after the date of birth of the child.

(d) If the bureau of vital statistics has received from the clerk of the court notice under Chapter 108 of a decree terminating the parent-child relationship between the person applying to register and the child, the bureau shall notify the person that the person's parent-child relationship with the child has been terminated and may not enter into the registry a notice of intent to claim paternity filed by the person.

History of Fam §160.256: Acts 1997, 75th Leg., ch. 561, §6, eff. Sept. 1, 1997. Deleted by Acts 2001, 77th Leg., ch. 821, §1.01, eff. June 14, 2001.

FAM §160.257. DENIAL OF REGISTRANT'S PATERNITY; NOTIFICATION

(a) Not later than the 30th day after the date of the receipt of notification from the bureau of vital statistics that a notice of intent to claim paternity has been filed, the mother of the child may deny the registrant's claim of paternity on a form provided by the bureau and signed and acknowledged before a notary public.

(b) If the mother denies that the registrant is the father of the child, the bureau of vital statistics shall immediately notify the registrant of the denial and of the registrant's right to file a legal action to establish paternity.

History of Fam §160.257: Acts 1997, 75th Leg., ch. 561, §6, eff. Sept. 1, 1997. Deleted by Acts 2001, 77th Leg., ch. 821, §1.01, eff. June 14, 2001.

FAM §160.258. EFFECT OF FAILURE TO FILE NOTICE OF INTENT

Except as provided by Chapter 102 and Chapter 161, a man who fails to file a notice of intent to claim paternity before the 30th day after the date of the birth of the child may not assert an interest in the child other than by filing a suit to establish paternity before the termination of the man's parental rights.

History of Fam §160.258: Acts 1997, 75th Leg., ch. 561, §6, eff. Sept. 1, 1997. Deleted by Acts 2001, 77th Leg., ch. 821, §1.01, eff. June 14, 2001.

FAM §160.259. CHANGE OR REVOCATION OF REGISTRY INFORMATION

(a) A man who files a notice of intent to claim paternity with the registry shall promptly notify the registry in writing of any change in the information, including a change of address.

(b) A man who files a notice of intent to claim paternity may at any time revoke the notice by sending the registry a written statement signed and acknowledged by the registrant before a notary public. The statement must include a declaration that, to the best of the registrant's knowledge and belief:

(1) the registrant is not the father of the named child; or

(2) a court has adjudicated paternity and a person other than the registrant has been determined to be the father of the child.

History of Fam §160.259: Acts 1997, 75th Leg., ch. 561, §6, eff. Sept. 1, 1997. Deleted by Acts 2001, 77th Leg., ch. 821, §1.01, eff. June 14, 2001.

FAM §160.260. FURNISHING OF CERTIFICATE OF REGISTRY SEARCH

On request, the bureau of vital statistics shall furnish a certificate, signed by the state registrar of vital statistics, attesting to the results of a search of the registry regarding a notice of intent to claim paternity to:

(1) a court;

(2) the mother of a child;

(3) an authorized agency;

(4) a licensed child-placing agency;

(5) an attorney licensed to practice law in this state who is participating or assisting in an adoption; or

(6) any other person or entity the bureau of vital statistics considers to have a legitimate interest in the information.

History of Fam §160.260 Acts 1997, 75th Leg., ch. 561, §6, eff. Sept. 1, 1997. Deleted by Acts 2001, 77th Leg., ch. 821, §1.01, eff. June 14, 2001.

FAM §160.261. REMOVAL OF REGISTRANT'S NAME

If a court determines that a registrant is not the father of the child, the court shall order the bureau of vital statistics to remove the registrant's name from the registry. On receipt of an order for the removal of a registrant's name, the bureau of vital statistics shall remove the name from the registry.

History of Fam §160.261: Acts 1997, 75th Leg., ch. 561, §6, eff. Sept. 1, 1997. Deleted by Acts 2001, 77th Leg., ch. 821, §1.01, eff. June 14, 2001.

FAM §160.262. REGISTRY FEES

(a) A fee may not be charged for filing with the registry a notice of intent to claim paternity of a child or a denial of a registrant's paternity.

(b) Except as provided by Subsection (c), the Texas Department of Health may charge a fee for processing a search of the paternity registry and for furnishing a certificate under Section 160.260.

(c) The Department of Protective and Regulatory Services and the Title IV-D agency are not required to pay a fee under Subsection (b).

History of Fam §160.262: Acts 1997, 75th Leg., ch. 561, §6, eff. Sept. 1, 1997. Deleted by Acts 2001, 77th Leg., ch. 821, §1.01, eff. June 14, 2001.

FAM §160.263. ADMISSIBILITY OF INFORMATION MAINTAINED BY REGISTRY

Information maintained by the paternity registry is admissible in a proceeding in a court or administrative tribunal of this state for any purpose, including for the establishment of the registrant's paternity or an action to terminate parental rights.

History of Fam §160.263: Acts 1997, 75th Leg., ch. 561, §6, eff. Sept. 1, 1997. Deleted by Acts 2001, 77th Leg., ch. 821, §1.01, eff. June 14, 2001.

CHAPTER 161. TERMINATION OF THE PARENT-CHILD RELATIONSHIP

Subchapter A. Grounds

Subchapter B. Procedures

Subchapter C. Hearing & Order

SUBCHAPTER A. GROUNDS

FAM §161.001. INVOLUNTARY TERMINATION OF PARENT-CHILD RELATIONSHIP

The court may order termination of the parent-child relationship if the court finds by clear and convincing evidence:

(1) that the parent has:

(A) voluntarily left the child alone or in the possession of another not the parent and expressed an intent not to return;

(B) voluntarily left the child alone or in the possession of another not the parent without expressing an intent to return, without providing for the adequate support of the child, and remained away for a period of at least three months;

(C) voluntarily left the child alone or in the possession of another without providing adequate support of the child and remained away for a period of at least six months;

(D) knowingly placed or knowingly allowed the child to remain in conditions or surroundings which endanger the physical or emotional well-being of the child;

(E) engaged in conduct or knowingly placed the child with persons who engaged in conduct which endangers the physical or emotional well-being of the child;

(F) failed to support the child in accordance with the parent's ability during a period of one year ending within six months of the date of the filing of the petition;

(G) abandoned the child without identifying the child or furnishing means of identification, and the child's identity cannot be ascertained by the exercise of reasonable diligence;

(H) voluntarily, and with knowledge of the pregnancy, abandoned the mother of the child beginning at a time during her pregnancy with the child and continuing through the birth, failed to provide adequate support or medical care for the mother during the period of abandonment before the birth of the child, and remained apart from the child or failed to support the child since the birth;

(I) contumaciously refused to submit to a reasonable and lawful order of a court under Subchapter D, Chapter 261;

(J) been the major cause of:

(i) the failure of the child to be enrolled in school as required by the Education Code; or

(ii) the child's absence from the child's home without the consent of the parents or guardian for a substantial length of time or without the intent to return;

(K) executed before or after the suit is filed an unrevoked or irrevocable affidavit of relinquishment of parental rights as provided by this chapter;

(L) been convicted or has been placed on community supervision, including deferred adjudication community supervision, for being criminally responsible for the death or serious injury of a child under the following sections of the Penal Code or adjudicated under Title 3 for conduct that caused the death or serious injury of a child and that would constitute a violation of one of the following Penal Code sections:

(i) Section 19.02 (murder);

(ii) Section 19.03 (capital murder);

(iii) Section 19.04 (manslaughter);

(iv) Section 21.11 (indecency with a child);

(v) Section 22.01 (assault);

(vi) Section 22.011 (sexual assault);

(vii) Section 22.02 (aggravated assault);

(viii) Section 22.021 (aggravated sexual assault);

(ix) Section 22.04 (injury to a child, elderly individual, or disabled individual);

(x) Section 22.041 (abandoning or endangering child);

(xi) Section 25.02 (prohibited sexual conduct);

(xii) Section 43.25 (sexual performance by a child); and

(xiii) Section 43.26 (possession or promotion of child pornography);

(M) had his or her parent-child relationship terminated with respect to another child based on a finding that the parent's conduct was in violation of Paragraph (D) or (E) or substantially equivalent provisions of the law of another state;

(N) constructively abandoned the child who has been in the permanent or temporary managing conservatorship of the Department of Protective and Regulatory Services or an authorized agency for not less than six months, and:

(i) the department or authorized agency has made reasonable efforts to return the child to the parent;

(ii) the parent has not regularly visited or maintained significant contact with the child; and

(iii) the parent has demonstrated an inability to provide the child with a safe environment;

(O) failed to comply with the provisions of a court order that specifically established the actions necessary for the parent to obtain the return of the child who has been in the permanent or temporary managing conservatorship of the Department of Protective and Regulatory Services for not less than nine months as a result of the child's removal from the parent under Chapter 262 for the abuse or neglect of the child;

(P) used a controlled substance, as defined by Chapter 481, Health and Safety Code, in a manner that endangered the health or safety of the child, and:

(i) failed to complete a court-ordered substance abuse treatment program; or

(ii) after completion of a court-ordered substance abuse treatment program, continued to abuse a controlled substance;

(Q) knowingly engaged in criminal conduct that has resulted in the parent's:

(i) conviction of an offense; and

(ii) confinement or imprisonment and inability to care for the child for not less than two years from the date of filing the petition;

(R) been the cause of the child being born addicted to alcohol or a controlled substance, other than a controlled substance legally obtained by prescription, as defined by Section 261.001; or

A (S) voluntarily delivered the child to a designated emergency infant care provider under Section 262.302 without expressing an intent to return for the child; and

(2) that termination is in the best interest of the child.

History of Fam §161.001: Acts 1995, 74th Leg., ch. 20, §1, eff. April 20, 1995. Amended by Acts 1995, 74th Leg., ch. 709, §1 (eff. Sept. 1, 1995), ch. 751, §65 (eff. Sept. 1, 1995); Acts 1997, 75th Leg., ch. 575, §9 (eff. Sept. 1, 1997), ch. 1022, §60 (eff. Sept. 1, 1997); Acts 1999, 76th Leg., ch. 1390, §18 (eff. Sept. 1, 1999), ch. 1087, §1 (eff. Sept. 1, 1999); Acts 2001, 77th Leg., ch. 1090, §1, eff. Sept. 1, 2001. Source: Former Fam §§11.15(b), 15.02(a).

Generally

Holick v. Smith, 685 S.W.2d 18, 20 (Tex.1985). "The natural right existing between parents and their children is of constitutional dimensions. ... A termination decree is complete, final, irrevocable and divests for all time that natural right as well as all legal rights, privileges, duties and powers with respect to each other except for the child's right to inherit. ... Consequently, termination proceedings should be strictly scrutinized, and involuntary termination statutes are strictly construed in favor of the parent."

Wiley v. Spratlan, 543 S.W.2d 349, 352 (Tex.1976). "Actions which break the ties between a parent and child 'can never be justified without the most solid and substantial reasons.' Particularly in an action which permanently sunders those ties, should the proceedings be strictly scrutinized. This court has always recognized the strong presumption that the best interest of a minor is usually served by keeping custody in the natural parents. [¶] 'The presumption is based upon a logical belief that the ties of the natural relationship of parent and child ordinarily furnish strong assurance of genuine efforts on the part of the custodians to provide the child with the best care and opportunities possible, and, as well, the best atmosphere for the mental, moral and emotional development of the child.'"

In re J.F.C., 57 S.W.3d 66, 72 (Tex.App.—Waco 2001, pet. granted 3-21-02). "[W]e are not persuaded that application of [TRAP] 33.1 in an involuntary termination-of-parental-rights case to preclude review of a claim of charge error about a 'core issue,' in this case 'best interest of the child,' affords the parent due process. To terminate parental rights—a Fourteenth Amendment liberty interest—when there is a fundamentally erroneous charge on a 'core issue,' only because the complaint was not preserved in the trial court, does not adhere to Fourteenth Amendment procedural due process. There is no '[strict] scrutiny' ... in such an approach. Therefore, because we are constitutionally required to follow the directives of the United States Supreme Court when they differ with state procedural law, we will not apply Rule 33.1. [¶] We believe the better—and constitutional—approach is to review such a charge complaint. Our holding is limited to complaints raised on appeal about 'core issues' in the court's charge in an involuntary termination case. We hold that when such a challenge to the charge is made on appeal, and no motion, request, or objection was made at the trial court which would have preserved the complaint for appellate review, we will nevertheless review the complaint."

In re A.V., 57 S.W.3d 51, 58 (Tex.App.—Waco 2001, pet. filed 9-25-01). "[W]e review involuntary termination-of-parental-rights cases according to the following standards: [¶] 1. The two 'core issues' are (1) whether at least one of the statutory grounds for termination in §161.001 ... has occurred, and (2) whether termination is in the 'best interest' of the child. [¶] 2. To comport with procedural due process, we will review unpreserved complaints about the legal and factual sufficiency of the evidence regarding 'core issues.' [¶] 3. To comport with procedural due process, we will review unpreserved complaints about jury-charge errors concerning 'core issues.' [¶] 4. As a matter of procedural due process, the jury charge, by instructions or individual questions, must ensure that 'core issues' are decided by the same ten (or more) jurors. [¶] 5. Parents have a procedural due-process right to 'effective assistance of counsel.'" *See also* ***In re A.P.***, 42 S.W.3d 248, 256 (Tex.App.—Waco 2001, no pet.). *But see* ***In re I.V.***, 61 S.W.3d 789, 794 n.3 (Tex.App.—Corpus Christi 2001, n.p.h.).

In re A.M.C., 2 S.W.3d 707, 711 (Tex.App.—Waco 1999, no pet.). "In proceedings to terminate the parent-child relationship brought under §161.001 ... the petitioner must establish two elements. First, petitioner must prove one or more acts or omissions enumerated under the first subsection of the statute. Second, petitioner must prove, that termination of the parent-child relationship is in the best interest of the child. Both elements must be established, with regard to each child, and proof of one element does not relieve the petitioner of the burden of proving the other."

In re T.R.R., 986 S.W.2d 31, 36 (Tex.App.—Corpus Christi 1998, no pet.). "Before parental rights may be terminated, there must be a finding of *specific* conduct under §161.001(a), as well as a finding that termination is in the best interest of the child. The trial court may not terminate the parent-child relationship solely on the finding that it is in the best interest of the child. [¶] Neither the [movant's] original petition nor the court's judgment recite any of the statutory grounds for termination set out in §161.001.... *At 37:* A parent whose rights are involuntarily terminated is entitled to sufficiently specific findings so that she will know upon what conduct the court terminated her rights. [¶] Because the petition failed to state any statutory ground for the termination, and the decree failed to delineate any statutory basis for the termination, we find [respondent] established a prima facia meritorious defense."

Avery v. State, 963 S.W.2d 550, 553 (Tex.App.—Houston [1st Dist.] 1997, no pet.). "The parental conduct to be examined in considering termination of parental rights includes what the parents did before and after the birth of the child."

Wetzel v. Wetzel, 715 S.W.2d 387, 391 (Tex.App.—Dallas 1986, no writ). In a "termination suit, acts done in the distant past, without showing a present or future danger to a child, cannot be sufficient to terminate parental rights."

Clear & Convincing Evidence

Meadows v. Green, 524 S.W.2d 509, 510 (Tex. 1975). "[T]he Court of Civil Appeals has sought to apply a third standard of reviewing the evidence presented at trial—the 'clear and convincing' standard. In Texas there are but two standards by which evidence is reviewed: factual sufficiency and legal sufficiency. The requirement of clear and convincing evidence is merely another method of stating that a cause of action must be supported by factually sufficient evidence."

In re S.F., 32 S.W.3d 318, 321 (Tex.App.—San Antonio 2000, no pet.). "This intermediate standard colors our review of the factual sufficiency of the evidence in a termination case. Applying this standard to our review of a trial judge's findings, we ask whether sufficient evidence was presented to produce in the mind of a rational fact finder a 'firm belief or conviction as to the truth of the allegations sought to be established.'" *See also* ***Spurlock v. Texas DPRS***, 904 S.W.2d 152, 155-56 (Tex.App.—Austin 1995, writ denied). *But see* ***In re King***, below; ***In re J.R.***, 991 S.W.2d 318, 320 (Tex. App.—Fort Worth 1999, no pet.).

In re King, 15 S.W.3d 272, 275 (Tex.App.—Texarkana 2000, pet. denied). The "courts of appeals have disagreed on whether this intermediate standard of proof requires the application of a corresponding intermediate standard of appellate review. [W]e reassert our position that the clear and convincing standard of proof at the trial court level does not alter the fundamental standards of appellate review." *See also* ***Spangler v. Texas DPRS***, below. *But see* ***In re S.F.***, above.

Spangler v. Texas DPRS, 962 S.W.2d 253, 256 (Tex.App.—Waco 1998, no pet.). "Termination of parental rights is a drastic remedy and is of such weight and gravity that due process requires the petitioner to justify termination by 'clear and convincing evidence.' This standard is defined as 'that measure or degree of proof which will produce in the mind of the trier of fact a firm belief or conviction as to the truth or the allegations sought to be established.' Although the clear and convincing standard of proof required at the trial level is well settled, the standard of appellate review to be applied by this court is not as well defined. *At 257:* [T]he rule adopted by this court is stated as follows: When the trier of fact is required to make a finding by clear and convincing evidence, the court of appeals will only sustain a point of error alleging insufficient evidence if the trier of fact could not reasonably find the existence of the fact to be established by clear and convincing evidence. [¶] Therefore, just as the clear and convincing standard of proof is an intermediate standard, falling between the preponderance standard of ordinary civil proceedings and the reasonable doubt standard of criminal proceedings, this standard of appellate review is an intermediate standard. This intermediate standard of review is necessary to protect the fundamental constitutional rights involved by termination of parental rights."

Juries

Texas DHS v. E.B., 802 S.W.2d 647, 649 (Tex.1990). "The charge in parental rights cases should be the same as in other civil cases. The controlling question in this case was whether the parent-child relationship between the mother and each of her two children should be terminated, not what specific ground or grounds under §15.02 [now §161.001] the jury relied on to answer affirmatively the questions posed. All ten jurors agree that the mother had endangered the child by doing one or the other of the things listed in §15.02. Petitioner argues that the charge, as presented to the jury, violates her due process right by depriving a natural mother of her fundamental right to the care, custody and management of her children. Recognizing her rights does not change the form of submission. The standard for review of the charge is abuse of discretion, and abuse of discretion occurs only when the trial court acts without reference to any guiding principle. Here the trial court tracked the statutory language in the instruction and then asked the controlling question. This simply does not amount to abuse of discretion."

In re B.L.D., 56 S.W.3d 203, 217 (Tex.App.—Waco 2001, no pet.). "We hold that in termination cases, procedural due process requires a strict application of [TRCP] 292's requirement of accord by ten or more jurors."

§161.001(1)(A)

In re R.D.S., 902 S.W.2d 714, 718-19 (Tex.App.—Amarillo 1995, no writ). A "statute vests the trial judge with authority to end a parent-child relationship if it finds that 'the parent ... voluntarily left the child alone or in the possession of another not the parent and expressed an intent not to return.' There is no specified time frame within which these pivotal indicia must arise. Though some authority suggests that the underlying misconduct may not be too remote in time, it is certain that it need not immediately precede the final hearing. [¶] Furthermore, discontinuing the misconduct does not necessarily prevent the court from acting. Once activity within the parameters of §15.02(a) [now §161.001(1)] occurs, a parent's change of heart does not stay the court's hand. ... Thus, if the evidence at bar established that [mother] voluntarily left her son with someone other than his biological father while expressing an intent not to return, the court was entitled to sever the parent-child relationship, notwithstanding her later attempt to renounce her decision."

Swinney v. Mosher, 830 S.W.2d 187, 195 (Tex. App.—Fort Worth 1992, writ denied). There is no "evidence that [respondent] abandoned [daughter] as contemplated by §15.02(1)(A) [now §161.001(1)(A)]. [Respondent's] actions of surrendering possession of [daughter] and execution of the affidavit relinquishing her parental rights were done in contemplation of her adoption ... not with an intent to abandon.... Also, there is [no] evidence that [respondent] expressed 'an intent not to return' as that language was intended to be applied by the legislature. [Respondent's] actions were done in furtherance of her original agreement to allow [petitioners] to adopt [her daughter], which under 15.03(d) [now §161.103] [respondent] had a right to revoke. [Respondent's] prompt notice to the [adopting couple] of her intent to revoke the affidavit coupled with her prompt retention of a lawyer, her attendance at all hearings concerning her termination, and her weekly visitation [with her daughter], when it was permitted, establishes conclusively that [respondent] did not intend to abandon [her daughter] under §15.02(1)(A). Any finding to the contrary would render §15.03(d) null and void. [¶] A finding that parental rights could be involuntarily terminated based on the actions consistent with an open adoption would be contrary to the history of Texas law prior to the Family Code and a subversion of the legislatures' intent...."

Smith v. McLin, 632 S.W.2d 390, 392 (Tex.App.—Austin 1982, writ ref'd n.r.e.). Adopting parents "provided [respondent] with an affidavit of relinquishment. The instrument, which [respondent] signed before a notary, manifested a clear intent to completely sever her ties with the child. Because the instrument was defective it could not, standing alone, serve as the proof necessary for termination. It is, however, evidentiary as to [respondent's] expressed intent not to return."

§161.001(1)(B)

Brokenleg v. Butts, 559 S.W.2d 853, 856 (Tex. App.—El Paso 1977, writ ref'd n.r.e.). "[T]here are four elements to [§15.02(1)(B), now §161.001(1)(B)]. They are: (1) voluntarily leaving the child; (2) without expressing an intent to return; (3) without providing for the adequate support of the child; and (4) remaining away for a period of at least three months. [T]he standard for determining nonsupport under Subparagraph (B) is whether or not there is provision for adequate support of the child, rather than the parent's ability to support the child as in Subparagraph (F). The evidence in this case all reflects that the grandparents were able to and did in fact adequately support the child.... They testified themselves that they provided for all of her physical and medical needs and that she was well-fed, clothed, and in good health during the time she remained in their custody. Since the test under this Subparagraph is not whether or not the parent actually supported the child, but whether or not arrangements were made for the adequate support of the child, and the evidence is undisputed that they were, we conclude that §15.02(1)(B) is not applicable...."

§161.001(1)(C)

Holick v. Smith, 685 S.W.2d 18, 21 (Tex.1985). Respondents "argue that the legislature intended to require parents to personally 'provide adequate support' under (1)(C) because (1)(B) contains the language 'provide *for the* adequate support.' [¶] We believe that subsection (1)(C) is capable of two interpretations. 'Provide' is defined to mean 'to furnish; supply' or 'to fit out with means to an end.' Thus, subsection (1)(C) is susceptible to an interpretation which would merely require that the parent make arrangements for adequate support rather than personally support the child. [¶] We hold that under §15.02(1)(C) [now §161.001(1)(C)], [mother] was required to make arrangements for the adequate support rather than personally support the children."

In re D.L.N., 958 S.W.2d 934, 937 (Tex.App.—Waco 1997, pet. denied). "We must look at the plain and common meaning of 'remained away for a period of at least six months' to determine if the law requires that these be six consecutive months of absence. The language used in this subsection indicates that a parent must remain away from a child for a minimum of six months, without providing adequate support, in order to have his or her parental rights terminated under this provision. Thus, because a parent should not face a termination on this ground until the minimum time-period of six months has passed, we believe the legislature intended that the six month time-period consist of six consecutive months. In addition to the plain language of the statute, other appellate courts have concluded that when a parent's rights are terminated for failing to support a child for one year under §161.001(1)(F) the 'year' referred to in the statute means twelve consecutive months. Finally, our interpretation of §161.001(1)(C) to require six consecutive months of absence is consistent with the Supreme Court's directive that involuntary termination statutes be strictly construed in favor of the parent."

In re B.T., 954 S.W.2d 44, 49 (Tex.App.—San Antonio 1997, writ denied). Respondent "claims in his brief that he did not voluntarily leave [child] with the Department since he was in jail most of the time. Mere imprisonment does not constitute intentional abandonment of the child as a matter of law. However, imprisonment is a factor to consider along with the other evidence."

In re S.K.S., 648 S.W.2d 402, 404 (Tex.App.—San Antonio 1983, no writ). Under §161.001(1)(C), "[i]nability to provide support during some months would not interrupt the running of the [limitations] period if no effort is made to pay support during other months in which there is clear ability to pay."

In re Guillory, 618 S.W.2d 948, 951 (Tex.App.—Houston [1st Dist.] 1981, no writ). "The prerequisites for parental rights to be terminated on grounds of nonsupport are that the evidence must establish not only that the parent failed to support the child for [six] consecutive months, but also that the parent had the ability to contribute to the support of the child for [six] consecutive months. This rule applies even where the inability to pay is the result of the parent's conscious choice."

§161.001(1)(D)

Doyle v. Texas DPRS, 16 S.W.3d 390, 394 (Tex. App.—El Paso 2000, pet. denied). "Section 161.001(1)(D) requires a showing that the environment in which the child is placed endangered the child's physical or emotional well-being. This provision addresses the child's surroundings and environment rather than parental misconduct…."

In re S.D., 980 S.W.2d 758, 763 (Tex.App.—San Antonio 1998, pet. denied). "An environment which routinely subjects a child to the probability that she will be left alone because her parents are once again jailed, whether because of the continued violation of probationary conditions or because of a new offense growing out of a continued use of illegal drugs, or because the parents are once again committed to a rehabilitation program, endangers both the physical and emotional well-being of a child. Conduct that results in such disability, and conduct that subjects a child to a life of uncertainty and instability, endangers the physical and emotional well-being of a child."

Ybarra v. Texas DHS, 869 S.W.2d 574, 577-78 (Tex.App.—Corpus Christi 1993, no writ). "A parent who knowingly places or knowingly allows a child to remain in conditions or surroundings which endanger the physical or emotional well-being of the child violates §15.02(1)(D) [now §161.001(1)(D)]. [To endanger a child is] 'to expose to loss or injury or to jeopardize a child's emotional or physical health.' This provision addresses the child's surroundings and environment, rather than parental conduct. [¶] Because of the higher level of deprivation involved in termination, [courts should] look to *specific* conditions or surroundings and determine whether they endanger the child. [¶] The State must show that the child's living conditions pose a threat of injury or harm. The concern in §15.02(1)(D) is 'the *cause* of the resulting danger to the child's physical or emotional well-being.' There must be a connection between the conditions and the resulting danger to the child's emotional or physical wellbeing."

§161.001(1)(E)

In re M.C., 917 S.W.2d 268, 270 (Tex.1996). "Although there is no evidence that [the respondent] inflicted direct physical abuse on her children, there is evidence that she neglected their physical needs, and neglect can be just as dangerous to the well-being of a child as direct physical abuse."

Texas DHS v. Boyd, 727 S.W.2d 531, 533 (Tex. 1987). "While we agree that 'endanger' means more than a threat of metaphysical injury or the possible ill effects of a less-than-ideal family environment, it is not necessary that the conduct be directed at the child or that the child actually suffers injury. Rather, 'endanger' means to expose to loss or injury [or] to jeopardize[,] and imprisonment is certainly a factor to be considered by the trial court on the issue of endangerment. *At 534:* We hold that if the evidence, including the imprisonment, shows a course of conduct which has the effect of endangering the physical or emotional well-being of the child, a finding under section 15.02(1)(E) [now §161.001(1)(E)] is supportable."

In re R.G., 61 S.W.3d 661, 667-68 (Tex.App.—Waco 2001, n.p.h.). "It is beyond question that sexual abuse is conduct that endangers a child's physical or emotional well-being. ... Parental knowledge that an actual offense has occurred is not necessary; it is sufficient that the parent was aware of the potential for danger and disregarded that risk."

In re AWT, 61 S.W.3d 87, 89 (Tex.App.—Amarillo 2001, no pet.). "[I]ntentional criminal activity which exposed the parent to incarceration is relevant evidence tending to establish a course of conduct endangering the emotional and physical well being of the child. Thus, the evidence regarding [parent's] recent history of criminal behavior ... was admissible...."

In re D.M., 58 S.W.3d 801, 811 (Tex.App.—Fort Worth 2001, n.p.h.). "Subsection E requires us to look at the parent's conduct alone, including actions, omissions, or the parent's failure to act. *At 812:* It is inconsequential that the parental conduct considered in a termination proceeding occurred before the child's birth. Rather, courts look to what the parent did both before and after the child's birth to determine whether termination is necessary. [¶] Additionally, termination under subsection E must be based on more than a single act or omission; a voluntary, deliberate, and conscious 'course of conduct' by the parent is required."

Doyle v. Texas DPRS, 16 S.W.3d 390, 395 (Tex. App.—El Paso 2000, pet. denied). "Under §161.001(1)(E), the cause of the danger to the child must be the parent's conduct alone, as evidenced not only by the parent's actions but also by the parent's omission or failure to act. *At 398:* The [TDPRS] urges that [respondent's] failure to locate and maintain stable employment so that she could provide for the children's needs and her failure to provide a stable home for the children violates §161.001(1)(E). Ordinarily, the stability of the home is one of the factors that should be examined in ascertaining the best interest of a child. Depending on the evidence, it is possible that a parent's failure to provide a stable home and otherwise provide for the children's needs may contribute to a finding that termination is appropriate."

In re King, 15 S.W.3d 272, 276 (Tex.App.—Texarkana 2000, pet. denied). "The aggravated sexual assault of a child living in the home with the child whose parental rights are in question is conduct that we may infer will endanger or jeopardize the well-being, both physical and emotional, of other children in the home who may discover the abuse or be abused themselves. Section 161.001(1)(E) does not require such actual injury before a parent's parental rights may be terminated. *At 277:* Another court of appeals interpreting §161.001(1)(E) has held that similar evidence of sexual abuse of one child living in the home and evidence that the conduct is likely to be repeated is sufficient evidence to support a finding of endangerment to other children living in the home. Other courts of appeals have held that evidence of the abuse of one child is sufficient to support a finding of endangerment to other children. In some cases, such evidence is sufficient even where the child is unborn at the time of the abuse."

In re J.N.R., 982 S.W.2d 137, 142 (Tex.App.—Houston [1st Dist.] 1998, no. pet.). "Mere imprisonment will not, standing alone, constitute engaging in conduct that endangers the physical or emotional well-being of the child. However, if all the evidence, including imprisonment shows a course of conduct that has the effect of endangering the physical or emotional well being of the child, a finding under §161.001(1)(E) is supportable. If the imprisonment of the parent displays a voluntary, deliberate, and conscious course of conduct, it qualifies as conduct that endangers the emotional well being of the child. The conduct need not be directed toward the child or cause the child physical injury to constitute conduct that endangers the emotional well being of the child." *See also* ***In re D.T.***, 34 S.W.3d 625, 634 (Tex.App.—Fort Worth 2000, pet. denied).

Hann v. Texas DPRS, 969 S.W.2d 77, 82 (Tex.App.—El Paso 1998, pet. denied). "Section 161.001(1)(E) of the statute does not require a showing that a parent's conduct caused an actual adverse effect upon the child. It is sufficient to establish endangerment that the child's well-being be jeopardized or exposed to loss or injury. In addition, the specific danger to the child's well-being need not be established as an independent proposition, but may instead be inferred from parental misconduct."

In re B.R., 950 S.W.2d 113, 119 (Tex.App.—El Paso 1997, no writ). "Violent or negligent conduct directed at the other parent or other children, even though not committed in the child's presence, may also be sufficient to demonstrate a course of conduct under §161.001(1)(E)." *See also* ***In re B.B.***, 971 S.W.2d 160, 169 (Tex.App.—Beaumont 1998, pet. denied) (overruling ***Lane v. Jefferson Cty. Child Welfare Unit***, 564 S.W.2d 130, 132 (Tex.App.—Beaumont 1978, writ ref'd n.r.e.); ***Lucas v. Texas DPRS***, 949 S.W.2d 500, 503 (Tex.App.—Waco 1997, writ denied).

Edwards v. Texas DPRS, 946 S.W.2d 130, 138 (Tex.App.—El Paso 1997, no writ). "The use of drugs during pregnancy may be conduct which endangers the physical and emotional well-being of the child. One parent's drug-related endangerment of the child may be imputed to the other parent. "

In re B.J.B., 546 S.W.2d 674, 677 (Tex.App.—Texarkana 1977, writ ref'd n.r.e.). "It is not mandated therein that the children observed the conduct."

Carter v. Dallas Cty. Child Welfare Unit, 532 S.W.2d 140, 141-42 (Tex.App.—Dallas 1975, no writ). "We agree with [mother] that mental incompetence or mental illness alone is not grounds for termination of the parent-child relationship. [¶] When a parent's mental state allows or forces him to engage in conduct which endangers the physical or emotional well-being of his child or children, that conduct is evidence which bears upon the advisability of terminating the parent-child relationship."

§161.001(1)(F)

Lumbis v. Texas DPRS, 65 S.W.3d 844 (Tex.App.—Austin 2002, n.p.h.). "Once it is established by clear and convincing evidence that the affidavit [of relinquishment] was properly executed, the affidavit may only be set aside upon a finding, by the preponderance of the evidence, that it was procured by coercion, duress, fraud, deception, undue influence, or overreaching."

In re J.M.T., 39 S.W.3d 234, 238-39 (Tex.App.—Waco 1999, no pet.). "One of the acts upon which termination can be based is a showing of failure to support the child in accordance with one's ability for a period of one year ending within six months of the date of the filing of the petition. [¶] It was undisputed at trial that [father] had paid no child support for two years. Evidence of failure to pay alone is not adequate to support a violation of the statute. There must be some evidence of ability to support, and that the support was not provided. [¶] When the trial court establishes the amount of child support to be paid by a parent, the court must consider the ability to contribute to the child's support. The child support order includes within it an implied finding that the obligor has the means or ability to pay the amount ordered."

In re Z.W.C., 856 S.W.2d 281, 283 (Tex.App.—Fort Worth 1993, no writ). "One year means twelve consecutive months, and the ability to pay support must exist each month during the twelve-month period." *See also* ***In re M.A.N.M.***, ___ S.W.3d ___ (Tex.App.—San Antonio 2002, n.p.h.) (No. 04-01-00295-CV; 2-6-02).

In re S.K.S., 648 S.W.2d 402, 404 (Tex.App.—San Antonio 1983, no writ). "Inability to provide support during some months would not interrupt the running of the one-year period if no effort is made to pay support during other months in which there is clear ability to pay."

Hellman v. Kincy, 632 S.W.2d 216, 218 (Tex.App.—Fort Worth 1982, no writ). "We find that even though there is no consecutive twelve month period when [father] failed to pay the $140.00 payments as ordered, the requisite period of time was satisfied in which the additional arrearage payment was not made."

Brazier v. Brazier, 597 S.W.2d 442, 444 (Tex. App.—Beaumont 1980, no writ). Respondent "contends the beginning date in computing the time for 'failure to support' is determined by the date of the filing of [petitioner's] second amended petition—December 12,

1978.... [Petitioner] contends the beginning date is the date of the filing of the original petition. We do not agree with either contention. [¶] The original petition, filed June 13, 1978, prayed for divorce, managing conservatorship of only three minors, omitting any reference to the two children.... The first amended petition, filed September 14, 1978, for the first time named the two children and sought termination of [respondent's] parental rights. This was the first time an action for termination of such rights was instituted and constituted the 'filing of the petition' within the meaning of that term as used in §15.02(1)(F) [now §161.001(1)(F)]. The third amended petition, filed April 2, 1979, superseded and completely supplanted the pleadings which were amended. The third amended petition relates back to the time of filing the first amended petition. Therefore, the beginning date for the 'non-support' period would be March 14, 1977."

McGowen v. State, 558 S.W.2d 561, 566 (Tex. App.—Houston [14th Dist.] 1977, writ ref'd n.r.e.). The respondents argue that "the statute does not apprise parents who have not been ordered to pay support of their legal duty to support, and does not inform them of the amount or degree of support that is required. We reject this contention. 'Support' is a legal concept that has acquired a well defined and understood meaning. The term encompasses the contribution of money or services necessary for the maintenance of a person."

§161.001(1)(H)

In re T.M.Z., 665 S.W.2d 184, 187 (Tex.App.—San Antonio 1984, no writ). "Although the evidence clearly shows it was the mother who left the scene when violence erupted during her seventh month of pregnancy, we do not agree there was no 'voluntary abandonment' by the father as the result of her departure. The father knew where his pregnant wife went; he knew her parents and the location of their house. Testimony indicates he did go to that house on occasion, but he never provided any support either to his wife or his child. He was not prohibited from tendering support through the mails. He was not prohibited from going to the attending doctor's office to arrange payment for prenatal care. Nor was he denied entrance to the business office of the hospital to arrange payment for hospital care for his wife and for delivery of his child. [¶] Abandonment can mean more than a physical leave-taking. It can also mean to turn one's back on a duty that one has."

Allred v. Harris Cty. Child Welfare Unit, 615 S.W.2d 803, 807 (Tex.App.—Houston [1st Dist.] 1980, writ ref'd n.r.e.). "The evidence that [father] entered into a course of wilful criminal activity with knowledge of his wife's pregnancy and of the possible consequences of his course of conduct implied a conscious disregard and indifference to his parental responsibilities and the subsequent imprisonment for such conduct constituted 'voluntary abandonment.'"

§161.001(1)(K)

Neal v. Texas DHS, 814 S.W.2d 216, 218-19 (Tex.App.—San Antonio 1991, writ denied). "Section 15.02(1)(K) [now §161.001(1)(K)] allows the court to grant a petition terminating the parent-child relationship with respect to a petitioner who is not a parent if the court finds that the parent has executed before or after the suit is filed an unrevoked or irrevocable affidavit of relinquishment of parental rights as provided by §15.03 [now §161.103]. The affidavit referred to in §15.03 is identified as an 'affidavit for voluntary relinquishment of parental rights.' Because of the very nature of a voluntary relinquishment of parental rights, we find that it is implicit in the language of §15.03 that such an affidavit be executed voluntarily. Accordingly, we hold that only a voluntarily executed §15.03 affidavit will support a finding under §15.02(1)(K). ... Stated another way, we hold that an involuntarily executed affidavit is a complete defense to a termination suit or decree based solely upon a finding under §15.02(1)(K)...."

Ivy v. Edna Gladney Home, 783 S.W.2d 829, 832 (Tex.App.—Fort Worth 1990, no writ). "Even though ... §15.02 [now §161.001] and the case law do not expressly state that an affidavit of waiver of interest in a child is sufficient to uphold a termination judgment by the court, we again think the legislature did not intend to give more protection to fathers signing an affidavit of waiver of interest in child than they did to parents signing affidavits of relinquishment, and therefore, we hold the executed 'Affidavit of Waiver of Interest in Child,' in and of itself, was sufficient to uphold the termination judgment signed by the court."

In re B.B.F., 595 S.W.2d 873, 874 (Tex.App.—San Antonio 1980, no writ). "Since execution of an affidavit of relinquishment of parental rights is a proper basis for terminating those rights in a subsequent suit to terminate the parent-child relationship, and a waiver of process may be included in the affidavit, it is clear that a waiver of citation may be signed prior to the filing of suit. Thus, the Family Code provides an exception to the general rule that a waiver of citation is proper only if executed after suit is brought. There is a sound reason for this exception. After executing an unrevoked or irrevocable affidavit of relinquishment of parental rights, a natural parent is no longer an interested party in a suit to terminate the parent-child relationship. Consequently, neither due process nor logic require that a person who has voluntarily relinquished parental rights and waived service of citation be given notice of a subsequent suit to terminate the parent-child relationship."

§161.001(1)(L)

Vidaurri v. Ensey, 58 S.W.3d 142, 145 (Tex.App.—Amarillo 2001, no pet.). The prospective adoptive parents urged that the *serious injury* contemplated by the statute must "necessarily be inferred, based on the way the statute was written and the particular language the enacting legislature chose to use....' [¶] One rule of construction obligates us to afford meaning to every word and phrase in a statute. In that at bar appears the phrase 'death or serious injury of a child'. Thus, we cannot ignore it. Furthermore, the phrase is used in relation to the parent (whose parental rights are in jeopardy) having been criminally responsible for same. That is, the edict directs that termination may be permitted 'if the court finds ... that the parent has ... been convicted or has been placed on community supervision ... for being criminally responsible for the death or serious injury of a child....' And, when the crimes enumerated in the statute are placed in context with the aforementioned words, we cannot but conclude that termination is permissible only if 1) the parent has committed acts constituting a violation of one of the crimes enumerated in §161.001(1)(l)(i) through (xiii), 2) the parent's guilt for committing the crime has been adjudicated or the adjudication of that guilt has been deferred, and 3) the parent, in committing the acts which underlie the crime, was responsible for a child's death or serious injury. [¶] As to the contention that serious injury 'must necessarily be inferred' from the mere commission of an enumerated crime, we again note the dearth of citation supporting their argument. [W]e find nothing in the statute itself expressly directing a court to infer the existence of death or serious injury to a child simply because a parent was convicted of or granted deferred adjudication viz-a-viz an enumerated crime. Indeed, such could not be inferred from some of the crimes itemized, especially that involved at bar." *See also* ***In re L.S.R.***, 60 S.W.3d 376, 378 (Tex.App.—Fort Worth 2001, n.p.h.).

§161.001(1)(M)

Avery v. State, 963 S.W.2d 550, 552-53 (Tex.App.—Houston [1st Dist.] 1997, no pet.). "Section 161.001(1)(M) provides that a trial court may order termination of the parent-child relationship if the parent has had her parent-child relationship terminated with another child based on a finding that her conduct was in violation of paragraphs (D) or (E). Although [respondent] admitted that her parental rights were terminated with another child 17 years ago based upon paragraph (D) and (E), she claims that termination is too remote in time, and, therefore, is irrelevant to her current capacity to care for [child]. [¶] [T]he evidence shows that [respondent's] endangering conduct still persists. Her criminal record shows a pattern of criminal activity beginning in 1979 and continuing after [child's] birth. [¶] Based upon this evidence, we hold the trial court could find by clear and convincing evidence that [respondent's] problems with crime and drug abuse still existed."

§161.001(1)(N)

In re D.T., 34 S.W.3d 625, 633 (Tex.App.—Fort Worth 2000, pet. denied). "The elements of constructive abandonment are: (1) the child has been in the permanent or temporary managing conservatorship of TDPRS for not less than six months; (2) the department has made reasonable efforts to return the child to the parent; (3) the parent has not regularly visited or maintained significant contact with the child; and (4) the parent has demonstrated an inability to provide the child with a safe environment. If there is no evidence of one or more of these elements, then the finding of constructive abandonment fails."

§161.001(1)(O)

In re M.C.M., 57 S.W.3d 27, 32 (Tex.App.—Houston [1st Dist.] 2001, pet. denied). Respondents "do not challenge the constitutionality of §161.001(1)(O). Instead, they seem to argue that violation of a court order can *only* be an act of criminal contempt, and, therefore, they are entitled to all the protections afforded a person being held in contempt of court. [¶] We disagree. Violation of the trial court's temporary orders in this case may be a ground for criminal contempt, but it is also a ground for termination of [respondents'] parental rights. The fact is, [respondents] were not held in contempt of court, and their parental rights were not terminated as a *punishment* for refusing to comply with the court's order. [¶] The trial court, in its temporary orders, determined that to obtain the return of their children, [respondents] should participate in psychotherapy and substance abuse treatment. [Respondents] did not do so. Thus, §161.001(1)(O) was included in the court's charge as a ground for termination. [Respondents] are not being punished for violating the court's order; their parental rights are being terminated because [respondents] refused to take the steps necessary to obtain the return of the children."

§161.001(1)(Q)

In re Caballero, 53 S.W.3d 391, 395-96 (Tex.App.—Amarillo 2001, pet. denied). Petitioner's argument is that "the term 'care' in §161.001(1)(Q) is limited to the parent's personal care of the child. We do not agree with that view. [¶] Subsection (Q) was added to §161.001(1) by the 75th Legislature. We have found no published opinion construing the term 'care' in subsection (Q). However, a long line of cases have recognized the rule that incarceration alone cannot support a termination of parental rights. The [petitioner] argues these cases are inapplicable because they were decided prior to the adoption of subsection (Q). We disagree. There is nothing in the text of subsection (Q) or in the bill analysis that would indicate the legislature intended to change or alter the established rule. Because incarceration is inherently inconsistent with providing personal care for a child, the legislature's inclusion of the phrase "and inability to care for the child" would be meaningless unless care encompassed arranging for care to be provided by another. Without a clear indication of legislative intent to alter the established rule, we decline to adopt the Department's position." *See also **In re A.R.R.***, 61 S.W.3d 691, 700-01 (Tex.App.—Fort Worth 2001, pet. denied).

§161.001(2)

Holley v. Adams, 544 S.W.2d 367, 371-72 (Tex. 1976). "An extended number of factors have been considered by the courts in ascertaining the best interest of the child. Included among these are the following: (A) the desires of the child; (B) the emotional and physical needs of the child now and in the future; (C) the emotional and physical danger to the child now and in the future; (D) the parental abilities of the individuals seeking custody; (E) the programs available to assist these individuals to promote the best interest of the child; (F) the plans for the child by these individuals or by the agency seeking custody; (G) the stability of the home or proposed placement; (H) the acts or omissions of the parent which may indicate that the existing parent-child relationship is not a proper one; and (I) any excuse for the acts or omissions of the parent. This listing is by no means exhaustive, but does indicate a number of considerations which either have been or would appear to be pertinent." *See also **Swate v. Swate***, 72 S.W.3d 763, 769 (Tex.App.—Waco 2002, n.p.h.) (stepparent's desire for adoption is another factor); ***Salas v. Texas DPRS***, 71 S.W.3d 783, 792 (Tex. App.—El Paso 2002, n.p.h.) (child's young age is another factor).

In re M.A.N.M., ___ S.W.3d ___ (Tex.App.—San Antonio 2002, n.p.h.) (No. 04-01-00295-CV; 2-6-02). "Quite often, the best interest of the child is infused with the statutory offensive behavior. While there are instances where the offending behavior will demand termination of parental rights, there are also those cases where the best interest determination must have a firm basis in facts standing apart from the offending behavior. Although such behavior may reasonably suggest that a child would be better off with a new family, the best interest standard does not permit termination merely because a child might be better off living elsewhere." (Internal quotations omitted.)

In re K.C.M., 4 S.W.3d 392, 395 (Tex.App.—Houston [1st Dist.] 1999, pet. denied). "There is a strong presumption that the best interest of the child is served by keeping custody in the natural parent. It is the TDPRS's burden to rebut this presumption." *See also **Horvatich v. Texas DPRS***, ___ S.W.3d ___ (Tex.App.—Austin 2002, n.p.h.) (No. 03-01-00248-CV; 5-16-02).

Trevino v. Texas DPRS, 893 S.W.2d 243, 246 (Tex.App.—Austin 1995, no writ). "To support a trial court's judgment, the petitioner must prove that the parent engaged in conduct described in §15.02(a)(1) [now §161.001(a)(1)] *and* that it was in the best interest of the child to terminate the parental rights. The trial court has no authority to terminate a parent-child relationship solely because it would be in the best interest of the child."

FAM §161.002. TERMINATION OF THE RIGHTS OF AN ALLEGED BIOLOGICAL FATHER

A *Subsections (a) through (e) below are effective for motions or requests for relief made in parentage or paternity proceedings commenced on or after June 14, 2001.*

(a) The procedural and substantive standards for termination of parental rights apply to the termination of the rights of an alleged father.

(b) The rights of an alleged father may be terminated if:

(1) after being served with citation, he does not respond by timely filing an admission of paternity or a counterclaim for paternity under Chapter 160;

(2) he has not registered with the paternity registry under Chapter 160, and after the exercise of due diligence by the petitioner:

(A) his identity and location are unknown; or

(B) his identity is known but he cannot be located; or

(3) he has registered with the paternity registry under Chapter 160, but the petitioner's attempt to personally serve citation at the address provided to the registry and at any other address for the alleged father known by the petitioner has been unsuccessful, despite the due diligence of the petitioner.

(c) The termination of the rights of an alleged father under Subsection (b)(2) rendered on or after January 1, 1998, does not require personal service of citation or citation by publication on the alleged father.

(d) The termination of rights of an alleged father under Subsection (b)(3) does not require service of citation by publication on the alleged father.

(e) The court shall not render an order terminating parental rights under Subsection (b)(2) unless the court, after reviewing the petitioner's sworn affidavit describing the petitioner's effort to identify and locate the alleged father and considering any evidence submitted by the attorney ad litem for the alleged father, has found that the petitioner exercised due diligence in attempting to identify and locate the alleged father. The order shall contain specific findings regarding due diligence of the petitioner.

Subsections (a) through (e) below are effective for motions or requests for relief made in parentage or paternity proceedings commenced before June 14, 2001.

(a) The procedural and substantive standards for termination of parental rights apply to the termination of the rights of an alleged biological father.

(b) The rights of an alleged biological father may be terminated if:

(1) after being served with citation, he does not respond by timely filing an admission of paternity or a counterclaim for paternity under Chapter 160 prior to the final hearing in the suit;

(2) he has not registered with the paternity registry under Subchapter D, Chapter 160, and after the exercise of due diligence by the petitioner:

(A) his identity and location are unknown; or

(B) his identity is known but he cannot be located; or

(3) he has registered with the paternity registry under Subchapter D, Chapter 160, but the petitioner's attempt to personally serve citation at the address provided to the registry and at any other address for the alleged father known by the petitioner has been unsuccessful, despite the due diligence of the petitioner.

(c) The termination of the rights of an alleged biological father under Subsection (b)(2) rendered on or after January 1, 1998, does not require personal service of citation or citation by publication on the alleged father.

(d) The termination of rights of an alleged biological father under Subsection (b)(3) does not require service of citation by publication on the alleged father.

(e) The court shall not render an order terminating parental rights under Subsection (b)(2) unless the court, after reviewing the petitioner's sworn affidavit describing the petitioner's effort to identify and locate the alleged biological father and considering any evidence submitted by the attorney ad litem for the alleged biological father, has found that the petitioner exercised due diligence in attempting to identify and locate the alleged biological father. The order shall contain specific findings regarding due diligence of the petitioner.

(f) The court shall not render an order terminating parental rights under Subsection (b)(3) unless the court, after reviewing the petitioner's sworn affidavit describing the petitioner's effort to obtain personal service of citation on the alleged father and considering any evidence submitted by the attorney ad litem for the alleged father, has found that the petitioner exercised due diligence in attempting to obtain service on the alleged father. The order shall contain specific findings regarding the exercise of due diligence of the petitioner.

History of Fam §161.002: Acts 1995, 74th Leg., ch. 20, §1, eff. April 20, 1995. Amended by Acts 1995, 74th Leg., ch. 751, §66, eff. Sept. 1, 1995; Acts 1997, 75th Leg., ch. 561, §7, eff. Sept. 1, 1997; Acts 2001, 77th Leg., ch. 821, §2.16 (eff. June 14, 2001), ch. 1090, §1 (eff. Sept. 1, 2001). Source: Former Fam §15.023.

In re J.W.T., 872 S.W.2d 189, 198 (Tex.1994). "We do not say that our Constitution guarantees every natural father ties with his illegitimate offspring. We do say that one who is arbitrarily prevented from attempting to establish any relationship with his natural child, after making early and unqualified acceptance of parental duties as [the father] has done, is denied due course of law under §19 of our Texas Bill of Rights."

Attorney Gen. v. Lavan, 833 S.W.2d 952, 954 (Tex. 1992). "We ... find nothing in the Code that expressly prohibits the State from bringing a claim under chapter 12 [now chapter 151] to disestablish the paternity of a presumed father in the same suit in which it brings a claim under chapter 13 [now chapter 160] to establish paternity in an alleged biological father. To allow both claims ... to be joined in one suit advances the best interest of the child by eliminating any period of time a child would be left without the benefit of a legal father. ... Conversely, we find no countervailing benefit from a requirement that the paternity of a presumed father be disestablished in a final judgment in a separate proceeding before proceeding with a second suit to establish the paternity of an alleged biological father."

In re Baby McLean, 725 S.W.2d 696, 698 (Tex. 1987). We "conclude that the Equal Rights Amendment is more extensive and provides more specific protection than both the United States and Texas due process and equal protection guarantees. [¶] We...choose not to adopt a per se standard which would automatically invalidate gender-based distinctions, but rather seek a standard to be used to reach the evils which it was designed to combat. Our reading of the [ERA] elevates sex to a suspect classification. Sex is clearly listed in the amendment along with other classifications afforded maximum constitutional protection. [¶] The appropriate standard is thus one which recognizes that the [ERA] does not yield except to compelling state interests. Further, it is not enough to say that the state has an important interest furthered by the discriminatory law. Even the loftiest goal does not justify sex-based discrimination in light of the clear constitutional prohibition. Under our model of strict judicial scrutiny, such discrimination is allowed only when the proponent of the discrimination can prove that there is no other manner to protect the state's compelling interest. [¶] In this case, the state no doubt has a significant interest in protecting the welfare of a child born to a mother not married to the child's father. [¶] Nevertheless, the state's interest can be protected without discriminating solely on the basis of sex. The state goal of protecting children's welfare is better served by keying that interest to the father's relationship to the child. A father who steps forward, willing and able to shoulder the responsibilities of raising a child should not be required to meet a higher burden of proof solely because he is male."

Phillips v. Texas DPRS, 25 S.W.3d 348, 357 (Tex. App.—Austin 2000, no pet.). "Theoretically, if a married woman were to name several different men as the potential father of her child, the [DPRS] could include the presumed father (the husband) and all the other alleged biological fathers in one suit and seek to terminate the parental rights, if any, of each according to §§161.001 and 161.002. Section 161.002 does not require a definitive *biological* determination of paternity before an alleged biological father's rights can be terminated. The statutory scheme anticipates that there can be more than one candidate for paternity and allows the court to terminate, in the same proceeding, whatever parental rights they may have."

FAM §161.003. INVOLUNTARY TERMINATION: INABILITY TO CARE FOR CHILD

(a) The court may order termination of the parent-child relationship in a suit filed by the Department of Protective and Regulatory Services if the court finds that:

(1) the parent has a mental or emotional illness or a mental deficiency that renders the parent unable to provide for the physical, emotional, and mental needs of the child;

(2) the illness or deficiency, in all reasonable probability, proved by clear and convincing evidence, will continue to render the parent unable to provide for the child's needs until the 18th birthday of the child;

A *Subsection (3) below is effective for suits to terminate the parent-child relationship filed by the DPRS on or after Sept. 1, 2001.*

(3) the department has been the temporary or sole managing conservator of the child of the parent for at least six months preceding the date of the hearing on the termination held in accordance with Subsection (c);

Subsection (3) below is effective for suits to terminate the parent-child relationship filed by the DPRS before Sept. 1, 2001.

(3) the department has been the temporary or sole managing conservator of the child of the parent for the six months preceding the filing of the petition;

(4) the department has made reasonable efforts to return the child to the parent; and

(5) the termination is in the best interest of the child.

(b) Immediately after the filing of a suit under this section, the court shall appoint an attorney ad litem to represent the interests of the parent against whom the suit is brought.

(c) A hearing on the termination may not be held earlier than 180 days after the date on which the suit was filed.

(d) An attorney appointed under Subsection (b) shall represent the parent for the duration of the suit unless the parent, with the permission of the court, retains another attorney.

History of Fam §161.003: Acts 1995, 74th Leg., ch. 20, §1, eff. April 20, 1995. Amended by Acts 1995, 74th Leg., ch. 751, §67, eff. Sept. 1, 1995; Acts 2001, 77th Leg., ch. 1090, §2 (eff. Sept. 1, 2001), ch. 496, §1 (eff. Sept. 1, 2001). Source: Former Fam §15.024.

Spurlock v. Texas DPRS, 904 S.W.2d 152, 158 (Tex.App.—Austin 1995, writ denied). "[T]he trial court's judgment that *in all reasonable probability* [respondent] will not be able to care for her children until they reach the age of eighteen is supported by factually sufficient evidence. The statute does not require scientific certainty, but rather reasonable probability. According to the evidence produced at trial, [respondent's] condition will not improve with time absent future advances in research and medication; even if such advances occur, her condition will improve only if [respondent], who has a history of noncompliance with medication, takes the medication." *See also* ***Salas v. Texas DPRS***, 71 S.W.3d 783, 790 (Tex.App.—El Paso 2002, n.p.h.).

FAM §161.004. TERMINATION OF PARENTAL RIGHTS AFTER DENIAL OF PRIOR PETITION TO TERMINATE

(a) The court may terminate the parent-child relationship after rendition of an order that previously denied termination of the parent-child relationship if:

(1) the petition under this section is filed after the date the order denying termination was rendered;

(2) the circumstances of the child, parent, sole managing conservator, possessory conservator, or other party affected by the order denying termination have materially and substantially changed since the date that the order was rendered;

(3) the parent committed an act listed under Section 161.001 before the date the order denying termination was rendered; and

(4) termination is in the best interest of the child.

(b) At a hearing under this section, the court may consider evidence presented at a previous hearing in a suit for termination of the parent-child relationship of the parent with respect to the same child.

History of Fam §161.004: Acts 1995, 74th Leg., ch. 20, §1, eff. April 20, 1995. Source: Former Fam §15.025.

FAM §161.005. TERMINATION WHEN PARENT IS PETITIONER

(a) A parent may file a suit for termination of the petitioner's parent-child relationship. The court may order termination if termination is in the best interest of the child.

(b) If the petition designates the Department of Protective and Regulatory Services as managing conservator, the department shall be given service of citation. The court shall notify the department if the court appoints the department as the managing conservator of the child.

History of Fam §161.005: Acts 1995, 74th Leg., ch. 20, §1, eff. April 20, 1995. Amended by Acts 1995, 74th Leg., ch. 751, §68, eff. Sept. 1, 1995. Source: Former Fam §15.01.

In re T.S.S., 61 S.W.3d 481, 483-84 (Tex.App.—San Antonio 2001, n.p.h.). Petitioner "seeks to terminate his parental responsibilities under ... §161.005 (a).... [***Nichols v. Nichols***, 803 S.W.2d 484 (Tex.App.—El Paso 1991, no writ)] construed this provision as permitting a parent to petition the court to terminate its own rights and responsibilities in the parent-child relationship, 'but the petition is to be *granted* only if the courts finds that the termination is in the best interest of the child.' In dicta, the court recognized that a child under such circumstances might want to raise defenses 'such as res judicata or collateral attack on the prior divorce decree.' *At 487:* In the present action, [petitioner] seeks to terminate his future responsibilities to a child he has raised for fourteen years because he says he now has proof that he is not the biological father and this has destroyed his paternal feelings toward the child. This was an issue that could have been litigated in 1989 at the time of the divorce. ... Now he has responded to a motion to modify child support with his own independent action to terminate the parent-child relationship. The basis of the action is alleged DNA evidence that he is not the biological father. That evidence could have been obtained in 1989 before the divorce decree was entered. [Petitioner] attempts to do an end-run around a final decree by filing this action, and he seeks to relitigate a fact issue that was essential to the judgment in the prior decree. [¶] That being the case, ... the issue of parentage is precluded by collateral estoppel...."

FAM §161.006. TERMINATION AFTER ABORTION

(a) A petition requesting termination of the parent-child relationship with respect to a parent who is not the petitioner may be granted if the child was born alive as the result of an abortion.

(b) In this code, "abortion" means an intentional expulsion of a human fetus from the body of a woman induced by any means for the purpose of causing the death of the fetus.

(c) The court or the jury may not terminate the parent-child relationship under this section with respect to a parent who:

(1) had no knowledge of the abortion; or

(2) participated in or consented to the abortion for the sole purpose of preventing the death of the mother.

History of Fam §161.006: Acts 1995, 74th Leg., ch. 20, §1, eff. April 20, 1995. Source: Former Fam §15.022.

FAM §161.007. TERMINATION WHEN PREGNANCY RESULTS FROM CRIMINAL ACT

The court may order the termination of the parent-child relationship of a parent and a child if the court finds that:

(1) the parent has been convicted of an offense committed under Section 22.011, 22.021, or 25.02, Penal Code;

(2) as a direct result of the commission of the offense by the parent, the victim of the offense became pregnant with the parent's child; and

(3) termination is in the best interest of the child.

History of Fam §161.007: Acts 1997, 75th Leg., ch. 561, §8, eff. Sept. 1, 1997.

Sections 161.008-161.100 reserved for expansion

SUBCHAPTER B. PROCEDURES

FAM §161.101. PETITION ALLEGATIONS

A petition for the termination of the parent-child relationship is sufficient without the necessity of specifying the underlying facts if the petition alleges in the statutory language the ground for the termination and that termination is in the best interest of the child.

History of Fam §161.101: Acts 1995, 74th Leg., ch. 20, §1, eff. April 20, 1995. Source: Former Fam §11.08(e).

In re B.B., 971 S.W.2d 160, 163 (Tex.App.—Beaumont 1998, pet. denied). "While under §161.001(1)(A), (B), (F), (N)(i), (ii) and (iii), these are grounds for termination, they must be pleaded in order to support the trial court's judgment."

In re S.R.M., 601 S.W.2d 766, 769 (Tex.App.—Amarillo 1980, no writ). "[W]e conclude that the word 'must' as used in §11.08(b)(10) [now §102.008] denotes a mandatory statutory requirement; and therefore, the statutory grounds for termination must be stated in the petition."

FAM §161.102. FILING SUIT FOR TERMINATION BEFORE BIRTH

(a) A suit for termination may be filed before the birth of the child.

(b) If the suit is filed before the birth of the child, the petition shall be styled "In the Interest of an Unborn Child." After the birth, the clerk shall change the style of the case to conform to the requirements of Section 102.008.

History of Fam §161.102: Acts 1995, 74th Leg., ch. 20, §1, eff. April 20, 1995. Source: Former Fam §15.021(a), (c).

FAM §161.103. AFFIDAVIT OF VOLUNTARY RELINQUISHMENT OF PARENTAL RIGHTS

(a) An affidavit for voluntary relinquishment of parental rights must be:

(1) signed after the birth of the child, but not before 48 hours after the birth of the child, by the parent, whether or not a minor, whose parental rights are to be relinquished;

(2) witnessed by two credible persons; and

(3) verified before a person authorized to take oaths.

(b) The affidavit must contain:

(1) the name, address, and age of the parent whose parental rights are being relinquished;

(2) the name, age, and birth date of the child;

(3) the names and addresses of the guardians of the person and estate of the child, if any;

(4) a statement that the affiant is or is not presently obligated by court order to make payments for the support of the child;

(5) a full description and statement of value of all property owned or possessed by the child;

(6) an allegation that termination of the parent-child relationship is in the best interest of the child;

(7) one of the following, as applicable:

(A) the name and address of the other parent;

(B) a statement that the parental rights of the other parent have been terminated by death or court order; or

(C) a statement that the child has no presumed father and that an affidavit of status of the child has been executed as provided by this chapter;

(8) a statement that the parent has been informed of parental rights and duties;

(9) a statement that the relinquishment is revocable, that the relinquishment is irrevocable, or that the relinquishment is irrevocable for a stated period of time;

(10) if the relinquishment is revocable, a statement in boldfaced type concerning the right of the parent signing the affidavit to revoke the relinquishment only if the revocation is made before the 11th day after the date the affidavit is executed;

(11) if the relinquishment is revocable, the name and address of a person to whom the revocation is to be delivered; and

(12) the designation of a prospective adoptive parent, the Department of Protective and Regulatory Services, if the department has consented in writing to the designation, or a licensed child-placing agency to serve as managing conservator of the child and the address of the person or agency.

(c) The affidavit may contain:

(1) a waiver of process in a suit to terminate the parent-child relationship filed under this chapter or in a suit to terminate joined with a petition for adoption; and

(2) a consent to the placement of the child for adoption by the Department of Protective and Regulatory Services or by a licensed child-placing agency.

(d) A copy of the affidavit shall be provided to the parent at the time the parent signs the affidavit.

(e) The relinquishment in an affidavit that designates the Department of Protective and Regulatory Services or a licensed child-placing agency to serve as the managing conservator is irrevocable. A relinquishment in any other affidavit of relinquishment is revocable unless it expressly provides that it is irrevocable for a stated period of time not to exceed 60 days after the date of its execution.

(f) A relinquishment in an affidavit of relinquishment of parental rights that fails to state that the relinquishment is irrevocable for a stated time is revocable as provided by Section 161.1035.

(g) To revoke a relinquishment under Subsection (e) the parent must sign a statement witnessed by two credible persons and verified before a person authorized to take oaths. A copy of the revocation shall be delivered to the person designated in the affidavit. If a parent attempting to revoke a relinquishment under this subsection has knowledge that a suit for termination of the parent-child relationship has been filed based on the parent's affidavit of relinquishment of parental rights, the parent shall file a copy of the revocation with the clerk of the court.

History of Fam §161.103: Acts 1995, 74th Leg., ch. 20, §1, eff. April 20, 1995. Amended by Acts 1995, 74th Leg., ch. 751, §69, eff. Sept. 1, 1995; Acts 1997, 75th Leg., ch. 561, §9, eff. Sept. 1, 1997. Source: Former Fam §15.03.

Brown v. McLennan Cty. Children's Protective Servs., 627 S.W.2d 390, 393 (Tex.1982). "Looking to §15.03(c)(2) [now §161.103(c)(1)], it provides for waiver of citation within the affidavit of relinquishment if the suit for termination of relationship is brought.... Section 15.02(1)(K) [now §161.001(1)(K)] is the provision creating the right to termination when the parent has executed an affidavit of relinquishment either before or after the suit is filed. [¶] These provisions have been upheld as a permissible exception to the prohibition against pre-suit waiver. [¶] In this cause, [respondent] voluntarily executed the affidavit in question in the presence of two witnesses, before a notary. The affidavit clearly sets out she is relinquishing all parental rights, that suit will be filed to terminate her rights, that she will not be further informed about the suit, and that this act is irrevocable. Certainly this Court recognizes the parent-child relationship as a basic civil right due a high degree of protection. However, when a parent voluntarily terminates this [P-C] bond, the best interests of the child become paramount."

In re V.R.W., 41 S.W.3d 183, 192-93 (Tex.App.—Houston [14th Dist.] 2001, no pet.). "[B]ecause an affidavit of relinquishment waives a constitutional right, it must be made voluntarily, knowingly, intelligently, and with full awareness of its legal consequences. The proponent of the affidavit has the burden to establish by clear and convincing evidence that the affidavit was executed according to the terms of §161.103.... Once the proponent has met that burden, the burden then shifts to the affiant to establish by a preponderance of the evidence that the affidavit was executed as a result of coercion, duress, fraud, deception, undue influence or overreaching. An involuntarily executed affidavit is a complete defense to a termination decree."

In re Bruno, 974 S.W.2d 401, 405 (Tex.App.—San Antonio 1998, no pet.). "The Texas family code requires that an affidavit of relinquishment of parental rights be witnessed by two credible persons. However, there is no requirement that the credibility of the witnesses be affirmatively proven or even that the witnesses be present when the document is signed."

In re R.D.S., 902 S.W.2d 714, 721 (Tex.App.—Amarillo 1995, no writ). We are not ready to say that "revoking an affidavit of voluntary relinquishment under §15.03 [now §161.103] [does not] *per se* strip[] the document of all probative value. If the parent truly intended to 'not return' when it signed the affidavit, the fact that the parent *had* that intent is frozen. Rescinding the document simply evinces a changed mind. It does not have the effect of creating a time gate through which the parent may travel back and erase established fact. The affidavit remains indicative of the preexisting intent."

In re D.E.W., 654 S.W.2d 33, 35 (Tex.App.—Fort Worth 1983, writ ref'd n.r.e.). "There is no requirement that the witnesses be present when the document is signed. It is also well established that the notary need not be physically present at the time the signature is made. *At 36:* The only grounds for overturning a properly notarized document is fraud or imposition which must be alleged and proven."

In re B.B.F., 595 S.W.2d 873, 875 (Tex.App.—San Antonio 1980, no writ). "There is no requirement in §15.03 [now §161.103] or anywhere else that an affidavit of relinquishment affirmatively show the credibility of the attesting witnesses. Moreover, an affidavit of relinquishment of parental rights, in proper form, is prima facie evidence of its validity. Thus, it is not necessary for a proponent of an affidavit to offer direct testimony that the attesting witnesses are credible."

FAM §161.1035. REVOCABILITY OF CERTAIN AFFIDAVITS

An affidavit of relinquishment of parental rights or affidavit of waiver of interest in a child that fails to state that the relinquishment or waiver is irrevocable for a stated time is:

(1) revocable only if the revocation is made before the 11th day after the date the affidavit is executed; and

(2) irrevocable on or after the 11th day after the date the affidavit is executed.

History of Fam §161.1035: Acts 1997, 75th Leg., ch. 561, §10, eff. Sept. 1, 1997.

FAM §161.104. RIGHTS OF DESIGNATED MANAGING CONSERVATOR PENDING COURT APPOINTMENT

A person, licensed child-placing agency, or authorized agency designated managing conservator of a child in an irrevocable or unrevoked affidavit of relinquishment has a right to possession of the child superior to the right of the person executing the affidavit, the right to consent to medical, surgical, dental, and psychological treatment of the child, and the rights and duties given by Chapter 153 to a possessory conservator until such time as these rights and duties are modified or terminated by court order.

History of Fam §161.104: Acts 1995, 74th Leg., ch. 20, §1, eff. April 20, 1995. Amended by Acts 1995, 74th Leg., ch. 751, §70, eff. Sept. 1, 1995. Source: Former Fam §14.02(d).

FAM §161.105. AFFIDAVIT OF STATUS OF CHILD

(a) If the child has no presumed father, an affidavit shall be:

(1) signed by the mother, whether or not a minor;

(2) witnessed by two credible persons; and

(3) verified before a person authorized to take oaths.

(b) The affidavit must:

(1) state that the mother is not and has not been married to the alleged father of the child;

(2) state that the mother and alleged father have not attempted to marry under the laws of this state or another state or nation;

(3) state that paternity has not been established under the laws of any state or nation; and

(4) contain one of the following, as applicable:

(A) the name and whereabouts of a man alleged to be the father;

(B) the name of an alleged father and a statement that the affiant does not know the whereabouts of the father;

(C) a statement that an alleged father has executed an acknowledgment of paternity under Chapter 160 and an affidavit of relinquishment of parental rights under this chapter and that both affidavits have been filed with the court; or

(D) a statement that the name of an alleged father is unknown.

(c) The affidavit of status of child may be executed at any time after the first trimester of the pregnancy of the mother.

History of Fam §161.105: Acts 1995, 74th Leg., ch. 20, §1, eff. April 20, 1995. Amended by Acts 1999, 76th Leg., ch. 556, §40, eff. Sept. 1, 1999. Source: Former Fam §15.04.

FAM §161.106. AFFIDAVIT OF WAIVER OF INTEREST IN CHILD

(a) A man may sign an affidavit disclaiming any interest in a child and waiving notice or the service of citation in any suit filed or to be filed affecting the parent-child relationship with respect to the child.

(b) The affidavit may be signed before the birth of the child.

(c) The affidavit shall be:

(1) signed by the man, whether or not a minor;

(2) witnessed by two credible persons; and

(3) verified before a person authorized to take oaths.

(d) The affidavit may contain a statement that the affiant does not admit being the father of the child or having had a sexual relationship with the mother of the child.

(e) An affidavit of waiver of interest in a child may be used in a suit in which the affiant attempts to establish an interest in the child. The affidavit may not be used in a suit brought by another person, licensed child-placing agency, or authorized agency to establish the affiant's paternity of the child.

(f) A waiver in an affidavit under this section that designates the Department of Protective and Regulatory Services or a licensed child-placing agency to serve as the managing conservator is irrevocable. A waiver in any other affidavit under this section is revocable unless it expressly provides that it is irrevocable for a stated period not to exceed 60 days after the date of execution.

(g) A waiver in an affidavit under this section that fails to state that the waiver is irrevocable for a stated time is revocable as provided by Section 161.1035.

(h) An affidavit under this section that contains a waiver that is revocable must contain:

(1) a statement in boldfaced type concerning the right of the person who executed the affidavit to revoke the affidavit only if the revocation is made before the 11th day after the date the affidavit is executed; and

(2) the name and address of the person to whom the revocation is to be delivered.

(i) A copy of the affidavit shall be provided to the person who executed the affidavit at the time the person signs the affidavit.

(j) To revoke a waiver, the person who executed the affidavit must sign a statement witnessed by two credible persons and verified before a person authorized to take oaths. A copy of the revocation shall be delivered to the person designated in the affidavit of waiver of interest in a child. If a person attempting to revoke an affidavit under this subsection has knowledge that a suit for termination of the parent-child relationship based on the person's waiver of interest in a child has been filed, the person shall file a copy of the revocation with the clerk of the court.

History of Fam §161.106: Acts 1995, 74th Leg., ch. 20, §1, eff. April 20, 1995. Amended by Acts 1997, 75th Leg., ch. 561, §11, eff. Sept. 1, 1997. Source: Former Fam §15.041(a)-(d).

FAM §161.107. MISSING PARENT OR RELATIVE

(a) In this section:

(1) "Parent" means a parent whose parent-child relationship with a child has not been terminated.

(2) "Relative" means a parent, grandparent, or adult sibling or child.

(b) If a parent of the child has not been personally served in a suit in which the Department of Protective and Regulatory Services seeks termination, the department must make a diligent effort to locate that parent.

(c) If a parent has not been personally served and cannot be located, the department shall make a diligent effort to locate a relative of the missing parent to give the relative an opportunity to request appointment as the child's managing conservator.

(d) If the department is not able to locate a missing parent or a relative of that parent and sufficient information is available concerning the physical whereabouts of the parent or relative, the department shall request the state agency designated to administer a statewide plan for child support to use the parental locator service established under 42 U.S.C. Section 653 to determine the location of the missing parent or relative.

(e) The department shall be required to provide evidence to the court to show what actions were taken by the department in making a diligent effort to locate the missing parent and relative of the missing parent.

History of Fam §161.107: Acts 1995, 74th Leg., ch. 20, §1, eff. April 20, 1995. Amended by Acts 1995, 74th Leg., ch. 751, §71, eff. Sept. 1, 1995. Source: Former Fam §15.051.

FAM §161.108. RELEASE OF CHILD FROM HOSPITAL OR BIRTHING CENTER

(a) Before or at the time an affidavit of relinquishment of parental rights under Section 161.103 is executed, the mother of a newborn child may authorize the release of the child from the hospital or birthing center to a licensed child-placing agency, the Department of Protective and Regulatory Services, or another designated person.

(b) A release under this section must be:

(1) executed in writing;

(2) witnessed by two credible adults; and

(3) verified before a person authorized to take oaths.

(c) A hospital or birthing center shall comply with the terms of a release executed under this section without requiring a court order.

History of Fam §161.108: Acts 1997, 75th Leg., ch. 561, §12, eff. Sept. 1, 1997.

FAM §161.109. REQUIREMENT OF PATERNITY REGISTRY CERTIFICATE

(a) If an affidavit of status of child as provided by this chapter states that the father of the child is unknown and no probable father is known, a certificate from the bureau of vital statistics signed by the registrar that a diligent search has been made of the paternity registry maintained by the bureau and that a registration has not been found pertaining to the father of the child in question must be filed with the court before a trial on the merits in the suit for termination may be held.

(b) In a proceeding to terminate parental rights in which the alleged or probable father has not been personally served with citation or signed an affidavit of relinquishment or an affidavit of waiver of interest, the court may not terminate the parental rights of the alleged or probable father, whether known or unknown, unless a certificate from the bureau of vital statistics signed by the registrar states that a diligent search has been made of the paternity registry maintained by the bureau and that a filing or registration has not been found pertaining to the father of the child in question.

History of Fam §161.109: Acts 1997, 75th Leg., ch. 561, §12, eff. Sept. 1, 1997.

Sections 161.110-161.200 reserved for expansion

SUBCHAPTER C. HEARING & ORDER

FAM §161.201. REPEALED

Repealed by Acts 2001, 77th Leg., ch. 130, §1, eff. Sept. 1, 2001.

FAM §161.201. NO FINAL ORDER UNTIL CHILD FIVE DAYS OLD

Section 161.201 below is effective for suits to terminate the parent-child relationship filed before Sept. 1, 2001.

If the petition in a suit for termination is filed before the birth of the child, the court may not conduct a hearing in the suit nor render an order other than a temporary order until the child is at least five days old.

In re Baby Girl T, 671 S.W.2d 654, 656 (Tex.App.—Fort Worth 1984, writ ref'd n.r.e.). Respondent "maintains that the language of §15.021 [now §161.201] is mandatory and that any order entered in violation thereof, within five days of the birth of the child, is totally void. [¶] We need not get into semantics and concern ourselves with whether 'may', 'shall', or 'must' was used in this section; the clear meaning of §15.021 is that no hearing is to be held nor permanent orders terminating parental rights issued within five days of the birth of the child. The words used are clearly prohibitive and preclude such action by the court."

FAM §161.2011. CONTINUANCE; ACCESS TO CHILD

Ⓐ (a) A parent whose rights are subject to termination in a suit affecting the parent-child relationship and against whom criminal charges are filed that directly relate to the grounds for which termination is sought may file a motion requesting a continuance of the final trial in the suit until the criminal charges are resolved. The court may grant the motion only if the court finds that a continuance is in the best interest of the child. Notwithstanding any continuance granted, the court shall conduct status and permanency hearings with respect to the child as required by Chapter 263 and shall comply with the dismissal date under Section 263.401.

(b) Nothing in this section precludes the court from issuing appropriate temporary orders as authorized in this code.

(c) The court in which a suit to terminate the parent-child relationship is pending may render an order denying a parent access to a child if the parent is indicted for criminal activity that constitutes a ground for terminating the parent-child relationship under Section 161.001. The denial of access under this section shall continue until the date the criminal charges for which the parent was indicted are resolved and the court renders an order providing for access to the child by the parent.

History of Fam §161.2011: Acts 1997, 75th Leg., ch. 1022, §61, eff. Sept. 1, 1997. Amended by Acts 2001, 77th Leg., ch. 1090, §1.01, eff. June 14, 2001.

In re Texas DPRS, 71 S.W.3d 446, 450 (Tex.App.—Fort Worth 2002, orig. proceeding). "TDPRS contends that … the amendment to §161.2011 that prohibits a continuance or stay of a termination proceeding beyond the 180-day time period in [Family Code] §263.401(b) applies retroactively, and that, therefore, the trial court abused its discretion in not granting the TDPRS's motion to vacate the stay, to the extent it continues the case beyond 180 days after the original deadline of August 13, 2001. *At 451:* If a statute is procedural or remedial in nature, '[i]t is the settled law that a litigant has no vested right in a remedy, and that remedial statutes are valid and control the litigation from the date they become a law, and all proceedings taken thereafter must be under the new law.' [¶] We hold that the 2001 amendment to §161.2011 … does not involve a vested substantive right, but is procedural or remedial in nature. Accordingly, the amended statute controlled the underlying case from its effective date, September 1, 2001."

In re M.C.M., 57 S.W.3d 27, 36 (Tex.App.—Houston [1st Dist.] 2001, pet. denied). "[W]e believe that §161.2011 should be read as a stay provision. That is, the 18-month deadline will be stayed by the pendency of criminal charges against the parent. The effect of the stay is to halt all action in the SAPCR and toll the running of the applicable time limits. Once the criminal proceedings against the parent terminate, the time period for resolving the SAPCR continues. Under this interpretation, compliance with §161.2011 would not cause the trial court to miss the dismissal deadline imposed by §263.401."

FAM §161.202. PREFERENTIAL SETTING

Ⓐ *Section 161.202 below is effective for SAPCRs filed on or after Sept. 1, 2001.*

In a termination suit, after a hearing, the court shall grant a motion for a preferential setting for a final hearing on the merits filed by a party to the suit or by the attorney or guardian ad litem for the child and shall give precedence to that hearing over other civil cases if:

(1) termination would make the child eligible for adoption; and

(2) discovery has been completed or sufficient time has elapsed since the filing of the suit for the completion of all necessary and reasonable discovery if diligently pursued.

History of Fam §161.202: Acts 1995, 74th Leg., ch. 20, §1, eff. April 20, 1995. Amended by Acts 2001, 77th Leg., ch. 133, §5, eff. Sept. 1, 2001. Source: Former Fam §11.14(h).

FAM §161.202. PREFERENTIAL SETTING; SUIT BY GOVERNMENTAL ENTITY

Section 161.202 below is effective for SAPCRs filed before Sept. 1, 2001.

In a termination suit filed by a governmental entity, licensed child-placing agency, or authorized agency, after a hearing, the court shall grant a motion for a preferential setting for a final hearing on the merits filed by a party to the suit or by the attorney or guardian ad litem for the child and shall give precedence to that hearing over other civil cases if:

(1) termination would make the child eligible for adoption; and

(2) discovery has been completed or sufficient time has elapsed since the filing of the suit for the completion of all necessary and reasonable discovery if diligently pursued.

Ⓐ FAM §161.203. DISMISSAL OF PETITION

A suit to terminate may not be dismissed nor may a nonsuit be taken unless the dismissal or nonsuit is approved by the court. The dismissal or nonsuit approved by the court is without prejudice.

History of Fam §161.203: Acts 1995, 74th Leg., ch. 20, §1, eff. April 20, 1995. Amended by Acts 2001, 77th Leg., ch. 1090, §4, eff. Sept. 1, 2001. Source: Former Fam §15.06.

Ⓐ FAM §161.204. TERMINATION BASED ON AFFIDAVIT OF WAIVER OF INTEREST

In a suit for termination, the court may render an order terminating the parent-child relationship between a child and a man who has signed an affidavit of waiver of interest in the child, if the termination is in the best interest of the child.

History of Fam §161.204: Acts 1995, 74th Leg., ch. 20, §1, eff. April 20, 1995. Amended by Acts 2001, 77th Leg., ch. 1090, §6, eff. Sept. 1, 2001. Source: Former Fam §15.041(e).

Ⓐ FAM §161.205. ORDER DENYING TERMINATION

If the court does not order termination of the parent-child relationship, the court shall:

(1) deny the petition; or

(2) render any order in the best interest of the child.

History of Fam §161.205: Acts 1995, 74th Leg., ch. 20, §1, eff. April 20, 1995. Amended by Acts 2001, 77th Leg., ch. 1090, §6, eff. Sept. 1, 2001. Source: Former Fam §15.05(c).

FAM §161.206. ORDER TERMINATING PARENTAL RIGHTS

(a) If the court finds by clear and convincing evidence grounds for termination of the parent-child relationship, it shall render an order terminating the parent-child relationship.

(b) An order terminating the parent-child relationship divests the parent and the child of all legal rights and duties with respect to each other, except that the child retains the right to inherit from and through the parent unless the court otherwise provides.

(c) Nothing in this chapter precludes or affects the rights of a biological or adoptive maternal or paternal grandparent to reasonable access under Chapter 153.

History of Fam §161.206: Acts 1995, 74th Leg., ch. 20, §1, eff. April 20, 1995. Amended by Acts 1995, 74th Leg., ch. 709, §2 (eff. Sept. 1, 1995), ch. 751, §72 (eff. Sept. 1, 1995). Source: Former Fam §§11.15(b), 15.05(a), 15.07.

Texas DHS v. E.B., 802 S.W.2d 647, 649 (Tex.1990). "The charge in parental rights cases should be the same as in other civil cases. The controlling question in this case was whether the parent-child relationship between the mother and each of her two children should be terminated, not what specific ground or grounds under §15.02 [now §161.001] the jury relied on to answer affirmatively the questions posed. All ten jurors agree that the mother had endangered the child by doing one or the other of the things listed in §15.02. [Respondent] argues that the charge, as presented to the jury, violates her due process right by depriving a natural mother of her fundamental right to the care, custody and management of her children. Recognizing her rights does not change the form of submission. The standard for review of the charge is abuse of discretion, and abuse of discretion occurs only when the trial court acts without reference to any guiding principle. Here the trial court tracked the statutory language in the instruction and then asked the controlling question. This simply does not amount to abuse of discretion."

Durham v. Barrow, 600 S.W.2d 756, 760 (Tex. 1980). The Family Code "provides that an individual who has been divested of parental rights by a termination decree loses all legal rights and interest in the children who were the subject of the termination proceeding [and] that a person whose parental rights have been terminated is not entitled to notice of a subsequent adoption. Therefore, if the termination judgment was valid, [a biological parent] has no standing to bring a bill of review as a party to [an] adoption."

Swate v. Swate, 72 S.W.3d 763, 771 (Tex.App.—Waco 2002, n.p.h.) "Reading §161.206(b) ... to absolve child support arrearage would eliminate the purpose of §151.001(c).... The delinquent parent could refuse to pay child support until termination of parental rights was ultimately ordered, thus defeating the statute and the court's original order to pay child support."

In re J.R., 991 S.W.2d 318, 320 (Tex.App.—Fort Worth 1999, no pet.). The clear and convincing evidence standard "is an intermediate standard that falls between the preponderance standard of ordinary civil proceedings and the reasonable doubt standard of criminal proceedings. While the proof must weigh heavier than merely the greater weight of the credible evidence, there is no requirement that the evidence be unequivocal or undisputed. Termination proceedings should be strictly scrutinized, and involuntary termination statutes are strictly construed in favor of the parent. [¶] This higher burden of proof in the trial court does not alter the appellate standard of review for factual sufficiency. Accordingly, to prevail on an assertion that the evidence supporting the termination of parental rights is 'factually insufficient,' the evidence supporting the finding must be so weak or the evidence to the contrary must be so overwhelming that the finding should be set aside and a new trial ordered. We are required to consider all of the evidence in the case in making this determination."

FAM §161.207. APPOINTMENT OF MANAGING CONSERVATOR ON TERMINATION

(a) If the court terminates the parent-child relationship with respect to both parents or to the only living parent, the court shall appoint a suitable, competent adult, the Department of Protective and Regulatory Services, a licensed child-placing agency, or an authorized agency as managing conservator of the child. An agency designated managing conservator in an unrevoked or irrevocable affidavit of relinquishment shall be appointed managing conservator.

(b) The order of appointment may refer to the docket number of the suit and need not refer to the parties nor be accompanied by any other papers in the record.

History of Fam §161.207: Acts 1995, 74th Leg., ch. 20, §1, eff. April 20, 1995. Source: Former Fam §15.05(b).

In re J.R.P., 55 S.W.3d 147, 152 (Tex.App.—Corpus Christi 2001, pet. denied). Section 161.207 "does not specifically include grandparents and allows the trial court to balance the best interests of the children in appointing managing conservators. There is no support in this statute, nor does [grandfather] provide us with any authority for his contention that there is a presumption that a grandparent should be given custody in a suit between non-parents."

In re Ruiz, 16 S.W.3d 921, 925 (Tex.App.—Waco 2000, orig. proceeding). "Under the 1907 version of the statute, Texas courts held that 'the trial court had the authority to award custody of the children to any suitable person or agency.' [¶] Because of the substantial similarities between the 1907 statute and §161.207, we presume that the Legislature intended for this construction of the statute to continue. Accordingly, we conclude that Respondent could have appointed any suitable person or agency to be [child's] managing conservator, regardless of whether such person or agency filed pleadings requesting such appointment."

FAM §161.208. APPOINTMENT OF DEPARTMENT OF PROTECTIVE & REGULATORY SERVICES AS MANAGING CONSERVATOR

If a parent of the child has not been personally served in a suit in which the Department of Protective and Regulatory Services seeks termination, the court that terminates a parent-child relationship may not appoint the Department of Protective and Regulatory Services as permanent managing conservator of the child unless the court determines that:

(1) the department has made a diligent effort to locate a missing parent who has not been personally served and a relative of that parent; and

(2) a relative located by the department has had a reasonable opportunity to request appointment as managing conservator of the child or the department has not been able to locate the missing parent or a relative of the missing parent.

History of Fam §161.208: Acts 1995, 74th Leg., ch. 20, §1, eff. April 20, 1995. Source: Former Fam §15.051(b).

FAM §161.209. COPY OF ORDER OF TERMINATION

A copy of an order of termination rendered under Section 161.206 is not required to be mailed to parties as provided by Rules 119a and 239a, Texas Rules of Civil Procedure.

History of Fam §161.209: Acts 1995, 74th Leg., ch. 20, §1, eff. April 20, 1995. Source: Former Fam §11.16.

FAM §161.210. SEALING OF FILE

The court, on the motion of a party or on the court's own motion, may order the sealing of the file, the minutes of the court, or both, in a suit for termination.

History of Fam §161.210: Acts 1995, 74th Leg., ch. 20, §1, eff. April 20, 1995. Source: Former Fam §11.17(f).

FAM §161.211. DIRECT OR COLLATERAL ATTACK ON TERMINATION ORDER

(a) Notwithstanding Rule 329, Texas Rules of Civil Procedure, the validity of an order terminating the parental rights of a person who has been personally served or who has executed an affidavit of relinquishment of parental rights or an affidavit of waiver of interest in a child or whose rights have been terminated under Section 161.002(b) is not subject to collateral or direct attack after the sixth month after the date the order was signed.

(b) Notwithstanding Rule 329, Texas Rules of Civil Procedure, the validity of an order terminating the parental rights of a person who is served by citation by publication is not subject to collateral or direct attack after the sixth month after the date the order was signed.

(c) A direct or collateral attack on an order terminating parental rights based on an unrevoked affidavit of relinquishment of parental rights or affidavit of waiver of interest in a child is limited to issues relating to fraud, duress, or coercion in the execution of the affidavit.

History of Fam §161.211: Acts 1997, 75th Leg., ch. 601, §2 (eff. Sept. 1, 1997), ch. 600, §1 (eff. Sept. 1, 1997). Amended by Acts 1999, 76th Leg., ch. 1390, §19, eff. Sept. 1, 1999.

CHAPTER 162. ADOPTION

Subchapter A. Adoption of a Child

Subchapter B. Interstate Compact on the Placement of Children

Subchapter C. Interstate Compact on Adoption & Medical Assistance

Subchapter D. Adoption Services by the Department of Protective & Regulatory Services

Subchapter E. Voluntary Adoption Registries

Subchapter F. Adoption of an Adult

SUBCHAPTER A. ADOPTION OF A CHILD

FAM §162.001. WHO MAY ADOPT & BE ADOPTED

(a) Subject to the requirements for standing to sue in Chapter 102, an adult may petition to adopt a child who may be adopted.

(b) A child residing in this state may be adopted if:

(1) the parent-child relationship as to each living parent of the child has been terminated or a suit for termination is joined with the suit for adoption;

(2) the parent whose rights have not been terminated is presently the spouse of the petitioner and the proceeding is for a stepparent adoption;

(3) the child is at least two years old, the parent-child relationship has been terminated with respect to one parent, the person seeking the adoption is the child's former stepparent and has been a managing conservator or has had actual care, possession, and control of the child for a period of six months preceding the adoption, and the nonterminated parent consents to the adoption; or

(4) the child is at least two years old, the parent-child relationship has been terminated with respect to one parent, and the person seeking the adoption is the child's former stepparent and has been a managing conservator or has had actual care, possession, and control of the child for a period of one year preceding the adoption.

(c) If an affidavit of relinquishment of parental rights contains a consent for the Department of Protective and Regulatory Services or a licensed child-placing agency to place the child for adoption and appoints the department or agency managing conservator of the child, further consent by the parent is not required and the adoption order shall terminate all rights of the parent without further termination proceedings.

History of Fam §162.001: Acts 1995, 74th Leg., ch. 20, §1, eff. April 20, 1995. Amended by Acts 1997, 75th Leg., ch. 561, §14, eff. Sept. 1, 1997. Source: Former Fam §§16.01, 16.02, 16.03(b)-(d).

Trevino v. Garcia, 627 S.W.2d 147, 148 (Tex.1982). Petitioners "claim they are entitled to custody of [child] because they have adopted her by estoppel. We disagree. *At 149:* [S]ection 16.03 [now §162.001] provides that a valid adoption must be preceded by either a judicial termination of the rights of the natural parents, or an irrevocable relinquishment of parental rights by affidavit meeting the requirements of §15.03(b) [now §161.103]. The Family Code requires a judicial order for adoption."

Durham v. Barrow, 600 S.W.2d 756, 761 (Tex. 1980). Plaintiff "has no standing to attack the adoption by virtue of his being guardian ad litem in the termination proceeding. A guardian ad litem's representation is limited to matters related to the suit for which he was appointed. Termination suits are separate from any other [SAPCR], and a termination judgment is a final, appealable judgment. Therefore, [plaintiff] does not have standing to attack the adoption as a necessary party to that suit, and he was not entitled to notice of those proceedings under §11.09 [now §102.009]. [¶] Although the children were the subject of the adoption suit, they were not participants in the suit, and were not necessary parties to the adoption. Since the children themselves were not necessary parties to the adoption, a next friend would not have standing to attack the adoption by bill of review. *At 761 n.6:* In Texas, as in other jurisdictions, a total stranger may not bring a bill of review to set aside an adoption."

In re W.E.R., 663 S.W.2d 887, 888 (Tex.App.—San Antonio 1983), *rev'd on other grounds*, 669 S.W.2d 716 (Tex.1984). "Any adult in Texas may adopt an adoptable child. The statute says nothing about a one-parent versus a two-parent home."

FAM §162.002. PREREQUISITES TO PETITION

(a) If a petitioner is married, both spouses must join in the petition for adoption.

(b) A petition in a suit for adoption or a suit for appointment of a nonparent managing conservator with authority to consent to adoption of a child must include:

(1) a verified allegation that there has been compliance with Subchapter B; or

(2) if there has not been compliance with Subchapter B, a verified statement of the particular reasons for noncompliance.

History of Fam §162.002: Acts 1995, 74th Leg., ch. 20, §1, eff. April 20, 1995. Source: Former Fam §§11.08(d), 16.03(a).

FAM §162.0025. REPEALED

Repealed by Acts 2001, 77th Leg., ch. 133, §7, eff. Sept. 1, 2001.

FAM §162.0025. ADOPTIVE HOME SCREENING

Section 162.0025 below is effective for SAPCRs filed before Sept. 1, 2001.

(a) The court shall order an adoptive home screening to evaluate each party who requests the adoption. The screening must be completed before a child may be placed in an applicant's home unless the child is being adopted by a member of the child's family related by the second degree of consanguinity or affinity. The screening must comply with the rules adopted by the Board of Protective and Regulatory Services providing minimum requirements for the screening.

(b) The court may appoint an investigator to conduct the screening required by this section who has the qualifications established by rule of the Board of Protective and Regulatory Services providing minimum qualifications for persons who may perform adoptive home screenings.

(c) The cost of an adoptive home study shall be paid by an applicant who seeks to adopt a child.

FAM §162.003. PRE-ADOPTIVE HOME SCREENING & POST-PLACEMENT REPORT

Ⓐ *Section 162.003 below is effective for SAPCRs filed on or after Sept. 1, 2001.*

In a suit for adoption, a pre-adoptive home screening and post-placement report must be conducted as provided in Chapter 107.

History of Fam §162.003: Acts 1995, 74th Leg., ch. 20, §1, eff. April 20, 1995. Amended by Acts 1995, 74th Leg., ch. 751, §73 (eff. Sept. 1, 1995), ch. 800, §1 (eff. Sept. 1, 1995); Acts 2001, 77th Leg., ch. 133, §6, eff. Sept. 1, 2001. Source: Former Fam §16.031(a).

FAM §162.003. SOCIAL STUDY

Section 162.003 below is effective for SAPCRs filed before Sept. 1, 2001.

(a) In a suit for adoption, including a suit in which a private agency or individual is responsible for placing the child for adoption, the court shall order a social study as provided in Chapter 107.

(b) The social study required by this section must include a complete investigation of the circumstances and condition of the home of a person petitioning for the adoption of a child under this chapter.

(c) The court shall order that the cost of the social study be paid by the person seeking to adopt the child who is the subject of the social study.

Green v. Remling, 608 S.W.2d 905, 909-10 (Tex. 1980). "Although §11.14 [now §104.001] provides that in [SAPCRs] the rules of evidence apply as in other civil cases, we are not persuaded that the legislature intended that the trial court could not consider the social study when it has been ordered and filed and is contained in the record. The Family Code clearly provides in §11.12 [now Family Code §107.054] for a social study when made, to be filed with the court and become a part of the record. The social study is mandatory in adoption cases under §16.031 [now §162.003]. It would defeat the purpose of the statute to deprive the court of potentially valuable information submitted by an independent investigator by holding that the trial court may not consider the report until it is formally introduced in evidence by one of the parties. [¶] [W]e conclude that the legislature intended for the trial judge to have full access to the contents of the social study. [¶] Consideration of the contents of the report by the jury on the other hand is a different matter. Section 11.12(c) [now Family Code §107.055(a)] provides: 'The report shall be made a part of the record; however, the disclosure of its contents to the jury is subject to the rules of evidence.' This provision clearly indicates that a different rule applies to the consideration of the report when the hearing is before the judge and when it is before the jury. We note that the statute uses the term 'disclosure' rather than admissibility. The inclusion of the social study in the 'record' makes it unnecessary to formally introduce it in evidence. It is before the court for all purposes, but only those portions of the study which are admissible under the rules of evidence may be disclosed to the jury."

Hopper v. Brittain, 612 S.W.2d 636, 638 (Tex. App.—Houston [14th Dist.] 1981, no writ). "We ... hold the trial judge in the case at bar was free to consider the social study notwithstanding a portion of the report may contain hearsay evidence, and despite the fact it may never have been properly admitted in evidence. The trial judge was at liberty to consider the report and was able to use his discretion in determining the weight to be given to it. To deprive the court of this type of valuable information could be detrimental to the child's best interest."

FAM §162.004. REPEALED

Repealed by Acts 2001, 77th Leg., ch. 133, §7, eff. Sept. 1, 2001.

FAM §162.004. TIME FOR HEARING

Section 162.004 below is effective for SAPCRs filed before Sept. 1, 2001.

(a) The court shall set the date for the hearing on the adoption at a time not before the 40th day after the later of the date the social study is ordered or the date criminal history record information is requested under Section 162.0085.

(b) The court may set the hearing at any time before the time provided by Subsection (a) if the hearing date provides adequate time for filing the social study and notifying the court of the criminal history record information for a person seeking to adopt the child.

FAM §162.0045. PREFERENTIAL SETTING

The court shall grant a motion for a preferential setting for a final hearing on an adoption and shall give precedence to that hearing over all other civil cases not given preference by other law if the social study has been filed and the criminal history for the person seeking to adopt the child has been obtained.

History of Fam §162.0045: Acts 1997, 75th Leg., ch. 561, §15, eff. Sept. 1, 1997.

FAM §162.005. PREPARATION OF HEALTH, SOCIAL, EDUCATIONAL, & GENETIC HISTORY REPORT

(a) This section does not apply to an adoption by the child's:

(1) grandparent;

(2) aunt or uncle by birth, marriage, or prior adoption; or

(3) stepparent.

(b) Before placing a child for adoption, the Department of Protective and Regulatory Services, a licensed child-placing agency, or the child's parent or guardian shall compile a report on the available health, social, educational, and genetic history of the child to be adopted.

(c) The report shall include a history of physical, sexual, or emotional abuse suffered by the child, if any.

(d) If the child has been placed for adoption by a person or entity other than the department, a licensed child-placing agency, or the child's parent or guardian, it is the duty of the person or entity who places the child for adoption to prepare the report.

(e) The person or entity who places the child for adoption shall provide the prospective adoptive parents a copy of the report as early as practicable before the first meeting of the adoptive parents with the child. The copy of the report shall be edited to protect the identity of birth parents and their families.

(f) The department, licensed child-placing agency, parent, guardian, person, or entity who prepares and files the original report is required to furnish supplemental medical, psychological, and psychiatric information to the adoptive parents if that information becomes available and to file the supplemental information where the original report is filed. The supplemental information shall be retained for as long as the original report is required to be retained.

History of Fam §162.005: Acts 1995, 74th Leg., ch. 20, §1, eff. April 20, 1995. Source: Former Fam §16.032(a), (f). (*l*).

FAM §162.006. RIGHT TO EXAMINE RECORDS

(a) The department, licensed child-placing agency, person, or entity placing a child for adoption shall inform the prospective adoptive parents of their right to examine the records and other information relating to the history of the child. The person or entity placing the child for adoption shall edit the records and information to protect the identity of the biological parents and any other person whose identity is confidential.

(b) The department, licensed child-placing agency, or court retaining a copy of the report shall provide a copy of the report that has been edited to protect the identity of the birth parents and any other person whose identity is confidential to the following persons on request:

(1) an adoptive parent of the adopted child;

(2) the managing conservator, guardian of the person, or legal custodian of the adopted child;

(3) the adopted child, after the child is an adult;

(4) the surviving spouse of the adopted child if the adopted child is dead and the spouse is the parent or guardian of a child of the deceased adopted child; or

(5) a progeny of the adopted child if the adopted child is dead and the progeny is an adult.

(c) A copy of the report may not be furnished to a person who cannot furnish satisfactory proof of identity and legal entitlement to receive a copy.

(d) A person requesting a copy of the report shall pay the actual and reasonable costs of providing a copy and verifying entitlement to the copy.

(e) The report shall be retained for 99 years from the date of the adoption by the department or licensed child-placing agency placing the child for adoption. If the agency ceases to function as a child-placing agency, the agency shall transfer all the reports to the department or, after giving notice to the department, to a transferee agency that is assuming responsibility for the preservation of the agency's adoption records. If the child has not been placed for adoption by the department or a licensed child-placing agency and if the child is being adopted by a person other than the child's stepparent, grandparent, aunt, or uncle by birth, marriage, or prior adoption, the person or entity who places the child for adoption shall file the report with the department, which shall retain the copies for 99 years from the date of the adoption.

History of Fam §162.006: Acts 1995, 74th Leg., ch. 20, §1, eff. April 20, 1995. Source: Former Fam §16.032(g), (i)-(k), (a).

See also 25 TAC §181.32.

FAM §162.007. CONTENTS OF HEALTH, SOCIAL, EDUCATIONAL, & GENETIC HISTORY REPORT

(a) The health history of the child must include information about:

(1) the child's health status at the time of placement;

(2) the child's birth, neonatal, and other medical, psychological, psychiatric, and dental history information;

(3) a record of immunizations for the child; and

(4) the available results of medical, psychological, psychiatric, and dental examinations of the child.

(b) The social history of the child must include information, to the extent known, about past and existing relationships between the child and the child's siblings, parents by birth, extended family, and other persons who have had physical possession of or legal access to the child.

(c) The educational history of the child must include, to the extent known, information about:

(1) the enrollment and performance of the child in educational institutions;

(2) results of educational testing and standardized tests for the child; and

(3) special educational needs, if any, of the child.

(d) The genetic history of the child must include a description of the child's parents by birth and their parents, any other child born to either of the child's parents, and extended family members and must include, to the extent the information is available, information about:

(1) their health and medical history, including any genetic diseases and disorders;

(2) their health status at the time of placement;

(3) the cause of and their age at death;

(4) their height, weight, and eye and hair color;

(5) their nationality and ethnic background;

(6) their general levels of educational and professional achievements, if any;

(7) their religious backgrounds, if any;

(8) any psychological, psychiatric, or social evaluations, including the date of the evaluation, any diagnosis, and a summary of any findings;

(9) any criminal conviction records relating to a misdemeanor or felony classified as an offense against the person or family or public indecency or a felony violation of a statute intended to control the possession or distribution of a substance included in Chapter 481, Health and Safety Code; and

(10) any information necessary to determine whether the child is entitled to or otherwise eligible for state or federal financial, medical, or other assistance.

History of Fam §162.007: Acts 1995, 74th Leg., ch. 20, §1, eff. April 20, 1995. Source: Former Fam §16.032(b)-(e).

Little v. Smith, 943 S.W.2d 414, 418 (Tex.1997). "Under §162.007, the adoption records are to include information about the biological parents' health and medical history; any genetic diseases or disorders; their height, weight, eye, and hair color; nationality and ethnic background; general levels of education; religious backgrounds; and psychological, psychiatric, or social evaluations. However, the identity of the biological parents must be edited from the public records."

FAM §162.008. FILING OF HEALTH, SOCIAL, EDUCATIONAL, & GENETIC HISTORY REPORT

(a) This section does not apply to an adoption by the child's:

(1) grandparent;

(2) aunt or uncle by birth, marriage, or prior adoption; or

(3) stepparent.

(b) A petition for adoption may not be granted until the following documents have been filed:

(1) a copy of the health, social, educational, and genetic history report signed by the child's adoptive parents; and

(2) if the report is required to be submitted to the bureau of vital statistics under Section 162.006(e), a certificate from the bureau acknowledging receipt of the report.

(c) A court having jurisdiction of a suit affecting the parent-child relationship may by order waive the making and filing of a report under this section if the child's biological parents cannot be located and their absence results in insufficient information being available to compile the report.

History of Fam §162.008: Acts 1995, 74th Leg., ch. 20, §1, eff. April 20, 1995. Amended by Acts 1999, 76th Leg., ch. 1390, §20, eff. Sept. 1, 1999. Source: Former Fam §16.032(h), (m).

FAM §162.0085. CRIMINAL HISTORY REPORT REQUIRED

(a) In a suit affecting the parent-child relationship in which an adoption is sought, the court shall order each person seeking to adopt the child to obtain that person's own criminal history record information. The court shall accept under this section a person's criminal history record information that is provided by the Department of Protective and Regulatory Services or by a licensed child-placing agency that received the information from the department if the information was obtained not more than one year before the date the court ordered the history to be obtained.

(b) A person required to obtain information under Subsection (a) shall obtain the information in the manner provided by Section 411.128, Government Code.

History of Fam §162.0085: Acts 1995, 74th Leg., ch. 751, §75 (eff. Sept. 1, 1995), ch. 908, §2 (eff. Sept. 1, 1995). Amended by Acts 1997, 75th Leg., ch. 561, §16, eff. Sept. 1, 1997.

FAM §162.009. RESIDENCE WITH PETITIONER

(a) The court may not grant an adoption until the child has resided with the petitioner for not less than six months.

(b) On request of the petitioner, the court may waive the residence requirement if the waiver is in the best interest of the child.

History of Fam §162.009: Acts 1995, 74th Leg., ch. 20, §1, eff. April 20, 1995. Source: Former Fam §16.04.

FAM §162.010. CONSENT REQUIRED

(a) Unless the managing conservator is the petitioner, the written consent of a managing conservator to the adoption must be filed. The court may waive the requirement of consent by the managing conservator if the court finds that the consent is being refused or has been revoked without good cause. A hearing on the issue of consent shall be conducted by the court without a jury.

(b) If a parent of the child is presently the spouse of the petitioner, that parent must join in the petition for adoption and further consent of that parent is not required.

(c) A child 12 years of age or older must consent to the adoption in writing or in court. The court may waive this requirement if it would serve the child's best interest.

History of Fam §162.010: Acts 1995, 74th Leg., ch. 20, §1, eff. April 20, 1995. Amended by Acts 1995, 74th Leg., ch. 751, §76, eff. Sept. 1, 1995. Source: Former Fam §16.05.

Chapman v. Home, 561 S.W.2d 265, 267 (Tex. App.—Fort Worth 1978, no writ). "In agency adoption situations, consent of the managing conservator must be expressed in writing pursuant to the literal terms of §16.05(a) [now §162.010(a)], and will not be inferred from the fact of placement or subsequent acts allowing a child to remain in the possession of would-be adoptive parents. [¶] The managing conservator has good cause for withholding consent whenever it has good reason to believe in good faith that the adoptive placement is not working out satisfactorily or that the best interest of the child requires that it withhold or revoke consent. [¶] The burden of proof of establishing the managing conservator's lack of good cause for withholding or revoking consent rests upon the party seeking waiver of the consent requirement. [¶] The trial court may, in one hearing, consider whether or not the managing conservator has withheld consent without good cause, whether or not the child should be restored to the possession of the prospective adoptive parents, whether or not the adoption should be granted, and, if not, whether or not the managing conservator should have authority to place the child in the home of third parties pending appeal of an adverse decision by the original prospective adoptive parents."

FAM §162.011. REVOCATION OF CONSENT

At any time before an order granting the adoption of the child is rendered, a consent required by Section 162.010 may be revoked by filing a signed revocation.

History of Fam §162.011: Acts 1995, 74th Leg., ch. 20, §1, eff. April 20, 1995. Source: Former Fam §16.06.

Hendricks v. Curry, 401 S.W.2d 796, 800 (Tex. 1966). "It is settled law in this State that consent to adoption of a child, where required, can be withdrawn at any time before an adoption decree is entered. It follows that the acts of a parent in executing a consent to adoption and delivery of possession of a child pursuant thereto are done with the reserved legal right to withdraw consent at any time before entry of an adoption decree."

FAM §162.012. DIRECT OR COLLATERAL ATTACK

(a) Notwithstanding Rule 329, Texas Rules of Civil Procedure, the validity of an adoption order is not subject to attack after six months after the date the order was signed.

(b) The validity of a final adoption order is not subject to attack because a health, social, educational, and genetic history was not filed.

History of Fam §162.012: Acts 1995, 74th Leg., ch. 20, §1, eff. April 20, 1995. Amended by Acts 1997, 75th Leg., ch. 601, §1 (eff. Sept. 1, 1997), ch. 600, §2 (eff. Jan. 1, 1998). Source: Former Fam §16.12.

FAM §162.013. ABATEMENT OR DISMISSAL

(a) If the sole petitioner dies or the joint petitioners die, the court shall dismiss the suit for adoption.

(b) If one of the joint petitioners dies, the proceeding shall continue uninterrupted.

(c) If the joint petitioners divorce, the court shall abate the suit for adoption. The court shall dismiss the petition unless the petition is amended to request adoption by one of the original petitioners.

History of Fam §162.013: Acts 1995, 74th Leg., ch. 20, §1, eff. April 20, 1995. Source: Former Fam §16.11.

FAM §162.014. ATTENDANCE AT HEARING REQUIRED

(a) If the joint petitioners are husband and wife and it would be unduly difficult for one of the petitioners to appear at the hearing, the court may waive the attendance of that petitioner if the other spouse is present.

(b) A child to be adopted who is 12 years of age or older shall attend the hearing. The court may waive this requirement in the best interest of the child.

History of Fam §162.014: Acts 1995, 74th Leg., ch. 20, §1, eff. April 20, 1995. Source: Former Fam §16.07.

FAM §162.015. RACE OR ETHNICITY

(a) In determining the best interest of the child, the court may not deny or delay the adoption or otherwise discriminate on the basis of race or ethnicity of the child or the prospective adoptive parents.

(b) This section does not apply to a person, entity, tribe, organization, or child custody proceeding subject to the Indian Child Welfare Act of 1978 (25 U.S.C. Section 1901 et seq.). In this subsection "child custody proceeding" has the meaning provided by 25 U.S.C. Section 1903.

History of Fam §162.015: Acts 1995, 74th Leg., ch. 20, §1, eff. April 20, 1995. Amended by Acts 1995, 74th Leg., ch. 751, §77, eff. Sept. 1, 1995. Source: Former Fam §16.081.

FAM §162.016. ADOPTION ORDER

(a) If a petition requesting termination has been joined with a petition requesting adoption, the court shall also terminate the parent-child relationship at the same time the adoption order is rendered. The court must make separate findings that the termination is in the best interest of the child and that the adoption is in the best interest of the child.

(b) If the court finds that the requirements for adoption have been met and the adoption is in the best interest of the child, the court shall grant the adoption.

(c) The name of the child may be changed in the order if requested.

History of Fam §162.016: Acts 1995, 74th Leg., ch. 20, §1, eff. April 20, 1995. Source: Former Fam §16.08.

Green v. Remling, 608 S.W.2d 905, 907 (Tex.1980). "The paramount considerations in adoption proceedings are the rights and welfare of the children involved and these statutes are to be liberally construed in favor of the minor to effectuate their beneficial purpose. *At 908:* Section 16.08(a) [now §162.016] indicates that the court may decree an adoption only when it is satisfied that adoption is in the best interests of the child. To effectuate this provision, the trial court in adoption cases is invested with broad discretionary power in determining the best interests of the children. The trial judge is better situated to weigh all of the surrounding circumstances and arrive at a judgment which in his discretion will best protect the best interests of the child. No right to a jury exists in an adoption hearing. The judgment of the trial court should not be disturbed unless it appears from the record as a whole that there was an abuse of discretion."

FAM §162.017. EFFECT OF ADOPTION

(a) An order of adoption creates the parent-child relationship between the adoptive parent and the child for all purposes.

(b) An adopted child is entitled to inherit from and through the child's adoptive parents as though the child were the biological child of the parents.

(c) The terms "child," "descendant," "issue," and other terms indicating the relationship of parent and child include an adopted child unless the context or express language clearly indicates otherwise.

(d) Nothing in this chapter precludes or affects the rights of a biological or adoptive maternal or paternal grandparent to reasonable access, as provided in Chapter 153.

History of Fam §162.017: Acts 1995, 74th Leg., ch. 20, §1, eff. April 20, 1995. Source: Former Fam §16.09(a), (d)-(f).

Penland v. Agnich, 940 S.W.2d 324, 326 (Tex. App.—Dallas 1997, writ denied). "Currently, the law provides that an adopted person is regarded as a 'child' of his adoptive parent in wills unless other language indicates an intent to exclude children by adoption. This presumption applies even to instruments executed by third persons."

Raines v. Sugg, 930 S.W.2d 912, 916 (Tex.App.—Fort Worth 1996, no writ). The court holds that "notwithstanding §16.09(a) [now §162.017(a)], under §16.09(f) [now §162.017(d)], the [plaintiffs] are the grandparents of [adopted child] as contemplated by §14.03(e) [now §153.342] and are in all ways entitled to avail themselves of the grandchild access benefits of that section."

FAM §162.018. ACCESS TO INFORMATION

(a) The adoptive parents are entitled to receive copies of the records and other information relating to the history of the child maintained by the department, licensed child-placing agency, person, or entity placing the child for adoption.

(b) The adoptive parents and the adopted child, after the child is an adult, are entitled to receive copies of the records that have been edited to protect the identity of the biological parents and any other person whose identity is confidential and other information relating to the history of the child maintained by the department, licensed child-placing agency, person, or entity placing the child for adoption.

(c) It is the duty of the person or entity placing the child for adoption to edit the records and information to protect the identity of the biological parents and any other person whose identity is confidential.

(d) At the time an adoption order is rendered, the court shall provide to the parents of an adopted child information provided by the bureau of vital statistics that describes the functions of the voluntary adoption registry under Subchapter E. The licensed child-placing agency shall provide to each of the child's biological parents known to the agency, the information when the parent signs an affidavit of relinquishment of parental rights, affidavit of status of child, or affidavit of waiver of interest in a child. The information shall include the right of the child or biological parent to refuse to participate in the registry. If the adopted child is 14 years old or older the court shall provide the information to the child.

History of Fam §162.018: Acts 1995, 74th Leg., ch. 20, §1, eff. April 20, 1995. Amended by Acts 1997, 75th Leg., ch. 561, §17, eff. Sept. 1, 1997. Source: Former Fam §§16.032(f), (i), 16.09(b), (c).

FAM §162.019. COPY OF ORDER

A copy of the adoption order is not required to be mailed to the parties as provided in Rules 119a and 239a, Texas Rules of Civil Procedure.

History of Fam §162.019: Acts 1995, 74th Leg., ch. 20, §1, eff. April 20, 1995. Source: Former Fam §11.16.

FAM §162.020. WITHDRAWAL OR DENIAL OF PETITION

If a petition requesting adoption is withdrawn or denied, the court may order the removal of the child from the proposed adoptive home if removal is in the child's best interest and may enter any order necessary for the welfare of the child.

History of Fam §162.020: Acts 1995, 74th Leg., ch. 20, §1, eff. April 20, 1995. Source: Former Fam §16.10.

FAM §162.021. SEALING FILE

(a) The court, on the motion of a party or on the court's own motion, may order the sealing of the file and the minutes of the court, or both, in a suit requesting an adoption.

(b) Rendition of the order does not relieve the clerk from the duty to send information regarding adoption to the bureau of vital statistics as required by this subchapter and Chapter 108.

History of Fam §162.021: Acts 1995, 74th Leg., ch. 20, §1, eff. April 20, 1995. Amended by Acts 1995, 74th Leg., ch. 751, §78, eff. Sept. 1, 1995. Source: Former Fam §11.17(f).

FAM §162.022. CONFIDENTIALITY MAINTAINED BY CLERK

The records concerning a child maintained by the district clerk after entry of an order of adoption are confidential. No person is entitled to access to the records or may obtain information from the records except for good cause under an order of the court that issued the order.

History of Fam §162.022: Acts 1995, 74th Leg., ch. 20, §1, eff. April 20, 1995. Source: Former Fam §11.17(d).

FAM §§162.023, 162.024. REPEALED

Repealed by Acts 1995, 74th Leg., ch. 751, §1.28, eff. Sept. 1, 1995.

FAM §162.025. PLACEMENT BY UNAUTHORIZED PERSON; OFFENSE

(a) A person who is not the natural or adoptive parent of the child, the legal guardian of the child, or a child-placing agency licensed under Chapter 42, Human Resources Code, commits an offense if the person:

(1) serves as an intermediary between a prospective adoptive parent and an expectant parent or parent of a minor child to identify the parties to each other; or

(2) places a child for adoption.

(b) It is not an offense under this section if a professional provides legal or medical services to:

(1) a parent who identifies the prospective adoptive parent and places the child for adoption without the assistance of the professional; or

(2) a prospective adoptive parent who identifies a parent and receives placement of a child for adoption without the assistance of the professional.

(c) An offense under this section is a Class B misdemeanor.

History of Fam §162.025: Acts 1995, 74th Leg., ch. 411, §1, eff. Sept. 1, 1995. Amended by Acts 1997, 75th Leg., ch. 561, §18, eff. Sept. 1, 1997.

Sections 162.026-162.100 reserved for expansion

SUBCHAPTER B. INTERSTATE COMPACT ON THE PLACEMENT OF CHILDREN

FAM §162.101. DEFINITIONS

In this subchapter:

(1) "Appropriate public authorities," with reference to this state, means the executive director.

(2) "Appropriate authority in the receiving state," with reference to this state, means the executive director.

(3) "Compact" means the Interstate Compact on the Placement of Children.

(4) "Executive head," with reference to this state, means the governor.

History of Fam §162.101: Acts 1995, 74th Leg., ch. 20, §1, eff. April 20, 1995. Amended by Acts 1995, 74th Leg., ch. 846, §2, eff. June 16, 1995. Source: Former Hum. Res. Code §§45.001, 45.022.

FAM §162.102. ADOPTION OF COMPACT; TEXT

The Interstate Compact on the Placement of Children is adopted by this state and entered into with all other jurisdictions in form substantially as provided by this subchapter.

INTERSTATE COMPACT
ON THE PLACEMENT OF CHILDREN

ARTICLE I. PURPOSE AND POLICY

It is the purpose and policy of the party states to cooperate with each other in the interstate placement of children to the end that:

(a) Each child requiring placement shall receive the maximum opportunity to be placed in a suitable environment and with persons or institutions having appropriate qualifications and facilities to provide a necessary and desirable degree and type of care.

(b) The appropriate authorities in a state where a child is to be placed may have full opportunity to ascertain the circumstances of the proposed placement, thereby promoting full compliance with applicable requirements for the protection of the child.

(c) The proper authorities of the state from which the placement is made may obtain the most complete information on the basis on which to evaluate a projected placement before it is made.

(d) Appropriate jurisdictional arrangements for the care of children will be promoted.

ARTICLE II. DEFINITIONS

As used in this compact:

(a) "Child" means a person who, by reason of minority, is legally subject to parental, guardianship, or similar control.

(b) "Sending agency" means a party state, officer, or employee thereof; a subdivision of a party state, or officer or employee thereof; a court of a party state; a person, corporation, association, charitable agency, or other entity which sends, brings, or causes to be sent or brought any child to another party state.

(c) "Receiving state" means the state to which a child is sent, brought, or caused to be sent or brought, whether by public authorities or private persons or agencies, and whether for placement with state or local public authorities or for placement with private agencies or persons.

(d) "Placement" means the arrangement for the care of a child in a family free or boarding home or in a child-caring agency or institution but does not include any institution caring for the mentally ill, mentally defective, or epileptic or any institution primarily educational in character, and any hospital or other medical facility.

ARTICLE III. CONDITIONS FOR PLACEMENT

(a) No sending agency shall send, bring, or cause to be sent or brought into any other party state any child for placement in foster care or as a preliminary to a possible adoption unless the sending agency shall comply with each and every requirement set forth in this article and with the applicable laws of the receiving state governing the placement of children therein.

(b) Prior to sending, bringing, or causing any child to be sent or brought into a receiving state for placement in foster care or as a preliminary to a possible adoption, the sending agency shall furnish the appropriate public authorities in the receiving state written notice of the intention to send, bring, or place the child in the receiving state. The notice shall contain:

(1) the name, date, and place of birth of the child;

(2) the identity and address or addresses of the parents or legal guardian;

(3) the name and address of the person, agency, or institution to or with which the sending agency proposes to send, bring, or place the child;

(4) a full statement of the reasons for such proposed action and evidence of the authority pursuant to which the placement is proposed to be made.

(c) Any public officer or agency in a receiving state which is in receipt of a notice pursuant to Paragraph (b) of this article may request of the sending agency, or any other appropriate officer or agency of or in the sending agency's state, and shall be entitled to receive therefrom, such supporting or additional information as it may deem necessary under the circumstances to carry out the purpose and policy of this compact.

(d) The child shall not be sent, brought, or caused to be sent or brought into the receiving state until the appropriate public authorities in the receiving state shall notify the sending agency, in writing, to the effect that the proposed placement does not appear to be contrary to the interests of the child.

ARTICLE IV. PENALTY FOR ILLEGAL PLACEMENT

The sending, bringing, or causing to be sent or brought into any receiving state of a child in violation of the terms of this compact shall constitute a violation of the laws respecting the placement of children of both the state in which the sending agency is located or from which it sends or brings the child and of the receiving state. Such violation may be punished or subjected to penalty in either jurisdiction in accordance with its laws. In addition to liability for any such punishment or penalty, any such violation shall constitute full and sufficient grounds for the suspension or revocation of any license, permit, or other legal authorization held by the sending agency which empowers or allows it to place or care for children.

ARTICLE V. RETENTION OF JURISDICTION

(a) The sending agency shall retain jurisdiction over the child sufficient to determine all matters in relation to the custody, supervision, care, treatment, and disposition of the child which it would have had if the child had remained in the sending agency's state, until the child is adopted, reaches majority, becomes self-supporting, or is discharged with the concurrence of the appropriate authority in the receiving state. Such jurisdiction shall also include the power to effect or cause the return of the child or its transfer to another location and custody pursuant to law. The sending agency shall continue to have financial responsibility for support and maintenance of the child during the period of the placement. Nothing contained herein shall defeat a claim of jurisdiction by a receiving state sufficient to deal with an act of delinquency or crime committed therein.

(b) When the sending agency is a public agency, it may enter into an agreement with an authorized public or private agency in the receiving state providing for the performance of one or more services in respect of such case by the latter as agent for the sending agency.

(c) Nothing in this compact shall be construed to prevent a private charitable agency authorized to place children in the receiving state from performing services or acting as agent in that state for a private charitable agency of the sending state; nor to prevent the agency in the receiving state from discharging financial responsibility for the support and maintenance of a child who has been placed on behalf of the sending agency without relieving the responsibility set forth in Paragraph (a) hereof.

ARTICLE VI. INSTITUTIONAL CARE OF DELINQUENT CHILDREN

A child adjudicated delinquent may be placed in an institution in another party jurisdiction pursuant to this compact but no such placement shall be made unless the child is given a court hearing on notice to the parent or guardian with opportunity to be heard, prior to his being sent to such other party jurisdiction for institutional care and the court finds that:

(1) equivalent facilities for the child are not available in the sending agency's jurisdiction; and

(2) institutional care in the other jurisdiction is in the best interest of the child and will not produce undue hardship.

ARTICLE VII. COMPACT ADMINISTRATOR

The executive head of each jurisdiction party to this compact shall designate an officer who shall be general coordinator of activities under this compact in his jurisdiction and who, acting jointly with like officers of other party jurisdictions, shall have power to promulgate rules and regulations to carry out more effectively the terms and provisions of this compact.

ARTICLE VIII. LIMITATIONS

This compact shall not apply to:

(a) the sending or bringing of a child into a receiving state by his parent, stepparent, grandparent, adult brother or sister, adult uncle or aunt, or his guardian and leaving the child with any such relative or nonagency guardian in the receiving state; or

(b) any placement, sending, or bringing of a child into a receiving state pursuant to any other interstate compact to which both the state from which the child is sent or brought and the receiving state are party, or to any other agreement between said states which has the force of law.

ARTICLE IX. ENACTMENT AND WITHDRAWAL

This compact shall be open to joinder by any state, territory, or possession of the United States, the District of Columbia, the Commonwealth of Puerto Rico, and, with the consent of congress, the government of Canada or any province thereof. It shall become effective with respect to any such jurisdiction when such jurisdiction has enacted the same into law. Withdrawal from this compact shall be by the enactment of a statute repealing the same, but shall not take effect until two years after the effective date of such statute and until written notice of the withdrawal has been given by the withdrawing state to the governor of each other party jurisdiction. Withdrawal of a party state shall not affect the rights, duties, and obligations under this compact of any sending agency therein with respect to a placement made prior to the effective date of withdrawal.

ARTICLE X. CONSTRUCTION AND SEVERABILITY

The provisions of this compact shall be liberally construed to effectuate the purposes thereof. The provisions of this compact shall be severable and if any phrase, clause, sentence, or provision of this compact is declared to be contrary to the constitution of any party state or of the United States or the applicability thereof to any government, agency, person, or circumstance is held invalid, the validity of the remainder of this compact and the applicability thereof to any government, agency, person, or circumstance shall not be affected thereby. If this compact shall be held contrary to the constitution of any state party thereto, the compact shall remain in full force and effect as to the remaining states and in full force and effect as to the state affected as to all severable matters.

History of Fam §162.102: Acts 1995, 74th Leg., ch. 20, §1, eff. April 20, 1995. Renumbered from §162.108 and amended by Acts 1995, 74th Leg., ch. 846, §3, eff. June 16, 1995. Source: Former Hum. Res. Code §45.021.

History of Former Fam §162.102: Acts 1995, 74th Leg., ch. 20, §1, eff. April 20, 1995. Repealed by Acts 1995, 74th Leg., ch. 846, §10, eff. June 16, 1995. Source: Former Hum. Res. Code §45.002(a)-(c), (e).

See also 40 TAC §§700.1901-700.1902.

Broyles v. Ashworth, 782 S.W.2d 31, 33-34 (Tex. App.—Fort Worth 1989, orig. proceeding). "We interpret [§162.102, art. V(a)] as meaning that whatever authority the sending agency might have with respect to custody and disposition of the child, prior to one of the listed events, is to be determined according to the law of the sending agency's state. We do not interpret the section to mean that a natural mother, if she is the sending agency, has the absolute right to regain custody of a child which she has placed in another state for adoption, merely upon her demand."

FAM §162.103. FINANCIAL RESPONSIBILITY FOR CHILD

(a) Financial responsibility for a child placed as provided in the compact is determined, in the first instance, as provided in Article V of the compact. After partial or complete default of performance under the provisions of Article V assigning financial responsibility, the executive director may bring suit under Chapter 154 and may file a complaint with the appropriate prosecuting attorney, claiming a violation of Section 25.05, Penal Code.

(b) After default, if the executive director determines that financial responsibility is unlikely to be assumed by the sending agency or the child's parents, the executive director may cause the child to be returned to the sending agency.

(c) After default, the department shall assume financial responsibility for the child until it is assumed by the child's parents or until the child is safely returned to the sending agency.

History of Fam §162.103: Acts 1995, 74th Leg., ch. 20, §1, eff. April 20, 1995. Renumbered from §162.109 and amended by Acts 1995, 74th Leg., ch. 846, §4, eff. June 16, 1995. Source: Former Hum. Res. Code §45.023.

History of Former Fam §162.103: Acts 1995, 74th Leg., ch. 20, §1, eff. April 20, 1995. Repealed by Acts 1995, 74th Leg., ch. 846, §10, eff. June 16, 1995. Source: Former Hum. Res. Code §45.003(a)-(d).

FAM §162.104. APPROVAL OF PLACEMENT

The executive director may not approve the placement of a child in this state without the concurrence of the individuals with whom the child is proposed to be placed or the head of an institution with which the child is proposed to be placed.

History of Fam §162.104: Acts 1995, 74th Leg., ch. 20, §1, eff. April 20, 1995. Renumbered from §162.110 and amended by Acts 1995, 74th Leg., ch. 846, §5, eff. June 16, 1995. Source: Former Hum. Res. Code §45.024.

History of Former Fam §162.104: Acts 1995, 74th Leg., ch. 20, §1, eff. April 20, 1995. Repealed by Acts 1995, 74th Leg., ch. 846, §10, eff. June 16, 1995. Source: Former Hum. Res. Code §45.004.

FAM §162.105. PLACEMENT IN ANOTHER STATE

A juvenile court may place a delinquent child in an institution in another state as provided by Article VI of the compact. After placement in another state, the court retains jurisdiction of the child as provided by Article V of the compact.

History of Fam §162.105: Acts 1995, 74th Leg., ch. 20, §1, eff. April 20, 1995. Renumbered from §162.111 by Acts 1995, 74th Leg., ch. 846, §6, eff. June 16, 1995. Source: Former Hum. Res. Code §45.025.

History of Former Fam §162.105: Acts 1995, 74th Leg., ch. 20, §1, eff. April 20, 1995. Repealed by Acts 1995, 74th Leg., ch. 846, §10, eff. June 16, 1995. Source: Former Hum. Res. Code §45.005.

FAM §162.106. COMPACT AUTHORITY

(a) The governor shall appoint the executive director of the Department of Protective and Regulatory Services as compact administrator.

(b) The executive director shall designate a deputy compact administrator and staff necessary to execute the terms of the compact in this state.

History of Fam §162.106: Acts 1995, 74th Leg., ch. 20, §1, eff. April 20, 1995. Renumbered from §162.112 and amended by Acts 1995, 74th Leg., ch. 846, §7, eff. June 16, 1995. Source: Former Hum. Res. Code §45.026.

History of Former Fam §162.106: Acts 1995, 74th Leg., ch. 20, §1, eff. April 20, 1995. Repealed by Acts 1995, 74th Leg., ch. 846, §10, eff. June 16, 1995. Source: Former Hum. Res. Code §45.006.

FAM §162.107. OFFENSES; PENALTIES

(a) An individual, agency, corporation, or child-care facility that violates a provision of the compact commits an offense. An offense under this subsection is a Class B misdemeanor.

(b) An individual, agency, corporation, child-care facility, or child-care institution in this state that violates Article IV of the compact commits an offense. An offense under this subsection is a Class B misdemeanor. On conviction, the court shall revoke any license to operate as a child-care facility or child-care institution issued by the department to the entity convicted and shall revoke any license or certification of the individual, agency, or corporation necessary to practice in the state.

History of Fam §162.107: Acts 1995, 74th Leg., ch. 20, §1, eff. April 20, 1995. Renumbered from §162.113 and amended by Acts 1995, 74th Leg., ch. 846, §8, eff. June 16, 1995.

History of Former Fam §162.107: Acts 1995, 74th Leg., ch. 20, §1, eff. April 20, 1995. Repealed by Acts 1995, 74th Leg., ch. 846, §10, eff. June 16, 1995. Source: Former Hum. Res. Code §45.007.

FAM §§162.108 TO 162.113. RENUMBERED

Renumbered as §§162.103-162.107 by Acts 1995, 74th Leg., ch. 846, §§2-8, eff. June 16, 1995.

FAM §162.114. REPEALED

Repealed by Acts 1995, 74th Leg., ch. 846, §10, eff. June 16, 1995.

Sections 162.115-162.200 reserved for expansion

SUBCHAPTER C. INTERSTATE COMPACT ON ADOPTION & MEDICAL ASSISTANCE

FAM §162.201. ADOPTION OF COMPACT; TEXT

The Interstate Compact on Adoption and Medical Assistance is adopted by this state and entered into with all other jurisdictions joining in the compact in form substantially as provided under this subchapter.

INTERSTATE COMPACT
ON ADOPTION AND MEDICAL ASSISTANCE

ARTICLE I. FINDINGS

The legislature finds that:

(a) Finding adoptive families for children for whom state assistance is desirable, under Subchapter D, Chapter 162, and assuring the protection of the interest of the children affected during the entire assistance period require special measures when the adoptive parents move to other states or are residents of another state.

(b) The provision of medical and other necessary services for children, with state assistance, encounters special difficulties when the provision of services takes place in other states.

ARTICLE II. PURPOSES

The purposes of the compact are to:

(a) authorize the Department of Protective and Regulatory Services, with the concurrence of the Health and Human Services Commission, to enter into interstate agreements with agencies of other states for the protection of children on behalf of whom adoption assistance is being provided by the Department of Protective and Regulatory Services; and

(b) provide procedures for interstate children's adoption assistance payments, including medical payments.

ARTICLE III. DEFINITIONS

In this compact:

(a) "Adoption assistance state" means the state that signs an adoption assistance agreement in a particular case.

(b) "Residence state" means the state in which the child resides by virtue of the residence of the adoptive parents.

(c) "State" means a state of the United States, the District of Columbia, the Commonwealth of Puerto Rico, the Virgin Islands, Guam, the Commonwealth of the Northern Mariana Islands, or a territory or possession of or a territory or possession administered by the United States.

ARTICLE IV. COMPACTS AUTHORIZED

The Department of Protective and Regulatory Services, through its executive director, is authorized to develop, participate in the development of, negotiate, and enter into one or more interstate compacts on behalf of this state with other states to implement one or more of the purposes of this compact. An interstate compact authorized by this article has the force and effect of law.

ARTICLE V. CONTENTS OF COMPACTS

A compact entered into under the authority conferred by this compact shall contain:

(1) a provision making the compact available for joinder by all states;

(2) a provision for withdrawal from the compact on written notice to the parties, with a period of one year between the date of the notice and the effective date of the withdrawal;

(3) a requirement that protections under the compact continue for the duration of the adoption assistance and apply to all children and their adoptive parents who on the effective date of the withdrawal are receiving adoption assistance from a party state other than the one in which they reside and have their principal place of abode;

(4) a requirement that each case of adoption assistance to which the compact applies be covered by a written adoption assistance agreement between the adoptive parents and the state child welfare agency of the state that provides the adoption assistance and that the agreement be expressly for the benefit of the adopted child and enforceable by the adoptive parents and the state agency providing the adoption assistance; and

(5) other provisions that are appropriate for the proper administration of the compact.

ARTICLE VI. OPTIONAL CONTENTS OF COMPACTS

A compact entered into under the authority conferred by this compact may contain the following provisions, in addition to those required under Article V of this compact:

(1) provisions establishing procedures and entitlement to medical, developmental, child-care, or other social services for the child in accordance with applicable laws, even if the child and the adoptive parents are in a state other than the one responsible for or providing the services or the funds to defray part or all of the costs thereof; and

(2) other provisions that are appropriate or incidental to the proper administration of the compact.

ARTICLE VII. MEDICAL ASSISTANCE

(a) A child with special needs who resides in this state and who is the subject of an adoption assistance agreement with another state is entitled to receive a medical assistance identification from this state on the filing in the state medical assistance agency of a certified copy of the adoption assistance agreement obtained from the adoption assistance state. In accordance with rules of the state medical assistance agency, the adoptive parents, at least annually, shall show that the agreement is still in effect or has been renewed.

(b) The state medical assistance agency shall consider the holder of a medical assistance identification under this article as any other holder of a medical assistance identification under the laws of this state and shall process and make payment on claims on the holder's account in the same manner and under the same conditions and procedures as for other recipients of medical assistance.

(c) The state medical assistance agency shall provide coverage and benefits for a child who is in another state and who is covered by an adoption assistance agreement made by the Department of Protective and Regulatory Services for the coverage or benefits, if any, not provided by the residence state. The adoptive parents acting for the child may submit evidence of payment for services or benefit amounts not payable in the residence state and shall be reimbursed for those amounts. Services or benefit amounts covered under any insurance or other third-party medical contract or arrangement held by the child or the adoptive parents may not be reimbursed. The state medical assistance agency shall adopt rules implementing this subsection. The additional coverage and benefit amounts provided under this subsection are for services for which there is no federal contribution or services that, if federally aided, are not provided by the residence state. The rules shall include procedures for obtaining prior approval for services in cases in which prior approval is required for the assistance.

(d) The submission of a false, misleading, or fraudulent claim for payment or reimbursement for services or benefits under this article or the making of a false, misleading, or fraudulent statement in connection with the claim is an offense under this subsection if the person submitting the claim or making the statement knows or should know that the claim or statement is false, misleading, or fraudulent. A person who commits an offense under this subsection may be liable for a fine not to exceed $10,000 or imprisonment for not more than two years, or both the fine and the imprisonment. An offense under this subsection that also constitutes an offense under other law may be punished under either this subsection or the other applicable law.

(e) This article applies only to medical assistance for children under adoption assistance agreements with states that have entered into a compact with this state under which the other state provides medical assistance to children with special needs under adoption assistance agreements made by this state. All other children entitled to medical assistance under adoption assistance agreements entered into by this state are eligible to receive the medical assistance in accordance with the laws and procedures that apply to the agreement.

ARTICLE VIII. FEDERAL PARTICIPATION

Consistent with federal law, the Department of Protective and Regulatory Services and the Health and Human Services Commission, in connection with the administration of this compact or a compact authorized by this compact, shall include the provision of adoption assistance and medical assistance for which the federal government pays some or all of the cost in any state plan made under the Adoption Assistance and Child Welfare Act of 1980 (Pub. L. No. 96-272), Titles IV-E and XIX of the Social Security Act, and other applicable federal laws. The Department of Protective and Regulatory Services and the Health and Human Services Commission shall apply for and administer all relevant federal aid in accordance with law.

History of Fam §162.201: Acts 1995, 74th Leg., ch. 846, §9, eff. June 16, 1995.

FAM §162.202. AUTHORITY OF DEPARTMENT OF PROTECTIVE & REGULATORY SERVICES

The Department of Protective and Regulatory Services, with the concurrence of the Health and Human Services Commission, may develop, participate in the development of, negotiate, and enter into one or more interstate compacts on behalf of this state with other states to implement one or more of the purposes of this subchapter. An interstate compact authorized by this article has the force and effect of law.

History of Fam §162.202: Acts 1995, 74th Leg., ch. 846, §9, eff. June 16, 1995.

FAM §162.203. COMPACT ADMINISTRATION

The executive director of the Department of Protective and Regulatory Services shall serve as the compact administrator. The administrator shall cooperate with all departments, agencies, and officers of this state and its subdivisions in facilitating the proper administration of the compact and any supplemental agreements entered into by this state. The executive director and the commissioner of human services shall designate deputy compact administrators to represent adoption assistance services and medical assistance services provided under Title XIX of the Social Security Act.

History of Fam §162.203: Acts 1995, 74th Leg., ch. 846, §9, eff. June 16, 1995.

FAM §162.204. SUPPLEMENTARY AGREEMENTS

The compact administrator may enter into supplementary agreements with appropriate officials of other states under the compact. If a supplementary agreement requires or authorizes the use of any institution or facility of this state or requires or authorizes the provision of a service by this state, the supplementary agreement does not take effect until approved by the head of the department or agency under whose jurisdiction the institution or facility is operated or whose department or agency will be charged with rendering the service.

History of Fam §162.204: Acts 1995, 74th Leg., ch. 846, §9, eff. June 16, 1995.

FAM §162.205. PAYMENTS BY STATE

The compact administrator, subject to the approval of the chief state fiscal officer, may make or arrange for payments necessary to discharge financial obligations imposed on this state by the compact or by a supplementary agreement entered into under the compact.

History of Fam §162.205: Acts 1995, 74th Leg., ch. 846, §9, eff. June 16, 1995.

FAM §162.206. PENALTIES

A person who, under a compact entered into under this subchapter, knowingly obtains or attempts to obtain or aids or abets any person in obtaining, by means of a wilfully false statement or representation or by impersonation or other fraudulent device, any assistance on behalf of a child or other person to which the child or other person is not entitled, or assistance in an amount greater than that to which the child or other person is entitled, commits an offense. An offense under this section is a Class B misdemeanor. An offense under this section that also constitutes an offense under other law may be punished under either this section or the other applicable law.

History of Fam §162.206: Acts 1995, 74th Leg., ch. 846, §9, eff. June 16, 1995.

Sections 162.207-162.300 reserved for expansion

SUBCHAPTER D. ADOPTION SERVICES BY THE DEPARTMENT OF PROTECTIVE & REGULATORY SERVICES

FAM §162.301. DEFINITIONS

In this subchapter:

(1) "Adoption assistance agreement" means a written agreement, binding on the parties to the agreement, between the department and the prospective adoptive parents that specifies the nature and amount of any payment, services, or assistance to be provided under the agreement and stipulates that the agreement will remain in effect without regard to the state in which the prospective adoptive parents reside at any particular time.

(2) "Child" means a child who cannot be placed for adoption with appropriate adoptive parents without the provision of adoption assistance because of factors including ethnic background, age, membership in a minority or sibling group, the presence of a medical condition, or a physical, mental, or emotional disability.

(3) "Department" means the Department of Protective and Regulatory Services.

History of Fam §162.301: Acts 1995, 74th Leg., ch. 20, §1, eff. April 20, 1995. Amended by Acts 1995, 74th Leg., ch. 412, §1, eff. Aug. 28, 1995. Source: Former Hum. Res. Code §47.001.

FAM §162.302. ADOPTION ASSISTANCE PROGRAM

(a) The department shall administer a program designed to promote the adoption of children by providing information to prospective adoptive parents concerning the availability and needs of the children, assisting the parents in completing the adoption process, and providing adoption assistance necessary for the parents to adopt the children.

(b) The legislature intends that the program benefit children residing in foster homes at state or county expense by providing them with the stability and security of permanent homes and that the costs paid by the state and counties for foster home care for the children be reduced.

(c) The program shall be carried out by licensed child-placing agencies or county child-care or welfare units under rules adopted by the department.

(d) The department shall keep records necessary to evaluate the program's effectiveness in encouraging and promoting the adoption of children.

E (e) It is the intent of the legislature that the department in providing adoption services, when it is in the children's best interest, keep siblings together and whenever possible place siblings in the same adoptive home.

History of Fam §162.302: Acts 1995, 74th Leg., ch. 20, §1, eff. April 20, 1995. Amended by Acts 1995, 74th Leg., ch. 412, §2, eff. Aug. 28, 1995; Acts 2001, 77th Leg., ch. 744, §1, eff. June 13, 2001. Source: Former Hum. Res. Code §47.002.

FAM §162.303. DISSEMINATION OF INFORMATION

The department, county child-care or welfare units, and licensed child-placing agencies shall disseminate information to prospective adoptive parents concerning the availability and needs of children for adoption and the existence of adoption assistance for parents who adopt them. Special effort shall be made to disseminate the information to families that have lower income levels or that belong to disadvantaged groups.

History of Fam §162.303: Acts 1995, 74th Leg., ch. 20, §1, eff. April 20, 1995. Amended by Acts 1995, 74th Leg., ch. 412, §3, eff. Aug. 28, 1995. Source: Former Hum. Res. Code §47.003.

FAM §162.304. FINANCIAL & MEDICAL ASSISTANCE

(a) The department shall enter into adoption assistance agreements with the adoptive parents of a child as authorized by Part E of Title IV of the federal Social Security Act, as amended (42 U.S.C. Section 673).

(b) The adoption of a child may be subsidized by the department. The need for and amount of the subsidy shall be determined by the department under its rules.

(c) In addition to the subsidy under Subsection (b), the department may subsidize the cost of medical care for a child. The department shall determine the amount and need for the subsidy.

(d) The county may pay a subsidy under Subsection (b) or (c) if the county is responsible for the child's foster care at the time of the child's adoptive placement.

(e) If the child is receiving supplemental security income from the federal government, the state may pay the subsidy regardless of whether the state is the managing conservator for the child.

History of Fam §162.304: Acts 1995, 74th Leg., ch. 20, §1, eff. April 20, 1995. Amended by Acts 1995, 74th Leg., ch. 412, §4, eff. Aug. 28, 1995. Source: Former Hum. Res. Code §47.004.

See also 40 TAC §§700.337-700.344.

E FAM §162.3041. CONTINUATION OF ASSISTANCE AFTER CHILD'S 18TH BIRTHDAY

(a) The department shall, in accordance with department rules, offer adoption assistance after a child's 18th birthday to the child's adoptive parents under an existing adoption assistance agreement entered into under Section 162.304 until:

(1) the first day of the month of the child's 21st birthday if the department determines, as provided by department rules, that:

(A) the child has a mental or physical disability that warrants the continuation of that assistance;

(B) the child, or the child's adoptive parent on behalf of the child, has applied for federal benefits under the supplemental security income program (42 U.S.C. Section 1381 et seq.), as amended; and

(C) the child's adoptive parents are providing the child's financial support; or

(2) if the child does not meet the requirements of Subdivision (1), the earlier of:

(A) the date the child ceases to regularly attend high school or a vocational or technical program;

(B) the date the child obtains a high school diploma or high school equivalency certificate;

(C) the date the child's adoptive parents stop providing financial support to the child; or

(D) the first day of the month of the child's 19th birthday.

(b) In determining whether a child meets the requirements of Subdivision (a)(1), the department may conduct an assessment of the child's mental or physical disability or may contract for the assessment to be conducted.

(c) The department and any person with whom the department contracts to conduct an assessment under Subsection (b) shall:

(1) inform the adoptive parents of the child for whom the assessment is conducted of the application requirement under Subsection (a)(1)(B) for federal benefits for the child under the supplemental security income program (42 U.S.C. Section 1381 et seq.), as amended;

(2) provide assistance to the adoptive parents and the child in preparing an application for benefits under that program; and

(3) provide ongoing consultation and guidance to the adoptive parents and the child throughout the eligibility determination process for benefits under that program.

(d) If the legislature does not appropriate sufficient money to provide adoption assistance to the adoptive parents of all children described by Subsection (a), the department shall provide adoption assistance only to the adoptive parents of children described by Subsection (a)(1).

History of Fam §162.3041: Enacted by Acts 2001, 77th Leg., ch. 1449, §1, eff. Sept. 1, 2001.

FAM §162.305. FUNDS

The department and other state agencies shall actively seek and use federal funds available for the purposes of this subchapter.

History of Fam §162.305: Acts 1995, 74th Leg., ch. 20, §1, eff. April 20, 1995. Amended by Acts 1995, 74th Leg., ch. 412, §5, eff. Aug. 28, 1995. Source: Hum. Res. Code §47.005.

FAM §162.306. POSTADOPTION SERVICES

(a) The department may provide services after adoption to adoptees and adoptive families for whom the department provided services before the adoption.

(b) The department may provide services under this section directly or through contract.

(c) The services may include financial assistance, respite care, placement services, parenting programs, support groups, counseling services, crisis intervention, and medical aid.

History of Fam §162.306: Acts 1995, 74th Leg., ch. 20, §1, eff. April 20, 1995. Amended by Acts 1995, 74th Leg., ch. 412, §6, eff. Aug. 28, 1995. Source: Former Hum. Res. Code §47.031.

See also 40 TAC §700.1726.

FAM §162.307. REPEALED

Repealed by Acts 1995, 74th Leg., ch. 412, §7, eff. Aug. 28, 1995.

FAM §162.308. RACE OR ETHNICITY

(a) The department, a county child-care or welfare unit, or a licensed child-placing agency may not make an adoption placement decision on the presumption that placing a child in a family of the same race or ethnicity as the race or ethnicity of the child is in the best interest of the child.

(b) Unless an independent psychological evaluation specific to a child indicates that placement with a family of a particular race or ethnicity would be detrimental to the child, the department, county child-care or welfare unit, or licensed child-placing agency may not deny, delay, or prohibit the adoption of a child because the department, county, or agency is attempting to locate a family of a particular race or ethnicity.

(c) This section does not prevent or limit the recruitment of minority families as adoptive families, but the recruitment of minority families may not be a reason to delay placement of a child with an available family of a race or ethnicity different from that of the child.

(d) A state or county employee who violates this section is subject to immediate dismissal. A licensed child-placing agency that violates this section is subject to action by the licensing agency as a ground for revocation or suspension of the agency's license.

(e) A district court, on the application for an injunction or the filing of a petition complaining of a violation of this section by any person residing in the county in which the court has jurisdiction, shall enforce this section by issuing appropriate orders. An action for an injunction is in addition to any other action, proceeding, or remedy authorized by law. An applicant or petitioner who is granted an injunction or given other appropriate relief under this section is entitled to the costs of the suit, including reasonable attorney's fees.

History of Fam §162.308: Acts 1995, 74th Leg., ch. 20, §1, eff. April 20, 1995. Amended by Acts 1995, 74th Leg., ch. 879, §1, eff. June 16, 1995. Source: Former Hum. Res. Code §47.041.

FAM §162.309. ADVISORY COMMITTEE ON PROMOTING ADOPTION OF MINORITY CHILDREN

(a) An advisory committee on promoting the adoption of and provision of services to minority children is established within the department.

(b) The committee is composed of 12 members appointed by the board of the Department of Protective and Regulatory Services. The board shall appoint to the committee individuals who in the aggregate have knowledge of and experience in community education, cultural relations, family support, counseling, and parenting skills and education. At least six members must be ordained members of the clergy.

(c) A committee member serves for a two-year term and may be appointed for additional terms.

(d) A member of the committee receives no compensation but is entitled to reimbursement for actual and necessary expenses incurred in performing the member's duties under this section.

(e) The committee shall elect one member to serve as presiding officer. The presiding officer serves for a two-year term and may be elected for additional terms.

(f) The department shall set the time and place of the first committee meeting. The committee shall meet at least quarterly.

(g) The department shall pay the expenses of the committee and shall supply necessary personnel and supplies.

(h) To promote the adoption of and provision of services to minority children, the committee shall:

(1) study, develop, and evaluate programs and projects relating to community awareness and education, family support, counseling, parenting skills and education, and reform of the child welfare system;

(2) consult with churches and other cultural and civic organizations; and

(3) report to the department at least annually the committee's recommendations for department programs and projects that will promote the adoption of and provision of services to minority children.

(i) On receiving the committee's recommendations, the department may adopt rules to implement a program or project recommended under this section. The department may solicit, accept, and use gifts and donations to implement a program or project recommended by the committee.

(j) The department shall report to the legislature not later than November 1 of each even-numbered year following the first year in which it receives recommendations under this section regarding committee recommendations and action taken by the department under this section.

(k) The recruitment of minority families may not be a reason to delay placement of a child with an available family of a race or ethnicity different from that of the child.

History of Fam §162.309: Acts 1997, 75th Leg., ch. 165, §7.17(a), eff. Sept. 1, 1997. Source: Former Hum. Res. Code §47.006.

Sections 162.310-162.400 reserved for expansion

SUBCHAPTER E. VOLUNTARY ADOPTION REGISTRIES

FAM §162.401. PURPOSE

The purpose of this subchapter is to provide for the establishment of mutual consent voluntary adoption registries through which adoptees, birth parents, and biological siblings may voluntarily locate each other. It is not the purpose of this subchapter to inhibit or prohibit persons from locating each other through other legal means or to inhibit or affect in any way the provision of postadoptive services and education, by adoption agencies or others, that go further than the procedures set out for registries established under this subchapter.

History of Fam §162.401: Acts 1995, 74th Leg., ch. 20, §1, eff. April 20, 1995. Source: Former Hum. Res. Code §49.001.

Little v. Smith, 943 S.W.2d 414, 418-19 (Tex.1997). "An adoptee who wants to know the identity of his or her biological parents, a parent whose child has been adopted and wants to locate that child, or a biological sibling may file an application with a registry. The statute spells out processes for establishing these registries, for making application to them, and for determining if applications 'match.' When a 'match' is found, the registry is required by statute to remind the registrants that they may withdraw the registration before disclosure is made, and each registrant is required to sign a consent to disclosure. Even after the death of a registrant, identifying information will not be released unless the registrant had specifically consented in writing to a posthumous disclosure of a match and that consent remained in effect and valid at the time of death. [¶] These procedures are designed to maintain the confidentiality of the identities of adoptees, their natural parents, and biological siblings unless there is a *mutual* desire for that information to be disclosed. The statutes contain no indication that an adoptee can circumvent these procedures simply by asking a court to open the adoption records so that any inheritance rights can be asserted."

FAM §162.402. DEFINITIONS

In this subchapter:

(1) "Administrator" means the administrator of a mutual consent voluntary adoption registry established under this subchapter.

(2) "Adoptee" means a person 18 years of age or older who has been legally adopted in this state or another state or country.

(3) "Adoption" means the act of creating the legal relationship of parent and child between a person and a child who is not the biological child of that person. The term does not include the act of establishing the legal relationship of parent and child between a man and a child through proof of paternity or voluntary legitimation proceedings.

(4) "Adoption agency" means a person, other than a natural parent or guardian of a child, who plans for the placement of or places a child in the home of a prospective adoptive parent.

(5) "Adoptive parent" means an adult who is a parent of an adoptee through a legal process of adoption.

(6) "Alleged father" means a man who is not deemed by law to be or who has not been adjudicated to be the biological father of an adoptee and who claims or is alleged to be the adoptee's biological father.

(7) "Authorized agency" means a public agency authorized to care for or to place children for adoption or a private entity approved for that purpose by the department through a license, certification, or other means. The term includes a licensed child-placing agency or a previously licensed child-placing agency that has ceased operations and has transferred its adoption records to the bureau or an agency authorized by the department to place children for adoption and a licensed child-placing agency that has been acquired by, merged with, or

otherwise succeeded by an agency authorized by the department to place children for adoption.

(8) "Biological parent" means a man or woman who is the father or mother of genetic origin of a child.

(9) "Biological siblings" means persons who share a common birth parent.

(10) "Birth parent" means:

(A) the biological mother of an adoptee;

(B) the man adjudicated or presumed under Chapter 151 to be the biological father of an adoptee; and

(C) a man who has signed a consent to adoption, affidavit of relinquishment, affidavit of waiver of interest in child, or other written instrument releasing the adoptee for adoption, unless the consent, affidavit, or other instrument includes a sworn refusal to admit or a denial of paternity. The term includes a birth mother and birth father but does not include a person adjudicated by a court of competent jurisdiction as not being the biological parent of an adoptee.

(11) "Central registry" means the mutual consent voluntary adoption registry established and maintained by the bureau under this subchapter.

(12) "Department" means the Department of Protective and Regulatory Services.

(13) "Registry" means a mutual consent voluntary adoption registry established under this subchapter.

(14) "Bureau" means the bureau of vital statistics.

History of Fam §162.402: Acts 1995, 74th Leg., ch. 20, §1, eff. April 20, 1995. Amended by Acts 1995, 74th Leg., ch. 968, §§1, 11, eff. Sept. 1, 1995; Acts 1997, 75th Leg., ch. 561, §19, eff. Sept. 1, 1997. Source: Former Hum. Res. Code §49.002.

FAM §162.403. ESTABLISHMENT OF VOLUNTARY ADOPTION REGISTRIES

(a) The bureau shall establish and maintain a mutual consent voluntary adoption registry.

(b) Except as provided by Subsection (c), an agency authorized by the department to place children for adoption and an association comprised exclusively of those agencies may establish a mutual consent voluntary adoption registry. An agency may contract with any other agency authorized by the department to place children for adoption or with an association comprised exclusively of those agencies to perform registry services on its behalf.

(c) An authorized agency that did not directly or by contract provide registry services as required by this subchapter on January 1, 1984, may not provide its own registry service. The bureau shall operate through the central registry those services for agencies not permitted to provide a registry under this section.

History of Fam §162.403: Acts 1995, 74th Leg., ch. 20, §1, eff. April 20, 1995. Amended by Acts 1997, 75th Leg., ch. 561, §20, eff. Sept. 1, 1997. Source: Former Hum. Res. Code §49.003(a)-(c).

FAM §162.404. REQUIREMENT TO SEND INFORMATION TO CENTRAL REGISTRY

An authorized agency that is permitted to provide a registry under this subchapter or that participates in a mutual consent voluntary adoption registry with an association of authorized agencies shall send to the central registry a duplicate of all information the registry maintains in the agency's registry or sends to the registry in which the agency participates.

History of Fam §162.404: Acts 1997, 75th Leg., ch. 561, §21, eff. Sept. 1, 1997.

History of Former Fam §162.404: Acts 1995, 74th Leg., ch. 20, §1, eff. April 20, 1995. Repealed by Acts 1995, 74th Leg., ch. 968, §11, eff. Sept. 1, 1995. Source: Former Hum. Res. Code §49.004.

See also 25 TAC §181.43.

FAM §162.405. DETERMINATION OF APPROPRIATE REGISTRY

(a) The administrator of the central registry shall determine the appropriate registry to which an applicant is entitled to apply.

(b) On receiving an inquiry by an adoptee, birth parent, or sibling who has provided satisfactory proof of age and identity and paid all required inquiry fees, the administrator of the central registry shall review the information on file in the central index and consult with the administrators of other registries in the state to determine the identity of any appropriate registry through which the adoptee, birth parent, or sibling may register.

(c) Each administrator shall, not later than the 30th day after the date of receiving an inquiry from the administrator of the central registry, respond in writing to the inquiry that the registrant was not placed for adoption by an agency served by that registry or that the registrant was placed for adoption by an agency served by that registry. If the registrant was placed for adoption by an agency served by the registry, the administrator shall file a report with the administrator of the central registry including:

(1) the name of the adopted child as shown in the final adoption decree;

(2) the birth date of the adopted child;

(3) the docket number of the adoption suit;

(4) the identity of the court that granted the adoption;

(5) the date of the final adoption decree;

(6) the identity of the agency, if any, through which the adopted child was placed; and

(7) the identity, address, and telephone number of the registry through which the adopted child may register as an adoptee.

(d) After completing the investigation, the administrator of the central registry shall issue an official certificate stating:

(1) the identity of the registry through which the adoptee, birth parent, or biological sibling may apply for registration, if known; or

(2) if the administrator cannot make a conclusive determination, that the adoptee, birth parent, or biological sibling is entitled to apply for registration through the central registry.

History of Fam §162.405: Acts 1995, 74th Leg., ch. 20, §1, eff. April 20, 1995. Amended by Acts 1995, 74th Leg., ch. 751, §79 (eff. Sept. 1, 1995), ch. 968, §2 (eff. Sept. 1, 1995). Source: Former Hum. Res. Code §49.005.

FAM §162.406. REGISTRATION ELIGIBILITY

(a) An adoptee who is 18 years of age or older may apply to a registry for information about the adoptee's birth parents and biological siblings.

(b) A birth parent who is 18 years of age or older may apply to a registry for information about an adoptee who is a child by birth of the birth parent.

(c) An alleged father who is 18 years of age or older and who acknowledges paternity but is not, at the time of application, a birth father may register as a birth father but may not otherwise be recognized as a birth father for the purposes of this subchapter unless:

(1) the adoptee's birth mother in her application identifies him as the adoptee's biological father; and

(2) additional information concerning the adoptee obtained from other sources is not inconsistent with his claim of paternity.

(d) A biological sibling who is 18 years of age or older may apply to a registry for information about the person's adopted biological siblings.

(e) Only birth parents, adoptees, and biological siblings may apply for information through a registry.

(f) A person, including an authorized agency, may not apply for information through a registry as an agent, attorney, or representative of an adoptee, birth parent, or biological sibling.

History of Fam §162.406: Acts 1995, 74th Leg., ch. 20, §1, eff. April 20, 1995. Amended by Acts 1995, 74th Leg., ch. 968, §3, eff. Sept. 1, 1995. Source: Former Hum. Res. Code §49.006.

See also 25 TAC §181.45.

FAM §162.407. REGISTRATION

(a) The administrator shall require each registration applicant to sign a written application.

(b) An adoptee adopted or placed through an authorized agency may register through the registry maintained by that agency or the registry to which the agency has delegated registry services or through the central registry maintained by the bureau.

(c) Birth parents and biological siblings shall register through:

(1) the registry of the authorized agency through which the adoptee was adopted or placed; or

(2) the central registry.

(d) The administrator may not accept an application for registration unless the applicant:

(1) provides proof of identity as provided by Section 162.408;

(2) establishes the applicant's eligibility to register; and

(3) pays all required registration fees.

(e) A registration remains in effect until the 99th anniversary of the date the registration is accepted unless a shorter period is specified by the applicant or the registration is withdrawn before that time.

(f) A registrant may withdraw the registrant's registration in writing without charge at any time.

(g) After a registration is withdrawn or expires, the registrant shall be treated as if the person has not previously registered.

(h) A completed registry application must be accepted or rejected before the 46th day after the date the application is received. If an application is rejected, the administrator shall provide the applicant with a written statement of the reason for the rejection.

History of Fam §162.407: Acts 1995, 74th Leg., ch. 20, §1, eff. April 20, 1995. Amended by Acts 1995, 74th Leg., ch. 968, §4, eff. Sept. 1, 1995; Acts 1997, 75th Leg., ch. 561, §22, eff. Sept. 1, 1997. Source: Former Hum. Res. Code §49.007(a)-(c).

See also 25 TAC §181.45.

FAM §162.408. PROOF OF IDENTITY

The rules and minimum standards of the Texas Board of Health for the bureau must provide for proof of identity in order to facilitate the purposes of this subchapter and to protect the privacy rights of adoptees, adoptive parents, birth parents, biological siblings, and their families.

History of Fam §162.408: Acts 1995, 74th Leg., ch. 20, §1, eff. April 20, 1995. Amended by Acts 1997, 75th Leg., ch. 561, §23, eff. Sept. 1, 1997. Source: Former Hum. Res. Code §49.008.

FAM §162.409. APPLICATION

(a) An application must contain:

(1) the name, address, and telephone number of the applicant;

(2) any other name or alias by which the applicant has been known;

(3) the age, date of birth, and place of birth of the applicant;

(4) the original name of the adoptee, if known;

(5) the adoptive name of the adoptee, if known;

(6) a statement that the applicant is willing to allow the applicant's identity to be disclosed to a registrant who is eligible to learn the applicant's identity;

(7) the name, address, and telephone number of the agency or other entity, organization, or person placing the adoptee for adoption, if known, or, if not known, a statement that the applicant does not know that information;

(8) an authorization to the administrator and the administrator's designees to inspect all vital statistics records, court records, and agency records, including confidential records, relating to the birth, adoption, marriage, and divorce of the applicant or to the birth and death of any child or sibling by birth or adoption of the applicant;

(9) the specific address to which the applicant wishes notice of a successful match to be mailed;

(10) a statement that the applicant either does or does not consent to disclosure of identifying information about the applicant after the applicant's death;

(11) a statement that the registration is to be effective for 99 years or for a stated shorter period selected by the applicant; and

(12) a statement that the adoptee applicant either does or does not desire to be informed that registry records indicate that the applicant has a biological sibling who has registered under this subchapter.

(b) The application may contain the applicant's social security number if the applicant, after being advised of the right not to supply the number, voluntarily furnishes it.

(c) The application of a birth parent must include:

(1) the original name and date of birth or approximate date of birth of each adoptee with respect to whom the parent is registering;

(2) the names of all other birth children, including maiden names, aliases, dates and places of birth, and names of the birth parents;

(3) each name known or thought by the applicant to have been used by the adoptee's other birth parent;

(4) the last known address of the adoptee's other birth parent; and

(5) other available information through which the other birth parent may be identified.

(d) The application of a biological sibling must include:

(1) a statement explaining the applicant's basis for believing that the applicant has one or more biological siblings;

(2) the names, including maiden and married names, and aliases of all the applicant's siblings by birth and adoption and their dates and places of birth, if known;

(3) the names of the applicant's legal parents;

(4) the names of the applicant's birth parents, if known; and

(5) any other information known to the applicant through which the existence and identity of the applicant's biological siblings can be confirmed.

(e) An application may also contain additional information through which the applicant's identity and eligibility to register may be ascertained.

(f) The administrator shall assist the applicant in filling out the application if the applicant is unable to complete the application without assistance, but the administrator may not furnish the applicant with any substantive information necessary to complete the application.

History of Fam §162.409: Acts 1995, 74th Leg., ch. 20, §1, eff. April 20, 1995. Amended by Acts 1995, 74th Leg., ch. 968, §5, eff. Sept. 1, 1995. Source: Former Hum. Res. Code §49.007(e).

FAM §162.410. REPEALED

Repealed by Acts 1995, 74th Leg., ch. 968, §11, eff. Sept. 1, 1995.

FAM §162.411. FEES

(a) The costs of establishing, operating, and maintaining a registry may be recovered in whole or in part through users' fees charged to applicants and registrants.

(b) Each registry shall establish a schedule of fees for services provided by the registry. The fees shall be reasonably related to the direct and indirect costs of establishing, operating, and maintaining the registry.

(c) A fee may not be charged for withdrawing a registration.

(d) The fees collected by the bureau shall be deposited in a special fund in the general revenue fund. Funds in the special fund may be appropriated only for the administration of the central registry.

(e) The administrator may waive users' fees in whole or in part if the applicant provides satisfactory proof of financial inability to pay the fees.

History of Fam §162.411: Acts 1995, 74th Leg., ch. 20, §1, eff. April 20, 1995. Amended by Acts 1995, 74th Leg., ch. 968, §6, eff. Sept. 1, 1995; Acts 1997, 75th Leg., ch. 561, §24, eff. Sept. 1, 1997. Source: Former Hum. Res. Code §49.011.

See also 25 TAC §181.49.

FAM §162.412. SUPPLEMENTAL INFORMATION

(a) A registrant may amend the registrant's registration and submit additional information to the administrator. A registrant shall notify the administrator of any change in the registrant's name or address that occurs after acceptance of the application.

(b) The administrator does not have a duty to search for a registrant who fails to register a change of name or address.

History of Fam §162.412: Acts 1995, 74th Leg., ch. 20, §1, eff. April 20, 1995. Source: Former Hum. Res. Code §49.012.

FAM §162.413. COUNSELING

The applicant must participate in counseling for not less than one hour with a social worker or mental health professional with expertise in postadoption counseling after the administrator has accepted the application for registration and before the release of confidential information.

History of Fam §162.413: Acts 1995, 74th Leg., ch. 20, §1, eff. April 20, 1995. Amended by Acts 1995, 74th Leg., ch. 968, §7, eff. Sept. 1, 1995. Source: Former Hum. Res. Code §49.013.

FAM §162.414. MATCHING PROCEDURES

(a) The administrator shall process each registration in an attempt to match the adoptee and the adoptee's birth parents or the adoptee and the adoptee's biological siblings.

(b) The administrator shall determine that there is a match if the adult adoptee and the birth mother or the birth father have registered or if a biological sibling has registered.

(c) To establish or corroborate a match, the administrator shall request confirmation of a possible match from the bureau. If the agency operating the registry has in its own records sufficient information through which the match may be confirmed, the administrator may, but is not required to, request confirmation from the bureau. The bureau may confirm or deny the match without breaching the duty of confidentiality to the adoptee, adoptive parents, birth parents, or biological siblings and without a court order.

(d) To establish a match, the administrator may also request confirmation of a possible match from the agency, if any, that has possession of records concerning the adoption of an adoptee or from the court that granted the adoption, the hospital where the adoptee or any biological sibling was born, the physician who delivered the adoptee or biological sibling, or any other person who has knowledge of the relevant facts. The agency, court, hospital, physician, or person with knowledge may confirm or deny the match without breaching any duty of confidentiality to the adoptee, adoptive parents, birth parents, or biological siblings.

(e) If a match is denied by a source contacted under Subsection (d), the administrator shall make a full and complete investigation into the reliability of the denial. If the match is corroborated by other reliable sources and the administrator is satisfied that the denial is erroneous, the administrator may make disclosures but shall report to the adoptee, birth parents, and biological siblings involved that the match was not confirmed by all information sources.

History of Fam §162.414: Acts 1995, 74th Leg., ch. 20, §1, eff. April 20, 1995. Amended by Acts 1995, 74th Leg., ch. 968, §8, eff. Sept. 1, 1995; Acts 1997, 75th Leg., ch. 561, §25, eff. Sept. 1, 1997. Source: Former Hum. Res. Code §49.014.

FAM §162.415. REPEALED

Repealed by Acts 1995, 74th Leg., ch. 968, §11, eff. Sept. 1, 1995.

FAM §162.416. DISCLOSURE OF IDENTIFYING INFORMATION

(a) When a match has been made and confirmed to the administrator's satisfaction, the administrator shall mail to each registrant, at the registrant's last known address, by fax or registered or certified mail, return receipt requested, delivery restricted to addressee only, a written notice:

(1) informing the registrant that a match has been made and confirmed;

(2) reminding the registrant that the registrant may withdraw the registration before disclosures are made, if desired; and

(3) notifying the registrant that before any identifying disclosures are made, the registrant must:

(A) sign a written consent to disclosure that allows the disclosure of identifying information about the other registrants to the registrant and allows the disclosure of identifying information about the registrant to other registrants;

(B) participate in counseling for not less than one hour with a social worker or mental health professional who has expertise in postadoption counseling; and

(C) provide the administrator with written certification that the counseling required under Subdivision (B) has been completed.

(b) Identifying information about a registrant shall be released without the registrant's having consented after the match to disclosure if the registrant is dead, the registrant's registration was valid at the time of death, and the registrant had in writing specifically authorized the postdeath disclosure in the registrant's application or in a supplemental statement filed with the administrator.

(c) Identifying information about a deceased birth parent may not be released until each surviving child of the deceased birth parent is an adult or until each child's surviving parent, guardian, managing conservator, or legal custodian consents in writing to the disclosure.

(d) The administrator shall prepare and release written disclosure statements identifying information about each of the registrants if the registrants complied with Subsection (a) and, before the 60th day after the date notification of match was mailed, the registrant or registrants have not withdrawn their registrations.

(e) If the administrator establishes that a match cannot be made because of the death of an adoptee, birth parent, or biological sibling, the administrator shall promptly notify the affected registrant. The administrator shall disclose the reason why a match cannot be made and may disclose nonidentifying information concerning the circumstances of the person's death.

History of Fam §162.416: Acts 1995, 74th Leg., ch. 20, §1, eff. April 20, 1995. Amended by Acts 1995, 74th Leg., ch. 968, §9, eff. Sept. 1, 1995. Source: Former Hum. Res. Code §49.016.

See also 25 TAC §§181.46-181.47.

FAM §§162.417, 162.418. REPEALED

Repealed by Acts 1995, 74th Leg., ch. 968, §11, eff. Sept. 1, 1995.

FAM §162.419. REGISTRY RECORDS CONFIDENTIAL

(a) All applications, registrations, records, and other information submitted to, obtained by, or otherwise acquired by a registry are confidential and may not be disclosed to any person or entity except in the manner authorized by this subchapter.

(b) Information acquired by a registry may not be disclosed under freedom of information or sunshine legislation, rules, or practice.

(c) A person may not file or prosecute a class action litigation to force a registry to disclose identifying information.

History of Fam §162.419: Acts 1995, 74th Leg., ch. 20, §1, eff. April 20, 1995. Source: Former Hum. Res. Code §49.020.

See also 25 TAC §181.48.

FAM §162.420. RULEMAKING

(a) The Texas Board of Health shall make rules and adopt minimum standards for the bureau to:

(1) administer the provisions of this subchapter; and

(2) ensure that each registry respects the right to privacy and confidentiality of an adoptee, birth parent, and biological sibling who does not desire to disclose the person's identity.

(b) The bureau shall conduct a comprehensive review of all rules and standards adopted under this subchapter not less than every six years.

(c) In order to provide the administrators an opportunity to review proposed rules and standards and send written suggestions to the Texas Board of Health, the board shall, before adopting rules and minimum standards, send a copy of the proposed rules and standards not less than 60 days before the date they take effect to:

(1) the administrator of each registry established under this subchapter; and

(2) the administrator of each agency authorized by the department to place children for adoption.

History of Fam §162.420: Acts 1995, 74th Leg., ch. 20, §1, eff. April 20, 1995. Amended by Acts 1997, 75th Leg., ch. 561, §26, eff. Sept. 1, 1997. Source: Former Hum. Res. Code §49.021.

See also 25 TAC §§181.41-181.49.

FAM §162.421. PROHIBITED ACTS; CRIMINAL PENALTIES

(a) This subchapter does not prevent the bureau from making known to the public, by appropriate means, the existence of voluntary adoption registries.

(b) Information received by or in connection with the operation of a registry may not be stored in a data bank used for any purpose other than operation of the registry.

(c) A person commits an offense if the person knowingly or recklessly discloses information from a registry application, registration, record, or other information submitted to, obtained by, or otherwise acquired by a registry in violation of this subchapter. This subsection may not be construed to penalize the disclosure of information from adoption agency records. An offense under this subsection is a felony of the second degree.

(d) A person commits an offense if the person with criminal negligence causes or permits the disclosure of information from a registry application, registration, record, or other information submitted to, obtained by, or otherwise acquired by a registry in violation of this subchapter. This subsection may not be construed to penalize the disclosure of information from adoption agency records. An offense under this subsection is a Class A misdemeanor.

(e) A person commits an offense if the person impersonates an adoptee, birth parent, or biological sibling with the intent to secure confidential information from a registry established under this subchapter. An offense under this subsection is a felony of the second degree.

(f) A person commits an offense if the person impersonates an administrator, agent, or employee of a registry with the intent to secure confidential information from a registry established under this subchapter. An offense under this subsection is a felony of the second degree.

(g) A person commits an offense if the person, with intent to deceive and with knowledge of the statement's meaning, makes a false statement under oath in connection with the operation of a registry. An offense under this subsection is a felony of the third degree.

History of Fam §162.421: Acts 1995, 74th Leg., ch. 20, §1, eff. April 20, 1995. Amended by Acts 1995, 74th Leg., ch. 968, §10, eff. Sept. 1, 1995; Acts 1997, 75th Leg., ch. 561, §27, eff. Sept. 1, 1997. Source: Former Hum. Res. Code §49.022.

FAM §162.422. IMMUNITY FROM LIABILITY

(a) The bureau or authorized agency establishing or operating a registry is not liable to any person for obtaining or disclosing identifying information about a birth parent, adoptee, or biological sibling within the scope of this subchapter and under its provisions.

(b) An employee or agent of the bureau or of an authorized agency establishing or operating a registry under this subchapter is not liable to any person for obtaining or disclosing identifying information about a birth parent, adoptee, or biological sibling within the scope of this subchapter and under its provisions.

(c) A person or entity furnishing information to the administrator or an employee or agent of a registry is not liable to any person for disclosing information about a birth parent, adoptee, or biological sibling within the scope of this subchapter and under its provisions.

(d) A person or entity is not immune from liability for performing an act prohibited by Section 162.421.

History of Fam §162.422: Acts 1995, 74th Leg., ch. 20, §1, eff. April 20, 1995. Amended by Acts 1997, 75th Leg., ch. 561, §28, eff. Sept. 1, 1997. Source: Former Hum. Res. Code §49.023.

Sections 162.423-162.500 reserved for expansion

SUBCHAPTER F. ADOPTION OF AN ADULT

FAM §162.501. ADOPTION OF ADULT

The court may grant the petition of an adult residing in this state to adopt another adult according to this subchapter.

History of Fam §162.501: Acts 1995, 74th Leg., ch. 20, §1, eff. April 20, 1995. Source: Former Fam §16.51.

FAM §162.502. JURISDICTION

The petitioner shall file a suit to adopt an adult in the district court or a statutory county court granted jurisdiction in family law cases and proceedings by Chapter 25, Government Code, in the county of the petitioner's residence.

History of Fam §162.502: Acts 1995, 74th Leg., ch. 20, §1, eff. April 20, 1995. Source: Former Fam §16.51.

FAM §162.503. REQUIREMENTS OF PETITION

(a) A petition to adopt an adult shall be entitled "In the Interest of __________, An Adult."

(b) If the petitioner is married, both spouses must join in the petition for adoption.

History of Fam §162.503: Acts 1995, 74th Leg., ch. 20, §1, eff. April 20, 1995. Source: Former Fam §16.53.

FAM §162.504. CONSENT

A court may not grant an adoption unless the adult consents in writing to be adopted by the petitioner.

History of Fam §162.504: Acts 1995, 74th Leg., ch. 20, §1, eff. April 20, 1995. Source: Former Fam §16.52.

FAM §162.505. ATTENDANCE REQUIRED

The petitioner and the adult to be adopted must attend the hearing. For good cause shown, the court may waive this requirement, by written order, if the petitioner or adult to be adopted is unable to attend.

History of Fam §162.505: Acts 1995, 74th Leg., ch. 20, §1, eff. April 20, 1995. Source: Former Fam §16.54.

FAM §162.506. ADOPTION ORDER

The court shall grant the adoption if the court finds that the requirements for adoption of an adult are met.

History of Fam §162.506: Acts 1995, 74th Leg., ch. 20, §1, eff. April 20, 1995.

FAM §162.507. EFFECT OF ADOPTION

(a) The adopted adult is the son or daughter of the adoptive parents for all purposes.

(b) The adopted adult is entitled to inherit from and through the adopted adult's adoptive parents as though the adopted adult were the biological child of the adoptive parents.

(c) The adopted adult retains the right to inherit from the adult's biological parents. However, a biological parent may not inherit from or through an adopted adult.

History of Fam §162.507: Acts 1995, 74th Leg., ch. 20, §1, eff. April 20, 1995. Source: Former Fam §16.55.

Sections 162.508-162.600 blank

SUBCHAPTER G. MISCELLANEOUS PROVISIONS

FAM §162.601. INCENTIVES FOR LICENSED CHILD-PLACING AGENCIES

(a) Subject to the availability of funds, the Department of Protective and Regulatory Services shall pay, in addition to any other amounts due, a monetary incentive to a licensed child-placing agency for the completion of an adoption:

(1) of a child, as defined by Section 162.301, receiving or entitled to receive foster care at department expense; and

(2) arranged with the assistance of the agency.

(b) The incentive may not exceed 25 percent of the amount the department would have spent to provide one year of foster care for the child, determined according to the child's level of care at the time the adoption is completed.

(c) For purposes of this section, an adoption is completed on the date on which the court issues the adoption order.

History of Fam §162.601: Acts 1997, 75th Leg., ch. 1309, §1, eff. Sept. 1, 1997.

Chapters 163-200 reserved for expansion

SUBTITLE C. JUDICIAL RESOURCES & SERVICES

CHAPTER 201. ASSOCIATE JUDGE; CHILD SUPPORT MASTER

Subchapter A. Associate Judge

Subchapter B. Child Support Master & Court Monitor

Subchapter C. Associate Judge for Substitute Care & Child Protective Services Cases

SUBCHAPTER A. ASSOCIATE JUDGE

FAM §201.001. APPOINTMENT

(a) A judge of a court having jurisdiction of a suit under this title or Title 1 or 4 may appoint a full-time or part-time associate judge to perform the duties authorized by this chapter if the commissioners court of a county in which the court has jurisdiction authorizes the employment of an associate judge.

(b) If a court has jurisdiction in more than one county, an associate judge appointed by that court may serve only in a county in which the commissioners court has authorized the associate judge's appointment.

(c) If more than one court in a county has jurisdiction of a suit under this title or Title 1 or 4 the commissioners court may authorize the appointment of an associate judge for each court or may authorize one or more associate judges to share service with two or more courts.

(d) If an associate judge serves more than one court, the associate judge's appointment must be made with the unanimous approval of all the judges under whom the associate judge serves.

(e) This section does not apply to a master appointed under Subchapter B or an associate judge appointed under Subchapter C.

History of Fam §201.001: Acts 1995, 74th Leg., ch. 20, §1, eff. April 20, 1995. Amended by Acts 1999, 76th Leg., ch. 1302, §1, eff. Sept. 1, 1999. Source: Former Govt Code §54.001.

FAM §201.002. QUALIFICATIONS

To be eligible for appointment as an associate judge, a person must meet the requirements and qualifications to serve as a judge of the court or courts for which the associate judge is appointed.

History of Fam §201.002: Acts 1995, 74th Leg., ch. 20, §1, eff. April 20, 1995. Source: Former Govt Code §54.002.

FAM §201.003. COMPENSATION

(a) An associate judge shall be paid a salary determined by the commissioners court of the county in which the associate judge serves.

(b) If an associate judge serves in more than one county, the associate judge shall be paid a salary as determined by agreement of the commissioners courts of the counties in which the associate judge serves.

(c) The associate judge's salary is paid from the county fund available for payment of officers' salaries.

(d) This section does not apply to a master appointed under Subchapter B or an associate judge appointed under Subchapter C.

History of Fam §201.003: Acts 1995, 74th Leg., ch. 20, §1, eff. April 20, 1995. Amended by Acts 1999, 76th Leg., ch. 1302, §2, eff. Sept. 1, 1999. Source: Former Govt Code §54.003.

FAM §201.004. TERMINATION OF ASSOCIATE JUDGE

(a) An associate judge who serves a single court serves at the will of the judge of that court.

(b) The employment of an associate judge who serves more than two courts may only be terminated by a majority vote of all the judges of the courts which the associate judge serves.

(c) The employment of an associate judge who serves two courts may be terminated by either of the judges of the courts which the associate judge serves.

(d) This section does not apply to a master appointed under Subchapter B or an associate judge appointed under Subchapter C.

History of Fam §201.004: Acts 1995, 74th Leg., ch. 20, §1, eff. April 20, 1995. Amended by Acts 1999, 76th Leg., ch. 1302, §3, eff. Sept. 1, 1999. Source: Former Govt Code §54.004.

FAM §201.005. CASES THAT MAY BE REFERRED

(a) Except as provided by this section, a judge of a court may refer to an associate judge any aspect of a suit over which the court has jurisdiction under this title or Title 1 or 4 including any matter ancillary to the suit.

(b) Unless a party files a written objection to the associate judge hearing a trial on the merits, the judge may refer the trial to the associate judge. A trial on the merits is any final adjudication from which an appeal may be taken to a court of appeals.

(c) A party must file an objection to an associate judge hearing a trial on the merits or presiding at a jury trial not later than the 10th day after the date the party receives notice that the associate judge will hear the trial. If an objection is filed, the referring court shall hear the trial on the merits or preside at a jury trial.

(d) The requirements of Subsections (b) and (c) shall apply whenever a judge has authority to refer the trial of a suit under this title, Title 1, or Title 4 to an associate judge, master, or other assistant judge regardless of whether the assistant judge is appointed under this subchapter.

History of Fam §201.005: Acts 1995, 74th Leg., ch. 20, §1, eff. April 20, 1995. Amended by Acts 1999, 76th Leg., ch. 1302, §4, eff. Sept. 1, 1999. Source: Former Govt Code §54.005.

FAM §201.006. ORDER OF REFERRAL

(a) In referring a case to an associate judge, the judge of the referring court shall render:

(1) an individual order of referral; or

(2) a general order of referral specifying the class and type of cases to be heard by the associate judge.

(b) The order of referral may limit the power or duties of an associate judge.

History of Fam §201.006: Acts 1995, 74th Leg., ch. 20, §1, eff. April 20, 1995. Source: Former Govt Code §54.006.

FAM §201.007. POWERS OF ASSOCIATE JUDGE

(a) Except as limited by an order of referral, an associate judge may:

(1) conduct a hearing;

(2) hear evidence;

(3) compel production of relevant evidence;

(4) rule on the admissibility of evidence;

(5) issue a summons for the appearance of witnesses;

(6) examine a witness;

(7) swear a witness for a hearing;

(8) make findings of fact on evidence;

(9) formulate conclusions of law;

(10) recommend an order to be rendered in a case;

(11) regulate all proceedings in a hearing before the associate judge;

(12) order the attachment of a witness or party who fails to obey a subpoena;

(13) order the detention of a witness or party found guilty of contempt, pending approval by the referring court as provided by Section 201.013; and

(14) take action as necessary and proper for the efficient performance of the associate judge's duties.

(b) An associate judge may, in the interest of justice, refer a case back to the referring court regardless of whether a timely objection to the associate judge hearing the trial on the merits or presiding at a jury trial has been made by any party.

History of Fam §201.007: Acts 1995, 74th Leg., ch. 20, §1, eff. April 20, 1995. Amended by Acts 1999, 76th Leg., ch. 1302, §5, eff. Sept. 1, 1999. Source: Former Govt Code §54.007.

Stein v. Stein, 868 S.W.2d 902, 904 (Tex.App.—Houston [14th Dist.] 1994, no writ). Section 201.007 "sets out the powers and duties of family law associate judges. Such powers include making findings of fact, formulating conclusions of law, and *recommending* the judgment to be made in a case. The listed powers do not include rendering judgment. In fact, the referring court is free to adopt or reject the recommendation of the master, and the findings and recommendations of the master become the decree or order of the referring court only on the referring court's signing an order or decree conforming to the master's report. We hold that an associate judge of the family law court does not have the power to render judgment. Rendition occurs only when the referring court adopts the master's report, or if no report is generated, when the trial judge signs the final judgment."

Pinkley v. Vega, 768 S.W.2d 473, 475 (Tex.App.—El Paso 1989, no writ). Under §201.007, "the court master [now associate judge] has as several of his powers and duties, the duty to hear evidence and the power to make findings of fact on such evidence. In the exercise of these responsibilities, he is nothing more than an independent fact finder, similar in that respect to the function of a jury. What the court master heard, found and recommended as a result of a previous hearing became a nullity upon the granting of the new trial."

FAM §201.008. ATTENDANCE OF BAILIFF

A bailiff may attend a hearing by an associate judge if directed by the referring court.

History of Fam §201.008: Acts 1995, 74th Leg., ch. 20, §1, eff. April 20, 1995. Source: Former Govt Code §54.008.

FAM §201.009. COURT REPORTER

(a) A court reporter may be provided during a hearing held by an associate judge appointed under this chapter. A court reporter is required to be provided when the associate judge presides over a jury trial or a final termination hearing.

(b) A party, the associate judge, or the referring court may provide for a reporter during the hearing, if one is not otherwise provided.

(c) The record may be preserved in the absence of a court reporter by any other means approved by the associate judge.

(d) The referring court or associate judge may tax the expense of preserving the record under Subsection (c) as costs.

(e) On appeal of the associate judge's report or proposed order, the referring court may consider testimony or other evidence in the record, if the record is taken by a court reporter, in addition to witnesses or other matters presented under Section 201.015.

History of Fam §201.009: Acts 1995, 74th Leg., ch. 20, §1, eff. April 20, 1995. Amended by Acts 1999, 76th Leg., ch. 1302, §6, eff. Sept. 1, 1999. Source: Former Govt Code §54.018.

FAM §201.010. WITNESS

(a) A witness appearing before an associate judge is subject to the penalties for perjury provided by law.

(b) A referring court may fine or imprison a witness who:

(1) failed to appear before an associate judge after being summoned; or

(2) improperly refused to answer questions if the refusal has been certified to the court by the associate judge.

History of Fam §201.010: Acts 1995, 74th Leg., ch. 20, §1, eff. April 20, 1995. Source: Former Govt Code §54.009.

FAM §201.011. REPORT

(a) The associate judge's report may contain the associate judge's findings, conclusions, or recommendations, including a proposed order. The associate judge's report must be in writing in the form directed by the referring court. The form may be a notation on the referring court's docket sheet.

(b) After a hearing, the associate judge shall provide the parties participating in the hearing notice of the substance of the associate judge's report. The notice may be given in the form of a proposed order.

(c) Notice may be given to the parties:

(1) in open court, by an oral statement or a copy of the associate judge's written report, including any proposed order; or

(2) by certified mail, return receipt requested.

(d) The associate judge shall certify the date of mailing of notice by certified mail. Notice is considered given on the third day after the date of mailing.

(e) After a hearing conducted by an associate judge, the associate judge shall send the associate judge's signed and dated report, including any proposed order, and all other papers relating to the case to the referring court.

History of Fam §201.011: Acts 1995, 74th Leg., ch. 20, §1, eff. April 20, 1995. Amended by Acts 1999, 76th Leg., ch. 1302, §7, eff. Sept. 1, 1999. Source: Former Govt Code §§54.010(a), (b), 54.012(c).

FAM §201.012. NOTICE OF RIGHT TO APPEAL

(a) Notice of the right of appeal to the judge of the referring court shall be given to all parties.

(b) The notice may be given:

(1) by oral statement in open court;

(2) by posting inside or outside the courtroom of the referring court; or

(3) as otherwise directed by the referring court.

History of Fam §201.012: Acts 1995, 74th Leg., ch. 20, §1, eff. April 20, 1995. Source: Former Govt Code §54.010(c).

FAM §201.013. ORDER OF COURT

(a) Pending appeal of the associate judge's report, including any proposed order, to the referring court, the decisions and recommendations of the associate judge are in full force and effect and are enforceable as an order of the referring court, except for orders providing for the appointment of a receiver.

(b) If an appeal to the referring court is not filed or the right to an appeal to the referring court is waived, the findings and recommendations of the associate judge become the order of the referring court only on the referring court's signing an order conforming to the associate judge's report.

(c) An order by an associate judge for the temporary detention or incarceration of a witness or party shall be presented to the referring court on the day the witness or party is detained or incarcerated. The referring court, without prejudice to the right of appeal provided by Section 201.015, may approve the temporary detention or incarceration or may order the release of the party or witness, with or without bond, pending appeal. If the referring court is not immediately available, the associate judge may order the release of the party or witness, with or without bond, pending appeal or may continue the person's detention or incarceration for not more than 72 hours.

History of Fam §201.013: Acts 1995, 74th Leg., ch. 20, §1, eff. April 20, 1995. Amended by Acts 1999, 76th Leg., ch. 1302, §8, eff. Sept. 1, 1999. Source: Former Govt Code §§54.013, 54.015.

Attorney Gen. v. Orr, 989 S.W.2d 464, 468 n.2 (Tex. App.—Austin 1999, no pet.). "We view the purpose of §201.013(a) to be allowing temporary orders to be in effect pending trial before the referring court. Despite the continuing validity of the associate judge's recommendations for that limited purpose, the judgment of the referring court on the issues appealed will be based solely on evidence presented at the de novo hearing."

Ex parte Christensen, 868 S.W.2d 376, 380 (Tex. App.—Houston [1st Dist.] 1993, orig. proceeding). [T]he "[associate judge's] findings and recommendations become the court's order or decree only when the court signs an order or decree conforming to the [associate judge's] report. The language of the statute demonstrates that the operative date is when the referring court signs an order that conforms to the [associate judge's] report. Prior to that time, the [associate judge's] report merely consists of findings and recommendations. There is no specified period in which the trial court must adopt the [associate judge's] report. The court's plenary power extends 30 days after the signing of the final decree."

FAM §201.014. JUDICIAL ACTION ON ASSOCIATE JUDGE'S REPORT

Unless a party files a written notice of appeal, the referring court may:

(1) adopt, modify, or reject the associate judge's report, including any proposed order;

(2) hear further evidence; or

(3) recommit the matter to the associate judge for further proceedings.

History of Fam §201.014: Acts 1995, 74th Leg., ch. 20, §1, eff. April 20, 1995. Amended by Acts 1999, 76th Leg., ch. 1302, §9, eff. Sept. 1, 1999. Source: Former Govt Code §54.011.

FAM §201.015. APPEAL TO REFERRING COURT

(a) A party may appeal an associate judge's report by filing notice of appeal not later than the third day after the date the party receives notice of the substance of the associate judge's report as provided by Section 201.011.

(b) An appeal to the referring court must be in writing specifying the findings and conclusions of the associate judge to which the party objects. The appeal is limited to the specified findings and conclusions.

(c) On appeal to the referring court, the parties may present witnesses as in a hearing de novo on the issues raised in the appeal. The court may also consider the record from the hearing before the associate judge, including the charge to and verdict returned by a jury, if the record was taken by a court reporter.

(d) Notice of an appeal to the referring court shall be given to the opposing attorney under Rule 21a, Texas Rules of Civil Procedure.

(e) If an appeal to the referring court is filed by a party, any other party may file an appeal to the referring court not later than the seventh day after the date the initial appeal was filed.

(f) The referring court, after notice to the parties, shall hold a hearing on all appeals not later than the 30th day after the date on which the initial appeal was filed with the referring court.

(g) Before the start of a hearing by an associate judge, the parties may waive the right of appeal to the referring court in writing or on the record.

(h) Denial of an appeal under this section or waiver of the right to appeal to the referring court does not affect the right of a party to file a motion for new trial, motion for judgment notwithstanding the verdict, or other post-trial motion.

(i) A party may not demand a second jury on appeal of an associate judge's report, including any proposed order, resulting from a jury trial.

History of Fam §201.015: Acts 1995, 74th Leg., ch. 20, §1, eff. April 20, 1995. Amended by Acts 1999, 76th Leg., ch. 1302, §10, eff. Sept. 1, 1999. Source: Former Govt Code §54.012(a), (d)-(i).

State ex rel. Latty v. Owens, 907 S.W.2d 484, 485 (Tex.1995). "Although the district court should have held a hearing on [respondent's] appeal before signing an order adopting the master's report, its failure to do so did not deprive it of jurisdiction to issue the order or make the order void. A judgment is void only when it is clear that the court rendering the judgment had no jurisdiction over the parties or subject matter, no jurisdiction to render judgment, or no capacity to act as a court. Mere failure to follow proper procedure will not render a judgment void. [¶] An order which purports to dispose of all issues and all parties, like the district court's first order, is a final appealable order. Errors other than lack of jurisdiction must be attacked within the prescribed time limits. When [respondent] did not timely appeal from the first order, it became final."

In re E.M., 54 S.W.3d 849, 852 (Tex.App.—Corpus Christi 2001, no pet.). "[T]o be entitled to a *de novo* hearing on appeal of an associate judge's recommendations to the referring court, a party must timely file a written notice of appeal containing the associate judge's findings and conclusions to which the party objects. [¶] Although appellant's notice of appeal was timely filed, it did not contain his objections to any specific findings or conclusions. Because appellant failed to comply with the requirements under §201.015, we conclude he is not entitled to a *de novo* hearing of his appeal of the associate judge's recommendation."

Fountain v. Knebel, 45 S.W.3d 736, 739 (Tex. App.—Dallas 2001, no pet.). "A party who timely appeals from the report of an associate judge is entitled to a hearing de novo before the referring court. Section 201.015 ... requires the referring court to hold a hearing on the appeal within thirty days. The purpose of this section is to require the prompt resolution of appeals from an associate judge's rulings. Nonetheless, the referring court does not lose its jurisdiction if it fails to hear an appeal within thirty days after the appeal is filed. Rather, the thirty-day provision affords a party the right to compel the district court to hear the case promptly. The requirement is a deadline for the trial court, not the parties. Once a party has filed a notice of appeal, the party has completed the prerequisites necessary to be entitled to a de novo hearing."

Attorney Gen. v. Orr, 989 S.W.2d 464, 467-68 (Tex. App.—Austin 1999, no pet.). "For purposes of the final determination of the merits of the case ... filing a notice of appeal to the referring court cuts off the earlier proceedings, and evidence is presented anew to the referring court; in making its decision, the referring court may not rely on what occurred before the associate judge. Although in the absence of a notice of appeal the referring court's action continues a process begun before the associate judge, filing a notice of appeal breaks that continuity and begins an entirely new process. [¶] [A] party whose case is heard by an associate judge and who files a notice of appeal from the report could fail to attend the de novo hearing before the referring court. Given that filing a notice of appeal initiates a new process before the referring court, such a defaulting party stands in the same position as one who fails to attend an ordinary trial on the merits after answering the petition."

Harrell v. Harrell, 986 S.W.2d 629, 631 (Tex.App.—El Paso 1998, no pet.). "It is clear that the purpose of §201.015(f) is to require the prompt resolution of appeals from associate judge's rulings. We also interpret the word 'shall' in §201.015(f) to be mandatory. The referring court does not lose its jurisdiction if it fails to hear an appeal from a master's recommendation within thirty days after the appeal is filed. [¶] Because §201.015(f) is not a jurisdictional prerequisite to a de novo hearing, the referring court is not statutorily precluded from conducting the de novo hearing outside the thirty day window."

Peacock v. Humble, 933 S.W.2d 341, 342 (Tex. App.—Austin 1996, order on mot.). "A party may appeal an associate judge's report by filing a written notice of appeal to the referring district court not later than the third day after the date the party receives notice of the substance of the associate judge's report.... *At 343:* Because the three-day filing period in the present case is statutory, the Code Construction Act's method for computing time applies rather than the method contained in [TRCP] 4."

FAM §201.016. APPELLATE REVIEW

(a) Failure to appeal to the referring court, by waiver or otherwise, the approval by the referring court of an associate judge's report does not deprive a party of the right to appeal to or request other relief from a court of appeals or the supreme court.

(b) The date an order or judgment by the referring court is signed is the controlling date for the purposes of appeal to or request for other relief from a court of appeals or the supreme court.

History of Fam §201.016: Acts 1995, 74th Leg., ch. 20, §1, eff. April 20, 1995. Source: Former Govt Code §54.012(j).

FAM §201.017. IMMUNITY

An associate judge appointed under this subchapter has the judicial immunity of a district judge. All existing immunity granted an associate judge by law, express or implied, continues in full force and effect.

History of Fam §201.017: Acts 1995, 74th Leg., ch. 20, §1, eff. April 20, 1995. Source: Former Govt Code §54.017.

FAM §201.018. VISITING ASSOCIATE JUDGE

(a) If an associate judge appointed under this subchapter is temporarily unable to perform the judge's official duties because of absence or illness, injury, or other disability, a judge of a court having jurisdiction of a suit under this title or Title 1 or 4 may appoint a visiting associate judge to perform the duties of the associate judge during the period of the associate judge's absence or disability if the commissioners court of a county in which the court has jurisdiction authorizes the employment of a visiting associate judge.

A *Subsection (b) below is effective for appointments of visiting associate judges made on or after Sept. 1, 2001.*

(b) To be eligible for appointment under this section, a person must have served as an associate judge for at least two years.

Subsection (b) below is effective for appointments of visiting associate judges made before Sept. 1, 2001.

(b) To be eligible for appointment under this section, a person must have served as an associate judge for at least six years.

(c) Sections 201.001 through 201.017 apply to a visiting associate judge appointed under this section.

(d) This section does not apply to a master appointed under Subchapter B.

History of Fam §201.018: Acts 1999, 76th Leg., ch. 1355, §1, eff. Aug. 30, 1999. Amended by Acts 2001, 77th Leg., ch. 308, §1, eff. Sept. 1, 2001.

Sections 201.019-201.100 reserved for expansion

SUBCHAPTER B. CHILD SUPPORT MASTER & COURT MONITOR

FAM §201.101. AUTHORITY OF PRESIDING JUDGE

(a) The presiding judge of each administrative judicial region, after conferring with the judges of courts in the region having jurisdiction of Title IV-D cases, shall determine which courts require the appointment of a full-time or part-time master to complete each Title IV-D case within the time specified in this subchapter.

(b) The presiding judge may limit the appointment to a specified time period and may terminate an appointment at any time.

(c) A master appointed under this subchapter may be appointed to serve more than one court. Two or more judges of administrative judicial regions may jointly appoint one or more masters to serve the regions.

(d) If the presiding judge determines that a court requires a master, the presiding judge shall appoint a master. If a master is appointed for a court, all Title IV-D cases shall be referred to the master by a general order for each county issued by the judge of the court for which the master is appointed, or, in the absence of that order, by a general order issued by the presiding judge who appointed the master. Referral of Title IV-D cases may not be made for individual cases or case by case.

History of Fam §201.101: Acts 1995, 74th Leg., ch. 20, §1, eff. April 20, 1995. Amended by Acts 1999, 76th Leg., ch. 1072, §1, eff. Sept. 1, 1999. Source: Former Fam §14.82(a), (b).

FAM §201.102. APPLICATION OF LAW GOVERNING ASSOCIATE JUDGES

(a) The provisions of Subchapter A relating to the qualifications, powers, and immunity of an associate judge apply to a master appointed under this subchapter, except that a master:

(1) may reside anywhere within the administrative judicial region in which the court to which the master is appointed is located or, if a master is appointed to serve in two or more administrative judicial regions, may reside anywhere within the regions; and

(2) may not be designated as an associate judge.

(b) Except as provided by this subchapter, the provisions of Subchapter A relating to an associate judge apply to a master appointed under this subchapter.

History of Fam §201.102: Acts 1995, 74th Leg., ch. 20, §1, eff. April 20, 1995. Amended by Acts 1999, 76th Leg., ch. 556, §41 (eff. Sept. 1, 1999), ch. 1302, §11 (eff. Sept. 1, 1999). Source: Former Fam §14.82(c), (e).

FAM §201.103. DESIGNATION OF HOST COUNTY

(a) The presiding judges of the administrative judicial regions by majority vote shall determine the host county of a master appointed under this subchapter.

(b) The host county shall provide an adequate courtroom and quarters, including furniture, necessary utilities, and telephone equipment and service, for the master and other personnel assisting the master.

(c) A master is not required to reside in the host county.

History of Fam §201.103: Acts 1995, 74th Leg., ch. 20, §1, eff. April 20, 1995. Source: Former Fam §14.82(d).

FAM §201.104. POWERS & DUTIES OF MASTER

(a) On motion of a party, a master may refer a complex case back to the judge for final disposition after the master has recommended temporary support.

(b) A master shall take testimony and make a record in all Title IV-D cases as provided by this chapter.

(c) A master may render and sign any order that is not a final order on the merits of the case.

(d) A master may recommend to the referring court any order after a trial on the merits.

E *Subsection (e) below is effective for SAPCRs commenced on or after Sept. 1, 2001.*

(e) Only the referring court may render an order for postjudgment relief, including an order for a new trial.

History of Fam §201.104: Acts 1995, 74th Leg., ch. 20, §1, eff. April 20, 1995. Amended by Acts 1999, 76th Leg., ch. 556, §42, eff. Sept. 1, 1999; Acts 2001, 77th Leg., ch. 1023, §46, eff. Sept. 1, 2001. Source: Former Fam §14.82(f), (g).

FAM §201.1041. JUDICIAL ACTION ON MASTER'S REPORT

(a) If an appeal to the referring court is not filed or the right to appeal is waived, a recommendation of the master, other than a recommendation of enforcement by contempt or a recommendation of the immediate incarceration of a party, shall become an order of the referring court by operation of law without ratification by the referring court.

(b) A master's report that recommends enforcement by contempt or the immediate incarceration of a party becomes an order of the referring court only if:

(1) the referring court signs an order adopting the master's recommendation; and

E *Subsection (2) below is effective for modification or enforcement proceedings commenced on or after Sept. 1, 2001.*

(2) the order meets the requirements of Section 157.166.

(c) Except as provided by Subsection (b), the decisions and recommendations of the master have full force and effect and are enforceable as an order of the referring court during an appeal of the master's report to the referring court.

History of Fam §201.1041: Acts 1999, 76th Leg., ch. 556, §43, eff. Sept. 1, 1999. Amended by Acts 2001, 77th Leg., ch. 1023, §47, eff. Sept. 1, 2001.

FAM §201.1042. APPEAL TO REFERRING COURT

(a) Except as provided in this section, Section 201.015 applies to an appeal of the master's recommendations.

(b) The party appealing a master's recommendation shall file notice with the referring court and the clerk of the court.

(c) A respondent who timely files an appeal of a master's report recommending incarceration after a finding of contempt shall be brought before the referring court not later than the first working day after the date of filing the appeal. The referring court shall determine whether the respondent should be released on bond or whether the respondent's appearance in court at a designated time and place can be otherwise assured.

(d) If the respondent under Subsection (c) is released on bond or other security, the referring court shall condition the bond or other security on the respondent's promise to appear in court for a hearing on the appeal at a designated date, time, and place, and the referring court shall give the respondent notice of the hearing in open court. No other notice to the respondent is required.

(e) If the respondent under Subsection (c) is released without posting bond or security, the court shall set a hearing on the appeal at a designated date, time, and place and give the respondent notice of the hearing in open court. No other notice to the respondent is required.

(f) If the referring court is not satisfied that the respondent's appearance in court can be assured and the respondent remains incarcerated, a hearing on the appeal shall be held as soon as practicable, but not later than the fifth day after the date the respondent's notice of appeal was filed, unless the respondent and, if represented, the respondent's attorney waive the accelerated hearing.

E *Subsection (g) below is effective for modification or enforcement proceedings commenced on or after Sept. 1, 2001.*

(g) Until a hearing is held on a timely filed appeal under this section, a master may not hold a hearing on the respondent's compliance with conditions in the master's report for suspension of incarceration.

History of Fam §201.1042: Acts 1999, 76th Leg., ch. 556, §43, eff. Sept. 1, 1999. Amended by Acts 2001, 77th Leg., ch. 1023, §48, eff. Sept. 1, 2001.

Phagan v. Aleman, 29 S.W.3d 632, 634 (Tex.App.—Houston [1st Dist.] 2000, no pet.). "Any party may appeal the recommendation of a child support master by filing a notice of appeal with the trial judge within three days of receiving notice of the recommendation. Once the notice of appeal is filed, the trial judge must conduct a hearing de novo addressing the issues raised. *At 635:* The Family Code's requirement that a trial judge hold a hearing de novo, when a timely notice of appeal is filed, is mandatory. The failure to hold such a hearing is presumed harmful."

FAM §201.105. COMPENSATION OF MASTER

(a) A master appointed under this subchapter is entitled to a salary to be determined by a majority vote of the presiding judges of the administrative judicial regions. The salary may not exceed 90 percent of the salary paid to a district judge as set by the state general appropriations act.

(b) The master's salary shall be paid from the county fund available for payment of officers' salaries or from funds available from the state and federal government as provided in Section 201.107.

History of Fam §201.105: Acts 1995, 74th Leg., ch. 20, §1, eff. April 20, 1995. Source: Former Fam §14.83(a), (b).

FAM §201.106. CHILD SUPPORT COURT MONITOR & OTHER PERSONNEL

(a) The presiding judge of an administrative judicial region or the presiding judges of the administrative judicial regions, by majority vote, may appoint other personnel, including a child support court monitor for each master appointed under this subchapter, as needed to implement and administer the provisions of this subchapter.

(b) The salary of the personnel and court monitors shall be paid from the county fund available for payment of officers' salaries or from funds available from the state and federal government as provided by Section 201.107.

History of Fam §201.106: Acts 1995, 74th Leg., ch. 20, §1, eff. April 20, 1995. Amended by Acts 1999, 76th Leg., ch. 1072, §2, eff. Sept. 1, 1999. Source: Former Fam §14.83(c).

FAM §201.1065. DUTIES OF CHILD SUPPORT COURT MONITOR

(a) A child support court monitor appointed under Section 201.106 shall monitor child support cases in which the obligor is placed on probation for failure to comply with the requirements of a child support order.

(b) In monitoring a child support case, a court monitor shall:

(1) conduct an intake assessment of the needs of an obligor that, if addressed, would enable the obligor to comply with a child support order;

(2) refer an obligor to employment services offered by the employment assistance program under Section 302.0035, Labor Code, if appropriate;

(3) provide mediation services or referrals to services, if appropriate;

(4) schedule periodic contacts with an obligor to assess compliance with the child support order and whether additional support services are required; and

(5) monitor the amount and timeliness of child support payments owed and paid by an obligor.

History of Fam §201.1065: Acts 1999, 76th Leg., ch. 1072, §3, eff. Sept. 1, 1999.

Ⓐ FAM §201.1066. SUPERVISION OF MASTERS

(a) Not later than January 1, 2000, the office of court administration and the presiding judges of the administrative judicial regions shall report to the legislature a plan to improve the efficiency of the masters appointed under this subchapter and the masters' participation in the child support enforcement program in the state.

(b) The plan must:

(1) contain written personnel performance standards and require annual performance evaluations for the masters and other personnel appointed under this subchapter;

(2) require uniform practices;

(3) address training needs and resource requirements of the masters;

(4) ensure accountability of the masters for complying with applicable federal and state law, including statutes regarding a minimum 40-hour workweek and working hours under Chapter 658, Government Code; and

(5) require a uniform process for receiving, handling, and resolving complaints about individual masters or the child support masters program under this subchapter.

(c) The office of court administration shall assist the presiding judges in monitoring the masters' compliance with job performance standards and federal and state laws and policies.

History of Fam §201.1066: Acts 1999, 76th Leg., ch. 556, §44, eff. Sept. 1, 1999. Renumbered from §201.1065 by Acts 2001, 77th Leg., ch. 1420, §21.001(31), eff. Sept. 1, 2001.

FAM §201.107. STATE & FEDERAL FUNDS

(a) The office of court administration may contract with the Title IV-D agency for available state and federal funds under Title IV-D and may employ personnel needed to implement and administer this subchapter. A master, a court monitor for each master, and other personnel appointed under this subchapter are state employees for all purposes, including accrual of leave time, insurance benefits, retirement benefits, and travel regulations.

(b) The presiding judges of the administrative judicial regions, state agencies, and counties may contract with the Title IV-D agency for available federal funds under Title IV-D to reimburse costs and salaries associated with masters, court monitors, and personnel appointed under this subchapter and may also use available state funds and public or private grants.

(c) The presiding judges and the Title IV-D agency shall act and are authorized to take any action necessary to maximize the amount of federal funds available under the Title IV-D program.

History of Fam §201.107: Acts 1995, 74th Leg., ch. 20, §1, eff. April 20, 1995. Amended by Acts 1999, 76th Leg., ch. 556, §45 (eff. Sept. 1, 1999), ch. 1072, §4 (eff. Sept. 1, 1999). Source: Former Fam §14.83(d), (e).

FAM §201.108. MANDATORY APPOINTMENT OF MASTER

The presiding judge shall appoint a master for each court handling Title IV-D cases for which the state has not been granted an exemption from the expedited process of Title IV-D cases required by federal law.

History of Fam §201.108: Acts 1995, 74th Leg., ch. 20, §1, eff. April 20, 1995. Source: Former Fam §14.84.

FAM §201.1085. REPEALED

Repealed by Acts 1999, 76th Leg., ch. 1302, §14 (eff. Sept. 1, 1999), ch. 62, §6.26 (eff. Sept. 1, 1999).

FAM §201.109. EXEMPTION FROM APPOINTMENT OF MASTER

(a) If a presiding judge of an administrative judicial region does not require the appointment of a master for a court, the presiding judge shall provide to the Title IV-D agency the information required by the secretary of health and human services to grant the court an exemption from the expedited process requirement for Title IV-D cases.

(b) On receipt of sufficient information, the Title IV-D agency shall immediately apply to the secretary for an exemption from the expedited process requirement for Title IV-D cases for the district court.

(c) The Title IV-D agency shall promptly notify the presiding judge of the administrative judicial region in which the court is located of any information received from the secretary concerning the application for the exemption.

(d) If the secretary does not grant an exemption for a court or if the secretary revokes an exemption for a court, the presiding judge of the administrative judicial region in which the court is located shall appoint a master as prescribed by this subchapter not later than the 30th day after the date the judge receives notice that the exemption was denied or revoked.

(e) The presiding judge of an administrative judicial region shall require each court within the judicial region to provide information and data to the presiding judge, the office of court administration, and the Title IV-D agency regarding the processing of Title IV-D cases necessary to:

(1) establish the need for an exemption as provided by Subsection (a); and

(2) comply with federal law.

(f) The Title IV-D agency and the office of court administration shall provide assistance to the presiding judge in obtaining and storing the information and data provided under this section.

(g) Any information or data required under this section may be provided as required by the presiding judge.

History of Fam §201.109: Acts 1995, 74th Leg., ch. 20, §1, eff. April 20, 1995. Source: Former Fam §14.85.

FAM §201.110. TIME FOR DISPOSITION OF TITLE IV-D CASES

(a) Title IV-D cases must be completed from the time of successful service to the time of disposition within the following time:

(1) 90 percent within three months;

(2) 98 percent within six months; and

(3) 100 percent within one year.

(b) Title IV-D cases shall be given priority over other cases.

(c) A clerk or judge may not restrict the number of Title IV-D cases that are filed or heard in the courts.

History of Fam §201.110: Acts 1995, 74th Leg., ch. 20, §1, eff. April 20, 1995. Source: Former Fam §14.81.

FAM §201.111. TIME TO ACT ON MASTER'S REPORT THAT INCLUDES FINDING OF CONTEMPT

(a) Not later than the 10th day after the date a master's report recommending a finding of contempt is filed, the referring court shall:

(1) adopt, approve, or reject the master's report;

(2) hear further evidence; or

(3) recommit the matter for further proceedings.

(b) The time limit in Subsection (a) does not apply if a party has filed a written notice of appeal to the referring court.

History of Fam §201.111: Acts 1995, 74th Leg., ch. 751, §80, eff. Sept. 1, 1995. Amended by Acts 1999, 76th Leg., ch. 556, §46, eff. Sept. 1, 1999. Source: Former Fam §14.82(h).

FAM §201.112. LIMITATION ON LAW PRACTICE BY MASTER

A master may not engage in the private practice of law.

History of Fam §201.112: Acts 1999, 76th Leg., ch. 556, §47, eff. Sept. 1, 1999.

FAM §201.113. VISITING CHILD SUPPORT MASTER

E *Section 201.113 below is effective for SAPCRs commenced on or after Sept. 1, 2001.*

(a) If a child support master appointed under this subchapter is temporarily unable to perform the master's official duties because of absence resulting from family circumstances, illness, injury, or disability, the presiding judge of the administrative judicial region in which the master serves may appoint a visiting child support master to perform the duties of the master during the period the master is unable to perform the master's duties.

(b) A person is not eligible for appointment under this section unless the person has served as a child support master or associate judge for at least two years before the date of appointment.

(c) A visiting master appointed under this section is subject to each provision of this chapter that applies to a child support master serving under a regular appointment. A visiting master appointed under this section is entitled to compensation to be determined by a majority vote of the presiding judges of the administrative judicial regions through use of funds under Section 201.105(b). A visiting judge is not considered a state employee for any purpose.

History of Fam §201.113: Enacted by Acts 2001, 77th Leg., ch. 1023, §49, eff. Sept. 1, 2001.

Sections 201.114-201.200 blank

SUBCHAPTER C. ASSOCIATE JUDGE FOR SUBSTITUTE CARE & CHILD PROTECTIVE SERVICES CASES

FAM §201.201. AUTHORITY OF PRESIDING JUDGE

(a) The presiding judge of each administrative judicial region, after conferring with the judges of courts in the region having family law jurisdiction and a substitute care caseload, shall determine which courts require the appointment of a full-time or part-time associate judge to complete each case within the times specified in Chapters 262 and 263.

(b) The presiding judge may limit the appointment to a specified period and may terminate an appointment at any time.

(c) An associate judge appointed under this subchapter may be appointed to serve more than one court. Two or more judges of administrative judicial regions may jointly appoint one or more associate judges to serve the regions.

(d) If the presiding judge determines that a court requires an associate judge, the presiding judge shall appoint an associate judge. If an associate judge is appointed for a court, all substitute care cases shall be referred to the associate judge by a general order for each county issued by the judge of the court for which the associate judge is appointed or, in the absence of that order, by a general order issued by the presiding judge who appointed the associate judge.

(e) This section does not limit the jurisdiction of a court to issue orders under Chapter 262 or 263.

History of Fam §201.201: Acts 1999, 76th Leg., ch. 1302, §12, eff. Sept. 1, 1999.

FAM §201.202. APPLICATION OF LAW GOVERNING ASSOCIATE JUDGES

(a) Except as provided by this subchapter, Subchapter A applies to an associate judge appointed under this subchapter.

(b) An associate judge may reside anywhere in the administrative judicial region in which the court to which the associate judge is appointed is located. An associate judge appointed to serve in two or more administrative judicial regions may reside anywhere in the regions.

History of Fam §201.202: Acts 1999, 76th Leg., ch. 1302, §12, eff. Sept. 1, 1999.

FAM §201.203. DESIGNATION OF HOST COUNTY

(a) Subject to the approval of the commissioners court of the proposed host county, the presiding judges of the administrative judicial regions by majority vote shall determine the host county of an associate judge appointed under this subchapter.

(b) The host county shall provide an adequate courtroom and quarters, including furniture, necessary utilities, and telephone equipment and service, for the associate judge and other personnel assisting the associate judge.

(c) An associate judge is not required to reside in the host county.

History of Fam §201.203: Acts 1999, 76th Leg., ch. 1302, §12, eff. Sept. 1, 1999.

FAM §201.204. GENERAL POWERS & DUTIES OF ASSOCIATE JUDGE

(a) On the motion of a party, an associate judge may refer a complex case back to the referring court for final disposition after recommending temporary orders for the protection of a child.

(b) An associate judge shall take testimony and make a record in a case as provided by this chapter.

History of Fam §201.204: Acts 1999, 76th Leg., ch. 1302, §12, eff. Sept. 1, 1999.

FAM §201.205. COMPENSATION OF ASSOCIATE JUDGE

(a) An associate judge appointed under this subchapter is entitled to a salary as determined by a majority vote of the presiding judges of the administrative judicial regions. The salary may not exceed 90 percent of the salary paid to a district judge as set by the state General Appropriations Act.

(b) The associate judge's salary shall be paid from county funds available for payment of officers' salaries subject to the approval of the commissioners court or from funds available from the state and federal governments as provided in Section 201.207.

History of Fam §201.205: Acts 1999, 76th Leg., ch. 1302, §12, eff. Sept. 1, 1999.

FAM §201.206. PERSONNEL

(a) The presiding judge of an administrative judicial region or the presiding judges of the administrative judicial regions, by majority vote, may appoint personnel as needed to implement and administer the provisions of this subchapter.

(b) The salary of the personnel shall be paid from county funds available for payment of officers' salaries subject to the approval of the commissioners court or from funds available from the state and federal governments as provided by Section 201.207.

History of Fam §201.206: Acts 1999, 76th Leg., ch. 1302, §12, eff. Sept. 1, 1999.

FAM §201.207. STATE & FEDERAL FUNDS; PERSONNEL

(a) The office of court administration may contract for available state and federal funds from any source and may employ personnel needed to implement and administer this subchapter. An associate judge and other personnel appointed under this subsection are state employees for all purposes, including accrual of leave time, insurance benefits, retirement benefits, and travel regulations.

(b) The presiding judges of the administrative judicial regions, state agencies, and counties may contract for available federal funds from any source to reimburse costs and salaries associated with associate judges and personnel appointed under this section and may also use available state funds and public or private grants.

(c) The presiding judges and the office of court administration in cooperation with other agencies shall take action necessary to maximize the amount of federal money available to fund the use of associate judges under this subchapter.

History of Fam §201.207: Acts 1999, 76th Leg., ch. 1302, §12, eff. Sept. 1, 1999.

FAM §201.208. APPOINTMENT OF ASSOCIATE JUDGE FOR CHILD PROTECTION CASES

(a) The presiding judge of an administrative judicial region may appoint an associate judge for a court handling child protection cases.

(b) This chapter does not limit the authority of a presiding judge to appoint visiting or retired judges to assist in processing cases in a reasonable time.

History of Fam §201.208: Acts 1999, 76th Leg., ch. 1302, §12, eff. Sept. 1, 1999.

CHAPTER 202. FRIEND OF THE COURT

FAM §202.001. APPOINTMENT

(a) After an order for child support or possession of or access to a child has been rendered, a court may appoint a friend of the court on:

(1) the request of a person alleging that the order has been violated; or

(2) its own motion.

(b) A court may appoint a friend of the court in a proceeding under Part D of Title IV of the federal Social Security Act (42 U.S.C. Section 651 et seq.) only if the Title IV-D agency agrees in writing to the appointment.

(c) The duration of the appointment of a friend of the court is as determined by the court.

(d) In the appointment of a friend of the court, the court shall give preference to:

(1) a local domestic relations office;

(2) a local child support collection office;

(3) the local court official designated to enforce actions as provided in Chapter 159; or

(4) an attorney in good standing with the State Bar of Texas.

(e) In the execution of a friend of the court's duties under this subchapter, a friend of the court shall represent the court to ensure compliance with the court's order.

History of Fam §202.001: Acts 1995, 74th Leg., ch. 20, §1, eff. April 20, 1995. Source: Former Fam §14.91.

FAM §202.002. AUTHORITY & DUTIES

(a) A friend of the court may coordinate nonjudicial efforts to improve compliance with a court order relating to child support or possession of or access to a child by use of:

(1) telephone communication;

(2) written communication;

(3) one or more volunteer advocates under Chapter 107;

(4) informal pretrial consultation;

(5) one or more of the alternate dispute resolution methods under Chapter 154, Civil Practice and Remedies Code;

(6) a certified social worker;

(7) a family mediator; and

(8) employment agencies, retraining programs, and any similar resources to ensure that both parents can meet their financial obligations to the child.

(b) A friend of the court, not later than the 15th day of the month following the reporting month:

(1) shall report to the court or monitor reports made to the court on:

(A) the amount of child support collected as a percentage of the amount ordered; and

(B) efforts to ensure compliance with orders relating to possession of or access to a child; and

(2) may file an action to enforce, clarify, or modify a court order relating to child support or possession of or access to a child.

(c) A friend of the court may file a notice of delinquency and a request for a writ of income withholding under Chapter 158 in order to enforce a child support order.

History of Fam §202.002: Acts 1995, 74th Leg., ch. 20, §1, eff. April 20, 1995. Amended by Acts 1995, 74th Leg., ch. 751, §81, eff. Sept. 1, 1995; Acts 1997, 75th Leg., ch. 702, §9, eff. Sept. 1, 1997. Source: Former Fam §14.92.

FAM §202.003. DUTY OF LOCAL OFFICES & OFFICIALS TO REPORT

A local domestic relations office, a local registry, or a court official designated to receive child support under a court order shall, if ordered by the court, report to the court or a friend of the court on a monthly basis:

(1) any delinquency and arrearage in child support payments; and

(2) any violation of an order relating to possession of or access to a child.

History of Fam §202.003: Acts 1995, 74th Leg., ch. 20, §1, eff. April 20, 1995. Source: Former Fam §14.93.

FAM §202.004. ACCESS TO INFORMATION

A friend of the court may arrange access to child support payment records by electronic means if the records are computerized.

History of Fam §202.004: Acts 1995, 74th Leg., ch. 20, §1, eff. April 20, 1995. Source: Former Fam §14.94.

FAM §202.005. COMPENSATION

(a) A friend of the court is entitled to compensation for services rendered and for expenses incurred in rendering the services.

(b) The court may assess the amount that the friend of the court receives in compensation against a party to the suit in the same manner as the court awards costs under Chapter 106.

(c) A friend of the court or a person who acts as the court's custodian of child support records, including the clerk of a court, may apply for and receive funds from the child support and court management account under Section 21.007, Government Code.

(d) A friend of the court who receives funds under Subsection (c) shall use the funds to reimburse any compensation the friend of the court received under Subsection (b).

History of Fam §202.005: Acts 1995, 74th Leg., ch. 20, §1, eff. April 20, 1995. Source: Former Fam §14.95.

CHAPTER 203. DOMESTIC RELATIONS OFFICES

FAM §203.001. DEFINITIONS

In this chapter:

(1) "Administering entity" means a commissioners court, juvenile board, or other entity responsible for

administering a domestic relations office under this chapter.

(2) "Domestic relations office" means a county office that serves families, county departments, and courts to ensure effective implementation of this title.

History of Fam §203.001: Acts 1995, 74th Leg., ch. 20, §1, eff. April 20, 1995. Amended by Acts 1995, 74th Leg., ch. 475, §1, eff. Sept. 1, 1995. Source: Former Hum. Res. Code §151.003(a).

FAM §203.002. ESTABLISHMENT OF DOMESTIC RELATIONS OFFICE

A commissioners court may establish a domestic relations office.

History of Fam §203.002: Acts 1995, 74th Leg., ch. 20, §1, eff. April 20, 1995. Renumbered from §203.003 and amended by Acts 1995, 74th Leg., ch. 475, §1, eff. Sept. 1, 1995. Source: Former Hum. Res. Code §151.001.

FAM §203.003. ADMINISTRATION

(a) A domestic relations office shall be administered:

(1) as provided by the commissioners court; or

(2) if the commissioners court does not otherwise provide for the administration of the office, by the juvenile board that serves the county in which the domestic relations office is located.

(b) The administering entity shall appoint and assign the duties of a director who shall be responsible for the day-to-day administration of the office. A director serves at the pleasure of the administering entity.

(c) The administering entity shall determine the amount of money needed to operate the office.

(d) A commissioners court that establishes a domestic relations office under this chapter may execute a bond for the office. A bond under this subsection must be:

(1) executed with a solvent surety company authorized to do business in the state; and

(2) conditioned on the faithful performance of the duties of the office.

(e) The administering entity shall establish procedures for the acceptance and use of a grant or donation to the office.

History of Fam §203.003: Acts 1995, 74th Leg., ch. 20, §1, eff. April 20, 1995. Renumbered from §203.004 and amended by Acts 1995, 74th Leg., ch. 475, §1, eff. Sept. 1, 1995. Source: Former Hum. Res. Code §151.002(a).

FAM §203.004. POWERS & DUTIES

(a) A domestic relations office may:

(1) collect and disburse child support payments that are ordered by a court to be paid through a domestic relations registry;

(2) maintain records of payments and disbursements made under Subdivision (1);

(3) file a suit, including a suit to:

(A) establish paternity;

(B) enforce a court order for child support or for possession of and access to a child; and

(C) modify or clarify an existing child support order;

(4) provide an informal forum in which:

(A) mediation is used to resolve disputes in an action under Subdivision (3); or

(B) an agreed repayment schedule for delinquent child support is negotiated as an alternative to filing a suit to enforce a court order for child support under Subdivision (3);

(5) prepare a court-ordered social study;

(6) represent a child as guardian ad litem in a suit in which:

(A) termination of the parent-child relationship is sought; or

(B) conservatorship of or access to a child is contested;

(7) serve as a friend of the court;

(8) provide predivorce counseling ordered by a court;

(9) provide community supervision services under Chapter 157;

(10) provide information to assist a party in understanding, complying with, or enforcing the party's duties and obligations under Subdivision (3); and

E *Subsection (11) below is effective for modification or enforcement proceedings commenced on or after Sept. 1, 2001.*

(11) provide, directly or through a contract, visitation services, including supervision of court-ordered visitation, visitation exchange, or other similar services.

(b) A court having jurisdiction in a proceeding under this title, Title 3, or Section 25.05, Penal Code, may order that child support payments be made through a domestic relations office.

(c) A domestic relations office may:

(1) hire or contract for the services of attorneys to assist the office in providing services under this chapter; and

E *Subsection (2) below is effective for modification or enforcement proceedings commenced on or after Sept. 1, 2001.*

(2) employ community supervision officers or court monitors.

History of Fam §203.004: Acts 1995, 74th Leg., ch. 20, §1, eff. April 20, 1995. Renumbered from §203.005 and amended by Acts 1995, 74th Leg., ch. 475, §1, eff. Sept. 1, 1995. Amended by Acts 1997, 75th Leg., ch. 702, §10, eff. Sept. 1, 1997; Acts 1999, 76th Leg., ch. 1191, §1 (eff. June 19, 1999), ch. 859, §3 (eff. Sept. 1, 1999); Acts 2001, 77th Leg., ch. 1023, §50, eff. Sept. 1, 2001. Source: Former Hum. Res. Code §151.004.

FAM §203.005. FEES & CHARGES

(a) The administering entity may authorize a domestic relations office to assess and collect:

(1) an initial operations fee not to exceed $15 to be paid to the domestic relations office on the filing of a suit;

(2) in a county that has a child support enforcement cooperative agreement with the Title IV-D agency, an initial child support service fee not to exceed $36 to be paid to the domestic relations office on the filing of a suit;

(3) a reasonable application fee to be paid by an applicant requesting services from the office;

(4) a reasonable attorney's fee and court costs incurred or ordered by the court;

A *Subsection (5) below is effective for modification or enforcement proceedings commenced on or after Sept. 1, 2001.*

(5) a monthly service fee not to exceed $3 to be paid annually in advance by a managing conservator and possessory conservator for whom the domestic relations office provides services;

Subsection (5) below is effective for modification or enforcement proceedings commenced before Sept. 1, 2001.

(5) a monthly child support service fee not to exceed $3 to be paid by a managing conservator and possessory conservator for whom the domestic relations office acts as a local child support registry;

(6) community supervision fees as provided by Chapter 157 if community supervision officers are employed by the domestic relations office; and

(7) a reasonable fee for preparation of a court-ordered social study.

(b) The first payment of a fee under Subsection (a)(4) is due on the date that the person required to pay support is ordered to begin child support, alimony, or separate maintenance payments. Subsequent payments of the fee are due annually and in advance.

(c) The director of a domestic relations office shall attempt to collect all fees in an efficient manner.

(d) The administering entity may provide for an exemption from the payment of a fee authorized under this section if payment of the fee is not practical or in the interest of justice. Fees that may be exempted under this subsection include fees related to:

(1) spousal and child support payments made under an interstate pact;

(2) a suit brought by the Texas Department of Human Services;

(3) activities performed by the Department of Protective and Regulatory Services or another governmental agency, a private adoption agency, or a charitable organization; and

(4) services for a person who has applied for or who receives public assistance under the laws of this state.

History of Fam §203.005: Acts 1995, 74th Leg., ch. 20, §1, eff. April 20, 1995. Renumbered from §203.009 and amended by Acts 1995, 74th Leg., ch. 475, §1, eff. Sept. 1, 1995. Amended by Acts 1999, 76th Leg., ch. 556, §48, eff. Sept. 1, 1999; Acts 2001, 77th Leg., ch. 1023, §51, eff. Sept. 1, 2001. Source: Former Hum. Res. Code §151.008.

FAM §203.006. FUND

(a) As determined by the administering entity, fees collected or received by a domestic relations office shall be deposited in:

(1) the general fund for the county in which the domestic relations office is located; or

(2) the office fund established for the domestic relations office.

(b) The administering entity shall use the domestic relations office fund to provide money for services authorized by this chapter.

(c) A domestic relations office fund may be supplemented as necessary from the county's general fund or from other money available from the county.

History of Fam §203.006: Acts 1995, 74th Leg., ch. 20, §1, eff. April 20, 1995. Renumbered from §203.010 and amended by Acts 1995, 74th Leg., ch. 475, §1, eff. Sept. 1, 1995. Amended by Acts 1997, 75th Leg., ch. 702, §11, eff. Sept. 1, 1997. Source: Former Hum. Res. Code §151.009.

FAM §203.007. ACCESS TO RECORDS; OFFENSE

(a) A domestic relations office may obtain the records described by Subsections (b), (c), (d), and (e) that relate to a person who has:

(1) been ordered to pay child support;

(2) been designated as a possessory conservator or managing conservator of a child;

(3) been designated to be the father of a child; or

(4) executed an acknowledgment of paternity.

(b) A domestic relations office is entitled to obtain from the Department of Public Safety records that relate to:

(1) a person's date of birth;

(2) a person's most recent address;

(3) a person's current driver's license status;

(4) motor vehicle accidents involving a person; and

(5) reported traffic-law violations of which a person has been convicted.

(c) A domestic relations office is entitled to obtain from the Texas Workforce Commission records that relate to:

(1) a person's address;

(2) a person's employment status and earnings;

(3) the name and address of a person's current or former employer; and

(4) unemployment compensation benefits received by a person.

(d) To the extent permitted by federal law, a domestic relations office is entitled to obtain from the National Directory of New Hires[1] established under 42 U.S.C. Section 653(i), as amended, records that relate to a person described by Subsection (a), including records that relate to:

(1) the name, telephone number, and address of the person's employer;

(2) information provided by the person on a W-4 form; and

(3) information provided by the person's employer on a Title IV-D form.

(e) To the extent permitted by federal law, a domestic relations office is entitled to obtain from the state case registry records that relate to a person described by Subsection (a), including records that relate to:

(1) the street and mailing address and the social security number of the person;

(2) the name, telephone number, and address of the person's employer;

(3) the location and value of real and personal property owned by the person; and

(4) the name and address of each financial institution in which the person maintains an account and the account number for each account.

(f) An agency required to provide records under this section may charge a domestic relations office a fee for providing the records in an amount that does not exceed the amount paid for those records by the agency responsible for Title IV-D cases.

(g) The Department of Public Safety, the Texas Workforce Commission, or the office of the secretary of state may charge a domestic relations office a fee not to exceed the charge paid by the Title IV-D agency for furnishing records under this section.

(h) Information obtained by a domestic relations office under this section that is confidential under a constitution, statute, judicial decision, or rule is privileged and may be used only by that office.

(i) A person commits an offense if the person releases or discloses confidential information obtained under this section without the consent of the person to whom the information relates. An offense under this subsection is a Class C misdemeanor.

(j) A domestic relations office is entitled to obtain from the office of the secretary of state the following information about a registered voter to the extent that the information is available:

(1) complete name;

(2) current and former street and mailing address;

(3) sex;

(4) date of birth;

(5) social security number; and

(6) telephone number.

[1] Acts 1999, 76th Leg., ch. 859, §4 does not capitalize National Directory of New Hires.

History of Fam §203.007: Acts 1995, 74th Leg., ch. 20, §1, eff. April 20, 1995. Renumbered from §203.012 and amended by Acts 1995, 74th Leg., ch. 475, §1, eff. Sept. 1, 1995. Amended by Acts 1995, 74th Leg., ch. 803, §1, eff. Sept. 1, 1995; Acts 1997, 75th Leg., ch. 165, §7.18, eff. Sept. 1, 1997; Acts 1999, 76th Leg., ch. 859, §4 (eff. Sept. 1, 1999), ch. 1191, §2 (eff. June 19, 1999), ch. 556, §49 (eff. Sept. 1, 1999). Source: Former Hum. Res. Code §151.011.

FAM §203.008. DELETED

Deleted by Acts 1995, 74th Leg., ch. 475, §1, eff. Sept. 1, 1995.

FAM §§203.009, 203.010. RENUMBERED

Renumbered as §§203.005 & 203.006 by Acts 1995, 74th Leg., ch. 475, §1, eff. Sept. 1, 1995.

FAM §203.011. DELETED

Deleted by Acts 1995, 74th Leg., ch. 475, §1, eff. Sept. 1, 1995.

FAM §203.012. RENUMBERED

Renumbered as §203.007 by Acts 1995, 74th Leg., ch. 475, §1, eff. Sept. 1, 1995.

CHAPTER 204. CHILD SUPPORT COLLECTION BY PRIVATE ENTITY

FAM §204.001. APPLICABILITY

This chapter applies only to a county that did not have the authority to contract with a private entity to receive, disburse, and record payments or restitution of child support on January 1, 1997.

History of Fam §204.001: Amended by Acts 1999, 76th Leg., ch. 118, §1, eff. Sept. 1, 1999. Source: Former Hum. Res. Code §153.001.

FAM §204.002. AUTHORITY TO CONTRACT

A county, acting through its commissioners court or domestic relations office, may contract with a private entity to:

(1) enforce, collect, receive, and disburse:

(A) child support payments;

(B) other amounts due under a court order containing an order to pay child support; and

(C) fees, including fees provided by this chapter;

(2) maintain appropriate records, including records of child support and other amounts and fees that are due, past due, paid, or delinquent;

(3) locate absent parents;

(4) furnish statements to parents accounting for payments that are due, past due, paid, or delinquent;

(5) send billings and other appropriate notices to parents;

(6) perform any duty or function that a local registry is authorized to perform;

(7) perform any duty or function in connection with the state case registry; or

(8) provide another child support or visitation enforcement service authorized by the commissioners court, including mediation of disputes related to child support or visitation.

History of Fam §204.002: Amended by Acts 1999, 76th Leg., ch. 118, §1, eff. Sept. 1, 1999. Source: Former Hum. Res. Code §153.002.

FAM §204.003. TERMS & CONDITIONS OF CONTRACT

The commissioners court or domestic relations office shall include all appropriate terms and conditions in the contract that it determines are reasonable to secure the services of a private entity as provided by this chapter, including:

(1) provisions specifying the services to be provided by the entity;

(2) the method, conditions, and amount of compensation for the entity;

(3) provisions for the security of funds collected as child support, fees, or other amounts under the contract or that otherwise provide reasonable assurance to the county of the entity's full and faithful performance of the contract;

(4) provisions specifying the records to be kept by the entity, including any records necessary to fully account for all funds received and disbursed as child support, fees, or other amounts;

(5) requirements governing the inspection, verification, audit, or explanation of the entity's accounting or other records;

(6) the county's right to terminate the contract on 30 days' notice to the private entity if the private entity engages in an ongoing pattern of child support enforcement that constitutes wilful and gross misconduct subjecting delinquent obligors to unconscionable duress, abuse, or harassment;

(7) provisions permitting an obligor and obligee to jointly waive the monitoring procedure, if not required by law, by written request approved by order of the court having jurisdiction of the suit in which the child support order was issued; and

(8) provisions for the disclosure or nondisclosure of information or records maintained or known to the entity as a result of contract performance, including a requirement for the private entity to:

(A) disclose to any child support obligor that the private entity is attempting to enforce the obligor's child support obligation; and

(B) make no disclosure of the information or records other than in furtherance of the effort to enforce the child support order.

History of Fam §204.003: Amended by Acts 1999, 76th Leg., ch. 118, §1, eff. Sept. 1, 1999. Source: Former Hum. Res. Code §153.003.

FAM §204.004. FUNDING

(a) To provide or recover the costs of providing services authorized by this chapter, a commissioners court, on its behalf or on behalf of the domestic relations office, may:

(1) provide by order for the assessment and collection of a reasonable fee at the time a party files a suit affecting the parent-child relationship;

(2) provide by order for the assessment and collection of a fee of $3 per month at a time specified for payment of child support;

(3) provide by order for the assessment and collection of a late payment fee of $4 per month to be imposed if an obligor does not make a payment of child support in full when due;

(4) accept or receive funds from public grants or private sources available for providing services authorized by this chapter; or

(5) use any combination of funding sources specified by this subsection.

(b) The commissioners court, on its behalf or on behalf of the domestic relations office, may:

(1) provide by order for reasonable exemptions from the collection of fees authorized by Subsection (a); and

(2) require payment of a fee authorized by Subsection (a)(2) annually and in advance.

(c) The commissioners court may not charge a fee under Subsection (a)(2) if the amount of child support ordered to be paid is less than the equivalent of $100 per month.

(d) The fees established under Subsection (a) may be collected by any means provided for the collection of child support. The commissioners court may provide by order, on its behalf or on behalf of the domestic relations office, for the manner of collection of fees and the apportionment of payments received to meet fee obligations.

History of Fam §204.004: Amended by Acts 1999, 76th Leg., ch. 118, §1, eff. Sept. 1, 1999. Source: Former Hum. Res. Code §153.004.

FAM §204.005. CUMULATIVE EFFECT OF CHAPTER

A power or duty conferred on a county, county official, or county instrumentality by this chapter is cumulative of the powers and duties created or conferred by other law.

History of Fam §204.005: Amended by Acts 1999, 76th Leg., ch. 118, §1, eff. Sept. 1, 1999. Source: Former Hum. Res. Code §153.005.

Chapters 205-230 reserved for expansion

SUBTITLE D. ADMINISTRATIVE SERVICES

CHAPTER 231. TITLE IV-D SERVICES

Subchapter A. Administration of Title IV-D Program

Subchapter B. Services Provided by Title IV-D Program

SUBCHAPTER A. ADMINISTRATION OF TITLE IV-D PROGRAM

FAM §231.001. DESIGNATION OF TITLE IV-D AGENCY

The office of the attorney general is designated as the state's Title IV-D agency.

History of Fam §231.001: Acts 1995, 74th Leg., ch. 20, §1, eff. April 20, 1995. Source: Former Hum. Res. Code §76.001.

FAM §231.0011. DEVELOPMENT OF STATEWIDE INTEGRATED SYSTEM FOR CHILD SUPPORT & MEDICAL SUPPORT ENFORCEMENT

(a) The Title IV-D agency shall have final approval authority on any contract or proposal for delivery of Title IV-D services under this section and in coordination with the Texas Judicial Council, the Office of Court Administration of the Texas Judicial System, the federal Office of Child Support Enforcement, and state, county, and local officials, shall develop and implement a statewide integrated system for child support and medical support enforcement, employing federal, state, local, and private resources to:

(1) unify child support registry functions;

(2) record and track all child support orders entered in the state;

(3) establish an automated enforcement process which will use delinquency monitoring, billing, and other enforcement techniques to ensure the payment of current support;

(4) incorporate existing enforcement resources into the system to obtain maximum benefit from state and federal funding; and

(5) ensure accountability for all participants in the process, including state, county, and local officials, private contractors, and the judiciary.

(b) Counties and other providers of child support services shall be required, as a condition of participation in the unified system, to enter into a contract with the Title IV-D agency, to comply with all federal requirements for the Title IV-D program, and to maintain at least the current level of funding for activities which are proposed to be included in the integrated child support system.

(c) The Title IV-D agency may contract with any county meeting technical system requirements necessary to comply with federal law for provision of Title IV-D services in that county. All new cases in which support orders are entered in such county after the effective date of a monitoring contract shall be Title IV-D cases. Any other case in the county, subject to federal requirements and the agreement of the county and the Title IV-D agency, may be included as a Title IV-D case. Any obligee under a support order may refuse Title IV-D enforcement services unless required to accept such services pursuant to other law.

(d) Counties participating in the unified enforcement system shall monitor all child support registry cases and on delinquency may, subject to the approval of the Title IV-D agency, provide enforcement services through:

(1) direct provision of services by county personnel;

(2) subcontracting all or portions of the services to private entities or attorneys; or

(3) such other methods as may be approved by the Title IV-D agency.

(e) The Title IV-D agency may phase in the integrated child support registry and enforcement system, and the requirement to implement the system shall be contingent on the receipt of locally generated funds and federal reimbursement. Locally generated funds include but are not limited to funds contributed by counties and cities.

(f) The Title IV-D agency shall adopt rules to implement this section.

(g) Participation in the statewide integrated system for child support and medical support enforcement by a county is voluntary, and nothing in this section shall be construed to mandate participation.

(h) This section does not limit the ability of the Title IV-D agency to enter into an agreement with a county for the provision of services as authorized under Section 231.002.

History of Fam §231.0011: Acts 1995, 74th Leg., ch. 341, §1.01, eff. Sept. 1, 1995. Amended by Acts 1997, 75th Leg., ch. 702, §12, eff. Sept. 1, 1997; Acts 1999, 76th Leg., ch. 556, §50, eff. Sept. 1, 1999.

FAM §231.0012. CHILD SUPPORT ENFORCEMENT MANAGEMENT

The person appointed by the attorney general as the person responsible for managing the Title IV-D agency's child support enforcement duties shall report directly to the attorney general.

History of Fam §231.0012: Acts 1997, 75th Leg., ch. 420, §16, eff. Sept. 1, 1997.

FAM §231.0013. DEDICATION OF FUNDS

Appropriations made to the Title IV-D agency for child support enforcement may be expended only for the purposes for which the money was appropriated.

History of Fam §231.0013: Acts 1997, 75th Leg., ch. 420, §16, eff. Sept. 1, 1997.

FAM §231.002. POWERS & DUTIES

(a) The Title IV-D agency may:

(1) accept, transfer, and expend funds, subject to the General Appropriations Act, made available by the federal or state government or by another public or private source for the purpose of carrying out this chapter;

(2) adopt rules for the provision of child support services;

(3) initiate legal actions needed to implement this chapter; and

(4) enter into contracts or agreements necessary to administer this chapter.

(b) The Title IV-D agency may perform the duties and functions necessary for locating children under agreements with the federal government as provided by 42 U.S.C. Section 663.

(c) The Title IV-D agency may enter into agreements or contracts with federal, state, or other public or private agencies or individuals for the purpose of carrying out this chapter. The agreements or contracts between the agency and other state agencies or political subdivisions of the state are not subject to Chapter 771 or 783, Government Code.

(d) Consistent with federal law and any international treaty or convention to which the United States is a party and that has been ratified by the United States Congress, the Title IV-D agency may:

(1) on approval by and in cooperation with the governor, pursue negotiations and enter into reciprocal arrangements with the federal government, another state, or a foreign country or a political subdivision of the federal government, state, or foreign country to:

(A) establish and enforce child support obligations; and

(B) establish mechanisms to enforce an order providing for possession of or access to a child rendered under Chapter 153;

(2) spend money appropriated to the agency for child support enforcement to engage in international child support enforcement; and

(3) spend other money appropriated to the agency necessary for the agency to conduct the agency's activities under Subdivision (1).

(e) The Title IV-D agency may take the following administrative actions with respect to the location of a parent, the determination of parentage, and the establishment, modification, and enforcement of child support and medical support orders required by 42 U.S.C. Section 666(c), without obtaining an order from any other judicial or administrative tribunal:

(1) issue an administrative subpoena, as provided by Section 231.303, to obtain financial or other information;

(2) order genetic testing for parentage determination, as provided by Chapter 233;

(3) order income withholding, as provided by Chapter 233, and issue an administrative writ of withholding, as provided by Chapter 158; and

(4) take any action with respect to execution, collection, and release of a judgment or lien for child support necessary to satisfy the judgment or lien, as provided by Chapter 157.

(f) The Title IV-D agency shall recognize and enforce the authority of the Title IV-D agency of another state to take actions similar to the actions listed in this section.

(g) The Title IV-D agency shall develop and use procedures for the administrative enforcement of interstate cases meeting the requirements of 42 U.S.C. Section 666(a)(14) under which the agency:

(1) shall promptly respond to a request made by another state for assistance in a Title IV-D case; and

(2) may, by electronic or other means, transmit to another state a request for assistance in a Title IV-D case.

(h) In each Title IV-D case in which the total amount of a child support obligor's child support delinquency is at least $5,000 and the obligor owns property in the state or resides in the state, the Title IV-D agency shall enforce the child support obligation by filing a child support lien under Subchapter G, Chapter 157. This subsection does not prohibit the Title IV-D agency from filing a child support lien in any other case in which a lien may be filed under Subchapter G, Chapter 157.

History of Fam §231.002: Acts 1995, 74th Leg., ch. 20, §1, eff. April 20, 1995. Amended by Acts 1997, 75th Leg., ch. 874, §1 (eff. Sept. 1, 1997), ch. 911, §68 (eff. Sept. 1, 1997); Acts 1999, 76th Leg., ch. 556, §51 (eff. Sept. 1, 1999), ch. 62, §6.27 (eff. Sept. 1, 1999). Source: Former Hum. Res. Code §§76.002(a), (d), (f), 76.004(b).

See also 1 TAC, Ch. 55.

FAM §231.003. FORMS & PROCEDURES

The Title IV-D agency shall by rule promulgate any forms and procedures necessary to comply fully with the intent of this chapter.

History of Fam §231.003: Acts 1995, 74th Leg., ch. 20, §1, eff. April 20, 1995. Source: Former Fam §14.86.

See also 1 TAC §§55.111-55.119.

FAM §231.004. REPEALED

Repealed by Acts 1997, 75th Leg., ch. 911, §97(a), eff. Sept. 1, 1997.

FAM §231.005. BIENNIAL REPORT REQUIRED

(a) The Title IV-D agency shall report to the legislature each biennium on:

(1) the effectiveness of the agency's child support enforcement activity in reducing the state's public assistance obligations;

(2) the use and effectiveness of all enforcement tools authorized by state or federal law or otherwise available to the agency; and

(3) the progress and impact of the Title IV-D agency's efforts to use private contractors to perform Title IV-D program functions.

(b) The agency shall develop a method for estimating the costs and benefits of the child support enforcement program and the effect of the program on appropriations for public assistance.

History of Fam §231.005: Acts 1995, 74th Leg., ch. 20, §1, eff. April 20, 1995. Amended by Acts 1999, 76th Leg., ch. 556, §51, eff. Sept. 1, 1999. Source: Former Hum. Res. Code §76.002(i).

FAM §231.006. INELIGIBILITY TO RECEIVE STATE GRANTS OR LOANS OR RECEIVE PAYMENT ON STATE CONTRACTS

(a) A child support obligor who is more than 30 days delinquent in paying child support and a business entity in which the obligor is a sole proprietor, partner, shareholder, or owner with an ownership interest of at least 25 percent is not eligible to:

(1) receive payments from state funds under a contract to provide property, materials, or services; or

(2) receive a state-funded grant or loan.

(b) A child support obligor or business entity ineligible to receive payments under Subsection (a) remains ineligible until:

(1) all arrearages have been paid; or

(2) the obligor is in compliance with a written repayment agreement or court order as to any existing delinquency.

(c) A bid or an application for a contract, grant, or loan paid from state funds must include the name and social security number of the individual or sole proprietor and each partner, shareholder, or owner with an ownership interest of at least 25 percent of the business entity submitting the bid or application.

(d) A contract, bid, or application subject to the requirements of this section must include the following statement:

"Under Section 231.006, Family Code, the vendor or applicant certifies that the individual or business entity named in this contract, bid, or application is not ineligible to receive the specified grant, loan, or payment and acknowledges that this contract may be terminated and payment may be withheld if this certification is inaccurate."

(e) If a state agency determines that an individual or business entity holding a state contract is ineligible to receive payment under Subsection (a), the contract may be terminated.

(f) If the certificate required under Subsection (d) is shown to be false, the vendor is liable to the state for attorney's fees, the costs necessary to complete the contract, including the cost of advertising and awarding a second contract, and any other damages provided by law or contract.

(g) This section does not create a cause of action to contest a bid or award of a state grant, loan, or contract. This section does not impose a duty on the Title IV-D agency to collect information to send to the comptroller to withhold a payment to a business entity. The Title IV-D agency and other affected agencies are encouraged to develop a system by which the Title IV-D agency may identify a business entity that is ineligible to receive a state payment under Subsection (a) and to ensure that a state payment to the entity is not made. This system should be implemented using existing funds and only if the Title IV-D agency, comptroller, and other affected agencies determine that it will be cost-effective.

(h) This section does not apply to a contract between governmental entities.

(i) The Title IV-D agency may adopt rules or prescribe forms to implement any provision of this section.

(j) A state agency may accept a bid that does not include the information required under Subsection (c) if the state agency collects the information before the contract, grant, or loan is executed.

History of Fam §231.006: Acts 1995, 74th Leg., ch. 20, §1, eff. April 20, 1995. Amended by Acts 1995, 74th Leg., ch. 751, §82, eff. Sept. 1, 1995; Acts 1999, 76th Leg., ch. 28, §1, eff. Sept. 1, 1999. Source: Former Fam §14.52.

FAM §231.007. DEBTS TO STATE

(a) A person obligated to pay child support in a case in which the Title IV-D agency is providing services under this chapter who does not pay the required support is indebted to the state for the purposes of Section 403.055, Government Code, if the Title IV-D agency has reported the person to the comptroller under that section properly.

(b) The amount of a person's indebtedness to the state under Subsection (a) is equal to the sum of:

(1) the amount of the required child support that has not been paid; and

(2) any interest, fees, court costs, or other amounts owed by the person because the person has not paid the support.

(c) The Title IV-D agency is the sole assignee of all payments, including payments of compensation, by the state to a person indebted to the state under Subsection (a).

(d) On request of the Title IV-D agency:

(1) the comptroller shall make payable and deliver to the agency any payments for which the agency is the assignee under Subsection (c), if the comptroller is responsible for issuing warrants or initiating electronic funds transfers to make those payments; and

(2) a state agency shall make payable and deliver to the Title IV-D agency any payments for which the Title IV-D agency is the assignee under Subsection (c) if the comptroller is not responsible for issuing warrants or initiating electronic funds transfers to make those payments.

(e) A person indebted to the state under Subsection (a) may eliminate the debt by:

(1) paying the entire amount of the debt; or

(2) resolving the debt in a manner acceptable to the Title IV-D agency.

(f) The comptroller or a state agency may rely on a representation by the Title IV-D agency that:

(1) a person is indebted to the state under Subsection (a); or

(2) a person who was indebted to the state under Subsection (a) has eliminated the debt.

(g) Except as provided by Subsection (h), the payment of workers' compensation benefits to a person indebted to the state under Subsection (a) is the same for the purposes of this section as any other payment made to the person by the state. Notwithstanding Section 408.203, Labor Code, an order or writ to withhold income from workers' compensation benefits is not required before the benefits are withheld or assigned under this section.

(h) The amount of weekly workers' compensation benefits that may be withheld or assigned under this section may not exceed the percentage of the person's benefits that would apply if the benefits equalled the person's monthly net resources as provided by Chapter 154, except that in no event may more than 50 percent of the person's weekly compensation benefits be withheld or assigned. The comptroller or a state agency may rely on a representation by the Title IV-D agency that a withholding or assignment under this section would not violate this subsection.

Ⓐ (i) Section 403.055(d), Government Code, does not authorize the comptroller to issue a warrant or initiate an electronic funds transfer to pay the compensation or remuneration of an individual who is indebted to the state under Subsection (a).

Ⓐ (j) Section 2107.008(h), Government Code, does not authorize a state agency to pay the compensation or remuneration of an individual who is indebted to the state under Subsection (a).

(k) In this section, "compensation," "state agency," and "state officer or employee" have the meanings assigned by Section 403.055, Government Code.

History of Fam §231.007: Acts 1995, 74th Leg., ch. 20, §1, eff. April 20, 1995. Amended by Acts 1995, 74th Leg., ch. 751, §83, eff. Sept. 1, 1995; Acts 1997, 75th Leg., ch. 165, §7.19, eff. Sept. 1, 1997; Acts 1999, 76th Leg., ch. 1467, §1.07, eff. Jan. 1, 2000; Acts 2001, 77th Leg., ch. 1158, §6, eff June 15, 2001. Source: Former Hum. Res. Code §76.0041.

FAM §231.008. DISPOSITION OF FUNDS

(a) The Title IV-D agency shall deposit money received under assignments or as fees in a special fund in the state treasury. The agency may spend money in the fund for the administration of this chapter, subject to the General Appropriations Act.

(b) All other money received under this chapter shall be deposited in a special fund in the state treasury.

(c) Sections 403.094 and 403.095, Government Code, do not apply to a fund described by this section.

History of Fam §231.008: Acts 1995, 74th Leg., ch. 20, §1, eff. April 20, 1995. Source: Former Hum. Res. Code §76.005.

FAM §231.009. PAYMENT OF PENALTIES

From funds appropriated for the Title IV-D agency, the agency shall reimburse the Texas Department of Human Services for any penalty assessed under Title IV-A of the federal Social Security Act (42 U.S.C. Section 651 et seq.) that is assessed because of the agency's administration of this chapter.

History of Fam §231.009: Acts 1995, 74th Leg., ch. 20, §1, eff. April 20, 1995. Source: Former Hum. Res. Code §76.008.

FAM §231.010. REPEALED

Repealed by Acts 2001, 77th Leg., ch. 1023, §76, eff. Sept. 1, 2001.

FAM §231.010. CASE PROCESSING PILOT PROGRAM

Section 231.010 below is effective for SAPCRs and modification or enforcement proceedings commenced before Sept. 1, 2001.

(a) As part of the development of a statewide integrated system for child support and medical support enforcement under Section 231.0011, the Title IV-D agency shall establish a pilot program to improve the efficiency of court processing of family welfare cases, including child support, medical support, and foster care cases. The Title IV-D agency shall consult with the Department of Protective and Regulatory Services in establishing the pilot program with respect to the processing of foster care cases.

(b) The Title IV-D agency shall identify at least two counties that have a population of more than one million and that are voluntarily participating in the statewide integrated system under Section 231.0011 for the development and establishment of pilot programs during each fiscal year of the 1998-1999 biennium. A county shall be selected on the basis of the county's ability to achieve the automation goals of the pilot program.

(c) A pilot program must include processes for:

(1) electronic case filing;

(2) automated reporting of appropriate orders to the state case registry required under 42 U.S.C. Section 654a;

(3) automated case tracking;

(4) automated child support delinquency monitoring; and

(5) automated statistical reporting to the state case registry.

(d) The pilot program authorized under this section shall be developed and implemented in cooperation with representatives of the counties identified under Subsection (b), including representatives of the county's judiciary.

(e) As part of the pilot program, the Title IV-D agency shall review county assessments of needs related to processing child support, medical support, and foster care cases and shall provide technical assistance to county and district clerks as requested.

(f) The Title IV-D agency shall provide funding for the pilot program from funds appropriated to operate the agency and from any available federal funds.

(g) Not later than January 15, 1999, the agency shall submit a report regarding the status of the pilot program to the governor, the lieutenant governor, the speaker of the house of representatives, and the comptroller. On request, the Title IV-D agency shall make the report available to any member of the legislature.

FAM §231.011. INTERAGENCY WORK GROUP

(a) The Title IV-D agency shall convene a standing work group to develop and maintain an interagency partnership strategy. The director of the Title IV-D agency shall lead the work group.

(b) The work group shall consist of representatives from the Department of Protective and Regulatory Services, the Texas Department of Human Services, the Texas Department of Health, the Texas Workforce Commission, and the office of the comptroller. The executive head of each agency shall appoint the agency's representative. If the work group addresses an issue that is under the authority of the Health and Human Services Commission, the work group shall include a representative from that commission when addressing that issue.

(c) The interagency partnership strategy shall:

(1) identify methods to improve the exchange of data between the agencies represented in the work group;

(2) develop procedures to coordinate the child support efforts of each agency in the work group;

(3) identify the benefits of contracts under which a state agency provides child support services related to the agency's core competency to the Title IV-D agency;

(4) identify ways to improve client intake and client referral;

(5) develop methods to enhance foster care child support collections;

(6) increase the recovery of Medicaid for the Title IV-D agency and the Texas Department of Health; and

(7) examine the benefits of contracts under which the comptroller or a private entity provides services regarding the receipt and payment of child support.

(d) Each agency represented on the work group shall identify specific child support services that are related to the agency's areas of core competence and may be provided by the agency under a contract. The state auditor and the State Council on Competitive Government shall assist:

(1) the agencies in identifying the child support services that are within the agency's core competency; and

(2) the work group in developing strategies to obtain child support services from the agencies.

History of Fam §231.011: Acts 1999, 76th Leg., ch. 556, §51, eff. Sept. 1, 1999.

FAM §231.012. COUNTY ADVISORY WORK GROUP

(a) The director of the Title IV-D agency shall establish a county advisory work group to assist the Title IV-D agency in developing and changing child support programs that affect counties. The work group shall consist of at least one of each of the following:

(1) county judge;

(2) county commissioner;

(3) district clerk;

(4) domestic relations officer;

(5) Title IV-D master; and

(6) district court judge.

(b) The director of the Title IV-D agency shall appoint the members of the work group after consulting with the relevant professional or trade associations of the professions that are represented on the work group. The director of the Title IV-D agency shall determine the number of members of the work group and shall designate the presiding officer of the group.

(c) The work group shall:

(1) advise the director of the Title IV-D agency of the impact on counties that a proposed child support program or a change in a program may have;

(2) establish a state-county child support improvement plan;

(3) advise the Title IV-D agency on the operation of the state disbursement unit;

(4) plan for monetary incentives for county partnership programs;

(5) expand the number of agreements with counties for enforcement services; and

(6) work with relevant statewide associations on a model partnership agreement.

(d) A work group member or the member's designee may not receive compensation but is entitled to reimbursement for actual and necessary expenses incurred in performing the member's duties under this section.

(e) The work group is not an advisory committee as defined by Section 2110.001, Government Code. Chapter 2110, Government Code, does not apply to the work group.

History of Fam §231.012: Acts 1999, 76th Leg., ch. 556, §51, eff. Sept. 1, 1999.

FAM §231.013. INFORMATION RESOURCES STEERING COMMITTEE

(a) The Title IV-D agency shall create an information resources steering committee to:

(1) oversee information resource project development for the Title IV-D agency;

(2) make strategic prioritization recommendations;

(3) facilitate development of accurate information for the director of the Title IV-D agency; and

(4) perform other functions as determined by the director of the Title IV-D agency.

(b) The steering committee must include a senior management executive representing each significant function of the Title IV-D agency. The steering committee may include a person representing:

(1) counties; or

(2) a vendor contracting with the Title IV-D agency.

(c) The director of the Title IV-D agency shall appoint the members of the steering committee after consulting with the Department of Information Resources.

History of Fam §231.013: Acts 1999, 76th Leg., ch. 556, §51, eff. Sept. 1, 1999.

FAM §231.014. PERSONNEL

The director of the Title IV-D agency shall provide to the employees of the Title IV-D agency, as often as necessary, information regarding the requirements for employment under this title, including information regarding a person's responsibilities under applicable laws relating to standards of conduct for state employees.

History of Fam §231.014: Acts 1999, 76th Leg., ch. 556, §51, eff. Sept. 1, 1999.

FAM §231.015[A*]. INSURANCE REPORTING PILOT PROGRAM

☠ E *In 2001, the Legislature enacted this section without reference to the conflicting renumbering of another section to 231.015. Section 231.015 below was enacted by Acts 2001, 77th Leg., ch. 1023, §52, effective Sept. 1, 2001. The [A*] has been added by the editor to distinguish this section 231.015 from the other, which is marked with [B*]. In 2003, the Legislature is expected to correct the duplicate numbering. Section 231.015 below is effective for SAPCRs and modification or enforcement proceedings commenced on or after Sept. 1, 2001.*

(a) In consultation with the Texas Department of Insurance and representatives of the insurance industry in this state, including insurance trade associations, the Title IV-D agency by rule shall establish a pilot program to improve the use of child support liens under Chapter 157. The pilot program shall develop processes under which insurance companies may voluntarily cooperate with the Title IV-D agency in identifying obligors who are subject to liens for child support arrearages to intercept certain liability insurance settlements or awards for claims in satisfaction of the arrearage amounts.

(b) An insurance company that provides information or otherwise responds to a notice of child support lien or levy under Subchapter G, Chapter 157, or acts in good faith to comply with procedures established in the pilot program under this section is not liable for those acts under any law to any person.

History of Fam §231.015: Enacted by Acts 2001, 77th Leg., ch. 1023, §52, eff. Sept. 1, 2001.

FAM §231.015[B*]. COOPERATION WITH DEPARTMENT OF PROTECTIVE & REGULATORY SERVICES

☠ A *In 2001, the Legislature renumbered this section without reference to the conflicting enactment of another section 231.015. Section 231.015 below was renumbered from §231.011 by Acts 2001, 77th Leg., ch. 1420, §21.001(32), effective Sept. 1, 2001. The [B*] has been added by the editor to distinguish this section 231.015 from the other, which is marked with [A*]. In 2003, the Legislature is expected to correct the duplicate numbering.*

(a) In this section, "department" means the Department of Protective and Regulatory Services.

(b) To the extent possible, the Title IV-D agency shall:

(1) provide to the department access to all of the Title IV-D agency's available child support locating resources;

(2) allow the department to use the Title IV-D agency's child support enforcement system to track child support payments and to have access to the agency's management reports that show payments made;

(3) make reports on Title IV-E, Social Security Act (42 U.S.C. Section 670 et seq.), foster care collections available to the department in a timely manner; and

(4) work with the department to obtain child support payments for protective services cases in which the department is responsible for providing care for children under temporary and final orders.

History of Fam §231.015: Acts 1999, 76th Leg., ch. 228, §1, eff. Sept. 1, 1999. Renumbered from §231.011 by Acts 2001, 77th Leg., ch. 1420, §21.001(32), eff. Sept. 1, 2001.

Sections 231.016-231.100 reserved for expansion

SUBCHAPTER B. SERVICES PROVIDED BY TITLE IV-D PROGRAM

FAM §231.101. TITLE IV-D CHILD SUPPORT SERVICES

(a) The Title IV-D agency may provide all services required or authorized to be provided by Part D of Title IV of the federal Social Security Act (42 U.S.C. Section 651 et seq.), including:

(1) parent locator services;

(2) paternity determination;

(3) child support and medical support establishment;

(4) review and adjustment of child support orders;

(5) enforcement of child support and medical support orders; and

(6) collection and distribution of child support payments.

(b) At the request of either the obligee or obligor, the Title IV-D agency shall review a child support order once every three years and, if appropriate, adjust the support amount to meet the requirements of the child support guidelines under Chapter 154.

(c) Except as notice is included in the child support order, a party subject to a support order shall be provided notice not less than once every three years of the party's right to request that the Title IV-D agency review and, if appropriate, adjust the amount of ordered support.

(d) The Title IV-D agency may review a support order at any time on a showing of a material and substantial change in circumstances, taking into consideration the best interests of the child.

(e) The Title IV-D agency shall distribute a child support payment received by the agency from an employer within two working days after the date the agency receives the payment.

History of Fam §231.101: Acts 1995, 74th Leg., ch. 20, §1, eff. April 20, 1995. Amended by Acts 1997, 75th Leg., ch. 702, §13 (eff. Sept. 1, 1997), ch. 911, §69 (eff. Sept. 1, 1997); Acts 1999, 76th Leg., ch. 62, §19.01(22), eff. Sept. 1, 1999. Source: Former Hum. Res. Code §76.002(e).

FAM §231.102. ELIGIBILITY FOR CHILD SUPPORT SERVICES

The Title IV-D agency on application or as otherwise authorized by law may provide services for the benefit of a child without regard to whether the child has received public assistance.

History of Fam §231.102: Acts 1995, 74th Leg., ch. 20, §1, eff. April 20, 1995.

FAM §231.103. APPLICATION FEE

(a) The Title IV-D agency may charge a reasonable application fee and recover costs for the services provided.

(b) An application fee may not be charged in a case in which the Title IV-D agency provides services because the family receives public assistance.

(c) An application fee may not exceed a maximum amount established by federal law.

History of Fam §231.103: Acts 1995, 74th Leg., ch. 20, §1, eff. April 20, 1995. Source: Former Hum. Res. Code §76.004.

FAM §231.104. ASSIGNMENT OF RIGHT TO SUPPORT

A *Subsection (a) below is effective for SAPCRs and modification or enforcement proceedings commenced on or after Sept. 1, 2001.*

(a) To the extent authorized by federal law, the approval of an application for or the receipt of financial assistance as provided by Chapter 31, Human Resources Code, constitutes an assignment to the Title IV-D agency of any rights to support from any other person that the applicant or recipient may have personally or for a child for whom the applicant or recipient is claiming assistance.

Subsection (a) below is effective for SAPCRs and modification or enforcement proceedings commenced before Sept. 1, 2001.

(a) To the extent authorized by law, the approval of an application for or the receipt of financial assistance as provided by Chapter 31, Human Resources Code, constitutes an assignment to the Title IV-D agency of any rights to support from any other person that the applicant or recipient may have personally or for a child for whom the applicant or recipient is claiming assistance, including the right to the amount accrued at the time the application is filed or the assistance is received.

(b) An application for child support services is an assignment of support rights, to the extent permitted by federal law, to enable the Title IV-D agency to establish and enforce child support and medical support obligations, but an assignment is not a condition of eligibility for services.

History of Fam §231.104: Acts 1995, 74th Leg., ch. 20, §1, eff. April 20, 1995. Amended by Acts 1997, 75th Leg., ch. 911, §70, eff. Sept. 1, 1997; Acts 2001, 77th Leg., ch. 1023, §53, eff. Sept. 1, 2001. Source: Former Hum. Res. Code §76.003(a).

In re K.E.T., 974 S.W.2d 760, 762 (Tex.App.—San Antonio 1998, no pet.). "[D]uring the course of the four years that [obligee] was receiving public assistance, she received $11,645 from the State for the support of the children. The law provides that the State is entitled to recoup that amount from child support owed by [obligor]. The State argued that amounts paid to the children by the Social Security Administration can not be used to satisfy [obligor's] debt to the State. [¶] In this case, the arrearages at issue are owed to the State as assignee of [obligee's] right to receive child support obligations. However, under federal law, social security benefits are to be paid directly to the family and may not be assigned. Consequently, if [obligor's] arrearages were to be completely offset by the social security benefits in this case, the State would be left without a remedy because they never could have and cannot collect social security benefits in satisfaction of the assignment. Because [obligor] was obligated to pay his child support obligation directly to the State during the period of assignment, the social security benefits could not be used to satisfy his obligation to the State where those benefits have to be paid directly to the family and are unassignable."

FAM §231.105. NOTICE OF CHANGE OF PAYEE

Ⓐ *Subsections (a) & (b) below are effective for SAPCRs and modification or enforcement proceedings commenced on or after Sept. 1, 2001.*

(a) Child support payments for the benefit of a child whose support rights have been assigned to the Title IV-D agency under Section 231.104 shall be made payable to the Title IV-D agency and transmitted to the state disbursement unit as provided by Chapter 234.

(b) If a court has ordered support payments to be made to an applicant for or recipient of financial assistance or to an applicant for or recipient of Title IV-D services, the Title IV-D agency shall, on providing notice to the obligee and the obligor, direct the obligor or other payor to make support payments payable to the Title IV-D agency and to transmit the payments to the state disbursement unit. The Title IV-D agency shall file a copy of the notice with the court ordering the payments and with the child support registry. The notice must include:

(1) a statement that the child is an applicant for or recipient of financial assistance, or a child other than a recipient child for whom Title IV-D services are provided;

(2) the name of the child and the caretaker for whom support has been ordered by the court;

(3) the style and cause number of the case in which support was ordered; and

(4) instructions for the payment of ordered support to the agency.

Subsections (a) & (b) below are effective for SAPCRs and modification or enforcement proceedings commenced before Sept. 1, 2001.

(a) Child support payments for the benefit of a child whose support rights have been assigned to the Title IV-D agency shall be made payable to and transmitted to the Title IV-D agency.

(b) If a court has ordered support payments to be made to an applicant for or recipient of financial assistance or to a person other than the applicant or recipient, the Title IV-D agency shall, on providing notice to the obligee and the obligor, direct the obligor or other payor to make support payments payable to the Title IV-D agency and to transmit the payments to the agency. The Title IV-D agency shall file a copy of the notice with the court ordering the payments and with the child support registry. The notice must include:

(1) a statement that the child is an applicant for or recipient of financial assistance, or a child other than a recipient child for whom services are provided;

(2) the name of the child and the caretaker for whom support has been ordered by the court;

(3) the style and cause number of the case in which support was ordered; and

(4) instructions for the payment of ordered support to the agency.

(c) On receipt of a copy of the notice under Subsection (b), the clerk of the court shall file the notice in the appropriate case file.

History of Fam §231.105: Acts 1995, 74th Leg., ch. 20, §1, eff. April 20, 1995. Amended by Acts 1997, 75th Leg., ch. 911, §71, eff. Sept. 1, 1997; Acts 2001, 77th Leg., ch. 1023, §54, eff. Sept. 1, 2001. Source: Former Hum. Res. Code §76.003(b).

FAM §231.106. NOTICE OF TERMINATION OF ASSIGNMENT

(a) On termination of support rights to the Title IV-D agency, the Title IV-D agency shall, after providing notice to the obligee and the obligor, send a notice of termination of assignment to the obligor or other payor, which may direct that all or a portion of the payments be made payable to the agency and to other persons who are entitled to receive the payments.

(b) The Title IV-D agency shall send a copy of the notice of termination of assignment to the court ordering the support and to the child support registry, and on receipt of the notice the clerk of the court shall file the notice in the appropriate case file. The clerk may not require an order of the court to terminate the assignment and direct support payments to the person entitled to receive the payment.

History of Fam §231.106: Acts 1995, 74th Leg., ch. 20, §1, eff. April 20, 1995. Amended by Acts 1997, 75th Leg., ch. 911, §72, eff. Sept. 1, 1997; Acts 1999, 76th Leg., ch. 556, §52, eff. Sept. 1, 1999. Source: Former Hum. Res. Code §76.003(e).

FAM §231.107. CERTIFICATE OF ASSIGNMENT OR OF TERMINATION OF ASSIGNMENT

If an abstract of judgment or a child support lien on support amounts assigned to the Title IV-D agency under this chapter has previously been filed of record, the agency shall file for recordation, with the county clerk of each county in which such abstract or lien has been filed, a certificate that a notice of change of payee or a notice of termination of assignment has been issued by the agency.

History of Fam §231.107: Acts 1995, 74th Leg., ch. 20, §1, eff. April 20, 1995. Amended by Acts 1997, 75th Leg., ch. 911, §73, eff. Sept. 1, 1997. Source: Former Hum. Res. Code §76.003(f).

FAM §231.108. CONFIDENTIALITY OF RECORDS & PRIVILEGED COMMUNICATIONS

(a) Except as provided by Subsection (c), all files and records of services provided under this chapter, including information concerning a custodial parent, noncustodial parent, child, and an alleged or presumed father, are confidential.

(b) Except as provided by Subsection (c), all communications made by a recipient of financial assistance under Chapter 31, Human Resources Code, or an applicant for or recipient of services under this chapter are privileged.

(c) The Title IV-D agency may use or release information from the files and records, including information that results from a communication made by a recipient of financial assistance under Chapter 31, Human Resources Code, or by an applicant for or recipient of services under this chapter, for purposes directly connected with the administration of the child support, paternity determination, parent locator, or aid to families with dependent children programs. The Title IV-D agency may release information from the files and records to a consumer reporting agency in accordance with Section 231.114.

(d) The Title IV-D agency by rule may provide for the release of information to public officials.

(e) The Title IV-D agency may not release information on the physical location of a person if:

(1) a protective order has been entered with respect to the person; or

(2) there is reason to believe that the release of information may result in physical or emotional harm to the person.

(f) The Title IV-D agency, by rule, may provide for the release of information to persons for purposes not prohibited by federal law.

History of Fam §231.108: Acts 1995, 74th Leg., ch. 20, §1, eff. April 20, 1995. Amended by Acts 1995, 74th Leg., ch. 341, §1.08, eff. Sept. 1, 1995; Acts 1997, 75th Leg., ch. 911, §74, eff. Sept. 1, 1997; Acts 1999, 76th Leg., ch. 556, §53, eff. Sept. 1, 1999. Source: Former Hum. Res. Code §76.006.

FAM §231.109. ATTORNEYS REPRESENTING STATE

(a) Attorneys employed by the Title IV-D agency may represent this state or another state in an action brought under the authority of federal law or this chapter.

(b) The Title IV-D agency may contract with private attorneys, other private entities, or political subdivisions of the state to provide services in Title IV-D cases.

(c) The Title IV-D agency shall provide copies of all contracts entered into under this section to the Legislative Budget Board and the Governor's Office of Budget and Planning, along with a written justification of the need for each contract, within 60 days after the execution of the contract.

(d) An attorney employed to provide Title IV-D services represents the interest of the state and not the interest of any other party. The provision of services by an attorney under this chapter does not create an attorney-client relationship between the attorney and any other party. The agency shall, at the time an application for child support services is made, inform the applicant that neither the Title IV-D agency nor any attorney who provides services under this chapter is the applicant's attorney and that the attorney providing services under this chapter does not provide legal representation to the applicant.

(e) An attorney employed by the Title IV-D agency or as otherwise provided by this chapter may not be appointed or act as a guardian ad litem or attorney ad litem for a child or another party.

History of Fam §231.109: Acts 1995, 74th Leg., ch. 20, §1, eff. April 20, 1995. Amended by Acts 1995, 74th Leg., ch. 341, §1.02, eff. Sept. 1, 1995. Source: Former Hum. Res. Code §76.007(a)-(e).

FAM §231.110. AUTHORIZATION OF SERVICE

The provision of services by the Title IV-D agency under this chapter or Part D of Title IV of the federal Social Security Act (42 U.S.C. Section 651 et seq.) does not authorize service on the agency of any legal notice that is required to be served on any party other than the agency.

History of Fam §231.110: Acts 1995, 74th Leg., ch. 20, §1, eff. April 20, 1995. Source: Former Hum. Res. Code §76.007(f).

FAM §231.111. DISQUALIFICATION OF AGENCY

A court shall not disqualify the Title IV-D agency in a legal action filed under this chapter or Part D of Title IV of the federal Social Security Act (42 U.S.C. Section 651 et seq.) on the basis that the agency has previously provided services to a party whose interests may now be adverse to the relief requested.

History of Fam §231.111: Acts 1995, 74th Leg., ch. 20, §1, eff. April 20, 1995. Source: Former Hum. Res. Code §76.007(g).

FAM §231.112. INFORMATION ON PATERNITY ESTABLISHMENT

On notification by the state registrar under Section 192.005(d), Health and Safety Code, that the items relating to the child's father are not completed on a birth certificate filed with the state registrar, the Title IV-D agency may provide to:

(1) the child's mother and, if possible, the man claiming to be the child's biological father written information necessary for the man to complete an acknowledgment of paternity as provided by Chapter 160; and

(2) the child's mother written information:

(A) explaining the benefits of having the child's paternity established; and

(B) regarding the availability of paternity establishment and child support enforcement services.

History of Fam §231.112: Acts 1995, 74th Leg., ch. 20, §1, eff. April 20, 1995. Amended by Acts 1999, 76th Leg., ch. 556, §54, eff. Sept. 1, 1999. Source: Former Fam §13.015.

FAM §231.113. ENFORCEMENT OF SUPPORT OBLIGATIONS IN PUBLIC ASSISTANCE CASES

To the extent possible, the Title IV-D agency shall enforce a child support obligation in a case involving a child who receives financial assistance under Chapter 31, Human Resources Code, not later than the first anniversary of the date the agency receives from the Texas Department of Human Services the information the department is required to provide to assist in the enforcement of that obligation.

History of Fam §231.113: Acts 1995, 74th Leg., ch. 341, §1.03, eff. Sept. 1, 1995.

FAM §231.114. REPORTS OF CHILD SUPPORT PAYMENTS TO CONSUMER REPORTING AGENCIES

(a) The Title IV-D agency shall make information available in accordance with this section to a consumer reporting agency regarding the amount of child support owed and the amount paid by an obligor in a Title IV-D case.

(b) Before disclosing the information to consumer reporting agencies, the Title IV-D agency shall send the obligor a notice by mail to the obligor's last known address. The notice must include:

(1) the information to be released, including the amount of the obligor's child support obligation and delinquency, if any, that will be reported;

(2) the procedure available for the obligor to contest the accuracy of the information; and

(3) a statement that the information will be released if the obligor fails to contest the disclosure before the 30th day after the date of mailing of the notice.

(c) If the obligor does not contest the disclosure within the period specified by Subsection (b), the Title IV-D agency shall make the information available to the consumer reporting agency.

(d) The Title IV-D agency shall regularly update the information released to a consumer reporting agency under this section to ensure the accuracy of the released information.

(e) The Title IV-D agency may charge a consumer reporting agency a reasonable fee for making information available under this section, including all applicable mailing costs.

(f) In this section:

(1) "Consumer reporting agency" means any person that regularly engages in whole or in part in the practice of assembling or evaluating consumer credit information or other information on consumers for monetary fees, for dues, or on a cooperative nonprofit basis, to furnish consumer reports to third parties.

(2) "Obligor" means any person required to make payments under the terms of a support order for a child.

(3) "Title IV-D case" means a case in which services are being provided by the Title IV-D agency under Part D of Title IV of the federal Social Security Act (42 U.S.C. Section 651 et seq.) seeking to locate an absent parent, determine parentage, or establish, modify, enforce, or monitor a child support obligation.

History of Fam §231.114: Acts 1995, 74th Leg., ch. 341, §1.03, eff. Sept. 1, 1995.

See also 1 TAC §§55.102, 55.103.

FAM §231.115. NONCOOPERATION BY RECIPIENT OF PUBLIC ASSISTANCE

(a) The failure by a person who is a recipient of public assistance under Chapter 31, Human Resources Code, to provide accurate information as required by Section 31.0315, Human Resources Code, shall serve as the basis for a determination by the Title IV-D agency that the person did not cooperate with the Title IV-D agency.

(b) The Title IV-D agency shall:

(1) identify the actions or failures to act by a recipient of public assistance that constitute noncooperation with the Title IV-D agency;

(2) adopt rules governing noncompliance; and

(3) send noncompliance determinations to the Texas Department of Human Services for immediate imposition of sanctions.

(c) In adopting rules under this section that establish the basis for determining that a person has failed to cooperate with the Title IV-D agency, the Title IV-D agency shall consider whether:

(1) good cause exists for the failure to cooperate;

(2) the person has failed to disclose the name and location of an alleged or probable parent of the child, if known by the person, at the time of applying for public assistance or at a subsequent time; and

(3) the person named a man as the alleged father and the man was subsequently excluded by parentage testing as being the father if the person has previously named another man as the child's father.

History of Fam §231.115: Acts 1997, 75th Leg., ch. 911, §75, eff. Sept. 1, 1997. Amended by Acts 1999, 76th Leg., ch. 556, §54, eff. Sept. 1, 1999.

See also 1 TAC §55.3.

FAM §231.116. INFORMATION ON INTERNET

The Title IV-D agency shall place on the Internet for public access child support information to assist the public in child support matters, including application forms, child support collection in other states, and profiles of certain obligors who are in arrears in paying child support.

History of Fam §231.116: Acts 1997, 75th Leg., ch. 420, §18, eff. Sept. 1, 1997.

E FAM §231.1165. INFORMATION ON SERVICE OF CITATION

The Title IV-D agency shall update the agency's child support automated system to inform the parties in a suit of the service of citation in the suit not later than the first business day after the date the agency receives notice that citation has been served. The information required by this section must be available by telephone and on the Internet.

History of Fam §213.1165: Enacted by Acts 2001, 77th Leg., ch. 141, §1, eff Sept. 1, 2001.

FAM §231.117. UNEMPLOYED & UNDEREMPLOYED OBLIGORS

(a) The Title IV-D agency shall refer to appropriate state and local entities that provide employment services any unemployed or underemployed obligor who is in arrears in court-ordered child support payments

(b) A referral under Subsection (a) may include:

(1) skills training and job placement through:

(A) the Texas Workforce Commission; or

(B) the agency responsible for the food stamp employment and training program (7 U.S.C. Section 2015(d));

(2) referrals to education and literacy classes; and

(3) counseling regarding:

(A) substance abuse;

(B) parenting skills;

(C) life skills; and

(D) mediation techniques.

(c) The Title IV-D agency may require an unemployed or underemployed obligor to complete the training, classes, or counseling to which the obligor is referred under this section. The agency shall suspend under Chapter 232 the license of an obligor who fails to comply with the requirements of this subsection.

(d) A court or the Title IV-D agency may issue an order that requires the parent to either work, have a plan to pay overdue child support, or participate in work activities appropriate to pay the overdue support.

History of Fam §231.117: Acts 1997, 75th Leg., ch. 165, §7.20(a), eff. Sept. 1, 1997. Renumbered from §231.115 by Acts 1999, 76th Leg., ch. 62, §19.01(23) (eff. Sept. 1, 1999) and ch. 307, §54 (eff. Sept. 1, 1999) and amended by ch. 556, §54 (eff. Sept. 1, 1999) and ch. 1072, §5 (eff. Sept. 1, 1999). Source: Former Hum. Res. Code §76.012.

FAM §231.118. SERVICE OF CITATION

(a) The Title IV-D agency may contract with private process servers to serve a citation, a subpoena, an order, or any other document required or appropriate under law to be served a party.

(b) For the purposes of Rule 103 of the Texas Rules of Civil Procedure, a person who serves a citation or any other document under this section is authorized to serve the document without a written court order authorizing the service.

(c) Issuance and return of the process shall be made in accordance with law and shall be verified by the person serving the document.

History of Fam §231.118: Acts 1999, 76th Leg., ch. 556, §54, eff. Sept. 1, 1999.

FAM §231.119. OMBUDSMAN PROGRAM

(a) The Title IV-D agency shall establish an ombudsman program to process and track complaints against the Title IV-D agency. The director of the Title IV-D agency shall:

(1) designate an employee to serve as chief ombudsman to manage the ombudsman program; and

(2) designate an employee in each field office to act as the ombudsman for the office.

(b) The Title IV-D agency shall develop and implement a uniform process for receiving and resolving complaints against the Title IV-D agency throughout the state. The process shall include statewide procedures to inform the public and recipients of Title IV-D services of the right to file a complaint against the Title IV-D agency, including the mailing addresses and telephone numbers of appropriate Title IV-D agency personnel responsible for receiving complaints and providing related assistance.

(c) The ombudsman in each field office shall ensure that an employee in the field office responds to and attempts to resolve each complaint that is filed with the field office. If a complaint cannot be resolved at the field office level, the ombudsman in the field office shall refer the complaint to the chief ombudsman.

(d) The Title IV-D agency shall maintain a file on each written complaint filed with the Title IV-D agency. The file must include:

(1) the name of the person who filed the complaint;

(2) the date the complaint is received by the Title IV-D agency;

(3) the subject matter of the complaint;

(4) the name of each person contacted in relation to the complaint;

(5) a summary of the results of the review or investigation of the complaint; and

(6) an explanation of the reason the file was closed, if the agency closed the file without taking action other than to investigate the complaint.

(e) The Title IV-D agency, at least quarterly until final disposition of the complaint, shall notify the person filing the complaint and each person who is a subject of the complaint of the status of the investigation of the complaint unless the notice would jeopardize an undercover investigation.

(f) The Title IV-D agency shall provide to the person filing the complaint and to each person who is a subject of the complaint a copy of the Title IV-D agency's policies and procedures relating to complaint investigation and resolution.

History of Fam §231.119: Acts 1999, 76th Leg., ch. 556, §54, eff. Sept. 1, 1999.

FAM §231.120. TOLL-FREE TELEPHONE NUMBER FOR EMPLOYERS

The Title IV-D agency shall maintain a toll-free telephone number at which personnel are available during normal business hours to answer questions from employers responsible for withholding child support. The Title IV-D agency shall inform employers about the toll-free telephone number.

History of Fam §231.120: Acts 1999, 76th Leg., ch. 556, §54, eff. Sept. 1, 1999.

E **FAM §231.121. AVAILABILITY OF BROCHURES**

The Title IV-D agency shall ensure that all Title IV-D brochures published by the agency are available to the public at courthouses where family law cases are heard in the state.

History of Fam §231.121: Enacted by Acts 2001, 77th Leg., ch. 141, §2, eff. Sept 1, 2001.

Sections 231.122-231.200 reserved for expansion

SUBCHAPTER C. PAYMENT OF FEES & COSTS

FAM §231.201. DEFINITIONS

In this subchapter:

(1) "Federal share" means the portion of allowable expenses for fees and other costs that will be reimbursed by the federal government under federal law and regulations regarding the administration of the Title IV-D program.

(2) "State share" means the portion of allowable expenses for fees and other costs that remain after receipt of the federal share of reimbursement and that is to be reimbursed by the state or may be contributed by certified public expenditure by a county.

History of Fam §231.201: Acts 1995, 74th Leg., ch. 20, §1, eff. April 20, 1995. Source: Former Hum. Res. Code §76.009(g).

FAM §231.202. AUTHORIZED COSTS & FEES IN TITLE IV-D CASES

In a Title IV-D case filed under this title, the Title IV-D agency shall pay:

(1) filing fees and fees for issuance and service of process as provided by Chapter 110 of this code and by Sections 51.317, 51.318(b)(2), and 51.319(2), Government Code;

(2) fees for transfer as provided by Chapter 110;

(3) fees for the issuance and delivery of orders and writs of income withholding in the amounts provided by Chapter 110;

(4) a fee of $45 for each item of process to each individual on whom service is required, including service by certified or registered mail, to be paid to a sheriff, constable, or clerk whenever service of process is required; and

E *Subsection (5) below is effective for Title IV-D cases filed on or after Sept. 1, 2001.*

(5) the fee for filing an administrative writ of withholding under Section 158.503(d).

History of Fam §231.202: Acts 1995, 74th Leg., ch. 20, §1, eff. April 20, 1995. Amended by Acts 1995, 74th Leg., ch. 641, §2.02 (eff. Sept. 1, 1995), ch. 341, §1.04 (eff. Sept. 1, 1995); Acts 1997, 75th Leg., ch. 165, §7.21(a), eff. Sept. 1, 1997; Acts 2001, 77th Leg., ch. 116, §2, eff. Sept. 1, 2001. Source: Former Hum. Res. Code §76.009(a).

In re Lee Children, 36 S.W.3d 702, 706 (Tex.App.—Waco 2001, no pet.). "In this case, the clerk is attempting to collect [from the attorney general as a Title IV-D agency] the normal filing fee of $125. This fee is composed of two components as follows: (1) $100 as fees and cost; and (2) $25 as additional filing fee for basic civil legal services for indigents. [¶] We believe [the $25] is purely 'a judicial fund fee' specifically excepted by §231.204. Thus, the clerk is prohibited from collecting this $25 fee from the IV-D agency. However, because §231.202(1) specifically requires the IV-D agency to pay 'filing fees,' this operates as a specific exception to §231.204 as provided for, in the opening words of the section; 'Except as provided by this subchapter....' Thus, under §231.202(1), the Attorney General is specifically required to pay the general $100 filing fee imposed by §51.207 [of the Government Code]."

FAM §231.2025. CONTINGENCY FEES

The Title IV-D agency may pay a contingency fee in a contract or agreement between the agency and a private agency or individual authorized under Section 231.002(c).

History of Fam §231.2025: Acts 1997, 75th Leg., ch. 420, §19, eff. Sept. 1, 1997.

FAM §231.203. STATE EXEMPTION FROM BOND NOT AFFECTED

This subchapter does not affect, nor is this subchapter affected by, the exemption from bond provided by Section 6.001, Civil Practice and Remedies Code.

History of Fam §231.203: Acts 1995, 74th Leg., ch. 20, §1, eff. April 20, 1995. Source: Former Hum. Res. Code §76.009(h).

FAM §231.204. PROHIBITED FEES IN TITLE IV-D CASES

Except as provided by this subchapter, an appellate court, a clerk of an appellate court, a district or county clerk, sheriff, constable, or other government officer or employee may not charge the Title IV-D agency or a private attorney or political subdivision that has entered into a contract to provide Title IV-D services any fees or other amounts otherwise imposed by law for services rendered in, or in connection with, a Title IV-D case, including:

(1) a fee payable to a district clerk for:

(A) performing services related to the estates of deceased persons or minors;

(B) certifying copies; or

(C) comparing copies to originals;

(2) a court reporter fee, except as provided by Section 231.209;

(3) a judicial fund fee;

(4) a fee for a child support registry, enforcement office, or domestic relations office;

(5) a fee for alternative dispute resolution services; and

E *Subsection (6) below is effective for SAPCRs and modification or enforcement proceedings commenced on or after Sept. 1, 2001.*

(6) a filing fee or other costs payable to a clerk of an appellate court.

History of Fam §231.204: Acts 1995, 74th Leg., ch. 20, §1, eff. April 20, 1995. Amended by Acts 1999, 76th Leg., ch. 556, §55, eff. Sept. 1, 1999; Acts 2001, 77th Leg., ch. 1023, §55, eff. Sept. 1, 2001. Source: Former Hum. Res. Code §76.009(b).

In re Lee Children, 36 S.W.3d 702, 706 (Tex.App.—Waco 2001, no pet.). See Annotation in FAM §231.202.

FAM §231.205. LIMITATIONS ON LIABILITY OF ATTORNEY GENERAL FOR AUTHORIZED FEES & COSTS

(a) The Title IV-D agency is liable for a fee or cost under this subchapter only to the extent that an express, specific appropriation is made to the agency exclusively for that purpose. To the extent that state funds are not available, the amount of costs and fees that are not reimbursed by the federal government and that represent the state share shall be paid by certified public expenditure by the county through the clerk of the court, sheriff, or constable. This section does not prohibit the agency from spending other funds appropriated for child support enforcement to provide the initial expenditures necessary to qualify for the federal share.

(b) The Title IV-D agency is liable for the payment of the federal share of reimbursement for fees and costs under this subchapter only to the extent that the federal share is received, and if an amount is paid by the agency and that amount is disallowed by the federal government or the federal share is not otherwise received, the clerk of the court, sheriff, or constable to whom the payment was made shall return the amount to the agency not later than the 30th day after the date on which notice is given by the agency.

History of Fam §231.205: Acts 1995, 74th Leg., ch. 20, §1, eff. April 20, 1995. Source: Former Hum. Res. Code §76.009(e), (f).

FAM §231.206. RESTRICTION ON FEES FOR CHILD SUPPORT OR REGISTRY SERVICES IN TITLE IV-D CASES

A district clerk, a county child support registry or enforcement office, or a domestic relations office may not assess or collect fees for processing child support payments or for child support services from the Title IV-D agency, a managing conservator, or a possessory conservator in a Title IV-D case, except as provided by this subchapter.

History of Fam §231.206: Acts 1995, 74th Leg., ch. 20, §1, eff. April 20, 1995. Source: Former Hum. Res. Code §76.009(i) [A*].

FAM §231.207. METHOD OF BILLING FOR ALLOWABLE FEES

(a) To be entitled to reimbursement under this subchapter, the clerk of the court, sheriff, or constable must submit one monthly billing to the Title IV-D agency.

(b) The monthly billing must be in the form and manner prescribed by the Title IV-D agency and be approved by the clerk, sheriff, or constable.

History of Fam §231.207: Acts 1995, 74th Leg., ch. 20, §1, eff. April 20, 1995. Source: Former Hum. Res. Code §76.009(c).

In re Lee Children, 36 S.W.3d 702, 708 (Tex.App.—Waco 2001, no pet.). "The Legislature provided the specific mechanism for collection of the fees from the Title IV-D agency [under §231.207]. Thus, the Attorney General cannot use [CPRC] §6.001 as an exemption from paying the fee in the manner provided."

FAM §231.208. AGREEMENTS FOR REIMBURSEMENT IN LIEU OF FEES

(a) The Title IV-D agency and a qualified county may enter into a written agreement under which reimbursement for salaries and certain other actual costs incurred by the clerk, sheriff, or constable in Title IV-D cases is provided to the county.

(b) A county may not enter into an agreement for reimbursement under this section unless the clerk, sheriff, or constable providing service has at least two full-time employees each devoted exclusively to providing services in Title IV-D cases.

(c) Reimbursement made under this section is in lieu of all costs and fees provided by this subchapter.

History of Fam §231.208: Acts 1995, 74th Leg., ch. 20, §1, eff. April 20, 1995. Source: Former Hum. Res. Code §76.009(d).

FAM §231.209. PAYMENT FOR SERVICES NOT AFFECTED BY THIS SUBCHAPTER

Without regard to this subchapter and specifically Section 231.205, the Title IV-D agency may pay the costs for:

(1) the services of an official court reporter for the preparation of statements of facts;

(2) the costs for the publication of citation served by publication; and

(3) mileage or other reasonable travel costs incurred by a sheriff or constable when traveling out of the county to execute an outstanding warrant or capias, to be reimbursed at a rate not to exceed the rate provided for mileage or other costs incurred by state employees in the General Appropriations Act.

History of Fam §231.209: Acts 1995, 74th Leg., ch. 20, §1, eff. April 20, 1995. Amended by Acts 1995, 74th Leg., ch. 341, §1.05, eff. Sept. 1, 1995. Source: Former Hum. Res. Code §76.009(i) [B*].

FAM §231.210. AUTHORITY TO PAY LITIGATION EXPENSES

(a) The Title IV-D agency may pay all fees, expenses, costs, and bills necessary to secure evidence and to take the testimony of a witness, including advance payments or purchases for transportation, lodging, meals, and incidental expenses of custodians of evidence or witnesses whose transportation is necessary and proper for the production of evidence or the taking of testimony in a Title IV-D case.

(b) In making payments under this section, the Title IV-D agency shall present vouchers to the comptroller that have been sworn to by the custodian or witness and approved by the agency. The voucher shall be sufficient to authorize payment without the necessity of a written contract.

(c) The Title IV-D agency may directly pay a commercial transportation company or commercial lodging establishment for the expense of transportation or lodging of a custodian or witness.

History of Fam §231.210: Acts 1995, 74th Leg., ch. 20, §1, eff. April 20, 1995. Source: Former Hum. Res. Code §76.002(g).

Attorney Gen. v. O'Quinn, 938 S.W.2d 542, 543-44 (Tex.App.—Beaumont 1997, no writ.). "In a Title IV-D case… 'the court may assess attorney fees and all court costs as authorized by law, except that the court may not assess those amounts against the attorney general … or any party to whom the attorney general has provided services under this chapter.' [¶] [Defendant] contends the award may be sustained pursuant to the statute which authorizes the attorney general's office to pay all fees, expenses, costs, and bills necessary to secure evidence and to take witness testimony. This statute authorizes submission of vouchers to the Comptroller's office for payment of expenses, but has nothing to do with civil liability for a respondent's attorney fees and court costs. As we have already noted, the statute regarding court costs specifically prohibits assessment of court costs."

FAM §231.211. AWARD OF COST AGAINST NONPREVAILING PARTY IN TITLE IV-D CASE

(a) At the conclusion of a Title IV-D case, the court may assess attorney's fees and all court costs as authorized by law against the nonprevailing party, except that the court may not assess those amounts against the Title IV-D agency or a private attorney or political subdivision that has entered into a contract under this chapter or any party to whom the agency has provided services under this chapter. Such fees and costs may not exceed reasonable and necessary costs as determined by the court.

(b) The clerk of the court may take any action necessary to collect any fees or costs assessed under this section.

History of Fam §231.211: Acts 1995, 74th Leg., ch. 20, §1, eff. April 20, 1995. Source: Former Fam §11.181.

Sections 231.212-231.300 reserved for expansion

SUBCHAPTER D. LOCATION OF PARENTS & RESOURCES

FAM §231.301. TITLE IV-D PARENT LOCATOR SERVICES

(a) The parent locator service conducted by the Title IV-D agency shall be used to obtain information for:

(1) child support establishment and enforcement purposes regarding the identity, social security number, location, employer and employment benefits, income, and assets or debts of any individual under an obligation to pay child or medical support or to whom a support obligation is owed; or

(2) the establishment of paternity.

(b) As authorized by federal law, the following persons may receive information under this section:

(1) a person or entity that contracts with the Title IV-D agency to provide services authorized under Title IV-D or an employee of the Title IV-D agency;

(2) an attorney who has the duty or authority, by law, to enforce an order for possession of or access to a child;

(3) a court, or an agent of the court, having jurisdiction to render or enforce an order for possession of or access to a child;

(4) the resident parent, legal guardian, attorney, or agent of a child who is not receiving public assistance; and

(5) a state agency that administers a program operated under a state plan as provided by 42 U.S.C. Section 653(c).

History of Fam §231.301: Acts 1995, 74th Leg., ch. 20, §1, eff. April 20, 1995. Amended by Acts 1997, 75th Leg., ch. 911, §76, eff. Sept. 1, 1997; Acts 1999, 76th Leg., ch. 556, §56, eff. Sept. 1, 1999. Source: Former Hum. Res. Code §77.001(a).

FAM §231.302. INFORMATION TO ASSIST IN LOCATION OF PERSONS OR PROPERTY

(a) The Title IV-D agency of this or another state may request and obtain information relating to the identity, location, employment, compensation, benefits, income, and property holdings or other assets of any person from a state or local government agency, private company, institution, or other entity as necessary to establish, modify, or enforce a support order.

A *Subsection (b) below is effective for SAPCRs and modification or enforcement proceedings commenced on or after Sept. 1, 2001.*

(b) A government agency, private company, institution, or other entity shall provide the information requested under Subsection (a) directly to the Title IV-D agency, without the requirement of payment of a fee for the information, and shall, subject to safeguards on privacy and information security, provide the information in the most efficient and expeditious manner available, including electronic or automated transfer and interface. Any individual or entity disclosing information under this section in response to a request from a Title IV-D agency may not be held liable in any civil action or proceeding to any person for the disclosure of information under this subsection.

Subsection (b) below is effective for SAPCRs and modification or enforcement proceedings commenced before Sept. 1, 2001.

(b) A government agency, private company, institution, or other entity shall provide the information requested under Subsection (a) and shall, subject to safeguards on privacy and information security, provide the information in the most efficient and expeditious manner available, including electronic or automated transfer and interface. Any individual or entity disclosing information under this section in response to a request from a Title IV-D agency may not be held liable in any civil action or proceeding to any person for the disclosure of information under this subsection.

(c) To assist in the administration of laws relating to child support enforcement under Parts A and D of Title IV of the federal Social Security Act (42 U.S.C. Sections 601-617 and 651-669):

(1) each licensing authority shall request and each applicant for a license shall provide the applicant's social security number;

(2) each agency administering a contract that provides for a payment of state funds shall request and each individual or entity bidding on a state contract shall provide the individual's or entity's social security number as required by Section 231.006, Family Code; and

(3) each agency administering a state-funded grant or loan program shall request and each applicant for a grant or loan shall provide the applicant's social security number as required by Section 231.006, Family Code.

(d) This section does not limit the right of an agency or licensing authority to collect and use a social security number under another provision of law.

(e) Except as provided by Subsection (d), a social security number provided under this section is confidential and may be disclosed only for the purposes of responding to a request for information from an agency operating under the provisions of Part A or D of Title IV of the federal Social Security Act (42 U.S.C. Sections 601 et seq. and 651 et seq.).

(f) Information collected by the Title IV-D agency under this section may be used only for child support purposes.

(g) In this section, "licensing authority" has the meaning assigned by Section 232.001.

History of Fam §231.302: Acts 1995, 74th Leg., ch. 20, §1, eff. April 20, 1995. Amended by Acts 1995, 74th Leg., ch. 751, §84, eff. Sept. 1, 1995; Acts 1997, 75th Leg., ch. 420, §20 (eff. Sept. 1, 1997), ch. 911, §77 (eff. Sept. 1, 1997); Acts 1999, 76th Leg., ch. 62, §6.28, eff. Sept. 1, 1999; Acts 2001, 77th Leg., ch. 1023, §56, eff. Sept. 1, 2001. Source: Former Hum. Res. Code §77.001(b).

FAM §231.303. TITLE IV-D ADMINISTRATIVE SUBPOENA

(a) The Title IV-D agency of this state or another state may issue an administrative subpoena to any individual or private or public entity in this state to furnish information necessary to carry out the purposes of child support enforcement under 42 U.S.C. Section 651 et seq. or this chapter.

(b) An individual or entity receiving an administrative subpoena under this section shall comply with the subpoena. The Title IV-D agency may impose a fine in an amount not to exceed $500 on an individual or entity that fails without good cause to comply with an administrative subpoena. An alleged or presumed father or a parent who fails to comply with a subpoena without good cause may also be subject to license suspension under Chapter 232.

(c) A court may compel compliance with an administrative subpoena and with any administrative fine for failure to comply with the subpoena and may award attorney's fees and costs to the Title IV-D agency in enforcing an administrative subpoena on proof that an individual or organization failed without good cause to comply with the subpoena.

(d) An individual or organization may not be liable in a civil action or proceeding for disclosing financial or other information to a Title IV-D agency under this section. The Title IV-D agency may disclose information in a financial record obtained from a financial institution only to the extent necessary:

(1) to establish, modify, or enforce a child support obligation; or

(2) to comply with Section 233.001, as added by Chapter 420, Acts of the 75th Legislature, Regular Session, 1997.

History of Fam §231.303: Acts 1995, 74th Leg., ch. 20, §1, eff. April 20, 1995. Amended by Acts 1997, 75th Leg., ch. 911, §78, eff. Sept. 1, 1997; Acts 1999, 76th Leg., ch. 859, §5, eff. Sept. 1, 1999. Source: Former Hum. Res. Code §77.001(c).

FAM §231.304. REPEALED

Repealed by Acts 1997, 75th Leg., ch. 911, §97(b), eff. Oct. 1, 1998.

FAM §231.305. MEMORANDUM OF UNDERSTANDING ON CHILD SUPPORT FOR CHILDREN RECEIVING PUBLIC ASSISTANCE

(a) The Title IV-D agency and the Texas Department of Human Services by rule shall adopt a memorandum of understanding governing the establishment and enforcement of court-ordered child support in cases involving children who receive financial assistance under Chapter 31, Human Resources Code. The memorandum shall require the agency and the department to:

(1) develop procedures to ensure that the information the department is required to collect to establish and enforce child support:

(A) is collected from the person applying to receive the financial assistance at the time the application is filed;

(B) is accurate and complete when the department forwards the information to the agency;

(C) is not information previously reported to the agency; and

(D) is forwarded to the agency in an expeditious manner;

(2) develop procedures to ensure that the agency does not duplicate the efforts of the department in gathering necessary information;

(3) clarify each agency's responsibilities in the establishment and enforcement of child support;

(4) develop guidelines for use by eligibility workers and child support enforcement officers in obtaining from an applicant the information required to establish and enforce child support for that child;

(5) develop training programs for appropriate department personnel to enhance the collection of information for child support enforcement;

(6) develop a standard time, not to exceed 30 days, for the department to initiate a sanction on request from the agency;

(7) develop procedures for agency participation in department appeal hearings relating to noncompliance sanctions;

(8) develop performance measures regarding the timeliness and the number of sanctions resulting from agency requests for noncompliance sanctions; and

(9) prescribe:

(A) the time in which the department is required to forward information under Subdivision (1)(D); and

(B) what constitutes complete information under Subdivision (1)(B).

(b) The Title IV-D agency and the Texas Department of Human Services shall review and renew or modify the memorandum not later than January 1 of each even-numbered year.

History of Fam §231.305: Acts 1995, 74th Leg., ch. 341, §1.07, eff. Sept. 1, 1995. Amended by Acts 1999, 76th Leg., ch. 556, §57, eff. Sept. 1, 1999.

FAM §231.306. MAXIMIZING MEDICAL SUPPORT ESTABLISHMENT & COLLECTION BY THE TITLE IV-D AGENCY

(a) On the installation of an automated child support enforcement system, the Title IV-D agency is strongly encouraged to:

(1) maximize the collection of medical support; and

(2) establish cash medical support orders for children eligible for medical assistance under the state Medicaid program for whom private insurance coverage is not available.

(b) In this section, "medical support" has the meaning assigned by Section 101.020.

History of Fam §231.306: Acts 1995, 74th Leg., ch. 341, §2.03, eff. Sept. 1, 1995.

FAM §231.307. FINANCIAL INSTITUTION DATA MATCHES

Ⓐ *Subsection (a) below is effective for SAPCRs and modification or enforcement proceedings commenced on or after Sept. 1, 2001.*

(a) The Title IV-D agency shall develop a system meeting the requirements of federal law (42 U.S.C. Sections 666(a)(4) and (17)) for the exchange of data with financial institutions doing business in the state to identify an account of an obligor owing past-due child support and to enforce support obligations against the obligor, including the imposition of a lien and a levy and execution on an obligor's assets held in financial institutions as required by federal law (42 U.S.C. Section 666(c)(1)(G)).

Subsection (a) below is effective for SAPCRs and modification or enforcement proceedings commenced before Sept. 1, 2001.

(a) The Title IV-D agency shall develop a system meeting the requirements of 42 U.S.C. Section 666(a)(17) for the quarterly exchange of data with financial institutions doing business in the state to identify an account of an obligor owing past-due child support and enforce support obligations against the obligor.

(b) The Title IV-D agency by rule shall establish procedures for data matches authorized under this section.

(c) The Title IV-D agency may enter into an agreement with one or more states to create a consortium for data matches authorized under this section. The Title IV-D agency may contract with a vendor selected by the consortium to perform data matches with financial institutions.

(d) A financial institution providing information or responding to a notice of child support lien provided under Subchapter G, Chapter 157, or otherwise acting in good faith to comply with the Title IV-D agency's procedures under this section may not be liable under any federal or state law for any damages that arise from those acts.

Ⓐ *Subsection (e) below is effective for SAPCRs and modification or enforcement proceedings commenced on or after Sept. 1, 2001.*

(e) In this section:

(1) "Financial institution" has the meaning assigned by Section 157.311; and

(2) "Account" has the meaning assigned by Section 157.311.

Subsection (e) below is effective for SAPCRs and modification or enforcement proceedings commenced before Sept. 1, 2001.

(e) In this section:

(1) "Financial institution" has the meaning assigned by 42 U.S.C. Section 669a(d)(1); and

(2) "Account" means a demand deposit account, checking or negotiable withdrawal order account, savings account, time deposit account, or money market mutual fund account.

Ⓔ *Subsection (f) below is effective for SAPCRs and modification or enforcement proceedings commenced on or after Sept. 1, 2001.*

(f) A financial institution participating in data matches authorized by this section may provide the Title IV-D agency an address for the purpose of service of notices or process required in actions under this section or Subchapter G, Chapter 157.

History of Fam §231.307: Acts 1997, 75th Leg., ch. 911, §79, eff. Sept. 1, 1997. Amended by Acts 1999, 76th Leg., ch. 556, §58, eff. Sept. 1, 1999; Acts 2001, 77th Leg., ch. 1023, §57, eff. Sept. 1, 2001.

FAM §231.308. PUBLIC IDENTIFICATION OF CERTAIN OBLIGORS

(a) The Title IV-D agency shall develop a program to identify publicly certain child support obligors who are delinquent in the payment of child support. The program shall include the displaying of photographs and profiles of obligors in public and private locations.

The Title IV-D agency shall use posters, the news media, and other cost-effective methods to display photographs and profiles of certain obligors who are in arrears in paying child support. The Title IV-D agency shall divide the state into at least six regions for local identification of certain child support obligors who are delinquent in the payment of child support.

(b) The Title IV-D agency may not disclose information under this section that is by law required to remain confidential.

History of Fam §231.308: Acts 1997, 75th Leg., ch. 420, §21, eff. Sept. 1, 1997.

FAM §231.309. REWARDS FOR INFORMATION

(a) The Title IV-D agency may offer a reward to an individual who provides information to the agency that leads to the collection of child support owed by an obligor who is delinquent in paying support.

(b) The Title IV-D agency shall adopt rules providing for the amounts of rewards offered under this section and the circumstances under which an individual providing information described in Subsection (a) is entitled to receive a reward.

(c) A reward paid under this section shall be paid from the child support retained collections account.

History of Fam §231.309: Acts 1997, 75th Leg., ch. 420, §21, eff. Sept. 1, 1997.

FAM §231.310. INTERAGENCY WORK GROUP

(a) The Title IV-D agency shall establish a work group to facilitate the sharing of data and resources to locate parents and relatives of children served by the Title IV-D agency and other health and human services agencies.

(b) The work group shall consist of representatives from the Title IV-D agency, the Department of Protective and Regulatory Services, the Texas Department of Human Services, the Texas Department of Health, the Texas Workforce Commission, the Texas Department of Public Safety, the Texas Rehabilitation Commission, and the Texas Department of Criminal Justice.

(c) The commissioner of human services or the commissioner's designee shall serve as the work group's presiding officer.

(d) The work group shall evaluate the procedures used by each agency in the work group to locate parents and relatives of children served by the agencies and develop a mechanism to ensure that each agency in the work group, or any private contractor performing location functions for an agency, is able to access information in the database of each other agency without paying a fee.

(e) The work group shall evaluate opportunities for using outside contracting and coordinating efforts with other community resources.

(f) To the extent possible, the Department of Protective and Regulatory Services and the Title IV-D agency shall use outside contractors and community resources to locate parents in child protection and child support cases.

History of Fam §231.310: Acts 1999, 76th Leg., ch. 228, §2, eff. Sept. 1, 1999.

Sections 231.311-231.400 reserved for expansion

FAM §§231.401, 231.429. RENUMBERED

Renumbered as §§233.001-233.029 by Acts 1997, 75th Leg., ch. 911, §80, eff. Sept. 1, 1997.

FAM §§231.430, 231.431. REPEALED

Repealed by Acts 1997, 75th Leg., ch. 911, §97(a), eff. Sept. 1, 1997.

A CHAPTER 232. SUSPENSION OF LICENSE

FAM §232.001. DEFINITIONS

In this chapter:

(1) "License" means a license, certificate, registration, permit, or other authorization that:

(A) is issued by a licensing authority;

(B) is subject before expiration to suspension, revocation, forfeiture, or termination by the issuing licensing authority; and

(C) a person must obtain to:

(i) practice or engage in a particular business, occupation, or profession;

(ii) operate a motor vehicle; or

(iii) engage in any other regulated activity, including hunting, fishing, or other recreational activity for which a license or permit is required.

(2) "Licensing authority" means a department, commission, board, office, or other agency of the state or a political subdivision of the state that issues a license.

(3) "Order suspending license" means an order issued by the Title IV-D agency or a court directing a licensing authority to suspend a license.

Ⓐ *Subsection (4) below is effective for modification or enforcement proceedings commenced on or after Sept. 1, 2001.*

(4) "Subpoena" means a judicial or administrative subpoena issued in a parentage determination or child support proceeding under this title.

Subsection (4) below is effective for modification or enforcement proceedings commenced before Sept. 1, 2001.

(4) "Subpoena" means a subpoena issued in a parentage determination or child support proceeding under this title.

History of Fam §232.001: Acts 1995, 74th Leg., ch. 655, §5.03 (eff. Sept. 1, 1995), ch. 751, §85 (eff. Sept. 1, 1995). Amended by Acts 1997, 75th Leg., ch. 911, §82, eff. Sept. 1, 1997; Acts 2001, 77th Leg., ch. 1023, §58 (eff. Sept. 1, 2001), ch. 724, §1 (eff. Sept. 2001).

FAM §232.002. LICENSING AUTHORITIES SUBJECT TO CHAPTER

The following are licensing authorities subject to this chapter:

(1) Department of Agriculture;

(2) Texas Commission on Alcohol and Drug Abuse;

(3) Texas Alcoholic Beverage Commission;

(4) Texas Appraiser Licensing and Certification Board;

(5) Texas Board of Architectural Examiners;

(6) State Board of Barber Examiners;

(7) Texas Board of Chiropractic Examiners;

(8) Comptroller of Public Accounts;

(9) Texas Cosmetology Commission;

(10) Court Reporters Certification Board;

(11) State Board of Dental Examiners;

(12) Texas State Board of Examiners of Dietitians;

(13) Texas Funeral Service Commission;

(14) Texas Department of Health;

(15) Texas Department of Human Services;

(16) Texas Board of Professional Land Surveying;

(17) Texas Department of Licensing and Regulation;

(18) Texas State Board of Examiners of Marriage and Family Therapists;

(19) Texas State Board of Medical Examiners;

(20) Midwifery Board;

(21) Texas Natural Resource Conservation Commission;

(22) Board of Nurse Examiners;

(23) Texas Board of Occupational Therapy Examiners;

(24) Texas Optometry Board;

(25) Parks and Wildlife Department;

(26) Texas State Board of Examiners of Perfusionists;

(27) Texas State Board of Pharmacy;

(28) Texas Board of Physical Therapy Examiners;

(29) Texas State Board of Plumbing Examiners;

(30) Texas State Board of Podiatric Medical Examiners;

(31) Polygraph Examiners Board;

Ⓐ (32) Texas Commission on Private Security;

(33) Texas State Board of Examiners of Professional Counselors;

(34) Texas Board of Professional Engineers;

(35) Department of Protective and Regulatory Services;

(36) Texas State Board of Examiners of Psychologists;

(37) Texas State Board of Public Accountancy;

(38) Department of Public Safety of the State of Texas;

(39) Public Utility Commission of Texas;

(40) Railroad Commission of Texas;

(41) Texas Real Estate Commission;

(42) State Bar of Texas;

(43) Texas State Board of Social Worker Examiners;

(44) State Board of Examiners for Speech-Language Pathology and Audiology;

(45) Texas Structural Pest Control Board;

(46) Board of Tax Professional Examiners;

(47) Secretary of State;

(48) Supreme Court of Texas;

(49) Texas Transportation Commission;

(50) State Board of Veterinary Medical Examiners;

(51) Board of Vocational Nurse Examiners;

(52) Texas Ethics Commission;

(53) Advisory Board of Athletic Trainers;

(54) State Committee of Examiners in the Fitting and Dispensing of Hearing Instruments;

(55) Texas Board of Licensure for Professional Medical Physicists;

(56) Texas Department of Insurance;

(57) Texas Board of Orthotics and Prosthetics;

A (58) savings and loan commissioner;

A (59) Texas Juvenile Probation Commission; and

E (60) Texas Lottery Commission under Chapter 466, Government Code.

History of Fam §232.002: Acts 1995, 74th Leg., ch. 655, §5.03 (eff. Sept. 1, 1995), ch. 751, §85 (eff. Sept. 1, 1995). Amended by Acts 1997, 75th Leg., ch. 165, §7.22 (eff. Sept. 1, 1997), ch. 1280, §1.02 (eff. Sept. 1, 1997), ch. 1288, §2 (eff. Sept. 1, 1997); Acts 1999, 76th Leg., ch. 1477, §23 (eff. Sept. 1, 1999), ch. 1254, §4 (eff. Sept. 1, 1999); Acts 2001, 77th Leg., ch. 394, §2 (eff. Sept. 1, 2001), ch. 1420, §14.744 (eff. Sept. 1, 2001).

E FAM §232.0021. APPLICATION OF CHAPTER TO TEXAS LOTTERY COMMISSION

With respect to the Texas Lottery Commission, this chapter applies only to a lottery ticket sales agent license issued under Chapter 466, Government Code.

History of Fam §232.0021: Enacted by Acts 2001, 77th Leg., ch. 394, §3, eff. Sept. 1, 2001.

FAM §232.003. SUSPENSION OF LICENSE

A *Subsections (a) & (b) below are effective for modification or enforcement proceedings commenced on or after Sept. 1, 2001.*

(a) A court or the Title IV-D agency may issue an order suspending a license as provided by this chapter if an individual who is an obligor:

(1) owes overdue child support in an amount equal to or greater than the total support due for three months under a support order;

(2) has been provided an opportunity to make payments toward the overdue child support under a court-ordered or agreed repayment schedule; and

(3) has failed to comply with the repayment schedule.

(b) A court or the Title IV-D agency may issue an order suspending a license as provided by this chapter if a parent or alleged parent has failed, after receiving appropriate notice, to comply with a subpoena.

Subsections (a) & (b) below are effective for modification or enforcement proceedings commenced before Sept. 1, 2001.

(a) A court or the Title IV-D agency may issue an order suspending a license as provided by this chapter if an individual who is an obligor:

(1) has a child support arrearage equal to or greater than the total support due for 90 days under a support order;

(2) has been provided an opportunity to make payments toward the child support arrearage under a court order or an agreed repayment schedule; and

(3) has failed to comply with the repayment schedule.

(b) A court or the Title IV-D agency may issue an order suspending license as provided by this chapter if an individual has failed, after receiving appropriate notice, to comply with a subpoena.

E (c) A court may issue an order suspending license as provided by this chapter for an individual for whom a court has rendered an enforcement order under Chapter 157 finding that the individual has failed to comply with the terms of a court order providing for the possession of or access to a child.

History of Fam §232.003: Acts 1995, 74th Leg., ch. 655, §5.03 (eff. Sept. 1, 1995), ch. 751, §85 (eff. Sept. 1, 1995). Amended by Acts 1997, 75th Leg., ch. 420, §§22, 23 (eff. Sept. 1, 1997), ch. 911, §83 (eff. Sept. 1, 1997); Acts 1999, 76th Leg., ch. 556, §59, eff. Sept. 1, 1999; Acts 2001, 77th Leg., ch. 724, §2 (eff. Sept. 1, 2001), ch. 1023, §59 (eff. Sept. 1, 2001).

FAM §232.004. PETITION FOR SUSPENSION OF LICENSE

(a) A child support agency or obligee may file a petition to suspend, as provided by this chapter, a license of an obligor who has an arrearage equal to or greater than the total support due for 90 days under a support order.

(b) In a Title IV-D case, the petition shall be filed with the Title IV-D agency, the court of continuing jurisdiction, or the tribunal in which a child support order has been registered under Chapter 159. The tribunal in which the petition is filed obtains jurisdiction over the matter.

(c) In a case other than a Title IV-D case, the petition shall be filed in the court of continuing jurisdiction or the court in which a child support order has been registered under Chapter 159.

(d) A proceeding in a case filed with the Title IV-D agency under this chapter is governed by the contested case provisions of Chapter 2001, Government Code, except that Section 2001.054 does not apply to the proceeding. The director of the Title IV-D agency or the director's designee may render a final decision in a contested case proceeding under this chapter.

History of Fam §232.004: Acts 1995, 74th Leg., ch. 655, §5.03 (eff. Sept. 1, 1995), ch. 751, §85 (eff. Sept. 1, 1995). Amended by Acts 1997, 75th Leg., ch. 420, §24 (eff. Sept. 1, 1997), ch. 911, §84 (eff. Sept. 1, 1997); Acts 1999, 76th Leg., ch. 556, §60, eff. Sept. 1, 1999.

See also 1 TAC §§55.203(a), (b), 55.205.

FAM §232.005. CONTENTS OF PETITION

(a) A petition under this chapter must state that license suspension is required under Section 232.003 and allege:

(1) the name and, if known, social security number of the individual;

A *Subsection (2) below is effective for modification or enforcement proceedings commenced on or after Sept. 1, 2001.*

(2) with regard to each license, the type, and if known, number of any license the individual is believed to hold and the name of the licensing authority that issued the license; and

Subsection (2) below is effective for modification or enforcement proceedings commenced before Sept. 1, 2001.

(2) the type, and if known, number of any license the individual is believed to hold and the name of the licensing authority that issued the license; and

(3) the amount of arrearages owed under the child support order or the facts associated with the individual's failure to comply with:

(A) a subpoena; or

E (B) the terms of a court order providing for the possession of or access to a child.

(b) A petition under this chapter may include as an attachment a copy of:

(1) the record of child support payments maintained by the Title IV-D registry or local registry;

(2) the subpoena with which the individual has failed to comply, together with proof of service of the subpoena; or

E (3) with respect to a petition for suspension under Section 232.003(c):

(A) the enforcement order rendered under Chapter 157 describing the manner in which the individual was found to have not complied with the terms of a court order providing for the possession of or access to a child; and

(B) the court order containing the provisions that the individual was found to have violated.

History of Fam §232.005: Acts 1995, 74th Leg., ch. 655, §5.03 (eff. Sept. 1, 1995), ch. 751, §85 (eff. Sept. 1, 1995). Amended by Acts 1997, 75th Leg., ch. 911, §85, eff. Sept. 1, 1997; Acts 2001, 77th Leg., ch. 724, §3 (eff. Sept. 1, 2001), ch. 1023, §60 (eff. Sept. 1, 2001).

FAM §232.006. NOTICE

(a) On the filing of a petition under Section 232.004, the clerk of the court or the Title IV-D agency shall deliver to the individual:

(1) notice of the individual's right to a hearing before the court or agency;

(2) notice of the deadline for requesting a hearing; and

(3) a hearing request form if the proceeding is in a Title IV-D case.

(b) Notice under this section may be served as in civil cases generally.

(c) The notice must contain the following prominently displayed statement in boldfaced type, capital letters, or underlined:

"AN ACTION TO SUSPEND ONE OR MORE LICENSES ISSUED TO YOU HAS BEEN FILED. YOU MAY EMPLOY AN ATTORNEY TO REPRESENT YOU IN THIS ACTION. IF YOU OR YOUR ATTORNEY DO NOT REQUEST A HEARING BEFORE THE 21ST DAY AFTER THE DATE OF SERVICE OF THIS NOTICE, AN ORDER OF LICENSE SUSPENSION MAY BE RENDERED."

History of Fam §232.006: Acts 1995, 74th Leg., ch. 655, §5.03 (eff. Sept. 1, 1995), ch. 751, §85 (eff. Sept. 1, 1995). Amended by Acts 1997, 75th Leg., ch. 911, §86 (eff. Sept. 1, 1997), ch. 976, §7 (eff. Sept. 1, 1997); Acts 1999, 76th Leg., ch. 178, §11, eff. Aug. 30, 1999.

FAM §232.007. HEARING ON PETITION TO SUSPEND LICENSE

(a) A request for a hearing and motion to stay suspension must be filed with the court or Title IV-D agency by the individual not later than the 20th day after the date of service of the notice under Section 232.006.

(b) If a request for a hearing is filed, the court or Title IV-D agency shall:

(1) promptly schedule a hearing;

(2) notify each party of the date, time, and location of the hearing; and

(3) stay suspension pending the hearing.

(c) In a case involving support arrearages, a record of child support payments made by the Title IV-D agency or a local registry is evidence of whether the payments were made. A copy of the record appearing regular on its face shall be admitted as evidence at a hearing under this chapter, including a hearing on a motion to revoke a stay. Either party may offer controverting evidence.

(d) In a case in which an individual has failed to comply with a subpoena, proof of service is evidence of delivery of the subpoena.

History of Fam §232.007: Acts 1995, 74th Leg., ch. 655, §5.03 (eff. Sept. 1, 1995), ch. 751, §85 (eff. Sept. 1, 1995). Amended by Acts 1997, 75th Leg., ch. 911, §87, eff. Sept. 1, 1997.
See also 1 TAC §§55.203(c), 55.207-55.212.

FAM §232.008. ORDER SUSPENDING LICENSE FOR FAILURE TO PAY CHILD SUPPORT

(a) On making the findings required by Section 232.003, the court or Title IV-D agency shall render an order suspending the license unless the individual:

(1) proves that all arrearages and the current month's support have been paid;

Ⓐ (2) shows good cause for failure to comply with the subpoena or the terms of the court order providing for the possession of or access to a child; or

(3) establishes an affirmative defense as provided by Section 157.008(c).

(b) The court or Title IV-D agency may stay an order suspending a license conditioned on the individual's compliance with:

(1) a reasonable repayment schedule that is incorporated in the order;

(2) the requirements of a reissued and delivered subpoena; or

Ⓔ (3) the requirements of any court order pertaining to the possession of or access to a child.

(c) An order suspending a license with a stay of the suspension may not be served on the licensing authority unless the stay is revoked as provided by this chapter.

(d) A final order suspending license rendered by a court or the Title IV-D agency shall be forwarded to the appropriate licensing authority by the clerk of the court or Title IV-D agency. The clerk shall collect from an obligor a fee of $5 for each order mailed.

(e) If the court or Title IV-D agency renders an order suspending license, the individual may also be ordered not to engage in the licensed activity.

(f) If the court or Title IV-D agency finds that the petition for suspension should be denied, the petition shall be dismissed without prejudice, and an order suspending license may not be rendered.

History of Fam §232.008: Acts 1995, 74th Leg., ch. 655, §5.03 (eff. Sept. 1, 1995), ch. 751, §85 (eff. Sept. 1, 1995). Amended by Acts 1997, 75th Leg., ch. 911, §88 (eff. Sept. 1, 1997), ch. 976, §8 (eff. Sept. 1, 1997); Acts 1999, 76th Leg., ch. 556, §61, 76th Leg., eff. Sept. 1, 1999; Acts 2001, 77th Leg., ch. 724, §4, eff. Sept. 1, 2001.

FAM §232.009. DEFAULT ORDER

Ⓐ *Section 232.009 below is effective for modification or enforcement proceedings commenced on or after Sept. 1, 2001.*

The court or Title IV-D agency shall consider the allegations of the petition for suspension to be admitted and shall render an order suspending the license of an obligor without the requirement of a hearing if the court or Title IV-D agency determines that the individual failed to respond to a notice issued under Section 232.006 by:

(1) requesting a hearing; or

(2) appearing at a scheduled hearing.

History of Fam §232.009: Acts 1995, 74th Leg., ch. 655, §5.03 (eff. Sept. 1, 1995), ch. 751, §85 (eff. Sept. 1, 1995). Amended by Acts 1997, 75th Leg., ch. 420, §25 (eff. Sept. 1, 1997), ch. 911, §89 (eff. Sept. 1, 1997); Acts 2001, 77th Leg., ch. 1023, §61, eff. Sept. 1, 2001.

FAM §232.009. DEFAULT ORDER

Section 232.009 below is effective for modification or enforcement proceedings commenced before Sept. 1, 2001.

The court or Title IV-D agency shall consider the allegations of the petition for suspension to be admitted and shall render an order suspending the license of an obligor without the requirement of a hearing if the court or Title IV-D agency determines that the individual failed to:

(1) respond to a notice issued under Section 232.006;

(2) request a hearing; or

(3) appear at a hearing.

FAM §232.010. REVIEW OF FINAL ADMINISTRATIVE ORDER

An order issued by a Title IV-D agency under this chapter is a final agency decision and is subject to review under the substantial evidence rule as provided by Chapter 2001, Government Code.

History of Fam §232.010: Acts 1995, 74th Leg., ch. 655, §5.03 (eff. Sept. 1, 1995), ch. 751, §85 (eff. Sept. 1, 1995).

FAM §232.011. ACTION BY LICENSING AUTHORITY

(a) On receipt of a final order suspending license, the licensing authority shall immediately determine if the authority has issued a license to the individual named on the order and, if a license has been issued:

(1) record the suspension of the license in the licensing authority's records;

(2) report the suspension as appropriate; and

(3) demand surrender of the suspended license if required by law for other cases in which a license is suspended.

(b) A licensing authority shall implement the terms of a final order suspending license without additional review or hearing. The authority may provide notice as appropriate to the license holder or to others concerned with the license.

(c) A licensing authority may not modify, remand, reverse, vacate, or stay an order suspending license issued under this chapter and may not review, vacate, or reconsider the terms of a final order suspending license.

(d) An individual who is the subject of a final order suspending license is not entitled to a refund for any fee or deposit paid to the licensing authority.

(e) An individual who continues to engage in the business, occupation, profession, or other licensed activity after the implementation of the order suspending license by the licensing authority is liable for the same civil and criminal penalties provided for engaging in the licensed activity without a license or while a license is suspended that apply to any other license holder of that licensing authority.

(f) A licensing authority is exempt from liability to a license holder for any act authorized under this chapter performed by the authority.

(g) Except as provided by this chapter, an order suspending license or dismissing a petition for the suspension of a license does not affect the power of a licensing authority to grant, deny, suspend, revoke, terminate, or renew a license.

(h) The denial or suspension of a driver's license under this chapter is governed by this chapter and not by the general licensing provisions of Chapter 521, Transportation Code.

E *Subsection (i) below is effective for modification or enforcement proceedings commenced on or after Sept. 1, 2001.*

(i) An order issued under this chapter to suspend a license applies to each license issued by the licensing authority subject to the order for which the obligor is eligible. The licensing authority may not issue or renew any other license for the obligor until the court or the Title IV-D agency renders an order vacating or staying an order suspending license.

History of Fam §232.011: Acts 1995, 74th Leg., ch. 655, §5.03 (eff. Sept. 1, 1995), ch. 751, §85 (eff. Sept. 1, 1995). Amended by Acts 1997, 75th Leg., ch. 165, §30.184 (eff. Sept. 1, 1997), ch. 911, §90 (eff. Sept. 1, 1997); Acts 2001, 77th Leg., ch. 1023, §62, eff. Sept. 1, 2001.

FAM §232.012. MOTION TO REVOKE STAY

(a) The obligee, support enforcement agency, court, or Title IV-D agency may file a motion to revoke the stay of an order suspending license if the individual who is subject of an order suspending license does not comply with:

(1) the terms of a reasonable repayment plan entered into by the individual;

(2) the requirements of a reissued subpoena; or

E (3) the terms of any court order pertaining to the possession of or access to a child.

(b) Notice to the individual of a motion to revoke stay under this section may be given by personal service or by mail to the address provided by the individual, if any, in the order suspending license. The notice must include a notice of hearing. The notice must be provided to the individual not less than 10 days before the date of the hearing.

A (c) A motion to revoke stay must allege the manner in which the individual failed to comply with the repayment plan, the reissued subpoena, or the court order pertaining to possession of or access to a child.

A (d) If the court or Title IV-D agency finds that the individual is not in compliance with the terms of the repayment plan, reissued subpoena, or court order pertaining to possession of or access to a child, the court or agency shall revoke the stay of the order suspending license and render a final order suspending license.

History of Fam §232.012: Acts 1995, 74th Leg., ch. 655, §5.03 (eff. Sept. 1, 1995), ch. 751, §85 (eff. Sept. 1, 1995). Amended by Acts 1997, 75th Leg., ch. 911, §91, eff. Sept. 1, 1997; Acts 2001, 77th Leg., ch. 724, §5, eff. Sept. 1, 2001.

FAM §232.013. VACATING OR STAYING ORDER SUSPENDING LICENSE

(a) The court or Title IV-D agency may render an order vacating or staying an order suspending license if the individual has:

(1) paid all delinquent child support or has established a satisfactory payment record;

(2) complied with the requirements of a reissued subpoena; or

E (3) complied with the terms of any court order providing for the possession of or access to a child.

(b) The clerk of the court or Title IV-D agency shall promptly deliver an order vacating or staying an order suspending license to the appropriate licensing authority. The clerk shall collect from an obligor a fee of $5 for each order mailed.

(c) On receipt of an order vacating or staying an order suspending license, the licensing authority shall promptly issue the affected license to the individual if the individual is otherwise qualified for the license.

(d) An order rendered under this section does not affect the right of the child support agency or obligee to any other remedy provided by law, including the right to seek relief under this chapter. An order rendered under this section does not affect the power of a licensing authority to grant, deny, suspend, revoke, terminate, or renew a license as otherwise provided by law.

History of Fam §232.013: Acts 1995, 74th Leg., ch. 655, §5.03 (eff. Sept. 1, 1995), ch. 751, §85 (eff. Sept. 1, 1995). Amended by Acts 1997, 75th Leg., ch. 911, §92 (eff. Sept. 1, 1997), ch. 976, §9 (eff. Sept. 1, 1997); Acts 2001, 77th Leg., ch. 724, §6, eff. Sept. 1, 2001.

FAM §232.014. FEE BY LICENSING AUTHORITY

A licensing authority may charge a fee to an individual who is the subject of an order suspending license in an amount sufficient to recover the administrative costs incurred by the authority under this chapter.

History of Fam §232.014: Acts 1995, 74th Leg., ch. 655, §5.03 (eff. Sept. 1, 1995), ch. 751, §85 (eff. Sept. 1, 1995). Amended by Acts 1997, 75th Leg., ch. 911, §93, eff. Sept. 1, 1997.

FAM §232.015. COOPERATION BETWEEN LICENSING AUTHORITIES & TITLE IV-D AGENCY

(a) The Title IV-D agency may request from each licensing authority the name, address, social security number, license renewal date, and other identifying information for each individual who holds, applies for, or renews a license issued by the authority.

A *Subsection (b) below is effective for modification or enforcement proceedings commenced on or after Sept. 1, 2001.*

(b) A licensing authority shall provide the requested information in the form and manner identified by the Title IV-D agency.

Subsection (b) below is effective for modification or enforcement proceedings commenced before Sept. 1, 2001.

(b) A licensing authority shall provide the requested information in the manner agreed to by the Title IV-D agency and the licensing authority.

(c) The Title IV-D agency may enter into a cooperative agreement with a licensing authority to administer this chapter in a cost-effective manner.

(d) The Title IV-D agency may adopt a reasonable implementation schedule for the requirements of this section.

(e) The Title IV-D agency, the comptroller, and the Texas Alcoholic Beverage Commission shall by rule specify additional prerequisites for the suspension of licenses relating to state taxes collected under Title 2, Tax Code. The joint rules must be adopted not later than March 1, 1996.

History of Fam §232.015: Acts 1995, 74th Leg., ch. 751, §85 (eff. Sept. 1, 1995), ch. 655, §5.03 (eff. Sept. 1, 1995). Amended by Acts 1997, 75th Leg., ch. 165, §7.23, eff. Sept. 1, 1997; Acts 2001, 77th Leg., ch. 1023, §63, eff. Sept. 1, 2001.

FAM §232.016. RULES, FORMS, & PROCEDURES

The Title IV-D agency by rule shall prescribe forms and procedures for the implementation of this chapter.

History of Fam §232.016: Acts 1995, 74th Leg., ch. 655, §5.03 (eff. Sept. 1, 1995), ch. 751, §85 (eff. Sept. 1, 1995).

See also 1 TAC §§55.201-55.216.

CHAPTER 233. CHILD SUPPORT REVIEW PROCESS TO ESTABLISH OR ENFORCE SUPPORT OBLIGATIONS

FAM §233.001. PURPOSE

(a) The purpose of the procedures specified in the child support review process authorized by this chapter is to enable the Title IV-D agency to take expedited administrative actions to establish, modify, and enforce child support and medical support obligations, to determine parentage, or to take any other action authorized or required under Part D, Title IV, of the federal Social Security Act (42 U.S.C. Section 651 et seq.), and Chapter 231.

(b) A child support review order issued under this chapter and confirmed by a court constitutes an order of the court and is enforceable by any means available for the enforcement of child support obligations under this code, including withholding income, filing a child support lien, and suspending a license under Chapter 232.

History of Fam §233.001: Acts 1995, 74th Leg., ch. 20, §1, eff. April 20, 1995. Amended by Acts 1995, 74th Leg., ch. 341, §2.04, eff. Sept. 1, 1995. Renumbered from §231.401 and amended by Acts 1997 75th Leg., ch. 911, §80, eff. Sept. 1, 1997. Source: Former Fam §14.802(a).

FAM §233.002. AGREEMENTS ENCOURAGED

To the extent permitted by this chapter, the Title IV-D agency shall encourage agreement of the parties.

History of Fam §233.002: Acts 1995, 74th Leg., ch. 20, §1, eff. April 20, 1995. Amended by Acts 1995, 74th Leg., ch. 341, §2.04, eff. Sept. 1, 1995. Renumbered from §231.402 and amended by Acts 1997, 75th Leg., ch. 911, §80, eff. Sept. 1, 1997. Source: Former Fam §14.802(a).

FAM §233.003. BILINGUAL FORMS REQUIRED

A notice or other form used to implement administrative procedures under this chapter shall be printed in both Spanish and English.

History of Fam §233.003: Acts 1995, 74th Leg., ch. 20, §1, eff. April 20, 1995. Amended by Acts 1995, 74th Leg., ch. 341, §2.04, eff. Sept. 1, 1995. Renumbered from §231.403 and amended by Acts 1997 75th Leg., ch. 911, §80, eff. Sept. 1, 1997. Source: Former Fam §14.802(g).

FAM §233.004. INTERPRETER REQUIRED

If a party participating in an administrative proceeding under this chapter does not speak English or is hearing impaired, the Title IV-D agency shall provide for interpreter services at no charge to the party.

History of Fam §233.004: Acts 1995, 74th Leg., ch. 20, §1, eff. April 20, 1995. Amended by Acts 1995, 74th Leg., ch. 341, §2.04, eff. Sept. 1, 1995. Renumbered from §231.404 and amended by Acts 1997 75th Leg., ch. 911, §80, eff. Sept. 1, 1997. Source: Former Fam §14.802(g).

FAM §233.005. INITIATING ADMINISTRATIVE ACTIONS

An administrative action under this chapter may be initiated by issuing a notice of child support review under Section 233.006 or a notice of proposed child support review order under Section 233.009 or 233.0095 to each party entitled to notice.

History of Fam §233.005: Acts 1995, 74th Leg., ch. 20, §1, eff. April 20, 1995. Amended by Acts 1995, 74th Leg., ch. 341, §2.04, eff. Sept. 1, 1995. Renumbered from §231.405 and amended by Acts 1997 75th Leg., ch. 911, §80, eff. Sept. 1, 1997. Amended by Acts 1999, 76th Leg., ch. 556, §63, eff. Sept. 1, 1999. Source: Former Fam §§14.802(b), 14.803(a).

FAM §233.006. CONTENTS OF NOTICE OF CHILD SUPPORT REVIEW

A *Section 233.006 below is effective for modification or enforcement proceedings commenced on or after Sept. 1, 2001.*

(a) The notice of child support review issued by the Title IV-D agency must:

(1) describe the procedure for a child support review, including the procedures for requesting a negotiation conference;

(2) inform the recipient that the recipient may be represented by legal counsel during the review process or at a court hearing; and

(3) inform the recipient that the recipient may refuse to participate or cease participation in the child support review process, but that the refusal by the recipient to participate will not prevent the completion of the process or the filing of a child support review order.

(b) In addition to the information required by Subsection (a), the notice of child support review may inform the recipient that:

(1) an affidavit of financial resources included with the notice must be executed by the recipient and returned to the Title IV-D agency not later than the 15th day after the date the notice is received or delivered; and

(2) if the requested affidavit of financial resources is not returned as required, the agency may:

(A) proceed with the review using the information that is available to the agency; and

(B) file a legal action without further notice to the recipient, except as otherwise required by law.

History of Fam §233.006: Acts 1995, 74th Leg., ch. 20, §1, eff. April 20, 1995. Amended by Acts 1995, 74th Leg., ch. 341, §2.04, eff. Sept. 1, 1995. Renumbered from §231.406 and amended by Acts 1997 75th Leg., ch. 911, §80, eff. Sept. 1, 1997; Acts 2001, 77th Leg., ch. 1023, §64, eff. Sept. 1, 2001. Source: Former Fam §14.803(b), (c).

FAM §233.006. CONTENTS OF NOTICE OF CHILD SUPPORT REVIEW

Section 233.006 below is effective for modification and enforcement proceedings commenced before Sept. 1, 2001.

(a) The notice of child support review issued by the Title IV-D agency must:

(1) describe the procedure for a child support review, including the procedures for requesting a negotiation conference;

(2) inform the recipient that the recipient may be represented by legal counsel during the review process or at a court hearing;

(3) inform the recipient that the recipient may refuse to participate or cease participation in the child support review process, but that the refusal by the recipient to participate will not prevent the completion of the process or the filing of a child support review order;

(4) include an affidavit of financial resources to be executed by the recipient; and

(5) include a request that the recipient designate, on a form provided by the Title IV-D agency, an address for mailing any subsequent notice to the recipient.

(b) In addition to the information required by Subsection (a), the notice of child support review must inform the recipient that:

(1) the information requested on the form must be returned to the Title IV-D agency not later than the 15th day after the date the notice is received or delivered; and

(2) if the requested information is not returned as required, the agency may:

(A) proceed with the review using the information that is available to the agency; and

(B) file a legal action without further notice to the recipient, except as otherwise required by law.

FAM §233.007. SERVICE OF NOTICE

(a) A notice required in an administrative action under this chapter may be delivered by personal service or first class mail on each party entitled to citation or notice as provided by Chapter 102.

(b) This section does not apply to notice required on filing of a child support review order or to later judicial actions.

History of Fam §233.007: Acts 1995, 74th Leg., ch. 20, §1, eff. April 20, 1995. Amended by Acts 1995, 74th Leg., ch. 341, §2.04, eff. Sept. 1, 1995. Renumbered from §231.407 and amended by Acts 1997 75th Leg., ch. 911, §80, eff. Sept. 1, 1997. Source: Former Fam §14.802(e), (f).

FAM §233.008. ADMINISTRATIVE SUBPOENA IN CHILD SUPPORT REVIEW

In a child support review under this chapter, the Title IV-D agency may issue an administrative subpoena authorized under Chapter 231 to any individual or organization believed to have financial or other information needed to establish, modify, or enforce a support order.

History of Fam §233.008: Acts 1995, 74th Leg., ch. 20, §1, eff. April 20, 1995. Amended by Acts 1995, 74th Leg., ch. 341, §2.04, eff. Sept. 1, 1995. Renumbered from §231.408 and amended by Acts 1997 75th Leg., ch. 911, §80, eff. Sept. 1, 1997. Source: Former Fam §14.802(c).

FAM §233.009. NOTICE OF PROPOSED CHILD SUPPORT REVIEW ORDER; NEGOTIATION CONFERENCE

(a) After an investigation and assessment of financial resources, the Title IV-D agency may serve on the parties a notice of proposed child support review order in enforcing or modifying an existing order.

(b) The notice of proposed child support review order shall state:

(1) the amount of periodic payment of child support due, the amount of any overdue support that is owed as an arrearage as of the date of the notice, and the amounts that are to be paid by the obligor for current support due and in payment on the arrearage owed;

(2) that the person identified in the notice as the party responsible for payment of the support amounts may contest the notice order on the grounds that:

(A) the respondent is not the responsible party;

(B) the dependent child is no longer entitled to child support; or

(C) the amount of monthly support or arrearage is incorrectly stated; and

(3) that, if the person identified in the notice as the party responsible for payment of the support amounts does not contest the notice in writing or request a negotiation conference to discuss the notice not later than the 15th day after the date the notice was delivered, the Title IV-D agency may file a child support review order for child support and for medical support for the child as provided by Chapter 154 according to the information available to the agency.

(c) The Title IV-D agency may schedule a negotiation conference without a request from a party.

(d) The Title IV-D agency shall schedule a negotiation conference on the timely request of a party.

(e) The agency may conduct a negotiation conference, or any part of a negotiation conference, by telephone conference call, by video conference, as well as in person and may adjourn the conference for a reasonable time to permit mediation of issues that cannot be resolved by the parties and the agency.

E *Subsection (f) below is effective for SAPCRs and modification or enforcement proceedings commenced on or after Sept. 1, 2001.*

(f) Notwithstanding any other provision of this chapter, if the parties have agreed to the terms of a proposed child support review order and each party has signed the order, including a waiver of the right to service of process as provided by Section 233.018, the Title IV-D agency may immediately present the order and waiver to the court for confirmation without conducting a negotiation conference or requiring the production of financial information.

History of Fam §233.009: Acts 1995, 74th Leg., ch. 20, §1, eff. April 20, 1995. Amended by Acts 1995, 74th Leg., ch. 341, §2.04, eff. Sept. 1, 1995. Renumbered from §231.409 and amended by Acts 1997 75th Leg., ch. 911, §80, eff. Sept. 1, 1997. Amended by Acts 2001, 77th Leg., ch. 1023, §65, eff. Sept. 1, 2001. Source: Former Fam §14.804(a).

FAM §233.0095. NOTICE OF PROPOSED CHILD SUPPORT REVIEW ORDER IN CASES OF ACKNOWLEDGED PATERNITY

(a) If an individual has signed the acknowledgment of paternity as the father of the child or executed a statement of paternity, the Title IV-D agency may serve on the parties a notice of proposed child support review order.

(b) The notice of proposed child support review order shall state:

(1) the amount of periodic payment of child support due;

(2) that the person identified in the notice as the party responsible for payment of the support amounts may only contest the amount of monthly support; and

(3) that, if the person identified in the notice as the party responsible for payment of the support amounts does not contest the notice in writing or request a negotiation conference to discuss the notice not later than the 15th day after the date the notice was delivered, the Title IV-D agency may file the child support order for child support and for medical support for the child as provided by Chapter 154 according to the information available to the agency.

(c) The Title IV-D agency may schedule a negotiation conference without a request from a party.

(d) The Title IV-D agency shall schedule a negotiation conference on the timely request of a party.

(e) The Title IV-D agency may conduct a negotiation conference, or any part of a negotiation conference, by telephone conference call, by video conference, or in person and may adjourn the conference for a reasonable time to permit mediation of issues that cannot be resolved by the parties and the agency.

E *Subsection (f) below is effective for SAPCRs and modification or enforcement proceedings commenced on or after Sept. 1, 2001.*

(f) Notwithstanding any other provision of this chapter, if paternity has been acknowledged, the parties have agreed to the terms of a proposed child support review order, and each party has signed the order, including a waiver of the right to service of process as provided by Section 233.018, the Title IV-D agency may immediately present the order and waiver to the court for confirmation without conducting a negotiation conference or requiring the production of financial information.

History of Fam §233.0095: Acts 1999, 76th Leg., ch. 556, §64, eff. Sept. 1, 1999. Amended by Acts 2001, 77th Leg., ch. 1023, §66, eff. Sept. 1, 2001.

FAM §233.010. NOTICE OF NEGOTIATION CONFERENCE; FAILURE TO ATTEND CONFERENCE

(a) The Title IV-D agency shall notify all parties entitled to notice of the negotiation conference of the date, time, and place of the conference not later than the 10th day before the date of the conference.

(b) If a party fails to attend the scheduled conference, the agency may proceed with the review and file a child support review order according to the information available to the agency.

History of Fam §233.010: Acts 1995, 74th Leg., ch. 20, §1, eff. April 20, 1995. Amended by Acts 1995, 74th Leg., ch. 341, §2.04, eff. Sept. 1, 1995. Renumbered from §231.410 and amended by Acts 1997 75th Leg., ch. 911, §80, eff. Sept. 1, 1997. Source: Former Fam §14.804(b), (c).

FAM §233.011. RESCHEDULING NEGOTIATION CONFERENCE; NOTICE REQUIRED

(a) The Title IV-D agency may reschedule or adjourn a negotiation conference on the request of any party.

(b) The Title IV-D agency shall give all parties notice of a rescheduled conference not later than the third day before the date of the rescheduled conference.

History of Fam §233.011: Acts 1995, 74th Leg., ch. 20, §1, eff. April 20, 1995. Amended by Acts 1995, 74th Leg., ch. 341, §2.04, eff. Sept. 1, 1995. Renumbered from §231.411 and amended by Acts 1997 75th Leg., ch. 911, §80, eff. Sept. 1, 1997. Source: Former Fam §14.804(d).

FAM §233.012. INFORMATION REQUIRED TO BE PROVIDED AT NEGOTIATION CONFERENCE

At the beginning of the negotiation conference, the child support review officer shall review with the parties participating in the conference information provided in the notice of child support review and inform the parties that:

(1) the purpose of the negotiation conference is to provide an opportunity to reach an agreement on a child support order;

(2) if the parties reach an agreement, the review officer will prepare an agreed review order to be effective immediately on being confirmed by the court, as provided by Section 233.024;

(3) a party does not have to sign a review order prepared by the child support review officer but that the Title IV-D agency may file a review order without the agreement of the parties;

(4) the parties may sign a waiver of the right to service of process;

(5) a party may request a court hearing on a nonagreed order at any time before the 20th day after the date a petition for confirmation of the order is filed; and

(6) a party may file a motion for a new trial at any time before the 30th day after an order is confirmed by the court.

History of Fam §233.012: Acts 1995, 74th Leg., ch. 20, §1, eff. April 20, 1995. Amended by Acts 1995, 74th Leg., ch. 341, §2.04, eff. Sept. 1, 1995. Renumbered from §231.412 and amended by Acts 1997 75th Leg., ch. 911, §80, eff. Sept. 1, 1997. Source: Former Fam §14.804(e).

FAM §233.013. DETERMINING SUPPORT AMOUNT; MODIFICATION

(a) The Title IV-D agency may use any information obtained by the agency from the parties or any other source and shall apply the child support guidelines provided by this code to determine the appropriate amount of child support.

(b) If it has been three years since a child support order was rendered or last modified and the amount of the child support award under the order differs by either 20 percent or $100 from the amount that would be awarded under the child support guidelines, the Title IV-D agency shall file an appropriate child support review order, including an order that has the effect of modifying an existing court or administrative order for child support without the necessity of filing a motion to modify.

History of Fam §233.013: Acts 1995, 74th Leg., ch. 20, §1, eff. April 20, 1995. Amended by Acts 1995, 74th Leg., ch. 341, §2.04, eff. Sept. 1, 1995. Renumbered from §231.413 and amended by Acts 1997 75th Leg., ch. 911, §80, eff. Sept. 1, 1997. Source: Former Fam §14.802(d).

FAM §233.014. RECORD OF PROCEEDINGS

(a) For the purposes of this chapter, documentary evidence relied on by the child support review officer, including an affidavit of a party, together with the child support review order is a sufficient record of the proceedings.

(b) The Title IV-D agency is not required to make any other record or transcript of the negotiation conference.

History of Fam §233.014: Acts 1995, 74th Leg., ch. 20, §1, eff. April 20, 1995. Amended by Acts 1995, 74th Leg., ch. 341, §2.04, eff. Sept. 1, 1995. Renumbered from §231.414 and amended by Acts 1997 75th Leg., ch. 911, §80, eff. Sept. 1, 1997. Source: Former Fam §14.804(f).

FAM §233.015. ISSUANCE OF CHILD SUPPORT REVIEW ORDER OR FINDING THAT NO ORDER SHOULD BE ISSUED; EFFECT

(a) If a negotiation conference does not result in agreement by all parties to the child support review order, the Title IV-D agency shall render a final decision in the form of a child support review order or a determination that the agency should not issue a child support review order not later than the fifth day after the date of the negotiation conference.

(b) If the Title IV-D agency determines that the agency should not issue a child support order, the agency shall immediately provide each party with notice of the determination by personal delivery or by first class mail.

(c) A determination that a child support order should not be issued must include a statement of the reasons that an order is not being issued and a statement that the agency's determination does not affect the right of the Title IV-D agency or a party to request any other remedy provided by law.

History of Fam §233.015: Acts 1995, 74th Leg., ch. 20, §1, eff. April 20, 1995. Amended by Acts 1995, 74th Leg., ch. 341, §2.04, eff. Sept. 1, 1995. Renumbered from §231.415 and amended by Acts 1997 75th Leg., ch. 911, §80, eff. Sept. 1, 1997. Source: Former Fam §14.804(h)-(j).

FAM §233.016. VACATING CHILD SUPPORT REVIEW ORDER

(a) The Title IV-D agency may vacate a child support review order at any time before the order is filed with the court.

(b) A new negotiation conference, with notice to all parties, may be scheduled or the Title IV-D agency may make a determination that a child support review order should not be issued and give notice of that determination as provided by this chapter.

History of Fam §233.016: Acts 1995, 74th Leg., ch. 20, §1, eff. April 20, 1995. Amended by Acts 1995, 74th Leg., ch. 341, §2.04, eff. Sept. 1, 1995. Renumbered from §231.416 and amended by Acts 1997 75th Leg., ch. 911, §80, eff. Sept. 1, 1997. Source: Former Fam §14.804(k).

FAM §233.017. CONTENTS OF CHILD SUPPORT REVIEW ORDER

(a) An order issued under this chapter must be reviewed and signed by an attorney of the Title IV-D agency and must contain all provisions that are appropriate for an order under this title, including current child support, medical support, a determination of any arrearages or retroactive support, and, if not otherwise ordered, income withholding.

(b) A child support review order providing for the enforcement of an order may not contain a provision that imposes incarceration or a fine or contains a finding of contempt.

(c) A child support review order that establishes or modifies an amount of previously ordered support must include the findings required by Section 154.130.

(d) A child support review order that is not agreed to by all the parties may specify and reserve for the court at the confirmation hearing unresolved issues relating to conservatorship or possession of a child.

History of Fam §233.017: Acts 1995, 74th Leg., ch. 20, §1, eff. April 20, 1995. Amended by Acts 1995, 74th Leg., ch. 341, §2.04, eff. Sept. 1, 1995. Renumbered from §231.417 and amended by Acts 1997 75th Leg., ch. 911, §80, eff. Sept. 1, 1997. Source: Former Fam §14.805.

FAM §233.018. ADDITIONAL CONTENTS OF AGREED CHILD SUPPORT REVIEW ORDER

(a) If a negotiation conference results in an agreement of the parties, each party must sign the child support review order and the order must contain as to each party:

(1) a waiver by the party of the right to service of process and a court hearing and the making of a record on the petition for confirmation;

(2) the mailing address of the party; and

A *Subsection (3) below is effective for SAPCRs and modification or enforcement proceedings commenced on or after Sept. 1, 2001.*

(3) the following statement printed on the order in boldfaced type, in capital letters, or underlined:

"I ACKNOWLEDGE THAT I HAVE READ AND UNDERSTAND THIS CHILD SUPPORT REVIEW ORDER. I UNDERSTAND THAT IF I SIGN THIS ORDER, IT WILL BE CONFIRMED BY THE COURT WITHOUT FURTHER NOTICE TO ME. I KNOW THAT I HAVE A RIGHT TO REQUEST THAT A COURT RECONSIDER THE ORDER BY FILING A MOTION FOR A NEW TRIAL AT ANY TIME BEFORE THE 30TH DAY AFTER THE DATE OF THE CONFIRMATION OF THE ORDER BY THE COURT. I KNOW THAT IF I DO NOT OBEY THE TERMS OF THIS ORDER I MAY BE HELD IN CONTEMPT OF COURT."

Subsection (3) below is effective for SAPCRs and modification or enforcement proceedings commenced before Sept. 1, 2001.

(3) the following statement printed on the order in boldfaced type, in capital letters, or underlined:

"I KNOW THAT I DO NOT HAVE TO SIGN THIS CHILD SUPPORT REVIEW ORDER. I UNDERSTAND

THAT IF I SIGN THIS ORDER, IT WILL BE CONFIRMED BY THE COURT WITHOUT FURTHER NOTICE TO ME. I KNOW THAT I HAVE A RIGHT TO REQUEST THAT A COURT RECONSIDER THE ORDER BY FILING A MOTION FOR A NEW TRIAL AT ANY TIME BEFORE THE 30TH DAY AFTER THE DATE OF THE CONFIRMATION OF THE ORDER BY THE COURT. I KNOW THAT IF I DO NOT OBEY THE TERMS OF THIS ORDER I MAY BE HELD IN CONTEMPT OF COURT."

(b) If a negotiation conference results in an agreement on some but not all issues in the case, the parties may sign a waiver of service along with an agreement to appear in court at a specified date and time for a determination by the court of all unresolved issues. Notice of the hearing is not required.

History of Fam §233.018: Acts 1995, 74th Leg., ch. 20, §1, eff. April 20, 1995. Amended by Acts 1995, 74th Leg., ch. 341, §2.04, eff. Sept. 1, 1995. Renumbered from §231.418 and amended by Acts 1997 75th Leg., ch. 911, §80, eff. Sept. 1, 1997. Amended by Acts 1999, 76th Leg., ch. 556, §65, eff. Sept. 1, 1999; Acts 2001, 77th Leg., ch. 1023, §67, eff. Sept. 1, 2001. Source: Former Fam §14.804(g).

FAM §233.019. FILING OF AGREED REVIEW ORDER

(a) The Title IV-D agency shall file an agreed child support review order and a waiver of service signed by the parties with the clerk of the court having continuing jurisdiction of the child who is the subject of the order.

(b) If there is not a court of continuing jurisdiction, the Title IV-D agency shall file the agreed review order with the clerk of a court having jurisdiction under this title.

(c) If applicable, an acknowledgment of paternity or a written report of a parentage testing expert and any documentary evidence relied upon by the agency shall be filed with the agreed review order as an exhibit to the order.

History of Fam §233.019: Acts 1995, 74th Leg., ch. 20, §1, eff. April 20, 1995. Amended by Acts 1995, 74th Leg., ch. 341, §2.04, eff. Sept. 1, 1995. Renumbered from §231.419 and amended by Acts 1997 75th Leg., ch. 911, §80, eff. Sept. 1, 1997. Amended by Acts 1999, 76th Leg., ch. 556, §66, eff. Sept. 1, 1999. Source: Former Fam §14.806(a).

FAM §233.020. CONTENTS OF PETITION FOR CONFIRMATION OF NONAGREED ORDER

(a) A petition for confirmation of a child support review order not agreed to by the parties:

(1) must include the final review order as an attachment to the petition; and

(2) may include a waiver of service executed under Section 233.018(b) and an agreement to appear in court for a hearing.

(b) Documentary evidence relied on by the Title IV-D agency, including, if applicable, an acknowledgment of paternity or a written report of a parentage testing expert, shall be filed with the clerk as exhibits to the petition, but are not required to be served on the parties. The petition must identify the exhibits that are filed with the clerk.

History of Fam §233.020: Acts 1995, 74th Leg., ch. 20, §1, eff. April 20, 1995. Amended by Acts 1995, 74th Leg., ch. 341, §2.04, eff. Sept. 1, 1995. Renumbered from §231.420 and amended by Acts 1997 75th Leg., ch. 911, §80, eff. Sept. 1, 1997. Amended by Acts 1999, 76th Leg., ch. 556, §67, eff. Sept. 1, 1999. Source: Former Fam §14.806(b).

FAM §233.021. DUTIES OF CLERK OF COURT

(a) On the filing of an agreed child support review order or of a petition for confirmation of a nonagreed order issued by the Title IV-D agency, the clerk of court shall endorse on the order or petition the date and time the order or petition is filed.

(b) In an original action, the clerk shall endorse the appropriate court and cause number on the agreed review order or on the petition for confirmation of a nonagreed order.

(c) The clerk shall deliver by personal service a copy of the petition for confirmation of a nonagreed review order and a copy of the order, to each party entitled to service who has not waived service.

(d) A clerk of a district court is entitled to collect in a child support review case the fees authorized in a Title IV-D case by Chapter 231.

History of Fam §233.021: Acts 1995, 74th Leg., ch. 20, §1, eff. April 20, 1995. Amended by Acts 1995, 74th Leg., ch. 341, §2.04, eff. Sept. 1, 1995. Renumbered from §231.421 and amended by Acts 1997 75th Leg., ch. 911, §80, eff. Sept. 1, 1997. Source: Former Fam §14.806(c), (d).

FAM §233.022. FORM TO REQUEST A COURT HEARING ON NONAGREED ORDER

(a) A court shall consider any responsive pleading that is intended as an objection to confirmation of a child support review order not agreed to by the parties, including a general denial, as a request for a court hearing.

(b) The Title IV-D agency shall:

(1) make available to each clerk of court copies of the form to request a court hearing on a nonagreed review order; and

(2) provide the form to request a court hearing to a party to the child support review proceeding on request of the party.

(c) The clerk shall furnish the form to a party to the child support review proceeding on the request of the party.

History of Fam §233.022: Acts 1995, 74th Leg., ch. 20, §1, eff. April 20, 1995. Amended by Acts 1995, 74th Leg., ch. 341, §2.04, eff. Sept. 1, 1995. Renumbered from §231.422 and amended by Acts 1997 75th Leg., ch. 911, §80, eff. Sept. 1, 1997. Source: Former Fam §14.806(e).

FAM §233.023. TIME TO REQUEST A COURT HEARING

A party may file a request for a court hearing not later than the 20th day after the date the petition for confirmation of a nonagreed child support review order is delivered to the party.

History of Fam §233.023: Acts 1995, 74th Leg., ch. 20, §1, eff. April 20, 1995. Amended by Acts 1995, 74th Leg., ch. 341, §2.04, eff. Sept. 1, 1995. Renumbered from §231.423 and amended by Acts 1997 75th Leg., ch. 911, §80, eff. Sept. 1, 1997. Source: Former Fam §14.807(e).

FAM §233.024. CONFIRMATION OF AGREED ORDER

A *Subsection (a) below is effective for SAPCRs and modification or enforcement proceedings commenced on or after Sept. 1, 2001.*

(a) If the court finds that all parties have appropriately agreed to a child support review order and that there is waiver of service, the court shall sign the order not later than the third day after the filing of the order. The court may sign the order before filing the order, but the signed order shall immediately be filed.

Subsection (a) below is effective for SAPCRs and modification or enforcement proceedings commenced before Sept. 1, 2001.

(a) If the court finds that all parties have appropriately agreed to a child support review order and that there is waiver of service, the court shall sign the order not later than the third day after the filing of the order.

(b) On confirmation by the court, the Title IV-D agency shall immediately deliver to each party a copy of the signed agreed review order.

History of Fam §233.024: Acts 1995, 74th Leg., ch. 20, §1, eff. April 20, 1995. Amended by Acts 1995, 74th Leg., ch. 341, §2.04, eff. Sept. 1, 1995. Renumbered from §231.424 and amended by Acts 1997 75th Leg., ch. 911, §80, eff. Sept. 1, 1997; Acts 2001, 77th Leg., ch. 1023, §68, eff. Sept. 1, 2001. Source: Former Fam §14.807(b), (c).

FAM §233.025. EFFECT OF REQUEST FOR HEARING ON NONAGREED ORDER; PLEADING

(a) A request for hearing or an order setting a hearing on confirmation of a nonagreed child support review order stays confirmation of the order pending the hearing.

(b) At a hearing on confirmation, any issues in dispute shall be heard in a trial de novo.

(c) The petition for confirmation and the child support review order constitute a sufficient pleading by the Title IV-D agency for relief on any issue addressed in the petition and order.

(d) The request for hearing may limit the scope of the de novo hearing by specifying the issues that are in dispute.

History of Fam §233.025: Acts 1995, 74th Leg., ch. 20, §1, eff. April 20, 1995. Amended by Acts 1995, 74th Leg., ch. 341, §2.04, eff. Sept. 1, 1995. Renumbered from §231.425 and amended by Acts 1997 75th Leg., ch. 911, §80, eff. Sept. 1, 1997. Source: Former Fam §14.807(d), (f).

FAM §233.026. TIME FOR COURT HEARING

A court shall hold a hearing on the confirmation of a child support review order that has not been agreed to by the parties not later than the 30th day after the date the last party to be served files a timely request for a court hearing.

History of Fam §233.026: Acts 1995, 74th Leg., ch. 20, §1, eff. April 20, 1995. Amended by Acts 1995, 74th Leg., ch. 341, §2.04, eff. Sept. 1, 1995. Renumbered from §231.426 and amended by Acts 1997 75th Leg., ch. 911, §80, eff. Sept. 1, 1997. Source: Former Fam §14.807(g).

FAM §233.027. ORDER AFTER HEARING; EFFECT OF CONFIRMATION ORDER

(a) After the hearing on the confirmation of a nonagreed child support review order, the court shall:

(1) if the court finds that the order should be confirmed, immediately sign a confirmation order and enter the order as an order of the court;

(2) if the court finds that the relief granted in the child support review order is inappropriate, sign an appropriate order at the conclusion of the hearing or as soon after the conclusion of the hearing as is practical and enter the order as an order of the court; or

(3) if the court finds that all relief should be denied, enter an order that denies relief and includes specific findings explaining the reasons that relief is denied.

(b) On the signing of a confirmation order by the judge of the court, the child support review order becomes a final order of the court.

History of Fam §233.027: Acts 1995, 74th Leg., ch. 20, §1, eff. April 20, 1995. Amended by Acts 1995, 74th Leg., ch. 341, §2.04, eff. Sept. 1, 1995. Renumbered from §231.427 and amended by Acts 1997 75th Leg., ch. 911, §80, eff. Sept. 1, 1997. Source: Former Fam §14.807(h), (i).

FAM §233.0271. CONFIRMATION OF NONAGREED ORDER WITHOUT HEARING

(a) If a request for hearing has not been timely received, the court shall confirm and sign a nonagreed child support review order not later than the 30th day after the date the petition for confirmation was delivered to the last party entitled to service.

(b) The Title IV-D agency shall immediately deliver a copy of the confirmed nonagreed review order to each party, together with notice of right to file a motion for a new trial not later than the 30th day after the date the order was confirmed by the court.

History of Fam §233.0271: Acts 1997, 75th Leg., ch. 911, §80, eff. Sept. 1, 1997.

FAM §233.028. SPECIAL CHILD SUPPORT REVIEW PROCEDURES RELATING TO ESTABLISHMENT OF PARENTAGE

(a) If the parentage of a child has not been established, the notice of child support review delivered to the parties must include an allegation that the recipient is a biological parent of the child. The notice shall inform the parties that:

(1) not later than the 15th day after the date of delivery of the notice, the alleged parent of the child shall either sign a statement of paternity or an acknowledgment of paternity or deny in writing that the alleged parent is the biological parent of the child;

(2) either party may request that scientifically accepted parentage testing be conducted to assist in determining the identities of the child's parents;

(3) if the alleged parent timely denies parentage of the child, the Title IV-D agency shall order parentage testing; and

(4) if the alleged parent does not deny parentage of the child, the Title IV-D agency may conduct a negotiation conference.

(b) If all parties agree to the child's parentage, the agency may file an agreed child support review order as provided by this chapter.

(c) If a party denies parentage, the Title IV-D agency shall order parentage testing and give each party notice of the time and place of testing. If either party fails or refuses to participate in administrative parentage testing, the Title IV-D agency may file a child support review order resolving the question of parentage against that party. The court shall confirm the child support review order as a temporary or final order of the court only after an opportunity for parentage testing has been provided.

A *Subsection (d) below is effective for motions or other requests for relief made in parentage or paternity proceedings commenced on or after June 14, 2001.*

(d) If genetic testing identifies the alleged parent as the parent of the child and the results of a verified written report of a genetic testing expert meet the requirements of Chapter 160 for issuing a temporary order, the Title IV-D agency may conduct a negotiation conference to resolve any issues of support and file with the court a child support review order.

Subsection (d) below is effective for motions or other requests for relief made in parentage or paternity proceedings commenced before June 14, 2001.

(d) If parentage testing does not exclude the alleged parent and the results of a verified written report of a parentage testing expert meet the requirements of Chapter 160 for issuing a temporary order, the Title IV-D agency may conduct a negotiation conference to resolve any issues of support and file with the court a child support review order.

(e) If the results of parentage testing exclude an alleged parent from being the biological parent of the child, the Title IV-D agency shall issue and provide to each party a child support review order that declares that the excluded person is not a parent of the child.

(f) Any party may file a petition for confirmation of a child support review order issued under this section.

History of Fam §233.028: Acts 1995, 74th Leg., ch. 20, §1, eff. April 20, 1995. Amended by Acts 1995, 74th Leg., ch. 341, §2.04, eff. Sept. 1, 1995. Renumbered from §231.428 and amended by Acts 1997 75th Leg., ch. 911, §80, eff. Sept. 1, 1997. Amended by Acts 2001, 77th Leg., ch. 821, §2.17, eff. June 14, 2001. Source: Former Fam §14.808.

FAM §233.029. ADMINISTRATIVE PROCEDURE LAW NOT APPLICABLE

The child support review process under this chapter is not governed by Chapter 2001, Government Code.

History of Fam §233.029: Acts 1995, 74th Leg., ch. 20, §1, eff. April 20, 1995. Amended by Acts 1995, 74th Leg., ch. 341, §2.04, eff. Sept. 1, 1995. Renumbered from §231.429 and amended by Acts 1997 75th Leg., ch. 911, §80, eff. Sept. 1, 1997. Source: Former Fam §14.801.

CHAPTER 234. STATE CASE REGISTRY, DISBURSEMENT UNIT, & DIRECTORY OF NEW HIRES

Subchapter A. Unified State Case Registry & Disbursement Unit

SUBCHAPTER A. UNIFIED STATE CASE REGISTRY & DISBURSEMENT UNIT

FAM §234.001. ESTABLISHMENT & OPERATION OF STATE CASE REGISTRY & STATE DISBURSEMENT UNIT

A *Subsection (a) below is effective for SAPCRs and modification or enforcement proceedings commenced on or after Sept. 1, 2001.*

(a) The Title IV-D agency shall establish and operate a state case registry and state disbursement unit meeting the requirements of 42 U.S.C. Sections 654a(e) and 654b and this subchapter.

Subsection (a) below is effective for SAPCRs and modification or enforcement proceedings commenced before Sept. 1, 2001.

(a) The Title IV-D agency shall establish and operate a state case registry and state disbursement unit meeting the requirements of 42 U.S.C. Sections 654a(e) and 654b.

(b) The state case registry shall maintain records of child support orders in Title IV-D cases and in other cases in which a child support order has been established or modified in this state on or after October 1, 1998.

(c) The state disbursement unit shall:

A *Subsections (1) & (2) below are effective for SAPCRs and modification or enforcement proceedings commenced on or after Sept. 1, 2001.*

(1) receive, maintain, and furnish records of child support payments in Title IV-D cases and other cases as authorized by law;

(2) forward child support payments as authorized by law;

Subsections (1) & (2) below are effective for SAPCRs and modification or enforcement proceedings commenced before Sept. 1, 2001.

(1) receive, maintain, and furnish records of child support payments in Title IV-D cases and other cases as required by law;

(2) forward child support payments as required by law;

(3) maintain child support payment records made through the state disbursement unit; and

(4) make available to a local registry each day in a manner determined by the Title IV-D agency with the assistance of the work group established under Section 234.003 the following information:

(A) the cause number of the suit under which withholding is required;

(B) the payor's name and social security number;

(C) the payee's name and, if available, social security number;

(D) the date the disbursement unit received the payment;

(E) the amount of the payment; and

(F) the instrument identification information.

E *Subsection (d) below is effective for SAPCRs and modification or enforcement proceedings commenced on or after Sept. 1, 2001.*

(d) A certified child support payment record produced by the state disbursement unit is admissible as evidence of the truth of the information contained in the record and does not require further authentication or verification.

History of Fam §234.001: Acts 1997, 75th Leg., ch. 911, §94, eff. Sept. 1, 1997. Amended by Acts 1999, 76th Leg., ch. 556, §68, eff. Sept. 1, 1999; Acts 2001, 77th Leg., ch. 1023, §69, eff. Sept. 1, 2001.

FAM §234.002. INTEGRATED SYSTEM FOR CHILD SUPPORT & MEDICAL SUPPORT ENFORCEMENT

The statewide integrated system for child support and medical support enforcement under Chapter 231 shall be part of the state case registry and state disbursement unit authorized by this subchapter.

History of Fam §234.002: Acts 1997, 75th Leg., ch. 911, §94, eff. Sept. 1, 1997. Amended by Acts 1999, 76th Leg., ch. 556, §68, eff. Sept. 1, 1999.

FAM §234.003. EXPIRED

FAM §234.004. CONTRACTS & COOPERATIVE AGREEMENTS

(a) The Title IV-D agency may enter into contracts and cooperative agreements as necessary to establish and operate the state case registry and state disbursement unit authorized under this subchapter.

E *Subsection (b) below is effective for SAPCRs and modification or enforcement proceedings commenced on or after Sept. 1, 2001.*

(b) To the extent funds are available for this purpose, the Title IV-D agency may enter into contracts or cooperative agreements to process through the state disbursement unit child support collections in cases not otherwise eligible under 42 U.S.C. Section 654b.

History of Fam §234.004: Acts 1997, 75th Leg., ch. 911, §94, eff. Sept. 1, 1997. Amended by Acts 2001, 77th Leg., ch. 1023, §70, eff. Sept. 1, 2001.

FAM §234.005. EXPIRED

FAM §234.006. EFFECTIVE DATE & PROCEDURES

A *Section 234.006 below is effective for SAPCRs and modification or enforcement proceedings commenced on or after Sept. 1, 2001.*

The Title IV-D agency, in cooperation with the work group established under Section 234.003, may adopt rules in compliance with federal law for the operation of the state case registry and the state disbursement unit.

History of Fam §234.006: Acts 1999, 76th Leg., ch. 556, §68, eff. Sept. 1, 1999. Amended by Acts 2001, 77th Leg., ch. 1023, §71, eff. Sept. 1, 2001.

FAM §234.006. EFFECTIVE DATE & PROCEDURES

Section 234.006 below is effective for SAPCRs and modification or enforcement proceedings commenced before Sept. 1, 2001.

The Title IV-D agency shall, in cooperation with the work group established under Section 234.003, adopt rules, in compliance with federal law, that establish the definitions for, and the date of and the procedures for:

(1) the operation of the state case registry and the state disbursement unit; and

(2) the return of payments made in error or delivered to the state disbursement unit with insufficient information for disbursement.

FAM §234.007. NOTICE OF PLACE OF PAYMENT

(a) The Title IV-D agency shall notify the courts that the state disbursement unit has been established. After receiving notice of the establishment of the state disbursement unit, a court that orders income to be withheld for child support shall order that all income withheld for child support be paid to the state disbursement unit.

(b) In order to redirect payments from a local registry to the state disbursement unit after the date of the establishment of the state disbursement unit, the Title IV-D agency shall issue a notice of place of payment informing the obligor, obligee, and employer that income withheld for child support is to be paid to the state disbursement unit.

(c) A copy of the notice under Subsection (b) shall be filed with the court of continuing jurisdiction and with the local child support registry.

(d) The notice under Subsection (b) must include:

(1) the name of the child for whom support is ordered and of the person to whom support is ordered by the court to be paid;

(2) the style and cause number of the case in which support is ordered; and

(3) instructions for the payment of ordered support to the state disbursement unit.

(e) On receipt of a copy of the notice under Subsection (b), the clerk of the court shall file the notice in the appropriate case file.

History of Fam §234.007: Acts 1999, 76th Leg., ch. 556, §68, eff. Sept. 1, 1999.

FAM §234.008. DEPOSIT, DISTRIBUTION, & ISSUANCE OF PAYMENTS

(a) Not later than the second business day after the date the state disbursement unit receives a child support payment, the state disbursement unit shall distribute the payment to the Title IV-D agency or the obligee.

(b) The state disbursement unit shall deposit daily all child support payments in a trust fund with the state comptroller. Subject to the agreement of the comptroller, the state disbursement unit may issue checks from the trust fund.

History of Fam §234.008: Acts 1999, 76th Leg., ch. 556, §68, eff. Sept. 1, 1999.

FAM §234.009. OFFICIAL CHILD SUPPORT PAYMENT RECORD

(a) The record of child support payments maintained by a local registry is the official record of a payment received directly by the local registry.

(b) The record of child support payments maintained by the state disbursement unit is the official record of a payment received directly by the unit.

(c) After the date child support payments formerly received by a local registry are redirected to the state disbursement unit, a local registry may accept a record of payments furnished by the state disbursement unit and may add the payments to the record of payments maintained by the local registry so that a complete payment record is available for use by the court.

(d) If the local registry does not add payments received by the state disbursement unit to the record maintained by the registry as provided by Subsection (c), the official record of child support payments consists of the record maintained by the local registry for payments received directly by the registry and the record maintained by the state disbursement unit for payments received directly by the unit.

History of Fam §234.009: Acts 1999, 76th Leg., ch. 556, §68, eff. Sept. 1, 1999.

Ⓐ FAM §234.010. DIRECT DEPOSIT OF CHILD SUPPORT PAYMENTS

(a) The state disbursement unit authorized under this chapter may transmit a child support payment to an obligee by electronic funds transfer if the obligee maintains an account with a financial institution.

(b) The work group convened under this subchapter may develop a plan to assist an obligee who does not have an account with a financial institution to obtain an account.

(c) The work group may determine whether it is feasible and cost-effective for the state to administer an electronic benefits transfer system for child support obligees and may recommend implementation of such a system to the Title IV-D agency.

(d) After receiving any recommendations by the work group under Subsection (c), the Title IV-D agency or the vendor selected by the Title IV-D agency to operate the state disbursement unit may provide for electronic benefits transfer, if the request for proposals issued by the Title IV-D agency and any contract resulting from the selection of a vendor to provide the services specified in the request for proposals provides for electronic benefits transfer.

(e) The work group may recommend and the Title IV-D agency may establish procedures to implement this section.

(f) The Title IV-D agency, after receiving the recommendation of the work group, may require an obligee to receive payments by direct deposit to the obligee's bank account or by electronic benefits transfer to an account established by the Title IV-D agency or the state disbursement unit if the account is established at no cost to the obligee.

History of Fam §234.010: Acts 1999, 76th Leg., ch. 1072, §6, eff. Sept. 1, 1999. Renumbered from §234.006 by Acts 2001, 77th Leg., ch. 1420, §21.001(33), eff. Sept. 1, 2001.

Ⓐ FAM §234.011. USE OF ELECTRONIC BENEFITS TRANSFER FOR CHILD SUPPORT PAYMENTS

The Title IV-D agency, in coordination with the Texas Department of Human Services and the comptroller of public accounts, shall study the use of an existing electronic benefits transfer system to determine the advisability of and method for implementation of a debit card child support system. If it is determined that such a system is feasible and cost-effective, these agencies shall begin implementation of such a system. These agencies must report their findings and progress to the legislature by December 1, 2000.

History of Fam §234.011: Acts 1999, 76th Leg., ch. 1072, §6, eff. Sept. 1, 1999. Renumbered from §234.007 by Acts 2001, 77th Leg., ch. 1420, §21.001(34), eff. Sept. 1, 2001.

Sections 234.012-234.100 reserved for expansion

SUBCHAPTER B. STATE DIRECTORY OF NEW HIRES

FAM §234.101. DEFINITIONS

In this subchapter:

(1) "Employee" means an individual who is an employee within the meaning of Chapter 24 of the Internal Revenue Code of 1986 (26 U.S.C. Section 3401(c)). The term does not include an employee of a state agency performing intelligence or counterintelligence functions if the head of the agency has determined that reporting employee information under this subchapter could endanger the safety of the employee or compromise an ongoing investigation or intelligence activity.

(2) "Employer" has the meaning given that term by Section 3401(d) of the Internal Revenue Code of 1986 (26 U.S.C. Section 3401(d)) and includes a governmental entity and a labor organization, as that term is identified in Section 2(5) of the National Labor Relations Act (29 U.S.C. Section 152(5)), including an entity, also known as a "hiring hall," used by the labor organization and an employer to carry out requirements of an agreement between the organization and an employer described in Section 8(f)(3) of that Act (29 U.S.C. Section 158(f)(3)).

History of Fam §234.101: Acts 1997, 75th Leg., ch. 911, §94, eff. Sept. 1, 1997.

FAM §234.102. OPERATION OF NEW HIRE DIRECTORY

In cooperation with the Texas Workforce Commission, the Title IV-D agency shall develop and operate a state directory to which employers in the state shall report each newly hired or rehired employee in accordance with the requirements of 42 U.S.C. Section 653a.

History of Fam §234.102: Acts 1997, 75th Leg., ch. 911, §94, eff. Sept. 1, 1997. Amended by Acts 1999, 76th Leg., ch. 178, §12, eff. Aug. 30, 1999.

FAM §234.103. CONTRACTS & COOPERATIVE AGREEMENTS

The Title IV-D agency may enter into cooperative agreements and contracts as necessary to create and operate the directory authorized under this subchapter.

History of Fam §234.103: Acts 1997, 75th Leg., ch. 911, §94, eff. Sept. 1, 1997. Amended by Acts 1999, 76th Leg., ch. 178, §13, eff. Aug. 30, 1999.

FAM §234.104. PROCEDURES

The Title IV-D agency by rule shall establish procedures for reporting employee information and for operating a state directory of new hires meeting the requirements of federal law.

History of Fam §234.104: Acts 1997, 75th Leg., ch. 911, §94, eff. Sept. 1, 1997. Amended by Acts 1999, 76th Leg., ch. 178, §14, eff. Aug. 30, 1999.
See also 1 TAC §§55.310-55.308.

CHAPTER 235. SHARING INFORMATION IN STATE CASE REGISTRY

FAM §235.001. REQUEST FOR INFORMATION

(a) The state case registry shall provide information under this chapter on the written request of a custodial parent whose case:

(1) is included in the state case registry established under 42 U.S.C. Section 654a and for whom the Title IV-D agency is not providing enforcement services; or

(2) would otherwise not be required to be included in the state case registry under 42 U.S.C. Section 654a but who has applied for inclusion under Section 235.002.

(b) The state case registry shall provide to a custodial parent under Subsection (a) who makes a request for information or, to the extent provided by federal law, to an attorney, friend of the court, guardian ad litem, or domestic relations office designated by the parent any information in the registry required by 42 U.S.C. Section 654a(e) concerning the parent's case.

(c) To the extent permitted by federal law, the state case registry shall provide the information described by Subsection (b) to a domestic relations office or friend of the court that requests information regarding a case described by Subsection (a).

History of Fam §235.001: Acts 1997, 75th Leg., ch. 420, §26, eff. Sept. 1, 1997. Amended by Acts 1999, 76th Leg., ch. 556, §62 eff. Sept. 1, 1999. Renumbered from §233.001 by Acts 1999, 76th Leg., ch. 62, §§19.01(24), 19.02(4), eff. Sept. 1, 1999.

FAM §235.002. REQUEST TO INCLUDE CASE IN REGISTRY

The case of a custodial parent whose case would otherwise not be included in the state case registry under 42 U.S.C. Section 654a may be included in the state case registry by making a written request to the registry either directly or through an attorney, friend of the court, guardian ad litem, or domestic relations office designated by the custodial parent. The request must be accompanied by a certified copy of the court order requiring the payment of child support.

History of Fam §235.002: Acts 1997, 75th Leg., ch. 420, §26, eff. Sept. 1, 1997. Renumbered from §233.002 by Acts 1999, 76th Leg., ch. 62, §19.01(24), eff. Sept. 1, 1999.

FAM §235.003. APPLICATION FOR SERVICES NOT REQUIRED

The Title IV-D agency may not require an application for services as a condition for:

(1) releasing information under Section 235.001; or

(2) including a case in the state case registry under Section 235.002.

History of Fam §235.003: Acts 1997, 75th Leg., ch. 420, §26, eff. Sept. 1, 1997. Renumbered from §233.003 by Acts 1999, 76th Leg., ch. 62, §§19.01(24), 19.02(5), eff. Sept. 1, 1999. Amended by Acts 1999, 76th Leg., ch. 859, §6 (eff. Sept. 1, 1999), ch. 1191, §3 (eff. June 18, 1999).

FAM §235.004. FEES

(a) The state case registry may charge a fee for:

(1) including in the registry a child support case entered in the registry under Section 235.002; and

(2) providing information concerning a case as authorized by Section 235.001.

(b) The amount of a fee under this section may not exceed the actual costs incurred by the state case registry in providing the services.

History of Fam §235.004: Acts 1997, 75th Leg., ch. 420, §26, eff. Sept. 1, 1997. Renumbered from §233.004 by Acts 1999, 76th Leg., ch. 62, §§19.01(24), 19.02(6), eff. Sept. 1, 1999.

CHAPTER 236. COMPETITIVE BIDDING FOR CHILD SUPPORT COLLECTION SERVICES

FAM §236.001. DEFINITION

In this chapter, "council" means the State Council on Competitive Government.

History of Fam §236.001: Acts 1997, 75th Leg., ch. 420, §27, eff. Sept. 1, 1997. Renumbered from §234.001 by Acts 1999, 76th Leg., ch. 62, §19.01(25), eff. Sept. 1, 1999.

FAM §236.002. POWERS & DUTIES OF COUNCIL

(a) The council shall:

(1) establish an initiative called "Kids Can't Wait" to increase child support enforcement;

(2) identify child support enforcement functions performed by the Title IV-D agency that may be competitively bid;

(3) establish guidelines for referral of child support enforcement cases to a contractor;

(4) after consulting with the Title IV-D agency, make recommendations regarding competitive bidding of child support enforcement functions that are identified under Subdivision (2);

(5) consider the benefits of the state's participation in an electronic parent locator network or a similar national service designed to locate parents who owe child support;

(6) study the feasibility of cost recovery options in child support collection actions for children who do not receive public assistance; and

(7) engage in other activities necessary for the administration of this chapter.

(b) The Title IV-D agency shall coordinate with the council regarding competitive bidding of child support enforcement functions identified under this section.

(c) A member of the council may designate an employee of the state agency represented by the member to perform any of the member's powers or duties under this section.

(d) The Title IV-D agency shall cooperate with the council if requested by the council.

(e) The council and the Title IV-D agency shall report not later than October 1, 1998, to the presiding officer of each house of the legislature the results of the council's efforts under this section.

History of Fam §236.002: Acts 1997, 75th Leg., ch. 420, §27, eff. Sept. 1, 1997. Renumbered from §234.002 by Acts 1999, 76th Leg., ch. 62, §19.01(25), eff. Sept. 1, 1999.

FAM §236.003. CHILD SUPPORT COLLECTION AGREEMENT

The Title IV-D agency or a contractor awarded a contract under this chapter to collect child support may enter into an agreement with a person liable for the payment of child support. The agreement may relate to any matter that may be adjudicated by a court, including:

(1) the determination of paternity;

(2) the determination of the amount of child support due;

(3) the method of making child support payments;

(4) the imposition of income garnishment or withholding;

(5) the payment of fees;

(6) the reimbursement of costs; and

(7) other child support enforcement matters permitted by state or federal law.

History of Fam §236.003: Acts 1997, 75th Leg., ch. 420, §27, eff. Sept. 1, 1997. Renumbered from §234.003 by Acts 1999, 76th Leg., ch. 62, §19.01(25), eff. Sept. 1, 1999.

Chapters 237-260 reserved for expansion

SUBTITLE E. PROTECTION OF THE CHILD

CHAPTER 261. INVESTIGATION OF REPORT OF CHILD ABUSE OR NEGLECT

Subchapter A. General Provisions

Subchapter B. Report of Abuse or Neglect; Immunities

SUBCHAPTER A. GENERAL PROVISIONS

FAM §261.001. DEFINITIONS

In this chapter:

(1) "Abuse" includes the following acts or omissions by a person:

(A) mental or emotional injury to a child that results in an observable and material impairment in the child's growth, development, or psychological functioning;

(B) causing or permitting the child to be in a situation in which the child sustains a mental or emotional injury that results in an observable and material impairment in the child's growth, development, or psychological functioning;

(C) physical injury that results in substantial harm to the child, or the genuine threat of substantial harm from physical injury to the child, including an injury that is at variance with the history or explanation given and excluding an accident or reasonable discipline by a parent, guardian, or managing or possessory conservator that does not expose the child to a substantial risk of harm;

(D) failure to make a reasonable effort to prevent an action by another person that results in physical injury that results in substantial harm to the child;

A (E) sexual conduct harmful to a child's mental, emotional, or physical welfare, including conduct that constitutes the offense of indecency with a child under Section 21.11, Penal Code, sexual assault under Section 22.011, Penal Code, or aggravated sexual assault under Section 22.021, Penal Code;

(F) failure to make a reasonable effort to prevent sexual conduct harmful to a child;

(G) compelling or encouraging the child to engage in sexual conduct as defined by Section 43.01, Penal Code;

(H) causing, permitting, encouraging, engaging in, or allowing the photographing, filming, or depicting of the child if the person knew or should have known that the resulting photograph, film, or depiction of the child is obscene as defined by Section 43.21, Penal Code, or pornographic;

(I) the current use by a person of a controlled substance as defined by Chapter 481, Health and Safety Code, in a manner or to the extent that the use results in physical, mental, or emotional injury to a child;

(J) causing, expressly permitting, or encouraging a child to use a controlled substance as defined by Chapter 481, Health and Safety Code; or

E (K) causing, permitting, encouraging, engaging in, or allowing a sexual performance by a child as defined by Section 43.25, Penal Code.

(2) "Department" means the Department of Protective and Regulatory Services.

(3) "Designated agency" means the agency designated by the court as responsible for the protection of children.

(4) "Neglect" includes:

(A) the leaving of a child in a situation where the child would be exposed to a substantial risk of physical or mental harm, without arranging for necessary care for the child, and the demonstration of an intent not to return by a parent, guardian, or managing or possessory conservator of the child;

(B) the following acts or omissions by a person:

(i) placing a child in or failing to remove a child from a situation that a reasonable person would realize requires judgment or actions beyond the child's level of maturity, physical condition, or mental abilities and that results in bodily injury or a substantial risk of immediate harm to the child;

(ii) failing to seek, obtain, or follow through with medical care for a child, with the failure resulting in or presenting a substantial risk of death, disfigurement, or bodily injury or with the failure resulting in an observable and material impairment to the growth, development, or functioning of the child;

(iii) the failure to provide a child with food, clothing, or shelter necessary to sustain the life or health of the child, excluding failure caused primarily by financial inability unless relief services had been offered and refused; or

(iv) placing a child in or failing to remove the child from a situation in which the child would be exposed to a substantial risk of sexual conduct harmful to the child; or

(C) the failure by the person responsible for a child's care, custody, or welfare to permit the child to return to the child's home without arranging for the necessary care for the child after the child has been absent from the home for any reason, including having been in residential placement or having run away.

(5) "Person responsible for a child's care, custody, or welfare" means a person who traditionally is responsible for a child's care, custody, or welfare, including:

(A) a parent, guardian, managing or possessory conservator, or foster parent of the child;

(B) a member of the child's family or household as defined by Chapter 71;

(C) a person with whom the child's parent cohabits;

(D) school personnel or a volunteer at the child's school; or

(E) personnel or a volunteer at a public or private child-care facility that provides services for the child or at a public or private residential institution or facility where the child resides.

(6) "Report" means a report that alleged or suspected abuse or neglect of a child has occurred or may occur.

(7) "Board" means the Board of Protective and Regulatory Services.

(8) "Born addicted to alcohol or a controlled substance" means a child:

(A) who is born to a mother who during the pregnancy used a controlled substance, as defined by Chapter 481, Health and Safety Code, other than a controlled substance legally obtained by prescription, or alcohol; and

(B) who, after birth as a result of the mother's use of the controlled substance or alcohol:

(i) experiences observable withdrawal from the alcohol or controlled substance;

(ii) exhibits observable or harmful effects in the child's physical appearance or functioning; or

(iii) exhibits the demonstrable presence of alcohol or a controlled substance in the child's bodily fluids.

History of Fam §261.001: Acts 1995, 74th Leg., ch. 20, §1, eff. April 20, 1995. Amended by Acts 1995, 74th Leg., ch. 751, §86, eff. Sept. 1, 1995; Acts 1997, 75th Leg., ch. 575, §10 (eff. Sept. 1, 1997), ch. 1022, §63 (eff. Sept. 1, 1997); Acts 1999, 76th Leg., ch. 62, §19.01(26), eff. Sept. 1, 1999; Acts 2001, 77th Leg., ch. 59, §1, eff. Sept. 1, 2001. Source: Former Fam §34.012.

See also 37 TAC §349.101.

FAM §261.002. CENTRAL REGISTRY

(a) The department shall establish and maintain in Austin a central registry of reported cases of child abuse or neglect.

(b) The department may adopt rules necessary to carry out this section. The rules shall provide for cooperation with local child service agencies, including hospitals, clinics, and schools, and cooperation with other states in exchanging reports to effect a national registration system.

History of Fam §261.002: Acts 1995, 74th Leg., ch. 20, §1, eff. April 20, 1995. Source: Former Fam §34.06.

See also 40 TAC §700.104.

FAM §261.003. APPLICATION TO STUDENTS IN SCHOOL FOR DEAF OR SCHOOL FOR BLIND & VISUALLY IMPAIRED

This chapter applies to the investigation of a report of abuse or neglect of a student, without regard to the age of the student, in the Texas School for the Deaf or the Texas School for the Blind and Visually Impaired.

History of Fam §261.003: Acts 1995, 74th Leg., ch. 20, §1, eff. April 20, 1995. Source: Former Fam §34.013.

FAM §261.004. STATISTICS OF ABUSE & NEGLECT OF CHILDREN

(a) The department shall prepare and disseminate statistics by county relating to the department's activities under this subtitle and include the information specified in Subsection (b) in an annual report available to the public.

(b) The department shall report the following information:

(1) the number of initial phone calls received by the department alleging abuse and neglect;

(2) the number of children reported to the department as having been abused and neglected;

(3) the number of reports received by the department alleging abuse or neglect and assigned by the department for investigation;

(4) of the children to whom Subdivision (2) applies:

(A) the number for whom the report was substantiated;

(B) the number for whom the report was unsubstantiated;

(C) the number for whom the report was determined to be false;

(D) the number who did not receive services from the department under a state or federal program;

(E) the number who received services, including preventative services, from the department under a state or federal program; and

(F) the number who were removed from the child's home during the preceding year;

(5) the number of families in which the child was not removed, but the child or family received services from the department;

(6) the number of children who died during the preceding year as a result of child abuse or neglect;

(7) of the children to whom Subdivision (6) applies, the number who were in foster care at the time of death;

(8) the number of child protective services workers responsible for report intake, assessment, or investigation;

(9) the response time by the department with respect to conducting an initial investigation of a report of child abuse or neglect;

(10) the response time by the department with respect to commencing services to families and children for whom an allegation of abuse or neglect has been made;

(11) the number of children who were returned to their families or who received family preservation services and who, before the fifth anniversary of the date of return or receipt, were the victims of substantiated reports of child abuse or neglect, including abuse or neglect resulting in the death of the child;

(12) the number of cases pursued by the department in each stage of the judicial process, including civil and criminal proceedings and the results of each proceeding; and

(13) the number of children for whom a person was appointed by the court to represent the best interests of the child and the average number of out-of-court contacts between the person and the child.

(c) The department shall compile the information specified in Subsection (b) for the preceding year in a report to be submitted to the legislature and the general public not later than February 1 of each year.

History of Fam §261.004: Acts 1997, 75th Leg., ch. 1022, §64, eff. Sept. 1, 1997.

Sections 261.005-261.100 reserved for expansion

SUBCHAPTER B. REPORT OF ABUSE OR NEGLECT; IMMUNITIES

FAM §261.101. PERSONS REQUIRED TO REPORT; TIME TO REPORT

(a) A person having cause to believe that a child's physical or mental health or welfare has been adversely affected by abuse or neglect by any person shall immediately make a report as provided by this subchapter.

A (b) If a professional has cause to believe that a child has been abused or neglected or may be abused or neglected, or that a child is a victim of an offense under Section 21.11, Penal Code, and the professional has cause to believe that the child has been abused as defined by Section 261.001, the professional shall make a report not later than the 48th hour after the hour the professional first suspects that the child has been or may be abused or neglected or is a victim of an offense under Section 21.11, Penal Code. A professional may not delegate to or rely on another person to make the report. In this subsection, "professional" means an individual who is licensed or certified by the state or who is an employee of a facility licensed, certified, or operated by the state and who, in the normal course of official duties or duties for which a license or certification is required, has direct contact with children. The term includes teachers, nurses, doctors, day-care employees, employees of a clinic or health care facility that provides reproductive services, juvenile probation officers, and juvenile detention or correctional officers.

(c) The requirement to report under this section applies without exception to an individual whose personal communications may otherwise be privileged, including an attorney, a member of the clergy, a medical practitioner, a social worker, a mental health professional, and an employee of a clinic or health care facility that provides reproductive services.

(d) Unless waived in writing by the person making the report, the identity of an individual making a report under this chapter is confidential and may be disclosed only:

(1) as provided by Section 261.201; or

(2) to a law enforcement officer for the purposes of conducting a criminal investigation of the report.

History of Fam §261.101: Acts 1995, 74th Leg., ch. 20, §1, eff. April 20, 1995. Amended by Acts 1995, 74th Leg., ch. 751, §87, eff. Sept. 1, 1995; Acts 1997, 75th Leg., ch. 162, §1 (eff. Sept. 1, 1997), ch. 575, §11 (eff. Sept. 1, 1997), ch. 1022, §65 (eff. Sept. 1, 1997); Acts 1999, 76th Leg., ch. 1390, §21 (eff. Sept. 1, 1999), ch. 1150, §2 (eff. Sept. 1, 1999), ch. 62, §6.29 (eff. Sept. 1, 1999); Acts 2001, 77th Leg., ch. 1420, §5.003, eff. Sept. 1, 2001. Source: Former Fam §§34.01, 34.02(d).

See also 19 TAC §61.1051 (teachers), 40 TAC §700.501 (others).

Marshall v. First Baptist Ch., 949 S.W.2d 504, 508 (Tex.App.—Houston [14th Dist.] 1997, no writ.). "The statute only creates a duty to report the abuse or neglect of a *child*. Thus, [appellee]'s duty to report the molestation of [victim] no longer existed as of the day he turned eighteen...."

FAM §261.102. MATTERS TO BE REPORTED

A report should reflect the reporter's belief that a child has been or may be abused or neglected or has died of abuse or neglect.

History of Fam §261.102: Acts 1995, 74th Leg., ch. 20, §1, eff. April 20, 1995. Amended by Acts 1995, 74th Leg., ch. 751, §88, eff. Sept. 1, 1995. Source: Former Fam §34.02(a).

FAM §261.103. REPORT MADE TO APPROPRIATE AGENCY

Ⓐ *Subsection (a) below is effective for criminal conduct that occurs on or after Sept. 1, 2001.*

(a) Except as provided by Subsection (b) and Section 261.405, a report shall be made to:

Subsection (a) below is effective for criminal conduct in which any element of the conduct occurred before Sept. 1, 2001.

(a) Except as provided by Subsection (b), a report shall be made to:

(1) any local or state law enforcement agency;

(2) the department if the alleged or suspected abuse involves a person responsible for the care, custody, or welfare of the child;

(3) the state agency that operates, licenses, certifies, or registers the facility in which the alleged abuse or neglect occurred; or

(4) the agency designated by the court to be responsible for the protection of children.

(b) A report may be made to the Texas Youth Commission instead of the entities listed under Subsection (a) if the report is based on information provided by a child while under the supervision of the commission concerning the child's alleged abuse of another child.

History of Fam §261.103: Acts 1995, 74th Leg., ch. 20, §1, eff. April 20, 1995. Amended by Acts 1995, 74th Leg., ch. 751, §89, eff. Sept. 1, 1995; Acts 1999, 76th Leg., ch. 1477, §24, eff. Sept. 1, 1999; Acts 2001, 77th Leg., ch. 1297, §46, eff. Sept. 1, 2001. Source: Former Fam §34.02(a).

FAM §261.104. CONTENTS OF REPORT

The person making a report shall identify, if known:

(1) the name and address of the child;

(2) the name and address of the person responsible for the care, custody, or welfare of the child; and

(3) any other pertinent information concerning the alleged or suspected abuse or neglect.

History of Fam §261.104: Acts 1995, 74th Leg., ch. 20, §1, eff. April 20, 1995. Amended by Acts 1995, 74th Leg., ch. 751, §90, eff. Sept. 1, 1995. Source: Former Fam §34.02(b).

Dominguez v. Kelly, 786 S.W.2d 749, 752 (Tex. App.—El Paso 1990, writ denied). Plaintiff abuser "contends the reports were not entitled to immunity as the written report did not conform to the explicit form requirement of §34.02 [now §261.104], namely there is no name and address of the child or the person responsible for the child. He also contends there is no stated designation that the written report is the required follow-up report. Imprecise compliance with form requirements, per se, will not vitiate an immunity provision. There was substantial compliance in this case."

FAM §261.105. REFERRAL OF REPORT BY DEPARTMENT OR LAW ENFORCEMENT

(a) All reports received by a local or state law enforcement agency that allege abuse or neglect by a person responsible for a child's care, custody, or welfare shall be referred immediately to the department or the designated agency.

(b) The department or designated agency shall immediately notify the appropriate state or local law enforcement agency of any report it receives, other than a report from a law enforcement agency, that concerns the suspected abuse or neglect of a child or death of a child from abuse or neglect.

(c) In addition to notifying a law enforcement agency, if the report relates to a child in a facility operated, licensed, certified, or registered by a state agency, the department shall refer the report to the agency for investigation.

(d) If the department initiates an investigation and determines that the abuse or neglect does not involve a person responsible for the child's care, custody, or welfare, the department shall refer the report to a law enforcement agency for further investigation.

(e) In cooperation with the department, the Texas Youth Commission by rule shall adopt guidelines for identifying a report made to the commission under Section 261.103(b) that is appropriate to refer to the department or a law enforcement agency for investigation. Guidelines adopted under this subsection must require the commission to consider the severity and immediacy of the alleged abuse or neglect of the child victim.

History of Fam §261.105: Acts 1995, 74th Leg., ch. 20, §1, eff. April 20, 1995. Amended by Acts 1997, 75th Leg., ch. 1022, §66, eff. Sept. 1, 1997; Acts 1999, 76th Leg., ch. 1477, §25, eff. Sept. 1, 1999. Source: Former Fam §34.02(c).

See also 40 TAC §700.506.

FAM §261.1055. NOTIFICATION OF DISTRICT ATTORNEYS

(a) A district attorney may inform the department or designated agency that the district attorney wishes to receive notification of some or all reports of suspected abuse or neglect of children who were in the county at the time the report was made or who were in the county at the time of the alleged abuse or neglect.

(b) If the district attorney makes the notification under this section, the department or designated agency shall, on receipt of a report of suspected abuse or neglect, immediately notify the district attorney as requested and the department or designated agency shall forward a copy of the reports to the district attorney on request.

History of Fam §261.1055: Acts 1997, 75th Leg., ch. 1022, §67, eff. Sept. 1, 1997.

FAM §261.106. IMMUNITIES

(a) A person acting in good faith who reports or assists in the investigation of a report of alleged child abuse or neglect or who testifies or otherwise participates in a judicial proceeding arising from a report, petition, or investigation of alleged child abuse or neglect is immune from civil or criminal liability that might otherwise be incurred or imposed.

(b) Immunity from civil and criminal liability extends to an authorized volunteer of the department or a law enforcement officer who participates at the request of the department in an investigation of alleged or suspected abuse or neglect or in an action arising from an investigation if the person was acting in good faith and in the scope of the person's responsibilities.

(c) A person who reports the person's own abuse or neglect of a child or who acts in bad faith or with malicious purpose in reporting alleged child abuse or neglect is not immune from civil or criminal liability.

History of Fam §261.106: Acts 1995, 74th Leg., ch. 20, §1, eff. April 20, 1995. Amended by Acts 1995, 74th Leg., ch. 751, §91, eff. Sept. 1, 1995. Source: Former Fam §34.03.

Rodriguez v. State, 47 S.W.3d 86, 89 (Tex. App.—Houston [14th Dist.] 2001, pet. ref'd). "To be entitled to immunity, one must have assisted in the investigation of the report in good faith."

Walker v. Pollock, 981 S.W.2d 226, 227 (Tex. App.—Houston [1st Dist.] 1998, no pet.). Defendant "'otherwise participated' in this judicial proceeding by examining [child] pursuant to a court order and reporting to the court. [Defendant] was, therefore, entitled to immunity."

Laub v. Pesikoff, 979 S.W.2d 686, 690 n.2 (Tex. App.—Houston [1st Dist.] 1998, pet. denied). Spouse "argues that the existence of §261.106 of the Family Code and §571.019 of the Health and Safety Code provides evidence that the judicial communication privilege is not absolute. However, we find that the qualified privileges addressed in those statutes serve different purposes from those of the judicial communications privilege, and, thus, do not act to modify the common law."

Blum v. Julian, 977 S.W.2d 819, 822 (Tex.App.—Fort Worth 1998, no pet.). Plaintiff "asserts various causes of action that are all related to [defendant]'s investigation, diagnosis, and report of alleged child sexual abuse concerning [plaintiff]'s daughters and stepdaughters. Although [plaintiff] categorizes his claims in terms of conspiracy and intentional malfeasance, this is exactly the type of suit the Family Code immunity provisions are designed to prevent. ... Thus, [defendant] is entitled to immunity unless she acted in bad faith or with malice."

Gonzalez v. Avalos, 866 S.W.2d 346, 351 (Tex. App.—El Paso 1993), *writ dism'd*, 907 S.W.2d 443 (Tex.1995). Defendant "claims that as a person who investigates and determines the validity of child abuse allegations generally, he is absolutely immune. Of course, the language of the statute grants immunity to a person who assists in the investigation, not in investigations generally. [Defendant] by deciding to close the ... case without investigation was not 'a person ... assisting in the investigation of a report.' Because of that fact, we conclude that [defendant] cannot claim immunity under §34.03 [now §261.106]."

Dominguez v. Kelly, 786 S.W.2d 749, 752-53 (Tex. App.—El Paso 1990, writ denied). "If a person has probable cause to believe an act of child abuse has occurred, his reporting of that belief pursuant to the guidelines set forth in Chapter 34 [now Chapter 261] would entitle him to immunity, regardless of whether he was actuated by any malice. In this case, the doctor reported certain bruises were made by large hands on the thighs, 'presumably pulling them apart to sexually abuse her.' Section 34.02 [now §261.102] calls for nonaccusatory reports. The purpose of the reporting is to foster protection for abused children and not to cause penalty to others. The type of accusation impliedly condemned by the language of §34.02 concerns the expression of which person may have committed the act of abuse. The expression of the belief and facts underlying that belief that a type of abuse had been committed does not violate the intent of the reporting statutes. It merely enhances the probability of proper investigation for and the ascertainment of abuse by the authorities."

Austin v. Hale, 711 S.W.2d 64, 67-68 (Tex.App.—Waco 1986, no writ). "Although there are some mandatory provisions in §34.05 [now §261.301 et seq.] which indicate that the investigation may involve some ministerial acts, the section is not completely mandatory. For instance, §34.05(b)(7) specifies that, in addition to the information listed in (1) through (6), the department shall determine 'all other pertinent data.' Thus, the person or persons conducting the investigation have the freedom to conduct each investigation in an individual way and to determine, using their own discretion, what other information they may need to acquire before deciding what action should be taken. In §34.05(c) [now §261.302], the legislature also provided that an investigator has discretion in choosing where and when to interview and examine the child that is the subject of the report. Furthermore, the legislature provided in that section that the investigator, in his discretion, 'may' want to interview the child's parents or have a psychological or psychiatric examination of all of the children in the home. Additionally, §34.05(d) outlines a procedure whereby the investigator 'may' remove the child from the home even before he completes the investigation. This subsection, more than any other subsection within §34.05, indicates that the investigation under §34.05 is not merely a ministerial act being performed by an employee who is in a quasi-judicial position. Rather, the investigator may exercise his discretion as an integral part of the investigation before deciding what action should be taken. Therefore, the evidence conclusively established that [defendants] occupied quasi-judicial positions as employees of DHR and that they were acting within their authority and were performing quasi-judicial acts when they conducted the investigation of the report that [child] had been abused."

FAM §261.107. FALSE REPORT; PENALTY

(a) A person commits an offense if the person knowingly or intentionally makes a report as provided in this chapter that the person knows is false or lacks factual foundation. An offense under this section is a Class A misdemeanor unless it is shown on the trial of the offense that the person has previously been convicted under this section, in which case the offense is a state jail felony.

(b) A finding by a court in a suit affecting the parent-child relationship that a report made under this chapter before or during the suit was false or lacking factual foundation may be grounds for the court to modify an order providing for possession of or access to the child who was the subject of the report by restricting further access to the child by the person who made the report.

(c) The appropriate county prosecuting attorney shall be responsible for the prosecution of an offense under this section.

History of Fam §261.107: Acts 1995, 74th Leg., ch. 20, §1, eff. April 20, 1995. Amended by Acts 1995, 74th Leg., ch. 751, §92, eff. Sept. 1, 1995; Acts 1997, 75th Leg., ch. 1022, §68 (eff. Sept. 1, 1997), ch. 575, §2 (eff. Sept. 1, 1997); Acts 1999, 76th Leg., ch. 62, §6.30, eff. Sept. 1, 1999. Source: Former Fam §34.031.

FAM §261.108. FRIVOLOUS CLAIMS AGAINST PERSON REPORTING

(a) In this section:

(1) "Claim" means an action or claim by a party, including a plaintiff, counterclaimant, cross-claimant, or third-party plaintiff, requesting recovery of damages.

(2) "Defendant" means a party against whom a claim is made.

(b) A court shall award a defendant reasonable attorney's fees and other expenses related to the defense of a claim filed against the defendant for damages or other relief arising from reporting or assisting in the investigation of a report under this chapter or participating in a judicial proceeding resulting from the report if:

(1) the court finds that the claim is frivolous, unreasonable, or without foundation because the defendant is immune from liability under Section 261.106; and

(2) the claim is dismissed or judgment is rendered for the defendant.

(c) To recover under this section, the defendant must, at any time after the filing of a claim, file a written motion stating that:

(1) the claim is frivolous, unreasonable, or without foundation because the defendant is immune from liability under Section 261.106; and

(2) the defendant requests the court to award reasonable attorney's fees and other expenses related to the defense of the claim.

History of Fam §261.108: Acts 1995, 74th Leg., ch. 20, §1, eff. April 20, 1995. Source: Former Fam §34.032.

FAM §261.109. FAILURE TO REPORT; PENALTY

(a) A person commits an offense if the person has cause to believe that a child's physical or mental health or welfare has been or may be adversely affected by abuse or neglect and knowingly fails to report as provided in this chapter.

(b) An offense under this section is a Class B misdemeanor.

History of Fam §261.109: Acts 1995, 74th Leg., ch. 20, §1, eff. April 20, 1995. Source: Former Fam §34.07.

Perry v. S.N., 973 S.W.2d 301, 309 (Tex.1998). "Because a decision to impose negligence per se could not be limited to cases charging serious misconduct ..., but rather would impose immense potential liability under an ill-defined standard on a broad class of individuals whose relationship to the abuse was extremely indirect, we hold that it is not appropriate to adopt ... §261.109(a) as establishing a duty and standard of conduct in tort. Therefore, [parents] may not maintain a claim for negligence per se or gross negligence based on defendants' violation of the child abuse reporting statute."

Morris v. State, 833 S.W.2d 624, 629 (Tex.App.—Houston [14th Dist.] 1992, writ refused). Defendant "was charged under §34.07 [now §261.109], which makes it a misdemeanor offense for failing to report child abuse. Since it was unnecessary for the state to allege in the information the ... agencies [listed in §261.103] to which a person may report, the trial court did not err in denying appellant's request to include those agencies in the application paragraph of the jury charge."

FAM §261.110. EMPLOYER RETALIATION PROHIBITED

E *Section 261.110 below is effective for reports of child abuse or neglect made on or after Sept. 1, 2001.*

(a) In this section, "professional" has the meaning assigned by Section 261.101(b).

(b) An employer may not suspend or terminate the employment of, or otherwise discriminate against, a person who is a professional and who in good faith:

(1) reports child abuse or neglect to:

(A) the person's supervisor;

(B) an administrator of the facility where the person is employed;

(C) a state regulatory agency; or

(D) a law enforcement agency; or

(2) initiates or cooperates with an investigation or proceeding by a governmental entity relating to an allegation of child abuse or neglect.

(c) A person whose employment is suspended or terminated or who is otherwise discriminated against in violation of this section may sue for injunctive relief, damages, or both.

(d) A plaintiff who prevails in a suit under this section may recover:

(1) actual damages, including damages for mental anguish even if an injury other than mental anguish is not shown;

(2) exemplary damages under Chapter 41, Civil Practice and Remedies Code, if the employer is a private employer;

(3) court costs; and

(4) reasonable attorney's fees.

(e) In addition to amounts recovered under Subsection (d), a plaintiff who prevails in a suit under this section is entitled to:

(1) reinstatement to the person's former position or a position that is comparable in terms of compensation, benefits, and other conditions of employment;

(2) reinstatement of any fringe benefits and seniority rights lost because of the suspension, termination, or discrimination; and

(3) compensation for wages lost during the period of suspension or termination.

(f) A public employee who alleges a violation of this section may sue the employing state or local governmental entity for the relief provided for by this section. Sovereign immunity is waived and abolished to the extent of liability created by this section. A person having a claim under this section may sue a governmental unit for damages allowed by this section.

(g) In a suit under this section against an employing state or local governmental entity, a plaintiff may not recover compensatory damages for future pecuniary losses, emotional pain, suffering, inconvenience, mental anguish, loss of enjoyment of life, and other nonpecuniary losses in an amount that exceeds:

(1) $50,000, if the employing state or local governmental entity has fewer than 101 employees in each of 20 or more calendar weeks in the calendar year in which the suit is filed or in the preceding year;

(2) $100,000, if the employing state or local governmental entity has more than 100 and fewer than 201 employees in each of 20 or more calendar weeks in the calendar year in which the suit is filed or in the preceding year;

(3) $200,000, if the employing state or local governmental entity has more than 200 and fewer than 501 employees in each of 20 or more calendar weeks in the calendar year in which the suit is filed or in the preceding year; and

(4) $250,000, if the employing state or local governmental entity has more than 500 employees in each of 20 or more calendar weeks in the calendar year in which the suit is filed or in the preceding year.

(h) If more than one subdivision of Subsection (g) applies to an employing state or local governmental entity, the amount of monetary damages that may be recovered from the entity in a suit brought under this section is governed by the applicable provision that provides the highest damage award.

(i) A plaintiff suing under this section has the burden of proof, except that there is a rebuttable presumption that the plaintiff's employment was suspended or terminated or that the plaintiff was otherwise discriminated against for reporting abuse or neglect if the suspension, termination, or discrimination occurs before the 61st day after the date on which the person made a report in good faith.

(j) A suit under this section may be brought in a district or county court of the county in which:

(1) the plaintiff was employed by the defendant; or

(2) the defendant conducts business.

(k) It is an affirmative defense to a suit under Subsection (b) that an employer would have taken the action against the employee that forms the basis of the suit based solely on information, observation, or evidence that is not related to the fact that the employee reported child abuse or neglect or initiated or cooperated with an investigation or proceeding relating to an allegation of child abuse or neglect.

(*l*) A public employee who has a cause of action under Chapter 554, Government Code, based on conduct described by Subsection (b) may not bring an action based on that conduct under this section.

(m) This section does not apply to a person who reports the person's own abuse or neglect of a child or who initiates or cooperates with an investigation or proceeding by a governmental entity relating to an allegation of the person's own abuse or neglect of a child.

History of Fam §261.110: Enacted by Acts 2001, 77th Leg., ch. 896, §1, eff. Sept. 1, 2001.

Sections 261.111-261.200 reserved for expansion

SUBCHAPTER C. CONFIDENTIALITY & PRIVILEGED COMMUNICATION

FAM §261.201. CONFIDENTIALITY & DISCLOSURE OF INFORMATION

(a) The following information is confidential, is not subject to public release under Chapter 552, Government Code, and may be disclosed only for purposes consistent with this code and applicable federal or state law or under rules adopted by an investigating agency:

(1) a report of alleged or suspected abuse or neglect made under this chapter and the identity of the person making the report; and

(2) except as otherwise provided in this section, the files, reports, records, communications, audiotapes, videotapes, and working papers used or developed in an investigation under this chapter or in providing services as a result of an investigation.

(b) A court may order the disclosure of information that is confidential under this section if:

(1) a motion has been filed with the court requesting the release of the information;

(2) a notice of hearing has been served on the investigating agency and all other interested parties; and

(3) after hearing and an in camera review of the requested information, the court determines that the disclosure of the requested information is:

(A) essential to the administration of justice; and

(B) not likely to endanger the life or safety of:

(i) a child who is the subject of the report of alleged or suspected abuse or neglect;

(ii) a person who makes a report of alleged or suspected abuse or neglect; or

(iii) any other person who participates in an investigation of reported abuse or neglect or who provides care for the child.

(c) In addition to Subsection (b), a court, on its own motion, may order disclosure of information that is confidential under this section if:

(1) the order is rendered at a hearing for which all parties have been given notice;

(2) the court finds that disclosure of the information is:

(A) essential to the administration of justice; and

(B) not likely to endanger the life or safety of:

(i) a child who is the subject of the report of alleged or suspected abuse or neglect;

(ii) a person who makes a report of alleged or suspected abuse or neglect; or

(iii) any other person who participates in an investigation of reported abuse or neglect or who provides care for the child; and

(3) the order is reduced to writing or made on the record in open court.

(d) The adoptive parents of a child who was the subject of an investigation and an adult who was the subject of an investigation as a child are entitled to examine and make copies of any report, record, working paper, or other information in the possession, custody, or control of the state that pertains to the history of the child. The department may edit the documents to protect the identity of the biological parents and any other person whose identity is confidential.

(e) Before placing a child who was the subject of an investigation, the department shall notify the prospective adoptive parents of their right to examine any report, record, working paper, or other information in the possession, custody, or control of the state that pertains to the history of the child.

(f) The department shall provide prospective adoptive parents an opportunity to examine information under this section as early as practicable before placing a child.

(g) Notwithstanding Subsection (b), the department, on request and subject to department rule, shall provide to the parent, managing conservator, or other legal representative of a child who is the subject of reported abuse or neglect information concerning the reported abuse or neglect that would otherwise be confidential under this section if the department has edited the information to protect the confidentiality of the identity of the person who made the report and any other person whose life or safety may be endangered by the disclosure.

(h) This section does not apply to an investigation of child abuse or neglect in a home or facility regulated under Chapter 42, Human Resources Code.

History of Fam §261.201: Acts 1995, 74th Leg., ch. 20, §1, eff. April 20, 1995. Amended by Acts 1995, 74th Leg., ch. 751, §93, eff. Sept. 1, 1995; Acts 1997, 75th Leg., ch. 575, §12 (eff. Sept. 1, 1997), ch. 1022, §69 (eff. Sept. 1, 1997); Acts 1999, 76th Leg., ch. 1390, §22 (eff. Sept. 1, 1999), ch. 1150, §3 (eff. Sept. 1, 1999). Source: Former Fam §34.08.

See also 40 TAC §§700.203-700.206.

Texas DHS v. Benson, 893 S.W.2d 236, 241 (Tex. App.—Austin 1995, writ denied). The DHS's "refusal to protect the confidentiality of professionals and collateral sources who are not the first to report abuse contravenes the mandate of … §34.08 [now §261.201] that reports be held confidential and 'be disclosed only for purposes consistent with the purpose of this code *under regulations adopted by the investigating agency*.' *At 242:* [T]he trial court properly declared that confidentiality is central to the Family Code provisions governing the reporting of child abuse. Those provisions reflect a legislative determination that granting immunity and confidentiality to complainants will encourage the reporting of child abuse. … The Department must protect all individuals who report child abuse, without distinction between professionals and nonprofessionals and without limitation to who calls first."

Coachman v. State, 692 S.W.2d 940, 945 (Tex. App.—Houston [1st Dist.] 1985, writ refused). Under §34.08, now §261.201, "all reports, records, and working papers used or developed in an investigation of child abuse are confidential and may be disclosed only for purposes consistent with the intent of the Texas Family Code. In the absence of a showing of necessity, the confidential nature of child abuse case reports should be maintained."

FAM §261.202. PRIVILEGED COMMUNICATION

In a proceeding regarding the abuse or neglect of a child, evidence may not be excluded on the ground of privileged communication except in the case of communications between an attorney and client.

History of Fam §261.202: Acts 1995, 74th Leg., ch. 20, §1, eff. April 20, 1995. Source: Former Fam §34.04.

Texas DHS v. Benson, 893 S.W.2d 236, 242 n.7 (Tex.App.—Austin 1995, writ denied). "The only privileged communications recognized by the Family Code provisions governing child abuse are confidential communications between attorney and client."

Sections 261.203-261.300 reserved for expansion

SUBCHAPTER D. INVESTIGATIONS

FAM §261.301. INVESTIGATION OF REPORT

(a) With assistance from the appropriate state or local law enforcement agency, the department or designated agency shall make a prompt and thorough investigation of a report of child abuse or neglect allegedly committed by a person responsible for a child's care, custody, or welfare. The investigation shall be conducted without regard to any pending suit affecting the parent-child relationship.

(b) A state agency shall investigate a report that alleges abuse or neglect occurred in a facility operated, licensed, certified, or registered by that agency as provided by Subchapter E. In conducting an investigation for a facility operated, licensed, certified, registered, or listed by the department, the department shall perform the investigation as provided by:

(1) Subchapter E; and

(2) the Human Resources Code.

(c) The department is not required to investigate a report that alleges child abuse or neglect by a person other than a person responsible for a child's care, custody, or welfare. The appropriate state or local law enforcement agency shall investigate that report if the agency determines an investigation should be conducted.

(d) The department may by rule assign priorities and prescribe investigative procedures for investigations based on the severity and immediacy of the alleged harm to the child.

The primary purpose of the investigation shall be the protection of the child.

(e) As necessary to provide for the protection of the child, the department or designated agency shall determine:

(1) the nature, extent, and cause of the abuse or neglect;

(2) the identity of the person responsible for the abuse or neglect;

(3) the names and conditions of the other children in the home;

(4) an evaluation of the parents or persons responsible for the care of the child;

(5) the adequacy of the home environment;

(6) the relationship of the child to the persons responsible for the care, custody, or welfare of the child; and

(7) all other pertinent data.

(f) An investigation of a report to the department of serious physical or sexual abuse of a child shall be conducted jointly by an investigator from the appropriate local law enforcement agency and the department or agency responsible for conducting an investigation under Subchapter E.

(g) The inability or unwillingness of a local law enforcement agency to conduct a joint investigation under Subsection (f) does not constitute grounds to prevent or prohibit the department from performing its duties under this subtitle. The department shall document any instance in which a law enforcement agency is unable or unwilling to conduct a joint investigation under Subsection (f).

History of Fam §261.301: Acts 1995, 74th Leg., ch. 20, §1, eff. April 20, 1995. Amended by Acts 1995, 74th Leg., ch. 751, §94 (eff. Sept. 1, 1995), ch. 943, §2 (eff. Sept. 1, 1995); Acts 1997, 75th Leg., ch. 1022, §70 (eff. Sept. 1, 1997), ch. 1137, §1 (eff. Sept. 1, 1997); Acts 1999, 76th Leg., ch. 1390, §23 (eff. Sept. 1, 1999), ch. 1150, §4 (eff. Sept. 1, 1999). Source: Former Fam §34.05(a), (b).

See also 40 TAC §§700.501-700.523.

Gonzalez v. Avalos, 866 S.W.2d 346, 350 (Tex. App.—El Paso 1993), *writ dism'd*, 907 S.W.2d 443 (Tex.1995). On the question of official immunity for a [DHS] investigator, plaintiff contends "that [DHS investigator] did not act within the scope of his discretionary authority because he had no discretion under ... §34.05(a) [now §261.301] to decide whether or not to investigate [witness's] allegations of abuse. We agree. ... It is obvious from a reading of the statute that the legislature chose the uses of the mandatory 'shall' and the discretionary 'may' very carefully. We hold that those provisions that use 'shall' in relation to investigations and by their wording leave the employee no choice are mandatory. The provision requiring DHS to make a thorough investigation leaves no room for an employee to decide that no investigation is necessary when child abuse has been reported. Thus, [DHS investigator's] decision not to investigate was not within the scope of his authority and discretion. On the other hand, those provisions of §34.05 that use 'may' or clearly give the employee some choice in how much investigation is necessary and what action is to be taken after completion of the investigation are discretionary."

FAM §261.3015. FLEXIBLE RESPONSE SYSTEM

(a) In assigning priorities and prescribing investigative procedures based on the severity and immediacy of the alleged harm to a child under Section 261.301(d), the board by rule shall establish a flexible response system to allow the department to allocate resources by investigating serious cases of abuse and neglect and providing assessment and family preservation services in less serious cases.

(b) The classification under the flexible response system of a case may be changed as warranted by the circumstances.

(c) The department may implement the flexible response system by establishing a pilot program in a single department service region. The department shall study the results of the system in the region in determining the method by which to implement the system statewide.

History of Fam §261.3015: Acts 1997, 75th Leg., ch. 1022, §71, eff. Sept. 1, 1997.

FAM §261.3019. EXPIRED

FAM §261.302. CONDUCT OF INVESTIGATION

(a) The investigation may include:

(1) a visit to the child's home, unless the alleged abuse or neglect can be confirmed or clearly ruled out without a home visit; and

(2) an interview with and examination of the subject child, which may include a medical, psychological, or psychiatric examination.

(b) The interview with and examination of the child may:

(1) be conducted at any reasonable time and place, including the child's home or the child's school;

(2) include the presence of persons the department or designated agency determines are necessary; and

(3) include transporting the child for purposes relating to the interview or investigation.

(c) The investigation may include an interview with the child's parents and an interview with and medical, psychological, or psychiatric examination of any child in the home.

(d) If, before an investigation is completed, the investigating agency believes that the immediate removal of a child from the child's home is necessary to protect the child from further abuse or neglect, the investigating agency shall file a petition or take other action under Chapter 262 to provide for the temporary care and protection of the child.

(e) An interview with a child alleged to be a victim of physical abuse or sexual abuse shall be audiotaped or videotaped unless the investigating agency determines that good cause exists for not audiotaping or videotaping the interview in accordance with rules of the agency. Good cause may include, but is not limited to, such considerations as the age of the child and the nature and seriousness of the allegations under investigation. Nothing in this subsection shall be construed as prohibiting the investigating agency from audiotaping or videotaping an interview of a child on any case for which such audiotaping or videotaping is not required under this subsection. The fact that the investigating agency failed to audiotape or videotape an interview is admissible at the trial of the offense that is the subject of the interview.

History of Fam §261.302: Acts 1995, 74th Leg., ch. 20, §1, eff. April 20, 1995. Amended by Acts 1995, 74th Leg., ch. 751, §95, eff. Sept. 1, 1995; Acts 1997, 75th Leg., ch. 575, §§13, 14 (eff. Sept. 1, 1997), ch. 1022, §73 (eff. Sept. 1, 1997). Source: Former Fam §34.05(c), (d).

See also 40 TAC §§700.507, 700.508, 700.522.

FAM §261.303. INTERFERENCE WITH INVESTIGATION; COURT ORDER

(a) A person may not interfere with an investigation of a report of child abuse or neglect conducted by the department or designated agency.

(b) If admission to the home, school, or any place where the child may be cannot be obtained, then for good cause shown the court having family law jurisdiction shall order the parent, the person responsible for the care of the children, or the person in charge of any place where the child may be to allow entrance for the interview, examination, and investigation.

(c) If a parent or person responsible for the child's care does not consent to release of the child's prior medical, psychological, or psychiatric records or to a medical, psychological, or psychiatric examination of the child that is requested by the department or designated agency, the court having family law jurisdiction shall, for good cause shown, order the records to be released or the examination to be made at the times and places designated by the court.

(d) A person, including a medical facility, that makes a report under Subchapter B shall release to the department or designated agency, as part of the required report under Section 261.103, records that directly relate to the suspected abuse or neglect without requiring parental consent or a court order.

History of Fam §261.303: Acts 1995, 74th Leg., ch. 20, §1, eff. April 20, 1995. Amended by Acts 1995, 74th Leg., ch. 751, §96, eff. Sept. 1, 1995; Acts 1999, 76th Leg., ch. 1390, §24 (eff. Sept. 1, 1999), ch. 1150, §5 (eff. Sept. 1, 1999). Source: Former Fam §34.05(c).

FAM §261.304. INVESTIGATION OF ANONYMOUS REPORT

(a) If the department receives an anonymous report of child abuse or neglect by a person responsible for a child's care, custody, or welfare, the department shall conduct a preliminary investigation to determine whether there is any evidence to corroborate the report.

(b) An investigation under this section may include a visit to the child's home and an interview with and examination of the child and an interview with the child's parents. In addition, the department may interview any other person the department believes may have relevant information.

(c) Unless the department determines that there is some evidence to corroborate the report of abuse, the department may not conduct the thorough investigation required by this chapter or take any action against the person accused of abuse.

History of Fam §261.304: Acts 1995, 74th Leg., ch. 20, §1, eff. April 20, 1995. Source: Former Fam §34.053.

FAM §261.305. ACCESS TO MENTAL HEALTH RECORDS

(a) An investigation may include an inquiry into the possibility that a parent or a person responsible for the care of a child who is the subject of a report under Subchapter B has a history of medical or mental illness.

(b) If the parent or person does not consent to an examination or allow the department or designated agency to have access to medical or mental health records requested by the department or agency, the court having family law jurisdiction, for good cause shown, shall order the examination to be made or that the department or agency be permitted to have access to the records under terms and conditions prescribed by the court.

(c) If the court determines that the parent or person is indigent, the court shall appoint an attorney to represent the parent or person at the hearing. The fees for the appointed attorney shall be paid as provided by Chapter 107.

(d) A parent or person responsible for the child's care is entitled to notice and a hearing when the department or designated agency seeks a court order to allow a medical, psychological, or psychiatric examination or access to medical or mental health records.

(e) This access does not constitute a waiver of confidentiality.

History of Fam §261.305: Acts 1995, 74th Leg., ch. 20, §1, eff. April 20, 1995. Amended by Acts 1997, 75th Leg., ch. 575, §15, eff. Sept. 1, 1997; Acts 1999, 76th Leg., ch. 1390, §25 (eff. Sept. 1, 1999), ch. 1150, §6 (eff. Sept. 1, 1999). Source: Former Fam §34.05(c).

See also 40 TAC §700.509.

FAM §261.306. REMOVAL OF CHILD FROM STATE

(a) If the department or designated agency has reason to believe that a person responsible for the care, custody, or welfare of the child may remove the child from the state before the investigation is completed, the department or designated agency may file an application for a temporary restraining order in a district court without regard to continuing jurisdiction of the child as provided in Chapter 155.

(b) The court may render a temporary restraining order prohibiting the person from removing the child from the state pending completion of the investigation if the court:

(1) finds that the department or designated agency has probable cause to conduct the investigation; and

(2) has reason to believe that the person may remove the child from the state.

History of Fam §261.306: Acts 1995, 74th Leg., ch. 20, §1, eff. April 20, 1995. Source: Former Fam §34.05(g).

FAM §261.307. INFORMATION RELATING TO INVESTIGATION PROCEDURE

As soon as possible after initiating an investigation of a parent or other person having legal custody of a child, the department shall provide to the person a brief and easily understood summary of:

(1) the department's procedures for conducting an investigation of alleged child abuse or neglect, including:

(A) a description of the circumstances under which the department would request to remove the child from the home through the judicial system; and

(B) an explanation that the law requires the department to refer all reports of alleged child abuse or neglect to a law enforcement agency for a separate determination of whether a criminal violation occurred;

(2) the person's right to file a complaint with the department or to request a review of the findings made by the department in the investigation;

(3) the person's right to review all records of the investigation unless the review would jeopardize an ongoing criminal investigation;

(4) the person's right to seek legal counsel;

(5) references to the statutory and regulatory provisions governing child abuse and neglect and how the person may obtain copies of those provisions; and

(6) the process the person may use to acquire access to the child if the child is removed from the home.

History of Fam §261.307: Acts 1995, 74th Leg., ch. 20, §1, eff. April 20, 1995. Source: Former Fam §34.051.

FAM §261.308. SUBMISSION OF INVESTIGATION REPORT

(a) The department or designated agency shall make a complete written report of the investigation.

(b) If sufficient grounds for filing a suit exist, the department or designated agency shall submit the report, together with recommendations, to the court, the district attorney, and the appropriate law enforcement agency.

(c) On receipt of the report and recommendations, the court may direct the department or designated agency to file a petition requesting appropriate relief as provided in this title.

History of Fam §261.308: Acts 1995, 74th Leg., ch. 20, §1, eff. April 20, 1995. Amended by Acts 1995, 74th Leg., ch. 751, §97, eff. Sept. 1, 1995. Source: Former Fam §34.05(e), (f).

FAM §261.309. REVIEW OF DEPARTMENT INVESTIGATIONS

(a) The department shall by rule establish policies and procedures to resolve complaints relating to and conduct reviews of child abuse or neglect investigations conducted by the department.

(b) If a person under investigation for allegedly abusing or neglecting a child requests clarification of the status of the person's case or files a complaint relating to the conduct of the department's staff or to department policy, the department shall conduct an informal review to clarify the person's status or resolve the complaint. The immediate supervisor of the employee who conducted the child abuse or neglect investigation or against whom the complaint was filed shall conduct the informal review as soon as possible but not later than the 14th day after the date the request or complaint is received.

(c) If, after the department's investigation, the person who is alleged to have abused or neglected a child disputes the department's determination of whether child abuse or neglect occurred, the person may request an administrative review of the findings. A department employee in administration who was not involved in or did not directly supervise the investigation shall conduct the review. The review must sustain, alter, or reverse the department's original findings in the investigation.

(d) Unless a civil or criminal court proceeding or an ongoing criminal investigation relating to the alleged abuse or neglect investigated by the department is pending, the department employee shall conduct the review prescribed by Subsection (c) as soon as possible but not later than the 45th day after the date the department receives the request. If a civil or criminal court proceeding or an ongoing criminal investigation is pending, the department may postpone the review until the court proceeding is completed.

(e) A person is not required to exhaust the remedies provided by this section before pursuing a judicial remedy provided by law.

(f) This section does not provide for a review of an order rendered by a court.

History of Fam §261.309: Acts 1995, 74th Leg., ch. 20, §1, eff. April 20, 1995. Source: Former Fam §34.052.

FAM §261.310. INVESTIGATION STANDARDS

(a) The department shall by rule develop and adopt voluntary standards for persons who investigate suspected child abuse or neglect at the state or local level. The standards shall encourage professionalism and consistency in the investigation of suspected child abuse or neglect.

(b) The standards must provide for a minimum number of hours of annual professional training for interviewers and investigators of suspected child abuse or neglect.

(c) The professional training curriculum developed under this section shall include information concerning:

(1) physical abuse and neglect, including distinguishing physical abuse from ordinary childhood injuries;

(2) psychological abuse and neglect;

(3) available treatment resources; and

(4) the incidence and types of reports of child abuse and neglect that are received by the investigating agencies, including information concerning false reports.

(d) The standards shall recommend:

(1) that videotaped and audiotaped interviews with a suspected victim be uninterrupted;

(2) a maximum number of interviews with and examinations of a suspected victim;

(3) procedures to preserve evidence, including the original notes, videotapes, and audiotapes; and

(4) that an investigator of suspected child abuse or neglect make a reasonable effort to locate and inform each parent of a child of any report of abuse or neglect relating to the child.

History of Fam §261.310: Acts 1995, 74th Leg., ch. 20, §1, eff. April 20, 1995. Source: Former Fam §34.054.

See also 40 TAC §700.519.

FAM §261.311. NOTICE OF REPORT

(a) When during an investigation of a report of suspected child abuse or neglect a representative of the department or the designated agency conducts an interview with or an examination of a child, the department or designated agency shall make a reasonable effort before 24 hours after the time of the interview or examination to notify each parent of the child and the child's legal guardian, if one has been appointed, of the nature of the allegation and of the fact that the interview or examination was conducted.

(b) If a report of suspected child abuse or neglect is administratively closed by the department or designated agency as a result of a preliminary investigation that did not include an interview or examination of the child, the department or designated agency shall make a reasonable effort before the expiration of 24 hours after the time the investigation is closed to notify each parent and legal guardian of the child of the disposition of the investigation.

(c) The notice required by Subsection (a) or (b) is not required if the department or agency determines that the notice is likely to endanger the safety of the child who is the subject of the report, the person who made the report, or any other person who participates in the investigation of the report.

(d) The notice required by Subsection (a) or (b) may be delayed at the request of a law enforcement agency if notification during the required time would interfere with an ongoing criminal investigation.

History of Fam §261.311: Acts 1995, 74th Leg., ch. 20, §1, eff. April 20, 1995. Amended by Acts 1997, 75th Leg., ch. 1022, §74, eff. Sept. 1, 1997. Source: Former Fam §34.055.

FAM §261.312. REVIEW TEAMS; OFFENSE

(a) The department shall establish review teams to evaluate department casework and decision-making related to investigations by the department of child abuse or neglect. The department may create one or more review teams for each region of the department for child protective services. A review team is a citizen review panel or a similar entity for the purposes of federal law relating to a state's child protection standards.

(b) A review team consists of five members who serve staggered two-year terms. Review team members are appointed by the director of the department and consist of community representatives and private citizens who live in the region for which the team is established. Each member must be a parent who has not been convicted of or indicted for an offense involving child abuse or neglect, has not been determined by the department to have engaged in child abuse or neglect, or is not under investigation by the department for child abuse or neglect. A member of a review team is a department volunteer for the purposes of Section 411.114, Government Code.

(c) A review team conducting a review of an investigation may conduct the review by examining the facts of the case as outlined by the department caseworker and law enforcement personnel. A review team member acting in the member's official capacity may receive information made confidential under Section 40.005, Human Resources Code, or Section 261.201.

(d) A review team shall report to the department the results of the team's review of an investigation. The review team's report may not include confidential information. The findings contained in a review team's report are subject to disclosure under Chapter 552, Government Code. This section does not require a law enforcement agency to divulge information to a review team that the agency believes would compromise an ongoing criminal case, investigation, or proceeding.

(e) A member of a review team commits an offense if the member discloses confidential information. An offense under this subsection is a Class C misdemeanor.

History of Fam §261.312: Acts 1995, 74th Leg., ch. 943, §3, eff. Sept. 1, 1995. Amended by Acts 1997, 75th Leg., ch. 575, §16, eff. Sept. 1, 1997.

FAM §261.3125. INVESTIGATIONS COORDINATOR

(a) The department shall employ in each region of the department for child protective services at least one child protective services investigations coordinator. The job responsibilities of the investigations coordinator must focus only on child abuse and neglect investigation issues, including reports of child abuse required by Section 261.101, to achieve a greater compliance with that section, and on assessing and improving the effectiveness of the department in providing for the protection of children in the region.

(b) The duties of a child protective services investigations coordinator must include the duty to:

(1) conduct staff reviews and evaluations of cases determined to involve a high risk to the health or safety of a child, including cases of abuse reported under Section 261.101;

(2) monitor cases in which there have been multiple referrals to the department of child abuse or neglect involving the same family, child, or person alleged to have committed the abuse or neglect; and

(3) approve decisions and assessments related to investigations of cases of child abuse or neglect that involve a high risk to the health or safety of a child.

History of Fam §261.3125: Acts 1999, 76th Leg., ch. 1490, §1, eff. Sept. 1, 1999.

Section 261.313 reserved for expansion

FAM §261.314. TESTING

(a) The department shall provide testing as necessary for the welfare of a child who the department believes, after an investigation under this chapter, has been sexually abused, including human immunodeficiency virus (HIV) testing of a child who was abused in a manner by which HIV may be transmitted.

(b) Except as provided by Subsection (c), the results of a test under this section are confidential.

(c) If requested, the department shall report the results of a test under this section to:

(1) a court having jurisdiction of a proceeding involving the child or a proceeding involving a person suspected of abusing the child;

(2) a person responsible for the care and custody of the child as a foster parent; and

(3) a person seeking to adopt the child.

History of Fam §261.314: Acts 1995, 74th Leg., ch. 943, §7, eff. Sept. 1, 1995.

FAM §261.315. REMOVAL OF CERTAIN INVESTIGATION INFORMATION FROM RECORDS

(a) At the conclusion of an investigation in which the department determines that the person alleged to have abused or neglected a child did not commit abuse or neglect, the department shall notify the person of the person's right to request the department to remove information about the person's alleged role in the abuse or neglect report from the department's records.

(b) On request under Subsection (a) by a person whom the department has determined did not commit abuse or neglect, the department shall remove information from the department's records concerning the person's alleged role in the abuse or neglect report.

(c) The board shall adopt rules necessary to administer this section.

History of Fam §261.315: Acts 1997, 75th Leg., ch. 1022, §75, eff. Sept. 1, 1997.
See also 40 TAC §700.523.

FAM §261.316. EXEMPTION FROM FEES FOR MEDICAL RECORDS

The department is exempt from the payment of a fee otherwise required or authorized by law to obtain a medical record from a hospital or health care provider if the request for a record is made in the course of an investigation by the department.

History of Fam §261.316: Acts 1997, 75th Leg., ch. 575, §17, eff. Sept. 1, 1997. Renumbered from 261.315 by Acts 1999, 76th Leg., ch. 62, §19.01(27), eff. Sept. 1, 1999.

Sections 261.317-261.400 reserved for expansion

Ⓐ SUBCHAPTER E. INVESTIGATIONS OF ABUSE, NEGLECT, OR EXPLOITATION IN CERTAIN FACILITIES

FAM §261.401. AGENCY INVESTIGATION

Ⓔ (a) Notwithstanding Section 261.001, in this section:

(1) "Abuse" means an intentional, knowing, or reckless act or omission by an employee, volunteer, or other individual working under the auspices of a facility that causes or may cause emotional harm or physical injury to, or the death of, a child served by the facility as further described by rule or policy.

(2) "Exploitation" means the illegal or improper use of a child or of the resources of a child for monetary or personal benefit, profit, or gain by an employee, volunteer, or other individual working under the auspices of a facility as further described by rule or policy.

(3) "Neglect" means a negligent act or omission by an employee, volunteer, or other individual working under the auspices of a facility, including failure to comply with an individual treatment plan, plan of care, or individualized service plan, that causes or may cause substantial emotional harm or physical injury to, or the death of, a child served by the facility as further described by rule or policy.

Ⓐ (b) A state agency that operates, licenses, certifies, or registers a facility in which children are located shall make a prompt, thorough investigation of a report that a child has been or may be abused, neglected, or exploited in the facility. The primary purpose of the investigation shall be the protection of the child.

Ⓐ (c) A state agency shall adopt rules relating to the investigation and resolution of reports received as provided by this subchapter. The Health and Human Services Commission shall review and approve the rules of agencies other than the Texas Department of Criminal Justice, Texas Youth Commission, or Texas Juvenile Probation Commission to ensure that those agencies implement appropriate standards for the conduct of investigations and that uniformity exists among agencies in the investigation and resolution of reports.

Ⓔ (d) The Texas School for the Blind and Visually Impaired and the Texas School for the Deaf shall adopt policies relating to the investigation and resolution of reports received as provided by this subchapter. The Health and Human Services Commission shall review and approve the policies to ensure that the Texas School for the Blind and Visually Impaired and the Texas School for the Deaf adopt those policies in a manner consistent with the minimum standards adopted by the Health and Human Services Commission under Section 261.407.

History of Fam §261.401: Acts 1995, 74th Leg., ch. 20, §1, eff. April 20, 1995. Amended by Acts 1995, 74th Leg., ch. 751, §98, eff. Sept. 1, 1995; Acts 2001, 77th Leg., ch. 355, §2, eff. Sept. 1, 2001. Source: Former Fam §34.22.
See also 25 TAC §§1.201-1.207.

Ⓐ FAM §261.402. INVESTIGATIVE REPORTS

(a) A state agency shall prepare and keep on file a complete written report of each investigation conducted by the agency under this subchapter.

(b) A state agency shall immediately notify the appropriate state or local law enforcement agency of any report the agency receives, other than a report from a law enforcement agency, that concerns the suspected abuse, neglect, or exploitation of a child or the death of a child from abuse or neglect. If the state agency finds evidence indicating that a child may have been abused, neglected, or exploited, the agency shall report the evidence to the appropriate law enforcement agency.

(c) A state agency that licenses, certifies, or registers a facility in which children are located shall compile, maintain, and make available statistics on the incidence of child abuse, neglect, and exploitation in the facility.

(d) A state agency shall compile, maintain, and make available statistics on the incidence of child abuse, neglect, and exploitation in a facility operated by the state agency.

History of Fam §261.402: Acts 1995, 74th Leg., ch. 20, §1, eff. April 20, 1995. Amended by Acts 1995, 74th Leg., ch. 751, §99, eff. Sept. 1, 1995; Acts 2001, 77th Leg., ch. 355, §3, eff. Sept. 1, 2001. Source: Former Fam §34.23.

FAM §261.403. COMPLAINTS

(a) If a state agency receives a complaint relating to an investigation conducted by the agency concerning a facility operated by that agency in which children are located, the agency shall refer the complaint to the agency's board.

Ⓐ (b) The board of a state agency that operates a facility in which children are located shall ensure that the procedure for investigating abuse, neglect, and exploitation allegations and inquiries in the agency's facility is periodically reviewed under the agency's internal audit program required by Chapter 2102, Government Code.

History of Fam §261.403: Acts 1995, 74th Leg., ch. 20, §1, eff. April 20, 1995. Amended by Acts 2001, 77th Leg., ch. 355, §4, eff. Sept. 1, 2001. Source: Former Fam §34.24.

FAM §261.404. INVESTIGATIONS IN FACILITIES UNDER DEPARTMENT OF MENTAL HEALTH & MENTAL RETARDATION

(a) The department shall investigate a report of abuse, neglect, or exploitation of a child receiving services:

(1) in a facility operated by the Texas Department of Mental Health and Mental Retardation;

(2) in or from a community center, a local mental health authority, or a local mental retardation authority; or

(3) through a program providing services to that child by contract with a facility operated by the Texas Department of Mental Health and Mental Retardation, a community center, a local mental health authority, or a local mental retardation authority.

(b) The department shall investigate the report under rules developed jointly between the department and the Texas Department of Mental Health and Mental Retardation.

(c) The definitions of "abuse" and "neglect" prescribed by Section 261.001 do not apply to an investigation under this section.

(d) In this section, "community center," "local mental health authority," and "local mental retardation authority" have the meanings assigned by Section 531.002, Health and Safety Code.

History of Fam §261.404: Acts 1995, 74th Leg., ch. 751, §100, eff. Sept. 1, 1995. Amended by Acts 1999, 76th Leg., ch. 907, §39, eff. Sept. 1, 1999.

See also 25 TAC §§404.41-404.55.

FAM §261.405. INVESTIGATIONS IN JUVENILE JUSTICE PROGRAMS & FACILITIES

Ⓐ *Section 261.405 below is effective for criminal conduct that occurs on or after Sept. 1, 2001.*

(a) In this section:

(1) "Juvenile justice facility" means a facility operated wholly or partly by the juvenile board or by a private vendor under a contract with the juvenile board or county that serves juveniles under juvenile court jurisdiction. The term includes:

(A) a public or private juvenile pre-adjudication secure detention facility, including a holdover facility;

(B) a public or private juvenile post-adjudication secure correctional facility except for a facility operated solely for children committed to the Texas Youth Commission; and

(C) a public or private non-secure juvenile post-adjudication residential treatment facility that is not licensed by the Department of Protective and Regulatory Services or the Texas Commission on Alcohol and Drug Abuse.

(2) "Juvenile justice program" means a program operated wholly or partly by the juvenile board or by a private vendor under a contract with a juvenile board that serves juveniles under juvenile court jurisdiction. The term includes:

(A) a juvenile justice alternative education program; and

(B) a non-residential program that serves juvenile offenders under the jurisdiction of the juvenile court.

(b) A report of alleged abuse or neglect in any juvenile justice program or facility shall be made to the Texas Juvenile Probation Commission and a local law enforcement agency for investigation.

(c) The Texas Juvenile Probation Commission shall conduct an investigation as provided by this chapter if the commission receives a report of alleged abuse or neglect in any juvenile justice program or facility.

(d) In an investigation required under this section, the investigating agency shall have access to medical and mental health records as provided by Subchapter D.

History of Fam §261.405: Acts 1995, 74th Leg., ch. 751, §100, eff. Sept. 1, 1995. Amended by Acts 1997, 75th Leg., ch. 162, §2 (eff. Sept. 1, 1997), ch. 1374, §8 (eff. Sept. 1, 1997); Acts 1999, 76th Leg., ch. 1390, §26 (eff. Sept. 1, 1999), ch. 1477, §26 (eff. Sept. 1, 1999), ch. 1150, §7 (eff. Sept. 1, 1999); Acts 2001, 77th Leg., ch. 1297, §47, eff. Sept. 1, 2001.

See also 37 TAC, ch. 349.

FAM §261.405. INVESTIGATIONS IN JUVENILE JUSTICE PROGRAMS & FACILITIES

Section 261.405 below is effective for criminal conduct in which any element of the conduct occurred before Sept. 1, 2001.

(a) A report of alleged abuse or neglect in a public or private juvenile pre-adjudication secure detention facility, including hold-over facilities, or public or private juvenile post-adjudication secure correctional facility, except for a facility operated solely for children committed to the Texas Youth Commission, shall be made to a local law enforcement agency for investigation. The local law enforcement agency shall immediately notify the Texas Juvenile Probation Commission of any report the agency receives.

(b) The Texas Juvenile Probation Commission shall conduct an investigation as provided by this chapter if the commission receives a report of alleged abuse or neglect in any program, including a juvenile justice alternative education program, operated wholly or partly by:

(1) a local juvenile probation department; or

(2) a private vendor operating under the authority of a county juvenile board in accordance with the standards adopted by the commission.

(c) In an investigation required under this section, the investigating agency shall have access to medical and mental health records as provided by Subchapter D.

FAM §261.406. INVESTIGATIONS IN SCHOOLS

(a) On receipt of a report of alleged or suspected abuse or neglect of a child in a public or private school under the jurisdiction of the Texas Education Agency, the department shall perform an investigation as provided by this chapter.

(b) The department shall send a written report of the department's investigation, as appropriate, to the Texas Education Agency, the agency responsible for teacher certification, the local school board or the school's governing body, and the school principal or director, unless the principal or director is alleged to have committed the abuse or neglect, for appropriate action. On request, the department shall provide a copy of the report of investigation to the parent, managing conservator, or legal guardian of a child who is the subject of the investigation and to the person alleged to have committed the abuse or neglect. The report of investigation shall be edited to protect the identity of the persons who made the report of abuse or neglect. Section 261.201(b) applies to the release of confidential information relating to the investigation of a report of abuse or neglect under this section and to the identity of the person who made the report of abuse or neglect.

(c) Nothing in this section may prevent a law enforcement agency from conducting an investigation of a report made under this section.

(d) The Board of Protective and Regulatory Services shall adopt rules necessary to implement this section.

History of Fam §261.406: Acts 1995, 74th Leg., ch. 751, §100, eff. Sept. 1, 1995. Amended by Acts 1997, 75th Leg., ch. 575, §18, eff. Sept. 1, 1997; Acts 1999, 76th Leg., ch. 1150, §8 (eff. Sept. 1, 1999), ch. 1390, §27 (eff. Sept. 1, 1999).

See also 40 TAC §§700.401-700.413.

E FAM §261.407. MINIMUM STANDARDS

(a) The Health and Human Services Commission by rule shall adopt minimum standards for the investigation under Section 261.401 of suspected child abuse, neglect, or exploitation in a facility.

(b) A rule or policy adopted by a state agency or institution under Section 261.401 must be consistent with the minimum standards adopted by the Health and Human Services Commission.

(c) This section does not apply to a facility under the jurisdiction of the Texas Department of Criminal Justice, Texas Youth Commission, or Texas Juvenile Probation Commission.

History of Fam §261.407: Enacted by Acts 2001, 77th Leg., ch. 355, §5, eff. Sept. 1, 2001.

E FAM §261.408. INFORMATION COLLECTION

(a) The Health and Human Services Commission by rule shall adopt uniform procedures for collecting information under Section 261.401, including procedures for collecting information on deaths that occur in facilities.

(b) The department shall receive and compile information on investigations in facilities. An agency submitting information to the department is responsible for ensuring the timeliness, accuracy, completeness, and retention of the agency's reports.

(c) This section does not apply to a facility under the jurisdiction of the Texas Department of Criminal Justice, Texas Youth Commission, or Texas Juvenile Probation Commission.

History of Fam §261.408: Enacted by Acts 2001, 77th Leg., ch. 355, §5, eff. Sept. 1, 2001.

E

FAM §261.409. INVESTIGATIONS IN FACILITIES UNDER TEXAS YOUTH COMMISSION JURISDICTION

The board of the Texas Youth Commission by rule shall adopt standards for:

(1) the investigation under Section 261.401 of suspected child abuse, neglect, or exploitation in a facility under the jurisdiction of the Texas Youth Commission; and

(2) compiling information on those investigations.

History of Fam §261.409: Enacted by Acts 2001, 77th Leg., ch. 355, §6, eff. Sept. 1, 2001.

CHAPTER 262. PROCEDURES IN SUIT BY GOVERNMENTAL ENTITY TO PROTECT HEALTH & SAFETY OF CHILD

SUBCHAPTER A. GENERAL PROVISIONS

FAM §262.001. AUTHORIZED ACTIONS BY GOVERNMENTAL ENTITY

(a) A governmental entity with an interest in the child may file a suit affecting the parent-child relationship requesting an order or take possession of a child without a court order as provided by this chapter.

(b) In determining the reasonable efforts that are required to be made with respect to preventing or eliminating the need to remove a child from the child's home or to make it possible to return a child to the child's home, the child's health and safety is the paramount concern.

History of Fam §262.001: Acts 1995, 74th Leg., ch. 20, §1, eff. April 20, 1995. Amended by Acts 1999, 76th Leg., ch. 1390, §29 (eff. Sept. 1, 1999), ch. 1150, §10 (eff. Sept. 1, 1999). Source: Former Fam §17.01.

FAM §262.002. JURISDICTION

A suit brought by a governmental entity requesting an order under this chapter may be filed in a court with jurisdiction to hear the suit in the county in which the child is found.

History of Fam §262.002: Acts 1995, 74th Leg., ch. 20, §1, eff. April 20, 1995. Amended by Acts 1999, 76th Leg., ch. 1390, §30 (eff. Sept. 1, 1999), ch. 1150, §11 (eff. Sept. 1, 1999). Source: Former Fam §17.05(a).

FAM §262.003. CIVIL LIABILITY

A person who takes possession of a child without a court order is immune from civil liability if, at the time possession is taken, there is reasonable cause to believe there is an immediate danger to the physical health or safety of the child.

History of Fam §262.003: Acts 1995, 74th Leg., ch. 20, §1, eff. April 20, 1995. Source: Former Fam §17.08.

FAM §262.004. ACCEPTING VOLUNTARY DELIVERY OF POSSESSION OF CHILD

A law enforcement officer or a juvenile probation officer may take possession of a child without a court order on the voluntary delivery of the child by the parent, managing conservator, possessory conservator, guardian, caretaker, or custodian who is presently entitled to possession of the child.

History of Fam §262.004: Acts 1995, 74th Leg., ch. 20, §1, eff. April 20, 1995. Amended by Acts 1995, 74th Leg., ch. 751, §101, eff. Sept. 1, 1995. Source: Former Fam §17.03(a)(2).

FAM §262.005. FILING PETITION AFTER ACCEPTING VOLUNTARY DELIVERY OF POSSESSION OF CHILD

When possession of the child has been acquired through voluntary delivery of the child to a law enforcement officer or juvenile probation officer, the law enforcement officer or juvenile probation officer taking the child into possession shall cause a suit to be filed not later than the 60th day after the date the child is taken into possession.

History of Fam §262.005: Acts 1995, 74th Leg., ch. 20, §1, eff. April 20, 1995. Amended by Acts 1995, 74th Leg., ch. 751, §102, eff. Sept. 1, 1995. Source: Former Fam §17.03(g).

FAM §262.006. LIVING CHILD AFTER ABORTION

(a) An authorized representative of the Department of Protective and Regulatory Services may assume the care, control, and custody of a child born alive as the result of an abortion as defined by Chapter 161.

(b) The department shall file a suit and request an emergency order under this chapter.

(c) A child for whom possession is assumed under this section need not be delivered to the court except on the order of the court.

History of Fam §262.006: Acts 1995, 74th Leg., ch. 20, §1, eff. April 20, 1995. Source: Former Fam §17.011.

FAM §262.007. POSSESSION & DELIVERY OF MISSING CHILD

(a) A law enforcement officer who, during a criminal investigation relating to a child's custody, discovers that a child is a missing child and believes that a person may flee with or conceal the child shall take possession of the child and provide for the delivery of the child as provided by Subsection (b).

(b) An officer who takes possession of a child under Subsection (a) shall deliver or arrange for the delivery of the child to a person entitled to possession of the child.

(c) If a person entitled to possession of the child is not immediately available to take possession of the child, the law enforcement officer shall deliver the child to the Department of Protective and Regulatory Services. Until a person entitled to possession of the child takes possession of the child, the department may, without a court order, retain possession of the child not longer than five days after the date the child is delivered to the department. While the department retains possession of a child under this subsection, the department may place the child in foster home care. If a parent or other person entitled to possession of the child does not take possession of the child before the sixth day after the date the child is delivered to the department, the department shall proceed under this chapter as if the law enforcement officer took possession of the child under Section 262.104.

History of Fam §262.007: Acts 1995, 74th Leg., ch. 776, §1, eff. Sept. 1, 1995. Amended by Acts 1999, 76th Leg., ch. 685, §6 (eff. Sept. 1, 1999), ch. 1150, §12 (eff. Sept. 1, 1999), ch. 1390, §31 (eff. Sept. 1, 1999).

FAM §262.008. ABANDONED CHILDREN

(a) An authorized representative of the Department of Protective and Regulatory Services may assume the care, control, and custody of a child:

(1) who is abandoned without identification or a means for identifying the child; and

(2) whose identity cannot be ascertained by the exercise of reasonable diligence.

(b) The department shall immediately file a suit to terminate the parent-child relationship of a child under Subsection (a).

(c) A child for whom possession is assumed under this section need not be delivered to the court except on the order of the court.

History of Fam §262.008: Acts 1997, 75th Leg., ch. 600, §4, eff. Jan. 1, 1998.

Sections 262.009-262.100 reserved for expansion

SUBCHAPTER B. TAKING POSSESSION OF CHILD

FAM §262.101. FILING PETITION BEFORE TAKING POSSESSION OF CHILD

A *Section 262.101 below is effective for SAPCRs requesting orders to take possession of a child filed on or after Sept. 1, 2001, or for children taken into possession without a court order on or after Sept. 1, 2001.*

An original suit filed by a governmental entity that requests permission to take possession of a child without prior notice and a hearing must be supported by an affidavit sworn to by a person with personal knowledge and stating facts sufficient to satisfy a person of ordinary prudence and caution that:

(1) there is an immediate danger to the physical health or safety of the child or the child has been a victim of neglect or sexual abuse and that continuation in the home would be contrary to the child's welfare;

(2) there is no time, consistent with the physical health or safety of the child, for a full adversary hearing under Subchapter C; and

(3) reasonable efforts, consistent with the circumstances and providing for the safety of the child, were made to prevent or eliminate the need for the removal of the child.

History of Fam §262.101: Acts 1995, 74th Leg., ch. 20, §1, eff. April 20, 1995. Amended by Acts 1995, 74th Leg., ch. 751, §103, eff. Sept. 1, 1995; Acts 1997, 75th Leg., ch. 752, §1, eff. June 17, 1997; Acts 1999, 76th Leg., ch. 1390, §32 (eff. Sept. 1, 1999), ch. 1150, §§13 & 14 (eff. Sept. 1, 1999); Acts 2001, 77th Leg., ch. 849, §1, eff. Sept. 1, 2001. Source: Former Fam §17.02(b).

FAM §262.101. FILING PETITION BEFORE TAKING POSSESSION OF CHILD

Section 262.101 below is effective for SAPCRs requesting orders to take possession of a child filed before Sept. 1, 2001, or for children taken into possession without a court order before Sept. 1, 2001.

An original suit filed by a governmental entity that requests permission to take possession of a child without prior notice and a hearing must be supported by an affidavit sworn to by a person with personal knowledge and stating facts sufficient to satisfy a person of ordinary prudence and caution that:

(1) there is an immediate danger to the physical health or safety of the child or the child has been a victim of neglect or sexual abuse and that continuation in the home would be contrary to the child's welfare; and

(2) there is no time, consistent with the physical health or safety of the child, for an adversary hearing or to make reasonable efforts to prevent or eliminate the need for the removal of the child.

FAM §262.1015. REMOVAL OF ALLEGED PERPETRATOR; OFFENSE

(a) If the department determines after an investigation that child abuse has occurred and that the child would be protected in the child's home by the removal of the alleged perpetrator of the abuse, the department shall file a petition for the removal of the alleged perpetrator from the residence of the child rather than attempt to remove the child from the residence.

(b) A court may issue a temporary restraining order in a suit by the department for the removal of an alleged perpetrator under Subsection (a) if the department's petition states facts sufficient to satisfy the court that:

(1) there is an immediate danger to the physical health or safety of the child or the child has been a victim of sexual abuse;

(2) there is no time, consistent with the physical health or safety of the child, for an adversary hearing;

(3) the child is not in danger of abuse from a parent or other adult with whom the child will continue to reside in the residence of the child; and

(4) the issuance of the order is in the best interest of the child.

(c) The order shall be served on the alleged perpetrator and on the parent or other adult with whom the child will continue to reside.

(d) A temporary restraining order under this section expires not later than the 14th day after the date the order was rendered.

(e) A temporary restraining order under this section and any other order requiring the removal of an alleged perpetrator from the residence of a child shall require that the parent or other adult with whom the child will continue to reside in the child's home make a reasonable effort to monitor the residence and report to the department and the appropriate law enforcement agency any attempt by the alleged perpetrator to return to the residence.

(f) The court shall order the removal of an alleged perpetrator if the court finds that the child is not in danger of abuse from a parent or other adult with whom the child will continue to reside in the child's residence and that:

(1) the presence of the alleged perpetrator in the child's residence constitutes a continuing danger to the physical health or safety of the child; or

(2) the child has been the victim of sexual abuse and there is a substantial risk that the child will be the victim of sexual abuse in the future if the alleged perpetrator remains in the residence.

(g) A person commits an offense if the person is a parent or other person with whom a child resides, the person is served with an order containing the requirement specified by Subsection (e), and the person fails to make a reasonable effort to monitor the residence of the child or to report to the department and the appropriate law enforcement agency an attempt by the alleged perpetrator to return to the residence. An offense under this section is a Class A misdemeanor.

(h) A person commits an offense if, in violation of a court order under this section, the person returns to the residence of the child the person is alleged to have abused. An offense under this subsection is a Class A misdemeanor, except that the offense is a felony of the third degree if the person has previously been convicted under this subsection.

History of Fam §262.1015: Acts 1995, 74th Leg., ch. 943, §4, eff. Sept. 1, 1995. Amended by Acts 1997, 75th Leg., ch. 575, §19, eff. Sept. 1, 1997.

FAM §262.102. EMERGENCY ORDER AUTHORIZING POSSESSION OF CHILD

A *Subsection (a) below is effective for SAPCRs requesting orders to take possession of a child filed on or after Sept. 1, 2001, or for children taken into possession without a court order on or after Sept. 1, 2001.*

(a) Before a court may, without prior notice and a hearing, issue a temporary restraining order or attachment of a child in a suit brought by a governmental entity, the court must find that:

(1) there is an immediate danger to the physical health or safety of the child or the child has been a victim of neglect or sexual abuse and that continuation in the home would be contrary to the child's welfare;

(2) there is no time, consistent with the physical health or safety of the child and the nature of the emergency, for a full adversary hearing under Subchapter C; and

(3) reasonable efforts, consistent with the circumstances and providing for the safety of the child, were made to prevent or eliminate the need for removal of the child.

Subsection (a) below is effective for SAPCRs requesting orders to take possession of a child filed before Sept. 1, 2001, or for children taken into possession without a court order before Sept. 1, 2001.

(a) Before a court may, without prior notice and a hearing, issue a temporary restraining order or attachment of a child in a suit brought by a governmental entity, the court must find that:

(1) there is an immediate danger to the physical health or safety of the child or the child has been a victim of neglect or sexual abuse and that continuation in the home would be contrary to the child's welfare; and

(2) there is no time, consistent with the physical health or safety of the child and the nature of the emergency, to hold an adversary hearing or to make reasonable efforts to prevent or eliminate the need for removal of the child.

(b) In determining whether there is an immediate danger to the physical health or safety of a child, the court may consider whether the child's household includes a person who has:

(1) abused or neglected another child in a manner that caused serious injury to or the death of the other child; or

(2) sexually abused another child.

(c) If, based on the recommendation of or a request by the department, the court finds that child abuse or neglect has occurred and that the child requires protection from family violence by a member of the child's family or household, the court shall render a temporary order under Chapter 71 for the protection of the child. In this subsection, "family violence" has the meaning assigned by Section 71.01.

History of Fam §262.102: Acts 1995, 74th Leg., ch. 20, §1, eff. April 20, 1995. Amended by Acts 1995, 74th Leg., ch. 751, §104, eff. Sept. 1, 1995; Acts 1997, 75th Leg., ch. 752, §2, eff. June 17, 1997; Acts 1999, 76th Leg., ch. 1390, §34 (eff. Sept. 1, 1999), ch. 1150, §15 (eff. Sept. 1, 1999); Acts 2001, 77th Leg., ch. 849, §2, eff. Sept. 1, 2001. Source: Former Fam §17.02(a), (d).

Vidaurri v. Ensey, 58 S.W.3d 142, 147 (Tex.App.—Amarillo 2001, no pet.). "The term 'immediate danger' insinuates the potential for harm yet to come, as opposed to harm that has already occurred. Thus, removal due to the prospect of future harm is not evidence that anyone has already suffered harm or injury."

FAM §262.103. DURATION OF TEMPORARY RESTRAINING ORDER & ATTACHMENT

A temporary restraining order or attachment of the child issued under this chapter expires not later than 14 days after the date it is issued unless it is extended as provided by the Texas Rules of Civil Procedure.

History of Fam §262.103: Acts 1995, 74th Leg., ch. 20, §1, eff. April 20, 1995. Source: Former Fam §17.02(c).

FAM §262.104. TAKING POSSESSION OF A CHILD IN EMERGENCY WITHOUT A COURT ORDER

If there is no time to obtain a temporary restraining order or attachment before taking possession of a child consistent with the health and safety of that child, an authorized representative of the Department of Protective and Regulatory Services, a law enforcement officer, or a juvenile probation officer may take possession of a child without a court order under the following conditions, only:

(1) on personal knowledge of facts that would lead a person of ordinary prudence and caution to believe that there is an immediate danger to the physical health or safety of the child;

(2) on information furnished by another that has been corroborated by personal knowledge of facts and all of which taken together would lead a person of ordinary prudence and caution to believe that there is an immediate danger to the physical health or safety of the child;

(3) on personal knowledge of facts that would lead a person of ordinary prudence and caution to believe that the child has been the victim of sexual abuse;

(4) on information furnished by another that has been corroborated by personal knowledge of facts and all of which taken together would lead a person of ordinary prudence and caution to believe that the child has been the victim of sexual abuse; or

(5) on information furnished by another that has been corroborated by personal knowledge of facts and all of which taken together would lead a person of ordinary prudence and caution to believe that the parent or person who has possession of the child is currently using a controlled substance as defined by Chapter 481, Health and Safety Code, and the use constitutes an immediate danger to the physical health or safety of the child.

History of Fam §262.104: Acts 1995, 74th Leg., ch. 20, §1, eff. April 20, 1995. Amended by Acts 1997, 75th Leg., ch. 575, §20, eff. Sept. 1, 1997. Source: Former Fam §17.03(a)(3)-(6).

FAM §262.105. FILING PETITION AFTER TAKING POSSESSION OF CHILD IN EMERGENCY

(a) When a child is taken into possession without a court order, the person taking the child into possession, without unnecessary delay, shall:

(1) file a suit affecting the parent-child relationship;

(2) request the court to appoint an attorney ad litem for the child; and

(3) request an initial hearing to be held by no later than the first working day after the date the child is taken into possession.

E (b) If the Department of Protective and Regulatory Services files a suit affecting the parent-child relationship required under Subsection (a)(1) seeking termination of the parent-child relationship, the department shall file the suit not later than the 45th day after the date the department assumes the care, control, and custody of a child under Section 262.303.

History of Fam §262.105: Acts 1995, 74th Leg., ch. 20, §1, eff. April 20, 1995. Amended by Acts 2001, 77th Leg., ch. 809, §2, eff. Sept. 1, 2001. Source: Former Fam §17.03(b).

FAM §262.106. INITIAL HEARING AFTER TAKING POSSESSION OF CHILD IN EMERGENCY WITHOUT COURT ORDER

(a) The court in which a suit has been filed after a child has been taken into possession without a court order by a governmental entity shall hold an initial hearing on or before the first working day after the date the child is taken into possession. The court shall render orders that are necessary to protect the physical health and safety of the child. If the court is unavailable for a hearing on the first working day, then, and only in that event, the hearing shall be held no later than the first working day after the court becomes available, provided that the hearing is held no later than the third working day after the child is taken into possession.

(b) The initial hearing may be ex parte and proof may be by sworn petition or affidavit if a full adversary hearing is not practicable.

(c) If the initial hearing is not held within the time required, the child shall be returned to the parent, managing conservator, possessory conservator, guardian, caretaker, or custodian who is presently entitled to possession of the child.

(d) For the purpose of determining under Subsection (a) the first working day after the date the child is taken into possession, the child is considered to have been taken into possession by the Department of Protective and Regulatory Services on the expiration of the five-day period permitted under Section 262.007(c) or 262.110(b), as appropriate.

History of Fam §262.106: Acts 1995, 74th Leg., ch. 20, §1, eff. April 20, 1995. Amended by Acts 1999, 76th Leg., ch. 1390, §35 (eff. Sept. 1, 1999), ch. 1150, §16 (eff. Sept. 1, 1999). Source: Former Fam §17.03(c).

FAM §262.107. STANDARD FOR DECISION AT INITIAL HEARING AFTER TAKING POSSESSION OF CHILD WITHOUT A COURT ORDER IN EMERGENCY

(a) The court shall order the return of the child at the initial hearing regarding a child taken in possession without a court order by a governmental entity unless the court is satisfied that:

(1) there is a continuing danger to the physical health or safety of the child if the child is returned to the parent, managing conservator, possessory conservator, guardian, caretaker, or custodian who is presently entitled to possession of the child or the evidence shows that the child has been the victim of sexual abuse on one or more occasions and that there is a substantial risk that the child will be the victim of sexual abuse in the future;

A *Subsections (2) & (3) below are effective for SAPCRs requesting orders to take possession of a child filed on or after Sept. 1, 2001, or for children taken into possession without a court order on or after Sept. 1, 2001.*

(2) continuation of the child in the home would be contrary to the child's welfare; and

(3) reasonable efforts, consistent with the circumstances and providing for the safety of the child, were made to prevent or eliminate the need for removal of the child.

Subsection (2) below is effective for SAPCRs requesting orders to take possession of a child filed before Sept. 1, 2001, or for children taken into possession without a court order before Sept. 1, 2001.

(2) the nature of the emergency and the continuing danger to the welfare of the child make efforts to allow the child to remain with or return to the person entitled to possession of the child impossible or unreasonable.

(b) In determining whether there is a continuing danger to the physical health or safety of a child, the court may consider whether the household to which the child would be returned includes a person who has:

(1) abused or neglected another child in a manner that caused serious injury to or the death of the other child; or

(2) sexually abused another child.

History of Fam §262.107: Acts 1995, 74th Leg., ch. 20, §1, eff. April 20, 1995. Amended by Acts 1995, 74th Leg., ch. 751, §105, eff. Sept. 1, 1995; Acts 2001, 77th Leg., ch. 849, §3, eff. Sept. 1, 2001. Source: Former Fam §17.03(d), (e), (i).

FAM §262.108. UNACCEPTABLE FACILITIES FOR HOUSING CHILD

When a child is taken into possession under this chapter, that child may not be held in isolation or in a jail, juvenile detention facility, or other secure detention facility.

History of Fam §262.108: Acts 1995, 74th Leg., ch. 20, §1, eff. April 20, 1995. Amended by Acts 1997, 75th Leg., ch. 1374, §9, eff. Sept. 1, 1997. Source: Former Fam §17.03(h).

FAM §262.109. NOTICE TO PARENT, CONSERVATOR, OR GUARDIAN

(a) The department or other agency must give written notice as prescribed by this section to each parent of the child or to the child's conservator or legal guardian when a representative of the Department of Protective and Regulatory Services or other agency takes possession of a child under this chapter.

(b) The written notice must be given as soon as practicable, but in any event not later than the first working day after the date the child is taken into possession.

(c) The written notice must include:

(1) the reasons why the department or agency is taking possession of the child and the facts that led the department to believe that the child should be taken into custody;

(2) the name of the person at the department or agency that the parent, conservator, or other custodian may contact for information relating to the child or a legal proceeding relating to the child;

(3) a summary of legal rights of a parent, conservator, guardian, or other custodian under this chapter and an explanation of the probable legal procedures relating to the child; and

(4) a statement that the parent, conservator, or other custodian has the right to hire an attorney.

(d) The written notice may be waived by the court at the initial hearing:

(1) on a showing that:

(A) the parents, conservators, or other custodians of the child could not be located; or

E (B) the department took possession of the child under Subchapter D; or

(2) for other good cause.

History of Fam §262.109: Acts 1995, 74th Leg., ch. 20, §1, eff. April 20, 1995. Amended by Acts 1997, 75th Leg., ch. 1022, §76, eff. Jan. 1, 1998; Acts 1999, 76th Leg., ch. 1390, §36 (eff. Sept. 1, 1999), ch. 1150, §17 (eff. Sept. 1, 1999); Acts 2001, 77th Leg., ch. 809, §3, eff. Sept. 1, 2001. Source: Former Fam §17.031(b).

FAM §262.110. TAKING POSSESSION OF CHILD IN EMERGENCY WITH INTENT TO RETURN HOME

(a) An authorized representative of the Department of Protective and Regulatory Services, a law enforcement officer, or a juvenile probation officer may take temporary possession of a child without a court order on discovery of a child in a situation of danger to the child's physical health or safety when the sole purpose is to deliver the child without unnecessary delay to the parent, managing conservator, possessory conservator, guardian, caretaker, or custodian who is presently entitled to possession of the child.

(b) Until a parent or other person entitled to possession of the child takes possession of the child, the department may retain possession of the child without a court order for not more than five days. On the expiration of the fifth day, if a parent or other person entitled to possession does not take possession of the child, the department shall take action under this chapter as if the department took possession of the child under Section 262.104.

History of Fam §262.110: Acts 1995, 74th Leg., ch. 20, §1, eff. April 20, 1995. Amended by Acts 1999, 76th Leg., ch. 1390, §37 (eff. Sept. 1, 1999), ch. 1150, §18 (eff. Sept. 1, 1999). Source: Former Fam §17.03(a)(1).

FAM §262.111. REPEALED

Repealed by Acts 2001, 77th Leg., ch. 849, §10, eff. Sept. 1, 2001.

FAM §262.111. FINDING THAT CHILD CANNOT REMAIN IN OR BE RETURNED TO HOME

Section 262.111 below is effective for SAPCRs requesting orders to take possession of a child filed before Sept. 1, 2001, or for children taken into possession without a court order before Sept. 1, 2001.

In the absence of a specific finding to the contrary, the issuance of a temporary restraining order or attachment pending a full adversary hearing or the issuance of an order after a full adversary hearing constitutes a finding by the court that for the child to remain in the home is contrary to the child's welfare or safety and that the emergency made efforts to prevent or eliminate the need for the removal of the child impossible or unreasonable.

FAM §262.112. EXPEDITED HEARING & APPEAL

(a) The Department of Protective and Regulatory Services is entitled to an expedited hearing under this chapter in any proceeding in which a hearing is required if the department determines that a child should be removed from the child's home because of an immediate danger to the physical health or safety of the child.

(b) In any proceeding in which an expedited hearing is held under Subsection (a), the department, parent, guardian, or other party to the proceeding is entitled to an expedited appeal on a ruling by a court that the child may not be removed from the child's home.

(c) If a child is returned to the child's home after a removal in which the department was entitled to an expedited hearing under this section and the child is the subject of a subsequent allegation of abuse or neglect, the department or any other interested party is entitled to an expedited hearing on the removal of the child from the child's home in the manner provided by Subsection (a) and to an expedited appeal in the manner provided by Subsection (b).

History of Fam §262.112: Acts 1995, 74th Leg., ch. 943, §1, eff. Sept. 1, 1995. Renumbered from §262.111 by Acts 1997, 75th Leg., ch. 165, §31.01(29), eff. Sept. 1, 1997.

FAM §262.113. FILING SUIT WITHOUT TAKING POSSESSION OF CHILD

An original suit filed by a governmental entity that requests to take possession of a child after notice and a hearing must be supported by an affidavit sworn to by a person with personal knowledge and stating facts sufficient to satisfy a person of ordinary prudence and caution that:

(1) reasonable efforts have been made to prevent or eliminate the need to remove the child from the child's home; and

(2) allowing the child to remain in the home would be contrary to the child's welfare.

History of Fam §262.113: Acts 1999, 76th Leg., ch. 1390, §38 (eff. Sept. 1, 1999), ch. 1150, §19 (eff. Sept. 1, 1999).

Sections 262.114-262.200 reserved for expansion

SUBCHAPTER C. ADVERSARY HEARING

FAM §262.201. FULL ADVERSARY HEARING; FINDINGS OF THE COURT

(a) Unless the child has already been returned to the parent, managing conservator, possessory conservator, guardian, caretaker, or custodian entitled to possession and the temporary order, if any, has been dissolved, a full adversary hearing shall be held not later than the 14th day after the date the child was taken into possession by the governmental entity.

(b) At the conclusion of the full adversary hearing, the court shall order the return of the child to the parent, managing conservator, possessory conservator, guardian, caretaker, or custodian entitled to possession unless the court finds sufficient evidence to satisfy a person of ordinary prudence and caution that:

(1) there was a danger to the physical health or safety of the child which was caused by an act or failure to act of the person entitled to possession and for the child to remain in the home is contrary to the welfare of the child;

A *Subsections (2) & (3) below are effective for SAPCRs requesting orders to take possession of a child filed on or after Sept. 1, 2001, or for children taken into possession without a court order on or after Sept. 1, 2001.*

(2) the urgent need for protection required the immediate removal of the child and reasonable efforts, consistent with the circumstances and providing for the safety of the child, were made to eliminate or prevent the child's removal; and

(3) reasonable efforts have been made to enable the child to return home, but there is a substantial risk of a continuing danger if the child is returned home.

Subsections (2) & (3) below are effective for SAPCRs requesting orders to take possession of a child filed before Sept. 1, 2001, or for children taken into possession without a court order before Sept. 1, 2001.

(2) the urgent need for protection required the immediate removal of the child and makes efforts to eliminate or prevent the child's removal impossible or unreasonable; and

(3) notwithstanding reasonable efforts to eliminate the need for the child's removal and enable the child to return home, there is a substantial risk of a continuing danger if the child is returned home.

A *Subsection (c) below is effective for children placed in custody of the DPRS on or after Sept. 1, 2001.*

(c) If the court finds sufficient evidence to satisfy a person of ordinary prudence and caution that there is a continuing danger to the physical health or safety of the child and for the child to remain in the home is contrary to the welfare of the child, the court shall issue an appropriate temporary order under Chapter 105. The court shall require each parent, alleged father, or relative of the child before the court to provide the Department of Protective and Regulatory Services with information necessary to locate any other absent parent, alleged father, or relative of the child. The court shall inform each parent in open court that parental and custodial rights and duties may be subject to restriction or to termination unless the parent or parents are willing and able to provide the child with a safe environment. If the court finds that the child requires protection from family violence by a member of the child's family or household, the court shall render a protective order under Title 4 for the child. In this subsection, "family violence" has the meaning assigned by Section 71.004.

Subsection (c) below is effective for children placed in custody of the DPRS before Sept. 1, 2001.

(c) If the court finds sufficient evidence to satisfy a person of ordinary prudence and caution that there is a continuing danger to the physical health or safety of the child and for the child to remain in the home is contrary to the welfare of the child, the court shall issue an appropriate temporary order under Chapter 105 and inform each parent in open court that parental and custodial rights and duties may be subject to restriction or to termination unless the parent or parents are willing and able to provide the child with a safe environment. If the court finds that the child requires protection from family violence by a member of the child's family or household, the court shall render a protective order under Title 4 for the child. In this subsection, "family violence" has the meaning assigned by Section 71.004.

(d) In determining whether there is a continuing danger to the physical health or safety of the child, the court may consider whether the household to which the child would be returned includes a person who:

(1) has abused or neglected another child in a manner that caused serious injury to or the death of the other child; or

(2) has sexually abused another child.

(e) The court shall place a child removed from the child's custodial parent with the child's noncustodial parent or with a relative of the child if placement with the noncustodial parent is inappropriate, unless placement with the noncustodial parent or a relative is not in the best interest of the child.

(f) When citation by publication is needed for a parent or alleged or probable father in an action brought under this chapter because the location of the parent, alleged father, or probable father is unknown, the court may render a temporary order without delay at any time after the filing of the action without regard to whether notice of the citation by publication has been published.

(g) For the purpose of determining under Subsection (a) the 14th day after the date the child is taken into possession, a child is considered to have been taken into possession by the department on the expiration of the five-day period permitted under Section 262.007(c) or 262.110(b), as appropriate.

History of Fam §262.201: Acts 1995, 74th Leg., ch. 20, §1, eff. April 20, 1995. Amended by Acts 1995, 74th Leg., ch. 751, §107, eff. Sept. 1, 1995; Acts 1997, 75th Leg., ch. 575, §21 (eff. Sept. 1, 1997), ch. 600, §5 (eff. Jan, 1, 1998), ch. 603, §1 (eff. Jan. 1, 1998), ch. 752, §3 (eff. June 17, 1997), ch. 1022, §77 (eff. Jan. 1, 1998), ch. 1022, §78 (eff. Sept. 1, 1997); Acts 1999, 76th Leg., ch. 1390, §39 (eff. Sept. 1, 1999), ch. 1150, §20 (eff. Sept. 1, 1999), ch. 62, §§6.31(a) & (b) (eff. Sept. 1, 1999); Acts 2001, 77th Leg., ch. 306, §1 (eff. Sept. 1, 2001), ch. 849, §4 (eff. Sept. 1, 2001). Source: Former Fam §§17.03(f), 17.04.

FAM §262.2015. AGGRAVATED CIRCUMSTANCES

Ⓐ *Subsection (a) below is effective for SAPCRs requesting orders to take possession of a child filed on or after Sept. 1, 2001, or for children taken into possession without a court order on or after Sept. 1, 2001.*

(a) The court may waive the requirement of a service plan and the requirement to make reasonable efforts to return the child to a parent and may accelerate the trial schedule to result in a final order for a child under the care of the department at an earlier date than provided by Subchapter D, Chapter 263, if the court finds that the parent has subjected the child to aggravated circumstances.

Subsection (a) below is effective for SAPCRs requesting orders to take possession of a child filed before Sept. 1, 2001, or for children taken into possession without a court order before Sept. 1, 2001.

(a) The court may waive the requirement of a service plan and the requirement to make reasonable efforts to return the child to a parent and may accelerate the trial schedule to result in a final order for a child under the care of the department at an earlier date than provided by Subchapter D, Chapter 263, if the court finds that all reasonable efforts have been made to return the child to a parent or that the parent has subjected the child to aggravated circumstances.

(b) The court may find under Subsection (a) that a parent has subjected the child to aggravated circumstances if:

(1) the parent abandoned the child without identification or a means for identifying the child;

(2) the child is a victim of serious bodily injury or sexual abuse inflicted by the parent or by another person with the parent's consent;

Ⓐ *Subsection (3) below is effective for SAPCRs requesting orders to take possession of a child filed on or after Sept. 1, 2001, or for children taken into possession without a court order on or after Sept. 1, 2001.*

(3) the parent has engaged in conduct against the child that would constitute an offense under the following provisions of the Penal Code:

Subsection (3) below is effective for SAPCRs requesting orders to take possession of a child filed before Sept. 1, 2001, or for children taken into possession without a court order before Sept. 1, 2001.

(3) the parent has engaged in conduct against the child or against another child of the parent that would constitute an offense under the following provisions of the Penal Code:

(A) Section 19.02 (murder);

(B) Section 19.03 (capital murder);

(C) Section 19.04 (manslaughter);

(D) Section 21.11 (indecency with a child);

(E) Section 22.011 (sexual assault);

(F) Section 22.02 (aggravated assault);

(G) Section 22.021 (aggravated sexual assault);

(H) Section 22.04 (injury to a child, elderly individual, or disabled individual);

(I) Section 22.041 (abandoning or endangering child);

(J) Section 25.02 (prohibited sexual conduct);

(K) Section 43.25 (sexual performance by a child); or

(L) Section 43.26 (possession or promotion of child pornography);

(4) the parent voluntarily left the child alone or in the possession of another person not the parent of the child for at least six months without expressing an intent to return and without providing adequate support for the child;

(5) the parent's parental rights with regard to another child have been involuntarily terminated based on a finding that the parent's conduct violated Section 161.001(1)(D) or (E) or a substantially equivalent provision of another state's law; or

E *Subsection (6) below is effective for SAPCRs requesting orders to take possession of a child filed on or after Sept. 1, 2001, or for children taken into possession without a court order on or after Sept. 1, 2001.*

(6) the parent has been convicted for:

(A) the murder of another child of the parent and the offense would have been an offense under 18 U.S.C. Section 1111(a) if the offense had occurred in the special maritime or territorial jurisdiction of the United States;

(B) the voluntary manslaughter of another child of the parent and the offense would have been an offense under 18 U.S.C. Section 1112(a) if the offense had occurred in the special maritime or territorial jurisdiction of the United States;

(C) aiding or abetting, attempting, conspiring, or soliciting an offense under Subdivision (A) or (B); or

(D) the felony assault of the child or another child of the parent that resulted in serious bodily injury to the child or another child of the parent.

A *Subsection (c) below is effective for SAPCRs requesting orders to take possession of a child filed on or after Sept. 1, 2001, or for children taken into possession without a court order on or after Sept. 1, 2001.*

(c) On finding that reasonable efforts to make it possible for the child to safely return to the child's home are not required, the court shall at any time before the 30th day after the date of the finding, conduct an initial permanency hearing under Subchapter D, Chapter 263. Separate notice of the permanency plan is not required but may be given with a notice of a hearing under this section.

Subsection (c) below is effective for SAPCRs requesting orders to take possession of a child filed before Sept. 1, 2001, or for children taken into possession without a court order before Sept. 1, 2001.

(c) On finding that reasonable efforts to prevent or eliminate the need to remove the child or to make it possible for the child to safely return to the child's home are not required, the court shall at any time before the 30th day after the date of the finding, conduct an initial permanency hearing under Subchapter D, Chapter 263. Separate notice of the permanency plan is not required but may be given with a notice of a hearing under this section.

(d) The Department of Protective and Regulatory Services shall make reasonable efforts to finalize the permanent placement of a child for whom the court has made the finding described by Subsection (c). The court shall set the suit for trial on the merits as required by Subchapter D, Chapter 263, in order to facilitate final placement of the child.

History of Fam §262.2015: Acts 1997, 75th Leg., ch. 1022, §79, eff. Sept. 1, 1997. Amended by Acts 1999, 76th Leg., ch. 1390, §40 (eff. Sept. 1, 1999), ch. 1150, §21 (eff. Sept. 1, 1999); Acts 2001, 77th Leg., ch. 849, §5, eff. Sept. 1, 2001.

FAM §262.202. IDENTIFICATION OF COURT OF CONTINUING, EXCLUSIVE JURISDICTION

If at the conclusion of the full adversary hearing the court renders a temporary order, the governmental entity shall request identification of a court of continuing, exclusive jurisdiction as provided by Chapter 155.

History of Fam §262.202: Acts 1995, 74th Leg., ch. 20, §1, eff. April 20, 1995. Source: Former Fam §17.05(b).

FAM §262.203. TRANSFER OF SUIT

(a) On the motion of a party or the court's own motion, if applicable, the court that rendered the temporary order shall in accordance with procedures provided by Chapter 155:

(1) transfer the suit to the court of continuing, exclusive jurisdiction, if any;

(2) if grounds exist for mandatory transfer from the court of continuing, exclusive jurisdiction under Section 155.201, order transfer of the suit from that court; or

(3) if grounds exist for transfer based on improper venue, order transfer of the suit to the court having venue of the suit under Chapter 103.

(b) Notwithstanding Section 155.204, a motion to transfer relating to a suit filed under this chapter may be filed separately from the petition and is timely if filed while the case is pending.

(c) Notwithstanding Sections 6.407 and 103.002, a court exercising jurisdiction under this chapter is not required to transfer the suit to a court in which a parent has filed a suit for dissolution of marriage before a final order for the protection of the child has been rendered under Subchapter E, Chapter 263.

History of Fam §262.203: Acts 1995, 74th Leg., ch. 20, §1, eff. April 20, 1995. Amended by Acts 1997, 75th Leg., ch. 575, §22, eff. Sept. 1, 1997; Acts 1999, 76th Leg., ch. 1390, §41 (eff. Sept. 1, 1999), ch. 1150, §22 (eff. Sept. 1, 1999). Source: Former Fam §17.06(a).

FAM §262.204. TEMPORARY ORDER IN EFFECT UNTIL SUPERSEDED

(a) A temporary order rendered under this chapter is valid and enforceable until properly superseded by a court with jurisdiction to do so.

(b) A court to which the suit has been transferred may enforce by contempt or otherwise a temporary order properly issued under this chapter.

History of Fam §262.204: Acts 1995, 74th Leg., ch. 20, §1, eff. April 20, 1995. Source: Former Fam §17.06(b), (c).

FAM §262.205. HEARING WHEN CHILD NOT IN POSSESSION OF GOVERNMENTAL ENTITY

(a) In a suit requesting possession of a child after notice and hearing, the court may render a temporary restraining order as provided by Section 105.001. The suit shall be promptly set for hearing.

(b) After the hearing, the court may grant the request to remove the child from the parent, managing conservator, possessory conservator, guardian, caretaker, or custodian entitled to possession of the child if the court finds sufficient evidence to satisfy a person of ordinary prudence and caution that:

(1) reasonable efforts have been made to prevent or eliminate the need to remove the child from the child's home; and

(2) allowing the child to remain in the home would be contrary to the child's welfare.

(c) If the court orders removal of the child from the child's home, the court shall:

(1) issue an appropriate temporary order under Chapter 105; and

(2) inform each parent in open court that parental and custodial rights and duties may be subject to restriction or termination unless the parent is willing and able to provide a safe environment for the child.

(d) If citation by publication is required for a parent or alleged or probable father in an action under this chapter because the location of the person is unknown, the court may render a temporary order without regard to whether notice of the citation has been published.

(e) Unless it is not in the best interest of the child, the court shall place a child who has been removed under this section with:

(1) the child's noncustodial parent; or

(2) another relative of the child if placement with the noncustodial parent is inappropriate.

(f) If the court finds that the child requires protection from family violence by a member of the child's family or household, the court shall render a protective order for the child under Title 4.

History of Fam §262.205: Acts 1999, 76th Leg., ch. 1390, §42 (eff. Sept. 1, 1999), ch. 1150, §23 (eff. Sept. 1, 1999).

Sections 262.206-262.300 blank

SUBCHAPTER D. EMERGENCY POSSESSION OF CERTAIN ABANDONED CHILDREN

E FAM §262.301. DEFINITIONS

In this chapter:

(1) "Designated emergency infant care provider" means:

(A) an emergency medical services provider;

(B) a hospital; or

(C) a child-placing agency licensed by the Department of Protective and Regulatory Services under Chapter 42, Human Resources Code, that:

(i) agrees to act as a designated emergency infant care provider under this subchapter; and

(ii) has on staff a person who is licensed as a registered nurse under Chapter 301, Occupations Code, or who provides emergency medical services under Chapter 773, Health and Safety Code, and who will examine and provide emergency medical services to a child taken into possession by the agency under this subchapter.

(2) "Emergency medical services provider" has the meaning assigned that term by Section 773.003, Health and Safety Code.

History of Fam §262.301: Enacted by Acts 2001, 77th Leg., ch. 809, §4, eff. Sept. 1, 2001.

A FAM §262.302. ACCEPTING POSSESSION OF CERTAIN ABANDONED CHILDREN

(a) A designated emergency infant care provider shall, without a court order, take possession of a child who appears to be 60 days old or younger if the child is voluntarily delivered to the provider by the child's parent and the parent did not express an intent to return for the child.

(b) A designated emergency infant care provider who takes possession of a child under this section has no legal duty to detain or pursue the parent and may not do so unless the child appears to have been abused or neglected. The designated emergency infant care provider has no legal duty to ascertain the parent's identity and the parent may remain anonymous. However, the parent may be given a form for voluntary disclosure of the child's medical facts and history.

(c) A designated emergency infant care provider who takes possession of a child under this section shall perform any act necessary to protect the physical health or safety of the child. The designated emergency infant care provider is not liable for damages related to the provider's taking possession of, examining, or treating the child, except for damages related to the provider's negligence.

History of Fam §262.302: Acts 1999, 76th Leg., ch. 1087, §2, eff. Sept. 1, 1999. Renumbered from §262.301 and amended by Acts 2001, 77th Leg., ch. 809, §4, eff. Sept. 1, 2001.

FAM §262.303. NOTIFICATION OF POSSESSION OF ABANDONED CHILD

Ⓐ (a) Not later than the close of the first business day after the date on which a designated emergency infant care provider takes possession of a child under Section 262.302, the provider shall notify the Department of Protective and Regulatory Services that the provider has taken possession of the child.

(b) The department shall assume the care, control, and custody of the child immediately on receipt of notice under Subsection (a).

History of Fam §262.303: Acts 1999, 76th Leg., ch. 1087, §2, eff. Sept. 1, 1999. Renumbered from §262.302 and amended by Acts 2001, 77th Leg., ch. 809, §4, eff. Sept. 1, 2001.

Ⓐ FAM §262.304. FILING PETITION AFTER ACCEPTING POSSESSION OF ABANDONED CHILD

A child for whom the Department of Protective and Regulatory Services assumes care, control, and custody under Section 262.303 shall be treated as a child taken into possession without a court order, and the department shall take action as required by Section 262.105 with regard to the child.

History of Fam §262.304: Acts 1999, 76th Leg., ch. 1087, §2, eff. Sept. 1, 1999. Renumbered from §262.303 and amended by Acts 2001, 77th Leg., ch. 809, §4, eff. Sept. 1, 2001.

Ⓔ FAM §262.305. REPORT TO LAW ENFORCEMENT AGENCY; INVESTIGATION

(a) Immediately after assuming care, control, and custody of a child under Section 262.303, the Department of Protective and Regulatory Services shall report the child to appropriate state and local law enforcement agencies as a potential missing child.

(b) A law enforcement agency that receives a report under Subsection (a) shall investigate whether the child is reported as missing.

History of Fam §262.305: Enacted by Acts 2001, 77th Leg., ch. 809, §4, eff. Sept. 1, 2001.

Ⓔ FAM §262.306. NOTICE

Each designated emergency infant care provider shall post in a conspicuous location a notice stating that the provider is a designated emergency infant care provider location and will accept possession of a child in accordance with this subchapter.

History of Fam §262.306: Enacted by Acts 2001, 77th Leg., ch. 809, §4, eff. Sept. 1, 2001.

Ⓔ FAM §262.307. REIMBURSEMENT FOR CARE OF ABANDONED CHILD

The department shall reimburse a designated emergency infant care provider that takes possession of a child under Section 262.302 for the cost to the provider of assuming the care, control, and custody of the child.

History of Fam §262.307: Enacted by Acts 2001, 77th Leg., ch. 809, §4, eff. Sept. 1, 2001.

CHAPTER 263. REVIEW OF PLACEMENT OF CHILDREN UNDER CARE OF DEPARTMENT OF PROTECTIVE & REGULATORY SERVICES

SUBCHAPTER A. GENERAL PROVISIONS

FAM §263.001. DEFINITIONS

(a) In this chapter:

(1) "Department" means the Department of Protective and Regulatory Services.

(2) "Child's home" means the place of residence of at least one of the child's parents.

(3) "Household" means a unit composed of persons living together in the same dwelling, without regard to whether they are related to each other.

(4) "Substitute care" means the placement of a child who is in the conservatorship of the department or an authorized agency in care outside the child's home. The term includes foster care, institutional care, adoption, or placement with a relative of the child.

(b) In the preparation and review of a service plan under this chapter, a reference to the parents of the child includes both parents of the child unless the child has only one parent or unless, after due diligence by the department in attempting to locate a parent, only one parent is located, in which case the reference is to the remaining parent.

History of Fam §263.001: Acts 1995, 74th Leg., ch. 20, §1, eff. April 20, 1995. Amended by Acts 1995, 74th Leg., ch. 751, §108, eff. Sept. 1, 1995. Source: Former Fam §18.01.

FAM §263.002. REVIEW OF PLACEMENTS BY COURT

In a suit affecting the parent-child relationship in which the department or an authorized agency has been appointed by the court or designated in an affidavit of relinquishment of parental rights as the temporary or permanent managing conservator of a child, the court shall hold a hearing to review the conservatorship appointment and substitute care.

History of Fam §263.002: Acts 1995, 74th Leg., ch. 20, §1, eff. April 20, 1995. Amended by Acts 1995, 74th Leg., ch. 751, §109, eff. Sept. 1, 1995. Source: Former Fam §18.02.

FAM §§263.003, 263.004. REPEALED

Repealed by Acts 1999, 76th Leg., ch. 1390, §50 (eff. Sept. 1, 1999), ch. 1150, §31 (eff. Sept. 1, 1999).

FAM §263.005. ENFORCEMENT OF FAMILY SERVICE PLAN

The department shall designate existing department personnel to ensure that the parties to a family service plan comply with the plan.

History of Fam §263.005: Acts 1995, 74th Leg., ch. 943, §5, eff. Sept. 1, 1995.

FAM §263.006. WARNING TO PARENTS

At the status hearing under Subchapter C and at each permanency hearing under Subchapter D held after the court has rendered a temporary order appointing the department as temporary managing conservator, the court shall inform each parent in open court that parental and custodial rights and duties may be subject to restriction or to termination unless the parent or parents are willing and able to provide the child with a safe environment.

History of Fam §263.006: Acts 1997, 75th Leg., ch. 600, §6, eff. Jan. 1, 1998; Acts 1997, 75th Leg., ch. 603, §2 (eff. Jan. 1, 1998), ch. 1022, §80 (eff. Jan. 1, 1998).

Sections 263.007-263.100 reserved for expansion

SUBCHAPTER B. SERVICE PLAN

FAM §263.101. DEPARTMENT TO FILE SERVICE PLAN

Not later than the 45th day after the date the court renders a temporary order appointing the department as temporary managing conservator of a child under Chapter 262, the department or other agency appointed as the managing conservator of a child shall file a service plan.

History of Fam §263.101: Acts 1995, 74th Leg., ch. 20, §1, eff. April 20, 1995. Amended by Acts 1999, 76th Leg., ch. 1390, §43 (eff. Sept. 1, 1999), ch. 1150, §24 (eff. Sept. 1, 1999). Source: Former Fam §18.03(a).

See also 40 TAC §§700.1331-700.1333.

FAM §263.1015. SERVICE PLAN NOT REQUIRED

A service plan is not required under this subchapter in a suit brought by the department for the termination of the parent-child relationship for a child who has been abandoned without identification and whose identity cannot be determined.

History of Fam §263.1015: Acts 1997, 75th Leg., ch. 600, §7, eff. Jan. 1, 1998.

FAM §263.102. SERVICE PLAN; CONTENTS

(a) The service plan must:

(1) be specific;

(2) be in writing;

(3) be prepared by the department or other agency in conference with the child's parents;

(4) state appropriate deadlines;

(5) state whether the goal of the plan is:

(A) return of the child to the child's parents;

(B) termination of parental rights and placement of the child for adoption; or

(C) because of the child's special needs or exceptional circumstances, continuation of the child's care out of the child's home;

(6) state steps that are necessary to:

(A) return the child to the child's home if the placement is in foster care;

(B) enable the child to remain in the child's home with the assistance of a service plan if the placement is in the home under the department's or other agency's supervision; or

(C) otherwise provide a permanent safe placement for the child;

(7) state the actions and responsibilities that are necessary for the child's parents to take to achieve the plan goal during the period of the service plan and the assistance to be provided to the parents by the department or other authorized agency toward meeting that goal;

(8) state the name of the person with the department or other agency whom the child's parents may contact for information relating to the child if other than the person preparing the plan; and

(9) prescribe any other term or condition that the department or other agency determines to be necessary to the service plan's success.

(b) The service plan shall include the following statement:

TO THE PARENT: THIS IS A VERY IMPORTANT DOCUMENT. ITS PURPOSE IS TO HELP YOU PROVIDE YOUR CHILD WITH A SAFE ENVIRONMENT WITHIN THE REASONABLE PERIOD SPECIFIED IN THE PLAN. IF YOU ARE UNWILLING OR UNABLE TO PROVIDE YOUR CHILD WITH A SAFE ENVIRONMENT, YOUR PARENTAL AND CUSTODIAL DUTIES AND RIGHTS MAY BE RESTRICTED OR TERMINATED OR YOUR CHILD MAY NOT BE RETURNED TO YOU. THERE WILL BE A COURT HEARING AT WHICH A JUDGE WILL REVIEW THIS SERVICE PLAN.

(c) If both parents are available but do not live in the same household and do not agree to cooperate with one another in the development of a service plan for the child, the department in preparing the service plan may provide for the care of the child in the home of either parent or the homes of both parents as the best interest of the child requires.

History of Fam §263.102: Acts 1995, 74th Leg., ch. 20, §1, eff. April 20, 1995. Source: Former Fam §18.03(b)-(d).

See also 40 TAC §§700.1331-700.1333.

FAM §263.103. SERVICE PLAN: SIGNING & TAKING EFFECT

(a) Before the service plan is signed, the child's parents and the representative of the department or other agency shall discuss each term and condition of the plan.

(b) The child's parents and the person preparing the service plan shall sign the plan, and the department shall give each parent a copy of the service plan.

(c) If the department or other authorized agency determines that the child's parents are unable or unwilling to sign the service plan, the department may file the plan without the parents' signatures.

(d) The plan takes effect when:

(1) the child's parents and the appropriate representative of the department or other authorized agency sign the plan; or

(2) the department or other authorized agency files the plan without the parents' signatures.

(e) The service plan is in effect until amended by the court.

History of Fam §263.103: Acts 1995, 74th Leg., ch. 20, §1, eff. April 20, 1995. Source: Former Fam §18.04.

FAM §263.104. AMENDED SERVICE PLAN

(a) The service plan may be amended at any time.

(b) The amended service plan supersedes the previously filed service plan and takes effect when:

(1) the child's parents and the appropriate representative of the department or other authorized agency sign the plan; or

(2) the department or other authorized agency determines that the child's parents are unable or unwilling to sign the amended plan and files it without the parents' signatures.

(c) The amended service plan remains in effect until amended by the court.

story of Fam §263.104: Acts 1995, 74th Leg., ch. 20, §1, eff. April 20, 1995. Source: Former Fam §18.05.

FAM §263.105. REVIEW OF SERVICE PLAN

(a) The service plan currently in effect shall be filed with the court.

(b) The court shall review the plan at the next required hearing under this chapter after the plan is filed.

History of Fam §263.105: Acts 1995, 74th Leg., ch. 20, §1, eff. April 20, 1995. Amended by Acts 1999, 76th Leg., ch. 1390, §44 (eff. Sept. 1, 1999), ch. 1150, §25 (eff. Sept. 1, 1999). Source: Former Fam §18.06.

FAM §263.106. COURT IMPLEMENTATION OF SERVICE PLAN

The court may render appropriate orders to implement or require compliance with an original or amended service plan.

History of Fam §263.106: Acts 1995, 74th Leg., ch. 20, §1, eff. April 20, 1995.

Sections 263.107-263.200 reserved for expansion

SUBCHAPTER C. STATUS HEARING

FAM §263.201. STATUS HEARING; TIME

(a) Not later than the 60th day after the date the court renders a temporary order appointing the department as temporary managing conservator of a child, the court shall hold a status hearing to review the child's status and the service plan developed for the child.

(b) A status hearing is not required if the court holds an initial permanency hearing under Section 262.2015 before the date a status hearing is required by this section.

History of Fam §263.201: Acts 1995, 74th Leg., ch. 20, §1, eff. April 20, 1995. Amended by Acts 1997, 75th Leg., ch. 600, §8 (eff. Jan. 1, 1998), ch. 603, §3 (eff. Jan. 1, 1998), ch. 1022, §81 (eff. Jan. 1, 1998); Acts 1999, 76th Leg., ch. 1390, §45 (eff. Sept. 1, 1999), ch. 1150, §26 (eff. Sept. 1, 1999). Source: Former Fam §18.07(a).

FAM §263.202. STATUS HEARING; FINDINGS

(a) If all parties entitled to citation and notice under this chapter were not served, the court shall make findings as to whether:

(1) the department or other agency has exercised due diligence to locate all necessary persons; and

A *Subsection (2) below is effective for children placed in custody of the DPRS on or after Sept. 1, 2001.*

(2) each custodial parent, alleged father, or relative of the child before the court has furnished to the department all available information necessary to locate another absent parent, alleged father, or relative of the child through exercise of due diligence.

Subsection (2) below is effective for children placed in custody of the DPRS before Sept. 1, 2001.

(2) if only one parent is before the court, that parent has furnished to the department all available information necessary to locate an absent parent through the parental locator service.

(b) A status hearing shall be limited to matters related to the contents and execution of the service plan filed with the court. The court shall review the service plan that the department or other agency filed under this chapter for reasonableness, accuracy, and compliance with requirements of court orders and make findings as to whether:

(1) a plan that has the goal of returning the child to the child's parents adequately ensures that reasonable efforts are made to enable the child's parents to provide a safe environment for the child; and

(2) the child's parents have reviewed and understand the service plan and have been advised that unless the parents are willing and able to provide the child with a safe environment, even with the assistance of a service plan, within the reasonable period of time specified in the plan, the parents' parental and custodial duties and rights may be subject to restriction or to termination under this code or the child may not be returned to the parents.

(c) The court shall advise the parties that progress under the service plan will be reviewed at all subsequent hearings.

(d) If a service plan with respect to a parent has not been filed with the court, the court shall consider whether to waive the service plan under Section 262.2015.

History of Fam §263.202: Acts 1995, 74th Leg., ch. 20, §1, eff. April 20, 1995. Amended by Acts 1995, 74th Leg., ch. 751, §111, eff. Sept. 1, 1995; Acts 1999, 76th Leg., ch. 1390, §46 (eff. Sept. 1, 1999), ch. 1150, §27 (eff. Sept. 1, 1999); Acts 2001, 77th Leg., ch. 306, §2, eff. Sept. 1, 2001. Source: Former Fam §18.07(b)-(d).

Sections 263.203-263.300 reserved for expansion

SUBCHAPTER D. PERMANENCY HEARINGS

FAM §263.301. NOTICE

(a) Notice of a permanency hearing shall be given as provided by Rule 21a, Texas Rules of Civil Procedure, to all persons entitled to notice of the hearing.

(b) The following persons are entitled to at least 10 days' notice of a permanency hearing and are entitled to present evidence and be heard at the hearing:

(1) the department;

A (2) the foster parent, preadoptive parent, relative of the child providing care, or director of the group home or institution where the child is residing;

(3) each parent of the child;

(4) the managing conservator or guardian of the child;

(5) an attorney ad litem appointed for the child under Chapter 107;

(6) a volunteer advocate appointed for the child under Chapter 107; and

(7) any other person or agency named by the court to have an interest in the child's welfare.

(c) If a person entitled to notice under Chapter 102 or this section has not been served, the court shall review the department's or other agency's efforts at attempting to locate all necessary persons and requesting service of citation and the assistance of a parent in providing information necessary to locate an absent parent.

History of Fam §263.301: Acts 1995, 74th Leg., ch. 20, §1, eff. April 20, 1995. Amended by Acts 1997, 75th Leg., ch. 600, §10 (eff. Jan. 1, 1998), ch. 603, §5 (eff. Jan. 1, 1998), ch. 1022, §83 (eff. Jan. 1, 1998); Acts 2001, 77th Leg., ch. 849, §6, eff. Sept. 1, 2001. Source: Former Fam §§18.08(b), (c), 18.12.

FAM §263.302. CHILD'S ATTENDANCE AT HEARING

The child shall attend each permanency hearing unless the court specifically excuses the child's attendance. Failure by the child to attend a hearing does not affect the validity of an order rendered at the hearing.

History of Fam §263.302: Acts 1995, 74th Leg., ch. 20, §1, eff. April 20, 1995. Amended by Acts 1997, 75th Leg., ch. 600, §11 (eff. Jan. 1, 1998), ch. 603, §6 (eff. Jan. 1, 1998), ch. 1022, §84 (eff. Jan. 1, 1998). Source: Former Fam §18.14.

FAM §263.3025. PERMANENCY PLAN

(a) The department shall prepare a permanency plan for a child for whom the department has been appointed temporary managing conservator. The department shall give a copy of the plan to each person entitled to notice under Section 263.301(b) not later than the 10th day before the date of the child's first permanency hearing.

(b) In addition to the requirements of the department rules governing permanency planning, the permanency plan must contain the information required to be included in a permanency progress report under Section 263.303.

(c) The department shall modify the permanency plan for a child as required by the circumstances and needs of the child.

E (d) In preparing the permanency plan for a child taken into possession under Subchapter D, Chapter 262, the department is not required to conduct a search for or give preference to the child's relatives for purposes of permanent placement if the department does not have information concerning the child's identity or the identities of the child's parents.

History of Fam §263.3025: Acts 1997, 75th Leg., ch. 600, §12 (eff. Jan. 1, 1998), ch. 603, §7 (eff. Jan. 1, 1998), ch. 1022, §85 (eff. Jan. 1, 1998). Amended by Acts 2001, 77th Leg., ch. 809, §5, eff. Sept. 1, 2001.

See also 40 TAC §700.1310.

FAM §263.303. PERMANENCY PROGRESS REPORT

(a) Not later than the 10th day before the date set for each permanency hearing other than the first permanency hearing, the department or other authorized agency shall file with the court and provide to each party, the child's attorney ad litem, and the child's volunteer advocate a permanency progress report unless the court orders a different period for providing the report.

(b) The permanency progress report must:

(1) recommend that the suit be dismissed; or

(2) recommend that the suit continue, and:

(A) identify the date for dismissal of the suit under this chapter;

(B) provide:

(i) the name of any person entitled to notice under Chapter 102 who has not been served;

(ii) a description of the efforts by the department or another agency to locate and request service of citation; and

(iii) a description of each parent's assistance in providing information necessary to locate an unserved party;

(C) evaluate the parties' compliance with temporary orders and with the service plan;

(D) evaluate whether the child's placement in substitute care meets the child's needs and recommend other plans or services to meet the child's special needs or circumstances;

(E) describe the permanency plan for the child and recommend actions necessary to ensure that a final order consistent with that permanency plan is rendered before the date for dismissal of the suit under this chapter; and

(F) with respect to a child 16 years of age or older, identify the services needed to assist the child in the transition to adult life.

(c) A parent whose parental rights are the subject of a suit affecting the parent-child relationship, the attorney for that parent, or the child's attorney ad litem or guardian ad litem may file a response to the department's or other agency's report filed under Subsection (b). A response must be filed not later than the third day before the date of the hearing.

History of Fam §263.303: Acts 1995, 74th Leg., ch. 20, §1, eff. April 20, 1995. Amended by Acts 1995, 74th Leg., ch. 751, §112, eff. Sept. 1, 1995; Acts 1997, 75th Leg., ch. 600, §13 (eff. Jan. 1, 1998), ch. 603, §8 (eff. Jan. 1, 1998), ch. 1022, §86 (eff. Jan. 1, 1998). Source: Former Fam §18.10(b), (c).

FAM §263.304. INITIAL PERMANENCY HEARING; TIME

(a) Not later than the 180th day after the date the court renders a temporary order appointing the department as temporary managing conservator of a child, the court shall hold a permanency hearing to review the status of, and permanency plan for, the child to ensure that a final order consistent with that permanency plan is rendered before the date for dismissal of the suit under this chapter.

E *Subsection (b) below is effective for SAPCRs pending on Sept. 1, 2001.*

(b) The court shall set a final hearing under this chapter on a date that allows the court to render a final order before the date for dismissal of the suit under this chapter. Any party to the suit or an attorney ad litem for the child may seek a writ of mandamus to compel the court to comply with the duties imposed by this subsection.

History of Fam §263.304: Acts 1995, 74th Leg., ch. 20, §1, eff. April 20, 1995. Amended by Acts 1995, 74th Leg., ch. 751, §113, eff. Sept. 1, 1995; Acts 1997, 75th Leg., ch. 600, §14 (eff. Jan. 1, 1998), ch. 603, §9 (eff. Jan. 1, 1998), ch. 1022, §87 (eff. Jan. 1, 1998); Acts 2001, 77th Leg., ch. 1090, §7, eff. Sept. 1, 2001. Source: Former Fam §18.08(a).

FAM §263.305. SUBSEQUENT PERMANENCY HEARINGS

A subsequent permanency hearing before entry of a final order shall be held not later than the 120th day after the date of the last permanency hearing in the suit. For good cause shown or on the court's own motion, the court may order more frequent hearings.

History of Fam §263.305: Acts 1995, 74th Leg., ch. 20, §1, eff. April 20, 1995. Amended by Acts 1997, 75th Leg., ch. 600, §15 (eff. Jan. 1, 1998), ch. 603, §10 (eff. Jan. 1, 1998), ch. 1022, §88 (eff. Jan. 1, 1998). Source: Former Fam §18.10(a).

FAM §263.306. PERMANENCY HEARINGS: PROCEDURE

(a) At each permanency hearing the court shall:

(1) identify all persons or parties present at the hearing or those given notice but failing to appear;

(2) review the efforts of the department or another agency in:

(A) attempting to locate all necessary persons;

(B) requesting service of citation; and

A *Subsection (C) below is effective for children placed in custody of the DPRS on or after Sept. 1, 2001.*

(C) obtaining the assistance of a parent in providing information necessary to locate an absent parent, alleged father, or relative of the child;

Subsection (C) below is effective for children placed in custody of the DPRS before Sept. 1, 2001.

(C) obtaining the assistance of a parent in providing information necessary to locate an absent parent;

E *Subsection (3) below is effective for children placed in custody of the DPRS on or after Sept. 1, 2001.*

(3) review the efforts of each custodial parent, alleged father, or relative of the child before the court in providing information necessary to locate another absent parent, alleged father, or relative of the child;

(4) return the child to the parent or parents if the child's parent or parents are willing and able to provide the child with a safe environment and the return of the child is in the child's best interest;

(5) place the child with a person or entity, other than a parent, entitled to service under Chapter 102 if the person or entity is willing and able to provide the child with a safe environment and the placement of the child is in the child's best interest;

(6) evaluate the department's efforts to identify relatives who could provide the child with a safe environment, if the child is not returned to a parent or another person or entity entitled to service under Chapter 102;

(7) evaluate the parties' compliance with temporary orders and the service plan;

(8) determine whether:

(A) the child continues to need substitute care;

A (B) the child's current placement is appropriate for meeting the child's needs, including with respect to a child who has been placed outside of the state, whether that placement continues to be in the best interest of the child; and

(C) other plans or services are needed to meet the child's special needs or circumstances;

(9) if the child is placed in institutional care, determine whether efforts have been made to ensure placement of the child in the least restrictive environment consistent with the best interest and special needs of the child;

(10) if the child is 16 years of age or older, order services that are needed to assist the child in making the transition from substitute care to independent living if the services are available in the community;

(11) determine plans, services, and further temporary orders necessary to ensure that a final order is rendered before the date for dismissal of the suit under this chapter; and

(12) determine the date for dismissal of the suit under this chapter and give notice in open court to all parties of:

(A) the dismissal date;

(B) the date of the next permanency hearing; and

(C) the date the suit is set for trial.

(b) The court shall also review the service plan, permanency report, and other information submitted at the hearing to:

(1) determine:

(A) the safety of the child;

(B) the continuing necessity and appropriateness of the placement;

(C) the extent of compliance with the case plan;

(D) the extent of progress that has been made toward alleviating or mitigating the causes necessitating the placement of the child in foster care; and

E *Subsection (E) below is effective for children for whom the DPRS is providing permanency planning on or after Sept. 1, 2001.*

(E) whether the department has made reasonable efforts to finalize the permanency plan that is in effect for the child; and

(2) project a likely date by which the child may be returned to and safely maintained in the child's home, placed for adoption, or placed in permanent managing conservatorship.

History of Fam §263.306: Acts 1995, 74th Leg., ch. 20, §1, eff. April 20, 1995. Amended by Acts 1995, 74th Leg., ch. 751, §114, eff. Sept. 1, 1995; Acts 1997, 75th Leg., ch. 600, §16 (eff. Jan. 1, 1998), ch. 603, §11 (eff. Jan. 1, 1998), ch. 1022, §89 (eff. Jan. 1, 1998); Acts 1999, 76th Leg., ch. 1390, §47, 76th Leg., eff. Sept. 1, 1999; Acts 2001, 77th Leg., ch. 306, §3 (eff. Sept. 1, 2001), ch. 849, §7 (eff. Sept. 1, 2001). Source: Former Fam §18.09(a), (b).

FAM §263.307. FACTORS IN DETERMINING BEST INTEREST OF CHILD

(a) In considering the factors established by this section, the prompt and permanent placement of the child in a safe environment is presumed to be in the child's best interest.

(b) The following factors should be considered by the court, the department, and other authorized agencies in determining whether the child's parents are willing and able to provide the child with a safe environment:

(1) the child's age and physical and mental vulnerabilities;

(2) the frequency and nature of out-of-home placements;

(3) the magnitude, frequency, and circumstances of the harm to the child;

(4) whether the child has been the victim of repeated harm after the initial report and intervention by the department or other agency;

(5) whether the child is fearful of living in or returning to the child's home;

(6) the results of psychiatric, psychological, or developmental evaluations of the child, the child's parents, other family members, or others who have access to the child's home;

(7) whether there is a history of abusive or assaultive conduct by the child's family or others who have access to the child's home;

(8) whether there is a history of substance abuse by the child's family or others who have access to the child's home;

(9) whether the perpetrator of the harm to the child is identified;

(10) the willingness and ability of the child's family to seek out, accept, and complete counseling services and to cooperate with and facilitate an appropriate agency's close supervision;

(11) the willingness and ability of the child's family to effect positive environmental and personal changes within a reasonable period of time;

(12) whether the child's family demonstrates adequate parenting skills, including providing the child and other children under the family's care with:

(A) minimally adequate health and nutritional care;

(B) care, nurturance, and appropriate discipline consistent with the child's physical and psychological development;

(C) guidance and supervision consistent with the child's safety;

(D) a safe physical home environment;

(E) protection from repeated exposure to violence even though the violence may not be directed at the child; and

(F) an understanding of the child's needs and capabilities; and

(13) whether an adequate social support system consisting of an extended family and friends is available to the child.

(c) In the case of a child 16 years of age or older, the following guidelines should be considered by the court in determining whether to adopt the permanency plan submitted by the department:

(1) whether the permanency plan submitted to the court includes the services planned for the child to make the transition from foster care to independent living; and

(2) whether this transition is in the best interest of the child.

History of Fam §263.307: Acts 1995, 74th Leg., ch. 20, §1, eff. April 20, 1995. Source: Former Fam §18.15.

In re Verbois, 10 S.W.3d 825, 830 (Tex.App.—Waco 2000, orig. proceeding). "In a suit commenced by DPRS involving children suspected to be victims of abuse or neglect, the Family Code expressly permits a trial court to consider the results of psychological evaluations of the parents' and the parents' willingness to submit to counseling when deciding whether the parents are willing and able to provide the child with a safe environment. [¶] Relators have wholly refused to submit to the psychological evaluations ordered because of a concern they might be asked a question which requires an incriminating answer. This is an impermissible blanket assertion of the privilege against self-incrimination. [¶] [T]he Supreme Court has clearly defined Relators' remedy. If the psychologist agreed to by the parties asks a question which either parent believes calls for an answer that might reasonably present a hazard of self-incrimination to the parent, he may refuse to answer upon the ground of the privilege. Respondent must then determine whether that refusal is justified under the circumstances. Respondent must be perfectly clear, from a careful consideration of all the circumstances in the case, that the witness is mistaken, and that the answer(s) cannot possibly have such tendency to incriminate before he can compel either parent to answer. If Respondent orders a parent to answer, the parent may challenge that directive in a habeas or mandamus proceeding (as warranted)." (Internal quotations omitted.)

FAM §§263.308, 263.309. REPEALED

Repealed by Acts 1997, 75th Leg., ch. 603, §13, eff. Jan. 1, 1998; Acts 1997, 75th Leg., ch. 1022, §104(a), eff. Sept. 1, 1997.

Sections 263.310-263.400 blank

SUBCHAPTER E. FINAL ORDER FOR CHILD UNDER DEPARTMENT CARE

FAM §263.401. DISMISSAL AFTER ONE YEAR; EXTENSION

(a) Unless the court has rendered a final order or granted an extension under Subsection (b), on the first Monday after the first anniversary of the date the court rendered a temporary order appointing the department as temporary managing conservator, the court shall dismiss the suit affecting the parent-child relationship filed by the department that requests termination of the parent-child relationship or requests that the department be named conservator of the child.

A (b) The court may retain the suit on the court's docket for a period not to exceed 180 days after the time described by Subsection (a), if the court finds that continuing the appointment of the department as temporary managing conservator is in the best interest of the child. If the court retains the suit on the court's docket, the court shall render an order in which the court:

(1) schedules the new date for dismissal of the suit not later than the 180th day after the time described by Subsection (a);

(2) makes further temporary orders for the safety and welfare of the child as necessary to avoid further delay in resolving the suit; and

E *Subsection (3) below is effective for SAPCRs pending on Sept. 1, 2001.*

(3) sets a final hearing on a date that allows the court to render a final order before the required date for dismissal of the suit under this subsection.

A (c) If the court grants an extension but does not render a final order or dismiss the suit on or before the required date for dismissal under Subsection (b), the court shall dismiss the suit. The court may not grant an additional extension that extends the suit beyond the required date for dismissal under Subsection (b).

(d) For purposes of this section, a final order is an order that:

(1) requires that a child be returned to the child's parent;

(2) names a relative of the child or another person as the child's managing conservator;

(3) without terminating the parent-child relationship, appoints the department as the managing conservator of the child; or

(4) terminates the parent-child relationship and appoints a relative of the child, another suitable person, or the department as managing conservator of the child.

History of Fam §263.401: Acts 1997, 75th Leg., ch. 600, §17 (eff. Sept. 1, 1997), ch. 603, §12 (eff. Jan. 1, 1998), ch. 1022, §90 (eff. Jan. 1, 1998). Amended by Acts 2001, 77th Leg., ch. 1090, §8, eff. Sept. 1, 2001.

In re T.M., 33 S.W.3d 341, 346-47 (Tex.App.—Amarillo 2000, no pet.). Section 263.401 mandates "the dismissal of the proceeding when the 180 day extension expired.... The trial court had neither the discretion nor authority to do otherwise. [¶] Nor could the litigants negate this legislative mandate through a [TRCP] Rule 11 agreement. [G]iven the clear public policy encompassed within the time restrictions of §263.401(a) and the fact that the parties through the Rule 11 agreement at bar attempted to bypass those restrictions, we conclude the [Rule 11] agreement was unenforceable. [¶] [A]uthority holds that a dismissal under §263.401 does not constitute an adjudication on the merits. So too does it conclude that the DPRS may refile the case and assert the same grounds for *termination* as originally alleged. However, the right to rely upon the same grounds for termination does not permit the entity to use the same facts as the basis for removing the child from her parents or maintaining her in a foster home pending resolution of the suit. New facts justifying the temporary relief must be propounded. *At ___ n.5:* The suit contemplated in §263.401 could be likened to one involving a statutory cause of action in favor of the DPRS. In creating it, the legislature had the authority to determine its parameters. So too could it dictate the effect of exceeding or failing to abide by those parameters, such as mandating the loss and dismissal of the cause due to the passage of time."

In re Ruiz, 16 S.W.3d 921, 924 (Tex.App.—Waco 2000, orig. proceeding). "[T]he issue before us is whether [the judge's] signed docket notation constitutes rendition of judgment by written memorandum. The docket notation states in pertinent part, Decree of termination to be entered as to both parents per jury's verdict. This notation fails to satisfy either of the requirements of a subdivision (d)(4) final order. The notation does not grant DPRS's petition, nor does it order or decree that ... parental rights be terminated. Rather, it indicates the court's intent to render a termination decree in the future. [¶] Even assuming that rendition of a termination decree could be implied from the docket notation, the writing fails to address the appointment of a managing conservator for [the child], which subdivision (d)(4) requires in a 'final order.' *At 926:* This Court has determined that mandamus is an appropriate vehicle for enforcement of §263.401 because the relators in such a case have no adequate legal remedy by which they can otherwise obtain timely compliance with the statute. *At 927:* Justice demands a speedy resolution of child custody and child support issues. The Supreme Court recognized in ***Proffer*** that an appeal is frequently inadequate to protect the rights of parents and children in these cases. Applying these principles to [this] case and the legislative purpose for §263.401, we believe that an appeal is inadequate to obtain timely compliance with the statute." (Internal quotations omitted.)

In re Bishop, 8 S.W.3d 412, 419 (Tex.App.—Waco 1999, orig. proceeding). "[W]e construe §263.402 to permit a temporary order retaining jurisdiction of the suit beyond the scheduled dismissal date only if such an order is rendered on or before the dismissal date mandated by §263.401. [¶] DPRS contends that §263.401(a) does not provide for an 'automatic dismissal.' We agree that the suit is not automatically dismissed on the statutory dismissal date if no final order, extension order, or §263.402 retention order is rendered by that date. However, if the dismissal date passes without the rendition of such an order, the court 'shall dismiss the suit.' Thus, the court has no discretion in the matter. [¶] Relators filed a motion asking the court to dismiss DPRS's suit under the provisions of §263.401. This is sufficient to support their request for mandamus relief."

In re Neal, 4 S.W.3d 443, 445 (Tex.App.—Houston [1st Dist.] 1999, orig. proceeding). Section 263.401(a) "provides that unless the trial court renders a final order on the first Monday after the first anniversary of the date the trial court rendered a temporary order appointing DPRS as temporary managing conservator in a [SAPCR], the trial court '**shall** dismiss the [SAPCR] suit.' There are two exceptions to the 'one year final order or dismiss' rule. [¶] The first is that before expiration of the one-year period, the trial court may extend its jurisdiction of the SAPCR suit in an extension order for a period no longer than 180 days after the 'first Monday after the first anniversary.' [¶] The second exception occurs under ... §263.402(a) [now §263.403(a)], known as the 'return and monitor' statute. There is no limit on the number of temporary orders that may be rendered under §263.402(a). Any de facto extension in the 'one year final order or dismiss' rule of §263.401(a) that results from a §263.402(a) temporary order does not prevent a one-time extension under §263.401(b). *At 447:* Sections 263.401 and 263.402 [now §263.403] represent a scheme adopted by the 1997 Legislature to ensure that children would remain under the temporary care of DPRS for no longer than one year, with an extension not to exceed 180 days beyond that under the two exceptions outlined above."

FAM §263.402. LIMIT ON EXTENSION; WAIVER

E *Section 263.402 below is effective for SAPCRs pending on Sept. 1, 2001.*

(a) The parties to a suit under this chapter may not extend the deadlines set by the court under this subchapter by agreement or otherwise.

(b) A party to a suit under this chapter who fails to make a timely motion to dismiss the suit or to make a motion requesting the court to render a final order before the deadline for dismissal under this subchapter waives the right to object to the court's failure to dismiss the suit. A motion to dismiss under this subsection is timely if the motion is made before the department has introduced all of the department's evidence, other than rebuttal evidence, at the trial on the merits.

History of Fam §263.402: Enacted by Acts 2001, 77th Leg., ch. 1090, §9, eff. Sept. 1, 2001.

A FAM §263.403. MONITORED RETURN OF CHILD TO PARENT

(a) Notwithstanding Section 263.401, the court may retain jurisdiction and not dismiss the suit or render a final order as required by that section if the court renders a temporary order that:

(1) finds that retaining jurisdiction under this section is in the best interest of the child;

(2) orders the department to return the child to the child's parent;

(3) orders the department to continue to serve as temporary managing conservator of the child; and

(4) orders the department to monitor the child's placement to ensure that the child is in a safe environment.

(b) If the court renders an order under this section, the court shall:

(1) include in the order specific findings regarding the grounds for the order; and

(2) schedule a new date, not later than the 180th day after the date the temporary order is rendered, for dismissal of the suit.

(c) If a child placed with a parent under this section must be moved from that home by the department before the dismissal of the suit or the rendering of a final order, the court shall, at the time of the move, schedule a new date for dismissal of the suit. The new dismissal date may not be later than the original dismissal date established under Section 263.401 or the 180th day after the date the child is moved under this subsection, whichever date is later.

(d) If the court renders an order under this section, the court must include in the order specific findings regarding the grounds for the order.

History of Fam §263.403: Acts 1997, 75th Leg., ch. 600, §17 (eff. Sept. 1, 1997), ch. 603, §12 (eff. Jan. 1, 1997), ch. 1022, §90 (eff. Jan. 1, 1997). Amended by Acts 1999, 76th Leg., ch. 1390, §48, eff. Sept. 1, 1999. Renumbered from §263.402 by Acts 2001, 77th Leg., ch. 1090, §9, eff. Sept. 1, 2001.

In re Bishop, 8 S.W.3d 412, 419 (Tex.App.—Waco 1999, orig. proceeding). "[W]e construe §263.402 [now

§263.403] to permit a temporary order retaining jurisdiction of the suit beyond the scheduled dismissal date only if such an order is rendered on or before the dismissal date mandated by §263.401. [¶] DPRS contends that §263.401(a) does not provide for an 'automatic dismissal.' We agree that the suit is not automatically dismissed on the statutory dismissal date if no final order, extension order, or §263.402 retention order is rendered by that date. However, if the dismissal date passes without the rendition of such an order, the court 'shall dismiss the suit.' Thus, the court has no discretion in the matter."

In re Neal, 4 S.W.3d 443, 445 (Tex.App.—Houston [1st Dist.] 1999, orig. proceeding). "There is no limit on the number of temporary orders that may be rendered under §263.402(a) [now §263.403(a)]. Any de facto extension in the 'one year final order or dismiss' rule of §263.401(a) that results from a §263.402(a) temporary order does not prevent a one-time extension under §263.401(b). *At 447:* Sections 263.401 and 263.402 [now §263.403] represent a scheme adopted by the 1997 Legislature to ensure that children would remain under the temporary care of DPRS for no longer than one year, with an extension not to exceed 180 days beyond that under the two exceptions outlined above."

A FAM §263.404. FINAL ORDER APPOINTING DEPARTMENT AS MANAGING CONSERVATOR WITHOUT TERMINATING PARENTAL RIGHTS

(a) The court may render a final order appointing the department as managing conservator of the child without terminating the rights of the parent of the child if the court finds that:

(1) appointment of a parent as managing conservator would not be in the best interest of the child because the appointment would significantly impair the child's physical health or emotional development; and

(2) it would not be in the best interest of the child to appoint a relative of the child or another person as managing conservator.

(b) In determining whether the department should be appointed as managing conservator of the child without terminating the rights of a parent of the child, the court shall take the following factors into consideration:

(1) that the child will reach 18 years of age in not less than three years;

(2) that the child is 12 years of age or older and has expressed a strong desire against termination or being adopted;

(3) that the child has special medical or behavioral needs that make adoption of the child unlikely; and

(4) the needs and desires of the child.

History of Fam §263.404: Acts 1997, 75th Leg., ch. 600, §17 (eff. Sept. 1, 1997), ch. 603, §12 (eff. Jan. 1, 1998), ch. 1022, §90 (eff. Jan. 1, 1998). Renumbered from §263.403 by Acts 2001, 77th Leg., ch. 1090, §9, eff. Sept. 1, 2001.

FAM §263.405[A*]. FINAL ORDER APPOINTING DEPARTMENT AS MANAGING CONSERVATOR OF CERTAIN ABANDONED CHILDREN; TERMINATION OF PARENTAL RIGHTS

☠ E *In 2001, the Legislature enacted two sections 263.405. Section 263.405 below was enacted by Acts 2001, 77th Leg., ch. 809, §6, effective Sept. 1, 2001. The [A*] has been added by the editor to distinguish this section 263.405 from the other, which is marked with [B*]. In 2003, the Legislature is expected to correct the duplicate numbering. Section 263.405[A*] below is effective for suits for termination of the parent-child relationship filed on or after Sept. 1, 2001.*

(a) In a suit to terminate the parent-child relationship, there is a rebuttable presumption that a parent who delivers a child to a designated emergency infant care provider in accordance with Subchapter D, Chapter 262, consents to the termination of parental rights with regard to the child.

(b) If a person claims to be the parent of a child taken into possession under Subchapter D, Chapter 262, before the court renders a final order terminating the parental rights of the child's parents, the court shall order genetic testing for parentage determination unless parentage has previously been established. The court shall hold the petition for termination of the parent-child relationship in abeyance for a period not to exceed 60 days pending the results of the genetic testing.

History of Fam §263.405[A*]: Enacted by Acts 2001, 77th Leg., ch. 809, §6, eff. Sept. 1, 2001.

FAM §263.405[B*]. APPEAL OF FINAL ORDER

☠ E *In 2001, the Legislature enacted two sections 263.405. Section 263.405 below was enacted by Acts 2001, 77th Leg., ch. 1090, §9, effective Sept. 1, 2001. The [B*] has been added by the editor to distinguish this section 263.405 from the other, which is marked with [A*]. In 2003, the Legislature is expected to correct the duplicate numbering. Section 263.405[B*] below is effective* *for appeals of a final order under Chapter 263, Subchapter E, filed on or after Sept. 1, 2001.*

(a) An appeal of a final order rendered under this subchapter is governed by the rules of the supreme court for accelerated appeals in civil cases and the procedures provided by this section. The appellate court shall render its final order or judgment with the least possible delay.

(b) Not later than the 15th day after the date a final order is signed by the trial judge, a party intending to appeal the order must file with the trial court a statement of the point or points on which the party intends to appeal. The statement may be combined with a motion for a new trial.

(c) A motion for a new trial, a request for findings of fact and conclusions of law, or any other post-trial motion in the trial court does not extend the deadline for filing a notice of appeal under Rule 26.1(b), Texas Rules of Appellate Procedure, or the deadline for filing an affidavit of indigence under Rule 20, Texas Rules of Appellate Procedure.

(d) The trial court shall hold a hearing not later than the 30th day after the date the final order is signed to determine whether:

(1) a new trial should be granted;

(2) a party's claim of indigence, if any, should be sustained; and

(3) the appeal is frivolous as provided by Section 13.003(b), Civil Practice and Remedies Code.

(e) If a party claims indigency and requests the appointment of an attorney, the court shall require the person to file an affidavit of indigency and shall hear evidence to determine the issue of indigency. If the court does not render a written order denying the claim of indigence or requiring the person to pay partial costs before the 36th day after the date the final order being appealed is signed, the court shall consider the person to be indigent and shall appoint counsel to represent the person.

(f) The appellate record must be filed in the appellate court not later than the 60th day after the date the final order is signed by the trial judge, unless the trial court, after a hearing, grants a new trial or denies a request for a trial court record at no cost.

(g) The appellant may appeal the court's order denying the appellant's claim of indigence or the court's finding that the appeal is frivolous by filing with the appellate court the reporter's record and clerk's record of the hearing held under this section, both of which shall be provided without advance payment, not later than the 10th day after the date the court makes the decision. The appellate court shall review the records and may require the parties to file appellate briefs on the issues presented, but may not hear oral argument on the issues. The appellate court shall render appropriate orders after reviewing the records and appellate briefs, if any.

(h) Except on a showing of good cause, the appellate court may not extend the time for filing a record or appellate brief.

History of Fam §263.405: Enacted by Acts 2001, 77th Leg., ch. 1090, §9, eff. Sept. 1, 2001.

Ⓐ FAM §263.406. COURT INFORMATION SYSTEM

The Office of Court Administration of the Texas Judicial System shall consult with the courts presiding over cases brought by the department for the protection of children to develop an information system to track compliance with the requirements of this subchapter for the timely disposition of those cases.

History of Fam §263.406: Acts 1997, 75th Leg., ch. 600, §17, eff. Sept. 1, 1997. Renumbered from §263.404 by Acts 2001, 77th Leg., ch. 1090, §9, eff. Sept. 1, 2001.

Sections 263.407-263.500 reserved for expansion

SUBCHAPTER F. PLACEMENT REVIEW HEARINGS

FAM §263.501. PLACEMENT REVIEW AFTER FINAL ORDER

(a) If the department has been named as a child's managing conservator in a final order that does not include termination of parental rights, the court shall conduct a placement review hearing at least once every six months until the child becomes an adult.

(b) If the department has been named as a child's managing conservator in a final order that terminates a parent's parental rights, the court shall conduct a placement review hearing at least once every six months until the date the child is adopted or the child becomes an adult.

(c) Notice of a placement review hearing shall be given as provided by Rule 21a, Texas Rules of Civil Procedure, to each person entitled to notice of the hearing.

(d) The following are entitled to not less than 10 days' notice of a placement review hearing:

(1) the department;

A (2) the foster parent, preadoptive parent, relative of the child providing care, or director of the group home or institution in which the child is residing;

(3) each parent of the child;

(4) each possessory conservator or guardian of the child;

(5) the child's attorney ad litem and volunteer advocate, if the appointments were not dismissed in the final order; and

(6) any other person or agency named by the court as having an interest in the child's welfare.

(e) The court may dispense with the requirement that the child attend a placement review hearing.

History of Fam §263.501: Acts 1997, 75th Leg., ch. 600, §17 (eff. Sept. 1, 1997), ch. 603, §12 (eff. Jan. 1, 1998), ch. 1022, §90 (eff. Jan. 1, 1997). Amended by Acts 2001, 77th Leg., ch. 849, §8, eff. Sept. 1, 2001.

FAM §263.502. PLACEMENT REVIEW REPORT

(a) Not later than the 10th day before the date set for a placement review hearing, the department or other authorized agency shall file a placement review report with the court and provide a copy to each person entitled to notice under Section 263.501(d).

(b) For good cause shown, the court may order a different time for filing the placement review report or may order that a report is not required for a specific hearing.

(c) The placement review report must:

(1) evaluate whether the child's current placement is appropriate for meeting the child's needs;

(2) evaluate whether efforts have been made to ensure placement of the child in the least restrictive environment consistent with the best interest and special needs of the child if the child is placed in institutional care;

(3) identify the services that are needed to assist a child who is at least 16 years of age in making the transition from substitute care to independent living if the services are available in the community;

(4) identify other plans or services that are needed to meet the child's special needs or circumstances; and

(5) describe the efforts of the department or authorized agency to place the child for adoption if parental rights to the child have been terminated and the child is eligible for adoption.

History of Fam §263.502: Acts 1997, 75th Leg., ch. 600, §17 (eff. Sept. 1, 1997), ch. 603, §12 (eff. Jan. 1, 1998), ch. 1022, §90 (eff. Jan. 1, 1998).

FAM §263.503. PLACEMENT REVIEW HEARINGS; PROCEDURE

At each placement review hearing, the court shall determine whether:

A (1) the child's current placement is necessary, safe, and appropriate for meeting the child's needs, including with respect to a child placed outside of the state, whether the placement continues to be appropriate and in the best interest of the child;

(2) efforts have been made to ensure placement of the child in the least restrictive environment consistent with the best interest and special needs of the child if the child is placed in institutional care;

(3) the services that are needed to assist a child who is at least 16 years of age in making the transition from substitute care to independent living are available in the community;

(4) other plans or services are needed to meet the child's special needs or circumstances;

(5) the department or authorized agency has exercised due diligence in attempting to place the child for adoption if parental rights to the child have been terminated and the child is eligible for adoption; and

E *Subsection (6) below is effective for children for whom the DPRS is providing permanency planning on or after Sept. 1, 2001.*

(6) the department or authorized agency has made reasonable efforts to finalize the permanency plan that is in effect for the child.

History of Fam §263.503: Acts 1997, 75th Leg., ch. 600, §17 (eff. Sept. 1, 1997), ch. 603, §12 (eff. Jan. 1, 1998), ch. 1022, §90 (eff. Jan. 1, 1998). Amended by Acts 2001, 77th Leg., ch. 849, §9, eff. Sept. 1, 2001.

CHAPTER 264. CHILD WELFARE SERVICES

SUBCHAPTER A. GENERAL PROVISIONS

FAM §264.001. DEFINITION

In this chapter, "department" means the Department of Protective and Regulatory Services.

History of Fam §264.001: Acts 1995, 74th Leg., ch. 20, §1, eff. April 20, 1995. Source: Former Fam §34.50; Hum. Res. Code §11.001(2).

FAM §264.002. DUTIES OF DEPARTMENT

(a) The department shall:

(1) promote the enforcement of all laws for the protection of abused and neglected children; and

(2) take the initiative in all matters involving the interests of children where adequate provision has not already been made.

(b) The department shall give special attention to the dissemination of information through bulletins and visits, where practical, to all agencies operating under a provision of law affecting the welfare of children.

(c) Through the county child welfare boards, the department shall work in conjunction with the commissioners courts, juvenile boards, and all other officers and agencies involved in the protection of children. The department may use and allot funds for the establishment and maintenance of homes, schools, and institutions for the care, protection, education, and training of children in conjunction with a juvenile board, a county or city board, or any other agency.

(d) The department shall visit and study the conditions in state-supported eleemosynary institutions for children and shall make actions for the management and operation of the institutions that ensure that the children receive the best possible training in contemplation of their earliest discharge from the institutions.

(e) The department may not spend state funds to accomplish the purposes of this chapter unless the funds have been specifically appropriated for those purposes.

History of Fam §264.002: Acts 1995, 74th Leg., ch. 20, §1, eff. April 20, 1995. Source: Former Hum. Res. Code §41.001.

FAM §264.003. REPEALED

Repealed by Acts 2001, 77th Leg., ch. 114, §3, eff. Sept. 1, 2001. See Gov't Code §531.055.

FAM §264.004. ALLOCATION OF STATE FUNDS

(a) The department shall establish a method of allocating state funds for children's protective services programs that encourages and rewards the contribution of funds or services from all persons, including local governmental entities.

(b) Except as provided by this subsection, if a contribution of funds or services is made to support a children's protective services program in a particular county, the department shall use the contribution to benefit that program. The department may use the contribution for another purpose only if the commissioners court of the county gives the department written permission.

(c) The department may use state and federal funds to provide benefits or services to children and families who are otherwise eligible for the benefits or services, including foster care, adoption assistance, medical assistance, family reunification services, and other child protective services and related benefits without regard to the immigration status of the child or the child's family.

History of Fam §264.004: Acts 1995, 74th Leg., ch. 20, §1, eff. April 20, 1995. Amended by Acts 1997, 75th Leg., ch. 575, §23, eff. Sept. 1, 1997. Source: Former Hum. Res. Code §41.0012.

FAM §264.005. COUNTY CHILD WELFARE BOARDS

(a) The commissioners court of a county may appoint a child welfare board for the county. The commissioners court and the department shall determine the size of the board and the qualifications of its members. However, a board must have not less than seven and not more than 15 members, and the members must be residents of the county. The members shall serve at the pleasure of the commissioners court and may be removed by the court for just cause. The members serve without compensation.

(b) With the approval of the department, two or more counties may establish a joint child welfare board if that action is found to be more practical in accomplishing the purposes of this chapter. A board representing more than one county has the same powers as a board representing a single county and is subject to the same conditions and liabilities.

(c) The members of a county child welfare board shall select a presiding officer and shall perform the duties required by the commissioners court and the department to accomplish the purposes of this chapter.

(d) A county child welfare board is an entity of the department for purposes of providing coordinated state and local public welfare services for children and their families and for the coordinated use of federal, state, and local funds for these services. The child welfare board shall work with the commissioners court.

(e) A county child welfare board is a governmental unit for the purposes of Chapter 101, Civil Practice and Remedies Code.

(f) A county child protective services board member may receive information that is confidential under

Section 40.005, Human Resources Code, or Section 261.201 when the board member is acting in the member's official capacity.

(g) A child welfare board may conduct a closed meeting under Section 551.101, Government Code, to discuss, consider, or act on a matter that is confidential under Section 40.005, Human Resources Code, or Section 261.201.

History of Fam §264.005: Acts 1995, 74th Leg., ch. 20, §1, eff. April 20, 1995. Amended by Acts 1997, 75th Leg., ch. 575, §24, eff. Sept. 1, 1997. Source: Former Hum. Res. Code §41.002.

FAM §264.006. COUNTY FUNDS

The commissioners court of a county may appropriate funds from its general fund or any other fund for the administration of its county child welfare board. The court may provide for services to and support of children in need of protection and care without regard to the immigration status of the child or the child's family.

History of Fam §264.006: Acts 1995, 74th Leg., ch. 20, §1, eff. April 20, 1995. Amended by Acts 1997, 75th Leg., ch. 575, §25, eff. Sept. 1, 1997. Source: Former Hum. Res. Code §41.003.

FAM §264.007. COOPERATION WITH DEPARTMENT OF HEALTH & HUMAN SERVICES

The department is the state agency designated to cooperate with the United States Department of Health and Human Services in:

(1) establishing, extending, and strengthening public welfare services for the protection and care of abused or neglected children;

(2) developing state services for the encouragement and assistance of adequate methods of community child welfare organizations and paying part of the cost of district, county, or other local child welfare services in rural areas and in other areas of special need; and

(3) developing necessary plans to implement the services contemplated in this section and to comply with the rules of the United States Department of Health and Human Services under the federal Social Security Act (42 U.S.C. Section 651 et seq.).

History of Fam §264.007: Acts 1995, 74th Leg., ch. 20, §1, eff. April 20, 1995. Source: Former Hum. Res. Code §41.004.

FAM §264.008. CHILD WELFARE SERVICE FUND

The child welfare service fund is a special fund in the state treasury. The fund shall be used to administer the child welfare services provided by the department.

History of Fam §264.008: Acts 1995, 74th Leg., ch. 20, §1, eff. April 20, 1995. Source: Former Hum. Res. Code §41.006.

FAM §264.009. LEGAL REPRESENTATION OF DEPARTMENT

(a) Except as provided by Subsection (b), (c), or (f), in any action under this code, the department shall be represented in court by the county attorney of the county where the action is brought, unless the district attorney or criminal district attorney of the county elects to provide representation.

(b) If the county attorney, district attorney, or criminal district attorney is unable to represent the department in an action under this code because of a conflict of interest or because special circumstances exist, the attorney general shall represent the department in the action.

(c) If the attorney general is unable to represent the department in an action under this code, the attorney general shall deputize an attorney who has contracted with the department under Subsection (d) or an attorney employed by the department under Subsection (e) to represent the department in the action.

(d) Subject to the approval of the attorney general, the department may contract with a private attorney to represent the department in an action under this code.

(e) The department may employ attorneys to represent the department in an action under this code.

(f) In a county with a population of 2.8 million or more, in an action under this code, the department shall be represented in court by the attorney who represents the state in civil cases in the district or county court of the county where the action is brought. If such attorney is unable to represent the department in an action under this code because of a conflict of interest or because special circumstances exist, the attorney general shall represent the department in the action.

History of Fam §264.009: Acts 1995, 74th Leg., ch. 20, §1, eff. April 20, 1995. Amended by Acts 1995, 74th Leg., ch. 751, §116, eff. Sept. 1, 1995; Acts 1997, 75th Leg., ch. 1022, §91, eff. Sept. 1, 1997. Source: Former Fam §11.20.

FAM §264.010. CHILD ABUSE PLAN; LIMITATION ON EXPENDITURE OF FUNDS

(a) Funds appropriated for protective services, child and family services, and the purchased service system for the department may only be spent on or after March 1, 1996, in a county that provides the department with a child abuse prevention and protection plan. If a plan is not submitted to the department under this section, the department shall document the county's failure to submit a plan and may spend appropriated funds in the county to carry out the department's duties under this subtitle.

(b) A child abuse prevention and protection plan may be submitted by the governing body of a county or of a regional council of governments in which the county is an active participant.

(c) The department may not require a child abuse prevention and protection plan to exceed five double-spaced letter-size pages. The county or council of governments may voluntarily provide a longer plan.

(d) A child abuse prevention and protection plan must:

(1) specify the manner of communication between entities who are parties to the plan, including the department, the Texas Department of Human Services, local law enforcement agencies, the county and district attorneys, members of the medical and social service community, foster parents, and child advocacy groups; and

(2) provide other information concerning the prevention and investigation of child abuse in the area for which the plan is adopted.

History of Fam §264.010: Acts 1995, 74th Leg., ch. 943, §6, eff. Sept. 1, 1995.

FAM §264.011. LOCAL ACCOUNTS

(a) The department may establish and maintain local bank or savings accounts for a child who is under the managing conservatorship of the department as necessary to administer funds received in trust for or on behalf of the child.

(b) Funds maintained in an account under this section may be used by the department to support the child, including for the payment of foster care expenses, or may be paid to a person providing care for the child.

History of Fam §264.011: Acts 1997, 75th Leg., ch. 575, §26, eff. Sept. 1, 1997.

E FAM §264.0111. MONEY EARNED BY CHILD

(a) A child for whom the department has been appointed managing conservator and who has been placed by the department in a foster home or child-care institution as defined by Chapter 42, Human Resources Code, is entitled to keep any money earned by the child during the time of the child's placement.

(b) The child may deposit the money earned by the child in a bank or savings account subject to the sole management and control of the child as provided by Section 34.305, Finance Code. The child is the sole and absolute owner of the deposit account.

(c) If a child earns money as described by this section and is returned to the child's parent or guardian, the child's parent or guardian may not interfere with the child's authority to control, transfer, draft on, or make a withdrawal from the account.

(d) In this section, a reference to money earned by a child includes any interest that accrues on the money.

(e) The department may adopt rules to implement this section.

History of Fam §264.0111: Enacted by Acts 2001, 77th Leg., ch. 964, §3, eff. Sept. 1, 2001.

FAM §264.012. BURIAL EXPENSES FOR CHILD IN FOSTER CARE

(a) The department shall request that the parents pay reasonable and necessary burial expenses for a child for whom the department has been appointed managing conservator and who dies in foster care, including a request that if the parents have an insurance policy or a bank account for the child, that the parents spend the proceeds from the policy or money in the account on the burial expenses. If the parents cannot pay all or part of the burial expenses, the department shall spend funds appropriated for the child protective services program to pay reasonable and necessary burial expenses for the child.

(b) The department may accept donations, gifts, or in-kind contributions to cover the costs of any burial expenses for children for whom the department has been appointed managing conservator.

(c) This section does not apply to a foster parent.

History of Fam §264.012: Acts 1997, 75th Leg., ch. 575, §26, eff. Sept. 1, 1997. Amended by Acts 1999, 76th Leg., ch. 1248, §1, eff. Sept. 1, 1999.

Sections 264.013-264.100 reserved for expansion

SUBCHAPTER B. FOSTER CARE

FAM §264.101. FOSTER CARE PAYMENTS

(a) The department may pay the cost of foster care for a child:

(1) for whom the department has initiated a suit and has been named managing conservator under an order rendered under this title,

who is a resident of the state, and who has been placed by the department in a foster home or child-care institution, as defined by Chapter 42, Human Resources Code; or

(2) who is under the placement and care of a state agency or political subdivision with which the department has entered into an agreement to reimburse the cost of care and supervision of the child.

(b) The department may not pay the cost of protective foster care for a child for whom the department has been named managing conservator under an order rendered solely under Section 161.001(1)(J).

(c) The payment of foster care, including medical care, for a child as authorized under this subchapter shall be made without regard to the child's eligibility for federally funded care.

(d) The Board of Protective and Regulatory Services may adopt rules that establish criteria and guidelines for the payment of foster care, including medical care, for a child and for providing care for a child after the child becomes 18 years of age if the child is regularly attending high school, an institution of higher education, or a vocational or technical program.

(e) The department may accept and spend funds available from any source to pay for foster care, including medical care, for a child in the department's care.

(f) In this section, "child" means a person who:

(1) is under 22 years of age and for whom the department has been appointed managing conservator of the child before the date the child became 18 years of age; or

(2) is the responsibility of an agency with which the department has entered into an agreement to provide care and supervision of the child.

History of Fam §264.101: Acts 1995, 74th Leg., ch. 20, §1, eff. April 20, 1995. Amended by Acts 1997, 75th Leg., ch. 575, §27, eff. Sept. 1, 1997. Source: Former Hum. Res. Code §41.021.

See also 40 TAC §§700.315-700.334.

FAM §264.1015. LIABILITY OF CHILD'S ESTATE FOR FOSTER CARE

(a) The cost of foster care provided for a child, including medical care, is an obligation of the estate of the child and the estate is liable to the department for the cost of the care.

(b) The department may take action to recover from the estate of the child the cost of foster care for the child.

History of Fam §264.1015: Acts 1997, 75th Leg., ch. 575, §28, eff. Sept. 1, 1997.

FAM §264.102. COUNTY CONTRACTS

(a) The department may contract with a county commissioners court to administer the funds authorized by this subchapter for eligible children in the county and may require county participation.

(b) The payments provided by this subchapter do not abrogate the responsibility of a county to provide child welfare services.

History of Fam §264.102: Acts 1995, 74th Leg., ch. 20, §1, eff. April 20, 1995. Source: Former Hum. Res. Code §41.022.

FAM §264.103. DIRECT PAYMENTS

The department may make direct payments for foster care to a foster parent residing in a county with which the department does not have a contract authorized by Section 264.102.

History of Fam §264.103: Acts 1995, 74th Leg., ch. 20, §1, eff. April 20, 1995. Source: Former Hum. Res. Code §41.023.

FAM §264.104. PARENT OR GUARDIAN LIABILITY

(a) The parent or guardian of a child is liable to the state or to the county for a payment made by the state or county for foster care of a child under this subchapter.

(b) The cost of foster care for a child, including medical care, is a legal obligation of the child's parents, and the estate of a parent of the child is liable to the department for payment of the costs.

(c) The funds collected by the state under this section shall be used by the department for child welfare services.

History of Fam §264.104: Acts 1995, 74th Leg., ch. 20, §1, eff. April 20, 1995. Amended by Acts 1997, 75th Leg., ch. 575, §29, eff. Sept. 1, 1997. Source: Former Hum. Res. Code §41.024.

FAM §264.105. MEDICAL SERVICES PAYMENTS

The department shall attempt to maximize the use of federal funding to provide medical care payments authorized by Section 264.101(c) for children for whom the department has been named managing conservator.

History of Fam §264.105: Acts 1995, 74th Leg., ch. 20, §1, eff. April 20, 1995. Amended by Acts 1997, 75th Leg., ch. 575, §30, eff. Sept. 1, 1997. Source: Former Hum. Res. Code §41.025.

FAM §264.106. CONTRACTS FOR SUBSTITUTE CARE SERVICES

(a) The department shall:

(1) assess the need for substitute care services throughout the state; and

(2) contract with substitute care providers only to the extent necessary to meet the need for those services.

(b) Before contracting with a substitute care provider, the department shall determine whether:

(1) community resources are available to support children placed under the provider's care; and

(2) the appropriate public school district has sufficient resources to support children placed under the provider's care if the children will attend public school.

(c) In addition to the requirements of Section 40.058(b), Human Resources Code, a contract with a substitute care provider must include provisions that:

(1) enable the department to monitor the effectiveness of the provider's services; and

(2) authorize the department to terminate the contract or impose sanctions for a violation of a provision of the contract that specifies performance criteria.

(d) In determining whether to contract with a substitute care provider, the department shall consider the provider's performance under any previous contract for substitute care services between the department and the provider.

(e) In this section, "substitute care provider" means a person who provides residential care for children for 24 hours a day, including:

(1) a child-care institution, as defined by Section 42.002, Human Resources Code;

(2) a child-placing agency, as defined by Section 42.002, Human Resources Code;

(3) a foster group home or foster family home, as defined by Section 42.002, Human Resources Code; and

(4) an agency group home or agency home, as defined by Section 42.002, Human Resources Code, other than an agency group home, agency home, or a foster home verified or certified by the department.

History of Fam §264.106: Acts 1995, 74th Leg., ch. 20, §1, eff. April 20, 1995. Amended by Acts 1997, 75th Leg., ch. 1022, §92, eff. Sept. 1, 1997. Source: Former Hum. Res. Code §41.026.

See also 40 TAC §§700.1301-700.1355.

FAM §264.1061. FOSTER PARENT PERFORMANCE

The department shall monitor the performance of a foster parent who has been verified by the department in the department's capacity as a child-placing agency. The method under which performance is monitored must include the use of objective criteria by which the foster parent's performance may be assessed. The department shall include references to the criteria in a written agreement between the department and the foster parent concerning the foster parent's services.

History of Fam §264.1061: Acts 1997, 75th Leg., ch. 1022, §92, eff. Sept. 1, 1997.

FAM §264.107. PLACEMENT OF CHILDREN

(a) The department shall use a system for the placement of children in contract residential care, including foster care, that conforms to the levels of care adopted and maintained by the Health and Human Services Commission.

(b) The department shall use the standard application for the placement of children in contract residential care as adopted and maintained by the Health and Human Services Commission.

History of Fam §264.107: Acts 1995, 74th Leg., ch. 20, §1, eff. April 20, 1995. Source: Former Hum. Res. Code §41.027.

FAM §264.1075. USE OF ASSESSMENT SERVICES

Before placing a child in substitute care, the department shall use assessment services provided by a child-care facility or child-placing agency in accordance with Section 42.0425, Human Resources Code, to determine the appropriate substitute care for the child.

History of Fam §264.1075: Acts 1997, 75th Leg., ch. 1022, §93, eff. Sept. 1, 1997.

FAM §264.108. RACE OR ETHNICITY

(a) The department may not make a foster care placement decision on the presumption that placing a child in a family of the same race or ethnicity as the race or ethnicity of the child is in the best interest of the child.

(b) Unless an independent psychological evaluation specific to a child indicates that placement or continued living with a family of a particular race or ethnicity would be detrimental to the child, the department may not:

(1) deny, delay, or prohibit placement of a child in foster care because the department is attempting to locate a family of a particular race or ethnicity; or

(2) remove a child from foster care with a family that is of a race or ethnicity different from that of the child.

(c) The department may not remove a child from foster care with a family that is of a race or ethnicity different from that of the child for the sole reason that continued foster care with that family may:

(1) strengthen the emotional ties between the child and the family; or

(2) increase the potential of the family's desire to adopt the child because of the amount of time the child and the family are together.

(d) This section does not prevent or limit the department's recruitment of minority families as foster care families, but the recruitment of minority families may not be a reason to delay placement of a child in foster care with an available family of a race or ethnicity different from that of the child.

(e) An employee who violates this section is subject to immediate dismissal.

(f) The department by rule shall define what constitutes a delay under Subsections (b) and (d).

(g) A district court, on the application for an injunction or the filing of a petition complaining of a violation of this section by any person residing in the county in which the court has jurisdiction, shall enforce this section by issuing appropriate orders. An action for an injunction is in addition to any other action, proceeding, or remedy authorized by law. An applicant or petitioner who is granted an injunction or given other appropriate relief under this section is entitled to the costs of the suit, including reasonable attorney's fees.

History of Fam §264.108: Acts 1995, 74th Leg., ch. 20, §1, eff. April 20, 1995. Amended by Acts 1995, 74th Leg., ch. 879, §2, eff. June 16, 1995. Source: Former Hum. Res. Code §41.028.

FAM §264.109. ASSIGNMENT OF SUPPORT RIGHTS IN SUBSTITUTE CARE CASES

(a) The placement of a child in substitute care by the department constitutes an assignment to the state of any support rights attributable to the child as of the date the child is placed in substitute care.

(b) If a child placed by the department in substitute care is entitled under federal law to Title IV-D child support enforcement services without the requirement of an application for services, the department shall immediately refer the case to the Title IV-D agency. If an application for Title IV-D services is required and the department has been named managing conservator of the child, then an authorized representative of the department shall be the designated individual entitled to apply for services on behalf of the child and shall promptly apply for the services.

(c) The department and the Title IV-D agency shall execute a memorandum of understanding for the implementation of the provisions of this section and for the allocation between the department and the agency, consistent with federal laws and regulations, of any child support funds recovered by the Title IV-D agency in substitute care cases. All child support funds recovered under this section and retained by the department or the Title IV-D agency and any federal matching or incentive funds resulting from child support collection efforts in substitute care cases shall be in excess of amounts otherwise appropriated to either the department or the Title IV-D agency by the legislature.

History of Fam §264.109: Acts 1995, 74th Leg., ch. 751, §117, eff. Sept. 1, 1995.

FAM §264.110. ADOPTIVE PARENT REGISTRY

(a) The department shall establish a registry of persons who are willing to accept foster care placement of a child in the care of the department. The child may be placed temporarily with a person registered under this section pending termination of the parent-child relationship.

(b) A person registered under this section must satisfy requirements adopted by rule by the department.

(c) The department shall maintain a list of persons registered under this section and shall make a reasonable effort to place a child with the first available qualified person on the list if a qualified extended family member is not available for the child.

(d) Before a child may be placed with a person under this section, the person must sign a written statement in which the person agrees to the immediate removal of the child by the department under circumstances determined by the department.

(e) A person registered under this section is not entitled to compensation during the time the child is placed in the person's home but may receive support services provided for the child by the department.

(f) A person registered under this section has the right to be considered first for the adoption of a child placed in the person's home if the parent-child relationship is terminated with regard to the child.

(g) The department may refuse to place a child with a person registered under this section only for a reason permitted under criteria adopted by department rule.

(h) The department shall make the public aware of the existence and benefits of the adoptive parent registry through appropriate existing department communication methods.

History of Fam §264.110: Acts 1995, 74th Leg., ch. 943, §8, eff. Sept. 1, 1995. Renumbered from §264.109 by Acts 1997, 75th Leg., ch. 165, §31.01(30), eff. Sept. 1, 1997.

FAM §264.111. ADOPTION & SUBSTITUTE INFORMATION

(a) The department shall maintain in the department's central database information concerning children placed in the department's custody, including:

(1) for each formal adoption of a child in this state:

(A) the length of time between the date of the permanency plan decision of adoption and the date of the actual placement of the child with an adoptive family;

(B) the length of time between the date of the placement of the child for adoption and the date a final order of adoption was rendered;

(C) if the child returned to the department's custody after the date a final order of adoption was rendered for the child, the time between the date the final adoption order was rendered and the date the child returned to the department's custody; and

(D) for the adoptive family of a child under Paragraph (C), whether the family used postadoption program services before the date the child returned to the department's custody; and

(2) for each placement of a child in substitute care:

(A) the level of care the child was determined to require;

(B) whether the child was placed in an appropriate setting based on the level of care determined for the child;

(C) the number of moves for the child in substitute care and the reasons for moving the child;

(D) the length of stay in substitute care for the child from the date of initial placement to the date of approval of a permanency plan for the child;

(E) the length of time between the date of approval of a permanency plan for the child and the date of achieving the plan;

(F) whether the child's permanency plan was long-term substitute care;

(G) whether the child's achieved permanency plan was placement with an appropriate relative or another person, other than a foster parent, having standing; and

(H) whether the child was adopted by the child's foster parents.

(b) In addition to the information required in Subsection (a), the department shall compile information on:

(1) the number of families that used postadoption program services to assist in maintaining adoptive placements;

(2) the number of children returned to the department's custody after placement with an adoptive family but before a final adoption order was rendered;

(3) the number of children returned to the department's custody after the date a final order of adoption was rendered for the child;

(4) the number of adoptive families who used postadoption program services before the date a child placed with the family returned to the department's custody;

(5) the percentage of children who were placed in an appropriate setting based on the level of care determined for the child;

(6) the percentage of children placed in a department foster home;

(7) the percentage of children placed in a private child-placing agency;

(8) the number of children whose permanency plan was long-term substitute care;

(9) the number of children whose achieved permanency plan was placement with an appropriate relative or another person, other than a foster parent, having standing;

(10) the number of children adopted by the child's foster parents; and

(11) the number of children whose achieved permanency plan was removal of the disabilities of minority.

(c) The department shall make the information maintained under this section, other than information that is required by law to be confidential, available to the public by computer.

History of Fam §264.111: Acts 1997, 75th Leg., ch. 600, §18, eff. Sept. 1, 1997.

FAM §264.112. REPORT ON CHILDREN IN SUBSTITUTE CARE

(a) The department shall report the status for children in substitute care to the Board of Protective and Regulatory Services at least once every 12 months.

(b) The report shall analyze the length of time each child has been in substitute care and the barriers to placing the child for adoption or returning the child to the child's parent or parents.

History of Fam §264.112: Acts 1997, 75th Leg., ch. 600, §18, eff. Sept. 1, 1997.

Sections 264.113-264.200 reserved for expansion

SUBCHAPTER C. CHILD & FAMILY SERVICES

FAM §264.201. SERVICES BY DEPARTMENT

(a) When the department provides services directly or by contract to an abused or neglected child and the child's family, the services shall be designed to:

(1) prevent further abuse;

(2) alleviate the effects of the abuse suffered;

(3) prevent removal of the child from the home; and

(4) provide reunification services when appropriate for the return of the child to the home.

(b) The department shall emphasize ameliorative services for sexually abused children.

(c) The department shall provide or contract for necessary services to an abused or neglected child and the child's family without regard to whether the child remains in or is removed from the family home. If parental rights have been terminated, services may be provided only to the child.

(d) The services may include in-home programs, parenting skills training, youth coping skills, and individual and family counseling.

(e) The department may not provide and a court may not order the department to provide supervision for visitation in a child custody matter unless the department is a petitioner or intervenor in the underlying suit.

History of Fam §264.201: Acts 1995, 74th Leg., ch. 20, §1, eff. April 20, 1995. Amended by Acts 1999, 76th Leg., ch. 1390, §49 (eff. Sept. 1, 1999), ch. 1150, §28 (eff. Sept. 1, 1999). Source: Former Fam §34.51.

See also 40 TAC §§700.701-700.705.

FAM §264.202. STANDARDS & EFFECTIVENESS

(a) The department, with assistance from national organizations with expertise in child protective services, shall define a minimal baseline of in-home and foster care services for abused or neglected children that meets the professionally recognized standards for those services. The department shall attempt to provide services at a standard not lower than the minimal baseline standard.

(b) The department, with assistance from national organizations with expertise in child protective services, shall develop outcome measures to track and monitor the effectiveness of in-home and foster care services.

History of Fam §264.202: Acts 1995, 74th Leg., ch. 20, §1, eff. April 20, 1995. Source: Former Fam §34.52.

FAM §264.203. REQUIRED PARTICIPATION

(a) Except as provided by Subsection (d), the court on request of the department may order the parent, managing conservator, guardian, or other member of the abused or neglected child's household to participate in the services the department provides or purchases for alleviating the effects of the abuse or neglect and to permit the child and any siblings of the child to receive the services.

(b) The department may request the court to order the parent, managing conservator, guardian, or other member of the child's household to participate in the services whether the child resides in the home or has been removed from the home.

(c) If the person ordered to participate in the services fails to follow the court's order, the court may impose community service as a sanction for contempt.

(d) If the court does not order the person to participate, the court in writing shall specify the reasons for not ordering participation.

History of Fam §264.203: Acts 1995, 74th Leg., ch. 20, §1, eff. April 20, 1995. Source: Former Fam §34.53.

FAM §264.204. REPEALED

Repealed by Acts 1995, 74th Leg., ch. 262, eff. Jan. 1, 1996.

FAM §264.205. SWIFT ADOPTION TEAMS

A *Subsection (a) below is effective for children placed in custody of the DPRS on or after Sept. 1, 2001.*

(a) The department shall develop swift adoption teams to expedite the process of placing a child under the jurisdiction of the department for adoption. Swift adoption teams developed under this section shall, in performing their duties, attempt to place a child for adoption with an appropriate relative of the child.

Subsection (a) below is effective for children placed in custody of the DPRS before Sept. 1, 2001.

(a) The department shall develop swift adoption teams to expedite the process of placing a child under the jurisdiction of the department for adoption.

(b) A swift adoption team shall consist of department personnel who shall operate under policies adopted by rule by the department. The department shall set priorities for the allocation of department resources to enable a swift adoption team to operate successfully under the policies adopted under this subsection.

(c) The department shall, using a system of measurement developed by the department, report to the legislature on the success of swift adoption teams in expediting the administrative procedures and the length of time in placing children for adoption. The report shall include recommendations by the department concerning legislation that would enable the department to further improve adoption placements. The department shall report under this section on or before December 1 of each even-numbered year.

History of Fam §264.205: Acts 1995, 74th Leg., ch. 943, §9, eff. Sept. 1, 1995. Amended by Acts 2001, 77th Leg., ch. 306, §4, eff. Sept. 1, 2001.

FAM §264.206. SEARCH FOR ADOPTIVE PARENTS

(a) The department shall begin its efforts to locate qualified persons to adopt a child, including persons registered with the adoptive parent registry under Subchapter B, at the time the department's permanency plan for the child becomes the termination of the parent-child relationship and adoption of the child.

(b) The department shall report to the court in which the department petitions for termination of the parent-child relationship on the child's adoptability and the department's search for prospective adoptive parents for the child, including information relating to the department's efforts to work with licensed child-placing agencies.

History of Fam §264.206: Acts 1997, 75th Leg., ch. 600, §19, (eff. Sept. 1, 1997), ch. 1022, §94 (eff. Sept. 1, 1997).

FAM §264.207. DEPARTMENT PLANNING & ACCOUNTABILITY

(a) The department shall adopt policies that provide for the improvement of the department's services for children and families, including policies that provide for conducting a home study within four months after the date an applicant is approved for an adoption and documenting the results of the home study within 30 days after the date the study is completed. The policies adopted under this section must:

(1) be designed to increase the accountability of the department to individuals who receive services and to the public; and

(2) assure consistency of services provided by the department in the different regions of the state.

(b) To accomplish the goals stated in Subsection (a), the department shall:

(1) establish time frames for the initial screening of families seeking to adopt children;

(2) provide for the evaluation of the effectiveness of the department's management-level employees in expeditiously making permanent placements for children;

(3) establish, as feasible, comprehensive assessment services in various locations in the state to determine the needs of children and families served by the department;

(4) emphasize and centralize the monitoring and promoting of the permanent placement of children receiving department services;

(5) establish goals and performance measures in the permanent placement of children;

(6) seek private licensed child-placing agencies to place a child in the department's managing conservatorship who has been available for permanent placement for more than 90 days;

(7) provide information to private licensed child-placing agencies concerning children under Subdivision (6);

(8) provide incentives for a private licensed child-placing agency that places a child, as defined by Section 162.301, under Subdivision (6);

(9) encourage foster parents to be approved by the department as both foster parents and adoptive parents;

(10) address failures by the department's service regions in making permanent placements for children in a reasonable time; and

(11) require the department's service regions to participate in the Texas Adoption Resources Exchange.

History of Fam §264.207: Acts 1997, 75th Leg., ch. 600, §19 (eff. Sept. 1, 1997), ch. 1022, §94 (eff. Sept. 1, 1997).

FAM §264.208. LOCATION OF PARENTS

(a) The department shall create a division staffed by personnel trained in locating parents and relatives of children throughout the state.

(b) The department shall use outside contractors and volunteer resources to the extent feasible to perform its responsibilities under this section.

History of Fam §264.208: Acts 1999, 76th Leg., ch. 228, §3, eff. Sept. 1, 1999.

Sections 264.209-264.300 reserved for expansion

SUBCHAPTER D. SERVICES TO AT-RISK YOUTH

FAM §264.301. SERVICES FOR AT-RISK YOUTH

(a) The department shall operate a program to provide services for children in at-risk situations and for the families of those children.

(b) The services under this section may include:

(1) crisis family intervention;

(2) emergency short-term residential care;

(3) family counseling;

(4) parenting skills training;

(5) youth coping skills training;

(6) mentoring; and

(7) advocacy training.

History of Fam §264.301: Acts 1995, 74th Leg., ch. 20, §1, eff. April 20, 1995. Amended by Acts 1995, 74th Leg., ch. 262, §58, eff. Jan. 1, 1996.

FAM §264.302. EARLY YOUTH INTERVENTION SERVICES

(a) This section applies to a child who:

(1) is seven years of age or older and under 17 years of age; and

(2) has not had the disabilities of minority for general purposes removed under Chapter 31.

(b) The department shall operate a program under this section to provide services for children in at-risk situations and for the families of those children.

(c) The department may not provide services under this section to a child who has:

(1) at any time been referred to juvenile court for engaging in conduct that violates a penal law of this state of the grade of felony other than a state jail felony; or

(2) been found to have engaged in delinquent conduct under Title 3.

(d) The department may provide services under this section to a child who engages in conduct for which the child may be found by a court to be an at-risk child, without regard to whether the conduct violates a penal law of this state of the grade of felony other than a state jail felony, if the child was younger than 10 years of age at the time the child engaged in the conduct.

(e) The department shall provide services for a child and the child's family if a contract to provide services under this section is available in the county and the child is referred to the department as an at-risk child by:

(1) a court under Section 264.304;

(2) a juvenile court or probation department as part of a progressive sanctions program under Chapter 59;

(3) a law enforcement officer or agency under Section 52.03; or

A *Subsection (4) below is effective for children alleged to have engaged in conduct that occurs on or after Sept. 1, 2001.*

(4) a justice or municipal court under Article 45.057, Code of Criminal Procedure.

Subsection (4) below is effective for children alleged to have engaged in conduct in which every element of the conduct occurred before Sept. 1, 2001.

(4) a justice or municipal court under Section 54.022.

(f) The services under this section may include:

(1) crisis family intervention;

(2) emergency short-term residential care for children 10 years of age or older;

(3) family counseling;

(4) parenting skills training;

(5) youth coping skills training;

(6) advocacy training; and

(7) mentoring.

History of Fam §264.302: Acts 1995, 74th Leg., ch. 262, §58, eff. Jan. 1, 1996. Amended by Acts 1997, 75th Leg., ch. 1086, §30 (eff. Sept. 1, 1997), ch. 575, §31 (eff. Sept. 1, 1997); Acts 2001, 77th Leg., ch. 1514, §16, eff. Sept. 1, 2001.

FAM §264.303. COMMENCEMENT OF CIVIL ACTION FOR DETERMINATION OF AT-RISK CHILDREN

(a) The department may file a civil action to request any district court or county court, other than a juvenile court, to determine that a child is an at-risk child. A person with whom the department contracts to provide services under Section 264.302 may file an action under this section if the department has approved the filing.

(b) Notice of the action must be provided to:

(1) the child;

(2) the parent, managing conservator, or guardian of the child; and

(3) any other member of the child's household who may be affected by an order of the court if the court finds that the child is an at-risk child.

(c) A person served with notice of the action may, but is not required, to file a written answer. Any answer must be filed before the hearing on the action begins.

History of Fam §264.303: Acts 1995, 74th Leg., ch. 262, §58, eff. Jan. 1, 1996.

FAM §264.304. HEARING; DETERMINATION OF AT-RISK CHILD

(a) Unless a later date is requested by the department, the court shall set a date and time for the hearing not later than 30 days after the date the action is filed.

(b) The court is the trier of fact at the hearing.

(c) The court shall determine that the child is an at-risk child if the court finds that the child has engaged in the following conduct:

(1) conduct, other than a traffic offense and except as provided by Subsection (d), that violates:

(A) the penal laws of this state; or

(B) the penal ordinances of any political subdivision of this state;

(2) the unexcused voluntary absence of the child on 10 or more days or parts of days within a six-month period or three or more days or parts of days within a four-week period from school without the consent of the child's parent, managing conservator, or guardian;

(3) the voluntary absence of the child from the child's home without the consent of the child's parent, managing conservator, or guardian for a substantial length of time or without intent to return;

(4) conduct that violates the laws of this state prohibiting driving while intoxicated or under the influence of intoxicating liquor (first or second offense) or driving while under the influence of any narcotic drug or of any other drug to a degree that renders the child incapable of safely driving a vehicle (first or second offense); or

(5) conduct that evidences a clear and substantial intent to engage in any behavior described by Subdivisions (1)-(4).

(d) The court may not determine that a child is an at-risk child if the court finds that the child engaged in conduct violating the penal laws of this state of the grade of felony other than a state jail felony when the child was 10 years of age or older.

History of Fam §264.304: Acts 1995, 74th Leg., ch. 262, §58, eff. Jan. 1, 1996.

FAM §264.305. COURT ORDER FOR SERVICES

(a) Except as provided by Subsection (b), if the court finds that the child is an at-risk child under Section 264.304, the court may order the child, the child's parent, managing conservator, or guardian or any other member of the child's household to participate in services provided by the department under Section 264.302 and contained in a plan approved by the court.

(b) The court may order an at-risk child to participate in services involving emergency short-term residential care only if the court finds that the child engaged in conduct described by Section 264.304(c)(1), (2), (3), or (4).

(c) An order rendered by a court under this section expires not later than six months after the date the order was rendered.

History of Fam §264.305: Acts 1995, 74th Leg., ch. 262, §58, eff. Jan. 1, 1996.

FAM §264.306. SANCTIONS

(a) A child who violates a court order under Section 264.305 by failing to participate in services provided by the department engages in conduct indicating a need for supervision and the department shall refer the child to an appropriate juvenile authority for proceedings under Title 3 for that conduct.

(b) A parent, managing conservator, guardian, or other member of the child's household who violates a court order under Section 264.305 by failing to participate in services provided by the department is subject to contempt of court. The court may under its contempt powers impose a community service requirement.

History of Fam §264.306: Acts 1995, 74th Leg., ch. 262, §58, eff. Jan. 1, 1996.

Sections 264.307-264.400 reserved for expansion

SUBCHAPTER E. CHILDREN'S ADVOCACY CENTERS

FAM §264.401. DEFINITION

In this subchapter, "center" means a children's advocacy center.

History of Fam §264.401: Acts 1995, 74th Leg., ch. 255, §1, eff. Sept. 1, 1995.

FAM §264.402. ESTABLISHMENT OF CHILDREN'S ADVOCACY CENTER

(a) On the execution of a memorandum of understanding under Section 264.403, a children's advocacy center may be established by the participating entities.

(b) A center may be established to serve two or more contiguous counties.

History of Fam §264.402: Acts 1995, 74th Leg., ch. 255, §1, eff. Sept. 1, 1995.

FAM §264.403. INTERAGENCY MEMORANDUM OF UNDERSTANDING

(a) Before a center may be established under Section 264.402, a memorandum of understanding regarding participation in operation of the center must be executed among:

(1) the division of the department responsible for child abuse investigations;

(2) representatives of county and municipal law enforcement agencies that investigate child abuse in the area to be served by the center;

(3) the county or district attorney who routinely prosecutes child abuse cases in the area to be served by the center; and

(4) a representative of any other governmental entity that participates in child abuse investigations or offers services to child abuse victims that desires to participate in the operation of the center.

(b) A memorandum of understanding executed under this section shall include the agreement of each participating entity to cooperate in:

(1) developing a cooperative, team approach to investigating child abuse;

(2) reducing, to the greatest extent possible, the number of interviews required of a victim of child abuse to minimize the negative impact of the investigation on the child; and

(3) developing, maintaining, and supporting, through the center, an environment that emphasizes the best interests of children and that provides investigatory and rehabilitative services.

(c) A memorandum of understanding executed under this section may include the agreement of one or more participating entities to provide office space and administrative services necessary for the center's operation.

History of Fam §264.403: Acts 1995, 74th Leg., ch. 255, §1, eff. Sept. 1, 1995.

FAM §264.404. BOARD; ADMINISTRATION OF CENTER

(a) The executive officer or board of each participating entity executing a memorandum of understanding that establishes a center under this subchapter shall appoint a member to serve on the governing board of the center.

(b) A governing board member serves at the pleasure of the appointing executive officer or board.

(c) Service on a center's board by a public officer or employee is an additional duty of the office or employment.

History of Fam §264.404: Acts 1995, 74th Leg., ch. 255, §1, eff. Sept. 1, 1995.

FAM §264.405. DUTIES

A center shall:

(1) assess victims of child abuse and their families to determine their need for services relating to the investigation of child abuse;

(2) provide services determined to be needed under Subdivision (1);

(3) provide a facility at which a multidisciplinary team appointed under Section 264.406 can meet to facilitate the efficient and appropriate disposition of child abuse cases through the civil and criminal justice systems; and

(4) coordinate the activities of governmental entities relating to child abuse investigations and delivery of services to child abuse victims and their families.

History of Fam §264.405: Acts 1995, 74th Leg., ch. 255, §1, eff. Sept. 1, 1995.

FAM §264.406. MULTIDISCIPLINARY TEAM

(a) A center's board shall appoint a multidisciplinary team to work within the center to review new and pending child abuse cases for the purpose of coordinating the activities of entities involved in investigation, prosecution, and victim services.

(b) A multidisciplinary team may review a child abuse case in which the alleged perpetrator does not have custodial control or supervision of the child or is not responsible for the child's welfare or care.

(c) A multidisciplinary team shall consist of persons who are involved in the investigation or prosecution of child abuse cases or the delivery of services to child abuse victims and their families.

(d) A multidisciplinary team shall meet at the call of the board. The board shall call a meeting of the multidisciplinary team if:

(1) a new child abuse case is received; or

(2) a pending child abuse case requires attention.

(e) At each meeting, the multidisciplinary team shall discuss each active case and the actions of the entities involved in investigation, prosecution, and victim services.

(f) When acting in the member's official capacity, a multidisciplinary team member is authorized to receive information made confidential by Section 40.005, Human Resources Code, or Section 261.201 or 264.408.

History of Fam §264.406: Acts 1995, 74th Leg., ch. 255, §1, eff. Sept. 1, 1995. Amended by Acts 1997, 75th Leg., ch. 575, §32, eff. Sept. 1, 1997.

FAM §264.407. LIABILITY

(a) A person is not liable for civil damages for a recommendation made or an opinion rendered in good faith while acting in the official scope of the person's duties as a member of a multidisciplinary team or as a board member, staff member, or volunteer of a center.

(b) The limitation on civil liability of Subsection (a) does not apply if a person's actions constitute gross negligence.

History of Fam §264.407: Acts 1995, 74th Leg., ch. 255, §1, eff. Sept. 1, 1995.

FAM §264.408. USE OF INFORMATION & RECORDS; CONFIDENTIALITY & OWNERSHIP

(a) The files, reports, records, communications, and working papers used or developed in providing services under this chapter are confidential and not subject to public release under Chapter 552, Government Code, and may only be disclosed for purposes consistent with this chapter. Disclosure may be to:

(1) the department, department employees, law enforcement agencies, prosecuting attorneys, medical professionals, and other state agencies that provide services to children and families; and

(2) the attorney for the child who is the subject of the records and a court-appointed volunteer advocate appointed for the child under Section 107.031.

(b) Information related to the investigation of a report of abuse or neglect under Chapter 261 and services provided as a result of the investigation is confidential as provided by Section 261.201.

(c) The department, a law enforcement agency, and a prosecuting attorney may share with a center information that is confidential under Section 261.201 as needed to provide services under this chapter. Confidential information shared with or provided to a center remains the property of the agency that shared or provided the information to the center.

(d) A videotaped interview of a child made at a center is the property of the prosecuting attorney involved in the criminal prosecution of the case involving the child. If no criminal prosecution occurs, the videotaped interview is the property of the attorney involved in representing the department in a civil action alleging child abuse or neglect. If the matter involving the child is not prosecuted, the videotape is the property of the department if the matter is an investigation by the department of abuse or neglect. If the department is not investigating or has not investigated the matter, the videotape is the property of the agency that referred the matter to the center. If the center employs a custodian of records for videotaped interviews of children, the center is responsible for the custody of the videotape. A videotaped interview may be shared with other agencies under a written agreement.

(e) The department shall be allowed access to a center's videotaped interviews of children.

History of Fam §264.408: Acts 1997, 75th Leg., ch. 575, §33, eff. Sept. 1, 1997.

FAM §264.409. ADMINISTRATIVE CONTRACTS

(a) The department or the office of the attorney general may contract with a statewide organization of individuals or groups of individuals who have expertise in the establishment and operation of children's advocacy center programs. The statewide organization shall provide training, technical assistance, and evaluation services for local children's advocacy center programs.

(b) If the office of the attorney general enters into a contract under this section, the contract must provide that the statewide organization may not spend annually for administrative purposes more than 12 percent of the annual amount appropriated to the office of the attorney general for purposes of this section.

History of Fam §264.409: Acts 1997, 75th Leg., ch. 575, §33, eff. Sept. 1, 1997. Amended by Acts 1999, 76th Leg., ch. 347, §1, eff. Sept. 1, 1999.

FAM §264.410. CONTRACTS WITH CHILDREN'S ADVOCACY CENTERS

(a) The statewide organization with which the department or the office of the attorney general contracts under Section 264.409 shall contract for services with eligible centers to enhance the existing services of the programs.

(b) The contract under this section may not result in reducing the financial support a local center receives from another source.

(c) If the attorney general enters into a contract with a statewide organization under Section 264.409, the attorney general by rule shall adopt standards for eligible local centers. The statewide organization shall assist the attorney general in developing the standards.

History of Fam §264.410: Acts 1997, 75th Leg., ch. 575, §33, eff. Sept. 1, 1997. Amended by Acts 1999, 76th Leg., ch. 347, §2, eff. Sept. 1, 1999.

FAM §264.411. ELIGIBILITY FOR CONTRACTS

(a) A public entity or nonprofit entity is eligible for a contract under Section 264.410 if the entity:

(1) has a signed memorandum of understanding as provided by Section 264.403;

(2) operates under the authority of a governing board as provided by Section 264.404;

(3) has a multidisciplinary team of persons involved in the investigation or prosecution of child abuse cases or the delivery of services as provided by Section 264.406;

(4) holds regularly scheduled case reviews as provided by Section 264.406;

(5) operates in a neutral and physically separate space from the day-to-day operations of any public agency partner;

(6) has developed a method of statistical information gathering on children receiving services through the center and shares such statistical information with the statewide organization, the department, and the office of the attorney general when requested;

(7) has an in-house volunteer program;

(8) employs an executive director who is answerable to the board of directors of the entity and who is not the exclusive salaried employee of any public agency partner; and

(9) operates under a working protocol that includes a statement of:

(A) the center's mission;

(B) each agency's role and commitment to the center;

(C) the type of cases to be handled by the center; and

(D) procedure for case reviews.

(b) The statewide organization may waive the requirements specified in Subsection (a) if it determines that the waiver will not adversely affect the center's ability to carry out its duties under Section 264.405. Any waiver that is granted must be identified in the written contract with the center.

History of Fam §264.411: Acts 1997, 75th Leg., ch. 575, §33, eff. Sept. 1, 1997. Amended by Acts 1999, 76th Leg., ch. 347, §3, eff. Sept. 1, 1999.

Sections 164.412-264.500 reserved for expansion

SUBCHAPTER F. CHILD FATALITY REVIEW & INVESTIGATION

FAM §264.501. DEFINITIONS

A *Section 264.501 below does not affect or impair any act done, any obligation, right, criterion, standard, or requirement existing, or any investigation begun by the Children's Trust Fund of Texas Council before Sept. 1, 2001.*

In this subchapter:

(1) "Autopsy" and "inquest" have the meanings assigned by Article 49.01, Code of Criminal Procedure.

(2) "Bureau of vital statistics" means the bureau of vital statistics of the Texas Department of Health.

(3) "Child" means a person younger than 18 years of age.

(4) "Committee" means the child fatality review team committee.

(5) "Department" means the Department of Protective and Regulatory Services.

(6) "Health care provider" means any health care practitioner or facility that provides medical evaluation or treatment, including dental and mental health evaluation or treatment.

(7) "Meeting" means an in-person meeting or a meeting held by telephone or other electronic medium.

(8) "Preventable death" means a death that may have been prevented by reasonable medical, social, legal, psychological, or educational intervention. The term includes the death of a child from:

(A) intentional or unintentional injuries;

(B) medical neglect;

(C) lack of access to medical care;

(D) neglect and reckless conduct, including failure to supervise and failure to seek medical care; and

(E) premature birth associated with any factor described by Paragraphs (A) through (D).

(9) "Review" means a reexamination of information regarding a deceased child from relevant agencies, professionals, and health care providers.

(10) "Review team" means a child fatality review team established under this subchapter.

(11) "Unexpected death" includes a death of a child that, before investigation:

(A) appears to have occurred without anticipation or forewarning; and

(B) was caused by trauma, suspicious or obscure circumstances, sudden infant death syndrome, abuse or neglect, or an unknown cause.

History of Fam §264.501: Acts 1995, 74th Leg., ch. 255, §2, (eff. Sept. 1, 1995), ch. 878, §1 (eff. Sept. 1, 1995). Amended by Acts 2001, 77th Leg., ch. 957, §2, eff. Sept. 1, 2001.

FAM §264.501. DEFINITIONS

Section 264.501 below is effective for any act done, any obligation, right, criterion, standard, or requirement existing, or any investigation begun by the Children's Trust Fund of Texas Council before Sept. 1, 2001.

In this subchapter:

(1) "Autopsy" and "inquest" have the meanings assigned by Article 49.01, Code of Criminal Procedure.

(2) "Bureau of vital statistics" means the bureau of vital statistics of the Texas Department of Health.

(3) "Child" means a person younger than 18 years of age.

(4) "Committee" means the child fatality review team committee.

(5) "Council" means the Children's Trust Fund of Texas Council.

(6) "Department" means the Department of Protective and Regulatory Services.

(7) "Health care provider" means any health care practitioner or facility that provides medical evaluation or treatment, including dental and mental health evaluation or treatment.

(8) "Meeting" means an in-person meeting or a meeting held by telephone or other electronic medium.

(9) "Preventable death" means a death that may have been prevented by reasonable medical, social, legal, psychological, or educational intervention. The term includes the death of a child from:

(A) intentional or unintentional injuries;

(B) medical neglect;

(C) lack of access to medical care;

(D) neglect and reckless conduct, including failure to supervise and failure to seek medical care; and

(E) premature birth associated with any factor described by Paragraphs (A) through (D).

(10) "Review" means a reexamination of information regarding a deceased child from relevant agencies, professionals, and health care providers.

(11) "Review team" means a child fatality review team established under this subchapter.

(12) "Unexpected death" includes a death of a child that, before investigation:

(A) appears to have occurred without anticipation or forewarning; and

(B) was caused by trauma, suspicious or obscure circumstances, sudden infant death syndrome, abuse or neglect, or an unknown cause.

FAM §264.502. COMMITTEE

A *Subsections (a) & (b) below do not affect or impair any act done, any obligation, right, criterion, standard, or requirement existing, or any investigation begun by the Children's Trust Fund of Texas Council before Sept. 1, 2001.*

(a) The child fatality review team committee is composed of:

(1) a person appointed by and representing the state registrar for the bureau of vital statistics;

(2) a person appointed by and representing the director of protective services for families and children of the department;

(3) a person appointed by and representing the director of the bureau of epidemiology of the Texas Department of Health; and

(4) individuals selected under Subsection (b).

(b) The members of the committee who serve under Subsections (a)(1) through (3) shall select the following additional committee members:

(1) a criminal prosecutor involved in prosecuting crimes against children;

(2) a sheriff;

(3) a justice of the peace;

(4) a medical examiner;

(5) a police chief;

(6) a pediatrician experienced in diagnosing and treating child abuse and neglect;

(7) a child educator;

(8) a child mental health provider;

(9) a public health professional;

(10) a child protective services specialist;

(11) a sudden infant death syndrome family service provider;

(12) a neonatologist;

(13) a child advocate; and

(14) a chief juvenile probation officer.

Subsections (a) & (b) below are effective for any act done, any obligation, right criterion, standard, or requirement existing, or any investigation begun by the Children's Trust Fund of Texas Council before Sept. 1, 2001.

(a) The child fatality review team committee is composed of:

(1) a person appointed by and representing the state registrar for the bureau of vital statistics;

(2) a person appointed by and representing the director of protective services for families and children of the department;

(3) a person appointed by and representing the director of the bureau of epidemiology of the Texas Department of Health;

(4) a person appointed by and representing the executive director of the council; and

(5) individuals selected under Subsection (b).

(b) The members of the committee who serve under Subsections (a)(1) through (4) shall select the following additional committee members:

(1) a criminal prosecutor involved in prosecuting crimes against children;

(2) a sheriff;

(3) a justice of the peace;

(4) a medical examiner;

(5) a police chief;

(6) a pediatrician experienced in diagnosing and treating child abuse and neglect;

(7) a child educator;

(8) a child mental health provider;

(9) a public health professional;

(10) a child protective services specialist;

(11) a sudden infant death syndrome family service provider;

(12) a neonatologist;

(13) a child advocate; and

(14) a chief juvenile probation officer.

(c) Members of the committee selected under Subsection (b) serve two-year terms that expire on February 1 of each even-numbered year.

(d) Members selected under Subsection (b) must reflect the geographical, cultural, racial, and ethnic diversity of the state.

(e) An appointment to a vacancy on the committee shall be made in the same manner as the original appointment.

(f) Members of the committee shall select a presiding officer from the members of the committee.

(g) The presiding officer of the committee shall call the meetings of the committee, which shall be held at least quarterly.

A *Subsection (h) below does not affect or impair any act done, any obligation, right, criterion, standard, or requirement existing, or any investigation begun by the Children's Trust Fund of Texas Council before Sept. 1, 2001.*

(h) A member of the committee is not entitled to compensation for serving on the committee but is entitled to reimbursement for the member's travel expenses as provided in the General Appropriations Act. Reimbursement under this subsection for a person serving on the committee under Subsection (a)(1) or (3) shall be paid from funds appropriated to the Texas Department of Health. Reimbursement for other persons serving on the committee shall be paid from funds appropriated to the department.

Subsection (h) below is effective for any act done, any obligation, right, criterion, standard, or requirement existing, or any investigation begun by the Children's Trust Fund of Texas Council before Sept. 1, 2001.

(h) A member of the committee is not entitled to compensation for serving on the committee but is entitled to reimbursement for the member's travel expenses as provided in the General Appropriations Act. Reimbursement under this subsection for a person serving on the committee under Subsection (a)(1) or (3) shall be paid from funds appropriated to the Texas Department of Health. Reimbursement for other persons serving on the committee shall be paid equally from funds appropriated to the department and funds appropriated to the council.

History of Fam §264.502: Acts 1995, 74th Leg., ch. 255, §2 (eff. Sept. 1, 1995), ch. 878, §1 (eff. Sept. 1, 1995). Amended by Acts 2001, 77th Leg., ch. 957, §3, eff. Sept. 1, 2001.

FAM §264.503. PURPOSE & DUTIES OF COMMITTEE & SPECIFIED STATE AGENCIES

(a) The purpose of the committee is to:

(1) develop an understanding of the causes and incidence of child deaths in this state;

(2) identify procedures within the agencies represented on the committee to reduce the number of preventable child deaths; and

(3) promote public awareness and make recommendations to the governor and the legislature for changes in law, policy, and practice to reduce the number of preventable child deaths.

A *Subsection (b) below does not affect or impair any act done, any obligation, right, criterion, standard, or requirement existing, or any investigation begun by the Children's Trust Fund of Texas Council before Sept. 1, 2001.*

(b) To ensure that the committee achieves its purpose, the department and the Texas Department of Health shall perform the duties specified by this section.

Subsection (b) below is effective for any act done, any obligation, right, criterion, standard, or requirement existing, or any investigation begun by the Children's Trust Fund of Texas Council before Sept. 1, 2001.

(b) To ensure that the committee achieves its purpose, the department, the council, and the Texas Department of Health shall perform the duties specified by this section.

(c) The department shall:

(1) recognize the creation and participation of review teams;

(2) promote and coordinate training to assist the review teams in carrying out their duties;

(3) assist the committee in developing model protocols for:

(A) the reporting and investigating of child fatalities for law enforcement agencies, child protective services, justices of the peace and medical examiners, and other professionals involved in the investigations of child deaths;

(B) the collection of data regarding child deaths; and

(C) the operation of the review teams; and

(4) develop and implement procedures necessary for the operation of the committee.

A *Subsection (d) below does not affect or impair any act done, any obligation, right, criterion, standard, or requirement existing, or any investigation begun by the Children's Trust Fund of Texas Council before Sept. 1, 2001.*

(d) The department shall promote education of the public regarding the incidence and causes of child deaths, the public role in preventing child deaths, and specific steps the public can undertake to prevent child deaths. The committee shall enlist the support and assistance of civic, philanthropic, and public service organizations in the performance of the duties imposed under this subsection.

Subsection (d) below is effective for any act done, any obligation, right, criterion, standard, or requirement existing, or any investigation begun by the Children's Trust Fund of Texas Council before Sept. 1, 2001.

(d) The council shall promote education of the public regarding the incidence and causes of child deaths, the public role in preventing child deaths, and specific steps the public can undertake to prevent child deaths. The committee shall enlist the support and assistance of civic, philanthropic, and public service organizations in the performance of the duties imposed under this subsection.

(e) The Texas Department of Health shall:

(1) collect data under this subchapter and coordinate the collection of data under this subchapter with other data collection activities; and

(2) perform annual statistical studies of the incidence and causes of child fatalities using the data collected under this subchapter.

(f) The committee shall issue annual reports on the committee's activities, including findings and recommendations relating to each purpose and duty of the committee described by this section. Not later than December 1 of each even-numbered year, the committee shall publish the report and submit a copy of the report to the governor, lieutenant governor, and speaker of the house of representatives.

History of Fam §264.503: Acts 1995, 74th Leg., ch. 255, §2 (eff. Sept. 1, 1995), ch. 878, §1 (eff. Sept. 1, 1995). Amended by Acts 2001, 77th Leg., ch. 957, §4, eff. Sept. 1, 2001.

FAM §264.504. MEETINGS OF COMMITTEE

(a) Except as provided by Subsections (b), (c), and (d), meetings of the committee are subject to the open meetings law, Chapter 551, Government Code, as if the committee were a governmental body under that chapter.

(b) Any portion of a meeting of the committee during which the committee discusses an individual child's death is closed to the public and is not subject to the open meetings law, Chapter 551, Government Code.

(c) Information identifying a deceased child, a member of the child's family, a guardian or caretaker of the child, or an alleged or suspected perpetrator of abuse or neglect of the child may not be disclosed during a public meeting.

(d) Information regarding the involvement of a state or local agency with the deceased child or another person described by Subsection (c) may not be disclosed during a public meeting.

(e) The committee may conduct an open or closed meeting by telephone conference call or other electronic medium. A meeting held under this subsection is subject to the notice requirements applicable to other meetings. The notice of the meeting must specify as the location of the meeting the location where meetings of the committee are usually held. Each part of the meeting by telephone conference call that is required to be open to the public shall be audible to the public at the location specified in the notice of the meeting as the location of the meeting and shall be tape-recorded. The tape recording shall be made available to the public.

(f) This section does not prohibit the committee from requesting the attendance at a closed meeting of a person who is not a member of the committee and who has information regarding a deceased child.

History of Fam §264.504: Acts 1995, 74th Leg., ch. 255, §2 (eff. Sept. 1, 1995), ch. 878, §1 (eff. Sept. 1, 1995).

FAM §264.505. ESTABLISHMENT OF REVIEW TEAM

(a) A multidisciplinary and multiagency child fatality review team may be established for a county to review child deaths in that county. A review team for a county with a population of less than 50,000 may join with an adjacent county or counties to establish a combined review team.

(b) Any person who may be a member of a review team under Subsection (c) may initiate the establishment of a review team and call the first organizational meeting of the team.

(c) A review team may include:

(1) a criminal prosecutor involved in prosecuting crimes against children;

(2) a sheriff;

(3) a justice of the peace or medical examiner;

(4) a police chief;

(5) a pediatrician experienced in diagnosing and treating child abuse and neglect;

(6) a child educator;

(7) a child mental health provider;

(8) a public health professional;

(9) a child protective services specialist;

(10) a sudden infant death syndrome family service provider;

(11) a neonatologist;

(12) a child advocate; and

(13) a chief juvenile probation officer.

(d) Members of a review team may select additional team members according to community resources and needs.

(e) A review team shall select a presiding officer from its members.

History of Fam §264.505: Acts 1995, 74th Leg., ch. 255, §2 (eff. Sept. 1, 1995), ch. 878, §1 (eff. Sept. 1, 1995).

FAM §264.506. PURPOSE & DUTIES OF REVIEW TEAM

(a) The purpose of a review team is to decrease the incidence of preventable child deaths by:

(1) providing assistance, direction, and coordination to investigations of child deaths;

(2) promoting cooperation, communication, and coordination among agencies involved in responding to child fatalities;

(3) developing an understanding of the causes and incidence of child deaths in the county or counties in which the review team is located;

(4) recommending changes to agencies, through the agency's representative member, that will reduce the number of preventable child deaths; and

(5) advising the committee on changes to law, policy, or practice that will assist the team and the agencies represented on the team in fulfilling their duties.

(b) To achieve its purpose, a review team shall:

(1) adapt and implement, according to local needs and resources, the model protocols developed by the department and the committee;

(2) meet on a regular basis to review child fatality cases and recommend methods to improve coordination of services and investigations between agencies that are represented on the team;

(3) collect and maintain data as required by the committee; and

(4) submit to the bureau of vital statistics data reports on deaths reviewed as specified by the committee.

(c) A review team shall initiate prevention measures as indicated by the review team's findings.

History of Fam §264.506: Acts 1995, 74th Leg., ch. 255, §2 (eff. Sept. 1, 1995), ch. 878, §1 (eff. Sept. 1, 1995).

FAM §264.507. DUTIES OF PRESIDING OFFICER

The presiding officer of a review team shall:

(1) send notices to the review team members of a meeting to review a child fatality;

(2) provide a list to the review team members of each child fatality to be reviewed at the meeting;

(3) submit data reports to the bureau of vital statistics not later than the 30th day after the date on which the review took place; and

(4) ensure that the review team operates according to the protocols developed by the department and the committee, as adapted by the review team.

History of Fam §264.507: Acts 1995, 74th Leg., ch. 255, §2 (eff. Sept. 1, 1995), ch. 878, §1 (eff. Sept. 1, 1995).

FAM §264.508. REVIEW PROCEDURE

(a) The review team of the county in which the injury, illness, or event that was the cause of the death of the child occurred, as stated on the child's death certificate, shall review the death.

(b) On receipt of the list of child fatalities under Section 264.507, each review team member shall review the member's records and the records of the member's agency for information regarding each listed child.

History of Fam §264.508: Acts 1995, 74th Leg., ch. 255, §2 (eff. Sept. 1, 1995), ch. 878, §1 (eff. Sept. 1, 1995).

FAM §264.509. ACCESS TO INFORMATION

(a) A review team may request information and records regarding a deceased child as necessary to carry out the review team's purpose and duties. Records and information that may be requested under this section include:

(1) medical, dental, and mental health care information; and

(2) information and records maintained by any state or local government agency, including:

(A) a birth certificate;

(B) law enforcement investigative data;

(C) medical examiner investigative data;

(D) juvenile court records;

(E) parole and probation information and records; and

(F) child protective services information and records.

(b) On request of the presiding officer of a review team, the custodian of the relevant information and records relating to a deceased child shall provide those records to the review team.

(c) This subsection does not authorize the release of the original or copies of the mental health or medical records of any member of the child's family or the guardian or caretaker of the child or an alleged or suspected perpetrator of abuse or neglect of the child which are in the possession of any state or local government agency as provided in Subsection (a)(2). Information relating to the mental health or medical condition of a member of the child's family or the guardian or caretaker of the child or the alleged or suspected perpetrator of abuse or neglect of the child acquired as part of an investigation by a state or local government agency as provided in Subsection (a)(2) may be provided to the review team.

History of Fam §264.509: Acts 1995, 74th Leg., ch. 255, §2 (eff. Sept. 1, 1995), ch. 878, §1 (eff. Sept. 1, 1995).

FAM §264.510. MEETING OF REVIEW TEAM

(a) A meeting of a review team is closed to the public and not subject to the open meetings law, Chapter 551, Government Code.

(b) This section does not prohibit a review team from requesting the attendance at a closed meeting of a person who is not a member of the review team and who has information regarding a deceased child.

(c) Except as necessary to carry out a review team's purpose and duties, members of a review team and persons attending a review team meeting may not disclose what occurred at the meeting.

(d) A member of a review team participating in the review of a child death is immune from civil or criminal liability arising from information presented in or opinions formed as a result of a meeting.

History of Fam §264.510: Acts 1995, 74th Leg., ch. 255, §2 (eff. Sept. 1, 1995), ch. 878, §1 (eff. Sept. 1, 1995).

FAM §264.511. USE OF INFORMATION & RECORDS; CONFIDENTIALITY

(a) Information and records acquired by the committee or by a review team in the exercise of its purpose and duties under this subchapter are confidential and exempt from disclosure under the open records law, Chapter 552, Government Code, and may only be disclosed as necessary to carry out the committee's or review team's purpose and duties.

(b) A report of the committee or of a review team or a statistical compilation of data reports is a public record subject to the open records law, Chapter 552, Government Code, as if the committee or review team were a governmental body under that chapter, if the report or statistical compilation does not contain any information that would permit the identification of an individual.

(c) A member of a review team may not disclose any information that is confidential under this section.

(d) Information, documents, and records of the committee or of a review team that are confidential under this section are not subject to subpoena or discovery and may not be introduced into evidence in any civil or criminal proceeding, except that information, documents, and records otherwise available from other sources are not immune from subpoena, discovery, or introduction into evidence solely because they were presented during proceedings of the committee or a review team or are maintained by the committee or a review team.

History of Fam §264.511: Acts 1995, 74th Leg., ch. 255, §2 (eff. Sept. 1, 1995), ch. 878, §1 (eff. Sept. 1, 1995).

FAM §264.512. GOVERNMENTAL UNITS

The committee and a review team are governmental units for purposes of Chapter 101, Civil Practice and Remedies Code. A review team is a unit of local government under that chapter.

History of Fam §264.512: Acts 1995, 74th Leg., ch. 255, §2 (eff. Sept. 1, 1995), ch. 878, §1 (eff. Sept. 1, 1995).

FAM §264.513. REPORT OF DEATH OF CHILD

(a) A person who knows of the death of a child younger than six years of age shall immediately report the death to the medical examiner of the county in which the death occurs or, if the death occurs in a county that does not have a medical examiner's office or that is not part of a medical examiner's district, to a justice of the peace in that county.

(b) The requirement of this section is in addition to any other reporting requirement imposed by law, including any requirement that a person report child abuse or neglect under this code.

(c) A person is not required to report a death under this section that is the result of a motor vehicle accident. This subsection does not affect a duty imposed by another law to report a death that is the result of a motor vehicle accident.

History of Fam §264.513: Acts 1995, 74th Leg., ch. 255, §2 (eff. Sept. 1, 1995), ch. 878, §1 (eff. Sept. 1, 1995).

FAM §264.514. PROCEDURE IN THE EVENT OF REPORTABLE DEATH

(a) A medical examiner or justice of the peace notified of a death of a child under Section 264.513 shall hold an inquest under Chapter 49, Code of Criminal Procedure, to determine whether the death is unexpected or the result of abuse or neglect. An inquest is not required under this subchapter if the child's death is expected and is due to a congenital or neoplastic disease. A death caused by an infectious disease may be considered an expected death if:

(1) the disease was not acquired as a result of trauma or poisoning;

(2) the infectious organism is identified using standard medical procedures; and

(3) the death is not reportable to the Texas Department of Health under Chapter 81, Health and Safety Code.

(b) The medical examiner or justice of the peace shall immediately notify an appropriate local law enforcement agency if the medical examiner or justice of the peace determines that the death is unexpected or the result of abuse or neglect, and that agency shall investigate the child's death.

(c) In this section, the terms "abuse" and "neglect" have the meaning assigned those terms by Section 261.001.

History of Fam §264.514: Acts 1995, 74th Leg., ch. 255, §2, eff. Sept. 1, 1995; Acts 1995, 74th Leg., ch. 878, §1, eff. Sept. 1, 1995. Amended by Acts 1997, 75th Leg., ch. 1022, §95 (eff. Sept. 1, 1997), ch. 1301, §2 (eff. Sept. 1, 1997); Acts 1999, 76th Leg., ch. 785, §3, eff. Sept. 1, 1999.

FAM §264.515. INVESTIGATION

(a) The investigation required by Section 264.514 must include:

(1) an autopsy, unless an autopsy was conducted as part of the inquest;

(2) an inquiry into the circumstances of the death, including an investigation of the scene of the death and interviews with the parents of the child, any guardian or caretaker of the child, and the person who reported the child's death; and

(3) a review of relevant information regarding the child from an agency, professional, or health care provider.

(b) The review required by Subsection (a)(3) must include a review of any applicable medical record, child protective services record, record maintained by an emergency medical services provider, and law enforcement report.

(c) The committee shall develop a protocol relating to investigation of an unexpected death of a child under this section. In developing the protocol, the committee shall consult with individuals and organizations that have knowledge and experience in the issues of child abuse and child deaths.

History of Fam §264.515: Acts 1995, 74th Leg., ch. 255, §2 (eff. Sept. 1, 1995), ch. 878, §1 (eff. Sept. 1, 1995).

Sections 264.516-264.600 reserved for expansion

SUBCHAPTER G. COURT-APPOINTED VOLUNTEER ADVOCATE PROGRAMS

FAM §264.601. DEFINITIONS

In this subchapter:

(1) "Abused or neglected child" means a child who is:

(A) the subject of a suit affecting the parent-child relationship filed by a governmental entity; and

(B) under the control or supervision of the department.

(2) "Volunteer advocate program" means a volunteer-based, nonprofit program that provides advocacy services to abused or neglected children with the goal of obtaining a permanent placement for a child that is in the child's best interest.

History of Fam §264.601: Acts 1995, 74th Leg., ch. 20, §1, eff. April 20, 1995. Source: Former Fam §34.601.

FAM §264.602. CONTRACTS WITH ADVOCATE PROGRAMS

(a) The statewide organization with which the attorney general contracts under Section 264.603 shall contract for services with eligible volunteer advocate programs to expand the existing services of the programs.

(b) The contract under this section may not result in reducing the financial support a volunteer advocate program receives from another source.

(c) The attorney general shall develop a scale of state financial support for volunteer advocate programs that declines over a six-year period beginning on the date each individual contract takes effect. After the end of the six-year period, the attorney general may not provide more than 50 percent of the volunteer advocate program's funding.

(d) The attorney general by rule shall adopt standards for a local volunteer advocate program. The statewide organization shall assist the attorney general in developing the standards.

History of Fam §264.602: Acts 1995, 74th Leg., ch. 20, §1, eff. April 20, 1995. Amended by Acts 1995, 74th Leg., ch. 751, §118, eff. Sept. 1, 1995; Acts 1997, 75th Leg., ch. 1294, §7, eff. Sept. 1, 1997. Source: Former Fam §34.602.

FAM §264.603. ADMINISTRATIVE CONTRACTS

(a) The attorney general shall contract with one statewide organization of individuals or groups of individuals who have expertise in the dynamics of child abuse and neglect and experience in operating volunteer advocate programs to provide training, technical assistance, and evaluation services for the benefit of local volunteer advocate programs. The contract shall require measurable goals and objectives for expanding local volunteer child advocate programs to areas of the state in which those programs do not exist.

(b) The contract under this section shall provide that not more than 12 percent of the annual legislative appropriation to implement this subchapter may be spent for administrative purposes by the statewide organization with which the attorney general contracts under this section.

History of Fam §264.603: Acts 1995, 74th Leg., ch. 20, §1, eff. April 20, 1995. Amended by Acts 1995, 74th Leg., ch. 751, §119, eff. Sept. 1, 1995; Acts 1997, 75th Leg., ch. 600, §20, eff. Sept. 1, 1997. Source: Former Fam §34.603.

FAM §264.604. ELIGIBILITY FOR CONTRACTS

(a) A person is eligible for a contract under Section 264.602 only if the person is a public or private nonprofit entity that operates a volunteer advocate program that:

(1) uses individuals appointed as volunteer advocates or guardians ad litem by the court to provide for the needs of abused or neglected children;

(2) has provided court-appointed advocacy services for at least two years;

(3) provides court-appointed advocacy services for at least 10 children each month; and

(4) has demonstrated that the program has local judicial support.

(b) The statewide organization with which the attorney general contracts under Section 264.603 may not contract with a person that is not eligible under this section. However, the statewide organization may waive the requirement in Subsection (a)(3) for an established program in a rural area or under other special circumstances.

History of Fam §264.604: Acts 1995, 74th Leg., ch. 20, §1, eff. April 20, 1995. Amended by Acts 1995, 74th Leg., ch. 751, §120, eff. Sept. 1, 1995; Acts 1997, 75th Leg., ch. 1294, §8, eff. Sept. 1, 1997. Source: Former Fam §34.604.

FAM §264.605. CONTRACT FORM

A person shall apply for a contract under Section 264.602 on a form provided by the attorney general.

History of Fam §264.605: Acts 1995, 74th Leg., ch. 20, §1, eff. April 20, 1995. Source: Former Fam §34.605.

FAM §264.606. CRITERIA FOR AWARD OF CONTRACTS

The statewide organization with which the attorney general contracts under Section 264.603 shall consider the following in awarding a contract under Section 264.602:

(1) the volunteer advocate program's eligibility for and use of funds from local, state, or federal governmental sources, philanthropic organizations, and other sources;

(2) community support for the volunteer advocate program as indicated by financial contributions from civic organizations, individuals, and other community resources;

(3) whether the volunteer advocate program provides services that encourage the permanent placement of children through reunification with their families or timely placement with an adoptive family; and

(4) whether the volunteer advocate program has the endorsement and cooperation of the local juvenile court system.

History of Fam §264.606: Acts 1995, 74th Leg., ch. 20, §1, eff. April 20, 1995. Amended by Acts 1995, 74th Leg., ch. 751, §121, eff. Sept. 1, 1995. Source: Former Fam §34.606.

FAM §264.607. CONTRACT REQUIREMENTS

(a) The attorney general shall require that a contract under Section 264.602 require the volunteer advocate program to:

(1) make quarterly and annual financial reports on a form provided by the attorney general;

(2) cooperate with inspections and audits that the attorney general makes to ensure service standards and fiscal responsibility; and

(3) provide as a minimum:

(A) independent and factual information in writing to the court and to counsel for the parties involved regarding the child;

(B) advocacy through the courts for permanent home placement and rehabilitation services for the child;

(C) monitoring of the child to ensure the safety of the child and to prevent unnecessary movement of the child to multiple temporary placements;

(D) reports in writing to the presiding judge and to counsel for the parties involved;

(E) community education relating to child abuse and neglect;

(F) referral services to existing community services;

(G) a volunteer recruitment and training program, including adequate screening procedures for volunteers;

(H) procedures to assure the confidentiality of records or information relating to the child; and

(I) compliance with the standards adopted under Section 264.602.

(b) The statewide organization with which the attorney general contracts under Section 264.603 may require that a contract under Section 264.602 require the volunteer advocate program to use forms provided by the attorney general.

(c) The attorney general shall develop forms in consultation with a statewide organization of individuals or groups of individuals who have expertise in the dynamics of child abuse and neglect and experience in operating volunteer advocate programs.

History of Fam §264.607: Acts 1995, 74th Leg., ch. 20, §1, eff. April 20, 1995. Amended by Acts 1995, 74th Leg., ch. 751, §122, eff. Sept. 1, 1995; Acts 1997, 75th Leg., ch. 1294, §9, eff. Sept. 1, 1997. Source: Former Fam §34.607.

FAM §264.608. REPORT TO THE LEGISLATURE

(a) Before each regular session of the legislature, the attorney general shall publish a report that:

(1) summarizes reports from volunteer advocate programs under contract with the attorney general;

(2) analyzes the effectiveness of the contracts made by the attorney general under this chapter; and

(3) provides information on:

(A) the expenditure of funds under this chapter;

(B) services provided and the number of children for whom the services were provided; and

(C) any other information relating to the services provided by the volunteer advocate programs under this chapter.

(b) The attorney general shall submit copies of the report to the governor, lieutenant governor, speaker of the house of representatives, the Legislative Budget Board, and members of the legislature.

History of Fam §264.608: Acts 1995, 74th Leg., ch. 20, §1, eff. April 20, 1995. Source: Former Fam §34.608.

FAM §264.609. RULE-MAKING AUTHORITY

The attorney general may adopt rules necessary to implement this chapter.

History of Fam §264.609: Acts 1995, 74th Leg., ch. 20, §1, eff. April 20, 1995. Source: Former Fam §34.609.

FAM §264.610. CONFIDENTIALITY

The attorney general may not disclose information gained through reports, collected case data, or inspections that would identify a person working at or receiving services from a volunteer advocate program.

History of Fam §264.610: Acts 1995, 74th Leg., ch. 20, §1, eff. April 20, 1995. Source: Former Fam §34.610.

FAM §264.611. CONSULTATIONS

In implementing this chapter, the attorney general shall consult with individuals or groups of individuals who have expertise in the dynamics of child abuse and neglect and experience in operating volunteer advocate programs.

History of Fam §264.611: Acts 1995, 74th Leg., ch. 20, §1, eff. April 20, 1995. Source: Former Fam §34.611.

FAM §264.612. FUNDING

(a) The attorney general may solicit and receive grants or money from either private or public sources, including by appropriation by the legislature from the general revenue fund, to implement this chapter.

(b) The need for and importance of the implementation of this chapter by the attorney general requires priority and preferential consideration for appropriation.

(c) Repealed by Acts 1995, 74th Leg., ch. 751, Sec. 128, eff. Sept. 1, 1995.

History of Fam §264.612: Acts 1995, 74th Leg., ch. 20, §1, eff. April 20, 1995. Amended by Acts 1995, 74th Leg., ch. 751, §128, eff. Sept. 1, 1995. Source: Former Fam §34.612.

E FAM §264.613. USE OF INFORMATION & RECORDS; CONFIDENTIALITY

(a) The files, reports, records, communications, and working papers used or developed in providing services under this subchapter are confidential and not subject to disclosure under Chapter 552, Government Code, and may only be disclosed for purposes consistent with this subchapter.

(b) Information described by Subsection (a) may be disclosed to:

(1) the department, department employees, law enforcement agencies, prosecuting attorneys, medical professionals, and other state agencies that provide services to children and families;

(2) the attorney for the child who is the subject of the information; and

(3) eligible children's advocacy centers.

(c) Information related to the investigation of a report of abuse or neglect of a child under Chapter 261 and services provided as a result of the investigation are confidential as provided by Section 261.201.

History of Fam §264.613: Enacted by Acts 2001, 77th Leg., ch. 142, §1, eff. May 16, 2001.

Sections 264.614-264.700 blank

SUBCHAPTER H. CHILD ABUSE PROGRAM EVALUATION

FAM §264.701. CHILD ABUSE PROGRAM EVALUATION COMMITTEE

(a) The Child Abuse Program Evaluation Committee is established within the Department of Protective and Regulatory Services.

A *Subsections (b) & (c) below do not affect or impair any act done, any obligation, right, criterion, standard, or requirement existing, or any investigation begun by the Children's Trust Fund of Texas Council before Sept. 1, 2001.*

(b) The committee is appointed by the Board of Protective and Regulatory Services and is composed of the following 15 members:

(1) an officer or employee of the Texas Education Agency;

(2) two officers or employees of the Department of Protective and Regulatory Services;

(3) an officer or employee of the Texas Juvenile Probation Commission;

(4) an officer or employee of the Texas Department of Mental Health and Mental Retardation;

(5) an officer or employee of the Health and Human Services Commission;

(6) three members of the public who have knowledge of and experience in the area of delivery of services relating to child abuse and neglect;

(7) three members of the public who have knowledge of and experience in the area of evaluation of

programs relating to the prevention and treatment of child abuse and neglect; and

(8) three members of the public who are or have been recipients of services relating to the prevention or treatment of child abuse or neglect.

(c) In appointing members to the committee under Subsection (b)(8), the board shall consider appointing:

(1) an adult who as a child was a recipient of services relating to the prevention or treatment of child abuse or neglect; and

(2) a custodial and a noncustodial parent of a child who is or was a recipient of services relating to the prevention or treatment of child abuse or neglect.

Subsections (b) & (c) below are effective for any act done, any obligation, right, criterion, standard, or requirement existing, or any investigation begun by the Children's Trust Fund of Texas Council before Sept. 1, 2001.

(b) The committee is appointed by the Board of Protective and Regulatory Services and is composed of the following 15 members:

(1) an officer or employee of the Texas Education Agency;

(2) an officer or employee of the Department of Protective and Regulatory Services;

(3) an officer or employee of the Texas Juvenile Probation Commission;

(4) an officer or employee of the Texas Department of Mental Health and Mental Retardation;

(5) an officer or employee of the Children's Trust Fund of Texas Council;

(6) an officer or employee of the Health and Human Services Commission;

(7) three members of the public who have knowledge of and experience in the area of delivery of services relating to child abuse and neglect;

(8) three members of the public who have knowledge of and experience in the area of evaluation of programs relating to the prevention and treatment of child abuse and neglect; and

(9) three members of the public who are or have been recipients of services relating to the prevention or treatment of child abuse or neglect.

(c) In appointing members to the committee under Subsection (b)(9), the board shall consider appointing:

(1) an adult who as a child was a recipient of services relating to the prevention or treatment of child abuse or neglect; and

(2) a custodial and a noncustodial parent of a child who is or was a recipient of services relating to the prevention or treatment of child abuse or neglect.

(d) A committee member appointed to represent a state agency or entity serves at the pleasure of the board or until termination of the person's employment or membership with the agency or entity. The public members serve staggered six-year terms, with the terms of three public members expiring on September 1 of each even-numbered year.

(e) A member of the committee serves without compensation. A public member is entitled to reimbursement for travel expenses and per diem as provided by the General Appropriations Act.

(f) The committee shall elect from its members a presiding officer and any other officers considered necessary.

(g) Appointments to the committee shall be made without regard to the race, color, handicap, sex, religion, age, or national origin of an appointee.

(h) The committee shall:

(1) develop and adopt policies and procedures governing the system each state agency uses to evaluate the effectiveness of programs to prevent or treat child abuse or neglect with which the agency contracts;

(2) develop and adopt standard definitions of "child abuse treatment" and "child abuse prevention" to be used in implementing and administering the evaluation system created under this subchapter;

(3) develop and adopt standard models and guidelines for prevention and treatment of child abuse to be used in implementing and administering the evaluation system created under this subchapter;

(4) develop and adopt, in cooperation with each affected state agency, a schedule for each agency's adoption and implementation of the committee's evaluation system that considers each agency's budget cycle;

(5) develop and adopt a standard report form and a reporting schedule for the affected agencies;

(6) develop and adopt objective criteria by which the performance of child abuse programs may be measured after reports under this subchapter are submitted and evaluated; and

(7) report annually to the Board of Protective and Regulatory Services, governor, lieutenant governor, and speaker of the house of representatives on the results of the committee's evaluation process.

(i) In adopting an evaluation system under this subchapter, the committee shall allow the affected agencies as much latitude as possible in:

(1) the methods used to collect the required data; and

(2) the timetable for full implementation of the system, allowing for gradual implementation of the system according to classes of program providers.

(j) Each agency that contracts with a public or private entity for services relating to a program for the prevention or treatment of child abuse or neglect shall adopt and implement the committee's evaluation system and shall report to the committee as required by this subchapter.

History of Fam §264.701: Amended by Acts 1995, 74th Leg., ch. 943, §12, eff. Sept. 1, 1995. Amended by Acts 1997, 75th Leg., ch. 165, §6.10, eff. Sept. 1, 1997; Acts 2001, 77th Leg., ch. 957, §5, eff. Sept. 1, 2001. Source: Former Govt Code §772.007.

Sections 264.702-264.750 blank

SUBCHAPTER I. COMMUNITIES IN SCHOOLS PROGRAM

FAM §264.751. DEFINITIONS

In this subchapter:

(1) "Agency" means the Texas Education Agency.

(2) "Communities In Schools program" means an exemplary youth dropout prevention program.

(3) "Delinquent conduct" has the meaning assigned by Section 51.03.

(4) "Student at risk of dropping out of school" has the meaning assigned by Section 29.081, Education Code, or means a student who is eligible for a free or reduced lunch or is in family conflict or crisis.

History of Fam §264.751: Acts 1997, 75th Leg., ch. 165, §6.69, eff. Sept. 1, 1997. Amended by Acts 1999, 76th Leg., ch. 489, §3, eff. Sept. 1, 1999. Source: Former Labor Code §305.001.

FAM §264.752. STATEWIDE OPERATION OF PROGRAM

It is the intent of the legislature that the Communities In Schools program operate throughout this state. It is also the intent of the legislature that programs established under Chapter 305, Labor Code, and its predecessor statute, the Texas Unemployment Compensation Act (Article 5221b-9d, Vernon's Texas Civil Statutes), and programs established under this subchapter shall remain eligible to participate in the Communities In Schools program if funds are available and if their performance meets the criteria established by the department for renewal of their contracts.

History of Fam §264.752: Acts 1997, 75th Leg., ch. 165, §6.69, eff. Sept. 1, 1997. Amended by Acts 1999, 76th Leg., ch. 489, §3, eff. Sept. 1, 1999. Source: Former Labor Code §305.002.

FAM §264.753. STATE DIRECTOR

The executive director of the department shall designate a state director for the Communities In Schools program.

History of Fam §264.753: Acts 1997, 75th Leg., ch. 165, §6.69, eff. Sept. 1, 1997. Amended by Acts 1999, 76th Leg., ch. 489, §3, eff. Sept. 1, 1999. Source: Former Labor Code §305.011.

FAM §264.754. DUTIES OF STATE DIRECTOR

The state director shall:

(1) coordinate the efforts of the Communities In Schools program with other social service organizations and agencies and with public school personnel to provide services to students who are at risk of dropping out of school or engaging in delinquent conduct, including students who are in family conflict or emotional crisis;

(2) set standards for the Communities In Schools program and establish state performance goals, objectives, and measures for the program;

(3) obtain information to determine accomplishment of state performance goals, objectives, and measures;

(4) promote and market the program in communities in which the program is not established;

(5) help communities that want to participate in the program establish a local funding base; and

(6) provide training and technical assistance for participating communities and programs.

History of Fam §264.754: Acts 1997, 75th Leg., ch. 165, §6.69, eff. Sept. 1, 1997. Amended by Acts 1999, 76th Leg., ch. 489, §3, eff. Sept. 1, 1999. Source: Former Labor Code §305.012.

FAM §264.755. AGENCY COOPERATION; MEMORANDUM OF UNDERSTANDING

(a) The agency, the department, and Communities In Schools, Inc. shall work together to maximize the effectiveness of the Communities In Schools program.

(b) The agency and the department shall develop and mutually agree to a memorandum of understanding to clearly define the responsibilities of the agency and of the department under this subchapter. The memorandum must address:

(1) the role of the department in encouraging local business to participate in local Communities In Schools programs;

(2) the role of the agency in obtaining information from participating school districts;

(3) the use of federal or state funds available to the agency or the department for programs of this nature; and

(4) other areas identified by the agency and the department that require clarification.

(c) The agency and the department shall adopt rules to implement the memorandum and shall update the memorandum and rules annually.

History of Fam §264.755: Acts 1997, 75th Leg., ch. 165, §6.69, eff. Sept. 1, 1997. Amended by Acts 1999, 76th Leg., ch. 489, §3, eff. Sept. 1, 1999. Source: Former Labor Code §305.013.

FAM §264.756. FUNDING; EXPANSION OF PARTICIPATION

(a) The department shall develop and implement an equitable formula for the funding of local Communities In Schools programs. The formula may provide for the reduction of funds annually contributed by the state to a local program by an amount not more than 50 percent of the amount contributed by the state for the first year of the program. The formula must consider the financial resources of individual communities and school districts. Savings accomplished through the implementation of the formula may be used to extend services to counties and municipalities currently not served by a local program or to extend services to counties and municipalities currently served by an existing local program.

(b) Each local Communities In Schools program shall develop a funding plan which ensures that the level of services is maintained if state funding is reduced.

(c) A local Communities In Schools program may accept federal funds, state funds, private contributions, grants, and public and school district funds to support a campus participating in the program.

History of Fam §264.756: Acts 1997, 75th Leg., ch. 165, §6.69, eff. Sept. 1, 1997. Amended by Acts 1999, 76th Leg., ch. 489, §3, eff. Sept. 1, 1999. Source: Former Labor Code §305.021.

FAM §264.757. PARTICIPATION IN PROGRAM

An elementary or secondary school designated under Section 264.756 shall participate in a local Communities In Schools program if the number of students enrolled in the school who are at risk of dropping out of school is equal to at least 10 percent of the number of students in average daily attendance at the school, as determined by the agency.

History of Fam §264.757: Acts 1997, 75th Leg., ch. 165, §6.69, eff. Sept. 1, 1997. Amended by Acts 1999, 76th Leg., ch. 489, §3, eff. Sept. 1, 1999. Source: Former Labor Code §305.022.

FAM §264.758. DONATIONS TO PROGRAM

(a) The department may accept a donation of services or money or other property that the department determines furthers the lawful objectives of the department in connection with the Communities In Schools program.

(b) Each donation, with the name of the donor and the purpose of the donation, must be reported in the public records of the department.

History of Fam §264.758: Acts 1997, 75th Leg., ch. 165, §6.69, eff. Sept. 1, 1997. Amended by Acts 1999, 76th Leg., ch. 489, §3, eff. Sept. 1, 1999. Source: Former Labor Code §305.031.

CHAPTER 265. PREVENTION & EARLY INTERVENTION SERVICES

FAM §265.001. DEFINITIONS

In this chapter:

(1) "Department" means the Department of Protective and Regulatory Services.

(2) "Division" means the prevention and early intervention services division within the department.

(3) "Prevention and early intervention services" means programs intended to provide early intervention or prevent at-risk behaviors that lead to child abuse, delinquency, running away, truancy, and dropping out of school.

History of Fam §265.001: Acts 1999, 76th Leg., ch. 489, §2, eff. Sept. 1, 1999.

FAM §265.002. PREVENTION & EARLY INTERVENTION SERVICES DIVISION

The department shall operate a division to provide services for children in at-risk situations and for the families of those children and to achieve the consolidation of prevention and early intervention services within the jurisdiction of a single agency in order to avoid fragmentation and duplication of services and to increase the accountability for the delivery and administration of these services. The division shall be called the prevention and early intervention services division and shall have the following duties:

(1) to plan, develop, and administer a comprehensive and unified delivery system of prevention and early intervention services to children and their families in at-risk situations;

(2) to improve the responsiveness of services for at-risk children and their families by facilitating greater coordination and flexibility in the use of funds by state and local service providers;

(3) to provide greater accountability for prevention and early intervention services in order to demonstrate the impact or public benefit of a program by adopting outcome measures; and

(4) to assist local communities in the coordination and development of prevention and early intervention services in order to maximize federal, state, and local resources.

History of Fam §265.002: Acts 1999, 76th Leg., ch. 489, §2, eff. Sept. 1, 1999.

FAM §265.003. CONSOLIDATION OF PROGRAMS

(a) In order to implement the duties provided in Section 265.002, the department shall consolidate into the division programs with the goal of providing early intervention or prevention of at-risk behavior that leads to child abuse, delinquency, running away, truancy, and dropping out of school.

(b) The division may provide additional prevention and early intervention services in accordance with Section 265.002.

History of Fam §265.003: Acts 1999, 76th Leg., ch. 489, §2, eff. Sept. 1, 1999.

TEXAS RULES OF CIVIL PROCEDURE
ANNOTATED RULES
TABLE OF CONTENTS

TEXAS RULES OF CIVIL PROCEDURE
ANNOTATED RULES
TABLE OF CONTENTS

TEXAS RULES OF CIVIL PROCEDURE
ANNOTATED RULES
TABLE OF CONTENTS

Texas Rules of Civil Procedure
Annotated Rules
Table of Contents

TABLE OF CONTENTS

TEXAS RULES OF CIVIL PROCEDURE
ANNOTATED RULES
TABLE OF CONTENTS

TABLE OF CONTENTS

Texas Rules of Civil Procedure
Annotated Rules

The annotated cases and reference notes that follow the rules are not part of the official rules; they are copyrighted material included with the rules to assist in research.

TEXAS RULES OF PROCEDURE

PART I. GENERAL RULES

TRCP 1. OBJECTIVE OF RULES

The proper objective of rules of civil procedure is to obtain a just, fair, equitable and impartial adjudication of the rights of litigants under established principles of substantive law. To the end that this objective may be attained with as great expedition and dispatch and at the least expense both to the litigants and to the state as may be practicable, these rules shall be given a liberal construction.

See also *O'Connor's Texas Rules*, "Introduction to the Texas Rules," ch. 1-A.

Stelly v. Papania, 927 S.W.2d 620, 622 (Tex.1996). "The discovery rules were not designed as traps for the unwary, nor should we construe them to prevent a litigant from presenting the truth."

TRCP 2. SCOPE OF RULES

These rules shall govern the procedure in the justice, county, and district courts of the State of Texas in all actions of a civil nature, with such exceptions as may be hereinafter stated. Where any statute in effect immediately prior to September 1, 1941, prescribed a rule of procedure in lunacy, guardianship, or estates of decedents, or any other probate proceedings in the county court differing from these Rules, and not included in the "List of Repealed Statutes," such statute shall apply; and where any statute in effect immediately prior to September 1, 1941, and not included in the "List of Repealed Statutes," prescribed a rule of procedure in any special statutory proceeding differing from these rules, such statute shall apply. All statutes in effect immediately prior to September 1, 1941, prescribing rules of procedure in bond or recognizance forfeitures in criminal cases are hereby continued in effect as rules of procedure governing such cases, but where such statutes prescribed no rules of procedure in such cases, these rules shall apply. All statutes in effect immediately prior to September 1, 1941, prescribing rules of procedure in tax suits are hereby continued in effect as rules of procedure governing such cases, but where such statutes prescribed no rules of procedure in such cases, these rules shall apply; provided, however, that Rule 117a shall control with respect to citation in tax suits.

See also *O'Connor's Texas Rules*, "Introduction to the Texas Rules," ch. 1-A.

In re J.D.H., 661 S.W.2d 744, 748 (Tex.App.—Beaumont 1983, no writ). The "rule to be followed in child custody cases is that technical rules of civil procedure, as to practice and pleading, are not of controlling importance, since the controlling factor is the best interests of the child. It is because of our profound concern for the best interests of the child in issue that we have addressed this point of error, for we are not technically required to do so under TRCP 90 because appellant failed to preserve the alleged error by objection."

TRCP 3. CONSTRUCTION OF RULES

Unless otherwise expressly provided, the past, present or future tense shall each include the other; the masculine, feminine, or neuter gender shall each include the other; and the singular and plural number shall each include the other.

See also Govt Code §312.003.

TRCP 3a. LOCAL RULES

Each administrative judicial region, district court, county court, county court at law, and probate court may make and amend local rules governing practice before such courts, provided:

(1) that any proposed rule or amendment shall not be inconsistent with these rules or with any rule of the administrative judicial region in which the court is located;

(2) no time period provided by these rules may be altered by local rules;

(3) any proposed local rule or amendment shall not become effective until it is submitted and approved by the Supreme Court of Texas;

(4) any proposed local rule or amendment shall not become effective until at least thirty days after its publication in a manner reasonably calculated to bring it to the attention of attorneys practicing before the court or courts for which it is made;

(5) all local rules or amendments adopted and approved in accordance herewith are made available upon request to the members of the bar;

(6) no local rule, order, or practice of any court, other than local rules and amendments which fully comply with all requirements of this Rule 3a, shall ever be applied to determine the merits of any matter.

See also *Local Rules*, p. 1203-1258; Govt Code §51.807 (local rules for fax filing); Rules of Judicial Administration 10; *O'Connor's Texas Rules*, "Introduction to the Texas Rules," ch. 1-A.

TRCP 4. COMPUTATION OF TIME

In computing any period of time prescribed or allowed by these rules, by order of court, or by any applicable statute, the day of the act, event, or default after which the designated period of time begins to run is not to be included. The last day of the period so computed is to be included, unless it is a Saturday, Sunday or legal holiday, in which event the period runs until the end of the next day which is not a Saturday, Sunday or legal holiday. Saturdays, Sundays and legal holidays shall not be counted for any purpose in any time period of five days or less in these rules, except that Saturdays, Sundays and legal holidays shall be counted for purposes of the three-day periods in Rules 21 and 21a, extending other periods by three days when service is made by registered or certified mail or by telephonic document transfer, and for purposes of the five-day periods provided for under Rules 748, 749, 749a, 749b, and 749c.

See also Govt Code §311.014, "Computation of Time"; *O'Connor's Texas Rules*, "Rules for Filing Documents," ch. 1-C; "Rules for Serving Documents," ch. 1-D; "Motion for Summary Judgment," ch. 7-B.

Sosa v. Central Power & Light, 909 S.W.2d 893, 894 (Tex.1995). Plaintiffs "filed their second amended original petition [7 days before the hearing on the motion for summary judgment]. *At 895:* When [TRCP 4] is applied, the day on which [P] filed their amendment is not counted but the 7th day after it was filed is counted. … As we held in ***Lewis***, the last day counted from the date of the filing may be the date of the hearing. Therefore, [P] timely filed their second amended original petition."

Lewis v. Blake, 876 S.W.2d 314, 316 (Tex.1994). TRCP 4 "applies to *any* period of time prescribed by the rules of procedure…. Applying [TRCP] 4 to [TRCP] 166a(c), the … hearing on a motion for summary judgment may be set as early as the 21st day after the motion is served, or the 24th day if the motion is served by mail."

Peacock v. Humble, 933 S.W.2d 341, 342 (Tex. App.—Austin 1996, no writ). "The Code Construction Act and [TRCP] 4 … are not consistent in the manner in which they address Saturdays, Sundays, and legal holidays when computing time periods of 5 days or less. [¶] When a rule of procedure conflicts with a statute, the rule yields to the legislative enactment. *At 343:* Because the 3-day filing period in the present case is statutory, the Code Construction Act's method for computing time applies rather than the method contained in Rule 4."

TRCP 5. ENLARGEMENT OF TIME

When by these rules or by a notice given thereunder or by order of court an act is required or allowed to be done at or within a specified time, the court for cause shown may, at any time in its discretion (a) with or without motion or notice, order the period enlarged if application therefor is made before the expiration of the period originally prescribed or as extended by a previous order; or (b) upon motion permit the act to be done after the expiration of the specified period where good cause is shown for the failure to act. The court may not enlarge the period for taking any action under the rules relating to new trials except as stated in these rules.

If any document is sent to the proper clerk by first-class United States mail in an envelope or wrapper properly addressed and stamped and is deposited in the mail on or before the last day for filing same, the same, if received by the clerk not more than ten days tardily, shall be filed by the clerk and be deemed filed in time. A legible postmark affixed by the United States Postal Service shall be prima facie evidence of the date of mailing.

See also TRAP 4, "Time & Notice Provisions"; *O'Connor's Texas Rules*, "Rules for Filing Documents," ch. 1-C; "Motion for Continuance," ch. 5-D; "Requests for Admissions," ch. 6-G; "Motion for New Trial," ch. 10-B.

Stokes v. Aberdeen Ins. Co., 917 S.W.2d 267, 268 (Tex.1996). "[W]e hold that mailing the document to the proper court address is *conditionally effective* as mailing it to the proper court clerk's address. [¶] The clerk still must receive the document within 10 days to perfect the filing."

Miller Brewing Co. v. Villarreal, 829 S.W.2d 770, 771-72 (Tex.1992). A "party who finds the courthouse closed on the last day that a document must be filed … may mail the document that day, and if it is received by the clerk not more than ten days later it is timely filed. He may also locate the clerk or judge of the court and file the document with them. In some circumstances a party may also move for an enlargement of time."

Arnold v. Shuck, 24 S.W.3d 470, 472 (Tex.App.—Texarkana 2000, pet. denied). Under TRCP 5, "a document is deemed timely filed if (1) it is sent to the proper clerk, (2) by first-class United States mail, (3) in a properly addressed and stamped envelope, (4) on or before the last day for filing, and (5) it is received not more than ten days tardily. In addition, a legible postmark affixed by the U.S. Postal Service is prima facie evidence of the date of mailing."

Milam v. Miller, 891 S.W.2d 1, 2 (Tex.App.—Amarillo 1994, writ ref'd). "[O]nce the provision of [TRCP] 5 are met, the post office becomes a branch of the district clerk's office for purposes of filing pleadings."

TRCP 6. SUITS COMMENCED ON SUNDAY

No civil suit shall be commenced nor process issued or served on Sunday, except in cases of injunction, attachment, garnishment, sequestration, or distress proceedings; provided that citation by publication published on Sunday shall be valid.

See also *O'Connor's Texas Rules*, "Serving the Defendant with Suit," ch. 2-H; "Default Judgment," ch. 7-A.

Nichols v. Nichols, 857 S.W.2d 657, 659 (Tex. App.—Houston [1st Dist.] 1993, no writ). "Ms. Nichols [who was served on Sunday] was not served in strict compliance with the law. Service was invalid and the trial court's order was improper."

TRCP 7. MAY APPEAR BY ATTORNEY

Any party to a suit may appear and prosecute or defend his rights therein, either in person or by an attorney of the court.

See also *O'Connor's Texas Rules*, "Rules for Serving Documents," ch. 1-D; "The Lawyer," ch. 1-H; *O'Connor's Texas Forms*, FORMS 1I.

Kunstoplast v. Formosa Plastics Corp., 937 S.W.2d 455, 456 (Tex.1996). "Generally a corporation may be represented only by a licensed attorney .... We hold, however, that ... a nonlawyer [is not precluded] from performing the specific ministerial task of depositing cash with a clerk in lieu of a cost bond."

Ayres v. Canales, 790 S.W.2d 554, 557 (Tex.1990). "Ordering a party to be represented by an attorney violates [TRCP] 7."

Computize, Inc. v. NHS Comm. Group, Inc., 992 S.W.2d 608, 612 (Tex.App.—Texarkana 1999, no pet.). "[A] response to a motion for summary judgment by a corporation must be made through an attorney."

TRCP 8. ATTORNEY IN CHARGE

On the occasion of a party's first appearance through counsel, the attorney whose signature first appears on the initial pleadings for any party shall be the attorney in charge, unless another attorney is specifically designated therein. Thereafter, until such designation is changed by written notice to the court and all other parties in accordance with Rule 21a, said attorney in charge shall be responsible for the suit as to such party.

All communications from the court or other counsel with respect to a suit shall be sent to the attorney in charge.

See also *O'Connor's Texas Rules*, "Rules for Serving Documents," ch. 1-D; *O'Connor's Texas Forms*, FORMS 1H.

Gem Vending, Inc. v. Walker, 918 S.W.2d 656, 658 (Tex.App.—Fort Worth 1996, orig. proceeding). "Notice to an attorney is notice to a party. [O]nce an attorney has entered an appearance in a case, all communications *must* be sent to that attorney."

Reichhold Chem., Inc. v. Puremco Mfg., 854 S.W.2d 240, 246 (Tex.App.—Waco 1993, writ denied). Service of discovery answers on the co-counsel of the attorney in charge did not comply with rules.

Palmer v. Cantrell, 747 S.W.2d 39, 41 (Tex.App.—Houston [1st Dist.] 1988, no writ). "Where a single adverse party is represented by two attorneys who are not associated in a firm, we believe that it is sufficient to serve the attorney who is designated as lead counsel because he has 'control in the management of the cause....'"

TRCP 9. NUMBER OF COUNSEL HEARD

Not more than two counsel on each side shall be heard on any question or on the trial, except in important cases, and upon special leave of the court.

See also *O'Connor's Texas Rules*, "The Defendant's Responses & Pleadings," ch. 3.

TRCP 10. WITHDRAWAL OF ATTORNEY

An attorney may withdraw from representing a party only upon written motion for good cause shown. If another attorney is to be substituted as attorney for the party, the motion shall state: the name, address, telephone number, telecopier number, if any, and State Bar of Texas identification number of the substitute attorney; that the party approves the substitution; and that the withdrawal is not sought for delay only. If another attorney is not to be substituted as attorney for the party, the motion shall state: that a copy of the motion has been delivered to the party; that the party has been notified in writing of his right to object to the motion;

whether the party consents to the motion; the party's last known address and all pending settings and deadlines. If the motion is granted, the withdrawing attorney shall immediately notify the party in writing of any additional settings or deadlines of which the attorney has knowledge at the time of the withdrawal and has not already notified the party. The Court may impose further conditions upon granting leave to withdraw. Notice or delivery to a party shall be either made to the party in person or mailed to the party's last known address by both certified and regular first class mail. If the attorney in charge withdraws and another attorney remains or becomes substituted, another attorney in charge must be designated of record with notice to all other parties in accordance with Rule 21a.

See also *O'Connor's Texas Rules*, "The Lawyer," ch. 1-H; ***O'Connor's Texas Forms***, FORMS 1H.

Rogers v. Clinton, 794 S.W.2d 9, 10 n.1 (Tex.1990). "Although a client may discharge his attorney at any time even without cause ... an attorney may withdraw from representation of a client only if he satisfies the requirements of [TRCP] 10."

Walton v. Canon, Short & Gaston, P.C., 23 S.W.3d 143, 148 (Tex.App.—El Paso 2000, no pet.). "A trial court abuses its discretion when it grants a motion to withdraw that does not comply with the mandatory requirements of [TRCP] 10. Nevertheless, such error may be harmless if the court allows the party time to secure new counsel and time for the new counsel to investigate the case and prepare for trial." *See also* ***Williams v. Bank One***, 15 S.W.3d 110, 114 (Tex.App.—Waco 1999, no pet.).

In re News Am. Pub'g, Inc., 974 S.W.2d 97, 104 (Tex.App.—San Antonio 1998, orig. proceeding). "[T]his rule requires that the attorney of record have actual knowledge that his client has terminated their professional relationship. [T]herefore, ... 'if retained counsel has entered an appearance in a matter ... and remains counsel of record, ... the communicating lawyer may not communicate with the person until the lawyer has withdrawn her appearance.'"

TRCP 11. AGREEMENTS TO BE IN WRITING

Unless otherwise provided in these rules, no agreement between attorneys or parties touching any suit pending will be enforced unless it be in writing, signed and filed with the papers as part of the record, or unless it be made in open court and entered of record.

Caution: TRCP 11 is affected by the following sections in the Fam. Code: §§4.002, 4.104, 4.203, 7.006, 153.007, 153.133, 154.124.

See also TRCP 191.1 (agreements in discovery matters); ***O'Connor's Texas Rules***, "The Lawyer," ch. 1-H; "Settlement of the Suit," ch. 7-G; ***O'Connor's Texas Forms***, FORMS 1H.

Padilla v. LaFrance, 907 S.W.2d 454, 461 (Tex. 1995). "The ... filing requirement [in TRCP 11] is satisfied so long as the agreement is filed before it is sought to be enforced."

London Mkt. Cos. v. Schattman, 811 S.W.2d 550, 552 (Tex.1991). TRCP 11 "requires agreements between attorneys or parties concerning a pending suit to be in writing, signed and filed in the record of the cause to be enforceable. Once the existence of such an agreement becomes disputed, it is unenforceable unless it comports with these requirements."

CherCo Props., Inc. v. Law, Snakard & Gambill, P.C., 985 S.W.2d 262, 265 (Tex.App.—Fort Worth 1999, no pet.). A TRCP 11 "settlement agreement is not enforceable unless it is complete ... as to every material detail and contains all the essential elements of the agreement so the contract can be ascertained from the writing, without resort to oral testimony."

Clanin v. Clanin, 918 S.W.2d 673, 676-77 (Tex. App.—Fort Worth 1996, no writ). "An agreement for judgment will not be enforced unless the agreement is reduced to writing, signed and filed with the papers as part of the record, or unless it is made in open court and entered of record. Compliance with the 'open court and entered of record' portion of Rule 11 satisfies the Family Code §3.631 [now §7.006] requirement of written agreements in divorce cases. This is so because the sworn testimony of the parties given to the court reporter in open court memorializes the parties' consent and can also be reduced to writing. Therefore, this procedure has the same legal effect as a written agreement signed by the parties and, in fact, results in a written agreement that meets the requirements of ... §3.631 for agreements in divorce cases to be in writing."

Delaup v. Delaup, 917 S.W.2d 411, 413-14 (Tex. App.—Houston [14th Dist.] 1996, no writ). "Appellant argues that because the parties did not reduce the agreement to writing, but only read the agreement into the record of the court, the provision was not 'in writing.' [¶] Rule 11 of the [TRCPs] prohibits the enforcement of any agreement between the parties to a suit unless it be in writing and filed with the court or '*be made in open court and entered of record.*' The parties' settlement in the present case, including the contractual alimony provision, satisfied this rule."

Southwestern Bell Tel. Co. v. Perez, 904 S.W.2d 817, 821 (Tex.App.—San Antonio 1995, orig. proceeding). "[A]n oral agreement [to extend discovery deadlines] is unenforceable unless it is made in open court and entered of record."

McLendon v. McLendon, 847 S.W.2d 601, 607 (Tex. App.—Dallas 1992, writ denied). Appellant "contends that compliance with the 'open court and entered of record' portion of rule 11 does not satisfy any of the Family Code requirements of written agreements. *At 608:* The court reporter's transcription of the dictated agreement results in a written agreement, and the sworn testimony of the parties given to the court reporter in open court memorializes the parties' consent and can also be reduced to writing. We hold that this procedure has the same legal effect as a written agreement signed by the parties and, in fact, results in a written agreement that meets the requirements of [Family Code] §3.631 [now §7.006], §14.06 [now §§153.007 & 154.124], and §14.021 [now §153.133]."

TRCP 12. ATTORNEY TO SHOW AUTHORITY

A party in a suit or proceeding pending in a court of this state may, by sworn written motion stating that he believes the suit or proceeding is being prosecuted or defended without authority, cause the attorney to be cited to appear before the court and show his authority to act. The notice of the motion shall be served upon the challenged attorney at least ten days before the hearing on the motion. At the hearing on the motion, the burden of proof shall be upon the challenged attorney to show sufficient authority to prosecute or defend the suit on behalf of the other party. Upon his failure to show such authority, the court shall refuse to permit the attorney to appear in the cause, and shall strike the pleadings if no person who is authorized to prosecute or defend appears. The motion may be heard and determined at any time before the parties have announced ready for trial, but the trial shall not be unnecessarily continued or delayed for the hearing.

See also *O'Connor's Texas Rules*, "The Lawyer," ch. 1-H; *O'Connor's Texas Forms*, FORMS 1H.

In re Users Sys. Servs., Inc., 22 S.W.3d 331, 335 (Tex.1999). "[T]he procedure prescribed by [TRCP] 12 for requiring an attorney to show his authority to act for a party presupposes the possibility that an attorney can be counsel of record for a party he is not authorized to represent. The rules contemplate that authorization may not have existed or may cease before the attorney has withdrawn from the case."

City of San Antonio v. River City Cabaret, Ltd., 32 S.W.3d 291, 293 (Tex.App.—San Antonio 2000, pet. denied). TRCP "12 does not authorize the trial court to dismiss a lawsuit if an authorized person appears to prosecute or defend."

Coleson v. Bethan, 931 S.W.2d 706, 712 (Tex. App.—Fort Worth 1996, no writ). A challenge under TRCP 12 "would be appropriate where perhaps the attorney ad litem's duties had been fulfilled but the attorney ad litem continued to act and failed to seek his or her discharge...."

TRCP 13. EFFECT OF SIGNING OF PLEADINGS, MOTIONS & OTHER PAPERS; SANCTIONS

The signatures of attorneys or parties constitute a certificate by them that they have read the pleading, motion, or other paper; that to the best of their knowledge, information, and belief formed after reasonable inquiry the instrument is not groundless and brought in bad faith or groundless and brought for the purpose of harassment. Attorneys or parties who shall bring a fictitious suit as an experiment to get an opinion of the court, or who shall file any fictitious pleading in a cause for such a purpose, or shall make statements in pleading which they know to be groundless and false, for the purpose of securing a delay of the trial of the cause, shall be held guilty of a contempt. If a pleading, motion or other paper is signed in violation of this rule, the court, upon motion or upon its own initiative, after notice and hearing, shall impose an appropriate sanction available under Rule 215-2b, upon the person who signed it, a represented party, or both.

Courts shall presume that pleadings, motions, and other papers are filed in good faith. No sanctions under this rule may be imposed except for good cause, the particulars of which must be stated in the sanction order. "Groundless" for purposes of this rule means no basis in law or fact and not warranted by good faith argument for the extension, modification, or reversal of existing law. A general denial does not constitute a violation of this rule. The amount requested for damages does not constitute a violation of this rule.

See also CPRC chs. 9 & 10; *O'Connor's Texas Rules*, "Groundless or Frivolous Pleadings," ch. 1-B, §5; "Motion for Sanctions," ch. 5-J.

Scott & White Mem. Hosp. v. Schexnider, 940 S.W.2d 594, 596 (Tex.1996). "[A] trial court's plenary power to act in a case does not expire until 30 days after the court has signed the judgment. A trial court's power to decide a motion for sanctions pertaining to matters occurring before judgment is no different than its power to decide any other motion during its plenary jurisdiction."

GTE Comm. Sys. Corp. v. Tanner, 856 S.W.2d 725, 731 (Tex.1993). TRCP 13 "prescribes that courts presume that papers are filed in good faith. Thus, the burden is on the party moving for sanctions to overcome this presumption."

Texas-Ohio Gas, Inc. v. Mecom, 28 S.W.3d 129, 139 (Tex.App.—Texarkana 2000, no pet.). "Courts must presume that pleadings are filed in good faith, and the burden is on the party moving for sanctions to overcome this presumption. In deciding whether a pleading was filed in bad faith or for the purpose of harassment, the trial court must measure a litigant's conduct at the time the relevant pleading was signed. ... The plaintiff's petition alone cannot establish that a case was brought in bad faith or to harass. Rule 13 generally requires that the trial court hold an evidentiary hearing to make a determination about the motives and credibility of the person signing the petition."

Mattly v. Spiegel, Inc., 19 S.W.3d 890, 896 (Tex. App.—Houston [14th Dist.] 2000, no pet.). "Bad faith does not exist when a party exercises bad judgment or negligence; '[bad faith] is the conscious doing of a wrong for dishonest, discriminatory, or malicious purposes.'"

Murphy v. Friendswood Dev. Co., 965 S.W.2d 708, 709 (Tex.App.—Houston [1st Dist.] 1998, no pet.). "Rule 13 is clear—the particulars of good cause 'must be stated in the sanctions order.' *At 710:* [Because the] order here did not recite the particular reasons supporting good cause to issue the sanctions and did not include findings of fact and conclusions of law supporting good cause ... we hold that the sanction order does not comply with Rule 13."

TRCP 14. AFFIDAVIT BY AGENT

Whenever it may be necessary or proper for any party to a civil suit or proceeding to make an affidavit, it may be made by either the party or his agent or his attorney.

See also TRCP 197.2(d); *O'Connor's Texas Forms*, FORMS 1B.

Cantu v. Holiday Inns, Inc., 910 S.W.2d 113, 116 (Tex.App.—Corpus Christi 1995, writ denied). "A party's attorney may verify the pleading where he has knowledge of the facts, but does not have authority to verify based merely on his status as counsel. ... Here, counsel does not show any basis in the pleading or in her affidavit for her personal knowledge of relevant facts."

TRCP 14a. REPEALED

TRCP 14b. RETURN OR OTHER DISPOSITION OF EXHIBITS

The clerk of the court in which the exhibits are filed shall retain and dispose of the same as directed by the Supreme Court.

See also TRCP 75b.

Perez v. Bagous, 833 S.W.2d 671, 674 (Tex.App.—Corpus Christi 1992, no writ). "Once an exhibit has been admitted into evidence, ... if a party wishes to use it in some fashion, that party must give notice to opposing counsel and to the court, particularly when the admitted exhibit is used to create a new exhibit...."

SUPREME COURT ORDER RELATING TO RETENTION & DISPOSITION OF EXHIBITS

In compliance with the provisions of Rule 14b, the Supreme Court hereby directs that exhibits offered or admitted into evidence shall be retained and disposed of by the clerk of the court in which the exhibits are filed upon the following basis.

This order shall apply only to: (1) those cases in which judgment has been rendered on service of process by publication and in which no motion for new trial was filed within two years after judgment was signed; and, (2) all other cases in which judgment has been signed for one year and in which no appeal was perfected or in which a perfected appeal was dismissed or concluded by a final judgment as to all parties and the issuance of the appellate court's mandate such that the case is no longer pending on appeal or in the trial court.

After first giving all attorneys of record thirty days written notice that they have an opportunity to claim and withdraw the trial exhibits, the clerk, unless otherwise directed by the court, may dispose of the exhibits. If any such exhibit is desired by more than one attorney, the clerk shall make the necessary copies and prorate the cost among all the attorneys desiring the exhibit.

If the exhibit is not a document or otherwise capable of reproduction, the party who offered the exhibit shall be entitled to claim same; provided, however, that the party claiming the exhibit shall provide a photograph of said exhibit to any other party upon request and payment of the reasonable cost thereof by the other party.

TRCP 14c. DEPOSIT IN LIEU OF SURETY BOND

Wherever these rules provide for the filing of a surety bond, the party may in lieu of filing the bond deposit cash or other negotiable obligation of the government of the United States of America or any agency thereof, or with leave of court, deposit a negotiable obligation of any bank or savings and loan association chartered by the government of the United States of America or any state thereof that is insured by the government of the United States of America or any agency thereof, in the amount fixed for the surety bond, conditioned in the same manner as would be a surety bond for the protection of other parties. Any interest thereon shall constitute a part of the deposit.

Southwestern States Gen. Corp. v. McKenzie, 658 S.W.2d 850, 852 (Tex.App.—Dallas 1983, writ dism'd). "Because we read [TRCP] 14c as requiring no more than that the issuing bank will be one whose deposits are insured by an agency of the U.S. government, and because we can take judicial notice that Mercantile Bank at Dallas is so insured, we hold [the debtor]'s complaints about the adequacy of insurance to be without merit."

PART II. RULES OF PRACTICE IN DISTRICT & COUNTY COURTS

SECTION 1. GENERAL RULES

TRCP 15. WRITS & PROCESS

The style of all writs and process shall be "The State of Texas;" and unless otherwise specially provided by law or these rules every such writ and process shall be directed to any sheriff or any constable within the State of Texas, shall be made returnable on the Monday next after expiration of twenty days from the date of service thereof, and shall be dated and attested by the clerk with the seal of the court impressed thereon; and the date of issuance shall be noted thereon.

See also Local Govt Code §86.021; ***O'Connor's Texas Rules***, "Serving the Defendant with Suit," ch. 2-H; "Default Judgment," ch. 7-A; ***O'Connor's Texas Forms***, FORMS 2H.

Barker CATV Constr., Inc. v. Ampro, Inc., 989 S.W.2d 789, 792 (Tex.App.—Houston [1st Dist.] 1999, no pet.). TRCP 15 "seems to conflict with [TRCP] 99(b), which states the citation shall (1) be styled The State of Texas, and (8) *be directed to the defendant*.... [¶] The citation ... in this case is a preprinted form addressed to the sheriff or any constable of Texas, as well as to the defendant. The requirements of rules 15 and 99(b) can be harmonized by allowing the citations to be directed to both the sheriff or constable, as the officer serving it, and the defendant, as the person being served." (Internal quotations omitted.)

TRCP 16. SHALL ENDORSE ALL PROCESS

Every officer or authorized person shall endorse on all process and precepts coming to his hand the day and hour on which he received them, the manner in which he executed them, and the time and place the process was served and shall sign the returns officially.

See also TRCP 107; Local Govt Code §§85.021, 86.021; ***O'Connor's Texas Rules***, "Serving the Defendant with Suit," ch. 2-H; "Default Judgment," ch. 7-A; "Motion for New Trial," ch. 10-B.

Merritt v. Harris Cty., 775 S.W.2d 17, 23 (Tex. App.—Houston [14th Dist.] 1989, writ denied). "A constable is charged with the execution of all process, warrants, and precepts which are directed to him...."

TRCP 17. OFFICER TO EXECUTE PROCESS

Except where otherwise expressly provided by law or these rules, the officer receiving any process to be executed shall not be entitled in any case to demand his fee for executing the same in advance of such execution, but his fee shall be taxed and collected as other costs in the case.

See also ***O'Connor's Texas Rules***, "Default Judgment," ch. 7-A; ***O'Connor's Texas Forms***, FORMS 2H.

Rodeheaver v. Alridge, 601 S.W.2d 51, 54 (Tex. App.—Houston [1st Dist.] 1980, writ ref'd n.r.e.). "[T]here is no statutory authorization for the constable to require an advance deposit of fees for service of citation."

TRCP 18. WHEN JUDGE DIES DURING TERM, RESIGNS OR IS DISABLED

If the judge dies, resigns, or becomes unable to hold court during the session of court duly convened for the term, and the time provided by law for the holding of said court has not expired, such death, resignation, or inability on the part of the judge shall not operate to adjourn said court for the term, but such court shall be deemed to continue in session. If a successor to such judge shall qualify and assume office during the term, or if a judge be transferred to said district from some other judicial district, he may continue to hold said court for the term provided, and all motions undisposed of shall be heard and determined by him, and statements of facts and bills of exception shall be approved by him. If the time for holding such court expires before a successor shall qualify, and before a judge can be transferred to said district from some other judicial district, then all motions pending, including those for new trial, shall stand as continued in force until such successor has qualified and assumed office, or a judge has been transferred to said district who can hold said court, and thereupon such judge shall have power to act thereon at the succeeding term, or on an earlier day in vacation, on notice to all parties to the motion, and such orders shall have the same effect as if rendered in term time. The time for allowing statement of facts and bills of exception from such orders shall date from the time the motion was decided.

See also Govt Code §74.053.

W.C. Banks, Inc. v. Team, Inc., 783 S.W.2d 783, 786 (Tex.App.—Houston [1st Dist.] 1990, no writ). While TRCP 18 "specifically allows the successor judge to rule on motions pending, it does not allow rendition of judgment by a judge who has heard no evidence."

TRCP 18a. RECUSAL OR DISQUALIFICATION OF JUDGES

(a) At least ten days before the date set for trial or other hearing in any court other than the Supreme Court, the Court of Criminal Appeals or the court of appeals, any party may file with the clerk of the court a motion stating grounds why the judge before whom the case is pending should not sit in the case. The grounds may include any disability of the judge to sit in the case. The motion shall be verified and must state with particularity the grounds why the judge before whom the case is pending should not sit. The motion shall be made on personal knowledge and shall set forth such facts as would be admissible in evidence provided that facts may be stated upon information and belief if the grounds of such belief are specifically stated.

(b) On the day the motion is filed, copies shall be served on all other parties or their counsel of record, together with a notice that movant expects the motion to be presented to the judge three days after the filing of such motion unless otherwise ordered by the judge. Any other party may file with the clerk an opposing or concurring statement at any time before the motion is heard.

(c) Prior to any further proceedings in the case, the judge shall either recuse himself or request the presiding judge of the administrative judicial district to assign a judge to hear such motion. If the judge recuses himself, he shall enter an order of recusal and request the presiding judge of the administrative judicial district to assign another judge to sit, and shall make no further orders and shall take no further action in the case except for good cause stated in the order in which such action is taken.

(d) If the judge declines to recuse himself, he shall forward to the presiding judge of the administrative judicial district, in either original form or certified copy, an order of referral, the motion, and all opposing and concurring statements. Except for good cause stated in the order in which further action is taken, the judge shall make no further orders and shall take no further action in the case after filing of the motion and prior to a hearing on the motion. The presiding judge of the administrative judicial district shall immediately set a hearing before himself or some other judge designated by him, shall cause notice of such hearing to be given to all parties or their counsel, and shall make such other orders including orders on interim or ancillary relief in the pending cause as justice may require.

(e) If within ten days of the date set for trial or other hearing a judge is assigned to a case, the motion shall be filed at the earliest practicable time prior to the commencement of the trial or other hearing.

(f) If the motion is denied, it may be reviewed for abuse of discretion on appeal from the final judgment. If the motion is granted, the order shall not be reviewable, and the presiding judge shall assign another judge to sit in the case.

(g) The Chief Justice of the Supreme Court may also appoint and assign judges in conformity with this rule and pursuant to statute.

(h) If a party files a motion to recuse under this rule and it is determined by the presiding judge or the judge designated by him at the hearing and on motion of the opposite party, that the motion to recuse is brought solely for the purpose of delay and without sufficient cause, the judge hearing the motion may, in the interest of justice, impose any sanction authorized by Rule 215(2)(b).[1]

[1] Now TRCP 215.2(b).

See also Govt Code §§74.053, 74.059(c)(3); TRAP 16; *O'Connor's Texas Rules*, "Motion to Challenge the Trial Judge," ch. 5-C; *O'Connor's Texas Forms*, FORMS 5C.

In re Perritt, 992 S.W.2d 444, 445 (Tex.1999). "[A] judge designated by the presiding judge of the administrative judicial district to hear a recusal motion under [TRCP] 18a is also an assigned judge subject to objection and mandatory disqualification under [Gov't Code] §74.053(b)…."

In re Union Pac. Res. Co., 969 S.W.2d 427, 428 (Tex.1998). Mandamus is not available to review the denial of a motion to recuse made under the TRCPs. TRCP 18a(f) "expressly provide[s] for appellate review from a final judgment after denial of a recusal motion. If the appellate court determines … the trial judge should have been recused, the appellate court can reverse the trial court's judgment and remand for a new trial before a different judge."

In re M.C.M., 57 S.W.3d 27, 33 (Tex.App.—Houston [1st Dist.] 2001, pet. denied). "Where a party challenges a denial of a recusal motion based on alleged bias or impartiality, the party must show that this bias arose from an extrajudicial source and not from actions during the pendency of the trial court proceedings, unless these actions during proceedings indicate a high degree of favoritism or antagonism that renders fair judgment impossible."

Brosseau v. Ranzau, 28 S.W.3d 235, 238 (Tex. App.—Beaumont 2000, no pet.). "Consistent with [the] 'mandatory nature' [of TRCP 18a] is the recognition that the judge named in the motion not be permitted to act in *any* way other than the two options provided for in the rule. [I]f a trial court fails to comply with the strictures provided in Rule 18a, all actions taken by the judge subsequent to such violation are void."

Gill v. Texas Dept. of Crim. Justice, 3 S.W.3d 576, 579 (Tex.App.—Houston [1st Dist.] 1999, no pet.). TRCP 18a "requires that a motion for recusal or disqualification be verified and state with particularity why the judge before whom the case is pending should not sit. If a party does not comply with the mandatory requirements of Rule 18a, he waives his right to complain of a judge's refusal to recuse himself."

In re Rio Grande Valley Gas Co., 987 S.W.2d 167, 179 (Tex.App.—Corpus Christi 1999, orig. proceeding). TRCP 18a(d) and (f) and Gov't Code §74.059(c)(3) "clearly contemplate a hearing will be held on a motion to recuse. A hearing affords the movants an opportunity to develop a record regarding the motions to recuse."

TRCP 18b. GROUNDS FOR DISQUALIFICATION & RECUSAL OF JUDGES

(1) Disqualification. Judges shall disqualify themselves in all proceedings in which:

(a) they have served as a lawyer in the matter in controversy, or a lawyer with whom they previously practiced law served during such association as a lawyer concerning the matter; or

(b) they know that, individually or as a fiduciary, they have an interest in the subject matter in controversy; or

(c) either of the parties may be related to them by affinity or consanguinity within the third degree.

(2) Recusal. A judge shall recuse himself in any proceeding in which:

(a) his impartiality might reasonably be questioned;

(b) he has a personal bias or prejudice concerning the subject matter or a party, or personal knowledge of disputed evidentiary facts concerning the proceeding;

(c) he or a lawyer with whom he previously practiced law has been a material witness concerning it;

(d) he participated as counsel, adviser or material witness in the matter in controversy, or expressed an opinion concerning the merits of it, while acting as an attorney in government service;

(e) he knows that he, individually or as a fiduciary, or his spouse or minor child residing in his household, has a financial interest in the subject matter in controversy or in a party to the proceeding, or any other interest that could be substantially affected by the outcome of the proceeding;

(f) he or his spouse, or a person within the third degree of relationship to either of them, or the spouse of such a person:

(i) is a party to the proceeding, or an officer, director, or trustee of a party;

(ii) is known by the judge to have an interest that could be substantially affected by the outcome of the proceeding;

(iii) is to the judge's knowledge likely to be a material witness in the proceeding.

(g) he or his spouse, or a person within the first degree of relationship to either of them, or the spouse of such a person, is acting as a lawyer in the proceeding.

(3) A judge should inform himself about his personal and fiduciary financial interests, and make a reasonable effort to inform himself about the personal financial interests of his spouse and minor children residing in his household.

(4) In this rule:

(a) "proceeding" includes pretrial, trial, or other stages of litigation;

(b) the degree of relationship is calculated according to the civil law system;

(c) "fiduciary" includes such relationships as executor, administrator, trustee, and guardian;

(d) "financial interest" means ownership of a legal or equitable interest, however small, or a relationship as director, adviser, or other active participant in the affairs of a party, except that:

(i) ownership in a mutual or common investment fund that holds securities is not a "financial interest" in such securities unless the judge participates in the management of the fund;

(ii) an office in an educational, religious, charitable, fraternal, or civic organization is not a "financial interest" in securities held by the organization;

(iii) the proprietary interest of a policyholder in a mutual insurance company, of a depositor in a mutual savings association, or a similar proprietary interest, is a "financial interest" in the organization only if the outcome of the proceeding could substantially affect the value of the interest;

(iv) ownership of government securities is a "financial interest" in the issuer only if the outcome of the proceeding could substantially affect the value of the securities;

(v) an interest as a taxpayer or utility ratepayer, or any similar interest, is not a "financial interest" unless the outcome of the proceeding could substantially affect the liability of the judge or a person related to him within the third degree more than other judges.

(5) The parties to a proceeding may waive any ground for recusal after it is fully disclosed on the record.

(6) If a judge does not discover that he is recused under subparagraphs (2)(e) or (2)(f)(iii)* until after he has devoted substantial time to the matter, he is not required to recuse himself if he or the person related to him divests himself of the interest that would otherwise require recusal.

* Editor's Note: This should probably read "(2)(f)(ii)."

See also Tex. Const. art. 5, §11; Govt Code §§21.005, 74.053, 74.059(c)(3), 573.022, 573.025; TRAP 16; ***O'Connor's Texas Rules***, "Motion to Challenge the Trial Judge," ch. 5-C; ***O'Connor's Texas Forms***, FORMS 5C.

Sommers v. Concepcion, 20 S.W.3d 27, 42 (Tex. App.—Houston [14th Dist.] 2000, pet. denied). TRCP 18b(2)(c) "requires a judge to recuse himself in any proceeding in which he is called as a material witness. Here, the judge was not called as a material witness in this proceeding. Instead, ... the judge [was called] as a witness in another proceeding, a disciplinary proceeding. We do not believe recusal is required under these circumstances."

Pena v. Pena, 986 S.W.2d 696, 700 (Tex.App.—Corpus Christi 1998), *pet. denied*, 8 S.W.3d 639 (Tex.1999). "[T]he interest of a judge, in order that he may be disqualified, must, in general, be a direct pecuniary or property interest in the subject matter of litigation. [¶] [W]e conclude that the trial judge's attorney-client relationship with opposing counsel does not amount to a constitutional disqualification."

Ludlow v. Deberry, 959 S.W.2d 265, 271 (Tex. App.—Houston [14th Dist.] 1997, no writ). "[O]pinions formed by the judge on the basis of facts introduced or events occurring during proceedings do not constitute a basis for a recusal motion unless they display a deep-seated favoritism or antagonism that would make fair judgment impossible. [J]udicial remarks during the course of a trial that are critical or disapproving or even hostile to counsel, parties, or their cases, ordinarily do not support recusal. Such remarks may do so if they reveal an opinion deriving from an extrajudicial source and such remarks will do so if they reveal such a high degree of favoritism or antagonism as to make fair judgment impossible."

TRCP 18c. RECORDING & BROADCASTING OF COURT PROCEEDINGS

A trial court may permit broadcasting, televising, recording, or photographing of proceedings in the courtroom only in the following circumstances:

(a) in accordance with guidelines promulgated by the Supreme Court for civil cases, or

(b) when broadcasting, televising, recording, or photographing will not unduly distract participants or impair the dignity of the proceedings and the parties have consented, and consent to being depicted or recorded is obtained from each witness whose testimony will be broadcast, televised, or photographed, or

(c) the broadcasting, televising, recording, or photographing of investiture, or ceremonial proceedings.

Caution: TRCP 18c is affected by the following sections in the Fam. Code: §§104.002-104.005.

TRCP 19. NON-ADJOURNMENT OF TERM

Every term of court shall commence and convene by operation of law at the time fixed by statute without any act, order, or formal opening by a judge or other official thereof, and shall continue to be open at all times until and including the last day of the term unless sooner adjourned by the judge thereof.

TRCP 20. MINUTES READ & SIGNED

On the last day of the session, the minutes shall be read, corrected and signed in open court by the judge. Each special judge shall sign the minutes of such proceedings as were had by him.

TRCP 21. FILING & SERVING PLEADINGS & MOTIONS

Every pleading, plea, motion or application to the court for an order, whether in the form of a motion, plea or other form of request, unless presented during a hearing or trial, shall be filed with the clerk of the court in writing, shall state the grounds therefor, shall set forth the relief or order sought, and at the same time a true copy shall be served on all other parties, and shall be noted on the docket.

An application to the court for an order and notice of any hearing thereon, not presented during a hearing or trial, shall be served upon all other parties not less than three days before the time specified for the hearing unless otherwise provided by these rules or shortened by the court.

If there is more than one other party represented by different attorneys, one copy of such pleading shall be delivered or mailed to each attorney in charge.

The party or attorney of record, shall certify to the court compliance with this rule in writing over signature on the filed pleading, plea, motion or application.

After one copy is served on a party that party may obtain another copy of the same pleading upon tendering reasonable payment for copying and delivering.

See also *O'Connor's Texas Rules*, "Rules of Pleading," ch. 1-B; "Rules for Filing Documents," ch. 1-C; "Rules for Serving Documents," ch. 1-D; "Motion in Limine," ch. 5-E; "Motion to Seal Court Records," ch. 5-K.

Tate v. E.I. du Pont de Nemours & Co., 934 S.W.2d 83, 84 (Tex.1996). "[T]he filing [of plaintiff's motion for new trial] became complete when she later paid the filing fee [after the motion was overruled by operation of law, but within the trial court's plenary jurisdiction]. *At n.1:* However, we express no opinion about whether a motion for new trial extends the appellate timetable if the filing fee is not paid within the period of the trial court's plenary jurisdiction [or] about whether a motion for new trial ... properly *preserves error* for appeal if, as in this case, the filing fee is not paid until after the motion is overruled by operation of law."

Jamar v. Patterson, 868 S.W.2d 318, 319 (Tex. 1993). "[T]he date of filing is when the document is first tendered to the clerk [even though no filing fee was paid]. The filing was completed ... when Jamar paid the filing fee. *At n.3:* The filing is not completed until the fee is paid, and absent emergency or other rare circumstances, the court should not consider it before then."

TRCP 21a. METHODS OF SERVICE

Every notice required by these rules, and every pleading, plea, motion, or other form of request required to be served under Rule 21, other than the citation to be served upon the filing of a cause of action and except as otherwise expressly provided in these rules, may be served by delivering a copy to the party to be served, or the party's duly authorized agent or attorney of record, as the case may be, either in person or by agent or by courier receipted delivery or by certified or registered mail, to the party's last known address, or by telephonic document transfer to the recipient's current telecopier number, or by such other manner as the court in its discretion may direct. Service by mail shall be complete upon deposit of the paper, enclosed in a postpaid, properly addressed wrapper, in a post office or official depository under the care and custody of the United States Postal Service. Service by telephonic document transfer after 5:00 p.m. local time of the recipient shall be deemed served on the following day. Whenever a party has the right or is required to do some act within a prescribed period after the service of a notice or other paper upon him and the notice or paper is served upon by mail or by telephonic document transfer, three days shall be added to the prescribed period. Notice may be served by a party to the suit, an attorney of record, a sheriff or constable, or by any other person competent to testify. The party or attorney of record shall certify to the court compliance with this rule in writing over signature and on the filed instrument. A certificate by a party or an attorney of record, or the return of an officer, or the affidavit of any person showing service of a notice shall be prima facie evidence of the fact of service. Nothing herein shall preclude any party from offering proof that the notice or instrument was not received, or, if service was by mail, that it was not received within three days from the date of deposit in a post office or official depository under the care and custody of the United States Postal Service, and upon so finding, the court may extend the time for taking the action required of such party or grant such other relief as it deems just. The provisions hereof relating to the method of service of notice are cumulative of all other methods of service prescribed by these rules.

Caution: TRCP 21a is affected by the following sections in the Fam. Code: §§6.4035, 6.408, 6.409, 102.009, 102.010.

See also ***O'Connor's Texas Rules***, "Rules of Pleading," ch. 1-B; "Rules for Filing Documents," ch. 1-C; "Rules for Serving Documents," ch. 1-D; ***O'Connor's Texas Forms***, FORMS 1B:09, 1B:10.

Wembley Inv. Co. v. Herrera, 11 S.W.3d 924, 928 (Tex.1999). "[W]hen the sender of a document relies on office routine or custom to support an inference that the document was mailed, the sender must provide corroborating evidence that the practice was actually carried out. ... At best, [witness'] affidavit is only an 'opinion[] that the notice w[as] *probably* sent,' and does not controvert [D's] attorneys' affidavits attesting that the nonsuit motion was not received."

Thomas v. Ray, 889 S.W.2d 237, 238-39 (Tex.1994). "When a letter, properly addressed and postage prepaid, is mailed, there exists a presumption that the notice was duly received by the addressee. ... This presumption may be rebutted by an offer of proof of nonreceipt."

Lewis v. Blake, 876 S.W.2d 314, 315 (Tex.1994). TRCP 21a "extends that minimum notice by 3 days when the motion is served by mail. *At 316:* [The] hearing on a motion for summary judgment may be set as early as the 21st day after the motion is served, or the 24th day if the motion is served by mail."

Gonzales v. Surplus Ins. Servs., 863 S.W.2d 96, 102 (Tex.App.—Beaumont 1993, writ denied). "[W]here it is shown, as here, that a party has fully complied with the notice requirements set forth in [TRCP] 21a..., yet fails to establish actual receipt of notice upon opposing party or counsel, such notice shall be sufficient constructive notice where it is shown that the intended recipient engaged in instances of selective acceptance/refusal of certified mail relating to the case."

TRCP 21b. SANCTIONS FOR FAILURE TO SERVE OR DELIVER COPY OF PLEADINGS & MOTIONS

If any party fails to serve on or deliver to the other parties a copy of any pleading, plea, motion, or other application to the court for an order in accordance with Rules 21 and 21a, the court may in its discretion, after notice and hearing, impose an appropriate sanction available under Rule 215-2b.[1]

[1] Now TRCP 215.2(6).

See also ***O'Connor's Texas Rules***, "Rules for Filing Documents," ch. 1-C; "Rules for Serving Documents," ch. 1-D; "Motion for Sanctions," ch. 5-J; ***O'Connor's Texas Forms***, FORMS 5J.

Union City Body Co. v. Ramirez, 911 S.W.2d 196, 200 (Tex.App.—San Antonio 1995, orig. proceeding). "[I]f a party does not serve or deliver to other parties copies of pleadings, motions, or other papers as required by [TRCP] 21 and 21a, the court can impose sanctions. *At 201:* [A] complaint of inadequate notice under [TRCP] 21 or 21a is waived absent a timely and specific objection."

TRCP 21c. REPEALED

SECTION 2. INSTITUTION OF SUIT

TRCP 22. COMMENCED BY PETITION

A civil suit in the district or county court shall be commenced by a petition filed in the office of the clerk.

Caution: TRCP 22 is affected by Fam. Code §102.002.

See also *O'Connor's Texas Rules*, "Plaintiff's Original Petition," ch. 2-B; "Serving the Defendant with Suit," ch. 2-H; *O'Connor's Texas Forms*, FORMS 2B.

Billings v. Concordia Heritage Ass'n, 960 S.W.2d 688, 690 n.4 (Tex.App.—El Paso 1997, pet. denied). "In Texas an action is commenced in the district or county court by filing a petition in the office of the clerk. Judicial action without jurisdiction is void."

TRCP 23. SUITS TO BE NUMBERED CONSECUTIVELY

It shall be the duty of the clerk to designate the suits by regular consecutive numbers, called file numbers, and he shall mark on each paper in every case the file number of the cause.

See also *O'Connor's Texas Rules*, "Rules for Filing Documents," ch. 1-C.

TRCP 24. DUTY OF CLERK

When a petition is filed with the clerk he shall indorse thereon the file number, the day on which it was filed and the time of filing, and sign his name officially thereto.

See also TRCP 74; *O'Connor's Texas Rules*, "Rules for Filing Documents," ch. 1-C.

Biffle v. Morton Rubber Indus., Inc., 785 S.W.2d 143, 144 (Tex.1990). "An instrument is deemed in law filed at the time it is delivered to the clerk, regardless of whether the instrument is filemarked."

TRCP 25. CLERK'S FILE DOCKET

Each clerk shall keep a file docket which shall show in convenient form the number of the suit, the names of the attorneys, the names of the parties to the suit, and the nature thereof, and, in brief form, the officer's return on the process, and all subsequent proceedings had in the case with the dates thereof.

See also *O'Connor's Texas Rules*, "Rules for Filing Documents," ch. 1-C.

TRCP 26. CLERK'S COURT DOCKET

Each clerk shall also keep a court docket in a permanent record that shall include the number of the case and the names of parties, the names of the attorneys, the nature of the action, the pleas, the motions, and the ruling of the court as made.

See also *O'Connor's Texas Rules*, "Rules for Filing Documents," ch. 1-C.

First Nat'l Life Ins. Co. v. Herring, 318 S.W.2d 119, 123 (Tex.App.—Waco 1958, no writ). "The making of entries on the docket sheet is primarily the duty of the clerk."

TRCP 27. ORDER OF CASES

The cases shall be placed on the docket as they are filed.

See also *O'Connor's Texas Rules*, "Rules for Filing Documents," ch. 1-C.

SECTION 3. PARTIES TO SUITS

TRCP 28. SUITS IN ASSUMED NAME

Any partnership, unincorporated association, private corporation, or individual doing business under an assumed name may sue or be sued in its partnership, assumed or common name for the purpose of enforcing for or against it a substantive right, but on a motion by any party or on the court's own motion the true name may be substituted.

See also *O'Connor's Texas Rules*, "Plaintiff's Original Petition," ch. 2-B; *O'Connor's Texas Forms*, FORMS 2B. In 1995, the Legislature enacted the Texas Uniform Unincorporated Non-Profit Association Act (TUNA), which makes unincorporated non-profit associations legal entities responsible for their contracts and torts and relieves their members from individual liability. TRCS 1396-70.01 §7.

Chilkewitz v. Hyson, 22 S.W.3d 825, 830 (Tex. 1999). "Rule 28 is not a tolling provision when a party is sued in the name under which it conducts business and that party has actual notice of the suit. Rule 28 allows suit directly against the correct party in its assumed name. To the extent that ***Bailey*** [***v. Vanscot Concrete Co.***, 894 S.W.2d 757 (Tex.1995)] and certain court of appeals decisions indicate that Rule 28 is a tolling provision, we disapprove of them. [¶] Because the Association conducted business under the name of Morton Hyson, M.D., suit was commenced against the Association when suit was filed naming 'Morton Hyson, M.D.' as a defendant, and the Association was notified of the suit through its only officer and director, who also did business under the same name."

Cox v. Thee Evergreen Ch., 836 S.W.2d 167, 171 (Tex.1992). TRCP 28 "treat[s] unincorporated associations as legal entities. … Rule 28 generally does not affect substantive rights."

Holberg & Co. v. Citizens Nat'l Assur. Co., 856 S.W.2d 515, 517 (Tex.App.—Houston [1st Dist.] 1993, no writ). "When an individual is doing business under an assumed name, a judgment rendered against the unincorporated association is binding on the individual. *At 518:* Under [TRCP] 28, the trial court had the authority to substitute [the proprietor] for the [unincorporated sole proprietorship] on a motion by the plaintiff or on its own motion…."

TRCP 29. SUIT ON CLAIM AGAINST DISSOLVED CORPORATION

When no receiver has been appointed for a corporation which has dissolved, suit may be instituted on any claim against said corporation as though the same had not been dissolved, and service of process may be obtained on the president, directors, general manager, trustee, assignee, or other person in charge of the affairs of the corporation at the time it was dissolved, and judgment may be rendered as though the corporation had not been dissolved.

See also Business Corp. Act art. 7.12; TRCP 160.

TRCP 30. PARTIES TO SUITS

Assignors, endorsers and other parties not primarily liable upon any instruments named in the chapter of the Business and Commerce Code, dealing with commercial paper, may be jointly sued with their principal obligors, or may be sued alone in the cases provided for by statute.

See also *O'Connor's Texas Rules*, "Plaintiff's Original Petition," ch. 2-B; *O'Connor's Texas Forms*, FORMS 2B.

Reed v. Buck, 370 S.W.2d 867, 872 (Tex.1963). "We hold that when a party signs a note in the capacity of a maker, the payee (or one standing in the shoes of a payee) may sue such maker singly and proceed to judgment upon the note without joining in the suit another or others who may also appear upon the note as comakers."

TRCP 31. SURETY NOT TO BE SUED ALONE

No surety shall be sued unless his principal is joined with him, or unless a judgment has previously been rendered against his principal, except in cases otherwise provided for in the law and these rules.

See also CPRC §17.001; *O'Connor's Texas Rules*, "Motion to Abate," ch. 3-H.

McGrath v. Bank of the W., 786 S.W.2d 754, 757 (Tex.App.—Houston [1st Dist.] 1990, no writ). "[T]he Bank acquired and perfected a valid and enforceable security interest in the certificate of deposit as security for Armstrong's debt.... As such, the Bank was not required, under [TRCP] 31, to join Armstrong and attempt collection prior to exercising its rights in the collateral."

Hart v. First Fed. S.&L. Ass'n, 727 S.W.2d 723, 726 (Tex.App.—Austin 1987, no writ). "[T]he necessity of joining the principal debtor in the creditor's suit against the guarantor is subject to an exception for cases where the debtor is 'hopelessly insolvent.' *At n.1:* [TRCP] 31 incorporates, in effect, the provisions of [CPRC] §17.001."

TRCP 32. MAY HAVE QUESTION OF SURETYSHIP TRIED

When any suit is brought against two or more defendants upon any contract, any one or more of the defendants being surety for the other, the surety may cause the question of suretyship to be tried and determined upon the issue made for the parties defendant at the trial of the cause, or at any time before or after the trial or at a subsequent term. Such proceedings shall not delay the suit of the plaintiff.

See also Bus. & Com. Code, ch. 34; *O'Connor's Texas Rules*, "Motion to Abate," ch. 3-H.

Musey v. Dickinson Soc. Club, 466 S.W.2d 84, 86 (Tex.App.—Houston [1st Dist.] 1971, no writ). "Defendants argue they had a right ... under [TRCP] 32 to a determination of the principal-surety relationship they asserted between themselves and [one of the makers of the promissory note]. *At 87:* It is well settled that an accommodation maker is bound on the instrument without any resort to his principal. [¶] Since the payee or holder may proceed to judgment against a maker without joining other co-makers, he should be able to proceed to judgment following severance of the suit against a co-maker."

TRCP 33. SUITS BY OR AGAINST COUNTIES

Suits by or against a county or incorporated city, town or village shall be in its corporate name.

See also *O'Connor's Texas Rules*, "Plaintiff's Original Petition," ch. 2-B.

Scott v. Graham, 292 S.W.2d 324, 327 (Tex.1956). TRCP 33 "provides that suits by or against a county shall be in its corporate name. A county is not made a party to a suit by joining the commissioners and other officials of the county as parties."

TRCP 34. AGAINST SHERIFF, ETC.

Whenever a sheriff, constable, or a deputy or either has been sued for damages for any act done in his official character, and has taken an indemnifying bond for the acts upon which the suit is based, he may make the principal and surety on such bond parties defendant in such suit, and the cause may be continued to obtain service on such parties.

Agricultural Bond & Credit Corp. v. Shepherd, 69 S.W.2d 213, 215 (Tex.App.—Amarillo 1934, no writ). Under what is now TRCP 34, the sheriff has "a right to bring in the principal and surety on the indemnity bond given him."

TRCP 35. ON OFFICIAL BONDS

In suits brought by the State or any county, city, independent school district, irrigation district, or other political subdivision of the State, against any officer who has held an office for more than one term, or against any depository which has been such depository for more than one term, or has given more than one official bond, the sureties on each and all such bonds may be joined as defendants in the same suit whenever it is difficult to determine when the default sued for occurred and which set of sureties on such bonds is liable therefor.

Aetna Cas. & Sur. Co. v. State, 86 S.W.2d 826, 828 (Tex.App.—Fort Worth 1935, writ dism'd). "It is elementary that a surety bond given by a public official does not cover defaults which occurred prior to the date when it became effective, or defaults occurring after expiration of the term covered by the bond."

TRCP 36. DIFFERENT OFFICIALS & BONDSMEN

In suits by the State upon the official bond of a State officer, any subordinate officer who has given bond, payable either to the State or such superior officer, to cover all or part of the default sued for, together with the sureties on his official bond, may be joined as defendants with such superior officer and his bondsmen whenever it is alleged in the petition that both of such officers are liable for the money sued for.

TRCP 37. ADDITIONAL PARTIES

Before a case is called for trial, additional parties, necessary or proper parties to the suit, may be brought in, either by the plaintiff or the defendant, upon such terms as the court may prescribe; but not at a time nor in a manner to unreasonably delay the trial of the case.

See also *O'Connor's Texas Rules*, "Plaintiff's Original Petition," ch. 2-B; "The Answer—Denying Liability," ch. 3-E.

Gomez v. Kestermeier, 924 S.W.2d 210, 212 (Tex. App.—Eastland 1996, writ denied). Defendants urge "that the trial court erred by rendering judgment without the joinder of … the grantors. … [Ds] raised this issue in their motion for new trial and in their [motion for JNOV]. Even though they did raise the issue at trial, [Ds] did not preserve the issue for review because … they made no effort themselves to join [the grantors] as parties."

TRCP 38. THIRD-PARTY PRACTICE

(a) When defendant may bring in third party. At any time after commencement of the action a defending party, as a third-party plaintiff, may cause a citation and petition to be served upon a person not a party to the action who is or may be liable to him or to the plaintiff for all or part of the plaintiff's claim against him. The third-party plaintiff need not obtain leave to make the service if he files the third-party petition not later than thirty (30) days after he serves his original answer. Otherwise, he must obtain leave on motion upon notice to all parties to the action. The person served, hereinafter called the third-party defendant, shall make his defenses to the third-party plaintiff's claim under the rules applicable to the defendant, and his counterclaims against the third-party plaintiff and cross-claims against other third-party defendants as provided in Rule 97. The third-party defendant may assert against the plaintiff any defenses which the third-party plaintiff has to the plaintiff's claim. The third-party defendant may also assert any claim against the plaintiff arising out of the transaction or occurrence that is the subject matter of the plaintiff's claim against the third-party plaintiff. The plaintiff may assert any claim against the third-party defendant arising out of the transaction or occurrence that is the subject matter of the plaintiff's claim against the third-party plaintiff, and the third-party defendant thereupon shall assert his defenses and his counterclaims and cross-claims. Any party may move to strike the third-party claim, or for its severance or separate trial. A third-party defendant may proceed under this rule against any person not a party to the action who is or who may be liable to him or to the third-party plaintiff for all or part of the claim made in the action against the third-party defendant.

(b) When plaintiff may bring in third party. When a counterclaim is asserted against a plaintiff, he may cause a third party to be brought in under circumstances which under this rule would entitle a defendant to do so.

(c) This rule shall not be applied, in tort cases, so as to permit the joinder of a liability or indemnity insurance company, unless such company is by statute or contract liable to the person injured or damaged.

(d) This rule shall not be applied so as to violate any venue statute, as venue would exist absent this rule.

See also CPRC §33.004 (adding "responsible third party"); ***O'Connor's Texas Rules***, "Plaintiff's Original Petition," ch. 2-B; "The Answer—Denying Liability," ch. 3-E.

Smith v. Clary Corp., 917 S.W.2d 796, 797 (Tex. 1996). "[T]he legislature enacted Gov't Code §24.009, the aggregating statute, to allow multiple plaintiffs to aggregate their claims to achieve the minimum jurisdictional amount for a court, not to defeat jurisdiction for multiple defendants each of whose counterclaims is within the jurisdictional limit."

Getty Oil Co. v. Insurance Co. of N. Am., 845 S.W.2d 794, 801 (Tex.1992). Getty's claims against INA and Youell, the primary and excess carriers of a cross-defendant in the first suit, were not barred by res judicata in a second suit. TRCP 38(c) "prohibited Getty from joining INA and Youell in the [first] suit. [¶] Rule 38(c) has been held to prohibit the joinder of insurers in situations resembling this case [in a tort suit]. [¶] Since Getty could not have asserted its present claims against INA or Youell in the [first] suit, it is not now precluded by res judicata from bringing these claims."

TRCP 39. JOINDER OF PERSONS NEEDED FOR JUST ADJUDICATION

(a) Persons to be Joined if Feasible. A person who is subject to service of process shall be joined as a party in the action if (1) in his absence complete relief cannot be accorded among those already parties, or (2) he claims an interest relating to the subject of the action and is so situated that the disposition of the action in his absence may (i) as a practical matter impair or impede his ability to protect that interest or (ii) leave any of the persons already parties subject to a substantial risk of incurring double, multiple, or otherwise inconsistent obligations by reason of his claimed interest. If he has not been so joined, the court shall order that he be made a party. If he should join as a plaintiff but refuses to do so, he may be made a defendant, or, in a proper case, an involuntary plaintiff.

(b) Determination by Court Whenever Joinder Not Feasible. If a person as described in subdivision (a)(1)-(2) hereof cannot be made a party, the court shall determine whether in equity and good conscience the action should proceed among the parties before it, or should be dismissed, the absent person being thus regarded as indispensable. The factors to be considered by the court include: first, to what extent a judgment rendered in the person's absence might be prejudicial to him or those already parties; second, the extent to which, by protective provisions in the judgment, by the shaping of relief, or other measures, the prejudice can be lessened or avoided; third, whether a judgment rendered in the person's absence will be adequate; fourth, whether the plaintiff will have an adequate remedy if the action is dismissed for non-joinder.

(c) Pleading Reasons for Nonjoinder. A pleading asserting a claim for relief shall state the names, if known to the pleader, of any persons as described in subdivision (a)(1)-(2) hereof who are not joined, and the reasons why they are not joined.

(d) Exception of Class Actions. This rule is subject to the provisions of Rule 42.

Caution: TRCP 39 is affected by the following sections in the Fam. Code: §§1.105, 162.002.

See also TRCP 41, 51, 174; ***O'Connor's Texas Rules***, "Plaintiff's Original Petition," ch. 2-B; "Parties & Claims," ch. 2-E; "The Answer—Denying Liability," ch. 3-E; "Motion to Abate," ch. 3-H; "Motions for Severance & Separate Trials," ch. 5-H.

Smith v. Clary Corp., 917 S.W.2d 796, 799 (Tex. 1996). "The courts have not and should not apply aggregation [in Gov't Code §24.009] to divest a court of jurisdiction on counterclaims asserted by multiple defendants, whose joinder normally is not voluntary, and who have not chosen the forum."

Cooper v. Texas Gulf Indus., Inc., 513 S.W.2d 200, 204 (Tex.1974). "Under the provisions of our present [TRCP] 39 it would be rare indeed if there were a person whose presence was so indispensable in the sense that his absence deprives the court of jurisdiction to adjudicate between the parties already joined."

TRCP 40. PERMISSIVE JOINDER OF PARTIES

(a) Permissive Joinder. All persons may join in one action as plaintiffs if they assert any right to relief jointly, severally, or in the alternative in respect of or arising out of the same transaction, occurrence, or series of transactions or occurrences and if any question of law or fact common to all of them will arise in the action. All persons may be joined in one action as defendants if there is asserted against them jointly, severally, or in the alternative any right to relief in respect of or arising out of the same transaction, occurrence, or series of transactions or occurrences and if any question of law or fact common to all of them will arise in the action. A plaintiff or defendant need not be interested in obtaining or defending against all the relief demanded. Judgment may be given for one or more of the plaintiffs according to their respective rights to relief, and against one or more defendants according to their respective liabilities.

(b) Separate Trials. The court may make such orders as will prevent a party from being embarrassed, delayed, or put to expense by the inclusion of a party against whom he asserts no claim and who asserts no claim against him, and may order separate trials or make other orders to prevent delay or prejudice.

Caution: TRCP 40 is affected by Fam. Code §1.105.

See also TRCP 41, 51, 174; ***O'Connor's Texas Rules***, "Plaintiff's Original Petition," ch. 2-B; "Parties & Claims," ch. 2-E; "The Answer—Denying Liability," ch. 3-E; "Motion to Abate," ch. 3-H; "Motions for Severance & Separate Trials," ch. 5-H.

Landers v. East Tex. Salt Water Disposal Co., 248 S.W.2d 731, 734 (Tex.1952). "Where the tortious acts of 2 or more wrongdoers join to produce an indivisible injury ... all of the wrongdoers will be held jointly and severally liable for the entire damages and the injured party may proceed to judgment against any one separately or against all in one suit. If fewer than the whole number of wrongdoers are joined as defendants..., those joined may by proper cross action ... bring in those omitted."

TRCP 41. MISJOINDER & NON-JOINDER OF PARTIES

Misjoinder of parties is not ground for dismissal of an action. Parties may be dropped or added, or suits filed separately may be consolidated, or actions which have been improperly joined may be severed and each ground of recovery improperly joined may be docketed as a separate suit between the same parties, by order of the court on motion of any party or on its own initiative at any stage of the action, before the time of submission to the jury or to the court if trial is without a jury, on such terms as are just. Any claim against a party may be severed and proceeded with separately.

See also TRCP 40, 51, 174; ***O'Connor's Texas Rules***, "The Answer—Denying Liability," ch. 3-E.

State Dept. of Highways & Pub. Transp. v. Cotner, 845 S.W.2d 818, 819 (Tex.1993). TRCP 41 "does not 'permit a trial court to sever a case after it has been submitted to the trier of fact.' [¶] A partial new trial may be ordered notwithstanding the prohibition in Rule 41 against post-submission severances. [TRCP] 320 is thus an exception to [TRCP] 41."

Guaranty Fed. Sav. Bank v. Horseshoe Operating Co., 793 S.W.2d 652, 658 (Tex.1990). "A claim is properly severable if (1) the controversy involves more than one cause of action, (2) the severed claim is one that would be the proper subject of a lawsuit if independently asserted, and (3) the severed claim is not so interwoven with the remaining action that they involve the same facts and issues."

Duncan v. Calhoun Cty. Navigation Dist., 28 S.W.3d 707, 710 (Tex.App.—Corpus Christi 2000, pet. denied). "[S]everance of that portion of the lawsuit is not proper when it amounts to the splitting of a single cause of action. *At 711:* The filing of a motion for partial summary judgment is not an indication that an independent cause exists."

TRCP 42. CLASS ACTIONS

(a) Prerequisites to a Class Action. One or more members of a class may sue or be sued as representative parties on behalf of all only if (1) the class is so numerous that joinder of all members is impracticable, (2) there are questions of law or fact common to the class, (3) the claims or defenses of the representative parties are typical of the claims or defenses of the class, and (4) the representative parties will fairly and adequately protect the interests of the class.

Derivative Suit. In a derivative suit brought pursuant to Article 5.14 of the Texas Business Corporation Act, the petition shall contain the allegations (1) that the plaintiff was a record or beneficial owner of shares, or of an interest in a voting trust for shares at the time of the transaction of which he complains, or his shares or interest thereafter devolved upon him by operation of law from a person who was the owner at that time, and (2) with particularity, the efforts of the plaintiff to have suit brought for the corporation by the board of directors, or the reasons for not making any such efforts. The derivative suit may not be maintained if it appears that the plaintiff does not fairly and adequately represent the interests of the shareholders similarly situated in enforcing the right of the corporation. The suit shall not be dismissed or compromised without the approval of the court, and notice in the manner directed by the court of the proposed dismissal or compromise shall be given to shareholders.

(b) Class Actions Maintainable. An action may be maintained as a class action if the prerequisites of subdivision (a) are satisfied, and in addition:

(1) the prosecution of separate actions by or against individual members of the class would create a risk of

(A) inconsistent or varying adjudications with respect to individual members of the class which would establish incompatible standards of conduct for the party opposing the class, or

(B) adjudications with respect to individual members of the class which would as a practical matter be dispositive of the interests of the other members not parties to the adjudications or substantially impair or impede their ability to protect their interests; or

(2) the party opposing the class has acted or refused to act on grounds generally applicable to the class, thereby making appropriate final injunctive relief or corresponding declaratory relief with respect to the class as a whole; or

(3) where the object of the action is the adjudication of claims which do or may affect specific property involved in the action; or

(4) the court finds that the questions of law or fact common to the members of the class predominate over any questions affecting only individual members, and that a class action is superior to other available methods for the fair and efficient adjudication of the controversy. The matters pertinent to the findings include: (A) the interest of members of the class in individually controlling the prosecution or defense of separate actions; (B) the extent and nature of any litigation concerning the controversy already commenced by or against members of the class; (C) the desirability or undesirability of concentrating the litigation of the claims in the particular forum; (D) the difficulties likely to be encountered in the management of a class action.

(c) Determination by Order Whether Class Action to be Maintained; Notice; Judgment; Actions Conducted Partially as Class Actions.

(1) As soon as practicable after the commencement of an action brought as a class action, the court shall, after hearing, determine by order whether it is to be so maintained. This determination may be altered, amended, or withdrawn at any time before final judgment. The court may order the naming of additional parties in order to insure the adequacy of representation.

(2) After the court has determined that a class action may be maintained it shall order the party claiming the class action to direct to the members of the class the best notice practicable under the circumstances including individual notice to all members who can be identified through reasonable effort. In all class actions maintained under subdivisions (b)(1), (b)(2), and (b)(3), this notice shall advise the members of the class (A) the nature of the suit, (B) the binding effect of the judgment, whether favorable or not, and (C) the right of any member to appear before the court and challenge the court's determinations as to the class and its representatives. In all class actions maintained under subdivision (b)(4) this notice shall advise each member of the class (A) the nature of the suit; (B) that the court will exclude him from the class if he so requests by a specified date; (C) that the judgment, whether favorable or not, will include and bind all members who do not request exclusion by the specified date; and (D) that any member who does not request exclusion may if he desires, enter an appearance through his counsel.

(3) The judgment in an action maintained as a class action under subdivisions (b)(1), (b)(2), and (b)(3), whether or not favorable to the class, shall include, describe, and be binding upon all those whom the court finds to be members of the class and who received notice as provided in subdivision (c)(2). The judgment in an action maintained as a class action under subdivision (b)(4), whether or not favorable to the class, shall include and specify or describe those to whom the notice provided in subdivision (c)(2) was directed, and who have not requested exclusion, and whom the court finds to be members of the class.

(d) Actions Conducted Partially as Class Actions. When appropriate (1) an action may be brought or maintained as a class action with respect to particular issues, or (2) a class may be divided into subclasses and each subclass treated as a class, and the provisions of this rule shall then be construed and applied accordingly.

(e) Dismissal or Compromise. A class action shall not be dismissed or compromised without the approval of the court, and notice of the proposed dismissal or compromise shall be given to all members of the class in such manner as the court directs.

(f) Discovery. Unnamed members of a class action are not to be considered as parties for purposes of discovery.

(g) Effective Date. This rule shall be effective only with respect to actions commenced on or after September 1, 1977.

See also CPRC §51.014(a)(3); ***O'Connor's Texas Civil Appeals***, "Preliminary Issues to the Appeal," ch. 11.

TRCP 43. INTERPLEADER

Persons having claims against the plaintiff may be joined as defendants and required to interplead when their claims are such that the plaintiff is or may be exposed to double or multiple liability. It is not ground for objection to the joinder that the claims of the several claimants or the titles on which their claims depend do not have a common origin or are not identical but are adverse to and independent of one another, or that the plaintiff avers that he is not liable in whole or in part to any or all of the claimants. A defendant exposed to similar liability may obtain such interpleader by way of cross-claim or counterclaim. The provisions of this rule supplement and do not in any way limit the joinder of parties permitted in any other rules.

Great Am. Reserve Ins. Co. v. Sanders, 525 S.W.2d 956, 958 (Tex.1975). The insurance company "was entitled to maintain an interpleader suit if there existed a reasonable doubt, either of fact or law, as to which of the rival claimants was entitled to the proceeds of the policy."

Tri-State Pipe & Equip., Inc. v. Southern Cty. Mut. Ins. Co., 8 S.W.3d 394, 402 (Tex.App.—Texarkana 1999, no pet.). "A petitioner in interpleader must prove: (1) that he is subject to, or has reasonable grounds to anticipate, rival claims to the same fund or property; (2) that he has not unreasonably delayed in filing the interpleader action; and (3) that he has unconditionally tendered the funds into the court."

TRCP 44. MAY APPEAR BY NEXT FRIEND

Minors, lunatics, idiots, or persons non compos mentis who have no legal guardian may sue and be represented by "next friend" under the following rules:

(1) Such next friend shall have the same rights concerning such suits as guardians have, but shall give security for costs, or affidavits in lieu thereof, when required.

(2) Such next friend or his attorney of record may with the approval of the court compromise suits and agree to judgments, and such judgments, agreements and compromises, when approved by the court, shall be forever binding and conclusive upon the party plaintiff in such suit.

See also TRCP 173; ***O'Connor's Texas Rules***, "Plaintiff's Original Petition," ch. 2-B; "Motion to Abate," ch. 3-H.

American Gen. Fire & Cas. Co. v. Vandewater, 907 S.W.2d 491, 492-93 (Tex.1995). A "court should evaluate whether the minor's interests have been properly protected and whether a deficiency in notice or due process has been shown to determine whether a trial court has obtained personal jurisdiction over a minor. In this case, the answer of [the mother] in her capacity as [the minor's] next friend was sufficient indication that [the minor's] legal representative knew about the proceedings and could therefore defend against them."

Urbish v. 127th Judicial Dist. Court, 708 S.W.2d 429, 431-32 (Tex.1986). "When minors sue, trial courts have the responsibility to protect the minor's best interest. As part of this responsibility, trial courts are authorized to replace next friends and attorneys when it appears to the court that either has an interest adverse to the minor. The trial court's decision is within its discretion. When deciding whether to replace a next friend or attorney, trial courts should consider only the minor's best interest; the interests of the next friend and attorney are irrelevant."

Gracia v. RC Cola-7-Up Bottling Co., 667 S.W.2d 517, 519 (Tex.1984). "In a suit by a 'next friend,' the real party plaintiff is the child and not the next friend."

Massey v. Galvan, 822 S.W.2d 309, 319 (Tex.App.—Houston [14th Dist.] 1992, writ denied). TRCP 44 "clearly states that only when a minor has no legal guardian may that minor be represented by a next friend. [W]hen [appellant] contracted ... to represent the minors, the minors had a legal guardian, ... the natural mother. [T]he death of the managing conservator ends the conservatorship order and it no longer constitutes a valid subsisting order. [W]ithout an existing court order, conservatorship is vested in the natural parent to the exclusion of other interested parties. Thus, when ... the managing conservator died, conservatorship vested in ... the natural mother."

SECTION 4. PLEADING

A. GENERAL

TRCP 45. DEFINITION & SYSTEM

Pleadings in the district and county courts shall

(a) be by petition and answer;

(b) consist of a statement in plain and concise language of the plaintiff's cause of action or the defendant's grounds of defense. That an allegation be evidentiary or be of legal conclusion shall not be grounds for objection when fair notice to the opponent is given by the allegations as a whole;

(c) contain any other matter which may be required by any law or rule authorizing or regulating any particular action or defense;

(d) be in writing, on paper measuring approximately 8½ inches by 11 inches, and signed by the party or his attorney, and either the signed original together with any verification or a copy of said original and copy of any such verification shall be filed with the court. The use of recycled paper is strongly encouraged.

When a copy of the signed original is tendered for filing, the party or his attorney filing such copy is required to maintain the signed original for inspection by the court or any party incident to the suit, should a question be raised as to its authenticity.

All pleadings shall be construed so as to do substantial justice.

Caution: TRCP 45 is affected by the following sections in the Fam. Code: §§6.401, 6.402, 102.008, 161.101.

See also *O'Connor's Texas Rules*, "Rules of Pleading," ch. 1-B; "Rules for Filing Documents," ch. 1-C; "Plaintiff's Original Petition," ch. 2-B; "Special Exceptions," ch. 3-G; "Default Judgment," ch. 7-A.

Perez v. Briercroft Serv. Corp., 809 S.W.2d 216, 218 (Tex.1991). "[T]he purpose of pleading is to give the adversary parties notice of each [party's] claims and defenses, as well as notice of the relief sought."

Paramount Pipe & Sup. Co. v. Muhr, 749 S.W.2d 491, 494-95 (Tex.1988). "The purpose of the fair notice requirement is to provide the opposing party with sufficient information to enable him to prepare a defense. [¶] [TRCP] 45 does not require that the plaintiff set out in his pleadings the evidence upon which he relies to establish his asserted cause of action."

TRCP 46. PETITION & ANSWER; EACH ONE INSTRUMENT OF WRITING

The original petition, first supplemental petition, second supplemental petition, and every other, shall each be contained in one instrument of writing, and so with the original answer and each of the supplemental answers.

TRCP 47. CLAIMS FOR RELIEF

An original pleading which sets forth a claim for relief, whether an original petition, counterclaim, cross-claim, or third party claim, shall contain

(a) a short statement of the cause of action sufficient to give fair notice of the claim involved,

(b) in all claims for unliquidated damages only the statement that the damages sought are within the jurisdictional limits of the court, and

(c) a demand for judgment for all the other relief to which the party deems himself entitled.

Relief in the alternative or of several different types may be demanded; provided, further, that upon special exception the court shall require the pleader to amend so as to specify the maximum amount claimed.

Caution: TRCP 47 is affected by the following sections in the Fam. Code: §§6.401, 6.402, 102.008, 161.101.

See also *O'Connor's Texas Rules*, "Rules of Pleading," ch. 1-B; "Plaintiff's Original Petition," ch. 2-B; "Special Exceptions," ch. 3-G; "Default Judgment," ch. 7-A; *O'Connor's Texas Forms*, FORMS 2B.

Boyles v. Kerr, 855 S.W.2d 593, 601 (Tex.1993). "A court should uphold the petition as to a cause of action that may be reasonably inferred from what is specifically stated, even if an element of a cause of action is not specifically alleged."

Roark v. Allen, 633 S.W.2d 804, 810 (Tex.1982). "A petition is sufficient if it gives fair and adequate notice of the facts upon which the pleader bases his claim. The purpose of this rule is to give the opposing party information sufficient to enable him to prepare a defense."

TRCP 48. ALTERNATIVE CLAIMS FOR RELIEF

A party may set forth two or more statements of a claim or defense alternatively or hypothetically, either in one count or defense or in separate counts or defenses. When two or more statements are made in the alternative and one of them if made independently would be sufficient, the pleading is not made insufficient by the insufficiency of one or more of the alternative statements. A party may also state as many separate claims or defenses as he has regardless of consistency and whether based upon legal or equitable grounds or both.

See also *O'Connor's Texas Rules*, "Rules of Pleading," ch. 1-B.

Regency Advantage L.P. v. Bingo Idea-Watauga, Inc., 936 S.W.2d 275, 278 (Tex.1996). "[O]ur rules expressly permit parties to proceed on alternative theories of relief."

Birchfield v. Texarkana Mem. Hosp., 747 S.W.2d 361, 367 (Tex.1987). "[W]here the prevailing party fails to elect between alternative measures of damages, the court should utilize the findings affording the greater recovery and render judgment accordingly."

Household Credit Serv., Inc. v. Driscol, 989 S.W.2d 72, 80 (Tex.App.—El Paso 1998, pet. denied). "If a plaintiff pleads alternate theories of liability under [TRCP] 48, a judgment that awards damages based upon more than one theory does not amount to a double recovery if the theories of liability arise from two separate and distinct injuries, and there has been a separate and distinct finding of damages on both theories of liability."

TRCP 49. WHERE SEVERAL COUNTS

Where there are several counts in the petition, and entire damages are given, the verdict or judgment, as the case may be, shall be good, notwithstanding one or more of such counts may be defective.

TRCP 50. PARAGRAPHS, SEPARATE STATEMENTS

All averments of claim or defense shall be made in numbered paragraphs, the contents of each of which shall be limited as far as practicable to a statement of a single set of circumstances; and a paragraph may be referred to by number in all succeeding pleadings, so long as the pleading containing such paragraph has not been superseded by an amendment as provided by Rule 65. Each claim founded upon a separate transaction or occurrence and each defense other than denials shall be stated in a separate count or defense whenever a separation facilitates the clear presentation of the matters set forth.

See also *O'Connor's Texas Rules*, "Rules of Pleading," ch. 1-B; "Plaintiff's Original Petition," ch. 2-B.

TRCP 51. JOINDER OF CLAIMS & REMEDIES

(a) Joinder of Claims. The plaintiff in his petition or in a reply setting forth a counterclaim and the defendant in an answer setting forth a counterclaim may join either as independent or as alternate claims as many claims either legal or equitable or both as he may have against an opposing party. There may be a like joinder of claims when there are multiple parties if the requirements of Rules 39, 40, and 43 are satisfied. There may be a like joinder of cross claims or third-party claims if the requirements of Rules 38 and 97, respectively, are satisfied.

(b) Joinder of Remedies. Whenever a claim is one heretofore cognizable only after another claim has been prosecuted to a conclusion, the two claims may be joined in a single action; but the court shall grant relief in that action only in accordance with the relative substantive rights of the parties. This rule shall not be applied in tort cases so as to permit the joinder of a liability or indemnity insurance company, unless such company is by statute or contract directly liable to the person injured or damaged.

Caution: TRCP 51 is affected by the following sections in the Fam. Code: §§6.406, 102.001, 157.003.

See also TRCP 40, 41, 174.

Allison v. Arkansas La. Gas Co., 624 S.W.2d 566, 568 (Tex.1981). "Under [TRCP] 51(a), a plaintiff or defendant is permitted to join in the same proceeding 'as many claims either legal or equitable or both as he may have against an opposing party.'"

TRCP 52. ALLEGING A CORPORATION

An allegation that a corporation is incorporated shall be taken as true, unless denied by the affidavit of the adverse party, his agent or attorney, whether such corporation is a public or private corporation and however created.

See also TRCP 93(6); *O'Connor's Texas Rules*, "The Defendant's Responses & Pleadings," ch. 3; "Motion to Abate," ch. 3-H.

Dr. Pepper Co. v. Crow, 621 S.W.2d 464, 465 (Tex. App.—Waco 1981, no writ). "Plaintiff plead defendant was a corporation. Defendant did not deny by verified pleading pursuant to [TRCP] 52 and 93 ... that it was not a corporation; thus, such fact was established."

TRCP 53. SPECIAL ACT OR LAW

A pleading founded wholly or in part on any private or special act or law of this State or of the Republic of Texas need only recite the title thereof, the date of its approval, and set out in substance so much of such act or laws as may be pertinent to the cause of action or defense.

TRCP 54. CONDITIONS PRECEDENT

In pleading the performance or occurrence of conditions precedent, it shall be sufficient to aver generally that all conditions precedent have been performed or have occurred. When such performances or occurrences have been so plead, the party so pleading same shall be required to prove only such of them as are specifically denied by the opposite party.

See also *O'Connor's Texas Rules*, "Plaintiff's Original Petition," ch. 2-B; "The Defendant's Responses & Pleadings," ch. 3; "The Answer—Denying Liability," ch. 3-E; *O'Connor's Texas Forms*, FORMS 2B.

Associated Indem. Corp. v. CAT Contracting, Inc., 964 S.W.2d 276, 283 n.6 (Tex.1998). "Where a party avers generally that all conditions precedent have been performed or have occurred, he or she need only prove those that are specifically denied by the opposite party. This pleading rule, however, does not shift the burden of proof on those conditions which the opposite party denies."

Greathouse v. Charter Nat'l Bank-Southwest., 851 S.W.2d 173, 177 (Tex.1992). "[C]harter met its burden of pleading [that disposition of the collateral was commercially reasonable] by its general allegation that all conditions precedent had been performed. In answer, Greathouse did not specifically deny that Charter's disposition of the collateral was commercially unreasonable. Consequently, Charter was not required to prove commercial reasonableness at trial."

TRCP 55. JUDGMENT

In pleading a judgment or decision of a domestic or foreign court, judicial or quasi-judicial tribunal, or of a board or officer, it shall be sufficient to aver the judgment or decision without setting forth matter showing jurisdiction to render it.

See also CPRC, ch. 36.

Don Docksteader Motors, Ltd. v. Patal Enter., Ltd., 794 S.W.2d 760, 761 (Tex.1990). The Uniform Foreign Country Money-Judgment Recognition Act is constitutional because it "necessarily allows for the bringing of a common-law suit [to enforce the foreign judgment] and thereby allows for notice and hearing."

TRCP 56. SPECIAL DAMAGE

When items of special damage are claimed, they shall be specifically stated.

See also *O'Connor's Texas Rules*, "Plaintiff's Original Petition," ch. 2-B, §8.3.2.

Arthur Andersen & Co. v. Perry Equip. Corp., 945 S.W.2d 812, 816 (Tex.1997). Special damages are also known as consequential damages. "Consequential damages ... result naturally, but not necessarily, from the defendant's wrongful acts."

Harkins v. Crews, 907 S.W.2d 51, 61 (Tex.App.—San Antonio 1995, writ denied). When special damages are not pled, they are waived.

TRCP 57. SIGNING OF PLEADINGS

Every pleading of a party represented by an attorney shall be signed by at least one attorney of record in his individual name, with his State Bar of Texas identification number, address, telephone number, and, if available, telecopier number. A party not represented by an attorney shall sign his pleadings, state his address, telephone number, and, if available, telecopier number.

See also TRCP 191.3; *O'Connor's Texas Rules*, "Rules of Pleading," ch. 1-B; "Rules for Serving Documents," ch. 1-D; "Plaintiff's Original Petition," ch. 2-B; "Default Judgment," ch. 7-A; *O'Connor's Texas Forms*, FORMS 1B.

W.C. Turnbow Pet. Corp. v. Fulton, 194 S.W.2d 256, 257 (Tex.1946). "Counsel should sign their names to motions and pleadings 'to make themselves responsible for what is stated in them, and so as to leave no doubt as to the parties for whom they appear.' But ... the signature to a pleading is a formal requisite and ... failure to comply with the requirement is not fatal to the pleading."

TRCP 58. ADOPTION BY REFERENCE

Statements in a pleading may be adopted by reference in a different part of the same pleading or in another pleading or in any motion, so long as the pleading containing such statements has not been superseded by an amendment as provided by Rule 65.

See also *O'Connor's Texas Rules*, "Rules of Pleading," ch. 1-B.

Texas Gas Utils. Co. v. Barrett, 460 S.W.2d 409, 416 (Tex.1970). Because "[t]he original petition had been superseded by [the] First Amended Original Petition ... statements in the former were not subject to adoption by reference in the supplemental petitions."

TRCP 59. EXHIBITS & PLEADING

Notes, accounts, bonds, mortgages, records, and all other written instruments, constituting, in whole or in part, the claim sued on, or the matter set up in defense, may be made a part of the pleadings by copies thereof, or the originals, being attached or filed and referred to as such, or by copying the same in the body of the pleading in aid and explanation of the allegations in the petition or answer made in reference to said instruments and shall be deemed a part thereof for all purposes. Such pleadings shall not be deemed defective because of the lack of any allegations which can be supplied from said exhibit. No other instrument of writing shall be made an exhibit in the pleading.

Skepnek v. Mynatt, 8 S.W.3d 377, 381 (Tex.App.—El Paso 1999, pet. denied). "[T]he statements found in the affidavit, having been incorporated into the special appearance motion, became part of the motion, which was then signed and tendered by [attorney]. Therefore, we hold that the trial court did not abuse its discretion in imposing sanctions against [attorney] under [CPRC] Chapter 10" for filing a false affidavit.

Johnson v. Smith, 697 S.W.2d 625, 632 (Tex. App.—Houston [14th Dist.] 1985, no writ). "[T]he pleadings will not be considered defective if any missing allegations can be supplied from any attached exhibits."

TRCP 60. INTERVENOR'S PLEADINGS

Any party may intervene by filing a pleading, subject to being stricken out by the court for sufficient cause on the motion of any party.

Caution: TRCP 60 is affected by Fam. Code §102.004.

See also *O'Connor's Texas Rules*, "Joining an Ongoing Lawsuit," ch. 5-I; *O'Connor's Texas Forms*, FORMS 5I.

Guaranty Fed. Sav. Bank v. Horseshoe Operating Co., 793 S.W.2d 652, 657 (Tex.1990). "An intervenor is not required to secure the court's permission to intervene; the party who opposed the intervention has the burden to challenge it by a motion to strike. [¶] [I]t is an abuse of discretion to strike a plea in intervention if (1) the intervenor meets [the requirements of the rule], (2) the intervention will not complicate the case by an excessive multiplication of the issues, and (3) the intervention is almost essential to effectively protect the intervenor's interest." *See also* ***In re AG of Texas***, ___ S.W.3d ___ (Tex.App.—Houston [14th Dist.] 2002, orig. proceeding) (No. 14-01-00895-CV; 1-10-02) (motion to disqualify intervenor cannot be construed as motion to strike).

Mendez v. Brewer, 626 S.W.2d 498, 499-500 (Tex. 1982). TRCP 60 "provides in part that any party may intervene, subject to being stricken by the court for sufficient cause on the motion of the opposite party. [¶] The intervenor bears the burden to show a justiciable interest, legal or equitable, in the lawsuit. The only relationship the [foster parents] had with [child] was as agent for the Department under the written contract to provide foster home care for [child]. The [foster parents] admitted that the contract expressly provided that the Department, as temporary managing conservator of the child, retained the absolute right to remove the child for any of several reasons: to place it with another family, to return the child to his home, or to have the child adopted by other persons. [¶] The sole interest alleged by the [foster parents] in their petition in intervention was their wish to adopt the child if the parent-child relationship with the [biological parents] was terminated. Thus, the [foster parents'] interest was wholly contingent upon a judgment of termination. The [foster parents] alleged no additional grounds for termination and, in fact, adopted the Department's grounds for termination. We do not believe this was sufficient standing to entitle them to join in this suit...."

Grizzle v. Texas Commerce Bank, 38 S.W.3d 265, 272 (Tex.App.—Dallas 2001, pet. dism'd). "[A] petition in intervention is not subject to the requirements of [TRCP 63] concerning amendments and responses to pleadings, nor is it subject to the requirements of [TRCP 166a] concerning responses to motions for summary judgment. An intervention is proper at any time before a final decision on the merits."

Breazeale v. Casteel, 4 S.W.3d 434, 437 (Tex. App.—Austin 1999, pet. denied). "We hold that intervention is not necessarily barred after the trial court has rendered final judgment where the intervenor does not attack the substance of the judgment itself, but merely seeks to protect his interest in property that is the subject of a turnover motion."

TRCP 61. TRIAL: INTERVENORS: RULES APPLY TO ALL PARTIES

These rules of pleading shall apply equally, so far as it may be practicable to intervenors and to parties, when more than one, who may plead separately.

TRCP 62. AMENDMENT DEFINED

The object of an amendment, as contra-distinguished from a supplemental petition or answer, is to add something to, or withdraw something from, that which has been previously pleaded so as to perfect that which is or may be deficient, or to correct that which has been incorrectly stated by the party making the amendment, or to plead new matter, additional to that formerly pleaded by the amending party, which constitutes an additional claim or defense permissible to the suit.

Texas Gas Utils. Co. v. Barrett, 460 S.W.2d 409, 416 (Tex.1970). Because "[t]he original petition had been superseded by petitioner's First Amended Original Petition ... statements in the former were not subject to adoption by reference in the supplemental petitions."

J.M. Huber Corp. v. Santa Fe Energy Res., Inc., 871 S.W.2d 842, 844 (Tex.App.—Houston [14th Dist.] 1994, no writ). "An amended petition ... adds or withdraws from that which was previously pleaded for correction or to plead new matter.... An amended petition also supersedes all prior petitions and operates to dismiss parties and causes of action to the extent they are omitted from the amended pleading."

TRCP 63. AMENDMENTS & RESPONSIVE PLEADINGS

Parties may amend their pleadings, respond to pleadings on file of other parties, file suggestions of death and make representative parties, and file such other pleas as they may desire by filing such pleas with the clerk at such time as not to operate as a surprise to the opposite party; provided, that any pleadings, responses or pleas offered for filing within seven days of the date of trial or thereafter, or after such time as may be ordered by the judge under Rule 166, shall be filed only after leave of the judge is obtained, which leave shall be granted by the judge unless there is a showing that such filing will operate as a surprise to the opposite party.

See also *O'Connor's Texas Rules*, "Motion to Amend Pleadings—Pretrial," ch. 5-F; "Motion to Amend Pleadings—Trial and Post-Trial", ch. 8-F; *O'Connor's Texas Forms*, FORMS 5F.

Sosa v. Central Power & Light, 909 S.W.2d 893, 895 (Tex.1995). The plaintiffs "filed their second amended original petition exactly one week before a scheduled summary judgment hearing. [Under TRCP 4,] the day on which the [Ps] filed their amendment is not counted but the seventh day after it was filed is counted. [T]he last day counted from the date of the filing may be the date of the hearing. Therefore, the [Ps] timely filed their second amended original petition."

Chapin & Chapin, Inc. v. Texas Sand & Gravel Co., 844 S.W.2d 664, 665 (Tex.1992). Under TRCP "'63 and 66 a trial court has no discretion to refuse an amendment unless: 1) the opposing party presents evidence of surprise or prejudice...; or 2) the amendment asserts a new cause of action or defense, and thus is prejudicial on its face....' [¶] [W]e conclude that the trial court's refusal to allow [D] to verify its denial [less than 7 days before trial] was an abuse of discretion."

Greenhalgh v. Service Lloyds Ins. Co., 787 S.W.2d 938, 940 (Tex.1990). "[A] party's right to amend under [TRCP] 63 is subject only to the opposing party's right to show surprise."

Goswami v. Metropolitan S.&L. Ass'n, 751 S.W.2d 487, 490 (Tex.1988). "[I]n the absence of a sufficient showing of surprise by the opposing party, the failure to obtain leave of court when filing a late pleading may be cured by the trial court's action in considering the amended pleading. [¶] A summary judgment proceeding is a trial within the meaning of [TRCP] 63."

TRCP 64. AMENDED INSTRUMENT

The party amending shall point out the instrument amended, as "original petition," or "plaintiff's first supplemental petition," or as "original answer," or "defendant's first supplemental answer" or other instrument filed by the party and shall amend by filing a substitute therefor, entire and complete in itself, indorsed "amended original petition," or "amended first supplemental petition," or "amended original answer," or "amended first supplemental answer," accordingly as said instruments of pleading are designated.

TRCP 65. SUBSTITUTED INSTRUMENT TAKES PLACE OF ORIGINAL

Unless the substituted instrument shall be set aside on exceptions, the instrument for which it is substituted shall no longer be regarded as a part of the pleading in the record of the cause, unless some error of the court in deciding upon the necessity of the amendment, or otherwise in superseding it, be complained of, and exception be taken to the action of the court, or unless it be necessary to look to the superseded pleading upon a question of limitation.

See also *O'Connor's Texas Rules*, "Amending the Pleadings," ch. 1-B, §7; "Nonsuit by amendment," ch. 7-E, §2.8.1.

Drake Ins. Co. v. King, 606 S.W.2d 812, 817 (Tex. 1980). The "original petition in intervention contained a judicial admission.... [H]owever ... a first and then a second amended petition [was filed]. The original petition ... was thus superceded by the amended petitions and no longer constituted a pleading in the case. Having been superceded, it was no longer a judicial admission, but must be introduced into evidence as any other admission before it may be considered as evidence."

Randolph v. Jackson Walker L.L.P., 29 S.W.3d 271, 274 (Tex.App.—Houston [14th Dist.] 2000, pet. denied). "When a party's name is omitted from an amended pleading, he is as effectively dismissed as where a formal order of dismissal is entered."

TRCP 66. TRIAL AMENDMENT

If evidence is objected to at the trial on the ground that it is not within the issues made by the pleading, or if during the trial any defect, fault or omission in a pleading, either of form or substance, is called to the attention of the court, the court may allow the pleadings to be amended and shall do so freely when the presentation of the merits of the action will be subserved thereby and the objecting party fails to satisfy the court that the allowance of such amendment would prejudice him in maintaining his action or defense upon the merits. The court may grant a postponement to enable the objecting party to meet such evidence.

See also *O'Connor's Texas Rules*, "Motion to Amend Pleadings—Trial and Post-Trial," ch. 8-F; *O'Connor's Texas Forms*, FORMS 8F.

City of Fort Worth v. Zimlich, 29 S.W.3d 62, 73 (Tex.2000). "A trial amendment must be filed as a written pleading; an oral statement at trial is insufficient to modify the pleadings. However, a party waives its complaint of any defect, omission, or fault in the pleadings if the party fails to specifically object before the submission of the charge to the jury."

State Bar v. Kilpatrick, 874 S.W.2d 656, 658 (Tex. 1994). "A court may not refuse a trial amendment unless (1) the opposing party presents evidence of surprise or prejudice, or (2) the amendment asserts a new cause of action or defense, and thus is prejudicial on its face. ... The burden of showing surprise or prejudice rests on the party resisting the amendment." *See also* ***Greenhalgh v. Service Lloyds Ins. Co.***, 787 S.W.2d 938, 941 (Tex.1990).

In re Marriage of Loftis, 40 S.W.3d 160, 163 (Tex. App.—Texarkana 2001, no pet.). "The burden of showing surprise or prejudice rests on the party opposing the amendment. A party that opposes a trial amendment does not have to prove prejudice or surprise if the amendment is substantive, which would change the nature of the trial."

Weynand v. Weynand, 990 S.W.2d 843, 847 (Tex. App.—Dallas 1999, pet. denied). "An amendment that is prejudicial on its face has three defining characteristics. First, the pleading must assert new substantive matter that reshapes the nature of the trial itself. [¶] Second, the new matter asserted must be such that it could not have been anticipated by the opposing party in light of the development of the case. [¶] Finally, allowance of the amendment must not detrimentally affect the opposing party's case."

TRCP 67. AMENDMENTS TO CONFORM TO ISSUES TRIED WITHOUT OBJECTION

When issues not raised by the pleadings are tried by express or implied consent of the parties, they shall be treated in all respects as if they had been raised in the pleadings. In such case such amendment of the pleadings as may be necessary to cause them to conform to the evidence and to raise these issues may be made by leave of court upon motion of any party at any time up to the submission of the case to the Court or jury, but failure so to amend shall not affect the result of the trial of these issues; provided that written pleadings, before the time of submission, shall be necessary to the submission of questions, as is provided in Rules 277 and 279.

Bedgood v. Madalin, 600 S.W.2d 773, 775-76 (Tex. 1980). TRCP 67 "requires that written pleadings, before the time of submission, shall be necessary to the submission of special issues even where issues are tried by implied consent. Since there were no proper pleadings, the trial court erred in overruling [Ds'] objections to the introduction of evidence and the submission of special issues regarding damages sustained by [Ps] as a result of the death of their minor child."

Dickerson v. DeBarbieris, 964 S.W.2d 680, 689 (Tex.App.—Houston [14th Dist.] 1998, no pet.). "As to the lack of a pleading for such damages, ... the trial court found that before it announced its decision in favor of [P], [D] did not object at trial or in post-trial materials to the evidence introduced on civil damages. It concluded that the issue of civil damages was tried by consent."

RE/MAX, Inc. v. Katar Corp., 961 S.W.2d 324, 328 (Tex.App.—Houston [1st Dist.] 1997) *pet. denied*, 989 S.W.2d 363 (Tex.1999). TRCP 67 "provides for trial by consent. ... Trial by consent is intended to cover the exceptional case where it clearly appears from the record as a whole that the parties tried the [unpled] issue. ... To determine whether the issue was tried by consent, the Court must examine the record not for evidence of the issue, but rather for evidence of trial of the issue."

TRCP 68. COURT MAY ORDER REPLEADER

The court, when deemed necessary in any case, may order a repleader on the part of one or both of the parties, in order to make their pleadings substantially conform to the rules.

Caution: TRCP 68 is affected by Fam. Code §102.001.

Miller v. Kossey, 802 S.W.2d 873, 877 (Tex.App.—Amarillo 1991, writ denied). "[W]hen [P] failed to comply with the court's ... order to send a new notice establishing a necessary element of her cause of action, the court was authorized to dismiss her DTPA action. Consequently, the court did not err in dismissing the action."

TRCP 69. SUPPLEMENTAL PETITION OR ANSWER

Each supplemental petition or answer, made by either party, shall be a response to the last preceding pleading by the other party, and shall not repeat allegations formerly pleaded further than is necessary as an introduction to that which is stated in the pleading then being drawn up. These instruments, to wit, the original petition and its several supplements, and the original answer and its several supplements, shall respectively, constitute separate and distinct parts of the pleadings of each party; and the position and identity, by number and name, with the indorsement of each instrument, shall be preserved throughout the pleadings of either party.

J.M. Huber Corp. v. Santa Fe Energy Res., Inc., 871 S.W.2d 842, 844 (Tex.App.—Houston [14th Dist.] 1994, no writ). "A supplemental petition is a response to the last preceding pleading by the other party and does not repeat allegations previously pleaded unless such repetition is necessary."

TRCP 70. PLEADING: SURPRISE: COST

When either a supplemental or amended pleading is of such character and is presented at such time as to take the opposite party by surprise, the court may charge the continuance of the cause, if granted, to the party causing the surprise if the other party satisfactorily shows that he is not ready for trial because of the allowance of the filing of such supplemental or amended pleading, and the court may, in such event, in its discretion require the party filing such pleading to pay to the surprised party the amount of reasonable costs and expenses incurred by the other party as a result of the continuance, including attorney fees, or make such other order with respect thereto as may be just.

See also ***O'Connor's Texas Rules***, "Motion to Amend Pleadings—Pretrial," ch. 5-F; "Motion to Amend Pleadings—Trial and Post-Trial," ch. 8-F; ***O'Connor's Texas Forms***, FORMS 5F, 8F.

TRCP 71. MISNOMER OF PLEADING

When a party has mistakenly designated any plea or pleading, the court, if justice so requires, shall treat the plea or pleading as if it had been properly designated.

Pleadings shall be docketed as originally designated and shall remain identified as designated, unless the court orders redesignation. Upon court order filed with the clerk, the clerk shall modify the docket and all other clerk records to reflect redesignation.

State Bar v. Heard, 603 S.W.2d 829, 833 (Tex. 1980). "We look to the substance of a plea for relief to determine the nature of the pleading, not merely at the form of title given to it."

Wilson v. Kutler, 971 S.W.2d 557, 559 (Tex.App.—Dallas 1998, no pet.). "It is true that the court must look to the content of a filing rather than its title to determine its nature. ... Nothing in the ... request for a hearing suggests that it was intended to function as a motion for new trial."

TRCP 72 - 73. REPEALED

TRCP 74. FILING WITH THE COURT DEFINED

The filing of pleadings, other papers and exhibits as required by these rules shall be made by filing them with the clerk of the court, except that the judge may permit the papers to be filed with him, in which event he shall note thereon the filing date and time and forthwith transmit them to the office of the clerk.

See also TRCP 24; ***O'Connor's Texas Rules***, "Rules for Filing Documents," ch. 1-C.

Miller Brewing Co. v. Villarreal, 829 S.W.2d 770, 771 (Tex.1992). "Under our current rules, a party who finds the courthouse closed on the last day that a document must be filed ... may also locate the clerk or judge of the court and file the document with them."

Standard Fire Ins. Co. v. LaCoke, 585 S.W.2d 678, 680 (Tex.1979). "The rule is traditionally stated to be that an instrument is deemed in law filed at the time it is left with the clerk, regardless of whether or not a file mark is placed on the instrument and regardless of whether the file mark gives some other date of filing."

TRCP 75. FILED PLEADINGS; WITHDRAWAL

All filed pleadings shall remain at all times in the clerk's office or in the court or in custody of the clerk, except that the court may by order entered on the minutes allow a filed pleading to be withdrawn for a limited time whenever necessary, on leaving a certified copy on file. The party withdrawing such pleading shall pay the costs of such order and certified copy.

Trinity Indus., Inc. v. Rivera, 745 S.W.2d 525, 526 (Tex.App.—Corpus Christi 1988, no writ). A party cannot terminate a suit by withdrawing its pleadings. "Under our rules of civil procedure, a final order terminating a lawsuit may be accomplished by a judgment on the merits, a dismissal or a non-suit."

TRCP 75a. FILING EXHIBITS: COURT REPORTER TO FILE WITH CLERK

The court reporter or stenographer shall file with the clerk of the court all exhibits which were admitted in evidence or tendered on bill of exception during the course of any hearing, proceeding, or trial.

See also TRAP 13.1(b) & (c).

Walton v. Canon, Short & Gaston, P.C., 23 S.W.3d 143, 151 (Tex.App.—El Paso 2000, no pet.). TRCP 75a "provides that a court reporter shall file all exhibits admitted into evidence, so that a trial court may consider only evidence admitted at trial."

TRCP 75b. FILED EXHIBITS: WITHDRAWAL

All filed exhibits admitted in evidence or tendered on bill of exception shall, until returned or otherwise disposed of as authorized by Rule 14b, remain at all times in the clerk's office or in the court or in the custody of the clerk except as follows:

(a) The court may by order entered on the minutes allow a filed exhibit to be withdrawn by any party only upon such party's leaving on file a certified, photo, or other reproduced copy of such exhibit. The party withdrawing such exhibit shall pay the costs of such order and copy.

(b) The court reporter or stenographer of the court conducting the hearing, proceedings, or trial in which exhibits are admitted or offered in evidence, shall have the right to withdraw filed exhibits, upon giving the clerk proper receipt therefor, whenever necessary for the court reporter or stenographer to transmit such original exhibits to an appellate court under the provisions of Rule 379 or to otherwise discharge the duties imposed by law upon said court reporter or stenographer.

Perez v. Bagous, 833 S.W.2d 671, 674 (Tex.App.—Corpus Christi 1992, no writ). "Once a party has admitted an exhibit into evidence at trial, the exhibit may not be retrieved and used to create another during a jury recess without notifying opposing counsel or the court. It is wholly outside the scope of the rule to then enter this newly created exhibit into evidence without informing opposing counsel of the use of the entered exhibit."

TRCP 76. MAY INSPECT PAPERS

Each attorney at law practicing in any court shall be allowed at all reasonable times to inspect the papers and records relating to any suit or other matter in which he may be interested.

U.S. v. Marks, 949 S.W.2d 320, 326 (Tex.1997). Plaintiff "argues that sealing the transcript [of the ex parte hearing between the judge and federal prosecutor] violated [TRCP] 76.... This general rule is not absolute. Although not stated in the rule, there are exceptions, such as documents submitted *in camera* under a claim of privilege, documents subject to a protective order, or materials sealed under [TRCP] 76a. Rule 76 does not give [P] an absolute right to the transcript of the *in camera* hearing. *At 327:* However, the district court's order was overly broad in sealing the entire record rather than those portions that pertained to the grand jury proceeding."

Davenport v. Garcia, 834 S.W.2d 4, 24 (Tex.1992). "[A]ccess to [court records] is separately guaranteed to '[e]ach attorney at law practicing in any court ... at all reasonable times to inspect.' ... A court may not escape the strict obligations of [TRCP 76 and 76a] by tacitly closing the record through an unwritten order."

TRCP 76a. SEALING COURT RECORDS

1. Standard for Sealing Court Records. Court records may not be removed from court files except as permitted by statute or rule. No court order or opinion issued in the adjudication of a case may be sealed. Other court records, as defined in this rule, are presumed to be open to the general public and may be sealed only upon a showing of all of the following:

(a) a specific, serious and substantial interest which clearly outweighs:

(1) this presumption of openness;

(2) any probable adverse effect that sealing will have upon the general public health or safety;

(b) no less restrictive means than sealing records will adequately and effectively protect the specific interest asserted.

2. Court Records. For purposes of this rule, court records means:

(a) all documents of any nature filed in connection with any matter before any civil court, except:

(1) documents filed with a court in camera, solely for the purpose of obtaining a ruling on the discoverability of such documents;

(2) documents in court files to which access is otherwise restricted by law;

(3) documents filed in an action originally arising under the Family Code.

(b) settlement agreements not filed of record, excluding all reference to any monetary consideration, that seek to restrict disclosure of information concerning matters that have a probable adverse effect upon the general public health or safety, or the administration of public office, or the operation of government.

(c) discovery, not filed of record, concerning matters that have a probable adverse effect upon the general public health or safety, or the administration of public office, or the operation of government, except discovery in cases originally initiated to preserve bona fide trade secrets or other intangible property rights.

3. Notice. Court records may be sealed only upon a party's written motion, which shall be open to public inspection. The movant shall post a public notice at the place where notices for meetings of county governmental bodies are required to be posted, stating: that a hearing will be held in open court on a motion to seal court records in the specific case; that any person may intervene and be heard concerning the sealing of court records; the specific time and place of the hearing; the style and number of the case; a brief but specific description of both the nature of the case and the records which are sought to be sealed; and the identity of the movant. Immediately after posting such notice, the movant shall file a verified copy of the posted notice with the clerk of the court in which the case is pending and with the Clerk of the Supreme Court of Texas.

4. Hearing. A hearing, open to the public, on a motion to seal court records shall be held in open court as soon as practicable, but not less than fourteen days after the motion is filed and notice is posted. Any party may participate in the hearing. Non-parties may intervene as a matter of right for the limited purpose of participating in the proceedings, upon payment of the fee required for filing a plea in intervention. The court may inspect records in camera when necessary. The court may determine a motion relating to sealing or unsealing court records in accordance with the procedures prescribed by Rule 120a.

5. Temporary Sealing Order. A temporary sealing order may issue upon motion and notice to any parties who have answered in the case pursuant to Rules 21 and 21a upon a showing of compelling need from specific facts shown by affidavit or by verified petition that immediate and irreparable injury will result to a specific interest of the applicant before notice can be posted and a hearing held as otherwise provided herein. The temporary order shall set the time for the hearing required by paragraph 4 and shall direct that the movant immediately give the public notice required by paragraph 3. The court may modify or withdraw any temporary order upon motion by any party or intervenor, notice to the parties, and hearing conducted as soon as practicable. Issuance of a temporary order shall not reduce in any way the burden of proof of a party requesting sealing at the hearing required by paragraph 4.

6. Order on Motion to Seal Court Records. A motion relating to sealing or unsealing court records shall be decided by written order, open to the public, which shall state: the style and number of the case; the specific reasons for finding and concluding whether the showing required by paragraph 1 has been made; the specific portions of court records which are to be sealed; and the time period for which the sealed portions of the court records are to be sealed. The order shall not be included in any judgment or other order but shall be a separate document in the case; however, the failure to comply with this requirement shall not affect its appealability.

7. Continuing Jurisdiction. Any person may intervene as a matter of right at any time before or after judgment to seal or unseal court records. A court that issues a sealing order retains continuing jurisdiction to enforce, alter, or vacate that order. An order sealing or unsealing court records shall not be reconsidered on motion of any party or intervenor who had actual notice of the hearing preceding issuance of the order, without first showing changed circumstances materially affecting the order. Such circumstances need not be related to the case in which the order was issued. However, the burden of making the showing required by paragraph 1 shall always be on the party seeking to seal records.

8. Appeal. Any order (or portion of an order or judgment) relating to sealing or unsealing court records shall be deemed to be severed from the case and a final judgment which may be appealed by any party or intervenor who participated in the hearing preceding issuance of such order. The appellate court may abate the appeal and order the trial court to direct that further public notice be given, or to hold further hearings, or to make additional findings.

9. Application. Access to documents in court files not defined as court records by this rule remains governed by existing law. This rule does not apply to any court records sealed in an action in which a final judgment has been entered before its effective date. This rule applies to cases already pending on its effective date only with regard to:

(a) all court records filed or exchanged after the effective date;

(b) any motion to alter or vacate an order restricting access to court records, issued before the effective date.

Caution: TRCP 76a is affected by the following sections in the Fam. Code: §§58.001-58.007, 108.001, 108.005, 161.210, 264.509.

For definitions of trade secret, see Tex. Penal Code §31.05(a)(4). See also *O'Connor's Texas Rules*, "Motion to Seal Court Records," ch. 5-K; "Scope of Discovery," ch. 6-B; *O'Connor's Texas Forms*, FORMS 5K.

In re Continental Gen. Tire, Inc., 979 S.W.2d 609, 614 (Tex.1998). "We disagree with [the] premise that all discoverable trade secrets will likely constitute 'court records' under Rule 76a. Moreover, even if a trade secret produced under a protective order is later determined to be a court record, this does not necessarily mean that the information must be made public. Rule 76a allows the information to remain sealed upon a showing that it meets the criteria specified in Rule 76a(1). That a document contains trade secret information is a factor to be considered in applying this sealing standard."

General Tire, Inc. v. Kepple, 970 S.W.2d 520, 525 (Tex.1998). "[W]e hold that when a party seeks a protective order under [TRCP] 166b(5)(c) [now 192.6] to restrict the dissemination of unfiled discovery, and no party or intervenor contends that the discovery is a 'court record,' a trial court need not conduct a hearing or render any findings on that issue. If a party or intervenor opposing a protective order claims that the discovery is a 'court record,' the court must make a threshold determination on that issue. However, public notice and a [TRCP] 76a hearing are mandated only if the court finds that the documents are court records."

State Bar v. Jefferson, 942 S.W.2d 575, 576 (Tex. 1997). "[T]he Bar requests that all papers filed in the district court case be unsealed. The district court ordered the papers temporarily sealed under Rule 76a(5).... The order provides for further proceedings as required by Rule 76a. The Bar may yet obtain from the district court the relief it seeks, and if it does not, it may appeal under Rule 76a(8). Mandamus is therefore unavailable."

Dallas Morning News v. 5th Ct. of Appeals, 842 S.W.2d 655, 657 (Tex.1992). "The press and the public have a right to be present at all proceedings in the trial of the underlying case, and to report all that they observe."

Eli Lilly & Co. v. Marshall, 829 S.W.2d 157, 158 (Tex.1992). "[T]he trial court abused its discretion by refusing to conduct a hearing and render decision on the motion in compliance with [TRCP] 76a."

P.I.A., Inc. v. Sullivan, 837 S.W.2d 844, 845-46 (Tex.App.—Fort Worth 1992, no writ). "The Family Code mandates that when a family law case is voluntarily dismissed, the court does not retain any continuing jurisdiction. [¶] The real parties in interest contend that ***Ashpole*** was overruled by the ... recent enactment of [TRCP] 76a. This rule gives a court power and procedure to seal court records along with continuing jurisdiction to enforce, alter, or vacate a sealing order. However, rule 76a states that documents filed in an original action arising under the Family Code are not court records within rule 76a. The rule then specifically states: Access to documents in court files not defined as court records by this rule remains governed by existing law. This means that ***Ashpole*** is good law and governs these sealed documents because they were filed in an original action arising under the Family Code."

Ashpole v. Millard, 778 S.W.2d 169, 170-71 (Tex. App.—Houston [1st Dist.] 1989, no writ). "[T]he trial court's inherent power to control public access to its records does not extend beyond the period of its plenary power. [¶] After a court's plenary power over a judgment or order expires, it may only: (1) make nunc pro tunc corrections of clerical errors in a prior judgment or order; and (2) declare a previous judgment or order void because it was signed after the court's plenary power had expired."

TRCP 77. LOST RECORDS & PAPERS

When any papers or records are lost or destroyed during the pendency of a suit, the parties may, with the approval of the judge, agree in writing on a brief statement of the matters contained therein; or either party may supply such lost records or papers as follows:

a. After three days' notice to the adverse party or his attorney, make written sworn motion before the court stating the loss or destruction of such record or papers, accompanied by certified copies of the originals if obtainable, or by substantial copies thereof.

b. If, upon hearing, the court be satisfied that they are substantial copies of the original, an order shall be made substituting such copies or brief statement for the originals.

c. Such substituted copies or brief statement shall be filed with the clerk, constitute a part of the cause, and have the force and effect of the originals.

See also TRE 1003, 1004; ***O'Connor's Texas Rules***, "Lost pleadings," ch. 1-C, §12.4.

Coke v. Coke, 802 S.W.2d 270, 275 (Tex.App.—Dallas 1990, writ denied). The court overruled a party's objection to the trial court's reconstruction of the lost file from the other party's documents. The party "testified that as far as he could tell, the copies were true duplicates of the originals."

B. PLEADINGS OF PLAINTIFF

TRCP 78. PETITION; ORIGINAL & SUPPLEMENTAL; INDORSEMENT

The pleading of plaintiff shall consist of an original petition, and such supplemental petitions as may be necessary in the course of pleading by the parties to the suit. The original petition and the supplemental petitions shall be indorsed, so as to show their respective positions in the process of pleading, as "original petition," "plaintiff's first supplemental petition," "plaintiff's second supplemental petition," and so on, to be successively numbered, named, and indorsed.

Caution: TRCP 78 is affected by the following sections in the Fam. Code: §§6.401, 6.402, 45.002, 45.102, 102.008, 161.101.

TRCP 79. THE PETITION

The petition shall state the names of the parties and their residences, if known, together with the contents prescribed in Rule 47 above.

Caution: TRCP 79 is affected by the following sections in the Fam. Code: §§6.401, 6.402, 45.002, 45.102, 85.007, 102.008, 161.101.

See also *O'Connor's Texas Rules*, "Plaintiff's Original Petition," ch. 2-B; *O'Connor's Texas Forms*, FORMS 2B.

Enserch Corp. v. Parker, 794 S.W.2d 2, 4-5 (Tex. 1990). "If the plaintiff merely misnames the correct defendant (misnomer), limitations is tolled and a subsequent amendment ... relates back to the date of the original petition. If, however, the plaintiff is mistaken as to which of two defendants is the correct one and there is ... a corporation with the name of the erroneously named defendant (misidentification), then the plaintiff has sued the wrong party and limitations is not tolled."

TRCP 80. PLAINTIFF'S SUPPLEMENTAL PETITION

The plaintiff's supplemental petitions may contain special exceptions, general denials, and the allegations of new matter not before alleged by him, in reply to those which have been alleged by the defendant.

Moody-Rambin Interests v. Moore, 722 S.W.2d 790, 792 (Tex.App.—Houston [14th Dist.] 1987, no writ). The proper way to bring new parties into a suit is by an amended pleading, not a supplemental pleading. "An exception to this rule exists if the necessity for adding a new party arises from facts pled in the defendant's answer."

TRCP 81. DEFENSIVE MATTERS

When the defendant sets up a counter claim, the plaintiff may plead thereto under rules prescribed for pleadings of defensive matter by the defendant, so far as applicable. Whenever the defendant is required to plead any matter of defense under oath, the plaintiff shall be required to plead such matters under oath when relied on by him.

Greater Fort Worth v. Mims, 627 S.W.2d 149, 152 (Tex.1982). "If the plaintiff contesting the counterclaim does not intend to urge any defensive theory which must be verified or any affirmative defense under [TRCP] 94, he is not required to answer the defendant's counterclaim."

TRCP 82. SPECIAL DEFENSES

The plaintiff need not deny any special matter of defense pleaded by the defendant, but the same shall be regarded as denied unless expressly admitted.

Sanchez v. Matthews, 636 S.W.2d 455, 460 (Tex. App.—San Antonio 1982, writ ref'd n.r.e.). Under TRCP 82 the plaintiff was not required to plead a special denial to the affirmative defense of release.

C. PLEADINGS OF DEFENDANT

TRCP 83. ANSWER; ORIGINAL & SUPPLEMENTAL; INDORSEMENT

The answer of defendant shall consist of an original answer, and such supplemental answers as may be necessary, in the course of pleading by the parties to the suit. The original answer and the supplemental answers shall be indorsed, so as to show their respective positions in the process of pleading, as "original answer," "defendant's first supplemental answer," "defendant's second supplemental answer," and so on, to be successively numbered, named and indorsed.

Caution: TRCP 83 is affected by the following sections in the Fam. Code: §§6.403, 8.057, 8.059, 9.001, 9.302, 53.04, 82.021.

Smith v. Lippmann, 826 S.W.2d 137, 138 (Tex. 1992). "[A] defendant, who timely files a pro se answer by a signed letter that identifies the parties, the case, and the defendant's current address, has sufficiently appeared by answer and deserves notice of any subsequent proceedings in the case."

TRCP 84. ANSWER MAY INCLUDE SEVERAL MATTERS

The defendant in his answer may plead as many several matters, whether of law or fact, as he may think necessary for his defense, and which may be pertinent to the cause, and such matters shall be heard in such order as may be directed by the court, special appearance and motion to transfer venue, and the practice thereunder being excepted herefrom.

Glover v. Moser, 930 S.W.2d 940, 944 (Tex.App.—Beaumont 1996, writ denied). "We believe the clear intent of [TRCP] 84 was to prevent exactly what occurred in [this] case, i.e., the trial court proceeding on meritorious matters prior to its determination of whether venue is properly before it."

TRCP 85. ORIGINAL ANSWER; CONTENTS

The original answer may consist of motions to transfer venue, pleas to the jurisdiction, in abatement, or any other dilatory pleas; of special exceptions, of general denial, and any defense by way of avoidance or estoppel, and it may present a cross-action, which to that extent will place defendant in the attitude of a plaintiff. Matters in avoidance and estoppel may be stated together, or in several special pleas, each presenting a distinct defense, and numbered so as to admit of separate issues to be formed on them.

Caution: TRCP 85 is affected by Fam. Code §6.403.

See also *O'Connor's Texas Rules*, "The Answer—Denying Liability," ch. 3-E; *O'Connor's Texas Forms*, FORMS 3B to 3I.

Hines v. Hash, 843 S.W.2d 464, 469 (Tex.1992). "To be timely, the [D's] request for an abatement [under the DTPA] must be made while the purpose of notice—settlement and avoidance of litigation expense—remains viable. Thus, defendant must request an abatement with the filing of an answer or very soon thereafter. If the trial court determines that plaintiff has failed to give notice as required by the [DTPA] statute, the action must be abated."

TRCP 86. MOTION TO TRANSFER VENUE

1. Time to File. An objection to improper venue is waived if not made by written motion filed prior to or concurrently with any other plea, pleading or motion except a special appearance motion provided for in Rule 120a. A written consent of the parties to transfer the case to another county may be filed with the clerk of the court at any time. A motion to transfer venue because an impartial trial cannot be had in the county where the action is pending is governed by the provisions of Rule 257.

2. How to File. The motion objecting to improper venue may be contained in a separate instrument filed concurrently with or prior to the filing of the movant's first responsive pleading or the motion may be combined with other objections and defenses and included in the movant's first responsive pleading.

3. Requisites of Motion. The motion, and any amendments to it, shall state that the action should be transferred to another specified county of proper venue because:

(a) The county where the action is pending is not a proper county; or

(b) Mandatory venue of the action in another county is prescribed by one or more specific statutory provisions which shall be clearly designated or indicated.

The motion shall state the legal and factual basis for the transfer of the action and request transfer of the action to a specific county of mandatory or proper venue. Verification of the motion is not required. The motion may be accompanied by supporting affidavits as provided in Rule 87.

4. Response and Reply. Except as provided in paragraph 3(a) of Rule 87, a response to the motion to transfer is not required. Verification of a response is not required.

5. Service. A copy of any instrument filed pursuant to Rule 86 shall be served in accordance with Rule 21a.

Caution: TRCP 86 is affected by the following sections in the Fam. Code: §§6.407, 103.002, 103.003, 155.201 et seq., 155.301, 262.203.

See also CPRC ch. 15; *O'Connor's Texas Rules*, "Motion to Transfer—Challenging Venue," ch. 3-C; *O'Connor's Texas Forms*, FORMS 3C.

GeoChem Tech Corp. v. Verseckes, 962 S.W.2d 541, 544 (Tex.1998). "[U]nder the current venue statutes, the [P] has the 'first choice' of venue. However, the statutes do not say that the [P] may choose venue only once." *But see* ***Martinez***, below.

Wichita Cty. v. Hart, 917 S.W.2d 779, 781 (Tex. 1996). "A [D] raises the question of proper venue by objecting to a [P's] venue choice through a motion to transfer venue. ... The fact that mandatory venue lies in another county provides one ground for a motion to transfer venue. If the plaintiff's chosen venue rests on a permissive venue statute and the defendant files a meritorious motion to transfer based on a mandatory venue provision, the trial court must grant the motion. ... A trial court's erroneous denial of a motion to transfer venue requires reversal of the judgment and remand for a new trial. *But see* ***Martinez***, below.

Ruiz v. Conoco, Inc., 868 S.W.2d 752, 757 (Tex. 1993). "When the suit is dismissed for want of prosecution while the motion to transfer venue is pending, it is not effective to fix venue in the county named in the motion to transfer venue." *But see* ***Martinez***, below.

Martinez v. Flores, 820 S.W.2d 937, 938 (Tex. App.—Corpus Christi 1991, orig. proceeding). The "transfer procedures in the Family Code governing

[SAPCRs] are the exclusive mechanism for transferring [a] case or challenging venue and were designed to supplant the regular rules dealing with transfer of venue applicable in ordinary civil cases." *See* ***Mendez v. Attorney Gen.***, 761 S.W.2d 519, 521 (Tex.App.—Corpus Christi 1988, no writ).

TRCP 87. DETERMINATION OF MOTION TO TRANSFER

1. Consideration of Motion. The determination of a motion to transfer venue shall be made promptly by the court and such determination must be made in a reasonable time prior to commencement of the trial on the merits. The movant has the duty to request a setting on the motion to transfer. Except on leave of court each party is entitled to at least 45 days notice of a hearing on the motion to transfer.

Except on leave of court, any response or opposing affidavits shall be filed at least 30 days prior to the hearing of the motion to transfer. The movant is not required to file a reply to the response but any reply and any additional affidavits supporting the motion to transfer must, except on leave of court, be filed not later than 7 days prior to the hearing date.

2. Burden of Establishing Venue.

(a) *In General.* A party who seeks to maintain venue of the action in a particular county in reliance upon Section 15.001[1] (General Rule), Sections 15.011-15.017 (Mandatory Venue), Sections 15.031-15.040 (Permissive Venue), or Sections 15.061 and 15.062 (Multiple Claims), Civil Practice and Remedies Code, has the burden to make proof, as provided in paragraph 3 of this rule, that venue is maintainable in the county of suit. A party who seeks to transfer venue of the action to another specified county under Section 15.001[1] (General Rule), Sections 15.011-15.017 (Mandatory Venue), Sections 15.031-15.040 (Permissive Venue), or Sections 15.061 and 15.062 (Multiple Claims), Civil Practice and Remedies Code, has the burden to make proof, as provided in paragraph 3 of this rule, that venue is maintainable in the county to which transfer is sought. A party who seeks to transfer venue of the action to another specified county under Sections 15.011-15.017, Civil Practice and Remedies Code on the basis that a mandatory venue provision is applicable and controlling has the burden to make proof, as provided in paragraph 3 of this rule, that venue is maintainable in the county to which transfer is sought by virtue of one or more mandatory venue exceptions.

(b) *Cause of Action.* It shall not be necessary for a claimant to prove the merits of a cause of action, but the existence of a cause of action, when pleaded properly, shall be taken as established as alleged by the pleadings. When the defendant specifically denies the venue allegations, the claimant is required, by prima facie proof as provided in paragraph 3 of this rule, to support such pleading that the cause of action taken as established by the pleadings, or a part of such cause of action, accrued in the county of suit. If a defendant seeks transfer to a county where the cause of action or a part thereof accrued, it shall be sufficient for the defendant to plead that if a cause of action exists, then the cause of action or part thereof accrued in the specific county to which transfer is sought, and such allegation shall not constitute an admission that a cause of action in fact exists. But the defendant shall be required to support his pleading by prima facie proof as provided in paragraph 3 of this rule, that, if a cause of action exists, it or a part thereof accrued in the county to which transfer is sought.

(c) *Other Rules.* A motion to transfer venue based on the written consent of the parties shall be determined in accordance with Rule 255. A motion to transfer venue on the basis that an impartial trial cannot be had in the county where the action is pending shall be determined in accordance with Rules 258 and 259.

3. Proof.

(a) *Affidavit and Attachments.* All venue facts, when properly pleaded, shall be taken as true unless specifically denied by the adverse party. When a venue fact is specifically denied, the party pleading the venue fact must make prima facie proof of that venue fact; provided, however, that no party shall ever be required for venue purposes to support by prima facie proof the existence of a cause of action or part thereof, and at the hearing the pleadings of the parties shall be taken as conclusive on the issues of existence of a cause of action. Prima facie proof is made when the venue facts are properly pleaded and an affidavit, and any duly proved attachments to the affidavit, are filed fully and specifically setting forth the facts supporting such pleading. Affidavits shall be made on personal knowledge, shall set forth specific facts as would be admissible in evidence, and shall show affirmatively that the affiant is competent to testify.

(b) *The Hearing*. The court shall determine the motion to transfer venue on the basis of the pleadings, any stipulations made by and between the parties and such affidavits and attachments as may be filed by the parties in accordance with the preceding subdivision of this paragraph 3 or of Rule 88.

(c) If a claimant has adequately pleaded and made prima facie proof that venue is proper in the county of suit as provided in subdivision (a) of paragraph 3, then the cause shall not be transferred but shall be retained in the county of suit, unless the motion to transfer is based on the grounds that an impartial trial cannot be had in the county where the action is pending as provided in Rules 257-259 or on an established ground of mandatory venue. A ground of mandatory venue is established when the party relying upon a mandatory exception to the general rule makes prima facie proof as provided in subdivision (a) of paragraph 3 of this rule.

(d) In the event that the parties shall fail to make prima facie proof that the county of suit or the specific county to which transfer is sought is a county of proper venue, then the court may direct the parties to make further proof.

4. No Jury. All venue challenges shall be determined by the court without the aid of a jury.

5. Motion for Rehearing. If venue has been sustained as against a motion to transfer, or if an action has been transferred to a proper county in response to a motion to transfer, then no further motions to transfer shall be considered regardless of whether the movant was a party to the prior proceedings or was added as a party subsequent to the venue proceedings, unless the motion to transfer is based on the grounds that an impartial trial cannot be had under Rules 257-259 or on the ground of mandatory venue, provided that such claim was not available to the other movant or movants.

Parties who are added subsequently to an action and are precluded by this rule from having a motion to transfer considered may raise the propriety of venue on appeal, provided that the party has timely filed a motion to transfer.

6. There shall be no interlocutory appeals from such determination.

[1] Now CPRC §15.002.

Caution: TRCP 87 is affected by the following sections in the Fam. Code: §§6.407, 103.002, 103.003, 155.201 et seq., 155.301, 262.203.

The Legislature enacted new venue provisions in 1995 which legislatively modified or overruled parts of TRCP 87. See also CPRC, ch. 15; *O'Connor's Texas Rules*, "Choosing the Court—Venue," ch. 2-G; "Motion to Transfer—Challenging Venue," ch. 3-C; *O'Connor's Texas Forms*, FORMS 3C.

HCA Health Servs., Inc. v. Salinas, 838 S.W.2d 246, 247-48 (Tex.1992). "[I]t is an abuse of discretion, correctable by mandamus, for a trial court to rule on a motion to transfer venue without giving the parties the notice required by [TRCP 87(1)]." *But see* ***Martinez***, below.

Rodriguez v. Printone Color Corp., 982 S.W.2d 69, 71 (Tex.App.—Houston [1st Dist.] 1998, pet. denied). "[S]tatements such as '[D] specifically denies those venue facts pleaded in [P's] Petition' do not constitute a 'specific denial' as required by [TRCP] 87. Thus, [D] did not specifically deny [P's] allegations that he was a resident of Bexar County or that his injury occurred in Bexar County." *But see* ***Martinez***, below.

Bleeker v. Villarreal, 941 S.W.2d 163, 168 (Tex. App.—Corpus Christi 1997, writ dism'd). "The [P's] response to the motion to transfer venue did not comply with [TRCP] 87: neither an affidavit setting forth venue facts nor any duly proved attachments accompanied the response." *But see* ***Martinez***, below.

Martinez v. Flores, 820 S.W.2d 937, 938 (Tex. App.—Corpus Christi 1991, orig. proceeding). See Annotation in TRCP 86.

TRCP 88. DISCOVERY & VENUE

Discovery shall not be abated or otherwise affected by pendency of a motion to transfer venue. Issuing process for witnesses and taking depositions shall not constitute a waiver of a motion to transfer venue, but depositions taken in such case may be read in evidence in any subsequent suit between the same parties concerning the same subject matter in like manner as if taken in such subsequent suit. Deposition transcripts, responses to requests for admission, answers to interrogatories and other discovery products containing information relevant to a determination of proper venue may be considered by the court in making the venue determination when they are attached to, or incorporated by reference in, an affidavit of a party, a witness or an attorney who has knowledge of such discovery.

See also *O'Connor's Texas Rules*, "Motion to Transfer—Challenging Venue," ch. 3-C.

Montalvo v. 4th Ct. of Appeals, 917 S.W.2d 1, 2 (Tex.1995). "[T]he trial court set a shortened schedule for completing discovery related to venue, filing the

[P's] response to the motions to transfer, and the hearing. [The Ps] offered no argument or evidence that the limitation on discovery or the abbreviated schedule deprived them of any ability to develop evidence pertinent to the venue issue. Without a showing of such harm, the record is wholly insufficient to establish that the [Ps] lacked an adequate remedy by appeal."

Safety-Kleen Corp. v. Garcia, 945 S.W.2d 268, 270 (Tex.App.—San Antonio 1997, orig. proceeding). "Despite Judge Garcia's misgivings, he is the elected official assigned to hear this cause, and neither the case law … nor the Texas Code of Judicial Conduct give Judge Garcia the discretion to refuse to hear or rule on [P's] motion [to compel discovery] within a reasonable period of time. [P's] right to discovery cannot be abated or otherwise affected by the pendency of a motion to transfer venue."

TRCP 89. TRANSFERRED IF MOTION IS SUSTAINED

If a motion to transfer venue is sustained, the cause shall not be dismissed, but the court shall transfer said cause to the proper court; and the costs incurred prior to the time such suit is filed in the court to which said cause is transferred shall be taxed against the plaintiff. The clerk shall make up a transcript of all the orders made in said cause, certifying thereto officially under the seal of the court, and send it with the original papers in the cause to the clerk of the court to which the venue has been changed. Provided, however, if the cause be severable as to parties defendant and shall be ordered transferred as to one or more defendants but not as to all, the clerk, instead of sending the original papers, shall make certified copies of such filed papers as directed by the court and forward the same to the clerk of the court to which the venue has been changed. After the cause has been transferred, as above provided for the clerk of the court to which the cause has been transferred shall mail notification to the plaintiff or his attorney that transfer of the cause has been completed, that the filing fee in the proper court is due and payable within thirty days from the mailing of such notification, and that the case may be dismissed if the filing fee is not timely paid; and if such filing fee is timely paid, the cause will be subject to trial at the expiration of thirty days after the mailing of notification to the parties or their attorneys by the clerk that the papers have been filed in the court to which the cause has been transferred; and if the filing fee is not timely paid, any court of the transferee county to which the case might have been assigned, upon its own motion or the motion of a party, may dismiss the cause without prejudice to the refiling of same.

See also *O'Connor's Texas Rules*, "Motion to Transfer—Challenging Venue," ch. 3-C.

WTFO, Inc. v. Braithwaite, 899 S.W.2d 709, 718 (Tex.App.—Dallas 1995, no writ). "Where a cause of action is against several defendants jointly and severally, the trial court shall transfer the action as to those defendants whose motions are sustained. Comakers on a note are jointly and severally liable. Accordingly, because venue was proper in Dallas County, the trial court did not abuse its discretion in severing [D's] cause of action and transferring it to Dallas County."

TRCP 90. WAIVER OF DEFECTS IN PLEADING

General demurrers shall not be used. Every defect, omission or fault in a pleading either of form or of substance, which is not specifically pointed out by exception in writing and brought to the attention of the judge in the trial court before the instruction or charge to the jury or, in a non-jury case, before the judgment is signed, shall be deemed to have been waived by the party seeking reversal on such account; provided that this rule shall not apply as to any party against whom default judgment is rendered.

See also *O'Connor's Texas Rules*, "Special Exceptions," ch. 3-G.

Friesenhahn v. Ryan, 960 S.W.2d 656, 658 (Tex. 1998). "Special exceptions may be used to challenge the sufficiency of a pleading. When the trial court sustains special exceptions, it must give the pleader an opportunity to amend the pleading. If a party refuses to amend, or the amended pleading fails to state a cause of action, then summary judgment may be granted. Summary judgment may also be proper if a pleading deficiency is of the type that could not be cured by an amendment."

Shoemake v. Fogel, Ltd., 826 S.W.2d 933, 937 (Tex. 1992). The defendant "filed no special exceptions to clarify [the plaintiff's claim]. Thus, [D] cannot now complain that [P's] pleading was insufficiently specific."

Steves Sash & Door Co. v. Ceco Corp., 751 S.W.2d 473, 476 (Tex.1988). "If [P] considered the pleading obscure or non-specific, [P] had the right to file special exceptions to clarify [D's] counterclaims. By failing to file special exceptions, [P] waived any defect in [D's] pleadings, and the pleadings must be construed in favor of the pleader." *See also* ***Roark v. Allen***, 633 S.W.2d 804, 809 (Tex.1982).

In re J.D.H., 661 S.W.2d 744, 748 (Tex.App.—Beaumont 1983, no writ). The "rule to be followed in child custody cases is that technical rules of civil procedure, as to practice and pleading, are not of controlling importance, since the controlling factor is the best interests of the child. It is because of our profound concern for the best interests of the child in issue that we have addressed this point of error, for we are not technically required to do so under [TRCP] 90 because appellant failed to preserve the alleged error by objection."

TRCP 91. SPECIAL EXCEPTIONS

A special exception shall not only point out the particular pleading excepted to, but it shall also point out intelligibly and with particularity the defect, omission, obscurity, duplicity, generality, or other insufficiency in the allegations in the pleading excepted to.

Caution: TRCP 91 is affected by Family Code §6.402.

See also ***O'Connor's Texas Rules***, "Special Exceptions," ch. 3-G; ***O'Connor's Texas Forms***, FORMS 3G.

Friesenhahn v. Ryan, 960 S.W.2d 656, 658 (Tex. 1998). "If [after special exceptions are sustained] a party refuses to amend, or the amended pleading fails to state a cause of action, then summary judgment may be granted. Summary judgment may also be proper if a pleading deficiency is of the type that could not be cured by an amendment. *At 659:* Before a court may grant a 'no cause of action' summary judgment ... it must give the parties an adequate opportunity to plead a viable cause of action."

Peek v. Equip. Serv. Co., 779 S.W.2d 802, 805 (Tex. 1989). "[T]he omission of any allegation regarding the amount in controversy from plaintiff's petition did not deprive the court of jurisdiction, but was instead a defect in pleading subject to special exception and amendment."

Humphreys v. Meadows, 938 S.W.2d 750, 753 (Tex. App.—Fort Worth 1996, writ denied). "No provision in the [TRCPs] permits a trial court to dismiss a plaintiff's case because of insufficient pleadings. [¶] A trial court may not dismiss a plaintiff's case for pleading defects unless an opportunity is first afforded to amend and cure the defect."

Villarreal v. Martinez, 834 S.W.2d 450, 451 (Tex. App.—Corpus Christi 1992, no writ). "The purpose of special exceptions is to furnish the adverse party a medium by which to force clarification of pleadings when they are not clear or sufficiently specific."

TRCP 92. GENERAL DENIAL

A general denial of matters pleaded by the adverse party which are not required to be denied under oath, shall be sufficient to put the same in issue. When the defendant has pleaded a general denial, and the plaintiff shall afterward amend his pleading, such original denial shall be presumed to extend to all matters subsequently set up by the plaintiff.

When a counterclaim or cross-claim is served upon a party who has made an appearance in the action, the party so served, in the absence of a responsive pleading, shall be deemed to have pleaded a general denial of the counterclaim or cross-claim, but the party shall not be deemed to have waived any special appearance or motion to transfer venue. In all other respects the rules prescribed for pleadings of defensive matter are applicable to answers to counterclaims and cross-claims.

See also ***O'Connor's Texas Rules***, "The Answer—Denying Liability," ch. 3-E.

Shell Chem. Co. v. Lamb, 493 S.W.2d 742, 744 (Tex. 1973). "[A] general denial puts the plaintiff ... on proof of every fact essential to his case and issue is joined on all material facts asserted by plaintiff ... except those which are required to be denied under oath."

Texas DPS v. Moran, 949 S.W.2d 523, 526 (Tex. App.—San Antonio 1997, no writ). Plaintiff "contends he met his burden by filing a verified petition. Because the [D.A.] filed a general denial and appeared at the hearing, we disagree. ... Because a general denial was filed, the allegations in [P's] petition were not evidence; instead, the allegations were put into issue and [P] was required to prove he met the statutory conditions."

TRCP 93. CERTAIN PLEAS TO BE VERIFIED

A pleading setting up any of the following matters, unless the truth of such matters appear of record, shall be verified by affidavit.

1. That the plaintiff has not legal capacity to sue or that the defendant has not legal capacity to be sued.

2. That the plaintiff is not entitled to recover in the capacity in which he sues, or that the defendant is not liable in the capacity in which he is sued.

3. That there is another suit pending in this State between the same parties involving the same claim.

4. That there is a defect of parties, plaintiff or defendant.

5. A denial of partnership as alleged in any pleading as to any party to the suit.

6. That any party alleged in any pleading to be a corporation is not incorporated as alleged.

7. Denial of the execution by himself or by his authority of any instrument in writing, upon which any pleading is founded, in whole or in part and charged to have been executed by him or by his authority, and not alleged to be lost or destroyed. Where such instrument in writing is charged to have been executed by a person then deceased, the affidavit shall be sufficient if it states that the affiant has reason to believe and does believe that such instrument was not executed by the decedent or by his authority. In the absence of such a sworn plea, the instrument shall be received in evidence as fully proved.

8. A denial of the genuineness of the indorsement or assignment of a written instrument upon which suit is brought by an indorsee or assignee and in the absence of such a sworn plea, the indorsement or assignment thereof shall be held as fully proved. The denial required by this subdivision of the rule may be made upon information and belief.

9. That a written instrument upon which a pleading is founded is without consideration, or that the consideration of the same has failed in whole or in part.

10. A denial of an account which is the foundation of the plaintiff's action, and supported by affidavit.

11. That a contract sued upon is usurious. Unless such plea is filed, no evidence of usurious interest as a defense shall be received.

12. That notice and proof of loss or claim for damage has not been given as alleged. Unless such plea is filed such notice and proof shall be presumed and no evidence to the contrary shall be admitted. A denial of such notice or such proof shall be made specifically and with particularity.

13. In the trial of any case appealed to the court from the Industrial Accident Board the following, if pleaded, shall be presumed to be true as pleaded and have been done and filed in legal time and manner, unless denied by verified pleadings:

(a) Notice of injury.

(b) Claim for compensation.

(c) Award of the Board.

(d) Notice of intention not to abide by the award of the Board.

(e) Filing of suit to set aside the award.

(f) That the insurance company alleged to have been the carrier of the workers' compensation insurance at the time of the alleged injury was in fact the carrier thereof.

(g) That there was good cause for not filing claim with the Industrial Accident Board within the one year period provided by statute.

(h) Wage rate.

A denial of any of the matters set forth in subdivisions (a) or (g) of paragraph 13 may be made on information and belief.

Any such denial may be made in original or amended pleadings; but if in amended pleadings the same must be filed not less than seven days before the case proceeds to trial. In case of such denial the things so denied shall not be presumed to be true, and if essential to the case of the party alleging them, must be proved.

14. That a party plaintiff or defendant is not doing business under an assumed name or trade name as alleged.

15. In the trial of any case brought against an automobile insurance company by an insured under the provisions of an insurance policy in force providing protection against uninsured motorists, an allegation that the insured has complied with all the terms of the policy as a condition precedent to bringing the suit shall be presumed to be true unless denied by verified pleadings which may be upon information and belief.

16. Any other matter required by statute to be pleaded under oath.

See O'Connor's Texas Rules, "The Answer—Denying Liability," ch. 3-E; *O'Connor's Texas Forms*, FORMS 3E.

Nootsie, Ltd. v. Williamson Cty. Appr. Dist., 925 S.W.2d 659, 662 (Tex.1996). TRCP 93(1) "requires a party to file a verified pleading if it argues that 'the plaintiff has not legal capacity to sue or that the defendant has not legal capacity to be sued.' We have not hesitated in previous cases to hold that parties who do not follow rule 93's mandate waive any right to complain about the matter on appeal."

Werner v. Colwell, 909 S.W.2d 866, 870 (Tex.1995). "The failure to file [a verified] denial does waive any complaint of a judgment rendered in the capacity in which the party was sued. However, it does not allow the court to render judgment against the party in a capacity in which she was not sued."

Roark v. Stallworth Oil & Gas, Inc., 813 S.W.2d 492, 494 (Tex.1991). "[W]hen the defense is based on a claim enumerated in [TRCP] 93, [the party] must verify the pleading by affidavit."

Pledger v. Schoellkopf, 762 S.W.2d 145, 146 (Tex. 1988). "When capacity [to sue] is contested, [TRCP] 93(2) requires that a verified plea be filed anytime the record does not affirmatively demonstrate the plaintiff's or defendant's right to bring suit or be sued in *whatever* capacity he is suing."

Allison v. National Un. Fire Ins. Co., 703 S.W.2d 637, 638 (Tex.1986). "A proper challenge to a defect of parties is by way of verified plea."

Gutierrez v. Rodriguez, 30 S.W.3d 558, 562 (Tex. App.—Texarkana 2000, no pet.). TRCP 93(7) "requires that a party denying the execution of a document must file a verified pleading of [its] contentions. Absent such a verified pleading, the document is received into evidence as fully proved." *See also* ***Boyd v. Diversified Fin. Sys.***, 1 S.W.3d 888, 891 (Tex.App.—Dallas 1999, no pet.).

Boyd v. Diversified Fin. Sys., 1 S.W.3d 888, 891 (Tex.App.—Dallas 1999, no pet.). "Under [TRCP] 93(7), when a claim is founded on the execution of a written instrument, and the defendant does not deny under oath the execution of the instrument, 'the instrument shall be received in evidence as fully proved.'" *See also* ***Gutierrez v. Rodriguez***, 30 S.W.3d 558, 562 (Tex. App.—Texarkana 2000, no pet.).

TRCP 94. AFFIRMATIVE DEFENSES

In pleading to a preceding pleading, a party shall set forth affirmatively accord and satisfaction, arbitration and award, assumption of risk, contributory negligence, discharge in bankruptcy, duress, estoppel, failure of consideration, fraud, illegality, injury by fellow servant, laches, license, payment, release, res judicata, statute of frauds, statute of limitations, waiver, and any other matter constituting an avoidance or affirmative defense. Where the suit is on an insurance contract which insures against certain general hazards, but contains other provisions limiting such general liability, the party suing on such contract shall never be required to allege that the loss was not due to a risk or cause coming within any of the exceptions specified in the contract, nor shall the insurer be allowed to raise such issue unless it shall specifically allege that the loss was due to a risk or cause coming within a particular exception to the general liability; provided that nothing herein shall be construed to change the burden of proof on such issue as it now exists.

Caution: TRCP 94 is affected by the following sections in the Fam. Code: §§4.006, 6.008, 8.059, 42.007, 88.003, 157.006-157.008.

See also ***O'Connor's Texas Rules***, "The Answer—Denying Liability," ch. 3-E; ***O'Connor's Texas Forms***, FORMS 3E.

Kinnear v. Texas Comm'n on Human Rights, 14 S.W.3d 299, 300 (Tex.2000). "Immunity from liability, like other affirmative defenses to liability, must be pleaded, or else it is waived. Because the Commission never pleaded sovereign immunity from liability as an affirmative defense to the requested attorney fees, it waived the defense, and the court of appeals erred in overturning the attorney fees award on sovereign immunity grounds." *See also* ***Davis v. City of San Antonio***, 752 S.W.2d 518, 519 (Tex.1988).

Texas Beef Cattle Co. v. Green, 921 S.W.2d 203, 212 (Tex.1996). "[A]n affirmative defense ... is one of confession and avoidance. An affirmative defense does not seek to defend by merely denying the plaintiff's claims, but rather seeks to establish 'an independent reason why the plaintiff should not recover.'"

Dresser Indus. v. Page Pet., Inc., 853 S.W.2d 505, 508 (Tex.1993). Because a "release surrenders legal rights or obligations between the parties to an agreement [it] is expressly designated as an affirmative defense."

Shoemake v. Fogel, Ltd., 826 S.W.2d 933, 937 (Tex. 1992). "Rule 94's requirement of pleading is not absolute. [¶] [T]he defense of [parental] immunity ... is not waived by the failure to specifically plead it if it is apparent on the face of the petition and established as a matter of law."

Land Title Co. v. Stigler Inc., 609 S.W.2d 754, 756 (Tex.1980). "Ratification is a plea in avoidance and thus an affirmative defense which, absent trial by consent, is waived unless affirmatively pleaded."

Hall v. Diamond Shamrock Ref. Co., ___ S.W.3d ___ (Tex.App.—San Antonio 2001, n.p.h.) (No. 04-99-00370; 6-27-01). "[T]he exemplary damages cap [under CPRC §41.008] is not an affirmative defense."

TRCP 95. PLEAS OF PAYMENT

When a defendant shall desire to prove payment, he shall file with his plea an account stating distinctly the nature of such payment, and the several items thereof; failing to do so, he shall not be allowed to prove the same, unless it be so plainly and particularly described in the plea as to give the plaintiff full notice of the character thereof.

See also *O'Connor's Texas Rules*, "The Answer—Denying Liability," ch. 3-E.

Southwestern Fire & Cas. Co. v. Larue, 367 S.W.2d 162, 163 (Tex.1963). "Under [TRCP] 94 and [TRCP] 95, payment is ... an affirmative defense on which the defendant has the burden of proof, which must be specially pleaded, and may not be shown under a general denial."

TRCP 96. NO DISCONTINUANCE

Where the defendant has filed a counterclaim seeking affirmative relief, the plaintiff shall not be permitted by a discontinuance of his suit, to prejudice the right of the defendant to be heard on such counterclaim.

See also TRCP 162; *O'Connor's Texas Rules*, "Voluntary Dismissal—Nonsuit," ch. 7-E.

BHP Pet. Co. v. Millard, 800 S.W.2d 838, 840 (Tex. 1990). "The plaintiff's right to take a nonsuit is *unqualified and absolute* as long as the defendant has not made a claim for affirmative relief."

TRCP 97. COUNTERCLAIM & CROSS-CLAIM

(a) Compulsory Counterclaims. A pleading shall state as a counterclaim any claim within the jurisdiction of the court, not the subject of a pending action, which at the time of filing the pleading the pleader has against any opposing party, if it arises out of the transaction or occurrence that is the subject matter of the opposing party's claim and does not require for its adjudication the presence of third parties of whom the court cannot acquire jurisdiction; provided, however, that a judgment based upon a settlement or compromise of a claim of one party to the transaction or occurrence prior to a disposition on the merits shall not operate as a bar to the continuation or assertion of the claims of any other party to the transaction or occurrence unless the latter has consented in writing that said judgment shall operate as a bar.

(b) Permissive Counterclaims. A pleading may state as a counterclaim any claim against an opposing party whether or not arising out of the transaction or occurrence that is the subject matter of the opposing party's claim.

(c) Counterclaim Exceeding Opposing Claim. A counterclaim may or may not diminish or defeat the recovery sought by the opposing party. It may claim relief exceeding in amount or different in kind from that sought in the pleading of the opposing party, so long as the subject matter is within the jurisdiction of the court.

(d) Counterclaim Maturing or Acquired After Pleading. A claim which either matured or was acquired by the pleader after filing his pleading may be presented as a counterclaim by amended pleading.

(e) Cross-Claim Against Co-Party. A pleading may state as a cross-claim any claim by one party against a co-party arising out of the transaction or occurrence that is the subject matter either of the original action or of a counterclaim therein. Such cross-claim may include a claim that the party against whom it is asserted is or may be liable to the cross-claimant for all or part of a claim asserted in the action against the cross-claimant.

(f) Additional Parties. Persons other than those made parties to the original action may be made parties to a third party action, counterclaim or cross-claim in accordance with the provisions of Rules 38, 39 and 40.

(g) Tort shall not be the subject of set-off or counterclaim against a contractual demand nor a contractual demand against tort unless it arises out of or is incident to or is connected with same.

(h) Separate Trials; Separate Judgments. If the court orders separate trials as provided in Rule 174, judgment on a counterclaim or cross-claim may be rendered when the court has jurisdiction so to do, even if the claims of the opposing party have been dismissed or otherwise disposed of.

See also CPRC §33.004 (responsible third parties); *O'Connor's Texas Rules*, "The Answer—Denying Liability," ch. 3-E; *O'Connor's Texas Forms*, FORMS 3E.

State & Cty. Mut. Fire Ins. Co. v. Miller, 52 S.W.3d 693, 696 (Tex.2001). "[W]hen the parties are co-parties rather than opposing parties, the compulsory counterclaim rule and res judicata only act as a bar to a co-party's claim in a subsequent action if the co-parties had 'issues drawn between them' in the first action. For the purposes of res judicata, co-parties have issues drawn between them and become adverse when one co-party files a cross-action against a second co-party." *See also* ***Getty Oil Co. v. Insurance Co. of N. Am.***, 845 S.W.2d 794, 800 (Tex.1992).

Ingersoll-Rand Co. v. Valero Energy Corp., 997 S.W.2d 203, 207 (Tex.1999). "[A] counterclaim is compulsory only if: (1) it is within the jurisdiction of the court; (2) it is not at the time of filing the answer the subject of a pending action; (3) the claim is mature and owned by the defendant at the time of filing the answer; (4) it arose out of the same transaction or occurrence that is the subject matter of the opposing party's claim; (5) it is against an opposing party in the same capacity; and (6) it does not require the presence of third parties over whom the court cannot acquire jurisdiction. A claim having all of these elements must be asserted in the initial action and cannot be asserted in later actions."

Klein v. Dooley, 949 S.W.2d 307, 307 (Tex.1997). "When DTPA plaintiffs take a voluntary nonsuit and the trial court later rules that the defendants are not entitled to costs and fees under [the DTPA], does the trial court's judgment preclude the plaintiffs from filing their claims in a second suit, under [TRCP] 97(a) governing compulsory counterclaims? We hold ... the trial court's judgment in the first suit does not preclude the plaintiffs' claims in a second suit."

Bard v. Charles R. Myers Ins. Agency, 839 S.W.2d 791, 796 (Tex.1992). The compulsory counterclaim rule is "designed to avoid piecemeal or duplicative litigation. Its purpose is to provide that a potential counterclaimant with a justifiable interest arising out of the same transaction or occurrence at issue in the opposing party's claim bring the counterclaim in the same proceeding or it will be deemed waived. ... The 'compelling interest' underlying the compulsory counterclaim rule is solely in judicial economy; its purpose it to prevent multiple suits arising out of the same transactions or occurrences."

TRCP 98. SUPPLEMENTAL ANSWERS

The defendant's supplemental answers may contain special exceptions, general denial, and the allegations of new matter not before alleged by him, in reply to that which has been alleged by the plaintiff.

State ex rel. Grimes Cty. Taxpayers Ass'n v. Texas Mun. Power Agency, 565 S.W.2d 258, 277 (Tex. App.—Houston [1st Dist.] 1978, writ dism'd). "A supplemental answer is properly filed in response to any pleading of the plaintiff, regardless of whether it is an amended petition or a supplemental petition."

SECTION 5. CITATION

TRCP 99. ISSUANCE & FORM OF CITATION

a. Issuance. Upon the filing of the petition, the clerk, when requested, shall forthwith issue a citation and deliver the citation as directed by the requesting party. The party requesting citation shall be responsible for obtaining service of the citation and a copy of the petition. Upon request, separate or additional citations shall be issued by the clerk.

b. Form. The citation shall (1) be styled "The State of Texas," (2) be signed by the clerk under seal of court, (3) contain name and location of the court, (4) show date of filing of the petition, (5) show date of issuance of citation, (6) show file number, (7) show names of parties, (8) be directed to the defendant, (9) show the name and address of attorney for plaintiff, otherwise the address of plaintiff, (10) contain the time within which these rules require the defendant to file a written answer with the clerk who issued citation, (11) contain address of the clerk, and (12) shall notify the defendant that in case of failure of defendant to file an answer, judgment by default may be rendered for the relief demanded in the petition. The citation shall direct the defendant to file a written answer to the plaintiff's petition on or before 10:00 a.m. on the Monday next after the expiration of twenty days after the date of service thereof. The requirement of subsections 10 and 12 of this section shall be in the form set forth in section c of this rule.

c. Notice. The citation shall include the following notice to the defendant: "You have been sued. You may employ an attorney. If you or your attorney do not file a written answer with the clerk who issued this citation by 10:00 a.m. on the Monday next following the expiration of twenty days after you were served this citation and petition, a default judgment may be taken against you."

d. Copies. The party filing any pleading upon which citation is to be issued and served shall furnish the clerk with a sufficient number of copies thereof for use in serving the parties to be served, and when copies are so furnished the clerk shall make no charge for the copies.

Caution: TRCP 99 is affected by the following sections in the Fam. Code: §§3.304, 3.305, 5.105, 6.408, 6.409, 9.001, 9.102, 45.003, 82.043, 102.009, 102.010, 154.193, 156.003, 158.306, 158.505, 161.005, 233.007.

See also ***O'Connor's Texas Rules***, "Serving the Defendant with Suit," ch. 2-H; "Default Judgment," ch. 7-A; ***O'Connor's Texas Forms***, FORMS 2H.

Primate Constr., Inc. v. Silver, 884 S.W.2d 151, 153 (Tex.1994). "It is the responsibility of the one requesting service, not the process server, to see that service is properly accomplished. ... This responsibility extends to seeing that service is properly reflected in the record."

Roberts v. Padre Island Brewing Co., 28 S.W.3d 618, 621-22 (Tex.App.—Corpus Christi 2000, pet. denied). "Reliance on the process server does not constitute due diligence in attempting service of process. A reasonable person ... would have employed an alternate process server, a constable, or would have attempted service through other alternative court approved methods such as service through a court appointed third party. ... Although the existence of diligence is usually a question of fact, a lack of diligence exists as a matter of law because it is clear that [P] did not exhaust all of the alternatives available to achieve proper service."

Boyattia v. Hinojosa, 18 S.W.3d 729, 734 (Tex. App.—Dallas 2000, pet. denied). "Although a party may ordinarily rely on the clerk to perform his duty within a reasonable amount of time, an unexplained three-month delay is not a reasonable time for the clerk to deliver a citation as directed by a party. [¶] We conclude [P's] failure to act during the clerk's three-month delay constitutes a lack of diligence as a matter of law."

Barker CATV Constr., Inc. v. Ampro, Inc., 989 S.W.2d 789, 792 (Tex.App.—Houston [1st Dist.] 1999, no pet.). TRCP 15 "seems to conflict with [TRCP] 99(b), which states the citation shall (1) be styled The State of Texas, and (8) *be directed to the defendant*.... [¶] The citation ... in this case is a preprinted form addressed to the sheriff or any constable of Texas, as well as to the defendant. The requirements of rules 15 and 99(b) can be harmonized by allowing the citations to be directed to both the sheriff or constable, as the officer serving it, and the defendant, as the person being served." (Internal quotations omitted.)

TRCP 100 - 102. REPEALED

TRCP 103. WHO MAY SERVE

Citation and other notices may be served anywhere by (1) any sheriff or constable or other person authorized by law or, (2) by any person authorized by law or by written order of the court who is not less than eighteen years of age. No person who is a party to or interested in the outcome of a suit shall serve any process. Service by registered or certified mail and citation by publication shall, if requested, be made by the clerk of the court in which the case is pending. The order authorizing a person to serve process may be made without written motion and no fee shall be imposed for issuance of such order.

Caution: TRCP 103 is affected by the following section in the Fam. Code: §231.118.

See also ***O'Connor's Texas Rules***, "Serving the Defendant with Suit," ch. 2-H; "Default Judgment," ch. 7-A.

Mayfield v. Dean Witter Fin. Servs., Inc., 894 S.W.2d 502, 505 (Tex.App.—Austin 1995, writ denied). "[S]ervice of process by a private process server in Texas ... requires authorization by law or a written order of the court. *At 506:* The parties do not dispute that pursuant to [TRCP] 103, a standing court order authorized ... the private process server ... to serve citation and other notices in any lawsuit filed in the district court of Travis County in which he was not an interested party."

TRCP 104. REPEALED

TRCP 105. DUTY OF OFFICER OR PERSON RECEIVING

The officer or authorized person to whom process is delivered shall endorse thereon the day and hour on which he received it, and shall execute and return the same without delay.

See also ***O'Connor's Texas Rules***, "Serving the Defendant with Suit," ch. 2-H; "Default Judgment," ch. 7-A.

Melendez v. John R. Schatzman, Inc., 685 S.W.2d 137, 138 (Tex.App.—El Paso 1985, no writ). Service by certified mail "was attempted in the case before us; however, it does not appear that the officer receiving delivery of the process for service endorsed thereon the day and hour of receipt, nor was the return completed showing the execution by certified mail, all as required by Rule 105…."

TRCP 106. METHOD OF SERVICE

(a) Unless the citation or an order of the court otherwise directs, the citation shall be served by any person authorized by Rule 103 by

(1) delivering to the defendant, in person, a true copy of the citation with the date of delivery endorsed thereon with a copy of the petition attached thereto, or

(2) mailing to the defendant by registered or certified mail, return receipt requested, a true copy of the citation with a copy of the petition attached thereto.

(b) Upon motion supported by affidavit stating the location of the defendant's usual place of business or usual place of abode or other place where the defendant can probably be found and stating specifically the facts showing that service has been attempted under either (a)(1) or (a)(2) at the location named in such affidavit but has not been successful, the court may authorize service

(1) by leaving a true copy of the citation, with a copy of the petition attached, with anyone over sixteen years of age at the location specified in such affidavit, or

(2) in any other manner that the affidavit or other evidence before the court shows will be reasonably effective to give the defendant notice of the suit.

Caution: TRCP 106 is affected by the following sections in the Fam. Code: §§3.304, 3.305, 5.105, 6.408, 6.409, 9.001, 9.102, 45.003, 82.043, 102.009, 102.010, 154.193, 156.003, 158.306, 158.505, 161.005, 233.007.

See also ***O'Connor's Texas Rules***, "Serving the Defendant with Suit," ch. 2-H.

State Farm Fire & Cas. Co. v. Costley, 868 S.W.2d 298, 298-99 (Tex.1993). "Under [TRCP] 106(b) a court may authorize substituted service only after a plaintiff has unsuccessfully tried to effect personal service or service by mail, return receipt requested, as required by Rule 106(a). … Thus, to require proof of actual notice upon substituted service would frustrate Rule 106(b)'s purpose of providing alternate methods [of service]."

Wilson v. Dunn, 800 S.W.2d 833, 836 (Tex.1990). "[S]ubstitute service is not authorized under [TRCP] 106(b) without an affidavit which meets the requirements of the rule demonstrating the necessity for other than personal service."

Uvalde Country Club v. Martin Linen Sup. Co., 690 S.W.2d 884, 885 (Tex.1985). "There are no presumptions in favor of valid issuance, service, and return of citation in the face of a writ of error attack on a default judgment. … Moreover, failure to affirmatively show strict compliance with the [TRCPs] renders the attempted service of process invalid and of no effect."

TRCP 107. RETURN OF SERVICE

The return of the officer or authorized person executing the citation shall be endorsed on or attached to the same; it shall state when the citation was served and the manner of service and be signed by the officer officially or by the authorized person. The return of citation by an authorized person shall be verified. When the citation was served by registered or certified mail as authorized by Rule 106, the return by the officer or authorized person must also contain the return receipt with the addressee's signature. When the officer or authorized person has not served the citation, the return shall show the diligence used by the officer or authorized person to execute the same and the cause of failure to execute it, and where the defendant is to be found, if he can ascertain.

Where citation is executed by an alternative method as authorized by Rule 106, proof of service shall be made in the manner ordered by the court.

No default judgment shall be granted in any cause until the citation, or process under Rules 108 or 108a, with proof of service as provided by this rule or by Rules 108 or 108a, or as ordered by the court in the event citation is executed under Rule 106, shall have been on file with the clerk of the court ten days, exclusive of the day of filing and the day of judgment.

See also TRCP 16; ***O'Connor's Texas Rules***, "Serving the Defendant with Suit," ch. 2-H; ***O'Connor's Texas Forms***, FORMS 2H.

Primate Constr., Inc. v. Silver, 884 S.W.2d 151, 152-53 (Tex.1994). "The officer's return does not cease to be prima facie evidence of the facts of service simply because the facts are recited in a form rather than filled in by the officer. … If the facts as recited in the sheriff's return, pre-printed or otherwise, are incorrect and do not show proper service, the one requesting service must amend the return prior to judgment."

Union Pac. Corp. v. Legg, 49 S.W.3d 72, 78 (Tex. App.—Austin 2001, no pet.). "The clerk's return of the citation directed to [D] and the accompanying certified-mail receipt do not bear a file mark or other indication that they were in fact filed with the clerk on a particular day, or that they were, indeed, filed at all. Consequently, they do not show they were 'on file' for the requisite ten days before default judgment was granted. We hold this violates the strict-compliance requirement. *At 79:* Rule 107 also requires that the return receipt bear 'the addressee's signature' when service is by certified mail. The return receipt in this instance bears only a stamp rather than a handwritten signature.... We believe the return receipt does not bear the requisite addressee's signature. A stamped signature may be sufficient if shown to be authorized by proof in the record, but no such proof appears here. We hold the return fatally defective for the reason indicated."

Bautista v. Bautista, 9 S.W.3d 250, 251 (Tex. App.—San Antonio 1999, no pet.). "'Verified' for purposes of rule 107 has been defined as an acknowledgment of the instrument before a notary public. ... In this case, ... there is nothing on the return or attached to the return that can be considered a verification. Since the return was not verified, it did not comply with rule 107."

Onyx TV v. TV Strategy Group, LLC, 990 S.W.2d 427, 431 (Tex.App.—Texarkana 1999, no pet.). "The Secretary of State's certificate of process, [showing proof of service under the long-arm statute,] does not place on file the information [required under TRCP 99 and] contained in the citation sent to [D]. We hold that the filing of the Secretary of State's certificate does not comply with the requirement of [TRCP] 107 that the citation be on file."

Seib v. Bekker, 964 S.W.2d 25, 28 (Tex.App.—Tyler 1997, no writ). "[A] return of service of citation by a private process server must contain the fact of service, the time of service, and manner of service, and shall be sworn to by the private process server before a notary public and filed with the papers in the cause."

Maddison Dual Fuels, Inc. v. Southern Un. Co., 944 S.W.2d 735, 738 (Tex.App.—Corpus Christi 1997, no writ). "When a citation has been returned unserved, the officer's return must show the diligence used by the officer to execute the citation and the cause of his failure to execute it."

TRCP 108. DEFENDANT WITHOUT STATE

Where the defendant is absent from the State, or is a nonresident of the State, the form of notice to such defendant of the institution of the suit shall be the same as prescribed for citation to a resident defendant; and such notice may be served by any disinterested person competent to make oath of the fact in the same manner as provided in Rule 106 hereof. The return of service in such cases shall be endorsed on or attached to the original notice, and shall be in the form provided in Rule 107, and be signed and sworn to by the party making such service before some officer authorized by the laws of this State to take affidavits, under the hand and official seal of such officer. A defendant served with such notice shall be required to appear and answer in the same manner and time and under the same penalties as if he had been personally served with a citation within this State to the full extent that he may be required to appear and answer under the Constitution of the United States in an action either in rem or in personam.

See also *O'Connor's Texas Rules*, "Serving the Defendant with Suit," ch. 2-H.

Paramount Pipe & Sup. Co. v. Muhr, 749 S.W.2d 491, 495-96 (Tex.1988). TRCP 108 "is a valid procedural alternative to service under the long-arm statute. ... So long as the allegations confronting [D] were sufficient to satisfy due process requirements, the trial court had jurisdiction to render judgment by default against him. The only question ... is whether the jurisdictional allegations in the petitions were sufficient, under the Constitution of the U.S., to require [D] to answer."

World Distribs., Inc. v. Knox, 968 S.W.2d 474, 479 (Tex.App.—El Paso 1998, no pet.). "We have ... found no authority for the Secretary of State to serve process. [N]umerous statutes require the Secretary of State to act as agent for service, but no statute authorizes him to serve process. [¶] We fail to perceive how the Secretary of State may act as the defendant's agent for service and at the same time still qualify as a 'disinterested person.'"

TRCP 108a. SERVICE OF PROCESS IN FOREIGN COUNTRIES

(1) Manner. Service of process may be effected upon a party in a foreign country if service of the citation and petition is made: (a) in the manner prescribed by the law of the foreign country for service in that country in an action in any of its courts of general jurisdiction; or (b) as directed by the foreign authority in response to a letter rogatory or a letter of request; or (c) in the manner provided by Rule 106; or (d) pursuant to the terms and provisions of any applicable treaty or convention; or (e) by diplomatic or consular officials when authorized by the United States Department of State; or (f) by any other means directed by the court that is not prohibited by the law of the country where service is to be made. The method for service of process in a foreign country must be reasonably calculated, under all of the circumstances, to give actual notice of the proceedings to the defendant in time to answer and defend. A defendant served with process under this rule shall be required to appear and answer in the same manner and time and under the same penalties as if he had been personally served with citation within this state to the full extent that he may be required to appear and answer under the Constitution of the United States or under any applicable convention or treaty in an action either in rem or in personam.

(2) Return. Proof of service may be made as prescribed by the law of the foreign country, by order of the court, by Rule 107, or by a method provided in any applicable treaty or convention.

See also CPRC §§17.044, 17.045.

Commission of Contracts v. Arriba, Ltd., 882 S.W.2d 576, 584 (Tex.App.—Houston [1st Dist.] 1994, no writ). Plaintiffs "argue that service on a resident of a foreign country under the long-arm statute is improper, and that a resident of a foreign country can only be served according to the methods of service prescribed in [TRCP] 108a. *At 585:* We find a party in a foreign country may be served under the long-arm statute."

TRCP 109. CITATION BY PUBLICATION

When a party to a suit, his agent or attorney, shall make oath that the residence of any party defendant is unknown to affiant, and to such party when the affidavit is made by his agent or attorney, or that such defendant is a transient person, and that after due diligence such party and the affiant have been unable to locate the whereabouts of such defendant, or that such defendant is absent from or is a nonresident of the State, and that the party applying for the citation has attempted to obtain personal service of nonresident notice as provided for in Rule 108, but has been unable to do so, the clerk shall issue citation for such defendant for service by publication. In such cases it shall be the duty of the court trying the case to inquire into the sufficiency of the diligence exercised in attempting to ascertain the residence or whereabouts of the defendant or to obtain service of nonresident notice, as the case may be, before granting any judgment on such service.

Caution: TRCP 109 is affected by the following sections in the Fam. Code: §§3.305, 6.409, 82.043, 102.010.

See also ***O'Connor's Texas Rules***, "Serving the Defendant with Suit," ch. 2-H; "Motion for New Trial," ch. 10-B.

Wood v. Brown, 819 S.W.2d 799, 800 (Tex.1991). "In his affidavit, [P's] counsel stated that ... [D] had moved from his last known address in Oklahoma and that neighbors thought that [D] had moved to Florida. The affidavit, however, does not state that [D's] residence was unknown to [P's] attorney, that [D] was a transient person, that [D] was absent from Texas or that [D] did not reside in Texas. Therefore, the affidavit sworn by [P's] attorney did not meet any of the requirements for service by publication under [TRCP] 109."

In re A.Y., 16 S.W.3d 387, 389 (Tex.App.—El Paso 2000, no pet.). TRCP "109 requires the trial court to determine the diligence used by the plaintiff in trying to locate the defendant's residence. If the trial court finds a lack of diligence, then the plaintiff must undertake additional efforts to comply with Rule 109. If the plaintiff is successful in his efforts to locate the defendant, then regular service of process is required."

TRCP 109a. OTHER SUBSTITUTED SERVICE

Whenever citation by publication is authorized, the court may, on motion, prescribe a different method of substituted service, if the court finds, and so recites in its order, that the method so prescribed would be as likely as publication to give defendant actual notice. When such method of substituted service is authorized, the return of the officer executing the citation shall state particularly the manner in which service is accomplished, and shall attach any return receipt, returned mail, or other evidence showing the result of such service. Failure of defendant to respond to such citation shall not render the service invalid. When such substituted service has been obtained and the defendant has not appeared, the provisions of Rules 244 and 329 shall apply as if citation had been served by publication.

Caution: TRCP 109a is affected by the following sections in the Fam. Code: §§3.305, 6.409, 82.043, 102.010.

See also *O'Connor's Texas Rules*, "Serving the Defendant with Suit," ch. 2-H.

Howell v. Homecraft Land Dev., Inc., 749 S.W.2d 103, 112 (Tex.App.—Dallas 1987, writ denied). "The rules require a strict showing of the need for substituted service, and the trial court must order the substituted service."

TRCP 110. EFFECT OF RULES ON OTHER STATUTES

Where by statute or these rules citation by publication is authorized and the statute or rules do not specify the requisites of such citation or the method of service thereof, or where they direct that such citation be issued or served as in other civil actions, the provisions of these rules shall govern. Where, however, the statute authorizing citation by publication provides expressly for requisites of such citation or service thereof, or both, differing from the provisions of Rules 114, 115, and 116, these rules shall not govern, but the special statutory procedure shall continue in force; provided, however, that Rule 117a shall control with respect to citation in tax suits.

Caution: TRCP 110 is affected by the following sections in the Fam. Code: §§3.305, 6.409, 82.043, 102.010.

TRCP 111. CITATION BY PUBLICATION IN ACTION AGAINST UNKNOWN HEIRS OR STOCKHOLDERS OF DEFUNCT CORPORATIONS

If the plaintiff, his agent, or attorney, shall make oath that the names of the heirs or stockholders against whom an action is authorized by Section 17.004, Civil Practice and Remedies Code, are unknown to the affiant, the clerk shall issue a citation for service by publication. Such citation shall be addressed to the defendants by a concise description of their classification, as "the Unknown Heirs of A.B., deceased," or "Unknown Stockholders of __________ Corporation," as the case may be, and shall contain the other requisites prescribed in Rules 114 and 115 and shall be served as provided by Rule 116.

See also *O'Connor's Texas Rules*, "Serving the Defendant with Suit," ch. 2-H.

TRCP 112. PARTIES TO ACTIONS AGAINST UNKNOWN OWNERS OR CLAIMANTS OF INTEREST IN LAND

In suits authorized by Section 17.005, Civil Practice and Remedies Code, all persons claiming under such conveyance whose names are known to plaintiff shall be made parties by name and cited to appear, in the manner now provided by law as in other suits; all other persons claiming any interest in such land under such conveyance may be made parties to the suit and cited by publication under the designation "all persons claiming any title or interest in land under deed heretofore given to __________ of ______________ as grantee" (inserting in the blanks the name and residence of grantee as given in such conveyance). It shall be permissible to join in one suit all persons claiming under two or more conveyances affecting title to the same tract of land.

See also TRCP 113, CPRC §17.005; *O'Connor's Texas Rules*, "Serving the Defendant with Suit," ch. 2-H.

TRCP 113. CITATION BY PUBLICATION IN ACTIONS AGAINST UNKNOWN OWNERS OR CLAIMANTS OF INTEREST IN LAND

In suits authorized by Section 17.005, Civil Practice and Remedies Code, plaintiff, his agent or attorney shall make and file with the clerk of the court an affidavit, stating

(a) the name of the grantee as set out in the conveyance constituting source of title of defendants, and

(b) stating that affiant does not know the names of any persons claiming title or interest under such conveyance other than as stated in plaintiff's petition and

(c) if the conveyance is to a company or association name as grantee, further stating whether grantee is incorporated or unincorporated, if such fact is known, and if such fact is unknown, so stating.

Said clerk shall thereupon issue a citation for service upon all persons claiming any title or interest in such land under such conveyance. The citation in such cases shall contain the requisites and be served in the manner provided by Rules 114, 115 and 116.

See also CPRC §17.005; *O'Connor's Texas Rules*, "Serving the Defendant with Suit," ch. 2-H.

Quarles v. Champion Int'l Corp., 760 S.W.2d 792, 794 (Tex.App.—Beaumont 1988, writ denied). Service of citation by publication on a known party is improper, "[a]nd this notice requirement to a known party is of due process dimension."

TRCP 114. CITATION BY PUBLICATION; REQUISITES

Where citation by publication is authorized by these rules, the citation shall contain the requisites prescribed by Rules 15 and 99, in so far as they are not inconsistent herewith, provided that no copy of the plaintiff's petition shall accompany this citation, and the citation shall be styled "The State of Texas" and shall be directed to the defendant or defendants by name, if their names are known, or to the defendant or defendants as designated in the petition, if unknown, or such other classification as may be fixed by any statute or by these rules. Where there are two or more defendants or classes of defendants to be served by publication, the citation may be directed to all of them by name and classification, so that service may be completed by publication of the one citation for the required number of times. The citation shall contain the names of the parties, a brief statement of the nature of the suit (which need not contain the details and particulars of the claim) a description of any property involved and of the interest of the named or unknown defendant or defendants, and, where the suit involves land, the requisites of Rule 115. If issued from the district or county court, the citation shall command such parties to appear and answer at or before 10 o'clock a.m. of the first Monday after the expiration of 42 days from the date of issuance thereof, specifying the day of the week, the day of the month, and the time of day the defendant is required to answer. If issued from the justice of the peace court, such citation shall command such parties to appear and answer on or before the first day of the first term of court which convenes after the expiration of 42 days from the date of issue thereof, specifying the day of the week, and the day of the month, that such term will meet.

Caution: TRCP 114 is affected by the following sections in the Fam. Code: §§3.305, 6.409, 82.043, 102.010.

Wiebusch v. Wiebusch, 636 S.W.2d 540, 542 (Tex.App.—San Antonio 1982, no writ). The rule "mandates that ... the citation by publication *shall* contain 'a brief statement of the nature of the suit.' Thus, notice of the nature of the suit is essential to a valid citation by publication."

TRCP 115. FORM OF PUBLISHED CITATION IN ACTIONS INVOLVING LAND

In citations by publication involving land, it shall be sufficient in making the brief statement of the claim in such citation to state the kind of suit, the number of acres of land involved in the suit, or the number of the lot and block, or any other plat description that may be of record if the land is situated in a city or town, the survey on which and the county in which the land is situated, and any special pleas which are relied upon in such suit.

TRCP 116. SERVICE OF CITATION BY PUBLICATION

The citation, when issued, shall be served by the sheriff or any constable of any county of the State of Texas or by the clerk of the court in which the case is pending, by having the same published once each week for four (4) consecutive weeks, the first publication to be at least twenty-eight (28) days before the return day of the citation. In all suits which do not involve the title to land or the partition of real estate, such publication shall be made in the county where the suit is pending, if there be a newspaper published in said county, but if not, then in an adjoining county where a newspaper is published. In all suits which involve the title to land or partition of real estate, such publication shall be made in the county where the land, or a portion thereof, is situated, if there be a newspaper in such county, but if not, then in an adjoining county to the county where the land or a part thereof is situated, where a newspaper is published.

Caution: TRCP 116 is affected by the following sections in the Fam. Code: §§3.305, 6.409, 82.043, 102.010.

In re A.Y., 16 S.W.3d 387, 389 (Tex.App.—El Paso 2000, no pet.). "The Family Code allows for citation by publication as in other civil cases. Therefore, the [TRCPs] apply and Rule 116 makes citation by publication proper if published in the county where suit is pending."

Fleming v. Hernden, 564 S.W.2d 157, 159 (Tex. App.—El Paso 1978, writ ref'd n.r.e.). Citation by publication in San Antonio newspapers affecting title to land in Willacy County did not comply with TRCP 116.

TRCP 117. RETURN OF CITATION BY PUBLICATION

The return of the officer executing such citation shall be indorsed or attached to the same, and show how and when the citation was executed, specifying the dates of such publication, be signed by him officially and shall be accompanied by a printed copy of such publication.

TRCP 117a. CITATION IN SUITS FOR DELINQUENT AD VALOREM TAXES

In all suits for collection of delinquent ad valorem taxes, the rules of civil procedure governing issuance and service of citation shall control the issuance and service of citation therein, except as herein otherwise specially provided.

1. Personal Service: Owner and Residence Known, Within State. Where any defendant in a tax suit is a resident of the State of Texas and is not subject to citation by publication under subdivision 3 below, the process shall conform substantially to the form hereinafter set out for personal service and shall contain the essential elements and be served and returned and otherwise regulated by the provisions of Rules 99 to 107, inclusive.

2. Personal Service: Owner and Residence Known, Out of State. Where any such defendant is absent from the State or is a nonresident of the State and is not subject to citation by publication under subdivision 3 below, the process shall conform substantially to the form hereinafter set out for personal service and shall contain the essential elements and be served and returned and otherwise regulated by the provisions of Rule 108.

3. Service by Publication: Nonresident, Absent from State, Transient, Name Unknown, Residence Unknown, Owner Unknown, Heirs Unknown, Corporate Officers, Trustees, Receivers or Stockholders Unknown, Any Other Unknown Persons Owing or Claiming or Having an Interest. Where any defendant in a tax suit is a nonresident of the State, or is absent from the State, or is a transient person, or the name or the residence of any owner of any interest in any property upon which a tax lien is sought to be foreclosed, is unknown to the attorney requesting the issuance of process or filing the suit for the taxing unit, and such attorney shall make affidavit that such defendant is a nonresident of the State, or is absent from the State, or is a transient person, or that the name or residence of such owner is unknown and cannot be ascertained after diligent inquiry, each such person in every such class above mentioned, together with any and all other persons, including adverse claimants, owning or claiming or having any legal or equitable interest in or lien upon such property, may be cited by publication. All unknown owners of any interest in any property upon which any taxing unit seeks to foreclose a lien for taxes, including stockholders of corporations—defunct or otherwise—their successors, heirs, and assigns, may be joined in such suit under the designation of "unknown owners" and citation be had upon them as such; provided, however, that record owners of such property or of any apparent interest therein, including, without limitation, record lien holders, shall not be included in the designation of "unknown owners"; and provided further that where any record owner has rendered the property involved within five years before the tax suit is filed, citation on such record owner may not be had by publication or posting unless citation for personal service has been issued as to such record owner, with a notation thereon setting forth the same address as is contained on the rendition sheet made within such five years, and the sheriff or other person to whom citation has been delivered makes his return thereon that he is unable to locate the defendant. Where any attorney filing a tax suit for a taxing unit, or requesting the issuance of process in such suit, shall make affidavit that a corporation is the record owner of any interest in any property upon which a tax lien is sought to be foreclosed, and that he does not know, and after diligent inquiry has been unable to ascertain, the location of the place of business, if any, of such corporation, or the name or place of residence of any officer of such corporation upon whom personal service may be had, such corporation may be cited by publication as herein provided. All defendants of the classes enumerated above may be joined in the same citation by publication.

An affidavit which complies with the foregoing requirements therefor shall be sufficient basis for the citation above mentioned in connection with it but shall be held to be made upon the criminal responsibility of affiant.

Such citation by publication shall be directed to the defendants by names or by designation as hereinabove provided, and shall be issued and signed by the clerk of the court in which such tax suit is pending. It shall be sufficient if it states the file number and style of the case, the date of the filing of the petition, the names of all parties by name or by designation as hereinabove provided, and the court in which the suit is pending; shall command such parties to appear and defend such suit at or before 10 o'clock a.m. of the first Monday after the expiration of forty-two days from the date of the issuance thereof, specifying such date when such parties are required to answer; shall state the place of holding the court, the nature of the suit, and the date of the issuance of the citation; and shall be signed and sealed by the clerk.

The citation shall be published in the English language one time a week for two weeks in some newspaper published in the county in which the property is located, which newspaper must have been in general circulation for at least one year immediately prior to the first publication and shall in every respect answer the requirements of the law applicable to newspapers which are employed for such a purpose, the first publication to be not less than twenty-eight days prior to the return day fixed in the citation; and the affidavit of the editor or publisher of the newspaper giving the date of publication, together with a printed copy of the citation as published, shall constitute sufficient proof of due publication when returned and filed in court. If there is no newspaper published in the county, then the publication may be made in a newspaper in an adjoining county, which newspaper shall in every respect answer the requirements of the law applicable to newspapers which are employed for such a purpose. The maximum fee for publishing the citation shall be the lowest published word or line rate of that newspaper for classified advertising. If the publication of the citation cannot be had for this fee, chargeable as costs and payable upon sale of the property, as provided by law, and this fact is supported by the affidavit of the attorney for the plaintiff or the attorney requesting the issuance of the process, then service of the citation may be made by posting a copy at the courthouse door of the county in which the suit is pending, the citation to be posted at least twenty-eight days prior to the return day fixed in the citation. Proof of the posting of the citation shall be made by affidavit of the attorney for the plaintiff, or of the person posting it. When citation is served as here provided it shall be sufficient, and no other form of citation or notice to the named defendants therein shall be necessary.

4. Citation in Tax Suits: General Provisions. Any process authorized by this rule may issue jointly in behalf of all taxing units who are plaintiffs or intervenors in any tax suit. The statement of the nature of the suit, to be set out in the citation, shall be sufficient if it contains a brief general description of the property upon which the taxes are due and the amount of such taxes, exclusive of interest, penalties, and costs, and shall state, in substance, that in such suit the plaintiff and all other taxing units who may set up their claims therein seek recovery of the delinquent ad valorem taxes due on said property, and the (establishment and foreclosure) of liens, if any, securing the payment of same, as provided by law; that in addition to the taxes all interest, penalties, and costs allowed by law up to and including the day of judgment are included in the suit; and that all parties to the suit, including plaintiff, defendants, and intervenors, shall take notice that claims for any taxes on said property becoming delinquent subsequent to the filing of the suit and up to the day of judgment, together with all interest, penalties, and costs allowed by law thereon, may, upon request therefor, be recovered therein without further citation or notice to any parties thereto. Such citation need not be accompanied by a copy of plaintiff's petition and no such copy need be served. Such citation shall also show the names of all taxing units which assess and collect taxes on said property not made parties to such suit, and shall contain, in substance, a recitation that each party to such suit shall take notice of, and plead and answer to, all claims and pleadings then on file or thereafter filed in said cause by all other parties therein, or who may intervene therein and set up their respective tax claims against said property. After citation or notice has been given on behalf of any plaintiff or intervenor taxing unit, the court shall have jurisdiction to hear and determine the tax claims of all taxing units who are parties plaintiff, intervenor or defendant at the time such process is issued and of all taxing units intervening after such process is issued, not only for the taxes, interest, penalties, and costs which may be due on said property at the time the suit is filed, but those becoming delinquent thereon at any time thereafter up to and including the day of judgment, without the necessity of further citation or notice to any party to said suit; and any taxing unit having a tax claim against said property may, by answer or intervention, set up and have determined its tax claim without the necessity of further citation or notice to any parties to such suit.

5. Form of Citation by Publication or Posting. The form of citation by publication or posting shall be sufficient if it is in substantially the following form, with proper changes to make the same applicable to personal property, where necessary, and if the suit includes or is for the recovery of taxes assessed on personal property, a general description of such personal property shall be sufficient:

THE STATE OF TEXAS §
COUNTY OF __________ §

In the name and by the authority of the State of Texas

Notice is hereby given as follows:

To ______________________________

____

and any and all other persons, including adverse claimants, owning or having or claiming any legal or equitable interest in or lien upon the following described property delinquent to Plaintiff herein, for taxes, to-wit:

____

____

Which said property is delinquent to Plaintiff for taxes in the following amounts:

$_____, exclusive of interest, penalties, and costs, and there is included in this suit in addition to the taxes all said interest, penalties, and costs thereon, allowed by law up to and including the day of judgment herein.

You are hereby notified that suit has been brought by _____ as Plaintiffs, against ______ as Defendants, by petition filed on the ___ day of ____, 20__, in a certain suit styled ________ v. ________ for collection of the taxes on said property and that said suit is now pending in the District Court of _____ County, Texas, ____ Judicial District, and the file number of said suit is ____, that the names of all taxing units which assess and collect taxes on the property hereinabove described, not made parties to this suit, are ____________.

Plaintiff and all other taxing units who may set up their tax claims herein seek recovery of delinquent ad valorem taxes on the property hereinabove described, and in addition to the taxes all interest, penalties, and costs allowed by law thereon up to and including the day of judgment herein, and the establishment and foreclosure of liens, if any, securing the payment of same, as provided by law.

All parties to this suit, including plaintiff, defendants, and intervenors, shall take notice that claims not only for any taxes which were delinquent on said property at the time this suit was filed but all taxes becoming delinquent thereon at any time thereafter up to the day of judgment, including all interest, penalties, and costs allowed by law thereon, may, upon request therefor, be recovered herein without further citation or notice to any parties herein, and all said parties shall take notice of and plead and answer to all claims and pleadings now on file and which may hereafter be filed in said cause by all other parties herein, and all of those taxing units above named who may intervene herein and set up their respective tax claims against said property.

You are hereby commanded to appear and defend such suit on the first Monday after the expiration of forty-two (42) days from and after the date of issuance hereof, the same being the ___ day of ________, A.D., 20___ (which is the return day of such citation), before the honorable District Court of ____________ County, Texas, to be held at the courthouse thereof, then and there to show cause why judgment shall not be rendered for such taxes, penalties, interest, and costs, and condemning said property and ordering foreclosure of the constitutional and statutory tax liens thereon for taxes due the plaintiff and the taxing units parties hereto, and those who may intervene herein, together with all interest, penalties, and costs allowed by law up to and including the day of judgment herein, and all costs of this suit.

Issued and given under my hand and seal of said court in the City of ________, ________ County, Texas, this ___ day of ________, A.D., 20__.

____
Clerk of the District Court
___________ County, Texas,
___________ Judicial District.

6. Form of Citation by Personal Service in or out of State. The form of citation for personal service shall be sufficient if it is in substantially the following form, with proper changes to make the same applicable to personal property, where necessary, and if the suit includes or is for the recovery of taxes assessed on personal property, a general description of such personal property shall be sufficient:

THE STATE OF TEXAS

To ________, Defendant,
GREETING:

YOU ARE HEREBY COMMANDED to appear and answer before the Honorable District Court, ______ Judicial District, _____________ County, Texas, at the Courthouse of said county in ____________, Texas, at or before 10 o'clock a.m. of the Monday next after the expiration of 20 days from the date of service of this citation, then and there to answer the petition of ____________, Plaintiff, filed in said Court on the ___ day of _____, A.D., 20__, against _________, Defendant, said suit being number _________ on the docket of said Court, the nature of which demand is a suit to collect delinquent ad valorem taxes on the property hereinafter described.

The amount of taxes due Plaintiff, exclusive of interest, penalties, and costs, is the sum of $ _________, said property being described as follows, to-wit:

____

____

The names of all taxing units which assess and collect taxes on said property, not made parties to this suit, are:

____

Plaintiff and all other taxing units who may set up their tax claims herein seek recovery of delinquent ad valorem taxes on the property hereinabove described, and in addition to the taxes all interest, penalties, and costs allowed by law thereon up to and including the day of judgment herein, and the establishment and foreclosure of liens securing the payment of same, as provided by law.

All parties to this suit, including plaintiff, defendants, and intervenors, shall take notice that claims not only for any taxes which were delinquent on said property at the time this suit was filed but all taxes becoming delinquent thereon at any time thereafter up to the day of judgment, including all interest, penalties, and costs allowed by law thereon, may, upon request therefor, be recovered herein without further citation or notice to any parties herein, and all said parties shall take notice of and plead and answer to all claims and pleadings now on file and which may hereafter be filed in this cause by all other parties hereto, and by all of those taxing units above named, who may intervene herein and set up their respective tax claims against said property.

If this citation is not served within 90 days after the date of its issuance, it shall be returned unserved.

The officer executing this return shall promptly serve the same according to the requirements of law and the mandates hereof and make due return as the law directs.

Issued and given under my hand and seal of said Court at ____, Texas, this the ___ day of ______, A.D., 20__.

____
Clerk of the District Court
___________ County, Texas,
By ____________, Deputy

See also *O'Connor's Texas Rules*, "Serving the Defendant with Suit," ch. 2-H.

Anderson v. Collum, 514 S.W.2d 230, 231 (Tex. 1974). "[T]he failure to comply with [TRCP 117a] and the admitted lack of diligence to locate the defendants renders the service by publication ineffective."

TRCP 118. AMENDMENT

At any time in its discretion and upon such notice and on such terms as it deems just, the court may allow any process or proof of service thereof to be amended, unless it clearly appears that material prejudice would result to the substantial rights of the party against whom the process issued.

See also *O'Connor's Texas Rules*, "Serving the Defendant with Suit," ch. 2-H.

Higginbotham v. General Life & Acc. Ins. Co., 796 S.W.2d 695, 697 (Tex.1990). Because a trial court's order holding that service was proper was "tantamount to formal amendment of the return of citation, the record was sufficient to show valid service."

Union Pac. Corp. v. Legg, 49 S.W.3d 72, 77 (Tex. App.—Austin 2001, no pet.). "'If the facts as recited in the [officer's] return ... are incorrect and do not show proper service, the one requesting service must amend the return prior to judgment.' [¶] [T]he rules allow for liberal amendment of 'any process or proof of service' before a default judgment is taken."

TRCP 119. ACCEPTANCE OF SERVICE

The defendant may accept service of process, or waive the issuance or service thereof by a written memorandum signed by him, or by his duly authorized agent or attorney, after suit is brought, sworn to before a proper officer other than an attorney in the case, and filed among the papers of the cause, and such waiver or acceptance shall have the same force and effect as if the citation had been issued and served as provided by law. The party signing such memorandum shall be delivered a copy of plaintiff's petition, and the receipt of the same shall be acknowledged in such memorandum. In every divorce action such memorandum shall also include the defendant's mailing address.

Caution: TRCP 119 is affected by Fam. Code §6.4035.

See also CPRC §30.001; ***O'Connor's Texas Rules***, "Serving the Defendant with Suit," ch. 2-H; ***O'Connor's Texas Forms***, FORMS 2H.

Deen v. Kirk, 508 S.W.2d 70, 71 (Tex.1974). "Under the provisions of [TRCP] 119 ... a defendant may waive the issuance and service of citation by filing among the papers of the cause a verified written memorandum 'signed by him, or by his duly authorized agent or attorney, after suit is brought.' Article 2224 [now CPRC §30.001] prohibits the waiver of process by an instrument executed prior to institution of suit."

In re Bruno, 974 S.W.2d 401, 405 (Tex.App.—San Antonio 1998, no pet.). Mother "argues that, while she waived her right to receive service of citation, she was still entitled to receive a copy of the petition for termination pursuant to [TRCP] 119. However, by its very terms, Rule 119 requires the delivery of the original petition only when a party either accepts service or waives the issuance of citation *after suit is brought*. It does not apply in cases of pre-suit waiver."

Tidwell v. Tidwell, 604 S.W.2d 540, 541 (Tex. App.—Texarkana 1980, no writ). TRCP 119 makes "it absolutely clear that a waiver of service of process must be executed *after* suit is brought."

TRCP 119a. COPY OF DECREE

The district clerk shall forthwith mail a certified copy of the final divorce decree or order of dismissal to the party signing a memorandum waiving issuance or service of process. Such divorce decree or order of dismissal shall be mailed to the signer of the memorandum at the address stated in such memorandum or to the office of his attorney of record.

Caution: TRCP 119a is affected by the following section in the Fam. Code: §161.209.

TRCP 120. ENTERING APPEARANCE

The defendant may, in person, or by attorney, or by his duly authorized agent, enter an appearance in open court. Such appearance shall be noted by the judge upon his docket and entered in the minutes, and shall have the same force and effect as if the citation had been duly issued and served as provided by law.

Caution: TRCP 120 is affected by the following section in the Fam. Code: §157.063.

See also ***O'Connor's Texas Rules***, "Default Judgment," ch. 7-A.

Mays v. Perkins, 927 S.W.2d 222, 225 (Tex.App.—Houston [1st Dist.] 1996, no writ). "A defendant's appearance before a court generally indicates a submission to the court's jurisdiction. However, the mere presence in court by an attorney, retained as counsel by a person formerly a party to the lawsuit, does not constitute a general appearance, unless the attorney seeks a judgment or an adjudication on some question."

Gonzalez v. Phoenix Frozen Foods, Inc., 884 S.W.2d 587, 589 (Tex.App.—Corpus Christi 1994, no writ). "A defendant's appearance in open court shall have the same force and effect as if the citation had been duly issued and served as provided by law."

TRCP 120a. SPECIAL APPEARANCE

1. Notwithstanding the provisions of Rules 121, 122 and 123, a special appearance may be made by any party either in person or by attorney for the purpose of objecting to the jurisdiction of the court over the person or property of the defendant on the ground that such party or property is not amenable to process issued by the courts of this State. A special appearance may be made as to an entire proceeding or as to any severable claim involved therein. Such special appearance shall be made by sworn motion filed prior to motion to transfer venue or any other plea, pleading or motion; provided however, that a motion to transfer venue and any other plea, pleading, or motion may be contained in the same instrument or filed subsequent thereto without waiver of such special appearance; and may be amended to cure defects. The issuance of process for witnesses, the taking of depositions, the serving of requests for admissions, and the use of discovery processes, shall not constitute a waiver of such special appearance. Every appearance, prior to judgment, not in compliance with this rule is a general appearance.

2. Any motion to challenge the jurisdiction provided for herein shall be heard and determined before a motion to transfer venue or any other plea or pleading may be heard. No determination of any issue of fact in connection with the objection to jurisdiction is a determination of the merits of the case or any aspect thereof.

3. The court shall determine the special appearance on the basis of the pleadings, any stipulations made by and between the parties, such affidavits and attachments as may be filed by the parties, the results of discovery processes, and any oral testimony. The affidavits, if any, shall be served at least seven days before the hearing, shall be made on personal knowledge, shall set forth specific facts as would be admissible in evidence, and shall show affirmatively that the affiant is competent to testify.

Should it appear from the affidavits of a party opposing the motion that he cannot for reasons stated present by affidavit facts essential to justify his opposition, the court may order a continuance to permit affidavits to be obtained or depositions to be taken or discovery to be had or may make such other order as is just.

Should it appear to the satisfaction of the court at any time that any of such affidavits are presented in violation of Rule 13, the court shall impose sanctions in accordance with that rule.

4. If the court sustains the objection to jurisdiction, an appropriate order shall be entered. If the objection to jurisdiction is overruled, the objecting party may thereafter appear generally for any purpose. Any such special appearance or such general appearance shall not be deemed a waiver of the objection to jurisdiction when the objecting party or subject matter is not amenable to process issued by the courts of this State.

See also CPRC §§17.041-.042, 51.014(a)(7); *O'Connor's Texas Rules*, "Special Appearance," ch. 3-B; *O'Connor's Texas Forms*, FORMS 3B.

GFTA Trendanalysen B.G.A. Iterrdum GMBH & Co. v. Varme, 991 S.W.2d 785, 786 (Tex.1999). "[T]he court of appeals held that by challenging the method of service within the special appearance, [D] converted its special appearance into a general appearance and thereby consented to jurisdiction. [¶] [A] party [does not] waive[] a due process challenge for want of minimum contacts by challenging the method of service in the special appearance."

Dawson-Austin v. Austin, 968 S.W.2d 319, 322-23 (Tex.1998). The Supreme Court held: (1) an unverified special appearance may be amended to cure the defect, even after the trial court has overruled it, as long as the amendment is filed before the defendant enters a general appearance; and (2) it is not necessary for the answer and other motions filed in the same instrument with the special appearance to contain "subject to" language.

CMMC v. Salinas, 929 S.W.2d 435, 439 (Tex.1996). Manufacturer's "mere knowledge that its winepress was to be sold and used in Texas and its wiring the machine for use in the U.S. were not sufficient to subject CMMC to the jurisdiction of Texas courts. *At 440:* A manufacturer cannot fairly be expected to litigate in every part of the world where its products may end up; its contacts with the forum must be more purposeful ... before it can constitutionally be subjected to personal jurisdiction."

CSR Ltd. v. Link, 925 S.W.2d 591, 595-96 (Tex. 1996). "A defendant should not be subject to the jurisdiction of a foreign court based upon 'random,' 'fortuitous,' or 'attenuated' contacts. Minimum contacts are particularly important when the defendant is from a different country because of the unique and onerous burden placed on a party called upon to defend a suit in a foreign legal system. [¶] [T]he record contains no evidence that [the Australian company] took any act purposefully directed toward selling or distributing the raw asbestos fiber in Texas."

In re S.A.V., 837 S.W.2d 80, 84-85 (Tex.1992). "In his special appearance, the father challenged the trial court's subject matter jurisdiction to adjudicate custody as well as the court's personal jurisdiction over the father. The court of appeals determined that, by raising the issue of subject matter jurisdiction in his special appearance, the father made a general appearance before the trial court. We disagree. [¶] By challenging the court's subject matter jurisdiction over custody, the father challenged the satisfaction of the jurisdictional statute. As discussed earlier, in adjudications of custody, satisfaction of the jurisdictional statute confers 'personal jurisdiction' over the nonresident. As a result, the father's challenge to the court's subject matter jurisdiction over custody issues served as a challenge to the court's 'personal jurisdiction' over the father. This type of challenge is properly raised in a special appearance."

Schlobohm v. Schapiro, 784 S.W.2d 355, 358 (Tex. 1990). The Texas standard for jurisdiction over a nonresident defendant requires: "(1) The nonresident defendant or foreign corporation must purposefully do some act or consummate some transaction in the forum state; [¶] (2) The cause of action must arise from, or be connected with, such act or transaction; [¶] and (3) The assumption of jurisdiction by the forum state must not offend traditional notions of fair play and substantial justice.... [¶] [However], we modify the second part ... to state that jurisdiction may also arise from the continuing and systematic contacts of the [D] with Texas, even if the cause of action does not arise from a specific contact." *See also* **Guardian Royal Exch. Assur., Ltd. v. English China Clays, P.L.C.**, 815 S.W.2d 223, 226 (Tex.1991).

Case v. Grammar, 31 S.W.3d 304, 311 (Tex.App.—San Antonio 2000, no pet.). "The trial court ... erred in determining that [Ds] waived their special appearances by using the discovery process to seek information pertaining to the merits of the case."

Mouso v. Alworth, 777 S.W.2d 795, 797 (Tex. App.—Beaumont 1989, orig. proceeding). "We think it is axiomatic that before a court has the power to transfer a case under state statute, even one in the Family Code, that the court would have to possess the proper jurisdiction of the litigation, including in personam jurisdiction. We hold that Rule 120a is paramount and that a hearing on the special appearance must be held first."

Pleadings

Casino Magic Corp. v. King, 43 S.W.3d 14, 18 (Tex.App.—Dallas 2001, pet. denied). TRCP 120a "requires special appearances to be made by 'sworn motion.' Strict compliance with the rule is required. [¶] In this case, the special appearance was not sworn or verified. Although [D] attached an affidavit to the special appearance which set out various 'jurisdictional facts,' in that affidavit [D's] general counsel stated only that the allegations in the *affidavit* were true and correct, not that the facts set out in the *special appearance* were true and correct. [W]e conclude the affidavit did not strictly comply with rule 120a and it, therefore, could not serve to verify the special appearance."

TRCP 121. ANSWER IS APPEARANCE

An answer shall constitute an appearance of the defendant so as to dispense with the necessity for the issuance or service of citation upon him.

Burrows v. Arce, 997 S.W.2d 229, 246 (Tex.1999). "The filing of an answer dispenses with the necessity of service of citation."

Moody Nat'l Bank v. Riebschlager, 946 S.W.2d 521, 524 (Tex.App.—Houston [14th Dist.] 1997, writ denied). "In order for an act of the garnishee to constitute an appearance, it must seek a judgment or adjudication by the court on some issue.... When a garnishee appears for the purpose of filing a motion to quash the garnishment, such an appearance does not confer jurisdiction on the court for all purposes, and does not operate as a waiver of an objection as to jurisdiction."

TRCP 122. CONSTRUCTIVE APPEARANCE

If the citation or service thereof is quashed on motion of the defendant, such defendant shall be deemed to have entered his appearance at ten o'clock a.m. on the Monday next after the expiration of twenty (20) days after the day on which the citation or service is quashed, and such defendant shall be deemed to have been duly served so as to require him to appear and answer at that time, and if he fails to do so, judgment by default may be rendered against him.

See also *O'Connor's Texas Rules*, "Motion to Quash," ch. 3-I.

Kawasaki Steel Corp. v. Middleton, 699 S.W.2d 199, 202 (Tex.1985). "[A] non-resident defendant, like any other defendant, may move to quash the citation for defects in the process, but his only relief is additional time to answer rather than dismissal of the cause."

Moody Nat'l Bank v. Riebschlager, 946 S.W.2d 521, 524 (Tex.App.—Houston [14th Dist.] 1997, writ denied). "[F]iling a motion to quash in garnishment proceedings is not comparable to filing a motion to quash citation in ordinary suits.... Because the filing of a motion to quash in a garnishment proceeding does not constitute an appearance as in other civil proceedings, rule 122 is wholly inapplicable to this case...."

TRCP 123. REVERSAL OF JUDGMENT

Where the judgment is reversed on appeal or writ of error for the want of service, or because of defective service of process, no new citation shall be issued or served, but the defendant shall be presumed to have entered his appearance to the term of the court at which the mandate shall be filed.

See also *O'Connor's Texas Rules*, "Motion to Quash," ch. 3-I.

Ackerly v. Ackerly, 13 S.W.3d 454, 458 (Tex.App.—Corpus Christi 2000, no pet.). "By attacking the judgment, [respondent] has submitted himself to the jurisdiction of the district court. Therefore, upon remand, [respondent] is presumed to have entered his appearance, and no new citation is required to be issued or served."

TRCP 124. NO JUDGMENT WITHOUT SERVICE

In no case shall judgment be rendered against any defendant unless upon service, or acceptance or waiver of process, or upon an appearance by the defendant, as prescribed in these rules, except where otherwise expressly provided by law or these rules.

When a party asserts a counterclaim or a cross-claim against another party who has entered an appearance, the claim may be served in any manner prescribed for service of citation or as provided in Rule 21a.

See also *O'Connor's Texas Rules*, "Serving the Defendant with Suit," ch. 2-H; "Default Judgment," ch. 7-A.

Werner v. Colwell, 909 S.W.2d 866, 869-70 (Tex. 1995). "Judgment shall not be rendered against one who was neither named nor served as a party defendant. An exception exist when a person waives service by making a general appearance before the court. [W]e have never held and decline to hold today, that merely appearing as a witness in a cause serves as a general appearance, subjecting one to the jurisdiction of the court."

Spivey v. Holloway, 902 S.W.2d 46, 48 (Tex.App.—Houston [1st Dist.] 1995, no writ). "[E]ven without service or waiver of process, a judgment may be rendered upon appearance by the defendant. An appearance constitutes waiver of service. [W]e hold that [appellant]'s signing of the divorce decree constituted an appearance before the court pursuant to rule 124."

Strawder v. Thomas, 846 S.W.2d 51, 62 (Tex. App.—Corpus Christi 1992, no writ). "Rules relating to service of process are mandatory, and a failure to comply therewith, if a judgment be rendered against a party who was not served in accordance with those rules (and who did not waive service of citation or appear voluntarily) renders the judgment void."

SECTION 6. COSTS & SECURITY THEREFOR

TRCP 125. PARTIES RESPONSIBLE

Each party to a suit shall be liable to the officers of the court for all costs incurred by himself.

Caution: TRCP 125 is affected by the following sections in the Fam. Code: §§6.708, 9.013, 9.014, 9.205, 33.004, 33.007, 41.002, 41.0025, 42.009, 81.003, 85.064, 106.001, 106.002, 107.015, 107.056, 110.002, 152.312, 152.317, 154.012, 156.005, 157.167, 157.211, 157.323, 158.206, 159.305, 159.313, 231.202, 231.205, 231.209, 231.210, 231.211.

Gross v. Gross, 808 S.W.2d 215, 221 (Tex.App.—Houston [14th Dist.] 1991, no writ). Unsuccessful party argues "that courts do not have unlimited discretion under [Family Code] §11.18 [now §§106.001 & 106.002] to award attorney's fees and costs. He further argues that only a successful party can recover attorney's fees and costs, absent good cause. Initially, we note that not only is [he] not a successful party, but the provisions of the Family Code with respect to attorney's fees and costs were intended to supplant the Rules of Civil Procedure."

TRCP 126. FEE FOR EXECUTION OF PROCESS, DEMAND

No sheriff or constable shall be compelled to execute any process in civil cases coming from any county other than the one in which he is an officer, unless the fees allowed him by law for the service of such process shall be paid in advance; except when affidavit is filed, as provided by law or these rules. The clerk issuing the process shall indorse thereon the words "pauper oath filed," and sign his name officially below them; and the officer in whose hands such process is placed for service shall serve the same.

TRCP 127. PARTIES LIABLE FOR OTHER COSTS

Each party to a suit shall be liable for all costs incurred by him. If the costs cannot be collected from the party against whom they have been adjudged, execution may issue against any party in such suit for the amount of costs incurred by such party, but no more.

Caution: TRCP 127 is affected by the following sections in the Fam. Code: §§6.708, 9.013, 9.014, 9.205, 33.004, 33.007, 41.002, 41.0025, 42.009, 81.003, 85.064, 106.001, 106.002, 107.015, 107.056, 110.002, 152.312, 152.317, 154.012, 156.005, 157.167, 157.211, 157.323, 158.206, 159.305, 159.313, 231.202, 231.205, 231.209, 231.210, 231.211.

Gross v. Gross, 808 S.W.2d 215, 221 (Tex.App.—Houston [14th Dist.] 1991, no writ). See Annotation in TRCP 125.

TRCP 128. REPEALED

TRCP 129. HOW COSTS COLLECTED

If any party responsible for costs fails or refuses to pay the same within ten days after demand for payment, the clerk or justice of the peace may make certified copy of the bill of costs then due, and place the same in the hands of the sheriff or constable for collection. All taxes imposed on law proceedings shall be included in the bill of costs. Such certified bill of costs shall have the force and effect of an execution. The removal of a case by appeal shall not prevent the issuance of an execution for costs.

TRCP 130. OFFICER TO LEVY

The sheriff or constable upon demand and failure to pay said bill of costs, may levy upon a sufficient amount of property of the person from whom said costs are due to satisfy the same, and sell such property as under execution. Where such party is not a resident of the county where such suit is pending, the payment of such costs may be demanded of his attorney of record; and neither the clerk nor justice of the peace shall be allowed to charge any fee for making out such certified bill of costs, unless he is compelled to make a levy.

TRCP 131. SUCCESSFUL PARTY TO RECOVER

The successful party to a suit shall recover of his adversary all costs incurred therein, except where otherwise provided.

Caution: TRCP 131 is affected by the following sections in the Fam. Code: §§6.708, 85.064, 106.001, 106.002, 107.015, 152.312, 152.317, 154.012, 157.167, 158.206, 159.313.

See also CPRC §31.007; *O'Connor's Texas Rules*, "The Judgment," ch. 9-C.

Gross v. Gross, 808 S.W.2d 215, 221 (Tex.App.—Houston [14th Dist.] 1991, no writ). See Annotation in TRCP 125.

TRCP 132. REPEALED

TRCP 133. COSTS OF MOTION

The court may give or refuse costs on motions at its discretion, except where otherwise provided by law or these rules.

TRCP 134 - 135. REPEALED

TRCP 136. DEMAND REDUCED BY PAYMENTS

Where the plaintiff's demand is reduced by payment to an amount which would not have been within the jurisdiction of the court, the defendant shall recover his costs.

TRCP 137. IN ASSAULT & BATTERY, ETC.

In civil actions for assault and battery, slander and defamation of character, if the verdict or judgment shall be for the plaintiff, but for less than twenty dollars, the plaintiff shall not recover his costs, but each party shall be taxed with the costs incurred by him in such suit.

Maass v. Sefcik, 138 S.W.2d 897, 900 (Tex.App.—Austin 1940, no writ). "We hold that the statements made by appellee are slanderous per se [and] costs ... should have been assessed under the terms of [TRCP 137]."

TRCP 138. COST OF NEW TRIALS

The costs of new trials may either abide the result of the suit or may be taxed against the party to whom the new trial is granted, as the court may adjudge when he grants such new trial.

TRCP 139. ON APPEAL & CERTIORARI

When a case is appealed, if the judgment of the higher court be against the appellant, but for less amount than the original judgment, such party shall recover the costs of the higher court but shall be adjudged to pay the costs of the court below; if the judgment be against him for the same or a greater amount than in the court below, the adverse party shall recover the costs of both courts. If the judgment of the court above be in favor of the party appealing and for more than the original judgment, such party shall recover the costs of both courts; if the judgment be in his favor, but for the same or a less amount than in the court below, he shall recover the costs of the court below, and pay the costs of the court above.

Keene Corp. v. Gardner, 837 S.W.2d 224, 232 (Tex. App.—Dallas 1992, writ denied). "Because the appellate relief given [D] is *de minimis* compared to [Ps'] overall award affirmed on appeal, we assess all costs of this appeal against [D]."

TRCP 140. NO FEE FOR COPY

No fee for a copy of a paper not required by law or these rules to be copied shall be taxed in the bill of costs.

Crescendo Invs., Inc. v. Brice, 61 S.W.3d 465, 481 (Tex.App.—San Antonio 2001, pet. denied). "Awarding costs for certified copies of depositions which may be admitted at trial does not violate Rule 140."

TRCP 141. COURT MAY OTHERWISE ADJUDGE COSTS

The court may, for good cause, to be stated on the record, adjudge the costs otherwise than as provided by law or these rules.

Rogers v. Walmart Stores, Inc., 686 S.W.2d 599, 601 (Tex.1985). TRCP 141 "permits a court to assess costs on the prevailing party for good cause as shown on the face of the record." *But see* ***Billeaud***, below.

Billeaud v. Billeaud, 697 S.W.2d 652, 655 (Tex. App.—Houston [1st Dist.] 1985, no writ). Family Code §11.18(a), now §106.001, "does not require a family court judgment to state good cause for adjudging costs against the successful party as is required in other civil cases. By deleting that portion of the statute which required costs to be assessed 'as in other civil cases,' the legislature recognized the difficulty of deciding, in family cases, which party is successful."

TRCP 142. SECURITY FOR COSTS

The clerk shall require from the plaintiff fees for services rendered before issuing any process unless filing is requested pursuant to Rule 145 of these rules.

TRCP 143. RULE FOR COSTS

A party seeking affirmative relief may be ruled to give security for costs at any time before final judgment, upon motion of any party, or any officer of the court interested in the costs accruing in such suit, or by the court upon its own motion. If such rule be entered against any party and he failed to comply therewith on or before twenty (20) days after notice that such rule has been entered, the claim for affirmative relief of such party shall be dismissed.

See also CPRC, ch. 9.

TransAmerican Nat. Gas Corp. v. Mancias, 877 S.W.2d 840, 844 (Tex.App.—Corpus Christi 1994, orig. proceeding). TRCP 143 "generally allows the trial court to require a party to post security for costs that have already accrued, but not to fix a specific amount for anticipated costs which a party is required to pay or post security for prematurely." *See also* ***Hager v. Apollo Paper Corp.***, 856 S.W.2d 512, 515 (Tex.App.—Houston [1st Dist.] 1993, no writ).

TRCP 143a. COSTS ON APPEAL TO COUNTY COURT

If the appellant fails to pay the costs on appeal from a judgment of a justice of the peace or small claims court within twenty (20) days after being notified to do so by the county clerk, the appeal shall be deemed not perfected and the county clerk shall return all papers in said cause to the justice of the peace having original jurisdiction and the justice of the peace shall proceed as though no appeal had been attempted.

Farmer v. McGee Servs., Inc., 704 S.W.2d 927, 929 (Tex.App.—Tyler 1986, no writ). "Since no notice [of costs] had been given, the trial court erred in applying [TRCP] 143a to dismiss [D's] appeal."

TRCP 144. JUDGMENT ON COST BOND

All bonds given as security for costs shall authorize judgment against all the obligors in such bond for the said costs, to be entered in the final judgment of the cause.

Mosher v. Tunnell, 400 S.W.2d 402, 404 (Tex. App.—Houston [1st Dist.] 1966, writ ref'd n.r.e.). TRCP 144 "provides the bond shall authorize judgment against the obligors for said costs. This means such costs as shall be adjudged against the principal whatever be the amount."

TRCP 145. AFFIDAVIT OF INABILITY

In lieu of filing security for costs of an original action, a party who is unable to afford said costs shall file an affidavit as herein described. A "party who is unable to afford costs" is defined as a person who is presently receiving a governmental entitlement based on indigency or any other person who has no ability to pay costs. Said affidavit, and the party's action, shall be processed by the clerk in the manner prescribed by this rule.

1. Procedure. Upon the filing of the affidavit, the clerk shall docket the action, issue citation and provide such other customary services as are provided any party. After service of citation, the defendant may contest the affidavit by filing a written contest giving notice to all parties, provided that temporary hearings will not be continued pending the filing of the contest. If the court shall find at the first regular hearing in the course of the action that the party (other than a party receiving a governmental entitlement) is able to afford costs, the party shall pay the costs of the action. Reasons for such a finding shall be contained in an order. Except with leave of court, no further steps in the action will be taken by a party who is found able to afford costs until payment is made. If the party's action results in monetary award, and the court finds sufficient monetary award to reimburse costs, the party shall pay the costs of the action. If the court finds that another party to the suit can pay the costs of the action, the other party shall pay the costs of the action.

2. Affidavit. The affidavit shall contain complete information as to the party's identity, nature and amount of governmental entitlement income, nature and amount of employment income, other income, (interest, dividends, etc.), spouse's income if available to the party, property owned (other than homestead), cash or checking account, dependents, debts, and monthly expenses. The affidavit shall contain the following statements: "I am unable to pay the court costs. I verify that the statements made in this affidavit are true and correct." The affidavit shall be sworn before a Notary Public.

3. Attorney's Certification. If the party is represented by an attorney who is providing free legal services, without contingency, because of the party's indigency, said attorney may file an affidavit to that effect to assist the court in understanding the financial condition of the party.

See also CPRC, chs. 13, 14; ***O'Connor's Texas Rules***, "Suit by Indigent," ch. 2-I; ***O'Connor's Texas Forms***, FORMS 2I.

Griffin Indus., Inc. v. 13th Ct. of Appeals, 934 S.W.2d 349, 354 (Tex.1996). When a contingency fee agreement "provides that the attorney is to pay or advance costs, and the [party] makes no further showing [at a hearing to determine indigency status], the agreement would be some evidence that the [party] has a source of funds from which to pay costs. But, when the facts establish that the attorney will not or cannot pay those costs, … we cannot erect a legal fiction that an indigent has the ability to pay [costs]."

Equitable Gen. Ins. Co. v. Yates, 684 S.W.2d 669, 671 (Tex.1984). "An uncontested affidavit of inability to pay is conclusive as a matter of law."

Varkonyi v. Troche, 802 S.W.2d 63, 65 (Tex.App.—El Paso 1990, orig. proceeding). "The trial court's order of denial [of indigent status] failed to comply with [TRCP] 145 which requires that there should be contained in the denial order 'Reasons for such a finding….'"

TRCP 146. DEPOSIT FOR COSTS

In lieu of a bond for costs, the party required to give the same may deposit with the clerk of court or the justice of the peace such sum as the court or justice from time to time may designate as sufficient to pay the accrued costs.

Caution: TRCP 146 is affected by the following section in the Fam. Code: §110.002.

Mosher v. Tunnell, 400 S.W.2d 402, 404-05 (Tex. App.—Houston [1st Dist.]1966, writ ref'd n.r.e.). "The deposit of court costs, as distinguished from a bond as security for costs, is provided for by [TRCP] 146 and clearly contemplates a deposit only for accrued costs."

TRCP 147. APPLIES TO ANY PARTY

The foregoing rules as to security and rule for costs shall apply to any party who seeks a judgment against any other party.

Ex parte Shaffer, 649 S.W.2d 300, 302 (Tex.1983). "[O]ne who involuntarily comes into court and does not seek any affirmative relief cannot be required to post a cost bond."

TRCP 148. SECURED BY OTHER BOND

No further security shall be required if the costs are secured by the provisions of an attachment or other bond filed by the party required to give security for costs.

Buck v. Johnson, 495 S.W.2d 291, 298 (Tex.App.—Waco 1973, writ ref'd n.r.e.). "*[T]he option lies with the party ruled for costs, and not with the court*, as to whether a cost bond shall be furnished or a deposit in lieu of bond."

TRCP 149. EXECUTION FOR COSTS

When costs have been adjudged against a party and are not paid, the clerk or justice of the court in which the suit was determined may issue execution, accompanied by an itemized bill of costs, against such party to be levied and collected as in other cases; and said officer, on demand of any party to whom any such costs are due, shall issue execution for costs at once. This rule shall not apply to executors, administrators or guardians in cases where costs are adjudged against the estate of a deceased person or of a ward. No execution shall issue in any case for costs until after judgment rendered therefor by the court.

SECTION 7. ABATEMENT & DISCONTINUANCE OF SUIT

TRCP 150. DEATH OF PARTY

Where the cause of action is one which survives, no suit shall abate because of the death of any party thereto before the verdict or decision of the court is rendered, but such suit may proceed to judgment as hereinafter provided.

Caution: TRCP 150 is affected by the following section in the Fam. Code: §162.013.

See also *O'Connor's Texas Rules*, "Motion to Abate," ch. 3-H.

Palomino v. Palomino, 960 S.W.2d 899, 900-01 (Tex.App.—El Paso 1997, pet. denied). "The general rule in Texas is that a cause of action for divorce is purely personal and becomes moot and abates upon the death of either spouse. ... However, when a trial court has rendered judgment on the merits in a divorce case, the cause does not abate when a party dies, and the cause cannot be dismissed."

TRCP 151. DEATH OF PLAINTIFF

If the plaintiff dies, the heirs, or the administrator or executor of such decedent may appear and upon suggestion of such death being entered of record in open court, may be made plaintiff, and the suit shall proceed in his or their name. If no such appearance and suggestion be made within a reasonable time after the death of the plaintiff, the clerk upon the application of defendant, his agent or attorney, shall issue a scire facias for the heirs or the administrator or executor of such decedent, requiring him to appear and prosecute such suit. After service of such scire facias, should such heir or administrator or executor fail to enter appearance within the time provided, the defendant may have the suit dismissed.

Caution: TRCP 151 is affected by the following section in the Fam. Code: §162.013.

See also *O'Connor's Texas Rules*, "Motion to Abate," ch. 3-H.

Gracey v. West, 422 S.W.2d 913, 918 (Tex.1968). TRCP 151 "requires defendant to have a scire facias issued bringing in a deceased plaintiff's representative and his failure to appear before defendant can have the cause discontinued."

TRCP 152. DEATH OF DEFENDANT

Where the defendant shall die, upon the suggestion of death being entered of record in open court, or upon petition of the plaintiff, the clerk shall issue a scire facias for the administrator or executor or heir requiring him to appear and defend the suit and upon the return of such service, the suit shall proceed against such administrator or executor or heir.

Caution: TRCP 152 is affected by the following section in the Fam. Code: §162.013.

See also *O'Connor's Texas Rules*, "Motion to Abate," ch. 3-H.

Estate of Pollack v. McMurrey, 858 S.W.2d 388, 390 n.2 (Tex.1993). "Scire facias ... provides for substitution of any person or persons succeeding to the rights of the original party, whether executor, administrator, heir, or person holding the same practical relation."

Henson v. Estate of Crow, 734 S.W.2d 648, 649 (Tex.1987). After the death of the defendant, the plaintiff "filed an amended petition naming the Estate of Bruce L. Crow as defendant. The attorney who had represented Crow filed an amended answer on behalf of the Estate.... Trial was had on those pleadings." Held: The trial court had no jurisdiction, because the plaintiff did not sue the personal representative.

TRCP 153. WHEN EXECUTOR, ETC., DIES

When an executor or administrator shall be a party to any suit, whether as plaintiff or as defendant, and shall die or cease to be such executor or administrator, the suit may be continued by or against the person succeeding him in the administration, or by or against the heirs, upon like proceedings being had as provided in the two preceding rules, or the suit may be dismissed, as provided in Rule 151.

TRCP 154. REQUISITES OF SCIRE FACIAS

The scire facias and returns thereon, provided for in this section, shall conform to the requisites of citations and the returns thereon, under the provisions of these rules.

Mackintosh v. State, 845 S.W.2d 361, 363 (Tex. App.—Houston [1st Dist.] 1992, no writ). "[T]here is a provision for amending the scire facias documents if necessary and the court is apprised of the necessity. [¶] The [TRCPs] provide that scire facias shall conform to the requisites of citations under the rules."

TRCP 155. SURVIVING PARTIES

Where there are two or more plaintiffs or defendants, and one or more of them die, upon suggestion of such death being entered upon the record, the suit shall at the instance of either party proceed in the name of the surviving plaintiffs or against the surviving defendants, as the case may be.

First Nat'l Bank v. Hawn, 392 S.W.2d 377, 379 (Tex.App.—Dallas 1965, writ ref'd n.r.e.). "Having elected to proceed under [TRCP] 155 against the surviving [D], approving a judgment against that [D] ... and that judgment having become final [the P] had no right to ... suggest [the other D's] death and endeavor to reinstate the suit as to his legal representative."

TRCP 156. DEATH AFTER VERDICT OR CLOSE OF EVIDENCE

When a party in a jury case dies between verdict and judgment, or a party in a non-jury case dies after the evidence is closed and before judgment is pronounced, judgment shall be rendered and entered as if all parties were living.

Nacogdoches Mem. Hosp. v. Justice, 694 S.W.2d 204, 206 (Tex.App.—Tyler 1985, writ ref'd n.r.e.). "The obvious purpose of [TRCP] 156 is merely to avoid a mistrial in a jury case upon the death of [a] party occurring *after* a jury has resolved all material disputed issues of fact."

TRCP 157. REPEALED

TRCP 158. SUIT FOR THE USE OF ANOTHER

When a plaintiff suing for the use of another shall die before verdict, the person for whose use such suit was brought, upon such death being suggested on the record in open court, may prosecute the suit in his own name, and shall be as responsible for costs as if he brought the suit.

TRCP 159. SUIT FOR INJURIES RESULTING IN DEATH

In cases arising under the provisions of the title relating to injuries resulting in death, the suit shall not abate by the death of either party pending the suit, but in such case, if the plaintiff dies, where there is only one plaintiff, some one or more of the parties entitled to the money recovered may be substituted and the suit prosecuted to judgment in the name of such party or parties, for the benefit of the person entitled; if the defendant dies, his executor, administrator or heir may be made a party, and the suit prosecuted to judgment.

TRCP 160. DISSOLUTION OF CORPORATION

The dissolution of a corporation shall not operate to abate any pending suit in which such corporation is a defendant, but such suit shall continue against such corporation and judgment shall be rendered as though the same were not dissolved.

See also Business Corp. Act art. 7.12; TRCP 29.

TRCP 161. WHERE SOME DEFENDANTS NOT SERVED

When some of the several defendants in a suit are served with process in due time and others are not so served, the plaintiff may either dismiss as to those not so served and proceed against those who are, or he may take new process against those not served, or may obtain severance of the case as between those served and those not served, but no dismissal shall be allowed as to a principal obligor without also dismissing the parties secondarily liable except in cases provided by statute. No defendant against whom any suit may be so dismissed shall be thereby exonerated from any liability, but may at any time be proceeded against as if no such suit had been brought and no such dismissal ordered.

See also TRCP 240.

Osborne v. St. Luke's Episcopal Hosp., 915 S.W.2d 906, 908 (Tex.App.—Houston [1st Dist.] 1996, writ denied). "Although the November 19 summary judgment did not explicitly dispose of the 8 nonappearing defendants that were not properly sued or served, such a judgment is normally considered final for purposes of appeal and the case stands as if there had been a discontinuance as to the parties not served."

Young v. Hunderup, 763 S.W.2d 611, 612-13 (Tex. App.—Austin 1989, no writ). "Where the judgment disposes of all named parties except those which have not been served and have not appeared ... the judgment is considered final for purposes of appeal and the case stands as if there had been a discontinuance as to those parties not served." *Contra* ***Reed v. Gum Keepsake Diamond Ctr***, 657 S.W.2d 524, 525 (Tex.App.—Corpus Christi 1983, no writ) (judgment was not final because co-defendant was not served, did not waive the service, did not make an appearance, and was not dismissed).

TRCP 162. DISMISSAL OR NON-SUIT

At any time before the plaintiff has introduced all of his evidence other than rebuttal evidence, the plaintiff may dismiss a case, or take a non-suit, which shall be entered in the minutes. Notice of the dismissal or non-suit shall be served in accordance with Rule 21a on any party who has answered or has been served with process without necessity of court order.

Any dismissal pursuant to this rule shall not prejudice the right of an adverse party to be heard on a pending claim for affirmative relief or excuse the payment of all costs taxed by the clerk. A dismissal under this rule shall have no effect on any motion for sanctions, attorney's fees or other costs, pending at the time of dismissal, as determined by the court. Any dismissal pursuant to this rule which terminates the case shall authorize the clerk to tax court costs against dismissing party unless otherwise ordered by the court.

See also TRCP 96; ***O'Connor's Texas Rules***, "Voluntary Dismissal—Non-suit," ch. 7-E; ***O'Connor's Texas Forms***, FORMS 7F.

In re Bennett, 960 S.W.2d 35, 38 (Tex.1997). Plaintiffs "have the right under [TRCP] 162 to take a nonsuit at any time until they have introduced all evidence other than rebuttal evidence. Such a nonsuit may have the effect of vitiating earlier interlocutory orders and of precluding further action by the trial court.... [¶] Appellate timetables do not run from the date a nonsuit is filed, but rather from the date the trial court signs an order of dismissal."

Scott & White Mem. Hosp. v. Schexnider, 940 S.W.2d 594, 595 (Tex.1996). "Does the trial court have the power during its plenary jurisdiction to grant a motion for sanctions under [TRCP] 13 though the motion was not pending when a nonsuit is filed? [Yes.] *At 596:* A trial court need not reinstate a case in order to exercise its powers under Rule 13."

Farmer v. Ben E. Keith Co., 907 S.W.2d 495, 496 (Tex.1995). "When a judgment is interlocutory because unadjudicated parties or claims remain before the court, and when one moves to have such unadjudicated claims or parties removed by severance, dismissal, or nonsuit, the appellate timetable runs from the signing of a judgment or order disposing of those claims or parties. The appellate timetable *does not* commence to run other than by signed, written order, even when the signing of such an order is purely ministerial."

Hyundai Motor Co. v. Alvarado, 892 S.W.2d 853, 854-55 (Tex.1995). "In Texas, our general rule is that plaintiffs have the right to take a nonsuit at any time until they introduce all evidence other than rebuttal evidence. Such a nonsuit may have the effect of vitiating earlier interlocutory orders. A decision on the merits, such as a summary judgment, however, is not vitiated. This includes partial summary judgments."

Ex parte Brown, 382 S.W.2d 97, 98-99 (Tex.1964). "We agree with relators that the non-suit in the original divorce action did not deprive the Moore Court of power to make temporary orders for the protection of the interests of the child. Article V, Section 8, of the Texas Constitution ... confers upon the District Court original jurisdiction and general control over minors under such regulations as may be prescribed by law. 'While it has been held that a court may not take jurisdiction to adjudicate the custody of a minor on its own motion, it has also been held that a child becomes a ward of the court when it is brought before the court for any purpose. One cannot invoke the jurisdiction of the court to deal with the personal status or the person of a child and at the same time deny the power of the court, in that proceeding, to do with the child's person or his status whatever appears to the court to be for the best interest of the child.'"

Benavides v. Garcia, 687 S.W.2d 397, 398 (Tex. App.—San Antonio 1985, no writ). "On a timely motion, the plaintiff has an absolute unqualified right to take a non-suit before presentment of all plaintiff's evidence as long as the defendant has not already made a claim for affirmative relief. ... No specific procedures are required under [TRCP] 164. The mere filing of the motion with the clerk or an oral announcement in open court are sufficient. [¶] The defendant may defeat a plaintiff's right to discontinue the entire proceeding when the defendant seeks affirmative relief. However, he must do more than pray for affirmative relief. He must allege facts which show he has a cause of action, independent of the plaintiff's claim, on which he might recover even if the plaintiff abandons or fails to establish his cause of action."

TRCP 163. DISMISSAL AS TO PARTIES SERVED, ETC.

When it will not prejudice another party, the plaintiff may dismiss his suit as to one or more of several parties who were served with process, or who have answered, but no such dismissal shall in any case, be allowed as to a principal obligor, except in the cases provided for by statute.

See also *O'Connor's Texas Rules*, "Voluntary Dismissal—Nonsuit," ch. 7-E.

Texas Cab Co. v. Giles, 783 S.W.2d 695, 697 (Tex. App.—El Paso 1989, no writ). "Unless the settlement with the deleted defendant was properly presented to the trial court, there generally could have been no dismissal to that defendant under [TRCP] 162 or 163, as the dismissal would have prejudiced the codefendant...."

TRCP 164. REPEALED

TRCP 165. ABANDONMENT

A party who abandons any part of his claim or defense, as contained in the pleadings, may have that fact entered of record, so as to show that the matters therein were not tried.

See also *O'Connor's Texas Rules*, "Motion for Summary Judgment," ch. 7-B.

In re Shaw, 966 S.W.2d 174, 177 (Tex.App.—El Paso 1998, no pet.). "Whether a pleading has been abandoned is a question of law which we review de novo. Formal amendment of the pleadings is not required in order to show abandonment. Indeed, a stipulation may form the basis for abandonment."

In re R.G., 865 S.W.2d 504, 508 (Tex.App.—Corpus Christi 1993, no writ). TRCP 165 "permits the abandonment of claims; however, the rule has been interpreted to require abandonment '*before* but not *after* trial of the cause and entry of the judgment.' This is the same requirement as for the non-suit."

TRCP 165a. DISMISSAL FOR WANT OF PROSECUTION

1. Failure to Appear. A case may be dismissed for want of prosecution on failure of any party seeking affirmative relief to appear for any hearing or trial of which the party had notice. Notice of the court's intention to dismiss and the date and place of the dismissal hearing shall be sent by the clerk to each attorney of record, and to each party not represented by an attorney and whose address is shown on the docket or in the papers on file, by posting same in the United States Postal Service. At the dismissal hearing, the court shall dismiss for want of prosecution unless there is good cause for the case to be maintained on the docket. If the court determines to maintain the case on the docket, it shall render a pretrial order assigning a trial date for the case and setting deadlines for the joining of new parties, all discovery, filing of all pleadings, the making of a response or supplemental responses to discovery and other pretrial matters. The case may be continued thereafter only for valid and compelling reasons specifically determined by court order. Notice of the signing of the order of dismissal shall be given as provided in Rule 306a. Failure to mail notices as required by this rule shall not affect any of the periods mentioned in Rule 306a except as provided in that rule.

2. Non-Compliance With Time Standards. Any case not disposed of within time standards promulgated by the Supreme Court under its Administrative Rules may be placed on a dismissal docket.

3. Reinstatement. A motion to reinstate shall set forth the grounds therefor and be verified by the movant or his attorney. It shall be filed with the clerk within 30 days after the order of dismissal is signed or within the period provided by Rule 306a. A copy of the motion to reinstate shall be served on each attorney of record and each party not represented by an attorney whose address is shown on the docket or in the papers on file. The clerk shall deliver a copy of the motion to the judge, who shall set a hearing on the motion as soon as practicable. The court shall notify all parties or their attorneys of record of the date, time and place of the hearing.

The court shall reinstate the case upon finding after a hearing that the failure of the party or his attorney was not intentional or the result of conscious indifference but was due to an accident or mistake or that the failure has been otherwise reasonably explained.

In the event for any reason a motion for reinstatement is not decided by signed written order within seventy-five days after the judgment is signed, or, within such other time as may be allowed by Rule 306a, the motion shall be deemed overruled by operation of law. If a motion to reinstate is timely filed by any party, the trial court, regardless of whether an appeal has been perfected, has plenary power to reinstate the case until 30 days after all such timely filed motions are overruled, either by a written and signed order or by operation of law, whichever occurs first.

4. Cumulative Remedies. This dismissal and reinstatement procedure shall be cumulative of the rules and laws governing any other procedures available to the parties in such cases. The same reinstatement procedures and timetable are applicable to all dismissals for want of prosecution including cases which are dismissed pursuant to the court's inherent power, whether or not a motion to dismiss has been filed.

See also ***O'Connor's Texas Rules***, "Notice of Intent to Dismiss," ch. 7-F, §3; "Motion to Reinstate after DWOP," ch. 10-F; ***O'Connor's Texas Forms***, FORM 7F:01.

Villarreal v. San Antonio Truck & Equip., 994 S.W.2d 628, 630 (Tex.1999). "The trial court's authority to dismiss for want of prosecution stems from two sources: (1) [TRCP] 165a ... and (2) the court's inherent power. [¶] [A] party must be provided with notice and an opportunity to be heard before a court may dismiss a case for want of prosecution under either Rule 165a or its inherent authority. The failure to provide adequate notice of the trial court's intent to dismiss for want of prosecution requires reversal."

Smith v. Babcock & Wilcox Constr. Co., 913 S.W.2d 467, 468 (Tex.1995). "The operative standard [to reinstate after dismissal for want of prosecution] is essentially the same as that for setting aside a default judgment. A failure to appear is not intentional or due to conscious indifference within the meaning of the rule merely because it is deliberate; it must also be without adequate justification. Proof of such justification—accident, mistake or other reasonable explanation—negates the intent or conscious indifference for which reinstatement can be denied. Also, conscious indifference means more than mere negligence."

Thordson v. City of Houston, 815 S.W.2d 550, 550 (Tex.1991). Under the language in TRCP 165a(4), "it was not within the discretion of the trial court to fail to hold an oral hearing on the motion to reinstate."

McConnell v. May, 800 S.W.2d 194, 194 (Tex. 1990). "A proper motion to reinstate must be verified and filed with the clerk within 30 days of the signing of the order of dismissal. Since [the P] did not file a verified motion to reinstate within 30 days of the signing of the order of dismissal, the trial court's jurisdiction to reinstate the case expired."

In re Wal-Mart Stores, Inc., 20 S.W.3d 734, 740 (Tex.App.—El Paso 2000, orig. proceeding). "Rule 165a(3) requires that a case be reinstated by signed written order.... An oral pronouncement by the court reinstating the case, even when accompanied by a docket entry, is ordinarily inadequate to reinstate the case."

Burton v. Hoffman, 959 S.W.2d 351, 353 (Tex. App.—Austin 1998, no pet.). Under TRCP 165a "a trial court may dismiss a case for failure to appear at trial or a hearing, and the clerk is required to send notice of the court's intention to dismiss and the date and the place of the dismissal hearing to the attorney of record."

Texas DPS v. Deck, 954 S.W.2d 108, 111 (Tex. App.—San Antonio 1997, no writ). "[A] court, on its own, can reinstate a case after dismissal."

SECTION 8. PRETRIAL PROCEDURE

TRCP 166. PRETRIAL CONFERENCE

In an appropriate action, to assist in the disposition of the case without undue expense or burden to the parties, the court may in its discretion direct the attorneys for the parties and the parties or their duly authorized agents to appear before it for a conference to consider:

(a) All pending dilatory pleas, motions and exceptions;

(b) The necessity or desirability of amendments to the pleadings;

(c) A discovery schedule;

(d) Requiring written statements of the parties' contentions;

(e) Contested issues of fact and simplification of the issues;

(f) The possibility of obtaining stipulations of fact;

(g) The identification of legal matters to be ruled on or decided by the court;

(h) The exchange of a list of direct fact witnesses, other than rebuttal or impeaching witnesses the necessity of whose testimony cannot reasonably be anticipated before the time of trial, who will be called to testify at trial, stating their address and telephone number, and the subject of the testimony of each such witness;

(i) The exchange of a list of expert witnesses who will be called to testify at trial, stating their address and telephone number, and the subject of the testimony and opinions that will be proffered by each expert witness;

(j) Agreed applicable propositions of law and contested issues of law;

(k) Proposed jury charge questions, instructions, and definitions for a jury case or proposed findings of fact and conclusions of law for a nonjury case;

(*l*) The marking and exchanging of all exhibits that any party may use at trial and stipulation to the authenticity and admissibility of exhibits to be used at trial;

(m) Written trial objections to the opposite party's exhibits, stating the basis for each objection;

(n) The advisability of a preliminary reference of issues to a master or auditor for findings to be used as evidence when the trial is to be by jury;

(o) The settlement of the case, and to aid such consideration, the court may encourage settlement;

(p) Such other matters as may aid in the disposition of the action.

The court shall make an order that recites the action taken at the pretrial conference, the amendments allowed to the pleadings, the time within which same may be filed, and the agreements made by the parties as to any of the matters considered, and which limits the issues for trial to those not disposed of by admissions, agreements of counsel, or rulings of the court; and such order when issued shall control the subsequent course of the action, unless modified at the trial to prevent manifest injustice. The court in its discretion may establish by rule a pretrial calendar on which actions may be placed for consideration as above provided and may either confine the calendar to jury actions or extend it to all actions.

See also Govt Code §21.001(a); TRCP 248; *O'Connor's Texas Rules*, "The Pretrial Conference," ch. 5-A; *O'Connor's Texas Forms*, FORM 5A:01.

Koslow's v. Mackie, 796 S.W.2d 700, 703 (Tex. 1990). TRCP 166 "includes the power to order the parties through their attorneys (or through themselves if appearing pro se) to confer to narrow the issues for the written pretrial conference report."

Provident Life & Acc. Ins. Co. v. Hazlitt, 216 S.W.2d 805, 807 (Tex.1949). "The purpose of [TRCP 166] is to simplify and shorten the trial.... [N]o controverted issues of fact could be adjudicated at [the pretrial] conference, but orders could be entered disposing of issues which are founded upon admitted or undisputed facts."

In re Bledsoe, 41 S.W.3d 807, 812 (Tex.App.—Fort Worth 2001, orig. proceeding). "Rule 166 of the [TRCPs] permits trial courts to hold pretrial conferences and to enter orders establishing the agreements of the parties as to any of the matters considered, which control the subsequent course of the case up to trial. The trial court has power, implicit under rule 166, to sanction a party for failing to obey its pretrial orders."

Lindley v. Johnson, 936 S.W.2d 53, 55 (Tex.App.—Tyler 1996, writ denied). "When a trial court's pretrial scheduling order changes the deadlines set forth in a procedural rule, the trial court's order prevails."

Masterson v. Cox, 886 S.W.2d 436, 439 (Tex.App.—Houston [1st Dist.] 1994, no writ). There is "no rule or caselaw that authorizes the trial court to hear evidence of both liability and unliquidated damages in a pretrial conference and to dispose of a case on the merits...."

TRCP 166a. SUMMARY JUDGMENT

(a) For Claimant. A party seeking to recover upon a claim, counterclaim, or cross-claim or to obtain a declaratory judgment may, at any time after the adverse party has appeared or answered, move with or without supporting affidavits for a summary judgment in his favor upon all or any part thereof. A summary judgment, interlocutory in character, may be rendered on the issue of liability alone although there is a genuine issue as to amount of damages.

(b) For Defending Party. A party against whom a claim, counterclaim, or cross-claim is asserted or a declaratory judgment is sought may, at any time, move with or without supporting affidavits for a summary judgment in his favor as to all or any part thereof.

(c) Motion and Proceedings Thereon. The motion for summary judgment shall state the specific grounds therefor. Except on leave of court, with notice to opposing counsel, the motion and any supporting affidavits shall be filed and served at least twenty-one days before the time specified for hearing. Except on leave of court, the adverse party, not later than seven days prior to the day of hearing may file and serve opposing affidavits or other written response. No oral testimony shall be received at the hearing. The judgment sought shall be rendered forthwith if (i) the deposition transcripts, interrogatory answers, and other discovery responses referenced or set forth in the motion or response, and (ii) the pleadings, admissions, affidavits, stipulations of the parties, and authenticated or certified public records, if any, on file at the time of the hearing, or filed thereafter and before judgment with permission of the court, show that, except as to the amount of damages, there is no genuine issue as to any material fact and the moving party is entitled to judgment as a matter of law on the issues expressly set out in the motion or in an answer or any other response. Issues not expressly presented to the trial court by written motion, answer or other response shall not be considered on appeal as grounds for reversal. A summary judgment may be based on uncontroverted testimonial evidence of an interested witness, or of an expert witness as to subject matter concerning which the trier of fact must be guided solely by the opinion testimony of experts, if the evidence is clear, positive and direct, otherwise credible and free from contradictions and inconsistencies, and could have been readily controverted.

(d) Appendices, References and Other Use of Discovery Not Otherwise on File. Discovery products not on file with the clerk may be used as summary judgment evidence if copies of the material, appendices containing the evidence, or a notice containing specific references to the discovery or specific references to other instruments, are filed and served on all parties together with a statement of intent to use the specified discovery as summary judgment proofs: (i) at least twenty-one days before the hearing if such proofs are to be used to support the summary judgment; or (ii) at least seven days before the hearing if such proofs are to be used to oppose the summary judgment.

(e) Case Not Fully Adjudicated on Motion. If summary judgment is not rendered upon the whole case or for all the relief asked and a trial is necessary, the judge may at the hearing examine the pleadings and the evidence on file, interrogate counsel, ascertain what material fact issues exist and make an order specifying the facts that are established as a matter of law, and directing such further proceedings in the action as are just.

(f) Form of Affidavits; Further Testimony. Supporting and opposing affidavits shall be made on personal knowledge, shall set forth such facts as would be admissible in evidence, and shall show affirmatively that the affiant is competent to testify to the matters stated therein. Sworn or certified copies of all papers or parts thereof referred to in an affidavit shall be attached thereto or served therewith. The court may permit affidavits to be supplemented or opposed by depositions or by further affidavits. Defects in the form of affidavits or attachments will not be grounds for reversal unless specifically pointed out by objection by an opposing party with opportunity, but refusal, to amend.

(g) When Affidavits Are Unavailable. Should it appear from the affidavits of a party opposing the motion that he cannot for reasons stated present by affidavit facts essential to justify his opposition, the court may refuse the application for judgment or may order a continuance to permit affidavits to be obtained or depositions to be taken or discovery to be had or may make such other order as is just.

(h) Affidavits Made in Bad Faith. Should it appear to the satisfaction of the court at any time that any of the affidavits presented pursuant to this rule are presented in bad faith or solely for the purpose of delay, the court shall forthwith order the party employing them to pay to the other party the amount of the reasonable expenses which the filing of the affidavits caused him to incur, including reasonable attorney's fees, and any offending party or attorney may be adjudged guilty of contempt.

(i) No-Evidence Motion. After adequate time for discovery, a party without presenting summary judgment evidence may move for summary judgment on the ground that there is no evidence of one or more essential elements of a claim or defense on which an adverse party would have the burden of proof at trial. The motion must state the elements as to which there is no evidence. The court must grant the motion unless the respondent produces summary judgment evidence raising a genuine issue of material fact.

By Texas Supreme Court Order dated Aug. 15, 1997, the amendments to TRCP 166a(e) & (i) take effect September 1, 1997, and apply to all motions for summary judgment filed on or after that date. Unlike other notes and comments in the TRCP, the Notes & Comments to TRCP 166a(i), below, is intended to inform the construction and application of the rule.

Notes & Comments to TRCP 166a(i): This comment is intended to inform the construction and application of the rule. Paragraph (i) authorizes a motion for summary judgment based on the assertion that, after adequate opportunity for discovery, there is no evidence to support one or more specified elements of an adverse party's claim or defense. A discovery period set by pretrial order should be adequate opportunity for discovery unless there is a showing to the contrary, and ordinarily a motion under paragraph (i) would be permitted after the period but not before. The motion must be specific in challenging the evidentiary support for an element of a claim or defense; paragraph (i) does not authorize conclusory motions or general no-evidence challenges to an opponent's case. Paragraph (i) does not apply to ordinary motions for summary judgment under paragraphs (a) or (b), in which the movant must prove it is entitled to judgment by establishing each element of its own claim or defense as a matter of law. To defeat a motion made under paragraph (i), the respondent is not required to marshal its proof; its response need only point out evidence that raises a fact issue on the challenged elements. The existing rules continue to govern the general requirements of summary judgment practice. A motion under paragraph (i) is subject to sanctions provided by existing law (CPRC §§9.001-10.006) and rules (TRCP 13). The denial of a motion under paragraph (i) is no more reviewable by appeal or mandamus than the denial of a motion under paragraph (c).

See also *O'Connor's Texas Rules*, "Rules of Pleading," ch. 1-B; "Rules for Filing Documents," ch. 1-C; "Motion for Continuance," ch. 5-D; "Interrogatories," ch. 6-F; "Requests for Admissions," ch. 6-G; "Motion for Summary Judgment," ch. 7-B; *O'Connor's Texas Forms*, FORMS 7B.

SJ Notice & Hearing

Martin v. Martin, Martin & Richards, Inc., 989 S.W.2d 357, 359 (Tex.1998). "An oral hearing on a motion for summary judgment may be helpful ... just as oral argument is often helpful on appeal, but since oral testimony cannot be adduced in support of or opposition to a motion for summary judgment, an oral hearing is not mandatory. Notice of hearing or submission of a summary judgment motion, however, is required, although as the court of appeals said, it is not 'jurisdictional'. The hearing date determines the time for response to the motion; without notice of hearing, the respondent cannot know when the response is due."

Traditional SJ

Huckabee v. Time Warner Entm't Co., 19 S.W.3d 413, 421-22 (Tex.2000). "Requiring the trial court to determine at the summary judgment stage whether a reasonable juror could find the evidence to be clear and convincing suggests that the trial court must weigh the evidence. Texas law has always emphasized that trial courts must not weigh the evidence at the summary judgment stage. [A] trial court's only duty at the summary judgment stage is to determine if a material question of fact exists."

Park Place Hosp. v. Estate of Milo, 909 S.W.2d 508, 510 (Tex.1995). For defendants "to prevail, they were required to prove that there was no genuine issue as to any material fact and that they were entitled to judgment as a matter of law. In reviewing a summary judgment, we must accept as true evidence favoring the nonmovant, indulging every reasonable inference and resolving all doubts in the nonmovant's favor."

Cathey v. Booth, 900 S.W.2d 339, 341 (Tex.1995). "A defendant who conclusively negates at least one of the essential elements of each of the plaintiff's causes of action or who conclusively establishes all of the elements of an affirmative defense is entitled to summary judgment."

Medlock v. Commission for Lawyer Discipline, 24 S.W.3d 865, 870 (Tex.App.—Texarkana 2000, no pet.). "The trial court may not grant a summary judgment motion by default for lack of an answer or response by the nonmovant when the summary judgment proof is legally insufficient. The nonmovant is not required to file a response to defeat a motion for summary judgment if deficiencies in the movant's own proof or legal theories defeat its right to judgment as a matter of law. However, if the respondent fails to file a response, the only ground for reversal she may raise on appeal is the legal insufficiency of the movant's summary judgment motion or proof."

No-Evidence SJ

Michael v. Dyke, 41 S.W.3d 746, 751 (Tex.App.—Corpus Christi 2001, no pet.). "When it is not readily apparent to the trial court that summary judgment is sought under rule 166a(i), the court should presume that it is filed under the traditional summary judgment rule and analyze it according to those well-recognized standards. [The] order granting summary judgment should clarify whether the motion is granted on no-evidence grounds or traditional grounds. When an order fails to so clarify, a motion requesting such clarification should be filed with the trial court."

Specialty Retailers, Inc. v. Fuqua, 29 S.W.3d 140, 145 (Tex.App.—Houston [14th Dist.] 2000, pet. denied). TRCP 166a(i) "does not require that discovery must have been completed, only that there was 'adequate time.'"

Harrill v. A.J.'s Wrecker Serv., Inc., 27 S.W.3d 191, 193 (Tex.App.—Dallas 2000, pet. dism'd). "A no-evidence motion places the burden on the nonmovant to present evidence raising a genuine fact issue on the challenged elements. If the nonmovant is unable to produce summary judgment evidence raising a genuine issue of material fact on the challenged elements, the trial court must grant the motion."

Grant v. Southwestern Elec. Power Co., 20 S.W.3d 764, 768 (Tex.App.—Texarkana 2000), *rev'd on other grounds*, ___ S.W.3d ___ (Tex.2002) (No. 00-0625; 3-28-02). Defendant's "motion contained both a no-evidence summary judgment motion ... and an ordinary summary judgment motion.... The rules do not prohibit such a hybrid motion, but the better practice is either to file two separate motions ... or to file one document containing both motions but with the arguments and authorities for each clearly delineated and separate from one another."

Aguirre v. South Tex. Blood & Tissue Ctr., 2 S.W.3d 454, 456 (Tex.App.—San Antonio 1999, pet. denied). "A no-evidence summary judgment is the functional equivalent of a pretrial directed verdict...."

Saenz v. Southern Un. Gas Co., 999 S.W.2d 490, 493-94 (Tex.App.—El Paso 1999, pet. denied). "To marshal one's evidence is to arrange *all of the evidence* in the order that it will be presented at trial. A party is not required to present or arrange all of its evidence in response to a summary judgment motion."

Denton v. Big Spring Hosp. Corp., 998 S.W.2d 294, 298 (Tex.App.—Eastland 1999, no pet.). "The motion must specifically state the elements for which there is no evidence. ... The rule requires a motion to be specific in alleging a lack of evidence on an essential element of a plaintiff's cause of action, but it does not require that the motion specifically attack the evidentiary components that may prove an element of the cause of action."

SJ Evidence

Morgan v. Anthony, 27 S.W.3d 928, 929 (Tex. 2000). "The summary judgment evidence includes excerpts from two depositions of [P] and her answer to an interrogatory. Generally, a party cannot rely on its own answer to an interrogatory as summary judgment evidence. However, [P] was questioned in one of her depositions about her seven-page interrogatory answer ... and the interrogatory answer was attached to her deposition as an exhibit. ... The excerpts from her deposition about the interrogatory answer and the interrogatory answer itself were part of the summary judgment record. The interrogatory answer became competent summary judgment evidence when it became a deposition exhibit, [P] affirmed in her deposition that it was correct, and she was subject to cross-examination about the assertions in her interrogatory answer."

Wadewitz v. Montgomery, 951 S.W.2d 464, 466 (Tex.1997). "An expert's testimony will support summary judgment only if it is 'clear, positive and direct, otherwise credible and free from contradictions and inconsistencies, and could have been readily controverted.' Conclusory statements by an expert are insufficient to support or defeat summary judgment."

Trico Tech. Corp. v. Montiel, 949 S.W.2d 308, 310 (Tex.1997). "The mere fact that the affidavit is self-serving does not necessarily make the evidence an improper basis for summary judgment. Summary judgment based on the uncontroverted affidavit of an interested witness is proper if the evidence is clear, positive, direct, otherwise credible, free from contradictions and inconsistencies, and could have been readily controverted. 'Could have been readily controverted' does not mean that the summary judgment evidence could have been easily and conveniently rebutted, but rather indicates that the testimony could have been effectively countered by opposing evidence."

United Blood Servs. v. Longoria, 938 S.W.2d 29, 30 (Tex.1997). "When a party relies on expert testimony, this requirement includes proof of the expert's qualifications. [¶] Whether a witness is qualified to offer expert testimony is a matter committed to the trial court's discretion."

Benchmark Bank v. Crowder, 919 S.W.2d 657, 663 (Tex.1996). Accountant's "testimony is not part of the summary judgment record. [His] affidavit was filed 2 days before the summary judgment hearing. Summary judgment evidence may be filed late, but only with leave of court. There is no order in this record granting the [Ps] leave to file [the] affidavit late."

Wilson v. Burford, 904 S.W.2d 628, 629 (Tex.1995). "Defendants moved for summary judgment [but their] motion did not incorporate or refer to any specific summary judgment evidence. However, an accompanying brief referred to a deposition attached to the brief. [¶] The deposition transcript ... was ... proper summary judgment evidence on which both the [D] and the [P] could rely...."

McConathy v. McConathy, 869 S.W.2d 341, 341 (Tex.1994). "[D]eposition excerpts [and other discovery] submitted as summary judgment evidence need not be authenticated. *At 342:* All parties have ready access to depositions taken in a cause, and thus deposition excerpts submitted with a motion for summary judgment may be easily verified as to their accuracy."

Casso v. Brand, 776 S.W.2d 551, 558 (Tex.1989). "If the credibility of the affiant ... is likely to be a dispositive factor in the resolution of the case, then summary judgment is inappropriate. On the other hand, if the non-movant must, in all likelihood, come forth with independent evidence to prevail, then summary judgment may well be proper in the absence of such controverting proof."

Brewer & Pritchard, P.C. v. Johnson, 7 S.W.3d 862, 869 (Tex.App.—Houston [1st Dist.] 1999), *aff'd*, ___ S.W.3d ___ (Tex.2002) (No. 00-0081; 3-21-02). "[A]lthough it is true that [P] globally stated facts to support its conclusions as it sees them and cited to the record in support of those facts, it made no effort to connect any of the facts to the challenged elements of the causes of action. We believe rule 166a(i) requires the non-movant to make that connection."

Watts v. Hermann Hosp., 962 S.W.2d 102, 105 (Tex.App.—Houston [1st Dist.] 1997, no pet.). "Without a proper objection, defects in the authentication of attachments in support of a motion for summary judgment or response are waived."

Final vs. Partial SJ

McNally v. Guevara, 52 S.W.3d 195, 196 (Tex. 2001). "[A] party's omission of one of his claims from a motion for summary judgment does not waive the claim because a party can always move for partial summary judgment, and thus there can be no presumption that a motion for summary judgment addresses all of the movant's claims. Nothing in the trial court's judgment, other than its award of costs to the defendants, suggests that it intended to deny the defendants' claim for attorney fees. The award of costs, by itself, does not make the judgment final."

Lehmann v. Har-Con Corp., 39 S.W.3d 191, 192-93 (Tex.2001). "We no longer believe that a Mother Hubbard clause in an order or in a judgment issued without a full trial can be taken to indicate finality. We therefore hold that in cases in which only one final and appealable judgment can be rendered, a judgment issued without a conventional trial is final for purposes of appeal if and only if either it actually disposes of all claims and parties then before the court, regardless of its language, or it states with unmistakable clarity that it is a final judgment as to all claims and all parties."

Newco Drilling Co. v. Weyand, 960 S.W.2d 654, 656 (Tex.1998). "[A] plaintiff cannot avoid the effects of a partial summary judgment by subsequently filing a nonsuit, and any issues decided in the partial summary judgment are dismissed with prejudice. [A] plaintiff, who after suffering an adverse summary judgment allows his claims to be dismissed for want of prosecution, should likewise be barred from having a second bite at the apple."

Page v. Geller, 941 S.W.2d 101, 102 (Tex.1997). "[W]hen a trial court grants more relief than requested and, therefore makes an otherwise partial summary judgment final, that judgment, although erroneous, is final, and it is appealable. On appeal, the court of appeals must treat the judgment as any other final judgment. It is to consider all matters raised on appeal and reverse only those portions of the judgment that were rendered in error."

Cincinnati Life Ins. Co. v. Cates, 927 S.W.2d 623, 625 (Tex.1996). "Under [TRCP] 166a, a trial court cannot grant summary judgment for a reason that the movant does not present to the trial court in writing. [R]ule 166a does not prevent an appellate court from affirming the judgment on other grounds the parties properly raised before the trial court, when the trial court grants summary judgment specifically on fewer than all grounds asserted. Rather, our rules of appellate procedure give appellate courts the authority, when reviewing judgments of lower courts, to render the judgment or decree that the court below should have rendered."

Pleadings in SJ Cases

Sosa v. Central Power & Light, 909 S.W.2d 893, 895 (Tex.1995). "Because the [Ps] timely filed their second amended original petition, it superseded their first amended original petition containing the statements on which the defendants based their motion for summary judgment. Contrary to statements in live pleadings, those contained in superseded pleadings are not conclusive and indisputable judicial admissions. Therefore, the basis for the defendants' motion no longer existed and summary judgment was improper."

Laidlaw Waste Sys., Inc. v. City of Wilmer, 904 S.W.2d 656, 660 (Tex.1995). "Generally, pleadings are not competent evidence, even if sworn or verified."

Natividad v. Alexsis, Inc., 875 S.W.2d 695, 699 (Tex.1994). "A review of the pleadings [when a summary judgment is based on the pleadings] is *de novo*, with the reviewing court taking all allegations, facts, and inferences in the pleadings as true and viewing them in a light most favorable to the pleader. The reviewing court will affirm the summary judgment only if the pleadings are legally insufficient."

In re B.I.V., 870 S.W.2d 12, 13 (Tex.1994). "A summary judgment should not be based on a pleading deficiency that could be cured by amendment."

Motion for Continuance

Tenneco, Inc. v. Enterprise Prods. Co., 925 S.W.2d 640, 647 (Tex.1996). "When a party contends that it has not had an adequate opportunity for discovery before a summary judgment hearing, it must file either an affidavit explaining the need for further discovery or a verified motion for continuance. [¶] The determination to allow the Enterprise Parties more time for discovery was within the trial court's discretion."

TRCP 166b - 170. REPEALED

TRCP 171. MASTER IN CHANCERY

The court may, in exceptional cases, for good cause appoint a master in chancery, who shall be a citizen of this State, and not an attorney for either party to the action, nor related to either party, who shall perform all of the duties required of him by the court, and shall be under orders of the court, and have such power as the master of chancery has in a court of equity.

The order of reference to the master may specify or limit his powers, and may direct him to report only upon particular issues, or to do or perform particular acts, or to receive and report evidence only and may fix the time and place for beginning and closing the hearings, and for the filing of the master's report. Subject to the limitations and specifications stated in the order, the master has and shall exercise the power to regulate all proceedings in every hearing before him and to do all acts and take all measures necessary or proper for the efficient performance of his duties under the order. He may require the production before him of evidence upon all matters embraced in the reference, including the production of books, papers, vouchers, documents and other writings applicable thereto. He may rule upon the admissibility of evidence, unless otherwise directed by the order of reference and has the authority to put witnesses on oath, and may, himself, examine them, and may call the parties to the action and examine them upon oath. When a party so requests, the master shall make a record of the evidence offered and excluded in the same manner as provided for a court sitting in the trial of a case.

The clerk of the court shall forthwith furnish the master with a copy of the order of reference.

The parties may procure the attendance of witnesses before the master by the issuance and service of process as provided by law and these rules.

The court may confirm, modify, correct, reject, reverse or recommit the report, after it is filed, as the court may deem proper and necessary in the particular circumstances of the case. The court shall award reasonable compensation to such master to be taxed as costs of suit.

See also *O'Connor's Texas Rules*, "Master in Chancery," ch. 1-J.

Academy of Model Aeronautics, Inc. v. Packer, 860 S.W.2d 419, 419 (Tex.1993). "[T]he trial court abused its discretion in entering an order referring all pending and future discovery matters to a master."

Republic Ins. Co. v. Davis, 856 S.W.2d 158, 160 (Tex.1993). "Republic did not have the opportunity to object [to the master's report before the trial court adopted it]. Consequently, without reaching the question of whether an objection is required, we conclude that Republic has not waived error…."

Simpson v. Canales, 806 S.W.2d 802, 811 (Tex. 1991). TRCP 171 "permits appointment of a master only 'in exceptional cases, for good cause'. [T]his requirement cannot be met merely by showing that a case is complicated or time-consuming, or that the court is busy."

Mann v. Mann, 607 S.W.2d 243, 246 (Tex.1980). "The Master conducted lengthy hearings which included hearing evidence and inspecting the books and inventory of the salvage warehouse. The records and the unique nature of the salvage business were such that the Master had great difficulty in valuing the community property assets of the business. In addition, and because of the complex nature of the property involved in the divorce proceeding, the trial court appointed an auditor and a receiver. [¶] [A] trial court should be free to exercise its discretion in the appointments of a master and should be reversed only where there is a clear abuse of this discretion. [¶] The fact that [wife] had requested a jury trial does not preclude the appointment of a Master. Either party is entitled to a jury trial after a Master has filed his report. The present case involved numerous complex issues which involved the valuation of many types of dissimilar inventory having no regular market value. It was to the advantage and in the interest of all parties, including [husband], to have a complete accounting of all the community and separate property assets of the parties."

AIU Ins. Co. v. Mehaffy, 942 S.W.2d 796, 803 (Tex. App.—Beaumont 1997, orig. proceeding). "The cases construing [TRCP] 171 provide that if a party timely and formally objects to a master's ruling, that party is entitled to a de novo hearing before a judge or jury. We conclude this right is automatic and not subject to a harmless error analysis."

TRCP 172. AUDIT

When an investigation of accounts or examination of vouchers appears necessary for the purpose of justice between the parties to any suit, the court shall appoint an auditor or auditors to state the accounts between the parties and to make report thereof to the court as soon as possible. The auditor shall verify his report by his affidavit stating that he has carefully examined the state of the account between the parties, and that his report contains a true statement thereof, so far as the same has come within his knowledge. Exceptions to such report or of any item thereof must be filed within 30 days of the filing of such report. The court shall award reasonable compensation to such auditor to be taxed as costs of suit.

See also TRE 706.

AIU Ins. Co. v. Mehaffy, 942 S.W.2d 796, 800-01 (Tex.App.—Beaumont 1997, orig. proceeding). "[T]he order does not state what authority the court relied upon in appointing the auditor. ... Although the word 'auditor' is used, it does not appear [TRCP] 172 was the basis since this was not 'an investigation of accounts or examination of vouchers.'"

Lovelace v. Sabine Consol., Inc., 733 S.W.2d 648, 656 (Tex.App.—Houston [14th Dist.] 1987, writ denied). "The audit report before this court contains no ... affidavit as is required by [TRCP] 172. ... Further, 6 days before trial [P] filed an objection to the audit. Therefore, the trial court did not err in admitting evidence that contradicted and supplemented the auditor's report."

TRCP 173. GUARDIAN AD LITEM

When a minor, lunatic, idiot or a non-compos mentis may be a defendant to a suit and has no guardian within this State, or where such person is a party to a suit either as plaintiff, defendant or intervenor and is represented by a next friend or a guardian who appears to the court to have an interest adverse to such minor, lunatic, idiot or non-compos mentis, the court shall appoint a guardian ad litem for such person and shall allow him a reasonable fee for his services to be taxed as a part of the costs.

Caution: TRCP 173 is affected by the following sections in the Fam. Code: §§2.103, 31.004, 33.003, 33.006, 51.11, 107.001, 107.002, 107.003, 107.006.

See also *O'Connor's Texas Rules*, "Guardian Ad Litem Under TRCP 173," ch. 1-I.

Garcia v. Martinez, 988 S.W.2d 219, 222 (Tex. 1998). "A guardian ad litem is entitled to a reasonable fee for his services to be taxed as a part of the costs. [¶] Generally, trial courts employ the same factors used to determine the reasonableness of attorney's fees to ascertain an appropriate guardian ad litem fee. These factors include: (1) the time and labor required, the novelty and difficulty of the questions involved, and the skill required to perform the legal service properly; (2) the likelihood ... that the acceptance of the particular employment will preclude other employment by the lawyer; (3) the fee customarily charged in the locality for similar legal services; (4) the amount involved and the results obtained; (5) the time limitations imposed by the client or by the circumstances; (6) the nature and length of the professional relationship with the client; (7) the experience, reputation, and ability of the lawyer or lawyers performing the services; and (8) whether the fee is fixed or contingent on results obtained or uncertainty of collection before the legal services have been rendered."

American Gen. Fire & Cas. Co. v. Vandewater, 907 S.W.2d 491, 493 n.2 (Tex.1995). "A guardian ad litem is not an attorney for the child but an officer appointed by the court to assist in properly protecting the child's interests. A guardian ad litem is the personal representative of the minor appointed to protect the interests of the minor in a lawsuit in which the minor is a party. The guardian ad litem is required to participate in the case to the extent necessary to protect the minor."

Brownsville Valley Reg'l Med. Ctr. v. Gamez, 894 S.W.2d 753, 755 (Tex.1995). "The trial court can appoint a guardian ad litem pursuant to [TRCP] 173 only when there is a conflict of interest between the minor and next friend. When the conflict of interest no longer exists, the trial court should remove the guardian ad litem."

Delcourt v. Silverman, 919 S.W.2d 777, 784 (Tex. App.—Houston [14th Dist.] 1996, writ denied). "When an ad litem is appointed under Rule 173, he or she is not acting as an 'arm of the court' or performing functions the court normally performs, because trial courts do not act as advocates. The ad litem appointed under Rule 173 is acting as a personal representative and advocate for the interests of the minor; the fact that he or she was appointed by the court is merely procedural. Therefore, this type of ad litem is not and should not be entitled to absolute immunity."

TRCP 174. CONSOLIDATION; SEPARATE TRIALS

(a) Consolidation. When actions involving a common question of law or fact are pending before the court, it may order a joint hearing or trial of any or all the matters in issue in the actions; it may order all the actions consolidated; and it may make such orders concerning proceedings therein as may tend to avoid unnecessary costs or delay.

(b) Separate Trials. The court in furtherance of convenience or to avoid prejudice may order a separate trial of any claim, cross-claim, counterclaim, or third-party claim, or of any separate issue or of any number of claims, cross-claims, counterclaims, third-party claims, or issues.

See also TRCP 40, 41, 51; ***O'Connor's Texas Rules***, "Motions for Severance & Separate Trials," ch. 5-H; "Joining an Ongoing Lawsuit," ch. 5-I.

In re Ethyl Corp., 975 S.W.2d 606, 611-12 (Tex. 1998). "The maximum number of claims that can be aggregated is not an absolute, and the particular circumstances determine the outer limits beyond which trial courts cannot go. [¶] While considerations of judicial economy are a factor, '[c]onsiderations of convenience and economy must yield to a paramount concern for a fair and impartial trial.'"

Liberty Nat'l Fire Ins. Co. v. Akin, 927 S.W.2d 627, 630 (Tex.1996). "A severance may ... be necessary in some bad faith [and contract] cases. A trial court will ... confront instances in which evidence admissible only on the bad faith claim would prejudice the insurer to such an extent that a fair trial on the contract claim would become unlikely. One example would be when the insurer has made a settlement offer on the disputed contract claim."

Transportation Ins. Co. v. Moriel, 879 S.W.2d 10, 30 (Tex.1994). "[A] trial court, if presented with a timely motion, should bifurcate the determination of the amount of punitive damages from the remaining issues. Under this approach, the jury first hears evidence relevant to liability for actual damages, the amount of actual damages, and liability for punitive damages ... and then returns findings on these issues."

Owens-Corning Fiberglas Corp. v. Martin, 942 S.W.2d 712, 716 (Tex.App.—Dallas 1997, no writ). TRCP 174 "gives the trial court broad discretion to consolidate cases with common issues of law or fact. [¶] In deciding whether to consolidate, the trial court must balance the judicial economy and convenience that may be gained by the consolidation against the risk of an unfair outcome because of prejudice or jury confusion. [¶] Even if the cases share common questions of law and fact, an abuse of discretion may be found if the consolidation results in prejudice to the complaining party."

TRCP 175. ISSUE OF LAW & DILATORY PLEAS

When a case is called for trial in which there has been no pretrial hearing as provided by Rule 166, the issues of law arising on the pleadings, all pleas in abatement and other dilatory pleas remaining undisposed of shall be determined; and it shall be no cause for postponement of a trial of the issues of law that a party is not prepared to try the issues of fact.

Garcia v. TEIA, 622 S.W.2d 626, 630 n.3 (Tex. App.—Amarillo 1981, writ ref'd n.r.e.). "The language of [TRCP] 175 imposes on the party relying upon a dilatory plea a duty to demand action by the court thereon at the time the rule requires action by the court, and his failure to do so is a waiver of the plea."

SECTION 9. EVIDENCE & DISCOVERY

Explanatory Statement Accompanying the 1999 Amendments to the Rules of Civil Procedure Governing Discovery

The rules pertaining to discovery have been substantively revised and reorganized to clarify and streamline discovery procedures and to reduce costs and delays associated with discovery practice. The notes and comments appended to the rules, unlike most other notes and comments in the Rules of Civil Procedure, are intended to inform their construction and application by both courts and practitioners.

Discovery in civil cases is founded on the principle that justice is best served when litigants may obtain information not in their possession to prosecute and defend claims. Discovery provides access to that information, but at a price. Recent years' experience has shown that discovery may be misused to deny justice to parties by driving up the costs of litigation until it is unaffordable and stalling resolution of cases. As any litigant on a budget knows, the benefits to be gained by discovery in a particular case must be weighed against its costs. The rules of procedure must provide both adequate access to information and effective means of curbing discovery when appropriate to preserve litigation as a viable, affordable, and expeditious dispute resolution mechanism.

These revisions recognize the importance of discovery as well as the necessity for reasonable limits. The scope of discovery, always broad, is unchanged. All the forms of discovery under the prior rules are retained, and a new one—disclosure—is added. Disclosure is not required unless requested and thus does not burden cases in which it is not sought. When requested, it provides ready access to basic information without objection. At the same time, the necessity of a discovery control plan in each case, whether by rule or by order, is intended to focus courts and parties on both the need for discovery and its costs in each case. The Level 1 plan allows a party seeking recovery of no more than $50,000 to insist that discovery be minimal. The Level 2 plan will provide adequate discovery in most cases, and Level 3 is available for cases needing special attention. No single set of rules can address so diverse and changing a practice as discovery, and thus the rules maintain the ability of parties by agreement and courts by order to tailor discovery to individual cases.

Presentation of objections and assertions of privilege are streamlined under these rules. A party who objects to only part of a discovery request must usually comply with the rest of the request. Assertions of privilege are not to be made prophylactically against the threat of waiver, but only when information is actually withheld. Documents produced in discovery are now presumed to be authentic for use against the party producing them, thus avoiding the cost of proving authentication when there is no dispute. Procedures for oral depositions are revised to encourage focused examination by imposing time limits and to discourage colloquy between counsel.

An important aspect of these revisions has been the regrouping of provisions in a more logical sequence and the elimination of archaic and confusing language.

A. EVIDENCE

TRCP 176. SUBPOENAS

176.1 Form. Every subpoena must be issued in the name of "The State of Texas" and must:

(a) state the style of the suit and its cause number;

(b) state the court in which the suit is pending;

(c) state the date on which the subpoena is issued;

(d) identify the person to whom the subpoena is directed;

(e) state the time, place, and nature of the action required by the person to whom the subpoena is directed, as provided in Rule 176.2;

(f) identify the party at whose instance the subpoena is issued, and the party's attorney of record, if any;

(g) state the text of Rule 176.8(a); and

(h) be signed by the person issuing the subpoena.

176.2 Required Actions. A subpoena must command the person to whom it is directed to do either or both of the following:

(a) attend and give testimony at a deposition, hearing, or trial;

(b) produce and permit inspection and copying of designated documents or tangible things in the possession, custody, or control of that person.

176.3 Limitations.

(a) ***Range.*** A person may not be required by subpoena to appear or produce documents or other things in a county that is more than 150 miles from where the person resides or is served. However, a person whose appearance or production at a deposition may be compelled by notice alone under Rules 199.3 or 200.2 may be required to appear and produce documents or other things at any location permitted under Rules 199.2(b)(2).

(b) ***Use for discovery.*** A subpoena may not be used for discovery to an extent, in a manner, or at a time other than as provided by the rules governing discovery.

176.4 Who May Issue. A subpoena may be issued by:

(a) the clerk of the appropriate district, county, or justice court, who must provide the party requesting the subpoena with an original and a copy for each witness to be completed by the party;

(b) an attorney authorized to practice in the State of Texas, as an officer of the court; or

(c) an officer authorized to take depositions in this State, who must issue the subpoena immediately on a request accompanied by a notice to take a deposition under Rules 199 or 200, or a notice under Rule 205.3, and who may also serve the notice with the subpoena.

176.5 Service.

(a) ***Manner of service.*** A subpoena may be served at any place within the State of Texas by any sheriff or constable of the State of Texas, or any person who is not a party and is 18 years of age or older. A subpoena must be served by delivering a copy to the witness and tendering to that person any fees required by law. If the witness is a party and is represented by an attorney of record in the proceeding, the subpoena may be served on the witness's attorney of record.

(b) ***Proof of service.*** Proof of service must be made by filing either:

(1) the witness's signed written memorandum attached to the subpoena showing that the witness accepted the subpoena; or

(2) a statement by the person who made the service stating the date, time, and manner of service, and the name of the person served.

176.6 Response.

(a) ***Compliance required.*** Except as provided in this subdivision, a person served with a subpoena must comply with the command stated therein unless discharged by the court or by the party summoning such witness. A person commanded to appear and give testimony must remain at the place of deposition, hearing, or trial from day to day until discharged by the court or by the party summoning the witness.

(b) ***Organizations.*** If a subpoena commanding testimony is directed to a corporation, partnership, association, governmental agency, or other organization, and the matters on which examination is requested are described with reasonable particularity, the organization must designate one or more persons to testify on its behalf as to matters known or reasonably available to the organization.

(c) ***Production of documents or tangible things.*** A person commanded to produce documents or tangible things need not appear in person at the time and place of production unless the person is also commanded to attend and give testimony, either in the same subpoena or a separate one. A person must produce documents as they are kept in the usual course of business or must organize and label them to correspond with the categories in the demand. A person may withhold material or information claimed to be privileged but must comply with Rule 193.3. A nonparty's production of a document authenticates the document for use against the nonparty to the same extent as a party's production of a document is authenticated for use against the party under Rule 193.7.

(d) ***Objections.*** A person commanded to produce and permit inspection or copying of designated documents and things may serve on the party requesting issuance of the subpoena—before the time specified for compliance—written objections to producing any or all of the designated materials. A person need not comply with the part of a subpoena to which objection is made as provided in this paragraph unless ordered to do so by the court. The party requesting the subpoena may move for such an order at any time after an objection is made.

(e) ***Protective orders.*** A person commanded to appear at a deposition, hearing, or trial, or to produce and permit inspection and copying of designated documents and things, and any other person affected by the subpoena, may move for a protective order under Rule 192.6(b)—before the time specified for compliance—either in the court in which the action is pending or in a district court in the county where the subpoena was served. The person must serve the motion on all parties in accordance with Rule 21a. A person need not comply with the part of a subpoena from which protection is sought under this paragraph unless ordered to do so by the court. The party requesting the subpoena may seek such an order at any time after the motion for protection is filed.

(f) ***Trial subpoenas.*** A person commanded to attend and give testimony, or to produce documents or things, at a hearing or trial, may object or move for protective order before the court at the time and place specified for compliance, rather than under paragraphs (d) and (e).

176.7 Protection of Person from Undue Burden and Expense. A party causing a subpoena to issue must take reasonable steps to avoid imposing undue burden or expense on the person served. In ruling on objections or motions for protection, the court must provide a person served with a subpoena an adequate time for compliance, protection from disclosure of privileged material or information, and protection from undue burden or expense. The court may impose reasonable conditions on compliance with a subpoena, including compensating the witness for undue hardship.

176.8 Enforcement of Subpoena.

(a) ***Contempt.*** Failure by any person without adequate excuse to obey a subpoena served upon that person may be deemed a contempt of the court from which the subpoena is issued or a district court in the county in which the subpoena is served, and may be punished by fine or confinement, or both.

(b) ***Proof of payment of fees required for fine or attachment.*** A fine may not be imposed, nor a person served with a subpoena attached, for failure to comply with a subpoena without proof by affidavit of the party requesting the subpoena or the party's attorney of record that all fees due the witness by law were paid or tendered.

Comments to 1999 change:

1. This rule combines the former rules governing subpoenas for trial and discovery. When a subpoena is used for discovery, the protections from undue burden and expense apply, just as with any discovery.

2. Rule 176.3(b) prohibits the use of a subpoena to circumvent the discovery rules. Thus, for example, a deposition subpoena to a party is subject to the procedures of Rules 196, 199, and 200, and a deposition subpoena to a nonparty is subject to the procedures of Rule 205.

See also CPRC §22.001; ***O'Connor's Texas Rules***, "Subpoenas," ch. 1-K; "Depositions," ch. 6-E.

Automatic Drilling Machs., Inc. v. Miller, 515 S.W.2d 256, 259 (Tex.1974). "On motion … the court is authorized by Rule 177a [now TRCP 176.7] to quash or modify the subpoena if it is unreasonable or oppressive or condition denial of the motion on advancement of reasonable costs by the party in whose behalf the subpoena was issued."

St. Luke's Episcopal Hosp. v. Garcia, 928 S.W.2d 307, 310 (Tex.App.—Houston [14th Dist.] 1996, orig. proceeding). "In determining whether a deposition notice or subpoena duces tecum is unreasonable and oppressive, the following factors are relevant: '(1) the quantity of materials subpoenaed, (2) the ease or difficulty of collecting and transporting the materials, (3) the length of time before the deposition, (4) the availability of the information from other sources, and (5) the relevance of the materials.'"

Dr. Pepper Co. v. Davis, 745 S.W.2d 470, 471 (Tex. App.—Austin 1988, orig. proceeding). "The uncontroverted proof is that [the witness] is a resident of Dallas and that the distance between Austin and Dallas is approximately 200 miles. It follows that [the witness] is beyond the subpoena power of the district court of Travis County."

Kieffer v. Miller, 560 S.W.2d 431, 432 (Tex.App.—Beaumont 1977, writ ref'd n.r.e.). "Plaintiffs' motion for a writ of attachment for [the witness] contained no affidavit that 'all lawful fees' had been paid or tendered to [the witness]. This, in and of itself, was adequate grounds for the trial judge to deny plaintiffs' request for a writ of attachment for [the witness]."

TRCP 177-179. REPEALED

TRCP 180. REFUSAL TO TESTIFY

Any witness refusing to give evidence may be committed to jail, there to remain without bail until such witness shall consent to give evidence.

Caution: TRCP 180 is affected by the following sections in the Fam. Code: §§6.704, 6.705.

See also TRCP 176; *O'Connor's Texas Rules*, "Subpoenas," ch. 1-K; "Depositions," ch. 6-E.

TRCP 181. PARTY AS WITNESS

Either party to a suit may examine the opposing party as a witness, and shall have the same process to compel his attendance as in the case of any other witness.

Caution: TRCP 181 is affected by the following sections in the Fam. Code: §§6.704, 104.002 et seq.

See also TRCP 176, 199-201; *O'Connor's Texas Rules*, "Subpoenas," ch. 1-K; "Depositions," ch. 6-E.

TRCP 182 - 182a. REPEALED

TRCP 183. INTERPRETERS

The court may appoint an interpreter of its own selection and may fix the interpreter's reasonable compensation. The compensation shall be paid out of funds provided by law or by one or more of the parties as the court may direct, and may be taxed ultimately as costs, in the discretion of the court.

See also TRCP 200.4; TRE 604; *O'Connor's Texas Rules*, "Depositions," ch. 6-E.

TRCP 184 - 184a. REPEALED

TRCP 185. SUIT ON ACCOUNT

When any action or defense is founded upon an open account or other claim for goods, wares and merchandise, including any claim for a liquidated money demand based upon written contract or founded on business dealings between the parties, or is for personal service rendered, or labor done or labor or materials furnished, on which a systematic record has been kept, and is supported by the affidavit of the party, his agent or attorney taken before some officer authorized to administer oaths, to the effect that such claim is, within the knowledge of affiant, just and true, that it is due, and that all just and lawful offsets, payments and credits have been allowed, the same shall be taken as prima facie evidence thereof, unless the party resisting such claim shall file a written denial, under oath. A party resisting such a sworn claim shall comply with the rules of pleading as are required in any other kind of suit, provided, however, that if he does not timely file a written denial, under oath, he shall not be permitted to deny the claim, or any item therein, as the case may be. No particularization or description of the nature of the component parts of the account or claim is necessary unless the trial court sustains special exceptions to the pleadings.

See also *O'Connor's Texas Rules*, "Plaintiff's Original Petition," ch. 2-B; "The Answer—Denying Liability," ch. 3-E; *O'Connor's Texas Forms*, FORMS 2B, 3E.

Vance v. Holloway, 689 S.W.2d 403, 403-04 (Tex. 1985). "The petition and affidavit filed by [P] clearly met the requirements of [TRCP] 185. [D] answered by way of an unverified general denial only. He failed to meet the requirements of [TRCP] 185 and 93(10) which state that a written denial of the plaintiff's action must be verified. [¶] [D] therefore, waived his right to dispute the amount and ownership of the account."

Rizk v. Financial Guardian Ins. Agency, Inc., 584 S.W.2d 860, 862 (Tex.1979). "In the absence of a sworn denial meeting the requirements of the rule, the account is received as prima facie evidence as against a defendant sued thereon, and the defendant may not dispute the receipt of the items or services, or the correctness of the stated charges...."

Powers v. Adams, 2 S.W.3d 496, 498 (Tex.App.—Houston [14th Dist.] 1999, no pet.). "Under [TRCP 185], a plaintiff's petition on sworn account must contain a systematic, itemized statement of the goods or services sold, reveal offsets made to the account, and be supported by an affidavit stating the claim is within the affiant's knowledge, and that it is 'just and true.'"

Bird v. First Deposit Nat'l Bank, 994 S.W.2d 280, 282 (Tex.App.—El Paso 1999, pet. denied). "We find that a credit card issued by a financial institution does not create the sort of debtor-creditor relationship required in order to bring suit under [TRCP] 185."

Worley v. Butler, 809 S.W.2d 242, 245 (Tex.App.—Corpus Christi 1990, no writ). "To prevail in a cause of action on sworn account, a party must show: (1) that there was a sale and delivery of the merchandise or performance of the services; (2) that the amount of the account is just, that is, that the prices were charged in accordance with an agreement or in the absence of an agreement, they are the usual, customary and reasonable prices for that merchandise or services; and (3) that the amount is unpaid."

B. DISCOVERY

TRCP 186 - 189. REPEALED

TRCP 190. DISCOVERY LIMITATIONS

190.1 **Discovery Control Plan Required.** Every case must be governed by a discovery control plan as provided in this Rule. A plaintiff must allege in the first numbered paragraph of the original petition whether discovery is intended to be conducted under Level 1, 2, or 3 of this Rule.

190.2 **Discovery Control Plan—Suits Involving $50,000 or Less (Level 1).**

(a) ***Application.*** This subdivision applies to:

(1) any suit in which all plaintiffs affirmatively plead that they seek only monetary relief aggregating $50,000 or less, excluding costs, pre-judgment interest and attorneys' fees, and

(2) any suit for divorce not involving children in which a party pleads that the value of the marital estate is more than zero but not more than $50,000.

(b) ***Exceptions.*** This subdivision does not apply if:

(1) the parties agree that Rule 190.3 should apply;

(2) the court orders a discovery control plan under Rule 190.4; or

(3) any party files a pleading or an amended or supplemental pleading that seeks relief other than that to which this subdivision applies.

A pleading, amended pleading (including trial amendment), or supplemental pleading that renders this subdivision no longer applicable may not be filed without leave of court less than 45 days before the date set for trial. Leave may be granted only if good cause for filing the pleading outweighs any prejudice to an opposing party.

(c) ***Limitations.*** Discovery is subject to the limitations provided elsewhere in these rules and to the following additional limitations:

(1) *Discovery period.* All discovery must be conducted during the discovery period, which begins when the suit is filed and continues until 30 days before the date set for trial.

(2) *Total time for oral depositions.* Each party may have no more than six hours in total to examine and cross-examine all witnesses in oral depositions. The parties may agree to expand this limit up to ten hours in total, but not more except by court order. The court may modify the deposition hours so that no party is given unfair advantage.

(3) *Interrogatories.* Any party may serve on any other party no more than 25 written interrogatories, excluding interrogatories asking a party only to identify or authenticate specific documents. Each discrete subpart of an interrogatory is considered a separate interrogatory.

(d) ***Reopening discovery.*** When the filing of a pleading or an amended or supplemental pleading renders this subdivision no longer applicable, the discovery period reopens, and discovery must be completed within the limitations provided in Rules 190.3 or 190.4, whichever is applicable. Any person previously deposed may be redeposed. On motion of any party, the court should continue the trial date if necessary to permit completion of discovery.

190.3 Discovery Control Plan—By Rule (Level 2).

(a) ***Application.*** Unless a suit is governed by a discovery control plan under Rules 190.2 or 190.4, discovery must be conducted in accordance with this subdivision.

(b) ***Limitations.*** Discovery is subject to the limitations provided elsewhere in these rules and to the following additional limitations:

(1) *Discovery period.* All discovery must be conducted during the discovery period, which begins when suit is filed and continues until:

(A) 30 days before the date set for trial, in cases under the Family Code; or

(B) in other cases, the earlier of

(i) 30 days before the date set for trial, or

(ii) nine months after the earlier of the date of the first oral deposition or the due date of the first response to written discovery.

(2) *Total time for oral depositions.* Each side may have no more than 50 hours in oral depositions to examine and cross-examine parties on the opposing side, experts designated by those parties, and persons who are subject to those parties' control. "Side" refers to all the litigants with generally common interests in the litigation. If one side designates more than two experts, the opposing side may have an additional six hours of total deposition time for each additional expert designated. The court may modify the deposition hours and must do so when a side or party would be given unfair advantage.

(3) *Interrogatories.* Any party may serve on any other party no more than 25 written interrogatories, excluding interrogatories asking a party only to identify or authenticate specific documents. Each discrete subpart of an interrogatory is considered a separate interrogatory.

190.4 Discovery Control Plan—By Order (Level 3).

(a) ***Application.*** The court must, on a party's motion, and may, on its own initiative, order that discovery be conducted in accordance with a discovery control plan tailored to the circumstances of the specific suit. The parties may submit an agreed order to the court for its consideration. The court should act on a party's motion or agreed order under this subdivision as promptly as reasonably possible.

(b) ***Limitations.*** The discovery control plan ordered by the court may address any issue concerning discovery or the matters listed in Rule 166, and may change any limitation on the time for or amount of discovery set forth in these rules. The discovery limitations of Rule 190.2, if applicable, or otherwise of Rule 190.3 apply unless specifically changed in the discovery control plan ordered by the court. The plan must include:

(1) a date for trial or for a conference to determine a trial setting;

(2) a discovery period during which either all discovery must be conducted or all discovery requests must be sent, for the entire case or an appropriate phase of it;

(3) appropriate limits on the amount of discovery; and

(4) deadlines for joining additional parties, amending or supplementing pleadings, and designating expert witnesses.

190.5 Modification of Discovery Control Plan. The court may modify a discovery control plan at any time and must do so when the interest of justice requires. The court must allow additional discovery:

(a) related to new, amended or supplemental pleadings, or new information disclosed in a discovery response or in an amended or supplemental response, if:

(1) the pleadings or responses were made after the deadline for completion of discovery or so nearly before that deadline that an adverse party does not have an adequate opportunity to conduct discovery related to the new matters, and

(2) the adverse party would be unfairly prejudiced without such additional discovery;

(b) regarding matters that have changed materially after the discovery cutoff if trial is set or postponed so that the trial date is more than three months after the discovery period ends.

190.6 Certain Types of Discovery Excepted. This rule's limitations on discovery do not apply to or include discovery conducted under Rule 202 ("Depositions Before Suit or to Investigate Claims"), or Rule 621a ("Discovery and Enforcement of Judgment"). But Rule 202 cannot be used to circumvent the limitations of this rule.

Comments to 1999 change:

1. This rule establishes three tiers of discovery plans and requires that every case be in one at all times. A case is in Level 1 if it is pleaded by the plaintiff so as to invoke application of Level 1, as provided by Rule 190.2(a). If a plaintiff does not or cannot plead the case in compliance with Rule 190.2(a) so as to invoke the application of Level 1, the case is automatically in Level 2. A case remains in Level 1 or Level 2, as determined by the pleadings, unless and until it is moved to Level 3. To be in Level 3, the court must order a specific plan for the case, either on a party's motion or on the court's own initiative. The plan may be one agreed to by the parties and submitted as an agreed order. A Level 3 plan may simply adopt Level 1 or Level 2 restrictions. Separate Level 3 plans for phases of the case may be appropriate. The initial pleading required by Rule 190.1 is merely to notify the court and other parties of the plaintiff's intention; it does not determine the applicable discovery level or bind the court or other parties. Thus, a plaintiff's failure to state in the initial pleading that the case should be in Level 1, as provided in Rule 190.1, does not alone make the case subject to Level 2 because the discovery level is determined by Rule 190.2. Likewise, a plaintiff's statement in the initial paragraph of the petition that the case is to be governed by Level 3 does not make Level 3 applicable, as a case can be in Level 3 only by court order. A plaintiff's failure to plead as required by Rule 190.1 is subject to special exception.

2. Rule 190.2 does not apply to suits for injunctive relief or divorces involving children. The requirement of an affirmative pleading of limited relief (*e.g.*: "Plaintiff affirmatively pleads that he seeks only monetary relief aggregating $50,000 or less, excluding costs, pre-judgment interest and attorneys' fees") does not conflict with other pleading requirements, such as Rule 47 and Tex. Rev. Civ. Stat. Ann. art. 4590i, §5.01. In a suit to which Rule 190.2 applies, the relief awarded cannot exceed the limitations of Level 1 because the purpose of the rule, unlike Rule 47, is to bind the pleader to a maximum claim. To this extent, the rule in *Greenhalgh v. Service Lloyds Ins. Co.*, 787 S.W.2d 938 (Tex. 1990), does not apply.

3. "Discrete subparts" of interrogatories are counted as single interrogatories, but not every separate factual inquiry is a discrete subpart. See also FRCP 33(a). While not susceptible of precise definition, see *Braden v. Downey*, 811 S.W.2d 922, 927-928 (Tex.1991), a "discrete subpart" is, in general, one that calls for information that is not logically or factually related to the primary interrogatory. The number of sets of interrogatories is no longer limited to two.

4. As other rules make clear, unless otherwise ordered or agreed, parties seeking discovery must serve requests sufficiently far in advance of the end of the discovery period that the deadline for responding will be within the discovery period. The court may order a deadline for sending discovery requests in lieu of or in addition to a deadline for completing discovery.

5. Use of forms of discovery other than depositions and interrogatories, such as requests for disclosure, admissions, or production of documents, are not restricted in Levels 1 and 2. But depositions on written questions cannot be used to circumvent the limits on interrogatories.

6. The concept of "side" in Rule 190.3(b)(2) borrows from Rule 233, which governs the allocation of peremptory strikes, and from FRCP 30(a)(2). In most cases there are only two sides—plaintiffs and defendants. In complex cases, however, there may be more than two sides, such as when defendants have sued third parties not named by plaintiffs, or when defendants have sued each other. As an example, if P1 and P2 sue D1, D2, and D3, and D1 sues D2 and D3, Ps would together be entitled to depose Ds and others permitted by the rule (i.e., Ds' experts and persons subject to Ds' control) for 50 hours, and Ds would together be entitled to depose Ps and others for 50 hours. D1 would also be entitled to depose D2 and D3 and others for 50 hours on matters in controversy among them, and D2 and D3 would together be entitled to depose D1 and others for 50 hours.

7. Any matter listed in Rule 166 may be addressed in an order issued under Rule 190.4. A pretrial order under Rule 166 may be used in individual cases regardless of the discovery level.

8. For purposes of defining discovery periods, "trial" does not include summary judgment.

See also *O'Connor's Texas Rules*, "General Rules for Discovery," ch. 6-A.

In re Van Waters & Rogers, Inc., 62 S.W.3d 197, 200 (Tex.2001). "[T]he [Ps] have failed to show why after seven years of litigation they should not be required to provide the ... basic information regarding their individual injuries and the causative chemicals.... While ... a trial court must be given latitude in managing discovery ..., that latitude is not unbounded. *At 201:* [T]he trial court's discovery order denies defendants 'discovery that goes to the heart of the litigation.'"

In re Alford Chevrolet-Geo, 997 S.W.2d 173, 181 (Tex.1999). "[C]ourts may limit discovery pending resolution of threshold issues like venue, jurisdiction, forum non conveniens, and official immunity."

TRCP 191. MODIFYING DISCOVERY PROCEDURES & LIMITATIONS; CONFERENCE REQUIREMENT; SIGNING DISCLOSURES, DISCOVERY REQUESTS, RESPONSES, & OBJECTIONS; FILING REQUIREMENTS

191.1 Modification of Procedures. Except where specifically prohibited, the procedures and limitations set forth in the rules pertaining to discovery may be modified in any suit by the agreement of the parties or by court order for good cause. An agreement of the parties is enforceable if it complies with Rule 11 or, as it affects an oral deposition, if it is made a part of the record of the deposition.

191.2 Conference. Parties and their attorneys are expected to cooperate in discovery and to make any agreements reasonably necessary for the efficient disposition of the case. All discovery motions or requests for hearings relating to discovery must contain a certificate by the party filing the motion or request that a reasonable effort has been made to resolve the dispute without the necessity of court intervention and the effort failed.

191.3 Signing of Disclosures, Discovery Requests, Notices, Responses, and Objections.

(a) ***Signature required.*** Every disclosure, discovery request, notice, response, and objection must be signed:

(1) by an attorney, if the party is represented by an attorney, and must show the attorney's State Bar of Texas identification number, address, telephone number, and fax number, if any; or

(2) by the party, if the party is not represented by an attorney, and must show the party's address, telephone number, and fax number, if any.

(b) ***Effect of signature on disclosure.*** The signature of an attorney or party on a disclosure constitutes a certification that to the best of the signer's knowledge, information, and belief, formed after a reasonable inquiry, the disclosure is complete and correct as of the time it is made.

(c) ***Effect of signature on discovery request, notice, response, or objection.*** The signature of an attorney or party on a discovery request, notice, response, or objection constitutes a certification that to the best of the signer's knowledge, information, and belief, formed after a reasonable inquiry, the request, notice, response, or objection:

(1) is consistent with the rules of civil procedure and these discovery rules and warranted by existing law or a good faith argument for the extension, modification, or reversal of existing law;

(2) has a good faith factual basis;

(3) is not interposed for any improper purpose, such as to harass or to cause unnecessary delay or needless increase in the cost of litigation; and

(4) is not unreasonable or unduly burdensome or expensive, given the needs of the case, the discovery already had in the case, the amount in controversy, and the importance of the issues at stake in the litigation.

(d) ***Effect of failure to sign.*** If a request, notice, response, or objection is not signed, it must be stricken unless it is signed promptly after the omission is called to the attention of the party making the request, notice, response, or objection. A party is not required to take any action with respect to a request or notice that is not signed.

(e) ***Sanctions.*** If the certification is false without substantial justification, the court may, upon motion or its own initiative, impose on the person who made the certification, or the party on whose behalf the request, notice, response, or objection was made, or both, an appropriate sanction as for a frivolous pleading or motion under Chapter 10 of the Civil Practice and Remedies Code.

191.4 Filing of Discovery Materials.

(a) ***Discovery materials not to be filed.*** The following discovery materials must not be filed:

(1) discovery requests, deposition notices, and subpoenas required to be served only on parties;

(2) responses and objections to discovery requests and deposition notices, regardless on whom the requests or notices were served;

(3) documents and tangible things produced in discovery; and

(4) statements prepared in compliance with Rule 193.3(b) or (d).

(b) ***Discovery materials to be filed.*** The following discovery materials must be filed:

(1) discovery requests, deposition notices, and subpoenas required to be served on nonparties;

(2) motions and responses to motions pertaining to discovery matters; and

(3) agreements concerning discovery matters, to the extent necessary to comply with Rule 11.

(c) ***Exceptions.*** Notwithstanding paragraph (a)—

(1) the court may order discovery materials to be filed;

(2) a person may file discovery materials in support of or in opposition to a motion or for other use in a court proceeding; and

(3) a person may file discovery materials necessary for a proceeding in an appellate court.

(d) ***Retention requirement for persons.*** Any person required to serve discovery materials not required to be filed must retain the original or exact copy of the materials during the pendency of the case and any related appellate proceedings begun within six months after judgment is signed, unless otherwise provided by the trial court.

(e) ***Retention requirement for courts.*** The clerk of the court shall retain and dispose of deposition transcripts and depositions upon written questions as directed by the Supreme Court.

191.5 Service of Discovery Materials.

Every disclosure, discovery request, notice, response, and objection required to be served on a party or person must be served on all parties of record.

Comments to 1999 change:

1. Rule 191.1 preserves the ability of parties by agreement and trial courts by order to adapt discovery to different circumstances. That ability is broad but not unbounded. Parties cannot merely by agreement modify a court order without the court's concurrence. Trial courts cannot simply "opt out" of these rules by form orders or approve or order a discovery control plan that does not contain the matters specified in Rule 190.4, but trial courts may use standard or form orders for providing discovery plans, scheduling, and other pretrial matters. In individual instances, courts may order, or parties may agree, to use discovery methods other than those prescribed in these rules if appropriate. Because the general rule is stated here, it is not repeated in each context in which it applies. Thus, for example, parties can agree to enlarge or shorten the time permitted for a deposition and to change the manner in which a deposition is conducted, notwithstanding Rule 199.5, although parties could not agree to be abusive toward a witness.

2. Rule 191.2 expressly states the obligation of parties and their attorneys to cooperate in conducting discovery.

3. The requirement that discovery requests, notices, responses, and objections be signed also applies to documents used to satisfy the purposes of such instruments. An example is a statement that privileged material or information has been withheld, which may be separate from a response to the discovery request but is nevertheless part of the response.

See also CPRC §10.001; TRCP 11, 13, 57; *O'Connor's Texas Rules*, "General Rules for Discovery," ch. 6-A; "Requests for Disclosure," ch. 6-D; "Depositions," ch. 6-E; "Interrogatories," ch. 6-F.

Groves v. Gabriel, 874 S.W.2d 660, 661 n.3 (Tex. 1994). Plaintiff "complains that [D's] motion to compel discovery did not contain the certificate of conference required under [TRCP 191.2]. Because this rule is for the benefit of the trial court, the court's failure to require a certificate of conference does not justify mandamus relief."

USAA v. Thomas, 893 S.W.2d 628, 629 (Tex.App.—Corpus Christi 1994, writ denied). TRCP 191.2 "ensures that parties will make good faith efforts to settle discovery disputes before filing sanctions motions and that sanctions motions will be filed only when court intervention is absolutely necessary. *At 630:* We hold that the trial court abused its discretion by granting the motion for sanctions without the required certificate of conference."

TRCP 192. PERMISSIBLE DISCOVERY: FORMS & SCOPE; WORK PRODUCT; PROTECTIVE ORDERS; DEFINITIONS

192.1 Forms of Discovery. Permissible forms of discovery are:

(a) requests for disclosure;

(b) requests for production and inspection of documents and tangible things;

(c) requests and motions for entry upon and examination of real property;

(d) interrogatories to a party;

(e) requests for admission;

(f) oral or written depositions; and

(g) motions for mental or physical examinations.

192.2 Sequence of Discovery. The permissible forms of discovery may be combined in the same document and may be taken in any order or sequence.

192.3 Scope of Discovery.

(a) ***Generally.*** In general, a party may obtain discovery regarding any matter that is not privileged and is relevant to the subject matter of the pending action, whether it relates to the claim or defense of the party seeking discovery or the claim or defense of any other party. It is not a ground for objection that the information sought will be inadmissible at trial if the information sought appears reasonably calculated to lead to the discovery of admissible evidence.

(b) ***Documents and tangible things.*** A party may obtain discovery of the existence, description, nature, custody, condition, location, and contents of documents and tangible things (including papers, books, accounts, drawings, graphs, charts, photographs, electronic or videotape recordings, data, and data compilations) that constitute or contain matters relevant to the subject matter of the action. A person is required to produce a document or tangible thing that is within the person's possession, custody, or control.

(c) ***Persons with knowledge of relevant facts.*** A party may obtain discovery of the name, address, and telephone number of persons having knowledge of relevant facts, and a brief statement of each identified person's connection with the case. A person has knowledge of relevant facts when that person has or may have knowledge of any discoverable matter. The person need not have admissible information or personal knowledge of the facts. An expert is "a person with knowledge of relevant facts" only if that knowledge was obtained firsthand or if it was not obtained in preparation for trial or in anticipation of litigation.

(d) ***Trial witnesses.*** A party may obtain discovery of the name, address, and telephone number of any person who is expected to be called to testify at trial. This paragraph does not apply to rebuttal or impeaching witnesses the necessity of whose testimony cannot reasonably be anticipated before trial.

(e) ***Testifying and consulting experts.*** The identity, mental impressions, and opinions of a consulting expert whose mental impressions and opinions have not been reviewed by a testifying expert are not discoverable. A party may discover the following information regarding a testifying expert or regarding a consulting expert whose mental impressions or opinions have been reviewed by a testifying expert:

(1) the expert's name, address, and telephone number;

(2) the subject matter on which a testifying expert will testify;

(3) the facts known by the expert that relate to or form the basis of the expert's mental impressions and opinions formed or made in connection with the case in which the discovery is sought, regardless of when and how the factual information was acquired;

(4) the expert's mental impressions and opinions formed or made in connection with the case in which discovery is sought, and any methods used to derive them;

(5) any bias of the witness;

(6) all documents, tangible things, reports, models, or data compilations that have been provided to, reviewed by, or prepared by or for the expert in anticipation of a testifying expert's testimony;

(7) the expert's current resume and bibliography.

(f) ***Indemnity and insuring agreements.*** Except as otherwise provided by law, a party may obtain discovery of the existence and contents of any indemnity or insurance agreement under which any person may be liable to satisfy part or all of a judgment rendered in the action or to indemnify or reimburse for payments made to satisfy the judgment. Information concerning the indemnity or insurance agreement is not by reason of disclosure admissible in evidence at trial.

(g) ***Settlement agreements.*** A party may obtain discovery of the existence and contents of any relevant portions of a settlement agreement. Information concerning a settlement agreement is not by reason of disclosure admissible in evidence at trial.

(h) ***Statements of persons with knowledge of relevant facts.*** A party may obtain discovery of the statement of any person with knowledge of relevant facts—a "witness statement"—regardless of when the statement was made. A witness statement is (1) a written statement signed or otherwise adopted or approved in writing by the person making it, or (2) a stenographic, mechanical, electrical, or other type of recording of a witness's oral statement, or any substantially verbatim transcription of such a recording. Notes taken during a conversation or interview with a witness are not a witness statement. Any person may obtain, upon written request, his or her own statement concerning the lawsuit, which is in the possession, custody or control of any party.

(i) ***Potential parties.*** A party may obtain discovery of the name, address, and telephone number of any potential party.

(j) ***Contentions.*** A party may obtain discovery of any other party's legal contentions and the factual bases for those contentions.

192.4 Limitations on Scope of Discovery. The discovery methods permitted by these rules should be limited by the court if it determines, on motion or on its own initiative and on reasonable notice, that:

(a) the discovery sought is unreasonably cumulative or duplicative, or is obtainable from some other source that is more convenient, less burdensome, or less expensive; or

(b) the burden or expense of the proposed discovery outweighs its likely benefit, taking into account the needs of the case, the amount in controversy, the parties' resources, the importance of the issues at stake in the litigation, and the importance of the proposed discovery in resolving the issues.

192.5 Work Product.

(a) ***Work product defined.*** Work product comprises:

(1) material prepared or mental impressions developed in anticipation of litigation or for trial by or for a party or a party's representatives, including the party's attorneys, consultants, sureties, indemnitors, insurers, employees, or agents; or

(2) a communication made in anticipation of litigation or for trial between a party and the party's representatives or among a party's representatives, including the party's attorneys, consultants, sureties, indemnitors, insurers, employees, or agents.

(b) ***Protection of work product.***

(1) *Protection of core work product—attorney mental processes.* Core work product—the work product of an attorney or an attorney's representative that contains the attorney's or the attorney's representative's mental impressions, opinions, conclusions, or legal theories—is not discoverable.

(2) *Protection of other work product.* Any other work product is discoverable only upon a showing that the party seeking discovery has substantial need of the materials in the preparation of the party's case and that

the party is unable without undue hardship to obtain the substantial equivalent of the material by other means.

(3) *Incidental disclosure of attorney mental processes.* It is not a violation of subparagraph (1) if disclosure ordered pursuant to subparagraph (2) incidentally discloses by inference attorney mental processes otherwise protected under subparagraph (1).

(4) *Limiting disclosure of mental processes.* If a court orders discovery of work product pursuant to subparagraph (2), the court must—insofar as possible—protect against disclosure of the mental impressions, opinions, conclusions, or legal theories not otherwise discoverable.

(c) ***Exceptions.*** Even if made or prepared in anticipation of litigation or for trial, the following is not work product protected from discovery:

(1) information discoverable under Rule 192.3 concerning experts, trial witnesses, witness statements, and contentions;

(2) trial exhibits ordered disclosed under Rule 166 or Rule 190.4;

(3) the name, address, and telephone number of any potential party or any person with knowledge of relevant facts;

(4) any photograph or electronic image of underlying facts (*e.g.*, a photograph of the accident scene) or a photograph or electronic image of any sort that a party intends to offer into evidence; and

(5) any work product created under circumstances within an exception to the attorney-client privilege in Rule 503(d) of the Rules of Evidence.

(d) ***Privilege.*** For purposes of these rules, an assertion that material or information is work product is an assertion of privilege.

192.6 Protective Orders.

(a) ***Motion.*** A person from whom discovery is sought, and any other person affected by the discovery request, may move within the time permitted for response to the discovery request for an order protecting that person from the discovery sought. A person should not move for protection when an objection to written discovery or an assertion of privilege is appropriate, but a motion does not waive the objection or assertion of privilege. If a person seeks protection regarding the time or place of discovery, the person must state a reasonable time and place for discovery with which the person will comply. A person must comply with a request to the extent protection is not sought unless it is unreasonable under the circumstances to do so before obtaining a ruling on the motion.

(b) ***Order.*** To protect the movant from undue burden, unnecessary expense, harassment, annoyance, or invasion of personal, constitutional, or property rights, the court may make any order in the interest of justice and may—among other things—order that:

(1) the requested discovery not be sought in whole or in part;

(2) the extent or subject matter of discovery be limited;

(3) the discovery not be undertaken at the time or place specified;

(4) the discovery be undertaken only by such method or upon such terms and conditions or at the time and place directed by the court;

(5) the results of discovery be sealed or otherwise protected, subject to the provisions of Rule 76a.

192.7 Definitions. As used in these rules—

(a) *Written discovery* means requests for disclosure, requests for production and inspection of documents and tangible things, requests for entry onto property, interrogatories, and requests for admission.

(b) *Possession, custody, or control* of an item means that the person either has physical possession of the item or has a right to possession of the item that is equal or superior to the person who has physical possession of the item.

(c) A *testifying expert* is an expert who may be called to testify as an expert witness at trial.

(d) A *consulting expert* is an expert who has been consulted, retained, or specially employed by a party in anticipation of litigation or in preparation for trial, but who is not a testifying expert.

Comments to 1999 change:

1. While the scope of discovery is quite broad, it is nevertheless confined by the subject matter of the case and reasonable expectations of obtaining information that will aid resolution of the dispute. The rule must be read and applied in that context. See also *In re American Optical Corp.*, 988 S.W.2d 711 (Tex.1998) (per curiam); *K-Mart v. Sanderson*, 937 S.W.2d 429 (Tex.1996) (per curiam); *Dillard Dept. Stores v. Hall*, 909 S.W.2d 491 (Tex.1995) (per curiam); *Texaco, Inc. v. Sanderson*, 898 S.W.2d 813 (Tex.1995) (per curiam); *Loftin v. Martin*, 776 S.W.2d 145, 148 (Tex.1989).

2. The definition of documents and tangible things has been revised to clarify that things relevant to the subject matter of the action are within the scope of discovery regardless of their form.

3. Rule 192.3(c) makes discoverable a "brief statement of each identified person's connection with the case." This provision does not contemplate a narrative statement of the facts the person knows, but at most a few words

describing the person's identity as relevant to the lawsuit. For instance: "treating physician," "eyewitness," "chief financial officer," "director," "plaintiff's mother and eyewitness to accident." The rule is intended to be consistent with *Axelson v. McIlhany*, 798 S.W.2d 550 (Tex.1990).

4. Rule 192.3(g) does not suggest that settlement agreements in other cases are relevant or irrelevant.

5. Rule 192.3(j) makes a party's legal and factual contentions discoverable but does not require more than a basic statement of those contentions and does not require a marshaling of evidence.

6. The sections in former Rule 166b concerning land and medical records are not included in this rule. They remain within the scope of discovery and are discussed in other rules.

7. The court's power to limit discovery based on the needs and circumstances of the case is expressly stated in Rule 192.4. The provision is taken from Rule 26(b)(2) of the Federal Rules of Civil Procedure. Courts should limit discovery under this rule only to prevent unwarranted delay and expense as stated more fully in the rule. A court abuses its discretion in unreasonably restricting a party's access to information through discovery.

8. Work product is defined for the first time, and its exceptions stated. Work product replaces the "attorney work product" and "party communication" discovery exemptions from former Rule 166b.

9. Elimination of the "witness statement" exemption does not render all witness statements automatically discoverable but subjects them to the same rules concerning the scope of discovery and privileges applicable to other documents or tangible things.

See also ***O'Connor's Texas Rules***, "General Rules for Discovery," ch. 6-A; "Scope of Discovery," ch. 6-B; "Securing Discovery from Experts," ch. 6-C; "Requests for Disclosure," ch. 6-D; "Depositions," ch. 6-E; "Interrogatories," ch. 6-F; "Requests for Admissions," ch. 6-G; "Securing Documents & Tangible Things," ch. 6-H; "Medical Records," ch. 6-I; "Entry on Land," ch. 6-J; ***O'Connor's Texas Forms***, FORMS 6A-6H.

Definition

GTE Comm. Sys. Corp. v. Tanner, 856 S.W.2d 725, 729 (Tex.1993). "The phrase, 'possession, custody or control,' within the meaning of [TRCP 192.7(b)], includes not only actual physical possession, but constructive possession, and the right to obtain possession from a third party, such as an agent or representative."

Scope of Discovery

In re City of Georgetown, 53 S.W.3d 328, 334 (Tex.2001). The TRCPs "expressly provide that a party is not required to disclose the identity, mental impressions, and opinions of consulting experts. *At 337:* [I]f documents are privileged or confidential under the [TRCPs] or [TREs], they are within a 'category of information [that] is expressly made confidential under other law' within the meaning of [Gov't Code] §552.022 of the Public Information Act."

G.M. Corp. v. Gayle, 951 S.W.2d 469, 474 (Tex. 1997). "'The policy behind the consulting expert privilege is to encourage parties to seek expert advice in evaluating their case and to prevent a party from receiving undue benefit from an adversary's efforts and diligence.' [¶] Without the consulting-expert privilege, parties would be reluctant to test an uncertain theory, for fear that it would provide evidence for the other side. *At 476:* [W]e conclude that the trial court's crash-test order constitutes an abuse of discretion by infringing on General Motors' consulting-expert privilege."

K-Mart Corp. v. Sanderson, 937 S.W.2d 429, 431 (Tex.1996). "A reference in [another court opinion] suggests that interrogatories and depositions may properly be used for a fishing expedition when a request for production of documents cannot. We reject the notion that any discovery device can be used to 'fish.'"

Irving Healthcare Sys. v. Brooks, 927 S.W.2d 12, 18 (Tex.1996). "[R]outine business records of a health-care entity such as a patient's medical records do not become privileged and are not shielded from discovery simply because a medical peer review committee has reviewed or considered them."

Ford Motor Co. v. Leggat, 904 S.W.2d 643, 649 (Tex.1995). "Settlement agreements are discoverable, to the extent they are relevant. Settlement agreements themselves, of course, are not admissible at trial to prove liability."

Monsanto Co. v. May, 889 S.W.2d 274, 276 (Tex. 1994). "A party is entitled to discovery that is relevant to the subject matter of the claim, and which appears reasonably calculated to lead to the discovery of admissible evidence." *See also* ***Volkswagen, A.G. v. Valdez***, 909 S.W.2d 900, 902 (Tex.1995); ***Texaco, Inc. v. Sanderson***, 898 S.W.2d 813, 814 (Tex.1995).

Aluminum Co. of Am. v. Bullock, 870 S.W.2d 2, 4 (Tex.1994). TRCP 192.3(e) "provides for discovery of not only the identity, but also the expected substance of the testimony of expert witnesses who will testify at trial.... When [the expert's] opinion concerning [D's] negligence changed due to the review of additional facts, [Ps] then had a duty to supplement their discovery responses to disclose the material change."

Housing Auth. of El Paso v. Rodriguez-Yepez, 843 S.W.2d 475, 476 (Tex.1992). "The broad scope of discovery is tempered by the trial court's discretion, properly invoked under [TRCP 192.6], to narrow the scope of discovery on a case by case basis with a protective order."

Jampole v. Touchy, 673 S.W.2d 569, 573 (Tex. 1984), *overruled on other grounds*, ***Walker v. Packer***, 827 S.W.2d 833 (Tex.1992). "[T]he ultimate purpose of discovery is to seek the truth, so that disputes may be decided by what the facts reveal, not by what facts are concealed. For this reason, discovery is not limited to information that will be admissible at trial. To increase the likelihood that all relevant evidence will be disclosed and brought before the trier of fact, the law circumscribes a significantly larger class of discoverable evidence to include anything reasonably calculated to lead to the discovery of material evidence."

Limitations on Scope of Discovery

In re Alford Chevrolet-Geo, 997 S.W.2d 173, 182 (Tex.1999). "[I]t is within the trial court's discretion to schedule discovery and decide whether and how much discovery is warranted to determine any [class] certification questions. Factors in determining the scope of precertification discovery include the importance, benefit, burden, expense, and time needed to produce the proposed discovery."

Protective Orders

General Tire, Inc. v. Kepple, 970 S.W.2d 520, 524 (Tex.1998). "To the extent that discovery, whether filed or unfiled, is a 'court record' under [TRCP] 76a, the court must follow the stricter standards of that rule to limit its dissemination. *At 525:* [W]e hold that when a party seeks a protective order under [TRCP 192.6] to restrict the dissemination of unfiled discovery, and no party or intervenor contends that the discovery is a 'court record,' a trial court need not conduct a hearing or render any findings on that issue. If a party or intervenor opposing a protective order claims that the discovery is a 'court record,' the court must make a threshold determination on that issue. However, public notice and a Rule 76a hearing are mandated only if the court finds that the documents are court records."

Crown Cent. Pet. Corp. v. Garcia, 904 S.W.2d 125, 128 (Tex.1995). "When a party seeks to depose a ... high level corporate official [apex deposition] and that official (or the corporation) files a motion for protective order ... denying any knowledge of relevant facts, the trial court should first determine whether the party seeking the deposition has arguably shown that the official has any unique or superior personal knowledge of discoverable information. If the party seeking the deposition cannot [so] show ... the trial court should grant the motion for protective order and first require the party seeking the deposition to attempt to obtain the discovery through less intrusive methods."

In re Amaya, 34 S.W.3d 354, 356-57 (Tex.App.—Waco 2001, orig. proceeding). "A trial judge may exercise some discretion in the granting of a protective order and in controlling the nature and form of discovery. ... A party seeking to avoid discovery must show particular, specific and demonstrable injury by facts sufficient to justify a protective order. 'So long as the discovery sought is within the scope of Rule 166b [now 192], a trial court may not grant a protective order limiting discovery unless the party seeking such protection has met this burden.' Conclusory allegations are not adequate. [¶] Any party who seeks to exclude matters from discovery on grounds that the requested information is unduly burdensome, costly or harassing to produce, has the affirmative duty to plead and prove the work necessary to comply with discovery."

Work Product

In re City of Georgetown, 53 S.W.3d 328, 334 (Tex. 2001). "The rules of civil procedure delineate a category for consulting experts whose mental impressions and opinions have not been reviewed by a testifying expert. The rules expressly provide that a party is not required to disclose the identity, mental impressions, and opinions of consulting experts. A law does not have to use the word 'confidential' to expressly impose confidentiality. The rules of procedure make it abundantly clear that information about consulting experts is confidential. [¶] The rules of procedure also define with some precision the categories of documents that comprise work product. Again, the rules do not have to use the word 'confidential' to make information confidential. The rules expressly provide that certain types of work product do not have to be disclosed, which means they are confidential."

Goode v. Shoukfeh, 943 S.W.2d 441, 449 (Tex. 1997). "Work product of counsel may not be considered by the factfinder unless the privilege has been waived or one of the [TRE] 503(d) exceptions applies."

Occidental Chem. Corp. v. Banales, 907 S.W.2d 488, 490 (Tex.1995). "The attorney work product privilege protects two related but different concepts. First, the privilege protects the attorney's thought process, which includes strategy decisions and issue formulation, and notes or writings evincing those mental processes. Second, the privilege protects the mechanical compilation of information to the extent such compilation reveals the attorney's thought processes. The work product exemption is of continuing duration."

National Un. Fire Ins. Co. v. Valdez, 863 S.W.2d 458, 461 (Tex.1993). "[N]o legitimate purpose is served by allowing a party to discover an opponent's litigation file. Our decision today does not prevent a party from requesting specific documents or categories of documents relevant to issues in a pending case, even though some or all of the documents may be contained in an attorney's files."

In re Monsanto Co., 998 S.W.2d 917, 929 (Tex. App.—Waco 1999, orig. proceeding). "Both the attorney-client privilege and the work product privilege have been recently expanded—the former by changing from the control-group test to the subject-matter test and the latter by combining privileges and eliminating of the 'subsequent to the occurrence' and 'particular pending suit' requirements."

In re Team Transp., Inc., 996 S.W.2d 256, 259 (Tex. App.—Houston [14th Dist.] 1999, orig. proceeding). "The work product privilege protects 'core work product,' which includes the attorney's 'mental impressions, opinions, conclusions or legal theories.' It also protects 'other work product' unless the party seeking discovery shows a 'substantial need' for the materials and 'undue hardship' in obtaining the substantial equivalent of the materials by other means. 'Witness statements' are not work product, however, even if made or prepared in anticipation of litigation or trial."

TRCP 193. WRITTEN DISCOVERY: RESPONSE; OBJECTION; ASSERTION OF PRIVILEGE; SUPPLEMENTATION & AMENDMENT; FAILURE TO TIMELY RESPOND; PRESUMPTION OF AUTHENTICITY

193.1 Responding to Written Discovery; Duty to Make Complete Response. A party must respond to written discovery in writing within the time provided by court order or these rules. When responding to written discovery, a party must make a complete response, based on all information reasonably available to the responding party or its attorney at the time the response is made. The responding party's answers, objections, and other responses must be preceded by the request to which they apply.

193.2 Objecting to Written Discovery.

(a) ***Form and time for objections.*** A party must make any objection to written discovery in writing—either in the response or in a separate document—within the time for response. The party must state specifically the legal or factual basis for the objection and the extent to which the party is refusing to comply with the request.

(b) ***Duty to respond when partially objecting; objection to time or place of production.*** A party must comply with as much of the request to which the party has made no objection unless it is unreasonable under the circumstances to do so before obtaining a ruling on the objection. If the responding party objects to the requested time or place of production, the responding party must state a reasonable time and place for complying with the request and must comply at that time and place without further request or order.

(c) ***Good faith basis for objection.*** A party may object to written discovery only if a good faith factual and legal basis for the objection exists at the time the objection is made.

(d) ***Amendment.*** An objection or response to written discovery may be amended or supplemented to state an objection or basis that, at the time the objection or response initially was made, either was inapplicable or was unknown after reasonable inquiry.

(e) ***Waiver of objection.*** An objection that is not made within the time required, or that is obscured by numerous unfounded objections, is waived unless the court excuses the waiver for good cause shown.

(f) ***No objection to preserve privilege.*** A party should not object to a request for written discovery on the grounds that it calls for production of material or information that is privileged but should instead comply with Rule 193.3. A party who objects to production of privileged material or information does not waive the privilege but must comply with Rule 193.3 when the error is pointed out.

193.3 Asserting a Privilege. A party may preserve a privilege from written discovery in accordance with this subdivision.

(a) ***Withholding privileged material or information.*** A party who claims that material or information responsive to written discovery is privileged may withhold the privileged material or information from the response. The party must state—in the response (or an amended or supplemental response) or in a separate document—that:

(1) information or material responsive to the request has been withheld,

(2) the request to which the information or material relates, and

(3) the privilege or privileges asserted.

(b) ***Description of withheld material or information.*** After receiving a response indicating that material or information has been withheld from production, the party seeking discovery may serve a written request that the withholding party identify the information and material withheld. Within 15 days of service of that request, the withholding party must serve a response that:

(1) describes the information or materials withheld that, without revealing the privileged information itself or otherwise waiving the privilege, enables other parties to assess the applicability of the privilege, and

(2) asserts a specific privilege for each item or group of items withheld.

(c) ***Exemption.*** Without complying with paragraphs (a) and (b), a party may withhold a privileged communication to or from a lawyer or lawyer's representative or a privileged document of a lawyer or lawyer's representative—

(1) created or made from the point at which a party consults a lawyer with a view to obtaining professional legal services from the lawyer in the prosecution or defense of a specific claim in the litigation in which discovery is requested, and

(2) concerning the litigation in which the discovery is requested.

(d) ***Privilege not waived by production.*** A party who produces material or information without intending to waive a claim of privilege does not waive that claim under these rules or the Rules of Evidence if—within ten days or a shorter time ordered by the court, after the producing party actually discovers that such production was made—the producing party amends the response, identifying the material or information produced and stating the privilege asserted. If the producing party thus amends the response to assert a privilege, the requesting party must promptly return the specified material or information and any copies pending any ruling by the court denying the privilege.

193.4 Hearing and Ruling on Objections and Assertions of Privilege.

(a) ***Hearing.*** Any party may at any reasonable time request a hearing on an objection or claim of privilege asserted under this rule. The party making the objection or asserting the privilege must present any evidence necessary to support the objection or privilege. The evidence may be testimony presented at the hearing or affidavits served at least seven days before the hearing or at such other reasonable time as the court permits. If the court determines that an *in camera* review of some or all of the requested discovery is necessary, that material or information must be segregated and produced to the court in a sealed wrapper within a reasonable time following the hearing.

(b) ***Ruling.*** To the extent the court sustains the objection or claim of privilege, the responding party has no further duty to respond to that request. To the extent the court overrules the objection or claim of privilege, the responding party must produce the requested material or information within 30 days after the court's ruling or at such time as the court orders. A party need not request a ruling on that party's own objection or assertion of privilege to preserve the objection or privilege.

(c) ***Use of material or information withheld under claim of privilege.*** A party may not use—at any hearing or trial—material or information withheld from discovery under a claim of privilege, including a claim sustained by the court, without timely amending or supplementing the party's response to that discovery.

193.5 Amending or Supplementing Responses to Written Discovery.

(a) ***Duty to amend or supplement.*** If a party learns that the party's response to written discovery was incomplete or incorrect when made, or, although complete and correct when made, is no longer complete and correct, the party must amend or supplement the response:

(1) to the extent that the written discovery sought the identification of persons with knowledge of relevant facts, trial witnesses, or expert witnesses, and

(2) to the extent that the written discovery sought other information, unless the additional or corrective information has been made known to the other parties in writing, on the record at a deposition, or through other discovery responses.

(b) ***Time and form of amended or supplemental response.*** An amended or supplemental response must be made reasonably promptly after the party discovers the necessity for such a response. Except as otherwise provided by these rules, it is presumed that an amended or supplemental response made less than 30 days before trial was not made reasonably promptly. An amended or supplemental response must be in the same form as the initial response and must be verified by the party if the original response was required to be verified by the party, but the failure to comply with this requirement does not make the amended or supplemental response untimely unless the party making the response refuses to correct the defect within a reasonable time after it is pointed out.

193.6 Failing to Timely Respond—Effect on Trial.

(a) ***Exclusion of evidence and exceptions.*** A party who fails to make, amend, or supplement a discovery response in a timely manner may not introduce in evidence the material or information that was not timely disclosed, or offer the testimony of a witness (other than a named party) who was not timely identified, unless the court finds that:

(1) there was good cause for the failure to timely make, amend, or supplement the discovery response; or

(2) the failure to timely make, amend, or supplement the discovery response will not unfairly surprise or unfairly prejudice the other parties.

(b) ***Burden of establishing exception.*** The burden of establishing good cause or the lack of unfair surprise or unfair prejudice is on the party seeking to introduce the evidence or call the witness. A finding of good cause or of the lack of unfair surprise or unfair prejudice must be supported by the record.

(c) ***Continuance.*** Even if the party seeking to introduce the evidence or call the witness fails to carry the burden under paragraph (b), the court may grant a continuance or temporarily postpone the trial to allow a response to be made, amended, or supplemented, and to allow opposing parties to conduct discovery regarding any new information presented by that response.

193.7 Production of Documents Self-Authenticating. A party's production of a document in response to written discovery authenticates the document for use against that party in any pretrial proceeding or at trial unless—within ten days or a longer or shorter time ordered by the court, after the producing party has actual notice that the document will be used—the party objects to the authenticity of the document, or any part of it, stating the specific basis for objection. An objection must be either on the record or in writing and must have a good faith factual and legal basis. An objection made to the authenticity of only part of a document does not affect the authenticity of the remainder. If objection is made, the party attempting to use the document should be given a reasonable opportunity to establish its authenticity.

Comments to 1999 change:

1. This rule imposes a duty upon parties to make a complete response to written discovery based upon all information reasonably available, subject to objections and privileges.

2. An objection to written discovery does not excuse the responding party from complying with the request to the extent no objection is made. But a party may object to a request for "all documents relevant to the lawsuit" as overly broad and not in compliance with the rule requiring specific requests for documents and refuse to comply with it entirely. See also *Loftin v. Martin*, 776 S.W.2d 145 (Tex.1989). A party may also object to a request for a litigation file on the ground that it is overly broad and may assert that on its face the request seeks only materials protected by privilege. See also *National Union Fire Ins. Co. v. Valdez*, 863 S.W.2d 458 (Tex.1993). A party who objects to production of documents from a remote time period should produce documents from a more recent period unless that production would be burdensome and duplicative should the objection be overruled.

3. This rule governs the presentation of all privileges including work product. It dispenses with objections to written discovery requests on the basis that responsive information or materials are protected by a specific privilege from discovery. Instead, the rule requires parties to state that information or materials have been withheld and to identify the privilege upon which the party relies. The statement should not be made prophylactically, but only when specific information and materials have been withheld. The party must amend or supplement the statement if additional privileged information or material is found subsequent to the initial response. Thus, when large numbers of documents are being produced, a party may amend the initial response when documents are found as to which the party claims privilege. A party need not state that material created by or for lawyers for the litigation has been withheld as it can be assumed that such material will be withheld from virtually any request on the grounds of attorney-client privilege or work product. However, the rule does not prohibit a party from specifically requesting the material or information if the party has a good faith basis for asserting that it is discoverable. An example would be material or information described by Rule 503(d)(1) of the Rules of Evidence.

4. Rule 193.3(d) is a new provision that allows a party to assert a claim of privilege to material or information produced inadvertently without intending to waive the privilege. The provision is commonly used in complex cases to reduce costs and risks in large document productions. The focus is on the intent to waive the privilege, not the intent to produce the material or information. A party who fails to diligently screen documents before producing them does not waive a claim of privilege. This rule is thus broader than TRE 511 and overturns *Granada Corp. v. First Court of Appeals*, 844 S.W.2d 223 (Tex.1992), to the extent the two conflict. The ten-day period (which may be shortened by the court) allowed for an amended response does not run from the production of the material or information but from the party's first awareness of the mistake. To avoid complications at trial, a party may identify prior to trial the documents intended to be offered, thereby triggering the obligation to assert any overlooked privilege under this rule. A trial court may also order this procedure.

5. This rule imposes no duty to supplement or amend deposition testimony. The only duty to supplement deposition testimony is provided in Rule 195.6.

6. Any party can request a hearing in which the court will resolve issues brought up in objections or withholding statements. The party seeking to avoid discovery has the burden of proving the objection or privilege.

7. The self-authenticating provision is new. Authentication is, of course, but a condition precedent to admissibility and does not establish admissibility. See also TRE 901(a). The ten-day period allowed for objection to authenticity (which period may be altered by the court in appropriate circumstances) does not run from the production of the material or information but from the party's actual awareness that the document will be used. To avoid complications at trial, a party may identify prior to trial the documents intended to be offered, thereby

triggering the obligation to object to authenticity. A trial court may also order this procedure. An objection to authenticity must be made in good faith.

See also *O'Connor's Texas Rules*, "General Rules for Discovery," ch. 6-A; "Scope of Discovery," ch. 6-B; "Requests for Disclosure," ch. 6-D; "Interrogatories," ch. 6-F; "Securing Documents & Tangible Things," ch. 6-H; "Medical Records," ch. 6-I; "Entry on Land," ch. 6-J.

193.2 – Objections

G.M. Corp. v. Tanner, 892 S.W.2d 862, 863 (Tex. 1995). "As the party objecting to the request, [P] was required to provide evidence in support of his objection."

193.3 – Privileges

In re Union Pac. Res. Co., 22 S.W.3d 338, 340 (Tex.1999). "'Any party who seeks to deny the production of evidence must claim a specific privilege against such production. The burden is on the party asserting a privilege from discovery to produce evidence *concerning the applicability of a particular privilege*.'"

Humphreys v. Caldwell, 888 S.W.2d 469, 470 (Tex. 1994). "A party who seeks to exclude any matter from discovery on the basis of an exemption or immunity from discovery, must specifically plead the particular exemption or immunity relied on and produce evidence supporting such claim in the form of affidavits or live testimony at a hearing."

In re Monsanto Co., 998 S.W.2d 917, 926 (Tex. App.—Waco 1999, orig. proceeding). "The mere listing of a specific privilege in a response or a privilege log does not prove that privilege. The response and log are the vehicles by which the privilege is claimed. Proof of the facts that justify the claim of privilege is necessary."

193.5 – Supplementing Discovery

Titus Cty. Hosp. Dist. v. Lucas, 988 S.W.2d 740, 740 (Tex.1998). TRCP 193.5 "requires supplementation of a response to a request for discovery. An interrogatory answer is a response to a request for discovery, but testimony in a deposition is not. A general duty to supplement deposition testimony (as opposed to a narrow duty for certain expert testimony, for example) would impose too great a burden on litigants. We therefore disapprove the court of appeals' holding that deposition testimony must be supplemented."

State Farm Fire & Cas. Co. v. Morua, 979 S.W.2d 616, 619 (Tex.1998). "[S]upplemental answers to interrogatories must be verified."

Exxon Corp. v. West Tex. Gathering Co., 868 S.W.2d 299, 304 (Tex.1993). "Our rules do not prevent experts from refining calculations and perfecting reports through the time of trial. The testimony of an expert should not be barred because a change in some minor detail of the person's work has not been disclosed a month before trial. The additional supplementation requirement of [TRCP 193.5] does require that opposing parties have sufficient information about an expert's opinion to prepare a rebuttal with their own experts and cross-examination, and that they be promptly and fully advised when further developments have rendered past information incorrect or misleading."

Sharp v. Broadway Nat'l Bank, 784 S.W.2d 669, 671 (Tex.1990). "Identification of witnesses in response to discovery must be in writing; oral notice is not proper."

Snider v. Stanley, 44 S.W.3d 713, 715 (Tex.App.—Beaumont 2001, pet. denied). "'An amended or supplemental response must be made reasonably promptly after the party discovers the necessity for such a response.' It is presumed that response made within 30 days of trial is not reasonably promptly made. [D's] response, made 30 days before trial, is not subject to the presumption. [Ps] argue that the opposite presumption applies, that is, the supplementation was made reasonably promptly. We disagree. Had such a presumption been intended, it would have been incorporated into the rules."

193.6 – Effect of Failing to Respond

Mares v. Ford Motor Co., 53 S.W.3d 416, 419 (Tex. App.—San Antonio 2001, no pet.). Even though D filed a general statement of the nature of the expert's opinions, the trial court did not abuse its discretion in permitting D's expert to testify because "the trial court limited the testimony of [D's] experts to the testimony provided at the earlier trial or in response to earlier discovery [and] the substance of that testimony had been fully disclosed to [Ps]."

193.6 – Good Cause

Alvarado v. Farah Mfg., 830 S.W.3d 911, 914 (Tex. 1992). The salutary purpose of TRCP 193.6 "is to require complete responses to discovery so as to promote responsible assessment of settlement and prevent trial by ambush. The rule is mandatory, and its sole sanction—exclusion of evidence—is automatic, unless there is good cause to excuse its imposition. The good cause exception permits a trial court to excuse a failure to comply with discovery in difficult or impossible circumstances. The trial court has discretion to determine whether the offering party has met his burden of showing good cause to admit the testimony; but the trial court has no discretion to admit testimony excluded by the rule without a showing of good cause."

Ersek v. Davis & Davis, P.C., 69 S.W.3d 268, 271 (Tex.App.—Austin 2002, pet. denied). Plaintiff "contends he met the requirements for late designation of his expert witness based on rule 193.6. ... First, we consider good cause for the late designation. [Plaintiff] was required to provide expert testimony to establish his cause of action. The suit was filed November 12, 1999. [Expert witness] was designated December 7, 2000." Held: No abuse of discretion in concluding that plaintiff did not establish good cause by failing for more than one year to designate an expert witness to support his cause of action.

Northwestern Nat. Cty. Mutual Ins. Co. v. Rodriguez, 18 S.W.3d 718, 722 n.1 (Tex.App.—San Antonio 2000, no pet.). TRCP 193.6 "states that a party who fails to respond to a discovery request to name a witness may not offer the testimony of a witness who was not so identified, unless the court can find good cause *or* that the failure to timely make the discovery response will not unfairly surprise *or* unfairly prejudice the other parties. The Supreme Court's inclusion of the coordinating conjunction, 'or,' means that a party, who is seeking to introduce a witness, must merely meet the burden of showing either good cause *or* lack of unfair surprise *or* lack of unfair prejudice and support it with the record."

Wal-Mart Stores, Inc. v. Tinsley, 998 S.W.2d 664, 671 (Tex.App.—Texarkana 1999, pet. denied). "The trial court has the discretion to determine whether the offering party has met his burden of showing good cause to admit the testimony. The ruling of the trial court here does not expressly state that [P] demonstrated good cause in failing to supplement [witness's] address. We find, however, that the trial court implicitly found good cause. The facts show that [D] was not misled to its detriment; it did not contact the [Ps'] counsel to inquire into [witness's] whereabouts; and it refused a mistrial and a delay with an opportunity to depose [witness] before trial."

TRCP 194. REQUESTS FOR DISCLOSURE

194.1 Request. A party may obtain disclosure from another party of the information or material listed in Rule 194.2 by serving the other party—no later than 30 days before the end of any applicable discovery period—the following request: "Pursuant to Rule 194, you are requested to disclose, within 30 days of service of this request, the information or material described in Rule [state rule, e.g., 194.2, or 194.2(a), (c), and (f), or 194.2(d)-(g)]."

194.2 Content. A party may request disclosure of any or all of the following:

(a) the correct names of the parties to the lawsuit;

(b) the name, address, and telephone number of any potential parties;

(c) the legal theories and, in general, the factual bases of the responding party's claims or defenses (the responding party need not marshal all evidence that may be offered at trial);

(d) the amount and any method of calculating economic damages;

(e) the name, address, and telephone number of persons having knowledge of relevant facts, and a brief statement of each identified person's connection with the case;

(f) for any testifying expert:

(1) the expert's name, address, and telephone number;

(2) the subject matter on which the expert will testify;

(3) the general substance of the expert's mental impressions and opinions and a brief summary of the basis for them, or if the expert is not retained by, employed by, or otherwise subject to the control of the responding party, documents reflecting such information;

(4) if the expert is retained by, employed by, or otherwise subject to the control of the responding party:

(A) all documents, tangible things, reports, models, or data compilations that have been provided to, reviewed by, or prepared by or for the expert in anticipation of the expert's testimony; and

(B) the expert's current resume and bibliography;

(g) any indemnity and insuring agreements described in Rule 192.3(f);

(h) any settlement agreements described in Rule 192.3(g);

(i) any witness statements described in Rule 192.3(h);

(j) in a suit alleging physical or mental injury and damages from the occurrence that is the subject of the case, all medical records and bills that are reasonably related to the injuries or damages asserted or, in lieu thereof, an authorization permitting the disclosure of such medical records and bills;

(k) in a suit alleging physical or mental injury and damages from the occurrence that is the subject of the case, all medical records and bills obtained by the responding party by virtue of an authorization furnished by the requesting party.

194.3 Response. The responding party must serve a written response on the requesting party within 30 days after service of the request, except that:

(a) a defendant served with a request before the defendant's answer is due need not respond until 50 days after service of the request, and

(b) a response to a request under Rule 194.2(f) is governed by Rule 195.

194.4 Production. Copies of documents and other tangible items ordinarily must be served with the response. But if the responsive documents are voluminous, the response must state a reasonable time and place for the production of documents. The responding party must produce the documents at the time and place stated, unless otherwise agreed by the parties or ordered by the court, and must provide the requesting party a reasonable opportunity to inspect them.

194.5 No Objection or Assertion of Work Product. No objection or assertion of work product is permitted to a request under this rule.

194.6 Certain Responses Not Admissible. A response to requests under Rule 194.2(c) and (d) that has been changed by an amended or supplemental response is not admissible and may not be used for impeachment.

Comments to 1999 change:

1. Disclosure is designed to afford parties basic discovery of specific categories of information, not automatically in every case, but upon request, without preparation of a lengthy inquiry, and without objection or assertion of work product. In those extremely rare cases when information ordinarily discoverable should be protected, such as when revealing a person's residence might result in harm to the person, a party may move for protection. A party may assert any applicable privileges other than work product using the procedures of Rule 193.3 applicable to other written discovery. Otherwise, to fail to respond fully to a request for disclosure would be an abuse of the discovery process.

2. Rule 194.2(c) and (d) permit a party further inquiry into another's legal theories and factual claims than is often provided in notice pleadings. So-called "contention interrogatories" are used for the same purpose. Such interrogatories are not properly used to require a party to marshal evidence or brief legal issues. Paragraphs (c) and (d) are intended to require disclosure of a party's basic assertions, whether in prosecution of claims or in defense. Thus, for example, a plaintiff would be required to disclose that he or she claimed damages suffered in a car wreck caused by defendant's negligence in speeding, and would be required to state how loss of past earnings and future earning capacity was calculated, but would not be required to state the speed at which defendant was allegedly driving. Paragraph (d) does not require a party, either a plaintiff or a defendant, to state a method of calculating non-economic damages, such as for mental anguish. In the same example, defendant would be required to disclose his or her denial of the speeding allegation and any basis for contesting the damage calculations.

3. Responses under Rule 194.2(c) and (d) that have been amended or supplemented are inadmissible and cannot be used for impeachment, but other evidence of changes in position is not likewise barred.

See also *O'Connor's Texas Rules*, "General Rules for Discovery," ch. 6-A; "Securing Discovery from Experts," ch. 6-C; "Requests for Disclosure," ch. 6-D; *O'Connor's Texas Forms*, FORMS 6C.

In re K.S., ___ S.W.3d ___ (Tex.App.—Amarillo 2002, n.p.h.) (No. 07-00-0470-CV; 1-3-02). "The record shows that the TRCP 194 Request for Disclosure on which [parents] based their objection to the TDPRS witnesses was served only on behalf of [mother]. At the time the request was served, [father] had not made an appearance in the lawsuit and the document specified that [mother] was making the discovery request. The trial court did not abuse its discretion in denying the objection of [father] to testimony of the TDPRS witnesses when the witnesses had not been disclosed in response to a TRCP 194 request made only by [mother]."

Castellanos v. Littlejohn, 945 S.W.2d 236, 239 (Tex.App.—San Antonio 1997, orig. proceeding). Plaintiff's expert "was retained as a consulting-only expert and was designated as a testifying expert only because of a clerical error. The issue presented ... is whether a party who has inadvertently listed a consulting-only expert as a testifying expert may 'de-designate' him to reflect his proper status. We believe the party can do so, so long as the 'de-designation' does not constitute 'an offensive and unacceptable use of discovery mechanisms' or 'violate[ ] the clear purpose and policy underlying the rules of discovery.'"

TRCP 195. DISCOVERY REGARDING TESTIFYING EXPERT WITNESSES

195.1 Permissible Discovery Tools. A party may request another party to designate and disclose information concerning testifying expert witnesses only through a request for disclosure under Rule 194 and through depositions and reports as permitted by this rule.

195.2 Schedule for Designating Experts. Unless otherwise ordered by the court, a party must designate experts—that is, furnish information requested under Rule 194.2(f)—by the later of the following two dates: 30 days after the request is served, or—

(a) with regard to all experts testifying for a party seeking affirmative relief, 90 days before the end of the discovery period;

(b) with regard to all other experts, 60 days before the end of the discovery period.

195.3 Scheduling Depositions.

(a) ***Experts for party seeking affirmative relief.*** A party seeking affirmative relief must make an expert retained by, employed by, or otherwise in the control of the party available for deposition as follows:

(1) *If no report furnished.* If a report of the expert's factual observations, tests, supporting data, calculations, photographs, and opinions is not produced when the expert is designated, then the party must make the expert available for deposition reasonably promptly after the expert is designated. If the deposition cannot—due to the actions of the tendering party—reasonably be concluded more than 15 days before the deadline for designating other experts, that deadline must be extended for other experts testifying on the same subject.

(2) *If report furnished.* If a report of the expert's factual observations, tests, supporting data, calculations, photographs, and opinions is produced when the expert is designated, then the party need not make the expert available for deposition until reasonably promptly after all other experts have been designated.

(b) ***Other experts.*** A party not seeking affirmative relief must make an expert retained by, employed by, or otherwise in the control of the party available for deposition reasonably promptly after the expert is designated and the experts testifying on the same subject for the party seeking affirmative relief have been deposed.

195.4 Oral Deposition. In addition to disclosure under Rule 194, a party may obtain discovery concerning the subject matter on which the expert is expected to testify, the expert's mental impressions and opinions, the facts known to the expert (regardless of when the factual information was acquired) that relate to or form the basis of the testifying expert's mental impressions and opinions, and other discoverable matters, including documents not produced in disclosure, only by oral deposition of the expert and by a report prepared by the expert under this rule.

195.5 Court-Ordered Reports. If the discoverable factual observations, tests, supporting data, calculations, photographs, or opinions of an expert have not been recorded and reduced to tangible form, the court may order these matters reduced to tangible form and produced in addition to the deposition.

195.6 Amendment and Supplementation. A party's duty to amend and supplement written discovery regarding a testifying expert is governed by Rule 193.5. If an expert witness is retained by, employed by, or otherwise under the control of a party, that party must also amend or supplement any deposition testimony or written report by the expert, but only with regard to the expert's mental impressions or opinions and the basis for them.

195.7 Cost of Expert Witnesses. When a party takes the oral deposition of an expert witness retained by the opposing party, all reasonable fees charged by the expert for time spent in preparing for, giving, reviewing, and correcting the deposition must be paid by the party that retained the expert.

Comments to 1999 change:

1. This rule does not limit the permissible methods of discovery concerning consulting experts whose mental impressions or opinions have been reviewed by a testifying expert. See also Rule 192.3(e). Information concerning purely consulting experts, of course, is not discoverable.

2. This rule and Rule 194 do not address depositions of testifying experts who are not retained by, employed by, or otherwise subject to the control of the responding party, nor the production of the materials identified in Rule 192.3(e)(5) and (6) relating to such experts. Parties may obtain this discovery, however, through Rules 176 and 205.

3. In scheduling the designations and depositions of expert witnesses, the rule attempts to minimize unfair surprise and undue expense. A party seeking affirmative relief must either produce an expert's report or tender the expert for deposition before an opposing party is required to designate experts. A party who does not wish to incur the expense of a report may simply tender the expert for deposition, but a party who wishes an expert to have the benefit of an opposing party's expert's opinions before being deposed may trigger designation by providing a report. Rule 191.1 permits a trial court, for good cause, to modify the order or deadlines for designating and deposing experts and the allocation of fees and expenses.

See also *O'Connor's Texas Rules*, "General Rules for Discovery," ch. 6-A; "Scope of Discovery," ch. 6-B; "Securing Discovery from Experts," ch. 6-C; "Requests for Disclosure," ch. 6-D; "Depositions," ch. 6-E.

TRCP 196. REQUESTS FOR PRODUCTION & INSPECTION TO PARTIES; REQUESTS & MOTIONS FOR ENTRY UPON PROPERTY

196.1 Request for Production and Inspection to Parties.

(a) ***Request.*** A party may serve on another party—no later than 30 days before the end of the discovery period—a request for production or for inspection, to inspect, sample, test, photograph and copy documents or tangible things within the scope of discovery.

(b) ***Contents of request.*** The request must specify the items to be produced or inspected, either by individual item or by category, and describe with reasonable particularity each item and category. The request must specify a reasonable time (on or after the date on which the response is due) and place for production. If the requesting party will sample or test the requested items, the means, manner and procedure for testing or sampling must be described with sufficient specificity to inform the producing party of the means, manner, and procedure for testing or sampling.

(c) ***Requests for production of medical or mental health records regarding nonparties.***

(1) *Service of request on nonparty.* If a party requests another party to produce medical or mental health records regarding a nonparty, the requesting party must serve the nonparty with the request for production under Rule 21a.

(2) *Exceptions.* A party is not required to serve the request for production on a nonparty whose medical records are sought if:

(A) the nonparty signs a release of the records that is effective as to the requesting party;

(B) the identity of the nonparty whose records are sought will not directly or indirectly be disclosed by production of the records; or

(C) the court, upon a showing of good cause by the party seeking the records, orders that service is not required.

(3) *Confidentiality.* Nothing in this rule excuses compliance with laws concerning the confidentiality of medical or mental health records.

196.2 Response to Request for Production and Inspection.

(a) ***Time for response.*** The responding party must serve a written response on the requesting party within 30 days after service of the request, except that a defendant served with a request before the defendant's answer is due need not respond until 50 days after service of the request.

(b) ***Content of response.*** With respect to each item or category of items, the responding party must state objections and assert privileges as required by these rules, and state, as appropriate, that:

(1) production, inspection, or other requested action will be permitted as requested;

(2) the requested items are being served on the requesting party with the response;

(3) production, inspection, or other requested action will take place at a specified time and place, if the responding party is objecting to the time and place of production; or

(4) no items have been identified—after a diligent search—that are responsive to the request.

196.3 Production.

(a) ***Time and place of production.*** Subject to any objections stated in the response, the responding party must produce the requested documents or tangible things within the person's possession, custody or control at either the time and place requested or the time and place stated in the response, unless otherwise agreed by the parties or ordered by the court, and must provide the requesting party a reasonable opportunity to inspect them.

(b) ***Copies.*** The responding party may produce copies in lieu of originals unless a question is raised as to the authenticity of the original or in the circumstances it would be unfair to produce copies in lieu of originals. If originals are produced, the responding party is entitled to retain the originals while the requesting party inspects and copies them.

(c) ***Organization.*** The responding party must either produce documents and tangible things as they are kept in the usual course of business or organize and label them to correspond with the categories in the request.

196.4 Electronic or Magnetic Data. To obtain discovery of data or information that exists in electronic or magnetic form, the requesting party must specifically request production of electronic or magnetic data and specify the form in which the requesting party wants it produced. The responding party must produce the electronic or magnetic data that is responsive to the request and is reasonably available to the responding party in its ordinary course of business. If the responding party cannot—through reasonable efforts—retrieve the data or information requested or produce it in the form requested, the responding party must state an objection complying with these rules. If the court orders the responding party to comply with the request, the court must also order that the requesting party pay the reasonable expenses of any extraordinary steps required to retrieve and produce the information.

196.5 Destruction or Alteration. Testing, sampling or examination of an item may not destroy or materially alter an item unless previously authorized by the court.

196.6 Expenses of Production. Unless otherwise ordered by the court for good cause, the expense of producing items will be borne by the responding party and the expense of inspecting, sampling, testing, photographing, and copying items produced will be borne by the requesting party.

196.7 Request or Motion for Entry Upon Property.

(a) ***Request or motion.*** A party may gain entry on designated land or other property to inspect, measure, survey, photograph, test, or sample the property or any designated object or operation thereon by serving—no later than 30 days before the end of any applicable discovery period—

(1) a request on all parties if the land or property belongs to a party, or

(2) a motion and notice of hearing on all parties and the nonparty if the land or property belongs to a nonparty. If the identity or address of the nonparty is unknown and cannot be obtained through reasonable diligence, the court must permit service by means other than those specified in Rule 21a that are reasonably calculated to give the nonparty notice of the motion and hearing.

(b) ***Time, place, and other conditions.*** The request for entry upon a party's property, or the order for entry upon a nonparty's property, must state the time, place, manner, conditions, and scope of the inspection, and must specifically describe any desired means, manner, and procedure for testing or sampling, and the person or persons by whom the inspection, testing, or sampling is to be made.

(c) ***Response to request for entry.***

(1) *Time to respond.* The responding party must serve a written response on the requesting party within 30 days after service of the request, except that a defendant served with a request before the defendant's answer is due need not respond until 50 days after service of the request.

(2) *Content of response.* The responding party must state objections and assert privileges as required by these rules, and state, as appropriate, that:

(A) entry or other requested action will be permitted as requested;

(B) entry or other requested action will take place at a specified time and place, if the responding party is objecting to the time and place of production; or

(C) entry or other requested action cannot be permitted for reasons stated in the response.

(d) ***Requirements for order for entry on nonparty's property.*** An order for entry on a nonparty's property may issue only for good cause shown and only if the land, property, or object thereon as to which discovery is sought is relevant to the subject matter of the action.

Comments to 1999 change:

1. "Document and tangible things" are defined in Rule 192.3(b).
2. A party requesting sampling or testing must describe the procedure with sufficient specificity to enable the responding party to make any appropriate objections.
3. A party requesting production of magnetic or electronic data must specifically request the data, specify the form in which it wants the data produced, and specify any extraordinary steps for retrieval and translation. Unless ordered otherwise, the responding party need only produce the data reasonably available in the ordinary course of business in reasonably usable form.
4. The rule clarifies how the expenses of production are to be allocated absent a court order to the contrary.
5. The obligation of parties to produce documents within their possession, custody or control is explained in Rule 192.3(b).
6. Parties may request production and inspection of documents and tangible things from nonparties under Rule 205.3.
7. Rule 196.3(b) is based on TRE 1003.
8. Rule 196.1(c) is merely a notice requirement and does not expand the scope of discovery of a nonparty's medical records.

See also ***O'Connor's Texas Rules***, "General Rules for Discovery," ch. 6-A; "Scope of Discovery," ch. 6-B; "Depositions," ch. 6-E; "Securing Documents & Tangible Things," ch. 6-H; "Medical Records," ch. 6-I; "Entry on Land," ch. 6-J; ***O'Connor's Texas Forms***, FORMS 6G-6I.

In re Colonial Pipeline Co., 968 S.W.2d 938, 942 (Tex.1998). "While the [Ps] may be entitled to production of any relevant discovery from the related cases 'as they are kept in the usual course of business,' [Ds] cannot be forced to prepare an inventory of the documents for plaintiffs."

G.M. Corp. v. Gayle, 951 S.W.2d 469, 475-76 (Tex. 1997). Plaintiffs "rely on Rule 167(1)(b) [now TRCP 196.7(a)] to support their claim to attend [D's crash] testing. ... The rule allowing entry upon land does not render discoverable items which are privileged under [TRCP 193.3]. For example, [TRCP 196.7(a)] obviously does not authorize a party to enter into opposing counsel's office to inspect privileged work product documents. Similarly, it does not authorize the [Ps] to enter into testing facilities under [D's] control to view privileged tests."

Dillard Dept. Stores, Inc. v. Hall, 909 S.W.2d 491, 492 (Tex.1995). Plaintiff "admits that he wants the document production to explore whether he can in good faith allege racial discrimination. This is the very kind of 'fishing expedition' that is not allowable under [TRCP 196.1]."

Schein v. American Rest. Group, Inc., 852 S.W.2d 496, 497 (Tex.1993). "If a party does not comply with a discovery request pursuant to [TRCP 196 & 197], the party may be prohibited from introducing a requested document or evidence at trial."

Sears, Roebuck & Co. v. Ramirez, 824 S.W.2d 558, 559 (Tex.1992). The trial court ordered [D] to produce its annual reports *and* its federal income tax statements. The Supreme Court held there was "no justification for requiring [D] to produce the same information in different form."

In re Diversicare Gen. Partner, Inc., 41 S.W.3d 788, 795 (Tex.App.—Corpus Christi 2001, orig. proceeding). "[W]hile rule 196.1(c) contemplates redaction of identifying information from nonparty medical records or a showing of good cause in order to avoid service on the nonparty, it is only a notice requirement rule and in no way addresses the parameters of the substantive confidentiality of the records."

TRCP 197. INTERROGATORIES TO PARTIES

197.1 Interrogatories. A party may serve on another party—no later than 30 days before the end of the discovery period—written interrogatories to inquire about any matter within the scope of discovery except matters covered by Rule 195. An interrogatory may inquire whether a party makes a specific legal or factual contention and may ask the responding party to state the legal theories and to describe in general the factual bases for the party's claims or defenses, but interrogatories may not be used to require the responding party to marshal all of its available proof or the proof the party intends to offer at trial.

197.2 Response to Interrogatories.

(a) ***Time for response.*** The responding party must serve a written response on the requesting party within 30 days after service of the interrogatories, except that a defendant served with interrogatories before the defendant's answer is due need not respond until 50 days after service of the interrogatories.

(b) ***Content of response.*** A response must include the party's answers to the interrogatories and may include objections and assertions of privilege as required under these rules.

(c) ***Option to produce records.*** If the answer to an interrogatory may be derived or ascertained from public records, from the responding party's business records, or from a compilation, abstract or summary of the responding party's business records, and the burden of deriving or ascertaining the answer is substantially the same for the requesting party as for the responding party, the responding party may answer the interrogatory by specifying and, if applicable, producing the records or compilation, abstract or summary of the records. The records from which the answer may be derived or ascertained must be specified in sufficient detail to permit the requesting party to locate and identify them as readily as can the responding party. If the responding party has specified business records, the responding party must state a reasonable time and place for examination of the documents. The responding party must produce the documents at the time and place stated, unless otherwise agreed by the parties or ordered by the court, and must provide the requesting party a reasonable opportunity to inspect them.

(d) ***Verification required; exceptions.*** A responding party—not an agent or attorney as otherwise permitted by Rule 14—must sign the answers under oath except that:

(1) when answers are based on information obtained from other persons, the party may so state, and

(2) a party need not sign answers to interrogatories about persons with knowledge of relevant facts, trial witnesses, and legal contentions.

197.3 Use. Answers to interrogatories may be used only against the responding party. An answer to an interrogatory inquiring about matters described in Rule 194.2(c) and (d) that has been amended or supplemented is not admissible and may not be used for impeachment.

Comments to 1999 change:

1. Interrogatories about specific legal or factual assertions—such as, whether a party claims a breach of implied warranty, or when a party contends that limitations began to run—are proper, but interrogatories that ask a party to state all legal and factual assertions are improper. As with requests for disclosure, interrogatories may be used to ascertain basic legal and factual claims and defenses but may not be used to force a party to marshal evidence. Use of the answers to such interrogatories is limited, just as the use of similar disclosures under Rule 194.6 is.

2. Rule 191's requirement that a party's attorney sign all discovery responses and objections applies to interrogatory responses and objections. In addition, the responding party must sign some interrogatory answers under oath, as specified by the rule. Answers in amended and supplemental responses must be signed by the party under oath only if the original answers were required to be signed under oath. The failure to sign or verify answers is only a formal defect that does not otherwise impair the answers unless the party refuses to sign or verify the answers after the defect is pointed out.

See also *O'Connor's Texas Rules*, "General Rules for Discovery," ch. 6-A; "Scope of Discovery," ch. 6-B; "Interrogatories," ch. 6-F; *O'Connor's Texas Forms*, FORMS 6F.

Morgan v. Anthony, 27 S.W.3d 928, 929 (Tex. 2000). "Generally, a party cannot rely on its own answer to an interrogatory as summary judgment evidence. ... The interrogatory answer became competent summary judgment evidence when it became a deposition exhibit, [P] affirmed in her deposition that it was correct, and she was subject to cross-examination about [it]."

Smith v. Southwest Feed Yards, 835 S.W.2d 89, 91 (Tex.1992). "[W]here the answer to another query in a single, short set of interrogatories plainly indicated that the individual responding had knowledge of relevant facts, the trial court abused its discretion by failing to find 'good cause' to permit that party's testimony."

Ticor Title Ins. Co. v. Lacy, 803 S.W.2d 265, 266 (Tex.1991). "'A party must be able to rely on the interrogatories and answers of other parties in the same suit. Otherwise, a multi-party case would require redundant interrogatories with identical questions and answers.'"

TRCP 198. REQUESTS FOR ADMISSIONS

198.1 Request for Admissions. A party may serve on another party—no later than 30 days before the end of the discovery period—written requests that the other party admit the truth of any matter within the scope of discovery, including statements of opinion or of fact or of the application of law to fact, or the genuineness of any documents served with the request or otherwise made available for inspection and copying. Each matter for which an admission is requested must be stated separately.

198.2 Response to Requests for Admissions.

(a) *Time for response.* The responding party must serve a written response on the requesting party within 30 days after service of the request, except that a defendant served with a request before the defendant's answer is due need not respond until 50 days after service of the request.

(b) *Content of response.* Unless the responding party states an objection or asserts a privilege, the responding party must specifically admit or deny the request or explain in detail the reasons that the responding party cannot admit or deny the request. A response must fairly meet the substance of the request. The responding party may qualify an answer, or deny a request in part, only when good faith requires. Lack of information or knowledge is not a proper response unless the responding party states that a reasonable inquiry was made but that the information known or easily obtainable is insufficient to enable the responding party to admit or deny. An assertion that the request presents an issue for trial is not a proper response.

(c) *Effect of failure to respond.* If a response is not timely served, the request is considered admitted without the necessity of a court order.

198.3 Effect of Admissions; Withdrawal or Amendment. Any admission made by a party under this rule may be used solely in the pending action and not in any other proceeding. A matter admitted under this rule is conclusively established as to the party making the admission unless the court permits the party to withdraw or amend the admission. The court may permit the party to withdraw or amend the admission if:

(a) the party shows good cause for the withdrawal or amendment; and

(b) the court finds that the parties relying upon the responses and deemed admissions will not be unduly prejudiced and that the presentation of the merits of the action will be subserved by permitting the party to amend or withdraw the admission.

See also *O'Connor's Texas Rules*, "General Rules for Discovery," ch. 6-A; "Scope of Discovery," ch. 6-B; "Requests for Admissions," ch. 6-G; *O'Connor's Texas Forms*, FORMS 6G.

Wal-Mart Stores, Inc. v. Deggs, 968 S.W.2d 354, 356 (Tex.1998). "'Good cause' is established when the failure to respond is accidental or the result of a mistake, rather than intentional or the result of conscious indifference."

Sanders v. Harder, 227 S.W.2d 206, 208 (Tex.1950). "The primary purpose of [TRCP 169, now TRCP 198] is to simplify trials by eliminating matters about which there is no real controversy, but which may be difficult or expensive to prove. It was never intended to be used as a demand upon a plaintiff or defendant to admit that he had no cause of action or ground of defense."

Payton v. Ashton, 29 S.W.3d 896, 898 (Tex.App.—Amarillo 2000, no pet.). "[C]ombining our interpretation of Rule 21a with that of Rule 198.2(a), we ... hold that a party's duty to respond to requests for admission is dependent upon receipt of those requests. ... In short, the requests cannot be deemed admitted if service was not perfected."

Pinal v. Carnevale, 964 S.W.2d 311, 313-14 (Tex. App.—Corpus Christi 1998, no pet.). "Because the language of [TRCP 198] provides no basis for requiring verification of answers to requests for admission, we hold that the requested matters could not be deemed admitted and summary judgment could not be granted on the ground that the answers were not verified."

TRCP 199. DEPOSITIONS UPON ORAL EXAMINATION

199.1 Oral Examination; Alternative Methods of Conducting or Recording.

(a) ***Generally.*** A party may take the testimony of any person or entity by deposition on oral examination before any officer authorized by law to take depositions. The testimony, objections, and any other statements during the deposition must be recorded at the time they are given or made.

(b) ***Depositions by telephone or other remote electronic means.*** A party may take an oral deposition by telephone or other remote electronic means if the party gives reasonable prior written notice of intent to do so. For the purposes of these rules, an oral deposition taken by telephone or other remote electronic means is considered as having been taken in the district and at the place where the witness is located when answering the questions. The officer taking the deposition may be located with the party noticing the deposition instead of with the witness if the witness is placed under oath by a person who is present with the witness and authorized to administer oaths in that jurisdiction.

(c) ***Nonstenographic recording.*** Any party may cause a deposition upon oral examination to be recorded by other than stenographic means, including videotape recording. The party requesting the nonstenographic recording will be responsible for obtaining a person authorized by law to administer the oath and for assuring that the recording will be intelligible, accurate, and trustworthy. At least five days prior to the deposition, the party must serve on the witness and all parties a notice, either in the notice of deposition or separately, that the deposition will be recorded by other than stenographic means. This notice must state the method of nonstenographic recording to be used and whether the deposition will also be recorded stenographically. Any other party may then serve written notice designating another method of recording in addition to the method specified, at the expense of such other party unless the court orders otherwise.

199.2 Procedure for Noticing Oral Deposition.

(a) ***Time to notice deposition.*** A notice of intent to take an oral deposition must be served on the witness and all parties a reasonable time before the deposition is taken. An oral deposition may be taken outside the discovery period only by agreement of the parties or with leave of court.

(b) ***Content of notice.***

(1) *Identity of witness; organizations.* The notice must state the name of the witness, which may be either an individual or a public or private corporation, partnership, association, governmental agency, or other organization. If an organization is named as the witness, the notice must describe with reasonable particularity the matters on which examination is requested. In response, the organization named in the notice must—a reasonable time before the deposition—designate one or more individuals to testify on its behalf and set forth, for each individual designated, the matters on which the individual will testify. Each individual designated must testify as to matters that are known or reasonably available to the organization. This subdivision does not preclude taking a deposition by any other procedure authorized by these rules.

(2) *Time and place.* The notice must state a reasonable time and place for the oral deposition. The place may be in:

(A) the county of the witness's residence;

(B) the county where the witness is employed or regularly transacts business in person;

(C) the county of suit, if the witness is a party or a person designated by a party under Rule 199.2(b)(1);

(D) the county where the witness was served with the subpoena, or within 150 miles of the place of service, if the witness is not a resident of Texas or is a transient person; or

(E) subject to the foregoing, at any other convenient place directed by the court in which the cause is pending.

(3) *Alternative means of conducting and recording.* The notice must state whether the deposition is to be taken by telephone or other remote electronic means and identify the means. If the deposition is to be recorded by nonstenographic means, the notice may include the notice required by Rule 199.1(c).

(4) *Additional attendees.* The notice may include the notice concerning additional attendees required by Rule 199.5(a)(3).

(5) *Request for production of documents.* A notice may include a request that the witness produce at the deposition documents or tangible things within the scope of discovery and within the witness's possession, custody, or control. If the witness is a nonparty, the request must comply with Rule 205 and the designation of materials required to be identified in the subpoena must be attached to, or included in, the notice. The nonparty's response to the request is governed by Rules 176 and 205. When the witness is a party or subject to the control of a party, document requests under this subdivision are governed by Rules 193 and 196.

199.3 Compelling Witness to Attend. A party may compel the witness to attend the oral deposition by serving the witness with a subpoena under Rule 176. If the witness is a party or is retained by, employed by, or otherwise subject to the control of a party, however, service of the notice of oral deposition upon the party's attorney has the same effect as a subpoena served on the witness.

199.4 Objections to Time and Place of Oral Deposition. A party or witness may object to the time and place designated for an oral deposition by motion for protective order or by motion to quash the notice of deposition. If the motion is filed by the third business day after service of the notice of deposition, an objection to the time and place of a deposition stays the oral deposition until the motion can be determined.

199.5 Examination, Objection, and Conduct During Oral Depositions.

(a) *Attendance.*

(1) *Witness.* The witness must remain in attendance from day to day until the deposition is begun and completed.

(2) *Attendance by party.* A party may attend an oral deposition in person, even if the deposition is taken by telephone or other remote electronic means. If a deposition is taken by telephone or other remote electronic means, the party noticing the deposition must make arrangements for all persons to attend by the same means. If the party noticing the deposition appears in person, any other party may appear by telephone or other remote electronic means if that party makes the necessary arrangements with the deposition officer and the party noticing the deposition.

(3) *Other attendees.* If any party intends to have in attendance any persons other than the witness, parties, spouses of parties, counsel, employees of counsel, and the officer taking the oral deposition, that party must give reasonable notice to all parties, either in the notice of deposition or separately, of the identity of the other persons.

(b) ***Oath; examination.*** Every person whose deposition is taken by oral examination must first be placed under oath. The parties may examine and cross-examine the witness. Any party, in lieu of participating in the examination, may serve written questions in a sealed envelope on the party noticing the oral deposition, who must deliver them to the deposition officer, who must open the envelope and propound them to the witness.

(c) ***Time limitation.*** No side may examine or cross-examine an individual witness for more than six hours. Breaks during depositions do not count against this limitation.

(d) ***Conduct during the oral deposition; conferences.*** The oral deposition must be conducted in the same manner as if the testimony were being obtained in court during trial. Counsel should cooperate with and be courteous to each other and to the witness. The witness should not be evasive and should not unduly delay the examination. Private conferences between the witness and the witness's attorney during the actual taking of the deposition are improper except for the purpose of determining whether a privilege should be asserted. Private conferences may be held, however, during agreed recesses and adjournments. If the lawyers and witnesses do not comply with this rule, the court may allow in evidence at trial statements, objections, discussions, and other occurrences during the oral deposition that reflect upon the credibility of the witness or the testimony.

(e) ***Objections.*** Objections to questions during the oral deposition are limited to "Objection, leading" and "Objection, form." Objections to testimony during the oral deposition are limited to "Objection, nonresponsive." These objections are waived if not stated as phrased during the oral deposition. All other objections need not be made or recorded during the oral deposition to be later raised with the court. The objecting party must give a clear and concise explanation of an objection if requested by the party taking the oral deposition, or the objection is waived. Argumentative or suggestive objections or explanations waive objection and may be grounds for terminating the oral deposition or assessing costs or other sanctions. The officer taking the oral deposition will not rule on objections but must record them for ruling by the court. The officer taking the oral deposition must not fail to record testimony because an objection has been made.

(f) ***Instructions not to answer.*** An attorney may instruct a witness not to answer a question during an oral deposition only if necessary to preserve a privilege, comply with a court order or these rules, protect a witness from an abusive question or one for which any answer would be misleading, or secure a ruling pursuant to paragraph (g). The attorney instructing the witness not to answer must give a concise, nonargumentative, nonsuggestive explanation of the grounds for the instruction if requested by the party who asked the question.

(g) ***Suspending the deposition.*** If the time limitations for the deposition have expired or the deposition is being conducted or defended in violation of these rules, a party or witness may suspend the oral deposition for the time necessary to obtain a ruling.

(h) ***Good faith required.*** An attorney must not ask a question at an oral deposition solely to harass or mislead the witness, for any other improper purpose, or without a good faith legal basis at the time. An attorney must not object to a question at an oral deposition, instruct the witness not to answer a question, or suspend the deposition unless there is a good faith factual and legal basis for doing so at the time.

199.6 Hearing on Objections. Any party may, at any reasonable time, request a hearing on an objection or privilege asserted by an instruction not to answer or suspension of the deposition; provided the failure of a party to obtain a ruling prior to trial does not waive any objection or privilege. The party seeking to avoid discovery must present any evidence necessary to support the objection or privilege either by testimony at the hearing or by affidavits served on opposing parties at least seven days before the hearing. If the court determines that an *in camera* review of some or all of the requested discovery is necessary to rule, answers to the deposition questions may be made in camera, to be transcribed and sealed in the event the privilege is sustained, or made in an affidavit produced to the court in a sealed wrapper.

Comments to 1999 change:

1. Rule 199.2(b)(5) incorporates the procedures and limitations applicable to requests for production or inspection under Rule 196, including the 30-day deadline for responses, as well as the procedures and duties imposed by Rule 193.

2. For purposes of Rule 199.5(c), each person designated by an organization under Rule 199.2(b)(1) is a separate witness.

3. The requirement of Rule 199.5(d) that depositions be conducted in the same manner as if the testimony were being obtained in court is a limit on the conduct of the lawyers and witnesses in the deposition, not on the scope of the interrogation permitted by Rule 192.

4. An objection to the form of a question includes objections that the question calls for speculation, calls for a narrative answer, is vague, is confusing, or is ambiguous. Ordinarily, a witness must answer a question at a deposition subject to the objection. An objection may therefore be inadequate if a question incorporates such unfair assumptions or is worded so that any answer would necessarily be misleading. A witness should not be required to answer whether he has yet ceased conduct he denies ever doing, subject to an objection to form (i.e., that the question is confusing or assumes facts not in evidence) because any answer would necessarily be misleading on account of the way in which the question is put. The witness may be instructed not to answer. Abusive questions include questions that inquire into matters clearly beyond the scope of discovery or that are argumentative, repetitious, or harassing.

See also CPRC §20.001; Govt Code §§52.021, 52.031, 52.059 (imposes joint and several liability for the cost of the deposition on the lawyer who asks the first question and the lawyer's firm); TRE 603; ***O'Connor's Texas Rules***, "General Rules for Discovery," ch. 6-A; "Scope of Discovery," ch. 6-B; "Depositions," ch. 6-E; ***O'Connor's Texas Forms***, FORMS 6E. Lawyers can find important information about the conduct of the deposition in the Supreme Court's rules regarding court reporters in the Uniform Format Manual for Texas Court Reporters §12 cmt., ¶3, which can be found at <http://www.supreme.courts.state.tx.us/rules/reporter>.

Wal-Mart Stores, Inc. v. Street, 754 S.W.2d 153, 154-55 (Tex.1988). The trial court abused its discretion when it ordered Sam Walton, the former president of the defendant corporation, to travel to Fort Worth from Arkansas to be deposed. TRCP 199 required the deposition to be taken in the Arkansas county where Walton lived.

Lindsey v. O'Neill, 689 S.W.2d 400, 402 (Tex.1985). TRCP 199.2(b)(1) "requires that a deposition notice of a corporation describe with reasonable particularity the matters on which examination is requested."

TRCP 200. DEPOSITIONS UPON WRITTEN QUESTIONS

200.1 Procedure for Noticing Deposition Upon Written Questions.

(a) ***Who may be noticed; when.*** A party may take the testimony of any person or entity by deposition on written questions before any person authorized by law to take depositions on written questions. A notice of intent to take the deposition must be served on the witness and all parties at least 20 days before the deposition is taken. A deposition on written questions may be taken outside the discovery period only by agreement of the parties or with leave of court. The party noticing the deposition must also deliver to the deposition officer a copy of the notice and of all written questions to be asked during the deposition.

(b) ***Content of notice.*** The notice must comply with Rules 199.1(b), 199.2(b), and 199.5(a)(3). If the witness is an organization, the organization must comply with the requirements of that provision. The notice also may include a request for production of documents as permitted by Rule 199.2(b)(5), the provisions of which will govern the request, service, and response.

200.2 Compelling Witness to Attend. A party may compel the witness to attend the deposition on written questions by serving the witness with a subpoena under Rule 176. If the witness is a party or is retained by, employed by, or otherwise subject to the control of a party, however, service of the deposition notice upon the party's attorney has the same effect as a subpoena served on the witness.

200.3 Questions and Objections.

(a) ***Direct questions.*** The direct questions to be propounded to the witness must be attached to the notice.

(b) ***Objections and additional questions.*** Within ten days after the notice and direct questions are served, any party may object to the direct questions and serve cross-questions on all other parties. Within five days after cross-questions are served, any party may object to the cross-questions and serve redirect questions on all other parties. Within three days after redirect questions are served, any party may object to the redirect questions and serve recross questions on all other parties. Objections to recross questions must be served within five days after the earlier of when recross questions are served or the time of the deposition on written questions.

(c) ***Objections to form of questions.*** Objections to the form of a question are waived unless asserted in accordance with this subdivision.

200.4 Conducting the Deposition Upon Written Questions. The deposition officer must: take the deposition on written questions at the time and place designated; record the testimony of the witness under oath in response to the questions; and prepare, certify, and deliver the deposition transcript in accordance with Rule 203. The deposition officer has authority when necessary to summon and swear an interpreter to facilitate the taking of the deposition.

Comments to 1999 change:

1. The procedures for asserting objections during oral depositions under Rule 199.5(e) do not apply to depositions on written questions.

2. Section 20.001 of the CPRC provides that a deposition on written questions of a witness who is alleged to reside or to be in this state may be taken by a clerk of a district court, a judge or clerk of a county court, or a notary public of this state.

See also CPRC §20.001; Govt Code §§52.021, 52.031; ***O'Connor's Texas Rules***, "General Rules for Discovery," ch. 6-A; "Scope of Discovery," ch. 6-B; "Depositions," ch. 6-D; ***O'Connor's Texas Forms***, FORMS 6E.

St. Luke's Episcopal Hosp. v. Garcia, 928 S.W.2d 307, 310 (Tex.App.—Houston [14th Dist.] 1996, orig. proceeding). "Because relator has no objection to the form of TMC's written questions, relator claims the provision in [TRCP 200] regarding timeliness of objections is inapplicable. We agree. In its objections to the deposition notice and subpoena duces tecum, relator's primary objections are substantive objections relating to privilege. We hold that the ten-day limitation in [TRCP 200] is inapplicable to substantive objections."

Fibreboard Corp. v. Pool, 813 S.W.2d 658, 677 (Tex.App.—Texarkana 1991, writ denied). "[T]he trial court limited [D's] examination of [two witnesses] to 50 cross-questions. [¶] Until the [Ds] exhaust the number of questions allotted to them …, they cannot be heard to complain that they were denied the right to ask additional questions."

TRCP 201. DEPOSITIONS IN FOREIGN JURISDICTIONS FOR USE IN TEXAS PROCEEDINGS; DEPOSITIONS IN TEXAS FOR USE IN FOREIGN PROCEEDINGS

201.1 Depositions in Foreign Jurisdictions for Use in Texas Proceedings.

(a) *Generally.* A party may take a deposition on oral examination or written questions of any person or entity located in another state or a foreign country for use in proceedings in this State. The deposition may be taken by:

(1) notice;

(2) letter rogatory, letter of request, or other such device;

(3) agreement of the parties; or

(4) court order.

(b) *By notice.* A party may take the deposition by notice in accordance with these rules as if the deposition were taken in this State, except that the deposition officer may be a person authorized to administer oaths in the place where the deposition is taken.

(c) *By letter rogatory.* On motion by a party, the court in which an action is pending must issue a letter rogatory on terms that are just and appropriate, regardless of whether any other manner of obtaining the deposition is impractical or inconvenient. The letter must:

(1) be addressed to the appropriate authority in the jurisdiction in which the deposition is to be taken;

(2) request and authorize that authority to summon the witness before the authority at a time and place stated in the letter for examination on oral or written questions; and

(3) request and authorize that authority to cause the witness's testimony to be reduced to writing and returned, together with any items marked as exhibits, to the party requesting the letter rogatory.

(d) *By letter of request or other such device.* On motion by a party, the court in which an action is pending, or the clerk of that court, must issue a letter of request or other such device in accordance with an applicable treaty or international convention on terms that are just and appropriate. The letter or other device must be issued regardless of whether any other manner of obtaining the deposition is impractical or inconvenient. The letter or other device must:

(1) be in the form prescribed by the treaty or convention under which it is issued, as presented by the movant to the court or clerk; and

(2) must state the time, place, and manner of the examination of the witness.

(e) *Objections to form of letter rogatory, letter of request, or other such device.* In issuing a letter rogatory, letter of request, or other such device, the court must set a time for objecting to the form of the device. A party must make any objection to the form of the device in writing and serve it on all other parties by the time set by the court, or the objection is waived.

(f) *Admissibility of evidence.* Evidence obtained in response to a letter rogatory, letter of request, or other such device is not inadmissible merely because it is not a verbatim transcript, or the testimony was not taken under oath, or for any similar departure from the requirements for depositions taken within this State under these rules.

(g) *Deposition by electronic means.* A deposition in another jurisdiction may be taken by telephone, videoconference, teleconference, or other electronic means under the provisions of Rule 199.

201.2 Depositions in Texas for Use in Proceedings in Foreign Jurisdictions. If a court of record of any other state or foreign jurisdiction issues a mandate, writ, or commission that requires a witness's oral or written deposition testimony in this State, the witness may be compelled to appear and testify in the same manner and by the same process used for taking testimony in a proceeding pending in this State.

Comments to 1999 change:

1. Rule 201.1 sets forth procedures for obtaining deposition testimony of a witness in another state or foreign jurisdiction for use in Texas court proceedings. It does not, however, address whether any of the procedures listed are, in fact, permitted or recognized by the law of the state or foreign jurisdiction where the witness is located. A party must first determine what procedures are permitted by the jurisdiction where the witness is located before using this rule.

2. Section 20.001 of the CPRC provides a nonexclusive list of persons who are qualified to take a written deposition in Texas and who may take depositions (oral or written) in another state or outside the United States.

3. Rule 201.2 is based on Section 20.002 of the CPRC.

See also CPRC §§20.001-20.002; *O'Connor's Texas Rules*, "General Rules for Discovery," ch. 6-A; "Scope of Discovery," ch. 6-B; "Depositions," ch. 6-E; *O'Connor's Texas Forms*, FORMS 6E.

Clone Component Distrib., Inc. v. State, 819 S.W.2d 593, 598 (Tex.App.—Dallas 1991, no writ). Regarding a telephone deposition in another state: "[W]e hold that the requirement of [TRCP 201.1(b)] that the deposition be taken 'before' a person authorized to take oaths was satisfied by the court reporter's being in the vocal and aural presence of the deponent through the use of the telephone."

Latham v. Thornton, 806 S.W.2d 347, 349-50 (Tex. App.—Fort Worth 1991, orig. proceeding). "[A]s regards the person whose deposition is sought, if that person is not a party, the order may only be sought in the court where the deposition is to be taken. In this particular case under the authority of [TRCP] 201, that place is the county of the witness's residence…."

TRCP 202. DEPOSITIONS BEFORE SUIT OR TO INVESTIGATE CLAIMS

202.1 Generally. A person may petition the court for an order authorizing the taking of a deposition on oral examination or written questions either:

(a) to perpetuate or obtain the person's own testimony or that of any other person for use in an anticipated suit; or

(b) to investigate a potential claim or suit.

202.2 Petition. The petition must:

(a) be verified;

(b) be filed in a proper court of any county:

(1) where venue of the anticipated suit may lie, if suit is anticipated; or

(2) where the witness resides, if no suit is yet anticipated;

(c) be in the name of the petitioner;

(d) state either:

(1) that the petitioner anticipates the institution of a suit in which the petitioner may be a party; or

(2) that the petitioner seeks to investigate a potential claim by or against petitioner;

(e) state the subject matter of the anticipated action, if any, and the petitioner's interest therein;

(f) if suit is anticipated, either:

(1) state the names of the persons petitioner expects to have interests adverse to petitioner's in the anticipated suit, and the addresses and telephone numbers for such persons; or

(2) state that the names, addresses, and telephone numbers of persons petitioner expects to have interests adverse to petitioner's in the anticipated suit cannot be ascertained through diligent inquiry, and describe those persons;

(g) state the names, addresses and telephone numbers of the persons to be deposed, the substance of the testimony that the petitioner expects to elicit from each, and the petitioner's reasons for desiring to obtain the testimony of each; and

(h) request an order authorizing the petitioner to take the depositions of the persons named in the petition.

202.3 Notice and Service.

(a) ***Personal service on witnesses and persons named.*** At least 15 days before the date of the hearing on the petition, the petitioner must serve the petition and a notice of the hearing—in accordance with Rule 21a—on all persons petitioner seeks to depose and, if suit is anticipated, on all persons petitioner expects to have interests adverse to petitioner's in the anticipated suit.

(b) ***Service by publication on persons not named.***

(1) *Manner.* Unnamed persons described in the petition whom the petitioner expects to have interests adverse to petitioner's in the anticipated suit, if any, may be served by publication with the petition and notice of the hearing. The notice must state the place for the hearing and the time it will be held, which must be more than 14 days after the first publication of the notice. The petition and notice must be published once each week for two consecutive weeks in the newspaper of broadest circulation in the county in which the petition is filed, or if no such newspaper exists, in the newspaper of broadest circulation in the nearest county where a newspaper is published.

(2) *Objection to depositions taken on notice by publication.* Any interested party may move, in the proceeding or by bill of review, to suppress any deposition, in whole or in part, taken on notice by publication, and may also attack or oppose the deposition by any other means available.

(c) ***Service in probate cases.*** A petition to take a deposition in anticipation of an application for probate of a will, and notice of the hearing on the petition, may be served by posting as prescribed by Section 33(f)(2) of the Probate Code. The notice and petition must be directed to all parties interested in the testator's estate and must comply with the requirements of Section 33(c) of the Probate Code insofar as they may be applicable.

(d) ***Modification by order.*** As justice or necessity may require, the court may shorten or lengthen the notice periods under this rule and may extend the notice period to permit service on any expected adverse party.

202.4 Order.

(a) ***Required findings.*** The court must order a deposition to be taken if, but only if, it finds that:

(1) allowing the petitioner to take the requested deposition may prevent a failure or delay of justice in an anticipated suit; or

(2) the likely benefit of allowing the petitioner to take the requested deposition to investigate a potential claim outweighs the burden or expense of the procedure.

(b) ***Contents.*** The order must state whether a deposition will be taken on oral examination or written questions. The order may also state the time and place at which a deposition will be taken. If the order does not state the time and place at which a deposition will be taken, the petitioner must notice the deposition as required by Rules 199 or 200. The order must contain any protections the court finds necessary or appropriate to protect the witness or any person who may be affected by the procedure.

202.5 Manner of Taking and Use. Except as otherwise provided in this rule, depositions authorized by this rule are governed by the rules applicable to depositions of nonparties in a pending suit. The scope of discovery in depositions authorized by this rule is the same as if the anticipated suit or potential claim had been filed. A court may restrict or prohibit the use of a deposition taken under this rule in a subsequent suit to protect a person who was not served with notice of the deposition from any unfair prejudice or to prevent abuse of this rule.

Comments to 1999 change:

1. This rule applies to all discovery before suit covered by former rules governing depositions to perpetuate testimony and bills of discovery.

2. A deposition taken under this rule may be used in a subsequent suit as permitted by the rules of evidence, except that a court may restrict or prohibit its use to prevent taking unfair advantage of a witness or others. The bill of discovery procedure, which Rule 202 incorporates, is equitable in nature, and a court must not permit it to be used inequitably.

See also CPRC §§20.001, 20.002; Govt Code §§52.021, 52.031, 52.059; ***O'Connor's Texas Rules***, "General Rules for Discovery," ch. 6-A; "Scope of Discovery," ch. 6-B; "Depositions," ch. 6-E; ***O'Connor's Texas Forms***, FORMS 6E.

U.S. v. Marks, 949 S.W.2d 320, 322 (Tex.1997). TRCP 202 "authorizes a court to order the taking of a deposition to perpetuate testimony in anticipation of litigation."

Office Employees Int'l Un. v. Southwestern Drug Corp., 391 S.W.2d 404, 406 (Tex.1965). "[A] proceeding to perpetuate testimony is not of itself an independent suit, but is in aid of and incident to an anticipated suit."

In re Akzo Nobel Chem., Inc., 24 S.W.3d 919, 921 (Tex.App.—Beaumont 2000, orig. proceeding). "Neither by its language nor by implication can we construe [TRCP] 202 to authorize a trial court, before suit is filed, to order any form of discovery but deposition."

TRCP 203. SIGNING, CERTIFICATION & USE OF ORAL & WRITTEN DEPOSITIONS

203.1 Signature and Changes.

(a) ***Deposition transcript to be provided to witness.*** The deposition officer must provide the original deposition transcript to the witness for examination and signature. If the witness is represented by an attorney at the deposition, the deposition officer must provide the transcript to the attorney instead of the witness.

(b) ***Changes by witness; signature.*** The witness may change responses as reflected in the deposition transcript by indicating the desired changes, in writing, on a separate sheet of paper, together with a statement of the reasons for making the changes. No erasures or obliterations of any kind may be made to the original deposition transcript. The witness must then sign the transcript under oath and return it to the deposition officer. If the witness does not return the transcript to the deposition officer within 20 days of the date the transcript was provided to the witness or the witness's attorney, the witness may be deemed to have waived the right to make the changes.

(c) ***Exceptions.*** The requirements of presentation and signature under this subdivision do not apply:

(1) if the witness and all parties waive the signature requirement;

(2) to depositions on written questions; or

(3) to nonstenographic recordings of oral depositions.

203.2 Certification. The deposition officer must file with the court, serve on all parties, and attach as part of the deposition transcript or nonstenographic recording of an oral deposition a certificate duly sworn by the officer stating:

(a) that the witness was duly sworn by the officer and that the transcript or nonstenographic recording of the oral deposition is a true record of the testimony given by the witness;

(b) that the deposition transcript, if any, was submitted to the witness or to the attorney for the witness for examination and signature, the date on which the transcript was submitted, whether the witness returned the transcript, and if so, the date on which it was returned.

(c) that changes, if any, made by the witness are attached to the deposition transcript;

(d) that the deposition officer delivered the deposition transcript or nonstenographic recording of an oral deposition in accordance with Rule 203.3;

(e) the amount of time used by each party at the deposition;

(f) the amount of the deposition officer's charges for preparing the original deposition transcript, which the clerk of the court must tax as costs; and

(g) that a copy of the certificate was served on all parties and the date of service.

203.3 Delivery.

(a) ***Endorsement; to whom delivered.*** The deposition officer must endorse the title of the action and "Deposition of (name of witness)" on the original deposition transcript (or a copy, if the original was not returned) or the original nonstenographic recording of an oral deposition, and must return:

(1) the transcript to the party who asked the first question appearing in the transcript, or

(2) the recording to the party who requested it.

(b) ***Notice.*** The deposition officer must serve notice of delivery on all other parties.

(c) ***Inspection and copying; copies.*** The party receiving the original deposition transcript or nonstenographic recording must make it available upon reasonable request for inspection and copying by any other party. Any party or the witness is entitled to obtain a copy of the deposition transcript or nonstenographic recording from the deposition officer upon payment of a reasonable fee.

203.4 Exhibits. At the request of a party, the original documents and things produced for inspection during the examination of the witness must be marked for identification by the deposition officer and annexed to the deposition transcript or nonstenographic recording. The person producing the materials may produce copies instead of originals if the party gives all other parties fair opportunity at the deposition to compare the copies with the originals. If the person offers originals rather than copies, the deposition officer must, after the conclusion of the deposition, make copies to be attached to the original deposition transcript or nonstenographic recording, and then return the originals to the person who produced them. The person who produced the originals must preserve them for hearing or trial and make them available for inspection or copying by any other party upon seven days' notice. Copies annexed to the original deposition transcript or nonstenographic recording may be used for all purposes.

203.5 Motion to Suppress. A party may object to any errors and irregularities in the manner in which the testimony is transcribed, signed, delivered, or otherwise dealt with by the deposition officer by filing a motion to suppress all or part of the deposition. If the deposition officer complies with Rule 203.3 at least one day before the case is called to trial, with regard to a deposition transcript, or 30 days before the case is called to trial, with regard to a nonstenographic recording, the party must file and serve a motion to suppress before trial commences to preserve the objections.

203.6 Use.

(a) ***Nonstenographic recording; transcription.*** A nonstenographic recording of an oral deposition, or a written transcription of all or part of such a recording, may be used to the same extent as a deposition taken by stenographic means. However, the court, for good cause shown, may require that the party seeking to use a nonstenographic recording or written transcription first obtain a complete transcript of the deposition recording from a certified court reporter. The court reporter's transcription must be made from the original or a certified copy of the deposition recording. The court reporter must, to the extent applicable, comply with the provisions of this rule, except that the court reporter must deliver the original transcript to the attorney requesting the transcript, and the court reporter's certificate must include a statement that the transcript is a true record of the nonstenographic recording. The party to whom the court reporter delivers the original transcript must make the transcript available, upon reasonable request, for inspection and copying by the witness or any party.

(b) ***Same proceeding.*** All or part of a deposition may be used for any purpose in the same proceeding in which it was taken. If the original is not filed, a certified copy may be used. "Same proceeding" includes a proceeding in a different court but involving the same subject matter and the same parties or their representatives or successors in interest. A deposition is admissible against a party joined after the deposition was taken if:

(1) the deposition is admissible pursuant to Rule 804(b)(1) of the Rules of Evidence, or

(2) that party has had a reasonable opportunity to redepose the witness and has failed to do so.

(c) ***Different proceeding.*** Depositions taken in different proceedings may be used as permitted by the Rules of Evidence.

See also Govt Code §52.021; ***O'Connor's Texas Rules***, "General Rules for Discovery," ch. 6-A; "Depositions," ch. 6-E. Lawyers can find important information about the conduct of the deposition in the Supreme Court's rules regarding court reporters in the Uniform Format Manual for Texas Court Reporters §12 cmt., ¶3, which can be found at <http://www.supreme.courts.state.tx.us/rules/reporters>.

Jones v. Colley, 820 S.W.2d 863, 866 (Tex.App.—Texarkana 1991, writ denied). "No rule requires that a deposition be read into the record or played before the jury in chronological order. A party, as a matter of trial strategy, is entitled to present his evidence in the order he believes constitutes the most effective presentation of his case, provided that it does not convey a *distinctly false* impression."

Klorer v. Block, 717 S.W.2d 754, 759 (Tex.App.—San Antonio 1986, writ ref'd n.r.e.). "The statement in [TRCP 203.5] that a deposition shall have been filed at least one entire day before the day of trial is a condition precedent to the filing of a *written* motion to suppress. This rule does not require that *all* depositions must be filed at least one entire day before the day of trial."

TRCP 204. PHYSICAL & MENTAL EXAMINATIONS

204.1 Motion and Order Required.

(a) ***Motion.*** A party may—no later than 30 days before the end of any applicable discovery period—move for an order compelling another party to:

(1) submit to a physical or mental examination by a qualified physician or a mental examination by a qualified psychologist; or

(2) produce for such examination a person in the other party's custody, conservatorship or legal control.

(b) ***Service.*** The motion and notice of hearing must be served on the person to be examined and all parties.

(c) ***Requirements for obtaining order.*** The court may issue an order for examination only for good cause shown and only in the following circumstances:

(1) when the mental or physical condition (including the blood group) of a party, or of a person in the custody, conservatorship or under the legal control of a party, is in controversy; or

(2) except as provided in Rule 204.4, an examination by a psychologist may be ordered when the party responding to the motion has designated a psychologist as a testifying expert or has disclosed a psychologist's records for possible use at trial.

(d) ***Requirements of order.*** The order must be in writing and must specify the time, place, manner, conditions, and scope of the examination and the person or persons by whom it is to be made.

204.2 Report of Examining Physician or Psychologist.

(a) ***Right to report.*** Upon request of the person ordered to be examined, the party causing the examination to be made must deliver to the person a copy of a detailed written report of the examining physician or psychologist setting out the findings, including results of all tests made, diagnoses and conclusions, together with like reports of all earlier examinations of the same condition. After delivery of the report, upon request of the party causing the examination, the party against whom the order is made must produce a like report of any examination made before or after the ordered examination of the same condition, unless the person examined is not a party and the party shows that the party is unable to obtain it. The court on motion may limit delivery of a report on such terms as are just. If a physician or psychologist fails or refuses to make a report the court may exclude the testimony if offered at the trial.

(b) ***Agreements; relationship to other rules.*** This subdivision applies to examinations made by agreement of the parties, unless the agreement expressly provides otherwise. This subdivision does not preclude discovery of a report of an examining physician or psychologist or the taking of a deposition of the physician or psychologist in accordance with the provisions of any other rule.

204.3 Effect of No Examination. If no examination is sought either by agreement or under this subdivision, the party whose physical or mental condition is in controversy must not comment to the court or jury concerning the party's willingness to submit to an examination, or on the right or failure of any other party to seek an examination.

204.4 Cases Arising Under Titles II or V, Family Code. In cases arising under Family Code Titles II or V, the court may—on its own initiative or on motion of a party—appoint:

(a) one or more psychologists or psychiatrists to make any and all appropriate mental examinations of the children who are the subject of the suit or of any other parties, and may make such appointment irrespective of whether a psychologist or psychiatrist has been designated by any party as a testifying expert;

(b) one or more experts who are qualified in paternity testing to take blood, body fluid, or tissue samples to conduct paternity tests as ordered by the court.

204.5 Definition. For the purpose of this rule, a psychologist is a person licensed or certified by a state or the District of Columbia as a psychologist.

See also TRE 510(d)(5); ***O'Connor's Texas Rules***, "General Rules for Discovery," ch. 6-A; "Scope of Discovery," ch. 6-B; "Medical Records," ch. 6-I; ***O'Connor's Texas Forms***, FORMS 6I.

Coates v. Whittington, 758 S.W.2d 749, 751 (Tex. 1988). TRCP 204, "by its express language, places an affirmative burden on the movant to meet a two pronged test: (1) the movant must show that the party's mental condition is 'in controversy'; and (2) the movant must demonstrate that there is 'good cause' for a compulsory mental examination. In the absence of an affirmative showing of both prongs of the test, a trial court may not order an examination pursuant to [TRCP 204.1]."

In re Caballero, 36 S.W.3d 143, 145 (Tex.App.—Corpus Christi 2000, orig. proceeding). Good cause "requires an affirmative showing of three components: (1) that an examination is relevant to issues that are genuinely in controversy in the case; (2) that a reasonable nexus exists between the condition in controversy and the examination sought; and (3) that it is not possible to obtain the desired information through means that are less intrusive than a compelled examination."

In re Doe, 22 S.W.3d 601, 606 (Tex.App.—Austin 2000, orig. proceeding). "A court may compel a [P] to submit to a mental examination only if *the [P] asserts a mental injury that exceeds the common emotional reaction to an injury or loss.*"

Laub v. Millard, 925 S.W.2d 363, 365 (Tex.App.—Houston [1st Dist.] 1996, orig. proceeding). "If [petitioner] plans to call these experts as witnesses, [respondent] should be given the opportunity to have a mental health expert, other than those employed by [petitioner], examine [her] to evaluate her mental competency during the years in question. [O]therwise, [respondent] will be at a severe disadvantage in the 'battle of experts.'"

Delcourt v. Silverman, 919 S.W.2d 777, 782-83 (Tex.App.—Houston [14th Dist.] 1996, writ denied). "Under Rule 167a(d) [now 204.4], the court, in cases arising under Title II of the Texas Family Code, may appoint one or more psychologists to make any and all appropriate mental examinations of the child or children who are the subject of the suit or any other parties to the suit. [¶] Numerous courts have extended absolute immunity to psychiatrists and other mental health experts assisting the court in criminal cases. The consistent reasoning given by the courts in these cases is that the psychiatrist or mental health professional performed a special task closely related to the judicial process pursuant to a court directive. We believe this reasoning also applies to mental health experts appointed to provide psychological expertise in child custody suits. Many courts recognize that psychiatrists and psychologists performing court-ordered custody evaluations perform a judicial function and enjoy absolute immunity. When a court appoints a mental health professional to examine the child and the parents in a custody proceeding, the professional is acting as a fact finder for the court. The court relies on the professional to provide information essential to the decision-making process. Without the protection of absolute immunity, such professionals would be, at the very least, reluctant to accept these appointments."

TRCP 205. DISCOVERY FROM NONPARTIES

205.1 Forms of Discovery; Subpoena Requirement. A party may compel discovery from a nonparty—

that is, a person who is not a party or subject to a party's control—only by obtaining a court order under Rules 196.7, 202, or 204, or by serving a subpoena compelling:

(a) an oral deposition;

(b) a deposition on written questions;

(c) a request for production of documents or tangible things, pursuant to Rule 199.2(b)(5) or Rule 200.1(b), served with a notice of deposition on oral examination or written questions; and

(d) a request for production of documents and tangible things under this rule.

205.2 Notice. A party seeking discovery by subpoena from a nonparty must serve, on the nonparty and all parties, a copy of the form of notice required under the rules governing the applicable form of discovery. A notice of oral or written deposition must be served before or at the same time that a subpoena compelling attendance or production under the notice is served. A notice to produce documents or tangible things under Rule 205.3 must be served at least 10 days before the subpoena compelling production is served.

205.3 Production of Documents and Tangible Things Without Deposition.

(a) *Notice; subpoena.* A party may compel production of documents and tangible things from a nonparty by serving—a reasonable time before the response is due but no later than 30 days before the end of any applicable discovery period—the notice required in Rule 205.2 and a subpoena compelling production or inspection of documents or tangible things.

(b) *Contents of notice.* The notice must state:

(1) the name of the person from whom production or inspection is sought to be compelled;

(2) a reasonable time and place for the production or inspection; and

(3) the items to be produced or inspected, either by individual item or by category, describing each item and category with reasonable particularity, and, if applicable, describing the desired testing and sampling with sufficient specificity to inform the nonparty of the means, manner, and procedure for testing or sampling.

(c) *Requests for production of medical or mental health records of other nonparties.* If a party requests a nonparty to produce medical or mental health records of another nonparty, the requesting party must serve the nonparty whose records are sought with the notice required under this rule. This requirement does not apply under the circumstances set forth in Rule 196.1(c)(2).

(d) *Response.* The nonparty must respond to the notice and subpoena in accordance with Rule 176.6.

(e) *Custody, inspection and copying.* The party obtaining the production must make all materials produced available for inspection by any other party on reasonable notice, and must furnish copies to any party who requests at that party's expense.

(f) *Cost of production.* A party requiring production of documents by a nonparty must reimburse the nonparty's reasonable costs of production.

Comments to 1999 change: Under this rule, a party may subpoena production of documents and tangible things from nonparties without need for a motion or oral or written deposition.

See also *O'Connor's Texas Rules*, "General Rules for Discovery," ch. 6-A; "Scope of Discovery," ch. 6-B; "Depositions," ch. 6-E; "Securing Documents & Tangible Things," ch. 6-H.

Automatic Drilling Machs., Inc. v. Miller, 515 S.W.2d 256, 259 (Tex.1974). "Under the general provisions of [TRCP 205], a subpoena may be issued in a proper case to require a witness to produce, at the time and place of giving his deposition, documents and other tangible things which constitute or contain evidence relating to any of the matters.... The subpoena is, however, subject to the provisions of [TRCP 176 & 192]."

In re Diversicare Gen. Partner, Inc., 41 S.W.3d 788, 794 (Tex.App.—Corpus Christi 2001, orig. proceeding). "[P]ersonal and clinical records do not have to be in the nonparty's possession to be described as nonparty records, they only have to be personal and clinical records *regarding* the nonparty."

TRCP 206 - 214. REPEALED

TRCP 215. ABUSE OF DISCOVERY; SANCTIONS

215.1 Motion for Sanctions or Order Compelling Discovery. A party, upon reasonable notice to other parties and all other persons affected thereby, may apply for sanctions or an order compelling discovery as follows:

(a) *Appropriate court.* On matters relating to a deposition, an application for an order to a party may be made to the court in which the action is pending, or to any district court in the district where the deposition is being taken. An application for an order to a deponent who is not a party shall be made to the court in the district where the deposition is being taken. As to all other discovery matters, an application for an order will be made to the court in which the action is pending.

(b) ***Motion.***

(1) If a party or other deponent which is a corporation or other entity fails to make a designation under Rules 199.2(b)(1) or 200.1(b); or

(2) if a party, or other deponent, or a person designated to testify on behalf of a party or other deponent fails:

(A) to appear before the officer who is to take his deposition, after being served with a proper notice; or

(B) to answer a question propounded or submitted upon oral examination or upon written questions; or

(3) if a party fails:

(A) to serve answers or objections to interrogatories submitted under Rule 197, after proper service of the interrogatories; or

(B) to answer an interrogatory submitted under Rule 197; or

(C) to serve a written response to a request for inspection submitted under Rule 196, after proper service of the request; or

(D) to respond that discovery will be permitted as requested or fails to permit discovery as requested in response to a request for inspection submitted under Rule 196;

the discovering party may move for an order compelling a designation, an appearance, an answer or answers, or inspection or production in accordance with the request, or apply to the court in which the action is pending for the imposition of any sanction authorized by Rule 215.2(b) without the necessity of first having obtained a court order compelling such discovery.

When taking a deposition on oral examination, the proponent of the question may complete or adjourn the examination before he applies for an order.

If the court denies the motion in whole or in part, it may make such protective order as it would have been empowered to make on a motion pursuant to Rule 192.6.

(c) ***Evasive or incomplete answer.*** For purposes of this subdivision an evasive or incomplete answer is to be treated as a failure to answer.

(d) ***Disposition of motion to compel: award of expenses.*** If the motion is granted, the court shall, after opportunity for hearing, require a party or deponent whose conduct necessitated the motion or the party or attorney advising such conduct or both of them to pay, at such time as ordered by the court, the moving party the reasonable expenses incurred in obtaining the order, including attorney fees, unless the court finds that the opposition to the motion was substantially justified or that other circumstances make an award of expenses unjust. Such an order shall be subject to review on appeal from the final judgment.

If the motion is denied, the court may, after opportunity for hearing, require the moving party or attorney advising such motion to pay to the party or deponent who opposed the motion the reasonable expenses incurred in opposing the motion, including attorney fees, unless the court finds that the making of the motion was substantially justified or that other circumstances make an award of expenses unjust.

If the motion is granted in part and denied in part, the court may apportion the reasonable expenses incurred in relation to the motion among the parties and persons in a just manner.

In determining the amount of reasonable expenses, including attorney fees, to be awarded in connection with a motion, the trial court shall award expenses which are reasonable in relation to the amount of work reasonably expended in obtaining an order compelling compliance or in opposing a motion which is denied.

(e) ***Providing person's own statement.*** If a party fails to comply with any person's written request for the person's own statement as provided in Rule 192.3(h), the person who made the request may move for an order compelling compliance. If the motion is granted, the movant may recover the expenses incurred in obtaining the order, including attorney fees, which are reasonable in relation to the amount of work reasonably expended in obtaining the order.

215.2 Failure to Comply with Order or with Discovery Request.

(a) ***Sanctions by court in district where deposition is taken.*** If a deponent fails to appear or to be sworn or to answer a question after being directed to do so by a district court in the district in which the deposition is being taken, the failure may be considered a contempt of that court.

(b) ***Sanctions by court in which action is pending.*** If a party or an officer, director, or managing agent of a party or a person designated under Rules

199.2(b)(1) or 200.1(b) to testify on behalf of a party fails to comply with proper discovery requests or to obey an order to provide or permit discovery, including an order made under Rules 204 or 215.1, the court in which the action is pending may, after notice and hearing, make such orders in regard to the failure as are just, and among others the following:

(1) an order disallowing any further discovery of any kind or of a particular kind by the disobedient party;

(2) an order charging all or any portion of the expenses of discovery or taxable court costs or both against the disobedient party or the attorney advising him;

(3) an order that the matters regarding which the order was made or any other designated facts shall be taken to be established for the purposes of the action in accordance with the claim of the party obtaining the order;

(4) an order refusing to allow the disobedient party to support or oppose designated claims or defenses, or prohibiting him from introducing designated matters in evidence;

(5) an order striking out pleadings or parts thereof, or staying further proceedings until the order is obeyed, or dismissing with or without prejudice the action or proceedings or any part thereof, or rendering a judgment by default against the disobedient party;

(6) in lieu of any of the foregoing orders or in addition thereto, an order treating as a contempt of court the failure to obey any orders except an order to submit to a physical or mental examination;

(7) when a party has failed to comply with an order under Rule 204 requiring him to appear or produce another for examination, such orders as are listed in paragraphs (1), (2), (3), (4) or (5) of this subdivision, unless the person failing to comply shows that he is unable to appear or to produce such person for examination.

(8) In lieu of any of the foregoing orders or in addition thereto, the court shall require the party failing to obey the order or the attorney advising him, or both, to pay, at such time as ordered by the court, the reasonable expenses, including attorney fees, caused by the failure, unless the court finds that the failure was substantially justified or that other circumstances make an award of expenses unjust. Such an order shall be subject to review on appeal from the final judgment.

(c) ***Sanction against nonparty for violation of Rules 196.7 or 205.3.*** If a nonparty fails to comply with an order under Rules 196.7 or 205.3, the court which made the order may treat the failure to obey as contempt of court.

215.3 Abuse of Discovery Process in Seeking, Making, or Resisting Discovery. If the court finds a party is abusing the discovery process in seeking, making or resisting discovery or if the court finds that any interrogatory or request for inspection or production is unreasonably frivolous, oppressive, or harassing, or that a response or answer is unreasonably frivolous or made for purposes of delay, then the court in which the action is pending may, after notice and hearing, impose any appropriate sanction authorized by paragraphs (1), (2), (3), (4), (5), and (8) of Rule 215.2(b). Such order of sanction shall be subject to review on appeal from the final judgment.

215.4 Failure to Comply with Rule 198.

(a) ***Motion.*** A party who has requested an admission under Rule 198 may move to determine the sufficiency of the answer or objection. For purposes of this subdivision an evasive or incomplete answer may be treated as a failure to answer. Unless the court determines that an objection is justified, it shall order that an answer be served. If the court determines that an answer does not comply with the requirements of Rule 198, it may order either that the matter is admitted or that an amended answer be served. The provisions of Rule 215.1(d) apply to the award of expenses incurred in relation to the motion.

(b) ***Expenses on failure to admit.*** If a party fails to admit the genuineness of any document or the truth of any matter as requested under Rule 198 and if the party requesting the admissions thereafter proves the genuineness of the document or the truth of the matter, he may apply to the court for an order requiring the other party to pay him the reasonable expenses incurred in making that proof, including reasonable attorney fees. The court shall make the order unless it finds that (1) the request was held objectionable pursuant to Rule 193, or (2) the admission sought was of no substantial importance, or (3) the party failing to admit had a reasonable ground to believe that he might prevail on the matter, or (4) there was other good reason for the failure to admit.

215.5 Failure of Party or Witness to Attend or to Serve Subpoena; Expenses.

(a) ***Failure of party giving notice to attend.*** If the party giving the notice of the taking of an oral deposition fails to attend and proceed therewith and another party attends in person or by attorney pursuant to the notice, the court may order the party giving the notice to pay such other party the reasonable expenses incurred by him and his attorney in attending, including reasonable attorney fees.

(b) ***Failure of witness to attend.*** If a party gives notice of the taking of an oral deposition of a witness and the witness does not attend because of the fault of the party giving the notice, if another party attends in person or by attorney because he expects the deposition of that witness to be taken, the court may order the party giving the notice to pay such other party the reasonable expenses incurred by him and his attorney in attending, including reasonable attorney fees.

215.6 Exhibits to Motions and Responses. Motions or responses made under this rule may have exhibits attached including affidavits, discovery pleadings, or any other documents.

Comments to 1999 change: The references in this rule to other discovery rules are changed to reflect the revisions in those rules, and former Rule 203 is added as Rule 215.5 in place of the former provision, which is superseded by Rule 193.6.

See also CPRC §§10.001-10.006; TRCP 13; ***O'Connor's Texas Rules***, "Motion for Sanctions," ch. 5-J; "General Rules for Discovery," ch. 6-A; "Depositions," ch. 6-E; "Interrogatories," ch. 6-F; "Securing Documents & Tangible Things," ch. 6-H; ***O'Connor's Texas Forms***, FORMS 6A.

Hamill v. Level, 917 S.W.2d 15, 16 (Tex.1996). "At issue in this case is whether the trial court properly dismissed the [P's] claims with prejudice for failing to comply with the [D's] discovery requests. ... Because the imposition of a 'death penalty' sanction in this case is excessive, we reverse the judgment of the court of appeals and remand this case to the trial court for further proceedings consistent with this opinion. [¶] Here, the sanction of dismissal with prejudice conflicts with ***TransAmerican*** [***Nat. Gas Corp. v. Powell***, 811 S.W.2d 913 (Tex.1999)] and its progeny because the sanction imposed in this case is more severe than necessary to satisfy its legitimate purpose and the sanctioned conduct does not justify the presumption that Hamill's claims are meritless."

Occidental Chem. Corp. v. Banales, 907 S.W.2d 488, 490 (Tex.1995). "The sanction imposed for discovery abuse should be no more severe than necessary to satisfy the legitimate purposes of the discovery process offended. The work product privilege is essential to the attorney-client relationship. Requiring the production of the attorney's notes from interviews of witnesses is a severe sanction and should receive an appropriately strict review. Piercing the work product privilege, like the 'death penalty' sanction, should apply only when lesser sanctions are inadequate to correct the discovery abuse that has occurred, *i.e.*, when it is the only appropriate sanction. Here the record does not reflect why lesser traditional sanctions might not cure the discovery abuse."

Global Serv., Inc. v. Bianchi, 901 S.W.2d 934, 938 (Tex.1995). "We recognize that it is often difficult to prove that a party has withheld documents from discovery. Direct evidence of such conduct is seldom available, and it may be necessary to rely entirely upon circumstantial evidence. But an imposition of sanctions cannot be based merely on a party's bald assertions. There must be some evidence to show an abuse of discovery before sanctions can be imposed. [The district] court ordered [D] to keep trying to produce all the documents requested, and prohibited [D] from conducting any discovery of its own until it complied. ... Thus, the effect of the sanction is to prohibit [D] from conducting any discovery."

Department of Pub. Safety Officers Ass'n v. Denton, 897 S.W.2d 757, 763 (Tex.1995). "A trial court has limited authority to dismiss a cause of action on its own initiative."

Remington Arms Co. v. Caldwell, 850 S.W.2d 167, 170 (Tex.1993). "[I]f pretrial discovery abuse is not revealed until after the trial has begun, or even after trial, a party cannot be said to have waived a claim for sanctions."

Chrysler Corp. v. Blackmon, 841 S.W.2d 844, 849 (Tex.1992). "Two factors mark the bounds of the trial court's discretion in order for sanctions to be just: first, a direct relationship between the offensive conduct and the sanction imposed must exist; and second, the sanction imposed must not be excessive. [¶] A permissible sanction should, therefore, be no more severe than required to satisfy legitimate purposes. This means that a court must consider relatively less stringent sanctions first to determine whether lesser sanctions will fully promote compliance, deterrence, and discourage further abuse."

TransAmerican Nat. Gas Corp. v. Powell, 811 S.W.2d 913, 917 (Tex.1991). "The punishment [for discovery abuse] should fit the crime. *At 918:* Discovery sanctions cannot be used to adjudicate the merits of a party's claims or defenses unless a party's hindrance of the discovery process justifies a presumption that its claims or defenses lack merit."

In re P.M.B., 2 S.W.3d 618, 624-25 (Tex.App.—Houston [14th Dist.] 1999, no pet.). "However, in determining issues regarding the conservatorship of, possession of, and access to a child, the court's primary consideration is always the best interest of the child. Compared to the best interest of the child, technical rules of pleading and practice are of little importance in determining child custody issues. This is also true with regard to rule 215 discovery sanctions. Moreover, courts have recognized that the exclusion of essential evidence, like the striking of pleadings, can equate to a death penalty sanction, and should not be used without considering whether lesser sanctions are adequate to accomplish the needed compliance, deterrence and punishment. [¶] We believe that the best interest of a child can only be attained when a court's decision is as well-informed as the circumstances allow. A decision on custody, possession, or access can rarely be well-informed without consideration of the evidence and perspectives of both parents. Because the exclusion of any important evidence as a discovery sanction can only produce a less-informed decision, contrary to the best interest of the child, we believe that it should be resorted to only where lesser sanctions are either impracticable or have been attempted and proven unsuccessful."

Saxton v. Daggett, 864 S.W.2d 729, 734 (Tex. App.—Houston [1st Dist.] 1993, orig. proceeding). "A failure to obey a court order under §11.11(a)(5) [now §105.005] of the Family Code to pay interim attorney's fees by a specific date does not involve the issue of any abuse of discovery."

Ismail v. Ismail, 702 S.W.2d 216, 224 (Tex.App.—Houston [1st Dist.] 1985, writ ref'd n.r.e.). "The Family Code provides that the trial court may issue temporary orders requiring either party to file a sworn inventory. If a party fails to comply with a temporary order, the party may be punished under the court's contempt power. We hold that the request for an inventory in a divorce case is a specie of discovery, and that the sanctions provided for in [TRCP] 215, as well as those granted in §3.58(c)(1) [now §6.502], are available to the trial court to punish or secure compliance with its order to furnish an inventory."

TRCP 215a - 215c. REPEALED

SECTION 10. THE JURY IN COURT

TRCP 216. REQUEST & FEE FOR JURY TRIAL

a. Request. No jury trial shall be had in any civil suit, unless a written request for a jury trial is filed with the clerk of the court a reasonable time before the date set for trial of the cause on the non-jury docket, but not less than thirty days in advance.

b. Jury Fee. Unless otherwise provided by law, a fee of ten dollars if in the district court and five dollars if in the county court must be deposited with the clerk of the court within the time for making a written request for a jury trial. The clerk shall promptly enter a notation of the payment of such fee upon the court's docket sheet.

Caution: TRCP 216 is affected by the following sections in the Fam. Code: §§6.703, 105.002.

See also U.S. Const. amend. 7; Tex. Const. art. 1, §15; Govt Code §51.604; *O'Connor's Texas Rules*, "Request for Jury Trial," ch. 5-B; *O'Connor's Texas Forms*, FORMS 5B.

G.M. Corp. v. Gayle, 951 S.W.2d 469, 476 (Tex. 1997). "Even where a party does not timely pay the jury fee, courts have held that a trial court should accord the right to jury trial if it can be done without interfering with the court's docket, delaying the trial, or injuring the opposing party. *At 477:* [D] established that a 30-day continuance to perfect [D's] jury trial demand would not cause [Ps] any injury or delay. [T]he trial court's seriatim trial schedule seems only a sham to hold [D] to its mistake in not paying the jury fee without penalizing the other side. Under these particular and unusual circumstances, we hold that the trial court abused its discretion by not granting a continuance to allow [D's] jury request and fee to become timely."

Ricardo N., Inc. v. Turcios de Argueta, 907 S.W.2d 423, 429 (Tex.1995). "Assuming [D's] request for a jury in advance of the first trial setting was not timely made, that request had certainly become timely when the case was remanded from federal court 4 years later."

Halsell v. DeHoyos, 810 S.W.2d 371, 371 (Tex. 1991). "A [jury] request in advance of the 30-day deadline [of TRCP 216] is presumed to have been made a reasonable time before trial."

In re V.R.W., 41 S.W.3d 183, 194-95 (Tex.App.—Houston [14th Dist.] 2001, no pet.). "A request for a jury trial made in advance of the 30-day deadline is presumed to have been made a reasonable time before trial. That presumption may be rebutted by showing that the granting of a jury trial would operate to injure the adverse party, disrupt the court's docket, or impede the ordinary handling of the court's business. 'Such evidence must appear in the record.' [¶] The refusal to grant a timely requested jury trial is harmless error only if the record shows that no material issues of fact exist[ ] and an instructed verdict would not have been justified. In the absence of a timely request, it is within the trial court's discretion to deny a jury trial."

Bell Helicopter Textron, Inc. v. Abbott, 863 S.W.2d 139, 140 (Tex.App.—Texarkana 1993, writ denied). "[T]he court must give at least 45 days' notice of a first setting for trial, but may reset the case to a later date on any reasonable notice. [¶] As the first trial setting here gave only 24 days' notice, it did not comply with [TRCP] 245. *At 141:* It was not harmless ... because it made it impossible for [D], after receiving notice of the setting, to comply with the time limit for paying the jury fee."

TRCP 217. OATH OF INABILITY

The deposit for a jury fee shall not be required when the party shall within the time for making such deposit, file with the clerk his affidavit to the effect that he is unable to make such deposit, and that he cannot, by the pledge of property or otherwise, obtain the money necessary for that purpose; and the court shall then order the clerk to enter the suit on the jury docket.

See also *O'Connor's Texas Rules*, "Request for Jury Trial," ch. 5-B.

TRCP 218. JURY DOCKET

The clerks of the district and county courts shall each keep a docket, styled, "The Jury Docket," in which shall be entered in their order the cases in which jury fees have been paid or affidavit in lieu thereof has been filed as provided in the two preceding rules.

Higginbotham v. Collateral Protection, Inc., 859 S.W.2d 487, 489 n.2 (Tex.App.—Houston [1st Dist.] 1993, writ denied). "The clerk is required to enter a notation on the court's docket sheet that the jury fee was paid."

TRCP 219. JURY TRIAL DAY

The court shall designate the days for taking up the jury docket and the trial of jury cases. Such order may be revoked or changed in the court's discretion.

TRCP 220. WITHDRAWING CAUSE FROM JURY DOCKET

When any party has paid the fee for a jury trial, he shall not be permitted to withdraw the cause from the jury docket over the objection of the parties adversely interested. If so permitted, the court in its discretion may by an order permit him to withdraw also his jury fee deposit. Failure of a party to appear for trial shall be deemed a waiver by him of the right to trial by jury.

See also *O'Connor's Texas Rules*, "Request for Jury Trial," ch. 5-B.

Mercedes-Benz Credit Corp. v. Rhyne, 925 S.W.2d 664, 666 (Tex.1996). "Only when a party demands a jury *and* pays the fee can the opposing party rely on those actions. In such a case, the trial court may not remove the case from the jury docket over the objections of the opposing party."

Green v. Grace Mfg. Co., 422 S.W.2d 723, 726 (Tex. 1968). "We hold that a party, who does not timely demand a jury and pay the fee must object to the withdrawal of the case from the jury docket under [TRCP] 220."

Taylor v. Taylor, 63 S.W.3d 93, 102 (Tex.App.—Waco 2001, no pet.). Wife does "not dispute that [husband] was incarcerated at the time of trial and could not voluntarily appear. [Husband] filed a pleading one month before trial asking the judge to issue a bench warrant so he could participate at trial. In view of the 'sacred' nature of the right to jury trial, we hold that a deemed waiver under Rule 220 occurs only when a party's failure to appear is voluntary. Because [husband] did not voluntarily fail to appear for trial, we conclude that he cannot be deemed to have waived his right to jury trial."

TRCP 221. CHALLENGE TO THE ARRAY

When the jurors summoned have not been selected by jury commissioners or by drawing the names from a jury wheel, any party to a suit which is to be tried by a jury may, before the jury is drawn challenge the array upon the ground that the officer summoning the jury has acted corruptly, and has wilfully summoned jurors known to be prejudiced against the party challenging or biased in favor of the adverse party. All such challenges must be in writing setting forth distinctly the grounds of such challenge and supported by the affidavit of the party or some other credible person. When such challenge is made, the court shall hear evidence and decide without delay whether or not the challenge shall be sustained.

See also Govt Code §62.001; *O'Connor's Texas Rules*, "Jury Selection," ch. 8-A.

State ex rel Hightower v. Smith, 671 S.W.2d 32, 36 (Tex.1984). "The courts of Smith County operate under the interchangeable jury system of [Gov't Code §62.016]. Objections to the jury panel therefore must be presented to the judge charged with organizing and impaneling the jurors for the week. [The defendant's] motion to the trial judge after the panels were organized was not timely."

Mann v. Ramirez, 905 S.W.2d 275, 280 (Tex.App.—San Antonio 1995, writ denied). "It is undisputed that irregularities in the granting and documentation of exemptions and excuses occurred. *At 283:* We conclude that the trial court abused its discretion in denying a mistrial and erred in failing to grant a new trial, in light of the totality of the record and the evidence adduced at the posttrial hearings."

TRCP 222. WHEN CHALLENGE IS SUSTAINED

If the challenge be sustained, the array of jurors summoned shall be discharged, and the court shall order other jurors summoned in their stead, and shall direct that the officer who summoned the persons so discharged, and on account of whose misconduct the challenge has been sustained, shall not summon any other jurors in the case.

See also Govt Code §§62.101-62.110 (juror qualifications).

Martinez v. City of Austin, 852 S.W.2d 71, 73 (Tex. App.—Austin 1993, writ denied). A challenge to the array "alleges a defect in the juror selection and summons procedure or a violation of the jury-wheel statute. If the movant is successful, the entire array is dismissed and a new array summoned. The challenge [to the array] must be presented in a written motion supported by affidavit to the particular judge in charge of the local jury system."

TRCP 223. JURY LIST IN CERTAIN COUNTIES

In counties governed as to juries by the laws providing for interchangeable juries, the names of the jurors shall be placed upon the general panel in the order in which they are randomly selected, and jurors shall be assigned for service from the top thereof, in the order in which they shall be needed, and jurors returned to the general panel after service in any of such courts shall be enrolled at the bottom of the list in the order of their respective return; provided, however, after such assignment to a particular court, the trial judge of such court, upon the demand prior to voir dire examination by any party or attorney in the case reached for trial in such court, shall cause the names of all members of such assigned jury panel in such case to be placed in a receptacle, shuffled, and drawn, and such names shall be transcribed in the order drawn on the jury list from which the jury is to be selected to try such case. There shall be only one shuffle and drawing by the trial judge in each case.

See also Govt Code §§62.016, 62.017 (interchangeable juries in certain counties); *O'Connor's Texas Rules*, "Jury Selection," ch. 8-A.

Rivas v. Liberty Mut. Ins. Co., 480 S.W.2d 610, 612 (Tex.1972). "The court of civil appeals recognized the listing and reshuffle provisions of [TRCP] 223 are designed to insure a random selection of jurors. While the method used here did not conform to the method prescribed by the rule, it did insure a degree of randomness in the listing of the jurors."

Carr v. Smith, 22 S.W.3d 128, 134 (Tex.App.—Fort Worth 2000, pet. denied). "After the venire panel has been sworn and once substantive inquiry begins and responses have been observed or made available to the parties or their counsel, whether verbally or in writing, voir dire has begun."

Whiteside v. Watson, 12 S.W.3d 614, 619 (Tex. App.—Eastland 2000, pet. granted w.r.m.). "[T]he first shuffle was not performed in compliance with the mandatory procedures set forth in [TRCP] 223. Whether it substantially complied with the underlying purpose of Rule 223 is irrelevant to the determination of whether it was error. Rule 223 sets forth a mandatory procedure for shuffling the jury panel, and failure to comply with that procedure is error. [¶] [However], even if the trial court erred by conducting the second shuffle, the error was harmless."

TRCP 224. PREPARING JURY LIST

In counties not governed as to juries by the laws providing for interchangeable juries, when the parties have announced ready for trial the clerk shall write the name of each regular juror entered of record for that week on separate slips of paper, as near the same size and appearance as may be, and shall place the slips in a box and mix them well. The clerk shall draw from the box, in the presence of the court, the names of twenty-four jurors, if in the district court, or so many as there may be, if there be a less number in the box; and the names of twelve jurors if in the county court, or so many as there may be, and write the names as drawn upon two slips of paper and deliver one slip to each party to the suit or his attorney.

See also *O'Connor's Texas Rules*, "Jury Selection," ch. 8-A.

Southwestern Pub. Serv. Co. v. Morris, 380 S.W.2d 648, 649 (Tex.App.—Amarillo 1964, no writ). "[E]rror was committed by the court in refusing condemnor's request that the jury panel be drawn before the selection of the jury." Such error may be harmless.

TRCP 225. SUMMONING TALESMAN

When there are not as many as twenty-four names drawn from the box, if in the district court, or as many as twelve, if in the county court, the court shall direct the sheriff to summon such number of qualified persons as the court deems necessary to complete the panel. The names of those thus summoned shall be placed in the box and drawn and entered upon the slips as provided in the preceding rules.

TRCP 226. OATH TO JURY PANEL

Before the parties or their attorneys begin the examination of the jurors whose names have thus been listed, the jurors shall be sworn by the court or under its direction, as follows: "You, and each of you, do solemnly swear that you will true answers give to all questions propounded to you concerning your qualifications as a juror, so help you God."

See also *O'Connor's Texas Rules*, "Jury Selection," ch. 8-A.

Barron v. State, 378 S.W.2d 144, 147 (Tex.App.—San Antonio 1964, no writ). "[F]ailure to swear the jury panel prior to the voir dire examination as required by [TRCP] 226 ... was waived by [the] failure to timely complain of same."

TRCP 226a. ADMONITORY INSTRUCTIONS TO JURY PANEL & JURY

The court shall give such admonitory instructions to the jury panel and to the jury as may be prescribed by the Supreme Court in an order or orders entered for that purpose.

See also *O'Connor's Texas Rules*, "Jury Selection," ch. 8-A; *O'Connor's Texas Forms*, FORMS 8A, 8I.

APPROVED INSTRUCTIONS

Pursuant to the provisions of Rule 226a, Texas Rules of Civil Procedure, it is ordered [July 20, 1966] by the Supreme Court of Texas, effective January 1, 1967; January 1, 1971; February 1, 1973; December 5, 1983, effective April 1, 1984; July 15, 1987; Jan. 1, 1988:

I.

That the following oral instructions, with such modifications as the circumstances of the particular case may require, shall be given by the court to the jurors after they have been sworn as provided in Rule 226 and before the voir dire examination:

Ladies and Gentlemen of the Jury Panel:

The case that is now on trial is _____ vs. _____. This is a civil action which will be tried before a jury. Your duty as jurors will be to decide the disputed facts. It is the duty of the judge to see that the case is tried in accordance with the rules of law. In this case, as in all cases, the actions of the judge, parties, witnesses, attorneys and jurors must be according to law. The Texas law permits proof of any violation of the rules of proper jury conduct. By this I mean that jurors and others may be called upon to testify in open court about acts of jury misconduct. I instruct you, therefore, to follow carefully all instructions which I am now going to give you, as well as others which you will receive while this case is on trial. If you do not obey the instructions I am about to give you, it may become necessary for another jury to re-try this case with all of the attendant waste of your time here and the expense to the litigants and the taxpayers of this county for another trial. These instructions are as follows:

1. Do not mingle with nor talk to the lawyers, the witnesses, the parties, or any other person who might be connected with or interested in this case, except for casual greetings. They have to follow these same instructions and you will understand it when they do.

2. Do not accept from, nor give to, any of those persons any favors however slight, such as rides, food or refreshments.

3. Do not discuss anything about this case, or even mention it to anyone whomsoever, including your wife or husband, nor permit anyone to mention it in your hearing until you are discharged as jurors or excused from this case. If anyone attempts to discuss the case, report it to me at once.

4. The parties through their attorneys have the right to direct questions to each of you concerning your qualifications, background, experiences and attitudes. In questioning you, they are not meddling in your personal affairs, but are trying to select fair and impartial jurors who are free from any bias or prejudice in this particular case.

a. Do not conceal information or give answers which are not true. Listen to the questions and give full and complete answers.

b. If the attorneys ask some questions directed to you as a group which require an answer on your part individually, hold up your hand until you have answered the questions.

Do you understand these instructions? If not, please let me know now.

Whether you are selected as a juror for this case or not, you are performing a significant service which only free people can perform. We shall try the case as fast as possible consistent with justice, which requires a careful and correct trial. If selected on the jury, unless I instruct you differently, you will be permitted to separate at recesses and for meals, and at night.

The attorneys will now proceed with their examination.

II.

That the following oral and written instructions, with such modifications as the circumstances of the particular case may require shall be given by the court to the jury immediately after the jurors are selected for the case:

Oral Instructions

Ladies and Gentlemen:

By the oath which you take as jurors, you become officials of this court and active participants in the public administration of justice. I now give you further instructions which you must obey throughout this trial.

It is your duty to listen to and consider the evidence and to determine fact issues later submitted to you, but I, as judge, will decide matters of the law. You will now receive written instructions which you will observe during this trial, together with such other instructions as I may hereafter give, or as heretofore I have given to you.

(A copy of the written instructions set out below in this Section II shall thereupon be handed to each juror.)

As you examine the instructions which have just been handed to you, we will go over them briefly together. The first three instructions have previously been stated, and you will continue to observe them throughout the trial. These and the other instructions just handed to you are as follows:

(The written instructions set out below in this Section II shall thereupon be read by the court to the jury.)

Counsel, you may proceed.

Written Instructions

1. Do not mingle with nor talk to the lawyers, the witnesses, the parties, or any other person who might be connected with or interested in this case, except for casual greetings. They have to follow these same instructions and you will understand it when they do.

2. Do not accept from, nor give to, any of those persons any favors however slight, such as rides, food or refreshments.

3. Do not discuss anything about this case, or even mention it to anyone whomsoever, including your wife or husband nor permit anyone to mention it in your hearing until you are discharged as jurors or excused from this case. If anyone attempts to discuss the case, report it to me at once.

4. Do not even discuss this case among yourselves until after you have heard all of the evidence, the court's charge, the attorneys' arguments and until I have sent you to the jury room to consider your verdict.

5. Do not make any investigation about the facts of this case. Occasionally we have a juror who privately seeks out information about a case on trial. This is improper. All evidence must be presented in open court so that each side may question the witnesses and make proper objection. This avoids a trial based upon secret evidence. These rules apply to jurors the same as they apply to the parties and to me. If you know of, or learn anything about, this case except from the evidence admitted during the course of this trial, you should tell me about it at once. You have just taken an oath that you will render a verdict on the evidence submitted to you under my rulings.

6. Do not make personal inspections, observations, investigations, or experiments nor personally view premises, things or articles not produced in court. Do not let anyone else do any of these things for you.

7. Do not tell other jurors your own personal experiences nor those of other persons, nor relate any special information. A juror may have special knowledge of matters such as business, technical or professional matters or he may have expert knowledge or opinions, or he may know what happened in this or some other lawsuit.

To tell the other jurors any of this information is a violation of these instructions.

8. Do not discuss or consider attorney's fees unless evidence about attorney's fees is admitted.

9. Do not consider, discuss, nor speculate whether or not any party is or is not protected in whole or in part by insurance of any kind.

10. Do not seek information contained in law books, dictionaries, public or private records or elsewhere, which is not admitted in evidence.

At the conclusion of all the evidence, I may submit to you a written charge asking you some specific questions. You will not be asked, and you should not consider, whether one party or the other should win. Since you will need to consider all of the evidence admitted by me, it is important that you pay close attention to the evidence as it is presented.

The Texas law permits proof of any violation of the rules of proper jury conduct. By this I mean that jurors and others may be called upon to testify in open court about acts of jury misconduct. I instruct you, therefore, to follow carefully all instructions which I have given you, as well as others which you later receive while this case is on trial.

You may keep these instructions and review them as the case proceeds. A violation of these instructions should be reported to me.

III.

That the following written instructions, with such modifications as the circumstances of the particular case may require, shall be given by the court to the jury as part of the charge:

Ladies and Gentlemen of the Jury:

This case is submitted to you by asking questions about the facts, which you must decide from the evidence you have heard in this trial. You are the sole judges of the credibility of the witnesses and the weight to be given their testimony, but in matters of law, you must be governed by the instructions in this charge. In discharging your responsibility on this jury, you will observe all the instructions which have previously been given you. I shall now give you additional instructions which you should carefully and strictly follow during your deliberations.

1. Do not let bias, prejudice or sympathy play any part in your deliberations.

2. In arriving at your answers, consider only the evidence introduced here under oath and such exhibits, if any, as have been introduced for your consideration under the rulings of the Court, that is, what you have seen and heard in this courtroom, together with the law as given you by the court. In your deliberations, you will not consider or discuss anything that is not represented by the evidence in this case.

3. Since every answer that is required by the charge is important, no juror should state or consider that any required answer is not important.

4. You must not decide who you think should win, and then try to answer the questions accordingly. Simply answer the questions, and do not discuss nor concern yourselves with the effect of your answers.

5. You will not decide the answer to a question by lot or by drawing straws, or by any other method of chance. Do not return a quotient verdict. A quotient verdict means that the jurors agree to abide by the result to be reached by adding together each juror's figures and dividing by the number of jurors to get an average. Do not do any trading on your answers; that is, one juror should not agree to answer a certain question one way if others will agree to answer another question another way.

6. You may render your verdict upon the vote of ten or more members of the jury. The same ten or more of you must agree upon all of the answers made and to the entire verdict. You will not, therefore, enter into an agreement to be bound by a majority or any other vote of less than ten jurors. If the verdict and all of the answers therein are reached by unanimous agreement, the presiding juror shall sign the verdict for the entire jury. If any juror disagrees as to any answer made by the verdict, those jurors who agree to all findings shall each sign the verdict.

These instructions are given you because your conduct is subject to review the same as that of the witnesses, parties, attorneys and the judge. If it should be found that you have disregarded any of these instructions, it will be jury misconduct and it may require another trial by another jury; then all of our time will have been wasted.

The presiding juror or any other who observes a violation of the court's instructions shall immediately warn the one who is violating the same and caution the juror not to do so again.

(Definitions, questions and special instructions given to the jury will be transcribed here.)

After you retire to the jury room, you will select your own presiding juror. The first thing the presiding juror will do is to have this complete charge read aloud and then you will deliberate upon your answers to the questions asked.

____

Judge Presiding

CERTIFICATE

We, the jury, have answered the above and foregoing questions as herein indicated, and herewith return same into court as our verdict.

(To be signed by the presiding juror if unanimous.)

____

Presiding Juror

(To be signed by those rendering the verdict if not unanimous.)

________________ ________________
________________ ________________
________________ ________________
________________ ________________
________________ ________________
____

IV.

That the following oral instructions shall be given by the court to the jury after the verdict has been accepted by the court and before the jurors are discharged:

The court has previously instructed you that you should observe strict secrecy during the trial and during your deliberations, and that you should not discuss this case with anyone except other jurors during your deliberations. I am now about to discharge you. After your discharge, you are released from your secrecy. You will then be free to discuss the case and your deliberations with anyone. However, you are also free to decline to discuss the case and your deliberations if you wish.

After you are discharged, it is lawful for the attorneys or other persons to question you to determine whether any of the standards for jury conduct which I have given you in the course of this trial were violated and to ask you to give an affidavit to that effect. You are free to discuss or not to discuss these matters and to give or not to give an affidavit.

Pharo v. Chambers Cty., 922 S.W.2d 945, 949 (Tex. 1996). "[N]ot every employee of a county is automatically 'interested' in a case in which the county is a party. ... Collier, however, was a member of the Sheriff's Department, the division of county government whose conduct was being scrutinized at trial. [D]etermining whether [he] was connected with or interested in the case within the meaning of Rule 226a is a factually intensive inquiry, committed to the sound discretion of the trial court."

Woods v. Crane Carrier Co., 693 S.W.2d 377, 379 (Tex.1985). "[W]hen terms requiring definitions are used more than once in a charge, it is preferable that the definition or instruction occur immediately after the general instructions required by [TRCP] 226a...."

Phippen v. Deere & Co., 965 S.W.2d 713, 718 (Tex. App.—Texarkana 1998, no pet.). TRCP 226a "provides in relevant part that if a verdict is unanimous, it shall be signed by the presiding juror, and if not unanimous, then those jurors who agree with all of the findings shall sign the verdict. *At 719:* Because the appellants ... failed to raise their objections to the exemplary damages verdict at trial before the jury was discharged, so that the trial court could have instructed the jury to enter a corrected verdict, we conclude that appellants waived their objection...."

TRCP 227. CHALLENGE TO JUROR

A challenge to a particular juror is either a challenge for cause or a peremptory challenge. The court shall decide without delay any such challenge, and if sustained, the juror shall be discharged from the particular case. Either such challenge may be made orally on the formation of a jury to try the case.

See also Govt Code §§62.101-62.110 (juror qualifications); ***O'Connor's Texas Rules***, "Jury Selection," ch. 8-A.

Lopez v. Southern P.T. Co., 847 S.W.2d 330, 333 (Tex.App.—El Paso 1993, no writ). "A party exercises its peremptory challenges by delivering its list of peremptory challenges to the court."

TRCP 228. "CHALLENGE FOR CAUSE" DEFINED

A challenge for cause is an objection made to a juror, alleging some fact which by law disqualifies him to serve as a juror in the case or in any case, or which in the opinion of the court, renders him an unfit person to sit on the jury. Upon such challenge the examination is not confined to the answers of the juror, but other evidence may be heard for or against the challenge.

See also ***O'Connor's Texas Rules***, "Jury Selection," ch. 8-A.

Compton v. Henrie, 364 S.W.2d 179, 182 (Tex. 1963). "[T]he statutory disqualification of bias or prejudice extends not only to the litigant personally, but to the subject matter of the litigation as well."

TRCP 229. CHALLENGE FOR CAUSE

When twenty-four or more jurors, if in the district court, or twelve or more, if in the county court, are drawn, and the lists of their names delivered to the parties, if either party desires to challenge any juror for cause, the challenge shall then be made. The name of a juror challenged and set aside for cause shall be erased from such lists.

See also Govt Code §§62.101-62.110 (juror qualifications); *O'Connor's Texas Rules*, "Jury Selection," ch. 8-A.

Hallett v. Houston Northwest Med. Ctr., 689 S.W.2d 888, 890 (Tex.1985). To preserve error in the denial of challenges for cause, "[i]t was incumbent upon [P], prior to exercising her peremptory challenges, to advise the trial court of two things: (1) that she would exhaust her peremptory challenges; and, (2) that after exercising her peremptory challenges, specific objectionable jurors would remain on the jury list."

Lucas v. Titus Cty. Hosp. Dist., 964 S.W.2d 144, 157-58 (Tex.App.—Texarkana 1998), *pet. denied*, 988 S.W.2d 740 (Tex.1998). "[A] trial court's refusal to excuse an unqualified juror does not necessarily constitute harmful error. Harm occurs only if the party uses all of their peremptory challenges and is thus prevented from striking other objectionable jurors because he has no additional peremptory challenges. Additionally, the complaining party must inform the court that objectionable jurors will be chosen. Failure to notify the trial court of these two facts constitutes a waiver of the right to complain of the trial court's refusal to discharge a juror challenged for cause."

TRCP 230. CERTAIN QUESTIONS NOT TO BE ASKED

In examining a juror, he shall not be asked a question the answer to which may show that he has been convicted of an offense which disqualifies him, or that he stands charged by some legal accusation with theft or any felony.

See also *O'Connor's Texas Rules*, "Jury Selection," ch. 8-A.

Palmer Well Servs., Inc. v. Mack Trucks, Inc., 776 S.W.2d 575, 576 (Tex.1989). Gov't Code §62.102 "disqualifies a person to serve as a petit juror if he is 'under indictment or other legal accusation of misdemeanor or felony theft, or any other felony.'"

TRCP 231. NUMBER REDUCED BY CHALLENGES

If the challenges reduce the number of jurors to less than twenty-four, if in the district court, or to less than twelve, if in the county court, the court shall order other jurors to be drawn from the wheel or from the central jury panel or summoned, as the practice may be in the particular county, and their names written upon the list instead of those set aside for cause. Such jurors so summoned may likewise be challenged for cause.

Williams v. State, 631 S.W.2d 955, 957 (Tex.App.—Austin 1982, no writ). TRCP 231 "authorizes the calling of additional individuals to supplement a jury panel rendered insufficient (by disqualifications or peremptory strikes) to supply a jury of twelve."

TRCP 232. MAKING PEREMPTORY CHALLENGES

If there remain on such lists not subject to challenge for cause, twenty-four names, if in the district court, or twelve names, if in the county court, the parties shall proceed to make their peremptory challenges. A peremptory challenge is made to a juror without assigning any reason therefor.

See also *O'Connor's Texas Rules*, "Jury Selection," ch. 8-A.

Goode v. Shoukfeh, 943 S.W.2d 441, 445-46 (Tex. 1997). "At the first step of the [***Batson***] process, the opponent of the peremptory challenge must establish a prima facie case of racial discrimination. [¶] During the second step of the process, the burden shifts to the party who has exercised the strike to come forward with a race-neutral explanation. ... The issue ... at this juncture is the facial validity of the explanation. ... It is not until the third step that the persuasiveness of the justification for the challenge becomes relevant. At the third step of the process, the trial court must determine if the party challenging the strike has proven purposeful racial discrimination, and the trial court may believe or not believe the explanation offered by the party who exercised the peremptory challenge. It is at this stage that implausible justifications for striking potential jurors 'may (and probably will) be found [by the trial court] to be pretexts for purposeful discrimination.'"

Powers v. Palacios, 813 S.W.2d 489, 491 (Tex. 1991). "We hold that equal protection is denied when race is a factor in counsel's exercise of a peremptory challenge to a prospective juror."

TRCP 233. NUMBER OF PEREMPTORY CHALLENGES

Except as provided below, each party to a civil action is entitled to six peremptory challenges in a case tried in the district court, and to three in the county court.

Alignment of the Parties. In multiple party cases, it shall be the duty of the trial judge to decide whether any of the litigants aligned on the same side of the docket are antagonistic with respect to any issue to be submitted to the jury, before the exercise of peremptory challenges.

Definition of Side. The term "side" as used in this rule is not synonymous with "party," "litigant," or "person." Rather, "side" means one or more litigants who have common interests on the matters with which the jury is concerned.

Motion to Equalize. In multiple party cases, upon motion of any litigant made prior to the exercise of peremptory challenges, it shall be the duty of the trial judge to equalize the number of peremptory challenges so that no litigant or side is given unfair advantage as a result of the alignment of the litigants and the award of peremptory challenges to each litigant or side. In determining how the challenges should be allocated the court shall consider any matter brought to the attention of the trial judge concerning the ends of justice and the elimination of an unfair advantage.

See also *O'Connor's Texas Rules*, "Jury Selection," ch. 8-A.

Garcia v. Central Power & Light Co., 704 S.W.2d 734, 736 (Tex.1986). "The existence of antagonism [between litigants on the same side of a lawsuit] is a question of law. If no antagonism exists, each side must receive the same number of strikes. *At 737:* [I]n determining whether antagonism exists, the trial court must consider the pleadings, information disclosed by pretrial discovery, information and representations made during voir dire of the jury panel, and any other information brought to the attention of the trial court before the exercise of the strikes by the parties."

TRCP 234. LISTS RETURNED TO THE CLERK

When the parties have made or declined to make their peremptory challenges, they shall deliver their lists to the clerk. The clerk shall, if the case be in the district court, call off the first twelve names on the lists that have not been erased; and if the case be in the county court, he shall call off the first six names on the lists that have not been erased; those whose names are called shall be the jury.

See also *O'Connor's Texas Rules*, "Jury Selection," ch. 8-A.

Lopez v. Southern P.T. Co., 847 S.W.2d 330, 333 (Tex.App.—El Paso 1993, no writ). To preserve error when the court refuses to strike a panelist for cause, the party must name the objectionable panelist before giving its peremptory strikes to the clerk.

TRCP 235. IF JURY IS INCOMPLETE

When by peremptory challenges the jury is left incomplete, the court shall direct other jurors to be drawn or summoned to complete the jury; and such other jurors shall be impaneled as in the first instance.

See also *O'Connor's Texas Rules*, "Jury Selection," ch. 8-A.

Thomas v. City of O'Donnell, 811 S.W.2d 757, 759 (Tex.App.—Amarillo, 1991, no writ). "Under the mandatory provisions of [TRCP 235], the onus is on the court to direct that additional prospective jurors be drawn or summoned. The trial court erred in overruling [P's] motion to call additional jurors in accordance with Rule 235."

TRCP 236. OATH TO JURY

The jury shall be sworn by the court or under its direction, in substance as follows: "You, and each of you, do solemnly swear that in all cases between parties which shall be to you submitted, you will a true verdict render, according to the law, as it may be given you in charge by the court, and to the evidence submitted to you under the rulings of the court. So help you God."

Traders & Gen. Ins. Co. v. Diebel, 188 S.W.2d 411, 414 (Tex.App.—Dallas 1945, writ ref'd). "Jurors are sworn to render a verdict according to submitted evidence...."

SECTION 11. TRIAL OF CAUSES

A. APPEARANCE & PROCEDURE

TRCP 237. APPEARANCE DAY

If a defendant, who has been duly cited, is by the citation required to answer on a day which is in term time, such day is appearance day as to him. If he is so required to answer on a day in vacation, he shall plead or answer accordingly, and the first day of the next term is appearance day as to him.

See also *O'Connor's Texas Rules*, "Default Judgment," ch. 7-A.

Texas Alcoholic Beverage Comm'n v. Wilson, 573 S.W.2d 832, 835 (Tex.App.—Beaumont 1978, writ ref'd n.r.e.). The TABC "had no valid notice that a hearing would be held prior to appearance day.... Any judgment entered before the time at which a defendant is commanded by the citation to appear and answer is erroneous and must be set aside."

TRCP 237a. CASES REMANDED FROM FEDERAL COURT

When any cause is removed to the Federal Court and is afterwards remanded to the state court, the plaintiff shall file a certified copy of the order of remand with the clerk of the state court and shall forthwith give written notice of such filing to the attorneys of record for all adverse parties. All such adverse parties shall have fifteen days from the receipt of such notice within which to file an answer. No default judgment shall be rendered against a party in a removed action remanded from federal court if that party filed an answer in federal court during removal.

See also *O'Connor's Texas Rules*, "Default Judgment," ch. 7-A.

Quaestor Invs., Inc. v. State of Chiapas, 997, S.W.2d 226, 229 (Tex.1999). "[W]e hold that jurisdiction revests in the state court when the federal district court executes the remand order and mails a certified copy to the state court. [¶] We are ... persuaded that nothing more is required to recommence the appellate timetable than the state court's reaquiring jurisdiction over a case. ... The court of appeals erred when it inferred from [TRCP] 237a ... that any further affirmative action was needed."

HBA East, Ltd. v. JEA Boxing Co., 796 S.W.2d 534, 538 (Tex.App.—Houston [1st Dist.] 1990, writ denied). "Reading [TRCP] 237a and 239 together, we conclude that a default judgment cannot be granted against a defendant following remand of a case from federal to state court until 15 days have expired from the defendant's receipt of the remand notice from the plaintiff."

TRCP 238. CALL OF APPEARANCE DOCKET

On the appearance day of a particular defendant and at the hour named in the citation, or as soon thereafter as may be practicable, the court or clerk in open court shall call, in their order, all the cases on the docket in which such day is appearance day as to any defendant, or, the court or clerk failing therein, any such case shall be so called on request of the plaintiff's attorney.

See also *O'Connor's Texas Rules*, "Default Judgment," ch. 7-A.

TRCP 239. JUDGMENT BY DEFAULT

Upon such call of the docket, or at any time after a defendant is required to answer, the plaintiff may in term time take judgment by default against such defendant if he has not previously filed an answer, and provided that the citation with the officer's return thereon shall have been on file with the clerk for the length of time required by Rule 107.

Caution: TRCP 239 is affected by the following sections in the Fam. Code: §§85.006, 157.066, 157.115, 232.009.

See also *O'Connor's Texas Rules*, "Default Judgment," ch. 7-A; "Motion for New Trial," ch. 10-B; *O'Connor's Texas Forms*, FORMS 7A.

LeBlanc v. LeBlanc, 778 S.W.2d 865, 865 (Tex. 1989). "***Craddock*** has general application to all judgments of default, both those 'entered on failure of a defendant to file an answer and those entered on failure to appear for trial.'" *But see **Lowe***, below.

Lopez v. Lopez, 757 S.W.2d 721, 723 (Tex.1988). "Because the record here establishes that [D] had no actual or constructive notice of the trial setting, the lower courts erred in requiring him to show that he had a meritorious defense as a condition to granting his motion for new trial." *But see **Lowe***, below.

Craddock v. Sunshine Bus Lines, Inc., 133 S.W.2d 124, 126 (Tex.1939). "A default judgment should be set aside and a new trial ordered in any case in which the failure of the defendant to answer before judgment was not intentional, or the result of conscious indifference on his part, but was due to a mistake or accident; provided the motion for new trial sets up a meritorious defense and is filed at a time when the granting thereof will occasion no delay or otherwise work an injury to the plaintiff." *But see **Lowe***, below.

Lowe v. Lowe, 971 S.W.2d 720, 723 (Tex.App.—Houston [14th Dist.] 1998, pet. denied). "Since 1939, ***Craddock*** has been the seminal case setting forth the elements of proof a defaulting party must show to obtain a new trial following a default judgment. *At 725:* Although we have found that [appellant] met the three prongs of the ***Craddock*** test, we feel obligated to note our reluctance to apply it to a suit affecting the parent-child relationship. [¶] The most important reason

Craddock is not appropriate in a suit affecting the parent-child relationship is because ***Craddock*** was designed to be applied to traditional civil litigation—personal injury, products liability, consumer, and commercial litigation—in which only two competing interests—the plaintiff's and the defendant's—are involved. ... But in suits involving the parent-child relationship, we have more than two interests involved, we have three interests: the mother's interests, the father's interests, and, of paramount importance, the child's interests. Under our family code, the ultimate question to ask is what is in the best interest of the child. Yet, invariably, when the ***Craddock*** test is applied, it only takes into consideration the actions of the father and/or the mother, whichever happens to be the defaulting party. ***Craddock*** does not inquire into the child's interests and leaves no maneuvering room for a judge to consider the child's interests. *At 726:* We also find that the second prong of ***Craddock*** does not neatly fit the family law area. Unlike other suits, where clear defenses and claims exist, in family law, we have only factors to be considered by the court in determining best interest. ... There is, in other words, no clear, meritorious defense in this area. [¶] Additionally, another reason exists for not applying ***Craddock*** in this context, the ***Craddock*** test assumes an adversarial relationship between the parties. And yet, our legislature has made great attempts to rid family law proceedings of an adversarial nature."

TRCP 239a. NOTICE OF DEFAULT JUDGMENT

At or immediately prior to the time an interlocutory or final default judgment is rendered, the party taking the same or his attorney shall certify to the clerk in writing the last known mailing address of the party against whom the judgment is taken, which certificate shall be filed among the papers in the cause. Immediately upon the signing of the judgment, the clerk shall mail written notice thereof to the party against whom the judgment was rendered at the address shown in the certificate, and note the fact of such mailing on the docket. The notice shall state the number and style of the case, the court in which the case is pending, the names of the parties in whose favor and against whom the judgment was rendered, and the date of the signing of the judgment. Failure to comply with the provisions of this rule shall not affect the finality of the judgment.

See also *O'Connor's Texas Rules*, "Default Judgment," ch. 7-A; "The Judgment," ch. 9-C; "Motion to Extend Postjudgment Deadlines," ch. 10-G.

John v. State, 826 S.W.2d 138, 140 (Tex.1992). TRCP 239a "specifically states that 'failure to comply with the provisions of the rule shall not affect the finality of the judgment.'"

TRCP 240. WHERE ONLY SOME ANSWER

Where there are several defendants, some of whom have answered or have not been duly served and some of whom have been duly served and have made default, an interlocutory judgment by default may be entered against those who have made default, and the cause may proceed or be postponed as to the others.

See also TRCP 161; *O'Connor's Texas Rules*, "Default Judgment," ch. 7-A; "The Judgment," ch. 9-C.

TRCP 241. ASSESSING DAMAGES ON LIQUIDATED DEMANDS

When a judgment by default is rendered against the defendant, or all of several defendants, if the claim is liquidated and proved by an instrument in writing, the damages shall be assessed by the court, or under its direction, and final judgment shall be rendered therefor, unless the defendant shall demand and be entitled to a trial by jury.

See also *O'Connor's Texas Rules*, "Default Judgment," ch. 7-A.

Novosad v. Cunningham, 38 S.W.3d 767, 773 (Tex. App.—Houston [14th Dist.] 2001, no pet.). Under TRCP 241 "proof is required only with respect to damages which are either unliquidated or not proven by a written instrument. A claim is liquidated if the amount of damages can be accurately calculated by the court from the factual, as opposed to the conclusory, allegations in the petition and an instrument in writing."

Hanners v. State Bar, 860 S.W.2d 903, 911 (Tex. App.—Dallas 1993, no writ). TRCP 241 "provides that when a default judgment is rendered against a defendant and the claim is liquidated or proven by a written instrument, the court shall assess the damages, unless the defendant is entitled to a jury trial."

TRCP 242. REPEALED

TRCP 243. UNLIQUIDATED DEMANDS

If the cause of action is unliquidated or be not proved by an instrument in writing, the court shall hear evidence as to damages and shall render judgment therefor, unless the defendant shall demand and be entitled to a trial by jury in which case the judgment by default shall be noted, a writ of inquiry awarded, and the cause entered on the jury docket.

See also *O'Connor's Texas Rules*, "Motion for Sanctions," ch. 5-J; "Default Judgment," ch. 7-A.

Texas Commerce Bank v. New, 3 S.W.3d 515, 516 (Tex.1999). "We conclude that because unobjected-to hearsay is, as a matter of law, probative evidence, affidavits can be evidence for purposes of an unliquidated-damages hearing pursuant to [TRCP] 243."

Holt Atherton Indus., Inc. v. Heine, 835 S.W.2d 80, 86 (Tex.1992). "After a default judgment is granted, the trial court must hear evidence of unliquidated damages. ... Therefore, when an appellate court sustains a no evidence point after an *uncontested* hearing on unliquidated damages following a no-answer default judgment, the appropriate disposition is a remand for a new trial on the issue of unliquidated damages."

Marr v. Marr, 905 S.W.2d 331, 333-34 (Tex.App.—Waco 1995, no writ). "The question before us is whether Rule 243 applies in divorce cases.... Rule 243 recognizes, first, the importance of a party's right to a trial by jury, and, second, that the determination of the amount of damages is a question primarily for the jury. It assures defaulting defendants, provided they properly request and do not waive a trial by jury, that they will be afforded their right to have a jury weigh the facts underlying the plaintiff's complaint for unliquidated damages and ascertain from those facts the amount of their damages. [¶] We believe Rule 243 applies in cases involving the division of marital property as well as the proper characterization of the parties' assets as either community or separate. The prominent role of a jury in divorce cases is readily apparent. Parties to divorce proceedings are entitled to a jury trial upon proper request; the jury alone decides whether contested assets will be characterized as either community or separate; and, while the question of a just and right division of the marital estate rests solely within the sound discretion of the court, the jury's findings on the factual issues underlying the division of the marital estate, including the valuation of the assets, are conclusive. Given the right of parties to a jury trial in divorce cases and the pronounced functions of the jury in the property division and characterization aspects of divorce cases, we believe the nature of the property division to be sufficiently akin to the unliquidated damages referred to in Rule 243 so as to require defaulting parties in divorce cases be provided sufficient notice of a hearing before a jury on the issue of the property division, unless, of course, the defaulting party somehow waives his request for a jury."

TRCP 244. ON SERVICE BY PUBLICATION

Where service has been made by publication, and no answer has been filed nor appearance entered within the prescribed time, the court shall appoint an attorney to defend the suit in behalf of the defendant, and judgment shall be rendered as in other cases; but, in every such case a statement of the evidence, approved and signed by the judge, shall be filed with the papers of the cause as a part of the record thereof. The court shall allow such attorney a reasonable fee for his services, to be taxed as part of the costs.

Caution: TRCP 244 is affected by the following sections of the Fam. Code: §§6.409(e), 102.010.

See also *O'Connor's Texas Rules*, "Motion for New Trial," ch. 10-B.

Cahill v. Lyda, 826 S.W.2d 932, 933 (Tex.1992). TRCP 244 "requires that a trial court appoint an attorney ad litem to represent defendants served with citation by publication who fail to file an answer or appear before the court. [TRCP] 244 also requires that the attorney ad litem be paid a reasonable fee for his services, which is to be taxed as part of the costs. The attorney ad litem must exhaust all remedies available to his client and, if necessary, represent his client's interest on appeal."

Isaac v. Westheimer Colony Ass'n, 933 S.W.2d 588, 591 (Tex.App.—Houston [1st Dist.] 1996, writ denied). "[T]here is no evidence in the record of the trial court having appointed an attorney ad litem in [D's] behalf. Absent strict compliance with the essential requirements of [TRCP] 244, a trial court commits reversible error."

Barnes v. Domain, 875 S.W.2d 32, 33 (Tex.App.—Houston [14th Dist.] 1994, no writ). "Neither the case law nor the language of [TRCP 244] reveals any indication that the burden is on the attorney to move the court to make such appointment."

TRCP 245. ASSIGNMENT OF CASES FOR TRIAL

The Court may set contested cases on written request of any party, or on the court's own motion, with reasonable notice of not less than forty-five days to the parties of a first setting for trial, or by agreement of the parties; provided, however, that when a case previously has been set for trial, the Court may reset said contested case to a later date on any reasonable notice to the parties or by agreement of the parties. Noncontested cases may be tried or disposed of at any time whether set or not, and may be set at any time for any other time.

A request for trial setting constitutes a representation that the requesting party reasonably and in good faith expects to be ready for trial by the date requested, but no additional representation concerning the completion of pretrial proceedings or of current readiness for trial shall be required in order to obtain a trial setting in a contested case.

See also Tex. Const. art. 1, §19; ***O'Connor's Texas Rules***, "Default Judgment," ch. 7-A; "Motion for New Trial," ch. 10-B.

In re Carter, 958 S.W.2d 919, 925 (Tex.App.—Amarillo 1997, orig. proceeding). TRCP 245 "indicates that once a written request for a trial setting has been filed no others need be proffered. [B]y making a written request ... the requesting party is implicitly telling the court that the cause will be ready to be tried on the dates suggested. [T]he court is entitled to rely upon the representation in ordering its docket, and the parties need not again reassure the court of their preparedness. But, the same cannot be said when the court has relied upon such requests only to find that the parties could not appear on the dates selected. [W]hen that occurs, the court is empowered to take measure to reduce the disruption by again demanding notification of the parties' preparedness."

Hardin v. Hardin, 932 S.W.2d 566, 567 (Tex.App.—Tyler 1995, no writ). TRCP 245 "was amended in 1990 to require 45 days' notice in order to harmonize it with [TRCP] 216 (request and fee for jury trial), and to require notice of trial setting before the time for demanding a jury. [¶] Since the trial setting notice in the instant case only gave [respondent] 6 days notice, it failed to comply with the current version of Rule 245. The language of the rule is mandatory."

Harmon v. Harmon, 879 S.W.2d 213, 215 (Tex.App.—Houston [14th Dist.] 1994, writ denied). Defendant "complains that the case was tried without notice in violation of Rule 245, which requires not less than 45-days notice of a first trial setting. [¶] Since [D] did not answer, this was a *noncontested* case, and [D] was vulnerable to a default judgment. [D] was not entitled notice of a trial setting. [¶] [D] contends that the case was 'contested' until the 60-day waiting period required by Texas Family Code §3.60 [now §6.702] had elapsed. We disagree. ... It is true that the 60-day statutory waiting period precluded a divorce judgment, default or otherwise, from being rendered.... But this does not mean that the case was 'contested' for purposes of Rule 245. The case became noncontested when [D] failed to answer."

State Farm Fire & Cas. Co. v. Price, 845 S.W.2d 427, 431-32 (Tex.App.—Amarillo 1992, writ dism'd). "By the clear language of [TRCP] 245, the 45 day notice applies only to the first setting of the trial. By failing to timely and specifically object to the first setting on the basis of insufficiency of notice under rule 245, [D] failed to preserve any error for our review."

TRCP 246. CLERK TO GIVE NOTICE OF SETTINGS

The clerk shall keep a record in his office of all cases set for trial, and it shall be his duty to inform any nonresident attorney of the date of setting of any case upon request by mail from such attorney, accompanied by a return envelope properly addressed and stamped. Failure of the clerk to furnish such information on proper request shall be sufficient ground for continuance or for a new trial when it appears to the court that such failure has prevented the attorney from preparing or presenting his claim or defense.

Bruneio v. Bruneio, 890 S.W.2d 150, 156 n.2 (Tex.App.—Corpus Christi 1994, no writ). TRCP 246 "merely provides an additional vehicle for notice to any of the various attorneys who may be working on the case and want direct notification.... Accordingly, Rule 246 [expands] the requirements of notice to include nonresident attorneys who would not otherwise be entitled to direct notification of the setting under Rule 245 as the attorney in charge."

TRCP 247. TRIED WHEN SET

Every suit shall be tried when it is called, unless continued or postponed to a future day or placed at the end of the docket to be called again for trial in its regular order. No cause which has been set upon the trial docket of the court shall be taken from the trial docket for the date set except by agreement of the parties or for good cause upon motion and notice to the opposing party.

See also *O'Connor's Texas Rules*, "Motion for Continuance," ch. 5-D.

Brooks v. Brooks, 561 S.W.2d 949, 951 (Tex.App.—Tyler 1978, no writ). "It was the legal duty of the [P] to keep himself posted as to the setting of the case for trial, and to be present to testify and aid his counsel."

TRCP 248. JURY CASES

When a jury has been demanded, questions of law, motions, exceptions to pleadings, and other unresolved pending matters shall, as far as practicable, be heard and determined by the court before the trial commences, and jurors shall be summoned to appear on the day so designated.

See also TRCP 166.

Gaines v. Gaines, 677 S.W.2d 727, 730 (Tex.App.—Corpus Christi 1984, no writ). TRCP 166 and 248 "are directory procedures that are designed to help streamline the disposition of pre-trial issues."

TRCP 249. CALL OF NON-JURY DOCKET

The non-jury docket shall be taken up at such times as not unnecessarily to interfere with the dispatch of business on the jury docket.

TRCP 250. REPEALED

B. CONTINUANCE & CHANGE OF VENUE

TRCP 251. CONTINUANCE

No application for a continuance shall be heard before the defendant files his defense, nor shall any continuance be granted except for sufficient cause supported by affidavit, or by consent of the parties, or by operation of law.

See also *O'Connor's Texas Rules*, "Motion for Continuance," ch. 5-D; *O'Connor's Texas Forms*, FORMS 5D.

Tenneco, Inc. v. Enterprise Prods. Co., 925 S.W.2d 640, 647 (Tex.1996). "When a party contends that it has not had an adequate opportunity for discovery before a summary judgment hearing, it must file either an affidavit explaining the need for further discovery or a verified motion for continuance."

Villegas v. Carter, 711 S.W.2d 624, 626 (Tex.1986). "Generally, when movants fail to comply with [TRCP] 251's requirement that the motion for continuance be 'supported by affidavit,' we presume that the trial court did not abuse its discretion in denying the motion."

Favaloro v. Commission for Lawyer Discipline, 13 S.W.3d 831, 838 (Tex.App.—Dallas 2000, no pet.). "The record contains Favaloro's oral request for a continuance in order to designate witnesses. This oral motion does not satisfy the provisions of [TRCP] 251."

TRCP 252. APPLICATION FOR CONTINUANCE

If the ground of such application be the want of testimony, the party applying therefor shall make affidavit that such testimony is material, showing the materiality thereof, and that he has used due diligence to procure such testimony, stating such diligence, and the cause of failure, if known; that such testimony cannot be procured from any other source; and, if it be for the absence of a witness, he shall state the name and residence of the witness, and what he expects to prove by him; and also state that the continuance is not sought for delay only, but that justice may be done; provided that, on a first application for a continuance, it shall not be necessary to show that the absent testimony cannot be procured from any other source.

The failure to obtain the deposition of any witness residing within 100 miles of the courthouse of the county in which the suit is pending shall not be regarded as want of diligence when diligence has been used to secure the personal attendance of such witness under the rules of law, unless by reason of age, infirmity or sickness, or official duty, the witness will be unable to attend the court, or unless such witness is about to leave, or has left, the State or county in which the suit is pending and will not probably be present at the trial.

See also *O'Connor's Texas Rules*, "Rules for Filing Documents," ch. 1-C; "Motion for Continuance," ch. 5-D; "Motion for Summary Judgment," ch. 7-B; *O'Connor's Texas Forms*, FORMS 5D.

State v. Wood Oil Distrib., Inc., 751 S.W.2d 863, 865 (Tex.1988). "[T]he failure of a litigant to diligently utilize the rules of civil procedure for discovery purposes will not authorize the granting of a continuance."

Ramirez v. State, 973 S.W.2d 388, 391 (Tex.App.—El Paso 1998, no pet.). Defendant's continuance "motion failed to specify the information and testimony he sought or why it was material. [D] did not state the names of the witnesses from whom he sought testimony, nor did he state what he expected to prove from said witnesses."

Verkin v. Southwest Ctr. One, Ltd., 784 S.W.2d 92, 94 (Tex.App.—Houston [1st Dist.] 1989, writ denied). When a motion for continuance is: (1) in substantial compliance with the rule; (2) verified; and (3) uncontroverted, the court "must accept the statements in the motion as true."

TRCP 253. ABSENCE OF COUNSEL AS GROUND FOR CONTINUANCE

Except as provided elsewhere in these rules, absence of counsel will not be good cause for a continuance or postponement of the cause when called for trial, except it be allowed in the discretion of the court, upon cause shown or upon matters within the knowledge or information of the judge to be stated on the record.

See also *O'Connor's Texas Rules*, "Motion for Continuance," ch. 5-D; *O'Connor's Texas Forms*, FORMS 5D.

Villegas v. Carter, 711 S.W.2d 624, 626 (Tex.1986). "[T]he trial court abused its discretion because the evidence shows that [the party] was not negligent or at fault in causing his attorney's withdrawal. The court granted [the party's] attorney's motion to voluntarily withdraw 2 days before trial—too short a time for [the party] to find a new attorney and for that new attorney to investigate the case and prepare for trial."

Rehabilitation Facility, Inc. v. Cooper, 962 S.W.2d 151, 155-56 (Tex.App.—Austin 1998, no pet.). "In general, absence of counsel is not good cause for a continuance. The court does have the discretion, however, to allow a continuance if good cause is shown. [¶] [A]nother attorney from the same law firm ... had signed pleadings and conducted discovery in this case before trial. Nothing in the record suggests that attorney was incapable of rendering adequate representation."

TRCP 254. ATTENDANCE ON LEGISLATURE

In all civil actions, including matters of probate, and in all matters ancillary to such suits which require action by or the attendance of an attorney, including appeals but excluding temporary restraining orders, at any time within thirty days of a date when the legislature is to be in session, or at any time the legislature is in session, or when the legislature sits as a Constitutional Convention, it shall be mandatory that the court continue the cause if it shall appear to the court, by affidavit, that any party applying for continuance, or any attorney for any party to the cause, is a member of either branch of the legislature, and will be or is in actual attendance on a session of the same. If the member of the legislature is an attorney for a party to the cause, his affidavit shall contain a declaration that it is his intention to participate actively in the preparation and/or presentation of the case. Where a party to any cause, or an attorney for any party to a cause, is a member of the legislature, his affidavit need not be corroborated. On the filing of such affidavit, the court shall continue the cause until thirty days after adjournment of the legislature and the affidavit shall be proof of the necessity for the continuance, and the continuance shall be deemed one of right and shall not be charged against the movant upon any subsequent application for continuance.

The right to a continuance shall be mandatory, except only where the attorney was employed within ten days of the date the suit is set for trial, the right to continuance shall be discretionary.

Caution: TRCP 254 is affected by the following section in the Fam. Code: §84.005.

See also CPRC §30.003, for other requirements of a legislative continuance; *O'Connor's Texas Rules*, "Motion for Continuance," ch. 5-D; *O'Connor's Texas Forms*, FORMS 5D.

Waites v. Sondock, 561 S.W.2d 772, 773 (Tex. 1977). "We granted leave to file in order that we might consider the constitutional question ... whether the legislature constitutionally may require mandatory continuances of causes or suits involving legislators when the party opposing the continuance or a person in their charge faces irreparable harm from the delay in enforcing existing rights. We now hold that mandatory continuances under such circumstances violate the due process clause of the Fourteenth Amendment of the United States Constitution and Article I, §§13 and 19 of the Texas Constitution. *At 774-75:* Article 2168a [now TRCP 254] effectively withdraws the common law remedy of litigants who, in emergency situations, seek to enforce court decrees and obtain other relief other than by a temporary restraining order. Although article 2168a appears on its face merely to postpone pending suits and matters ancillary thereto, in the present case the delay in enforcement caused by the legislative continuance allegedly inflicts harm that is not susceptible to remedy at a later date. The mother here claims that the support payments are critical to her ability to feed and support her children. The trial court, after the expiration of the continuance, may force the father to pay any overdue sums, but these payments will not compensate the child for any injury resulting from the mother's present inability to care for the child. *At 776:* [A] legislative continuance is mandatory except in those cases in which the party opposing the continuance alleges that a substantial existing right will be defeated or abridged by delay. In cases of this type the trial court has a duty to conduct a hearing on the allegations. If the allegations are shown to be meritorious the court should deny the continuance."

TRCP 255. CHANGE OF VENUE BY CONSENT

Upon the written consent of the parties filed with the papers of the cause, the court, by an order entered on the minutes, may transfer the same for trial to the court of any other county having jurisdiction of the subject matter of such suit.

See also CPRC §15.020; *O'Connor's Texas Rules*, "Agreement to Transfer," ch. 3-C, §5; *O'Connor's Texas Forms*, FORMS 3C.

Farris v. Ray, 895 S.W.2d 351, 352 (Tex.1995). "[A] signed written agreement filed in the record of the *transferee* court meets all the requirements of [TRCP] 11. Such an agreement, enforceable against the signatories under the terms of the rule, operates as an express waiver of any error there may have been in the initial transfer."

TRCP 256. REPEALED

TRCP 257. GRANTED ON MOTION

A change of venue may be granted in civil causes upon motion of either party, supported by his own affidavit and the affidavit of at least three credible persons, residents of the county in which the suit is pending, for any following cause:

(a) That there exists in the county where the suit is pending so great a prejudice against him that he cannot obtain a fair and impartial trial.

(b) That there is a combination against him instigated by influential persons, by reason of which he cannot expect a fair and impartial trial.

(c) That an impartial trial cannot be had in the county where the action is pending.

(d) For other sufficient cause to be determined by the court.

Caution: TRCP 257 is affected by the following sections in the Fam. Code: §§103.002, 103.003.

See also *O'Connor's Texas Rules*, "Motion to Transfer—Challenging Venue," ch. 3-C.

Acker v. Denton Publ'g Co., 937 S.W.2d 111, 118 (Tex.App.—Fort Worth 1996, writ vacated). "The inability to obtain a fair and impartial trial of a civil case may be grounds for a change of venue. A motion on those grounds must be supported by competent affidavits of the party seeking the transfer and 3 credible residents of the county where the suit is pending." *See also* ***Dorchester Gas Prod'g Co. v. Harlow Corp.***, 743 S.W.2d 243, 253 n.6 (Tex.App.—Amarillo 1987, no writ); ***Tenneco, Inc. v. Salyer***, 739 S.W.2d 448, 449 (Tex. App.—Corpus Christi 1987, orig. proceeding).

TRCP 258. SHALL BE GRANTED

Where such motion to transfer venue is duly made, it shall be granted, unless the credibility of those making such application, or their means of knowledge or the truth of the facts set out in the said application are attacked by the affidavit of a credible person; when thus attacked, the issue thus formed shall be tried by the judge; and the application either granted or refused. Reasonable discovery in support of, or in opposition to, the application shall be permitted, and such discovery as is relevant, including deposition testimony on file, may be attached to, or incorporated by reference in, the affidavit of a party, a witness, or an attorney who has knowledge of such discovery.

See also *O'Connor's Texas Rules*, "Motion to Transfer—Challenging Venue," ch. 3-C.

City of Abilene v. Downs, 367 S.W.2d 153, 155 (Tex. 1963). TRCP 258 "by its terms is mandatorily operative. It provides the only means by which issue can be joined."

Lone Star Steel Co. v. Scott, 759 S.W.2d 144, 146 (Tex.App.—Texarkana 1988, writ denied). "[I]f the motion for transfer is duly filed and is not challenged as provided in [TRCP 258] the trial judge is required to transfer the case."

TRCP 259. TO WHAT COUNTY

If the motion under Rule 257 is granted, the cause shall be removed:

(a) If from a district court, to any county of proper venue in the same or an adjoining district;

(b) If from a county court, to any adjoining county of proper venue;

(c) If (a) or (b) are not applicable, to any county of proper venue;

(d) If a county of proper venue (other than the county of suit) cannot be found, then if from

(1) A district court, to any county in the same or an adjoining district or to any district where an impartial trial can be had;

(2) A county court, to any adjoining county or to any district where an impartial trial can be had;

but the parties may agree that venue shall be changed to some other county, and the order of the court shall conform to such agreement.

See also ***O'Connor's Texas Rules***, "Motion to Transfer—Challenging Venue," ch. 3-C.

Dorchester Gas Prod'g Co. v. Harlow Corp., 743 S.W.2d 243, 253 (Tex.App.—Amarillo 1987, no writ). "[W]hen the trial court determined that [one party] could not obtain a fair and impartial trial in that county, the court had two options under [TRCP] 259(d)—either to remove the case to any county in the same or an adjoining district or to any district where an impartial trial could be had."

TRCP 260. REPEALED

TRCP 261. TRANSCRIPT ON CHANGE

When a change of venue has been granted, the clerk shall immediately make out a correct transcript of all the orders made in said cause, certifying thereto officially under the seal of the court, and send the same, with the original papers in the cause, to the clerk of the court to which the venue has been changed.

C. THE TRIAL

TRCP 262. TRIAL BY THE COURT

The rules governing the trial of causes before a jury shall govern in trials by the court in so far as applicable.

Qantel Bus. Sys., Inc. v. Custom Controls Co., 761 S.W.2d 302, 304 (Tex.1988). "When a plaintiff rests, he indicates that he does not desire to put on further evidence, except by rebuttal testimony, and that he has fully developed his case." In a nonjury case, the court is presumed to have ruled on the sufficiency of the evidence when it grants judgment for the defendant after the plaintiff rests.

TRCP 263. AGREED CASE

Parties may submit matters in controversy to the court upon an agreed statement of facts filed with the clerk, upon which judgment shall be rendered as in other cases; and such agreed statement signed and certified by the court to be correct and the judgment rendered thereon shall constitute the record of the cause.

See also ***O'Connor's Texas Rules***, "Motion for Judgment on Agreed Statement of Facts," ch. 7-D.

Trevino & Gonzalez Co. v. R.F. Muller Co., 949 S.W.2d 39, 41 (Tex.App.—San Antonio 1997, no writ). Under TRCP 263 "parties to a lawsuit may submit matters in controversy to the court upon an agreed statement of facts. [N]o evidence is admitted or considered by the trial court and the trial court's decision is based upon the papers on file and the arguments of counsel. Therefore, ... we indulge no presumptions in favor of the judgment in such a case because the trial court had no factual issues to resolve."

Tarrant Appr. Rev. Bd. v. Martinez Bros. Invs., 946 S.W.2d 914, 917 (Tex.App.—Fort Worth 1997, no writ). "Because this case was submitted to the trial court on an agreed statement of facts and the trial court certified the agreed statement of facts as correct, the stipulated facts are binding on the parties and on this court. ... The court's judgment must declare only the law necessarily arising from the stipulated facts."

City of Galveston v. Giles, 902 S.W.2d 167, 170 n.2 (Tex.App.—Houston [1st Dist.] 1995, no writ). "Findings of fact have no place in the trial of an agreed case. Once the parties stipulate to all the facts, the court may not make additional fact findings."

TRCP 264. VIDEOTAPE TRIAL

By agreement of the parties, the trial court may allow that all testimony and such other evidence as may be appropriate be presented at trial by videotape. The expenses of such videotape recordings shall be taxed as costs. If any party withdraws agreement to a videotape trial, the videotape costs that have accrued will be taxed against the party withdrawing from the agreement.

TRCP 265. ORDER OF PROCEEDINGS ON TRIAL BY JURY

The trial of cases before a jury shall proceed in the following order unless the court should, for good cause stated in the record, otherwise direct:

(a) The party upon whom rests the burden of proof on the whole case shall state to the jury briefly the nature of his claim or defense and what said party expects to prove and the relief sought. Immediately thereafter, the adverse party may make a similar statement, and intervenors and other parties will be accorded similar rights in the order determined by the court.

(b) The party upon whom rests the burden of proof on the whole case shall then introduce his evidence.

(c) The adverse party shall briefly state the nature of his claim or defense and what said party expects to prove and the relief sought unless he has already done so.

(d) He shall then introduce his evidence.

(e) The intervenor and other parties shall make their statement, unless they have already done so, and shall introduce their evidence.

(f) The parties shall then be confined to rebutting testimony on each side.

(g) But one counsel on each side shall examine and cross-examine the same witness, except on leave granted.

Producer's Constr. Co. v. Muegge, 669 S.W.2d 717, 719 (Tex.1984). "The trial court erred in rendering judgment before [the D] had an opportunity to present evidence and rest its case."

TRCP 266. OPEN & CLOSE—ADMISSION

Except as provided in Rule 269 the plaintiff shall have the right to open and conclude both in adducing his evidence and in the argument, unless the burden of proof on the whole case under the pleadings rests upon the defendant, or unless the defendant or all of the defendants, if there should be more than one, shall, after the issues of fact are settled and before the trial commences, admit that the plaintiff is entitled to recover as set forth in the petition, except so far as he may be defeated, in whole or in part, by the allegations of the answer constituting a good defense, which may be established on the trial; which admission shall be entered of record, whereupon the defendant, or the defendants, if more than one, shall have the right to open and conclude in adducing the evidence and in the argument of the cause. The admission shall not serve to admit any allegation which is inconsistent with such defense, which defense shall be one that defendant has the burden of establishing, as for example, and without excluding other defenses: accord and satisfaction, adverse possession, arbitration and award, contributory negligence, discharge in bankruptcy, duress, estoppel, failure of consideration, fraud, release, res judicata, statute of frauds, statute of limitations, waiver, and the like.

See also *O'Connor's Texas Rules*, "Opening Statement," ch. 8-B; "Final Argument," ch. 8-J.

4M Linen & Uniform Sup. Co. v. W.P. Ballard & Co., 793 S.W.2d 320, 324 (Tex.App.—Houston [1st Dist.] 1990, writ denied). TRCP 266 "provides that the plaintiff has the right to open and close argument. There are two exceptions.... First, a defendant has the right to open and close if the burden of proof for the entire case under the pleadings is on defendant. Second, a defendant has the right to open and close if, before trial begins, defendant admits that plaintiff is entitled to recover, subject to proof of defensive allegations."

TRCP 267. WITNESSES PLACED UNDER RULE

a. At the request of either party, in a civil case, the witnesses on both sides shall be sworn and removed out of the courtroom to some place where they cannot hear the testimony as delivered by any other witness in the cause. This is termed placing witnesses under the rule.

b. This rule does not authorize exclusion of (1) a party who is a natural person or the spouse of such natural person, or (2) an officer or employee of a party that is not a natural person and who is designated as its representative by its attorney, or (3) a person whose presence is shown by a party to be essential to the presentation of the cause.

c. If any party be absent, the court in its discretion may exempt from the rule a representative of such party.

d. Witnesses, when placed under Rule 614 of the Texas Rules of Civil Evidence, shall be instructed by the court that they are not to converse with each other or with any other person about the case other than the attorneys in the case, except by permission of the court, and that they are not to read any report of or comment upon the testimony in the case while under the rule.

e. Any witness or other person violating such instructions may be punished for contempt of court.

See also TRE 614; *O'Connor's Texas Rules*, "Objecting to Evidence," ch. 8-D.

Drilex Sys., Inc. v. Flores, 1 S.W.3d 112, 118-19 (Tex.1999). "Although an expert witness may *typically* be found exempt under the essential presence exception, experts are not *automatically* exempt. Instead, [TRE] 614 and [TRCP] 267 vest in trial judges broad discretion to determine whether a witness is essential. *At 120:* We acknowledge that the court never expressly placed [P's expert] under the Rule and never instructed him not to discuss the case with others. However, a court may, in its discretion, exclude the testimony of a prospective witness who technically violates the Rule even though the witness was never actually placed under the Rule."

TRCP 268. MOTION FOR INSTRUCTED VERDICT

A motion for directed verdict shall state the specific grounds therefor.

See also *O'Connor's Texas Rules*, "Motion for Directed Verdict," ch. 8-G; *O'Connor's Texas Forms*, FORMS 8G.

S.V. v. R.V., 933 S.W.2d 1, 8 (Tex.1996). "In reviewing a directed verdict, we examine the evidence in the light most favorable to the person suffering an adverse judgment."

Szczepanik v. First S. Trust Co., 883 S.W.2d 648, 649 (Tex.1994). "In reviewing … an instructed verdict, we must determine whether there is any evidence of probative force to raise a fact issue on the material questions presented. … If there is any conflicting evidence of probative value on any theory of recovery, an instructed verdict is improper…."

Mills v. Angel, 995 S.W.2d 262, 266 (Tex.App.—Texarkana 1999, no pet.). "A directed verdict … is proper only under limited circumstances, e.g., where (1) a specifically indicated defect in the opponent's pleading makes it insufficient to support a judgment; or (2) the evidence proves conclusively the truth of fact propositions which, under the substantive law, establish the right of the movant or negate the right of his opponent to judgment; or (3) the evidence is insufficient to raise an issue of fact as to one or more fact propositions which must be established for the opponent to be entitled to judgment."

TRCP 269. ARGUMENT

(a) After the evidence is concluded and the charge is read, the parties may argue the case to the jury. The party having the burden of proof on the whole case, or on all matters which are submitted by the charge, shall be entitled to open and conclude the argument; where there are several parties having separate claims or defenses, the court shall prescribe the order of argument between them.

(b) In all arguments, and especially in arguments on the trial of the case, the counsel opening shall present his whole case as he relies on it, both of law and facts, and shall be heard in the concluding argument only in reply to the counsel on the other side.

(c) Counsel for an intervenor shall occupy the position in the argument assigned by the court according to the nature of the claim.

(d) Arguments on questions of law shall be addressed to the court, and counsel should state the substance of the authorities referred to without reading more from books than may be necessary to verify the statement. On a question on motions, exceptions to the evidence, and other incidental matters, the counsel will be allowed only such argument as may be necessary to present clearly the question raised, and refer to authorities on it, unless further discussion is invited by the court.

(e) Arguments on the facts should be addressed to the jury, when one is impaneled in a case that is being tried, under the supervision of the court. Counsel shall be required to confine the argument strictly to the evidence and to the arguments of opposing counsel. Mere personal criticism by counsel upon each other shall be avoided, and when indulged in shall be promptly corrected as a contempt of court.

(f) Side-bar remarks, and remarks by counsel of one side, not addressed to the court, while the counsel on the other side is examining a witness or arguing any question to the court, or addressing the jury, will be rigidly repressed by the court.

(g) The court will not be required to wait for objections to be made when the rules as to arguments are violated; but should they not be noticed and corrected by the court, opposing counsel may ask leave of the court to rise and present his point of objection. But the court shall protect counsel from any unnecessary interruption made on frivolous and unimportant grounds.

(h) It shall be the duty of every counsel to address the court from his place at the bar, and in addressing the court to rise to his feet; and while engaged in the trial of a case, he shall remain at his place in the bar.

See also *O'Connor's Texas Rules*, "Final Argument," ch. 8-J.

Standard Fire Ins. Co. v. Reese, 584 S.W.2d 835, 839 (Tex.1979). "There are only rare instances of incurable harm from improper argument."

Wal-Mart Stores, Inc. v. Reece, 32 S.W.3d 339, 347-48 (Tex.App.—Waco 2000, pet. granted 10-18-01, argued 2-6-02). "Although it is true that [TRCP] 269(f) specifically provides that such inappropriate side-bar remarks must be 'rigidly repressed,' this does not excuse counsel from complying with the basic rules for preservation of error. [¶] [T]he Supreme Court [has] held that no error [is] preserved because [of the failure] to obtain an express ruling on [an] objection to the side-bar comments at issue."

National Un. Fire Ins. Co. v. Soto, 819 S.W.2d 619, 624 (Tex.App.—El Paso 1991, writ denied). "Counsel are admonished to keep their arguments within the parameters of [TRCP] 269, avoiding personal criticism of opposing counsel and refraining from side-bar remarks and interrupting opposing counsel when making a motion or objection."

TEIA v. Guerrero, 800 S.W.2d 859, 867 (Tex.App.—San Antonio 1990, writ denied). TRCP 269 "commands courts to correct improper argument sua sponte...."

TRCP 270. ADDITIONAL TESTIMONY

When it clearly appears to be necessary to the due administration of justice, the court may permit additional evidence to be offered at any time; provided that in a jury case no evidence on a controversial matter shall be received after the verdict of the jury.

See also *O'Connor's Texas Rules*, "Motion to Reopen for Additional Evidence," ch. 8-H; *O'Connor's Texas Forms*, FORM 8H:01.

Lopez v. Lopez, 55 S.W.3d 194, 201 (Tex.App.—Corpus Christi 2001, no pet.). "Rule 270 allows, but does not require, the court to permit additional evidence. In determining whether to grant a motion to reopen, the trial court considers whether: (1) the moving party showed due diligence in obtaining the evidence, (2) the proffered evidence is decisive, (3) reception of such evidence will cause undue delay, and (4) granting the motion will cause an injustice. ... [A] trial court does not abuse its discretion by refusing to reopen a case after evidence is closed if the party seeking to reopen has not shown diligence in attempting to produce the evidence in a timely fashion. The trial court should exercise its discretion liberally 'in the interest of permitting both sides to fully develop the case in the interest of justice.'"

Estrello v. Elboar, 965 S.W.2d 754, 759 (Tex. App.—Fort Worth 1998, no pet.). "[A] trial court does not abuse its discretion by refusing to reopen a case after evidence is closed if the party seeking to reopen has not shown diligence in attempting to produce the evidence in a timely fashion."

Apresa v. Montfort Ins. Co., 932 S.W.2d 246, 249 (Tex.App.—El Paso 1996, no writ). "After having rested his case, the right of a party to reopen it and introduce additional evidence is a question addressed to the sound discretion of the trial court. The trial judge should liberally exercise his discretion to permit both sides to fully develop their case. The trial court's decision should only be overturned for clear abuse."

D. CHARGE TO THE JURY

TRCP 271. CHARGE TO THE JURY

Unless expressly waived by the parties, the trial court shall prepare and in open court deliver a written charge to the jury.

See also *O'Connor's Texas Rules*, "The Charge," ch. 8-I.

TRCP 272. REQUISITES

The charge shall be in writing, signed by the court, and filed with the clerk, and shall be a part of the record of the cause. It shall be submitted to the respective parties or their attorneys for their inspection, and a reasonable time given them in which to examine and present objections thereto outside the presence of the jury, which objections shall in every instance be presented to the court in writing, or be dictated to the court reporter in the presence of the court and opposing counsel, before the charge is read to the jury. All objections not so presented shall be considered as waived. The court shall announce its rulings thereon before reading the charge to the jury and shall endorse the rulings on the objections if written or dictate same to the court reporter in the presence of counsel. Objections to the charge and the court's rulings thereon may be included as a part of any transcript or statement of facts on appeal and, when so included in either, shall constitute a sufficient bill of exception to the rulings of the court thereon. It shall be presumed, unless otherwise noted in the record, that the party making such objections presented the same at the proper time and excepted to the ruling thereon.

See also *O'Connor's Texas Rules*, "The Charge," ch. 8-I.

State Farm Life Ins. Co. v. Beaston, 907 S.W.2d 430, 440 (Tex.1995). "[N]either the trial court nor [P's] counsel had the opportunity to change the conditional submission structure of the court's charge, because [D] made no objection before the verdict. This is precisely what [TRCP] 272 and 274 are intended to prevent. [¶] The failure to object to the conditional submission of the damages issue waives error as to form and substance of the submission."

Reinhart v. Young, 906 S.W.2d 471, 473 (Tex.1995). "This was not a close case, where a superfluous instruction would be more likely to influence the jury improperly. *At 474:* [A]nd even more important, the charge contained an instruction concerning the doctrine of sudden emergency. ... Plaintiffs made no objection whatsoever to this instruction, even though it reiterates much of the unavoidable accident instruction."

City of Brownsville v. Alvarado, 897 S.W.2d 750, 752 (Tex.1995). "Submission of an improper jury question can be harmless error if the jury's answers to other questions render the improper question immaterial. A jury question is considered immaterial when its answer can be found elsewhere in the verdict or when its answer cannot alter the effect of the verdict."

State Dept. of Highways & Pub. Transp. v. Payne, 838 S.W.2d 235, 241 (Tex.1992). "The procedure for preparing and objecting to the charge has lost its philosophical moorings. There should be but one test for determining if a party has preserved error in the jury charge, and that is whether the party made the trial court aware of the complaint, timely and plainly, and obtained a ruling."

TRCP 273. JURY SUBMISSIONS

Either party may present to the court and request written questions, definitions, and instructions to be given to the jury; and the court may give them or a part thereof, or may refuse to give them, as may be proper. Such requests shall be prepared and presented to the court and submitted to opposing counsel for examination and objection within a reasonable time after the charge is given to the parties or their attorneys for examination. A request by either party for any questions, definitions, or instructions shall be made separate and apart from such party's objections to the court's charge.

See also *O'Connor's Texas Rules*, "The Charge," ch. 8-I.

Galveston Cty. Fair & Rodeo, Inc. v. Glover, 940 S.W.2d 585, 586-87 (Tex.1996). "The court of appeals ... held that [D] 'did not separately request in writing any definitions or instructions on' 'what constitutes wrongful disqualification' as required by [TRCP] 273.... We disagree. [D's] written request was separate from its oral objection. This request fully complied with Rule 273."

Lester v. Logan, 907 S.W.2d 452, 453 (Tex.1995). Disapproved of the court of appeals' opinion that held a request on one piece of paper that included 5 related matters—one question, 2 instructions, and 2 definitions—was improper.

Alaniz v. Jones & Neuse, Inc., 907 S.W.2d 450, 451 (Tex.1995). TRCP 273 "does not prohibit including the request in a complete charge as long as it is not obscured."

Jarrin v. Sam White Oldsmobile Co., 929 S.W.2d 21, 25 (Tex.App.—Houston [1st Dist.] 1996, writ denied). "To complain of the trial court's omission of a requested instruction on appeal, a party is obliged to make a written request to the trial court.... Dictating a requested instruction to the court reporter is not sufficient to support an appeal based on the trial court's refusal to submit requested material."

TRCP 274. OBJECTIONS & REQUESTS

A party objecting to a charge must point out distinctly the objectionable matter and the grounds of the objection. Any complaint as to a question, definition, or instruction, on account of any defect, omission, or fault in pleading, is waived unless specifically included in the objections. When the complaining party's objection, or requested question, definition, or instruction is, in the opinion of the appellate court, obscured or concealed by voluminous unfounded objections, minute differentiations or numerous unnecessary requests, such objection or request shall be untenable. No objection to one part of the charge may be adopted and applied to any other part of the charge by reference only.

See also *O'Connor's Texas Rules*, "The Charge," ch. 8-I.

Universal Servs. Co. v. Ung, 904 S.W.2d 638, 640 (Tex.1995). A party cannot complain on appeal that the trial court did not submit an instruction or definition with the correct cluster if the party did not request it as part of that cluster.

General Chem. Corp. v. De La Lastra, 852 S.W.2d 916, 920 (Tex.1993). Defendant "requested the very issues that it now seeks to avoid. Parties may not invite error by requesting an issue and then objecting to its submission."

Byrne v. Harris Adacom Network Servs., Inc., 11 S.W.3d 244, 253 (Tex.App.—Texarkana 1999, pet. denied). "The purpose of [TRCP 274] is to afford the trial courts an opportunity to correct errors in the charge by requiring objections to clearly specify the error and explain the grounds for objection. An objection that does not meet both requirements is properly overruled and will not preserve error on appeal. [P] has not provided us with any authority providing that a party must object to a question conditionally submitted *unless* the party has already objected to the question on which the question complained of was conditioned."

TRCP 275. CHARGE READ BEFORE ARGUMENT

Before the argument is begun, the trial court shall read the charge to the jury in the precise words in which it was written, including all questions, definitions, and instructions which the court may give.

See also *O'Connor's Texas Rules*, "The Charge," ch. 8-I.

Board of Regents v. S&G Constr. Co., 529 S.W.2d 90, 98 (Tex.App.—Austin 1975, writ ref'd n.r.e.), *overruled on other grounds*, ***Federal Sign v. TSU***, 951 S.W.2d 401, 408 (Tex.1997). A trial court does not violate TRCP 275 by amending the written charge to correct errors after oral argument.

TRCP 276. REFUSAL OR MODIFICATION

When an instruction, question, or definition is requested and the provisions of the law have been complied with and the trial judge refuses the same, the judge shall endorse thereon "Refused," and sign the same officially. If the trial judge modifies the same the judge shall endorse thereon "Modified as follows: (stating in what particular the judge has modified the same) and given, and exception allowed" and sign the same officially. Such refused or modified instruction, question, or definition, when so endorsed shall constitute a bill of exceptions, and it shall be conclusively presumed that the party asking the same presented it at the proper time, excepted to its refusal or modification, and that all the requirements of law have been observed, and such procedure shall entitle the party requesting the same to have the action of the trial judge thereon reviewed without preparing a formal bill of exceptions.

See also *O'Connor's Texas Rules*, "The Charge," ch. 8-I.

Dallas Mkt. Ctr. Dev. Co. v. Liedeker, 958 S.W.2d 382, 386 (Tex.1997), *overruled on other grounds*, ***Torrington Co. v. Stutzman***, 46 S.W.3d 829 (Tex.2000). TRCP 276 "requires a trial court to endorse refused requests 'Refused,' and sign the same officially. The rule provides that such endorsement preserves error. [¶] This Court has never held that the trial court's endorsement is the only means of preserving error in refusing charge requests." (Internal quotations omitted.)

Acord v. G.M. Corp., 669 S.W.2d 111, 114 (Tex. 1984). "We interpret the presumptive provision of [TRCP] 272 to mean that if an objection is articulated and the trial court makes no change in the charge, the objection is, of necessity, overruled."

TRCP 277. SUBMISSION TO THE JURY

In all jury cases the court shall, whenever feasible, submit the cause upon broad-form questions. The court shall submit such instructions and definitions as shall be proper to enable the jury to render a verdict.

Inferential rebuttal questions shall not be submitted in the charge. The placing of the burden of proof may be accomplished by instructions rather than by inclusion in the question.

In any cause in which the jury is required to apportion the loss among the parties the court shall submit a question or questions inquiring what percentage, if any, of the negligence or causation, as the case may be, that caused the occurrence or injury in question is attributable to each of the persons found to have been culpable. The court shall also instruct the jury to answer the damage question or questions without any reduction because of the percentage of negligence or causation, if any, of the person injured. The court may predicate the damage question or questions upon affirmative findings of liability.

The court may submit a question disjunctively when it is apparent from the evidence that one or the other of the conditions or facts inquired about necessarily exists.

The court shall not in its charge comment directly on the weight of the evidence or advise the jury of the effect of their answers, but the court's charge shall not be objectionable on the ground that it incidentally constitutes a comment on the weight of the evidence or advises the jury of the effect of their answers when it is properly a part of an instruction or definition.

See also *O'Connor's Texas Rules*, "The Charge," ch. 8-I.

Crown Life Ins. Co. v. Casteel, 22 S.W.3d 378, 389 (Tex.1999). Plaintiff "argues that [TRCP] 277 required the trial court to submit all liability theories in a single broad-form question, and that the verdict should not be overturned because the trial court simply followed that rule. *At 390:* Rule 277 is not absolute; rather, it mandates broad-form submission 'whenever feasible.' [W]hen the trial court is unsure whether it should submit a particular theory of liability, separating liability theories best serves the policy of judicial economy underlying Rule 277 by avoiding the need for a new trial when the basis for liability cannot be determined." *See also **Texas Dept. of Human Servs. v. Hinds***, 904 S.W.2d 629, 637 (Tex.1995).

Hyundai Motor Co. v. Rodriguez, 995 S.W.2d 661, 664 (Tex.1999). "[S]ubmission of a single question relating to multiple theories may be necessary to avoid the risk that the jury will become confused and answer questions inconsistently. The goal of the charge is to submit to the jury the issues for decision logically, simply, clearly, fairly, correctly, and completely."

State Farm Lloyds v. Nicolau, 951 S.W.2d 444, 451 (Tex.1997). TRCP 277 "affords the trial court considerable discretion in deciding what instructions are necessary and proper in submitting issues to the jury." *See also **Wichita Cty. v. Hart***, 917 S.W.2d 779, 783-84 (Tex. 1996).

Texas DHS v. E.B., 802 S.W.2d 647, 649 (Tex.1990). TRCP 277 "unequivocally requires broad-form submission whenever feasible. Unless extraordinary circumstances exist, a court must submit such broad-form questions."

In re M.E.C., 66 S.W.3d 449, 458 (Tex.App.—Waco 2001, no pet.). TRCP 277 "provides that '[t]he court shall not in its charge comment directly on the weight of the evidence.' Although Rule 277 concerns the court's charge, appellate courts have applied the principle expressed therein to a court's verbal statements. [¶] A trial judge's statement during the course of trial impermissibly comments on the weight of the evidence if 'it indicates the judge's opinion concerning a matter to be determined by the jury.'"

In re M.C.M., 57 S.W.3d 27, 30 (Tex.App.—Houston [1st Dist.] 2001, pet. denied). Parents argue "the broad-form submission of jury questions is not proper in [a SAPCR proceeding to terminate parental rights]. They claim that, unless the jury makes a specific finding for each ground alleged for termination, as well as a separate finding that termination would be in the best interest of the child, their parental rights cannot be terminated. *At 31:* [I]t is not necessary for the trial court to submit separate questions in parental termination cases."

Toennies v. Quantum Chem. Corp., 998 S.W.2d 374, 377 (Tex.App.—Houston [1st Dist.] 1999), *aff'd*, 47 S.W.3d 473 (Tex.2001). "When liability is asserted based upon a provision of a statute or regulation, a jury charge should track the language of the provision as closely as possible."

TRCP 278. SUBMISSION OF QUESTIONS, DEFINITIONS, & INSTRUCTIONS

The court shall submit the questions, instructions and definitions in the form provided by Rule 277, which are raised by the written pleadings and the evidence. Except in trespass to try title, statutory partition proceedings, and other special proceedings in which the pleadings are specially defined by statutes or procedural rules, a party shall not be entitled to any submission of any question raised only by a general denial and not raised by affirmative written pleading by that party. Nothing herein shall change the burden of proof from what it would have been under a general denial. A judgment shall not be reversed because of the failure to submit other and various phases or different shades of the same question. Failure to submit a question shall not be deemed a ground for reversal of the judgment, unless its submission, in substantially correct wording, has been requested in writing and tendered by the party complaining of the judgment; provided, however, that objection to such failure shall suffice in such respect if the question is one relied upon by the opposing party. Failure to submit a definition or instruction shall not be deemed a ground for reversal of the judgment unless a substantially correct definition or instruction has been requested in writing and tendered by the party complaining of the judgment.

See also *O'Connor's Texas Rules*, "The Charge," ch. 8-I.

Texas Workers' Comp. Ins. Fund v. Mandlbauer, 34 S.W.3d 909, 912 (Tex.2000). "When a trial court refuses to submit a requested instruction, the question on appeal is whether the request was reasonably necessary to enable the jury to render a proper verdict. Further, for an instruction to be proper, it must (1) assist the jury; (2) accurately state the law; and (3) find support in the pleadings and the evidence." *Cf.* ***Plainsman Trading Co. v. Crews***, 898 S.W.2d 786, 791 (Tex.1995).

Green Int'l, Inc. v. Solis, 951 S.W.2d 384, 390 (Tex.1997). "Assuming the trial court erred in failing to permit an amendment of the trial pleadings, the trial court did not err in failing to submit the accompanying jury questions. Each requested jury question must be supported by the evidence."

Texas DHS v. Hinds, 904 S.W.2d 629, 637-38 (Tex. 1995). Defendant "did not request the instruction that should have been given, but instead requested [another] instruction. ... We believe this request nevertheless preserved error for 2 reasons. First, [D] took the instruction from the concurring opinion in ***Winters*** [***v. Houston Chronicle Publ'g Co.***, 795 S.W.2d 723 (Tex.1990)]. Second, the request called the trial court's attention to the causation element missing in Question No. 2."

Triplex Comm., Inc. v. Riley, 900 S.W.2d 716, 718 (Tex.1995). "If an issue is properly pleaded and is supported by some evidence, a litigant is entitled to have controlling questions submitted to the jury." *See also* ***Elbaor v. Smith***, 845 S.W.2d 240, 243 (Tex.1992).

Southwestern Bell Tel. Co. v. John Carlo Tex., Inc., 843 S.W.2d 470, 472 (Tex.1992). "The court of appeals ... held the error [in refusing to define justification] harmless. We disagree. Virtually the entire factual dispute between the parties has been over whether Bell's conduct was justified. To ask the jury to resolve this dispute without a proper legal definition to the essential legal issue was reversible error."

Robertson Cty. v. Wymola, 17 S.W.3d 334, 342 (Tex.App.—Austin 2000, pet. denied). "A fact issue that is established with uncontroverted evidence and is not in dispute should not be submitted to the jury."

Fairfield Estates L.P. v. Griffin, 986 S.W.2d 719, 724 (Tex.App.—Eastland 1999, no pet.). "The record shows that, at the jury charge conference, defendants objected to the lack of an instruction on the measure of damages and requested an instruction on temporary damages. However, the record contains only an oral request, not a written request. Because defendants' request was not made 'in writing,' it was waived."

TRCP 279. OMISSIONS FROM THE CHARGE

Upon appeal all independent grounds of recovery or of defense not conclusively established under the evidence and no element of which is submitted or requested are waived. When a ground of recovery or defense consists of more than one element, if one or more of such elements necessary to sustain such ground of recovery or defense, and necessarily referable thereto, are submitted to and found by the jury, and one or more of such elements are omitted from the charge, without request or objection, and there is factually sufficient evidence to support a finding thereon, the trial court, at the request of either party, may after notice and hearing and at any time before the judgment is rendered, make and file written findings on such omitted element or elements in support of the judgment. If no such written findings are made, such omitted element or elements shall be deemed found by the court in such manner as to support the judgment. A claim that the evidence was legally or factually insufficient to warrant the submission of any question may be made for the first time after verdict, regardless of whether the submission of such question was requested by the complainant.

See also *O'Connor's Texas Rules*, "The Charge," ch. 8-I.

Maritime Overseas Corp. v. Ellis, 971 S.W.2d 402, 417 (Tex.1998). Federal procedure requires a judgment as a matter of law "be made before the case is submitted to the jury 'to assure the responding party an opportunity to cure any deficiency in that party's proof that may have been overlooked until called to the party's attention.' Texas procedure does not afford parties the same protection."

State Farm Life Ins. Co. v. Beaston, 907 S.W.2d 430, 437 (Tex.1995). "Where ... a jury awards damages based on a charge that omits an element necessary to sustain a ground of recovery, the trial court can either file a written finding regarding the missing element or render judgment without one. If the trial court does not file a written finding, the omitted element is deemed found in support of the judgment as long as no objection was made and the evidence supports such a finding."

T.O. Stanley Boot Co. v. Bank of El Paso, 847 S.W.2d 218, 222-23 (Tex.1992). Plaintiff "failed to submit or request any element of its affirmative claim to the jury. Unless the [P's] affirmative claim is conclusively established under the evidence, the ground of recovery is waived upon appeal."

Ramos v. Frito-Lay, Inc., 784 S.W.2d 667, 668 (Tex. 1990). "Where ... issues are omitted which constitute only a part of a complete and independent ground and other issues necessarily referable to that ground are submitted and answered, the omitted elements are deemed found in support of the judgment if no objection is made and they are supported by some evidence."

Wal-Mart Stores, Inc. v. Renteria, 52 S.W.3d 848, 850 (Tex.App.—San Antonio 2001, pet. denied). "[R]ule 279 does not require that the submitted element and the omitted element be 'necessarily referable' to each other. Rule 279 only requires that the submitted element or elements be 'necessarily referable' to the cause of action."

E. CASE TO THE JURY

TRCP 280. PRESIDING JUROR OF JURY

Each jury shall appoint one of their body presiding juror.

TRCP 281. PAPERS TAKEN TO JURY ROOM

The jury may, and on request shall, take with them in their retirement the charges and instructions, general or special, which were given and read to them, and any written evidence, except the depositions of witnesses, but shall not take with them any special charges which have been refused. Where part only of a paper has been read in evidence, the jury shall not take the same with them, unless the part so read to them is detached from that which was excluded.

First Employees Ins. Co. v. Skinner, 646 S.W.2d 170, 172 (Tex.1983). TRCP 281 "is mandatory and ... the trial court is required to send all exhibits admitted into evidence to the jury room during the deliberations of the jury. Furthermore, this rule is self-operative and requires no request from the jurors or counsel."

Speier v. Webster Coll., 616 S.W.2d 617, 619 (Tex. 1981). "The fact that a chart happens to summarize testimony on damages does not remove its admissibility from the discretion of the trial court. The type of testimony summarized is only one of many factors a trial court must consider in exercising its discretion."

Harvey v. Culpepper, 801 S.W.2d 596, 601 (Tex. App.—Corpus Christi 1990, no writ). "The admission of depositions into evidence is prohibited. The trial court should not have allowed the jury to retire with the depositions."

TRCP 282. JURY KEPT TOGETHER

The jury may either decide a case in court or retire for deliberation. If they retire, they shall be kept together in some convenient place, under the charge of an officer, until they agree upon a verdict or are discharged by the court; but the court in its discretion may permit them to separate temporarily for the night and at their meals, and for other proper purposes.

Union City Transfer v. Adams, 248 S.W.2d 256, 260 (Tex.App.—Fort Worth 1952, writ ref'd n.r.e.). "Permitting the jury to separate temporarily for their meal was within the discretion of the court."

TRCP 283. DUTY OF OFFICER ATTENDING JURY

The officer in charge of the jury shall not make nor permit any communication to be made to them, except to inquire if they have agreed upon a verdict, unless by order of the court; and he shall not before their verdict is rendered communicate to any person the state of their deliberations or the verdict agreed upon.

Logan v. Grady, 482 S.W.2d 313, 322 (Tex.App.—Fort Worth 1972, no writ). "[T]he jury bailiff violated [TRCP] 283 and 285 ... when he did not make the jury's wish as communicated to him known to the court and also when he instructed the jury that its members already had in the jury room all that it needed in order to answer Issue No. 14."

TRCP 284. JUDGE TO CAUTION JURY

If permitted to separate, either during the trial or after the case is submitted to them, the jury shall be admonished by the court that it is their duty not to converse with, or permit themselves to be addressed by any other person, on any subject connected with the trial.

TRCP 285. JURY MAY COMMUNICATE WITH COURT

The jury may communicate with the court by making their wish known to the officer in charge, who shall inform the court, and they may then in open court, and through their presiding juror, communicate with the court, either verbally or in writing. If the communication is to request further instructions, Rule 286 shall be followed.

See also *O'Connor's Texas Rules*, "The Charge," ch. 8-I.

Ross v. TEIA, 267 S.W.2d 541, 542 (Tex.1954). TRCP 285 "provides that the jury may communicate with the trial judge through its foreman in open court, and [TRCP] 286 provides that when the jury desires further instructions it shall appear in open court in a body, shall make a request in writing through its foreman, and, if additional instructions are given, they shall be in writing."

TRCP 286. JURY MAY RECEIVE FURTHER INSTRUCTIONS

After having retired, the jury may receive further instructions from the court touching any matter of law, either at their request or upon the court's own motion. For this purpose they shall appear before the judge in open court in a body, and if the instruction is being given at their request, they shall through their presiding juror state to the court, in writing, the particular question of law upon which they desire further instruction. The court shall give such instruction in writing, but no instruction shall be given except in conformity with the rules relating to the charge. Additional argument may be allowed in the discretion of the court.

See also *O'Connor's Texas Rules*, "The Charge," ch. 8-I.

Stevens v. Travelers Ins. Co., 563 S.W.2d 223, 229 (Tex.1978). "[E]ven though there is a latent danger of coercion, supplemental, verdict-urging instructions are not, in and of themselves, erroneous, so long as the particular charge given is not otherwise objectionable. *At 226 n.1:* Under [TRCP] 286 the supplemental charge should have been given in writing and not orally."

Lochinvar Corp. v. Meyers, 930 S.W.2d 182, 187 (Tex.App.—Dallas 1996, no writ). Plaintiff, "by failing to object to the charge prior to its being read to the jury, waived his objections under [TRCP] 272. However, [TRCP] 286 allows a court the opportunity to correct an error by modifying its charge. ... The instruction was given to the jury in writing [but the trial court did not] reassemble the jury in the courtroom. [D] did not object to the court's failure to reassemble the jury and read the modified charge." Thus, defendant waived the error.

TRCP 287. DISAGREEMENT AS TO EVIDENCE

If the jury disagree as to the statement of any witness, they may, upon applying to the court, have read to them from the court reporter's notes that part of such witness' testimony on the point in dispute; but, if there be no such reporter, or if his notes cannot be read to the jury, the court may cause such witness to be again brought upon the stand and the judge shall direct him to repeat his testimony as to the point in dispute, and no other, as nearly as he can in the language used on the trial; and on their notifying the court that they disagree as to any portion of a deposition or other paper not permitted to be carried with them in their retirement, the court may, in like manner, permit such portion of said deposition or paper to be again read to the jury.

Krishnan v. Ramirez, 42 S.W.3d 205, 225 (Tex.App.—Corpus Christi 2001, pet. denied). "The judge is given broad discretion in determining what portions of the testimony are relevant to the jury's request to have testimony re-read."

Steinberger v. Archer Cty., 621 S.W.2d 838, 843 (Tex.App.—Fort Worth 1981, no writ). Under TRCP 287 "the jury is entitled to hear only the specific part of the testimony relevant to the point in dispute, and only when the jury notifies the court, that it disagrees upon the statement made by the witness. In the absence of disagreement between the jurors, the court is not obligated to have any witness' testimony read back to the jury...."

TRCP 288. COURT OPEN FOR JURY

The court, during the deliberations of the jury, may proceed with other business or recess from time to time, but shall be deemed open for all purposes connected with the case before the jury.

TRCP 289. DISCHARGE OF JURY

The jury to whom a case has been submitted may be discharged by the court when they cannot agree and the parties consent to their discharge, or when they have been kept together for such time as to render it altogether improbable that they can agree, or when any calamity or accident may, in the opinion of the court, require it, or when by sickness or other cause their number is reduced below the number constituting the jury in such court.

The cause shall again be placed on the jury docket and shall again be set for trial as the court directs.

See also ***O'Connor's Texas Rules***, "The Charge," ch. 8-I.

Shaw v. Greater Houston Transp. Co., 791 S.W.2d 204, 205-10 (Tex.App.—Corpus Christi 1990, no writ). It was coercive for the trial court to refuse to release the jury after they stated three times they were deadlocked.

F. VERDICT

TRCP 290. DEFINITION & SUBSTANCE

A verdict is a written declaration by a jury of its decision, comprehending the whole or all the issues submitted to the jury, and shall be either a general or special verdict, as directed, which shall be signed by the presiding juror of the jury.

A general verdict is one whereby the jury pronounces generally in favor of one or more parties to the suit upon all or any of the issues submitted to it. A special verdict is one wherein the jury finds the facts only on issues made up and submitted to them under the direction of the court.

A special verdict shall, as between the parties, be conclusive as to the facts found.

Wal-Mart Stores, Inc. v. Alexander, 868 S.W.2d 322, 328 (Tex.1993). "A jury's marginal notations generally may not be considered on appeal. They reflect the jury's mental processes, but they are not part of its verdict."

Houston Fire & Cas. Ins. Co. v. Gerhardt, 281 S.W.2d 176, 178 (Tex.App.—San Antonio 1955, orig. proceeding). "A verdict form reflecting answers to special issues but not signed by the foreman may or may not be a verdict, and presents a question which must be determined by the hearing of evidence."

TRCP 291. FORM OF VERDICT

No special form of verdict is required, and the judgment shall not be arrested or reversed for mere want of form therein if there has been substantial compliance with the requirements of the law in rendering a verdict.

TRCP 292. VERDICT BY PORTION OF ORIGINAL JURY

A verdict may be rendered in any cause by the concurrence, as to each and all answers made, of the same ten members of an original jury of twelve or of the same five members of an original jury of six. However, where as many as three jurors die or be disabled from sitting and there are only nine of the jurors remaining of an original jury of twelve, those remaining may render and return a verdict. If less than the original twelve or six jurors render a verdict, the verdict must be signed by each juror concurring therein.

See also ***O'Connor's Texas Rules***, "The Verdict," ch. 8-K.

Yanes v. Sowards, 996 S.W.2d 849, 850 (Tex.1999). "The Texas Constitution and [TRCPs] require a district-court jury to consist of 12 original jurors, but as few as 9 may render and return a verdict if the others die or become disabled from sitting. [T]rial courts have broad discretion in determining whether a juror is disabled from sitting when there is evidence of constitutional disqualification. But not just any inconvenience or delay is a disability. A constitutional disability must be in the nature of an actual physical or mental incapacity." (Internal quotations omitted.)

In re B.L.D., 56 S.W.3d 203, 217 (Tex.App.—Waco 2001, no pet.). "We hold that in termination cases, procedural due process requires a strict application of Rule 292's requirement of accord by 10 or more jurors."

Schlafly v. Schlafly, 33 S.W.3d 863, 870 (Tex. App.—Houston [14th Dist.] 2000, pet. denied). "The alternate juror hears the same evidence that a regular juror hears and ... 'has the same functions, powers and privileges.' There is no reason to treat a jury comprised of 12 members, one of whom is an alternate, any differently than a jury comprised of 12 regular members. ...

We find 'original jurors' means all the jurors empaneled, both regular members and alternates."

McDaniel v. Yarbrough, 898 S.W.2d 251, 253 (Tex. 1995). "No evidence of record suggests that [the juror] became 'disabled from sitting' within the [meaning of the constitution]. She was not mentally incompetent or sick, nor did she have some other physical or mental incapacity. On the contrary, she was temporarily detained by flooding caused by heavy rain, which is at most a transient physical barrier. Her dismissal from the jury as 'disabled' was improper. [¶] Depriving the [Ps] of a full jury of 12 members, absent an exception authorized by the constitution or applicable rules, is a denial of the right to jury trial guaranteed by the Texas Constitution."

Fiore v. Fiore, 946 S.W.2d 436, 438 (Tex.App.—Fort Worth 1997, writ denied). "[W]hen a trial court dismisses a juror who is not 'disabled,' and there is no agreement to proceed with 11 jurors, it is an abuse of discretion to deny a motion for mistrial."

TRCP 293. WHEN THE JURY AGREE

When the jury agree upon a verdict, they shall be brought into court by the proper officer, and they shall deliver their verdict to the clerk; and if they state that they have agreed, the verdict shall be read aloud by the clerk. If the verdict is in proper form, no juror objects to its accuracy, no juror represented as agreeing thereto dissents therefrom, and neither party requests a poll of the jury, the verdict shall be entered upon the minutes of the court.

Thomas v. Oil & Gas Bldg., Inc., 582 S.W.2d 873, 880 (Tex.App.—Corpus Christi 1979, writ ref'd n.r.e.). TRCP 293, "in essence, provides that when a verdict is accurate and in proper form, that it 'shall be entered upon the minutes of the court.'"

TRCP 294. POLLING THE JURY

Any party shall have the right to have the jury polled. A jury is polled by reading once to the jury collectively the general verdict, or the questions and answers thereto consecutively, and then calling the name of each juror separately and asking the juror if it is the juror's verdict. If any juror answers in the negative when the verdict is returned signed only by the presiding juror as a unanimous verdict, or if any juror shown by the juror's signature to agree to the verdict should answer in the negative, the jury shall be retired for further deliberation.

See also *O'Connor's Texas Rules*, "Request to Poll the Jury," ch. 8-K, §4.

Pate v. Texline Feed Mills, Inc., 689 S.W.2d 238, 243 (Tex.App.—Amarillo 1985, writ ref'd n.r.e.). "Once the request is promptly made before the jury is discharged, the trial court has no discretion but to poll the jury, and the requesting party's motive is immaterial."

TRCP 295. CORRECTION OF VERDICT

If the purported verdict is defective, the court may direct it to be reformed. If it is incomplete, or not responsive to the questions contained in the court's charge, or the answers to the questions are in conflict, the court shall in writing instruct the jury in open court of the nature of the incompleteness, unresponsiveness, or conflict, provide the jury such additional instructions as may be proper, and retire the jury for further deliberations.

Elbar, Inc. v. Claussen, 774 S.W.2d 45, 55 (Tex. App.—Dallas 1989, no writ). "[B]ecause the charge was defective, the trial court was ... authorized to give the jury such additional instructions as it thought proper."

G. FINDINGS BY COURT

TRCP 296. REQUESTS FOR FINDINGS OF FACTS & CONCLUSIONS OF LAW

In any case tried in the district or county court without a jury, any party may request the court to state in writing its findings of fact and conclusions of law. Such request shall be entitled "Request for Findings of Fact and Conclusions of Law" and shall be filed within twenty days after judgment is signed with the clerk of the court, who shall immediately call such request to the attention of the judge who tried the case. The party making the request shall serve it on all other parties in accordance with Rule 21a.

Caution: TRCP 296 is affected by the following sections in the Fam. Code: §§6.711, 154.130.

See also *O'Connor's Texas Rules*, "Request for Findings of Fact," ch. 10-E; *O'Connor's Texas Forms*, FORMS 10E.

Tenery v. Tenery, 932 S.W.2d 29, 30 (Tex.1996). Under TRCP 296, "harm to the complaining party is presumed unless the contrary appears on the face of the record when the party makes a proper and timely request for findings and the trial court fails to comply.

Error is harmful if it prevents an appellant from properly presenting a case to the appellate court."

Black v. Dallas Cty. Child Welfare Unit, 835 S.W.2d 626, 630 n.10 (Tex.1992). "If no findings of fact or conclusions of law are filed, the reviewing court must imply all necessary fact findings in support of the trial court's judgment."

Cherne Indus., Inc. v. Magallanes, 763 S.W.2d 768, 772 (Tex.1989). "[T]he trial court's duty to file findings and conclusions is mandatory, [and] the failure to respond when all requests have been properly made is presumed harmful, unless 'the record before appellate court affirmatively shows that the complaining party has suffered no injury.'" *See also* ***Harco Energy, Inc. v. Re-Entry People, Inc.***, 23 S.W.3d 389, 392 (Tex.App.—Amarillo 2000, no pet.).

Rutledge v. Staner, 9 S.W.3d 469, 470 (Tex.App.—Tyler 1999, pet. denied). "It is well-settled that an appellate court cannot construe comments the trial judge may have made at the conclusion of the bench trial as findings of fact and conclusions of law."

Roberts v. Roberts, 999 S.W.2d 424, 433 (Tex. App.—El Paso 1999, no pet.). "Findings of fact and conclusions of law as a general rule are not available after a jury trial. [TRCP] 296 provides that findings and conclusions are available in any case tried in the district or county court without a jury. ... Given the assumption that findings and conclusions are appropriate in a bench trial but not in a jury trial, what happens when the two are combined? Perhaps the suit involves domestic torts and the jury will determine the personal injury or fraud issues while the judge will decide the ultimate division of property. Also, it is not unusual for the court to permit separate trials on the issues of property and custody, with a jury deciding issues of conservatorship and the judge deciding issues of characterization, valuation, and division of property. If one party chooses to appeal from the property division, is s/he entitled to findings and conclusions? If the jury and nonjury portions of the case are conducted via separate trials, findings and conclusions are available in the nonjury trial. When the judgment of the court differs substantially from or exceeds the scope of the jury verdict, findings are also available. ... If at least one of the issues tried in the court below was tried to the jury, the entire trial was to a jury within the meaning of the rules." *See also* ***Limbaugh v. Limbaugh***, 71 S.W.3d 1, 6 (Tex.App.—Houston [1st Dist.] 2002, n.p.h.).

Kenedy Mem. Found. v. Dewhurst, 994 S.W.2d 285, 308 (Tex.App.—Austin 1999), *aff'd*, ___ S.W.3d ___ (Tex.2000) (No. 99-0667; 12-21-00). "Findings of fact set out in a trial-court memorandum are not findings of fact as contemplated by [TRCPs] 296-299. ... We do not review an opinion written by a trial court and it has no persuasive value for an appellate court."

TRCP 297. TIME TO FILE FINDINGS OF FACT & CONCLUSIONS OF LAW

The court shall file its findings of fact and conclusions of law within twenty days after a timely request is filed. The court shall cause a copy of its findings and conclusions to be mailed to each party in the suit.

If the court fails to file timely findings of fact and conclusions of law, the party making the request shall, within thirty days after filing the original request, file with the clerk and serve on all other parties in accordance with Rule 21a a "Notice of Past Due Findings of Fact and Conclusions of Law" which shall be immediately called to the attention of the court by the clerk. Such notice shall state the date the original request was filed and the date the findings and conclusions were due. Upon filing this notice, the time for the court to file findings of fact and conclusions of law is extended to forty days from the date the original request was filed.

See also *O'Connor's Texas Rules*, "Request for Findings of Fact," ch. 10-E.

Curtis v. Commission for Lawyer Discipline, 20 S.W.3d 227, 232 (Tex.App.—Houston [14th Dist.] 2000, no pet.). "The failure to file a notice of past due findings of fact waives the right to complain about the trial court's failure to file findings of fact and conclusions of law." *See also* ***Salinas v. Beaudrie***, 960 S.W.2d 314, 317 (Tex.App.—Corpus Christi 1997, no pet.).

Vargas v. Texas Dept. of Protective & Reg. Servs., 973 S.W.2d 423, 425 (Tex.App.—Austin 1998, pet. granted w.r.m.). "If findings of fact and conclusions of law are properly requested, the trial court has a mandatory duty to file [them]. The trial court's failure to comply with a proper request to prepare and file findings and conclusions is presumed harmful, unless the record affirmatively shows that the complaining party suffered no injury."

TRCP 298. ADDITIONAL OR AMENDED FINDINGS OF FACT & CONCLUSIONS OF LAW

After the court files original findings of fact and conclusions of law, any party may file with the clerk of the court a request for specified additional or amended findings or conclusions. The request for these findings shall be made within ten days after the filing of the original findings and conclusions by the court. Each request made pursuant to this rule shall be served on each party to the suit in accordance with Rule 21a.

The court shall file any additional or amended findings and conclusions that are appropriate within ten days after such request is filed, and cause a copy to be mailed to each party to the suit. No findings or conclusions shall be deemed or presumed by any failure of the court to make any additional findings or conclusions.

See also *O'Connor's Texas Rules*, "Request for Findings of Fact," ch. 10-E; *O'Connor's Texas Forms*, FORMS 10E.

In re R.D.Y., 51 S.W.3d 314, 322 (Tex.App.—Houston [1st Dist.] 2001, pet. denied). "Additional findings are not required if the original findings of fact and conclusions of law 'properly and succinctly relate the ultimate findings of fact and law necessary to apprise [the party] of adequate information for the preparation of his or her appeal.' ... [D] must show the trial court's refusal to file the requested additional findings caused the rendition of an improper judgment. If the refusal to file additional findings does not prevent [D] from adequately presenting her argument on appeal, there is no reversible error."

Johnston v. McKinney Am., Inc., 9 S.W.3d 271, 277 (Tex.App.—Houston [14th Dist.] 1999, pet. denied). "The court shall file any additional findings and conclusions *that are appropriate* within ten days after a request is filed. ... Where refusal [to make additional findings] does not prevent the adequate presentation of the matter being complained of on appeal, no reversible error has occurred."

Vickery v. Commission for Lawyer Discipline, 5 S.W.3d 241, 254 (Tex.App.—Houston [14th Dist.] 1999, pet. denied). "[B]efore the failure to grant additional findings will impede an appellate court from presuming implied findings, the omission must be made manifest to the trial court. ... If the trial court is not specifically made aware of the missing element, the omission is presumed to be inadvertent."

TRCP 299. OMITTED FINDINGS

When findings of fact are filed by the trial court they shall form the basis of the judgment upon all grounds of recovery and of defense embraced therein. The judgment may not be supported upon appeal by a presumed finding upon any ground of recovery or defense, no element of which has been included in the findings of fact; but when one or more elements thereof have been found by the trial court, omitted unrequested elements, when supported by evidence, will be supplied by presumption in support of the judgment. Refusal of the court to make a finding requested shall be reviewable on appeal.

See also *O'Connor's Texas Rules*, "Request for Findings of Fact," ch. 10-E.

Black v. Dallas Cty. Child Welfare Unit, 835 S.W.2d 626, 630 n.10 (Tex.1992). "[A]n omitted finding, supported by the evidence, may be supplied by a presumption that it supports the judgment."

Vickery v. Commission for Lawyer Discipline, 5 S.W.3d 241, 252 (Tex.App.—Houston [14th Dist.] 1999, pet. denied). "When a court makes findings of fact, but inadvertently omits an essential element of a ground of recovery or defense, the presumption of validity will supply the omitted element by implication. However, if the record demonstrates the trial judge deliberately omitted the element, the presumption is refuted and the element cannot logically be supplied by implication."

Boy Scouts v. Responsive Terminal Sys., Inc., 790 S.W.2d 738, 742 (Tex.App.—Dallas 1990, writ denied). "[T]he provisions of [TRCP 299] which allow omitted findings to be deemed to support the judgment of the trial court ... only apply to omitted *unrequested* elements. [¶] If a party makes a request for additional or amended findings of fact ... and the trial court fails to make such findings, its failure is tantamount to a refusal."

TRCP 299a. FINDINGS OF FACT TO BE SEPARATELY FILED & NOT RECITED IN A JUDGMENT

Findings of fact shall not be recited in a judgment. If there is a conflict between findings of fact recited in a judgment in violation of this rule and findings of fact made pursuant to Rules 297 and 298, the latter findings will control for appellate purposes. Findings of fact shall be filed with the clerk of the court as a document or documents separate and apart from the judgment.

See also *O'Connor's Texas Rules*, "The Judgment," ch. 9-C; "Request for Findings of Fact," ch. 10-E.

Pena v. Garza, 61 S.W.3d 529, 531-32 (Tex.App.—San Antonio 2001, no pet.). Boyfriend "contends the trial court erred by not responding to his timely motions for written findings of fact and conclusions of law, and that he was harmed by the omission. The State argues there is an inherent conflict between [TRCP] 299a and Family Code §85.001. Rule 299a states that findings of fact should not be recited in a judgment but should be filed as a separate document. In contrast, §85.001 directs the court to find whether family violence has occurred and is likely to occur in the future, and to include these findings in the protective order. The rules of procedure are general rules; statutes are specific. Thus, when the two conflict, the statute trumps the rule. In its protective order, the trial court found that [boyfriend] committed family violence, that such violence was likely to occur in the future, and that a protective order was in the best interest of the household. The recitation of these findings complied with §85.001, thus the trial court did not err in refusing to file additional findings of fact and conclusions of law."

Tate v. Tate, 55 S.W.3d 1, 9 (Tex.App.—El Paso 2000, no pet.). TRCP 299a "provides that findings of fact are to be separately filed and not recited in the judgment. If there is a conflict between findings of fact recited in a judgment in violation of this rule and findings of fact made pursuant to [TRCPs] 297 and 298, the latter findings will control for appellate purposes."

Sutherland v. Cobern, 843 S.W.2d 127, 131 n.7 (Tex.App.—Texarkana 1992, writ denied). "Findings of fact contained in the body of a judgment may not be considered on appeal. Therefore, for our purposes, we review this case as one in which no findings of fact were made."

H. JUDGMENTS

TRCP 300. COURT TO RENDER JUDGMENT

Where a special verdict is rendered, or the conclusions of fact found by the judge are separately stated the court shall render judgment thereon unless set aside or a new trial is granted, or judgment is rendered notwithstanding verdict or jury finding under these rules.

Astec Indus., Inc. v. Suarez, 921 S.W.2d 794, 798 (Tex.App.—Fort Worth 1996, no writ). "In order for a judge's ministerial duty to render judgment under [TRCP] 300 to arise, the jury must first return a sufficient verdict for the judge to receive."

TRCP 301. JUDGMENTS

The judgment of the court shall conform to the pleadings, the nature of the case proved and the verdict, if any, and shall be so framed as to give the party all the relief to which he may be entitled either in law or equity. Provided, that upon motion and reasonable notice the court may render judgment non obstante veredicto if a directed verdict would have been proper, and provided further that the court may, upon like motion and notice, disregard any jury finding on a question that has no support in the evidence. Only one final judgment shall be rendered in any cause except where it is otherwise specially provided by law. Judgment may, in a proper case, be given for or against one or more of several plaintiffs, and for or against one or more of several defendants or intervenors.

Caution: TRCP 301 is affected by the following section in the Fam. Code: §105.002.

See also *O'Connor's Texas Rules*, "Motion for JNOV," ch. 9-B; "The Judgment," ch. 9-C; *O'Connor's Texas Forms*, FORMS 9B, 9C.

Holland v. Wal-Mart Stores, Inc., 1 S.W.3d 91, 95 (Tex.1999). Defendant "specifically challenged the availability of attorney's fees [in a motion for JNOV] before the error resulted. The court of appeals, therefore, erred in concluding that [D] waived its right to challenge the propriety of an award of attorney's fees…."

Wal-Mart Stores, Inc. v. McKenzie, 997 S.W.2d 278, 280 (Tex.1999). "Whether a particular remedy is available under a statute is a question of law for the court. Accordingly, the jury's findings are immaterial to the ultimate issue of whether compensatory and punitive damages are available under [the statute]. [D]'s response to [P]'s motion for judgment on the verdict was timely and sufficiently specific to give the trial court an opportunity to resolve the legal issue before rendering judgment."

Brown v. Bank of Galveston, 963 S.W.2d 511, 513 (Tex.1998). "A trial court may grant a judgment notwithstanding the verdict if there is no evidence to support one or more of the jury findings on issues necessary to liability. In determining whether [to] uphold the [JNOV], we consider the evidence in the light most favorable to the verdict and reasonable inferences that tend to support it."

In re Marriage of Moore, 890 S.W.2d 821, 838 n.10 (Tex.App.—Amarillo 1994, no writ). "A motion to disregard the jury's findings, with notice, is usually required to enable a court to disregard a finding and to preserve alleged error if the court fails to do so. However, in a marital relations case, such a motion is only necessary when the trial court is attempting to disregard a jury's finding as to the value of certain community property or the character or status of property possessed by the parties. This is true because the jury's findings as to the characterization and valuation of property are binding upon the trial court."

Stewart v. USA Custom Paint & Body Shop, Inc., 870 S.W.2d 18, 20 (Tex.1994). "A judgment must be sufficiently definite and certain to define and protect the rights of all litigants, or it should provide a definite means of ascertaining such rights, to the end that ministerial officers can carry the judgment into execution without ascertainment of facts not therein stated."

Fort Bend Cty. Drainage Dist. v. Sbrusch, 818 S.W.2d 392, 394 (Tex.1991). "A court may render judgment n.o.v. if a directed verdict would have been proper."

TRCP 302. ON COUNTERCLAIM

If the defendant establishes a demand against the plaintiff upon a counterclaim exceeding that established against him by the plaintiff, the court shall render judgment for defendant for such excess.

Building Concepts, Inc. v. Duncan, 667 S.W.2d 897, 904 (Tex.App.—Houston [14th Dist.] 1984, writ ref'd n.r.e.). "[A]s a matter of law the court was required to offset the amount of damages established by the [Ps] against the amount of [the D's] counterclaim, and to render judgment in favor of [the D] for the excess."

TRCP 303. ON COUNTERCLAIM FOR COSTS

When a counterclaim is pleaded, the party in whose favor final judgment is rendered shall also recover the costs, unless it be made to appear on the trial that the counterclaim of the defendant was acquired after the commencement of the suit, in which case, if the plaintiff establishes a claim existing at the commencement of the suit, he shall recover his costs.

See also TRCP 141.

Building Concepts, Inc. v. Duncan, 667 S.W.2d 897, 906 (Tex.App.—Houston [14th Dist.] 1984, writ ref'd n.r.e.). Relying on TRCP 303 and 141: "It is apparent from the record that the judge assessed costs as he did because *both* parties successfully prosecuted their claims."

TRCP 304. JUDGMENT UPON RECORD

Judgments rendered upon questions raised upon citations, pleadings, and all other proceedings, constituting the record proper as known at common law, must be entered at the date of each term when pronounced.

TRCP 305. PROPOSED JUDGMENT

Any party may prepare and submit a proposed judgment to the court for signature.

Each party who submits a proposed judgment for signature shall serve the proposed judgment on all other parties to the suit who have appeared and remain in the case, in accordance with Rule 21a.

Failure to comply with this rule shall not affect the time for perfecting an appeal.

See also *O'Connor's Texas Rules*, "The Judgment," ch. 9-C.

First Nat'l Bank v. Fojtik, 775 S.W.2d 632, 633 (Tex.1989). A party's motion requesting the trial court to enter judgment does not waive its right to complain about that judgment. "There must be a method by which a party who desires to initiate the appellate process may move the trial court to render judgment without being bound by its terms."

Dikeman v. Snell, 490 S.W.2d 183, 185-86 (Tex. 1973). Even though prepared by a party, a mistake in a rendered judgment is a judicial error.

TRCP 306. RECITATION OF JUDGMENT

The entry of the judgment shall contain the full names of the parties, as stated in the pleadings, for and against whom the judgment is rendered.

See also *O'Connor's Texas Rules*, "The Judgment," ch. 9-C.

Crystal City ISD v. Wagner, 605 S.W.2d 743, 747 (Tex.App.—San Antonio 1980, writ ref'd n.r.e.). "Undoubtedly, the better practice is to recite the names of all the parties in the judgment, in accordance with

TRCP 306. Nevertheless, when ... the names of all the parties and the relief each is entitled to is easily ascertainable from the record, it would be a useless thing to remand the entire cause for the purpose of amending the judgment to include the names of all the parties."

TRCP 306a. PERIODS TO RUN FROM SIGNING OF JUDGMENT

1. Beginning of periods. The date of judgment or order is signed as shown of record shall determine the beginning of the periods prescribed by these rules for the court's plenary power to grant a new trial or to vacate, modify, correct or reform a judgment or order and for filing in the trial court the various documents that these rules authorize a party to file within such periods including, but not limited to, motions for new trial, motions to modify judgment, motions to reinstate a case dismissed for want of prosecution, motions to vacate judgment and requests for findings of fact and conclusions of law; but this rule shall not determine what constitutes rendition of a judgment or order for any other purpose.

2. Date to be shown. Judges, attorneys and clerks are directed to use their best efforts to cause all judgments, decisions and orders of any kind to be reduced to writing and signed by the trial judge with the date of signing stated therein. If the date of signing is not recited in the judgment or order, it may be shown in the record by a certificate of the judge or otherwise; provided, however, that the absence of a showing of the date in the record shall not invalidate any judgment or order.

3. Notice of judgment. When the final judgment or other appealable order is signed, the clerk of the court shall immediately give notice to the parties or their attorneys of record by first-class mail advising that the judgment or order was signed. Failure to comply with the provisions of this rule shall not affect the periods mentioned in paragraph (1) of this rule, except as provided in paragraph (4).

4. No notice of judgment. If within twenty days after the judgment or other appealable order is signed, a party adversely affected by it or his attorney has neither received the notice required by paragraph (3) of this rule nor acquired actual knowledge of the order, then with respect to that party all the periods mentioned in paragraph (1) shall begin on the date that such party or his attorney received such notice or acquired actual knowledge of the signing, whichever occurred first, but in no event shall such periods begin more than ninety days after the original judgment or other appealable order was signed.

5. Motion, notice and hearing. In order to establish the application of paragraph (4) of this rule, the party adversely affected is required to prove in the trial court, on sworn motion and notice, the date on which the party or his attorney first either received a notice of the judgment or acquired actual knowledge of the signing and that this date was more than twenty days after the judgment was signed.

6. Nunc pro tunc order. When a corrected judgment has been signed after expiration of the court's plenary power pursuant to Rule 316, the periods mentioned in paragraph (1) of this rule shall run from the date of signing the corrected judgment with respect to any complaint that would not be applicable to the original document.

7. When process served by publication. With respect to a motion for new trial filed more than thirty days after the judgment was signed pursuant to Rule 329 when process has been served by publication, the periods provided by paragraph (1) shall be computed as if the judgment were signed on the date of filing the motion.

See also *O'Connor's Texas Rules*, "Default Judgment," ch. 7-A; "The Judgment," ch. 9-C; "Motion for New Trial," ch. 10-B; "Motion to Reinstate after DWOP" ch. 10-F; "Motion to Extend Postjudgment Deadlines," ch. 10-G; "Motion for Judgment Nunc Pro Tunc," ch. 10-H.

Bastrop ISD v. Toungate, 958 S.W.2d 365, 367 (Tex.1997). "We note that the trial court should have submitted the modified judgment to the clerk immediately upon signing it to avoid the burden of a notification hearing."

Martinez v. Humble Sand & Gravel, Inc., 875 S.W.2d 311, 312 (Tex.1994). When "an otherwise final judgment fails to dispose of all parties, the court may make the judgment final for purposes of appeal by severing the causes and parties disposed of by the judgment into a different cause. *At 313:* When a severance order takes effect, the appellate timetable runs from the signing date of the order that made the judgment severed 'final' and appealable."

Burns v. Bishop, 48 S.W.3d 459, 465 (Tex.App.—Houston [14th] Dist. 2001, no pet.). "Signing and rendition are not synonymous. Signing an order is not among the official steps that would fall within the common meaning of 'proceedings.' Drafting and signing the judgment [are] preparatory, *administrative* acts that ... authenticate the record of the court's rendition.

Rendition occurs when the trial court officially announces its decision (1) in open court in a manner that objectively reflects its intention to render or (2) by written memorandum *filed with the clerk*."

Cannon v. ICO Tubular Servs., 905 S.W.2d 380, 388 (Tex.App.—Houston [1st Dist.] 1995, no writ). TRCP 306a "specifically require[s] the clerk of the court to send notice of the court's intent to dismiss a case for want of prosecution and order of dismissal to *each attorney of record*. *At 387:* Once the order of dismissal is signed, Rule 306a requires the clerk to give immediate notice to the parties or their attorneys by first-class mail advising them of the judgment."

No Notice of Judgment

John v. Marshall Health Servs., Inc., 58 S.W.3d 738, 741 (Tex.2001). Rule 306a(5) "does not prohibit a motion from being filed at any time within the trial court's plenary jurisdiction measured from the date determined under Rule 306a(4). [TRCP] 306a simply imposes no deadline, and none can be added by decision, other than the deadline of the expiration of the trial court's jurisdiction."

Estate of Howley v. Haberman, 878 S.W.2d 139, 140 (Tex.1994). "A party who does not have actual knowledge of an order of dismissal within 90 days of the date it is signed cannot move for reinstatement. ... Since [P] did not learn of the dismissal within this period, the order of dismissal for want of prosecution was final. [P's] only possible recourse is a bill of review." *See also* ***Levit v. Adams***, 850 S.W.2d 469, 470 (Tex.1993).

Grondona v. Sutton, 991 S.W.2d 90, 92 (Tex. App.—Austin 1998, pet. denied). "Grondona filed his motion 84 days after the date he claims to have learned of the default judgment. Neither [TRCP] 306a nor [TRAP] 4 states when a party must move for a determination of late notice. [¶] This Court ... has concluded that a party can file such a motion more than 30 days after receiving notice, as long as he files it within the court's plenary power counted from the date of notice."

TRCP 306b. REPEALED

TRCP 306c. PREMATURELY FILED DOCUMENTS

No motion for new trial or request for findings of fact and conclusions of law shall be held ineffective because prematurely filed; but every such motion shall be deemed to have been filed on the date of but subsequent to the time of signing of the judgment the motion assails, and every such request for findings of fact and conclusions of law shall be deemed to have been filed on the date of but subsequent to the time of signing of the judgment.

See also TRAP 27; *O'Connor's Texas Rules*, "Motion for New Trial," ch. 10-B.

Fredonia State Bank v. General Am. Life Ins. Co., 881 S.W.2d 279, 281 (Tex.1994). "[A] motion for new trial relating to an earlier judgment may be considered applicable to a second judgment when the substance of the motion could properly be raised with respect to the corrected judgment."

Harris Cty. Hosp. Dist. v. Estrada, 831 S.W.2d 876, 878 (Tex.App.—Houston [1st Dist.] 1992, order on mot.). The court found the defendant's "prematurely filed motion for new trial, which was also prematurely overruled, extended the appellate timetable for perfecting appeal to 90 days after the [second] judgment."

TRCP 306d. REPEALED

TRCP 307. EXCEPTIONS, ETC., TRANSCRIPT

In non-jury cases, where findings of fact and conclusions of law are requested and filed, and in jury cases, where a special verdict is returned, any party claiming that the findings of the court or the jury, as the case may be, do not support the judgment, may have noted in the record an exception to said judgment and thereupon take an appeal or writ of error, where such writ is allowed, without a statement of facts or further exceptions in the transcript, but the transcript in such cases shall contain the conclusions of law and fact or the special verdict and the judgment rendered thereon.

TRCP 308. COURT SHALL ENFORCE ITS DECREES

The court shall cause its judgments and decrees to be carried into execution; and where the judgment is for personal property, and it is shown by the pleadings and evidence and the verdict, if any, that such property has an especial value to the plaintiff, the court may award a special writ for the seizure and delivery of such property to the plaintiff; and in such case may enforce its judgment by attachment, fine and imprisonment.

Bridas Corp. v. Unocal Corp., 16 S.W.3d 887, 889 (Tex.App.—Houston [14th Dist.] 2000, pet. dism'd).

"The trial court is vested with the inherent judicial authority to enforce its orders and decrees. Additionally, it is vested with explicit statutory authority to enforce its judgments, including the issuance of an injunction."

TRCP 308a. IN SUITS AFFECTING THE PARENT-CHILD RELATIONSHIP

When the court has ordered child support or possession of or access to a child and it is claimed that the order has been violated, the person claiming that a violation has occurred shall make this known to the court. The court may appoint a member of the bar to investigate the claim to determine whether there is reason to believe that the court order has been violated. If the attorney in good faith believes that the order has been violated, the attorney shall take the necessary action as provided under Chapter 14, Family Code.[1] On a finding of a violation, the court may enforce its order as provided in Chapter 14, Family Code.[1]

Except by order of the court, no fee shall be charged by or paid to the attorney representing the claimant. If the court determines that an attorney's fee should be paid, the fee shall be adjudged against the party who violated the court's order. The fee may be assessed as costs of court, or awarded by judgment, or both.

[1] Now Chapter 157 of the Family Code

Ex parte Herring, 438 S.W.2d 801, 803 (Tex.1969). TRCP 308a "contemplates that service under any of the applicable portions of [TRCP] 21a including service upon the attorney would constitute a compliance with the rules. [¶] [I]t is a denial of due process to commit a person to prison for contempt who is not shown to be avoiding deliberately the service of process, and who has had *no* personal notice or knowledge of the show-cause hearing…." Relator discharged.

In re A.M., 974 S.W.2d 857, 865 (Tex.App.—San Antonio 1998, no pet.). TRCP "308a governs enforcement actions for [SAPCRs]. That rule states that, in an enforcement action, no fee shall be charged or paid to an attorney, except by order of the court. In the event that attorney's fees are ordered, the rule states, '[T]he fee shall be adjudged against the party who violated the court's order.' The Family Code states that, in enforcement proceedings on child support payments, the court 'shall' order respondent to pay the movant's reasonable attorney's fees, unless good cause is stated in the court's findings. [¶] Rule 308a speaks only to enforcement proceedings. We note that several courts have held that, in non-enforcement proceedings under the Family Code, the trial court need not state good cause for awarding fees to the non-prevailing party. We agree that, because in family law cases involving children, the best interests of the children are paramount, it may not always be appropriate to award costs and fees to the prevailing party."

TRCP 309. IN FORECLOSURE PROCEEDINGS

Judgments for the foreclosure of mortgages and other liens shall be that the plaintiff recover his debt, damages and costs, with a foreclosure of the plaintiff's lien on the property subject thereto, and, except in judgments against executors, administrators and guardians, that an order of sale shall issue to any sheriff or any constable within the State of Texas, directing him to seize and sell the same as under execution, in satisfaction of the judgment; and, if the property cannot be found, or if the proceeds of such sale be insufficient to satisfy the judgment, then to take the money or any balance thereof remaining unpaid, out of any other property of the defendant, as in case of ordinary executions.

TRCP 310. WRIT OF POSSESSION

When an order foreclosing a lien upon real estate is made in a suit having for its object the foreclosure of such lien, such order shall have all the force and effect of a writ of possession as between the parties to the foreclosure suit and any person claiming under the defendant to such suit by any right acquired pending such suit; and the court shall so direct in the judgment providing for the issuance of such order. The sheriff or other officer executing such order of sale shall proceed by virtue of such order of sale to place the purchaser of the property sold thereunder in possession thereof within thirty days after the day of sale.

TRCP 311. ON APPEAL FROM PROBATE COURT

Judgment on appeal or certiorari from any county court sitting in probate shall be certified to such county court for observance.

TRCP 312. ON APPEAL FROM JUSTICE COURT

Judgments on appeal or certiorari from a justice court shall be enforced by the county or district court rendering the judgment.

TRCP 313. AGAINST EXECUTORS, ETC.

A judgment for the recovery of money against an executor, administrator or guardian, as such, shall state that it is to be paid in the due course of administration. No execution shall issue thereon, but it shall be certified to the county court, sitting in matters of probate, to be there enforced in accordance with law, but judgment against an executor appointed and acting under a will dispensing with the action of the county court in reference to such estate shall be enforced against the property of the testator in the hands of such executor, by execution, as in other cases.

TRCP 314. CONFESSION OF JUDGMENT

Any person against whom a cause of action exists may, without process, appear in person or by attorney, and confess judgment therefor in open court as follows:

(a) A petition shall be filed and the justness of the debt or cause of action be sworn to by the person in whose favor the judgment is confessed.

(b) If the judgment is confessed by attorney, the power of attorney shall be filed and its contents be recited in the judgment.

(c) Every such judgment duly made shall operate as a release of all errors in the record thereof, but such judgment may be impeached for fraud or other equitable cause.

See also ***O'Connor's Texas Rules***, "Plaintiff's Original Petition," ch. 2-B; "The Answer—Denying Liability," ch. 3-E.

I. REMITTITUR & CORRECTION

TRCP 315. REMITTITUR

Any party in whose favor a judgment has been rendered may remit any part thereof in open court, or by executing and filing with the clerk a written remittitur signed by the party or the party's attorney of record, and duly acknowledged by the party or the party's attorney. Such remittitur shall be a part of the record of the cause. Execution shall issue for the balance only of such judgment.

See also ***O'Connor's Texas Rules***, "Motion for Remittitur," ch. 10-C; ***O'Connor's Texas Forms***, FORMS 10C.

Larson v. Cactus Util. Co., 730 S.W.2d 640, 641 (Tex.1987). "A court of appeals should uphold a trial court remittitur only when the evidence is factually insufficient to support the verdict. [¶] If a court of appeals holds that there is no evidence to support a damages verdict, it should render a take nothing judgment as to that amount. If part of a damage verdict lacks sufficient evidentiary support, the proper course is to suggest a remittitur of that part of the verdict."

TRCP 316. CORRECTION OF CLERICAL MISTAKES IN JUDGMENT RECORD

Clerical mistakes in the record of any judgment may be corrected by the judge in open court according to the truth or justice of the case after notice of the motion therefor has been given to the parties interested in such judgment, as provided in Rule 21a, and thereafter the execution shall conform to the judgment as amended.

See also ***O'Connor's Texas Rules***, "Motion for Judgment Nunc Pro Tunc," ch. 10-H.

Escobar v. Escobar, 711 S.W.2d 230, 231 (Tex. 1986). "After the trial court loses its jurisdiction over a judgment, it can correct only clerical errors in the judgment by judgment nunc pro tunc. In this regard, the trial court has plenary power to correct a clerical error made in *entering* final judgment. [¶] A judicial error is an error which occurs in the *rendering* as opposed to the *entering* of a judgment."

Andrews v. Koch, 702 S.W.2d 584, 585 (Tex.1986). "[A]fter a judgment has become final, the trial court may only correct clerical errors by nunc pro tunc judgment and may not correct judicial errors. The salient distinction between 'clerical' and 'judicial' errors lies in the exercise of the judgmental offices of the court. A clerical error is one which does not result from judicial reasoning or determination."

In re Bridges, 28 S.W.3d 191, 195 (Tex.App.—Fort Worth 2000, orig. proceeding). "A trial court can enter a judgment nunc pro tunc to correct a clerical error at any time, even after it has lost jurisdiction over the case. This court has previously determined that a trial court commits a clerical error when it grants a motion for nonsuit and dismisses a defendant the plaintiff did not move to nonsuit. Such an order is void to the extent it purports or attempts to dismiss the lawsuit against a defendant who was not nonsuited."

TRCP 317 - 319. REPEALED

J. NEW TRIALS

TRCP 320. MOTION & ACTION OF COURT THEREON

New trials may be granted and judgment set aside for good cause, on motion or on the court's own motion on such terms as the court shall direct. New trials may be granted when the damages are manifestly too small or too large. When it appears to the court that a new trial should be granted on a point or points that affect only a part of the matters in controversy and that such part is clearly separable without unfairness to the parties, the court may grant a new trial as to that part only, provided that a separate trial on unliquidated damages alone shall not be ordered if liability issues are contested. Each motion for new trial shall be in writing and signed by the party or his attorney.

See also *O'Connor's Texas Rules*, "Motion for New Trial," ch. 10-B; *O'Connor's Texas Forms*, FORMS 10B.

Old Republic Ins. Co. v. Scott, 846 S.W.2d 832, 833 (Tex.1993). "The *filing* of a motion for new trial in order to extend the appellate timetable is a matter of right, whether or not there is any sound or reasonable basis for the conclusion that a further motion is necessary."

State Dept. of Highways & Pub. Transp. v. Cotner, 845 S.W.2d 818, 819 (Tex.1993). "A partial new trial may be ordered notwithstanding the prohibition in [TRCP] 41 against post-submission severances. [TRCP] 320 is thus an exception to Rule 41."

TRCP 321. FORM

Each point relied upon in a motion for new trial or in arrest of judgment shall briefly refer to that part of the ruling of the court, charge given to the jury, or charge refused, admission or rejection of evidence, or other proceedings which are designated to be complained of, in such a way that the objection can be clearly identified and understood by the court.

See also *O'Connor's Texas Rules*, "Motion for New Trial," ch. 10-B; *O'Connor's Texas Forms*, FORMS 10B.

Marino v. Hartfield, 877 S.W.2d 508, 513 (Tex. App.—Beaumont 1994, writ denied). TRCP 321 "requires that the motion for new trial briefly refer to the ruling of the court, the charge, the evidence, or other proceedings complained of so that the objection can be identified and understood by the court."

TRCP 322. GENERALITY TO BE AVOIDED

Grounds of objections couched in general terms—as that the court erred in its charge, in sustaining or overruling exceptions to the pleadings, and in excluding or admitting evidence, the verdict of the jury is contrary to law, and the like—shall not be considered by the court.

See also *O'Connor's Texas Rules*, "Motion for New Trial," ch. 10-B.

D/FW Commercial Roofing Co. v. Mehra, 854 S.W.2d 182, 189 (Tex.App.—Dallas 1993, no writ). "The purpose of a motion for new trial is to provide an opportunity for the trial court to cure any errors by granting a new trial. Therefore, the allegations in a motion for new trial must be sufficiently specific to enable the trial court to clearly understand what is being alleged as error."

TRCP 323. REPEALED

TRCP 324. PREREQUISITES OF APPEAL

(a) Motion for New Trial Not Required. A point in a motion for new trial is not a prerequisite to a complaint on appeal in either a jury or a nonjury case, except as provided in subdivision (b).

(b) Motion for New Trial Required. A point in a motion for new trial is a prerequisite to the following complaints on appeal:

(1) A complaint on which evidence must be heard such as one of jury misconduct or newly discovered evidence or failure to set aside a judgment by default;

(2) A complaint of factual insufficiency of the evidence to support a jury finding;

(3) A complaint that a jury finding is against the overwhelming weight of the evidence;

(4) A complaint of inadequacy or excessiveness of the damages found by the jury; or

(5) Incurable jury argument if not otherwise ruled on by the trial court.

(c) Judgment Notwithstanding Findings; Cross-Points. When judgment is rendered non obstante veredicto or notwithstanding the findings of a jury on one or more questions, the appellee may bring forward by cross-point contained in his brief filed in the Court of Appeals any ground which would have vitiated the verdict or would have prevented an affirmance of the judgment had one been rendered by the trial court in harmony with the verdict, including although not limited to the ground that one or more of the jury's findings have insufficient support in the evidence or are against the overwhelming preponderance of the evidence as a matter of fact, and the ground that the verdict and judgment based thereon should be set aside because of improper argument of counsel.

The failure to bring forward by cross-points such grounds as would vitiate the verdict shall be deemed a waiver thereof; provided, however, that if a cross-point is upon a ground which requires the taking of evidence in addition to that adduced upon the trial of the cause, it is not necessary that the evidentiary hearing be held until after the appellate court determines that the cause be remanded to consider such a cross-point.

See also *O'Connor's Texas Rules*, "Motion in Limine," ch. 5-E; "Motion for JNOV," ch. 9-B; "Motion for New Trial," ch. 10-B.

State Farm Lloyds v. Nicolau, 951 S.W.2d 444, 452 (Tex.1997). Defendant was not entitled to a new trial based on newly discovered evidence because it "has not shown any likelihood that the new evidence, if introduced at trial, would have resulted in a different verdict on any of the [P's] claims."

Tate v. E.I. du Pont de Nemours & Co., 934 S.W.2d 83, 84 (Tex.1996). "[B]ecause the filing is not complete until the fee is paid, the trial court should not consider the motion [for new trial] before then, absent emergency or other rare circumstances. [T]he failure to pay the [filing] fee before the motion is overruled by operation of law may forfeit altogether the movant's opportunity to have the trial court consider the motion; it does not, however, retroactively invalidate the conditional filing for purposes of the appellate timetable."

Horrocks v. Dept. of Transp., 852 S.W.2d 498, 498-99 (Tex.1993). "The court of appeals erred in rendering judgment based on a no evidence point preserved solely in the State's motion for new trial. Ordinarily, an appellate court should render judgment after sustaining a complaint as to the legal sufficiency of the evidence. ... Here, the State ... failed to lay [the] predicate [for rendition]."

Cecil v. Smith, 804 S.W.2d 509, 510 (Tex.1991). "A point in a motion for new trial is a prerequisite to complain on appeal that the evidence is factually insufficient to support a jury finding and that a jury finding is against the overwhelming weight of the evidence."

Lee v. Braeburn Valley W. Civic Ass'n, 786 S.W.2d 262, 263 (Tex.1990). "[A] motion for new trial is not a prerequisite for an appeal of a summary judgment proceeding."

Jackson v. Van Winkle, 660 S.W.2d 807, 809 (Tex. 1983). "It is incumbent upon a party who seeks a new trial on the ground of newly discovered evidence to satisfy the court first, that the evidence has come to his knowledge since the trial; second, that it was not owing to the want of due diligence that it did not come sooner; third, that it is not cumulative; fourth, that it is so material that it would probably produce a different result if a new trial were granted."

TRCP 325. REPEALED

TRCP 326. NOT MORE THAN TWO

Not more than two new trials shall be granted either party in the same cause because of insufficiency or weight of the evidence.

TRCP 327. FOR JURY MISCONDUCT

a. When the ground of a motion for new trial, supported by affidavit, is misconduct of the jury or of the officer in charge of them, or because of any communication made to the jury, or that a juror gave an erroneous or incorrect answer on voir dire examination, the court shall hear evidence thereof from the jury or others in open court, and may grant a new trial if such misconduct proved, or the communication made, or the erroneous or incorrect answer on voir dire examination, be material, and if it reasonably appears from the evidence both on the hearing of the motion and the trial of the case and from the record as a whole that injury probably resulted to the complaining party.

b. A juror may not testify as to any matter or statement occurring during the course of the jury's deliberations or to the effect of anything upon his or any other juror's mind or emotions as influencing him to assent to or dissent from the verdict concerning his mental processes in connection therewith, except that a juror may testify whether any outside influence was improperly brought to bear upon any juror. Nor may his affidavit or evidence of any statement by him concerning a matter about which he would be precluded from testifying be received for these purposes.

See also TRE 606(b); *O'Connor's Texas Rules*, "Rules of Pleading," ch. 1-B; "Jury Selection," ch. 8-A; "Motion for New Trial," ch. 10-B; *O'Connor's Texas Forms*, FORMS 10B.

Golden Eagle Archery, Inc. v. Jackson, 24 S.W.3d 362, 370 (Tex.2000). "A juror may testify about jury misconduct provided it does not require delving into deliberations. [¶] [TRCP 327(b) and TRE 606(b)] contemplate that an 'outside influence' originates from sources other than the jurors themselves. *At 371:* [An] alleged conversation between [jurors] during a trial break ... should not be considered 'deliberations' and therefore barred by [TRE] 606(b) and [TRCP] 327(b). [TRCPs] use the term 'deliberations' as meaning formal jury deliberations – when the jury weighs the evidence to arrive at a verdict. [¶] Clearly, [TRCP 327(b)] refers to formal deliberations and not incidental discussions that might occur between jurors during trial."

Pharo v. Chambers Cty., 922 S.W.2d 945, 950 (Tex. 1996). "[T]he bailiff's ... misconduct ... justifies a new trial only if it reasonably appears from the record that injury probably resulted to the complaining party. To show probable injury, there must be some indication in the record that the alleged misconduct most likely caused a juror to vote differently than he would otherwise have done on one or more issues vital to the judgment. Determining the existence of probable injury is a question of law." (Internal quotations omitted.)

Crowson v. Kansas City S. Ry., 11 S.W.3d 300, 305 (Tex.App.—Eastland 1999, no pet.). We "hold that the use of the discount formula by the jury in this case did not constitute an outside influence and that, therefore, there was no evidence of jury misconduct that could be considered by the trial court."

Kiefer v. Continental Airlines, Inc., 10 S.W.3d 34, 40 (Tex.App.—Houston [14th Dist.] 1999, pet. denied). "To establish jury misconduct on grounds that the venire person concealed information during voir dire, a party must obtain proof of concealment from a source other than jury deliberations."

Doucet v. Owens-Corning Fiberglas Corp., 966 S.W.2d 161, 163 (Tex.App.—Beaumont 1998, pet. denied). "To obtain a new trial on the ground of jury misconduct, the complaining party must show (1) that the misconduct occurred; (2) that it was material; and (3) that, based on the record as a whole, the misconduct resulted in harm to them."

TRCP 328. REPEALED

TRCP 329. MOTION FOR NEW TRIAL ON JUDGMENT FOLLOWING CITATION BY PUBLICATION

In cases in which judgment has been rendered on service of process by publication, when the defendant has not appeared in person or by attorney of his own selection:

(a) The court may grant a new trial upon petition of the defendant showing good cause, supported by affidavit, filed within two years after such judgment was signed. The parties adversely interested in such judgment shall be cited as in other cases.

(b) Execution of such judgment shall not be suspended unless the party applying therefor shall give a good and sufficient bond payable to the plaintiff in the judgment, in an amount fixed in accordance with Appellate Rule 47 relating to supersedeas bonds, to be approved by the clerk, and conditioned that the party will prosecute his petition for new trial to effect and will perform such judgment as may be rendered by the court should its decision be against him.

(c) If property has been sold under the judgment and execution before the process was suspended, the defendant shall not recover the property so sold, but shall have judgment against the plaintiff in the judgment for the proceeds of such sale.

(d) If the motion is filed more than thirty days after the judgment was signed, the time period shall be computed pursuant to Rule 306a(7).

See also *O'Connor's Texas Rules*, "Motion for New Trial," ch. 10-B.

Stock v. Stock, 702 S.W.2d 713, 714 (Tex.App.—San Antonio 1985, no writ). "Because [D] was cited by publication for the modification hearing, he had 2 years in which to file the motion for new trial."

TRCP 329a. COUNTY COURT CASES

If a case or other matter is on trial or in the process of hearing when the term of the county court expires, such trial, hearing or other matter may be proceeded with at the next or any subsequent term of court and no motion or plea shall be considered as waived or overruled, because not acted upon at the term of court at which it was filed, but may be acted upon at any time the judge may fix or at which it may have been postponed or continued by agreement of the parties with leave of the court. This subdivision is not applicable to original or amended motions for new trial which are governed by Rule 329b.

TRCP 329b. TIME FOR FILING MOTIONS

The following rules shall be applicable to motions for new trial and motions to modify, correct, or reform judgments (other than motions to correct the record under Rule 316) in all district and county courts:

(a) A motion for new trial, if filed, shall be filed prior to or within thirty days after the judgment or other order complained of is signed.

(b) One or more amended motions for new trial may be filed without leave of court before any preceding motion for new trial filed by the movant is overruled and within thirty days after the judgment or other order complained of is signed.

(c) In the event an original or amended motion for new trial or a motion to modify, correct or reform a judgment is not determined by written order signed within seventy-five days after the judgment was signed, it shall be considered overruled by operation of law on expiration of that period.

(d) The trial court, regardless of whether an appeal has been perfected, has plenary power to grant a new trial or to vacate, modify, correct, or reform the judgment within thirty days after the judgment is signed.

(e) If a motion for new trial is timely filed by any party, the trial court, regardless of whether an appeal has been perfected, has plenary power to grant a new trial or to vacate, modify, correct, or reform the judgment until thirty days after all such timely-filed motions are overruled, either by a written and signed order or by operation of law, whichever occurs first.

(f) On expiration of the time within which the trial court has plenary power, a judgment cannot be set aside by the trial court except by bill of review for sufficient cause, filed within the time allowed by law; provided that the court may at any time correct a clerical error in the record of a judgment and render judgment nunc pro tunc under Rule 316, and may also sign an order declaring a previous judgment or order to be void because signed after the court's plenary power had expired.

(g) A motion to modify, correct, or reform a judgment (as distinguished from motion to correct the record of a judgment under Rule 316), if filed, shall be filed and determined within the time prescribed by this rule for a motion for new trial and shall extend the trial court's plenary power and the time for perfecting an appeal in the same manner as a motion for new trial. Each such motion shall be in writing and signed by the party or his attorney and shall specify the respects in which the judgment should be modified, corrected, or reformed. The overruling of such a motion shall not preclude the filing of a motion for new trial, nor shall the overruling of a motion for new trial preclude the filing of a motion to modify, correct, or reform.

(h) If a judgment is modified, corrected or reformed in any respect, the time for appeal shall run from the time the modified, corrected, or reformed judgment is signed, but if a correction is made pursuant to Rule 316 after expiration of the period of plenary power provided by this rule, no complaint shall be heard on appeal that could have been presented in an appeal from the original judgment.

See also *O'Connor's Texas Rules*, "Rules for Filing Documents," ch. 1-C; "Motion for JNOV," ch. 9-B; "The Judgment," ch. 9-C; "Motion for New Trial," ch. 10-B; "Motion to Modify the Judgment," ch. 10-D; "Request for Findings of Fact," ch. 10-E; "Motion for Judgment Nunc Pro Tunc," ch. 10-H.

Plenary Power

Lane Bank Equip. Co. v. Smith S. Equip., Inc., 10 S.W.3d 308, 312 (Tex.2000). A "motion made after judgment to incorporate a sanction as a part of the final judgment does propose a change to that judgment. Such a motion is, on its face, a motion to modify, correct or reform the existing judgment within the meaning of [TRCP] 329b(g). *At 314:* We ... hold that [such a motion] qualifies as a motion to modify under Rule 329b(g), thus extending the trial court's plenary jurisdiction and the appellate timetable."

Bastrop ISD v. Toungate, 958 S.W.2d 365, 367 (Tex.1997). Plaintiff "filed a timely motion to modify or reform the judgment, and the trial court signed the modified judgment in favor of [P] well within its plenary power. Upon signing the modified judgment, the trial court then had plenary power to set aside or to further modify or reform that judgment within 30 days, absent another motion extending the time periods."

Scott & White Mem. Hosp. v. Schexnider, 940 S.W.2d 594, 596 (Tex.1996). "A trial court's power to decide a motion for sanctions pertaining to matters occurring before judgment is no different than its power to decide any other motion during its plenary jurisdiction. [T]he time during which the trial court has authority to impose sanctions on such a motion is limited to when it retains plenary jurisdiction."

L.M. Healthcare, Inc. v. Childs, 929 S.W.2d 442, 443 (Tex.1996). "That the trial court overruled [P's] motion for new trial does not shorten the trial court' plenary power to resolve a motion to modify the judgment. *At 444:* [TRCP 329b(g) & (e)] provide that a timely filed motion to modify judgment extends the trial court's plenary power, separate and apart from a motion for new trial."

In re T.G., 68 S.W.3d 171, 176 (Tex.App.—Houston [1st Dist.] 2002, n.p.h.). "Parties may extend the trial court's initial 30-day plenary power to change its judgment by filing an appropriate post-judgment motion within the 30 day period. Appropriate motions include a motion for new trial, pursuant to [TRCP] 329b(e) …, which the [Ds] filed, or a motion to modify, correct, or reform the judgment under rule 329b(g). Although any change in the trial court's judgment will restart the appellate-timetable and plenary-power rules under rule 329b(h), a rule 329b motion for new trial or to modify, correct, or reform the judgment, or a motion that has the same effect, is the only means by which a party may extend the appellate timetables and the trial court's plenary power over its judgment. Amending a rule 329b motion does not extend the trial court's plenary power."

Appellate Deadlines

Thomas v. Oldham, 895 S.W.2d 352, 356 (Tex. 1995). "Under Texas procedure, a plaintiff's suit does not end with rendition of judgment. Rather, the parties may file one or more motions for new trial within 30 days after rendition of judgment. The trial court may in its discretion grant such a motion within 75 days after the judgment is signed, continuing the action for a new trial. … If a motion for new trial or motion to modify the judgment is overruled, the trial court still retains plenary power to vacate, modify, correct or reform the judgment for an additional 30 day period."

In re Boyd, 34 S.W.3d 708, 710 (Tex.App.—Fort Worth 2000, orig. proceeding). Relator contends that Family Code §6.709 provides "the exclusive authority for the trial court to render the [temporary] order, and that the order is void because, under §6.709, the trial court lost jurisdiction to render the order 30 days after he perfected his appeal. [Real party in interest] responds that the trial court had plenary power to render the order under TRCP 329b, and that the trial court did not abuse its discretion by rendering the order, even though it was rendered more than 30 days after [relator] perfected his appeal. *At 711:* The trial court's power to render the [temporary] order derived exclusively from §6.709, which requires that all such orders be entered within 30 days of the perfection of a party's appeal. Because the order was entered more than 30 days from the date [relator] perfected his appeal, the trial court's power to act under the statute had terminated."

Written Order

Fruehauf Corp. v. Carrillo, 848 S.W.2d 83, 84 (Tex. 1993). "A trial court has plenary power over its judgment until it becomes final. The trial court also retains continuing control over interlocutory orders and has the power to set those orders aside any time before final judgment is entered."

K. CERTAIN DISTRICT COURTS

TRCP 330. RULES OF PRACTICE & PROCEDURE IN CERTAIN DISTRICT COURTS

The following rules of practice and procedure shall govern and be followed in all civil actions in district courts in counties where the only district court of said county vested with civil jurisdiction, or all the district courts thereof having civil jurisdiction, have successive terms in said county throughout the year, without more than two days intervening between any of such terms, whether or not any one or more of such district courts include one or more other counties within its jurisdiction.

(a) Appealed Cases. In cases appealed to said district courts from inferior courts, the appeal, including transcript, shall be filed in the district court within thirty (30) days after the rendition of the judgment or order appealed from, and the appellee shall enter his appearance on the docket or answer to said appeal on or before ten o'clock a.m. of the Monday next after the expiration of twenty (20) days from the date the appeal is filed in the district court.

(b) Repealed by order of July 22, 1975, eff. Jan. 1, 1976 (525-526 S.W.2d (Tex.Cases) li).

(c) Postponement or Continuance. Cases may be postponed or continued by agreement with the approval of the court, or upon the court's own motion or for cause. When a case is called for trial and only one party is ready, the court may for good cause either continue the case for the term or postpone and reset it for a later day in the same or succeeding term.

(d) Cases May Be Reset. A case that is set and reached for trial may be postponed for a later day in the term or continued and reset for a day certain in the succeeding term on the same grounds as an application for continuance would be granted in other district courts.

After any case has been set and reached in its due order and called for trial two (2) or more times and not tried, the court may dismiss the same unless the parties agree to a postponement or continuance but the court shall respect written agreements of counsel for postponement and continuance if filed in the case when or before it is called for trial unless to do so will unreasonably delay or interfere with other business of the court.

(e) Exchange and Transfer. Where in such county there are two or more district courts having civil jurisdiction, the judges of such courts may, in their discretion, exchange benches or districts from time to time, and may transfer cases and other proceedings from one court to another, and any of them may in his own courtroom try and determine any case or proceeding pending in another court without having the case transferred, or may sit in any other of said courts and there hear and determine any case there pending, and every judgment and order shall be entered in the minutes of the court in which the case is pending and at the time the judgment or order is rendered, and two (2) or more judges may try different cases in the same court at the same time, and each may occupy his own courtroom or the room of any other court. The judge of any such court may issue restraining orders and injunctions returnable to any other judge or court, and any judge may transfer any case or proceeding pending in his court to any other of said courts, and the judge of any court to which a case or proceeding is transferred shall receive and try the same, and in turn shall have power in his discretion to transfer any such case to any other of said courts and any other judge may in his courtroom try any case pending in any other of such courts.

(f) Cases Transferred to Judges Not Occupied. Where in such counties there are two or more district courts having civil jurisdiction, when the judge of any such court shall become disengaged, he shall notify the presiding judge, and the presiding judge shall transfer to the court of the disengaged judge the next case which is ready for trial in any of said courts. Any judge not engaged in his own court may try any case in any other court.

(g) Judge May Hear Only Part of Case. Where in such counties there are two or more district courts having civil jurisdiction, any judge may hear any part of any case or proceeding pending in any of said courts and determine the same, or may hear and determine any question in any case, and any other judge may complete the hearing and render judgment in the case.

(h) Any Judge May Hear Dilatory Pleas. Where in such county there are two or more district courts having civil jurisdiction, any judge may hear and determine motions, petitions for injunction, applications for appointment of receivers, interventions, pleas of privilege, pleas in abatement, all dilatory pleas and special exceptions, motions for a new trial and all preliminary matters, questions and proceedings and may enter judgment or order thereon in the court in which the case is pending without having the case transferred to the court of the judge acting, and the judge in whose court the case is pending may thereafter proceed to hear, complete and determine the case or other matter, or any part thereof, and render final judgment therein. Any judgment rendered or action taken by any judge in any of said courts in the county shall be valid and binding.

(i) Acts in Succeeding Terms. If a case or other matter is on trial, or in the process of hearing when the term of court expires, such trial, hearing or other matter may be proceeded with at the next or any subsequent term of court and no motion or plea shall be considered as waived or overruled, because not acted upon at the term of court at which it was filed, but may be acted upon at any time the judge may fix or at which it may have been postponed or continued by agreement of the parties with leave of the court. This subdivision is not applicable to original or amended motions for new trial which are governed by Rule 329b.

See also Govt Code §24.003; ***O'Connor's Texas Rules***, "Default Judgment," ch. 7-A.

Wilson v. Dunn, 800 S.W.2d 833, 835 n.6 (Tex. 1990). "The 236th District Court and the 67th District Court both sit in Tarrant County. They are permitted to, and do, hear each other's civil cases under [TRCP] 330."

In re Rio Grande Valley Gas Co., 987 S.W.2d 167, 173 (Tex.App.—Corpus Christi 1999, orig. proceeding). "[L]itigants do not have a protected proprietary interest in having their cases heard by a particular district judge or court within the county of filing."

Starnes v. Holloway, 779 S.W.2d 86, 96 (Tex. App.—Dallas 1989, writ denied). TRCP 330(e) is "consistent with [Tex. Const. art. 5, §11]. The rule ... make[s] each district judge the judge of any other district court in the county."

TRCP 331 - 351. REPEALED

PART III. RULES OF PROCEDURE FOR THE COURTS OF APPEALS

TRCP 352 - 473. REPEALED

PART IV. RULES OF PRACTICE FOR THE SUPREME COURT

TRCP 474 - 522. REPEALED

PART V. RULES OF PRACTICE IN JUSTICE COURTS

SECTION 1. GENERAL

TRCP 523. DISTRICT COURT RULES GOVERN

All rules governing the district and county courts shall also govern the justice courts, insofar as they can be applied, except where otherwise specifically provided by law or these rules.

SECTION 2. INSTITUTION OF SUIT

TRCP 524. DOCKET

Each justice shall keep a civil docket in which he shall enter:

(a) The title of all suits commenced before him.

(b) The time when the first process was issued against the defendant, when returnable, and the nature thereof.

(c) The time when the parties, or either of them, appeared before him, either with or without a citation.

(d) A brief statement of the nature of the plaintiff's demand or claim, and the amount claimed, and a brief statement of the nature of the defense made by the defendant, if any.

(e) Every adjournment, stating at whose request and to what time.

(f) The time when the trial was had, stating whether the same was by a jury or by the justice.

(g) The verdict of the jury, if any.

(h) The judgment signed by the justice and the time of signing same.

(i) All applications for setting aside judgments or granting new trials and the order of the justice thereon, with the date thereof.

(j) The time of issuing execution, to whom directed and delivered, and the amount of debt, damages and costs; and, when any execution is returned, he shall note such return on said docket, with the manner in which it was executed.

(k) All stays and appeals that may be taken, and the time when taken, the amount of the bond and the names of the sureties.

(*l*) He shall also keep such other dockets, books and records as may be required by law or these rules, and shall keep a fee book in which shall be taxed all costs accruing in every suit commenced before him.

TRCP 525. ORAL PLEADINGS

The pleadings shall be oral, except where otherwise specially provided; but a brief statement thereof may be noted on the docket; provided that after a case has been appealed and is docketed in the county (or district) court all pleadings shall be reduced to writing.

TRCP 526. SWORN PLEADINGS

An answer or other pleading setting up any of the matters specified in Rule 93 shall be in writing and signed by the party or his attorney and verified by affidavit.

TRCP 527. MOTION TO TRANSFER

A motion to transfer filed in the justice court shall contain the requisites prescribed in Rule 86; and in addition shall set forth the precinct to which transfer is sought.

TRCP 528. VENUE CHANGED ON AFFIDAVIT

If any party to a suit before any justice shall make an affidavit supported by the affidavit of two other credible persons, citizens of the county, that they have good reason to believe, and do believe, that such party cannot have a fair and impartial trial before such justice or in such justice's precinct, the justice shall transfer such suit to the court of the nearest justice within the county not subject to the same or some other disqualification.

See also CPRC §§15.081-15.100.

TRCP 529. "NEAREST JUSTICE" DEFINED

By the term "nearest justice," as used in this section, is meant the justice whose place of holding his court is nearest to that of the justice before whom the proceeding is pending or should have been brought.

TRCP 530. BY CONSENT

The venue may also be changed to the court of any other justice of the county, upon the written consent of the parties or their attorneys, filed with the papers of the cause.

TRCP 531. ORDER OF TRANSFER

The order of transfer in such cases shall state the cause of the transfer, and the name of the court to which the transfer is made, and shall require the parties and witnesses to appear before such court at its next ensuing term.

TRCP 532. TRANSCRIPT

When such order of transfer is made, the justice who made the order shall immediately make out a true and correct transcript of all the entries made on his docket in the cause, certify thereto officially, and send it, with a certified copy of the bill of costs taken from his fee book, and the original papers in the cause, to the justice of the precinct to which the same has been transferred.

TRCP 533. REQUISITES OF PROCESS

Every writ or process from the justice courts shall be issued by the justice, shall be in writing and signed by him officially. The style thereof shall be "The State of Texas." It shall, except where otherwise specially provided by law or these rules be directed to the person or party upon whom it is to be served, be made returnable to some regular term of court, and have noted thereon the date of its issuance.

TRCP 534. ISSUANCE & FORM OF CITATION

a. **Issuance.** When a claim or demand is lodged with a justice for suit, the clerk when requested shall forthwith issue a citation and deliver the citation as directed by the requesting party. The party requesting citation shall be responsible for obtaining service of the citation and a copy of the petition if any is filed. Upon request, separate or additional citations shall be issued by the clerk.

b. **Form.** The citation shall (1) be styled "The State of Texas", (2) be signed by the clerk under seal of court or by the Justice of the Peace, (3) contain name and location of the court, (4) show date of filing of the petition if any is filed, (5) show date of issuance of citation, (6) show file number and names of parties, (7) state the nature of plaintiff's demand, (8) be directed to the defendant, (9) show name and address of attorney for plaintiff, otherwise the address of plaintiff, (10) contain the time within which these rules require defendant to file a written answer with the clerk who issued citation, (11) contain address of the clerk, and (12) shall notify defendant that in case of failure of defendant to file an answer, judgment by default may be rendered for the relief demanded in the petition. The citation shall direct defendant to file a written answer to plaintiff's petition on or before 10:00 a.m. on the Monday next after the expiration of ten days after the date of service thereof. The requirement of subsections 10 and 12 of this rule shall be in the form set forth in section c of this rule.

c. **Notice.** The citation shall include the following notice to defendant: "You have been sued. You may employ an attorney. If you or your attorney do not file a written answer with the clerk who issued this citation by 10:00 a.m. on the Monday next following the expiration of ten days after you were served this citation and petition, a default judgment may be taken against you."

d. **Copies.** The party filing any pleading upon which citation is to be issued and served shall furnish the clerk with a sufficient number of copies thereof for use in serving the parties to be served, and when copies are so furnished the clerk shall make no charge for the copies.

TRCP 535. ANSWER FILED

Where citation has been personally served at least ten days before appearance day, exclusive of the day of service and of return, the answer of the defendant shall be filed at or before ten o'clock a.m. on such day. Where citation has been served by publication, and the first publication has been made at least twenty-eight days before appearance day, the answer of the defendant shall be filed at or before ten o'clock a.m. on the first day of the first term which shall convene after the expiration of forty-two days from the date of issuance of such citation.

TRCP 536. WHO MAY SERVE & METHOD OF SERVICE

(a) Citation and other notices may be served anywhere by (1) any sheriff or constable or other person authorized by law or, (2) any person authorized by law or by written order of the court who is not less than eighteen years of age. No person who is a party to or interested in the outcome of a suit shall serve any process. Service by registered or certified mail and citation by publication shall, if requested, be made by the clerk of the court in which the case is pending. The order authorizing a person to serve process may be made without written motion and no fee shall be imposed for issuance of such order.

(b) Unless the citation or an order of the court otherwise directs, the citation shall be served by any person authorized by this rule by:

(1) delivering to the defendant, in person, a true copy of the citation with the date of delivery endorsed thereon with a copy of the petition attached thereto, or

(2) mailing to the defendant by registered or certified mail, return receipt requested, a true copy of the citation with a copy of the petition attached thereto if any is filed.

(c) Upon motion supported by affidavit stating the location of the defendant's usual place of business or usual place of abode or other place where the defendant can probably be found and stating specifically the facts showing that service has been attempted under either (a)(1) or (a)(2) at the location named in such affidavit but has not been successful, the court may authorize service:

(1) by leaving a true copy of the citation, with a copy of the petition attached, with anyone over sixteen years of age at the location specified in such affidavit, or

(2) in any other manner that the affidavit or other evidence before the court shows will be reasonably effective to give the defendant notice of the suit.

TRCP 536a. DUTY OF OFFICER OR PERSON RECEIVING & RETURN OF CITATION

The officer or authorized person to whom process is delivered shall endorse thereon the day and hour on which he received it, and shall execute and return the same without delay.

The return of the officer or authorized person executing the citation shall be endorsed on or attached to the same; it shall state when the citation was served and the manner of service and be signed by the officer officially or by the authorized person. The return of citation by an authorized person shall be verified. When the citation was served by registered or certified mail as authorized by Rule 536, the return by the officer or authorized person must also contain the receipt with the addressee's signature. When the officer or authorized person has not served the citation, the return shall show the diligence used by the officer or authorized person to execute the same and the cause of failure to execute it, and where the defendant is to be found, if he can ascertain.

Where citation is executed by an alternative method as authorized by Rule 536, proof of service shall be made in the manner ordered by the court.

No default judgment shall be granted in any cause until the citation with proof of service as provided by this rule, or as ordered by the court in the event citation is executed under Rule 536, shall have been on file with the clerk of the court three (3) days, exclusive of the day of filing and the day of judgment.

SECTION 3. APPEARANCE & TRIAL

TRCP 537. APPEARANCE DAY

If a defendant who has been duly cited is required by the citation to answer on a day which is in term time, such day is appearance day as to him. If he is so required to answer on a day in vacation, the first day of the next term is appearance day as to him. Where service of citation has been had by publication, the first day of the term of court which convenes after the expiration of 42 days from the date of issuance of the citation shall be appearance day.

TRCP 538. IF DEFENDANT FAILS TO APPEAR

If the defendant who has been duly served with a citation shall fail to appear at, or before, ten o'clock a.m. on appearance day, the justice shall proceed in the following manner:

(a) If the plaintiff's claim be liquidated and proved by an instrument of writing purporting to have been executed by the defendant, or be upon an open account duly verified by affidavit, the justice shall, whether the plaintiff appear or not, render judgment in his favor against the defendant for the amount of such written obligation or sworn account, after deducting all credits indorsed thereon.

(b) If the plaintiff's claim is not so liquidated, and the plaintiff appears in person or by attorney, the justice shall proceed to hear the testimony; and, if it appears therefrom that the plaintiff is entitled to recover, judgment shall be rendered against the defendant for such amount as the testimony shows the plaintiff entitled to; otherwise, judgment shall be rendered for the defendant.

TRCP 539. APPEARANCE NOTED

If the defendant appear, the same shall be noted on the docket, and the cause shall stand for trial in its order.

TRCP 540. IF NO DEMAND FOR JURY

If neither party shall demand and be entitled to a jury, the justice shall try the cause without a jury.

TRCP 541. CONTINUANCE

The justice for good cause shown, supported by affidavit, may continue any suit pending before him to the next regular term of his court, or postpone the same to some other day of the term.

TRCP 542. CALL OF NON-JURY DOCKET

The docket of cases to be tried by the justice shall be called regularly, and the cases shall be tried when called unless continued or postponed.

TRCP 543. DISMISSAL

If the plaintiff shall fail to appear when the cause is called in its order for trial, the justice, on motion of the defendant, may dismiss the suit.

TRCP 544. JURY TRIAL DEMANDED

Either party shall be entitled to a trial by jury. Except in forcible entry and detainer cases, the party desiring a jury shall before the case is called for trial not less than one day in advance of the date set for trial of the cause make a demand for a jury, and also deposit a jury fee of five dollars, which shall be noted on the docket; and the case shall be set down as a jury case.

TRCP 545. JURY TRIAL DAY

The justice shall, on the first day of the term, fix a day for taking up the jury cases, if any, pending for trial at such term, and he may fix said first day of the term for that purpose.

TRCP 546. CALL OF JURY DOCKET

When the required number of jurors is present, the jury cases set for trial shall be called.

TRCP 547. CHALLENGE TO THE ARRAY

When the parties to a jury case have announced themselves for trial, either party may challenge the array of jurors. The cause and the manner of making such challenge, the decision thereof and the proceedings, when such challenge is sustained, shall be as provided for similar proceedings in the district and county courts.

TRCP 548. DRAWING JURY

If no challenge to the array is made, the justice shall write the names of all the jurors present on separate slips of paper, as nearly alike as may be, and shall place them in a box and mix them well, and shall then draw the names one by one from the box, and write them down as they are drawn, upon several slips of paper, and deliver one slip to each of the parties, or their attorneys.

TRCP 549. CHALLENGE FOR CAUSE

If either party desires to challenge any juror for cause, such challenge shall now be made. The causes of such challenge, and the manner of making it and the decision thereof, and the proceedings, when such challenge is sustained, shall be as provided for similar proceedings in the district and county courts.

TRCP 550. PEREMPTORY CHALLENGE

When a juror has been challenged for cause, and the challenge has been sustained, his name shall be erased from the slips furnished to the parties; and, if as many as twelve names remain on such slips, the parties may make their peremptory challenges governed by the rules prescribed for the district and county courts. Each party shall be entitled to three peremptory challenges.

See also *O'Connor's Texas Rules*, "Jury Selection," ch. 8-A.

TRCP 551. THE JURY

When the peremptory challenges are made, they shall deliver their slips to the justice, who shall call off the first six names on the slips that have not been erased, and these shall be the jury to try the case.

TRCP 552. IF JURY IS INCOMPLETE

If the jury by peremptory challenges is left incomplete, the justice shall direct the sheriff or constable to summon others to complete the jury; and the same proceedings shall be had in selecting and impaneling such jurors as are had in the first instance.

TRCP 553. JURY SWORN

When the jury has been selected, such of them as have not been previously sworn for the trial of civil cases shall be sworn by the justice. The form of the oath shall be in substance as follows: "You and each of you do solemnly swear that in all cases between parties which shall be to you submitted you will a true verdict render, according to the law and the evidence. So help you God."

TRCP 554. JUSTICE SHALL NOT CHARGE JURY

The justice of the peace shall not charge the jury in any cause tried in his court before a jury.

TRCP 555. VERDICT

When the suit is for the recovery of specific articles, the jury shall, if they find for the plaintiff, assess the value of each of such articles separately, according to the proof.

SECTION 4. JUDGMENT

TRCP 556. JUDGMENT UPON VERDICT

Where the case has been tried by a jury and a verdict has been returned by them, the justice shall announce the same in open court and note it in his docket, and shall proceed to render judgment thereon.

TRCP 557. CASE TRIED BY JUSTICE

When the case has been tried by the justice without a jury, he shall announce his decision in open court and note the same in his docket and render judgment thereon.

TRCP 558. JUDGMENT

The judgment shall be recorded at length in the justice's docket, and shall be signed by the justice. It shall clearly state the determination of the rights of the parties in the subject matter in controversy and the party who shall pay the costs, and shall direct the issuance of such process as may be necessary to carry the judgment into execution.

TRCP 559. COSTS

The successful party in the suit shall recover his costs, except in cases where it is otherwise expressly provided.

TRCP 560. JUDGMENT FOR SPECIFIC ARTICLES

Where the judgment is for the recovery of specific articles, their value shall be separately assessed, and the judgment shall be that the plaintiff recover such specific articles, if they can be found, and if not, then their value as assessed with interest thereon at the rate of six per cent from the date of judgment.

TRCP 561. TO ENFORCE JUDGMENT

The court shall cause its judgments to be carried into execution, and where the judgment is for personal property and the verdict, if any, is that such property has an especial value to the plaintiff the court may award a special writ for the seizure and delivery of such property to the plaintiff, and may, in addition to the other relief granted in such cases, enforce its judgment by attachment, fine and imprisonment.

TRCP 562. NO JUDGMENT WITHOUT CITATION

No judgment, other than judgment by confession, shall be rendered by the justice of the peace against any party who has not entered an appearance or accepted service, unless such party has been duly cited.

TRCP 563. CONFESSION OF JUDGMENT

Any party may appear in person, or by an agent or attorney, before any justice of the peace, without the issuance or service of process, and confess judgment for any amount within the jurisdiction of the justice court; and such judgment shall be entered on the justice's docket as in other cases; but, in such cases, the plaintiff, his agent or attorney shall make and file an affidavit signed by him, to the justness of his claim.

TRCP 564. WARRANT OF ATTORNEY

Where such judgment is confessed by an agent or attorney, the warrant of attorney shall be in writing and filed with the justice and noted in the judgment.

TRCP 565. RULES GOVERNING

The rules governing the district and county courts in relation to judgment and confession thereof, shall also apply to justice courts, insofar as they do not conflict with some provision of the rules applicable to justice courts.

SECTION 5. NEW TRIAL

TRCP 566. JUDGMENTS BY DEFAULT

A justice may within ten days after a judgment by default or of dismissal is signed, set aside such judgment, on motion in writing, for good cause shown, supported by affidavit. Notice of such motion shall be given to the opposite party at least one full day prior to the hearing thereof.

TRCP 567. NEW TRIALS

The justice, within ten days after the rendition of a judgment in any suit tried before him, may grant a new trial therein on motion in writing showing that justice has not been done in the trial of the cause.

If the grounds of the motion be other than that the verdict or judgment is contrary to the law or the evidence, or that the justice erred in some matter of law, the motion shall be supported by affidavit.

TRCP 568. REPEALED

TRCP 569. NOTICE

All motions to set aside a judgment or to grant a new trial, under the two preceding rules, shall be made within five days after the rendition of judgment and one day's notice thereof shall be given the opposite party or his attorney.

TRCP 570. BUT ONE NEW TRIAL

But one new trial may be granted to either party.

SECTION 6. APPEAL

TRCP 571. APPEAL BOND

The party appealing, his agent or attorney, shall within ten days from the date a judgment or order overruling motion for new trial is signed, file with the justice a bond, with two or more good and sufficient sureties, to be approved by the justice, in double the amount of the judgment, payable to the appellee, conditioned that appellant shall prosecute his appeal to effect, and shall pay off and satisfy the judgment which may be rendered against him on appeal; or if the appeal is by the plaintiff by reason of judgment denying in whole or in part his claim, he shall file with the justice a bond in the same ten-day period, payable to the appellee, with two or more good and sufficient sureties, to be approved by the justice, in double the amount of the costs incurred in the justice court and estimated costs in the county court, less such sums as may have been paid by the plaintiff on the costs, conditioned that he shall prosecute his appeal to effect and shall pay off and satisfy such costs if judgment for costs be rendered against him on appeal. When such bond has been filed with the justice, the appeal shall be held to be thereby perfected and all parties to said suit or to any suit so appealed shall make their appearance at the next term of court to which said case has been appealed. Within five days following the filing of such appeal bond, the party appealing shall give notice as provided in Rule 21a of the filing of such bond to all parties to the suit who have not filed such bond. No judgment shall be taken by default against any party in the court to which the cause has been appealed without first showing that this rule has been complied with. The appeal shall not be dismissed for defects or irregularities in procedure, either of form or substance, without allowing appellant five days after notice within which to correct or amend same.

TRCP 572. AFFIDAVIT OF INABILITY

Where appellant is unable to pay the costs of appeal, or give security therefor, he shall nevertheless be entitled to appeal by making strict proof of such inability within five days after the judgment or order overruling motion for new trial is signed, which shall consist of his affidavit filed with the justice of the peace stating his inability to pay such costs, or any part thereof, or to give security, which may be contested within five days after the filing of such affidavit and notice thereof to the opposite party or his attorney of record by any officer of court or party to the suit, whereupon it shall be the duty of the justice of the peace in whose court the suit is pending to hear evidence and determine the right of the party to appeal, and he shall enter his finding on the docket as a part of the record. It will be presumed prima facie that the affidavit speaks the truth, and, unless contested within five days after the filing and notice thereof, the presumption shall be deemed conclusive; but if a contest is filed, the burden shall then be on the appellant to prove his alleged inability by competent evidence other than by the affidavit above referred to. If the justice of the peace denies the right of appeal, appellant may, within five days thereafter, bring the matter before the county judge of the county for final decision, and, on request, the justice shall certify to the county judge appellant's affidavit, the contest thereof, and all documents and papers pertaining thereto. The county judge shall set a day for hearing, not later than ten days, and shall hear the contest de novo, and if the appeal is granted, shall direct the justice to transmit to the clerk of the county court, the transcript, records and papers of the case, as provided in these rules.

TRCP 573. APPEAL PERFECTED

When the bond, or the affidavit in lieu thereof, provided for in the rules applicable to justice courts, has been filed and the previous requirements have been complied with, the appeal shall be held to be perfected.

TRCP 574. TRANSCRIPT

Whenever an appeal has been perfected from the justice court, the justice who made the order, or his successor, shall immediately make out a true and correct copy of all the entries made on his docket in the cause, and certify thereto officially, and immediately send it together with a certified copy of the bill of costs taken from his fee book, and the original papers in the cause, to the clerk of the county court of his county, or other court having jurisdiction.

TRCP 574a. NEW MATTER MAY BE PLEADED

Either party may plead any new matter in the county or district court which was not presented in the court below, but no new ground of recovery shall be set up by the plaintiff, nor shall any set-off or counterclaim be set up by the defendant which was not pleaded in the court below. The pleading thereof shall be in writing and filed in the cause before the parties have announced ready for trial.

TRCP 574b. TRIAL DE NOVO

The cause shall be tried de novo in the county or district court; and judgment shall be rendered.

SECTION 7. CERTIORARI

TRCP 575. ORDER FOR WRIT

The writ of certiorari shall be issued by order of the county court or the judge thereof (or district court or judge thereof, if jurisdiction is transferred to the district court) as provided in these rules.

TRCP 576. REQUISITES OF WRIT

The writ shall command the justice to immediately make and certify a copy of the entries in the cause on his docket, and immediately transmit the same, with the papers in his possession and a certified copy of the bill of costs to the proper court.

TRCP 577. AFFIDAVIT OF SUFFICIENT CAUSE

The writ shall not be granted unless the applicant or some person for him having knowledge of the facts, shall make affidavit setting forth sufficient cause to entitle him thereto.

See also *O'Connor's Texas Rules*, "The Answer—Denying Liability," ch. 3-E.

TRCP 578. APPLICATION FOR CERTIORARI

To constitute a sufficient cause, the facts stated must show that either the justice of the peace had not jurisdiction, or that injustice was done to the applicant by the final determination of the suit or proceeding, and that such injustice was not caused by his own inexcusable neglect.

TRCP 579. WITHIN WHAT TIME GRANTED

Such writ shall not be granted after ninety days from the time the final judgment is signed.

TRCP 580. BOND WITH SURETIES REQUIRED

The writ shall not be issued unless the applicant shall first cause to be filed a bond with two or more good and sufficient sureties, to be approved by the clerk, payable to the adverse party, in such sum as the judge shall direct, to the effect that the party applying therefor will perform the judgment of the county or district court, if the same shall be against him.

TRCP 581. BOND, AFFIDAVIT & ORDER

The bond and affidavit, with the order of the judge, when made in vacation, shall be filed with the clerk of the court to which the same is returnable.

TRCP 582. WRIT TO ISSUE INSTANTER

As soon as such affidavit, order of the judge, and bond, shall have been filed, the clerk shall issue a writ of certiorari.

TRCP 583. JUSTICE SHALL STAY PROCEEDINGS

Upon service of such writ of certiorari being made upon the justice of the peace, he shall stay further proceedings on the judgment and forthwith comply with said writ.

TRCP 584. CITATION AS IN OTHER CASES

Whenever a writ of certiorari has been issued, the clerk shall forthwith issue a citation for the party adversely interested.

TRCP 585. CAUSE DOCKETED

The action shall be docketed in the name of the original plaintiff, as plaintiff, and of the original defendant, as defendant.

TRCP 586. MOTION TO DISMISS

Within thirty days after the service of citation on the writ of certiorari, the adverse party may move to dismiss the certiorari for want of sufficient cause appearing in the affidavit, or for want of sufficient bond.

TRCP 587. AMENDMENT OF BOND OR OATH

The affidavit or bond may be amended in the discretion of the court in which it is filed.

TRCP 588. JUDGMENT OF DISMISSAL

If the certiorari be dismissed, the judgment shall direct the justice to proceed with the execution of the judgment below.

TRCP 589. PLEADING

After the transcript of the proceedings in the justice court, together with the original papers and a bill of costs, have been filed in the county (or district) court, all pleadings in the cause which are not already written shall be reduced to writing.

TRCP 590. NEW MATTER MAY BE PLEADED

Either party may plead any new matter in the county or district court which was not presented in the court below, but no new ground of recovery shall be set up by the plaintiff, nor shall any set-off or counterclaim be set up by the defendant which was not pleaded in the court below. The pleading thereof shall be in writing and filed in the cause before the parties have announced ready for trial.

TRCP 591. TRIAL DE NOVO

The cause shall be tried de novo in the county or district court; and judgment shall be rendered as in cases appealed from justice courts.

PART VI. RULES RELATING TO ANCILLARY PROCEEDINGS

SECTION 1. ATTACHMENT

TRCP 592. APPLICATION FOR WRIT OF ATTACHMENT & ORDER

Either at the commencement of a suit or at any time during its progress the plaintiff may file an application for the issuance of a writ of attachment. Such application shall be supported by affidavits of the plaintiff, his agent, his attorney, or other persons having knowledge of relevant facts. The application shall comply with all statutory requirements and shall state the grounds for issuing the writ and the specific facts relied upon by the plaintiff to warrant the required findings by the court. The writ shall not be quashed because two or more grounds are stated conjunctively or disjunctively. The application and any affidavits shall be made on personal knowledge and shall set forth such facts as would be admissible in evidence; provided that facts may be stated based upon information and belief if the grounds of such belief are specifically stated.

No writ shall issue except upon written order of the court after a hearing, which may be ex parte. The court, in its order granting the application, shall make specific findings of facts to support the statutory grounds found to exist, and shall specify the maximum value of property that may be attached, and the amount of bond required of plaintiff, and, further shall command that the attached property be kept safe and preserved subject to further orders of the court. Such bond shall be in an amount which, in the opinion of the court, will adequately compensate the defendant in the event plaintiff fails to prosecute his suit to effect, and to pay all damages and costs which may be adjudged against him for wrongfully suing out the writ of attachment. The court shall further find in its order the amount of bond required of defendant to replevy, which, unless the defendant chooses to exercise his option as provided in Rule 599, shall be the amount of plaintiff's claim, one year's accrual of interest if allowed by law on the claim, and the estimated costs of court. The order may direct the issuance of several writs at the same time, or in succession, to be sent to different counties.

TRCP 592a. BOND FOR ATTACHMENT

No writ of attachment shall issue until the party applying therefor has filed with the officer authorized to issue such writ a bond payable to the defendant in the amount fixed by the court's order, with sufficient surety or sureties as provided by statute to be approved by such officer, conditioned that the plaintiff will prosecute his suit to effect and pay to the extent of the penal amount of the bond all damages and costs as may be adjudged against him for wrongfully suing out such writ of attachment.

After notice to the opposite party, either before or after the issuance of the writ, the defendant or plaintiff may file a motion to increase or reduce the amount of such bond, or to question the sufficiency of the sureties thereon, in the court in which such suit is pending. Upon hearing, the court shall enter its order with respect to such bond and sufficiency of the sureties.

TRCP 592b. FORM OF ATTACHMENT BOND

The following form of bond may be used:

"The State of Texas,

"County of ________,

"We, the undersigned, ________ as principal, and ________ and ________ as sureties, acknowledge ourselves bound to pay to C.D. the sum of ________ dollars, conditioned that the above bound plaintiff in attachment against the said C.D., defendant, will prosecute his said suit to effect, and that he will pay all such damages and costs to the extent of the penal amount of this bond as shall be adjudged against him for wrongfully suing out such attachment. Witness our hands this ___ day of ________, 20___."

TRCP 593. REQUISITES FOR WRIT

A writ of attachment shall be directed to the sheriff or any constable within the State of Texas. It shall command him to attach and hold, unless replevied, subject to the further order of the court, so much of the property of the defendant, of a reasonable value in approximately the amount fixed by the court, as shall be found within his county.

TRCP 594. FORM OF WRIT

The following form of writ may be issued:

"The State of Texas.

"To the Sheriff or any Constable of any County of the State of Texas, greeting:

"We command you that you attach forthwith so much of the property of C.D., if it be found in your county, repleviable on security, as shall be of value sufficient to make the sum of ________ dollars, and the probable costs of suit, to satisfy the demand of A.B., and that you keep and secure in your hands the property so attached, unless replevied, that the same may be liable to further proceedings thereon to be had before our court in ________, County of ________. You will true return make of this writ on or before 10 a.m. of Monday, the ________ day of ________, 20___, showing how you have executed the same."

TRCP 595. SEVERAL WRITS

Several writs of attachment may, at the option of the plaintiff, be issued at the same time, or in succession, and sent to different counties, until sufficient property shall be attached to satisfy the writ.

TRCP 596. DELIVERY OF WRIT

The writ of attachment shall be dated and tested as other writs, and may be delivered to the sheriff or constable by the officer issuing it, or he may deliver it to the plaintiff, his agent or attorney, for that purpose.

TRCP 597. DUTY OF OFFICER

The sheriff or constable receiving the writ shall immediately proceed to execute the same by levying upon so much of the property of the defendant subject to the writ, and found within his county, as may be sufficient to satisfy the command of the writ.

TRCP 598. LEVY, HOW MADE

The writ of attachment shall be levied in the same manner as is, or may be, the writ of execution upon similar property.

TRCP 598a. SERVICE OF WRIT ON DEFENDANT

The defendant shall be served in any manner prescribed for service of citation, or as provided in Rule 21a, with a copy of the writ of attachment, the application, accompanying affidavits, and orders of the court as soon as practicable following the levy of the writ. There shall be prominently displayed on the face of the copy of the writ served on the defendant, in ten-point type and in a manner calculated to advise a reasonably attentive person of its contents, the following:

"To ________, Defendant:

"You are hereby notified that certain properties alleged to be owned by you have been attached. If you claim any rights in such property, you are advised:

"YOU HAVE A RIGHT TO REGAIN POSSESSION OF THE PROPERTY BY FILING A REPLEVY BOND. YOU HAVE A RIGHT TO SEEK TO REGAIN POSSESSION OF THE PROPERTY BY FILING WITH THE COURT A MOTION TO DISSOLVE THIS WRIT."

TRCP 599. DEFENDANT MAY REPLEVY

At any time before judgment, should the attached property not have been previously claimed or sold, the defendant may replevy the same, or any part thereof, or the proceeds from the sale of the property if it has been sold under order of the court, by giving bond with sufficient surety or sureties as provided by statute, to be approved by the officer who levied the writ, payable to plaintiff, in the amount fixed by the court's order, or, at the defendant's option, for the value of the property sought to be replevied (to be estimated by the officer), plus one year's interest thereon at the legal rate from the date of the bond, conditioned that the defendant shall satisfy, to the extent of the penal amount of the bond, any judgment which may be rendered against him in such action.

On reasonable notice to the opposing party (which may be less than three days) either party shall have the right to prompt judicial review of the amount of bond required, denial of bond, sufficiency of sureties, and estimated value of the property, by the court which authorized issuance of the writ. The court's determination may be made upon the basis of affidavits, if uncontroverted, setting forth such facts as would be admissible in evidence; otherwise, the parties shall submit evidence. The court shall forthwith enter its order either approving or modifying the requirements of the officer or of the court's prior order, and such order of the court shall supersede and control with respect to such matters.

On reasonable notice to the opposing party (which may be less than three days) the defendant shall have the right to move the court for a substitution of property, of equal value as that attached, for the property attached. Provided that there has been located sufficient property of the defendants to satisfy the order of attachment, the court may authorize substitution of one or more items of defendant's property for all or for part of the property attached. The court shall first make findings as to the value of the property to be substituted. If property is substituted, the property released from attachment shall be delivered to defendant, if such property is personal property, and all liens upon such property from the original order of attachment or modification thereof shall be terminated. Attachment of substituted property shall be deemed to have existed from the date of levy on the original property attached, and no property on which liens have become affixed since the date of levy on the original property may be substituted.

TRCP 600. SALE OF PERISHABLE PROPERTY

Whenever personal property which has been attached shall not have been claimed or replevied, the judge, or justice of the peace, out of whose court the writ was issued, may, either in term time or in vacation, order the same to be sold, when it shall be made to appear that such property is in danger of serious and immediate waste or decay, or that the keeping of the same until the trial will necessarily be attended with such expense or deterioration in value as greatly to lessen the amount likely to be realized therefrom.

TRCP 601. TO PROTECT INTERESTS

In determining whether the property attached is perishable, and the necessity or advantage of ordering a sale thereof, the judge or justice of the peace may act upon affidavits in writing or oral testimony, and may by a preliminary order entered of record, with or without notice to the parties as the urgency of the case in his opinion requires, direct the sheriff or constable to sell such property at public auction for cash, and thereupon the officer shall sell it accordingly.

TRCP 602. BOND OF APPLICANT FOR SALE

If the application for an order of sale be filed by any person or party other than the defendant from whose possession the property was taken by levy, the court shall not grant such order unless the applicant shall file with such court a bond payable to such defendant, with two or more good and sufficient sureties, to be approved by said court, conditioned that they will be responsible to the defendant for such damages as he may sustain in case such sale be illegally and unjustly applied for, or be illegally and unjustly made.

TRCP 603. PROCEDURE FOR SALE

Such sale of attached perishable personal property shall be conducted in the same manner as sales of personal property under execution; provided, however, that the time of the sale, and at the time of advertisement thereof, may be fixed by the judge or justice of the peace at a time earlier than ten days, according to the exigency of the case, and in such event notice thereof shall be given in such manner as directed by the order.

TRCP 604. RETURN OF SALE

The officer making such sale of perishable property shall promptly pay the proceeds of such sale to the clerk of such court or justice of the peace, as the case may be, and shall make written return of the order of sale signed by him officially, stating the time and place of the sale, the name of the purchaser, and the amount of money received, with an itemized account of the expenses attending the sale. Such return shall be filed with the papers of the case.

TRCP 605. JUDGE MAY MAKE NECESSARY ORDERS

When the perishable personal property levied on under the attachment writ has not been claimed or replevied, the judge or justice of the peace may make such orders, either in term time or vacation, as may be necessary for its preservation or use.

TRCP 606. RETURN OF WRIT

The officer executing the writ of attachment shall return the writ, with his action endorsed thereon, or attached thereto, signed by him officially, to the court from which it issued, at or before 10 o'clock a.m. of the Monday next after the expiration of fifteen days from the date of issuance of the writ. Such return shall describe the property attached with sufficient certainty to identify it, and state when the same was attached, and whether any personal property attached remains still in his hands, and, if not, the disposition made of the same. When property has been replevied he shall deliver the replevy bond to the clerk or justice of the peace to be filed with the papers of the cause.

TRCP 607. REPORT OF DISPOSITION OF PROPERTY

When the property levied on is claimed, replevied or sold, or otherwise disposed of after the writ has been returned, the officer having the custody of the same shall immediately make a report in writing, signed by him officially, to the clerk, or justice of the peace, as the case may be, showing such disposition of the property. Such report shall be filed among the papers of the cause.

TRCP 608. DISSOLUTION OR MODIFICATION OF WRIT OF ATTACHMENT

A defendant whose property has been attached or any intervening party who claims an interest in such property, may by sworn written motion, seek to vacate, dissolve, or modify the writ, and the order directing its issuance, for any grounds or cause, extrinsic or intrinsic. Such motion shall admit or deny each finding of the order directing the issuance of the writ except where the movant is unable to admit or deny the finding, in which case movant shall set forth the reasons why he cannot admit or deny. Unless the parties agree to an extension of time, the motion shall be heard promptly, after reasonable notice to the plaintiff (which may be less than three days), and the issue shall be determined not later than ten days after the motion is filed. The filing of the motion shall stay any further proceedings under the writ, except for any orders concerning the care, preservation, or sale of perishable property, until a hearing is had and the issue is determined. The writ shall be dissolved unless at such hearing, the plaintiff shall prove the grounds relied upon for its issuance, but the court may modify its previous order granting the writ and the writ issued pursuant thereto. The movant shall, however, have the burden to prove that the reasonable value of the property attached exceeds the amount necessary to secure the debt, interest for one year, and probable costs. He shall also have the burden to prove the facts to justify substitution of property.

The court's determination may be made upon the basis of affidavits, if uncontroverted, setting forth such facts as would be admissible in evidence; otherwise, the parties shall submit evidence. The court may make all such orders, including orders concerning the care, preservation, or disposition of the property (or the proceeds therefrom if the same has been sold), as justice may require. If the movant has given a replevy bond, an order to vacate or dissolve the writ shall vacate the replevy bond and discharge the sureties thereon, and if the court modifies its order or the writ issued pursuant thereto, it shall make such further orders with respect to the bond as may be consistent with its modification.

TRCP 609. AMENDMENT

Clerical errors in the affidavit, bond, or writ of attachment, or the officer's return thereof, may upon application in writing to the judge or justice of the court in which the suit is filed, and after notice to the opponent, be amended in such manner and on such terms as the judge or justice shall authorize by an order entered in the minutes of the court or noted on the docket of the justice of the peace, provided the amendment does not change or add to the grounds of such attachment as stated in the affidavit, and provided such amendment appears to the judge or justice to be in furtherance of justice.

SECTION 2. DISTRESS WARRANT

TRCP 610. APPLICATION FOR DISTRESS WARRANT & ORDER

Either at the commencement of a suit or at any time during its progress the plaintiff may file an application for the issuance of a distress warrant with the justice of the peace. Such application may be supported by affidavits of the plaintiff, his agent, his attorney, or other persons having knowledge of relevant facts, but shall include a statement that the amount sued for is rent, or advances described by statute, or shall produce a writing signed by the tenant to that effect, and shall further swear that such warrant is not sued out for the purpose of vexing and harassing the defendant. The application shall comply with all statutory requirements and shall state the grounds for issuing the warrant and the specific facts relied upon by the plaintiff to warrant the required findings by the justice of the peace. The warrant shall not be quashed because two or more grounds are stated conjunctively or disjunctively. The application and any affidavits shall be made on personal knowledge and shall set forth such facts as would be admissible in evidence provided that facts may be stated based upon information and belief if the grounds of such belief are specifically stated.

No warrant shall issue before final judgment except on written order of the justice of the peace after a hearing, which may be ex parte. Such warrant shall be made returnable to a court having jurisdiction of the amount in controversy. The justice of the peace in his order granting the application shall make specific findings of fact to support the statutory grounds found to exist, and shall specify the maximum value of property that may be seized, and the amount of bond required of plaintiff, and, further shall command that property be kept safe and preserved subject to further orders of the court having jurisdiction. Such bond shall be in an amount which, in the opinion of the court, shall adequately compensate defendant in the event plaintiff fails to prosecute his suit to effect, and pay all damages and costs as shall be adjudged against him for wrongfully suing out the warrant. The justice of the peace shall further find in his order the amount of bond required to replevy, which, unless the defendant chooses to exercise his option as provided in Rule 614, shall be the amount of plaintiff's claim, one year's accrual of interest if allowed by law on the claim, and the estimated costs of court. The order may direct the issuance of several warrants at the same time, or in succession, to be sent to different counties.

TRCP 611. BOND FOR DISTRESS WARRANT

No distress warrant shall issue before final judgment until the party applying therefor has filed with the justice of the peace authorized to issue such warrant a bond payable to the defendant in an amount approved by the justice of the peace, with sufficient surety or sureties as provided by statute, conditioned that the plaintiff will prosecute his suit to effect and pay all damages and costs as may be adjudged against him for wrongfully suing out such warrant.

After notice to the opposite party, either before or after the issuance of the warrant, the defendant or plaintiff may file a motion to increase or reduce the amount of such bond, or to question the sufficiency of the sureties thereon, in a court having jurisdiction of the subject matter. Upon hearing, the court shall enter its order with respect to such bond and sufficiency of the sureties.

TRCP 612. REQUISITES FOR WARRANT

A distress warrant shall be directed to the sheriff or any constable within the State of Texas. It shall command him to attach and hold, unless replevied, subject to the further orders of the court having jurisdiction, so much of the property of the defendant, not exempt by statute, of reasonable value in approximately the amount fixed by the justice of the peace, as shall be found within his county.

TRCP 613. SERVICE OF WARRANT ON DEFENDANT

The defendant shall be served in any manner prescribed for service of citation, or as provided in Rule 21a, with a copy of the distress warrant, the application, accompanying affidavits, and orders of the justice of the peace as soon as practicable following the levy of the warrant. There shall be prominently displayed on the face of the copy of the warrant served on the defendant, in 10-point type and in a manner calculated to advise a reasonably attentive person of its contents, the following:

"To __________, Defendant:

"You are hereby notified that certain properties alleged to be owned by you have been seized. If you claim any rights in such property, you are advised:

"YOU HAVE A RIGHT TO REGAIN POSSESSION OF THE PROPERTY BY FILING A REPLEVY BOND. YOU HAVE A RIGHT TO SEEK TO REGAIN POSSESSION OF THE PROPERTY BY FILING WITH THE COURT A MOTION TO DISSOLVE THIS WARRANT."

TRCP 614. DEFENDANT MAY REPLEVY

At any time before judgment, should the seized property not have been previously claimed or sold, the defendant may replevy the same, or any part thereof, or the proceeds from the sale of the property if it has been sold under order of the court, by giving bond with sufficient surety or sureties as provided by statute, to be approved by a court having jurisdiction of the amount in controversy payable to plaintiff in double the amount of the plaintiff's debt, or, at the defendant's option for not less than the value of the property sought to be replevied, plus one year's interest thereon at the legal rate from the date of the bond, conditioned that the defendant shall satisfy to the extent of the penal amount of the bond any judgment which may be rendered against him in such action.

On reasonable notice to the opposing party (which may be less than three days) either party shall have the right to prompt judicial review of the amount of bond required, denial of bond, sufficiency of sureties, and estimated value of the property, by a court having jurisdiction of the amount in controversy. The court's determination may be made upon the basis of affidavits if uncontroverted setting forth such facts as would be admissible in evidence, otherwise the parties shall submit evidence. The court shall forthwith enter its order either approving or modifying the requirements of the order of the justice of the peace, and such order of the court shall supersede and control with respect to such matters.

On reasonable notice to the opposing party (which may be less than three days) the defendant shall have the right to move the court for a substitution of property, of equal value as that attached, for the property seized. Provided that there has been located sufficient property of the defendant's to satisfy the order of seizure, the court may authorize substitution of one or more items of defendant's property for all or part of the property seized. The court shall first make findings as to the value of the property to be substituted. If property is substituted, the property released from seizure shall be delivered to defendant, if such property is personal property, and all liens upon such property from the original order of seizure or modification thereof shall be terminated. Seizure of substituted property shall be deemed to have existed from the date of levy on the original property seized, and no property on which liens have become affixed since the date of levy on the original property may be substituted.

TRCP 614a. DISSOLUTION OR MODIFICATION OF DISTRESS WARRANT

A defendant whose property has been seized or any intervening claimant who claims an interest in such property, may by sworn written motion, seek to vacate, dissolve, or modify the seizure, and the order directing its issuance, for any grounds or cause, extrinsic or intrinsic. Such motion shall admit or deny each finding of the order directing the issuance of the warrant except where the movant is unable to admit or deny the finding, in which case movant shall set forth the reasons why he cannot admit or deny. Unless the parties agree to an extension of time, the motion shall be heard promptly, after reasonable notice to the plaintiff (which may be less than three days), and the issue shall be determined not later than 10 days after the motion is filed. The filing of the motion shall stay any further proceedings under the warrant, except for any orders concerning the care, preservation, or sale of any perishable property, until a hearing is had, and the issue is determined. The warrant shall be dissolved unless, at such hearing, the plaintiff shall prove the specific facts alleged and the grounds relied upon for its issuance, but the court may modify the order of the justice of the peace granting the warrant and the warrant issued pursuant thereto. The movant shall however have the burden to prove that the reasonable value of the property seized exceeds the amount necessary to secure the debt, interest for one year, and probable costs. He shall also have the burden to prove the facts to justify substitution of property.

The court's determination may be made upon the basis of affidavits setting forth such facts as would be admissible in evidence, but additional evidence, if tendered by either party shall be received and considered. The court may make all such orders, including orders concerning the care, preservation, or disposition of the property (or the proceeds therefrom if the same has been sold), as justice may require. If the movant has given a replevy bond, an order to vacate or dissolve the warrant shall vacate the replevy bond and discharge the sureties thereon, and if the court modifies the order of the justice of the peace or the warrant issued pursuant thereto, it shall make such further orders with respect to the bond as may be consistent with its modification.

TRCP 615. SALE OF PERISHABLE PROPERTY

Whenever personal property which has been levied on under a distress warrant shall not have been claimed or replevied, the judge, or justice of the peace, to whose court such writ is made returnable may, either in term time or in vacation, order the same to be sold, when it shall be made to appear that such property is in danger of serious and immediate waste or decay, or that the keeping of the same until the trial will necessarily be attended with such expense or deterioration in value as greatly to lessen the amount likely to be realized therefrom.

TRCP 616. TO PROTECT INTERESTS

In determining whether the property levied upon is perishable, and the necessity or advantage of ordering a sale thereof, the judge or justice of the peace may act upon affidavits in writing or oral testimony, and may by a preliminary order entered of record with or without notice to the parties as the urgency of the case in his opinion requires, direct the sheriff or constable to sell such property at public auction for cash, and thereupon the sheriff or constable shall sell it accordingly. If the application for an order of sale be filed by any person or party other than the defendant from whose possession the property was taken by levy, the court shall not grant such order, unless the applicant shall file with such court a bond payable to such defendant, with two or more good and sufficient sureties, to be approved by said court, conditioned that they will be responsible to the defendant for such damages as he may sustain in case such sale be illegally and unjustly applied for, or be illegally and unjustly made.

TRCP 617. PROCEDURE FOR SALE

Such sale of perishable personal property shall be conducted in the same manner as sales of personal property under execution; provided, however, that the time of the sale, and the time of advertisement thereof, may be fixed by the judge or justice of the peace at a time earlier than ten days, according to the exigency of the case, and in such event notice thereof shall be given in such manner as directed by the order.

TRCP 618. RETURN OF SALE

The officer making such sale of perishable property shall promptly pay the proceeds of such sale to the clerk of such court or to the justice of the peace, as the case may be, and shall make written return of the order of sale, signed by him officially, stating the time and place of the sale, the name of the purchaser, and the amount of money received, with an itemized account of the expenses attending the sale. Such return shall be filed with the papers of the case.

TRCP 619. CITATION FOR DEFENDANT

The justice at the time he issues the warrant shall issue a citation to the defendant requiring him to answer before such justice at the first day of the next succeeding term of court, stating the time and place of holding the same, if he has jurisdiction to finally try the cause, and upon its being returned served, to proceed to judgment as in ordinary cases; and, if he has not such jurisdiction, the citation shall require the defendant to answer before the court to which the warrant was made returnable at or before ten o'clock a.m. of the Monday next after the expiration of twenty days from the date of service thereof, stating the place of holding the court, and shall be returned with the other papers to such court. If the defendant has removed from the county without service, the proper officer shall state this fact in his return on the citation; and the court shall proceed to try the case ex parte, and may enter judgment.

TRCP 620. PETITION

When the warrant is made returnable to the district or county court, the plaintiff shall file his petition within ten days from the date of the issuance of the writ.

SECTION 3. EXECUTIONS

TRCP 621. ENFORCEMENT OF JUDGMENT

The judgments of the district, county, and justice courts shall be enforced by execution or other appropriate process. Such execution or other process shall be returnable in thirty, sixty, or ninety days as requested by the plaintiff, his agent or attorney.

TRCP 621a. DISCOVERY & ENFORCEMENT OF JUDGMENT

At any time after rendition of judgment, and so long as said judgment has not been suspended by a supersedeas bond or by order of a proper court and has not become dormant as provided by Article 3773, V.A.T.S., the successful party may, for the purpose of obtaining information to aid in the enforcement of such judgment, initiate and maintain in the trial court in the same suit in which said judgment was rendered any discovery proceeding authorized by these rules for pre-trial matters. Also, at any time after rendition of judgment, either party may, for the purpose of obtaining information relevant to motions allowed by Texas Rules of Appellate Procedure 47[1] and 49[1] initiate and maintain in the trial court in the same suit in which said judgment was rendered any discovery proceeding authorized by these rules for pre-trial matters. The rules governing and related to such pre-trial discovery proceedings shall apply in like manner to discovery proceedings after judgment. The rights herein granted to the parties shall inure to their successors or assignees, in whole or in part. Judicial supervision of such discovery proceedings after judgment shall be the same as that provided by law or these rules for pre-trial discovery and proceedings insofar as applicable.

[1] Now TRAP 24 (effective Sept. 1, 1997).

TRCP 622. EXECUTION

An execution is a process of the court from which it is issued. The clerk of the district or county court or the justice of the peace, as the case may be, shall tax the costs in every case in which a final judgment has been rendered and shall issue execution to enforce such judgment and collect such costs. The execution and subsequent executions shall not be addressed to a particular county, but shall be addressed to any sheriff or any constable within the State of Texas.

TRCP 623. ON DEATH OF EXECUTOR

When an executor, administrator, guardian or trustee of an express trust dies, or ceases to be such executor, administrator, guardian or trustee after judgment, execution shall issue on such judgment in the name of his successor, upon an affidavit of such death or termination being filed with the clerk of the court or the justice of the peace, as the case may be, together with the certificate of the appointment of such successor under the hand and seal of the clerk of the court wherein the appointment was made.

TRCP 624. ON DEATH OF NOMINAL PLAINTIFF

When a person in whose favor a judgment is rendered for the use of another dies after judgment, execution shall issue in the name of the party for whose use the suit was brought upon an affidavit of such death being filed with the clerk of the court or the justice of the peace.

TRCP 625. ON MONEY OF DECEASED

If a sole defendant dies after judgment for money against him, execution shall not issue thereon, but the judgment may be proved up and paid in due course of administration.

TRCP 626. ON PROPERTY OF DECEASED

In any case of judgment other than a money judgment, where the sole defendant, or one or more of several joint defendants, shall die after judgment, upon an affidavit of such death being filed with the clerk, together with the certificate of the appointment of a representative of such decedent under the hand and seal of the clerk of the court wherein such appointment was made, the proper process on such judgment shall issue against such representative.

TRCP 627. TIME FOR ISSUANCE

If no supersedeas bond or notice of appeal, as required of agencies exempt from filing bonds, has been filed and approved, the clerk of the court or justice of the peace shall issue the execution upon such judgment upon application of the successful party or his attorney after the expiration of thirty days from the time a final judgment is signed. If a timely motion for new trial or in arrest of judgment is filed, the clerk shall issue the execution upon the judgment on application of the party or his attorney after the expiration of thirty days from the time the order overruling the motion is signed or from the time the motion is overruled by operation of law.

See also CPRC §65.013 et seq.

TRCP 628. EXECUTION WITHIN THIRTY DAYS

Such execution may be issued at any time before the thirtieth day upon the filing of an affidavit by the plaintiff in the judgment or his agent or attorney that the defendant is about to remove his personal property subject to execution by law out of the county, or is about to transfer or secrete such personal property for the purpose of defrauding his creditors.

See also CPRC §65.013 et seq.

TRCP 629. REQUISITES OF EXECUTION

The style of the execution shall be "The State of Texas." It shall be directed to any sheriff or any constable within the State of Texas. It shall be signed by the clerk or justice officially, and bear the seal of the court, if issued out of the district or county court, and shall require the officer to execute it according to its terms, and to make the costs which have been adjudged against the defendant in execution and the further costs of executing the writ. It shall describe the judgment, stating the court in which, and the time when, rendered, and the names of the parties in whose favor and against whom the judgment was rendered. A correct copy of the bill of costs taxed against the defendant in execution shall be attached to the writ. It shall require the officer to return it within thirty, sixty, or ninety days, as directed by the plaintiff or his attorney.

See also CPRC §65.013 et seq.

TRCP 630. EXECUTION ON JUDGMENT FOR MONEY

When an execution is issued upon a judgment for a sum of money, or directing the payment simply of a sum of money, it must specify in the body thereof the sum recovered or directed to be paid and the sum actually due when it is issued and the rate of interest upon the sum due. It must require the officer to satisfy the judgment and costs out of the property of the judgment debtor subject to execution by law.

See also CPRC §65.013 et seq.

TRCP 631. EXECUTION FOR SALE OF PARTICULAR PROPERTY

An execution issued upon a judgment for the sale of particular chattels or personal property or real estate, must particularly describe the property, and shall direct the officer to make the sale by previously giving the public notice of the time and place of sale required by law and these rules.

See also CPRC §65.013 et seq.

TRCP 632. EXECUTION FOR DELIVERY OF CERTAIN PROPERTY

An execution issued upon a judgment for the delivery of the possession of a chattel or personal property, or for the delivery of the possession of real property, shall particularly describe the property, and designate the party to whom the judgment awards the possession. The writ shall require the officer to deliver the possession of the property to the party entitled thereto.

See also CPRC §65.013 et seq.

TRCP 633. EXECUTION FOR POSSESSION OR VALUE OF PERSONAL PROPERTY

If the judgment be for the recovery of personal property or its value, the writ shall command the officer, in case a delivery thereof cannot be had, to levy and collect the value thereof for which the judgment was recovered, to be specified therein, out of any property of the party against whom judgment was rendered, liable to execution.

See also CPRC §65.013 et seq.

TRCP 634. EXECUTION SUPERSEDED

The clerk or justice of the peace shall immediately issue a writ of supersedeas suspending all further proceedings under any execution previously issued when a supersedeas bond is afterward filed and approved within the time prescribed by law or these rules.

See also CPRC §65.013 et seq.

TRCP 635. STAY OF EXECUTION IN JUSTICE COURT

At any time within ten days after the rendition of any judgment in a justice court, the justice may grant a stay of execution thereof for three months from the date of such judgment, if the person against whom such judgment was rendered shall, with one or more good and sufficient sureties, to be approved by the justice, appear before him and acknowledge themselves and each of them bound to the successful party in such judgment for the full amount thereof, with interest and costs, which acknowledgment shall be entered in writing on the docket, and signed by the persons binding themselves as sureties; provided, no such stay of execution shall be granted unless the party applying therefor shall first file an affidavit with the justice that he has not the money with which to pay such judgment, and that the enforcement of same by execution prior to three months would be a hardship upon him and would cause a sacrifice of his property which would not likely be caused should said execution be stayed. Such acknowledgment shall be entered by the justice on his docket and shall constitute a judgment against the defendant and such sureties, upon which execution shall issue in case the same is not paid on or before the expiration of such day.

See also CPRC §65.013 et seq.

TRCP 636. INDORSEMENTS BY OFFICER

The officer receiving the execution shall indorse thereon the exact hour and day when he received it. If he receives more than one on the same day against the same person he shall number them as received.

TRCP 637. LEVY OF EXECUTION

When an execution is delivered to an officer he shall proceed without delay to levy the same upon the property of the defendant found within his county not exempt from execution, unless otherwise directed by the plaintiff, his agent or attorney. The officer shall first call upon the defendant, if he can be found, or, if absent, upon his agent within the county, if known, to point out property to be levied upon, and the levy shall first be made upon the property designated by the defendant, or his agent. If in the opinion of the officer the property so designated will not sell for enough to satisfy the execution and costs of sale, he shall require an additional designation by the defendant. If no property be thus designated by the defendant, the officer shall levy the execution upon any property of the defendant subject to execution.

TRCP 638. PROPERTY NOT TO BE DESIGNATED

A defendant in execution shall not point out property which he has sold, mortgaged or conveyed in trust, or property exempt from forced sale.

TRCP 639. LEVY

In order to make a levy on real estate, it shall not be necessary for the officer to go upon the ground but it shall be sufficient for him to indorse such levy on the writ. Levy upon personal property is made by taking possession thereof, when the defendant in execution is entitled to the possession. Where the defendant in execution has an interest in personal property, but is not entitled to the possession thereof, a levy is made thereon by giving notice thereof to the person who is entitled to the possession, or one of them where there are several.

TRCP 640. LEVY ON STOCK RUNNING AT LARGE

A levy upon livestock running at large in a range, and which cannot be herded and penned without great inconvenience and expense, may be made by designating by reasonable estimate the number of animals and describing them by their marks and brands, or either; such levy shall be made in the presence of two or more credible persons, and notice thereof shall be given in writing to the owner or his herder or agent, if residing within the county and known to the officer.

TRCP 641. LEVY ON SHARES OF STOCK

A levy upon shares of stock of any corporation or joint stock company for which a certificate is outstanding is made by the officer seizing and taking possession of such certificate. Provided, however, that nothing herein shall be construed as restricting any rights granted under Section 8.317* of the Texas Uniform Commercial Code.

* **Editor's Note:** Deleted by Acts 1995, 74th Leg., ch. 962, §1, eff. Sept. 1, 1995. See B&CC §8.112.

TRCP 642. REPEALED

TRCP 643. LEVY ON GOODS PLEDGED OR MORTGAGED

Goods and chattels pledged, assigned or mortgaged as security for any debt or contract, may be levied upon and sold on execution against the person making the pledge, assignment or mortgage subject thereto; and the purchaser shall be entitled to the possession when it is held by the pledgee, assignee or mortgagee, on complying with the conditions of the pledge, assignment or mortgage.

TRCP 644. MAY GIVE DELIVERY BOND

Any personal property taken in execution may be returned to the defendant by the officer upon the delivery by the defendant to him of a bond, payable to the plaintiff, with two or more good and sufficient sureties, to be approved by the officer, conditioned that the property shall be delivered to the officer at the time and place named in the bond, to be sold according to law, or for the payment to the officer of a fair value thereof, which shall be stated in the bond.

TRCP 645. PROPERTY MAY BE SOLD BY DEFENDANT

Where property has been replevied, as provided in the preceding rule, the defendant may sell or dispose of the same, paying the officer the stipulated value thereof.

TRCP 646. FORFEITED DELIVERY BOND

In case of the non-delivery of the property according to the terms of the delivery bond, and non-payment of the value thereof, the officer shall forthwith indorse the bond "Forfeited" and return the same to the clerk of the court or the justice of the peace from which the execution issued; whereupon, if the judgment remain unsatisfied in whole or in part, the clerk or justice shall issue execution against the principal debtor and the sureties on the bond for the amount due, not exceeding the stipulated value of the property, upon which execution no delivery bond shall be taken, which instruction shall be indorsed by the clerk or justice on the execution.

TRCP 646a. SALE OF REAL PROPERTY

Real property taken by virtue of any execution shall be sold at public auction, at the courthouse door of the county, unless the court orders that such sale be at the place where the real property is situated, on the first Tuesday of the month, between the hours of ten o'clock, a.m. and four o'clock, p.m.

TRCP 647. NOTICE OF SALE OF REAL ESTATE

The time and place of sale of real estate under execution, order of sale, or venditioni exponas, shall be advertised by the officer by having the notice thereof published in the English language once a week for three consecutive weeks preceding such sale, in some newspaper published in said county. The first of said publications shall appear not less than twenty days immediately preceding the day of sale. Said notice shall contain a statement of the authority by virtue of which the sale is to be made, the time of levy, and the time and place of sale; it shall also contain a brief description of the property to be sold, and shall give the number of acres, original survey, locality in the county, and the name by which the land is most generally known, but it shall not be necessary for it to contain field notes. Publishers of newspapers shall charge the legal rate of Two (2) Cents per word for the first insertion of such publication and One (1) Cent per word for such subsequent insertions, or such newspapers shall be entitled to charge for such publication at a rate equal to but not in excess of the published word or line rate of that newspaper for such class of advertising. If there be no newspaper published in the county, or none which will publish the notice of sale for the compensation herein fixed, the officer shall then post such notice in writing in three public places in the county, one of which shall be at the courthouse door of such county, for at least twenty days successively next before the day of sale. The officer making the levy shall give the defendant, or his attorney, written notice of such sale, either in person or by mail, which notice shall substantially conform to the foregoing requirements.

TRCP 648. "COURTHOUSE DOOR" DEFINED

By the term "courthouse door" of a county is meant either of the principal entrances to the house provided by the proper authority for the holding of the district court. If from any cause there is no such house, the door of the house where the district court was last held in that county shall be deemed to be the courthouse door. Where the courthouse, or house used by the court, has been destroyed by fire or other cause, and another has not been designated by the proper authority, the place where such house stood shall be deemed to be the courthouse door.

TRCP 649. SALE OF PERSONAL PROPERTY

Personal property levied on under execution shall be offered for sale on the premises where it is taken in execution, or at the courthouse door of the county, or at some other place if, owing to the nature of the property, it is more convenient to exhibit it to purchasers at such place. Personal property susceptible of being exhibited shall not be sold unless the same be present and subject to the view of those attending the sale, except shares of stock in joint stock or incorporated companies, and in cases where the defendant in execution has merely an interest without right to the exclusive possession in which case the interest of defendant may be sold and conveyed without the presence or delivery of the property. When a levy is made upon livestock running at large on the range, it is not necessary that such stock, or any part thereof, be present at the place of sale, and the purchaser at such sale is authorized to gather and pen such stock and select therefrom the number purchased by him.

TRCP 650. NOTICE OF SALE OF PERSONAL PROPERTY

Previous notice of the time and place of the sale of any personal property levied on under execution shall be given by posting notice thereof for ten days successively immediately prior to the day of sale at the courthouse door of any county and at the place where the sale is to be made.

TRCP 651. WHEN EXECUTION NOT SATISFIED

When the property levied upon does not sell for enough to satisfy the execution, the officer shall proceed anew, as in the first instance, to make the residue.

TRCP 652. PURCHASER FAILING TO COMPLY

If any person shall bid off property at any sale made by virtue of an execution, and shall fail to comply with the terms of the sale, he shall be liable to pay the plaintiff in execution twenty per cent on the value of the property thus bid off, besides costs, to be recovered on motion, five days notice of such motion being given to such purchaser; and should the property on a second sale bring less than on the former, he shall be liable to pay to the defendant in execution all loss which he sustains thereby, to be recovered on motion as above provided.

TRCP 653. RESALE OF PROPERTY

When the terms of the sale shall not be complied with by the bidder the levying officer shall proceed to sell the same property again on the same day, if there be sufficient time; but if not, he shall readvertise and sell the same as in the first instance.

TRCP 654. RETURN OF EXECUTION

The levying officer shall make due return of the execution, in writing and signed by him officially, stating concisely what such officer has done in pursuance of the requirements of the writ and of the law. The return shall be filed with the clerk of the court or the justice of the peace as the case may be. The execution shall be returned forthwith if satisfied by the collection of the money or if ordered by the plaintiff or his attorney indorsed thereon.

TRCP 655. RETURN OF EXECUTION BY MAIL

When an execution is placed in the hands of an officer of a county other than the one in which the judgment is rendered, return may be made by mail; but money cannot be thus sent except by direction of the party entitled to receive the same or his attorney of record.

TRCP 656. EXECUTION DOCKET

The clerk of each court shall keep an execution docket in which he shall enter a statement of all executions as they are issued by him, specifying the names of the parties, the amount of the judgment, the amount due thereon, the rate of interest when it exceeds six per cent, the costs, the date of issuing the execution, to whom delivered, and the return of the officer thereon, with the date of such return. Such docket entries shall be taken and deemed to be a record. The clerk shall keep an index and cross-index to the execution docket. When execution is in favor or against several persons, it shall be indexed in the name of each person. Any clerk who shall fail to keep said execution docket and index thereto, or shall neglect to make the entries therein, shall be liable upon his official bond to any person injured for the amount of damages sustained by such neglect.

SECTION 4. GARNISHMENT

TRCP 657. JUDGMENT FINAL FOR GARNISHMENT

In the case mentioned in subsection 3, section 63.001, Civil Practice and Remedies Code, the judgment whether based upon a liquidated demand or an unliquidated demand, shall be deemed final and subsisting for the purpose of garnishment from and after the date it is signed, unless a supersedeas bond shall have been approved and filed in accordance with Texas Rule of Appellate Procedure 47.[1]

[1] Now TRAP 24 (effective Sept. 1, 1997).

TRCP 658. APPLICATION FOR WRIT OF GARNISHMENT & ORDER

Either at the commencement of a suit or at any time during its progress the plaintiff may file an application for a writ of garnishment. Such application shall be supported by affidavits of the plaintiff, his agent, his attorney, or other person having knowledge of relevant facts. The application shall comply with all statutory requirements and shall state the grounds for issuing the writ and the specific facts relied upon by the plaintiff to warrant the required findings by the court. The writ shall not be quashed because two or more grounds are stated conjunctively or disjunctively. The application and any affidavits shall be made on personal knowledge and shall set forth such facts as would be admissible in evidence; provided that facts may be stated based upon information and belief if the grounds of such belief are specifically stated.

No writ shall issue before final judgment except upon written order of the court after a hearing, which may be ex parte. The court in its order granting the application shall make specific findings of facts to support the statutory grounds found to exist, and shall specify the maximum value of property or indebtedness that may be garnished and the amount of bond required of plaintiff. Such bond shall be in an amount which, in the opinion of the court, shall adequately compensate defendant in the event plaintiff fails to prosecute his suit to effect, and pay all damages and costs as shall be adjudged against him for wrongfully suing out the writ of garnishment. The court shall further find in its order the amount of bond required of defendant to replevy, which, unless defendant exercises his option as provided under Rule 664, shall be the amount of plaintiff's claim, one year's accrual of interest if allowed by law on the claim, and the estimated costs of court. The order may direct the issuance of several writs at the same time, or in succession, to be sent to different counties.

TRCP 658a. BOND FOR GARNISHMENT

No writ of garnishment shall issue before final judgment until the party applying therefor has filed with the officer authorized to issue such writ a bond payable to the defendant in the amount fixed by the court's order, with sufficient surety or sureties as provided by statute, conditioned that the plaintiff will prosecute his suit to effect and pay to the extent of the penal amount of the bond all damages and costs as may be adjudged against him for wrongfully suing out such writ of garnishment.

After notice to the opposite party, either before or after the issuance of the writ, the defendant or plaintiff may file a motion to increase or reduce the amount of such bond, or to question the sufficiency of the sureties. Upon hearing, the court shall enter its order with respect to such bond and the sufficiency of the sureties.

Should it be determined from the garnishee's answer if such is not controverted that the garnishee is indebted to the defendant, or has in his hands effects belonging to the defendant, in an amount or value less than the amount of the debt claimed by the plaintiff, then after notice to the defendant the court in which such garnishment is pending upon hearing may reduce the required amount of such bond to double the sum of the garnishee's indebtedness to the defendant plus the value of the effects in his hands belonging to the defendant.

TRCP 659. CASE DOCKETED

When the foregoing requirements of these rules have been complied with, the judge, or clerk, or justice of the peace, as the case may be, shall docket the case in the name of the plaintiff as plaintiff and of the garnishee as defendant; and shall immediately issue a writ of garnishment directed to the garnishee, commanding him to appear before the court out of which the same is issued at or before 10 o'clock a.m. of the Monday next following the expiration of twenty days from the date the writ was served, if the writ is issued out of the district or county court; or the Monday next after the expiration of ten days from the date the writ was served, if the writ is issued out of the justice court. The writ shall command the garnishee to answer under oath upon such return date what, if anything, he is indebted to the defendant, and was when the writ was served, and what effects, if any, of the defendant he has in his possession, and had when such writ was served, and what other persons, if any, within his knowledge, are indebted to the defendant or have effects belonging to him in their possession.

TRCP 660. REPEALED

TRCP 661. FORM OF WRIT

The following form of writ may be used:

"The State of Texas.

"To E.F., Garnishee, greeting:

"Whereas, in the ______ Court of ____________ County (if a justice court, state also the number of the precinct), in a certain cause wherein A.B. is plaintiff and C.D. is defendant, the plaintiff, claiming an indebtedness against the said C.D. of ___________ dollars, besides interest and costs of suit, has applied for a writ of garnishment against you, E.F.; therefore you are hereby commanded to be and appear before said court at _________ in said county (if the writ is issued from the county or district court, here proceed: 'at 10 o'clock a.m. on the Monday next following the expiration of twenty days from the date of service hereof.' If the writ is issued from a justice of the peace court, here proceed: 'at or before 10 o'clock a.m. on the Monday next after the expiration of ten days from the date of service hereof.' In either event, proceed as follows:) then and there to answer upon oath what, if anything, you are indebted to the said C.D., and were when this writ was served upon you, and what effects, if any, of the said C.D. you have in your possession, and had when this writ was served, and what other persons, if any, within your knowledge, are indebted to the said C.D. or have effects belonging to him in their possession. You are further commanded NOT to pay to defendant any debt or to deliver to him any effects, pending further order of this court. Herein fail not, but make due answer as the law directs."

TRCP 662. DELIVERY OF WRIT

The writ of garnishment shall be dated and tested as other writs, and may be delivered to the sheriff or constable by the officer who issued it, or he may deliver it to the plaintiff, his agent or attorney, for that purpose.

TRCP 663. EXECUTION & RETURN OF WRIT

The sheriff or constable receiving the writ of garnishment shall immediately proceed to execute the same by delivering a copy thereof to the garnishee, and shall make return thereof as of other citations.

TRCP 663a. SERVICE OF WRIT ON DEFENDANT

The defendant shall be served in any manner prescribed for service of citation or as provided in Rule 21a with a copy of the writ of garnishment, the application, accompanying affidavits and orders of the court as soon as practicable following the service of the writ. There shall be prominently displayed on the face of the copy of the writ served on the defendant, in ten-point type and in a manner calculated to advise a reasonably attentive person of its contents, the following:

"To __________, Defendant:

"You are hereby notified that certain properties alleged to be owned by you have been garnished. If you claim any rights in such property, you are advised:

"YOU HAVE A RIGHT TO REGAIN POSSESSION OF THE PROPERTY BY FILING A REPLEVY BOND. YOU HAVE A RIGHT TO SEEK TO REGAIN POSSESSION OF THE PROPERTY BY FILING WITH THE COURT A MOTION TO DISSOLVE THIS WRIT."

TRCP 664. DEFENDANT MAY REPLEVY

At any time before judgment, should the garnished property not have been previously claimed or sold, the defendant may replevy the same, or any part thereof, or the proceeds from the sale of the property if it has been sold under order of the court, by giving bond with sufficient surety or sureties as provided by statute, to be approved by the officer who levied the writ, payable to plaintiff, in the amount fixed by the court's order, or, at the defendant's option, for the value of the property or indebtedness sought to be replevied (to be estimated by the officer), plus one year's interest thereon at the legal rate from the date of the bond, conditioned that the defendant, garnishee, shall satisfy, to the extent of the penal amount of the bond, any judgment which may be rendered against him in such action.

On reasonable notice to the opposing party (which may be less than three days) either party shall have the right to prompt judicial review of the amount of bond required, denial of bond, sufficiency of sureties, and estimated value of the property, by the court which authorized issuance of the writ. The court's determination may be made upon the basis of affidavits, if uncontroverted, setting forth such facts as would be admissible in evidence; otherwise, the parties shall submit evidence. The court shall forthwith enter its order either approving or modifying the requirements of the officer or of the court's prior order, and such order of the court shall supersede and control with respect to such matters.

On reasonable notice to the opposing party (which may be less than three days) the defendant shall have the right to move the court for a substitution of property, of equal value as that garnished, for the property garnished. Provided that there has been located sufficient property of the defendant's to satisfy the order of garnishment, the court may authorize substitution of one or more items of defendant's property for all or for part of the property garnished. The court shall first make findings as to the value of the property to be substituted. If property is substituted, the property released from garnishment shall be delivered to defendant, if such property is personal property, and all liens upon such property from the original order of garnishment or modification thereof shall be terminated. Garnishment of substituted property shall be deemed to have existed from date of garnishment on the original property garnished, and no property on which liens have become affixed since the date of garnishment of the original property may be substituted.

TRCP 664a. DISSOLUTION OR MODIFICATION OF WRIT OF GARNISHMENT

A defendant whose property or account has been garnished or any intervening party who claims an interest in such property or account, may by sworn written motion, seek to vacate, dissolve or modify the writ of garnishment, and the order directing its issuance, for any grounds or cause, extrinsic or intrinsic. Such motion shall admit or deny each finding of the order directing the issuance of the writ except where the movant is unable to admit or deny the finding, in which case movant shall set forth the reasons why he cannot admit or deny. Unless the parties agree to an extension of time, the motion shall be heard promptly, after reasonable notice to the plaintiff (which may be less than three days), and the issue shall be determined not later than ten days after the motion is filed. The filing of the motion shall stay any further proceedings under the writ, except for any orders concerning the care, preservation or sale of any perishable property, until a hearing is had, and the issue is determined. The writ shall be dissolved unless, at such hearing, the plaintiff shall prove the grounds relied upon for its issuance, but the court may modify its previous order granting the writ and the writ issued pursuant thereto. The movant shall, however, have the burden to prove that the reasonable value of the property garnished exceeds the amount necessary to secure the debt, interest for one year, and probable costs. He shall also have the burden to prove facts to justify substitution of property.

The court's determination may be made upon the basis of affidavits, if uncontroverted, setting forth such facts as would be admissible in evidence; otherwise, the parties shall submit evidence. The court may make all such orders including orders concerning the care, preservation or disposition of the property (or the proceeds therefrom if the same has been sold), as justice may require. If the movant has given a replevy bond, an order to vacate or dissolve the writ shall vacate the replevy bond and discharge the sureties thereon, and if the court modifies its order or the writ issued pursuant thereto, it shall make such further orders with respect to the bond as may be consistent with its modification.

TRCP 665. ANSWER TO WRIT

The answer of the garnishee shall be under oath, in writing and signed by him, and shall make true answers to the several matters inquired of in the writ of garnishment.

See also *O'Connor's Texas Rules*, "The Answer—Denying Liability," ch. 3-E.

TRCP 666. GARNISHEE DISCHARGED

If it appears from the answer of the garnishee that he is not indebted to the defendant, and was not so indebted when the writ of garnishment was served upon him, and that he has not in his possession any effects of the defendant and had not when the writ was served, and if he has either denied that any other persons within his knowledge are indebted to the defendant or have in their possession effects belonging to the defendant, or else has named such persons, should the answer of the garnishee not be controverted as hereinafter provided, the court shall enter judgment discharging the garnishee.

TRCP 667. JUDGMENT BY DEFAULT

If the garnishee fails to file an answer to the writ of garnishment at or before the time directed in the writ, it shall be lawful for the court, at any time after judgment shall have been rendered against the defendant, and on or after appearance day, to render judgment by default, as in other civil cases, against such garnishee for the full amount of such judgment against the defendant together with all interest and costs that may have accrued in the main case and also in the garnishment proceedings. The answer of the garnishee may be filed as in any other civil case at any time before such default judgment is rendered.

TRCP 668. JUDGMENT WHEN GARNISHEE IS INDEBTED

Should it appear from the answer of the garnishee or should it be otherwise made to appear and be found by the court that the garnishee is indebted to the defendant in any amount, or was so indebted when the writ of garnishment was served, the court shall render judgment for the plaintiff against the garnishee for the amount so admitted or found to be due to the defendant from the garnishee, unless such amount is in excess of the amount of the plaintiff's judgment against the defendant with interest and costs, in which case, judgment shall be rendered against the garnishee for the full amount of the judgment already rendered against the defendant, together with interest and costs of the suit in the original case and also in the garnishment proceedings. If the garnishee fail or refuse to pay such judgment rendered against him, execution shall issue thereon in the same manner and under the same conditions as is or may be provided for the issuance of execution in other cases.

TRCP 669. JUDGMENT FOR EFFECTS

Should it appear from the garnishee's answer, or otherwise, that the garnishee has in his possession, or had when the writ was served, any effects of the defendant liable to execution, including any certificates of stock in any corporation or joint stock company, the court shall render a decree ordering sale of such effects under execution in satisfaction of plaintiff's judgment and directing the garnishee to deliver them, or so much thereof as shall be necessary to satisfy plaintiff's judgment, to the proper officer for that purpose.

TRCP 670. REFUSAL TO DELIVER EFFECTS

Should the garnishee adjudged to have effects of the defendant in his possession, as provided in the preceding rule, fail or refuse to deliver them to the sheriff or constable on such demand, the officer shall immediately make return of such failure or refusal, whereupon on motion of the plaintiff, the garnishee shall be cited to show cause upon a date to be fixed by the court why he should not be attached for contempt of court for such failure or refusal. If the garnishee fails to show some good and sufficient excuse for such failure or refusal, he shall be fined for such contempt and imprisoned until he shall deliver such effects.

TRCP 671. REPEALED

TRCP 672. SALE OF EFFECTS

The sale so ordered shall be conducted in all respects as other sales of personal property under execution; and the officer making such sale shall execute a transfer of such effects or interest to the purchaser, with a brief recital of the judgment of the court under which the same was sold.

TRCP 673. MAY TRAVERSE ANSWER

If the plaintiff should not be satisfied with the answer of any garnishee, he may controvert the same by his affidavit stating that he has good reason to believe, and does believe, that the answer of the garnishee is incorrect, stating in what particular he believes the same to be incorrect. The defendant may also, in like manner, controvert the answer of the garnishee.

TRCP 674. TRIAL OF ISSUE

If the garnishee whose answer is controverted, is a resident of the county in which the proceeding is pending, an issue shall be formed under the direction of the court and tried as in other cases.

TRCP 675. DOCKET & NOTICE

The clerk of the court or the justice of the peace, on receiving certified copies filed in the county of the garnishee's residence under the provisions of the statutes, shall docket the case in the name of the plaintiff as plaintiff, and of the garnishee as defendant, and issue a notice to the garnishee, stating that his answer has been so controverted, and that such issue will stand for trial on the docket of such court. Such notice shall be directed to the garnishee, be dated and tested as other process from such court, and served by delivering a copy thereof to the garnishee. It shall be returnable, if issued from the district or county court, at ten o'clock a.m. of the Monday next after the expiration of twenty days from the date of its service; and if issued from the justice court, to the next term of such court convening after the expiration of twenty days after the service of such notice.

TRCP 676. ISSUE TRIED AS IN OTHER CASES

Upon the return of such notice served, an issue shall be formed under the direction of the court and tried as in other cases.

TRCP 677. COSTS

Where the garnishee is discharged upon his answer, the costs of the proceeding, including a reasonable compensation to the garnishee, shall be taxed against the plaintiff; where the answer of the garnishee has not been controverted and the garnishee is held thereon, such costs shall be taxed against the defendant and included in the execution provided for in this section; where the answer is contested, the costs shall abide the issue of such contest.

TRCP 678. GARNISHEE DISCHARGED ON PROOF

It shall be a sufficient answer to any claim of the defendant against the garnishee founded on an indebtedness of such garnishee, or on the possession by him of any effects, for the garnishee to show that such indebtedness has been paid, or such effects, including any certificates of stock in any incorporated or joint stock company, have been delivered to any sheriff or constable as provided for in Rule 669.

TRCP 679. AMENDMENT

Clerical errors in the affidavit, bond, or writ of garnishment or the officer's return thereof, may upon application in writing to the judge or justice of the court in which the suit is filed, and after notice to the opponent, be amended in such manner and on such terms as the judge or justice shall authorize by an order entered in the minutes of the court (or noted on the docket of the justice of the peace), provided such amendment appears to the judge or justice to be in furtherance of justice.

SECTION 5. INJUNCTIONS

TRCP 680. TEMPORARY RESTRAINING ORDER

No temporary restraining order shall be granted without notice to the adverse party unless it clearly appears from specific facts shown by affidavit or by the verified complaint that immediate and irreparable injury, loss, or damage will result to the applicant before notice can be served and a hearing had thereon. Every temporary restraining order granted without notice shall be endorsed with the date and hour of issuance; shall be filed forthwith in the clerk's office and entered of record; shall define the injury and state why it is irreparable and why the order was granted without notice; and shall expire by its terms within such time after signing, not to exceed fourteen days, as the court fixes, unless within the time so fixed the order, for good cause shown, is extended for a like period or unless the party against whom the order is directed consents that it may be extended for a longer period. The reasons for the extension shall be entered of record. No more than one extension may be granted unless subsequent extensions are unopposed. In case a temporary restraining order is granted without notice, the application for a temporary injunction shall be set down for hearing at the earliest possible date and takes precedence of all matters except older matters of the same character; and when the application comes on for hearing the party who obtained the temporary restraining order shall proceed with the application for a temporary injunction and, if he does not do so, the court shall dissolve the temporary restraining order. On two days' notice to the party who obtained the temporary restraining order without notice or on such shorter notice to that party as the court may prescribe, the adverse party may appear and move its dissolution or modification and in that event the court shall proceed to hear and determine such motion as expeditiously as the ends of justice require.

Every restraining order shall include an order setting a certain date for hearing on the temporary or permanent injunction sought.

Caution: TRCP 680 is affected by the following sections in the Fam. Code: §§6.501, 6.503, 105.001.

See also CPRC ch. 65; *O'Connor's Texas Rules*, "Plaintiff's Pleadings for Injunctive Relief," ch. 2-C; *O'Connor's Texas Forms*, FORMS 2C.

Author's Comment: Temporary restraining orders under Fam. Code §§6.501 and 105.001 are not required to (1) define the injury, (2) state why it is irreparable, (3) state why the order was granted without notice, or (4) include an order setting the suit for trial on the merits. Fam. Code §§6.503, 105.001(b).

Ex Parte Lesikar, 899 S.W.2d 654, 654 (Tex.1995). "Extensions of temporary restraining orders, absent some special statutory authority ... must meet the limitations of [TRCP] 680, including in particular written orders and written extensions. An oral extension of a TRO is ineffective, and the contemnor must have notice of the actual written extension before he can be charged with contempt."

Isuani v. Manske-Sheffield Radiology Group, 802 S.W.2d 235, 236 (Tex.1991). "If, while on the appeal of the granting or denying of the temporary injunction, the trial court renders final judgment, the case on appeal becomes moot."

Davis v. Huey, 571 S.W.2d 859, 862 (Tex.1978). "At a hearing upon the request for a temporary injunction the only question before the trial court is whether the applicant is entitled to preservation of the status quo of the subject matter of the suit pending trial on the merits. On appeal the reviewing court is limited in its consideration as to whether the trial court abused its discretion in making the foregoing determination."

Commonwealth Mortg. Corp. v. Wadkins, 709 S.W.2d 679, 680 (Tex.App.—Houston [14th Dist.] 1985, no writ). "Section 3.58 [now §6.501] of the Family Code ... authorizes a domestic relations court to grant temporary orders for the 'preservation of the property and the protection of the parties.' The orders may be directed to one or both parties and need not define the injury or state why it is irreparable or state why the order was granted without notice. "

TRCP 681. TEMPORARY INJUNCTIONS: NOTICE

No temporary injunction shall be issued without notice to the adverse party.

See also CPRC §51.014(a)(4) (interlocutory appeal of temporary injunction).

State v. Cook United, Inc., 469 S.W.2d 709, 712 (Tex.1971). "In the absence of notice to or service of citation upon the Attorney General of the State of Texas ... the temporary injunction is hereby modified to enjoin only the county and district attorneys of Tarrant and McLennan Counties [who had notice], and shall have no effect on the Attorney General of the State of Texas or the other district and county attorneys in this State."

PILF Invs., Inc. v. Arlitt, 940 S.W.2d 255, 260 (Tex. App.—San Antonio 1997, no writ). "[N]otice on a motion for injunctive relief is inadequate to the extent a non-movant party, who is ultimately enjoined, is not served with notice of the hearing."

TRCP 682. SWORN PETITION

No writ of injunction shall be granted unless the applicant therefor shall present his petition to the judge verified by his affidavit and containing a plain and intelligible statement of the grounds for such relief.

Caution: TRCP 682 is affected by the following sections in the Fam. Code: §§6.503, 105.001.

See also ***O'Connor's Texas Rules***, "Plaintiff's Pleadings for Injunctive Relief," ch. 2-C; ***O'Connor's Texas Forms***, FORMS 2C.

Author's Comment: Most temporary restraining orders and temporary injunctions under Fam. Code §§6.501, 6.502, and 105.001 do not require a sworn affidavit or a verified pleading stating specific facts showing immediate and irreparable injury. Fam. Code §§6.503, 105.001(b). However, temporary injunctions require a verified pleading or affidavit if they (1) attach the body of the child, (2) take the child into the possession of the court or of a parent, or (3) exclude a parent from possession of or access to a child. Fam. Code §105.001(c).

Walling v. Metcalfe, 863 S.W.2d 56, 57 (Tex.1993). "A trial court may grant a temporary writ of injunction to preserve the status quo pending trial even though the applicant's prayer does not include a claim for equitable relief following determination of the merits. In such cases, however, a temporary injunction should only issue if the applicant establishes a probable right on final trial to the relief sought, and a probable injury in the interim."

Town of Palm Valley v. Johnson, 17 S.W.3d 281, 288 (Tex.App.—Corpus Christi 2000), *pet. denied*, ___ S.W.3d ___ (Tex.2001) (No.00-0650; 9-20-01). "A verified petition for injunctive relief is not required, however, when a full evidentiary hearing on evidence independent of the petition has been held."

Crystal Media, Inc. v. HCI Acquisition Corp., 773 S.W.2d 732, 734 (Tex.App.—San Antonio 1989, no writ). "If the insufficiency of the verification is not objected to prior to the introduction of evidence the defect has been waived. [¶] Further, the court allowed an amendment of the verification…."

TRCP 683. FORM & SCOPE OF INJUNCTION OR RESTRAINING ORDER

Every order granting an injunction and every restraining order shall set forth the reasons for its issuance; shall be specific in terms; shall describe in reasonable detail and not by reference to the complaint or other document, the act or acts sought to be restrained; and is binding only upon the parties to the action, their officers, agents, servants, employees, and attorneys, and upon those persons in active concert or participation with them who receive actual notice of the order by personal service or otherwise.

Every order granting a temporary injunction shall include an order setting the cause for trial on the merits with respect to the ultimate relief sought. The appeal of a temporary injunction shall constitute no cause for delay of the trial.

Caution: TRCP 683 is affected by the following sections in the Fam. Code: §§6.501, 6.502, 6.503, 105.001.

See also ***O'Connor's Texas Rules***, "Plaintiff's Original Petition," ch. 2-B; "Request for Findings of Fact," ch. 10-E.

Author's Comment: Temporary restraining orders and injunctions under Fam. Code §§6.501, 6.502, and 105.001 do not require an order setting the cause for trial on the merits. Fam. Code §§6.503, 105.001(b)(3).

Qwest Comm. Corp. v. AT&T Corp., 24 S.W.3d 334, 337 (Tex.2000). "The [TRCPs] require that an order granting a temporary injunction set the cause for trial on the merits and fix the amount of security to be given by the applicant. These procedural requirements are mandatory, and an order granting a temporary injunction that does not meet them is subject to being declared void and dissolved."

InterFirst Bank San Felipe v. Paz Constr. Co., 715 S.W.2d 640, 641 (Tex.1986). "The requirements of [TRCP] 683 are mandatory and must be strictly followed. When a temporary injunction order does not adhere to the requirements of Rule 683 the injunction order is subject to being declared void and dissolved."

Ex parte Slavin, 412 S.W.2d 43, 44 (Tex.1967). An injunction decree "must spell out the details of compliance in clear, specific and unambiguous terms so that such person will readily know exactly what duties or obligations are imposed upon him."

Evans v. C. Woods, Inc., 34 S.W.3d 581, 583 (Tex. App.—Tyler 1999, no pet.). "[W]e … hold that [CPRC] §51.014(b) does not absolve the trial court from its mandatory rule 683 duty to include within its temporary injunction order an order setting the cause for trial on the merits."

Fasken v. Darby, 901 S.W.2d 591, 592-93 (Tex. App.—El Paso 1995, no writ). "[T]he trial court must state in the injunction the reasons why the court deems it proper to issue the injunction, including the reasons why the applicant will suffer injury if the injunction is not issued. An injunction that fails to identify the harm that will be suffered if it does not issue must be declared void and be dissolved. This rule operates to invalidate an injunction even when the complaining party fails to bring the error to the trial court's attention."

Wells v. Wells, 539 S.W.2d 220, 222 (Tex.App.—Houston [1st Dist.] 1976, writ dism'd). "The trial court in a divorce proceeding is authorized by statute to grant temporary relief as it may deem necessary and equitable with respect to the parties and their property. The order in question recited that its provisions were necessary and equitable for the preservation of the parties' rights. This was sufficient compliance with Rule 683, ... requiring that every injunctive order set forth the reasons for its issuance."

TRCP 684. APPLICANT'S BOND

In the order granting any temporary restraining order or temporary injunction, the court shall fix the amount of security to be given by the applicant. Before the issuance of the temporary restraining order or temporary injunction the applicant shall execute and file with the clerk a bond to the adverse party, with two or more good and sufficient sureties, to be approved by the clerk, in the sum fixed by the judge, conditioned that the applicant will abide the decision which may be made in the cause, and that he will pay all sums of money and costs that may be adjudged against him if the restraining order or temporary injunction shall be dissolved in whole or in part.

Where the temporary restraining order or temporary injunction is against the State, a municipality, a State agency, or a subdivision of the State in its governmental capacity, and is such that the State, municipality, State agency, or subdivision of the State in its governmental capacity, has no pecuniary interest in the suit and no monetary damages can be shown, the bond shall be allowed in the sum fixed by the judge, and the liability of the applicant shall be for its face amount if the restraining order or temporary injunction shall be dissolved in whole or in part. The discretion of the trial court in fixing the amount of the bond shall be subject to review. Provided that under equitable circumstances and for good cause shown by affidavit or otherwise the court rendering judgment on the bond may allow recovery for less than its full face amount, the action of the court to be subject to review.

Caution: TRCP 684 is affected by the following sections in the Fam. Code: §§6.503, 105.001.

See also TRCP 693a, 695a.

Author's Comment: The court may dispense with the requirement of a bond involving temporary orders under Fam. Code §§6.501, 6.502, and 105.001; see TRCP 693a.

DeSantis v. Wackenhut Corp., 793 S.W.2d 670, 685-86 (Tex.1990). "To prevail upon [a suit on a bond], the claimant must prove that the [TRO] or temporary injunction was issued or perpetuated when it should not have been, and that it was later dissolved. The claimant need not prove that the [TRO] or temporary injunction was obtained maliciously or without probable cause."

Ex parte Jordan, 787 S.W.2d 367, 368 (Tex.1990). Jordan "argues the order [for temporary injunction] is void because it does not require a separate bond as required by [TRCP] 684. We agree." *But see* ***Wells***, below.

Ex parte Lesher, 651 S.W.2d 734, 736 (Tex.1983). "[T]he provisions of [TRCP] 684 are mandatory and an order of injunction issued without a bond is void on its face." *But see* ***Wells***, below.

Wells v. Wells, 539 S.W.2d 220, 222 (Tex.App.—Houston [1st Dist.] 1976, writ dism'd). "In a divorce case, the trial court is specifically empowered to dispense with the necessity of a bond in connection with an ancillary injunction by one spouse against the other. It is not essential to the validity of the order that the court's determination in this respect be evidenced on the face of the order."

TRCP 685. FILING & DOCKETING

Upon the grant of a temporary restraining order or an order fixing a time for hearing upon an application for a temporary injunction, the party to whom the same is granted shall file his petition therefor, together with the order of the judge, with the clerk of the proper court; and, if such orders do not pertain to a pending suit in said court, the cause shall be entered on the docket of the court in its regular order in the name of the party applying for the writ as plaintiff and of the opposite party as defendant.

TRCP 686. CITATION

Upon the filing of such petition and order not pertaining to a suit pending in the court, the clerk of such court shall issue a citation to the defendant as in other civil cases, which shall be served and returned in like manner as ordinary citations issued from said court; provided, however, that when a temporary restraining order is issued and is accompanied with a true copy of plaintiff's petition, it shall not be necessary for the citation in the original suit to be accompanied with a copy of plaintiff's petition, nor contain a statement of the nature of plaintiff's demand, but it shall be sufficient for said citation to refer to plaintiff's claim as set forth in a true copy of plaintiff's petition which accompanies the temporary restraining order; and provided further that the court may have a hearing upon an application for a temporary restraining order or temporary injunction at such time and upon such reasonable notice given in such manner as the court may direct.

TRCP 687. REQUISITES OF WRIT

The writ of injunction shall be sufficient if it contains substantially the following requisites:

(a) Its style shall be, "The State of Texas."

(b) It shall be directed to the person or persons enjoined.

(c) It must state the names of the parties to the proceedings, plaintiff and defendant, and the nature of the plaintiff's application, with the action of the judge thereon.

(d) It must command the person or persons to whom it is directed to desist and refrain from the commission or continuance of the act enjoined, or to obey and execute such order as the judge has seen proper to make.

(e) If it is a temporary restraining order, it shall state the day and time set for hearing, which shall not exceed fourteen days from the date of the court's order granting such temporary restraining order; but if it is a temporary injunction, issued after notice, it shall be made returnable at or before ten o'clock a.m. of the Monday next after the expiration of twenty days from the date of service thereof, as in the case of ordinary citations.

(f) It shall be dated and signed by the clerk officially and attested with the seal of his office and the date of its issuance must be indorsed thereon.

TRCP 688. CLERK TO ISSUE WRIT

When the petition, order of the judge and bond have been filed, the clerk shall issue the temporary restraining order or temporary injunction, as the case may be, in conformity with the terms of the order, and deliver the same to the sheriff or any constable of the county of the residence of the person enjoined, or to the applicant, as the latter shall direct. If several persons are enjoined, residing in different counties, the clerk shall issue such additional copies of the writ as shall be requested by the applicant.

Schliemann v. Garcia, 685 S.W.2d 690, 693 (Tex. App.—San Antonio 1984, orig. proceeding). The "order was improper for several reasons. ... The injunction was not properly issued or served."

TRCP 689. SERVICE & RETURN

The officer receiving a writ of injunction shall indorse thereon the date of its receipt by him, and shall forthwith execute the same by delivering to the party enjoined a true copy thereof. The original shall be returned to the court from which it issued on or before the return day named therein with the action of the officer indorsed thereon or annexed thereto showing how and when he executed the same.

TRCP 690. THE ANSWER

The defendant to an injunction proceeding may answer as in other civil actions; but no injunction shall be dissolved before final hearing because of the denial of the material allegations of the plaintiff's petition, unless the answer denying the same is verified by the oath of the defendant.

See also *O'Connor's Texas Rules*, "The Answer—Denying Liability," ch. 3-E.

Executive Tele-Comm. Sys., Inc. v. Buchbaum, 669 S.W.2d 400, 403 (Tex.App.—Dallas 1984, no writ). "The only prescribed response for a defendant to a temporary injunction proceeding is pronounced in [TRCP] 690, and the failure to answer does not impair the defendant's right to a full hearing. [A] party seeking an injunction cannot rely on the verified pleading rules to limit the defense of the nonmovant."

TRCP 691. BOND ON DISSOLUTION

Upon the dissolution of an injunction restraining the collection of money, by an interlocutory order of the court or judge, made in term time or vacation, if the petition be continued over for trial, the court or judge shall require of the defendant in such injunction proceedings a bond, with two or more good and sufficient sureties, to be approved by the clerk of the court, payable to the complainant in double the amount of the sum enjoined, and conditioned to refund to the complainant the amount of money, interest and costs which may be collected of him in the suit or proceeding enjoined if such injunction is made perpetual on final hearing. If such injunction is so perpetuated, the court, on motion of the complainant, may enter judgment against the principal and sureties in such bond for such amount as may be shown to have been collected from such defendant.

TRCP 692. DISOBEDIENCE

Disobedience of an injunction may be punished by the court or judge, in term time or in vacation, as a contempt. In case of such disobedience, the complainant, his agent or attorney, may file in the court in which such injunction is pending or with the judge in vacation, his affidavit stating what person is guilty of such disobedience and describing the acts constituting the same; and thereupon the court or judge shall cause to be issued an attachment for such person, directed to the sheriff or any constable of any county, and requiring such officer to arrest the person therein named if found within his county and have him before the court or judge at the time and place named in such writ; or said court or judge may issue a show cause order, directing and requiring such person to appear on such date as may be designated and show cause why he should not be adjudged in contempt of court. On return of such attachment or show cause order, the judge shall proceed to hear proof; and if satisfied that such person has disobeyed the injunction, either directly or indirectly, may commit such person to jail without bail until he purges himself of such contempt, in such manner and form as the court or judge may direct.

City of San Antonio v. Singleton, 858 S.W.2d 411, 412 (Tex.1993). "A trial court generally retains jurisdiction to review, open, vacate or modify a permanent injunction upon a showing of changed conditions. The authority to exercise that jurisdiction, however, must be balanced against principles of res judicata. Whether right or wrong, an injunction 'is not subject to impeachment in its application to the conditions that existed at its making.' [¶] There is no evidence in the record that conditions affecting the trial court's judgment have changed since the time it was originally rendered."

Ex parte Jackman, 663 S.W.2d 520, 524 (Tex. App.—Dallas 1983, orig. proceeding). "The injunction must be obeyed irrespective of the ultimate validity of the order, and a defendant cannot avoid compliance with the commands, or excuse his violation, of the injunction by simply moving to dissolve it or by the pendency of a motion to modify it."

TRCP 693. PRINCIPLES OF EQUITY APPLICABLE

The principles, practice and procedure governing courts of equity shall govern proceedings in injunctions when the same are not in conflict with these rules or the provisions of the statutes.

State v. Texas Pet Foods, Inc., 591 S.W.2d 800, 804 (Tex.1979). "[I]njunctive relief is proper when the trial court finds it justified under the rules of equity, notwithstanding a defendant's cessation of the activity or solemn promises to cease the activity. *At 805:* When it is determined that [a] statute is being violated, it is within the province of the district court to restrain it. The doctrine of balancing the equities has no application to ... statutorily authorized injunctive relief."

TRCP 693a. BOND IN DIVORCE CASE

In a divorce case the court in its discretion may dispense with the necessity of a bond in connection with an ancillary injunction in behalf of one spouse against the other.

Caution: TRCP 693a is affected by the following sections in the Fam. Code: §6.503, 105.001.

Author's Comment: The court may dispense with the requirement of a bond involving temporary orders under Fam. Code §§6.501, 6.502, and 105.001.

Eichelberger v. Hayton, 814 S.W.2d 179, 182 n.4 (Tex.App.—Houston [1st Dist.] 1991, writ denied). TRCP 693a "provides that in a divorce case, the court may dispense with the necessity of a bond in connection with an ancillary injunction in behalf of one spouse against the other. We note that the present cause of action is neither a divorce case, nor are the parties presently spouses. Thus, rule 693a is inapplicable."

Hopkins v. Hopkins, 539 S.W.2d 242, 246 (Tex. App.—Fort Worth 1976, writ dism'd). Since there was a third-party defendant, "the provisions of law entitling the trial court to waive requirement of bond in connection with injunctions deemed necessary as applied to petitioners and respondents in divorce cases are without application."

SECTION 6. MANDAMUS

TRCP 694. NO MANDAMUS WITHOUT NOTICE

No mandamus shall be granted by the district or county court on ex parte hearing, and any peremptory mandamus granted without notice shall be abated on motion.

SECTION 7. RECEIVERS

TRCP 695. NO RECEIVER OF IMMOVABLE PROPERTY APPOINTED WITHOUT NOTICE

Except where otherwise provided by statute, no receiver shall be appointed without notice to take charge of property which is fixed and immovable. When an application for appointment of a receiver to take possession of property of this type is filed, the judge or court shall set the same down for hearing and notice of such hearing shall be given to the adverse party by serving notice thereof not less than three days prior to such hearing. If the order finds that the defendant is a nonresident or that his whereabouts is unknown, the notice may be served by affixing the same in a conspicuous manner and place upon the property or if that is impracticable it may be served in such other manner as the court or judge may require.

See also *O'Connor's Texas Rules*, "Motion for New Trial," ch. 10-B.

Gray v. PHI Res., Ltd., 710 S.W.2d 566, 567 (Tex.1986). "In this case, no citation was issued, but instead, notice was provided by a 3-day posting of the petition. [T]he September 7 order did not comply with the terms of [TRCP 695]. *At 568:* Nonetheless, the 3-day posting of the petition is analogous to citation by publication … or other substituted service. Thus, the successors to [one of the D's] interest were entitled to bring their motion for new trial within two years from the date the judgment was signed."

Rusk v. Rusk, 5 S.W.3d 299, 309 (Tex.App.—Houston [14th Dist.] 1999, pet. denied). "We would hold that [TRCP] 695 is applicable to the appointment of receivers in marriage dissolution cases involving fixed and immovable property. Otherwise, every divorce proceeding could give rise to un-noticed, non-pled, last-second arguments for appointment of a receiver, as occurred in this case."

Continental Homes Co. v. Hilltown Prop. Owners Ass'n, 529 S.W.2d 293, 296 (Tex.App.—Fort Worth 1975, no writ). "Real estate is 'fixed and immovable property' within the meaning of [TRCP] 695, and the trial court committed reversible error in this case in appointing a receiver over the defendants' real estate … without giving the defendants the notice required by Rule 695…."

TRCP 695a. BOND, & BOND IN DIVORCE CASE

No receiver shall be appointed with authority to take charge of property until the party applying therefor has filed with the clerk of the court a good and sufficient bond, to be approved by such clerk, payable to the defendant in the amount fixed by the court, conditioned for the payment of all damages and cost in such suit, in case it should be decided that such receiver was wrongfully appointed to take charge of such property. The amount of such bond shall be fixed at a sum sufficient to cover all such probable damages and costs. In a divorce case the court or judge, as a matter of discretion, may dispense with the necessity of a bond.

Sclafani v. Sclafani, 870 S.W.2d 608, 609 (Tex.App.—Houston [1st Dist.] 1993, writ denied). Respondent "contends that the trial court erred … in ordering the receiver to sell the property because [movant] did not file an applicant's bond, in violation of [TRCP] 695a. *At 609 n.2:* [W]hile this proceeding was pending in this Court, [movant] filed an applicant's bond, making [respondent's] complaint about the lack of a bond moot."

Young v. Young, 765 S.W.2d 440, 444 (Tex.App.—Dallas 1988, no writ). "When the trial court appoints a receiver in a divorce case, it may, at its discretion, dispense with the necessity of a bond."

SECTION 8. SEQUESTRATION

TRCP 696. APPLICATION FOR WRIT OF SEQUESTRATION & ORDER

Either at the commencement of a suit or at any time during its progress the plaintiff may file an application for a writ of sequestration. The application shall be supported by affidavits of the plaintiff, his agent, his attorney, or other persons having knowledge of relevant facts. The application shall comply with all statutory requirements and shall state the grounds for issuing the writ, including the description of the property to be sequestered with such certainty that it may be identified and distinguished from property of a like kind, giving the value of each article of the property and the county in which it is located, and the specific facts relied upon by the plaintiff to warrant the required findings by the court. The writ shall not be quashed because two or more grounds are stated conjunctively or disjunctively. The application and any affidavits shall be made on personal knowledge and shall set forth such facts as would be admissible in evidence; provided that facts may be stated based upon information and belief if the grounds of such belief are specifically stated.

No writ shall issue except upon written order of the court after a hearing, which may be ex parte. The court, in its order granting the application, shall make specific findings of facts to support the statutory grounds found to exist, and shall describe the property to be sequestered with such certainty that it may be identified and distinguished from property of a like kind, giving the value of each article of the property and the county in which it is located. Such order shall further specify the amount of bond required of plaintiff which shall be in an amount which, in the opinion of the court, shall adequately compensate defendant in the event plaintiff fails to prosecute his suit to effect and pay all damages and costs as shall be adjudged against him for wrongfully suing out the writ of sequestration including the elements of damages stated in Sections 62.044 and 62.045, Civil Practice and Remedies Code. The court shall further find in its order the amount of bond required of defendant to replevy, which shall be in an amount equivalent to the value of the property sequestered or to the amount of plaintiff's claim and one year's accrual of interest if allowed by law on the claim, whichever is the lesser amount, and the estimated costs of court. The order may direct the issuance of several writs at the same time, or in succession, to be sent to different counties.

See also CPRC §62.001.

TRCP 697. PETITION

If the suit be in the district or county court, no writ of sequestration shall issue, unless a petition shall have been first filed therein, as in other suits in said courts.

TRCP 698. BOND FOR SEQUESTRATION

No writ of sequestration shall issue until the party applying therefor has filed with the officer authorized to issue such writ a bond payable to the defendant in the amount fixed by the court's order, with sufficient surety or sureties as provided by statute to be approved by such officer, conditioned that the plaintiff will prosecute his suit to effect and pay to the extent of the penal amount of the bond all damages and costs as may be adjudged against him for wrongfully suing out such writ of sequestration, and plaintiff may further condition the bond pursuant to the provisions of Rule 708, in which case he shall not be required to give additional bond to replevy unless so ordered by the court.

After notice to the opposite party, either before or after the issuance of the writ, the defendant or plaintiff may file a motion to increase or reduce the amount of such bond, or to question the sufficiency of the sureties thereon, in the court in which such suit is pending. Upon hearing, the court shall enter its order with respect to such bond and sufficiency of the sureties as justice may require.

TRCP 699. REQUISITES OF WRIT

The writ of sequestration shall be directed "To the Sheriff or any Constable within the State of Texas" (not naming a specific county) and shall command him to take into his possession the property, describing the same as it is described in the application or affidavits, if to be found in his county, and to keep the same subject to further orders of the court, unless the same is replevied. There shall be prominently displayed on the face of the writ, in ten-point type and in a manner calculated to advise a reasonably attentive person of its contents, the following:

"YOU HAVE A RIGHT TO REGAIN POSSESSION OF THE PROPERTY BY FILING A REPLEVY BOND. YOU HAVE A RIGHT TO SEEK TO REGAIN POSSESSION OF THE PROPERTY BY FILING WITH THE COURT A MOTION TO DISSOLVE THIS WRIT."

See also CPRC §§62.061-62.063.

TRCP 700. AMENDMENT

Clerical errors in the affidavit, bond, or writ of sequestration or the officer's return thereof may upon application in writing to the judge of the court in which the suit is filed and after notice to the opponent, be amended in such manner and on such terms as the judge shall authorize by an order entered in the minutes of the court, provided the amendment does not change or add to the grounds of such sequestration as stated in the affidavit, and provided such amendment appears to the judge to be in furtherance of justice.

TRCP 700a. SERVICE OF WRIT ON DEFENDANT

The defendant shall be served in any manner provided for service of citation or as provided in Rule 21a, with a copy of the writ of sequestration, the application, accompanying affidavits, and orders of the court as soon as practicable following the levy of the writ. There shall also be prominently displayed on the face of the copy of the writ served on defendant, in ten-point type and in a manner calculated to advise a reasonably attentive person of its contents, the following:

"To ____________________, Defendant:

"You are hereby notified that certain properties alleged to be claimed by you have been sequestered. If you claim any rights in such property, you are advised:

"YOU HAVE A RIGHT TO REGAIN POSSESSION OF THE PROPERTY BY FILING A REPLEVY BOND. YOU HAVE A RIGHT TO SEEK TO REGAIN POSSESSION OF THE PROPERTY BY FILING WITH THE COURT A MOTION TO DISSOLVE THIS WRIT."

TRCP 701. DEFENDANT MAY REPLEVY

At any time before judgment, should the sequestered property not have been previously claimed, replevied, or sold, the defendant may replevy the same, or any part thereof, or the proceeds from the sale of the property if it has been sold under order of the court, by giving bond, with sufficient surety or sureties as provided by statute, to be approved by the officer who levied the writ, payable to plaintiff in the amount fixed by the court's order, conditioned as provided in Rule 702 or Rule 703.

On reasonable notice to the opposing party (which may be less than three days) either party shall have the right to prompt judicial review of the amount of bond required, denial of bond, sufficiency of sureties, and estimated value of the property, by the court which authorized issuance of the writ. The court's determination may be made upon the basis of affidavits, if uncontroverted, setting forth such facts as would be admissible in evidence; otherwise, the parties shall submit evidence. The court shall forthwith enter its order either approving or modifying the requirements of the officer or of the court's prior order, and such order of the court shall supersede and control with respect to such matters.

TRCP 702. BOND FOR PERSONAL PROPERTY

If the property to be replevied be personal property, the condition of the bond shall be that the defendant will not remove the same out of the county, or that he will not waste, ill-treat, injure, destroy, or dispose of the same, according to the plaintiff's affidavit, and that he will have such property, in the same condition as when it is replevied, together with the value of the fruits, hire or revenue thereof, forthcoming to abide the decision of the court, or that he will pay the value thereof, or the difference between its value at the time of replevy and the time of judgment and of the fruits, hire or revenue of the same in case he shall be condemned to do so.

TRCP 703. BOND FOR REAL ESTATE

If the property be real estate, the condition of such bond shall be that the defendant will not injure the property, and that he will pay the value of the rents of the same in case he shall be condemned so to do.

TRCP 704. RETURN OF BOND & ENTRY OF JUDGMENT

The bond provided for in the three preceding rules shall be returned with the writ to the court from whence the writ issued. In case the suit is decided against the defendant, final judgment shall be rendered against all the obligors in such bond, jointly and severally, for the value of the property replevied as of the date of the execution of the replevy bond, and the value of the fruits, hire, revenue, or rent thereof, as the case may be.

TRCP 705. DEFENDANT MAY RETURN SEQUESTERED PROPERTY

Within ten days after final judgment for personal property the defendant may deliver to the plaintiff, or to the officer who levied the sequestration or to his successor in office the personal property in question, and such officer shall deliver same to plaintiff upon his demand therefor; or such defendant shall deliver such property to the officer demanding same under execution issued therefor upon a judgment for the title or possession of the same; and such officer shall receipt the defendant for such property; provided, however, that such delivery to the plaintiff or to such officer shall be without prejudice to any rights of the plaintiff under the replevy bond given by the defendant. Where a mortgage or other lien of any kind is foreclosed upon personal property sequestered and replevied, the defendant shall deliver such property to the officer calling for same under order of sale issued upon a judgment foreclosing such mortgage or other lien, either in the county of defendant's residence or in the county where sequestered, as demanded by such officer; provided, however, that such delivery by the defendant shall be without prejudice to any rights of the plaintiff under the replevy bond given by the defendant.

TRCP 706. DISPOSITION OF THE PROPERTY BY OFFICER

When the property is tendered back by the defendant to the officer who sequestered the same or to the officer calling for same under an order of sale, such officer shall receive said property and hold or dispose of the same as ordered by the court; provided, however, that such return to and receipt of same by the officer and any sale or disposition of said property by the officer under order or judgment of the court shall not affect or limit any rights of the plaintiff under the bond provided for in Rule 702.

TRCP 707. EXECUTION

If the property be not returned and received, as provided in the two preceding rules, execution shall issue upon said judgment for the amount due thereon, as in other cases.

TRCP 708. PLAINTIFF MAY REPLEVY

When the defendant fails to replevy the property within ten days after the levy of the writ and service of notice on defendant, the officer having the property in possession shall at any time thereafter and before final judgment, deliver the same to the plaintiff upon his giving bond payable to defendant in a sum of money not less than the amount fixed by the court's order, with sufficient surety or sureties as provided by statute to be approved by such officer. If the property to be replevied be personal property, the condition of the bond shall be that he will have such property, in the same condition as when it is replevied, together with the value of the fruits, hire or revenue thereof, forthcoming to abide the decision of the court, or that he will pay the value thereof, or the difference between its value at the time of replevy and the time of judgment (regardless of the cause of such difference in value, and of the fruits, hire or revenue of the same in case he shall be condemned to do so). If the property be real estate, the condition of such bond shall be that the plaintiff will not injure the property, and that he will pay the value of the rents of the same in case he shall be condemned to do so.

On reasonable notice to the opposing party (which may be less than three days) either party shall have the right to prompt judicial review of the amount of bond required, denial of bond, sufficiency of sureties, and estimated value of the property, by the court which authorized issuance of the writ. The court's determination may be made upon the basis of affidavits, if uncontroverted, setting forth such facts as would be admissible in evidence; otherwise, the parties shall submit evidence. The court shall forthwith enter its order either approving or modifying the requirements of the officer or of the court's prior order, and such order of the court shall supersede and control with respect to such matters.

TRCP 709. WHEN BOND FORFEITED

The bond provided for in the preceding rule shall be returned by the officer to the court issuing the writ immediately after he has approved same, and in case the suit is decided against the plaintiff, final judgment shall be entered against all the obligors in such bond, jointly and severally for the value of the property replevied as of the date of the execution of the replevy bond, and the value of the fruits, hire, revenue or rent thereof as the case may be. The same rules which govern the discharge or enforcement of a judgment against the obligors in the defendant's replevy bond shall be applicable to and govern in case of a judgment against the obligors in the plaintiff's replevy bond.

TRCP 710. SALE OF PERISHABLE GOODS

If after the expiration of ten days from the levy of a writ of sequestration the defendant has failed to replevy the same, if the plaintiff or defendant shall make affidavit in writing that the property levied upon, or any portion thereof, is likely to be wasted or destroyed or greatly depreciated in value by keeping, and if the officer having possession of such property shall certify to the truth of such affidavit, it shall be the duty of the judge or justice of the peace to whose court the writ is returnable, upon the presentation of such affidavit and certificate, either in term time or vacation, to order the sale of said property or so much thereof as is likely to be so wasted, destroyed or depreciated in value by keeping, but either party may replevy the property at any time before such sale.

TRCP 711. ORDER OF SALE FOR

The judge or justice granting the order provided for in the preceding rule shall issue an order directed to the officer having such property in possession, commanding such officer to sell such property in the same manner as under execution.

TRCP 712. RETURN OF ORDER

The officer making such sale shall, within five days thereafter, return the order of sale to the court from whence the same issued, with his proceedings thereon, and shall, at the time of making such return, pay over to the clerk or justice of the peace the proceeds of such sale.

TRCP 712a. DISSOLUTION OR MODIFICATION OF WRIT OF SEQUESTRATION

A defendant whose property has been sequestered or any intervening party who claims an interest in such property, may by sworn written motion, seek to vacate, dissolve, or modify the writ and the order directing its issuance, for any grounds or cause, extrinsic or intrinsic, including a motion to reduce the amount of property sequestered when the total amount described and authorized by such order exceeds the amount necessary to secure the plaintiff's claim, one year's interest if allowed by law on the claim, and costs. Such motion shall admit or deny each finding of the order directing the issuance of the writ except where the movant is unable to admit or deny the finding, in which case movant shall set forth the reasons why he cannot admit or deny. Unless the parties agree to an extension of time, the motion shall be heard promptly, after reasonable notice to the plaintiff (which may be less than three days), and the issue shall be determined not later than ten days after the motion is filed. The filing of the motion shall stay any further proceedings under the writ, except for any orders concerning the care, preservation, or sale of any perishable property, until a hearing is had, and the issue is determined. The writ shall be dissolved unless, at such hearing, the plaintiff shall prove the grounds relied upon for its issuance, but the court may modify its previous order granting the writ and the writ issued pursuant thereto. The movant shall, however, have the burden to prove that the reasonable value of the property sequestered exceeds the amount necessary to secure the debt, interest for one year, and probable costs.

The court's determination may be made upon the basis of affidavits, if uncontroverted, setting forth such facts as would be admissible in evidence; otherwise, the parties shall submit evidence. The court may make all such orders, including orders concerning the care, preservation, or disposition of the property (or the proceeds therefrom if the same has been sold) as justice may require. If the movant has given a replevy bond, an order to vacate or dissolve the writ shall vacate the replevy bond and discharge the sureties thereon, and if the court modifies its order or the writ issued pursuant thereto, it shall make such further orders with respect to the bond as may be consistent with its modification.

See also CPRC §62.045.

TRCP 713. SALE ON DEBT NOT DUE

If the suit in which the sequestration issued be for a debt or demand not yet due, and the property sequestered be likely to be wasted, destroyed or greatly depreciated in value by keeping, the judge or justice of the peace shall, under the regulations hereinbefore provided, order the same to be sold, giving credit on such sale until such debt or demand shall become due.

See also CPRC §62.003.

TRCP 714. PURCHASER'S BOND

In the case of a sale as provided for in the preceding rule, the purchaser of the property shall execute his bond, with two or more good and sufficient sureties, to be approved by the officer making the sale, and payable to such officer, in a sum not less than double the amount of the purchase money, conditioned that such purchaser shall pay such purchase money at the expiration of the time given.

TRCP 715. RETURN OF BOND

The bond provided for in the preceding rule shall be returned by the officer taking the same to the clerk or justice of the peace from whose court the order of sale issued, with such order, and shall be filed among the papers in the cause.

TRCP 716. RECOVERY ON BOND

In case the purchaser does not pay the purchase money at the expiration of the time given, judgment shall be rendered against all the obligors in such bond for the amount of such purchase money, interest thereon and all costs incurred in the enforcement and collection of the same; and execution shall issue thereon in the name of the plaintiff in the suit, as in other cases, and the money when collected shall be paid to the clerk or justice of the peace to abide the final decision of the cause.

SECTION 9. TRIAL OF RIGHT OF PROPERTY

TRCP 717. CLAIMANT MUST MAKE AFFIDAVIT

Whenever a distress warrant, writ of execution, sequestration, attachment, or other like writ is levied upon personal property, and such property, or any part thereof, shall be claimed by any claimant who is not a party to such writ, such claimant may make application that such claim is made in good faith, and file such application with the court in which such suit is pending. Such application may be supported by affidavits of the claimant, his agent, his attorney, or other persons having knowledge of relevant facts. The application shall comply with all statutory requirements and shall state the grounds for such claim and the specific facts relied upon by the claimant to warrant the required findings by the court.

The claim shall not be quashed because two or more grounds are stated conjunctively or disjunctively. The application and any affidavits shall be made on personal knowledge and shall set forth such facts as would be admissible in evidence; provided that facts may be stated based upon information and belief if the grounds of such belief are specifically stated.

No property shall be delivered to the claimant except on written order of the court after a hearing pursuant to Rule 718. The court in its order granting the application shall make specific findings of facts to support the statutory grounds found to exist and shall specify the amount of the bond required of the claimant.

TRCP 718. PROPERTY DELIVERED TO CLAIMANT

Any claimant who claims an interest in property on which a writ has been levied may, by sworn written motion, seek to obtain possession of such property. Such motion shall admit or deny each finding of the order directing the issuance of the writ except where the claimant is unable to admit or deny the finding, in which case claimant shall set forth the reasons why he cannot admit or deny. Such motion shall also contain the reasons why the claimant has superior right or title to the property claimed as against the plaintiff in the writ. Unless the parties agree to an extension of time, the motion shall be heard promptly, after reasonable notice to the plaintiff (which may be less than three days), and the issue shall be determined not later than 10 days after the motion is filed. The filing of the motion shall stay any further proceedings under the writ, except for any orders concerning the care, preservation, or sale of any perishable property, until a hearing is had, and the issue is determined. The claimant shall have the burden to show superior right or title to the property claimed as against the plaintiff and defendant in the writ.

The court's determination may be made upon the basis of affidavits, if uncontroverted, setting forth such facts as would be admissible in evidence, but additional evidence, if tendered by either party shall be received and considered. The court may make all such orders, including orders concerning the care, preservation, or disposition of the property, or the proceeds therefrom if the same has been sold, as justice may require, and if the court modifies its order or the writ issued pursuant thereto, it shall make such further orders with respect to the bond as may be consistent with its modification.

TRCP 719. BOND

No property shall be put in the custody of the claimant until the claimant has filed with the officer who made the levy, a bond in an amount fixed by the court's order equal to double the value of the property so claimed, payable to the plaintiff in the writ, with sufficient surety or sureties as provided by statute to be approved by such officer, conditioned that the claimant will return the same to the officer making the levy, or his successor, in as good condition as he received it, and shall also pay the reasonable value of the use, hire, increase and fruits thereof from the date of said bond, or, in case he fails so to return said property and pay for the use of the same, that he shall pay the plaintiff the value of said property, with legal interest thereon from the date of the bond, and shall also pay all damages and costs that may be awarded against him for wrongfully suing out such claim.

The plaintiff or claimant may file a motion to increase or reduce the amount of such bond, or to question the sufficiency of the sureties thereon, in the court in which such suit is pending. Upon hearing, the court shall enter its order with respect to such bond and sufficiency of the sureties.

TRCP 720. RETURN OF BOND

Whenever any person shall claim property and shall duly make the application and give the bond, if the writ under which the levy was made was issued by a justice of the peace or a court of the county where such levy was made, the officer receiving such application and bond shall endorse on the writ that such claim has been made and application and bond given, and by whom; and shall also endorse on such bond the value of the property as assessed by himself, and shall forthwith return such bond with a copy of the writ to the proper court having jurisdiction to try such claim.

TRCP 721. OUT-COUNTY LEVY

Whenever any person shall claim property and shall make the application and give the bond as provided for herein, if the writ under which such levy was made was issued by a justice of the peace or a court of another county than that in which such levy was made, then the officer receiving such bond shall endorse on such bond the value of the property as assessed by himself, and shall forthwith return such bond with a copy of the writ, to the proper court having jurisdiction to try such claim.

TRCP 722. RETURN OF ORIGINAL WRIT

The officer taking such bond shall also endorse on the original writ, if in his possession, that such claim has been made and application and bond given, stating by whom, the names of the surety or sureties, and to what justice or court the bond has been returned; and he shall forthwith return such original writ to the tribunal from which it issued.

TRCP 723. DOCKETING CAUSE

Whenever any bond for the trial of the right of property shall be returned, the clerk of the court, or such justice of the peace, shall docket the same in the original writ proceeding in the name of the plaintiff in the writ as the plaintiff, and the claimant of the property as intervening claimant.

TRCP 724. ISSUE MADE UP

After the claim proceedings have been docketed, and on the hearing day set by the court, then the court, or the justice of the peace, as the case may be, shall enter an order directing the making and joinder of issues by the parties. Such issues shall be in writing and signed by each party or his attorney. The plaintiff shall make a brief statement of the authority and right by which he seeks to subject the property levied on to the process, and it shall be sufficient for the claimant and other parties to make brief statements of the nature of their claims thereto.

TRCP 725. JUDGMENT BY DEFAULT

If the plaintiff appears and the claimant fails to appear or neglects or refuses to join issue under the direction of the court or justice within the time prescribed for pleading, the plaintiff shall have judgment by default.

TRCP 726. JUDGMENT OF NON-SUIT

If the plaintiff does not appear, he shall be non-suited.

TRCP 727. PROCEEDINGS

The proceedings and practice on the trial shall be as nearly as may be the same as in other cases before such court or justice.

TRCP 728. BURDEN OF PROOF

If the property was taken from the possession of the claimant pursuant to the original writ, the burden of proof shall be on the plaintiff in the writ. If it was taken from the possession of the defendant in such writ, or any other person than the claimant, the burden of proof shall be on the claimant.

TRCP 729. COPY OF WRIT EVIDENCE

In all trials of the right of property, under the provisions of this section in any county other than that in which the writ issued under which the levy was made, the copy of the writ herein required to be returned by the officer making the levy shall be received in evidence in like manner as the original could be.

TRCP 730. FAILURE TO ESTABLISH TITLE

Where any claimant has obtained possession of property, and shall ultimately fail to establish his right thereto, judgment may be rendered against him and his sureties for the value of the property, with legal interest thereon from the date of such bond. Such judgment shall be rendered in favor of the plaintiff or defendant in the writ, or of the several plaintiffs or defendants, if more than one, and shall fix the amount of the claim of each.

TRCP 731. EXECUTION SHALL ISSUE

If such judgment should not be satisfied by a return of the property, then after the expiration of ten days from the date of the judgment, execution shall issue thereon in the name of the plaintiff or defendant for the amount of the claim, or of all the plaintiffs or defendants for the sum of their several claims, provided the amount of such judgment shall inure to the benefit of any person who shall show superior right or title to the property claimed as against the claimant; but if such judgment be for a less amount than the sum of the several plaintiffs' or defendants' claims, then the respective rights and priorities of the several plaintiffs or defendants shall be fixed and adjusted in the judgment.

TRCP 732. RETURN OF PROPERTY BY CLAIMANT

If, within ten days from the rendition of said judgment, the claimant shall return such property in as good condition as he received it, and pay for the use of the same together with the damages and costs, such delivery and payment shall operate as a satisfaction of such judgment.

TRCP 733. CLAIM IS A RELEASE OF DAMAGES

A claim made to the property, under the provisions of this section, shall operate as a release of all damages by the claimant against the officer who levied upon said property.

TRCP 734. LEVY ON OTHER PROPERTY

Proceedings for the trial of right of property under these rules shall in no case prevent the plaintiff in the writ from having a levy made upon any other property of the defendant.

PART VII. RULES RELATING TO SPECIAL PROCEEDINGS

SECTION 1. PROCEDURES RELATED TO HOME EQUITY & CERTAIN REVERSE MORTGAGE FORECLOSURE

Ⓐ TRCP 735. PROCEDURES

A party seeking to foreclose a lien created under Tex. Const. art. XVI, §50(a)(6), for a home equity loan, or Tex. Const. art. XVI, §50(a)(7), for a reverse mortgage, that is to be foreclosed on grounds other than Tex. Const. art. XVI, §§50(k)(6)(A) or (B), may file: (1) a suit seeking judicial foreclosure; (2) a suit or counterclaim seeking a final judgment which includes an order allowing foreclosure under the security instrument and Tex. Prop. Code §51.002; or (3) an application under Rule 736 for an order allowing foreclosure.

Comment to 2000 change: Rules 735 and 736 do not change duties of a lender seeking foreclosure. These rules do not preclude a respondent from timely proceeding in district court to contest the right to foreclose or abate a Rule 736 proceeding.

See also Tex. Const. art. XVI, §50; Property Code §51.002.

Ⓐ TRCP 736. EXPEDITED FORECLOSURE PROCEEDING

1. Application. A party filing an application under Rule 736 seeking a court order allowing the foreclosure of a lien under Tex. Const. art. XVI, §50(a)(6)(D), for a home equity loan, or §50(k)(11), for a reverse mortgage, shall initiate such in rem proceeding by filing a verified application in the district court in any county where all or any part of the real property encumbered by the lien sought to be foreclosed (the "property") is located. The application shall:

(A) be styled: "In re: Order for Foreclosure Concerning (*Name of person to receive notice of foreclosure*) and (*Property Mailing Address*)";

(B) identify by name the party who, according to the records of the holder of the debt, is obligated to pay the debt secured by the property;

(C) identify the property by mailing address and legal description;

(D) identify the security instrument encumbering the property by reference to volume and page, clerk's file number or other identifying recording information found in the official real property records of the county where all or any part of the property is located or attach a legible copy of the security instrument;

(E) allege that:

(1) a debt exists;

(2) the debt is secured by a lien created under Tex. Const. art. XVI, §50(a)(6), for a home equity loan, or §50(a)(7), for a reverse mortgage;

(3) a default under the security instrument exists;

(4) the applicant has given the requisite notices to cure the default and accelerate the maturity of the debt under the security instrument, Tex. Prop. Code §51.002, Tex. Const. art. XVI, §50(k)(10), for a reverse mortgage, and applicable law;

(F) describe facts which establish the existence of a default under the security instrument; and

(G) state that the applicant seeks a court order required by Tex. Const. art. XVI, §50(a)(6)(D), for a home equity loan, or §50(k)(11), for a reverse mortgage, to sell the property under the security instrument and Tex. Prop. Code §51.002.

A notice required by Tex. Const. art. XVI, §50(k)(10), for a reverse mortgage, may be combined or incorporated in any other notice referenced in Rule

736(1)(E)(4). The verified application and any supporting affidavit shall be made on personal knowledge and shall set forth such facts as would be admissible in evidence, provided that facts may be stated based upon information and belief if the grounds of such belief are specifically stated.

2. Notice.

(A) *Service.* Every application filed with the clerk of the court shall be served by the party filing the application. Service of the application and notice shall be by delivery of a copy to the party to be served by certified and first class mail addressed to each party who, according to the records of the holder of the debt is obligated to pay the debt. Service shall be complete upon the deposit of the application and notice, enclosed in a postage prepaid and properly addressed wrapper, in a post office or official depository under the care and custody of the United States Postal Service. If the respondent is represented by an attorney and the applicant's attorney has knowledge of the name and address of the attorney, an additional copy of the application and notice shall be sent to respondent's attorney.

(B) *Certificate of Service.* The applicant or applicant's attorney shall certify to the court compliance with the service requirements of Rule 736. The applicant shall file a copy of the notice and the certificate of service with the clerk of the court. The certificate of service shall be prima facie evidence of the fact of service.

(C) *Form of Notice.* The notice shall be sufficient if it is in substantially the following form in at least ten point type:

Example 1: Form of Notice

Cause No. ________

In re: Order for ForeclosureIn the District Court
Concerning

____*(1)____ Of ________ County
and
____* (2)____ Judicial District

NOTICE TO: ____*(3)____
____
____

An application has been filed by________, as Applicant, on ____*(4)____, in a proceeding described as:

"In re: Order for Foreclosure Concerning ____*(1)____ and ____*(2)____."

The attached application alleges that you, the Respondent, are in default under a security instrument creating a lien on your homestead under Tex. Const. art. XVI, §50(a)(6), for a home equity loan, or §50(a)(7), for a reverse mortgage. This application is now pending in this court.

Applicant seeks a court order, as required by Tex. Const. art. XVI, §50(a)(6)(D) or §50(k)(11), to allow it to sell at public auction the property described in the attached application under the security instrument and Tex. Prop. Code §51.002.

You may employ an attorney. If you or your attorney do not file a written response with the clerk of the court at ____*(5)____ on or before 10:00 a.m. on ____*(6)____ an order authorizing a foreclosure sale may be signed. If the court grants the application, the foreclosure sale will be conducted under the security instrument and Tex. Prop. Code §51.002.

You may file a response setting out as many matters, whether of law or fact, as you consider may be necessary and pertinent to contest the application. If a response is filed, the court will hold a hearing at the request of the applicant or respondent.

In your response to this application, you must provide your mailing address. In addition, you must send a copy of your response to ____*(7)____

ISSUED

By ________________
(Applicant or Applicant's Attorney)

CERTIFICATE OF SERVICE

I certify that a true and correct copy of this notice with a copy of the application was sent certified and regular mail to ____*(3)____ on the ___ day of ________________.

(signature)
(Applicant or Applicant's Attorney)

*(1) name of respondent
*(2) mailing address of property
*(3) name and address of respondent
*(4) date application filed
*(5) address of clerk of court
*(6) response due date

*(7) name and address of applicant or applicant's attorney ____________

(D) The applicant shall state in the notice the date the response is due in accordance with Rule 736(3).

(E) The application and notice may be accompanied by any other notice required by state or federal law.

3. Response Due Date. A response is due on or before 10:00 a.m. on the first Monday after the expiration of thirty-eight (38) days after the date of mailing of the application and notice to respondent, exclusive of the date of mailing, as set forth in the certificate of service.

4. Response.

(A) The respondent may file a response setting out as many matters, whether of law or fact, as respondent deems necessary or pertinent to contest the application. Such response and any supporting affidavit shall be made on personal knowledge and shall set forth such facts as would be admissible in evidence, provided that facts may be stated based upon information and belief if the grounds of such belief are specifically stated.

(B) The response shall state the respondent's mailing address.

(C) The response shall be filed with the clerk of the court. The respondent shall also send a copy of the response to the applicant or the applicant's attorney at the address set out in the notice.

5. Default. At any time after a response is due, the court shall grant the application without further notice or hearing if:

(A) the application complies with Rule 736(1);

(B) the respondent has not previously filed a response; and

(C) a copy of the notice and the certificate of service shall have been on file with the clerk of the court for at least ten days exclusive of the date of filing.

6. Hearing When Response Filed. On the filing of a response, the application shall be promptly heard after reasonable notice to the applicant and the respondent. No discovery of any kind shall be permitted in a proceeding under Rule 736. Unless the parties agree to an extension of time, the issue shall be determined by the court not later than ten business days after a request for hearing by either party. At the hearing, the applicant shall have the burden to prove by affidavits on file or evidence presented the grounds for the granting of the order sought in the application.

7. Only Issue. The only issue to be determined under Rule 736 shall be the right of the applicant to obtain an order to proceed with foreclosure under the security instrument and Tex. Prop. Code §51.002.

8. Order to Proceed with Notice of Sale and Sale.

(A) *Grant or denial.* The court shall grant the application if the court finds applicant has proved the elements of Rule 736(1)(E). Otherwise, the court shall deny the application. The granting or denial of the application is not an appealable order.

(B) *Form of order.* The order shall recite the mailing address and legal description of the property, direct that foreclosure proceed under the security instrument and Tex. Prop. Code §51.002, provide that a copy of the order shall be sent to respondent with the notice of sale, provide that applicant may communicate with the respondent and all third parties reasonably necessary to conduct the foreclosure sale, and, if respondent is represented by counsel, direct that notice of the foreclosure sale date shall also be mailed to counsel by certified mail.

(C) *Filing of order.* The applicant is to file a certified copy of the order in the real property records of the county where the property is located within ten business days of the entry of the order. Failure to timely record the order shall not affect the validity of the foreclosure or defeat the presumption of Tex. Const. art. XVI, §50(i).

9. Nonpreclusive Effect of Order. No order or determination of fact or law under Rule 736 shall be res judicata or constitute collateral estoppel or estoppel by judgment in any other proceeding or suit. The granting of an application under these rules shall be without prejudice to the right of the respondent to seek relief at law or in equity in any court of competent jurisdiction. The denial of an application under these rules shall be without prejudice to the right of the applicant to re-file the application or seek other relief at law or in equity in any court of competent jurisdiction.

10. Abatement and Dismissal. A proceeding under Rule 736 is automatically abated if, before the signing of the order, notice is filed with the clerk of the court in which the application is pending that respondent has filed a petition contesting the right to foreclose in a district court in the county where the application is pending. A proceeding that has been abated shall be dismissed.

Comment to 2000 changes: Rules 735 and 736 do not change duties of a lender seeking foreclosure. These rules do not preclude a respondent from timely proceeding in district court to contest the right to foreclose or abate a Rule 736 proceeding.

See also Tex. Const. art. XVI, §50; Property Code §51.002.

SECTION 2. BILL OF DISCOVERY

TRCP 737. REPEALED

SECTION 3. FORCIBLE ENTRY & DETAINER

TRCP 738. MAY SUE FOR RENT

A suit for rent may be joined with an action of forcible entry and detainer, wherever the suit for rent is within the jurisdiction of the justice court. In such case the court in rendering judgment in the action of forcible entry and detainer, may at the same time render judgment for any rent due the landlord by the renter; provided the amount thereof is within the jurisdiction of the justice court.

See also CPRC §15.084; Prop. Code §24.004.

TRCP 739. CITATION

When the party aggrieved or his authorized agent shall file his written sworn complaint with such justice, the justice shall immediately issue citation directed to the defendant or defendants commanding him to appear before such justice at a time and place named in such citation, such time being not more than ten days nor less than six days from the date of service of the citation.

The citation shall inform the parties that, upon timely request and payment of a jury fee no later than five days after the defendant is served with citation, the case shall be heard by a jury.

TRCP 740. COMPLAINANT MAY HAVE POSSESSION

The party aggrieved may, at the time of filing his complaint, or thereafter prior to final judgment in the justice court, execute and file a possession bond to be approved by the justice in such amount as the justice may fix as the probable amount of costs of suit and damages which may result to defendant in the event that the suit has been improperly instituted, and conditioned that the plaintiff will pay defendant all such costs and damages as shall be adjudged against plaintiff.

The defendant shall be notified by the justice court that plaintiff has filed a possession bond. Such notice shall be served in the same manner as service of citation and shall inform the defendant of all of the following rules and procedures:

(a) Defendant may remain in possession if defendant executes and files a counterbond prior to the expiration of six days from the date defendant is served with notice of the filing of plaintiff's bond. Said counterbond shall be approved by the justice and shall be in such amount as the justice may fix as the probable amount of costs of suit and damages which may result to plaintiff in the event possession has been improperly withheld by defendant;

(b) Defendant is entitled to demand and he shall be granted a trial to be held prior to the expiration of six days from the date defendant is served with notice of the filing of plaintiff's possession bond;

(c) If defendant does not file a counterbond and if defendant does not demand that trial be held prior to the expiration of said six-day period, the constable of the precinct or the sheriff of the county where the property is situated, shall place the plaintiff in possession of the property promptly after the expiration of six days from the date defendant is served with notice of the filing of plaintiff's possession bond; and

(d) If, in lieu of a counterbond, defendant demands trial within said six-day period, and if the justice of the peace rules after trial that plaintiff is entitled to possession of the property, the constable or sheriff shall place the plaintiff in possession of the property five days after such determination by the justice of the peace.

TRCP 741. REQUISITES OF COMPLAINT

The complaint shall describe the lands, tenements or premises, the possession of which is claimed, with sufficient certainty to identify the same, and it shall also state the facts which entitled the complainant to the possession and authorize the action under Sections 24.001-24.004, Texas Property Code.

TRCP 742. SERVICE OF CITATION

The officer receiving such citation shall execute the same by delivering a copy of it to the defendant, or by leaving a copy thereof with some person over the age of sixteen years, at his usual place of abode, at least six days before the return day thereof; and on or before the day assigned for trial he shall return such citation, with his action written thereon, to the justice who issued the same.

TRCP 742a. SERVICE BY DELIVERY TO PREMISES

If the sworn complaint lists all home and work addresses of the defendant which are known to the person filing the sworn complaint and if it states that such person knows of no other home or work addresses of the defendant in the county where the premises are located, service of citation may be by delivery to the premises in question as follows:

If the officer receiving such citation is unsuccessful in serving such citation under Rule 742, the officer shall no later than five days after receiving such citation execute a sworn statement that the officer has made diligent efforts to serve such citation on at least two occasions at all addresses of the defendant in the county where the premises are located as may be shown on the sworn complaint, stating the times and places of attempted service. Such sworn statement shall be filed by the officer with the justice who shall promptly consider the sworn statement of the officer. The justice may then authorize service according to the following:

(a) The officer shall place the citation inside the premises by placing it through a door mail chute or by slipping it under the front door; and if neither method is possible or practical, the officer shall securely affix the citation to the front door or main entry to the premises.

(b) The officer shall that same day or the next day deposit in the mail a true copy of such citation with a copy of the sworn complaint attached thereto, addressed to defendant at the premises in question and sent by first class mail;

(c) The officer shall note on the return of such citation the date of delivery under (a) above and the date of mailing under (b) above; and

(d) Such delivery and mailing to the premises shall occur at least six days before the return day of the citation; and on or before the day assigned for trial he shall return such citation with his action written thereon, to the justice who issued the same.

It shall not be necessary for the aggrieved party or his authorized agent to make request for or motion for alternative service pursuant to this rule.

TRCP 743. DOCKETED

The cause shall be docketed and tried as other cases. If the defendant shall fail to enter an appearance upon the docket in the justice court or file answer before the case is called for trial, the allegations of the complaint may be taken as admitted and judgment by default entered accordingly. The justice shall have authority to issue subpoenas for witnesses to enforce their attendance, and to punish for contempt.

TRCP 744. DEMANDING JURY

Any party shall have the right of trial by jury, by making a request to the court on or before five days from the date the defendant is served with citation, and by paying a jury fee of five dollars. Upon such request, a jury shall be summoned as in other cases in justice court.

TRCP 745. TRIAL POSTPONED

For good cause shown, supported by affidavit of either party, the trial may be postponed not exceeding six days.

TRCP 746. ONLY ISSUE

In case of forcible entry or of forcible detainer under Sections 24.001-24.008, Texas Property Code, the only issue shall be as to the right to actual possession; and the merits of the title shall not be adjudicated.

See also Prop. Code §24.001 et seq.

TRCP 747. TRIAL

If no jury is demanded by either party, the justice shall try the case. If a jury is demanded by either party, the jury shall be empaneled and sworn as in other cases; and after hearing the evidence it shall return its verdict in favor of the plaintiff or the defendant as it shall find.

TRCP 747a. REPRESENTATION BY AGENTS

In forcible entry and detainer cases for non-payment of rent or holding over beyond the rental term, the parties may represent themselves or be represented by their authorized agents in justice court.

TRCP 748. JUDGMENT & WRIT

If the judgment or verdict be in favor of the plaintiff, the justice shall give judgment for plaintiff for possession of the premises, costs, and damages; and he shall award his writ of possession. If the judgment or verdict be in favor of the defendant, the justice shall give judgment for defendant against the plaintiff for costs and any damages. No writ of possession shall issue until the expiration of five days from the time the judgment is signed.

See also *O'Connor's Texas Rules*, "Rules for Filing Documents," ch. 1-C.

TRCP 749. MAY APPEAL

In appeals in forcible entry and detainer cases, no motion for new trial shall be filed.

Either party may appeal from a final judgment in such case, to the county court of the county in which the judgment is rendered by filing with the justice within five days after the judgment is signed, a bond to be approved by said justice, and payable to the adverse party, conditioned that he will prosecute his appeal with effect, or pay all costs and damages which may be adjudged against him.

The justice shall set the amount of the bond to include the items enumerated in Rule 752.

Within five days following the filing of such bond, the party appealing shall give notice as provided in Rule 21a of the filing of such bond to the adverse party. No judgment shall be taken by default against the adverse party in the court to which the cause has been appealed without first showing substantial compliance with this rule.

See also *O'Connor's Texas Rules*, "Rules for Filing Documents," ch. 1-C.

TRCP 749a. PAUPER'S AFFIDAVIT

If appellant is unable to pay the costs of appeal, or file a bond as required by Rule 749, he shall nevertheless be entitled to appeal by making strict proof of such inability within five days after the judgment is signed, which shall consist of his affidavit filed with the justice of the peace stating his inability to pay such costs, or any part thereof, or to give security, which may be contested within five days after the filing of such affidavit and notice thereof to the opposite party or his attorney of record by any officer of the court or party to the suit, whereupon it shall be the duty of the justice of the peace in whose court the suit is pending to hear evidence and determine the right of the party to appeal, and he shall enter his finding on the docket as part of the record. Upon the filing of a pauper's affidavit the justice of the peace or clerk of the court shall notice the opposing party of the filing of the affidavit of inability within one working day of its filing by written notification accomplished through first class mail. It will be presumed prima facie that the affidavit speaks the truth, and, unless contested within five days after the filing and notice thereof, the presumption shall be deemed conclusive; but if a contest is filed, the burden shall then be on the appellant to prove his alleged inability by competent evidence other than by the affidavit above referred to. When a pauper's affidavit is timely contested by the appellee, the justice shall hold a hearing and rule on the matter within five days.

If the justice of the peace disapproves the pauper's affidavit, appellant may, within five days thereafter bring the matter before the county judge for a final decision, and, on request, the justice shall certify to the county judge appellant's affidavit, the contest thereof, and all documents, and papers thereto. The county judge shall set a day for hearing, not later than five days, and shall hear the contest de novo. If the pauper's affidavit is approved by the county judge, he shall direct the justice to transmit to the clerk of the county court, the transcript, records and papers of the case.

A pauper's affidavit will be considered approved upon one of the following occurrences: (1) the pauper's affidavit is not contested by the other party; (2) the pauper's affidavit is contested by the other party and upon a hearing the justice determines that the pauper's affidavit is approved; or (3) upon a hearing by the justice disapproving of the pauper's affidavit the appellant appeals to the county judge who then, after a hearing, approves the pauper's affidavit.

No writ of possession may issue pending the hearing by the county judge of the appellant's right to appeal on a pauper's affidavit. If the county judge disapproves the pauper's affidavit, appellant may perfect his appeal by filing an appeal bond in the amount as required by Rule 749 within five days thereafter. If no appeal bond is filed within five days, a writ of possession may issue.

See also *O'Connor's Texas Rules*, "Rules for Filing Documents," ch. 1-C.

TRCP 749b. PAUPER'S AFFIDAVIT IN NONPAYMENT OF RENT APPEALS

In a nonpayment of rent forcible detainer case a tenant/appellant who has appealed by filing a pauper's affidavit under these rules shall be entitled to stay in possession of the premises during the pendency of the appeal, by complying with the following procedure:

(1) Within five days of the date that the tenant/appellant files his pauper's affidavit, he must pay into the justice court registry one rental period's rent under the terms of the rental agreement.

(2) During the appeal process as rent becomes due under the rental agreement, the tenant/appellant shall pay the rent into the county court registry within five days of the due date under the terms of the rental agreement.

(3) If the tenant/appellant fails to pay the rent into the court registry within the time limits prescribed by these rules, the appellee may file a notice of default in county court. Upon sworn motion by the appellee and a showing of default to the judge, the court shall issue a writ of restitution.

(4) Landlord/appellee may withdraw any or all rent in the county court registry upon a) sworn motion and hearing, prior to final determination of the case, showing just cause, b) dismissal of the appeal, or c) order of the court upon final hearing.

(5) All hearings and motions under this rule shall be entitled to precedence in the county court.

See also *O'Connor's Texas Rules*, "Rules for Filing Documents," ch. 1-C.

TRCP 749c. APPEAL PERFECTED

When an appeal bond has been timely filed in conformity with Rule 749 or a pauper's affidavit approved in conformity with Rule 749a, the appeal shall be perfected.

See also *O'Connor's Texas Rules*, "Rules for Filing Documents," ch. 1-C.

TRCP 750. FORM OF APPEAL BOND

The appeal bond authorized in the preceding article may be substantially as follows:

"The State of Texas,

"County of ________

"Whereas, upon a writ of forcible entry (or forcible detainer) in favor of A.B., and against C.D., tried before ________, a justice of the peace of ________ county, a judgment was rendered in favor of the said A.B. on the ___ day of ________, A.D. ______, and against the said C.D., from which the said C.D. has appealed to the county court; now, therefore, the said C.D. and ______ his sureties, covenant that he will prosecute his said appeal with effect and pay all costs and damages which may be adjudged against him, provided the sureties shall not be liable in an amount greater than $ ______, said amount being the amount of the bond herein.

"Given under our hands this _____ day of ________, A.D. ________."

TRCP 751. TRANSCRIPT

When an appeal has been perfected, the justice shall stay all further proceedings on the judgment, and immediately make out a transcript of all the entries made on his docket of the proceedings had in the case; and he shall immediately file the same, together with the original papers and any money in the court registry, including sums tendered pursuant to Rule 749b(1), with the clerk of the county court of the county in which the trial was had, or other court having jurisdiction of such appeal. The clerk shall docket the cause, and the trial shall be de novo.

The clerk shall immediately notify both appellant and the adverse party of the date of receipt of the transcript and the docket number of the cause. Such notice shall advise the defendant of the necessity for filing a written answer in the county court when the defendant has pleaded orally in the justice court.

The trial, as well as all hearings and motions, shall be entitled to precedence in the county court.

TRCP 752. DAMAGES

On the trial of the cause in the county court the appellant or appellee shall be permitted to plead, prove and recover his damages, if any, suffered for withholding or defending possession of the premises during the pendency of the appeal.

Damages may include but are not limited to loss of rentals during the pendency of the appeal and reasonable attorney fees in the justice and county courts provided, as to attorney fees, that the requirements of Section 24.006 of the Texas Property Code have been met. Only the party prevailing in the county court shall be entitled to recover damages against the adverse party. He shall also be entitled to recover court costs. He shall be entitled to recover against the sureties on the appeal bond in cases where the adverse party has executed such bond.

TRCP 753. JUDGMENT BY DEFAULT

Said cause shall be subject to trial at any time after the expiration of eight full days after the date the transcript is filed in the county court. If the defendant has filed a written answer in the justice court, the same shall be taken to constitute his appearance and answer in the county court, and such answer may be amended as in other cases. If the defendant made no answer in writing in the justice court, and if he fails to file a written answer within eight full days after the transcript is filed in the county court, the allegations of the complaint may be taken as admitted and judgment by default may be entered accordingly.

TRCP 754. BLANK

TRCP 755. WRIT OF POSSESSION

The writ of possession, or execution, or both, shall be issued by the clerk of the county court according to the judgment rendered, and the same shall be executed by the sheriff or constable, as in other cases; and such writ of possession shall not be suspended or superseded in any case by appeal from such final judgment in the county court, unless the premises in question are being used as the principal residence of a party.

SECTION 4. PARTITION OF REAL ESTATE

TRCP 756. PETITION

The plaintiff's petition shall state:

(a) The names and residence, if known, of each of the other joint owners, or joint claimants, of such property.

(b) The share or interest which the plaintiff and the other joint owners, or joint claimants, of same own or claim so far as known to the plaintiff.

(c) The land sought to be partitioned shall be so described as that the same may be distinguished from any other and the estimated value thereof stated.

See also Property Code §23.001.

Yoast v. Yoast, 649 S.W.2d 289, 292 (Tex.1983). "The court of appeals mischaracterized this case as a partition suit. [P's suit was for] trespass to try title. ... Partition issues may be resolved in a trespass to try title suit once the controversy as to title or right to possession is settled. That, however, does not convert the cause of action to a partition suit. [¶] A partition suit is based on the theory of common title, rather than disputed ownership."

TRCP 757. CITATION & SERVICE

Upon the filing of a petition for partition, the clerk shall issue citation for each of the joint owners, or joint claimants, named therein, as in other cases, and such citations shall be served in the manner and for the time provided for the service of citations in other cases.

Carper v. Halamicek, 610 S.W.2d 556, 557 (Tex. App.—Tyler 1980, writ ref'd n.r.e.). "This rule and past cases indicate that the joinder of all owners is mandatory and that no valid, binding decree of partition can be made in their absence."

TRCP 758. WHERE DEFENDANT IS UNKNOWN OR RESIDENCE IS UNKNOWN

If the plaintiff, his agent or attorney, at the commencement of any suit, or during the progress thereof, for the partition of land, shall make affidavit that an undivided portion of the land described in plaintiff's petition in said suit is owned by some person unknown to affiant, or that the place of residence of any known party owning an interest in land sought to be partitioned is unknown to affiant, the Clerk of the Court shall issue citation for publication, conforming to the requirements of Rules 114 and 115, and served in accordance with the directions of Rule 116. In case of unknown residence or party, the affidavit shall include a statement that after due diligence plaintiff and the affiant have been unable to ascertain the name or locate the residence of such party, as the case may be, and in such case it shall be the duty of the court trying the action to inquire into the sufficiency of the diligence so stated before granting any judgment.

TRCP 759. JUDGMENT WHERE DEFENDANT CITED BY PUBLICATION

When the defendant has been duly cited by publication in accordance with the preceding rule, and no appearance is entered within the time prescribed for pleadings, the court shall appoint an attorney to defend in behalf of such owner or owners, and proceed as in other causes where service is made by publication. It shall be the special duty of the court in all cases to see that its decree protects the rights of the unknown parties thereto. The judge of the court shall fix the fee of the attorney so appointed, which shall be entered and collected as costs against said unknown owner or owners.

TRCP 760. COURT SHALL DETERMINE, WHAT

Upon the hearing of the cause, the court shall determine the share or interest of each of the joint owners or claimants in the real estate sought to be divided, and all questions of law or equity affecting the title to such land which may arise.

See also TRCP 769.

Johnson v. Johnson-McHenry, 978 S.W.2d 142, 144 (Tex.App.—Austin 1998, no pet.). "[I]n a partition suit, the trial court determines whether the partition will be by sale or in kind, the share or interest of the joint owners or claimants, and all questions of law or equity affecting title. The court then allocates to the parties their rightful shares or tracts. A trial court may also exercise equitable powers in a partition suit."

Thomas v. McNair, 882 S.W.2d 870, 876 (Tex. App.—Corpus Christi 1994, no writ). "'In a partition suit two judgments are rendered. The first decree determines: the share or interest of each of the joint owners or claimants; all questions of law or equity affecting title; and appoints commissioners and gives them directions as may be necessary and appropriate. ... The rights and matters determined in the first decree are final, and it is appealable as a final judgment.'"

TRCP 761. APPOINTMENT OF COMMISSIONERS

The court shall determine before entering the decree of partition whether the property, or any part thereof, is susceptible of partition; and, if the court determines that the whole, or any part of such property is susceptible of partition, then the court for that part of such property held to be susceptible of partition shall enter a decree directing the partition of such real estate, describing the same, to be made in accordance with the respective shares or interests of each of such parties entitled thereto, specify in such decree the share or interest of each party, and shall appoint three or more competent and disinterested persons as commissioners to make such partition in accordance with such decree and the law, a majority of which commissioners may act.

Benson v. Fox, 589 S.W.2d 823, 826 (Tex.App.—Tyler 1979, no writ). "The law makes it the duty of the court, before entering a decree of partition, to determine whether the property is susceptible of partition. It is evident that [TRCP] 761 employs the word 'partition' in a restricted sense as synonymous with the phrase 'partition in kind.'"

TRCP 762. WRIT OF PARTITION

The clerk shall issue a writ of partition, directed to the sheriff or any constable of the county, commanding such sheriff or constable to notify each of the commissioners of their appointment as such, and shall accompany such writ with a certified copy of the decree of the court directing the partition.

TRCP 763. SERVICE OF WRIT OF PARTITION

The writ of partition shall be served by reading the same to each of the persons named therein as commissioners, and by delivering to any one of them the accompanying certified copy of the decree of the court.

TRCP 764. MAY APPOINT SURVEYOR

The court may, should it be deemed necessary, appoint a surveyor to assist the commissioners in making the partition, in which case the writ of partition shall name such surveyor, and shall be served upon him by reading the same to him.

TRCP 765. RETURN OF WRIT

A writ of partition, unless otherwise directed by the court, shall be made returnable twenty days from date of service on the commissioner last served; and the officer serving it shall endorse thereon the time and manner of such service.

TRCP 766. SHALL PROCEED TO PARTITION

The commissioners, or a majority of them, shall proceed to partition the real estate described in the decree of the court, in accordance with the directions contained in such decree and with the provisions of law and these rules.

Mansfield v. Davenport, 362 S.W.2d 912, 913 (Tex. App.—San Antonio 1962, writ ref'd n.r.e.). "By its first order or judgment in a partition suit, a court may properly give such directions as may be necessary and appropriate."

TRCP 767. MAY CAUSE SURVEY

If the commissioners deem it necessary, they may cause to be surveyed the real estate to be partitioned into several tracts or parcels.

TRCP 768. SHALL DIVIDE REAL ESTATE

The commissioners shall divide the real estate to be partitioned into as many shares as there are persons entitled thereto, as determined by the court, each share to contain one or more tracts or parcels, as the commissioners may think proper, having due regard in the division to the situation, quantity and advantages of each share, so that the shares may be equal in value, as nearly as may be, in proportion to the respective interests of the parties entitled. The commissioners shall then proceed by lot to set apart to each of the parties entitled one of said shares, as determined by the decrees of the court.

Grimes v. Hall, 211 S.W.2d 956, 958 (Tex.App.—Eastland 1948, no writ). "Where the interests of the parties in the realty to be partitioned are unequal, selection of owners of shares by lot is not required."

TRCP 769. REPORT OF COMMISSIONERS

When the commissioners have completed the partition, they shall report the same in writing and under oath to the court, which report shall show:

(a) The property divided, describing the same.

(b) The several tracts or parcels into which the same was divided by them, describing each particularly.

(c) The number of shares and the land which constitutes each share, and the estimated value of each share.

(d) The allotment of each share.

(e) The report shall be accompanied by such field notes and maps as may be necessary to make the same intelligible.

The clerk shall immediately mail written notice of the filing of the report to all parties.

Thomas v. McNair, 882 S.W.2d 870, 876 (Tex. App.—Corpus Christi 1994, no writ). "'The second decree [in a partition suit] approves the report of the commissioners and allocates to the respective parties their separate shares or tracts.'"

TRCP 770. PROPERTY INCAPABLE OF DIVISION

Should the court be of the opinion that a fair and equitable division of the real estate, or any part thereof, cannot be made, it shall order a sale of so much as is incapable of partition, which sale shall be for cash, or upon such other terms as the court may direct, and shall be made as under execution or by private or public sale through a receiver, if the court so order, and the proceeds thereof shall be returned into court and be partitioned among the persons entitled thereto, according to their respective interests.

Cecola v. Ruley, 12 S.W.3d 848, 853-54 (Tex.App.—Texarkana 2000, no pet.). "Whether a piece of land can fairly be partitioned in kind is a question of fact for the court or jury to decide. The law favors partition in kind over partition by sale. Therefore, at trial the burden of proof falls on the party opposing partitioning in kind and seeking a partition by sale. Because [D] opposed the partition in kind and sought a partition by sale, the burden of proof was upon him to show that an in-kind partition would not be fair."

Thomas v. McNair, 882 S.W.2d 870, 876 (Tex. App.—Corpus Christi 1994, no writ). "Pursuant to [TRCP] 770, a trial court must order the sale of property incapable of partition and determine the respective interests or shares of the person entitled thereto. After the sale, the court enters an order of disbursement dividing the proceeds of the sale among the persons entitled thereto, according to their respective interests."

TRCP 771. OBJECTIONS TO REPORT

Either party to the suit may file objections to any report of the commissioners in partition within thirty days of the date the report is filed, and in such case a trial of the issues thereon shall be had as in other cases. If the report be found to be erroneous in any material respect, or unequal and unjust, the same shall be rejected, and other commissioners shall be appointed by the Court, and the same proceedings had as in the first instance.

Ellis v. First City Nat'l Bank, 864 S.W.2d 555, 557 (Tex.App.—Tyler 1993, no writ). "If the trial court finds the report of the commissioners is [erroneous or unequal] it must reject the report and appoint other commissioners. The party objecting to the commissioners' report had the burden of proving that it is materially erroneous or that it unequally and unjustly partitions the property."

SECTION 5. PARTITION OF PERSONAL PROPERTY

TRCP 772. PROCEDURE

An action seeking partition of personal property as authorized by Section 23.001, Texas Property Code, shall be commenced in the same manner as other civil suits, and the several owners or claimants of such property shall be cited as in other cases.

TRCP 773. VALUE ASCERTAINED

The separate value of each article of such personal property, and the allotment in kind to which each owner is entitled, shall be ascertained by the court, with or without a jury.

Price v. Price, 394 S.W.2d 855, 858 (Tex.App.—Tyler 1965, writ ref'd n.r.e.). "The fact that the property has now been transformed into personal property in the form of money would not alter the application rule, but would only make the property more susceptible to a partition in kind."

TRCP 774. DECREE OF COURT EXECUTED

When partition in kind of personal property is ordered by the judgment of the court, a writ shall be issued in accordance with such judgment, commanding the sheriff or constable of the county where the property may be to put the parties forthwith in possession of the property allotted to each respectively.

TRCP 775. PROPERTY SOLD

When personal property will not admit of a fair and equitable partition, the court shall ascertain the proportion to which each owner thereof is entitled, and order the property to be sold, and execution shall be issued to the sheriff or any constable of the county where the property may be describing such property and commanding such officer to sell the same as in other cases of execution, and pay over the proceeds of sale to the parties entitled thereto, in the proportion ascertained by the judgment of the court.

SECTION 6. PARTITION: MISCELLANEOUS PROVISIONS

TRCP 776. CONSTRUCTION

No provision of the statutes or rules relating to partition shall affect the mode of proceeding prescribed by law for the partition of estates of decedents among the heirs and legatees, nor preclude partition in any other manner authorized by the rules of equity, which rules shall govern in proceedings for partition in all respects not provided for by law or these rules.

TRCP 777. PLEADING & PRACTICE

The same rules of pleading, practice and evidence which govern in other civil actions shall govern in suits for partition, when not in conflict with any provisions of the law or these rules relating to partition.

Rayson v. Johns, 524 S.W.2d 380, 382 (Tex.App.—Texarkana 1975, writ ref'd n.r.e.). "[I]n whatever posture the question has arisen, the courts have treated disputed issues of fact in partition proceedings as being for the jury when one has been properly demanded. [¶] The law does not favor compelling an owner to sell his property against his will, but prefers a division in kind when such can be fairly and equitably made."

TRCP 778. COSTS

The court shall adjudge the costs in a partition suit to be paid by each party to whom a share has been allotted in proportion to the value of such share.

Ellis v. First City Nat'l Bank, 864 S.W.2d 555, 557-58 (Tex.App.—Tyler 1993, no writ). TRCP 778 "provides that the court shall adjudge the costs in proportion to the *value* of each share. ... [Ds] concede that there was no testimony ... regarding the value of the several shares. ... We conclude that the record contains no evidence of value sufficient to an apportionment of costs in the manner required by [TRCP] 778." Remanded to adjudge costs.

SECTION 7. QUO WARRANTO

TRCP 779. JOINDER OF PARTIES

When it appears to the court or judge that the several rights of diverse parties to the same office or franchise may properly be determined on one information, the court or judge may give leave to join all such persons in the same information in order to try their respective rights to such office or franchise.

TRCP 780. CITATION TO ISSUE

When such information is filed, the clerk shall issue citation as in civil actions, commanding the defendant to appear and answer the relator in an information in the nature of a quo warranto.

TRCP 781. PROCEEDINGS AS IN CIVIL CASES

Every person or corporation who shall be cited as hereinbefore provided shall be entitled to all the rights in the trial and investigation of the matters alleged against him, as in cases of trial in civil cases in this State. Either party may prosecute an appeal or writ of error from any judgment rendered, as in other civil cases, subject, however, to the provisions of Rule 42[1], Texas Rules of Appellate Procedure, and the appellate court shall give preference to such case, and hear and determine the same as early as practicable.

[1] Now TRAP 28 (effective Sept. 1, 1997).

TRCP 782. REMEDY CUMULATIVE

The remedy and mode of procedure hereby prescribed shall be construed to be cumulative of any now existing.

SECTION 8. TRESPASS TO TRY TITLE

TRCP 783. REQUISITES OF PETITION

The petition shall state:

(a) The real names of the plaintiff and defendant and their residences, if known.

(b) A description of the premises by metes and bounds, or with sufficient certainty to identify the same, so that from such description possession thereof may be delivered, and state the county or counties in which the same are situated.

(c) The interest which the plaintiff claims in the premises, whether it be a fee simple or other estate; and, if he claims an undivided interest, the petition shall state the same and the amount thereof.

(d) That the plaintiff was in possession of the premises or entitled to such possession.

(e) That the defendant afterward unlawfully entered upon and dispossessed him of such premises, stating the date, and withholds from him the possession thereof.

(f) If rents and profits or damages are claimed, such facts as show the plaintiff to be entitled thereto and the amount thereof.

(g) It shall conclude with a prayer for the relief sought.

TRCP 784. THE POSSESSOR SHALL BE DEFENDANT

The defendant in the action shall be the person in possession if the premises are occupied, or some person claiming title thereto in case they are unoccupied.

TRCP 785. MAY JOIN AS DEFENDANTS, WHEN

The plaintiff may join as a defendant with the person in possession, any other person who, as landlord, remainderman, reversioner or otherwise, may claim title to the premises, or any part thereof, adversely to the plaintiff.

TRCP 786. WARRANTOR, ETC., MAY BE MADE A PARTY

When a party is sued for lands, the real owner or warrantor may make himself, or may be made, a party defendant in the suit, and shall be entitled to make such defense as if he had been the original defendant in the action.

TRCP 787. LANDLORD MAY BECOME DEFENDANT

When such action shall be commenced against a tenant in possession, the landlord may enter himself as the defendant, or he may be made a party on motion of such tenant; and he shall be entitled to make the same defense as if the suit had been originally commenced against him.

TRCP 788. MAY FILE PLEA OF "NOT GUILTY" ONLY

The defendant in such action may file only the plea of "not guilty," which shall state in substance that he is not guilty of the injury complained of in the petition filed by the plaintiff against him, except that if he claims an allowance for improvements, he shall state the facts entitling him to the same.

TRCP 789. PROOF UNDER SUCH PLEA

Under such plea of "not guilty" the defendant may give in evidence any lawful defense to the action except the defense of limitations, which shall be specially pleaded.

TRCP 790. ANSWER TAKEN AS ADMITTING POSSESSION

Such plea or any other answer to the merits shall be an admission by the defendant, for the purpose of that action, that he was in possession of the premises sued for, or that he claimed title thereto at the time of commencing the action, unless he states distinctly in his answer the extent of his possession or claim, in which case it shall be an admission to such extent only.

TRCP 791. MAY DEMAND ABSTRACT OF TITLE

After answer filed, either party may, by notice in writing, duly served on the opposite party or his attorney of record, not less than ten days before the trial of the cause, demand an abstract in writing of the claim or title to the premises in question upon which he relies.

TRCP 792. TIME TO FILE ABSTRACT

Such abstract of title shall be filed with the papers of the cause that within thirty days after the service of the notice, or within such further time that the court on good cause shown may grant; and in default thereof, the court may, after notice and hearing prior to the beginning of trial, order that no written instruments which are evidence of the claim or title of such opposite party be given on trial.

TRCP 793. ABSTRACT SHALL STATE, WHAT

The abstract mentioned in the two preceding rules shall state:

(a) The nature of each document or written instrument intended to be used as evidence and its date; or

(b) If a contract or conveyance, its date, the parties thereto and the date of the proof of acknowledgment, and before what officer the same was made; and

(c) Where recorded, stating the book and page of the record.

(d) If not recorded in the county when the trial is had, copies of such instrument, with the names of the subscribing witnesses, shall be included. If such unrecorded instrument be lost or destroyed it shall be sufficient to state the nature of such instrument and its loss or destruction.

TRCP 794. AMENDED ABSTRACT

The court may allow either party to file an amended abstract of title, under the same rules, which authorize the amendment of pleadings so far as they are applicable; but in all cases the documentary evidence of title shall at the trial be confined to the matters contained in the abstract of title.

TRCP 795. RULES IN OTHER CASES OBSERVED

The trial shall be conducted according to the rules of pleading, practice and evidence in other cases in the district court and conformable to the principles of trial by ejectment, except as otherwise provided by these rules.

TRCP 796. SURVEYOR APPOINTED, ETC.

The judge of the court may, either in term time or in vacation, at his own discretion, or on motion of either party to the action appoint a surveyor, who shall survey the premises in controversy pursuant to the order of the court, and report his action under oath to such court. If said report be not rejected for good cause shown, the same shall be admitted as evidence on the trial.

TRCP 797. SURVEY UNNECESSARY, WHEN

Where there is no dispute as to the lines or boundaries of the land in controversy, or where the defendant admits that he is in possession of the lands or tenements included in the plaintiff's claim, or title, an order of survey shall be unnecessary.

TRCP 798. COMMON SOURCE OF TITLE

It shall not be necessary for the plaintiff to deraign title beyond a common source. Proof of a common source may be made by the plaintiff by certified copies of the deeds showing a chain of title to the defendant emanating from and under such common source. Before any such certified copies shall be read in evidence, they shall be filed with the papers of the suit three days before the trial, and the adverse party served with notice of such filing as in other cases. Such certified copies shall not be evidence of title in the defendant unless offered in evidence by him. The plaintiff may make any legal objection to such certified copies, or the originals thereof, when introduced by the defendant.

TRCP 799. JUDGMENT BY DEFAULT

If the defendant, who has been personally served with citation according to law or these rules fails to appear and answer by himself or attorney within the time prescribed by law or these rules for other actions in the district court, then judgment by default may be entered against him and in favor of the plaintiff for the title to the premises, or the possession thereof, or for both, according to the petition, and for all costs, without any proof of title by the plaintiff.

TRCP 800. PROOF EX PARTE

If the defendant has been cited only by publication, and fails to appear and answer by himself, or by attorney of his own selection, or if any defendant, having answered, fails to appear by himself or attorney when the case is called for trial on its merits, the plaintiff shall make such proof as will entitle him prima facie to recover, whereupon the proper judgment shall be entered.

TRCP 801. WHEN DEFENDANT CLAIMS PART ONLY

Where the defendant claims part of the premises only, the answer shall be equivalent to a disclaimer of the balance.

TRCP 802. WHEN PLAINTIFF PROVES PART

Where the defendant claims the whole premises, and the plaintiff shows himself entitled to recover part, the plaintiff shall recover such part and costs.

TRCP 803. MAY RECOVER A PART

When there are two or more plaintiffs or defendants any one or more of the plaintiffs may recover against one or more of the defendants the premises, or any part thereof, or any interest therein, or damages, according to the rights of the parties.

TRCP 804. THE JUDGMENT

Upon the finding of the jury, or of the court where the case is tried by the court, in favor of the plaintiff for the whole or any part of the premises in controversy, the judgment shall be that the plaintiff recover of the defendant the title or possession, or both, as the case may be, of such premises, describing them, and where he recovers the possession, that he have his writ of possession.

TRCP 805. DAMAGES

Where it is alleged and proved that one of the parties is in possession of the premises, the court or jury, if they find for the adverse party, shall assess the damages for the use and occupation of the premises. If special injury to the property be alleged and proved, the damages for such injury shall also be assessed, and the proper judgment shall be entered therefor, on which execution may issue.

TRCP 806. CLAIM FOR IMPROVEMENTS

When the defendant or person in possession has claimed an allowance for improvements in accordance with Sections 22.021-22.024, Texas Property Code, the claim for use and occupation and damages mentioned in the preceding rule shall be considered and acted on in connection with such claim by the defendant or person in possession.

TRCP 807. JUDGMENT WHEN CLAIM FOR IMPROVEMENTS IS MADE

When a claim for improvements is successfully made under Sections 22.021-22.024, Texas Property Code, the judgment shall recite the estimated value of the premises without the improvements, and shall also include the conditions, stipulations and directions contained in Sections 22.021-22.024, Texas Property Code so far as applicable to the case before the court.

TRCP 808. THESE RULES SHALL NOT GOVERN, WHEN

Nothing in Sections 22.001-22.045, Texas Property Code, shall be so construed as to alter, impair or take away the rights of parties, as arising under the laws in force before the introduction of the common law, but the same shall be decided by the principles of the law under which the same accrued, or by which the same were regulated or in any manner affected.

TRCP 809. THESE RULES SHALL NOT GOVERN, WHEN

Nothing in these rules relating to trespass to try title shall be so construed as to alter, impair or take away the rights of parties, as arising under the laws in force before the introduction of the common law, but the same shall be decided by the principles of the law under which the same accrued, or by which the same were regulated or in any manner affected.

SECTION 9. SUITS AGAINST NON-RESIDENTS

TRCP 810. REQUISITES OF PLEADINGS

The petition in actions authorized by Section 17.003, Civil Practice and Remedies Code, shall state the real names of the plaintiff and defendant, and shall describe the property involved with sufficient certainty to identify the same, the interest which the plaintiff claims, and such proceedings shall be had in such action as may be necessary to fully settle and determine the question of right or title in and to said property between the parties to said suit, and to decree the title or right of the party entitled thereto; and the court may issue the appropriate order to carry such decree, judgment or order into effect; and whenever such petition has been duly filed and citation thereon has been duly served by publication as required by Rules 114-116, the plaintiff may, at any time prior to entering the decree by leave of court first had and obtained, file amended and supplemental pleadings that do not subject additional property to said suit without the necessity of reciting the defendants so cited as aforesaid.

TRCP 811. SERVICE BY PUBLICATION IN ACTIONS UNDER §17.003, CIVIL PRACTICE & REMEDIES CODE

In actions authorized by Section 17.003, Civil Practice and Remedies Code, service on the defendant or defendants may be made by publication as is provided by Rules 114-116 or by service of notice of the character and in the manner provided by Rule 108.

TRCP 812. NO JUDGMENT BY DEFAULT

No judgment by default shall be taken in such case when service has been had by publication, but in such case the facts entitling the plaintiff to judgment shall be exhibited to the court on the trial; and a statement of facts shall be filed as provided by law and these rules in suits against nonresidents of this State served by publication, where no appearance has been made by them.

TRCP 813. SUIT TO EXTINGUISH LIEN

If said suit shall be for the extinguishment of a lien or claim for money on said property that may be held by the defendant, the amount thereof, with interest, shall be ascertained by the court; and the same deposited in the registry of the court, subject to be drawn by the parties entitled thereto; but in such case no decree shall be entered until said sum is deposited; which fact shall be noted in said decree.

PART VIII. CLOSING RULES

TRCP 814. EFFECTIVE DATE

These rules shall take effect on September 1st, 1941. They shall govern all proceedings in actions brought after they take effect, and also all further proceedings in actions then pending, except to the extent that in the opinion of the court their application in a particular action pending when the rules take effect would not be feasible or would work injustice, in which event the former procedure shall apply. All things properly done under any previously existing rule or statutes prior to the taking effect of these rules shall be treated as valid. Where citation or other process is issued and served in compliance with existing rules or laws prior to the taking effect of these rules, the party upon whom such citation or other process has been served shall have the time provided for under such previously existing rules or laws in which to comply therewith.

TRCP 815. SUBSTANTIVE RIGHTS UNAFFECTED

These rules shall not be construed to enlarge or diminish any substantive rights or obligations of any parties to any civil action.

See also Govt Code §22.004(a).

McLendon v. McLendon, 847 S.W.2d 601, 608 (Tex.App.—Dallas 1992, writ denied). "[T]he supreme court's rulemaking power may not [adopt rules that] 'abridge, enlarge, or modify the substantive rights of a litigant.' "

TRCP 816. JURISDICTION & VENUE UNAFFECTED

These rules shall not be construed to extend or limit the jurisdiction of the courts of the State of Texas nor the venue of actions therein.

TRCP 817. RENUMBERED

TRCP 818. REFERENCE TO FORMER STATUTES

Wherever any statute or rule refers to any practice or procedure in any law, laws, statute or statutes, or to a title, chapter, section, or article of the statutes, or contains any reference of any such nature, and the matter referred to has been supplanted in whole or in part by these rules, every such reference shall be deemed to be to the pertinent part or parts of these rules.

TRCP 819. PROCEDURE CONTINUED

All procedure prescribed by statutes of the State of Texas not specifically listed in the accompanying enumeration of repealed articles shall, insofar as the same is not inconsistent with the provisions of these rules, continue in accordance with the provisions of such statutes as rules of court. In case of inconsistency between the provisions of these rules and any statutory procedure not specifically listed as repealed, these rules shall apply.

Moore v. Johnson, 785 S.W.2d 176, 179 (Tex. App.—Waco 1990, orig. proceeding). TRCP 819 "clearly provides that in the event of an inconsistency between any statutory procedural matter which is given the effect of a court rule and a specific Rule of Civil Procedure, the Rule of Civil Procedure controls."

TRCP 820. WORKERS' COMPENSATION LAW

All portions of the Workers' Compensation Law, Articles 8306-8309-1, Revised Civil Statutes, and amendments thereto, which relate to matters of practice and procedure are hereby adopted and retained in force and effect as rules of court.

TRCP 821. PRIOR COURT RULES REPEALED

These rules shall supersede all Court Rules heretofore promulgated for any court; and all of said prior Court Rules are hereby repealed; provided, however, any rules of procedure heretofore adopted by a particular county or district court or by any Court of Appeals which were not of general application but were solely to regulate procedure in the particular court promulgating such rules are to remain in force and effect insofar as they are not inconsistent with these rules.

TRCP 822. TITLE

These rules may be known and cited as the Texas Rules of Civil Procedure.

TEXAS RULES OF EVIDENCE

ANNOTATED RULES

TABLE OF CONTENTS

TEXAS RULES OF EVIDENCE

ARTICLE I. GENERAL PROVISIONS

TRE 101. TITLE & SCOPE

(a) Title. These rules shall be known and cited as the Texas Rules of Evidence.

(b) Scope. Except as otherwise provided by statute, these rules govern civil and criminal proceedings (including examining trials before magistrates) in all courts of Texas, except small claims courts.

(c) Hierarchical Governance in Criminal Proceedings. Hierarchical governance shall be in the following order: the Constitution of the United States, those federal statutes that control states under the supremacy clause, the Constitution of Texas, the Code of Criminal Procedure and the Penal Code, civil statutes, these rules, and the common law. Where possible, inconsistency is to be removed by reasonable construction.

(d) Special Rules of Applicability in Criminal Proceedings.

(1) *Rules not applicable in certain proceedings.* These rules, except with respect to privileges, do not apply in the following situations:

(A) the determination of questions of fact preliminary to admissibility of evidence when the issue is to be determined by the court under Rule 104;

(B) proceedings before grand juries;

(C) proceedings in an application for habeas corpus in extradition, rendition, or interstate detainer;

(D) a hearing under Code of Criminal Procedure article 46.02, by the court out of the presence of a jury, to determine whether there is sufficient evidence of incompetency to require a jury determination of the question of incompetency;

(E) proceedings regarding bail except hearings to deny, revoke or increase bail;

(F) a hearing on justification for pretrial detention not involving bail;

(G) proceedings for the issuance of a search or arrest warrant; or

(H) proceedings in a direct contempt determination.

(2) *Applicability of privileges.* These rules with respect to privileges apply at all stages of all actions, cases, and proceedings.

(3) *Military justice hearings.* Evidence in hearings under the Texas Code of Military Justice, Tex. Gov't Code §432.001-432.195, shall be governed by that Code.

Comment to 1998 change: "Criminal proceedings" rather than "criminal cases" is used since that was the terminology used in the prior Rules of Criminal Evidence. In subpart (b), the reference to "trials before magistrates" comes from prior Criminal Rule 1101(a). In the prior Criminal Rules, both Rule 101 and Rule 1101 dealt with the same thing—the applicability of the rules. Thus, Rules 101(c) and (d) have been written to incorporate the provisions of former Criminal Rule 1101 and that rule is omitted.

See also Cochran, ***Texas Rules of Evidence Handbook***, p. 65 (2001).

TRE 102. PURPOSE & CONSTRUCTION

These rules shall be construed to secure fairness in administration, elimination of unjustifiable expense and delay, and promotion of growth and development of the law of evidence to the end that the truth may be ascertained and proceedings justly determined.

See also Cochran, ***Texas Rules of Evidence Handbook***, p. 78 (2001).

TRE 103. RULINGS ON EVIDENCE

(a) Effect of Erroneous Ruling. Error may not be predicated upon a ruling which admits or excludes evidence unless a substantial right of the party is affected, and

(1) *Objection.* In case the ruling is one admitting evidence, a timely objection or motion to strike appears of record, stating the specific ground of objection, if the specific ground was not apparent from the context. When the court hears objections to offered evidence out of the presence of the jury and rules that such evidence be admitted, such objections shall be deemed to apply to such evidence when it is admitted before the jury without the necessity of repeating those objections.

(2) *Offer of proof.* In case the ruling is one excluding evidence, the substance of the evidence was made known to the court by offer, or was apparent from the context within which questions were asked.

(b) Record of Offer and Ruling. The offering party shall, as soon as practicable, but before the court's charge is read to the jury, be allowed to make, in the absence of the jury, its offer of proof. The court may add any other or further statement which shows the character of the evidence, the form in which it was offered, the objection made, and the ruling thereon. The court may, or at the request of a party shall, direct the making of an offer in question and answer form.

(c) Hearing of Jury. In jury cases, proceedings shall be conducted, to the extent practicable, so as to prevent inadmissible evidence from being suggested to the jury by any means, such as making statements or offers of proof or asking questions in the hearing of the jury.

(d) Fundamental Error in Criminal Cases. In a criminal case, nothing in these rules precludes taking notice of fundamental errors affecting substantial rights although they were not brought to the attention of the court.

Comment to 1998 change: The exception to the requirement of an offer of proof for matters that were apparent from the context within which questions were asked, found in paragraph (a)(2), is now applicable to civil as well as criminal cases.

See also TRAP 44.1; ***O'Connor's Texas Rules***, "Motion in Limine," ch. 5-E; "Objecting to Evidence," ch. 8-D; "Offer of Proof & Bill of Exceptions," ch. 8-E; Cochran, ***Texas Rules of Evidence Handbook***, p. 79 (2001).

Bean v. Baxter Healthcare Corp., 965 S.W.2d 656, 660 (Tex.App.—Houston [14th Dist.] 1998, no pet.). Plaintiff "preserved error after its initial offer of the videotape. If exclusion of evidence is based on the substance of the evidence, however, the offering party must reoffer it if it again becomes relevant. This may occur when the evidence is pertinent to rebuttal. Error is waived if the offering party fails to reoffer evidence for a limited purpose after it has been excluded pursuant to a general objection."

Hill v. Heritage Res., Inc., 964 S.W.2d 89, 136 (Tex.App.—El Paso 1997, pet. denied). "To obtain a reversal of judgment based upon a trial court's decision to admit or exclude evidence, the [D] must show: (1) that the trial court abused its discretion in making the decision; and (2) that the error was reasonably calculated to cause and probably did cause rendition of an improper judgment. [¶] It has been held that when evidence is sharply conflicting and the case is hotly contested, any error of law by the trial court will be reversible...."

Ludlow v. Deberry, 959 S.W.2d 265, 270 (Tex. App.—Houston [14th Dist.] 1997, no writ). "The primary purpose of the offer of proof is to enable an appellate court to determine whether the exclusion was erroneous and harmful. A secondary purpose is to permit the trial judge to reconsider his ruling in light of the actual evidence. An offer of proof is sufficient if it apprised the court of the substance of the testimony and may be presented in the form of a concise statement.... When the trial court excludes evidence, failure to make an offer of proof waives any complaint about the exclusion on appeal."

Chance v. Chance, 911 S.W.2d 40, 52 (Tex.App.—Beaumont 1995, writ denied). "[T]he rule requiring that proffered evidence be incorporated in a bill of exception does not apply to cross-examination of an adverse witness.... When cross-examination testimony is excluded, appellant need not show the answer to be expected but only need show that the substance of the evidence was apparent form the context within which the question was asked."

Rendleman v. Clarke, 909 S.W.2d 56, 58 (Tex. App.—Houston [14th Dist.] 1995, writ dism'd). "We do not reach the merits of the admissibility of evidence of other falls because in each case, [D] either failed to object, or objected only after the testimony had been offered and received. To preserve a complaint for appellate review, a party must present to the trial court a *timely* request, objection, or motion, state the specific grounds therefor[e], and obtain a ruling before the testimony is offered and received."

TRE 104. PRELIMINARY QUESTIONS

(a) Questions of Admissibility Generally. Preliminary questions concerning the qualification of a person to be a witness, the existence of a privilege, or the admissibility of evidence shall be determined by the court, subject to the provisions of subdivision (b). In making its determination the court is not bound by the rules of evidence except those with respect to privileges.

(b) Relevancy Conditioned on Fact. When the relevancy of evidence depends upon the fulfillment of a condition of fact, the court shall admit it upon, or subject to, the introduction of evidence sufficient to support a finding of the fulfillment of the condition.

(c) Hearing of Jury. In a criminal case, a hearing on the admissibility of a confession shall be conducted out of the hearing of the jury. All other civil or criminal hearings on preliminary matters shall be conducted out of the hearing of the jury when the interests of justice so require or in a criminal case when an accused is a witness and so requests.

(d) Testimony by Accused Out of the Hearing of the Jury. The accused in a criminal case does not, by testifying upon a preliminary matter out of the hearing of the jury, become subject to cross-examination as to other issues in the case.

(e) Weight and Credibility. This rule does not limit the right of a party to introduce before the jury evidence relevant to weight or credibility.

See also *O'Connor's Texas Rules*, "Motion in Limine," ch. 5-E; "Objecting to Evidence," ch. 8-D; Cochran, ***Texas Rules of Evidence Handbook***, p. 99 (2001).

Bourjaily v. U.S., 483 U.S. 171, 175, 107 S.Ct. 2775, 2778-2779 (1987). "We are ... guided by our prior decisions regarding admissibility determinations that hinge on preliminary factual questions. We have traditionally required that these matters be established by a preponderance of proof. Evidence is placed before the jury when it satisfies the technical requirements of the evidentiary Rules, which embody certain legal and policy determinations. The inquiry made by a court concerned with these matters is not whether the proponent of the evidence wins or loses his case on the merits, but whether the evidentiary Rules have been satisfied. Thus, the evidentiary standard is unrelated to the burden of proof on the substantive issues, be it a criminal case ... or a civil case. The preponderance standard ensures that before admitting evidence, the court will have found it more likely than not that the technical issues and policy concerns addressed by the Federal Rules of Evidence have been afforded due consideration."

Broders v. Heise, 924 S.W.2d 148, 151 (Tex.1996). "The qualification of a witness as an expert is within the trial court's discretion. [T]he party offering the expert's testimony bears the burden to prove that the witness is qualified under [TRE] 702.

E.I. du Pont de Nemours & Co. v. Robinson, 923 S.W.2d 549, 556 (Tex.1995). "The trial court is responsible for making the preliminary determination of whether the proffered testimony meets the standards set forth [for experts]."

Lofton v. Texas Brine Corp., 777 S.W.2d 384, 386 (Tex.1989). "Testimony by an interested witness may establish a fact as a matter of law only if the testimony could be readily contradicted if untrue, and is clear, direct and positive, and there are no circumstances tending to discredit or impeach it."

TRE 105. LIMITED ADMISSIBILITY

(a) Limiting Instruction. When evidence which is admissible as to one party or for one purpose but not admissible as to another party or for another purpose is admitted, the court, upon request, shall restrict the evidence to its proper scope and instruct the jury accordingly; but, in the absence of such request the court's action in admitting such evidence without limitation shall not be a ground for complaint on appeal.

(b) Offering Evidence for Limited Purpose. When evidence referred to in paragraph (a) is excluded, such exclusion shall not be a ground for complaint on appeal unless the proponent expressly offers the evidence for its limited, admissible purpose or limits its offer to the party against whom it is admissible.

See also *O'Connor's Texas Rules*, "Request for limited admissibility," ch. 8-D, §6.1.3(1); Cochran, ***Texas Rules of Evidence Handbook***, p. 109 (2001).

Horizon v. Auld, 34 S.W.3d 887, 906 (Tex.2000). Defendant "did not request a limiting instruction as to the general admission of the survey reports. Thus, if the survey reports were admissible by any party or for any purpose, the court of appeals did not err in affirming the trial court's admission of the reports."

Larson v. Cactus Util. Co., 730 S.W.2d 640, 642 (Tex.1987). "Where tendered evidence should be considered for only one purpose, it is the opponent's burden to secure a limiting instruction. Absent a requested limiting instruction, [the opponent of the evidence] waived his grounds for complaint."

TRE 106. REMAINDER OF OR RELATED WRITINGS OR RECORDED STATEMENTS

When a writing or recorded statement or part thereof is introduced by a party, an adverse party may at that time introduce any other part or any other writing or recorded statement which ought in fairness to be considered contemporaneously with it. "Writing or recorded statement" includes depositions.

This rule is the same as FRE 106, with one modification. Under FRE 106, a party may require its opponent to introduce evidence contrary to the latter's own case. The Committee believed it was better to permit the party to introduce such evidence contemporaneously with the introduction of the incomplete evidence. TRCE 106 does not in any way circumscribe the right of a party to develop fully the matter on cross-examination or as part of his own case. *Cf.* Tex. Code Crim. P. art. 38.24. Nor does it alter the common law doctrine that the rule of optional completeness, as to writings, oral conversations, or other matters, may take precedence over exclusionary doctrines such as the hearsay or best evidence rule or the first-hand knowledge requirement.

See also Cochran, ***Texas Rules of Evidence Handbook***, p. 113 (2001).

Jones v. Colley, 820 S.W.2d 863, 866 (Tex.App.—Texarkana 1991, writ denied). TRE 106, the rule of optional completeness, "is not enforced by excluding the partial statement, but by allowing the opposing party to contemporaneously introduce any other part of the statement that should be considered with the portion introduced by the proponent."

TRE 107. RULE OF OPTIONAL COMPLETENESS

When part of an act, declaration, conversation, writing or recorded statement is given in evidence by one party, the whole on the same subject may be inquired into by the other, and any other act, declaration, writing or recorded statement which is necessary to make it fully understood or to explain the same may also be given in evidence, as when a letter is read, all letters on the same subject between the same parties may be given. "Writing or recorded statement" includes depositions.

Comment to 1998 change: This rule is the former Criminal Rule 107 except that the example regarding "when a letter is read" has been relocated in the rule so as to more accurately indicate the provision it explains. While this rule appeared only in the prior criminal rules, it is made applicable to civil cases because it accurately reflects the common law rule of optional completeness in civil cases.

See also Cochran, ***Texas Rules of Evidence Handbook***, p. 116 (2001).

ARTICLE II. JUDICIAL NOTICE

TRE 201. JUDICIAL NOTICE OF ADJUDICATIVE FACTS

(a) Scope of Rule. This rule governs only judicial notice of adjudicative facts.

(b) Kinds of Facts. A judicially noticed fact must be one not subject to reasonable dispute in that it is either (1) generally known within the territorial jurisdiction of the trial court or (2) capable of accurate and ready determination by resort to sources whose accuracy cannot reasonably be questioned.

(c) When Discretionary. A court may take judicial notice, whether requested or not.

(d) When Mandatory. A court shall take judicial notice if requested by a party and supplied with the necessary information.

(e) Opportunity to Be Heard. A party is entitled upon timely request to an opportunity to be heard as to the propriety of taking judicial notice and the tenor of the matter noticed. In the absence of prior notification, the request may be made after judicial notice has been taken.

(f) Time of Taking Notice. Judicial notice may be taken at any stage of the proceeding.

(g) Instructing Jury. In civil cases, the court shall instruct the jury to accept as conclusive any fact judicially noticed. In criminal cases, the court shall instruct the jury that it may, but is not required to, accept as conclusive any fact judicially noticed.

See also CPRC §38.004; ***O'Connor's Texas Rules***, "Motion for Judicial Notice," ch. 5-L; Cochran, ***Texas Rules of Evidence Handbook***, p. 122 (2001).

Office of Pub. Util. Counsel v. PUC, 878 S.W.2d 598, 600 (Tex.1994). "To be the proper subject of judicial notice, a fact must be 'capable of accurate and ready determination by resort to sources whose accuracy cannot reasonably be questioned.' Judicial notice is mandatory if 'requested by a party and [the court is] supplied with the necessary information.' A court of appeals has the power to take judicial notice for the first time on appeal. … The authenticity and contents of the PUC ratemaking order are capable of accurate and ready determination…."

Higginbotham v. General Life & Acc. Ins. Co., 796 S.W.2d 695, 696 (Tex.1990). "The trial court could properly take judicial notice that 12:01 p.m. on March 18, 1986 was an early afternoon on a Tuesday that was not a statutory holiday."

Coward v. Gateway Nat'l Bank, 525 S.W.2d 857, 859 (Tex.1975). CPRC chapter 38 "applies only in suits on one or more of the claims described in [CPRC §38.001]. [¶] [T]he Legislature authorized the court, in non-jury cases, to take judicial notice of [attorney fees]. [T]he court may examine the case file and is to make a determination of the amount of attorney's fees even if no other evidence is offered. This responsibility may be discharged by the trial judge in his role of trier of fact in the conventional trial of a non-jury case but not in passing on a motion for summary judgment."

Krishnan v. Ramirez, 42 S.W.3d 205, 222-23 (Tex. App.—Corpus Christi 2001, pet. denied). "Rule 201(b) allows a court to take judicial notice of a fact that is not subject to reasonable dispute. So long as a party provides proof of another court's records, a court can take judicial notice of another court's records."

Magee v. Ulery, 993 S.W.2d 332, 338-39 (Tex.App.—Houston [14th Dist.] 1999, no pet.). Plaintiffs "furnished information to the trial court that the Texas Medical Examiners Board advised [P's expert] of [P's treating physician's] birth date, place of practice, his status as a general practitioner, and his date of death. Accordingly, we find the facts were capable of accurate and ready determination by resort to a source whose accuracy cannot be reasonably questioned. Because the trial court was furnished with the 'necessary information,' it was error not to notice these facts under [TRE] 201(d)."

Trimble v. Texas DPRS, 981 S.W.2d 211, 215 (Tex. App.—Houston [14th Dist.] 1998, no pet.). "[A] trial court may take judicial notice of its own records in matters that are generally known, easily proven, and not reasonably disputed. [¶] The trial court acted within its discretion in taking judicial notice of the evidence and its previous rulings, and in admitting the statement of facts from previous rulings into the record at the hearing on application for permanent guardianship."

1.70 Acres v. State, 935 S.W.2d 480, 489 (Tex. App.—Beaumont 1996, no writ). "Although such variables as a vehicle's speed, road construction or repairs, weather, traffic, or accidents may be matters in someone's personal knowledge, they are not necessarily matters subject to judicial review. Personal knowledge is not judicial knowledge, and a judge may personally know a fact of which he cannot take judicial knowledge."

Tschirhart v. Tschirhart, 876 S.W.2d 507, 508 (Tex. App.—Austin 1994, no writ). "A court may not ... take judicial notice of the truth of allegations in its records."

Apostolic Ch. v. American Honda Motor Co., 833 S.W.2d 553, 555-56 (Tex.App.—Tyler 1992, writ denied). "Highway nomenclature and designations within the trial court's jurisdiction are matters of common knowledge and proper subjects for judicial notice. ... In matters involving geographical knowledge, it is not necessary that a formal request for judicial notice be made by a party."

TRE 202. DETERMINATION OF LAW OF OTHER STATES

A court upon its own motion may, or upon the motion of a party shall, take judicial notice of the constitutions, public statutes, rules, regulations, ordinances, court decisions, and common law of every other state, territory, or jurisdiction of the United States. A party requesting that judicial notice be taken of such matter shall furnish the court sufficient information to enable it properly to comply with the request, and shall give all parties such notice, if any, as the court may deem necessary, to enable all parties fairly to prepare to meet the request. A party is entitled upon timely request to an opportunity to be heard as to the propriety of taking judicial notice and the tenor of the matter noticed. In the absence of prior notification, the request may be made after judicial notice has been taken. Judicial notice of such matters may be taken at any stage of the proceeding. The court's determination shall be subject to review as a ruling on a question of law.

See also *O'Connor's Texas Rules*, "Motion for Judicial Notice," ch. 5-L; Cochran, *Texas Rules of Evidence Handbook*, p. 150 (2001).

Daugherty v. Southern P.T. Co., 772 S.W.2d 81, 83 (Tex.1989). "The failure to plead sister-state law does not preclude a court from judicially noticing that law. [TRE] 202 requires the moving party to furnish sufficient information to the trial court for it to determine the foreign law's applicability to the case and to furnish all parties any notice that the court finds necessary."

Pittsburgh Corning Corp. v. Walters, 1 S.W.3d 759, 769 (Tex.App.—Corpus Christi 1999, pet. denied). "The issue of a choice-of-law determination is distinct from the court's power to generally take judicial notice of a foreign state's law. [T]he mere fact that the court may take judicial notice of foreign laws does not mean that choice-of-law issues may be raised at any point in the proceeding. A preliminary motion is, therefore, necessary to assure the application of the laws of another jurisdiction. The court may undertake a choice of law analysis *sua sponte*, but [TRE] 202 does not compel this action."

TRE 203. DETERMINATION OF THE LAWS OF FOREIGN COUNTRIES

A party who intends to raise an issue concerning the law of a foreign country shall give notice in the pleadings or other reasonable written notice, and at least 30 days prior to the date of trial such party shall furnish all parties copies of any written materials or sources that the party intends to use as proof of the foreign law. If the materials or sources were originally written in a language other than English, the party intending to rely upon them shall furnish all parties both a copy of the foreign language text and an English translation. The court, in determining the law of a foreign nation, may consider any material or source, whether or not submitted by a party or admissible under the rules of evidence, including but not limited to affidavits, testimony, briefs, and treatises. If the court considers sources other than those submitted by a party, it shall give all parties notice and a reasonable opportunity to comment on the sources and to submit further materials for review by the court. The court, and not a jury, shall determine the laws of foreign countries. The court's determination shall be subject to review as a ruling on a question of law.

See also *O'Connor's Texas Rules*, "Motion for Judicial Notice," ch. 5-L; Cochran, *Texas Rules of Evidence Handbook*, p. 154 (2001).

Long Distance Int'l, Inc. v. Telefonos de Mexico, S.A., 49 S.W.3d 347, 351 (Tex.2001). "Rule 203 has been aptly characterized as a hybrid rule by which the presentation of the foreign law to the court resembles the presentment of evidence but which ultimately is decided as a question of law. Summary judgment is not precluded when experts disagree on the law's meaning if, as here, the parties do not dispute that all the pertinent foreign law was properly submitted in evidence. When experts disagree on how the foreign law applies to the facts, the court is presented with a question of law."

Bridas Corp. v. Unocal Corp., 16 S.W.3d 893, 896 (Tex.App.—Houston [14th Dist.] 2000, pet. denied). "Rule 203 is a hybrid rule by which presentation of the law to the court resembles presentment of evidence, but which the court ultimately decides as a matter of law. The determination of the law of a foreign country may present the court with a mixed question of law and fact. Summary judgment is not precluded when experts disagree on the interpretation of the law if, as in this case, the parties have not disputed that all of the pertinent foreign law was properly submitted in evidence. Where experts disagree on application of the law to the facts, the court is presented with a question of law."

Reading & Bates Constr. Co. v. Baker Energy Resources Corp., 976 S.W.2d 702, 707 (Tex.App.—Houston [1st Dist.] 1998, pet. denied). TRE 203 "facilitates a trial court's determination of a particular law of a foreign country. Although it is contained within the article designated, 'Judicial Notice,' the rule itself does not refer to judicial notice. It sets forth the procedural mechanism for raising an issue concerning the law of a foreign country, for giving notice to the other parties, and for furnishing materials concerning the foreign law."

TRE 204. DETERMINATION OF TEXAS CITY & COUNTY ORDINANCES, THE CONTENTS OF THE TEXAS REGISTER, & THE RULES OF AGENCIES PUBLISHED IN THE ADMINISTRATIVE CODE

A court upon its own motion may, or upon the motion of a party shall, take judicial notice of the ordinances of municipalities and counties of Texas, of the contents of the Texas Register, and of the codified rules of the agencies published in the Administrative Code. Any party requesting that judicial notice be taken of such matter shall furnish the court sufficient information to enable it properly to comply with the request, and shall give all parties such notice, if any, as the court may deem necessary, to enable all parties fairly to prepare to meet the request. A party is entitled upon timely request to an opportunity to be heard as to the propriety of taking judicial notice and the tenor of the matter noticed. In the absence of prior notification, the request may be made after judicial notice has been taken. The court's determination shall be subject to review as a ruling on a question of law.

See also *O'Connor's Texas Rules*, "Motion for Judicial Notice," ch. 5-L; Cochran, *Texas Rules of Evidence Handbook*, p. 158 (2001).

ARTICLE III. PRESUMPTIONS

[No rules adopted at this time.]

ARTICLE IV. RELEVANCY & ITS LIMITS

TRE 401. DEFINITION OF "RELEVANT EVIDENCE"

"Relevant evidence" means evidence having any tendency to make the existence of any fact that is of consequence to the determination of the action more probable or less probable than it would be without the evidence.

See also Cochran, *Texas Rules of Evidence Handbook*, p. 193.

E.I. du Pont de Nemours & Co. v. Robinson, 923 S.W.2d 549, 556 (Tex.1995). "[T]o constitute scientific knowledge which will assist the trier of fact, the proposed [scientific] testimony must be relevant and reliable. [¶] The requirement that the proposed testimony be relevant incorporates traditional relevancy analysis under [TRE] 401 and 402.... To be relevant, the proposed testimony must be 'sufficiently tied to the facts of the case that it will aid the jury in resolving a factual dispute.'"

Transportation Ins. Co. v. Moriel, 879 S.W.2d 10, 24-25 (Tex.1994). "Simply because a piece or pieces of evidence are material in the sense that they make a 'fact that is of consequence to the determination of the action more ... or less probable,' does not render the evidence legally sufficient. As Professor McCormick succinctly put it, 'a brick is not a wall.'"

Castillo v. State, 939 S.W.2d 754, 758 (Tex.App.—Houston [14th Dist.] 1997, writ ref'd). "The evidence need not prove or disprove a particular fact; the evidence is sufficiently relevant if it provides 'a small nudge' towards proving or disproving any fact of consequence. Furthermore, 'the motives which operate upon the mind of a witness when he testifies are never regarded as immaterial or collateral matters.'"

TRE 402. RELEVANT EVIDENCE GENERALLY ADMISSIBLE; IRRELEVANT EVIDENCE INADMISSIBLE

All relevant evidence is admissible, except as otherwise provided by Constitution, by statute, by these rules, or by other rules prescribed pursuant to statutory authority. Evidence which is not relevant is inadmissible.

See also *O'Connor's Texas Rules*, "Objecting to Evidence," ch. 8-D; Cochran, *Texas Rules of Evidence Handbook*, p. 193.

E.I. du Pont de Nemours & Co. v. Robinson, 923 S.W.2d 549, 556 (Tex.1995). "Evidence that has no relationship to any of the issues in the case is irrelevant and does not satisfy [TRE] 702's requirement that the testimony be of assistance to the jury. It is thus inadmissible under [TRE] 702 as well as under [TRE] 401 and 402."

Lunsford v. Morris, 746 S.W.2d 471, 473 (Tex. 1988). The rules of evidence do not "contemplate exclusion of otherwise relevant proof unless the evidence proffered is unfairly prejudicial, privileged, incompetent, or otherwise *legally* inadmissible. We do not circumscribe, however, a trial judge's authority to consider on motion whether a party's discovery request involves unnecessary harassment or invasion of personal or property rights."

Jampole v. Touchy, 673 S.W.2d 569, 573 (Tex. 1984), *overruled on other grounds*, ***Walker v. Packer***, 827 S.W.2d 833 (Tex.1992). "To increase the likelihood that all relevant evidence will be disclosed and brought before the trier of fact, the law circumscribes a significantly larger class of discoverable evidence [than admissible evidence] to include anything reasonably calculated to lead to the discovery of material evidence."

TRE 403. EXCLUSION OF RELEVANT EVIDENCE ON SPECIAL GROUNDS

Although relevant, evidence may be excluded if its probative value is substantially outweighed by the danger of unfair prejudice, confusion of the issues, or misleading the jury, or by considerations of undue delay, or needless presentation of cumulative evidence.

See also *O'Connor's Texas Rules*, "Objecting to Evidence," ch. 8-D; Cochran, *Texas Rules of Evidence Handbook*, p. 210.

Owens-Corning Fiberglas Corp. v. Malone, 972 S.W.2d 35, 41 (Tex.1998). "Evidence that is not relevant, or is unduly prejudicial, and thus, not admissible to mitigate punitive damages, includes actual damage amounts paid by settlements or by judgments; the number of pending claims filed against a [D] for the same conduct; the number of anticipated claims for the same conduct; insurance coverage; unpaid punitive damages awards for the same course of conduct; and evidence of punitive damages that may be levied in the future."

Ford Motor Co. v. Miles, 967 S.W.2d 377, 389 (Tex. 1998). "[R]elevant photographic evidence is admissible unless it is merely calculated to arouse the sympathy, prejudice or passion [of] the jury where the photographs do not serve to illustrate disputed issues or aid the jury in understanding the case. The videos were calculated to arouse the sympathy and passions of the jury." (Internal quotations omitted.)

Allstate Tex. Lloyds v. Potter, 30 S.W.3d 658, 662 (Tex.App.—Texarkana 2000, no pet.). TRE "403 does not require that the balancing test be performed on the record. The trial judge is assumed to have conducted the balancing test and determined that the evidence is inadmissible."

Pittsburgh Corning Corp. v. Walters, 1 S.W.3d 759, 772 (Tex.App.—Corpus Christi 1999, pet. denied). "The fact that evidence has some prejudicial effect is insufficient to warrant its exclusion. Instead, there must be a demonstration that introduction of the evidence would be *unfairly* prejudicial to the objecting party. Moreover, to be excluded, 'evidence must not only create a danger of unfair prejudice, but such danger must substantially outweigh its relevance.'"

Boswell v. Brazos Elec. Power Coop., 910 S.W.2d 593, 602 n.3 (Tex.App.—Fort Worth 1995, pet. denied). "In making its determination under [TRE] 403, the trial court must: (i) identify the probative value of the proffered evidence; (ii) identify the costs of admitting the evidence; and (iii) weigh one against the other."

TRE 404. CHARACTER EVIDENCE NOT ADMISSIBLE TO PROVE CONDUCT; EXCEPTIONS; OTHER CRIMES

(a) Character Evidence Generally. Evidence of a person's character or character trait is not admissible for the purpose of proving action in conformity therewith on a particular occasion, except:

(1) *Character of accused.* Evidence of a pertinent character trait offered:

(A) by an accused in a criminal case, or by the prosecution to rebut the same, or

(B) by a party accused in a civil case of conduct involving moral turpitude, or by the accusing party to rebut the same;

(2) *Character of victim.* In a criminal case and subject to Rule 412, evidence of a pertinent character trait of the victim of the crime offered by an accused, or by the prosecution to rebut the same, or evidence of peaceable character of the victim offered by the prosecution in a homicide case to rebut evidence that the victim was the first aggressor; or in a civil case, evidence of character for violence of the alleged victim of assaultive conduct offered on the issue of self-defense by a party accused of the assaultive conduct, or evidence of peaceable character to rebut the same;

(3) *Character of witness.* Evidence of the character of a witness, as provided in rules 607, 608 and 609.

(b) Other Crimes, Wrongs or Acts. Evidence of other crimes, wrongs or acts is not admissible to prove the character of a person in order to show action in conformity therewith. It may, however, be admissible for other purposes, such as proof of motive, opportunity, intent, preparation, plan, knowledge, identity, or absence of mistake or accident, provided that upon timely request by the accused in a criminal case, reasonable notice is given in advance of trial of intent to introduce in the State's case-in-chief such evidence other than that arising in the same transaction.

See also ***O'Connor's Texas Rules***, "Motion in Limine," ch. 5-E; Cochran, ***Texas Rules of Evidence Handbook***, p. 242 (2001).

State Bar v. Evans, 774 S.W.2d 656, 658 (Tex. 1989). "Since [the attorney] was accused of conduct involving moral turpitude, he was allowed to offer evidence of a pertinent trait of his character, which he did; the State Bar was then allowed to offer rebuttal testimony, which it did."

In re M.R., 975 S.W.2d 51, 55 (Tex.App.—San Antonio 1998, pet. denied). "Rule 404(b) ... allows evidence of 'other' wrongs or acts to be admitted when they are not admitted to prove character in order to show that that person acted in conformity with the prior conduct. Here, the Family Code mandates that such evidence be admitted for another purpose—in order to establish what is in the best interest of the child. [Mother] was not trying to prove that [father] committed acts in conformity with a prior act of violence. Instead, she was trying to establish that [his] violent act made it less in the best interest of the child that he be named sole managing conservator."

In re S.G., 935 S.W.2d 919, 924 (Tex.App.—San Antonio 1996, writ dism'd). "The philosophical basis for these exclusionary rules is that this type of character evidence tends to inject into a trial a dangerous baggage of prejudice, distraction from the issues, time consumption, and hazard of surprise." (Internal quotations omitted.)

Bexar Cty. Appr. Review Bd. v. First Baptist Ch., 846 S.W.2d 554, 562 (Tex.App.—San Antonio 1993, writ denied). "[T]he court ... allowed the church to elicit ... testimony about several of [the company's] charitable works. [¶] No one contends that [the company's] character was an issue.... The church argues that it is 'just good lawyering' to humanize and personalize a corporate entity. ... Under such a system, trials would turn into contests about which party has the better charitable record. [T]he rules strictly limit the admissibility of evidence of good or bad character."

TRE 405. METHODS OF PROVING CHARACTER

(a) Reputation or Opinion. In all cases in which evidence of a person's character or character trait is admissible, proof may be made by testimony as to reputation or by testimony in the form of an opinion. In a criminal case, to be qualified to testify at the guilt stage of trial concerning the character or character trait of an accused, a witness must have been familiar with the reputation, or with the underlying facts or information upon which the opinion is based, prior to the day of the offense. In all cases where testimony is admitted under this rule, on cross-examination inquiry is allowable into relevant specific instances of conduct.

(b) Specific Instances of Conduct. In cases in which a person's character or character trait is an essential element of a charge, claim or defense, proof may also be made of specific instances of that person's conduct.

See also *O'Connor's Texas Rules*, "Motion in Limine," ch. 5-E; Cochran, *Texas Rules of Evidence Handbook*, p. 243 (2001).

In re G.M.P., 909 S.W.2d 198, 209 (Tex.App.—Houston [14th Dist.] 1995, no writ). "[W]hen a witness testifies as to the character of the accused, [TRE] 405(a) allows 'do you know' questions to be asked of the witness to test the basis for his personal opinion. Here, by making the statement 'My son wouldn't do that,' [father of the accused] became a character witness, espousing his opinion about [the accused's] propensity to commit the crime."

International Sec. Life Ins. Co. v. Melancon, 463 S.W.2d 762, 767 (Tex.App.—Beaumont 1971, writ ref'd n.r.e.). In interrogating a witness on the subject of reputation, the only proper questions to ask are: "'Whether he knows the general character or reputation of the witness intended to be impeached in point of truth among his neighbors? If so, then what that character is, whether good or bad? We think the proper practice should be, that, after the impeaching witness has, prima facie, thus first qualified himself to speak of the general reputation of the other witness, (this to be decided by the court) then, before he answers the question as to what that reputation is, the opposite party, if he demands it, should have the right to cross-examine as to his means of knowledge....'"

TRE 406. HABIT; ROUTINE PRACTICE

Evidence of the habit of a person or of the routine practice of an organization, whether corroborated or not and regardless of the presence of eyewitnesses, is relevant to prove that the conduct of the person or organization on a particular occasion was in conformity with the habit or routine practice.

See also Cochran, *Texas Rules of Evidence Handbook*, p. 293 (2001).

Acker v. Water Comm'n, 790 S.W.2d 299, 302 (Tex. 1990). Both water commissioners who had been accused of holding an ex parte meeting in the restroom "testified by affidavit that they had no recollection of any conversation outside the hearing, and that considering their past behavior and habit at the Texas Water Commission, the occurrence of such a conversation was highly unlikely. The habit or custom of a person doing a particular act is relevant in determining his conduct on the occasion in question."

McClure v. Landis, 959 S.W.2d 679, 681 (Tex. App.—Austin 1997, pet. denied). "The two instances suggested by [D about P's conduct] do not establish a habit or pattern and have, therefore, no probative force whatever as contradicting the testimony and affidavits supplied by [D]."

TRE 407. SUBSEQUENT REMEDIAL MEASURES; NOTIFICATION OF DEFECT

(a) Subsequent Remedial Measures. When, after an event, measures are taken which, if taken previously, would have made the event less likely to occur, evidence of the subsequent remedial measures is not admissible to prove negligence or culpable conduct in connection with the event. This rule does not require the exclusion of evidence of subsequent remedial measures when offered for another purpose, such as proving ownership, control or feasibility of precautionary measures, if controverted, or impeachment. Nothing in this rule shall preclude admissibility in products liability cases based on strict liability.

(b) Notification of Defect. A written notification by a manufacturer of any defect in a product produced by such manufacturer to purchasers thereof is admissible against the manufacturer on the issue of existence of the defect to the extent that it is relevant.

See also *O'Connor's Texas Rules*, "Motion in Limine," ch. 5-E; Cochran, *Texas Rules of Evidence Handbook*, p. 300 (2001).

Beavers v. Northrop Worldwide Aircraft Servs., Inc., 821 S.W.2d 669, 677 (Tex.App.—Amarillo 1991, writ denied). "[W]e hold the exclusion under [TRE] 407(a) does not apply to evidence of subsequent remedial measures taken by third parties when offered to show that a [D] was not the cause of [P's] injury."

E.V.R. II Assocs. v. Brundige, 813 S.W.2d 552, 556 (Tex.App.—Dallas 1991, no writ). "Evidence of subsequent remedial repair is inadmissible to establish negligence. The rule is one of policy and good sense to avoid discouraging safety measures. [T]he rule is inapplicable where the evidence would be valid as to other issues which also exist in the case."

TRE 408. COMPROMISE & OFFERS TO COMPROMISE

Evidence of (1) furnishing or offering or promising to furnish or (2) accepting or offering or promising to accept, a valuable consideration in compromising or attempting to compromise a claim which was disputed as to either validity or amount is not admissible to prove liability for or invalidity of the claim or its amount. Evidence of conduct or statements made in compromise negotiations is likewise not admissible. This rule does not require the exclusion of any evidence otherwise discoverable merely because it is presented in the course of compromise negotiations. This rule also does not require exclusion when the evidence is offered for another purpose, such as proving bias or prejudice or interest of a witness or a party, negativing a contention of undue delay, or proving an effort to obstruct a criminal investigation or prosecution.

See also *O'Connor's Texas Rules*, "Motion in Limine," ch. 5-E; Cochran, *Texas Rules of Evidence Handbook*, p. 310 (2001).

Ford Motor Co. v. Leggat, 904 S.W.2d 643, 649 (Tex.1995). "Settlement agreements are discoverable ... to the extent they are relevant. Settlement agreements themselves ... are not admissible at trial to prove liability." *See also* ***Birchfield v. Texarkana Mem. Hosp.***, 747 S.W.2d 361, 365 (Tex.1987).

Stam v. Mack, 984 S.W.2d 747, 752 (Tex.App.—Texarkana 1999, no pet.). "Settlement agreements may be admissible ... if offered for other purposes, such as proving bias or prejudice. One kind of settlement agreement that is admissible is a 'Mary Carter' agreement. ... These agreements are admissible to show the true alignment of the parties."

Tarrant Cty. v. English, 989 S.W.2d 368, 377 (Tex. App.—Fort Worth 1998, pet. denied). "The [TREs] prohibit the admission of settlement negotiations to prove a party's liability. But evidence of settlement negotiations may be admitted for other purposes, such as establishing that statements made during the negotiations were misrepresentations. In this case, the trial court admitted the letter for the limited purpose of showing [P's] state of mind."

State Farm Mut. Auto. Ins. Co. v. Wilborn, 835 S.W.2d 260, 261 (Tex.App.—Houston [14th Dist.] 1992, orig. proceeding). "[O]ffers of settlement and compromise are excluded in order to allow a party to buy his peace and encourage settlement of claims outside of the courthouse."

Ochs v. Martinez, 789 S.W.2d 949, 959 (Tex.App.—San Antonio 1990, writ denied). "The [TRE] 408 exception allowing for admission of evidence of bias or prejudice [even if statement is made during settlement negotiations] is a narrow one drafted in consideration of strong Texas judicial policy favoring the disclosure of conflicts of interest among parties to a lawsuit...."

TRE 409. PAYMENT OF MEDICAL & SIMILAR EXPENSES

Evidence of furnishing or offering or promising to pay medical, hospital, or similar expenses occasioned by an injury is not admissible to prove liability for the injury.

See also *O'Connor's Texas Rules*, "Motion in Limine," ch. 5-E; Cochran, *Texas Rules of Evidence Handbook*, p. 332 (2001).

Port Neches ISD v. Soignier, 702 S.W.2d 756, 757 (Tex.App.—Beaumont 1986, writ ref'd n.r.e.). A letter from an insurance company authorizing medical expenses for a workers' compensation plaintiff and stating that all future medical bills should be sent to the insurance company goes beyond TRE 409 and actually admits coverage, and thus is admissible.

TRE 410. INADMISSIBILITY OF PLEAS, PLEA DISCUSSIONS & RELATED STATEMENTS

Except as otherwise provided in this rule, evidence of the following is not admissible against the defendant who made the plea or was a participant in the plea discussions:

(1) a plea of guilty that was later withdrawn;

(2) in civil cases, a plea of *nolo contendere*, and in criminal cases, a plea of *nolo contendere* that was later withdrawn;

(3) any statement made in the course of any proceedings under Rule 11 of the Federal Rules of Criminal Procedure or comparable state procedure regarding, in a civil case, either a plea of guilty that was later withdrawn or a plea of *nolo contendere*, or in a criminal case, either a plea of guilty that was later withdrawn or a plea of *nolo contendere* that was later withdrawn; or

(4) any statement made in the course of plea discussions with an attorney for the prosecuting authority, in a civil case, that do not result in a plea of guilty or that

result in a plea of guilty later withdrawn, or in a criminal case, that do not result in a plea of guilty or a plea of *nolo contendere* or that results in a plea, later withdrawn, of guilty or *nolo contendere*.

However, such a statement is admissible in any proceeding wherein another statement made in the course of the same plea or plea discussions has been introduced and the statement ought in fairness be considered contemporaneously with it.

See also *O'Connor's Texas Rules*, "Motion in Limine," ch. 5-E; Cochran, *Texas Rules of Evidence Handbook*, p. 336 (2001).

Cox v. Bohman, 683 S.W.2d 757, 758 (Tex.App.—Corpus Christi 1984, writ ref'd n.r.e.). "Unless a plea of guilty to a traffic offense was made in open court ... evidence of such guilty plea is not admissible in a civil suit for damages arising out of negligence giving rise to the charge.... A plea of *nolo contendere* to a traffic violation cannot be admitted into evidence in a civil suit for damages arising out of the same incident."

TRE 411. LIABILITY INSURANCE

Evidence that a person was or was not insured against liability is not admissible upon the issue whether the person acted negligently or otherwise wrongfully. This rule does not require the exclusion of evidence of insurance against liability when offered for another issue, such as proof of agency, ownership, or control, if disputed, or bias or prejudice of a witness.

See also Cochran, *Texas Rules of Evidence Handbook*, p. 349 (2001).

Thornhill v. Ronnie's I-45 Truck Stop, Inc., 944 S.W.2d 780, 794 (Tex.App.—Beaumont 1997, writ dism'd). TRE 411 "only prohibits the admission of 'liability insurance,' not 'property insurance.' [¶] [TRE] 411 only prohibits the admission of evidence that a person was or was not insured against liability upon the issue of whether he acted negligently or otherwise wrongfully. [TRE] 411 ... 'does not require the exclusion of evidence of insurance against liability when offered for another issue, such as proof of agency, ownership, or *control*.'"

Beall v. Ditmore, 867 S.W.2d 791, 795 (Tex.App.—El Paso 1993, writ denied). "The mere mention of insurance during trial before a jury, though erroneous, does not result in an automatic mistrial or reversal."

TRE 412. EVIDENCE OF PREVIOUS SEXUAL CONDUCT IN CRIMINAL CASES

(a) Reputation or Opinion Evidence. In a prosecution for sexual assault or aggravated sexual assault, or attempt to commit sexual assault or aggravated sexual assault, reputation or opinion evidence of the past sexual behavior of an alleged victim of such crime is not admissible.

(b) Evidence of Specific Instances. In a prosecution for sexual assault or aggravated sexual assault, or attempt to commit sexual assault or aggravated sexual assault, evidence of specific instances of an alleged victim's past sexual behavior is also not admissible, unless:

(1) such evidence is admitted in accordance with paragraphs (c) and (d) of this rule;

(2) it is evidence:

(A) that is necessary to rebut or explain scientific or medical evidence offered by the State;

(B) of past sexual behavior with the accused and is offered by the accused upon the issue of whether the alleged victim consented to the sexual behavior which is the basis of the offense charged;

(C) that relates to the motive or bias of the alleged victim;

(D) is admissible under Rule 609; or

(E) that is constitutionally required to be admitted; and

(3) its probative value outweighs the danger of unfair prejudice.

(c) Procedure for Offering Evidence. If the defendant proposes to introduce any documentary evidence or to ask any question, either by direct examination or cross-examination of any witness, concerning specific instances of the alleged victim's past sexual behavior, the defendant must inform the court out of the hearing of the jury prior to introducing any such evidence or asking any such question. After this notice, the court shall conduct an in camera hearing, recorded by the court reporter, to determine whether the proposed evidence is admissible under paragraph (b) of this rule. The court shall determine what evidence is admissible and shall accordingly limit the questioning. The defendant shall not go outside these limits or refer to any evidence ruled inadmissible in camera without prior approval of the court without the presence of the jury.

(d) Record Sealed. The court shall seal the record of the in camera hearing required in paragraph (c) of this rule for delivery to the appellate court in the event of an appeal.

(e) Sexual Conduct of Child as Defense.[1] This rule does not limit the right of the accused to produce evidence of promiscuous sexual conduct of a child 14 years old or older as a defense to sexual assault, aggravated sexual assault, indecency with a child or an attempt to commit any of the foregoing crimes. If such evidence is admitted, the court shall instruct the jury as to the purpose of the evidence and as to its limited use.

[1] Editor's note: Former TRCrE 412(e), now TRE 412(e), was disapproved by the Texas Legislature in Acts 1993, 73rd Leg., ch. 900, §1.17 (eff. Sept. 1, 1994). *See* Govt Code §22.109(b) (authority to disapprove rules of evidence in criminal cases).

See also Cochran, ***Texas Rules of Evidence Handbook***, p. 357 (2001).

In re Doe, 22 S.W.3d 601, 611-12 (Tex.App.—Austin 2000, orig. proceeding). Plaintiff "argues that the 'rape victims shield laws,' incorporated in [TRE] 412, should apply despite the fact that the Rule specifically applies only in criminal cases. [¶] At this early stage of the litigation and considering the fact that [P] pleads that this was a forcible assault and the grand jury indicted [D's employee] under the criminal statutes for the crime of sexual assault, we hold that until the record is more fully developed and these issues are clarified the rape shield laws ought to protect the victim ... at this time. We hold that the trial court abused its discretion by failing to issue a protective order preventing [D] from questioning [P] about her past and present sexual activity."

ARTICLE V. PRIVILEGES

TRE 501. PRIVILEGES RECOGNIZED ONLY AS PROVIDED

Except as otherwise provided by Constitution, by statute, by these rules, or by other rules prescribed pursuant to statutory authority, no person has a privilege to:

(1) refuse to be a witness;

(2) refuse to disclose any matter;

(3) refuse to produce any object or writing; or

(4) prevent another from being a witness or disclosing any matter or producing any object or writing.

Caution: TRE 501 is affected by the following sections in the Fam. Code: §§6.704, 6.705, 152.310, 159.314, 159.316, 231.108, 261.101, 261.201, 261.202.

See also ***O'Connor's Texas Rules***, "Scope of Discovery," ch. 6-B; Cochran, ***Texas Rules of Evidence Handbook***, p. 374 (2001).

Volkswagen, A.G. v. Valdez, 909 S.W.2d 900, 902-03 (Tex.1995). The trial court must weigh the following factors when evaluating a privilege of a foreign county: (1) the importance of the discovery request to the investigation or litigation; (2) the degree of specificity of the request; (3) whether the information originated in the U.S.; (4) the availability of alternative means of securing the information; and (5) the extent to which noncompliance with the request would undermine important interests of the U.S., or the extent to which compliance would undermine important interests of the foreign jurisdiction where the information is located.

State v. Lowry, 802 S.W.2d 669, 671 (Tex.1991). "Only in certain narrow circumstances is it appropriate to obstruct the search for truth by denying discovery. Very limited exceptions to the strongly preferred policy of openness are recognized in our state procedural rules and statutes."

Oyster Creek Fin. Corp. v. Richwood Invs., II, Inc., 957 S.W.2d 640, 646 (Tex.App.—Amarillo 1997, pet. denied). "[B]ecause evidence is presumed discoverable, the party resisting discovery ... bears the burden of establishing the privilege and, therefore, must plead it and present evidence which establishes that the document(s) in question qualify for the privilege as a matter of law."

TRE 502. REQUIRED REPORTS PRIVILEGED BY STATUTE

A person, corporation, association, or other organization or entity, either public or private, making a return or report required by law to be made has a privilege to refuse to disclose and to prevent any other person from disclosing the return or report, if the law requiring it to be made so provides. A public officer or agency to whom a return or report is required by law to be made has a privilege to refuse to disclose the return or report if the law requiring it to be made so provides. No privilege exists under this rule in actions involving perjury, false statements, fraud in the return or report, or other failure to comply with the law in question.

See also *O'Connor's Texas Rules*, "Scope of Discovery," ch. 6-B; Cochran, *Texas Rules of Evidence Handbook*, p. 377 (2001).

Star-Telegram, Inc. v. Schattman, 784 S.W.2d 109, 111 (Tex.App.—Fort Worth 1990, no writ). TRE 502 "only protects reports 'required by law to be made' if the law requiring the report to be made makes such report privileged. Reports are not required under the EEOC sexual harassment guidelines … and certainly are not made privileged.… Rule 502 thus provides no privilege here."

TRE 503. LAWYER-CLIENT PRIVILEGE

(a) Definitions. As used in this rule:

(1) A "client" is a person, public officer, or corporation, association, or other organization or entity, either public or private, who is rendered professional legal services by a lawyer, or who consults a lawyer with a view to obtaining professional legal services from that lawyer.

(2) A "representative of the client" is:

(A) a person having authority to obtain professional legal services, or to act on advice thereby rendered, on behalf of the client, or

(B) any other person who, for the purpose of effectuating legal representation for the client, makes or receives a confidential communication while acting in the scope of employment for the client.

(3) A "lawyer" is a person authorized, or reasonably believed by the client to be authorized, to engage in the practice of law in any state or nation.

(4) A "representative of the lawyer" is:

(A) one employed by the lawyer to assist the lawyer in the rendition of professional legal services; or

(B) an accountant who is reasonably necessary for the lawyer's rendition of professional legal services.

(5) A communication is "confidential" if not intended to be disclosed to third persons other than those to whom disclosure is made in furtherance of the rendition of professional legal services to the client or those reasonably necessary for the transmission of the communication.

(b) Rules of Privilege.

(1) *General rule of privilege.* A client has a privilege to refuse to disclose and to prevent any other person from disclosing confidential communications made for the purpose of facilitating the rendition of professional legal services to the client:

(A) between the client or a representative of the client and the client's lawyer or a representative of the lawyer;

(B) between the lawyer and the lawyer's representative;

(C) by the client or a representative of the client, or the client's lawyer or a representative of the lawyer, to a lawyer or a representative of a lawyer representing another party in a pending action and concerning a matter of common interest therein;

(D) between representatives of the client or between the client and a representative of the client; or

(E) among lawyers and their representatives representing the same client.

(2) *Special rule of privilege in criminal cases.* In criminal cases, a client has a privilege to prevent the lawyer or lawyer's representative from disclosing any other fact which came to the knowledge of the lawyer or the lawyer's representative by reason of the attorney-client relationship.

(c) Who May Claim the Privilege. The privilege may be claimed by the client, the client's guardian or conservator, the personal representative of a deceased client, or the successor, trustee, or similar representative of a corporation, association, or other organization, whether or not in existence. The person who was the lawyer or the lawyer's representative at the time of the communication is presumed to have authority to claim the privilege but only on behalf of the client.

(d) Exceptions. There is no privilege under this rule:

(1) *Furtherance of crime or fraud.* If the services of the lawyer were sought or obtained to enable or aid anyone to commit or plan to commit what the client knew or reasonably should have known to be a crime or fraud;

(2) *Claimants through same deceased client.* As to a communication relevant to an issue between parties who claim through the same deceased client, regardless of whether the claims are by testate or intestate succession or by inter vivos transactions;

(3) *Breach of duty by a lawyer or client.* As to a communication relevant to an issue of breach of duty by a lawyer to the client or by a client to the lawyer;

(4) *Document attested by a lawyer.* As to a communication relevant to an issue concerning an attested document to which the lawyer is an attesting witness; or

(5) *Joint clients.* As to a communication relevant to a matter of common interest between or among two or more clients if the communication was made by any of them to a lawyer retained or consulted in common, when offered in an action between or among any of the clients.

Comment to 1998 change: The addition of subsection (a)(2)(B) adopts a subject matter test for the privilege of an entity, in place of the control group test previously used. See also *National Tank Co. v. Brotherton*, 851 S.W.2d 193, 197-198 (Tex.1993).

Caution: TRE 503 is affected by the following sections in the Fam. Code: §§261.101, 261.202.

See also ***O'Connor's Texas Rules***, "Scope of Discovery," ch. 6-B; Cochran, ***Texas Rules of Evidence Handbook***, p. 379 (2001).

Generally

Duncan v. Board of Disciplinary Appeals, 898 S.W.2d 759, 762 (Tex.1995). "Our rules recognize that our system of justice relies on a client's privilege to speak frankly and candidly with his or her attorney."

Boales v. Brighton Builders, Inc., 29 S.W.3d 159, 168 (Tex.App.—Houston [14th Dist.] 2000, pet. denied). "Under the lawyer-client privilege, the client may refuse to disclose and may prevent any other person from disclosing confidential communications made for the purpose of facilitating rendition of legal services to client. The privilege extends to all matters concerning litigation or business transactions, regardless of whether the matters are pertinent to the matter for which the attorney was employed. The statements and advice of the attorney to the client are as protected as the communications of the client to the attorney."

In re Monsanto Co., 998 S.W.2d 917, 930 (Tex. App.—Waco 1999, orig. proceeding). "We recognize that it might be argued [under TRE 503(a)(2)(B)] that all communications between corporate representatives could be claimed as privileged on the basis that 'the legal department can better represent us if we keep them informed.' We reject that assertion. We do not believe that it is necessary for the legal department to be advised of every development out in the field, no matter how minute. Thus, we applied common sense to the contents of the documents."

In re Texas Farmers Ins., 990 S.W.2d 337, 340 (Tex. App.—Texarkana 1999, orig. proceeding). The attorney-client "privilege does not apply if the attorney is acting in a capacity other than that of an attorney. *At 341:* Based on the evidence presented at the hearing, the trial court did not abuse its discretion in determining that [the attorney] was acting as an investigator and was conducting a routine investigation of a fire of suspicious origin."

Markowski v. City of Marlin, 940 S.W.2d 720, 726 (Tex.App.—Waco 1997, writ denied). "[A] governmental body has as much right as an individual to consult with its attorney without risking the disclosure of important confidential information."

Perez v. Kirk & Carrigan, 822 S.W.2d 261, 265 (Tex. App.—Corpus Christi 1991, writ denied). "An agreement to form an attorney-client relationship may be implied from the conduct of the parties. Moreover, the relationship does not depend upon the payment of a fee, but may exist as a result of rendering services gratuitously."

Borden, Inc. v. Valdez, 773 S.W.2d 718, 720 (Tex. App.—Corpus Christi 1989, orig. proceeding). "An attorney may not avoid a deposition [on grounds of attorney-client privilege] merely because some matters may be privileged, but must object when those inquiries are raised during the deposition."

Exceptions to Privilege

Granada Corp. v. 1st Ct. of Appeals, 844 S.W.2d 223, 227 (Tex.1992). "The crime-fraud exception [to the attorney-client privilege in TRE 503(d)(1)] applies only if a prima facie case is made of contemplated fraud. Additionally, there must be a relationship between the document for which the privilege is challenged and the prima facie proof offered."

Vinson & Elkins v. Moran, 946 S.W.2d 381, 394 (Tex.App.—Houston [14th Dist.] 1997, writ dism'd). "When an attorney is sued by his own client, the attorney is permitted to reveal confidential information so far as necessary to defend himself."

Offensive use

Republic Ins. Co. v. Davis, 856 S.W.2d 158, 163 (Tex.1993). "In an instance in which the privilege is being used as a sword rather than a shield, the privilege may be waived. Privileges, however, represent society's desire to protect certain relationships, and an offensive use waiver of a privilege should not lightly be found. For that reason, the following factors should guide the trial court in determining whether a waiver has occurred. [¶] First, before a waiver may be found the party asserting the privilege must seek affirmative relief. Second, the privileged information sought must be such that, if believed by the fact finder, in all probability it would be outcome determinative of the cause of action asserted. Mere relevance is insufficient. A contradiction in position without more is insufficient. The confidential communication must go to the very heart of the affirmative relief sought. Third, disclosure of the confidential communication must be the only means by which the aggrieved party may obtain the evidence. If any one of these requirements is lacking, the trial court must uphold the privilege."

TRE 504. HUSBAND-WIFE PRIVILEGES

(a) Confidential Communication Privilege.

(1) *Definition.* A communication is confidential if it is made privately by any person to the person's spouse and it is not intended for disclosure to any other person.

(2) *Rule of privilege.* A person, whether or not a party, or the guardian or representative of an incompetent or deceased person, has a privilege during marriage and afterwards to refuse to disclose and to prevent another from disclosing a confidential communication made to the person's spouse while they were married.

(3) *Who may claim the privilege.* The confidential communication privilege may be claimed by the person or the person's guardian or representative, or by the spouse on the person's behalf. The authority of the spouse to do so is presumed.

(4) *Exceptions.* There is no confidential communication privilege:

(A) *Furtherance of crime or fraud.* If the communication was made, in whole or in part, to enable or aid anyone to commit or plan to commit a crime or fraud.

(B) *Proceeding between spouses in civil cases.* In (A)[1] a proceeding brought by or on behalf of one spouse against the other spouse, or (B)[2] a proceeding between a surviving spouse and a person who claims through the deceased spouse, regardless of whether the claim is by testate or intestate succession or by inter vivos transaction.

(C) *Crime against spouse or minor child.* In a proceeding in which the party is accused of conduct which, if proved, is a crime against the person of the spouse, any minor child, or any member of the household of either spouse.

(D) *Commitment or similar proceeding.* In a proceeding to commit either spouse or otherwise to place that person or that person's property, or both, under the control of another because of an alleged mental or physical condition.

(E) *Proceeding to establish competence.* In a proceeding brought by or on behalf of either spouse to establish competence.

(b) Privilege not to Testify in Criminal Case.

(1) *Rule of privilege.* In a criminal case, the spouse of the accused has a privilege not to be called as a witness for the state. This rule does not prohibit the spouse from testifying voluntarily for the state, even over objection by the accused. A spouse who testifies on behalf of an accused is subject to cross-examination as provided in rule 611(b).

(2) *Failure to call as witness.* Failure by an accused to call the accused's spouse as a witness, where other evidence indicates that the spouse could testify to relevant matters, is a proper subject of comment by counsel.

(3) *Who may claim the privilege.* The privilege not to testify may be claimed by the person or the person's guardian or representative but not by that person's spouse.

(4) *Exceptions.* The privilege of a person's spouse not to be called as a witness for the state does not apply:

(A) *Certain criminal proceedings.*[3] In any proceeding in which the person is charged with a crime against the person's spouse, a member of the household of either spouse, or any minor.

(B) *Matters occurring prior to marriage.* As to matters occurring prior to the marriage.

1 Editor's Note: This should probably read "(i)".

2 Editor's Note: This should probably read "(ii)".

3 Editor's Note: Former TRCrE 504(2)(b)(1), now TRE 504(b)(4)(A), was disapproved by the Texas Legislature in Acts 1995, 74th Leg., ch. 67, §6 (eff. Sept. 1, 1995). *See* Govt Code §22.109(b) (authority to disapprove rules of evidence in criminal cases).

Comment to 1998 change: The rule eliminates the spousal testimonial privilege for prosecutions in which the testifying spouse is the alleged victim of a crime by the accused. This is intended to be consistent with Code of Criminal Procedure article 38.10, effective September 1, 1995.

Caution: TRE 504 is affected by the following sections in the Fam. Code: §§6.704, 152.310, 159.316.

See also ***O'Connor's Texas Rules***, "Scope of Discovery," ch. 6-B; Cochran, ***Texas Rules of Evidence Handbook***, p. 417 (2001).

Marshall v. Ryder Sys., Inc., 928 S.W.2d 190, 195 (Tex.App.—Houston [14th Dist.] 1996, writ denied). In civil cases, "[t]he marital privilege is limited to *confidential* communications between spouses. Only in criminal cases is there a broad, general privilege protecting a person from being a witness against his or her spouse."

Earthman's, Inc. v. Earthman, 526 S.W.2d 192, 206 (Tex.App.—Houston [1st Dist.] 1975, no writ). "We do not regard as error the trial court's ruling which allowed evidence of communications between [the parties] based on conversations prior to and after their divorce. This testimony insofar as relevant to the existing controversy between them was admissible notwithstanding the marital privilege."

TRE 505. COMMUNICATIONS TO MEMBERS OF THE CLERGY

(a) Definitions. As used in this rule:

(1) A "member of the clergy" is a minister, priest, rabbi, accredited Christian Science Practitioner, or other similar functionary of a religious organization or an individual reasonably believed so to be by the person consulting with such individual.

(2) A communication is "confidential" if made privately and not intended for further disclosure except to other persons present in furtherance of the purpose of the communication.

(b) General Rule of Privilege. A person has a privilege to refuse to disclose and to prevent another from disclosing a confidential communication by the person to a member of the clergy in the member's professional character as spiritual adviser.

(c) Who May Claim the Privilege. The privilege may be claimed by the person, by the person's guardian or conservator, or by the personal representative of the person if the person is deceased. The member of the clergy to whom the communication was made is presumed to have authority to claim the privilege but only on behalf of the communicant.

See also *O'Connor's Texas Rules*, "Scope of Discovery," ch. 6-B; Cochran, ***Texas Rules of Evidence Handbook***, p. 440 (2001).

Simpson v. Tennant, 871 S.W.2d 301, 306 (Tex. App.—Houston [14th Dist.] 1994, orig. proceeding). "The real issue in this case is whether the scope of the communications-to-clergymen privilege encompasses the *identity* of the communicant. We hold, on the facts in this case, that it does."

Nicholson v. Wittig, 832 S.W.2d 681, 685 (Tex. App.—Houston [1st Dist.] 1992, orig. proceeding). The clergy-communicant "privilege attaches when a person makes a communication with a reasonable expectation of confidentiality to a member of the clergy acting in his or her professional or spiritual capacity. [¶] An individual may invoke a privilege regardless of the nature of the underlying proceeding. *At 686:* Rule 505 makes no reference to the content of the communication; rather, the rule focuses on the counseling opportunity."

TRE 506. POLITICAL VOTE

Every person has a privilege to refuse to disclose the tenor of the person's vote at a political election conducted by secret ballot unless the vote was cast illegally.

See also ***O'Connor's Texas Rules***, "Scope of Discovery," ch. 6-B; Cochran, ***Texas Rules of Evidence Handbook***, p. 446 (2001).

TRE 507. TRADE SECRETS

A person has a privilege, which may be claimed by the person or the person's agent or employee, to refuse to disclose and to prevent other persons from disclosing a trade secret owned by the person, if the allowance of the privilege will not tend to conceal fraud or otherwise work injustice. When disclosure is directed, the judge shall take such protective measure as the interests of the holder of the privilege and of the parties and the furtherance of justice may require.

See also TRCP 193; Penal Code §31.05(a)(4); ***O'Connor's Texas Rules***, "Scope of Discovery," ch. 6-B; Cochran, ***Texas Rules of Evidence Handbook***, p. 446 (2001).

TRE 508. IDENTITY OF INFORMER

(a) Rule of Privilege. The United States or a state or subdivision thereof has a privilege to refuse to disclose the identity of a person who has furnished information relating to or assisting in an investigation of a possible violation of a law to a law enforcement officer or member of a legislative committee or its staff conducting an investigation.

(b) Who May Claim. The privilege may be claimed by an appropriate representative of the public entity to which the information was furnished, except the privilege shall not be allowed in criminal cases if the state objects.

(c) Exceptions.

(1) *Voluntary disclosure; informer a witness.* No privilege exists under this rule if the identity of the informer or the informer's interest in the subject matter of the communication has been disclosed to those who would have cause to resent the communication by a holder of the privilege or by the informer's own action, or if the informer appears as a witness for the public entity.

(2) *Testimony on merits.* If it appears from the evidence in the case or from other showing by a party that

an informer may be able to give testimony necessary to a fair determination of a material issue on the merits in a civil case to which the public entity is a party, or on guilt or innocence in a criminal case, and the public entity invokes the privilege, the court shall give the public entity an opportunity to show in camera facts relevant to determining whether the informer can, in fact, supply that testimony. The showing will ordinarily be in the form of affidavits, but the court may direct that testimony be taken if it finds that the matter cannot be resolved satisfactorily upon affidavit. If the court finds that there is a reasonable probability that the informer can give the testimony, and the public entity elects not to disclose the informer's identity, the court in a civil case may make any order that justice requires, and in a criminal case shall, on motion of the defendant, and may, on the court's own motion, dismiss the charges as to which the testimony would relate. Evidence submitted to the court shall be sealed and preserved to be made available to the appellate court in the event of an appeal, and the contents shall not otherwise be revealed without consent of the public entity. All counsel and parties shall be permitted to be present at every stage of proceedings under this subdivision except a showing in camera, at which no counsel or party shall be permitted to be present.

(3) *Legality of obtaining evidence.* If information from an informer is relied upon to establish the legality of the means by which evidence was obtained and the court is not satisfied that the information was received from an informer reasonably believed to be reliable or credible, it may require the identity of the informer to be disclosed. The court shall, on request of the public entity, direct that the disclosure be made in camera. All counsel and parties concerned with the issue of legality shall be permitted to be present at every stage of proceedings under this subdivision except a disclosure in camera, at which no counsel or party shall be permitted to be present. If disclosure of the identity of the informer is made in camera, the record thereof shall be sealed and preserved to be made available to the appellate court in the event of an appeal, and the contents shall not otherwise be revealed without consent of the public entity.

See also ***O'Connor's Texas Rules***, "Scope of Discovery," ch. 6-B; Cochran, ***Texas Rules of Evidence Handbook***, p. 449 (2001).

TRE 509. PHYSICIAN-PATIENT PRIVILEGE

(a) Definitions. As used in this rule:

(1) A "patient" means any person who consults or is seen by a physician to receive medical care.

(2) A "physician" means a person licensed to practice medicine in any state or nation, or reasonably believed by the patient so to be.

(3) A communication is "confidential" if not intended to be disclosed to third persons other than those present to further the interest of the patient in the consultation, examination, or interview, or those reasonably necessary for the transmission of the communication, or those who are participating in the diagnosis and treatment under the direction of the physician, including members of the patient's family.

(b) Limited Privilege in Criminal Proceedings. There is no physician-patient privilege in criminal proceedings. However, a communication to any person involved in the treatment or examination of alcohol or drug abuse by a person being treated voluntarily or being examined for admission to treatment for alcohol or drug abuse is not admissible in a criminal proceeding.

(c) General Rule of Privilege in Civil Proceedings. In a civil proceeding:

(1) Confidential communications between a physician and a patient, relative to or in connection with any professional services rendered by a physician to the patient are privileged and may not be disclosed.

(2) Records of the identity, diagnosis, evaluation, or treatment of a patient by a physician that are created or maintained by a physician are confidential and privileged and may not be disclosed.

(3) The provisions of this rule apply even if the patient received the services of a physician prior to the enactment of the Medical Liability and Insurance Improvement Act, Tex. Rev. Civ. Stat. art. 4590i.

(d) Who May Claim the Privilege in a Civil Proceeding. In a civil proceeding:

(1) The privilege of confidentiality may be claimed by the patient or by a representative of the patient acting on the patient's behalf.

(2) The physician may claim the privilege of confidentiality, but only on behalf of the patient. The authority to do so is presumed in the absence of evidence to the contrary.

(e) Exceptions in a Civil Proceeding. Exceptions to confidentiality or privilege in administrative proceedings or in civil proceedings in court exist:

(1) when the proceedings are brought by the patient against a physician, including but not limited to malpractice proceedings, and in any license revocation proceeding in which the patient is a complaining witness and in which disclosure is relevant to the claims or defense of a physician;

(2) when the patient or someone authorized to act on the patient's behalf submits a written consent to the release of any privileged information, as provided in paragraph (f);

(3) when the purpose of the proceedings is to substantiate and collect on a claim for medical services rendered to the patient;

(4) as to a communication or record relevant to an issue of the physical, mental or emotional condition of a patient in any proceeding in which any party relies upon the condition as a part of the party's claim or defense;

(5) in any disciplinary investigation or proceeding of a physician conducted under or pursuant to the Medical Practice Act, Tex. Rev. Civ. Stat. art. 4495b[1], or of a registered nurse under or pursuant to Tex. Rev. Civ. Stat. arts. 4525[2], 4527a[2], 4527b[2], and 4527c[2], provided that the board shall protect the identity of any patient whose medical records are examined, except for those patients covered under subparagraph (e)(1) or those patients who have submitted written consent to the release of their medical records as provided by paragraph (f);

(6) in an involuntary civil commitment proceeding, proceeding for court-ordered treatment, or probable cause hearing under Tex. Health & Safety Code ch. 462; tit. 7, subtit. C; and tit. 7, subtit. D;

(7) in any proceeding regarding the abuse or neglect, or the cause of any abuse or neglect, of the resident of an "institution" as defined in Tex. Health & Safety Code §242.002.

(f) Consent.

(1) Consent for the release of privileged information must be in writing and signed by the patient, or a parent or legal guardian if the patient is a minor, or a legal guardian if the patient has been adjudicated incompetent to manage personal affairs, or an attorney ad litem appointed for the patient, as authorized by Tex. Health & Safety Code tit. 7, subtits. C and D; Tex. Prob. Code ch. V; and Tex. Fam. Code §107.011; or a personal representative if the patient is deceased, provided that the written consent specifies the following:

(A) the information or medical records to be covered by the release;

(B) the reasons or purposes for the release; and

(C) the person to whom the information is to be released.

(2) The patient, or other person authorized to consent, has the right to withdraw consent to the release of any information. Withdrawal of consent does not affect any information disclosed prior to the written notice of the withdrawal.

(3) Any person who received information made privileged by this rule may disclose the information to others only to the extent consistent with the authorized purposes for which consent to release the information was obtained.

[1] Now Occ. Code, title 3, subtitle B-C.
[2] Now Occ. Code, chapter 301.

Comment to 1998 change: This comment is intended to inform the construction and application of this rule. Prior Criminal Rules of Evidence 509 and 510 are now in subparagraph (b) of this Rule. This rule governs disclosures of patient-physician communications only in judicial or administrative proceedings. Whether a physician may or must disclose such communications in other circumstances is governed by TRCS art. 4495b, § 5.08 [now Occ. Code ch. 159]. Former subparagraph (d)(6) of the Civil Evidence Rules, regarding disclosures in a suit affecting the parent-child relationship, is omitted, not because there should be no exception to the privilege in suits affecting the parent-child relationship, but because the exception in such suits is properly considered under subparagraph (e)(4) of the new rule (formerly subparagraph (d)(4)), as construed in *R.K. v. Ramirez*, 887 S.W.2d 836 (Tex.1994). In determining the proper application of an exception in such suits, the trial court must ensure that the precise need for the information is not outweighed by legitimate privacy interests protected by the privilege. Subparagraph (e) of the new rule does not except from the privilege information relating to a nonparty patient who is or may be a consulting or testifying expert in the suit.

See also ***O'Connor's Texas Rules***, "Scope of Discovery," ch. 6-B; "Medical Records," ch. 6-H; Cochran, ***Texas Rules of Evidence Handbook***, p. 458 (2001).

R.K. v. Ramirez, 887 S.W.2d 836, 842 (Tex.1994). "[T]he patient-litigant exception to the [TRE 509 & 510] privileges applies when a party's condition relates in a significant way to a party's claim or defense. *At 843 n.7:* Whether a condition is a part of a claim or defense should be determined on the face of the pleadings, without reference to the evidence that is allegedly privileged. *At 843:* [T]he exceptions to the medical and mental health privileges apply when (1) the records sought to be discovered are relevant to the condition at issue, and (2) the condition is relied upon as a part of a party's claim or defense, meaning that the condition itself is a fact that carries some legal significance."

Groves v. Gabriel, 874 S.W.2d 660, 661 (Tex.1994). "[A] trial court's order compelling release of medical records should be restrictively drawn so as to maintain the privilege with respect to records or communications not relevant to the underlying suit. The global release in this case does not meet the *Mutter* standard."

Mutter v. Wood, 744 S.W.2d 600, 601 (Tex.1988). "Even in the interest of broad discovery directed at seeking the truth, no privilege should be totally ignored." A court order requiring the plaintiffs to waive the physician-patient privilege was too broad.

Rios v. Texas Dept. of MHMR, 58 S.W.3d 167, 169-70 (Tex.App.—San Antonio 2001, no pet.). Plaintiffs "complain that opposing counsel's *ex parte* contact with [P's physician] was improper and should be declared impermissible because it conflicts with a physician's fiduciary duty of loyalty to his patient and invites improper influence that threatens the relationship of trust confidence. ... [Ps] presented no evidence that [D] elicited confidential, privileged medical information as a result of its interview with [P's physician]. [Ds] contacted [P's physician] more than four years following his consultation with [P], and at a time when the doctor did not consider himself a 'treating physician' to [P]."

Hogue v. Kroger Store, 875 S.W.2d 477, 480 (Tex. App.—Houston [1st Dist.] 1994, writ denied). "The disclosure of physician-patient communications in judicial or administrative proceedings is governed by [TRE] 509, and [TRCS] art. 4495b, §5.08(g)[now Occ. Code §159.003]. Generally, confidential communications between a physician and patient are privileged and may not be disclosed."

TRE 510. CONFIDENTIALITY OF MENTAL HEALTH INFORMATION IN CIVIL CASES

(a) Definitions. As used in this rule:

(1) "Professional" means any person:

(A) authorized to practice medicine in any state or nation;

(B) licensed or certified by the State of Texas in the diagnosis, evaluation or treatment of any mental or emotional disorder;

(C) involved in the treatment or examination of drug abusers; or

(D) reasonably believed by the patient to be included in any of the preceding categories.

(2) "Patient" means any person who:

(A) consults, or is interviewed by, a professional for purposes of diagnosis, evaluation, or treatment of any mental or emotional condition or disorder, including alcoholism and drug addiction; or

(B) is being treated voluntarily or being examined for admission to voluntary treatment for drug abuse.

(3) A representative of the patient is:

(A) any person bearing the written consent of the patient;

(B) a parent if the patient is a minor;

(C) a guardian if the patient has been adjudicated incompetent to manage the patient's personal affairs; or

(D) the patient's personal representative if the patient is deceased.

(4) A communication is "confidential" if not intended to be disclosed to third persons other than those present to further the interest of the patient in the diagnosis, examination, evaluation, or treatment, or those reasonably necessary for the transmission of the communication, or those who are participating in the diagnosis, examination, evaluation, or treatment under the direction of the professional, including members of the patient's family.

(b) General Rule of Privilege.

(1) Communication between a patient and a professional is confidential and shall not be disclosed in civil cases.

(2) Records of the identity, diagnosis, evaluation, or treatment of a patient which are created or maintained by a professional are confidential and shall not be disclosed in civil cases.

(3) Any person who received information from confidential communications or records as defined herein, other than a representative of the patient acting on the patient's behalf, shall not disclose in civil cases the information except to the extent that disclosure is consistent with the authorized purposes for which the information was first obtained.

(4) The provisions of this rule apply even if the patient received the services of a professional prior to the enactment of Tex. Rev. Civ. Stat. art. 5561h (Vernon Supp. 1984) (now codified as Tex. Health & Safety Code §§611.001-611.008).

(c) Who May Claim the Privilege.

(1) The privilege of confidentiality may be claimed by the patient or by a representative of the patient acting on the patient's behalf.

(2) The professional may claim the privilege of confidentiality but only on behalf of the patient. The authority to do so is presumed in the absence of evidence to the contrary.

(d) Exceptions. Exceptions to the privilege in court or administrative proceedings exist:

(1) when the proceedings are brought by the patient against a professional, including but not limited to malpractice proceedings, and in any license revocation proceedings in which the patient is a complaining witness and in which disclosure is relevant to the claim or defense of a professional;

(2) when the patient waives the right in writing to the privilege of confidentiality of any information, or when a representative of the patient acting on the patient's behalf submits a written waiver to the confidentiality privilege;

(3) when the purpose of the proceeding is to substantiate and collect on a claim for mental or emotional health services rendered to the patient;

(4) when the judge finds that the patient after having been previously informed that communications would not be privileged, has made communications to a professional in the course of a court-ordered examination relating to the patient's mental or emotional condition or disorder, providing that such communications shall not be privileged only with respect to issues involving the patient's mental or emotional health. On granting of the order, the court, in determining the extent to which any disclosure of all or any part of any communication is necessary, shall impose appropriate safeguards against unauthorized disclosure;

(5) as to a communication or record relevant to an issue of the physical, mental or emotional condition of a patient in any proceeding in which any party relies upon the condition as a part of the party's claim or defense;

(6) in any proceeding regarding the abuse or neglect, or the cause of any abuse or neglect, of the resident of an institution as defined in Tex. Health and Safety Code §242.002.

Comment to 1998 change: This comment is intended to inform the construction and application of this rule. This rule governs disclosures of patient-professional communications only in judicial or administrative proceedings. Whether a professional may or must disclose such communications in other circumstances is governed by Tex. Health & Safety Code §§ 611.001-611.008. Former subparagraph (d)(6) of the Civil Evidence Rules, regarding disclosures in a suit affecting the parent-child relationship, is omitted, not because there should be no exception to the privilege in suits affecting the parent-child relationship, but because the exception in such suits is properly considered under subparagraph (d)(5), as construed in *R.K. v. Ramirez*, 887 S.W.2d 836 (Tex. 1994). In determining the proper application of an exception in such suits, the trial court must ensure that the precise need for the information is not outweighed by legitimate privacy interests protected by the privilege. Subparagraph (d) does not except from the privilege information relating to a nonparty patient who is or may be a consulting or testifying expert in the suit.

See also ***O'Connor's Texas Rules***, "Scope of Discovery," ch. 6-B; "Medical Records," ch. 6-H; Cochran, ***Texas Rules of Evidence Handbook***, p. 476 (2001).

R.K. v. Ramirez, 887 S.W.2d 836, 843 (Tex.1994). "As a general rule, a mental condition will be a 'part' of a claim or defense if the pleadings indicate that the jury must make a factual determination concerning the condition itself. *At n.7:* Whether a condition is a party of a claim or defense should be determined on the face of the pleadings, without reference to the evidence that is allegedly privileged."

Groves v. Gabriel, 874 S.W.2d 660, 661 (Tex.1994). "Because [P] alleges severe emotional damages, including 'post-traumatic stress disorder,' [she] waived the privilege as to any medical records relevant to her claim for emotional damages."

Ginsberg v. 5th Ct. of Appeals, 686 S.W.2d 105, 107 (Tex.1985). Plaintiff "has invoked the jurisdiction of the courts in search of affirmative relief against [D]; yet she would attempt, on the basis of [psychotherapist-patient] privilege, to deny [D] the benefit of evidence which would materially weaken or defeat her claims against him. This is an offensive, rather than defensive, use of the privilege, and it lies outside the intended scope of [TRE] 510...."

TRE 511. WAIVER OF PRIVILEGE BY VOLUNTARY DISCLOSURE

A person upon whom these rules confer a privilege against disclosure waives the privilege if:

(1) the person or a predecessor of the person while holder of the privilege voluntarily discloses or consents to disclosure of any significant part of the privileged matter unless such disclosure itself is privileged; or

(2) the person or a representative of the person calls a person to whom privileged communications have been made to testify as to the person's character or character trait insofar as such communications are relevant to such character or character trait.

See also ***O'Connor's Texas Rules***, "Waiver of objections & privileges," ch. 6-A, §23.3; Cochran, ***Texas Rules of Evidence Handbook***, p. 505 (2001).

Axelson, Inc. v. McIlhany, 798 S.W.2d 550, 553-54 (Tex.1990). Defendant "also resists discovery based on the attorney-client privilege under [TRE] 503(b) and the work product privilege under [TRCP 192.5]. Since there was evidence that the investigation was disclosed to the FBI, IRS, and the *Wall Street Journal*, the court of appeals properly held that these privileges had been waived."

Jordan v. 4th Ct. of Appeals, 701 S.W.2d 644, 649 (Tex.1985). "If the matter for which a privilege is sought has been disclosed to a third party, thus raising the question of waiver of the privilege, the party asserting the privilege has the burden of proving that no waiver has occurred."

TRE 512. PRIVILEGED MATTER DISCLOSED UNDER COMPULSION OR WITHOUT OPPORTUNITY TO CLAIM PRIVILEGE

A claim of privilege is not defeated by a disclosure which was (1) compelled erroneously or (2) made without opportunity to claim the privilege.

See also *O'Connor's Texas Rules*, "General Rules for Discovery," ch. 6-A; Cochran, *Texas Rules of Evidence Handbook*, p. 515 (2001).

TRE 513. COMMENT UPON OR INFERENCE FROM CLAIM OF PRIVILEGE; INSTRUCTION

(a) Comment or Inference Not Permitted. Except as permitted in Rule 504(b)(2), the claim of a privilege, whether in the present proceeding or upon a prior occasion, is not a proper subject of comment by judge or counsel, and no inference may be drawn therefrom.

(b) Claiming Privilege Without Knowledge of Jury. In jury cases, proceedings shall be conducted, to the extent practicable, so as to facilitate the making of claims of privilege without the knowledge of the jury.

(c) Claim of Privilege Against Self-Incrimination in Civil Cases. Paragraphs (a) and (b) shall not apply with respect to a party's claim, in the present civil proceeding, of the privilege against self-incrimination.

(d) Jury Instruction. Except as provided in Rule 504(b)(2) and in paragraph (c) of this Rule, upon request any party against whom the jury might draw an adverse inference from a claim of privilege is entitled to an instruction that no inference may be drawn therefrom.

Comment to 1998 change: Subdivision (d) regarding a party's entitlement to a jury instruction about a claim of privilege is made applicable to civil cases.

See also Cochran, *Texas Rules of Evidence Handbook*, p. 519 (2001).

In re L.S., 748 S.W.2d 571, 575 (Tex.App.—Amarillo 1988, no writ). TRE 513(b) "reflects a desire to protect the parties from any adverse inference drawn by the jurors who witness the invocation of the privilege against self-incrimination. 'It is reasonable to anticipate that in most instances, planned reliance upon the privilege will be known in advance and the mandate of Rule 513(b) can be implemented through the use of motions in limine.'"

ARTICLE VI. WITNESSES

TRE 601. COMPETENCY & INCOMPETENCY OF WITNESSES

(a) General Rule. Every person is competent to be a witness except as otherwise provided in these rules. The following witnesses shall be incompetent to testify in any proceeding subject to these rules:

(1) *Insane persons.* Insane persons who, in the opinion of the court, are in an insane condition of mind at the time when they are offered as a witness, or who, in the opinion of the court, were in that condition when the events happened of which they are called to testify.

(2) *Children.* Children or other persons who, after being examined by the court, appear not to possess sufficient intellect to relate transactions with respect to which they are interrogated.

(b) "Dead Man's Rule" in Civil Actions. In civil actions by or against executors, administrators, or guardians, in which judgment may be rendered for or against them as such, neither party shall be allowed to testify against the others as to any oral statement by the testator, intestate or ward, unless that testimony to the oral statement is corroborated or unless the witness is called at the trial to testify thereto by the opposite party; and, the provisions of this article shall extend to and include all actions by or against the heirs or legal representatives of a decedent based in whole or in part on such oral statement. Except for the foregoing, a witness is not precluded from giving evidence of or concerning any transaction with, any conversations with, any admissions of, or statement by, a deceased or insane party or person merely because the witness is a party to the action or a person interested in the event thereof. The trial court shall, in a proper case, where this rule prohibits an interested party or witness from testifying, instruct the jury that such person is not permitted by the law to give evidence relating to any oral statement by the deceased or ward unless the oral statement is corroborated or unless the party or witness is called at the trial by the opposite party.

Caution: TRE 601 is affected by the following sections in the Fam. Code: §§6.704, 6.705.

See also *O'Connor's Texas Rules*, "Motion in Limine," ch. 5-E; "Objecting to Evidence," ch. 8-D; Cochran, *Texas Rules of Evidence Handbook*, p. 527 (2001).

Lunsford v. Morris, 746 S.W.2d 471, 473 (Tex. 1988). "[T]he rules of evidence [do not] contemplate exclusion of otherwise relevant proof unless the evidence proffered is unfairly prejudicial, privileged, incompetent, or otherwise *legally* inadmissible."

Quitta v. Fossati, 808 S.W.2d 636, 641 (Tex.App.—Corpus Christi 1991, writ denied). Because the plaintiffs "are neither heirs nor legal representatives of [the deceased], but [are successors in interest to the deceased, t]he Dead Man's Statute ... does not apply to prevent the [Ds] from testifying to their conversations with [the deceased] concerning the modification."

TRE 602. LACK OF PERSONAL KNOWLEDGE

A witness may not testify to a matter unless evidence is introduced sufficient to support a finding that the witness has personal knowledge of the matter. Evidence to prove personal knowledge may, but need not, consist of the testimony of the witness. This rule is subject to the provisions of Rule 703, relating to opinion testimony by expert witnesses.

See also *O'Connor's Texas Rules*, "Introducing Evidence," ch. 8-C; "Objecting to Evidence," ch. 8-D; Cochran, *Texas Rules of Evidence Handbook*, p. 538 (2001).

Anderson Prod'g, Inc. v. Koch Oil Co., 929 S.W.2d 416, 425 (Tex.1996). Defendant "argues that the trial court erred [because P's attorney] failed to demonstrate personal knowledge supporting the testimony. The record reflects that [P's attorney's] testimony was based on his review of the documents executed by [Ds], and that [one of the Ds] had ample opportunity to cross-examine [P's attorney] regarding the basis of his conclusion. Under these circumstances, the trial court did not abuse its discretion in failing to strike the testimony."

Radio Station KSCS v. Jennings, 750 S.W.2d 760, 762 (Tex.1988). The affidavit of an inmate confined to TDC "fails to show how [the inmate] became familiar with the facts in the affidavit. [The inmate] does not claim to have worked for any radio station or record company. [¶] We hold that the [inmate's] affidavit controverting the [D's] motion for summary judgment fails to establish personal knowledge of the business practices of record companies or of the radio station."

City of Dallas v. GTE Southwest, Inc., 980 S.W.2d 928, 935 (Tex.App.—Fort Worth 1998, pet. denied). "A person proffered as a fact witness may not testify, absent personal knowledge of the matter to be testified about."

TRE 603. OATH OR AFFIRMATION

Before testifying, every witness shall be required to declare that the witness will testify truthfully, by oath or affirmation administered in a form calculated to awaken the witness' conscience and impress the witness' mind with the duty to do so.

See also Cochran, *Texas Rules of Evidence Handbook*, p. 541 (2001).

Banda v. Garcia, 955 S.W.2d 270, 272 (Tex.1997). "Normally, an attorney's statements must be under oath to be considered evidence. [H]owever, the opponent of the testimony can waive the oath requirement by failing to object when the opponent knows or should know that an objection is necessary. [¶] [Petitioner's] attorney ... did not take an oath before discussing the existence and terms of the oral settlement agreement. Nevertheless, [respondent's attorney] should have known to object to [attorney's] unsworn statements. The record shows that [petitioner's attorney] was clearly attempting to prove the existence and terms of the settlement agreement, including the agreement to extend the deadline, at the hearing. In fact, [petitioner's attorney] stated at the conclusion of her presentation that 'as an officer of the court I can just state under oath what—what I am telling the court and what my representations were....' She also said that 'this agreement that *I'm testifying* to today before the court as an officer of the court....' [Petitioner's attorney] therefore clearly placed [respondent's] attorney on notice that she was attempting to prove the existence and terms of the oral agreement."

Glenn v. C&G Elec., Inc., 977 S.W.2d 686, 689 (Tex. App.—Fort Worth 1998, pet. denied). The "requirement [to testify truthfully under oath] applies not only to those who will testify in person in the courtroom, but also to those whose testimony at the trial will be presented by deposition."

TRE 604. INTERPRETERS

An interpreter is subject to the provisions of these rules relating to qualification as an expert and the administration of an oath or affirmation to make a true translation.

See also TRCP 183, regarding appointment and compensation of interpreters; Cochran, ***Texas Rules of Evidence Handbook***, p. 543 (2001).

International Commercial Bank v. Hall-Fuston Corp., 767 S.W.2d 259, 261 (Tex.App.—Beaumont 1989, no writ). Where a foreign company attempts to introduce into evidence business records that are not written in English, it may have one of its corporate representatives orally interpret the documents under oath after being qualified as an expert.

TRE 605. COMPETENCY OF JUDGE AS A WITNESS

The judge presiding at the trial may not testify in that trial as a witness. No objection need be made in order to preserve the point.

See also Cochran, ***Texas Rules of Evidence Handbook***, p. 545 (2001).

In re M.S., ___ S.W.3d ___ (Tex.App.—Beaumont 2002, n.p.h.) (No. 09-01-037 CV; 4-11-02). Appellant "cites ***In re T.T.*** as support for her argument that admission of a court order violates Rule 605. [¶] [T]he Texas Court of Criminal Appeals has strictly construed Rule 605. In holding that the rule did not encompass future proceedings over which the judge was not presently presiding, it stated, 'The phrase the judge presiding at *the* trial may not testify in *that* trial means that the judge who is presiding over a proceeding may not step down from the bench and become a witness in the very same proceeding over which he is currently presiding.' [¶] [I]t seems to us ... that the problem should be addressed under Texas Rule of Evidence 403, not Rule 605. (Internal quotations omitted). *But see* ***In re T.T.***, below.

In re T.T., 39 S.W.3d 355, 359 (Tex.App.—Houston [1st Dist.] 2001, no pet.). "The effect of admitting the judge's written statements in the [temporary] order was the same as if the judge had violated Rule 605 by testifying to those statements. [¶] We hold that admitting the trial judge's temporary order was error because it ... violated Rule 605." *But see* ***In re M.S.***, above.

Orion Enter. v. Pope, 927 S.W.2d 654, 660 (Tex. App.—San Antonio 1996, orig. proceeding). "[M]erely because a judge is *competent* to testify under [TRE] 605 does not mean he or she may *properly* do so within the confines of Canon 2 of the Code of Judicial Conduct. ... Under these circumstances, we believe [the presiding judge's] affidavit, provided ... apparently as the result of ex parte communications with the [Ps'] counsel, was improper."

Duvall v. Sadler, 711 S.W.2d 369, 376 (Tex.App.—Texarkana 1986, writ ref'd n.r.e.). "Disregard of the testimony [of the presiding judge] is justified upon the grounds that it nullifies an involvement in the case by the judge that is destructive of impartiality and enforces the policy underlying the rule."

TRE 606. COMPETENCY OF JUROR AS A WITNESS

(a) At the Trial. A member of the jury may not testify as a witness before that jury in the trial of the case in which the juror is sitting as a juror. If the juror is called so to testify, the opposing party shall be afforded an opportunity to object out of the presence of the jury.

(b) Inquiry Into Validity of Verdict or Indictment. Upon an inquiry into the validity of a verdict or indictment, a juror may not testify as to any matter or statement occurring during the jury's deliberations, or to the effect of anything on any juror's mind or emotions or mental processes, as influencing any juror's assent to or dissent from the verdict or indictment. Nor may a juror's affidavit or any statement by a juror concerning any matter about which the juror would be precluded from testifying be admitted in evidence for any of these purposes. However, a juror may testify: (1) whether any outside influence was improperly brought to bear upon any juror; or (2) to rebut a claim that the juror was not qualified to serve.

See also TRCP 327(b); ***O'Connor's Texas Rules***, "MNT Based on Jury or Bailiff Misconduct," ch. 10-B, §13; Cochran, ***Texas Rules of Evidence Handbook***, p. 548 (2001).

Golden Eagle Archery, Inc. v. Jackson, 24 S.W.3d 362, 371 (Tex.2000). An "alleged conversation between [jurors] during a trial break ... should not be considered 'deliberations' and therefore barred by [TRE] 606(b) and [TRCP] 327(b). [TRCPs] use the term 'deliberations' as meaning formal jury deliberations—when the jury weighs the evidence to arrive at a verdict."

Crowson v. Kansas City S. Ry., 11 S.W.3d 300, 305 (Tex.App.—Eastland 1999, no pet.). We "hold that the use of the discount formula by the jury in this case did not constitute an outside influence and that, therefore, there was no evidence of jury misconduct that could be considered by the trial court."

Perry v. Safeco Ins. Co., 821 S.W.2d 279, 281 (Tex. App.—Houston [1st Dist.] 1991, writ denied). "Information gathered by a juror and introduced to other jurors by that juror—even if it were introduced to prejudice the vote—does not constitute outside influence. [¶] Further, the coercive influence of one juror upon the rest of the panel is not 'outside influence.' Proof of coercive statements and their effect on the jury is barred by the rules."

TRE 607. WHO MAY IMPEACH

The credibility of a witness may be attacked by any party, including the party calling the witness.

See also *O'Connor's Texas Rules*, "Introducing Evidence," ch. 8-C; Cochran, ***Texas Rules of Evidence Handbook***, p. 563 (2001).

Allied Chem. Co. v. DeHaven, 824 S.W.2d 257, 265 (Tex.App.—Houston [14th Dist.] 1992, no writ). TRE 607 "allows the credibility of a witness to be attacked by the party calling him." *See also* ***Loyd Elec. Co. v. Millett***, 767 S.W.2d 476, 479 (Tex.App.—San Antonio 1989, no writ).

TRE 608. EVIDENCE OF CHARACTER & CONDUCT OF A WITNESS

(a) Opinion and Reputation Evidence of Character. The credibility of a witness may be attacked or supported by evidence in the form of opinion or reputation, but subject to these limitations:

(1) the evidence may refer only to character for truthfulness or untruthfulness; and

(2) evidence of truthful character is admissible only after the character of the witness for truthfulness has been attacked by opinion or reputation evidence or otherwise.

(b) Specific Instances of Conduct. Specific instances of the conduct of a witness, for the purpose of attacking or supporting the witness' credibility, other than conviction of crime as provided in Rule 609, may not be inquired into on cross-examination of the witness nor proved by extrinsic evidence.

See also *O'Connor's Texas Rules*, "Motion in Limine," ch. 5-E; "Introducing Evidence," ch. 8-C; Cochran, ***Texas Rules of Evidence Handbook***, p. 568 (2001).

Closs v. Goose Creek Consol. ISD, 874 S.W.2d 859, 870 n.7 (Tex.App.—Texarkana 1994, no writ). "The credibility of a witness may be attacked by evidence in the form of an opinion or reputation. Specific instances of the conduct of a witness, other than conviction for a crime, may not be inquired into nor proved by extrinsic evidence for purposes of attacking the credibility of the witness."

Service Lloyds Ins. Co. v. Martin, 855 S.W.2d 816, 823 (Tex.App.—Dallas 1993, no writ). "Under [TRE] 608(a), a witness's credibility can be attacked by either opinion or reputation evidence. The evidence, however, must relate only to the witness's character for truthfulness or untruthfulness."

Rose v. Intercontinental Bank, 705 S.W.2d 752, 757 (Tex.App.—Houston [1st Dist.] 1986, writ ref'd n.r.e.). Under TRE 608(a), "the witness' reputation for truthfulness must first be attacked before [the party] can offer rehabilitating evidence."

TRE 609. IMPEACHMENT BY EVIDENCE OF CONVICTION OF CRIME

(a) General Rule. For the purpose of attacking the credibility of a witness, evidence that the witness has been convicted of a crime shall be admitted if elicited from the witness or established by public record but only if the crime was a felony or involved moral turpitude, regardless of punishment, and the court determines that the probative value of admitting this evidence outweighs its prejudicial effect to a party.

(b) Time Limit. Evidence of a conviction under this rule is not admissible if a period of more than ten years has elapsed since the date of the conviction or of the release of the witness from the confinement imposed for that conviction, whichever is the later date, unless the court determines, in the interests of justice, that the probative value of the conviction supported by specific facts and circumstances substantially outweighs its prejudicial effect.

(c) Effect of Pardon, Annulment, or Certificate of Rehabilitation. Evidence of a conviction is not admissible under this rule if:

(1) based on the finding of the rehabilitation of the person convicted, the conviction has been the subject of a pardon, annulment, certificate of rehabilitation, or other equivalent procedure, and that person has not been convicted of a subsequent crime which was classified as a felony or involved moral turpitude, regardless of punishment;

(2) probation has been satisfactorily completed for the crime for which the person was convicted, and that person has not been convicted of a subsequent crime which was classified as a felony or involved moral turpitude, regardless of punishment; or

(3) based on a finding of innocence, the conviction has been the subject of a pardon, annulment, or other equivalent procedure.

(d) Juvenile Adjudications. Evidence of juvenile adjudications is not admissible, except for proceedings conducted pursuant to Title III, Family Code, in which the witness is a party, under this rule unless required to be admitted by the Constitution of the United States or Texas.

(e) Pendency of Appeal. Pendency of an appeal renders evidence of a conviction inadmissible.

(f) Notice. Evidence of a conviction is not admissible if after timely written request by the adverse party specifying the witness or witnesses, the proponent fails to give to the adverse party sufficient advance written notice of intent to use such evidence to provide the adverse party with a fair opportunity to contest the use of such evidence.

See also *O'Connor's Texas Rules*, "Motion in Limine," ch. 5-E; "Introducing Evidence," ch. 8-C; Cochran, *Texas Rules of Evidence Handbook*, p. 577 (2001).

In re M.R., 975 S.W.2d 51, 55 (Tex.App.—San Antonio 1998, pet. denied). TRE 609 "exists to establish when and within what parameters a prior conviction may be introduced. It does not *require* a conviction in order to admit some testimony. [¶] [T]he Family Code itself does not require a conviction in order to introduce evidence of family violence. Instead, it requires that the evidence be 'credible.'"

Porter v. Nemir, 900 S.W.2d 376, 382 (Tex.App.—Austin 1995, no writ). "[T]he danger of unfair prejudice was particularly great because the extraneous conduct involved sexual abuse of a child. [¶] [D's] conviction for sexual abuse of a child was not admissible under [TRE] 609 [and] the court did not abuse its discretion in concluding that the probative value *was substantially outweighed* by the danger of unfair prejudice…."

Borden, Inc. v. Rios, 850 S.W.2d 821, 834 (Tex. App.—Corpus Christi 1993), *writ granted w.r.m.*, 859 S.W.2d 70 (Tex.1993). "Evidence of a conviction is not admissible under [TRE] 609 if the person successfully completes probation for the crime and has not been convicted for a subsequent crime. Evidence of other wrongs or acts is not admissible to prove the character of a person in order to show that he acted in conformity therewith. Evidence of the habit of a person or of the routine practice of an organization is relevant to prove that the conduct of the person or organization on a particular occasion was in conformity with the habit or routine practice."

TRE 610. RELIGIOUS BELIEFS OR OPINIONS

Evidence of the beliefs or opinions of a witness on matters of religion is not admissible for the purpose of showing that by reason of their nature the witness' credibility is impaired or enhanced.

Comment to 1998 change: This is prior Rule of Criminal Evidence 615.

See also *O'Connor's Texas Rules*, "Motion in Limine," ch. 5-E; "Objecting to Evidence," ch. 8-D; Cochran, *Texas Rules of Evidence Handbook*, p. 594 (2001).

TRE 611. MODE & ORDER OF INTERROGATION & PRESENTATION

(a) Control by Court. The court shall exercise reasonable control over the mode and order of interrogating witnesses and presenting evidence so as to (1) make the interrogation and presentation effective for the ascertainment of the truth, (2) avoid needless consumption of time, and (3) protect witnesses from harassment or undue embarrassment.

(b) Scope of Cross-Examination. A witness may be cross-examined on any matter relevant to any issue in the case, including credibility.

(c) Leading Questions. Leading questions should not be used on the direct examination of a witness except as may be necessary to develop the testimony of the witness. Ordinarily leading questions should be permitted on cross-examination. When a party calls a hostile witness, an adverse party, or a witness identified with an adverse party, interrogation may be by leading questions.

See also *O'Connor's Texas Rules*, "Introducing Evidence," ch. 8-C; Cochran, *Texas Rules of Evidence Handbook*, p. 595 (2001).

Stam v. Mack, 984 S.W.2d 747, 752 (Tex.App.—Texarkana 1999, no pet.). "The trial court interrupted [P's] cross-examination because it felt that [P] was questioning the witness on immaterial issues and he was going into areas that were improper. The trial court's interruption of the cross-examination was not improper, but was a proper action to maintain control and promote expedition."

Cecil v. T.M.E. Invs., 893 S.W.2d 38, 47 (Tex.App.—Corpus Christi 1994, no writ). The defendant, in cross-examining its own witness who had been called by the plaintiff, should not have been able to "lead" the witness. See comment to TRE 611, in the history note above. The error was harmless.

Sims v. Brackett, 885 S.W.2d 450, 455 (Tex.App.—Corpus Christi 1994, writ denied). "The trial judge has the power and obligation to control his courtroom for the purposes of ascertaining the truth, promoting judicial economy, and protecting witnesses.... The court has some leeway in the order of proceedings in multi-party cases. [¶] The control given the trial judge must be exercised reasonably; a party must be given a fair opportunity to present its case so the jury may ascertain the truth."

GAB Bus. Servs., Inc. v. Moore, 829 S.W.2d 345, 351 (Tex.App.—Texarkana 1992, no writ). TRE 611 "gives the trial judge the discretion to limit the use of leading questions in cross-examining a friendly witness. [¶] A question framed so that a yes or no answer will enable the witness to merely echo the words of counsel is leading."

TRE 612. WRITING USED TO REFRESH MEMORY

If a witness uses a writing to refresh memory for the purpose of testifying either

(1) while testifying;

(2) before testifying, in civil cases, if the court in its discretion determines it is necessary in the interests of justice; or

(3) before testifying, in criminal cases;

an adverse party is entitled to have the writing produced at the hearing, to inspect it, to cross-examine the witness thereon, and to introduce in evidence those portions which relate to the testimony of the witness. If it is claimed that the writing contains matters not related to the subject matter of the testimony the court shall examine the writing in camera, excise any portion not so related, and order delivery of the remainder to the party entitled thereto. Any portion withheld over objections shall be preserved and made available to the appellate court in the event of an appeal. If a writing is not produced or delivered pursuant to order under this rule, the court shall make any order justice requires, except that in criminal cases when the prosecution elects not to comply, the order shall be one striking the testimony or, if the court in its discretion determines that the interests of justice so require, declaring a mistrial.

See also Cochran, ***Texas Rules of Evidence Handbook***, p. 603 (2001).

Goode v. Shoukfeh, 943 S.W.2d 441, 449 (Tex. 1997). "If a witness uses the writing while testifying the adverse party must be given access to it, but if the writing is used before the witness testifies, the court has the discretion to order the writing disclosed to the adverse party."

TRE 613. PRIOR STATEMENTS OF WITNESSES: IMPEACHMENT & SUPPORT

(a) Examining Witness Concerning Prior Inconsistent Statement. In examining a witness concerning a prior inconsistent statement made by the witness, whether oral or written, and before further cross-examination concerning, or extrinsic evidence of, such statement may be allowed, the witness must be told the contents of such statement and the time and place and the person to whom it was made, and must be afforded an opportunity to explain or deny such statement. If written, the writing need not be shown to the witness at that time, but on request the same shall be shown to opposing counsel. If the witness unequivocally admits having made such statement, extrinsic evidence of same shall not be admitted. This provision does not apply to admissions of a party-opponent as defined in Rule 801(e)(2).

(b) Examining Witness Concerning Bias or Interest. In impeaching a witness by proof of circumstances or statements showing bias or interest on the part of such witness, and before further cross-examination concerning, or extrinsic evidence of, such bias or interest may be allowed, the circumstances supporting such claim or the details of such statement, including the contents and where, when and to whom made, must be made known to the witness, and the witness must be given an opportunity to explain or to deny such circumstances or statement. If written, the writing need not be shown to the witness at that time, but on request the same shall be shown to opposing counsel. If the witness unequivocally admits such bias or interest, extrinsic evidence of same shall not be admitted. A party shall be permitted to present evidence rebutting any evidence impeaching one of said party's witnesses on grounds of bias or interest.

(c) Prior Consistent Statements of Witnesses. A prior statement of a witness which is consistent with the testimony of the witness is inadmissible except as provided in Rule 801(e)(1)(B).

See also *O'Connor's Texas Rules*, "Introducing Evidence," ch. 8-C; Cochran, *Texas Rules of Evidence Handbook*, p. 609 (2001).

Walker v. Packer, 827 S.W.2d 833, 839 n.5 (Tex. 1992). "Evidence of bias is not admissible if the witness 'unequivocally admits such bias or interest' at trial. To date, however, [D's witness] has not admitted any bias, but rather has flatly denied it. In this situation, such evidence should be discoverable."

Downen v. Texas Gulf Shrimp Co., 846 S.W.2d 506, 512 (Tex.App.—Corpus Christi 1993, writ denied). "[T]o impeach a witness with a prior statement, a proper foundation must be established [which] includes establishing where, when, and to whom the statement was made. Additionally, the party ... must allow the witness to admit or deny making the prior statement. If ... the witness admits unequivocally having made the statement the impeachment is complete and the prior statement is not admissible."

TRE 614. EXCLUSION OF WITNESSES

At the request of a party the court shall order witnesses excluded so that they cannot hear the testimony of other witnesses, and it may make the order of its own motion. This rule does not authorize exclusion of:

(1) a party who is a natural person or in civil cases the spouse of such natural person;

(2) an officer or employee of a party in a civil case or a defendant in a criminal case that is not a natural person designated as its representative by its attorney;

(3) a person whose presence is shown by a party to be essential to the presentation of the party's cause; or

(4) the victim in a criminal case, unless the victim is to testify and the court determines that the victim's testimony would be materially affected if the victim hears other testimony at the trial.

See also TRCP 267; *O'Connor's Texas Rules*, "Introducing Evidence," ch. 8-C; Cochran, *Texas Rules of Evidence Handbook*, p. 623 (2001).

Drilex Systems, Inc. v. Flores, 1 S.W.3d 112, 118-19 (Tex.1999). Defendant "argues that all expert witnesses are exempt from the Rule under the essential presence exception in [TRE] 614 and [TRCP] 267, and therefore [D's expert] was exempt. [D] is correct that this exception is often relied on to allow expert witnesses to be exempt from the Rule. But nothing in Rules 614 or 267 suggests that all expert witnesses qualify for exemption. Although an expert witness may typically be found exempt under the essential presence exception, experts are not automatically exempt. Instead, Rules 614 and 267 vest in trial judges broad discretion to determine whether a witness is essential."

Elbar, Inc. v. Claussen, 774 S.W.2d 45, 51 (Tex. App.—Dallas 1989, writ dism'd). TRE 614, "commonly referred to as 'the rule,' provides for the exclusion of witnesses from the courtroom so that they cannot hear and be influenced by the testimony of other witnesses."

TRE 615. PRODUCTION OF STATEMENTS OF WITNESSES IN CRIMINAL CASES

(a) Motion for Production. After a witness other than the defendant has testified on direct examination, the court, on motion of a party who did not call the witness, shall order the attorney for the state or the defendant and defendant's attorney, as the case may be, to produce, for the examination and use of the moving party, any statement of the witness that is in their possession and that relates to the subject matter concerning which the witness has testified.

(b) Production of Entire Statement. If the entire contents of the statement relate to the subject matter concerning which the witness has testified, the court shall order that the statement be delivered to the moving party.

(c) Production of Excised Statement. If the other party claims that the statement contains matter that does not relate to the subject matter concerning which the witness has testified, the court shall order that it be delivered to the court in camera. Upon inspection, the court shall excise the portions of the statement that do not relate to the subject matter concerning which the witness has testified, and shall order that the statement, with such material excised, be delivered to the moving party. Any portion withheld over objection shall be preserved and made available to the appellate court in the event of appeal.

(d) Recess for Examination of Statement. Upon delivery of the statement to the moving party, the court, upon application of that party, shall recess proceedings in the trial for a reasonable examination of such statement and for preparation for its use in the trial.

(e) Sanction for Failure to Produce Statement. If the other party elects not to comply with an order to deliver a statement to the moving party, the court shall order that the testimony of the witness be stricken from the record and that the trial proceed, or, if it is the attorney for the state who elects not to comply, shall declare a mistrial if required by the interest of justice.

(f) Definition. As used in this rule, a "statement" of a witness means:

(1) a written statement made by the witness that is signed or otherwise adopted or approved by the witness;

(2) a substantially verbatim recital of an oral statement made by the witness that is recorded contemporaneously with the making of the oral statement and that is contained in a stenographic, mechanical, electrical, or other recording or a transcription thereof; or

(3) a statement, however taken or recorded, or a transcription thereof, made by the witness to a grand jury.

Comment to 1998 change: This is prior Rule of Criminal Evidence 614. See also Cochran, ***Texas Rules of Evidence Handbook***, p. 629 (2001).

ARTICLE VII. OPINIONS & EXPERT TESTIMONY

TRE 701. OPINION TESTIMONY BY LAY WITNESSES

If the witness is not testifying as an expert, the witness' testimony in the form of opinions or inferences is limited to those opinions or inferences which are (a) rationally based on the perception of the witness and (b) helpful to a clear understanding of the witness' testimony or the determination of a fact in issue.

See also Cochran, ***Texas Rules of Evidence Handbook***, p. 640 (2001).

Porras v. Craig, 675 S.W.2d 503, 504-05 (Tex.1984). "[F]or a property owner to qualify as a witness to the damages to his property, his testimony must show that it refers to market, rather than intrinsic or some other value of the property. This requirement is usually met by asking the witness if he is familiar with the market value of his property."

Coker v. Burghardt, 833 S.W.2d 306, 309 (Tex. App.—Dallas 1992, writ denied). "A witness who familiarizes himself with the reasonable car repair costs in a given county can give his opinion about what those costs might be."

Laprade v. Laprade, 784 S.W.2d 490, 492 (Tex. App.—Fort Worth 1990, writ denied). Husband "in his brief, admits that the owner of property can testify as to its value. However, he argues that the determining factor of whether or not a witness is qualified to give testimony concerning the value of property is not if they own the property or not, but whether or not they have any basis of knowledge of the value of the property. [Husband] argues that there is no evidence which would indicate that [wife] had any knowledge about the business other than the day-to-day office procedure. [¶] To the contrary, we note that the evidence shows [wife] had knowledge of the business accounts receivable; she ran the business for five years; she knew what was paid for each of their trucks; and she knew the value of other smaller, similar businesses for sale. ... Furthermore, it is largely discretionary with the judge as to whether a witness is qualified to testify as to market value, and the admission of such testimony should not be disturbed on appeal unless a clear abuse of discretion is shown."

City of San Antonio v. Vela, 762 S.W.2d 314, 321 (Tex.App.—San Antonio 1988, writ denied). "'In general, a witness need not be an expert in medical matters to state an opinion as to his own physical health.'"

Guaranty Cty. Mut. Ins. Co. v. Williams, 732 S.W.2d 57, 60 (Tex.App.—Amarillo 1987, no writ). "[E]ven if the owner is not asked if he is familiar with the market value of his property, his opinion testimony of value is sufficient if it shows that it refers to market value."

TRE 702. TESTIMONY BY EXPERTS

If scientific, technical, or other specialized knowledge will assist the trier of fact to understand the evidence or to determine a fact in issue, a witness qualified as an expert by knowledge, skill, experience, training, or education may testify thereto in the form of an opinion or otherwise.

See also ***O'Connor's Texas Rules***, "Introducing Evidence," ch. 8-C; "Objecting to Evidence," ch. 8-D; Cochran, ***Texas Rules of Evidence Handbook***, p. 653 (2001).

Kumho Tire Co. v. Carmichael, 526 U.S. 137, 141-42, 119 S.Ct. 1167, 1171 (1999). "***Daubert***'s general holding—setting forth the trial judge's general 'gatekeeping' obligation—applies not only to testimony based on 'scientific' knowledge, but also to testimony based on 'technical' and 'other specialized' knowledge. [A] trial court *may* consider one or more of the more specific factors that ***Daubert*** mentioned when doing so will help determine that testimony's reliability. But ... the test of reliability is 'flexible.' and ***Daubert***'s list of specific factors neither necessarily nor exclusively applies to all experts or in every case. *At 153, 1176:* [W]hether ***Daubert***'s specific factors are, or are not, reasonable measures of reliability in a particular case is a matter that the law grants the trial judge broad latitude to determine."

Daubert v. Merrell Dow Pharm., Inc., 509 U.S. 579, 592-94, 113 S.Ct. 2786, 2796-97 (1993). "Faced with a proffer of expert scientific testimony ... the trial judge must determine at the outset ... whether the expert is proposing to testify to (1) scientific knowledge that (2) will assist the trier of fact.... This entails a preliminary assessment of whether the reasoning or methodology underlying the testimony is scientifically valid and of whether that reasoning or methodology properly can be applied to the facts in issue. ... Many factors will bear on the inquiry, and we do not presume to set out a definitive checklist or test. But some general observations are appropriate. [¶] Ordinarily, a key question to be answered in determining whether a theory or technique is scientific knowledge that will assist the trier of fact will be whether it can be (and has been) tested. [¶] Another pertinent consideration is whether the theory or technique has been subjected to peer review and publication. [¶] Additionally, ... the court ordinarily should consider the known or potential rate of error, and the existence and maintenance of standards controlling the technique's operation. [¶] Finally, 'general acceptance' can yet have a bearing on the inquiry. A 'reliability assessment does not require, although it does permit, explicit identification of a relevant scientific community and an express determination of a particular degree of acceptance within that community."

K-Mart Corp. v. Honeycutt, 24 S.W.3d 357, 360 (Tex.2000). "'Rule 702 makes inadmissible expert testimony as to a matter which obviously is within the common knowledge of jurors because such testimony, almost by definition, can be of no assistance.'"

GTE Southwest, Inc. v. Bruce, 998 S.W.2d 605, 620 (Tex.1999). "Except in highly unusual circumstances, expert testimony concerning extreme and outrageous conduct would not meet [the standards of TRE 702]. Where, as here, the issue involves only general knowledge and experience rather than expertise, it is within the province of the jury to decide, and admission of expert testimony on the issue is error."

Gammill v. Jack Williams Chevrolet, Inc., 972 S.W.2d 713, 726 (Tex.1998). "Nothing in the language of [TRE 702] suggests that opinions based on scientific knowledge should be treated any differently than opinions based on technical or other specialized knowledge. It would be an odd rule of evidence that insisted that some expert opinions be reliable but not others. All expert testimony should be shown to be reliable before it is admitted. [¶] That said, it is equally clear that the considerations listed in ***Daubert*** and in ***Robinson*** for assessing the reliability of scientific evidence cannot always be used with other kinds of expert testimony." *See also* ***Helena Chem. Co. v. Wilkins***, 475 S.W.3d 486, 499 (Tex.2001) (reaffirming ***Gammill***).

Maritime Overseas Corp. v. Ellis, 971 S.W.2d 402, 409 (Tex.1998). "To preserve a complaint that scientific evidence is unreliable and thus, no evidence, a party must object to the evidence before trial or when the evidence is offered. Without requiring a timely objection to the reliability of the scientific evidence, the offering party is not given an opportunity to cure any defect that may exist, and will be subject to trial and appeal by ambush."

Nenno v. State, 970 S.W.2d 549, 560 (Tex.Crim.App. 1998), *overruled on other grounds*, ***State v. Terrazas***, 4 S.W.3d 720 (Tex.Crim.App.1999). "Although ***Kelly*** involved novel scientific evidence, we later concluded that the standard established in that case applied to *all* scientific evidence, whether or not it was novel. The question we confront today is whether ***Kelly*** is applicable to *nonscientific* expert testimony (i.e. that involving technical or other specialized knowledge). The answer to that question is a qualified 'yes.' *At 561:* When addressing fields of study aside from the hard sciences, such as the social sciences or fields that are based primarily upon experience and training as opposed to the scientific method, ***Kelly***'s requirement of reliability applies but with less rigor than to the hard sciences. To speak of the validity of a 'theory' or 'technique' in these fields may be roughly accurate but somewhat misleading. The appropriate questions are: (1) whether the field of expertise is a legitimate one, (2) whether the subject matter of the expert's testimony is within the scope of that field, and (3) whether the expert's testimony properly relies upon and/or utilizes the principles involved in the field. These questions are merely an appropriately tailored translation of the *Kelly* test to areas outside of hard science. And, hard science methods of validation, such as assessing the potential rate of error or subjecting a theory to peer review, may often be inappropriate for testing the reliability of fields of expertise outside the hard sciences."

Merrell Dow Pharm., Inc. v. Havner, 953 S.W.2d 706, 712 (Tex.1997). "[T]o say that the expert's testimony is some evidence under our standard of review [of a challenge to the legal sufficiency of the evidence] simply because the expert testified that the underlying technique or methodology supporting his or her opinion is generally accepted by the scientific community is putting the cart before the horse. *At 714:* If the foundational data underlying opinion testimony are unreliable, ... any opinion drawn from that data is likewise unreliable. Further, an expert's testimony is unreliable even when the underlying data are sound if the expert draws conclusions from that data based on flawed methodology. A flaw in the expert's reasoning from the data may render reliance on a study unreasonable and render the inferences drawn therefrom dubious. Under that circumstance, the expert's scientific testimony is unreliable and, legally, no evidence."

United Blood Servs. v. Longoria, 938 S.W.2d 29, 30 (Tex.1997). "Whether a witness is qualified to offer expert testimony is a matter committed to the trial court's discretion."

Broders v. Heise, 924 S.W.2d 148, 152 (Tex.1996). "[G]iven the increasingly specialized and technical nature of medicine, ... every licensed medical doctor [is not] automatically qualified to testify as an expert on every medical question. *At 153:* Our holding does not mean that only a neurosurgeon can testify about the cause in fact of death from an injury to the brain, or even that an emergency room physician could never so testify. What is required is that the offering party establish that the expert has 'knowledge, skill, experience, training, or education' regarding the specific issue before the court which would qualify the expert to give an opinion on that particular subject."

E.I. du Pont de Nemours & Co. v. Robinson, 923 S.W.2d 549, 557 (Tex.1995). "There are many factors that a trial court may consider in making the threshold determination of admissibility [of scientific knowledge] under [TRE] 702. These factors include, but are not limited to: (1) the extent to which the theory has been or can be tested; (2) the extent to which the technique relies upon the subjective interpretation of the expert; (3) whether the theory has been subjected to peer review and/or publication; (4) the technique's potential rate of error; (5) whether the underlying theory or technique has been generally accepted as valid by the relevant scientific community; and (6) the non-judicial uses which have been made of the theory or technique. *At 558:* [T]he trial court's role is to make the initial determination whether the expert's opinion is relevant and whether the methods and research upon which it is based are reliable."

Yount v. State, 872 S.W.2d 706, 709-10 (Tex.Crim. App.1993). "We ... question whether a psychologist who specializes in child sexual abuse cases is an 'expert' on credibility. While a witness may possess 'scientific, technical, or other specialized knowledge' concerning sexually abused children, we seriously question whether any such person also possesses 'scientific, technical or other specialized knowledge,' beyond the realm of the jury, regarding the truthfulness of those children. 'Psychologists and psychiatrists are not, and do not claim to be, experts at discerning truth. Psychiatrists are trained to accept facts provided by their patients, not to act as judges of patients' credibility.' *At 711:* We ... conclude that expert testimony that a particular witness is truthful is inadmissible under Rule 702. [¶] The further question in this case is whether the same holds true for expert testimony as to the credibility of a *class* of persons to which the complainant belongs. ... An expert who testifies that a class of persons to which the victim belongs is truthful is essentially telling the jury that they can believe the victim in the instant case as well. This is not 'expert' testimony of the kind which will assist the jury under Rule 702. *At 712:* We hold that Rule 702 does not permit an expert to give an opinion that the complainant or class of persons to which the complainant belongs is truthful."

Havner v. E-Z Mart Stores, Inc., 825 S.W.2d 456, 460 n.4 (Tex.1992). "An investigating officer may properly testify as to causation."

Kelly v. State, 824 S.W.2d 568, 573 (Tex.Crim.App. 1992). "How does the proponent of novel scientific evidence prove it to be reliable? As a matter of common

TRE 702

sense, evidence derived from a scientific theory, to be considered reliable, must satisfy three criteria in any particular case: (a) the underlying scientific theory must be valid; (b) the technique applying the theory must be valid; and (c) the technique must have been properly applied on the occasion in question. Under Rule 104(a) and (c) and Rule 702, *all three criteria must be proven to the trial court*, outside the presence of the jury, before the evidence may be admitted."

Gainsco Cty. Mut. Ins. Co. v. Martinez, 27 S.W.3d 97, 104 (Tex.App.—San Antonio 2000, pet. granted w.r.m.). "Generally, a law enforcement officer is not qualified to render an expert opinion regarding an accident simply by virtue of his position. However, an officer may offer expert testimony in accident cases if the party proffering the testimony demonstrates that the officer is trained in the science about which he will testify and possesses the high degree of knowledge sufficient to qualify him as an expert."

In re M.D.S., 1 S.W.3d 190, 203 (Tex.App.—Amarillo 1999, no pet.). "Dr. Wurtsbaugh testified that he was a medical doctor and had completed a full residency in psychiatry. He testified that his practice experience was in clinical psychiatry. He did not testify that he had any training or experience with termination of parent-child relationships. Dr. Wurtsbaugh may well have been qualified to give expert opinion testimony in regard to termination of parent-child relationships. This record, however, does not demonstrate those qualifications. In the face of proper challenge, an expert must be proved to have qualification in the specific issue before the court."

Chance v. Chance, 911 S.W.2d 40, 51 (Tex.App.—Beaumont 1995, writ denied). Mother "contends that it was error to allow Dr. Gripon to base his opinion, at least on part, on statements contained in a tape-recording of [her child]. This tape-recording was made by [the father] of a conversation between himself and his son.... [¶] For an expert's opinion to be admissible as evidence, the witness must be qualified in the area of his opinion, his opinion must have a sufficient evidentiary foundation, and the opinion must assist the fact finder. There is no contest that Dr. Gripon qualified as an expert in the field of psychiatry. For the evidentiary base, Dr. Gripon relied on [father's] history, which included Dr. Gripon's interview of [father], another doctor's records, the tape recording in question, interviews with [father] during his office visits, tests, evaluations, and treatment. As an expert, Dr. Gripon could base his opinion at least in part on inadmissible opinions if the facts are of a nature that other experts in the field reasonably rely on same. Even if the tape of the conversation with [child] is inadmissible Dr. Gripon's opinion would remain admissible."

In re G.M.P., 909 S.W.2d 198, 206 (Tex.App.—Houston [14th Dist.] 1995, no writ). "A determination of who is telling the truth is the sole province of the jury. [U]nder [TRE] 702, the trial court erred in allowing [the witness] to testify that, in his expert opinion [the complainant] was telling the truth."

In re A.V., 849 S.W.2d 393, 395 (Tex.App.—Fort Worth 1993, no writ). "Appellee called as a witness John Brogden, a supervisor of a sexual abuse unit with Child Protective Services. ... Brogden testified that in his practice he uses the results of a penile plethysmograph to evaluate the absence or presence of deviant arousal in a patient, and to measure whether someone is making progress in treatment. *At 399:* [W]e have grave reservations whether appellee has established that the penile plethysmograph is a reliable test of a person's alleged sexual deviancy, and whether such a test is generally accepted in the scientific community as a valid indicator of sexual preferences or disorders. There was no medical testimony presented on the issue of reliability, and Brogden himself admitted that a person of high intelligence who does some reading can easily manipulate the results of the penile plethysmograph. Based upon the record before us, we are unable to conclude that appellee has established the reliability of the penile plethysmograph."

TRE 703. BASES OF OPINION TESTIMONY BY EXPERTS

The facts or data in the particular case upon which an expert bases an opinion or inference may be those perceived by, reviewed by, or made known to the expert at or before the hearing. If of a type reasonably relied upon by experts in the particular field in forming opinions or inferences upon the subject, the facts or data need not be admissible in evidence.

Comment to 1998 change: The former Civil Rule referred to facts or data "perceived by or reviewed by" the expert. The former Criminal Rule referred to facts or data "perceived by or made known to" the expert. The terminology is now conformed, but no change in meaning is intended.

See also *O'Connor's Texas Rules*, "Introducing Evidence," ch. 8-C; "Objecting to Evidence," ch. 8-D; Cochran, ***Texas Rules of Evidence Handbook***, p. 685 (2001).

Merrell Dow Pharms., Inc. v. Havner, 953 S.W.2d 706, 711 (Tex.1997). "The substance of the [expert's] testimony must be considered. *At 712:* [A]n expert's bald assurance of validity is not enough. *At 713:* The underlying data should be independently evaluated in determining if the opinion itself is reliable."

Stam v. Mack, 984 S.W.2d 747, 750 (Tex.App.—Texarkana 1999, no pet.). See Annotation in TRE 705.

Sosa ex rel Gant v. Koshy, 961 S.W.2d 420, 427 (Tex.App.—Houston [1st Dist.] 1997, pet. denied). "Under rule 703, Officer Null, as an expert on accident reconstruction, properly relied on hearsay evidence provided by eyewitnesses to the accident if experts in his field would reasonably rely on such evidence."

TRE 704. OPINION ON ULTIMATE ISSUE

Testimony in the form of an opinion or inference otherwise admissible is not objectionable because it embraces an ultimate issue to be decided by the trier of fact.

See also *O'Connor's Texas Rules*, "Objecting to Evidence," ch. 8-D; Cochran, ***Texas Rules of Evidence Handbook***, p. 697 (2001).

Birchfield v. Texarkana Mem. Hosp., 747 S.W.2d 361, 365 (Tex.1987). "Fairness and efficiency dictate that an expert may state an opinion on a mixed question of law and fact as long as the opinion is confined to the relevant issues and is based on proper legal concepts." An expert may testify that conduct constituted "negligence" and "gross negligence," and that certain acts were "proximate causes" of the plaintiff's injuries.

Dickerson v. DeBarbieris, 964 S.W.2d 680, 690 (Tex.App.—Houston [14th Dist.] 1998, no pet.). "Although rule 704 allows an expert to state an opinion on a mixed question of law and fact, it does not permit an expert to state an opinion or conclusion on a pure question of law because such a question is exclusively for the court to decide and is not an ultimate issue to be decided by the trier of fact."

Isern v. Watson, 942 S.W.2d 186, 193 (Tex.App.—Beaumont 1997, pet. denied). "[B]efore a testifying expert's opinion can be rendered [on negligence, gross negligence, or proximate cause], a predicate must be laid showing that the expert is familiar with the proper legal definition in question."

TRE 705. DISCLOSURE OF FACTS OR DATA UNDERLYING EXPERT OPINION

(a) Disclosure of Facts or Data. The expert may testify in terms of opinion or inference and give the expert's reasons therefor without prior disclosure of the underlying facts or data, unless the court requires otherwise. The expert may in any event disclose on direct examination, or be required to disclose on cross-examination, the underlying facts or data.

(b) Voir dire. Prior to the expert giving the expert's opinion or disclosing the underlying facts or data, a party against whom the opinion is offered upon request in a criminal case shall, or in a civil case may, be permitted to conduct a *voir dire* examination directed to the underlying facts or data upon which the opinion is based. This examination shall be conducted out of the hearing of the jury.

(c) Admissibility of opinion. If the court determines that the underlying facts or data do not provide a sufficient basis for the expert's opinion under Rule 702 or 703, the opinion is inadmissible.

(d) Balancing test; limiting instructions. When the underlying facts or data would be inadmissible in evidence, the court shall exclude the underlying facts or data if the danger that they will be used for a purpose other than as explanation or support for the expert's opinion outweighs their value as explanation or support or are unfairly prejudicial. If otherwise inadmissible facts or data are disclosed before the jury, a limiting instruction by the court shall be given upon request.

Comment to 1998 change: Paragraphs (b), (c), and (d) are based on the former Criminal Rule and are made applicable to civil cases. This rule does not preclude a party in any case from conducting a *voir dire* examination into the qualifications of an expert.

See also Cochran, ***Texas Rules of Evidence Handbook***, p. 704 (2001).

Weiss v. Mechanical Assoc. Servs., 989 S.W.2d 120, 124-25 (Tex.App.—San Antonio 1999, pet. denied). "The non-exclusive list of factors the court may consider in deciding admissibility [under TRE 705(c)] includes the extent to which the theory has been or can be tested, the extent to which the technique relies upon the subjective interpretation of the expert, whether the theory has been subjected to peer review and/or publication, the technique's potential rate of error, whether the underlying theory or technique has been generally accepted as valid by the relevant scientific community, and the non-judicial uses that have been made of the theory or technique."

Stam v. Mack, 984 S.W.2d 747, 750 (Tex.App.—Texarkana 1999, no pet.). TRE 703 and 705 "now allow a testifying expert to relate on direct examination the reasonably reliable facts and data on which he relied in forming his opinion, subject to an objection under [TRE] 403 that the probative value of such facts and data is outweighed by the risk of undue prejudice. ... The details of those facts and data may be brought out on cross-examination pursuant to [TRE] 705(a), 705(b), and 705(d). Moreover, the opponent of such evidence may ask for a limiting instruction if he fears the evidence may be used for a purpose other than support for the testifying expert's opinion."

TRE 706. AUDIT IN CIVIL CASES

Despite any other evidence rule to the contrary, verified reports of auditors prepared pursuant to Rule of Civil Procedure 172, whether in the form of summaries, opinions, or otherwise, shall be admitted in evidence when offered by any party whether or not the facts or data in the reports are otherwise admissible and whether or not the reports embrace the ultimate issues to be decided by the trier of fact. Where exceptions to the reports have been filed, a party may contradict the reports by evidence supporting the exceptions.

See also Cochran, ***Texas Rules of Evidence Handbook***, p. 720 (2001).

Lovelace v. Sabine Consol., Inc., 733 S.W.2d 648, 656 (Tex.App.—Houston [14th Dist.] 1987, writ denied). "The audit report before this court contains no such affidavit as is required by [TRCP] 172. ... Further, 6 days before trial [P] filed an objection to the audit. Therefore, the trial court did not err in admitting evidence that contradicted and supplemented the auditor's report."

ARTICLE VIII. HEARSAY

TRE 801. DEFINITIONS

The following definitions apply under this article:

(a) Statement. A "statement" is (1) an oral or written verbal expression or (2) nonverbal conduct of a person, if it is intended by the person as a substitute for verbal expression.

(b) Declarant. A "declarant" is a person who makes a statement.

(c) Matter Asserted. "Matter asserted" includes any matter explicitly asserted, and any matter implied by a statement, if the probative value of the statement as offered flows from declarant's belief as to the matter.

(d) Hearsay. "Hearsay" is a statement, other than one made by the declarant while testifying at the trial or hearing, offered in evidence to prove the truth of the matter asserted.

(e) Statements Which Are Not Hearsay. A statement is not hearsay if:

(1) *Prior statement by witness.* The declarant testifies at the trial or hearing and is subject to cross-examination concerning the statement, and the statement is:

(A) inconsistent with the declarant's testimony, and was given under oath subject to the penalty of perjury at a trial, hearing, or other proceeding except a grand jury proceeding in a criminal case, or in a deposition;

(B) consistent with the declarant's testimony and is offered to rebut an express or implied charge against the declarant of recent fabrication or improper influence or motive;

(C) one of identification of a person made after perceiving the person; or

(D) taken and offered in a criminal case in accordance with Code of Criminal Procedure article 38.071.

(2) *Admission by party-opponent.* The statement is offered against a party and is:

(A) the party's own statement in either an individual or representative capacity;

(B) a statement of which the party has manifested an adoption or belief in its truth;

(C) a statement by a person authorized by the party to make a statement concerning the subject;

(D) a statement by the party's agent or servant concerning a matter within the scope of the agency or employment, made during the existence of the relationship; or

(E) a statement by a co-conspirator of a party during the course and in furtherance of the conspiracy.

(3) *Depositions.* In a civil case, it is a deposition taken in the same proceeding, as same proceeding is defined in Rule of Civil Procedure 203.6(b). Unavailability of deponent is not a requirement for admissibility.

Caution: TRE 801 is affected by the following section in the Fam. Code: §104.006.

See also *O'Connor's Texas Rules*, "Depositions," ch. 6-E; "Requests for Admissions," ch. 6-G; Cochran, ***Texas Rules of Evidence Handbook***, p. 729 (2001).

Note: The definitions in TRCE 801(a), (b), (c) and (d) combined bring within the hearsay rule four categories of conduct; these are described and illustrated below.

(1) A verbal (oral or written) explicit assertion. Illustration. Witness testifies that declarant said "A shot B." Declarant's conduct is a statement because it is an oral expression. Because it is an explicit assertion, the matter asserted is that A shot B. Finally, the statement is hearsay because it was not made while testifying at the trial and is offered to prove the truth of the matter asserted.

(2) A verbal (oral or written) explicit assertion, not offered to prove the matter explicitly asserted, but offered for the truth of a matter implied by the statement, the probative value of the statement flowing from declarant's belief as to the matter. Illustration. The only known remedy for X disease is medicine Y and the only known use of medicine Y is to cure X disease. To prove that Oglethorpe had X disease, witness testifies that declarant, a doctor, stated, "The best medicine for Oglethorpe is Y." The testimony is to a statement because it was a verbal expression. The matter asserted was that Oglethorpe had X disease because that matter is implied from the statement, the probative value of the statement as offered flowing from declarant's belief as to the matter. Finally, the statement is hearsay because it was not made while testifying at the trial and is offered to prove the truth of the matter asserted.

(3) Non-assertive verbal conduct offered for the truth of a matter implied by the statement, the probative value of the statement flowing from declarant's belief as to the matter. Illustration. In a rape prosecution to prove that Richard, the defendant, was in the room at the time of the rape, W testifies that declarant knocked on the door to the room and shouted, "Open the door, Richard." The testimony is to a statement because it was a verbal expression. The matter asserted was that Richard was in the room because that matter is implied from the statement, the probative value of the statement as offered flowing from declarant's belief as to the matter. Finally, the statement is hearsay because it was not made while testifying at the trial and is offered to prove the truth of the matter asserted.

(4) Nonverbal assertive conduct intended as a substitute for verbal expression. Illustration. W testifies that A asked declarant "Which way did X go?" and declarant pointed north. This nonverbal conduct of declarant was intended by him as a substitute for verbal expression and so is a statement. The matter asserted is that X went north because that is implied from the statement and the probative value of the statement as offered flows from declarant's belief that X went north. Finally, the statement is hearsay because it was not made at trial and is offered to prove the truth of the matter asserted. Source: FRE 801.

Author's Comment: Example of nonhearsay statement: X testifies that Y said "I am William Shakespeare." The purpose of the testimony is to provide evidence of the fact that Y *said* he is William Shakespeare—not that he *is* William Shakespeare. Therefore, the statement is not offered as proof of the truth of the matter asserted and not hearsay.

TRE 801(d)

McCraw v. Maris, 828 S.W.2d 756, 757 (Tex.1992). "Out-of-court statements are not hearsay if offered for a purpose other than to prove the truth of the matter asserted. Since the duplicate beneficiary designation form was offered only to prove its existence, we conclude that it was not hearsay."

In re. J.A.M., 945 S.W.2d 320, 323 (Tex.App.—San Antonio 1997, no writ). "Depositions used in the same proceeding are not hearsay."

City of Austin v. H.L. & P. Co., 844 S.W.2d 773, 791 (Tex.App.—Dallas 1992, writ denied). "Generally, Texas courts consider newspaper articles inadmissible hearsay. [N]ewspaper articles not offered for the truth of the matters asserted but used merely to show notice of those matters are not hearsay."

TRE 801(e)

Tome v. U.S., 513 U.S. 150, 156, 115 S.Ct. 696, 701 (1995) (criminal case interpreting federal rule). If a witness was cross-examined about the statement, a party may introduce a earlier consistent statement to rebut the charge of recent fabrication or improper influence by proving through another witness, that (1) before testifying, the testifying witness made out-of-court statement consistent with testimony, and (2) the statement was made before the testifying witness had reason to fabricate.

In re M.S., ___ S.W.3d ___ (Tex.App.—Beaumont 2002, n.p.h.) (No. 09-01-037 CV; 4-11-02). "The 'Memorandum of Agreement' set forth the acts that [mother] would undertake; CPS agreed to return the children to [mother] if she complied with the agreement. That agreement is not hearsay. First, the memorandum was not offered for the truth of matters stated therein, but for the fact that the agreement was made. To the extent that it could be argued to fit within Rule 801(d), a statement by [mother] contained in the agreement would not be hearsay because it was an admission by the party opponent under Rule 801(e). To the extent that the memorandum, which was adopted by the trial court as an order, could be argued to include statements of belief by the trial court or any of the parties to the agreement, it would be admissible as a public record, and as a statement against civil interest."

McEwen v. Wal-Mart Stores, Inc., 975 S.W.2d 25, 28 (Tex.App.—San Antonio 1998, pet. denied). "An admission by a party opponent is not hearsay. ... Rule 801(e)(2)(D) includes as non-hearsay statements made by an 'agent or servant' regarding matters within the scope of their agency or employment during the existence of that relationship."

Worley v. Butler, 809 S.W.2d 242, 245 (Tex.App.—Corpus Christi 1990, no writ). TRE 801(e)(2) "provides that a statement is not hearsay if it is offered against a party and is his own statement in either his individual or representative capacity. [D's] prior testimony concerning his employment agreement and fee arrangement is being offered against him as a party-opponent. Further, [D] made these statements in his individual capacity."

Reviea v. Marine Drilling Co., 800 S.W.2d 252, 257 (Tex.App.—Corpus Christi 1990, writ denied). Defendant's witness "testified at trial and was subject to cross-examination concerning his statement about [P's] prior knee injury. Thus, his statement to [the claims investigator] was consistent with his trial testimony regarding [P's] prior knee injury. We find that the prior consistent statement of [D's witness] concerning [P's] admission of a prior injury was not hearsay, as it was offered to rebut [P's] implied charge of recent fabrication."

TRE 802. HEARSAY RULE

Hearsay is not admissible except as provided by statute or these rules or by other rules prescribed pursuant to statutory authority. Inadmissible hearsay admitted without objection shall not be denied probative value merely because it is hearsay.

Caution: TRE 802 is affected by the following section in the Fam. Code: §104.006.

See also Cochran, ***Texas Rules of Evidence Handbook***, p. 772 (2001).

Texas Commerce Bank v. New, 3 S.W.3d 515, 517 (Tex.1999). "Nothing in [TRE] 802 limits its application to contested hearings. The rule is not ambiguous and requires no explication." Thus, an affidavit containing unobjected-to hearsay can establish facts in a default judgment case.

Birchfield v. Texarkana Mem. Hosp., 747 S.W.2d 361, 365 (Tex.1987). "Ordinarily an expert witness should not be permitted to recount a hearsay conversation with a third person, even if that conversation forms part of the basis of his opinion."

Schleuter v. City of Ft. Worth, 947 S.W.2d 920, 930 (Tex.App.—Fort Worth 1997, pet. denied). Defendant "timely objected to admission of the affidavits as hearsay [but the] court overruled the objection.... Admission of these out-of-court statements without a showing that the declarants were unavailable or that a hearsay exception applied was error."

TRE 803. HEARSAY EXCEPTIONS; AVAILABILITY OF DECLARANT IMMATERIAL

The following are not excluded by the hearsay rule, even though the declarant is available as a witness:

(1) Present Sense Impression. A statement describing or explaining an event or condition made while the declarant was perceiving the event or condition, or immediately thereafter.

(2) Excited Utterance. A statement relating to a startling event or condition made while the declarant was under the stress of excitement caused by the event or condition.

(3) Then Existing Mental, Emotional, or Physical Condition. A statement of the declarant's then existing state of mind, emotion, sensation, or physical condition (such as intent, plan, motive, design, mental feeling, pain, or bodily health), but not including a statement of memory or belief to prove the fact remembered or believed unless it relates to the execution, revocation, identification, or terms of declarant's will.

(4) Statements for Purposes of Medical Diagnosis or Treatment. Statements made for purposes of medical diagnosis or treatment and describing medical history, or past or present symptoms, pain, or sensations, or the inception or general character of the cause or external source thereof insofar as reasonably pertinent to diagnosis or treatment.

(5) Recorded Recollection. A memorandum or record concerning a matter about which a witness once had personal knowledge but now has insufficient recollection to enable the witness to testify fully and accurately, shown to have been made or adopted by the witness when the matter was fresh in the witness' memory and to reflect that knowledge correctly, unless the circumstances of preparation cast doubt on the document's trustworthiness. If admitted, the memorandum or record may be read into evidence but may not itself be received as an exhibit unless offered by an adverse party.

(6) Records of Regularly Conducted Activity. A memorandum, report, record, or data compilation, in any form, of acts, events, conditions, opinions, or diagnoses, made at or near the time by, or from information transmitted by, a person with knowledge, if kept in the course of a regularly conducted business activity, and if it was the regular practice of that business activity to make the memorandum, report, record, or data compilation, all as shown by the testimony of the custodian or other qualified witness, or by affidavit that complies with Rule 902(10), unless the source of information or the method or circumstances of preparation indicate lack of trustworthiness. "Business" as used in this paragraph includes any and every kind of regular organized activity whether conducted for profit or not.

(7) Absence of Entry in Records Kept in Accordance With the Provisions of Paragraph (6). Evidence that a matter is not included in the memoranda, reports, records, or data compilations, in any form, kept in accordance with the provisions of paragraph (6), to prove the nonoccurrence or nonexistence of the matter, if the matter was of a kind of which a memorandum, report, record, or data compilation was regularly made and preserved, unless the sources of information or other circumstances indicate lack of trustworthiness.

(8) Public Records and Reports. Records, reports, statements, or data compilations, in any form, of public offices or agencies setting forth:

(A) the activities of the office or agency;

(B) matters observed pursuant to duty imposed by law as to which matters there was a duty to report, excluding in criminal cases matters observed by police officers and other law enforcement personnel; or

(C) in civil cases as to any party and in criminal cases as against the state, factual findings resulting from an investigation made pursuant to authority granted by law;

unless the sources of information or other circumstances indicate lack of trustworthiness.

(9) Records of Vital Statistics. Records or data compilations, in any form, of births, fetal deaths, deaths, or marriages, if the report thereof was made to a public office pursuant to requirements of law.

(10) Absence of Public Record or Entry. To prove the absence of a record, report, statement, or data compilation, in any form, or the nonoccurrence or nonexistence of a matter of which a record, report, statement, or data compilation, in any form, was regularly made and preserved by a public office or agency, evidence in the form of a certification in accordance with Rule 902, or testimony, that diligent search failed to disclose the record, report statement, or data compilation, or entry.

(11) Records of Religious Organizations. Statements of births, marriages, divorces, deaths, legitimacy, ancestry, relationship by blood or marriage, or other similar facts of personal or family history, contained in a regularly kept record of a religious organization.

(12) Marriage, Baptismal, and Similar Certificates. Statements of fact contained in a certificate that the maker performed a marriage or other ceremony or administered a sacrament, made by a member of the clergy, public official, or other person authorized by the rules or practices of a religious organization or by law to perform the act certified, and purporting to have been issued at the time of the act or within a reasonable time thereafter.

(13) Family Records. Statements of fact concerning personal or family history contained in family Bibles, genealogies, charts, engravings on rings, inscriptions on family portraits, engravings on urns, crypts, or tombstones, or the like.

(14) Records of Documents Affecting an Interest in Property. The record of a document purporting to establish or affect an interest in property, as proof of the content of the original recorded document and its execution and delivery by each person by whom it purports to have been executed, if the record is a record of a public office and an applicable statute authorizes the recording of documents of that kind in that office.

(15) Statements in Documents Affecting an Interest in Property. A statement contained in a document purporting to establish or affect an interest in property if the matter stated was relevant to the purpose of the document, unless dealings with the property since the document was made have been inconsistent with the truth of the statement or the purport of the document.

(16) Statements in Ancient Documents. Statements in a document in existence twenty years or more the authenticity of which is established.

(17) Market Reports, Commercial Publications. Market quotations, tabulations, lists, directories, or other published compilations, generally used and relied upon by the public or by persons in particular occupations.

(18) Learned Treatises. To the extent called to the attention of an expert witness upon cross-examination or relied upon by the expert in direct examination, statements contained in published treatises, periodicals, or pamphlets on a subject of history, medicine, or other science or art established as a reliable authority by the testimony or admission of the witness or by other expert testimony or by judicial notice. If admitted, the statements may be read into evidence but may not be received as exhibits.

(19) Reputation Concerning Personal or Family History. Reputation among members of a person's family by blood, adoption, or marriage, or among a person's associates, or in the community, concerning a person's birth, adoption, marriage, divorce, death, legitimacy, relationship by blood, adoption, or marriage, ancestry, or other similar fact of personal or family history.

(20) Reputation Concerning Boundaries or General History. Reputation in a community, arising before the controversy, as to boundaries of or customs affecting lands in the community, and reputation as to events of general history important to the community or state or nation in which located.

(21) Reputation as to Character. Reputation of a person's character among associates or in the community.

(22) Judgment of Previous Conviction. In civil cases, evidence of a judgment, entered after a trial or upon a plea of guilty (but not upon a plea of *nolo contendere*), judging a person guilty of a felony, to prove any fact essential to sustain the judgment of conviction. In criminal cases, evidence of a judgment, entered after a trial or upon a plea of guilty or nolo contendere, adjudging a person guilty of a criminal offense, to prove any fact essential to sustain the judgment of conviction, but not including, when offered by the state for purposes other than impeachment, judgments against persons other than the accused. In all cases, the pendency of an appeal renders such evidence inadmissible.

(23) Judgment as to Personal, Family, or General History, or Boundaries. Judgments as proof of matters of personal, family or general history, or boundaries, essential to the judgment, if the same would be provable by evidence of reputation.

(24) Statement Against Interest. A statement which was at the time of its making so far contrary to the declarant's pecuniary or proprietary interest, or so far tended to subject the declarant to civil or criminal liability, or to render invalid a claim by the declarant against another, or to make the declarant an object of hatred, ridicule, or disgrace, that a reasonable person in declarant's position would not have made the statement unless believing it to be true. In criminal cases, a statement tending to expose the declarant to criminal liability is not admissible unless corroborating circumstances clearly indicate the trustworthiness of the statement.

Caution: TRE 803 is affected by the following sections in the Fam. Code: §§54.031, 104.006, 107.055.

See also Cochran, ***Texas Rules of Evidence Handbook***, p. 775 (2001).

Generally

Robinson v. Harkins & Co., 711 S.W.2d 619, 621 (Tex.1986). "All hearsay exceptions require a showing of trustworthiness."

Texas DPS v. Gratzer, 982 S.W.2d 88, 90 (Tex. App.—Houston [1st Dist.] 1998, no pet.). "We are unaware of any authority that holds a party's affidavit cannot be based in part on a preprinted form. [The officer] swore to the truth of the *entire* [affidavit], so there is no question of double hearsay. [¶] We conclude the county court erred in finding that … the probable cause affidavit … was improperly admitted [into evidence]."

TRE 803(1)

1.70 Acres v. State, 935 S.W.2d 480, 488 (Tex. App.—Beaumont 1996, no writ). "Present sense impressions are those comments made at the time the declarant is receiving the impression or immediately thereafter. They possess the following safeguards which render them reliable: 1) the report at the moment of the thing then seen, heard, etc. is safe from any error from defect of memory of the declarant; 2) there is little or no time for a calculated misstatement; 3) the statement will usually be made to another—the witness who reports it—who would have equal opportunity to observe and hence to check a misstatement."

TRE 803(2)

Templeton v. Dreiss, 961 S.W.2d 645, 668 (Tex. App.—San Antonio 1998, pet. denied). "[A]ll declarations or exclamations which are made under circumstances which raise a reasonable presumption that they are the spontaneous utterances of thoughts created by or springing out of the transaction itself and so soon thereafter as to exclude the presumption that they are the result of premeditation or design are admissible as res gestae. [¶] Moreover, for declarations to be admissible in evidence as part of the res gestae they must be made in connection with an act proven. In other words, there must be evidence of an act itself admissible in the case independently of the declaration that encompasses it."

Almaraz v. Burke, 827 S.W.2d 80, 83 (Tex.App.—Fort Worth 1992, writ denied). "Although [***First Southwest Lloyds***, cited below] states that the witness's statement was a narrative account, given after he had returned to the scene of the fire, the opinion does not reflect whether the witness was still excited from the fire and the chase at the time the statement was given, nor does it state whether that mattered in reaching the result. If the witness in that case were still excited from the event at the time he told the fire marshall what had just happened, we would have held that the evidence qualified as an exception to the hearsay rule in accordance with rule 803(2). On the other hand, if there were no evidence that the witness was still under the excitement of the preceding events, we would agree with the opinion."

First Southwest Lloyds Ins. Co. v. MacDowell, 769 S.W.2d 954, 959 (Tex.App.—Texarkana 1989, writ denied). "A statement that is simply a narrative of past acts or events, as distinguished from a spontaneous utterance, does not qualify as an excited utterance regardless of how soon after the event that it is made. The circumstances must show that it was the event speaking through the person and not the person speaking about the event."

TRE 803(3)

Ochs v. Martinez, 789 S.W.2d 949, 959 (Tex.App.—San Antonio 1990, writ denied). "Statements admitted under [TRE 803(3)] are usually spontaneous remarks about pain or some other sensation, made by the declarant while the sensation, not readily observable by a third party, is being experienced. The exception does not extend to statements of past external facts or conditions."

Posner v. Dallas Cty. Child Welfare Unit, 784 S.W.2d 585, 587 (Tex.App.—Eastland 1990, writ denied). A child's hearsay statement "was not offered to prove the truth of the [statement]. Rather, it was offered to show that [the child] made the statement which was relevant to the issue of her emotional well-being and state of mind. Hence, the statement clearly falls within the hearsay exception…."

TRE 803(4)

In re L.S., 748 S.W.2d 571, 576 (Tex.App.—Amarillo 1988, no writ). "The crucial issue under [TRE 803(4)] is whether the out-of-court statement was reasonably pertinent to diagnosis or treatment. [¶] [A] statement made by a victim of child abuse identifying the alleged perpetrator is pertinent to both physical and psychological diagnosis and treatment."

TRE 803(6)

Burroughs Wellcome Co. v. Crye, 907 S.W.2d 497, 500 (Tex.1995). "The diagnoses contained in [P's] medical and hospital records are admissible. However, to constitute evidence of causation, an expert opinion must rest in reasonable medical probability. [¶] The context of the opinions contained in the medical records … indicates that these statements are merely recitations of medical history or opinion as to causation provided by other records, [P], or [her doctor]." Held: no evidence of causation.

Freeman v. American Motorists Ins. Co., 53 S.W.3d 710, 715 (Tex.App.—Houston [1st Dist.] 2001, no pet.) The letter from plaintiff's physician to P's attorney was dated over "10 years after the cause of action accrued and a mere 10 days before the summary judgment hearing. This time frame indicates a lack of trustworthiness. In the absence of [P's physician's] remaining records, it appears that he wrote the letter solely in response to a request from [P's] attorney. [The letter] does not qualify as a routine entry in [P's] medical history; therefore, it is inadmissible as a business record under rule 803(6)."

Rodriguez-Narrera v. Ridinger, 19 S.W.3d 531, 532 (Tex.App.—Fort Worth 2000, no pet.). Plaintiff's "medical bills and expenses, verified by custodians' affidavits, were admissible as business records. … However, those exhibits would have been admissible solely to prove the amount, not the reasonableness or necessity, of the expenses. Proof of amounts charged or paid is not proof of reasonableness…."

GT & MC, Inc. v. Texas City Ref., Inc., 822 S.W.2d 252, 258 (Tex.App.—Houston [1st Dist.] 1991, writ denied). The defendant claimed evidence admitted as the plaintiff's business records were not business records because they were invoices created by another entity and sent to the plaintiff. "Though the documents in question were initially authored by outside vendors, employees of [P] placed numerous markings on the invoices after receipt by [P]. … Thus, the invoices became [P's] primary record of information about the underlying transaction."

TRE 803(7)

Coleman v. United Sav. Ass'n, 846 S.W.2d 128, 131 (Tex.App.—Fort Worth 1993, no writ). "Testimony that is offered as evidence that a matter is not included in records to prove the nonoccurrence or nonexistence of

TRE 803

the matter is inadmissible hearsay evidence unless [TRE] 803(7) is satisfied. The initial foundational predicate of rule 803(7) is that the records that would include the matter, if it were not absent from those records, are kept in accordance with the provisions of rule 803(6). [D's] affidavit does not even attempt to satisfy the requirements of rule 803(6) and therefore cannot support the summary judgment."

TRE 803(8)

In re T.T., 39 S.W.3d 355, 358 (Tex.App.—Houston [1st Dist.] 2001, no pet.). Parties "contend the trial judge's temporary order in this case, which was admitted in evidence upon final trial, was inadmissible hearsay and was an improper comment on the weight of the evidence. We agree. *At 359:* The State contends that the temporary order was not excluded by the hearsay rule because of the exception in Rule 803(8)(C).... [¶] We decline to hold that the exception in Rule 803(8)(C) would allow the admission of this temporary order. First, that rule was not meant to allow a jury to hear hearsay statements from the presiding judge about the merits of the case on trial. Even direct testimony by the presiding judge is expressly prohibited by Rule 605. It is inconceivable that the authors of the Texas Rules of Evidence would have meant to allow the presiding judge's hearsay statements into evidence while Rule 605 prohibits the judge from testifying in person. The prohibition in Rule 605 is stronger than any other in our rules of evidence; no other rule provides that objection is unnecessary to preserve the error for appellate review."

Robinson v. Warner-Lambert, 998 S.W.2d 407, 412 (Tex.App.—Waco 1999, no pet.). "[T]he evidence at issue here is an article and not a record, report, statement, or data compilation of a public office or agency. The information contained within the article may summarize a study, but cannot be said to be a report of an agency. Thus, the article is not admissible under [TRE] 803(8)(C)."

TRE 803(10)

Towne Square Assocs. v. Angelina Cty. Appr. Dist., 709 S.W.2d 776, 777 (Tex.App.—Beaumont 1986, no writ). "In support of the motion for summary judgment, [Ds] filed affidavits.... Each of these affidavits stated that, after a diligent search, [Ds] could find no notice of appeal filed in the records. [Ps] assert these affidavits are insufficient in that they contain hearsay and do not have some of the predicate language required for a business record in accordance with [TRE] 902. [Ps'] complete reliance on this rule is misplaced. The affidavits are controlled by [TRE] 803(10).... While it is true the affidavits do not meet the authentication requirements of Rule 902, they do contain testimony that a diligent search failed to disclose the notice of appeal."

TRE 803(14) & (15)

Compton v. WWV Enter., 679 S.W.2d 668, 671 (Tex. App.—Eastland 1984, no writ). "Hearsay exceptions [TRE 803(14) & (15)] must ... be construed to relate to recitals or statements made in deeds, leases, mortgages and other such 'documents affecting an interest in property' and not to affidavits of heirship which more properly fall within the hearsay exception stated under [TRE] 804(b)(3)."

TRE 803(16)

Guthrie v. Suiter, 934 S.W.2d 820, 825 (Tex.App.—Houston [1st Dist.] 1996, no writ). "Statements contained in documents 20 years old or older qualify as an exception to the hearsay rule, provided the documents are properly authenticated. To qualify for this exception, the document must be shown (1) in such condition as to create no suspicion concerning its authenticity; (2) that it was in a place where it would likely be if it were authentic; and (3) that it has been in existence 20 years or more at the time it is offered."

TRE 803(17)

New Braunfels Factory Outlet Ctr. v. IHOP Rlty. Corp., 872 S.W.2d 303, 310 (Tex.App.—Austin 1994, no writ). "The hearsay exception provided by [TRE] 803(17) permits the admission of certain objective data.... At common law, survey results were also admissible *provided* that the party opposing admission was given the opportunity to cross-examine the person who had conducted the survey."

TRE 803(18)

King v. Bauer, 767 S.W.2d 197, 199-200 (Tex. App.—Corpus Christi 1989, writ denied). Under TRE 803(18), plaintiff introduced a medical textbook that was published two years after plaintiff's therapy, but the earlier edition of which was recognized by defendant as a learned treatise. "The fact that the 3rd edition [of the textbook] was not published until 1980 does not serve to disqualify the evidence which was aimed at illustrating an appropriate treatment plan for [P] in 1978. Treatises which directly refer to the standard of care in use at the time of the occurrence are material, relevant and therefore admissible."

TRE 803(20)

Roberts v. Allison, 836 S.W.2d 185, 191 (Tex. App.—Tyler 1992, writ denied). "A reason for the exception [in TRE 803(20)] is '[t]he fact that a prolonged observation and discussion of certain matters of general interest by a whole community will sift possible errors and bring the result down to us in a fairly trustworthy form furnishes a guarantee of correctness.' [Ps'] proposed testimony pertains to an individual family's assertion of an easement; there is no contention of the ... community's knowledge of [Ps'] claim to access [D's] property. ... There was no proof of the recognized 'vehicles of reputation', such as 'declarations of residents, old maps, surveys, deeds and leases' of the claimed easement. ... The trial court did not abuse its discretion in excluding [the] testimony of a claimed oral agreement granting an easement to [Ps] over the subject property."

TRE 803(22)

McCormick v. Texas Commerce Bank, 751 S.W.2d 887, 890 (Tex.App.—Houston [14th Dist.] 1988, writ denied). "Where (i) the issue at stake was identical to that in the criminal case, (ii) the issue had been actually litigated, and (iii) determination of the issue was a critical and necessary part of the prior judgment, the judgment is established by offensive collateral estoppel and is within the hearsay exception of [FRE] 803(22). [¶] Applying the standards of the federal judiciary to [TRE] 803(22), we hold that the trial court did not err in refusing to permit [D] to explain the circumstances of his criminal conviction."

TRE 803(24)

State v. Arnold, 778 S.W.2d 68, 69 (Tex.1989). Under TRE 803(24), a "statement may be self-serving in one respect but contrary to another interest. The court must balance these competing interests to determine their predominant nature and ultimately the level of trustworthiness to be accorded."

Green v. Reyes, 836 S.W.2d 203, 213 (Tex.App.—Houston [14th Dist.] 1992, no writ). "[A]ffidavits of persons who thereby admit under oath an action which can subject them to criminal liability may be properly admitted at trial as an exception to the hearsay rule as statements against their interest."

TRE 804. HEARSAY EXCEPTIONS; DECLARANT UNAVAILABLE

(a) Definition of Unavailability. "Unavailability as a witness" includes situations in which the declarant:

(1) is exempted by ruling of the court on the ground of privilege from testifying concerning the subject matter of the declarant's statement;

(2) persists in refusing to testify concerning the subject matter of the declarant's statement despite an order of the court to do so;

(3) testifies to a lack of memory of the subject matter of the declarant's statement;

(4) is unable to be present or to testify at the hearing because of death or then existing physical or mental illness or infirmity; or

(5) is absent from the hearing and the proponent of the declarant's statement has been unable to procure the declarant's attendance or testimony by process or other reasonable means.

A declarant is not unavailable as a witness if the declarant's exemption, refusal, claim of lack of memory, inability, or absence is due to the procurement or wrong-doing of the proponent of the declarant's statement for the purpose of preventing the witness from attending or testifying.

(b) Hearsay Exceptions. The following are not excluded if the declarant is unavailable as a witness:

(1) *Former testimony.* In civil cases, testimony given as a witness at another hearing of the same or a different proceeding, or in a deposition taken in the course of another proceeding, if the party against whom the testimony is now offered, or a person with a similar interest, had an opportunity and similar motive to develop the testimony by direct, cross, or redirect examination. In criminal cases, testimony given as a witness at another hearing of the same or a different proceeding, if the party against whom the testimony is now offered had an opportunity and similar motive to develop the testimony by direct, cross, or redirect examination. In criminal cases the use of depositions is controlled by Chapter 39 of the Code of Criminal Procedure.

(2) *Dying declarations.* A statement made by a declarant while believing that the declarant's death was imminent, concerning the cause or circumstances of what the declarant believed to be impending death.

(3) *Statement of personal or family history.*

(A) A statement concerning the declarant's own birth, adoption, marriage, divorce, legitimacy, relationship by blood, adoption, or marriage, ancestry, or other similar fact of personal or family history even though declarant had no means of acquiring personal knowledge of the matter stated; or

(B) A statement concerning the foregoing matters, and death also, of another person, if the declarant was related to the other by blood, adoption, or marriage or was so intimately associated with the other's family as to be likely to have accurate information concerning the matter declared.

See also ***O'Connor's Texas Rules***, "Depositions," ch. 6-E; Cochran, ***Texas Rules of Evidence Handbook***, p. 832 (2001).

Natural Gas Pipeline Co. v. Pool, 30 S.W.3d 618, 631 (Tex.App.—Amarillo 2000, pet. granted, argued 3-6-02). "We believe [the witness'] refusal to testify on the advice of his counsel made the witness 'unavailable' for purposes of this trial. There is nothing in the record to show that his refusal to testify on the advise of his counsel was not true [thus, his] deposition was properly admitted."

Fuller-Austin Insulation Co. v. Bilder, 960 S.W.2d 914, 921 (Tex.App.—Beaumont 1998, pet. granted w.r.m.). "Unavailability of a witness [as defined in TRE 804(a)] means the witness is dead, has become insane, is physically unable to testify, is beyond the jurisdiction of the court, is unable to be found after a diligent search, or has been kept away from the trial by the adverse party. [¶] 'Mere comments by an attorney are not sufficient proof of a declarant's unavailability.' [T]he fact that [the witness] was uncooperative in attending trial did not mean he could not give his deposition.... Although [the witness] may have been beyond the subpoena power of the court, [D] did not establish it was unable to take his deposition or otherwise procure his testimony in this cause."

Thompson v. Mayes, 707 S.W.2d 951, 957 (Tex. App.—Eastland 1986, writ ref'd n.r.e.). Under TRE 804(b)(2), "dying declarations which concern the cause or the circumstances of what the declarant believed to be his impending death are admissible as exceptions to the hearsay rule."

TRE 805. HEARSAY WITHIN HEARSAY

Hearsay included within hearsay is not excluded under the hearsay rule if each part of the combined statements conforms with an exception to the hearsay rule provided in these rules.

See also Cochran, ***Texas Rules of Evidence Handbook***, p. 845 (2001).

H.L. & P. Co. v. Klein ISD, 739 S.W.2d 508, 519 (Tex.App.—Houston [14th Dist.] 1987, writ denied). "[C]harts summarizing studies of power lines and health effects [were] objected to ... as hearsay because the underlying studies were hearsay."

TRE 806. ATTACKING & SUPPORTING CREDIBILITY OF DECLARANT

When a hearsay statement, or a statement defined in Rule 801(e)(2)(C), (D), or (E), or in civil cases a statement defined in Rule 801(e)(3), has been admitted in evidence, the credibility of the declarant may be attacked, and if attacked may be supported by any evidence which would be admissible for those purposes if declarant had testified as a witness. Evidence of a statement or conduct by the declarant at any time, offered to impeach the declarant, is not subject to any requirement that the declarant may have been afforded an opportunity to deny or explain. If the party against whom a hearsay statement has been admitted calls the declarant as a witness, the party is entitled to examine the declarant on the statement as if under cross-examination.

See also Cochran, ***Texas Rules of Evidence Handbook***, p. 847 (2001).

Anthony Pools, Inc. v. Charles & David, Inc., 797 S.W.2d 666, 676 (Tex.App.—Houston [14th Dist.] 1990, writ denied). "Texas courts long have allowed the use of affidavits to impeach a witness. The jury could have been allowed to consider any inconsistencies between the affidavit and the deposition as damaging to the credibility of [the witness'] deposition, but not as substantive evidence. [¶] Upon timely request and objection ... the court was required to instruct the jury of the limited use to be made of the affidavit."

Victor M. Solis Underground Util. & Paving Co. v. City of Laredo, 751 S.W.2d 532, 537 (Tex.App.—San Antonio 1988, writ denied). "If a declarant is unavailable as a witness, [TRE] 806 ... provides that testimony by that person at a former hearing is not excluded as hearsay if the party against whom the testimony is offered, 'or a person with similar interest, had an opportunity and similar motive to develop the testimony by direct, cross, or redirect examination.'"

ARTICLE IX. AUTHENTICATION & IDENTIFICATION

TRE 901. REQUIREMENT OF AUTHENTICATION OR IDENTIFICATION

(a) General Provision. The requirement of authentication or identification as a condition precedent to admissibility is satisfied by evidence sufficient to support a finding that the matter in question is what its proponent claims.

(b) Illustrations. By way of illustration only, and not by way of limitation, the following are examples of authentication or identification conforming with the requirements of this rule:

(1) *Testimony of witness with knowledge.* Testimony that a matter is what it is claimed to be.

(2) *Nonexpert opinion on handwriting.* Nonexpert opinion as to the genuineness of handwriting, based upon familiarity not acquired for purposes of the litigation.

(3) *Comparison by trier or expert witness.* Comparison by the trier of fact or by expert witness with specimens which have been found by the court to be genuine.

(4) *Distinctive characteristics and the like.* Appearance, contents, substance, internal patterns, or other distinctive characteristics, taken in conjunction with circumstances.

(5) *Voice identification.* Identification of a voice, whether heard firsthand or through mechanical or electronic transmission or recording, by opinion based upon hearing the voice at anytime under circumstances connecting it with the alleged speaker.

(6) *Telephone conversations.* Telephone conversations, by evidence that a call was made to the number assigned at the time by the telephone company to a particular person or business, if:

(A) in the case of a person, circumstances, including self-identification, show the person answering to be the one called; or

(B) in the case of a business, the call was made to a place of business and the conversation related to business reasonably transacted over the telephone.

(7) *Public records or reports.* Evidence that a writing authorized by law to be recorded or filed and in fact recorded or filed in a public office, or a purported public record, report, statement, or data compilation, in any form, is from the public office where items of this nature are kept.

(8) *Ancient documents or data compilation.* Evidence that a document or data compilation, in any form, (A) is in such condition as to create no suspicion concerning its authenticity, (B) was in a place where it, if authentic, would likely be, and (C) has been in existence twenty years or more at the time it is offered.

(9) *Process or system.* Evidence describing a process or system used to produce a result and showing that the process or system produces an accurate result.

(10) *Methods provided by statute or rule.* Any method of authentication or identification provided by statute or by other rule prescribed pursuant to statutory authority.

See also ***O'Connor's Texas Rules***, "Introducing Evidence," ch. 8-C; Cochran, ***Texas Rules of Evidence Handbook***, p. 853 (2001).

G.M. Corp. v. Gayle, 951 S.W.2d 469, 475 (Tex. 1997). "Any tests that a party ... offer[s] at trial will be admissible only if the trial court determines that there is a substantial similarity between the test conditions and the accident conditions."

In re Estate of Watson, 720 S.W.2d 806, 808 (Tex. 1986). TRE 901(b) "provides a variety of methods to authenticate a writing...."

In re G.F.O., 874 S.W.2d 729, 731 (Tex.App.—Houston [1st Dist.] 1994, no writ). TRE 901(a) "requires the authentication or identification as a condition precedent to admissibility; the requirement is satisfied by evidence sufficient to support a finding that the matter in question is what its proponent claims. [¶] A document is considered authentic if a sponsoring witness vouches for its authenticity or if the document meets the requirements of self-authentication."

Durkay v. Madco Oil Co., Inc., 862 S.W.2d 14, 24 (Tex.App.—Corpus Christi 1993, writ denied). "Even if the report was admissible ... the report was still subject to the requirement of authentication. [No] witness testified to the completeness of the report, how it was prepared, its accuracy, or the basis for the calculations contained within it. The report is not a self authenticating document under the provisions of [TRE] 902 and must be authenticated in some other manner."

TRE 902. SELF-AUTHENTICATION

Extrinsic evidence of authenticity as a condition precedent to admissibility is not required with respect to the following:

(1) Domestic Public Documents Under Seal. A document bearing a seal purporting to be that of the United States, or of any State, district, Commonwealth, territory, or insular possession thereof, or the Panama Canal Zone, or the Trust Territory of the Pacific Islands, or of a political subdivision, department, officer, or agency thereof, and a signature purporting to be an attestation or execution.

(2) Domestic Public Documents Not Under Seal. A document purporting to bear the signature in the official capacity of an officer or employee of any entity included in paragraph (1) hereof, having no seal, if a public officer having a seal and having official duties in the district or political subdivision of the officer or employee certifies under seal that the signer has the official capacity and that the signature is genuine.

(3) Foreign Public Documents. A document purporting to be executed or attested in an official capacity by a person, authorized by the laws of a foreign country to make the execution or attestation, and accompanied by a final certification as to the genuineness of the signature and official position (A) of the executing or attesting person, or (B) of any foreign official whose certificate of genuineness of signature and official position relates to the execution or attestation or is in a chain of certificates of genuineness of signature and official position relating to the execution or attestation. A final certification may be made by a secretary of embassy or legation, consul general, consul, vice consul, or consular agent of the United States, or a diplomatic or consular official of the foreign country assigned or accredited to the United States. If reasonable opportunity has been given to all parties to investigate the authenticity and accuracy of official documents, the court may, for good cause shown, order that they be treated as presumptively authentic without final certification or permit them to be evidenced by an attested summary with or without final certification. The final certification shall be dispensed with whenever both the United States and the foreign country in which the official record is located are parties to a treaty or convention that abolishes or displaces such requirement, in which case the record and the attestation shall be certified by the means provided in the treaty or convention.

(4) Certified Copies of Public Records. A copy of an official record or report or entry therein, or of a document authorized by law to be recorded or filed and actually recorded or filed in a public office, including data compilations in any form certified as correct by the custodian or other person authorized to make the certification, by certificate complying with paragraph (1), (2) or (3) of this rule or complying with any statute or other rule prescribed pursuant to statutory authority.

(5) Official Publications. Books, pamphlets, or other publications purporting to be issued by public authority.

(6) Newspapers and Periodicals. Printed materials purporting to be newspapers or periodicals.

(7) Trade Inscriptions and the Like. Inscriptions, signs, tags, or labels purporting to have been affixed in the course of business and indicating ownership, control, or origin.

(8) Acknowledged Documents. Documents accompanied by a certificate of acknowledgment executed in the manner provided by law by a notary public or other officer authorized by law to take acknowledgments.

(9) Commercial Paper and Related Documents. Commercial paper, signatures thereon, and documents relating thereto to the extent provided by general commercial law.

(10) Business Records Accompanied by Affidavit.

(a) *Records or photocopies; admissibility; affidavit; filing.* Any record or set of records or photographically reproduced copies of such records, which would be admissible under Rule 803(6) or (7) shall be admissible in evidence in any court in this state upon the affidavit of the person who would otherwise provide the prerequisites of Rule 803(6) or (7), that such records attached to such affidavit were in fact so kept as required by Rule 803(6) or (7), provided further, that such record or records along with such affidavit are filed with the clerk of the court for inclusion with the papers in the cause in which the record or records are sought to be used as evidence at least fourteen days prior to the day upon which trial of said cause commences, and provided the other parties to said cause are given prompt notice by the party filing same of the filing of such record or records and affidavit, which notice shall identify the name and employer, if any, of the person making the affidavit and such records shall be made available to the counsel for other parties to the action or litigation for inspection and copying. The expense for copying shall be borne by the party, parties or persons who desire copies and not by the party or parties who file the records and serve notice of said filing, in compliance with this rule. Notice shall be deemed to have been promptly given if it is served in the manner contemplated by Rule of Civil Procedure 21a fourteen days prior to commencement of trial in said cause.

(b) *Form of affidavit.* A form for the affidavit of such person as shall make such affidavit as is permitted in paragraph (a) above shall be sufficient if it follows this form though this form shall not be exclusive, and an affidavit which substantially complies with the provisions of this rule shall suffice, to-wit:

No.__________

John Doe	§	IN THE ________
(Name of Plaintiff)	§	COURT IN AND FOR
v.	§	
John Roe	§	______ COUNTY,
(Name of Defendant)	§	TEXAS

AFFIDAVIT

Before me, the undersigned authority, personally appeared ____________, who, being by me duly sworn, deposed as follows:

My name is __________, I am of sound mind, capable of making this affidavit, and personally acquainted with the facts herein stated:

I am the custodian of the records of ____________. Attached hereto are _____ pages of records from ______. These said ____ pages of records are kept by ________ in the regular course of business, and it was the regular course of business of ___________ for an employee or representative of _________, with knowledge of the act, event, condition, opinion, or diagnosis, recorded to make the record or to transmit information thereof to be included in such record; and the record was made at or near the time or reasonably soon thereafter. The records attached hereto are the original or exact duplicates of the original.

____
Affiant

SWORN TO AND SUBSCRIBED before me on the _________ day of __________, 20 ____.

____
Notary Public, State of Texas
Notary's printed name:

____

My commission expires:

____

(11) Presumptions Under Statutes or Other Rules. Any signature, document, or other matter declared by statute or by other rules prescribed pursuant to statutory authority to be presumptively or prima facie genuine or authentic.

See also *O'Connor's Texas Rules*, "Motion for Summary Judgment," ch. 7-B; "Introducing Evidence," ch. 8-C; Cochran, ***Texas Rules of Evidence Handbook***, p. 878 (2001).

Texas DPS v. Silva, 988 S.W.2d 873, 877 (Tex. App.—San Antonio 1999, pet. denied). Defendant "cites no authority, nor have we found any requirement that the [seal] state what the document is certifying or that the [seal] be from the county where the documents were prepared."

Mathis v. State, 930 S.W.2d 203, 206 (Tex.App.—Houston [14th Dist.] 1996, no writ). "Certified copies have traditionally been permitted to prove public records because of reluctance to remove originals from their proper custody and the inconvenience of requiring testimony of the custodian in order to authenticate either an original or a copy."

Director v. Lara, 901 S.W.2d 635, 638 (Tex.App.—El Paso 1995, writ denied). TRE 902(4) "speaks only to the authenticity of certain documentary evidence. That a document is authentic does not make it admissible...."

Shaw v. Kennedy, Ltd., 879 S.W.2d 240, 246 (Tex. App.—Amarillo 1994, no writ). "The copies of the application for, and order accepting, the closing of [the] bankruptcy proceedings [that] were certified by the bankruptcy court ... were properly authenticated pursuant to [TRE] 902, ... and were competent summary judgment evidence...."

Fullick v. City of Baytown, 820 S.W.2d 943, 945 (Tex.App.—Houston [1st Dist.] 1991, no writ). "[T]he tax statements were not self-authenticating under [TRE] 902(4).... However, the record reflects that the tax statements were properly self-authenticated under [TRE] 902(10)."

March v. Victoria Lloyds Ins. Co., 773 S.W.2d 785, 789 (Tex.App.—Fort Worth 1989, writ denied). "[T]he requirements for authentication under [TRE] 803(6) and 902(10) do not require the sponsoring witness or affiant to testify as to the trustworthiness of the report. The witness or affiant is to set forth the facts upon which an assessment of trustworthiness can be made by the court."

TRE 903. SUBSCRIBING WITNESS' TESTIMONY UNNECESSARY

The testimony of a subscribing witness is not necessary to authenticate a writing unless required by the laws of the jurisdiction whose laws govern the validity of the writing.

See also Cochran, ***Texas Rules of Evidence Handbook***, p. 899 (2001).

ARTICLE X. CONTENTS OF WRITINGS, RECORDINGS, & PHOTOGRAPHS

TRE 1001. DEFINITIONS

For purposes of this article the following definitions are applicable:

(a) Writings and Recordings. "Writings" and "recordings" consist of letters, words, or numbers or their equivalent, set down by handwriting, typewriting, printing, photostating, photographing, magnetic impulse, mechanical or electronic recording, or other form of data compilation.

(b) Photographs. "Photographs" include still photographs, X-ray films, video tapes, and motion pictures.

(c) Original. An "original" of a writing or recording is the writing or recording itself or any counterpart intended to have the same effect by a person executing or issuing it. An "original" of a photograph includes the negative or any print therefrom. If data are stored in a computer or similar device, any printout or other output readable by sight, shown to reflect the data accurately, is an "original."

(d) Duplicate. A "duplicate" is a counterpart produced by the same impression as the original, or from the same matrix, or by means of photography, including enlargements and miniatures, or by mechanical or electronic re-recording, or by chemical reproduction, or by other equivalent techniques which accurately reproduce the original.

See also ***O'Connor's Texas Rules***, "Introducing Evidence," ch. 8-C; Cochran, ***Texas Rules of Evidence Handbook***, p. 903 (2001).

S.D.G. v. State, 936 S.W.2d 371, 381 (Tex.App.—Houston [14th Dist.] 1996, writ denied). "The predicate for introduction of a photograph and a videotape not accompanied by a sound recording requires proof of (1) its accuracy as a correct representation of the subject at a given time, and (2) its relevance to a material issue.... Any witness who observed the object or the scene depicted in the photograph may lay the predicate."

TRE 1002. REQUIREMENT OF ORIGINALS

To prove the content of a writing, recording, or photograph, the original writing, recording, or photograph is required except as otherwise provided in these rules or by law.

See also Cochran, ***Texas Rules of Evidence Handbook***, p. 904 (2001).

White v. Bath, 825 S.W.2d 227, 231 (Tex.App.—Houston [14th Dist.] 1992, writ denied). "[O]nly when one seeks to prove the contents of a document [does] the best evidence rule [apply]. When the document and its contents are only collaterally related to the issues in the case, the best evidence rule does not apply."

Ramsey v. Jones Enters., 810 S.W.2d 902, 905 (Tex. App.—Beaumont 1991, writ denied). "The best evidence of the content of documents is the documents themselves. The trial court erred in admitting hearsay testimony to prove up the content of documents without a proper showing that the subject documents were unavailable through no fault or failure on the part of the party offering same."

TRE 1003. ADMISSIBILITY OF DUPLICATES

A duplicate is admissible to the same extent as an original unless (1) a question is raised as to the authenticity of the original or (2) in the circumstances it would be unfair to admit the duplicate in lieu of the original.

See also ***O'Connor's Texas Rules***, "Introducing Evidence," ch. 8-C; Cochran, ***Texas Rules of Evidence Handbook***, p. 904 (2001).

Ford Motor Co. v. Leggat, 904 S.W.2d 643, 646 (Tex.1995). "[I]n the absence of a challenge to the authenticity of the affidavit, submission of a copy is not grounds for rejecting it."

Closs v. Goose Creek Consol. ISD, 874 S.W.2d 859, 868 (Tex.App.—Texarkana 1994, no writ). "A duplicate is admissible to the same extent as the original unless a question is raised as to the authenticity of the original or it would otherwise be unfair to submit the duplicate in lieu of the original."

TRE 1004. ADMISSIBILITY OF OTHER EVIDENCE OF CONTENTS

The original is not required, and other evidence of the contents of a writing, recording, or photograph is admissible if:

(a) Originals Lost or Destroyed. All originals are lost or have been destroyed, unless the proponent lost or destroyed them in bad faith;

(b) Original Not Obtainable. No original can be obtained by any available judicial process or procedure;

(c) Original Outside the State. No original is located in Texas;

(d) Original in Possession of Opponent. At a time when an original was under the control of the party against whom offered, that party was put on notice, by the pleadings or otherwise, that the content would be a subject of proof at the hearing, and that party does not produce the original at the hearing; or

(e) Collateral Matters. The writing, recording or photograph is not closely related to a controlling issue.

See also TRCP 77; *O'Connor's Texas Rules*, "Rules for Filing Documents," ch. 1-C; "Introducing Evidence," ch. 8-C; Cochran, ***Texas Rules of Evidence Handbook***, p. 920 (2001).

Coke v. Coke, 802 S.W.2d 270, 275 (Tex.App.—Dallas 1990, writ denied). "Under [TRE] 1004, an original document is not required if the original is lost or destroyed without the fault of the proponent. Copies are admissible if 'there is a reasonable account for [the originals'] absence or if there is no question of their authenticity.'"

TRE 1005. PUBLIC RECORDS

The contents of an official record or of a document authorized to be recorded or filed and actually recorded or filed, including data compilations in any form, if otherwise admissible, may be proved by copy, certified as correct in accordance with Rule 902 or testified to be correct by a witness who has compared it with the original. If a copy which complies with the foregoing cannot be obtained by the exercise of reasonable diligence, then other evidence of the contents may be given.

See also *O'Connor's Texas Rules*, "Introducing Evidence," ch. 8-C; Cochran, ***Texas Rules of Evidence Handbook***, p. 925 (2001).

ESIS, Inc. v. Johnson, 908 S.W.2d 554, 561 (Tex. App.—Fort Worth 1995, writ denied). "A copy of a public record is considered authentic if a sponsoring witness vouches for its authenticity or if the document meets the certification requirements for self-authentication contained in [TRE] 902."

Hickson v. Martinez, 707 S.W.2d 919, 926 (Tex. App.—Dallas 1985), *writ ref'd n.r.e.*, 716 S.W.2d 499 (Tex.1986). A photocopy of federal regulations that a witness stated was correct when compared with "the original" was admissible under TRE 1005, even though the document from which it was copied is not an "original" under TRE 1001(3), if there is nothing in the witness' testimony to indicate that the reference document was a photocopy.

TRE 1006. SUMMARIES

The contents of voluminous writings, recordings, or photographs, otherwise admissible, which cannot conveniently be examined in court may be presented in the form of a chart, summary, or calculation. The originals, or duplicates, shall be made available for examination or copying, or both, by other parties at a reasonable time and place. The court may order that they be produced in court.

See also Cochran, ***Texas Rules of Evidence Handbook***, p. 928 (2001).

Aquamarine Assocs. v. Burton Shipyard, Inc., 659 S.W.2d 820, 821 (Tex.1983). "In cases involving voluminous records, the trial court has discretion to relax the best evidence rule and allow the admission of summaries.... The party sponsoring the summary must, however, lay the proper predicate for its admission."

Black Lake Pipe Line Co. v. Union Constr. Co., 538 S.W.2d 80, 92-93 (Tex.1976), *overruled on other grounds*, ***Sterner v. Marathon Oil Co.***, 767 S.W.2d 686 (Tex.1989). "Although the best evidence rule has been relaxed to permit secondary evidence of voluminous records, we have required, as a condition, that the underlying records be brought into court or at least be made available to the opposing party in order that the correctness of the evidence may be tested by inspection or that the material for cross-examination may be available."

Welder v. Welder, 794 S.W.2d 420, 429 (Tex.App.—Corpus Christi 1990, no writ). "In order to bring a summary within the guidelines of [TRE] 1006, the party sponsoring the summary must lay the proper predicate for its admission, by demonstrating that the underlying records were voluminous, were made available to the opposing party for inspection and use in cross examination, and were admissible under the Texas Business Records Act."

TRE 1007. TESTIMONY OR WRITTEN ADMISSION OF PARTY

Contents of writings, recordings, or photographs may be proved by the testimony or deposition of the party against whom offered or by that party's written admission, without accounting for the nonproduction of the original.

See also Cochran, *Texas Rules of Evidence Handbook*, p. 932 (2001).

TRE 1008. FUNCTIONS OF COURT & JURY

When the admissibility of other evidence of contents of writings, recordings, or photographs under these rules depends upon the fulfillment of a condition of fact, the question whether the condition has been fulfilled is ordinarily for the court to determine in accordance with the provisions of Rule 104. However, when an issue is raised (a) whether the asserted writing ever existed, or (b) whether another writing, recording, or photograph produced at the trial is the original, or (c) whether other evidence of contents correctly reflects the contents, the issue is for the trier of fact to determine as in the case of other issues of fact.

See also Cochran, *Texas Rules of Evidence Handbook*, p. 934 (2001).

TRE 1009. TRANSLATION OF FOREIGN LANGUAGE DOCUMENTS

(a) Translations. A translation of foreign language documents shall be admissible upon the affidavit of a qualified translator setting forth the qualifications of the translator and certifying that the translation is fair and accurate. Such affidavit, along with the translation and the underlying foreign language documents, shall be served upon all parties at least 45 days prior to the date of trial.

(b) Objections. Any party may object to the accuracy of another party's translation by pointing out the specific inaccuracies of the translation and by stating with specificity what the objecting party contends is a fair and accurate translation. Such objection shall be served upon all parties at least 15 days prior to the date of trial.

(c) Effect of Failure to Object or Offer Conflicting Translation. If no conflicting translation or objection is timely served, the court shall admit a translation submitted under paragraph (a) without need of proof, provided however that the underlying foreign language documents are otherwise admissible under the Texas Rules of Evidence. Failure to serve a conflicting translation under paragraph (a) or failure to timely and properly object to the accuracy of a translation under paragraph (b) shall preclude a party from attacking or offering evidence contradicting the accuracy of such translation at trial.

(d) Effect of Objections or Conflicting Translations. In the event of conflicting translations under paragraph (a) or if objections to another party's translation are served under paragraph (b), the court shall determine whether there is a genuine issue as to the accuracy of a material part of the translation to be resolved by the trier of fact.

(e) Expert Testimony of Translator. Except as provided in paragraph (c), this Rule does not preclude the admission of a translation of foreign language documents at trial either by live testimony or by deposition testimony of a qualified expert translator.

(f) Varying of Time Limits. The court, upon motion of any party and for good cause shown, may enlarge or shorten the time limits set forth in this Rule.

(g) Court Appointment. The court, if necessary, may appoint a qualified translator, the reasonable value of whose services shall be taxed as court costs.

Comment to 1998 change: This is a new rule.
See also Cochran, *Texas Rules of Evidence Handbook*, p. 936 (2001).

Civil Practice & Remedies Code
Selected Provisions
Table of Contents

For the complete Civil Practice & Remedies Code annotated, see ***O'Connor's Civil Practice & Remedies Code Plus*** (2002-2003). To order, call 1-800-OCONNOR (1-800-626-6667) or visit <http://www.jonesmcclure.com/>.

TITLE 2. TRIAL, JUDGMENT, & APPEAL

SUBTITLE B. TRIAL MATTERS

CHAPTER 16. LIMITATIONS

SUBCHAPTER A. LIMITATIONS OF PERSONAL ACTIONS

CPRC §16.003. TWO-YEAR LIMITATIONS PERIOD

(a) Except as provided by Sections 16.010 and 16.0045, a person must bring suit for trespass for injury to the estate or to the property of another, conversion of personal property, taking or detaining the personal property of another, personal injury, forcible entry and detainer, and forcible detainer not later than two years after the day the cause of action accrues.

(b) A person must bring suit not later than two years after the day the cause of action accrues in an action for injury resulting in death. The cause of action accrues on the death of the injured person.

History of CPRC §16.003: Acts 1985, 69th Leg., ch. 959, §1, eff. Sept. 1, 1985. Amended by Acts 1995, 74th Leg., ch. 739, §2, eff. June 15, 1995; Acts 1997, 75th Leg., ch. 26, §2, eff. May 1, 1997.

CPRC §16.003

SUBCHAPTER D. MISCELLANEOUS PROVISIONS

CPRC §16.068. AMENDED & SUPPLEMENTAL PLEADINGS

If a filed pleading relates to a cause of action, cross action, counterclaim, or defense that is not subject to a plea of limitation when the pleading is filed, a subsequent amendment or supplement to the pleading that changes the facts or grounds of liability or defense is not subject to a plea of limitation unless the amendment or supplement is wholly based on a new, distinct, or different transaction or occurrence.

History of CPRC §16.068: Acts 1985, 69th Leg., ch. 959, §1, eff. Sept. 1, 1985.

CPRC §16.069. COUNTERCLAIM OR CROSS CLAIM

(a) If a counterclaim or cross claim arises out of the same transaction or occurrence that is the basis of an action, a party to the action may file the counterclaim or cross claim even though as a separate action it would be barred by limitation on the date the party's answer is required.

(b) The counterclaim or cross claim must be filed not later than the 30th day after the date on which the party's answer is required.

History of CPRC §16.069: Acts 1985, 69th Leg., ch. 959, §1, eff. Sept. 1, 1985.

CPRC §16.072. SATURDAY, SUNDAY, OR HOLIDAY

If the last day of a limitations period under any statute of limitations falls on a Saturday, Sunday, or holiday, the period for filing suit is extended to include the next day that the county offices are open for business.

History of CPRC §16.072: Acts 1985, 69th Leg., ch. 959, §1, eff. Sept. 1, 1985. See also *O'Connor's Texas Rules*, "Rules for Filing Documents," ch. 1-C.

SUBTITLE C. JUDGMENTS

CHAPTER 35. ENFORCEMENT OF JUDGMENTS OF OTHER STATES

CPRC §35.001. DEFINITION

In this chapter, "foreign judgment" means a judgment, decree, or order of a court of the United States or of any other court that is entitled to full faith and credit in this state.

History of CPRC §35.001: Acts 1985, 69th Leg., ch. 959, §1, eff. Sept. 1, 1985.

CPRC §35.002. SHORT TITLE

This chapter may be cited as the Uniform Enforcement of Foreign Judgments Act.

History of CPRC §35.002: Acts 1985, 69th Leg., ch. 959, §1, eff. Sept. 1, 1985.

CPRC §35.003. FILING & STATUS OF FOREIGN JUDGMENTS

(a) A copy of a foreign judgment authenticated in accordance with an act of congress or a statute of this state may be filed in the office of the clerk of any court of competent jurisdiction of this state.

(b) The clerk shall treat the foreign judgment in the same manner as a judgment of the court in which the foreign judgment is filed.

(c) A filed foreign judgment has the same effect and is subject to the same procedures, defenses, and proceedings for reopening, vacating, staying, enforcing, or satisfying a judgment as a judgment of the court in which it is filed.

History of CPRC §35.003: Acts 1985, 69th Leg., ch. 959, §1, eff. Sept. 1, 1985.

CPRC §35.004. AFFIDAVIT; NOTICE OF FILING

(a) At the time a foreign judgment is filed, the judgment creditor or the judgment creditor's attorney shall file with the clerk of the court an affidavit showing the name and last known post office address of the judgment debtor and the judgment creditor.

(b) The clerk shall promptly mail notice of the filing of the foreign judgment to the judgment debtor at the address given and shall note the mailing in the docket.

(c) The notice must include the name and post office address of the judgment creditor and if the judgment creditor has an attorney in this state, the attorney's name and address.

History of CPRC §35.004: Acts 1985, 69th Leg., ch. 959, §1, eff. Sept. 1, 1985.

CPRC §35.005. ALTERNATE NOTICE OF FILING—JUDGMENT CREDITOR

(a) The judgment creditor may mail a notice of the filing of the judgment to the judgment debtor and may file proof of mailing with the clerk.

(b) A clerk's lack of mailing the notice of filing does not affect the enforcement proceedings if proof of mailing by the judgment creditor has been filed.

History of CPRC §35.005: Acts 1985, 69th Leg., ch. 959, §1, eff. Sept. 1, 1985.

CPRC §35.006. STAY

(a) If the judgment debtor shows the court that an appeal from the foreign judgment is pending or will be taken or that a stay of execution has been granted and proves that the judgment debtor has furnished the security for the satisfaction of the judgment required by the state in which it was rendered, the court shall stay enforcement of the foreign judgment until the appeal is concluded, the time for appeal expires, or the stay of execution expires or is vacated.

(b) If the judgment debtor shows the court a ground on which enforcement of a judgment of the court of this state would be stayed, the court shall stay enforcement of the foreign judgment for an appropriate period and require the same security for satisfaction of the judgment that is required in this state.

History of CPRC §35.006: Acts 1985, 69th Leg., ch. 959, §1, eff. Sept. 1, 1985.

CPRC §35.007. FEES

(a) A person filing a foreign judgment shall pay to the clerk of the court the amount as otherwise provided by law for filing suit in the courts of this state.

(b) Filing fees are due and payable at the time of filing.

(c) Fees for other enforcement proceedings are as provided by law for judgments of the courts of this state.

History of CPRC §35.007: Acts 1985, 69th Leg., ch. 959, §1, eff. Sept. 1, 1985.

CPRC §35.008. OPTIONAL PROCEDURE

A judgment creditor retains the right to bring an action to enforce a judgment instead of proceeding under this chapter.

History of CPRC §35.008: Acts 1985, 69th Leg., ch. 959, §1, eff. Sept. 1, 1985.

CHAPTER 36. ENFORCEMENT OF JUDGMENTS OF OTHER COUNTRIES

CPRC §36.001. DEFINITIONS

In this chapter:

(1) "Foreign country" means a governmental unit other than:

(A) the United States;

(B) a state, district, commonwealth, territory, or insular possession of the United States;

(C) the Panama Canal Zone; or

(D) the Trust Territory of the Pacific Islands.

(2) "Foreign country judgment" means a judgment of a foreign country granting or denying a sum of money other than a judgment for:

(A) taxes, a fine, or other penalty; or

(B) support in a matrimonial or family matter.

History of CPRC §36.001: Acts 1985, 69th Leg., ch. 959, §1, eff. Sept. 1, 1985.

CPRC §36.002. APPLICABILITY

(a) This chapter applies to a foreign country judgment:

(1) that is final and conclusive and enforceable where rendered, even though an appeal is pending or the judgment is subject to appeal; or

(2) that is in favor of the defendant on the merits of the cause of action and is final and conclusive where rendered, even though an appeal is pending or the judgment is subject to appeal.

(b) This chapter does not apply to a judgment rendered before June 17, 1981.

History of CPRC §36.002: Acts 1985, 69th Leg., ch. 959, §1, eff. Sept. 1, 1985.

CPRC §36.003. SHORT TITLE

This chapter may be cited as the Uniform Foreign Country Money-Judgment Recognition Act.

History of CPRC §36.003: Acts 1985, 69th Leg., ch. 959, §1, eff. Sept. 1, 1985.

CPRC §36.004. RECOGNITION & ENFORCEMENT

Except as provided by Section 36.005, a foreign country judgment that is filed with notice given as provided by this chapter, that meets the requirements of Section 36.002, and that is not refused recognition under Section 36.0044 is conclusive between the parties to the extent that it grants or denies recovery of a sum of money. The judgment is enforceable in the same manner as a judgment of a sister state that is entitled to full faith and credit.

History of CPRC §36.004: Acts 1985, 69th Leg., ch. 959, §1, eff. Sept. 1, 1985. Amended by Acts 1989, 71st Leg., ch. 402, §1, eff. June 14, 1989.

CPRC §36.0041. FILING

A copy of a foreign country judgment authenticated in accordance with an act of congress, a statute of this state, or a treaty or other international convention to which the United States is a party may be filed in the office of the clerk of a court in the county of residence of the party against whom recognition is sought or in any other court of competent jurisdiction as allowed under the Texas venue laws.

History of CPRC §36.0041: Acts 1989, 71st Leg., ch. 402, §2, eff. June 14, 1989.

CPRC §36.0042. AFFIDAVIT; NOTICE OF FILING

(a) At the time a foreign country judgment is filed, the party seeking recognition of the judgment or the party's attorney shall file with the clerk of the court an affidavit showing the name and last known post office address of the judgment debtor and the judgment creditor.

(b) The clerk shall promptly mail notice of the filing of the foreign country judgment to the party against whom recognition is sought at the address given and shall note the mailing in the docket.

(c) The notice must include the name and post office address of the party seeking recognition and that party's attorney, if any, in this state.

History of CPRC §36.0042: Acts 1989, 71st Leg., ch. 402, §3, eff. June 14, 1989.

CPRC §36.0043. ALTERNATE NOTICE OF FILING

(a) The party seeking recognition may mail a notice of the filing of the foreign country judgment to the other party and may file proof of mailing with the clerk.

(b) A clerk's lack of mailing the notice of filing does not affect the conclusive recognition of the foreign country judgment under this chapter if proof of mailing by the party seeking recognition has been filed.

History of CPRC §36.0043: Acts 1989, 71st Leg., ch. 402, §4, eff. June 14, 1989.

CPRC §36.0044. CONTESTING RECOGNITION

(a) A party against whom recognition of a foreign country judgment is sought may contest recognition of the judgment if, not later than the 30th day after the date of service of the notice of filing, the party files with the court, and serves the opposing party with a copy of, a motion for nonrecognition of the judgment on the basis of one or more grounds under Section 36.005. If the party is domiciled in a foreign country, the party must file the motion for nonrecognition not later than the 60th day after the date of service of the notice of filing.

(b) The party filing the motion for nonrecognition shall include with the motion all supporting affidavits, briefs, and other documentation.

(c) A party opposing the motion must file any response, including supporting affidavits, briefs, and other documentation, not later than the 20th day after the date of service on that party of a copy of the motion for nonrecognition.

(d) The court may, on motion and notice, grant an extension of time, not to exceed 20 days unless good cause is shown, for the filing of a response or any document that is required to establish a ground for nonrecognition but that is not available within the time for filing the document.

(e) A party filing a motion for nonrecognition or responding to the motion may request an evidentiary hearing that the court may allow in its discretion.

(f) The court may at any time permit or require the submission of argument, authorities, or supporting material in addition to that provided for by this section.

(g) The court may refuse recognition of the foreign country judgment if the motions, affidavits, briefs, and other evidence before it establish grounds for nonrecognition as specified in Section 36.005, but the court may not, under any circumstances, review the foreign country judgment in relation to any matter not specified in Section 36.005.

History of CPRC §36.0044: Acts 1989, 71st Leg., ch. 402, §5, eff. June 14, 1989.

CPRC §36.005. GROUNDS FOR NONRECOGNITION

(a) A foreign country judgment is not conclusive if:

(1) the judgment was rendered under a system that does not provide impartial tribunals or procedures compatible with the requirements of due process of law;

(2) the foreign country court did not have personal jurisdiction over the defendant; or

(3) the foreign country court did not have jurisdiction over the subject matter.

(b) A foreign country judgment need not be recognized if:

(1) the defendant in the proceedings in the foreign country court did not receive notice of the proceedings in sufficient time to defend;

(2) the judgment was obtained by fraud;

(3) the cause of action on which the judgment is based is repugnant to the public policy of this state;

(4) the judgment conflicts with another final and conclusive judgment;

(5) the proceeding in the foreign country court was contrary to an agreement between the parties under which the dispute in question was to be settled otherwise than by proceedings in that court;

(6) in the case of jurisdiction based only on personal service, the foreign country court was a seriously inconvenient forum for the trial of the action; or

(7) it is established that the foreign country in which the judgment was rendered does not recognize judgments rendered in this state that, but for the fact that they are rendered in this state, conform to the definition of "foreign country judgment."

History of CPRC §36.005: Acts 1985, 69th Leg., ch. 959, §1, eff. Sept. 1, 1985.

CPRC §36.006. PERSONAL JURISDICTION

(a) A court may not refuse to recognize a foreign country judgment for lack of personal jurisdiction if:

(1) the defendant was served personally in the foreign country;

(2) the defendant voluntarily appeared in the proceedings, other than for the purpose of protecting property seized or threatened with seizure in the proceedings or of contesting the jurisdiction of the court over him;

(3) the defendant prior to the commencement of the proceedings had agreed to submit to the jurisdiction of the foreign country court with respect to the subject matter involved;

(4) the defendant was domiciled in the foreign country when the proceedings were instituted or, if the defendant is a body corporate, had its principal place of business, was incorporated, or had otherwise acquired corporate status in the foreign country;

(5) the defendant had a business office in the foreign country and the proceedings in the foreign country court involved a cause of action arising out of business done by the defendant through that office in the foreign country; or

(6) the defendant operated a motor vehicle or airplane in the foreign country and the proceedings involved a cause of action arising out of operation of the motor vehicle or airplane.

(b) A court of this state may recognize other bases of jurisdiction.

History of CPRC §36.006: Acts 1985, 69th Leg., ch. 959, §1, eff. Sept. 1, 1985.

CPRC §36.007. STAY IN CASE OF APPEAL

If the defendant satisfies the court either that an appeal is pending or that the defendant is entitled and intends to appeal from the foreign country judgment, the court may stay the proceedings until the appeal has been determined or until a period of time sufficient to enable the defendant to prosecute the appeal has expired.

History of CPRC §36.007: Acts 1985, 69th Leg., ch. 959, §1, eff. Sept. 1, 1985.

CPRC §36.008. OTHER FOREIGN COUNTRY JUDGMENTS

This chapter does not prevent the recognition of a foreign country judgment in a situation not covered by this chapter.

History of CPRC §36.008: Acts 1985, 69th Leg., ch. 959, §1, eff. Sept. 1, 1985.

TITLE 3. EXTRAORDINARY REMEDIES

CHAPTER 64. RECEIVERSHIP

SUBCHAPTER A. GENERAL PROVISIONS

CPRC §64.001. AVAILABILITY OF REMEDY

(a) A court of competent jurisdiction may appoint a receiver:

(1) in an action by a vendor to vacate a fraudulent purchase of property;

(2) in an action by a creditor to subject any property or fund to his claim;

(3) in an action between partners or others jointly owning or interested in any property or fund;

(4) in an action by a mortgagee for the foreclosure of the mortgage and sale of the mortgaged property;

(5) for a corporation that is insolvent, is in imminent danger of insolvency, has been dissolved, or has forfeited its corporate rights; or

(6) in any other case in which a receiver may be appointed under the rules of equity.

(b) Under Subsection (a)(1), (2), or (3), the receiver may be appointed on the application of the plaintiff in the action or another party. The party must have a probable interest in or right to the property or fund, and the property or fund must be in danger of being lost, removed, or materially injured.

(c) Under Subsection (a)(4), the court may appoint a receiver only if:

(1) it appears that the mortgaged property is in danger of being lost, removed, or materially injured; or

(2) the condition of the mortgage has not been performed and the property is probably insufficient to discharge the mortgage debt.

(d) A court having family law jurisdiction or a probate court located in the county in which a missing person, as defined by Article 63.001, Code of Criminal Procedure, resides or, if the missing person is not a resident of this state, located in the county in which the majority of the property of a missing person's estate is located may, on the court's own motion or on the application of an interested party, appoint a receiver for the missing person if:

(1) it appears that the estate of the missing person is in danger of injury, loss, or waste; and

(2) the estate of the missing person is in need of a representative.

History of CPRC §64.001: Acts 1985, 69th Leg., ch. 959, §1, eff. Sept. 1, 1985. Amended by Acts 1997, 75th Leg., ch. 1376, §4, eff. Sept. 1, 1997; Acts 1999, 76th Leg., ch. 1081, §§1, 3, eff. Sept. 1, 1999.

CPRC §64.002. PERSONS NOT ENTITLED TO APPOINTMENT

(a) A court may not appoint a receiver for a corporation, partnership, or individual on the petition of the same corporation, partnership, or individual.

(b) A court may appoint a receiver for a corporation on the petition of one or more stockholders of the corporation.

(c) This section does not prohibit:

(1) appointment of a receiver for a partnership in an action arising between partners; or

(2) appointment of a receiver over all or part of the marital estate in a suit filed under Title 1 or 5, Family Code.

History of CPRC §64.002: Acts 1985, 69th Leg., ch. 959, §1, eff. Sept. 1, 1985. Amended by Acts 1987, 70th Leg., ch. 167, §3.12(a), eff. Sept. 1, 1987; Acts 1997, 75th Leg., ch. 165, §7.06, eff. Sept. 1, 1997.

CPRC §64.003. FOREIGN APPOINTMENT

A court outside this state may not appoint a receiver for:

(1) a person who resides in this state and for whom appointment of a receiver has been applied for in this state; or

(2) property located in this state.

History of CPRC §64.003: Acts 1985, 69th Leg., ch. 959, §1, eff. Sept. 1, 1985.

CPRC §64.004. APPLICATION OF EQUITY RULES

Unless inconsistent with this chapter or other general law, the rules of equity govern all matters relating to the appointment, powers, duties, and liabilities of a receiver and to the powers of a court regarding a receiver.

History of CPRC §64.004: Acts 1985, 69th Leg., ch. 959, §1, eff. Sept. 1, 1985.

Sections 64.005-64.020 reserved for expansion

SUBCHAPTER B. QUALIFICATIONS, OATH, & BOND

CPRC §64.021. QUALIFICATIONS; RESIDENCE REQUIREMENT

(a) To be appointed as a receiver for property that is located entirely or partly in this state, a person must:

(1) be a citizen and qualified voter of this state at the time of appointment; and

(2) not be a party, attorney, or other person interested in the action for appointment of a receiver.

(b) The appointment of a receiver who is disqualified under Subsection (a)(1) is void as to property in this state.

(c) A receiver must maintain actual residence in this state during the receivership.

History of CPRC §64.021: Acts 1985, 69th Leg., ch. 959, §1, eff. Sept. 1, 1985.

CPRC §64.022. OATH

Before a person assumes the duties of a receiver, he must be sworn to perform the duties faithfully.

History of CPRC §64.022: Acts 1985, 69th Leg., ch. 959, §1, eff. Sept. 1, 1985.

CPRC §64.023. BOND

Before a person assumes the duties of a receiver, he must execute a good and sufficient bond that is:

(1) approved by the appointing court;

(2) in an amount fixed by the court; and

(3) conditioned on faithful discharge of his duties as receiver in the named action and obedience to the orders of the court.

History of CPRC §64.023: Acts 1985, 69th Leg., ch. 959, §1, eff. Sept. 1, 1985.

Sections 64.024-64.030 reserved for expansion

SUBCHAPTER C. POWERS & DUTIES

CPRC §64.031. GENERAL POWERS & DUTIES

Subject to the control of the court, a receiver may:

(1) take charge and keep possession of the property;

(2) receive rents;

(3) collect and compromise demands;

(4) make transfers; and

(5) perform other acts in regard to the property as authorized by the court.

History of CPRC §64.031: Acts 1985, 69th Leg., ch. 959, §1, eff. Sept. 1, 1985.

CPRC §64.032. INVENTORY

As soon as possible after appointment, a receiver shall return to the appointing court an inventory of all property received.

History of CPRC §64.032: Acts 1985, 69th Leg., ch. 959, §1, eff. Sept. 1, 1985.

CPRC §64.033. SUITS BY RECEIVER

A receiver may bring suits in his official capacity without permission of the appointing court.

History of CPRC §64.033: Acts 1985, 69th Leg., ch. 959, §1, eff. Sept. 1, 1985.

CPRC §64.034. INVESTMENTS, LOANS, & CONTRIBUTIONS OF FUNDS

(a) Except as provided by Subsection (b), on an order of the court to which all parties consent, a receiver may invest for interest any funds that he holds.

(b) A receiver appointed for a missing person under Section 64.001(d) who has on hand an amount of money belonging to the missing person in excess of the amount needed for current necessities and expenses may, on order of the court, invest, lend, or contribute all or a part of the excess amount in the manner provided by Subpart L, Part 4, Chapter XIII, Texas Probate Code, for investments, loans, or contributions by guardians. The receiver shall report to the court all transactions involving the excess amount in the manner that reports are required of guardians.

History of CPRC §64.034: Acts 1985, 69th Leg., ch. 959, §1, eff. Sept. 1, 1985. Amended by Acts 1999, 76th Leg., ch. 1081, §4, eff. Sept. 1, 1999.

CPRC §64.035. DEPOSIT OF CERTAIN RAILROAD FUNDS

If a receiver operates a railroad that lies wholly within this state, the receiver shall deposit all money that comes into his hands, from operation of the railroad or otherwise, in a place in this state directed by the court. The money shall remain on deposit until properly disbursed. If any portion of the railroad lies in another state, the court shall require the receiver to deposit in this state a share of the funds that is at least proportionate to the value of the property of the company in this state.

History of CPRC §64.035: Acts 1985, 69th Leg., ch. 959, §1, eff. Sept. 1, 1985.

CPRC §64.036. RECEIVERSHIP PROPERTY HELD BY FINANCIAL INSTITUTION

Service or delivery of a notice of receivership, or a demand or instruction by or on behalf of a receiver, relating to receivership property held by a financial institution in the name of or on behalf of a customer of the financial institution is governed by Section 59.008, Finance Code.

History of CPRC §64.036: Acts 1999, 76th Leg., ch. 344, §7.005, eff. Sept. 1, 1999.

Sections 64.037-64.050 reserved for expansion

SUBCHAPTER D. CLAIMS & LIABILITIES

CPRC §64.051. APPLICATION OF FUNDS; PREFERENCES

(a) A receiver shall apply the earnings of property held in receivership to the payment of the following claims in the order listed:

(1) court costs of suit;

(2) wages of employees due by the receiver;

(3) debts owed for materials and supplies purchased by the receiver for the improvement of the property held as receiver;

(4) debts due for improvements made during the receivership to the property held as receiver;

(5) claims and accounts against the receiver on contracts made by the receiver, personal injury claims and claims for stock against the receiver accruing during the receivership, and judgments rendered against the receiver for personal injuries and for stock killed; and

(6) judgments recovered in suits brought before the receiver was appointed.

(b) Claims listed in this section have a preference lien on the earnings of the property held by the receiver.

(c) The court shall ensure that the earnings are paid in the order of preference listed in this section.

History of CPRC §64.051: Acts 1985, 69th Leg., ch. 959, §1, eff. Sept. 1, 1985.

CPRC §64.052. SUITS AGAINST RECEIVER

(a) A receiver who holds property in this state may be sued in his official capacity in a court of competent jurisdiction without permission of the appointing court.

(b) A suit against a receiver may be brought where the person whose property is in receivership resides.

(c) In a suit against a receiver, citation may be served on the receiver or on any agent of the receiver who resides in the county in which the suit is brought.

(d) The discharge of a receiver does not abate a suit against the receiver or affect the right of a party to sue the receiver.

History of CPRC §64.052: Acts 1985, 69th Leg., ch. 959, §1, eff. Sept. 1, 1985.

CPRC §64.053. PAYMENT OF JUDGMENT AGAINST RECEIVER

The court that appointed a receiver shall order any judgment against the receiver to be paid from funds held by the receiver.

History of CPRC §64.053: Acts 1985, 69th Leg., ch. 959, §1, eff. Sept. 1, 1985.

CPRC §64.054. JUDGMENT LIEN

A judgment rendered against a receiver in a cause of action arising during the receivership is a lien on all property held by the receiver. The lien is superior to the mortgage lien of a mortgagee who instituted the receivership.

History of CPRC §64.054: Acts 1985, 69th Leg., ch. 959, §1, eff. Sept. 1, 1985.

CPRC §64.055. EXECUTION ON JUDGMENT

(a) To obtain payment on a judgment against a receiver, the owner of the judgment may apply to the court that appointed the receiver for an order that the receiver pay the judgment. If the receiver possesses money that is subject to payment of the judgment, but the court refuses to order payment, the owner of the judgment may apply to the court that issued the judgment for execution on the judgment.

(b) The owner of the judgment must file with the court that issued the judgment an affidavit reciting that:

(1) he applied to the court that appointed the receiver for an order of payment;

(2) it was shown to the appointing court that the receiver had money subject to payment of the judgment at that time; and

(3) the appointing court refused to order the receiver to pay the judgment.

(c) The court that issued the judgment shall issue execution that may be levied on any property held by the receiver. The property shall be sold as under ordinary execution, and the sale of the property conveys title to the purchaser.

History of CPRC §64.055: Acts 1985, 69th Leg., ch. 959, §1, eff. Sept. 1, 1985.

CPRC §64.056. LIABILITY OF PERSONS RECEIVING RECEIVERSHIP PROPERTY

(a) A person to whom a receiver delivers property held in receivership, including the owner of the property, a person who receives it for the owner, or an assignee of the owner is liable to the extent of the value of the property for the liabilities of the receiver arising during the receivership that are unpaid at the time of the receiver's discharge. The person receiving the property may be made a defendant to a suit against the receiver, and if judgment is rendered against the receiver, the court shall also render judgment against that defendant.

(b) A judgment against a receiver or an unpaid claim that arose during the receivership and has not been sued on at the date the receiver is discharged constitutes a preference lien on the property held by the receiver on the date of discharge. The lien is superior to the mortgage lien of a mortgagee who instituted the receivership. The person who received the property is liable on the judgment or claim to the extent of the value of the property.

History of CPRC §64.056: Acts 1985, 69th Leg., ch. 959, §1, eff. Sept. 1, 1985.

Sections 64.057-64.070 reserved for expansion

Subchapter E. Provisions Relating to Receivership of Corporations

CPRC §64.071. VENUE FOR APPOINTMENT

An action to have a receiver appointed for a corporation with property in this state shall be brought in the county in which the principal office of the corporation is located.

History of CPRC §64.071: Acts 1985, 69th Leg., ch. 959, §1, eff. Sept. 1, 1985.

CPRC §64.072. LIMITED DURATION

(a) Except as provided by this section, a court may not administer a corporation in receivership for more than three years after the date the receiver is appointed, and the court shall wind up the affairs of the corporation within that period.

(b) A court may, from time to time, extend the duration of a corporate receivership if:

(1) litigation prevents the court from winding up the affairs of the corporation within three years; or

(2) the receiver is operating the corporation as a going concern.

(c) To extend the duration of a corporate receivership, the court must have received an application for the extension and, following notice to all attorneys of record, must conduct a hearing on the extension. As required by the best interests of all concerned parties, the court may prescribe conditions for the extension and extend it for a term within the limits provided by Subsection (d). The court shall enter into its minutes the proper order extending the receivership.

(d) A court may not extend a corporate receivership for more than five years beyond the original three years, except that the court may extend for any additional period the receivership of a corporation organized and existing under Article 3.05(A)(2), Texas Miscellaneous Corporation Laws Act (Article 1302-3.05, Vernon's Texas Civil Statutes), or Title 112, Revised Statutes.

History of CPRC §64.072: Acts 1985, 69th Leg., ch. 959, §1, eff. Sept. 1, 1985.

CPRC §64.0721. TERMINATION OF RAILROAD RECEIVERSHIP

(a) A receiver of a railroad company located wholly within this state that has been in receivership for more than 50 years may apply to the court that appointed the receiver requesting the court to:

(1) terminate the receivership; and

(2) disburse any assets of the railroad company remaining after the payment of the company's debts to one or more nonprofit charitable organizations chosen by the receiver for use in providing services within the county in which the receiver was appointed.

(b) After a receiver makes an application under Subsection (a), the receiver shall publish notice of the proposed termination of the receivership for seven consecutive days in a newspaper of general circulation in the county in which the receivership is located. The notice must state that a person with an interest in the assets of the railroad company may file a claim with the court that appointed the receiver not later than the 90th day after the final day of the publication of the notice.

(c) After the expiration of the period for filing claims provided by Subsection (b) and after the court resolves all claims filed with the court relating to the railroad company, the court shall disburse any remaining assets of the receivership to the nonprofit charitable organizations chosen by the receiver that are acceptable to the court in its discretion.

(d) Any noncash assets of a railroad company that exist when its receivership is terminated under this section escheat to the state.

History of CPRC §64.0721: Acts 1997, 75th Leg., ch. 821, §1, eff. June. 17, 1997.

CPRC §64.073. EARNINGS ON IMPROVED PROPERTY LIABLE FOR DEBTS

(a) A corporation in receivership shall contribute to the payment of any floating debts against it an amount equal to the full value of current earnings spent by the receiver for:

(1) improvements to the corporate property held by the receiver, the purchase of rolling stock or machinery, and other improvements that increase the value of the property; or

(2) the extension of a road or the acquisition of land in connection with a road.

(b) If property of a corporation in receivership is sold under court order in a lien foreclosure, the court shall order the clerk to retain from the sale proceeds an amount equal to the value of improvements made by the receiver to the property sold and shall order that money to be paid to persons with a claim, debt, or judgment against the corporation. The courts shall require an amount of cash sufficient for that purpose to be paid in at the date of sale.

History of CPRC §64.073: Acts 1985, 69th Leg., ch. 959, §1, eff. Sept. 1, 1985.

CPRC §64.074. CLAIMS PREFERENCE AGAINST CURRENT EARNINGS

A judgment or claim existing against a corporation at the time the receiver is appointed or a judgment in an action existing at that time shall be paid out of the earnings of the corporation earned during the receivership in preference to the mortgage of a mortgagee who instituted the receivership. The judgment or claim is a lien on those earnings.

History of CPRC §64.074: Acts 1985, 69th Leg., ch. 959, §1, eff. Sept. 1, 1985.

CPRC §64.075. FORFEITURE OF CHARTER FOR UNQUALIFIED RECEIVER

If a person who is not a citizen and qualified voter of this state is appointed receiver for a domestic corporation that owns property in this state, the corporation forfeits its charter. The attorney general shall immediately bring suit in the nature of quo warranto for forfeiture of the charter.

History of CPRC §64.075: Acts 1985, 69th Leg., ch. 959, §1, eff. Sept. 1, 1985.

CPRC §64.076. SUITS AGAINST RAILROAD RECEIVER: VENUE & SERVICE

An action against the receiver of a railroad company may be brought in any county through or into which the railroad is constructed, and citation may be served on the receiver, the general or division superintendent, or an agent of the receiver who resides in the county in which the suit is brought. If no agent of the receiver resides in the county in which the suit is brought, citation may be served on any agent of the receiver in this state.

History of CPRC §64.076: Acts 1985, 69th Leg., ch. 959, §1, eff. Sept. 1, 1985.

Sections 64.077-64.090 reserved for expansion

SUBCHAPTER F. RECEIVER FOR CERTAIN MINERAL INTERESTS

CPRC §64.091. RECEIVER FOR MINERAL INTERESTS OWNED BY NONRESIDENT OR ABSENTEE

(a) The purpose of this section is to encourage the exploration and development of mineral resources.

Subsection (b) below was enacted by Acts 1985, 69th Leg., ch. 959, §1, eff. Sept. 1, 1985, without reference to the other subsection (b) in the same enactment.

(b) In the following actions, a district court may appoint a receiver for the mineral interest or leasehold interest under a mineral lease owned by a nonresident or absent defendant:

(1) an action that is brought by a person claiming or owning an undivided mineral interest in land in this state or an undivided leasehold interest under a mineral lease of land in this state and that has one or more defendants who have, claim, or own an undivided mineral interest in the same property; or

(2) an action that is brought by a person claiming or owning an undivided leasehold interest under a mineral lease of land in this state and that has one or more defendants who have, claim, or own an undivided leasehold interest under a mineral lease of the same property.

Subsection (b) below was enacted by Acts 1985, 69th Leg., ch. 959, §1, eff. Sept. 1, 1985, without reference to the other subsection (b) in the same enactment.

(b) The defendant for whom the receiver is sought must:

(1) be a person whose residence or identity is unknown or a nonresident; and

(2) have not paid taxes on the interest or rendered it for taxes during the five-year period immediately preceding the filing of the action.

(c) The plaintiff in the action must allege by verified petition and prove that he:

(1) has made a diligent but unsuccessful effort to locate the defendant; and

(2) will suffer substantial damage or injury unless the receiver is appointed.

(d) In an action under Subsection (b)(1):

(1) the plaintiff, in the verified petition, must name the last known owner or the last record owner of the interest as defendant;

(2) the plaintiff must serve notice on the defendant by publication as provided by the Texas Rules of Civil Procedure;

(3) the court may appoint as receiver the county judge and his successors, the county clerk and his successors, or any other resident of the county in which the land is located;

(4) notwithstanding the Texas Rules of Civil Procedure, the applicant is not required to post bond; and

(5) the receiver is not required to post bond.

(e) A receivership created under this subchapter continues as long as the defendant or his heirs, assigns, or personal representatives fail to appear in court in person or by agent or attorney to claim the defendant's interest.

(f) As ordered by the court, the receiver shall immediately:

(1) execute and deliver to a lessee or successive lessees mineral leases on the outstanding undivided mineral interests;

(2) execute and deliver to a lessee or successive lessees an assignment of the outstanding undivided leasehold interest; and

(3) enter into a unitization agreement authorized by the Railroad Commission of Texas.

(g) A lease executed by a receiver under this section may authorize the lessee to pool and unitize land subject to the lease with adjacent land into a unit not to exceed 160 acres for an oil well or 640 acres for a gas well plus 10 percent tolerance or into a unit that substantially conforms to a larger unit prescribed or permitted by governmental rule.

(h) Money consideration paid for the execution of a lease, assignment, or unitization agreement by the receiver must be paid to the clerk of the court in which the case is pending before the receiver executes the instrument. The court shall apply the money to the costs accruing in the case and retain any balance for the use and benefit of the nonresident or person of unknown residence who owns the mineral or leasehold interest. Payments made at a later time under the lease, assignment, or unitization agreement shall be paid into the registry of the court and impounded for the use and benefit of the owner of the mineral or leasehold interest.

(i) This section is cumulative of other laws relating to removal of a cloud from title or appointment of a receiver.

(j) In this section:

(1) "Mineral lease" includes any lease of oil, gas, or other minerals that contains provisions necessary or incident to the orderly exploration, development, and recovery of oil, gas, or other minerals.

(2) "Leasehold interest" includes ownership created under a mineral lease or carved out of a leasehold estate granted under a mineral lease, including production payments, overriding royalty interests, and working interests.

(3) "Lessee" includes an assignee under an assignment of a mineral lease.

(k) To the extent that Subsection (d)(2) conflicts with the Texas Rules of Civil Procedure, Subsection (d)(2) controls. Notwithstanding Section 22.004, Government Code, the supreme court may not amend or adopt rules in conflict with Subsection (d)(2).

History of CPRC §64.091: Acts 1985, 69th Leg., ch. 959, §1, eff. Sept. 1, 1985. Amended by Acts 1989, 71st Leg., ch. 492, §1 (eff. June 14, 1989), ch. 998, §1 (eff. Sept. 1, 1989); Acts 1991, 72nd Leg., ch. 16, §3.01, eff. Aug. 26, 1991.

CPRC §64.092. RECEIVER FOR CONTINGENT INTERESTS IN MINERALS

(a) On the application of a person who has a vested, contingent, or possible interest in land or an estate subject to a contingent future interest, a district court of the county in which all or part of the land is located may appoint a receiver for the land or estate, pending the occurrence of the contingency and the vesting of the future interest, if:

(1) the land or estate is susceptible to drainage of oil, gas, or other minerals;

(2) lease of the land for oil, gas, or mineral development and the safe and proper investment of the proceeds will inure to the benefit and advantage of the persons entitled to the proceeds; or

(3) lease of the land for the production of oil, gas, or other minerals is necessary for the conservation, preservation, or protection of the land or estate or of a present, contingent, or future interest in the land or estate.

(b) As authorized or directed by the court, a receiver appointed under Subsection (a) may:

(1) lease the land for the development of oil, gas, or other minerals at public or private sale and on terms and conditions directed by the court; and

(2) receive, hold, and invest the proceeds of the lease for the benefit of persons who are entitled or may become entitled to those proceeds according to their respective rights and interests.

(c) On the application of a person who has a vested, contingent, or possible interest in land or an estate that is under an oil, gas, or mineral lease and is subject to a contingent future interest, a district court of the county in which all or part of the land is located may appoint a receiver for the contingent future interests, pending the occurrence of the contingency and the vesting of the future interest, if:

(1) the lease fails to provide for pooling or contains pooling provisions that are ineffective as to the contingent future interest covered by the lease; and

(2) the pooling of the contingent future interest:

(A) is necessary to protect correlative rights;

(B) is necessary to prevent the physical or economic waste of oil, gas, or other minerals;

(C) will inure to the benefit and advantage of the persons entitled to the future interest; or

(D) is necessary for the conservation, preservation, or protection of the land or estate or of a present, contingent, or future interest in the land or estate.

(d) The lessee or an assignee of the lessee may apply for appointment of a receiver under Subsection (c). As authorized or directed by the court, the receiver appointed under that subsection may:

(1) amend the lease to authorize pooling for the contingent future interest on terms and conditions and for additional consideration directed by the court; and

(2) receive, hold, and invest the additional consideration for the benefit of the persons who are entitled or may become entitled to that consideration, according to their respective rights and interests.

(e) A court appointing a receiver under this section may confer on the receiver all powers necessary to the exercise of the receiver's authority.

(f) A lease executed or amended by a receiver under this section may authorize the lessee and his assigns to pool all or part of the land subject to the lease with adjacent land into a unit not to exceed 160 acres for an oil well or 640 acres for a gas well plus 10 percent tolerance or into a unit that substantially conforms to a larger unit prescribed or permitted by governmental rule.

(g) In an action for appointment of a receiver under this section, a person who has a vested, contingent, or possible interest in the land must be cited in the manner and for the time provided for in actions concerning title to land. A person not in being must be cited in the manner and for the time provided in actions against unknown owners or claimants of interest in land. In an action brought under Subsection (c), a person is not a necessary party if:

(1) the person's interest in the land subject to the lease is effectively subject to pooling authority under the lease; and

(2) enlargement of the pooling authority as to the person's interest is not sought.

(h) The court appointing a receiver under this section may order that, after payment of court costs, money paid to the receiver be deposited in the registry of the court for the use and benefit of the persons who are entitled or may become entitled to the money, according to their respective rights and interests. If the court then discharges the receiver, it may order that later payments under the lease accruing to the contingent future interest be deposited in the same manner and for the same purpose.

(i) This section does not apply to a mineral lease on land on which drilling began before October 5, 1949. This section does not authorize a lease of mineral interests on land subject to existing homestead rights without the written consent of the owner of the homestead rights given in the manner provided by law for the conveyance of homesteads.

(j) In this section, "contingent future interest" means a legal or equitable interest arising by way of remainder, reversion, possibility of reverter, executory devise, on the occurrence of a condition subsequent, or otherwise.

History of CPRC §64.092: Acts 1985, 69th Leg., ch. 959, §1, eff. Sept. 1, 1985.

CPRC §64.093. RECEIVER FOR ROYALTY INTERESTS OWNED BY NONRESIDENT OR ABSENTEE

(a) A district court may appoint a receiver for the royalty interest owned by a nonresident or absent defendant in an action that:

(1) is brought by a person claiming or owning an undivided mineral interest in land in this state or an undivided leasehold interest under a mineral lease of land in the state; and

(2) has one or more defendants who have, claim, or own an undivided royalty interest in that property.

(b) The defendant for whom the receiver is sought must:

(1) be a person whose residence or identity is unknown or a nonresident; and

(2) not have paid taxes on the interest or rendered it for taxes during the five-year period immediately preceding the filing of the action.

(c) The plaintiff in the action must allege by verified petition and prove that the plaintiff:

(1) has made a diligent but unsuccessful effort to locate the defendant; and

(2) will suffer substantial damage or injury unless the receiver is appointed.

(d) In an action under Subsection (a):

(1) the plaintiff, in the petition, must name the last known owner or the last record owner of the interest as defendant;

(2) the plaintiff must serve notice on the defendant by publication as provided by the Texas Rules of Civil Procedure;

(3) the court may appoint as receiver the county judge, the county clerk, or any other resident of the county in which the land is located;

(4) notwithstanding the Texas Rules of Civil Procedure, the applicant is not required to post bond; and

(5) the receiver is not required to post bond.

(e) A receivership created under this section continues as long as the defendant or the defendant's heirs, assigns, or personal representatives fail to appear in court in person or by agent or attorney to claim the defendant's interest.

(f) As ordered by the court, the receiver shall immediately:

(1) ratify a mineral lease executed by a person owning an undivided mineral interest in the property;

(2) ratify a pooling agreement executed by a person owning an undivided mineral interest in the property or an undivided leasehold interest in the property; or

(3) enter into a unitization agreement authorized by the Railroad Commission of Texas.

(g) A lease ratified by a receiver under this section may authorize the lessee to pool and unitize land subject to the lease with adjacent land into a unit not to exceed 160 acres for an oil well or 640 acres for a gas well plus 10 percent tolerance or into a unit that substantially conforms to a larger unit prescribed or permitted by governmental rule. A pooling agreement ratified by a receiver under this section may allow a pooled unit not to exceed 160 acres for an oil well or 640 acres for a gas well plus 10 percent tolerance or into a unit that substantially conforms to a larger unit prescribed or permitted by governmental rule.

(h) The monetary consideration, if any, due for the execution of a ratification, pooling agreement, or unitization agreement by the receiver must be paid to the clerk of the court in which the case is pending before the receiver executes the instrument. It is, however, recognized that, because ratifications, pooling agreements, and unitization agreements are typically entered into in consideration of the future benefits accruing to the grantor thereof, an initial monetary consideration is not typically paid for the execution of such instruments. The court shall apply the money to the costs accruing in the case and retain any balance for the owner of the royalty interest. Payments made at a later time under the lease, pooled unit, or unitization agreement shall be paid into the registry of the court and impounded for the owner of the royalty interest.

(i) This section is cumulative of other laws relating to removal of a cloud from title or appointment of a receiver.

(j) In this section:

(1) "Mineral lease" includes any lease of oil, gas, or other minerals that contains provisions necessary or incident to the orderly exploration, development, and recovery of oil, gas, or other minerals.

(2) "Leasehold interest" includes ownership created under a mineral lease or carved out of a leasehold estate granted under a mineral lease, including production payments, overriding royalty interests, and working interests.

(3) "Pooling agreement" includes any agreement that pools or unitizes land with adjacent land for production of oil, gas, or other minerals.

(4) "Royalty interest" includes any interest in the lands entitled to share in the production of oil, gas, or other minerals that is not required to execute a mineral lease or any other instrument in order to vest in the mineral interest owner or mineral leasehold interest owner the right and power, as to that interest, to develop oil, gas, or other minerals produced solely from those lands.

(k) To the extent that Subsection (d)(2) conflicts with the Texas Rules of Civil Procedure, Subsection (d)(2) controls. Notwithstanding Section 22.004, Government Code, the supreme court may not amend or adopt rules in conflict with Subsection (d)(2).

History of CPRC §64.093: Acts 1999, 76th Leg., ch. 1483, §1, eff. Aug. 30, 1999.

Sections 64.094-64.100 blank

SUBCHAPTER G. RECEIVER FOR CERTAIN MISSING PERSONS

CPRC §64.101. NOTICE & CITATION FOR RECEIVERSHIP FOR CERTAIN MISSING PERSONS

(a) On the filing of an application for the appointment of a receiver for a missing person under Section 64.001(d), the court clerk shall issue a citation that states that the application for receivership was filed and includes:

(1) the name of the missing person; and

(2) the name of the applicant.

(b) The citation must cite all persons interested in the welfare of the missing person to appear at the time and place stated in the notice for purposes of contesting the application. The citation shall be posted.

(c) The citation shall be published in a newspaper of general circulation:

(1) once in the county in which the missing person resides; and

(2) once in each county in which property of the missing person's estate is located.

History of CPRC §64.101: Acts 1999, 76th Leg., ch. 1081, §5, eff. Sept. 1, 1999.

CPRC §64.102. PROCEEDING TO APPOINT RECEIVER

(a) The court shall appoint an attorney ad litem to represent the interests of a missing person at a proceeding to appoint a receiver for the missing person under Section 64.001(d). To be eligible for appointment as an attorney ad litem under this subsection, a person must be certified in the same manner and to the same extent as a person who is appointed as an attorney ad litem for a proposed ward under Section 646, Texas Probate Code.

(b) The court may appoint a guardian ad litem for a missing person if the court determines that the appointment would be in the best interest of the missing person. A guardian ad litem appointed under this subsection is an officer of the court. The guardian ad litem shall protect the missing person in a manner that will enable the court to determine the appropriate action to take in relation to the best interest of the missing person.

(c) An attorney ad litem or a guardian ad litem appointed under this section is entitled to reasonable compensation for services in an amount set by the court to be charged as costs in the proceeding.

(d) The cost of a proceeding instituted for the appointment of a receiver for a missing person under Section 64.001(d) shall be paid from the receivership, if a receivership is created. If the court denies an application for appointment of a receiver, the applicant shall pay the costs of the proceeding.

(e) The term of a receivership for a missing person granted under Section 64.001(d) may not exceed six months unless, before the expiration of the term and for good cause shown, the court extends the receivership for another term not to exceed six months.

History of CPRC §64.102: Acts 1999, 76th Leg., ch. 1081, §5, eff. Sept. 1, 1999.

CPRC §64.103. BOND

The bond under Section 64.023 required to be executed by a receiver for a missing person appointed under Section 64.001(d) must be set in an amount the court considers necessary to protect the estate of the missing person.

History of CPRC §64.103: Acts 1999, 76th Leg., ch. 1081, §5, eff. Sept. 1, 1999.

CPRC §64.104. EXPENDITURES BY RECEIVER

If, during the receivership for a missing person under Section 64.001(d), the needs of the spouse or dependent children of the missing person require the use of the income or corpus of the estate for education, clothing, or subsistence, the court may, with or without application, by order entered in the minutes of the court, appropriate an amount of the income or corpus sufficient for that purpose. The income or corpus shall be used by the receiver to pay claims for education, clothing, or subsistence that are presented to the court and approved and ordered to be paid.

History of CPRC §64.104: Acts 1999, 76th Leg., ch. 1081, §5, eff. Sept. 1, 1999.

CPRC §64.105. RECEIVER'S EXPENSES, ACCOUNT, & COMPENSATION

(a) All necessary expenses incurred by a receiver appointed under Section 64.001(d) for a missing person in administering the property shall be reported to the court at intervals not longer than six months in length, as required by the court, and shall be reported in an annual report filed not later than the 60th day after the end of each calendar year if the court extends the receivership in accordance with Section 64.102(e). The report shall be made to the court by a sworn statement of account, including a report of:

(1) the receiver's acts;

(2) the condition of the property;

(3) the status of the threatened danger to the property; and

(4) the progress made toward abatement of the threatened danger.

(b) If the court is satisfied that the statement is correct and reasonable in all respects, the court shall promptly by order approve the report and authorize the reimbursement of the receiver from the funds under the receiver's control.

(c) For official services rendered, the receiver is entitled to be compensated in the same manner and amount as is provided by Chapter XIII, Texas Probate Code, for similar services rendered by guardians of estates.

History of CPRC §64.105: Acts 1999, 76th Leg., ch. 1081, §5, eff. Sept. 1, 1999.

CPRC §64.106. CLOSING RECEIVERSHIP

When the threatened danger has abated and the estate of a missing person for whom a receiver was appointed under Section 64.001(d) is no longer liable to injury, loss, or waste for the lack of a representative or when the receivership terminates under Section 64.102(e), whichever occurs earlier, the receiver shall:

(1) report to the court; and

CPRC §64.102

(2) file with the clerk a full and final sworn account of:

(A) all property received by the receiver;

(B) all sums paid out;

(C) all acts performed by the receiver with respect to the property; and

(D) all property remaining in the receiver's control.

History of CPRC §64.106: Acts 1999, 76th Leg., ch. 1081, §5, eff. Sept. 1, 1999.

CPRC §64.107. ACTION OF COURT

(a) If, on hearing the report and account required under Section 64.106, the court is satisfied that the danger of injury, loss, or waste has abated and that the report and account are correct, the court shall render an order finding that the danger has abated and that the report and account are correct and shall direct the receiver to deliver the property to the person from whom the receiver took possession as receiver, to the missing person, or to another person the court finds to be entitled to possession of the estate. The person to whom the property is delivered shall execute and file with the clerk an appropriate receipt for the property delivered.

(b) The order of the court shall discharge the receiver and the receiver's sureties.

(c) If the court is not satisfied that the danger has abated, or is not satisfied with the report and account, the court shall render an order continuing the receivership in effect until the court is satisfied that the danger has abated and that the report and account are correct, subject to the limitation prescribed by Section 64.102(e) for the extension of a receivership.

History of CPRC §64.107: Acts 1999, 76th Leg., ch. 1081, §5, eff. Sept. 1, 1999.

CPRC §64.108. RECORDATION OF PROCEEDINGS

All orders, bonds, reports, accounts, and notices in the receivership proceedings under this subchapter shall be recorded in the minutes of the court.

History of CPRC §64.108: Acts 1999, 76th Leg., ch. 1081, §5, eff. Sept. 1, 1999.

TITLE 7. ALTERNATE METHODS OF DISPUTE RESOLUTION

CHAPTER 154. ALTERNATIVE DISPUTE RESOLUTION PROCEDURES

SUBCHAPTER A. GENERAL PROVISIONS

CPRC §154.001. DEFINITIONS

In this chapter:

(1) "Court" includes an appellate court, district court, constitutional county court, statutory county court, family law court, probate court, municipal court, or justice of the peace court.

(2) "Dispute resolution organization" means a private profit or nonprofit corporation, political subdivision, or public corporation, or a combination of these, that offers alternative dispute resolution services to the public.

History of CPRC §154.001: Acts 1987, 70th Leg., ch. 1121, §1, eff. June 20, 1987.

See also *O'Connor's Texas Rules*, "The ADR System," ch. 4-A.

CPRC §154.002. POLICY

It is the policy of this state to encourage the peaceable resolution of disputes, with special consideration given to disputes involving the parent-child relationship, including the mediation of issues involving conservatorship, possession, and support of children, and the early settlement of pending litigation through voluntary settlement procedures.

History of CPRC §154.002: Acts 1987, 70th Leg., ch. 1121, §1, eff. June 20, 1987.

See also *O'Connor's Texas Rules*, "The ADR System," ch. 4-A.

CPRC §154.003. RESPONSIBILITY OF COURTS & COURT ADMINISTRATORS

It is the responsibility of all trial and appellate courts and their court administrators to carry out the policy under Section 154.002.

History of CPRC §154.003: Acts 1987, 70th Leg., ch. 1121, §1, eff. June 20, 1987.

Sections 154.004-154.020 reserved for expansion

SUBCHAPTER B. ALTERNATIVE DISPUTE RESOLUTION PROCEDURES

CPRC §154.021. REFERRAL OF PENDING DISPUTES FOR ALTERNATIVE DISPUTE RESOLUTION PROCEDURE

(a) A court may, on its own motion or the motion of a party, refer a pending dispute for resolution by an alternative dispute resolution procedure including:

(1) an alternative dispute resolution system established under Chapter 26, Acts of the 68th Legislature, Regular Session, 1983 (Article 2372aa, Vernon's Texas Civil Statutes*);

(2) a dispute resolution organization; or

(3) a nonjudicial and informally conducted forum for the voluntary settlement of citizens' disputes through the intervention of an impartial third party, including those alternative dispute resolution procedures described under this subchapter.

(b) The court shall confer with the parties in the determination of the most appropriate alternative dispute resolution procedure.

* Repealed. See generally CPRC ch. 152.

History of CPRC §154.021: Acts 1987, 70th Leg., ch. 1121, §1, eff. June 20, 1987.

See also *O'Connor's Texas Rules*, "The ADR System," ch. 4-A; *O'Connor's Texas Forms*, FORMS 4A.

CPRC §154.022. NOTIFICATION & OBJECTION

(a) If a court determines that a pending dispute is appropriate for referral under Section 154.021, the court shall notify the parties of its determination.

(b) Any party may, within 10 days after receiving the notice under Subsection (a), file a written objection to the referral.

(c) If the court finds that there is a reasonable basis for an objection filed under Subsection (b), the court may not refer the dispute under Section 154.021.

History of CPRC §154.022: Acts 1987, 70th Leg., ch. 1121, §1, eff. June 20, 1987.

See also *O'Connor's Texas Rules*, "The ADR System," ch. 4-A; *O'Connor's Texas Forms*, FORM 4A:03.

CPRC §154.023. MEDIATION

(a) Mediation is a forum in which an impartial person, the mediator, facilitates communication between parties to promote reconciliation, settlement, or understanding among them.

(b) A mediator may not impose his own judgment on the issues for that of the parties.

E **(c)** Mediation includes victim-offender mediation by the Texas Department of Criminal Justice described in Article 56.13, Code of Criminal Procedure.

History of CPRC §154.023: Acts 1987, 70th Leg., ch. 1121, §1, eff. June 20, 1987. Amended by Acts 2001, 77th Leg., ch. 1034, §12, eff. Sept. 1, 2001.

See also *O'Connor's Texas Rules*, "The ADR System," ch. 4-A, "Mediation," ch. 4-B; *O'Connor's Texas Forms*, FORM 4A:04.

CPRC §154.024. MINI-TRIAL

(a) A mini-trial is conducted under an agreement of the parties.

(b) Each party and counsel for the party present the position of the party, either before selected representatives for each party or before an impartial third party, to define the issues and develop a basis for realistic settlement negotiations.

(c) The impartial third party may issue an advisory opinion regarding the merits of the case.

(d) The advisory opinion is not binding on the parties unless the parties agree that it is binding and enter into a written settlement agreement.

History of CPRC §154.024: Acts 1987, 70th Leg., ch. 1121, §1, eff. June 20, 1987.

See also *O'Connor's Texas Rules*, "The ADR System," ch. 4-A; *O'Connor's Texas Forms*, FORM 4A:07.

CPRC §154.025. MODERATED SETTLEMENT CONFERENCE

(a) A moderated settlement conference is a forum for case evaluation and realistic settlement negotiations.

(b) Each party and counsel for the party present the position of the party before a panel of impartial third parties.

(c) The panel may issue an advisory opinion regarding the liability or damages of the parties or both.

(d) The advisory opinion is not binding on the parties.

History of CPRC §154.025: Acts 1987, 70th Leg., ch. 1121, §1, eff. June 20, 1987.

See also *O'Connor's Texas Rules*, "The ADR System," ch. 4-A; *O'Connor's Texas Forms*, FORM 4A:05.

CPRC §154.026. SUMMARY JURY TRIAL

(a) A summary jury trial is a forum for early case evaluation and development of realistic settlement negotiations.

(b) Each party and counsel for the party present the position of the party before a panel of jurors.

(c) The number of jurors on the panel is six unless the parties agree otherwise.

(d) The panel may issue an advisory opinion regarding the liability or damages of the parties or both.

(e) The advisory opinion is not binding on the parties.

History of CPRC §154.026: Acts 1987, 70th Leg., ch. 1121, §1, eff. June 20, 1987.

See also *O'Connor's Texas Rules*, "The ADR System," ch. 4-A; *O'Connor's Texas Forms*, FORM 4A:06.

CPRC §154.027. ARBITRATION

(a) Nonbinding arbitration is a forum in which each party and counsel for the party present the position of the party before an impartial third party, who renders a specific award.

(b) If the parties stipulate in advance, the award is binding and is enforceable in the same manner as any contract obligation. If the parties do not stipulate in advance that the award is binding, the award is not binding and serves only as a basis for the parties' further settlement negotiations.

History of CPRC §154.027: Acts 1987, 70th Leg., ch. 1121, §1, eff. June 20, 1987.

See also *O'Connor's Texas Rules*, "The ADR System," ch. 4-A, "Arbitration," ch. 4-C.

Sections 154.028-154.050 reserved for expansion

SUBCHAPTER C. IMPARTIAL THIRD PARTIES

CPRC §154.051. APPOINTMENT OF IMPARTIAL THIRD PARTIES

(a) If a court refers a pending dispute for resolution by an alternative dispute resolution procedure under Section 154.021, the court may appoint an impartial third party to facilitate the procedure.

(b) The court may appoint a third party who is agreed on by the parties if the person qualifies for appointment under this subchapter.

(c) The court may appoint more than one third party under this section.

History of CPRC §154.051: Acts 1987, 70th Leg., ch. 1121, §1, eff. June 20, 1987.

See also *O'Connor's Texas Rules*, "The ADR System," ch. 4-A.

CPRC §154.052. QUALIFICATIONS OF IMPARTIAL THIRD PARTY

(a) Except as provided by Subsections (b) and (c), to qualify for an appointment as an impartial third party under this subchapter a person must have completed a minimum of 40 classroom hours of training in dispute resolution techniques in a course conducted by an alternative dispute resolution system or other dispute resolution organization approved by the court making the appointment.

(b) To qualify for an appointment as an impartial third party under this subchapter in a dispute relating to the parent-child relationship, a person must complete the training required by Subsection (a) and an additional 24 hours of training in the fields of family dynamics, child development, and family law.

(c) In appropriate circumstances, a court may in its discretion appoint a person as an impartial third party who does not qualify under Subsection (a) or (b) if the court bases its appointment on legal or other professional training or experience in particular dispute resolution processes.

History of CPRC §154.052: Acts 1987, 70th Leg., ch. 1121, §1, eff. June 20, 1987.

See also *O'Connor's Texas Rules*, "The ADR System," ch. 4-A.

CPRC §154.053. STANDARDS & DUTIES OF IMPARTIAL THIRD PARTIES

(a) A person appointed to facilitate an alternative dispute resolution procedure under this subchapter shall encourage and assist the parties in reaching a settlement of their dispute but may not compel or coerce the parties to enter into a settlement agreement.

(b) Unless expressly authorized by the disclosing party, the impartial third party may not disclose to either party information given in confidence by the other and shall at all times maintain confidentiality with respect to communications relating to the subject matter of the dispute.

(c) Unless the parties agree otherwise, all matters, including the conduct and demeanor of the parties and their counsel during the settlement process, are confidential and may never be disclosed to anyone, including the appointing court.

(d) Each participant, including the impartial third party, to an alternative dispute resolution procedure is subject to the requirements of Subchapter B, Chapter 261, Family Code, and Subchapter C, Chapter 48, Human Resources Code.

History of CPRC §154.053: Acts 1987, 70th Leg., ch. 1121, §1, eff. June 20, 1987. Amended by Acts 1999, 76th Leg., ch. 1150, §29, eff. Sept. 1, 1999.

See also *O'Connor's Texas Rules*, "The ADR System," ch. 4-A; "Mediation," ch. 4-B.

CPRC §154.054. COMPENSATION OF IMPARTIAL THIRD PARTIES

(a) The court may set a reasonable fee for the services of an impartial third party appointed under this subchapter.

(b) Unless the parties agree to a method of payment, the court shall tax the fee for the services of an impartial third party as other costs of suit.

History of CPRC §154.054: Acts 1987, 70th Leg., ch. 1121, §1, eff. June 20, 1987.

See also *O'Connor's Texas Rules*, "The ADR System," ch. 4-A.

CPRC §154.055. QUALIFIED IMMUNITY OF IMPARTIAL THIRD PARTIES

(a) A person appointed to facilitate an alternative dispute resolution procedure under this subchapter or under Chapter 152 relating to an alternative dispute resolution system established by counties, or appointed by the parties whether before or after the institution of formal judicial proceedings, who is a volunteer and who does not act with wanton and wilful disregard of the rights, safety, or property of another, is immune from civil liability for any act or omission within the course and scope of his or her duties or functions as an impartial third party. For purposes of this section, a volunteer impartial third party is a person who does not receive compensation in excess of reimbursement for expenses incurred or a stipend intended as reimbursement for expenses incurred.

(b) This section neither applies to nor is it intended to enlarge or diminish any rights or immunities enjoyed by an arbitrator participating in a binding arbitration pursuant to any applicable statute or treaty.

History of CPRC §154.055: Acts 1993, 73rd Leg., ch. 875, §1, eff. Sept. 1, 1993.

Sections 154.056-154.070 reserved for expansion

SUBCHAPTER D. MISCELLANEOUS PROVISIONS

CPRC §154.071. EFFECT OF WRITTEN SETTLEMENT AGREEMENT

(a) If the parties reach a settlement and execute a written agreement disposing of the dispute, the agreement is enforceable in the same manner as any other written contract.

(b) The court in its discretion may incorporate the terms of the agreement in the court's final decree disposing of the case.

(c) A settlement agreement does not affect an outstanding court order unless the terms of the agreement are incorporated into a subsequent decree.

History of CPRC §154.071: Acts 1987, 70th Leg., ch. 1121, §1, eff. June 20, 1987.

See also Family Code §153.0071; ***O'Connor's Texas Rules***, "The ADR System," ch. 4-A, "Enforceable Settlement Agreements," ch. 7-F, §6.

CPRC §154.072. STATISTICAL INFORMATION ON DISPUTES REFERRED

The Texas Supreme Court shall determine the need and method for statistical reporting of disputes referred by the courts to alternative dispute resolution procedures.

History of CPRC §154.072: Acts 1987, 70th Leg., ch. 1121, §1, eff. June 20, 1987.

CPRC §154.073. CONFIDENTIALITY OF CERTAIN RECORDS & COMMUNICATIONS

Ⓐ **(a)** Except as provided by Subsections (c), (d), (e), and (f), a communication relating to the subject matter of any civil or criminal dispute made by a participant in an alternative dispute resolution procedure, whether before or after the institution of formal judicial proceedings, is confidential, is not subject to disclosure, and may not be used as evidence against the participant in any judicial or administrative proceeding.

(b) Any record made at an alternative dispute resolution procedure is confidential, and the participants or the third party facilitating the procedure may not be required to testify in any proceedings relating to or arising out of the matter in dispute or be subject to process requiring disclosure of confidential information or data relating to or arising out of the matter in dispute.

(c) An oral communication or written material used in or made a part of an alternative dispute resolution procedure is admissible or discoverable if it is admissible or discoverable independent of the procedure.

(d) A final written agreement to which a governmental body, as defined by Section 552.003, Government Code, is a signatory that is reached as a result of a dispute resolution procedure conducted under this chapter is subject to or excepted from required disclosure in accordance with Chapter 552, Government Code.

(e) If this section conflicts with other legal requirements for disclosure of communications, records, or materials, the issue of confidentiality may be presented to the court having jurisdiction of the proceedings to determine, in camera, whether the facts, circumstances, and context of the communications or materials sought to be disclosed warrant a protective order of the court or whether the communications or materials are subject to disclosure.

Ⓐ **(f)** This section does not affect the duty to report abuse or neglect under Subchapter B, Chapter 261, Family Code, and abuse, exploitation, or neglect under Subchapter C, Chapter 48, Human Resources Code.

Ⓔ **(g)** This section applies to a victim-offender mediation by the Texas Department of Criminal Justice as described in Article 56.13, Code of Criminal Procedure.

History of CPRC §154.073: Acts 1987, 70th Leg., ch. 1121, §1, eff. June 20, 1987. Amended by Acts 1999, 76th Leg., ch. 1352, §6 (eff. Sept. 1, 1999), ch. 1150, §30 (eff. Sept. 1, 1999); Acts 2001, 77th Leg., ch. 1034, §13 (eff. Sept. 1, 2001), ch. 1420, §21.001(6) & §21.002(3) (eff. Sept. 1, 2001).

See also ***O'Connor's Texas Rules***, "The ADR System," ch. 4-A, "Mediation," ch. 4-B.

GOVERNMENT CODE
SELECTED PROVISIONS
TABLE OF CONTENTS

TITLE 2. JUDICIAL BRANCH

SUBTITLE A. COURTS

CHAPTER 24. DISTRICT COURTS

SUBCHAPTER A. GENERAL PROVISIONS

E GOVT §24.022. EFFECT OF TRANSFER OF CERTAIN CASES FOLLOWING CREATION OF ADDITIONAL COURT

(a) On the creation of an additional district court in a county, an existing district court in the county may transfer to the new court a case regarding a child who is subject to the continuing exclusive jurisdiction of the existing court under Title 5, Family Code, regardless of whether the case is pending in the existing court or the existing court rendered a final order in the case.

(b) The district court to which the case is transferred under this section acquires continuing exclusive jurisdiction under Title 5, Family Code, over the child.

History of Govt §24.022: Enacted by Acts 2001, 77th Leg., ch. 1148, §1, eff. June 15, 2001.

SUBTITLE F. COURT ADMINISTRATION

CHAPTER 74. COURT ADMINISTRATION ACT

SUBCHAPTER C. ADMINISTRATIVE JUDICIAL REGIONS

GOVT §74.053. OBJECTION TO ASSIGNED JUDGE

(a) When a judge is assigned under this chapter the presiding judge shall, if it is reasonable and practicable and if time permits, give notice of the assignment to each attorney representing a party to the case that is to be heard in whole or part by the assigned judge.

(b) If a party to a civil case files a timely objection to the assignment, the judge shall not hear the case. Except as provided by Subsection (d), each party to the case is only entitled to one objection under this section for that case.

(c) An objection under this section must be filed before the first hearing or trial, including pretrial hearings, over which the assigned judge is to preside.

(d) A former judge or justice who was not a retired judge may not sit in a case if either party objects to the judge or justice.

History of Govt §74.053: Acts 1987, 70th Leg., ch. 148, §2.93(a), eff. Sept. 1, 1987. Amended by Acts 1989, 71st Leg., ch. 2, §8.37(a) (eff. Aug. 28, 1989), ch. 270, §1 (eff. Aug. 28, 1989); Acts 1991, 72nd Leg., ch. 785, §2, eff. June 16, 1991.

TITLE 3. LEGISLATIVE BRANCH

SUBTITLE B. LEGISLATION

CHAPTER 311. CODE CONSTRUCTION ACT

SUBCHAPTER A. GENERAL PROVISIONS

GOVT §311.001. SHORT TITLE

This chapter may be cited as the Code Construction Act.

History of Govt §311.001: Acts 1985, 69th Leg., ch. 479, §1, eff. Sept. 1, 1985.

GOVT §311.002. APPLICATION

This chapter applies to:

(1) each code enacted by the 60th or a subsequent legislature as part of the state's continuing statutory revision program;

(2) each amendment, repeal, revision, and reenactment of a code or code provision by the 60th or a subsequent legislature;

(3) each repeal of a statute by a code; and

(4) each rule adopted under a code.

History of Govt §311.002: Acts 1985, 69th Leg., ch. 479, §1, eff. Sept. 1, 1985.

GOVT §311.003. RULES NOT EXCLUSIVE

The rules provided in this chapter are not exclusive but are meant to describe and clarify common situations in order to guide the preparation and construction of codes.

History of Govt §311.003: Acts 1985, 69th Leg., ch. 479, §1, eff. Sept. 1, 1985.

GOVT §311.004. CITATION OF CODES

A code may be cited by its name preceded by the specific part concerned. Examples of citations are:

(1) Title 1, Business & Commerce Code;

(2) Chapter 5, Business & Commerce Code;

(3) Section 9.304, Business & Commerce Code;

(4) Section 15.06(a), Business & Commerce Code; and

(5) Section 17.18(b)(1)(B)(ii), Business & Commerce Code.

History of Govt §311.004: Acts 1985, 69th Leg., ch. 479, §1, eff. Sept. 1, 1985. Amended by Acts 1985, 69th Leg., ch. 117, §13(b), eff. Sept. 1, 1985.

GOVT §311.005. GENERAL DEFINITIONS

The following definitions apply unless the statute or context in which the word or phrase is used requires a different definition:

(1) "Oath" includes affirmation.

(2) "Person" includes corporation, organization, government or governmental subdivision or agency, business trust, estate, trust, partnership, association, and any other legal entity.

(3) "Population" means the population shown by the most recent federal decennial census.

(4) "Property" means real and personal property.

(5) "Rule" includes regulation.

(6) "Signed" includes any symbol executed or adopted by a person with present intention to authenticate a writing.

(7) "State," when referring to a part of the United States, includes any state, district, commonwealth, territory, and insular possession of the United States and any area subject to the legislative authority of the United States of America.

(8) "Swear" includes affirm.

(9) "United States" includes a department, bureau, or other agency of the United States of America.

(10) "Week" means seven consecutive days.

(11) "Written" includes any representation of words, letters, symbols, or figures.

(12) "Year" means 12 consecutive months.

(13) "Includes" and "including" are terms of enlargement and not of limitation or exclusive enumeration, and use of the terms does not create a presumption that components not expressed are excluded.

History of Govt §311.005: Acts 1985, 69th Leg., ch. 479, §1, eff. Sept. 1, 1985. Amended by Acts 1989, 71st Leg., ch. 340, §1, eff. Aug. 28, 1989.

GOVT §311.006. INTERNAL REFERENCES

In a code:

(1) a reference to a title, chapter, or section without further identification is a reference to a title, chapter, or section of the code; and

(2) a reference to a subtitle, subchapter, subsection, subdivision, paragraph, or other numbered or lettered unit without further identification is a reference to a unit of the next larger unit of the code in which the reference appears.

History of Govt §311.006: Acts 1993, 73rd Leg., ch. 131, §1, eff. May 11, 1993.

Sections 311.007-311.010 reserved for expansion

SUBCHAPTER B. CONSTRUCTION OF WORDS & PHRASES

GOVT §311.011. COMMON & TECHNICAL USAGE OF WORDS

(a) Words and phrases shall be read in context and construed according to the rules of grammar and common usage.

(b) Words and phrases that have acquired a technical or particular meaning, whether by legislative definition or otherwise, shall be construed accordingly.

History of Govt §311.011: Acts 1985, 69th Leg., ch. 479, §1, eff. Sept. 1, 1985.

GOVT §311.012. TENSE, NUMBER, & GENDER

(a) Words in the present tense include the future tense.

(b) The singular includes the plural and the plural includes the singular.

(c) Words of one gender include the other genders.

History of Govt §311.012: Acts 1985, 69th Leg., ch. 479, §1, eff. Sept. 1, 1985.

GOVT §311.013. AUTHORITY & QUORUM OF PUBLIC BODY

(a) A grant of authority to three or more persons as a public body confers the authority on a majority of the number of members fixed by statute.

(b) A quorum of a public body is a majority of the number of members fixed by statute.

History of Govt §311.013: Acts 1985, 69th Leg., ch. 479, §1, eff. Sept. 1, 1985.

GOVT §311.014. COMPUTATION OF TIME

(a) In computing a period of days, the first day is excluded and the last day is included.

(b) If the last day of any period is a Saturday, Sunday, or legal holiday, the period is extended to include the next day that is not a Saturday, Sunday, or legal holiday.

(c) If a number of months is to be computed by counting the months from a particular day, the period ends on the same numerical day in the concluding month as the day of the month from which the computation is begun, unless there are not that many days in the concluding month, in which case the period ends on the last day of that month.

History of Govt §311.014: Acts 1985, 69th Leg., ch. 479, §1, eff. Sept. 1, 1985.

GOVT §311.015. REFERENCE TO A SERIES

If a statute refers to a series of numbers or letters, the first and last numbers or letters are included.

History of Govt §311.015: Acts 1985, 69th Leg., ch. 479, §1, eff. Sept. 1, 1985.

GOVT §311.016. "MAY," "SHALL," "MUST," ETC.

The following constructions apply unless the context in which the word or phrase appears necessarily requires a different construction or unless a different construction is expressly provided by statute:

(1) "May" creates discretionary authority or grants permission or a power.

(2) "Shall" imposes a duty.

(3) "Must" creates or recognizes a condition precedent.

(4) "Is entitled to" creates or recognizes a right.

(5) "May not" imposes a prohibition and is synonymous with "shall not."

(6) "Is not entitled to" negates a right.

(7) "Is not required to" negates a duty or condition precedent.

History of Govt §311.016: Acts 1997, 75th Leg., ch. 220, §1, eff. May 23, 1997.

Sections 311.017-311.020 reserved for expansion

SUBCHAPTER C. CONSTRUCTION OF STATUTES

GOVT §311.021. INTENTION IN ENACTMENT OF STATUTES

In enacting a statute, it is presumed that:

(1) compliance with the constitutions of this state and the United States is intended;

(2) the entire statute is intended to be effective;

(3) a just and reasonable result is intended;

(4) a result feasible of execution is intended; and

(5) public interest is favored over any private interest.

History of Govt §311.021: Acts 1985, 69th Leg., ch. 479, §1, eff. Sept. 1, 1985.

GOVT §311.022. PROSPECTIVE OPERATION OF STATUTES

A statute is presumed to be prospective in its operation unless expressly made retrospective.

History of Govt §311.022: Acts 1985, 69th Leg., ch. 479, §1, eff. Sept. 1, 1985.

GOVT §311.023. STATUTE CONSTRUCTION AIDS

In construing a statute, whether or not the statute is considered ambiguous on its face, a court may consider among other matters the:

(1) object sought to be attained;

(2) circumstances under which the statute was enacted;

(3) legislative history;

(4) common law or former statutory provisions, including laws on the same or similar subjects;

(5) consequences of a particular construction;

(6) administrative construction of the statute; and

(7) title (caption), preamble, and emergency provision.

History of Govt §311.023: Acts 1985, 69th Leg., ch. 479, §1, eff. Sept. 1, 1985.

GOVT §311.024. HEADINGS

The heading of a title, subtitle, chapter, subchapter, or section does not limit or expand the meaning of a statute.

History of Govt §311.024: Acts 1985, 69th Leg., ch. 479, §1, eff. Sept. 1, 1985.

GOVT §311.025. IRRECONCILABLE STATUTES & AMENDMENTS

(a) Except as provided by Section 311.031(d), if statutes enacted at the same or different sessions of the legislature are irreconcilable, the statute latest in date of enactment prevails.

(b) Except as provided by Section 311.031(d), if amendments to the same statute are enacted at the same session of the legislature, one amendment without reference to another, the amendments shall be harmonized, if possible, so that effect may be given to each. If the amendments are irreconcilable, the latest in date of enactment prevails.

(c) In determining whether amendments are irreconcilable, text that is reenacted because of the requirement of Article III, Section 36, of the Texas Constitution is not considered to be irreconcilable with additions or omissions in the same text made by another amendment. Unless clearly indicated to the contrary, an amendment that reenacts text in compliance with that constitutional requirement does not indicate legislative intent that the reenacted text prevail over changes in the same text made by another amendment, regardless of the relative dates of enactment.

(d) In this section, the date of enactment is the date on which the last legislative vote is taken on the bill enacting the statute.

(e) If the journals or other legislative records fail to disclose which of two or more bills in conflict is latest in date of enactment, the date of enactment of the respective bills is considered to be, in order of priority:

(1) the date on which the last presiding officer signed the bill;

(2) the date on which the governor signed the bill; or

(3) the date on which the bill became law by operation of law.

History of Govt §311.025: Acts 1985, 69th Leg., ch. 479, §1, eff. Sept. 1, 1985. Amended by Acts 1989, 71st Leg., ch. 340, §2, eff. Aug. 28, 1989; Acts 1997, 75th Leg., ch. 220, §2, eff. May 23, 1997.

GOVT §311.026. SPECIAL OR LOCAL PROVISION PREVAILS OVER GENERAL

(a) If a general provision conflicts with a special or local provision, the provisions shall be construed, if possible, so that effect is given to both.

(b) If the conflict between the general provision and the special or local provision is irreconcilable, the special or local provision prevails as an exception to the general provision, unless the general provision is the later enactment and the manifest intent is that the general provision prevail.

History of Govt §311.026: Acts 1985, 69th Leg., ch. 479, §1, eff. Sept. 1, 1985.

GOVT §311.027. STATUTORY REFERENCES

Unless expressly provided otherwise, a reference to any portion of a statute or rule applies to all reenactments, revisions, or amendments of the statute or rule.

History of Govt §311.027: Acts 1985, 69th Leg., ch. 479, §1, eff. Sept. 1, 1985. Amended by Acts 1993, 73rd Leg., ch. 131, §2, eff. May 11, 1993.

GOVT §311.028. UNIFORM CONSTRUCTION OF UNIFORM ACTS

A uniform act included in a code shall be construed to effect its general purpose to make uniform the law of those states that enact it.

History of Govt §311.028: Acts 1985, 69th Leg., ch. 479, §1, eff. Sept. 1, 1985.

GOVT §311.029. ENROLLED BILL CONTROLS

If the language of the enrolled bill version of a statute conflicts with the language of any subsequent printing or reprinting of the statute, the language of the enrolled bill version controls.

History of Govt §311.029: Acts 1985, 69th Leg., ch. 479, §1, eff. Sept. 1, 1985.

GOVT §311.030. REPEAL OF REPEALING STATUTE

The repeal of a repealing statute does not revive the statute originally repealed nor impair the effect of any saving provision in it.

History of Govt §311.030: Acts 1985, 69th Leg., ch. 479, §1, eff. Sept. 1, 1985.

GOVT §311.031. SAVING PROVISIONS

(a) Except as provided by Subsection (b), the reenactment, revision, amendment, or repeal of a statute does not affect:

(1) the prior operation of the statute or any prior action taken under it;

(2) any validation, cure, right, privilege, obligation, or liability previously acquired, accrued, accorded, or incurred under it;

(3) any violation of the statute or any penalty, forfeiture, or punishment incurred under the statute before its amendment or repeal; or

(4) any investigation, proceeding, or remedy concerning any privilege, obligation, liability, penalty, forfeiture, or punishment; and the investigation, proceeding, or remedy may be instituted, continued, or enforced, and the penalty, forfeiture, or punishment imposed, as if the statute had not been repealed or amended.

(b) If the penalty, forfeiture, or punishment for any offense is reduced by a reenactment, revision, or amendment of a statute, the penalty, forfeiture, or punishment, if not already imposed, shall be imposed according to the statute as amended.

(c) The repeal of a statute by a code does not affect an amendment, revision, or reenactment of the statute by the same legislature that enacted the code. The amendment, revision, or reenactment is preserved and given effect as part of the code provision that revised the statute so amended, revised, or reenacted.

(d) If any provision of a code conflicts with a statute enacted by the same legislature that enacted the code, the statute controls.

History of Govt §311.031: Acts 1985, 69th Leg., ch. 479, §1, eff. Sept. 1, 1985.

GOVT §311.032. SEVERABILITY OF STATUTES

(a) If any statute contains a provision for severability, that provision prevails in interpreting that statute.

(b) If any statute contains a provision for nonseverability, that provision prevails in interpreting that statute.

(c) In a statute that does not contain a provision for severability or nonseverability, if any provision of the statute or its application to any person or circumstance is held invalid, the invalidity does not affect other provisions or applications of the statute that can be given effect without the invalid provision or application, and to this end the provisions of the statute are severable.

History of Govt §311.032: Acts 1985, 69th Leg., ch. 479, §1, eff. Sept. 1, 1985.

E GOVT §311.034. WAIVER OF SOVEREIGN IMMUNITY

In order to preserve the legislature's interest in managing state fiscal matters through the appropriations process, a statute shall not be construed as a waiver of sovereign immunity unless the waiver is effected by clear and unambiguous language. In a statute, the use of "person," as defined by Section 311.005 to include governmental entities, does not indicate legislative intent to waive sovereign immunity unless the context of the statute indicates no other reasonable construction.

History of Govt §311.034: Enacted by Acts 2001, 77th Leg., ch. 1158, §8, eff. June 15, 2001.

TITLE 8. PUBLIC RETIREMENT SYSTEMS

SUBTITLE A. PROVISIONS GENERALLY APPLICABLE TO PUBLIC RETIREMENT SYSTEMS

CHAPTER 804. DOMESTIC RELATIONS ORDERS & SPOUSAL CONSENT

SUBCHAPTER A. QUALIFIED DOMESTIC RELATIONS ORDERS

GOVT §804.001. DEFINITIONS

In this chapter:

(1) "Alternate payee" means a spouse, former spouse, child, or other dependent of a member or retiree who is recognized by a domestic relations order as having a right to receive all or a portion of the benefits payable by a public retirement system with respect to such member or retiree.

(2) "Domestic relations order" means any judgment, decree, or order, including approval of a property settlement agreement, which relates to the provision of child support, alimony payments, or marital property rights to a spouse, former spouse, child, or other dependent of a member or retiree, and is made pursuant to a domestic relations law, including a community property law of the State of Texas or of another state.

(3) "Public retirement system" means the Employees Retirement System of Texas, the Judicial Retirement System of Texas Plan One, the Judicial Retirement System of Texas Plan Two, the Teacher Retirement System of Texas, the Texas County and District Retirement System, the Texas Municipal Retirement System, and any other continuing, organized program of service retirement, disability retirement, or death benefits for officers or employees of the state or a political subdivision or of an agency or instrumentality of the state or a political subdivision and includes the optional retirement program governed by Chapter 830. Public retirement system does not include:

(A) a program, other than the optional retirement program, for which benefits are administered by a life insurance company;

(B) a program providing only workers' compensation benefits;

(C) a program administered by the federal government;

(D) an individual retirement account or individual retirement annuity within the meaning of Section 408, or a retirement bond within the meaning of Section 409, of the Internal Revenue Code of 1986;

(E) a plan described by Subsection (d) of Section 401 of the Internal Revenue Code of 1986;

(F) a group or an individual account plan consisting of an annuity contract described by Subsection (b) of Section 403 of the Internal Revenue Code of 1986, other than a 403(b) contract or plan under the optional retirement program;

(G) an eligible state deferred compensation plan described by Subsection (b) of Section 457 of the Internal Revenue Code of 1986; or

(H) the program established by Chapter 615.

(4) "Qualified domestic relations order" means a domestic relations order which creates or recognizes the existence of an alternate payee's right or assigns to an alternate payee the right to receive all or a portion of the benefits payable with respect to a member or retiree under a public retirement system, which directs the

public retirement system to disburse benefits to the alternate payee, and which meets the requirements of Section 804.003.

(5) "Statewide retirement system" means the Employees Retirement System of Texas, the Judicial Retirement System of Texas Plan One, the Judicial Retirement System of Texas Plan Two, the Teacher Retirement System of Texas, the Texas County and District Retirement System, or the Texas Municipal Retirement System.

History of Govt §804.001: Acts 1991, 72nd Leg., ch. 16, §11.02(a), eff. Aug. 26, 1991. Amended by Acts 1995, 74th Leg., ch. 76, §5.95(32), eff. Sept. 1, 1995.

GOVT §804.002. APPLICATION OF CHAPTERS

This subchapter and Subchapter C apply to each statewide retirement system and to the optional retirement program governed by Chapter 830. This subchapter and Subchapter C also apply to each other public retirement system for which the board of trustees of the system elects to adopt the provisions of this subchapter and Subchapter C. An election under this section must be by order or resolution and need not set out the text of this subchapter or Subchapter C. A board of trustees may not elect to adopt only this subchapter or Subchapter C.

History of Govt §804.002: Acts 1991, 72nd Leg., ch. 16, §11.02(a), eff. Aug. 26, 1991.

GOVT §804.003. QUALIFIED DOMESTIC RELATIONS ORDERS

(a) Sections 811.005, 821.005, 831.004, 836.004, 841.006, and 851.006 and any similar antialienation provisions contained in any other public retirement system shall apply to the creation, assignment, recognition, or enforcement of a right to any benefit payable with respect to a member or retiree of a public retirement system to which the section applies pursuant to a domestic relations order unless the order is determined to be a qualified domestic relations order.

(b) Except as provided in Subsection (d), the administrative head of a public retirement system to which this chapter applies and to which a domestic relations order is submitted or his designee has exclusive authority to determine whether a domestic relations order is a qualified domestic relations order. A determination by the administrative head or his designee under this section may be appealed only to the board of trustees of the public retirement system. An appeal to the board of trustees of a statewide retirement system is a contested case under Chapter 2001. However, the board of a statewide retirement system by rule may waive the requirement of an appeal to the board. On appeal of a decision made by the board of trustees or by the administrative head if there is no appeal to the board under this section, the standard of review is by substantial evidence.

(c) Except as provided in Subsection (d), a court does not have jurisdiction over a public retirement system to which this chapter applies with respect to a divorce or other domestic relations action in which an alternate payee's right to receive all or a portion of the benefits payable to a member or retiree under the public retirement system is created or established. A party to such an action who attempts to make a public retirement system a party to the action contrary to the provision of this subsection shall be liable to the public retirement system for its costs and attorney's fees.

(d) Under the optional retirement program, applicable carriers shall determine whether a domestic relations order is a qualified domestic relations order. If a dispute arises over the determination of whether a domestic relations order is a qualified domestic relations order which cannot be resolved by the procedure described in Subsection (g), the court which issued the order or which otherwise has jurisdiction over the matter shall resolve the dispute with respect to a divorce or other domestic relations action in which an alternate payee's right to receive all or a portion of the benefits payable to a member or retiree under the optional retirement program is created or established.

(e) For the purposes of this section, benefits payable with respect to a member or retiree under the retirement system include the types of benefits payable by a public retirement system and a withdrawal of contributions from a public retirement system.

(f) A domestic relations order is a qualified domestic relations order only if such order:

(1) clearly specifies the name, social security number, and last known mailing address, if any, of the member or retiree and the name, social security number, and mailing address of each alternate payee covered by the order;

(2) clearly specifies the amount or percentage of the member's or retiree's benefits to be paid by a public retirement system to each such alternate payee or the

manner in which such amount or percentage is to be determined;

(3) clearly specifies the number of payments or the period to which such order applies;

(4) clearly specifies that such order applies to a designated public retirement system;

(5) does not require the public retirement system to provide any type or form of benefit or any option not otherwise provided under the plan;

(6) does not require the public retirement system to provide increased benefits determined on the basis of actuarial value;

(7) does not require the payment of benefits to an alternate payee which are required to be paid to another alternate payee under another order previously determined to be a qualified domestic relations order; and

(8) does not require the payment of benefits to an alternate payee before the retirement of a member, the distribution of a withdrawal of contributions to a member, or other distribution to a member required by law.

(g) A public retirement system may reject a domestic relations order as a qualified domestic relations order unless the order:

(1) provides for a proportional reduction of the amount awarded to an alternate payee in the event of the retirement of the member before normal retirement age;

(2) does not purport to require the designation of a particular person as the recipient of benefits in the event of a member's or annuitant's death;

(3) does not purport to require the selection of a particular benefit payment plan or option;

(4) provides clearly for each possible benefit distribution under plan provisions;

(5) does not require any action on the part of the retirement system contrary to its governing statutes or plan provision other than the direct payment of the benefit awarded to an alternate payee;

(6) does not make the award of an interest contingent on any condition other than those conditions resulting in the liability of a retirement system for payments under its plan provisions;

(7) does not purport to award any future benefit increases that are provided or required by the legislature; and

(8) provides for a proportional reduction of the amount awarded to an alternate payee in the event that benefits available to the retiree or member are reduced by law.

(h) The administrative head of a public retirement system to which this chapter applies or his designee (or applicable carrier, if under the optional retirement program), upon receipt of a certified copy of a domestic relations order, shall determine whether such order is a qualified domestic relations order and shall notify the member or retiree and each alternate payee of such determination. If the order is determined to be a qualified domestic relations order, the public retirement system (or applicable carrier, if under the optional retirement program), shall pay benefits in accordance with the order. If the order is determined not to be a qualified domestic relations order, the member or retiree or any alternate payee named in the order may appeal the administrative head's determination in the manner specified in Subsection (b) or the optional retirement program carrier's determination in the manner specified in Subsection (d) and may petition the court which issued the order to amend the order so that it will be qualified. The court which issued the order or which would otherwise have jurisdiction over the matter has jurisdiction to amend the order so that it will be qualified even though all other matters incident to the action or proceeding have been fully and finally adjudicated.

(i) During any period in which the issue of whether a domestic relations order is a qualified domestic relations order is being determined by the agency administrative head, his designee, the board of trustees, a court of competent jurisdiction, optional retirement program carrier, or otherwise, the public retirement system shall separately account for the amounts, in this section referred to as the "segregated amounts," which would have been payable to the alternate payee during such period if the order had been determined to be a qualified domestic relations order.

(j) If a domestic relations order is determined to be a qualified domestic relations order, then the public retirement system (or applicable carrier, if under the optional retirement program) shall pay the segregated amounts without interest to the person or persons entitled thereto and shall thereafter pay benefits pursuant to the order.

(k) If a domestic relations order is determined not to be a qualified domestic relations order or if within 18 months of the date a domestic relations order is received by the public retirement system (or applicable carrier, if under the optional retirement program) the issue as to whether such order is a qualified domestic relations order is not resolved, then the public retirement system (or applicable carrier, if under the optional retirement program) shall pay the segregated amounts without interest and shall thereafter pay benefits to the person or persons who would have been entitled to such amounts if there had been no order. This subsection shall not be construed to limit or otherwise affect any liability, responsibility, or duty of a party with respect to any other party to the action out of which the order arose.

(*l*) Any determination that an order is a qualified domestic relations order which is made after the close of the 18-month period shall be applied prospectively only.

(m) The public retirement system, the board of trustees, and officers and employees of the public retirement system (or applicable carrier, if under the optional retirement program) shall not be liable to any person for making payments of any benefits in accordance with a domestic relations order in a cause in which a member or a retiree was a party or for making payments in accordance with Subsection (k).

(n) The board of trustees of a public retirement system may promulgate rules it deems necessary to implement the provisions of this section.

(o) Except as specifically provided in this subtitle or by any other statute, public employment does not confer special privileges or immunities on a public employee. An ownership or beneficial interest in any retirement, pension, or other financial plan not included in the definition of "public retirement system" as set forth in Section 804.001 held in whole or in part by an officer or employee of the state or a political subdivision or of an agency or an instrumentality of either, whether obtained in connection with that employment or otherwise, shall be subject to the requirements of the federal laws governing qualified domestic relations orders.

History of Govt §804.003: Acts 1991, 72nd Leg., ch. 16, §11.02(a), eff. Aug. 26, 1991. Amended by Acts 1995, 74th Leg., ch. 76, §5.95(50), eff. Sept. 1, 1995.

See also 34 TAC, ch. 74.

GOVT §804.004. LIFE ANNUITY OR LUMP-SUM PAYMENT IN LIEU OF BENEFITS AWARDED BY A QUALIFIED DOMESTIC RELATIONS ORDER

(a) The board of trustees of a public retirement system to which this chapter applies may by rule provide that, in lieu of paying an alternate beneficiary the interest awarded by a qualified domestic relations order, the system may pay the alternate beneficiary an amount that is the actuarial equivalent of such interest in the form of:

(1) an annuity payable in equal monthly installments for the life of the alternate payee; or

(2) a lump sum.

(b) The determination of whether to pay an amount authorized by this section in lieu of the interest awarded by the qualified domestic relations order shall be at the sole discretion of the public retirement system.

(c) If a public retirement system elects to pay the alternate payee pursuant to this section, the benefit payable by the system to the member, retiree, or beneficiary shall be reduced by the interest in the benefit awarded to the alternate payee by the qualified domestic relations order.

(d) If the public retirement system pays the alternate payee pursuant to this section, the retirement system shall be entitled to rely on a beneficiary designation or benefit option selection made or changed pursuant to its plan without regard to any domestic relations order.

History of Govt §804.004: Acts 1991, 72nd Leg., ch. 16, §11.02(a), eff. Aug. 26, 1991.

GOVT §804.005. PAYMENT IN CERTAIN CIRCUMSTANCES IN LIEU OF BENEFITS AWARDED BY QUALIFIED DOMESTIC RELATIONS ORDER

(a) This section applies only to the Employees Retirement System of Texas and the Teacher Retirement System of Texas.

(b) A public retirement system to which this section applies shall pay an alternate payee of a member of the retirement system who is described by Subsection (c), if the alternate payee so elects and in lieu of the interest awarded by a qualified domestic relations order on or after January 1, 1985, an amount that is the alternate payee's portion of the actuarial equivalent of the accrued retirement benefit of the member of the retirement system, determined as if the member retired on the date of the alternate payee's election. The amount becomes payable at the time the actuarial equivalent is determined, and the amount is payable in the form of an annuity payable in equal monthly installments for the life of the alternate payee.

(c) A member whose benefits are subject to partial payment under this section is one who has not retired from the retirement system, has attained the greater of the age of 62 or normal retirement age and the service requirements for service retirement, and retains credit and contributions in the retirement system attributable to that service.

(d) If an alternate payee elects to be paid under this section, the retirement system shall reduce the benefit payable by the system to the member or the member's beneficiary by the alternate payee's portion of the actuarial equivalent determined under Subsection (b).

(e) In determining under Subsection (b) the actuarial equivalent of an accrued retirement benefit, the system shall consider the member's benefit as a normal age standard service retirement annuity, without regard to any optional annuity chosen or beneficiary designated by the member.

(f) The beginning of monthly payments under this section terminates any interest that the alternate payee who receives the payment might otherwise have in benefits that accrue to the account of the member after the date the initial payment to the alternate payee is made.

(g) A public retirement system may adopt rules for administration of this section.

History of Govt §804.005: Acts 1993, 73rd Leg., ch. 867, §1, eff. Sept. 1, 1993.

Sections 804.006 to 804.050 reserved for expansion

SUBCHAPTER B. SPOUSAL CONSENT REQUIREMENTS

GOVT §804.051. AUTHORITY TO REQUIRE SPOUSAL CONSENT

A public retirement system may adopt rules to require spousal consent for the selection of a service retirement annuity other than a joint and survivor annuity that pays benefits to the member's spouse on the death of the member or for the selection of a death benefits plan that pays benefits in the form of an annuity to a person other than the member's spouse on the death of the member.

History of Govt §804.051: Acts 1991, 72nd Leg., ch. 16, §11.02(a), eff. Aug. 26, 1991.

Sections 804.052 to 804.100 reserved for expansion

SUBCHAPTER C. TERMINATION OF INTERESTS IN PUBLIC RETIREMENT SYSTEM

GOVT §804.101. TERMINATION OF INTEREST IN PUBLIC RETIREMENT SYSTEM

The death of an alternate payee as defined in Section 804.001 or the death of a spouse of a member or retiree of a public retirement system to which this chapter applies shall terminate the interest of the alternate payee or spouse in that public retirement system. This section shall not affect an interest in a public retirement system accrued to an individual as a member of the public retirement system.

History of Govt §804.101: Acts 1991, 72nd Leg., ch. 16, §11.02(a), eff. Aug. 26, 1991.

For the complete Penal Code annotated, see ***O'Connor's Criminal Codes Plus*** (2002-2003). To order, call 1-800-OCONNOR (1-800-626-6667) or visit <http://www.jonesmcclure.com/>.

TITLE 6. OFFENSES AGAINST THE FAMILY

TITLE 9. OFFENSES AGAINST PUBLIC ORDER & DECENCY

TITLE 10. OFFENSES AGAINST PUBLIC HEALTH, SAFETY, & MORALS

TITLE 6. OFFENSES AGAINST THE FAMILY

CHAPTER 25. OFFENSES AGAINST THE FAMILY

PENAL §25.01. BIGAMY

(a) An individual commits an offense if:

(1) he is legally married and he:

(A) purports to marry or does marry a person other than his spouse in this state, or any other state or foreign country, under circumstances that would, but for the actor's prior marriage, constitute a marriage; or

(B) lives with a person other than his spouse in this state under the appearance of being married; or

(2) he knows that a married person other than his spouse is married and he:

(A) purports to marry or does marry that person in this state, or any other state or foreign country, under circumstances that would, but for the person's prior marriage, constitute a marriage; or

(B) lives with that person in this state under the appearance of being married.

(b) For purposes of this section, "under the appearance of being married" means holding out that the parties are married with cohabitation and an intent to be married by either party.

(c) It is a defense to prosecution under Subsection (a)(1) that the actor reasonably believed that his marriage was void or had been dissolved by death, divorce, or annulment.

(d) For the purposes of this section, the lawful wife or husband of the actor may testify both for or against the actor concerning proof of the original marriage.

(e) An offense under this section is a Class A misdemeanor.

History of Penal §25.01: Acts 1973, 63rd Leg., ch. 399, §1, eff. Jan. 1, 1974. Amended by Acts 1993, 73rd Leg., ch. 900, §1.01, eff. Sept. 1, 1994.

PENAL §25.02. PROHIBITED SEXUAL CONDUCT

(a) An individual commits an offense if he engages in sexual intercourse or deviate sexual intercourse with a person he knows to be, without regard to legitimacy:

(1) his ancestor or descendant by blood or adoption;

(2) his stepchild or stepparent, while the marriage creating that relationship exists;

(3) his parent's brother or sister of the whole or half blood;

(4) his brother or sister of the whole or half blood or by adoption; or

(5) the children of his brother or sister of the whole or half blood or by adoption.

(b) For purposes of this section:

(1) "Deviate sexual intercourse" means any contact between the genitals of one person and the mouth or anus of another person with intent to arouse or gratify the sexual desire of any person.

(2) "Sexual intercourse" means any penetration of the female sex organ by the male sex organ.

(c) An offense under this section is a felony of the third degree.

History of Penal §25.02: Acts 1973, 63rd Leg., ch. 399, §1, eff. Jan. 1, 1974. Amended by Acts 1993, 73rd Leg., ch. 900, §1.01, eff. Sept. 1, 1994.

See also *O'Connor's Criminal Codes Plus*, CCP arts. 38.072, 38.37; PenC §3.03.

PENAL §25.03. INTERFERENCE WITH CHILD CUSTODY

Ⓐ (a) A person commits an offense if the person takes or retains a child younger than 18 years when the person:

(1) knows that the person's taking or retention violates the express terms of a judgment or order of a court disposing of the child's custody; or

(2) has not been awarded custody of the child by a court of competent jurisdiction, knows that a suit for divorce or a civil suit or application for habeas corpus to dispose of the child's custody has been filed, and takes the child out of the geographic area of the counties composing the judicial district if the court is a district court or the county if the court is a statutory county court, without the permission of the court and with the intent to deprive the court of authority over the child.

A (b) A noncustodial parent commits an offense if, with the intent to interfere with the lawful custody of a child younger than 18 years, the noncustodial parent knowingly entices or persuades the child to leave the custody of the custodial parent, guardian, or person standing in the stead of the custodial parent or guardian of the child.

(c) It is a defense to prosecution under Subsection (a)(2) that the actor returned the child to the geographic area of the counties composing the judicial district if the court is a district court or the county if the court is a statutory county court, within three days after the date of the commission of the offense.

(d) An offense under this section is a state jail felony.

History of Penal §25.03: Acts 1973, 63rd Leg., ch. 399, §1, eff. Jan. 1, 1974. Amended by Acts 1979, 66th Leg., ch. 527, §1, eff. Aug. 27, 1979; Acts 1987, 70th Leg., ch. 444, §1, eff. Sept. 1, 1987; Acts 1989, 71st Leg., ch. 830, §1, eff. Sept. 1, 1989; Acts 1993, 73rd Leg., ch. 900, §1.01, eff. Sept. 1, 1994; Acts 2001, 77th Leg., ch. 332, §1, eff. May 24, 2001.

PENAL §25.031. AGREEMENT TO ABDUCT FROM CUSTODY

(a) A person commits an offense if the person agrees, for remuneration or the promise of remuneration, to abduct a child younger than 18 years of age by force, threat of force, misrepresentation, stealth, or unlawful entry, knowing that the child is under the care and control of a person having custody or physical possession of the child under a court order or under the care and control of another person who is exercising care and control with the consent of a person having custody or physical possession under a court order.

(b) An offense under this section is a state jail felony.

History of Penal §25.031: Acts 1987, 70th Leg., ch. 444, §3, eff. Sept. 1, 1987. Amended by Acts 1993, 73rd Leg., ch. 900, §1.01, eff. Sept. 1, 1994.

PENAL §25.04. ENTICING A CHILD

(a) A person commits an offense if, with the intent to interfere with the lawful custody of a child younger than 18 years, he knowingly entices, persuades, or takes the child from the custody of the parent or guardian or person standing in the stead of the parent or guardian of such child.

(b) An offense under this section is a Class B misdemeanor, unless it is shown on the trial of the offense that the actor intended to commit a felony against the child, in which event an offense under this section is a felony of the third degree.

History of Penal §25.04: Acts 1973, 63rd Leg., ch. 399, §1, eff. Jan. 1, 1974. Amended by Acts 1999, 76th Leg., ch. 685, §7, eff. Sept. 1, 1999.

PENAL §25.05. CRIMINAL NONSUPPORT

A (a) An individual commits an offense if the individual intentionally or knowingly fails to provide support for the individual's child younger than 18 years of age, or for the individual's child who is the subject of a court order requiring the individual to support the child.

(b) For purposes of this section, "child" includes a child born out of wedlock whose paternity has either been acknowledged by the actor or has been established in a civil suit under the Family Code or the law of another state.

(c) Under this section, a conviction may be had on the uncorroborated testimony of a party to the offense.

A (d) It is an affirmative defense to prosecution under this section that the actor could not provide support for the actor's child.

(e) The pendency of a prosecution under this section does not affect the power of a court to enter an order for child support under the Family Code.

(f) An offense under this section is a state jail felony.

History of Penal §25.05: Acts 1973, 63rd Leg., ch. 399, §1, eff. Jan. 1, 1974. Amended by Acts 1987, 70th Leg., 2nd C.S., ch. 73, §13, eff. Nov. 1, 1987; Acts 1993, 73rd Leg., ch. 900, §1.01, eff. Sept. 1, 1994; Acts 2001, 77th Leg., ch. 375, §1, eff. May 25, 2001.

See also Family Code ch. 157, "Enforcement," ch. 232, "Suspension of License for Failure to Pay Child Support or Comply with Subpoena;" Govt Code §21.002; 42 U.S.C. §651, et seq.

PENAL §25.06. HARBORING RUNAWAY CHILD

(a) A person commits an offense if he knowingly harbors a child and he is criminally negligent about whether the child:

(1) is younger than 18 years; and

(2) has escaped from the custody of a peace officer, a probation officer, the Texas Youth Council, or a detention facility for children, or is voluntarily absent from the child's home without the consent of the child's parent or guardian for a substantial length of time or without the intent to return.

(b) It is a defense to prosecution under this section that the actor was related to the child within the second degree by consanguinity or affinity, as determined under Chapter 573, Government Code.

(c) It is a defense to prosecution under this section that the actor notified:

(1) the person or agency from which the child escaped or a law enforcement agency of the presence of the child within 24 hours after discovering that the child had escaped from custody; or

(2) a law enforcement agency or a person at the child's home of the presence of the child within 24 hours after discovering that the child was voluntarily absent from home without the consent of the child's parent or guardian.

(d) An offense under this section is a Class A misdemeanor.

(e) On the receipt of a report from a peace officer, probation officer, the Texas Youth Council, a foster home, or a detention facility for children that a child has escaped its custody or upon receipt of a report from a parent, guardian, conservator, or legal custodian that a child is missing, a law enforcement agency shall immediately enter a record of the child into the National Crime Information Center.

History of Penal §25.06: Acts 1979, 66th Leg., ch. 558, §1, eff. Sept. 1, 1979. Amended by Acts 1983, 68th Leg., ch. 831, §1, eff. Sept. 1, 1983; Acts 1991, 72nd Leg., ch. 561, §40, eff. Aug. 26, 1991. Renumbered from §25.07 by Acts 1993, 73rd Leg., ch. 900, §1.01, eff. Sept. 1, 1994; Acts 1995, 74th Leg., ch. 76, §5.95(27), eff. Sept. 1, 1995.

PENAL §25.07. VIOLATION OF PROTECTIVE ORDER OR MAGISTRATE'S ORDER

(a) A person commits an offense if, in violation of an order issued under Section 6.504 or Chapter 85, Family Code, under Article 17.292, Code of Criminal Procedure, or by another jurisdiction as provided by Chapter 88, Family Code, the person knowingly or intentionally:

(1) commits family violence or an act in furtherance of an offense under Section 42.072;

(2) communicates:

(A) directly with a protected individual or a member of the family or household in a threatening or harassing manner;

(B) a threat through any person to a protected individual or a member of the family or household; and

(C) in any manner with the protected individual or a member of the family or household except through the person's attorney or a person appointed by the court, if the order prohibits any communication with a protected individual or a member of the family or household;

(3) goes to or near any of the following places as specifically described in the order:

(A) the residence or place of employment or business of a protected individual or a member of the family or household; or

(B) any child care facility, residence, or school where a child protected by the order normally resides or attends; or

E (4) possesses a firearm.

A (b) For the purposes of this section:

(1) "Family violence," "family," "household," and "member of a household" have the meanings assigned by Chapter 71, Family Code.

E (2) "Firearm" has the meaning assigned by Chapter 46.

(c) If conduct constituting an offense under this section also constitutes an offense under another section of this code, the actor may be prosecuted under either section or under both sections.

(d) Reconciliatory actions or agreements made by persons affected by an order do not affect the validity of the order or the duty of a peace officer to enforce this section.

(e) A peace officer investigating conduct that may constitute an offense under this section for a violation of an order may not arrest a person protected by that order for a violation of that order.

(f) It is not a defense to prosecution under this section that certain information has been excluded, as provided by Section 85.007, Family Code, or Article 17.292, Code of Criminal Procedure, from an order to which this section applies.

(g) An offense under this section is a Class A misdemeanor unless it is shown on the trial of the offense that the defendant has previously been convicted under this section two or more times or has violated the protective order by committing an assault or the offense of stalking, in which event the offense is a third degree felony.

History of Penal §25.07: Acts 1983, 68th Leg., p. 4049, ch. 631, §3, eff. Sept. 1, 1983. Amended by Acts 1985, 69th Leg., ch. 583, §3, eff. Sept. 1, 1985; Acts 1987, 70th Leg., ch. 170, §1 (eff. Sept. 1, 1987), ch. 677, §8 (eff. Sept. 1, 1987); Acts 1989, 71st Leg., ch. 614, §§23 to 26 (eff. Sept. 1, 1989), ch. 739, §§4 to 7 (eff. Sept. 1, 1989); Acts 1991, 72nd Leg., ch. 366, §2, eff. Sept. 1, 1991. Renumbered from §25.08 and amended by Acts 1993, 73rd Leg., ch. 900, §1.01, eff. Sept. 1, 1994. Amended by Acts 1995, 74th Leg., ch. 658, §§2, 3 (eff. June 14, 1995), ch. 660, §§1, 2 (eff. Sept. 1, 1995), ch. 1024, §23 (eff. Sept. 1, 1995); Acts 1997, 75th Leg., ch. 1, §2 (eff. Jan. 28, 1997), ch. 1193, §21 (eff. Sept. 1, 1997); Acts 1999, 76th Leg., ch. 62, §15.02(e), eff. Sept. 1, 1999; Acts 2001, 77th Leg., ch. 23, §1, eff. Sept. 1, 2001.

Section 25.071 omitted by editor

PENAL §25.08. SALE OR PURCHASE OF CHILD

(a) A person commits an offense if he:

(1) possesses a child younger than 18 years of age or has the custody, conservatorship, or guardianship of a child younger than 18 years of age, whether or not he has actual possession of the child, and he offers to accept, agrees to accept, or accepts a thing of value for the delivery of the child to another or for the possession of the child by another for purposes of adoption; or

(2) offers to give, agrees to give, or gives a thing of value to another for acquiring or maintaining the possession of a child for the purpose of adoption.

A *Subsection (b) below is effective for convictions under §25.08 becoming final on or after Sept. 1, 2001.*

(b) It is an exception to the application of this section that the thing of value is:

(1) a fee or reimbursement paid to a child-placing agency as authorized by law;

(2) a fee paid to an attorney, social worker, mental health professional, or physician for services rendered in the usual course of legal or medical practice or in providing adoption counseling;

(3) a reimbursement of legal or medical expenses incurred by a person for the benefit of the child; or

E (4) a necessary pregnancy-related expense paid by a child-placing agency for the benefit of the child's parent during the pregnancy or after the birth of the child as permitted by the minimum standards for child-placing agencies and Department of Protective and Regulatory Services rules.

Subsection (b) below is effective for convictions under §25.08 becoming final before Sept. 1, 2001.

(b) It is an exception to the application of this section that the thing of value is:

(1) a fee paid to a child-placing agency as authorized by law;

(2) a fee paid to an attorney or physician for services rendered in the usual course of legal or medical practice; or

(3) a reimbursement of legal or medical expenses incurred by a person for the benefit of the child.

(c) An offense under this section is a felony of the third degree.

History of Penal §25.08: Acts 1977, 65th Leg., ch. 38, §1, eff. March 30, 1977. Amended by Acts 1981, 67th Leg., ch. 514, §1, eff. Sept. 1, 1981. Renumbered from §25.06 by Acts 1987, 70th Leg., ch. 167, §5.01(a)(44). Renumbered from §25.11 and amended by Acts 1993, 73rd Leg., ch. 900, §1.01, eff. Sept. 1, 1994. Amended by Acts 2001, 77th Leg., ch. 134, §1, eff. Sept. 1, 2001.

PENAL §25.09. ADVERTISING FOR PLACEMENT OF CHILD

(a) A person commits an offense if the person advertises in the public media that the person will place a child for adoption or will provide or obtain a child for adoption.

(b) This section does not apply to a licensed child-placing agency that is identified in the advertisement as a licensed child-placing agency.

(c) An offense under this section is a Class A misdemeanor unless the person has been convicted previously under this section, in which event the offense is a felony of the third degree.

(d) In this section:

(1) "Child" has the meaning assigned by Section 101.003, Family Code.

(2) "Public media" has the meaning assigned by Section 38.01. The term also includes communications through the use of the Internet or another public computer network.

History of Penal §25.09: Acts 1997, 75th Leg., ch. 561, §31, eff. Sept. 1, 1997.

TITLE 9. OFFENSES AGAINST PUBLIC ORDER & DECENCY

CHAPTER 42. DISORDERLY CONDUCT & RELATED OFFENSES

PENAL §42.07. HARASSMENT

A *Section 42.07 below is effective for offenses committed on or after Sept. 1, 2001.*

(a) A person commits an offense if, with intent to harass, annoy, alarm, abuse, torment, or embarrass another, he:

(1) initiates communication by telephone, in writing, or by electronic communication and in the course of

the communication makes a comment, request, suggestion, or proposal that is obscene;

(2) threatens, by telephone, in writing, or by electronic communication, in a manner reasonably likely to alarm the person receiving the threat, to inflict bodily injury on the person or to commit a felony against the person, a member of his family or household, or his property;

(3) conveys, in a manner reasonably likely to alarm the person receiving the report, a false report, which is known by the conveyor to be false, that another person has suffered death or serious bodily injury;

(4) causes the telephone of another to ring repeatedly or makes repeated telephone communications anonymously or in a manner reasonably likely to harass, annoy, alarm, abuse, torment, embarrass, or offend another;

(5) makes a telephone call and intentionally fails to hang up or disengage the connection;

(6) knowingly permits a telephone under the person's control to be used by another to commit an offense under this section; or

E (7) sends repeated electronic communications in a manner reasonably likely to harass, annoy, alarm, abuse, torment, embarrass, or offend another.

(b) In this section:

E (1) "Electronic communication" means a transfer of signs, signals, writing, images, sounds, data, or intelligence of any nature transmitted in whole or in part by a wire, radio, electromagnetic, photoelectronic, or photo-optical system. The term includes:

(A) a communication initiated by electronic mail, instant message, network call, or facsimile machine; and

(B) a communication made to a pager.

E (2) "Family" and "household" have the meaning assigned by Chapter 71, Family Code.

(3) "Obscene" means containing a patently offensive description of or a solicitation to commit an ultimate sex act, including sexual intercourse, masturbation, cunnilingus, fellatio, or anilingus, or a description of an excretory function.

(c) An offense under this section is a Class B misdemeanor, except that the offense is a Class A misdemeanor if the actor has previously been convicted under this section.

History of Penal §42.07: Acts 1973, 63rd Leg., ch. 399, §1, eff. Jan. 1, 1974. Amended by Acts 1983, 68th Leg., p. 2204, ch. 411, §1, eff. Sept. 1, 1983; Acts 1993, 73rd Leg., ch. 10, §1 (eff. March 19, 1993), ch. 900, §1.01 (eff. Sept. 1, 1994); Acts 1995, 74th Leg., ch. 657, §1, eff. June 14, 1995; Acts 1999, 76th Leg., ch. 62, §15.02(d), eff. Sept. 1, 1999; Acts 2001, 77th Leg., ch. 1222, §1, eff. Sept. 1, 2001.

PENAL §42.07. HARASSMENT

Section 42.07 below is effective for offenses in which any element of the offense was committed before Sept. 1, 2001.

(a) A person commits an offense if, with intent to harass, annoy, alarm, abuse, torment, or embarrass another, he:

(1) initiates communication by telephone or in writing and in the course of the communication makes a comment, request, suggestion, or proposal that is obscene;

(2) threatens, by telephone or in writing, in a manner reasonably likely to alarm the person receiving the threat, to inflict bodily injury on the person or to commit a felony against the person, a member of his family, or his property;

(3) conveys, in a manner reasonably likely to alarm the person receiving the report, a false report, which is known by the conveyor to be false, that another person has suffered death or serious bodily injury;

(4) causes the telephone of another to ring repeatedly or makes repeated telephone communications anonymously or in a manner reasonably likely to harass, annoy, alarm, abuse, torment, embarrass, or offend another;

(5) makes a telephone call and intentionally fails to hang up or disengage the connection; or

(6) knowingly permits a telephone under his control to be used by a person to commit an offense under this section.

(b) For purposes of Subsection (a)(1), "obscene" means containing a patently offensive description of or a solicitation to commit an ultimate sex act, including sexual intercourse, masturbation, cunnilingus, fellatio, or anilingus, or a description of an excretory function. In this section, "family" has the meaning assigned by Section 71.003, Family Code.

(c) An offense under this section is a Class B misdemeanor.

PENAL §42.072. STALKING

(a) A person commits an offense if the person, on more than one occasion and pursuant to the same scheme or course of conduct that is directed specifically at another person, knowingly engages in conduct, including following the other person, that:

(1) the actor knows or reasonably believes the other person will regard as threatening:

(A) bodily injury or death for the other person;

(B) bodily injury or death for a member of the other person's family or household; or

(C) that an offense will be committed against the other person's property;

(2) causes the other person or a member of the other person's family or household to be placed in fear of bodily injury or death or fear that an offense will be committed against the other person's property; and

(3) would cause a reasonable person to fear:

(A) bodily injury or death for himself or herself;

(B) bodily injury or death for a member of the person's family or household; or

(C) that an offense will be committed against the person's property.

A *Subsection (b) below is effective for offenses committed on or after Sept. 1, 2001.*

(b) An offense under this section is a felony of the third degree, except that the offense is a felony of the second degree if the actor has previously been convicted under this section.

Subsection (b) below is effective for offenses in which any element of the offense was committed before Sept. 1, 2001.

(b) An offense under this section is a Class A misdemeanor, except that the offense is a felony of the third degree if the actor has previously been convicted under this section.

(c) In this section, "family," "household," and "member of a household" have the meanings assigned by Chapter 71, Family Code.

History of Penal §42.072: Acts 1997, 75th Leg., ch. 1, §1, eff. Jan. 28, 1997. Amended by Acts 1999, 76th Leg., ch. 62, §15.02(e), eff. Sept. 1, 1999; Acts 2001, 77th Leg., ch. 1222, §2, eff. Sept. 1, 2001.

TITLE 10. OFFENSES AGAINST PUBLIC HEALTH, SAFETY, & MORALS

CHAPTER 46. WEAPONS

A §46.04. UNLAWFUL POSSESSION OF FIREARM

(a) A person who has been convicted of a felony commits an offense if he possesses a firearm:

(1) after conviction and before the fifth anniversary of the person's release from confinement following conviction of the felony or the person's release from supervision under community supervision, parole, or mandatory supervision, whichever date is later; or

(2) after the period described by Subdivision (1), at any location other than the premises at which the person lives.

E (b) A person who has been convicted of an offense under Section 22.01, punishable as a Class A misdemeanor and involving a member of the person's family or household, commits an offense if the person possesses a firearm before the fifth anniversary of the later of:

(1) the date of the person's release from confinement following conviction of the misdemeanor; or

(2) the date of the person's release from community supervision following conviction of the misdemeanor.

E (c) A person, other than a peace officer, as defined by Section 1.07, actively engaged in employment as a sworn, full-time paid employee of a state agency or political subdivision, who is subject to an order issued under Section 6.504 or Chapter 85, Family Code, under Article 17.292, Code of Criminal Procedure, or by another jurisdiction as provided by Chapter 88, Family Code, commits an offense if the person possesses a firearm after receiving notice of the order and before expiration of the order.

E (d) In this section, "family," "household," and "member of a household" have the meanings assigned by Chapter 71, Family Code.

A (e) An offense under Subsection (a) is a felony of the third degree. An offense under Subsection (b) or (c) is a Class A misdemeanor.

History of Penal Code §46.04: Acts 1973, 63rd Leg., ch. 399, §1, eff. Jan. 1, 1974. Renumbered from §46.05 and amended by Acts 1993, 73rd Leg., ch. 900, §1.01, eff. Sept. 1, 1994. Amended by Acts 2001, 77th Leg., ch. 23, §2, eff. Sept. 1, 2001.

For the complete Code of Criminal Procedure annotated, see ***O'Connor's Criminal Codes Plus*** (2002-2003). To order, call 1-800-OCONNOR (1-800-626-6667) or visit <http://www.jonesmcclure.com/>.

CHAPTER 5. FAMILY VIOLENCE PREVENTION

ART. 5.01. LEGISLATIVE STATEMENT

(a) Family violence is a serious danger and threat to society and its members. Victims of family violence are entitled to the maximum protection from harm or abuse or the threat of harm or abuse as is permitted by law.

(b) In any law enforcement, prosecutorial, or judicial response to allegations of family violence, the responding law enforcement or judicial officers shall protect the victim, without regard to the relationship between the alleged offender and victim.

History of Art. 5.01: Acts 1985, 69th Leg., ch. 583, §1, eff. Sept. 1, 1985.

ART. 5.02. DEFINITIONS

In this chapter, "family violence," "family," "household," and "member of a household" have the meanings assigned by Section 71.01, Family Code.

History of Art. 5.02: Acts 1985, 69th Leg., ch. 583, §1, eff. Sept. 1, 1985.

ART. 5.03. FAMILY OR HOUSEHOLD RELATIONSHIP DOES NOT CREATE AN EXCEPTION TO OFFICIAL DUTIES

A general duty prescribed for an officer by Chapter 2 of this code is not waived or excepted in any family violence case or investigation because of a family or household relationship between an alleged violator and the victim of family violence. A peace officer's or a magistrate's duty to prevent the commission of criminal offenses, including acts of family violence, is not waived or excepted because of a family or household relationship between the potential violator and victim.

History of Art. 5.03: Acts 1985, 69th Leg., ch. 583, §1, eff. Sept. 1, 1985.

ART. 5.04. DUTIES OF PEACE OFFICERS

(a) The primary duties of a peace officer who investigates a family violence allegation or who responds to a disturbance call that may involve family violence are to protect any potential victim of family violence, enforce the law of this state, enforce a protective order from another jurisdiction as provided by Chapter 88, Family Code, and make lawful arrests of violators.

(b) A peace officer who investigates a family violence allegation or who responds to a disturbance call that may involve family violence shall advise any possible adult victim of all reasonable means to prevent further family violence, including giving written notice of a victim's legal rights and remedies and of the availability of shelter or other community services for family violence victims.

(c) A written notice required by Subsection (b) of this article is sufficient if it is in substantially the following form with the required information in English and in Spanish inserted in the notice:

"NOTICE TO ADULT VICTIMS OF FAMILY VIOLENCE

"It is a crime for any person to cause you any physical injury or harm EVEN IF THAT PERSON IS A MEMBER OR FORMER MEMBER OF YOUR FAMILY OR HOUSEHOLD.

"Please tell the investigating peace officer:

"IF you, your child, or any other household resident has been injured; or

"IF you feel you are going to be in danger when the officer leaves or later.

"You have the right to:

"ASK the local prosecutor to file a criminal complaint against the person committing family violence; and

"APPLY to a court for an order to protect you (you should consult a legal aid office, a prosecuting attorney, or a private attorney). If a family or household member assaults you and is arrested, you may request that a magistrate's order for emergency protection be issued. Please inform the investigating officer if you want an order for emergency protection. You need not be present when the order is issued. You cannot be charged a fee by a court in connection with filing, serving, or entering a protective order. For example, the court can enter an order that:

"(1) the abuser not commit further acts of violence;

"(2) the abuser not threaten, harass, or contact you at home;

"(3) directs the abuser to leave your household; and

"(4) establishes temporary custody of the children and directs the abuser not to interfere with the children or any property.

"A VIOLATION OF CERTAIN PROVISIONS OF COURT-ORDERED PROTECTION (such as (1) and (2) above) MAY BE A FELONY.

"CALL THE FOLLOWING VIOLENCE SHELTERS OR SOCIAL ORGANIZATIONS IF YOU NEED PROTECTION:

"____________________

"____________________."

History of Art. 5.04: Acts 1985, 69th Leg., ch. 583, §1, eff. Sept. 1, 1985. Amended by Acts 1991, 72nd Leg., ch. 366, §4, eff. Sept. 1, 1991; Acts 1995, 74th Leg., ch. 1024, §24, eff. Sept. 1, 1995; Acts 1997, 75th Leg., ch. 610, §2 (eff. Sept. 1, 1997), ch. 1193, §23 (eff. Sept. 1, 1997).

ART. 5.045. STANDBY ASSISTANCE; LIABILITY

(a) In the discretion of a peace officer, the officer may stay with a victim of family violence to protect the victim and allow the victim to take the personal property of the victim or of a child in the care of the victim to a place of safety in an orderly manner.

(b) A peace officer who provides assistance under Subsection (a) of this article is not:

(1) civilly liable for an act or omission of the officer that arises in connection with providing the assistance or determining whether to provide the assistance; or

(2) civilly or criminally liable for the wrongful appropriation of any personal property by the victim.

History of Art. 5.045: Acts 1995, 74th Leg., ch. 565, §1, eff. June 14, 1995.

ART. 5.05. REPORTS & RECORDS

(a) A peace officer who investigates a family violence incident or who responds to a disturbance call that may involve family violence shall make a written report, including but not limited to:

(1) the names of the suspect and complainant;

(2) the date, time, and location of the incident;

(3) any visible or reported injuries; and

(4) a description of the incident and a statement of its disposition.

(b) Each local law enforcement agency shall establish a departmental code for identifying and retrieving family violence reports as outlined in Subsection (a) of this section. A district or county attorney or an assistant district or county attorney exercising authority in the county where the law enforcement agency maintains records under this section is entitled to access to the records.

(c) In order to ensure that officers responding to calls are aware of the existence and terms of protective orders, each municipal police department and sheriff shall establish procedures within the department or office to provide adequate information or access to information for law enforcement officers of the names of persons protected by a protective order and of persons to whom protective orders are directed.

(d) Each law enforcement officer shall accept a certified copy of an original or modified protective order as proof of the validity of the order and it is presumed the order remains valid unless:

(1) the order contains a termination date that has passed;

(2) it is more than one year after the date the order was issued; or

(3) the law enforcement officer has been notified by the clerk of the court vacating the order that the order has been vacated.

(e) A peace officer who makes a report under Subsection (a) of this article shall provide information concerning the incident or disturbance to the bureau of identification and records of the Department of Public Safety for its recordkeeping function under Section 411.042, Government Code. The bureau shall prescribe the form and nature of the information required to be reported to the bureau by this article.

History of Art. 5.05: Acts 1985, 69th Leg., ch. 583, §1, eff. Sept. 1, 1985. Amended by Acts 1989, 71st Leg., ch. 614, §27 (eff. Sept. 1, 1989), ch. 739, §8 (eff. Sept. 1, 1989); Acts 1993, 73rd Leg., ch. 900, §8.01, eff. Sept. 1, 1993.

ART. 5.06. DUTIES OF PROSECUTING ATTORNEYS & COURTS

(a) Neither a prosecuting attorney nor a court may:

(1) dismiss or delay any criminal proceeding that involves a prosecution for an offense that constitutes

family violence because a civil proceeding is pending or not pending; or

(2) require proof that a complaining witness, victim, or defendant is a party to a suit for the dissolution of a marriage or a suit affecting the parent-child relationship before presenting a criminal allegation to a grand jury, filing an information, or otherwise proceeding with the prosecution of a criminal case.

(b) A prosecuting attorney's decision to file an application for a protective order under Chapter 71, Family Code, should be made without regard to whether a criminal complaint has been filed by the applicant. A prosecuting attorney may require the applicant to provide information for an offense report, relating to the facts alleged in the application, with a local law enforcement agency.

(c) The prosecuting attorney having responsibility under Section 71.04(c), Family Code, for filing applications for protective orders under Chapter 71, Family Code, shall provide notice of that responsibility* to all law enforcement agencies within the jurisdiction of the prosecuting attorney for the prosecuting attorney.

History of Art. 5.06: Acts 1985, 69th Leg., ch. 583, §1, eff. Sept. 1, 1985. Amended by Acts 1989, 71st Leg., ch. 614, §28 (eff. Sept. 1, 1989), ch. 739, §9 (eff. Sept. 1, 1989); Acts 1995, 74th Leg., ch. 564, §2 (eff. Sept. 1, 1995), ch. 1024, §25 (eff. Sept. 1, 1995).

* Enacted as "those responsibilities" by Acts 1995, ch. 1024, §25, eff. Sept. 1, 1995.

ART. 5.07. VENUE FOR PROTECTIVE ORDER OFFENSES

The venue for an offense under Section 25.07, Penal Code, is in the county in which the order was issued or, without regard to the identity or location of the court that issued the protective order, in the county in which the offense was committed.

History of Art. 5.07: Acts 1989, 71st Leg., ch. 614, §29 (eff. Sept. 1, 1989), ch. 739, §10 (eff. Sept. 1, 1989). Amended by Acts 1995, 74th Leg., ch. 76, §14.16, eff. Sept. 1, 1995.

ART. 5.08. MEDIATION IN FAMILY VIOLENCE CASES

Notwithstanding Article 26.13(g) or Section 11(a)(16), Article 42.12, of this code, in a criminal prosecution arising from family violence, as that term is defined by Section 71.004, Family Code, a court shall not refer or order the victim or the defendant involved to mediation, dispute resolution, arbitration, or other similar procedures.

History of Art. 5.08: Acts 1999, 76th Leg., ch. 389, §1, eff. Aug. 30, 1999.

CHAPTER 14. ARREST WITHOUT WARRANT

ART. 14.03. AUTHORITY OF PEACE OFFICERS

(a) Any peace officer may arrest, without warrant:

(1) persons found in suspicious places and under circumstances which reasonably show that such persons have been guilty of some felony, violation of Title 9, Chapter 42, Penal Code, breach of the peace, or offense under Section 49.02, Penal Code, or threaten, or are about to commit some offense against the laws;

(2) persons who the peace officer has probable cause to believe have committed an assault resulting in bodily injury to another person and the peace officer has probable cause to believe that there is danger of further bodily injury to that person;

(3) persons who the peace officer has probable cause to believe have committed the offense defined by Section 25.07, Penal Code (violation of Protective Order), if the offense is not committed in the presence of the peace officer; or

(4) persons who the peace officer has probable cause to believe have committed an assault resulting in bodily injury to a member of the person's family or household.

(b) A peace officer shall arrest, without a warrant, a person the peace officer has probable cause to believe has committed an offense under Section 25.07, Penal Code (violation of Protective Order), if the offense is committed in the presence of the peace officer.

(c) If reasonably necessary to verify an allegation of a violation of a protective order or of the commission of an assault against a member of the family or household, a peace officer shall remain at the scene of the investigation to verify the allegation and to prevent the further commission of family violence.

(d) A peace officer who is outside his jurisdiction may arrest, without warrant, a person who commits an offense within the officer's presence or view, if the offense is a felony, a violation of Title 9, Chapter 42, Penal Code, a breach of the peace, or an offense under Section 49.02, Penal Code. A peace officer making an arrest under this subsection shall, as soon as practicable after making the arrest, notify a law enforcement agency having jurisdiction where the arrest was made. The law enforcement agency shall then take custody of the person committing the offense and take the person before a magistrate in compliance with Article 14.06 of this code.

(e) The justification for conduct provided under Section 9.21, Penal Code, applies to a peace officer when the peace officer is performing a duty required by this article.

(f) In this article, "family," "household," and "member of a household" have the meanings assigned to those terms by Section 71.01, Family Code.

(g) A peace officer listed in Subdivision (1), (2), (3), (4), or (5), Article 2.12, who is licensed under Chapter 415, Government Code, and is outside of the officer's jurisdiction may arrest without a warrant a person who commits any offense within the officer's presence or view, except that an officer who is outside the officer's jurisdiction may arrest a person for a violation of Subtitle C, Title 7, Transportation Code, only if the officer is listed in Subdivision (4), Article 2.12. A peace officer making an arrest under this subsection shall as soon as practicable after making the arrest notify a law enforcement agency having jurisdiction where the arrest was made. The law enforcement agency shall then take custody of the person committing the offense and take the person before a magistrate in compliance with Article 14.06.

History of Art. 14.03: Acts 1965, 59th Leg., vol. 2, ch. 722. Amended by Acts 1967, 60th Leg., ch. 659, §9, eff. Aug. 28, 1967; Acts 1981, 67th Leg., ch. 442, §1, eff. Aug. 31, 1981; Acts 1985, 69th Leg., ch. 583, §2, eff. Sept. 1, 1985; Acts 1987, 70th Leg., ch. 68, §1, eff. Sept. 1, 1987; Acts 1989, 71st Leg., ch. 740, §1, eff. Aug. 28, 1989; Acts 1991, 72nd Leg., ch. 542, §9, eff. Sept. 1, 1991; Acts 1993, 73rd Leg., ch. 900, §3.02, eff. Sept. 1, 1994; Acts 1995, 74th Leg., ch. 76, §14.17 (eff. Sept. 1, 1995), ch. 829, §1 (eff. Aug. 28, 1995); Acts 1999, 76th Leg., ch. 210, §2 (eff. May 24, 1999), ch. 62, §3.02 (eff. Sept. 1, 1999).

CHAPTER 17. ACCUSED LIBERATED

ART. 17.29. ACCUSED LIBERATED

(a) When the accused has given the required bond, either to the magistrate or the officer having him in custody, he shall at once be set at liberty.

(b) Before releasing on bail a person arrested for an offense under Section 42.072, Penal Code, or a person arrested or held without warrant in the prevention of family violence, the law enforcement agency holding the person shall make a reasonable attempt to give personal notice of the imminent release to the victim of the alleged offense or to another person designated by the victim to receive the notice. An attempt by an agency to give notice to the victim or the person designated by the victim at the victim's or person's last known telephone number or address, as shown on the records of the agency, constitutes a reasonable attempt to give notice under this subsection. If possible, the arresting officer shall collect the address and telephone number of the victim at the time the arrest is made and shall communicate that information to the agency holding the person.

(c) A law enforcement agency or an employee of a law enforcement agency is not liable for damages arising from complying or failing to comply with Subsection (b) of this article.

(d) In this article, "family violence" has the meaning assigned by Section 71.01, Family Code.

History of Art. 17.29: Acts 1965, 59th Leg., vol. 2, ch. 722. Amended by Acts 1995, 74th Leg., ch. 656, §1 (eff. June 14, 1995), ch. 661, §1 (eff. Aug. 28, 1995); Acts 1997, 75th Leg., ch. 1, §3, eff. Jan. 28, 1997.

ART. 17.291. FURTHER DETENTION OF CERTAIN PERSONS

(a) In this article:

(1) "family violence" has the meaning assigned to that phrase by Section 71.01(b)(2), Family Code; and

(2) "magistrate" has the meaning assigned to it by Article 2.09 of this code, as amended by Chapters 25, 79, 916, and 1068, Acts of the 71st Legislature, Regular Session, 1989.

(b) Article 17.29 does not apply when a person has been arrested or held without a warrant in the prevention of family violence if there is probable cause to believe the violence will continue if the person is immediately released. The head of the agency arresting or holding such a person may hold the person for a period of not more than four hours after bond has been posted. This detention period may be extended for an additional period not to exceed 48 hours, but only if authorized in a writing directed to the person having custody of the detained person by a magistrate who concludes that:

(1) the violence would continue if the person is released; and

(2) if the additional period exceeds 24 hours, probable cause exists to believe that the person committed the instant offense and that, during the 10-year period preceding the date of the instant offense, the person has been arrested:

(A) on more than one occasion for an offense involving family violence; or

(B) for any other offense, if a deadly weapon, as defined by Section 1.07, Penal Code, was used or exhibited during commission of the offense or during immediate flight after commission of the offense.

History of Art. 17.291: Acts 1991, 72nd Leg., ch. 552, §2, eff. June 16, 1991. Amended by Acts 1999, 76th Leg., ch. 1341, §1, eff. Sept. 1, 1999.

ART. 17.292. MAGISTRATE'S ORDER FOR EMERGENCY PROTECTION

(a) At a defendant's appearance before a magistrate after arrest for an offense involving family violence or an offense under Section 42.072, Penal Code, the magistrate may issue an order for emergency protection on the magistrate's own motion or on the request of:

(1) the victim of the offense;

(2) the guardian of the victim;

(3) a peace officer; or

(4) the attorney representing the state.

(b) At a defendant's appearance before a magistrate after arrest for an offense involving family violence, the magistrate shall issue an order for emergency protection if the arrest is for an offense that also involves:

(1) serious bodily injury to the victim; or

(2) the use or exhibition of a deadly weapon during the commission of an assault.

(c) The magistrate in the order for emergency protection may prohibit the arrested party from:

(1) committing:

(A) family violence or an assault on the person protected under the order; or

(B) an act in furtherance of an offense under Section 42.072, Penal Code;

(2) communicating:

(A) directly with a member of the family or household or with the person protected under the order in a threatening or harassing manner; or

(B) a threat through any person to a member of the family or household or to the person protected under the order;

(3) going to or near:

(A) the residence, place of employment, or business of a member of the family or household or of the person protected under the order; or

(B) the residence, child care facility, or school where a child protected under the order resides or attends; or

E (4) possessing a firearm, unless the person is a peace officer, as defined by Section 1.07, Penal Code, actively engaged in employment as a sworn, full-time paid employee of a state agency or political subdivision.

(d) The victim of the offense need not be present in court when the order for emergency protection is issued.

(e) In the order for emergency protection the magistrate shall specifically describe the prohibited locations and the minimum distances, if any, that the party must maintain, unless the magistrate determines for the safety of the person or persons protected by the order that specific descriptions of the locations should be omitted.

(f) To the extent that a condition imposed by an order for emergency protection issued under this article conflicts with an existing court order granting possession of or access to a child, the condition imposed under this article prevails for the duration of the order for emergency protection.

A (g) An order for emergency protection issued under this article must contain the following statements printed in bold-face type or in capital letters:

"A VIOLATION OF THIS ORDER BY COMMISSION OF AN ACT PROHIBITED BY THE ORDER MAY BE PUNISHABLE BY A FINE OF AS MUCH AS $4,000 OR BY CONFINEMENT IN JAIL FOR AS LONG AS ONE YEAR OR BY BOTH. AN ACT THAT RESULTS IN FAMILY VIOLENCE OR A STALKING OFFENSE MAY BE PROSECUTED AS A SEPARATE MISDEMEANOR OR FELONY OFFENSE. IF THE ACT IS PROSECUTED AS A SEPARATE FELONY OFFENSE, IT IS PUNISHABLE BY CONFINEMENT IN PRISON FOR AT LEAST TWO YEARS. THE POSSESSION OF A FIREARM BY A PERSON, OTHER THAN A PEACE OFFICER, AS DEFINED BY SECTION 1.07, PENAL CODE, ACTIVELY ENGAGED IN EMPLOYMENT AS A SWORN, FULL-TIME PAID EMPLOYEE OF A STATE AGENCY OR POLITICAL SUBDIVISION, WHO IS SUBJECT TO THIS ORDER MAY BE PROSECUTED AS A SEPARATE OFFENSE PUNISHABLE BY CONFINEMENT OR IMPRISONMENT.

"NO PERSON, INCLUDING A PERSON WHO IS PROTECTED BY THIS ORDER, MAY GIVE PERMISSION TO ANYONE TO IGNORE OR VIOLATE ANY PROVISION OF THIS ORDER. DURING THE TIME IN WHICH THIS ORDER IS VALID, EVERY PROVISION OF THIS ORDER IS IN FULL FORCE AND EFFECT UNLESS A COURT CHANGES THE ORDER."

(h) The magistrate issuing an order for emergency protection under this article shall send a copy of the order to the chief of police in the municipality where the member of the family or household or individual protected by the order resides, if the person resides in a municipality, or to the sheriff of the county where the person resides, if the person does not reside in a municipality. If the victim of the offense is not present when the order is issued, the magistrate issuing the order shall order an appropriate peace officer to make a good faith effort to notify, within 24 hours, the victim that the order has been issued by calling the victim's residence and place of employment. The clerk of the court shall send a copy of the order to the victim.

(i) If an order for emergency protection issued under this article prohibits a person from going to or near a child care facility or school, the magistrate shall send a copy of the order to the child care facility or school.

(j) An order for emergency protection issued under this article is effective on issuance, and the defendant shall be served a copy of the order in open court. An order for emergency protection issued under this article remains in effect up to the 61st day but not less than 31 days after the date of issuance.

(k) To ensure that an officer responding to a call is aware of the existence and terms of an order for emergency protection issued under this article, each municipal police department and sheriff shall establish a procedure within the department or office to provide adequate information or access to information for peace officers of the names of persons protected by an order for emergency protection issued under this article and of persons to whom the order is directed. The police department or sheriff may enter an order for emergency protection issued under this article in the department's or office's record of outstanding warrants as notice that the order has been issued and is in effect.

(*l*) In the order for emergency protection, the magistrate may suspend a license to carry a concealed handgun issued under Section 411.177, Government Code, that is held by the defendant.

A (m) In this article:

(1) "Family," "family violence," and "household" have the meanings assigned by Chapter 71, Family Code.

E (2) "Firearm" has the meaning assigned by Chapter 46, Penal Code.

History of Art. 17.292: Acts 1995, 74th Leg., ch. 658, §1, eff. June 14, 1995. Amended by Acts 1997, 75th Leg., ch. 610, §1 (eff. Sept. 1, 1997), ch. 1, §4 (eff. Jan. 28, 1997); Acts 1999, 76th Leg., ch. 1412, §1, (eff. Sept. 1, 1999), ch. 514, §1, (eff. Sept. 1, 1999); Acts 2001, 77th Leg., ch. 23, §4, eff. Sept. 1, 2001.

Art. 17.293. Delivery of Order for Emergency Protection to Other Persons

The magistrate or the clerk of the magistrate's court issuing an order for emergency protection under Article 17.292 that suspends a license to carry a concealed handgun shall immediately send a copy of the order to the appropriate division of the Department of Public Safety at its Austin headquarters. On receipt of the order suspending the license, the department shall:

(1) record the suspension of the license in the records of the department;

(2) report the suspension to local law enforcement agencies, as appropriate; and

(3) demand surrender of the suspended license from the license holder.

History of Art. 17.293: Acts 1999, 76th Leg., ch. 1412, §1, eff. Sept. 1, 1999.

Chapter 42. Judgment & Sentence

Art. 42.23. Notification of Court of Family Violence Conviction

E *Article 42.23 below is effective for actions to modify orders in SAPCRs pending on or filed on or after Sept. 1, 2001.*

(a) In this article, "family violence" has the meaning assigned by Section 71.004, Family Code.

(b) If the attorney representing the state in a criminal case involving family violence learns that the defendant is subject to the jurisdiction of another court relating to an order that provides for the appointment of a conservator or that sets the terms and conditions of conservatorship or for possession of or access to a child, the attorney representing the state shall notify the court in which the defendant is being tried of the existence of the order and the identity of the court of continuing jurisdiction.

(c) On the conviction or entry of an order deferring adjudication of a defendant for an offense involving family violence, the convicting court or the court entering the order shall notify the court of continuing jurisdiction of the conviction or deferred adjudication.

History of Art. 42.23: Acts 2001, 77th Leg., ch. 1289, §11, eff. Sept. 1, 2001.

TITLE 7. MENTAL HEALTH & MENTAL RETARDATION

Subtitle E. Special Provisions Relating to Mental Illness & Mental Retardation

Chapter 611. Mental Health Records

TITLE 7. MENTAL HEALTH & MENTAL RETARDATION

SUBTITLE E. SPECIAL PROVISIONS RELATING TO MENTAL ILLNESS & MENTAL RETARDATION

CHAPTER 611. MENTAL HEALTH RECORDS

H&S §611.001. DEFINITIONS

In this chapter:

(1) "Patient" means a person who consults or is interviewed by a professional for diagnosis, evaluation, or treatment of any mental or emotional condition or disorder, including alcoholism or drug addiction.

(2) "Professional" means:

(A) a person authorized to practice medicine in any state or nation;

(B) a person licensed or certified by this state to diagnose, evaluate, or treat any mental or emotional condition or disorder; or

(C) a person the patient reasonably believes is authorized, licensed, or certified as provided by this subsection.

History of H&SC §611.001: Acts 1991, 72nd Leg., ch. 76, §1, eff. Sept. 1, 1991.

H&S §611.002. CONFIDENTIALITY OF INFORMATION & PROHIBITION AGAINST DISCLOSURE

(a) Communications between a patient and a professional, and records of the identity, diagnosis, evaluation, or treatment of a patient that are created or maintained by a professional, are confidential.

(b) Confidential communications or records may not be disclosed except as provided by Section 611.004 or 611.0045.

(c) This section applies regardless of when the patient received services from a professional.

History of H&SC §611.002: Acts 1991, 72nd Leg., ch. 76, §1, eff. Sept. 1, 1991. Amended by Acts 1993, 73rd Leg., ch. 903, §1.11, eff. Aug. 30, 1993.

H&S §611.003. PERSONS WHO MAY CLAIM PRIVILEGE OF CONFIDENTIALITY

(a) The privilege of confidentiality may be claimed by:

(1) the patient;

(2) a person listed in Section 611.004(a)(4) or (a)(5) who is acting on the patient's behalf; or

(3) the professional, but only on behalf of the patient.

(b) The authority of a professional to claim the privilege of confidentiality on behalf of the patient is presumed in the absence of evidence to the contrary.

History of H&SC §611.003: Acts 1991, 72nd Leg., ch. 76, §1, eff. Sept. 1, 1991.

H&S §611.004. AUTHORIZED DISCLOSURE OF CONFIDENTIAL INFORMATION OTHER THAN IN JUDICIAL OR ADMINISTRATIVE PROCEEDING

(a) A professional may disclose confidential information only:

(1) to a governmental agency if the disclosure is required or authorized by law;

(2) to medical or law enforcement personnel if the professional determines that there is a probability of imminent physical injury by the patient to the patient or others or there is a probability of immediate mental or emotional injury to the patient;

(3) to qualified personnel for management audits, financial audits, program evaluations, or research, in accordance with Subsection (b);

(4) to a person who has the written consent of the patient, or a parent if the patient is a minor, or a guardian if the patient has been adjudicated as incompetent to manage the patient's personal affairs;

(5) to the patient's personal representative if the patient is deceased;

(6) to individuals, corporations, or governmental agencies involved in paying or collecting fees for mental or emotional health services provided by a professional;

(7) to other professionals and personnel under the professionals' direction who participate in the diagnosis, evaluation, or treatment of the patient;

(8) in an official legislative inquiry relating to a state hospital or state school as provided by Subsection (c);

(9) to designated persons or personnel of a correctional facility in which a person is detained if the disclosure is for the sole purpose of providing treatment and health care to the person in custody;

(10) to an employee or agent of the professional who requires mental health care information to provide mental health care services or in complying with statutory, licensing, or accreditation requirements, if the professional has taken appropriate action to ensure that the employee or agent:

(A) will not use or disclose the information for any other purposes; and

(B) will take appropriate steps to protect the information; or

(11) to satisfy a request for medical records of a deceased or incompetent person pursuant to Section 4.01(e), Medical Liability and Insurance Improvement Act of Texas (Article 4590i, Vernon's Texas Civil Statutes).

(b) Personnel who receive confidential information under Subsection (a)(3) may not directly or indirectly identify or otherwise disclose the identity of a patient in a report or in any other manner.

(c) The exception in Subsection (a)(8) applies only to records created by the state hospital or state school or by the employees of the hospital or school. Information or records that identify a patient may be released only with the patient's proper consent.

(d) A person who receives information from confidential communications or records may not disclose the information except to the extent that disclosure is consistent with the authorized purposes for which the person first obtained the information. This subsection does not apply to a person listed in Subsection (a)(4) or (a)(5) who is acting on the patient's behalf.

History of H&SC §611.004: Acts 1991, 72nd Leg., ch. 76, §1, eff. Sept. 1, 1991. Amended by Acts 1995, 74th Leg., ch. 856, §8, eff. Sept. 1, 1995; Acts 1999, 76th Leg., ch. 1264, §1, eff. Sept. 1, 1999.

H&S §611.0045. RIGHT TO MENTAL HEALTH RECORD

(a) Except as otherwise provided by this section, a patient is entitled to have access to the content of a confidential record made about the patient.

(b) The professional may deny access to any portion of a record if the professional determines that release of that portion would be harmful to the patient's physical, mental, or emotional health.

(c) If the professional denies access to any portion of a record, the professional shall give the patient a signed and dated written statement that having access to the record would be harmful to the patient's physical, mental, or emotional health and shall include a copy of the written statement in the patient's records. The statement must specify the portion of the record to which access is denied, the reason for denial, and the duration of the denial.

(d) The professional who denies access to a portion of a record under this section shall redetermine the necessity for the denial at each time a request for the denied portion is made. If the professional again denies access, the professional shall notify the patient of the denial and document the denial as prescribed by Subsection (c).

(e) If a professional denies access to a portion of a confidential record, the professional shall allow examination and copying of the record by another professional if the patient selects the professional to treat the patient for the same or a related condition as the professional denying access.

(f) The content of a confidential record shall be made available to a person listed by Section 611.004(a)(4) or (5) who is acting on the patient's behalf.

(g) A professional shall delete confidential information about another person who has not consented to the release, but may not delete information relating to the patient that another person has provided, the identity of the person responsible for that information, or the identity of any person who provided information that resulted in the patient's commitment.

(h) If a summary or narrative of a confidential record is requested by the patient or other person requesting release under this section, the professional shall prepare the summary or narrative.

(i) The professional or other entity that has possession or control of the record shall grant access to any portion of the record to which access is not specifically denied under this section within a reasonable time and may charge a reasonable fee.

A (j) Notwithstanding Section 159.002, Occupations Code, this section applies to the release of a confidential record created or maintained by a professional, including a physician, that relates to the diagnosis, evaluation, or treatment of a mental or emotional condition or disorder, including alcoholism or drug addiction.

(k) The denial of a patient's access to any portion of a record by the professional or other entity that has possession or control of the record suspends, until the release of that portion of the record, the running of an applicable statute of limitations on a cause of action in which evidence relevant to the cause of action is in that portion of the record.

History of H&SC §611.045: Acts 1993, 73rd Leg., ch. 903, §1.12, eff. Aug. 30, 1993. Amended by Acts 2001, 77th Leg., ch. 1420, §14.806, eff. Sept. 1, 2001.

H&S §611.005. LEGAL REMEDIES FOR IMPROPER DISCLOSURE OR FAILURE TO DISCLOSE

(a) A person aggrieved by the improper disclosure of or failure to disclose confidential communications or records in violation of this chapter may petition the district court of the county in which the person resides for appropriate relief, including injunctive relief. The person may petition a district court of Travis County if the person is not a resident of this state.

(b) In a suit contesting the denial of access under Section 611.0045, the burden of proving that the denial was proper is on the professional who denied the access.

(c) The aggrieved person also has a civil cause of action for damages.

History of H&SC §611.005: Acts 1991, 72nd Leg., ch. 76, §1, eff. Sept. 1, 1991. Amended by Acts 1993, 73rd Leg., ch. 903, §1.13, eff. Aug. 30, 1993.

H&S §611.006. AUTHORIZED DISCLOSURE OF CONFIDENTIAL INFORMATION IN JUDICIAL OR ADMINISTRATIVE PROCEEDING

(a) A professional may disclose confidential information in:

(1) a judicial or administrative proceeding brought by the patient or the patient's legally authorized representative against a professional, including malpractice proceedings;

(2) a license revocation proceeding in which the patient is a complaining witness and in which disclosure is relevant to the claim or defense of a professional;

(3) a judicial or administrative proceeding in which the patient waives the patient's right in writing to the privilege of confidentiality of information or when a representative of the patient acting on the patient's behalf submits a written waiver to the confidentiality privilege;

(4) a judicial or administrative proceeding to substantiate and collect on a claim for mental or emotional health services rendered to the patient;

(5) a judicial proceeding if the judge finds that the patient, after having been informed that communications would not be privileged, has made communications to a professional in the course of a court-ordered examination relating to the patient's mental or emotional condition or disorder, except that those communications may be disclosed only with respect to issues involving the patient's mental or emotional health;

(6) a judicial proceeding affecting the parent-child relationship;

(7) any criminal proceeding, as otherwise provided by law;

(8) a judicial or administrative proceeding regarding the abuse or neglect, or the cause of abuse or neglect, of a resident of an institution, as that term is defined by Chapter 242;

(9) a judicial proceeding relating to a will if the patient's physical or mental condition is relevant to the execution of the will;

(10) an involuntary commitment proceeding for court-ordered treatment or for a probable cause hearing under:

(A) Chapter 462;

(B) Chapter 574; or

(C) Chapter 593; or

(11) a judicial or administrative proceeding where the court or agency has issued an order or subpoena.

(b) On granting an order under Subsection (a)(5), the court, in determining the extent to which disclosure of all or any part of a communication is necessary, shall impose appropriate safeguards against unauthorized disclosure.

History of H&SC §611.006: Acts 1995, 74th Leg., ch. 856, §9, eff. Sept. 1, 1995.

H&S §611.007. REVOCATION OF CONSENT

(a) Except as provided by Subsection (b), a patient or a patient's legally authorized representative may revoke a disclosure consent to a professional at any time. A revocation is valid only if it is written, dated, and signed by the patient or legally authorized representative.

(b) A patient may not revoke a disclosure that is required for purposes of making payment to the professional for mental health care services provided to the patient.

(c) A patient may not maintain an action against a professional for a disclosure made by the professional in good faith reliance on an authorization if the professional did not have notice of the revocation of the consent.

History of H&SC §611.007: Acts 1995, 74th Leg., ch. 856, §9, eff. Sept. 1, 1995.

H&S §611.008. REQUEST BY PATIENT

(a) On receipt of a written request from a patient to examine or copy all or part of the patient's recorded mental health care information, a professional, as promptly as required under the circumstances but not later than the 15th day after the date of receiving the request, shall:

(1) make the information available for examination during regular business hours and provide a copy to the patient, if requested; or

(2) inform the patient if the information does not exist or cannot be found.

(b) Unless provided for by other state law, the professional may charge a reasonable fee for retrieving or copying mental health care information and is not required to permit examination or copying until the fee is paid unless there is a medical emergency.

(c) A professional may not charge a fee for copying mental health care information under Subsection (b) to the extent the fee is prohibited under Subchapter M, Chapter 161.

History of H&SC §611.008: Acts 1995, 74th Leg., ch. 856, §9, eff. Sept. 1, 1995.

TITLE 5. EXEMPT PROPERTY & LIENS

Subtitle A. Property Exempt from Creditor's Claims

Chapter 41. Interests in Land

Subchapter A. Exemptions in Land Defined

Subchapter B. Designation of a Homestead in Aid of Enforcement of a Judgment Debt

Chapter 42. Personal Property

TITLE 5. EXEMPT PROPERTY & LIENS

SUBTITLE A. PROPERTY EXEMPT FROM CREDITOR'S CLAIMS

CHAPTER 41. INTERESTS IN LAND

SUBCHAPTER A. EXEMPTIONS IN LAND DEFINED

PROP §41.001. INTERESTS IN LAND EXEMPT FROM SEIZURE

(a) A homestead and one or more lots used for a place of burial of the dead are exempt from seizure for the claims of creditors except for encumbrances properly fixed on homestead property.

(b) Encumbrances may be properly fixed on homestead property for:

(1) purchase money;

(2) taxes on the property;

(3) work and material used in constructing improvements on the property if contracted for in writing as provided by Sections 53.254(a), (b), and (c);

(4) an owelty of partition imposed against the entirety of the property by a court order or by a written agreement of the parties to the partition, including a debt of one spouse in favor of the other spouse resulting from a division or an award of a family homestead in a divorce proceeding;

(5) the refinance of a lien against a homestead, including a federal tax lien resulting from the tax debt of both spouses, if the homestead is a family homestead, or from the tax debt of the owner;

E (6) an extension of credit that meets the requirements of Section 50(a)(6), Article XVI, Texas Constitution; or

E (7) a reverse mortgage that meets the requirements of Sections 50(k)-(p), Article XVI, Texas Constitution.

(c) The homestead claimant's proceeds of a sale of a homestead are not subject to seizure for a creditor's claim for six months after the date of sale.

History of Prop §41.001: Acts 1983, 68th, Leg., ch. 576, §1, eff. Jan. 1, 1984. Amended by Acts 1984, 68th Leg., 2nd C.S., ch. 18, §2(b), eff. Oct. 2, 1984; Acts 1985, 69th Leg., ch. 840, §1, eff. June 15, 1985; Acts 1993, 73rd Leg., ch. 48, §2, eff. Sept. 1, 1993; Acts 1995, 74th Leg., ch. 121, §1.01, eff. May 17, 1995; Acts 1995, 74th Leg., ch. 121, §2.01; Acts 1997, 75th Leg., ch. 526, §1, eff. Sept. 1, 1997; Acts 2001, 77th Leg., ch. 516, §1, eff. Sept. 1, 2001.

PROP §41.002. DEFINITION OF HOMESTEAD

(a) If used for the purposes of an urban home or as a place to exercise a calling or business both an urban home and the homestead of a family or a single, adult person, not otherwise entitled to a homestead, shall consist of not more than ten acres of land which may be in one or more contiguous lots, together with any improvements thereon.

(b) If used for the purposes of a rural home, the homestead shall consist of:

(1) for a family, not more than 200 acres, which may be in one or more parcels, with the improvements thereon; or

(2) for a single, adult person, not otherwise entitled to a homestead, not more than 100 acres, which may be in one or more parcels, with the improvements thereon.

(c) A homestead is considered to be urban if, at the time the designation is made, the property is:

(1) located within the limits of a municipality or its extraterritorial jurisdiction or a platted subdivision; and

(2) served by police protection, paid or volunteer fire protection, and at least three of the following services provided by a municipality or under contract to a municipality:

(A) electric;

(B) natural gas;

(C) sewer;

(D) storm sewer; and

(E) water.

(d) The definition of a homestead as provided in this section applies to all homesteads in this state whenever created.

History of Prop §41.002: Acts 1983, 68th Leg., ch. 576, §1, eff. Jan. 1, 1984. Amended by Acts 1985, 69th Leg., ch. 840, §1, eff. June 15, 1985; Acts 1989, 71st Leg., ch. 391, §2, eff. Aug. 28, 1989; Acts 1999, 76th Leg., ch. 1510, §1 (eff. Jan. 1, 2000), ch. 1510, §2 (eff. Sept. 1, 1999).

PROP §41.003. TEMPORARY RENTING OF A HOMESTEAD

Temporary renting of a homestead does not change its homestead character if the homestead claimant has not acquired another homestead.

History of Prop §41.003: Acts 1983, 68th Leg., ch. 576, §1, eff. Jan. 1, 1984. Amended by Acts 1985, 69th Leg., ch. 840, §1, eff. June 15, 1985.

PROP §41.004. ABANDONMENT OF A HOMESTEAD

If a homestead claimant is married, a homestead cannot be abandoned without the consent of the claimant's spouse.

History of Prop §41.004: Acts 1985, 69th Leg., ch. 840, §1, eff. June 15, 1985.

PROP §41.005. VOLUNTARY DESIGNATION OF HOMESTEAD

(a) If a rural homestead of a family is part of one or more parcels containing a total of more than 200 acres, the head of the family and, if married, that person's spouse may voluntarily designate not more than 200 acres of the property as the homestead. If a rural homestead of a single adult person, not otherwise entitled to a homestead, is part of one or more parcels containing a total of more than 100 acres, the person may voluntarily designate not more than 100 acres of the property as the homestead.

(b) If an urban homestead of a family, or an urban homestead of a single adult person not otherwise entitled to a homestead, is part of one or more contiguous lots containing a total of more than 10 acres, the head of the family and, if married, that person's spouse or the single adult person, as applicable, may voluntarily designate not more than 10 acres of the property as the homestead.

(c) Except as provided by Subsection (e) or Subchapter B, to designate property as a homestead, a person or persons, as applicable, must make the designation in an instrument that is signed and acknowledged or proved in the manner required for the recording of other instruments. The person or persons must file the designation with the county clerk of the county in which all or part of the property is located. The clerk shall record the designation in the county deed records. The designation must contain:

(1) a description sufficient to identify the property designated;

(2) a statement by the person or persons who executed the instrument that the property is designated as the homestead of the person's family or as the homestead of a single adult person not otherwise entitled to a homestead;

(3) the name of the current record title holder of the property; and

(4) for a rural homestead, the number of acres designated and, if there is more than one survey, the number of acres in each.

(d) A person or persons, as applicable, may change the boundaries of a homestead designated under Subsection (c) by executing and recording an instrument in the manner required for a voluntary designation under that subsection. A change under this subsection does not impair rights acquired by a party before the change.

(e) Except as otherwise provided by this subsection, property on which a person receives an exemption from taxation under Section 11.43, Tax Code, is considered to have been designated as the person's homestead for purposes of this subchapter if the property is listed as the person's residence homestead on the most recent appraisal roll for the appraisal district established for the county in which the property is located. If a person designates property as a homestead under Subsection (c) or Subchapter B and a different property is considered to have been designated as the person's homestead under this subsection, the designation under Subsection (c) or Subchapter B, as applicable, prevails for purposes of this chapter.

(f) If a person or persons, as applicable, have not made a voluntary designation of a homestead under this section as of the time a writ of execution is issued against the person, any designation of the person's or persons' homestead must be made in accordance with Subchapter B.

(g) An instrument that made a voluntary designation of a homestead in accordance with prior law and that is on file with the county clerk on September 1,

1987, is considered a voluntary designation of a homestead under this section.

History of Prop §41.005: Acts 1987, 70th Leg., ch. 727, §1, eff. Aug. 31, 1987. Amended by Acts 1993, 73rd Leg., ch. 48, §3, eff. Sept. 1, 1993; Acts 1993, 73rd Leg., ch. 297, §1, eff. Aug. 1, 1993; Acts 1997, 75th Leg., ch. 846, §1, eff. Sept. 1, 1997; Acts 1999, 76th Leg., ch. 1510, §3, eff. Jan. 1, 2000.

E PROP §41.0051. DISCLAIMER REQUIRED

(a) A person may not deliver a written advertisement offering, for a fee, to designate property as a homestead as provided by Section 41.005 unless there is a disclaimer on the advertisement that is conspicuous and printed in 14-point boldface type or 14-point uppercase typewritten letters that makes the following statement or a substantially similar statement:

THIS DOCUMENT IS AN ADVERTISEMENT OF SERVICES. IT IS NOT AN OFFICIAL DOCUMENT OF THE STATE OF TEXAS.

(b) A person's failure to provide a disclaimer on an advertisement as required by Subsection (a) is considered a false, misleading, or deceptive act or practice for purposes of Section 17.46(a), Business & Commerce Code, and is subject to action by the consumer protection division of the attorney general's office as provided by Section 17.46(a), Business & Commerce Code.

History of Prop §41.0051: Enacted by Acts 2001, 77th Leg., ch. 341, §1, eff. Sept. 1, 2001.

PROP §41.006. CERTAIN SALES OF HOMESTEAD

(a) Except as provided by Subsection (c), any sale or purported sale in whole or in part of a homestead at a fixed purchase price that is less than the appraised fair market value of the property at the time of the sale or purported sale, and in connection with which the buyer of the property executes a lease of the property to the seller at lease payments that exceed the fair rental value of the property, is considered to be a loan with all payments made from the seller to the buyer in excess of the sales price considered to be interest subject to Title 4, Finance Code.

(b) The taking of any deed in connection with a transaction described by this section is a deceptive trade practice under Subchapter E, Chapter 17, Business & Commerce Code, and the deed is void and no lien attaches to the homestead property as a result of the purported sale.

(c) This section does not apply to the sale of a family homestead to a parent, stepparent, grandparent, child, stepchild, brother, half brother, sister, half sister, or grandchild of an adult member of the family.

History of Prop §41.006: Acts 1987, 70th Leg., ch. 1130, §1, eff. Sept. 1, 1987. Amended by Acts 1999, 76th Leg., ch. 62, §7.84, eff. Sept. 1, 1999.

PROP §41.007. HOME IMPROVEMENT CONTRACT

(a) A contract described by Section 41.001(b)(3) must contain the following warning conspicuously printed, stamped, or typed in a size equal to at least 10-point bold type or computer equivalent, next to the owner's signature line on the contract:

"IMPORTANT NOTICE: You and your contractor are responsible for meeting the terms and conditions of this contract. If you sign this contract and you fail to meet the terms and conditions of this contract, you may lose your legal ownership rights in your home. KNOW YOUR RIGHTS AND DUTIES UNDER THE LAW."

(b) A violation of Subsection (a) of this section is a false, misleading, or deceptive act or practice within the meaning of Section 17.46, Business & Commerce Code, and is actionable in a public or private suit brought under the provisions of the Deceptive Trade Practices-Consumer Protection Act (Subchapter E, Chapter 17, Business & Commerce Code).

History of Prop §41.007: Acts 1987, 70th Leg., ch. 116, §1, eff. Sept. 1, 1987. Renumbered from §41.005 by Acts 1989, 71st Leg., ch. 2, §16.01(30), eff. Aug. 28, 1989. Amended by Acts 1993, 73rd Leg., ch. 48, §4, eff. Sept. 1, 1993.

PROP §41.008. CONFLICT WITH FEDERAL LAW

To the extent of any conflict between this subchapter and any federal law that imposes an upper limit on the amount, including the monetary amount or acreage amount, of homestead property a person may exempt from seizure, this subchapter prevails to the extent allowed under federal law.

History of Prop §41.008: Acts 1999, 76th Leg., ch. 1510, §4, eff. Sept. 1, 1999.

Sections 41.009–41.020 reserved for expansion

SUBCHAPTER B. DESIGNATION OF A HOMESTEAD IN AID OF ENFORCEMENT OF A JUDGMENT DEBT

PROP §41.021. NOTICE TO DESIGNATE

If an execution is issued against a holder of an interest in land of which a homestead may be a part and the judgment debtor has not made a voluntary designation of a homestead under Section 41.005, the judgment creditor may give the judgment debtor notice to designate the homestead as defined in Section 41.002. The notice shall state that if the judgment debtor fails to designate the homestead within the time allowed by Section 41.022, the court will appoint a commissioner to make the designation at the expense of the judgment debtor.

History of Prop §41.021: Acts 1983, 68th Leg., ch. 576, §31, eff. Jan. 1, 1984. Amended by Acts 1985, 69th Leg., ch. 840, §1, eff. June 15, 1985; Acts 1987, 70th Leg., ch. 727, §2, eff. Aug. 31, 1987.

PROP §41.022. DESIGNATION BY HOMESTEAD CLAIMANT

At any time before 10 a.m. on the Monday next after the expiration of 20 days after the date of service of the notice to designate, the judgment debtor may designate the homestead as defined in Section 41.002 by filing a written designation, signed by the judgment debtor, with the justice or clerk of the court from which the writ of execution was issued, together with a plat of the area designated.

History of Prop §41.022: Acts 1983, 68th Leg., ch, 576, §31, eff. Jan. 1, 1984. Amended by Acts 1985, 69th Leg., ch. 840, §1, eff. June 15, 1985.

PROP §41.023. DESIGNATION BY COMMISSIONER

(a) If a judgment debtor who has not made a voluntary designation of a homestead under Section 41.005 does not designate a homestead as provided in Section 41.022, on motion of the judgment creditor, filed within 90 days after the issuance of the writ of execution, the court from which the writ of execution issued shall appoint a commissioner to designate the judgment debtor's homestead. The court may appoint a surveyor and others as may be necessary to assist the commissioner. The commissioner shall file his designation of the judgment debtor's homestead in a written report, together with a plat of the area designated, with the justice or clerk of the court not more than 60 days after the order of appointment is signed or within such time as the court may allow.

(b) Within 10 days after the commissioner's report is filed, the judgment debtor or the judgment creditor may request a hearing on the issue of whether the report should be confirmed, rejected, or modified as may be deemed appropriate in the particular circumstances of the case. The commissioner's report may be contradicted by evidence from either party, when exceptions to it or any item thereof have been filed before the hearing, but not otherwise. After the hearing, or if there is no hearing requested, the court shall designate the homestead as deemed appropriate and order sale of the excess.

(c) The commissioner, a surveyor, and others appointed to assist the commissioner are entitled to such fees and expenses as are deemed reasonable by the court. The court shall tax these fees and expenses against the judgment debtor as part of the costs of execution.

History of Prop §41.023: Acts 1983, 68th Leg., ch. 576, §1, eff. Jan. 1, 1984. Amended by Acts 1985, 69th Leg., ch. 840, §1, eff. June 15, 1985; Acts 1987, 70th Leg., ch. 727, §3, eff. Aug. 31, 1987.

PROP §41.024. SALE OF EXCESS

An officer holding an execution sale of property of a judgment debtor whose homestead has been designated under this chapter may sell the excess of the judgment debtor's interest in land not included in the homestead.

History of Prop §41.024: Amended by Acts 1985, 69th Leg., ch. 840, §1, eff. June 15, 1985; Acts 1987, 70th Leg., ch. 727, §4, eff. Aug. 31, 1987.

CHAPTER 42. PERSONAL PROPERTY

PROP §42.001. PERSONAL PROPERTY EXEMPTION

(a) Personal property, as described in Section 42.002, is exempt from garnishment, attachment, execution, or other seizure if:

(1) the property is provided for a family and has an aggregate fair market value of not more than $60,000, exclusive of the amount of any liens, security interests, or other charges encumbering the property; or

(2) the property is owned by a single adult, who is not a member of a family, and has an aggregate fair market value of not more than $30,000, exclusive of the amount of any liens, security interests, or other charges encumbering the property.

(b) The following personal property is exempt from seizure and is not included in the aggregate limitations prescribed by Subsection (a):

(1) current wages for personal services, except for the enforcement of court-ordered child support payments;

(2) professionally prescribed health aids of a debtor or a dependent of a debtor; and

(3) alimony, support, or separate maintenance received or to be received by the debtor for the support of the debtor or a dependent of the debtor.

(c) This section does not prevent seizure by a secured creditor with a contractual landlord's lien or other security in the property to be seized.

(d) Unpaid commissions for personal services not to exceed 25 percent of the aggregate limitations prescribed by Subsection (a) are exempt from seizure and are included in the aggregate.

History of Prop §42.001: Acts 1983, 68th Leg., ch. 576, §1, eff. Jan. 1, 1984. Amended by Acts 1991, 72nd Leg., ch. 175, §1, eff. May 24, 1991; Acts 1997, 75th Leg., ch. 1046, §1, eff. Sept. 1, 1997.

PROP §42.002. PERSONAL PROPERTY

(a) The following personal property is exempt under Section 42.001(a):

(1) home furnishings, including family heirlooms;

(2) provisions for consumption;

(3) farming or ranching vehicles and implements;

(4) tools, equipment, books, and apparatus, including boats and motor vehicles used in a trade or profession;

(5) wearing apparel;

(6) jewelry not to exceed 25 percent of the aggregate limitations prescribed by Section 42.001(a);

(7) two firearms;

(8) athletic and sporting equipment, including bicycles;

(9) a two-wheeled, three-wheeled, or four-wheeled motor vehicle for each member of a family or single adult who holds a driver's license or who does not hold a driver's license but who relies on another person to operate the vehicle for the benefit of the nonlicensed person;

(10) the following animals and forage on hand for their consumption:

(A) two horses, mules, or donkeys and a saddle, blanket, and bridle for each;

(B) 12 head of cattle;

(C) 60 head of other types of livestock; and

(D) 120 fowl; and

(11) household pets.

Subsection (b) is effective for transactions or liens entered into before July 1, 2001. However, there are numerous exceptions to the effective date. See Bus. & Com. Code §9.701-9.709.

(b) Personal property, unless precluded from being encumbered by other law, may be encumbered by a security interest under Subchapter B, Chapter 9, Business & Commerce Code, or Subchapter F, Chapter 501, Transportation Code, or by a lien fixed by other law, and the security interest or lien may not be avoided on the ground that the property is exempt under this chapter.

Subsection (b) below is effective for transactions or liens until July 1, 2001. Parties to valid liens that were entered into before July 1, 2001, and which are not the subject of litigation may use either the earlier law or the amended law to govern the lien.

(b) Personal property, unless precluded from being encumbered by other law, may be encumbered by a security interest under Section 9.203, Business & Commerce Code, or Subchapter F, Chapter 501, Transportation Code, or by a lien fixed by other law, and the security interest or lien may not be avoided on the ground that the property is exempt under this chapter.

History of Prop §42.002: Acts 1983, 68th Leg., ch. 576, §1, eff. Jan. 1, 1984. Amended by Acts 1991, 72nd Leg., ch. 175, §1, eff. May 24, 1991; Acts 1993, 73rd Leg., ch. 216, §1, eff. May, 17, 1993; Acts 1997, 75th Leg., ch. 165, §30.245, eff. Sept. 1, 1997; Acts 1999, 76th Leg., ch. 414, §2.36 (eff. July 1, 2001), ch. 846, §1 (eff. Aug. 30, 1999).

PROP §42.0021. ADDITIONAL EXEMPTION FOR RETIREMENT PLAN

(a) In addition to the exemption prescribed by Section 42.001, a person's right to the assets held in or to receive payments, whether vested or not, under any stock bonus, pension, profit-sharing, or similar plan, including a retirement plan for self-employed individuals, and under any annuity or similar contract purchased with assets distributed from that type of plan, and under any retirement annuity or account described by Section 403(b) or 408A of the Internal Revenue Code of 1986, and under any individual retirement account or any individual retirement annuity, including a simplified employee pension plan, is exempt from attachment, execution, and seizure for the satisfaction of debts unless the plan, contract, or account does not qualify under the applicable provisions of the Internal Revenue Code of 1986. A person's right to the assets held in or to receive payments, whether vested or not, under a government or church plan or contract is also exempt unless the plan or contract does not qualify under the definition of a government or church plan under the applicable provisions of the federal Employee Retirement Income Security Act of 1974. If this subsection is held invalid or preempted by federal law in whole or in part or in certain circumstances, the subsection remains in effect in all other respects to the maximum extent permitted by law.

(b) Contributions to an individual retirement account, other than contributions to a Roth IRA described in Section 408A, Internal Revenue Code of 1986, or annuity that exceed the amounts deductible under the applicable provisions of the Internal Revenue Code of 1986 and any accrued earnings on such contributions are not exempt under this section unless otherwise exempt by law. Amounts qualifying as nontaxable rollover contributions under Section 402(a)(5), 403(a)(4), 403(b)(8), or 408(d)(3) of the Internal Revenue Code of 1986 before January 1, 1993, are treated as exempt amounts under Subsection (a). Amounts treated as qualified rollover contributions under Section 408A, Internal Revenue Code of 1986, are treated as exempt amounts under Subsection (a). In addition, amounts qualifying as nontaxable rollover contributions under Section 402(c), 402(e)(6), 402(f), 403(a)(4), 403(a)(5), 403(b)(8), 403(b)(10), 408(d)(3), or 408A of the Internal Revenue Code of 1986 on or after January 1, 1993, are treated as exempt amounts under Subsection (a).

(c) Amounts distributed from a plan or contract entitled to the exemption under Subsection (a) are not subject to seizure for a creditor's claim for 60 days after the date of distribution if the amounts qualify as a nontaxable rollover contribution under Subsection (b).

(d) A participant or beneficiary of a stock bonus, pension, profit-sharing, retirement plan, or government plan is not prohibited from granting a valid and enforceable security interest in the participant's or beneficiary's right to the assets held in or to receive payments under the plan to secure a loan to the participant or beneficiary from the plan, and the right to the assets held in or to receive payments from the plan is subject to attachment, execution, and seizure for the satisfaction of the security interest or lien granted by the participant or beneficiary to secure the loan.

(e) If Subsection (a) is declared invalid or preempted by federal law, in whole or in part or in certain circumstances, as applied to a person who has not brought a proceeding under Title 11, United States Code, the subsection remains in effect, to the maximum extent permitted by law, as to any person who has filed that type of proceeding.

(f) A reference in this section to a specific provision of the Internal Revenue Code of 1986 includes a subsequent amendment of the substance of that provision.

History of Prop §42.0021: Acts 1987, 70th Leg., ch. 376, §1, eff. Sept. 1, 1987. Amended by Acts 1989, 71st Leg., ch. 1122, §1, eff. Sept. 1, 1989; Acts 1995, 74th Leg., ch. 963, §1, eff. Aug. 28, 1995; Acts 1999, 76th Leg., ch. 106, §1, eff. Sept. 1, 1999.

PROP §42.003. DESIGNATION OF EXEMPT PROPERTY

(a) If the number or amount of a type of personal property owned by a debtor exceeds the exemption allowed by Section 42.002 and the debtor can be found in the county where the property is located, the officer making a levy on the property shall ask the debtor to designate the personal property to be levied on. If the debtor cannot be found in the county or the debtor fails to make a designation within a reasonable time after the officer's request, the officer shall make the designation.

(b) If the aggregate value of a debtor's personal property exceeds the amount exempt from seizure under Section 42.001(a), the debtor may designate the portion of the property to be levied on. If, after a court's request, the debtor fails to make a designation within a reasonable time or if for any reason a creditor contests that the property is exempt, the court shall make the designation.

History of Prop §42.003: Acts 1983, 68th Leg., ch. 576, §1, eff. Jan. 1, 1984. Amended by Acts 1991, 72nd Leg., ch. 175, §1, eff. May 24, 1991.

PROP §42.004. TRANSFER OF NONEXEMPT PROPERTY

(a) If a person uses the property not exempt under this chapter to acquire, obtain an interest in, make improvement to, or pay an indebtedness on personal property which would be exempt under this chapter with the intent to defraud, delay, or hinder an interested person from obtaining that to which the interested person is or may be entitled, the property, interest, or improvement acquired is not exempt from seizure for the satisfaction of liabilities. If the property, interest, or improvement is acquired by discharging an encumbrance held by a third person, a person defrauded, delayed, or hindered is subrogated to the rights of the third person.

(b) A creditor may not assert a claim under this section more than two years after the transaction from which the claim arises. A person with a claim that is unliquidated or contingent at the time of the transaction may not assert a claim under this section more than one year after the claim is reduced to judgment.

(c) It is a defense to a claim under this section that the transfer was made in the ordinary course of business by the person making the transfer.

History of Prop §42.004: Acts 1983, 68th Leg., ch. 576, §1, eff. Jan. 1, 1984. Amended by Acts 1991, 72nd Leg., ch. 175, §1, eff. May 24, 1991.

PROP §42.005. CHILD SUPPORT LIENS

Sections 42.001, 42.002, and 42.0021 of this code do not apply to a child support lien established under Subchapter G, Chapter 157, Family Code.

History of Prop §42.005: Acts 1991, 72nd Leg., 1st C.S., ch. 15, §4.07, eff. Sept. 1, 1991. Amended by Acts 1997, 75th Leg., ch. 165, §7.56, eff. Sept. 1, 1997.

CONTENTS

ARTICLE 1
Bill of Rights

ARTICLE 16
General Provisions

ARTICLE 1
BILL OF RIGHTS

§3a. EQUALITY UNDER THE LAW

Equality under the law shall not be denied or abridged because of sex, race, color, creed, or national origin. This amendment is self-operative.

ARTICLE 16
GENERAL PROVISIONS

§15. SEPARATE & COMMUNITY PROPERTY OF HUSBAND & WIFE

All property, both real and personal, of a spouse owned or claimed before marriage, and that acquired afterward by gift, devise or descent, shall be the separate property of that spouse; and laws shall be passed more clearly defining the rights of the spouses, in relation to separate and community property; provided that persons about to marry and spouses, without the intention to defraud pre-existing creditors, may by written instrument from time to time partition between themselves all or part of their property, then existing or to be acquired, or exchange between themselves the community interest of one spouse or future spouse in any property for the community interest of the other spouse or future spouse in other community property then existing or to be acquired, whereupon the portion or interest set aside to each spouse shall be and constitute a part of the separate property and estate of such spouse or future spouse; spouses also may from time to time, by written instrument, agree between themselves that the income or property from all or part of the separate property then owned or which thereafter might be acquired by only one of them, shall be the separate property of that spouse; if one spouse makes a gift of property to the other that gift is presumed to include all the income or property which might arise from that gift of property; spouses may agree in writing that all or part of their community property becomes the property of the surviving spouse on the death of a spouse; and spouses may agree in writing that all or part of the separate property owned by either or both of them shall be the spouses' community property.

§28. GARNISHMENT OF WAGES

No current wages for personal service shall ever be subject to garnishment, except for the enforcement of court-ordered:

(1) child support payments; or

(2) spousal maintenance.

§50. HOMESTEAD; PROTECTION FROM FORCED SALE; MORTGAGES, TRUST DEEDS & LIENS

(a) The homestead of a family, or of a single adult person, shall be, and is hereby protected from forced sale, for the payment of all debts except for:

(1) the purchase money thereof, or a part of such purchase money;

(2) the taxes due thereon;

(3) an owelty of partition imposed against the entirety of the property by a court order or by a written agreement of the parties to the partition, including a debt of one spouse in favor of the other spouse resulting from a division or an award of a family homestead in a divorce proceeding;

(4) the refinance of a lien against a homestead, including a federal tax lien resulting from the tax debt of both spouses, if the homestead is a family homestead, or from the tax debt of the owner;

(5) work and material used in constructing new improvements thereon, if contracted for in writing, or work and material used to repair or renovate existing improvements thereon if:

(A) the work and material are contracted for in writing, with the consent of both spouses, in the case of a family homestead, given in the same manner as is required in making a sale and conveyance of the homestead;

(B) the contract for the work and material is not executed by the owner or the owner's spouse before the 5th day after the owner makes written application for any extension of credit for the work and material, unless the work and material are necessary to complete immediate repairs to conditions on the homestead property that materially affect the health or safety of the owner or person residing in the homestead and the owner of the homestead acknowledges such in writing;

(C) the contract for the work and material expressly provides that the owner may rescind the contract without penalty or charge within three days after the execution of the contract by all parties, unless the work and material are necessary to complete immediate repairs to conditions on the homestead property that materially affect the health or safety of the owner or person residing in the homestead and the owner of the homestead acknowledges such in writing; and

(D) the contract for the work and material is executed by the owner and the owner's spouse only at the office of a third-party lender making an extension of credit for the work and material, an attorney at law, or a title company;

(6) an extension of credit that:

(A) is secured by a voluntary lien on the homestead created under a written agreement with the consent of each owner and each owner's spouse;

(B) is of a principal amount that when added to the aggregate total of the outstanding principal balances of all other indebtedness secured by valid encumbrances of record against the homestead does not exceed 80 percent of the fair market value of the homestead on the date the extension of credit is made;

(C) is without recourse for personal liability against each owner and the spouse of each owner, unless the owner or spouse obtained the extension of credit by actual fraud;

(D) is secured by a lien that may be foreclosed upon only by a court order;

(E) does not require the owner or the owner's spouse to pay, in addition to any interest, fees to any person that are necessary to originate, evaluate, maintain, record, insure, or service the extension of credit that exceed, in the aggregate, three percent of the original principal amount of the extension of credit;

(F) is not a form of open-end account that may be debited from time to time or under which credit may be extended from time to time;

(G) is payable in advance without penalty or other charge;

(H) is not secured by any additional real or personal property other than the homestead;

(I) is not secured by homestead property designated for agricultural use as provided by statutes governing property tax, unless such homestead property is used primarily for the production of milk;

(J) may not be accelerated because of a decrease in the market value of the homestead or because of the owner's default under other indebtedness not secured by a prior valid encumbrance against the homestead;

(K) is the only debt secured by the homestead at the time the extension of credit is made unless the other debt was made for a purpose described by Subsections (a)(1)-(a)(5) of this section;

(L) is scheduled to be repaid in substantially equal successive monthly installments beginning no later than two months from the date the extension of credit is made, each of which equals or exceeds the amount of accrued interest as of the date of the scheduled installment;

(M) is closed not before:

(i) the 12th day after the later of the date that the owner of the homestead submits an application to the lender for the extension of credit or the date that the lender provides the owner a copy of the notice prescribed by Subsection (g) of this section; and

(ii) the first anniversary of the closing date of any other extension of credit described by Subsection (a)(6) of this section secured by the same homestead property;

(N) is closed only at the office of the lender, an attorney at law, or a title company;

(O) permits a lender to contract for and receive any fixed or variable rate of interest authorized under statute;

(P) is made by one of the following that has not been found by a federal regulatory agency to have engaged in the practice of refusing to make loans because the applicants for the loans reside or the property proposed to secure the loans is located in a certain area:

(i) a bank, savings and loan association, savings bank, or credit union doing business under the laws of this state or the United States;

(ii) a federally chartered lending instrumentality or a person approved as a mortgagee by the United States government to make federally insured loans;

(iii) a person licensed to make regulated loans, as provided by statute of this state;

(iv) a person who sold the homestead property to the current owner and who provided all or part of the financing for the purchase; or

(v) a person who is related to the homestead property owner within the second degree of affinity or consanguinity; and

(Q) is made on the condition that:

(i) the owner of the homestead is not required to apply the proceeds of the extension of credit to repay another debt except debt secured by the homestead or debt to another lender;

(ii) the owner of the homestead not assign wages as security for the extension of credit;

(iii) the owner of the homestead not sign any instrument in which blanks are left to be filled in;

(iv) the owner of the homestead not sign a confession of judgment or power of attorney to the lender or to a third person to confess judgment or to appear for the owner in a judicial proceeding;

(v) the lender, at the time the extension of credit is made, provide the owner of the homestead a copy of all documents signed by the owner related to the extension of credit;

(vi) the security instruments securing the extension of credit contain a disclosure that the extension of credit is the type of credit defined by Section 50(a)(6), Article XVI, Texas Constitution;

(vii) within a reasonable time after termination and full payment of the extension of credit, the lender cancel and return the promissory note to the owner of the homestead and give the owner, in recordable form, a release of the lien securing the extension of credit or a copy of an endorsement and assignment of the lien to a lender that is refinancing the extension of credit;

(viii)the owner of the homestead and any spouse of the owner may, within three days after the extension of credit is made, rescind the extension of credit without penalty or charge;

(ix) the owner of the homestead and the lender sign a written acknowledgment as to the fair market value of the homestead property on the date the extension of credit is made; and

(x) the lender or any holder of the note for the extension of credit shall forfeit all principal and interest of the extension of credit if the lender or holder fails to comply with the lender's or holder's obligations under the extension of credit within a reasonable time after the lender or holder is notified by the borrower of the lender's failure to comply;

(7) a reverse mortgage; or

(8) the conversion and refinance of a personal property lien secured by a manufactured home to a lien on real property, including the refinance of the purchase price of the manufactured home, the cost of installing the manufactured home on the real property, and the refinance of the purchase price of the real property.

(b) An owner or claimant of the property claimed as homestead may not sell or abandon the homestead without the consent of each owner and the spouse of each owner, given in such manner as may be prescribed by law.

(c) No mortgage, trust deed, or other lien on the homestead shall ever be valid unless it secures a debt described by this section, whether such mortgage, trust deed, or other lien, shall have been created by the owner alone, or together with his or her spouse, in case the owner is married. All pretended sales of the homestead involving any condition of defeasance shall be void.

(d) A purchaser or lender for value without actual knowledge may conclusively rely on an affidavit that designates other property as the homestead of the affiant and that states that the property to be conveyed or encumbered is not the homestead of the affiant.

(e) A refinance of debt secured by a homestead and described by any subsection under Subsections (a)(1)-(a)(5) that includes the advance of additional funds may not be secured by a valid lien against the homestead unless:

(1) the refinance of the debt is an extension of credit described by Subsection (a)(6) of this section; or

(2) the advance of all the additional funds is for reasonable costs necessary to refinance such debt or for a purpose described by Subsection (a)(2), (a)(3), or (a)(5) of this section.

(f) A refinance of debt secured by the homestead, any portion of which is an extension of credit described by Subsection (a)(6) of this section, may not be secured by a valid lien against the homestead unless the refinance of the debt is an extension of credit described by Subsection (a)(6) of this section.

(g) An extension of credit described by Subsection (a)(6) of this section may be secured by a valid lien against homestead property if the extension of credit is not closed before the 12th day after the lender provides the owner with the following written notice on a separate instrument:

"NOTICE CONCERNING EXTENSIONS OF CREDIT DEFINED BY SECTION 50(a)(6), ARTICLE XVI, TEXAS CONSTITUTION:

"SECTION 50(a)(6), ARTICLE XVI, OF THE TEXAS CONSTITUTION ALLOWS CERTAIN LOANS TO BE SECURED AGAINST THE EQUITY IN YOUR HOME. SUCH LOANS ARE COMMONLY KNOWN AS EQUITY LOANS. IF YOU DO NOT REPAY THE LOAN OR IF YOU FAIL TO MEET THE TERMS OF THE LOAN, THE LENDER MAY FORECLOSE AND SELL YOUR HOME. THE CONSTITUTION PROVIDES THAT:

"(A) THE LOAN MUST BE VOLUNTARILY CREATED WITH THE CONSENT OF EACH OWNER OF YOUR HOME AND EACH OWNER'S SPOUSE;

"(B) THE PRINCIPAL LOAN AMOUNT AT THE TIME THE LOAN IS MADE MUST NOT EXCEED AN AMOUNT THAT, WHEN ADDED TO THE PRINCIPAL BALANCES OF ALL OTHER LIENS AGAINST YOUR HOME, IS MORE THAN 80 PERCENT OF THE FAIR MARKET VALUE OF YOUR HOME;

"(C) THE LOAN MUST BE WITHOUT RECOURSE FOR PERSONAL LIABILITY AGAINST YOU AND YOUR SPOUSE UNLESS YOU OR YOUR SPOUSE OBTAINED THIS EXTENSION OF CREDIT BY ACTUAL FRAUD;

"(D) THE LIEN SECURING THE LOAN MAY BE FORECLOSED UPON ONLY WITH A COURT ORDER;

"(E) FEES AND CHARGES TO MAKE THE LOAN MAY NOT EXCEED 3 PERCENT OF THE LOAN AMOUNT;

"(F) THE LOAN MAY NOT BE AN OPEN-END ACCOUNT THAT MAY BE DEBITED FROM TIME TO TIME OR UNDER WHICH CREDIT MAY BE EXTENDED FROM TIME TO TIME;

"(G) YOU MAY PREPAY THE LOAN WITHOUT PENALTY OR CHARGE;

"(H) NO ADDITIONAL COLLATERAL MAY BE SECURITY FOR THE LOAN;

"(I) THE LOAN MAY NOT BE SECURED BY AGRICULTURAL HOMESTEAD PROPERTY, UNLESS THE AGRICULTURAL HOMESTEAD PROPERTY IS USED PRIMARILY FOR THE PRODUCTION OF MILK;

"(J) YOU ARE NOT REQUIRED TO REPAY THE LOAN EARLIER THAN AGREED SOLELY BECAUSE THE FAIR MARKET VALUE OF YOUR HOME DECREASES OR BECAUSE YOU DEFAULT ON ANOTHER LOAN THAT IS NOT SECURED BY YOUR HOME;

"(K) ONLY ONE LOAN DESCRIBED BY SECTION 50(a)(6), ARTICLE XVI, OF THE TEXAS CONSTITUTION MAY BE SECURED WITH YOUR HOME AT ANY GIVEN TIME;

"(L) THE LOAN MUST BE SCHEDULED TO BE REPAID IN PAYMENTS THAT EQUAL OR EXCEED THE AMOUNT OF ACCRUED INTEREST FOR EACH PAYMENT PERIOD;

"(M) THE LOAN MAY NOT CLOSE BEFORE 12 DAYS AFTER YOU SUBMIT A WRITTEN APPLICATION TO THE LENDER OR BEFORE 12 DAYS AFTER YOU RECEIVE THIS NOTICE, WHICHEVER DATE IS LATER; AND IF YOUR HOME WAS SECURITY FOR THE SAME TYPE OF LOAN WITHIN THE PAST YEAR, A NEW LOAN SECURED BY THE SAME PROPERTY MAY NOT CLOSE BEFORE ONE YEAR HAS PASSED FROM THE CLOSING DATE OF THE OTHER LOAN;

"(N) THE LOAN MAY CLOSE ONLY AT THE OFFICE OF THE LENDER, TITLE COMPANY, OR AN ATTORNEY AT LAW;

"(O) THE LENDER MAY CHARGE ANY FIXED OR VARIABLE RATE OF INTEREST AUTHORIZED BY STATUTE;

"(P) ONLY A LAWFULLY AUTHORIZED LENDER MAY MAKE LOANS DESCRIBED BY SECTION 50(a)(6), ARTICLE XVI, OF THE TEXAS CONSTITUTION; AND

"(Q) LOANS DESCRIBED BY SECTION 50(a)(6), ARTICLE XVI, OF THE TEXAS CONSTITUTION MUST:

"(1) NOT REQUIRE YOU TO APPLY THE PROCEEDS TO ANOTHER DEBT THAT IS NOT SECURED BY YOUR HOME OR TO ANOTHER DEBT TO THE SAME LENDER;

"(2) NOT REQUIRE THAT YOU ASSIGN WAGES AS SECURITY;

"(3) NOT REQUIRE THAT YOU EXECUTE INSTRUMENTS WHICH HAVE BLANKS LEFT TO BE FILLED IN;

"(4) NOT REQUIRE THAT YOU SIGN A CONFESSION OF JUDGMENT OR POWER OF ATTORNEY TO ANOTHER PERSON TO CONFESS JUDGMENT OR APPEAR IN A LEGAL PROCEEDING ON YOUR BEHALF;

"(5) PROVIDE THAT YOU RECEIVE A COPY OF ALL DOCUMENTS YOU SIGN AT CLOSING;

"(6) PROVIDE THAT THE SECURITY INSTRUMENTS CONTAIN A DISCLOSURE THAT THIS LOAN IS

A LOAN DEFINED BY SECTION 50(a)(6), ARTICLE XVI, OF THE TEXAS CONSTITUTION;

"(7) PROVIDE THAT WHEN THE LOAN IS PAID IN FULL, THE LENDER WILL SIGN AND GIVE YOU A RELEASE OF LIEN OR AN ASSIGNMENT OF THE LIEN, WHICHEVER IS APPROPRIATE;

"(8) PROVIDE THAT YOU MAY, WITHIN 3 DAYS AFTER CLOSING, RESCIND THE LOAN WITHOUT PENALTY OR CHARGE;

"(9) PROVIDE THAT YOU AND THE LENDER ACKNOWLEDGE THE FAIR MARKET VALUE OF YOUR HOME ON THE DATE THE LOAN CLOSES; AND

"(10) PROVIDE THAT THE LENDER WILL FORFEIT ALL PRINCIPAL AND INTEREST IF THE LENDER FAILS TO COMPLY WITH THE LENDER'S OBLIGATIONS."

If the discussions with the borrower are conducted primarily in a language other than English, the lender shall, before closing, provide an additional copy of the notice translated into the written language in which the discussions were conducted.

(h) A lender or assignee for value may conclusively rely on the written acknowledgment as to the fair market value of the homestead property made in accordance with Subsection (a)(6)(Q)(ix) of this section if:

(1) the value acknowledged to is the value estimate in an appraisal or evaluation prepared in accordance with a state or federal requirement applicable to an extension of credit under Subsection (a)(6); and

(2) the lender or assignee does not have actual knowledge at the time of the payment of value or advance of funds by the lender or assignee that the fair market value stated in the written acknowledgment was incorrect.

(i) This subsection shall not affect or impair any right of the borrower to recover damages from the lender or assignee under applicable law for wrongful foreclosure. A purchaser for value without actual knowledge may conclusively presume that a lien securing an extension of credit described by Subsection (a)(6) of this section was a valid lien securing the extension of credit with homestead property if:

(1) the security instruments securing the extension of credit contain a disclosure that the extension of credit secured by the lien was the type of credit defined by Section 50(a)(6), Article XVI, Texas Constitution;

(2) the purchaser acquires the title to the property pursuant to or after the foreclosure of the voluntary lien; and

(3) the purchaser is not the lender or assignee under the extension of credit.

(j) Subsection (a)(6) and Subsections (e)-(i) of this section are not severable, and none of those provisions would have been enacted without the others. If any of those provisions are held to be preempted by the laws of the United States, all of those provisions are invalid. This subsection shall not apply to any lien or extension of credit made after January 1, 1998, and before the date any provision under Subsection (a)(6) or Subsections (e)-(i) is held to be preempted.

(k) "Reverse mortgage" means an extension of credit:

(1) that is secured by a voluntary lien on homestead property created by a written agreement with the consent of each owner and each owner's spouse;

(2) that is made to a person who is or whose spouse is 62 years or older;

(3) that is made without recourse for personal liability against each owner and the spouse of each owner;

(4) under which advances are provided to a borrower based on the equity in a borrower's homestead;

(5) that does not permit the lender to reduce the amount or number of advances because of an adjustment in the interest rate if periodic advances are to be made;

(6) that requires no payment of principal or interest until:

(A) all borrowers have died;

(B) the homestead property securing the loan is sold or otherwise transferred;

(C) all borrowers cease occupying the homestead property for a period of longer than 12 consecutive months without prior written approval from the lender; or

(D) the borrower:

(i) defaults on an obligation specified in the loan documents to repair and maintain, pay taxes and assessments on, or insure the homestead property;

(ii) commits actual fraud in connection with the loan; or

(iii) fails to maintain the priority of the lender's lien on the homestead property, after the lender gives notice to the borrower, by promptly discharging any lien that has priority or may obtain priority over the lender's lien within 10 days after the date the borrower receives the notice, unless the borrower:

(a) agrees in writing to the payment of the obligation secured by the lien in a manner acceptable to the lender;

(b) contests in good faith the lien by, or defends against enforcement of the lien in, legal proceedings so as to prevent the enforcement of the lien or forfeiture of any part of the homestead property; or

(c) secures from the holder of the lien an agreement satisfactory to the lender subordinating the lien to all amounts secured by the lender's lien on the homestead property;

(7) that provides that if the lender fails to make loan advances as required in the loan documents and if the lender fails to cure the default as required in the loan documents after notice from the borrower, the lender forfeits all principal and interest of the reverse mortgage, provided, however, that this subdivision does not apply when a governmental agency or instrumentality takes an assignment of the loan in order to cure the default;

(8) that is not made unless the owner of the homestead attests in writing that the owner received counseling regarding the advisability and availability of reverse mortgages and other financial alternatives;

(9) that requires the lender, at the time the loan is made, to disclose to the borrower by written notice the specific provisions contained in Subdivision (6) of this subsection under which the borrower is required to repay the loan;

(10) that does not permit the lender to commence foreclosure until the lender gives notice to the borrower, in the manner provided for a notice by mail related to the foreclosure of liens under Subsection (a)(6) of this section, that a ground for foreclosure exists and gives the borrower at least 30 days, or at least 20 days in the event of a default under Subdivision (6)(D)(iii) of this subsection, to:

(A) remedy the condition creating the ground for foreclosure;

(B) pay the debt secured by the homestead property from proceeds of the sale of the homestead property by the borrower or from any other sources; or

(C) convey the homestead property to the lender by a deed in lieu of foreclosure; and

(11) that is secured by a lien that may be foreclosed upon only by a court order, if the foreclosure is for a ground other than a ground stated by Subdivision (6)(A) or (B) of this subsection.

(*l*) Advances made under a reverse mortgage and interest on those advances have priority over a lien filed for record in the real property records in the county where the homestead property is located after the reverse mortgage is filed for record in the real property records of that county.

(m) A reverse mortgage may provide for an interest rate that is fixed or adjustable and may also provide for interest that is contingent on appreciation in the fair market value of the homestead property. Although payment of principal or interest shall not be required under a reverse mortgage until the entire loan becomes due and payable, interest may accrue and be compounded during the term of the loan as provided by the reverse mortgage loan agreement.

(n) A reverse mortgage that is secured by a valid lien against homestead property may be made or acquired without regard to the following provisions of any other law of this state:

(1) a limitation on the purpose and use of future advances or other mortgage proceeds;

(2) a limitation on future advances to a term of years or a limitation on the term of open-end account advances;

(3) a limitation on the term during which future advances take priority over intervening advances;

(4) a requirement that a maximum loan amount be stated in the reverse mortgage loan documents;

(5) a prohibition on balloon payments;

(6) a prohibition on compound interest and interest on interest;

(7) a prohibition on contracting for, charging, or receiving any rate of interest authorized by any law of this state authorizing a lender to contract for a rate of interest; and

(8) a requirement that a percentage of the reverse mortgage proceeds be advanced before the assignment of the reverse mortgage.

(o) For the purposes of determining eligibility under any statute relating to payments, allowances, benefits, or services provided on a means-tested basis by this state, including supplemental security income, low-income energy assistance, property tax relief, medical assistance, and general assistance:

(1) reverse mortgage loan advances made to a borrower are considered proceeds from a loan and not income; and

(2) undisbursed funds under a reverse mortgage loan are considered equity in a borrower's home and not proceeds from a loan.

(p) The advances made on a reverse mortgage loan under which more than one advance is made must be made according to the terms established by the loan documents by one or more of the following methods:

(1) at regular intervals;

(2) at regular intervals in which the amounts advanced may be reduced, for one or more advances, at the request of the borrower; or

(3) at any time by the lender, on behalf of the borrower, if the borrower fails to timely pay any of the following that the borrower is obligated to pay under the loan documents to the extent necessary to protect the lender's interest in or the value of the homestead property:

(A) taxes;

(B) insurance;

(C) costs of repairs or maintenance performed by a person or company that is not an employee of the lender or a person or company that directly or indirectly controls, is controlled by, or is under common control with the lender;

(D) assessments levied against the homestead property; and

(E) any lien that has, or may obtain, priority over the lender's lien as it is established in the loan documents.

(q) To the extent that any statutes of this state, including without limitation, Section 41.001 of the Texas Property Code, purport to limit encumbrances that may properly be fixed on homestead property in a manner that does not permit encumbrances for extensions of credit described in Subsection (a)(6) or (a)(7) of this section, the same shall be superseded to the extent that such encumbrances shall be permitted to be fixed upon homestead property in the manner provided for by this amendment.

(r) The supreme court shall promulgate rules of civil procedure for expedited foreclosure proceedings related to the foreclosure of liens under Subsection (a)(6) of this section and to foreclosure of a reverse mortgage lien that requires a court order.

(s) The Finance Commission of Texas shall appoint a director to conduct research on the availability, quality, and prices of financial services and research the practices of business entities in the state that provide financial services under this section. The director shall collect information and produce reports on lending activity of those making loans under this section. The director shall report his or her findings to the legislature not later than December 1 of each year.

§51. AMOUNT OF HOMESTEAD; USES

The homestead, not in a town or city, shall consist of not more than two hundred acres of land, which may be in one or more parcels, with the improvements thereon; the homestead in a city, town or village, shall consist of lot or contiguous lots amounting to not more than 10 acres of land, together with any improvements on the land; provided, that the homestead in a city, town or village shall be used for the purposes of a home, or as both an urban home and a place to exercise a calling or business, of the homestead claimant, whether a single adult person, or the head of a family; provided also, that any temporary renting of the homestead shall not change the character of the same, when no other homestead has been acquired; provided further that a release or refinance of an existing lien against a homestead as to a part of the homestead does not create an additional burden on the part of the homestead property that is unreleased or subject to the refinance, and a new lien is not invalid only for that reason.

UNITED STATES CODE
SELECTED PROVISIONS
TABLE OF CONTENTS

UNITED STATES CODE
SELECTED PROVISIONS
TABLE OF CONTENTS

TITLE 10. ARMED FORCES

SUBTITLE A. GENERAL MILITARY LAW

PART II. PERSONNEL

CHAPTER 71. COMPUTATION OF RETIRED PAY

§1408. PAYMENT OF RETIRED OR RETAINER PAY IN COMPLIANCE WITH COURT ORDERS

(a) Definitions—In this section:

(1) The term "court" means—

(A) any court of competent jurisdiction of any State, the District of Columbia, the Commonwealth of Puerto Rico, Guam, American Samoa, the Virgin Islands, the Northern Mariana Islands, and the Trust Territory of the Pacific Islands;

(B) any court of the United States (as defined in section 451 of title 28) having competent jurisdiction;

(C) any court of competent jurisdiction of a foreign country with which the United States has an agreement requiring the United States to honor any court order of such country; and

(D) any administrative or judicial tribunal of a State competent to enter orders for support or maintenance (including a State agency administering a program under a State plan approved under part D of title IV of the Social Security Act [42 U.S.C. §651 et seq.]), and, for purposes of this subparagraph, the term "State" includes the District of Columbia, the Commonwealth of Puerto Rico, the Virgin Islands, Guam, and American Samoa.

(2) The term "court order" means a final decree of divorce, dissolution, annulment, or legal separation issued by a court, or a court ordered, ratified, or approved property settlement incident to such a decree (including a final decree modifying the terms of a previously issued decree of divorce, dissolution, annulment, or legal separation, or a court ordered, ratified, or approved property settlement incident to such previously issued decree), or a support order, as defined in section 453(p) of the Social Security Act (42 U.S.C. 653(p)), which—

(A) is issued in accordance with the laws of the jurisdiction of that court;

(B) provides for—

(i) payment of child support (as defined in section 459(i)(2) of the Social Security Act (42 U.S.C. 659(i)(2)));

(ii) payment of alimony (as defined in section 459(i)(3) of the Social Security Act (42 U.S.C. 659(i)(3))); or

(iii) division of property (including a division of community property); and

(C) in the case of a division of property, specifically provides for the payment of an amount, expressed in dollars or as a percentage of disposable retired pay, from the disposable retired pay of a member to the spouse or former spouse of that member.

(3) The term "final decree" means a decree from which no appeal may be taken or from which no appeal has been taken within the time allowed for taking such appeals under the laws applicable to such appeals, or a decree from which timely appeal has been taken and such appeal has been finally decided under the laws applicable to such appeals.

(4) The term "disposable retired pay" means the total monthly retired pay to which a member is entitled less amounts which—

(A) are owed by that member to the United States for previous overpayments of retired pay and for recoupments required by law resulting from entitlement to retired pay;

(B) are deducted from the retired pay of such member as a result of forfeitures of retired pay ordered by a court-martial or as a result of a waiver of retired pay required by law in order to receive compensation under title 5 or title 38;

(C) in the case of a member entitled to retired pay under chapter 61 of this title [10 U.S.C. §1201 et seq.], are equal to the amount of retired pay of the member under that chapter computed using the percentage of the member's disability on the date when the member was retired (or the date on which the member's name was placed on the temporary disability retired list); or

(D) are deducted because of an election under chapter 73 of this title [10 U.S.C. §1431 et seq.] to provide an annuity to a spouse or former spouse to whom payment of a portion of such member's retired pay is being made pursuant to a court order under this section.

(5) The term "member" includes a former member entitled to retired pay under section 12731 of this title.

(6) The term "spouse or former spouse" means the husband or wife, or former husband or wife, respectively, of a member who, on or before the date of a court order, was married to that member.

(7) The term "retired pay" includes retainer pay.

(b) Effective service of process.—For the purposes of this section—

(1) service of a court order is effective if—

(A) an appropriate agent of the Secretary concerned designated for receipt of service court orders under regulations prescribed pursuant to subsection (i) or, if no agent has been so designated, the Secretary concerned, is personally served or is served by facsimile or electronic transmission or by mail;

(B) the court order is regular on its face;

(C) the court order or other documents served with the court order identify the member concerned and include, if possible, the social security number of such member; and

(D) the court order or other documents served with the court order certify that the rights of the member under the Soldiers' and Sailors' Civil Relief Act of 1940 (50 U.S.C. App. 501 et seq.) were observed; and

(2) a court order is regular on its face if the order—

(A) is issued by a court of competent jurisdiction;

(B) is legal in form; and

(C) includes nothing on its face that provides reasonable notice that it is issued without authority of law.

(c) Authority for court to treat retired pay as property of the member and spouse.—

(1) Subject to the limitations of this section, a court may treat disposable retired pay payable to a member for pay periods beginning after June 25, 1981, either as property solely of the member or as property of the member and his spouse in accordance with the law of the jurisdiction of such court. A court may not treat retired pay as property in any proceeding to divide or partition any amount of retired pay of a member as the property of the member and the member's spouse or former spouse if a final decree of divorce, dissolution, annulment, or legal separation (including a court ordered, ratified, or approved property settlement incident to such decree) affecting the member and the member's spouse or former spouse (A) was issued before June 25, 1981, and (B) did not treat (or reserve jurisdiction to treat) any amount of retired pay of the member as property of the member and the member's spouse or former spouse.

(2) Notwithstanding any other provision of law, this section does not create any right, title, or interest which can be sold, assigned, transferred, or otherwise disposed of (including by inheritance) by a spouse or former spouse. Payments by the Secretary concerned under subsection (d) to a spouse or former spouse with respect to a division of retired pay as the property of a member and the member's spouse under this subsection may not be treated as amounts received as retired pay for service in the uniformed services.

(3) This section does not authorize any court to order a member to apply for retirement or retire at a particular time in order to effectuate any payment under this section.

(4) A court may not treat the disposable retired pay of a member in the manner described in paragraph (1) unless the court has jurisdiction over the member by reason of (A) his residence, other than because of military assignment, in the territorial jurisdiction of the court, (B) his domicile in the territorial jurisdiction of the court, or (C) his consent to the jurisdiction of the court.

(d) Payments by Secretary concerned to (or for benefit of) spouse or former spouse.—

(1) After effective service on the Secretary concerned of a court order providing for the payment of child support or alimony or, with respect to a division of property, specifically providing for the payment of an amount of the disposable retired pay from a member to the spouse or a former spouse of the member, the Secretary shall make payments (subject to the limitations of this section) from the disposable retired pay of the member to the spouse or former spouse (or for the benefit of such spouse or former spouse to a State disbursement unit established pursuant to section 454B of the Social Security Act [42 U.S.C. §654b] or other public payee designated by a State, in accordance with part D of title IV of the Social Security Act [42 U.S.C. §651 et seq.], as directed by court order, or as otherwise directed in accordance with such part D) in an amount sufficient to satisfy the amount of child support and alimony set forth in the court order and, with respect to a division of property, in the amount of disposable retired pay specifically provided for in the court order. In the case of a spouse or former spouse who, pursuant to section 408(a)(3) of the Social Security Act (42 U.S.C. 608(a)[(3)](4)), assigns to a State the rights of the spouse or former spouse to receive support, the Secretary concerned may make the child support payments referred to in the preceding sentence to that State in amounts consistent with that assignment of rights. In the case of a member entitled to receive retired pay on the date of the effective service of the court order, such payments shall begin not later than 90 days after the date of effective service. In the case of a member not entitled to receive retired pay on the date of the effective service of the court order, such payments shall begin not later than 90 days after the date on which the member first becomes entitled to receive retired pay.

(2) If the spouse or former spouse to whom payments are to be made under this section was not married to the member for a period of 10 years or more during which the member performed at least 10 years of service creditable in determining the member's eligibility for retired pay, payments may not be made under this section to the extent that they include an amount resulting from the treatment by the court under subsection (c) of disposable retired pay of the member as property of the member or property of the member and his spouse.

(3) Payments under this section shall not be made more frequently than once each month, and the Secretary concerned shall not be required to vary normal pay and disbursement cycles for retired pay in order to comply with a court order.

(4) Payments from the disposable retired pay of a member pursuant to this section shall terminate in accordance with the terms of the applicable court order, but not later than the date of the death of the member or the date of the death of the spouse or former spouse to whom payments are being made, whichever occurs first.

(5) If a court order described in paragraph (1) provides for a division of property (including a division of community property) in addition to an amount of child support or alimony or the payment of an amount of disposable retired pay as the result of the court's treatment of such pay under subsection (c) as property of the member and his spouse, the Secretary concerned shall pay (subject to the limitations of this section) from the disposable retired pay of the member to the spouse or former spouse of the member, any part of the amount payable to the spouse or former spouse under the division of property upon effective service of a final court order of garnishment of such amount from such retired pay.

A **(6)** In the case of a court order for which effective service is made on the Secretary concerned on or after Aug. 22, 1996 and which provides for payments from the disposable retired pay of a member to satisfy the amount of child support set forth in the order, the authority provided in paragraph (1) to make payments from the disposable retired pay of a member to satisfy the amount of child support set forth in a court order shall apply to payment of any amount of child support arrearages set forth in that order as well as to amounts of child support that currently become due.

(7)(A) The Secretary concerned may not accept service of a court order that is an out-of-State modification, or comply with the provisions of such a court order, unless the court issuing that order has jurisdiction in the manner specified in subsection (c)(4) over both the member and the spouse or former spouse involved.

(B) A court order shall be considered to be an out-of-State modification for purposes of this paragraph if the order—

(i) modifies a previous court order under this section upon which payments under this subsection are based; and

(ii) is issued by a court of a State other than the State of the court that issued the previous court order.

(e) Limitations.—

(1) The total amount of the disposable retired pay of a member payable under all court orders pursuant to subsection (c) may not exceed 50 percent of such disposable retired pay.

(2) In the event of effective service of more than one court order which provide for payment to a spouse and one or more former spouses or to more than one former spouse the disposable retired pay of the member shall be used to satisfy (subject to the limitations of paragraph (1)) such court orders on a first-come, first-served basis. Such court orders shall be satisfied (subject to the limitations of paragraph (1)) out of that amount of disposable retired pay which remains after the satisfaction of all court orders which have been previously served.

(3)(A) In the event of effective service of conflicting court orders under this section which assert to direct that different amounts be paid during a month to the same spouse or former spouse of the same member, the Secretary concerned shall—

(i) pay to that spouse from the member's disposable retired pay the least amount directed to be paid during that month by any such conflicting court order, but not more than the amount of disposable retired pay which remains available for payment of such courts orders based on when such court orders were effectively served and the limitations of paragraph (1) and subparagraph (B) of paragraph (4);

(ii) retain an amount of disposable retired pay that is equal to the lesser of—

(I) the difference between the largest amount required by any conflicting court order to be paid to the spouse or former spouse and the amount payable to the spouse or former spouse under clause (i); and

(II) the amount of disposable retired pay which remains available for payment of any conflicting court order based on when such court order was effectively served and the limitations of paragraph (1) and subparagraph (B) of paragraph (4); and

(iii) pay to that member the amount which is equal to the amount of that member's disposable retired pay (less any amount paid during such month pursuant to legal process served under section 459 of the Social Security Act (42 U.S.C. 659) and any amount paid during such month pursuant to court orders effectively served under this section, other than such conflicting court orders) minus—

(I) the amount of disposable retired pay paid under clause (i); and

(II) the amount of disposable retired pay retained under clause (ii).

(B) The Secretary concerned shall hold the amount retained under clause (ii) of subparagraph (A) until such time as that Secretary is provided with a court order which has been certified by the member and the spouse or former spouse to be valid and applicable to the retained amount. Upon being provided with such an order, the Secretary shall pay the retained amount in accordance with the order.

(4)(A) In the event of effective service of a court order under this section and the service of legal process pursuant to section 459 of the Social Security Act (42 U.S.C. 659), both of which provide for payments during a month from the same member, satisfaction of such court orders and legal process from the retired pay of the member shall be on a first-come, first-served basis. Such court orders and legal process shall be satisfied out of moneys which are subject to such orders and legal process and which remain available in accordance with the limitations of paragraph (1) and subparagraph (B) of this paragraph during such month after the satisfaction of all court orders or legal process which have been previously served.

(B) Notwithstanding any other provision of law, the total amount of the disposable retired pay of a member payable by the Secretary concerned under all court orders pursuant to this section and all legal processes pursuant to section 459 of the Social Security Act (42 U.S.C. 659) with respect to a member may not exceed 65 percent of the amount of the retired pay payable to such member that is considered under section 462 of the Social Security Act (42 U.S.C. 662) to be remuneration for employment that is payable by the United States.

(5) A court order which itself or because of previously served court orders provides for the payment of an amount which exceeds the amount of disposable retired pay available for payment because of the limit set forth in paragraph (1), or which, because of previously served court orders or legal process previously served under section 459 of the Social Security Act (42 U.S.C. 659), provides for payment of an amount that exceeds the maximum amount permitted under paragraph (1) or subparagraph (B) of paragraph (4), shall not be considered to be irregular on its face solely for that reason. However, such order shall be considered to be fully satisfied for purposes of this section by the payment to the spouse or former spouse of the maximum amount of disposable retired pay permitted under paragraph (1) and subparagraph (B) of paragraph (4).

(6) Nothing in this section shall be construed to relieve a member of liability for the payment of alimony, child support, or other payments required by a court order on the grounds that payments made out of disposable retired pay under this section have been made in the maximum amount permitted under paragraph (1) or subparagraph (B) of paragraph (4). Any such unsatisfied obligation of a member may be enforced by any means available under law other than the means provided under this section in any case in which the maximum amount permitted under paragraph (1) has been paid and under section 459 of the Social Security Act (42 U.S.C. 659) in any case in which the maximum amount permitted under subparagraph (B) of paragraph (4) has been paid.

(f) Immunity of officers and employees of United States.—

(1) The United States and any officer or employee of the United States shall not be liable with respect to any payment made from retired pay to any member, spouse, or former spouse pursuant to a court order that is regular on its face if such payment is made in accordance with this section and the regulations prescribed pursuant to subsection (i).

(2) An officer or employee of the United States who, under regulations prescribed pursuant to subsection (i), has the duty to respond to interrogatories shall not be subject under any law to any disciplinary action or civil or criminal liability or penalty for, or because of, any disclosure of information made by him in carrying out any of his duties which directly or indirectly pertain to answering such interrogatories.

(g) Notice to member of service of court order on Secretary concerned.—

A person receiving effective service of a court order under this section shall, as soon as possible, but not later than 30 days after the date on which effective service is made, send a written notice of such court order (together with a copy of such order) to the member affected by the court order at his last known address.

(h) Benefits for dependents who are victims of abuse by members losing right to retired pay.—

(1) If, in the case of a member or former member of the armed forces referred to in paragraph (2)(A), a court order provides (in the manner applicable to a division of property) for the payment of an amount from the disposable retired pay of that member or former member (as certified under paragraph (4)) to an eligible spouse or former spouse of that member or former member, the Secretary concerned, beginning upon effective service of such court order, shall pay that amount in accordance with this subsection to such spouse or former spouse.

(2) A spouse or former spouse of a member or former member of the armed forces is eligible to receive payment under this subsection if—

(A) the member or former member, while a member of the armed forces and after becoming eligible to be retired from the armed forces on the basis of years of service, has eligibility to receive retired pay terminated as a result of misconduct while a member involving abuse of a spouse or dependent child (as defined in regulations prescribed by the Secretary of Defense or, for the Coast Guard when it is not operating as a service in the Navy, by the Secretary of Transportation); and

(B) the spouse or former spouse—

(i) was the victim of the abuse and was married to the member or former member at the time of that abuse; or

(ii) is a natural or adopted parent of a dependent child of the member or former member who was the victim of the abuse.

(3) The amount certified by the Secretary concerned under paragraph (4) with respect to a member or former member of the armed forces referred to in paragraph (2)(A) shall be deemed to be the disposable retired pay of that member or former member for the purposes of this subsection.

(4) Upon the request of a court or an eligible spouse or former spouse of a member or former member of the armed forces referred to in paragraph (2)(A) in connection with a civil action for the issuance of a court order in the case of that member or former member, the Secretary concerned shall determine and certify the amount of the monthly retired pay that the member or former member would have been entitled to receive as of the date of the certification—

(A) if the member or former member's eligibility for retired pay had not been terminated as described in paragraph (2)(A); and

(B) if, in the case of a member or former member not in receipt of retired pay immediately before that termination of eligibility for retired pay, the member or former member had retired on the effective date of that termination of eligibility.

(5) A court order under this subsection may provide that whenever retired pay is increased under section 1401a of this title (or any other provision of law), the amount payable under the court order to the spouse or former spouse of a member or former member described in paragraph (2)(A) shall be increased at the same time by the percent by which the retired pay of the member or former member would have been increased if the member or former member were receiving retired pay.

(6) Notwithstanding any other provision of law, a member or former member of the armed forces referred to in paragraph (2)(A) shall have no ownership interest in, or claim against, any amount payable under

this section to a spouse or former spouse of the member or former member.

(7)(A) If a former spouse receiving payments under this subsection with respect to a member or former member referred to in paragraph (2)(A) marries again after such payments begin, the eligibility of the former spouse to receive further payments under this subsection shall terminate on the date of such marriage.

(B) A person's eligibility to receive payments under this subsection that is terminated under subparagraph (A) by reason of remarriage shall be resumed in the event of the termination of that marriage by the death of that person's spouse or by annulment or divorce. The resumption of payments shall begin as of the first day of the month in which that marriage is so terminated. The monthly amount of the payments shall be the amount that would have been paid if the continuity of the payments had not been interrupted by the marriage.

(8) Payments in accordance with this subsection shall be made out of funds in the Department of Defense Military Retirement Fund established by section 1461 of this title or, in the case of the Coast Guard, out of funds appropriated to the Department of Transportation for payment of retired pay for the Coast Guard.

(9)(A) A spouse or former spouse of a member or former member of the armed forces referred to in paragraph (2)(A), while receiving payments in accordance with this subsection, shall be entitled to receive medical and dental care, to use commissary and exchange stores, and to receive any other benefit that a spouse or a former spouse of a retired member of the armed forces is entitled to receive on the basis of being a spouse or former spouse, as the case may be, of a retired member of the armed forces in the same manner as if the member or former member referred to in paragraph (2)(A) was entitled to retired pay.

(B) A dependent child of a member or former member referred to in paragraph (2)(A) who was a member of the household of the member or former member at the time of the misconduct described in paragraph (2)(A) shall be entitled to receive medical and dental care, to use commissary and exchange stores, and to have other benefits provided to dependents of retired members of the armed forces in the same manner as if the member or former member referred to in paragraph (2)(A) was entitled to retired pay.

(C) If a spouse or former spouse or a dependent child eligible or entitled to receive a particular benefit under this paragraph is eligible or entitled to receive that benefit under another provision of law, the eligibility or entitlement of that spouse or former spouse or dependent child to such benefit shall be determined under such other provision of law instead of this paragraph.

(10)(A) For purposes of this subsection, in the case of a member of the armed forces who has been sentenced by a court-martial to receive a punishment that will terminate the eligibility of that member to receive retired pay if executed, the eligibility of that member to receive retired pay may, as determined by the Secretary concerned, be considered terminated effective upon the approval of that sentence by the person acting under section 860(c) of this title (article 60(c) of the Uniform Code of Military Justice).

(B) If each form of the punishment that would result in the termination of eligibility to receive retired pay is later remitted, set aside, or mitigated to a punishment that does not result in the termination of that eligibility, a payment of benefits to the eligible recipient under this subsection that is based on the punishment so vacated, set aside, or mitigated shall cease. The cessation of payments shall be effective as of the first day of the first month following the month in which the Secretary concerned notifies the recipient of such benefits in writing that payment of the benefits will cease. The recipient may not be required to repay the benefits received before that effective date (except to the extent necessary to recoup any amount that was erroneous when paid).

(11) In this subsection, the term "dependent child", with respect to a member or former member of the armed forces referred to in paragraph (2)(A), means an unmarried legitimate child, including an adopted child or a stepchild of the member or former member, who—

(A) is under 18 years of age;

(B) is incapable of self-support because of a mental or physical incapacity that existed before becoming 18 years of age and is dependent on the member or former member for over one-half of the child's support; or

(C) if enrolled in a full-time course of study in an institution of higher education recognized by the Secretary of Defense for the purposes of this subparagraph, is under 23 years of age and is dependent on the member or former member for over one-half of the child's support.

(i) Certification date.—It is not necessary that the date of a certification of the authenticity or completeness of a copy of a court order for child support received by the Secretary concerned for the purposes of this section be recent in relation to the date of receipt by the Secretary.

(j) Regulations.—The Secretaries concerned shall prescribe uniform regulations for the administration of this section.

(k) Relationship to other laws.—In any case involving an order providing for payment of child support (as defined in section 459(i)(2) of the Social Security Act [42 U.S.C. §659(i)(2)]) by a member who has never been married to the other parent of the child, the provisions of this section shall not apply, and the case shall be subject to the provisions of section 459 of such Act [42 U.S.C. §659].

History of 10 U.S.C. §1408: Added Sept. 8, 1982, P.L. 97-252, §1002(a), 96 Stat. 730; Oct. 19, 1984, P.L. 98-525, §643(a)-(d), 98 Stat. 2547; Nov. 14, 1986, P.L. 99-661, §644(a), 100 Stat. 3887; April 21, 1987, P.L. 100-26, §§3(3) in part, 7(h)(1) in part, 101 Stat. 273, 282; Nov. 29, 1989, P.L. 101-189, §653(a)(5), §1622(e)(6), 103 Stat. 1462, 1605; Nov. 5, 1990, P.L. 101-510, §555(a)-(d), (f), (g), 104 Stat. 1569, 1570; Dec. 5, 1991, P.L. 102-190, §1061(a)(7), 105 Stat. 1472; Oct. 23, 1992, P.L. 102-484, §653(a), 106 Stat. 2426; Nov. 30, 1993, P.L. 103-160, §555(a), (b), §1182(a)(2), 107 Stat. 1666, 1771; Feb. 10, 1996, P.L. 104-106, §1501(c)(16), 110 Stat. 499; Aug. 22, 1996, P.L. 104-193, §§362(c), 363(c)(1)-(3), 110 Stat. 2246, 2249; Sept. 23, 1996, P.L. 104-201, §636, 110 Stat. 2579; Nov. 18, 1997, P.L. 105-85, §1073(a)(24), (25), 111 Stat. 1901; Dec. 28, 2001, P.L. 107-107, §1048(c)(9), 115 Stat. 1226.

CHAPTER 73. ANNUITIES BASED ON RETIRED OR RETAINER PAY

SUBCHAPTER II. SURVIVOR BENEFIT PLAN

§1447. DEFINITIONS

In this subchapter:

(1) Plan.—The term "Plan" means the Survivor Benefit Plan established by this subchapter.

(2) Standard annuity.—The term "standard annuity" means an annuity provided by virtue of eligibility under section 1448(a)(1)(A) of this title.

(3) Reserve-component annuity.—The term "reserve-component annuity" means an annuity provided by virtue of eligibility under section 1448(a)(1)(B) of this title.

(4) Retired pay.—The term "retired pay" includes retainer pay paid under section 6330 of this title.

(5) Reserve-component retired pay.—The term "reserve-component retired pay" means retired pay under chapter 1223 of this title [10 U.S.C. §12731 et seq.] (or under chapter 67 of this title [former 10 U.S.C. §1331 et seq.] as in effect before the effective date of the Reserve Officer Personnel Management Act).

(6) Base amount.—The term "base amount" means the following:

(A) Full amount under standard annuity.—In the case of a person who dies after becoming entitled to retired pay, such term means the amount of monthly retired pay (determined without regard to any reduction under section 1409(b)(2) of this title) to which the person—

(i) was entitled when he became eligible for that pay; or

(ii) later became entitled by being advanced on the retired list, performing active duty, or being transferred from the temporary disability retired list to the permanent disability retired list.

(B) Full amount under reserve-component annuity.—In the case of a person who would have become eligible for reserve-component retired pay but for the fact that he died before becoming 60 years of age, such term means the amount of monthly retired pay for which the person would have been eligible—

(i) if he had been 60 years of age on the date of his death, for purposes of an annuity to become effective on the day after his death in accordance with a designation made under section 1448(e) of this title; or

(ii) upon becoming 60 years of age (if he had lived to that age), for purposes of an annuity to become effective on the 60th anniversary of his birth in accordance with a designation made under section 1448(e) of this title.

(C) Reduced amount.—Such term means any amount less than the amount otherwise applicable under subparagraph (A) or (B) with respect to an annuity provided under the Plan but which is not less than $300 and which is designated by the person (with the concurrence of the person's spouse, if required under section 1448(a)(3) of this title) providing the annuity on or before—

(i) the first day for which he becomes eligible for retired pay, in the case of a person providing a standard annuity, or

(ii) the end of the 90-day period beginning on the date on which he receives the notification required by section 12731(d) of this title that he has completed the years of service required for eligibility for reserve-component retired pay, in the case of a person providing a reserve-component annuity.

(7) Widow.—The term "widow" means the surviving wife of a person who, if not married to the person at the time he became eligible for retired pay—

(A) was married to him for at least one year immediately before his death; or

(B) is the mother of issue by that marriage.

(8) Widower.—The term "widower" means the surviving husband of a person who, if not married to the person at the time she became eligible for retired pay—

(A) was married to her for at least one year immediately before her death; or

(B) is the father of issue by that marriage.

(9) Surviving spouse.—The term "surviving spouse" means a widow or widower.

(10) Former spouse.—The term "former spouse" means the surviving former husband or wife of a person who is eligible to participate in the Plan.

(11) Dependent child.—

(A) In general.—The term "dependent child" means a person who—

(i) is unmarried;

(ii) is (I) under 18 years of age, (II) at least 18, but under 22, years of age and pursuing a full-time course of study or training in a high school, trade school, technical or vocational institute, junior college, college, university, or comparable recognized educational institution, or (III) incapable of self support because of a mental or physical incapacity existing before the person's eighteenth birthday or incurred on or after that birthday, but before the person's twenty-second birthday, while pursuing such a full-time course of study or training; and

(iii) is the child of a person to whom the Plan applies, including (I) an adopted child, and (II) a stepchild, foster child, or recognized natural child who lived with that person in a regular parent-child relationship.

(B) Special rules for college students.—For the purpose of subparagraph (A), a child whose twenty-second birthday occurs before July 1 or after August 31 of a calendar year, and while regularly pursuing such a course of study or training, is considered to have become 22 years of age on the first day of July after that birthday. A child who is a student is considered not to have ceased to be a student during an interim between school years if the interim is not more than 150 days and if the child shows to the satisfaction of the Secretary of Defense that the child has a bona fide intention of continuing to pursue a course of study or training in the same or a different school during the school semester (or other period into which the school year is divided) immediately after the interim.

(C) Foster children.—A foster child, to qualify under this paragraph as the dependent child of a person to whom the Plan applies, must, at the time of the death of that person, also reside with, and receive over one-half of his support from, that person, and not be cared for under a social agency contract. The temporary absence of a foster child from the residence of that person, while a student as described in this paragraph, shall not be considered to affect the residence of such a foster child.

(12) Court.—The term "court" has the meaning given that term by section 1408(a)(1) of this title.

(13) Court order.—

(A) In general.—The term "court order" means a court's final decree of divorce, dissolution, or annulment or a court ordered, ratified, or approved property settlement incident to such a decree (including a final decree modifying the terms of a previously issued decree of divorce, dissolution, annulment, or legal separation, or of a court ordered, ratified, or approved property settlement agreement incident to such previously issued decree).

(B) Final decree.—The term "final decree" means a decree from which no appeal may be taken or from which no appeal has been taken within the time allowed for the taking of such appeals under the laws applicable to such appeals, or a decree from which timely appeal has been taken and such appeal has been finally decided under the laws applicable to such appeals.

(C) Regular on its face.—The term "regular on its face", when used in connection with a court order, means a court order that meets the conditions prescribed in section 1408(b)(2) of this title.

History of 10 U.S.C. §1447: Added Sept. 21, 1972, P.L. 92-425, §1(3), 86 Stat. 706; Oct. 14, 1976, P.L. 94-496, §1(1), 90 Stat. 2375; Sept. 30, 1978, P.L. 95-397, §201, 92 Stat. 843; Oct. 9, 1980, P.L. 96-402, §2, 94 Stat. 1705; Sept. 8, 1982, P.L. 97-252, §1003(a), 96 Stat. 735; Sept. 24, 1983, P.L. 98-94, §941(c)(1), 97 Stat. 653; Nov. 8, 1985, P.L. 99-145, §719(1), (2), §721(b), 99 Stat. 675, 676; July 1, 1986, P.L. 99-348, §301(a)(1), 100 Stat. 702; Nov. 14, 1986, P.L. 99-661, §1343(a)(8)(A), 100 Stat. 3992; Dec. 4, 1987, P.L. 100-180, §1231(17), 101 Stat. 1161; Nov. 29, 1989, P.L. 101-189, §1407(a)(1)-(3), 103 Stat. 1588; Nov. 5, 1990, P.L. 101-510, §1484(*l*)(4)(C)(i), 104 Stat. 1720; Oct. 5, 1994, P.L. 103-337, §1671(d)(1), (2), 108 Stat. 3014, 3015; Sept. 23, 1996, P.L. 104-201, §634, 110 Stat. 2551.

§1448. APPLICATION OF PLAN

(a) General rules for participation in the Plan.—

(1) Name of Plan; eligible participants.—The program established by this subchapter shall be known as the Survivor Benefit Plan. The following persons are eligible to participate in the Plan:

(A) Persons entitled to retired pay.

(B) Persons who would be eligible for reserve-component retired pay but for the fact that they are under 60 years of age.

(2) Participants in the Plan.—The Plan applies to the following persons, who shall be participants in the Plan:

(A) Standard annuity participants.—A person who is eligible to participate in the Plan under paragraph (1)(A) and who is married or has a dependent child when he becomes entitled to retired pay, unless he elects (with his spouse's concurrence, if required under paragraph (3)) not to participate in the Plan before the first day for which he is eligible for that pay.

(B) Reserve-component annuity participants.—A person who (i) is eligible to participate in the Plan under paragraph (1)(B), and (ii) is married or has a dependent child when he is notified under section 12731(d) of this title that he has completed the years of service required for eligibility for reserve-component retired pay, unless the person elects (with his spouse's concurrence, if required under paragraph (3)) not to participate in the Plan before the end of the 90-day period beginning on the date on which he receives that notification.

A person who elects under subparagraph (B) not to participate in the Plan remains eligible, upon reaching 60 years of age and otherwise becoming entitled to retired pay, to participate in the Plan in accordance with eligibility under paragraph (1)(A).

(3) Elections.—

(A) Spousal consent for certain elections respecting standard annuity.—A married person who is eligible to provide a standard annuity may not without the concurrence of the person's spouse elect—

(i) not to participate in the Plan;

(ii) to provide an annuity for the person's spouse at less than the maximum level; or

(iii) to provide an annuity for a dependent child but not for the person's spouse.

(B) Spousal consent for certain elections respecting reserve-component annuity.—A married person who is eligible to provide a reserve-component annuity may not without the concurrence of the person's spouse elect—

(i) not to participate in the Plan;

(ii) to designate under subsection (e)(2) the effective date for commencement of annuity payments under the Plan in the event that the member dies before becoming 60 years of age to be the 60th anniversary of the member's birth (rather than the day after the date of the member's death);

(iii) to provide an annuity for the person's spouse at less than the maximum level; or

(iv) to provide an annuity for a dependent child but not for the person's spouse.

(C) Exception when spouse unavailable.—A person may make an election described in subparagraph (A) or (B) without the concurrence of the person's spouse if the person establishes to the satisfaction of the Secretary concerned—

(i) that the spouse's whereabouts cannot be determined; or

(ii) that, due to exceptional circumstances, requiring the person to seek the spouse's consent would otherwise be inappropriate.

(D) Construction with former spouse election provisions.—This paragraph does not affect any right or obligation to elect to provide an annuity for a former spouse (or for a former spouse and dependent child) under subsection (b)(2).

(E) Notice to spouse of election to provide former spouse annuity.—If a married person who is eligible to provide a standard annuity elects to provide an annuity for a former spouse (or for a former spouse and dependent child) under subsection (b)(2), that person's spouse shall be notified of that election.

(4) Irrevocability of elections.—

(A) Standard annuity.—An election under paragraph (2)(A) is irrevocable if not revoked before the date on which the person first becomes entitled to retired pay.

(B) Reserve-component annuity.—An election under paragraph (2)(B) is irrevocable if not revoked before the end of the 90-day period referred to in that paragraph.

(5) Participation by person marrying after retirement, etc.—

(A) Election to participate in Plan.—A person who is not married and has no dependent child upon becoming eligible to participate in the Plan but who later marries or acquires a dependent child may elect to participate in the Plan.

(B) Manner and time of election.—Such an election must be written, signed by the person making the election, and received by the Secretary concerned within one year after the date on which that person marries or acquires that dependent child.

(C) Limitation on revocation of election.—Such an election may not be revoked except in accordance with subsection (b)(3).

(D) Effective date of election.—The election is effective as of the first day of the first calendar month following the month in which the election is received by the Secretary concerned.

(E) Designation if RCSBP election.—In the case of a person providing a reserve-component annuity, such an election shall include a designation under subsection (e).

(6) Election out of Plan by person with spouse coverage who remarries.—

(A) General rule.—A person—

(i) who is a participant in the Plan and is providing coverage under the Plan for a spouse (or a spouse and child);

(ii) who does not have an eligible spouse beneficiary under the Plan; and

(iii) who remarries,

may elect not to provide coverage under the Plan for the person's spouse.

(B) Effect of election on retired pay.—If such an election is made, reductions in the retired pay of that person under section 1452 of this title shall not be made.

(C) Terms and conditions of election.—An election under this paragraph—

(i) is irrevocable;

(ii) shall be made within one year after the person's remarriage; and

(iii) shall be made in such form and manner as may be prescribed in regulations under section 1455 of this title.

(D) Notice to spouse.—If a person makes an election under this paragraph—

(i) not to participate in the Plan;

(ii) to provide an annuity for the person's spouse at less than the maximum level; or

(iii) to provide an annuity for a dependent child but not for the person's spouse,

the person's spouse shall be notified of that election.

(E) Construction with former spouse election provisions.—This paragraph does not affect any right or obligation to elect to provide an annuity to a former spouse under subsection (b).

(b) Insurable interest and former spouse coverage.—

(1) Coverage for person with insurable interest.—

(A) General rule.—A person who is not married and does not have a dependent child upon becoming eligible to participate in the Plan may elect to provide an annuity under the Plan to a natural person with an insurable interest in that person. In the case of a person providing a reserve-component annuity, such an election shall include a designation under subsection (e).

(B) Termination of coverage.—An election under subparagraph (A) for a beneficiary who is not the former spouse of the person providing the annuity may be terminated. Any such termination shall be made by a participant by the submission to the Secretary concerned of a request to discontinue participation in the Plan, and such participation in the Plan shall be discontinued effective on the first day of the first month following the month in which the request is received by the Secretary concerned. Effective on such date, the Secretary concerned shall discontinue the reduction being made in such person's retired pay on account of participation in the Plan or, in the case of a person who has been required to make deposits in the Treasury on account of participation in the Plan, such person may discontinue making such deposits effective on such date.

(C) Form for discontinuation.—A request under subparagraph (B) to discontinue participation in the Plan shall be in such form and shall contain such information as may be required under regulations prescribed by the Secretary of Defense.

(D) Withdrawal of request for discontinuation.—The Secretary concerned shall furnish promptly to each person who submits a request under subparagraph (B) to discontinue participation in the Plan a written statement of the advantages and disadvantages of participating in the Plan and the possible disadvantages of discontinuing participation. A person may withdraw the request to discontinue participation if withdrawn within 30 days after having been submitted to the Secretary concerned.

(E) Consequences of discontinuation.—Once participation is discontinued, benefits may not be paid in conjunction with the earlier participation in the Plan and premiums paid may not be refunded. Participation in the Plan may not later be resumed except through a qualified election under paragraph (5) of subsection (a).

(2) Former spouse coverage upon becoming a participant in the Plan.—

(A) General rule.—A person who has a former spouse upon becoming eligible to participate in the Plan may elect to provide an annuity to that former spouse.

(B) Effect of former spouse election on spouse or dependent child.—In the case of a person with a spouse or a dependent child, such an election prevents payment of an annuity to that spouse or child (other than a child who is a beneficiary under an election under paragraph (4)), including payment under subsection (d).

(C) Designation if more than one former spouse.—If there is more than one former spouse, the person shall designate which former spouse is to be provided the annuity.

(D) Designation if RCSBP election.—In the case of a person providing a reserve-component annuity, such an election shall include a designation under subsection (e).

(3) Former spouse coverage by persons already participating in Plan.—

(A) Election of coverage.—

(i) Authority for election.—A person—

(I) who is a participant in the Plan and is providing coverage for a spouse or a spouse and child (even though there is no beneficiary currently eligible for such coverage), and

(II) who has a former spouse who was not that person's former spouse when that person became eligible to participate in the Plan,

may (subject to subparagraph (B)) elect to provide an annuity to that former spouse.

(ii) Termination of previous coverage.—Any such election terminates any previous coverage under the Plan.

(iii) Manner and time of election.—Any such election must be written, signed by the person making the election, and received by the Secretary concerned within one year after the date of the decree of divorce, dissolution, or annulment.

(B) Limitation on election.—A person may not make an election under subparagraph (A) to provide an annuity to a former spouse who that person married after becoming eligible for retired pay unless—

(i) the person was married to that former spouse for at least one year, or

(ii) that former spouse is the parent of issue by that marriage.

(C) Irrevocability, etc.—An election under this paragraph may not be revoked except in accordance with section 1450(f) of this title. This paragraph does not provide the authority to change a designation previously made under subsection (e).

(D) Notice to spouse.—If a person who is married makes an election to provide an annuity to a former spouse under this paragraph, that person's spouse shall be notified of the election.

(E) Effective date of election.—An election under this paragraph is effective as of—

(i) the first day of the first month following the month in which the election is received by the Secretary concerned; or

(ii) in the case of a person required (as described in section 1450(f)(3)(B) of this title) to make the election by reason of a court order or filing the date of which is after October 16, 1998 the first day of the first month which begins after the date of that court order or filing.

(4) Former spouse and child coverage.—A person who elects to provide an annuity for a former spouse under paragraph (2) or (3) may, at the time of the election, elect to provide coverage under that annuity for both the former spouse and a dependent child, if the child resulted from the person's marriage to that former spouse.

(5) Disclosure of whether election of former spouse coverage is required.—A person who elects to provide an annuity to a former spouse under paragraph (2) or (3) shall, at the time of making the election, provide the Secretary concerned with a written statement (in a form to be prescribed by that Secretary and signed by such person and the former spouse) setting forth—

(A) whether the election is being made pursuant to the requirements of a court order; or

(B) whether the election is being made pursuant to a written agreement previously entered into voluntarily by such person as a part of, or incident to, a proceeding of divorce, dissolution, or annulment and (if so) whether such voluntary written agreement has been incorporated in, or ratified or approved by, a court order.

(c) Persons on temporary disability retired list.—The application of the Plan to a person whose name is on the temporary disability retired list terminates when his name is removed from that list and he is no longer entitled to disability retired pay.

(d) Coverage for survivors of members who die on active duty.—

A **(1) Surviving spouse annuity.**—The Secretary concerned shall pay an annuity under this subchapter to the surviving spouse of—

(A) a member who dies while on active duty after—

(i) becoming eligible to receive retired pay;

(ii) qualifying for retired pay except that the member has not applied for or been granted that pay; or

(iii) completing 20 years of active service but before the member is eligible to retire as a commissioned officer because the member has not completed 10 years of active commissioned service; or

(B) a member not described in subparagraph (A) who dies in line of duty while on active duty.

(2) Dependent child annuity.—The Secretary concerned shall pay an annuity under this subchapter to the dependent child of a member described in paragraph (1) if there is no surviving spouse or if the member's surviving spouse subsequently dies.

(3) Mandatory former spouse annuity.—If a member described in paragraph (1) is required under a court order or spousal agreement to provide an annuity to a former spouse upon becoming eligible to be a participant in the Plan or has made an election under subsection (b) to provide an annuity to a former spouse, the Secretary—

(A) may not pay an annuity under paragraph (1) or (2); but

(B) shall pay an annuity to that former spouse as if the member had been a participant in the Plan and had made an election under subsection (b) to provide an annuity to the former spouse, or in accordance with that election, as the case may be, if the Secretary receives a written request from the former spouse concerned that the election be deemed to have been made in the same manner as provided in section 1450(f)(3) of this title.

(4) Priority.—An annuity that may be provided under this subsection shall be provided in preference to an annuity that may be provided under any other provision of this subchapter on account of service of the same member.

(5) Computation.—The amount of an annuity under this subsection is computed under section 1451(c) of this title.

(e) Designation for commencement of reserve-component annuity.—In any case in which a person is required to make a designation under this subsection, the person shall designate whether, in the event he dies before becoming 60 years of age, the annuity provided shall become effective on—

(1) the day after the date of his death; or

(2) the 60th anniversary of his birth.

(f) Coverage of survivors of persons dying when eligible to elect reserve-component annuity.—

(1) Surviving spouse annuity.—The Secretary concerned shall pay an annuity under this subchapter to the surviving spouse of a person who is eligible to provide a reserve-component annuity and who dies—

(A) before being notified under section 12731(d) of this title that he has completed the years of service required for eligibility for reserve-component retired pay; or

(B) during the 90-day period beginning on the date he receives notification under section 12731(d) of this title that he has completed the years of service required for eligibility for reserve-component retired pay if he had not made an election under subsection (a)(2)(B) to participate in the Plan.

(2) Dependent child annuity.—The Secretary concerned shall pay an annuity under this subchapter to the dependent child of a person described in paragraph (1) if there is no surviving spouse or if the person's surviving spouse subsequently dies.

(3) Mandatory former spouse annuity.—If a person described in paragraph (1) is required under a court order or spousal agreement to provide an annuity to a former spouse upon becoming eligible to be a participant in the Plan or has made an election under subsection (b) to provide an annuity to a former spouse, the Secretary—

(A) may not pay an annuity under paragraph (1) or (2); but

(B) shall pay an annuity to that former spouse as if the person had been a participant in the Plan and had made an election under subsection (b) to provide an annuity to the former spouse, or in accordance with that election, as the case may be, if the Secretary receives a written request from the former spouse concerned that the election be deemed to have been made in the same manner as provided in section 1450(f)(3) of this title.

(4) Computation.—The amount of an annuity under this subsection is computed under section 1451(c) of this title.

(g) Election to increase coverage upon remarriage.—

(1) Election.—A person—

(A) who is a participant in the Plan and is providing coverage under subsection (a) for a spouse or a spouse and child, but at less than the maximum level; and

(B) who remarries,

may elect, within one year of such remarriage, to increase the level of coverage provided under the Plan to a level not in excess of the current retired pay of that person.

(2) Payment required.—Such an election shall be contingent on the person paying to the United States the amount determined under paragraph (3) plus interest on such amount at a rate determined under regulations prescribed by the Secretary of Defense.

(3) Amount to be paid.—The amount referred to in paragraph (2) is the amount equal to the difference between—

(A) the amount that would have been withheld from such person's retired pay under section 1452 of this title if the higher level of coverage had been in effect from the time the person became a participant in the Plan; and

(B) the amount of such person's retired pay actually withheld.

(4) Manner of making election.—An election under paragraph (1) shall be made in such manner as the Secretary shall prescribe and shall become effective upon receipt of the payment required by paragraph (2).

(5) Disposition of payments.—A payment received under this subsection by the Secretary of Defense shall be deposited into the Department of Defense Military Retirement Fund. Any other payment received under this subsection shall be deposited in the Treasury as miscellaneous receipts.

History of 10 U.S.C. §1448: Added Sept. 21, 1972, P.L. 92-425, §1(3), 86 Stat. 707; Oct. 14, 1976, P.L. 94-496, §1(2), 90 Stat. 2375; Sept. 30, 1978, P.L. 95-397, §202, 92 Stat. 844; Sept. 8, 1982, P.L. 97-252, §1003(b), 96 Stat. 735; Oct. 12, 1982, P.L. 97-295, §1(18), 96 Stat. 1290; Sept. 24, 1983, P.L. 98-94, §941(a)(1), (2), (c)(2), 97 Stat. 652, 653; Nov. 8, 1985, P.L. 99-145, §513(b), §§712(a), 713(a), 715, 716(a), 719(3), (8)(A) in part, §721(a), 99 Stat. 628, 670, 671, 673-676; Nov. 14, 1986, P.L. 99-661, §§641(b)(1), 642(a), §1343(a)(8)(B), 100 Stat. 3885, 3886, 3992; Nov. 29, 1989, P.L. 101-189, §1407(a)(2), (3), 103 Stat. 1588; Oct. 5, 1994, P.L. 103-337, §638, §1671(d)(2), 108 Stat. 2791, 3015; Sept. 23, 1996, P.L. 104-201, §634, 110 Stat. 2553; Nov. 18, 1997, P.L. 105-85, §1073(a)(27), 111 Stat. 1901; Oct. 17, 1998, P.L., 105-261; §643(a), 112 Stat. 2047; Oct. 5, 1999, P.L. 106-65, §1066(a)(12), 113 Stat. 771; Oct. 30, 2000, P.L. 106-398, §§655, 1087(a)(10), 114 Stat. 1654A-165, 1654A-166, 1654A-290; Dec. 28, 2001, P.L. 107-107, §642(a), (c)(1), 115 Stat. 1151, 1152.

§1448a. ELECTION TO DISCONTINUE PARTICIPATION: ONE-YEAR OPPORTUNITY AFTER SECOND ANNIVERSARY OF COMMENCEMENT OF PAYMENT OF RETIRED PAY

(a) Authority.—A participant in the Plan may, subject to the provisions of this section, elect to discontinue participation in the Plan at any time during the one-year period beginning on the second anniversary of the date on which payment of retired pay to the participant commences.

(b) Concurrence of spouse.—

(1) Concurrence required.—A married participant may not (except as provided in paragraph (2)) make an election under subsection (a) without the concurrence of the participant's spouse.

(2) Exceptions.—A participant may make such an election without the concurrence of the participant's spouse by establishing to the satisfaction of the Secretary concerned that one of the conditions specified in section 1448(a)(3)(C) of this title exists.

(3) Form of concurrence.—The concurrence of a spouse under paragraph (1) shall be made in such written form and shall contain such information as may be required under regulations prescribed by the Secretary of Defense.

(c) Limitation on election when former spouse coverage in effect.—The limitation set forth in section 1450(f)(2) of this title applies to an election to discontinue participation in the Plan under subsection (a).

(d) Withdrawal of election to discontinue.—Section 1448(b)(1)(D) of this title applies to an election under subsection (a).

(e) Consequences of discontinuation.—Section 1448(b)(1)(E) of this title applies to an election under subsection (a).

(f) Notice to affected beneficiaries.—The Secretary concerned shall notify any former spouse or other natural person previously designated under section 1448(b) of this title of an election to discontinue participation under subsection (a).

(g) Effective date of election.—An election under subsection (a) is effective as of the first day of the first calendar month following the month in which the election is received by the Secretary concerned.

(h) Inapplicability of irrevocability provisions.—Paragraphs (4)(B) and (5)(C) of section 1448(a) of this title do not apply to prevent an election under subsection (a).

History of 10 U.S.C. §1448a: Added Nov. 18, 1997, P.L. 105-85, §641(a)(1), 111 Stat. 1797.

§1450. PAYMENT OF ANNUITY: BENEFICIARIES

(a) In general.—Effective as of the first day after the death of a person to whom section 1448 of this title applies (or on such other day as that person may provide under subsection (j)), a monthly annuity under section 1451 of this title shall be paid to the person's beneficiaries under the Plan, as follows:

(1) Surviving spouse or former spouse.—The eligible surviving spouse or the eligible former spouse.

(2) Surviving children.—The surviving dependent children in equal shares, if the eligible surviving spouse or the eligible former spouse is dead, dies, or otherwise becomes ineligible under this section.

(3) Dependent children.—The dependent children in equal shares if the person to whom section 1448 of this title applies (with the concurrence of the person's spouse, if required under section 1448(a)(3) of this title) elected to provide an annuity for dependent children but not for the spouse or former spouse.

(4) Natural person designated under "insurable interest" coverage.—The natural person designated under section 1448(b)(1) of this title, unless the election to provide an annuity to the natural person has been changed as provided in subsection (f).

(b) Termination of annuity for death, remarriage before age 55, etc.—

(1) General rule.—An annuity payable to the beneficiary terminates effective as of the first day of the month in which eligibility is lost.

(2) Termination of spouse annuity upon death or remarriage before age 55.—An annuity for a surviving spouse or former spouse shall be paid to the surviving spouse or former spouse while the surviving spouse or former spouse is living or, if the surviving spouse or former spouse remarries before reaching age 55, until the surviving spouse or former spouse remarries.

(3) Effect of termination of subsequent marriage before age 55.—If the surviving spouse or former spouse remarries before reaching age 55 and that marriage is terminated by death, annulment, or divorce, payment of the annuity shall be resumed effective as of the first day of the month in which the marriage is so terminated. However, if the surviving spouse or former spouse is also entitled to an annuity under the Plan based upon the marriage so terminated, the surviving spouse or former spouse may not receive both annuities but must elect which to receive.

(c) Offset for amount of dependency and indemnity compensation.—

(1) Required offset.—If, upon the death of a person to whom section 1448 of this title applies, the surviving spouse or former spouse of that person is also entitled to dependency and indemnity compensation under section 1311(a) of title 38, the surviving spouse or former spouse may be paid an annuity under this section, but only in the amount that the annuity otherwise payable under this section would exceed that compensation.

(2) Effective date of offset.—A reduction in an annuity under this section required by paragraph (1) shall be effective on the date of the commencement of the period of payment of such dependency and indemnity compensation under title 38.

(d) Limitation on payment of annuities when coverage under civil service retirement elected.—If, upon the death of a person to whom section 1448 of this title applies, that person had in effect a waiver of that person's retired pay for the purposes of subchapter III of chapter 83 of title 5 [5 U.S.C. §8331 et seq.], an annuity under this section shall not be payable unless, in accordance with section 8339(j) of title 5, that person notified the Office of Personnel Management that he did not desire any spouse surviving him to receive an annuity under section 8341(b) of that title.

(e) Refund of amounts deducted from retired pay when DIC offset is applicable.—

(1) Full refund when DIC greater than SBP annuity.—If an annuity under this section is not payable because of subsection (c), any amount deducted from the retired pay of the deceased under section 1452 of this title shall be refunded to the surviving spouse or former spouse.

(2) Partial refund when SBP annuity reduced by DIC.—If, because of subsection (c), the annuity payable is less than the amount established under section 1451 of this title, the annuity payable shall be recalculated under that section. The amount of the reduction in the retired pay required to provide that recalculated annuity shall be computed under section 1452 of this title, and the difference between the amount deducted before the computation of that recalculated annuity and the amount that would have been deducted on the basis of that recalculated annuity shall be refunded to the surviving spouse or former spouse.

(f) Change in election of insurable interest or former spouse beneficiary.—

(1) Authorized changes.—

(A) Election in favor of spouse or child.—A person who elects to provide an annuity to a person designated by him under section 1448(b) of this title may, subject to paragraph (2), change that election and provide an annuity to his spouse or dependent child.

(B) Notice.—The Secretary concerned shall notify the former spouse or other natural person previously designated under section 1448(b) of this title of any change of election under subparagraph (A).

(C) Procedures, effective date, etc.—Any such change of election is subject to the same rules with respect to execution, revocation, and effectiveness as are set forth in section 1448(a)(5) of this title (without regard to the eligibility of the person making the change of election to make such an election under that section). Notwithstanding the preceding sentence, a change of election under this subsection to provide an annuity to a spouse instead of a former spouse may (subject to paragraph (2)) be made at any time after the person providing the annuity remarries without regard to the time limitation in section 1448(a)(5)(B) of this title.

(2) Limitation on change in beneficiary when former spouse coverage in effect.—A person who, incident to a proceeding of divorce, dissolution, or annulment, is required by a court order to elect under section 1448(b) of this title to provide an annuity to a former spouse (or to both a former spouse and child), or who enters into a written agreement (whether voluntary or required by a court order) to make such an election, and who makes an election pursuant to such order or agreement, may not change that election under paragraph (1) unless, of the following requirements, whichever are applicable in a particular case are satisfied:

(A) In a case in which the election is required by a court order, or in which an agreement to make the election has been incorporated in or ratified or approved by a court order, the person—

(i) furnishes to the Secretary concerned a certified copy of a court order which is regular on its face and which modifies the provisions of all previous court orders relating to such election, or the agreement to make such election, so as to permit the person to change the election; and

(ii) certifies to the Secretary concerned that the court order is valid and in effect.

(B) In a case of a written agreement that has not been incorporated in or ratified or approved by a court order, the person—

(i) furnishes to the Secretary concerned a statement, in such form as the Secretary concerned may prescribe, signed by the former spouse and evidencing the former spouse's agreement to a change in the election under paragraph (1); and

(ii) certifies to the Secretary concerned that the statement is current and in effect.

(3) Required former spouse election to be deemed to have been made.—

(A) Deemed election upon request by former spouse.—If a person described in paragraph (2) or (3) of section 1448(b) of this title is required (as described in subparagraph (B)) to elect under section 1448(b) of this title to provide an annuity to a former spouse and such person then fails or refuses to make such an election, such person shall be deemed to have made such an election if the Secretary concerned receives the following:

(i) Request from former spouse.—A written request, in such manner as the Secretary shall prescribe, from the former spouse concerned requesting that such an election be deemed to have been made.

(ii) Copy of court order or other official statement.—Either—

(I) a copy of the court order, regular on its face, which requires such election or incorporates, ratifies, or approves the written agreement of such person; or

(II) a statement from the clerk of the court (or other appropriate official) that such agreement has been filed with the court in accordance with applicable State law.

(B) Persons required to make election.—A person shall be considered for purposes of subparagraph (A) to be required to elect under section 1448(b) of this title to provide an annuity to a former spouse if—

(i) the person enters, incident to a proceeding of divorce, dissolution, or annulment, into a written agreement to make such an election and the agreement (I) has been incorporated in or ratified or approved by a court order, or (II) has been filed with the court of appropriate jurisdiction in accordance with applicable State law; or

(ii) the person is required by a court order to make such an election.

(C) Time limit for request by former spouse.—An election may not be deemed to have been made under subparagraph (A) in the case of any person unless the Secretary concerned receives a request from the former spouse of the person within one year of the date of the court order or filing involved.

(D) Effective date of deemed election.—An election deemed to have been made under subparagraph (A) shall become effective on the day referred to in section 1448(b)(3)(E)(ii) of this title.

(4) Former spouse coverage may be required by court order.—A court order may require a person to elect (or to enter into an agreement to elect) under section 1448(b) of this title to provide an annuity to a former spouse (or to both a former spouse and child).

(g) Limitation on changing or revoking elections.—

(1) In general.—An election under this section may not be changed or revoked.

(2) Exceptions.—Paragraph (1) does not apply to—

(A) a revocation of an election under section 1449(b) of this title; or

(B) a change in an election under subsection (f).

(h) Treatment of annuities under other laws.—Except as provided in section 1451 of this title, an annuity under this section is in addition to any other payment to which a person is entitled under any other provision of law. Such annuity shall be considered as income under laws administered by the Secretary of Veterans Affairs.

(i) Annuities exempt from certain legal process.—Except as provided in subsection (*l*)(3)(B), an annuity under this section is not assignable or subject to execution, levy, attachment, garnishment, or other legal process.

(j) Effective date of reserve-component annuities.—

(1) Persons making section 1448(e) designation.—A reserve-component annuity shall be effective in accordance with the designation made under section 1448(e) of this title by the person providing the annuity.

(2) Persons dying before making section 1448(e) designation.—An annuity payable under section 1448(f) of this title shall be effective on the day after the date of the death of the person upon whose service the right to the annuity is based.

(k) Adjustment of spouse or former spouse annuity upon loss of dependency and indemnity compensation.—

(1) Readjustment if beneficiary 55 years of age or more.—If a surviving spouse or former spouse whose annuity has been adjusted under subsection (c) subsequently loses entitlement to dependency and indemnity compensation under section 1311(a) of title 38 because of the remarriage of the surviving spouse, or former spouse, and if at the time of such remarriage the surviving spouse or former spouse is 55 years of age or more, the amount of the annuity of the surviving spouse or former spouse shall be readjusted, effective on the effective date of such loss of dependency and indemnity compensation, to the amount of the annuity which would be in effect with respect to the surviving spouse or former spouse if the adjustment under subsection (c) had never been made.

(2) Repayment of amounts previously refunded.—

(A) General rule.—A surviving spouse or former spouse whose annuity is readjusted under paragraph (1) shall repay any amount refunded under subsection (e) by reason of the adjustment under subsection (c).

(B) Interest required if repayment not a lump sum.—If the repayment is not made in a lump sum, the surviving spouse or former spouse shall pay interest on the amount to be repaid. Such interest shall commence on the date on which the first such payment is due and shall be applied over the period during which any part of the repayment remains to be paid.

(C) Manner of repayment; rate of interest.—The manner in which such repayment shall be made, and the rate of any such interest, shall be prescribed in regulations under section 1455 of this title.

(D) Deposit of amounts repaid.—An amount repaid under this paragraph (including any such interest) received by the Secretary of Defense shall be deposited into the Department of Defense Military Retirement Fund. Any other amount repaid under this paragraph shall be deposited into the Treasury as miscellaneous receipts.

(*l*) Participants in the Plan who are missing.—

(1) Authority to presume death of missing participant.—

(A) In general.—Upon application of the beneficiary of a participant in the Plan who is missing, the Secretary concerned may determine for purposes of this subchapter that the participant is presumed dead.

(B) Participant who is missing.—A participant in the Plan is considered to be missing for purposes of this subsection if—

(i) the retired pay of the participant has been suspended on the basis that the participant is missing; or

(ii) in the case of a participant in the Plan who would be eligible for reserve-component retired pay but for the fact that he is under 60 years of age, his retired pay, if he were entitled to retired pay, would be suspended on the basis that he is missing.

(C) Requirements applicable to presumption of death.—Any such determination shall be made in accordance with regulations prescribed under section 1455 of this title. The Secretary concerned may not make a determination for purposes of this subchapter that a participant who is missing is presumed dead unless the Secretary finds that—

(i) the participant has been missing for at least 30 days; and

(ii) the circumstances under which the participant is missing would lead a reasonably prudent person to conclude that the participant is dead.

(2) Commencement of annuity.—Upon a determination under paragraph (1) with respect to a participant in the Plan, an annuity otherwise payable under this subchapter shall be paid as if the participant died on the date as of which the retired pay of the participant was suspended.

(3) Effect of person not being dead.—

(A) Termination of annuity.—If, after a determination under paragraph (1), the Secretary concerned determines that the participant is alive—

(i) any annuity being paid under this subchapter by reason of this subsection shall be terminated; and

(ii) the total amount of any annuity payments made by reason of this subsection shall constitute a debt to the United States.

(B) Collection from participant of annuity amounts erroneously paid.—A debt under subparagraph (A)(ii) may be collected or offset—

(i) from any retired pay otherwise payable to the participant;

(ii) if the participant is entitled to compensation under chapter 11 of title 38 [38 U.S.C. §1101 et seq.], from that compensation; or

(iii) if the participant is entitled to any other payment from the United States, from that payment.

(C) Collection from beneficiary.—If the participant dies before the full recovery of the amount of annuity payments described in subparagraph (A)(ii) has been made by the United States, the remaining amount of such annuity payments may be collected from the participant's beneficiary under the Plan if that beneficiary was the recipient of the annuity payments made by reason of this subsection.

History of 10 U.S.C. §1450: Added Sept. 21, 1972, P.L. 92-425, §1(3), 86 Stat. 708; Oct. 14, 1976, P.L. 94-496, §1(3), (4), 90 Stat. 2375; Sept. 30, 1978, P.L. 95-397, §§203, 207(b), (c) 92 Stat. 845, 848; July 10, 1981, P.L. 97-22, §11(a)(3) in part 95, Stat. 137; Sept. 8, 1982, P.L. 97-252, §1003(c), (d), 96 Stat. 736; Sept. 24, 1983, P.L. 98-94, §941 (a)(3), (c)(3), 97 Stat. 653, 654; Oct. 19, 1984, P.L. 98-525, §§642(b), 644, 98 Stat. 2546, 2548; Nov. 8, 1985, P.L. 99-145, §§713(b), 717,

718, 719(4)-(6), (8)(A) in part, §722, 723(a), (b), §1303(a)(11), 99 Stat. 672, 674-677, 739; Nov. 14, 1986, P.L. 99-661, §§641(a), (b)(2), (3), 643(a), §1343(a)(8)(C), 100 Stat. 3885, 3886, 3992; April 21, 1987, P.L. 100-26, §3(3) in part, 101 Stat. 273; Dec. 4, 1987, P.L. 100-180, §636(a), 101 Stat. 1106; Dec. 30, 1987, P.L. 100-224, §5(b)(1), 101 Stat. 1538; Nov. 29, 1989, P.L. 101-189, §1407(a)(2)-(4); §1621(a)(1), 103 Stat. 1588, 1602; Oct. 5, 1994, P.L. 103-337, §1070(e)(3), 108 Stat. 2859; Sept. 23, 1996, P.L. 104-201, §634, 110 Stat. 2561; Nov. 18, 1997, P.L. 105-85, §642(a), 111 Stat. 1799; Oct. 17, 1998, P.L. 105-261, §643(b), 112 Stat. 2048; Oct. 30, 2000, P.L. 106-398, §1, 114 Stat. 1654A-165, 1654A-166.

TITLE 18. CRIMES & CRIMINAL PROCEDURE

PART I. CRIMES

CHAPTER 11A. CHILD SUPPORT

§228. FAILURE TO PAY LEGAL CHILD SUPPORT OBLIGATIONS

(a) Offense.—Any person who—

(1) willfully fails to pay a support obligation with respect to a child who resides in another State, if such obligation has remained unpaid for a period longer than 1 year, or is greater than $5,000;

(2) travels in interstate or foreign commerce with the intent to evade a support obligation, if such obligation has remained unpaid for a period longer than 1 year, or is greater than $5,000; or

(3) willfully fails to pay a support obligation with respect to a child who resides in another State, if such obligation has remained unpaid for a period longer than 2 years, or is greater than $10,000;

shall be punished as provided in subsection (c).

(b) Presumption.—The existence of a support obligation that was in effect for the time period charged in the indictment or information creates a rebuttable presumption that the obligor has the ability to pay the support obligation for that time period.

(c) Punishment.—The punishment for an offense under this section is—

(1) in the case of a first offense under subsection (a)(1), a fine under this title, imprisonment for not more than 6 months, or both; and

(2) in the case of an offense under paragraph (2) or (3) of subsection (a), or a second or subsequent offense under subsection (a)(1), a fine under this title, imprisonment for not more than 2 years, or both.

(d) Mandatory restitution.—Upon a conviction under this section, the court shall order restitution under section 3663A in an amount equal to the total unpaid support obligation as it exists at the time of sentencing.

(e) Venue.—With respect to an offense under this section, an action may be inquired of and prosecuted in a district court of the United States for—

(1) the district in which the child who is the subject of the support obligation involved resided during a period during which a person described in subsection (a) (referred to in this subsection as an "obliger") failed to meet that support obligation;

(2) the district in which the obliger resided during a period described in paragraph (1); or

(3) any other district with jurisdiction otherwise provided for by law.

(f) Definitions.—As used in this section—

(1) the term "Indian tribe" has the meaning given that term in section 102 of the Federally Recognized Indian Tribe List Act of 1994 (25 U.S.C. 479a);

(2) the term "State" includes any State of the United States, the District of Columbia, and any commonwealth, territory, or possession of the United States; and

(3) the term "support obligation" means any amount determined under a court order or an order of an administrative process pursuant to the law of a State or of an Indian tribe to be due from a person for the support and maintenance of a child or of a child and the parent with whom the child is living.

History of 18 U.S.C. §228: Added Oct. 25, 1992, P.L. 102-521, §2(a), 106 Stat. 3403; Oct. 11, 1996, P.L. 104-294, §607(1), 1100 Stat. 3512; June 24, 1998, P.L. 105-187, §2, 112 Stat. 618.

CHAPTER 44. FIREARMS

§921. DEFINITIONS

(a) As used in this chapter [18 U.S.C. §921 et seq.]—

(1) The term "person" and the term "whoever" include any individual, corporation, company, association, firm, partnership, society, or joint stock company.

(2) The term "interstate or foreign commerce" includes commerce between any place in a State and any place outside of that State, or within any possession of the United States (not including the Canal Zone) or the District of Columbia, but such term does not include commerce between places within the same State but through any place outside of that State. The term "State" includes the District of Columbia, the Commonwealth of Puerto Rico, and the possessions of the United States (not including the Canal Zone).

(3) The term "firearm" means (A) any weapon (including a starter gun) which will or is designed to or may readily be converted to expel a projectile by the action of an explosive; (B) the frame or receiver of any such weapon; (C) any firearm muffler or firearm silencer; or (D) any destructive device. Such term does not include an antique firearm.

(4) The term "destructive device" means—

(A) any explosive, incendiary, or poison gas—

(i) bomb,

(ii) grenade,

(iii) rocket having a propellant charge of more than four ounces,

(iv) missile having an explosive or incendiary charge of more than one-quarter ounce,

(v) mine, or

(vi) device similar to any of the devices described in the preceding clauses;

(B) any type of weapon (other than a shotgun or a shotgun shell which the Secretary finds is generally recognized as particularly suitable for sporting purposes) by whatever name known which will, or which may be readily converted to, expel a projectile by the action of an explosive or other propellant, and which has any barrel with a bore of more than one-half inch in diameter; and

(C) any combination of parts either designed or intended for use in converting any device into any destructive device described in subparagraph (A) or (B) and from which a destructive device may be readily assembled.

The term "destructive device" shall not include any device which is neither designed nor redesigned for use as a weapon; any device, although originally designed for use as a weapon, which is redesigned for use as a signaling, pyrotechnic, line throwing, safety, or similar device; surplus ordinance sold, loaned, or given by the Secretary of the Army pursuant to the provisions of section 4684(2), 4685, or 4686 of title 10; or any other device which the Secretary of the Treasury finds is not likely to be used as a weapon, is an antique, or is a rifle which the owner intends to use solely for sporting, recreational or cultural purposes.

(5) The term "shotgun" means a weapon designed or redesigned, made or remade, and intended to be fired from the shoulder and designed or redesigned and made or remade to use the energy of an explosive to fire through a smooth bore either a number of ball shot or a single projectile for each single pull of the trigger.

(6) The term "short-barreled shotgun" means a shotgun having one or more barrels less than eighteen inches in length and any weapon made from a shotgun (whether by alteration, modification, or otherwise) if such weapon as modified has an overall length of less than twenty-six inches.

(7) The term "rifle" means a weapon designed or redesigned, made or remade, and intended to be fired from the shoulder and designed or redesigned and made or remade to use the energy of an explosive to fire only a single projectile through a rifled bore for each single pull of the trigger.

(8) The term "short-barreled rifle" means a rifle having one or more barrels less than sixteen inches in length and any weapon made from a rifle (whether by alteration, modification, or otherwise) if such weapon, as modified, has an overall length of less than twenty-six inches.

Subsections (9)-(15) omitted by editor

(16) The term "antique firearm" means—

(A) any firearm (including any firearm with a matchlock, flintlock, percussion cap, or similar type of ignition system) manufactured in or before 1898; or

(B) any replica of any firearm described in subparagraph (A) if such replica—

(i) is not designed or redesigned for using rimfire or conventional centerfire fixed ammunition, or

(ii) uses rimfire or conventional centerfire fixed ammunition which is no longer manufactured in the United States and which is not readily available in the ordinary channels of commercial trade; or

(C) any muzzle loading rifle, muzzle loading shotgun, or muzzle loading pistol, which is designed to use black powder, or a black powder substitute, and which cannot use fixed ammunition. For purposes of this subparagraph, the term antique firearm shall not include any weapon which incorporates a firearm frame or receiver, any firearm which is converted into a muzzle loading weapon, or any muzzle loading weapon which can be readily converted to fire fixed ammunition by replacing the barrel, bolt, breechblock, or any combination thereof.

(17) (A) The term "ammunition" means ammunition or cartridge cases, primers, bullets, or propellant powder designed for use in any firearm.

Subsections (B) & (C) omitted by editor

Subsections (18)-(23) omitted by editor

(24) The terms "firearm silencer" and "firearm muffler" mean any device for silencing, muffling, or diminishing the report of a portable firearm, including any combination of parts, designed or redesigned, and intended for use in assembling or fabricating a firearm silencer or firearm muffler, and any part intended only for use in such assembly or fabrication.

Subsections (25)-(31) omitted by editor

(32) The term "intimate partner" means, with respect to a person, the spouse of the person, a former spouse of the person, an individual who is a parent of a child of the person, and an individual who cohabitates or has cohabited with the person.

(33) (A) Except as provided in subparagraph (C), the term "misdemeanor crime of domestic violence" means an offense that—

(i) is a misdemeanor under Federal or State law; and

(ii) has, as an element, the use or attempted use of physical force, or the threatened use of a deadly weapon, committed by a current or former spouse, parent, or guardian of the victim, by a person with whom the victim shares a child in common, by a person who is cohabiting with or has cohabited with the victim as a spouse, parent, or guardian, or by a person similarly situated to a spouse, parent, or guardian of the victim.

(B) (i) A person shall not be considered to have been convicted of such an offense for purposes of this chapter [18 U.S.C. §921 et seq.], unless—

(I) the person was represented by counsel in the case, or knowingly and intelligently waived the right to counsel in the case; and

(II) in the case of a prosecution for an offense described in this paragraph for which a person was entitled to a jury trial in the jurisdiction in which the case was tried, either

(aa) the case was tried by a jury, or

(bb) the person knowingly and intelligently waived the right to have the case tried by a jury, by guilty plea or otherwise.

(ii) A person shall not be considered to have been convicted of such an offense for purposes of this chapter [18 U.S.C. §921 et seq.] if the conviction has been expunged or set aside, or is an offense for which the person has been pardoned or has had civil rights restored (if the law of the applicable jurisdiction provides for the loss of civil rights under such an offense) unless the pardon, expungement, or restoration of civil rights expressly provides that the person may not ship, transport, possess, or receive firearms.

Subsection (34) omitted by editor

Subsection (b) omitted by editor

History of 18 USC §921: Added June 19, 1968, P.L. 90-351, §902, 82 Stat. 226; Oct. 22, 1968, P.L. 90-618, §102, 82 Stat. 1214; Jan. 4, 1975, P.L. 93-639, §102, 88 Stat. 2217; May 19, 1986, P.L. 99-308, §101, 100 Stat. 449; July 8, 1986, P.L. 99-360, §1(b), 100 Stat 766; Aug. 28, 1986, P.L. 99-408, §1, 100 Stat. 920; Nov. 29, 1990, P.L. 101-647, §1702(b)(2), §2204(a), 104 Stat. 4845; Nov. 30, 1993, P.L. 103-159, 107 Stat. 1539; Sept. 13, 1994, P.L. 103-322, §§110102(b), 110103(b), 110401(a), 110519, 330021(1), 108 Stat. 1997, 1999, 2014, 2020, 2150; Dec. 29, 1995, P.L. 104-88, §303(1), 109 Stat. 943; Sept. 30, 1996, P.L. 104-208, §101(f) [§658(a)], 110 Stat. 3009-371; Oct. 21, 1998, P.L. 105-277, §101(b) [§119(a)], §101(h) [§115], 112 Stat. 2681-69, 2681-490.

§922. UNLAWFUL ACTS

Subsections (a)-(c) omitted by editor

(d) It shall be unlawful for any person to sell or otherwise dispose of any firearm or ammunition to any person knowing or having reasonable cause to believe that such person—

Subsections (1)-(7) omitted by editor

(8) is subject to a court order that restrains such person from harassing, stalking, or threatening an intimate partner of such person or child of such intimate partner or person, or engaging in other conduct that would place an intimate partner in reasonable fear of bodily injury to the partner or child, except that this paragraph shall only apply to a court order that—

(A) was issued after a hearing of which such person received actual notice, and at which such person had the opportunity to participate; and

(B) (i) includes a finding that such person represents a credible threat to the physical safety of such intimate partner or child; or

(ii) by its terms explicitly prohibits the use, attempted use, or threatened use of physical force against such intimate partner or child that would reasonably be expected to cause bodily injury; or

(9) has been convicted in any court of a misdemeanor crime of domestic violence.

Subsections (e) & (f) omitted by editor

(g) It shall be unlawful for any person—

Subsections (1)-(7) omitted by editor

(8) who is subject to a court order that—

(A) was issued after a hearing of which such person received actual notice, and at which such person had an opportunity to participate;

(B) restrains such person from harassing, stalking, or threatening an intimate partner of such person or child of such intimate partner or person, or engaging in other conduct that would place an intimate partner in reasonable fear of bodily injury to the partner or child; and

(C) **(i)** includes a finding that such person represents a credible threat to the physical safety of such intimate partner or child; or

(ii) by its terms explicitly prohibits the use, attempted use, or threatened use of physical force against such intimate partner or child that would reasonably be expected to cause bodily injury; or

(9) who has been convicted in any court of a misdemeanor crime of domestic violence,

to ship or transport in interstate or foreign commerce, or possess in or affecting commerce, any firearm or ammunition; or to receive any firearm or ammunition which has been shipped or transported in interstate or foreign commerce.

(h) It shall be unlawful for any individual, who to that individual's knowledge and while being employed for any person described in any paragraph of subsection (g) of this section, in the course of such employment—

(1) to receive, possess, or transport any firearm or ammunition in or affecting interstate or foreign commerce; or

(2) to receive any firearm or ammunition which has been shipped or transported in interstate or foreign commerce.

Subsections (i)-(x) omitted by editor

Appendix A omitted by editor

History of 18 USC §922: Added June 19, 1968, P.L. 90-351, §902, 82 Stat. 228; Oct. 22, 1968, P.L. 90-618, §102, 82 Stat. 1216; Dec. 21, 1982, P.L. 97-377, §165(a), 96 Stat. 1923; May 19, 1986, P.L. 99-308, §102, 100 Stat. 451; Aug. 28, 1986, P.L. 99-408, §2, 100 Stat. 920; Nov. 11, 1988, P.L. 100-649, §2(a), 102 Stat. 3816; Nov. 18, 1988, P.L. 100-690, §7060(c), 102 Stat. 4404; Nov. 29, 1990, P.L. 101-647, §1702(b)(1), §§2201, 2202, 2204(b), §3524 104 Stat. 4844, 4856, 4857, 4924; Nov. 30, 1993, P.L. 103-159, §102(a)(1), (b), §302(a)-(c), 107 Stat. 1536, 1539, 1545; Sept. 13, 1994, P.L. 103-322, §§110102(a), 110103(a), 110106, 110201(a), 110401(b), (c), §§110511, 110514, §§320904, 320927, §330011(i), 108 Stat. 1996, 1998, 2000, 2010, 2014, 2019, 2125, 2131, 2145. Amended Oct. 11, 1996, P.L. 104-294, §603(b), (c)(1), (d), (e), (f)(1), (g), 110 Stat. 3503, 3504; Sept. 30, 1996, P.L. 104-208, §101(f) §§657, 658(b)], 110 Stat. 3009-369, 3009-372; Oct. 21, 1998, P.L. 105-277, §101(b), 112 Stat. 2681-71.

CHAPTER 55. KIDNAPPING

§1204. INTERNATIONAL PARENTAL KIDNAPPING

(a) Whoever removes a child from the United States or retains a child (who has been in the United States) outside the United States with intent to obstruct the lawful exercise of parental rights shall be fined under this title or imprisoned not more than 3 years, or both.

(b) As used in this section—

(1) the term "child" means a person who has not attained the age of 16 years; and

(2) the term "parental rights", with respect to a child, means the right to physical custody of the child—

(A) whether joint or sole (and includes visiting rights); and

(B) whether arising by operation of law, court order, or legally binding agreement of the parties.

(c) It shall be an affirmative defense under this section that—

(1) the defendant acted within the provisions of a valid court order granting the defendant legal custody or visitation rights and that order was obtained pursuant to the Uniform Child Custody Jurisdiction Act and was in effect at the time of the offense;

(2) the defendant was fleeing an incidence or pattern of domestic violence;

(3) the defendant had physical custody of the child pursuant to a court order granting legal custody or visitation rights and failed to return the child as a result of circumstances beyond the defendant's control, and the defendant notified or made reasonable attempts to notify the other parent or lawful custodian of the child of such circumstances within 24 hours after the visitation period had expired and returned the child as soon as possible.

(d) This section does not detract from The Hague Convention on the Civil Aspects of International Parental Child Abduction, done at The Hague on October 25, 1980.

History of 18 U.S.C. §1204: Dec. 2, 1993, P.L. 103-173, §2(a), 107 Stat. 1998.

CHAPTER 110A. DOMESTIC VIOLENCE & STALKING

§2261. INTERSTATE DOMESTIC VIOLENCE

(a) Offenses.—

(1) Travel or conduct of offender.—A person who travels in interstate or foreign commerce or enters or leaves Indian country with the intent to kill, injure, harass, or intimidate a spouse or intimate partner, and who, in the course of or as a result of such travel, commits or attempts to commit a crime of violence against that spouse or intimate partner, shall be punished as provided in subsection (b).

(2) Causing travel of victim.—A person who causes a spouse or intimate partner to travel in interstate or foreign commerce or to enter or leave Indian country by force, coercion, duress, or fraud, and who, in the course of, as a result of, or to facilitate such conduct or travel, commits or attempts to commit a crime of violence against that spouse or intimate partner, shall be punished as provided in subsection (b).

(b) Penalties.—A person who violates this section or section 2261A shall be fined under this title, imprisoned—

(1) for life or any term of years, if death of the victim results;

(2) for not more than 20 years if permanent disfigurement or life threatening bodily injury to the victim results;

(3) for not more than 10 years, if serious bodily injury to the victim results or if the offender uses a dangerous weapon during the offense;

(4) as provided for the applicable conduct under chapter 109A [18 U.S.C. §2241 et seq.] if the offense would constitute an offense under chapter 109A [18 U.S.C. §2241 et seq.] (without regard to whether the offense was committed in the special maritime and territorial jurisdiction of the United States or in a Federal prison); and

(5) for not more than 5 years, in any other case, or both fined and imprisoned.

History of 18 USC §2261: Added Sept. 13, 1994, P.L. 103-322, Ch 2, §40221(a), 108 Stat. 1926; Sept. 23, 1996, P.L. 104-201, §1069(b)(1), (2), 110 Stat. 2656; Oct. 28, 2000, P.L. 106-386, §1107(a), 114 Stat. 1497.

§2261A. INTERSTATE STALKING

Whoever—

(1) travels in interstate or foreign commerce or within the special maritime and territorial jurisdiction of the United States, or enters or leaves Indian country, with the intent to kill, injure, harass, or intimidate another person, and in the course of, or as a result of, such travel places that person in reasonable fear of the death of, or serious bodily injury to, that person, a member of the immediate family (as defined in section 115) of that person, or the spouse or intimate partner of that person; or

(2) with the intent—

(A) to kill or injure a person in another State or tribal jurisdiction or within the special maritime and territorial jurisdiction of the United States; or

(B) to place a person in another State or tribal jurisdiction, or within the special maritime and territorial jurisdiction of the United States, in reasonable fear of the death of, or serious bodily injury to—

(i) that person;

(ii) a member of the immediate family (as defined in section 115) of that person; or

(iii) a spouse or intimate partner of that person,

uses the mail or any facility of interstate or foreign commerce to engage in a course of conduct that places that person in reasonable fear of the death of, or serious bodily injury to, any of the persons described in clauses (i) through (iii),

shall be punished as provided in section 2261(b).

History of 18 USC §2261A: Added Sept. 23, 1996, P.L. 104-201, §1069(a), 110 Stat. 2655; Oct. 28, 2000, P.L. 106-386, §1107(b), 114 Stat. 1498.

§2262. INTERSTATE VIOLATION OF PROTECTIVE ORDER

(a) Offenses.—

(1) Travel or conduct of offender.—A person who travels in interstate or foreign commerce, or enters or leaves Indian country, with the intent to engage in conduct that violates the portion of a protection order that prohibits or provides protection against violence, threats, or harassment against, contact or communication with, or physical proximity to, another person, or that would violate such a portion of a protection order in the jurisdiction in which the order was issued, and subsequently engages in such conduct, shall be punished as provided in subsection (b).

(2) Causing travel of victim.—A person who causes another person to travel in interstate or foreign commerce or to enter or leave Indian country by force, coercion, duress, or fraud, and in the course of, as a result of, or to facilitate such conduct or travel engages in conduct that violates the portion of a protection order that prohibits or provides protection against violence, threats, or harassment against, contact or communication with, or physical proximity to, another person, or that would violate such a portion of a protection order in the jurisdiction in which the order was issued, shall be punished as provided in subsection (b).

(b) Penalties.—A person who violates this section shall be fined under this title, imprisoned—

(1) for life or any term of years, if death of the victim results;

(2) for not more than 20 years if permanent disfigurement or life threatening bodily injury to the victim results;

(3) for not more than 10 years, if serious bodily injury to the victim results or if the offender uses a dangerous weapon during the offense;

(4) as provided for the applicable conduct under chapter 109A if the offense would constitute an offense under chapter 109A (without regard to whether the offense was committed in the special maritime and territorial jurisdiction of the United States or in a Federal prison); and

(5) for not more than 5 years, in any other case,

or both fined and imprisoned.

History of 18 USC §2262: Added Sept. 13, 1994, P.L. 103-322, Ch 2, §40221(a), 108 Stat. 1927; Sept. 23, 1996, P.L. 104-201, §1069(b)(2), 110 Stat. 2656; Oct. 11, 1996, P.L. 104-294, §605(d), 110 Stat. 3509; Oct. 28, 2000, P.L. 106-386, §1107(c), 114 Stat. 1498.

§2265. FULL FAITH & CREDIT GIVEN TO PROTECTION ORDERS

(a) Full faith and credit.—Any protection order issued that is consistent with subsection (b) of this section by the court of one State or Indian tribe (the issuing State or Indian tribe) shall be accorded full faith and credit by the court of another State or Indian tribe (the enforcing State or Indian tribe) and enforced as if it were the order of the enforcing State or tribe.

(b) Protection order.—A protection order issued by a State or tribal court is consistent with this subsection if—

(1) such court has jurisdiction over the parties and matter under the law of such State or Indian tribe; and

(2) reasonable notice and opportunity to be heard is given to the person against whom the order is sought sufficient to protect that person's right to due process. In the case of ex parte orders, notice and opportunity to be heard must be provided within the time required by State or tribal law, and in any event within a reasonable time after the order is issued, sufficient to protect the respondent's due process rights.

(c) Cross or counter petition.—A protection order issued by a State or tribal court against one who has petitioned, filed a complaint, or otherwise filed a written pleading for protection against abuse by a spouse or intimate partner is not entitled to full faith and credit if—

(1) no cross or counter petition, complaint, or other written pleading was filed seeking such a protection order; or

(2) a cross or counter petition has been filed and the court did not make specific findings that each party was entitled to such an order.

(d) Notification and registration.—

(1) Notification.—A State or Indian tribe according full faith and credit to an order by a court of another State or Indian tribe shall not notify or require notification of the party against whom a protection order has been issued that the protection order has been registered or filed in that enforcing State or tribal jurisdiction unless requested to do so by the party protected under such order.

(2) No prior registration or filing as prerequisite for enforcement.—Any protection order that is otherwise consistent with this section shall be accorded full faith and credit, notwithstanding failure to comply with any requirement that the order be registered or filed in the enforcing State or tribal jurisdiction.

(e) Tribal court jurisdiction.—For purposes of this section, a tribal court shall have full civil jurisdiction to enforce protection orders, including authority to enforce any orders through civil contempt proceedings, exclusion of violators from Indian lands, and other appropriate mechanisms, in matters arising within the authority of the tribe.

History of 18 U.S.C. §2265: Added Sept. 13, 1994, P.L. 103-322, Ch 2, §40221(a), 108 Stat. 1930; Oct. 28, 2000, P.L. 106-386, Div B, §1101(b)(4), 114 Stat. 1493.

§2266. DEFINITIONS

In this chapter:

(1) Bodily injury.—The term "bodily injury" means any act, except one done in self-defense, that results in physical injury or sexual abuse.

(2) Course of conduct.—The term "course of conduct" means a pattern of conduct composed of 2 or more acts, evidencing a continuity of purpose.

(3) Enter or leave Indian country.—The term "enter or leave Indian country" includes leaving the jurisdiction of 1 tribal government and entering the jurisdiction of another tribal government.

(4) Indian country.—The term "Indian country" has the meaning stated in section 1151 of this title.

(5) Protection order.—The term "protection order" includes any injunction or other order issued for the purpose of preventing violent or threatening acts or harassment against, or contact or communication with or physical proximity to, another person, including any temporary or final order issued by a civil and criminal court (other than a support or child custody order issued pursuant to State divorce and child custody laws, except to the extent that such an order is entitled to full faith and credit under other Federal law) whether obtained by filing an independent action or as a pendente lite order in another proceeding so long as any civil order was issued in response to a complaint, petition, or motion filed by or on behalf of a person seeking protection.

(6) Serious bodily injury.—The term "serious bodily injury" has the meaning stated in section 2119(2).

(7) Spouse or intimate partner.—The term "spouse or intimate partner" includes—

(A) for purposes of—

(i) sections other than 2261A, a spouse or former spouse of the abuser, a person who shares a child in common with the abuser, and a person who cohabits or has cohabited as a spouse with the abuser; and

(ii) section 2261A, a spouse or former spouse of the target of the stalking, a person who shares a child in common with the target of the stalking, and a person who cohabits or has cohabited as a spouse with the target of the stalking; and

(B) any other person similarly situated to a spouse who is protected by the domestic or family violence laws of the State or tribal jurisdiction in which the injury occurred or where the victim resides.

(8) State.—The term "State" includes a State of the United States, the District of Columbia, and a commonwealth, territory, or possession of the United States.

(9) Travel in interstate or foreign commerce.—The term "travel in interstate or foreign commerce" does not include travel from 1 State to another by an individual who is a member of an Indian tribe and who remains at all times in the territory of the Indian tribe of which the individual is a member.

History of 18 U.S.C. §2266: Added Sept. 13, 1994, P.L. 103-322, Ch 2, §40221(a), 108 Stat. 1931; Oct. 28, 2000, P.L. 106-386, Div B, §1107(d), 114 Stat. 1499.

TITLE 25. INDIANS

CHAPTER 21. INDIAN CHILD WELFARE

§1901. CONGRESSIONAL FINDINGS

Recognizing the special relationship between the United States and the Indian tribes and their members and the Federal responsibility to Indian people, the Congress finds—

(1) that clause 3, section 8, article I of the United States Constitution provides that "The Congress shall have Power ... To regulate Commerce ... with Indian [T]ribes" and, through this and other constitutional authority, Congress has plenary power over Indian affairs;

(2) that Congress, through statutes, treaties, and the general course of dealing with Indian tribes, has assumed the responsibility for the protection and preservation of Indian tribes and their resources;

(3) that there is no resource that is more vital to the continued existence and integrity of Indian tribes than their children and that the United States has a direct interest, as trustee, in protecting Indian children who are members of or are eligible for membership in an Indian tribe;

(4) that an alarmingly high percentage of Indian families are broken up by the removal, often unwarranted, of their children from them by nontribal public and private agencies and that an alarmingly high percentage of such children are placed in non-Indian foster and adoptive homes and institutions; and

(5) that the States, exercising their recognized jurisdiction over Indian child custody proceedings through administrative and judicial bodies, have often failed to recognize the essential tribal relations of Indian people and the cultural and social standards prevailing in Indian communities and families.

History of 25 U.S.C. §1901: Nov. 8, 1978, P.L. 95-608, §2, 92 Stat. 3069.

§1902. CONGRESSIONAL DECLARATION OF POLICY

The Congress hereby declares that it is the policy of this Nation to protect the best interests of Indian children and to promote the stability and security of Indian tribes and families by the establishment of minimum Federal standards for the removal of Indian children from their families and the placement of such children in foster or adoptive homes which will reflect the unique values of Indian culture, and by providing for assistance to Indian tribes in the operation of child and family service programs.

History of 25 U.S.C. §1902: Nov. 8, 1978, P.L. 95-608, §3, 92 Stat. 3069.

§1903. DEFINITIONS

For the purposes of this Act [25 U.S.C. §1901 et seq.], except as may be specifically provided otherwise, the term—

(1) "child custody proceeding" shall mean and include—

(i) "foster care placement" which shall mean any action removing an Indian child from its parent or Indian custodian for temporary placement in a foster home or institution or the home of a guardian or conservator where the parent or Indian custodian cannot have the child returned upon demand, but where parental rights have not been terminated;

(ii) "termination of parental rights" which shall mean any action resulting in the termination of the parent-child relationship;

(iii) "preadoptive placement" which shall mean the temporary placement of an Indian child in a foster home or institution after the termination of parental rights, but prior to or in lieu of adoptive placement; and

(iv) "adoptive placement" which shall mean the permanent placement of an Indian child for adoption, including any action resulting in a final decree of adoption.

Such term or terms shall not include a placement based upon an act which, if committed by an adult, would be deemed a crime or upon an award, in a divorce proceeding, of custody to one of the parents.

(2) "extended family member" shall be as defined by the law or custom of the Indian child's tribe or, in the absence of such law or custom, shall be a person who has reached the age of eighteen and who is the Indian child's grandparent, aunt or uncle, brother or sister, brother-in-law or sister-in-law, niece or nephew, first or second cousin, or stepparent;

(3) "Indian" means any person who is a member of an Indian tribe, or who is an Alaska Native and a member of a Regional Corporation as defined in section 7 of the Alaska Native Claims Settlement Act (85 Stat. 688, 689) [43 U.S.C. §1606];

(4) "Indian child" means any unmarried person who is under age eighteen and is either (a) a member of an Indian tribe or (b) is eligible for membership in an Indian tribe and is the biological child of a member of an Indian tribe;

(5) "Indian child's tribe" means (a) the Indian tribe in which an Indian child is a member or eligible for membership or (b), in the case of an Indian child who is a member of or eligible for membership in more than one tribe, the Indian tribe with which the Indian child has the more significant contacts;

(6) "Indian custodian" means any Indian person who has legal custody of an Indian child under tribal law or custom or under State law or to whom temporary physical care, custody, and control has been transferred by the parent of such child;

(7) "Indian organization" means any group, association, partnership, corporation, or other legal entity owned or controlled by Indians, or a majority of whose members are Indians;

(8) "Indian tribe" means any Indian tribe, band, nation, or other organized group or community of Indians recognized as eligible for the services provided to Indians by the Secretary because of their status as Indians, including any Alaska Native village as defined in section 3(c) of the Alaska Native Claims Settlement Act (85 Stat. 688, 689), as amended [42 U.S.C. §1602(c)];

(9) "parent" means any biological parent or parents of an Indian child or any Indian person who has lawfully adopted an Indian child, including adoptions under tribal law or custom. It does not include the unwed father where paternity has not been acknowledged or established;

(10) "reservation" means Indian country as defined in section 1151 of title 18, and any lands, not covered under such section, title to which is either held by the United States in trust for the benefit of any Indian tribe or individual or held by any Indian tribe or individual subject to a restriction by the United States against alienation;

(11) "Secretary" means the Secretary of the Interior; and

(12) "tribal court" means a court with jurisdiction over child custody proceedings and which is either a Court of Indian Offenses, a court established and operated under the code or custom of an Indian tribe, or any other administrative body of a tribe which is vested with authority over child custody proceedings.

History of 25 U.S.C. §1903: Nov. 8, 1978, P.L. 95-608, §4, 92 Stat. 3069.

SUBCHAPTER I. CHILD CUSTODY PROCEEDINGS

§1911. INDIAN TRIBE JURISDICTION OVER INDIAN CHILD CUSTODY PROCEEDINGS

(a) Exclusive jurisdiction.—An Indian tribe shall have jurisdiction exclusive as to any State over any child custody proceeding involving an Indian child who resides or is domiciled within the reservation of such tribe, except where such jurisdiction is otherwise vested in the State by existing Federal law. Where an Indian child is a ward of a tribal court, the Indian tribe shall retain exclusive jurisdiction, notwithstanding the residence or domicile of the child.

(b) Transfer of proceedings; declination by tribal court.—In any State court proceeding for the foster care placement of, or termination of parental rights to, an Indian child not domiciled or residing within the reservation of the Indian child's tribe, the court, in the absence of good cause to the contrary, shall transfer such proceeding to the jurisdiction of the tribe, absent objection by either parent, upon the petition of either parent or the Indian custodian or the Indian child's tribe: Provided, that such transfer shall be subject to declination by the tribal court of such tribe.

(c) State court proceedings; intervention.—In any State court proceeding for the foster care placement of, or termination of parental rights to, an Indian child, the Indian custodian of the child and the Indian child's tribe shall have a right to intervene at any point in the proceeding.

(d) Full faith and credit to public acts, records, and judicial proceedings of Indian tribes.—The United States, every State, every territory or possession of the United States, and every Indian tribe shall give full faith and credit to the public acts, records, and judicial proceedings of any Indian tribe applicable to Indian child custody proceedings to the same extent that such entities give full faith and credit to the public acts, records, and judicial proceedings of any other entity.

History of 25 U.S.C. §1911: Nov. 8, 1978, P.L. 95-608, §101, 92 Stat. 3071.

§1912. PENDING COURT PROCEEDINGS

(a) Notice; time for commencement of proceedings; additional time for preparation.—In any involuntary proceeding in a State court, where the court knows or has reason to know that an Indian child is involved, the party seeking the foster care placement of, or termination of parental rights to, an Indian child shall notify the parent or Indian custodian and the Indian child's tribe, by registered mail with return receipt requested, of the pending proceedings and of their right of intervention. If the identity or location of the parent or Indian custodian and the tribe cannot be determined, such notice shall be given to the Secretary in like manner, who shall have fifteen days after receipt to provide the requisite notice to the parent or Indian custodian and the tribe. No foster care placement or termination of parental rights proceeding shall be held until at least ten days after receipt of notice by the parent or Indian custodian and the tribe or the Secretary: Provided, That the parent or Indian custodian or the tribe shall, upon request, be granted up to twenty additional days to prepare for such proceeding.

(b) Appointment of counsel.—In any case in which the court determines indigency, the parent or Indian custodian shall have the right to court-appointed counsel in any removal, placement, or termination proceeding. The court may, in its discretion, appoint counsel for the child upon a finding that such appointment is in the best interest of the child. Where State law makes no provision for appointment of counsel in such proceedings, the court shall promptly notify the Secretary upon appointment of counsel, and the Secretary, upon certification of the presiding judge, shall pay reasonable fees and expenses out of funds which may be appropriated pursuant to the Act of November 2, 1921 (42 Stat. 208; 25 U.S.C. 13).

(c) Examination of reports or other documents.—Each party to a foster care placement or termination of parental rights proceeding under State law involving an Indian child shall have the right to examine all reports or other documents filed with the court upon which any decision with respect to such action may be based.

(d) Remedial services and rehabilitative programs; preventive measures.—Any party seeking to effect a foster care placement of, or termination of parental rights to, an Indian child under State law shall satisfy the court that active efforts have been made to provide remedial services and rehabilitative programs designed to prevent the breakup of the Indian family and that these efforts have proved unsuccessful.

(e) Foster care placement orders; evidence; determination of damage to child.—No foster care placement may be ordered in such proceeding in the absence of a determination, supported by clear and convincing evidence, including testimony of qualified expert witnesses, that the continued custody of the child by the parent or Indian custodian is likely to result in serious emotional or physical damage to the child.

(f) Parental rights termination orders; evidence; determination of damage to child.—No termination of parental rights may be ordered in such proceeding in the absence of a determination, supported by evidence beyond a reasonable doubt, including testimony of qualified expert witnesses, that the continued custody of the child by the parent or Indian custodian is likely to result in serious emotional or physical damage to the child.

History of 25 U.S.C. §1912: Nov. 8, 1978, P.L. 95-608, §102, 92 Stat. 3071.

§1913. PARENTAL RIGHTS; VOLUNTARY TERMINATION

(a) Consent; record; certification matters; invalid consents.—Where any parent or Indian custodian voluntarily consents to a foster care placement or to termination of parental rights, such consent shall not be valid unless executed in writing and recorded before a judge of a court of competent jurisdiction and accompanied by the presiding judge's certificate that the terms and consequences of the consent were fully explained in detail and were fully understood by the parent or Indian custodian. The court shall also certify that either the parent or Indian custodian fully understood the explanation in English or that it was interpreted into a language that the parent or Indian custodian understood. Any consent given prior to, or within ten days after, birth of the Indian child shall not be valid.

(b) Foster care placement; withdrawal of consent.—Any parent or Indian custodian may withdraw consent to a foster care placement under State law at any time and, upon such withdrawal, the child shall be returned to the parent or Indian custodian.

(c) Voluntary termination of parental rights or adoptive placement; withdrawal of consent; return of custody.—In any voluntary proceeding for termination of parental rights to, or adoptive placement of, an Indian child, the consent of the parent may be withdrawn for any reason at any time prior to the entry of a final decree of termination or adoption, as the case may be, and the child shall be returned to the parent.

(d) Collateral attack; vacation of decree and return of custody; limitations.—After the entry of a final decree of adoption of an Indian child in any State court, the parent may withdraw consent thereto upon the grounds that consent was obtained through fraud or duress and may petition the court to vacate such decree. Upon a finding that such consent was obtained through fraud or duress, the court shall vacate such decree and return the child to the parent. No adoption which has been effective for at least two years may be invalidated under the provisions of this subsection unless otherwise permitted under State law.

History of 25 U.S.C. §1913: Nov. 8, 1978, P.L. 95-608, §103, 92 Stat. 3072.

§1914. PETITION TO COURT OF COMPETENT JURISDICTION TO INVALIDATE ACTION UPON SHOWING OF CERTAIN VIOLATIONS

Any Indian child who is the subject of any action for foster care placement or termination of parental rights under State law, any parent or Indian custodian from whose custody such child was removed, and the Indian child's tribe may petition any court of competent jurisdiction to invalidate such action upon a showing that such action violated any provision of sections 101, 102, and 103 of this Act [25 U.S.C. §§1911, 1912, and 1913].

History of 25 U.S.C. §1914: Nov. 8, 1978, P.L. 95-608, §104, 92 Stat. 3072.

§1915. PLACEMENT OF INDIAN CHILDREN

(a) Adoptive placements; preferences.—In any adoptive placement of an Indian child under State law, a preference shall be given, in the absence of good cause to the contrary, to a placement with—

(1) a member of the child's extended family;

(2) other members of the Indian child's tribe; or

(3) other Indian families.

(b) Foster care or preadoptive placements; criteria; preferences.—Any child accepted for foster care or preadoptive placement shall be placed in the least restrictive setting which most approximates a family and in which his special needs, if any, may be met. The child shall also be placed within reasonable proximity to his or her home, taking into account any special needs of the child. In any foster care or preadoptive placement, a preference shall be given, in the absence of good cause to the contrary, to a placement with—

(i) a member of the Indian child's extended family;

(ii) a foster home licensed, approved, or specified by the Indian child's tribe;

(iii) an Indian foster home licensed or approved by an authorized non-Indian licensing authority; or

(iv) an institution for children approved by an Indian tribe or operated by an Indian organization which has a program suitable to meet the Indian child's needs.

(c) Tribal resolution for different order of preference; personal preference considered; anonymity in application of preferences.—In the case of a placement under subsection (a) or (b) of this section, if the Indian child's tribe shall establish a different order of preference by resolution, the agency or court effecting the placement shall follow such order so long as the placement is the least restrictive setting appropriate to the particular needs of the child, as provided in subsection (b) of this section. Where appropriate, the preference of the Indian child or parent shall be considered: Provided, That where a consenting parent evidences a desire for anonymity, the court or agency shall give weight to such desire in applying the preferences.

(d) Social and cultural standards applicable.—The standards to be applied in meeting the preference requirements of this section shall be the prevailing social and cultural standards of the Indian community in which the parent or extended family resides or with which the parent or extended family members maintain social and cultural ties.

(e) Record of placement; availability.—A record of each such placement, under State law, of an Indian child shall be maintained by the State in which the placement was made, evidencing the efforts to comply with the order of preference specified in this section. Such record shall be made available at any time upon the request of the Secretary or the Indian child's tribe.

History of 25 U.S.C. §1915: Nov. 8, 1978, P.L. 95-608, §105, 92 Stat. 3073.

§1916. RETURN OF CUSTODY

(a) Petition; best interests of child.—Notwithstanding State law to the contrary, whenever a final decree of adoption of an Indian child has been vacated or set aside or the adoptive parents voluntarily consent to the termination of their parental rights to the child, a biological parent or prior Indian custodian may petition for return of custody and the court shall grant such petition unless there is a showing, in a proceeding subject to the provisions of section 102 of this Act [25 U.S.C. §1912], that such return of custody is not in the best interests of the child.

(b) Removal from foster care home; placement procedure.—Whenever an Indian child is removed from a foster care home or institution for the purpose of further foster care, preadoptive, or adoptive placement, such placement shall be in accordance with the provisions of this Act [25 U.S.C. §1901 et seq.], except in the case where an Indian child is being returned to the parent or Indian custodian from whose custody the child was originally removed.

History of 25 U.S.C. §1916: Nov. 8, 1978, P.L. 95-608, §106, 92 Stat. 3073.

§1917. TRIBAL AFFILIATION INFORMATION & OTHER INFORMATION FOR PROTECTION OF RIGHTS FROM TRIBAL RELATIONSHIP; APPLICATION OF SUBJECT OF ADOPTIVE PLACEMENT; DISCLOSURE BY COURT

Upon application by an Indian individual who has reached the age of eighteen and who was the subject of an adoptive placement, the court which entered the final decree shall inform such individual of the tribal affiliation, if any, of the individual's biological parents and provide such other information as may be necessary to protect any rights flowing from the individual's tribal relationship.

History of 25 U.S.C. §1917: Nov. 8, 1978, P.L. 95-608, §107, 92 Stat. 3073.

§1918. REASSUMPTION OF JURISDICTION OVER CHILD CUSTODY PROCEEDINGS

(a) Petition; suitable plan; approval by Secretary.—Any Indian tribe which became subject to State jurisdiction pursuant to the provisions of the Act of August 15, 1953 (67 Stat. 588), as amended by title IV of the Act of April 11, 1968 (82 Stat. 73, 78), or pursuant to any other Federal law, may reassume jurisdiction over child custody proceedings. Before any Indian tribe may reassume jurisdiction over Indian child custody proceedings, such tribe shall present to the Secretary for approval a petition to reassume such jurisdiction which includes a suitable plan to exercise such jurisdiction.

(b) Criteria applicable to consideration by Secretary; partial retrocession.—

(1) In considering the petition and feasibility of the plan of a tribe under subsection (a), the Secretary may consider, among other things:

(i) whether or not the tribe maintains a membership roll or alternative provision for clearly identifying the persons who will be affected by the reassumption of jurisdiction by the tribe;

(ii) the size of the reservation or former reservation area which will be affected by retrocession and reassumption of jurisdiction by the tribe;

(iii) the population base of the tribe, or distribution of the population in homogeneous communities or geographic areas; and

(iv) the feasibility of the plan in cases of multitribal occupation of a single reservation or geographic area.

(2) In those cases where the Secretary determines that the jurisdictional provisions of section 101(a) of this Act [25 U.S.C. §1911(a)] are not feasible, he is authorized to accept partial retrocession which will enable tribes to exercise referral jurisdiction as provided in section 101(b) of this Act [25 U.S.C. §1911(b)], or, where appropriate, will allow them to exercise exclusive jurisdiction as provided in section 101(a) [25 U.S.C. §1911(a)] over limited community or geographic areas without regard for the reservation status of the area affected.

(c) Approval of petition; publication in Federal Register; notice; reassumption period; correction of causes for disapproval.—If the Secretary approves any petition under subsection (a), the Secretary shall publish notice of such approval in the Federal Register and shall notify the affected State or States of such approval. The Indian tribe concerned shall reassume jurisdiction sixty days after publication in the Federal Register of notice of approval. If the Secretary disapproves any petition under subsection (a), the Secretary shall provide such technical assistance as may be necessary to enable the tribe to correct any deficiency which the Secretary identified as a cause for disapproval.

(d) Pending actions or proceedings unaffected.—Assumption of jurisdiction under this section shall not affect any action or proceeding over which a court has already assumed jurisdiction, except as may be provided pursuant to any agreement under section 109 of this Act [25 U.S.C. §1919].

History of 25 U.S.C. §1918: Nov. 8, 1978, P.L. 95-608, §108, 92 Stat. 3074.

§1919. AGREEMENTS BETWEEN STATES & INDIAN TRIBES

(a) Subject coverage.—States and Indian tribes are authorized to enter into agreements with each other respecting care and custody of Indian children and jurisdiction over child custody proceedings, including agreements which may provide for orderly transfer of jurisdiction on a case-by-case basis and agreements which provide for concurrent jurisdiction between States and Indian tribes.

(b) Revocation; notice; actions or proceedings unaffected.—Such agreements may be revoked by either party upon one hundred and eighty days' written notice to the other party. Such revocation shall not affect any action or proceeding over which a court has already assumed jurisdiction, unless the agreement provides otherwise.

History of 25 U.S.C. §1919: Nov. 8, 1978, P.L. 95-608, §109, 92 Stat. 3074.

§1920. IMPROPER REMOVAL OF CHILD FROM CUSTODY; DECLINATION OF JURISDICTION; FORTHWITH RETURN OF CHILD: DANGER EXCEPTION

Where any petitioner in an Indian child custody proceeding before a State court has improperly removed the child from custody of the parent or Indian custodian or has improperly retained custody after a visit or other temporary relinquishment of custody, the court shall decline jurisdiction over such petition and shall forthwith return the child to his parent or Indian custodian unless returning the child to his parent or custodian would subject the child to a substantial and immediate danger or threat of such danger.

History of 25 U.S.C. §1920: Nov. 8, 1978, P.L. 95-608, §110, 92 Stat. 3075.

§1921. HIGHER STATE OR FEDERAL STANDARD APPLICABLE TO PROTECT RIGHTS OF PARENT OR INDIAN CUSTODIAN OF INDIAN CHILD

In any case where State or Federal law applicable to a child custody proceeding under State or Federal law provides a higher standard of protection to the rights of the parent or Indian custodian of an Indian child than the rights provided under this title [particularly 25 U.S.C. §1911 et seq.], the State or Federal court shall apply the State or Federal standard.

History of 25 U.S.C. §1921: Nov. 8, 1978, P.L. 95-608, §111, 92 Stat. 3075.

§1922. EMERGENCY REMOVAL OR PLACEMENT OF CHILD; TERMINATION; APPROPRIATE ACTION

Nothing in this title [particularly 25 U.S.C. §1911 et seq.] shall be construed to prevent the emergency removal of an Indian child who is a resident of or is domiciled on a reservation, but temporarily located off the reservation, from his parent or Indian custodian or the emergency placement of such child in a foster home or institution, under applicable State law, in order to prevent imminent physical damage or harm to the child. The State authority, official, or agency involved shall insure that the emergency removal or placement terminates immediately when such removal or placement is no longer necessary to prevent imminent physical damage or harm to the child and shall expeditiously initiate a child custody proceeding subject to the provisions of this title [particularly 25 U.S.C. §1911 et seq.], transfer the child to the jurisdiction of the appropriate Indian tribe, or restore the child to the parent or Indian custodian, as may be appropriate.

History of 25 U.S.C. §1922: Nov. 8, 1978, P.L. 95-608, §112, 92 Stat. 3075.

§1923. EFFECTIVE DATE

None of the provisions of this title [particularly 25 U.S.C. §1911 et seq.], except sections 101(a), 108, and 109 [25 U.S.C. §§1911(a), 1918, and 1919], shall affect a proceeding under State law for foster care placement, termination of parental rights, preadoptive placement, or adoptive placement which was initiated or completed prior to one hundred and eighty days after the enactment of this Act [enacted Nov. 8, 1978], but shall apply to any subsequent proceeding in the same matter or subsequent proceedings affecting the custody or placement of the same child.

History of 25 U.S.C. §1923: Nov. 8, 1978, P.L. 95-608, §113, 92 Stat. 3075.

TITLE 26. INTERNAL REVENUE CODE

SUBTITLE A. INCOME TAXES

CHAPTER 1. NORMAL TAXES & SURTAXES

SUBCHAPTER B. COMPUTATION OF TAXABLE INCOME

PART I. DEFINITION OF GROSS INCOME, ADJUSTED GROSS INCOME, TAXABLE INCOME, ETC.

§66. TREATMENT OF COMMUNITY INCOME

(a) Treatment of community income where spouses live apart.—If—

(1) 2 individuals are married to each other at any time during a calendar year;

(2) such individuals—

(A) live apart at all times during the calendar year, and

(B) do not file a joint return under section 6013 with each other for a taxable year beginning or ending in the calendar year;

(3) one or both of such individuals have earned income for the calendar year which is community income; and

(4) no portion of such earned income is transferred (directly or indirectly) between such individuals before the close of the calendar year,

then, for purposes of this title, any community income of such individuals for the calendar year shall be treated in accordance with the rules provided by section 879(a) [26 U.S.C. §879(a)].

(b) Secretary may disregard community property laws where spouse not notified of community income.—The Secretary may disallow the benefits of any community property law to any taxpayer with respect to any income if such taxpayer acted as if solely entitled to such income and failed to notify the taxpayer's spouse before the due date (including extensions) for filing the return for the taxable year in which the income was derived of the nature and amount of such income.

(c) Spouse relieved of liability in certain other cases.—Under regulations prescribed by the Secretary, if—

(1) an individual does not file a joint return for any taxable year,

(2) such individual does not include in gross income for such taxable year an item of community income properly includible therein which, in accordance with the rules contained in section 879(a) [26 U.S.C. §879(a)], would be treated as the income of the other spouse,

(3) the individual establishes that he or she did not know of, and had no reason to know of, such item of community income, and

(4) taking into account all facts and circumstances, it is inequitable to include such item of community income in such individual's gross income,

then, for purposes of this title, such item of community income shall be included in the gross income of the other spouse (and not in the gross income of the individual). Under procedures prescribed by the Secretary, if, taking into account all the facts and circumstances, it is inequitable to hold the individual liable for any unpaid tax or any deficiency (or any portion of either) attributable to any item for which relief is not available under the preceding sentence, the Secretary may relieve such individual of such liability.

(d) Definitions.—For purposes of this section—

(1) Earned income.—The term "earned income" has the meaning given to such term by section 911(d)(2).

(2) Community income.—The term "community income" means income which, under applicable community property laws, is treated as community income.

(3) Community property laws.—The term "community property laws" means the community property laws of a State, a foreign country, or a possession of the United States.

History of 26 U.S.C. §66: Added Dec. 28, 1980, P.L. 96-605, §101(a), 94 Stat. 3521; July 18, 1984, Pub. 98-369, §424(b)(1), (2)(A), (B), 98 Stat. 802, 803; Dec. 19, 1989, P.L. 101-239, §7841(d)(8), 103 Stat. 2428; July 22, 1998, P.L. 105-206, §3201(b), 112 Stat. 739.

PART II. ITEMS SPECIFICALLY INCLUDED IN GROSS INCOME

§71. ALIMONY & SEPARATE MAINTENANCE PAYMENTS

(a) General rule.—Gross income includes amounts received as alimony or separate maintenance payments.

(b) Alimony or separate maintenance payments defined.—For purposes of this section—

(1) In general.—The term "alimony or separate maintenance payment" means any payment in cash if—

(A) such payment is received by (or on behalf of) a spouse under a divorce or separation instrument,

(B) the divorce or separation instrument does not designate such payment as a payment which is not includible in gross income under this section and not allowable as a deduction under section 215 [26 U.S.C. §215],

(C) in the case of an individual legally separated from his spouse under a decree of divorce or of separate maintenance, the payee spouse and the payor spouse are not members of the same household at the time such payment is made, and

(D) there is no liability to make any such payment for any period after the death of the payee spouse and there is no liability to make any payment (in cash or property) as a substitute for such payments after the death of the payee spouse.

(2) Divorce or separation instrument.—The term "divorce or separation instrument" means—

(A) a decree of divorce or separate maintenance or a written instrument incident to such a decree,

(B) a written separation agreement, or

(C) a decree (not described in subparagraph (A)) requiring a spouse to make payments for the support or maintenance of the other spouse.

(c) Payments to support children.—

(1) In general.—Subsection (a) shall not apply to that part of any payment which the terms of the divorce or separation instrument fix (in terms of an amount of money or a part of the payment) as a sum which is payable for the support of children of the payor spouse.

(2) Treatment of certain reductions related to contingencies involving child.—For purposes of paragraph (1), if any amount specified in the instrument will be reduced—

(A) on the happening of a contingency specified in the instrument relating to a child (such as attaining a specified age, marrying, dying, leaving school, or a similar contingency), or

(B) at a time which can clearly be associated with a contingency of a kind specified in subparagraph (A), an amount equal to the amount of such reduction will be treated as an amount fixed as payable for the support of children of the payor spouse.

(3) Special rule where payment is less than amount specified in instrument.—For purposes of this subsection, if any payment is less than the amount specified in the instrument, then so much of such payment as does not exceed the sum payable for support shall be considered a payment for such support.

(d) Spouse.—For purposes of this section, the term "spouse" includes a former spouse.

(e) Exception for joint returns.—This section and section 215 [26 U.S.C. §215] shall not apply if the spouses make a joint return with each other.

(f) Recomputation where excess front-loading of alimony payments.—

(1) In general.—If there are excess alimony payments—

(A) the payor spouse shall include the amount of such excess payments in gross income for the payor spouse's taxable year beginning in the 3rd post-separation year, and

(B) the payee spouse shall be allowed a deduction in computing adjusted gross income for the amount of such excess payments for the payee's taxable year beginning in the 3rd post-separation year.

(2) Excess alimony payments.—For purposes of this subsection, the term "excess alimony payments" mean the sum of—

(A) the excess payments for the 1st post-separation year, and

(B) the excess payments for the 2nd post-separation year.

(3) Excess payments for 1st post-separation year.—For purposes of this subsection, the amount of the excess payments for the 1st post-separation year is the excess (if any) of—

(A) the amount of the alimony or separate maintenance payments paid by the payor spouse during the 1st post-separation year, over

(B) the sum of—

(i) the average of—

(I) the alimony or separate maintenance payments paid by the payor spouse during the 2nd post-separation year, reduced by the excess payments for the 2nd post-separation year, and

(II) the alimony or separate maintenance payments paid by the payor spouse during the 3rd post-separation year, plus

(ii) $15,000.

(4) Excess payments for 2nd post-separation year.—For purposes of this subsection, the amount of the excess payments for the 2nd post-separation year is the excess (if any) of—

(A) the amount of the alimony or separate maintenance payments paid by the payor spouse during the 2nd post-separation year, over

(B) the sum of—

(i) the amount of the alimony or separate maintenance payments paid by the payor spouse during the 3rd post-separation year, plus

(ii) $15,000.

(5) Exceptions.—

(A) Where payment ceases by reason of death or remarriage.—Paragraph (1) shall not apply if—

(i) either spouse dies before the close of the 3rd post-separation year, or the payee spouse remarries before the close of the 3rd post-separation year, and

(ii) the alimony or separate maintenance payments cease by reason of such death or remarriage.

(B) Support payments.—For purposes of this subsection, the term "alimony or separate maintenance payment" shall not include any payment received under a decree described in subsection (b)(2)(C).

(C) Fluctuating payments not within control of payor spouse.—For purposes of this subsection, the term "alimony or separate maintenance payment" shall not include any payment to the extent it is made pursuant to a continuing liability (over a period of not less than 3 years) to pay a fixed portion or portions of the income from a business or property or from compensation for employment or self-employment.

(6) Post-separation years.—For purposes of this subsection, the term "1st post-separation years" means the 1st calendar year in which the payor spouse paid to the payee spouse alimony or separate maintenance payments to which this section applies. The 2nd and 3rd post-separation years shall be the 1st and 2nd succeeding calendar years, respectively.

(g) Cross references.—

(1) For deduction of alimony or separate maintenance payments, see section 215 [26 U.S.C. §215].

(2) For taxable status of income of an estate or trust in the case of divorce, etc., see section 682 [26 U.S.C. §682].

History of 26 U.S.C. §71: Aug. 16, 1954, ch. 736, 68A Stat. 19; July 18, 1984, P.L. 98-369, §422(a), 98 Stat. 795; Oct. 22, 1986, P.L. 99-514, §1843(a)-(c)(1), (d), 100 Stat. 2853, 2855.

PART III. ITEMS SPECIFICALLY EXCLUDED FROM GROSS INCOME

§121. EXCLUSION OF GAIN FROM SALE OF PRINCIPAL RESIDENCE

(a) Exclusion.—Gross income shall not include gain from the sale or exchange of property if, during the 5-year period ending on the date of the sale or exchange, such property has been owned and used by the taxpayer as the taxpayer's principal residence for periods aggregating 2 years or more.

(b) Limitations.—

(1) In general.—The amount of gain excluded from gross income under subsection (a) with respect to any sale or exchange shall not exceed $250,000.

(2) Special rules for joint returns.—In the case of a husband and wife who make a joint return for the taxable year of the sale or exchange of the property—

(A) $500,000 Limitation for certain joint returns.—Paragraph (1) shall be applied by substituting "$500,000" for "$250,000" if—

(i) either spouse meets the ownership requirements of subsection (a) with respect to such property;

(ii) both spouses meet the use requirements of subsection (a) with respect to such property; and

(iii) neither spouse is ineligible for the benefits of subsection (a) with respect to such property by reason of paragraph (3).

(B) Other joint returns.—If such spouses do not meet the requirements of subparagraph (A), the limitation under paragraph (1) shall be the sum of the limitations under paragraph (1) to which each spouse would be entitled if such spouses had not been married. For purposes of the preceding sentence, each spouse shall be treated as owning the property during the period that either spouse owned the property.

(3) Application to only 1 sale or exchange every 2 years.—

(A) In general.—Subsection (a) shall not apply to any sale or exchange by the taxpayer if, during the 2-year period ending on the date of such sale or exchange, there was any other sale or exchange by the taxpayer to which subsection (a) applied.

(B) Pre-May 7, 1997, sales not taken into account.—Subparagraph (A) shall be applied without regard to any sale or exchange before May 7, 1997.

(c) Exclusion for taxpayers failing to meet certain requirements.—

(1) In general.—In the case of a sale or exchange to which this subsection applies, the ownership and use requirements of subsection (a), and subsection (b)(3), shall not apply; but the dollar limitation under paragraph (1) or (2) of subsection (b), whichever is applicable, shall be equal to—

(A) the amount which bears the same ratio to such limitation (determined without regard to this paragraph) as

(B)(i) the shorter of—

(I) the aggregate periods, during the 5-year period ending on the date of such sale or exchange, such property has been owned and used by the taxpayer as the taxpayer's principal residence; or

(II) the period after the date of the most recent prior sale or exchange by the taxpayer to which subsection (a) applied and before the date of such sale or exchange, bears to

(ii) 2 years.

(2) Sales and exchanges to which subsection applies.—This subsection shall apply to any sale or exchange if—

(A) subsection (a) would not (but for this subsection) apply to such sale or exchange by reason of—

(i) a failure to meet the ownership and use requirements of subsection (a), or

(ii) subsection (b)(3), and

(B) such sale or exchange is by reason of a change in place of employment, health, or, to the extent provided in regulations, unforeseen circumstances.

(d) Special rules.*—

(1) Joint returns.—If a husband and wife make a joint return for the taxable year of the sale or exchange of the property, subsections (a) and (c) shall apply if either spouse meets the ownership and use requirements of subsection (a) with respect to such property.

(2) Property of deceased spouse.—For purposes of this section, in the case of an unmarried individual whose spouse is deceased on the date of the sale or exchange of property, the period such unmarried individual owned and used such property shall include the period such deceased spouse owned and used such property before death.

(3) Property owned by spouse or former spouse.—For purposes of this section—

(A) Property transferred to individual from spouse or former spouse.—In the case of an individual holding property transferred to such individual in a transaction described in section 1041(a) [26 U.S.C. §1041(a)], the period such individual owns such property shall include the period the transferor owned the property.

(B) Property used by former spouse pursuant to divorce decree, etc.—Solely for purposes of this section, an individual shall be treated as using property as such individual's principal residence during any period of ownership while such individual's spouse or former spouse is granted use of the property under a divorce or separation instrument (as defined in section 71(b)(2) [26 U.S.C. §71(b)(2)]).

(4) Tenant-stockholder in cooperative housing corporation.—For purposes of this section, if the taxpayer holds stock as a tenant-stockholder (as defined in section 216 [26 U.S.C. §216 (b)(2)]) in a cooperative housing corporation (as defined in such section), then—

(A) the holding requirements of subsection (a) shall be applied to the holding of such stock, and

(B) the use requirements of subsection (a) shall be applied to the house or apartment which the taxpayer was entitled to occupy as such stockholder.

(5) Involuntary conversions.—

(A) In general.—For purposes of this section, the destruction, theft, seizure, requisition, or condemnation of property shall be treated as the sale of such property.

(B) Application of section 1033.—In applying section 1033 [26 U.S.C. §1033] (relating to involuntary conversions), the amount realized from the sale or exchange of property shall be treated as being the amount determined without regard to this section, reduced by the amount of gain not included in gross income pursuant to this section.

(C) Property acquired after involuntary conversion.—If the basis of the property sold or exchanged is determined (in whole or in part) under section 1033(b) [26 U.S.C. §1033(b)] (relating to basis of property acquired through involuntary conversion), then the holding and use by the taxpayer of the converted property shall be treated as holding and use by the taxpayer of the property sold or exchanged.

(6) Recognition of gain attributable to depreciation.—Subsection (a) shall not apply to so much of the gain from the sale of any property as does not exceed the portion of the depreciation adjustments (as defined in section 1250(b)(3) [26 U.S.C. §1250(b)(3)]) attributable to periods after May 6, 1997, in respect of such property.

(7) Determination of use during periods of out-of-residence care.—In the case of a taxpayer who—

(A) becomes physically or mentally incapable of self-care, and

(B) owns property and uses such property as the taxpayer's principal residence during the 5-year period described in subsection (a) for periods aggregating at least 1 year,

then the taxpayer shall be treated as using such property as the taxpayer's principal residence during any time during such 5-year period in which the taxpayer owns the property and resides in any facility (including a nursing home) licensed by a State or political subdivision to care for an individual in the taxpayer's condition.

(8) Sales of remainder interests.—For purposes of this section—

(A) In general.—At the election of the taxpayer, this section shall not fail to apply to the sale or exchange of an interest in a principal residence by reason of such interest being a remainder interest in such residence, but this section shall not apply to any other interest in such residence which is sold or exchanged separately.

(B) Exception for sales to related parties.—Subparagraph (A) shall not apply to any sale to, or exchange with, any person who bears a relationship to the taxpayer which is described in section 267(b) or 707(b) [26 U.S.C. §267(b) or §707(b)].

(e) Denial of exclusion for expatriates.—This section shall not apply to any sale or exchange by an individual if the treatment provided by section 877(a)(1) [26 U.S.C. §877a)(1)] applies to such individual.

(f) Election to have section not apply.—This section shall not apply to any sale or exchange with respect to which the taxpayer elects not to have this section apply.

(g) Residences acquired in rollovers under section 1034.—For purposes of this section, in the case of property the acquisition of which by the taxpayer resulted under section 1034 [26 U.S.C. §1034] (as in effect on the day before the date of the enactment of this section) in the nonrecognition of any part of the gain realized on the sale or exchange of another residence, in determining the period for which the taxpayer has owned and used such property as the taxpayer's principal residence, there shall be included the aggregate periods for which such other residence (and each prior residence taken into account under section 1223(7) [26 U.S.C. §1223(7)] in determining the holding period of such property) had been so owned and used.

History of 26 U.S.C. §121: Added Feb. 26, 1964, P.L. 88-272, §206(a), 78 Stat. 38; Oct. 4, 1976, P.L. 94-455, §1404(a), §1906(b)(13)(A), 90 Stat. 1733; Nov. 6, 1978, P.L. 95-600, §404(a)-(c)(2), 92 Stat. 2869, 2870, Aug. 13, 1981, P.L. 97-34, §123(a), 95 Stat. 197; Nov.10, 1988, P.L. 100-647, §6011(a), 102 Stat. 3691, Aug. 5, 1977, P.L. 105-34, §312(a), 111 Stat. 836; July 22, 1998, P.L. 105-206, §6005(e)(1), (2), 112 Stat. 805.

* P.L. 107-16 §542(c) adds subsection (d)(9), effective Dec. 31, 2009.

PART V. DEDUCTIONS FOR PERSONAL EXEMPTIONS

§152. DEPENDENT DEFINED

(a) General definition.—For purposes of this subtitle, the term "dependent" means any of the following individuals over half of whose support, for the calendar year in which the taxable year of the taxpayer begins, was received from the taxpayer (or is treated under subsection (c) or (e) as received from the taxpayer):

(1) A son or daughter of the taxpayer, or a descendant of either,

(2) A stepson or stepdaughter of the taxpayer,

(3) A brother, sister, stepbrother, or stepsister of the taxpayer,

(4) The father or mother of the taxpayer, or an ancestor of either,

(5) A stepfather or stepmother of the taxpayer,

(6) A son or daughter of a brother or sister of the taxpayer,

(7) A brother or sister of the father or mother of the taxpayer,

(8) A son-in-law, daughter-in-law, father-in-law, mother-in-law, brother-in-law, or sister-in-law of the taxpayer, or

(9) An individual (other than an individual who at any time during the taxable year was the spouse, determined without regard to section 7703 [26 U.S.C. §7703], of the taxpayer) who, for the taxable year of the taxpayer, has as his principal place of abode the home of the taxpayer and is a member of the taxpayer's household.

(b) Rules relating to general definition.—For purposes of this section—

(1) The terms "brother" and "sister" include a brother or sister by the halfblood.

(2) In determining whether any of the relationships specified in subsection (a) or paragraph (1) of this subsection exists, a legally adopted child of an individual (and a child who is a member of an individual's household, if placed with such individual by an authorized placement agency for legal adoption by such individual), or a foster child of an individual (if such child satisfies the requirements of subsection (a)(9) with respect to such individual), shall be treated as a child of such individual by blood.

(3) The term "dependent" does not include any individual who is not a citizen or national of the United States unless such individual is a resident of the United States or of a country contiguous to the United States. The preceding sentence shall not exclude from the definition of "dependent" any child of the taxpayer legally adopted by him, if, for the taxable year of the taxpayer, the child has as his principal place of abode the home of the taxpayer and is a member of the taxpayer's household, and if the taxpayer is a citizen or national of the United States.

(4) A payment to a wife which is includible in the gross income of the wife under section 71 or 682 [26 U.S.C. §71 or §682] shall not be treated as a payment by her husband for the support of any dependent.

(5) An individual is not a member of the taxpayer's household if at any time during the taxable year of the taxpayer the relationship between such individual and the taxpayer is in violation of local law.

(c) Multiple support agreements.—For purposes of subsection (a), over half of the support of an individual for a calendar year shall be treated as received from the taxpayer if—

(1) no one person contributed over half of such support;

(2) over half of such support was received from persons each of whom, but for the fact that he did not contribute over half of such support, would have been entitled to claim such individual as a dependent for a taxable year beginning in such calendar year;

(3) the taxpayer contributed over 10 percent of such support; and

(4) each person described in paragraph (2) (other than the taxpayer) who contributed over 10 percent of such support files a written declaration (in such manner and form as the Secretary may by regulations prescribe) that he will not claim such individual as a dependent for any taxable year beginning in such calendar year.

(d) Special support test in case of students.—For purposes of subsection (a), in the case of any individual who is—

(1) a son, stepson, daughter, or stepdaughter of the taxpayer (within the meaning of this section), and

(2) a student (within the meaning of section 151(c)(4)[26 U.S.C. §151(c)(4)]),

amounts received as scholarships for study at an educational organization described in section 170(b)(1)(A)(ii) [26 U.S.C. §170(b)(1)(A)(ii)] shall not be taken into account in determining whether such individual received more than half of his support from the taxpayer.

(e) Support test in case of child of divorced parents, etc.—

(1) Custodial parent gets exemption.—Except as otherwise provided in this subsection, if—

(A) a child (as defined in section 151(c)(3)[26 U.S.C. §151(c)(3)]) receives over half of his support during the calendar year from his parents—

(i) who are divorced or legally separated under a decree of divorce or separate maintenance,

(ii) who are separated under a written separation agreement, or

(iii) who live apart at all times during the last 6 months of the calendar year, and

(B) such child is in the custody of one or both of his parents for more than one-half of the calendar year,

such child shall be treated, for purposes of subsection (a), as receiving over half of his support during the calendar year from the parent having custody for a greater portion of the calendar year (hereinafter in this subsection referred to as the "custodial parent").

(2) Exception where custodial parent releases claim to exemption for the year.—A child of parents described in paragraph (1) shall be treated as having received over half of his support during a calendar year from the noncustodial parent if—

(A) the custodial parent signs a written declaration (in such manner and form as the Secretary may by regulations prescribe) that such custodial parent will not claim such child as a dependent for any taxable year beginning in such calendar year, and

(B) the noncustodial parent attaches such written declaration to the noncustodial parent's return for the taxable year beginning during such calendar year.

For purposes of this subsection, the term "noncustodial parent" means the parent who is not the custodial parent.

(3) Exception for multiple-support agreement.—This subsection shall not apply in any case where over half of the support of the child is treated as having been received from a taxpayer under the provisions of subsection (c).

(4) Exception for certain pre-1985 instruments.—

(A) In general.—A child of parents described in paragraph (1) shall be treated as having received over half his support during a calendar year from the noncustodial parent if—

(i) a qualified pre-1985 instrument between the parents applicable to the taxable year beginning in such calendar year provides that the noncustodial parent shall be entitled to any deduction allowable under section 151 [26 U.S.C. §151] for such child, and

(ii) the noncustodial parent provides at least $600 for the support of such child during such calendar year.

For purposes of this subparagraph, amounts expended for the support of a child or children shall be treated as received from the noncustodial parent to the extent that such parent provided amounts for such support.

(B) Qualified pre-1985 instrument.—For purposes of this paragraph, the term "qualified pre-1985 instrument" means any decree of divorce or separate maintenance or written agreement—

(i) which is executed before January 1, 1985,

(ii) which on such date contains the provision described in subparagraph (A)(i), and

(iii) which is not modified on or after such date in a modification which expressly provides that this paragraph shall not apply to such decree or agreement.

(5) Special rule for support received from new spouse of parent.—For purposes of this subsection, in the case of the remarriage of a parent, support of a child received from the parent's spouse shall be treated as received from the parent.

(6) Cross reference.—For provision treating child as dependent of both parents for purposes of medical expense deduction, see section 213(d)(5) [26 U.S.C. §213(d)(5)].

History of 26 U.S.C. §152: Aug. 16, 1954, ch. 736, 68A Stat. 43; Aug. 9, 1955, ch. 693, (2, 69 Stat. 626; Sept. 2, 1958, P.L. 85-866, (4(a)-(c), 72 Stat. 1607; Sept. 23, 1959, P.L. 86-376, (1(a), 73 Stat. 699; Aug. 31, 1967, P.L. 90-78, (1, 81 Stat. 191; Dec. 30, 1969, P.L. 91-192, (912(a), 83 Stat. 722; Oct. 27, 1972, P.L. 92-580, (1(a), 86 Stat. 1276; Oct. 4, 1976, P.L. 94-455, ((1901(a)(24), (b)(7)(B), (8)(A), 1906(b)(13)(A), (2139(a), 90 Stat. 1767, 1794, 1834, 1932; July 18, 1984, P.L. 98-369, ((423(a), 482(b)(2), 98 Stat. 799, 848; Oct. 22, 1986, P.L. 99-514, (104(b)(1)(B), (3), (1301(j)(8), 100 Stat. 2104, 2105, 2658.

PART VII. ADDITIONAL ITEMIZED DEDUCTIONS FOR INDIVIDUALS

§215. ALIMONY, ETC., PAYMENTS

(a) General rule.—In the case of an individual, there shall be allowed as a deduction an amount equal to the alimony or separate maintenance payments paid during such individual's taxable year.

(b) Alimony or separate maintenance payments defined.—For purposes of this section, the term "alimony or separate maintenance payment" means any alimony or separate maintenance payment (as defined in section 71(b) [26 U.S.C. §71(b)]) which is includible in the gross income of the recipient under section 71 [26 U.S.C. §71(b)].

(c) Requirement of identification number.—The Secretary may prescribe regulations under which—

(1) any individual receiving alimony or separate maintenance payments is required to furnish such individual's taxpayer identification number to the individual making such payments, and

(2) the individual making such payments is required to include such taxpayer identification number on such individual's return for the taxable year in which such payments are made.

(d) Coordination with section 682.—No deduction shall be allowed under this section with respect to any payment if, by reason of section 682 [26 U.S.C. §682] (relating to income of alimony trusts), the amount thereof is not includible in such individual's gross income.

History of 26 U.S.C. §215: Aug. 16, 1954, ch. 736, 68A Stat. 71; July 18, 1984, P.L. 98-369, §422(b), 98 Stat. 797.

SUBCHAPTER O. GAIN OR LOSS ON DISPOSITION OF PROPERTY

PART III. COMMON NONTAXABLE EXCHANGES

§1041. TRANSFERS OF PROPERTY BETWEEN SPOUSES OR INCIDENT TO DIVORCE

(a) General rule.—No gain or loss shall be recognized on a transfer of property from an individual to (or in trust for the benefit of)—

(1) a spouse, or

(2) a former spouse, but only if the transfer is incident to the divorce.

(b) Transfer treated as gift; transferee has transferor's basis.—In the case of any transfer of property described in subsection (a)—

(1) for purposes of this subtitle, the property shall be treated as acquired by the transferee by gift, and

(2) the basis of the transferee in the property shall be the adjusted basis of the transferor.

(c) Incident to divorce.—For purposes of subsection (a)(2), a transfer of property is incident to the divorce if such transfer—

(1) occurs within 1 year after the date on which the marriage ceases, or

(2) is related to the cessation of the marriage.

(d) Special rule where spouse is nonresident alien.—Subsection (a) shall not apply if the spouse (or former spouse) of the individual making the transfer is a nonresident alien.

(e) Transfers in trust where liability exceeds basis.—Subsection (a) shall not apply to the transfer of property in trust to the extent that—

(1) the sum of the amount of the liabilities assumed, plus the amount of the liabilities to which the property is subject, exceeds

(2) the total of the adjusted basis of the property transferred.

Proper adjustment shall be made under subsection (b) in the basis of the transferee in such property to take into account gain recognized by reason of the preceding sentence.

History of 26 U.S.C. §1041: July 18, 1984, P.L. 98-369, §421(a), 98 Stat. 793; Oct. 22, 1986, P.L. 99-514, §1842(b), 100 Stat. 2853; Nov. 10, 1988, P.L. 100-647, §1018(1)(3), 102 Stat. 3584.

SUBTITLE F. PROCEDURE & ADMINISTRATION

CHAPTER 61. INFORMATION & RETURNS

SUBCHAPTER A. RETURNS & RECORDS

PART II. TAX RETURNS OR STATEMENTS

SUBPART B. INCOME TAX RETURNS

§6015. RELIEF FROM JOINT & SEVERAL LIABILITY ON JOINT RETURN

(a) In general.—Notwithstanding section 6013(d)(3) [26 U.S.C. §6013(d)(3)]—

(1) an individual who has made a joint return may elect to seek relief under the procedures prescribed under subsection (b); and

(2) if such individual is eligible to elect the application of subsection (c), such individual may, in addition to any election under paragraph (1), elect to limit such individual's liability for any deficiency with respect to such joint return in the manner prescribed under subsection (c).

Any determination under this section shall be made without regard to community property laws.

(b) Procedures for relief from liability applicable to all joint filers.—

(1) In general.—Under procedures prescribed by the Secretary, if—

(A) a joint return has been made for a taxable year;

(B) on such return there is an understatement of tax attributable to erroneous items of one individual filing the joint return;

(C) the other individual filing the joint return establishes that in signing the return he or she did not know, and had no reason to know, that there was such understatement;

(D) taking into account all the facts and circumstances, it is inequitable to hold the other individual liable for the deficiency in tax for such taxable year attributable to such understatement; and

(E) the other individual elects (in such form as the Secretary may prescribe) the benefits of this subsection not later than the date which is 2 years after the date the Secretary has begun collection activities with respect to the individual making the election,

then the other individual shall be relieved of liability for tax (including interest, penalties, and other amounts) for such taxable year to the extent such liability is attributable to such understatement.

(2) Apportionment of relief.—If an individual who, but for paragraph (1)(C), would be relieved of liability under paragraph (1), establishes that in signing the return such individual did not know, and had no reason to know, the extent of such understatement, then such individual shall be relieved of liability for tax (including interest, penalties, and other amounts) for such taxable year to the extent that such liability is attributable to the portion of such understatement of which such individual did not know and had no reason to know.

(3) Understatement.—For purposes of this subsection, the term "understatement" has the meaning given to such term by section 6662(d)(2)(A) [26 U.S.C. §6662(d)(2)(A)].

(c) Procedures to limit liability for taxpayers no longer married or taxpayers legally separated or not living together.—

(1) In general.—Except as provided in this subsection, if an individual who has made a joint return for any taxable year elects the application of this subsection, the individual's liability for any deficiency which is assessed with respect to the return shall not exceed the portion of such deficiency properly allocable to the individual under subsection (d).

(2) Burden of proof.—Except as provided in subparagraph (A)(ii) or (C) of paragraph (3), each individual who elects the application of this subsection shall have the burden of proof with respect to establishing the portion of any deficiency allocable to such individual.

(3) Election.—

(A) Individuals eligible to make election.—

(i) In general.—An individual shall only be eligible to elect the application of this subsection if—

(I) at the time such election is filed, such individual is no longer married to, or is legally separated from, the individual with whom such individual filed the joint return to which the election relates; or

(II) such individual was not a member of the same household as the individual with whom such joint return was filed at any time during the 12-month period ending on the date such election is filed.

(ii) Certain taxpayers ineligible to elect.—If the Secretary demonstrates that assets were transferred between individuals filing a joint return as part of a fraudulent scheme by such individuals, an election under this subsection by either individual shall be invalid (and section 6013(d)(3) [26 U.S.C. §6013(d)(3)] shall apply to the joint return).

(B) Time for election.—An election under this subsection for any taxable year may be made at any time after a deficiency for such year is asserted but not later than 2 years after the date on which the Secretary has begun collection activities with respect to the individual making the election.

(C) Election not valid with respect to certain deficiencies.—If the Secretary demonstrates that an individual making an election under this subsection had actual knowledge, at the time such individual signed the return, of any item giving rise to a deficiency (or portion thereof) which is not allocable to such individual under subsection (d), such election shall not apply to such deficiency (or portion). This subparagraph shall not apply where the individual with actual knowledge establishes that such individual signed the return under duress.

(4) Liability increased by reason of transfers of property to avoid tax.—

(A) In general.—Notwithstanding any other provision of this subsection, the portion of the deficiency for which the individual electing the application of this subsection is liable (without regard to this paragraph) shall be increased by the value of any disqualified asset transferred to the individual.

(B) Disqualified asset.—For purposes of this paragraph—

(i) In general.—The term "disqualified asset" means any property or right to property transferred to an individual making the election under this subsection with respect to a joint return by the other individual filing such joint return if the principal purpose of the transfer was the avoidance of tax or payment of tax.

(ii) Presumption.—

(I) In general.—For purposes of clause (i), except as provided in subclause (II), any transfer which is made after the date which is 1 year before the date on which the first letter of proposed deficiency which allows the taxpayer an opportunity for administrative review in the Internal Revenue Service Office of Appeals is sent shall be presumed to have as its principal purpose the avoidance of tax or payment of tax.

(II) Exceptions.—Subclause (I) shall not apply to any transfer pursuant to a decree of divorce or separate maintenance or a written instrument incident to such a decree or to any transfer which an individual establishes did not have as its principal purpose the avoidance of tax or payment of tax.

(d) Allocation of deficiency.—For purposes of subsection (c)—

(1) In general.—The portion of any deficiency on a joint return allocated to an individual shall be the amount which bears the same ratio to such deficiency as the net amount of items taken into account in computing the deficiency and allocable to the individual under paragraph (3) bears to the net amount of all items taken into account in computing the deficiency.

(2) Separate treatment of certain items.—If a deficiency (or portion thereof) is attributable to—

(A) the disallowance of a credit; or

(B) any tax (other than tax imposed by section 1 or 55) required to be included with the joint return;

and such item is allocated to one individual under paragraph (3), such deficiency (or portion) shall be allocated to such individual. Any such item shall not be taken into account under paragraph (1).

(3) Allocation of items giving rise to the deficiency.—For purposes of this subsection—

(A) In general.—Except as provided in paragraphs (4) and (5), any item giving rise to a deficiency on a joint return shall be allocated to individuals filing the return in the same manner as it would have been allocated if the individuals had filed separate returns for the taxable year.

(B) Exception where other spouse benefits.—Under rules prescribed by the Secretary, an item otherwise allocable to an individual under subparagraph (A) shall be allocated to the other individual filing the joint return to the extent the item gave rise to a tax benefit on the joint return to the other individual.

(C) Exception for fraud.—The Secretary may provide for an allocation of any item in a manner not prescribed by subparagraph (A) if the Secretary establishes that such allocation is appropriate due to fraud of one or both individuals.

(4) Limitations on separate returns disregarded.—If an item of deduction or credit is disallowed in its entirety solely because a separate return is filed, such disallowance shall be disregarded and the item shall be computed as if a joint return had been filed and then allocated between the spouses appropriately. A similar rule shall apply for purposes of section 86.

(5) Child's liability.—If the liability of a child of a taxpayer is included on a joint return, such liability shall be disregarded in computing the separate liability of either spouse and such liability shall be allocated appropriately between the spouses.

(e) Petition for review by Tax Court.—

(1) In general.—In the case of an individual against whom a deficiency has been asserted and who elects to have subsection (b) or (c) apply—

(A) In general.—In addition to any other remedy provided by law, the individual may petition the Tax Court (and the Tax Court shall have jurisdiction) to determine the appropriate relief available to the individual under this section if such petition is filed—

(i) at any time after the earlier of—

(I) the date the Secretary mails, by certified or registered mail to the taxpayer's last known address, notice of the Secretary's final determination of relief available to the individual, or

(II) the date which is 6 months after the date such election is filed with the Secretary, and

(ii) not later than the close of the 90th day after the date described in clause (i)(I).

(B) Restrictions applicable to collection of assessment.—

(i) In general.—Except as otherwise provided in section 6851 or 6861 [26 U.S.C. §6851 or §6861], no levy or proceeding in court shall be made, begun, or prosecuted against the individual making an election under subsection (b) or (c) for collection of any assessment to which such election relates until the close of the 90th day referred to in subparagraph (A)(ii), or, if a petition has been filed with the Tax Court under subparagraph (A), until the decision of the Tax Court has become final. Rules similar to the rules of section 7485 [26 U.S.C. §7485] shall apply with respect to the collection of such assessment.

(ii) Authority to enjoin collection actions.—Notwithstanding the provisions of section 7421(a) [26 U.S.C. §7421(a)], the beginning of such levy or proceeding during the time the prohibition under clause (i) is in force may be enjoined by a proceeding in the proper court, including the Tax Court. The Tax Court shall have no jurisdiction under this subparagraph to enjoin any action or proceeding unless a timely petition has been filed under subparagraph (A) and then only in respect of the amount of the assessment to which the election under subsection (b) or (c) relates.

(2) Suspension of running of period of limitations.—The running of the period of limitations in section 6502 [26 U.S.C. §6502] on the collection of the assessment to which the petition under paragraph (1)(A) relates shall be suspended—

(A) for the period during which the Secretary is prohibited by paragraph (1)(B) from collecting by levy or a proceeding in court and for 60 days thereafter, and

(B) if a waiver under paragraph (5) is made, from the date the claim for relief was filed until 60 days after the waiver is filed with the Secretary.

(3) Limitation on tax court jurisdiction.—If a suit for refund is begun by either individual filing the joint return pursuant to section 6532 [26 U.S.C. §6532]—

(A) the Tax Court shall lose jurisdiction of the individual's action under this section to whatever extent jurisdiction is acquired by the district court or the United States Court of Federal Claims over the taxable years that are the subject of the suit for refund; and

(B) the court acquiring jurisdiction shall have jurisdiction over the petition filed under this subsection.

(4) Notice to other spouse.—The Tax Court shall establish rules which provide the individual filing a joint return but not making the election under subsection (b) or (c) with adequate notice and an opportunity to become a party to a proceeding under either such subsection.

(5) Waiver.—An individual who elects the application of subsection (b) or (c) (and who agrees with the Secretary's determination of relief) may waive in writing at any time the restrictions in paragraph (1)(B) with respect to collection of the outstanding assessment (whether or not a notice of the Secretary's final determination of relief has been mailed).

(f) Equitable relief.—Under procedures prescribed by the Secretary, if—

(1) taking into account all the facts and circumstances, it is inequitable to hold the individual liable for any unpaid tax or any deficiency (or any portion of either); and

(2) relief is not available to such individual under subsection (b) or (c), the Secretary may relieve such individual of such liability.

(g) Credits and refunds.—

(1) In general.—Except as provided in paragraphs (2) and (3), notwithstanding any other law or rule of law (other than section 6511, 6512(b), 7121, or 7122 [26 U.S.C. §§6511, 6512(b), 7121 or 7122]), credit or refund shall be allowed or made to the extent attributable to the application of this section.

(2) Res judicata.—In the case of any election under subsection (b) or (c), if a decision of a court in any prior proceeding for the same taxable year has become final, such decision shall be conclusive except with respect to the qualification of the individual for relief which was not an issue in such proceeding. The exception contained in the preceding sentence shall not apply if the court determines that the individual participated meaningfully in such prior proceeding.

(3) Credit and refund not allowed under subsection (c).—No credit or refund shall be allowed as a result of an election under subsection (c).

(h) Regulations.—The Secretary shall prescribe such regulations as are necessary to carry out the provisions of this section, including—

(1) regulations providing methods for allocation of items other than the methods under subsection (d)(3); and

(2) regulations providing the opportunity for an individual to have notice of, and an opportunity to participate in, any administrative proceeding with respect to an election made under subsection (b) or (c) by the other individual filing the joint return.

History of 26 U.S.C. §6015: Added July 22, 1998, P.L. 105-206, §3201(a), 112 Stat. 734. Amended Oct. 21, 1998, P.L. 105-277, §4002(c)(2), 112 Stat. 2681-906; Dec. 21, 2000, P.L. 106-554. §1(a)(7), 114 Stat. 2763.

TITLE 28. JUDICIARY & JUDICIAL PROCEDURE

PART V. PROCEDURE

CHAPTER 115. EVIDENCE; DOCUMENTARY

§1738. STATE & TERRITORIAL STATUTES & JUDICIAL PROCEEDINGS; FULL FAITH & CREDIT

The Acts of legislature of any State, Territory, or Possession of the United States, or copies thereof, shall be authenticated by affixing the seal of such State, Territory or Possession thereto.

The records and judicial proceedings of any court of any such State, Territory or Possession, or copies thereof, shall be proved or admitted in other courts within the United States and its Territories and Possessions by the attestation of the clerk and seal of the court annexed, if a seal exists, together with a certificate of a judge of the court that the said attestation is in proper form.

Such Acts, records and judicial proceedings or copies thereof, so authenticated, shall have the same full faith and credit in every court within the United States and its Territories and Possessions as they have by law or usage in the courts of such State, Territory or Possession from which they are taken.

History of 28 U.S.C. §1738: June 25, 1948, ch 646, §1, 62 Stat. 947.

§1738a. FULL FAITH & CREDIT GIVEN TO CHILD CUSTODY DETERMINATIONS

(a) The appropriate authorities of every State shall enforce according to its terms, and shall not modify except as provided in subsections (f), (g), and (h) of this section, any custody determination or visitation determination made consistently with the provisions of this section by a court of another State.

(b) As used in this section, the term—

(1) "child" means a person under the age of eighteen;

(2) "contestant" means a person, including a parent or grandparent, who claims a right to custody or visitation of a child;

(3) "custody determination" means a judgment, decree, or other order of a court providing for the custody of a child, and includes permanent and temporary orders, and initial orders and modifications;

(4) "home State" means the State in which, immediately preceding the time involved, the child lived with his parents, a parent, or a person acting as parent, for at least six consecutive months, and in the case of a child less than six months old, the State in which the child lived from birth with any of such persons. Periods of temporary absence of any of such persons are counted as part of the six-month or other period;

(5) "modification" and "modify" refer to a custody or visitation determination which modifies, replaces, supersedes, or otherwise is made subsequent to, a prior custody or visitation determination concerning the same child, whether made by the same court or not;

(6) "person acting as a parent" means a person, other than a parent, who has physical custody of a child and who has either been awarded custody by a court or claims a right to custody;

(7) "physical custody" means actual possession and control of a child;

(8) "State" means a State of the United States, the District of Columbia, the Commonwealth of Puerto Rico, or a territory or possession of the United States; and

(9) "visitation determination" means a judgment, decree, or other order of a court providing for the visitation of a child and includes permanent and temporary orders and initial orders and modifications.

(c) A child custody or visitation determination made by a court of a State is consistent with the provisions of this section only if—

(1) such court has jurisdiction under the law of such State; and

(2) one of the following conditions is met:

(A) such State (i) is the home State of the child on the date of the commencement of the proceeding, or (ii) had been the child's home State within six months before the date of the commencement of the proceeding and the child is absent from such State because of his removal or retention by a contestant or for other reasons, and a contestant continues to live in such State;

(B)(i) it appears that no other State would have jurisdiction under subparagraph (A), and (ii) it is in the best interest of the child that a court of such State assume jurisdiction because (I) the child and his parents, or the child and at least one contestant, have a significant connection with such State other than mere physical presence in such State, and (II) there is available in such State substantial evidence concerning the child's present or future care, protection, training, and personal relationships;

(C) the child is physically present in such State and (i) the child has been abandoned, or (ii) it is necessary in an emergency to protect the child because the child, a sibling, or parent of the child has been subjected to or threatened with mistreatment or abuse;

(D)(i) it appears that no other State would have jurisdiction under subparagraph (A), (B), (C), or (E), or another State has declined to exercise jurisdiction on the ground that the State whose jurisdiction is in issue is the more appropriate forum to determine the custody or visitation of the child, and (ii) it is in the best interest of the child that such court assume jurisdiction; or

(E) the court has continuing jurisdiction pursuant to subsection (d) of this section.

(d) The jurisdiction of a court of a State which has made a child custody or visitation determination consistently with the provisions of this section continues as long as the requirement of subsection (c)(1) of this section continues to be met and such State remains the residence of the child or of any contestant.

(e) Before a child custody or visitation determination is made, reasonable notice and opportunity to be heard shall be given to the contestants, any parent whose parental rights have not been previously terminated and any person who has physical custody of a child.

(f) A court of a State may modify a determination of the custody of the same child made by a court of another State, if—

(1) it has jurisdiction to make such a child custody determination; and

(2) the court of the other State no longer has jurisdiction, or it has declined to exercise such jurisdiction to modify such determination.

(g) A court of a State shall not exercise jurisdiction in any proceeding for a custody or visitation determination commenced during the pendency of a proceeding in a court of another State where such court of that other State is exercising jurisdiction consistently with the provisions of this section to make a custody or visitation determination.

(h) A court of a State may not modify a visitation determination made by a court of another State unless the court of the other State no longer has jurisdiction to modify such determination or has declined to exercise jurisdiction to modify such determination.

History of 28 U.S.C. §1738A: Added Dec. 28, 1980, P.L. 96-611, §8(a), 94 Stat. 3569; Nov. 12, 1998, P.L. 105-374, §1,112 Stat. 3838; Oct. 28, 2000, P.L. 106-386, §1303(c), 114 Stat. 1512.

§1738b. FULL FAITH & CREDIT FOR CHILD SUPPORT ORDERS

(a) General rule.—The appropriate authorities of each State—

(1) shall enforce according to its terms a child support order made consistently with this section by a court of another State; and

(2) shall not seek or make a modification of such an order except in accordance with subsections (e), (f), and (i).

(b) Definitions.—In this section:

"child" means—

(A) a person under 18 years of age; and

(B) a person 18 or more years of age with respect to whom a child support order has been issued pursuant to the laws of a State.

"child's State" means the State in which a child resides.

"child's home State" means the State in which a child lived with a parent or a person acting as parent for at least 6 consecutive months immediately preceding the time of filing of a petition or comparable pleading for support and, if a child is less than 6 months old, the State in which the child lived from birth with any of them. A period of temporary absence of any of them is counted as part of the 6-month period.

"child support" means a payment of money, continuing support, or arrearages or the provision of a benefit (including payment of health insurance, child care, and educational expenses) for the support of a child.

"child support order"—

(A) means a judgment, decree, or order of a court requiring the payment of child support in periodic amounts or in a lump sum; and

(B) includes—

(i) a permanent or temporary order; and

(ii) an initial order or a modification of an order.

"contestant" means—

(A) a person (including a parent) who—

(i) claims a right to receive child support;

(ii) is a party to a proceeding that may result in the issuance of a child support order; or

(iii) is under a child support order; and

(B) a State or political subdivision of a State to which the right to obtain child support has been assigned.

"court" means a court or administrative agency of a State that is authorized by State law to establish the amount of child support payable by a contestant or make a modification of a child support order.

"modification" means a change in a child support order that affects the amount, scope, or duration of the order and modifies, replaces, supersedes, or otherwise is made subsequent to the child support order.

"State" means a State of the United States, the District of Columbia, the Commonwealth of Puerto Rico, the territories and possessions of the United States, and Indian country (as defined in section 1151 of title 18).

(c) Requirements of child support orders.—A child support order made by a court of a State is made consistently with this section if—

(1) a court that makes the order, pursuant to the laws of the State in which the court is located and subsections (e), (f), and (g)—

(A) has subject matter jurisdiction to hear the matter and enter such an order; and

(B) has personal jurisdiction over the contestants; and

(2) reasonable notice and opportunity to be heard is given to the contestants.

(d) Continuing jurisdiction.—A court of a State that has made a child support order consistently with this section has continuing, exclusive jurisdiction over the order if the State is the child's State or the residence of any individual contestant unless the court of another State, acting in accordance with subsections (e) and (f), has made a modification of the order.

(e) **Authority to modify orders.**—A court of a State may modify a child support order issued by a court of another State if—

(1) the court has jurisdiction to make such a child support order pursuant to subsection (i); and

(2)(A) the court of the other State no longer has continuing, exclusive jurisdiction of the child support order because that State no longer is the child's State or the residence of any individual contestant; or

(B) each individual contestant has filed written consent with the State of continuing, exclusive jurisdiction for a court of another State to modify the order and assume continuing, exclusive jurisdiction over the order.

(f) **Recognition of child support orders.**—If 1 or more child support orders have been issued with regard to an obligor and a child, a court shall apply the following rules in determining which order to recognize for purposes of continuing, exclusive jurisdiction and enforcement:

(1) If only 1 court has issued a child support order, the order of that court must be recognized.

(2) If 2 or more courts have issued child support orders for the same obligor and child, and only 1 of the courts would have continuing, exclusive jurisdiction under this section, the order of that court must be recognized.

(3) If 2 or more courts have issued child support orders for the same obligor and child, and more than 1 of the courts would have continuing, exclusive jurisdiction under this section, an order issued by a court in the current home State of the child must be recognized, but if an order has not been issued in the current home State of the child, the order most recently issued must be recognized.

(4) If 2 or more courts have issued child support orders for the same obligor and child, and none of the courts would have continuing, exclusive jurisdiction under this section, a court having jurisdiction over the parties shall issue a child support order, which must be recognized.

(5) The court that has issued an order recognized under this subsection is the court having continuing, exclusive jurisdiction under subsection (d).

(g) **Enforcement of modified orders.**—A court of a State that no longer has continuing, exclusive jurisdiction of a child support order may enforce the order with respect to nonmodifiable obligations and unsatisfied obligations that accrued before the date on which a modification of the order is made under subsections (e) and (f).

(h) **Choice of law.**—

(1) **In general.**—In a proceeding to establish, modify, or enforce a child support order, the forum State's law shall apply except as provided in paragraphs (2) and (3).

(2) **Law of State of issuance of order.**—In interpreting a child support order including the duration of current payments and other obligations of support, a court shall apply the law of the State of the court that issued the order.

(3) **Period of limitation.**—In an action to enforce arrears under a child support order, a court shall apply the statute of limitation of the forum State or the State of the court that issued the order, whichever statute provides the longer period of limitation.

(i) **Registration for modification.**—If there is no individual contestant or child residing in the issuing State, the party or support enforcement agency seeking to modify, or to modify and enforce, a child support order issued in another State shall register that order in a State with jurisdiction over the nonmovant for the purpose of modification.

History of 28 U.S.C. §1738B: Added Oct. 20, 1994, P.L. 103-383, §3(a), 108 Stat. 4064; Aug. 22, 1996, P.L. 104-193, §322, 110 Stat. 2221; Aug. 5, 1997, P.L. 105-33, Ch 3, §5554, 111 Stat. 636.

§1738c. CERTAIN ACTS, RECORDS, & PROCEEDINGS & THE EFFECT THEREOF

No State, territory, or possession of the United States, or Indian tribe, shall be required to give effect to any public act, record, or judicial proceeding of any other State, territory, possession, or tribe respecting a relationship between persons of the same sex that is treated as a marriage under the laws of such other State, territory, possession, or tribe, or a right or claim arising from such relationship.

History of 28 U.S.C. §1738C: Added Sept. 21, 1996, P.L. 104-199, §2(a), 110 Stat. 2419.

TITLE 29. LABOR

CHAPTER 18. EMPLOYEE RETIREMENT INCOME SECURITY PROGRAM

SUBCHAPTER I. PROTECTION OF EMPLOYEE BENEFIT RIGHTS

SUBTITLE B. REGULATORY PROVISIONS

PART II. PARTICIPATION & VESTING

§1055. REQUIREMENT OF JOINT & SURVIVOR ANNUITY & PRERETIREMENT SURVIVOR ANNUITY

(a) Required contents for applicable plans.—Each pension plan to which this section applies shall provide that—

(1) in the case of a vested participant who does not die before the annuity starting date, the accrued benefit payable to such participant shall be provided in the form of a qualified joint and survivor annuity, and

(2) in the case of a vested participant who dies before the annuity starting date and who has a surviving spouse, a qualified preretirement survivor annuity shall be provided to the surviving spouse of such participant.

(b) Applicable plans.—

(1) This section shall apply to—

(A) any defined benefit plan,

(B) any individual account plan which is subject to the funding standards of section 302 [29 U.S.C. §1082], and

(C) any participant under any other individual account plan unless—

(i) such plan provides that the participant's nonforfeitable accrued benefit (reduced by any security interest held by the plan by reason of a loan outstanding to such participant) is payable in full, on the death of the participant, to the participant's surviving spouse (or, if there is no surviving spouse or the surviving spouse consents in the manner required under subsection (c)(2), to a designated beneficiary),

(ii) such participant does not elect the payment of benefits in the form of a life annuity, and

(iii) with respect to such participant, such plan is not a direct or indirect transferee (in a transfer after December 31, 1984) of a plan which is described in subparagraph (A) or (B) or to which this clause applied with respect to the participant.

Clause (iii) of subparagraph (C) shall apply only with respect to the transferred assets (and income therefrom) if the plan separately accounts for such assets and any income therefrom.

(2)(A) In the case of—

(i) a tax credit employee stock ownership plan (as defined in section 409(a) of the Internal Revenue Code of 1986 [26 U.S.C. §409(a)], or

(ii) an employee stock ownership plan (as defined in section 4975(e)(7) of such Code [26 U.S.C. §4975(e)(7)]), subsection (a)

shall not apply to that portion of the employee's accrued benefit to which the requirements of section 409(h) of such Code [26 U.S.C. §409(h)] apply.

(B) Subparagraph (A) shall not apply with respect to any participant unless the requirements of clause[s] (i), (ii), and (iii) of paragraph (1)(C) are met with respect to such participant.

[(3)] This section shall not apply to a plan which the Secretary of the Treasury or his delegate has determined is a plan described in section 404(c) of the Internal Revenue Code of 1986 [26 U.S.C. §404(c)](or a continuation thereof) in which participation is substantially limited to individuals who, before January 1, 1976, ceased employment covered by the plan.

(4) A plan shall not be treated as failing to meet the requirements of paragraph (1)(C) or (2) merely because the plan provides that benefits will not be payable to the surviving spouse of the participant unless the participant and such spouse had been married throughout the 1-year period ending on the earlier of the participant's annuity starting date or the date of the participant's death.

(c) Plans meeting requirements of section.—

(1) A plan meets the requirements of this section only if—

(A) under the plan, each participant—

(i) may elect at any time during the applicable election period to waive the qualified joint and survivor annuity form of benefit or the qualified preretirement survivor annuity form of benefit (or both), and

(ii) may revoke any such election at any time during the applicable election period, and

(B) the plan meets the requirements of paragraphs (2), (3), and (4).

(2) Each plan shall provide that an election under paragraph (1)(A)(i) shall not take effect unless—

(A)(i) the spouse of the participant consents in writing to such election, (ii) such election designates a beneficiary (or a form of benefits) which may not be changed without spousal consent (or the consent of the spouse expressly permits designations by the participant without any requirement of further consent by the spouse), and (iii) the spouse's consent acknowledges the effect of such election and is witnessed by a plan representative or a notary public, or

(B) it is established to the satisfaction of a plan representative that the consent required under subparagraph (A) may not be obtained because there is no spouse, because the spouse cannot be located, or because of such other circumstances as the Secretary of the Treasury may by regulations prescribe.

Any consent by a spouse (or establishment that the consent of a spouse may not be obtained) under the preceding sentence shall be effective only with respect to such spouse.

(3)(A) Each plan shall provide to each participant within a reasonable period of time before the annuity starting date (and consistent with such regulations as the Secretary of the Treasury may prescribe) a written explanation of—

(i) the terms and conditions of the qualified joint and survivor annuity,

(ii) the participant's right to make, and the effect of, an election under paragraph (1) to waive the joint and survivor annuity form of benefit,

(iii) the rights of the participant's spouse under paragraph (2), and

(iv) the right to make, and the effect of, a revocation of an election under paragraph (1).

(B)(i) Each plan shall provide to each participant, within the applicable period with respect to such participant (and consistent with such regulations as the Secretary may prescribe), a written explanation with respect to the qualified preretirement survivor annuity comparable to that required under subparagraph (A).

(ii) For purposes of clause (i), the term "applicable period" means, with respect to a participant, whichever of the following periods ends last:

(I) The period beginning with the first day of the plan year in which the participant attains age 32 and ending with the close of the plan year preceding the plan year in which the participant attains age 35.

(II) A reasonable period after the individual becomes a participant.

(III) A reasonable period ending after paragraph (5) ceases to apply to the participant.

(IV) A reasonable period ending after section 205 [this section] applies to the participant.

In the case of a participant who separates from service before attaining age 35, the applicable period shall be a reasonable period after separation.

(4) Each plan shall provide that, if this section applies to a participant when part or all of the participant's accrued benefit is to be used as security for a loan, no portion of the participant's accrued benefit may be used as security for such loan unless—

(A) the spouse of the participant (if any) consents in writing to such use during the 90-day period ending on the date on which the loan is to be so secured, and

(B) requirements comparable to the requirements of paragraph (2) are met with respect to such consent.

(5)(A) The requirements of this subsection shall not apply with respect to the qualified joint and survivor annuity form of benefit or the qualified preretirement survivor annuity form of benefit, as the case may be, if such benefit may not be waived (or another beneficiary selected) and if the plan fully subsidizes the costs of such benefit.

(B) For purposes of subparagraph (A), a plan fully subsidizes the costs of a benefit if under the plan the failure to waive such benefit by a participant would not result in a decrease in any plan benefits with respect to such participant and would not result in increased contributions from such participant.

(6) If a plan fiduciary acts in accordance with part 4 of this subtitle [29 U.S.C. §101 et seq.] in—

(A) relying on a consent or revocation referred to in paragraph (1)(A), or

(B) making a determination under paragraph (2),

then such consent, revocation, or determination shall be treated as valid for purposes of discharging the plan from liability to the extent of payments made pursuant to such Act.

(7) For purposes of this subsection, the term "applicable election period" means—

(A) in the case of an election to waive the qualified joint and survivor annuity form of benefit, the 90-day period ending on the annuity starting date, or

(B) in the case of an election to waive the qualified preretirement survivor annuity, the period which begins on the first day of the plan year in which the participant attains age 35 and ends on the date of the participant's death.

In the case of a participant who is separated from service, the applicable election period under subparagraph (B) with respect to benefits accrued before the date of such separation from service shall not begin later than such date.

(8) Notwithstanding any other provision of this subsection—

(A)(i) A plan may provide the written explanation described in paragraph (3)(A) after the annuity starting date. In any case to which this subparagraph applies, the applicable election period under paragraph (7) shall not end before the 30th day after the date on which such explanation is provided.

(ii) The Secretary of the Treasury may by regulations limit the application of clause (i), except that such regulations may not limit the period of time by which the annuity starting date precedes the provision of the written explanation other than by providing that the annuity starting date may not be earlier than termination of employment.

(B) A plan may permit a participant to elect (with any applicable spousal consent) to waive any requirement that the written explanation be provided at least 30 days before the annuity starting date (or to waive the 30-day requirement under subparagraph (A)) if the distribution commences more than 7 days after such explanation is provided.

(d) "Qualified joint and survivor annuity" defined.—For purposes of this section, the term "qualified joint and survivor annuity" means an annuity—

(1) for the life of the participant with a survivor annuity for the life of the spouse which is not less than 50 percent of (and is not greater than 100 percent of) the amount of the annuity which is payable during the joint lives of the participant and the spouse, and

(2) which is the actuarial equivalent of a single annuity for the life of the participant.

Such term also includes any annuity in a form having the effect of an annuity described in the preceding sentence.

(e) "Qualified preretirement survivor annuity" defined.—For purposes of this section—

(1) Except as provided in paragraph (2), the term "qualified preretirement survivor annuity" means a survivor annuity for the life of the surviving spouse of the participant if—

(A) the payments to the surviving spouse under such annuity are not less than the amounts which would be payable as a survivor annuity under the qualified joint and survivor annuity under the plan (or the actuarial equivalent thereof) if—

(i) in the case of a participant who dies after the date on which the participant attained the earliest retirement age, such participant had retired with an immediate qualified joint and survivor annuity on the day before the participant's date of death, or

(ii) in the case of a participant who dies on or before the date on which the participant would have attained the earliest retirement age, such participant had—

(I) separated from service on the date of death,

(II) survived to the earliest retirement age,

(III) retired with an immediate qualified joint and survivor annuity at the earliest retirement age, and

(IV) died on the day after the day on which such participant would have attained the earliest retirement age, and

(B) under the plan, the earliest period for which the surviving spouse may receive a payment under such annuity is not later than the month in which the participant would have attained the earliest retirement age under the plan.

In the case of an individual who separated from service before the date of such individual's death, subparagraph (A)(ii)(I) shall not apply.

(2) In the case of any individual account plan or participant described in subparagraph (B) or (C) of subsection (b)(1), the term "qualified preretirement survivor annuity" means an annuity for the life of the surviving spouse the actuarial equivalent of which is not less than 50 percent of the portion of the account balance of the participant (as of the date of death) to which the participant had a nonforfeitable right (within the meaning of section 203 [29 U.S.C. §1053]).

(3) For purposes of paragraphs (1) and (2), any security interest held by the plan by reason of a loan outstanding to the participant shall be taken into account in determining the amount of the qualified preretirement survivor annuity.

(f) Marriage requirements for plan.—

(1) Except as provided in paragraph (2), a plan may provide that a qualified joint and survivor annuity (or a qualified preretirement survivor annuity) will not be provided unless the participant and spouse had been married throughout the 1-year period ending on the earlier of—

(A) the participant's annuity starting date, or

(B) the date of the participant's death.

(2) For purposes of paragraph (1), if—

(A) a participant marries within 1 year before the annuity starting date, and

(B) the participant and the participant's spouse in such marriage have been married for at least a 1-year period ending on or before the date of the participant's death,

such participant and such spouse shall be treated as having been married throughout the 1-year period ending on the participant's annuity starting date.

(g) Distribution of present value of annuity; written consent; determination of present value.—

Ⓐ **(1)** A plan may provide that the present value of a qualified joint and survivor annuity or a qualified preretirement survivor annuity will be immediately distributed if such value does not exceed the amount that can be distributed without the participant's consent under section 203(e) [29 U.S.C. §1053(e)]. No distribution may be made under the preceding sentence after the annuity starting date unless the participant and the spouse of the participant (or where the participant has died, the surviving spouse) consent in writing to such distribution.

(2) If—

Ⓐ **(A)** the present value of the qualified joint and survivor annuity or the qualified preretirement survivor annuity exceeds the amount that can be distributed without the participant's consent under section 203(e) [29 U.S.C. §1053(e)], and

(B) the participant and the spouse of the participant (or where the participant has dies, the surviving spouse) consent in writing to the distribution,

the plan may immediately distribute the present value of such annuity.

(3) Determination of present value.—

(A) In general.—

(i) Present value.—

Except as provided in subparagraph.. (B), for purposes of paragraphs (1) and (2), the present value shall not be less than the present value calculated by using the applicable mortality table and the applicable interest rate.

(ii) Definitions.—

For purposes of clause (i)—

(I) Applicable mortality table.—

The term "applicable mortality table" means the table prescribed by the Secretary of the Treasury. Such table shall be based on the prevailing commissioners' standard table (described in section 807(d)(5)(A) of the Internal Revenue Code of 1986 [26 U.S.C. §807(d)(5)(A)]) used to determine reserves for group annuity contracts issued on the date as of which present value is being determined (without regard to any other subparagraph of section 807(d)(5) of such Code [26 U.S.C. §807(d)(5)]).

(II) Applicable interest rate.—

The term "applicable interest rate" means the annual rate of interest on 30-year Treasury securities for the month before the date of distribution or such other time as the Secretary of the Treasury may by regulations prescribe.

(B) Exception.—

In the case of a distribution from a plan that was adopted and in effect prior to the date of the enactment of the Retirement Protection Act of 1994 [enacted Dec. 8, 1994], the present value of any distribution made before the earlier of—

(i) the later of when a plan amendment applying subparagraph (A) is adopted or made effective, or

(ii) the first day of the first plan year beginning after December 31, 1999,

shall be calculated, for purposes of paragraphs (1) and (2), using the interest rate determined under the regulations of the Pension Benefit Guaranty Corporation for determining the present value of a lump sum distribution on plan termination that were in effect on September 1, 1993, and using the provisions of the plan as in effect on the day before such date of enactment but only if such provisions of the plan met the requirements of section 205(g)(3) [this paragraph] as in effect on the day before such date of enactment [December 8, 1994].

(h) Definitions.—For purposes of this section—

(1) The term "vested participant" means any participant who has a nonforfeitable right (within the meaning of section 3(19) [29 U.S.C. §1002(19)]) to any portion of such participant's accrued benefit.

(2)(A) The term "annuity starting date" means—

(i) the first day of the first period for which an amount is payable as an annuity, or

(ii) in the case of a benefit not payable in the form of an annuity, the first day on which all events have occurred which entitle the participant to such benefit.

(B) For purposes of subparagraph (A), the first day of the first period for which a benefit is to be received by reason of disability shall be treated as the annuity starting date only if such benefit is not an auxiliary benefit.

(3) The term "earliest retirement age" means the earliest date on which, under the plan, the participant could elect to receive retirement benefits.

(i) Increased costs from providing annuity.—A plan may take into account in any equitable manner (as determined by the Secretary of the Treasury) any increased costs resulting from providing a qualified joint or survivor annuity or a qualified preretirement survivor annuity.

(j) Use of participant's accrued benefit as security for loan as not preventing distribution.—If the use of any participant's accrued benefit (or any portion thereof) as security for a loan meets the requirements of subsection (c)(4), nothing in this section shall prevent any distribution required by reason of a failure to comply with the terms of such loan.

(k) Spousal consent.—No consent of a spouse shall be effective for purposes of subsection (g)(1) or (g)(2) (as the case may be) unless requirements comparable to the requirements for spousal consent to an election under subsection (c)(1)(A) are met.

(*l*) Regulations; consultation of Secretary of the Treasury with Secretary of Labor.—In prescribing regulations under this section, the Secretary of the Treasury shall consult with the Secretary of Labor.

History of 29 U.S.C. §1055: Sept. 2, 1974, P.L. 93-406, §205, 88 Stat. 862; Aug. 23, 1984, P.L. 98-397, §103(a), 98 Stat. 1429; Oct. 22, 1986, P.L. 99-514, §§1139(c)(2), 1145(b), Ch 2, §1898(b)(1)(B), (2)(B), (3)(B), (4)(B), (5)(B), (6)(B), (7)(B), (8)(B), (9)(B), (10)(B), (11)(B), (12)(B), (13)(B), (14)(B), 100 Stat. 2488, 2491, 2945-2951; Dec. 19, 1989, P.L. 101-239, Subpart A, §§7861(d)(2), 7862(d)(1)(B), (3), (6)-(9), Subpart D, §§7891(a)(1), (b)(3), (c), (e), 7894(c)(7)(A), 103 Stat. 2431, 2434, 2445, 2447, 2449; Dec. 8, 1994, P.L. 103-465, Subpart C, §767(c)(2), 108 Stat. 5039; Aug. 20, 1996, P.L. 104-188, Ch 2, Subch B, §1451(b), 110 Stat. 1815; Aug. 5, 1997, P.L. 105-34, §1071(b)(2), §1601(d)(5), 111 Stat. 948, 1089; March 9, 2002, P.L. 107-147, §411(r)(2), 116 Stat. 511.

§1056. FORM & PAYMENT OF BENEFITS

(a) Commencement date for payment of benefits.—

Each pension plan shall provide that unless the participant otherwise elects, the payment of benefits under the plan to the participant shall begin not later than the 60th day after the latest of the close of the plan year in which—

(1) occurs the date on which the participant attains the earlier of age 65 or the normal retirement age specified under the plan,

(2) occurs the 10th anniversary of the year in which the participant commenced participation in the plan, or

(3) the participant terminates his service with the employer.

In the case of a plan which provides for the payment of an early retirement benefit, such plan shall provide that a participant who satisfied the service requirements for such early retirement benefit, but separated from the service (with any nonforfeitable right to an accrued benefit) before satisfying the age requirement for such early retirement benefit, is entitled upon satisfaction of such age requirement to receive a benefit not less than the benefit to which he would be entitled at the normal retirement age, actuarially reduced under regulations prescribed by the Secretary of the Treasury.

(b) Decrease in plan benefits by reason of increases in benefit levels under Social Security Act or Railroad Retirement Act of 1937.—If—

(1) a participant or beneficiary is receiving benefits under a pension plan, or

(2) a participant is separated from the service and has nonforfeitable rights to benefits,

a plan may not decrease benefits of such a participant by reason of any increase in the benefit levels payable under title II of the Social Security Act [42 U.S.C. §401 et seq.] or the Railroad Retirement Act of 1937, or any increase in the wage base under such title II [42 U.S.C. §401 et seq.], if such increase takes place after the date of the enactment of this Act [enacted Sept. 2, 1974] or (if later) the earlier of the date of first entitlement of such benefits or the date of such separation.

(c) Forfeitures of accrued benefits derived from employer contributions.—

No pension plan may provide that any part of a participant's accrued benefit derived from employer contributions (whether or not otherwise nonforfeitable) is forfeitable solely because of withdrawal by such participant of any amount attributable to the benefit derived from contributions made by such participant. The preceding sentence shall not apply (1) to the accrued benefit of any participant unless, at the time of such withdrawal, such participant has a nonforfeitable right to at least 50 percent of such accrued benefit, or (2) to the extent that an accrued benefit is permitted to be forfeited in accordance with section 203(a)(3)(D)(iii) [29 U.S.C. §1053(a)(3)(D)(iii)].

(d) Assignment or alienation of plan benefits.—

(1) Each pension plan shall provide that benefits provided under the plan may not be assigned or alienated.

(2) For the purposes of paragraph (1) of this subsection, there shall not be taken into account any voluntary and revocable assignment of not to exceed 10 percent of any benefit payment, or of any irrevocable assignment or alienation of benefits executed before the date of enactment of this Act [enacted Sept. 2, 1974]. The preceding sentence shall not apply to any assignment or alienation made for the purposes of defraying plan administration costs. For purposes of this paragraph a loan made to a participant or beneficiary shall not be treated as an assignment or alienation if such loan is secured by the participant's accrued nonforfeitable benefit and is exempt from the tax imposed by section 4975 of the Internal Revenue Code of 1986 [26 U.S.C. §4975] (relating to tax on prohibited transactions) by reason of section 4975(d)(1) of such Code [26 U.S.C. §4975(d)(1)].

(3)(A) Paragraph (1) shall apply to the creation, assignment, or recognition of a right to any benefit payable with respect to a participant pursuant to a domestic relations order, except that paragraph (1) shall not apply if the order is determined to be a qualified domestic relations order. Each pension plan shall provide for the payment of benefits in accordance with the applicable requirements of any qualified domestic relations order.

(B) For purposes of this paragraph—

(i) the term "qualified domestic relations order" means a domestic relations order—

(I) which creates or recognizes the existence of an alternate payee's right to, or assigns to an alternate payee the right to, receive all or a portion of the benefits payable with respect to a participant under a plan, and

(II) with respect to which the requirements of subparagraphs (C) and (D) are met, and

(ii) the term "domestic relations order" means any judgment, decree, or order (including approval of a property settlement agreement) which—

(I) relates to the provision of child support, alimony payments, or marital property rights to a spouse, former spouse, child, or other dependent of a participant, and

(II) is made pursuant to a State domestic relations law (including a community property law).

(C) A domestic relations order meets the requirements of this subparagraph only if such order clearly specifies—

(i) the name and the last known mailing address (if any) of the participant and the name and mailing address of each alternate payee covered by the order,

(ii) the amount or percentage of the participant's benefits to be paid by the plan to each such alternate payee, or the manner in which such amount or percentage is to be determined,

(iii) the number of payments or period to which such order applies, and

(iv) each plan to which such order applies.

(D) A domestic relations order meets the requirements of this subparagraph only if such order—

(i) does not require a plan to provide any type or form of benefit, or any option, not otherwise provided under the plan,

(ii) does not require the plan to provide increased benefits (determined on the basis of actuarial value), and

(iii) does not require the payment of benefits to an alternate payee which are required to be paid to another alternate payee under another order previously determined to be a qualified domestic relations order.

(E)(i) A domestic relations order shall not be treated as failing to meet the requirements of clause (i) of subparagraph (D) solely because such order requires that payment of benefits be made to an alternate payee—

(I) in the case of any payment before a participant has separated from service, on or after the date on which the participant attains (or would have attained) the earliest retirement age,

(II) as if the participant had retired on the date on which such payment is to begin under such order (but taking into account only the present value of benefits actually accrued and not taking into account the present value of any employer subsidy for early retirement), and

(III) in any form in which such benefits may be paid under the plan to the participant (other than in the form of a joint and survivor annuity with respect to the alternate payee and his or her subsequent spouse).

For purposes of subclause (II), the interest rate assumption used in determining the present value shall be the interest rate specified in the plan or, if no rate is specified, 5 percent.

(ii) For purposes of this subparagraph, the term "earliest retirement age" means the earlier of—

(I) the date on which the participant is entitled to a distribution under the plan, or

(II) the later of the date of the participant attains age 50 or the earliest date on which the participant could begin receiving benefits under the plan if the participant separated from service.

(F) To the extent provided in any qualified domestic relations order—

(i) the former spouse of a participant shall be treated as a surviving spouse of such participant for purposes of section 205 [29 U.S.C. §1055] (and any spouse of the participant shall not be treated as a spouse of the participant for such purposes), and

(ii) if married for at least 1 year, the surviving former spouse shall be treated as meeting the requirements of section 205(f) [29 U.S.C. §1055(f)].

(G)(i) In the case of any domestic relations order received by a plan—

(I) the plan administrator shall promptly notify the participant and each alternate payee of the receipt of such order and the plan's procedures for determining the qualified status of domestic relations orders, and

(II) within a reasonable period after receipt of such order, the plan administrator shall determine whether such order is a qualified domestic relations order and notify the participant and each alternate payee of such determination.

(ii) Each plan shall establish reasonable procedures to determine the qualified status of domestic relations orders and to administer distributions under such qualified orders. Such procedures—

(I) shall be in writing,

(II) shall provide for the notification of each person specified in a domestic relations order as entitled to payment of benefits under the plan (at the address included in the domestic relations order) of such procedures promptly upon receipt by the plan of the domestic relations order, and

(III) shall permit an alternate payee to designate a representative for receipt of copies of notices that are sent to the alternate payee with respect to a domestic relations order.

(H)(i) During any period in which the issue of whether a domestic relations order is a qualified domestic relations order is being determined (by the plan administrator, by a court of competent jurisdiction, or otherwise), the plan administrator shall separately account for the amounts (hereinafter in this subparagraph referred to as the "segregated amounts") which would have been payable to the alternate payee during such period if the order had been determined to be a qualified domestic relations order.

(ii) If within the 18-month period described in clause (v) the order (or modification thereof) is determined to be a qualified domestic relations order, the plan administrator shall pay the segregated amounts (including any interest thereon) to the person or persons entitled thereto.

(iii) If within the 18-month period described in clause (v)—

(I) it is determined that the order is not a qualified domestic relations order, or

(II) the issue as to whether such order is a qualified domestic relations order is not resolved,

then the plan administrator shall pay the segregated amounts (including any interest thereon) to the person or persons who would have been entitled to such amounts if there had been no order.

(iv) Any determination that an order is a qualified domestic relations order which is made after the close of the 18-month period described in clause (v) shall be applied prospectively only.

(v) For purposes of this subparagraph, the 18-month period described in this clause is the 18-month period beginning with the date on which the first payment would be required to be made under the domestic relations order.

(I) If a plan fiduciary acts in accordance with part 4 of this subtitle [29 U.S.C. §1101 et seq.] in—

(i) treating a domestic relations order as being (or not being) a qualified domestic relations order, or

(ii) taking action under subparagraph (H),

then the plan's obligation to the participant and each alternate payee shall be discharged to the extent of any payment made pursuant to such Act.

(J) A person who is an alternate payee under a qualified domestic relations order shall be considered for purposes of any provision of this Act a beneficiary under the plan. Nothing in the preceding sentence shall permit a requirement under section 4001 [29 U.S.C. §1301] of the payment of more than 1 premium with respect to a participant for any period.

(K) The term "alternate payee" means any spouse, former spouse, child, or other dependent of a participant who is recognized by a domestic relations order as having a right to receive all, or a portion of, the benefits payable under a plan with respect to such participant.

(L) This paragraph shall not apply to any plan to which paragraph (1) does not apply.

(M) Payment of benefits by a pension plan in accordance with the applicable requirements of a qualified domestic relations order shall not be treated as garnishment for purposes of section 303(a) of the Consumer Credit Protection Act [15 U.S.C. §1673(a)].

(N) In prescribing regulations under this paragraph, the Secretary shall consult with the Secretary of the Treasury.

(4) Paragraph (1) shall not apply to any offset of a participant's benefits provided under an employee pension benefit plan against an amount that the participant is ordered or required to pay to the plan if—

(A) the order or requirement to pay arises—

(i) under a judgment of conviction for a crime involving such plan,

(ii) under a civil judgment (including a consent order or decree) entered by a court in an action brought in connection with a violation (or alleged violation) of part 4 of this subtitle [29 U.S.C. §1101 et seq.], or

(iii) pursuant to a settlement agreement between the Secretary and the participant, or a settlement agreement between the Pension Benefit Guaranty Corporation and the participant, in connection with a violation (or alleged violation) of part 4 of this subtitle [29 U.S.C. §1101 et seq.] by a fiduciary or any other person,

(B) the judgment, order, decree, or settlement agreement expressly provides for the offset of all or part of the amount ordered or required to be paid to the plan against the participant's benefits provided under the plan, and

(C) in a case in which the survivor annuity requirements of section 205 [29 U.S.C. §1055] apply with respect to distributions from the plan to the participant, if the participant has a spouse at the time at which the offset is to be made—

(i) either—

(I) such spouse has consented in writing to such offset and such consent is witnessed by a notary public or representative of the plan (or it is established to the satisfaction of a plan representative that such consent may not be obtained by reason of circumstances described in section 205(c)(2)(B) [29 U.S.C. §1055(c)(2)(B)]), or

(II) an election to waive the right of the spouse to a qualified joint and survivor annuity or a qualified preretirement survivor annuity is in effect in accordance with the requirements of section 205(c) [29 U.S.C. §1055(c)],

(ii) such spouse is ordered or required in such judgment, order, decree, or settlement to pay an amount to the plan in connection with a violation of part 4 of this subtitle [29 U.S.C. §1101 et seq.], or

(iii) in such judgment, order, decree, or settlement, such spouse retains the right to receive the survivor annuity under a qualified joint and survivor annuity provided pursuant to section 205(a)(1) [29 U.S.C. §1055(a)(1)] and under a qualified preretirement survivor annuity provided pursuant to section 205(a)(2) [29 U.S.C. §1055(a)(2)], determined in accordance with paragraph (5).

A plan shall not be treated as failing to meet the requirements of section 205 [29 U.S.C. §1055] solely by reason of an offset under this paragraph.

(5)(A) The survivor annuity described in paragraph (4)(C)(iii) shall be determined as if—

(i) the participant terminated employment on the date of the offset,

(ii) there was no offset,

(iii) the plan permitted commencement of benefits only on or after normal retirement age,

(iv) the plan provided only the minimum-required qualified joint and survivor annuity, and

(v) the amount of the qualified preretirement survivor annuity under the plan is equal to the amount of the survivor annuity payable under the minimum-required qualified joint and survivor annuity.

(B) For purposes of this paragraph, the term "minimum-required qualified joint and survivor annuity" means the qualified joint and survivor annuity which is the actuarial equivalent of the participant's accrued benefit (within the meaning of section 3(23) [29 U.S.C. §1002(23)]) and under which the survivor annuity is 50 percent of the amount of the annuity which is payable during the joint lives of the participant and the spouse.

(e) Limitation on distributions other than life annuities paid by the plan.—

(1) In general.—Notwithstanding any other provision of this part, the fiduciary of a pension plan that is subject to the additional funding requirements of section 302(d) [29 U.S.C. §1082(d)] shall not permit a prohibited payment to be made from a plan during a period in which such plan has a liquidity shortfall (as defined in section 302(e)(5) [29 U.S.C. §1082(e)(5)]).

(2) Prohibited payment.—For purposes of paragraph (1), the term "prohibited payment" means—

(A) any payment, in excess of the monthly amount paid under a single life annuity (plus any social security supplements described in the last sentence of section 204(b)(1)(G) [29 U.S.C. §1054(b)(1)(G)]), to a participant or beneficiary whose annuity starting date (as defined in section 205(h)(2) [29 U.S.C. §1055(h)(2)]), that occurs during the period referred to in paragraph (1),

(B) any payment for the purchase of an irrevocable commitment from an insurer to pay benefits, and

(C) any other payment specified by the Secretary of the Treasury by regulations.

(3) Period of shortfall.—For purposes of this subsection, a plan has a liquidity shortfall during the period that there is an underpayment of an installment under section 302(e) [29 U.S.C. §1082(e)] by reason of paragraph (5)(A) thereof.

(4) Coordination with other provisions.—Compliance with this subsection shall not constitute a violation of any other provision of this Act.

(f) Missing participants in terminated plans.—In the case of a plan covered by Title IV [29 U.S.C. §1301 et seq.], the plan shall provide that, upon termination of the plan, benefits of missing participants shall be treated in accordance with section 4050 [29 U.S.C. §1350].

History of 29 U.S.C. §1056: Sept. 2, 1974, P.L. 93-406, §206, 88 Stat. 864; Aug. 23, 1984, P.L. 98-397, §104(a), 98 Stat. 1433; Oct. 22, 1986, P.L. 99-514, Ch 2, §1898(c)(2)(B), (4)(B), (5), (6)(B), (7)(B), 100 Stat. 2952-2954; Dec. 19, 1989, P.L. 101-239, Subpart D, §§7891(a)(1), 7894(c)(8), (9)(A), 103 Stat. 2445, 2449; Dec. 8, 1994, P.L. 103-465, Subpart B, §761(a)(9)(B)(i), §776(c)(2), 108 Stat. 5033, 5048; Aug. 5, 1997, P.L. 105-34, §1502(a), 111 Stat. 1058.

PART VI. CONTINUATION COVERAGE & ADDITIONAL STANDARDS FOR GROUP HEALTH PLANS

§1169. ADDITIONAL STANDARDS FOR GROUP HEALTH PLANS

(a) Group health plan coverage pursuant to medical child support orders.—

(1) In general.—Each group health plan shall provide benefits in accordance with the applicable requirements of any qualified medical child support order. A qualified medical child support order with respect to any participant or beneficiary shall be deemed to apply to each group health plan which has received such order, from which the participant or beneficiary is eligible to receive benefits, and with respect to which the requirements of paragraph (4) are met.

(2) Definitions.—For purposes of this subsection—

(A) Qualified medical child support order.—The term "qualified medical child support order" means a medical child support order—

(i) which creates or recognizes the existence of an alternate recipient's right to, or assigns to an alternate recipient the right to, receive benefits for which a participant or beneficiary is eligible under a group health plan, and

(ii) with respect to which the requirements of paragraphs (3) and (4) are met.

(B) Medical child support order.—

The term "medical child support order" means any judgment, decree, or order (including approval of a settlement agreement) which—

(i) provides for child support with respect to a child of a participant under a group health plan or provides for health benefit coverage to such a child, is made pursuant to a State domestic relations law (including a community property law), and relates to benefits under such plan, or

(ii) is made pursuant to a law relating to medical child support described in section 1908 of the Social Security Act [42 U.S.C. §1396g-1] (as added by section 13822 [§13623(b)] of the Omnibus Budget Reconciliation Act of 1993) with respect to a group health plan,

if such judgment, decree, or order (I) is issued by a court of competent jurisdiction or (II) is issued through an administrative process established under State law and has the force and effect of law under applicable State law. For purposes of this subparagraph, an administrative notice which is issued pursuant to an administrative process referred to in subclause (II) of the preceding sentence and which has the effect of an order described in clause (i) or (ii) of the preceding sentence shall be treated as such an order.

(C) Alternate recipient.—The term "alternate recipient" means any child of a participant who is recognized under a medical child support order as having a right to enrollment under a group health plan with respect to such participant.

(D) Child.—The term "child" includes any child adopted by, or placed for adoption with, a participant of a group health plan.

(3) Information to be included in qualified order.—A medical child support order meets the requirements of this paragraph only if such order clearly specifies—

(A) the name and the last known mailing address (if any) of the participant and the name and mailing address of each alternate recipient covered by the order, except that, to the extent provided in the order, the name and mailing address of an official of a State or a political subdivision thereof may be substituted for the mailing address of any such alternate recipient,

(B) a reasonable description of the type of coverage to be provided to each such alternate recipient, or the manner in which such type of coverage is to be determined, and

(C) the period to which such order applies.

(4) Restriction on new types or forms of benefits.—A medical child support order meets the requirements of this paragraph only if such order does not require a plan to provide any type or form of benefit, or any option, not otherwise provided under the plan, except to the extent necessary to meet the requirements of a law relating to medical child support described in section 1908 of the Social Security Act [42 U.S.C. §1396g-1] (as added by §13822 [§13623(b)] of the Omnibus Budget Reconciliation Act of 1993).

(5) Procedural requirements.—

(A) Timely notifications and determinations.—In the case of any medical child support order received by a group health plan—

(i) the plan administrator shall promptly notify the participant and each alternate recipient of the receipt of such order and the plan's procedures for determining whether medical child support orders are qualified medical child support orders, and

(ii) within a reasonable period after receipt of such order, the plan administrator shall determine whether such order is a qualified medical child support order and notify the participant and each alternate recipient of such determination.

(B) Establishment of procedures for determining qualified status of orders.—Each group health plan shall establish reasonable procedures to determine whether medical child support orders are qualified medical child support orders and to administer the provision of benefits under such qualified orders. Such procedures—

(i) shall be in writing,

(ii) shall provide for the notification of each person specified in a medical child support order as eligible to receive benefits under the plan (at the address included in the medical child support order) of such procedures promptly upon receipt by the plan of the medical child support order, and

(iii) shall permit an alternate recipient to designate a representative for receipt of copies of notices that are sent to the alternate recipient with respect to a medical child support order.

(C) National Medical Support Notice deemed to be a qualified medical child support order.—

(i) In general.—If the plan administrator of a group health plan which is maintained by the employer of a noncustodial parent of a child or to which such an employer contributes receives an appropriately completed National Medical Support Notice promulgated pursuant to section 401(b) of the Child Support Performance and Incentive Act of 1998 [42 U.S.C. §651 note] in the case of such child, and the Notice meets the requirements of paragraphs (3) and (4), the Notice shall be deemed to be a qualified medical child support order in the case of such child.

(ii) Enrollment of child in plan.—In any case in which an appropriately completed National Medical Support Notice is issued in the case of a child of a participant under a group health plan who is a noncustodial parent of the child, and the Notice is deemed under clause (i) to be a qualified medical child support order, the plan administrator, within 40 business days after the date of the Notice, shall—

(I) notify the State agency issuing the Notice with respect to such child whether coverage of the child is available under the terms of the plan and, if so, whether such child is covered under the plan and either the effective date of the coverage or, if necessary, any steps to be taken by the custodial parent (or by the official of a State or political subdivision thereof substituted for the name of such child pursuant to paragraph (3)(A)) to effectuate the coverage; and

(II) provide to the custodial parent (or such substituted official) a description of the coverage available and any forms or documents necessary to effectuate such coverage.

(iii) Rule of construction.—Nothing in this subparagraph shall be construed as requiring a group health plan, upon receipt of a National Medical Support Notice, to provide benefits under the plan (or eligibility for such benefits) in addition to benefits (or eligibility for benefits) provided under the terms of the plan as of immediately before receipt of such Notice.

(6) Actions taken by fiduciaries.—If a plan fiduciary acts in accordance with part 4 of this subtitle [29 U.S.C. §1101 et seq.] in treating a medical child support order as being (or not being) a qualified medical child support order, then the plan's obligation to the participant and each alternate recipient shall be discharged to the extent of any payment made pursuant to such act of the fiduciary.

(7) Treatment of alternate recipients.—

(A) Treatment as beneficiary generally.—A person who is an alternate recipient under a qualified medical child support order shall be considered a beneficiary under the plan for purposes of any provision of this Act.

(B) Treatment as participant for purposes of reporting and disclosure requirements.—A person who is an alternate recipient under any medical child support order shall be considered a participant under the plan for purposes of the reporting and disclosure requirements of part 1 [29 U.S.C. §1021 et seq.].

(8) Direct provision of benefits provided to alternate recipients.—Any payment for benefits made by a group health plan pursuant to a medical child support order in reimbursement for expenses paid by an alternate recipient or an alternate recipient's custodial parent or legal guardian shall be made to the alternate recipient or the alternate recipient's custodial parent or legal guardian.

(9) Payment to State official treated as satisfaction of plan's obligation to make payment to alternate recipient.—Payment of benefits by a group health plan to an official of a State or a political subdivision thereof whose name and address have been substituted for the address of an alternate recipient in a qualified medical child support order, pursuant to paragraph (3)(A), shall be treated, for purposes of this title [29 U.S.C. §1001 et seq.], as payment of benefits to the alternate recipient.

(b) Rights of States with respect to group health plans where participants or beneficiaries thereunder are eligible for Medicaid benefits.—

(1) Compliance by plans with assignment of rights.—A group health plan shall provide that payment for benefits with respect to a participant under the plan will be made in accordance with any assignment of rights made by or on behalf of such participant or a beneficiary of the participant as required by a State plan for medical assistance approved under title XIX of the Social Security Act [42 U.S.C. §1396 et seq.] pursuant to section 1912(a)(1)(A) of such Act [42 U.S.C. §1396k(a)(1)(A)] (as in effect on the date of the enactment of the Omnibus Budget Reconciliation Act of 1993 [enacted Aug. 10, 1993]).

(2) Enrollment and provision of benefits without regard to Medicaid eligibility.—A group health plan shall provide that, in enrolling an individual as a participant or beneficiary or in determining or making any payments for benefits of an individual as a participant or beneficiary, the fact that the individual is eligible for or is provided medical assistance under a State plan for medical assistance approved under title XIX of the Social Security Act [42 U.S.C. §1396 et seq.] will not be taken into account.

(3) Acquisition by States of rights of third parties.—A group health plan shall provide that, to the extent that payment has been made under a State plan for medical assistance approved under title XIX of the Social Security Act [42 U.S.C. §1396 et seq.] in any case in which a group health plan has a legal liability to make payment for items or services constituting such assistance, payment for benefits under the plan will be made in accordance with any State law which provides that the State has acquired the rights with respect to a participant to such payment for such items or services.

(c) Group health plan coverage of dependent children in cases of adoption.—

(1) Coverage effective upon placement for adoption.—In any case in which a group health plan provides coverage for dependent children of participants or beneficiaries, such plan shall provide benefits to dependent children placed with participants or beneficiaries for adoption under the same terms and conditions as apply in the case of dependent children who are natural children of participants or beneficiaries under the plan, irrespective of whether the adoption has become final.

(2) Restrictions based on preexisting conditions at time of placement for adoption prohibited.—A group health plan may not restrict coverage under the plan of any dependent child adopted by a participant or beneficiary, or placed with a participant or beneficiary for adoption, solely on the basis of a preexisting condition of such child at the time that such child would otherwise become eligible for coverage under the plan, if the adoption or placement for adoption occurs while the participant or beneficiary is eligible for coverage under the plan.

(3) Definitions.—For purposes of this subsection—

(A) Child.—The term "child" means, in connection with any adoption, or placement for adoption, of the child, an individual who has not attained age 18 as of the date of such adoption or placement for adoption.

(B) Placement for adoption.—The term "placement", or being "placed", for adoption, in connection with any placement for adoption of a child with any person, means the assumption and retention by such person of a legal obligation for total or partial support of such child in anticipation of adoption of such child. The child's placement with such person terminates upon the termination of such legal obligation.

(d) Continued coverage of costs of a pediatric vaccine under group health plans.—A group health plan may not reduce its coverage of the costs of pediatric vaccines (as defined under section 1928(h)(6) of the Social Security Act [42 U.S.C. §1396s(h)(6)] as amended by section 13830 [§13631(b)] of the Omnibus Budget Reconciliation Act of 1993) below the coverage it provided as of May 1, 1993.

(e) Regulations.—Any regulations prescribed under this section shall be prescribed by the Secretary of Labor, in consultation with the Secretary of Health and Human Services.

History of 29 U.S.C. §1169: Sept. 2, 1974, P.L. 93-406, §609, as added Aug. 10, 1993, P.L. 103-66, §4301(a), 107 Stat. 371; Aug. 22, 1996, P.L. 104-193, §381(a), 110 Stat. 2257; Aug. 5, 1997, P.L. 105-33, Ch 7, §§5611(a), (b), 5612(a), 5613(a), (b), 111 Stat. 647; July 16, 1998, P.L. 105-200, §401(d), (h)(2)(A)(iii), (2)(B), (3)(A), 112 Stat. 662, 668.

TITLE 42. THE PUBLIC HEALTH & WELFARE

CHAPTER 7. SOCIAL SECURITY

SUBCHAPTER IV. GRANTS TO STATES FOR AID & SERVICES TO NEEDY FAMILIES WITH CHILDREN & FOR CHILD-WELFARE SERVICES

PART D. CHILD SUPPORT & ESTABLISHMENT OF PATERNITY

§651. AUTHORIZATION OF APPROPRIATIONS

For the purpose of enforcing the support obligations owed by noncustodial parents to their children and the spouse (or former spouse) with whom such children are living, locating noncustodial parents, establishing paternity, obtaining child and spousal support, and assuring that assistance in obtaining support will be available under this part [42 U.S.C. §651 et seq.] to all children (whether or not eligible for assistance under a State program funded under part A [42 U.S.C. §601 et seq.]) for whom such assistance is requested, there is hereby authorized to be appropriated for each fiscal year a sum sufficient to carry out the purposes of this part [42 U.S.C. §651 et seq.].

History of 42 U.S.C. §651: Aug. 14, 1935, ch 531, §451, as added Jan. 4, 1975, P.L. 93-647, §101(a), 88 Stat. 2351; Aug. 13, 1981, P.L. 97-35, ch 2, §2332(a), 95 Stat. 861; Aug. 16, 1984, P.L. 98-378, §2, 98 Stat. 1305; Aug. 22, 1996, P.L. 104-193, §108(c)(1), §395(d)(1)(A), 110 Stat. 2165, 2259.

§654. STATE PLAN FOR CHILD & SPOUSAL SUPPORT

A State plan for child and spousal support must—

(1) provide that it shall be in effect in all political subdivisions of the State;

(2) provide for financial participation by the State;

(3) provide for the establishment or designation of a single and separate organizational unit, which meets such staffing and organizational requirements as the Secretary may by regulation prescribe, within the State to administer the plan;

(4) provide that the State will—

(A) provide services relating to the establishment of paternity or the establishment, modification, or enforcement of child support obligations, as appropriate, under the plan with respect to—

(i) each child for whom (I) assistance is provided under the State program funded under part A of this title [42 U.S.C. §601 et seq.], (II) benefits or services for foster care maintenance are provided under the State program funded under part E of this title [42 U.S.C. §670 et seq.], (III) medical assistance is provided under the State plan approved under title XIX [42 U.S.C. §1396 et seq.], or (IV) cooperation is required pursuant to section 6(*l*)(1) of the Food Stamp Act of 1977 (7 U.S.C. 2015(*l*)(1)), unless, in accordance with paragraph (29), good cause or other exceptions exist;

(ii) any other child, if an individual applies for such services with respect to the child; and

(B) enforce any support obligation established with respect to—

(i) a child with respect to whom the State provides services under the plan; or

(ii) the custodial parent of such a child;

(5) provide that (A) in any case in which support payments are collected for an individual with respect to whom an assignment pursuant to section 408(a)(3) [42 U.S.C. §608(a)(3)] is effective, such payments shall be made to the State for distribution pursuant to section 457 [42 U.S.C. §657] and shall not be paid directly to the family, and the individual will be notified on a monthly basis (or on a quarterly basis for so long as the Secretary determines with respect to a State that requiring such notice on a monthly basis would impose an unreasonable administrative burden) of the amount of the support payments collected, and (B) in case in which support payments are collected for an individual pursuant to the assignment made under section 1912 [42 U.S.C. §1396k], such payments shall be made to the State for distribution pursuant to section 1912 [42 U.S.C. §1396k], except that this clause shall not apply to such payments for any month after the month in which the individual ceases to be eligible for medical assistance;

(6) provide that—

(A) services under the plan shall be made available to residents of other States on the same terms as to residents of the State submitting the plan;

(B) an application fee for furnishing such services shall be imposed on an individual, other than an individual receiving assistance under a State program funded under part A or E [42 U.S.C. §601 et seq. or 670 et seq.], or under a State plan approved under title XIX [42 U.S.C. §1396 et seq.], or who is required by the State to cooperate with the State agency administering the program under this part [42 U.S.C. §651 et seq.] pursuant to subsection (*l*) or (m) of section 6 of the Food Stamp Act of 1977 [7 U.S.C. §2015(*l*) or (m)], and shall be paid by the individual applying for such services, or recovered from the absent parent, or paid by the State out of its own funds (the payment of which from State funds shall not be considered as an administrative cost of the State for the operation of the plan, and shall be considered income to the program), the amount of which

(i) will not exceed $25 (or such higher or lower amount (which shall be uniform for all States) as the Secretary may determine to be appropriate for any fiscal year to reflect increases or decreases in administrative costs), and

(ii) may vary among such individuals on the basis of ability to pay (as determined by the State);

(C) a fee of not more than $25 may be imposed in any case where the State requests the Secretary of the Treasury to withhold past-due support owed to or on behalf of such individual from a tax refund pursuant to section 464(a)(2) [42 U.S.C. §664(a)(2)];

(D) a fee (in accordance with regulations of the Secretary) for performing genetic tests may be imposed on any individual who is not a recipient of assistance under a State program funded under part A [42 U.S.C. §601 et seq.]; and

(E) any costs in excess of the fees so imposed may be collected—

(i) from the parent who owes the child or spousal support obligation involved; or

(ii) at the option of the State, from the individual to whom such services are made available, but only if such State has in effect a procedure whereby all persons in such State having authority to order child or spousal support are informed that such costs are to be collected from the individual to whom such services were made available;

(7) provide for entering into cooperative arrangements with appropriate courts and law enforcement officials and Indian tribes or tribal organizations (as defined in subsections (e) and (*l*) of section 4 of the Indian Self-Determination and Education Assistance Act (25 U.S.C. 450b)) (A) to assist the agency administering the plan, including the entering into of financial arrangements with such courts and officials in order to assure optimum results under such program, and (B) with respect to any other matters of common concern to such courts or officials and the agency administering the plan;

(8) provide that, for the purpose of establishing parentage, establishing, setting the amount of, modifying, or enforcing child support obligations, or making or enforcing a child custody or visitation determination, as defined in section 463(d)(1) [42 U.S.C. §653(d)(1)] the agency administering the plan will establish a service to locate parents utilizing—

(A) all sources of information and available records; and

(B) the Federal Parent Locator Service established under section 453 [42 U.S.C. §653],

and shall, subject to the privacy safeguards required under paragraph (26), disclose only the information described in sections 453 and 463 [42 U.S.C. §653, 663] to the authorized persons specified in such sections for the purposes specified in such sections;

(9) provide that the State will, in accordance with standards prescribed by the Secretary, cooperate with any other State—

(A) in establishing paternity, if necessary;

(B) in locating a noncustodial parent residing in the State (whether or not permanently) against whom any action is being taken under a program established under a plan approved under this part [42 U.S.C. §651 et seq.] in another State;

(C) in securing compliance by a noncustodial parent residing in such State (whether or not permanently) with an order issued by a court of competent jurisdiction against such parent for the support and maintenance of the child or children or the parent of such child or children with respect to whom aid is being provided under the plan of such other State;

(D) in carrying out other functions required under a plan approved under this part [42 U.S.C. §651 et seq.]; and

(E) not later than March 1, 1997, in using the forms promulgated pursuant to section 452(a)(11) [42 U.S.C. §652(a)(11)] for income withholding, imposition of liens, and issuance of administrative subpoenas in interstate child support cases;

(10) provide that the State will maintain a full record of collections and disbursements made under the plan and have an adequate reporting system;

(11)(A) provide that amounts collected as support shall be distributed as provided in section 457 [42 U.S.C. §657]; and

(B) provide that any payment required to be made under section 456 or 457 [42 U.S.C. §656 or §657] to a family shall be made to the resident parent, legal guardian, or caretaker relative having custody of or responsibility for the child or children;

(12) provide for the establishment of procedures to require the State to provide individuals who are applying for or receiving services under the State plan, or who are parties to cases in which services are being provided under the State plan—

(A) with notice of all proceedings in which support obligations might be established or modified; and

(B) with a copy of any order establishing or modifying a child support obligation, or (in the case of a petition for modification) a notice of determination that there should be no change in the amount of the child support award, within 14 days after issuance of such order or determination;

(13) provide that the State will comply with such other requirements and standards as the Secretary determines to be necessary to the establishment of an effective program for locating noncustodial parents, establishing paternity, obtaining support orders, and collecting support payments and provide that information requests by parents who are residents of other

States be treated with the same priority as requests by parents who are residents of the State submitting the plan;

(14)(A) comply with such bonding requirements, for employees who receive, disburse, handle, or have access to, cash, as the Secretary shall by regulations prescribe;

(B) maintain methods of administration which are designed to assure that persons responsible for handling cash receipts shall not participate in accounting or operating functions which would permit them to conceal in the accounting records the misuse of cash receipts (except that the Secretary shall by regulations provide for exceptions to this requirement in the case of sparsely populated areas where the hiring of unreasonable additional staff would otherwise be necessary);

(15) provide for—

(A) a process for annual reviews of and reports to the Secretary on the State program operated under the State plan approved under this part [42 U.S.C. §651 et seq.], including such information as may be necessary to measure State compliance with Federal requirements for expedited procedures, using such standards and procedures as are required by the Secretary, under which the State agency will determine the extent to which the program is operated in compliance with this part [42 U.S.C. §651 et seq.]; and

(B) a process of extracting from the automated data processing system required by paragraph (16) and transmitting to the Secretary data and calculations concerning the levels of accomplishment (and rates of improvement) with respect to applicable performance indicators (including paternity establishment percentages) to the extent necessary for purposes of sections 452(g) and 458 [42 U.S.C. §§652(g), 658];

(16) provide for the establishment and operation by the State agency, in accordance with an (initial and annually updated) advance automated data processing planning document approved under section 452(d) [42 U.S.C. §652(d)], of a statewide automated data processing and information retrieval system meeting the requirements of section 454A [42 U.S.C. §654a] designed effectively and efficiently to assist management in the administration of the State plan, so as to control, account for, and monitor all the factors in the support enforcement collection and paternity determination process under such plan;

(17) provide that the State will have in effect an agreement with the Secretary entered into pursuant to section 463 [42 U.S.C. §663] for the use of the Parent Locator Service established under section 453 [42 U.S.C. §653], and provide that the State will accept and transmit to the Secretary requests for information authorized under the provisions of the agreement to be furnished by such Service to authorized persons, will impose and collect (in accordance with regulations of the Secretary) a fee sufficient to cover the costs to the State and to the Secretary incurred by reason of such requests, will transmit to the Secretary from time to time (in accordance with such regulations) so much of the fees collected as are attributable to such costs to the Secretary so incurred, and during the period that such agreement is in effect will otherwise comply with such agreement and regulations of the Secretary with respect thereto;

(18) provide that the State has in effect procedures necessary to obtain payment of past-due support from overpayments made to the Secretary of the Treasury as set forth in section 464 [42 U.S.C. §664], and take all steps necessary to implement and utilize such procedures;

(19) provide that the agency administering the plan—

(A) shall determine on a periodic basis, from information supplied pursuant to section 508 of the Unemployment Compensation Amendments of 1976 [29 U.S.C. §49b; 42 U.S.C. §603a], whether any individuals receiving compensation under the State's unemployment compensation law (including amounts payable pursuant to any agreement under any Federal unemployment compensation law) owe child support obligations which are being enforced by such agency; and

(B) shall enforce any such child support obligations which are owed by such an individual but are not being met—

(i) through an agreement with such individual to have specified amounts withheld from compensation otherwise payable to such individual and by submitting a copy of any such agreement to the State agency administering the unemployment compensation law; or

(ii) in the absence of such an agreement, by bringing legal process (as defined in section 459(i)(5) of this Act [42 U.S.C. §659(i)(5)]) to require the withholding of amounts from such compensation;

(20) provide, to the extent required by section 466 [42 U.S.C. §666], that the State (A) shall have in effect all of the laws to improve child support enforcement effectiveness which are referred to in that section, and (B) shall implement the procedures which are prescribed in or pursuant to such laws;

(21)(A) at the option of the State, impose a late payment fee on all overdue support (as defined in section 466(e) [42 U.S.C. §666(e)]) under any obligation being enforced under this part [42 U.S.C. §651 et seq.], in an amount equal to a uniform percentage determined by the State (not less than 3 percent nor more than 6 percent) of the overdue support, which shall be payable by the noncustodial parent owing the overdue support; and

(B) assure that the fee will be collected in addition to, and only after full payment of, the overdue support, and that the imposition of the late payment fee shall not directly or indirectly result in a decrease in the amount of the support which is paid to the child (or spouse) to whom, or on whose behalf, it is owed;

(22) in order for the State to be eligible to receive any incentive payments under section 458 [42 U.S.C. §658], provide that, if one or more political subdivisions of the State participate in the costs of carrying out activities under the State plan during any period, each such subdivision shall be entitled to receive an appropriate share (as determined by the State) of any such incentive payments made to the State for such period, taking into account the efficiency and effectiveness of the activities carried out under the State plan by such political subdivision;

(23) provide that the State will regularly and frequently publicize, through public service announcements, the availability of child support enforcement services under the plan and otherwise, including information as to any application fees for such services and a telephone number or postal address at which further information may be obtained and will publicize the availability and encourage the use of procedures for voluntary establishment of paternity and child support by means the State deems appropriate;

(24) provide that the State will have in effect an automated data processing and information retrieval system—

(A) by October 1, 1997, which meets all requirements of this part [42 U.S.C. §651 et seq.] which were enacted on or before the date of enactment of the Family Support Act of 1988 [enacted Oct. 13, 1988]; and

(B) by October 1, 2000, which meets all requirements of this part enacted on or before the date of the enactment of the Personal Responsibility and Work Opportunity Reconciliation Act of 1996 [enacted Aug. 22, 1996], except that such deadline shall be extended by 1 day for each day (if any) by which the Secretary fails to meet the deadline imposed by section 344(a)(3) of the Personal Responsibility and Work Opportunity Reconciliation Act of 1996 [42 U.S.C. §654a note];

(25) provide that if a family with respect to which services are provided under the plan ceases to receive assistance under the State program funded under part A [42 U.S.C. §601 et seq.], the State shall provide appropriate notice to the family and continue to provide such services, subject to the same conditions and on the same basis as in the case of other individuals to whom services are furnished under the plan, except that an application or other request to continue services shall not be required of such a family and paragraph (6)(B) shall not apply to the family;

(26) have in effect safeguards, applicable to all confidential information handled by the State agency, that are designed to protect the privacy rights of the parties, including—

(A) safeguards against unauthorized use or disclosure of information relating to proceedings or actions to establish paternity, or to establish, modify, or enforce support, or to make or enforce a child custody determination;

(B) prohibitions against the release of information on the whereabouts of 1 party or the child to another party against whom a protective order with respect to the former party or the child has been entered;

(C) prohibitions against the release of information on the whereabouts of 1 party or the child to another person if the State has reason to believe that the release of the information to that person may result in physical or emotional harm to the party or the child;

(D) in cases in which the prohibitions under subparagraphs (B) and (C) apply, the requirement to notify the Secretary, for purposes of section 453(b)(2) [42 U.S.C. §653(b)(2)], that the State has reasonable evidence of domestic violence or child abuse against a party or the child and that the disclosure of such information could be harmful to the party or the child; and

(E) procedures providing that when the Secretary discloses information about a parent or child to a State court or an agent of a State court described in section 453(c)(2) or 463(d)(2)(B) [42 U.S.C. §653(c)(2) or 663(d)(2)(B)], and advises that court or agent that the Secretary has been notified that there is reasonable evidence of domestic violence or child abuse pursuant to section 453(b)(2) [42 U.S.C. §653(b)(2)], the court shall determine whether disclosure to any other person of information received from the Secretary could be harmful to the parent or child and, if the court determines that disclosure to any other person could be harmful, the court and its agents shall not make any such disclosure;

(27) provide that, on and after October 1, 1998, the State agency will—

(A) operate a State disbursement unit in accordance with section 454B [42 U.S.C. §654b]; and

(B) have sufficient State staff (consisting of State employees) and (at State option) contractors reporting directly to the State agency to—

(i) monitor and enforce support collections through the unit in cases being enforced by the State pursuant to section 454(4) [42 U.S.C. §654(4)] (including carrying out the automated data processing responsibilities described in section 454A(g) [42 U.S.C. §654(4)]); and

(ii) take the actions described in section 466(c)(1) [42 U.S.C. §666(c)(1)] in appropriate cases;

(28) provide that, on and after October 1, 1997, the State will operate a State Directory of New Hires in accordance with section 453A [42 U.S.C. §653a];

(29) provide that the State agency responsible for administering the State plan—

(A) shall make the determination (and redetermination at appropriate intervals) as to whether an individual who has applied for or is receiving assistance under the State program funded under part A [42 U.S.C. §601 et seq.], the State program under part E [42 U.S.C. §670 et seq.], the State program under title XIX [42 U.S.C. §1396 et seq.], or the food stamp program, as defined under section 3(h) of the Food Stamp Act of 1977 (7 U.S.C. 2012(h)), is cooperating in good faith with the State in establishing the paternity of, or in establishing, modifying, or enforcing a support order for, any child of the individual by providing the State agency with the name of, and such other information as the State agency may require with respect to, the noncustodial parent of the child, subject to good cause and other exceptions which—

(i) in the case of the State program funded under part A [42 U.S.C. §601 et seq.], the State program under part E [42 U.S.C. §670 et seq.], or the State program under title XIX [42 U.S.C. §1396 et seq.] shall, at the option of the State, be defined, taking into account the best interests of the child, and applied in each case, by the State agency administering such program; and

(ii) in the case of the food stamp program, as defined under section 3(h) of the Food Stamp Act of 1977 (7 U.S.C. 2012(h)), shall be defined and applied in each case under that program in accordance with section 6(*l*)(2) of the Food Stamp Act of 1977 (7 U.S.C. 2015(*l*)(2));

(B) shall require the individual to supply additional necessary information and appear at interviews, hearings, and legal proceedings;

(C) shall require the individual and the child to submit to genetic tests pursuant to judicial or administrative order;

(D) may request that the individual sign a voluntary acknowledgment of paternity, after notice of the rights and consequences of such an acknowledgment, but may not require the individual to sign an acknowledgment or otherwise relinquish the right to genetic tests as a condition of cooperation and eligibility for assistance under the State program funded under part A [42 U.S.C. §601 et seq.], the State program under part E [42 U.S.C. §670 et seq.], the State program under title XIX [42 U.S.C. §1396 et seq.], or the food stamp program, as defined under section 3(h) of the Food Stamp Act of 1977 (7 U.S.C. 2012(h)); and

(E) shall promptly notify the individual and the State agency administering the State program funded under part A [42 U.S.C. §601 et seq.], the State agency administering the State program under part E [42 U.S.C. §670 et seq.], the State agency administering the State program under title XIX [42 U.S.C. §1396 et seq.], or the State agency administering the food stamp program, as defined under section 3(h) of the Food Stamp Act of 1977 (7 U.S.C. 2012(h)), of each such determination, and if noncooperation is determined, the basis therefor;

(30) provide that the State shall use the definitions established under section 452(a)(5) [42 U.S.C.

§652(a)(5)] in collecting and reporting information as required under this part [42 U.S.C. §651 et seq.];

(31) provide that the State agency will have in effect a procedure for certifying to the Secretary, for purposes of the procedure under section 452(k) [42 U.S.C. §652(k)], determinations that individuals owe arrearages of child support in an amount exceeding $5,000, under which procedure—

(A) each individual concerned is afforded notice of such determination and the consequences thereof, and an opportunity to contest the determination; and

(B) the certification by the State agency is furnished to the Secretary in such format, and accompanied by such supporting documentation, as the Secretary may require;

(32)(A) provide that any request for services under this part [42 U.S.C. §651 et seq.] by a foreign reciprocating country or a foreign country with which the State has an arrangement described in section 459A(d) [42 U.S.C. §659a(d)] shall be treated as a request by a State;

(B) provide, at State option, notwithstanding paragraph (4) or any other provision of this part [42 U.S.C. §651 et seq.], for services under the plan for enforcement of a spousal support order not described in paragraph (4)(B) entered by such a country (or subdivision); and

(C) provide that no applications will be required from, and no costs will be assessed for such services against, the foreign reciprocating country or foreign obligee (but costs may at State option be assessed against the obligor); and

(33) provide that a State that receives funding pursuant to section 428 [42 U.S.C. §628] and that has within its borders Indian country (as defined in section 1151 of title 18, United States Code) may enter into cooperative agreements with an Indian tribe or tribal organization (as defined in subsections (e) and (*l*) of section 4 of the Indian Self-Determination and Education Assistance Act (25 U.S.C. 450b)), if the Indian tribe or tribal organization demonstrates that such tribe or organization has an established tribal court system or a Court of Indian Offenses with the authority to establish paternity, establish, modify, or enforce support orders, or to enter support orders in accordance with child support guidelines established or adopted by such tribe or organization, under which the State and tribe or organization shall provide for the cooperative delivery of child support enforcement services in Indian country and for the forwarding of all collections pursuant to the functions performed by the tribe or organization to the State agency, or conversely, by the State agency to the tribe or organization, which shall distribute such collections in accordance with such agreement.

The State may allow the jurisdiction which makes the collection involved to retain any application fee under paragraph (6)(B) or any late payment fee under paragraph (21). Nothing in paragraph (33) shall void any provision of any cooperative agreement entered into before the date of the enactment of such paragraph, nor shall such paragraph deprive any State of jurisdiction over Indian country (as so defined) that is lawfully exercised under section 402 of the Act entitled "An Act to prescribe penalties for certain acts of violence or intimidation, and for other purposes", approved April 11, 1968 (25 U.S.C. 1322).

History of 42 U.S.C. §654: Aug. 14, 1935, ch. 531, §454, as added Jan. 4, 1975, P.L. 93-647, §101(a), 88 Stat. 2354; Aug. 9, 1975, P.L. 94-88, §208(b),(c), 89 Stat. 436; May 23, 1977, P.L. 95-30, §502(a), 91 Stat. 162; June 9, 1980, P.L. 96-265, §405(b), 94 Stat. 463; Dec. 28, 1980, P.L. 96-611, §9(a), 94 Stat. 3571; Aug. 13, 1981, P.L. 97-35, ch 2, §§2331(b), 2332(d)(2)-(7), 2333(a), (b), 2335(a), 95 Stat. 860, 862, 863; Sept. 3, 1982, P.L. 97-248, §§171(a), (b)(1), 173(a), 96 Stat. 401, 403; July 18, 1984, P.L. 98-369, Division B, §2663(c)(14), (j)(2)(B)(x), 98 Stat. 1166, 1170; Aug. 16, 1984, P.L. 98-378, §§3(a), (c)-(f), 5(b), 6(a), 11(b)(1), 12(a), (b), 14(a), 21(d), 98 Stat. 1306, 1310, 1311, 1314, 1318-1320, 1324; Dec. 22, 1987, P.L. 100-203, §§9141(a)(2), 9142(a), 101 Stat. 1330-321; Oct. 13, 1988, P.L. 100-485, §104(b), §111(c), §123(a), (d), 102 Stat. 2348, 2349, 2352; Oct. 12, 1995, P.L. 104-35, §1(a), 109 Stat. 294; Aug. 22, 1996, P.L. 104-193, §108(c)(11), (12), §§301(a), (b), 302(b)(2), 303(a), 304(a), §§312(a), 313(a), 316(g)(1), §324(b), §§332, 333, §§342(a), 343(b), 344(a)(1), (4), §§370(a)(2), 371(b), 375(a), (c), §395(d)(1)(D), (2)(B), 110 Stat. 2166, 2199, 2204, 2205, 2207, 2209, 2218, 2223, 2230, 2233, 2234, 2236, 2252, 2254, 2256, 2259, 2260; Aug. 5, 1997, P.L. 105-33, Ch 3, §§5531, 5542(c), 5545, 5546(a), 5548, 5552, 5556(b), 111 Stat. 625, 631, 633, 635, 637; Dec. 14, 1999, P.L. 106-169, §401(g), (h), 113 Stat. 1858.

§656. SUPPORT OBLIGATION AS OBLIGATION TO STATE; AMOUNT; DISCHARGE IN BANKRUPTCY

(a) Collection processes.—

(1) The support rights assigned to the State pursuant to section 408(a)(3) [42 U.S.C. §608(a)(3)] or secured on behalf of a child receiving foster care maintenance payments shall constitute an obligation owed to such State by the individual responsible for providing such support. Such obligation shall be deemed for collection purposes to be collectible under all applicable State and local processes.

(2) The amount of such obligation shall be—

(A) the amount specified in a court order which covers the assigned support rights, or

(B) if there is no court order, an amount determined by the State in accordance with a formula approved by the Secretary.

(3) Any amounts collected from a noncustodial parent under the plan shall reduce, dollar for dollar, the amount of his obligation under subparagraphs (A) and (B) of paragraph (2).

(b) Nondischargeability.—A debt (as defined in section 101 of title 11 of the United States Code) owed under State law to a State (as defined in such section) or municipality (as defined in such section) that is in the nature of support and that is enforceable under this part [42 U.S.C. §651 et seq.] is not released by a discharge in bankruptcy under title 11 of the United States Code.

History of 42 U.S.C. §656: Aug. 14, 1935, ch 531, §456, as added Jan. 4, 1975, P.L. 93-647, §101(a), 88 Stat. 2356; Nov. 6, 1978, P.L. 95-598, §328, 92 Stat. 2679; Aug. 13, 1981, P.L. 97-35, ch 2, §2334(a), 95 Stat. 863; July 18, 1984, P.L. 98-369, Division B, §2663(c)(15), 98 Stat. 1167; Aug, 16, 1984, P.L. 98-378, §11(b)(2), 98 Stat. 1318; Aug. 22, 1996, P.L. 104-193, §108(c)(13), §374(b), §395(d)(2)(C), 110 Stat. 2166, 2255, 2260; Aug. 5, 1997, P.L. 105-33, Ch 1, §5513(a)(3), Ch 3, §5556(d), 111 Stat. 619, 637.

§664. COLLECTION OF PAST-DUE SUPPORT FROM FEDERAL TAX REFUNDS

(a) Procedures applicable; distribution.—

(1) Upon receiving notice from a State agency administering a plan approved under this part [42 U.S.C. §651 et seq.] that a named individual owes past-due support which has been assigned to such State pursuant to section 408(a)(3) or 471(a)(17) [42 U.S.C. §608(a)(3) or §671(a)(17)], the Secretary of the Treasury shall determine whether any amounts, as refunds of Federal taxes paid, are payable to such individual (regardless of whether such individual filed a tax return as a married or unmarried individual). If the Secretary of the Treasury finds that any such amount is payable, he shall withhold from such refunds an amount equal to the past-due support, shall concurrently send notice to such individual that the withholding has been made (including in or with such notice a notification to any other person who may have filed a joint return with such individual of the steps which such other person may take in order to secure his or her proper share of the refund), and shall pay such amount to the State agency (together with notice of the individual's home address) for distribution in accordance with section 457 [42 U.S.C. §657]. This subsection may be executed by the disbursing official of the Department of the Treasury.

(2)(A) Upon receiving notice from a State agency administering a plan approved under this part [42 U.S.C. §651 et seq.] that a named individual owes past-due support (as that term is defined for purposes of this paragraph under subsection (c)) which such State has agreed to collect under section 454(4)(A)(ii) [42 U.S.C. §654(4)(A)(ii)], and that the State agency has sent notice to such individual in accordance with paragraph (3)(A), the Secretary of the Treasury shall determine whether any amounts, as refunds of Federal taxes paid, are payable to such individual (regardless of whether such individual filed a tax return as a married or unmarried individual). If the Secretary of the Treasury finds that any such amount is payable, he shall withhold from such refunds an amount equal to such past-due support, and shall concurrently send notice to such individual that the withholding has been made, including in or with such notice a notification to any other person who may have filed a joint return with such individual of the steps which such other person may take in order to secure his or her proper share of the refund. The Secretary of the Treasury shall pay the amount withheld to the State agency, and the State shall pay to the Secretary of the Treasury any fee imposed by the Secretary of the Treasury to cover the costs of the withholding and any required notification. The State agency shall, subject to paragraph (3)(B), distribute such amount to or on behalf of the child to whom the support was owed in accordance with section 457 [42 U.S.C. §657]. This subsection may be executed by the Secretary of the Department of the Treasury or his designee.

(B) This paragraph shall apply only with respect to refunds payable under section 6402 of the Internal Revenue Code of 1954 [26 U.S.C. §6402] after December 31, 1985.

(3)(A) Prior to notifying the Secretary of the Treasury under paragraph (1) or (2) that an individual owes past-due support, the State shall send notice to such individual that a withholding will be made from any refund otherwise payable to such individual. The notice shall also (i) instruct the individual owing the past-due support of the steps which may be taken to contest the State's determination that past-due support is owed or the amount of the past-due support, and (ii) provide information, as may be prescribed by the Secretary of Health and Human Services by regulation in consultation with the Secretary of the Treasury, with respect to procedures to be followed, in the case of a joint return, to protect the share of the refund which may be payable to another person.

(B) If the Secretary of the Treasury determines that an amount should be withheld under paragraph (1) or (2), and that the refund from which it should be withheld is based upon a joint return, the Secretary of the Treasury shall notify the State that the withholding is being made from a refund based upon a joint return, and shall furnish to the State the names and addresses of each taxpayer filing such joint return. In the case of a withholding under paragraph (2), the State may delay distribution of the amount withheld until the State has been notified by the Secretary of the Treasury that the other person filing the joint return has received his or her proper share of the refund, but such delay may not exceed six months.

(C) If the other person filing the joint return with the named individual owing the past-due support takes appropriate action to secure his or her proper share of a refund from which a withholding was made under paragraph (1) or (2), the Secretary of the Treasury shall pay such share to such other person. The Secretary of the Treasury shall deduct the amount of such payment from amounts subsequently payable to the State agency to which the amount originally withheld from such refund was paid.

(D) In any case in which an amount was withheld under paragraph (1) or (2) and paid to a State, and the State subsequently determines that the amount certified as past-due support was in excess of the amount actually owed at the time the amount withheld is to be distributed to or on behalf of the child, the State shall pay the excess amount withheld to the named individual thought to have owed the past-due support (or, in the case of amounts withheld on the basis of a joint return, jointly to the parties filing such return).

(b) Regulations; contents, etc.—

(1) The Secretary of the Treasury shall issue regulations, approved by the Secretary of Health and Human Services, prescribing the time or times at which states must submit notices of past-due support, the manner in which such notices must be submitted, and the necessary information that must be contained in or accompany the notices. The regulations shall be consistent with the provisions of subsection (a)(3), shall specify the minimum amount of past-due support to which the offset procedure established by subsection (a) may be applied, and the fee that a State must pay to reimburse the Secretary of the Treasury for the full cost of applying the offset procedure, and shall provide that the Secretary of the Treasury will advise the Secretary of Health and Human Services, not less frequently than annually, of the States which have furnished notices of past-due support under subsection (a), the number of cases in each State with respect to which such notices have been furnished, the amount of support sought to be collected under this subsection by each State, and the amount of such collections actually made in the case of each State. Any fee paid to the Secretary of the Treasury pursuant to this subsection may be used to reimburse appropriations which bore all or part of the cost of applying such procedure.

(2) In the case of withholdings made under subsection (a)(2), the regulations promulgated pursuant to this subsection shall include the following requirements:

(A) The withholding shall apply only in the case where the State determines that the amount of the past-due support which will be owed at the time the withholding is to be made, based upon the pattern of payment of support and other enforcement actions being pursued to collect the past-due support, is equal to or greater than $500. The State may limit the $500 threshold amount to amounts of past-due support accrued since the time that the State first began to enforce the child support order involved under the State plan, and may limit the application of the withholding to past-due support accrued since such time.

(B) The fee which the Secretary of the Treasury may impose to cover the costs of the withholding and notification may not exceed $25 per case submitted.

(c) "Past-due support" defined.—

(1) Except as provided in paragraph (2), as used in this part [42 U.S.C. §651 et seq.] the term "past-due support" means the amount of a delinquency, determined under a court order, or an order of an administrative process established under State law, for support and maintenance of a child, or of a child and the parent with whom the child is living.

(2) For purposes of subsection (a)(2), the term "past-due support" means only past-due support owed to or on behalf of a qualified child (or a qualified child and the parent with whom the child is living if the same support order includes support for the child and the parent).

(3) For purposes of paragraph (2), the term "qualified child" means a child—

(A) who is a minor; or

(B)(i) who, while a minor, was determined to be disabled under title II or XVI [42 U.S.C. §401 et seq. or 1381 et seq.]; and

(ii) for whom an order of support is in force.

History of 42 U.S.C. §664: Aug. 14, 1935, ch 531, §464, as added Aug. 13, 1981, P.L. 97-35, ch 2, §2331(a), 95 Stat. 860; Aug. 16, 1984, P.L. 98-378, §§11(d), 21 (a)-(c), 98 Stat. 1318, 1322; Oct. 22, 1986, P.L. 99-514, Ch 1, §1883(b)(8), 100 Stat. 2917; Nov. 5, 1990, P.L. 101-508, ch 1, §5011(a), (b), 104 Stat. 1388-220; April 26, 1996, P.L. 104-134, Ch 10, §31001(v)(2), 110 Stat. 1321-375; Aug. 22, 1996, P.L. 104-193, §302(b)(1), 110 Stat. 2204; Aug. 5, 1997, P.L. 105-33, Ch 1, §5513(a)(4), Ch 3, §§5531(b), 5532(i)(1), 111 Stat. 620, 626, 627.

§666. REQUIREMENT OF STATUTORILY PRESCRIBED PROCEDURES TO IMPROVE EFFECTIVENESS OF CHILD SUPPORT ENFORCEMENT

(a) Types of procedures required.—In order to satisfy section 454(20)(A) [42 U.S.C. §654(20)(A)], each State must have in effect laws requiring the use of the following procedures, consistent with this section and with regulations of the Secretary, to increase the effectiveness of the program which the State administers under this part [42 U.S.C. §651 et seq.]:

(1)(A) Procedures described in subsection (b) for the withholding from income of amounts payable as support in cases subject to enforcement under the State plan.

(B) Procedures under which the income of a person with a support obligation imposed by a support order issued (or modified) in the State before January 1, 1994, if not otherwise subject to withholding under subsection (b), shall become subject to withholding as provided in subsection (b) if arrearages occur, without the need for a judicial or administrative hearing.

(2) Expedited administrative and judicial procedures (including the procedures specified in subsection (c)) for establishing paternity and for establishing, modifying, and enforcing support obligations. The Secretary may waive the provisions of this paragraph with respect to one or more political subdivisions within the State on the basis of the effectiveness and timeliness of support order issuance and enforcement or paternity establishment within the political subdivision (in accordance with the general rule for exemptions under subsection (d)).

(3) Procedures under which the State child support enforcement agency shall request, and the State shall provide, that for the purpose of enforcing a support order under any State plan approved under this part [42 U.S.C. §651 et seq.]—

(A) any refund of State income tax which would otherwise be payable to a noncustodial parent will be reduced, after notice has been sent to that noncustodial parent of the proposed reduction and the procedures to be followed to contest it (and after full compliance with all procedural due process requirements of the State), by the amount of any overdue support owed by such noncustodial parent;

(B) the amount by which such refund is reduced shall be distributed in accordance with section 457 [42 U.S.C. §657] in the case of overdue support assigned to a State pursuant to section 408(a)(3) or 471(a)(17) [42 U.S.C. §608(a)(3) or §671(a)(17)], or, in any other case, shall be distributed, after deduction of any fees imposed by the State to cover the costs of collection, to the child or parent to whom such support is owed; and

(C) notice of the noncustodial parent's social security account number (or numbers, if he has more than one such number) and home address shall be furnished to the State agency requesting the refund offset, and to the State agency enforcing the order.

(4) Liens.—Procedures under which—

(A) liens arise by operation of law against real and personal property for amounts of overdue support owed by a noncustodial parent who resides or owns property in the State; and

(B) the State accords full faith and credit to liens described in subparagraph (A) arising in another State, when the State agency, party, or other entity seeking to enforce such a lien complies with the procedural rules relating to recording or serving liens that arise within the State, except that such rules may not require judicial notice or hearing prior to the enforcement of such a lien.

(5) Procedures concerning paternity establishment.—

(A) Establishment process available from birth until age 18.—

(i) Procedures which permit the establishment of the paternity of a child at any time before the child attains 18 years of age.

(ii) As of August 16, 1984, clause (i) shall also apply to a child for whom paternity has not been established or for whom a paternity action was brought but dismissed because a statute of limitations of less than 18 years was then in effect in the State.

(B) Procedures concerning genetic testing.—

(i) Genetic testing required in certain contested cases.—Procedures under which the State is required, in a contested paternity case (unless otherwise barred by State law) to require the child and all other parties (other than individuals found under section 454(29) [42 U.S.C. §654(29)] to have good cause and other exceptions for refusing to cooperate) to submit to genetic tests upon the request of any such party, if the request is supported by a sworn statement by the party—

(I) alleging paternity, and setting forth facts establishing a reasonable possibility of the requisite sexual contact between the parties; or

(II) denying paternity, and setting forth facts establishing a reasonable possibility of the nonexistence of sexual contact between the parties.

(ii) Other requirements.—Procedures which require the State agency, in any case in which the agency orders genetic testing—

(I) to pay costs of such tests, subject to recoupment (if the State so elects) from the alleged father if paternity is established; and

(II) to obtain additional testing in any case if an original test result is contested, upon request and advance payment by the contestant.

(C) Voluntary paternity acknowledgment.—

(i) Simple civil process.—Procedures for a simple civil process for voluntarily acknowledging paternity under which the State must provide that, before a mother and a putative father can sign an acknowledgment of paternity, the mother and the putative father must be given notice, orally, or through the use of video or audio equipment, and in writing, of the alternatives to, the legal consequences of, and the rights (including, if 1 parent is a minor, any rights afforded due to minority status) and responsibilities that arise from, signing the acknowledgment.

(ii) Hospital-based program.—Such procedures must include a hospital-based program for the voluntary acknowledgment of paternity focusing on the period immediately before or after the birth of a child.

(iii) Paternity establishment services.—

(I) State-offered services.—Such procedures must require the State agency responsible for maintaining birth records to offer voluntary paternity establishment services.

(II) Regulations.—

(aa) Services offered by hospitals and birth record agencies.—The Secretary shall prescribe regulations governing voluntary paternity establishment services offered by hospitals and birth record agencies.

(bb) Services offered by other entities.—The Secretary shall prescribe regulations specifying the types of other entities that may offer voluntary paternity establishment services, and governing the provision of such services, which shall include a requirement that such an entity must use the same notice provisions used by, use the same materials used by, provide the personnel providing such services with the same training provided by, and evaluate the provision of such services in the same manner as the provision of such services is evaluated by, voluntary paternity establishment programs of hospitals and birth record agencies.

(iv) Use of paternity acknowledgment affidavit.—Such procedures must require the State to develop and use an affidavit for the voluntary acknowledgment of paternity which includes the minimum requirements of the affidavit specified by the Secretary under section 452(a)(7) [42 U.S.C. §652(a)(7)] for the voluntary acknowledgment of paternity, and to give full faith and credit to such an affidavit signed in any other State according to its procedures.

(D) Status of signed paternity acknowledgment.—

(i) Inclusion in birth records.—Procedures under which the name of the father shall be included on the record of birth of the child of unmarried parents only if—

(I) the father and mother have signed a voluntary acknowledgment of paternity; or

(II) a court or an administrative agency of competent jurisdiction has issued an adjudication of paternity.

Nothing in this clause shall preclude a State agency from obtaining an admission of paternity from the father for submission in a judicial or administrative proceeding, or prohibit the issuance of an order in a judicial or administrative proceeding which bases a legal finding of paternity on an admission of paternity by the father and any other additional showing required by State law.

(ii) Legal finding of paternity.—Procedures under which a signed voluntary acknowledgment of paternity is considered a legal finding of paternity, subject to the right of any signatory to rescind the acknowledgment within the earlier of—

(I) 60 days; or

(II) the date of an administrative or judicial proceeding relating to the child (including a proceeding to establish a support order) in which the signatory is a party.

(iii) Contest.—Procedures under which, after the 60-day period referred to in clause (ii), a signed voluntary acknowledgment of paternity may be challenged in court only on the basis of fraud, duress, or material mistake of fact, with the burden of proof upon the challenger, and under which the legal responsibilities (including child support obligations) of any signatory arising from the acknowledgment may not be suspended during the challenge, except for good cause shown.

(E) Bar on acknowledgment ratification proceedings.—Procedures under which judicial or administrative proceedings are not required or permitted to ratify an unchallenged acknowledgment of paternity.

(F) Admissibility of genetic testing results.—Procedures—

(i) requiring the admission into evidence, for purposes of establishing paternity, of the results of any genetic test that is—

(I) of a type generally acknowledged as reliable by accreditation bodies designated by the Secretary; and

(II) performed by a laboratory approved by such an accreditation body;

(ii) requiring an objection to genetic testing results to be made in writing not later than a specified number of days before any hearing at which the results may be introduced into evidence (or, at State option, not later than a specified number of days after receipt of the results); and

(iii) making the test results admissible as evidence of paternity without the need for foundation testimony or other proof of authenticity or accuracy, unless objection is made.

(G) Presumption of paternity in certain cases.—Procedures which create a rebuttable or, at the option of the State, conclusive presumption of paternity upon genetic testing results indicating a threshold probability that the alleged father is the father of the child.

(H) Default orders.—Procedures requiring a default order to be entered in a paternity case upon a showing of service of process on the defendant and any additional showing required by State law.

(I) No right to jury trial.—Procedures providing that the parties to an action to establish paternity are not entitled to a trial by jury.

(J) Temporary support order based on probable paternity in contested cases.—Procedures which require that a temporary order be issued, upon motion by a party, requiring the provision of child support pending an administrative or judicial determination of parentage, if there is clear and convincing evidence of paternity (on the basis of genetic tests or other evidence).

(K) Proof of certain support and paternity establishment costs.—Procedures under which bills for pregnancy, childbirth, and genetic testing are admissible as evidence without requiring third-party foundation testimony, and shall constitute prima facie evidence of amounts incurred for such services or for testing on behalf of the child.

(L) Standing of putative fathers.—Procedures ensuring that the putative father has a reasonable opportunity to initiate a paternity action.

(M) Filing of acknowledgments and adjudications in state registry of birth records.—Procedures under which voluntary acknowledgments and adjudications of paternity by judicial or administrative processes are filed with the State registry of birth records for comparison with information in the State case registry.

(6) Procedures which require that a noncustodial parent give security, post a bond, or give some other guarantee to secure payment of overdue support, after notice has been sent to such noncustodial parent of the proposed action and of the procedures to be followed to contest it (and after full compliance with all procedural due process requirements of the State).

(7) Reporting arrearages to credit bureaus.—

(A) In general.—Procedures (subject to safeguards pursuant to subparagraph (B)) requiring the State to report periodically to consumer reporting agencies (as defined in section 603(f) of the Fair Credit Reporting Act (15 U.S.C. 1681a(f))) the name of any noncustodial parent who is delinquent in the payment of support, and the amount of overdue support owed by such parent.

(B) Safeguards.—Procedures ensuring that, in carrying out subparagraph (A), information with respect to a noncustodial parent is reported—

(i) only after such parent has been afforded all due process required under State law, including notice and a reasonable opportunity to contest the accuracy of such information; and

(ii) only to an entity that has furnished evidence satisfactory to the State that the entity is a consumer reporting agency (as so defined).

(8)(A) Procedures under which all child support orders not described in subparagraph (B) will include provision for withholding from income, in order to assure that withholding as a means of collecting child support is available if arrearages occur without the necessity of filing application for services under this part [42 U.S.C. §651 et seq.].

(B) Procedures under which all child support orders which are initially issued in the State on or after January 1, 1994, and are not being enforced under this part [42 U.S.C. §651 et seq.] will include the following requirements:

(i) The income of a noncustodial parent shall be subject to withholding, regardless of whether support payments by such parent are in arrears, on the effective date of the order; except that such income shall not be subject to withholding under this clause in any case where (I) one of the parties demonstrates, and the court (or administrative process) finds, that there is good cause not to require immediate income withholding, or (II) a written agreement is reached between both parties which provides for an alternative arrangement.

(ii) The requirements of subsection (b)(1) (which shall apply in the case of each noncustodial parent against whom a support order is or has been issued or modified in the State, without regard to whether the order is being enforced under the State plan).

(iii) The requirements of paragraphs (2), (5), (6), (7), (8), (9), and (10) of subsection (b), where applicable.

(iv) Withholding from income of amounts payable as support must be carried out in full compliance with all procedural due process requirements of the State.

(9) Procedures which require that any payment or installment of support under any child support order, whether ordered through the State judicial system or through the expedited processes required by paragraph (2), is (on and after the date it is due)—

(A) a judgment by operation of law, with the full force, effect, and attributes of a judgment of the State, including the ability to be enforced,

(B) entitled as a judgment to full faith and credit in such State and in any other State, and

(C) not subject to retroactive modification by such State or by any other State;

except that such procedures may permit modification with respect to any period during which there is pending a petition for modification, but only from the date that notice of such petition has been given, either directly or through the appropriate agent, to the obligee or (where the obligee is the petitioner) to the obligor.

(10) Review and adjustment of support orders upon request.—

(A) 3-year cycle.—

(i) In general.—Procedures under which every 3 years (or such shorter cycle as the State may determine), upon the request of either parent, or, if there is an assignment under part A [42 U.S.C. §601 et seq.], upon the request of the State agency under the State plan or of either parent, the State shall with respect to a support order being enforced under this part [42 U.S.C. §651 et seq.], taking into account the best interests of the child involved—

(I) review and, if appropriate, adjust the order in accordance with the guidelines established pursuant to section 467(a) [42 U.S.C. §667(a)] if the amount of the child support award under the order differs from the amount that would be awarded in accordance with the guidelines;

(II) apply a cost-of-living adjustment to the order in accordance with a formula developed by the State; or

(III) use automated methods (including automated comparisons with wage or State income tax data) to identify orders eligible for review, conduct the review, identify orders eligible for adjustment, and apply the appropriate adjustment to the orders eligible for adjustment under any threshold that may be established by the State.

(ii) Opportunity to request review of adjustment.—If the State elects to conduct the review under subclause (II) or (III) of clause (i), procedures which permit either party to contest the adjustment, within 30 days after the date of the notice of the adjustment, by making a request for review and, if appropriate, adjustment of the order in accordance with the child support guidelines established pursuant to section 467(a) [42 U.S.C. §667(a)].

(iii) No proof of change in circumstances necessary in 3-year cycle review.—Procedures which provide that any adjustment under clause (i) shall be made without a requirement for proof or showing of a change in circumstances.

(B) Proof of substantial change in circumstances necessary in request for review outside 3-year cycle.—Procedures under which, in the case of a request for a review, and if appropriate, an adjustment outside the 3-year cycle (or such shorter cycle as the State may determine) under clause (i), the State shall review and, if the requesting party demonstrates a substantial change in circumstances, adjust the order in accordance with the guidelines established pursuant to section 467(a) [42 U.S.C. §667(a)].

(C) Notice of right to review.—Procedures which require the State to provide notice not less than once every 3 years to the parents subject to the order informing the parents of their right to request the State to review and, if appropriate, adjust the order pursuant to this paragraph. The notice may be included in the order.

(11) Procedures under which a State must give full faith and credit to a determination of paternity made by any other State, whether established through voluntary acknowledgment or through administrative or judicial processes.

(12) Locator information from interstate networks.—Procedures to ensure that all Federal and State agencies conducting activities under this part have access to any system used by the State to locate an individual for purposes relating to motor vehicles or law enforcement.

(13) Recording of social security numbers in certain family matters.—Procedures requiring that the social security number of—

(A) any applicant for a professional license, driver's license, occupational license, recreational license, or marriage license be recorded on the application;

(B) any individual who is subject to a divorce decree, support order, or paternity determination or acknowledgment be placed in the records relating to the matter; and

(C) any individual who has died be placed in the records relating to the death and be recorded on the death certificate.

For purposes of subparagraph (A), if a State allows the use of a number other than the social security number to be used on the face of the document while the social security number is kept on file at the agency, the State shall so advise any applicants.

(14) High-volume, automated administrative enforcement in interstate cases.—

(A) In general.—Procedures under which—

(i) the State shall use high-volume automated administrative enforcement, to the same extent as used for intrastate cases, in response to a request made by another State to enforce support orders, and shall promptly report the results of such enforcement procedure to the requesting State;

(ii) the State may, by electronic or other means, transmit to another State a request for assistance in enforcing support orders through high-volume, automated administrative enforcement, which request—

(I) shall include such information as will enable the State to which the request is transmitted to compare the information about the cases to the information in the data bases of the State; and

(II) shall constitute a certification by the requesting State—

(aa) of the amount of support under an order the payment of which is in arrears; and

(bb) that the requesting State has complied with all procedural due process requirements applicable to each case;

(iii) if the State provides assistance to another State pursuant to this paragraph with respect to a case, neither State shall consider the case to be transferred to the caseload of such other State; and

(iv) the State shall maintain records of—

(I) the number of such requests for assistance received by the State;

(II) the number of cases for which the State collected support in response to such a request; and

(III) the amount of such collected support.

(B) High-volume automated administrative enforcement.—In this part [42 U.S.C. §651 et seq.], the term "high-volume automated administrative enforcement", in interstate cases, means, on request of another State, the identification by a State, through automated data matches with financial institutions and other entities where assets may be found, of assets owned by persons who owe child support in other States, and the seizure of such assets by the State, through levy or other appropriate processes.

(C) to (D) Repealed by P.L. 105-33, Title V, §5550(a), 111 Stat. 634.

(15) Procedures to ensure that persons owing overdue support work or have a plan for payment of such support.—Procedures under which the State has the authority, in any case in which an individual owes overdue support with respect to a child receiving assistance under a State program funded under part A [42 U.S.C. §601 et seq.], to issue an order or to request that a court or an administrative process established pursuant to State law issue an order that requires the individual to—

(A) pay such support in accordance with a plan approved by the court, or, at the option of the State, a plan approved by the State agency administering the State program under this part [42 U.S.C. §651 et seq.]; or

(B) if the individual is subject to such a plan and is not incapacitated, participate in such work activities (as defined in section 407(d) [42 U.S.C. §607(d)]) as the court, or, at the option of the State, the State agency administering the State program under this part [42 U.S.C. §651 et seq.], deems appropriate.

(16) Authority to withhold or suspend licenses.—Procedures under which the State has (and uses in appropriate cases) authority to withhold or suspend, or to restrict the use of driver's licenses, professional and occupational licenses, and recreational and sporting licenses of individuals owing overdue support or failing, after receiving appropriate notice, to comply with subpoenas or warrants relating to paternity or child support proceedings.

(17) Financial institution data matches.—

(A) In general.—Procedures under which the State agency shall enter into agreements with financial institutions doing business in the State—

(i) to develop and operate, in coordination with such financial institutions, and the Federal Parent Locator Service in the case of financial institutions doing business in two or more States, a data match system, using automated data exchanges to the maximum extent feasible, in which each such financial institution is required to provide for each calendar quarter the name, record address, social security number or other taxpayer identification number, and other identifying information for each noncustodial parent who maintains an account at such institution and who owes past-due support, as identified by the State by name and social security number or other taxpayer identification number; and

(ii) in response to a notice of lien or levy, encumber or surrender, as the case may be, assets held by such institution on behalf of any noncustodial parent who is subject to a child support lien pursuant to paragraph (4).

(B) Reasonable fees.—The State agency may pay a reasonable fee to a financial institution for conducting the data match provided for in subparagraph (A)(i), not to exceed the actual costs incurred by such financial institution.

(C) Liability.—A financial institution shall not be liable under any Federal or State law to any person—

(i) for any disclosure of information to the State agency under subparagraph (A)(i);

(ii) for encumbering or surrendering any assets held by such financial institution in response to a notice of lien or levy issued by the State agency as provided for in subparagraph (A)(ii); or

(iii) for any other action taken in good faith to comply with the requirements of subparagraph (A).

(D) Definitions.—For purposes of this paragraph—

(i) Financial institution.—The term "financial institution" has the meaning given to such term by section 469A(d)(1) [42 U.S.C. §669a(d)(1)].

(ii) Account.—The term "account" means a demand deposit account, checking or negotiable withdrawal order account, savings account, time deposit account, or money-market mutual fund account.

(18) Enforcement of orders against paternal or maternal grandparents.—Procedures under which, at the State's option, any child support order enforced under this part [42 U.S.C. §651 et seq.] with respect to a child of minor parents, if the custodial parent of such child is receiving assistance under the State program under part A [42 U.S.C. §601 et seq.], shall be enforceable, jointly and severally, against the parents of the noncustodial parent of such child.

(19) Health care coverage.—Procedures under which—

(A) effective as provided in section 401(c)(3) [42 U.S.C. §601(c)(3)] of the Child Support Performance and Incentive Act of 1998, all child support orders enforced pursuant to this part which include a provision for the health care coverage of the child are enforced, where appropriate, through the use of the National Medical Support Notice promulgated pursuant to section 401(b) of the Child Support Performance and Incentive Act of 1998 [42 U.S.C. §601(b)] (and referred to in section 609(a)(5)(C) of the Employee Retirement Income Security Act of 1974 [29 U.S.C. §1169(a)(5)(C)] in connection with group health plans covered under title I of such Act, in section 401(e)(3)(C) [42 U.S.C. §601(e)(3)(C)] of the Child Support Performance and Incentive Act of 1998 in connection with State or local group health plans, and in section 401(f)(5)(C) of such Act [42 U.S.C. §601(f)(5)(C)] in connection with church group health plans);

(B) unless alternative coverage is allowed for in any order of the court (or other entity issuing the child support order), in any case in which a noncustodial parent is required under the child support order to provide such health care coverage and the employer of such noncustodial parent is known to the State agency—

(i) the State agency uses the National Medical Support Notice to transfer notice of the provision for the health care coverage of the child to the employer;

(ii) within 20 business days after the date of the National Medical Support Notice, the employer is required to transfer the Notice, excluding the severable employer withholding notice described in section 401(b)(2)(C) of the Child Support Performance and Incentive Act of 1998 [42 U.S.C. §601(b)(2)(C)], to the appropriate plan providing any such health care coverage for which the child is eligible;

(iii) in any case in which the noncustodial parent is a newly hired employee entered in the State Directory of New Hires pursuant to section 453A(e) [42 U.S.C. §653a(e)], the State agency provides, where appropriate, the National Medical Support Notice, together with an income withholding notice issued pursuant to section 466(b) [42 U.S.C. §466(b)], within two days after the date of the entry of such employee in such Directory; and

(iv) in any case in which the employment of the noncustodial parent with any employer who has received a National Medical Support Notice is terminated, such employer is required to notify the State agency of such termination; and

(C) any liability of the noncustodial parent to such plan for employee contributions which are required under such plan for enrollment of the child is effectively subject to appropriate enforcement, unless the noncustodial parent contests such enforcement based on a mistake of fact.

Notwithstanding section 454(20)(B) [42 U.S.C. §654(20)(B)], the procedures which are required under paragraphs (3), (4), (6), (7), and (15) need not be used or applied in cases where the State determines (using guidelines which are generally available within the State and which take into account the payment record of the noncustodial parent, the availability of other remedies, and other relevant considerations) that such use or application would not carry out the purposes of this part [42 U.S.C. §651 et seq.] or would be otherwise inappropriate in the circumstances.

(b) [Withholding from income of amounts payable as support.]— The procedures referred to in subsection (a)(1)(A) (relating to the withholding from income of amounts payable as support) must provide for the following:

(1) In the case of each noncustodial parent against whom a support order is or has been issued or modified in the State, and is being enforced under the State plan, so much of such parent's income must be withheld, in accordance with the succeeding provisions of this subsection, as is necessary to comply with the order and provide for the payment of any fee to the employer which may be required under paragraph (6)(A), up to the maximum amount permitted under section 303(b) of the Consumer Credit Protection Act (15 U.S.C. 1673(b)). If there are arrearages to be collected, amounts withheld to satisfy such arrearages, when added to the amounts withheld to pay current support and provide for the fee, may not exceed the limit permitted under such section 303(b) [15 U.S.C. §1673(b)], but the State need not withhold up to the maximum amount permitted under such section in order to satisfy arrearages.

(2) Such withholding must be provided without the necessity of any application therefor in the case of a child (whether or not eligible for assistance under a State program funded under part A [42 U.S.C. §601 et seq.]) with respect to whom services are already being provided under the State plan under this part [42 U.S.C. §651 et seq.], and must be provided in accordance with this subsection on the basis of an application for services under the State plan in the case of any other child in whose behalf a support order has been issued or modified in the State. In either case such withholding must occur without the need for any amendment to the support order involved or for any further action (other than those actions required under this part [42 U.S.C. §651 et seq.]) by the court or other entity which issued such order.

(3)(A) The income of a noncustodial parent shall be subject to such withholding, regardless of whether support payments by such parent are in arrears, in the case of a support order being enforced under this part [42 U.S.C. §651 et seq.] that is issued or modified on or after the first day of the 25th month beginning after the date of the enactment of this paragraph [enacted Oct. 13, 1988], on the effective date of the order; except that such income shall not be subject to such withholding under this subparagraph in any case where (i) one of the parties demonstrates, and the court (or administrative process) finds, that there is good cause not to require immediate income withholding, or (ii) a written agreement is reached between both parties which provides for an alternative arrangement.

(B) The income of a noncustodial parent shall become subject to such withholding, in the case of income not subject to withholding under subparagraph (A), on the date on which the payments which the noncustodial parent has failed to make under a support order are at least equal to the support payable for one month or, if earlier, and without regard to whether there is an arrearage, the earliest of—

(i) the date as of which the noncustodial parent requests that such withholding begin,

(ii) the date as of which the custodial parent requests that such withholding begin, if the State determines, in accordance with such procedures and standards as it may establish, that the request should be approved, or

(iii) such earlier date as the State may select.

(4)(A) Such withholding must be carried out in full compliance with all procedural due process requirements of the State, and the State must send notice to each noncustodial parent to whom paragraph (1) applies—

(i) that the withholding has commenced; and

(ii) of the procedures to follow if the noncustodial parent desires to contest such withholding on the grounds that the withholding or the amount withheld is improper due to a mistake of fact.

(B) The notice under subparagraph (A) of this paragraph shall include the information provided to the employer under paragraph (6)(A).

(5) Such withholding must be administered by the State through the State disbursement unit established pursuant to section 454B [42 U.S.C. §654b], in accordance with the requirements of section 454B [42 U.S.C. §654b].

(6)(A)(i) The employer of any noncustodial parent to whom paragraph (1) applies, upon being given notice as described in clause (ii), must be required to withhold from such noncustodial parent's income the amount specified by such notice (which may include a fee, established by the State, to be paid to the employer unless waived by such employer) and pay such amount (after deducting and retaining any portion thereof which represents the fee so established) to the State disbursement unit within 7 business days after the date the amount would (but for this subsection) have been paid or credited to the employee, for distribution in accordance with this part [42 U.S.C. §651 et seq.]. The employer shall withhold funds as directed in the notice, except that when an employer receives an income withholding order issued by another State, the employer shall apply the income withholding law of the State of the obligor's principal place of employment in determining—

(I) the employer's fee for processing an income withholding order;

(II) the maximum amount permitted to be withheld from the obligor's income;

(III) the time periods within which the employer must implement the income withholding order and forward the child support payment;

(IV) the priorities for withholding and allocating income withheld for multiple child support obligees; and

(V) any withholding terms or conditions not specified in the order.

An employer who complies with an income withholding notice that is regular on its face shall not be subject to civil liability to any individual or agency for conduct in compliance with the notice.

(ii) The notice given to the employer shall be in a standard format prescribed by the Secretary, and contain only such information as may be necessary for the employer to comply with the withholding order.

(iii) As used in this subparagraph, the term "business day" means a day on which State offices are open for regular business.

(B) Methods must be established by the State to simplify the withholding process for employers to the greatest extent possible, including permitting any employer to combine all withheld amounts into a single payment to each appropriate agency or entity (with the portion thereof which is attributable to each individual employee being separately designated).

(C) The employer must be held liable to the State for any amount which such employer fails to withhold from income due an employee following receipt by such employer of proper notice under subparagraph (A), but such employer shall not be required to vary the normal pay and disbursement cycles in order to comply with this paragraph.

(D) Provision must be made for the imposition of a fine against any employer who—

(i) discharges from employment, refuses to employ, or takes disciplinary action against any noncustodial parent subject to income withholding required by this subsection because of the existence of such withholding and the obligations or additional obligations which it imposes upon the employer; or

(ii) fails to withhold support from income or to pay such amounts to the State disbursement unit in accordance with this subsection.

(7) Support collection under this subsection must be given priority over any other legal process under State law against the same income.

(8) For purposes of subsection (a) and this subsection, the term "income" means any periodic form of payment due to an individual, regardless of source, including wages, salaries, commissions, bonuses, worker's compensation, disability, payments pursuant to a pension or retirement program, and interest.

(9) The State must extend its withholding system under this subsection so that such system will include withholding from income derived within such State in cases where the applicable support orders were issued in other States, in order to assure that child support owed by noncustodial parents in such State or any other State will be collected without regard to the residence of the child for whom the support is payable or of such child's custodial parent.

(10) Provision must be made for terminating withholding.

(11) Procedures under which the agency administering the State plan approved under this part [42 U.S.C. §651 et seq.] may execute a withholding order without advance notice to the obligor, including issuing the withholding order through electronic means.

(c) Expedited procedures.—The procedures specified in this subsection are the following:

(1) Administrative action by State agency.—Procedures which give the State agency the authority to take the following actions relating to establishment of paternity or to establishment, modification, or enforcement of support orders, without the necessity of obtaining an order from any other judicial or administrative tribunal, and to recognize and enforce the authority of State agencies of other States to take the following actions:

(A) Genetic testing.—To order genetic testing for the purpose of paternity establishment as provided in section 466(a)(5) [42 U.S.C. §666(a)(5)].

(B) Financial or other information.—To subpoena any financial or other information needed to establish, modify, or enforce a support order, and to impose penalties for failure to respond to such a subpoena.

(C) Response to State agency request.—To require all entities in the State (including for-profit, nonprofit, and governmental employers) to provide promptly, in response to a request by the State agency of that or any other State administering a program under this part [42 U.S.C. §651 et seq.], information on the employment, compensation, and benefits of any individual employed by such entity as an employee or contractor, and to sanction failure to respond to any such request.

(D) Access to information contained in certain records.—To obtain access, subject to safeguards on privacy and information security, and subject to the nonliability of entities that afford such access under this subparagraph, to information contained in the following records (including automated access, in the case of records maintained in automated data bases):

(i) Records of other State and local government agencies, including—

(I) vital statistics (including records of marriage, birth, and divorce);

(II) State and local tax and revenue records (including information on residence address, employer, income and assets);

(III) records concerning real and titled personal property;

(IV) records of occupational and professional licenses, and records concerning the ownership and control of corporations, partnerships, and other business entities;

(V) employment security records;

(VI) records of agencies administering public assistance programs;

(VII) records of the motor vehicle department; and

(VIII) corrections records.

(ii) Certain records held by private entities with respect to individuals who owe or are owed support (or against or with respect to whom a support obligation is sought), consisting of—

(I) the names and addresses of such individuals and the names and addresses of the employers of such individuals, as appearing in customer records of public utilities and cable television companies, pursuant to an administrative subpoena authorized by subparagraph (B); and

(II) information (including information on assets and liabilities) on such individuals held by financial institutions.

(E) Change in payee.—In cases in which support is subject to an assignment in order to comply with a requirement imposed pursuant to part A, part E, or section 1912 [42 U.S.C. §601 et seq., §670 et seq., or §1396k], or to a requirement to pay through the State disbursement unit established pursuant to section 454B [42 U.S.C. §654b], upon providing notice to obligor and obligee, to direct the obligor or other payor to change the payee to the appropriate government entity.

(F) Income withholding.—To order income withholding in accordance with subsections (a)(1)(A) and (b).

(G) Securing assets.—In cases in which there is a support arrearage, to secure assets to satisfy any current support obligation and the arrearage by—

(i) intercepting or seizing periodic or lump-sum payments from—

(I) a State or local agency, including unemployment compensation, workers' compensation, and other benefits; and

(II) judgments, settlements, and lotteries;

(ii) attaching and seizing assets of the obligor held in financial institutions;

(iii) attaching public and private retirement funds; and

(iv) imposing liens in accordance with subsection (a)(4) and, in appropriate cases, to force sale of property and distribution of proceeds.

(H) Increase monthly payments.—For the purpose of securing overdue support, to increase the amount of monthly support payments to include amounts for arrearages, subject to such conditions or limitations as the State may provide.

Such procedures shall be subject to due process safeguards, including (as appropriate) requirements for notice, opportunity to contest the action, and opportunity for an appeal on the record to an independent administrative or judicial tribunal.

(2) Substantive and procedural rules.—The expedited procedures required under subsection (a)(2) shall include the following rules and authority, applicable with respect to all proceedings to establish paternity or to establish, modify, or enforce support orders:

(A) Locator information; presumptions concerning notice.—Procedures under which—

(i) each party to any paternity or child support proceeding is required (subject to privacy safeguards) to file with the State case registry upon entry of an order, and to update as appropriate, information on location and identity of the party, including social security number, residential and mailing addresses, telephone number, driver's license number, and name, address, and telephone number of employer; and

(ii) in any subsequent child support enforcement action between the parties, upon sufficient showing that diligent effort has been made to ascertain the location of such a party, the court or administrative agency of competent jurisdiction shall deem State due process requirements for notice and service of process to be met with respect to the party, upon delivery of written notice to the most recent residential or employer address filed with the State case registry pursuant to clause (i).

(B) Statewide jurisdiction.—Procedures under which—

(i) the State agency and any administrative or judicial tribunal with authority to hear child support and paternity cases exerts statewide jurisdiction over the parties; and

(ii) in a State in which orders are issued by courts or administrative tribunals, a case may be transferred between local jurisdictions in the State without need for any additional filing by the petitioner, or service of process upon the respondent, to retain jurisdiction over the parties.

(3) Coordination with ERISA.—Notwithstanding subsection (d) of section 514 of the Employee Retirement Income Security Act of 1974 [29 U.S.C. §1144(d)] (relating to effect on other laws), nothing in this subsection shall be construed to alter, amend, modify, invalidate, impair, or supersede subsections (a), (b), and (c) of such section 514 [29 U.S.C. §1144(a), (b), (c)] as it applies with respect to any procedure referred to in paragraph (1) and any expedited procedure referred to in paragraph (2), except to the extent that such procedure would be consistent with the requirements of section 206(d)(3) of such Act [29 U.S.C. §1056(d)(3)] (relating to qualified domestic relations orders) or the requirements of section 609(a) of such Act [29 U.S.C. §1169(a)] (relating to qualified medical child support orders) if the reference in such section 206(d)(3) [29 U.S.C. §1056(d)(3)] to a domestic relations order and the reference in such section 609(a) [29 U.S.C. §1169(a)] to a medical child support order were a reference to a support order referred to in paragraphs (1) and (2) relating to the same matters, respectively.

(d) Exemption of States.—If a State demonstrates to the satisfaction of the Secretary, through the presentation to the Secretary of such data pertaining to caseloads, processing times, administrative costs, and average support collections, and such other data or estimates as the Secretary may specify, that the enactment of any law or the use of any procedure or procedures requires by or pursuant to this section will not increase the effectiveness and efficiency of the State child support enforcement program, the Secretary may exempt the State, subject to the Secretary's continuing review and to termination of the exemption should circumstances change, from the requirement to enact the law or use the procedure or procedures involved.

(e) "Overdue support" defined.—For purposes of this section, the term "overdue support" means the amount of a delinquency pursuant to an obligation determined under a court order, or an order of an administrative process established under State law, for support and maintenance of a minor child which is owed to or on behalf of such child, or for support and maintenance of the noncustodial parent's spouse (or former spouse) with whom the child is living if and to the extent that spousal support (with respect to such spouse or former spouse) would be included for purposes of section 454(4) [42 U.S.C. §654(4)]. At the option of the State, overdue support may include amounts which otherwise meet the definition in the first sentence of this subsection but which are owed to or on behalf of a child who is not a minor child. The option to include support owed to children who are not minors shall apply independently to each procedure specified under this section.

(f) Uniform Interstate Family Support Act.—In order to satisfy section 454(20)(A) [42 U.S.C. §654(20)(A)], on and after January 1, 1998, each State must have in effect the Uniform Interstate Family Support Act, as approved by the American Bar Association on February 9, 1993, and as in effect on August 22, 1996, including any amendments officially adopted as of such date by the National Conference of Commissioners on Uniform State Laws.

(g) Laws voiding fraudulent transfers.—In order to satisfy section 454(20)(A) [42 U.S.C. §654(20)(A)], each State must have in effect—

(1)(A) the Uniform Fraudulent Conveyance Act of 1981;

(B) the Uniform Fraudulent Transfer Act of 1984; or

(C) another law, specifying indicia of fraud which create a prima facie case that a debtor transferred income or property to avoid payment to a child support creditor, which the Secretary finds affords comparable rights to child support creditors; and

(2) procedures under which, in any case in which the State knows of a transfer by a child support debtor with respect to which such a prima facie case is established, the State must—

(A) seek to void such transfer; or

(B) obtain a settlement in the best interests of the child support creditor.

History of 42 U.S.C. §666: Aug. 14, 1935, ch 531, §466, as added Aug. 16, 1984, P.L. 98-378, §3(b), 98 Stat. 1306; Oct. 21, 1986, P.L. 99-509, §9103(a), 100 Stat. 1973; Oct. 13, 1988, P.L. 100-485, §§101(a), (b), 103(c), §111(b), (e), 102 Stat. 2344-2346, 2349, 2350; Nov. 10, 1988, P.L. 100-647, §8105(4), 102 Stat. 3797; Aug. 10, 1993, P.L. 103-66, Ch 2, Subch C, §13721(b), 107 Stat. 659; Oct. 31, 1994, P.L. 103-432, §212(a), 108 Stat. 4460; Aug. 22, 1996, P.L. 104-193, §108(c)(14), (15), §301(c)(3), (4), §§314, 315, 317, §§321, 323, 325(a), §331(a), §351, §§364, 365, 367-369, 372, 373, §382, §395(d)(1)(H), (2)(D), 110 Stat. 2166, 2200, 2212, 2220, 2221, 2222, 2224, 2227, 2239, 2249-2251, 2254, 2255, 2257, 2259, 2260; Aug. 5, 1997, P.L. 105-33, Ch 3, §§5532(i)(2), 5536-5539, 5544, 5550(a), 5551, 5556(a), (e), 111 Stat. 627, 629, 631, 633, 634, 637; July 16, 1998, P.L. 105-200, §§401(c)(1), 404(a), 406(a), 112 Stat. 661, 671; Dec. 14, 1999, P.L. 106-169, §401(f), (m), (n), 113 Stat. 1858, 1859.

§667. STATE GUIDELINES FOR CHILD SUPPORT AWARDS

(a) Establishment of guidelines; method.—Each State, as a condition for having its State plan approved under this part [42 U.S.C. §651 et seq.] must establish guidelines for child support award amounts within the State. The guidelines may be established by law or by judicial or administrative action, and shall be reviewed at least once every 4 years to ensure that their application results in the determination of appropriate child support award amounts.

(b) Availability of guidelines; rebuttable presumption.—

(1) The guidelines established pursuant to subsection (a) shall be made available to all judges and other officials who have the power to determine child support awards within such State.

(2) There shall be a rebuttable presumption, in any judicial or administrative proceeding for the award of child support, that the amount of the award which would result from the application of such guidelines is the correct amount of child support to be awarded. A written finding or specific finding on the record that the application of the guidelines would be unjust or inappropriate in a particular case, as determined under criteria established by the State, shall be sufficient to rebut the presumption in that case.

(c) Technical assistance to States; State to furnish Secretary with copies.—The Secretary shall furnish technical assistance to the States for establishing the guidelines, and each State shall furnish the Secretary with copies of its guidelines.

History of 42 U.S.C. §667: Aug. 14, 1935, ch 531, §467, as added Aug. 16, 1984, P.L. 98-378, §18(a), 98 Stat. 1321; Oct. 13, 1988, P.L. 100-485, §103(a), (b), 102 Stat. 2346.

CHAPTER 121. INTERNATIONAL CHILD ABDUCTION REMEDIES

§11601. FINDINGS & DECLARATIONS

(a) Findings.—The Congress makes the following findings:

(1) The international abduction or wrongful retention of children is harmful to their well-being.

(2) Persons should not be permitted to obtain custody of children by virtue of their wrongful removal or retention.

(3) International abductions and retentions of children are increasing, and only concerted cooperation pursuant to an international agreement can effectively combat this problem.

(4) The Convention on the Civil Aspects of International Child Abduction, done at The Hague on October 25, 1980, establishes legal rights and procedures for the prompt return of children who have been wrongfully removed or retained, as well as for securing the exercise of visitation rights. Children who are wrongfully removed or retained within the meaning of the Convention are to be promptly returned unless one of the narrow exceptions set forth in the Convention applies. The Convention provides a sound treaty framework to help resolve the problem of international abduction and retention of children and will deter such wrongful removals and retentions.

(b) Declarations.—The Congress makes the following declarations:

(1) It is the purpose of this Act to establish procedures for the implementation of the Convention in the United States.

(2) The provisions of this Act are in addition to and not in lieu of the provisions of the Convention.

(3) In enacting this Act the Congress recognizes—

(A) the international character of the Convention; and

(B) the need for uniform international interpretation of the Convention.

(4) The Convention and this Act empower courts in the United States to determine only rights under the Convention and not the merits of any underlying child custody claims.

History of 42 U.S.C. §11601: April 29, 1988, P.L. 100-300, §2, 102 Stat. 437.

§11602. DEFINITIONS

For the purposes of this Act—

(1) the term "applicant" means any person who, pursuant to the Convention, files an application with the United States Central Authority or a Central Authority of any other party to the Convention for the return of a child alleged to have been wrongfully removed or retained or for arrangements for organizing or securing the effective exercise of rights of access pursuant to the Convention;

(2) the term "Convention" means the Convention on the Civil Aspects of International Child Abduction, done at The Hague on October 25, 1980;

(3) the term "Parent Locator Service" means the service established by the Secretary of Health and Human Services under section 453 of the Social Security Act (42 U.S.C. 653);

(4) the term "petitioner" means any person who, in accordance with this Act, files a petition in court seeking relief under the Convention;

(5) the term "person" includes any individual, institution, or other legal entity or body;

(6) the term "respondent" means any person against whose interests a petition is filed in court, in accordance with this Act, which seeks relief under the Convention;

(7) the term "rights of access" means visitation rights;

(8) the term "State" means any of the several States, the District of Columbia, and any commonwealth, territory, or possession of the United States; and

(9) the term "United States Central Authority" means the agency of the Federal Government designated by the President under section 7(a) [42 U.S.C. §11606(a)].

History of 42 U.S.C. §11602: April 29, 1988, P.L. 100-300, §3, 102 Stat. 438.

§11603. JUDICIAL REMEDIES

(a) Jurisdiction of the courts.—The courts of the States and the United States district courts shall have concurrent original jurisdiction of actions arising under the Convention.

(b) Petitions.—Any person seeking to initiate judicial proceedings under the Convention for the return of a child or for arrangements for organizing or securing the effective exercise of rights of access to a child may do so by commencing a civil action by filing a petition for the relief sought in any court which has jurisdiction of such action and which is authorized to exercise its jurisdiction in the place where the child is located at the time the petition is filed.

(c) Notice.—Notice of an action brought under subsection (b) shall be given in accordance with the applicable law governing notice in interstate child custody proceedings.

(d) Determination of case.—The court in which an action is brought under subsection (b) shall decide the case in accordance with the Convention.

(e) Burdens of proof.—

(1) A petitioner in an action brought under subsection (b) shall establish by a preponderance of the evidence—

(A) in the case of an action for the return of a child, that the child has been wrongfully removed or retained within the meaning of the Convention; and

(B) in the case of an action for arrangements for organizing or securing the effective exercise of rights of access, that the petitioner has such rights.

(2) In the case of an action for the return of a child, a respondent who opposes the return of the child has the burden of establishing—

(A) by clear and convincing evidence that one of the exceptions set forth in article 13b or 20 of the Convention applies; and

(B) by a preponderance of the evidence that any other exception set forth in article 12 or 13 of the Convention applies.

(f) Application of the Convention.—For purposes of any action brought under this Act—

(1) the term "authorities", as used in article 15 of the Convention to refer to the authorities of the state of the habitual residence of a child, includes courts and appropriate government agencies;

(2) the terms "wrongful removal or retention" and "wrongfully removed or retained", as used in the Convention, include a removal or retention of a child before the entry of a custody order regarding that child; and

(3) the term "commencement of proceedings", as used in article 12 of the Convention, means, with respect to the return of a child located in the United States, the filing of a petition in accordance with subsection (b) of this section.

(g) Full faith and credit.—Full faith and credit shall be accorded by the courts of the States and the courts of the United States to the judgment of any other such court ordering or denying the return of a child, pursuant to the Convention, in an action brought under this Act.

(h) Remedies under Convention not exclusive.—The remedies established by the Convention and this Act shall be in addition to remedies available under other laws or international agreements.

History of 42 U.S.C. §11603: April 29, 1988, P.L. 100-300, §4, 102 Stat. 438.

§11604. PROVISIONAL REMEDIES

(a) Authority of courts.—In furtherance of the objectives of article 7(b) and other provisions of the Convention, and subject to the provisions of subsection (b) of this section, any court exercising jurisdiction of an action brought under section 4(b) of this Act [42 U.S.C. §11630(b)] may take or cause to be taken measures under Federal or State law, as appropriate, to protect the well-being of the child involved or to prevent the child's further removal or concealment before the final disposition of the petition.

(b) Limitation on authority.—No court exercising jurisdiction of an action brought under section 4(b) [42 U.S.C. §11603(b)] may, under subsection (a) of this section, order a child removed from a person having physical control of the child unless the applicable requirements of State law are satisfied.

History of 42 U.S.C. §11604: April 29, 1988, P.L. 100-300, §5, 102 Stat. 439.

§11605. ADMISSIBILITY OF DOCUMENTS

With respect to any application to the United States Central Authority, or any petition to a court under section 4 [42 U.S.C. §11603], which seeks relief under the Convention, or any other documents or information included with such application or petition or provided after such submission which relates to the application or petition, as the case may be, no authentication of such application, petition, document, or information shall be required in order for the application, petition, document, or information to be admissible in court.

History of 42 U.S.C. §11605: April 29, 1988, P.L. 100-300, §6, 102 Stat. 439.

§11606. UNITED STATES CENTRAL AUTHORITY

(a) Designation.—The President shall designate a Federal agency to serve as the Central Authority for the United States under the Convention.

(b) Functions.—The functions of the United States Central Authority are those ascribed to the Central Authority by the Convention and this Act.

(c) Regulatory authority.—The United States Central Authority is authorized to issue such regulations as may be necessary to carry out its functions under the Convention and this Act.

(d) Obtaining information from Parent Locator Service.—The United States Central Authority may, to the extent authorized by the Social Security Act [42 U.S.C. §301 et seq.], obtain information from the Parent Locator Service.

(e) Grant authority.—The United States Central Authority is authorized to make grants to, or enter into contracts or agreements with, any individual, corporation, other Federal, State, or local agency, or private entity or organization in the United States for purposes of accomplishing its responsibilities under the Convention and this Act.

History of 42 U.S.C. §11606: April 29, 1988, P.L. 100-300, §7, 102 Stat. 439.

§11607. COSTS & FEES

(a) Administrative costs.—No department, agency, or instrumentality of the Federal Government or of any State or local government may impose on an applicant any fee in relation to the administrative processing of applications submitted under the Convention.

(b) Costs incurred in civil actions.—

(1) Petitioners may be required to bear the costs of legal counsel or advisors, court costs incurred in connection with their petitions, and travel costs for the return of the child involved and any accompanying persons, except as provided in paragraphs (2) and (3).

(2) Subject to paragraph (3), legal fees or court costs incurred in connection with an action brought under section 4 [42 U.S.C. §11603] shall be borne by the petitioner unless they are covered by payments from Federal, State, or local legal assistance or other programs.

(3) Any court ordering the return of a child pursuant to an action brought under section 4 [42 U.S.C. §11603] shall order the respondent to pay necessary expenses incurred by or on behalf of the petitioner, including court costs, legal fees, foster home or other care during the course of proceedings in the action, and transportation costs related to the return of the child, unless the respondent establishes that such order would be clearly inappropriate.

History of 42 U.S.C. §11607: April 29, 1988, P.L. 100-300, §8, 102 Stat. 440.

§11608. COLLECTION, MAINTENANCE, & DISSEMINATION OF INFORMATION

(a) In general.—In performing its functions under the Convention, the United States Central Authority may, under such conditions as the Central Authority prescribes by regulation, but subject to subsection (c), receive from or transmit to any department, agency, or instrumentality of the Federal Government or of any State or foreign government, and receive from or transmit to any applicant, petitioner, or respondent, information necessary to locate a child or for the purpose of otherwise implementing the Convention with respect to a child, except that the United States Central Authority—

(1) may receive such information from a Federal or State department, agency, or instrumentality only pursuant to applicable Federal and State statutes; and

(2) may transmit any information received under this subsection notwithstanding any provision of law other than this Act.

(b) Requests for information.—Requests for information under this section shall be submitted in such manner and form as the United States Central Authority may prescribe by regulation and shall be accompanied or supported by such documents as the United States Central Authority may require.

(c) Responsibility of government entities.—Whenever any department, agency, or instrumentality of the United States or of any State receives a request from the United States Central Authority for information authorized to be provided to such Central Authority under subsection (a), the head of such department, agency, or instrumentality shall promptly cause a search to be made of the files and records maintained by such department, agency, or instrumentality in order to determine whether the information requested is contained in any such files or records. If such search discloses the information requested, the head of such department, agency, or instrumentality shall immediately transmit such information to the United States Central Authority, except that any such information the disclosure of which—

(1) would adversely affect the national security interests of the United States or the law enforcement interests of the United States or of any State; or

(2) would be prohibited by section 9 of title 13, United States Code; shall not be transmitted to the Central Authority. The head of such department, agency, or instrumentality shall, immediately upon completion of the requested search, notify the Central Authority of the results of the search, and whether an exception set forth in paragraph (1) or (2) applies. In the event that the United States Central Authority receives information and the appropriate Federal or State department, agency, or instrumentality thereafter notifies the Central Authority that an exception set forth in paragraph (1) or (2) applies to that information, the Central Authority may not disclose that information under subsection (a).

(d) Information available from Parent Locator Service.—To the extent that information which the United States Central Authority is authorized to obtain under the provisions of subsection (c) can be obtained through the Parent Locator Service, the United States Central Authority shall first seek to obtain such information from the Parent Locator Service, before requesting such information directly under the provisions of subsection (c) of this section.

(e) Recordkeeping.—The United States Central Authority shall maintain appropriate records concerning its activities and the disposition of cases brought to its attention.

History of 42 U.S.C. §11608: April 29, 1988, P.L. 100-300, §9, 102 Stat. 440.

§11608a. OFFICE OF CHILDREN'S ISSUES

(a) Director requirements.—The Secretary of State shall fill the position of Director of the Office of Children's Issues of the Department of State (in this section referred to as the "Office") with an individual of senior rank who can ensure long-term continuity in the management and policy matters of the Office and has a strong background in consular affairs.

(b) Case officer staffing.—Effective April 1, 2000, there shall be assigned to the Office of Children's Issues of the Department of State a sufficient number of case officers to ensure that the average caseload for each officer does not exceed 75.

(c) Embassy contact.—The Secretary of State shall designate in each United States diplomatic mission an employee who shall serve as the point of contact for matters relating to international abductions of children by parents. The Director of the Office shall regularly inform the designated employee of children of United States citizens abducted by parents to that country.

(d) Reports to parents.—

(1) In general.—Except as provided in paragraph (2), beginning 6 months after the date of enactment of this Act [enacted Nov. 29, 1999], and at least once every 6 months thereafter, the Secretary of State shall report to each parent who has requested assistance regarding an abducted child overseas. Each such report shall include information on the current status of the abducted child's case and the efforts by the Department of State to resolve the case.

(2) Exception.—The requirement in paragraph (1) shall not apply in a case of an abducted child if—

(A) the case has been closed and the Secretary of State has reported the reason the case was closed to the parent who requested assistance; or

(B) the parent seeking assistance requests that such reports not be provided.

History of 42 U.S.C. §11608A: Nov. 29, 1999, P.L. 106-113, Div B, §1000(a)(7), 113 Stat. 1536.

§11609. INTERAGENCY COORDINATING GROUP

The Secretary of State, the Secretary of Health and Human Services, and the Attorney General shall designate Federal employees and may, from time to time, designate private citizens to serve on an interagency coordinating group to monitor the operation of the Convention and to provide advice on its implementation to the United States Central Authority and other Federal agencies. This group shall meet from time to time at the request of the United States Central Authority. The agency in which the United States Central Authority is located is authorized to reimburse such private citizens for travel and other expenses incurred in participating at meetings of the interagency coordinating group at rates not to exceed those authorized under subchapter I of chapter 57 of title 5, United States Code [5 U.S.C. §5701 et seq.], for employees of agencies.

History of 42 U.S.C. §11609: April 29, 1988, P.L. 100-300, §10, 102 Stat. 441.

§11610. AUTHORIZATION OF APPROPRIATIONS

There are authorized to be appropriated for each fiscal year such sums as may be necessary to carry out the purposes of the Convention and this Act.

History of 42 U.S.C. §11610: April 29, 1988, P.L. 100-300, §12, 102 Stat. 442.

TITLE 50. WAR & NATIONAL DEFENSE

TITLE 50, APPENDIX—WAR & NATIONAL DEFENSE SOLDIERS' & SAILORS' CIVIL RELIEF ACT OF 1940

ARTICLE I. GENERAL PROVISIONS

§511. DEFINITIONS

(1) The term "person in the military service", the term "persons in military service", and the term "persons in the military service of the United States", as used in this Act [50 U.S.C. App. §501 et seq.], shall include the following persons and no others: All members of the Army of the United States, the United States Navy, the Marine Corps, the Air Force, the Coast Guard, and all officers of the Public Health Service detailed by proper authority for duty either with the Army or the Navy. The term "military service", as used in this Act [50 U.S.C. App. §501 et seq.], shall signify Federal service on active duty with any branch of service heretofore referred to or mentioned as well as training or education under the supervision of the United States preliminary to induction into the military service. The terms "active service" or "active duty" shall include the period during which a person in military service is absent from duty on account of sickness, wounds, leave, or other lawful cause.

(2) The term "period of military service", as used in this Act [50 U.S.C. App. §501 et seq.], means, in the case of any person, the period beginning on the date on which the person enters active service and ending on the date of the person's release from active service or death while in active service, but in no case later than the date when this Act [50 U.S.C. App. §501 et seq.] ceases to be in force.

(3) The term "person", when used in this Act [50 U.S.C. App. §501 et seq.], with reference to the holder of any right alleged to exist against a person in military service or against a person secondarily liable under such right, shall include individuals, partnerships, corporations, and any other forms of business association.

(4) The term "court", as used in this Act [50 U.S.C. App. §501 et seq.], shall include any court of competent jurisdiction of the United States or of any State, whether or not a court of record.

History of 50 U.S.C. App. §511: Oct. 17, 1940, ch 888, §101, 54 Stat. 1179; Oct. 24, 1972, P.L. 92-540, §504(1), 86 Stat. 1098; March 18, 1991, P.L. 102-12, §9(1), 105 Stat. 39.

§512. TERRITORIAL APPLICATION; JURISDICTION OF COURTS; FORM OF PROCEDURE

(1) The provisions of this Act [50 U.S.C. App. §501 et seq.] shall apply to the United States, the several States and Territories, the District of Columbia, and all territory subject to the jurisdiction of the United States and to proceedings commenced in any court therein, and shall be enforced through the usual forms of procedure obtaining in such courts or under such regulations as may be by them prescribed.

(2) When under this Act [50 U.S.C. App. §501 et seq.] any application is required to be made to a court in which no proceeding has already been commenced with respect to the matter, such application may be made to any court.

History of 50 U.S.C. App. §512: Oct. 17, 1940, ch 888, §102, 54 Stat. 1179; March 18, 1991, P.L. 102-12, §9(2), 105 Stat. 39.

§515. NOTICE OF BENEFITS TO PERSONS IN & PERSONS ENTERING MILITARY SERVICE

The Secretary of Defense and the Secretary of Transportation, with respect to the Coast Guard when it is not operating as a service in the Navy, shall ensure the giving of notice of the benefits accorded by this Act [50 U.S.C. App. §501 et seq.] to persons in and to persons entering military service. The Director of Selective Service shall cooperate with the Secretary of Defense and the Secretary of Transportation in carrying out the provisions of this section.

History of 50 U.S.C. App. §515: Oct. 17, 1940, ch 888, §105, as added Oct. 6, 1942, ch 581, §4, 56 Stat. 770; March 18, 1991, P.L. 102-12, §9(4), 105 Stat. 39.

ARTICLE II. GENERAL RELIEF

§520. DEFAULT JUDGMENTS; AFFIDAVITS; BONDS; ATTORNEYS FOR PERSONS IN SERVICE

(1) In any action or proceeding commenced in any court, if there shall be a default of any appearance by the defendant, the plaintiff, before entering judgment shall file in the court an affidavit setting forth facts showing that the defendant is not in military service. If unable to file such affidavit plaintiff shall in lieu thereof file an affidavit setting forth either that the defendant is in the military service or that plaintiff is not able to determine whether or not defendant is in such service. If an affidavit is not filed showing that the defendant is not in the military service, no judgment shall be entered without first securing an order of court directing such entry, and no such order shall be made if the defendant is in such service until after the court shall have appointed an attorney to represent defendant and protect his interest, and the court shall on application make such appointment. Unless it appears that the defendant is not in such service the court may require, as a condition before judgment is entered, that the plaintiff file a bond approved by the court conditioned to indemnify the defendant, if in military service, against any loss or damage that he may suffer by reason of any judgment should the judgment be thereafter set aside in whole or in part. And the court may make such other and further order or enter such judgment as in its opinion may be necessary to protect the rights of the defendant under this Act [50 U.S.C. App. §501 et seq.]. Whenever, under the laws applicable with respect to any court, facts may be evidenced, established, or proved by an unsworn statement, declaration, verification, or certificate, in writing, subscribed and certified or declared to be true under penalty of perjury, the filing of such an unsworn statement, declaration, verification, or certificate shall satisfy the requirement of this [subdivision] that facts be established by affidavit.

(2) Any person who shall make or use an affidavit required under this section, or a statement, declaration, verification, or certificate certified or declared to be true under penalty of perjury permitted under [subdivision] (1), knowing it to be false, shall be guilty of a misdemeanor and shall be punishable by imprisonment not to exceed one year or by fine not to exceed $1,000, or both.

(3) In any action or proceeding in which a person in military service is a party if such party does not personally appear therein or is not represented by an authorized attorney, the court may appoint an attorney to represent him; and in such case a like bond may be required and an order made to protect the rights of such person. But no attorney appointed under this Act [50 U.S.C. App. §501 et seq.] to protect a person in military service shall have power to waive any right of the person for whom he is appointed or bind him by his acts.

(4) If any judgment shall be rendered in any action or proceeding governed by this section against any person in military service during the period of such service or within thirty days thereafter, and it appears that such person was prejudiced by reason of his military service in making his defense thereto, such judgment may,

upon application, made by such person or his legal representative, not later than ninety days after the termination of such service, be opened by the court rendering the same and such defendant or his legal representative let in to defend; provided it is made to appear that the defendant has a meritorious or legal defense to the action or some part thereof. Vacating, setting aside, or reversing any judgment because of any of the provisions of this Act [50 U.S.C. App. §501 et seq.] shall not impair any right or title acquired by any bona fide purchaser for value under such judgment.

History of 50 U.S.C. App. §520: Oct. 17, 1940, ch 888, §200, 54 Stat. 1180; Sept. 8, 1960, P.L. 86-721, §§1, 2, 74 Stat. 820.

§521. STAY OF PROCEEDINGS WHERE MILITARY SERVICE AFFECTS CONDUCT THEREOF

At any stage thereof any action or proceeding in any court in which a person in military service is involved, either as plaintiff or defendant, during the period of such service or within sixty days thereafter may, in the discretion of the court in which it is pending, on its own motion, and shall, on application to it by such person or some person on his behalf, be stayed as provided in this Act [50 U.S.C. App. §501 et seq.], unless, in the opinion of the court, the ability of plaintiff to prosecute the action or the defendant to conduct his defense is not materially affected by reason of his military service.

History of 50 U.S.C. App. §521: Oct. 17, 1940, ch 888, §201, 54 Stat. 1181.

§525. STATUTES OF LIMITATIONS AS AFFECTED BY PERIOD OF SERVICE

The period of military service shall not be included in computing any period now or hereafter to be limited by any law, regulation, or order for the bringing of any action or proceeding in any court, board, bureau, commission, department, or other agency of government by or against any person in military service or by or against his heirs, executors, administrators, or assigns, whether such cause of action or the right or privilege to institute such action or proceeding shall have accrued prior to or during the period of such service, nor shall any part of such period which occurs after October 6, 1942 be included in computing any period now or hereafter provided by any law for the redemption of real property sold or forfeited to enforce any obligation, tax, or assessment.

History of 50 U.S.C. App. §525: Oct. 17, 1940, ch 888, §205, 54 Stat. 1181; Oct. 6, 1942, ch 581, §5, 56 Stat. 770; March 18, 1991, P.L. 102-12, §9(6), 105 Stat. 39.

§527. LIMITATIONS PRESCRIBED BY INTERNAL REVENUE LAWS AS AFFECTED BY PERIOD OF SERVICE

Section 205 of this Act [50 U.S.C. App. §525] shall not apply with respect to any period of limitation prescribed by or under the internal revenue laws of the United States.

History of 50 U.S.C. App. §527: Oct. 17, 1940, ch 888, §207, as added Oct. 21, 1942, ch 619, §507(b)(2)(B), 56 Stat. 964.

TITLE 26—INTERNAL REVENUE

Chapter I—Internal Revenue Service, Department of the Treasury (continued)

Computation of Taxable Income—Table of Contents

TITLE 26—INTERNAL REVENUE

CHAPTER I—INTERNAL REVENUE SERVICE, DEPARTMENT OF THE TREASURY (CONTINUED)

COMPUTATION OF TAXABLE INCOME—TABLE OF CONTENTS

CFR §1.71-1T ALIMONY & SEPARATE MAINTENANCE PAYMENTS (TEMPORARY)

Section 1.71T below does not reflect changes made by P.L 99-515 (1986).

(a) In general.

Q-1 What is the income tax treatment of alimony or separate maintenance payments?

A-1 Alimony or separate maintenance payments are, under section 71, included in the gross income of the payee spouse and, under section 215, allowed as a deduction from the gross income of the payor spouse.

Q-2 What is an alimony or separate maintenance payment?

A-2 An alimony or separate maintenance payment is any payment received by or on behalf of a spouse (which for this purpose includes a former spouse) of the payor under a divorce or separation instrument that meets all of the following requirements:

(a) The payment is in cash (see A-5).

(b) The payment is not designated as a payment which is excludible from the gross income of the payee and nondeductible by the payor (see A-8).

(c) In the case of spouses legally separated under a decree of divorce or separate maintenance, the spouses are not members of the same household at the time the payment is made (see A-9).

(d) The payor has no liability to continue to make any payment after the death of the payee (or to make any payment as a substitute for such payment) and the divorce or separation instrument states that there is no such liability (see A-10).

(e) The payment is not treated as child support (see A-15).

(f) To the extent that one or more annual payments exceed $10,000 during any of the 6-post-separation years, the payor is obligated to make annual payments in each of the 6-post-separation years (see A-19).

Q-3 In order to be treated as alimony or separate maintenance payments, must the payments be "periodic" as that term was defined prior to enactment of the Tax Reform Act of 1984 or be made in discharge of a legal obligation of the payor to support the payee arising out of a marital or family relationship?

A-3 No. The Tax Reform Act of 1984 replaces the old requirements with the requirements described in A-2 above. Thus, the requirements that alimony or separate maintenance payments be "periodic" and be made in discharge of a legal obligation to support arising out of a marital or family relationship have been eliminated.

Q-4 Are the instruments described in section 71(a) of prior law the same as divorce or separation instruments described in section 71, as amended by the Tax Reform Act of 1984?

A-4 Yes.

(b) Specific requirements.

Q-5 May alimony or separate maintenance payments be made in a form other than cash?

A-5 No. Only cash payments (including checks and money orders payable on demand) qualify as alimony or separate maintenance payments. Transfers of services or property (including a debt instrument of a third party or an annuity contract), execution of a debt instrument by the payor, or the use of property of the payor do not qualify as alimony or separate maintenance payments.

Q-6 May payments of cash to a third party on behalf of a spouse qualify as alimony or separate maintenance payments if the payments are pursuant to the terms of a divorce or separation instrument?

A-6 Yes. Assuming all other requirements are satisfied, a payment of cash by the payor spouse to a third party under the terms of the divorce or separation instrument will qualify as a payment of cash which is received "on behalf of a spouse". For example, cash payments of rent, mortgage, tax, or tuition liabilities of the payee spouse made under the terms of the divorce or separation instrument will qualify as alimony or separate maintenance payments. Any payments to maintain property owned by the payor spouse and used by the payee spouse (including mortgage payments, real estate taxes and insurance premiums) are not payments on behalf of a spouse even if those payments are made pursuant to the terms of the divorce or separation instrument. Premiums paid by the payor spouse for term or whole life insurance on the payor's life made under the terms of the divorce or separation instrument will qualify as payments on behalf of the payee spouse to the extent that the payee spouse is the owner of the policy.

Q-7 May payments of cash to a third party on behalf of a spouse qualify as alimony or separate maintenance payments if the payments are made to the third party at the written request of the payee spouse?

A-7 Yes. For example, instead of making an alimony or separate maintenance payment directly to the payee, the payor spouse may make a cash payment to a charitable organization if such payment is pursuant to the written request, consent or ratification of the payee spouse. Such request, consent or ratification must state that the parties intend the payment to be treated as an alimony or separate maintenance payment to the payee spouse subject to the rules of section 71, and must be received by the payor spouse prior to the date of filing of the payor's first return of tax for the taxable year in which the payment was made.

Q-8 How may spouses designate that payments otherwise qualifying as alimony or separate maintenance payments shall be excludible from the gross income of the payee and nondeductible by the payor?

A-8 The spouses may designate that payments otherwise qualifying as alimony or separate maintenance payments shall be nondeductible by the payor and excludible from gross income by the payee by so providing in a divorce or separation instrument (as defined in section 71(b)(2)). If the spouses have executed a written separation agreement (as described in section 71(b)(2)(B)), any writing signed by both spouses which designates otherwise qualifying alimony or separate maintenance payments as nondeductible and excludible and which refers to the written separation agreement will be treated as a written separation agreement (and thus a divorce or separation instrument) for purposes of the preceding sentence. If the spouses are subject to temporary support orders (as described in section 71(b)(2)(C)), the designation of otherwise qualifying alimony or separate payments as nondeductible and excludible must be made in the original or a subsequent temporary support order. A copy of the instrument containing the designation of payments as not alimony or separate maintenance payments must be attached to the payee's first filed return of tax (Form 1040) for each year in which the designation applies.

Q-9 What are the consequences if, at the time a payment is made, the payor and payee spouses are members of the same household?

A-9 Generally, a payment made at the time when the payor and payee spouses are members of the same household cannot qualify as an alimony or separate maintenance payment if the spouses are legally separated under a decree of divorce or of separate maintenance. For purposes of the preceding sentence, a dwelling unit formerly shared by both spouses shall not be considered two separate households even if the spouses physically separate themselves within the dwelling unit. The spouses will not be treated as members of the same household if one spouse is preparing to depart from the household of the other spouse, and does depart not more than one month after the date the payment is made. If the spouses are not legally separated under a decree of divorce or separate maintenance, a payment under a written separation agreement or a decree described in section 71(b)(2)(C) may qualify as an alimony or separate maintenance payment notwithstanding that the payor and payee are members of the same household at the time the payment is made.

Q-10 Assuming all other requirements relating to the qualification of certain payments as alimony or separate maintenance payments are met, what are the consequences if the payor spouse is required to continue to make the payments after the death of the payee spouse?

A-10 None of the payments before (or after) the death of the payee spouse qualify as alimony or separate maintenance payments.

Q-11 What are the consequences if the divorce or separation instrument fails to state that there is no liability for any period after the death of the payee spouse to continue to make any payments which would otherwise qualify as alimony or separate maintenance payments?

A-11 If the instrument fails to include such a statement, none of the payments, whether made before or after the death of the payee spouse, will qualify as alimony or separate maintenance payments.

Example (1).—A is to pay B $10,000 in cash each year for a period of 10 years under a divorce or separation instrument which does not state that the payments will terminate upon the death of B. None of the payments will qualify as alimony or separate maintenance payments.

Example (2).—A is to pay B $10,000 in cash each year for a period of 10 years under a divorce or separation instrument which states that the payments will terminate upon the death of B. In addition, under the instrument, A is to pay B or B's estate $20,000 in cash each year for a period of 10 years. Because the $20,000 annual payments will not terminate upon the death of B, these payments will not qualify as alimony or separate maintenance payments. However, the separate $10,000 annual payments will qualify as alimony or separate maintenance payments.

Q-12 Will a divorce or separation instrument be treated as stating that there is no liability to make payments after the death of the payee spouse if the liability to make such payments terminates pursuant to applicable local law or oral agreement?

A-12 No. Termination of the liability to make payments must be stated in the terms of the divorce or separation instrument.

Q-13 What are the consequences if the payor spouse is required to make one or more payments (in cash or property) after the death of the payee spouse as a substitute for the continuation of pre-death payments which would otherwise qualify as alimony or separate maintenance payments?

A-13 If the payor spouse is required to make any such substitute payments, none of the otherwise qualifying payments will qualify as alimony or separate maintenance payments. The divorce or separation instrument need not state, however, that there is no liability to make any such substitute payment.

Q-14 Under what circumstances will one or more payments (in cash or property) which are to occur after the death of the payee spouse be treated as a substitute for the continuation of payments which would otherwise qualify as alimony or separate maintenance payments?

A-14 To the extent that one or more payments are to begin to be made, increase in amount, or become accelerated in time as a result of the death of the payee spouse, such payments may be treated as a substitute for the continuation of payments terminating on the death of the payee spouse which would otherwise qualify as alimony or separate maintenance payments. The determination of whether or not such payments are a substitute for the continuation of payments which would otherwise qualify as alimony or separate maintenance payments, and of the amount of the otherwise qualifying alimony or separate maintenance payments for which any such payments are a substitute, will depend on all of the facts and circumstances.

Example (1).—Under the terms of a divorce decree, A is obligated to make annual alimony payments to B of $30,000, terminating on the earlier of the expiration of 6 years or the death of B. B maintains custody of the minor children of A and B. The decree provides that at the death of B, if there are minor children of A and B remaining, A will be obligated to make annual payments of $10,000 to a trust, the income and corpus of which are to be used for the benefit of the children until the youngest child attains the age of majority. These facts indicate that A's liability to make annual $10,000 payments in trust for the benefit of his minor children upon the death of B is a substitute for $10,000 of the $30,000 annual payments to B. Accordingly, $10,000 of each of the $30,000 annual payments to B will not qualify as alimony or separate maintenance payments.

Example (2).—Under the terms of a divorce decree, A is obligated to make annual alimony payments to B of $30,000, terminating on the earlier of the expiration of 15 years or the death of B. The divorce decree provides that if B dies before the expiration of the 15 year period, A will pay to B's estate the difference between the total amount that A would have paid had B survived, minus the amount actually paid. For example, if B dies at the end of the 10th year in which payments are made, A will pay to B's estate $150,000 ($450,000-$300,000). These facts indicate that A's liability to make a lump sum payment to B's estate upon the death of B is a substitute for the full amount of each of the annual $30,000 payments to B. Accordingly, none of the annual $30,000 payments to B will qualify as alimony or separate maintenance payments. The result would be the same if the lump sum payable at B's death were discounted by an appropriate interest factor to account for the prepayment.

(c) Child support payments.

Q-15 What are the consequences of a payment which the terms of the divorce or separation instrument fix as payable for the support of a child of the payor spouse?

A-15 A payment which under the terms of the divorce or separation instrument is fixed (or treated as fixed) as payable for the support of a child of the payor spouse does not qualify as an alimony or separate maintenance payment. Thus, such a payment is not deductible by the payor spouse or includible in the income of the payee spouse.

Q-16 When is a payment fixed (or treated as fixed) as payable for the support of a child of the payor spouse?

A-16 A payment is fixed as payable for the support of a child of the payor spouse if the divorce or separation instrument specifically designates some sum or portion (which sum or portion may fluctuate) as payable for the support of a child of the payor spouse. A payment will be treated as fixed as payable for the support of a child of the payor spouse if the payment is reduced (a) on the happening of a contingency relating to a child of the payor, or (b) at a time which can clearly be associated with such a contingency. A payment may be treated as fixed as payable for the support of a child of the payor spouse even if other separate payments specifically are designated as payable for the support of a child of the payor spouse.

Q-17 When does a contingency relate to a child of the payor?

A-17 For this purpose, a contingency relates to a child of the payor if it depends on any event relating to that child, regardless of whether such event is certain or likely to occur. Events that relate to a child of the payor include the following: the child's attaining a specified age or income level, dying, marrying, leaving school, leaving the spouse's household, or gaining employment.

Q-18 When will a payment be treated as to be reduced at a time which can clearly be associated with the happening of a contingency relating to a child of the payor?

A-18 There are two situations, described below, in which payments which would otherwise qualify as alimony or separate maintenance payments will be presumed to be reduced at a time clearly associated with the happening of a contingency relating to a child of the payor. In all other situations, reductions in payments will not be treated as clearly associated with the happening of a contingency relating to a child of the payor.

The first situation referred to above is where the payments are to be reduced not more than 6 months before or after the date the child is to attain the age of 18, 21, or local age of majority. The second situation is where the payments are to be reduced on two or more occasions which occur not more than one year before or after a different child of the payor spouse attains a certain age between the ages of 18 and 24, inclusive. The certain age referred to in the preceding sentence must be the same for each such child, but need not be a whole number of years.

The presumption in the two situations described above that payments are to be reduced at a time clearly associated with the happening of a contingency relating to a child of the payor may be rebutted (either by the Service or by taxpayers) by showing that the time at which the payments are to be reduced was determined independently of any contingencies relating to the children of the payor. The presumption in the first situation will be rebutted conclusively if the reduction is a complete cessation of alimony or separate maintenance payments during the sixth post-separation year (described in A-21) or upon the expiration of a 72-month period. The presumption may also be rebutted in other circumstances, for example, by showing that alimony payments are to be made for a period customarily provided in the local jurisdiction, such as a period equal to one-half the duration of the marriage.

Example.—A and B are divorced on July 1, 1985, when their children, C (born July 15, 1970) and D (born September 23, 1972), are 14 and 12, respectively. Under the divorce decree, A is to make alimony payments to B of $2,000 per month. Such payments are to be reduced to $1,500 per month on January 1, 1991 and to $1,000 per month on January 1, 1995. On January 1, 1991, the date of the first reduction in payments, C will be 20 years 5 months and 17 days old. On January 1, 1995, the date of the second reduction in payments, D will be 22 years 3 months and 9 days old. Each of the reductions in payments is to occur not more than one year before or after a different child of A attains the age of 21 years and 4 months. (Actually, the reductions are to occur not more than one year before or after C and D attain any of the ages 21 years 3 months and 9 days through 21 years 5 months and 17 days.) Accordingly, the reductions will be presumed to clearly be associated with the happening of a contingency relating to C and D. Unless this presumption is rebutted, payments under the divorce decree equal to the sum of the reduction ($1,000 per month) will be treated as fixed for the support of the children of A and therefore will not qualify as alimony or separate maintenance payments.

(d) Excess front-loading rules.

Q-19 What are the excess front-loading rules?

A-19 The excess front-loading rules are two special rules which may apply to the extent that payments in any calendar year exceed $10,000. The first rule is a minimum term rule, which must be met in order for any annual payment, to the extent in excess of $10,000, to qualify as an alimony or separate maintenance payment (see A-2(f)). This rule requires that alimony or separate maintenance payments be called for, at a minimum, during the 6 "post-separation years". The second rule is a recapture rule which characterizes payments retrospectively by requiring a recalculation and inclusion in income by the payor and deduction by the payee of previously paid alimony or separate maintenance payment to the extent that the amount of such payments during any of the 6 "post-separation years" falls short of the amount of payments during a prior year by more than $10,000.

Q-20 Do the excess front-loading rules apply to payments to the extent that annual payments never exceed $10,000?

A-20 No. For example, A is to make a single $10,000 payment to B. Provided that the other requirements of section 71 are met, the payment will qualify as an alimony or separate maintenance payment. If A were to make a single $15,000 payment to B, $10,000 of the payment would qualify as an alimony or separate maintenance payment and $5,000 of the payment would be disqualified under the minimum term rule because payments were not to be made for the minimum period.

Q-21 Do the excess front-loading rules apply to payments received under a decree described in section 71(b)(2)(C)?

A-21 No. Payments under decrees described in section 71(b)(2)(C) are to be disregarded entirely for purposes of applying the excess front-loading rules.

Q-22 Both the minimum term rule and the recapture rule refer to 6 "post-separation years". What are the 6 "post separation years"?

A-22 The 6 "post-separation years" are the 6 consecutive calendar years beginning with the first calendar year in which the payor pays to the payee an alimony or separate maintenance payment (except a payment made under a decree described in section 71(b)(2)(C)). Each year within this period is referred to as a "post-separation year". The 6-year period need not commence with the year in which the spouses separate or divorce, or with the year in which payments under the divorce or separation instrument are made, if no payments during such year qualify as alimony or separate maintenance payments. For example, a decree for the divorce of A and B is entered in October, 1985. The decree requires A to make monthly payments to B commencing November 1, 1985, but A and B are members of the same household until February 15, 1986 (and as a result, the payments prior to January 16, 1986, do not qualify as alimony payments). For purposes of applying the excess front-loading rules to payments from A to B, the 6 calendar years 1986 through 1991 are post-separation years. If a spouse has been making payments pursuant to a divorce or separation instrument described in section 71(b)(2) (A) or (B), a modification of the instrument or the substitution of a new instrument (for example, the substitution of a divorce decree for a written separation agreement) will not result in the creation of additional post-separation years. However, if a spouse has been making payments pursuant to a divorce or separation instrument described in section 71(b)(2)(C), the 6-year period does not begin until the first calendar year in which alimony or separate maintenance payments are made under a divorce or separation instrument described in section 71(b)(2) (A) or (B).

Q-23 How does the minimum term rule operate?

A-23 The minimum term rule operates in the following manner. To the extent payments are made in excess of $10,000, a payment will qualify as an alimony or separate maintenance payment only if alimony or separate maintenance payments are to be made in each of the 6 post-separation years. For example, pursuant to a divorce decree, A is to make alimony payments to B of $20,000 in each of the 5 calendar years 1985 through 1989. A is to make no payment in 1990. Under the minimum term rule, only $10,000 will qualify as an alimony payment in each of the calendar years 1985 through 1989. If the divorce decree also required A to make a $1 payment in 1990, the minimum term rule would be satisfied and $20,000 would be treated as an alimony payment in each of the calendar years 1985 through 1989. The recapture rule would, however, apply for 1990. For purposes of determining whether alimony or separate maintenance payments are to be made in any year, the possible termination of such payments upon the happening of a contingency (other than the passage of time) which has not yet occurred is ignored (unless such contingency may cause all or a portion of the payment to be treated as a child support payment).

Q-24 How does the recapture rule operate?

A-24 The recapture rule operates in the following manner. If the amount of alimony or separate maintenance payments paid in any post-separation year (referred to as the "computation year") falls short of the amount of alimony or separate maintenance payments paid in any prior post-separation year by more than $10,000, the payor must compute an "excess amount" for the computation year. The excess amount for any computation year is the sum of excess amounts determined with respect to each prior post-separation year. The excess amount determined with respect to a prior post-separation year is the excess of (1) the amount of alimony or separate maintenance payments paid by the payor spouse during such prior post-separation year, over (2) the amount of the alimony or separate maintenance payments paid by the payor spouse during the computation year plus $10,000. For purposes of this calculation, the amount of alimony or separate maintenance payments made by the payor spouse during any post-separation year preceding the computation year is reduced by any excess amount previously determined with respect to such year. The rules set forth above may be illustrated by the following example. A makes alimony payments to B of $25,000 in 1985 and $12,000 in 1986. The excess amount with respect to 1985 that is recaptured in 1986 is $3,000 ($25,000-($12,000+$10,000)). For purposes of subsequent computation years, the amount deemed paid in 1985 is $22,000. If A makes alimony payments to B of $1,000 in 1987, the excess amount that is recaptured in 1987 will be $12,000. This is the sum of an $11,000 excess amount with respect to 1985 ($22,000-$1,000+$10,000)) and a $1,000 excess amount with respect to 1986 ($12,000-($1,000+$10,000)). If, prior to the end of 1990, payments decline further, additional recapture will occur. The payor spouse must include the excess amount in gross income for his/her taxable year beginning with or in the computation year. The payee spouse is allowed a deduction for the excess amount in computing adjusted gross income for his/her taxable year beginning with or in the computation year. However, the payee spouse must compute the excess amount by reference to the date when payments were made and not when payments were received.

Q-25 What are the exceptions to the recapture rule?

A-25 Apart from the $10,000 threshold for application of the recapture rule, there are three exceptions to the recapture rule. The first exception is for payments received under temporary support orders described in section 71(b)(2)(C) (see A-21). The second exception is for any payment made pursuant to a continuing liability over the period of the post-separation years to pay a fixed portion of the payor's income from a business or property or from compensation for employment or self-employment. The third exception is where the alimony or separate maintenance payments in any post- separation year cease by reason of the death of the payor or payee or the remarriage (as defined under applicable local law) of the payee before the close of the computation year. For example, pursuant to a divorce decree, A is to make cash payments to B of $30,000 in each of the calendar years 1985 through 1990. A makes cash payments of $30,000 in 1985 and $15,000 in 1986, in which year B remarries and A's alimony payments cease. The recapture rule does not apply for 1986 or any subsequent year. If alimony or separate maintenance payments made by A decline or cease during a post-separation year for any other reason (including a failure by the payor to make timely payments, a modification of the divorce or separation instrument, a reduction in the support needs of the payee, or a reduction in the ability of the payor to provide support) excess amounts with respect to prior post-separation years will be subject to recapture.

(e) Effective dates.

Q-26 When does section 71, as amended by the Tax Reform Act of 1984, become effective?

A-26 Generally, section 71, as amended, is effective with respect to divorce or separation instruments (as defined in section 71(b)(2)) executed after December 31, 1984. If a decree of divorce or separate maintenance executed after December 31, 1984, incorporates or adopts without change the terms of the alimony or separate maintenance payments under a divorce or separation instrument executed before January 1, 1985, such decree will be treated as executed before January 1, 1985. A change in the amount of alimony or separate maintenance payments or the time period over which such payments are to continue, or the addition or deletion of any contingencies or conditions relating to such payments is a change in the terms of the alimony or separate maintenance payments. For example, in November 1984, A and B executed a written separation agreement. In February 1985, a decree of divorce is entered in substitution for the written separation agreement. The decree of divorce does not change the terms of the alimony A pays to B. The decree of divorce will be treated as executed before January 1, 1985 and hence alimony payments under the decree will be subject to the rules of section 71 prior to amendment by the Tax Reform Act of 1984. If the amount or time period of the alimony or separate maintenance payments are not specified in the pre-1985 separation agreement or if the decree of divorce changes the amount or term of such payments, the decree of divorce will not be treated as executed before January 1, 1985, and alimony payments under the decree will be subject to the rules of section 71, as amended by the Tax Reform Act of 1984.

Section 71, as amended, also applies to any divorce or separation instrument executed (or treated as executed) before January 1, 1985 that has been modified on or after January 1, 1985, if such modification expressly provides that section 71, as amended by the Tax Reform Act of 1984, shall apply to the instrument as modified. In this case, section 71, as amended, is effective with respect to payments made after the date the instrument is modified.

History of 26 CFR §1.71-1T: 49 FR 34455, Aug. 31, 1984; 49 FR 36645, Sept. 19, 1984.

CFR §1.152-4T DEPENDENCY EXEMPTION IN THE CASE OF A CHILD OF DIVORCED PARENTS, ETC. (TEMPORARY)

(a) In general.

Q-1 Which parent may claim the dependency exemption in the case of a child of divorced or separated parents?

A-1 Provided the parents together would have been entitled to the dependency exemption had they been married and filing a joint return, the parent having custody of a child for the greater portion of the year (the custodial parent) will generally be entitled to the dependency exemption. This rule applies to parents not living together during the last 6 months of the calendar year, as well as those divorced or separated under a separation agreement.

Q-2 Are there any exceptions to the general rule in A-1?

A-2 Yes, there are three exceptions. The general rule does not apply (i) if a multiple support agreement is in effect (see section 152(c)), (ii) if a decree or agreement executed prior to January 1, 1985 provides that the custodial parent has agreed to release his or her claim to the dependency exemption to the noncustodial parent and the noncustodial parent provides at least $600 of support to the child (see section 152(e)(4)), or (iii) if the custodial parent relinquishes the exemption in the manner described in A-3.

Q-3 How may the exemption for a dependent child be claimed by a noncustodial parent?

A-3 A noncustodial parent may claim the exemption for a dependent child only if the noncustodial parent attaches to his/her income tax return for the year of the exemption a written declaration from the custodial parent stating that he/she will not claim the child as a dependent for the taxable year beginning in such calendar year. The written declaration may be made on a form to be provided by the Service for this purpose. Once the Service has released the form, any declaration made other than on the official form shall conform to the substance of such form.

Q-4 For what period may a custodial parent release to the noncustodial parent a claim to the exemption for a dependent child?

A-4 The exemption may be released for a single year, for a number of specified years (for example, alternate years), or for all future years, as specified in the declaration. If the exemption is released for more than one year, the original release must be attached to the return of the noncustodial spouse and a copy of such release must be attached to his/her return for each succeeding taxable year for which he/she claims the dependency exemption.

Q-5 May only the custodial parent claim a deduction under section 213(d) for medical expenses paid by the parent or an income exclusion under section 105(b) for medical expenses paid by an employer for a dependent child?

A-5 No. Under the new rules, if a child receives over half of his support during the calendar year from his parents who are divorced or legally separated under a decree of divorce or separate maintenance, or who are separated under a written separation agreement, that child will be treated as a dependent of both parents for purposes of sections 105(b) and 213(d). Thus, a parent can deduct medical expenses paid by that parent for a child even though a dependency exemption for the child is claimed by the other parent. The special rule of sections 105(b) and 213(d) does not apply where over half of the support of a child is treated as having been received from a person under the provisions of section 152(c) (relating to multiple support agreements).

Q-6 When does section 152(e), as amended by the Tax Reform Act of 1984, become effective?

A-6 Section 152(e), as amended, is effective with respect to dependency exemptions for taxable years beginning after December 31, 1984.

History of 26 CFR §1.152-4T: 49 FR 34459, Aug. 31, 1984.

PART 1—INCOME TAXES

CFR §1.215-1 PERIODIC ALIMONY, ETC., PAYMENTS

(a) A deduction is allowable under section 215 with respect to periodic payments in the nature of, or in lieu of, alimony or an allowance for support actually paid by the taxpayer during his taxable year and required to be included in the income of the payee wife or former wife, as the case may be, under section 71. As to the amounts required to be included in the income of such wife or former wife, see section 71 and the regulations thereunder. For definition of husband and wife see section 7701(a) (17).

(b) The deduction under section 215 is allowed only to the obligor spouse. It is not allowed to an estate, trust, corporation, or any other person who may pay the alimony obligation of such obligor spouse. The obligor spouse, however, is not allowed a deduction for any periodic payment includible under section 71 in the income of the wife or former wife, which payment is attributable to property transferred in discharge of his obligation and which, under section 71(d) or section 682, is not includible in his gross income.

(c) The following examples, in which both H and W file their income tax returns on the basis of a calendar year, illustrate cases in which a deduction is or is not allowed under section 215:

Example (1).—Pursuant to the terms of a decree of divorce, H, in 1956, transferred securities valued at $100,000 in trust for the benefit of W, which fully discharged all his obligations to W. The periodic payments made by the trust to W are required to be included in W's income under section 71. Such payments are stated in section 71(d) not to be includible in H's income and, therefore, under section 215 are not deductible from his income.

Example (2).—A decree of divorce obtained by W from H incorporated a previous agreement of H to establish a trust, the trustees of which were instructed to pay W $5,000 a year for the remainder of her life. The court retained jurisdiction to order H to provide further payments if necessary for the support of W. In 1956 the trustee paid to W $4,000 from the income of the trust and $1,000 from the corpus of the trust. Under the provisions of sections 71 and 682(b), W would include $5,000 in her income for 1956. H would not include any part of the $5,000 in his income nor take a deduction therefore. If H had paid the $1,000 to W pursuant to court order rather than allowing the trustees to pay it out of corpus, he would have been entitled to a deduction of $1,000 under the provisions of section 215.

(d) For other examples, see sections 71 and 682 and the regulations thereunder.

CFR §1.215-1T ALIMONY, ETC., PAYMENTS (TEMPORARY)

Q-1 What information is required by the Internal Revenue Service when an alimony or separate maintenance payment is claimed as a deduction by a payor?

A-1 The payor spouse must include on his/her first filed return of tax (Form 1040) for the taxable year in which the payment is made the payee's social security number, which the payee is required to furnish to the payor. For penalties applicable to a payor spouse who fails to include such information on his/her return of tax or to a payee spouse who fails to furnish his/her social security number to the payor spouse, see section 6676.

History of 26 CFR §1.215-1T: 49 FR 34458, Aug. 31, 1984.

CFR §1.1041-1T. TREATMENT OF TRANSFER OF PROPERTY BETWEEN SPOUSES OR INCIDENT TO DIVORCE (TEMPORARY)

Q-1 How is the transfer of property between spouses treated under section 1041?

A-1 Generally, no gain or loss is recognized on a transfer of property from an individual to (or in trust for the benefit of) a spouse or, if the transfer is incident to a divorce, a former spouse. The following questions and answers describe more fully the scope, tax consequences and other rules which apply to transfers of property under section 1041.

(a) Scope of section 1041 in general.

Q-2 Does section 1041 apply only to transfers of property incident to divorce?

A-2 No. Section 1041 is not limited to transfers of property incident to divorce. Section 1041 applies to any transfer of property between spouses regardless of whether the transfer is a gift or is a sale or exchange between spouses acting at arm's length (including a transfer in exchange for the relinquishment of property or marital rights or an exchange otherwise governed by another nonrecognition provision of the Code). A divorce or legal separation need not be contemplated between the spouses at the time of the transfer nor must a divorce or legal separation ever occur.

Example (1).—A and B are married and file a joint return. A is the sole owner of a condominium unit. A sale or gift of the condominium from A to B is a transfer which is subject to the rules of section 1041.

Example (2).—A and B are married and file separate returns. A is the owner of an independent sole proprietorship, X Company. In the ordinary course of business, X Company makes a sale of property to B. This sale is a transfer of property between spouses and is subject to the rules of section 1041.

Example (3).—Assume the same facts as in example (2), except that X Company is a corporation wholly owned by A. This sale is not a sale between spouses subject to the rules of section 1041. However, in appropriate circumstances, general tax principles, including the step-transaction doctrine, may be applicable in recharacterizing the transaction.

Q-3 Do the rules of section 1041 apply to a transfer between spouses if the transferee spouse is a nonresident alien?

A-3 No. Gain or loss (if any) is recognized (assuming no other nonrecognition provision applies) at the time of a transfer of property if the property is transferred to a spouse who is a nonresident alien.

Q-4 What kinds of transfers are governed by section 1041?

A-4 Only transfers of property (whether real or personal, tangible or intangible) are governed by section 1041. Transfers of services are not subject to the rules of section 1041.

Q-5 Must the property transferred to a former spouse have been owned by the transferor spouse during the marriage?

A-5 No. A transfer of property acquired after the marriage ceases may be governed by section 1041.

(b) Transfer incident to the divorce.

Q-6 When is a transfer of property incident to the divorce?

A-6 A transfer of property is incident to the divorce in either of the following 2 circumstances—

(1) The transfer occurs not more than one year after the date on which the marriage ceases, or

(2) The transfer is related to the cessation of the marriage.

Thus, a transfer of property occurring not more than one year after the date on which the marriage ceases need not be related to the cessation of the marriage to qualify for section 1041 treatment. (See A-7 for transfers occurring more than one year after the cessation of the marriage.)

Q-7 When is a transfer of property *related to the cessation of the marriage*?

A-7 A transfer of property is treated as related to the cessation of the marriage if the transfer is pursuant to a divorce or separation instrument, as defined in section 71(b)(2), and the transfer occurs not more than 6 years after the date on which the marriage ceases. A divorce or separation instrument includes a modification or amendment to such decree or instrument. Any transfer not pursuant to a divorce or separation instrument and any transfer occurring more than 6 years after the cessation of the marriage is presumed to be not related to the cessation of the marriage. This presumption may be rebutted only by showing that the transfer was made to effect the division of property owned by the former spouses at the time of the cessation of the marriage. For example, the presumption may be rebutted by showing that (a) the transfer was not made within the one- and six-year periods described above because of factors which hampered an earlier transfer of the property, such as legal or business impediments to transfer or disputes concerning the value of the property owned at the time of the cessation of the marriage, and (b) the transfer is effected promptly after the impediment to transfer is removed.

Q-8 Do annulments and the cessations of marriages that are void ab initio due to violations of state law constitute divorces for purposes of section 1041?

A-8 Yes.

(c) Transfers on behalf of a spouse.

Q-9 May transfers of property to third parties on behalf of a spouse (or former spouse) qualify under section 1041?

A-9 Yes. There are three situations in which a transfer of property to a third party on behalf of a spouse (or former spouse) will qualify under section 1041, provided all other requirements of the section are satisfied. The first situation is where the transfer to the third party is required by a divorce or separation instrument. The second situation is where the transfer to the third party is pursuant to the written request of the other spouse (or former spouse). The third situation is where the transferor receives from the other spouse (or former spouse) a written consent or ratification of the transfer to the third party. Such consent or ratification must state that the parties intend the transfer to be treated as a transfer to the nontransferring spouse (or former spouse) subject to the rules of section 1041 and must be received by the transferor prior to the date of filing of the transferor's first return of tax for the taxable year in which the transfer was made. In the three situations described above, the transfer of property will be treated as made directly to the nontransferring spouse (or former spouse) and the nontransferring spouse will be treated as immediately transferring the property to the third party. The deemed transfer from the nontransferring spouse (or former spouse) to the third party is not a transaction that qualifies for nonrecognition of gain under section 1041.

(d) Tax consequences of transfers subject to section 1041.

Q-10 How is the transferor of property under section 1041 treated for income tax purposes?

A-10 The transferor of property under section 1041 recognizes no gain or loss on the transfer even if the transfer was in exchange for the release of marital rights or other consideration. This rule applies regardless of whether the transfer is of property separately owned by the transferor or is a division (equal or unequal) of community property. Thus, the result under section 1041 differs from the result in *United States v. Davis*, 370 U.S. 65 (1962).

Q-11 How is the transferee of property under section 1041 treated for income tax purposes?

A-11 The transferee of property under section 1041 recognizes no gain or loss upon receipt of the transferred property. In all cases, the basis of the transferred property in the hands of the transferee is the adjusted basis of such property in the hands of the transferor immediately before the transfer. Even if the transfer is a bona fide sale, the transferee does not acquire a basis in the transferred property equal to the transferee's cost (the fair market value). This carryover basis rule applies whether the adjusted basis of the transferred property is less than, equal to, or greater than its fair market value at the time of transfer (or the value of any consideration provided by the transferee) and applies for purposes of determining loss as well as gain upon the subsequent disposition of the property by the transferee. Thus, this rule is different from the rule applied in section 1015(a) for determining the basis of property acquired by gift.

Q-12 Do the rules described in A-10 and A-11 apply even if the transferred property is subject to liabilities which exceed the adjusted basis of the property?

A-12 Yes. For example, assume A owns property having a fair market value of $10,000 and an adjusted basis of $1,000. In contemplation of making a transfer of this property incident to a divorce from B, A borrows $5,000 from a bank, using the property as security for the borrowing. A then transfers the property to B and B assumes, or takes the property subject to, the liability to pay the $5,000 debt. Under section 1041, A recognizes no gain or loss upon the transfer of the property, and the adjusted basis of the property in the hands of B is $1,000.

Q-13 Will a transfer under section 1041 result in a recapture of investment tax credits with respect to the property transferred?

A-13 In general, no. Property transferred under section 1041 will not be treated as being disposed of by, or ceasing to be section 38 property with respect to, the transferor. However, the transferee will be subject to investment tax credit recapture if, upon or after the transfer, the property is disposed of by, or ceases to be section 38 property with respect to, the transferee. For example, as part of a divorce property settlement, B receives a car from A that has been used in A's business for two years and for which an investment tax credit was taken by A. No part of A's business is transferred to B and B's use of the car is solely personal. B is subject to recapture of the investment tax credit previously taken by A.

(e) Notice and recordkeeping requirement with respect to transactions under section 1041.

Q-14 Does the transferor of property in a transaction described in section 1041 have to supply, at the time of the transfer, the transferee with records sufficient to determine the adjusted basis and holding period of the property at the time of the transfer and (if applicable) with notice that the property transferred under section 1041 is potentially subject to recapture of the investment tax credit?

A-14 Yes. A transferor of property under section 1041 must, at the time of the transfer, supply the transferee with records sufficient to determine the adjusted basis and holding period of the property as of the date of the transfer. In addition, in the case of a transfer of property which carries with it a potential liability for investment tax credit recapture, the transferor must, at the time of the transfer, supply the transferee with records sufficient to determine the amount and period of such potential liability. Such records must be preserved and kept accessible by the transferee.

(f) Property settlements—effective dates, transitional periods and elections.

Q-15 When does section 1041 become effective?

A-15 Generally, section 1041 applies to all transfers after July 18, 1984. However, it does not apply to transfers after July 18, 1984 pursuant to instruments in effect on or before July 18, 1984. (See A-16 with respect to exceptions to the general rule.)

Q-16 Are there any exceptions to the general rule stated in A-15 above?

A-16 Yes. Two transitional rules provide exceptions to the general rule stated in A-15. First, section 1041 will apply to transfers after July 18, 1984 under instruments that were in effect on or before July 18, 1984 if both spouses (or former spouses) elect to have section 1041 apply to such transfers. Second, section 1041 will apply to all transfers after December 31, 1983 (including transfers under instruments in effect on or before July 18, 1984) if both spouses (or former spouses) elect to have section 1041 apply. (See A-18 relating to the time and manner of making the elections under the first or second transitional rule.)

Q-17 Can an election be made to have section 1041 apply to some, but not all, transfers made after December 31, 1983, or some but not all, transfers made after July 18, 1984 under instruments in effect on or before July 18, 1984?

A-17 No. Partial elections are not allowed. An election under either of the two elective transitional rules applies to all transfers governed by that election whether before or after the election is made, and is irrevocable.

(g) Property settlements—time and manner of making the elections under section 1041.

Q-18 How do spouses (or former spouses) elect to have section 1041 apply to transfers after December 31, 1983, or to transfers after July 18, 1984 under instruments in effect on or before July 18, 1984?

A-18 In order to make an election under section 1041 for property transfers after December 31, 1983, or property transfers under instruments that were in effect on or before July 18, 1984, both spouses (or former spouses) must elect the application of the rules of section 1041 by attaching to the transferor's first filed income tax return for the taxable year in which the first transfer occurs, a statement signed by both spouses (or former spouses) which includes each spouse's social security number and is in substantially the form set forth at the end of this answer.

In addition, the transferor must attach a copy of such statement to his or her return for each subsequent taxable year in which a transfer is made that is governed by the transitional election. A copy of the signed statement must be kept by both parties.

The election statements shall be in substantially the following form:

In the case of an election regarding transfers after 1983:

Section 1041 Election

The undersigned hereby elect to have the provisions of section 1041 of the Internal Revenue Code apply to all qualifying transfers of property after December 31, 1983. The undersigned understand that section 1041 applies to all property transferred between spouses, or former spouses incident to divorce. The parties further understand that the effects for Federal income tax purposes of having section 1041 apply are that (1) no gain or loss is recognized by the transferor spouse or former spouse as a result of this transfer; and (2) the basis of the transferred property in the hands of the transferee is the adjusted basis of the property in the hands of the transferor immediately before the transfer, whether or not the adjusted basis of the transferred property is less than, equal to, or greater than its fair market value at the time of the transfer. The undersigned understand that if the transferee spouse or former spouse disposes of the property in a transaction in which gain is recognized, the amount of gain which is taxable may be larger than it would have been if this election had not been made.

In the case of an election regarding preexisting decrees:

Section 1041 Election

The undersigned hereby elect to have the provisions of section 1041 of the Internal Revenue Code apply to all qualifying transfers of property after July 18, 1984 under any instrument in effect on or before July 18, 1984. The undersigned understand that section 1041 applies to all property transferred between spouses, or former spouses incident to the divorce. The parties further understand that the effects for Federal income tax purposes of having section 1041 apply are that (1) no gain or loss is recognized by the transferor spouse or former spouse as a result of this transfer; and (2) the basis of the transferred property in the hands of the transferee is the adjusted basis of the property in the hands of the transferor immediately before the transfer, whether or not the adjusted basis of the transferred property is less than, equal to, or greater than its fair market value at the time of the transfer. The undersigned understand that if the transferee spouse or former spouse disposes of the property in a transaction in which gain is recognized, the amount of gain which is taxable may be larger than it would have been if this election had not been made.

History of 26 CFR §1.4041-1T: 49 FR 34452, Aug. 31, 1984.

HAGUE CONFERENCE ON PRIVATE INTERNATIONAL LAW

CONVENTION ON THE CIVIL ASPECTS OF INTERNATIONAL CHILD ABDUCTION

The States signatory to the present Convention,

Firmly convinced that the interests of children are of paramount importance in matters relating to their custody,

Desiring to protect children internationally from the harmful effects of their wrongful removal or retention and to establish procedures to ensure their prompt return to the State of their habitual residence, as well as to secure protection for rights of access,

Have resolved to conclude a Convention to this effect, and have agreed upon the following provisions –

CHAPTER I — SCOPE OF THE CONVENTION

Article 1

The objects of the present Convention are—

a) to secure the prompt return of children wrongfully removed to or retained in any Contracting State; and

b) to ensure that rights of custody and of access under the law of one Contracting State are effectively respected in the other Contracting States.

Article 2

Contracting States shall take all appropriate measures to secure within their territories the implementation of the objects of the Convention. For this purpose they shall use the most expeditious procedures available.

Article 3

The removal or the retention of a child is to be considered wrongful where—

a) it is in breach of rights of custody attributed to a person, an institution or any other body, either jointly or alone, under the law of the State in which the child was habitually resident immediately before the removal or retention; and

b) at the time of removal or retention those rights were actually exercised, either jointly or alone, or would have been so exercised but for the removal or retention.

The rights of custody mentioned in sub-paragraph a) above, may arise in particular by operation of law or by reason of a judicial or administrative decision, or by reason of an agreement having legal effect under the law of that State.

Article 4

The Convention shall apply to any child who was habitually resident in a Contracting State immediately before any breach of custody or access rights. The Convention shall cease to apply when the child attains the age of 16 years.

Article 5

For the purposes of this Convention—

a) "rights of custody" shall include rights relating to the care of the person of the child and, in particular, the right to determine the child's place of residence;

b) "rights of access" shall include the right to take a child for a limited period of time to a place other than the child's habitual residence.

CHAPTER II — CENTRAL AUTHORITIES

Article 6

A Contracting State shall designate a Central Authority to discharge the duties which are imposed by the Convention upon such authorities.

Federal States, States with more than one system of law or States having autonomous territorial organizations shall be free to appoint more than one Central Authority and to specify the territorial extent of their powers. Where a State has appointed more than one Central Authority, it shall designate the Central Authority to which applications may be addressed for transmission to the appropriate Central Authority within that State.

Article 7

Central Authorities shall co-operate with each other and promote co-operation amongst the competent authorities in their respective State to secure the prompt return of children and to achieve the other objects of this Convention.

In particular, either directly or through any intermediary, they shall take all appropriate measures—

a) to discover the whereabouts of a child who has been wrongfully removed or retained;

b) to prevent further harm to the child or prejudice to interested parties by taking or causing to be taken provisional measures;

c) to secure the voluntary return of the child or to bring about an amicable resolution of the issues;

d) to exchange, where desirable, information relating to the social background of the child;

e) to provide information of a general character as to the law of their State in connection with the application of the Convention;

f) to initiate or facilitate the institution of judicial or administrative proceedings with a view to obtaining the return of the child and, in a proper case, to make arrangements for organizing or securing the effective exercise of rights of access;

g) where the circumstances so require, to provide or facilitate the provision of legal aid and advice, including the participation of legal counsel and advisers;

h) to provide such administrative arrangements as may be necessary and appropriate to secure the safe return of the child;

i) to keep each other informed with respect to the operation of this Convention and, as far as possible, to eliminate any obstacles to its application.

CHAPTER III — RETURN OF CHILDREN

Article 8

Any person, institution or other body claiming that a child has been removed or retained in breach of custody rights may apply either to the Central Authority of the child's habitual residence or to the Central Authority of any other Contracting State for assistance in securing the return of the child.

The application shall contain—

a) information concerning the identity of the applicant, of the child and of the person alleged to have removed or retained the child;

b) where available, the date of birth of the child;

c) the grounds on which the applicant's claim for return of the child is based;

d) all available information relating to the whereabouts of the child and the identity of the person with whom the child is presumed to be.

The application may be accompanied or supplemented by—

e) an authenticated copy of any relevant decision or agreement;

f) a certificate or an affidavit emanating from a Central Authority, or other competent authority of the State of the child's habitual residence, or from a qualified person, concerning the relevant law of that State;

g) any other relevant document.

Article 9

If the Central Authority which receives an application referred to in Article 8 has reason to believe that the child is in another Contracting State, it shall directly and without delay transmit the application to the Central Authority of that Contracting State and inform the requesting Central Authority, or the applicant, as the case may be.

Article 10

The Central Authority of the State where the child is shall take or cause to be taken all appropriate measures in order to obtain the voluntary return of the child.

Article 11

The judicial or administrative authorities of Contracting States shall act expeditiously in proceedings for the return of children.

If the judicial or administrative authority concerned has not reached a decision within six weeks from the date of commencement of the proceedings, the applicant or the Central Authority of the requested State, on its own initiative or if asked by the Central Authority of the requesting State, shall have the right to request a statement of the reasons for the delay. If a reply is received by the Central Authority of the requested State, that Authority shall transmit the reply to the Central Authority of the requesting State, or to the applicant, as the case may be.

Article 12

Where a child has been wrongfully removed or retained in terms of Article 3 and, at the date of the commencement of the proceedings before the judicial or administrative authority of the Contracting State where the child is, a period of less than one year has elapsed from the date of the wrongful removal or retention, the authority concerned shall order the return of the child forthwith.

The judicial or administrative authority, even where the proceedings have been commenced after the expiration of the period of one year referred to in the preceding paragraph, shall also order the return of the child, unless it is demonstrated that the child is now settled in its new environment.

Where the judicial or administrative authority in the requested State has reason to believe that the child has been taken to another State, it may stay the proceedings or dismiss the application for the return of the child.

Article 13

Notwithstanding the provisions of the preceding Article, the judicial or administrative authority of the requested State is not bound to order the return of the child if the person, institution or other body which opposes its return establishes that—

a) the person, institution or other body having the care of the person of the child was not actually exercising the custody rights at the time of removal or retention, or had consented to or subsequently acquiesced in the removal or retention; or

b) there is a grave risk that his or her return would expose the child to physical or psychological harm or otherwise place the child in an intolerable situation.

The judicial or administrative authority may also refuse to order the return of the child if it finds that the child objects to being returned and has attained an age and degree of maturity at which it is appropriate to take account of its views.

In considering the circumstances referred to in this Article, the judicial and administrative authorities shall take into account the information relating to the social background of the child provided by the Central Authority or other competent authority of the child's habitual residence.

Article 14

In ascertaining whether there has been a wrongful removal or retention within the meaning of Article 3, the judicial or administrative authorities of the requested State may take notice directly of the law of, and of judicial or administrative decisions, formally recognized or not in the State of the habitual residence of the child, without recourse to the specific procedures for the proof of that law or for the recognition of foreign decisions which would otherwise be applicable.

Article 15

The judicial or administrative authorities of a Contracting State may, prior to the making of an order for the return of the child, request that the applicant obtain from the authorities of the State of the habitual residence of the child a decision or other determination that the removal or retention was wrongful within the meaning of Article 3 of the Convention, where such a decision or determination may be obtained in that State. The Central Authorities of the Contracting States shall so far as practicable assist applicants to obtain such a decision or determination.

Article 16

After receiving notice of a wrongful removal or retention of a child in the sense of Article 3, the judicial or administrative authorities of the Contracting State to which the child has been removed or in which it has been retained shall not decide on the merits of rights of custody until it has been determined that the child is not to be returned under this Convention or unless an application under this Convention is not lodged within a reasonable time following receipt of the notice.

Article 17

The sole fact that a decision relating to custody has been given in or is entitled to recognition in the requested State shall not be a ground for refusing to return a child under this Convention, but the judicial or administrative authorities of the requested State may take account of the reasons for that decision in applying this Convention.

Article 18

The provisions of this Chapter do not limit the power of a judicial or administrative authority to order the return of the child at any time.

Article 19

A decision under this Convention concerning the return of the child shall not be taken to be a determination on the merits of any custody issue.

Article 20

The return of the child under the provisions of Article 12 may be refused if this would not be permitted by the fundamental principles of the requested State relating to the protection of human rights and fundamental freedoms.

CHAPTER IV — RIGHTS OF ACCESS

Article 21

An application to make arrangements for organizing or securing the effective exercise of rights of access may be presented to the Central Authorities of the Contracting States in the same way as an application for the return of a child.

The Central Authorities are bound by the obligations of co-operation which are set forth in Article 7 to promote the peaceful enjoyment of access rights and the fulfilment of any conditions to which the exercise of those rights may be subject. The Central Authorities shall take steps to remove, as far as possible, all obstacles to the exercise of such rights.

The Central Authorities, either directly or through intermediaries, may initiate or assist in the institution of proceedings with a view to organizing or protecting these rights and securing respect for the conditions to which the exercise of these rights may be subject.

CHAPTER V — GENERAL PROVISIONS

Article 22

No security, bond or deposit, however described, shall be required to guarantee the payment of costs and expenses in the judicial or administrative proceedings falling within the scope of this Convention.

Article 23

No legalization or similar formality may be required in the context of this Convention.

Article 24

Any application, communication or other document sent to the Central Authority of the requested State shall be in the original language, and shall be accompanied by a translation into the official language or one of the official languages of the requested State or, where that is not feasible, a translation into French or English.

However, a Contracting State may, by making a reservation in accordance with Article 42, object to the use of either French or English, but not both, in any application, communication or other document sent to its Central Authority.

Article 25

Nationals of the Contracting States and persons who are habitually resident within those States shall be entitled in matters concerned with the application of this Convention to legal aid and advice in any other Contracting State on the same conditions as if they themselves were nationals of and habitually resident in that State.

Article 26

Each Central Authority shall bear its own costs in applying this Convention.

Central Authorities and other public services of Contracting States shall not impose any charges in relation to applications submitted under this Convention. In particular, they may not require any payment from the applicant towards the costs and expenses of the proceedings or, where applicable, those arising from the participation of legal counsel or advisers. However, they may require the payment of the expenses incurred or to be incurred in implementing the return of the child.

However, a Contracting State may, by making a reservation in accordance with Article 42, declare that it shall not be bound to assume any costs referred to in the preceding paragraph resulting from the participation of legal counsel or advisers or from court proceedings, except insofar as those costs may be covered by its system of legal aid and advice.

Upon ordering the return of a child or issuing an order concerning rights of access under this Convention, the judicial or administrative authorities may, where appropriate, direct the person who removed or retained the child, or who prevented the exercise of rights of access, to pay necessary expenses incurred by or on behalf of the applicant, including travel expenses, any costs incurred or payments made for locating the child, the costs of legal representation of the applicant, and those of returning the child.

Article 27

When it is manifest that the requirements of this Convention are not fulfilled or that the application is otherwise not well founded, a Central Authority is not bound to accept the application. In that case, the Central Authority shall forthwith inform the applicant or the Central Authority through which the application was submitted, as the case may be, of its reasons.

Article 28

A Central Authority may require that the application be accompanied by a written authorization empowering it to act on behalf of the applicant, or to designate a representative so to act.

Article 29

This Convention shall not preclude any person, institution or body who claims that there has been a breach of custody or access rights within the meaning of Article 3 or 21 from applying directly to the judicial or administrative authorities of a Contracting State, whether or not under the provisions of this Convention.

Article 30

Any application submitted to the Central Authorities or directly to the judicial or administrative authorities of a Contracting State in accordance with the terms of this Convention, together with documents and any other information appended thereto or provided by a Central Authority, shall be admissible in the courts or administrative authorities of the Contracting States.

Article 31

In relation to a State which in matters of custody of children has two or more systems of law applicable in different territorial units—

a) any reference to habitual residence in that State shall be construed as referring to habitual residence in a territorial unit of that State;

b) any reference to the law of the State of habitual residence shall be construed as referring to the law of the territorial unit in that State where the child habitually resides.

Article 32

In relation to a State which in matters of custody of children has two or more systems of law applicable to different categories of persons, any reference to the law of that State shall be construed as referring to the legal system specified by the law of that State.

Article 33

A State within which different territorial units have their own rules of law in respect of custody of children shall not be bound to apply this Convention where a State with a unified system of law would not be bound to do so.

Article 34

This Convention shall take priority in matters within its scope over the Convention of 5 October 1961 concerning the powers of authorities and the law applicable in respect of the protection of minors, as between parties to both Conventions. Otherwise the present Convention shall not restrict the application of an international instrument in force between the State of origin and the State addressed or other law of the State addressed for the purposes of obtaining the return of a child who has been wrongfully removed or retained or of organizing access rights.

Article 35

This Convention shall apply as between Contracting States only to wrongful removals or retentions occurring after its entry into force in those States.

Where a declaration has been made under Article 39 or 40, the reference in the preceding paragraph to a Contracting State shall be taken to refer to the territorial unit or units in relation to which this Convention applies.

Article 36

Nothing in this Convention shall prevent two or more Contracting States, in order to limit the restrictions to which the return of the child may be subject, from agreeing among themselves to derogate from any provisions of this Convention which may imply such a restriction.

CHAPTER VI — FINAL CLAUSES

Article 37

The Convention shall be open for signature by the States which were Members of the Hague Conference on Private International Law at the time of its Fourteenth Session.

It shall be ratified, accepted or approved and the instruments of ratification, acceptance or approval shall be deposited with the Ministry of Foreign Affairs of the Kingdom of the Netherlands.

Article 38

Any other State may accede to the Convention.

The instrument of accession shall be deposited with the Ministry of Foreign Affairs of the Kingdom of the Netherlands.

The Convention shall enter into force for a State acceding to it on the first day of the third calendar month after the deposit of its instrument of accession.

The accession will have effect only as regards the relations between the acceding State and such Contracting States as will have declared their acceptance of the accession. Such a declaration will also have to be made by any Member State ratifying, accepting or approving the Convention after an accession. Such declaration shall be deposited at the Ministry of Foreign Affairs of the Kingdom of the Netherlands; this Ministry shall forward, through diplomatic channels, a certified copy to each of the Contracting States.

The Convention will enter into force as between the acceding State and the State that has declared its acceptance of the accession on the first day of the third calendar month after the deposit of the declaration of acceptance.

Article 39

Any State may, at the time of signature, ratification, acceptance, approval or accession, declare that the Convention shall extend to all the territories for the international relations of which it is responsible, or to one or more of them. Such a declaration shall take effect at the time the Convention enters into force for that State.

Such declaration, as well as any subsequent extension, shall be notified to the Ministry of Foreign Affairs of the Kingdom of the Netherlands.

Article 40

If a Contracting State has two or more territorial units in which different systems of law are applicable in relation to matters dealt with in this Convention, it may at the time of signature, ratification, acceptance, approval or accession declare that this Convention shall extend to all its territorial units or only to one or more of them and may modify this declaration by submitting another declaration at any time.

Any such declaration shall be notified to the Ministry of Foreign Affairs of the Kingdom of the Netherlands and shall state expressly the territorial units to which the Convention applies.

Article 41

Where a Contracting State has a system of government under which executive, judicial and legislative powers are distributed between central and other authorities within that State, its signature or ratification, acceptance or approval of, or accession to this Convention, or its making of any declaration in terms of Article 40 shall carry no implication as to the internal distribution of powers within that State.

Article 42

Any State may, not later than the time of ratification, acceptance, approval or accession, or at the time of making a declaration in terms of Article 39 or 40, make one or both of the reservations provided for in Article 24 and Article 26, third paragraph. No other reservation shall be permitted.

Any State may at any time withdraw a reservation it has made. The withdrawal shall be notified to the Ministry of Foreign Affairs of the Kingdom of the Netherlands.

The reservation shall cease to have effect on the first day of the third calendar month after the notification referred to in the preceding paragraph.

Article 43

The Convention shall enter into force on the first day of the third calendar month after the deposit of the third instrument of ratification, acceptance, approval or accession referred to in Articles 37 and 38.

Thereafter the Convention shall enter into force—

(1) for each State ratifying, accepting, approving or acceding to it subsequently, on the first day of the third calendar month after the deposit of its instrument of ratification, acceptance, approval or accession;

(2) for any territory or territorial unit to which the Convention has been extended in conformity with Article 39 or 40, on the first day of the third calendar month after the notification referred to in that Article.

Article 44

The Convention shall remain in force for five years from the date of its entry into force in accordance with the first paragraph of Article 43 even for States which subsequently have ratified, accepted, approved it or acceded to it.

If there has been no denunciation, it shall be renewed tacitly every five years.

Any denunciation shall be notified to the Ministry of Foreign Affairs of the Kingdom of the Netherlands at least six months before the expiry of the five year period. It may be limited to certain of the territories or territorial units to which the Convention applies.

The denunciation shall have effect only as regards the State which has notified it. The Convention shall remain in force for the other Contracting States.

Article 45

The Ministry of Foreign Affairs of the Kingdom of the Netherlands shall notify the States Members of the Conference, and the States which have acceded in accordance with Article 38, of the following—

(1) the signatures and ratifications, acceptances and approvals referred to in Article 37;

(2) the accessions referred to in Article 38;

(3) the date on which the Convention enters into force in accordance with Article 43;

(4) the extensions referred to in Article 39;

(5) the declarations referred to in Articles 38 and 40;

(6) the reservations referred to in Article 24 and Article 26, third paragraph, and the withdrawals referred to in Article 42;

(7) the denunciations referred to in Article 44.

IN WITNESS WHEREOF the undersigned, being duly authorised thereto, have signed this Convention.

DONE at The Hague, on the 25th day of October, 1980, in the English and French languages, both texts being equally authentic, in a single copy which shall be deposited in the archives of the Government of the Kingdom of the Netherlands, and of which a certified copy shall be sent, through diplomatic channels, to each of the States Members of the Hague Conference on Private International Law at the date of its Fourteenth Session.

Entered into force for the United States July 1, 1988.

The following are Signatories to the Hague Convention on Service Abroad. Because the Hague Convention allows a Signatory to modify or object to articles of the Convention, a party seeking to secure the return of a child from a Signatory State should consult the website of the Hague Conference on Private International Law <http://www.hcch.net/e/status/> to determine how that state applies the Convention.

Argentina, Australia, Austria, Belgium, Brazil, Bulgaria, Canada, Chile, China, Croatia, Cyprus, Czech Republic, Denmark, Egypt, Estonia, Finland, Former Yugoslav Republic of Macedonia, France, Georgia, Germany, Greece, Hungary, Ireland, Israel, Italy, Japan, Hashemite Kingdom of Jordan, Republic of Korea, Latvia, Luxembourg, Malta, Mexico, Monaco, Morocco, Netherlands, Norway, Peru, Poland, Portugal, Romania, Slovakia, Slovenia, Spain, Suriname, Sweden, Switzerland, Turkey, United Kingdom of Great Britain and Northern Ireland, United States of America, Uruguay, Venezuela, Federal Republic of Yugoslavia.

Parental Notification Rules

Table of Contents

Texas Parental Notification Rules

Rule 1. General Provisions

Rule 2. Proceedings in the Trial Court

Rule 3. Appeal from Denial of Application

Rule 4. Appeal to the Supreme Court

TEXAS PARENTAL NOTIFICATION RULES & FORMS

Effective January 1, 2000; amended March 1, 2001.

Editor's note: References to parental notification forms in the rules below are not included in this edition. Please look for them in ***O'Connor's Texas Family Law Forms***, forthcoming.

Explanatory Statement

Chapter 33 of the Texas Family Code, adopted by Act of May 25, 1999, 76th Leg., R.S., ch. 395, 1999 Tex. Gen. Laws 2466 (S.B. 30), provides for judicial authorization of an unemancipated minor to consent to an abortion in Texas without notice to her parents, managing conservator, or guardian. Section 2 of the Act states: "The Supreme Court of Texas shall issue promptly such rules as may be necessary in order that the process established by Sections 33.003 and 33.004, Family Code, as added by this Act, may be conducted in a manner that will ensure confidentiality and sufficient precedence over all other pending matters to ensure promptness of disposition." *See also* Tex. Fam. Code §§33.003(l), 33.004(c). Section 6 of the Act adds: "The clerk of the Supreme Court of Texas shall adopt the application form and notice of appeal form to be used under Sections 33.003 and 33.004, Family Code, as added by this Act, not later than December 15, 1999." *See also* Tex. Fam. Code §§33.003(m), 33.004(d).

The following rules and forms are promulgated as directed by the Act without any determination that the Act or any part of it comports with the United States Constitution or the Texas Constitution. During the public hearings and debates on the rules and forms, questions were raised concerning the constitutionality of Chapter 33, among which were whether the statute can make court rulings secret, and whether the statute can require courts to act within the specified, short deadlines it imposes. Because such issues should not be resolved outside an adversarial proceeding with full briefing and argument, the rules and forms merely track statutory requirements of the Legislature. Adoption of these rules does not, of course, imply that abortion is or is not permitted in any specific situation. *See, e.g., Roe v. Wade*, 410 U.S. 113 (1973); Tex. Rev. Civ. Stat. Ann. art. 4495b, §4.011 (restrictions on third trimester abortions of viable fetuses).

The notes and comments appended to the rules are intended to inform their construction and application by courts and practitioners.

RULE 1. GENERAL PROVISIONS

1.1 Applicability of These Rules. These rules govern proceedings for obtaining a court order authorizing a minor to consent to an abortion without notice to either of her parents or a managing conservator or guardian under Chapter 33, Family Code (or as amended). Other Texas court rules—including the Rules of Civil Procedure, Rules of Evidence, Rules of Appellate Procedure, Rules of Judicial Administration, and local rules approved by the Supreme Court—also apply, but when the application of another rule would be inconsistent with the general framework or policy of Chapter 33, Family Code, or these rules, these rules control.

1.2 Expedition Required.

(a) ***Proceedings.*** A court must give proceedings under these rules precedence over all other pending matters to the extent necessary to assure that applications and appeals are adjudicated as soon as possible and within the time required by Rules 2.4(a), 2.5(d), and 3.3(c).

(b) ***Prompt actual notice required.*** Without compromising the confidentiality and anonymity required by statute and these rules, courts and clerks must serve orders, decisions, findings, and notices required under these rules in a manner designed to give prompt actual notice in order that the deadlines imposed by Chapter 33, Family Code, can be met.

(c) ***Instanter.*** "Instanter" means immediately, without delay. An action required by these rules to be taken instanter should be done at the first possible time and with the most expeditious means available.

1.3 Anonymity of Minor Protected.

(a) ***Generally.*** Proceedings under these rules must be conducted in a way that protects the anonymity of the minor.

(b) ***No reference to minor's identity in proceeding.*** With the exception of the verification page required under Rule 2.1(c)(2) and the communications required under Rule 2.2(e), no reference may be made in any order, decision, finding, or notice, or on the record, to the name of the minor, her address, or other information by which she might be identified by persons not participating in the proceedings. Instead, the minor must be referred to as "Jane Doe" in a numbered cause.

(c) ***Notice required to minor's attorney.*** With the exception of orders and rulings released under Rule 1.4(b), all service and communications from the court to the minor must be directed to the minor's attorney. This requirement takes effect when an attorney appears for the minor, or when the clerk has notified the minor of the appointment of an attorney.

1.4 Confidentiality of Proceedings Required; Exceptions.

(a) ***Generally.*** All officials and court personnel involved in the proceedings must ensure that the minor's contact with the clerk and court is confidential and expeditious. Except as permitted by law, no officials or court personnel involved in the proceedings may ever disclose to anyone outside the proceedings—including the minor's parent, managing conservator, or legal guardian—that the minor is or has ever been pregnant, or that she wants or has ever wanted an abortion.

(b) ***Documents and information pertaining to the proceeding.*** As required by Chapter 33, Family Code, the application and all other court documents and information pertaining to the proceedings are confidential and privileged and are not subject to disclosure under Chapter 552, Government Code, or to discovery, subpoena, or other legal process. But documents and information may be disclosed when expressly authorized by these rules, and an order, ruling, opinion, or clerk's certificate may be released to:

(1) the minor;

(2) the minor's guardian ad litem;

(3) the minor's attorney;

(4) a person designated in writing by the minor to receive the order, ruling, opinion, or certificate;

(5) a governmental agency or governmental attorney, in connection with a criminal or administrative action seeking to assert or protect the minor's interests; or

(6) another court, judge, or clerk in the same or related proceedings.

(c) ***Filing of court reporter's notes permitted.*** To assure confidentiality, court reporter notes, in whatever form, may be filed with other court documents in the proceeding.

(d) ***Duty to report possible sexual abuse.*** A court, guardian ad litem, or attorney ad litem who reasonably believes, based on information obtained in the proceeding, that a violation of Section 22.011, 22.021, or 25.02, Penal Code, has occurred must report the information to the appropriate officials or agencies as required by Section 33.009, Family Code.

(e) ***Department of Protective and Regulatory Services to disclose certain information in proceeding.*** The Department of Protective and Regulatory Services may disclose to the court, the attorney ad litem, and the guardian ad litem any information obtained under Section 33.008, Family Code, without being ordered to do so. The trial court may order the Department to disclose such information to such persons, and the Department must comply.

1.5 Electronic Transmission of Documents; Hearings Conducted By Remote Electronic Means; Electronic Record Allowed When Necessary.

(a) ***Electronic filing.*** Documents may be filed by facsimile or other electronic data transmission. If the sender communicates directly with the clerk the time at which the transmission will occur, the clerk must take all reasonable steps to assure that the confidentiality of the received transmission will be maintained.

(b) ***Electronic transmission by court and clerk.*** The court and clerk may transmit orders, rulings, notices, and other documents by facsimile or other electronic data transmission. But before the transmission is initiated, the sender must take all reasonable steps to assure that the confidentiality of the received transmission will be maintained. The time and date of a transmission by the court is the time and date when it was initiated.

(c) ***Hearings by electronic means.*** Consistent with the anonymity and confidentiality requirements of these rules, with the court's permission, the attorney ad litem, the guardian ad litem, and any witnesses may participate in hearings under these rules by video conferencing, telephone, or other remote electronic means. The minor must appear before the court in person unless the court determines that the minor's appearance by video conferencing will allow the court to view the minor during the hearing sufficiently well to assess her credibility and demeanor.

(d) ***Record of hearing made by electronic means if necessary.*** If the court determines that a court reporter is unavailable for a hearing, the court may have a record of the hearing made by audio recording or other electronic means. If a notice of appeal is filed, the court must have the recording transcribed if possible. The person transcribing the recording must certify to the accuracy of the transcription. The court must transmit both the recording and the transcription to the court of appeals.

1.6 Disqualification, Recusal, or Objection to a Judge.

(a) ***Time for filing and ruling.*** An objection to a trial judge, or a motion to recuse or disqualify a trial judge, must be filed before 10:00 a.m. of the first business day after an application is filed or promptly after the assignment of a judge to hear the case is made known to the minor or her attorney, whichever is later. An objection to an appellate judge, or a motion to recuse or disqualify an appellate judge must be filed before 10 a.m. of the first business day after a notice of appeal is filed. A judge who chooses to recuse voluntarily must do so instanter. An objection to a judge or a motion to disqualify or recuse does not extend the deadline for ruling on the minor's application.

(b) ***Voluntary disqualification or recusal, or objection.*** A judge to whom objection is made under Chapter 74, Government Code, or a judge or justice who voluntarily does not sit, must notify instanter the appropriate authority for assigning another judge by local rules or by statute. That authority must instanter assign a judge or justice to the proceeding.

(c) ***Involuntary disqualification or recusal.*** A judge or justice who refuses to remove himself or herself voluntarily from a proceeding in response to a motion must instanter refer the motion to the appropriate judge or justice, pursuant to local rule, rule, or statute, for determination. The judge or justice to whom the motion is referred must rule on it as soon as possible and may do so with or without a hearing. If the motion is granted, the judge or justice to whom the motion was referred must instanter assign a judge or justice to the proceeding.

(d) ***Only one objection or motion to recuse permitted.*** A minor who objects to a judge assigned to the proceeding may not thereafter file a motion to recuse or disqualify, and a minor who files a motion to recuse or disqualify a judge may not thereafter object to a judge assigned to the proceeding.

(e) ***Issues on appeal.*** Any error in the denial of a motion to recuse or disqualify, or any error in the disallowance of an objection, or any challenge to a judge that a minor is precluded from making by subsections (a) or (d), may be raised only on appeal from the court's denial of the application.

1.7 Rules and Forms to be Made Available. A copy of these rules, and a copy of the attached forms in English and Spanish, must be made available to any person without charge in the clerk's offices of all courts in which applications or appeals may be filed under these rules, on the Texas Judiciary Internet site at www.courts.state.tx.us, and by the Office of Court Administration upon request. A copy of a court's local rules relating to proceedings under Chapter 33, Family Code, must be made available to any person without charge in the office of the clerk for that court where applications may be filed. Rules and forms may be copied.

1.8 Duties of Attorneys Ad Litem. An attorney ad litem must represent the minor in the trial court in the proceeding in which the attorney is assigned, and in any appeal under these rules to the court of appeals or the Supreme Court. But an attorney ad litem is not required to represent the minor in any other court or any other proceeding.

1.9 Fees & Costs.

(a) ***No fees or costs charged to minor.*** No filing fee or court cost may be assessed against a minor for any proceeding in a trial or appellate court.

(b) ***State ordered to pay fees and costs.***

(1) Fees and costs that may be paid. The State may be ordered to pay the reasonable and necessary fees and expenses of the attorney ad litem, the reasonable and necessary fees and expenses of the guardian ad litem, the court reporter's fee as certified by the court reporter, and trial court filing fees and costs as certified by the clerk. Court costs include the expenses of an interpreter (Form 2H) but do not include the fees or expenses of a witness. Court costs do not include fees which must be remitted to the state treasury.

(2) To whom order directed and sent. The order must be directed to the Comptroller of Public Accounts but should be sent by the clerk to the Director, Fiscal Division, of the Texas Department of Health.

(3) Form and contents of the order. The order must state the amounts to be awarded the attorney ad litem and the guardian ad litem. The order must be separate from any other order in the proceeding and must not address any subject other than the assessment of costs. A trial court may use Forms 2F and 2G, but it is not required to do so.

(4) Time for signing and sending order. To be valid, the order must be signed by the judge and sent by the clerk to the Department of Health not later than the ninetieth day after the date of the final ruling in a proceeding, whether the application is granted, deemed granted, or denied, or the proceeding is dismissed or nonsuited.

(c) ***Motion to reconsider; time for filing.*** Within thirty days of actual receipt of the order, the Comptroller or any other person adversely affected by the order may file a motion in the trial court to reconsider the assessment of costs. The trial court retains jurisdiction of the case to hear and determine any timely filed motion to reconsider.

(d) ***Appeal.*** The Comptroller or any other person adversely affected by the order may appeal from the trial court's ruling on the motion to reconsider as from any other final judgment of the court.

(e) ***Report to the Office of Court Administration.*** The Department of Health must transmit to the Office of Court Administration a copy of every order assessing costs in a proceeding under Chapter 33, Family Code. Such orders are not subject to the Amended Order of the Supreme Court of Texas, dated September 21, 1994, in Misc. Docket No. 94-9143, regarding mandatory reports of judicial appointments and fees.

(f) ***Confidentiality.*** When transmitting an order awarding costs to the Department of Health, the clerk must take reasonable steps to preserve its confidentially. The confidentiality of an order awarding costs—as prescribed by Chapter 33, Family Code—is not affected by its transmission to the Comptroller, Texas Department of Health, or the Office of Court Administration, nor is the order subject to public disclosure in response to a request under any statute, rule, or other law. But these rules do not preclude the Comptroller, Texas Department of Health, and the Office of Court Administration from disclosing summary information from orders assessing costs for statistical or other such purposes.

1.10 Amicus Briefs. Amicus briefs may be submitted and received by a court—but not filed—under either of the following procedures.

(a) ***Confidential, Case-Specific Briefs.*** A nonparty who is authorized to attend or participate in a particular proceeding under Chapter 33, Family Code may submit an amicus brief addressing matters, including confidential matters, specific to the proceeding. The brief and the manner in which it is submitted must comply with Rules 1.3 and 1.4 and be directed to the court in which the proceeding is pending. The person must submit the original brief and the same number of copies required for other submissions to the court, and must serve a copy of the brief on the minor's attorney. The court to which the brief is submitted must maintain the brief as part of the confidential case file in accordance with Rule 1.4.

(b) ***Public or General Briefs.*** Any person may submit a brief addressing any matter relating to proceedings under Chapter 33, Family Code. Such a brief must not contain any information in violation of Rules 1.3 and 1.4. The person must submit the original brief and the same number of copies required for other submissions to the court. If the brief is submitted to a court of appeals, the original and eleven copies of the brief, plus a computer disk containing the brief, must also be submitted to the Supreme Court of Texas. When an appeal of a proceeding is filed, the clerk of the court of appeals or the Supreme Court must notify the parties to the appeal of the existence of any brief filed under this subsection and must make the brief available for inspection and copying. Upon submission, the Clerk of the Supreme Court must, as soon as practicable, have the brief posted on the Texas Judiciary Internet site and make it available to the public for inspection and copying.

Notes & Comments

1. Rule 1.1 contemplates that other court rules of procedure and administration remain as a "default" governing matters not addressed in these rules. Thus, for example, these rules do not state a deadline for filing notices of appeal, so the ordinary 30-day deadline controls, *see* Tex. R. App. P. 26.1, but these rules control over inconsistent provisions in the appellate rules governing the docketing statement, the record, and briefing.

2. Rule 1.1 also contemplates that individual jurisdictions may enact local rules pursuant to Tex. R. Civ. P. 3a, Tex. R. App. P. 1.2, or Tex. R. Jud. Admin. 10, to the extent consistent with Chapter 33, Family Code, and with these rules, to tailor the implementation of the statute and these rules to local needs and preferences. Local rules may address, for example, the specific location or office where applications are to be filed, how applications are to be assigned for hearing, and whether an appellate court will permit or require briefing or oral argument. *See also* Rule 2, Comment 1.

3. Any judge involved in a proceeding, whether as the judge assigned to hear and decide the application, the judge assigned to hear and decide any disqualification, recusal or objection, a judge authorized to transfer the application or assign another judge to it, or an appellate judge, may have access to all information (including the verification page) in the proceeding or any related proceeding, such as a prior filing by the minor. Similarly, a minor's attorney and guardian ad litem must, of course, have access to the case file to the extent necessary to perform their respective duties.

4. Section 33.008, Family Code, requires a physician who suspects that a minor has been physically or sexually abused by a person responsible for the minor's care to report the matter to the Texas Department of Protective and Regulatory Services. That section also requires the Department to investigate and to assist the minor in making an application, if appropriate. Section 33.010 makes confidential—"[n]otwithstanding any other law"—all information obtained by the Department under Section 33.008 except to the extent necessary to prove certain criminal conduct. Rule 1.4(e) construes Section 33.010 in harmony with Section 33.008. If Section 33.010 precluded the Department from disclosing information obtained under Section 33.008 to the court, the attorney ad litem, and the guardian ad litem in proceedings under section 33.003, the Department's statutorily mandated role in such proceedings would be seriously impaired. The Department could be required by Section 33.008 to assist a minor in filing an application but prohibited by Section 33.010 from providing the court with information supporting the application. The disclosure permitted and required by Rule 1.4(e) avoids this result.

5. Rule 1.5(a) constitutes the approval required by Section 51.803, Government Code, for electronic filing of documents in proceedings under these rules. To facilitate expedition of proceedings, restrictions imposed on electronic filing in other cases are not imposed here. However, electronic filing is only permitted, not required, and Rule 1.5(a) does not necessitate the provision of means for electronic filing. A person filing by electronic means cannot, of course, expect that the document will be treated confidentiality upon receipt unless the recipient has been told the time the transmission will occur.

6. Rule 1.6 controls to the extent that it conflicts with other provisions regarding the disqualification or recusal of judges, such as Tex. R. Civ. P. 18a, Tex. R. App. P. 16, and Tex. Govt Code 25.00255. But the rule incorporates the referral and reassignment processes otherwise applicable by local rule, rule, or statute.

7. The archival requirements relating to proceedings under Chapter 33, Family Code, and these rules is governed by Sections 441.158 and 441.185, Government Code, and the schedules promulgated by the Texas State Library and Archives Commission pursuant to those authorities.

8. Because orders awarding costs contain information made confidential by Chapter 33, Family Code, that confidentiality should not be affected by the transmission to the Texas Department of Health and the Comptroller, which is necessary to effectuate payment, or to the Office of Court Administration, which

is necessary to oversee the costs associated with the proceedings. Rule 1.9(f) does not preclude either the Comptroller, Texas Department of Health, or the Office of Court Administration from disclosing total amounts paid for all proceedings, or average amount per proceeding, or other such statistical summaries or analyses which do not impair the confidentiality of the proceedings.

9. Rule 1.10 adds a procedure for filing amicus curiae briefs uniquely designed for the expedited and confidential nature of parental notification cases.

RULE 2. PROCEEDINGS IN THE TRIAL COURT

2.1 Where to File an Application; Court Assignment and Transfer; Application Form.

(a) *Counties in which an application may be filed.* An application for an order under Section 33.003, Family Code, may be filed in any county, regardless of the minor's residence or where the abortion sought is to be performed.

(b) *Courts in which an application may be filed; assignment and transfer.*

(1) *Courts with jurisdiction.* An application may be filed in a district court (including a family district court), a county court-at-law, or a court having probate jurisdiction.

(2) *Application filed with district or county clerk.* An application must be filed with either the district clerk or the county clerk, who will assign the application to a court as provided by local rule or these rules. The clerk to whom the application is tendered cannot refuse to accept it because of any local rule or other rule or law that provides for filing and assignment of such applications but must accept the application and transfer it instanter to the proper clerk, advising the person tendering the application where it is being transferred.

(3) *Court assignment and transfer by local rule.* The courts in a county that have jurisdiction to hear applications may determine by local rule how applications will be assigned between or among them. A local rule must be approved by the Supreme Court under Rule 3a, Texas Rules of Civil Procedure.

(4) *Initial court assignment if no local rule.* Absent a local rule, the clerk that files an application—whether the district clerk or the county clerk—must assign it as follows:

(i) to a district court, if the active judge of the court, or a judge assigned to it, is then present in the county;

(ii) if the application cannot be assigned under (i), then to a statutory county or probate court, if the active judge of the court, or a judge assigned to it, is then present in the county;

(iii) if the application cannot be assigned under (i) or (ii), then to the constitutional county court, if it has probate jurisdiction, and if the active judge of the court, or a judge assigned to it, is then present in the county;

(iv) if the application cannot be assigned under (i), (ii), or (iii), then to the district court.

(5) *Judges who may hear and determine applications.* An application may be heard and determined (i) by the active judge of the court to which the application is assigned, or (ii) by any judge authorized to sit for the active judge, or (iii) by any judge who may be assigned to the court in which the application is pending. An application may not be heard or determined, or any proceedings under these rules conducted, by a master or magistrate.

(c) *Application form.* An application consists of two pages: a cover page and a separate verification page.

(1) *Cover page.* The cover page may be submitted on Form 2A, but use of the form is not required. The cover page must be styled "In re Jane Doe" and must not disclose the name of the minor or any information from which the minor's identity could be derived. The cover page must state:

(A) that the minor is pregnant;

(B) that the minor is unmarried, is under 18 years of age, and has not had her disabilities removed under Chapter 31, Family Code;

(C) that the minor wishes to have an abortion without notifying either of her parents or a managing conservator or guardian, and the statutory ground or grounds on which she relies;

(D) whether the minor has retained an attorney, and if so, the attorney's name, address, and telephone number;

(E) whether the minor requests the court to appoint a particular person as her guardian ad litem; and

(F) whether, concerning her current pregnancy, the minor has previously filed an application that was denied, and if so, where the application was filed.

(2) *Verification page.* The verification page may be submitted on Form 2B, but use of the form is not required. The verification page must be separate from the cover page, must be signed under oath by the person completing the application, and must state:

(A) the minor's full name and date of birth;

(B) the name, address, telephone number, and relationship to the minor of any person the minor requests the court to appoint as her guardian ad litem;

(C) a telephone or pager number—whether that of the minor or someone else (such as a physician, friend, or relative)—at which the minor may be contacted immediately and confidentially until an attorney is appointed to represent her; and

(D) that all information contained in the application, including both the cover page and the verification page, is true.

(d) ***Time of filing.*** An application is filed when it is actually received by the district or county clerk.

2.2 Clerk's Duties.

(a) ***Assistance in filing.*** The clerk must give prompt assistance—in a manner designed to protect the minor's confidentiality and anonymity—to persons seeking to file an application. If requested, the clerk must administer the oath required for the verification page or provide a person authorized to do so. The clerk should also redact from the cover page any information identifying the minor. The clerk should ensure that both the cover page and the separate verification page are completed in full.

(b) ***Filing procedure.*** The clerk must assign the application a cause number and affix it to both the cover page and the verification page. The clerk must then provide a certified copy of the verification page to the person filing the application. The clerk must file the verification page under seal in a secure place where access is limited to essential court personnel.

(c) ***Distribution.*** When an application is filed, the clerk must distribute the cover page and verification page, or a copy of them, to the appropriate court instanter. If appointment of a specific person as guardian ad litem has been requested, the clerk must also communicate the information to the appropriate court instanter.

(d) ***If judge of assigned court not present in county.*** The clerk must determine instanter whether the judge of the court to which the application is assigned is present in the county. If that judge is not present in the county, the clerk must instanter notify the local administrative judge or judges and the presiding judge of the administrative judicial region and must send them any information requested, including the cover page and verification page.

(e) ***Notice of hearing and appointments.*** When the clerk is advised by the court of a time for hearing or an appointment of a guardian ad litem or attorney ad litem, the clerk must instanter give notice—as directed in the verification page and to each appointee—of the hearing time or appointment. A court coordinator or other court personnel may give notice instead of the clerk.

(f) ***Orders.*** The clerk must provide the minor and the attorney ad litem with copies of all court orders, including findings of fact and conclusions of law.

(g) ***Certificate of court's failure to rule within time prescribed by statute.*** If the court fails to rule on an application within the time required by Section 33.002(g) and (h), Family Code, upon the minor's request, the clerk must instanter issue a certificate to that effect, stating that the application is deemed by statute to be granted. The clerk may use Form 2E but is not required to do so.

2.3 Court's Duties.

Upon receipt of an application from the clerk, the court must promptly:

(a) appoint a qualified person to serve as guardian ad litem for the minor;

(b) appoint an attorney for the minor, who may be the same person appointed guardian ad litem if that person is an attorney admitted to practice law in Texas and there is no conflict of interest in the same person serving as attorney ad litem and guardian ad litem;

(c) set a hearing on the application in accordance with Rule 2.4(a); and

(d) advise the clerk of the appointment or appointments and the hearing time.

2.4 Hearing.

(a) ***Time.*** The court must conduct a hearing in time to rule on the application as required by Rule 2.5(d). But the minor may postpone the hearing by written request to the clerk when the application is filed or thereafter. The request may be submitted on Form 2C, but use of the form is not required. The request must either specify a date on which the minor will be ready for the hearing, or state that the minor will later provide a date on which she will be ready for the hearing. Once the minor determines when she will be ready for the hearing, she must notify the clerk of that time in writing. The postponed hearing must be conducted in time for the court to rule on the application as required by Rule 2.5(d).

(b) ***Place.*** The hearing should be held in a location, such as a judge's chambers, that will assure confidentiality. The hearing may be held away from the courthouse.

(c) ***Persons attending.*** Hearings must be closed to the public. Only the judge, the court reporter and any other essential court personnel, the minor, her attorney, her guardian ad litem, and witnesses on the minor's behalf may be present.

(d) ***Record.*** If the minor appeals, or if there is evidence of past or potential abuse of the minor, the hearing must be transcribed instanter.

(e) ***Hearing to be informal.*** The court should attempt to rule on the application without regard to technical defects in the application or the evidence. Affidavits of persons other than applicants are admissible. Statements in the application cannot be offered as evidence to support the application. If necessary, the court may assist the minor in remedying technical defects in the application and in presenting relevant and material facts.

2.5 Ruling.

(a) ***Form of ruling.*** The court's ruling on the application must include a signed order and written findings of fact and conclusions of law. The findings and conclusions may be included in the order. The court may use Form 2D, but it is not required to do so.

(b) ***Grounds for granting application.*** The court must grant the application if the minor establishes, by a preponderance of the evidence, that:

(1) the minor is mature and sufficiently well informed to make the decision to have an abortion performed without notifying either of the minor's parents, the minor's managing conservator, or the minor's legal guardian, as the case may be;

(2) notifying either of the minor's parents, the minor's managing conservator, or the minor's legal guardian, as the case may be, would not be in the minor's best interest; or

(3) notifying either of the minor's parents, the minor's managing conservator, or the minor's legal guardian, as the case may be, may lead to physical, sexual, or emotional abuse of the minor.

(c) ***Grounds for denying application.*** If the minor can establish none of the grounds in Rule 2.5(b) by a preponderance of the evidence, the court must deny the application. If the court, the guardian ad litem, or the attorney ad litem are unable to contact the minor before the hearing despite diligent attempts to do so, or if the minor does not attend the hearing, the court must deny the application without prejudice.

(d) ***Time for ruling.*** The court must rule on an application as soon as possible after it is filed, subject to any postponement requested by the minor, and immediately after the hearing is concluded. Section 33.003(h), Family Code, states that a court must rule on an application by 5:00 p.m. on the second business day after the day the application is filed, or if the minor requests a postponement, after the date the minor states she is ready for the hearing, and that if the court does not rule within this time, the application is deemed to be granted.

(e) ***Notification of right to appeal.*** If the court denies the application, it must inform the minor of her right to appeal under Rule 3 and furnish her with the notice of appeal form, Form 3A.

Notes & Comments

1. Section 33.003(b), Family Code, permits an application to be filed in "any county court at law, court having probate jurisdiction, or district court, including a family district court, in this state." The initial assignment of an application to a specific court in a county is made by the clerk with whom the application is filed (not by the minor). Given the diversity of needs and circumstances among Texas courts, these rules allow the courts in each county to tailor the procedures for filing, handling, and assigning applications prescribed by these rules to best meet those needs and circumstances. Chapter 74, Subchapter C, Government Code, affords the presiding judge of an administrative judicial region broad discretion to assign active judges within the region, as well as visiting judges, to hear matters pending in courts within the region. *See* Tex. Govt. Code §§74.054, 74.056; *see also id.*, §74.056(b) (presiding judges may request judges from other judicial regions for assignment); §74.057 (Chief Justice may assign judges from one judicial region to another). Section 25.0022, Government Code, provides for assignment of probate judges. Furthermore, Chapter 74, Subchapter D, Government Code, authorizes district and statutory county court judges within a county to hear matters pending in any district or statutory county court in the county. *Id.*, §74.094(a). Finally, Section 74.121, Government Code, permits courts within a county to transfer cases among courts having jurisdiction over the case. If no local rule governs assignments, then Rule 2.1(b)(4) controls.

2. Because an application is considered filed when it is actually received by the clerk, the timing provisions relating to filing by mail of Tex. R. Civ. P. 21a are inapplicable.

3. Section 33.003(f), Family Code, provides that a guardian ad litem may be (1) a person who may consent to treatment for the minor under Sections 32.001(a)(1)-(3), Family Code; (2) a psychiatrist or an individual licensed or certified as a psychologist under the Psychologist's Licensing Act, Article 4512c, Vernon's Texas Civil Statutes; (3) an appropriate employee of the Department of Protective or Regulatory Services; (4) a member of the clergy; or (5) another appropriate person selected by the court. The trial court may also consider appointing a qualified person requested by the minor. Although not directly applicable to these proceedings, the standards embodied in Chapter 107, Family

Code, reflect legislative intent that competent and qualified persons be appointed to serve as ad litems and may provide general guidance concerning the nature of those qualifications. Appointment of an employee of the Department of Protective and Regulatory Services to serve as guardian ad litem may give rise to a conflict of interest not immediately apparent at the time since the Department may be involved with the minor's family due to an abuse or neglect investigation, or may be party to a suit affecting the parent-child relationship, or may already be serving as the child's managing conservator.

4. The duties of guardians ad litem are not susceptible of precise definition. Generally, a guardian ad litem should interview the minor and conduct any investigation the guardian believes to be appropriate, without violating Rules 1.3 and 1.4, to assist the court in arriving at an opinion whether the minor is mature and sufficiently well informed to make the decision to have an abortion performed without notification to either of her parents or a managing conservator or guardian, whether notification would not be in the best interest of the minor, or whether notification may lead to physical, sexual, or emotional abuse of the minor. In making these determinations, the following factors have been considered in other jurisdictions with similar parental notification statutes:

- Whether the minor has been examined by a doctor of medicine, doctor of osteopathy, or registered nurse—who is licensed to practice in Texas—and has given that health care provider an accurate and complete statement of her medical history.
- Whether the minor has been provided with information or counseling bearing on her decision to have an abortion.
- Whether the minor desires further counseling.
- Whether, based on the information or counseling provided to the minor, she is able to give informed consent.
- Whether the minor is attending school, or is or has been employed.
- Whether the minor has previously filed an application that was denied.
- Whether the minor lives with her parents.
- Whether the minor desires an abortion or has been threatened, intimidated or coerced into having an abortion.
- Whether the pregnancy resulted from sexual assault, sexual abuse, or incest.
- Whether there is a history or pattern of family violence.
- Whether the minor fears for her safety.

These considerations may not be relevant in every case, are not exclusive, and may not be sufficient to discharge the guardian ad litem's responsibilities in every case. Use of these factors as a basis for civil liability or as a statement of the standard of care is contrary to their intended purpose. Nothing in this comment alters existing standards of conduct under the Texas Disciplinary Rules of Professional Conduct, the Texas Rules of Disciplinary Procedure, or the Code of Judicial Conduct.

In addition to these general guidelines, Chapter 107, Family Code, sets forth duties of guardians and attorneys ad litem appointed in suits affecting the parent-child relationship. These duties are not directly applicable to proceedings under Chapter 33, Family Code, and may be incompatible with the nature of such proceedings, but they reflect general legislative intent concerning the responsibilities of ad litems.

5. Under Rule 2.5(b), once a court concludes that an application should be granted on a single ground, it need not address other grounds. But in addressing any ground, the court should attempt to ascertain, among other factors, whether the pregnancy resulted from sexual assault, sexual abuse, or incest. The legislative history of Chapter 33, Family Code, indicates that one of the principal purposes of the statute was to screen for sexual crimes and abuse of minors so as to protect them against further victimization.

RULE 3. APPEAL FROM DENIAL OF APPLICATION

3.1 How to Appeal. To appeal the denial of an application, the minor must simultaneously file a notice of appeal with the clerk of the court that denied the application, file a copy of the notice of appeal with the clerk of the court of appeals to which an appeal is to be taken, and advise the clerk of the court of appeals by telephone that an appeal is being taken under Chapter 33, Family Code. The minor may use Form 3A but is not required to do so. The notice of appeal must:

(a) be styled "In re Jane Doe";

(b) state the number of the cause in the trial court;

(c) be addressed to a court of appeals with jurisdiction in the county in which the application was filed;

(d) state an intention to appeal; and

(e) be signed by the minor's attorney or attorney ad litem appointed by the trial court.

3.2 Clerk's Duties.

(a) ***Assistance in filing.*** The trial court clerk must give prompt assistance—in a manner designed to protect the minor's confidentiality—to persons seeking to file an appeal. Such assistance must include assuring that the notice of appeal is addressed to the proper court of appeals and that the minor's name and identifying information are not disclosed.

(b) ***Forwarding record to court of appeals.*** Upon receipt of a notice of appeal, the trial court clerk must instanter forward to the clerk of the court of appeals the notice of appeal, the clerk's record (original papers or copies) excluding the verification page, and the reporter's record. The trial court clerk must not send the record to the clerk of the court of appeals by mail but must, if feasible, deliver it by hand or transmit it by facsimile or other electronic means. If neither of these methods is feasible, then the record may be sent by overnight delivery.

(c) ***Certificate of court's failure to rule within time prescribed by statute.*** If the court of appeals fails to rule on an application within the time required by Section 33.004(b), Family Code, upon the minor's request, the clerk of the court of appeals must instanter issue a certificate to that effect, stating that the trial court's order is reversed and judgment is rendered that the application is deemed by statute to be granted. The clerk may use Form 3D but is not required to do so.

3.3 Proceedings in the Court of Appeals.

(a) ***Briefing and argument.*** A minor may request to be allowed to submit a brief and to present oral argument, but the Court may decide to rule without a brief or oral argument.

(b) ***Ruling.*** The court of appeals—sitting in a three-judge panel—must issue a judgment affirming or reversing the trial court's order denying the application. The court may use Form 3C but is not required to do so.

(c) ***Time for ruling.*** The court of appeals must rule on an appeal as soon as possible, subject to any postponement requested by the minor. Section 33.004(b), Family Code, states that a court must rule on an appeal by 5:00 p.m. on the second business day after the notice of appeal is filed with the court that denied the application, or if the minor requests a postponement, after the date the minor states she is ready to proceed, and that if the court does not rule within this time, the appeal is deemed to be granted.

(d) ***Postponement by minor.*** The minor may postpone the time of ruling by written request filed either with the trial court clerk at the time she files the notice of appeal or thereafter with the court of appeals clerk. The request may be submitted on Form 3B, but use of the form is not required. The request must either specify a date on which the minor will be ready to proceed to ruling, or state that the minor will later provide a date on which she will be ready to proceed to ruling. Once the minor determines when she will be ready to proceed to ruling, she must notify the court of appeals clerk of that date in writing.

(e) ***Opinion.***

(1) *Opinion optional.* A court of appeals may issue an opinion explaining its ruling, but it is not required to do so.

(2) *Time.* Any opinion must issue not later than:

(A) ten business days after the day on which a notice of appeal is filed in the Supreme Court, if an appeal is taken to the Supreme Court; or

(B) sixty days after the day on which the court of appeals issued its judgment, if no appeal is taken to the Supreme Court.

(3) *Confidential transmission to Supreme Court.* When the court of appeals issues an opinion, the clerk must confidentially transmit it instanter to the Supreme Court and to the trial court.

Notes & Comments

1. Chapter 33, Family Code, provides for no appeal from an order granting an application.

2. A request to postpone the ruling of the court of appeals may be used in conjunction with a request for oral argument or to submit briefing.

3. Neither Chapter 33, Family Code, nor these rules prescribes the appellate standard of review.

4. Although publication of appellate court opinions is prohibited by statute, the Supreme Court may amend these rules to address issues arising from their application and interpretation.

RULE 4. APPEAL TO THE SUPREME COURT

4.1 How to Appeal to the Supreme Court. To appeal from the court of appeals to the Supreme Court, the minor must simultaneously file a notice of appeal with the Clerk of the Supreme Court, file a copy of the notice of appeal with the clerk of the court of appeals, and advise the clerk of each court by telephone that an appeal is being taken under Chapter 33, Family Code. The minor may use Form 4A but is not required to do so. The notice of appeal must:

(a) be styled "In re Jane Doe";

(b) state the number of the cause in the court of appeals;

(c) state an intention to appeal; and

(d) be signed by the minor's attorney or attorney ad litem appointed by the trial court.

4.2 Clerk's Duties.

(a) ***Assistance in filing.*** The Clerk of the Supreme Court must give prompt assistance—in a manner designed to protect the minor's confidentiality—to persons seeking to file an appeal. Such assistance must include assuring that the notice of appeal is addressed to the Supreme Court and that the minor's name and identifying information are not disclosed.

(b) ***Forwarding record to Supreme Court.*** Upon receipt of a notice of appeal to the Supreme Court, the clerks of the court of appeals and Supreme Court must instanter have forwarded to the Supreme Court the record that was before the court of appeals.

4.3 Proceedings in the Supreme Court. A minor may request to be allowed to submit a brief and to present oral argument, but the Court may decide to rule without a brief or oral argument. The Court must rule as soon as possible.

Editor's Note: The local rules included below are not the complete set of rules for the counties listed, but instead are specific to family law cases. The rules are current as of the date of this book's publication. Because local rules for district courts are subject to amendment at any time, attorneys should contact the district clerk's office to determine if any amendments have been submitted to the Supreme Court for approval since the effective date. Also, some of the rules below contain references to appendixes, exhibits, or addendums, most of which have not been included. Attorneys should contact the district clerk's office for any appendix, exhibit, or addendum referenced and not included.

TABLE OF CONTENTS

BLANCO - BURNET - LLANO - SAN SABA COUNTIES

LOCAL RULES OF ADMINISTRATION OF THE 33RD JUDICIAL DISTRICT

Effective March 2, 1989

Editor's note: *As of the date of publication, proposed amendments were open for public comment. See http://www.courts.state.tx.us/District/33rd.*

SECTION 6. DOMESTIC RELATIONS & FAMILY LAW MATTERS

6.1. In all domestic relations and family law cases involving both temporary and permanent child support and/or visitation, together with any modification thereof, such support and/or visitation shall be at the Court's discretion, provided that the support and visitation guidelines and formulas contained in *Appendix C, Parent-Child Relationship Guidelines*, will be followed by the Court unless clear and convincing evidence supports an exception thereto. Agreement of the parties regarding support and visitation is encouraged and should be within the guidelines set forth in the above mentioned attachment unless clear and convincing evidence supports an exception and such exception is approved by the Court. The guidelines and formulas set out in the attachment are intended to provide information to the parties and attorneys so that child support and visitation may be predictable, reasonable, simple to calculate, without prejudice and reflect the duty of both parents to support their children commensurate with their ability and are intended to provide the non-custodial parent with reasonable access to and visitation with their children.

6.2. In all domestic relations and family law cases wherein either the setting of support or modification of support is requested, the moving party shall include in any order setting hearing the following:

"All parties to this action shall file with the Clerk and deliver a copy to all counsel or pro se parties on or before the date and time set for hearing on any support matter a statement showing all income and expenses claimed by the parties, a form for which is attached to this order. Submission of a completed Financial Information Sheet shall be furnished at the hearing on support as the minimum evidence to be considered by the Court."

6.3. The moving party seeking support shall attach a copy of the Financial Information Sheet form, contained in *Appendix D*, to the copy of the order setting hearing which is to be served on a party and shall furnish a copy of same to each counsel or pro se party not served with such order. All parties are required to file Financial Information Sheets as set out herein.

6.4. Financial Information Sheets shall be signed by the party and by counsel for such party. Such Financial Information Sheets shall be received as evidence in any proceedings involving the issue of support.

6.5. Within thirty (30) days from the date of the filing of an answer to a suit for divorce or annulment, each party shall file in the records of the case, with copies being furnished to opposing counsel and pro se parties, a sworn inventory and appraisement of all separate and community property of the parties, including any property claimed to belong to the children of the parties. In the event of a substantial disparity in property evaluation filed by parties to a proceeding, within ten (10) days after the filing of the original inventories and appraisements, the parties shall file a sworn statement setting forth the reasons for the evaluations assigned by each party. In the event of dispute as to the character of property, each party's contention shall be supported by affidavit and documents, if any, filed at least ten (10) days prior to trial.

6.6. In cases where division of the property is in dispute, each party shall, at least ten (10) days prior to trial, prepare and file in the case a Proposed Property Division (a form for which is contained in *Appendix E*) with a copy thereof being furnished to opposing counsel and pro se parties.

6.7. The failure to timely file the inventories and appraisements, affidavits or statements or proposed property divisions, as set out herein above, may result, in addition to other sanctions provided by law, in the continuance of temporary support or in the discontinuance of same, depending on the party failing to comply with these rules.

6.8. In the event of the filing of an agreement incident to divorce settling the property of the parties to such actions and all other matters in issue, including custody, support and visitation matters, it shall not be necessary to file such inventories and appraisements and proposed property division forms.

6.9. In domestic relations and family law cases, ex parte orders:

See note on p. 1157.

A. May not include a provision that:

(1) Requires a sworn inventory and appraisement of all property;

(2) Requires the support of either of the spouses;

(3) Requires the production of books, papers, documents and tangible things by any party;

(4) Orders payment of attorney's fees and expenses;

(5) Appoints a receiver for the preservation and protection of the property of the parties;

(6) Awards one spouse exclusive occupancy of the residence during the pendency of the case;

(7) Prohibits the parties from spending funds for reasonable and necessary living expenses;

(8) Awards one spouse exclusive control of a party's usual business or occupation;

(9) Excludes a spouse from occupancy of the residence where the party is living;

(10) Prohibits a party from engaging in acts reasonable and necessary to the conduct of that party's usual business and occupation.

B. May be set for hearing in any of the five counties within the District.

6.10. Immediately following the hearing on temporary orders, counsel for the petition and/or movant or pro se petitioner and/or movant, shall prepare and submit an order to opposing counsel and/or pro se parties for their approval. In the event opposing counsel and/or parties fail to refuse to approve such order and return same to counsel for the moving party within five (5) days, such order will be signed by the Judge upon presentation by the moving party.

6.11. Requests for setting of a case for final trial in contested domestic relations or family law cases shall be in writing and directed to the Court Coordinator of this district, with a copy to opposing counsel and any pro se parties. Such request shall, in addition to the requirements set forth in Section 2 of these rules, certify that all parties have fully complied with the requirements under Section 6 of these rules and shall contain a statement by the requesting party of the contested issues and an estimate of the time required to hear the case.

6.12. Counsel shall consult with client and opposing counsel and/or pro se parties prior to trial time. Announcements requesting time to consult with client or opposing counsel shall be placed at the end of the docket for the day, or in the Court's discretion, passed to another day.

6.13. The Court may order a pre-trial conference in contested domestic relations and family law cases, as provided in Section 4 of these rules.

6.14. In the event an agreement is reached in domestic relations or family law cases on temporary orders, parties and counsel shall execute and file the Court an Agreement for Temporary Orders, a form for which appears in *Appendix F*.

6.15. The Court may, on its own motion or the motion of a party, refer a pending dispute for resolution by an alternative dispute resolution proceeding provided for in Chapters 151, 152 or 154 of the Texas Civil Practice and Remedies Code. Any party may, within 10 days after receiving notification of a referral, file a written objection which sets forth a reasonable basis for the party's objection to referral.

BRAZOS COUNTY

LOCAL RULES OF ADMINISTRATION OF THE DISTRICT COURTS & COUNTY COURTS AT LAW

Effective February 1, 1990.

RULE 4. FAMILY LAW CASES

4.10. TIME STANDARDS FOR FAMILY LAW CASE DISPOSITION

Each court shall, so far as reasonably possible, ensure that all family law and juvenile cases are brought to trial or final disposition in conformity with the following time standards.

a. Family Law Cases

(1) Contested Family Law Cases. Within six (6) months from appearance date or within six (6) months from the expiration of the waiting period provided by the Family Code where such is required, whichever is later.

(2) Uncontested Family Law Cases. Within three (3) months from appearance date or within three (3) months from the expiration of the waiting period provided by the Family Code where such is required, whichever is later.

b. Juvenile Cases. In addition to Title 3, Texas Family Code:

See note on p. 1157.

(1) Detention Hearings. On the next business day following admission to any detention facility.

(2) Adjudicatory or Transfer (Waiver) Hearings.

(a) Concerning a juvenile in a detention facility: Not later than 10 days following admission to such a facility, except for good cause shown of record.

(b) Concerning a juvenile not in a detention facility: Not later than 30 days following the filing of the petition, except for good cause shown of record.

(3) Disposition Hearings. Not later than 15 days following the adjudicatory hearing. The court may grant additional time in exceptional cases that require more complex evaluation.

(4) Nothing herein shall prevent a judge from recessing a juvenile hearing at any stage of the proceeding where the parties are agreeable or when, in the opinion of the judge presiding in the case, the best interests of the child and of society shall be served.

4.11. ANCILLARY PROCEEDINGS, TEMPORARY ORDERS, & EMERGENCY MATTERS

In the event a bona fide emergency exists or a matter requires special attention and the judge of the court where the case is pending is unavailable, the attorney or party seeking relief shall contact any judge who has jurisdiction and the judge can consider the matter, but the case shall remain in the court originally filed.

4.12. DISPOSITION PROPOSALS

(a) To expedite disposition, it shall be the duty of each attorney to confer, prior to trial, with each other attorney regarding settlement, stipulations, estimated time of trial, waiver of jury, the extent description, character and value of the property in question, amount of support, amount of monthly income, conservatorship, periods of possession and/or access, rights, duties and powers of the conservators, and contested issues.

(b) Each attorney shall submit a Proposed Property Division (form furnished by the clerk, court coordinator or see Appendix for form) including property claimed or recognized as separate property, to the court and opposing counsel not later than the commencement of trial.

4.13. UNCONTESTED MATTERS

Requests for hearing uncontested matters and ex parte matters may be made in person, by telephone or in writing to the court coordinator for the court in which the matter is pending. The court coordinator will set the matter for the next available uncontested docket or at any other time that may be convenient to the parties and the court. The requesting party shall, when required by these rules or other applicable law, notify all attorneys of record or parties pro se of such setting.

4.14. FINANCIAL INFORMATION STATEMENTS

A Financial Information Statement (furnished by the clerk, court coordinator or see Appendix for form) shall be furnished to the Court and opposing counsel not later than the commencement of a hearing or trial in which the payment of support or property rights will be an issue.

4.15. CHILD SUPPORT GUIDELINES

The amount of child support payable to the obligor parent shall be set in accordance with the current Child Support Guidelines adopted by the Supreme Court of Texas.

4.18. AD LITEM APPOINTMENTS

The attorneys requesting appointment of attorneys and guardians ad litem may recommend a suitable, qualified person for such appointment. Proposed orders of appointment should accompany each such request.

COLLIN COUNTY

RULES OF PRACTICE DISTRICT COURTS

Effective May 29, 1998.

PART FIVE (FAMILY LAW MATTERS)

5.1 HEARINGS ON TEMPORARY ORDERS

Each party at any hearing on temporary orders shall be limited to twenty (20) minutes total to present its evidence, cross-examine, rebut, and argue its case, unless the Judge affirmatively orders otherwise.

5.2 SEMINAR FOR DIVORCING PARENTS

The Court may require the parties to a suit affecting the parent-child relationship to successfully complete the "For Kids' Sake" Seminar (972-519-8720).

See note on p. 1157.

COMAL - HAYS - CALDWELL COUNTIES

LOCAL RULES OF PRACTICE FOR THE 22ND, 207TH & 274TH JUDICIAL DISTRICT COURTS OF TEXAS

Effective September 6, 1989.

SECTION THREE. DOMESTIC RELATIONS

RULE 6. UNCONTESTED CASES

In all uncontested Domestic Relations cases, all forms and preferably the final judgment should be ready at the time of trial.

RULE 7. SUPPORT & TEMPORARY SPOUSAL ALIMONY

A) Financial Information Statement. Before any contested trial or hearing involving child support or temporary spousal alimony, each party shall prepare and file with the Court a financial information statement in the form provided by the Clerk.

B) Obligor's Place of Payment. Unless waived by the Court, all support and temporary spousal alimony payments shall be made through the Office of the District Clerk and forwarded to the Obligee.

C) Envelopes. The Obligee shall provide self-addressed, postage prepaid envelopes to the District Clerk in order for payments to be forwarded to the Obligee.

RULE 8. SOCIAL STUDIES

A) Adoptions. Arrangements for the preparation of a social study shall be made on all adoptions before the case will be set for trial.

B) Arrangements for Payment. In contested domestic relation cases involving custody of children wherein a social study is requested, the anticipated costs of preparation must be deposited with the District Clerk or other satisfactory arrangements made to guarantee payment to the person preparing the social study. Without such arrangements the preparation of a social study will not be ordered.

RULE 9. GUIDELINES

Copies of the Supreme Court Family Code Guidelines on Support and the local Guidelines on Visitation may be obtained from the District Clerk.

See note on p. 1157.

DALLAS COUNTY

LOCAL RULES OF THE FAMILY DISTRICT COURTS

Effective May 11, 1999.

PART I: FILING, ASSIGNMENT & TRANSFER

1.01. RANDOM ASSIGNMENT TO FAMILY COURTS

Except as provided in 1.02, the following cases shall be docketed numerically in order of filing and assigned in random order to the 301st, 302nd, 303rd, 330th, 254th, 255th and 256th District Courts (and Courts hereafter created giving preference to Family Law matters): divorce, annulment, suit to declare a marriage void, suits affecting the parent-child relationship concerning paternity/legitimation, managing conservatorship, termination and adoption, possessory conservatorship; possession and access to a child, support for a minor or disabled child, actions for breach, enforcement or interpretation of an agreement incident to divorce and/or decrees of divorce, pre-marital and partition agreements, protective orders (other than those filed by the District Attorney), uniform interstate family support cases, and all other cases arising under the Texas Family Code when there is no court of continuing jurisdiction, and all matters incident to or originating from such cases including suits for attorneys fees.

1.02. RANDOM ASSIGNMENT TO JUVENILE COURTS

When there is no court of continuing jurisdiction, the following cases shall be docketed numerically in order of filing and assigned in random order to the 304th and 305th District Courts (and district courts hereafter designated to handle juvenile matters): protection of children in an emergency, removal of infant from hospital, juvenile name change, minority disability removal, delinquency, children in need of supervision and, when Petitioner is the Texas Department of Protective & Regulatory Services, suits affecting the parent-child relationship concerning Managing Conservatorship, Paternity/Legitimation, Termination or Adoption.

1.03. ASSIGNMENT TO COURT OF CONTINUING JURISDICTION

If there is a court of continuing jurisdiction, all requests or petitions for Further action, including but not limited to modification, habeas corpus, contempt or enforcement, clarification, protective orders or other relief under the Texas Family Code, shall be filed in the court of continuing jurisdiction.

1.04. BILLS OF REVIEW

Every suit or proceeding in the nature of a bill of review or otherwise, which seeks to attack, avoid or set aside any judgment, order or decree of a Family District Court of Dallas County, shall be assigned to the Court in which such judgment, order or decree was rendered.

1.05. ANCILLARY PROCEEDINGS

Every ancillary action suit shall be assigned to the Family District Court to which the matter is ancillary. Every garnishment, turnover or other collection-remedy after judgment or any action arising out of a decree/judgment or Agreement Incident to Divorce shall be filed in the Family District Court to which rendered the judgment upon which the action is founded.

1.06. CASES SUBJECT TO TRANSFER

a. Every motion for transfer, consolidation or joint hearing of two or more cases under Rule 174(a), Texas Rules of Civil Procedure, shall be filed in the earliest filed case. The Motion shall have the cause number and style of each applicable case. Notice of the hearing shall be given to all parties in all actions pursuant to Texas Rules of Civil Procedure 21 and 21a. If granted, the other District Court or Family District Court shall enter an order transferring all other actions into the earliest filed case, except in situations where a SAPCR is pending and a subsequent divorce is filed involving a parent of a child of the SAPCR. Upon motion, the SAPCR action shall be transferred and consolidated into the divorce action, in which case the transfer or consolidation shall be done pursuant to the Texas Family Code.

b. If any action is dismissed by any party or the Court, and is refiled within one hundred eighty (180) days of the date of dismissal and assigned to a different Court, either party or the Court may move within thirty (30) days of the filing of an answer to transfer the case to the first Court and, upon hearing, the transfer shall be granted.

1.07. CASES TRANSFERRED TO DALLAS COUNTY

Whenever a case is transferred to Dallas County by a Court of another county, and the order of transfer specifies the particular court to which the case is transferred, such specification shall be disregarded and the case shall be assigned in the manner provided in Part I of these rules.

1.08. SEVERED CASES

Whenever a motion to sever is granted, the severed claim shall be filed as a new case in the same Court and shall be assigned a new cause number by the District Clerk. A filing fee is required as in all new cases and the attorneys must provide copies of the severed pleadings at the time of filing.

PART II: EX PARTE ORDERS

2.01. PRESENTING EX PARTE ORDERS

All applications for ex parte orders shall first be presented for determination to the Court (Associate Judge) in which the case is pending, and only if the Court is unavailable to promptly review same may it be presented to another Court.

2.02. CERTIFICATES TO EX PARTE ORDERS

Prior to presentment, all applications for ex parte orders shall certify in writing, signed by the party or attorney, one of the following:

I hereby certify as follows: (check off and fill in blanks as required)

1. To the best of my knowledge, there is no attorney of record representing any opposing party at this time; or

2. Prior to presenting this matter to an Associate Judge for approval, I contacted all attorneys of record, transmitted a copy of the pleadings and proposed order in this matter, and notified them that I was requesting such ex parte relief, and:

A. After conferring, no attorney of record wishes to be heard prior to the presentment of this request for ex parte relief; or,

B. We were unable to reach an agreement, at which time I notified all attorneys of record that I would present this matter to the Associate Judge at (time) on, ______, (date) in the (court) and invited them to attend and be heard prior to signing; or,

C. I was unable to speak with the opposing attorney(s) and I left word with a staff person for each attorney that I would present this matter to the Associate Judge at (time) on, (date) in the (court) and invited them to attend and be heard prior to signing; or,

D. After diligent attempts, I was unable to reach the opposing attorney(s) and was further unable to

See note on p. 1157.

leave any message with counsels office regarding the presentment of this matter to the Associate Judge.

For purposes of this rule, representation of prior counsel ends upon the entry of a final order.

PART III: SETTING HEARINGS

3.01. CERTIFICATES OF CONFERENCE

No motion or special exceptions, other than those listed in Rules 3.03, 3.04 and 3.06, will be set for hearing until the moving party shall first communicate with opposing counsel to determine whether a contemplated motion will be opposed. If not opposed, the moving party shall accompany the motion with a proposed order signed by all counsel indicating approval of same. If the motion will be opposed, the following certificate shall be attached to the motion and signed by the attorney in charge (or party pro se):

CERTIFICATE OF CONFERENCE

I, the undersigned attorney (or party pro se), hereby certify to the Court that:

1. I have conferred with opposing counsel in an effort to resolve the issues contained in this motion without the necessity of Court intervention, or

2. At (time) on (date), I attempted to reach opposing counsel and left a specific message that the purpose of my call was to attempt to resolve the issues contained in this motion without the necessity of Court intervention or could not leave a message because __________ ______________________________.

Such efforts have been unsuccessful, and it is necessary to set a hearing on this motion.

3.02. MOTIONS/ORDERS REQUIRING ASSOCIATE JUDGES & JUDGES SIGNATURES

The following documents require the approval of an Associate Judge and original signature of a Judge (but no certificate of conference) before it can be set by the Court Clerk/Administrator for hearing:

a. Show cause order on contempt;

b. Order granting a writ of habeas corpus;

c. Motion to modify filed within one year;

d. Any motion to modify in which a request for temporary orders is made at the time the motion to modify is filed;

e. Writ of attachment;

f. Writ of garnishment;

g. Application for any kind of injunctive relief;

h. Application for protective order;

i. Order Extending TRO;

j. Motion for continuance; and

k. Motion to reinstate

3.03. NOTICE FOR ALL OTHER HEARINGS

The following form should be used to set hearings on all matters (except as otherwise required by law):

NOTICE OF HEARING

The above motion is set for hearing on the Associate Judges/Judges docket of the Judicial District Court at ______ o'clock ___.m. on the day of _________, __________.

CLERK/ADMINISTRATOR OF COURT

By the Clerks/Administrators stamped signature, on the above Notice of Hearing, the Court Clerk/Administrator shall set the following matters for hearing, without a Judges signature, Associate Judges approval or certificate of conference:

a. Motion for summary judgment;

b. Rule 13 motions for sanctions;

c. Motion to show authority;

d. Motion to extend TRO;

e. Motion to transfer venue;

f. Special appearance;

g. Plea in bar;

h. Plea to the subject matter jurisdiction of the court;

i. Motion for new trial or to correct, modify or amend an order;

j. Motion for rehearing;

k. Appeal from associate judges recommendation;

l. Motion for entry of order, with order sought attached if transmittal letter & provided;

m. "Trial motions" (Motion in limine; motion affecting order of proceeding; motion related to strikes or challenges of jurors);

n. Motion for temporary orders; and

o. Motion for pretrial hearing

3.04. REMOVAL/RESET OF HEARINGS

A party or counsel setting a non-final or non-special set hearing may remove or reset such setting only (1) upon agreement of all opposing sides or (2) after

See note on p. 1157.

reasonable notice to all opposing sides per Texas Rules of Civil Procedure Rule 21. Failure to comply with this rule may result in costs being assessed.

3.05. FINAL HEARINGS

a. A Clerk/Administrator may set final hearings on the merits without a certificate of conference or fiat.

b. Any person who obtains a setting for a final hearing before a District Judge or Associate Judge shall have the duty to send all opposing parties written notice of such setting within two (2) business days of the date they obtained such setting. This rule does not change the obligations for notice in the Texas Rules of Civil Procedure, including but not limited to Rules 12, 21, 21a, 166a and 245.

3.06. SPECIALLY SET CASE

Cases specially set shall take precedence over all other matters in all other Family District Courts, except matters entitled to preference by law and matters commenced but not completed in the preceding week. Other engagements of counsel or parties shall not be grounds for postponement of a case specially set, unless good cause is shown on a timely filed motion. No more than one case shall be specially set for any particular docket call. No party shall specially set a case that conflicts with another court setting of said party or his attorney. If a person with a special setting obtains a subsequent setting which conflicts with such special setting, that person must, within two (2) business days, notify the court setting the later matter and opposing party of the conflict.

3.07. MOTIONS TO BE HEARD TEN OR MORE DAYS BEFORE TRIAL

Dilatory pleas, special exceptions and other, motions or exceptions (excluding motions in limine and other trial motions) shall be heard no less than ten (10) days before the date on which the case is set for final hearing, provided that the pleadings to which same are directed are on file.

PART IV: SPECIAL EXCEPTIONS

4.01. SPECIAL EXCEPTIONS

The Court shall deny special exceptions complaining of a pleading which sets out its cause of action using language consistent with the Texas Family Code.

PART V: PRE-TRIAL CONFERENCE

5.01. PURPOSE OF PRE-TRIAL CONFERENCE

Counsel or parties pro se will be expected at pre-trial to advise the Court which issues will be disputed and to be familiar with the authorities applicable to the questions of law raised at pre-trial. Failure to conform to this rule shall be ground for postponement of the trial, setting of further pre-trial hearings, or other appropriate action.

5.02. WHO SHALL ATTEND PRE-TRIAL CONFERENCE

Counsel attending the pre-trial shall either be the attorney in charge or shall be familiar with the case and be fully authorized to state the party's position on the law and the facts and to make stipulations of fact. Counsel may not send to pre-trial in his stead a legal assistant, paralegal, investigator, secretary or other non-attorney. Parties appearing pro se must attend pre-trial in person.

5.03. CONSEQUENCES FOR FAILURE TO ATTEND PRE-TRIAL CONFERENCE

When counsel or a party pro se, after notice, fails to appear at pretrial the Court may:

a. Rule on all motions, dilatory pleas and exceptions in absence of such person;

b. Declare any motions, dilatory pleas, or exceptions of such absent party waived;

c. Advance or delay the trial setting according to the convenience of persons present;

d. Pass and reset the pre-trial;

e. Decline to set the case for trial, cancel a setting previously made;

f. Dismiss the case for want of prosecution or grant a default judgment, if attorneys were ordered to appear, especially where there has been a previous failure to appear or where no amendment has been filed after exceptions were previously sustained; and/or

g. Grant sanctions or other relief.

PART VI: DISCOVERY

Reserved for expansion.

PART VII: ANNOUNCEMENT FOR TRIAL

7.01. APPEARANCE AT DOCKET CALL

Docket call is the trial setting. In all contested matters set for final hearing, at the time of docket call for a

See note on p. 1157.

particular week, all counsel or parties pro so are required to appear at docket call and make their announcements to the Court concerning their readiness for trial unless they have previously appeared at the pretrial and received a specific date and time for trial. Any unqualified announcement of "ready" or "ready subject to" another court engagement shall be made to the Judge, or if so instructed by the Judge, to the Court Coordinator.

7.02. CONTINUANCES

Every ground for postponement or continuance shall be brought to the Courts attention at or before the docket call on the date the case is set for trial. No request for pass, postponement or reset of any trial, pretrial, or other hearing shall be granted unless counsel for all parties involved consent, or unless all parties not joining in such request or their counsel have been notified and have had opportunity to object; provided however, that failure to make an announcement at docket call shall be taken as consent to pass, postpone, reset or dismiss for want of prosecution any case set for trial the following week. All motions for continuance shall be presented in the form and manner provided by the Texas Rules of Civil Procedure.

7.03. APPEARANCE FOR NON-FINAL MATTERS

For all non-final matters and cases set on either the Judges daily docket or Associate Judges docket, all parties and counsel shall appear at the time and place set for the hearing and make their announcement as provided in 7.01. Failure to appear shall be treated as failure to announce under 7.02.

7.04 CONFLICTING ENGAGEMENT OF COUNSEL

a. Where counsel for either party has a conflicting trial or appeal setting, the Court may hold the case over until the trial or appeal has been completed.

b. If counsel is engaged in trial or appeal in another court, counsel shall be obligated to advise the clerk of the Court in which he is set for trial or which is holding the case over of counsels availability immediately upon completion of such other trial or appeal.

c. Mediation settings confirmed by letter from the Mediator and presented to the Court at docket call should take precedence over all cases except those cases previously given a special setting.

PART VIII: DISMISSAL FOR WANT OF PROSECUTION

8.01. ACTIONS RESULTING IN A CASE BEING DISMISSED FOR WANT OF PROSECUTION

a. Failure of a party to request a setting or take other appropriate action after notice from the Court Administrator that the case has been pending without action for more than 180 days, provided that upon giving the first notice (which shall be at least 30 days in advance of the date set for dismissal) of intent to dismiss for want of prosecution, the Court shall remove the matter from its dismissal docket if counsel for either side does contact the Court in person;

b. Failure of moving party or his counsel to appear for trial, pretrial or other preliminary hearing;

c. Failure to comply with Rule 8.02; or

d. For any other reason provided for by these rules and/or the Texas Rules of Civil Procedure.

Subject to other provisions of these rules, the Clerk shall mail a written notice of such dismissal to all parties or their counsel of record.

8.02. DWP AFTER RENDITION OR ANNOUNCED SETTLEMENT

Unless ordered otherwise, within thirty days after rendition or an announced settlement by the parties, they shall cause decisions or settlements of any kind to be reduced to writing. Upon failure to furnish the Court Clerk/Administrator with such a judgment or order finally disposing of a case, or to request extension of the filing or to set a motion for entry, the Court shall enter an order of dismissal without prejudice with costs taxed at the Judges discretion;

The Court will not sign an order that does not contain either the signature of all attorneys as to form or proof of notice that said order has been presented to all attorneys of record requesting same to file written objections within ten (10) days.

PART IX: WITHDRAWAL / SUBSTITUTION OF COUNSEL

9.01. CIRCUMSTANCES UNDER WHICH ATTORNEY MAY WITHDRAW

No attorney of record shall be permitted to withdraw from any case without presenting a motion and obtaining from the Court an order granting leave to withdraw pursuant to Texas Rules of Civil Procedure 10. The letter required under TRCP shall be sent to the client advising that the client has ten (10) days after the date of

See note on p. 1157.

mailing the letter to make any objection to such withdrawal to the Court, in writing, and that if not done and no objection raised, the motion shall be granted. A copy of the motion shall be delivered or mailed to opposing counsel. No such motion shall be presented within thirty (30) days of the trial date or at such time as to require delay of the trial. After leave is granted, the withdrawing attorney shall send his client, the Court and opposing counsel a letter notifying of the last known mailing address of his client and of any settings. Notice to the client shall be by certified and regular mail.

9.02. ATTORNEY SUBSTITUTING FOR PRIOR ATTORNEY

If an attorney is substituting in as new counsel or attorney in charge for a party, the Court shall sign an order withdrawing the prior attorney in charge and substituting in the new counsel. Upon the filing of a motion requesting such relief signed by the party and the attorney substituting in as attorney in charge, the motion and order must be sent to all opposing parties and to the former attorney in charge, pursuant to Texas Rules of Civil Procedure 21 and 21a.

PART X: INFORMATION FROM CLERK

10.01. INFORMATION THE COURT CLERK WILL NOT PROVIDE TO PARTIES OR COUNSEL

a. The Court Clerk will not state whether a case has been filed; and

b. No information will be given on a case unless a case number is known and provided. If the party or counsel does not know the case number, they will be referred to the public terminals in the records department of the District Clerks Office.

10.02. INFORMATION THE COURT CLERK WILL PROVIDE TO PARTIES OR COUNSEL IF A CASE NUMBER IS GIVEN

a. What action is on file, the date of filing, the names addresses and telephone numbers of all attorneys in charge, and the specific court to which the case is assigned;

b. Returns of service and the dates of such returns;

c. Correct style of a case; and

d. Any settings in a case.

10.03. COURT CLERK/ ADMINISTRATOR WILL TAKE MESSAGES FOR THE JUDGE

The Court Clerk/Administrator shall take and timely deliver messages, including those related to an attorney being delayed for an appearance, and shall promptly notify the Judge of same.

PART XI: FILING OF PLEADINGS

11.01. PLEADINGS MUST BE TITLED & HAVE HOLES PUNCHED

All pleadings, motions, orders and other papers, including exhibits attached thereto, when offered for filing or entry shall comply with TRCP Rule 45 and shall be descriptively titled and pre-punched at the top of the page to accommodate the Clerks 2 3/4" center-to-center flat-filing system. Each instrument shall, at the bottom of each page, be numbered and titled, *i.e.*, Petitioners Original Petition-page 2. Motions shall be separate documents from orders and judgments. The Clerk may not sign or amend any instrument for a party or attorney.

11.02. USE OF FAX MACHINES

Any party pro se or attorney who does not have a fax machine but who uses one to send correspondence to the other party or parties must indicate the number of the facsimile machine they are using, and they shall thereafter in the case be deemed to have designated such fax number as a number for receiving same.

PART XII: ACCESS TO FILES

12.01. NO PART OF A FILE CAN BE REMOVED FROM COURT

No pleadings or paper belonging to the files of the Court shall be taken from the office or custody of the Clerk, except upon order of the Court or with the Courts permission.

12.02. ORDER LIMITING ACCESS TO A FILE

Any party or attorney may obtain an order limiting access to the files in any pending action by applying to the Court in which the action is filed and upon showing good cause for such action, the motion shall be granted. Upon the entry of an order limiting access to a file, the Clerk shall comply with the order and shall prevent all persons, except those therein designated, from having access to the file.

See note on p. 1157.

PART XIII: ATTORNEYS

13.01. AD LITEM ENTITLED TO ALL PLEADINGS

When the court appoints a guardian or attorney ad litem, all counsel shall provide such appointee with copies of their pleadings, orders, and reports filed with the Court, within five days (5) of notice of the appointment.

13.02. APPOINTMENT OF MEDIATOR

In a case selected for mediation, the Court encourages parties to choose their own mediator. The Court, if requested, shall appoint an attorney-mediator who has substantial family law litigation experience.

13.03. LAWYERS CREED & CODE OF JUDICIAL CONDUCT

Counsel and parties shall treat the Court, court personnel, each other and trial participants in a manner consistent with the Texas Lawyers Creed.

The Court and court personnel shall treat attorneys, parties and trial participants in a manner consistent with the Texas Code of Judicial Conduct.

13.04. VACATION LETTERS

Each attorney in charge shall have the right to designate vacation days and days of continuing legal education provided he notifies the clerk of the court and all opposing counsel in writing by separate letters in each case at ten (10) days, prior to such designated dates, and provided said dates do not conflict with a current setting for trial, hearing, deposition, inspection, mediation or discovery deadline in the case. During the dates designated in said letter, opposing parties shall not set any matter for hearing in the case and any such setting is void. If a true emergency situation exists, the Court may grant ex parte emergency relief during the designated time period.

13.05. PRO SE LITIGANTS

Rules for attorneys apply equally to pro se litigants.

All requirements of these rules applicable to attorneys or counsel; apply with equal force to pro se litigants. Pro se litigants are required to provide addresses and telephone listings at which they can be reached by court personnel and opposing counsel. Failure to accept delivery or to pick up mail addressed to the address provided by pro se litigants will be considered constructive receipt of the mail or delivered document which may be established by postal service receipt, certified or registered mail receipt, or comparable proof of delivery.

PART XIV: COURTROOM DECORUM

14.01. ATTORNEYS TO INFORM CLIENT OF PROPER COURTROOM DECORUM

All attorneys shall be responsible for advising their clients and witnesses of appropriate courtroom conduct, attire, and policy regarding children.

14.02. PAGERS, BEEPERS & TELEPHONES

Pagers, beepers, and telephones should be turned off when a person is in the courtroom. If the beeper can be on without making a sound (except the vibration) it may remain on if kept in that mode. Failure to follow this rule may result in forfeiture of the device emitting sound.

14.03. APPROPRIATE DRESS FOR COURT APPEARANCES

The following shall not be acceptable in the courtroom: hats, bandannas or other headgear, shorts, bare midriffs, tank tops, tattered or dirty clothing.

14.04. CONDUCT IN THE COURTROOM

a. No magazines, newspapers or other such reading material may be read in the courtroom while court is in session.

b. There will be no eating, drinking or chewing gum in the courtroom unless the Court has expressly stated otherwise.

c. There will be no outbursts, disturbances, threats, obscene language, or gestures.

Violation of this rule shall result in immediate expulsion and/or direct contempt.

14.05. CHILDREN IN THE COURTROOM

No child is to be brought to the courthouse unless the Judge or Associate Judge has specifically requested the child be brought at a time certain for interview or testimony.

14.06. CONSEQUENCES OF VIOLATING RULES UNDER PART XIV

Violation of the courtroom decorum rules of Part XIV will result in immediate expulsion of the person who is violating the same. They will not be permitted to return until they have conformed to these rules. Such expulsion will not be grounds for a continuance or delay, and the case will proceed.

See note on p. 1157.

DALLAS COUNTY

PART XV: RULES

15.01. RULES

These local rules shall supersede any other local rules and shall constitute the Local Rules of Practice for the Family District Courts of Dallas County, Texas, as adopted by the seven (7) Family District Courts but shall not in anyway supersede or pre-empt any standing order promulgated by any Family District Judge as to a particular policy of that court.

DENTON COUNTY

ADMINISTRATIVE RULES

Effective March 1, 1994; amended July 26, 2000.

1.0. DOCKETING & SETTINGS OF TRIALS & HEARINGS

1.1 Setting Civil Cases. A request for trial shall be made by any party in writing within ninety days after appearance date.

...

1.14 In the event a request for setting is not made in a Family Code case, the clerk shall set the matter for final disposition no later than 75 days after the appearance date or within 75 days from the expiration of the waiting period provided by the Family Code where such is required, whichever is later unless a shorter period is required by law.

5.0. SPECIAL RULES FOR FAMILY LAW CASES

5.1 Conclusion Of Contested Family Code Cases. Contested Family Code cases should be concluded within six months from the appearance date or within six months from the expiration of the waiting period provided by the Family Code where such is required.

5.2 Conclusion Of Uncontested Family Code Cases. Uncontested Family Code cases should be concluded within 3 months from appearance date or within 3 months from the expiration of the waiting period provided by the Family Code where such is required, whichever is later.

5.3 Divorce Cases.

5.31 A sworn inventory and appraisement of all property, both real and personal, owned or claimed by the parties, and a list of all debts and liabilities owed by the parties shall be filed by the petitioner and any party seeking affirmative relief within three months after the appearance date. Unless leave of court is granted for a late filing of the sworn inventory and list of debts, the action will be dismissed for want of prosecution.

5.32 A sworn statement of income and monthly expenses shall be filed by the petitioner within three months after the appearance date. Unless leave of court is granted for a late filling of the sworn statement of income and monthly expenses, the action will be dismissed for want of prosecution.

5.4 Contested Conservatorship Cases. A social study shall be submitted to the Court and opposing counsel at least fifteen (15) days prior to trial by the litigant obtaining the trial setting.

EL PASO COUNTY

LOCAL RULES

Effective May 11, 1993.

PART FOUR—FAMILY LAW CASES

RULE 4.01. FILING OF FAMILY LAW CASES

(A) Juvenile cases are to be filed separately as Family district court cases.

(B) Family law cases shall be heard by associate judges upon orders of referral from the district courts and county courts at law pursuant to Chapter 54 of the Government Code.

RULE 4.02. ANCILLARY PROCEEDINGS, TEMPORARY ORDERS, & EMERGENCY MATTERS

(A) Notwithstanding a timely filed objection to referral to the trial on the merits, ancillary proceedings and temporary order hearings shall be scheduled and heard by associate judges and not by the referring court unless otherwise directed.

(B) The duration of such hearings is limited to no more than one half hour unless otherwise specifically requested at time of scheduling.

RULE 4.03. UNCONTESTED MATTERS

Uncontested matters shall be handled by an uncontested docket as directed by the associate judges. No schedule setting will be required for such dockets.

See note on p. 1157.

RULE 4.04. FINANCIAL INFORMATION STATEMENTS; INVENTORY & APPRAISEMENT; & PRETRIAL PROCEDURE

The associate judges shall establish policies to govern financial information statements, inventories and appraisements, and pretrial proceedings.

RULE 4.05. JURY DEMAND & WITHDRAWAL OF JURY DEMAND

A copy of the jury demand or withdrawal of jury demand shall be provided to the referring court and to the associate judges by the attorney filing same when filed with the district clerk.

RULE 4.06. OBJECTION TO REFERRAL

Objection to referral shall apply to trial on the merits only. A copy of the filed objection shall be provided to the referring court and to the associate judges by the attorney filing same when filed with the district clerk.

RULE 4.07. WITHDRAWAL OF OBJECTION

All withdrawals of objection to referral shall be made with the concurrence of all parties and a copy shall be provided to the referring court and to the associate judges when filed with the district clerk.

RULE 4.08. CANCELLATION OF COURT SETTING

Cancellations of court settings shall be in writing, unless expressly excused, and only with the concurrence of both parties. The cancellation notice shall state the parties' concurrence.

RULE 4.09. REQUEST FOR SETTING

Settings will be arranged through the family law court coordinator. Requests for settings may be required to be in writing, may specify the amount of time needed, and may be filed with the clerk, as directed by the associate judges.

RULE 4.10. CONFIRMATION OF LENGTHY HEARINGS

Attorneys shall confirm in writing with the family law court coordinator at least one week in advance of scheduled hearings of a duration of three hours or more that said hearings are still intended to be held. Failure to so confirm may result in cancellation of the hearing.

RULE 4.11. PROPOSED ORDERS OR DECREES

All proposed orders or decrees submitted to an associate judge which must be ratified or approved by the referring court shall include a signature line for the "Judge Presiding."

RULE 4.12. JANE DOE

Pursuant to Texas parental notification rules and forms effective date January 1, 2000, Rule 2.1(b)3—court assignment and transfer by local rule.

(A) Applications will be filed with the district clerk who will assign the application to a family law court in rotation. Applications filed with anyone other than the district clerk's office shall be filed instanter with the district clerk's office.

(B) Upon application, the district clerk will hand deliver the application and verification in a red folder to the court coordinator, should the assigned court be closed for business, then the district clerk will hand deliver the application to one of the other court coordinators/judges of the family law courts.

(C) The court coordinator will immediately deliver the application to the judge of said court. If the judge is not available the court coordinator will hand deliver the application to one of the court coordinators/judges of the other family law courts, should all family law judges be unavailable to hear cases, then the court coordinator or district clerk shall hand deliver the application to the court coordinator/presiding judge of the council of judges.

(D) The presiding judge of the council of judges will then assign one of the other district courts to hear the application and have the application hand delivered to that court coordinator/judge.

(E) If the presiding judge of the Council of Judges is not available, then the application will be hand delivered to the senior presiding judge to assign a court and have the application hand delivered to that court coordinator/judge.

FORT BEND COUNTY

RULES OF THE 328TH & 387TH DISTRICT COURTS

Effective September 18, 2000.

RULE 1. OBJECTIVE

1.1 Purpose of the Rules. Obtaining a fair, just and impartial adjudication of the rights of the parties and the children is the purpose of these rules. These rules encourage using alternate dispute resolution in all appropriate cases.

See note on p. 1157.

1.2 The rules shall apply equally to attorneys, parties and parties appearing pro se.

RULE 2. TRANSFER OF CASES

2.1 Transfer. Continuing, Exclusive Jurisdiction. All provisions of the Texas Family Code ("TFC") regarding continuing, exclusive jurisdiction and transfer shall take priority over these rules, provided that all such cases ending in an odd cause number shall be heard in the 387th District Court, except that all cases filed by the Texas Department of Protective and Regulatory Services shall be heard in the 328th District Court, per General Transfer Order signed August 27, 1999. All such cases ending in an even number shall be heard in the 328th District Court.

2.2 Multiple Suits. Subject to paragraph 2.1, when a suit is filed in the 328th or the 387th District Court of Fort Bend County (referred to as Family District courts) and is in any way terminated (by non-suit or otherwise), a subsequent suit or cause of action involving substantially the same parties or the same subject matter shall be filed in, or transferred to, the court that first had jurisdiction of the parties or subject matter. This rule applies to all controversies, including divorce, support, conservatorship and all matters incident to them, whether sought by original proceedings or by modification, clarification or enforcement of a former order, judgment or settlement agreement. When such a situation is disclosed for the first time after the hearing begins, the judge of the court shall immediately order the suit transferred to the court in which the prior suit was filed.

2.3 Enforcement of Consent Decree or Contract. Subject to paragraph 2.1 any action for the enforcement of a consent decree or contract arising out of or in conjunction with any action previously filed in any of the family District Courts shall be filed in the same court.

2.4 Consolidation. A motion to consolidate cases shall be heard in the court where the lowest numbered case is pending. If the motion is granted, the consolidated case will be given the number of the lowest numbered case and assigned to the appropriate court.

2.5 Severance. If a severance is granted, the new case remains assigned to the court where the original case is pending, bearing the same file date and the same number as the original case with a letter suffix.

2.6 Presiding for Another. In all cases where a judge signs an order on behalf of another court, the case shall remain in the original court.

2.7 Improper Court. If a case is improperly placed on the docket of one Family District Court, the judge of that court shall transfer the case to the proper court.

RULE 3. FLOW OF CASES

3.1 Appearance of Counsel. Any attorney representing a party or pro se party in a case shall file an appropriate initial pleading with the court, be it a Petition, Answer, Notice of Appearance as Attorney of Record, or Motion and Order for Substitution of Counsel and promptly furnish a true copy thereof to opposing attorney or pro se party, as applicable. The pleading shall contain all information required under the Texas Rules of Civil Procedure ("T.R.C.P.") Rule 57.

3.2. Docket Call Procedures.

3.2.1 Attorneys who will be late for court must give the court and opposing side notice of their estimated time of arrival at court and the reason for the delay. If the attorney is late because he or she must appear in another court at the same time, the clerk must be notified not only that the attorney will be late (as above) but also the specific court(s) in which the attorney will be appearing.

3.2.2 If an attorney does not appear in the courtroom within thirty (30) minutes of docket call, that party's motion may be ruled upon by the court and/or sanctions issued consistent with the Texas Rules of Civil Procedure, at the request of the opponent.

3.3 Telephone conferences. Use of telephone hearings between judges or associate judges and all attorneys in a case is encouraged for non-evidentiary matters. Telephone hearings shall be scheduled through the court coordinator.

3.4 Interview of Child/Child's Testimony. In all cases in which the court deems testimony of a child to be necessary or required by statute, the attorney wishing to have the child interviewed shall arrange a specific time through the court coordinator for the court to interview the child. No party is to bring a child to the courthouse to testify without prior arrangement pursuant to this rule, unless the child's attendance is required by court order including a writ of habeas corpus or attachment. The attorney who is responsible for the child's attendance at court shall immediately notify the

See note on p. 1157.

court coordinator of the child's presence in the courthouse. The child shall not be brought into the courtroom without the express consent of the judge or associate judge.

3.5 Scheduling Orders. It shall be the duty of an attorney or pro se party entering a pending case to ascertain from the court whether a Scheduling Order has issued and if so, to obtain a copy of the Scheduling Order from the District Clerk's office. Notwithstanding the foregoing, it shall also be the duty of the Petitioner or Movant in a pending case in which a Scheduling Order has been issued to provide a copy of the Scheduling Order to each party who has made or makes a general appearance in the pending case.

3.6 Trials.

3.6.1 Manner of Setting. Cases shall be set for trial by order of the court.

3.6.2 Date of Setting. Cases shall be set for trial for a date certain. If a case is not assigned to trial by the Friday after the date it was set, whether because of a continuance or because it was not reached, the court shall reset the case to a date certain. Unless all parties agree otherwise, the first setting must comply with all requisites of T.R.C.P. Rule 245.

3.6.3 Assignment to Trial. A case is assigned to trial when counsel is called to the court to commence the jury or non-jury trial on the merits. For the purposes of engaged counsel, no court may have more than two cases assigned to trial at any one time.

3.6.4 Continuances. Continuances shall be governed by T.R.C.P. Rules 251 through 254.

3.7 Decrees, Judgments and Orders. All judgments and orders must be submitted to the court for signing within 14 days of the rendition date, unless otherwise directed by the court. The party who is directed to prepare the judgment or order shall furnish all opposing parties with a copy of the proposed judgment or order at least five (5) days prior to entry date. All judgments or orders in uncontested matters (except for settlements made pursuant to (T.R.C.P. Rule 11) and in default matters (where citation has been served and there has been no answer filed or other general appearance) must be presented at the time of hearing. All forms required by governmental entities shall be submitted, along with orders for withholding, QDROs and the like, as appropriate.

3.8 Parent Education. All parties required by paragraph 11.1 herein to attend a parent education course shall file with the court a certificate verifying the party's attendance at such course. The certificates shall be filed no later than the date the case is set for final hearing.

RULE 4. DISCLOSURE OF PROPERTY & FINANCIAL INFORMATION

4.1 Temporary Orders. In any hearing for temporary orders in which child support or spousal support is an issue, completion and exchange of Financial Information Statements, copies of income tax returns for the past two years, and the three most recent payroll stubs shall be exchanged prior to the commencement of the hearing. This rule providing for the exchange of information shall constitute a discovery request and failure to comply with this rule may be grounds for sanctions, as provided by T.R.C.P. Rule 215.

4.2 Final Information. A party's final Inventory, Financial Information Statement and financial information required under the Family Code (including, but not limited to, the party's income tax returns for the past two years and the party's three most recent payroll stubs), as well as suggested findings regarding child support and a proposed division of property shall be exchanged no later than ten (10) days before trial, and shall be filed with the court at the commencement of trial. If children are involved in the proceeding, the inventory shall contain sufficient information so the court may render a qualified medical child support order regarding health insurance for the children. This rule providing for the exchange of information shall constitute a discovery request and failure to comply with this rule may be grounds for sanctions.

4.3 Inventory. Each inventory shall list each item of property and its value, and shall also list each liability, together with the amount of the liability, the number of periodic payments in arrears, if any, the property securing its payment, and the name of the creditor. Any property or liability shall likewise be characterized as separate or community. All beneficial interests in insurance and all benefits arising from a party's employment (such as pensions, profit sharing plans, savings or thrift plans, whether vested or non-vested) shall be identified. Each party shall incorporate as an exhibit to the inventory the last information furnished to the employee about to the employee's rights and monetary interest in

See note on p. 1157.

the retirement and savings plans. Each party shall also furnish sufficient information so the court may render a qualified domestic relations order, if applicable. The inventory shall list and total, in columnar format, the property values and liabilities. Each inventory shall show the net worth of the community estate.

RULE 5. REQUIREMENTS FOR CERTAIN DOCUMENTS

5.1 Certificate of Conference.

5.1.1 Unopposed motions shall be labeled "Unopposed" in the caption.

5.1.2 Opposed motions shall contain a certificate that:

1) states that the movant and respondent have conferred with each other and in good faith have attempted to resolve the matter and

2) identifies the basis of disagreement between counsel; or

3) states that the parties have not been able to confer, and states in detail all efforts made to confer, including dates and methods of attempted communication.

5.1.3 The provisions of subparagraph 5.1.2 do not apply to motions for summary judgment, default judgments, motions for voluntary dismissal or non-suit, and motions involving service of citation.

5.2 Orders, Judgments and Decrees.

5.2.1 All Orders, including Decrees or Judgments, shall be submitted to the opposing attorney or pro se party for approval at least as to form, prior to filing with the court.

5.2.2 Orders based upon agreement of the parties shall also be submitted to the parties for approval as to substance.

RULE 6. REFERRAL TO ASSOCIATE JUDGE

6.1 Referral. All pending cases and cases filed after the date of the adoption of these rules are hereby referred to the associate judge of each court pursuant to T. F. C. section 201.006, subject to limitations imposed by chapter 201.

6.2 Order of Referral. This Rule shall constitute the Order of Referral required by TFC section 201.006(a)(2), to any pending or future cases under Title 1, 2, 4, or 5.

RULE 7. ALTERNATE DISPUTE RESOLUTION

7.1 Temporary Hearings. In cases involving disputed custody or visitation issues, the court shall make referrals for mediation to the Dispute Resolution Center or private mediators, or as agreed upon by the parties and attorneys. Additional issues may be mediated by agreement of the parties and attorneys. Attorneys of record may attend all mediations. Except for good cause shown, no temporary hearings involving disputed custody or visitation issues will be conducted until the issues have been mediated.

7.2 Final Trial. Except for good cause shown, all cases shall be submitted for alternate dispute resolution procedures before trial, as provided in paragraph 7.1.

7.3 Settlement Weeks. Referral of appropriate cases to alternate dispute resolution procedures shall also be made at one or more settlement weeks each year, as provided by law.

RULE 8. CONFLICTING ENGAGEMENTS

8.1 Inter-County. The Rules of the Second Administrative Judicial Region control conflicts in settings of all cases between a Fort Bend County court and a non-Fort Bend County court.

8.2 Intra-County. Among the trial courts sitting in Fort Bend County:

8.2.1 Trial/Trial. An assigned trial setting takes precedence over a conflicting trial setting not yet assigned;

8.2.2 Trial/Non-Trial. An assigned trial setting takes precedence over conflicting non-trial settings, except as to a court-ordered mediation that is scheduled prior to the assignment to trial;

8.2.3 Non-Trial/Pre-Trial Intra-Court. The matter which was first filed, regardless of cause number, shall take precedence over subsequently filed non-trial settings, non-court-ordered alternate dispute resolution and non-court-ordered depositions.

8.3 Judge or Associate judge. This rule is applicable whether the matter is assigned to the judge or the associate judge of a court.

8.4 Waiver. The court lacking priority shall yield.

8.5 Lead Counsel. This rule operates only where lead counsel, as defined by T.R.C.P. Rule 8, is affected, unless the court expands coverage to other counsel.

See note on p. 1157.

8.6 Engaged Counsel. Counsel is deemed engaged and unavailable for trial if he or she is participating in the actual trial or hearing of another case or in court-ordered alternate dispute resolution or court-ordered deposition.

8.7 Reporting of Conflicting Engagements. It is the duty of an attorney to report promptly to the court immediately upon learning of a conflicting engagement that might preclude that attorney's availability. Failure to do so may result in sanctions.

RULE 9. VACATIONS OF ATTORNEYS

9.1 General Rule. Subject to the provisions of paragraph 9.2 of this rule, an attorney may designate not more than four weeks of vacation during a calendar year, during which time that attorney will not be assigned to trial or required to engage in any pretrial proceedings. This rule operates only where lead counsel, as defined by T.R.C.P. Rule 8, is affected, unless the court expands coverage to other counsel. The vacation designation shall be honored only if it is filed in writing with the District Clerk, and is accompanied by the attorney's designation of at least one attorney who has consented to act for the vacationing attorney. The designated attorney shall be called upon to act only if the client consents to the designated attorney's representation, and then only if the court requests the designated attorney's participation due to an emergency.

9.2 Time for Designation. Written designation for vacation weeks during June, July, or August must be filed with the District Clerk by May 15 of that year. Written designation for vacation weeks in months other than June, July, or August must be filed with the District Clerk at least 60 days in advance. Designated vacation weeks protect the attorney from trials or pretrial proceedings during those weeks, unless a setting order was signed and the case was assigned to trial before the vacation designation was filed.

RULE 10. UNIFORMITY

10.1 Letters and Orders. In managing their dockets under T.R.C.P. Rules 165a and 166, Family Trial Division judges shall endeavor to use form letters and orders approved by the district judges of Fort Bend County.

10.2 Policies and Procedures. The district judges of Fort Bend County shall establish common policies and procedures on pertinent court business. Such policies and procedures shall be made available through the district clerk. Each court may additionally establish policies and procedures particular to that court.

RULE 11. PARENT EDUCATION COURSE

11.1 Except for good cause shown, all parents or other individuals requesting appointment as a conservator are required to attend a parent education course, whether the suit is an original suit or a modification.

RULE 12. APPLICABILITY

12.1 Effective Date. These rules shall become effective on ____________, 2000 or upon their approval by the Texas Supreme Court pursuant to T.R.C.P. 3a, whichever comes later.

12.2 Cross-Reference. Any reference in these rules to a statute or a court rule shall also apply to any successor statute or court rule, whether recodification, revision or amendment.

12.3 Applicability. These rules are applicable to both jury and non-jury cases.

GALVESTON COUNTY

LOCAL RULES OF THE DISTRICT COURTS

Effective January 1, 1993.

RULE 4—DISPOSITION OF FAMILY LAW & JUVENILE CASES

RULE 4.1. GENERAL

All suits authorized under the Family code shall be filed by order of the 306th Family District Court. These rules shall be applicable to all family law cases filed in Galveston County.

Rule 4.1.1 Time Standards for Family Law Case Disposition.

A. Family Law Cases.

1. Contested Family Law Cases. Within 6 months from the appearance date or within 6 months from the expiration of the waiting period provided by the Family code where such is required, whichever is later.

2. Uncontested Family Law Cases. Within 3 months from the appearance date or within 3 months from the expiration of the waiting period provided by the Family Code where such is required, whichever is later.

B. Juvenile Cases. In addition to the requirements of Title 3, Texas Family Code

See note on p. 1157.

1. **Detention Hearings.** On the next business day following admission to any detention facility.

2. **Adjudicatory or Transfer (Waiver) Hearings.**

a. concerning a juvenile in detention facility: Not later than 10 days following admission to such a facility, except for good cause shown of record.

b. concerning a juvenile not in a detention facility: Not later than 30 days following the filing of the petition, except for good cause shown of record.

3. **Disposition Hearing.** Not later than 15 days following the Adjudicatory hearing. The Court may grant additional time in exceptional cases that require more complex evaluation.

4. Nothing herein shall prevent a judge from recessing a juvenile hearing at any stage of the proceedings where the parties are agreeable or when in the opinion of the judge presiding in the case the best interests of the child and of society shall be served.

C. **Complex Cases.** It is recognized that in especially complex cases or special circumstances it may not be possible to adhere to these standards.

Rule 4.1.2 Juvenile Disposition Provisions.

No provision is made in these rules for the disposition of juvenile cases other than setting out time standards as provided by Rule 4.10 hereof, since juvenile cases are heard by the 306th Family District Court, and the County Courts at Law No. One and Two. Rules for the disposition of juvenile cases will be adopted by the aforementioned courts.

RULE 4.2. FINANCIAL INFORMATION STATEMENTS

In all domestic relations cases related to divorce or modification of support, the following shall be included in all orders granted ex parte setting a hearing on temporary orders involving any support or alimony or setting a hearing on support modification:

All parties to this action shall file with the Clerk and deliver a copy to the judge and all counsel or pro se parties a Statement of income and Expense, pay receipts for one month and/or statement of income from employer.

Rule 4.2.1. The Clerk shall attach a copy of the Statement of Income and Expense form to each Notice of Temporary Hearing or Citation on Modification which is served on a party and shall furnish a copy of same to each counsel or pro se party not served with the Order. All parties are required to file Statement of Income and Expense as set out in these rules.

Rule 4.2.2. Statement of Income and Expense shall be verified by the party and signed by counsel for such party. Counsel and parties are encouraged to prepare such statements of Income and Expense in such manner that they can be presented as evidence in lieu of direct testimony. Counsel and parties are encouraged to offer the same as evidence in such proceeding.

Rule 4.2.3. Compliance with this rule may be by the completion of a Statement of Income and Expense in the form attached hereto. Counsel are responsible for accuracy and timeliness.

RULE 4.3. INVENTORY & APPRAISEMENT

Within seventy-five days of filing of each divorce or annulment case, each party shall file with the Clerk, a copy being furnished to the Judge, opposing counsel and pro se parties, a sworn inventory and appraisement of all property (both separate and community) of the parties, including any property belonging to children of the parties. In the event of a substantial disparity in property evaluation filed by parties to a proceeding, within ten days after the filing of the original inventories and appraisements, the parties shall file a sworn statement setting forth the reason for the evaluations assigned by each such party. In the event a dispute as to character of property, each party's contention shall be supported by affidavit and documents, if any, filed at least ten days prior to trial.

Rule 4.3.1. In the event of the filing of a written agreement completely settling the property of the parties to such action and all custody and support matters, it shall not be necessary to file such inventories and appraisements.

Rule 4.3.2. The failure to timely file such inventories and appraisements, affidavits or statements set out in these rules may result, in addition to sanctions provided by law, in the continuance of temporary alimony and/or support or the discontinuation of same, or dismissal of the case for want of prosecution.

RULE 4.4. EX PARTE RESTRAINING ORDERS & PROTECTIVE ORDERS

Except as otherwise provided by law, ex parte protective orders shall be granted only when presented by attorney accompanied by client (306th District Court only).

See note on p. 1157.

Rule 4.4.1. No ex parte restraining order shall evict a party from the home unless filed in conjunction with Chapter 71 T.F.C.

Rule 4.4.2. No ex parte order shall restrain a parent from having access to that person's child(ren) except upon affirmation showing that the interest of the children require such restraint.

RULE 4.5. POSSESSION OF & ACCESS TO A CHILD

Possession of and access to a child, including temporary orders, shall be pursuant to T.F.C. Section 14.03-14.04. See Family Code §105.001 (temporary orders) & §153.001 et seq. (possession & access).

RULE 4.6. CHILD SUPPORT

The setting of child support, including temporary child support, shall be pursuant to T.F.C. Section 14.05-14.08, and 14.061. See Family Code §105.001 (temporary orders) & §154.001 et seq. (child support) & §156.001 et seq. (modification).

RULE 4.7. TEMPORARY ORDERS

All temporary orders shall be presented to the Court within seven (7) days of the hearing or the case shall be subject to dismissal. Such orders need not be submitted to other counsel for approval, but a copy of the order delivered to the Court shall be forwarded to opposing counsel in a timely fashion.

RULE 4.8. FINAL HEARINGS

Rule 4.8.1. Notice of all first settings shall be pursuant to Rule 245 of the Texas Rules of Civil Procedure. (*i.e.*, 45 days notice)

Rule 4.8.2 Jury trials (306th). Due to the crowded non-jury docket, jury trials shall be set as follows: Upon proper request and payment of a jury fee pursuant to Rule 216 T.R.C.P., cases shall be set for jury trial on the first available calendar opening corresponding to a scheduled jury week. Cases shall be called in the order in which they are requested. If not reached, the case shall be reset by the Court for the next calendar opening corresponding to a scheduled jury week.

Rule 4.8.3 Docket Control Orders. Upon payment of the jury fee and submission of a jury request, the Court will complete a docket control order and forward to each party who will be bound thereto. Any objection to dates set out shall be by motion and hearing thereon.

Rule 4.8.4 Non-Jury Trials. Requests for settings for final hearings in all contested family law cases shall be in writing and directed to the Judge's office with copies to opposing counsel and the Clerk of the Court. In all cases where there is community property, a sworn inventory and appraisement must be filed with the District Clerk's office before the case will be set for trial. If a party fails to file an inventory, the one filed will be taken as uncontested. Such request shall, in addition to the requirements set forth in these rules, certify that all parties have fully complied with Rule 4.3 (inventories) and shall contain a general statement of the contested issues (*i.e.*, property, conservatorship, support) as well as an estimate of the time required to hear the entire matter.

Rule 4.8.5 Alternative Dispute Resolution.

A. In all child custody cases, the parties shall view the film, "Don't Forget the Children" which is on file in the County Law Library. After viewing film, parties shall certify same to Court by filing proof thereof with the District Clerk on a form provided by the librarian.

B. In all child custody cases, the parties shall first attend mediation unless objection made pursuant to Civil Practice and Remedies Code 154.022 is sustained.

Subsequent to A and B above, the parties may request setting of final hearing.

Rule 4.8.6 Uncontested Matters. Uncontested matters are heard in County Court No. 2 from 8:00-9:00 a.m., and in 306th District Court from 8:30-9:00 a.m., Monday through Friday or later in the day, at the Court's discretion.

Rule 4.8.7 Default Judgments. No default judgments in cases involving children or property shall be granted without proof of attempted notice of final hearing to opposing party.

Rule 4.8.8 Exhibits. All exhibits shall be premarked prior to beginning of hearing or trial.

Rule 4.9 Continuances. No continuances shall be granted, in any case, except upon good cause shown, in writing, signed by the attorneys and the clients and approved by the Court, and in accordance with T.R.C.P. Rule 251.

Rule 4.10 Dead Week. The week of the Advanced Family Law Course (usually in August) shall be a dead week for family law.

See note on p. 1157.

Rule 4.11 Entry Date. Entry date for all final orders and decrees is no later than 21 days post hearing at 9:00 a.m. unless granted an extension by the Court. Failure to appear may subject case to be dismissed for want of prosecution.

GREGG COUNTY

LOCAL RULES 307TH FAMILY DISTRICT COURT

Effective January 1, 1999.

LOCAL COURT RULES FOR TRIAL SETTINGS & DOCKET MANAGEMENT

These rules apply to Family Law Cases on file in the office of the District Clerk of Gregg County, and all such cases are to be governed hereby. These rules are adopted to achieve efficiency in the management of Family Law cases filed with the District Clerk of Gregg County, Texas, in each of the following ways:

1) Systematic ongoing dismissals for want of prosecution of dormant cases.

2) Provisions for presenting agreed matters, default hearings and waiver hearings at stated times;

3) Automatic setting of temporary orders, enforcement and juvenile court hearings, according to an understandable and predictable scheme;

4) Provision for special settings of contested final hearings;

5) Jury request procedures to insure effective use of the central jury panel.

6) Provisions for discovery, settlement and setting conferences for complex cases.

7) Providing simplified procedure for identifying those cases to be relieved from the time requirements and dismissal process.

8) Providing for alternative dispute resolution in appropriate cases.

RULE 1. ATTORNEYS' & PARTIES' RESPONSIBILITY

Attorneys and persons not represented by attorneys shall be charged with knowledge of and responsible for observing the requirements of these rules. Disregard, abuse or violation of these rules shall be subject to sanction by the Court. Sanctions shall include denial of the right to practice under the rules, and contempt of court and/or any other remedy deemed equitable by the Court under the circumstances.

When a party is represented by more than one attorney or firm of attorneys, the "attorney in charge" shall be determined and governed by Rule 8, TX RULES CIV PRO.

RULE 2. REQUISITES OF PLEADINGS

All pleadings shall be governed by the requisites set forth in TX RULES CIVIL PROCEDURE. A person not represented by an attorney shall sign his pleadings and state his address and telephone number. The stated address shall serve as the address of record for such individual and all notices sent to that address shall be deemed received absent notification to the District Clerk of a change of such address.

RULE 3. RESPONSIBILITY FOR ADHERENCE TO TIME STANDARDS

Exception from the case controls prescribed by the Supreme Court shall be permitted only on motion in writing, stating the reasons why the ends of justice require an exception and a finding by the Court that the circumstances in the case make an exception necessary.

In accordance with the Rules of Judicial Administration of the Supreme Court of Texas, Rule 6, the Court will, as far as reasonably possible, ensure that all cases are brought to trial or final disposition in conformity with the following time standards:

(1) Contested Family Law Cases—Within 6 months from appearance date or within 6 months from the expiration of the waiting period provided by the Family Code where such is required, whichever is later.

(2) Uncontested Family Law Cases—Within 3 months from appearance date or within 3 months from the expiration of the waiting period provided by the Family Code where such is required, whichever is later.

It is recognized that in especially complex cases or special circumstances it may not be possible to adhere to these standards. The judge shall determine whether a case should be excepted from these time requirements.

RULE 4. HEARINGS ON DEFAULT, WAIVERS & UNCONTESTED MATTERS

The Court will hear defaults, waivers and uncontested matters on Monday, Tuesday, Wednesday and Friday at 9:00 a.m., or by previous appointment in exceptional situations, at other times when the court is in session. No appointment is necessary for the 9:00 a.m.

See note on p. 1157.

docket; however, it is recommended that attorneys call the court coordinator to verify the Court will be in session on the desired day. If you notify the coordinator, she will have the court's file at her desk. If you do not schedule with the court coordinator, you must pick up the court's file at the District Clerk's office and bring it to the court coordinator.

RULE 5. PROTECTIVE ORDERS, TEMPORARY RESTRAINING ORDERS, TEMPORARY INJUNCTIONS & TEMPORARY ORDERS

All PO'S, TRO'S and settings for temporary order hearings will be returnable for hearing at 9:00 a.m. on the first Thursday after three days after service. Until service is obtained, all PO'S should be extended by notation and initial of the Judge on the docket sheet every fourteen days. Counsel for the moving party should bring said order to the attention of the judge. Any party receiving notice of a PO or TRO may, through counsel, obtain a hearing or conference by the next working day after service to modify or to make a mutual TRO. The hearing or conference may be obtained by contacting the court coordinator or the Judge, who will notify the attorney in whose client's favor the TRO runs. If this matter can be taken care of by conference between counsel and the Judge in person or by telephone, it will be followed by a memorandum for the Judge's signature as to the ruling out of the conference.

TEMPORARY ORDER HEARINGS

All hearings for temporary orders will be held at 9:00 a.m. on Thursdays. If you anticipate a lengthy temporary order hearing, for example, contested temporary conservatorship of a child, please notify the court coordinator as early as possible. The Court may arrange a more convenient time to have the hearing. The Court may refer the case for mediation of temporary orders through the Domestic Relations Office.

At the temporary hearing, each party shall produce for the court any copies of past IRS returns in their possession, a listing of the property in their possession, a listing of the debts of the parties and a statement of the earnings of the parties, verified by the employer. The statement of earnings may be by production of the latest pay stub showing cumulative gross earnings and amounts withheld from gross earnings. All show cause orders or orders setting hearing for temporary orders shall contain notice to the respondent to produce such items.

Protective Orders and Temporary Injunctions regarding persons or property shall be entered on or before the next working day after the hearing. If an agreed order containing the injunction has not been signed before the first Friday immediately following the hearing, at 1:15 p.m., all counsel and any pro se litigants shall appear for a hearing on entry of the order.

All other Temporary Orders should be presented for the Court's signature within three working days of the Court's pronouncement of the order.

Temporary orders should also contain any agreement by counsel or orders of the Court relating to discovery or scheduling deadlines.

ENFORCEMENT HEARINGS

All enforcement and contempt hearings will be held on the first Thursday 10 days after service at 1:15 p.m. in the auxiliary courtroom, unless otherwise previously arranged with the judge. The prosecuting attorney shall give notice to other parties.

All show cause orders shall command the respondent to produce the last two years' tax returns and a statement of the year to date earnings of the respondent, verified by his employer.

RULE 6. TRIAL SETTING NON-JURY CALENDAR

A. Causes of action shall placed on the non-jury trial calendar in the following manner: Upon the court's own motion, or Upon request of any interested party through his attorney of record, who shall give notice to all other parties to the cause of the time and date of such trial. Such notice shall be given by United States mail, postage prepaid, or by hand delivering same to all parties or their attorneys, unless otherwise directed by the Presiding Judge.

B. A setting for trial on the merits will be made by telephone directly to the court coordinator between the hours of 10:00 a.m. and 12:00 noon and 1:00 PM and 5:00 PM each weekday, except Thursdays.

It is suggested that anyone calling for a setting arrange a conference call between his/her office and the office of opposing counsel for scheduling a hearing. If opposing counsel cannot be reached, the coordinator shall set the hearing not less than 45 days hence.

The party requesting a setting shall reasonably and in good faith expect to be ready for trial by the date requested. The requesting party shall give the court coordinator an estimated time for trial and a brief statement

See note on p. 1157.

of the issues to be tried. If there are pre-trial matters pending, the court will, upon any party's request, set a pre-trial hearing not less than ten days prior to the date of the trial setting.

C. All parties in divorce cases involving children and any other case ordered by the presiding judge shall complete the "For Kids Sake" program or an equivalent course approved by the judge prior to a final hearing. In cases of default by respondent, petitioner shall attend the seminar and the court will order appropriate sanctions for respondent, which may include an action for contempt of court, suspension of visitation until completion of the course and assessment of additional attorney fees. Any party seeking an exception to this rule for good cause, shall schedule a pretrial hearing on the matter; no exceptions will be granted at the final hearing.

Each party, except one who is indigent, shall pay his or her fees in connection with the course. Indigents will be admitted on a reduced rate.

D. All contested child custody cases or property cases requiring more than two hours of court time must participate in good faith in mediation before a final hearing is scheduled. Upon the filing of a motion and showing of good cause (ex: spousal abuse or battering, alcoholism or drug abuse) the court may waive mediation. The cost of mediation shall be borne equally by the parties unless there is a showing that a party is unable to pay, in which case a financially aided mediation may be arranged. In any case where all issues are not resolved by the mediation, the parties shall identify and sign in the presence of the mediator a detailed statement of issues that will be contested at trial. Mediation will not be considered complete until such statement is completed and filed with the court.

JURY TRIAL CALENDAR

A. Requests for jury trial settings must be presented in writing to the Judge or Court Coordinator. The jury request shall be filed not less than 30 days in advance of the assigned trial date; provided that, if one party obtains a non-jury setting on less than 30 days notice to opposing counsel, then opposing counsel has two working days from receipt of notice of setting in which to request a jury trial and to inform the court and opposing counsel, in writing, of the issues expected to be submitted to the jury. The attorney paying the jury fee shall notify the Court Coordinator immediately that a jury fee has been paid, and the court coordinator shall set the same for pre-trial conference on the first Friday 5 days after request at 1:15, at which time the judge shall set the case for trial.

It is the duty of the requesting party to notify all other parties in the case, of the date and time of the pre-trial hearing. Failure to appear for the pre-trial conference may result in the case being stricken from the jury docket or other appropriate sanctions.

B. No case will proceed to jury trial until the parties in good faith have participated in mediation. All rules regarding mediation set forth above shall apply to jury trial mediations.

C. Cases shall be set on the jury trial docket in the order in which they are requested, with the exception of a "priority" or preferential setting by the judge. Priority shall be determined by the judge on the basis of the definition of "priority" in these rules and as governed by statute.

D. Counsel shall inform the Court, in a request for jury trial setting, what issues will be submitted to the jury. The court does not ordinarily furnish a jury trial on purely advisory issues.

RULE 7. AGREEMENTS TO PASS & MOTIONS FOR CONTINUANCE

1. No contested setting shall be passed except by:

A. settlement of the entire case;

B. agreement of all parties;

C. a motion for continuance granted by the court.

When a case is settled the attorneys shall immediately notify the court coordinator. No case may be passed by agreement less than 3 working days before a setting without approval of the judge.

2. No agreement to pass or continue a jury case shall be honored by the Court if announced after noon on Friday of the week preceding trial. In the event a case is not going to proceed to trial, one of the attorneys of record shall notify the court coordinator not later than 12:00 noon on Wednesday preceding the Monday of the week the cases are set for a jury trial. In the event one of the attorneys of record does NOT notify the court coordinator's office, and the case does NOT proceed to trial when called by the Court, the Court may assess the actual cost of the entire jury panel against the parties in such proportions as it deems proper. The Court shall not assess any such costs if the panel is sworn for the trial of another case.

See note on p. 1157.

Motions for Continuance in jury cases will be heard by the Court at 1:15 p.m. Friday ten days preceding the Monday of the week during which the case is set for trial, or at such other time set by the Court. Only matters arising subsequent to such date shall be grounds for any motion for continuance less than ten days prior to trial.

Motions for continuance in all other instances shall be heard at 1:15 p.m. on the first Friday following filing of such motion or at a time determined by the Court. A motion for continuance shall be filed by Thursday preceding the week during which a case is set for trial. Only matters arising subsequent to such a date shall be grounds for any motion for continuance.

Where a party is represented by more than one attorney or a firm of attorneys, a conflict in settings shall not be a ground for continuance when the motion for continuance is contested, until after a hearing has been held to determine that another attorney in the firm cannot handle the matter.

RULE 8. PRETRIAL CONFERENCES

Pretrial conferences will be set in matters designated by the Court as complex cases and any matters in which estimated time of trial is greater than 2 hours.

In other cases, pretrial conferences may be requested by either party or set by the Judge on his/her own motion. Unless the attorney deems that the presence of a party is necessary, they will be held with only the attorneys and Judge present.

At a pretrial conference, the Court may consider and make orders regarding any matters under TX RULES CIV PRO 166.

RULE 9. SUBMISSION OF ORDERS, JUDGMENTS, INSTRUMENTS

All Judgments, Decrees and Orders pronounced by the Court shall be reduced to writing by counsel for the prevailing party, or by counsel as directed by the Court, and submitted to the Court for signature within ten days of the pronouncement, or as directed by the Court, with a true and correct copy of same sent to all other counsel or pro se party by mail, postage prepaid. Any party objecting to such order shall, within five (5) days, raise any objection in writing to the Court and opposing counsel or pro se party. In any case in which a final judgment has not been signed within 20 days after pronouncement, the matter will be set for hearing on the following Friday at 1:15 p.m. at which time each party shall present to the Court a substantially correct decree.

At the hearing the Court may sign whichever order the Court deems appropriate, or draft and sign an order of the Court's own choice. Nothing herein shall prevent or preclude the attorneys and parties from entering an agreed judgment or order.

All orders, judgments and decrees shall be submitted to the court coordinator for presentment to the Judge for signature.

Any reports required to be filed with the state submitted with all final orders, judgments and decrees. They will be submitted to the clerk after the order, judgment or decree has been signed by the Judge.

RULE 10. PRIORITY OF CASE

The Court will, to the best of it's ability, try the cases set for hearing in the order in which they are set; however, some cases involving children shall have priority over other cases. When necessary to rearrange settings, cases shall be heard in the following priority:

1) Writs for possession of children;

2) Child Protective Services Ex Parte orders or 14-day hearings;

3) Any other matters involving custody, possession or welfare of children.

RULE 11. DISCOVERY

A. All discovery shall be conducted in accordance with the TX RULES CIVIL PROCEDURE.

RULE 12. RULE OF COURT ATTENDANCE

Counsel with scheduled matters in the 307th Family District Court will check in with the court coordinator on or before the time of their scheduled hearing and will not leave until the Judge of the Court has excused them.

RULE 13. CHILDREN IN COURT

When custody or possession of a child is in question the person having physical possession of the child at the time of the hearing shall have the child in court at each hearing or available to be brought to the court within 30 minutes upon telephone notice, unless the Court specifically states to each attorney that it is not necessary to have the child present.

If a child is to be called as a witness, the court coordinator and opposing counsel will be notified in writing

See note on p. 1157.

and a guardian ad litem will be appointed for the child. The fee for the guardian ad litem will be taxed as costs and apportioned by the Court.

RULE 14. SETTLEMENT NEGOTIATIONS

Before any contested final hearing, each party, or his/her attorney, shall certify to the Court that all pleadings are in order, that all necessary discovery has been completed, that all pretrial matters have been disposed of and that the parties have made a good faith effort to negotiate a settlement, or, if not, the reasons these have not been completed.

RULE 15. MISCELLANEOUS RULES OF PRACTICE

Child Support

The Court will follow the guidelines set forth in the Texas Family Code, §154 in setting child support.

Visitation

The Court will, in the absence of an agreement or in unusual circumstances, set visitation periods in accordance with the guidelines in Texas Family Code §153.

The Court commends to the parties the use of local services for safe exchange of children.

Alternate Dispute Resolutions

The Court will approve any agreement for alternate dispute resolutions and will entertain any motion for referral for alternate dispute resolutions sanctioned by the Texas Family Code.

Child Support Hearings

In every case involving support for children, whether the case is an original case, modification, or motion for contempt for back child support, each party must bring to each hearing the last two years' income tax returns, a statement of current earnings with a year-to-date figure showing gross pay and deductions, of if such statement cannot be obtained, then any form that is convenient for the employer to furnish will be accepted, so long as that statement shows the latest paycheck amount and to date accumulated earnings and deductions.

Nothing in these Rules shall restrict the authority of the Court to enter whatever order is necessary for the management of the docket or any specific case thereon.

HARRIS COUNTY

RULES OF THE JUDICIAL DISTRICT COURTS—FAMILY TRIAL DIVISION

Effective December 22, 1998.

RULE 1. OBJECTIVE

1.1 Purpose of the Rules. Obtaining a just, fair, and impartial adjudication of the parties' and the children's rights is the purpose of these rules. To achieve this goal efficiently and inexpensively, while complying with procedural rules and substantive law, these rules encourage using alternate dispute resolution in all appropriate cases.

RULE 2. TRANSFER OF CASES

2.1 Multiple Suits. When a suit filed in a Family Trial Division court is in any way terminated (by nonsuit or otherwise), a subsequent suit or cause of action involving the same parties or the same subject matter shall be filed in, or transferred to, the court that first had jurisdiction of the parties or subject matter. This rule applies to all controversies, including divorce, support, conservatorship, and all matters incident to them, whether sought by original proceedings or by modification, clarification or enforcement of a former order, judgment or settlement agreement. When such a situation is disclosed for the first time after the hearing begins, the judge of the court shall immediately order the suit transferred to the court in which the prior suit was filed.

2.2 Enforcement of Consent Decree or Contract. In accordance with General Assignment Order of September 1, 1977, any action for the enforcement of a consent decree or contract arising out of or in conjunction with any action previously filed in any of the courts of the Family Trial Division shall be filed in the same court.

2.3 Transfer.

2.3.1 Continuing, Exclusive Jurisdiction. All provisions of the Texas Family Code ("Tex. Fam. Code") regarding continuing, exclusive jurisdiction and transfer shall take precedence over these rules.

2.3.2 Later Filed Case. If a case is filed in which there is a substantial identity of parties or subject matter as in a previously non-suited or dismissed case, the later case shall be assigned to the court where the prior case was pending. When such a situation is disclosed for the first time after the hearing begins, the

See note on p. 1157.

judge of the court shall immediately order the suit transferred to the court in which the prior suit was pending.

2.4 Consolidation. A motion to consolidate cases shall be heard in the court where the lowest numbered case is pending. If the motion is granted, the consolidated case will be given the number of the lowest numbered case and assigned to that court.

2.5 Severance. If a severance is granted, the new case remains assigned to the court where the original case is pending, bearing the same file date and the same number as the original case with a letter designation; provided, however, that when a severed case has previously been consolidated from another court, the case shall upon severance be assigned to the court from which it was consolidated.

2.6 Presiding for Another. In all cases where a judge signs an order on behalf of another court, the case shall remain in the original court.

2.7 Improper Court. If a case is on the docket of a court by any manner other than as prescribed by these rules, the Administrative Judge of the Family Trial Division shall transfer the case to the proper court.

RULE 3. FLOW OF CASES

3.1 Appearances of Counsel. Any attorney representing a party in a case shall file an appropriate initial pleading with the court, be it a Petition, Answer, Notice of Appearance as Attorney of Record, or Motion and Order for Substitution of Counsel. The pleading shall contain all information required under Rule 57 of the Texas Rules of Civil Procedure ("T.R.C.P.").

3.2 Ancillary Matters.

3.2.1 Ancillary Docket. The ancillary docket consists of:

1) Temporary injunctions;

2) Temporary orders in original proceedings;

3) Writs of habeas corpus;

4) Motions for enforcement including contempts, except those brought under Title 5, Subtitle D, Chapter 231, Tex. Fam. Code;

5) Temporary receiverships;

6) Motions to transfer;

7) In the discretion of the court, as may be limited by the Tex. Fam. Code, hearings for temporary orders in suits for modification of a final order; and

8) All matters preliminary to trial on the merits.

3.2.2 Preference for ADR. In the discretion of the court, preference in setting hearings shall be given to matters in which the parties have participated in alternate dispute resolution procedures.

3.3 Docket Call Procedures.

3.3.1 Attorneys and pro se litigants who do not expect to be on time or present in the courtroom during docket call must notify the court and the opposing side of this fact.

3.3.2 Attorneys and pro se parties who will be late for docket call must give the court and opposing side notice of their estimated time of arrival at court and the reason for the delay. If the attorney is late because he or she must appear in another court at the same time, the clerk must be notified not only that the attorney will be late (as above), but also the specific court(s) in which the attorney will be appearing.

3.3.3 If the moving party (if pro se) or the party's attorney does not appear in the courtroom within thirty (30) minutes of docket call, that party's motion may be passed by the court at the request of the responding party.

3.4 Telephone Conferences. Use of telephone conferences between judges or associate judges and all attorneys in a case is encouraged for non-evidentiary matters. Telephone conferences shall be scheduled through the court coordinator.

3.5 Interview of Child / Child's Testimony. In all cases in which the court deems testimony of a child to be necessary or required by statute, the attorney wishing to have the child interviewed shall arrange a specific time through the court coordinator for the court to interview the child. No party is to bring a child to the courthouse to testify without prior arrangement pursuant to this rule, unless the child's attendance is required by court order including a writ of habeas corpus or attachment. The attorney or pro se party who is responsible for the child's attendance at court shall immediately notify the court coordinator of the child's presence in the courthouse. The child shall not be brought into the courtroom without the express consent of the judge or associate judge.

3.6 Scheduling Orders. It shall be the duty of an attorney or pro se party entering a pending case to ascertain from the court whether a Scheduling Order has

See note on p. 1157.

issued and if so, to obtain a copy of the Scheduling Order from the District Clerk's office. Notwithstanding the foregoing, it shall also be the duty of the Petitioner or Movant's attorney of record in a pending case in which a Scheduling Order has issued to provide a copy of the Scheduling Order to any pro se party who has made or makes a general appearance in the pending case.

3.7 Trials.

3.7.1 Manner of Setting. Cases shall be set for trial by order of the court.

3.7.2 Date of Setting. Cases shall be set for trial for a date certain. If a case is not assigned to trial by the second Friday after the date it was set, whether because of a continuance or because it was not reached, the court shall reset the case to a date certain. Unless all parties agree otherwise, the setting must comply with all requisites of T.R.C.P, 245.

3.7.3 Preference for ADR. In the discretion of the court, preference in setting cases for trial shall be given to matters in which the parties have participated in alternate dispute resolution procedures.

3.7.4 Assignment to Trial. A case is assigned to trial when counsel are called to the court to commence the jury or non-jury trial on the merits. For the purposes of engaged counsel, no court may have more than two cases assigned to trial at any one time, one before the judge and one before the associate judge.

3.7.5 Open Weeks. Except with the consent of all parties, and the court, no cases will be assigned to trial on the merits nor for ancillary hearings during:

1) The week of the Second Administrative Judicial Region Conference (March);

2) The week of the State Bar Convention (June);

3) The week of the State Bar of Texas Advanced Family Law Course (August);

4) The week of the Conference of the Judicial Section (September); and

5) The last two weeks of December.

3.7.6 Continuances. Continuances shall be governed by T.R.C.P. 251 through 254.

3.8 Judgments and Orders. All judgments and orders must be submitted to the court for signing within ten (10) days from the date of rendition, unless otherwise directed by the court. The party who is directed to prepare the judgment or order shall furnish all opposing parties with a copy of the proposed judgment or order at least five (5) days prior to entry date. All judgments and orders submitted for entry must be signed by the judge within seven (7) working days from the date that the judgments or orders are submitted for entry, unless the judgment or order is rejected by the court. All judgments or orders in uncontested matters (except for settlements made pursuant to T.R.C.P. 11) and in default matters (where citation has been served and there has been no answer filed or other general appearance) must be presented at the time of hearing on the uncontested or default matter. All forms required by governmental entities shall be submitted at the time the judgment or order is submitted.

RULE 4. DISCLOSURE OF PROPERTY & FINANCIAL INFORMATION

4.1 Temporary Orders. In any hearing for temporary orders in which child support or spousal support is an issue, completion and exchange of Financial Information Statements, copies of income tax returns for the past two years, and the two most recent payroll stubs are required prior to the commencement of the hearing. This rule providing for the exchange of information shall constitute a discovery request under the T.R.C.P., and failure to comply with this rule may be grounds for sanctions, as provided by Rule 215 of the T.R.C.P. Sanctions shall not issue if the judge or associate judge determines that the failure to comply was not willful.

4.2 Final Information. A party's final Inventory, Financial Information Statement and financial information required under the Tex. Fam. Code including, but not limited to, the party's income tax returns for the past two years and the party's two most recent payroll stubs, as well as suggested findings regarding child support and a proposed division of property shall be exchanged no later than ten (10) days before trial, and shall be filed before the commencement of trial. If children are involved in the proceeding, the inventory shall contain sufficient information so the court may render a qualified medical child support order regarding health insurance for the children. This rule providing for the exchange of information shall constitute a discovery request under the T.R.C.P., and failure to comply with this rule may be grounds for sanctions.

See note on p. 1157.

4.3 Inventory. Each inventory shall list each item of property and its value, and shall also list each liability, together with the amount of the liability, the number of periodic payments in arrears, if any, the property securing its payment, and the name of the creditor. Any property or liability claimed to be separate property shall be so characterized. All beneficial interests in insurance and all benefits arising from a party's employment (such as pensions, profit sharing plans, savings or thrift plans, whether vested or non-vested) shall be identified. Each party shall incorporate as an exhibit to the inventory the last information furnished about to the employee's rights and monetary interest in the retirement and savings plans. Each party shall also furnish sufficient information so the court may render a qualified domestic relations order, if applicable. A summary attached to the inventory shall list and total, in columnar format, the property values and liabilities. Each inventory shall show the net worth of the community estate and the net worth of any claimed separate estate.

4.4 Duty of Disclosure. Without waiting for a discovery request, each party to a suit for divorce, annulment, or a suit in which child or spousal support is in issue, has a duty of disclosure of certain information to the other party. "Disclosure" includes providing for inspection and copying the information in the party's "possession, custody or control," as that phrase is defined in Rule 166b(2)(b) of the T.R.C.P. Different types of suits require disclosure of different information.

4.4.1 Disclosure in Suit for Divorce or Annulment. Each party to a suit for divorce or annulment shall, without waiting for a discovery request, provide to the other party the following information about property in which the party claims an interest:

1) all documents pertaining to real estate;

2) all documents pertaining to any pension, retirement, profit-sharing, or other employee benefit plan, together with the most recent account statement for any plan;

3) all documents pertaining to any life, casualty, liability, and health insurance;

4) the most recent account statement pertaining to any account located with any financial institution including, but not limited to, banks, savings & loans, credit unions, and brokerage firms.

4.4.2 Disclosure in Suit in which Child or Spousal Support is in Issue. Each party to a suit in which child support or spousal support is in issue shall, without waiting for a discovery request, provide to the other party the following information:

1) all policies, statements, and description of benefits which reflect any and all medical and health insurance coverage that is or would be available for the child or the spouse;

2) Unless the information has previously been exchanged in connection with a temporary hearing (Rule 4.1), a Financial Information Statement for the party, together with that party's previous two years income tax returns and two most recent payroll check stubs, or, if no payroll check stubs are available, the party's latest Form MT-2.

4.4.3 Failure to Comply. This rule providing for the duty of disclosure shall constitute a discovery request under T.R.C.P., and failure to comply with this rule (or any of its subparts) may be grounds for sanctions, as prescribed by Rule 215 of T.R.C.P.

4.4.4 Method of Disclosure.

1) **Timing of Disclosure.** Disclosure required under this rule shall be made as follows:

a) by a Petitioner or Movant within 30 days after the Respondent files Respondent's first pleading or makes a general appearance in the case;

b) by a Respondent within 30 days after he or she files Respondent's first pleading or makes a general appearance in the case, whichever occurs first.

2) **Delivery of Disclosure.** The disclosures required under this rule shall be made by furnishing the information to the opposing party's attorney of record or, if the opposing party is pro se, by furnishing the disclosures to the opposing party at the party's address. Each party making a disclosure shall promptly file a notice with the court advising that the required disclosure has taken place.

4.4.5 Duty to Supplement. After disclosure is made pursuant to this rule, each party shall be under a duty to reasonably supplement or to amend the information it the party obtains information on the basis of which he or she knows that the information disclosed was either incomplete or incorrect when made, or is no longer complete or true.

HARRIS COUNTY

See note on p. 1157.

4.4.6 Rule 11. The provisions of this role may be modified by agreement pursuant to Rule 11 or T.R.C.P.

RULE 5. REQUIREMENTS FOR CERTAIN DOCUMENTS

5.1 Certificate of Conference.

5.1.1 Unopposed motions shall be labeled "Unopposed" in the caption.

5.1.2 Opposed motions shall contain a certificate that:

1) states that the movant and respondent have conferred with each other and in good faith have attempted to resolve the matter; and

2) identifies the basis of disagreement between counsel; or

3) states that the parties have not been able to confer, and states in detail all efforts made to confer, including dates and methods of attempted communication.

5.1.3 The clerk of each court is directed not to submit opposed motions to the judge which do not comply with this rule.

5.1.4 The provisions of subparts 5.1.2 and 5.1.3 do not apply to motions for summary judgment, default judgments, agreed judgments, motions for voluntary dismissal or non suit, and motions involving service of citation.

RULE 6. REFERRAL TO ASSOCIATE JUDGE

6.1 Referral. All pending cases and cases filed after the date of the adoption of these rules are hereby referred to the associate judge of each court pursuant to Chapter 201, Tex. Fam. Code, subject to limitations imposed by that same chapter.

6.2 Order of Referral. This Rule shall constitute the Order of Referral required by 201.006, Tex. Fam. Code, as to any pending or future cases under Title 1, 2, 4, or 5, Tex. Fam. Code.

RULE 7. ALTERNATE DISPUTE RESOLUTION

7.1 Temporary Hearings. In appropriate cases involving disputed custody or visitation issues, the court shall make referrals for mediation to Family Court Services or other private mediators agreed upon by the parties and attorneys. Additional issues may be mediated by agreement of the parties and attorneys. Attorneys may attend all mediations.

7.2 Final Trial. Except for good cause shown, cases shall be submitted for alternate dispute resolution procedures before trial.

7.3 Settlement Weeks. Referral of appropriate cases to alternate dispute resolution procedures shall be made at one or more settlement weeks each year as provided by law.

RULE 8. CONFLICTING ENGAGEMENTS

8.1 Inter-County. The Rules of the Second Administrative Judicial Region control conflicts in settings of all cases between of all cases between a Harris County court and a court not in Harris County.

8.2 Intra-County. Among the trial courts sitting in Harris County:

8.2.1 Trial/Trial. A trial setting not yet assigned takes precedence over a conflicting trial setting not yet assigned;

8.2.2 Trial/Non-Trial. Trial settings take precedence over conflicting non-trial settings except as to court-ordered mediations which are scheduled prior to the assignment to trial;

8.2.3 Non-Trial/Pre-Trial. The matter which was first filed, regardless of cause number, shall take precedence over non-trial settings, non-court-ordered alternate dispute resolution and non-court-ordered depositions.

8.3 Judge or Associate judge. This rule is applicable whether the matter is assigned to the judge or the associate judge of a court.

8.4 Waiver. The court with precedence may yield.

8.5 Lead Counsel. This rule operates only where lead counsel, as defined by T.R.C.P. 8, is affected, unless the court expands coverage to other counsel.

8.6 Engaged Counsel. Counsel is deemed engaged and unavailable for trial if he or she participates in the actual trial or hearing of another case or in court-ordered alternate dispute resolution or court-ordered deposition.

8.7 Reporting of Conflicting Engagements. It is the duty of counsel to report promptly to the court immediately upon learning of a conflicting engagement that might preclude that counsel's availability for trial. Failure to do so may result in sanctions.

RULE 9. VACATIONS OF COUNSEL

9.1 General Rule. Subject to the provisions of 9.2 of this rule, an attorney may designate not more than

See note on p. 1157.

four weeks of vacation during a calendar year as vacation, during which that attorney will not be assigned to trial or required to engage in any pretrial proceedings. This rule operates only where lead counsel, as defined by T.R.C.P. 8, is affected, unless the court expands coverage to other counsel. The vacation designation shall be honored only if it is made on the vacation letter form approved by the Board of District judges of the Family Trial Division and is accompanied by the attorney's designation of at least one attorney who has consented to act for the vacationing attorney. The designated attorney shall be called upon to act only if the client consents to the designated attorney's representation, and then only if the court requests the designated attorney's participation due to an emergency.

9.2 Time for Designation. Written designation for vacation weeks during June, July, or August must be filed with the District Clerk by May 15. Written designation for vacation weeks in months other than June, July, or August must be filed with the District Clerk by February 1. Designated vacation weeks protect the attorney from trials or pretrial proceedings during those weeks, unless an order setting the case for trial was signed and the case was assigned to trial before the vacation designation was filed.

RULE 10. UNIFORMITY

10.1 Letters and Orders. In managing their dockets under T.RC.P. 165a and 166, Family Trial Division judges shall use form letters and orders approved by the Board of District Judges of the Family Trial Division.

10.2 Policies and Procedures. The Board of District Judges of the Family Trial Division shall establish common policies and procedures on pertinent court business. If practical, policies and procedures shall be posted outside the entrance of each court.

RULE 11. ADMINISTRATION OF FAMILY TRIAL DIVISION

11.1 Presiding Judge. Each Family Trial Division judge, except the Administrative Judge, serves as Presiding Judge for a calendar month in rotation in order of judicial district numbers.

11.2 Administrative Judge of the Family Trial Division.

11.2.1 Term. At their regular May meeting, the Family Trial Division judges shall elect the Administrative Judge of the Family Trial Division for a one-year term beginning June 1 and ending the next May 31.

11.2.2 Substitute. The Administrative Judge of the Family Trial Division may, by written order, designate any other judge of the Division to ad for the Administrative Judge if the judge is absent or unable to act. The substitute administrative judge shall have all the duties and authority granted by these rules to the Administrative Judge during the period of the designation.

11.3 Meetings. The Family Trial Division judges shall meet regularly each month at times and places as the Administrative judge of the Family Trial Division may direct by a written notice distributed, except in case of emergency, at least 72 hours in advance of the meeting.

11.4 Reports to the Administrative Judge. On a monthly basis, the District Clerk shall supply to the Administrative Judge of the Family Trial Division information concerning the number of filings, dispositions, trials and other judicial activities in each Family Trial Division court.

RULE 12. PARENT EDUCATION & COUNSELING

12.1 Except for good cause shown, in all divorces joined with suits affecting the parent-child relationship, the court shall require parents to attend an educational program for divorcing parents. In its discretion, the court may also refer parents involved in modification or enforcement litigation, or a child involved in any type of custody litigation, to an education course or for counseling. In protective order cases authorized by Chapter 85, Tex. Fam. Code the court may refer a party to a batterers' treatment program.

RULE 13. APPLICABILITY

13.1 Effective Date. These rules shall become effective on January 1, 1998, or upon their approval by the Texas Supreme Court pursuant to T.R.C.P. 3a, whichever comes later.

13.2 Cross-Reference. Any reference in these rules to a statute or a court rule shall also apply to any successor statute or court rule; whether recodification, revision or amendment.

13.3 Applicability. These rules are applicable to both jury and non-jury cases.

See note on p. 1157.

JEFFERSON COUNTY

LOCAL RULES OF THE DISTRICT COURTS FOR FAMILY LAW PROCEEDINGS

Effective June 1, 1997.

TITLE 1. RULES GOVERNING ALL FAMILY LAW PRACTICE & PROCEEDINGS

RULE 1.1. CONDUCT & COURTROOM DECORUM

a. Policy. Judges and attorneys have a duty to uphold the highest standards of conduct and to earn and promote public respect for the judiciary, the legal profession and the American system of justice. Case disposition shall be accomplished effectively and efficiently consistent with applicable rules for the prompt administration of justice.

b. The Texas Lawyer's Creed. The Standards of Professional Conduct in Section IV of The Texas Lawyer's Creed, as promulgated by the Texas Supreme Court and the Texas Court of Criminal Appeals are adopted and incorporated herein by reference as guidelines for participating in family law litigation in the District Courts of Jefferson County, Texas.

c. Conduct Required of Counsel

1. Counsel shall timely appear before the Court at each setting and following each recess.

2. Counsel shall be appropriately attired for all court proceedings.

Male attorneys shall be dressed neatly in business suits or sportcoats, with dress shirt and tie.

Female attorneys shall be dressed in conservative dress or business attire.

3. Counsel shall rise and remain standing while addressing the Court.

4. Counsel shall address all statements, requests and objections to the Court and not to opposing counsel.

5. Counsel shall not argue objections in the presence of the jury without prior leave of Court.

6. Counsel shall not interrupt or talk over opposing counsel, except to state formal objections.

7. Counsel shall remain behind counsel table while examining witnesses. If requested by counsel, counsel may stand at a podium while examining witnesses.

8. Counsel shall neither make nor insinuate derogatory or insulting remarks about opposing counsel.

9. Counsel shall address the Court as "Your Honor" or "Judge" and except with leave of Court, shall refer to all counsel, parties and witnesses (except children) by their surnames, using such titles as Mr., Mrs., Miss, Dr., etc., as appropriate, and not by first names or nicknames, or any discriminatory or inappropriate classification.

10. Counsel shall request leave of Court before approaching the bench or to approach the witness when necessary to work with documentary or tangible evidence.

11. Counsel shall advise counsel's clients, witnesses and others subject to counsel's control of these rules of conduct and courtroom decorum.

12. At all times it shall be the duty of the attorneys to promptly advise the Court of any settlements and/or agreements that may affect the docket of the Court.

d. Conduct Required of All Persons. All persons in the courtroom during trials and other proceedings shall be attentive to the proceedings and shall refrain from any action that may disrupt the proceedings. Therefore, all persons shall comply with the following:

1. All persons shall be appropriately attired for court proceedings. Except with the permission of the Court, all persons entering the courtroom shall be dressed in clothing reasonably befitting the dignity and solemnity of court proceedings. Tank tops, T-shirts, shorts, thongs, and clothing that is tattered or soiled are among those items of clothing not considered appropriate courtroom attire. No hats, caps or sunglasses shall be worn in the courtroom.

2. No tobacco use in any form is permitted.

3. No bottles, beverage containers, paper cups or edibles are allowed in the courtroom, except as permitted by the Court.

4. No gum chewing is permitted.

5. No talking or unnecessary noise that interferes with the court proceeding is permitted.

6. All persons shall rise when the Judge enters the courtroom, and at such other times as the bailiff shall instruct.

See note on p. 1157.

7. No person shall bring radios, tape recorders, computers, cameras, cellular telephones, pagers or other electronic devices into the courtroom unless the device is required for the court proceeding and prior approval has been given by the bailiff or the Court.

e. Enforcement. The bailiff of the Court shall enforce the rules of conduct and courtroom decorum.

RULE 1.2. REQUESTS FOR CONTINUANCE OR POSTPONEMENT

a. Consent or Notice Required. No request for a continuance, to pass, postpone or reset any trial, pretrial, or other hearing shall be granted unless counsel for all parties consent, or unless all parties not joining in such request have been notified and have had an opportunity to object.

b. Contents of Motion. Unless counsel for all parties consents in writing to the request for a continuance and the same is approved by the Court, a motion must be filed pursuant to Rule 251, et seq. of The Texas Rules of Civil Procedure, as amended, or Article 29.01, Texas Code of Criminal Procedure, as applicable, and the motion must be accompanied by an order setting the motion for a hearing. Any motion that does not meet these requirements will be denied without prejudice to the right to refile.

RULE 1.3. CONFLICT IN TRIAL SETTINGS

a. Duty of Counsel to Notify Court. Whenever an attorney has two or more cases on trial dockets for trial at the same time, it shall be the duty of the attorney to bring the matter to the attention of the Courts concerned immediately upon learning of the conflicting settings.

b. Priority of Cases in Event of Conflict. Insofar as practicable, the affected Courts shall attempt to agree upon which case shall have priority.

RULE 1.4. WITHDRAWAL OF COUNSEL

a. Withdrawal. Withdrawal of counsel shall be governed by Rule 10 of the Texas Rules of Civil Procedure, as amended, and the following rules.

b. Notice to Client. If another attorney is not to be substituted as attorney for the party, or if the party does not consent to the motion to withdraw, the withdrawing attorney shall notify the client in writing and set the motion to withdraw for a hearing with notice of the date and time of the hearing provided to the client.

c. Orders. All orders granting withdrawal of counsel shall require withdrawing counsel to notify his or her client of all pending settings and deadlines known to withdrawing counsel.

d. No Delay of Trial. Unless allowed in the discretion of the Court, no motion to withdraw shall be granted when it is presented within thirty (30) days of the trial date or at such a time as to require a delay of trial.

RULE 1.5. ALTERNATIVE DISPUTE RESOLUTION

a. Policy. In family law matters, it shall be the policy of the District Courts of Jefferson County, Texas to encourage the peaceable resolution of disputes and early settlement of pending litigation, including family law litigation, by referral to alternative dispute resolution (ADR) pursuant to the Texas Alternative Dispute Resolution Procedures Act, Texas Civil Practice and Remedies Code, Chapter 154.

b. ADR Mandatory. No jury or nonjury trial which is expected to exceed three (3) hours of court time shall be conducted in any case (except juvenile delinquency cases) until all contested issues have been referred to an ADR procedure and ADR has been unsuccessful, or the Court has determined that ADR is inappropriate for the case.

c. Manner of Referral. It is anticipated that the parties shall cooperate in referring such issues to an ADR procedure under terms and conditions as are mutually agreeable, without the need for Court intervention. If the parties are unable to cooperate or agree to a referral of such issues to an ADR procedure, then upon written notification to the Court by one of the parties that efforts to coordinate a referral have been unsuccessful, the Court, without a hearing, shall enter an order of referral to an ADR procedure, and under such terms and conditions selected by the Court.

d. Objection to Referral. If the Court enters an order of referral to an ADR procedure, any party may object to such referral pursuant to Texas Civil Practice and Remedies Code, Chapter 154. Upon the filing of an objection, the Court shall schedule a hearing. If the Court finds that there is a reasonable basis for the objection, the Court shall order that the case not be referred to an

See note on p. 1157.

ADR procedure and order the case set for trial on the merits.

RULE 1.6. PRIORITY OF JURY CASES

The Courts shall give priority of court time to jury cases, recognizing the personal sacrifices jurors make to further the administration of justice. All jury trials will be conducted with punctuality and dispatch. All cases in conflict with the time allocated to a jury trial shall be re-set or heard in another court upon agreement of the affected courts.

RULE 1.7. FILING OF SUITS

a. Notice of Status Hearing. At the time a suit is filed seeking relief from the 279th or 317th District Courts, the District Clerk, with the approval of the Court, shall set the case for a "Status Hearing" by impressing on the first page of the initial pleading a stamp in the form set forth in Appendix 1 hereto which gives notice of the date and time of the Status Hearing.

b. Exceptions from Notice of Status Hearing. Suits filed initially by the Attorney General of the State of Texas and suits filed by the Jefferson County Criminal District Attorney do not require a Status Hearing unless specifically ordered by the Court. The District Clerk will not affix a Notice of Status Hearing to such suits.

c. Status Hearing. The Status Hearing will be set approximately 75 to 85 days after the suit is filed. Prior to the Status Hearing, the parties may seek temporary orders, proceed with discovery, set the case for hearings or final trial in accord with the Texas Rules of Civil Procedure and these rules.

If the Status Hearing is scheduled for a date when an attorney is unavailable due to a "vacation," it shall be the responsibility of such attorney to reschedule the Status Hearing with opposing counsel and the Court.

d. Scheduling Order. At the time of the Status Hearing, or by agreement prior to the date of the Status Hearing, a Scheduling Order will be entered scheduling the case for trial and setting forth deadlines and agreements of the parties necessary to prepare the case for trial. The Scheduling Order shall be in the form described in Appendix 2.

If an attorney otherwise fails to appear at a Status Hearing without good cause, the Scheduling Order may be entered in his or her absence.

RULE 1.8. APPLICATION FOR EX PARTE ORDERS

Counsel presenting any application for an ex parte order shall, at the time the application is presented to the Court, certify in writing that:

a. to the best of counsel's knowledge, the party against whom the relief is sought is not represented by counsel; or

b. [i]f the party against whom the relief is sought is represented by counsel, that (i) such counsel has been notified of the application and does not wish to be heard by the Court thereon; or (ii) counsel presenting the application has diligently attempted to notify opposing counsel, has been unable to do so, and the circumstances do not permit additional efforts to give such notice.

RULE 1.9. TEMPORARY HEARINGS

a. Scheduling. All temporary hearings shall be set on a date and at a time scheduled by the Court. At the time set for the temporary hearing, counsel shall make an announcement of the estimate of time required to present the case.

b. Notice Required When Responding Party Seeking Affirmative Relief. An application to the Court for a temporary order and notice of any hearing thereon which is presented by a party responding to an application for temporary orders in which that party is seeking affirmative relief shall be served on the adverse party in accordance with Rule 5 and Rule 21a of the Texas Rules of Civil Procedure, as amended.

c. Time Limits. In all matters in issue, the parties shall be granted a reasonable amount of time to present the case. Counsel should request a special setting at the time the application for temporary relief is presented to the Court for scheduling when, because of unusual circumstances, the time allotted for hearings in any particular working day are unworkable or inappropriate. The Court shall determine the amount of time that shall be allotted for the hearing on a case-by-case basis after consultation with the attorneys on the case.

d. Order of Cases. All cases in which counsel announces a settlement shall be heard first. All other cases shall be docketed according to counsel's announcement, with those matters requiring the least amount of time to be heard first.

See note on p. 1157.

e. Documents Required. In all cases in which temporary support of a spouse and/or the child is in issue, each party shall be required to furnish:

1. A statement of monthly income and expenses in a form substantially similar to that attached to these rules as Appendix 3.

2. Copies of that party's federal income tax returns for the two calendar years prior to the temporary hearing.

3. All payroll statements, pay stubs, W2 forms, and 1099 forms which evidence that party's earnings for the calendar year prior to the temporary hearing and from January 1 of the current year through the date of the temporary hearing.

RULE 1.10. SEMINAR FOR PARENTS

a. Seminar Mandatory. All parties in divorce suits involving a suit affecting the parent-child relationship, who are parents of a child the subject of the suit, shall attend and complete an educational seminar or course approved by the Court in which the suit is pending. The Courts of this County have determined that it is in the best interest of children of divorce to require parents to attend a seminar or course to enhance their parenting abilities and to better understand the effects of divorce on children. The content of the seminar or course shall include, but not be limited to:

1. the emotional effects of divorce on parents;

2. the emotional and behavioral reactions to divorce by young children and adolescents;

3. parenting issues relating to the concerns and needs of children at different developmental stages;

4. stress indicators in young children and adolescents;

5. conflict management;

6. family stabilization through development of a coparenting relationship;

7. the financial responsibilities of parenting;

8. family violence, spousal abuse, and child abuse and neglect; and

9. the availability of community services and resources.

A course or service taken in compliance with Section 105.009 of The Texas Family Code, as amended, satisfies the requires [sic] of this Rule.

b. Fees. Each party shall attend the seminar or approved service of equal value at that party's sole cost and expense. The fee shall be payable to the service provider at the time of registration. The fee for the seminar shall be reduced or waived in cases of indigence, in the manner provided by the Texas Rules of Civil Procedure.

c. Deadline for Completion. Each party shall complete the seminar or approved service of equal value within sixty (60) days after the date the respondent parent is served with process or executes a waiver of citation in the case, and prior to a final hearing on the merits of the case.

d. Verification of Attendance. Each party completing the seminar shall be provided with a certificate of attendance which that party shall present to the referring Court prior to final hearing of the case.

e. Sanctions. The Court may take appropriate action with regard to a party who fails to attend or complete a course or seminar ordered by the Court, including holding the party in contempt of Court, striking pleadings, or invoking any sanction provided by Rule 215, Texas Rules of Civil Procedure.

RULE 1.11. PRETRIAL & TRIAL SETTINGS

a. By Request. Except in settings ordered in Scheduling Order (Rule 1.7d of these rules), settings of contested cases shall be made ONLY upon the dated, written request of any attorney of record by delivering or mailing such request to the Clerk of Court. A copy of the request for setting shall be served, pursuant to Rule 21a, T.R.C.P., upon all attorneys of record in the case and all parties not represented by counsel. The written request shall be in substantially the same form as the form described in Appendix 4.

b. Uncontested Cases. In the 279th District Court, all uncontested matters will be heard at 8:30 a.m., Monday through Friday. In the 317th District Court, all uncontested matters will be heard at 9:00 a.m., Monday through Friday. Attorneys desiring to have uncontested matters heard at the above times should be in the appropriate court at the appropriate time.

Attorneys desiring to have their uncontested cases heard at the beginning of the morning docket of each Court (8:30 a.m. for the 279th and 9:00 a.m. for the

See note on p. 1157.

317th), should contact the Clerk of Court before 3:00 p.m. at least one (1) day prior to the setting.

If there is ANY issue that is not settled, the case will be considered to be a contested case and handled as such.

RULE 1.12. TRIALS IN EXCESS OF THREE (3) HOURS

All trials projected to require more than three (3) hours of court time will require a pre-trial hearing and will require an approved ADR procedure as set out in Rule 1.5 of these rules.

RULE 1.13. INVENTORY & APPRAISEMENT

a. Inventory and Appraisement Required. In all cases in which the character, value or division of property or debts is in issue, each party shall file, not less than thirty (30) days prior to trial, a sworn inventory and appraisement of all of the separate and community property owned or claimed by the parties and all debts and liabilities owed by the parties. It is recommended that each party file this inventory in a form substantially similar to the form attached as Appendix 5.

b. Composite Inventory and Appraisement. After each party's sworn inventory and appraisement has been filed, the parties shall file a composite inventory and appraisement in a form substantially similar to that attached as Appendix 5, which will include all items on each party's sworn inventory and appraisement. The petitioner shall initiate the composite inventory and forward it to the respondent for completion not less than seven (7) days prior to trial. The respondent shall complete and file the composite inventory with the Court and serve a copy of the same on the petitioner not less than three (3) days prior to trial. On the composite inventory, each party will indicate in the space provided any asset or liability he or she requests as an award from the Court. All values assigned by the parties will be assumed by the Court to fairly represent the value each party assigns to the asset or liability described.

c. Sanctions for Failure to File. If a party or the parties fail to prepare and/or file the initial inventory or the composite inventory as required, the Court may conduct a pretrial hearing and make such orders with regard to the failure as are just, including but not limited to, sanctions pursuant to Rule 215(2)(b) of the Texas Rules of Civil Procedure, as amended.

RULE 1.14. DISCOVERY

a. Child Support Cases. In all suits involving child support, each party who is a parent shall furnish to the Court the information described for determination of child support set out in Section 154.063, Texas Family Code, as amended.

b. Requests for Disclosure. In all suits for divorce, the parties may submit a Request for Disclosure in the form of the document described in Appendix 6, subject to sanctions provided for failure to properly reply as set forth in the Texas Rules of Civil Procedure.

c. Other Discovery. All other discovery shall be obtained by agreement or in compliance with the Texas Rules of Civil Procedure.

RULE 1.15. ORDERS & DECREES

a. Reduction to Writing Within Thirty (30) Days. Within no more than thirty (30) days after rendition, announcement of the Court's ruling or announcement of settlement by counsel, counsel shall cause all judgments, decrees or orders of any kind to be reduced to writing, forwarded to opposing counsel for approval as to form, and delivered to the Court for signing. At the end of each hearing or trial, the Court may set a date for receipt of written documents reflecting the judgment or order of the Court.

b. Dismissal if Written Order Not Furnished. Upon failure to furnish the Court with a judgment, order or decree disposing of the case within the thirty (30) day period, the case may be dismissed and costs may be taxed at the Court's discretion.

c. Procedure for Entry of Order. If counsel is unable to secure all opposing counsel's approval as to form, counsel may:

1. file a motion for entry of the proposed judgment, order or decree and secure a hearing for the same, with notice to all opposing counsel pursuant to Rule 21a, Texas Rules of Civil Procedure. At a hearing, the Court may assess costs and attorney's fees within the Court's discretion; or

2. present the Court with the proposed judgment, decree or order, together with a letter requesting the Court to sign the same if the Court has not received a written objection from opposing counsel within ten (10) days from the date of the letter. Each party who submits a proposed judgment for signature shall serve the proposed judgment and a copy of the letter on all

JEFFERSON COUNTY

See note on p. 1157.

other parties who have appeared and remain in the case, in accordance with Rule 21a, Texas Rules of Civil Procedure. If the Court or the proponent of the proposed judgment receives a written objection from opposing counsel within the stated times, the proponent of the judgment, decree or order shall schedule a hearing for entry of the same pursuant to subdivision 1 of this rule.

RULE 1.16. DISMISSAL FOR WANT OF PROSECUTION

a. Dismissal Docket. The court may set a "Try or Dismiss" Docket in any month, except June, July or August. All cases which have been on file for more than one (1) year may be dismissed for want of prosecution unless retained on the docket by order of the Court.

b. Other Dismissals for Want of Prosecution. The Court, on its own motion, may dismiss a case for want of prosecution. The procedure provided in Rule 165a of the Texas Rules of Civil Procedure, as amended, shall apply.

c. Reasons for Dismissal. A case may be dismissed for want of prosecution for any of the following reasons:

1. Failure of a party seeking affirmative relief to take appropriate action when the case has been pending for six months.

2. Failure of counsel for a party seeking affirmative relief to appear for a pretrial, scheduling or preliminary hearing, particularly if there has been a previous failure to appear or no motion has been timely filed to meet the exceptions previously sustained.

3. Failure of a party seeking affirmative relief to make an announcement as scheduled when the case has been set for trial.

TITLE 2. MISCELLANEOUS

RULE 2.1. AUTHORITY FOR RULES

These rules are adopted pursuant to Rule 3a of the Texas Rules of Civil Procedure, as amended, and the constitutional, statutory and inherent powers of the courts to regulate proceedings before them and to provide for the orderly and efficient dispatch of litigation.

RULE 2.2. TITLE & CITATION

These rules shall be known as the Local Rules of the District Courts of Jefferson County, Texas for Family Law Proceedings.

RULE 2.3. PARTIAL CIVIL INVALIDITY

In the event any of the foregoing rules or any part thereof is held to be invalid for any reason, such invalidity shall not affect the validity of the remaining rules and parts of rules, all of which have been separately numbered and adopted.

RULE 2.4 TERMS

The terms *counsel*, *lawyer*, and *attorney of record* as used in these rules shall apply to an individual litigant in the event a party appears *pro se*.

RULE 2.5. CONSTRUCTION OF RULES

Unless otherwise expressly provided, the past, present or future tense shall each include the other; the masculine, feminine or neuter gender shall each include the other; and the singular and plural shall each include the other.

RULE 2.6. APPLICATION OF RULES

These rules supersede any prior local rules of practice specific to family law matters in the District Courts of Jefferson County, Texas. These rules shall become effective upon approval by the Texas Supreme Court.

LUBBOCK COUNTY

LOCAL ADMINISTRATIVE RULES OF THE DISTRICT COURTS & COUNTY COURTS-AT-LAW

Effective May 21, 2002

RULE 4—FAMILY LAW CASES

RULE 4.10. PARENTAL NOTIFICATION

An application for an order under Section 33.003, Family Code, may be filed in a district court, a county court-at-law, or a court having probate jurisdiction. The application must be filed with the district clerk of Lubbock County, who will assign the application to a court as provided by these local rules. If the county clerk receives an application under this rule, the application must be accepted, but the county clerk must then transfer it instanter to the district clerk, and must advise the person tendering the application where it is being transferred.

The district clerk will assign the application to the appropriate court utilizing a rotating system. Each of the eligible courts will be assigned applications under

See note on p. 1157.

LUBBOCK COUNTY

this section for a period of one calendar month pursuant to the following schedule:

Month 1:	72nd District Court
Month 2:	99th District Court
Month 3:	137th District Court
Month 4:	140th District Court
Month 5:	237th District Court
Month 6:	364th District Court
Month 7:	County Court at Law No. 1
Month 8:	County Court at Law No. 2
Month 9:	County Court at Law No. 3
Month 10:	County Court
Month 11:	72nd District Court
Month 12 and beyond:	repeat rotation

If the judge of the assigned court is unavailable, then the district clerk shall assign the application to a judge selected by the local administrative judge.

RULE 4.20. POLICY STATEMENT

It is the goal of these rules that case disposition in family law matters shall be accomplished as effectively and efficiently as possible, in a just and timely manner. To achieve this goal, cases will be assigned a level according to the anticipated complexity of the case. The Judges recognize that family law cases have peculiarities which require special consideration such as reconciliation efforts and counseling. Each court retains the right to schedule a case as it deems appropriate and must do so when the interest of justice requires, taking into consideration the complexity and circumstances of the case pursuant to Rule 190.5 of the Texas Rules of Civil Procedure, as amended.

These rules are not intended to conflict with any applicable statute or the Texas Rules of Civil Procedure. In the event of such conflict, the applicable statute or Texas Rules of Civil Procedure shall prevail.

RULE 4.25. CASE LEVEL & TIME STANDARDS FOR CASE DISPOSITION

(A) Level One: Any suit for divorce not involving children in which a party pleads that the value of the marital estate is more than zero but not more than $50,000 should be concluded at the trial level within three months from the answer due date.

(B) Level Two: Any suit brought under Title 1, 2, or 5 of the Texas Family Code and/or substantial property issues should be concluded at the trial level no later than nine months from the answer due date.

(C) Level Three: Any suit brought under Title 1, 2, or 5 of the Texas Family Code and/or substantial property issues, and/or complex legal or factual issues should be concluded at the trial level no later than 12 months from the answer due date.

RULE 4.30. SCHEDULING CONFERENCE & ORDER

(A) Scheduling Conference. A scheduling conference will be set approximately 30 to 60 days after the answer due date. Prior to the scheduling conference, the parties may seek temporary orders, proceed with discovery, set the case for hearings or final trial in accord with the Texas Rules of Civil Procedure and these rules.

(B) Scheduling Order. At the time of the scheduling conference, or by agreement prior to the date of the scheduling conference, a scheduling order will be entered scheduling the case for trial and setting forth deadlines and agreements of the parties necessary to prepare the case for trial.

If an attorney or a pro se party fails to appear at a scheduling conference without good cause, the scheduling order may be entered in his or her absence.

RULE 4.35. ANCILLARY PROCEEDINGS, TEMPORARY ORDERS & EMERGENCY MATTERS

(A) An associate judge has been duly appointed for the district courts and county courts-at-law of Lubbock County and the following will be heard originally by the associate judge:

(1) motions to modify child support;

(2) motions to modify visitation orders;

(3) motions for temporary restraining orders and motions for temporary orders in suits for divorce or annulment;

(4) motions for temporary restraining orders and motions for temporary orders in suits affecting the parent-child relationship;

(5) a habeas corpus proceeding;

(6) motions to enforce child support;

(7) hearings requested pursuant to Title 4 of the Texas Family Code;

(8) hearings required by Chapter 262 and 263 of the Texas Family Code;

(9) motions to transfer;

(10) motions to withdraw;

(11) motions to dismiss;

See note on p. 1157.

(12) any other matter referred to the associate judge by the presiding judge.

(B) All motions on ancillary proceedings, temporary orders and emergency matters shall be presented to the court coordinator of the associate judge for scheduling for hearing before the associate judge. A request for hearing document shall accompany the order setting hearing. Orders setting hearings are to be signed by the associate judge or trial judge. Proper notice or service shall be the responsibility of the moving attorney or pro se party. A scheduling order shall not be required for hearings set out above unless ordered by the Judge.

RULE 4.40. REFERRAL TO MASTER

(A) A master has been duly appointed for the district courts and county courts-at-law of Lubbock County and the following will be heard originally by the master:

(1) All cases filed pursuant to Title IV-D of 42 U.S.C. Sections 651, et seq., by direction of §201.101 et seq. of the Family Code;

(2) All support, contempt, and visitation matters in which the Texas Department of Human Resources is represented by the Texas Attorney General's Office;

(3) Any other matter referred to a master by the presiding judge.

(B) Time for Disposition of Title IV-D Cases.

Title IV-D cases must be completed in accordance with §201.110 of the Texas Family Code.

RULE 4.45. ALTERNATIVE DISPUTE RESOLUTION

(A) Policy. In family law matters, it shall be the policy of the Board of Judges of Lubbock County, Texas to encourage the peaceable resolution of disputes and early settlement of pending litigation, including family law litigation, by referral to alternative dispute resolution (ADR) pursuant to the Texas Alternative Dispute Resolution Procedures Act, Texas Civil Practice and Remedies Code, Chapter 154.

(B) ADR Mandatory. No jury or nonjury trial shall be conducted in any case (except juvenile delinquency cases) until all contested issues have been referred to an ADR procedure and ADR has been unsuccessful, or the Court has determined that ADR is inappropriate for the case. ADR shall be completed no later than 30 days before trial.

(C) Manner of Referral. It is anticipated that the parties shall cooperate in an ADR procedure, under the terms and conditions ordered by the Court. After a date of completion for ADR is provided in the scheduling order, the Dispute Resolution Center (DRC) shall contact the parties by letter regarding the scheduling of mediation. Should the parties agree to use a selected neutral for this case, they shall notify the DRC and court within seven (7) days naming a neutral of their choice. The case will proceed according to the scheduling order. The selected neutral shall report the outcome of the ADR procedure to the DRC and court consistent with the provisions of the Tex. Civ. Prac. & Rem. Code Ann. Section 154.

(D) Objection to Referral. If the court enters an order of referral to an ADR procedure, any party may object to such referral pursuant to Texas Civil Practice and Remedies Code, Chapter 154. Upon the filing of an objection, the court shall schedule a hearing. If the Court finds that there is a reasonable basis for the objection, the court shall order that the case not be referred to an ADR procedure and order the case set for trial on the merits.

RULE 4.55. DOCUMENTS REQUIRED

(A) A "Case Information Sheet" must be filed along with a new petition, and a "Response Information Sheet" must be filed along with an original answer. The District Clerk and County Clerk will accept new filings on new cases without a completed "Case Information Sheet" being attached, however, the clerks will inform the filing party that the "Case Information Sheet" must be filed within ten (10) days of the date of filing the petition or the case will be placed on a "Dismiss for Want of Prosecution" docket by the court. The District Clerk and County Clerk will accept answers for filing without a completed "Response Information Sheet", but will inform the filing party that a completed "Response Information Sheet" must be filed within ten (10) days of the filing of the answer.

(B) In all cases in which support of a spouse and/or child(ren) is in issue, whether temporary or final, each party shall be required to furnish to the court and opposing party:

(1) A statement of monthly income and expenses.

(2) Copies of that party's federal income tax returns for the two calendar years prior to the hearing.

(3) All payroll statements, pay stubs, W2 forms, and 1099 forms which evidence that party's earnings for the calendar year prior to the hearing and from January 1 of the current year through the date of the hearing.

See note on p. 1157.

(4) Copies of any financial statements filed by that party with any financial institution in the two years prior to the hearing.

(C) In all suits involving child support, each party who is a parent shall furnish to the court the information described for determination of child support set out in Section 154.063, Texas Family Code, as amended.

(D) Inventory and Appraisement.

(1) Inventory and Appraisement Required. In all cases in which the character, value or division of property or debts is in issue, each party shall file, not less than thirty (30) days prior to final hearing, a sworn inventory and appraisement of all of the separate and community property owned or claimed by the parties and all debts and liabilities owed by the parties.

(2) Composite Inventory and Appraisement. After each party's sworn inventory and appraisement has been filed, the parties shall file a composite inventory and appraisement, which will include all items on each party's sworn inventory and appraisement. The petitioner shall initiate the composite inventory and forward it to the respondent for completion not less than seven (7) days prior to trial. The respondent shall complete and file the composite inventory with the court and serve a copy of the same on the petitioner not less than three (3) days prior to trial. On the composite inventory, each party will indicate in the space provided any asset or liability he or she requests as an award from the court. All values assigned by the parties will be assumed by the court to fairly represent the value each party assigns to the asset or liability described.

(3) Sanctions for Failure to File. If a party or the parties fail to prepare and/or file the initial inventory as required, the court may conduct a pretrial hearing and make sure orders with regard to the failure as are just, including but not limited to, sanctions pursuant to Rule 215(2)(b) of the Texas Rules of Civil Procedure, as amended.

RULE 4.60. DURATION OF ORDERS

No temporary order shall exceed one year in duration from the date the order is signed, except by agreement of the parties or order of the court.

RULE 4.65. PARENT EDUCATION & FAMILY STABILIZATION COURSE

(A) Seminar Mandatory.

(1) All parties in original suits affecting the parent-child relationship or in suits to modify existing orders of conservatorship or possession shall attend and complete an educational seminar. The content of the seminar or course shall include, but not be limited to:

(a) the emotional effect of divorce on parents;

(b) the emotional and behavioral reaction to divorce by young children and adolescents;

(c) parenting issues relating to the concerns and needs of children at different developmental stages;

(d) stress indicators in young children and adolescents;

(e) conflict management;

(f) family stabilization through development of a co-parenting relationship;

(g) the financial responsibilities of parenting;

(h) family violence, spousal abuse, and child abuse and neglect; and

(i) the availability of community services and resources.

(2) A course taken in compliance with Section 105.009 of the Texas Family Code, as amended, satisfies the requirements of this rule. A list of approved programs and dates and times for such programs can be obtained from the Associate's Judges office at 904 Broadway, Room 306. Parties who which [sic] to satisfy the requirement with another program may submit information regarding the program to the Associate Judge for approval prior to enrollment in the program. The requirement of a parenting program may be waived by the referring court for good cause shown.

(3) Fees. Each party shall attend the seminar or approved service of equal value at that party's sole cost and expense. The fee shall be payable to the service provider prior to the program date. The fee for the seminar shall be reduced or waived in cases of indigency as determined by the court.

(4) Deadline for Completion. The seminar shall be initiated within thirty days from the answer due date, and evidence of completion filed with the court at least seven days prior to the final hearing.

(5) Verification of Attendance. Each party completing the seminar shall be provided with a certificate of attendance which that party shall present to the court prior to final hearing of the case.

(6) Sanctions. The court may take appropriate action with regard to a party who fails to attend or complete a course or seminar ordered by the court,

See note on p. 1157.

including holding the party in contempt of court, striking pleadings, or invoking any sanction provided by Rule 215, Texas Rules of Civil Procedure, as amended.

RULE 4.70. DISMISSAL FOR WANT OF PROSECUTION

(A) Dismissal Docket.

The court may set a "Try or Dismiss" Docket. All cases which have been on file for more than one (1) year may be dismissed for want of prosecution unless retained on the docket by order of the court.

(B) Other Dismissals for Want of Prosecution.

The court, on its own motion, may dismiss a case for want of prosecution. The procedure provided in Rule 165a of the Texas Rules of Civil Procedure, as amended shall apply.

RULES FOR MANDATORY PARENTING PROGRAM IN THE COURTS OF LUBBOCK COUNTY

Effective April 29, 1998.

ORDER

The District Courts and County Courts at Law of Lubbock County hereby order the following:

Parenting: Program Required. All parties in original suits affecting the parent-child relationship or in suits to modify existing orders of conservatorship or possession are ordered to successfully complete a parenting program. This order applies to all persons seeking to become a managing or possessory conservator, whether sole, joint, temporary or permanent. The program shall include but not be limited to:

1. the developmental stages of childhood,
2. the needs of children at different ages,
3. stress indicators in children,
4. age appropriate expectations of children,
5. the grief process,
6. reducing stress for children the subject of a suit affecting the parent-child relationship,
7. the changing parental and marital roles as a result of divorce,
8. visitation recommendations to enhance the child's relationship with both parents,
9. the financial obligations of child rearing; and
10. conflict management and dispute resolution.

A list of approved programs and dates and times for such programs call [sic] be obtained from the Associate Judge's office at 904 Broadway, Room 305. Parties who wish to satisfy the requirement with another program may submit information regarding the program to the Associate Judge for approval prior to enrollment in the program. The requirement of a parenting program may be waived by the referring court for good cause shown.

Fees. Each party shall attend the parenting program at the party's sole cost and expense. The fee shall be payable to the program provider prior to the program date. Fees shall be reduced or waived in cases of indigency as determined by the court.

Notification Procedure. The attorney filing the case shall provide a copy of this order to the petitioner/movant. The District Clerk shall provide a copy of this order to all pro se parties. Additionally, the District Clerk shall attach a copy of this order to each citation or notice of hearing which is to be served in any suit affecting the parent-child relationship. Any person filing a waiver of citation or service shall provide a copy of this order to the person signing the waiver and shall file a statement confirming compliance with this order.

Deadline for Completion. The program shall be initiated within thirty days from the answer due date evidence of completion filed with the court at least seven days prior to the final hearing.

Sanctions. A party's failure to successfully complete the program pursuant to this order may result in the Court not appointing the party managing conservator or possessory conservator, or in the Court not granting specified periods of possession or access until the Court is supplied with evidence of successful completion of this program. The Court may take appropriate action for failing to comply with this order, including but not limited to actions for contempt.

MONTGOMERY COUNTY

LOCAL RULES OF THE DISTRICT COURTS

RULE 4 FAMILY LAW CASES

RULE 4.1. GENERAL

The filing, assignment, and transfer of cases under the Family Code shall be filed in accordance with Rule 1 of these rules. All cases filed pursuant to the Family Code with the exception of Title 3 of the Family Code shall be governed by Rule 3 of these rules.

See note on p. 1157.

RULE 4.2. TIME STANDARDS FOR FAMILY LAW CASE DISPOSITION

Cases shall be tried or dismissed within 6 months from the appearance date or within 6 months from the expiration of the waiting period provided by the Family Code where such is required, whichever is later.

RULE 4.3. JUVENILE DISPOSITION

Rules for the disposition of juvenile cases will be adopted by the Juvenile Court in conformity with Rule 1 of the Second Administrative Judicial Region of Texas Regional Rules of Administration and Title 3 of the Texas Family Code.

RULE 4.4. DEPARTMENT OF REGULATORY SERVICES CASES

Disposition of Texas Department of Protective and Regulatory Services cases shall be in conformity with those provisions set forth in Title 5 of the Texas Family Code.

RULE 4.5. INVENTORIES & FINANCIAL INFORMATION STATEMENTS

A. Initial Filing.

Inventories and Financial Information Statements shall be filed in all domestic relations cases related to divorce. Financial Information Statements shall be filed in all cases involving modification of conservatorship, support or periods of possession.

B. Temporary Orders.

In any hearing for temporary orders in which child support or spousal support is an issue, completion and exchange of Financial Information Statements is required prior to commencement of the hearing.

C. Trial.

A party's final Inventory, Financial Information Statement and financial information required under the Family Code, as well as suggested findings regarding child support and a proposed division of property shall be exchanged no later than thirty (30) days before trial, or as required by the docket control order, and filed with the court before the commencement of trial. If children are involved in the proceeding, the inventory shall contain sufficient information so the court may render a qualified medical child support order regarding health insurance for such children.

D. Failure to file Financial Information Statements and Inventories.

Failure of either party to file Financial Information Statements or Inventories will result in the court adopting as stipulated the information filed by the complying party. The non-complying party will be prohibited from contesting the accuracy of the information presented by the complying party. If both parties fail to comply with these rules, the court may strike the case from the docket.

RULE 4.6. PARENT EDUCATION & COUNSELING

Referral shall be made in suits affecting the parent-child relationship requiring the parents' attendance at an educational program for divorcing parents, except for good cause shown. In the discretion of the court, such a referral may also be made for parents involved in modification or enforcement litigation. Counseling may also be ordered in appropriate cases as authorized by the Family Code, including referral to a family violence program pursuant to a protective order under Chapter 71 of the Family Code.

RULE 4.7. EX PARTE RESTRAINING ORDERS, PROTECTIVE ORDERS & TEMPORARY ORDERS

A. Ex Parte Restraining Orders and Protective Orders.

Ex Parte Restraining Orders and Protective Orders shall be presented to the court in which it has been assigned. If the presiding judge of said court is not available, then the Ex Parte Order or Protective Order may be presented to any sitting District or County Court at Law Judge available. In all cases, only the court coordinator/administrator of the court to which the case is assigned may set the hearing.

B. Temporary Orders Entry.

All temporary orders shall be presented to the court for entry within ten (10) days after the hearing or at the entry date set by the court. Failure to comply could subject the case to dismissal.

RULE 4.8. DISCOVERY

A. Mandated Discovery.

In all cases the following items shall be exchanged without objection upon a written request of counsel.

1. Parties or individual income tax returns for two years preceding the year of the request.

2. Copies of all insurance polices, including home, auto, life and medical.

See note on p. 1157.

3. Copies of all promissory notes, deeds of trust and deeds evidencing ownership of real estate, including contract for deeds and time sharing contracts.

4. Copies of all stocks, mutual fund participation and investment portfolios held by the parties, in the name of the parties, or for the benefit of the parties.

5. Copies of all documents concerning employee benefits, retirement benefits and pension funds.

6. The preceding six (6) months statements for all credit card accounts in the name of the parties, or either party.

7. Wage statements or statement showing year to date earnings of the party.

4.9. CHILD SUPPORT LOCAL REGISTRY

Pursuant to §154.241 of the Texas Family Code, the District Clerk of Montgomery County is designated as the Local Registry to receive a court ordered child support payment or payment otherwise authorized by law.

NUECES COUNTY

LOCAL RULES OF ADMINISTRATION

RULE 20. JUDICIAL BYPASS PROCEDURES UNDER CHAPTER 33, FAMILY CODE

RULE 20.01. DEFINITIONS

a. "Court" or "courts" means and includes the District Courts and the County Courts at Law of Nueces County.

b. "Judge" means the Judge of any of the District Courts and the County Courts at Law of Nueces County.

c. "Application" means an application for a court order authorizing a minor to consent to the performance of an abortion without notification to either of her parents or a managing conservator or guardian.

RULE 20.02. FILING OF APPLICATION

a. An application shall be filed with the District Clerk during business hours.

b. The Clerk shall assign a cause number to an application as follows: the first number shall note the year in which the application is filed, followed by the letters "MA," followed by a four digit number given sequentially each year, and concluding with the letter or number designating the court to which the application is assigned.

RULE 20.03. ASSIGNMENT TO A COURT

a. The Clerk shall randomly assign the application among the courts in equal proportions.

b. After a court is assigned on application, that Court shall not be assigned another application until all thirteen courts have been assigned an application.

RULE 20.04. DELIVERY OF APPLICATION TO COURT

a. After assignment of an application to a court, the Clerk shall immediately personally deliver the application to the assigned Judge and a copy of the application to the Local Administrative District Judge. The Clerk shall note the time of delivery to each Judge.

b. If the assigned Judge is not immediately available, the Clerk shall wait for the Judge to become available; however, the Clerk shall not wait for more than one hour.

c. If the assigned Judge is not available after an hour from the time that the Clerk attempted to personally deliver the application or if the assigned Judge is otherwise absent, the Clerk shall immediately inform the Local Administrative District Judge of that fact. The Local Administrative District Judge shall then direct the Clerk to randomly reassign the cause.

d. The District Clerk shall designate a particular Clerk to handle and dispose of all applications.

RULE 20.05. APPOINTMENT OF GUARDIAN AD LITEM & ATTORNEY FOR MINOR

a. Upon receipt of the application, the Judge shall appoint a guardian ad litem for the minor.

b. If the minor has not retained an attorney, the Judge shall appoint an attorney to represent the minor.

c. The Local Administrative District Judge shall maintain a list of persons and attorneys who have indicated an interest in being appointed and in serving as guardians ad litem and/or appointed counsel in these proceedings. Said Judge shall make the list available to all Judges.

RULE 20.06. HEARING

a. The Court shall promptly set the cause for hearing.

b. The Court shall give precedence to proceedings on the application over all other pending matters to the extent necessary to assure that the Court reaches a decision promptly.

See note on p. 1157.

c. All proceedings shall be recorded by the Reporter.

d. All proceedings shall be closed to the public to assure the confidentiality of the minor.

e. The Court may conduct all proceedings in chambers.

RULE 20.07. COURT'S RULING

a. The Court shall rule—issue an order granting or denying the application, as well as findings of fact and conclusions of law—immediately after the hearing is concluded and not later than 5:00 p.m. on the second business day after the date the application is filed with the Court.

RULE 20.08. REPORTER'S RECORD

a. At the conclusion of the hearing on an application, the Reporter shall file the original notes, including any computer disks containing such notes, of the hearing in the file of the cause.

b. In the event of an appeal, the Reporter shall prepare the record according to the designation of record notice, shall file the record on appeal in a sealed envelope as in other appeals, and shall provide a copy thereof to the Clerk, who shall place the copy in the sealed file of the cause. On a separate sheet attached to the sealed envelope, the Reporter shall give notice to the Clerk of the Court of Appeals that the envelope contains the record of a Chapter 33, Family Code proceeding.

RULE 20.09. CONFIDENTIALITY OF ORDER

a. An Order of the Court regarding an application is confidential and privileged and is not subject to disclosure.

b. The Order may not be released to any person, except the following:

1. The pregnant minor;

2. The pregnant minor's guardian ad litem;

3. The pregnant minor's attorney;

4. Another person designated by the minor to receive the Order; or,

5. A governmental agency or attorney in a criminal or administrative action seeking to assert or protect the interest of the minor.

c. Before the Clerk may release a copy of the Order, the Clerk shall require the person to sign a statement showing receipt of the Order. The Clerk shall file the signed statement in the file.

RULE 20.10. CONFIDENTIALITY OF RECORDS

a. The Clerk shall establish and maintain a separate and secure filing and numbering system for all applications.

b. The Clerk shall deny access, including computer access, to all records of applications filed under Chapter 33, Fam.C.

c. The Clerk shall keep all final and closed applications in a place separate from all other files kept in storage.

d. The Clerk may destroy an application in the time and manner provided by law.

RULE 20.11. SEALED RECORDS

a. Notwithstanding the provisions of Rule 76a, Tx.R.Civ.P., and pursuant to the legislative directive that all Chapter 33 proceedings are confidential and privileged and not subject to disclosure or to discovery, subpoena or other legal process, the Clerk shall keep the application, all pleadings, exhibits, written findings and conclusions, Orders and all other documents in the cause in a sealed envelop [sic] at all times, except when the cause is in the possession of the Judge.

b. No person shall unseal or open a sealed cause other than the assigned Judge or a person authorized by the Judge.

c. The Judge or a person authorized to unseal or open a sealed cause shall sign a statement on the file that the person unsealed or opened the file.

RULE 20.12. DUTIES OF LOCAL ADMINISTRATIVE DISTRICT JUDGE

a. The Local Administrative District Judge shall supervise the filing, assignment and confidentiality of all applications filed pursuant to Chapter 33, Fam.C.

b. In the absence of the Local Administrative District Judge, the Local Administrative County Court at Law Judge shall act as provided in these Rules. In the absence of both the Local Administrative District Judge and Local Administrative County Court at Law Judge, their respective designees shall act as provided in these Rules.

RULE 20.13. STANDARD FORMS

a. The Courts shall adopt standard forms either as promulgated by the Supreme Court of Texas or as prepared locally.

See note on p. 1157.

b. The forms may provide for orders to reassign a case, appointment of guardian ad litem and/or attorney for the minor, setting the cause for hearing, findings of fact and conclusions of law, the final Order, compensation of guardian ad litem and/or attorney for minor, and any other written document deemed necessary in any proceeding.

c. Not withstanding the preceding Rule, a Court may use non-standard forms or Orders in any proceeding.

RULE 20.14. STATISTICAL INFORMATION

a. The Clerk shall maintain statistical records of all applications containing the following information, without identifying the applicants or any person named in an application:

1. The number of applications filed;
2. The assignment of applications among the Courts;
3. The number of applications granted;
4. The number of applications denied;
5. The number of applications in which the Court failed to timely rule;
6. The number of cases in which a Judge refused to consider the application; and,
7. The number of cases in which notice of appeal was filed.

b. The Clerk shall distribute of [sic] copies of report on monthly and annual bases to the Local Administrative District Judge.

SMITH COUNTY

LOCAL RULES OF PRACTICE FAMILY LAW CASES

1. RULES OF CIVIL PROCEDURE

If there is a conflict between these rules and the Texas Rules of Civil Procedure, the Texas Rules of Civil Procedure shall control.

2. FILING, ASSIGNMENT & TRANSFER

A. These rules shall apply to apply to [sic] all pending cases and are effective beginning April 1, 1999 or upon their approval by the Texas Supreme Court pursuant to T.R.C.P. 3a whichever occurs last.

B. All cases filed by the Texas Department of Regulatory and Protective Services shall be filed in the 321st District Court.

C. All new family law cases shall be filed by the District Clerk in random order pursuant to the last adopted case assignment order of the Smith County Council of Judges (50%-321st, 30%-County Court at Law and 20%-County Court at Law #2).

D. All subsequent proceedings shall be assigned to the court of continuing jurisdiction, with the exception of all subsequent proceedings in the 241st District Court which shall be assigned to the County Court at Law #2.

E. Transfer of cases:

(1) The presiding judge may, upon notice and hearing, or upon agreement of the parties, transfer any case from the Court in which same is pending to any other Court having subject matter jurisdiction. The judge of the receiving Court must approve the transfer and an order transferring the suit must be filed prior to any hearings by the receiving Court.

(2) Whenever any pending case is so related to another case previously filed in or disposed of by another family law court in Smith that a transfer of the later case to such other court would facilitate orderly and efficient disposition of the litigation, the Judge of the court in which the earlier case was pending may, upon notice and hearing, or by agreement of the parties, transfer the later case to such Court.

(3) Signing of the pleadings—every pleading of a party, represented by an attorney, before being filed shall be signed by at least one attorney of record in accordance with the Texas Rules of Civil Procedure. A party not represented by an attorney shall sign in like manner stating address and telephone number. The court personnel may not sign or amend any instrument for a party or attorney.

3. FLOW OF CASES

A. **Multiple Suits.** In all instances where a suit is filed in one of the courts in the Family Trial Division, and thereafter the suit is in any way terminated (by nonsuit or otherwise) and in a subsequent suit or case [sic] of action involving the same parties or the same subject matter is filed, the same shall be filed in or transferred to the court that first had jurisdiction of the said parties or subject matter. It is the purpose and intent of this rule that its applicable [sic] be made to all

See note on p. 1157.

controversies, including divorce support, conservatorship, and all matters incident thereto whether sought by original proceedings or by modification, clarification or enforcement of a former order, judgment or settlement agreement. When such a situation is disclosed for the first time after the hearing begins, the judge of the court shall immediately order the suit transferred to the court in which the earlier suit was filed.

B. **Severance.** If a severance is granted, the new case remains assigned to the court where the original case is pending, bearing the same file date and the same number as the original case with a letter designation; provided, however, that when a severed case has previously been consolidated from another court, the case shall upon severance be assigned to the court from which it was consolidated.

C. **Presiding for Another.** In all cases where a judge signed an order on behalf of another court, the case shall remain in the original court.

D. **Improper Court.** [I]f a case is on the docket of a court by any manner other than as prescribed by these rules, the Administrative Judge of Smith County shall transfer the case to the proper court.

4. TEMPORARY ORDERS

A. Except in emergencies when the District clerk's office is not open for business, no application for immediate or temporary relief shall be presented to a Judge until it has been filed and assigned to a Court. If the Judge of the court to which such case is assigned is absent or is occupied with other matters, the coordinator of the assigned Court shall insert a date and hour for hearing in any form of a proposed order before such application may be presented to any other Judge, who may sit for the Judge of the Court in which the case is pending and shall make all writs and process returnable to the assigned court.

B. Whenever immediate action of a Judge is required in an emergency when the clerk's office is not open for business, the case shall at the earliest practicable time be docketed and assigned to a Court, and all writs and process shall be returnable to the assigned court. If the Judge of such Court is not available to hear the application for temporary relief at the time set, any court with jurisdiction may preside in this case.

5. EX PARTE ORDERS

A. All applications for ex parte relief shall be presented to the Court to which the case is assigned, unless emergency circumstances exist and then shall be presented in accordance with Paragraph 3.

B. In any case in which counsel of record for the nonmoving party has been designated, said application shall be presented to said counsel, by fax, hand delivery, or other method of service designed to give opposing counsel immediate notification, in addition to the requirements of notification of Texas Rules of Civil Procedure 21a.

6. STANDING RESTRAINING ORDER

A. The Court hereby ORDERS that in all divorce suits filed, a Standing Temporary Restraining Order in the form attached hereto as Addendum "1" is imposed on all parties to the suit. All petitions for divorce shall contain a statement signed by Petitioner evidencing receipt of a copy of the Standing Temporary Restraining Order, and in the absence of such paragraph, it shall be DEEMED that Petitioner, by invoking the Court's jurisdiction, has constructive notice to the Standing Temporary Restraining Order and subject himself/herself to it.

B. The Clerk of this Court shall attach, to each citation to be served, a copy of the Standing Temporary Restraining Order. Said Standing Temporary Restraining Order shall become effective on the Respondent when citation is served, a waiver of citation is signed, or actual notice in some other manner is received.

C. The Standing Restraining Order remains effective until the temporary hearing, if any, or if no temporary hearing is requested by either party, until the final hearing. Should a temporary hearing be requested by either party, then the Court shall determine whether the Standing Restraining Order shall remain in effect until the final hearing, and absent a ruling on the Court to the contrary, the Standing Restraining Order shall remain effective until the final hearing.

7. SEMINAR FOR DIVORCING PARENTS

A. All parties in a suit affecting the parent-child relationship are encouraged to successfully complete an approved seminar listed in Addendum "2."

B. All parties in a contested suit affecting the parent child relationship shall complete the seminar prior to requesting a setting in the matter.

C. Pro Bono clients shall make application with the seminar director for a fee waiver.

See note on p. 1157.

8. PREREQUISITES FOR A TRIAL SETTING IN OTHER DEFAULT CASES

A. Attendance by all parties at a settlement conference.

B. Attendance at a seminar for divorcing parents in a suit affecting the parent child relationship.

C. Attendance by all parties at mediation. In the event the parties are financially unable to secure the services of a private mediator, attendance at settlement week mediation shall be satisfactory to comply with this requirement. As settlement week is intended to benefit clients who are financially unable to obtain the services of a private mediator, all other cases shall be submitted to a private mediator.

D. Submission to the Court of that form attached as Addendum "3."

9. MOTIONS FOR CONTINUANCE

A. An agreed continuance is not automatic and must be approved by the Court.

B. All contested motions for continuance must be filed before trial and a hearing had on the motion prior to the trial setting, except on good cause shown.

10. MOTIONS DURING PENDENCY OF CAUSE

A. All motions filed with the Court shall include a certificate of conference.

B. All unopposed motions shall be submitted with an agreed order signed by the attorneys of record.

11. EXCHANGE OF INFORMATION

A. Temporary Hearings. [P]rior to the hearing all parties shall exchange wage information and expense sheets. (Expense Sheet—Addendum "4").

B. At the temporary hearing, the Court shall be furnished the information described in 11A above.

C. Final Hearing. [P]rior to final hearing all parties shall exchange wage information, inventory and appraisement, proposed division of property, proposed resolutions of child custody, child support, visitation and any other pertinent matters.

D. At the final hearing, the Court shall be furnished all information set out in 11C.

12. EXHIBITS

A. All exhibits to be introduced shall be introduced with sufficient copies for all attorneys of record and the Court.

B. Counsel are encouraged to premark exhibits.

See note on p. 1157.

13. ORDERS

A. Within 10 days of the rendition of an order in a matter, the designated party shall submit a proposed order to the Court. If no objection is received within 10 days from the date the order is submitted, the Court shall enter it. If objection is received, the Court may set the matter for hearing.

Addendum 1

IN THE 321ST JUDICIAL DISTRICT COURT, COUNTY COURT AT LAW & COUNTY COURT AT LAW NUMBER TWO, SMITH COUNTY, TEXAS

STANDING TEMPORARY RESTRAINING ORDER

On the 1st day of February, 1999, came on to be considered the matter of issuance of temporary orders as provided by the Local Rules of these Courts (In supplement to the Texas Rules of Civil Procedures), effective February 1, 1999, and the Courts being of the opinion that all parties to original divorce proceedings in the 321st Judicial District Court, County Court at Law, and County Court at Law Number Two of Smith County, Texas, ought to be subject to a restraining order from the date of institution of suit or service thereof and it appearing to the said Courts appropriate to enter a STANDING TEMPORARY RESTRAINING ORDER and the Court does hereby enter this order which is henceforth to be effective with respect to all parties to original divorce proceedings receiving actual or constructive notice thereof, and each third party to original divorce proceedings, and IT IS THEREFORE ORDERED that Petitioner, Respondent, and all third parties to said proceedings ARE HEREBY RESTRAINED AND ENJOINED FROM:

1. Removing any minor child of the parties to a location beyond the jurisdiction of this Court unless authorized by this Court.

2. Consuming any illegal controlled substance (as that term is defined in the Texas Controlled Substance Act), 12 hours prior to and during any period of possession of the child(ren).

3. Engaging in any physical contact with a person with the intent to receive or arouse the sexual gratification of the party in possession of the child(ren) while in the presence or sphere of presence of the child(ren).

4. Doing, or attempting to do, or threatening to do any act of injury, embarrassment, molestation, or harassment to the other spouse or the child (or any of the

children) or any family member in possession of the child(ren) to which family member the parents relinquished possession of the child(ren) or acquiesced in said family member's possession of the child(ren) for at least six (6) months immediately preceding the filing of the divorce petition.

5. Making any derogatory or disparaging remarks against the other party to the child(ren) or within the child(ren)'s hearing range or presence nor shall either Party allow the child(ren) to be in the presence of anyone making disparaging or derogatory remarks against the other party or the child(ren).

6. Selling, encumbering, contracting to sell, damaging, destroying, negotiating, or otherwise disposing of or removing from the jurisdiction of this Court any of the property, including monies on account in any financial institution, which belong to the parties, except in the ordinary course of business or to make expenditures and incur indebtedness for reasonable attorney's fees, medical care, and for reasonable and necessary living expenses for food, clothing, shelter, and transportation.

7. Terminating or in any manner effecting the service of water, electricity, gas, telephone, cable television, at the customary residence of the other spouse or in any manner attempting to withdraw any deposits for service in connection with such services.

8. Intentionally excluding the other spouse from ingress and egress to the customary residence of said spouse.

9. Taking any action to terminate or limit credit or charge cards in the possession of the other spouse.

10. Incurring any credit purchase on any credit account or charge card in the name of either spouse except for the acquisition on credit or reasonable attorney's fees, medical care, and reasonable and necessary living expenses for food, clothing, shelter, and transportation.

11. Changing or in any manner altering the beneficiary designation on any life insurance policy on the life of either spouse.

12. Canceling, altering, or in any manner affecting any casualty, automobile, or health insurance policies insuring the parties' property or persons including the parties' minor child(ren).

13. Forging the name of the other spouse on any document.

TARRANT COUNTY

LOCAL RULES OF COURT

Effective September 8, 1994.

PART 4. RULES FOR DISPOSITION OF FAMILY LAW CASES

RULE 4.01: GENERAL DISPOSITION RULES

(a) ADR. It shall be the policy of the family law Courts of Tarrant Count to encourage the amicable resolution of family law litigation, including the use of alternative dispute resolution. On its own motion, motion of a party or by agreement of the parties, the Court may refer a case to alternative dispute resolution pursuant to Chapter 154, Texas Civil Practice and Remedies Code.

(b) Pre-Trial. Pre-trial hearings or orders will not be required in every case, but each Court may establish its own pre-trial procedures pursuant to Rule 166, Texas Rules of Civil Procedure. A pre-trial conference may be set on the Court's own motion or proper request of a party.

(c) Dilatory Pleas. Any party filing special exceptions, pleas in abatement or any other dilatory plea shall request and obtain a hearing on them at least 30 days prior to the final trial, or as soon as possible if the pleading is filed within 30 days of the final trial date. Any such matters not timely heard shall be waived.

(d) Stipulations. It is the responsibility of each attorney to stipulate to all the facts which are accurate and not in dispute, and to waive formal proof as to any document to be introduced about which there is no reasonable dispute as to authenticity.

(e) Notice. Unless otherwise ordered, all notice provisions and time periods provided by the Texas Rules of Civil Procedure, Family Code, Government Code, and any other applicable statute shall be followed. Unless specifically shortened by the Court, a party responding to a request for temporary relief contained in an original action shall be entitled to at least 3 days notice of any hearing. No hearing for temporary relief shall be set prior to answer date in any Motion to Modify child support and/or possession, unless special circumstances exist.

See note on p. 1157.

(f) Announcement of Time. When requested by the Court, it is the responsibility of each attorney to provide the Court with a reasonably accurate estimate of the time required for the Court to hear a manner. The Court may impose reasonable time limitation upon counsel and pro se parties to present their cases, with the confines of due process.

(g) DRO Fees. Every temporary or final order submitted to the Court for approval which contains provisions ordering the payment of child support shall contain a paragraph ordering the parties to pay the appropriate fees to the Tarrant County Child Support Office in such language as may be approved by each Court.

(h) Child Support Card. In every case in which child support is ordered payable through Tarrant County Child Support Office, a "Record of Order for Child Support" shall be completed and delivered to the Child Support Office using the forms provided. Such form shall be completed by the party appearing before the Court on an agreement prior to prove up, or by the Obligee immediately after a contested hearing.

(i) Forms. All appropriate state and local forms shall be completed and delivered to the Court Clerk with all proposed Orders or Decrees to be left with the Clerk for consideration by the Court.

RULE 4.02: PROVE-UPS & DEFAULT HEARINGS

(a) Times. Each Court shall routinely hear agreed cases and defaults at times set by each Court every morning. It is not necessary to schedule agreed prove-ups and default hearings with the Court, and such are heard on a first-come-first-served basis, except that the Court may first hear cases in which a party is appearing with counsel in order [to] save time for the party and minimize attorneys fees. A Court may cancel its morning prove-ups as may be required by other Court business, and notice of such cancellation shall be posted outside the Court. Agreed prove-ups and defaults may be heard at other times during the day if the Court is available.

(b) Presiding Judge. Agreed cases and default hearings should normally be heard by the District Judge sitting in the Court to which the case is assigned. If that Judge is not available, then it may be heard by any other District Judge who so consents. Unless otherwise directed by the Court, multiple prove-ups originating out of different Courts may be presented to one Court for hearing. Once a case has been presented to a Judge, and the Judge has made a ruling or deferred ruling, the same matter shall not be presented to any other Judge without the consent of the Judge to whom it was first presented. With the consent of the Court, agreed cases not requiring a record may be presented to the Associate Judge of the Court for hearing.

(c) Court's File. Any attorney presenting an agreed case or default to the Court for hearing shall obtain the Court's File on such case from the District Clerk's office prior to prove-up. The Court's File shall be delivered to the Court's bailiff, or other person designated by the Court, for consideration by the Court. When the File is so delivered, it shall contain the proposed Decree or Order with the appropriate number of copies, all other necessary pleadings, and the required State and local forms.

(d) Record. If a record of testimony is required, the attorney shall so notify the bailiff, or other person designated by the Court, and shall complete any additional forms as may be required by the Court to be delivered to the Court Reporter.

(e) Wage Withholdings. Except in unusual circumstances, every wage withholding order presented to the Court for approval shall have attached to it a receipt from the Tarrant County Child Support Office showing payment of the required fees.

RULE 4.03: TRIAL SETTINGS

(a) Final Trial. Cases will be set for final trial upon written request using the procedure and form as may be required by the specific Court. Each Court's procedure and setting request form shall be obtained from the Court's Court Coordinator.

(b) Associate Judge and IV-D Master. Upon agreement of the parties, the Court may refer a non-jury case for final trial by the Associate Judge of that Court or IV-D Master, if appropriate, if the parties agree to waive their right of appeal to the referring Court pursuant to Sect. 54.012(I), Texas Government Code, [see current Family Code §201.015 (associate judge) & §201.1042 (master)] prior to the commencement of trial.

RULE 4.04: ASSOCIATE JUDGES & IV-D MASTERS

(a) Cases Referred. Each Court may refer any aspect of a family law case to the Associate Judge or IV-D

See note on p. 1157.

Master that is consistent with Sect. 54.005, Texas Government Code, [now Family Code §201.005] Sect. 14.80 and Sect. 14.82, Texas Family Code. See current §101.001 et seq. & §201.101 et seq. Unless otherwise ordered by the Court, the following matters will *normally* be so referred:

(1) Requests for Temporary Orders in any case, including custody.

(2) Motions to Modify Temporary or Final Orders, except for final custody modifications.

(3) Motions to Transfer.

(4) Motions for Enforcement or Contempt.

(5) An action under Chapter 21, Texas Family Code.

(6) Applications for Protective Orders.

(7) An action under Chapter 46 or 76, Texas Human Resources Code.

(8) Discovery matters.

(9) Motions to Compel or for Sanctions.

(10) Motions for Judgment or to Sign Orders, if hearing the subject of the proposed Order was heard by the Associate Judge.

(11) Motions to Withdraw.

(12) Pre-Trial Conferences.

(13) An action under Chapter 13, Texas Family Code.

(14) Any other matter referred by the Court.

The Court will not refer to the IV-D Master, and the IV-D Master shall not hear, final trials involving divorce proceedings. The court *may* decline to refer to the IV-D Masters, and the IV-D Masters shall not hear, any matters listed above as is consistent with the relevant Code provisions.

(b) Settings. Hearings before the Associate Judge shall be obtained from the Court Coordinator of the appropriate Court and the appropriate written Order or Notice of Hearing shall be presented to the Coordinator at the time the hearing is requested. The Court, in its discretion, may allow the setting or resetting of a hearing without a written Order or Notice, but the attorney requesting said setting or resetting shall send the Coordinator and all parties written confirmation of the hearing date so set.

(c) Times. Hearings before the Associate Judge shall be held each morning at a specific time and place as directed by the Court. Each attorney and party appearing before the Associate judge shall timely report to the bailiff assigned to said Associate Judge on the date of the hearing, and the Associate Judge, at his or her discretion, may request an announcement from counsel or pro se parties as to the issues in controversy and estimates of time required.

RULE 4.05: TRIAL PROCEDURES

(a) Timely Appearance. It is the responsibility of every attorney to timely appear before the Judge, Associate Judge or IV-D Master, as appropriate, at the time of any hearing. Unless otherwise directed b the Court, counsel shall check-in with the Court or its bailiff at or before the time the hearing is set. If counsel is to be late for a hearing or is in another Court, counsel or counsel's staff shall, by telephone or otherwise, notify the Court or its bailiff, giving the reason for the delay in appearance and exactly which other Courts counsel is appearing before. Failure to appear or check-in with the Associate Judge's or IV-D Master's Court within 30 minutes of the scheduled hearing time shall result in a default being granted or the hearing being passed, as appropriate. Although it is the policy of the Courts to recognize the inevitable conflicts in an urban law practice and to be reasonably flexible, it is ultimately the responsibility of counsel to keep the Court accurately informed of counsel's whereabouts so that the Court's dockets will not be unduly disrupted. Violation of this Rule may result in sanctions against counsel.

(b) Documents Required. In all cases in which support of a spouse and/or child(ren) is in issue, whether temporary or final, each party shall be required to furnish the Court and opposing party true and correct copies of the following, at or before the time of hearing, if available:

(1) Summary statement of monthly income and expenses in a form substantially similar to any form that may be adopted by the Court.

(2) All payroll stubs or wage statements for the past 3 months.

(3) If self-employed, all Profit & Loss Statements, Balance Sheets, Income Statements or other evidence of earnings for the previous 12 months.

(4) Federal Income Tax Returns, including all attachments and schedules, for the two years immediately prior to the hearing, or if a return has not been prepared and filed for a particular year, all W-2's, 1099's, K-1's or other evidence of income for such a year.

See note on p. 1157.

(5) Financial statements filed by the parties with any financial institution within the past 3 years.

(6) Any other documents as ordered by the Court, or properly subpoenaed by a party.

(c) Inventories. When ordered by the Court, each party shall file a sworn inventory and appraisement within 60 days of the Court's order, unless the Court or the parties extend or shorten such period. An Inventory and Appraisement may be ordered in any case in which the character, value or division of property or debts is in issue, and should be filed in a form substantially similar to the form provided in the Texas Family Practice Manual of the State Bar of Texas. Additionally, each party shall at the time of trial prepare for the Court and opposing counsel a written summary of that party's proposed division of property and debts.

(d) Orders. Within 60 days after rendition by the Judge, Associate Judge or IV-D Master of a decision, counsel shall cause, unless ordered otherwise, all orders, decrees or judgments of any kind to be reduced to writing, approved as to form by opposing counsel, and to be delivered to the Court for signature. If counsel is unable to secure the approval as to form from opposing counsel, counsel shall file a motion for entry of a proposed order and secure a hearing on same. The party or counsel responding to such a motion shall at least 3 days prior to the hearing present to opposing counsel an alternative proposed order or a written list of objections to the first order. Failure to furnish the Court with a proposed order, decree or judgment or to schedule a hearing for entry within the 60 day period may result in the Court placing the case on the dismissal docket.

(e) Court Reporters. A Court Reporter will be furnished to the Associate Judges for hearings only on the days that Enforcement are to be heard, unless special arrangements are made with the referring Judge. Counsel shall be required to furnish his or her own Court Reporter, if desired, for all other hearings before the Associate Judge.

RULE 4.06: CONTINUANCES & RESETS

(a) Associate Judges and IV-D Masters. Unless otherwise directed by the Court, motions for continuance and resets may be presented to the Associate Judge or IV-D Master without the necessity of a written motion being filed. If not agreed by all parties, said motion for continuance or reset must be made to the Associate Judge or IV-D Master after all parties have been given notice and an opportunity to object.

(b) Presiding Judges. No request for a continuance or resetting shall be granted by the presiding Judge of a Court without the filing of a written motion, notice and hearing, unless agreed by all parties, with the consent of the Court. All other requests shall be in writing pursuant to the Texas Rules of Civil Procedure, filed with the Court, and shall be heard as may be scheduled by the Court after proper notice to all parties.

Rules 4.07 through 4.10: Reserved

RULE 4.11: DISCOVERY GUIDELINES

(a) Full Discovery. As provided in the Texas Rules of Civil Procedure and appellate court rulings, the Courts shall permit full, liberal and broad discovery, however such discovery shall not be unlimited, and the reasonable parameters contained in Rule 166b shall be applied in both letter and spirit.

(b) Disputes. Any discovery question, problem or dispute shall be attempted to be settled by counsel before intervention by the Court. Any discovery motion shall contain a certificate by the party or counsel filing same substantially as follows:

"A conference was held on (date) with (name of attorney for opposing party) on the merits of this motion. Agreement could not be reached. Therefore it is presented to the Court for determination."

or

"A conference was not held with (name of opposing attorney) on the merits of this motion because (explanation of inability to confer)."

No discovery motion shall be set for hearing or heard unless it contains such certificate, signed by counsel or a pro se party.

(c) Depositions. The following guidelines will *generally* be followed by the Courts on matters pertaining to oral depositions:

(1) A party filing an action in Tarrant County must give his or her deposition in Tarrant County, if requested.

(2) A Respondent properly sued in Tarrant County must give his or her deposition in Tarrant County, if requested.

(3) The party initiating a deposition may elect to take the deposition orally or on written questions and

See note on p. 1157.

the opposing party may elect to cross-examine orally or on written questions.

(4) Unless agreed otherwise, fees charged by an expert for giving of deposition testimony shall be paid by the party requesting the deposition. The fee for the preparation of an expert's report, not previously reduced to writing and sought under Rule 166(b)(2)(e)(4), Texas Rules of Civil Procedure, shall be paid by the party employing the expert.

(5) The following shall be presumed to be unreasonable unless otherwise agreed or ordered:

a. Notice of less than 10 days under Rules 21a and 200, Tex. Rules of Civ. Proc.

b. Depositions scheduled for Saturday, Sunday or legal holidays in which the County Courthouse is closed.

c. Depositions scheduled to begin before 8:00 a.m. or to extend past 6:00 p.m.

(6) A party initiating an oral deposition shall first attempt to communicate with all opposing counsels to determine whether agreement can be reached as to the date, time, place and materials to be furnished at the time of deposition. Any written notice of oral deposition shall state substantially as follows:

"A conference was held or attempted with the attorney for opposing party to agree on a date, time, place and materials to be furnished. Agreement could not be reached, or counsel will not respond, and the deposition is therefore being taken pursuant to this Notice (or) Agreement was reached and this Notice complies with the agreement."

Failure to hold such conference or to make adequate attempt to hold such conference prior to noticing a deposition shall be grounds to quash the deposition.

Notwithstanding the above guidelines, the parties may agree to a different procedure, and nothing shall preclude a party from submitting disputes as to such matters to the Court for determination by proper motion and hearing pursuant to the Texas Rules of Civil Procedure.

(d) Production. Unless otherwise ordered by the Court pursuant to Rule 167, Tex. Rules of Civ. Proc., or agreed by the parties, the following times and locations for production shall be presumed to be reasonable:

a. For non-voluminous production, counsel for the party from whom the production is requested shall make and deliver copies of the documents to the office of counsel for the requesting party within 30 days of receipt of the request.

b. For voluminous production, counsel for the party from whom the production is requested shall, within 30 days of the request, gather the documents at his or her office and inform requesting counsel that they are available. Requesting counsel shall then, at the option of requesting counsel, either pick up the documents to examine, copy and return within 5 working days, or to examine and copy the documents at the office of producing counsel, with the expense of examination and copying to be paid by requesting counsel.

TAYLOR COUNTY

RULES OF PRACTICE

326TH DISTRICT COURT

1989 Version.

RULE 4.10. TIME STANDARDS FOR FAMILY LAW CASE DISPOSITION

Dismissal dockets are prepared each April and October, therefore cases should be disposed of within six months of the date of filing.

RULE 4.11. ANCILLARY PROCEEDINGS, TEMPORARY ORDERS, & EMERGENCY MATTERS

All pleadings for ancillary, temporary and emergency matters shall first be filed with the Clerk and then brought to the attention of the Court Administrator.

RULE 4.12. DISPOSITION PROPOSALS

a. Requests for Settings: Non-jury: Requests for settings of contested final hearings shall be in writing and directed to the Court Administrator, with copies to the Clerk and opposing counsel, and shall:

1. Specify all matters to be heard; and,

2. Certify that counsel have attempted to settle the disputed issues by written, telephone or personal conference; and

3. Certify that both counsel have agreed to the estimated time requested to hear all matters.

Where setting requests do not so certify, opposing counsel has the obligation to inform the Court, in writing within 5 days of the request, that the amount of time requested is not sufficient.

Any party may request a setting.

See note on p. 1157.

b. Continuances: Requests for continuances must be in writing and will be set for hearing. The attorney obtaining a new hearing date shall confirm the setting in writing with opposing counsel and the Court.

c. Setting Conflicts: Having a case set with the Judge at the same time one is set with the Master is a setting conflict. In that event, the case which has the oldest setting shall take precedence and the later set case shall be reset for another time.

d. Request for Settings: Jury: Requests for jury trials must be made in writing and will not be placed on the docket until the jury fee is paid. Letters setting a pretrial hearing are routinely sent by the court administrator at least two weeks in advance of trial. Counsel shall attend such pretrial hearings to make announcements on their cases and present all pretrial motions.

RULE 4.13. UNCONTESTED MATTERS

Default, waiver and uncontested matters:

a. 9:00 a.m. – 9:30 a.m. Tuesday, Wednesday, Thursday and Friday will be set aside to hear uncontested matters only. No uncontested matters will be heard on Mondays. Files must be pulled and given to the Court Administrator or Bailiff before 9:15 a.m.

b. From time to time, notices will be posted in the District Clerk's Office and on the courtroom door indicating weeks during which no uncontested matters will be heard.

c. To facilitate collection of child support and to promote accuracy in the recording of payments, waivers of citation shall contain a place for the respondent's address, social security number and driver's license number, either in the body or under the signature.

RULE 4.14. FINANCIAL INFORMATION STATEMENTS

In all actions in which the Master or Judge is requested to set temporary alimony, child support or any other type of support, and in all actions involving a motion to increase or decrease support, each party shall prepare a financial disclosure form and deliver a copy of such form to the adverse party or his counsel and the Master or Judge prior to the hearing. Each party shall furnish two current pay stubs. Copies of the suggested forms are attached hereto as Exhibit A.

RULE 4.15. CHILD SUPPORT GUIDELINES

a. The guidelines of Art. 14.05 of the Family Code [see current §154.001 et seq.] and the rules thereunder apply to all original proceeding and motions to modify child support. All orders should direct that payments be made to the Taylor County Domestic Relations Office.

b. In cases involving more than one child, reductions in amount based on emancipation of older children, will be made proportionately, according to the guidelines, not equally by the number of children.

c. In all actions which the Master or Judge is requested to set child support and in all actions involving a motion to increase or decrease child support, each party shall prepare a financial disclosure form and deliver a copy of such form to the adverse party or his counsel and the Master or Judge prior to the hearing. Each party shall furnish two current pay stubs.

d. The Domestic Relations Office of Taylor County monitors all court ordered child support and visitation problems. Further information and forms can be obtained from that office.

RULE 4.16. POSSESSORY CONSERVATOR VISITATION GUIDELINES

Possessory conservator visitation is controlled by the Provisions of Section 14.033, Family Code, [see current §153.11 et seq.] Standard Possession Order.

RULE 4.17. INVENTORY & APPRAISEMENT

In cases involving an appreciable amount of property in dispute, counsel for each party shall prepare a list of property involved with estimates of value noted thereon. A copy of the list shall be presented to opposing counsel at least three days before trial and to the Court prior to any testimony being made.

RULE 4.18. AD LITEM APPOINTMENTS

In cases where attorneys or guardians ad litem are required by law, the request for an appointment of same shall be made in writing to the Court Administrator who will supply the attorney's name next appearing on the Court's rotating list.

RULE 4.19. CHILDREN'S INTEREST SEMINAR

Amended, effective October 12, 1995.

(a) This rule applies to all parties in all suits affecting the parent-child relationship filed in the 326th Judicial District Court, effective upon approval by the Supreme Court of Texas.

See note on p. 1157.

(b) The 326th Judicial District Court may require such parties to successfully complete a seminar that addresses the issues confronting children that are the subject of divorce, custody, and child support litigations. Exhibit "A" attached hereto and incorporated herein for all purposes describes the seminar. Each party is responsible for payment of the appropriate fee.

(c) The seminar shall be successfully completed within 60 days of the service of the original petition upon the respondent, or if service is waived, then within 60 days of waiver of citation.

(d) Upon a party's failure to successfully complete the seminar pursuant to this rule, the Court may take appropriate action, including contempt, striking of any pleading, or any of the sanctions listed in Rule 215 of the Texas Rules of Civil Procedure.

(e) For good cause shown, the Court may waive the requirement of completion of the seminar.

RULE 4.20. REFERRAL TO MASTER

a. Referrals: The Master shall hear all matters as set out in Article 54.005 of the Government Code, which includes all temporary orders, modifications, contempts and protective orders.

b. Objections: Objections to the Master will be considered untimely filed if filed fewer than 10 days before the trial date.

c. Settings:

(1) Proposed orders shall be presented with requests for hearing on temporary orders, contempts and applications for protective orders. If contempt actions are expected to be contested and lengthy, the Court Administrator should be advised at the time of the request for hearing. All orders should specify that the hearing will be before the Court Master.

(2) Requests for hearings on Motions to Modify shall be in writing and directed to the Court Administrator, with copies to the Clerk and opposing counsel, and shall certify that both counsel have conferred together and agreed to the estimated time requested to hear the entire matter. Where setting requests do not so certify, the allotted time will be divided equally between the parties.

(3) When continuances are granted by agreements of counsel, the attorney requesting the continuance must obtain a new hearing date and confirm the same with both the Court and opposing counsel. In resetting contempts, an order setting hearing is required.

(4) Having a case set with the Master at the same time one is set with the Judge is a setting conflict. In that event, the case which has the older setting will take preference and the later set case shall be reset for another time.

d. Written Orders: Written orders after the hearings by the Master shall provide appropriate signature spaces for both the Judge and the Master.

e. All Orders: Orders are appealable to the referring court. All appeals shall be in writing, specifying that portion of the master's ruling which is being appealed, and notice shall be given to opposing counsel. The notice shall also contain a request for a hearing and shall be filed and presented to the Court within three days after the recommendation is made by the Master.

All recommendations of the Master remain in full force and effect until the hearing is had on the appeal, except for incarceration for contempt.

Exhibits inserted here:

Financial Information Statement

Domestic Relations Office Data Sheet

Exhibit "A"

The seminar shall focus on fostering emotional health for children during periods of stress brought about by divorce and conflict between divorced parents.

The seminar administrator shall be designated by the Court. The Court has currently designated Family Outreach of Abilene/Taylor County, Inc., to be the seminar administrator.

The course content shall generally consist of the following:

(1) the development stages of childhood

(2) the needs of children at different ages

(3) stress indicators in children

(4) age appropriate expectations of children

(5) divorce as a growth stage

(6) the grief process

(7) reducing stress for children going through a divorce

(8) the changing parental and marital roles

(9) visitation recommendations to enhance the child's relationship with both parents

(10) financial obligations of child rearing

(11) conflict management and dispute resolution

See note on p. 1157.

Each seminar shall be a minimum of two hours and a maximum of four hours. The seminar may include the showing of appropriate videos.

The seminar shall be presented at such times and places as scheduled and announced by the seminar administrator.

A reasonable fee approved by the Court, unless waived by the Court, may be charged by the seminar administrator to be used to cover costs.

Each person completing the seminar and paying the appropriate fee shall receive a certificate to file with the Court.

The Court may require a certified peace officer to be in attendance at each seminar to provide security.

TRAVIS COUNTY

LOCAL RULES OF CIVIL PROCEDURE & RULES OF DECORUM

Effective November 26, 1990.

CHAPTER 6—PROCEEDINGS BEFORE ASSOCIATE JUDGES IN FAMILY LAW CASES

6.1 Pursuant to TEX.FAM.CODE.ANN. Chapter 201, the District Courts have appointed Associate Judges to hear certain matters specified by these Rules and by these Rules do refer such matters to the Associate Judges.

6.2 The following will be heard originally by an Associate Judge:

(a) All matters relating to suits over which the District Courts have jurisdiction under TEX.FAM. CODE.ANN. Titles 1, 4 and 5 except:

(1) matters on the uncontested docket;

(2) contested trials on the merits to terminate parental rights;

(3) contested trials on the merits that will require more than three hours, unless the parties in writing or on the record (i) consent to having the trial heard by an Associate Judge and (ii) waive the right to request a *de novo* hearing before a District Judge;

(4) proceedings in which Child Protective Services is a party;

(5) pretrial motions that, if granted, could have a dispositive effect on issues in the case e.g., pleas in abatement, special appearance, and summary judgment unless the parties in writing or on the record

(i) consent to having the motion heard by an Associate Judge, and

(ii) waive the right to request a de novo hearing before a District Judge;

(6) Motions for discovery sanctions with respect to any discovery issue where an order to compel has already been recommended by an Associate Judge; and

(b) Any other matter referred to an Associate Judge by a Judge (i) if the parties consent in writing or on the record or (ii) as otherwise provided by law.

(c) Adoptions and petitions to recognize foreign adoptions may not be heard at the uncontested docket. Uncontested adoptions and petitions to recognize foreign adoptions shall be set on the Associate Judges' settings docket.

6.3 All matters for which the Domestic Relations Office has responsibility shall be set by the Domestic Relations Office.

6.4 All other matters to be heard originally by an Associate Judge shall be set by the Court Administrator on the Associate Judges' settings docket. The Court Administrator may assign to another Associate Judge or to an available Judge. Any matter that cannot be reached by an Associate Judge at the time the case is called for hearing. An Associate Judge may refer any matter to the Court Administrator for a setting before a Judge. An Associate Judge will usually refer any matter requiring a lengthy hearing, unless the parties in writing or on the record waive their right to request a *de novo* hearing before a District Judge.

6.5 (a) A party may file an objection to the assignment of an Associate Judge to hear any trial on the merits. A trial on the merits is any trial in which a party seeks a final adjudication from which an appeal may be taken to a Court of Appeals. The objection must be in writing. The time for filing an objection pursuant to TEX.FAM.CODE.ANN. §201.005 shall be:

(1) on or before ten days from receipt of a notice of setting on the Associate Judges' docket;

(2) on or before the day a setting before a Judge is requested by the party seeking a hearing; or

(3) on or before ten days from receipt of notice that a Judge referred a specific case to an Associate Judge for a trial on the merits.

(b) A person filing an objection shall deliver a copy of the objection to all parties and to the Court Administrator on the same day the objection is filed with the

See note on p. 1157.

District Clerk. The Court Administrator shall remove any trial on the merits from the Associate Judges' docket after an objection is filed.

(c) A party may file a motion to have any other matter heard originally before a Judge instead of an Associate Judge. The motion must be in writing and must specify the grounds in support of the motion. The party filing the motion must set the motion for hearing by a Judge with notice to all parties as required by the applicable rules of civil procedure.

6.6 Matters set before an Associate Judge will be set on the days and times reflected on the docket schedule filed with the Court Administrator. Notice of the locations of the docket calls and hearings will be posted each day on the bulletin board outside of the District Clerk's office on the third floor of the courthouse.

6.7 The fact that the rules require that certain matters be heard originally by an Associate Judge does not affect a party's rights to have a Judge grant or extend a temporary restraining order or an *ex parte* protective order and does not prevent a temporary restraining order or an *ex parte* protective order from expiring. Until a Judge signs an order concerning the findings and recommendations of an Associate Judge, such findings and recommendations do not affect an existing temporary restraining order or *ex parte* protective order or the expiration or extension of such an order.

6.8 At the conclusion of any hearing conducted by an Associate Judge, the Associate Judge shall make findings, conclusions, and recommendations by making a written, signed and dated notation on the docket sheet of the case or on a separate document that will be placed in the file folder and noted on the docket sheet. The Associate Judge shall give to the parties participating in the hearing notice of the substance of the findings, conclusions, and recommendations. The notice may be given in open court or may be given by letter sent by certified mail return receipt requested. If the notice is by certified mail, the Associate Judge shall certify the date of mailing, and the notice is deemed to have been given on the third day after the date of mailing. **THE TIME FOR FILING A REQUEST FOR A *DE NOVO* HEARING BEFORE A JUDGE BEGINS ON THE FIRST DAY AFTER THIS NOTICE IS GIVEN OR DEEMED TO HAVE BEEN GIVEN.**

6.9 The Associate Judge shall give notice to all parties of the right to request a *de novo* hearing before a Judge. This notice shall be given in the Associate Judge's written report any by posting a copy of TEX.FAM.CODE.ANN. §§201.001-201.017 inside or outside the Associate Judge's courtroom.

6.10 After a hearing is concluded, the Associate Judge shall send to a Judge a written, signed report containing the Associate Judge's findings and recommendations. The report may be in the form of a written order prepared for a Judge's signature and accompanied by the Associate Judge's signed and dated statement that the order as prepared is recommended. The Judge shall promptly approve or disapprove the report in its entirety or set the matter for a hearing before a Judge.

6.11 Any party is entitled to a *de novo* hearing before a Judge if not later than the third day after the Associate Judge gives notice of his or her findings, conclusions, and recommendations, the party files with the District Clerk a written request for a *de novo* hearing. The right to a *de novo* hearing exists even if within said three-day period a Judge has signed an order approving the findings and recommendation of the Associate Judge.

6.12 Except for orders providing for incarceration or for the appointment of a receiver, a request for a *de novo* hearing does not stay, suspend, or affect the enforcement of an order of the Associate Judge pursuant to TEX.FAM.CODE.ANN. §201.013 pending a hearing before a District Judge on any appeal from the Associate Judge's report. A request for a *de novo* hearing does not stay, suspend, or prevent enforcement or contempt proceedings brought pursuant to an order requiring that the parties comply with an Associate Judge's decisions and recommendations pending a *de novo* hearing.

6.13 A request for a *de novo* hearing must state with particularity the specific findings conclusions and recommendations of the Associate Judge that are the subject of objections or the issue is deemed waived. The Judge to whom the *de novo* request is assigned for hearing may determine whether to consider other issues.

6.14 Any person requesting a *de novo* hearing before a Judge shall also deliver a copy of the request to the Court Administrator on the same day that the request is filed with the District Clerk. The Court Administrator shall set the matter for hearing on the Central Settings Docket on the first available date as determined by the

See note on p. 1157.

Court Administrator after seven days, but no later than thirty days, from the date the initial request was filed.

CHAPTER 7—PRE-TRIAL PROCEDURE IN FAMILY LAW CASES

7.1 Standing Pre-trial and Discovery Order. The District Courts have determined that the following procedures are necessary for the orderly disposition of certain family law matters, and pursuant to Rule 166, Texas Rules of Civil Procedure, it is hereby ordered that this Chapter 7 shall constitute a standing pre-trial and discovery order in all divorce cases, suits affecting the parent-child relationship, and suits to modify orders affecting the parent-child relationship. The term "party" as used below includes a party's counsel of record.

7.2 Pre-trial Procedure Before a Final Trial on the Merits. Before the final trial on the merits in any divorce suit, suit affecting the parent-child relationship, or suit to modify an order affecting the parent-child relationship each party shall prepare and deliver pre-trial forms as follows:

(1) Forms required depend on type of suit and issue at trial.

(a) In a divorce suit, each party shall prepare and deliver a Proposed Property Division in the form prescribed by these rules, fully completed and signed by the party, or a single agreed Proposed Property Division, signed by both parties.

(b) In any suit requiring a determination of child support or spousal maintenance, each party shall prepare and deliver a Proposed Support Decision and information in the form prescribed by these rules, fully completed and signed by the party, or a single agreed Proposed Support Decision and Information, signed by both parties.

(c) In any suit in which a Proposed Property Division or Proposed Support Decision and Information is required, then each party shall also prepare and deliver a Proposed Disposition of Other Issues, which shall state separately in brief complete sentences each trial decision that is sought by the party that is not covered by the Proposed Property Decision or Proposed Support Decision and Information.

(2) To whom forms are delivered. Each party shall deliver the required forms to the opposing party and to the Court Administrator.

(3) When forms are delivered. Each party shall deliver the required forms before 1:30 p.m. on the Thursday that is ten days prior to the Monday of the week of any trial on the merits.

7.3 Pre-trial Procedure Before a Temporary or Interim Orders Hearing. Before any hearing on temporary or interim orders in any divorce suit, suit affecting the parent-child relationship, or suit to modify an order affecting the parent-child relationship, each party shall prepare and deliver pre-trial forms as follows:

(1) Forms required depends on issues at hearing. In a hearing to determine child support or spousal maintenance, each party shall prepare and deliver a Proposed Support Decision and Information in the form prescribed by these rules, fully completed, and signed by the party.

(2) To whom form is delivered. Each party shall deliver the required form to the opposing party and to the Judge hearing the case.

(3) When form is delivered. Each party shall deliver the required form before the court calls the case for hearing.

7.4 Not Required in DRO, DRPS, AG or County Attorney Protective Order Hearings. Pre-trial forms are not required for any hearing at which attorneys from Travis County Domestic Relations Office, the Department of Protective and Regulatory Services, the Texas Attorney General's Office or the County Attorney Protective Order Division appear.

7.5 No Extensions or Waivers by Court Administrator or by Agreement. The Court Administrator is not authorized to extend the time for delivering pretrial forms. The parties may not by agreement waive or modify the provisions or requirements of these rules.

7.6 Handling of Forms. The Court Administrator will deliver pre-trial forms received prior to a final trial on the merits to the Judge to whom the case is assigned for trial. Pre-trial forms shall not be filed with the District Clerk at any time. The District Clerk is authorized to destroy any such forms found in the case file maintained by the Clerk.

7.7 Use of Evidence. Subject to applicable rules of evidence, the pre-trial forms required by these rules may be used during the trial or hearing and may be marked as exhibits and offered in evidence.

7.8 Consequences for Failure to Comply.

(1) All parties fail to comply. If all parties in a case fail to deliver pre-trial forms as required by these rules, the case will be moved to the bottom of the list of

See note on p. 1157.

cases set for the same time and will be heard only after all announced cases are heard and only if time permits.

(2) A party fails to comply. If it appears that any party in a case failed to deliver pre-trial forms as required by these rules, the Court shall conduct a pre-trial conference if requested and notice is given by any party, or the Court may conduct a pre-trial conference on its own motion. The Court may impose one or more of the sanctions authorized by Tex. R. Civ. Proc. 215 against any party or attorney responsible for such failure.

(3) Issues waived. All issues not stated in pre-trial forms as required by these rules will deemed waived except upon a showing of good cause for failure to comply with these rules.

7.9 No Limitation on Texas Rules of Civil Procedure. These rules shall not be construed as a substitute for, or as any limitation upon, any pre-trial or discovery right or proceeding pursuant to the Texas Rules of Civil Procedure. In cases subject to these local rules, as in other cases Texas pre-trial conference and discovery rules apply.

CHAPTER 8—FAMILY LAW SUPPORT & SHOW CAUSE ORDERS

8.1 The Domestic Relations Office of Travis County is hereby designated as the Registry of the Court for all of the District Courts for all spouse and child support payments, except for payment ordered pursuant to all Title IV-D Agency court orders or decrees signed on or after July 1, 2000.

Every draft of an order or decree requiring any such support payment must provide that all payments shall be made through the Domestic Relations Office of Travis County, Texas.

Every Title IV-D Agency order or decree signed on or after July 1, 2000, requiring child support payments must provide that all such payments be made through the Texas Child Support State Disbursement Unit, P.O. Box 659791, San Antonio, Texas 78265-9791.

At the time any support is ordered, the party who is to receive the support must provide to the Domestic Relations Office an Intake Sheet containing the information required by that office; and after the order or decree is signed, such party shall deliver to the Domestic Relations Office a conformed copy of the order or decree.

8.2 Every draft of a show cause order for a hearing before an Associate Judge must require the respondent to report to Room 511 in the Courthouse at 8:30 a.m.

The paragraph in the order stating this requirement should read as follows:

"It is ordered that the Clerk shall issue notice to Respondent, ______________________________, to appear, and said Respondent is hereby ordered to appear, by reporting to Room 511 of the Travis County Courthouse, 1000 Guadalupe, Austin, Texas, on the _____ day of ________________, ______, at 8:30 a.m."

Chapter 9—Omitted by Editor

CHAPTER 10—UNCONTESTED DIVORCES & OTHER UNCONTESTED MATTERS

10.1 On Monday through Friday of each week from 8:00 a.m. until approximately 8:50 a.m. and from 1:00 p.m. until approximately 1:50 p.m., at least one Judge will be available in a courtroom to sign orders and to hear uncontested divorces and other uncontested matters of very short duration.

These matters will ordinarily be considered in the order in which the pertinent files, docket sheets, and papers are brought to the courtroom clerk.

Court reporters will be available at the morning (8:00 a.m. to 8:50 a.m.) session only.

Notice of the location of this uncontested docket will be posted each day on the bulletin board outside of the District Clerk's office on the third floor of the Courthouse.

Comment Concerning Local Rule 10.1: The purpose of this Rule is to provide flexibility for attorneys in scheduling uncontested divorce hearings and to provide convenient access to a Judge for the signing of orders and for very brief uncontested hearings.

Attorneys should make use of this uncontested docket not only for uncontested divorces, but also for uncontested name changes, agreed orders in pending divorce cases, orders concerning service of citation, family law temporary restraining orders, show cause orders, and other such matters.

Special Instruction for Local Rule 10.1: Attorneys must obtain from the District Clerk's office and deliver to the courtroom all files and docket sheets, which may be needed for the matters, which they will present to the Judge.

When a request is to be made for withdrawal of funds maintained in the Registry of the Court for the benefit of a minor who has not yet reached legal age, the applicant shall bring to the Court with the motion a Summary of Minor's Bank Account obtained from the Office of the District Clerk reflecting the status of the minor's account, indicating previous withdrawals, if any.

CHAPTER 14—ADOPTIONS & TERMINATIONS

14.1 In the following proceedings, the District Clerk will maintain the files, docket sheets, and minutes as confidential records:

(a) every suit in which the petition includes a prayer seeking adoption of a child;

(b) every suit in which any authorized agency seeks termination of the parent-child relationship.

See note on p. 1157.

In all other suits seeking termination but not adoption, the files, docket sheets, and minutes will not be confidential or sealed unless otherwise ordered pursuant to Local Rule 14.03.

All social studies and reports filed pursuant to the Texas Family Code will be maintained as confidential records.

14.2 If confidential records relating to a request for further action concerning a child in the court of continuing jurisdiction are required by Texas Family Code, §155.104, to be filed under the same docket number as a prior proceeding in which records were not confidential or sealed, the District Clerk will place the petition in a separate file folder for the same suit, with the same docket number. The Clerk shall make a notation on the original file folder that there is a separate file folder containing confidential pleadings and orders.

14.3 In any pending proceeding brought by the Texas Department of Protective and Regulatory Services concerning a child and in any pending suit in which any party seeks termination of the parent-child relationship, the Court, on the application of a party or on the Court's own motion, may order that records shall be confidential.

After final judgment or decree in such a matter and in any proceeding in which adoption is sought, records may be sealed pursuant to §108.002 of the Texas Family Code.

14.4 In every suit in which there are confidential or sealed records, the petitioner's attorney must determine whether the records are correctly marked and maintained and must bring to the attention of the District Clerk any clerical action required.

14.5 The District Clerk is hereby authorized to use microfilm or other suitable means for maintaining inactive confidential records and sealed files.

14.6 The District Courts have determined that the following orders concerning appointments of guardians *ad litem* and the making of social studies are necessary for the orderly disposition of suits seeking termination of the parent-child relationship or adoption, or both.

Subject to any order that may be made in a particular cause, it is therefore ordered pursuant to Rule 166, Texas Rules of Civil Procedure, that Local Rules 14.07 and 14.08 shall constitute standing pre-trial orders in all cases to which said Rules apply.

14.7

(a) In every suit in which the petitioner seeks to terminate a parent-child relationship or to adopt a child, the Clerk shall forward a copy of the petition as soon as practicable to the Manager of the Family Services Unit of the Travis County Domestic Relations Office (Family Services Manager).

(b)(1) In each suit in which the Texas Department of Protective and Regulatory Services seeks to terminate the parent-child relationship, the Court shall appoint an attorney *ad litem* for each child by court order as soon as practicable after the suit is filed, and on a case-by-case basis as necessary the Court may appoint the Family Services Manager as guardian *ad litem* for each child.

(b)(2) In each suit in which a child-placing agency seeks to terminate the parent-child relationship (other than the Texas Department of Protective and Regulatory Services), the Family Services Manager shall as soon as practicable either (a) recommend that the child-placing agency be appointed guardian *ad litem* or (b) recommend that the Family Services Manager be appointed guardian *ad litem*.

(b)(3) In every other suit seeking termination of the parent-child relationship, the Family Services Manager is appointed by this standing order as guardian *ad litem* for each child.

(c)(1) In each suit seeking adoption of a child placed for adoption by the Texas Department of Protective and Regulatory Services, on a case-by-case basis as necessary the Court may appoint the Family Services Manager as guardian *ad litem* for each child.

(c)(2) In each suit seeking adoption of a child placed for adoption by a child-placing agency (other than the Texas Department of Protective and Regulatory Services), the Family Services Manager shall as soon as practicable either (a) recommend that the child-placing agency be appointed guardian *ad litem* or (b) recommend that the Family Services Manager be appointed guardian *ad litem*.

(c)(3) In every other suit seeking adoption of a child, the Family Services Manager is appointed by this standing order as guardian *ad litem* for each child.

(d) In all suits affecting the parent-child relationship in which the Texas Department of Protective and Regulatory Services has been named by the Court or seeks to be named by the Court, or has been named in

See note on p. 1157.

an affidavit of relinquishment, as the managing conservator of a child, the Family Services Manager shall to the extent practicable keep the following records for the information of the Court:

1) Cause Number.

2) Case Name.

3) Child Data—On each child: name, date of birth, place of birth, social security number, ethnicity, race, sex.

4) Child Placement Data—Name of facility or foster home, date of placement and removal, number of days at each placement special auspice of placement (e.g. Casey or Blair), type of placement facility school child is attending and grade level, addresses and phone numbers of facility and school, name of proprietor, and county of location.

5) Parent/Other Party Data—Names of parents, CASA volunteer and caseworker and supervisor, the Blair Foundation caseworker, and supervisor, and the DPRS caseworker and supervisor. The date when each volunteer, caseworker, or supervisor started working on the case, the date when that person's involvement ended, and addresses and phone numbers of all involved.

6) Home Study Data—Name of parent or other party requesting home study for child(ren)'s placement, including addresses and phone numbers for home and work.

7) Attorney Data—Name of all attorneys and their addresses, phone numbers, person(s) represented (including staff of the Attorney General).

8) Court Hearing Data—Date, type of hearing and order, name of the judge, and any special instructions; date and time of Chapter 18 reviews and any special instructions; type and date of last conservatorship and any special provisions.

9) Visitation Information—Type and frequency ordered for parents and siblings (if the siblings are placed apart).

10) Child Support Information—Amount ordered and terms, start date, payor/payee names, and Domestic Relations account number.

11) Court-Ordered Services—What type, name of agency providing, beginning date, party responsible for payment, transportation arrangements, and other instruction for service provision.

12) DPRS Plan of Service—Date of plan, who participated in development, timelines for implementation, plan for permanence, and whether filed with the Court.

13) Information on Service of Lawsuit—Persons to be served (parents and other parties), date of service, method of service, and dates service was attempted if unsuccessful.

14) Significant Incidents Information—Any information reported to the Court, in pleadings, court reports, statements, or testimony, concerning significant incidents which are alleged to have occurred during the child's care.

All parties are ordered to provide access to or produce the information necessary for the Family Services Manager to keep the required records.

The Family Services Manager shall permit all parties access to the records maintained pursuant to these Rules, except that if any party requests any particular information to be kept confidential, the Manager shall not disclose that information unless directed by the Court.

(e) As originally enacted, this standing order became effective October 1, 1984. The order is amended effective July 10, 1991. Each appointment under this order shall become effective on the date suit is filed. All appointments under the original order remain effective. In all cases in which the Family Services Manager was appointed under the terms of the original standing order but would not have been appointed under the terms of the amended standing order, the Family Services Manager shall continue as guardian *ad litem* until discharged by specific order of the Court.

(f) A decree terminating the parent-child relationship shall not discharge a guardian *ad litem* unless otherwise ordered.

14.8 In a suit in which the Texas Department of Protective and Regulatory Services seeks termination of the parent-child relationship, any social study that is ordered should be made by the petitioner Department.

Any party who seeks an order that the Family Services Manager make such a social study must submit a draft of the proposed order, approved and signed by the Family Services Manager, as well as the attorneys.

In each suit seeking adoption of a child placed for adoption by the Texas Department of Protective and Regulatory Services or an authorized agency, this is a

See note on p. 1157.

standing order that the agency or Department that placed the child for adoption shall make the social study required by §162.003 of the Texas Family Code.

In every other suit in which an adoption is sought, this is a standing order that the Family Services Manager shall make said social study.

Each social study made pursuant to this standing order shall be filed on a date set by, and shall be made according to criteria established by, the Family Services Manager, under the supervision of the District Judges.

In each suit in which an adoption is sought, this standing order shall be effective on the date the suit is filed, which date shall be "the date on which the investigator is appointed" for the purposes of setting the hearing pursuant to §162.004 of the Texas Family Code.

14.9 In suits seeking termination of the parent-child relationship or adoption, or both, and in all suits in which the Family Services Manager is guardian *ad litem*, the Family Services Manager may request that the matter be set for trial or a hearing.

WEBB COUNTY

LOCAL RULES OF ADMINISTRATION

Effective February 7, 1990.

RULE 4. FAMILY LAW CASES

RULE 4.10. TIME STANDARDS FOR FAMILY LAW CASE DISPOSITION:

A. Contested Family Law Cases—All contested family law cases hall be heard within six (6) months from appearance date or within six (6) months from the expiration of the waiting period provided by the Family Code where such is required, whichever is later. All parties and counsel must be ready for trial on the merits after ninety (90) days or on the date designated on the form attached to the petition and citation.

If no activity is reflected on the docket sheet, the case will be subject to a dismissal for want of prosecution.

If a case is complex and/or extraordinary requiring additional preparation, a motion can be filed in accordance with Rule 3.33.

B. 49th and 111th District Courts—Divorce cases are scheduled as all other civil cases.

C. County Court at Law and 341st District Court Cases:

1. The controlling date is the Friday of the week a divorce is filed.

2. Non-jury cases: The cases shall be automatically set for trial. The trial date shall be in writing on the citation to respondent.

3. Jury cases: A jury request must be submitted and the fee paid thirty (30) days before the initial schedule hearing.

4. The parties may ask for a continuance in writing at least ten (10) day before the non-jury trial date and thirty (30) days before the jury trial date. If the court grants a continuance, the case will be automatically set for pre-trial seven days following the original scheduled hearing date. The court will also set a trial date not to exceed thirty (30) days from the pre-trial hearing.

5. Submission of Judgments, Orders, Decrees, and Bureau of Vital Statistic Forms:

(a) As a matter of policy, petitioner's attorney shall prepare and submit the Bureau of Vital Statistics form and the divorce decree, unless otherwise agreed to by the parties.

(b) The support-receiving parties' attorney shall be responsible for filing the order of assignment of wages. This order shall conform so to the decree of divorce and must be properly completed, particularly as it relates to the employer and the amount to be paid weekly, biweekly, and monthly. Further, no order assigning wages is complete unless accompanied by notice to the employer and request for issuance of the order withholding.

(c) Before the date of hearing, all cases must have on file the Bureau of Vital Statistics form, (except date of hearing which will be filled in on date of hearing) and the order of assignment of wages. (Leave blank spaces for monetary amounts). There will be no exceptions.

(d) Parties not complying may be subject to sanctions.

(e) The case shall be set for entry of judgment two weeks following the date of hearing at 9:00 a.m. unless it is submitted beforehand.

RULE 4.11. ANCILLARY PROCEEDINGS, TEMPORARY ORDERS, & EMERGENCY MATTERS:

The provisions of Rule 3.32 will apply. [Rule 3.32 is included below.]

See note on p. 1157.

A. There shall be established an emergency docket for the handling of matters requiring immediate hearing or conferences in cases filed in the district courts of Webb County and the Webb County Court At Law. The local administrative judge shall assign to each of the district judges of Webb County, on an equal time basis, the responsibility for presiding over the emergency docket;

B. The emergency docket shall include only those cases involving hearings on applications for temporary Restraining orders, issuance of writs of sequestration, garnishment and attachment, whether such matters shall be heard ex-parte or otherwise, entries of default judgment and/or other writs and processes;

C. The court coordinator of the presiding judge of the court that has been assigned the emergency docket by the local administrative judge shall be responsible for maintaining the emergency docket for the period of assignment. Any attorney who requests any matter be placed on the emergency docket shall be responsible for communicating with the court coordinator of the presiding judge in order that the matter may be placed on the emergency docket by the court coordinator;

D. Whenever a matter is placed on the emergency docket, the court coordinator for the presiding judge is responsible for immediately coordinating with the district judge who has been assigned to the emergency docket for that period of time in order to establish the date, time, and place for hearing and to then notify the attorney(s) as to the date, time, and place of hearing;

E. The district judge assigned to the emergency docket during that period of time that any matter is placed on the emergency docket shall have the discretion to determine that any such matter should not be entitled to emergency disposition and remove the matter from emergency docket upon immediate notice to the attorney who requested that it be placed on the emergency docket;

F. In the event a matter has been removed from the emergency docket by the district judge assigned to the emergency docket for that period of time, any of the district judges of Webb County may preside over that matter upon request after proper notice to the court coordinator of that presiding judge;

G. Before any attorney shall request a matter be placed on the emergency docket, said attorney must first request the matter be heard by the judge in whose court the case is pending; and the attorney on all matters and documents being assigned to the emergency docket shall certify that the matter being placed on the emergency docket was not heard or disposed of by the judge in whose court the case or matter is pending.

RULE 4.13. UNCONTESTED MATTERS:

All uncontested family law cases shall be heard within three (3) months from appearance date or within three (3) months from the expiration of the waiting period provided by the Family Code where such is required, whichever is later. Uncontested cases or those that have been settled are processed and disposed of pursuant to Local Rule 3.14. Any person not filing an answer is subject to default.

RULE 4.14. FINANCIAL INFORMATION STATEMENTS:

If child support is a contested issue, a monthly financial statement of income and expenses shall be filed with the court seven days before a scheduled hearing on temporary child support or the final divorce hearing.

RULE 4.17. INVENTORY & APPRAISEMENT:

Petitioner shall have thirty (30) days to file a sworn inventory, list of claims, and debts from the date of filing of the original petition. Respondent shall have thirty (30) days to file sworn inventory, list of claims, and debts from date of filing of the original answer.

See note on p. 1157.

ATTORNEY FEES IN FAMILY LAW PROCEEDINGS

	Type of Action	Authority	When Permitted
		DISSOLUTION OF MARRIAGE	
1	Division of property—equitable factor	Fam. Code §7.001; ***Carle***, 234 S.W.2d 1002, 1005 (Tex.1950).	The allocation of attorney fees is a factor to be considered by the court in making an equitable division of the community estate.
2	Suit for dissolution of marriage—generally	Fam. Code §6.708; ***Hirczy***, 838 S.W.2d 783, 786 (C.C. 1992, writ denied).	May be awarded as costs if the awarded party pleaded for them, the parties tried the issue by consent, or the losing party waived the issue.
3	Temporary orders before final order	Fam. Code §6.502(a)(4)	May be awarded for the preservation of property and for the protection of the parties as deemed necessary and equitable while the suit for dissolution of marriage is pending.
4	Temporary orders during appeal	Fam. Code §6.709(a)(2)	May be awarded for the preservation of property and for the protection of the parties during the appeal.
		ENFORCEMENT	
5	Administrative subpoena issued by Title IV-D agency	Fam. Code §231.303(c)	The administrative subpoena is used to obtain information about the whereabouts and income of a parent with a support obligation. Attorney fees may be awarded if the individual or organization did not, without good cause, comply with the subpoena.
6	Agreements incident to divorce—breach of contract	CPRC §38.001; ***Praeger***, 721 S.W.2d 597, 601 (F.W. 1986, writ ref'd n.r.e.).	Mandatory if the claimant is the prevailing party and recovers damages.
7	Child custody—generally	TRCP 308a	Except by order of the court, no fee shall be charged by or paid to the attorney representing the claimant. If fee shall be paid it will be adjudged against the party who violated the order.
8	Child custody—interference with possessory interest in temporary or final order	Fam. Code §42.006(a)(1), §42.009 (frivolous claim)	
9	Child custody—UCCJEA	Fam. Code §152.312	Shall be awarded against the prevailing party unless it would clearly be inappropriate.
10.	Child support—generally	TRCP 308a	Except by order of the court, no fee shall be charged by or paid to the attorney representing the claimant. If fee shall be paid it will be adjudged against the party who violated the order.
11	Child or spousal support—UIFSA	Fam. Code §§159.305, 159.313(b) & (c)	May be awarded to a prevailing obligee but not to a prevailing obligor, except as provided by other law. Payment of fees by obligor is mandatory if hearing was requested primarily for delay.
12	Child support—foreclosure of lien	Fam. Code §157.323(c)(1)	An authorized official may execute and satisfy the lien, costs, and attorney fees by selling the property subject to the lien.
13	Child support—wage withholding order against employer	Fam. Code §158.206(b)(3)	Employer is liable for not complying with the wage withholding order. Includes orders directing that health insurance be provided for a child.

	Type of Action	Authority	When Permitted
14	Child support order	Fam. Code §157.167	Shall be awarded to the movant if the court finds that the respondent has not paid child support unless the respondent shows good cause and the court states its reasons supporting the finding.
15	Division of property—property divided in decree	Fam. Code §9.014; ***Jenkins***, 991 S.W.2d 440, 450 (F.W. 1999, pet. denied).	Party not required to have prevailed to be awarded attorney fees; the fee award must be reasonable under the circumstances of the case. When awarding attorney fees to the nonprevailing party, the court must state on the record or in its judgment the good cause substantiating the award.
16	Premarital & postmarital agreements—breach of contract	CPRC §38.001; *see **Praeger***, 721 S.W.2d 597, 601 (F.W. 1986, writ ref'd n.r.e.).	Mandatory if the claimant is the prevailing party and recovers damages.
	MARITAL PROPERTY		
17	Agreements incident to divorce—enforcement	See 6, above.	
18	Division of property—enforcement	See 13, above.	
19	Division of property—equitable factor in dissolution	See 1, above.	
20	Division of property—not previously divided	Fam. Code §9.205	May be ordered paid directly to the attorney, who may enforce the order for fees in own name by any means available for the enforcement of a judgment for debt.
21	Management of marital property under unusual circumstances	Fam. Code §3.303(c)	The costs of suit for the petitioning spouse shall include a reasonable fee for the attorney appointed to represent a respondent who is reported to be a prisoner of war or missing on public service.
22	Premarital & postmarital agreements—enforcement	See 14, above.	
23	Sale of homestead under unusual circumstances	Fam. Code §5.104(c)	The costs of suit for the petitioning spouse shall include a reasonable fee for the attorney appointed to represent a respondent who is reported to be a prisoner of war or missing on public service.
	POST-DECREE PROCEEDINGS		
24	Division of property—not previously divided	See 18, above.	
	PROTECTIVE ORDERS		
25	Application for protective order	Fam. Code §81.005	May be awarded for the services of a private or prosecuting attorney or an attorney employed by the Department of Protective and Regulatory Services against the party found to have committed family violence or the party against whom an agreed protective order is rendered.
	SAPCR		
26	Attorney ad litem appointed to represent a child or adult	Fam. Code §107.015	Entitled to reasonable fees and expenses.
27	False report of child abuse or neglect	Fam. Code §105.006(h)	Any party that knowingly makes a false allegation of child abuse in a SAPCR may be ordered to pay attorney fees.

	TYPE OF ACTION	AUTHORITY	WHEN PERMITTED
28	SAPCR—generally	Fam. Code §106.002; ***Nordstrom***, 965 S.W.2d 575, 583-84 (Hou. [1st Dist.] 1997, pet. denied); ***Roosth***, 889 S.W.2d 445, 455 (Hou. [14th Dist.] 1994, writ denied).	May be awarded as costs. Can be awarded to an unsuccessful party as necessaries or when in the best interest of the child.
29	Suit for modification of an order providing for the conservatorship, support, or possession of and access to a child	Fam. Code §156.005	Shall be taxed against applicant if suit held to be frivolous or harassing.
30	Temporary orders before final order	Fam. Code §105.001(a)(5)	May be awarded for the safety and welfare of the child.
31	Temporary orders during appeal	Fam. Code §109.001(a)(5)	May be awarded for the safety and welfare of the child.
32	Title IV-D suit	Fam. Code §231.211	May be awarded against the nonprevailing party except the Title IV-D agency or a private attorney or political subdivision that has entered into a contract to provide Title IV-D services.
	TEMPORARY ORDERS		
33	SAPCR—before final order	See 28, above.	
34	SAPCR—during appeal	See 29, above.	
35	Suit for dissolution—before final order	See 3, above.	
36	Suit for dissolution—during appeal	See 4, above.	
	MISCELLANEOUS PROVISIONS		
37	Attorney ad litem appointed to represent a child or adult	See 24, above.	
38	Civil suit—generally	TRCP 131; ***Casteel-Diebolt***, 912 S.W.2d 302, 305 (Hou. [14th Dist.] 1995, no writ); ***Gross***, 808 S.W.2d 215, 221 (Hou. [14th Dist.] 1991, no writ).	Family Code provisions on attorney fees and costs were intended to supplant the Texas Rules of Civil Procedure, including Rule 131, which requires that the successful party recover its costs.
39	Discrimination—adoption placement	Fam. Code §162.308(e)	Applicant entitled to fees if granted injunction or other appropriate relief.
40	Discrimination—foster care decision	Fam. Code §264.108(g)	Applicant entitled to fees if granted injunction or other appropriate relief.
41	Discrimination—wage withholding order	Fam. Code §§8.208(c), 158.209(c)	Applies both to termination and to refusal to hire. Action may be brought only by the employee.
42	Frivolous claim against party reporting child abuse or neglect	Fam. Code §261.108(b)	Shall be awarded to defendant when (1) the claim is found to be frivolous, unreasonable, or without foundation, and (2) the claim is dismissed or judgment is rendered for defendant.
43	Interference with possessory interest in child	Fam. Code §42.006	Attorney fees may be included as damages.
44	Property damage caused by the willful and malicious conduct of a child	Fam. Code §§41.001, 41.002, 41.0025 (inn or hotel)	Recoverable against a parent or other person who had a duty to control a child between the ages of 10 and 18.

Editor's Note: Unless otherwise provided, this chart does not include actions that have no limitations period.

	CAUSE OF ACTION	AUTHORITY	LIMITATIONS PERIOD	MISCELLANEOUS
	DISSOLUTION OF MARRIAGE			
1	Annulment—marriage occurring less than 72 hours after issuance of license	Fam. Code §6.110(b)	30 days from date of marriage	
2	Annulment—underage marriage by parent, guardian, or next friend	Fam. Code §6.101(c)-(d), §6.102(c), §6.103	90 days from date of marriage or 90 days after person's 14th birthday, whichever is later	Discovery rule contained in statute. If person is older than 14 but younger than 18 at time of marriage, suit may be brought by next friend within 90 days of the marriage; if person is younger than 14 at time of marriage, suit may be brought by next friend, parent or guardian within 90 days of date party knew or should have known about marriage or within 90 days of person's 14th birthday, whichever is later; suit may not be brought after person's 18th birthday
3	Informal marriage	Fam. Code §2.401(b)	No presumption that parties agreed to be married after 2 years from date on which parties separated or ceased living together	Proof may still be attempted after 2 years, but without the presumption
	ENFORCEMENT			
4	Child possession & access—contempt	Fam. Code §157.004	6 months after child becomes adult or 6 months after right of possession & access terminates	
5	Child support arrearages—judgment for	Fam. Code §157.005; *see* §159.604 (UIFSA)	Until the date all support is paid	
6	Child support—contempt	Fam. Code §157.005(a)	6 months after child becomes an adult or 6 months after obligation terminates	
7	Division of property—future property divided in decree	Fam. Code §9.003(b)	2 years from date the right to property matures or accrues or the decree becomes final, whichever is later	
8	Division of property—property divided in decree	Fam. Code §9.003(a)	2 years from date decree was signed or becomes final after appeal	
9	Premarital agreements	CPRC §16.004	4 years	Tolled during marriage. Fam. Code §4.008
	POST-DECREE DIVISION			
10	Division of property—not previously divided	Fam. Code §9.202(a)	2 years from date former spouse communicates an unequivocal repudiation of other spouse's ownership interest	Tolled for period a court of this state does not have jurisdiction over the spouses or the property. Fam. Code §9.202(b). Former §3.90(c) (now §9.202) does not bar otherwise valid partition under the Property Code. ***Carter***, 853 S.W.2d 667, 671 (Hou. [14th] 1993, no writ)

	CAUSE OF ACTION	AUTHORITY	LIMITATIONS PERIOD	MISCELLANEOUS
SUITS AFFECTING THE PARENT-CHILD RELATIONSHIP				
11	Generally—SAPCR filed by a person, other than a foster parent, who had actual care, control, and possession of child for 6 months	Fam. Code §102.003(a)(9)	Within 90 days after actual care, control, and possession has ended	
12	Generally—SAPCR filed by a person with whom the child and the child's guardian, managing conservator, or parent have resided for 6 months	Fam. Code §102.003(a)(11)	Within 90 days after residence has ended if child's guardian, managing conservator, or parent has died	
13	Generally—SAPCR filed by a foster parent of a child who was placed in foster parent's home for 12 months	Fam. Code §102.003(a)(12)	Within 90 days after placement of child has ended	
14	Adoption—attacking validity	Fam. Code §162.012	6 months after date order signed	
15	Parentage—adjudicating when child has presumed father	Fam. Code §§160.606-160.607	4 years from date of child's birth. A proceeding to disprove paternity may be filed at any time if presumed father and mother were not together at probable time of conception and presumed father never openly treated child as his own	
16	Parentage—adjudicating when child has no acknowledged, adjudicated, or presumed father	Fam. Code §160.606	Can be filed at any time	
17	Parentage—adjudicating when child has acknowledged or adjudicated father	Fam. Code §160.609(b)	4 years from effective date of acknowledgment or adjudication	
18	Parentage—challenging acknowledgement or denial of paternity by signatory	Fam. Code §160.609(a)	4 years from date when acknowledgement or denial was filed with bureau of vital statistics	
19	Parentage—challenging paternity when birth of child is by means of assisted reproduction	Fam. Code §160.705	4 years from learning of child's birth	If husband did not provide sperm, then paternity may be challenged at any time
20	Parentage—contesting voluntary statement of paternity executed before Sept. 1, 1999	Fam. Code §160.316	Before Sept. 1, 2003	
21	Parentage—rescinding acknowledgement or denial of paternity by signatory	Fam. Code §160.307	Before earlier of 60th day after effective date of acknowledgement or denial or date of first hearing to adjudicate an issue relating to the child	
22	Termination—attacking validity	Fam. Code §161.211	6 months after date order signed	

	CAUSE OF ACTION	AUTHORITY	LIMITATIONS PERIOD	MISCELLANEOUS
TORTS				
23	Assault/battery *See O'Connor's COA*, ch. 3, p. 21	CPRC §16.003(a)	2 years (except sexual assaults)	
24	Breach of fiduciary duty *See O'Connor's COA*, ch. 10, §2.2, p. 181	CPRC §16.004(a)(5)	4 years	Discovery rule contained in statute. ***Slay***, 187 S.W.2d 377, 394 (Tex.1945) Cause accrues when claimant knew or should have known of facts that in the exercise of reasonable diligence would have led to the discovery of the wrongful act. ***Little***, 943 S.W.2d 414, 421 (Tex.1997)
25	Breach of promise to marry	CPRC §16.002(a)	1 year	
26	Conversion of personal property *See O'Connor's COA*, ch. 6, p. 111	CPRC §16.003(a)	2 years	Discovery rule applies where possession initially lawful. ***Varel Mfg.***, 990 S.W.2d 486, 498 (C.C. 1999, no pet.). Generally, cause accrues at the time of the unlawful taking. *See* ***Pierson***, 829 S.W.2d 311, 314 (Austin 1992, no writ). Where possession is initially lawful, cause accrues upon demand and refusal or when unequivocal acts of conversion occur. ***Nelson***, 921 S.W.2d 411, 415 (C.C. 1996, no writ)
27	Fraud—common law *See O'Connor's COA*, ch. 11-A, p. 189	CPRC §16.004(A)(4)	4 years	
28	Illegal wiretapping	CPRC §16.003(a)	2 years	Suit is categorized as an invasion of privacy action. *See* ***Collins***, 904 S.W.2d 792, 804 (Hou. [1st] 1995), *denied* 923 S.W.2d 569 (Tex.1996)
29	Intentional infliction of emotional distress *See O'Connor's COA*, ch. 14, p. 349	CPRC §16.003(a)	2 years	Discovery rule does not apply. ***Patrick***, 904 S.W.2d 941, 944 (Austin 1995, no pet.) If the act causing the injury is itself a completed wrong, the cause accrues at the time the act is committed even where little or no damage occurs at that time. ***Sutton***, 915 S.W.2d 152, 157 (Ft. Worth 1996, denied)
30	Invasion of privacy *See O'Connor's COA*, ch. 11, p. 357	CPRC §16.003(a)	2 years	Discovery rule does not apply. ***Matlock***, 948 S.W.2d 308, 311 (S.A. 1997, no pet.)
31	Sexual abuse, negligent	CPRC §16.003(a)	2 years	Repressed memory of victim does not by itself toll limitations until discovery; objective verifiability also required. ***S.V.***, 933 S.W.2d 1, 23-24 (Tex.1996).
32	Sexual assault or aggravated sexual assault if conduct violates Penal Code §22.011 or §22.021	CPRC §16.0045(a)	5 years	If victim dies, cause accrues on death. CPRC §16.0045(b). Statute tolled by "John Doe" pleading. CPRC §16.0045(c)

STATUTES OF LIMITATIONS

DERIVATION TABLE
CURRENT TO FORMER

CURRENT	INTERIM (1999 - 1995)	PRE-1995
§1.001	Added ('97)	
§1.002	Added ('97)	
§1.003	Added ('97)	
§1.101		§2.01
§1.102		§2.01
§1.103		§4.01
§1.104		§4.03
§1.105		§4.04
§1.106		§4.05
§1.107		§4.06
§1.108	Added ('97). *See* BCC §26.01	
§2.001		§1.01
§2.002		§1.02
§2.003		§1.02(2)(B)
§2.004		§1.03
§2.005		§1.04
§2.006		§1.05(a), (b)
§2.007		§1.05(c)
§2.008		§1.06
§2.009		§1.07
§2.010		§1.07(e)
§2.011		§1.08
§2.012		§1.09
§2.013	Added ('99)	
§2.014	Added ('99)	
§2.101		§1.51
§2.102		§1.52
§2.103		§1.53
§2.201		§1.81(a)
§2.202		§1.83(a), (b)
§2.203		§1.82(a), (b)
§2.204		§1.82(c), (d)
§2.205		§1.83(c), (d)
§2.206		§1.84
§2.207		§1.81
§2.208		§1.85
§2.209		§1.86
§2.301		§2.02
§2.302		§2.03
§2.401		§1.91
§2.402		§1.92
§2.403		§1.93
§2.404		§1.94
§2.405		§1.95
§2.501		§4.02
§3.001		§5.01(a)
§3.002		§5.01(b)
§3.003		§5.02
§3.004		§5.03
§3.005		§5.04
(A) §3.006	Added ('99)	
§3.101		§5.21
§3.102		§5.22
(A) §3.103		§5.23
§3.104		§5.24
§3.201		§4.031
§3.202		§5.61
§3.203		§5.62
(A) §3.301		§5.25(a), (b)
§3.302		§5.26(a), (b)
§3.303		§5.25(c), §5.26(c)
§3.304		§5.25(d), §5.26(d)
§3.305		§5.25(e)
§3.306		§5.25(f), §5.26(e)
(A) §3.307		§5.25(g), §5.26(f)
§3.308		§5.25(h), §5.26(g)
§3.309		§5.27
(E) §3.401		
(E) §3.402		

Unless otherwise noted, all references are to the Family Code.
BCC = Texas Business Commerce Code
GC = Texas Government Code
HRC = Texas Human Resources Code
LC = Texas Labor Code

DERIVATION TABLE
CURRENT TO FORMER

	CURRENT	INTERIM (1999 - 1995)	PRE-1995
E	§3.403		
A	§3.404	§3.403 ('99)	
A	§3.405	§3.404 ('99)	
A	§3.406	Added ('99)	
E	§3.407		
E	§3.408		
E	§3.409		
E	§3.410		
	§4.001		§5.41
	§4.002		§5.42
	§4.003		§5.43
	§4.004		§5.44
	§4.005		§5.45
	§4.006		§5.46
	§4.007		§5.47
	§4.008		§5.48
	§4.009		§5.49
	§4.010		§5.50
	§4.101		§5.51
	§4.102		§5.52
	§4.103		§5.53
	§4.104		§5.54
	§4.105		§5.55
	§4.106		§5.56
	§§4.201-.206	Added ('99)	
	§5.001		§5.81
A	§5.002		§5.82
E	§5.003	§5.107 ('97)	§5.84
A	§5.101		§5.83(a), §5.831(a)
A	§5.102		§5.85(a), §5.87(a)
A	§5.103		§5.83(b), §5.831(b), §5.85(b), §5.87(b)
	§5.104		§5.83(b), §5.831(b), §5.85(b), §5.87(b)
	§5.105		§5.83(b), §5.831(b), §5.85(b), §5.87(b)
	§5.106		§5.83(c), §5.831(c), §5.85(c), §5.87(c)
	§5.108		§5.86

CURRENT	INTERIM (1999 - 1995)	PRE-1995
§6.001		§3.01
§6.002		§3.02
§6.003		§3.03
§6.004		§3.04
§6.005		§3.05
§6.006		§3.06
§6.007		§3.07
§6.008		§3.08
§6.101		§2.41(a)
§6.102		§2.41(b)
§6.103		§2.41(a), (b)
§6.104		§2.41(c)
§6.105		§2.42
§6.106		§2.43
§6.107		§2.44
§6.108		§2.45
§6.109		§2.46
§6.110		§2.48
§6.111		§2.47
§6.201		§2.21
§6.202		§2.22
§6.203		§2.23
§6.301		§3.21
§6.302		§3.24
§6.303		§3.22
§6.304		§3.23
§6.305		§3.26
§6.306		§3.25
§6.307		§2.24, §3.25
§6.308	Added ('97). *See* §102.012	
§6.401		§3.51
§6.402		§3.52
§6.403		§3.53
§6.4035	Added ('97)	
§6.404	§3.522[A] ('95)	
§6.405	§3.522[B] ('95)	
§6.406		§3.55(a), (b)

	CURRENT	INTERIM (1999 - 1995)	PRE-1995
	§6.407		§3.55(b), (c), (d)
	§6.408	Added ('97). *See* §102.009	
	§6.409		§3.521
	§6.501		§3.58(a), (b)
A	§6.502		§3.58(c), §3.59
	§6.503		§3.58(d), (e)
	§6.504		§3.581
	§6.505		§3.54(a)-(c)
	§6.506		§3.58(f)
	§6.507		§3.58(g)
	§6.601	Added ('97). *See* §153.0071(a), (b)	
	§6.602	Added ('97). *See* §153.0071(c)-(f)	
E	§6.603		
	§6.701		§3.53
	§6.702		§3.60
	§6.703		§3.61
	§6.704		§3.62
	§6.705		§3.54(b), (d)
	§6.706		§3.64
	§6.707		§3.57
	§6.708		§3.54(e), §3.65
	§6.709		§3.58(h), (i)
	§6.710	Added ('97)	
E	§6.711		
	§6.801		§3.66(a), (b)
	§6.802		§3.66(c)
	§7.001		§3.63(a)
A	§7.002		§3.63(b)
	§7.003		§3.633(a)
	§7.004		§3.632(a)
	§7.005		§3.632(d), (e)
	§7.006		§3.631
E	§7.007		
A	§8.001	§3.9601	
A	§8.051	§3.9602 ('95), §8.002(a) ('97)	
A	§8.052	§3.9603 ('95), §8.003 ('97)	
A	§8.053	§3.9604 ('95), §8.004 ('97)	
A	§8.054	§3.9605 ('95), §8.005 ('97)	
A	§8.055	§3.9606 ('95), §8.006 ('97)	
A	§8.056	§3.9607 ('95), §8.007 ('97)	
A	§8.057	§3.9608 ('95), §8.008 ('97)	
E	§8.058		
A	§8.059	§3.9609 ('95), §8.009 ('97)	
A	§8.060	§3.9610 ('95), §8.010 ('97)	
A	§8.061	§3.9611 ('95), §8.011 ('97)	
E	§§8.101-.305		
	§9.001		§3.70(a), (b)
	§9.002		§3.70(c)
	§9.003		§3.70(c)
	§9.004		§3.70(d)
	§9.005		§3.70(e)
	§9.006		§3.71(a)
	§9.007		§3.71
	§9.008		§3.72
	§9.009		§3.73
	§9.010		§3.74
	§9.011		§3.75
	§9.012		§3.76
	§9.013		§3.77
	§9.014		§3.77
	§9.101	§3.711(a), (b) ('95)	
	§9.102	§3.711(d) ('95)	
	§9.103	§3.711(a) ('95)	
	§9.104	§3.711(c) ('95)	
	§9.105	§3.711(e) ('95)	
	§9.201		§3.90(a), (b)

Derivation Table
Current to Former

CURRENT	INTERIM (1999 - 1995)	PRE-1995
§9.202		§3.90(c)
§9.203		§3.91
§9.204		§3.92
§9.205		§3.93
§9.301		§3.632(b), (c)
§9.302		§3.633(b)-(e)
§31.001		§31.01(a), (c)
§31.002		§31.02(a), (c)
§31.003		§31.03(a)
§31.004		§31.04
§31.005		§31.06
Ⓐ §31.006		§31.07
§31.007		§31.08
§32.001		§35.01
§32.002		§35.02
Ⓐ §32.003		§35.03(a)-(f)
§32.004		§35.03(g)
§32.005		§35.04
§32.101		§35.011
§32.102	§32.103 ('95)	§35.013
§32.103	§32.104 ('95)	§35.014
§32.201		§35.05
Chapter 33	Added ('99)	
Ⓐ §41.001		§33.01
§41.002		§33.02
§41.0025	Added ('97)	
§41.003		§33.03
§42.001		§36.01
§42.002		§36.02(a), (b)
§42.003		§36.02(c), (d)
§42.005		§36.05
§42.006		§36.03
§42.007		§36.04
§42.008		§36.06
§42.009		§36.08
§45.001		§32.01, §32.02(a)
§45.002		§32.02
§45.003		§32.03
§45.004		§32.04
§45.005		§32.05
§45.101		§32.21(a)
§45.102		§32.21(a), (b)
§45.103		§32.22
§45.104		§32.23
§45.105	Added ('97)	
§45.106	Added ('97)	
§71.001		§71.01(a)
§71.002		§71.01(b)(1)
Ⓔ §71.0021		
Ⓐ §71.003		§71.01(b)(3)
Ⓐ §71.004		§71.01(b)(2)
§71.005		§71.01(b)(5)
§71.006		§71.01(b)(4), (6)
§71.007	Added ('97)	
§81.001		§71.10(a), (b)
§81.002	§71.041(a) ('95)	
§81.003	§71.041(b) ('95)	
§81.004	§71.041(c) ('95)	
§81.005	§71.041(d) ('95)	
§81.006	§71.041(d) ('95)	
§81.007		§71.04(c)
§81.0075	Added ('97)	
§81.008		§71.19
§82.001		§71.02, §71.04(a)
Ⓐ §82.002		§71.04(b)
§82.003		§71.03
Ⓐ §82.004		§71.05(a)
§82.005		§71.06
§82.006		§71.05(c)
§82.007		§71.05(d)
§82.008		§71.05(f), (g)
§82.0085	Added ('99)	
§82.009		§71.05(e)
§82.021		§71.08
§82.022	§71.121(a) ('95)	§71.121(b)
§82.041		§71.07(d), (e)

DERIVATION TABLE

Derivation Table
Current to Former

	CURRENT	INTERIM (1999 - 1995)	PRE-1995
	§82.042		§71.07(b), (c)
	§82.043	§71.06(e) ('95)	§71.07(a), (f)-(h)
A	§83.001		§71.15(a)
	§83.002		§71.15(b), (c)
	§83.003		§71.15(d)
A	§83.004		§71.15(e)
	§83.005		§71.15(f)
	§83.006		§71.15(g), (h)
	§83.007		§71.15(j)
	§84.001		§71.09(a), §71.121(c)
	§84.002		§71.09(d)
	§84.003		§71.09(c)
	§84.004		§71.09(b)
	§84.005	Added ('99)	
A	§85.001	§71.121(d) ('95)	§71.10(a), (b)
	§85.002		§71.10(c)
	§85.003	§71.121 (e), (f) ('95)	§71.121(a)
	§85.004	§71.06(f) ('95)	
	§85.005	§71.10(d) ('95)	§71.12(a), (b), (d), (e)
	§85.006		§71.09(e)
A	§85.007		§71.111
	§85.009	§71.06(c) ('95)	
	§85.021		§71.11(a)(1)-(4), (6)
A	§85.022		§71.11(a)(5), (7), (b), (c)
	§85.023		§71.11(d)
	§85.024		§71.11(i)
	§85.025		§71.13
A	§85.026		§71.16
	§85.041	§71.17(a)-(d) ('95)	
A	§85.042	§71.17(e)-(g) ('95)	
	§§85.061-.065	Added ('97)	
	§86.001		§71.18(a), (b)
E	§86.0011		
	§86.002	§71.18(c)[A] ('95)	

	CURRENT	INTERIM (1999 - 1995)	PRE-1995
	§86.003	§71.18(c)[B] ('95)	
	§86.004	§71.18(d) ('95)	
A	§86.005	Added ('97)	
	§87.001		§71.14(a)
	§87.002		§71.14(b)
	§87.003	§71.14(c) ('95)	
	§87.004	Added ('97)	
E	§88.001		
E	§88.002		
E	§88.003		
E	§88.004		
E	§88.005		
E	§88.006		
E	§88.007		
E	§88.008		
	§91.001	§73.01 ('95)	
	§91.002	§73.02 ('95)	
	§91.003	§73.03 ('95)	
	§91.004	§73.05 ('95)	
	§92.001	§73.04 ('95)	
	§101.001		§11.01
E	§101.0010		
	§101.0011	Added ('97)	
E	§101.0015		
	§101.002		§11.01(7)
	§101.0021	Added ('99)	
	§101.003		§11.01(1)
	§101.004		§14.80(3)
	§101.005		§14.80(7)
	§101.006		§14.80(4)
	§101.007		§11.15(c)
	§101.008		§11.01(2)
	§101.009		§17.001
	§101.010		§14.30(a)(2)
	§101.011		§14.30(a)(1)
	§101.012		§14.30(a)(3)
	§101.0125	Added ('99)	

DERIVATION TABLE
CURRENT TO FORMER

	CURRENT	INTERIM (1999 - 1995)	PRE-1995
	§101.013	Added ('95)	
	§101.014		§11.01(8)
Ⓐ	§101.015		§14.061(d)
	§101.016		§14.021(b)
	§101.0161	Added ('97)	
	§101.017		§11.01(7); HRC §42.002(12)
	§101.018		§11.01(11)
	§101.019		§11.01(6)
	§101.020		§14.80(5)
	§101.0201	Added ('97)	
	§101.021		§11.01(10)
	§101.022		§11.01(9)
	§101.023	Added ('95)	
Ⓐ	§101.024		§11.01(3)
Ⓐ	§101.025		§11.01(4)
	§101.026	Added ('95)	
	§101.027		§15.051(a)(1)
	§101.028		§14.033(a)(1)
	§101.029		§14.033(a)(2)
	§101.030		§14.80(6), §21.01(19)
	§101.0301	Added ('97)	
	§101.0302	Added ('99)	
	§101.031	Added ('95)	
	§101.032		§11.01(5)
	§101.033		§14.80(2); HRC §76.001
	§101.034		§14.80(2)
	§101.035		§21.01(22)
	§102.001		§11.02
	§102.002		§11.07(a)
Ⓐ	§102.003		§11.03(a)
	§102.004		§11.03(b), (c)
	§102.005		§11.03(d)
Ⓐ	§102.006		§11.03(g), (h)
	§102.007		§11.03(i)
Ⓐ	§102.008		§11.08(a), (b)
	§102.0085	Added ('95)	

	CURRENT	INTERIM (1999 - 1995)	PRE-1995
Ⓐ	§102.009		§11.09(a)-(c), (f)
	§102.010		§11.09(d), (e)
	§102.011		§11.051
	§102.012	Added ('95)	
Ⓐ	§102.013		§11.07(c)
	§103.001		§11.04
	§103.002		§11.06(a), (c)
	§103.003		§11.061
	§104.001		§11.14(e)
	§104.002		§11.21(a), (b)
	§104.003		§11.21(d)
	§104.004		§11.21(c)
	§104.005		§11.21(e)
	§104.006	Added ('97)	
	§105.001		§11.11(a)-(d), (g), (h), §14.033(1), §14.055(e)
Ⓐ	§105.002		§11.13
	§105.003		§11.14(a), (b), (d), (f), (g)
	§105.004		§11.14(i)
	§105.005		§11.15(a)
Ⓐ	§105.006		§11.155
	§105.007		§14.045(a), (b)
	§105.008	Added ('97)	
	§105.009	Added ('99)	
	§106.001		§11.18(a)
	§106.002		§11.18(a), §11.22(j)
	§107.001		§11.10(a), (b)(1)
	§107.002	Added ('95)	
	§107.003	Added ('97)	
	§107.006	Added ('95)	
	§107.011		§11.10(b)(2), (c)
	§107.012		§11.10(d)
Ⓐ	§107.013		§11.10(d)
	§107.0135	§107.002(e) ('95)	
	§107.014	Added ('95)	
	§107.015		§11.10(a), (e)
	§107.016	Added ('95)	

DERIVATION TABLE
CURRENT TO FORMER

	CURRENT	INTERIM (1999 - 1995)	PRE-1995
	§107.031		§11.101
A	§107.051		§11.12(a), (b)
E	§107.0511		
A	§107.052		§11.12(b)
	§107.053		§11.12(b)
	§107.054		§11.12(c)
	§107.055		§11.12(c), §11.14(c)
	§107.056		§11.18(c)
	§108.001		§11.17(a), (d)
	§108.002		§11.17(b)
	§108.003		§11.17(b); HRC §49.003(d), §49.005(d)
	§108.004		§11.17(b)
	§108.005		§11.17(b)
	§108.006		§11.17(c), §11.171
	§108.007		§11.17(e)
	§108.008		§13.43(a)-(c)
A	§108.009		§13.43(e), (f)
	§108.110	Added ('99)	
A	§109.001		§11.11(e)-(g)
A	§109.002		§11.19
A	§109.003		§11.191
	§110.001	Added ('95)	
	§110.002		§14.13
	§110.003		§11.18(b)
	§110.004		§14.43(i), §14.45(h)
	§110.005		§11.06(*l*)
	§110.006	Added ('97)	
	§111.001		§14.03(j), §14.05(h), (i)
	§111.002		§14.032(e), (f), §14.052(c), (d)
	§111.003		§14.033(p), §14.058
A	§151.001	§151.003 ('95)	§4.02, §12.04
A	§151.002	§151.004 ('95)	§12.05
A	§151.003	§151.005 ('99)	
	§152.001	§152.001(a)(9), (b) ('95)	§11.51
	§152.002	Added ('99)	

	CURRENT	INTERIM (1999 - 1995)	PRE-1995
	§152.101	§152.025 ('95)	§11.75
	§152.102	§152.002 ('95)	§11.52
	§152.103	Added ('99)	
	§152.104	Added ('99)	
	§152.105	§152.023 ('95)	§11.73
	§152.106	§152.012 ('95)	§11.62
	§152.107	§152.024 ('95)	§11.74
	§152.108	§152.005 ('95)	§11.55
	§152.109	Added ('99)	
A	§152.110	Added ('99)	
	§152.111	§152.018 ('95)	§11.68
	§152.112	§152.019-.021 ('95)	§11.69-.71
	§152.201	§152.003 ('95)	§11.53
	§152.202	§152.003(d) ('95)	§11.53
	§152.203	§152.003(d) ('95)	§11.64
	§152.204	§152.003(e) ('95)	
	§152.205	§152.004, §152.010 ('95)	§11.54, §11.60
	§152.206	§152.006 ('95)	§11.56
	§152.207	§152.007 ('95)	§11.57
	§152.208	§152.008 ('95)	§11.58
	§152.209	§152.009 ('95)	§11.59
	§152.210	§152.011 ('95)	§11.61
	§152.301	Added ('99)	
	§152.302	Added ('99)	
	§152.303	Added ('99)	
	§152.304	Added ('99)	
	§152.305	§152.014, §152.016 ('95)	§11.66
	§152.306	§152.015 ('95)	§11.65
	§152.307	§152.006 ('95)	§11.56
	§152.308	Added ('99)	
	§152.309	Added ('99)	
	§152.310	Added ('99)	
	§152.311	Added ('99)	
	§152.312	Added ('99)	
	§152.313	§152.013 ('95)	§11.63
	§152.314	Added ('99)	

CURRENT	INTERIM (1999 - 1995)	PRE-1995
§152.315	Added ('99)	
§152.316	Added ('99)	
§152.317	Added ('99)	
§153.001		§14.021(a)
§153.002		§14.07(a)
§153.003		§14.01(c)(1), §14.032(d)
Ⓐ §153.004		§14.01(c)(2), §14.021(h), §14.03(d), (e)(3)
§153.005		§14.01(a)
§153.006		§14.03(a), (c)
§153.007		§14.06
§153.0071	Added ('95)	
Ⓔ §153.0072		
Ⓐ §153.008		§14.07(a)
Ⓐ §153.009		§14.07(c)
§153.010		§14.03(h)
§153.011		§14.03(i)
§153.012		§14.04(c)
§153.013		§34.031(b)
Ⓔ §153.014		
§153.071		§14.02(a)
§153.072		§14.02(b)
§153.073		§14.02(a), (b)(2)
§153.074		§14.02(b)(1)
§153.075		§14.03(d)
§153.076		§14.02(a)
§153.131		§14.01(b)(1)
§153.132		§14.02(b)(3)
§153.133		§14.021(c), (d)
§153.134		§14.021(e), (f)
§153.135		§14.021(b)
§153.136		§14.021(b)
§153.137		§14.034
§153.138		§14.021(g)
§153.191		§14.03(d)
§153.192		§14.03(b), §14.04
§153.193		§14.03(d)

CURRENT	INTERIM (1999 - 1995)	PRE-1995
§153.251		§14.032(a)
§153.252		§14.033(k)
§153.253		§14.033(k), (m)
§153.254		§14.032(b)
§153.255		§14.033(n)
§153.256		§14.032(c)
§153.257		§14.033(h)
§153.258		§14.033(k)
§153.311		§14.033(b)
§153.312		§14.033(c), (e)(4)-(7)
§153.313		§14.033(f)
§153.314		§14.033(e)(1)-(3), (8)-(10), (f)(2)
§153.315		§14.033(d)
§153.316		§14.033(g)
§153.317		§14.033(i)
§153.371		§14.02(c)
§153.372		§14.021(j)
§153.3721	Added ('99)	
§153.373		§14.01(b)(2)
§153.374		§14.01(d)
§153.375		§14.01(e)
§153.376		§14.04(a), (b)
§153.377		§14.04(c)
§153.431		§14.07(b)
§153.432		§14.03(e), (f)(1), (3)
§153.433		§14.03(e)
§153.434		§14.03(g)
§154.001		§14.05(a), (b), (d)
§154.002		§14.05(a)
§154.003		§14.05(a)
§154.004		§14.0503
§154.005		§14.05(c)
§154.006		§14.05(d)
§154.007		§14.05(e)
Ⓐ §154.008		§14.061(a)
Ⓐ §154.009		§14.062
§154.010		§14.05(g), §14.053(i)

	CURRENT	INTERIM (1999 - 1995)	PRE-1995
	§154.011	Added ('95)	
A	§154.012	Added ('99)	
E	§154.013[A*]		
E	§154.013[B*]		
	§154.061		§14.053(a), (h)
	§154.062		§14.053(b)
	§154.063		§14.053(g)
A	§154.064		§14.053(d)
	§154.065		§14.053(c)
	§154.066		§14.053(f)
	§154.067		§14.053(e)
	§154.068		§14.053(k)
	§154.069		§14.056(c)
	§154.070		§14.055(i)
	§154.121		§14.052(a)
	§154.122		§14.05(j), §14.055(a)
	§154.123		§14.052(b), §14.054
	§154.124		§14.053(j), §14.06
	§154.125		§14.055(a), (b)
	§154.126		§14.055(c)
	§154.127		§14.055(d)
	§154.128		§14.055(f)-(h)
	§154.129		§14.055(j)
A	§154.130		§14.057
A	§154.131		§14.053(l)
	§154.132	Added ('99)	
E	§154.133		
A	§154.181		§14.061
A	§154.182		§14.061(a), (b)
	§154.183		§14.053(d), §14.061(c)
	§154.184		§14.061(r)
A	§154.185		§14.061(e), (f)
	§154.186		§14.061(g)
	§154.187		§14.061(h)-(k), (p)
A	§154.188		§14.061(l)
	§154.189		§14.061(m)
	§154.190		§14.061(m)
	§154.191		§14.061(n), (o)

	CURRENT	INTERIM (1999 - 1995)	PRE-1995
	§154.192		§14.061(q)
	§154.193	Added ('97)	
	§154.241		§14.0501
	§154.242		§14.0502
	§154.243		§14.0504
	§154.301		§14.051(a)
	§154.302		§14.051(b)
	§154.303		§14.051(c)
	§154.304		§14.051(i)
	§154.305		§14.051(d)-(f)
	§154.306		§14.051(g)
	§154.307		§14.051(h)
	§154.308		§14.051(j), (k)
	§154.309	Added ('95)	
A	§155.001		§11.05(a), (b), (d), (e)
	§155.002		§11.05(a)
	§155.003		§11.05(g)
	§155.004		§11.05(b), (f), (g)
	§155.005		§11.05(h)
	§155.101		§11.071(a), (b)
	§155.102		§11.071(d)
	§155.103		§11.05(c)
	§155.104		§11.071(c)
	§155.201		§11.06(b), (c)
	§155.202		§11.06(b), (d)
	§155.203		§11.06(b)
	§155.204		§11.06(f)-(i)
A	§155.205		§11.05(h), §11.06(j)
	§155.206		§11.06(k)
A	§155.207		§11.06(j), (m)
	§155.301		§11.061
	§156.001		§11.05(g), §14.08(a)
	§156.002		§11.03(f), §14.08(a)
	§156.003		§11.09(c), §14.08(b)
	§156.004		§14.08(b)
	§156.005		§14.082
A	§156.006		§11.11(a), §14.08(g)
A	§156.101		§14.08(c)(1), (g)(3)

DERIVATION TABLE
CURRENT TO FORMER

	CURRENT	INTERIM (1999 - 1995)	PRE-1995
Ⓐ	§156.102		§14.08(d), (e)
Ⓔ	§156.103		
Ⓔ	§156.104		
Ⓔ	§156.1045		
	§156.401		§14.021(g), §14.08(c)(2)
	§156.402		§14.056(a), (b)
	§156.403		§14.056(b)
	§156.404		§14.056(c)
	§156.405		§14.056(c)
	§156.406		§14.056(d)
	§156.407		§14.08(h)
Ⓐ	§156.408	Added ('99)	
Ⓐ	§156.409	Added ('99)	
	§157.001		§14.30(b), §14.31, §14.40(a), §14.50(a)
	§157.002		§14.311(a)-(e), §14.312
	§157.003		§14.30(d), §14.313(a), §14.33(d)
	§157.004		§14.50(b)
	§157.005		§14.40(b), §14.41(b)
	§157.006		§14.40(h), §14.50(e)
	§157.007		§14.50(c)
	§157.008		§14.40(c), (g), §14.41(c)
	§157.061		§14.314(a), §14.32(d)
	§157.062		§14.314(a), (b), §14.315(b), (c)
	§157.063		§14.314(c)
	§157.064		§14.311(f)
	§157.065		§14.314(c)
	§157.066		§14.317(a)
	§157.101		§14.318(a), §14.32(e)
	§157.102		§14.317(d)
	§157.103		§14.317(e)
	§157.104		§14.318(b)
	§157.105		§14.318(c)

	CURRENT	INTERIM (1999 - 1995)	PRE-1995
	§157.106		§14.318(d)
	§157.107		§14.318(e)
	§157.108		§14.318(f)
	§157.109		§14.42(a), §14.51(a)
	§157.110		§14.42(b), (c), (f), §14.51(b), (c), (f)
	§157.111		§14.42(e), §14.51(e)
	§157.112		§14.42(d), §14.51(d)
	§157.113		§14.40(f), §14.32(e)
	§157.114		§14.317(a)
	§157.115		§14.317(a), (c)
	§157.161		§14.32(b)
	§157.162		§14.311(b), (c), §14.33(d)
	§157.163		§14.32(f)
	§157.164		§14.33(b)
	§157.165		§14.40(e)(1), §14.50(d)(1)
	§157.166		§14.33(a)
	§157.167		§14.33(c)
	§157.168	Added ('95)	
Ⓐ	§157.211		§14.40(e)(1), §14.50(d)(1)
	§157.212		§14.40(e)(2), §14.50(d)(2)
Ⓐ	§157.213		§14.40(e)(3), §14.50(d)(3)
Ⓐ	§157.214		§14.40(e)(4), §14.50(d)(4)
	§157.215		§14.40(e)(5), §14.50(d)(5)
	§157.216		§14.40(e)(6), §14.50(d)(6)
	§157.217		§14.40(e)(7), §14.50(d)(7)
	§157.261		§14.41(a)
Ⓐ	§157.262		§14.40(d), §14.41(a), (d)
	§157.263		§14.41(a), (e)
Ⓐ	§157.264		§14.41(a)
Ⓐ	§157.265		§14.34(a)

	CURRENT	INTERIM (1999 - 1995)	PRE-1995
	§157.266		§14.34(b)
	§157.267		§14.34(c)
A	§157.268		§14.34(c)
	§157.269	Added ('95)	
A	§157.311		§14.971(a), (b)
A	§157.312		§14.971(c), (d), §14.972(d)
A	§157.313		§14.973
A	§157.314		§14.974
E	§157.3145		
A	§157.315		§14.975
A	§157.316		§14.972(a)
A	§157.317		§14.972(b), (c)
A	§157.318		§14.972(e)
A	§157.319		§14.976(b)
	§157.320		§14.976(c), §14.977
A	§157.321		§14.980
A	§157.322		§14.978
A	§157.323		§14.979
A	§157.324		§14.981
A	§157.325		§14.982
A	§157.326		§14.983
E	§157.327		
E	§157.328		
E	§157.329		
E	§157.330		
E	§157.331		
	§157.371	Added ('95)	
	§157.372		§14.10(a), (b)
	§157.373		§14.10(c)
	§157.374		§14.10(d)
	§157.375		§14.10(e)
	§157.376		§14.10(f)
	§157.421		§11.22(a), (b), (g)
	§157.422		§11.22(h), (i)
	§157.423		§11.22(c)
	§157.424		§11.22(d)
	§157.425		§11.22(e)
	§157.426		§11.22(f)

	CURRENT	INTERIM (1999 - 1995)	PRE-1995
	§158.001		§14.05(e), §14.43(a)(1)
	§158.002		§14.43(a)(2)
	§158.003		§14.43(d)
	§158.004		§14.43(d)
	§158.005		§14.41(a), §14.43(d)
E	§158.0051		
	§158.006		§14.43(b)
	§158.007		§14.43(d)
	§158.008		§14.43(k)
	§158.009		§14.43(f)
	§158.010		§14.43(h)
	§158.011	Added ('95)	
	§158.101	Added ('95)	
	§158.102		§14.43(r)
A	§158.103		§14.43(e)
	§158.104		§14.43(g)
A	§158.105		§14.43(g), (h)
A	§158.106		§14.43(p), §14.44(f), §14.45(g)
	§158.201		§14.316
	§158.202		§14.43(h)
	§158.203		§14.43(h)
	§158.204		§14.43(i)
	§158.205		§14.43(j), §14.45(d)
A	§158.206		§14.43(l)
A	§158.207		§14.43(l)
	§158.208		§14.43(l)
	§158.209		§14.43(m)
	§158.210		§14.43(n)
	§158.211		§14.43(o)
	§158.212	Added ('99)	
	§158.301		§14.44(a)
	§158.302		§14.44(b)
	§158.303		§14.44(h)
	§158.304		§14.44(d)
	§158.306		§14.45(a). *See* §14.44(a)
	§158.307		§14.44(c)

Derivation Table

Current to Former

CURRENT	INTERIM (1999 - 1995)	PRE-1995
§158.308		§14.44(c)
§158.309		§14.44(d)
§158.310		§14.44(d)
§158.311		§14.43(a)(4), §14.44(a)
§158.312		§14.45(a)
§158.313		§14.45(a)
§158.314		§14.45(b)
§158.315		§14.45(c)
§158.316		§14.45(a)
§158.317		§14.44(e)
§158.319	Added ('95)	
§158.401		§14.43(q), §14.45(f)
§158.402	Added ('95)	
§158.403	Added ('95)	
§158.404		§14.43(q)
§158.405		§14.43(q)
(A) §§158.501-.507	Added ('97)	
§159.001	Added ('95)	
§159.101		§21.01
§159.102		§21.02
§159.103		§21.03
§159.201		§21.04
§159.202		§21.05
§159.203		§21.06
§159.204		§21.07
§159.205		§21.08
§159.206		§21.09
§159.207		§21.10
§159.208		§21.11
§159.209		§21.12
§159.301		§21.13
§159.302		§21.14
§159.303		§21.15
§159.304		§21.16
§159.305		§21.17
§159.306		§21.18
§159.307		§21.19
§159.308		§21.20
§159.309		§21.21
§159.310		§21.22
§159.311		§21.23
§159.312		§21.24
§159.313		§21.25
§159.314		§21.26
§159.315		§21.27
§159.316		§21.28
§159.317		§21.29
§159.318		§21.30
§159.319		§21.31
§159.401		§21.32
§159.501	§159.501(a) ('95)	§21.33(a)
§159.502	§159.501(a) ('95)	§21.33(a)
§159.503	Added ('97)	
§159.504	Added ('97)	
§159.505	Added ('97)	
§159.506	§159.501(b) ('95)	§21.33(b)
§159.507	§159.502 ('95)	§21.34
§159.601		§21.35
(A) §159.602		§21.36
§159.603		§21.37
§159.604		§21.38
§159.605		§21.39
§159.606		§21.40
§159.607		§21.41
§159.608		§21.42
§159.609		§21.43
§159.610		§21.44
(A) §159.611		§21.45
§159.612		§21.46
§159.613	Added ('97)	
§159.614	Added ('97)	
§159.701		§21.47
§159.801		§21.48
§159.802		§21.49
§159.901		§21.50
§159.902		§21.51
(E) Chapter 160		

Derivation Table
Current to Former

	Current	Interim (1999 - 1995)	Pre-1995
Ⓐ	§161.001		§11.15(b), §15.02(a)
Ⓐ	§161.002		§15.023
Ⓐ	§161.003		§15.024
	§161.004		§15.025
	§161.005		§15.01
	§161.006		§15.022
	§161.007	Added ('97)	
	§161.101		§11.08(e)
	§161.102		§15.021(a), (c)
	§161.103		§15.03
	§161.1035	Added ('97)	
	§161.104		§14.02(d)
	§161.105		§15.04
	§161.106		§15.041(a)-(d)
	§161.107		§15.051
	§161.108	Added ('97)	
	§161.109	Added ('97)	
Ⓐ	§161.2011	Added ('97)	
Ⓐ	§161.202		§11.14(h)
Ⓐ	§161.203		§15.06
Ⓐ	§161.204		§15.041(e)
Ⓐ	§161.205		§15.05(c)
	§161.206		§11.15(b), §15.05(a), §15.07
	§161.207		§15.05(b)
	§161.208		§15.051(b)
	§161.209		§11.16
	§161.210		§11.17(f)
	§161.211	Added ('97)	
	§162.001		§16.01, §16.02, §16.03(b)-(d)
	§162.002		§11.08(d), §16.03(a)
Ⓐ	§162.003		§16.031(a)
	§162.0045	Added ('97)	
	§162.005		§16.032(a), (f), (l)
	§162.006		§16.032(g), (i)-(k), (n)
	§162.007		§16.032(b)-(e)
	§162.008		§16.032(h), (m)
	§162.0085	Added ('95)	
	§162.009		§16.04
	§162.010		§16.05
	§162.011		§16.06
	§162.012		§16.12
	§162.013		§16.11
	§162.014		§16.07
	§162.015		§16.081
	§162.016		§16.08
	§162.017		§16.09(a), (d)-(f)
	§162.018		§16.032(f), (i), §16.09(b), (c)
	§162.019		§11.16
	§162.020		§16.10
	§162.021		§11.17(f)
	§162.022		§11.17(d)
	§162.025	Added ('95)	
	§162.101		HRC §45.022
	§162.102		HRC §45.021
	§162.103		HRC §45.023
	§162.104		HRC §45.024
	§162.105		HRC §45.025
	§162.106		HRC §45.026
	§162.107	Added ('95)	
	§§162.201-.206	Added ('95)	
	§162.301		HRC §47.001
Ⓐ	§162.302		HRC §47.002
	§162.303		HRC §47.003
	§162.304		HRC §47.004
Ⓔ	§162.3041		
	§162.305		HRC §47.005
	§162.306		HRC §47.031
	§162.308		HRC §47.041
	§162.309		HRC §47.006
	§162.401		HRC §49.001
	§162.402		HRC §49.002
	§162.403		HRC §49.003(a)-(c)
	§162.404	Added ('97)	
	§162.405		HRC §49.005

Derivation Table
Current to Former

CURRENT	INTERIM (1999 - 1995)	PRE-1995
§162.406		HRC §49.006
§162.407		HRC §49.007(a)-(c)
§162.408		HRC §49.008
§162.409		HRC §49.007(e)
§162.411		HRC §49.011
§162.412		HRC §49.012
§162.413		HRC §49.013
§162.414		HRC §49.014
§162.416		HRC §49.016
§162.419		HRC §49.020
§162.420		HRC §49.021
§162.421		HRC §49.022
§162.422		HRC §49.023
§162.501		§16.51
§162.502		§16.51
§162.503		§16.53
§162.504		§16.52
§162.505		§16.54
§162.506	Added ('95)	
§162.507		§16.55
§162.601	Added ('97)	
§201.001		GC §54.001
§201.002		GC §54.002
§201.003		GC §54.003
§201.004		GC §54.004
§201.005		GC §54.005. *See* GC §54.014
§201.006		GC §54.006
§201.007		GC §54.007
§201.008		GC §54.008
§201.009		GC §54.018
§201.010		GC §54.009
§201.011		GC §54.010(a), (b), §54.012(c)
§201.012		GC §54.010(c)
§201.013		GC §54.013, §54.015
§201.014		GC §54.011
§201.015		GC §54.012(a), §54.012 (d)-(i)
§201.016		GC §54.012(j)
§201.017		GC §54.017
Ⓐ §201.018	Added ('99)	
§201.101		§14.82(a), (b)
§201.102		§14.82(c), (e)
§201.103		§14.82(d)
Ⓐ §201.104		§14.82(f), (g)
Ⓐ §201.1041	Added ('99)	
Ⓐ §201.1042	Added ('99)	
§201.105		§14.83(a), (b)
§201.106		§14.83(c)
§201.1065	Added ('99)	
Ⓐ §201.1066	Added ('99)	
§201.107		§14.83(d), (e)
§201.108		§14.84
§201.109		§14.85
§201.110		§14.81
§201.111		§14.82(h)
§201.112	Added ('99)	
Ⓔ §201.113		
§§201.201-.208	Added ('99)	
§202.001		§14.91
§202.002		§14.92
§202.003		§14.93
§202.004		§14.94
§202.005		§14.95
§203.001		HRC §151.003(a)
§203.002		HRC §151.001
§203.003		HRC §151.002(a)
Ⓐ §203.004		HRC §151.004
Ⓐ §203.005		HRC §151.008
§203.006		HRC §151.009
§203.007		HRC §151.011
§204.001	HRC §153.001 ('95)	

	CURRENT	INTERIM (1999 - 1995)	PRE-1995
	§204.002	HRC §153.002 ('95)	
	§204.003	HRC §153.003 ('95)	
	§204.004	HRC §153.004 ('95)	
	§204.005	HRC §153.005 ('95)	
	§231.001		HRC §76.001
	§231.0011	Added ('95)	
	§231.0012	Added ('97)	
	§231.0013	Added ('97)	
	§231.002		HRC §76.002(a), (d), (f), §76.004(b)
	§231.003		§14.86
	§231.005		HRC §76.002(i)
	§231.006		§14.52
A	§231.007		HRC §76.0041
	§231.008		HRC §76.005
	§231.009		HRC §76.008
	§§231.011-.014	Added ('99)	
E	§231.015[A*]		
E	§231.015[B*]		
	§231.101		HRC §76.002(e)
	§231.102	Added ('95)	
	§231.103		HRC §76.004
A	§231.104		HRC §76.003(a)
A	§231.105		HRC §76.003(b)
	§231.106		HRC §76.003(e)
	§231.107		HRC §76.003(f)
	§231.108		HRC §76.006
	§231.109		HRC §76.007(a)-(e)
	§231.110		HRC §76.007(f)
	§231.111		HRC §76.007(g)
	§231.112		§13.015
	§231.113	Added ('95)	
	§231.114	Added ('95)	
	§231.115	Added ('97)	
	§231.116	Added ('97)	

	CURRENT	INTERIM (1999 - 1995)	PRE-1995
E	§231.1165		
	§231.117	§231.115 ('97); HRC §76.012 ('95)	
	§231.118	Added ('99)	
	§231.119	Added ('99)	
	§231.120	Added ('99)	
E	§231.121		
	§231.201		HRC §76.009(g)
A	§231.202		HRC §76.009(a)
	§231.2025	Added ('97)	
	§231.203		HRC §76.009(h)
A	§231.204		HRC §76.009(b)
	§231.205		HRC §76.009(e), (f)
	§231.206		HRC §76.009(i)[A*]
	§231.207		HRC §76.009(c)
	§231.208		HRC §76.009(d)
	§231.209		HRC §76.009(i)[B*]
	§231.210		HRC §76.002(g)
	§231.211		§11.181
	§231.301		HRC §77.001(a)
A	§231.302		HRC §77.001(b)
	§231.303		HRC §77.001(c)
	§231.305	Added ('95)	
	§231.306	Added ('95)	
A	§§231.307-.309	Added ('97)	
	§231.310	Added ('99)	
A	§232.001	Added ('95)	
A	§232.002	Added ('95)	
E	§232.0021		
A	§§232.003-.016	Added ('95)	
	§233.001	§231.401 ('95)	§14.802(a)
	§233.002	§231.402 ('95)	§14.802(a)
	§233.003	§231.403 ('95)	§14.802(g)
	§233.004	§231.404 ('95)	§14.802(g)
	§233.005	§231.405 ('95)	§14.802(b), §14.803(a)
A	§233.006	§231.406 ('95)	§14.803(b), (c)
	§233.007	§231.407 ('95)	§14.802(e), (f)

DERIVATION TABLE
CURRENT TO FORMER

	CURRENT	INTERIM (1999 - 1995)	PRE-1995
	§233.008	§231.408 ('95)	§14.802(c)
A	§233.009	§231.409 ('95)	§14.804(a)
A	§233.0095	Added ('99)	
	§233.010	§231.410 ('95)	§14.804(b), (c)
	§233.011	§231.411 ('95)	§14.804(d)
	§233.012	§231.412 ('95)	§14.804(e)
	§233.013	§231.413 ('95)	§14.802(d)
	§233.014	§231.414 ('95)	§14.804(f)
	§233.015	§231.415 ('95)	§14.804(h)-(j)
	§233.016	§231.416 ('95)	§14.804(k)
	§233.017	§231.417 ('95)	§14.805
A	§233.018	§231.418 ('95)	§14.804(g)
	§233.019	§231.419 ('95)	§14.806(a)
	§233.020	§231.420 ('95)	§14.806(b)
	§233.021	§231.421 ('95)	§14.806(c), (d)
	§233.022	§231.422 ('95)	§14.806(e)
	§233.023	§231.423 ('95)	§14.807(e)
A	§233.024	§231.424 ('95)	§14.807(b), (c)
	§233.025	§231.425 ('95)	§14.807(d), (f)
	§233.026	§231.426 ('95)	§14.807(g)
	§233.027	§231.427 ('95)	§14.807(h), (i)
	§233.0271	Added ('97)	
A	§233.028	§231.428 ('95)	§14.808
	§233.029	§231.429 ('95)	§14.801
A	§234.001, .002	Added ('97)	
A	§§234.004-.011	Added ('97)	
	§§234.101-.104	Added ('97)	
	§§235.001-.004	Added ('97)	
	§§236.001-.003	Added ('97)	
A	§261.001		§34.012
	§261.002		§34.06
	§261.003		§34.013
	§261.004	Added ('97)	
A	§261.101		§34.01, §34.02(d)
	§261.102		§34.02(a)
A	§261.103		§34.02(a)
	§261.104		§34.02(b)
	§261.105		§34.02(c)

	CURRENT	INTERIM (1999 - 1995)	PRE-1995
	§261.1055	Added ('97)	
	§261.106		§34.03
	§261.107		§34.031
	§261.108		§34.032
	§261.109		§34.07
E	§261.110		
	§261.201		§34.08
	§261.202		§34.04
	§261.301		§34.05(a), (b)
	§261.3015	Added ('97)	
	§261.3019	Added ('97)	
	§261.302		§34.05(c), (d)
	§261.303		§34.05(c)
	§261.304		§34.053
	§261.305		§34.05(c)
	§261.306		§34.05(g)
	§261.307		§34.051
	§261.308		§34.05(e), (f)
	§261.309		§34.052
	§261.310		§34.054
	§261.311		§34.055
	§261.312	Added ('95)	
	§261.3125	Added ('99)	
	§261.314	Added ('95)	
	§261.315	Added ('97)	
	§261.316	Added ('97)	
A	§261.401		§34.22
A	§261.402		§34.23
A	§261.403		§34.24
	§261.404	Added ('95)	
A	§261.405	Added ('95)	
	§261.406	Added ('95)	
E	§261.407		
E	§261.408		
E	§261.409		
	§262.001		§17.01
	§262.002		§17.05(a)
	§262.003		§17.08

Derivation Table
Current to Former

	CURRENT	INTERIM (1999 - 1995)	PRE-1995
	§262.004		§17.03(a)(2)
	§262.005		§17.03(g)
	§262.006		§17.011
	§262.007	Added ('95)	
	§262.008	Added ('97)	
A	§262.101		§17.02(b)
	§262.1015	Added ('95)	
A	§262.102		§17.02(a), (d)
	§262.103		§17.02(c)
	§262.104		§17.03(a)(3)-(6)
A	§262.105		§17.03(b)
	§262.106		§17.03(c)
A	§262.107		§17.03(d), (e), (i)
	§262.108		§17.03(h)
A	§262.109		§17.031(b)
	§262.110		§17.03(a)(1)
	§262.112	§262.111 ('95)	
	§262.113	Added ('99)	
A	§262.201		§17.03(f), §17.04
A	§262.2015	Added ('97)	
	§262.202		§17.05(b)
	§262.203		§17.06(a)
	§262.204		§17.06(b), (c)
	§262.205	Added ('99)	
E	§262.301		
A	§262.302	§262.301 ('99)	
A	§262.303	§262.302 ('99)	
A	§262.304	§262.303 ('99)	
E	§262.305		
E	§262.306		
E	§262.307		
	§263.001		§18.01
	§263.002		§18.02
	§263.005	Added ('95)	
	§263.006	Added ('97)	
	§263.101		§18.03(a)
	§263.1015	Added ('97)	
	§263.102		§18.03(b)-(d)
	§263.103		§18.04
	§263.104		§18.05
	§263.105		§18.06
	§263.106	Added ('95)	
	§263.201		§18.07(a)
A	§263.202		§18.07(b)-(d)
A	§263.301		§18.08(b), (c), §18.12
	§263.302		§18.14
A	§263.3025	Added ('97)	
	§263.303		§18.10(b), (c)
A	§263.304		§18.08(a)
	§263.305		§18.10(a)
A	§263.306		§18.09(a), (b)
	§263.307		§18.15
A	§263.401	Added ('97)	
E	§263.402		
A	§263.403	§263.402 ('97)	
A	§263.404	§263.403 ('97)	
E	§263.405[A*]		
E	§263.405[B*]		
E	§263.406	§263.404 ('97)	
A	§§263.501-.503	Added ('97)	
	§264.001		§34.50; HRC §11.001(2)
	§264.002		HRC §41.001
	§264.004		HRC §41.0012
	§264.005		HRC §41.002
	§264.006		HRC §41.003
	§264.007		HRC §§41.004
	§264.008		HRC §41.006
	§264.009		§11.20
	§264.010	Added ('95)	
	§264.011	Added ('97)	
E	§264.0111		
	§264.012	Added ('97)	
	§264.101		HRC §41.021
	§264.1015	Added ('97)	
	§264.102		HRC §41.022
	§264.103		HRC §41.023

	CURRENT	INTERIM (1999 - 1995)	PRE-1995
	§264.104		HRC §41.024
	§264.105		HRC §41.025
	§264.106		HRC §41.026
	§264.1061	Added ('97)	
	§264.107		HRC §41.027
	§264.1075	Added ('97)	
	§264.108		HRC §41.028
	§264.109	Added ('95)	
	§264.110	§264.109 ('95)	
	§264.111	Added ('97)	
	§264.112	Added ('97)	
	§264.201		§34.51
	§264.202		§34.52
	§264.203		§34.53
A	§264.205	Added ('95)	
	§264.206	Added ('97)	
	§264.207	Added ('97)	
	§264.208	Added ('99)	
	§§264.301-.407	Added ('95)	
	§§264.408-.411	Added ('97)	
A	§§264.501-.515	Added ('95)	
	§264.601		§34.601
	§264.602		§34.602
	§264.603		§34.603
	§264.604		§34.604
	§264.605		§34.605
	§264.606		§34.606
	§264.607		§34.607
	§264.608		§34.608
	§264.609		§34.609
	§264.610		§34.610
	§264.611		§34.611
	§264.612		§34.612
E	§264.613		
A	§264.701		GC §772.007
	§264.751	LC §305.001 ('95)	
	§264.752	LC §305.002 ('95)	
	§264.753	LC §305.011 ('95)	
	§264.754	LC §305.012 ('95)	

CURRENT	INTERIM (1999 - 1995)	PRE-1995
§264.755	LC §305.013 ('95)	
§264.756	LC §305.021 ('95)	
§264.757	LC §305.022 ('95)	
§264.758	LC §305.031 ('95)	
§265.001	Added ('99)	
§265.002	Added ('99)	
§265.003	Added ('99)	

Disposition Table
Former to Current

PRE-1995	INTERIM (1995-1999)	CURRENT
§1.01		§2.001
§1.02(2)(B)		§2.003
§1.02		§2.002
§1.03		§2.004
§1.04		§2.005
§1.05(a), (b)		§2.006
§1.05(c)		§2.007
§1.06		§2.008
§1.07		§2.009
§1.07(e)		§2.010
§1.08		§2.011
§1.09		§2.012
§1.51		§2.101
§1.52		§2.102
§1.53		§2.103
§1.81(a)		§2.201
§1.81(b)		§2.207
§1.82(a), (b)		§2.203
§1.82(c), (d)		§2.204
§1.83(a), (b)		§2.202
§1.83(c), (d)		§2.205
§1.84		§2.206
§1.85		§2.208
§1.86		§2.209
§1.91		§2.401
§1.92		§2.402
§1.93		§2.403
§1.94		§2.404
§1.95		§2.405
§2.01		§1.101, §1.102
§2.02		§2.301
§2.03		§2.302
§2.21		§6.201
§2.22		§6.202
§2.23		§6.203
§2.24		§6.307
§2.41(a)		§6.101, §6.103
§2.41(b)		§6.102, §6.103
§2.41(c)		§6.104

PRE-1995	INTERIM (1995-1999)	CURRENT
§2.42		§6.105
§2.43		§6.106
§2.44		§6.107
§2.45		§6.108
§2.46		§6.109
§2.47		§6.111
§2.48		§6.110
§3.01		§6.001
§3.02		§6.002
§3.03		§6.003
§3.04		§6.004
§3.05		§6.005
§3.06		§6.006
§3.07		§6.007
§3.08		§6.008
§3.21		§6.301
§3.22		§6.303
§3.23		§6.304
§3.24		§6.302
§3.25		§6.306, §6.307
§3.26		§6.305
	§3.403 ('99)	§3.404
	§3.404 ('99)	§3.405
§3.51		§6.401
§3.52		§6.402
§3.521		§6.409
	§3.522[A*] ('95)	§6.404
	§3.522[B*] ('95)	§6.405
§3.53		§6.403, §6.701
§3.54(a)-(c)		§6.505
§3.54(b), (d)		§6.705
§3.54(e)		§6.708
§3.55(a), (b)		§6.406
§3.55(b), (c), (d)		§6.407
§3.57		§6.707
§3.58(a), (b)		§6.501
§3.58(c)		§6.502
§3.58(d), (e)		§6.503

Disposition Table
Former to Current

PRE-1995	INTERIM (1995-1999)	CURRENT
§3.58(f)		§6.506
§3.58(g)		§6.507
§3.58(h), (i)		§6.709
§3.581		§6.504
§3.59		§6.502
§3.60		§6.702
§3.61		§6.703
§3.62		§6.704
§3.63(a)		§7.001
§3.63(b)		§7.002
§3.631		§7.006
§3.632(a)		§7.004
§3.632(b), (c)		§9.301
§3.632(d), (e)		§7.005
§3.633(a)		§7.003
§3.633(b)-(e)		§9.302
§3.64		§6.706
§3.65		§6.708
§3.66(a), (b)		§6.801
§3.66(c)		§6.802
§3.70(a), (b)		§9.001
§3.70(c)		§9.002, §9.003
§3.70(d)		§9.004
§3.70(e)		§9.005
§3.71		§9.007
§3.71(a)		§9.006
	§3.711(a) ('95)	§9.101, §9.103
	§3.711(b) ('95)	§9.101
	§3.711(c) ('95)	§9.104
	§3.711(d) ('95)	§9.102
	§3.711(e) ('95)	§9.105
§3.72		§9.008
§3.73		§9.009
§3.74		§9.010
§3.75		§9.011
§3.76		§9.012
§3.77		§9.013, §9.014
§3.90(a), (b)		§9.201
§3.90(c)		§9.202
§3.91		§9.203
§3.92		§9.204
§3.93		§9.205
	§3.9601 ('95), §8.001 ('97)	§8.001(1)
	§3.9602 ('95), §8.002 ('97)	§8.051
	§3.9603 ('95), §8.003 ('97)	§8.052
	§3.9604 ('95), §8.004 ('97)	§8.053
	§3.9605 ('95), §8.005 ('97)	§8.054
	§3.9606 ('95), §8.006 ('97)	§8.055
	§3.9607 ('95), §8.007 ('97)	§8.056
	§3.9608 ('95), §8.008 ('97)	§8.057
	§3.9609 ('95), §8.009 ('97)	§8.059
	§3.9610 ('95), §8.010 ('97)	§8.060
	§3.9611 ('95), §8.011 ('97)	§8.061
§4.01		§1.103
§4.02	§151.003('95), §2.501 ('97)	§151.001
§4.03		§1.104
§4.031		§3.201
§4.04		§1.105
§4.05		§1.106
§4.06		§1.107
§5.01(a)		§3.001
§5.01(b)		§3.002
§5.02		§3.003
§5.03		§3.004
§5.04		§3.005
	§5.107 ('97)	5.003
§5.21		§3.101
§5.22		§3.102
§5.23		§3.103

PRE-1995	INTERIM (1995-1999)	CURRENT
§5.24		§3.104
§5.25(a), (b)		§3.301
§5.25(c)		§3.303
§5.25(d)		§3.304
§5.25(e)		§3.305
§5.25(f)		§3.306
§5.25(g)		§3.307
§5.25(h)		§3.308
§5.26(a), (b)		§3.302
§5.26(c)		§3.303
§5.26(d)		§3.304
§5.26(e)		§3.306
§5.26(f)		§3.307
§5.26(g)		§3.308
§5.27		§3.309
§5.41		§4.001
§5.42		§4.002
§5.43		§4.003
§5.44		§4.004
§5.45		§4.005
§5.46		§4.006
§5.47		§4.007
§5.48		§4.008
§5.49		§4.009
§5.50		§4.010
§5.51		§4.101
§5.52		§4.102
§5.53		§4.103
§5.54		§4.104
§5.55		§4.105
§5.56		§4.106
§5.61		§3.202
§5.62		§3.203
§5.81		§5.001
§5.82		§5.002
§5.83(a)		§5.101
§5.83(b)		§5.103, §5.104, §5.105
§5.83(c)		§5.106
§5.831(a)		§5.101

PRE-1995	INTERIM (1995-1999)	CURRENT
§5.831(b)		§5.103, §5.104, §5.105
§5.831(c)		§5.106
§5.84	§5.107 ('97)	§5.003
§5.85(a)		§5.102
§5.85(b)		§5.103, §5.104, §5.105
§5.85(c)		§5.106
§5.86		§5.108
§5.87(a)		§5.102
§5.87(b)		§5.103, §5.104, §5.105
§5.87(c)		§5.106
	§8.002(a) ('97)	§8.051
	§8.002(b) ('97)	Omitted
	§8.003 ('97)	§8.052
	§8.004 ('97)	§8.053
	§8.005 ('97)	§8.054
	§8.006 ('97)	§8.055
	§8.007 ('97)	§8.056
	§8.008 ('97)	§8.057
	§8.009 ('97)	§8.059
	§8.010 ('97)	§8.060
	§8.011 ('97)	§8.061
§11.01		§101.001
§11.01(1)		§101.003
§11.01(2)		§101.008
§11.01(3)		§101.024
§11.01(4)		§101.025
§11.01(5)		§101.032
§11.01(6)		§101.019
§11.01(7)		§101.002, §101.017
§11.01(8)		§101.014
§11.01(9)		§101.022
§11.01(10)		§101.021
§11.01(11)		§101.018
§11.02		§102.001
§11.03(a)		§102.003
§11.03(b), (c)		§102.004
§11.03(d)		§102.005
§11.03(e)	Omitted	
§11.03(f)		§156.002

PRE-1995	INTERIM (1995-1999)	CURRENT
§11.03(g), (h)		§102.006
§11.03(i)		§102.007
§11.04		§103.001
§11.05(a)		§155.001, §155.002
§11.05(b)		§155.001, §155.004
§11.05(c)		§155.103
§11.05(d), (e)		§155.001
§11.05(f)		§155.004
§11.05(g)		§155.003, §155.004, §156.001
§11.05(h)		§155.005, §155.205
§11.051		§102.011
§11.06(a)		§103.002
§11.06(b)		§155.201, §155.202, §155.203
§11.06(c)		§103.002, §155.201(a)
§11.06(d)		§155.202
§11.06(e)	Omitted	
§11.06(f)-(i)		§155.204
§11.06(j)		§155.205, §155.207
§11.06(k)		§155.206
§11.06(l)		§110.005
§11.06(m)		§155.207
§11.061		§103.003, §155.301
§11.07(a)		§102.002
§11.07(b)	Omitted	
§11.07(c)		§102.013
§11.071(a), (b)		§155.101
§11.071(c)		§155.104
§11.071(d)		§155.102
§11.08(a), (b)		§102.008
§11.08(d)		§162.002
§11.08(e)		§161.101
§11.09(a)-(c), (f)		§102.009
§11.09(c)		§156.003
§11.09(d), (e)		§102.010
§11.10(a)		§107.001, §107.015
§11.10(b)(2), (c)		§107.011
§11.10(b)(1)		§107.001
§11.10(d)		§107.012, §107.013
§11.10(e)		§107.015
§11.101		§107.031
§11.11(a)		§156.006
§11.11(a)-(d), (g), (h)		§105.001
§11.11(e)-(g)		§109.001
§11.12(a)		§107.051
§11.12(b)		§107.051, §107.052, §107.053
§11.12(c)		§107.054, §107.055
§11.13		§105.002
§11.14(a), (b), (d), (f), (g)		§105.003
§11.14(c)		§107.055
§11.14(e)		§104.001
§11.14(h)		§161.202
§11.14(i)		§105.004
§11.14(j)	§160.108 ('95)	Deleted ('01)
§11.15(a)		§105.005
§11.15(b)		§161.001, §161.206
§11.15(c)		§101.007
§11.155		§105.006
§11.16		§161.209, §162.019
§11.17(a)		§108.001
§11.17(b)		§108.002, §108.003, §108.004, §108.005
§11.17(c)		§108.006
§11.17(d)		§108.001, §162.022
§11.17(e)		§108.007
§11.17(f)		§161.210, §162.021
§11.171		§108.006
§11.18(a)		§106.001, §106.002
§11.18(b)		§110.003
§11.18(c)		§107.056
§11.181		§231.211
§11.19		§109.002
§11.191		§109.003
§11.20		§264.009

DISPOSITION TABLE

Disposition Table
Former to Current

PRE-1995	INTERIM (1995-1999)	CURRENT
§11.21(a), (b)		§104.002
§11.21(c)		§104.004
§11.21(d)		§104.003
§11.21(e)		§104.005
§11.22(a), (b), (g)		§157.421
§11.22(c)		§157.423
§11.22(d)		§157.424
§11.22(e)		§157.425
§11.22(f)		§157.426
§11.22(h), (i)		§157.422
§11.22(j)		§106.002
§11.51		§152.001
§11.52		§152.102
§11.53		§152.201, §152.202
§11.54		§152.205
§11.55		§152.108
§11.56		§152.206, §152.307
§11.57		§152.207
§11.58		§152.208
§11.59		§152.209
§11.60		§152.205
§11.61		§152.210
§11.62		§152.106
§11.63		§152.313
§11.64		§152.203
§11.65		§152.306
§11.66		§152.305
§11.68		§152.111
§11.69-.71		§152.112
§11.73		§152.105
§11.74		§152.107
§11.75		§152.101
§12.01	§151.001 ('95)	Deleted ('01)
§12.02	§151.002 ('95)	Deleted ('01)
§12.02(b)	§160.110 ('95)	Deleted ('01)
§12.03	§151.101 ('95)	Deleted ('01)
§12.03A	§151.102 ('95)	Deleted ('01)
§12.03B	§151.103 ('95)	Deleted ('01)

PRE-1995	INTERIM (1995-1999)	CURRENT
§12.04	§151.003 ('95)	§151.001
§12.05	§151.004 ('95)	§151.002
§12.06(a), (b)	§160.101 ('95)	Deleted ('01)
§12.06(c)	§160.004 ('95)	Deleted ('01)
§13.01	§160.002 ('95)	Deleted ('01)
§13.015		§231.112
§13.02(a)	§160.102(a) ('95), §160.103 ('95)	Deleted ('01)
§13.02(b), (c)	§160.107 ('95)	Deleted ('01)
§13.02(d)	§160.102(b) ('95), §160.103 ('95)	Deleted ('01)
§13.03	§160.104 ('95)	Deleted ('01)
§13.04(a)-(e), (g)	§160.105 ('95)	Deleted ('01)
§13.04(f)	§160.004 ('95)	Deleted ('01)
§13.05	§160.106 ('95)	Deleted ('01)
§13.06(a)-(c), (f), (g)	§160.109 ('95)	Deleted ('01)
§13.06(c), (d)	§160.110 ('95)	Deleted ('01)
§13.06(e)	Omitted ('95)	
§13.07	§160.003 ('95)	Deleted ('01)
§13.08	§160.006 ('95)	Deleted ('01)
§13.09	§160.006 ('95)	Deleted ('01)
§13.21(a), (b)	§160.201 ('95)	Deleted ('01)
§13.21(c), (d)	Omitted ('95)	
§13.22	§160.202 ('95)	Deleted ('01)
§13.22(a), (e)	§160.204 ('95)	Deleted ('01)
§13.23	§160.203 ('95)	Deleted ('01)
§13.24	§160.205 ('95)	Deleted ('01)
§13.41		*See* §103.001
§13.42(a)	§160.004('95), §160.005 ('95)	Deleted ('01)
§13.42(b)		*See* 106.002(a)
§13.42(c)	Omitted ('95)	
§13.42(d)	§160.004 ('95)	Deleted ('01)
§13.43(a)-(c)		§108.008
§13.43(d)	§160.006 ('95)	Deleted ('01)
§13.43(e), (f)		§108.009
§13.44	§160.007 ('95)	Deleted ('01)
§14.01(a)		§153.005

PRE-1995	INTERIM (1995-1999)	CURRENT
§14.01(b)(1)		§153.131
§14.01(b)(2)		§153.373
§14.01(c)(1)		§153.003
§14.01(c)(2)		§153.004
§14.01(d)		§153.374
§14.01(e)		§153.375
§14.02(a)		§153.071, §153.073, §153.076
§14.02(b)(1)		§153.074
§14.02(b)(2)		§153.073
§14.02(b)(3)		§153.132
§14.02(b)		§153.072
§14.02(c)		§153.371
§14.02(d)		§161.104
§14.02(e)	§153.139 Repealed ('97)	
§14.021(a)		§153.001
§14.021(b)		§101.016, §153.135, §153.136
§14.021(c), (d)		§153.133
§14.021(e), (f)		§153.134
§14.021(g)		§153.138, §156.104, §156.401
§14.021(h)		§153.004
§14.021(i)	Omitted ('95)	
§14.021(j)		§153.372
§14.03(a)		§153.006
§14.03(b)		§153.192
§14.03(c)		§153.006
§14.03(d)		§153.004, §153.075, §153.191, §153.193
§14.03(e)		§153.432, §153.433
§14.03(e)(3)		§153.004
§14.03(f)(1), (3)		§153.432
§14.03(g)		§153.434
§14.03(h)		§153.010
§14.03(i)		§153.011
§14.03(j)		§111.001
§14.032(a)		§153.251
§14.032(b)		§153.254
§14.032(c)		§153.256
§14.032(d)		§153.003
§14.032(e), (f)		§111.002
§14.033(a)(1)		§101.028
§14.033(a)(2)		§101.029
§14.033(b)		§153.311
§14.033(c), (e)(4)-(7)		§153.312
§14.033(d)		§153.315
§14.033(e)(1)-(3)		§153.314
§14.033(e)(8)-(10)		§153.314
§14.033(f)(2)		§153.314
§14.033(f)		§153.313
§14.033(g)(7)	§156.301 ('95)	Repealed ('01)
§14.033(g)		§153.316
§14.033(h)		§153.257
§14.033(i)		§153.317
§14.033(k)		§153.252, §153.253, §153.258
§14.033(l)		§105.001
§14.033(m)		§153.253
§14.033(n)		§153.255
§14.033(o)	§156.302 ('95)	Repealed ('01)
§14.033(p)		§111.003
§14.034		§153.137
§14.04		§153.192
§14.04(a), (b)		§153.376
§14.04(c)		§153.012, §153.377
§14.045(a), (b)		§105.007
§14.045(c)		§105.007(b)
§14.05(a)		§154.001, §154.002, §154.003
§14.05(b)		§154.001
§14.05(c)		§154.005
§14.05(d)		§154.001, §154.006
§14.05(e)		§154.007, §158.001
§14.05(f)	Omitted ('95)	

DISPOSITION TABLE

DISPOSITION TABLE
FORMER TO CURRENT

PRE-1995	INTERIM (1995-1999)	CURRENT
§14.05(g)		§154.010
§14.05(h), (i)		§111.001
§14.05(j)		§154.122
§14.0501		§154.241
§14.0502		§154.242
§14.0503		§154.004
§14.0504		§154.243
§14.051(a)		§154.301
§14.051(b)		§154.302
§14.051(c)		§154.303
§14.051(d)-(f)		§154.305
§14.051(g)		§154.306
§14.051(h)		§154.307
§14.051(i)		§154.304
§14.051(j), (k)		§154.308
§14.052(a)		§154.121
§14.052(b)		§154.123
§14.052(c), (d)		§111.002
§14.052(d)		§111.002
§14.053(a)		§154.061
§14.053(b)		§154.062
§14.053(c)		§154.065
§14.053(d)		§154.064, §154.183
§14.053(e)		§154.067
§14.053(f)		§154.066
§14.053(g)		§154.063
§14.053(h)		§154.061
§14.053(i)		§154.010
§14.053(j)		§154.124
§14.053(k)		§154.068
§14.053(l)		§154.131
§14.054		§154.123
§14.055(a)		§154.122, §154.125
§14.055(b)		§154.125
§14.055(c)		§154.126
§14.055(d)		§154.127
§14.055(e)		§105.001
§14.055(f)-(h)		§154.128
§14.055(i)		§154.070

PRE-1995	INTERIM (1995-1999)	CURRENT
§14.055(j)		§154.129
§14.056(a)		§156.402
§14.056(b)		§156.402, §156.403
§14.056(c)		§154.069, §156.404, §156.405
§14.056(d)		§156.406
§14.057		§154.130
§14.058		§111.003
§14.06		§153.007, §154.124
§14.061		§154.181
§14.061(a)		§154.008, §154.182
§14.061(b)		§154.182
§14.061(c)		§154.183
§14.061(d)		§101.015
§14.061(e), (f)		§154.185
§14.061(g)		§154.186
§14.061(h)-(k)		§154.187
§14.061(l)		§154.188
§14.061(m)		§154.189, §154.190
§14.061(n), (o)		§154.191
§14.061(p)		§154.187
§14.061(q)		§154.192
§14.061(r)		§154.184
§14.062		§154.009
§14.07(a)		§153.002, §153.008
§14.07(b)		§153.431
§14.07(c)		§153.009
§14.08(a)		§156.001, §156.002
§14.08(b)		§156.003, §156.004
§14.08(c)(1)		§156.101
§14.08(c)(2)		§156.401
§14.08(c)(3)	§156.301 ('95)	Repealed ('01)
§14.08(c)(3)(C)	§156.303 ('95)	Repealed ('01)
§14.08(c)(4)	§156.103 ('95)	Deleted ('01)
§14.08(c)(5)	§156.104 ('95)	Deleted ('01)
§14.08(d), (e)		§156.102
§14.08(f)	Omitted ('95)	
§14.08(g)		§156.006

DISPOSITION TABLE

Disposition Table
Former to Current

PRE-1995	INTERIM (1995-1999)	CURRENT
§14.08(g)(3)		§156.101
§14.08(h)		§156.407
§14.08(i)	§156.105 ('95)	Repealed ('01)
§14.081(a)	Omitted ('95)	
§14.081(b)	§156.201 ('95)	Repealed ('01)
§14.081(c)	§156.202 ('95)	Repealed ('01)
§14.081(d)	§156.203 ('95)	Repealed ('01)
§14.082		§156.005
§14.10(a), (b)		§157.372
§14.10(c)		§157.373
§14.10(d)		§157.374
§14.10(e)		§157.375
§14.10(f)		§157.376
§14.11	Omitted	
§14.13		§110.002
§14.30(a)(1)		§101.011
§14.30(a)(2)		§101.010
§14.30(a)(3)		§101.012
§14.30(b)		§157.001
§14.30(c)		*See* §103.001, §103.002
§14.30(d)		§157.003
§14.31		§157.001
§14.311(a)-(e)		§157.002
§14.311(b)		§157.162
§14.311(c)		§157.162
§14.311(f)		§157.064
§14.312		§157.002
§14.313(a)		§157.003
§14.313(b)	Omitted ('95)	
§14.314(a)		§157.061, §157.062
§14.314(b)		§157.062
§14.314(c)		§157.063, §157.065
§14.315(b), (c)		§157.062
§14.316		§158.201
§14.317(a)		§157.066, §157.114, §157.115
§14.317(b)	Omitted ('95)	
§14.317(c)		§157.115
§14.317(d)		§157.102

PRE-1995	INTERIM (1995-1999)	CURRENT
§14.317(e)		§157.103
§14.318(a)		§157.101
§14.318(b)		§157.104
§14.318(c)		§157.105
§14.318(d)		§157.106
§14.318(e)		§157.107
§14.318(f)		§157.108
§14.32(a)	Omitted ('95)	
§14.32(b)		§157.161
§14.32(c)	Omitted ('95)	
§14.32(d)		§157.061
§14.32(e)		§157.101, §157.113
§14.32(f)		§157.163
§14.33(a)		§157.166
§14.33(b)		§157.164
§14.33(c)		§157.167
§14.33(d)		§157.003, §157.162
§14.34(a)		§157.265
§14.34(b)		§157.266
§14.34(c)		§157.267, §157.268
§14.40(a)		§157.001
§14.40(b)		§157.005
§14.40(c)		§157.008
§14.40(d)		§157.262
§14.40(e)(1)		§157.165, §157.211
§14.40(e)(2)		§157.212
§14.40(e)(3)		§157.213
§14.40(e)(4)		§157.214
§14.40(e)(5)		§157.215
§14.40(e)(6)		§157.216
§14.40(e)(7)		§157.217
§14.40(f)		§157.113
§14.40(g)		§157.008
§14.40(h)		§157.006
§14.41(a)		§157.261, §157.262, §157.263, §157.264, §158.005
§14.41(b)		§157.005
§14.41(c)		§157.008

PRE-1995	INTERIM (1995-1999)	CURRENT
§14.41(d)		§157.262
§14.41(e)		§157.263
§14.42(a)		§157.109
§14.42(b), (c), (f)		§157.110
§14.42(d)		§157.112
§14.42(e)		§157.111
§14.43(a)(1)		§158.001
§14.43(a)(2)		§158.002
§14.43(a)(4)		§158.311
§14.43(b)		§158.006
§14.43(c)	Omitted ('95)	
§14.43(d)		§158.003, §158.004, §158.005, §158.007
§14.43(e)		§158.103
§14.43(f)		§158.009
§14.43(g)		§158.104, §158.105
§14.43(h)		§158.010, §158.105, §158.202, §158.203
§14.43(i)		§110.004, §158.204
§14.43(j)		§158.205
§14.43(k)		§158.008
§14.43(l)		§158.206, §158.207, §158.208
§14.43(m)		§158.209
§14.43(n)		§158.210
§14.43(o)		§158.211
§14.43(p)		§158.106
§14.43(q)		§158.401, §158.404, §158.405
§14.43(r)		§158.102
§14.44(a)		§158.301, §158.311
§14.44(b)		§158.302
§14.44(c)		§158.307, §158.308
§14.44(d)		§158.304, §158.309, §158.310
§14.44(e)		§158.317
§14.44(f)		§158.106
§14.44(g)	§158.305 Repealed ('97)	
§14.44(h)		§158.303

PRE-1995	INTERIM (1995-1999)	CURRENT
§14.45(a)		§158.306, §158.312, §158.313, §158.316
§14.45(b)		§158.314
§14.45(c)		§158.315
§14.45(d)		§158.205
§14.45(e)	Omitted ('95)	
§14.45(f)		§158.401
§14.45(g)		§158.106
§14.45(h)		§110.004
§14.50(a)		§157.001
§14.50(b)		§157.004
§14.50(c)		§157.007
§14.50(d)(1)		§157.165, §157.211
§14.50(d)(2)		§157.212
§14.50(d)(3)		§157.213
§14.50(d)(4)		§157.214
§14.50(d)(5)		§157.215
§14.50(d)(6)		§157.216
§14.50(d)(7)		§157.217
§14.50(e)		§157.006
§14.51(a)		§157.109
§14.51(b), (c), (f)		§157.110
§14.51(d)		§157.112
§14.51(e)		§157.111
§14.52		§231.006
§14.80(1)	Omitted ('95)	
§14.80(2)		§101.033, §101.034
§14.80(3)		§101.004
§14.80(4)		§101.006
§14.80(5)		§101.020
§14.80(6)		§101.030
§14.80(7)		§101.005
§14.801		§233.029
§14.802(a)		§233.001, §233.002
§14.802(b)		§233.005
§14.802(c)		§233.008
§14.802(d)		§233.013
§14.802(e), (f)		§233.007

Disposition Table
Former to Current

PRE-1995	INTERIM (1995-1999)	CURRENT
§14.802(g)		§233.003, §233.004
§14.803(a)		§233.005
§14.803(b), (c)		§233.006
§14.804(a)		§233.009
§14.804(b), (c)		§233.010
§14.804(d)		§233.011
§14.804(e)		§233.012
§14.804(f)		§233.014
§14.804(g)		§233.018
§14.804(h)-(j)		§233.015
§14.804(k)		§233.016
§14.805		§233.017
§14.806(a)		§233.019
§14.806(b)		§233.020
§14.806(c)		§233.021
§14.806(d)		§233.021
§14.806(e)		§233.022
§14.807(a)	Omitted ('95)	
§14.807(b), (c)		§233.024
§14.807(d)		§233.025
§14.807(e)		§233.023
§14.807(f)		§233.025
§14.807(g)		§233.026
§14.807(h), (i)		§233.027
§14.808		§233.028
§14.81		§201.110
§14.82(a), (b)		§201.101
§14.82(c), (e)		§201.102
§14.82(d)		§201.103
§14.82(f)		§201.104
§14.82(g)		§201.104
§14.82(h)		§201.111
§14.83(a), (b)		§201.105
§14.83(c)		§201.106
§14.83(d), (e)		§201.107
§14.84		§201.108
§14.85		§201.109
§14.86		§231.003
§14.91		§202.001

PRE-1995	INTERIM (1995-1999)	CURRENT
§14.92		§202.002
§14.93		§202.003
§14.94		§202.004
§14.95		§202.005
§14.971(a), (b)		§157.311
§14.971(c), (d)		§157.312
§14.972(a)		§157.316
§14.972(b), (c)		§157.317
§14.972(d)		§157.312
§14.972(e)		§157.318
§14.973		§157.313
§14.974		§157.314
§14.975		§157.315
§14.976(a)		§157.318(c)
§14.976(b)		§157.319
§14.976(c)		§157.320
§14.977		§157.320
§14.978		§157.322
§14.979		§157.323
§14.98		§157.321
§14.981		§157.324
§14.982		§157.325
§14.983		§157.326
§15.01		§161.005
§15.02(a)		§161.001
§15.021(a), (c)		§161.102
§15.021(b)	§161.201 ('95)	Deleted ('01)
§15.022		§161.006
§15.023		§161.002
§15.024		§161.003
§15.025		§161.004
§15.03		§161.103
§15.04		§161.105
§15.041(a)-(d)		§161.106
§15.041(e)		§161.204
§15.05(a)		§161.206
§15.05(b)		§161.207
§15.05(c)		§161.205
§15.051		§161.107

Disposition Table
Former to Current

PRE-1995	INTERIM (1995-1999)	CURRENT
§15.051(a)(1)		§101.027
§15.051(b)		§161.208
§15.06		§161.203
§15.07		§161.206
§16.01		§162.001
§16.02		§162.001
§16.03(a)		§162.002
§16.03(b)-(d)		§162.001
§16.031(a)		§162.003
§16.031(b)	§162.004 ('95)	Repealed ('01)
§16.032(a)		§162.005
§16.032(b)-(e)		§162.007
§16.032(f)		§162.005, §162.018
§16.032(g)		§162.006
§16.032(h), (m)		§162.008
§16.032(i)		§162.018
§16.032(i)-(k), (n)		§162.006
§16.032(l)		§162.005
§16.04		§162.009
§16.05		§162.010
§16.06		§162.011
§16.07		§162.014
§16.08		§162.016
§16.081		§162.015
§16.09(a), (d)-(f)		§162.017
§16.09(b), (c)		§162.018
§16.10		§162.020
§16.11		§162.013
§16.12		§162.012
§16.51		§162.501, §162.502
§16.52		§162.504
§16.53		§162.503
§16.54		§162.505
§16.55		§162.507
§17.001		§101.009
§17.01		§262.001

PRE-1995	INTERIM (1995-1999)	CURRENT
§17.011		§262.006
§17.02(a), (d)		§262.102
§17.02(b)		§262.101
§17.02(c)		§262.103
§17.03(a)(1)		§262.110
§17.03(a)(2)		§262.004
§17.03(a)(3)-(6)		§262.104
§17.03(b)		§262.105
§17.03(c)		§262.106
§17.03(d), (e), (i)		§262.107
§17.03(f)		§262.201
§17.03(g)		§262.005
§17.03(h)		§262.108
§17.031(a)	Omitted ('95)	
§17.031(b)		§262.109
§17.04		§262.201
§17.05(a)		§262.002
§17.05(b)		§262.202
§17.06(a)		§262.203
§17.06(b), (c)		§262.204
§17.08		§262.003
§18.01		§263.001
§18.02		§263.002
§18.03(a)		§263.101
§18.03(b)-(d)		§263.102
§18.04		§263.103
§18.05		§263.104
§18.06		§263.105
§18.07(a)		§263.201
§18.07(b)-(d)		§263.202
§18.08(a)		§263.304
§18.08(b), (c)		§263.301
§18.09(a), (b)		§263.306
§18.09(c)	§263.308 Repealed ('97)	
§18.10(a)		§263.305
§18.10(b), (c)		§263.303

PRE-1995	INTERIM (1995-1999)	CURRENT
§18.12		§263.301
§18.14		§263.302
§18.15		§263.307
§18.16	§263.309 Repealed ('97)	
§21.01		§159.101
§21.01(19)		§101.030
§21.01(22)		§101.035
§21.02		§159.102
§21.03		§159.103
§21.04		§159.201
§21.05		§159.202
§21.06		§159.203
§21.07		§159.204
§21.08		§159.205
§21.09		§159.206
§21.10		§159.207
§21.11		§159.208
§21.12		§159.209
§21.13		§159.301
§21.14		§159.302
§21.15		§159.303
§21.16		§159.304
§21.17		§159.305
§21.18		§159.306
§21.19		§159.307
§21.20		§159.308
§21.21		§159.309
§21.22		§159.310
§21.23		§159.311
§21.24		§159.312
§21.25		§159.313
§21.26		§159.314
§21.27		§159.315
§21.28		§159.316
§21.29		§159.317
§21.30		§159.318
§21.31		§159.319
§21.32		§159.401

PRE-1995	INTERIM (1995-1999)	CURRENT
§21.33(a)		§159.501, §159.502
§21.33(b)		§159.506
§21.34		§159.507
§21.35		§159.601
§21.36		§159.602
§21.37		§159.603
§21.38		§159.604
§21.39		§159.605
§21.40		§159.606
§21.41		§159.607
§21.42		§159.608
§21.43		§159.609
§21.44		§159.610
§21.45		§159.611
§21.46		§159.612
§21.47		§159.701
§21.48		§159.801
§21.49		§159.802
§21.50		§159.901
§21.51		§159.902
§21.52	Omitted ('95)	
§§25.01-.09		§§60.001-.009
§31.01(a), (c)		§31.001
§31.01(b)	Omitted ('95)	
§31.02(a), (c)		§31.002
§31.02(b)	Omitted ('95)	
§31.03(a)		§31.003
§31.03(b)	Omitted ('95)	
§31.04		§31.004
§31.06		§31.005
§31.07		§31.006
§31.08		§31.007
§32.01		§45.001
§32.02		§45.002
§32.02(a)		§45.001
§32.03		§45.003
§32.04		§45.004
§32.05		§45.005
	§32.103 ('95)	§32.102

Disposition Table
Former to Current

PRE-1995	INTERIM (1995-1999)	CURRENT
	§32.104 ('95)	§32.103
§32.21(a)		§45.101, §45.102
§32.21(b)		§45.102
§32.21(c), (d)	Omitted ('95)	
§32.22		§45.103
§32.23		§45.104
§33.01		§41.001
§33.02		§41.002
§33.03		§41.003
§34.01		§261.101
§34.012		§261.001
§34.013		§261.003
§34.02(a)		§261.102, §261.103
§34.02(b)		§261.104
§34.02(c)		§261.105
§34.02(d)		§261.101
§34.03		§261.106
§34.031		§261.107
§34.031(b)		§153.013
§34.032		§261.108
§34.04		§261.202
§34.05(a), (b)		§261.301
§34.05(c)		§261.303, §261.305
§34.05(c), (d)		§261.302
§34.05(e), (f)		§261.308
§34.05(g)		§261.306
§34.051		§261.307
§34.052		§261.309
§34.053		§261.304
§34.054		§261.310
§34.055		§261.311
§34.06		§261.002
§34.07		§261.109
§34.08		§261.201
§34.22		§261.401
§34.23		§261.402
§34.24		§261.403
§34.50		§264.001
§34.51		§264.201

PRE-1995	INTERIM (1995-1999)	CURRENT
§34.52		§264.202
§34.53		§264.203
§34.601		§264.601
§34.602		§264.602
§34.603		§264.603
§34.604		§264.604
§34.605		§264.605
§34.606		§264.606
§34.607		§264.607
§34.608		§264.608
§34.609		§264.609
§34.610		§264.610
§34.611		§264.611
§34.612		§264.612
§35.01		§32.001
§35.011		§32.101
§35.013		§32.102
§35.014		§32.103
§35.02		§32.002
§35.03(a)-(f)		§32.003
§35.03(g)		§32.004
§35.04		§32.005
§35.05		§32.201
§36.01		§42.001
§36.02(a), (b)		§42.002
§36.02(c), (d)		§42.003
§36.03		§42.006
§36.04		§42.007
§36.05		§42.005
§36.06		§42.008
§36.08		§42.009
	§42.004 ('95)	Repealed ('99)
	§71.008 ('97)	Repealed ('01). *See* §88.002 (1); §88.003(d)
§71.01(a)		§71.001
§71.01(b)(1)		§71.002
§71.01(b)(3)		§71.003
§71.01(b)(2)		§71.004

Disposition Table

Former to Current

PRE-1995	INTERIM (1995-1999)	CURRENT
§71.01(b)(4), (6)		§71.006
§71.01(b)(5)		§71.005
§71.02		§82.001
§71.03		§82.003
§71.04(a)		§82.001
§71.04(b)		§82.002
§71.04(c)		§81.007
§71.04(d)-(f)	Repealed ('95)	
	§71.041(a) ('95)	§81.002
	§71.041(b) ('95)	§81.003
	§71.041(c) ('95)	§81.004
	§71.041(d) ('95)	§81.005, §81.006
§71.05(a)		§82.004
§71.05(b)	Omitted ('97)	
§71.05(c)		§82.006
§71.05(d)		§82.007
§71.05(e)		§82.009
§71.05(f), (g)		§82.008
§71.06		§82.005
	§71.06(c) ('95)	§85.009
	§71.06(e) ('95)	§82.043
	§71.06(f) ('95)	§85.004
§71.07(a)		§82.043
§71.07(b), (c)		§82.042
§71.07(d), (e)		§82.041
§71.07(f)-(h)		§82.043
§71.07(i)	Repealed ('95)	
§71.08		§82.021
§71.09(a)		§84.001
§71.09(b)		§84.004
§71.09(c)		§84.003
§71.09(d)		§84.002
§71.09(e)		§85.006
§71.10(a)		§81.001, §85.001
§71.10(b)		§81.001, §85.001
§71.10(c)		§85.002
§71.10(d)		§85.005

PRE-1995	INTERIM (1995-1999)	CURRENT
§71.11(a)(1)-(4), (6)		§85.021
§71.11(a)(5), (7)		§85.022
§71.11(b), (c)		§85.022
§71.11(d)		§85.023
§71.11(e)-(h)	Omitted ('95)	
§71.11(i)		§85.024
§71.111		§85.007
§71.12(a), (b)		§85.005
§71.12(c)	Omitted ('97)	
§71.12(d), (e)		§85.005
	§71.121(a) ('95)	§85.003
§71.121(a)		§82.022
§71.121(b)		§82.022
§71.121(c)		§84.001
§71.121(d)		§85.001
§71.121(e), (f)		§85.003
§71.13(a)		§85.025
§71.13(b), (c)	Repealed ('95)	
§71.14(a)		§87.001
§71.14(b)		§87.002
	§71.14(c) ('95)	§87.003
§71.15(a)		§83.001
§71.15(b), (c)		§83.002
§71.15(d)		§83.003
§71.15(e)		§83.004
§71.15(f)		§83.005
§71.15(g), (h)		§83.006
§71.15(i)		§86.003
§71.15(j)		§83.007
§71.16		§85.026
§71.17(a)-(d)		§85.041
§71.17(e)-(g)		§85.042
§71.18(a), (b)		§86.001
§71.18(c)[A]		§86.002
§71.18(c) [B]		§86.003
§71.18(d)		§86.004
§71.19		§81.008

Disposition Table
Former to Current

PRE-1995	INTERIM (1995-1999)	CURRENT
§§72.001-.004	Repealed ('95)	
	§73.01 ('95)	§91.001
	§73.02 ('95)	§91.002
	§73.03 ('95)	§91.003
	§73.04 ('95)	§92.001
	§73.05 ('95)	§91.004
	§88.001 ('97)	Deleted ('01)
	§88.002 ('97)	Deleted ('01)
	§88.003 ('97)	Deleted ('01)
	§88.004 ('97)	Deleted ('01)
	§107.002(e) ('95)	§107.0135
	§151.001 ('95)	Deleted ('01)
	§151.002 ('95)	Deleted ('01)
	§151.003 ('95)	§151.001
	§151.004 ('95)	§151.002
	§151.005 ('95)	§151.003
	§151.101 ('95)	Deleted ('01)
	§151.102 ('95)	Deleted ('01)
	§151.103 ('95)	Deleted ('01)
	§152.001 (a)(9), (b) ('95)	§152.001
	§152.002 ('95)	§152.102
	§152.003(d) ('95)	§152.202, §152.203
	§152.003(e) ('95)	§152.204
	§152.003 ('95)	§152.201
	§152.004 ('95)	§152.205
	§152.005 ('95)	§152.108
	§152.006 ('95)	§152.206, §152.307
	§152.007 ('95)	§152.207
	§152.008 ('95)	§152.208
	§152.009 ('95)	§152.209
	§152.010 ('95)	§152.205
	§152.011 ('95)	§152.210
	§152.012 ('95)	§152.106
	§152.013 ('95)	§152.313
	§152.014 ('95)	§152.305
	§152.015 ('95)	§152.306
	§152.016 ('95)	§152.305
	§152.018 ('95)	§152.111

PRE-1995	INTERIM (1995-1999)	CURRENT
	§§152.019-.021 ('95)	§152.112
	§152.023 ('95)	§152.105
	§152.024 ('95)	§152.107
	§152.025 ('95)	§152.101
	§153.139 ('95)	Repealed ('01)
	§§156.103-.104 ('95)	Deleted ('01)
	§156.105 ('95)	Repealed ('01)
	§156.201-.203 ('95)	Repealed ('01)
	§156.301-.304 ('95)	Repealed ('01)
	§158.107 ('95)	Repealed ('97)
	§158.305 ('95)	Repealed ('97)
	§158.508 ('97)	Repealed ('01)
	§159.501(a) ('95)	§159.501, §159.502
	§159.501(b) ('95)	§159.506
	§159.502 ('95)	§159.507
	§§160.001-.007 ('95)	Deleted ('01)
	§§160.101-.110 ('95)	Deleted ('01)
	§§160.201-.206 ('95)	Deleted ('01)
	§§160.207-.216 ('99)	Deleted ('01)
	§§160.251-.263 ('97)	Deleted ('01)
	§161.201 ('95)	Repealed ('01)
	§162.0025 ('97)	Repealed ('01)
	§162.004 ('95)	Repealed ('01)
	§201.1085 ('97)	Repealed ('99)
	§231.004 ('95)	Repealed ('97)
	§231.010 ('97)	Repealed ('01)
	§231.115 ('97)	§231.117
	§231.304 ('95)	Repealed ('97)
	§231.401 ('95)	§233.001
	§231.402 ('95)	§233.002
	§231.403 ('95)	§233.003
	§231.404 ('95)	§233.004
	§231.405 ('95)	§233.005
	§231.406 ('95)	§233.006
	§231.407 ('95)	§233.007
	§231.408 ('95)	§233.008
	§231.409 ('95)	§233.009
	§231.410 ('95)	§233.010
	§231.411 ('95)	§233.011

PRE-1995	INTERIM (1995-1999)	CURRENT
	§231.412 ('95)	§233.012
	§231.413 ('95)	§233.013
	§231.414 ('95)	§233.014
	§231.415 ('95)	§233.015
	§231.416 ('95)	§233.016
	§231.417 ('95)	§233.017
	§231.418 ('95)	§233.018
	§231.419 ('95)	§233.019
	§231.420 ('95)	§233.020
	§231.421 ('95)	§233.021
	§231.422 ('95)	§233.022
	§231.423 ('95)	§233.023
	§231.424 ('95)	§233.024
	§231.425 ('95)	§233.025
	§231.426 ('95)	§233.026
	§231.427 ('95)	§233.027
	§231.428 ('95)	§233.028
	§231.429 ('95)	§233.029
	§§231.430-.431 ('95)	Repealed ('97)
	§234.005 ('97)	Expired ('99)
	§262.111 [A*] ('95)	Repealed ('01)
	§262.111 [B*] ('95)	§262.112
	§262.301 ('99)	§262.302
	§262.302 ('99)	§262.303
	§262.303 ('99)	§262.304
	§§263.003-.004 ('95)	Repealed ('99)
	§§263.308-.309 ('95)	Repealed ('97)
	§263.402 ('97)	§263.403
	§263.403 ('97)	§263.404
	§264.003 ('95)	Repealed ('01)
	§264.109 ('95)	§264.110

TEXAS FAMILY LAW INFORMATION

Dallas Bar Association—Family Law Section <http://www.dallasfamilylawsection.org>

This site provides relevant references to legal resources and other web sites of use to family law practitioners in the DFW Metroplex. It also provides information regarding the policies, scheduling, assignment of duties, and staff for each of the Family District Courts in Dallas County.

Houston Bar Association—Family Law Section <http://www.hbafam.org>

This site contains general information on the family law division of the Houston Bar Association and links to helpful resources for family law practitioners in the Houston Metropolitan area.

State Bar of Texas—Family Law Section <http://www.sbotfam.org>

This site provides links to publications and general information regarding the family law division of the state bar, information on CLE, and other resources that may interest family law practitioners in Texas.

Texas Academy of Family Law Specialists <http://www.tafls.org>

This site includes links to useful family law sites, as well as links to various Texas and U.S. governmental organizations, online newspapers, and several search engines and legal directories.

Texas Attorney General—Child Support Program <http://www.oag.state.tx.us/child/mainchil.htm>

This site provides information on the role of the Texas Attorney General and Texas local agencies to collect child support, as well as links to other relevant governmental agencies and programs.

Texas Coalition for Adoption Resources & Education <http://www.txcare.org>

This site is dedicated to adoption issues and provides tracking of statutes in the Texas legislature related to adoption. It also has an adoption search registry for those born in or whose adoption was finalized in Texas.

Texas Collaborative Divorce <http://www.anchovypress.com/tcd>

This site features a listing of Texas attorneys trained in Collaborative Divorce.

Texas Council on Family Violence <http://www.tcfv.org>

This site contains information on laws and issues relevant to the prevention of violence against women, including forms for protective orders and magistrate's orders. It also provides links to similar state and national organizations.

Texas Department of Health—Bureau of Vital Statistics <http://www.tdh.state.tx.us/bvs>

This site provides information regarding births, adoptions, deaths, marriages and divorces in Texas, including information on how to obtain birth or death certificates and includes vital statistics reports, information on opening adoption records, and reporting forms for Suits Affecting the Parent-Child Relationship.

Texas Department of Human Services—Family Violence Shelters <http://www.dhs.state.tx.us/programs/familyviolence/shelters.html>

This site contains a statewide listing of family violence shelters and hotlines.

Texas Department of Protective & Regulatory Services <http://www.tdprs.state.tx.us>

This site provides information on the Texas Department of Protective and Regulatory Services, including information on adoption, adult protection, childcare, child protection, and a listing of relevant hotlines.

Texas Department of Public Safety—Missing Persons Clearinghouse <http://www.txdps.state.tx.us/mpch>

This site serves as a Central repository for information on missing and unidentified persons in Texas.

FEDERAL & NATIONAL FAMILY LAW INFORMATION

American Academy of Matrimonial Lawyers < http://www.aaml.org>

This site provides legal links and search engines, as well as an on-line divorce manual and a variety of articles related to marriage and divorce.

American Bar Association—Center on Children & the Law <http://www.abanet.org/child/home2.html>

This site contains information for family law practitioners, including on-line articles, federal statutes, and links to sites that discuss a variety of issues related to protecting and educating children.

American Bar Association—Commission on Domestic Violence <http://www.abanet.org/domviol>

This site features information on national organizations that aid victims of domestic violence, as well as links to related legal resources and other sites related to domestic violence.

American Bar Association—Family Law Section <http://www.abanet.org/family>

This site provides legal links aimed at practitioners, law students, and the general public, on-line discussion groups for family law section members, and a list of family law projects related to children's issues.

National Center for Missing & Exploited Children <http://www.missingkids.com>

This is the homepage of the National Center for Missing and Exploited Children. It includes NCMEC articles, a nationwide database with pictures of missing children, and resources for teaching children about safety.

National Child Support Enforcement Association <http://www.NCSEA.org>

This site contains information on child support issues and features a searchable database of citations, abstracts, and full documents of child support related articles, books, and reports to federal, state, and local governments, as well as a bill tracking chart for federal child support legislation and links to federal and state research initiatives.

Pension Benefit Guaranty Corporation <http://www.pbgc.gov>

This site features the "Divorce Order & PBGC Booklet," which provides general information to attorneys on QDROs submitted to PBGC after PBGC trustees a plan.

Support Guidelines <http://www.supportguidelines.com>

This site provides links to child support guidelines for all 50 states and Canada and links to on-line child support calculators, as well as numerous articles and case summaries.

U.S. Department of Defense—Military Mailing Addresses
<http://www.defenselink.mil/faq/pis/PC04MLTR.html>

This site provides a guide to locate individuals on active military service.

U.S. Department of Health & Human Services—Administration for Children & Families
<http://www.acf.dhhs.gov>

This site contains information on, and links to, the governmental programs and offices within the Administration for Children & Families.

U.S. Department of Justice—Violence Against Women Office
<http://www.ojp.usdoj.gov/vawo/regulations.htm>

This site provides updates on federal regulations and legislation relevant to the prevention of violence against women. It also provides contact information for the National Domestic Violence Hotline as well as information on state domestic violence hotlines and agencies.

U.S. Department of Labor—Pension & Welfare Benefits Administration <http://www.dol.gov/dol/pwba>

This site provides quick access to federal statutes, regulations, executive orders, advisory opinions, forms, news releases, compliance assistance information and other publications on pension and welfare benefits issues.

U.S. Department of State—Office of Children's Issues <http://travel.state.gov/children's_issues.html>

This site features information concerning enforcement of child support abroad, international parental child abduction, and international adoption. There are also links to other sites that deal with international children's issues.

GENERAL INFORMATION

ABA's Lawlink <http://www.abanet.org/lawlink>

This site provides links to legal research and information resources.

Bank rates <http://www.bankrate.com>

This site provides information, rates, news, and calculators for mortgages, auto loans, CD's, credit cards, among other topics.

Code of Federal Regulations <http://www.access.gpo.gov/nara/cfr/cfr-table-search.html>

This site features online access and search capabilities for rules and regulations adopted by federal agencies.

Congressional Record & U.S. House and Senate Bills <http://thomas.loc.gov>

This site includes records of weekly floor activities, a searchable listing of information on pending legislation, the Congressional Record, committee information, and other information on the legislative process.

Credit Reports <http://www.equifax.com> or <http://www.sarma.com>

These sites provide access to consumer credit reports.

Expert Witnesses <http://www.expertpages.com/family.htm>

This site features a directory to expert witnesses on most family law issues.

Federal Courts Finder <http://www.law.emory.edu/FEDCTS>

This site allows the user to search for federal appellate court decisions by circuit and provides a link to the U.S. Supreme Court.

Federal Judicial Center <http://www.fjc.gov>

This site is maintained by the federal judicial system's agency for research and continuing education and provides access to various publications on current legal issues, including alternative dispute resolution and civil litigation issues.

Findlaw <http://www.findlaw.com/>

This site provides an index to legal resources, including a legal subject index, state law resources, legal practice materials, cases, and codes.

Homes—Relocation <http://www.homefair.com>

This site provides finder services, cost-of-living and moving calculators, and school and crime reports for various cities.

Internal Revenue Service—Forms <http://www.irs.gov/pub/irs-pdf>

This site is the index to Internal Revenue Service forms.

Investigations—Locating Services—Free Service <http://www.docusearch.com> or <http://www.infospace.com> or <http://www.peoplesearch.net> or <http://www.knowx.com>

These sites feature database search capabilities to assist in locating individuals in the United States.

Investigations—Locating Services—Fee-For-Service <http://www.publicdata.com>

This site is a fee-for-service research service to assist in locating individuals.

Law and Politics Internet Guide <http://www.lpig.org>

This site serves as an Internet guide to law links, including book reviews, international law, law libraries, and legal research.

Lawsonline <http://www.lawsonline.com>

This site includes links to U.S. Supreme Court and state cases, federal and state rules and codes, an attorney listing, law schools, and law reviews, as well as other related links.

Medication <http://www.rxlist.com>

This site provides a searchable database on U.S. prescription products.

Meta-Index for U.S. Legal Research <http://gsulaw.gsu.edu/metaindex>

This site features a search engine for U.S. Supreme Court and federal circuit court decisions and additional legal sources.

Oyez Project—U.S. Supreme Court Multimedia Database <http://oyez.nwu.edu>

This site offers information about major constitutional cases heard and decided by the U.S. Supreme Court. Cases are organized by date, party, and subject.

Project Hermes <http://supct.law.cornell.edu/supct>

This site contains all U.S. Supreme Court opinions since May 1990, as well as a collection of over 600 historically important decisions rendered by the U.S. Supreme Court.

Texas Administrative Code <http://www.sos.state.tx.us/tac>

This site features online access to rules and regulations adopted by Texas state agencies.

Texas Attorney General—Opinions <http://www.oag.state.tx.us/opinopen/opinhome.htm>

This site features an index to and a searchable database of opinions issued by the Attorney General, an index to requests for an opinion, a status sheet on requests, and an overview of the request procedure.

Texas Ethics Commission <http://www.ethics.state.tx.us>

This site features a search engine for advisory opinions issued by the Texas Ethics Commission.

Texas Ethics Reporter <http://www.lawlib.uh.edu/ethics>

This site includes information about ethics rules governing lawyers and judges in Texas.

Texas Judiciary Online <http://www.courts.state.tx.us>

This site provides information about, and links to, the Texas Supreme Court, the court of criminal appeals, the appellate courts, and the trial courts.

Texas Law Librarians <http://www.geocities.com/CapitolHill/1802>

This site features an index of links to useful online legal research resources.

FAMILY CODE
ESSENTIAL WEBSITES

Texas Legislature Online <http://www.capitol.state.tx.us>

This site contains the complete text of Texas statutory law and a searchable database of bills passed by the Texas legislature dating back to 1995.

Texas Register <http://lamb.sos.state.tx.us/texreg>

This site is an online version of the Texas Register, with information on new and proposed regulations, open meetings, and gubernatorial appointments. Both current and back issues are accessible, and there are indexes beginning with 1997.

Texas State Law Library <http://www.sll.state.tx.us>

This site provides an online search of the library catalog and links to Texas legal resources.

U.S. Code <http://www4.law.cornell.edu/uscode>

This site provides the most current online version of the United States Code. The code is searchable by popular title, headings, and text.

U.S. Constitution <http://www.access.gpo.gov/congress/senate/constitution/toc.html>

This site contains the text and case annotations to the U.S. Constitution.

U.S. Court of Appeals for the Fifth Circuit <http://www.ca5.uscourts.gov>

This site features information about the Fifth circuit, including opinions of the court, case information, and links to courts within the Fifth circuit. It also contains information on the Fifth circuit library system.

U.S. House of Representatives Law Library <http://www.house.gov>

This site includes links to, and search mechanisms for, federal codes and regulations and includes contact information for each U.S. Representative.

Valuation—Automobiles <http://www.kbb.com>

This site provides a searchable database for blue book values of automobiles.

Valuation—Boats <http://www.boatvalue.com>

This site provides a fee-for-service approximate appraisal value of most makes and models of marine crafts.

Valuation—Bonds—U.S. Savings Bonds <http://www.publicdebt.treas.gov/sav/sav.htm>

This site provides general information on savings bonds and features a calculator for determining the value of the bond.

Valutation—Collectibles & Antiques <http://www.collect.com>

These sites provide pricing information on collectibles and antiques to registered users.

Valuation—Real Property <http://www.taxnetusa.com> or <http://www.txcountydata.com>

These sites provide property value and appraisal information.

Valuation—Stock Quotes <http://www.pcquote.com> or <http://www.bloomberg.com>

These sites provide stock pricing information.

World Wide Web Virtual Library: Law <http://www.law.indiana.edu/v-lib>

This site provides links to legal information organized by type and topic.

Texas Legislature Online <http://www.capitol.state.tx.us>
This site contains the complete text of Texas statutes [illegible] the status of bills passed by the Texas Legislature [illegible] 1995.

Texas Register <http://lamb.sos.state.tx.us/texreg>
This site is an online version of the Texas Register, [illegible] information on [illegible] proposed regulations, open meetings, and gubernatorial appointments. Both current and [illegible] indexes beginning with [illegible]

Texas State Law Library <http://www.sll.state.tx.us>
This site [illegible] online search of the library catalog and links to Texas legal resources.

U.S. Code <http://www4.law.cornell.edu/uscode>
This site provides [illegible] current online version of the United States Code [illegible] searchable by popular title, headings, and [illegible]

U.S. Constitution <http://www.access.gpo.gov/congress/senate/constitution/toc.html>
This site [illegible] text and case annotations to the U.S. Constitution.

U.S. Court of Appeals for the Fifth Circuit <http://www.ca5.uscourts.gov>
This site features information about the Fifth Circuit, including opinions of the court, general information, and links [illegible] the Fifth Circuit. It also contains information [illegible] Fifth Circuit [illegible]

U.S. House of Representatives Law Library <http://www.house.gov>
This site includes [illegible] and search engines for federal laws and regulations. It includes contact information for each House [illegible]

Valuation—Automobiles <http://www.kbb.com>
This site provides a searchable database for blue-book values of automobiles.

Valuation—[illegible] <http://www.nadaguides.com>
This site [illegible] to estimate [illegible] and values of marine crafts.

Valuation—Bonds—U.S. Savings Bonds <http://www.publicdebt.treas.gov>
This site provides information on savings bonds and features a calculator for determining the value of the bond.

Valuation—Collectibles & Antiques <http://www.[illegible]>
This site provides [illegible] information on collectibles and antiques to [illegible]

Valuation—Real Property <http://www.[illegible]>
These sites provide property value and appraisal information.

Valuation—Stock Prices <http://www.[illegible]> & <http://www.bloomberg.com>
These sites provide stock pricing information.

World Wide Web Virtual Library: Law <http://www.[illegible]>
This site provides links to legal information organized by topic.

INDEX

INDEX

INDEX